P9-EIE-697

HURON COUNTY LIBRARY

3 6492 00478284 0

796.962640922 Pod

Podnieks, A.
Players.

PRICE: $60.00 (3559/se   )

PLAYERS

PLAYERS

The Ultimate A-Z Guide
of Everyone Who Has Ever Played in the NHL

ANDREW PODNIEKS

FOREWORD BY
Chris Cuthbert

DOUBLEDAY CANADA

NOV 2 5 2003

Text copyright © Andrew Podnieks 2003
Design and Compilation © Otherwise Inc. 2003
Concept © Livingston Cooke Inc. 2003
Foreword copyright © Chris Cuthbert 2003

All rights reserved. The use of any part of this publication, reproduced, transmitted in any form or
by any means electronic, mechanical, photocopying, recording or otherwise, or stored in a retrieval
system without the prior written consent of the publisher – or, in the case of photocopying or
other reprographic copying, a license from the Canadian Copyright Licensing Agency – is an
infringement of the copyright law.

Doubleday Canada and colophon are trademarks.

National Library of Canada Cataloguing in Publication
Podnieks, Andrew
Players : the ultimate A-Z guide of everyone who has ever played in the NHL /
Andrew Podnieks ; foreword by Chris Cuthbert.

ISBN 0-385-25999-9

1. National Hockey League – Biography. 2. Hockey players – Biography. I. Title.

GV848.5.A1P638 2003   796.962'64'0922   C2003-902376-1

Jacket images: the Hockey Hall of Fame
Jacket and text design: 52 Pick-up Inc., Toronto
Printed and bound in Singapore

Published in Canada by
Doubleday Canada, a division of
Random House of Canada Limited

Visit Random House of Canada Limited's website: www. randomhouse.ca

10 9 8 7 6 5 4 3 2 1

CONTENTS

LA REVUE
SPORTIVE du *Forum* SPORTS
MAGAZINE

25¢

Jean
Béliveau

1960 CANADIENS ᵃⁿᵈ ROYALS 1961

FOREWORD

"The Dream" slumped into the seat beside me, breaking the monotony of one of the countless road trips across the bald, frozen Saskatchewan prairie. The Yorkton Terriers of the Saskatchewan Junior Hockey League were en route to an exotic hockey locale such as Estevan, Humboldt, or North Battleford. A generation ago, I was a fledgling play-by-play announcer; he, an apple-cheeked 15-year-old defenceman, with wide eyes and a bold vision.

"I'm Ken Daneyko, and I'm going to play in the NHL," he said, by way of introduction. Through the icy fog illuminated by the bus headlights, every Terrier could envisage a career in the National Hockey League. Daneyko's dream, however, was more explicit in the Edmonton native's words and imagination.

"Can you imagine me fighting Dave Semenko," he laughed incredulously. The prospects of this prodigious teen grappling with the Edmonton Oilers' heavyweight, who was just establishing his reputation as Wayne Gretzky's bodyguard, seemed comical then. But Ken understood that if his hockey ambition were to be realized, the nightmare of a showdown with Semenko was an obstacle that, eventually, he might be forced to confront.

In retrospect, nearly a quarter-century later, Daneyko was not surprised by his cocksure ambition. "Even at the age of seven I wanted it more than anything else," he says. "I said it so often in school, my teacher, Miss Ullman, finally called my mother. She was concerned that I was obsessed with it. She

thought my mother should get me focused on other things."

On October 5, 1983, Daneyko's childhood dream became a reality. He played his first NHL game against the New York Rangers. His mother, Ollie, with tears in her eyes, celebrated on the telephone. She called Miss Ullman with the news that Ken's magnificent obsession had come true.

Now a grizzled and chiselled veteran, Ken's boyish features have been eroded by the rigours of nearly 20 professional seasons and the battle scars of nearly 1,300 games, most in New Jersey Devils history. Daneyko has won the NHL's Masterton Trophy, awarded for perseverance, sportsmanship, and dedication to hockey. He has fulfilled another childhood dream, twice embracing hockey's greatest prize, the Stanley Cup. It has been a career that surpassed the boyhood vision – even if it never included that much anticipated showdown with Dave Semenko.

The Saskatchewan Junior League represents one of the lower rungs on the ladder to hockey's hierarchy. More players finish their hockey careers at this level than continue their ascent to college and the pros. Yet the league's rosters are brimming with prospects that dare to share Ken's dream. Of those, only a chosen few will realize it. Included in Daneyko's graduating class from the 1979–80 SAJHL season were future Hall of Fame defencemen Chris Chelios of Moose Jaw and Al MacInnis of the Regina Pat Blues, as well as Dave Tippett of Prince Albert, the current coach of the Dallas Stars.

"To you from failing hands we throw the torch. Be yours to hold it high." Those inspirational words from John McCrae's poignant poem, "In Flanders Fields," have been emblazoned on the walls of the Montreal Canadiens' dressing room for 50 years. The message has inspired Canadiens' legends from Rocket Richard to Jean Béliveau and Guy Lafleur.

In a broader context, a symbolic torch has been passed throughout the course of National Hockey League history. On the pages that follow are the stories of NHL players, past and present, who have grasped the torch. Fewer than 6,000 men have experienced the glory of reaching hockey's professional summit.

From a backyard rink in Brantford, Ontario, a prairie slough in Floral, Saskatchewan, and a frozen lake in Flin Flon, Manitoba, or Khabarovsk, Russia; from Parry Sound to Pardubice; from the small towns of the Canadian Shield to the hockey hamlets of Minnesota's Iron Range, their dream has emerged from humble beginnings, has been realized on a grand stage, and has been passed on from one generation to the next.

The hockey fraternity ranges from the dozens who were fortunate to have experienced but a single NHL game, to the mythical figures in the pantheon of hockey immortals, such as Gordie Howe, Bobby Orr, Wayne Gretzky, and Mario Lemieux. Their skills, backgrounds, and nationalities are disparate, but all share at least two essential traits; they have dared to dream and, in doing so, have inspired others.

The dream of playing in the NHL is grand and noble, its tangible fulfilment sometimes surreal. That's the way Don Cherry, the former Boston and Colorado coach and *Hockey Night in Canada* star, recalls his first and only NHL appearance. "It was like a dream where everything is bigger and brighter," Cherry recounts through misty eyes. "The ice was so white, the nets brand new, the red paint in the Forum so bright. To stand at centre ice and look across to see Jean Béliveau and Boom Boom Geoffrion, it just didn't seem real."

Cherry was a Boston reserve in the 1955 Stanley Cup playoffs. When Bruins defenceman Warren Godfrey was scratched with a wrist injury, the NHL's most famous one-game alumnus was thrust into action. Fittingly, his moment of NHL glory came at the Montreal Forum where his childhood hero had starred. "I went to bed every night looking at a colour picture of Ken Reardon," Grapes says.

The following summer, despite team orders to the contrary, Don pursued his other sporting passion, baseball. Diving for a ball, the Kingston native suffered a broken shoulder. His defiance of the orders, compounded by the injury, relegated Cherry to the minors for the next 15 years.

He played in an era without second chances, a victim of hockey's economic laws of supply and demand. "There were six teams in the NHL, six in the American League, six in the Central, and six in the Western league," Cherry points out. "Everybody that played in the minors back then would be playing in the NHL right now and there are still six teams left over."

Montreal Canadiens mastermind Sam Pollock once dubbed Cherry "a career minor leaguer." Nevertheless, neither Pollock nor anyone else can take away that one glorious night at the Montreal Forum when Don Cherry became an NHL veteran forever.

"As the old saying goes, build one bridge and you're a bridge builder," Grapes says proudly.

Clem Loughlin, like Cherry, was a rugged defenceman with an undistinguished NHL resumé, competing in 101 games from 1926 to 1929. After his playing days, Loughlin coached the Chicago Blackhawks for three seasons, before retiring to a farm in Viking, Alberta. Nearly a half century later, Loughlin would have his most profound impact on the game, as a coach and mentor for the Sutter brothers, hockey's most remarkable clan.

"Clem coached me in midget," Darryl Sutter, the current coach of the Calgary Flames, remembers. "He was 81 or 82 then. We'd known him since we were little boys. He was like an idol to us."

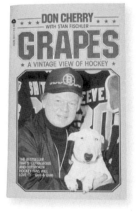

Sporting his old steel-blade skates with soft leather toes, which he wore as a Blackhawk, and bedecked with topcoat and fedora, Loughlin returned to the ice to demonstrate the subtleties of the game to the Sutter brood. "He was somebody I really looked up to," says Brian Sutter, the first of six Sutter brothers to play in the NHL. "He always had stories that would leave you thinking."

"We were good listeners," added Darryl. "Maybe that's why we learned a little about the game."

After watching Brian play a junior contest in Spruce Grove, Loughlin proclaimed that the eldest Sutter would indeed play in the NHL. "All it did was reaffirm what we had dreamed of doing since were little kids," Darryl recalls. "For Clem to say that gave us another tank of gas to go on."

At the age of six, Nicklas Lidstrom, a future Norris and Conn Smythe trophy winner, tapped the inspiration to become an NHL player. Lidstrom's source was the flush of pride he experienced watching countryman Borje Salming receive a prolonged standing ovation at Maple Leaf Gardens during the 1976 Canada Cup.

Salming wasn't the first Swedish-born NHL player. That distinction belongs to Gus Forsland. But it is Salming who all other Swedish players are measured against.

"He paved the way for all European players," Lidstrom acknowledges. "Opposing teams were tough on him, especially the Philadelphia Flyers. The way he handled himself made him a legend back in Sweden."

Fifteen years later Lidstrom, playing for Sweden, was paired on defence with his hero at the '91 Canada Cup. "Even late in his career he was a warrior, blocking shots, doing everything he could to win. It was a big thrill for me."

Further incentive was wrapped in the 1986 Stanley Cup final, a championship series that divided Swedish loyalties between Mats Naslund's Montreal Canadiens and Hakan Loob's Calgary Flames. Since the '86 Cup, NHL media coverage in Sweden has proliferated. In direct proportion, so too have the number of Swedish stars who have joined the

NHL's elite. Peter Forsberg, Markus Naslund, and Mats Sundin are among the premier players in the game. Every subsequent Swedish player, in Lidstrom's view, owes Salming a debt of gratitude. "He helped everyone else. It would have happened eventually, but he opened the door."

In neighbouring Finland, 14-year-old Teemu Selanne had a decision to make: whether to pursue a career as a soccer or hockey player. Teemu was equally accomplished in both sports, but the lure of hockey had one selling point that soccer couldn't counterbalance. A Finnish footballer had never enjoyed great success on the international stage. Meanwhile, the Flying Finn, Jari Kurri, was aligning with Wayne Gretzky to form the most dynamic offensive duo in NHL history.

"What Jari did in Edmonton gave me the courage to think I could do it too," Selanne reveals. "His success with the Oilers enhanced my dream. There were other Finnish players before him, but none who made the same impact he did."

As a youngster Selanne immersed himself in the Kurri mystique, completing a school project on his hero, working at his summer hockey school, and reading Kurri's best-selling biography. "The only book I've ever read," he says, with an impish grin.

Ultimately, Selanne would continue Kurri's legacy with other skilled and classy Finns such as Montreal Canadiens captain Saku Koivu and Jere Lehtinen of the Dallas Stars. Like Borje Salming in Sweden, Kurri paved the route to the NHL for future generations. "Now players in Finland feel so much closer to making it in the NHL," Selanne says. "The dream is stronger for those kids now."

Sergei Priakhin gained recognition as the first Soviet-trained player to play in the NHL when the unheralded winger joined the Calgary Flames in 1988. Priakhin, however, was merely a pawn in a bitter Soviet struggle to restrict its best players from abandoning Russian hockey for the spoils of capitalist North America. It took the erudite senior statesman of the Detroit Red Wings, Igor Larionov, to break down the restrictive, political walls of Soviet hockey.

MAPLE LEAFS

CARL BREWER defense

Unlike most NHL players, Larionov did not initially aspire to perform in the National Hockey League. In the closed Soviet society, he knew little of the North American game until he participated in the 1981 Canada Cup and the 1983 Super Series. "I became eager after that," Larionov recounts. "Every building was a sellout. The atmosphere was great and so was the hockey."

Larionov expressed his intentions through the media and was promptly banned from travelling for a year, deemed a risk to defect by Soviet officials. His value on the ice brought Larionov a reprieve and a 25-year Central Red Army contract with his signature forged by coach Viktor Tikhonov. "The longest contract in hockey history," Larionov says, with a cynical smile.

Following the 1988 Calgary Olympics, Larionov and veteran defenceman Vlacheslav Fetisov demanded their release in a public forum. "The politics in Russia were changing, so I wrote an open letter to Tikhonov, in a national magazine, saying it was time for players to get their freedom. We wanted to go before it was too late, while we were still at the top of our game."

A year later, with public support, if not Tikhonov's unconditional blessing, Larionov and Vladimir Krutov, two-thirds of the famed KLM line, were Vancouver Canucks. Their Soviet linemate, Sergei Makarov, was a Calgary Flame; Slava Fetisov joined the New Jersey Devils, and the NHL landscape was altered forever. Another triumphant troika, Pavel Bure, Sergei Fedorov, and Alexander Mogilny, have become key figures in the Russian evolution, joined recently by young gun Ilya Kovalchuk.

In just over a decade, the Russian hockey mindset has changed inexorably as well. Whereas a youthful Larionov knew little about the NHL, Russian youths now have their sights targeted on the western game. "I go back to my hometown every summer," Igor says of Voskresensk, an industrial city of 90,000 situated 80 kilometres south of Moscow. "I skate with kids 10 to 16 years old, three or four times a week. Every time you ask them about their futures, the NHL is now in their dreams. They know where the best hockey is played. They want to be a part of it."

The NHL's most lethal scorer of the 2001–02 NHL season was Jarome Iginla of the Calgary Flames. The son of a Nigerian immigrant, Jarome's feats marked the first time a black player has won the Art Ross trophy as the league scoring champion, as well as the Rocket Richard trophy for most goals. It was a remarkable achievement for any player, especially for one whose dream was discouraged because of his colour.

"I wanted to be an NHL player from the age of seven," Iginla says with a youthful grin. "Kids would tell me you can't be an NHL player. There aren't any black players in the NHL. But I would say that's not true. There's Claude Vilgrain, Tony McKegney, and Grant Fuhr."

Growing up in St. Albert, Alberta, Iginla was mesmerized by the exploits of the Edmonton Oilers. That a player of his race was starring in the Oilers' goal gave Jarome added impetus to succeed.

Unlike Iginla, Willie O'Ree, the Fredericton, New Brunswick, native didn't have the luxury of a black role model when he broke the NHL colour barrier on January 18, 1958, with the Boston Bruins. "Willie O'Ree's role was tough. I didn't face the barriers he faced," Jarome reflects. "I love to be a role model for young kids. I know what it meant to see a black player in the NHL."

The impact an NHL player has on his community was never more evident than at Bob Cole's celebrity golf tournament a few years ago in St. John's, Newfoundland. Cole, the play-by-play voice of *Hockey Night in Canada*, introduced a Hall of Fame lineup of participants, including Henri Richard, Pierre Pilote, Steve Shutt, and Scotty Bowman to an adoring throng. Finally, Cole welcomed Alex Faulkner, the first Newfoundlander to play in the NHL. The gathering at the

Ballyhaly Golf Club raised the roof with a tumultuous, heartfelt ovation. There were few dry eyes, even among the celebrity visitors, as an overwhelmed Faulkner received his due.

The Bishop's Falls native had been out of hockey for decades and his record paled beside his more illustrious peers. But for Newfoundlanders, Faulkner's achievements with Toronto and Detroit in the early '60s had made an indelible mark on their lives.

"He was playing on the same team as Howe, Delvecchio, and Sawchuk," Cole reminisces. "That was heavy stuff."

Enraptured by Faulkner's success, Cole spent many nights in his brother-in-law's driveway listening to the faint WJR Detroit radio signal of Red Wings broadcasts. "There would be others doing the same," Cole admits. "Sometimes we'd drive up to Signal Hill where the signal would come in stronger."

Following the 1963 Stanley Cup playoffs in which Faulkner netted five goals, Cole played a different radio role, broadcasting Faulkner's homecoming on VOCM. As Faulkner and his wife, Doris, made their way home on the Sydney to Port aux Basques ferry, on to Cornerbrook, Bishop's Falls, and St. John's, Cole would provide regular reports updating their progress. "We had a parade when he arrived in St. John's, a great turnout," Cole says. "Then, it was on to the Stadium for a ceremony with Premier Smallwood, the mayor, the whole works. This was a local-boy-makes-good-with-Gordie-Howe story. It was great."

Other Newfoundlanders have headed to the mainland and NHL glory since – Doug Grant, Joe Lundrigan, John Slaney, Dan Cleary, and Harold Druken among them. But Alex Faulkner will always have a special place in the hearts of Newfoundlanders, as the first of them who made it to the NHL.

In the remote Cree hamlet of Moose Factory, on the icy shore of James Bay in northern Ontario, native son Jonathan Cheechoo of the San Jose Sharks is the talk of the town. "There's quite a buzz around here every day after he's played," says his uncle, Charlie Cheechoo, deputy chief of the local First Nations band. "Everybody is getting a satellite dish so they can follow the Sharks."

It has been that way since Jonathan was selected 29th overall in the 1998 NHL entry draft. Hundreds of fans from Moose Factory converged on Buffalo for draft day, transforming his personal achievement into a festive community celebration.

Jonathan is Moose Factory's first-ever NHLer, realizing a prophetic vision of his childhood. "Back in school, I wrote a one-page essay on what I'd be doing in the year 2000," Jonathan recalls. "I wrote that I'd be playing in the NHL for the San Jose Sharks."

Now those aspirations are sifting through dream catchers throughout Moose Factory. "We have a lot of kids who dream of being like Jonathan now," says the elder Cheechoo. "They sense that they can do it. Before, there were road blocks for our kids. Jon had that special ingredient, the desire, that sparkle in his eye."

The hockey yearbook questionnaire was left out on the kitchen table, revealing a rare glimpse of my teenage son's thoughts and goals. Included in the survey were questions such as favourite aspect of high school (girls), pet peeve, (homework), favourite NHL player (Mike Comrie), and ultimate goal (NHL player).

The boy's hero, Mike Comrie, is living his childhood fantasy as a star centre with his hometown NHL team, the Edmonton Oilers. Comrie was weaned on the game during the Oilers' halcyon days of the '80s, inspired by an incomparable mentor, Wayne Gretzky.

"The way he saw the game, the way he anticipated, the way he made players around him so much better, he saw the game at a different level," Comrie notes. "For sure that rubs off. I would watch him and then try those moves at the next game or practice."

Benefiting from those Gretzky clinics, Comrie fast-tracked through the Edmonton minor hockey system to the St. Albert Saints of the Alberta Junior Hockey League, onto the University of Michigan, and the Western Hockey League's Kootenay Ice. He excelled at every level, but like his idol, critics were quick to identify perceived deficiencies, such as his diminutive stature.

Selected in the third round of the 1999 NHL entry draft, Comrie was one of the few early-round selections absent from the game's graduation exercises. "I didn't want to watch 90 guys walk up to the podium before me," he reveals. "I didn't believe they were better than me."

Eighteen months later, Comrie was awakened from a pregame slumber by a telephone call from his agent. The framework of a contract agreement had been finalized with the Oilers. Comrie was summoned from Cranbrook, where he'd been scheduled to play a junior game that night, to play his first NHL game for the Oilers against the Montreal Canadiens on *Hockey Night in Canada*.

"I remember skating around in the warmup trying not to fall," Mike recalls. " I had spent my whole life sitting in those stands and now I was one of the players the fans were watching. Here I am with Doug Weight and Ryan Smyth, who I'd been watching from the stands since I was 15 or 16. I felt like I'd won a lottery or raffle where the prize is to play a game with the Oilers. It didn't feel real."

Now, like Gretzky, Comrie is inspiring another generation of NHL hopefuls with his oil-slick moves. "Now I meet kids who say they dream of being me. That's pretty incredible."

I was driving one of those youngsters to the rink recently. "So you want to play in the NHL," I blurted out to my son, in reference to his yearbook questionnaire.

"Dad," he replied, rolling his eyes and speaking slowly for emphasis. "Every kid who has ever played hockey wants to play in the NHL."

Chris Cuthbert

PLAYERS

AALTO, Antti

b. Lappeenranta, Finland, March 4, 1975

Time is a-running out on the bloom of Aalto's youth and with it his chances of catching on with an NHL team full-time. Drafted by Anaheim in 1993, he continued to play Finnish league hockey until 1997, when he crossed the Atlantic to try his luck at the Pond. Alas, he played just three games with the Ducks that season, and after two full but unproductive years the centreman found himself fully ensconced in the minors for most of 2000-01. Previously, he had played internationally for his native Suomi at the World Junior Championships (1994 and '95) and the World Championships (1997 and 2000), earning but a bronze at the 2000 WC.

ABBOTT, George ("The Preacher")

b. Sydenham, Ontario, August 3, 1911

"Odd things take place in wartime hockey," wrote Andy Lytle in his report in the *Toronto Telegram* of the Toronto-Boston game of November 27, 1943. Indeed, he was referring to the presence of Abbott, practice goaltender for the Maple Leafs, tending the Bruins' goal! Boston's regular netminder, Bert Gardiner, fell ill at the last minute and couldn't play, so team manager Art Ross borrowed Abbott for the night's action at Maple Leaf Gardens. Abbott had played for the Dunnville Mudcats as a youngster, but his career more or less ended during a practice with the amateur Hamilton Tigers when a deflected shot hit him flush in the eye. He devoted his life to the Baptist ministry and during the war found himself assigned to the Toronto area. He approached Leafs coach Happy Day about keeping his pads in the game, so to speak, and Day gladly took him on as a spare goalie. In his only NHL appearance, the Preacher allowed 7 goals but was peppered with 52 shots, including one by Babe Pratt that knocked him out for a few minutes. The Leafs coasted to a 7-3 win.

ABBOTT, Reg

b. Winnipeg, Manitoba, February 4, 1930

An all-round athlete who played second base for the provincial champion Rosedales in Manitoba, Abbott was also a near-scratch golfer and a fine lacrosse player who decided to concentrate on hockey during his late teens. A popular young man, he played on the Brandon Wheat Kings' top line with Gus Juckes and Brian Roche. His big-league chance came when the Habs' Elmer Lach was injured and coach Dick Irvin called Abbott up from Victoria for a three-game trial – December 4, 6, and 7, 1952. He played on a line with Bernie Geoffrion and Paul Meger, just as he had at Montreal's training camp when he first impressed Irvin. Although Abbott was an excellent forechecker and stickhandler, those three games were to be his only time in the NHL, after which he played more than a dozen years in senior leagues across Canada. He had been scoring champion with Brandon in 1948-49, the year the Wheat Kings went to the Memorial Cup, and he later had a successful run with the Winnipeg Maroons. That team went to the Allan Cup finals three times to start the 1960s, winning in 1964, and a year later he played on Canada's nascent National Team at the World Championships, finishing in fourth

place. He was later inducted into the Manitoba Sports Hall of Fame.

ABEL, Clarence "Taffy"

b. Sault Ste. Marie, Michigan, May 28, 1900
d. Sault Ste. Marie, Michigan, August 1, 1964

Abel was the first American to make the NHL grade as a regular even though he didn't play organized hockey until he was 18. After four years playing in Michigan he joined the St. Paul Athletic Club and earned a spot on the 1924 U.S. Olympic team bound for Chamonix, France. He scored 15 times in 5 games during the Olympics, though he was held off the scoresheet in his team's 6-1 loss to Canada in the gold medal game. Abel returned to St. Paul and moved up to the CHL the following year, and when the New York Rangers began operations in 1926-27 he joined the expansion team to provide size and strength on the blueline. He stayed in New York for three seasons, often teamed with Ivan "Ching" Johnson, another formidable presence. In the team's second season, the Rangers won the Stanley Cup, but at the conclusion of the following season he was sold to Chicago for $15,000. Abel played the last five years of his pro career in the Windy City, usually teamed with Cy Wentorth or Art Coulter. In his final season, he won a second Cup as Chicago defeated Toronto in the finals. After retiring, he returned home to Sault Ste. Marie where he coached the local Americans for a number of years. After, he opened a tourist hotel called Taffy's Lodge, and it was there he passed away at age 64. His on-ice success, both in the NHL and internationally, led to his posthumous induction into the United States Hockey Hall of Fame in 1973.

ABEL, Gerry

b. Detroit, Michigan, December 25, 1944

The day Gerry was born, his father was playing a game down the road at the Olympia, leading the Red Wings to a 6-4 win over the visiting Leafs. "If I could be half as good as my dad, I'd be happy," Gerry said of his father, Sid, the day he signed his first pro contract with the Detroit Red Wings in the summer of 1965. Papa would have been doubly happy had this wish come true, partly because of his pride as a father, partly because he was general manager of the Wings! Such was not to be the case, however. Gerry's only NHL game came on March 8, 1967, an uneventful entry and finish to his NHL career. Of note, though, his father was by then coaching the team, and Sid, who played with Gordie Howe and Ted Lindsay some 15 years earlier on the Production Line, did get to see his son play with that same Howe and newcomer Doug Roberts. After two more seasons in minor pro, Gerry retired.

ABEL, Sid ("Boot Nose")

b. Melville, Saskatchewan, February 22, 1918
d. Detroit, Michigan, February 7, 2000

Sid Abel excelled in a number of capacities during his extended hockey career. On the ice he was an accomplished playmaking centre and team leader who contributed to three Stanley Cup championships in Detroit. The Red Wings' western Canada scout, Goldie Smith, signed Abel to his first

Antti Aalto

Reg Abbott

Gerry Abel

Sid Abel

Taffy Abel
(opposite page)

Dennis Abgrall

contract, but passed away just as he was about to mail the documents back to GM Jack Adams. Abel was performing well at his first pro camp when Adams informed the player of the problem. Abel joked, "I was hoping they wouldn't find the original because I figured I could sign again for more money." Adams soon found the contract, however, and Abel's NHL journey was underway. After spending a year each with the Saskatoon Wesleys and Flin Flon Bombers, Abel played 15 games with the Wings in 1938-39 and showed flashes of brilliance. He split the next season between Motown and Indianapolis of the AHL and made the Wings full-time the next year, 1940-41. In just his second full season, he averaged more than a point a game playing on the Liniment Line with Don Grosso and Eddie Wares and was voted to the Second All-Star Team. In 1942-43, he lead the team to Stanley Cup victory and at just age 24 served as the team's captain. Abel missed two years of playing time due to military service but returned for the final seven games of the 1945-46 season. In 1946-47 Abel was teamed with wingers Gordie Howe and Ted Lindsay for the first time. The line clicked almost immediately and was dubbed the Production Line in '48-'49. Abel led all Detroit scorers and won the Hart Trophy as the league's most valuable player, only the second Detroit player so honoured (after Ebbie Goodfellow in 1940). The next year, Abel set career highs with 34 goals and 69 points, he and his linemates finished 1-2-3 in the NHL scoring parade, and the Wings won the Cup. He earned his third championship with Detroit in 1951-52 before being traded to Chicago on July 22, 1952, one of the toughest moves GM Adams had ever made. During his two years in the Windy City, Abel was a playing coach and managed to get the team into the playoffs for the first time in nine years. Although his point production plummeted, he realized how much he enjoyed coaching. When he retired in 1954, however, he took some time off to figure out his next move. He tried his hand as a television broadcaster but decided he wasn't quite ready for this line of work. Midway through '57-'58, he became Red Wings coach when incumbent Jimmy Skinner resigned due to illness. Abel endured for a decade, and guided the team to four appearances in the Stanley Cup finals – 1961, '63, '64, and '66 – though he never won as bench boss. In 1962, he added GM to his portfolio when Jack Adams retired after having been with the team since 1927. He later became a scout for the expansion Kings in Los Angeles and GM in St. Louis before committing hockey suicide by taking over the Kansas City Scouts in 1974-75, one of the worst teams of all time. Abel later managed a restaurant and worked in sales for a heating business in Detroit. He also did commentary on Red Wings radio and TV. On April 12, 1995, his number 12 was raised to the rafters of the Joe Louis Arena to join Howe and Lindsay. Two years later, he received overwhelming support from fans when word spread of his struggles with cancer, emphysema, and a broken hip. He had earned his nickname a million years ago when he tried to help Gordie Howe in a fight with Rocket Richard and

Gene Achtymichuk

wound up being the most badly damaged. Abel was inducted into the Hockey Hall of Fame in 1969.

ABGRALL, Dennis
b. Moosomin, Saskatchewan, April 24, 1953
Abgrall's Hockey Index shot up and then down with a consistency so many players experienced. Los Angeles drafted him 70th overall in 1973 and he played 13 games with the Kings two years later. At season's end, he signed for money and greater opportunity with the WHA's Cinncinati Stingers after the Los Angeles Sharks went belly up. Two years later, the Winnipeg Jets claimed him back in the NHL's Expansion Draft, but he never got a chance to play. Instead, he continued his career another jump down, in Germany, and then another, in Belgium, before retiring in 1982.

ABRAHAMSSON, Thommy
b. Umea, Sweden, April 12, 1947
One of Sweden's greatest players of the 1970s, Thommy and his twin brother Christer signed with the WHA's New England Whalers for the 1974-75 season at the urging of team GM Jack Kelly. While Christer was dogged by injuries and never made it to the NHL, Thommy starred with the team and stayed in New England for three years before returning to Sweden in 1977, where he continued to play and ran a sporting goods store with Christer. After three seasons with Leksand, Thommy returned to North America. He signed with the Hartford Whalers for '80-'81 but played only 32 games because of a string of nagging injuries. At season's end, he was bought out. Thommy returned home to act as a part-time scout for Hartford and played a final year in the Swedish league. Abrahamsson played for Tre Kronor in five World Championships as well as the 1972 Olympic Winter Games. However, because because of his pro career, he was barred by the Swedish Ice Hockey Federation from representing his country at the inaugural Canada Cup in 1976. So incensed were the other players that they threatened to boycott the event were he not allowed to join the team. Thommy begged them to comply with his country's edict, and did not participate in the tournament.

ACHTYMICHUK, Gene ("Acky")
b. Lamont, Alberta, September 7, 1932
A prospect in the Montreal system, Acky was called up by the Habs in December 1957 to replace the injured Jean Béliveau. During his 16 games his linemates were Bernie Geoffrion and Bert Olmstead, and he registered 8 points. To replace him on their own roster, the junior Montreal Royals had to call up young Ralph Backstrom from the Ottawa-Hull Junior Canadiens. At the end of the season, Achtymichuk was traded to Detroit, and in '58-'59 again saw action as an emergency callup from the farm team in Edmonton. With the Wings, he played with two guys named Howe and Delvecchio for a dozen games, his last NHL stint. He roamed around in the minors for another decade, eventually becoming playing coach of the Long Island Ducks in June 1966 when head man John Muckler accepted

a job from the New York Rangers as director of player personnel.

ACOMB, Doug
b. Toronto, Ontario, May 15, 1949

A promising junior who rose through the sponsorship ranks of the Toronto Marlboros, Acomb played just two NHL games, both with the parent Maple Leafs, on March 7 and 11, 1970. He registered one assist. Acomb played four years with the Marlies, leading the OHA with 55 goals in 1968-69 in his last season after going to the Memorial Cup two years previously. He spent his last four years of pro hockey in the CHL and WHL, played briefly in Austria, and played senior hockey in Barrie before retiring in 1976.

ACTON, Keith
b. Stouffville, Ontario, April 15, 1958

"When I was growing up, I hated Montreal. Always." So spake Acton, the Canadiens' centre playing between Hall of Famers Steve Shutt and Guy Lafleur for his first three seasons in the NHL (1980-83). He started his first year on a line with Mario Tremblay and Yvon Lambert, but his feistiness, skill on faceoffs, and consistent play earned him a promotion to the number-one line in no time. Early in the 1983-84 season, he was traded to Minnesota, one of the weaker teams at the time, and felt betrayed. Five years later, he was traded again, but this time because of his play in Montreal. His remarkable performance in the 1981 playoffs during a series loss to the up-and-coming Edmonton Oilers impressed Glen Sather, GM of the Oilers. "I went into the room to shake hands," he recalled of eliminating the Canadiens, "and Keith Acton was heartbroken. That's what I remembered – how much he cared after they lost." Sure enough, that spring Sather got him, and the Oilers won another Cup. Sather traded Acton to Philadelphia the following year, and that summer he was involved in one of the stranger deals in league history. The Flyers sent him to Winnipeg only to acquire him five days later. Acton played more than 1,000 NHL games and represented Canada three times at the World Championships. After retiring, he became an assistant coach, ending up with Toronto for the 2000-01 season. During that time, he was diagnosed with testicular cancer, but never one to give in, he survived treatment and then ran the Canadian International Marathon in 4 hours, 26 minutes.

ADAM, Doug
b. Toronto, Ontario, September 7, 1929

Although he played just four NHL games with the Rangers, Adam became the first player in the Western

"When I was growing up, I hated Montreal. Always."
KEITH ACTON

Hockey League to score 200 goals for a career and he held numerous other league records using a stick with a number 9 lie. The Rangers called him up for games on February 5, 9, 11, and 12, 1950, before returning him to the Tacoma Rockets of the PCHL. He retired in 1957 after a year with Charlotte to return to Tacoma to sell automobiles, though he had wanted to coach in Philadelphia. Both ambitions, to retire and to coach, were ploys designed to extract more money from Charlotte, where he had just set a league record with 65 goals. In November 1957, he came to terms with the team and resumed his playing career. In 1958-59, he got his second wish and was named playing coach of the Philadelphia Ramblers. In January of that season, he caused a ruckus when he pulled his team off the ice and forfeited a game because of what he said were faulty goal nets. He was fined $250 for his actions, the largest fine in EHL history. Adam coached for three seasons and after a year's absence became the team's GM in 1963-64. Bud Poile then hired him as a part-time scout for the expansion Philadelphia Flyers in the NHL, but just three days after quitting his full-time civilian job to join Poile full-time, Poile himself was fired and Adam was forced to resign out of support.

ADAM, Russ
b. Windsor, Ontario, May 5, 1961

A fourth-line checker who played with a determination beyond his skill, Adam played with the Leafs for just eight games, from October 6 to November 3, 1982. Drafted 137th overall in 1980 by Toronto while a member of the Kitchener Rangers, he played on a decent line in junior that couldn't score with the same consistency in pro. Surrounding his time with the Leafs were three years in the minors, after which he descended to the IHL and eventually played senior hockey in Newfoundland. There he met the woman of his dreams and got married, though before he settled down altogether he played in Germany for five winters before calling St. John's his permanent home in 1992. He became an assistant coach with the St. John's Maple Leafs, Toronto's AHL affiliate.

ADAMS, Bryan
b. Fort St. James, British Columbia, March 30, 1977

This boy can't carry a tune, but he sure can carry a puck. Adams played four years of college hockey at Michigan State, reaching the Frozen Four in 1999, but his accomplishments never led to being drafted. Instead, the expansion Atlanta Thrashers signed him as a free agent and put him in his first NHL game on March 4, 2000, in Ottawa. He played most

Doug Acomb

Russ Adam

of the next two seasons in the "I" and AHL, becoming a steady performer hoping to get another shot in the big tent.

ADAMS, Craig
b. Brunei, Borneo (Malaysia), April 26, 1977
Born far from the hockey crowd because of his father's job, Adams grew up in more ice-friendly Calgary and was drafted 223rd overall in 1996 by Hartford. By the time he got into his first game on October 24, 2000, Hartford had become Carolina and Adams had graduated from Harvard University. Although young, he has missed large chunks of time due to serious injuries, one to his shoulder, another to his sternum.

ADAMS, Greg
b. Duncan, British Columbia, May 31, 1960

Greg Adams

Determination and perseverance alone got Adams to the NHL. Growing up on Vancouver Island, he had only one hockey rink to skate on and that was nine miles away in Chemainus. He begged every coach at the rink to let him practice with that team, even if it wasn't his age group. During summers as a teenager, he worked at a sawmill to pay for a hockey school he wanted to attend in Penticton. While his parents advised him to give up his dreams, Greg refused. He was enchanted by the story of Gene Carr, the first Island native to make it to the NHL, in 1971. Greg's determination paid off. Although undrafted after finishing junior with Victoria, he was signed by the Flyers as a free agent in 1980 and bounced between the minors and the NHL for five years. Likely his earliest career highlight was when he fought Gord Kluzak, one of the tough, new players in the league, three times in one game. In 1985-86, now with Washington, he played on a line with Alan Haworth and Craig Laughlin and scored a career-high 56 points. In the summer of 1988, he was involved in a motorcycle accident that required a metal plate and screws to be inserted into his left shoulder, though he made a full recovery and returned to the NHL. His first agent was Brian Burke, and when Burke became GM in Vancouver, he acquired Adams from the Caps. In all, Adams played 545 NHL games with 7 teams, not bad for a guy who seemed to have a "can't make it" tag in his youth.

ADAMS, Greg C.
b. Nelson, British Columbia, August 1, 1963

Greg C. Adams

Woe was him. Undrafted and unwanted. Adams was signed as a free agent by the New Jersey Devils in the summer of 1984 primarily because the Devils' GM, Tom McVie, had known Greg's father, Gus, for more than 30 years. A goaltender in his youth, Gus once played against the Trail Smoke Eaters in 1961, the year that great team went on to win gold at the World Championships. He sired five hockey-playing sons, of which Greg was the best. Greg played junior in Kelowna for two years before going to an obscure U.S. college – Northern Arizona University – for two more. He became only the second grad of that school (Bob Beers had been the first) to make the NHL. In his last year with the Lumberjacks, he was the NCAA's scoring champ. After one middling year with New Jersey, Adams resolved to build his upper body

strength, and by the time camp opened for the '85-'86 season he was a different player. He recorded 5 assists against Philadelphia in the first game of the year and went on to set team records for most goals (35), assists (42), and points (77) in a season. He was traded to Vancouver after two more years. He had nine 20-goal seasons with five teams, and his 1,056 games played is one of the greatest totals for players of the modern era who were never drafted.

ADAMS, Jack
("Jolly Jack"/ "Jolly Jawn")
b. Fort William, Ontario, June 14, 1895
d. Detroit, Michigan, May 1, 1968
Although he was inducted into the Hockey Hall of Fame as a player, Jack Adams spent the greater part of his career as coach and general manager of the Detroit Red Wings. He is the only man to have his name on the Stanley Cup as player, general manager, and coach. As a skater, his fame was established during the war when he played in Peterborough with the 247th Battalion. The next season, he joined the old Toronto Arenas during the inaugural NHL season, 1917-18, where he won his first Stanley Cup. After one more season with Toronto, he moved to Vancouver and played in the Pacific Coast league for the Millionaires for three years. In Vancouver, Adams did something no one has done before or since. In the last game of the 1920-21 season, against Victoria, he accidentally scored a goal on his own net. For reasons unknown, the referee nonetheless credited Adams with the goal, the only player ever to be so "honoured"! The next year, he won the scoring title in the PCHL. Adams returned east for the 1922-23 season, joining the Toronto St. Pats for four years before finishing his skating days with Ottawa in 1926-27. He ended his skating career as he had begun it, by winning a Stanley Cup. His teammates that year included a veritable who's who of the Hockey Hall of Fame – King Clancy, Frank Nighbor, Cy Denneny, Frank Finnigan, Alec Connell, and George Boucher. NHL president Frank Calder suggested to Adams that he coach the Detroit Falcons, a second-year team that had lost money and struggled badly its first year in the NHL. Adams accepted the challenge, and the team quickly improved. In 1934, the Red Wings, as Norris had nicknamed the team, made it to the finals before losing to Chicago. Two years later, in 1936, they won their first Stanley Cup, and repeated as champions in 1937. Adams was not only Detroit's on-ice authority but also its business manager, travelling secretary, and publicist. He was also loud and pugnacious, famous for storming the officials' room at the Olympia to berate the referees for calls he objected to. But in the off-season, he'd fight tooth and nail at the governors' meetings for pay raises for the officials. That was his style – tough and fair. After two Cups in the 1930s, the Wings had a tough time keeping pace with Toronto, Boston, and Montreal. They made it to the finals in 1941, where they lost to the Bruins. Then came the famous series in 1942 when Adams and his Wings blew a 3-0 lead and lost the Stanley Cup to Toronto when the Leafs won the last four in a row. The next year they lost in

the finals again to Boston, and in 1945 Toronto won in a series that saw Detroit fight back from 3-0 down to force a seventh game. The highlight of Jolly Jack's career came right after the war when the Wings finished in first place for seven successive years, 1948-55, and won four Stanley Cups – 1950, 1952, 1954, and 1955. By this time he had retired as a coach to concentrate on being general manager, and he became intent on developing a superior farm system and ensuring new talent would challenge old at every training camp. His pride and joy for the remainder of his days was Gordie Howe, the man he found, signed, developed, and helped mature into the greatest player of all time. His other great players included Ted Lindsay, Terry Sawchuk, Alex Delvecchio, and Red Kelly. Because of his success and longevity, the NHL named the coach of the year award in his honour.

ADAMS, John ("Jack")

b. Calgary, Alberta, May 5, 1920

Not to be confused with the Hall of Famer of Detroit note, this Jack Adams played but one full season in the NHL, with les Canadiens, in 1940-41. He scored six goals with a team that was uncharacteristically and summarily eliminated from the playoffs in the first round against Chicago. Adams left hockey to join the army that summer, staying in the military until 1945. When he was discharged, he was traded to Buffalo with Moe White for Murdo MacKay and never made it back to the NHL. He retired in 1949.

ADAMS, John

b. Port Arthur, Ontario, July 27, 1946

San Diego coach Jack Evans called Adams "the best goaltender I've seen in this league," the WHL, that is, which is faint praise at best. The remarks came after the goaler blocked 56 shots in his league-leading 66th game of the '73-'74 season for the shutout. Adams had been in the Boston system but did himself no favours at training camp when he showed up overweight and was immediately plunged into the Central league for the year. The next camp, he was leaner, but strayed too far from his goal for coach Johnson's liking. Nonetheless, Adams got into his first game in December 1972, a 3-3 tie with Montreal, and earned a shutout his next start, against Atlanta. He played 14 games for Bobby Orr and the Bruins, but was with San Diego the year after. He was acquired by the hapless Caps in their inaugural season and coughed up an enormous 46 goals in 8 games, an average of 6.90. A career that had begun with four trips to the Memorial Cup with Port Arthur in the mid-1960s ended with a lengthy stint in senior hockey in Thunder Bay.

Because of his success and longevity, the NHL named the coach of the year award in his honour.
JACK ADAMS

ADAMS, Kevyn ("Ads")

b. Washington, D.C., October 8, 1974

Drafted by Boston 25th overall in 1993, Adams played four years for the Redskins at the University of Maine-Ohio where he helped the team to a CCHA title in '93 as a freshman, graduating four years later. He spent a year with Grand Rapids in the IHL, but Boston never gave him an NHL chance and he signed with Toronto as a free agent in 1997. He played mostly in the minors for the next two years, but the Leafs called him up for brief appearances, including his first game, opening night of the 1997-98 season. Adams' big break came during the 1999 playoffs when he recorded two assists and demonstrated excellent two-way play. He made the team the following season and was an effective fourth-line player, taking key faceoffs, facing tough opponents, and killing penalties. That summer, the Leafs left Adams exposed and the Columbus Blue Jackets claimed him on June 23, 2000. Overnight, he went from the fourth line to the first. However, he scored just 8 times in his first 66 games and was traded to Florida with a draft choice for Ray Whitney.

ADAMS, Stewart

b. Calgary, Alberta, September 16, 1904

d. Calgary, Alberta, May 18, 1978

A seven-year veteran of junior hockey in Calgary and minor pro with the Minneapolis Millers, Adams was acquired by the Chicago Black Hawks during the 1929-30 season and played much of the next three years there. Early in the '32-'33 season, he was sold to Toronto and sent to the team's minor-league affiliate in Syracuse. Adams saw his first action as a member of the Leafs on December 29, 1932, replacing the injured Charlie Conacher on the Kid Line. He was given a warm ovation by the Gardens' crowd after one fine rush, though during his 19 games with the team earned but 2 assists. As a junior in Calgary, Adams played in three Memorial Cups in four years, losing each time. He then turned pro with Minneapolis in 1925 where he stayed for nearly five years. His career ended in perfect reflection: From Toronto he went back to Minneapolis, then Calgary, where he worked for Thomas Adams Distillers until his retirement in 1974.

ADDUONO, Rick

b. Thunder Bay, Ontario, January 25, 1955

Married at 16 with a child, Adduono embarked on a pro career by playing three seasons (1972-75) with St. Catharines in the OHA. In his second year, he led the league in assists (84) and points (135), and looked to be one of the better NHL prospects. However, he

John Adams (b. 1920)

John Adams (b. 1946)

Kevyn Adams

was hampered by injuries during his final season of junior, and his stock dropped by the time he became draft eligible. He went 60th overall to Boston in 1975 but played only one game with the Bruins during the '75-'76 season. After two more seasons with Rochester in the AHL, he joined Birmingham of the WHA and returned to the NHL for three games with Atlanta in 1979-80. His NHL career clearly over, Adduono played in the minors and then Austria before turning to coaching, starting with South Carolina in the ECHL in 1998 and then with Greensboro.

AEBISCHER, David ("Abi")
b. Fribourg, Switzerland, February 7, 1978

David Aebischer is at the forefront of Swiss hockey history for almost everything he does. He was the first Swiss goalie ever drafted into the NHL, 161st overall by Colorado in 1997; he backstopped the Swiss to a bronze medal at the 1998 World Junior championships, the nation's first-ever medal at that tournament; and he became the first man to take the Stanley Cup to that neutral country, in the summer of 2001. While Switzerland has long been known as a country where old Canadians go to prolong their playing careers, it has only recently established any sort of comprehensive national program to develop its own stars. Aebischer personifies the greatest success of the country. In his first start in the NHL, he beat Columbus; in his second, he shut out Chicago. As backup to Patrick Roy, he's not likely to play more than 15 games, but he's learning from one of the best. He also was part of the Avs' 2001 Stanley Cup victory, and got his day with the Cup. He took it to Fribourg and Tafers and shared the day with his house league team, Fribourg-Gotteron.

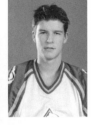

David Aebischer

AFANASENKOV, Dmitry
b. Arkhangelsk, Soviet Union (Russia), May 12, 1980

A product of the Russian hockey system, Afanasenkov was selected 72nd overall in the 1998 draft by Tampa Bay, making his NHL debut on March 10, 2001. After that draft, he moved to North America and played junior in Quebec, scoring 56 goals in 1999-2000 with Sherbrooke. That season, he also played for Russia at the World Juniors, scoring five goals for a team that finished a disappointing sixth. He finished 2002-03 with Kloten in the Swiss league.

AFFLECK, Bruce ("Scratch")
b. Salmon Arm, British Columbia, May 5, 1954

In 1959, U.S. President Dwight D. Eisenhower named Affleck's future father-in-law, William F. Quinn, the first governor of Hawaii. Quinn was later re-elected, and in 1976 ran for Senator as a Republican. Affleck and his family spent that summer helping with the campaign. "I gave out pamphlets and did anything else that needed doing. He's a Republican in a Democratic state, and we worked hard," Affleck said. After playing junior hockey in Penticton, Affleck enrolled at the University of Denver, primarily because the coach of the hockey team was the well-respected Murray Armstrong. It was there that Affleck met his future wife, Cecily, but just before their wedding, in the summer of 1975, tragedy nearly struck. Affleck was driving a Jeep with two other members of the St. Louis Blues – Chuck Lefley and Jim McCrimmon – when he lost control of the car. It rolled three times, and Lefley suffered a broken shoulder (the others were uninjured). Although he had been drafted by California in 1974, Affleck was acquired by the Blues and in 1974-75 began his NHL career in a city that would become his home for many years. His was not a spectacular game, though, and after fewer than six years he was in the minors to stay, the exception being one game with the Islanders during the '83-'84 season. Affleck played two years in Switzerland and after retiring joined the firm of W.M. French, a business that helped corporations in the St. Louis area relocate. In 1987, he joined the Blues as director of group sales and also provided colour commentary for Blues' radio broadcasts. A short time later, he was named president of sales and became president of the team's alumni association. It was in St. Louis that he got his nickname. Because he was scratched routinely from the lineup when he first joined the team, Chuck Lefley affectionately started calling him Scratch.

Maxim Afinogenov

After playing junior hockey in Penticton, Affleck enrolled at the University of Denver.
BRUCE AFFLECK

AFINOGENOV, Maxim
b. Moscow, Soviet Union (Russia), September 4, 1979

With speed to burn, Afinogenov could be one of hockey's next superstars. With a pedigree like his, he has every chance. His mother, Raisa, was a seven-time champion in the 800 metres, and father, Sergei, was also a track star. His sister, Katia, is a teen phenom in tennis. Maxim played at the 1998 World Junior Championships, and at the '99 WJC in Winnipeg he was named the tournament's best forward. The year after, 1999-2000, he started in the minors but played his way onto the Sabres, his draft team, and never looked back. He has learned to cope with the size and speed of the NHL game, adapted to its defensive responsibilities, and become a leading scorer on a team thin with offensive talent. His maturity has also led to invitations to the World Championships in 1999 and 2000 and being named to Russia's team for the

2002 Olympics in Salt Lake City. His 2002-03 NHL season, though, was badly hampered by a concussion and subsequent slow recovery.

AGNEW, Jim
b. Hartney, Manitoba, March 21, 1966
Drafted 157th overall in 1984, by Vancouver, Agnew played to about the level this selection implied. After four seasons of junior out west, he proved to be a journeyman during his six-year NHL career, never playing a full season without demotion to the minors. During his years with Brandon and Portland in the WHL, Agnew was named to the West Division's First All-Star team and after leaving junior was assigned to the Canucks to Fredericton of the American league. He saw his first NHL action in '86-'87, but only for four games. Agnew was the proverbial tough customer, but his game was greatly affected after he suffered a serious knee injury midway through the '89-'90 season while in the IHL. He spent much of the next three years recovering, and the final blow came during an exhibition game on September 14, 1994, when he injured his knee one final time and was forced to retire.

AHERN, Fred
b. Boston, Massachusetts, February 12, 1952
Undrafted during his years at Bowdoin College in Boston, Ahern was an aspiring teacher and hockey coach before he was signed by the California Golden Seals in September 1974. He later played for two other inferior "C" teams – Cleveland Barons and Colorado Rockies – but during the off-season always returned to south Boston, "where his pretty wife works as a professional model," according to the Rockies' 1977-78 media guide. He played for the U.S. in the 1976 Canada Cup, and after a few years in the minors, retired in 1982 to work in business in Boston.

AHLIN, Tony
b. Eveleth, Minnesota, December 12, 1914
Although he was born in the same small city as future U.S. Hall of Famer Frank Brimsek, Ahlin shares little else in common with any star from the NHL. In fact, in a hockey career that lasted a decade, Ahlin played just one NHL game, for Chicago, during the 1937-38 season. Beyond that, he played almost exclusively in Eveleth and Kansas City before retiring in 1942.

AHOLA, Peter
b. Espoo, Finland, May 14, 1968
Ranked as one of the top waterskiers in Finland, Ahola led the L.A. Kings in +/- in his rookie season with a modest +12 in 1991-92. He had been signed by the Kings as a free agent, and he was one of the first Europeans to make his way to the NHL via an American college. He attended Boston University from 1989 to '91, playing at BU alongside Tony Amonte, Keith Tkachuk, and Joe Sacco. Early in '92-'93, he was sent to Pittsburgh for Jeff Chychrun, but his days in a Penguins uniform were limited to just ?? games. Later in the season he played for his third team when he was sent to San Jose for nothing more than future considerations, but after just 20 games he

was sent to Calgary in the summer for Dave Capuano. Ahola played only two games at the start of the '93-'94 season for the Flames before getting another phone call, his fourth in 11 months, and being told to report to Tampa Bay. He didn't play a single game for the Bolts and returned to his native Finland in 1994, where he has enjoyed a successful career ever since.

AHRENS, Chris
b. San Bernadino, California, July 31, 1952
From the land of surf came a player who made his way to Kitchener, Ontario, to play junior hockey. Totally. Ahrens captained the Rangers in 1971-72 and was then drafted by Minnesota that summer. Although he played most of his career with the North Stars, this time amounted to just 52 games over 5 seasons. He played most of those years in the minors and finished his playing career with the Oilers in '77-'78, playing four games at the end of the season after an interleague trade sent him from Minnesota to Edmonton with Pierre Jarry for future considerations.

AIKEN, John
b. Arlington, Minnesota, January 1, 1932
It was a pretty incredible way to get into an NHL game. John Aiken was a 26-year-old mathematician working for the U.S. Air Force and living in the Boston area. After transferring from West Point to Boston University, he had to miss a year of hockey because of eligibility rules, and in the interim he became the practice goalie for the Bruins. He was also the standby goalie who attended every game at the Boston Garden in the unlikely event one of the two starting goalies was injured and could not continue. That's exactly what happened on March 13, 1958. Montreal was in town, and in the second period the Bruins held a slim 1-0 lead when Habs' goaler Jacques Plante was injured at the 6:15 mark. His own defenceman, Doug Harvey, had pushed Bruins forward Vic Stasiuk into Plante, who lost his balance and hit his head hard against the crossbar. Plante was taken to hospital, where he was kept for observation for a few days with a concussion. The Habs had two men in the penalty box at the time, and Aiken was summoned from the crowd to replace Plante. Nervous and overwhelmed, he gave up four goals in the first five minutes of play before settling down. In the third period, he allowed only one more puck to get by him, but the home team coasted to a 7-3 win. At the final bell, a number of the Habs ruffled his hair and swatted his pads in appreciation for his game effort. Just a week earlier, Aiken had led his own amateur team, the Arlington Canadiens, to the South Shore Senior League championship for the third year running.

AILSBY, Lloyd
b. Lac Pelletier, Saskatchewan, May 11, 1917
Although he played just three games with the New York Rangers in 1951-52 – December 19, 23, and 25 – Ailsby was one of the greatest defencemen the Eastern Hockey League had ever seen. He began his career playing junior with Moose Jaw, going to the Memorial Cup in 1935 where his Canucks lost to the Winnipeg Monarchs. From there he signed with

Fred Ahern

Peter Ahola

the Rovers and then journeyed around the continent until 1942 when he enlisted in the army. Ailsby later became a star in the fledgling United States Hockey League where he was named to either the First or Second All-Star Team in five out of six years, 1946-51. He could provide offence from the blueline, but when the Rangers summoned him he didn't bring his scoring stick and was soon back in the minors. Although he played many years with the New York Rovers, he also had success with the Johnstown Jets and coached both teams during the 1950s. He became full-time coach of the Rovers for the '60-'61 season, but was fired during the year and replaced by John Muckler, a 27-year-old defenceman on the team who went on to Stanley Cup success with the Edmonton Oilers in the 1980s.

AITKEN, Brad
b. Scarborough, Ontario,
October 30, 1967
Drafted 46th overall by Pittsburgh in 1986, Aitken played just 11 games with the Penguins and 3 more with the Oilers in the NHL. He split his junior career evenly between Peterborough and the Soo, and in his last year scored 27 goals as an apparent late bloomer. But when he got to the Penguins' camp in 1987, he found himself on the outside and played the year in Muskegon, with the exception of a five-game callup during which he managed to score a goal. He made a name for himself as a tough guy with the Lumberjacks but even that was not enough to get him back to the parent club. Aitken continued to play, but his next NHL appearance was to come almost four years later, and on March 5, 1991, he was traded to Edmonton for Kim Issel. The Oilers were Cup champs and used Aitken for just three games. Although the Leafs signed him in the off-season, he never made it beyond the farm club. Aitken retired in 1993.

AITKEN, Johnathan
b. Edmonton, Alberta, May 24, 1978
Here's a reverse story, if ever there was one: a Canadian who can't make it in the NHL goes to the Czech Republic to continue his career! Aitken started life as a typical good ol' boy, playing four years of junior in the WHL before the Bruins drafted him a very ambitious 8th overall in 1996. Impressed by his size and toughness – 6'4", 215 pounds, and triple-digit penalty minutes every year – they invited him to camp in 1998 before sending him to the minors for a year. He played three games with the Bruins in 1999-2000 but then packed up and headed Czech-ward for the next year, playing with Sparta Praha.

Aldcorn once scored a goal by shooting the puck between his legs with his back to the goal.
GARY ALDCORN

AITKENHEAD, Andy
b. Glasgow, Scotland, March 6, 1904
d. Portland, Oregon, 1968
A standout with the New York Rangers from 1932 to '34, Aitkenhead took over the starting job from John Ross Roach and for two full seasons was a solid and sometimes spectacular goaltender. He had played for 10 years with various minor leagues out west, most notably appearing in the Allan Cup finals in 1924 and '26 with Saskatoon, where he started as backup to George Hainsworth. When he wasn't playing, he would stand behind the net to study other goalies' play. He was famous for wearing a dirty, worn cap during all games. Aitkenhead's rookie season of 1932-33 was a Stanley Cup – winning one as he played all eight games of the playoffs for the Broadway Blueshirts en route to the championship in four games over Toronto. At 29, Aitkenhead looked to be the team's goalie of the future. After playing every game the following season, though, the team was eliminated from the playoffs quickly and he lost the starter's job the next season to Davey Kerr. Aitkenhead played just 10 games that season and spent the next 6 years in the PCHL, retiring in 1941.

AIVAZOFF, Micah
b. Powell River, British Columbia, May 4, 1969
Aivazoff's four-year junior career with the Victoria Cougars in the WHL established him as a prospect of note, and the L.A. Kings selected him 109th overall in the 1988 draft just before his final year, in which he reached the 100-point mark. Life got tougher after he attended his first NHL training camp, though, and he spent the next four years in the minors before L.A. let him go and the Red Wings signed him as a free agent. After a measly four-goal season with Detroit, Pittsburgh claimed him in the Waiver Draft and then he was claimed again by Edmonton just a few minutes later when the Penguins exposed him in the same draft. Aivazoff saw little action with the Oilers the next year and he signed with the Islanders in the off-season. He spent most of the year in the IHL and again moved, this time to the Rangers, though he never played again in the NHL. He spent much of the next five years in the "I" and also played half a season in Germany. Uniquely, he was owned by six NHL teams, played for three, but was never traded.

ALATALO, Mika
b. Oulu, Finland, May 11, 1971
Although he was drafted by Winnipeg in 1990, Alatalo did not make his NHL debut until the end of the decade in 1999-2000. He had been playing in the

Micah Aivazoff

Mika Alatalo

Finnish league all the while and for two years in Sweden, but the left winger had only a minimal impact in the NHL. He scored 17 goals in 152 career games before returning home to continue a career that was highlighted by a bronze medal for Suomi at the 1994 Olympics in Lillehammer, Norway.

ALBELIN, Tommy
b. Stockholm, Sweden, May 21, 1964

Time keeps ticking, and Albelin keeps right on playing in perfect syncopation. Fast becoming one of the NHL's most senior players, he is one of Sweden's prized treasures, not for his NHL play as much as his international participation. Albelin played five years for Djurgarden in the Swedish elite league prior to making his NHL debut in 1987 with the Quebec Nordiques, the team that had drafted him a lowly 158th overall in 1983. Since then, he has played with just three NHL teams over a 15-year period. The Nordiques traded Albelin to the Devils for a 4th-round draft choice, and it was with the Devils that he got his name on the Cup for the team's 1995 victory. He played nearly eight years in the Meadowlands before being traded to Calgary with Cale Hulse and Jocelyn Lemieux for Phil Housley and Dan Keczmer. In his nearly six years with the Flames the team played just four playoff games. In the summer of 2001, Albelin re-signed with New Jersey as a free agent. For Tre Kronor, he has played in two World Junior Championships (1983 and '84), five World Championships (1985, '86, '87, '89, and '97, winning gold in '87 and silver in '97), the 1987 and '91 Canada Cups, the 1996 World Cup, and the 1998 Olympics in Nagano.

ALBRIGHT, Clint ("The Professor")
b. Winnipeg, Manitoba, February 28, 1926
d. Winnipeg, Manitoba, December 30, 1999

After starting his career by rising through the junior ranks and making it to the NHL, Albright retired after just one year with the New York Rangers in 1948-49 to concentrate on his schooling. He had begun his junior career with a flourish, going to the Memorial Cup with the Winnipeg Monarchs in 1945 (losing to St. Mike's) and then winning the tournament the following year. But rather than join the NHL, Albright enrolled at the University of Manitoba in 1946, where he played on the school team as well as the city's senior team, the Flyers, which made two successive appearances in the Allan Cup. Only then did he join the Rangers, but after a fine season of 14 goals, the 25-year-old informed GM Frank Boucher that he was going home to Winnipeg to finish his engineering degree. Although the bespectacled Albright played one more season of semi-pro, with St. Paul in 1950-51, he became a mechanical engineer for Cominco in Trail, British Columbia, Kimberley, B.C., and Calgary, a position he held for 34 years. He was a member of the Engineering Institute of Canada and the Association of Professional Engineers of British Columbia.

ALDCORN, Gary
b. Shaunavon, Saskatchewan, March 7, 1935

Aldcorn once scored a goal by shooting the puck between his legs with his back to the goal, but his NHL career was otherwise without incident. After retiring, he moved to Winnipeg and completed his Master of Arts degree at the University of Manitoba which he had been chipping away at during summers when he was playing. He graduated with a Master's in virology, and this led to his forming a company called National Biological Labs at which he worked in association with the U of M's medical school. He later worked for Hockey Canada as the director of programming, a job he was given to improve the quality of coaching in Canada. He also founded an instructional hockey magazine called *Hockey Player.* As president of Flak Equipment Co., he designed a jacket with an air bag that hockey and football players could use to absorb hard hits, and by the mid-1990s he had turned his efforts to sculpture, designing commemorative pieces for teams and players circa his Original Six days, starting with a three-foot bronze of Gordie Howe. In 1981, Aldcorn had been rumoured to join head coach Mike Nykoluk as an assistant with the Leafs (the two had known each other since their junior days with the Marlies), but GM Punch Imlach vetoed the hiring. As a player, Aldcorn's finest year was with the Rochester Americans in the AHL, playing on a line with Rudy Migay and Billy Hicke. He played for short stretches with the Leafs before being sent to Detroit, where he played briefly on a line with Gordie Howe and Murray Oliver. He finished the '60-'61 season with the Bruins and then returned to school.

ALDRIDGE, Keith
b. Detroit, Michigan, July 20, 1973

On the verge of being called a career minor leaguer, Aldridge played college hockey at Lake Superior State for four years without being drafted. He signed as a free agent with Baltimore in the American league, and soon slipped into the dreaded "I," from where few return. The Dallas Stars signed him at training camp in 1999-2000 and used him for four games that year, but beyond that he has only seen playing time in the International league.

ALEXANDER, Clare ("The Milkman")
b. Collingwood, Ontario, June 16, 1945

He gave up his job as a milkman in Orillia to join the Leafs down the highway in Toronto, but not before winning the Allan Cup with the local Terriers. Alexander made his NHL debut at age 29 after persistent calls from scout and former junior teammate Gerry McNamara. No one was more surprised by the promotion than Alexander himself. He had played in numerous leagues previously but had been rejected by umpteen more, and in between cuts and disappointments he managed to acquire a degree from IBM. On the strength of his booming shot, he once won a scoring championship playing senior hockey with the Collingwood Shipbuilders. In Toronto, he provided solid defensive play for an up-and-coming Leafs team, though he scored a hat trick in one game. After three partial seasons in Toronto, he was traded to Vancouver. He later signed as a free agent with the WHA Oilers, then moved to Germany for a two-year term. He coached a junior team there and another in Switzerland the year after. He returned home and played on the Toronto Metro Oldtimers,

Tommy Albelin

Clint Albright

Keith Aldridge

Clare Alexander

world champion for 1983. At the same time, he ran a sporting goods store in Orillia and developed an instructional program with Pat Stapleton called Fundamentals in Action. The Leafs hired Alexander to coach their AHL affiliate in St. Catharines in 1984, but he left the organization the next year when the team wanted him to become assistant coach to Dan Maloney at Maple Leaf Gardens. The Milkman balked at uprooting his family, though he later worked on construction sites throughout the city as an installer of exterior glass windows on major building projects. Meanwhile, his daughter, Buffy, developed into a successful rower for Canada, winning a silver medal in the women's eight at the 1997 world championships, a silver in the women's coxless four a year later, consecutive bronzes in the women's eight in '98 and '99, and a bronze at the 2000 Olympics in Sydney.

ALEXANDRE, Art
b. St. Jean, Quebec, March 2, 1909
d. 1976
Alexandre's career was as short and nondescript as he was small and slight. He played his way up through Montreal city teams in 1930-31 to join les Canadiens for 11 games over 2 seasons, but he spent most of his 8-year career in the minors. A left winger, Alexandre did not score a goal in the NHL, though he did net 13 with Springfield in '35-'36. He retired in 1938.

ALEXEEV, Nikita
b. Murmansk, Soviet Union (Russia), December 27, 1981
The giant right winger (6'5" and 210 pounds) has yet to fill out, but if he develops and gets bigger, Tampa Bay may have a force in the lineup. Alexeev was drafted 8th overall in 2000 and joined the Lightning the following year after three years in Erie. In 44 games, the rookie scored 4 goals.

ALFREDSSON, Daniel ("Alfie")
b. Goteborg, Sweden, December 11, 1972
Life was not always as easy as hockey for Alfredsson in his years before joining the NHL in 1995. His mother, Margareta, suffered from multiple sclerosis, and during the summers he worked many menial jobs, from operating a forklift to selling ads for Vastra Frolunda, his team during the season. The Senators drafted him in 1994 and a year later he came to Canada's capital after signing a contract for just $250,000. He dazzled with his moves and consistent, hard play, scoring 26 goals, appearing in the All-Star Game, and winning the Calder Trophy. He had an equally impressive second season, but in his third year he suffered injuries that cost him 27 games on the year. Nonetheless, he was a training camp holdout in the fall of 1997, and when the fighting was over he had signed a new four-year contract worth $10 million. As is frequently the case, he then had his worst year, scoring just 11 goals and 33 points in another injury-shortened season. Ironically, Alfredsson was named team captain in 1999 when Alexei Yashin refused to join the Sens until his contract was renegotiated, and Alfredsson filled the breach admirably during that controversy-filled season. Although the Sens routinely made it into the playoffs during his tenure there, they seldom went very far and Alfredsson developed the

Daniel Alfredsson

George Allen

unpleasant habit of disappearing, as they say, when the Cup was on the line. He played in the All-Star Game his first three years in the league but hasn't been back since 1998. Internationally, Alfredsson had his finest moment at the 1995 World Championships when he scored an overtime goal to beat Canada 3-2. He also played at the WC the next year as well as at the two NHL Olympics in 1998 and 2002.

ALLAN, Jeff
b. Hull, Quebec, May 17, 1957
A callup for four games with the Cleveland Barons, Allan was an obscure defenceman whose pro career was fleeting. Even in junior he played for three teams – Cornwall, Peterborough, and Hull – an oddity the Barons were unconcerned with when they drafted him 95th overall in 1977. Allan's first pro year, 1977-78, was remarkable: he played for five teams in five different leagues. He dressed for the Barons, then the WHA's Cinncinati Stingers, Hampton in the AHL, Phoenix in the Central league, and Toledo in the "I." His next season, in the minors, was less hectic. He retired in 1979.

ALLEN, Bryan
b. Kingston, Ontario, August 21, 1980
Allen is a hulking 6'4", 215-pounder out of the Oshawa Generals whom Vancouver drafted an ambitious 4th overall in the 1998 Entry Draft. He has some offensive ability but is better known for his toughness and defensive play. He missed much of his last junior year recovering from a serious knee injury and spent most of 2000-01 in the minors, though he did get into his first six NHL games, with the Canucks, during the season. He's still very much a work in progress for the Canucks.

ALLEN, Chris
b. Chatham, Ontario, May 8, 1978
Allen was a junior standout on defence with Kingston in the OHL, an offensive threat who scored 38 times in his final season and played big and tough inside his own blueline. His final year of junior culminated with being named to the Canadian Major Junior First All-Star Team, and the prospects of an NHL career looked good. Allen had been drafted by the Panthers back in 1996 and played his first two NHL games on the final day of his first two years of pro – April 18, 1998 and April 17, 1999. To date, those are his only excursions to the big time. He hasn't developed as the Floridas had hoped, and his first five years of pro have all been in the minors, save those two appearances.

ALLEN, George
b. Bayfield, New Brunswick, July 27, 1914
d. Red Deer, Alberta, March 27, 2000
Brother of Viv, George Trenholme Allen was born in the Maritimes, but he was a farmer all his life. At the age of four, he moved with his family to Dodsland, Saskatchewan, and bought 1,200 acres of land in nearby Kerrobert. His father set up a business called Transport Business, and it was in this small part of the world that George learned to play hockey. He developed in the local system until he won the

Western Canadian championship and was soon signed by the Rangers, who sent him to New Haven to develop further. In 1938-39, he again played in the minors, with Philadelphia, but injuries forced the Rangers to call him up. In his first game, Allen scored two goals and an assist, one of the greatest first games in NHL history. He remained in the NHL for the next eight years. He was sold to Chicago but missed the entire '44-'45 season because War Labour Board restrictions prevented players from crossing the border. He spent the year farming, and when he returned to the big time he found himself on defence instead of left wing. A trade to Montreal saw him finish his pro career in '46-'47, and after a few years in the minors he retired. Midway through 1950-51, the Regina Caps needed a coach, and Allen signed to play and boss the team for the rest of the year. He then returned to the peace of Kerrobert, where he and his brother ran a farm equipment business. He moved to Red Deer in 1983, and died in 2000, leaving his wife of 68 years.

ALLEN, Courtney "Keith" ("Bingo")
b. Saskatoon, Saskatchewan, August 21, 1923

A perfectly pedestrian two-year career in the NHL paved the way for a lifelong involvement in the game that culminated with Allen's induction into the Hockey Hall of Fame as a Builder in 1992. After some seven seasons in the AHL, he was called up to Detroit in 1953-54 when the Red Wings had a rash of injuries, sometimes playing defence with Gordie Howe en route to the Stanley Cup. The following season, he became playing coach of the Brandon Regals in the WHL, his league of choice for the next decade. When Philadelphia was granted one of the coveted six expansion teams for 1967, Allen became the Flyers' coach and, two and a half years later, their general manager. He helped build the violent but ultimately successful Broad Street Bullies, and to this day remains with the organization as vice-president. He also helped establish the Maine Mariners in the AHL, one of the more successful teams in hockey's minor pro leagues during the 1970s. He was awarded the Lester Patrick Award for contribution to hockey in the United States. Allen began playing junior in 1940, but in 1943 he enlisted in the Canadian Navy where he was stationed aboard the corvette *Nanaimo* for more than two years.

ALLEN, Peter
b. Calgary, Alberta, March 6, 1970

When you think hockey, you don't think Yale. But at Yale, you think more than you play hockey. Allen played for the Bulldogs for four years, but only Boston expressed any pro interest in the defenceman, and

then only via the dog's breakfast that is the Supplemental Draft, in 1991. Allen's tour of hockey duty took him many places, though, ironically, never to Boston. His contract with the Bruins elapsed, and he later signed with Pittsburgh and then with San Jose, in 1997. He spent 1994-95 with Team Canada and finished that season by winning a bronze medal at the World Championships under coach Tom Renney. The next year, he played mostly in the IHL, though the Pens did call him up for eight games. More time in the minors ensued until he spent another season with the Nationals, culminating in a second appearance at the Worlds, a fourth-place finish in 2000.

ALLEN, Viv ("Squee")
b. Bayfield, New Brunswick, September 9, 1916
d. 1995

A career minor-leaguer, right winger Viv played out west with his older brother, George. Viv was called up to the New York Americans from Springfield and played on November 21 (vs. the Leafs), 23 and 24 (vs. Canadiens), 28 (vs. Rangers), and 30 (vs. the Leafs), 1940. In his sixth NHL game – December 3, 1940, against Boston – he suffered an eye injury that forced him back to the minors. He spent the next decade in small American cities playing in leagues that would never help him get promoted to the NHL, retiring in 1949. A speedy skater, Allen had shown he could score, most notably with Pittsburgh in the AHL where he had 20 goals in 1941-42, his first full year after the injury. Later, with the Dallas Texans, he led the league with 34 goals in '46-'47, but two years later he suffered a leg injury that eventually led to his retirement at age 33. He was originally nicknamed Squeaky because of his high-pitched voice, but when he moved to North Battleford, Saskatchewan to play junior hockey the moniker was shortened to Squee because there was a well-known amateur skater in the area with that name.

ALLEY, Steve
b. Anoka, Minnesota, December 29, 1953

After four years with the University of Wisconsin patrolling the left wing for the Badgers, Alley had hoped to play for the Black Hawks, the team that drafted him 141st overall in 1973. That never happened. Instead, he joined the U.S. National Team and played at the 1975 Worlds, where the U.S. finished sixth. He stayed with the team to prepare for the 1976 Olympics in Innsbruck. Although he made the team, the U.S. finished fifth, out of the medals again. He played briefly with Birmingham in the

Keith Allen

Viv Allen

Allen's tour of hockey duty took him many places, though, ironically, never to Boston.
PETER ALLEN

Dave Allison

Jamie Allison

Jason Allison

Mike Allison

Ray Allison

WHA to start the '77-'78 season but was soon back in the minors. He played at the 1978 Worlds (another sixth-place finish) and finally cracked the NHL barrier in '79-'80 when he played seven games with Hartford, scoring a goal. In all, he played just 15 games with the Whalers over 2 years and retired in 1981.

ALLISON, Dave
b. Fort Frances, Ontario, April 14, 1959
"Some people call me a failure because I haven't been in the NHL. But I don't look at myself as a failure. I've tried my very best." So spoke Allison at age 28, all but dismissing the three games he played with the Canadiens at the end of the '83-'84 season. That's three more than 99.9 percent of the population plays, but unfortunately he signed with Montreal in 1979, when the team was in the middle of winning four Stanley Cups in a row. Chances of him making that lineup were slim to none, and he spent the better part of six years with the farm team in Nova Scotia. His rights were later acquired by the Rangers and Toronto, but he played for neither team. After retiring, Allison became coach of the P.E.I. Senators, farm team to Ottawa. He became head coach for the NHL Sens for 25 games during the '95-'96 season, a disastrous stretch that saw the team post a record of 2-22-1.

ALLISON, Jamie
b. Lindsay, Ontario, May 13, 1975
The NHL has produced a number of fine musicians over the years, from Windy O'Neill to Pat Burns. But it's still too early to determine whether country guitarist Jamie Allison's name will be added to the list at some point. Allison captained his Detroit Jr. Red Wings to the Memorial Cup playoffs in his final year of junior in 1995. He had been drafted 44th overall by Calgary in '93 and made his NHL debut with the Flames on January 22, 1995, though he played most of his first three years in the minors. Early in the 1998-99 season, he was traded to Chicago with Marty McInnis and Eric Andersson for Jeff Shantz and Steve Dubinsky. He managed to work his way into the Hawks' lineup full-time after recovering from a broken wrist incurred shortly after arriving in the Windy City. Big and tough, he won't score many goals or make fancy plays, but he's admired for his honest effort, size, and physical presence inside his own blueline.

ALLISON, Jason ("Alley")
b. North York, Ontario, May 29, 1975
After an outstanding junior career with the London Knights, Allison developed quickly in the NHL into one of the finest young power forwards in the game. As captain of the Knights, he was named Canada's best junior in 1994, and in both that year and the next he led Canada to a gold medal at the World Junior Championships. Washington drafted him 17th overall in 1993, but his first three seasons were fraught with difficulty and inconsistency. Three times he impressed in training camp; three times he was demoted before Christmas. Exasperated, he demanded either more playing time or a trade. He got the latter. It was called, at the time, one of the

more lopsided trades in recent years: Allison, Anson Carter, Jim Carey and a draft choice were traded for three bona fide superstars – Bill Ranford, Adam Oates, and Rick Tocchet. Allison's play alone, however, proved Boston GM Harry Sinden got the better of the deal. Allison finished ninth overall in the scoring race in '97-'98, and the year after was almost as impressive. The following year was a write-off, as he suffered two serious wrist injuries, but in 2000-01 he recorded 95 points, fifth best in the NHL and tops on the Bruins. Of course, he then became a Group 2 free agent, and this spelled doom in an organization known for pinching its pennies. After a brief holdout, he was traded to Los Angeles. Much to his dismay, he never received an invite for Canada's 2002 Olympic team.

ALLISON, Mike ("Red"/ "Red Dog")
b. Fort Frances, Ontario, March 28, 1961
Allison was a plodder and a grinder, a checker and a mediocre skater, but he was also a team man, a determined player proud of his defensive abilities. He possessed a competitive spirit that helped keep him in the game for a decade despite suffering injuries to almost every part of his body. In his 10 years in the league, he played just 499 of a possible 800 games, each season cut short due to injuries. His finest moments came during the 1987 playoffs when, as a member of the Leafs, he played superbly against St. Louis. The following year, though, he played his way into the press box and was traded to Los Angeles. Allison was drafted and played his first six years in the NHL with the Rangers; he retired in 1990 after three years in L.A., where he had the chance to play with Wayne Gretzky. Allison's father once played for the Brandon Wheat Kings, and his brother, Dave, made the NHL as well. Mike had the distinction of scoring his first NHL goal on his first shot in his first game, October 9, 1980. Two days later, against the Leafs, he recorded his first and only career hat trick. His best scoring season turned out to be his first, when he had 26 goals and 64 points.

ALLISON, Ray
b. Cranbrook, British Columbia, March 4, 1959
As a member of the Flyers, Allison, Brian Propp, and Bill Barber set a club record for the fastest three goals, scoring in 35 seconds against Quebec on November 7, 1982. Previously, he and Propp combined with Laurie Boschman in Brandon (WHL) to register 220 goals and 276 assists as a line, a junior record. As the 18th overall selection at the 1979 Entry Draft, Allison was expected to be a franchise player with the Hartford Whalers following his great junior career, in which he scored 450 points in his final three seasons. But after a mediocre rookie season, he played himself out of Hartford's plans and less than two years later he was traded to Philadelphia in a 10-player deal that featured mostly lesser lights. Allison had a career year in '82-'83, scoring 21 goals and registering a +30, but the following year he missed nearly half the season after sliding into the goalpost in a game and breaking his ankle. He was never the same after that, and in 1987 he moved to Switzerland to try to resuscitate his career. He retired in 1990.

ALLUM, Bill

b. Winnipeg, Manitoba, October 9, 1916
d. Winnipeg, Manitoba, March 14, 1992

One of the better shotblockers of his era, and one of the finest athletes to come out of Winterpeg, Allum played hockey for more than 20 years and lacrosse for even longer. He began with the local Elmwood team and then moved up to the Winnipeg Rangers before joining the Canada Packers, a senior outfit in the city. His first pro team was the New York Rovers, and his time in the NHL consisted of a single game with the New York Rangers in 1940-41. Allum joined the Royal Canadian Naval Volunteer Reserve in 1943, where he both played and coached, and two years later returned to a career in the American league. Every summer he returned home to Winnipeg to work as a telephone line salesman. He retired as a pro in 1948 and was reinstated as an amateur, winning the Allan Cup with the Owen Sound Mercurys in 1951. He also won a Mann Cup (Canada's national lacrosse championship) with Owen Sound before returning to the 'Peg. He coached junior hockey for 14 years, most notably with the St. Boniface Canadiens, Winnipeg Braves, and Selkirk Steelers, winning the Memorial Cup with the Braves in 1959. Allum was inducted into the Owen Sound Sports Hall of Fame, the Manitoba Lacrosse Hall of Fame, and the Manitoba Hockey Hall of Fame.

ALMAS, Ralph "Red"

b. Saskatoon, Saskatchewan, April 26, 1924
d. Regina, Saskatchewan, May 13, 2001

Almas started skating on outdoor rinks as a child in and around Saskatoon, and his first team was the Kinsmen Pee Wee League. After two years, he moved up to the midget and juvenile Junior Quakers, where Detroit bird dog Fred Pinkney saw him in goal and invited him to the Red Wings' training camp for the fall of 1942. Almas made enough of an impression to be named the team's practice goalie, but his career was put on hold because of the war. After two years of duty with the Canadian Army he resumed what he expected would be a minor-league career. But wait! Before Detroit's final game of the '46-'47 season, incumbent Harry Lumley suffered an injury and Almas was called up to play on March 23, 1947, against Toronto. Although the Wings lost 5-3, Almas was named the team's number-one goalie heading into the playoffs against those same Leafs. Toronto won the series in five games. In the final game, Almas pulled a groin muscle while stopping a Garth Boesch shot. He was replaced by Johnny Mowers, and Red was back in the minors to start the next season. He got another chance in the NHL, playing for Chicago on December 6, 1950, a 5-4 loss to

Boston. Then it was back to the minors until Detroit called him up on Christmas 1952, when the Wings and Hawks played to a 3-3 tie. Although his NHL days were numbered, Almas was long considered the finest goaler in the AHL during the post-war years. After retiring in 1955, he moved to Regina with the mechanical contracting firm of Waterman Waterbury, which later became Comstock Canada.

Red Almas

AMADIO, Dave

b. Glace Bay, Nova Scotia, April 23, 1939
d. Calgary, Alberta, April 10, 1981

Son of a coalminer, Amadio was a tough, hard-hitting defenceman who played two games with Detroit in 1957-58 as an 18-year-old and then was buried in the minors for a decade. Part Native, part Scotch, he played most of that time with Springfield, and although he was better known for toughness than soft hands he once scored five goals in a game, in 1964, an AHL record for defencemen. When the L.A. Kings joined the NHL in 1967, they acquired the Indians franchise from Eddie Shore. Kings coach Red Kelly, who remembered Amadio from their playing days with the Wings, summoned him to the NHL. He played two years with the Kings but such was his lack of confidence that he left his wife back in Springfield and rented an apartment in the City of Angels with three teammates, Eddie Joyal, Brian Smith, and Bryan Campbell. Sure enough, Amadio spent 1969-74 back in the minors and in 1975 became coach of the Calgary Centennials of the Western league as his career wound down.

Allum played hockey for more than 20 years and lacrosse for even longer.
BILL ALLUM

AMBROZIAK, Peter

b. Toronto, Ontario, September 15, 1971

A dozen games with the Buffalo Sabres was the only NHL action Ambroziak ever experienced. He played four years of junior with the Ottawa 67's, and Buffalo selected him 72nd overall in the 1991 Entry Draft. The left winger played three years in the minors in Rochester before being given a chance in the fire city, recording a single assist. The Sabres didn't renew Ambroziak's contract, and his trail grew fainter and fainter as he wended his way down from the AHL to IHL to UHL and finally to a team called the New Mexico Scorpions, for whom he both played and coached, in the Western Professional league.

AMODEO, Mike

b. Toronto, Ontario, June 22, 1952

He was a rising star by the time he left the Toronto Marlies to begin a pro career, but the California Golden Seals, the NHL team that drafted him 102nd overall in 1972, couldn't catch him because he

Mike Amodeo

preferred to stay in Canada and play in the WHA. He signed with the Ottawa Nationals and was transferred to the Toronto Toros two years later. Teamed with Carl Brewer on the blueline, he developed into a fine defenceman, but during the '75-'76 season he fell out with management, which proved to be the end-game of his pro career. In February 1976, Amodeo sued the Toros after they first demoted him and then bought out his contract. He played in Sweden for most of the next two years, though returned to play the end of each WHA season with Winnipeg. In 1978-79, the pattern reversed; he played one game in Sweden and most of the year with the Jets. In '79-'80, he returned to Canada permanently to play his only NHL games with the Jets, though he didn't register a point and was a disappointing -15 in 19 games. Two years later, he was out of hockey for good, though he used his dual citizenship (his parents were Italian) to play for Italy at the 1982 Worlds (a seventh-place finish in "A" pool). After retiring, he settled in Toronto as a beer salesman.

Dale Anderson

AMONTE, Tony

b. Hingham, Massachusetts, August 2, 1970

There was but a blink between the end of Amonte's college career and the start of his pro journey. In 1991, he and Boston University lost a triple overtime game to Northern Michigan for the NCAA championships, but just two days later he signed with the Rangers. He was called up to the team on April 11, 1991, game five of the New York–Washington series, and although the team lost, Amonte recorded an assist. In the fall, he scored a goal in his first game and went on to record 35 on the year. He played the better part of two more years with the Rangers, but at the trading deadline in 1994 he and Matthew Oates were sent to Chicago for Brian Noonan and Stephane Matteau, just weeks before the New Yorkers won the Stanley Cup. In Chicago the right winger developed into one of the premier scorers in the league and eventually became team captain. In his 12 years in the NHL, Amonte scored at least 30 goals 8 times. In the summer of 2002, he became a free agent and signed a large contract with Phoenix in the hopes of finally attaining some measure of playoff success. When the success failed to materialize in 2002-03, he was traded to Philaedlphia in a cost-cutting move. Although Amonte will become one of the highest American-born scorers in the league, his crowning glory came at the 1996 World Cup when he scored the game-winning goal in game three against Canada. He had also played at the WJC and WC for the U.S., as well as at the 1998 Olympics in Nagano and the 2002 Olympics in Salt Lake City, winning a silver medal in the latter.

His crowning glory came at the 1996 World Cup when he scored the game-winning goal in game three against Canada.
TONY AMONTE

ANDERSON, Bill ("Red")

b. Tillsonburg, Ontario, December 13, 1912
d. unknown

Some men get only the briefest glimpses of life in the NHL. Anderson started in the IHL and played in a series of leagues thereafter until the Boston Olympics signed him in 1942. The 1943 semifinals were going swimmingly for the Boston Bruins. They had defeated Montreal in each of the first three games of the best-of-seven and were in control. Coach Art Ross decided to dress rookie Bill Anderson for the game, but the team lost 4-0. Red was scratched for the next game, a 5-4 Bruins victory in overtime to win the series, and Anderson never played pro hockey again.

ANDERSON, Dale

b. Regina, Saskatchewan, March 5, 1932

A prairie boy by birth, Anderson played junior hockey out west before heading to the Soo in the Northern Ontario league in 1954. He became only the second player, after Larry Regan, to be promoted from that league to the NHL, in '56-'57, a move necessitated when regular Detroit defenceman Al Arbour was injured and Bucky Hollingworth was demoted. When Arbour got healthy, Gord Strate was demoted and Anderson stayed on as fifth defenceman, a promising show of confidence by coach Jimmy Skinner. However, the team went on a terrific losing streak and Anderson's playing time diminished. He hung around long enough to play twice in the '57 playoffs, but although he played another 500 pro games, not one more took place in the NHL. He played with Eddie Shore in Springfield for a few years, then headed back west, retiring in 1968 after a stint with the local Saskatoon Quakers.

ANDERSON, Doug ("Andy")

b. Edmonton, Alberta, October 20, 1927

His only two NHL games came in the 1953 playoffs for the Canadiens, and although neither took place in the finals, his name is on the Stanley Cup! Anderson's first outing came on March 26, 1953, a 4-3 victory over Chicago in a semifinals won by the Habs in seven games. He had been called up as a precautionary measure after an excellent year with Victoria in the WHL, but after his brief stint with Montreal he played almost 700 more games outside the NHL. He started his career in Edmonton, making it to the Memorial Cup in 1945-46, and won the Allan Cup with the Edmonton Flyers two years later.

Doug Anderson

ANDERSON, Earl

b. Rosseau, Minnesota, February 24, 1951

A fan favourite at the Boston Garden and one of coach Don Cherry's chosen, Anderson enjoyed a haltingly positive career until injuries got the better of him. He was drafted by Detroit in 1971 while at the University of North Dakota, and after graduating in 1973 he represented the U.S. at the Worlds (the country was in "B" pool at the time). From there, he joined the London Lions, Detroit's farm team that played in a European league out of Wembley Arena. Anderson played the first part of '74-'75 with the Red Wings but after an unimpressive start was sent to Boston with Hank Nowak for Walt McKechnie and a draft choice. The following season was almost a write-off for him. After five games, the pain from calcium deposits in his left thigh was too great and he missed the rest of the season. After an operation and extensive rehab, he returned to the Bruins for '76-'77, though he spent half this season and all of the next in the minors before retiring.

ANDERSON, Glenn ("Mork"/ "The Spaceman"/ "Andy")

b. Vancouver, British Columbia, October 2, 1960

When he retired in 1997, Anderson had five playoff overtime goals to his credit. Only Maurice Richard, with six, had more. This statistic tells the story of Anderson's success, a player who won six Stanley Cups during a Hall of Fame career, yet who also retired with 498 career regular-seasons goals, achingly close to the magic 500 that would have put him in the elite class of scorers. His career began unhappily, as a kid who hated early morning practices and gave up the game for years. When he decided to try again, at age 12, he did so with greater passion, and by the time he was in his teens, he was showing NHL-bound skills. He played a single year of college hockey, with U of Denver in '78-'79, but his desires were more international than professional. He wanted to play in the Olympics for Canada, travel and see the world, and then think about the rigours of an 80-game schedule. In '79-'80, he played with the National Team, including at the Olympics in Lake Placid, and a year later joined Edmonton, the team that had drafted him in 1979. Thus began a remarkable career fraught with pitfalls. In his first 8 seasons, he scored 30 goals each time. He had three 100-point seasons and played in 4 All-Star Games that the mighty Oilers dominated. Anderson, a left-hand shot, played the right wing, like Richard, and this gave him a better angle for cutting in on goal. And cut in he did. He showed no fear in skating hell-bent toward the goalie, with or without the puck, and he became infamous for his dirty, often vicious use of his stick. He was

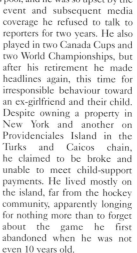

When he retired, Anderson had five playoff overtime goals to his credit.
GLENN ANDERSON

suspended numerous times for high-sticking infractions, but his reputation gave him more room than he might have had as a cleaner player. Anderson spent his first 11 seasons with the Oilers, but when he was traded to the Leafs in a major deal in 1991 it began a period of movement that persisted the rest of his career. He played not only for other NHL teams but a number of clubs in Europe, his desire to combine culture and hockey again taking control. Off the ice, he marched to the beat of a different drummer. Mork was a diminutive he hated, yet one apt because he was quirky, independent, and alien, in some ways, even to his teammates. He was particularly distraught at a Stanley Cup party in his own backyard in 1988. A good friend, George Varvis, died in hospital a few days after nearly drowning in Anderson's pool, and he was so upset by the event and subsequent media coverage he refused to talk to reporters for two years. He also played in two Canada Cups and two World Championships, but after his retirement he made headlines again, this time for irresponsible behaviour toward an ex-girlfriend and their child. Despite owning a property in New York and another on Providenciales Island in the Turks and Caicos chain, he claimed to be broke and unable to meet child-support payments. He lived mostly on the island, far from the hockey community, apparently longing for nothing more than to forget about the game he first abandoned when he was not even 10 years old.

Earl Anderson

ANDERSON, Jim ("Andy")

b. Pembroke, Ontario, December 1, 1930

So lifelong was his membership in the AHL that the hopes of Anderson ever playing in the NHL had long evaporated. Fifteen years he played in the minors before the godsend that was expansion in 1967 took him to the Los Angeles Kings at age 37. In all, he played 16 years with Eddie Shore's Springfield Indians, longer in years than most players survive in days. He was rookie of the year in 1954-55 and led the AHL in scoring on two occasions, 1960-61 with 43 goals, and 1963-64 with 40. The left winger played just seven games in the NHL, scoring a lone goal against future Hall of Famer Ed Giacomin before returning to the Indians. Each summer he worked in Springfield as a machinist, but after retiring he coached the Indians for a season and then became a scout for the Kings in 1969-70. He coached both Oklahoma City and Dayton and then served as scout for the Bruins until 1974, when the Washington Capitals hired him as their head coach on May 31, 1974. That gig lasted but 54 games, and Anderson's record of 4-45-5 remains one of the worst in league history.

ANDERSON, John ("Andy")

b. Toronto, Ontario, March 28, 1957

When he was three years old, John Anderson asked his grandmother to play goal so he could take shots on her. A little later, his father carried him around the East York Ice Arena after winning the city championships. At 16, he was playing with the Toronto Marlies, and two years later he was the team captain. Life was simple, life was sweet. Then, on the day he turned 18, he became a central part of the legal brouhaha that was the OHA's standard player's contract. With the arrival of the WHA in 1972 as a new professional league, teenagers could now sign a pro contract at age 18, even though the NHL didn't draft players (i.e., let them play) until 20. Anderson "retired" from the OHA rather than risk continuing his amateur career under the OHA's contract, which bound a player to that amateur team until age 20. However, he didn't receive an offer from the WHA, so returned to the Marlies and led them to the Memorial Cup. Drafted 11th overall by his dream-team Leafs, he matured slowly. By his third year he was a star on the new Kid Line featuring Laurie Boschman and Rockey Saganiuk, though the next year, 1980-81, he called them the Skid Line due to their poor season. One of the more popular Leafs of the 1970s, Anderson opened a chain of burger joints called, simply, John Anderson Burgers, one of which still operates in Toronto. Later in his Leafs career he played with Bill Derlago and Rick Vaive, again the team's top line, but after four consecutive 30-goal seasons he felt it was time to move on. He was traded to Quebec and then Hartford and spent the last five years of his career in the minors, the last two as playing assistant coach for the San Diego Gulls. In 1994, he quit coaching and worked for Mica Sportswear based in Bracebridge, Ontario, but the following year he returned to hockey as head coach of Winston-Salem in the Southern Hockey League. In 1996, he led the Quad City Mallards of the Colonial League to a championship and later coached the Chicago Wolves in the IHL for six years and counting, hoping for a shot as an NHL assistant.

ANDERSON, Lorne

b. Renfrew, Ontario, July 26, 1931
d. Renfrew, Ontario, March 20, 1984

His NHL career lasted three games at the end of a miserable season for a New York Rangers team that finished fifth out of six teams in 1951-52. Their brilliant goaler, Charlie Rayner, was lost midway through the year with a serious knee injury and was replaced by the diminutive Emile "the Cat" Francis.

For the final three games of the season – meaningless since the team had long been eliminated form the playoffs – Anderson had been given the starting job in the cage. He gave up four goals, then seven, and seven again on March 19, 20, and 23, numbers not likely to inspire an invitation to the following year's training camp. Gump Worsley was the goalie of the future for the Blueshirts, and Anderson was never heard of again in NHL circles, retiring with a round goals-against average of exactly 6.00. His career, though, was not done. He had been a northern Ontario boy all his life, playing with Renfrew and his hometown Pembroke, and in '52-'53 he starred for Sudbury, taking the Wolves to the Allan Cup the next spring. From there he moved around from one spot to the next before hanging up the pads for good in 1961.

ANDERSON, Murray

b. The Pas, Manitoba, August 28, 1949

A top prospect out of the Western league, Anderson was drafted 44th overall by Montreal in 1969 during his junior career with the Flin Flon Bombers. He failed to impress at training camp in 1971 and spent the next four years in the minors. Minnesota bought Anderson in 1973, but it wasn't until the lowly Washington Capitals ankle-skated into the league that he was given a chance to play in the NHL after the Caps claimed him in the Expansion Draft of '74. That first season, he was -40 in 40 games, not a good statistic for a defensive defenceman. He went back to the minors before retiring early in the '76-'77 season.

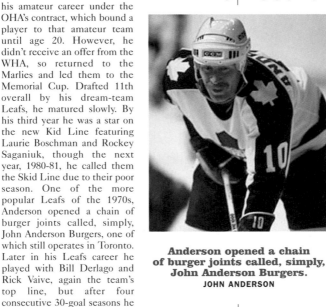

Anderson opened a chain of burger joints called, simply, John Anderson Burgers.
JOHN ANDERSON

ANDERSON, Perry ("Wheels")

b. Barrie, Ontario, October 14, 1961

Anderson was a superb ballplayer who had a tryout with the Toronto Blue Jays when he was 16. But like a good old Canadian, he decided to pursue a career on ice instead. To that end, he played for Kingston in the OHL and was drafted by St. Louis before his final season, 1980-81. Over the next four years, he slowly worked himself into the Blues' lineup, and his charitable work made him made him one of that city's most popular athletes. No sooner had he played his first full season, 1984-85, than he was traded to New Jersey for Rick Meagher and a draft choice. He spent the next five years with the Devils, a team that struggled to make the playoffs at that time. Anderson had outlived his usefulness to the team by 1989 and, after almost two years in the minors, he signed as a free agent with San Jose. After 48 games in the Shark Tank and some time in the minors, he retired. Anderson had exceptional speed (ergo his nickname) and was the consummate team player on ice and off.

Murray Anderson

Perry Anderson

ANDERSON, Ron ("Goings")

b. Red Deer, Alberta, July 29, 1945

Some players' greatest moments come in junior hockey, and then it's downhill from there. Case in point: Ron Anderson. During his four years with the Edmonton Oil Kings in the early 1960s, he went to the Memorial Cup each year, winning in his rookie season of 1963 and his graduating year of '66. But after a year of minor pro, he couldn't crack the Detroit lineup and the Wings traded him to Los Angeles after a total of just 25 games. He played much of '68-'69 with the Kings, but L.A. left him exposed in the Intra-League Draft and St. Louis grabbed the right winger. Same story with the Blues: After a year, he was traded to Buffalo, where he had his best season, scoring 14 goals in '70-'71. Anderson jumped to the WHA for two seasons and retired in 1977.

ANDERSON, Ron

b. Moncton, New Brunswick, January 21, 1950

His house league career is a who's who of championship teams, from Kinsmen Minor Hockey to the Moncton Junior Alpine Seals to the Keefe Cubs. Ever since he started skating on the frozen ponds around Moncton, Ron could go-go-go. In 1969, he ventured to Boston University to study and play when nary a scout darkened the arena of any American college. Sure enough, Anderson was never drafted. Nevertheless, his scoring abilities were noted by the Boston Bruins, who signed him as a free agent. He won rookie of the year honours with the Boston Braves of the AHL after scoring 41 goals, and he joined the Bruins for an exhibition game at the new Moncton Coliseum against Montreal before a crowd of 9,000. That night, the local hero received a bigger ovation than Bobby Orr. Anderson never played in the NHL for Boston, though, as Washington claimed him in the 1974 Expansion Draft. Just 28 games into his NHL career he tore knee ligaments and was gone for the year and from the NHL for good. In 1976, he moved to Vienna, Austria, to play until returning to Boston to work in a catering management business. He then joined Merrimack College as an assistant varsity and head junior coach, a position he held for 20 years. He was named NCAA coach of the year in 1996-97 and was inducted into the Moncton Hall of Fame in 1992.

ANDERSON, Russ ("The Enforcer")

b. Minneapolis, Minnesota, February 12, 1955

He was a battler and a fighter, a pugnacious and volatile player who married Miss America 1976, Dorothy Benman, and was named captain of the Hartford Whalers when a guy by the name of Dave Keon retired. While at the University of Minnesota, Anderson played on the football team – as a linebacker – while helping the hockey team to an NCAA championship in 1976. His coach there was Herb Brooks, and his defence partner was Reed Larson. When he got to Pittsburgh in the NHL, he was teamed on the blueline with Ron Stackhouse. During his first season, Anderson dislocated both shoulders and needed a double operation at season's end. During another season, he broke the same finger three times as a result of various fights. In one game – January 19, 1980 – he was assessed a total of 9 penalties and 51 minutes.

ANDERSON, Shawn

b. Montreal, Quebec, February 7, 1968

A defenceman with good puck-handling skills, Anderson was recruited by coach Shawn Walsh for his University of Maine Black Bears for 1985-86. Halfway through that season, Anderson left to join the Canadian National Team to play in the Spengler Cup over Christmas. He made the Buffalo Sabres the next fall as an 18-year-old under coach Scotty Bowman, but in his eight years in the league he never played a full season without demotion. The Sabres sent him to Washington after four and a half years, trading him on September 30, 1990. The very next day, the Caps exposed him in the Waiver Draft, and he was claimed by Quebec. Quebec traded him to Winnipeg on October 22, 1991, and the very next day he was sent back to Washington for future considerations. He has continued to play in recent years in Europe.

ANDERSON, Tom ("Cowboy")

b. Edinburgh, Scotland, July 9, 1910
d. Sylvan Lake, Alberta, September 15, 1971

Born in Scotland but raised in Calgary, Anderson had hockey in his blood and fire in his eyes during a career that carried him from the ice to the bench. He played in the NHL for the Red Wings and the New York Americans, winning the Hart Trophy in 1941-42 with the Amerks and in so doing becoming the first man to win the coveted trophy while playing for a last-place team. After three years with the Canadian Infantry Corps, Lieutenant Anderson finished his career with the Hollywood Wolves, where one of his teammates was Bill Barilko. In 1947, he hung up his sweater and immediately became coach of the Oshawa Generals. After three successful seasons, he became bench boss of the Pittsburgh Hornets, the prime minor-league affiliate for the Maple Leafs. Anderson had some offensive ability but usually played for a team that didn't go too far in the playoffs. Typical of his bad luck was his playing for the Wings in 1934-35, as the team went on to win the Cup the next two seasons. After Detroit sold him to the Americans, he recorded 4 seasons of at least 10 goals, but after the war that team was history and he couldn't find NHL work elsewhere. He became a coach with Calgary in the Pacific Coast league and later settled in Drumheller, Alberta, where he went into the plumbing business.

ANDERSSON, Erik

b. Stockholm, Sweden, August 19, 1971

One of a growing number of Europeans coming to train for the NHL via an American university, Andersson starred as a teen in Sweden and was drafted by Los Angeles in 1990. Over the next two years, the Kings could not get his signature on a contract and he became draft eligible in 1992. Problem was, no one wanted him by then. Andersson moved to Colorado and enrolled at the University of Denver, where he had four successful years. It wasn't until after he graduated, in 1997 at age 26, that he was re-drafted, 70th overall by Calgary. Almost no other player in draft history has such a gap between first and second time being selected. Andersson played but seven games with the Flames, scoring twice, but spent most of the next three years in the minors. He was traded to Chicago but never played

Ron "Goings"
Anderson

Ron Anderson
(b. 1950)

Russ Anderson

Shawn Anderson

Tom Anderson

**Kent-Erik
Andersson**

for the team, and with his star fading he returned to Sweden to continue his career.

ANDERSSON, Jonas
b. Stockholm, Sweden, February 24, 1981
After being drafted by Nashville in 1999, Andersson entered the OHL to learn the North American game, but has since played all his years in Milwaukee with the exception of five games with the Predators.

ANDERSSON, Kent-Erik
b. Orebro, Sweden, May 24, 1951
One of the few players to be traded twice in the same day, Andersson went from Hartford to Minnesota to the Rangers within hours on October 1, 1982. He had played six seasons for Farjestad in his native Sweden before joining the North Stars in 1977, and when he finally settled in with the Rangers he accounted for 48 points in two seasons. Andersson was a solid skater with excellent defensive commitment. He also played for Tre Kronor more than 50 times internationally, most notably in the 1981 Canada Cup. He won a silver medal at the '77 Worlds, though the following year the team finished a disappointing fourth. Andersson's best year in the NHL was '80-'81 when he had 17 goals and 41 points, but after '83-'84 he returned home to play his final two seasons of pro.

Niklas Andersson

ANDERSSON, Mikael
b. Malmo, Sweden, May 10, 1966
In an NHL career that spanned 16 seasons and 761 games, Andersson also managed to accomplish an enormous amount in minor and international hockey. Although he was but a part-time member of the Buffalo Sabres from 1985 to '89, he also won two Calder Cups in the AHL, one with the Rochester Americans, the other with Springfield. He also wore the blue and yellow sweater of Tre Kronor on numerous occasions, including three times at the World Juniors, a rare feat. He played in three World Championships (winning gold in 1992), the '91 Canada Cup, '96 World Cup, and '98 Olympics in Nagano. During the lockout-shortened '94-'95 season, he returned home to play a few games with Vastra Frolunda in the Swedish league. The number-one ranked European player in 1985, Andersson's entrance into the NHL was delayed after he damaged some tendons in his heel while playing touch football with his Sabres teammates that fall, forcing him back to the minors. For 2000-01, he moved back to Sweden to close out his career in Vastra Frolunda and captained the team to its first national championship in 38 years.

Peter Andersson

ANDERSSON, Niklas
b. Kungalv, Sweden, May 20, 1971
Younger brother of Mikael, Niklas also played with Vastra Frolunda before seeing any action in the NHL. He, too, played three successive years at the World Juniors, winning a silver in 1989. Andersson was drafted by Quebec 68th overall in 1989, and his first game came on January 5, 1993, after he finally agreed to leave Sweden to try the NHL. Two nights later, he registered his first point, an assist on an Owen Nolan goal. After that, though, he struggled to find a place on the team and the Nordiques let him go after almost two seasons in the minors. He signed with the

Steve Andrascik

Islanders, but again was let go after two years. He was later owned by San Jose, Toronto, the Islanders again, and Nashville, though he only played on Long Island. In 2000-01 Calgary signed him as a free agent and dressed him for 11 games.

ANDERSSON, Peter
b. Stockholm, Sweden, March 2, 1962
Andersson was a low draft choice (173rd overall by Washington in 1980) whose most starry moments came in international play. He played in the World Juniors twice (gold in 1981, fifth place in '82), the World Championships six times (including a gold in 1987 and '91 and a silver in '90), three Canada Cups, and two Olympics (bronze in '88). Washington had trouble convincing him to leave the comfort of home for the rigours of the NHL, but Andersson's English was excellent and the Caps already had a Swede on the team – Bengt Gustafsson – with whom he could talk. Besides, after such a distinguished career in his own country, he wanted the challenge of playing in the world's most demanding league, so over he came in '83 to try his luck. As it turned out, his time in the NHL was short. He played most of three seasons in Washington and then was traded to Quebec. But at the end of the '85-'86 season, he returned home to finish his career, retiring in 1995.

ANDERSSON, Peter
b. Orebro, Sweden, August 29, 1965
This Peter Andersson is Sweden's all-time leading scorer in World Junior Championship history. In his 56 international appearances, he has led his country to a silver medal at the 1993 World Championships in Germany and a silver at the '92 Olympics in Albertville. Although he was drafted 75th overall by the Rangers in 1983, it wasn't until nine years later that he played in the NHL. He played just 39 games over 2 years on Broadway before a trade to Florida gave him 9 more NHL starts. During this time, he also won a silver and bronze at the 1993 and '94 Worlds and returned to Europe to continue his career.

ANDRASCIK, Steve
b. Sherridon, Manitoba, November 6, 1948
He made a name for himself as an enforcer but played only once in the NHL, the playoff game of April 20, 1972, in which his Rangers beat Chicago 3-2. He had been drafted by Detroit after scoring 30 goals with Flin Flon, but the Wings traded him to Broadway for Don Luce before he got a chance to wear the Winged Wheel. His rights were later owned by Pittsburgh, but Andrascik chose the WHA for a brief time before retiring in 1978.

ANDREA, Paul ("Jigger"/"Squid")
b. North Sydney, Nova Scotia, July 31, 1941
One of only a handful of Nova Scotians to make it to the NHL, Andrea played four mostly part-time seasons in the big show and many more in the minors. However, his achievements were enough to earn him induction into the Cape Breton Sports Hall of Fame in 1987, in large measure because he survived 15 years of professional hockey. Andrea moved to Guelph to play junior hockey starting in 1958. He became Rangers

property and was called up for four games during the '65-'66 season. He proved to be an outstanding scorer in the CPHL and later played with Pittsburgh, California, and Buffalo at a time when expansion flooded the NHL with former minor-leaguers. Andrea played briefly in the WHA before finishing his career down east, retiring in 1975.

ANDREWS, Loyd ("Shrimp"/ "Andy")
b. Bromley Township, Ontario, December 26, 1900
d. unknown

The brief career of Loyd (with the funny spelling) Andrews was halted even before he could get going after he enlisted in the First World War while still a teenager. He returned to play senior hockey until the Toronto St. Pats signed him on January 23, 1922. Almost immediately he helped his NHL team win the Stanley Cup. He scored the game-winning goal in the St. Pats' 6-0 win over the Vancouver Millionaires in game four of the best-of-five finals in what was to be his only trip to the playoffs. Andrews then played minor pro for a number of years before retiring in 1934.

ANDREYCHUK, Dave ("The Shovel"/ "The Scoop"/ "Chucky")
b. Hamilton, Ontario, September 29, 1963

He's not the fastest player in the league, not the deftest stickhandler or most skilled or toughest, but inside 10 feet from the net, he might well be one of the greatest players of all time. He has a long reach and tremendous shot, a quick release and can absorb hits, and still get a shot away. Andreychuk has scored more than 600 goals and 1,200 points in more than 1,400 games played, and yet has never come close to winning the Stanley Cup and, amazingly, has played only ⸝2 international tournaments, the 1983 WJC and the 1986 Worlds. Andreychuk began as a rookie in '82-'83 with Buffalo, playing the last half of the season that began in junior with Oshawa. In '83-'84, his first full year, he scored 38 goals, his first of 15 consecutive 20-goal seasons. He was most effective on the power play, peaking in '92-'93 with 32 goals with the man advantage in a year in which he went from the Sabres to Toronto. (He was only the fourth player to score 30 or more on the power play.) That year, he also became part of a small group of players to score 50 goals in a season in which they were traded. He finished that year with 54, and the year after had 53, but soon finances dictated a trade to New Jersey. Since then, Andreychuk has bounced from team to team, an aging player teams look to for short term help. He never made an All-Star Team and has played in just two All-Star Games (1990 and '94) which poses a tricky question for the

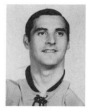

Paul Andrea

Hockey Hall of Fame when he retires. Andreychuk has Hall of Fame "numbers," but will he be regarded in perpetuity as a Hall of Fame player? Time will tell. On November 15, 2002, he scored his 250th career power-play goal, surpassing Phil Esposito as the all-time leader in that statistic.

ANDRIJEVSKI, Alexander
b. Moscow, Soviet Union (Belarus), August 10, 1968

A gangly, awkward giant of a player, Andrijevski struck out from Moscow, stick and bag slung over his shoulder, in the hopes of making it big in the NHL. This despite being drafted an unpromising 220th overall by Chicago in 1991. Unfortunately, he became a one-game wonder rather than a North American star. He played once for the Hawks in '92-'93, spending most of the next two years in the minors. In the post-perestroika age, though, he opted for Europe –Finland, Germany, and Italy, to be precise. In the off-hours, he enjoyed a successful international career playing for his new country, Belarus. Andrijevski played at the 1995 World Championships, helping Belarus win the tournament and gain promotion to "B" pool the following year, where he won a bronze medal. The year after, he won another gold that earned the nation a stunning promotion to "A" pool, and in 1998 the Belarussians finished a respectable eighth in their first year with hockey's elite. Additionally, Belarus placed a surprising fifth at the 1998 Olympics in Nagano, and Andrejevski holds the distinction of being one of a select few to play in "A," "B," and "C" pool at the Worlds.

On November 15, 2002, he scored his 250th career power-play goal.
DAVE ANDREYCHUK

ANDRUFF, Ron
b. Port Alberni, British Columbia, July 10, 1953

A career that started with promise and flourish ended with acrimony and disappointment. Montreal drafted him just as the team was readying itself to establish a new dynasty, and he was called up from the minors in both 1974-75 and '75-'76 to strut his stuff. In that second season, he won the AHL's scoring championship, and his stock was on the rise. Then the floor fell out from under him – he was traded to Colorado, the worst team in the league. Andruff figured, at the very least, he'd get plenty of ice time. Wrong. Coach Johnny Wilson never took a shine to him, and Andruff scored just 4 goals in 66 games. Midway through the next year, Wilson was fired, but Andruff didn't score any more as a result of the change. The next year, he was demoted and wound up in Germany the year after, his career on the downslope.

Ron Andruff

Greg Andrusak

Darrel Anholt

Bert Anslow

Mike Antonovich

ANDRUSAK, Greg

b. Cranbrook, British Columbia, November 14, 1969

To adapt Rodney Dangerfield's joke to hockey, one might say that if you look "journeyman" up in the dictionary, you'll see a picture of Greg Andrusak. But his career didn't start out that way. He played college hockey, at University of Minnesota-Duluth, and was drafted by Pittsburgh in 1988. He spent some time developing, with the Canadian National team and in minor pro, but he never stuck with a team. Pittsburgh called him up on four separate occasions during a six-year period for stints of three games, seven, two, and seven more. In between he played in the IHL and in Germany with a variety of teams. Once, in the Colonial league, his opponents were drunk: "There were guys throwing up over the boards… That was pretty well the lowest point of my career." His best shot came in the 1999 playoffs when he played in 12 games, including against Toronto. The Leafs liked his performance so much they signed him in the off-season, though he wore the blue and white for just nine games. Since then, it's been more of the IHL, though he did win a bronze medal with Canada at the 1995 World Championships.

ANGOTTI, Lou

b. Toronto, Ontario, January 16, 1938

It was with Chicago on March 12, 1966, that Angotti took his small place in hockey history. In a game against the Rangers, he stole the puck from Reggie Fleming and kicked it ahead to Bobby Hull before heading off on a line change. Hull took the puck, circled back into his own end as if winding himself up, then made a rink-long dash to score his 51st goal of the season, a new NHL record. Angotti, who earned the valued assist, watched the goal from the bench! Traded five times and claimed by teams on two other occasions during a decade in the NHL, Angotti was twice owned by the Blues before eventually playing for them in his final year, 1973-74. In one five-day span in June 1969 he was the property of Chicago, Philadelphia, St. Louis, and Pittsburgh. He didn't make his NHL debut, with the Rangers, until 1964 at age 26. It was during his second go-round with Chicago, in the early 1970s, that he had his greatest success. A fan favourite for his hustle and energy, he remained with the team for four years and two trips to the Stanley Cup finals. After a season with the Blues, he was hired to coach the team, but after just 32 games over 2 years he was let go. Intent on resuming his playing career, he joined the Chicago Cougars in the WHA for the rest of the season. Angotti returned to Chicago as a colour commentator for TV, started a car leasing business, and ran the Central Junior Hockey League of Illinois. He later coached in the AHL, with Erie and Baltimore, before moving up to coach the Pittsburgh Penguins. After one dismal year, he was fired. Angotti moved to Florida where he opened a bar called Pickles, in Pompano Beach. He is the cousin of Jim Pappin.

ANHOLT, Darrel

b. Hardisty, Alberta, November 23, 1962

A Rustler, a Wrangler, an Indian, a Black Hawk, and an Admiral, Anholt certainly came from the west and played a fair while out that way, too. Chicago drafted him in 1981, but he played just once in the NHL, in '83-'84, before retiring the next year.

Angotti opened a bar called Pickles, in Pompano Beach.
LOU ANGOTTI

ANSLOW, Bert ("Hub")

b. Pembroke, Ontario, March 23, 1926

Hub was talented, and Hub threw it all away. He played some good hockey in Pembroke, but at age 18 joined the navy and was out at sea for 10 months. When he returned, he had the opportunity to play with the New York Rovers, and he and Larry Kwong were called up to the Rangers for the final game of the '47-'48 season. Problem was, Bert liked his drink, and the drink liked him right back. He couldn't stay in decent shape, and so drifted around minor pro, far removed from the challenge and rigours of the NHL. He retired in 1960 and worked for Atomic Energy in Chalk River. His battles with alcohol continued, his marriage failed, and his bank account dried up, until he eventually returned to Pembroke and straightened himself out. He was lucky to find employment with the Board of Education in Ottawa as a bus driver, a job he held for a dozen years before he retired.

ANTONOVICH, Mike

b. Calumet, Minnesota, October 18, 1951

Antonovich had a peculiar and almost constant connection to his home state throughout his playing career. He spent three years at U of Minn, 1969-72, playing under coach Glen Sonmor and assistant Herb Brooks (both future coaches of the North Stars) and then bounced between the Stars of the NHL and the Fighting Saints of the WHA. Although he was drafted by the North Stars in 1971, it was the Fighting Saints he opted to play for after leaving university. He stayed four years until the team folded in March 1976, at which time he signed with the NHL Stars and played a dozen games before representing the U.S. at the '76 World Championships. The following season, the WHA franchise returned, and Antonovich immediately followed suit. His last WHA year came with the New

England Whalers in 1978-79, when he played on a dream line featuring Dave Keon and John McKenzie. At 5'6", he was the shortest player in the league, but he was also one of the scrappiest. He returned to play three more years with the Stars and after retiring became an assistant coach in the IHL before moving up to the St. Louis Blues in 1997 as a scout.

ANTOSKI, Shawn ("Moose"/ "Anton"/ "Room Service")

b. Brantford, Ontario, March 25, 1970

The prototypical tough guy in hockey, Antoski is anything but the feared villain away from the rink. He runs a summer camp in Sterling, Ontario for ailing children, organizes a golf tournament with former NHLer Rick Meagher, and has a hand in numerous other charitable causes. Antoski didn't start playing hockey until he was 12, living in Toronto and managing a paper route of his own. He made his way up through the ranks, but at every step it was his fighting talents that helped him the most. In North Bay, in junior, he averaged nearly 200 penalty minutes a year, and as a result Vancouver drafted him in 1990. For the next three years he fought his way to recognition in the minors, and by 1993 Antoski had made the Canucks as a regular. Early the next season, though, he was dealt to Philadelphia, and within two years he had added Pittsburgh and Anaheim to his NHL resumé. Antoski missed much of '96-'97 recovering from hernia surgery, but his career came to an end just nine games into the following season when he was involved in a serious car accident on November 24, 1997.

ANTROPOV, Nikolai "Nik"

b. Vost, Soviet Union (Kazakhstan), February 18, 1980

It's a long way from the streets of Ust Kamenogorsk to the Air Canada Centre in Toronto, and the brief success story that is Antropov is as improbable as almost any other in the game. His mother died of kidney disease when he was six; his father worked in a local factory and steered his son to sticks and skates as a means of escape. Still, it was only because of Leafs scouts Anders Hedberg and executive Mike Smith that Antropov was drafted 10th overall in the 1998 Entry Draft. The first time anyone in North America saw the teen play was at the 1999 World Junior Championships held in Winnipeg. The Kazakhs finished sixth that year, and the slight, rangy Antropov had eight points in six games. An awkward skater, he obviously possessed the puck

skills to play the game at a high level. He made his way to North America in the fall of '99 and made the Leafs team almost immediately. As a rookie he showed patience with the puck, and had an assist in his first game, October 13, 1999. On December 20, he became the first Leafs rookie in a decade to register a hat trick. But then he suffered a knee injury and his game fell to pieces. The 2000-01 was tentative at best for him; he lay prone on the ice in almost every game and finished the year with just six goals. Early in 2001-02, coach Pat Quinn sent him to the minors, to try to regain his rookie-season form, which he did the following season.

APPS, Syl ("Slippery Syl"/ "The Commish")

b. Paris, Ontario, January 18, 1915
d. Kingston, Ontario, December 24, 1998

It is impossible to point to an athlete who was a finer man, a hockey player who contributed more to society off the ice, a star who was as humble as he was generous. And, it is impossible to believe that there is some Being who looks out for us all when you see this extraordinary man spend his final years confined to a chair, unable to communicate except through the crude use of a letter board. Syl Apps defined hockey. He defined success and competitive and gentleman. As a youth, he was an outstanding football player, and while watching him play the pigskin game at McMaster University Leafs owner Conn Smythe signed him to a contract, never having seen Apps even skate! Apps refused to join the Leafs until after the 1936 Summer Olympics, in which he competed in the pole vault, finishing sixth, by which time he had also finished his degree in political economics. He had been British Empire champion with a jump of 12'6" in the days when one used a bamboo pole and landed in a pit of sand. Apps joined the Leafs that fall and began a 10-year career with the team that was interrupted by a stint in the army. He won the Calder Trophy for his outstanding rookie season, establishing himself as a centre with remarkable puck instincts and great determination inside the offensive blueline. Players made fun of his sporting conduct on ice, though, and in his second season he made clear that fighting wasn't his preference but he would not be taken for a patsy. Flash Hollett high-sticked Apps, removing two teeth, and Apps promptly beat the speedy defenceman to a pulp. No one bothered Apps again. He played mostly on a line with Gord Drillon and Bob Davidson, and in his first six seasons led the team to the Cup finals three

Apps refused to join the Leafs until after the 1936 Summer Olympics, in which he competed in the pole vault.
SYL APPS

Shawn Antoski

Nik Antropov

times. In the last of these, 1942, he won the sacred trophy with a bravura performance, a year in which he did not incur a single penalty and won the Lady Byng Trophy. Apps never swore, never drank, and when incited uttered expressions such as "by hum" to express his greatest anger. He became team captain in 1940 when Red Horner retired, and midway through the '42-'43 season the most incredible turn of events made him a hero in Smythe's eyes. Apps broke his leg during a game, and a week later came to see Smythe holding his paycheque. He gave it to the owner, saying he no longer deserved to be paid until he could contribute again to the team. Smythe, of course, ensured that his star player received every cent of his salary. A short time later, Smythe established the Sportsmen's Battery, a war division made up of NHL players. Apps was first in line and spent two years away from the NHL while helping in Canada's war efforts. He returned to the team in 1945 and had his best three seasons with the Leafs. He won the Cup in 1947 and then declared the next year would be his last. By the final game of the '47-'48 season, he had 198 career goals. He went out and scored a hat trick, pushing himself over what was then the historic 200-goal mark. In the playoffs, he scored a goal in his final game, one that ended with NHL president Clarence Campbell presenting captain Apps with the Stanley Cup. He was only 33, at the top of his game, and he went out a champion. Apps gave happily of every free moment of his time. He spoke at luncheons and dinners, signed autographs, and coached kids teams in the city. He helped neighbours build backyard rinks. He worked with charities and underprivileged children and was once voted Father of the Year in Canada. Away from the ice, Apps was no less extraordinary. In 1947, Ontario Premier George Drew appointed him athletic commissioner for sport. He later became a Conservative member of the legislature representing Kingston (1963-74), and was chairman of the select committee on youth. In 1971, he was appointed minister of correctional services. In business, he rose to president of the Milton Brick Company. In his later years, though, he was assaulted by an appalling disease that left him of sound mind but unable to walk much or talk at all. His son, Syl, went on to a fine career in the NHL, and his grandson also played pro hockey. Another grandson, Darren Barber, won Olympic gold in 1992 with Canada's eight in rowing, and a granddaughter, Gillian, is now one of Canada's finest prospects in women's hockey. Apps is the only member of three Halls of Fame: the Hockey Hall, the Canadian

Sports Hall, and the Canadian Amateur Athletics Hall. In 1993, his number 10 was honoured by the Leafs, and to this day no finer man has ever played in the NHL, not for one game or a thousand.

APPS, Syl, Jr.
b. Toronto, Ontario, August 1, 1947

Apps became the first son of an NHL player who appeared in an All-Star Game to play in the game himself, though the record was a year delayed. Syl Jr. was named to play in the 1974 classic but had to withdraw because of injury. The next year, he was named to the team again, and this time not only did he play, he scored two goals and was named the game's most valuable player. His father, the great Slippery Syl of the 1940s Maple Leafs, watched from the stands.

Syl Jr. didn't aspire to a pro career early on. Born just weeks after his dad had won the 1947 Cup with the Leafs, Junior played minor hockey in Toronto with the Scarborough Lions. One of his teammates was Brad Park, and one of his opponents in a tournament was Bobby Orr. Apps went to Princeton University on a scholarship, where he played under coach Johnny Wilson, but the scholarship didn't come close to covering expenses so he returned to Canada and attended Queen's University. The New York Rangers recruited him to turn pro with their affiliate in Omaha, and he wound up playing half the 1970-71 season. He was traded to Pittsburgh with Sheldon Kannegiesser for Glen Sather, and it was with the Pens that he developed into a solid

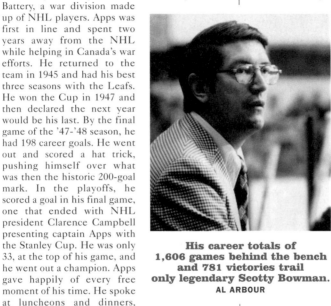

His career totals of 1,606 games behind the bench and 781 victories trail only legendary Scotty Bowman.
AL ARBOUR

player. For four years he was on the Century Line with Jean Pronovost and Lowell MacDonald, and the three were among the league's top scorers. Apps' play led to an astounding contract offer – five years, almost $1 million – and in '75-'76 he had 32 goals and 99 points. Perhaps the only sore point during his time with the Penguins was a lack of playoff success, the team never making it past the second round. In his most memorable game, he scored a penalty shot goal on Bernie Parent of Toronto at Maple Leaf Gardens while his father stood and cheered from the seats. Apps finished his career in Los Angeles in 1980 and was inducted into the Penguins Hall of Fame in 1994. He returned to Toronto to work as a bond trader, and his son, Syl Apps III, had a tryout with the Leafs in the fall of 1999.

ARBOUR, Alger "Al" ("Radar")
b. Sudbury, Ontario, November 1, 1932

He'll never be called the greatest defenceman of his generation, but Al Arbour certainly ranks as one of the great coaches. His career totals of 1,606 games

Syl Apps, Jr.

Syl Apps

behind the bench and 781 victories trail only the legendary Scotty Bowman. Arbour's genius catapulted the New York Islanders to success in the 1970s and to the club's subsequent run of four consecutive Stanley Cup wins from 1980 to '83. Arbour played defence on the junior Windsor Spitfires of the OHA. After distinguishing himself as an amateur, he was signed by the Detroit Red Wings and joined the pros with the Edmonton Flyers of the Western Hockey League in 1952-53. He split the next four years between Alberta, the Motor City, and Sherbrooke in the Quebec senior league. In 1957-58, Arbour played his first full NHL season with the Wings. He was then claimed by the Chicago Black Hawks, where he toiled for three years, including 1961, the year of the franchise's Stanley Cup victory. Arbour next played five seasons with the Toronto Maple Leafs and earned his second Stanley Cup ring in 1962, becoming one of few men to win consecutive Cups with two different teams. After spending the 1966-67 season in the AHL, he returned to the defence corps of the expansion St. Louis Blues in 1967-68, the team that had claimed him in the Expansion Draft. Early in 1970-71, he retired after playing some 600 games over 14 years. Arbour was also one of the few players in league history to wear glasses while playing. Upon retiring, Arbour was immediately hired to stand in as coach of the Blues for the remainder of the 1970-71 season. During the last 50 games, the team had a record of 21-15-14 before falling to the Minnesota North Stars in the quarter-finals of the playoffs. Arbour guided St. Louis on an interim basis over the next two seasons but jumped at the greatest challenge of his young coaching career in 1973. Prior to 1973-74, the New York Islanders hired him to sort out a second-year expansion team that had a mere 30 points in its first season in the NHL. Arbour's impact was immediate. The Isles improved to 56 points and began building a roster around talented defenceman Denis Potvin. The 1974-75 season saw the arrival of Arbour's Islanders as a competitive NHL franchise. They won 33 regular-season games and enjoyed a memorable playoff run in which they defeated Pittsburgh in a seven-game quarter-finals after losing the first three games. In the semifinals, they fell one game short of doing the same thing to the defending champion Philadelphia Flyers. During each of the next four seasons, the Islanders finished with more than 100 points. Following 1978-79, Arbour was presented the Jack Adams Award as the NHL's top coach. In 1979-80, the Islanders defeated the Philadelphia Flyers in six games to win the Stanley Cup in just their eighth season. They won again in each of the next three years to become only the second NHL club to win four straight titles (Montreal did it twice). Their drive for five consecutive championships fell short when they lost to the Edmonton Oilers in the 1984 finals. Afterward, Arbour marshalled the Islanders to solid if unspectacular results before stepping down following the 1985-86 season. He served as the organization's vice-president of player development before returning as the team's bench boss partway through the 1988-89 season. In 1992, he was awarded the Lester Patrick Trophy. The pinnacle of his second stint behind the New York bench occurred in 1992-93 when the Islanders upset the defending Stanley Cup champion Pittsburgh Penguins to reach the semifinals. Arbour retired in 1994 as the second winningest coach of all time, with 781 regular-season victories and 123 playoff wins to his credit. One of the major foundations in the history of the New York Islanders, Arbour was an obvious choice to enter the Hockey Hall of Fame Builders category in 1996.

Armos Arbour

ARBOUR, Armos ("Butch")

b. Waubaushene, Ontario, January 26, 1895
d. Orillia, Ontario, November 2, 1943

A butcher by trade and a long-time resident of Victoria Harbour, Armos Arbour played for the Cup-winning Montreal Canadiens of 1915-16 in the NHA, precursor to the NHL. Playing on a line with Goldie Prodgers and Louis Berlinquette, the left winger scored three goals in four games. Just weeks later, he joined the army and served overseas for two years. Upon returning, he rejoined the Habs before playing for Hamilton and Toronto in the newly formed NHL. He retired in 1924 to resume his career as a butcher.

ARBOUR, Ernest "Ty"

b. Waubaushene, Ontario, June 29, 1896
d. Waubaushene, Ontario, February 11, 1979

A sniper during the Great War, Ty was the older brother of Jack who had a similar, though slightly more successful, hockey career. Ty played many years in western Canada but stayed in the NHL for five years with Pittsburgh and Chicago (1926-31). After his playing days, he bought 250 acres of farmland in the Waubaushene/Port Severn area, where he had 50 head of cattle and hay that went back into the farm. Later in life he sold the farm and retired to Waubaushene.

Ty Arbour

ARBOUR, Jack

b. Waubaushene, Ontario, March 7, 1898
d. Calgary, Alberta, September 24, 1973

Twenty years of pro hockey got Arbour into the NHL for just 47 games over 2 seasons, first with Detroit and then with Toronto. He was a star in western Canada and was traded from Detroit to Toronto for Sailor Herberts, one of the bigger deals of the time. His stay with the Leafs was short, however, and he finished his career playing in the minors for another decade. Brother of Ty and related to Armos, Jack settled out west and worked on road maintenance for the City of Calgary. He also worked for the Calgary Stampede each year.

Jack Arbour

ARBOUR, John

b. Niagara Falls, Ontario, September 28, 1945

After four years of junior with the Niagara Falls Flyers, Arbour played two games with Boston in '65-'66. He later went to Pittsburgh, then to Vancouver, and finally to St. Louis under emergency circumstances. When defenceman Bill Plager was injured, coach Scotty Bowman was reduced to four defencemen. He called the Canucks, and bought Arbour in a strictly cash deal. When Plager recovered, Arbour was demoted to Denver and in his first game

John Arbour

Dave Archibald

**Ronald
Areshenkoff**

Bob Armstrong

Derek Armstrong

put the puck in his own net to give his new team a 4-3 loss. Arbour then went to the WHA for half a dozen seasons at the end of his career. A fighter, he was the stereotypical team man who stood up for his mates.

ARCHAMBAULT, Michel
b. St. Myacenthe, Quebec, September 27, 1950
He poured himself a cup of coffee with Chicago in '76-'77, but the Hawks wouldn't even let him add cream and sugar before sending him to the minors. This despite the fact that he had been a scorer of note in junior with Drummondville. He had played for the Quebec Nordiques during the first year of the WHA ('72-'73), and he retired in 1978.

ARCHIBALD, Dave ("Archie")
b. Chilliwack, British Columbia, April 14, 1969
At age 14, he was the youngest player in WHL history to register a point, and in his first NHL game, with Minnesota, he scored two ·goals. That was October 10, 1987, versus Philadelphia. Drafted 6th overall, he entered the NHL as an 18-year-old on a bad team and was supposed to be the North Stars' guiding light. When he didn't light up like he should have, his ice time dipped and his confidence slipped. His stock dropped, and three years later he was deemed a minor-leaguer. Archibald packed his bags and took his show international for two years, playing first with Canada's National Team in the 1991 World Championships (silver medal) and then in the 1992 Olympics in Albertville, where he led all scorers with seven goals. He played briefly in Italy and then made a moderate, subdued return to the NHL with the expansion Ottawa Senators. Then, history repeated itself. Four part-time years later, he was back in the minors and Europe.

ARCHIBALD, Jim
b. Cralk, Saskatchewan, June 6, 1961
The North Stars took a flyer on Archibald when they selected him 139th overall in 1981, and, in the end, they got what they paid for. He finished his four years at the University of North Dakota with a 37-goal season to go with his 197 penalty minutes. He played a handful of games with Minnesota over three years (1984-87) but his penalty-minute totals were the only impressive dimension he brought to the rink.

ARESHENKOFF, Ronald
b. Grand Forks, British Columbia, June 13, 1957
Owned by Buffalo, Edmonton, and Philadelphia at different times, Areshenkoff played just four games with the Oilers in his brief NHL career. He had scored 51 goals in his final year of junior with Medicine Hat and, as a result, was drafted a respectable 32nd overall by the Sabres in 1977. Trouble beset him, though, during his first year of pro, with the Sabres' farm team in Hershey – he suffered a serious shoulder injury that sidelined him for a year and a half. Buffalo let him go to Edmonton in the Expansion Draft, and the Oil later traded him to the Flyers. He retired in 1984.

ARKHIPOV, Denis ("Arkie")
b. Kazan, Soviet Union (Russia), May 19, 1979
A work in progress, young Arkhipov registered an assist in his first NHL game, January 8, 2001, for Nashville. He had been drafted by the new Preds in 1998 and played three years running in the World Juniors for Russia – 1997, '98, and '99 (bronze, silver, and gold respectively). At 6'3" and 210 pounds, he is expected to develop into a big forward with soft hands on a team that has little talent for the time being. He didn't help his cause by being charged with drunk driving after a pre-season game in 2002.

ARMSTRONG, Bill
b. London, Ontario, June 25, 1966
Undrafted, Armstrong was signed by Philly on a flyer after four years at U of Western Michigan. He wore number 58 for his one game, in 1990-91, and registered an assist. Then he played in the minors for a decade, never to return to the NHL. He later moved into coaching after a brain tumor ended his playing days in the summer of 1998, and moved from Providence to Trenton in 2002. Armstrong won the Calder Cup with Albany in '94-'95.

ARMSTRONG, Bob ("Satch")
b. Toronto, Ontario, April 7, 1931
d. Peterborough, Ontario, November 6, 1990
A bruising, hard-hitting defenceman, Armstrong anchored the blueline for every one of his 542 career games. He partnered with Bill Quackenbush as a rookie but teamed with Leo Boivin for the bulk of his years. He never rushed the puck, got into plenty of fights, and made it to the Stanley Cup finals twice. Prematurely bald, he wore a helmet for one game before deciding it wasn't worth the bother to cover what wasn't there. "He could tie guys up in such a way that wouldn't draw penalties," said Red Sullivan, a teammate and housemate from Armstrong's Bruins days. After retiring in 1963, Armstrong became a teacher of Canadian history and economics at Lakefield College, a private boys' school in southern Ontario. He coached the school's First Team from 1963 to 1989 and was also assistant coach for Roger Neilson in Peterborough. His son, Ian, played for the Petes and was drafted by the Bruins, though he never made it further than minor pro. Upon news of his death, Lakefield students wore an "RRA" patch for the year in his memory.

ARMSTRONG, Chris
b. Regina, Saskatchewan, June 26, 1975
The kid had size, toughness, and offensive talent from the blueline and was drafted a respectable 57th overall in 1993, but he was owned by four teams before he saw his first and only NHL action, and just three games at that. After Florida drafted him, Armstrong played for years in the minors and bounced to Nashville, San Jose, and, finally, Minnesota in his tour of expansion teams.

ARMSTRONG, Derek ("Army")
b. Ottawa, Ontario, April 23, 1973
A teammate of Michael Peca and Jamie Rivers in Sudbury of the OHL, Armstrong has loitered in the doorway of the NHL for years, mostly in New York with both teams, and also briefly with Ottawa. He was a decent scorer in junior, and the Islanders expected

more of the same when they drafted him. However, in 70 games he had just 7 goals. Ditto for stints on Broadway and with the Senators, though Armstrong led the AHL in assists and points in 2000-01 with Hartford. His reward? The Rangers didn't re-sign him, and he moved to Switzerland to continue playing.

ARMSTRONG, George ("Chief"/ "Chief-Shoot-the-Puck"/ "Army")
b. Skead, Ontario, July 6, 1930

George Armstrong grew up in tiny Falconbridge, near Sudbury, Ontario. He was of Irish-Algonquin heritage and his father worked in the nickel mines while young George worked at improving his hockey skills at the local rink. The Toronto Maple Leafs put Armstrong on their protected list while he was playing with the Copper Cliff Jr. Redmen of the NOHA in 1946-47. The following season, when the Leafs' Junior A affiliate in Stratford needed an additional player, Armstrong was promoted. He promptly led the league in scoring with 73 points in 36 games and won the MVP award. The Maple Leafs wasted no time in reassigning him to their main junior affiliate, the Toronto Marlboros of the OHA, for the 1948-49 season. Armstrong moved up to the senior Marlies in time for the 1949 Allan Cup series and stayed with the club on a full-time basis for 1949-50. He registered 64 goals in 45 games and a further 19 goals in 17 Allan Cup playdown games as the Marlboros captured the 1950 Canadian senior hockey championship. It was during the Allan Cup tournament that

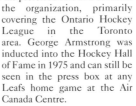

Armstrong was called by Conn Smythe "the best captain, as a captain, the Leafs have ever had."
GEORGE ARMSTRONG

the Marlies visited the Stoney Indian Reserve in Alberta. When the band heard of Armstrong's ancestral background they dubbed him Chief-Shoot-the-Puck and presented him with a ceremonial headdress. Chief played the majority of his first two pro seasons with the Leafs' AHL farm team in Pittsburgh before making the big club for good at the start of the 1952-53 season. Armstrong was never a great skater but was rarely out of position. He knew how to play the angles on the opposing forwards and was a great corner man in the offensive zone. He didn't survive in the NHL because of his scoring, but Armstrong brought determination, leadership, and humour to a Leafs team that was trying to escape the shadow of the Bill Barilko tragedy of 1951. Armstrong was named captain of the Leafs to start the 1957-58 season and was called by Conn Smythe "the best captain, as a captain, the Leafs have ever had." Smythe later honoured him by naming one of his horses Big Chief Army, something Smythe had done on only two other occasions, for Charlie Conacher and Jean Béliveau. He remained captain for a record 11 seasons and won 4 Stanley Cups in the 1960s with the

team. His empty-net goal to close out the '67 playoffs is emblematic of those Leafs teams, the Over-the-Hill Gang of Punch Imlach, and remains an integral part of Toronto's Stanley Cup history. In all, Armstrong holds many club records, notably playing his entire 21-year career with the team. After his retirement, he coached the Toronto Marlboros to Memorial Cup victories in 1972-73 and 1974-75 before accepting a scouting position with the Quebec Nordiques in 1978. Armstrong was with the Nordiques for nine years before returning to Toronto as assistant general manager and scout in 1988. His first year back was an eventful one and Armstrong found himself in the uncomfortable role of interim replacement coach for the final 47 games of the 1988-89 season. By the next year he had returned to his preferred role as a scout for the organization, primarily covering the Ontario Hockey League in the Toronto area. George Armstrong was inducted into the Hockey Hall of Fame in 1975 and can still be seen in the press box at any Leafs home game at the Air Canada Centre.

ARMSTRONG, Murray ("Army")
b. Manor, Saskatchewan, January 1, 1916

Raised in Regina by his blacksmith father, Army played junior in that city before making his way to the Toronto Maple Leafs for the '37-'38 season. Two years later, he was involved in one of the bigger deals of the decade. He, Busher Jackson, Buzz Boll, and Doc Romnes were sent to the New York Americans for scoring sensation Sweeney Schriner.

Murray Armstrong

Armstrong had three productive years on Broadway and then joined the Canadian Forces. While stationed at Regina, he played for and coached the Regina Army Caps, one of the finest teams of its kind ever assembled. The top line featured himself with Don Metz and Red Tilson. He was then signed by Jack Adams in Detroit but midway through his third year in Motown he was demoted when Adams decided to call up an 18-year-old named Gordon Howe. His style was always marked by sportsmanship and fair play; in 300 total NHL games, he earned just 74 penalty minutes. In '46-'47, Armstrong wound up on a team called the Dallas Texans. He was the coach and star player, leading the team to a championship and being named league MVP. He then returned to Regina to open two billiard halls, run a clothing business, and coach the local Pats, for whom he once played and which was part of the Montreal Canadiens junior system. He stayed with the Pats until 1956, when he accepted the head coaching job at the University of Denver. He led the Pioneers for 21 years until he retired to

Norm Armstrong

Tim Armstrong

Chuck Arnason

Scott Arniel

Venice, Florida. He won five NCAA championships in Denver, and his contributions to the game earned him the Lester Patrick Award in 1977. At a time when American universities were not seen as an NHL training ground, he sent a number of players on to the pro ranks, notably Keith Magnuson, Cliff Korroll, and Peter McNaborn.

ARMSTRONG, Norm ("Red")
b. Owen Sound, Ontario, October 17, 1938
d. Sault Ste. Marie, Ontario, July 23, 1974
Armstrong enjoyed body-checking and fighting equally, though his only call to the big time came when Bob Baun and Bob Nevin were injured and Toronto coach Punch Imlach summoned him from the farm. Trouble was, he had a tough time getting into his first game, December 15, 1962. When Imlach called for Red to jump onto the ice, out hopped Red Kelly. When he called for Armstrong, captain George Armstrong hustled over the boards. Third time lucky, Red Armstrong got his first shift. He carried the puck in over the blueline, shot, and scored. Just 25 seconds into his first shift, his was one of the fastest rookie goals ever. The next game, he got his only assist, and after five more less eventful games he was back in the minors. One of the greatest members of the Rochester Americans, Armstrong's contributions to the game are rooted in his AHL days. He played almost 9 full seasons and 500 games with the Americans. His number 6 was retired by the club in 1985, and a year later he was among the inaugural inductees into the Rochester Hockey Hall of Fame. He worked as a steelworker every summer, and as a result was one of the strongest players around. After retiring in 1973, he went to work for Algoma Steel in Sault Ste. Marie. One day at work, a year later, he lost his balance from a height and died from the fall. He was just 35 years old.

ARMSTRONG, Tim
b. Toronto, Ontario, May 12, 1967
After a fine junior career in which he averaged 83 points with the Toronto Marlies, Armstrong was drafted a lowly 211th overall by his hometown Leafs in 1985. He played most of the next 2 years with the farm team, and his lone callup to the team lasted just 11 games: December 29 and 31, 1988, and January 1, 6, 7, 9, 11, 21, 25, 28, 30, 1989. He scored once, and retired in 1991.

Collingwood tries to lord it over Wasaga claiming him as its own, but Arnott fervently remains committed to the Beach.
JASON ARNOTT

ARNASON, Chuck ("Rifleman")
b. Ashern, Manitoba, July 15, 1951
He had one of the hardest shots in the game, a skill he perfected in his home town of 450 souls some 160 clicks north of the 'Peg. He'd hammer shot after shot against his garage door – what else was there to do in the summer? – and eventually he used the shot to good effect in Flin Flon in the WHL, scoring a league-high 79 goals in 1970-71. But from there his career declined. He was drafted 7th overall by Montreal in the same year the Habs chose Guy Lafleur number one (1970), but he played only bits and pieces before being traded to Atlanta. Then he went to Pittsburgh, where he skated on the right side with Pierre Larouche and Bob Kelly. That was good for 26 goals, but the coaches wanted him to work on his defence. The Rifleman had the shot but not the commitment to his own end. Then the travel began as he moved to Kansas City, Colorado, Cleveland, Washington, and finally Germany, where he suffered a career-ending knee injury at training camp. Despite playing in 401 NHL games, he appeared in only 9 playoff games, the result of playing for so many poor teams.

ARNASON, Tyler
b. Oklahoma City, Oklahoma, March 16, 1979
While Chuck Arnason was playing in the CHL for the Oklahoma City Stars in '78-'79, he started a family. Son Tyler grew up in Winnipeg before going to St. Cloud State on scholarship. He made his NHL entrance with Chicago in 2001-02, but it is too soon to tell if he can outlast his dad, who played 401 games in the big league. His rookie season, though, suggested he could. He was one of the Hawks best players and Calder Trophy favourite.

ARNIEL, Scott
b. Kingston, Ontario, September 17, 1962
During a routine practice with his junior team, the Cornwall Royals, Arniel slid into the boards, swallowed his tongue, and stopped breathing. Quick-thinking trainer Steve Outerkirk came to the rescue, and Arniel recovered. He went on to win two Memorial Cups with the Royals in 1980 and '81 and played twice for Canada at the World Juniors, winning a gold medal the second time while on loan from his NHL team, the Winnipeg Jets. He had been the Jets' second pick in the 1981 draft (after Royals teammate Dale Hawerchuk), and he developed into a steady player, albeit below expectations. In almost five years with the Jest he averaged about 20 goals a year, but after annual playoff exits to the powerful Oilers he was traded to Buffalo in 1986, where he provided middling

play. His production slipped, he was dealt back to the 'Peg and then onto Boston. The Bruins sent him to the minors after 29 games, and for the next 8 years he skated in the AHL and IHL, even making a third stop in Winnipeg with the Moose. His blading days ended in 1999, but he remained with the Moose in an executive capacity.

ARNOTT, Jason ("Arnie")
b. Collingwood, Ontario, October 11, 1974
Ouch, that place of birth stings! Arnott remains a die-hard Wasaga Beachian, but because that sandy cove has no hospital, his mother had to go to nearby Collingwood for that special delivery in '74. As a result, Collingwood tries to lord it over Wasaga by claiming him as its own, but Arnott fervently remains committed to the Beach. When he returned home with the Cup in the summer of 2000, Wasaga had a parade for him, the showcase being the Arnott-mobile, a car covered in Jason memorabilia. He scored a goal in his first NHL game (October 6, 1993), but the road to respectability was fraught with potholes. He was a top-rated junior and won gold with Canada's world juniors in 1994 after being drafted 7th overall by Edmonton. When he arrived out west, he was seen as the next generation to follow Gretzky, Messier, and Coffey, but he was both inconsistent and too often injured. One game he would show remarkable potential, the next he would play distractedly, the next he'd take a puck to the face and miss games as a result. The Oilers traded him to Jersey and he slowly developed into one of the best power forwards in the game on the A-line with Peter Sykora and Patrik Elias. A consistent 20-goal scorer, he scored the Cup-winning goal at 8:20 of double overtime in game six against Dallas in 2000 and promptly held out the next camp for a better contract (which he got a few weeks into the season).

ARTHUR, Fred
b. Toronto, Ontario, March 6, 1961
This is the truth: Arthur never much liked playing hockey. Even in junior, he hated the bus trips, the long hours, the awful food, the small towns, the burden. Even while he was winning two Memorial Cups with the Cornwall Royals, he didn't have fun. But, he wanted to stick it out and see what he could do in the NHL. He was drafted very high – 8th overall in 1980 – but Hartford sent him to the Flyers in a 10-player deal after just 3 games. Arthur played one full season, 1981-82, but was demoted at the start of the next year. Rather than accept a move to the minors, he retired and went into medicine, pursuing a dream that had been in conflict with his hockey career ever since high school, when his average was 96.2 percent. As compensation for his early retirement, the Flyers received Hartford's 3rd-round draft choice in 1984 (John Stevens).

ARUNDEL, John
b. Winnipeg, Manitoba, November 4, 1927
d. Kemptville, Ontario, September 19, 2002
Recruited by the Leafs, Arundel joined St. Mike's in time to help secure the Memorial Cup in 1945. He played on another winning team out west, with

Winnipeg in 1948, and also won the Allan Cup with Sydney in '49. The only times Arundel's name appeared on NHL game sheets were December 31, 1949, and January 1 and 4, 1950. The Leafs lost the first two and tied the third, and Arundel was sent back to Pittsburgh in the AHL. He played in the minors until 1955, when he retired.

ARVEDSON, Magnus
b. Karlstad, Sweden, November 25, 1971
A late arrival to the NHL, Arvedson wasn't drafted until 1997, when he was 25 years old. At the time, he had a flourishing career with Farjestad back in Sweden, and when he came to Canada to play for the Senators he had just won a silver medal with Tre Kronor at the '97 World Championships. Although a talented left winger in a team laden with Europeans, he has struggled with injuries during the grind that is the 82-game NHL sked. Ironically, his best year for goals (21 in 1998-99) was the same year he was runner-up for the Frank Selke Trophy as the league's best defensive forward.

ASHAM, Arron ("Ash")
b. Portage la Prairie, Manitoba, April 13, 1978
Part of the new wave of Montreal player, Asham wears the undistinguished number 45 in a career so far of commensurate worth to the Habs. The right winger was drafted by Montreal in 1996 but has yet to put in a full season with the team, splitting his time between the NHL and AHL since graduating from junior (Red Deer) in 1998.

ASHBEE, Barry ("Ashcan"/ "Grumpy")
b. Weston, Ontario, July 28, 1939
d. Philadelphia, Pennsylvania, May 12, 1977
The short, happy life of the Ashcan lasted five NHL seasons, but by the time he died of leukemia in 1977 he was one of the most beloved Flyers of all time. He had played 14 games with Boston in '65-'66 but was soon returned to Hershey, where he was in the middle of a seven-year tour of duty. The Flyers acquired him from the Bears and he became not only one of the more reliable defencemen in the league but one of the more popular athletes in Philadelphia. He was as tough as any "Broad Street Bully" of that generation and in February 1973 was suspended for eight games for striking referee Bryan Lewis after a penalty call. Ashbee played on the '73-'74 team that won the Stanley Cup, but was absent from the clinching game due to an horrific career-ending eye injury he suffered on April 28, 1974. In a semifinals game against the Rangers, just days after being named to the NHL's second all-star team, he was hit flush in the eye by a Dale Rolfe shot. The following year, he became one of the team's assistant coaches after initially refusing the offer because of its perceived air of sympathy. On April 3, 1975, the club retired his number 4. In April 1977, doctors game him the devastating news that he had leukemia, and one month later he was dead. The team established a memorial scholarship fund in his honour, and the Barry Ashbee Trophy is awarded annually to the best defenceman on the Flyers. Ashbee is also a member of the team's Hall of Fame.

Fred Arthur

John Arundel

Magnus Arvedson

Arron Asham

Barry Ashbee

Frank Ashworth

"Ossie" Asmundson

Mark Astley

Hardy Astrom

ASHBY, Don ("Ants")
b. Kamloops, British Columbia, March 8, 1955
d. Penticton, British Columbia, May 30, 1981
A career that started with such promise and hope ended on a provincial highway near Penticton long after that hope had turned to disappointment. Drafted 6th overall by Toronto in 1975, Ashby became the number-one centre on the team just a few months later thanks to the departure of both Dave Keon and Norm Ullman. Ashby had a tough rookie season, scoring just six times, and only a slightly more encouraging sophomore year, with 19 goals. Demoted in each of his first three seasons with the Leafs, he quit briefly in 1978 before agreeing to keep at it. Traded to Colorado, then Edmonton, he ended up with the lowly Wichita Wind in the CHL, no place for a 6th overall selection to play. Making the best of a bad situation, he and teammates Don Murdoch and Tom Roulston led the Wind to the Adams Cup finals against Salt Lake before losing in seven games. He and his wife, Terry, drove home after the series, and just a few days into their languorous road trip were hit head-on by a pickup truck. Ashby died in hospital a few hours later from massive internal injuries, and Terry suffered a broken jaw. At the start of that season, Don had been a member of the NHL Players' Association and had bought extra insurance. The driver, Raymond Storteboom, admitted full liability, and both Roger Neilson and Glen Sather testified in court that Ashby could have played many more years in the NHL and Europe. As a result, Terry was awarded $644,480.43 in damages by the British Columbia Supreme Court.

ASHTON, Brent
b. Saskatoon, Saskatchewan, May 18, 1960
Got him. Need him. Got him. Got him. Need him. Got him. Brent Ashton was the Everyman of hockey cards. He played for 9 teams during a 14-year career and was traded an extraordinary 9 times: from Vancouver (the team that, a million years ago, drafted him) to Winnipeg, to Colorado, to Jersey, to Minnesota, to Quebec, to Detroit, back to the 'Peg, to Boston, and to Calgary. Along the way he had seven 20-goal seasons but missed the hallowed 1,000-game mark by just two appearances. He also won a silver medal with Canada at the 1989 Worlds.

ASHWORTH, Frank
b. Moose Jaw, Saskatchewan, October 16, 1927
Ashworth went to the Memorial Cup finals with Moose Jaw in both 1945 and '46, only to lose to the two powerhouses of Canadian hockey, St. Mike's and Winnipeg. Nonetheless, the hapless Chicago Black Hawks took a chance on him, and at 19 he was in the NHL. In 18 games, he had a fine run of 5 goals, but he was sent to the USHL and, at 19, was out of the NHL. He kicked around in the senior and western leagues for years, scoring 36 goals with Tulsa in '48-'49, a team to whom he refused to report two years later. He was suspended a full year as a result and this rift ended his USHL career. Ashworth returned to Canada to play for another decade, retiring in 1966. He opened a gas station in Calgary and later moved to British Columbia.

ASKEY, Tom
b. Kenmore, New York, October 4, 1974
He's getting a little long in the tooth for a goaler to establish himself in the NHL. Askey went 188th overall to Anaheim after a 4-year career at Ohio State, where he had an appalling record of 17 wins and 68 losses. He played his first game on March 13, 1998, but has played in the minors for most of his pro career. His brightest moment came when he played for the sixth-place USA team at the 1997 World Championships in Helsinki.

ASMUNDSON, Oscar "Ossie"
b. Red Deer, Alberta, November 17, 1908
Ossie played the 1931-32 season with an outfit that went by the moniker Bronx Tigers, and the next year he leaped on the downtown train and joined the Rangers for their triumphant march to the Stanley Cup. But after one more full year with New York, he played for four different NHL teams in three seasons before continuing in the shadows of the American league. He retired in 1945 and moved to Hollywood, becoming a lighting technician for movies and TV.

ASTASHENKO, Kaspars
b. Riga, Soviet Union (Latvia), February 7, 1975
Drafted at age 22 in 1999 by the horrid Tampa Bay Lightning, Kaspars has no better chance to establish himself than on a team that missed the playoffs six years running to close out the 20th century. He made his debut with the team in 2000-01 and at season's end represented Latvia at the World Championships.

ASTLEY, Mark ("Ash")
b. Calgary, Alberta, March 30, 1969
The Ash-man won a silver medal with Canada at the 1994 Olympics in Lillehammer, just a few months after making his NHL debut on October 12, 1993, with the Sabres. He had shown some scoring promise at Lake Superior University and played for Canada's National Team for two years leading up to the '94 Games. He played in Europe for a couple of years before making the NHL, and returned there after it became clear he was not going to become an NHL regular.

ASTROM, Hardy
b. Skelleftea, Sweden, March 29, 1951
Rangers GM John Ferguson scouted Astrom at the 1977 World Championships in Vienna, and the goaler stood up to the scrutiny, helping his native Sweden win a silver medal. Fergie put him on his team's negotiating list, and that fall Astrom became a Broadway Blueshirt. He played just four games that season, surrendering 14 goals, and moved to the minors and back to Sweden before joining the lowly Colorado Rockies for 1979-80. How bad was he in Denver? He had a record of 9-27-6, his coach, Don Cherry, told him he couldn't stop a beach ball, and his teammates begged management to trade him. But at year's end, the team nowhere near the playoffs, Cherry was fired and Astrom returned for an encore that proved to be every bit as brutal. He had a record of 6-15-6 and was soon in the minors. He then returned to Sweden to play out his career.

ATANAS, Walt ("Ants")
b. Hamilton, Ontario, December 22, 1922
d. August 8, 1991
The one and only Eddie Shore liked what he saw when he first scouted Atanas and assigned the right winger to his AHL team in Buffalo. While there, Ants displayed his trademark blistering shot and blazing speed and was a significant part of the Bisons' championship season. The next year, he moved up to the Rangers while their wartorn roster was fighting overseas and had a perfectly acceptable season with 13 goals. But the Rangers missed the playoffs and Atanas was buried in the minors for more than a decade before settling in with Shore's latest purchase, the Springfield Indians, in 1954. Atanas was a superb ballplayer and won four city championships in Hamilton during the off-season. He was a linesman in the NHL in 1961-62.

ATCHEYNUM, Blair ("Atch")
b. Estevan, Saskatchewan, April 20, 1969
It's not every player who gets traded for a draft choice named Zbynek Irgl, but that's what happened when Atch went from St. Louis to Nashville for a 2000 draft choice the previous year. He himself had been drafted a respectable 52nd overall in 1989, but from that date to 1997 he played exactly four NHL games, with Ottawa in 1992-93. Since then, he has worn more sweaters than years have passed, and at 33 and counting his game totals have just touched 200. Even in the minors he has played for a dozen teams over the last decade, a true journeyman who loves the game more than the place he plays it.

ATKINSON, Steve
b. Toronto, Ontario, October 16, 1948
An evermore promising career in junior with Niagara Falls led to just one game with Boston in '68-'69 before he was claimed by Buffalo in the Expansion Draft. Here was his chance to shine, but injuries – two concussions – led to lost confidence and run-ins with coach Joe Crozier. In four full seasons, his goal production diminished consistently – from 20 to 14, to 9, to 6 – and Mr. Atkinson went to Washington with the newest team in the league, the pitiful Capitals. He got so excited before his first exhibition game that he choked on his pre-game meal and had to be sent to hospital. GM Milt Schmidt called him a snail after one particular game and demoted him. He later played briefly for the Toros in the WHA before retiring in 1978.

ATTWELL, Bob
b. Spokane, Washington, December 26, 1959
On Mother's Day 1979, Bob gave his dad, Ron, a present that will last a lifetime. Playing for the Peterborough Petes, he scored an overtime goal to give his team the Memorial Cup. He banged in a Larry Murphy shot, and from that moment forward, their careers diverged. Murphy went on to become the NHL's all-time leader for games played by a defenceman; Attwell played just 22 times for the Colorado Rockies. Amazingly, father Ron had played that exact number of games during his brief NHL career in the 1960s. Perhaps more unusual, though, was that this father-son team played a mere 12 years apart, Ron playing in '67-'68, Bob in '79-'80. Neither appeared in a playoff game, and Ron outscored Bob by eight points to six. Bob kicked around the minors for a while, played in Europe for six years, and retired in 1990. He then returned to Peterborough with his wife and two children, getting a job in nearby Bolton with the Ontario Bus Industry.

ATTWELL, Ron
b. Humber Summit, Ontario, February 9, 1935
Father of Bob, and brother-in-law to Bill McCreary, Ron was a top-ranked junior in the Boston organization, tall, tough, and skilled. He played for the Junior Canadiens, but a callup to Providence lasted only three games after he suffered a separated shoulder. He played in Quebec for the better part of five years. The Canadiens bought the 19-year-old for $10,000, but he never played for the NHL team. After more years in the minors, he and Pat Quinn were sold to the expansion St. Louis Blues, and it was then that Attwell saw his first NHL action, 18 games' worth. He was traded to the Rangers, but after four games he was back in the minors to stay.

AUBIN, Jean-Sebastien
b. Montreal, Quebec, July 17, 1977
Timing can be everything. Had Aubin surfaced in Pittsburgh a decade ago with Tom Barrasso in his prime, he never would have seen the crease. But in 1998, Barrasso needed a rear-view mirror to see his prime and Aubin seized the moment. He played 17 times that season, and this experience helped get him the number-one gig the following season. In 1999-2000, he placed second in save percentage (.914) and first for wins among rookie goaltenders (23), but after one more season he couldn't fend off the challenge from another youngster, Johan Hedberg, and lost his pre-eminent status. A southpaw, Aubin came out of junior from the Quebec league, a veritable goalie factory in recent times.

AUBIN, Normand
b. St. Leonard, Quebec, July 26, 1960
Man oh man, could this guy score before he got to the

Walt Atanas

Blair Atcheynum

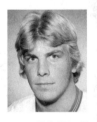

Bob Attwell

Ron Attwell

Normand Aubin

A career that started with such promise and hope ended on a provincial highway near Penticton.
DON ASHBY

NHL. Eight goals in one game for Verdun to break a record most recently held by Guy Lafleur. A total of 258 goals in 244 career junior games, and 43 in his first year in the AHL. But when the Maple Leafs asked him to do same in the big top, he responded with 7 goals in his first 11 games and then fizzled, scoring just 18 more in 69 games over 2 years. Demoted to St. Catharines, Aubin had one more story left in him. The Saints were in Glen Falls, New York, to play the Adirondack Red Wings, but the starting goalie, Bob Parent, had been suspended, leaving only Vincent Tremblay to mind the twine. Halfway through the first period, he pulled a hamstring and Aubin donned the pads for the rest of the game, giving up five goals in a 6-3 loss.

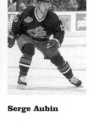

AUBIN, Serge
b. Val d'Or, Quebec, February 15, 1975
Pittsburgh drafted him in 1994 but never dressed him for a game. Colorado signed him on December 22, 1998, and nine days later he made his NHL entrance against Wayne Gretzky and the Rangers. He scored his first goal a year and a half later, but after the Avs were eliminated in the semifinals of the playoffs he was let go. Aubin signed with the Blue Jackets of Columbus and he has emerged as a front-line left winger in a 30-team NHL.

Serge Aubin

AUBRY, Pierre
b. Cap-de-la-Madeleine, Quebec, April 15, 1960
Numismatics is his passion, but scoring goals is what he does better. Aubry counted 138 goals in 139 games in his final 2 years of junior with Trois-Rivières, and in the Eastern league he had 66 more in just 71 games. These were eye-popping numbers NHL teams couldn't ignore – but they did. Undrafted, he signed with Quebec but justified the quiet appreciation scouts had had for him by scoring only 18 goals over 4 partial seasons. Ditto in Detroit after he was sold to the Wings. Then it was down to the minors and off to Europe for four years before returning to Quebec to take up a career as coach, which he has done since retiring in 1991.

Oscar Aubuchon

AUBUCHON, Oscar ("Ossie")
b. St. Hyacinthe, Quebec, January 1, 1917
Not to be confused with Ossie Asmundson, this Ossie started with the Montreal Jr. Canadiens before accepting an offer from Brighton to play in Britain. It was 1937 and Britain was abuzz with its country's gold medal upset of Canada at the 1936 Olympics in Garmisch-Partenkirchen. Many a fringe NHL-Canadian was being recruited, and quite a few accepted the offer of hockey and travel. Aubuchon returned to Canada at the start of the war, and it was because of the war that he got into his only NHL games, with the Bruins in 1942-43. He played briefly that season and spent most of '43-'44 as a wartime replacement before resuming a minor-league career.

AUCOIN, Adrian
b. Ottawa, Ontario, July 3, 1973
Aucoin's rise and fall in the NHL resembles the shape of a mountain, the peak coming in 1998-99 when he set a Vancouver team record with 23 goals as a defenceman, 18

Donald Audette

of which came on the power play to tie Denis Potvin's NHL record in that department. Aucoin went from provincial junior to Boston University on a scholarship, but after a year with BU he opted to join the Canadian National Team in 1992 with an eye toward the '94 Olympics in Lillehammer. He joined Vancouver briefly the following year, and rose steadily until '97-'98 when he missed more than half the year with ankle and groin injuries. Then came his great season, and then the descent. The year after he missed 20 games with a finger injury, salvaging the season by playing for Canada at the 2000 World Championships. In 2000-01, he was traded to Tampa Bay in mid-season, and the summit of his great offensive success looked farther and farther distant. Aucoin revived his career in 2002 when he went to the Islanders and led the league in ice time, averaging nearly 30 minutes a game.

AUDET, Philippe
b. Ottawa, Ontario, June 4, 1977
A Detroit draft choice in 1995 after a successful junior career in Granby, Audet had a tough time cracking a defence made up of aging thirty- and forty-somethings. He played without incident in four games in '98-'99 but was dealt at the 2000 deadline to Phoenix for Todd Gill, another of the thirties pack coach Scotty Bowman wanted patrolling his blueline. Since then, it's been nothing but the minors for Audet.

AUDETTE, Donald ("Donny")
b. Laval, Quebec, September 23, 1969
A big-time success story. Audette was drafted 183rd overall by Buffalo and looked to be filler for the minor-league team despite the fact he had just finished his junior career by scoring 76 goals and 161 points for Laval. In his first year in the minors, he scored 42 times, and the Sabres thought, Hmm, better have a look at him. He was called up early the next season to the Sabres, and after a red-hot start (four goals in eight games) he suffered a season-ending knee injury. The year after, healthy, he scored 31 times and made it clear he was a bona fide NHLer who had slipped through the cracks. Audette wrecked his knee in '92-'93 and again in '95-'96 but otherwise has been consistent for more than a decade. In fact, his best year came in 2000-01 when he scored 32 goals for Atlanta at the ripe old age of 32. He signed with Dallas in the summer of 2001, a team desperate for scoring.

AUGE, Les
b. St. Paul, Minnesota, May 16, 1953
d. St. Paul, Minnesota, September 13, 2002
An American through-and-through, Auge spent four years at the University of Minnesota, 1971-75, before commencing a career in the minors. He was never drafted, but the Colorado Rockies signed him as a free agent on July 15, 1979, after he had already been in the lower leagues for a number of years. He also played for the U.S. at the 1979 World Championships in the Soviet Union, finishing seventh. He stayed with the National Team the following year, hoping to make the Olympic squad for Lake Placid, but he was cut and missed the Miracle on Ice. The Rockies called him up for six games in '80-'81, his only time in the NHL before retiring in 1982.

AUGUSTA, Patrik

b. Jihlava, Czechoslovakia (Czech Republic), November 13, 1969

Augusta was a speedy forward drafted under the Cliff Fletcher-Anders Hedberg regime in Toronto. Hedberg knew Augusta's father, Josef, who played on the Czech national team in the 1970s as a member of that country's Canada Cup entry. Patrik played January 1 and 2, 1994, with the Leafs but spent the rest of his time in the minors, leading the AHL in scoring with 53 goals in that '93-'94 season. He slipped quickly into the IHL and eventually signed with Washington, where history repeated itself. After two games with the Caps, he was back in the minors. For 2000-01, he returned to Europe to continue his career.

AULD, Alex

b. Cold Lake, Alberta, January 7, 1981

Florida drafted him but Vancouver acquired him in a trade. Auld, a goalie, made his NHL debut with the Canucks in 2001-02, allowing two goals in a win during a season spent mostly in the minors.

AURIE, Larry ("Little Dempsey"/ "The Little Rag Man")

b. Sudbury, Ontario, February 8, 1905
d. Detroit, Michigan, December 12, 1952

His number 6 was retired by James Norris in 1938 as soon as Little Dempsey retired, the first Wings player so honoured and the only one until Gordie Howe some 30 years later. He was the last Red Wing to wear that number, yet it doesn't hang in the rafters of Joe Louis Arena. Instead, his sweater was put in a glass case in the lobby. However, while the Wings still won't allow any player to wear Aurie's number, they also formally refuse to acknowledge his importance. Strange. (The Wings were going to give number 6 to Cummy Burton, Aurie's nephew, but decided against it except for a few games.) One of the first moves Jack Adams made when he took over the team in 1927 was to sign Aurie, who became team captain in '32-'33, helped the Wings win their first two Stanley Cups in 1936 and '37, and played his entire career – 12 years – in Detroit. His only disappointment came toward the end of the '36-'37 season. A shoe-in to win the scoring title, he broke his leg, finished three points behind Sweeney Schriner, and missed the playoffs altogether. Aurie was a scorer who "ragged" the puck to kill penalties (thus the nickname), a team leader, and a member of the Wings' top line with Marty Barry and Herbie Lewis. Although he retired from the NHL in 1938, he played and coached in Pittsburgh the following season and returned to the Wings for one game in an emergency. He ended up scoring the winning goal. Although one of the smallest men ever to make the NHL (140 pounds soaking wet), he was one of the toughest. Adams called him "the most courageous player, pound for pound, in hockey." Aurie continued to coach, but in 1952 suffered a stroke while driving and died at Mt. Carmel Mercy Hospital in Detroit. He was 47.

AVERY, Sean

b. North York, Ontario, April 10, 1980

Tough and small, Avery was never drafted but

Detroit, annual Cup competitors, found his skills appealing and signed him in 1999. He has played mostly in the minors, but in 2001–02 he worked his way into the Wings lineup for nearly half a season, not quite enough to get his name on the Cup. He did get to take the Cup to his home in Toronto during the summer, though.

AWREY, DON ("Elbows"/ "Bugsy")

b. Kitchener, Ontario, July 18, 1943

A defence partner to Ted Green and Bobby Orr at various times, Awrey once went 153 games without scoring a goal. By then, he was lucky to be playing at all. An increasingly degenerative back became intolerably painful during his high school football days in Kitchener and he needed a serious operation that had him tied to a Striker Frame for three weeks, being turned on the hard bed while he recovered. Six months later, he could skate again, and tried out for the Niagara Falls Flyers the year after his brother, Bob, had played for the team. Slowly but surely he made his mark on Hap Emms and Milt Schmidt, the Boston decision-makers, and soon he was blocking shots and delivering bone-crunching checks for the Bruins. He was part of the two Boston Cup wins in 1970 and '72 and was named to Team Canada's roster for the historic Summit Series, playing two of the eight games. He won a final Stanley Cup with Montreal, sort of, in 1976. "Sort of" because although he played the full regular season with the team, he didn't dress for the playoffs. Rules at the time stipulated that a player had to appear in the playoffs to have his name on the Cup, so Awrey missed out on a third carving into the bowl. After retiring, he opened Don Awrey Sale Agency in Concord, New Hampshire and ran Sports Elite Distributing Company before moving back to Ontario and working for Berg and Baird Moving in the Toronto area. He resides in Florida for part of every year to act as off-ice official for the Florida Everglades Hockey League (ECHL) and has started refereeing.

AXELSSON, Per-Johan "PJ"

b. Kungalv, Sweden, February 26, 1975

On December 11, 1997, Axelsson changed his sweater number from 57 to 11, perhaps the most dramatic move he's made since coming to North America in 1997 to play in the NHL. Drafted by Boston, he has been with the team for his entire pro career after four seasons in the Swedish League. Axelsson won a bronze medal at the 1994 World Junior Championships and also played in the 2000 and '01 World Championships.

AYRES, Vern

b. Toronto, Ontario, April 27, 1909
d. Toronto, Ontario, February 18, 1968

At 6'2" and 220 pounds, he was a giant of a defenceman for his day. He hit and stayed close to his own goal, most notably for the New York Americans, for whom he played the majority of his 211 NHL games. In all his years, he never made the playoffs and retired in 1942 after a career in the minors. He died in Toronto while playing in a father-son hockey game at age 59.

Larry Aurie

Don Awrey

PJ Axelsson

BABANDO, Pete
b. Braeburn, Pennsylvania, May 10, 1925

Babando made NHL history on the night of April 23, 1950, when he scored at 8:31 of the second overtime in game seven of the Stanley Cup finals to give the Detroit Red Wings the Cup over the Rangers. It was the first game-seven OT goal to win the sacred trophy, and it came on a backhand along the ice that beat Charlie Rayner in goal. A year later, one of his juvenile teammates in Timmins, Bill Barilko, also won the Cup, for Toronto, in overtime. Babando was traded to Chicago as part of a nine-player deal, and he finished his career on Broadway in 1953. That summer, as always, he returned home to Porcupine, Ontario, where he played ball for the Porcupine Combines. He slid into second base during one game, broke his leg, and found himself in the minors at training camp in the fall, never fully recovering from the injury. Although he played just six years in the NHL, Babando went on to play another decade in the minors before retiring in 1967. He continued to play hockey all his life, skating with old friends who include Gus Mortson.

BABCOCK, Bob
b. Agincourt, Ontario, August 3, 1968

Twice as successful as a one-game wonder, Babcock was a sizable defenceman drafted by Washington in 1986 after a junior career spent with the Soo Greyhounds and Cornwall Royals. His most obvious ability was fistic, and outside his two games with the Caps his career went quickly and uneventfully, ending in 1994.

BABE, Warren
b. Medicine Hat, Alberta, July 9, 1968

He was front and centre, that's for sure. Drafted by Minnesota in 1986, he made his first NHL appearance the next season. On October 19, 1987, he was slashed viciously in the leg by Patrick Roy. The goalie was suspended for eight games, and Babe missed a month with the injury. But nothing compares to the game on September 21, 1989. That night, in a pre-season game, he was slashed by Shawn Cronin of Winnipeg and suffered a concussion, his 14th serious, documented head injury since he was 10 years old. On doctors' advice, he sat out a year, and on February 15, 1991, of the following season he got dinged again and wisely called it a career after just 21 NHL games spread over 4 injury-plagued seasons.

BABENKO, Yuri ("Babs")
b. Penza, Soviet Union (Russia), January 2, 1978

Babs played in his first career game, for the Avalanche, on November 22, 2000 and has played just three games to date. He was drafted by the team out of Russia but came to the OHL to play a final year of hockey while still junior eligible. From there he moved up to the AHL but has yet to establish himself as a regular centre on a club stacked with talented players down the middle. If he makes it in the NHL, it will likely be with another team.

BABIN, Mitch
b. Kapuskasing, Ontario, November 1, 1954

He came down from Ontario's North a goal scorer, a lanky centreman with quick hands drafted by St. Louis in 1974. But Babin appeared in only eight games for the Blues in '75–'76, then moved around in the minors briefly before accepting an offer to play in Vienna for a season. He retired in 1979 to work in Ottawa as a civil servant.

BABY, John
b. Sudbury, Ontario, May 18, 1957

A strong defenceman, Baby played junior in Ontario before being drafted in 1977 by the short-lived Cleveland Barons. He managed to play 24 games for that money-strapped franchise before it merged with Minnesota in the summer of 1978. The North Stars kept him on their roster for all of two games, and then he was sent to the minors to play out his days.

BABYCH, Dave
b. Edmonton, Alberta, May 23, 1961

Probably the best hockey player ever to be associated with the movie *Slap Shot*, Babych became technical adviser and hockey coordinator for *Slap Shot II* in 2001 after he retired. He actually played against one of the Hanson Brothers (Steve Carlson) in junior, but beyond that his hockey career was without much fanfare save the appreciation of coaches for the big and talented defenceman. He showed offensive ability early but as he got older he moved from "offensive" to "stay-at-home" as a blueliner. In his first four full seasons (1981-85), he scored 63 goals, a number he barely doubled in the ensuing 14 years of service with a total of five NHL teams. He represented Canada at the 1981 and '89 World Championships (winning a silver medal in the latter) and played 1,195 games altogether after being drafted a staggering 2nd overall in 1980 by Winnipeg. Brother of Wayne, Dave played in two All-Star Games ('83 and '84), and the closest he came to a Cup was with Vancouver in 1994, when the Canucks took the Rangers to seven games in the finals. On April 8, 1998, he broke his foot blocking a slapshot during a playoff game. He returned to the lineup quickly but was never the same again and retired in 1999. In early 2002, he took his team, the Flyers, and team doctors to court, arguing that his injury was misdiagnosed and he was forced to play while injured. Later in the year, a jury awarded him $1.3 million in lost earnings.

BABYCH, Wayne
b. Edmonton, Alberta, June 6, 1958

First the social: Wayne and brother Dave are not twins, but Wayne has a twin sister, Susan. Wayne and Dave married identical twins, Shelley and Sherry Buffie of Selkirk, Manitoba, in the summer of 1982. The twin girls had recently won a Miss International beauty pageant in Los Angeles, as a team, and their father is one of a set of twins. Not as big or strong as brother Dave, Wayne left the NHL in 1987 with a wreck of a body that had entered the NHL shiny and new. He finished his junior career in the Western league with consecutive 50-goal seasons and, like Dave, went high in the draft. In his case, that meant 3rd overall by St. Louis in 1978. Early in his career he won bronze with the World Juniors in 1978 and played for Canada the next year at the World Championships, but no one could have anticipated his meteoric rise in his first three NHL

Pete Babando

Bob Babcock

Dave Babych

Wayne Babych
(opposite page)

Jergus Baca

Ryan Bach

Mike Backman

Pete Backor

seasons. He scored 27 times as a rookie in '78–'79 despite missing a good part of the year with a broken ankle. He had 26 goals the next year despite missing 21 games with shoulder and knee injuries. He exploded with 54 goals in '80–'81 playing a full year, but then his bod lost control. His shoulder flared up the next year and required surgery, he broke his nose and cheekbone in a fight the year after, and the year after that he was down to 13 goals in a 70 game season. St. Louis traded him to Pittsburgh, and from there it was on to Quebec and Hartford, where more knee woes slowed him down further. He retired in 1987 after playing just 519 games.

BACA, Jergus
b. Liptovsky Mikulas, Czechoslovakia (Slovakia), January 4, 1965
A big defenceman with gobs of international experience, Baca could not refine his game for North America and lasted but 10 games with the Hartford Whalers in the early 1990s. He won a pair of bronze medals for CSSR at the Worlds in '89 and '90 and played in the '91 Canada Cup for the Czechs, and the '94 Olympics and '96 World Cup for Slovakia. He later represented his new country at two Worlds, in '97 and '98, as it struggled to establish itself as a strong "A" pool nation. More regularly, he has continued to thrive in European leagues as a rough-and-tumble force on the blueline.

BACH, Ryan
b. Sherwood Park, Alberta, October 21, 1973
At the time, Bach was the lowest goalie/draft choice ever selected to make it to the NHL. Chosen 262nd overall by Detroit in 1992 before he started a four-year career with Colorado College, he didn't make it with the Wings until 1998-99, when he played three games. Since then, he has been owned by Los Angeles and Florida but has yet to orchestrate a return to the NHL.

BACKMAN, Mike
b. Halifax, Nova Scotia, January 2, 1955
What he lacked in size he made up for in minor-league experience. At 5'10" and 175 pounds, Backman just wasn't a likely candidate to stay in the NHL for very long. Add to that fact that he played and studied at St. Mary's University down east, not a stop on any scout's regular itinerary. Nonetheless, the Rangers signed him as a free agent at the start of the 1979-80 season, and he did make it into 18 games over the next 4 years. Most of his time, though, was spent in the AHL before he retired in 1986.

BACKOR, Pete
b. Fort William (Thunder Bay), Ontario, April 29, 1919
d. Thunder Bay, Ontario, June 30, 1988
Pete grew up with a brother, Hank, who also played minor pro and aspired to make it to the NHL (he didn't). Pete got his one big chance in 1944-45 when many Maple Leafs were still at war and the team's roster was thin. He was called up to Maple Leaf Gardens and played in 36 games. Although he never made an appearance in the playoffs, the Leafs won the Cup that year and Backor had his name stamped in hockey's most hallowed hardware. By next season, though, most players had been discharged and regained their rightful

place on the team and Backor was back in the minors. The big defenceman had a long and distinguished career in the AHL with Pittsburgh, the Leafs' affiliate, before retiring in 1955. An avid gardener and golfer, Backor got a job with Great Lakes Forest Products that occupied the next 27 years of his life.

BACKSTROM, Ralph
b. Kirkland Lake, Ontario, September 18, 1937
Yes, he won six Stanley Cups with Montreal. Yes, he played pro for more than 20 years. And yes, he was one of the great unheralded players of his day. But the truth is, in some ways he is most famous for his part in arguably the smartest hockey trade ever made. By the start of 1970-71, he had been with the Canadiens for 15 seasons. He wanted a change and came close to retiring. Montreal GM Sam Pollock coveted the number one draft selection for the 1971 draft because he wanted Guy Lafleur. In the summer of 1970, he had acquired Oakland's number one pick, figuring that was the worst team in the league. But a funny thing happened during the '70-'71 season. Los Angeles was playing even more poorly than the Seals and looked certain to scupper Pollock's master plan by finishing last themselves. So, Silent Sam traded Backstrom to L.A.–gave him away, really–for Gord Labossiere and Ray Fortin, two players who stood no chance of making the Montreal roster even as a joke. Backstrom, happy for the change of scenery, played his heart out on the coast; L.A. rose above Oakland, and the Seals finished in last place. Pollock had his number one selection and, of course, chose Lafleur, the player who would lead Montreal to many Cups. Backstrom, meanwhile, left the NHL in 1973 to play four more years in the WHA before retiring. He immediately started coaching, joining the University of Denver in 1977 as an assistant coach for three years. He then became head coach for nine years and moved up to the IHL's Phoenix Roadrunners in 1990–91. More recently, he has been a special assignment scout for St. Louis, and is co-owner of a CHL team in Colorado.

BAILEY, Bob ("Bashin' Bob")
b. Kenora, Ontario, May 29, 1931
In a pro career that lasted 17 years, Bashin' Bob could have had a number of other nicknames, including Trader Bob, Minor-Pro Bob, and Here-and-There-and-Back Bob. But Bashin' Bob was particularly accurate because of his style of play, though he once did his bashin' with a referee during a Calder Cup game in 1956 and earned a suspension and a hefty fine. During the 1959-60 season, he was suspended 12 games for swinging his stick wildly at Ted Harris, a reaction, he said, to an incident the previous year when he had his own face sliced open by the stick of Larry Zeidel. In 1963-64, while with the Fort Wayne Komets, he again hit a referee, this time with his stick, and was suspended for the year. And then, at the age of 36, when most fellows seem to have mellowed, he went berserk while playing for the Dayton Gems of the IHL. On one play, referee Billy Purcell blew play dead on an offside, and Bashin' Bill went a-bashin'. He swore vociferously and repeatedly at the referee, earning a 10-minute misconduct. That penalty, of course, only made matters worse, and he threw his stick the length of the ice. Match misconduct. He then

attacked the referee, throwing a punch before being restrained by his own players and the linesmen. He was suspended for the year, and it turned out to be his final act of bashin' on a professional rink. Bailey was involved in trades for Bill Dineen on three separate occasions during his career and played with his brother, John, for a short time in Philadelphia in the EHL. He played 150 NHL games between 1953 and '58 with Toronto, Chicago, and Detroit.

BAILEY, Garnet "Ace"

b. Lloydminster, Saskatchewan, June 13, 1948
d. New York, New York, September 11, 2001

Every hockey player has a story about sleeping in late and missing a flight or team bus, arriving late for practice, or being fined for breaking curfew. If once, just once, Bailey had missed a flight instead of getting to the airport with minutes to spare, he'd still be alive today. On September 11, 2001, he slept in but managed to get to Logan airport in time to catch his Boston to Los Angeles fight, United Airlines 175, with protege Mark Bavis. Shortly after takeoff, the plane was hijacked and flown into the World Trade Center in New York. Bailey had started his post-NHL life as a coach in Edmonton's minor-league teams in Houston and Wichita. He then scouted for the Oil for 13 years and moved to L.A. to become director of pro scouting some 8 years previous, but like almost every member of the Boston Cup teams of 1970 and '72, he maintained close ties with his mates and with the city. Bailey might be the only man to have been teammates of both Bobby Orr and Wayne Gretzky.

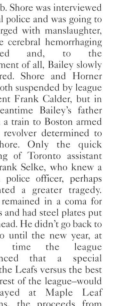

The night of December 12, 1933, changed the lives of Bailey and Eddie Shore, but also the very NHL itself.
ACE BAILEY

He played a decade in the NHL and his finest hour likely occurred at a crucial time in the '72 finals against the Rangers. Boston took a huge 5-1 lead and seemed poised to coast to victory, but the Blueshirts slowly chipped away at the score and tied the game in the third. Playing a hunch, coach Tom Johnson benched Eddie Westfall and inserted the little-used Bailey into the regular rotation of lines. Bailey took a pass from Shakey Walton, danced around the Rangers' best defenceman, Brad Park, and lifted a shot over the shoulder of future Hall of Famer Ed Giacomin to give the Bruins a 6-5 win and a 1-0 lead in the series. They won the Cup in six games, but the outcome might have been different had the B's lost that first game.

BAILEY, Irvine "Ace"

b. Bracebridge, Ontario, July 3, 1903
d. Toronto, Ontario, April 7, 1992

Never in the long and glorious history of hockey has so much good come out of so much bad. The night of December 12, 1933, changed the lives of Bailey and Eddie Shore, but also the very NHL itself. In a Toronto–Bruins game in Boston, Shore was making one of his great rushes when he was upended by Red Horner. Furious, he turned around to see Bailey, and figured Ace had been the culprit. As play moved back into the Boston end, Shore came up behind Bailey and flipped him in the air. Bailey landed on the ice headfirst, and the thud silenced the crowd instantly. Horner, the league's toughest man, then knocked Shore out with a punch, and two of the best players in the league lay unconscious, blood on the ice near their heads. Shore recovered and had his head stitched, but Bailey's injury was much more serious. He was taken to hospital and doctors were certain he was going to die. In the coming days, he underwent two brain operations, a priest was called to his side and it seemed a matter of hours before he would succumb. Shore was interviewed by local police and was going to be charged with manslaughter, but the cerebral hemorrhaging subsided and, to the amazement of all, Bailey slowly recovered. Shore and Horner were both suspended by league president Frank Calder, but in the meantime Bailey's father was on a train to Boston armed with a revolver determined to kill Shore. Only the quick thinking of Toronto assistant GM Frank Selke, who knew a Boston police officer, perhaps prevented a greater tragedy. Bailey remained in a coma for 15 days and had steel plates put in his head. He didn't go back to Toronto until the new year, at which time the league announced that a special game–the Leafs versus the best of the rest of the league–would be played at Maple Leaf Gardens, the proceeds from which would go to the Bailey family now that Ace's career was, without question, finished. At that game, February 14, 1934, Conn Smythe announced that no player would ever wear number 6 again, but the finest sporting gesture in hockey followed soon after. The All-Stars were introduced individually, greeting Bailey as they got their special sweater for the game. There was an eerie silence when number 2, Shore, was called, but Bailey, who had every right to snub the Boston great, shook his hand in exoneration. The crowd responded with deafening cheers. The success of that game paved the way for an annual All-Star Game started after the Second World War. In his eight years with the Leafs, Bailey had established himself as one of the league's top right wingers. He won the Paul Whiteman High Scoring Trophy in '28-'29 for his league-high 22 goals, his first of 3 consecutive seasons of 20 or more. In '31-'32, he helped the Leafs win the Cup in their first year at the Gardens, and in retirement he was the longest-standing fixture at the hallowed arena. He worked the penalty box almost until his death more than half a century later, and he also coached the U of T Blues for a decade. In business, he

Bob Bailey

"Ace" Bailey (left)

Reid Bailey

Scott Bailey

Joel Baillargeon

Bill Baker

Steve Baker

was also successful. He worked for O'Keefe Breweries, ran his own service station, and worked as an agency manager for Canada Mutual funds. In the 1960s, he became such a fan of a young player named Ron Ellis that he allowed Ellis to wear his number 6, though once Ellis retired the number went back up into the rafters, symbolically, at least. The number was to be retired before Bailey's eyes late in the '91-'92 season, but a players' strike prevented the ceremony from occurring and Bailey died just a few days later.

BAILEY, Reid ("Beetle")
b. Toronto, Ontario, May 28, 1956
Bailey got his nickname from his Philadelphia Flyers teammates, who likened their big, bad defenceman to the comic strip character Beetle Bailey. He got to the NHL on the strength of coach Bob McCammon, who knew Bailey from their days with the Port Huron Flags in 1977-78, but he played only 27 games on Broad Street before quick stops in Toronto and Hartford sent him out of the league. He became an executive with the WWF (World Wrestling Federation) and later worked as the vice-president of marketing for the CFC.

BAILEY, Scott
b. Calgary, Alberta, May 2, 1972
Go figure. One year he gets called up to the Bruins and goes 5-1-2 with a 3.26 average. The next year, same goalie, same team, but he has a record of 1-5-0 and a 3.65 average. Since then, he's been buried in the minors, no longer Bruins property.

BAILLARGEON, Joel
b. Quebec City, Quebec, October 6, 1964
Joel was the son of Quebec's famed Strongman, who once lifted a platform with an entire football team on it. Another time he climed a telephone pole while carrying a horse on his back. Baillargeon the Younger (and weaker) was also a physical presence, a defenceman known for his devastating bodychecks and whose first NHL point and assist made it into the record books only on the strength of a keen observer. The official scorer of a game between Baillargeon's Winnipeg Jets and the Washington Capitals back in 1986 watched the televised replay of a goal and noticed that the defenceman had touched the puck on its way to the scorer's stick dsuring a 3-3 game. Baillargeon was given due credit and the next morning received a telegram of congratulations from his former teammates in Sherbrooke. In all, he played 20 NHL games and had a second assist in '87-'88.

BAIRD, Ken
b. Flin Flon, Manitoba, February 1, 1951
A freckled, red-headed defenceman who looked like Opie from *The Andy Griffith Show*, Baird was anything but an innocent. He came out of the Bombers in junior to play 10 games for the yellow and blue California Golden Seals but then jumped to the WHA where his chances of making a go of it were far greater. Indeed, he had a 30-goal season with Edmonton in 1974–75, when Wayne Gretzky was still nowhere to be seen on the prairie landscape, and moved to Germany to play for three seasons after being released by Winnipeg a few winters later.

BAKER, Bill
b. Grand Rapids, Minnesota, November 29, 1956
Baker scored a seminal goal in the Americans' Miracle on Ice triumph at the 1980 Olympics in Lake Placid. He scored at 19:59 in the tournament's first game, against Sweden, to earn his country a tie and played a solid role on the blueline the rest of the way. Baker had long been a champion. He won the state crown with Grand Rapids and then won two NCAA titles with the University of Minnesota, where he was a top student and a West All-American. He had four brief stops in the NHL between 1980 and '83, and on one occasion in 1981 was traded to St. Louis by Colorado for Joe Micheletti and Dick Lamby. Micheletti had won the state championship two years previous to Baker and was a teammate with Baker at the U of M. He also had established the scoring record for defencemen that Baker surpassed in his final year.

BAKER, Jamie ("Bakes")
b. Ottawa, Ontario, August 31, 1966
There aren't many players who can boast of scoring two short-handed goals in a single period, but Baker is one of them. The feat came during the 1995-96 season against Los Angeles while he was with San Jose, and his six short-handed goals in that season was second only to Mario Lemieux. Baker had played at St. Lawrence University for four years, and after going unnoticed in the Entry Draft as a teen he was picked up by Quebec in the 1988 Supplemental Draft. He later played for Toronto, and he is the only player to date who can boast that his last NHL game occurred in Japan. He played for the Sharks in game one of the '98-'99 season against Calgary when those teams opened the season in the Far East.

BAKER, Steve
b. Boston, Massachusetts, May 6, 1957
Baker was so hot hot hot when he joined the Rangers in 1979-80 that he had a fan club before his career was 10 games old. A 20-foot banner promoting the Baker Fan Club hung from the rafters of Madison Square Garden and he went 9-1 in his first 10 games. But then the razzle-dazzle fizzled. He finished the season 9-8-6, and in each of the next three seasons his starts diminished, going from 27 to 21, to 6, to 3, and then he was off to the minors. Baker came to Canada to play a year of Junior B in '74-'75 and then attended Union College in Schenectady, New York, where he had a 27-5-1 record. However, he and several other players quit the team when popular coach Ned Harkness was forced to quit. Harkness had once sent a Cornell student named Ken Dryden on to the NHL.

BAKOVIC, Peter
b. Thunder Bay, Ontario, January 31, 1965
A late bloomer, they said. Give him time, they pleaded. He's always been slow to develop, but he'll come around, they argued. Well, the patience paid off with Bakovic at every level except the NHL. He didn't play in the OHL until he was 18, but he turned into a decent player. When Calgary signed him as a free agent, the team assigned him to the minors, where Terry Crisp was coaching the Moncton Golden Flames. Crisp knew him from junior, and gave him time. But then Vancouver acquired him, gave him

10 games in '87-'88 and sent him on his way. Bakovic played in the "I" for Milwaukee, retired in 1991, and stayed on to join the team's coaching staff.

BALA, Chris
b. Alexandria, Virginia, September 24, 1978
Not many Virginians grow up dreaming of the NHL, and even fewer ever get there. Bala impressed Ottawa after only a year at Harvard, and after he graduated and played in the minors the Sens called him up for five games in 2000-01. He's been in the minors ever since.

BALDERIS, Helmut
b. Riga, Soviet Union (Latvia), July 31, 1952
Balderis blew his chance to play on the vaunted Soviet national team at the 1976 Olympics in Innsbruck because of an ill-timed insult. A star winger with his hometown Dynamo Riga, he was later compared to Guy Lafleur for his magical skills. But Dynamo was a squad playing far removed from Moscow, and Balderis's coach was the tyrannical Viktor Tikhonov, a man who didn't suffer insubordination. During a league game in 1975, Balderis responded to Tikhonov's constant abuse by yelling the Latvian equivalent of "be fruitful and multiply," and then left the bench. Tikhonov swore revenge, and when orders arrived a few months later for Balderis to appear at training camp for the '76 Olympic team, the coach sent a telegram to the appropriate hockey authorities saying that Balderis had a drinking problem and was unfit to play for his country. Balderis discovered Tikhonov's treachery only after his country's victory in Innsbruck, one worth thousands of rubles in bonus money. Without options, Balderis continued to play for Tikhonov, both with the National team and the Central Army squad in Moscow. In 1977, he was arguably one of the best players in the world. Named MVP at the World Championships, he captured the Soviet league's scoring title. That didn't stop Tikhonov from throwing a punch at him after Balderis repeated his earlier insult, or from chasing the graceful but foul-mouthed winger off the ice by swinging a hockey stick at his head. Balderis, a figure skater in his youth, was known as Electruchka – Mr. Electricity or Electric Train – but by the time he was allowed to play in the NHL, in 1989, his engine was running on empty. He had retired four years earlier, and his comeback, with the Minnesota North Stars at the age of 37, lasted just 26 games.

BALDWIN, Doug
b. Winnipeg, Manitoba, November 2, 1922
Baldwin's timing was both good and bad. He got into the Leafs' lineup because injuries left the roster light a man, but after just 15 games he himself had to undergo an emergency appendectomy. By the time he recovered, he was back in Pittsburgh playing in the minors. Twice elsewise he was called up for brief stints, with Detroit and Chicago in successive years, but he never made a lasting impression. During the war, Baldwin made two Allan Cup appearances with the Quebec Aces, and after he continued to play for more than a decade.

BALES, Mike
b. Prince Albert, Saskatchewan, August 6, 1971
You just never know. In university, at Ohio State, Bales had a record of 28-57-10 over 3 years and a goals-against average over 5.00. Yet Boston drafted him 105th overall in 1990. He played just 25 minutes of a game with the B's in '92-'93 and signed with Ottawa in the summer of '94. He played a handful of games with the still-emerging Sens and later signed with Dallas while continuing a minor-league career. In all, he had a record of 2-15-1 in 23 NHL games.

BALFOUR, Earl ("Spider")
b. Toronto, Ontario, January 4, 1933
A travelling salesman by trade, Balfour couldn't sell Detroit GM Sid Abel on the idea of the Spider on left wing with Gordie Howe at right and Alex Delvecchio in the middle. The three played together for a blink during training camp in 1961, but the graft didn't take. That Balfour was in Detroit's camp was odd to start with. He had just won a Stanley Cup with Chicago but Boston claimed him in the summer's Intra-League Draft. After a run-in with coach Phil Watson, though, Balfour bolted the Bruins and headed for Motown. He wound up in the minors and then sought and received reinstatement as an amateur. A father of seven, he was a defensive specialist and penalty killer who began with Toronto, first with the Marlies in junior and then with the big club on a part-time basis for some seven years.

BALFOUR, Murray
b. Regina, Saskatchewan, August 24, 1936
d. Regina, Saskatchewan, May 30, 1965
Balfour was a member of the famed "Million Dollar Line" for Chicago and a playoff hero, but his life was cut short by cancer at age 28. After he was sold to Chicago from Montreal in 1959, he played on a forward combination with two stars earning sizable salaries – Bobby Hull and Bill Hay. The troika soon became known as the Million Dollar Line. Balfour repaid the Habs for the trade during the 1961 playoffs when he scored in triple overtime of game three of the semifinals. Chicago eliminated Montreal, ending the Habs' unprecedented run of five Cups in a row. Balfour, however, who outscored his wealthier linemates in the playoffs, had to watch the Cup-clinching game from the hospital after crashing into the Detroit net and breaking his arm in game five of the finals. The next year, he had an eight-inch steel rod inserted from his wrist to his elbow to support the arm, though it didn't slow down the rugged winger. A friend of his once said that Balfour was competitive and aggressive even while water-skiing, having seen him emerge bleeding but smiling after trying to ski over a rocky beach. Traded to the Boston Bruins in 1964, Balfour soon began complaining of constant fatigue. He was sent down to the minors and continued to experience health problems. Exploratory surgery in 1965 revealed an inoperable tumour in his lung. He died less than two months later. Nine hundred mourners attended his funeral in Regina, including million-dollar pallbearers Hull and Hay.

BALL, Terry
b. Selkirk, Manitoba, November 29, 1944
The NHL might be the finest league on the planet, but it is not the be-all and end-all of hockey. Terry Ball is living proof of that. Although he played just 74 games in the NHL, he skated for 15 years in various pro leagues around the continent and in Europe. He was small for a

Doug Baldwin

Mike Bales

Earl Balfour

Terry Ball

Maxim
Balmochnykh

Dave Balon

Steve Bancroft

Darren Banks

Murray
Bannerman

defenceman, 5'8" and 165 pounds, which accounts for his lack of NHL success, but he had a deadly slapshot and great stamina. He was a power play specialist on the point when Philadelphia called him up for most of the '69-'70 season, and when he joined the WHA in 1972 he used his skating and shot to full effect.

BALMOCHNYKH, Maxim
b. Lipetsk, Soviet Union (Russia), March 7, 1979
Winner of a bronze and silver medal at the '97 and '98 World Juniors for Russia, Balmochnykh is still young and adapting to life and ice in North America. He was drafted by Anaheim in 1997, played a little junior hockey in Quebec the year after, and has toiled mostly in the AHL since, appearing in six games with the Ducks in 1999-2000.

BALON, Dave
b. Wakaw, Saskatchewan, August 2, 1938
Dave Balon began to feel the symptoms of multiple sclerosis during his NHL days as a high-scoring left winger, though he wasn't diagnosed with the disease until after he retired. Fans and coaches alike watched him play and thought he had lost his drive and competitive edge that had helped him win Cups with Montreal in 1965 and '66 and become a scoring sensation with the Rangers a few years later playing on the "Bulldogs" line with Walt Tkaczuk and Bill Fairbairn. Once voted the most popular member of the team, his goal production dropped and he was soon out of the league. Balon first came to glory in junior with his brothers, Chick and Rudy, in the New York organization. He played for the team between 1960 and '63 and was then traded to Montreal with Gump Worsley, Leon Rochefort, and Len Ronson for Phil Goyette, Don Marshall, and Jacques Plante. After Montreal and the Rangers, he was traded to Vancouver, where fans booed him (but, hey, they also booed Team Canada in 1972). He retired in 1973 after a bref stint in the WHA and like many victims of MS was soon confined to a wheelchair. Undaunted, he owned and captained a tour boat in Prince Albert National Park in northern Saskatchewan and acted as part-time coach for a travelling oldtimers' team.

BALTIMORE, Bryon
b. Whitehorse, Yukon, August 26, 1952
Baltimore studied education at the University of Alberta in the early 1970s and almost got into an NHL game when he was called up from Springfield during the '74 playoffs. After that disappointment, he signed with the WHA and spent a number of years there, getting into his only two NHL games with Wayne Gretzky's Oilers in '79-'80, a memory he could take with him the rest of his life. His wife also performed on ice – she had been in the Ice Capades prior to their marriage. Baltimore later became a player agent, counting Jay Bouwmeester among his clients.

BALUIK, Stan
b. Port Arthur, Ontario, October 5, 1935
A golfer of extraordinary skill, Baluik played in his first of two Canadian Opens at the age of 16 back in 1952. Two years later, he won the Ontario junior golf title, the first player from Ontario's north to do so. He turned pro

at 19, and was club pro at Fort William Country Club from 1956 to 1963. He won numerous tournaments in the area, notably the Thunder Bay District Open in 1957, '60, and '61. In 1964, he accepted an offer to be club pro at Kirkbrae Country Club in Lincoln, Rhode Island, a position he has held to this day. Incidentally, he played pro hockey when snow covered the fairways and greens. He broke his leg in consecutive seasons (once in '57 and again in '58) and didn't get into his first NHL games until '59-'60, when Boston called him up for seven games. He went pointless and continued to play for Providence in the AHL until he accepted the Kirkbrae position.

BANCROFT, Steve
b. Toronto, Ontario, October 6, 1970
He was drafted, traded, signed as a free agent, and claimed during his decade and counting in hockey, but along the way the hockey gods gave him only one game in the NHL, an uneventful contest with Chicago in 1992-93. Although his activity besides has been confined to the IHL and AHL, Bancroft has played for some 17 teams and continues to skate for love of the game. Incredibly, he was called up to San Jose during the 2001-02 season for five games after Shawn Heins suffered a broken jaw. It was Bancroft's first NHL action in nine years.

BANDURA, Jeff
b. White Rock, British Columbia, February 4, 1957
A defenceman with good size and even better fists, Bandura was drafted by Vancouver in 1977 but played his only two NHL games with the Rangers in 1980-81. He won the Bob Gassoff Trophy as the most improved defenceman in the CHL, but after being demoted by New York he retired at year's end.

BANHAM, Frank
b. Calahoo, Alberta, April 14, 1975
The Duck from Calahoo couldn't do enough on the Pond, so he travelled to Finland to play with Espoo. Surprising, stunning really, considering that in his last three years of junior he scored 28, 50, and then 83 goals. But Washington drafted him and didn't play him and Anaheim played him but didn't keep him – just 27 games in the 4 seasons from 1996 to 2000. So, Banham moved overseas to continue his career.

BANKS, Darren
b. Toronto, Ontario, March 18, 1966
Big and strong, Banks put up huge numbers in the penalty-minute columns and binary code numbers in the goals and assists department. He played 20 NHL games with Boston in 1992-94 and beyond that has done his slugging in a myriad leagues and teams, including the Anaheim Bullfrogs and Long Island Jawz of Roller Hockey International league.

BANNERMAN, Murray
b. Fort Frances, Ontario, April 27, 1957
Bannerman is arguably the best "player to be named later" in the history of the NHL. On November 4, 1977, Vancouver acquired Pit Martin from Chicago for future considerations. Months later, the Canucks thought about sending Glen Hanlon to complete the

deal, but both teams then fixed on Murray Bannerman. He arrived in Chicago to find Tony Esposito holding fort, but slowly, as Esposito aged, their roles reversed and Bannerman became number one and Tony O the backup. Although he played well in the '82 playoffs for the Hawks, he encountered the scoring machine that was the Oilers in the '85 playoffs and was shelled for seven goals through two periods. That was, perhaps, the beginning of the end for him, although he played in both the 1983 and '84 All-Star Games and for a brief time was one of the league's steadier goalies. In 1987, he was sent to the minors, where he had a record of 6-21-5 with Baltimore. He retired at season's end and became the director of hockey operations for the Chicago Young Americans AAA Amateur Hockey Association as well as coach in the organization.

BANNISTER, Drew
b. Belleville, Ontario, September 4, 1974
Midway through a successful junior career, Bannister was charged with assault. He was in a parking lot after a high school prom with two women when someone called his friends "puck bunnies." A fight ensued, and two brothers charged the Soo Greyhound with assault. After two years in court and a $150,000 civil suit, Bannister was ordered to perform community service to gain a discharge, a vital arrangement because a conviction would have prevented his travelling to the U.S. For three years running the Greyhounds went to the Memorial Cup, winning in 1993. A year later, Bannister won gold with Team Canada at the World Juniors, but since then his career has been stalled. He has played for four teams in the last six years, but only one full season, 1996-97 with Tampa and Edmonton.

BARAHONA, Ralph
b. Lakewood, California, November 16, 1965
Despite scoring two goals in his first three NHL games when Boston called him up in 1990-91, Barahona has played both on ice and concrete many places outside the NHL. He went undrafted after four years at the University of Wisconsin-Stevens Point, a Division II school scouted by no one from the NHL. Barahona played three more games in 1991-92 (no goals), and the swift centre then began a tour of duty in ice hockey leagues as well as in-line and roller hockey leagues.

BARBE, Andre "Andy"
b. Coniston, Ontario, July 27, 1923
His lone NHL appearance came on January 18, 1951, for the Maple Leafs, but Barbe was much loved by his coach in the minors, King Clancy. The King swore the right winger had the hardest shot in all of hockey, and certainly Barbe proved he could score 20 goals in the AHL. He had joined the military as a teenager and scored 139 goals in three seasons with Los Angeles in the Pacific Coast league. But much as he adored life in LaLaLand, he knew that to further his career he had to move east, which he did, to join the Hornets.

BARBER, Bill
b. Callander, Ontario, July 11, 1952
Even when his knees were shot, Barber scored 20 goals. In fact, during his 12 years in the NHL, he never scored fewer than that number, a tribute to his abilities to put the puck in the net. He, Bernie Parent, and Bobby Clarke are the only three Hall of Famers from the gooning Philadelphia teams that won Stanley Cups in 1974 and '75. Ironically, he had his best season the year after, scoring 50 goals and 112 points. As a kid, he had an enormous backyard rink, complete with lights and hydro poles. He was drafted by the Flyers in 1972 and began the next year in Richmond. Just 11 games later, Bill Flett hurt his knee and Barber was recalled. He never went back. He scored 30 goals as a rookie playing left wing to Clarke's centre, which was Barber's natural position. He first hurt his knee in December 1982, and within two years it had deteriorated to the point that he had to retire. Although he was one of the few talented players on those Philadelphia teams, he was by no means lily pure. He was chippy and dirty at times, and introduced the NHL to the unsportsmanlike ability of diving to draw a penalty. He once kneed Bobby Orr on a rush, and was not at all averse to dirty play if, in his mind, the situation called for it. Barber immediately became a coach in the Flyers system, spending much of his time in Hershey before moving up to the NHL. He won the Jack Adams Award for his great year with the team in 2000-01, and soon after was fired by his former linemate Clarke.

BARBER, Don ("The Swan")
b. Victoria, British Columbia, December 2, 1964
Although he was a standout during his four years at Bowling Green University, Barber couldn't stick with Minnesota after a trade from Edmonton sent him to the North Stars in late 1985. He was owned by five teams between 1988 and '92 and in his final season played for three of them before retiring in 1993.

BARILKO, Bill
("The Kid"/ "Bashin' Bill")
b. Timmins, Ontario, March 25, 1927
d. Cochrane, Ontario, August 26, 1951
He called himself the Kid, but after watching him play his teammates and opponents alike called him Bashin' Bill. He came out of Ontario's North and made it to the NHL via the most improbable route – the Hollywood Wolves of the PCHL. When Conn Smythe called him up to the Leafs toward the end of the '46-'47 season, it was at the recommendation of the great Tommy Anderson, Barilko's legendary defence partner in California. Barilko travelled across the continent via trains, planes, and automobiles, culminating in a taxi ride from Buffalo to Varsity Arena in Toronto in a ferocious blizzard. He walked into the dressing room and hollered, "Boys, the sun is really shining!" He didn't score often, but he hit hard and harder, and in only five seasons of NHL hockey he won four Stanley Cups. As the Tragically Hip song "Fifty Mission Cap" says, "the last goal he ever scored/won the Leafs the Cup," a tribute to Barilko's untimely death. He scored the Cup winner in the 1951 finals against Montreal at 2:53 of overtime in game five of the series, the only one ever to go into overtime in each game. The goal occurred as the puck came into the slot and Barilko lunged for it to beat Gerry McNeil. Weeks later, Barilko and a family friend, Dr. Henry Hudson, a Timmins dentist, went on a fishing trip to Rupert House on James Bay. He never returned. Search party after search party

Drew Bannister

Ralph Barahona

Andy Barbe

Bill Barber

Bill Barilko

was sent out, only to come back without a trace of the men or their small plane. It wasn't until January 6, 1962, that the wreck was found, and a few months later the Leafs won the Stanley Cup, their first since 1951. Barilko died at just 24, leaving a Stanley Cup legacy and mythology behind, a mere boy stripped of life for reasons impossible to understand.

BARKLEY, Doug
b. Lethbridge, Alberta, January 6, 1937

Barkley's playing career ended when an on-ice accident left him without the use of his right eye. On January 30, 1966, just one week after he was named to the NHL's Second All-Star Team for the first half of the season, Barkley, a Detroit Red Wing, was battling with Chicago's Doug Mohns for a puck at the blueline. Mohns attempted to lift Barkley's stick but missed, and caught the bent-over Barkley directly in the right eye. The Detroit defender was rushed to the hospital, still in uniform, and was operated on immediately. He remained in hospital for two months and underwent three further operations, but the damage to the retina was too severe to salvage his vision. He never played again. Barkley had joined the Red Wings in 1963-64 after having played for Chicago briefly in '57-'58 and '59-'60. He finished second in Calder Trophy voting in the closest vote of all time in his first year with Detroit. Kent Douglas of Toronto received 99.4 weighted votes to Barkley's 99.2. After his injury, Barkley joined the Detroit front office, working in public relations and as a troubleshooter. He was appointed head coach of the Fort Worth farm team for Detroit in 1969 and a year later was behind the bench for the Wings, where he stayed for less than one season before quitting because of the team's poor start. He returned to coach the Wings in 1975 but immediately landed in trouble after punching a reporter from the *Newark Star Ledger* outside Detroit's dressing room during a heated discussion. Barkley lasted just 26 games before being fired and replaced by general manager Alex Delvecchio, his former teammate. Barkley became a scout for Detroit and later was the radio voice of the Calgary Flames.

BARLOW, Bob
b. Hamilton, Ontario, June 17, 1935

Barlow was 34 years old when he made his NHL debut, at the time the oldest rookie in the league's history. He scored six seconds into his second shift of that first game. "I waited 14 years for that shot," he said afterwards. Barlow had quietly played for independent teams in the AHL and WHL all those years, sometimes leading the league in scoring, sometimes playing like he'd never score again. Just when he seemed destined

to quit playing to devote more time to his rug business in Victoria, British Columbia, the Minnesota North Stars signed him to be a leader for their stable of young left wingers. He lasted a grand total of 77 games with Minnesota before he was sent down to the Phoenix Roadrunners in the WHL. By the time he retired, in 1976, he had played for 24 years and scored 522 goals in professional hockey, 16 of those in the NHL. He was soon coaching some of the teams he had scored for and against over the years, beginning with the Tucson Mavericks in the CHL.

BARNABY, Matthew
b. Ottawa, Ontario, May 4, 1973

He shoots the puck into opponents' nets during the pregame warmup; he smacked the walls at the Air Canada Centre before the drywall had been dry for very long; he fought Eric Cairns in the stands; and he is the über-master of trash talk on ice. You either love him or hate him, and most people, including his teammates, fall into the latter category. Barnaby has not been without skill. He scored 19 goals with Buffalo in '96-'97 and had 111 points in the Q in his final year of junior a few seasons' previous. He once had a four-point game (November 21, 1996, against Toronto) and on May 10, 1998, scored a hat trick in a playoff game against the Montreal Canadiens with his mother in the stands on Mother's Day. His penalty stats have been much more the focus of attention, and his on-ice time has gotten thin and has seen him move teams more than he might like.

Barkley became a scout for Detroit and later was the radio voice of the Calgary Flames.
DOUG BARKLEY

BARNES, Blair
b. Windsor, Ontario, September 21, 1960

Drafted at age 19 in 1979 by Edmonton during the first Entry Draft, Barnes went on to play a single NHL game, with Los Angeles, in 1982-83 during a brief pro career. He had been a terrific scorer in junior, and in his two years in the AHL he also found the net regularly, but he retired in 1984 without having made the impact the Oilers had hoped for.

BARNES, Norm
b. Toronto, Ontario, August 24, 1953

Barnes was drafted by Philly in 1973, but by 1979 he had played only three games for the team. He made the team in '79-'80, though, and quickly became the Flyers' best defenceman as the club embarked on a record-setting 35-game unbeaten streak. It wasn't difficult for him to get up for home games, because his wife, Sid, was a frequent anthem singer at the Spectrum at the time. (In fact, the team had a record of 8-0-2 when she sang!) Barnes also represented Canada at the 1981 World Championships when the team

Bob Barlow

Matthew Barnaby

Blair Barnes

Norm Barnes

finished fourth in Stockholm. At one point during the tournament, he noticed some memorabilia on a table outside the dressing room and signed a number of sticks. A short time later, Soviet trainers came by to collect their items and noticed this strange signature. Although embarrassing and awkward, the incident did not become a political event!

BARNES, Stu
b. Spruce Grove, Alberta, December 25, 1970
From the time he was 10 years old, folks out west referred to Barnes as the great kid scoring sensation, a reputation he lived up to all through junior in the WHL. But after being drafted 4th overall by Winnipeg in 1989, the Jets and then the Panthers turned him into a checker. It was only when he went to Pittsburgh, in 1996, that he got a chance to shine. With the retirement of Mario Lemieux, he was given Jaromir Jagr as a forward partner and responded with a 30-goal season, his first and only such outburst in the NHL.

BARON, Marco
b. Montreal, Quebec, April 8, 1959
Although Baron was trilingual (English, French, and Italian) no words could articulate his frustration during the early days of his career. No sooner had he thought he made the Bruins in 1980-81 than he was usurped by 1980 Olympic hero Jim Craig and ended up playing just 10 games that season. Late in one of those games, he lost a shutout bid at 19:59 of the third period on a goal by Rick Meagher of Hartford. The following year, he played 44 regular season games but not a-one in the playoffs. He later played for L.A. and Edmonton and finished his career in the trilingual capital of the world, Switzerland.

BARON, Murray ("Bear")
b. Prince George, British Columbia, June 1, 1967
Baron loves his motorcycles and every year takes part in Tony Twist's motorcycle tour to raise awareness of helmet use among the two-wheel set. Not surprisingly, he is one of the league's toughest hombres who was drafted by Philly but traded to St. Louis after a year and a half. His penalty-minute totals were always triple digit until the last couple of years, during which age seems to have mellowed the old warrior. In the off-season, he owns and operates a bar/restaurant in Prince George.

BARON, Normand
b. Verdun, Quebec, December 15, 1957
One day in 1983, Baron walked into the offices of les Canadiens and announced that he wanted to protect Guy Lafleur. The Habs had been beat and beaten up in the first round of each of the last three playoff years, and Baron felt he was the man to set things right. Who could argue? He could bench-press 600 pounds and was a serious bodybuilder who, in 1981, held the titles of Mr. Montreal and Mr. Quebec. Claude Ruel, the Canadiens' chief scout, guaranteed Baron a tryout if he lost 25 pounds. Later that year, Baron was assigned to the farm team in Nova Scotia and was called up for four games. He was traded to St. Louis the following year, and after 23 games with the Blues he retired from the skate game to continue the weight game.

BARR, Dave
b. Toronto, Ontario, November 30, 1960
Barr's three years of junior hockey out west were not considered impressive enough to merit being drafted, likely because four of his teammates all answered to the name Sutter. Barr signed with Boston as a free agent, but this was to be the first of eight teams he would play for in the next decade and a half. His best years came with Detroit (he scored 27 goals in '88-'89) but a short time later he wound up in New Jersey as compensation for Detroit's signing of Troy Crowder. The magic just wasn't there with the Devils and he was soon in the minors. Barr retired in 1997 and became a coach and later a manager with Houston in the IHL, where he had played his final three and a half seasons (with Orlando).

BARRASSO, Tom
b. Boston, Massachusetts, March 31, 1965
Perhaps the finest, if not the most arrogant, goalie to come out of the U.S., Barrasso burst onto the NHL scene in 1984. Still a high school student, he was drafted 5th overall by Buffalo and accepted an offer to attend Providence College in Rhode Island after he graduated. But a funny thing happened on his way to an education. He played in the 1984 Canada Cup for the Americans and then joined the Sabres right away. He won 26 games as a rookie and won the Calder and Vezina trophies to establish himself as the best young goaltender in the game. All was not well, though. His coach, Scotty Bowman, was having troubles of his own handling a team not already loaded with Stanley Cup talent. Bowman demoted Barrasso for five games the following year – because he could – but Barrasso still led the NHL with a GAA of 2.66. He suffered a letdown that persisted until a trade took him to Mario Lemieux's Penguins in Pittsburgh. Barrasso began to mature and his play was an important part of that team's back-to-back Stanley Cups in 1991 and '92. Injuries and inconsistent play crept into his game, to the point that in '96-'97 he played just five games. He became the first American to win 300 games, but a trade to Ottawa proved a disaster, culminating in the Senators' elimination from the first round of the 2000 playoffs and his uttering a swear word live on *Hockey Night in Canada*. Barrasso took the 2000-01 season off to care for his daughter, Ashley, who was undergoing a second round of bone marrow treatments. He returned the following season and signed with Carolina, a humbler, kinder veteran who could still play in the NHL In 2002-03, he had a disastrous stint with St. Louis.

BARRAULT, Doug
b. Golden, British Columbia, April 21, 1970
Despite being born in the mist and fog of B.C., Barrault played for the U.S. at the 1998 World Championships toward the end of his career with a team that finished a disastrous twelfth. He had been a low draft choice of Minnesota in 1990, but played only twice with that outfit in its final season and twice more with Florida the next year in its first season. Besides that, the right winger had a solid if unspectacular career in the IHL. A skilled penalty killer, he led that league in short-handed goals in '93-'94.

Stu Barnes

Marco Baron

Murray Baron

Dave Barr

Tom Barrasso

Fred Barrett

John Barrett

Doug Barrie

Ed Barry

Marty Barry

BARRETT, Fred ("Swoop")
b. Ottawa, Ontario, January 26, 1950

A defenceman with good lateral movement, Barrett's exploits in hockey read like a starter encyclopedia for a medical student. When he was 16, he split his kneecap and took six months to recuperate; the next year, he developed a large bone spur in his ankle and played just two games with the Marlies; at 18, he broke his hand. After he made Minnesota in 1970-71 (the team that had drafted him), he fractured his femur and the year after missed much of the year with a separated shoulder. In 1972-73, he broke his hand in training camp and hurt his ankle shortly after returning. The year after, he deflected a slapshot up into his own jaw, and the resultant break ended that season. A cracked ankle bone in '74-'75 and broken hand the year after followed. He retired in 1984, though not because of old age: he broke his hand again, and suffered a buildup of calcium deposits and a flareup of a back injury. Barrett settled in Minnesota to work for Spectrum Sports broadcasting and later as a custom home builder. He then became associated with a rollerblade company – this was still the 1980s, sadly – and tried unsuccessfully to get players to use blades for off-ice training. He then moved back to Ottawa to continue with the blading business, but ultimately the road wheels were too costly for most prospective buyers. He became president of the Ottawa-area NHL alumni, and since 1987 has worked for the Ottawa Fire Department, as does his brother, former NHLer John.

BARRETT, John ("Bear")
b. Ottawa, Ontario, July 1, 1958

A Dominion Day baby, John, like his brother, Fred, suffered from injuries from start to finish. With four seconds to go in a lopsided game against Vancouver on January 20, 1987, the Washington defenceman blocked a harmless-looking shot that found a hole in his equipment and struck him on the kneecap. The delicate bone was broken, but he worked hard to recover as quickly as possible. Just before he was due to return to action, he took a stress test and snap! The bone shattered again. Barrett tried gamely to come back, but even a trade to Minnesota could not salvage his career. Ironically, he got to the Caps in a trade from Detroit involving Greg Smith. Shortly after joining Washington, Smith broke his kneecap and two years later was out of the league. Barrett returned to Ottawa to work as a fireman with his brother, Fred.

BARRIE, Doug
b. Edmonton, Alberta, October 2, 1946

Trouble was Barrie's middle name. He had trouble getting into his first NHL game, being traded from Detroit to Toronto for cash, and then back to Detroit for more moolah, and then on to Pittsburgh for a further exchange of funds. The Pens used him but eight times in 1968-69 and he resurfaced with Buffalo in 1970. After a full season, life seemed to have steadied. Then he had a heated discussion with coach Punch Imlach and the next day was traded to the furthest place in NHL existence – Los Angeles. After that, he moved home and signed with the Oilers in the WHA, where he played the final five years of his career. Always pugnacious, he visited the penalty box regularly and was once called on the carpet in 1974 for pushing a linesman to the ice in a WHA game.

BARRIE, Len
b. Kimberley, British Columbia, June 4, 1969

Barrie's motto in life is simple: Keep skating and don't look back. He played his first NHL game the day he signed a contract with Philly while in the middle of a junior season with Kamloops that would see him earn 85 goals and 100 assists to lead the league in all scoring categories. But after two years in the minors and an ecstatic moment scoring his first goal, against Dominik Hasek in 1992-93, he proved himself worthy of not much more than the minors. Or did he? It seemed that every time he got called up, he was demoted for what seemed to be the last time. Yet he was always eventually recalled. He has signed as a free agent with NHL teams four times, and even a trip abroad for some Euro-hockey seems not to have dimmed his desire to keep at it NHL-wise. Amazingly, it wasn't until 13 years after that spectacular junior season that he played his most career games in a year, 60 with Florida in 2000-01. Keep moving the legs and good things will happen.

BARRY, Ed
b. Wellesley, Massachusetts, October 12, 1919

A Mass boy through and through, Barry spent the majority of his life in that state playing hockey. He played for the famed Boston Olympics in the early 1940s, the team that had defeated Canada for the 1933 World Championships, and after a year of war duty played 19 games for Boston in '46-'47. At the time, he was the fourth American in the NHL that season after Frank Brimsek, Johnny Mariucci, and Billy Moe. Barry then returned to the Olympics, retired in 1950, and began a long career as coach, first for that team and later for Boston University for 20 years.

BARRY, Marty
b. Quebec City, Quebec, December 8, 1905
d. Halifax, Nova Scotia, August 20, 1969

Although he was born in Quebec City, Barry grew up in Montreal where he was known as "goal a game" Barry because of his scoring ability. He made his NHL debut with the New York Americans in '27-'28, but also made his name with Boston and Detroit. He joined the Bruins in 1929, and in his 6 years with the team averaged 23 goals a season. Barry centred a line with Percy Galbraith and Harry Oliver, forming one of the top combinations in the league. He was not only a skilled player around the goal, but also an exceptional puckhandler. In the summer of 1935, he was involved in a major trade with Detroit that sent him and Art Giroux to the Red Wings for Cooney Weiland and Walt Buswell. Barry led the Wings to back-to-back Cups in his first two seasons (1935-37) playing on a line with Larrie Aurie and Herbie Lewis. Barry won the Lady Byng Trophy in '36-'37 and finished his career three years later with the Canadiens. In all his years in the NHL, he missed just two games. Barry went into coaching, leading the Halifax St. Mary's seniors for most of the 1940s. He later ran a grocery store in Dartmouth, on the other side of the bay, until suffering a fatal heart attack in his home. He was inducted into the Hockey Hall of Fame in 1965, truly one of the greats of Detroit's early years.

BARRY, Ray

b. Revere, Massachusetts, October 4, 1928

He was born but 10 minutes away from the old Boston Garden, but it would take 20 years for him to see the arena for the first time. Barry was still a baby when his father got a job in the oil business and moved the family to Edmonton. Ray became a fine player and received an invitation to the Bruins camp for 1947. There he met Joe Sadler, who talked eloquently of his years with the St. Mike's Majors in Toronto under the guidance of former Leafs great Joe Primeau. Barry resolved to make it to the NHL and moved to Toronto to play for Primeau's gang. Five times he went to Boston camp, and finally, in 1951, his dream came true. He played 18 games for Boston and scored a goal, though he eventually was sent back to the minors. He had had his moment and knew he wasn't an NHL regular, so he moved back west and played for the Calgary Stampeders for many years before coaching the Red Deer Rustlers in 1957-58.

BARTECKO, Lubos

b. Kezmarok, Czechoslovakia (Slovakia), July 14, 1976

The highs are often high and the lows are often low, and so it goes that Bartecko bounced from a Stanley Cup contender in St. Louis to a playoff-impossible Atlanta Thrashers team in one fell swoop. Although never drafted, he was one of a growing number of Eastern Europeans who came to Canada to play junior. He was signed by the Blues in 1997, and two years later he played on the famous Slovak line with Michal Handzus and Pavol Demitra. But even though that troika played well for much of the season, Bartecko was traded to the Thrashers in the summer and has had to continue his career in the ignominy of a team barely worthy of the NHL.

BARTEL, Robin

b. Drake, Saskatchewan, May 16, 1961

Someone should have given this guy a shake and told him how to get to the NHL. For someone with his talent, he did it all wrong. He played three years of provincial junior hockey and then attended U of Saskatchewan, played for the National Team, and played for the fourth-place Canadian team at the 1984 Olympics in Sarajevo. Undrafted all this time, he headed to Switzerland and only then did he sign with Calgary. After a single game with the Flames in '85-'86 and 40 more with Vancouver the following year, he was on the move again until retiring at age 29.

BARTLETT, Jim ("Rocky")

b. Verdun, Quebec, May 27, 1932

Playing in the NHL or AHL was a case of apples or oranges for Rocky, a left winger who scored more than 500 career goals in both leagues combined during a career that lasted more than 20 years. He set an AHL record by scoring goals five seconds apart (on Gerry McNeil, no less) and played his first NHL games at the end of the '54-'55 season with Montreal, replacing Rocket Richard who had been suspended for striking an official and clubbing Hal Laycoe on the head with his stick. The next year, Bartlett played some with the Rangers, but the majority of his career passed in the AHL, in Providence, where he played on the famous "B" line with Stan Baluik and Pierre Brillant. He almost lost an eye in 1963 when a stick caught him flush. The hemorrhaging was so severe doctors feared the eye might be lost, but Bartlett was back on skates in a matter of months. He earned his nickname in the AHL with Providence because of his willingness to fight, and with the Rangers he and Eddie Shack were called Nuts and Bolts for the same reason.

BARTON, Cliff

b. Sault Ste. Marie, Michigan, September 3, 1907
d. St. Louis, Missouri, September 14, 1969

Barton went straight from the Port Arthur Ports to the Pittsburgh Pirates of the NHL overnight, making his NHL debut in 1929 and making his exit two years later. A tiny right winger (5'7" and 155 pounds), he patrolled the ice lanes of minor league teams for years before skating three times for the Rangers in '39-'40. He remained in the game for another five years before calling it quits.

BARTOS, Peter

b. Martin, Czechoslovakia (Slovakia), September 5, 1973

Drafted at age 26 by Minnesota in 2000, Bartos had been a left winger in the Slovakian league for years before giving the NHL a shot for one season. He spent the majority of 2000-01 in the "I" with Cleveland, and played just 13 games with the Wild. At season's end, he returned home to play in the Czech league.

BASHKIROV, Andrei

b. Shelekhov, Soviet Union (Russia), June 22, 1970

One of those draft oddities, Bashkirov entered the NHL via Montreal after the Habs selected him in 1998 at the age of 28, one of the oldest players ever drafted. He stepped into the Canadiens' lineup, sort of, playing a handful of games that '98-'99 season and each since, but the left winger hasn't established himself as much of a scorer, checker, or anything else to separate him from the pack.

BASSEN, Bob

b. Calgary, Alberta, May 6, 1965

Son of Hank, the goalie. A great success story. Undrafted. Unwanted. Bob played junior in Medicine Hat, then helped Canada win a gold medal at the 1985 World Juniors in Helsinki. The Islanders signed him as a free agent, but they were on the downside of their dynasty years. He played 184 games on Long Island. Then he started to travel, team after team, year after year. Everyone needed a reliable and tough fourth-line centre, but no one wanted to keep one for too long. He played again at the 1992 Worlds for Canada. Bassen retired just as the 21st century began. Fifteen years in the NHL, seven teams. Not bad for someone no one wanted back in 1983.

BASSEN, Hank ("Red")

b. Calgary, Alberta, December 6, 1932

Sometimes called Mr. Emergency, Bassen the Elder had a tough go of it during a career that seemed fraught with bad timing. In his early years, with Chicago, he happened to be fighting Al Rollins for the starting job. It wasn't much of a fight though Bassen

Ray Barry

Lubos Bartecko

Jim Bartlett

Cliff Barton

Bob Bassen

Baz Bastien

Shawn Bates

Frank Bathe

Andy Bathgate

did set a WHL record with 63 penalty minutes with Calgary in '56-'57. Bassen played in the minors save for a handful of games. Then, when Detroit banished Ted Lindsay to Chicago, Bassen went the other way, to the Winged City, at a time when the Hawks were becoming a dominant team. He got the call for game six of the 1971 finals in the Detroit cage, but the Hawks stormed him and won the Cup that night with a 5-1 victory. Then Roger Crozier came up after the Leafs claimed the number-one man, a guy named Sawchuk. The Wings preferred Crozier to Bassen and he spent most of his puck-stopping hours in the minors for another six years. He did play in the 1966 playoffs but it was another tough 2-1 loss hung at his door. Then came the breath of fresh air that was the '67 expansion. Bassen played for Pittsburgh, and in one of his first games he surrendered Jean Béliveau's 400th career goal. At season's end he retired to Calgary to run an excavating business and coach the Calgary Wranglers. The Bassen name lived on, though, as his one son, Bob, played in the NHL and his other, Mark, ran amok in the minor pros.

BAST, Ryan
b. Spruce Grove, Alberta, August 27, 1975
Bast was a beast, but the best he has done so far was cause a ruckus in the boardrooms of the NHL. No team drafted him, and so after finishing junior hockey with Prince Albert he took his fists and skates to the minors, ending up with the Saint John Flames, affiliate of Calgary. Philadelphia signed him as a free agent on May 18, 1988, and then, for whatever reason, all hell broke loose. Calgary contended he was Flames property because of his minor-league affiliation. Four days later, the NHL pooh-poohed that idea, but also ruled that the contract offered to Bast exceeded the salary cap and was thus void. A trade was worked out – strange, since he wasn't Calgary property according to the NHL – that saw the Flames send Bast and an 8th-round draft choice in '99 to the Flyers for a 3rd-round selection in the same draft. Bast then played all of two games for Philly and has been buried in the minors ever since.

BASTIEN, Aldege "Baz"
b. Timmins, Ontario, August 29, 1919
d. Pittsburgh, Pennsylvania, March 15, 1983
He came down from the North as a Maple Leafs prospect, unable to make the NHL grade only because a guy named Turk Broda tended the twine at Maple Leaf Gardens. He played for the Marlies, but before he had much of a chance to start a pro career he entered the war. Two years later, he had a chance to shine with the Leafs because Broda himself had not yet been discharged. He played five games, went 0-4-1, and never saw the bigs again. At training camp in 1949 with the farm team, Pittsburgh Hornets, Bastien was hit flush in the eye by a puck and lost his vision in that optic. He retired, and a year later became that team's head coach (while working as the team's practise goalie as well!). In the ensuing years, he won three AHL championships and later ran the Hershey organization. For 10 years he served as general manager Sid Abel's assistant, first in Kansas City, then with the Red Wings. In 1977, Bastien became the GM for the Pittsburgh Penguins, but his life ended some

six years later. He attended the Pittsburgh chapter of the Professional Hockey Writers' Association dinner and had too much to drink. Nonetheless, he got into his car around midnight and collided with a motorcycle. Fortunately, the driver and passenger were unhurt, but Bastien died twenty minutes later in Mercy Hospital as a result of his injuries.

BATES, Shawn
b. Melrose, Massachusetts, April 3, 1975
There is no greater way to start an NHL career than scoring in your first game. Bates did that, on October 2, 1997, while playing for Boston. Strangely, it was more than a year before he got his first NHL assist. After a fine career in college with Boston University, Bates has yet to play a full season of pro hockey. After four part-time years with the Bruins, he became a free agent and signed with the resurgent Islanders on the recommendation of coach Peter Laviolette, who knew Bates from their mutual days at Providence in the AHL.

BATHE, Frank
b. Oshawa, Ontario, September 27, 1954
It's a physical game, they'll tell you. Live by the sword, die by the sword, they'll remind you. Kill or be killed is the guiding principle of the game. Bathe was big and tough; that's how he got to the NHL, and that's why he left the game at age 29. He played a little bit with Detroit in the 1970s and a little bit more with the Flyers a few years later, but the heavy-hitting defenceman discovered that his style of play, which made him so effective, also took a premature toll on his back. He retired after a single game in the '83-'84 season, unable to recover from surgery for a herniated disc enough to play his game at this level. Twice in his life he was first star in a game: once in a church-league contest played in a storm so thick no one actually saw the game, and the other time with the Flyers when he was at his hitting peak, in a 3-2 win over Minnesota.

BATHGATE, Andy
("Handy Andy"/ "Tubby")
b. Winnipeg, Manitoba, August 28, 1932
That Bathgate played for Guelph as a junior is neither here nor there. What is important is that on his first shift he suffered a debilitating knee injury that necessitated the insertion of a steel plate and forced him to wear a brace for the rest of his career. That that career lasted more than 20 years is a medical miracle of sorts. He won the Memorial Cup in 1952 with the Biltmores and turned pro with the Rangers the year after. He played a dozen years with the Blueshirts as a right winger on one of the worst teams in the league. Nonetheless, he was among the top scorers year after year, in large part because he was the first to champion the use of the slapshot, which, in his case, was also his most accurate shot. In '58-'59, he scored 40 goals and was named winner of the Hart Trophy, even though the team never made the playoffs. The next year, on November 1, 1959, he was an important part of hockey history. One of his patented slappers hit Jacques Plante flush in the face, and the goalie had to leave the ice to receive stitches. Plante refused to continue playing unless coach Toe Blake allowed him to wear a mask,

and, without alternative, Blake relented. Thus was born the use of the goalie mask on a nightly basis. Bathgate later played for three other NHL teams, most notably Toronto in the last part of the '63-'64 season, winning his first and only Cup. He played in eight All-Star Games and claimed to be the first man to use the curved stick, even before Stan Mikita (Mikita refuted the claim). Toward the end of his playing days, Bathgate ended up in the minors and then in Switzerland and Vancouver as a playing coach. He was inducted into the Hockey Hall of Fame in 1978. After hanging up the blades, he pulled out the sticks and turned his attention full-time to golf. He had spent much of his summer months playing in various tournaments, but became even more serious with more time on his hands. He became involved in a number of prosperous real estate investments in southern Ontario, most importantly buying the Indian Wells golf course.

BATHGATE, Frank

b. Winnipeg, Manitoba,
February 14, 1930
When Frank was in his third season of junior with the Guelph Biltmores, in 1949-50, he insisted kid brother Andy be given a tryout. Young Andy made an impression and made the team, and for a brief time the brothers played together on a line. From there, their careers crossed paths while the one went up and the other down. Frank had a two-game tryout with the Rangers in '52-'53, but later that season Andy got called up and never left. Six years later, Andy tried to return the Biltmore favour by arranging a tryout for Frank with the Rangers. The Blueshirts GM obliged, out of respect, but there was no contract forthcoming for Frank, who ended his career playing senior hockey in southern Ontario.

BATTAGLIA, Bates

b. Chicago, Illinois, December 13, 1975
Drafted by Anaheim but traded before he wore the vaunted colours of the Ducks, Battaglia has played all his NHL games with Carolina after three years with Lake Superior State. He's a big and strong left winger who can score a bit, and he has played for the U.S. at both the World Juniors and World Championships in his young career.

BATTERS, Jeff

b. Victoria, British Columbia, October 23, 1970
d. Canmore, Alberta, August 23, 1996
Batters went north to the University of Alaska in Anchorage to play college hockey in 1988 and a year later St. Louis drafted him. Between 1993 and '95 he played 16 games with the Blues, registering nary a point, but in the summer of 1996 he died from injuries sustained in a car crash. He was just 25 years old.

BATYRSHIN, Ruslan

b. Moscow, Soviet Union (Russia), February 19, 1975
If a player rises up to the stars and falls down to the earth in the blink of an eye, does he ever reach stardom? Batyrshin played for Dynamo at age 15 and worked his way up to the silver medal-winning national junior team by the time he was 19. He was drafted into the NHL, traded, and played two games with Los Angeles in '95-'96. He has since descended into the depths of the IHL and leagues even lower.

BAUER, Bobby

b. Waterloo, Ontario, February 16, 1915
d. Kitchener, Ontario, September 16, 1964
There are few men in hockey who have made a contribution as great as Bauer's both as a player and as an executive. Bauer came to prominence in 1931 at St. Mike's in Toronto. He played on a line with two other Kitchener-Waterloo boys, Milt Schmidt and Woody Dumart, unquestionably the most famous line in junior hockey history. The three played together for three years with the Majors and then many more in Boston, amazingly never playing for Toronto even though they played under the nose of Conn Smythe. They won the Memorial Cup in 1934 and Bauer carried on to the Bruins in 1936 where he scored a goal in his first game. It was his only game of the season, the line playing as a unit in Providence before being called up to Boston as a unit. The next year, they started the season together and were the class of the league. Backed by the Kraut Line, as they became known, the team won Cups in 1939 and '41, but perhaps there was never a more touching scene in the history of the game than in the latter stages of the '41-'42 season. The trio had joined the RCAF at the same time, and in their final game they received a tremendous ovation at the final bell. Then, the unthinkable happened. Members of the Habs, the dreaded enemy, lifted the three on their shoulders and paraded them around the ice for a final, emotional farewell. They were gone for three years, though they managed to stay together and play senior hockey, winning an Allan Cup with the Ottawa Flyers. Bauer played two more seasons after being discharged (1945-47), his last season his career best as he scored 30 goals for the first time and had 54 total points. He won three Lady Byng Trophies during his career. Bauer returned to Kitchener to coach and play, leading the K-W Dutchmen to two Allan Cups. During this time, he made a comeback of sorts with the Bruins, another remarkable and memorable night in Boston history. On March 18, 1952, the entire Kraut Line played a final game, and were honoured by the team. Even though he

Bauer came to prominence in 1931 at St. Mike's in Toronto.
BOBBY BAUER

Bates Battaglia

Jeff Batters

Ken Baumgartner

Mike Baumgartner

Nolan Baumgartner

Sergei Bautin

hadn't played in the NHL for five years, Bauer had a goal and an assist! His success with the K-W team led him to the 1956 Olympics in Cortina and the 1960 Olympics in Squaw Valley. He later became president of the Dutchmen and helped his brother, Father David Bauer, initiate and develop Canada's first national hockey program. Bauer was also involved in the skate business and was an active golfer. Through all his years and teams and successes, he maintained close ties with Schmidt and Dumart, friends not only on the ice but for life. In 1964, Bauer suffered a heart attack while on the links and died just a couple of days later in hospital.

BAUMAN, GARY
b. Innisfail, Alberta, July 21, 1940
After earning a degree in business administration from Michigan Tech on a hockey scholarship, goaler Bauman decided to pursue a career in the puck game. This was the 1960s, which meant a career mostly in the minors. He had his biggest moment of glory at the 1967 All-Star Game when he combined with Montreal teammate Charlie Hodge to defeat the best of the rest 3-0 and share the first, and still only, shutout in All-Star Game history. After two regular-season games with the Habs, he was claimed by Minnesota in the Expansion Draft, but after two years he was back in the minors. He first donned the pads while playing left wing on a team back in High River, Alberta. The goalie got hurt, and he offered to finish the game. He recorded a shutout and never looked back.

BAUMGARTNER, Ken ("Bomber")
b. Flin Flon, Manitoba, March 11, 1966
He once went 94 games without registering a single point, and he had a measly 54 total points compared to 2,244 penalty minutes. But heavy as he was on the ice with his fists, he was smart as a whip off it. During his years with the Islanders in the early 1990s, he studied business and finance at Hofstra University, and later became vice-president of the NHLPA. Although he won a Memorial Cup with Prince Albert in 1985, he was drafted a preposterous 245th overall that same summer, making him one of the lower draft picks ever to persevere in the NHL. After retiring in 1999, he served as assistant coach with the Bruins for a year and then enrolled full-time at the Harvard School of Business. After graduating in 2002, he moved to Los Angeles to work for Goldman Sachs, an investment firm.

BAUMGARTNER, Mike
b. Roseau, Minnesota, January 30, 1949
In the third period of a perfectly banal game in Kansas City on December 14, 1974, Vancouver defenceman Dennis Kearns sent a slapshot toward the Scouts net that hit Baumgartner near his left eye. In his 17th game with the team of his rookie NHL season, he was forced to call it a year. Scar tissue formed, and he returned home to Roseau, a town of 3000 near the Canadian border, to recuperate. But over the summer he had trouble playing baseball and at training camp he could follow a puck with no greater ease. He was sent to the minors, but in his first game he broke his nose. Doctors in both Boston and Kansas City told him he risked permanent damage to his eye if he continued to play, so he wisely retired. He returned home with his wife to his father's farm, knowing that his teaching certificate and degree in political science from the University of North Dakota could lead him off the land if he so desired.

BAUMGARTNER, Nolan
b. Calgary, Alberta, March 23, 1976
This has to rank up there as one of the mondo disappointments of recent drafts. Up to his time in the NHL, Baumgartner did everything imaginable, often twice. He won two Memorial Cups, with Kamloops, in 1994 and '95. He was a tournament all-star both years. He was defenceman of the year in Canadian junior hockey in '95, and he won consecutive gold medals at the World Juniors in '95 and '96. Naturally, he went high in the draft, 10th overall to Washington in 1994. And then, the big nothing. Eight games into his NHL career he dislocated his right shoulder and missed the year after surgery. Two years later, more serious surgery and another lost season. In five seasons of pro, he has played 26 games in all. The Caps eventually gave up on him and traded him to Chicago, but the size, intimidation, and confident play just haven't been there. Neither has the health.

BAUN, Bobby ("Boomer")
b. Lanigan, Saskatchewan, September 9, 1936
First things first: It was *not* a Stanley Cup-winning goal! Oh, yes, and another thing: He came back in the third period. No one seems to remember that, either. Oh, and something else: He didn't score on a broken leg! It was a big goal, an historic one, but the Cup didn't come out until a couple of nights later, back in Toronto. It was 1964 and the Leafs were in tight in the finals against Detroit. In the third period of game six, Detroit leading the series 3-2 and on the verge of winning the sacred bowl of hockey, Baun blocked a slapshot from Gordie Howe and fell to the ice in pain. He was carried off on a stretcher and most people thought he'd be lost for the series. But, no. Baun had his ankle frozen and returned near the end of the third period in a game that ended 3-3. At 2:43 of overtime, Baun smacked a bouncing puck on goal that eluded Terry Sawchuk, and the Leafs had tied the series. Back home, they won the Cup with a 4-0 shutout, Baun taking a regular shift despite a small crack in his ankle. Until the day he retired in 1973 and ever since, he has lived off that goal. A rugged, hard-hitting defenceman, he played his first eleven years with the Leafs, though the last, 1966-67, was bittersweet. He won his fourth and final Cup with the team, but he played little in the finals and was far out of the city the day the victory parade wended its way up Bay Street to city hall, so little did he feel part of that team. Expansion took him to Oakland, then to Detroit and then back to the Leafs for his final two years. Baun continued to live in the city, becoming the owner of numerous Tim Horton franchises as well as a golf course, forever a hero in the eyes of every Leafs fan who remembers that famous goal in '64.

BAUTIN, Sergei
b. Rogachev, USSR (Belarus), March 11, 1967
Indeed, 1992 was a good year for Bautin. He won a gold medal with Russia at the Olympics in Albertville, played at the World Championships a few months later, and was drafted by Winnipeg 17th overall a

month after that. The Jets liked him because, unlike most Soviets, he was big and tough and liked to mix it up, as they say. But he played just two years with the 'Peg and a single game each with Detroit and San Jose before returning to Europe to continue his career. He also played at the '97 and '99 Worlds.

BAWA, Robin
b. Chemainus, British Columbia, March 26, 1966
Goon is a job description sometimes euphemistically couched in kinder terms such as role player, team man, physical presence, policeman, handle himself, do what you have to, protect your star players, know when to step in, make a statement, stand up for your mates, stir things up, add some toughness. Bawa was all these rolled into one during his 61-game NHL career spread thin over four teams and five years (1989-94) and his minor-league career, which continued until the end of the '98-'99 season when he suffered a serious head injury in a game and has yet to play again.

BAXTER, Paul
b. Winnipeg, Manitoba, October 28, 1955
Fighting took on new meaning when Baxter entered the NHL. He arrived after ensconcing himself as the all-time penalty minutes leader in the WHA, and while playing for Quebec, Pittsburgh, and Calgary in the NHL he established records and antipathy that are, perhaps, unparalelled in the game. Though deeply religious, he had almost everyone in the league cursing him – and worse – in the name of getting even. On November 21, 1981, Chris Nilan of Montreal threw a puck at Baxter in the penalty box after an altercation, opening a cut that needed eight stitches. Nilan was suspended three games for his vulcanized fastball. Just 18 days later, Philadelphia's goon-to-end-goons, Paul Holmgren, punched referee Andy Van Hellemond in an attempt to get at Baxter. He was sentenced to a five-game quiet time. Five days after that, both Barry Beck and Nick Fotiu left the Rangers bench to get at Baxter, and both were suspended. Finally, the scoring star Blaine Stoughton was suspended for eight games after the league ruled that his repeated cross-checks to Baxter's head constituted a "deliberate attempt to injure." Baxter had overcome a serious injury before incurring all this wrath. In 1980, linesman Bob Hodges accidentally skated over his arm, severing four tendons in Baxter's wrist. In 1981-82, the fighter set a record with 409 penalty minutes (but still found time to score 8 goals). When he hung up his gloves for good, Baxter turned to the art of coaching. He became Bob Johnson's assistant in Calgary, which was fitting because Badger Bob had recruited Baxter for his University of Wisconsin team many years previous, but the player's

academic standing wasn't up to snuff. Baxter coached the farm team in Salt Lake City and was with Terry Crisp and the Flames when they won the Cup in 1989. Since then, Baxter has moved on to the Chicago and San Jose organizations.

BEADLE, Sandy
b. Regina, Saskatchewan, July 12, 1960
The Beadle-man was an All-American at Northeastern University in 1981 and decided to run headlong into the NHL before graduating. The impetus for this enthusiasm came from the Jets having drafted him the previous summer, but Beadle bedazzled the Jets for only six games in '80-'81 before being belittled with a demotion to the minors. He retired in 1984.

BEATON, Frank ("Seldom")
b. Antigonish, Nova Scotia, April 28, 1953
Seldom an NHLer and seldom well behaved, Beaton made his debut with the Rangers in 1978-79 under the most peculiar of circumstances. The left winger was playing a game with the Birmingham Bulls of the WHA. The night was February 19, 1978, and the team was in Cincinnati to play the Stingers. During the first period, he could see active movement by police in the crowd and during the intermission he raced to the dressing room and tried to scurry out the window. Two officers hauled him back inside and handcuffed him to a post. Beaton was wanted on a warrant for assaulting a service station attendant, Gabriel Fieno, who apparently spilled gas on the trunk of Beaton's sports car back in '76. The next day, Stingers coach Jacques Demers posted bond for his player's release. On April 30, 1978, Beaton was found guilty of assault. He was sentenced to 160 days in jail, but 155 were suspended. Beaton served his five days, and a few weeks later the Rangers signed him as a free agent. He played 25 games in 2 years on Broadway before being sent to the minors, where he continued to rack up penalty minutes until 1983.

BEATTIE, John "Red"
b. Ibstock, England, October 2, 1907
d. unknown
After a terrific rookie season in 1930-31, Beattie broke his leg in the second game of the next season and didn't return until the fall of 1932. He then played five complete seasons and was lucky enough to number Cooney Weiland, Dit Clapper, and Nels Stewart among his teammates. In 1935-36, he led the Bruins with 14 goals and tied Weiland with 18 assists and 32 points. Although he was born in England, he was raised in Edmonton and returned to the West after his NHL days came to an end in 1939 with the New York Americans.

A rugged, hard-hitting defenceman, he played his first eleven years with the Leafs, though the last, 1966-67, was bittersweet.
BOBBY BAUN

Robin Bawa

Paul Baxter

Sandy Beadle

Frank Beaton

Norm Beaudin

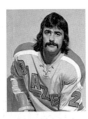

Serge Beaudoin

![Mark Beaufait action photo]

Mark Beaufait

![Don Beaupre goalie photo]

Don Beaupre

![Barry Beck photo]

Barry Beck

BEAUDIN, Norm
b. Montmartre, Saskatchewan, November 28, 1941

Everyone knows Bobby Hull was the first player to sign with the fledgling Winnipeg Jets of the new World Hockey Association back in 1972, right? Wrong. Norm Beaudin was the first. But his was not a name upon which to establish the reputation of a league and team, so the club withheld that small announcement until it had inked the "Golden Jet" to a lucrative deal. Nevertheless, the two played on the same line, centred by Christian Bordeleau and dubbed the Luxury Line during that first season. Despite suffering from arthritis, Beaudin still managed to collect 103 points that season and led the league in playoff points as well. Previously, he had kicked around in the minors for a decade after finishing junior out west, his only notable time coming with St. Louis and Minnesota. Those stints accounted for all of his 25 NHL games. Beaudin left the Jets and WHA after four years to accept the position of playing coach with a Swiss team.

BEAUDOIN, Eric
b. Ottawa, Ontario, May 3, 1980

His stock dropped even before he hit the NHL. Bedouin was drafted by Tampa Bay in the fourth round but traded to Florida for a seventh-round draft choice. He played eight games with the Panthers in 2001-02, although he missed a good part of the year after undergoing an emergency appendectomy.

BEAUDOIN, Serge
b. Montreal, Quebec, November 30, 1952

Referees, like players, have to earn their dues in the minors, and it might help those NHL-knowledgeable Kerry Fraser zealots to know that he once was pounded while working his way up. While playing in the Central Hockey League, Beaudoin either pushed Fraser aside to get at an opponent or picked him up and tossed him out of the way, depending on which version of the story is more precise. Either way, Beaudoin was suspended, and although he played in the NHL that year, he lasted but three games with Atlanta before his swift return whence he came. Fraser, meanwhile, continues to work in the NHL.

BEAUDOIN, Yves
b. Pointe-aux-trembles, Quebec, January 7, 1965

Young hockey players develop at erratic and inconsistent rates, thus rendering the Entry Draft more a crapshoot than anything else. Beaudoin was playing in the Q when Washington selected him 203rd overall in 1983, a clear indication he wasn't going far. Two years later, Beaudoin was considered one of the top juniors in the country; he made the Canadian team at the World Juniors and won a gold medal. But then, over the next three years, his maturation flatlined. He was recalled from the minors in '85-'86 to replace first Larry Murphy and then Rod Langway, injured veterans, but the defenceman went right back to the minors when they were healthy. This happened again the next year and the year after that, and by 1988, Beaudoin decided to take his game on the road, hoofing it to Europe to continue his career.

BEAUFAIT, Mark
b. Royal Oak, Michigan, May 13, 1970

Beaufait has played all but five of his pro games outside the NHL, that five-game exception coming with San Jose in 1992-93. A grad of Northern Michigan University, he took a year away from the moneyed ranks to play for the U.S. National Team and in the '94 Olympics in Lillehammer. Since then, he has played exclusively in the IHL until 2001, when Minnesota signed him and assigned him to Houston (AHL).

BEAUPRE, Don
b. Waterloo, Ontario, September 19, 1961

When his great-great-grandparents came to Canada from France during the First World War, they changed their name from Boppre to Beaupre, and many years later young Don had to explain the French pronunciation without the accent (bow-pray). Minnesota drafted him in 1980, and Beaupre stepped right in and won the starter's job from both Gilles Meloche and Gary Edwards. He was selected to play in the All-Star Game in his rookie season and quickly developed into one of the finer young goalies of the game, despite his slim build and small stature. "My job is to stop the puck, not beat it up," he would tell size-naysayers. But early in '88-'89, he fell into the team's bad books and was on his way to the minors. A trade took him to Washington, and it was there he enjoyed his finest years, though never with anything more than middling playoff success. He later went on to Ottawa and then to Toronto. With the Leafs, he was winless in his last 11 career games and was furious when he was sent to the minors to finish out the '96-'97 season.

BEAUREGARD, Stephane
b. Cowansville, Quebec, January 10, 1968

True to his name, Beauregard was highly admired by scouts as a junior. He was Canada's pre-eminent junior goalie in 1988, and looked to be one of the top prospects between the pipes. However, Beauregard had the difficult job of living down one of the more one-sided trades of all time. Winnipeg drafted him and he was sent to Buffalo. Then he went to Chicago with a 4th-round draft choice on August 7, 1992, for Dominik Hasek. Such was his swift drop in stock that just three days later he was sent to Winnipeg for Christian Ruuttu, and two months later he was traded to Philadelphia for nothing more than future considerations. Beauregard was out of the NHL by 1994; Hasek managed to hang around a little longer.

BECK, Barry ("Bubba")
b. Vancouver, British Columbia, June 3, 1957

Nicknamed after Bubba Smith of Baltimore Colts fame, at 6'3" and 215 pounds he was one of the biggest men to play in the NHL. But his shoulder was like concussions are for the modern player: one more hit and it's over. He got hit, and it was over. Teamed with defensive partner Brad Maxwell, Beck went to three successive Memorial Cups with the brawling New Westminster Bruins in the 1970s, and his combination of size, offensive talent, defensive ability, and leadership led to his being drafted 2nd overall in 1977 by Colorado. He didn't disappoint. Beck finished second to Mike Bossy in Calder Trophy voting and was an instant superstar in the league, but the lowly Rockies was not the place for him. The Rangers acquired him, and for a while he was the toast of Broadway, on ice and off. His tremendous open-ice hits, wicked slapshot, and overpowering defence made him one of the top all-round players in the game. But dishing out hits takes as much of a toll as receiving them. A recurring right shoulder injury accounted for surgery, lost games, and a change in style for Beck. In addition, problems with coach Ted Sator reached a boiling point in the '86 playoffs when Sator didn't dress him for a single game. Beck took a year off, though it proved to be three, to get away from Sator and rest his damaged shoulder. By the summer of 1989, he had had enough rest and got a tattoo of a Haida killer whale on the back of the injured shoulder to give it mystical strength. He signed with Los Angeles and was ready to hit the ice again. Just 52 games later, though, he retired from the game.

BECKETT, Bob ("B.B.")
b. Unionville, Ontario, April 8, 1936
Beckett's career came to a crashing halt in February 1964 when he slid into the boards while playing for Providence, the Boston farm team. He shattered his ankle, and after an operation discovered it still wasn't right. A year later, doctors told him to give up any hopes of returning. He had spent his whole career in the Bruins system, starting back in 1956-57 when the B's called him up for 18 games as a replacement. Big and strong, he failed to score a goal, so Boston sent him back down for further seasoning. Coach Phil Watson kept a watch over him and called him up whenever he had the chance. But despite being given four chances between '56 and '64, Beckett always managed to find his way back to the minors. And then came the career-ending injury.

BEDARD, Jim
b. Admiral, Saskatchewan, November 19, 1927
A relaxed man away from the rink, big Bedard was a heavy-hitting defenceman when he put on his equipment. He played junior hockey in the highly successful Moose Jaw system, but played only 22 games with Chicago from 1949 to '51. After that, he played primarily in New Westminster in the WHL, though Seattle acquired him in 1955 on loan with an option to buy, one the Americans didn't exercise. Bedard retired a couple of years later.

BEDARD, Jim
b. Niagara Falls, Ontario, November 14, 1956
He looked good to Washington, the horrible team that drafted him in 1976. And the next year, when the team had gone winless in 20 games, the Caps called Bedard up from the minors to try to staunch the bleeding. He did, stayed the year, and returned for a second term of punishment in '78-'79. Then, he, too, lost and lost and lost. The Caps eventually bought out his contract: For the next six years, Bedard would receive monthly payments, regardless of where he played or what he did. Bedard then attended the Maple Leafs training camp, but didn't make enough

of an impression and headed to Finland, where he stayed for 14 years. He played mostly in the second tier of Finnish league play and returned to North America in 1994, at which point he became a goaltending consultant for Detroit.

BEDDOES, Clayton
b. Bentley, Alberta, November 10, 1970
Although Beddoes had a fine final season at Lake Superior State University in 1993-94, he was never drafted into the NHL. Instead, Boston signed him as a free agent and assigned him to the farm team, which for the B's meant Providence. He didn't put up outstanding numbers, but he got the call to the big team for healthy chunks of the following two seasons, after which the Bruins decided not to renew his contract. Beddoes signed with Ottawa and a short time later took the long flight across the Atlantic to continue his career in Europe.

BEDNAR, Jaroslav
b. Prague, Czechoslovakia (Czech Republic), November 8, 1976
While he was playing happily in Czech and then Finland Bednar was drafted by Los Angeles at the ripe old age of 24. He joined the Kings in 2001 but spent most of the season in the minors. The right winger came to North America as a proven goal scorer in Europe, though he has yet to light the lamp with the same consistency in the pros here.

BEDNARSKI, John
b. Thunder Bay, Ontario, July 4, 1952
He could hit, skate, and score, and for a defenceman those were the three most important criteria. Nonetheless, he was free for the offing when the Rangers signed him in 1972 and he played for three seasons with the Blueshirts in the mid-1970s. He later signed with Edmonton and played one game with Gretzky and the boys in their first year, 1979-80. Although Buffalo later got his signature on a contract, he had seen his last NHL days. He played in the minors, including Rochester, and it was to that city he returned after retiring to begin a career as a radio and TV colour analyst.

BEECH, Kris
b. Salmon Arm, British Columbia, February 5, 1981
Still very much a work in progress, Beech was drafted 7th overall by Washington in 1999. Perhaps that selection and the fact that he was key to the package the Caps put together to obtain Jaromir Jagr in the summer of 2001 authenticate his value as a terrific promise. Whether he develops into a star or vanishes as a has-been will be determined in the next few years.

BEERS, Bob
b. Pittsburgh, Pennsylvania, May 20, 1967
Although Beers developed in the highly respected system of the University of Maine Black Bears, he didn't go in the 1985 draft until the 210th selection. Boston took him and developed him into a steady NHLer, not a superstar but a tough and reliable defenceman. However, that type is both valued and replaceable, so while Beers always had work, it was

Bob Beckett

Jim Bedard

John Bednarski

Kris Beech

Bob Beers

Eddy Beers

Marc Behrend

Frank Beisler

Derek Bekar

Wade Belak

frequently with a different team. From 1989 to '97 he played for four teams. Additionally, he represented the U.S. three times at the World Championships – 1993, 1994, and 1997 – though the results were always disappointing – sixth place, fourth, and sixth. After retiring, he moved into the broadcast booth of the Providence Bruins, where he had ended his playing days at age 30. However, he still longed for the game, and returned as a player a year later on a part-time basis.

BEERS, Eddy
b. Merritt, British Columbia, October 12, 1959

Here's an odd story of a player who warranted a suspension for his actions, but the team against whom those actions were committed went out of its way to make sure he *wasn't* suspended! In a Calgary – Vancouver game in March 1984, Eddy Beers of the Flames went to the penalty box with Harold Snepsts of the Canucks for roughing. Beers was furious, and while in the box threw his stick at Snepsts like a spear. Vancouver was in a tough race to the playoffs with Winnipeg, and Calgary's next game was with those very Jets. Vancouver wanted to ensure that Beers, Calgary's second-leading scorer, was in the lineup to maximize the Flames' chances of winning, thereby helping the Canucks! A year and a half later, Beers hurt his back during practice with Peoria and had to have a disc removed. No amount of rest or stretching helped, and he retired to pursue a career in teaching.

BEGIN, Steve
b. Trois Rivières, Quebec, June 14, 1978

Just a kid. When Begin was born, for goodness' sake, Gordie Howe had only two more seasons of professional hockey left. Drafted by Calgary in '96, he has been with the Flames ever since, though most of his time has been in the minors and just 22 games have been of the NHL flavour. Begin played for Canada at the 1998 World Juniors, when Canada had its worst showing ever – eighth place.

BEHLING, Clarence "Dick"
b. Berlin (Kitchener), Ontario, March 16, 1915
d. Kitchener, Ontario, July 24, 1994

Just five games in the NHL marred an otherwise perfectly clean minor pro sheet for Behling. He was born in Berlin, but by the time he was old enough to play in a league, the town's name had changed to Kitchener (Hitler had a good deal of influence in that decision), and it was in Kitchener that he both began and finished his pro career. In between, he played in Britain and in the AHL and served two years in the Canadian army. His lone forays in the NHL were with Detroit in '40-'41 and '42-'43.

BEHREND, Marc
b. Madison, Wisconsin, January 11, 1961

"He reminds me a lot of Glenn Hall," Winnipeg GM John Ferguson said of Behrend when he hoped the kid would join the Jets full-time. This was in Orwell's year, 1984. Well, Fergie never won a Cup as a GM. Behrend, in fact, almost quit the puck-stopping game in college when he was so far down the depth chart on the University of Wisconsin that he saw no hope. But

Badgers coach Bob Johnson encouraged him, and with some good fortune and injuries to other goalies, Behrend became the main man between the pipes for the school. He took the team to the NCAA championships in '81 and '83 and then played a year for the U.S. National Team, culminating with the 1984 Olympics in Sarajevo. At that point he joined the Jets. He earned his first shutout early the next season against Hartford, a team that featured Bob Johnson's son, Mark. From there, it was all downhill, and within two years his stock had gone from Wall Street to penny-share and nothing but nothing could have reminded Ferguson that Behrend looked like Glenn Hall, except for the fact that both 'tenders were retired.

BEISLER, Frank
b. New Haven, Connecticut, October 18, 1913
d. New Haven, Connecticut, September 8, 1973

The first Connecticutter to make it to the NHL, Beisler led a full and varied life that began with skates and ended in a funeral home. He played football, baseball, and hockey at Hillhouse High School in the late 1920s and focused on hockey a short time later. Beisler played his way up the ranks until he made the New Haven Eagles. At the same time, he opened a gas station in town that he ran in the summer and supervised in the winter. He played but two NHL games, one in '36-'37, the other during the '39-'40 season, after that he was sold to Springfield. During the war, he played only on weekends and worked at a defence plant. He eventually stopped playing altogether until the war was over. He retired in 1946 because of blood clots in his legs and turned to coaching, first with the Buffalo Bisons. In 1949, he was out of coaching and became a linesman in the AHL, but only for one season. His father died a short time later, and Frank Junior took over his dad's business, the Hamden Memorial Funeral Home, until he himself retired.

BEKAR, Derek
b. Burnaby, British Columbia, September 15, 1975

He was traded by St. Louis to Washington with future considerations for Mike Peluso and future considerations on November 29, 2000, and to date Bekar is a modern-day, active one-game wonder who has been mired in the minors since leaving the University of New Hampshire.

BELAK, Wade
b. Saskatoon, Saskatchewan, July 3, 1976

He was born Wade Aadland, but when his parents divorced and his mother remarried, Wade took his stepfather's surname. He grew up out west until Quebec took him in the first round of the '94 draft. When the Nords relocated to Denver, he was still part of the minor-league system and missed the run to the Stanley Cup, but over the next three years (1996-99) he saw limited action with the Avalanche. Colorado used him in the deal to get Theo Fleury and he was claimed off waivers by the Leafs in February 2001. Big and tough, Belak has seen action as both a sixth defenceman and a winger on occasion, though his hands are made more of sandpaper than something softer.

BELANGER, Alain ("Bam Bam")
b. St. Janvier, Quebec, January 18, 1956

Hockey is a sport of sometimes cruel irony. Any player will happily provide the sound bite that supports the theory that you do anything you can to help the team win. Belanger found out exactly what that meant the first time he was called to play in the NHL, with Toronto during the 1977 playoffs. There he was, a Leafs draft choice. He'd played most of two years in the minors; coach Red Kelly called him up for the playoffs, and he took the pre-game skate the night of April 7, 1977. A fighting right winger, he knew his role and was prepared to defend his mates if he had to. But he sat on the bench that night. Sat and sat. He watched defenceman Brian Glennie limp off with a knee injury during the second period, but Belanger was a winger, not a blueliner. Doctors said Glennie could continue only if he wore a knee brace, but one couldn't be found. Then a player piped up that Belanger wore one from a previous injury. The rookie undressed, handed his brace to Glennie, who returned to action, and watched the rest of the game from the bench. He played nine games for the Leafs the following season but never resurfaced after that.

BELANGER, Eric ("Belly")
b. Sherbrooke, Quebec, December 16, 1977

Talk about an introduction. In his first NHL game, October 6, 2000, his L.A. Kings were playing in Washington. The Kings won the game, and Belanger had a goal and two assists. In the next 61 games, he had but 18 more points, but, hey, it's not often a player walks into the NHL with that kind of a game.

BELANGER, Francis
b. Bellefeuille, Quebec, January 15, 1978

A bruiser is perhaps the best euphemism for this Belanger who was drafted by Philadelphia but signed by Montreal when the Flyers failed to use him or re-sign him. He appeared in 10 games for the Habs in 2000-01 and so far his NHL time has been limited to that action.

BELANGER, Jesse
b. St. Georges de Beauce, Quebec, June 15, 1969

In a career that has come full circle, Belanger signed with Montreal after finishing junior in 1990 with Granby, where he had three high-scoring seasons. From that point to this, though, he has failed to put down roots for too long, the common pattern for most modern hockeyists, journeymen and superstars both. He did play with the Habs in the '93 playoffs, and for

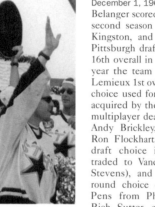

Belfour won his 400th game in 2002-03, the great hallmark of achievement for goalies.
ED BELFOUR (LEFT)

that he has his name on the Cup, Montreal's last. In addition, he has been owned by Edmonton, Florida, Vancouver, and Tampa Bay.

BELANGER, Ken
b. Sault Ste. Marie, Ontario, May 14, 1974

He could lift weights and skate, and even score an itty bit, but Belanger has remained in hockey because of his fists. That's why the Leafs traded for him; that's why the Islanders acquired him; and that's why Boston has hung on to him. However, after injuring his head in Toronto on November 11, 1999, Belanger was lucky to remember his phone number let alone play. He missed most of that season and recovered to join Boston the next.

BELANGER, Roger
b. St. Catharines, Ontario, December 1, 1965

Belanger scored 44 goals in his second season of junior, with Kingston, and on that merit Pittsburgh drafted him a high 16th overall in 1984, the same year the team selected Mario Lemieux 1st overall. The draft choice used for him had been acquired by the Penguins in a multiplayer deal that involved Andy Brickley, Mark Taylor, Ron Flockhart, a third-round draft choice in 1984 (later traded to Vancouver – Mike Stevens), and this '84 first-round choice coming to the Pens from Philadelphia for Rich Sutter, a second-round choice in '84 (Greg Smyth), and a third-round choice in '84 (David McLay). Although a complex deal, the results were simple: Belanger played 44 games with the Pens the next year and then had a short tour of duty in the minors before retiring.

BELANGER, Yves
b. Baie Comeau, Quebec, September 30, 1952

One in a series of goalies to come out of Quebec, Belanger had a modest NHL career during the 1970s with St. Louis, Atlanta, and Boston. He played as much in the minors as the NHL and retired in 1983 to upgrade his education. He graduated from the University of Moncton with a Business degree and worked in the Maritimes, Montreal, Toronto, and then Mississauga in the transportation industry.

BELFOUR, Ed ("Eddie the Eagle")
b. Carman, Manitoba, April 21, 1965

Any time a guy assaults a security guard, resists arrest, throws up on himself in the back of the cruiser, and offers police $1 billion not to put him in jail, you get the sense the guy in question is not playing with a full deck. All of which goes to say that goalie Ed Belfour is both supremely talented and a bit of a live wire. He has

Alain Belanger

Jesse Belanger

Ken Belanger

Roger Belanger

Yves Belanger

an obsession with fitness, his own Web site (www.belfour.com), and a healthy ego that gives him confidence when those around him aren't always sure that confidence is justified. He is also a tremendous success story, going from undrafted 22-year-old to Stanley Cup champion. Signed by Chicago, he played alongside Dominik Hasek in the early going and then became the Hawks' number-one goalie when the Dominator went to Buffalo. He blossomed into one of the best in the game with a reputation for not playing big in the big games, a regular-season wonder who seemed destined never to lead his team to the promised land of Lord Stanley. As a result, he was happy to leave Chicago and, after a few games with San Jose, he signed with Dallas and proved all naysayers wrong by leading the Stars to the Cup in his second season with the team. But his erratic personality came into conflict with the disciplined and regimented mandate of coach Ken Hitchcock. He lost and won back the starter's job on a few occasions – most notably after his run-in with security at a Dallas hotel – and although he was named a goalie for Canada's 2002 Olympics team, he continued to be more temperamental than consistent. Nonetheless, Belfour won his 400th game in 2002-03, the great hallmark of achievement for goalies, and he did it with Toronto, the team he signed with in 2002 and for whom he has succeeded Curtis Joseph admirably.

Michel Belhumeur

BELHUMEUR, Michel

b. Sorel, Quebec, September 2, 1949

The goalie with the mess of electric hair behind the mask received his NHL baptism by fire in 1972-73 when Philadelphia's starting goalie, Doug Favell, was shellacked for six goals in the first half of a game in Madison Square Garden. With nothing to lose, Flyers coach Fred Shero tossed Belhumeur to the wolves, and lo and behold the rookie shut out the Rangers for the rest of the way, 36 minutes in all. As a result, he earned a start in the next game, a 2-2 tie in Toronto, and in the game after that got his first win, 5-2 over Montreal. Belhumeur was the fourth player the Flyers had drafted in 1969; Bobby Clarke, Dave Schultz, and Don Saleski were the others. But after his flashy start with the team, his magic stick soon lost its gold dust and he was back in the minors to start the new year. Philadelphia left him exposed in the Expansion Draft in 1974, and he had the misfortune to be scooped by Washington, soon to be the worst team in NHL history. Believe it or not, Belhumeur played 42 games over 2 seasons with the Caps, and to this day he has yet to win another NHL game. His record was 0-29-4, and he allowed an average of more than 5 goals a game. Washington sent him to the minors, and it was there he closed out his career.

BELISLE, Dan

b. South Porcupine, Ontario, May 9, 1937

It's always odd to see a player with so few games to his credit do so well in those games. Belisle played just four games for the Rangers in 1960-61, but he scored two goals. Yet that wasn't enough to keep him in the NHL, and no team at a later date ever game him another chance. Belisle played 14 years of pro and then went into the unkindest business of all – coaching. He started with Des Moines in the IHL, his last team as a player, and then moved around the minors before taking on the impossible task of trying to guide the Washington Capitals to the occasional win. From 1978 to '80, when he was fired, he had a record of 28-51-17, an indictment more of the team than the man. Detroit hired him as an assistant after that, worthy exoneration for any man leaving the Caps of that era.

BÉLIVEAU, Jean ("Le Gros Bill")

b. Trois Rivières, Quebec, August 31, 1931

When he was five years old, his father gave him a pair of skates. He didn't take them off until 1971, by which time he had played his way into the very consciousness of Canadian culture, as a player and a man, a success and a gentleman of extraordinary talents. He played his first hockey in Victoriaville, and later played for the Quebec Aces, his first pro team. Béliveau was that rare specimen of the six-team NHL. He had no interest in playing in that league above all else, and he had no desire to be bullied and cornered by the team's owners. He was content to play with the Aces under coach Punch Imlach, and did so for three years (1950-53). During this time, the Canadiens were under relentless pressure to get Le Gros Bill (named after a popular French folk song of the day) to sign a contract. Béliveau demured. He was faithful to Quebec City, he was as well paid there as he would be in Montreal, and he was revered beyond words. For every hat trick he scored, local businesses would shower him with presents. He led the league in goals and points – there was no need for him to leave. He was called up for trials twice with the Habs. In his first two-game stint, he had a goal and assist; in his second three-game appearance, he scored five goals (he wasn't paid for this callup – instead, he was given a set of furniture by the team when he got married the next year). Béliveau was an unquestioned NHL star after just five games. The Canadiens did the only thing they legally could do – they bought the entire Quebec Hockey League, thus making Béliveau property of the Habs. Then, they signed him to the richest contract in league history, in 1953, and so began the NHL career of one of the greatest men the league has known. The contract ran for five years and paid a total of $100,000, but

He reached the 200 goal mark faster than anyone had done previously.
JEAN BÉLIVEAU

Dan Belisle

he was also hired by Molson at $10,000 a year in a side deal that had no particular duties attached save to work in promotions. In all, he played 20 seasons with the Habs. He could pass, shoot, score, play with grace, play with physical purpose, and lead by example. And, he could win. He was the key centreman to the team's five consecutive Cups (1956-60), replacing Elmer Lach as centre to Maurice Richard and Bert Olmstead. After the last of those Cups, when captain Maurice Richard retired, Béliveau inherited the hallowed "C." His methods as player and leader were direct, unassailable, and admirable. He controlled the dressing room and the on-ice decorum of the team, and he led the Habs to the so-called quiet dynasty of the 1960s, winning four more Cups. That decade was not altogether kind to him, though forgetful Montreal fans might not like to be reminded of their role in his unhappiness. In 1966, he was struck in the eye by Stan Mikita's banana blade, and although he recovered full use of it, doctors discovered that his heart was too small for his large body (he later required a pacemaker). His play suffered, and fans booed him relentlessly at times, though he played through the tough times with a character of which the spoiled fans can hardly boast. He retired after a final victory in '70-'71 when the team upset Boston en route to Béliveau's tenth Cup championship, a record eclipsed a few years later by Henri Richard. The honours for Béliveau were extraordinary. He was a First Team All-Star six times, Hart Trophy winner twice, Art Ross Trophy winner in '55-'56, and winner of the inaugural Conn Smythe Trophy in 1965. He played in 13 All-Star Games, scored 507 goals and 1,219 points. He reached the 200 goal mark faster than anyone had done previously. In retirement, he remained faithful to the club. He worked in publicity and became senior vice-president of corporate affairs, and he remained connected to Molson until 2002, some 49 years after his first contract with the beer giant. In 1981, he was named to the election committee of the Hockey Hall of Fame, and in 1994 he politely declined the most prestigious appointment in the land when he was offered the title of governor-general. Instead, he wanted to stay in Montreal and help raise his parentless grandchildren. He has been an ambassador for the Habs through good times and, more recently, bad, and he had advocated fair and skilled play above all else in hockey. Béliveau carries himself with a dignity that commands respect and awe, and his mere presence in the NHL has been to the game's immense benefit.

BELL, Billy
b. Lachine, Quebec, June 10, 1891
d. Lachine, Quebec, June 3, 1952
A forward in the NHL's earliest days, Bell played most of his games in Montreal, with the Wanderers and Canadiens. His tenure with the Wanderers was cut short when the arena burned down five games into the 1917-18 season and he was claimed by the Canadiens. In his last season, '23-'24, he won the Cup with the Canadiens. Bell later became a referee in the NHL and the Quebec Senior League, and worked at the Dominion Bridge Company in Lachine.

BELL, Bruce
b. Toronto, Ontario, February 15, 1965
Bell was four years old when he started skating in the West Hill district of Toronto, though his old man could have cared a hoot. An Englishman, Bill Bell would have preferred his boy play football (soccer), and when the family moved back to England in the 1970s, Bruce had no place to skate. But on returning to Canada, Bruce was encouraged by his grandfather, and eventually joined the Toronto Young Nats and then the OHL. Once drafted into the NHL, by Quebec, Bell's strengths were overshadowed by his weakness. He had been a left winger as a kid, but one year his coach put him on the blueline and he performed superbly. In the NHL, he was regarded as offensively capable – good skater, good speed, fine hands – but had troubles on defence. A fine rookie season was followed by a disastrous sophomore year, which led to an injury-hampered third year. His stock dropped quickly, but he continued his career in the minors, then back in his father's homeland and other parts of Europe. After retiring, Bell settled in Taber, Alberta, to coach kids' hockey and help his wife run a large turkey ranch.

Jean Béliveau

BELL, Gordie
b. Portage la Prairie, Manitoba, March 13, 1925
d. Belleville, Ontario, November 3, 1980
Prior to game two of the 1956 semifinals between the Rangers and Canadiens in Montreal, New York coach Phil Watson faced a conundrum as his number-one man in goal, Gump Worsley, had a groin pull too serious to allow him to play. Watson remembered having seen a puck-stopper a year ago playing for Springfield and managed to get him to the Forum in time for the game. Gordie Bell backstopped the Rangers to an improbable win, the team's first at Montreal in 19 tries. The Gumper came back for games three and four, both losses, and by the time Bell was put back in the crease for game five, his well of success had run dry. Montreal drove seven pucks past him and eliminated the Rangers from the playoffs. Bell had been playing in the minors for 11 years, and his only other NHL appearance had been near the start of the '45-'46 season in another emergency situation (he had been an Able Seaman with the Royal Canadian Naval Volunteer Reserve during the war). Regular Frank McCool had left the team in a contract dispute, and Turk Broda had not yet discharged from the army. So, for eight games, Bell filled the breach. When Turkey Face became available, Bell was sent down to begin his 11-year term. He was later reinstated as an amateur and played for Belleville McFarlands during their run to the 1959 gold medal at the World Championships.

Gordie Bell

BELL, Harry ("Huddy")
b. Regina, Saskatchewan, October 31, 1925
He had the most powerful slapshot around, and so the hefty Harry Bell was always in demand. A defenceman, he was in the Rangers organization for a number of years right after the war before settling down in his hometown to play senior hockey. He showed up for camp to start the '53-'54 season some 20 pounds over his playing weight of 200, and while coach Garth Boesch wasn't around to tell him, the owner suspended him until he lost some excess poundage. Bell never did, and he never played again.

Joe Bell

Neil Belland

Pete Bellefeuille

Andy Bellemer

Brian Bellows

BELL, Joe
b. Portage la Prairie, Manitoba, November 27, 1923

The Rangers raced through more minor leaguers during the war years than just about any other NHL team. Joe Bell was one of them, a career minor pro left winger who played a few games with the team in '42-'43 and who made the team full-time for '46-'47. At the end of that season, though, he was traded to Montreal, and the Habs buried him in the minors until he retired nine years later. His father had been a sergeant, based in Portage, and coached son Joe for a number of years.

BELL, Mark
b. St. Paul's, Ontario, August 5, 1980

A young 'un out of the Ottawa 67's, Bell played for Canada at the 2000 World Juniors and is still developing in the Chicago system after the Hawks took him 8th overall in the 1998 draft. He played his first NHL games in 2000-01.

BELLAND, Neil
b. Parry Sound, Ontario, April 3, 1961

There is one thing worse for a player than being bounced up and down between the NHL club and its AHL affiliate, and that is being bounced from an NHL team on the extreme west coast (Vancouver) to a farm team on the extreme east coast (Fredericton). Belland played an offensive game from the blueline (good) but his coaches felt he was not physical enough (bad) in his own end. As a result, he was up and down from coast to coast during his five years in the Canucks organization in the early 1980s. He later played briefly with Pittsburgh and then played for a number of years in Austria.

BELLEFEUILLE, Blake
b. Framingham, Massachusetts, December 27, 1977

It looks as if his best years might have been in high school, where Bellefeuille was a great scorer. During his four years at Boston College he had a solid but not spectacular career, and although no team drafted him he signed as a free agent with Columbus. He played his first two NHL games with the Blue Jackets in 2001-02 but has yet to make a regular place for himself on the team.

BELLEFEUILLE, Pierre "Pete" ("The Fleeting Frenchman")
b. Trois Rivières, Quebec, October 19, 1901
d. unknown

Bellefeuille's NHL career lasted from 1925 to '30, and little is known of him. He played 92 regular-season games, but not a-one in the playoffs, and the right winger was neither overly physical nor a terrific goal scorer.

BELLEMER, Andy (sometimes Bellehumeur)
b. Penetanguishene, Ontario, July 3, 1903
d. Toronto, Ontario, April 12, 1960

Midway through the 1958-59 season, the Windsor Bulldogs of the NOHA were in a mess. The team was losing, injuries were mounting, and the coach, Murph Chamberlain, had made no plea to drunk driving charges. As a result, he was told to step down for the good of the team, and former referee Andy Bellemer was installed behind the bench for the rest of the season. Bellemer had been an official in the OHA for

many years after retiring as a player during the war. He had played most of his junior hockey and early pro hockey in Windsor before being signed by the Montreal Maroons for 15 games in '32-'33. After that '58-'59 season with the Bulldogs, he fell ill and died just a year later after a lengthy stay in hospital. He changed the spelling of his surname when he turned pro.

BELLOWS, Brian
b. St. Catharines, Ontario, September 1, 1964

The scouts were drooling over this kid, as the saying goes, from the time he made the OHL as a 16-year-old and was named Kitchener's captain. He led the team to the Memorial Cup, went 2nd overall in the 1982 draft to Minnesota, and then put his name on a five-year, $1 million contract negotiated by his agent, one Alan Eagleson. The table was set; now all Bellows had to do was deliver the meal. And he did. Sort of. He scored 35 goals as a rookie, followed up with 40 the next year to quash fears of a sophomore jinx, and developed into a scoring star in an era when goals were going in more often than ever in the game's history. But for all his success, he didn't deliver the Stanley Cup to the North Stars. He came close, in 1991, when the team made it to the finals, but there was little consolation after Pittsburgh destroyed them 8-0 in the deciding game of the series. Bellows was traded to Montreal a year later and immediately promised to score 30 goals for his new team. Fortunately for Habs fans, he lied. He scored 40. And the team won the Cup to boot. Bellows' career then became more peripatetic, and along the way he played his 1,000th game and scored his 1,000th point. He missed 500 goals by a mere 15 before retiring in 1999.

BEND, Linthwaite "Lin"
b. Portage la Prairie, Manitoba, December 20, 1922
d. Winnipeg, Manitoba, April 6, 1978

John Linthwaite Bend was not big, but he did distinguish himself as an iron man who could play through pain. His pro career, surrounded by a year in the military with the Canadian Infantry Corps, was not long, but he rarely missed a game and played with a tenacity that belied his 5'10", 165-pound body. Bend played with a depleted Rangers team in '42-'43 but besides that played mostly in the USHL. He had won the Memorial Cup with Portage in 1941-42 and after retiring Bend returned to Poplar Point, where he grew up. He was active in minor hockey there until 1968 when he sold his farm and relocated to Charleswood. Bend became an investigative assistant to the ombudsman of Manitoba.

BENDA, Jan
b. Reef, Belgium, March 28, 1972

Although born in the land of the Mannequin Pis, Bend is Teutonic by heritage. His international resumé is as impressive for Germany as his NHL c.v. is pedestrian. After playing junior in Ontario (with Eric Lindros in Oshawa), he went back to Germany to play in that country's national league. He has played in the '94 and '98 Olympics, the '96 World Cup for Germany, and three World Championships. In the 1997-98 season, he decided to give North American hockey another chance, but after signing with Washington the Caps played him in only nine games before shipping him to the minors. After that, he returned to Europe.

BENEDICT, Clint
("Benny"/ "Praying Benny")
b. Ottawa, Ontario, September 26, 1892
d. Ottawa, Ontario, November 12, 1976

An early superstar of the cord cottage, Benedict got his nickname because of his penchant for falling down to make saves, an act strictly verboten in hockey's developing days. But because he did it so often, the NHL changed the rule, and so it is that all these decades later goalies such as Dominik Hasek can flop about like a swimmer on a frozen pool to keep the puck out of his goal. Benedict played all his years with the Ottawa Senators and Montreal Maroons. He won four Stanley Cups and was extraordinarily durable, playing every game for the first six years of the NHL's existence and missing few others until, ironically, his career was ended by injury. He led the league in wins six times, and in shutouts seven times, and backstopped the early Ottawa dynasty to Cups in 1920, '21, and '23 (his other Cup came in 1926 with the Maroons). Midway through the '29-'30 season, Benedict was hit in the face by a Howie Morenz shot and badly injured. He returned a few games later wearing a mask to protect a broken nose and cheekbone, but found the leather headgear too obstructive and discarded it. Just a short time later, he was hit in the throat by another Morenz drive, ending his season and his time in the NHL. He played in the International league the next year and then moved to the Maritimes to coach the Saint John Beavers. He moved to England to assume managerial duties for the Wembley Lions and four years later returned to his native Ottawa, where he worked for the municipal government until he retired. He was inducted into the Hockey Hall of Fame in 1965.

BENNETT, Adam
b. Georgetown, Ontario, March 30, 1971

Large and powerful, big and strong, Bennett was selected 6th overall in 1989 by Chicago, a hugely optimistic position for any player to enter the NHL. He had the proverbial size, toughness, and offence as a junior, but didn't make a great impression in the Windy City and was traded to Edmonton for Kevin Todd, a player who had been drafted 129th overall in '96. Bennett started the '93-'94 season with Cape Breton, but was quickly called up and played 48 games with the team until he blew out his left knee. He was lost for the year, and was never the same after. Just 15 minor-league games later, he was forced to retire.

BENNETT, Bill
b. Warwick, Rhode Island, May 31, 1953

One of the hockey-playing Bennetts, Bill was, quite simply, humongous. At 6'5" and 235 pounds, he was born to be a tough player, though he played left wing, not defence. His brothers Curt and Harvey also played in the NHL, and all three were sired by Harvey Sr., who was a player of note in a previous generation. Bill, though, was not the most accomplished skater of the lot; he was never drafted, and played just seven games with Boston in '78-'79 and a few games with Hartford a year later.

BENNETT, Curt
b. Regina, Saskatchewan, March 27, 1948

There were six Bennett boys. Curt, Harvey, and Bill

made the NHL. Jimmy played until college, John gave it up to attend medical school, and Peter, a child goalie, drowned in a skating accident at the tender age of 11. The three who went to the NHL were all born in different cities, but they were all Americans after father Harvey settled in the States once his playing days were over. Curt played for the U.S. at the 1976 Canada Cup and the '78 and '79 World Championships, but after a 10-year career in the NHL he and brother Harvey played in Japan for the Furukawa team in the heyday of Japan's "original six." Each team was allowed two foreigners, and the mix made for a contrapuntal combination of size and skill. One team, Oji, had the great Soviets Liapkin and Shadrin on it; Seibu featured Gary Monahan and Kokydo had Randy Gregg and a Finn, Markku Hakulinen; Jujo had Greg Body and Barry Wilcox, also former NHLers. Curt played there for two years before returning home and retiring from the game. Bennett graduated from Brown University in 1970 with a degree in Russian studies. In his third year of college, his team played in the ECAC Hockey Holiday Festival, a prestigious tournament for Ivy Leaguers, and lost to a Cornell team that featured Ken Dryden in goal. Bennett later went into commercial real estate in Alberta.

BENNETT, Frank
b. Toronto, Ontario, March 4, 1922

He played for the St. Mike's Majors prior to the war, prior to their glory years right after the war, but Bennett was called up to the Red Wings as a 19-year-old for 7 games and then never played again in the NHL. He played on October 31, and November 4, 7, 11, 13, 14, and 18, 1941, then retired from hockey altogether shortly after the war.

BENNETT, Harvey
b. Edington, Saskatchewan, July 23, 1925

He was great on breakaways, not so reliable on long shots. That was the book on this goalie. He was frequently jeered by fans in Providence, yet he stayed with the Reds for nine years. He was a tall, gangly goalie with an excellent reputation, but his only NHL time came in 1944-45 to the tune of 25 games with the Bruins. Bennett held the record for most games played by a goalie in the NHL (528). When put out to stud, he produced three offspring who went on to the NHL, though none as a goalie.

BENNETT, Harvey ("Too Tall")
b. Cranston, Rhode Island, August 9, 1952

Another of the Bennett siblings, Harvey, like Curt, attended Brown College and played hockey. He wasn't as naturally talented as his brothers and had to work for everything he got at the pro level. Pittsburgh signed him in 1974 as a free agent, and in the next five years he was traded five times and played for five teams. In 1980, he and brother Curt moved to Japan to play and coach for two years, then, like Curt, he returned home to a private life in 1982.

BENNETT, Max
b. Cobalt, Ontario, November 4, 1912
d. Buffalo, New York, January 12, 1972

A regular in the minors for many years, Bennett played only once in the NHL, in '35-'36, with les Canadiens.

Clint Benedict

Curt Bennett

Frank Bennett

Harvey Bennett

Max Bennett

Brian Benning

Jim Benning

Joe Benoit

Bill Benson

Bobby Benson

But although the *bleu, blanc, et rouge* were at their weakest that season, they sent Bennett to Springfield and he never made a return visit to the Forum.

BENNETT, Rick
b. Springfield, Massachusetts, July 24, 1967
Every native of Mass wants to play for the Bruins, but Bennett had to settle for the Rangers after he was acquired by the Blueshirts from Minnesota, the team that drafted him in 1986. He had played for Providence College for four years, getting the call to Broadway during his senior year. After graduating from high school, he played defence for Wilbraham Academy, a prep school that offered no future for any hockey player. But the Providence coach saw him and told him that if he improved his academic marks, a scholarship would be his. Bennett rose to the challenge, and in the process was converted to forward. Although the large left winger scored and hit with equal success in the minors, he never made an impact with a team close to its first Cup in half a century. Bennett continued to play in the minors, and in the summer donned his street blades and played roller hockey until 2000 when he returned to Providence as an assistant coach with the Friars.

BENNING, Brian
b. Edmonton, Alberta, June 10, 1966
It's a play the NHL has never tried to do anything about, a play so vicious, dirty, and dangerous – and common – that for the NHL and all other leagues not to enact legislation preventing it is almost criminal. While playing for Ken Hitchcock's Kamloops Blazers, Benning chased down an icing and was given a little tug. That's all it took. He slammed into the boards, broke his leg, and was gone for the season. The previous year, he missed most of the season with a broken wrist and, as a result, he was in no position to make the St. Louis Blues his first year in pro. He joined Canada's National Team and learned to take his game to the next level. The Blues called him up for the playoffs, and at next year's camp he proved worthy of a regular spot in the lineup. In the next decade, he was traded four times, often in multiplayer deals. On February 19, 1992, he went from Los Angeles to Pittsburgh to Philadelphia in a series of deals that involved some 10 players. He retired to Edmonton and bought an Interstate Batteries franchise.

BENNING, Jim ("Benji")
b. Edmonton, Alberta, April 29, 1963
Nineteen eighty was an excellent year; 1981 was a phenomenal year; 1982 was okay; 1986 was awful; 1990 was it. Defenceman Benning had 111 assists and 139 points in his final year of junior, and that summer he was drafted by the Toronto Maple Leafs. The Leafs took Bob McGill, Fred Boimistruck, and Benning in quick succession in the first round, a public declaration that this troika would anchor the Leafs' blueline for years to come. Boy, did that ever not happen. Benning didn't develop into the offensive force the team had expected and he was weak enough in his own end that he wasn't worth the trouble. In five seasons with Toronto, he was a -82. On December 2, 1986, he and Dan Hodgson were sent to Vancouver for Rick Lanz, and the Big Three experiment was over. Benning is now a scout for Buffalo.

BENOIT, Joe
b. St. Albert, Alberta, February 27, 1916
d. October 19, 1981
After the war, he was never the same. Yes, Montreal won the Cup in 1945-46, but Benoit just didn't contribute as he had before enlisting. In 1938, he won the World Championship gold medal with the Trail Smoke Eaters. From 1940 on, he centred the famous Punch Line with Toe Blake and Elmer Lach, a high-flying threesome that scored seemingly at will. In '42-'43, he had 30 goals. But after the war, and the Cup, Benoit was slowed by injuries. He finished his career in Springfield, and that would cause him some difficulty a year later. He coached the Spokane Flyers to a championship in '48-'49, but the next fall he wanted a richer contract. The Flyers were willing, but they wanted a playing coach and Benoit's skating rights were owned by Eddie Shore in Springfield. A cunning and harsh man, Shore would not part with those rights for nothing, and so Benoit couldn't play and his contract demands were out of line with what Spokane wanted. Benoit resigned.

BENSON, Bill
b. Winnipeg, Manitoba, July 29, 1920
Benson was a common name in Winnipeg at the time, testament to the Icelandic connection in the city. But this Benson was not related to the more famous Bobby. Bill played two seasons with New York's long-lost sister team, the New York/Brooklyn Americans, before the team disbanded in 1942 and left the NHL with six teams, the start of the golden era of the game. Bill was active in the military and played in the American league after the war for five years before retiring.

BENSON, Bobby
b. Winnipeg, Manitoba, May 18, 1894
d. Winnipeg, Manitoba, September 7, 1965
On March 20, 1916, still just 21 years of age, Bobby Benson enlisted in the war. He was assigned to the 27th Battalion and didn't wear his civvies again for three years. Almost immediately, he and a group of Icelandic-Canadians from that battalion formed the Winnipeg Falcons, one of the most dominant teams in the history of the game. The Falcons won the Allan Cup and then travelled to Europe to take part in the first international exhibition of hockey at the 1920 Summer Olympics in Antwerp, Belgium. It was no contest. Benson and the boys scored at will and returned to a hero's welcome. A shipper by trade, Benson continued to play hockey, at first in Calgary and later with the Boston Bruins for eight games in 1924-25. But at 5'3" and 130 pounds, he was hardly cut out for the NHL. He returned to the minor ranks after that and retired in 1931 to take up coaching. He guided the Kenora Thistles, and junior teams in Brandon and Portage la Prairie before settling down in the 'Peg as a clerk with the Timothy Eaton Company until he retired.

BENTLEY, Doug
b. Delisle, Saskatchewan, September 3, 1916
d. Saskatoon, Saskatchewan, November 24, 1972
The weekly groceries don't weigh much less than Bentley's 145 pounds. Yet he was an exceptional player in a league full of heavier, stronger, and tougher opponents. He started with Chicago in 1939, and a year

later brother Max joined him. The two played on a line together for their whole careers in Chicago, a time made historic in '42-'43 when brother Reggie was called up to the Hawks. The three Bentleys became the first forward-line combination of its kind, though Reggie lasted just 11 games. That year, Doug led the NHL in goals with 33 and points with 73 , and the year after his 38 goals was again tops. He played the entire '44-'45 season out of the NHL because Canadian authorities wouldn't let him cross back and forth to the U.S. The following season, though, he was back in fine form. He, Max, and Bill Mosienko formed the deadly Pony Line after the war, and although it lasted little more than a year, it was one of the great threesomes in the league. Doug played a total of 12 seasons with the Hawks. He finished his career with half a season in New York, but in 1950 was voted by the *Herald American* as the best Chicago hockey player in the first half of the century. He was accorded his own night by the team, but throughout his career he was beset by the team's almost total lack of playoff success. He played just 23 playoff games, coming closest to winning the Cup in 1944 when the Hawks were swept by Montreal in the finals. He made Saskatoon his home for the rest of his life, coaching and playing for the Quakers. In 1961, the 45-year-old came out of retirement to play for the Los Angeles Blades. He centred a line with Willie O'Ree and Earl Johnson, and enlivened fans out west as he had in Chicago and everywhere else the slim, ferocious left winger played. He was inducted into the Hockey Hall of Fame in 1964.

BENTLEY, Max ("The Dipsy Doodle Dandy from Delisle"/ "Muscles")
b. Delisle, Saskatchewan, March 1, 1920
d. Saskatoon, Saskatchewan, January 19, 1984
He was the toughest 155-pound player in the league and its most famous hypochondriac almost from his first day of serious hockey. At 16, Bentley tried out for the Bruins, but they thought he was much too slender to cut it in the NHL. He then went on to the Habs, and their doctor told him he had a heart problem. Forget about hockey, he said, or you're dead in a year. As a result, Bentley walked around with a plethora of medications, pills, and other revivifying substances, and he daily complained about a sore throat, upset stomach, burning eyes, or worse. Those were the days he'd have his best games. He left the Habs and played senior hockey before turning pro in 1940, joining his brother Doug in Chicago. There was a third brother, Reggie, who played with them briefly, and another, Marsh, who played professionally in Scotland. Max played more than five years with Doug in Chicago, but the team never performed well. He joined the Canadian Infantry Corps for two years, but upon his return not much had changed – he and Doug were superb, the team wasn't. Toronto's owner Conn Smythe made Bill Tobin an offer he couldn't refuse. At the start of the '47-'48 season, the Leafs acquired Max and a prospect, Cy Thomas, for five players – Gaye Stewart, Bob Goldham, Bud Poile, Gus Bodnar, and Ernie Dickens. Smythe was at first pilloried for the move but by season's end the Leafs were holding the Stanley Cup and the Hawks were out of the playoffs again. In his last full season with the Hawks, Max had won the scoring title (by one point

over Maurice Richard, on the final night of the season) and the Hart Trophy. Smythe knew what he was doing. In all, Max played six seasons with the Leafs, winning three Cups. He was a superb skater with the puck and extremely quick with it, deking this way and that, fending off bigger men with his speed. By the time he retired in 1954, his 245 career goals were second among active players to Richard. He returned to the farm in Saskatoon and played with his brother again, with the Quakers, before concentrating solely on wheat production. Conn Smythe called him the best power play centre of all time. The Hockey Hall of Fame inducted him in 1966, by which time he had sold the farm and settled in Saskatoon to maintain a government-subsidized apartment complex. He died of a heart attack at his home.

BENTLEY, Reg
b. Delisle, Saskatchewan, May 3, 1914
He's not Doug, and he's not Max, but for 11 magical games back in '42-'43 with Chicago, the three brothers from Delisle made hockey history as the first NHL brother-forward line. Reggie was the oldest of the three, but his career was the least formidable. He played pro for 16 years, but those nights with his brothers were his only time in the NHL. The three worked well together, and the publicity was over-the-moon gushing phenomenal, but in the end the weak Chicago team was no stronger than it had been when Reg was out of the big loop.

BENYSEK, Ladislav
b. Olomouc, Czechoslovakia (Czech Republic), March 24, 1975
When you're drafted 266th overall (in 1994), any time in the NHL is a miracle. Benysek experienced that miracle in '97-'98 when Edmonton played him for two games, but before and after that he played mostly in the Czech Republic. His life changed when Minnesota entered the NHL via that demon-beast expansion and he played 71 games in 2000-01. A defenceman with size, he played on the 2001 Czech team that won gold at the World Championships.

BERALDO, Paul
b. Hamilton, Ontario, October 5, 1967
Like any kid from southern Ontario, Beraldo played hockey growing up. He made it to the OHL and was drafted by Boston, but after that his career was, literally and figuratively, all over the map. He played 10 games with the Bruins between 1987 and '89, then toured Europe with a variety of teams and leagues. In the summer he played roller hockey. Like many Canadians, he played for the National Team for a brief time (in '89-'90), and like many Canadians, he also used his heritage to play internationally for Italy, in his case at the '94 World Championships with the *tricolore* of Italia.

BERANEK, Josef
b. Litvinov, Czechoslovakia (Czech Republic), October 25, 1969
He has been an NHLer since 1991, but more importantly he is a gold-medal winner with the Czech Republic at the 1998 Olympics in Nagano, the culmination of many years of international participation. Indeed, his is a puck life that can be traced through his

Max Bentley (right)

Reg Bentley

Josef Beranek

Bryan Berard

Drake Berehowsky

"Red" Berenson

Perry Berezan

Sergei Berezin

tournament success rather than NHL success. Beranek began in 1989 playing at the World Juniors, and two years later graduated to the World Championships and the 1991 Canada Cup. While he moved on to the NHL, his teams frequently missed the playoffs, leaving him free to return home for the Worlds again and again (four in all). At times, he played in both the NHL and the Czech league in the same season.

BERARD, Bryan ("B")
b. Woonsocket, Rhode Island, March 5, 1977
Whatever the opposite word for birthday is, that's how Berard will forever regard March 11. In the year 2000 on that date, he was defending Ottawa's Marian Hossa in front of his own goal. Hossa took a shot and followed through high with his stick, a play that occurs a hundred times a game. But this once, the stick caught Berard flush in the right eye. It was a sickening, horrifying moment – to lose an eye so violently, wastefully. No, he didn't technically lose all sight in the eye, but it was not an eye for playing hockey any longer. At least, that's what everyone but Berard himself thought. No. Just 23 years old, Berard was not ready to file his retirement papers, collect $6 million in insurance, and move on to the rest of his life. He underwent numerous operations, but still his vision could not be restored beyond a simple ability to identify light. Berard did not give up. He trained and prepared, and in the late summer of 2001 announced his intention to return to the game. The NHL reminded Berard of the 20/400 minimum vision requirements, but his agent, Tom Laidlaw, reminded the league that that league by-law almost certainly would be quashed in a court of law. Hockey's naysayers voiced their concerns, the Leafs announced they'd welcome him back, and the Rangers stepped up with a lucrative contract. Seeking a fresh start with a lesser team, Berard signed with Glen Sather in New York, and in a few short weeks proved he could still play. When Ottawa had drafted him 1st overall in 1995, he was considered a fluid skater with tremendous offensive potential from the blueline. With New York, and later Boston, he skated with defence first in his mind, ever-mindful that at any given moment he couldn't see half the ice. Berard's most improbable return has been tremendous for hockey.

BEREHOWSKY, Drake ("Bear")
b. Toronto, Ontario, January 3, 1972
At the 1990 draft, there were only nine players considered better than Berehowsky, yet time has proved that the reliable defenceman could have dropped a few places in the order. The Leafs were high on this native son, but Bear started slowly after he blew out a knee in 1989. Unfazed, the Leafs gave him ice time in the minors and called him up for brief stints at Maple Leaf Gardens. But he never caught on full-time with the Leafs and he went to Pittsburgh for Grant Jennings. He later played for teams called Cleveland Lumberjacks and San Antonio Dragons, but he persevered. "A bad day at the rink is still better than a great day at the office," was how he put it all in perspective. And sure enough, he experienced a renaissance. The new Nashville team acquired his services, and then Vancouver needed a big, tough, stay-at-home defenceman. And so his hockey life has been extended.

BERENSON, Gordon "Red" ("The Red Baron")
b. Regina, Saskatchewan, December 8, 1939
On November 7, 1968, Red Berenson scored six goals in a game, on the road, the first man to accomplish such a feat. After one period, his Blues were leading Philadelphia 5-0, and Berenson had scored all five goals! In the next two periods, he also hit a crossbar, and none of his scores came off a power play. Berenson had always been a decent scorer during his days with Regina in junior and at the University of Michigan, but obviously that night in 1968 was special. Not surprisingly, it helped him to a 35-goal year, his best of 17 seasons in the NHL. He had gone to the U of M to study business administration after turning down an offer of $16,000 from the Canadiens because he wanted an education first. Nonetheless, he later started out in the Montreal system, winning a Cup with the Habs despite limited action in '64-'65, but he was traded to the Rangers and soon after to St. Louis, where coach Scotty Bowman gave him as much ice time as he could handle. He later played for Detroit, but when he retired in 1978, it was to the Blues that he returned to begin the next stage of his life – coaching. He started as an assistant, but within a year and a half was the head man behind the St. Louis bench. In 1984, he accepted a job from his home away from home at U of Michigan, and he has been coaching the Wolverines ever since. He won a championship with the team in 1996 and has sent a number of players on to the NHL, notably Brendan Morrison and Bill Muckalt. Berenson also played in two games in the 1972 Summit Series and won a gold medal with Canada's team at the 1959 World Championships with the Belleville McFarlands.

BERENZWEIG, Andy ("Bubba")
b. Arlington Heights, Illinois, August 8, 1977
He's called Bubba more than Andy, though he's not by any stretch the biggest player in the league. Drafted by the Islanders in 1996 after his first year at the University of Michigan under coach Red Berenson, Berenzweig was traded to Nashville before ever playing on Long Island. He has spent all but a handful of games in the minors.

BEREZAN, Perry
b. Edmonton, Alberta, December 5, 1964
Injuries slowed him down but couldn't stop him. A serious case of the flu, food poisoning, a broken leg, all these marred his first couple of years with Calgary in 1984 when he joined the team from the University of North Dakota. In terms of point production, his first full year proved to be his best, though his teams never went far into the playoffs during his nine years in the league. He also played for Minnesota and San Jose before retiring in 1993. He returned to UND and earned a degree in commerce and later became an accredited financial planner. Berezan worked for Nesbitt Burns and then with Macleod Dixon as a financial consultant.

BEREZIN, Sergei
b. Voskresensk, Soviet Union (Russia), November 5, 1971
When Sergei Berezin played for Team Russia at the 1996 World Cup, he was the only man on his team who had yet to play in the NHL. That bit of trivia went out the window about two weeks later when he debuted

with Toronto. A late bloomer who wasn't drafted until he was 22, once Berezin put that Leafs sweater on, he introduced fans to a new and exciting style of play. In an era of hooking and holding and obstructing, Berezin still provided the classic end-to-end rush on a regular basis. Unfortunately he became predictable in his rushes, and, like a shinny star on an outdoor rink, he never passed the puck. Teams played him to hog the puck, and his team play suffered. Although he averaged some 20 goals a year, the Leafs traded him to Phoenix, where he suffered a knee injury and a drop in production. He later moved on to Montreal, Chicago and Washington in quick succession. Berezin is not big, but a smooth skater and expert stickhandler who can shoot without revealing his intentions. After a junior career in Russia, he moved to Germany to play, though he always returned to play for his homeland in international tournaments, including the '94 Olympics in Lillehammer and and three World Championships.

BERG, Aki-Petteri "Aki" ("Bergie")

b. Turku, Finland, July 28, 1977

Great name. In 1995, Aki Berg was chosen 3rd overall by Los Angeles in the draft, high praise indeed for a sure superstar on the horizon. He attended camp a couple of months later, made the team, and then … fizzled and sizzled. He went goalless in the 51 games he played, went down to the minors, and never developed. Ditto for the next season. He played all of '97–'98 with the team, and for Finland at the 1998 Olympics in Nagano, but the following season returned to Finland to play in his home league. In 2000-01, his relationship with coach Andy Murray proved strained at best. Berg sat in the press box, and when an offer came along from Toronto, the Kings jumped. So, too, did Berg, who caught the first plane out of town. When he landed, he was in a new country, physically and metaphorically. Coach Pat Quinn gave him a regular turn on the blueline, some power play time, and some confidence, and Berg has played the best hockey of his career (though it might not be 3rd overall-type hockey).

BERG, Bill

b. St. Catharines, Ontario, October 21, 1967

Berg grew up in small country southern Ontario, falling in love with the puck game at age five and never falling out of love with it during his career. Not even when he broke his leg in a fight with Igor Ulanov and missed much of the '94–'95 season. Berg was a pest, a guy who poked and jabbed and checked and nattered his way into many players' bad books, who hit hard and finished all his checks, and who played like his job was on the line every night. And it was. After starting out

In 1995, Aki Berg was chosen 3rd overall by Los Angeles in the draft.
AKI BERG

with the Islanders in 1988, he was claimed off waivers by the Leafs in 1992 and spent almost three years in the blue and white. It was his style that made him a terrific fourth-line player and helped the team make it to the semifinals in both '93 and '94. He finished his career in 1999, but all through his playing days he studied, first to complete grade 13 (which he did while playing for the Marlies) and later toward completing a degree in sociology from Brock University.

BERGDINON, Fred
see **BOURGDINON, Fred**

BERGEN, Todd

b. Prince Albert, Saskatchewan, July 11, 1963

Deal with Iron Mike or irons into the green? That was the question that burned inside this talented kid from out west. He never played in a league until he was 16, and even then only in an all-ages industrial gig that he and his father organized in Prince Albert. But soon provincial junior A teams came calling, and soon after that the Flyers drafted him in 1982. Two years later, Bergen was in his first year of pro, in the AHL, when the Flyers called him up near the end of the season. In the final 14 games of the regular schedule, Bergen had 11 goals and the team went undefeated. But then the playoffs hit and coach Mike Keenan – young, cruel, brutal Iron Mike – tried to motivate Bergen by verbally pummelling him. The love of the game vanished from Bergen's heart, and he refused to play for Philly the next year. He had always yearned to try his hand at golf, maybe go to a U.S. college on scholarship, give the pro tour a try. Since the Flyers were unwilling to trade him, and Keenan had just taken the team to the finals and wasn't leaving town any time soon, Bergen retired and declared he'd take up golf. But, he had suffered an abdominal injury that prevented him from swinging his sticks, so he holed up in his Minneapolis apartment and became a recluse. The Flyers finally traded him to Minnesota, and Bergen had surgery on his tummy and agreed to join the North Stars. Then he didn't. He picked up his clubs and started kicking around on satellite tours, finally landing a job as assistant pro at the Saskatoon Golf and Country Club. He could have been a somebody in the hockey world, but he refused to get there on someone else's terms.

BERGER, Mike

b. Edmonton, Alberta, June 2, 1967

A hard-hitting defenseman and career minor leaguer, Berger played 30 games with his drafted team, Minnesota, in '87-'88 and '88-'89. Although he was traded to Hartford shortly after, he never saw time with

Bill Berg

Todd Bergen

Mike Berger

Jean-Claude Bergeron

Michel Bergeron

Yves Bergeron

Tim Bergland

Bo Berglund

the Whalers but has continued his lengthy playing career in various minor leagues throughout the U.S.

BERGERON, Jean-Claude ("J.C.")
b. Hauterive, Quebec, October 14, 1968
He grew up in Quebec, watching Montreal win those Cups in the late 1970s, idolizing Ken Dryden and the great "C H" sweater. Bergeron's dreams came true when the Habs drafted him and tossed him into the cage for 18 games in '90-'91. This was after he won the prestigious Baz Bastien trophy for being the AHL's best goalie in 1989-90. His stint with the Habs was okay – not great, not horrible. But back then, okay still didn't cut it at the pre-shopping mall Forum. Bergeron moved on to Tampa Bay and L.A., but only as a callup or second man for brief spells.

BERGERON, Michel ("Le petit tigre")
b. Chicoutimi, Quebec, November 11, 1954
You mean he was a player? Yes, oh yes. Long before he strutted and stamped behind the bench of the Quebec Nordiques, Bergeron actually played in the NHL, with Detroit, the Islanders, and Washington. He even scored 32 goals in 1975-76 with the Red Wings, but he retired shortly thereafter to take up coaching. He was hired to guide the Nordiques in their second year in the NHL, '80-'81, and instantly the team developed a Bergeron character that defined it for most of the decade. It was a good run for the team, and the Quebec-Canadiens rivalry was perhaps the most bitterly contested one in the history of the league. Bergeron got the most out of his players and the team never missed the playoffs with him at the helm. But his popularity (some might argue that's a euphemism for ego) clashed with team president Marcel Aubut's popularity (read: ego) and so in an unusual move, Aubut traded his coach to the New York Rangers for a first-round draft choice and some cash. On Broadway, Bergeron missed the playoffs his first year and then with two games to go in '88-'89 GM Phil Esposito fired him. He returned to a hero's welcome in Quebec for the next season, though the welcome wore thin during a year in which the team posted a dismal record of 12-61-7. Bergeron stepped down as coach after suffering a heart attack, but he recovered and continues to work in Quebec doing television and radio colour commentary.

BERGERON, Yves
b. Malartic, Quebec, January 11, 1952
Small and speedy, Bergeron knew he wasn't destined to a long NHL career because of his size. At 5'9" and 165 pounds, he couldn't play with the bigger boys, so he signed with Quebec in 1972 when the WHA began. He didn't score the way he had in Quebec junior, and he moved on to the AHL and played three games with Pittsburgh between 1974 and '77. After that he moved to New Brunswick to coach senior hockey for a decade.

BERGEVIN, Marc
b. Montreal, Quebec, August 11, 1965
A thousand-game survivor of the NHL, that's what Bergevin is. He's got the proverbial size and strength that every defensive defenceman needs, but he also

has heart. He made the NHL as a teen, with Chicago in 1984, but after a few years, smack dab in the middle of his career, he found himself traded, and then in the minors for most of two full seasons. But he didn't give up. He re-established himself and continues to play his own style of game that has endured now through three decades.

BERGKVIST, Stefan
b. Leksand, Sweden, March 10, 1975
He gave it a try and it didn't work out, proof that although the NHL is becoming a worldwide dream, just as many Europeans as players from Canada or the States don't make it for one reason or another. Bergkvist was big and strong and Pittsburgh drafted him in 1993. He played another year at home and then moved to the OHL to prepare himself for a career in the NHL. But the Pens played him injust seven games, and after spending much of three seasons in the lowest depths of the IHL, he decided to return to the land of Tre Kronor if he wasn't going to play in the big tent. He has been there ever since.

BERGLAND, Tim
b. Crookstown, Minnesota, January 11, 1965
It's always noteworthy when a player records a point in his first NHL game, and Bergland made this list thanks to his assist on January 23, 1990, while playing for Washington. He had been drafted some seven years earlier and proceeded to have a fine college career at the University of Minnesota before moving on to minor pro and then the Caps. But in his five seasons of NHL play he split time between the big time and the minors each year, never proving himself worthy of full-time duty, but clearly something more than a career minor leaguer. Recently, though, he has remained away from the NHL and is no longer property of an NHL team.

BERGLOFF, Bob
b. Dickinson, North Dakota, July 26, 1958
Another graduate of the University of Minnesota Golden Gophers, Bergloff played just twice in the NHL, for Minnesota in '82-'83. Before and after that, he played minor pro, retiring at 30.

BERGLUND, Bo
b. Sjalevad, Sweden, April 6, 1955
In June 1983, 252 players were selected at that year's Entry Draft. Ten slots from the bottom, at 242, was the 28-year-old Berglund, a talented Swede with gobs of international and Swedish experience. He came to Canada – Quebec had selected him – and made an immediate impact, scoring four points in his first three games. But the long schedule was a killer. Previously, the most games he had played in a season was 36. That'll take you to Christmas in the NHL! Berglund finished the year with 43 points, but he was soon traded to Minnesota and then Philadelphia. He finished out the '85-'86 season in the minors and then returned home. Berglund had competed in two World Junior tournaments (in '74 and '75, when these were invitational and not official events) and played in the 1980 and '88 Olympics for Tre Kronor, winning bronze both times.

BERGLUND, Christian
b. Orebro, Sweden, March 12, 1980

Berglund was drafted in 1998 but unlike many of his compatriots was in no hurry to rush to the NHL. He continued to play in the Swedish league, and didn't come to North America until three years later. Berglund played a few games with the Devils in 2001-02 in a year spent mostly in the minors.

BERGMAN, Gary ("Bergie")
b. Kenora, Ontario, October 7, 1938
d. December 8, 2000

On November 3, 2000, most of the Canadian players from the 1972 Summit Series attended a function at the Hockey Hall of Fame to honour that team as Canada's Team of the Century, as selected by Canadian Press. Bergman was not there. He was at home dying from cancer that had reappeared on April 15. Six years earlier, he had a malignant melanoma removed from his back. The hero from the Summit Series, Paul Henderson, called Bergman one of the series' unsung warriors. From start to finish, Bergman was a good man, a proud player, and a dependable soul. That's why, of all the great defencemen in the league, he was among the chosen few in 1972. Between 1964 and 1976, he played mostly for Detroit, though his criticism of coach Ned Harkness led to his trade to Minnesota. He got his first chance in '64-'65 when he was called up to play for the injured Bill Gadsby; he never left. After retiring, he started his own building company in Detroit and worked with numerous charities that benefitted children. He coached the Michigan floor hockey team that competed in the Special Olympics and late into the 1990s served as the Wings' alumni president. In 1997, he was inducted into the Manitoba Sports Hall of Fame.

BERGMAN, Thommie
b. Munkfors, Sweden, December 10, 1947

Detroit scout Jack Patterson attended the 1972 Olympics in Sapporo on a scouting mission and came back with Bergman, one of Sweden's finest players. Detroit forked over $30,000 to Vastra Frolunda, his native team, to sign him, and the next fall he paired with Ron Stackhouse on the blueline. Bergman arrived in the Motor City to a new and different – though not necessarily better – life. Back home, he worked all day at an ad agency before playing at night. He had earned a master's degree in economics and had studied engineering. In the NHL, there were games and practices and road trips and… not much else. On ice, he proved his worth as the first Euro-trained pro to play regularly in the NHL, a year before Salming and Hammarstrom in Toronto. He got into a fight with Dave Schultz, scored a few goals, and became the top defenceman on the team. Perhaps the snuff he poked into his mouth before and during games helped. "It does not take down your condition like cigarettes, but it relaxes you," he tried to explain of his baseball-like habit of chewin' tabakee. As with many an early European star, though, the long schedule took its toll, and over the next few years injuries slowed him down. He played some in the WHA, participated in the 1976 Canada Cup with a lame knee, and eventually moved home to close out his career. After retiring in the early

1980s, he was hired as director of operations for the team in Gothenburg to elevate the status of the weak club. He later became the chief European scout for the Maple Leafs.

BERGQVIST, Jonas
b. Hassleholm, Sweden, September 26, 1962

Leksands and Bergqvist are synonymous with each other, each supporting and remaining loyal to the other for more than 20 years and counting. Part and parcel of this loyalty is Bergqvist's love of the national team, Tre Kronor. In all, he played some 272 international games, a Swedish record not likely to be broken for years to come. This includes nine World Championships, two Olympics, two Canada Cups, a World Cup, and a World Junior appearance. Bergqvist, Mats Sundin, and Tumba Johansson are the only three-time gold medalists in World Championships play for Sweden. His one, non-European blip occurred during the 1989-90 season, when he played 22 games for the Calgary Flames and a few more in the minors before returning to his homeland. After retiring as a player in 1999, he became the managing director (what in North America would be general manager) of Leksands, continuing one of the strongest relationships in Swedish league history. He had studied economics at university and during his years playing in the Swedish league he also worked at a bank.

Gary Bergman

BERLINQUETTE, Louis
b. Papineau, Quebec, 1887
d. Noranda, Quebec, June 2, 1959

Had the Frank Selke Award been around during the NHA and early years of the NHL, Berlinquette would have won it on numerous occasions. However, Selke himself was barely around then, so the Montreal Canadiens star left winger had to content himself with the respect accorded him as a superior defensive forward. He joined the Canadiens in 1911 and stayed with the team until 1923, winning a Stanley Cup in 1916 and playing in the tragic 1919 finals in Seattle, which were cancelled after Joe Hall died during the influenza epidemic. It was in part his speed and skating that gave those Canadiens teams the nickname "Flying Frenchmen."

Thommie Bergman

BERNHARDT, Tim ("Timber")
b. Sarnia, Ontario, January 17, 1958

Life is better lived in a kaleidoscope than a microscope, and Tim Bernhardt is living proof. To judge him by his NHL playing career alone would be to miss his finest moment entirely. Atlanta drafted the goaltender in 1978, but he didn't see action until four years later when the team had relocated to Calgary. In his six appearances that year, he had a perfectly clean record, 0-5-0. The Leafs signed him as a free agent, and although he played well enough to be the number-one goalie in '84-'85, he hurt his knee and missed the rest of the season. It was downhill from there, but the best was yet to come. He played in the minors, and after retiring in 1990 joined the NHL's Central Scouting department. The Dallas Stars hired him to do similar chores, and the team won the Cup in the spring of 1999. So there, right on Lord Stanley's bowl, is the name Tim Bernhardt, not as a player, but as a scout.

Tim Bernhardt

Serge Bernier

Bob Berry

Brad Berry

Doug Berry

Ken Berry

BERNIER, Serge
b. Padoue, Quebec, April 29, 1947

In the 1970 Expansion Draft, the Flyers protected Bernier and let Rosaire Paiement go even though the former had played exactly one NHL game. That's how high the team rated him. In his first full season, he justified that high regard. Playing on a line with Bill Lesuk and Jim Johnson, he scored 23 goals. But life didn't continue to be so painless. He was traded the next year to Los Angeles, and from the Kings he went to the WHA. There, he experienced a renaissance, and finished his career with the Quebec Nordiques. Bernier scored 54 goals in '74-'75 and won the Avco Cup with the Nords in 1977, and when the team joined the NHL a few years later, he stayed with it. His numbers dropped dramatically, though, and he injured his knee and missed many games. After retiring in 1981, his life fell apart. In 1985, he and three other men were charged by Quebec police with trafficking more than a thousand grams of cocaine with a street value of some $1.5 million. Because of lack of evidence, the court agreed to lesser charges and Bernier eventually pled guilty to conspiring to sell the cocaine.

BERRY, Bob
b. Montreal, Quebec, November 29, 1943

Hockey has been berry berry good to Bob over the years, from 1968 when he first played for the Montreal Canadiens right up to the present when he became a western scout for Ottawa. Good thing, too, because other sports had their crack at him. The Houston Astros invited him to training camp one year, and while he was at Sir George Williams in Montreal he played pro football for the Montreal Beavers of the Continental Football League as a flanker back. The only reason he attended George Williams was to obtain a liberal arts degree with a minor in psychology. He had turned down a football scholarship offer from the University of Kentucky. From there, he studied to get his teacher's certificate, but hockey became his obsession so he joined Canada's National Team for the end of the '66-'67 season and toured Europe and the Soviet Union. After two years in the minors and two games with the Habs, Berry was sold to Los Angeles and blossomed into a star. He scored 20 goals in 5 of 6 years, but he was on a team that was lucky to make the playoffs. He wound up in the minors, then turned to coaching. The Kings hired him in 1978, and after three successful seasons there he was hired by Montreal. At the end of his second season in Montreal, he was demoted to scout only to be re-hired as coach 38 days later. He later coached in Pittsburgh from 1984 to '87, Mario Lemieux's first three years in the league, and then moved on to St. Louis as a coach and, finally, to the Senators as a scout.

BERRY, Brad
b. Bashaw, Alberta, April 1, 1965

After a few partial seasons with the Winnipeg Jets, it seemed clear that Berry was not going to become an important part of the team as it had once hoped. Back in 1985, he was king. He won a gold medal with Canada at the World Juniors and was playing at U of North Dakota. The Jets had claimed him 29th overall back in '83 and called him up for the end of '85-'86 when he was still just 18, but he was up and down to the minors

for much of his five years in Winnipeg. He later signed with Minnesota and played a number of years in the minors before becoming a scout with the Dallas Stars.

BERRY, Doug
b. New Westminster, British Columbia, June 3, 1957

He was Don Cherry's kind of player, which was good if Grapes was the coach but not so good if he had been fired. A University of Denver grad, Berry played part of '78-'79 with Edmonton in the WHA and then joined the woeful Colorado Rockies the year after. The centreman had a decent season (7 goals, 30 points) under Cherry, but the next year, with Cherry gone, Berry played only 43 games before being demoted. He never made it back to the NHL, instead playing in Europe for the better part of the next decade. His brother, Ken, followed much the same path.

BERRY, Fred
b. Edmonton, Alberta, March 26, 1956

There should be another league in North America for small, skilled players who can skate and score and who don't fight and who can't handle the rough stuff. Such a league would be highly entertaining and feature someone like Berry. Not big (5'9", 175 pounds), he scored 59 goals and 146 points in his final year of junior with New Westminster, but the Detroit Red Wings were impressed enough to give him nothing more than a three-game trial. Once his contract had expired, no other NHL team offered him a deal, and so this perfectly talented player wound up in the IHL for the rest of his playing days.

BERRY, Ken ("Bears")
b. Burnaby, British Columbia, June 21, 1960

Once upon a time, in olden days, when there were players called amateurs, skaters aspired to play in the Olympics. Those were the days before the NHL got involved and professionalism tainted the participation of athletes. When Berry was growing up, he wanted to play for his country. Like brother Doug, he wasn't big or tough enough to duke out an NHL career forever, but that was okay. In 1979, Ken joined the National Team and played in the 1980 Lake Placid Games before embarking on a scattered pro career that featured 28 games with the Edmonton Oilers in their prime. Berry joined Canada again for much of '85-'88 to ready himself for the 1998 Olympics in Calgary, and he also played in both the Spengler Cup and Izvestia tournament for his country. In the late 1980s he moved to Germany to play there, alongside his brother Doug, at the end of his career.

BERRY, Rick ("Bears")
b. Birtle, Manitoba, November 4, 1978

Berry comes from a farming family, and he returns to the land every summer. Still young, he has both the privilege and the daunting task of trying to make the Colorado Avalanche. He played in the WHL with Seattle and helped the T-Birds to its first championship. Although he didn't play in enough games to get his name on the Cup for the Avs win in 2001, his hometown honoured him all the same – he was made Grand Marshal of the Birtle Town Fair Parade in the summer of 2001!

BERTHIAUME, Daniel ("The Bandit")
b. Longueuil, Quebec, January 26, 1966
He made his first appearance in a playoff game in 1986 but played so well that he became the favourite to become the number-one man the following year with Winnipeg. The Jets were in dire need of goaltending; each year they had an excellent regular season, each year the Oilers would eliminate them in the playoffs. GM John Ferguson invited nine goalies to camp in 1986, including Yannick Verstappen, who had led Belgium to a Group C gold medal at the World Championships and who could boast Jacques Plante as his former coach. Berthiaume won the job, though he didn't keep it for long. Over the next eight years he was traded four times, unusual for a goalie. In his last 8 seasons, he had a winning record only once, and only once did he play more than 37 games in a season. Nevertheless, he continued to play in the minors after Ottawa demoted him in 1993.

BERTRAND, Eric
b. St. Ephrem, Quebec, April 16, 1975
Since 1999, when he played his first game in the NHL, Bertrand has been owned by no fewer than five teams. No one wants to keep him. He played for four years with Albany trying to work himself into the New Jersey system, but this effort resulted in only four games with the Devils and a trade to Atlanta. After the Thrashers tossed him into eight games, he went on to Philadelphia and Nashville before the Habs, desperate for French-Canadian content, dressed him for a few games in 2001-02.

BERTUZZI, Todd
b. Sudbury, Ontario, February 2, 1975
Sometimes it's easy to forget just how young kids are when they join major junior hockey in Canada. Bertuzzi was 16, and he was young, fleshy, and not ready to handle all the pressures and rigours of preparing for a life as a pro player. But the skill? Oh, yes, he had that. He improved every year with Guelph and when he graduated in 1995 he joined the Islanders, the team that had drafted him two years earlier and signed him just hours before he was to become draft-eligible again. The maturity came after his father was nearly killed in a car accident. Big and fast with soft hands, Bertuzzi developed into a power forward of note, but on February 6, 1998, just before the NHL break for the Olympics in Nagano, he was traded to Vancouver. It was there he blossomed, yet he still shows signs that there might be one more gear, one more level to his game. He's a 25-goal scorer and a team leader, though he only skated in his first playoff game after 7 years of regular-season play. In 2002-03, he reached that next level, though, by scoring 46 goals and finishing among the scoring leaders.

BERUBE, Craig
b. Calahoo, Alberta, December 17, 1965
From his junior days to his minor pro days to his long and enduring NHL days, Berube is a name that evokes one image only – fighting. He has never had fewer than 100 penalty minutes in 15 seasons of play. He has played for Washington and Philadelphia twice each, as well as with Toronto, Calgary, and the Islanders, and is one of the few tough guys to last more than 1,000 NHL

games. In fact, he and Dale Hunter are the only 1,000-game players to have more than 3,000 penalty minutes.

BESLER, Phil
b. Melville, Saskatchewan, December 9, 1911
d. December 5, 1989
After playing in his home province until he was 21, Besler was signed by the Boston Cubs in 1934 with an eye to moving him up to the Bruins after some development. A year later, he played in eight games, but after that he moved into the Chicago organization and finally to Detroit after a trade. His only career goal came with the Hawks in '38-'39.

BESSONE, Pete
b. New Bradford, Massachusetts, January 13, 1913
d. December 5, 1989
Sons of an Italian railroad worker, Pete and his brother Amo were two peas in a pod growing up in Massachusetts. They would skate together every opportunity they got, and they took the game more seriously than any of their friends. Amo played in France for a year and then went to the University of Illinois, where he played under Vic Heyliger. Pete played professionally in Europe for four years (1931-35) in France and he became known as the Babe Ruth of hockey there. In February 1934, he was a last-minute addition to the U.S. national team that won a silver medal at the World Championships. In 1935, he returned to the U.S. to try his hand at a more sophisticated level of play. Amo later played in the AHL and after the war went into coaching, a job that became his vocation for the next 31 years (28 of which were spent at Michigan State). Pete continued to play. He was called up by Detroit for six games in '37-'38, but then played in the AHL for another decade. He returned to Italy, France, and Switzerland to play a little more and coach, and he even brought two Italian boys to the States to play in leagues there. After retiring, he and a good friend, Al Cavicchi, started a business called the Feeding Hills Club House, managing and bartending a restaurant at a golf course in suburban Massachusetts. He also acted as a recruiting officer for teams in the Italian hockey league.

BESTER, Allan ("Ernie"/ "Beast"/ "Worm")
b. Hamilton, Ontario, March 26, 1964
When Bester was drafted in 1983 by Toronto, he was coming to a great team at the very nadir of its existence. He and Ken Wregget were touted as the tandem that would take the Leafs out of their glum, basement dwelling and shoot them to the top of the standings. Bester, smaller and faster, developed more quickly, but not as far as the Leafs had hoped. Wregget, bigger and more positional, took longer, but he also failed to reach the level the team was counting on. The result was a form of torture for the pair. They often alternated games and split time for a number of seasons, but generally with sub-par records. Bester was eventually traded to Detroit, but he played only four games with the Wings before settling into the minors for most of the next eight years. His one final moment of glory came in '95-'96 when Dallas ran into goaltending injuries and signed

Daniel Berthiaume

Todd Bertuzzi

Craig Berube

Phil Besler

Allan Bester

John Bethel

Bester as a free agent, paying him on a per-game basis. He played 10 times for a powerful Stars team and performed admirably given that he had been away from the NHL for nearly 5 years. He and his family later settled in Orlando, Florida (he last played for the Solar Bears in the "I"), and he got a job as a regional salesman for Holiday Inn. He also does some goalie coaching for minor leaguers in the area and returns to Toronto for the occasional alumni game.

BETHEL, John
b. Montreal, Quebec, January 15, 1957
During his three years at Boston University, Bethel was drafted by the Rangers, in 1977. However, he missed much of the '78-'79 season with a serious knee injury and he never signed with the Rangers. Instead, the Winnipeg Jets took a chance on him, a chance that lasted just 17 games. Bethel spent the rest of his brief pro career in the minors.

BETIK, Karel
b. Karvina, Czechoslovakia (Czech Republic), October 28, 1978
He had two assists in his three games with Tampa back in '98-'99, but to date those are Betik's only numbers in the NHL. His contract has since expired, and he is now a minor-league nomad free for the asking should anyone choose to sign him.

Silvio Bettio

BETS, Maxim
b. Chelyabinsk, Soviet Union (Russia), January 31, 1974
He came, he played, and, failing to conquer, he returned home. Drafted by St. Louis but traded before he played for the Blues, Bets appeared in three games for Anaheim, moved around in the minors for a few years, and went back to Russia to continue to play. This after 2 superb seasons in Spokane during which he scored 49 and 46 goals.

BETTIO, Silvio "Sam"
b. Copper Cliff, Ontario, December 1, 1928
The "chunky speedster" came down from northern Ontario to play for the Boston Olympics in 1947, a team coached by Hago Harrington, and played on a line with Arnie Kullman and Steve Gaber. The following year he moved up to the Hershey Bears and played brilliantly, earning a chance to join the Bruins in 1949-50. His first goal was a game winner against Montreal, and he stuck around for 44 games that season. But Bettio was never a scorer; he was the model role player who hustled, led by example, killed penalties, and proved forever reliable. Although he never made it back to the NHL, he played mostly in the AHL for more than a decade. In '55-'56, he suffered a disgusting injury when Bill Folk's stick got into his mouth, lacerating his tongue and knocking out 14 teeth.

Jeff Beukeboom

BETTS, Blair
b. Edmonton, Alberta, February 16, 1980
A graduate of Prince George in the WHL, Betts started his career in the Calgary system, playing a few games with the Flames in 2001-02.

BEUKEBOOM, Jeff
b. Ajax, Ontario, March 28, 1965
In his 804-game career, Jeff Beukeboom had a total of 550 shots on goal, the same number Phil Esposito had in 78 games in 1970-71 when he set an NHL record. But there the comparisons end. Espo was a great and gifted scorer; Beukeboom was a heavy-hitting defensive defenceman who played his entire 14-year career with 2 teams, Edmonton and the Rangers. He won three Cups with the Oilers (in '87, '88, and '90), and then when GM Neil Smith tried to bring the entire Edmonton team to Manhattan (seven Oilers, in fact), Beukeboom won another with the Rangers in 1994. He was a tough competitor and physical player who both gave and absorbed many hits, none so violent, though, as the one he received the night of November 19, 1998, while playing against Los Angeles. In that game, he was sucker-punched by Matt Johnson and suffered a serious concussion. He came back after missing just two games, but on February 12, 1999, he suffered another concussion that caused him to miss the rest of the season. The post-concussion syndrome that followed was harrowing for him, and in the summer he retired.

His managerial reputation was such that he was appointed ticket manager for Expo '67 in Montreal.
PAUL BIBEAULT

BEVERIDGE, Bill
b. Ottawa, Ontario, July 1, 1909
d. Ottawa, Ontario, February 13, 1995
So many Ottawa-born players return to that city after their playing days, and Beveridge is certainly a tremendous example of a devoted Ottawan. He didn't play his whole career there, but he did get his start in the nation's capital and he played his final games with the historic Ottawa Commandos, one of the greatest short-lived teams of all time. Along the way, the goaltender played in 297 games, though because he always played for the league's weak sisters he had a poor record of 87-166-42 and appeared in only 5 playoff games in a 9-year career. After retiring at the close of the war, Beveridge settled in to a coaching position at Carleton College in Ottawa and even tossed his hat into the political arena at the civic level of government. He was a charter member of the South Ottawa Kiwanis and a lifetime member of the Chaudiere Lodge 264.

Bill Beveridge

BEVERLEY, Nick
b. Toronto, Ontario, April 21, 1947

Bobby Orr skated with a goodly number of players in his day, and the lanky defenceman Beverley was one of them, albeit briefly. They both played junior with Oshawa, and as a result both made their NHL debuts with Boston. In Beverley's case, that meant two games in '66-'67, two more in '69-'70, and a singleton in '71-'72. In those final two seasons, the B's won the Cup but Beverley was in the minors at the time. Funnily enough, he joined Orr full-time the next year but then was traded to Pittsburgh and wound up with five different teams in the coming seven seasons. Beverley became a coach in 1980 and has remained in the game ever since in one capacity or another. He joined the Kings in L.A. and worked his way up to general manager, then made his way home to Toronto where he was an interim coach late in the '95-'96 season. Since then he has scouted and worked as the director of player personnel. Most recently, he became assistant GM in Chicago.

BIALOWAS, Dwight
b. Regina, Saskatchewan, September 8, 1952

He had the big slapper from the point, the kind that always seemed to find the net or hurt someone in front or scare the bejesus out of opponents, at the very least. But, he just couldn't find the mark in the NHL night in and night out. Atlanta gave up on him in 1975 after just 48 games, and then he had a few troubles in Minnesota. Sent to the minors, he got his head in gear and returned to the North Stars with a fury, leading the defencemen in points despite playing only 58 games. But the next year, he had a rough start, finished in the minors, and retired a year later.

BIALOWAS, Frank ("The Animal")
b. Winnipeg, Manitoba, September 25, 1969

It was never any secret why he was called the animal, never any secret why he was never drafted, and never any secret why he played just three times in the NHL. Those three appearances occurred in '93-'94 with Toronto, and the rest of the year he was in St. John's, averaging – *averaging!* – five penalty minutes a game. In fact, that has been pretty much par for the course throughout his career, which, not surprisingly, continues.

BIANCHIN, Wayne
b. Nanaimo, British Columbia, September 6, 1953

When Wayne's parents arrived in Canada from Italy, they decided to drop the last letter of their name, Bianchini, and start a new life. Their son, meanwhile, almost ended his when he was just 20 years old and a top rookie with the Pittsburgh Penguins. After a solid season in 1973-74 to start his career, Wayne went to Hawaii to body-surf. He caught a violent wave that tossed him onto the beach and drove him into the sand headfirst. He broke his neck, lay on the beach paralyzed, and had to be brought home in a body cast by his mother. He underwent spinal fusion surgery and then had a delicate operation in which doctors had to move his voice box to the side of his neck. Within weeks, he was skating again. But this isn't a happy ending yet, and his tenacity in playing again was no

act of remarkable effort. He experienced dizziness on ice, suffered painful headaches, and often didn't know what he was supposed to do when the puck hit his stick. He took the remainder of the year off to recover properly, then made a truly remarkable comeback. He had scored 60 goals in his final year of junior in Flin Flon, playing on a line with Blaine Stoughton, and with the Penguins he had back-to-back 20-goal seasons. He was slowed by a back injury, though, and happy just to be able to skate and play he headed to Italy to put his dual citizenship to good use. He played for Italia at the 1981 World Championships ("B" pool) and in the Italian league for two seasons before returning to Nanaimo to become a stockbroker and coach the local Clippers.

BIBEAULT, Paul
b. Montreal, Quebec, April 13, 1919
d. Rigaud, Quebec, August 2, 1970

In a wartime career in which he was tossed from team to team, playing in four Original Six cities from 1940 to '47, Bibeault made more headlines at the altar than in the goal crease, for he married none other than Evelyn Selke, daughter of Toronto GM Frank. The two met during Bibeault's year with the Leafs (1943-44), when Evelyn was working as a telephone receptionist at Maple Leaf Gardens, and married in the spring of 1947 just after the end of the regular season. Bibeault drove like crazy from Chicago to get to the wedding (he was playing with the Hawks in what would be his last NHL season), and got a speeding ticket en route for his troubles. Bibeault never had much of a chance to stay in the NHL as the likes of Turk Broda and Frank Brimsek returned from war, but that did not diminish the length of his career, only its location. After playing his last NHL game with the Hawks in 1947, Bibeault went to the AHL and USHL, and was named top goalie in the latter league in 1948-49. That fall, he moved to the Cincinnati Mohawks as the team's spare goalie and the box office manager for the Cincinnati Gardens, an arena recently built and designed to be a miniature version of Maple Leaf Gardens. Bibeault remained the manager after retiring as a goalie, and in 1956 became arena manager for the Rochester War Memorial Arena for five years. He then moved back to Cincinnati, but in 1964 returned to his home province to become manager of the Pointe Claire Arena. His managerial reputation was such that he was appointed ticket manager for Expo '67 in Montreal. In 1970 he passed away at the Selke farm in Rigaud, succumbing to cancer at age 51.

BICANEK, Radim
b. Uherske Hradiste, Czechoslovakia (Czech Republic), January 18, 1975

He's played 6 partial years in the NHL with 3 teams for a total of 62 games and counting, but so far he hasn't scored a single NHL goal! The obvious comparison, then, is to Brad Marsh, though whether Bicanek is as jovial, funny, and enduring remains to be seen. Strangely, though, Bicanek has offensive ability from the blueline. He has scored in other leagues, notably the OHL, where he apprenticed after Ottawa drafted him in 1993.

Nick Beverley

Dwight Bialowas

Frank Bialowas

Wayne Bianchin

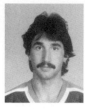

Todd Bidner

Zac Bierk

Larry Bignell

Gilles Bilodeau

Les Binkley

BICEK, Jiri

b. Kosice, Czechoslovakia (Slovakia), December 3, 1978
On the strength of his strong showings at the '96 and '97 World Juniors, Bicek was drafted by New Jersey in June 1997 and immediately moved to the U.S. to begin his pro career. He played three full seasons with Albany, but in 2000-01, a rash of injuries to the Devils gave him an NHL opportunity. His first game came on February 19, 2001, against Toronto, and he scored a goal. He played just five games during the regular season and stayed with the team briefly during that spring's playoffs.

BIDNER, Todd

b. Petrolia, Ontario, July 5, 1961
It took Bidner a quarter of a century to go from his first game in Petrolia to his last, but in between he played overseas longer than just about any Canadian in hockey history. He began his career with the traditional three stages of junior hockey, draft, and NHL, but after playing in the minors for a few years he decided to see the world and play at the same time. In 1985 he moved to Britain and for the next 12 years he played in leagues under the auspices of Queen Elizabeth II. He returned to play senior hockey for the Petrolia Chippewa Squires and settled into a job as a youth worker.

BIERK, Zac

b. Peterborough, Ontario, September 17, 1976
His older brother is Sebastian Bach, lead screamer for the band Skid Row, so it's no wonder Zac has an inner ear problem that doctors fear may be incurable. In fact, his whole career has been spackled with injuries, ranging from small wounds to hip surgery that forced him out of most of the 2001-02 season. A tall, quick goalie, he nonetheless was an important part of Minnesota's plans though his best NHL chance came in 2002-03 when he appeared in 16 games for Phoenix.

BIGGS, Don

b. Mississauga, Ontario, April 7, 1965
He wasn't big but they called him a little big man because he played with a fierceness and tenacity that belied his size. Although he played just a dozen NHL games in the 1980s with Minnesota and Philadelphia, he played pro for 15 seasons, culminating in 1992-93 when he led the AHL in scoring (54 goals, 138 points) and was named the league's MVP.

BIGNELL, Larry

b. Edmonton, Alberta, January 7, 1950
After overcoming a bout of mono and a broken hand in successive years in the minors, Bignell appeared in 20 games for Pittsburgh in '73-'74 and in 3 playoff games the year after. He signed with Denver in the WHA the following year, but that team quickly folded and moved to Ottawa to finish the year as the Civics.

BILLINGTON, Craig

b. London, Ontario, September 11, 1966
Sometimes a player gets a reputation and is typecast for the rest of his days, like a Hollywood bad guy or matinee idol. Billington had a terrific junior career, winning gold with Canada's World Juniors in 1985 and silver a year later. When he joined New Jersey the next year, he was happy to play the role of backup and ease his way into the starter's role. That's how it usually works. But not with Billington. He remained a backup, and stayed a backup, perhaps the best in the game. But no one considered him a number-one man languishing on a goalie-heavy team. Billington backed up Martin Brodeur in Jersey, Patrick Roy in Colorado, and Olaf Kolzig in Washington. In 1993-94 he started 63 games with Ottawa on a disastrous team and finished with an awful record of 11-41-4. Perhaps that was the year that sealed his fate. In 2002-03 with the Capitals, he was demoted to the minors and played only briefly in Washington before retiring and moving into a front-office job back in Colorado.

BILODEAU, Gilles

b. St. Prime, Quebec, July 31, 1955
Mayhem rules when this guy hits the ice. Never drafted by the NHL, he signed with the Toronto Toros of the WHA, who had selected him in that league's draft in 1975. He started the '75-'76 season with the St. George de Beauce Jaros and accrued a staggering 451 penalty minutes in 58 games before the Toros, impressed with his numbers, called him up to ratchet away on WHA opponents. He continued to play virtually glove-free hockey until Quebec acquired him the year the team joined the NHL, '79-'80. He fought in nine games for the Nords and disappeared shortly thereafter.

BINETTE, Andre

b. Montreal, Quebec, December 2, 1933
If you're born in Montreal, you worship les Canadiens. You want to play with them one day. For sure. You play goal and you make progress. And one day you get a call. The great Jacques Plante is injured. He cannot play. Can you be at the Forum tonight for the game? You are 20 years old. You cry, you shake, you get yourself to the Forum. Your team plays well and you recover your nerves to win the game 7-4 over Chicago. You never play another game in the NHL. Never come close. But it doesn't matter. For one night, you were Jacques Plante.

BINKLEY, Les ("Bink")

b. Owen Sound, Ontario, June 6, 1934
There was a reason Les Binkley began his life in hockey as a trainer – he couldn't see. He was minding his own business in the depths of the IHL when he got a call to play for Cleveland of the AHL because the regular goalie was fogged in in Toronto. Binkley accepted and made such a favourable impression that he received a tryout offer from the Barons for the next season. He made the club, but the contract he was offered involved being the team's backup goalie and trainer. He accepted, and late in the season the regular tender, Gil Mayer, was injured and Binkley came in for the final eight games. He was never a trainer after that. He was to toil yet another half-dozen years before he got into the NHL, and like so many others that opportunity came along first because of NHL expansion and then because of the WHA. Binkley was the first goaler to wear contact lenses, a requirement caused by his inability to see long shots, but he played five years for the Pittsburgh Penguins when they first joined the league. Then, for purely monetary reasons, he signed with the WHA, retired in 1975, and went on to become a scout for the Winnipeg Jets.

BIONDA, Jack ("Big Jack")
b. Huntsville, Ontario, September 18, 1933
d. Huntsville, Ontario, November 5, 1999

Even if he had never played an NHL game, even if he had never put on a pair of skates or held a hockey stick or flicked a puck in the air, Jack Bionda would still be regarded as one of the greatest athletes Canada has ever produced. He used to take shots against the garage door, all right, but it was with a lacrosse ball and stick that he made a noise. He considered hockey a job, playing because he was good at it and because he needed something to do in the winter. Although he played hockey for parts of four seasons with Toronto and Boston and numerous others in the WHL, he played lacrosse because he loved it and because he was one of its greatest proponents. He is in the Canada Sports Hall of Fame for lacrosse, and during his 20-year career in sports he felt his greatest moment was winning the 1962 Mann Cup with the New Westminster Salmon-bellies, when he scored the winning goal in OT. He won four Mann Cups besides and a ton of scoring championships, and could run down a street bouncing a ball off telephone poles without missing a beat. In truth, the lacrosse world called Gordie Howe the Jack Bionda of hockey. After retiring, he returned to Huntsville and bought a rug store from Doug Messier, Mark's father. Later, he owned and operated a series of restaurants, and invented the Bionda's Boomerang Ball which lacrosse players can use to practise on their own. He passed away too young, shortly after successful surgery to replace his sports-ravaged knees.

Jack Bionda

BIRON, Martin
b. Lac St. Charles, Quebec, August 15, 1977

Oh, but 1995 was a good year. Biron was named the best junior goalie in Canada and that June he was drafted by Buffalo. A year later, he made Canada's World Junior team and he was starting to get some time in the league. He also had the opportunity to learn from the number-one man with the Sabres, Dominik Hasek, and Biron was the beneficiary of great good fortune when the Dominator was traded to Detroit in the summer of 2001. With three years of pro under his belt, he had a chance to be the starting goalie. Well, so far it hasn't turned out entirely as he'd hoped, but he's still young. Without Hasek and Michael Peca, the Sabres are not nearly as good a team, and as a result Biron isn't winning with the same consistency. He's also not as good as Hasek – at least not yet.

BIRON, Mathieu
b. Lac St. Charles, Quebec, April 29, 1980

He had target practice as a kid, for his bro was none other than Buffalo's Martin Biron. Like Martin, Mathieu also played at the World Juniors and was a 1st-round draft choice. And like Martin, he is young and has yet to realize his potential as a defenceman with the Islanders.

BISSETT, Tom "Tim" ("Mahoney")
b. Seattle, Washington, March 13, 1966

Bissett tied Mike Zuke's record at Michigan Tech by playing in 163 consecutive games. Then in his second year of pro, he wrecked his knee and missed almost an entire season. After recovering, the Red Wings tossed him into five games and at season's end Bissett took his game to Europe where he has played for more than a decade, one of the very few Americans to play in national leagues overseas. He has also played for the U.S. at two World Championships (seventh place in 1992, sixth in '99).

BITTNER, Richard
b. New Haven, Connecticut, January 11, 1922
d. Columbus, Ohio, March 24, 2002

One man's groin injury is anther man's dream come true. Bittner was the very definition of a minor pro goalie who played every which way but up in bits and pieces during and after the war, but on February 12, 1950, he was allowed a moment of glory when Boston's Jack Gelineau couldn't play because of a painful groin injury. Bittner got the call from the Boston Olympics and played well in a 3-3 tie against Montreal. He allowed all three scores in the second period and once he returned to the minors he never made the NHL grade again.

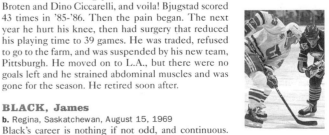

Bjugstad had a reputation for scoring goals with his incredible shot.
SCOTT BJUGSTAD

BJUGSTAD, Scott
b. St. Paul, Minnesota, June 2, 1961

From his days around Hillview Rink in St. Paul to Irondale High School to four years at the University of Minnesota, Bjugstad had a reputation for scoring goals with his incredible shot. But after playing in the 1984 Olympics in Sarajevo with the U.S., his stick went dry when he joined the Minnesota North Stars. Then coach Lorne Henning put him on a line with Neal Broten and Dino Ciccarelli, and voila! Bjugstad scored 43 times in '85-'86. Then the pain began. The next year he hurt his knee, then had surgery that reduced his playing time to 39 games. He was traded, refused to go to the farm, and was suspended by his new team, Pittsburgh. He moved on to L.A., but there were no goals left and he strained abdominal muscles and was gone for the season. He retired soon after.

Mathieu Biron

BLACK, James
b. Regina, Saskatchewan, August 15, 1969

Black's career is nothing if not odd, and continuous. Technically, he is an 11-year NHL veteran, but in that

James Black

Stephen Black

Bob Blackburn

Don Blackburn

Hank Blade

Andy Blair

time he has played just 352 games. There have been seasons of one game (his first two, '89-'90 and '90-'91) and full seasons ('96-'97, '98-'99), but mostly there have been seasons of shuffle where long periods in the minors have been rewarded with recalls to the NHL. A left winger, he has 57 career goals and counting, though they trickle rather than pour into the record books.

BLACK, Stephen
b. Fort William, Ontario, March 31, 1927
Although Black was born exactly one year before Gordie Howe, his NHL career ended 29 years earlier than Howe's. He came down from the Fort to play for Detroit in 1950 and played on the Cup-winning Wings team with Howe that year to get his name stamped on the great hockey bowl. The next season, though, Black was traded to Chicago with Lee Fogolin as both players wanted more ice time and weren't getting it with a Cup-strong team like Detroit. Although Black finished the year with the Hawks, it was his last in the NHL. He moved to Port Arthur, Ontario, and worked in the relative calm of a local liquor store.

BLACKBURN, Bob
b. Rouyn, Quebec, February 1, 1938
Master of shotblocking and logger of ice time, Blackburn was not a physical defenceman so much as a skilled craftsman who could keep opponents to the side and away from the net. He toiled in anonymity for years in minor pro until 1968-69 when, at 31, he made the AHL All-Star Team for the first time in his career under head coach Fred Shero. Not surprisingly, the Rangers put him in a few games that year as well, and the next two years Blackburn played almost exclusively in Pittsburgh after the Penguins claimed him in the Intra-League Draft. He finished his career with Rochester the following season.

BLACKBURN, Dan
b. Montreal, Quebec, May 20, 1983
Since the formation of the NHL in 1917, only three goaltenders have ever played their first game at a younger age than Blackburn: Harry Lumley, John Vanbiesbrouck, and Martin Biron. Young Danny was 18 years and 143 days when he started for the Rangers against Washington at Madison Square Garden on October 10, 2001. Not only that, he won the starter's job for a brief time over Mike Richter, and the two spent most of his first season sharing goaltending duties. The next year, which Richter missed because of a concussion, Blackburn played even more. Obviously, it's too soon to tell the extent of Blackburn's success, but he has already earned the respect of teammates and opponents alike.

BLACKBURN, Don
b. Kirkland Lake, Ontario, May 14, 1938
Typical for his time, Blackburn played six games in the Original Six era and 179 in the post-expansion era. The first half-dozen came with Boston, in '62-'63, and after toiling in the minors he was claimed by Philadelphia in 1967. He had been a decent scorer in lesser leagues but that didn't count for much in the NHL. He later moved to the WHA, and in '75-'76 he retired while playing for the New England Whalers to take over as coach. After just 10 weeks, he was removed as coach, reinstated as a player, and replaced behind the bench by Harry Neale.

At the end of '78-'79, he was again hired by the Whalers and led the team for its first 140 games of life in the NHL before being replaced by Larry Pleau. He remained an assistant for the rest of the year.

BLADE, Hank
b. Peterborough, Ontario, April 28, 1920
d. Peterborough, Ontario, February 8, 2003
He wasn't necessarily born with a stick in his hand, but he sure was born with one in his name. The son of an Imperial Oil employee, Hank was the only boy in a family with five sisters. He played junior hockey in Ottawa and managed to get into 24 games with Chicago in the years immediately after the Second World War. Blade's greatest games, though, were in Kansas City, where the balding left winger became a legend. He was the team's playing coach in 1949-50, and the team held a special "Blade Night" in his honour for five years of outstanding service. He later coached full-time after retiring.

BLADON, Tom ("Sparky"/ "Bomber")
b. Edmonton, Alberta, December 29, 1952
Four goals and four assists in a single game. Even Bobby Orr could only manage seven points in one outing. True, it was against the Cleveland Barons, but every other team played the Barons and no defenceman ever managed to get eight points in one game. In fact, his 42 points as a rookie eclipsed Orr's first year total of 41. And he won as many Stanley Cups as Orr – two, in '74 and '75. But that's where all comparisons end. Bladon was reliable and steady but not flashy, and certainly not a rushing defenceman in Orr's mould. Oddly, he played most of his career for the Flyers and Penguins, but in his final season (1980-81) he appeared in a few games for three teams before retiring. He settled in Victoria, B.C., and opened a trophy and sports store, and also worked for United Van Lines.

BLAINE, Garry
b. St. Boniface, Manitoba, April 19, 1933
d. Winnipeg, Manitoba, December 19, 1998
One of seven children growing up in Manitoba between the wars, Blaine was a talented skater who played in the Montreal organization in the 1950s. He appeared in one game for the Habs in '54-'55 before moving around a series of leagues and teams, and in the summer he was a noted baseball player in St. Boniface. He was inducted into the Manitoba Baseball Hall of Fame in 1998 and was an excellent golfer as well.

BLAIR, Andy
b. Winnipeg, Manitoba, February 27, 1908
d. Seattle, Washington, December 27, 1977
As a boy, Andrew Blair attended St. John's College in Manitoba, the same school that Red Dutton and Bill Cook had attended at a like age. He was awarded a letter for football at the University of Manitoba, and in the same year he achieved his B.A. he also won the Allan Cup with U of M's hockey team. He joined the Maple Leafs in 1928 and finished third in scoring that year behind Ace Bailey and Nels Stewart. A loner at first, he was convinced by coach Dick Irvin to move into a room at the Royal York Hotel (where Irvin, King Clancy, and Frank Finnigan all lived) to become one of the gang, as

it were. Although his reputation didn't rest in his goal-scoring prowess, he formed a superb second line with Bailey and Baldy Cotton on a team that featured the Kid Line of Conacher – Primeau – Jackson, the highest-scoring combination in the league. Blair scored two goals in the Cup-clinching game for the Leafs in 1932 and ended his career in 1937 after playing his final year with Chicago. Throughout his years in the NHL, he was the only mustachioed player and his whirling rushes were popular for their excitement. Blair then worked for the Hershey Pipe Company in Toronto for several years before moving to Winnipeg and then Vancouver to continue in the same capacity. He retired in 1969 and died of a heart attack while playing cards with his son, whom he was visiting in Seattle.

BLAIR, Chuck
b. Edinburgh, Scotland,
July 23, 1928
Brothers Chuck and George played hockey for many years following the war, though only intermittently on the same team. They were together in Oshawa in '47-'48, though they didn't play on the same line; briefly in Pittsburgh in '51-'52 when George was called up as an injury fill-in; and for much of '54-'55 with the Buffalo Bisons. Their longest brotherly stint came in Calgary, where they played from 1957 to '59 together. Both were forwards, and both were noted for their hustle and tenacity rather than finesse or offensive skill. Chuck played a single game with the Leafs, December 4, 1948, and after retiring coached for a number of years in the minors. In the summers, he often worked as a gold miner in Schumacher, Ontario.

BLAIR, George "Dusty"
b. South Porcupine, Ontario, September 15, 1929
Brother of Chuck and a minor-league sensation in his own right, Dusty played pro for some 15 years and doubled Chuck in NHL appearances. He played for the Leafs on December 30, 1950, and January 6, 1951, while on Christmas vacation from his junior team, St. Michael's.

BLAISDELL, Mike ("Blazer"/ "Wally")
b. Moose Jaw, Saskatchewan, January 18, 1960
Mike Blaisdell is a legend. He has won three Autumn Cups and is revered in Nottingham, though he was fired by the Wasps unceremoniously during the '92-'93 season. He weighs 12 stone, 5 pounds and continues to play the odd game when his team needs help. He is a longtime hero of Britain's Superleague, his league of choice since 1990. After a solid, nine-year career in the NHL, he moved to Britain as player with the Durham Wasps in 1990 and became the team's coach about a

year later. Over the next decade he played whenever there was a place in the lineup for a foreign player. The Autumn Cup is Britain's Stanley Cup, and because of his skill, commitment, and success he is loved by British fans who enjoy their "ice hockey."

BLAKE, Bob
b. Ashland, Wisconsin, August 16, 1914
Out of the land of football came a hockey star who rose to prominence with the Buffalo Bisons before and after the war. He played for that team during its inaugural season in the AHL, 1940-41, at which time he was moved from left wing back to defence by coach Tiny Thompson. Three years later, he played a major part in winning the championship. Blake then served for three years in the United States Air Corps before returning to the AHL, playing primarily with the Bisons again for a number of seasons.

BLAKE, Francis "Mickey"
b. Barriefield, Ontario,
October 31, 1912
d. unknown
Little is known about Blake outside his brief NHL career. This included single games with the Montreal Maroons in 1932-33 and the Leafs in '35-'36, and an eight-game stay with the St. Louis Eagles in '34-'35, the only year that team existed after leaving Ottawa at the end of the previous season.

BLAKE, Hector "Toe" ("The Old Lamplighter")
b. Victoria Mines, Ontario, August 21, 1912
d. Montreal, Quebec, May 17, 1995
Never before or since has a man combined Hall of Fame success as a player with Hall of Fame success as a coach. It all began in a small town just outside Sudbury when his father gave him a pair of skates to get to school and back. He was called Hector, but a brother couldn't wrap his tongue around the whole named and called him Toe for short. The name stuck. Blake played junior in Sudbury, senior in Hamilton, and turned pro with the Montreal Maroons. He won a Stanley Cup with that '34-'35 team despite playing just a few games for them. He was traded to the Canadiens, where he put down roots that lasted until the day he died. He played with the Habs for 13 years, most famously with Elmer Lach and Maurice Richard on the famous Punch Line. More than those stars, though, Blake was a complete player. He was used to kill penalties as well as work the power play. He skated well, worked in the corners, and had a great shot. His passing and stickhandling helped Richard score 50 goals in 50 games during the war years, and Blake was as tenacious as he was gentlemanly. The Habs made the playoffs every year but one, and won two Cups. In '38-'39 he led the league in scoring and

He was called Hector, but a brother couldn't wrap his tongue around the whole name and called him Toe for short.
TOE BLAKE

Chuck Blair

"Dusty" Blair

Mike Blaisdell

was named Hart Trophy winner, perhaps his finest year. He capped off the '43-'44 season by scoring the Cup-winning goal against Chicago. Blake was named to the First All-Star Team three times, but his career came to a crashing end on January 10, 1948, when Bill Juzda hit him hard and clean into the boards, shattering his leg and more or less finishing his playing days. He ended with 527 points, number one on the Canadiens all-time list, though he was later surpassed by both his linemates. He played very briefly in the minors, and then began a coaching career of unparalleled success. He coached in the minors until 1955, but when Dick Irvin stepped down as Habs coach, Blake was named his replacement, in large measure because management felt he was the one man Richard could respect and who could keep Richard in line. In 13 years with the Habs, Blake won an incredible 8 Stanley Cups, including 5 in a row to start his tenure as bench jockey. He retired immediately after the win in the 1968 playoffs with a lifetime post-season record of 82-37, surely a record that won't be surpassed. Known for his trademark fedora behind the bench, he loved coaching as much as he hated the ancillary duties of the job (interviews, etc.). He stayed in the organization for a while, and was later given a banquet in his honour. He also opened Blake's Tavern, a hugely popular hangout for the new generation of Habs who stopped by with the Cup during their parades in the 1970s. He was inducted into the Hockey Hall of Fame in 1966, and in 1982 was awarded the Order of Canada. He spent his final years fighting Alzheimer's, a battle he finally lost in 1995.

BLAKE, Jason
b. Moorhead, Minnesota, September 2, 1973
On April 18, 1999, Blake scored a goal in his first NHL contest. Signed as a free agent by Los Angeles after a college career in which he was nominated for the Hobey Baker Award, he also played for the U.S. in an embarrassing situation for the team. After finishing an atrocious twelfth in the 1998 World Championships, the nation had to play in a qualifying tournament to ensure their "A" pool status for the next Worlds. They accomplished as much, and two years later Blake played in the more prestigious championships, the highlight of his young career.

BLAKE, Mike
b. Kitchener, Ontario, April 6, 1956
Even the most cocky of trivia freaks would have trouble naming off the top of their head who the goalie was the night Wayne Gretzky scored his 92nd

and final goal toward the end of that miraculous, record-breaking season in 1981-82. The answer is Mike Blake. The nephew of legend Toe Blake, Mike signed as a free agent with Los Angeles in the hopes of moving up the Kings' depth charts faster than he might have with another team. Instead, as merely one of many goalies the team used over the three years he was there, and after bouncing around in the minors under these conditions, he retired, a decision made easier by his fifth knee operation, in 1985, at the age of 30. He returned home to Kitchener and became a sales rep for CHYM, a local radio station.

BLAKE, Rob ("Blakey")
b. Simcoe, Ontario, December 10, 1969
One of the giants of the current NHL game, Blake comes from a farming family where pride of character and strength of mind go hand in hand with physical attributes. He attended Bowling Green University and was drafted by Los Angeles after one year. Encouraged by one and all to turn pro with the Kings, Blake surely is one of the few to opt for college rather than the NHL – he didn't feel ready to play with the big boys, and he was correct. A year later, he was a much better player, more developed in all ways. When he got to L.A., he was awed by Wayne Gretzky. On the road, he roomed with Dave Taylor, who helped the country kid get used to life in the big cities. Blake quickly became the best young defenceman in the game and then one of the best players, period. He had tremendous size and strength, a great shot from the point, and offensive skill that matched his toughness in front of his own net. But the Kings rarely went far in the playoffs (with the exception of '93 when they went to the finals) and Blake suffered a number of injuries to his knees and shoulders that put him out for long stretches. He also had an almost annual opportunity to play for Canada at the World Championships. He played in five world tournaments during the 1990s, winning gold in '94 and '97, and also played for Canada at the 1998 Olympics in Nagano and the gold-medal team at Salt Lake City in 2002. During the 2000-01 season, as he approached unrestricted free agency, he demanded a trade by saying he almost certainly would not sign with the Kings when his services went on the open market. Dave Taylor, now the GM and a man who taught Blake too well, traded him to Colorado and the Avs won the Cup just a few weeks later. That summer, Blake signed the largest contract for a defenceman (about $10 million a year) to ensure his spot on the Avalanche blueline for many years to come. He also won gold with Canada at the 2002 Olympics at Salt Lake City.

Blake quickly became the best young defenceman in the game.
ROB BLAKE

Jason Blake

Mike Blake

BLIGHT, Rick
b. Portage la Prairie, Manitoba, October 17, 1955

A winger with size was what Vancouver wanted, and that's what they got when they selected Blight 10th overall at the 1975 Amateur Draft. His skating was suspect, his shot deadly, his attitude good, his history impressive. He scored buckets in Brandon, and in his first three years with Vancouver right out of junior he averaged 26 goals a season. Then his production dipped, he hurt his knee, and he wound up in the minors. His only three games with the Canucks in '80-'81 came when regular Bobby Schmautz was suspended and the team recalled him as a fill-in. He finished his career with L.A., playing twice in 1982-83. He was inducted into the Manitoba Sports Hall of Fame in 1995. Blight later worked as a stockbroker and managed the family farm and marketing business in Manitoba.

BLINCO, Russ ("Beaver")
b. Grand'Mere, Quebec, March 12, 1908
d. 1982

He was the first NHLer to wear glasses while playing. As a kid, he'd collect player cards from cigarette packages and cut them out. He'd line two teams into position and use a marble for a puck to script a game in which his hero, Frank Nighbor, usually ended up the idol. A few years later, while he was at Bishop's College in Lennoxville, he started his own career path to hockey stardom. When he got to the NHL, with the Montreal Maroons, he centred a line with Earl Robinson and Dave Trottier and led the team to the 1935 Stanley Cup. He played with the English-Montreal team for five years, but when times got tough for the owners, he, Robinson, and Baldy Northcott were sold to Chicago for $30,000. After one season in the Windy City, he retired. Blinco was a durable player who missed just 3 games in his career, and he had just 24 penalty minutes in 268 NHL games. In retirement, he ran a rink in Bedford, Quebec for many years, and later had an even greater influence on the Hershey Bears, running the team and arena.

BLOCK, Ken
b. Steinbach, Manitoba, March 18, 1944

On June 8, 1967, a friend of Ken Block's phoned him and told him he'd just heard on the radio that Block had been traded from Los Angeles to Toronto for the great Red Kelly. Block laughed, and bet his pal a case of beer that wasn't the case. Block's wife then phoned the station and was told, yes, that was the deal. Block then phoned another friend and told him he'd just been traded for Kelly. The friend laughed, and Block bet him a case of beer. In the end, it was a wash. But, yes, the deal occurred because the Kings wanted Kelly to retire and become the team's first coach. Kelly wanted nothing more than to do the same, but GM Punch Imlach refused to let a valuable piece of Leafs property just up and leave; he wanted something in return, and that something turned out to be Block. Beyond that, Block played in virtually every league conceivable in North America and got into the NHL history books by virtue of one game in 1970-71 with Vancouver, another new team for that season. Block later played in the WHA for seven years.

BLOEMBERG, Jeff
b. Listowel, Ontario, January 31, 1968

He was Rangers property from 1986 when he was drafted 93rd overall, but Bloemberg played only 43 games with the Blueshirts from 1988-92 before embarking on a lengthy tour of duty in the minors and Europe that continues. Amazingly, although his only NHL games are with New York, he has also been owned by Tampa Bay, Edmonton, Hartford, and Detroit.

BLOMQVIST, Timo
b. Helsinki, Finland, January 23, 1961

He was nearly 40 by the time he hung up his sweater, but along the way Blomqvist became a legend in Finland for his league play and participation with Suomi in international tournaments of every sort. He is one of a rare group to play in three World Juniors (1979, '80, and '81). He played at the '88 and '92 Olympics and the 1987 Canada Cup, and the 1985 World Championships. His NHL time was limited to 223 games with Washington and a further 20 with New Jersey, but the defenceman never had more than 1 goal or 20 points a year. He retired to become a coach back home in Helsinki.

BLOMSTEN, Arto
b. Vaasa, Finland, March 16, 1965

At 239th overall, Blomsten is one of the lower draft choices ever to play in the NHL. That it was for just 25 games is beside the point. That he was drafted at age 21 but didn't play with Winnipeg until he was 28 is also beside the point. He had a perfectly fine career going in Sweden, and he came to North America to give the league a try. He never scored a goal, and in 1996 he returned home to continue a career that endured until 2001 when he retired.

BLOOM, Mike
b. Ottawa, Ontario, April 12, 1952

When you're a left winger with Washington – the year is 1974-75 – and you play 67 games with a +/- rating of -54, you're not likely to stick around long. Bloom had been drafted by Boston, but the Beantowners left him high and dry in the Expansion Draft and he wound up on a team that had a record of 8-67-5, the worst season in NHL history. Fortunately, he was then traded to Detroit, where he played two and a half years before ending up in the minors.

BLOUIN, Sylvain ("Sly")
b. Montreal, Quebec, May 21, 1974

If his penalty minutes were a hitting average, he'd have been in Cooperstown years ago. As it is, the young member of the Wild continues to punish every chance he gets. In 1993 and '94, he won consecutive Memorial Cups with Laval and had 373 and 492 minutes in the penalty box. In the minors ever since, he's been healthily slugging 300, and in his few NHL games he's down to about 3 minutes a game. And yet, as a kid, he idolized Peter Stastny, one of the more skilled players ever to skate.

BLUE, John
b. Huntington Beach, California, February 19, 1966

When you've been playing serious hockey for 15 years

Rick Blight

Russ Blinco

Ken Block

Timo Blomqvist

Mike Bloom

John Blue

John Blum

Gregg Boddy

Gus Bodnar

Ron Boehm

or so and find out the only team that wants you is called the Austin Ice Bats, you kinda know it's time to pack it in. No disrespect to Ice Bats fans everywhere. Blue's story is a feel-good one, though – the kid from California making it in the ice game through perseverance and quick reflexes. He guarded the goal for 46 games (1992-96) with Boston and Buffalo and performed internationally for Team USA at the '90 and '97 World Championships before calling it quits.

BLUM, John
b. Detroit, Michigan, October 8, 1959

One winter, in baseball-mad Detroit, John's dad pushed him onto the ice and promised if he tried skating just once, he'd never want to stop. He was right. Blum played his way up through the ranks as a teen, but when it was time to decide on college or hockey, he was in a bind. He had no scholarship offers on the table, so he enrolled at the University of Michigan, the school he'd always loved as a kid. Once there, he wangled an invitation to try out for the hockey team, and he made it. But it wasn't until his senior year that he actually received a full scholarship. Upon graduation in 1981, he heard a great deal of silence. No draft, no phone calls, no interest from NHL teams. The Oilers signed him, but on a team chockfull of stars, he was destined for a career in the minors. A trade to Boston in 1984 was, if nothing else, a chance to play in the NHL. Blum was not a spectacular defenceman, merely big, tough, and reliable. He sought only to keep the puck out of the net, and he did that consistently well during a career that extended well into the 1990s.

BODAK, Bob
b. Thunder Bay, Ontario, May 28, 1961

The distance from Lakehead University to the Calgary Saddledome is so great that only a determined person could ever accomplish the trip. Bodak did just that. After graduating from LU in 1984, he signed with Springfield in the AHL. The Flames were impressed by his 20-goal season, signed him, and assigned him to their affiliate in Moncton. From there, he got the phone call all minor leaguers hope and dream about, and for three games in 1987-88, he was a member of the Calgary Flames. The same thing happened a couple of years later with Hartford, and these small NHL excursions constituted the pinnacle of his career.

BODDY, Gregg
b. Ponoka, Alberta, March 19, 1949

What do Scott McLeod, Gary Monahan, Vladimir Chadrin, and Gregg Boddy have in common? They were all among the leaders in assists in 1978-79 … in Japan. That's where Boddy ended his career. It all began in Edmonton a decade earlier. The defenceman was drafted by Los Angeles, but it wasn't until trades to Montreal and Vancouver that he ended up in the NHL with the second-year Canucks. Boddy played regularly for four and a half years and then migrated to the WHA briefly before heading to Japan to get a little culture with his hockey.

BODGER, Doug
b. Chemainus, British Columbia, June 18, 1966

When he was a young 'un, his grandmother would give him a dime for every lap of the local rink he made without falling down. Little Dougie did not get rich that way. But over time, he learned to skate and his love for the game grew. He moved to the big city – Kamloops – to play junior, and in 1984 the Penguins selected him 9th overall after selecting some guy named Mario 1st overall. Bodger was a rushing defenceman, a guy who loved Bobby Hull's slapshot and perfected his own, but a product of the Bobby Orr school of brilliance, watching number 4 go end to end with the puck. Bodger developed with Pittsburgh during the four and a half seasons he was there, but just as the team was turning into a Cup contender he was traded to Buffalo. He later played with 4 other teams, but by the time he retired he had played in 1,071 NHL games (though only 47 playoff matches, and only once did his team make it to the second round of the Cup chase). He also represented Canada at three World Championships.

BODNAR, August "Gus"
b. Fort William, Ontario, April 24, 1923

During his great years with the Leafs, Bodnar was one of the "Flying Forts," so called because of their birthplace, their speed, and, of course, their success. He joined Conn Smythe's men in 1943 and over the next four years won two Stanley Cups. He had tried to enter the army but failed the medical because of a heart murmur. Classified as 4F, he was told that he was taking his chances by playing hockey. Near the start of the '47-'48 season, another Cup year for the Leafs, Bodnar and four others were traded to Chicago for Max Bentley, one of Smythe's greatest trades. It would be six years before Bodner appeared in another playoff game. Although the Hawks had a weak team, Bodnar set an incredible record when he assisted on all three of the goals Bill Mosienko scored in just 21 seconds the night of March 23, 1952. He ended his career with Boston, then took a break from the game. He worked for Corman Engineering, the company that employed him every summer, during his career, and bought a hotel in Lindsay, Ontario. He worked as a sales rep for Dahmers Steel, then returned to hockey as coach of the Marlies. He moved to Salt Lake City after, then back to the OHL with Oshawa, but when Bill Torrey called him to be the first coach of the New York Islanders, in 1972, he turned the job down. Bodnar was later named one of three co-coaches for Canada's entry at the 1978 World Juniors, a talent-laden team featuring Wayne Gretzky and Mike Gartner that finished a disappointing third.

BOEHM, Ron
b. Saskatoon, Saskatchewan, August 14, 1943

Just a little guy, Boehm played 16 games with Oakland when the Seals joined the NHL in 1967-68. Besides that, he had a solid career in the minors. He had an excellent slapshot and was a versatile player who could score a bit, kill penalties, and skate well.

BOESCH, Garth
b. Milestone, Saskatchewan, October 7, 1920
d. California, May 13, 1998

He's the easiest player to recognize in old photos, because he's the only one sporting a moustache. Boesch started his NHL career late, finished it early, and in between won three successive Cups with the Leafs. He had planned on playing with the New York Americans but then enlisted as a flying officer in the Royal Canadian Air Force for four years. When he was discharged, the Amerks were gone and the Leafs had acquired his rights. He stepped right into the lineup in the fall of 1946 and won Cups in each of his first three years. When his father passed away, he moved back to the family 1,200-acre wheat farm in Riceton, Saskatchewan, though he gave up the land in 1964. He moved to California and became vice-president of a company that makes electric oil refiners for cars. Later in life, he had to have both his knees replaced.

BOGUNIECKI, Eric ("Bogie")
b. New Haven, Connecticut, May 6, 1975
The trade that sent Eric Boguniecki to St. Louis from Florida for Andrei Podkonicky on December 17, 2000, did not exactly rattle the hockey establishment, but it did bring one man's story full circle. Boguniecki had been drafted by the Blues in 1993 right out of high school, but after four years at the University of New Hampshire and two more in the IHL, the Blues never played him. He signed with Florida, but played most of 1999-2000 in the minors, finishing the year at the World Championships for the U.S. In 2001-02, he was named the AHL's MVP, and the year after, became one of the stars with the Blues, seemingly a late bloomer.

BOH, Rick
b. Kamloops, British Columbia, May 18, 1964
Boh played eight games with Minnesota in 1987-88 and then headed to Europe to play – in Holland, of all places. In his third year there, 1992-93, he was involved in an ugly incident in which he got his stick up and broke another player's jaw in three places. Boh was given a lengthy suspension, even though video replay showed the hit had been accidental. He returned to North America and set up Players Bench, a chain of stores that sells sporting goods throughout the southern U.S. and Canada. Having attended Colorado College, he also returned to that area and coached little-league hockey.

BOHONOS, Lonny ("Bo")
b. Winnipeg, Manitoba, May 20, 1973
How could he do it? How could he bury his country of birth like that? Actually, the answer is simple – the NHL let him. Bohonos wasn't big – there's that tag, again – but he could skate and shoot. That got him so far, a few games here and there in the NHL. He signed with Vancouver (of course, no one drafted him), and after 70 well-spaced games he was sent to Toronto for Brandon Convery, another smaller player the Leafs weren't playing. Although Bohonos had six points in six games with the Leafs in '97-'98, he was still sent to the minors. The next year, in the playoffs, he was phenomenal, with nine points in as many games. And still, back to the minors. The next year, with Manitoba of the IHL, he was leading the league in scoring when he broke his ankle. He came back, but still encountered no serious interest. Frustrated, he went to Switzerland and signed with HC (Hockey Club) Davos. It was there he proved his worth. He scored an overtime goal 62 seconds into the fourth period to give his club team a 4-3 win over Canada in the 2001 Spengler Cup finals. If an NHL team had wanted him, Canada likely would have won that game. At the 2002 Spengler Cup he was named tournament MVP, but this time Canada beat his Davos team. In 2002-03, he led the team to the Swiss league finals.

BOIKOV, Alexandre
b. Chelyabinsk, Soviet Union (Russia), February 7, 1975
Boikov's story is one of determination and perseverance, the kind one usually associates with some undersized Prairie kid bent on playing in the NHL. He was never drafted, but he had a mean streak in him that one doesn't normally expect from a Russian player. Undaunted, he packed his bags in search of the NHL dream, starting with a trip to the Western Hockey League in 1994. After two years, he had made enough of an impression that San Jose signed him, but after three years in the minors the Sharks had neither recalled him nor re-signed him. Nashville signed him that summer (1999) and a few months later he played his first two NHL games with the Predators. The year after, he played eight more, and although he seems to have been classified as a minor leaguer, one day he'll be able to return home and boast that he has, indeed, played in the NHL.

BOILEAU, Marc
b. Pointe Claire, Quebec, September 3, 1932
d. December 28, 2000
Unlike most Canadian kids, Boileau was not encouraged to play hockey as a boy. His uncle had played pro in the 1920s, and when the team went belly up, he was owed thousands of dollars. Marc's mom didn't want that happening to her boy. Nonetheless, he and his brothers played every chance they got, and Marc seemed determined to make a career of the game. That is, until he was 19, married, and playing for Cincinnati. He had a run-in with the coach and quit, and for a year and a half he was out of the game. After missing hockey, he moved out to Saint John and fell in love with the game again. He wound up in Indianapolis, and Detroit seemed his next destination. Then, he was assigned to Seattle, a step down, not up. Still, he kept at it and finally made the Red Wings in '61-'62 where he played most of the season. After that, he played in the minors for another decade before embarking on a coaching career that had a pattern opposite to most. He began in the NHL, with Pittsburgh for two and a half years, then coached in the WHA with Quebec, and finally in the junior ranks with the Seattle Thunderbirds.

BOILEAU, Patrick
b. Montreal, Quebec, February 22, 1975
He's getting on in years and doesn't seem to have made an impression during his brief stints in the NHL to date. Boileau has played five games for Washington but many more for the AHL affiliate Portland Pirates.

DOILEAU, Rene
b. Pointe Claire, Quebec, May 18, 1904
Uncle of Marc, who played a season with Detroit in 1961-62, Rene played seven games with the New York Americans in 1925-26 in a brief pro career.

Garth Boesch

Eric Boguniecki

Lonny Bohonos

Alexandre Boikov

Mark Boileau

Fred Boimistruck

Serge Boisvert

Claude Boivin

Leo Boivin

**Mike Boland
(b. 1954)**

BOIMISTRUCK, Fred
("Boimer"/ "Broomstick")
b. Sudbury, Ontario, January 14, 1962

There was a time, a long, long time ago, when the Allan Cup was more important than the Stanley Cup. The winners went on to represent Canada at the World Championships or Olympics, and the players were national heroes for their supremacy among Canada's amateur hockeyists. But those days are in the past, and when Boimistruck was on the Allan Cup–winning team of 1987, the victory caused barely a ripple. The name of the team was the Brantford Motts Clamatos, and the team had a simple rule: Players received $50 for a win, $5 for a loss. His teammates that year included Stan Weir, Stan Jonathan, and Don Edwards, former NHLers all. Boimistruck's NHL minutes came with the Leafs from '81–'83 after he had won fame with the Cornwall Royals, winners of the Memorial Cup in both 1980 and '81. After retiring, Boimistruck worked for the CNR and VIA Rail, now approaching twenty years of service with the company.

BOISVERT, Gilles
b. Trois Rivières, Quebec, February 15, 1933

Opening shot. The year is 1959, and the new hockey season is nicely underway. Boisvert is a goalie in Sudbury, but he gets a call to report to Cleveland because regular netminder Gil Mayer has fractured his jaw and is out of commission for a while. Boisvert, of course, reports. Cut to Ohio. The team travels by bus, and is on its way to Springfield for a game. New scene: the home of Terry Sawchuk, world-famous goalie of the Detroit Red Wings. He feels awful, his wife calls for an ambulance and then alerts the team. Doctors call it virus neuritis – he needs rest and whirlpool baths. Detroit plays that night. Daybreak. The office of GM Jack Adams. Adams calls the Ohio state police and explains that the Cleveland bus has to be found and stopped. State troopers – hockey fans – patrol the highways, find the bus, and tell the coach, Jackie Gordon, to call Detroit. He does. "Boisvert!" he hollers after putting down the phone, "Get to Detroit." And so he does, of course. The plane is delayed, and he arrives five minutes before the opening faceoff. Detroit is playing Montreal. The Habs win 4-2. Boisvert stays in goal for three games in all, then returns to a life in the minors.

BOISVERT, Serge
b. Drummondville, Quebec, June 1, 1959

Not many players can boast of having played for both Toronto and Montreal, but Boisvert is one, even though that boast consists of only 17 games with the former and 29 games with the latter in the 1980s. He was fortunate enough to have played a bit part on Montreal's '86 Cup team, and played most of '87–'88 with the National Team and at the 1988 Olympics in Calgary. Then, the travels began. He played in Sweden and Japan, eventually landing with the Frisk Tigers, in Norway where he continues as a coach.

BOIVIN, Claude
b. Ste. Foy, Quebec, March 1, 1970

From Vipiteno to the Pensacola Ice Pilots and everywhere in between, Boivin has been playing pro since 1990. He was drafted a remarkably optimistic 14th overall by Philadelphia at the '88 draft because of his size. But his physical attributes were greatly diminished after the night of January 2, 1993, when he destroyed his left knee. Two weeks later, he had reconstructive surgery, and for much of the next four years he struggled to regain proper use of the pin. During these struggles, he was traded to Ottawa, played a few games, and then made his way around the world of hockey.

BOIVIN, Leo
("Billy Boy Boivin"/ "Fireplug")
b. Prescott, Ontario, August 2, 1932

At 5'8" Boivin would hardly rattle the confidence of enemy forwards skating over the blueline in 21st-century hockey. But in his heyday, the 1950s and 1960s, he was considered the prototypical bodychecker, the defenceman who hit hard and cleanly and with effect night after night for 19 seasons. He played junior with Port Arthur and was signed by the Leafs, but at his first training camp at Maple Leaf Gardens in 1951 he decided to retire and drive a truck for a living. Conn Smythe talked Boivin out of his career change and convinced him to finish the season in the minors, and Boivin got into his first NHL games near the end of the '51-'52 season. He made the team as a regular the next fall, and for two seasons was a rock on the Leafs blueline. But Toronto felt it was strong on defence and lacking in talent up front and traded Boivin to Boston with Fern Flaman, Phil Maloney, and Ken Smith to acquire Bill Ezinicki and Vic Lynn. Boivin stayed a Bruins blueliner for the next 12 seasons, and on many nights was the only thing to cheer for on a weak team that missed the playoffs 8 of those 12 years. He also played in three All-Star Games (1961, '62, '64), testament to his value to the team as perceived by his league adversaries. He captained the Bruins from 1963 to '66, when he was traded to Detroit. The change was immediate in that he went to the Cup finals with the Wings at the end of that '65-'66 season. Boivin finished his career with 2 new teams in the 12-team NHL, Pittsburgh and Minnesota, and as soon as he retired from the North Stars in 1970 he began to scout for the team. He later scouted for St. Louis, during which time he served as interim coach in both the '75-'76 and '77-'78 seasons. He also coached briefly for the Ottawa 67's, but returned to scouting for the rest of his career. He was inducted into the Hockey Hall of Fame as a Veteran Player in 1986.

BOLAND, Mike
b. Montreal, Quebec, December 16, 1949

For a filmmaker, he was a heckuva hockey player. He played just two NHL games, with Philadelphia in '74-'75, and after a brief time in the minors turned his skills to the camera, making documentaries and helping his alma mater, St. Michael's, rejoin the OHL in the 1990s. In 1992, he was nominated for an Emmy in cinematography for a PBS series entitled "Millenium: Tribal Wisdom and the Modern World."

BOLAND, Mike
b. London, Ontario, October 29, 1954

Another tough guy trying to make the NHL, Boland's

career highlight came in 1978-79 when the Buffalo Sabres called him up for the final 22 games of the season. During that time, the team went on a lengthy unbeaten streak, but Boland never returned to the Sabres thereafter. He retired in 1981-82 to go into private business, but returned to hockey a year later to continue playing in the minors. His sister is married to Don Luce, another Sabres alumnus.

BOLDIREV, Ivan ("Ike")
b. Zranjanin, Yugoslavia, August 15, 1949
When little Ivan was only two, his parents moved the family from Yugoslavia to Sault Ste. Marie. They continued to speak the only language they knew, and Ivan learned his English the hard way, with friends, by listening to conversations, and through good old-fashioned practice. Boldirev started his career with Boston back in '70-'71, and the next year had the worst luck imaginable: He was traded from the Bruins, on the verge of winning the Stanley Cup, to Charles O. Finley's California Golden Seals, the worst team in the league. In the ensuing 15 years, he played for 5 teams and in more than 1,000 NHL games. He had nine 20-goal seasons but was weak defensively and frequently played on weaker teams, the one exception being 1981-82, when his Vancouver Canucks went to the finals. In his early days in the NHL, he acquired the nickname "D.P." (displaced person), a reflection of prejudices that Chicago teammate Stan Mikita had experienced (as another transplanted European). Nonetheless, Boldirev survived longer than most hurlers of the derogatory epithet before retiring in 1985. Detroit bought out his contract at season's end, and part of the settlement included a Little Caesar's pizza franchise from Red Wings owner and pizza entrepreneur Mike Ilitch. And so, Boldirev had a job to go to on the day he hung up his skates. He later established National Safety Associates, a home-security business in Indiana and Illinois.

BOLDUC, Danny
b. Waterville, Maine, April 6, 1953
During his three years at Harvard, Bolduc wrote a book on growing up in the States and wanting to be a hockey player. He left the prestigious university a year early to join the U.S. national team and play in the 1976 Olympics in Innsbruck, and after some time in the WHA and minors made it to Detroit for the better part of two seasons. He later played two games with Calgary and then stayed in the Flames system, first as a playing assistant coach and then dropping the "playing" from his title when the Moncton team had enough manpower to allow him to retire.

BOLDUC, Mike
b. Angegardien, Quebec, March 13, 1961
A big and tough defenceman, Bolduc played but 10 games in the NHL with the Quebec Nordiques in the early 1980s during a brief pro career that started in the QMJHL.

BOLL, Frank "Buzz"
b. Filmore, Saskatchewan, March 6, 1911
d. Mountlake Terrace, Shohomish, Washington, December 27, 2000
As a child, Frank's brother called him "Little Buzzer,"

but the term was soon reduced to "Buzz" and that became his nickname for life. When Buzz played in the 1930 Memorial Cup, he impressed Leafs scout Squib Walker and was offered a contract. Boll joined the Leafs during a decade in which the team went to the finals almost annually but never won. In the 1936 playoffs, he led all scorers with 7 goals and 10 points playing on a line with Bill Thoms and Frank Finnigan. After retiring, he returned to the family farm in Filmore and spent the rest of his working life growing wheat and barley.

BOLONCHUK, Larry
b. Winnipeg, Manitoba, February 26, 1952
For a brief, brief moment in time, Bolonchuk was a surprise NHLer, a defensive defenceman who couldn't rush the puck but who could, nonetheless, move the puck out of his end effectively. He was invited to Vancouver's camp in 1972, but no one expected him to make the team. He made the team. However, just 15 games later, he was demoted, and although he played a few more games with Washington when the Caps entered the league, he was out of the game by 1980.

BOLTON, Hugh ("Yug")
b. Toronto, Ontario, April 15, 1929
d. Toronto, Ontario, October 17, 1999
Toronto was his middle name. That's where he was born and that's where he passed away; that's where he played his junior hockey, with the Marlies; and that's where he lived all his life after hanging up the blades. Bolton played his whole NHL career with the Leafs during the 1950s, a decade that wasn't particularly good for the team. He suffered numerous injuries, notably a broken leg at the start of the '56-'57 season, which ended his career. Bolton then returned to school, earning a B.A. in electrical engineering from – where else? – the University of Toronto and complementing that with a teacher's certificate. He spent the rest of his life in the classroom in and around Toronto, teaching physics and science at Jarvis Collegiate, Bathurst Heights, and Scarlett Heights Collegiate. He passed away in his sleep at the age of 70.

BOMBARDIR, Brad ("Bomber")
b. Powell River, British Columbia, May 5, 1972
He captained the Minnesota Wild for two months in 2000-01, which might not seem like a long time, but in an era when coach Jacques Lemaire wanted a new captain every month to spread out the experience, being asked to keep the "C" was an honour for Bombardir. He had graduated from the University of North Dakota and put his time in with Albany, New Jersey's farm team, before playing a few games with the Devils in 1997-2000. He was on the Cup-winning team from 2000 but shortly after was traded to the Wild, where coach Lemaire (who knew him from their days in Jersey) welcomed him.

BONAR, Dan
b. Brandon, Manitoba, September 23, 1956
For three years, he came to training camp in Los Angeles, and for three years he was sent down to the minors. But on the fourth try, in September 1980, he made the team because of his hustle. He started off as a

Danny Bolduc

"Buzz" Boll

Larry Bolonchuk

Dan Bonar

Peter Bondra

Brian Bonin

Marcel Bonin

Radek Bonk

Dennis Bonvie

fourth-line checker, but his play so impressed coach Bob Berry that the small centre replaced Garry Unger on the second line. For two and a half seasons, he earned a regular spot in the lineup, but in December 1983 he was sold to Montreal and never made the NHL again.

BONDRA, Peter
b. Luck, Soviet Union (Ukraine), February 7, 1968
He was born in the Ukraine when it was still part of the Soviet Union and was raised in Czechoslovakia, but when his part of the world permitted its people freedom, he immediately became a citizen of Slovakia. And he immediately came to the NHL. That was 1990, and Washington had just drafted him. On February 5, 1994, he set a team record with four goals in a span of just 4:12, and scored another later in the game. That's what he has always done best – score. He has played all his NHL games with the Caps, scoring more than 400 goals with the team and becoming a true leader. He has also played for Slovakia at the 1996 World Cup and the 1998 and 2002 Olympics. In addition, he has also led the NHL in goals on two occasions and played in five All-Star Games. In May 2002, he scored the winning goal to give Slovakia its first gold medal at the World Championships.

BONIN, Brian
b. St. Paul, Minnesota, November 28, 1973
No longer young enough to be called a prospect, but not old enough to give up entirely on an NHL life, Bonin struggles to find him rhythm. He played four full years at the University of Minnesota, culminating with a Hobey Baker Award in 1996, but since then has played only a few games with Pittsburgh and Minnesota.

BONIN, Marcel
b. Montreal, Quebec, September 12, 1932
The story's details are a little murky, a bit mythological in narrative yet rooted in hard and simple fact. When Bonin was playing for Detroit in the mid-1950s, he became friends with a police officer who got the hockey player interested in guns. When Bonin retired from the NHL in 1962, he became a pistol shooting instructor with the police force in Joliette, Quebec, a job he had held part-time during his playing days. He was famous as a wrestler of bears in the off season and he could chew glass to the amazement of teammates. Bonin was very proud of his muscles – he was one of the earlier hockey-proponents of weightlifting – but during his minor-league games with Edmonton in 1954 he hurt his back. It was an ailment that grew more and more painful until February 1962, when he collided with Pete Goegan. He required an operation that kept him bedridden for two months and forced him to wear a corset for a long period afterwards. That's when he decided to retire. After all, the winger had won four Stanley Cups with Detroit in 1955 and Montreal in '58, '59, and '60. After retiring, he went back to Joliette to work as a security guard at a local school.

BONK, Radek
b. Krnov, Czechoslovakia (Czech Republic), January 9, 1976
Everything looks rosy now, but there was a time when

the thorns were more noticeable than the petals. Bonk arrived in North America as a 17-year-old in 1993 but opted to play in the IHL rather than junior or college. It was a precedent-setting decision, getting ready for the draft by playing against men rather than boys his own age, and he proved critics wrong when he scored 42 goals and 87 points in a league known for many things other than development. Bonk also accumulated 208 penalty minutes and won rookie-of-the-year honours. The year after, when he couldn't come to terms with Ottawa on a contract, he returned to the Las Vegas Thunder, but after a slow start, he signed with the Sens after all. His first four years were less than stellar, and many fans in Ottawa wondered if he was just a Czech version of Alexandre Daigle. Then, on March 3, 1998, he was charged with drinking and driving. To his credit, he overcame his difficulties on and off the ice and has emerged as one of the Senators' best players.

BONNI, Ryan
b. Winnipeg, Manitoba, February 18, 1979
At 6'4" and 220 pounds, Bonni is a large and tough defenceman still developing in the Vancouver organization. He had a brief trial with the Canucks in 1999-2000.

BONSIGNORE, Jason
b. Rochester, New York, April 15, 1976
When he was 15, he was the next Mario Lemieux. When he was 18, his stock was falling fast. When he was 23, he was out of the NHL. Bonsignore was a mammoth, smooth-skating American kid who idolized Mario. His bedroom was plastered with Mario memorabilia, and he had the size and smooth hands of le Magnifique. But as his draft year approached, he didn't develop. He played poorly at the '94 World Juniors, and although he went 4th overall to Edmonton that summer, it was a selection rooted more in hope and faith than hard evidence he was the next Next One. Sure enough, he played just 21 games with Edmonton before being packaged in a trade to Tampa. By the time he signed with Toronto as a free agent, he was yesterday's news. He was sent to St. John's, got into a fight with player coach Greg Smyth and was gone. He was playing hurt, his fitness centre was going bankrupt, and he retired. A year and a half later, he returned, to the AHL at age 26, to try to salvage a pro career.

BONVIE, Dennis
b. Antigonish, Nova Scotia, July 23, 1973
He was never drafted, and for good reason. He has yet to score an NHL goal in 56 career games over 6 seasons. For good reason. He also has yet to register an assist in those 56 games. For good reason. He is singularly equipped to play the game, and that skill lies inside his gloves. In the 1996-97 AHL season, he sat in the penalty box for 522 minutes. In every other season and for every other team, his penalty-minute totals are staggering testaments to his inability to play and his commensurate ability to fight.

BOO, Jim
b. Rolla, Montana, November 12, 1954
Boo played six games in the NHL, with Minnesota in 1977-78 during a brief pro career that ended in 1980.

BOONE, Carl "Buddy"
b. Kirkland Lake, Ontario, September 11, 1932
d. Kirkland Lake, Ontario, September 1, 1986

On April 4, 1957, Boone scored a goal that helped his Bruins eliminate Detroit from the semifinals in the fifth game of the series. He had sat on the bench the entire game, but coach Milt Schmidt put him out for one shift in the second period. He beat Glenn Hall with a great shot, and was back on the bench for the rest of the game. The next year, he played half a season with the B's, but his career shouldn't have been so fleeting. He was a top scorer in junior and in the minors, and continued to play for more than a decade. Always considered pudgy, he got by on his shot and scoring ability. In the summers, he always returned to Kirkland Lake to drive a taxi for his father's business.

BOOTHMAN, George ("Bow Ties"/ "Pruneface")
b. Calgary, Alberta, September 25, 1916

A wartime replacement renowned for his neckwear (ergo his nickname), Boothman played 58 games for the Leafs between 1942 and '44. His career ended after a few more years in the minors.

BORDELEAU, Christian
b. Noranda, Quebec, September 23, 1947

It all started in Noranda North, a poor suburb of a small mining city. The Bordeleaus – mother, father, three girls, four boys – had a small house, behind which was a small creek where the kids would scrape the ice and skate to their hearts' content. Christian wanted to play in the NHL with Montreal, as did Jean-Pierre, and Paulin, and Christian's dream came true in 1968 when he played briefly with the team and won a Stanley Cup with les Canadiens the next spring. He played only 205 games in the NHL before moving to a more lucrative situation in the WHA in 1972, one that ended awkwardly and painfully for the small, fleet forward. After years of playing with much larger opponents, he developed a bad shoulder. Doctors cautioned that the surgery only had a 20 percent success rate, and might not prolong his career. He retired, then un-retired and hung in there for a few more games before realizing he had no more to give.

BORDELEAU, Jean-Pierre "J.P."
b. Noranda, Quebec, June 13, 1949

Hockey is a sport that can occupy and consume a person for his entire life. The NHL might be the pinnacle of that endeavour, but hockey is such a large part of Canadian culture that it exists on many levels, from kids hockey to doughnuts. Jean-Pierre Bordeleau, like his brothers, hoped to play for the vaunted

Montreal Canadiens. Although he never did, he played many times at the Montreal Forum as an opponent and had a rich 10-year career with Chicago. He was never a scorer, but he was one of the best checkers and penalty killers in the league throughout the 1970s. At the start of the 1980-81 season, though, incoming coach Keith Magnuson sent Bordeleau to the minors, in Moncton. How such an insult could turn into a wonderful blessing reveals much about the sport itself. Bordeleau and his wife fell in love with Moncton, and after Bordeleau retired the next year they settled there and he worked as a life insurance agent for the next five years while coaching the Riverview Trappers, an Intermediate A team. He later moved to Dartmouth to coach in the MJHL and operate a Tim Hortons franchise.

"Buddy" Boone

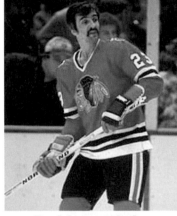

Bordeleau worked as a life insurance agent for five years while coaching the Riverview Trappers.
J.P. BORDELEAU

BORDELEAU, Paulin
b. Noranda, Quebec, January 29, 1953

Ironically, the least NHL-successful of the Bordeleau brothers was unquestionably the most well-travelled. He played three years with Vancouver (1973-76) after an enormously successful junior career that saw him complete the rare double, winning Memorial Cups with two different teams (Montreal Jr. Canadiens in 1970 and the Marlies in '73). He moved on to the WHA and then accepted a job as playing coach in Megeve, France. Using his family's ancestry, he was also able to play internationally for France, at the World Championships in 1986 and '87 in "B" pool, and at the 1988 Olympics in Calgary, the first time in 20 years the French had qualified for the Olympics.

George Boothman

Bordeleau stayed in Europe another four years as a scout for the Canadiens. He returned to Canada to coach Montreal's farm team in Fredericton and continues to coach to this day. His son, Sebastien, later played in the NHL and Europe.

BORDELEAU, Sebastien
b. Vancouver, British Columbia, February 15, 1975

While his dad was playing for the Canucks, his mom gave birth to little Sebastien who, 20 years later, would follow in his family's footsteps to the NHL. Sebastien played with the Canadiens in their post-glory days in the late 1990s, and after a trade to Nashville suffered a serious stomach injury that has, at least temporarily, put a crimp in his development. He played in Switzerland in '02-'03.

BOROTSIK, Jack
b. Brandon, Manitoba, November 26, 1949

A Brandon boy through and through, Borotsik played junior with the Wheat Kings and went on to appear in one game with the St. Louis Blues. He

Sebastien Bordeleau

Luciano Borsato

**Nikolai
Borschevsky**

Laurie Boschman

returned to Brandon to play and later coach senior hockey in Brandon.

BORSATO, Luciano
b. Richmond Hill, Ontario, January 7, 1966
From Richmond Hill to the Nurnberg Ice Tigers in 17 years, Borsato has played hockey all his life. After graduating from Clarkson University, he spent five very part-time years with St. Louis before going to Europe, where the playing was guaranteed, the schedule lighter, the culture enlightening, and the pay more than adequate. He won a bronze medal with Canada at the 1995 World Championships, and after retiring in 2002, settled in Toronto.

BORSCHEVSKY, Nikolai ("Nick the Stick")
b. Tomsk, Soviet Union (Russia), January 12, 1965
He scored the most important goal in Maple Leafs history since 1967, a goal that eliminated Detroit at home in game seven of the first-round playoff match in 1993 and a goal that affirmed the new era Leafs had arrived. Borschevsky had played for years in the Soviet Union, but he was a quality player who would never be allowed to leave freely for the West. But in 1992, at the age of 27, he was given permission to join Toronto, the team that had drafted him. Though not classified as a rookie, he had 34 goals that first year and, more importantly, scored that playoff goal to give GM Cliff Fletcher a huge lift during his massive overhaul of a club decimated by years of Harold Ballard's rule. But Borschevsky's life took another turn early the next season, on November 3, 1993. In a home game against Florida, he took a harmless-looking check that caused quite a lot of pain. As he sat on the bench unable to return to the ice, he knew something was wrong, and when team doctors examined him, they rushed him to the operating table. He had ruptured his spleen and blood was literally gushing into his abdomen. He lost half the blood in his body, but amazingly was up and skating within five weeks. Though he returned for the rest of this season and part of the next, he became less and less effective and wound up back in Europe playing out the rest of his days, happy just to be alive after that frightening night at the Gardens. After retiring, he returned to Toronto and started his own, very successful hockey school.

BOSCHMAN, Laurie ("Bosch")
b. Major, Saskatchewan, June 4, 1960
It just wasn't a good idea to find God when you were an employee of Harold Ballard, and certainly not a good idea to let people know about it. But perhaps in the case of Laurie Boschman it didn't much matter

because he was on the outs with the team anyway for what they considered unimpressive play. Boschman might have argued that the two went hand in hand, and certainly his numbers in Winnipeg certainly bore that out. He began as a high Leafs draft choice – 9th overall in 1979 – but had a tough time adjusting to the faster NHL. However, the public ridiculing Ballard subjected the youngster to destroyed his confidence and personality such that a trade to Edmonton proved a huge relief. He later had 4 seasons of 25 goals or more in a 5-year period and complemented his scoring ability with a toughness that belied both his spirituality and his size. After retiring in 1993, he took a year off and then joined Hockey Ministries International, a Christian organization that has 31 centres in 15 countries and combines the physical qualities of hockey with the spiritual qualities of religion.

He became the first man since Richard to hit 50 in 50.
MIKE BOSSY

BOSSY, Mike ("Boss")
b. Montreal, Quebec, January 22, 1957
Just as most kids go to school knowing that they are preparing for college or university, Bossy played kid hockey knowing that he would move up through the ranks – right to the NHL. As a youngster, he was a sensational scorer, once getting 23 goals in a game. At 16, he was playing junior for Laval, and the local media started to call him Michel, even though he was English and had been called Mike or Michael all his life. Laval retired his number 17 sweater because of his incredible four years with the team (1973-77) in which he averaged – *averaged!* – 77 goals a year. Somehow, it wasn't until the 15th selection at the 1977 draft that the Islanders chose him, and he came to training camp not hoping to make the team but planning on shattering all rookie scoring records. He did. The previous record for goals was 44, and Bossy improved that by more than 20 percent, finishing the year with 53 and winning the Calder Trophy. The next year, he led the league with 69 goals, and for the first 9 years of his career scored 51 or more each time. From early on he was paired on the ice with Bryan Trottier and Clark Gillies, Gillies a mucker, Trottier a passer, and Bossy a finisher deluxe. Off the ice, Bossy and Trottier became such good friends they were known as Bread and Butter, and although the knock against Bossy was his defence, the truth was that scoring goals and maintaining puck possession in the opponent's end was the best defence any coach could conjure. By the '80-'81 season, Bossy had his sights set on the most enduring and captivating scoring record of them all – Maurice Richard's feat in '44-'45 when he scored 50 goals in 50 games during the war era. Bossy was on target to repeat the accomplishment, but in the third period of his 50th game he still had just 48, a number he had been stuck on since game 47. With

just over 4 minutes to go against Washington, though, he scored on a power play – number 49 – and with under 2 minutes to go, his pal, passer, and centreman Trottier fired a perfect pass and Bossy one-timed the puck into the net. He became the first man since Richard to hit 50 in 50, and although Wayne Gretzky was to shatter that record by scoring 50 in 39 games a short time later, Bossy's achievement was still one for the ages. Through the years, his scoring skills were not selfishly accomplished. The Islanders won four consecutive Stanley Cups (1980-83), and he won the Conn Smythe Trophy in 1982. He starred on the 1981 and '84 Team Canada entries in the Canada Cup, scoring an overtime goal in the sudden-death semifinals of the latter to advance Canada to the finals. He was a First All-Star Team five times and an All-Star Game performer seven times, and also won the Lady Byng Trophy three times. Throughout his career – from Laval to the NHL – he had been a marked man, but Bossy refused to react to dirty hits and stick work with his own. Instead, he vowed publicly to respond with goals, and he was the first modern player to rail against on-ice violence that plagued the game and, by extension, was poisoning kids hockey as well. Rail though he might and counter with goals though he did, the physical abuse took its toll on his body in the form of deteriorating strength in his back. By the start of the '86-'87 season, he was in constant pain, and declined to play in Rendez-vous '87 in the hopes of resting his back. But before the season was out, he retired after scoring 38 goals in 63 games, the only year he never scored 50. In all, he had 573 goals and 1,126 points in just 752 career games, an extraordinary rate of point production reached by only a few of the greatest men to play. His 9 consecutive 50-goal seasons is still a record. After retiring, he continued to be actively involved in reducing violence in the game. He returned to Montreal, where he worked for radio station CJAD as a commentator. He also worked as a stockbroker and more recently has become director of public relations for Humpty Dumpty potato chips. He was inducted into the Hockey Hall of Fame in 1991 and his number 22 was later retired by the Islanders (along with those of linemates Trottier and Gillies).

BOSTROM, Helge
b. Winnipeg, Manitoba, January 9, 1894
d. Deer River, Minnesota, January 23, 1977
He didn't play in the NHA, in the days before the NHL formed in 1917, but he did play minor pro for long enough that when he made the NHL in 1929, he was 35 years old. The son of August and Anna, Helge joined the Canadian army in April 1918 and served overseas with the 1st Depot Battalion Manitoba Regiment. Upon his discharge, he played hockey out west before moving to Minneapolis and then the Chicago Black Hawks. He was a clerk by trade, and did not remain in hockey circles after his playing days.

BOTELL, Mark
b. Scarborough, Ontario, August 27, 1961
A large defenceman with limited offensive abilities, Botell skated around and about the minors in the early 1980s after being drafted by Philadelphia. He earned his Flyers stripes by playing 32 games in '81-'82 and later played for a year in Holland.

BOTHWELL, Tim
b. Vancouver, British Columbia, May 6, 1955
When Tim was young and answered his dad with a "yes, Father," he wasn't just being formal. His father was the Reverend John Bothwell, Anglican Bishop of Niagara in southern Ontario. Tim attended Brown University, and although he didn't attract interest in the draft, the Rangers signed the defenceman who had been blessed with talent. Thus began a 502-game NHL posting with 3 teams from 1978 to '89. After retiring, Bothwell became a coach in various minor pro leagues in the U.S. until he was fired by Phoenix in January 1994. He took some time off, but before he knew it the position of head coach at the University of Calgary was offered to him by Bob Corran, the athletic director. Together with assistant coach and former-NHLer Terry Johnson, the two made a formidable pairing for the Dinosaurs. Bothwell later joined Atlanta as an assistant coach.

BOTTERILL, Jason
b. Edmonton, Alberta, May 19, 1976
Jason is Jennifer's sister. He wouldn't mind admitting that and all it implies, for although Jason has made the NHL, Jennifer is a perennial all-star with Canada's national women's team. But Jason has nothing to be ashamed of. He won three successive gold medals with the junior team – 1994, '95, '96 – to tie an IIHF record. His draft position, 20th overall in 1994, promised more than he has delivered to date, and in four professional seasons he has played for a like number of NHL teams.

BOTTING, Cam
b. Kingston, Ontario, March 10, 1954
No wonder the fledgling Atlanta Flames selected Botting in the 1974 draft. He had just scored 40 goals and 96 points in only 48 games with Niagara Falls in junior hockey, and the team was desperate for offence. Unfortunately, Botting played just twice for the Flames before going down to the minors for a few short years.

BOUCHA, Henry ("Chief")
b. Warroad, Minnesota, June 1, 1951
Few times in the history of hockey has a stick been used as a weapon with the complete and utter contempt exhibited on January 4, 1975, when Dave Forbes butt-ended Boucha flush in the right eye. Boucha underwent three operations to try to correct his vision, without success. He retired after a few games in each of the next two seasons when it became perfectly clear to him that he couldn't tell how many pucks or players were on the ice. Forbes was suspended for all of 10 games, but Boucha won a small victory in the courts. Criminal charges against Forbes were dropped after the trial ended in a hung jury. The civil suit resulted in Boucha being awarded a monthly cheque for the next 30 years, but that's small consolation to someone who can't back out his driveway properly or reach for a pen on his desk. Boucha had been one of the more promising players to come out of the U.S. in the early 1970s. In three successive years he played at two World Championships and then at the 1972 Olympics in Sapporo, joining the Red Wings on his return. He showed promising offensive ability, and was a crowd favourite because of his flashy moustache and the red

Helge Bostrom

Jason Botterill

Henry Boucha

Dan Bouchard

"Butch" Bouchard

Joel Bouchard

Pierre Bouchard

headband he wore during games. Instead of a lengthy hockey career, he returned to Warroad at age 25, wrote a book on his life, and became a real estate agent.

BOUCHARD, Dan
b. Val d'Or, Quebec, December 12, 1950
The records don't show any obvious signs of hockey in Bouchard's blood, but they were there in spades below the surface of the numbers and the years. His father, Marcel, once played for Eddie Shore's Oakland Oaks; his uncle played goal in town; and Dan himself played in Ville la Salle for coach Emile Lemaire, Jacque's father. All these influences added up to a strong direction in goaltending and an NHL life. In a career that spanned some 655 games, Bouchard played mostly for Atlanta and Quebec, though he finished his career with a few games in Switzerland before suffering a knee injury. He later served as a goaltending coach for the Nordiques and became vice-president of a sports technology company in Atlanta. But it was his years as a goaltender with the Nordiques that had its own effect on the next generation. Growing up in Quebec was a small boy who revered Bouchard. In fact, he loved the goalie so much he slept every night with one of Bouchard's hockey sticks that he had been lucky enough to get at the Colisee one day. That boy's name was Patrick. Patrick Roy.

BOUCHARD, Dick
b. Lettelier, Manitoba, December 2, 1934
A one-game wonder for the Rangers in 1954-55, Bouchard also played minor pro for a number of years, mostly in Quebec and Minnesota, before retiring.

BOUCHARD, Edmond
b. Trois-Rivières, Quebec, May 24, 1892
d. Trois-Rivières, Quebec, July 18, 1953
Of the four teams for which Bouchard played in the 1920s, three became defunct: Hamilton, Pittsburgh, and the New York Americans. Like any player from Quebec, he started with les Canadiens in 1921 after a junior career in which he established himself as a scorer. But in the NHL he was primarily used as a defenceman or utility forward, and in 211 games he had only 19 goals.

BOUCHARD, Emile "Butch"
b. Montreal, Quebec, September 11, 1920
When a kid named Bouchard hit Montreal's training camp in 1941, his future teammates looked at his sizable body and figured he would skate himself into shape in the coming weeks. They quickly found that he was in impeccable shape and from day one was hitting players for keeps, as they say. They didn't much care for this roughhousing, but coach Dick Irvin most certainly did. Bouchard made the team, and for the next 15 years threw his large body at opponents with the same energy. He was not only one of the strongest players in the league, he was also one of its fairest. He broke up fights, refused to use his size to intimidate smaller players, and played to win when a player tried to get by him. Bouchard spent much of his career paired with Doug Harvey, the perfect stay-at-home match for the rushing Harvey. Despite his style of play, Bouchard was resilient and rarely missed games because of injury. He won four Cups with Montreal (1944, '46, '53, '56) and was named

to the First All-Star Team three times. The Habs made the playoffs every year he was in the league, and from 1948 until his retirement in 1956 he wore a "C" on his sweater. Maurice Richard took over as team leader, and Bouchard was a coaching candidate that very year, though he lost the job to another teammate, Toe Blake. Bouchard instead became active in junior hockey in Quebec. He also founded a junior baseball club and served as president of the Montreal Royals for years. In the early 1960s, he was elected alderman for Longueuil, a suburb of Montreal, and in 1968 he became president of the Metropolitan Junior A Hockey League. Bouchard later opened a restaurant and ran a beef cattle farm near Montreal with his son Pierre, who went on to have a career of his own with the Habs. Butch was inducted into the Hockey Hall of Fame in 1966 after playing all of his 785 career games with the Canadiens.

BOUCHARD, Joel
b. Montreal, Quebec, January 23, 1974
He plays in a band with Sebastien Bordeleau and Darren Turcotte, but his best gigs to date have been internationally. Bouchard won gold with the Canadian juniors in 1993 and '94, and won another gold with the men's team at the 1997 World Championships in Finland. In the NHL, he failed to find his groove until Nashville entered the league in 1998, though he has since played with Dallas and Phoenix. He was with the Stars when they went to the finals in 2000, but he didn't play because of meningitis. It was a life-threatening strain in his case, and he took months to recover. He was a Bill Masterton Trophy nominee in 2000-01 for his return to the NHL.

BOUCHARD, Pierre
b. Montreal, Quebec, February 20, 1948
Some say it was Jean Béliveau's fault. Others said it was a crazy series of NHL laws. Still others told the fans to relax; it was no big deal. Regardless, when Washington acquired Pierre Bouchard gratis, the *merde* hit the proverbial fan in Montreal. Bouchard was the son of Hall of Famer Butch, which was nice, but he was nowhere near Hall of Fame material himself. Even the austere Scotty Bowman said he empathized with Pierre having to follow in his father's footsteps, playing in his father's shadow at the Forum. Nonetheless, he survived for eight years and won five Stanley Cups, though he was merely a defensive specialist and never an overtime hero. Then the 1978 Waiver Draft occurred. Montreal left Bouchard exposed after agreeing to a deal with Washington in which the Caps would claim Bouchard and trade him right back for Rod Schutt, the player the Caps really wanted. And that's what happened, except that the league stepped in and pointed out a rule saying that a player claimed couldn't be traded back unless he first cleared waivers. This hadn't happened, and so president John Zeigler ruled that Bouchard was officially Washington property. Montreal fans were in an uproar and blamed everyone in the organization who was even the least bit accountable. Bouchard, disgusted, retired, though he ended up returning to the game and playing 106 games with Washington over the next 4 seasons. He later invested in a chain of restaurants and did colour commentary for RDS, the French-language arm of The Sports Network.

BOUCHER, Billy
b. Ottawa, Ontario, November 10, 1899
d. Ottawa, Ontario, November 10, 1958

He stood only 5'7" and tipped the Toledos at just 155 pounds, but Boucher was one of the scrappiest skilled players of the 1920s. He led the NHL in penalty minutes, won a Stanley Cup in 1924, and played on the right wing with Howie Morenz in the middle and Aurel Joliat port side (the latter with whom he had played as a 12-year-old at Crichton Street school). He was in his prime between 1921 and '25, leading the team in scoring with 31 points in '22-'23. He finished his career a few years later after brief times with Boston and the Americans, doing the family name proud. Brothers George, Frank, and Bobby all had fine NHL careers as well. Boucher became coach of the New Haven Eagles in 1931, but two years later he picked up a stick again to swoosh it around in the name of the Bronx Tigers. He returned home to coach the Quebec Aces, then became a scout for the Canadiens and coached junior in his home province. He moved to England for two years to coach the Brighton Tigers in 1937, but with the outbreak of the war returned home and joined the munitions and supply department in Ottawa as a purchasing agent. He was later transferred to the War Assets Department where he was named senior inspector (in the First World War he worked for the Imperial Munitions Board). He died of a heart attack on his fifty-ninth birthday.

BOUCHER, Bobby
b. Ottawa, Ontario, February 14, 1904
d. Ottawa, Ontario, June 9, 1931

He was just 27 when he died, this youngest member of the Boucher clan that was one of the more famous in all Canada. He had been the mascot for the Ottawa Senators as a small boy, but left his hometown to play in Iroquois Falls before returning to join the Gunners team. Bobby played with brother Billy during the Stanley Cup year of 1923-24, but after 1929 he became seriously ill and had to retire. He refereed a bit in and around Ottawa but was soon forced off his skates and passed away just a short time later. His wife, Kay Wilson, was a famous speed skater in her own right.

BOUCHER, Brian
b. Woonsocket, Rhode Island, January 2, 1977

His timing couldn't have been better and his entrance into the NHL more meteoric, but the young Boucher was quickly usurped by a surprise goalie, Roman Cechmanek. Boucher played for the U.S. at two World Juniors (1996 and '97), and his play for the local AHL Phantoms was so good he moved across the street to start 1999-2000 with the Flyers. But no sooner had he overtaken the veteran John Vanbiesbrouck than Cechmanek proved to be a number-one goalie. And so, without ever being number one, Boucher went from backup to starter to backup in less than a year.

BOUCHER, Clarence
b. North Bay, Ontario, November 1, 1896
d. Vancouver, British Columbia, April 1971

Besides playing 47 games with the New York Americans in 1926-27 and 1927-28, Boucher did not last in the pro ranks for very long. In that second season he finished third in the league in penalty minutes, but by 1929 he had left the game for good.

BOUCHER, Frank ("Raffles")
b. Ottawa, Ontario, October 7, 1901
d. Kemptville, Ontario, December 12, 1977

The Rideau Canal was the perfect place for any Ottawan to skate, and it's exactly where the Boucher family learned the game en masse. At one time, there were four Bouchers in pro hockey: George with Ottawa, Billy and Bob with Montreal, and Frank with Vancouver in the PCHL. When he was 17, Frank joined the North West Mounted Police, but after being assigned to Regina and playing brilliant hockey, he decided to try the pros rather than the cons, as it were. He had to buy his way out of the NWMP, for $50, a sum that took him a year to repay. It was worth it. He played '21-'22 with his hometown Senators and then accepted an offer from the Patrick brothers to play out west, and for the next four years he skated for the Maroons in Vancouver. But down in New York, the Cook brothers (Bill and Bun) implored Rangers management to acquire Boucher. It did, and the Cooks and Frank played on one of the highest-scoring lines of that generation, and certainly its longest surviving one. During the decade that they played as a forward combination, the Bread Line scored more than 1,000 points and brought 2 Stanley Cups to Manhattan, in 1928 and '33. In the 1928 finals, Boucher scored both goals in a 2-1 win over the Maroons to win New York's first Cup. Boucher, the passer, led the league in assists 3 times and twice scored more than 20 goals. By the time he retired in 1938, Boucher had accomplished something else extraordinary. He had won the Lady Byng Trophy seven times in eight years, a feat so impressive the NHL gave him the trophy and asked Lady Byng in England to craft another! Boucher coached the New York Rovers for a year and then returned to boss the Rangers bench in 1939. In his first year, the team won another Cup, and he stayed on as coach for a decade. During the '43-'44 season, though, the team was so depleted by players leaving to join the army that Boucher, now 42, came out of retirement for 15 games. In 1949, he became the team's GM, though he went behind the bench again for half of the '53-'54 season. During his playing days, he also served on the NHL's rules committee for 15 years. It was his suggestion to add a red line at centre ice to create more offence, a rule he later confessed had outlived its usefulness (previously, players had to skate the puck out of their end, but with the centre red line they were permitted to make passes halfway up ice, thus generating many breakaways). After his NHL career was over, Boucher returned to amateur hockey. He served as commissioner of the Saskatchewan Junior Hockey League (1959-67) and for a year in the same capacity for all junior hockey in Canada. He was posthumously named winner of the Lester Patrick Trophy in 1993 for his lifelong contributions to hockey in the United States, and was also elected to the Canada Sports Hall of Fame and the Ottawa Sports Hall of Fame. The Hockey Hall of Fame inducted him in 1958 for his obvious and remarkable achievements in the NHL. He died of cancer in 1977.

Billy Boucher

Bobby Boucher

Brian Boucher

Clarence Boucher

Frank Boucher

Philippe Boucher

BOUCHER, George "Buck"
b. Ottawa, Ontario, August 17, 1896
d. Ottawa, Ontario, October 17, 1960
In 1916, when George Boucher joined Canada's war efforts, he played football for a team at Camp Petawawa and played so well many thought he would make the grade as a pro. (Indeed, he played three years for the Ottawa Rough Riders.) In baseball, he was a superb catcher, but hockey was his true love and no other sport could, ultimately, take him from the ice. When Tommy Gorman was asked to take charge of the Senators in 1917 as that team entered the new NHL, his first priority was to recruit Boucher for the team. Boucher was a great stickhandler, but he could also play any position. He signed with Ottawa and played the first dozen years of his career in his own backyard, so to speak. He played forward for three years before switching to defence on the teams that were the first mini-dynasty of the new league, winning the Cup in 1920, '21, '23, and '27. He was paired with Eddie Gerard on the blueline, and Boucher turned out to be a fine scorer and a nasty bit of business when occasion called for it. He later played for the Maroons and Black Hawks before retiring in 1932, but his career in hockey was far from complete. Boucher became a playing coach with the Maroons in '30-'31 and then with the Boston Cubs. In 1933, he returned home to coach the Senators and went with the team to St. Louis the following season. He then coached a series of minor-league teams, notably the senior Senators in '48-'49 when they won the Allan Cup. During that year, he helped his brother Frank select players to represent Canada at the 1948 Olympics in St. Moritz, Switzerland. At season's end, he returned to the NHL, with Boston, after Dit Clapper suddenly retired. Boucher's one year with the Bruins wasn't particularly successful, and he returned to Ottawa to coach. He later developed throat cancer, which he suffered for six awful years. He was inducted into the Hockey Hall of Fame in 1960, but, too ill to attend the ceremonies, was presented with his insignia in hospital. He died three weeks later.

Bruce Boudreau

BOUCHER, Philippe
b. St. Apollinaire, Quebec, March 24, 1973
A hulking defensive defenceman, this Boucher has become a part of the Los Angeles revival in the post – Rob Blake scheme of things. He was drafted 13th overall by Buffalo in 1991, a sign of his superior reputation, and played parts of three years with the big squad in Firetown. He was then part of the huge deal that sent Grant Fuhr to LaLaLand in a seven-player deal, and he missed almost all of 1999-2000 with a serious foot injury.

Andre Boudrias

BOUCK, Tyler
b. Camrose, Alberta, January 13, 1980
His Dallas Stars were on the road in Tampa when Bouck celebrated his 21st birthday at a nightclub called Mons Venus. Unfortunately, that city was just days away from hosting the Super Bowl, and authorities in the city were trying to clamp down on vices pertaining to the ever-euphemistic adult entertainment. As a result, he and teammate Ted Donato were arrested on charges related to lap dancing, but a $250 bail had the boys out and safely on the streets again. Bouck had

Bob Boughner

made the Stars via Prince George in the WHL where he made a reputation as a power forward.

BOUDREAU, Bruce ("Gabby")
b. Toronto, Ontario, January 9, 1955
He set a junior record with 165 points in 1974-75 with the Toronto Marlies, and this earned him a contract with the WHA with the Minnesota Fighting Saints. The Saints put him in Johnstown for most of the year, though, and boy did that change his outlook on the game. The Johnstown Jets were the team upon which the movie *Slap Shot* was based, and it was Boudreau's apartment that was used as Paul Newman's in the flick. Boudreau even had a small part, but at season's end he signed with the Maple Leafs in the staid NHL. For the next seven seasons, he was bounced between the farm and big time more than any other NHLer. Up and down, up and down. When he was up, he performed no worse than many of the Leafs, but the knock that never subsided was that he was too small (5'9" 170, at best). The Hawks later signed him, but same thing. Along the way, he scored like a fiend in the AHL, and as his career wound down, he anticipated a career in management. He coached in the IHL, then became director of hockey operations in Mississippi with the legendary Sea Wolves, taking the team to the coveted Kelly Cup. Since 1999, he has been head coach of Lowell, and later Manchester, in the AHL.

BOUDRIAS, Andre
b. Montreal, Quebec, September 19, 1943
Like so many Montrealers growing up, little Andre wanted to play for the Habs. And, like so many, his dream was clouded by the deep deep pool of talent available to the team in those days long gone. He had an excellent junior career with the Canadiens, but played just seven games over four years with the team as it won a number of Cups in the mid- to late-1960s. As a result, he was traded to Minnesota, and eventually Vancouver where he defined his career as a goal scorer and leader. From 1970 to '73 he had seasons of 25, 27, and 30 goals and became captain in '75-'76, his last year with the Canucks before moving to the WHA. After rounding out his career with the Nordiques, he moved into the Canadiens' front office starting as an assistant coach for the farm team in Nova Scotia and moving up to assistant of the managing director and director of pro scouting. He also worked in the front office of the NHLPA.

BOUGHNER, Barry
b. Delhi, Ontario, January 29, 1948
After five years in the London junior system, Boughner wound up playing a handful of games with the Oakland/California franchise in 1969-71, an era of almost unparalleled futility in NHL history. He jumped around in the minors for a while and later wound up coaching the Niagara Falls Flyers in the OHL.

BOUGHNER, Bob
b. Windsor, Ontario, March 8, 1971
Anyone born in Windsor who wants to play in the NHL dreams of either Toronto or Detroit. For Boughner, who was drafted by the Red Wings in 1989, the latter seemed tenable… for a while. After leaving junior, though, he was ensconced in the minors, unable to

crack a strong Detroit blueline that included Vladimir Konstantinov and Niklas Lidstrom. He eventually wound up in Buffalo, and it was there he proved his worth as an NHL-calibre defenceman. Although he has moved a few times in recent years, his spot as a regular somewhere seems assured for a while longer.

BOUILLON, Francis
b. New York, New York, October 17, 1975
His father was Haitian, his mother French-Canadian, his place of birth Noo Yawk. Bouillon is a stocky fellow, short and thick and unwanted in the draft. He found a place in the IHL, but when the Canadiens found he was available they signed him. Coach Alain Vigneault called him to the Habs and kept him in the lineup, insisting the kid had earned a chance to prove his worth. This he has done, in fits and starts, since joining the Habs in 1999.

BOULERICE, Jesse
b. Plattsburgh, New York, August 10, 1978
Persistence pays off. Boulerice left junior hockey in 1998 and played most of the next four seasons in the minors before getting a three-game tryout with Philadelphia. He was traded to Carolina during the 2001-02 season, and although he didn't play for the 'Canes during their run to the Cup finals he did start the 2002-03 season with the team.

BOULTON, Eric
b. Halifax, Nova Scotia, August 17, 1976
Pretty much everyone but the cleaners had gone home when Boulton was drafted in 1994 by the Rangers just a couple of weeks after winning their first Stanley Cup in fifty years. The 234th pick overall, he never played on Broadway; instead, he skated around in the minors until the Sabres signed him, assigned him, and finally gave him a chance.

BOUMEDIENNE, Josef
b. Stockholm, Sweden, January 12, 1978
New Jersey was in a hurry to draft Boumedienne as soon as he was eligible at age 18, but he didn't play with the Devils until three years later. And, despite scoring a goal in his first game with the team, it turned out to be his only appearance as the Devils traded him to Tampa Bay soon after. Tampa later traded him to Ottawa, and so the one-year NHLer had already been owned by three teams.

BOURBONNAIS, Dan
b. Winnipeg, Manitoba, March 6, 1962
An Hartford draft choice, Bourbonnais played 59 games with the Whalers from 1981 to 1984. He later spent some time in the minors and then moved to Europe to continue his career.

BOURBONNAIS, Rick
b. Toronto, Ontario, April 20, 1955
Although he is unrelated to Dan, the careers of these two Bourbonnais are remarkably similar. In the case of Rick, it was St. Louis that drafted him and played him for his only 71 NHL games. And like Dan, he played for a bit in the minors before heading to Europe. Rick, though, played much longer overseas – close to a decade – before calling it a career.

BOURCIER, Conrad
b. Montreal, Quebec, May 28, 1916
d. unknown
The two brothers, Conrad and Jean, each left their little imprint in the history of the Montreal Canadiens when they played for a few games for the team in 1935-36. Beyond that, Conrad played virtually every game of his career with a Quebec team of one stripe or another.

BOURCIER, Jean
b. Montreal, Quebec, January 3, 1911
Not only did Jean and his brother play with the Canadiens in '35-'36, they stayed together for the better part of six years together in Verdun. Jean, older by five years, bowed out of the game early into the war and never returned.

BOURGDINON, Fred (sometimes Bergdinon)
b. Parry Sound, Ontario, 1906
d. 1995
A veritable ghost in the NHL's empty hallways of days long gone, Bourgdinon played twice for the Bruins in 1925-26. His career came to a sudden end thanks to a broken arm suffered in a brutal check. Bourgdinon later moved to Windsor and worked on the construction of the Ambassador Bridge.

BOURGEAULT, Leo
b. Sturgeon Falls, Ontario, January 17, 1903
d. Montreal, Quebec, November 1, 1965
He made a name for himself right off the bat as a teen with the North Bay Trappers, the team he captained in 1922-23. Bourgeault was a small player at 5'6" and 165 pounds but gained renown for his fiery spirit and unvanquishable tenacity. He turned pro with the Saskatoon Crescents where he played under coach Newsy Lalonde. He made his way East again to play for the Toronto St. Pats in '26-'27, but the team released him and he signed with the Rangers, where he enjoyed his finest seasons. He frequently teamed with either of the big boys – Ching Johnson or Taffy Abel – and helped the Rangers win the Cup in 1928. He returned home to Sturgeon Falls after that win to be feted by the Knights of Columbus, and at a banquet each menu had attached to it a picture of Bourgeault in his Rangers'

Bourgeault gained renown for his fiery spirit and unvanquishable tenacity.
LEO BOURGEAULT

Francis Bouillon

Dan Bourbonnais

Rick Bourbonnais

Conrad Bourcier

Jean Bourcier

Charlie Bourgeois

livery. He later played for Ottawa and the Canadiens before retiring in 1935. Bourgeault lived in Quebec and managed a tavern.

BOURGEOIS, Charlie ("Boo Boo")
b. Moncton, New Brunswick, November 19, 1959

Imagine the unimaginable. Try to picture a life both blessed and cursed, and you will understand that in life we cannot possibly be expected to understand everything. You're 13 years old. You live in tiny, perfect Moncton. You're skating on an outdoor rink your dad made for you. Dad's name is Aurelle. He's an RCMP officer in town. He routinely collects drunks and bums off the street and doesn't take them to jail; he brings them home, feeds them, sends them on their way. You skate this way and that, twist and twirl, stop, spray, make swirls in the clean white ice. Your older sister's husband comes up to you – tells you your dad is missing. Two days later, his body, and that of a colleague, is found in a grave he was forced to dig himself. He was investigating a kidnapping. Charlie's younger brother turned to drink and crime, but Charlie hugged hockey with all his strength. Hockey didn't always hug back. Charlie was determined, but he wasn't polished-smooth, skilled or a magician with the stick. He was dead-set on a career, that's all. Calgary signed him as a free agent, and he moved on to play for St. Louis and Hartford in a seven-year NHL career. Charlie moved to Europe to play, in Paris, and then coached the Chamonix Huskies in 1990. He returned two years later to be an assistant coach with the Moncton Hawks and became the director of marketing for Major Drilling Group International Inc. He ran clinics, performed charity work, ran the Charlie Bourgeois Golf Classic, gave back to the community that gave so much to him in his years of grief as a young teen. In 1996, he became an assistant at the University of Moncton where he himself had played briefly. Four years later, he became the team's head coach. He tried his hand at politics, but lost a provincial election in Moncton in 2001. To this day, he still carries a picture of his dad in his wallet.

BOURNE, Bob
b. Kindersley, Saskatchewan, June 21, 1954

Here's a good bit of Bournemania: although he played 964 NHL games and scored 258 goals in a 14-year career, it was not until game number 699, in his tenth season and three-30 goal years that he finally scored a hat trick. And he had one of each, an even strength, power play, and short-handed goal. And AND, he did the deed using a teammate's stick, Stefan Persson! Bourne was a much better player than any numbers show, though. His teammates and coaches all believed he could score 40 or 50 goals if he put his mind to it, but he passed more than he shot and played with second-line confidence rather than first line cockiness. He played on the four Islanders' Cups in the early 1980s and also played for Team Canada at the '84 Canada Cup. He had attended camp in 1981, but as a free agent he had no protection in case of injury so went home rather than risk his career. After retiring in 1988, he turned to coaching and has been a mainstay in the IHL, notably with the Utah Grizzlies. He has also become increasingly active in Islanders' alumni functions.

Bob Bourne

Phil Bourque

BOURQUE, Claude (sometimes Burke)
b. Oxford, Nova Scotia, March 31, 1915
d. May 13, 1982

Although he was born in Oxford, his parents moved the family to Moncton where his father ran a barber shop in the Main Street Subway Block. Claude played many years in Moncton, gaining national attention when he backstopped the team to the Memorial Cup. This got him as far as the Montreal Jr. Canadiens in 1933, a phenomenal achievement in itself for a Maritimer. He made the Habs in 1938, and for most of two seasons was the number one man in goal. However, these were not the Canadiens' salad days, and quickly found himself back in the minors where he played for Lachine and Calgary RCAF teams before retiring having injured his back in a car accident.

BOURQUE, Phil
b. Chelmsford, Massachusetts, June 8, 1962

He'll tell anyone who'll listen that he Ray Bourque's brother. Ray, that is, from Boston, not Montreal. He was a little wacky that way. He sometimes played goal in practise, and then there was the time later in his career, in 1994, when he broke his neck rock-climbing near the Grand Canyon at Lone Rock Canyon, from which he had to be helped by helicopter. It's always a special accomplishment to make the NHL after being ignored by all teams in the draft for two or three years. Bourque is one such example who signed as a freebie with Pittsburgh and stayed in the Pens' system for ten seasons, sometimes strictly as a minor leaguer, sometimes as a Penguins regular. He was around when the team won Cups in '91 and '92, and at one celebratory party at Mario Lemieux's place the Cup wound up with Bourque. He gave it a shake, thought he heard a bit of a rattle, and decided to take it apart. That was all fun and easy, but putting it back together was beyond his grasp, and the Hockey Hall of Fame had to give him a bit of a hand. He later played for Ottawa and the Rangers before venturing to Europe to continue his career.

BOURQUE, Ray
b. Montreal, Quebec, December 28, 1960

Of his 22 NHL seasons, Ray Bourque played more than 20 with Boston, the team with which he could never quite win a Stanley Cup. It wasn't until after demanding a trade to a Cup contender that he finally won with a squad that was poised to win anyway, the highly talented Colorado Avalanche, in 2000-01. Bourque had started his career way back in 1979 after the Bruins drafted him 8th overall. He had not had an astounding junior career in Verdun, but his strong skating and puckhandling abilities drew scouts to his play. Speaking almost no English, he made the team at age 18 and went on to become the all-time points leader for defencemen in NHL history, although he never hit the 100-point mark in any year as Orr, Coffey, and Potvin had. Like Adam Oates or Ron Francis, Bourque was the model of consistency for a long period of time. He didn't dominate the game from the blueline, but he moved the puck well and led the power play year after year. And, in what was to become his trademark, he could play 30 minutes a game and still keep going. His 65 points as a rookie set a record and earned him the Calder Trophy, and in '83-'84 he joined select company by scoring 31 goals, a rare feat for a defenceman. He wore "7" even though it was a sacred number that belonged to Phil Esposito, but he made up for it during a special ceremony on December 4, 1987 when the Bruins finally retired Espo's number. Bourque came to centre ice when the number was raised to the rafters, and then took off his own 7 to reveal 77, the number he wore for the rest of his career. Bourque helped the Bruins reach the playoffs for 17 consecutive seasons, from his rookie year through 1996, but it wasn't until 1988 that he first made it to the finals. He ran up against a vastly superior team in the Edmonton Oilers, and his dream was quashed after just four games (a fifth was postponed because of a power failure and didn't count in the series record). Bourque made it back to the finals two years later, but the Oilers again hammered the Bruins, this time in just five games. It was to be Bourque's last appearance in the finals until the Avalanche took him there in 2001. He won his first Norris Trophy in '86-'87 and won four more times in the next six years. In all, he had nine seasons of at least 20 goals and in 12 seasons he recorded more than 50 assists. By the middle of the 1999-2000 season, though, he was frustrated. He knew his career was coming to an end, and the Bruins were now on the downturn. He was part of a surging team when he joined Boston in 1979, but his failure to win a Cup frustrated him to the point that he asked to be traded. The Bruins sent him to Colorado, one of the top teams in the Western Conference, one that could be counted on to go to the finals in any given year. They didn't in 2000, but the

Bourque said no to playing with the best players in the country against the best from around the world.
RAY BOURQUE

next year, Joe Sakic, Patrick Roy, and Peter Forsberg led the team to victory, and Bourque hoisted the Cup on what turned out to be the final day of his career. He left the game having played in the All-Star Game every season of his career, but his international record was often like his Bruins record – close but no cigar. He played in the 1981 Canada Cup, the only time Canada lost, and then appeared in 1984 and '87 on winning teams. Without question, the low point of his career came in August 1996. Team Canada was getting ready for the World Cup, and Bourque had said no to playing with the best players in the country against the best from around the world. During the training camp, though, injuries hurt Canada's defence corps and Wayne Gretzky and Mark Messier phoned to ask him in the strongest terms possible to help out. Bourque declined and Canada lost the tournament. He played for Canada at the 1998 Olympics in Nagano, but Canada lost, and Bourque missed a penalty shot during the shootout in the semi-finals. Needless to say, Gretzky, as Canada's GM for the 2002 Olympics in Salt Lake City, did not name Bourque to the team. Bourque retired in 2001

with Hall of Fame numbers on his credentials. He is one of the all-time leaders in games played, and his points record will likely stand for quite some time. He is also the only defenceman to score more than 400 goals (410). At the start of the 2001-02 season, both Colorado and Boston retired his number 77, and during his speech in Denver he thanked the players for giving him what he had always wanted – the chance to raise the Stanley Cup above his head.

Pat Boutette

BOUTETTE, Pat ("Booter")
b. Windsor, Ontario, March 1, 1952
Just a little wee fellow, Boutette played with that all-important quality coaches sometimes called vinegar, a little bit old school term for "in yo face." He was a rare example of a player who shunned junior hockey to attend University of Minnesota-Duluth on scholarship to ensure he got an education in a world in which the hockey career was by no means fixed and guaranteed. Nonetheless, three years into a Phys Ed degree, he signed a contract with the Leafs and was on his way. He began his career playing 317 consecutive games before being scratched, and he later played for Hartford and Pittsburgh where he had three successive 20-goal seasons. Boutette also played for Canada at the 1981 World Championships (fourth place), and after retiring he remained in Toronto and became active in the Leafs' and NHL alumni activities.

Paul Boutilier

BOUTILIER, Paul ("Tree Trunk")
b. Sydney, Nova Scotia, May 3, 1963
The nickname came from his massive thighs conditioned by years of playing, officiating, running, and preparation for a hockey career. Paul's dad, Ernie, was the president of Sydney Steel Corporation. He trained with his son along the hills of Cape Breton and coached him through minor hockey. Paul turned into a fine player whom the Islanders drafted high in 1981, and over the next few years they groomed him to become one of their top blueliners. He had a fantastic shot but played only two full years on Long Island before being traded around over the next five seasons. Boutilier began his career winning gold with the juniors in 1982 and finished his career in Europe before settling in Halifax where he ran the World Curling Tour.

BOUTIN, Rollie
b. Westlock, Alberta, November 6, 1957
In his first 90 minutes in the NHL, Boutin surrendered an even ten goals. The next year, he settled in and got off to a flying start of 6-2-1 when the Caps of Washington called him up from Hershey, but playing on a team that allowed many more goals than it scored,

Rollie Boutin

Jason Bowen

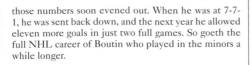

Johnny Bower

Johnny Bower

those numbers soon evened out. When he was at 7-7-1, he was sent back down, and the next year he allowed eleven more goals in just two full games. So goeth the full NHL career of Boutin who played in the minors a while longer.

BOUVRETTE, Lionel
b. Hawkesbury, Ontario, June 10, 1914
d. Delray Beach, Florida, February 8, 2000
An extended career in Quebec for this goalie resulted in one minor miracle, a chance to play in the NHL the night of March 18, 1943. The Rangers were in town to face Montreal, but their regular 'tender, Jimmy Franks, was injured and couldn't play. The Habs gave use of Bouvrette, a regular with the Quebec Aces, who played well in a 6-3 loss to the Habs. He won an Allan Cup the following year with the Aces, the pinnacle of his career. He passed away while on vacation in Florida, his wife of 54 years, Gisele, by his side.

BOWEN, Jason
b. Port Alice, British Columbia, November 9, 1973
Being drafted 15th overall is high praise, indeed, for any player. Not making it big time subsequently is a downer for the team doing the selecting, in Bowen's case Philadelphia in 1992. He was a big and strong defenceman, but try as they might the Flyers couldn't get him to fit into their system. His career was a perfect parabola: he was called up for a few games in his last year of junior; the next season he played full time; the years after mostly minors; and after some years strictly minor pro, he ventured to Britain to play in the Super League.

BOWER, Johnny
(née Kiszkan) ("The China Wall")
b. Prince Albert, Saskatchewan, November 8, 1924
How is it possible that a person can fight in the war for four years and, upon discharge, still be eligible to play junior hockey? Well, lying about your age helps, and that's what Johnny Kiszkan did in 1940. Born into the Kiszkan family, Johnny didn't take on the name of Bower until after the war, when he turned pro, and believed Kiszkan was too difficult to pronounce. He did his army training in British Columbia but was called up by the Queen's Own Cameron Highlanders and sent to England. In 1944, he became ill and was discharged, and played in goal that very season back in Prince Albert. The next year he turned pro in the AHL, starting the first of two full careers that were extraordinary achievements for a goalie. Between 1945 and 1958, Bower became the all-time leader in games played in the American league for a puckstopper. During those 13 seasons, he earned his nickname because he was older than the China wall – at least his teammates said so! For

three years he was named the league's best player, and five times he was named to the First All-Star Team in the league. Most of his time was with Cleveland, but Bower did have three callups with the New York Rangers. Two were very brief, but the third, in '53-'54, lasted the whole season. In fact, he played every game for the Rangers that year, but he was on a weak team, and the following year the Blueshirts opted to go with the younger Gump Worsley in goal, and Bower was relegated to the minors again. In 1958, his life took a dramatic turn. That summer, the Leafs claimed him in the Inter-League Draft and almost immediately he became their starting goalie at age 34, a time when most hockey players are thinking about retirement. But Bower wasn't just any player. He proved to be made of a substance not known to the league, something that could endure year after year of goaltending without a mask and under relentless pressure. Bower thrived on the intensity, and became more adamant about holding down his position when it was most threatened. He never had a GAA above 2.85 with the Leafs, and every time he considered retirement, coach Punch Imlach talked about a good young goalie coming up who could replace him. Before Imlach had finished his sentence, Bower was getting dressed. He backstopped the team to four Stanley Cups in the 1960s, but his performance wasn't just based on stopping the puck. The very fact that this "old" man was in goal inspired teammates 10 and 20 years younger, and it wasn't until 1969, when he was 45, that he finally hung up the pads, leaving with the distinction of being the oldest goalie to play in the NHL. During the '60s with the Leafs, Bower led the NHL in GAA on four occasions. He won a Vezina Trophy in '60-'61 and shared another with partner Terry Sawchuk in '64-'65. During his career he suffered every injury imaginable, including facial cuts too numerous to count, but it wasn't until his last few games that he ever wore a mask. He practised in one for years, but when the puck dropped to start a game, he was bare-faced and ready to sacrifice his good looks to get in the way of that black biscuit. Most notably, he was master of the pokecheck, a perfectly safe way to take the disc off an opponent for a skater, but a technique so hazardous that even the brave Original Six goalies couldn't do it as well as Bower. It was a move that required perfect timing and bravery, diving fully stretched toward an oncoming opponent with stick extended. The object was to surprise the player, and the result was a successful poke of the puck off the stick, but with the risk of the player skating right into the goalie's head. It was a move not for the faint of heart. Bower remained an integral part of the team after retiring. He worked as a scout and goalie coach, and when a goalie crisis occurred periodically, he

> **Born into the Kiszkan family, Johnny didn't take on the name of Bower until after the war.**
> **JOHNNY BOWER**

even threatened to put the pads on again as late as 1980. Bower was inducted into the Hockey Hall of Fame in 1976 and his number 1 was honoured by the Leafs. He left the game having had two full careers, a feat no other goalie can claim. He played in the AHL for 12 complete seasons and with the Rangers and Leafs another 15 (3 part time and 12 full time) in the NHL. Combining both leagues, Bower played a total of 1,207 regular-season games, a record no goalie will come close to – ever.

BOWLER, Bill
b. Toronto, Ontario, September 25, 1974
He finished junior in 1994 and played his first NHL game seven years later. With the Windsor Spitfires, Bowler established himself as one of the all-time scorers in the OHL, but when he attended New Jersey training camp as a walk-on, the Devils told him to shore up on defence and get into better shape. Instead, Bowler wound up playing in the IHL for most of the next six years before being signed by Columbus and claimed by Nashville. It was as a Predator that he made his NHL debut, which to date has been confined to one, nine-game stretch.

BOWMAN, Kirk
b. Leamington, Ontario, September 30, 1952
In an Eric Lindros career – that is, 88 games played – Bowman never had the impact he had had in the minors. His was not a typical career in that he never played junior. At 19, he signed with Columbus of the IHL in 1971, and played for years in the minors before the Chicago Black Hawks brought him up in 1976. He played parts of the next three years and then spent the better part of a decade in Europe before returning to Leamington. Once there, he established the Kirk Bowman Hockey School and has become a leader in development of skills in youth programs.

BOWMAN, Ralph ("Scotty")
b. Winnipeg, Manitoba, June 20, 1911
d. Flint, Michigan, October 22, 1990
In a career that featured just eight goals in seven years and 274 games, how unlikely that this defenceman would have been the first player in NHL history to score on a penalty shot! The goal came on November 13, 1934, against the legendary Alec Connell of the Maroons no less, in a 2-1 Montreal victory over Bowman and his St. Louis Eagles. Bowman had transferred to St. Loo with the rest of the financially-uncertain Ottawa Senators, but was traded to Detroit before the end of the season. It was with the Wings that he achieved his greatest success, winning back-to-back Cups with Jack Adams in 1936 and '37. After a number of years in the minors, Bowman later became a coach.

How unlikely that this defenceman would have been the first player in NHL history to score on a penalty shot!
RALPH "SCOTTY" BOWMAN

BOWNASS, Jack ("Red")
b. Winnipeg, Manitoba, July 27, 1930
He was but a part-time player with the Canadiens and later the Rangers from 1957 to 1962, but Jack Bownass had a full life in hockey that lasted a quarter of a century. He played 80 times in the NHL and many more in the minors, and when he had a chance to both play and coach, with Los Angeles in the WHL, he took it. From there he coached with the National Team when it was divided into two groups, and Eastern section and a Western group. Based it Ottawa, he led the Easterners for three years and then took off to Sweden for two seasons to coach. Upon his return, in 1973, he was hired by the Kingston Canadians, though he lasted less than two years before being fired in March 1975.

BOWNESS, Rick
b. Moncton, New Brunswick, January 25, 1955
The peripatetic life of a hockey player is nothing new to any fan of the game, but a nomadic coach is certainly a rarer breed. In 173 career games as a right winger, Bowness played for four teams in the 1970s and into the early part of the next decade. He retired as a player with Winnipeg and immediately became an assistant with the farm team in Sherbrooke. From there he rose to become the NHL team's coach, in '88-'89, the first of four head-coaching jobs he had in the next decade. Along the way, he compiled one of the worst records of all time – 121-277-45 – yet he always found favour with a new GM willing to give him another chance. More recently, he has become an assistant in Phoenix, a far more stable position.

BOYD, Bill
b. Belleville, Ontario, May 15, 1898
d. November 17, 1940
Born in a true hockey town, Boyd didn't hit his NHL stride until the ripe old age of 28. He served a year in the military in 1918 and after being discharged played for Minneapolis as a stepping stone to the Rangers. He was on the Cup team of 1927-28, and after one more part-time year joined the rival Americans, playing out of the same building in Manhattan before retiring.

BOYD, Irvin ("Yank")
b. Ardmore, Pennsylvania, November 13, 1908
First, the nickname. Nothing came easier, for he was the only American in the NHL when he appeared with Boston in 1931-32, although he had played his juvenile and junior hockey in Toronto. After 29 games with the Bruins, though, he was traded to the Can-Am league and didn't resurface until the Red Wings

Kirk Bowman

Jack Bownass

Rick Bowness

Bill Boyd

Irvin Boyd

Randy Boyd

Wally Boyer

Dan Boyle

Nick Boynton

bought him some two years later. Despite being a scorer in the minors, he had but two tallies in 42 games and was dispatched to the farm. Boyd spent the next eight years in the minors, but during the war, when teams were short of players and times were desperate, he squeezed in another 25 games with the B's before his playing days were over.

BOYD, Randy
b. Coniston, Ontario, January 23, 1962
No matter how many times they sent him down to the minors, he always found a way back to the NHL. Coming out of junior, Boyd had won the Kaminsky Trophy as the best defenceman in the OHL in 1979-80, prompting Pittsburgh to draft him that summer. He never played a full season for the Penguins, and although he went on to three other teams he spent more time in the lesser leagues than at the NHL level. He retired in 1993 and coached both hockey and roller hockey, the former with Memphis, the latter with an outfit called the Chicago Cheetahs.

BOYER, Wally
b. Cowan, Manitoba, September 27, 1937
He waited for the moment for a long time. That first NHL game came when he was 28 and had been toiling away in the minors while the stars of the Original Six shone brightest. But when he made the Leafs in 1965, he wasn't going to miss the chance. In that first game, Boyer scored a short-handed goal and added an assist, and proved he could play in the NHL. He wound up in Chicago the next year, then Oakland and Pittsburgh in succeeding seasons before finishing his career in the WHA. He settled in Midland, Ontario and ran the Midtown Tavern for a dozen years, then sold it and worked part-time as a draftsman. He never won the Stanley Cup, but he did play 365 NHL games.

BOYER, Zac
b. Inuvik, Northwest Territories, October 25, 1971
Not too many players come out of Inuvik to play in the NHL. To date, one, exactly. Boyer had tons of offensive skills in junior, leading Chicago to draft him in 1991. But like so many others, what he could do as a teenager and as a man in the minors he could not do in the NHL. He played three games with the Dallas Stars after signing with the team as a free agent, but then never made it back to the top. Even worse, his career was over after an IHL game between the Manitoba Moose and his Houston Aeros when he suffered a head injury late in the '98-'99 season and was forced to retire.

BOYKO, Darren ("Boyks"/ "DB 10")
b. Winnipeg, Manitoba, January 16, 1964
Although the lives of all NHLers cross at some point or in some way, their lives are all separate entities outside the NHL. Boyko played only once in the NHL, yet to this day he is the highest-scoring Canadian in Finnish league history. At 14, he played in the famous Quebec City Pee Wee tournament against Brett Hull's team. At 16, he was in provincial junior hockey and joined the WHL the following season. Two seasons with the Winnipeg Warriors, though, failed to attract interest in

NHL teams at the draft, so Boyko, now 19, enrolled at the University of Toronto and played CIAU hockey for two years under that team's most famous coaches – Mike Keenan and Tom Watt. In 1985, Boyko was offered both a contract to play in Finland and a two-way deal with Keenan and the Philadelphia Flyers. He took the former, and remained there for 11 seasons, eventually playing on a line with Sami Kapanen and Ville Peltonen. It was in 1988-89 that he played his one NHL game, with his hometown Jets, the same year he played a number of games with the farm team in Moncton under head coach Alpo Suhonen. Boyko played for Finland in a Spengler Cup and passed on a chance to play for Canada at the Izvestia tournament because he wanted to focus on earning his master's degree, which he did, in 1995, from the Helsinki International School of Economics. He played in Germany and Sweden in 1996-97 and then began an affiliation with the IIHF and Hockey Hall of Fame which endures to this day. Living in Toronto, he is the international consultant in public relations for the IIHF, working out of his Hall of Fame office.

BOYLE, Dan
b. Ottawa, Ontario, July 12, 1976
Another Canadian who went south to play and get an education, Boyle went to the University of Miami (in Ohio – go figure) where he played with future Florida Panthers teammate, Kevyn Adams. After four years, he remained undrafted and signed with the IHL before the Panthers offered him a contract. In the last four years, he his played his way onto the team full-time, though he lacks the size to be a dominating physical defenceman and has yet to show skill as an offensive blueliner.

BOYNTON, Nick
b. Etobicoke, Ontario, January 14, 1979
Sometimes players and player agents make poor judgments and time tells the true tale of a player's worth. Boynton was a hot hockey prospect as a teen, a defenceman with size and toughness and skill. But when Washington drafted him 9th overall in 1997, he wasn't content to make it with the Caps. He refused to sign with the team, and re-entered the draft two years later when he was chosen 21st overall by Boston. To finish his final season of junior, he led his Ottawa 67's to the Memorial Cup championship, and he was named that tournament's MVP. That was the pinnacle of his career to date. The Bruins have used him only occasionally in the past three years, and a junior career that offered such hope and promise of future glory has yet to deliver the goods.

BOZEK, Steve
b. Kelowna, British Columbia, November 26, 1960
Blessed with tremendous speed, Bozek cut short a career at Northern Michigan University to join the L.A. Kings, the team that drafted him in 1980. He had a terrific rookie season with 33 goals, but that total and his 56 points turned out to be career highs. Over the next decade, he played for four other teams and played briefly in Europe before retiring in 1993. He won a silver medal with Canada at the 1991 World Championships, but despite his offensive ability he never maintained a high profile in the NHL.

BOZON, Philippe
b. Chamonix, France, November 30, 1966

The most successful, famous, and decorated French player of all time, Bozon is a national hero in a country known for wine, cheese, and football. He learned what he knew from his father, Alain, one-time captain of France's national team, and at 16 Philippe was the youngest player ever to represent his country in hockey. His other formative influence was Paulin Bordeleau, who played in France after his NHL days were over. In the fall of 1983, Philippe attended training camp of the St. Jean Castors of the Quebec league, but he was unhappy with his performance and returned home for another year. In 1984, he was ready. Although he was never drafted, he signed with Peoria in the IHL in 1986 and then returned to France to play professionally for a number of years before the St. Louis Blues requested his services in 1992. He played parts of four years with the Blues, but his international career is where he has truly left his mark. His play in the 2002 Salt Lake City Games marked his fourth Olympics, and he has played in a staggering 12 World Championships for France. He has also played in pro leagues in Switzerland and Germany and remains the best player in France.

BRACKENBOROUGH, John ("Spider")
b. Parry Sound, Ontario, February 9, 1897
d. Dunedin, Florida, July 8, 1993

Brackenborough lost his right eye in a game on February 29, 1924 while playing senior hockey for the Hamilton Tigers yet went on to play seven games for the Bruins in the '25-'26 season. He never played professionally after that. Brackenborough later moved to Michigan where he worked as a supervisor for the Michigan Gas Co. and in 1972 he retired to Dunedin, Florida.

BRACKENBURY, Curt
b. Kapuskasing, Ontario, January 31, 1952

Asthma. Fighting. Triathlon. Sailing. Not terms most people could roll into one body, but Brackenbury managed it. He wasn't much of a hockey player, but in the WHA days you didn't have to be. He played in the Eastern League and shared a house with John Brophy and Jack McIlhargey, legends of the fistic side of the sport who influenced Brackenbury and gave him a chance to play in the pros. Brophy told him to fight, and fight he did, right into the WHA, where he amassed gobs of penalty minutes. Brackenbury had asthma, though, and had likely the shortest shifts in hockey's history. Nonetheless, he survived – five years in the WHA and four more in the NHL with Quebec, Edmonton, and St. Louis. After retiring in 1983, he settled in Chicago and became interested in triathlon, even though he was terrified of the water. He swam at the local YMCA, and after finishing his first Hawaii Ironman he met Steve Wallick, a crew man for Canada II ready to take part in the America's Cup. Wallick offered Brackenbury a job mid-deck as a grinder, adjusting the foresails on the 12-metre yacht. Knowing nothing of the task, Brackenbury, of course, accepted the challenge.

BRADLEY, Bart
b. Fort William, Ontario, July 29, 1930

A long and distinguished hockey career was marked by a single game in the NHL, in 1949-50 with Boston. Bradley began playing in Port Arthur before embarking on a pro career mostly out west, though he played for the Belleville McFarlands in 1959 the year they won the World Championships. In 1960-61, he moved to Dryden to coach the local Rockets but a year later was back playing in his old stomping ground of Port Arthur. In the fall of 1963, he replaced Lee Fogolin as coach, a position he held for two years.

BRADLEY, Brian
b. Kitchener, Ontario, January 21, 1965

In 1992-93, Bradley scored 42 goals in the NHL with Tampa Bay. By 1998, he had been suffering headaches for a year and couldn't exercise for 10 minutes without throwing up. His life changed forever on November 11, 1997, during a game in which he took a hard check while skating down the left wing. His head hit the Plexiglas, and he felt injured, but in the coming days doctors didn't identify his problem as a concussion. He played for another month, but when he had to lie down in the dressing room because he wasn't feeling well, he knew something was wrong. He stopped playing. Teammate Dino Ciccarelli called him a "gutless little puke," but Bradley continued to have painful and daily headaches. Later, X-rays revealed spots on his brain, and doctors were shocked to learn he had risked his life after the hit by continuing to play. Two years later, still unwell, he retired. He had played 651 NHL games with Calgary, Vancouver, and Toronto (besides Tampa Bay, for whom he played the final six years of his career). He never came close to 42 goals before or after his career-best year, but he had always been able to score at the NHL level. In the end, post-concussion syndrome affected him to such a degree that a return to the game was both unimaginable and undesirable.

BRADLEY, Lyle
b. Lloydminster, Saskatchewan, July 31, 1943

A wunderkind in every league except the NHL, Bradley played just six times in the top loop during a career in which he filled nets with pucks, notably the WHL and CHL. He was a rarity in that he attended the University of Denver in 1963 during an era when it was fashionable for an NHL aspirant to play junior in his native Canada. But Bradley was unwanted by the NHL during the six-team league and had played seven years of minor pro before the California Golden Seals gave him a four-game chance in '73-'74. Three years later, he played twice for the Cleveland Barons, and in between he set scoring records with Salt Lake, in '73-'74, by amassing 81 assists and 115 points. In all, he played five years with the Golden Eagles before retiring.

BRADLEY, Matt
b. Stittsville, Ontario, June 13, 1978

After playing almost three full seasons in the AHL, Bradley earned a callup to San Jose in October 2000, making the team out of camp. The Sharks had drafted him in 1996 during a fine career with Kingston in the OHL, a three-year stretch augmented by a trip to Switzerland with the Canadian National Junior team for the 1998 tournament.

Philippe Bozon

John Brackenborough

Curt Brackenbury

Bart Bradley

Lyle Bradley

Neil Brady

Rick Bragnalo

Andy Branigan

Per-Olov Brasar

Fred Brathwaite

BRADY, Neil
b. Montreal, Quebec, April 12, 1968
On opening night of the 1992-93 season, Brady scored the first goal in the history of the new Ottawa Senators' franchise. It was one of just seven goals the big centre scored that year after the Sens had acquired him in the off-season from New Jersey, where he had played the first three years of his career. Brady had been drafted 3rd overall by the Devils back in 1986, but for such a high draft choice he didn't leave much of a mark on the game. He played 89 NHL games in all, and since 1994 has been in the IHL, and later in the AHL, skating for a variety of teams.

BRAGNALO, Rick
b. Fort William, Ontario, December 1, 1951
He was skilled, fast, and had the "too small" tag stapled to his hockey stick. All that could mean only one thing – Europe. Bragnalo attended the University of Denver from 1970 to '74 under coach Murray Armstrong, studying physical education while developing his game on ice. But throughout his brief 145-game career in the NHL – all with lowly Washington – Bragnalo managed just 15 goals and didn't attract flies from other teams in the league. Thus began part two of his career: Rickie goes to Italy. For 12 years he played in the Chianti country, both in league play and as a member of the Italian national team in the World Championships, "A" pool (1982 and '83) and "B" pool (1981, '85, '86, and '87), eventually moving into coaching.

BRANIGAN, Andy
b. Winnipeg, Manitoba, April 11, 1922
d. Lincoln, Rhode Island, April 13, 1995
Branigan is the only player to both score a goal and play goal in the same game. It all happened on February 28, 1941, while he was playing for the New York Americans. Manager Red Dutton had signed him at the start of the season as a tough defenceman, but on the night in question regular goaltender Chuck Rayner suffered an injury and had to leave. Coach Art Chapman knew that Branigan had been a goalie in lacrosse and did not hesitate to put his rearguard in the nets. Branigan did not allow a goal, though his Amazing Amerks lost the game to Detroit, 5-4. That game was one of only six he played that season for the team, and the next year he played his final 21 NHL games when the team moved to Brooklyn (or, at least, when its name changed – the team continued to play out of Madison Square Garden). After that year, the Americans folded and Branigan enlisted with the RCAF. Three years later, he was discharged, but the NHL was a long way away for him. Nonetheless, he continued to play the

puck game for another 15 years, becoming the all-time leader in both games played and penalty minutes in the AHL. He retired in 1960 and later coached in the EHL.

BRASAR, Per-Olov
b. Falun, Sweden, September 30, 1950
He was named the team's most valuable player and best rookie, most liked player by fans, most Three Stars votes, and nominee for the Bill Masterton Trophy. He had 20 goals and 57 points on a team that missed the playoffs, but he was the cornerstone of the team's young and bright future. That first NHL year, 1977-78 with Minnesota, looked incredible for Brasar, and when he went off to the World Championships (his fifth) at season's end, GM Lou Nanne followed him to get him signed to a new contract. But the next year, Brasar had six goals, and the year after only one before being traded to Vancouver. The Canucks needed his services because their own Lars Lindgren had suffered a shoulder injury. Brasar recovered to score 22 goals in his first full year out west, but again fell to just six goals the year after. It was his last season in the NHL. He returned for a brief spell in Swedish league hockey before retiring.

BRASHEAR, Donald
b. Bedford, Indiana, January 7, 1972
He's an accomplished pianist. He wipes his hands derisively after beating up opponents in fights. He has played twice for the U.S. at the World Championships. He has three times been charged with assault for acts of violence in bars and his own home. He has clobbered many an opponent, been suspended for on-ice violence, and also been the victim of one of the most vicious hockey attacks of all time when, on the night of February 21, 2000, Marty McSorley knocked him unconscious with a blow from his stick. Brashear started fighting in the Quebec junior leagues before being signed by Montreal, but the Habs traded him to Vancouver and it was there he established himself as a regular. He continued to beat people up, but also improved as a player to the point that he was having a career year when McSorley belted him. McSorley was charged with assault and suspended for 23 games, a punishment that in effect ended his career. Brashear recovered and has continued to develop his skill while maintaining his reputation as a pugilist.

Brashear has played twice for the U.S. at the World Championships.
DONALD BRASHEAR

BRATHWAITE, Fred ("Shady B")
b. Ottawa, Ontario, November 24, 1972
It took him 11 games to win his first in the NHL, not a good way to begin a career given that the time from first to eleventh was nearly six months. Ever since, he has had trouble establishing himself

as number one, though he's certainly made a splash wherever he's been. In junior, he scored a goal in the playoffs. In the IHL, playing for Manitoba, he scored again from his own net. At the 1998 Spengler Cup, he was named the best goalie of the tournament. He played for Canada at the 2000 Worlds (though not particularly well), but just as he thought he was establishing himself as numero uno in Calgary, he was traded to St. Louis, where the Blues had a perfectly capable starter in Roman Turek. When the team acquired Chris Osgood in the 2003 trade deadline, he became redundant and was given outright release by the team. Small and quick, he has always relied on his reflexes for his success.

BRAYSHAW, Russ ("Buster")
b. Saskatoon, Saskatchewan, January 17, 1918
d. 1996

A left winger, Brayshaw signed with Chicago for the 1944-45 season, played most of the year, and then never saw the NHL again. He had played junior in Moose Jaw, and after his time with the Hawks played briefly in the AHL and a variety of minor pro leagues before retiring in 1949. He later coached the Edmonton Oil Kings.

BREAULT, Francois
b. Acton Vale, Quebec, May 11, 1967

Breault had the odd distinction of playing for three different junior teams in the Quebec league in the mid-1980s, a sign of things to come. He was never drafted and played more than two years in the minors before being given an NHL chance by Los Angeles. But over three seasons, the right winger played in only 27 games. His career didn't last much longer.

BREITENBACH, Ken
b. Welland, Ontario, January 9, 1955

On the morning of October 9, 1977, Ken Breitenbach was on top of the world. He had been drafted by Buffalo two years earlier and played part-time for the team since, but this training camp he looked to have made the team. By the end of the day, he couldn't walk and his career was in jeopardy. In the exhibition game that night, he suffered a serious broken leg that kept him out of the game for the entire season. He recovered in time to be available for the playoffs, but he didn't play until the next season. A year later, though, he was no longer the player he had been. After starting the year in the minors, he was called up to the Sabres for the final 30 games of the season. His recovery, though, was not complete, and at year's end he retired at age 24. He continues to play for the Sabres' alumni.

BRENDL, Pavel
b. Opocno, Czechoslovakia (Czech Republic), March 23, 1981

It's getting to be nearly time for Brendl to show his stuff. He was drafted 4th overall by the Rangers in 1999, and GM Glen Sather used Brendl as part of a package to acquire Eric Lindros from the Flyers. Brendl led the WHL in goals his first two seasons of junior, and in 2001 he led the Czech Republic to a gold medal at the World Juniors. His time is now. He

debuted with Philadelphia in 2001-02, but he has outgrown junior and the Flyers obviously think he is more than an AHL player. Brendl has to go out and prove it.

BRENNAN, Dan
b. Dawson Creek, British Columbia, October 1, 1962

A graduate of the University of North Dakota in 1984, Brennan played two games for the L.A. Kings at the end of his senior year. But after a full year in the minors, he played only six more games in '85–'86 with the Kings before retiring.

BRENNAN, Doug
b. Peterborough, Ontario, January 10, 1905

He wasn't around for very long, but he got his name on the Stanley Cup with the New York Rangers in 1933. Brennan played his early years in the Pacific Coast league before being recruited by the Rangers for the 1931-32 season. He was known as a fearless, rough defenceman, and in his first year the Rangers went to the Cup finals before losing to Toronto. The next year, the tables turned and it was Brennan's Blueshirts that defeated Conn Smythe's Blue and White. After one more season, though, Brennan wound up in the minors, and out of the game altogether a short time later. He settled in Havelock, Ontario, and became a conductor for the CNR.

BRENNAN, Kip
b. Kingston, Ontario, August 27, 1980

Left winger Brennan is the property of Los Angeles, but he has earned only a brief chance to play for the Kings, in 2001-02, since being drafted in 1998. A penalty-minute king, he is known for his fighting more than his scoring.

BRENNAN, Rich
b. Schenectady, New York, November 26, 1972

It just didn't happen for Brennan. He was drafted 46th by Quebec in 1991, but he played only 2 games with the franchise after it moved to Colorado. He played briefly with San Jose and the Rangers and L.A., but a career that began with promise at Boston University ended with an anonymity all too familiar for those who don't catch on in the NHL.

BRENNAN, Tom
b. Philadelphia, Pennsylvania, January 22, 1922

It was a confused play, and as is always the case, a freak play. The night was November 29, 1953, and Brennan was playing for Ste. Therese in the Quebec Pro league. His team was on the power play, but the defending team, St. Jérôme, almost cleared the puck out of the zone. Brennan started to skate back for the puck just as his defenceman kept it in with a backhand. The follow-through caught Brennan flush in the eye, and his life was forever altered. He suffered a fractured skull and needed 50 stitches to close the wound, but just a few days later doctors had to remove the eye. He had played 12 games with the Bruins from 1943 to '45 before having to miss the entire '45–'46 season with serious back surgery, and after a lengthy career in the minors that fateful night sabotaged his peaceful hockey existence.

Russ Brayshaw

Ken Breitenbach

Rich Brennan

BRENNEMAN, John

b. Fort Erie, Ontario, January 5, 1943

He scored his only goal with Chicago 30 seconds into his first shift playing on a line with Chico Maki and Phil Esposito, and after bouncing around with four Original Six teams in as many seasons in the 1960s he suffered an eventual career-ending injury with just two games left in the '67-'68 season. He crashed into the boards and damaged his vertebrae, an injury that affected his Achilles tendon. He tried unsuccessfully to return to full playing ability but was forced to retire. Brenneman went into the hotel and restaurant business and in 1978 joined Labatt's Breweries in Ontario, where he eventually became a sales rep for Mississauga.

BRETTO, Joe ("Brute")

b. Hibbing, Minnesota, November 29, 1913

He was one of the first Minnesotans to play in the NHL, three games in 1944-45 with Chicago during a time teams were desperate for players. Bretto hadn't played the previous two seasons, in fact, and did little to distinguish himself during his brief time with the Hawks. He had played mostly in the northeastern U.S. in minor pro leagues before the war.

BREWER, Carl

b. Toronto, Ontario, October 21, 1938

d. Toronto, Ontario, August 25, 2001

There is no greater irony in hockey than the career of Carl Brewer, one of the most complex men and complex lives the game has ever known. The man he reached out to at the height of his career, the man who revived his career when no one else would have dared, was the same man Brewer would spend years and much money successfully trying to put in jail many years later. He was a man of unequivocal emotion who said what he believed and acted according to his own creed, one he thought both tough and fair. He grew up playing hockey with Bob Nevin, and the two were on the great Marlies teams of the mid-1950s. Brewer had phenomenal acceleration, was one of the best skaters in the league, but his thoughts were often far away from the X's and O's of the dressing room chalkboard and his ears were often closed to the coach's whistle. He won three Stanley Cups with the Leafs during their last terrific flurry of greatness in the 1960s but fought bitterly with coach Punch Imlach and retired at training camp in 1966 because he could no longer abide the coach's dictatorial rule. He enrolled at the University of Toronto and finished his degree but he wanted to play hockey again, as an amateur. This was strictly forbidden unless he were to be reinstated as such, and the only one who could grant this

Brewer began a crusade that almost single-handedly resulted in the most dramatic court victory for players in the history of the NHL.
CARL BREWER

permission was NHL president Clarence Campbell. The prexy, of course, sided with Imlach and refused to help Brewer, so the player turned to a young Toronto lawyer named Alan Eagleson. Eagleson threatened Campbell with legal action and forced hockey's most powerful figure into submission. It was a victory that led to Eagleson's role as executive director of the soon-to-be-formed Players' Association. Brewer played for Canada at the 1967 World Championships and shortly after played and coached in Finland for a season while attending university there. He agreed to return to the NHL only after his rights were traded to Detroit, and after three years he retired again, only to return a year later to play in the WHA for the Toronto Toros. Five years later, he came out of retirement for a third time to play for the struggling Leafs in 1979-80 under his old coach, Imlach, though his return had more to do with his desire to finish his career as a Maple Leaf. His life took another turn in 1991, when he began to question why, after 11 years in the league, he was getting a paltry pension of $7,500 a year. His questions led him to answers that had the name Eagleson on them, and Brewer began a crusade that almost single-handedly resulted in the most dramatic court victory for players in the history of the NHL. In 1997, the NHL and its alumni reached a settlement that saw the old-timers receive US$ 41.1 million in a pension scandal that changed the business landscape of the game. But Brewer persisted until Eagleson was forced to face numerous charges of fraud in a Boston court, charges the Eagle pleaded guilty to and for which he served time in jail. In his later years, Brewer suffered from apnea, a condition that affects a person's breathing during sleep. By the time he died, he had proved himself a loud, forceful, belligerent man. He was always considered one of the fastest defencemen of his era, but in death he was remembered for his far, far greater contributions to the game off the ice. He brought a force of will that every NHLer is known for during a Stanley Cup finals into the living room and bank account of every player of the Original Six who had played, naively, for the love of the game.

BREWER, Eric

b. Vernon, British Columbia, April 17, 1979

Salt Lake City defined Brewer's early years as a player, gave him confidence, and gave him a platform to prove he was among the best young defencemen in the league. Tall, quick, and strong, he developed in the WHL and played for Canada at the 1998 World Juniors, a year after being drafted 5th overall by the Islanders. The Oilers stole him in a trade in which

Eric Brewer

they also got Josh Green and a draft choice and gave up Roman Hamrlik. In Alberta, Brewer took off. He was the seventh defenceman on Canada's entry at the 2002 Olympics in Salt Lake City, but he played his role perfectly and came home with a gold medal, assuring himself not only greater league-wide respect but almost certain invitation to the 2006 Games should NHLers be allowed to go. His play for Canada at the 2002 World Championships at season's end confirmed his place as a future star on the blueline.

BRICKLEY, Andy
b. Melrose, Massachusetts, August 9, 1961

Despite being drafted a distant 210th overall by Philly in 1980, Brickley managed to hang in there for 385 NHL games, though only 3 of those were with the Flyers. He was sent to Pittsburgh in '83-'84 and spent four games in the minors during the season as punishment for breaking curfew with Mike Bullard when the boys went out drinking and didn't get home on time. He also played for New Jersey, Boston, and Winnipeg, spending ever-increasing time in the minors until finally he was a full-fledged minor leaguer with no chance of being recalled. After retiring, he became a radio broadcaster in Boston. He won a Turner Cup with the Utah Grizzlies in 1995-96.

Andy Brickley

BRIDEN, Archie ("Bones")
b. Ottawa, Ontario, July 16, 1897
d. unknown

On May 4, 1916, 18-year-old Archibald Briden joined the 159th Battalion of the Canadian Expeditionary Force and headed overseas. An electrician by trade, he had played hockey prior to his departure and resumed a career on ice after his discharge. The 5'11", 175-pound left winger ended up on the west coast and eventually played briefly in the NHL with three teams, Boston and Detroit in '26-'27, and Pittsburgh in '29-'30. He later played in the international league before retiring in the early 1930s.

BRIDGMAN, Mel
b. Trenton, Ontario, April 28, 1955

Here's one for the how-low-can-you-go files. Bridgman was one of those scrappy, goon-like menaces that pervaded the Philadelphia teams of the 1970s under the guidance of captain Bobby Clarke. When Clarke stepped down in 1979 to assume duties as playing assistant coach, Bridgman wore the "C" for the team but quickly lost the respect of his teammates, who dubbed him "Captain Shampoo" because, it seems, his greatest concern was ensuring there was enough hair wash in the showers. That's a long way down from 1975, when he was considered

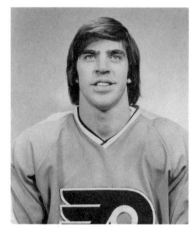

Bridgman was one of those scrappy, goon-like menaces.
MEL BRIDGMAN

one of the best juniors in the game. He later played for four other teams and after retiring in 1989 pursued management positions, culminating in 1992 when he was named first GM of the new Ottawa Senators. Bridgman received his MBA from the University of Pennsylvannia and became a player agent with IMG.

BRIERE, Daniel
b. Gatineau, Quebec, October 6, 1977

Not big, but fast, and he just keeps getting better. That's the line on this kid, Briere. His size hurts, but he's just too good not to play. He played junior hockey in Drummondville, led the league in goals (67), assists (96), and points (163) in 1995-96, and the next year helped Canada win gold at the World Juniors. Phoenix drafted him and kept him the whole of '98-'99, but with only 8 goals in 64 games Briere looked to have played himself to a minor league career. But he, like the Coyotes, rebounded in 2001-02, and he became one of the team's best scorers and key players.

Daniel Briere

BRIERE, Michel
b. Shawinigan Falls, Quebec, October 21, 1949
d. Montreal, Quebec, April 13, 1971

He played only two years of junior – 1967-68 and '68-'69 – and led the league in points both years. The year after, at age 19, he was playing for Pittsburgh in the NHL, and in his rookie season he had a perfectly respectable 12 goals and 44 points. Life looked good for the kid from Shawinigan, and after the season he bought himself a sports car with his playoff money. On May 15, 1970, his car skidded off the road and hit a tree near his home in Malartic in northwest Quebec. One of the three passengers was killed, the other two were injured, and Briere was left unconscious with serious brain damage. The roads had been slick and dangerous, so much so, in fact, that the ambulance that took Briere to the hospital itself struck and killed an 18-year-old pedestrian. Briere never recovered. He lay in a coma for a year until dying in a convalescent home after four unsuccessful operations. His number 21 was retired by the team in his honour and is constant reminder of a player who promised greatness but would never know it in this life.

Michel Briere

BRIGLEY, Travis
b. Coronation, Alberta, June 16, 1977

There isn't much to report on Brigley's career so far. Since being drafted in 1996, he has played only 19 NHL games, with Calgary, and each season he seems to get a bit farther away from the big show rather than closer to it. A left winger who showed an ability to score in junior and the minors, he has yet to fish that first-goal puck out of an NHL net.

Travis Brigley

Frank Brimsek

BRIMANIS, Aris
b. Cleveland, Ohio, March 14, 1972

From the home of the Rock and Roll Hall of Fame and Museum comes Brimanis, a hulking defenceman whose minor league career through the 1990s was punctuated by a smattering of appearances in the NHL, first with Philadelphia and later with the Islanders.

BRIMSEK, Frank ("Mister Zero")
b. Eveleth, Minnesota, September 26, 1915
d. Virginia, Minnesota, November 11, 1998

Just as Glenn Gould always wore gloves to protect his hands – his life, his career, his means to his art – so, too, did Brimsek hate to have his photograph taken for fear the flash would damage his eyes. Yet how could photographers resist taking images of one of the greatest goalies ever, and certainly the greatest American-born goalie until Tom Barrasso came along some 40 years later? Early in the '38-'39 season Brimsek replaced Tiny Thompson in the Boston goal, and in six of his first eight games he recorded a shutout, giving rise to his nickname. That rookie season, he led the NHL in wins (33) and shutouts (10), and won the Calder and Vezina trophies for his remarkable entrance into the league. He played 9 of his 10 seasons with the Bruins, and while the Kraut Line was doing all the damage up front, tiny Brimsek backstopped the teams to Stanley Cup victories in 1939 and '41. He was a patient, standup goalie, calm as a cucumber, who was famous for outwaiting his opponent. He missed two years in the middle of his career while serving in the army, and played his final season with a weak Chicago team in '49-'50. His 252 career wins and 40 shutouts were remarkable in that they were earned in just 514 regular-season games. He was, for decades, the only U.S.-born goalie to have won the Vezina Trophy, yet after he retired he left the game behind completely. He gave his equipment to Red Hamill's son and got a job as a fireman on the Pacific Railway running from Duluth to Winnipeg. Brimsek never saw a hockey game during all these years. He retired in 1976 to Virginia, where he spent his final years. He was inducted into the U.S. Hockey Hall of Fame in 1973 (located in his hometown, Eveleth) and the Hockey Hall of Fame in 1966.

BRIND'AMOUR, Rod
b. Ottawa, Ontario, August 9, 1970

Not too many times in a year does a player come along with the series of attributes to which Brind'Amour can lay claim. He has size and scoring ability, plays reliably defensively, and is a team man through and through.

Doug Brindley

Patrice Brisebois

That's what St. Louis liked about him when they drafted him in 1988 out of Notre Dame, that wonderful hockey school in Saskatchewan that has educated and raised so many NHLers-to-be. Brind'Amour scored 26 goals in his rookie season and 4 times had more than 33 goals in one year. In his early years he continued to go to university in the summers to earn a degree in business administration, and on ice he developed into one of the best forwards in the game. He played in the World Juniors for Canada in 1989, and later played four times in the World Championships. He also represented Canada at both the 1996 World Cup and the '98 Olympics in Nagano. With Philadelphia, he set a team Iron Man record by appearing in 484 consecutive games. In the 1997 playoffs, he set a league record by scoring 2 short-handed goals in just 54 seconds. That year, he led the league in playoff goals with 13. A physical player, he has been slowed by time but continues to play and lead, for Carolina, in a career that has now eclipsed 1,000 games.

In the 1997 playoffs, he set a league record by scoring 2 short-handed goals in just 54 seconds.
ROD BRIND'AMOUR

BRINDLEY, Doug
b. Walkerton, Ontario, June 8, 1949

Brindley rose quickly through the ranks from junior to the CHL and AHL before joining Toronto at Maple Leaf Gardens briefly in 1970-71 for a three-game tryout. After that, his descent was nearly as quick, though he stopped the fall briefly with a two-year stint in the WHA before finishing in lesser leagues and retiring in 1976. He settled in Orangeville, Ontario, and became a police officer.

BRINK, Milt ("Curly")
b. Hibbing, Minnesota, November 26, 1910
d. Eveleth, Minnesota, October 31, 1999

A lifelong native of Minnesota, Brink played five games with Chicago in 1936-37 during a brief pro career that was as pedestrian as it was anonymous.

BRISEBOIS, Patrice
b. Montreal, Quebec, January 27, 1971

It was a lifelong dream of every NHL forward to have Brisebois sign a long-term deal with the Habs, such was his reputation for being easily got around. Indeed, Montreal media nicknamed him "Breeze By" with that deprecation only they could muster. Yet it was an equally appalling sign of the time when in September 1998, his contract called for him to receive $6 million over three years. He actually had won gold with Canada's junior teams in 1990 and '91 and was a member of Montreal's last Cup win back in 1993, but his performance in recent years, and his stunning survival in the face of a rapidly declining team, provided much fodder for a city developing a taste for losing.

BRISSON, Gerry
b. St. Boniface, Manitoba, September 3, 1937

He may have played four games with Montreal in 1962-63, but Brisson's career highlight came five years earlier while playing for the Winnipeg Warriors. He skated on a line with legend Bill Mosienko and youngster Barrie Ross, and the threesome formed the highest-scoring unit in the WHL that year. Brisson later scored 44 goals with Spokane, earning a callup to Montreal, but after that his career was again minor league and not as star-studded.

BRITZ, Greg
b. Buffalo, New York, January 3, 1961

Sometimes an NHL career is simply the preamble to later success. Case in point: Britz. Talented by everyday standards, he was low down on the NHL food chain and managed to play just eight times with Toronto and Hartford in the mid-1980s. He retired in 1987 after finishing the year with Binghampton in the AHL and then took a road that led to a life in academia. He is currently the managing director and director of development of the Center for Documentary Studies at Duke University, a job that requires little in the way of slapshots and stops-and-starts as prerequisites for employment.

BROADBENT, Harry "Punch" ("Elbows")
b. Ottawa, Ontario, July 13, 1892
d. Ottawa, Ontario, March 5, 1971

There was an Elbows in hockey long before Gordie Howe, though the epithet conveyed a similar meaning. Harry Lawton Broadbent was as fine a player as there was in the NHL's early years, but he also knew how to crack an opponent with his elbow to good effect. He played hockey locally and joined the Senators of the NHA in 1912. Three years later the team went to Vancouver to challenge the Millionaires for possession of the Stanley Cup, though they lost three straight games. He then left the game to serve in the army, and he did so with distinction, earning the Military Medal. He returned to the Senators in 1918, only to find that the NHA had given way to the NHL. No matter. He played in the new league for 11 years, with commensurate distinction, winning three Cups with the Sens and another with the Maroons in '25-'26. He, Frank Nighbor, and Cy Denneny formed the heart of those Ottawa teams, an astounding goal-scoring threesome that carried the team to victory. Broadbent led the NHL in goals in '21-'22 with 32 but was soon traded to Montreal in a huge deal. He proved his continued worth by scoring five goals in one game and then winning a Cup with the English Montrealers just a short time later. He retired in 1929 and returned to

the RCAF. He was inducted into the Hockey Hall of Fame in 1962 and joined linemates Denneny and Nighbor in hockey's pantheon of greats.

BROCHU, Martin
b. Anjou, Quebec, March 10, 1973

If he's a goalie, he must be from Quebec. But in Brochu's case, that hasn't meant too much. He was never drafted, and only Montreal was willing to sign him as a free agent, in 1992. But after a few years in the minors, he never played well enough to be Patrick Roy's backup, and the Habs moved him to Washington for the proverbial future considerations. To date, he has played just twice, giving up six goals in two losses with the Caps, though he was named most valuable player in the AHL for the 1999-2000 season with the Portland Pirates.

BROCHU, Stephane
b. Sherbrooke, Quebec, August 15, 1967

There aren't many one-game wonders who have played more hockey outside the NHL than Brochu. His one chance in the NHL came in the '88-'89 season with the Rangers, but since then he has played more than 800 games of pro in a variety of under-leagues. For him, a good day is being called up to the AHL, but nevertheless he has played the pro puck game for 14 seasons now.

BRODA, Walter "Turk"
b. Brandon, Manitoba, May 15, 1914
d. Toronto, Ontario, October 17, 1972

As a kid, the freckles on his forehead gave friends the urge to call him Turkey Face, and over the years this was reduced merely to Turk. The media called him the Fabulous Fat Man, and most everyone who followed hockey and watched him play called Broda the best money goalie in the history of the game. He started out as a defenceman in Brandon, but his first coach decided the blueline corps was set. The team didn't have a goalie, so Turkey Face was sent to guard the twine. He did so the rest of his days. He started in the Detroit system but Conn Smythe saw him play with the Detroit Olympics in '35-'36 and bought him from Jack Adams, one of the finest deals Smythe ever engineered. Broda made the Leafs the next year and until 1951 he was the best there was. Small and chunky, he was also fearless and calm, attributes that helped him conquer opponents as much as quick hands or fast feet. He played his entire career with the Leafs, winning the first of five Stanley Cups in 1942 when the team came back from three games down to beat Detroit four games to three. Such was his extraordinary power that even when he went to war he was in demand and popular as ever. Both

Gerry Brisson

During his stay in England, he was hit in the mouth during a game and lost his front five teeth.
TURK BRODA

Greg Britz

"Punch" Broadbent

Martin Brochu

Connie Broden

Ken Broderick

Montreal and Toronto army teams tried to convince him to enlist in their areas so he could play hockey for them. Broda decided Montreal had made a better offer and took a train to Quebec to enlist. But just before the Ontario-Quebec border, the train lurched to a stop and Broda was arrested. He was brought back to Toronto, where he was forced to enlist, and so began the army duty of the most famous goalie in the world. He served for two and a half years, much of that time coming overseas as a gunner with the Royal Canadian Artillery. During his stay in England, he was hit in the mouth during a game and lost his front five teeth. He immediately wired Conn Smythe and announced his retirement, believing that if he couldn't stop a hot shot from an Englishman, he was no longer fit for the NHL. When he got off the train at Union Station in early 1946, though, he went directly to Maple Leaf Gardens and declared his intentions to return as soon as possible. Broda then went on to play 215 consecutive games. The streak ended on November 27, 1949, when Smythe benched Broda for being too fat. It was a publicity stunt as much as real punishment, and after one game and the loss of a few ounces, Turk was back guarding his cord cottage. During that streak, Broda won Cups in 1947, '48, and '49 (when he gave up just four goals in the finals). He won his last Cup in 1951 when he allowed just nine goals in eight games. He retired in 1951 with a playoff record of 60-39. On December 22, 1951, Conn Smythe gave his Fabulous Fat Man a special night at the Gardens, an honour accorded precious few Leafs over the years. Broda turned to coaching and was as good at that job as he had been at keeping the puck out of his own net. He coached the Marlies for a decade, winning two Memorial Cups, during which time he also sold sand for Conn Smythe at the gravel pits. Broda coached throughout the country besides, including for the Quebec Aces, Moncton, Newmarket, and London. He was inducted into the Hockey Hall of Fame in 1967 and later into the Manitoba Sports Hall of Fame, and passed away early as a result of a massive heart attack.

BRODEN, Connie
b. Montreal, Quebec, April 6, 1932

My, but 1958 was a fine year. Broden began the year in retirement, unsure if he wanted to continue a pro career that had "minors" written all over it. He had played three games with the Canadiens in '55-'56 and six more in '56-'57, but when the Habs asked him to report to Shawinigan again for the next year, he refused. Then the Whitby Dunlops phoned Montreal and asked about getting Ralph Backstrom. GM Frank Selke balked, and offered Broden instead. He stayed with the team as it traveled to Oslo, Norway, for the World Championships, and there he scored at least one goal in every game and helped the Dunnies win gold. When he got home, the news was good – Montreal wanted him for the NHL. Even better, the team won the Stanley Cup and he became the first – and still the only – man to win the greatest double championship in one season. He retired a year later and settled in Montreal, eventually becoming the vice-president and director of production services for Molson Breweries.

Len Broderick

BRODERICK, Ken
b. Toronto, Ontario, February 16, 1942

During a lengthy pro career spackled by NHL appearances, Broderick paid his dues, learned the game, and had some fun along the way. He played from 1963 to '68 almost exclusively with the Canadian National Team, appearing in both the '64 and '68 Olympics (he was named best goalie in the latter). He played a ton of minor pro hockey, but in 1971, when he was sent to San Diego, he established his roots and settled down. Although he continued to play and move around, he went into real estate and returned to San Diego after retiring in 1978. That December, he was offered the job of commissioner for the fledgling Pacific Hockey League. He took the bait, though there were days early on he must have regretted doing so. One game had to be cancelled when the referee didn't show up, two teams folded because of financial problems, and Broderick imposed a salary cap of $500 a week per player. Eventually, he turned the league around, though he shortly returned to real estate. He later became involved in numerous charities in the Niagara region of southern Ontario, notably playing in the annual Commisso Food Markets celebrity golf tournament.

BRODERICK, Len
b. Toronto, Ontario, October 11, 1938

Like a chosen few other young goalies, Broderick got into his one and only NHL game because of an injury to a visiting keeper. In Len's case, he was the replacement goalie the night of October 30, 1957, when Montreal was in town to play Toronto at Maple Leaf Gardens. Broderick was the starter for the Marlies, and his second duty was to show up for every Leafs game and be ready in case one of the two starters were hurt. That night, Jacques Plante was unable to start the game and Broderick had to play. Usually, the replacement goalie allows a few goals, keeps the game close, and loses. But the Habs were the dominant team in the league, and it didn't much matter who they put in goal. Broderick allowed only two pucks to elude him, and he won the game 6-2. He never played in the NHL again, though his brother, Ken, did.

BRODEUR, Martin
b. Montreal, Quebec, May 6, 1972

There is a chance – an outside chance, perhaps, but a chance just the same – that Brodeur could eclipse Terry Sawchuk's seemingly untouchable record of 103 career shutouts. There is every chance that Brodeur could be the winningest goalie of all time and have the lowest goals against average of all time. That's how incredible the first decade of Brodeur's career has been. His dad was a goalie: Denis played on the 1956 Canadian Olympic team that won bronze in Cortina, and he went on to become the photographer for the Canadiens. Martin's older brother, Claude, was a longtime pitcher with the Montreal Expos before an arm injury ended his career. And then Martin came along. New Jersey drafted him in 1990, and within three years he was their undisputed number-one goalie. Brodeur has played more than 70 games 5 times in his career. He is the only goalie to win 40 games on 4 occasions. He is the only goalie after Tony Esposito to win 30 games in 7 successive seasons. He already has 64 career shutouts. He won the Stanley Cup in 1995 and 2000 and a gold medal with Canada at Salt Lake City in 2002. And he scored a goal, in the playoffs, no less. On April 17, 1997, with the Devils leading Montreal 4-2, he made a perfect shot into an empty net to add to his collection of wonders. He still has many good years of hockey left; only time will tell if he can slow history down and catch it, but so far he's winning the race big time.

BRODEUR, Richard ("King Richard")
b. Longueuil, Quebec, September 15, 1952

It's not often you see a goalie so upset with a heckler that he tries to slice his stick between the panes of Plexiglas to get at the loudmouth. But that's what Brodeur did one night back in 1986. He was what coaches called an emotional goaltender. He was also mighty fine in his heyday. He began playing in the WHA, for the entire life of that league, in fact (1972-79) before joining the Islanders when the league merged with the NHL. He played just twice on Long Island and then was dealt to Vancouver, where he played eight years and dazzled fans who nicknamed him "King Richard." He took the Canucks to that improbable finals in 1982, and he was the number-one man year in, year out. He had one scary moment in 1983 at Maple Leaf Gardens when he turned his head on a Dan Daoust slapshot. The puck hit him on the ear, and he bled copiously on the ice. The shot damaged cartilage, punctured his eardrum, and required plastic surgery to repair. He recovered to return to his old form, but during the '87-'88 season he was demoted and then traded. Vancouver was playing poorly, and the team decided it needed a change. King Richard reigned no more. A few months later, he retired.

There is a chance that Brodeur could eclipse Terry Sawchuk's seemingly untouchable record of 103 career shutouts.
MARTIN BRODEUR

BROMLEY, Gary ("Bonesy")
b. Edmonton, Alberta, January 19, 1950

Certainly one of the strangest stats in goaltending history is the story of Bromley's first full year in Buffalo with the Sabres, 1974-75. He played 50 games during the regular season and had a phenomenal record of 26-11-11. He was their number-one guy, but in the playoffs he didn't see a minute of action. Coach Punch Imlach inexplicably benched him in favour of Roger Crozier, and that was the end of his career in the Fire City. He played once the next year in Buffalo and then made a dash to the WHA for two years before finishing with Vancouver. After retiring, he settled in Coquitlam and became a firefighter in Vancouver.

BROOKE, Bob
b. Melrose, Massachusetts, December 18, 1960

Not many American-born players from the 1980s played in the big three of international tournaments, but Brooke did. After an impressive rookie year at Yale and then the World Junior Championships in 1980, he was drafted by St. Louis. The Blues, however, couldn't get his name on a contract, so traded him to the Rangers. In the meantime he played most of '83-'84 with the USA National Team, culminating with the '84 Olympics in Sarajevo. He made his Rangers' debut near the end of the season. In the summer he worked for a plastics company in Leominster, Massachusetts, and joined the Blueshirts full-time that fall. He was a solid, third-line player who didn't score or fight to earn his keep but was, rather, a reliable big centre (6'2" and 207 pounds). He later played for Minnesota and New Jersey and twice played at the World Championships and at the 1987 Canada Cup for Team USA.

BROOKS, Art
b. Guelph, Ontario, 1892
d. unknown

Brooks has the distinction of playing in the first-ever NHL game for Toronto when the team was called the Arenas, a 10-9 loss to the Montreal Wanderers on December 19, 1917. He played in the first four games, but was released on January 6, 1918, when the team signed Hap Holmes. He never played in the NHL again.

BROOKS, Gord
b. Cobourg, Ontario, September 11, 1950

If variety is, indeed, the spice of life, then Brooks lived a spicy hockey life, to be sure. He went from junior to the NHL, but he never hung around too long in one place or for very long. He had two stints with St. Louis and another with Washington during its dreadful inaugural year, 1974-75, but for most of the next decade he wandered from team to league to country. En route, he led the AHL in scoring with 98 points in '77-'78 with the Philadelphia Firebirds.

BROOKS, Ross
b. Toronto, Ontario, October 17, 1937

Where to start? One of the most amazing stories the NHL has ever known. Brooks grew up in Islington, west Toronto, and played junior hockey in Barrie. This was the late 1950s. He was a good goalie, but the NHL had exactly six Hall of Fame goalies. That was no league for him. So he packed his pads and went a-wandering, through as many teams in the EHL and AHL as an atlas can mark. He kept this up for 14 years, during which he was a number-one goalie exactly three times. In 1971, he was out of work. He had been backup in Providence for seven years, and

Richard Brodeur

Gary Bromley

Bob Brooke

Gord Brooks

Ross Brooks

Willie Brossart

Aaron Broten

Neal Broten

the end seemed nigh. But, he still loved the game. He and his wife wrote to every pro team on the continent asking if it could use a goalie. Boston GM Milt Schmidt, of all people, said yes, and promptly assigned Brooks to the farm team. Then, in 1972, Gerry Cheevers fled to the WHA and Brooks found himself backup to Gilles Gilbert in the NHL. He replaced Gilbert in one game for which he took the loss, making his NHL debut at age 35. Then something amazing happened. He played and played again, and each time out he won. He won 14 straight games to tie the NHL record! The next year was the same. He spent some time in the minors and had a record of 16-3-0. The year after? Try 10-3-3. And, as he proudly noted, he was Jewish. In fact, he was nominated as Rhode Island's Jewish athlete of the year, but turned down the honour because he had played in only 16 games in his rookie year. He retired with an NHL record of 37-7-6 in 54 career games, one of the best win percentages of all time. He stayed on with the Bruins and became director of operations for the Providence Bruins, as well as running a bar in town called Brooksies.

BROPHY, Bernie
b. Collingwood, Ontario, August 9, 1905
d. unknown
Left winger Bernie Brophy had a moderately successful tenure in the minor pros but at the NHL level played just one full season, with the Detroit Cougars in 1928-29. He had made his first appearance with the Maroons three years earlier but spent much of the interim in the Can-Am league. Brophy later had his best success in the IHL and his career ended by the time the Second World War began.

BROPHY, Frank
b. Quebec City, Quebec, 1900
d. Quebec City, Quebec, June 29, 1930
A goalie in the NHL's earliest years, Brophy played most of the 1919-20 season for the Quebec Bulldogs. In 21 games that year, he gave up an atrocious 148 goals, an average of more than 7 a game. That was his only full season of professional hockey, and he died just a few years later.

BROSSART, Willie
b. Allan, Saskatchewan, May 29, 1949
His name is French but his parents were German, and as a small boy Willie didn't know a word of English until he went to school. He first put on skates when he was 4, and by the time he was 10 he couldn't think of another thing in life he wanted to do as much as play hockey. He had six sisters and brothers, but Willie was more determined than the others to pursue a career in sports, perhaps because his idol, and cousin, Ron Boehm, had a similar determination in playing in the NHL. Brossart dropped out of high school to play junior in the Western league, and he made it to the NHL with Philadelphia, the team that had drafted him in 1969. Despite being a part-timer, he was happy in Philly, and when he got married many Flyers attended; Bob Taylor and Dave Schultz were ushers. Then hockey life hit hard when he was traded to Toronto and then Washington; in neither place could he catch on. He retired in 1977.

BROTEN, Aaron
b. Roseau, Minnesota, November 14, 1960
His critics often pounded him, but Broten seldom rebutted their words with on-ice action. He was more skilled than his older brother, Neal, they would say. He was one of the best stickhandlers in the league, they would enthuse. He had as much potential as any American-born player coming into the NHL, they would declare. But game in, game out, Broten delivered hot and cold performances and over a season this spelled lack of determination and an abundance of complacency. He set records at the University of Minnesota with 106 points in his final year, 1980-81. In the NHL, he followed up a career-best 83-point year with seasons of 59 points and then 36 points. He played in five World Championships for Team USA, one World Juniors, and one Canada Cup. And then, six years after he retired in 1992, he donned the blades again to help his country qualify for the 1999 Worlds after an horrific twelfth-place finish the previous year. He lives in Minnesota and works as an investment broker. He also coaches kids' teams in the area.

BROTEN, Neal
b. Roseau, Minnesota, November 29, 1959
Any player who was on the Miracle on Ice team of 1980 holds a special place in the annals of hockey in the U.S., and 18 years after that historic win, the three Brotens – Neal, Aaron, and Paul – were back on skates to fortify an American team trying to qualify for "A" pool of the World Championships. In between, Neal played in the 1981 and '84 Canada Cups for the U.S. and the 1990 Worlds, though he was better known for his 1,099-game career in the NHL. He played almost every one of those games with the Minnesota/Dallas franchise, but also played a few games in New Jersey and Los Angeles. He scored more than 20 goals in a season 5 times and twice went to the Stanley Cup finals, in 1981 and 1991. Since retiring, he has become a rancher in River Falls, Wisconsin with his wife, and is also a goodwill ambassador for the Minnesota Wild.

BROTEN, Paul
b. Roseau, Minnesota, October 27, 1965
His career was shorter and less glamorous than his brothers' but Paul Broten still played in 322 NHL games. And, like his brothers, he played one final time, in 1998, to help the U.S. re-qualify for "A" pool of the World Championships. Paul was a right winger who came out of the University of Minnesota and was drafted by the Rangers. He played with the team for parts of four years, but after being put on waivers he was claimed by Dallas. He ended his NHL career with St. Louis and later played minor pro and then in Germany before his one final tournament with his brothers, the first international tournament of his career.

BROUSSEAU, Paul
b. Pierrefonds, Quebec, September 18, 1973
Brousseau is likely in the middle of a lengthy minor pro career that began with brief stints in Colorado and Tampa Bay. Although he had always been a decent scorer in junior, his goal stick betrayed him in the NHL, only to return when he scored 45 times for Adirondack in the AHL in '97-'98. After four years,

Paul Brousseau

he moved to Sweden to join AIK Stockholm in the Elite League.

BROWN, Adam ("The Flying Scotchman")
b. Johnstone, Scotland, February 4, 1920
d. Hamilton, Ontario, August 9, 1960

On the night of August 9, 1960, Brown attended a meeting to help organize a charity for a friend. When the meeting broke up, he offered to drive home a friend from Stoney Creek, Ontario, but for reasons unknown his car spun out of control en route, hit a sign, and crashed into a cement bridge. He was killed in the crash, though his passenger suffered only a cut lip. Brown acquired his nickname – The Flying Scotchman – during his teen years when Detroit scout Carson Cooper saw him play. Adam had come to Canada from near Glasgow with his brother, Andy, and parents at age seven and immediately took a liking to hockey. Cooper signed him almost on the spot because of his superb skating and his unwillingness to back down from rough play. He played for Detroit for much of 1941-47, winning a Cup in '43. He was later traded to Chicago and Boston before retiring in 1952. He was always proud of his son, Andy, a goalie, who was just 16 when Adam died. Andy went on to play in the NHL.

BROWN, Andy ("Moe")
b. Hamilton, Ontario, February 15, 1944

He's the answer to one of the great hockey trivia questions: who was the last NHL goalie to play without a mask? The season was 1973-74, his last in the NHL, and the team was Pittsburgh. Brown wore a mask in practice, but like all goalies from the previous generation, he said it interferred with his vision during games. Sort of like today's players and face shields. Brown also held the record for penalty minutes in a season with 60, and as if facing slapshots was not daredevil enough, he used to race cars in the summer months to keep his nerves on edge. He dreamed of the Indy 500, but had to settle for Cayuga Speedway and Speedway Park in Hamilton, where he won his fair share of races. He finished his playing career in the WHA, retiring at 33 because of spinal surgery from which he never fully recovered.

BROWN, Arnie ("Brownie")
b. Oshawa, Ontario, January 28, 1942

Life couldn't have been any better for Arnie Brown in the early 1960s. He won a Memorial Cup with St. Mike's in 1961 and the next year played a couple of games with the Maple Leafs. He hit a bump in the road when he was traded to the Rangers, but after a few years he was partnered with Brad Park and had back-to-back seasons of 10 and 15 goals after never before having more than 2. The Blueshirts expected this kind of Orrian production every year, and just as he was enjoying his best year, 1969-70, he injured both knees in Orrian fashion. It was all downhill from there. He had five operations on his pins in the ensuing years, slowing him down, and trades and change of scenery didn't help. He retired in 1974 and became a salesman for Monsanto Canada, a plastics manufacturer. In 1977, he quit that job to become

assistant coach to Orland Kurtenbach, an error if ever he made one, and the year after Monsanto took him back. He rose to the position of sales manager for central Canada based out of Toronto and still plays occasionally in old-timers' games.

BROWN, Brad ("Brownie")
b. Baie Verte, Newfoundland, December 27, 1975

It took Brown two teams and almost two years to record his first NHL point, but the big defenceman was never scouted for his soft hands or savvy in the enemy slot. Instead, he was all size and brawn and muscle as a defenceman in front of his own goaler. Although he is not yet 30, he has played for three Original Six teams – Montreal, Chicago, and New York.

BROWN, Cam
b. Saskatoon, Saskatchewan, May 15, 1969

Brown has played pro hockey for more than a decade, yet has seen NHL ice exactly once, during the '90-'91 season with Vancouver. Not surprisingly, he earned minor and major penalties in that game, a statistical mark he left at every port of call during his cruise through the minors. He beat up opponents in the Western league as a junior, and beat up players in the AHL, the IHL, and, most recently, the East Coast league, where he has become a mainstay.

BROWN, Patrick "Connie"
b. Vankleek Hill, Ontario, January 11, 1917
d. Ottawa, Ontario, June 3, 1966

At the end of the 1950-51 season, Connie Brown won the prestigious Lady Alexander Trophy as the player most valuable to his team in the Eastern Canada hockey league. This centre was also coach of his team in Ottawa, and he scored an amazing double by also being named best coach in the league! He had played five years with Detroit during 1938-43, winning the Cup with the Wings in his final season before returning to amateur hockey for the rest of his days.

BROWN, Curtis
b. Unity, Saskatchewan, February 12, 1976

After Buffalo drafted him in 1994, Brown had his best season in junior by scoring 51 goals for Moose Jaw, a year-long performance that earned him a one-game callup at season's end. In that game, he had a goal and an assist, and over the next three years he developed patiently in the Buffalo system to the point that he became a steady and reliable regular, despite being asthmatic. He also signed a long-term contract with the team ensuring his stay with his original club, a rarity in the modern game.

BROWN, Dave
b. Saskatoon, Saskatchewan, October 12, 1962

Unfortunately for Brown, the night of October 26, 1987, was so appalling that his career has been defined by an act of extreme violence. That night, he cross-checked Tomas Sandstrom of the Rangers flush across the face, an incident for which he received a 15-game suspension, the third longest in league history. Fans of the game decried the light sentence; supporters of Brown pointed out that he was a tough guy who had used his stick only once before (earning a five-game

Adam Brown

Arnie Brown

Brad Brown

Connie Brown

Doug Brown

George Brown

Greg Brown

Jeff Brown

Keith Brown

suspension). During the suspension, he accepted an offer to emcee two shows at the Comedy Factory Outlet in Philadelphia, perhaps an inappropriate diversion. Truth be told, he lacked merit and talent as a skater or scorer and was a fighter his entire career. He once went two full seasons without a single goal, a difficult task for any right winger who plays even semi-regularly, and in his last eight seasons in the league he scored but eight times. Yet he survived, and because every team needs a fighter he endured, from 1982 to '96.

BROWN, Doug
b. Southborough, Massachusetts, June 12, 1964
In today's NHL – so many teams, so many names – you can turn around and before you know it a guy like Brown has played 16 years and almost 1,000 games. In the old days, those would be Hall of Fame numbers. Now, it's just a long career. Brown has been a bit of a scorer and checker, a team guy who stays out of the penalty box. He played for New Jersey and Pittsburgh before landing with Detroit and being part of their Cup wins in '97 and '98. He played in two World Championships for the U.S. and the 1991 Canada Cup. And there you have it. An enduring career, but he could come and go without anyone even knowing it, save for the fact that brother Greg also played in the NHL and his father-in-law is Wellington Mara, owner of the NFL's New York Giants.

BROWN, Fred ("Baldy")
b. Kingston, Ontario, September 15, 1900
d. unknown
His was a brief career about which little is known save that he played 19 times with the old Montreal Maroons in the 1927-28 season. A speedy left winger, Brown was sold into the Can-Pro league and later finished his career in the International league.

BROWN, George
b. Winnipeg, Manitoba, May 17, 1912
He played for the Canadiens during the not-so-good years of the 1930s in a time when the Forum was nearly empty and the team on the verge of collapse. Brown played centre, and although he had been a scorer in Verdun, he couldn't produce the same kinds of numbers in the NHL. His career lasted from 1936 to '39 with the Habs, then continued for a few years in minor pro and finally with senior hockey in Quebec.

BROWN, Gerry
b. Edmonton, Alberta, July 7, 1917
d. Cornwall, Ontario, August 18, 1998
Everyone who makes it to the NHL possesses a remarkable skill in the game. Some make it their life's work; others toss it aside without a care. Brown played the game for many years despite playing only 23 games in the NHL with Detroit during wartime. (He later joined the Canadian Infantry Corps.) But he played in the minors until he had a chance to coach, and as a bench boss he moved from Oshawa to Quebec to Hamilton in junior A. He later accepted a position as scout for the Maple Leafs, and in 1962 became director of a hockey school for the Cornwall Recreation Department, teaching youngsters the fundamentals of the game.

BROWN, Greg
b. Hartford, Connecticut, March 7, 1968
Here's a guy hardly known in NHL circles but who has played the game for so long that he might well be the most decorated player for the U.S. internationally and the most international of Americans of the modern era. Between 1990 and '95 he played 94 NHL games with Buffalo, Pittsburgh, and Winnipeg, but he never played a full season and decided to see the world instead of slushing it out in the minors in his own backyard. He moved to Europe and played in Sweden and Germany, and he wore the USA sweater for the 1986 World Juniors up to the 1999 World Championships qualifying tournament. He played at the '92 Olympics in Albertville and in three World Championships besides.

BROWN, Harold "Hal"
b. Brandon, Manitoba, September 14, 1920
He was always known for his speed and ability to score goals, and that's why the Rangers called him up for 13 games in the '45-'46 season. He had led various leagues in goals and later became a fixture in the USHL until 1950-51, when he joined Denver. There, he was put on a line with Bing Juckes, and the two were asked to use their speed to check and prevent goals, a job the pair did admirably at the expense of their own production. Brown retired in 1953.

BROWN, Jeff
b. Ottawa, Ontario, April 30, 1966
Brown was a power-play specialist if ever there was such a beast. More than half his career points came on the power play, and 80 of his 154 career goals came with the man advantage. He was a big defenceman whom Quebec selected in the draft in 1984 and he quickly grew into his role as point man on the attack, often teamed with Normand Rochefort. He later moved on to other teams around the league, always contributing until he retired in 1998. His most notable foray in the playoffs came in 1994 when, with Vancouver, he played in game seven of the finals before losing to the Rangers.

BROWN, Jim
b. Phoenix, Arizona, March 1, 1960
Not too many players come out of the hazy glare of Arizona, but Jim Brown did, though not for long. After graduating from the University of Notre Dame, he played three games with Los Angeles in 1982-83 and was out of hockey a year later.

BROWN, Keith
b. Corner Brook, Newfoundland, May 6, 1960
He won the Pro Hockey Team Arm Wrestling championship in 1982 with partner John Marks by winning 6 matches in a row, but throughout his 16-year career he was slowed by serious injuries to his knees and shoulder. Brown played 14 of those years with Chicago before ending his NHL life with Florida in 1995. He went to the Stanley Cup finals in 1992, and four other times to the semis, but he never had the chance to hold the Cup for a sip of champagne. Brown stayed in Florida after retiring, and worked in real estate as well as doing work for the Christian community in West Palm Beach.

BROWN, Ken

b. Port Arthur, Ontario, December 19, 1948

Brown played goal for a total of 18 NHL minutes in a brief career, making his stay in the NHL one of the briefest even among the "one-game wonders" of the game. He allowed one goal for Chicago during a season he played mostly in the CHL, and he later played parts of two years in the WHA.

BROWN, Kevin

b. Birmingham, England, May 11, 1974

He has never played more than 23 games in a season, but Brown has been all over the hockey map since leaving junior in 1994. He had been drafted two years earlier by Los Angeles, but after just 30 games he was sent to Ottawa, Anaheim, and finally Hartford before getting another shot in the NHL. Since 1997 he has been a regular in the AHL, though after seven games with Edmonton in 1999-2000 his chances of getting another callup have gone from bad to worse.

BROWN, Larry

b. Brandon, Manitoba, April 14, 1947

New York, Detroit, New York. Got him, need him, got him. Brown did his fair share of bouncing from the time he joined the NHL in 1969 to the time he established himself with Los Angeles in 1972. By that point, he had missed most of the previous season with mono and his recuperation was further hampered by a summer bout of pneumonia. But once he got the old bod in order, he established himself as a perfectly reliable defenceman with the Kings became a regular for the next six years. Although he was claimed by the Oilers when they joined the NHL in 1979, he never got to play with Gretzky and the boys and finished his career in the minors a couple of years later.

BROWN, Mike

b. Surrey, British Columbia, April 27, 1979

Brown was a prospect who was part of the important trade between Vancouver and Florida that sent Pavel Bure to the land of the Keys and Ed Jovanovski to the Canucks. Brown played a single game with the Canucks in 2000-01, though he has yet to leave too deep an impression in the team's lineup.

BROWN, Rob

b. Kingston, Ontario, April 10, 1968

Sure, his dad, Bob, coached Kamloops, the team with which Rob played his junior hockey in the mid-1980s, but he put up numbers that rendered the coach's last name a moot point. Numbers? Try 173 and 212 points in his final two years of junior. He wasn't big – just 5'10" and 175 pounds – which is why he didn't go high in the draft, but when he got to Pittsburgh he played on a line with Mario Lemieux and helped number 66 win a scoring title or two. In Brown's second year, he had 49 goals and 115 points, but after that the bottom fell out of his career. He went down to 80, 58, and 47 points in succeeding years, and then the trades happened. In Hartford, he started off like a house on fire playing with Ron Francis and Pat Verbeek, but soon he was on the move again. He ended up in the minors, and his numbers improved. He led the IHL in assists and points three times, thus earning a reprieve

with Pittsburgh for the 1997-2000 period, only to return to the IHL thereafter. A huge talent not fully realized.

BROWN, Sean

b. Oshawa, Ontario, November 5, 1976

Since entering the NHL in 1996 with Edmonton, Brown has slowly developed into a steady, defensive defenceman for the Oilers, a proverbial tough customer who sticks up for his mates and clears the slot in front of his goalie. Now in the prime of his career, he'll not likely be named one of the Three Stars in any game soon, but his is the style of play every team needs to be successful.

BROWN, Dr. Stan ("Bus")

b. North Bay, Ontario, May 9, 1898

d. North Bay, Ontario, July 6, 1987

He was a rushing defenceman when there weren't any, a dentist who had a special flare with his hockey stick, and one of the fastest skaters of his era. He was born in North Bay, but lived almost all his life elsewhere, starting in 1915 when he played for Frank Selke's Berlin Union Jacks. He moved on to play for St. Mike's in Toronto and then attended U of T to study dentistry. From the day he graduated until the day his wife died in 1974, he practised dentistry first and played hockey second. He won the Allan Cup twice, and it was in the Soo that he first started to play professionally and work as a doctor. This was 1922. He was known as the Soo Flash because of his great speed, but he wound up in North Bay in 1926 without a team when the Detroit Greyhounds folded. By coincidence, Bill Cook of the Rangers was looking for a defenceman, and Brown jumped at the chance to play in New York in the NHL. That summer, he decided to set up his practice in the Walkerville area of Windsor and asked GM Lester Patrick for a trade to Detroit. A brash request, Patrick agreed only because of the quality of man who had asked for the favour. He played for the Cougars for half a season, then asked to be traded to Windsor of the International league. Jack Adams acquiesced. Brown won two championships with the Bulldogs and practised dentistry there for half a century, returning each summer to Lake Nipissing for a month. His wife passed away in 1974, and he returned to North Bay to bury her beside their adopted son, who had died in 1961. He retired to the Bay until his own death 13 years later.

BROWN, Wayne ("Weener")

b. Deloro, Ontario, November 16, 1930

The 1953-54 edition of the Seattle Bombers was a terrible team. It finished in last place in the WHL, but amazingly also produced the league's top two scorers – Guyle Fielder and Wayne Brown. Brown led the league with 49 goals, and his 81 points trailed only Fielder. As a reward for his great regular season, the Bruins called him up for four games in that year's semifinals against Montreal. Those were to be his only NHL games. He later was reinstated as an amateur and helped Canada win the gold medal at the 1959 World Championships with the Belleville McFarlands. He continued to play hockey for many years after, for the love of the game and not for the money.

Kevin Brown

Rob Brown

Sean Brown

Wayne Brown

Cecil Browne

Jack Brownschidle

Jeff Brubaker

Gordie Bruce

Murray Brumwell

BROWNE, Cecil ("Cece")

b. St. James, Manitoba, February 13, 1896
d. Winnipeg, Manitoba, August 13, 1985

Browne scored 2 goals in a 13-game NHL career with Chicago back in 1927-28, toward the end of his career. He had been bought by the Hawks after an outstanding season with Winnipeg in the AHA, and coming with him from that team was future Hall of Famer Charlie Gardiner. Browne was not as famous in the NHL, but in Manitoba he was the stuff of legend. After serving in the Royal Flying Corps during the First World War, he left his mark in his home province in baseball, football, lacrosse, and track and field. In 1970, he was named Manitoba's athlete of the century. He played in the CFL and later was a playing coach with Seattle in the PCHL toward the end of his hockey career.

BROWNSCHIDLE, Jack

b. Buffalo, New York, October 2, 1955

His strengths were skating and puckhandling; his weakness was a lack of self-will to push himself to the limit. His coach in St. Louis, Red Berenson, did what he could, but the defenceman proved both skilled and unpolished as the years flew by. Brownschidle was drafted by St. Louis in 1975 and joined the team after graduating from the University of Notre Dame two years later. St. Louis let him go on waivers on March 2, 1984, and he played his final 39 games with Hartford before ending up in the minors.

BROWNSCHIDLE, Jeff

b. Buffalo, New York, March 1, 1959

Younger brother of Jack, Jeff played but seven NHL games from 1981 to '83 with Hartford. He had graduated from the University of Notre Dame in '81, but was out of the game altogether just three years later.

BRUBAKER, Jeff ("Bru")

b. Frederick, Maryland, February 24, 1958

Brubaker accepted an offer from New England of the WHA in 1978 before he ever played for Boston, the NHL team that drafted him. He wound up going to Hartford the next year when the Whalers joined the NHL, but he knew he was nothing more than a fringe player and had counted on a brief minor league career before going into radio broadcasting. Surprisingly, teams kept looking to him for that clichéd toughness, and he kept fighting in the NHL for a variety of teams over the next decade.

BRUCE, David

b. Thunder Bay, Ontario, October 7, 1964

A career in hockey beset by serious injuries prevented Bruce from ever realizing what he could or could not do in the NHL. He missed much of the '87-'88 season due to mononucleosis, missed the end of the next season after tearing cartilage in his thumb, and missed much of two years from torn muscles in his stomach and groin. Yet when he was healthy, he scored 64 goals in 60 games in the IHL, and after being farmed out of the NHL for good in 1994, he still scored at an impressive rate in the minors for a few years.

BRUCE, Gordie

b. Ottawa, Ontario, May 9, 1919
d. Ottawa, Ontario, July 15, 1997

Bruce was a member of the Hershey Bears during their inaugural season, 1939-40, and won the Calder Cup with the team and later became its captain. He was a bit player with the Bruins the following year when they won the Stanley Cup, but after 15 games in '41-'42 his NHL days were almost over. He joined the Royal Canadian Army Service Corps and went overseas, playing hockey in England whenever possible. The Emerald Isle was his old stomping ground, for he had played with the Sudbury Tigers throughout Europe leading up to the 1938 World Championships in Prague (won by the Canadians). Upon being discharged, he was used for five more games by the Bruins, and then continued his career back in Hershey, eventually going into coaching.

BRUCE, Morley

b. North Gower, Ontario, March 7, 1896
d. Ottawa, Ontario, November 25, 1959

After beginning the 1917-18 season with Ottawa during the first year of the NHL's existence, Bruce visited a nearby registration centre and enlisted in the war on January 31, 1918, keeping him out of hockey for a year and a half. When he returned, he had the benefit of rejoining a Senators team that was about to become the first dynasty of sorts, winning Cups three times in four years (1920, 1921, 1923). Bruce was a member of the first two winning teams. He later retired to Ottawa and became secretary of the fire-prevention bureau of the Ottawa Fire Department.

BRULE, Steve

b. Montreal, Quebec, January 15, 1975

If you play for the love of the game, good things will happen. Just ask Brule. He was drafted by New Jersey in 1993, but didn't play his first game until the 2000 playoffs after five full years in the minors with the Albany River Rats. For that one game, he got his name on the Stanley Cup. Not a bad way to start a career. Or, perhaps, finish it. He was let go by the Devils in the summer, signed with Detroit, and has yet to return to the NHL.

BRUMWELL, Murray

b. Calgary, Alberta, March 31, 1960

Brumwell came and went without much fanfare. From 1980 to '88, he played snippets in the NHL while making a go of it in the CHL and AHL. All his 128 NHL games were with either New Jersey or Minnesota, though most of his last 9 years were of the minor-league sort.

BRUNET, Benoit

b. Ste. Anne de Bellevue, Quebec, August 24, 1968

In an age when players swap teams with regularity and no pangs of regret, Brunet managed to stay with Montreal from day one through the first dozen years of his career. He played junior in Quebec, was drafted by the Habs, developed in their system, and became a regular, winning the Cup in 1993 with the upstart team and continuing as the club fell into a funk. He has been the team's nominee for both the Bill

Masterton and King Clancy trophies and has averaged a point every two games throughout his career.

BRUNETEAU, Ed
b. St. Boniface, Manitoba, August 1, 1919
d. Omaha, Nebraska, July 30, 2002

Younger brother of the more famous Mud, Ed played parts of seven seasons in the NHL from 1940 to '49. In between, he won an Allan Cup with the Quebec Aces, and after his NHL days he continued to play in the minors, winding up with Omaha and playing under Mud, who had become the team's coach. Perhaps the highlight of his career came in the 1945 playoffs, when Detroit and Toronto went to seven games until the Leafs prevailed. In game six, Bruneteau scored the winner in overtime to extend the series and become hero for a night.

BRUNETEAU, Modere "Mud"
b. St. Boniface, Manitoba, November 28, 1914
d. Houston, Texas, April 15, 1982

As a kid in St. Boniface, young Modere attended DeAndreis High School. One of his teachers, Brother Vincent Brand, had trouble pronouncing Modere and nicknamed him Mud. The name stuck. He joined the Red Wings in 1935. In the first game of that season's semifinals, Bruneteau scored the only goal of the game at 16:30 of the sixth overtime period to end the longest game in NHL history. The Wings won the Cup that year and next, and Bruneteau went on to play his entire 11-year career with the Wings. He added a third Cup to his accomplishments in 1943. He played briefly in the minors to learn the ropes as a coach while still playing, and took over as Omaha's boss without skates in 1948. It was because of him that the United States league banned coaches from slamming their sticks against the side of the boards to get a referee's attention, a habit Bruneteau had developed much to the dismay of the on-ice officials. He settled in Omaha and later ran a bar.

BRUNETTA, Mario
b. Quebec City, Quebec, January 25, 1967

One of many, many Canadians to use his ancestry to play for Italy internationally, Brunetta played briefly for the Nordiques before moving to Italy to continue his career. He played in the 1995 and '98 World Championships for that country as well as in league play for almost a decade before trying teams in Sweden and Germany. The goalie started his junior career in Quebec before the Nordiques drafted him. In 40 career games with the team, he had a record of 12-17-1.

BRUNETTE, Andrew ("Bruno")
b. Sudbury, Ontario, August 24, 1973

Brunette had an outstanding final season of junior in 1992-93 when he led the OHL in goals (62), assists (100), and points (162). After playing his first three NHL seasons with Washington, he then embarked on an "expansion" career, playing for Nashville, Atlanta, and Minnesota in a span of four years. Although he didn't bring his scoring stick to the NHL, he did have goals in six successive games in the '97-'98 season and has developed into a reliable, second- or third-line left winger.

BRYDGE, Bill
b. Renfrew, Ontario, October 22, 1898
d. Kirkland Lake, Ontario, November 2, 1949

Although just over 5'7" Brydge tipped the Toledos at 190 pounds and was feared for his bone-crushing open-ice hits. His early career was postponed when he joined the army in 1917 in Sudbury but he returned to hockey upon being discharged. He came down from Port Arthur to play for the Toronto St. Pats in '26-'27, the year the team became the Leafs midway through the season. Two years later, he played for Detroit and then had a seven-year stay with the now-defunct New York Americans. Although he played 368 regular season games in 9 years, his teams never fared very well and he made only 2 appearances in the playoffs. After retiring, he moved to Kirkland Lake in 1937 to coach the Lake Shore Blue Devils and won the Allan Cup with that team. He later became an employee of the Donald Ropes and Wire Cloth Company of Hamilton for the Kirkland Lake area, but in 1947 became ill. He died in hospital two years later.

BRYDGES, Paul
b. Guelph, Ontario, June 21, 1965

A Guelph boy through and through, Brydges began playing hockey seriously with the Platers in the OHL, winning the Memorial Cup in 1986 with teammates Gary Roberts and Steve Chiasson. Although never drafted, he signed with Buffalo as a free agent and played his 15 NHL games with the Sabres in '86-'87. It became apparent his life was more minor than NHL, so after three more seasons he retired, at age 25, and returned home. He served as an assistant coach to the Guelph Storm for a year and then became a member of the city's fire department, a job he continues to hold.

BRYDSON, Glenn ("Swampy")
b. Swansea, Ontario, November 7, 1910
d. Rockwood, Ontario, December 8, 1993

The younger of the Brydsons had the longer of the careers in hockey. Glenn played junior in Toronto before signing with the Montreal Maroons in 1931. He stayed there some three and a half years and then was traded to Ottawa. But before he could play for the Senators, the team moved to St. Louis, and it was there Brydson continued his career in an ill-fated season with the team. Then it was on to commercial America – Chicago and New York – before he was relegated to the minors for the rest of his skating days. He settled in Toronto and ran his own hotel for many years after retiring.

BRYDSON, Gord
b. Toronto, Ontario, January 3, 1907
d. Mississauga, Ontario, February 4, 2001

Brydson left his mark on the hockey world for the eight games he played in Toronto during the 1929-30 season, but he left a far greater mark on this world for his life on the links, far removed from the ice lanes of the Arena Gardens. When he was seven years old, he ventured to the Toronto Golf Club to seek daily employment as a caddy, and for seven summers he dutifully bagged for the local wealthy. At 14, he retreated to Algonquin and Temagami, content to spend his days paddling and trapping his way to nightly fatigue. In the winters he

Ed Bruneteau

Mario Brunetta

Andrew Brunette

Bill Brydge

Glenn Brydson

Sergei Brylin

Jiri Bubla

Al Buchanan

Jeff Buchanan

Ron Buchanan

played hockey, but he always spent the sunny days on the golf course. He won the Ontario Open in 1930 and again in '44. He won the Canadian PGA Championship in 1944 and '48. And, most impressively, he placed second to Pat Fletcher in the 1954 Canadian Open. In 1961 and again in '65 he won the Canadian Senor PGA tournament. In 1931 he became golf pro at the Mississauga Golf Club, a position he held for the next 40 years. He even played a game for the Toronto Argonauts football club in 1926. He was always considered the finest dresser on any golf course and late in life was inducted into the Canadian Golf Hall of Fame. In 1969, his wife, Dorothy, became seriously ill, and Brydson took care of her for the remaining 13 years of her life. This devotion was not surprising given the circumstances under which they wed. The couple had planned a spring wedding in 1932. Trouble was, the team he was playing for, the Chicago Shamrocks, had advanced to the American league finals. Gord left the team and got married, without a care in the world about what anyone in hockey circles might have to say about his sudden departure.

BRYLIN, Sergei
b. Moscow, Soviet Union (Russia), January 13, 1974
It has taken Brylin a little time, but as he creeps toward the big three-oh he has established himself as one of New Jersey's best players. The Devils drafted him in 1992 and he played in two World Junior Championships for the mother country before coming to North America. In his first season, he joined a team that took advantage of the shortened 48-game schedule to win the Stanley Cup, and over the next three years he split his time between the farm team and the NHL. Since 1998, he has been a mainstay, and in 2000-01 had a career year with 23 goals after winning a second Cup the previous spring.

BRYZGALOV, Ilya
b. Togliatti, Soviet Union (Russia), June 22, 1980
Anaheim holds this goalie prospect in high regard and is in no hurry to rush him into the NHL. He played one game for the Ducks in 2001-02, and was also named as Russia's third goalie at the 2002 Olympics in Salt Lake City. He didn't play, but the experience of practising and being with the bronze-medal team was invaluable for the youngster.

BUBLA, Jiri
b. Usti nad Labem, Czechoslovakia (Czech Republic), January 27, 1950
Although Jiri Bubla attended nine World Championships as a player and established a record of international success almost unparalleled in Czech history, he should not have attended the 1987 Worlds in Vienna, Austria. He did quite a bit of travelling after his playing days (he was in the import business), but on this particular trip in '87 he was discovered by Austrian police to be importing four kilograms of heroin from Pakistan. He and a North Vancouver neighbour were charged and convicted, and Bubla was sentenced to five years in prison. His wife and two children, blind to his criminal ways, were left to fend for themselves in British Columbia. Bubla always talked about fruits and vegetables or crystal when pressed about the nature of

his imports, and it was known that he had few friends except for former teammate Ivan Hlinka. His conviction was stunning given the successes he had experienced as a player. In addition to his success at the Worlds, which included the stunning gold in 1971 at the expense of the Soviets, Bubla also played in two Olympics. He joined the Vancouver Canucks in 1981, where he played the last five years of his career. The defenceman retired in 1986 and fell into trouble with his neighbour, Joe Janda, who apparently convinced Bubla to get involved in smuggling drugs. Bubla's son, Jiri Slegr, later played in the NHL himself.

BUCHANAN, Al
b. Winnipeg, Manitoba, May 17, 1927
His was not a long stay in the NHL, four games all told between 1948 and '50 with the Leafs. Buchanan played for the vaunted Winnipeg Monarchs that won the 1946 Memorial Cup and later joined that team's greatest nemesis, the Marlies, in Toronto. After just a few seasons of the minors, though, Buchanan retired to pursue other interests.

BUCHANAN, Jeff
b. Swift Current, Saskatchewan, May 23, 1971
It took until he was 27 to realize a lifelong dream to play in the NHL, but finally, on his third team, Buchanan played with Colorado, one of the league's best teams. He came out of the west (Saskatoon, more precisely) and went straight to the IHL for six years. His rights were owned by Tampa Bay and Chicago along the way, but only the Avs would give him a shot. The ride lasted just nine games, but that's nine more than most hockey players enjoy.

BUCHANAN, Mike
b. Sault Ste. Marie, Ontario, March 1, 1932
He got it all wrong. He played in the NHL, and then he went to university! Buchanan played one game with Chicago in '51-'52, and after a brief time in the minors enrolled at the University of Michigan. After two years, he accepted an offer to play in Britain for a season, his last of any note on skates.

BUCHANAN, Ralph "Bucky"
b. Bout De L'Isle, Quebec, December 28, 1922
He was an incredible scorer in the minors and gave the NHL his son, Ron, a generation later, but Bucky managed just two harmless games of his own, with the Rangers in '48-'49. In the Pacific Coast league, he had scored 66 goals in one season, and after his stint with the Blueshirts he was a consistent scorer in the minors for a number of years.

BUCHANAN, Ron
b. Montreal, Quebec, November 15, 1944
While Bucky Buchanan was playing on the Montreal Navy team in '44-'45, his wife gave birth to a son, Ron, who went on to play in the NHL. Bucky and Ron hold a unique record: fewest NHL games played by a father-son team. Pa had played two, and Ron played five, three with Boston in '66-'67, and two with St. Louis in 1969-70. Ironically, Ron played with the Bruins in Bobby Orr's first year and then with St. Louis the year Orr scored his flying, diving goal to beat the Blues in

the 1970 Stanley Cup finals. After some time in the minors, he joined the WHA when that league formed in 1972 and spent four years there before retiring.

BUCHBERGER, Kelly
b. Langenburg, Saskatchewan, December 2, 1966
He had a large drop of oil tattooed on his butt (metaphorically speaking), so loyal a player was he for the Oilers from his entry in the NHL back in 1986. He was on two Cup teams with the Oil during the final hours of their heyday and developed into a team captain after Mark Messier signed his soul to the Rangers and Shayne Corson left. But all good things must pass, and Buchberger was made available by Edmonton in the 1999 Expansion Draft. He was scooped up by the Thrashers and quickly traded to Los Angeles, where he now has a crown tattooed on the other side of his butt (metaphorically speaking), though no new Cups are forthcoming in the foreseeable future.

BUCYK, Johnny ("The Beast"/ "Chief")
b. Edmonton, Alberta, May 12, 1935
You have to go back nearly half a century to find a reference to the name Bucyk that doesn't have Boston in the same sentence. He is everything the Bruins stand for, and he has been associated with that team since being traded from Detroit on June 10, 1957. Going the other way was a goalie named Sawchuk. Call it an even deal. Bucyk grew up in Edmonton before joining the Red Wings in 1955. The husky left winger had a promising start to his career, and when Sawchuk wanted to leave the Bruins, the deal proved workable for both parties. A cartoonist in the Hub gave Bucyk his nickname Chief because he thought the new player was an Indian. Bucyk wasn't, but he loved the name and it stuck. What did he not do in Boston? Over the next 21 years, he played most of his 1,540 career games there. He went far beyond 500 goals and 1,000 points. He captained the team, won 2 Stanley Cups, scored more than 20 goals 16 times. He played in seven All-Star Games and won two Lady Byng Trophies and a Lester Patrick Trophy. When he retired in 1978, his number 9 was retired and he has stayed with the organization from that day to this. He had his first wave of fame in the 1950s playing on the Uke Line with Bronco Horvath and Vic Stasiuk, a line so-called because all three were of Ukrainian heritage. Those were the days when there was little else to cheer about. The team never made the playoffs and was a decade away from success. Bucyk kept right on playing, though. By the time the Bruins had Orr, Esposito, and Sanderson, he was a veteran on the Cup-contending team, and incredibly he had his best

He was 36 when he scored 51 goals and 116 points in the '70-'71 season.
JOHNNY BUCYK

years late in life. He was 36 when he scored 51 goals and 116 points in the '70-'71 season, by far his best totals. A back injury jeopardized his career, but he wore a harness and produced a 40-goal season at age 38, a 31-goal season at 39, and a 20-goal year in his last full season when he was 42 years old. He had set up businesses in British Columbia in swimming pools and car repairs, believing these would occupy him when he retired. Instead, he remained in Boston, worked in TV and radio, and was a pioneer in the development of a team alumni, a job that has consumed him ever since.

BUCYK, Randy
b. Edmonton, Alberta, November 9, 1962
Being the nephew of Johnny Bucyk just wasn't as good as being the Chief himself. He was good, mind you, and went to Northeastern University on scholarship while studying civil engineering, but no one drafted him into the NHL. His first chance proved serendipitous, though, as Montreal signed him on January 15, 1986. Just a few months later, the Habs stunned the world by winning the Cup. Bucyk played only 17 regular-season games and 2 more in the playoffs on a line with Brian Skrudland and Lucien Deblois, but he got his name on the Cup. His NHL career lasted just two more games, two years later, with Calgary. Then it was down to the minors, in Salt Lake City, where he got to see the site of the 2002 Olympic Winter Games long before scandal rocked that city's successful bid.

BUHR, Doug
b. Vancouver, British Columbia, June 29, 1949
He played his entire career with the Kansas City Scouts. Six games in 1974-75. Got a couple of assists, not bad on such an awful team. He played a little in Trail, out west, then retired in '78.

BUKOVICH, Tony
b. Painesdale, Michigan, August 30, 1917
He never went quietly into any night, from start to finish. Bukovich got his NHL games in with Detroit, 17 in all during the war, but in 1947 he wanted what he wanted. Although he was playing for Cleveland in the AHL, he bought a tavern in Houghton, Michigan, and wanted to be released by the Barons so he could run his bar and play and coach for the local Portage Lake Pioneers in the Michigan-Wisconsin Hockey League. The Barons said, fine, go, but you're worth $3,000. Fans around Houghton went on a drive to raise the money to buy his contract, and sure enough, their efforts worked! He had pulled the same stunt just the year before, but the Barons had simply suspended him and he returned to the fold, though he finished that season with Minneapolis.

Kelly Buchberger

Randy Bucyk

Tony Bukovich

Jan Bulis

Mike Bullard

Hy Buller

Ted Bulley

Bruce Bullock

BULIS, Jan
b. Pardubice, Czechoslovakia (Czech Republic), March 18, 1978

Bulis started his career in Washington but went to Montreal in a multiplayer deal that sent Trevor Linden to the Caps. Jan had been the first man to reach 100 points in a season for the Barrie Colts back in junior, but the big centre joined a Habs team in flux. On a team renowned for its great players and numbers, he became part of a new generation of Canadiens players who wore crazy numbers, in his case 38.

BULLARD, Mike ("The Bullet")
b. Ottawa, Ontario, March 10, 1961

In his final two years of junior, Bullard scored 111 goals and 257 points, and after being drafted by Pittsburgh in 1980, he was one of the gifted players who came up to the NHL and continued to score. He reached his zenith in '83-'84 by recording 51 goals and 92 points with the Pens. The result was a long-term contract and the hallowed "C" for his sweater. Then his ego got in the way. Mario Lemieux arrived, and according to all reports Bullard didn't like the attention going from him to this 18-year-old hero. His production dipped as Mario became the world's second-greatest player, and after losing his temper one day in practice, coach Bob Berry took away his captaincy. Bullard demanded a trade, and a day later got it. He was on his way to Calgary, and Lemieux was on his way to the Stanley Cup. Ironically, Bullard had 103 points in his first full season with the Flames, but in that year's playoffs he fell victim to a Marty McSorley spear that nearly cost him his spleen. McSorley was suspended for three games for the barbaric act, and Bullard was traded again that summer, just before the Flames won the Cup. He went to St. Louis, then on to Philly, where Bobby Clarke told him to shed some of his 218 pounds. Bullard signed a large contract with the Leafs for '91-'92 under new GM Cliff Fletcher, but after one disappointing season he was out of the league and on his way to Europe, where he had a 10-year career, primarily in Germany.

BULLER, Hyman "Hy" ("The Blueline Blaster")
b. Montreal, Quebec, March 15, 1926
d. Cleveland, Ohio, August 1968

To be cute, many newspapers of Buller's day (the 1940s and '50s) called him "Hymie" to accentuate the Jewishness of his name and highlight his religious uniqueness in a league of Catholics and Protestants. Born in Montreal, he moved with his family to Saskatoon at age three, and as a kid he looked up to his older brother, Harry, who was a better hockey player on every level. Hy was an excellent swimmer and diver, but as he got older his other athletic endeavours fell by the wayside in favour of hockey. As the oldest boy, Harry had to find a job and gave up on hockey while Hy flourished. After getting two quick callups with Detroit during the war, he wound up in the American league and became one of the best defencemen around. NHL teams wanted Buller, but the Hershey Bears refused to part with him. The revered coach Frank Boucher compared Buller to Bill Quackenbush, a great rusher of the puck and

stickhandler. It was Boucher, with the Rangers, who finally got Buller back to the NHL in 1951, where he was paired with Allan Stanley on the blueline for three years. In the summer of 1954, Buller was traded to Montreal, but because he had established roots in Cleveland from his AHL days he decided to retire rather than report. During the summers with Hershey and Cleveland, he had sold sporting goods, and he went into that line of work immediately after returning home to Cleveland. He helped establish Ohio Boystown, a home where teenage boys could receive help. Buller died of cancer at age 42.

BULLEY, Ted
b. Windsor, Ontario, March 25, 1955

There could have been more there than there was, but what there was wasn't all bad. Bulley came out of junior in Quebec to play for Chicago in 1976, and it was there he had his two finest seasons, 1977-78 and '78-'79. The left winger had seasons of 23 and 27 goals, but in the summer of 1982 he was traded to Washington for nothing more than draft choices, always a bad sign. A year later he was in the minors. His greatest success came in the spring of '82 when the Hawks reached the semifinals in the playoffs. Bulley later became a firefighter in Chatham, Ontario.

BULLOCK, Bruce
b. Toronto, Ontario, May 9, 1949

A journeyman goaler, as they say, Bullock got into his first NHL game with Vancouver in his home and native Maple Leaf Gardens. He had been tending to his business in Seattle of the WHL when the Canucks' number-one man, Dunc Wilson, got hurt. Not confident with his backup, one Ed Dyck, Bullock was summoned from the Totems. In his first game, a 5-5 tie in December 1972, he wandered from his net, got caught, and threw his stick back to prevent a goal. The referee didn't whistle the mandatory penalty shot, and Bullock ended the strange game with a tie. He stuck around for another 13 games that season and played only 2 more NHL games, with Vancouver, over the next few years.

BURAKOVSKY, Robert
b. Malmo, Sweden, November 24, 1966

Burakovsky was drafted in 1985 by the Rangers but didn't make it to the NHL, with Ottawa, until eight years later at age 27. He stuck around for only half a season, spent the rest of his time in the minors, and then returned whence he came. He had started his career in Swedish league play, but after his failed NHL try he played all over Europe.

BURCH, Billy
b. Yonkers, New York, November 20, 1900
d. Toronto, Ontario, November 30, 1950

Technically, he was a New Yorker by birth, though Burch came to Toronto at a very young age and grew up there. As a kid, he was an outstanding athlete, excelling in football and lacrosse as well as hockey. He cut his teeth at the Aura Lee rink on Avenue Road just north of Davenport, at Jesse Ketchum Park not far away, and at Cottingham Square over toward Yonge Street. His childhood friends and teammates included Lionel Conacher and Roy Worters. Burch played football for the Central YMCA, quarterbacking the team to the Ontario Union championship. He played junior hockey with Aura Lee and later with the Toronto Canoe Club, where he won the OHA and Canadian championship. He joined the Hamilton Tigers in 1922 and remained with the team for two and a half years. In '24-'25, he was awarded the Hart Trophy, a season that ended in great controversy when the Tigers went on strike before the playoffs. They demanded more money, didn't get it, and were disqualified by the NHL. Tex Rickard bought the team and moved the Tigers to New York the next year, where they played as the New York Americans. Burch played seven seasons with New York's "other team" and because of his heritage was always a popular player. Dubbed Yonkers Billy Burch by the press, he was a scoring forward on a not very good team. He played out his career in '32-'33 with Boston and Chicago. Toward the end of that season, he broke his leg and decided to retire to Toronto. Burch was inducted into the Hockey Hall of Fame in 1950, the first of only six players to win both the Hart and Lady Byng trophies during their career (along with Buddy O'Connor, Stan Mikita, Bobby Hull, Wayne Gretzky, and Brett Hull).

BURCHELL, Fred ("The Pest"/ "The Skipper")
b. Montreal, Quebec, January 9, 1931
d. Verdun, Quebec, June 4, 1998
At 5'6" and 145 pounds, Burchell had a nasty bite to him for those who ignored his bark. As a kid, he was called Skippy, but in junior he became the Pest because he was always called on to shadow the enemy's best players, notably Jean Béliveau. When Fred got to the NHL, Skippy became the Skipper, perhaps for its more adult sound, but his role never changed. Although he played just four games with the Canadiens in the early '50s, he had a lengthy career in the minors, mostly in Quebec. So popular was he with the fans that he had his own cheering section that would follow his career and watch him play with religious zeal. He continued to play into the late 1960s, and in 1972 became coach of the Toledo Miners of the IHL. He was one of the first coaches to use four forwards on the power play, a move that added many goals to a weak-scoring team.

BURDON, Glen
b. Regina, Saskatchewan, August 4, 1954
When the Kansas City Scouts think highly of you, you know you're in trouble. And when they select you 20th overall in 1974, you'd better start thinking of a second career. Burdon came out of Regina, played 11 games with the Scouts, and then went on to a brief career in the minors.

BURE, Pavel ("The Russian Rocket")
b. Moscow, Soviet Union (Russia), March 31, 1971
It's a curious confusion of a nickname. On the one hand, it means he's the Russian version of the Canadian "Rocket," Maurice Richard, yet Bure has none of the insane competitive fire that drove Richard and gave him his greatest attribute. On the other hand, it refers simply to blazing speed, and that Bure has in spades. Five times he's scored 50 goals in the NHL – 60 goals twice – because of his speed. He is as exciting and dynamic a player as the league has seen, yet he is an enigma wrapped in a hockey sweater. His father, Vladimir, won three bronze medals and a silver at the 1968 and '72 Olympics as a swimmer, and from the time he was young, Pavel and brother Valeri were pushed by Vladimir to become athletes. The focus worked on a professional level, but it destroyed the family. Pavel burst onto the hockey scene at the 1989 World Junior Championships, playing on a line with Alexander Mogilny and Sergei Fedorov, the obvious heirs to the CCCP's famous KLM line of the previous era. Bure was terrified of defecting, fearing repercussions to his family, so they all left together in 1991. He dazzled with Vancouver from the get-go and became a fan favourite until the summer of 1998, when he demanded a trade and sat out the start of the following season until his wish was granted. He was sent to Florida, and although he continued to lead the league in goals he became *persona non grata* when the team failed to improve its place in the standings. When he went to the Rangers, he wore number 9 for the first time in honour of the

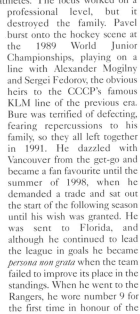

In 2000-01, he scored 29.5 percent of his squad's goals.
PAVEL BURE

Rocket. Along the way, Bure remained his own, isolated man. It has been many years since he last spoke to his father. He married a Los Angeles model but quickly left her. He has associated with Russian mobster Anzor Kikalishvili. His budding relationship with tennis star Anna Kournikova ended because of Sergei Fedorov. And he refuses to talk about his personal life. On ice, he has won umpteen international honours and has established his place in history as one of the NHL's greatest pure goal scorers. In 2000-01, he scored 29.5 percent of his squad's goals, a record for one man's contribution over a season to a team's total goals.

BURE, Valeri
b. Moscow, Soviet Union (Russia), June 13, 1974
Pavel Bure arrived in North America as one of the more talented players in the world not yet in the NHL. For Valeri, who arrived at the same time, his introduction to North America was more difficult. He had just turned 17, he was a prospect who had to apprentice in junior before going anywhere with his hockey career, and he had to follow in his brother's footsteps. From Spokane in

Billy Burch

Fred Burchell

Glen Burdon

Valeri Bure

Marc Bureau

the WHL he went on to the Montreal Canadiens, but the fit was far from perfect. Bure could not acclimatize to the media, and in '96-'97 he suffered two concussions and had his kidneys damaged. A trade, to Calgary, was the best thing that could have happened to him. He turned into an excellent scorer with the Flames, and in 1999-2000 he and Pavel set a record for most goals by two brothers in a season (Pavel had 93; Valeri had 35). In the summer of 2001, he was sent to Florida to join his brother, but this experiment proved less than successful and Pavel was traded to the Rangers. Days earlier, Valeri suffered a season-ending knee injury.

BUREAU, Marc
b. Trois Rivières, Quebec, May 19, 1966
How is it that a guy who can score oodles in junior managed so very little offence in the NHL? Bureau had size. He was given ice time. He scored in the IHL whenever he was sent down. But he just couldn't score with any of his NHL teams. Nonetheless, after 54 goals with Longueuil in 1986-87, Bureau has managed to survive in the NHL, going from team to team and chipping in half a dozen or so goals a year.

Bill Burega

BUREGA, Bill ("Wild Bill")
b. Winnipeg, Manitoba, March 13, 1932
The penalty king wherever he went and for whomever he played, Burega was one of the early proponents of helmets. He played four games with the Leafs in '55-'56 but beyond that had a career that spanned four decades, from junior in Winnipeg to senior hockey in Kingston. He routinely compiled more than 100 penalty minutes a season and became known as Wild Bill for his physical outbursts. No opposing forward went by him without feeling the wrath, and Burega's staying power proved the worth of his services.

Eddie Burke

BURKE, Eddie ("Shanty")
b. Toronto, Ontario, June 3, 1907
d. unknown
Burke developed with the Boston Tigers of the Can-Am league in the late 1920s and was called up to play for Boston during the '31-'32 season. He played 16 games for the Bruins and later went to the New York Americans, where he scored 20 goals in '33-'34. He was out of the league a year later and out of hockey altogether shortly after that.

Marty Burke

BURKE, Marty
b. Toronto, Ontario, January 28, 1905
d. March 7, 1968
Burke roomed with Howie Morenz for eight and a half years in Montreal and Chicago. Burke was a rough

In the space of two years, he played in the World Juniors, World Championships, and Olympics.
SEAN BURKE

defenceman. On the Canadiens, he paired with Sylvio Mantha, winning Stanley Cups in 1930 and '31. He had come to the Habs to replace Herb Gardiner, and his credentials were supplemented by an Allan Cup win the previous spring (1927) with Port Arthur. Although those were his only chances to drink from the bowl, Burke played in the NHL until 1938, when he moved to Saskatoon to coach the Quakers for a year. He then became manager of the Victoria Hotel in Calgary and part-owner of C.W. Boon and Co., a wholesale tobacco firm in Edmonton. While living in Calgary, he coached the local Stampeders and guided them to the Allan Cup in his first year, losing to the Kirkland Lake Blue Devils. After two more seasons, the league changed hands, so Burke kept active by organizing the HMCS Navy team. After the war, he took a greater interest in golf and curling, though the hotel was where his heart was. Hockey people from all over Canada visited this place of special renown and talked up Burke about the game. He was only too happy to oblige.

BURKE, Sean
b. Windsor, Ontario, January 29, 1967
Sean Burke's career is a tough one to pin down. His reputation is so very much stronger than his performance would indicate, his experience outdoing his results in equal measure. After graduating from the Marlies in 1986, Burke was the top young goalie prospect entering the NHL. He enhanced his reputation by playing internationally at every opportunity. In the space of two years, 1986-88, he played in the World Juniors, World Championships, and Olympics, and at the end of the '87-'88 season he played 13 games with New Jersey, posting an impressive record of 10-1-0. But Burke never developed. A big man, he was given extra time to prove himself, but wherever he went, mediocrity seemed to follow. After New Jersey traded him, Burke played for six more NHL teams, never once having a record better than .500. Since 1989, he has played in just 12 playoff games, though when he got to Phoenix he performed particularly well under new owner Wayne Gretzky. Nonetheless, Gretzky bypassed him for the 2002 Canadian Olympic team, and Burke's career, paradoxically, continues despite its lack of brilliance. His finest moment came in 1997 when he led Canada to a gold medal at the World Championships in Finland.

BURMEISTER, Roy
b. Collingwood, Ontario, August 12, 1906
d. unknown
He came down from the Owen Sound area and wound up in New Haven, where he had the chance to get

noticed by the New York Americans. Burmeister played the 1929-30 season with the Amerks and then small parts of the two successive years while maintaining a spot on the Eagles roster in the minors. He later played minor pro for a few more years before retiring in 1939.

BURNETT, Kelly
b. Lachine, Quebec, June 16, 1926
Burnett retired early in the 1960-61 season while a member of the Montreal Royals. Although he was only 34, he had suffered a bad back injury in the previous year's playoffs while leading the team to the championship, but the back hadn't healed as he had hoped and he wanted to pursue a career as a golf pro. Risking further injury would have jeopardized both sports careers. Burnett played all his hockey in the minors with the exception of three games with the Rangers in '52-'53. A small and speedy centre, he was equally a capable goal scorer and a set-up man throughout his career.

BURNS, Bobby
b. Manitoulin Island, Ontario, April 4, 1905
d. Madison, Wisconsin, August 12, 1995
Scotch, vermouth, and benedictine over cracked ice he is not. But he was a blade artist of some renown in the American Hockey Association throughout the 1930s. Burns played bits and pieces of three seasons in the late 1920s with Chicago in the NHL. The left winger failed to distinguish himself, and as a result had the opportunity to make his mark in the AHA. He later settled in Chicago and worked for Mirror Reflector in that city.

BURNS, Charlie
b. Detroit, Michigan, February 14, 1936
At practice in 1951 with the St. Michael's Buzzers, Burns fell headfirst into the boards at Ted Reeve Arena in Toronto and lost consciousness. After a week in hospital and still no signs of life, he was given last rites when hours of surgery didn't seem to revive him. But he came out of his coma, a steel plate in his head, and when doctors told him to focus on life and forget about hockey, he nodded. Within a few months, he was out looking for a helmet so he could play again. He joined the Marlies and won a Memorial Cup, then joined the Whitby Dunlops, with whom he won a gold medal at the 1958 World Championships. He was named most valuable player, and Detroit coach Jack Adams took note. Burns joined the Wings as a defensive centre and later played four years with Boston, during which time his reputation took a hit for the worse. In a home-and-home series with the Leafs, the Bruins received penalties for high-sticking, cross-checking, and fighting. Toronto coach Punch Imlach decreed his team would now treat Burns like any other player, implying they had taken things a little easy on him because of his previous head injury. Later that year, Chicago's Pierre Pilote hit him hard, and Burns wound up in the hospital with a concussion, though undeterred. Between 1963 and '67, Burns was in the minors full time and his career got going again only after expansion. In the six years after the NHL doubled in size in 1967, Burns played for Oakland, Pittsburgh, and Minnesota, establishing himself as perhaps the best defensive

forward in the game. He later coached the Stars in '74-'75 and then made his way to Connecticut, where he worked for a company that made Sikorsky helicopters.

BURNS, Gary
b. Cambridge, Massachusetts, January 16, 1955
The Leafs drafted him 191st overall in 1975, but they didn't want him. The Bruins signed him as a free agent on October 10, 1978, but they didn't want him. The Rangers signed him on September 16, 1980, and they used him, but only for 11 regular-season games in 1980-81 and 4 playoff games the next year. He averaged more than 20 goals a year in the minors, but never got back to the NHL.

BURNS, Normie
b. Youngstown, Alberta, February 20, 1918
d. Marion, Florida, February 23, 1995
It's a good thing Burns got his NHL games in at the start of the war because shortly thereafter he joined the Royal Canadian Air Force and never returned except to play in the minors. He played 11 games with the Rangers in '41-'42 and then played with a number of war teams before picking things up in the American league. After retiring in 1949, he settled in Hartford.

BURNS, Robin
b. Montreal, Quebec, August 27, 1946
He was always the funny guy, the guy who'd goof around in hotel lobbies and airport areas, keeping the team loosey-goosey. He wore number 13 just for the hell of it, and played on a pair of lousy teams during his career in the 1970s, first Pittsburgh and then the Scouts of Kansas City. With K.C., he played on a line with Simon Nolet and Dave Hudson, yet despite getting 31 goals in 2 seasons he was known for his sandpaper touch around the neck. One writer of the day observed that Burns couldn't score into the Grand Canyon. He later became vice-president of sales and marketing for Micron Sports Products.

BURR, Shawn
b. Sarnia, Ontario, July 1, 1966
Early in his career, scouts thought Burr resembled another player the Wings drafted, Steve Yzerman. Burr had size and speed and good hands, and had a competitive edge that separated him from many. All of this may have been the case, but early on in their careers, Yzerman proved he was no Shawn Burr. Stevie Y went on to establish himself as one of the greatest players of all time, and Burr became a reliable forward with the Wings for 11 years until he was traded to Tampa. He just missed out on the two Cups Detroit captured and instead found himself a veteran on a crummy team. He scored 20 goals three times with Detroit and also represented Canada at the 1990 World Championships, a fourth-place finish for the team.

BURRIDGE, Randy
b. Fort Erie, Ontario, January 7, 1966
Perhaps if size hadn't deterred so many teams and scouts from considering Burridge a legit NHL player, he never would have made it to the big loop. He stood 5'9" and weighed (generously) 188 pounds but he had a tenacity that reminded Boston coach Butch Goring of

Charlie Burns

Norm Burns

Robin Burns

Shawn Burr

Randy Burridge

Dave Burrows

Adam Burt

Cummy Burton

Eddie Bush

Rod Buskas

his own hardships breaking into the league a generation earlier. Boston drafted him, and Burridge became a feisty, skilled regular who thrived under Goring. He had seasons of 27 and 31 goals, and after two off years the B's traded him to Washington, where he revived briefly. Burridge played in the 1992 All-Star Game and scored a goal, but his next season was wrecked by a serious knee injury. He bounced back with two 25-goal seasons later on and kept right on playing until 1999.

BURROWS, Dave ("Bone Rack")
b. Toronto, Ontario, January 11, 1949
A workhorse was what he was called, a guy the coach would play for half a game or more, in all situations. A guy you needed if your team was going to win. That's what Pittsburgh had when it acquired Burrows in 1971, and for seven years he was a rock on defence and a heart in the eyes of the fans at the Igloo. He was traded to Toronto, and after a serious knee injury six games into his time with his new team, his game changed enough that the Leafs traded him two years later, even though he was supposed to be with the Blue and White for the rest of his career. He was sent back to the Penguins with Paul Gardner for Kim Davis and Paul Marshall, another in a series of horrific trades the Leafs made during this time. After retiring, Burrows settled in Brampton and started his own industrial maintenance business. He later worked in Parry Sound for the local Optimist Club.

BURRY, Berthold "Bert"
b. Toronto, Ontario, 1909
d. unknown
Little is known about Burry beyond the fact that he played four games for the old Ottawa Senators back in '32-'33 and little more elsewhere.

BURT, Adam
b. Detroit, Michigan, January 15, 1969
After captaining Team USA to a fifth-place finish at the 1989 World Junior Championships in Alaska, Burt began his career with Hartford, the franchise for whom he played more than a decade, including the '94-'95 season when he was team captain. He was a big, strong defenceman who established himself almost immediately as NHL calibre, but in his ten and a half seasons with the team he played exactly four playoff games. He was later traded to Philadelphia and then to Atlanta. Burt also played for the U.S. at the World Championships in 1993 (seventh-place finish) and 1998 (twelfth-place finish). His career ended prematurely because of a herniated disc injury from which he could never fully recover. Burt joined the Champions for Christ, an organization that promotes athletics and the Bible.

BURTON, Cumming "Cummy"
b. Sudbury, Ontario, May 12, 1936
In 1960-61, Burton was a good two years beyond his last NHL game. He was down in the EPHL playing for Sudbury, when his goaler, Carl Wetzel, went berserk after referee Bruce Simms allowed a Seattle goal that Wetzel objected to. Wetzel smacked the ref with his stick and tossed the puck, earning a game misconduct. Winger Burton, who had scored two goals

in the game for the Wolves, donned the pads and was perfect the rest of the way in a 3-3 tie. In a more traditional vein, Burton played parts of three seasons with Detroit, a symbolic time given that his uncle was Larry Aurie, the great number 6 of the Red Wings during the 1930s. In fact, Burton lobbied long and hard to have Aurie's number retired officially, even though no one had worn 6 since. In fact, in '57-'58, Burton wore number 6 in tribute to his uncle, the one and only time from then until now that number has been used in Detroit.

BURTON, Nelson
b. Sydney, Nova Scotia, November 6, 1957
In junior, Burton combined a modicum of scoring talent with a maximum of fighting talent to make his presence known come the 1977 draft, when Washington chose the large left winger. But despite his double prowess, the Caps summoned him for only eight games over two seasons before trading him to Minnesota, and the Stars had no NHL use for him at all. Burton frequently had more than 300 penalty minutes in a given year and scored a career-high 20 goals with Erie in the EHL in 1980-81. He later returned to the Washington area and became head coach of the Washington Little Capitals, a major midget AAA all-star team for 16-year-olds.

BUSH, Eddie
b. Collingwood, Ontario, July 11, 1918
d. London, Ontario, May 31, 1984
For some 43 years, Eddie Bush held an NHL playoffs record no one could match, let alone top. On April 9, 1942, while his Red Wings played the Leafs in the finals, he scored a goal and had four assists, a five-point night that remained the standard until Paul Coffey improved the mark by one assist on May 14, 1985. Bush went to war shortly after his historic game and never played again in the NHL, though his career in hockey would last until 1978. During the war, Bush played for Toronto, Dartmouth, and the Oldham Mosquitoes in the RCAF, and he continued to play until 1950 when he began what would become a lengthy coaching career. As a player, he was known to be a tough hombre, once taping his stick to a broken arm so he could dress for a playoff game. As a coach, he became known as a disciplinarian who would brook no dissent or lax play. He coached in Collingwood, Kitchener, Pittsburgh, Memphis, and Hamilton, among other stops. While with Hamilton, he once got into a fight with Howie Young who was in the stands cheering too loudly, Bush felt, for the opposition. Young wound up in jail, and Bush was fined, though the coach eventually led those Red Wings to the Memorial Cup in 1962. He also coached the Guelph Biltmores while Rod Gilbert and Eddie Shack were there, and he later got a brief NHL chance with the hapless Kansas City Scouts. In 32 games, he had a record of just 1-23-8 before being let go. He died in a London hospital while undergoing treatment for lung cancer.

BUSKAS, Rod
b. Wetaskiwin, Alberta, January 7, 1961
A defenceman of size, Buskas scored but 19 goals in an 11-year NHL career, a sure sign hat he was wanted

for more than his slapshot. He was a late draft choice by Pittsburgh in 1981 but managed to make the team during the '82-'83 season and hang on to his job for seven years. He later played for three other teams, though his playoff success was nothing to brag about. Some 556 regular-season games gave way to only 18 in the playoffs. He finished his career in the IHL before retiring in 1995. Buskas relocated to Henderson, Nevada, where he teaches aviation.

BUSNIUK, Mike
b. Thunder Bay, Ontario, December 13, 1951
Education means options, and options mean freedom. Even if they are never exercised, knowing one has options allows one breathing room. Busniuk was a good hockey player, but he came out of the University of Denver with a teaching certificate and a minor in math, and for him this meant guaranteed employment after his playing days were over. And for him, that meant just about any time. He played four years in the minors, winning the championship each time. But after being drafted by Montreal, he knew there was no chance in Hades he'd be playing for les Habitants. Just as he was about to pack his bags and move to Europe, Behn Wilson, a Flyers defenceman, got hurt and Busniuk was called up to the NHL team. For two seasons, he was a tough and dependable regular, but he knew his NHL days were done after another season in the minors. He moved to Italy and played there for a few years, then returned home to coach in the AHL. His daughter, Kate, also got the hockey bug, and is the head coach of the Trinity College women's bantam team in West Hartford. Busniuk still returns to Thunder Bay occasionally to teach at women's hockey schools.

BUSNIUK, Ron
b. Fort William, Ontario, August 13, 1948
The older brother of Mike, Ron played just six NHL games before moving into the WHA for a four-year career. He finished with the Edmonton Oilers in '77-'78, just missing out on the arrival of Wayne Gretzky. He was a rightwinger with the proverbial toughness, and after he retired he moved to Thunder Bay. His son, Bryson, played hockey at the University of Vermont.

BUSWELL, Walt
b. Montreal, Quebec, November 6, 1907
d. St. Lustache, Quebec, October 16, 1991
Buswell made the Wings to start the '32-'33 season and established a reputation as a reliable defenceman. He was with the team for three years, but just before the Wings were about to win back-to-back Stanley Cups

he was traded to Montreal during that team's leanest years. Buswell partnered with Babe Siebert on the blueline, and after the Babe retired Buswell became Montreal captain for a year before himself retiring.

BUTCHER, Garth ("Butch")
b. Regina, Saskatchewan, January 8, 1963
His is a kaleidoscopic career. Look at it one way, and you see an offensive defenceman who could fight with the best of them. That was junior hockey. Look at it another way, and you see a devoted team man who went through walls for his mates. Another turn shows a survivor who managed to stay in the NHL for 14 years despite limited skills. Look at it again and you see a fighter, a guy who liked to drop the gloves, not the puck. His last year in junior saw him register an unlikely combination of points (92) and penalty minutes (318), and that led the Canucks to draft him 10th overall in 1981. He remained with Vancouver for 10 years, but the team had almost no playoff success and he was traded to St. Louis, where he became the most popular player on the team, a man who fought like a maniac on the ice, and on off-days visited hospitals and retirement homes. He retired in 1995 and settled in Bellingham, Washington, where he coaches and runs local minor hockey programs, while operating a real estate business in nearby Langley, B.C.

His last year in junior saw him register an unlikely combination of points (92) and penalty minutes (318).
GARTH BUTCHER

BUTENSCHON, Sven
b. Itzehoe, West Germany, March 22, 1976
Born in Germany but raised in Winnipeg, Butenschon played junior hockey in Brandon, where he won the WHL championship in 1995-96. He had been drafted by Pittsburgh two years earlier and played his first three years with the Penguins before being acquired by Edmonton on March 13, 2001, for Dan Lacouture. Nonetheless, the defenceman has spent the majority of his career so far in the minors.

BUTLER, Dick
b. Delisle, Saskatchewan, June 2, 1926
Little Dickie, as he was sometimes called, sure could fire the puck and score goals. Even when he was with Chicago for just seven games in 1947-48 he managed to score twice, and in the minors he routinely scored 20, sometimes 30, and once even 40 goals. But seven games was all he saw in the NHL.

BUTLER, Jerry ("Bugsy")
b. Sarnia, Ontario, February 27, 1951
In the 1974 playoffs, Butler's New York Rangers were fighting Philadelphia when Butler was hurt in a fight with Rick MacLeish. He didn't say a word, though, because he wanted to play. He played the next game,

Mike Busniuk

Ron Busniuk

Walt Buswell

Sven Butenschon

Dick Butler

Viacheslav
Butsayev

Yuri Butsayev

Gord Buttrey

Petr Buzek

Steve Buzinski

too, until the pain was so bad he couldn't move. The Rangers lost that game and were eliminated, and the next day Butler went to the team doctor. Tests were done that day and the next, and then the doctor hustled Butler into surgery to remove a ruptured spleen. Butler wasn't big, but he was hockey-tough, to be sure. He managed to stay in the NHL for 11 years as a checker, a fourth-liner who would play every shift against the Gretzkys of the league and agitate his opponents to distraction. But when he retired in 1983, he had nothing. He had finished grade 13 in Sarnia but dropped out of university when courses and hockey became too much. At the age of 31, he returned to high school – grade 12 – to upgrade his marks in order to qualify for the engineering program at the University of Manitoba. He did just that, went on to U of M, and graduated with a degree in civil engineering in 1986. He now works for the City of Winnipeg as a senior planner. His determination and strength on the ice translated to a commensurate will off it.

BUTSAYEV, Viacheslav
b. Togliatti, Soviet Union (Russia), June 13, 1970
His was not a career that reached full bloom in the NHL, but it was a full career regardless, notable for international and European play over and above his 132 NHL games. He skated for six teams in six years in the big time, but before and after Butsayev represented his native Russia frequently at the great tournaments. He played in three World Championships (1991, '93, and '97), one World Junior (1990), and one Olympics (1992) in addition to league play in both Russia and Sweden.

BUTSAYEV, Yuri
b. Togliatti, Soviet Union (Russia), October 11, 1978
Brother of Viacheslav, Yuri seems destined for a finer career than his sibling now that he has established himself as one of the new-generation Red Wings ready to inherit a position on a team getting old quickly. Although the Red Wings drafted him in 1997, they couldn't reach a deal with him for two years. During that time, he played in the Russian league, and in 1999 he finally joined the NHL, making the Detroit roster immediately. Since then, he has improved his skating and shown some speed and scoring ability.

BUTTERS, Bill
b. St. Paul, Minnesota, January 10, 1951
He started off as a fighter and finished as a Christian who sought peace and happiness. Butters attended the University of Minnesota, where he had consecutive seasons with 100 penalty minutes, a true oddity for U.S. college hockey. He left in 1973 and played in the minors for two years before signing with the Minnesota Fighting Saints, where he lived up to the fighting part of the name more than the saints part. He later wound up in New England with the Whalers, but a money dispute ended his time there. The Minnesota North Stars settled the $9,000 disagreement to take him on, and he played 72 games over the next 2 years in the NHL. He retired shortly thereafter and became involved in the Christian Athletes Hockey Camps, helping children ages 10 to 17 develop both their hockey skills and their life skills in a Christian environment.

BUTTREY, Gord
b. Regina, Saskatchewan, March 17, 1926
He played for Chicago during the war, 1943-44, 10 games that didn't change the world or even alter the Hawks' fortunes. But then again, he was only 17 at the time. Buttrey never developed enough to the satisfaction of any other NHL team and he spent the next dozen years in the minors, one of the youngest ever to play in the big leagues, and one of the quickest exits as well.

BUYNAK, Gord
b. Detroit, Michigan, March 19, 1954
No, he and Bruce Affleck were not joined at the hip, but they were joined at the airport, it seemed. Buynak and Affleck were sold to St. Louis by Vancouver on November 9, 1979, while both were playing for Dallas in the CHL. Four months later, both were sold right back to Vancouver! Buynak never played for the Canucks (Affleck played five games for them that year), though he had played four games with St. Louis back in '74-'75, his only NHL action.

BUZEK, Petr
b. Jihlava, Czechoslovakia (Czech Republic), April 26, 1977
If you need a story of inspiration, of human triumph and extraordinary perseverance, Buzek is your man. He was a teen who had it all, a tall, speedy hockey player who was a sure 1st-round draft choice in 1995. Then June 3, 1995, when he and a friend were driving home at night. Buzek fell asleep at the wheel. His car hit a tree, and his friend got off easy with a broken nose. Not Buzek. He broke both legs, a kneecap, a wrist, a cheekbone, his nose, his forehead, and suffered a concussion. He was unconscious for two days, and when he woke up doctors told him his right leg was going to have to be amputated. He refused. For four weeks, he fought for his life. Doctors told him he'd be wheelchair-bound. Meanwhile, back in the NHL, the Dallas Stars drafted Buzek 63rd overall. A preposterous choice given that he was in a wheelchair being told he wasn't going anywhere fast. Buzek worked and exercised and trained until finally he could put skates on. He had a long plate and 10 screws put in his left leg. He had two screws put in his right knee, seven screws and a plate put in his right ankle, two screws put in his left wrist. Airport security goes ballistic when he's anywhere near a departure gate. Just 15 months later, he was playing in the IHL, and the year after that he played two games for the Dallas Stars. He played twice more for them the next year, and then Atlanta claimed him in the Expansion Draft and turned him into a starting defenceman. In February 2000 in Toronto, he played at the All-Star Game. An heroic milestone for a once-dead guy.

BUZINSKI, Steve ("Buzzie")
b. Dunblane, Saskatchewan, October 15, 1917
d. Swift Current, Saskatchewan
A nickname, by definition, is a diminutive, a friendly, jokey, or alternate name. So the fact that someone called Buzinski "the puck goes inski" does not mean that's what his teammates called him in the dressing room or hotel lobby. Still, the phrase was apt. He truly

was an awful goalie, even by his own admission. He replaced Sugar Jim Henry in goal during the war, 1942-43 to be exact, and in only nine games Buzinski allowed 55 goals to pour past him. Fortunately, he also had a good sense of humour, and when the Rangers decided not to play him any more, they kept him on and listed him as a member of the public relations department. Truth was, though, he enlisted in the army at season's end, and after the war he returned to senior hockey in Saskatchewan, where he had been before being summoned to Broadway. After retiring in 1953, he lived in Swift Current and worked provincially for the Department of Agriculture.

BYAKIN, Ilja
b. Sverdlovsk, Soviet Union (Russia), February 2, 1963
He was one of the oldest draft choices in the history of the NHL. In 1993, at age 30, Byakin was selected 267th overall by Edmonton. Why? Well, the defenceman was a star in his native Russia. He had played in eight World Championships, an Olympics, and a World Junior tournament, and no NHL team had staked a claim to him. The Oilers got him to Edmonton for the '93-'94 season, and he had a decent season. Not decent enough, however, to stop the Oil from releasing him, and San Jose signed him as a free agent. He played 13 games during that lockout-shortened year and decided North America wasn't for him, returning to Europe to continue his career first in Sweden and then back in Russia.

BYCE, John
b. Madison, Wisconsin, August 9, 1967
Out of Wisconsin came a hockey player who wanted to see the world with stick in hand and puck at skates. Byce graduated from the University of Wisconsin to play briefly for Boston from 1989 to '92, but he couldn't crack the lineup and ended up in the minors. He played for a time in Sweden, then returned to the U.S. to play in the minors for a number of years, and then, in 1999, he accepted an offer to play in Britain, where he has happily remained ever since.

BYERS, Gord
b. Eganville, Ontario, March 11, 1930
Being a member of the One-Game Wonder club, even in the NHL, is not that exclusive. There are more than a hundred names on that list. But one-game wonders who have scored a point in their only NHL game is something else, a much shorter, more exclusive list. Byers is one such name, for when he played with the Boston Bruins in 1949-50 for a single contest, he picked up an assist. It's always a curious fact, because one would think anyone who achieved such a small but important milestone would surely be kept for a second game, even just to see how long his "hot streak" might last. Not so with Byers.

BYERS, Jerry
b. Kentville, Nova Scotia, March 29, 1952
It's not a good sign when a 11-year-old beats out an up-and-coming 21-year-old for a place on the roster at the start of a season, but such was the fate of Byers when he attended Minnesota camp in the fall of 1973. He lost his job to Dean Prentice, old man of the

league, and started the year in the minors, though he did play in 10 games for the Stars that year without registering a point. Therein lay the problem. Byers had scored 41 goals twice in junior with Kitchener, but he scored only 3 times in 43 career NHL games with Minnesota, Atlanta, and the Rangers. He later played in both Switzerland and Japan.

BYERS, Lyndon ("L.B.")
b. Nipawin, Saskatchewan, February 29, 1964
Only an odd duck could have a middle name of Svi, and a leap-year baby certainly qualifies. Byers played 10 years in the NHL according to the stats, but not once did he play a full season. Often he spent part of the year in the minors, but more frequently he spent part of the year in the hospital with injuries to various parts of his battered body. His foot took a pounding, forcing him to miss almost the entire '90-'91 season, and assorted other broken bones and pulls and strains took their toll and prevented him from reaching his full potential.

BYERS, Mike
b. Toronto, Ontario, September 11, 1946
Byers came out of Toronto with the Memorial Cup Marlies in 1967 to play briefly for the Leafs and Philadelphia, but it wasn't until he ended up in Los Angeles that he was given a chance to play on a regular basis. He had 27 goals for the Kings in '70-'71, but after just 28 games and 4 goals the following year he was traded to Buffalo. This was the beginning of the end for Byers. He played out the season with coach Joe Crozier, whom he came to despise, and rather than play another season under "Crow" decided to jump to the WHA. He happily joined the L.A. Sharks, but as soon as he realized how bush league the operation was he was just as happy to leave. After retiring a few years later, Byers settled in Los Angeles and became senior vice-president for a banking and investment company.

BYLSMA, Dan
b. Grand Haven, Michigan, September 19, 1970
He and his father have written three books to date, two on hockey: *So Your Son Wants to Be in the NHL*, *So You Want to Play in the NHL*, and *Pitcher's Hand Is Out*. Bylsma started out as Winnipeg Jets property back in 1989, but the Jets did nothing with him and he signed as a free agent with Los Angeles five years later. During the next five years, he played most of three seasons with the team, but the Kings struggled and Bylsma again was a free agent, this time signing with Anaheim in 2000. He also publishes his own newsletter and maintains a Web site, www.danbylsma.com in an attempt to provide advice and assistance to kids.

BYRAM, Shawn
b. Neepawa, Manitoba, September 12, 1968
The NHL didn't want him; he tired of the minors; the Brits took him into their fold happily. He played five NHL games from 1990 to '92, but after a career too deeply rooted in the minors, Byram took off for Europe, landing in Britain in '94 and becoming a fixture in Ayr, Scotland, three years later, where he continues to play.

John Byce

Jerry Byers

Lyndon Byers

Mike Byers

Dan Bylsma

CAFFERY, Jack

b. Kingston, Ontario, June 30, 1934
d. Toronto, Ontario, December 2, 1992

He was the first player to use a backward grip for face-offs (both hands in the same direction on the stick), and he was one of three NHLers of the era to reject pro baseball contracts in favour of hockey. While playing junior at St. Mike's, he was also being pursued by the Cleveland Indians who wanted him to play ball. Caffery had pitched for Evansville before signing with the Milwaukee Braves, but in 1957 made a clean break to focus on the ice sport. (Doug Harvey of Montreal had also signed with the Braves and the Hawks' Frank Martin had been approached by the Brooklyn Dodgers.) After three games with his hometown Leafs as an 18-year-old, Caffery was claimed by the Bruins and began his Boston life by scoring the game-winning goal, at Maple Leaf Gardens, against his old club with friends and family watching. The intent was to have him kill penalties, but he quickly found himself playing alongside Vic Stasiuk and John Peirson. His stay in Boston was short. A serious knee injury hurt both his skating and his fastball, though he wouldn't acknowledge the disability. Eddie Shore of Springfield bought his rights, and Caffery continued to juggle ball and ice, even throwing a few fastballs for the Milwaukee Braves down the stretch in 1960.

CAFFERY, Terry

b. Toronto, Ontario, April 1, 1949

The younger brother to Jack by some 15 years, Terry had no two-sport choices to make in life. Small, rugged, and fearless, he dreamed of the NHL from the get-go, though Jack's injuries also pointed to the ephemeral nature of a career in hockey. Alas, Terry blew his knee out in a game in '72–'73 and missed an entire season recovering. Drafted by Chicago, though assigned to play for the Marlies in Toronto, he played briefly with the Hawks and North Stars before establishing himself as a regular in the WHA. The knee never fully recovered, though, and he retired in 1976.

CAHAN, Larry ("Hank")

b. Fort William, Ontario, December 25, 1933
d. June 25, 1992

In a career that lasted some 24 years, Hank's rap sheet is speckled inconsistently with NHL glitter. A couple of seasons with Toronto, then the minors. Three with the Rangers, minors, more with New York, the minors. Then came expansion and Cahan was a wanted man… by the Oakland Seals, hockey's version of Siberia. Next: a trade to Los Angeles via Montreal, and a welcoming handshake from coach Red Kelly. When he joined the Kings, Cahan was the only man over 30 on the roster. An able passer, skater, and hitter, he provided daily lessons in life on the blueline for the team. Although he didn't intend to stay long with the Kings, when Bill White left the team Cahan was offered a lucrative three-year contract to shore up a depleted corps.

CAHILL, Chuck

b. Summerside, Prince Edward Island, January 4, 1904
d. Summerside, Prince Edward Island, June 5, 1954

An Islander, proud to make the NHL even if briefly, Cahill skated for Boston before being sent out to the Can-Am league to pasture.

CAIN, Francis ("Dutch")

b. Newmarket, Ontario, March 22, 1899
d. January 13, 1962

Not very much is known about Cain beyond his stats – which in themselves are hardly revealing. His two years in the NHL punctuated an uneventful career in the minor pros, and he retired in 1933.

CAIN, Herb

b. Newmarket, Ontario, December 24, 1913
d. Newmarket, Ontario, February 15, 1982

Born a year later than the records show, Cain was a tremendous player during his lengthy and successful career. His first team was the local St. John's Separate School squad. In Cain's only season, St. John's scored 56 goals – Cain scored them all! He was put on the negotiation list for the Canadiens, but they let the Maroons sign him in 1933. Coach T.P. Gorman formed the explosive Green Line – Cain, Bob Gracie, and Gus Marker – and the English Montrealers won the Stanley Cup in the spring of '35. In 1939, Cain was sent to Boston for Charlie Sands, and became one of the most popular players in town. At the time, Cain became the 13th player to score 200 career goals and win the scoring championship with a then-record 82 points. In 1947, he began a career in the AHL, playing for Hershey and winning the Calder Cup. He later coached the Junior Smoke Rings in Ontario for five years, winning three provincial championships. Then his life changed. In 1955 he was diagnosed with Hodgkins disease and there was little hope of survival. His weight plummeted from 205 to 130. But doctors in Ottawa were experimenting with a serum that had been used successfully with animals, and in desperation Cain agreed to try it himself. His health took a complete turn. He gained back most of the weight, settled in Newmarket, got a job with a sheet metal company, and lived another thirty years.

CAIRNS, Don

b. Calgary, Alberta, October 8, 1955

A complete bust for a 20th overall selection, but it was lowly Kansas City that did the selecting. A few games in the NHL (nine), a few seasons in the minors (three), a career ended quickly and quietly (in 1978) and a franchise that relocated first to Colorado and then moved on to Heaven.

CAIRNS, Eric

b. Oakville, Ontario, June 27, 1974

They didn't get him for his scoring, as the saying goes. A behemoth with a nasty streak, a blueliner with a wing-span that seems to reach from boards to boards, Cairns is a work-in-progress with the young and inexperienced Islanders after being claimed off waivers from cross-town rivals, the Rangers. He made his NHL debut on October 8, 1996, and scored his first goal almost four years later during which time he averaged more than three penalty minutes a game.

Larry Cahan

Francis Cain

Herb Cain

Eric Cairns

Jack Caffery
(opposite page)

Eric Calder

CALDER, Eric
b. Kitchener, Ontario, July 26, 1963
He played a game for Washington in '81-'82, and another for the Caps the next year, but that was all she wrote on the NHL front. Calder was also one of the youngest players to represent Canada at the World Juniors, in 1981, as a 17-year-old, though the team finished a disappointing seventh. He returned to university after his NHL days and moved to Europe where he had a long and successful career until taking up coaching in 1998 at the University of Waterloo in Ontario.

CALDER, Kyle
b. Mannville, Alberta, January 5, 1979
Very much a work in progress, Calder is with Chicago, a team trying to build on speed rather than size, which suits the smallish Calder just fine. He capped off a junior career out west with a silver medal with Canada at the 2000 World Juniors, and played briefly for the Hawks that season as well. In 2000-01, he played more than half the season in Chicago and developed a solid game defensively as well.

Kyle Calder

CALEY, Don
b. Dauphin, Manitoba, October 9, 1945
Although he played only half a game in the NHL with the newly-minted St. Louis Blues, Caley once had a shutout streak of 189 minutes with Phoenix in the WHL. He suffered serious whiplash in February 1970 when he stopped quickly at a crosswalk and a car rear-ended his. He missed the rest of the season but recovered in time for '70-'71. He retired at the end of the '72-'73 season to study to become a dentist, returned the next season when he felt he could juggle school and pucks at the same time, and retired permanently after seven games when he realized he couldn't handle the two preoccupations, as it were, together.

CALLADINE, Norm
b. Peterborough, Ontario, July 30, 1916
d. unknown
A wartime replacement for the numerous Bruins off to war, Calladine played most of '43-'44 and parts of the season before and after. In that one full season, he performed admirably, scoring 16 goals and averaging nearly a point per game, and in just 63 career NHL games he had an excellent 48 points.

John Callander

CALLANDER, Drew
b. Regina, Saskatchewan, August 17, 1956
No matter how persistent he was, Callander just couldn't catch on with the Flyers. Three times in the late 1970s he was called up to the big time, three times he was sent back down to the minors. Vancouver acquired him with Kevin McCarthy for Dennis Ververgaert, but a change of scenery didn't change his fortunes. After two partial seasons, he was in the minors for good. In 1982, Callander changed the scenery again himself, moving to Germany and playing in the Deutsche-Eishockey Liga.

CALLANDER, John ("Jock")
b. Regina, Saskatchewan, April 23, 1961
The younger brother of Drew, Jock replaced a small

Brett Callighen

NHL career with an historic one in the "I." He had brief stops with St. Louis, Pittsburgh, and Tampa, but with the Muskegon/Cleveland Lumberjacks he was sensational, breaking the IHL all-time points mark during the 1999-2000 season when he registered his 1,383rd career point. For much of his time in the "I" he was paired with best friend Dave Michayluk, another journeyman NHLer who became the IHL's all-time leading scorer, in large measure thanks to the passing of Callander. They lived near each other on Avon Lake, Ohio, their wives were best friends, and they played together for almost their entire IHL careers. They were both called up by Pittsburgh during the 1992 playoffs, along with another Muskegon forward, Mike Needham, and the three played together on what was appropriately dubbed the "Muskegon Line." Pittsburgh won the Stanley Cup that year.

CALLIGHEN, Brett
("Key"/ "Hummingbird")
b. Toronto, Ontario, May 15, 1953
It was the best of careers and the worst of careers, a life of hockey playing alongside Wayne Gretzky, a career cut short by a serious eye injury, a dreams-come-true story, a story ended too soon. Callighen played minor hockey in Toronto, but gave up the sport entirely at 16, intending instead to become a ski instructor. In 1973, he enrolled at Centennial College, took some courses in Hospitality, and then 21, played hockey on the school team. He was noticeably better than anyone else, so his coach, Dave McDowell, arranged a tryout with the Flint Generals. Callighen made the team, and moved up through the ranks quickly. New England signed him to a WHA contract in 1976 and during the season he was traded to the Oilers. There he stayed for six years, and when Gretzky arrived in '78-'79, coach Glen Sather formed Callighen, Gretzky, and Blair MacDonald into the "GMC Line." But in February 1980, in a game against Boston, Callighen was accidentally struck in the eye by the blade of Brad McCrimmon's stick. He missed six months of hockey, and when he returned, the vision in his left eye was still nowhere near perfect. He had two operations, played again in Lugano, Switzerland for two years, and then quit. He is now legally blind in that eye. Callighen continues to play oldtimers hockey in Toronto, and established The Hockey Institute, a school that runs programs for tykes and older children. He also works in commercial real estate for John W. Combs Ltd. in Toronto.

CALLIGHEN, Francis "Patsy"
b. Toronto, Ontario, February 13, 1906
d. unknown
He played just one full season in the NHL, with the Rangers, and didn't register a single point. Ditto for the playoffs. Amazingly, his team won the Stanley Cup in only its second year in the league. After a number of more years in the minor pros, he retired. One season, one Stanley Cup. He became a referee in the AHL, though he never made it back to the NHL as a whistle-tooter.

CALOUN, Jan
b. Ústí nad Labem, Czechoslovakia (Czech Republic), December 20, 1972
How's this for a record? Caloun scored on his first four

shots in the NHL. And even then, that only ties the record. After that beginning, however, he fell off the face of the earth faster than wind. He did play at the big three of international tournaments for the Czechs, though: the World Juniors in '92, the Worlds in '93, and the gold medal Olympic team in '98.

CAMAZZOLA, Jim
b. Vancouver, British Columbia, January 5, 1964
A successful career in the Italian League was prefaced by three games with the Blackhawks, all to no avail. A 196th draft choice in 1982, he pottered around in the minors briefly before starting a career-long sojourn in Europe that has lasted 14 years and counting. He has also played in two Olympics and one World Championships for Italy.

CAMAZZOLA, Tony
b. Vancouver, British Columbia, September 11, 1962
Older brother of Jim, with a similar career , Tony elected for a decent career in the IHL instead of one in Italy after his fleeting glory with the Washington Capitals, which consisted of three games in 1981-82.

CAMERON, Al
b. Edmonton, Alberta, October 21, 1955
A perfectly pedestrian player, perhaps, but tough and hard-working nonetheless. Cameron played three more or less full seasons in the NHL in a hockey life that saw him pinball up and down to the minors. Drafted by Detroit, the only other team he played for was Winnipeg after the Jets claimed him in the Expansion Draft in 1979.

Cameron played three seasons in the NHL.
AL CAMERON

CAMERON, Angus "Scotty"
b. Prince Albert, Saskatchewan, November 5, 1921
d. Calgary, Alberta, April 12, 1993
His parents came from Scotland, a fact that accounts for both his nickname and the fact that he was a scratch golfer. Cameron won the Saskatchewan Amateur Championship in 1942 despite a bad back that kept him off the Rangers' roster for a year. He seemed destined to join the Blueshirts in 1941 after having won the Allan Cup the previous year with the Regina Rangers, but his back was too painful and he spent most of the season convalescing. He was even rejected from the army because of his injury, though by 1945 he was healthy enough to be taken into the Canadian Forces. For many years, he worked at the Regina Golf Club, and upon being discharged from the military he resumed his career in the minor pros. He died suddenly, after hitting golf balls on a practice range.

CAMERON, Billy
b. Buckingham, Quebec, December 5, 1897
d. Buckingham, Quebec, January 28, 1972
A veteran of the Great War, Cameron played hockey for 15 years, darkening the doors of the NHL for 2 of those, first with the Habs, then with the "Amazing Amerks" in New York. He joined the 2nd Depot Battalion in October 1917 and remained in the army until after the war had ended. When he played for the Habs, briefly in the 1923-24 season, he won the Stanley Cup, though the Americans never made it to the playoffs two years later.

Billy Cameron

CAMERON, Craig ("Gunner")
b. Edmonton, Alberta, July 19, 1945
Brother of Al, Craig saw his career take a noticeable turn when he arrived with the Islanders. As a youngster, he was eased into the Detroit, St. Louis, and Minnesota lineups as a checker with not much expected of him offensively. That's how things started on Long Island, too, but when his checking linemates – Brian Lavender and Terry Crisp – were traded, Cameron started to look for more goals. Guess what? He found them. He scored a career-high 19 in his first season with the Isles, but the production was short-lived. The drought set in, but fortunately he could fall back on his defensive abilities, which likely would have gained him some Selke Trophy votes had the award been around at that time. As it was, New York traded him back to the North Stars for Jude Drouin, and he retired the next year.

Craig Cameron

CAMERON, Dave
b. Charlottetown, Prince Edward Island, July 29, 1958
There's just not very much to Cameron's hockey life. A student of the University of PEI, where he played for the school team, he is one of the few Islanders to go on to the NHL, albeit briefly. A steady, reliable skater, he was very much a replaceable player. After three part-time seasons with Colorado and New Jersey, he returned to PEI to play senior hockey and coach.

Dave Cameron

CAMERON, Harry ("Cammie")
b. Pembroke, Ontario, February 6, 1890
d. Vancouver, British Columbia, October 20, 1953
He was considered the first man to be able to curve his shot – with a straight stick, no less! – and long before Bobby Orr flew end to end with the puck ,Harry Cameron was the finest rushing defenseman and goal scorer of hockey's early pro years. He made his way up through the ranks from his local Pembroke Debaters team to Port Arthur, where he accepted a contract for $30 a week on condition he could bring his left-winger

Harry Cameron

Brian Campbell

Bryan Campbell

Colin Campbell

Don Campbell

Earl Campbell

Frank Nighbor. The Ports acquiesced, and the pair headed toward a pro career. Cameron joined the Toronto Blueshirts of the NHA the next year and stayed with the team when it became the Arenas upon the formation of the NHL in 1917. In Toronto he was teamed with Jack Marshall, the equally light, resilient, and talented blueliner. Together they won the Stanley Cup in 1914, and Cameron stayed on to win again with the Toronto Arenas in 1918, the first time an NHL team had won. He travelled to Ottawa and Montreal for a time before returning to Toronto, the franchise by now called the St. Pats, and sure enough he helped the team win another Cup, in 1922. In 1923 he moved out west to coach and play for the Saskatoon Sheiks, skating now as a forward with Harry Connor and Earl Miller. His curved shot became his trademark, and only a few other players have ever been credited with perfecting its use: Bill and Bun Cook, Dr. Gordie Roberts, and Didier Pitre. He continued to play until 1933, at which time he devoted his efforts fully to coaching the Saskatoon Standards in senior hockey. Later, he moved to Vancouver where many of his children lived, and it was there he spent his last year incapacitated by a stroke. He was inducted into the Hockey Hall of Fame in 1962.

CAMPBELL, Brian
b. Strathroy, Ontario, May 23, 1979
A beautifully fluid skater, Campbell capped a fine junior career with the Ottawa 67's by winning a silver medal with Canada at the 1999 World Juniors in Manitoba. He was also named the best junior player in Canada that season. The Sabres draft choice made his NHL debut the following year with Buffalo and is slowly establishing himself in the league, though he has yet to play a full season with the team.

CAMPBELL, Bryan
b. Sudbury, Ontario, March 27, 1944
His is not a household name, but for a few brief months during the 1970-71 season, Bryan Campbell played on one of the highest-scoring lines in the NHL. He began playing junior in Hamilton at age 16, captained the team, and won a Memorial Cup with the junior Red Wings in 1962. Unwanted by both Detroit and the Rangers, he thought Los Angeles would make him a player when they claimed him in the 1967 Expansion Draft. The Kings more or less committed him to the minors, though, and he was traded to Chicago in a huge deal with Bill White and Gerry Desjardins for Gilles Marotte, Jim Stanfield, and Denis DeJordy, a trade that built momentum in the Hawks. At the start of the next season, '70-'71, he was put on a line with Bobby Hull and Chicago Maki, and fans in the Windy City happily recalled the Million Dollar Line, also anchored by Hull a decade earlier. The line clicked, as they say, but the following season Campbell scored just five goals and found himself on his way out of town. He played on five WHA teams over the next six seasons, then retired to Florida where he opened two bars in Fort Lauderdale.

CAMPBELL, Colin ("Soupy"/ "Collie")
b. London, Ontario, January 28, 1953
Believe it or not, the NHL's executive vice-president

and director of hockey operations once played the game under a simpler moniker – plugger. He played junior in Peterborough under head coach Roger Neilson but went to the WHA initially before joining the Penguins in the NHL. In all, he dressed for five teams, accumulating more than 100 penalty minutes in almost every season he played. "Colin is afraid of no one," coach Glen Sather said of his new charge when he arrived in Edmonton. True enough, Campbell fought for the team, hit, checked, disturbed, and harassed his way to a regular job for more than a decade. One of his coaches in Vancouver, Harry Neale, saw him as a potential bench boss, and in 1985, Neale now in Detroit and Campbell not getting any younger, the player retired to become Neale's assistant. He moved on to the Rangers in 1990 in the same capacity, winning a Cup on Broadway under head man Mike Keenan. That summer, when Keenan bolted to St. Louis, Campbell became New York's head coach, a position he held for four years. In 1998 he was fired after the team failed to make the playoffs, but the NHL hired him, fancy titles aside, to adjudicate nefarious on-ice actions by players. Under his reign, Campbell has handed out increasingly lengthy suspensions, culminating with a 23-game ban for Marty McSorley, the longest suspension in league history. His son, Gregory, is one of the NHL's brightest teen prospects.

CAMPBELL, Dave
b. Brownsburg, Quebec, April 27, 1896
d. unknown
There was a time long ago when hockey was young, the rules different, the players smaller, and the puck the same size – when the Montreal Canadiens were not so vaunted, so *glorieux*, so *bleu, blanc, et rouge*. And it was during this time that the name Campbell graced the Montreal scoresheets for two games. That was it. No fanfare, no great moment. Two games and gone. He was briefly reinstated as an amateur the next season and played in Montreal for a few more years before turning to coaching. Campbell had twice served for Canada overseas, the first time from June to December 1915, the second from August 1916 until the war's conclusion.

CAMPBELL, Don
b. Drumheller, Alberta, July 12, 1925
Campbell played junior near home, in Portage, and made his way to Chicago for the '43-'44 season. Like so many players of the time, his enlistment into the army spelled the end of his NHL career. After being discharged, he played in the Pacific Coast league for a number of years, finishing with the Kimberley Dynamiters, the team that had brought glory to Canada many years earlier by winning the 1937 World Championships.

CAMPBELL, Earl ("Spiff")
b. Buckingham, Quebec, July 23, 1900
d. Rockcliffe, Ontario, February 11, 1953
Although he played his junior hockey in and around Ottawa, Campbell spent most of his pro career in western Canada, save his two years with the Senators in 1923-25. His only other NHL season came in '25-

'26 as a member of the New York Americans. Campbell spent most of his life in the military, and at his funeral Sergeant Campbell was accorded full military honours.

CAMPBELL, Jim ("Soup")
b. Worcester, Massachusetts, April 3, 1973
A career still in development, Campbell has done everything right toward becoming a solid NHLer. He started playing junior hockey in Quebec, even though he was raised in the U.S., a sign of his commitment to making a go of a pro life in the game. He represented his country at both the World Junior Championships and the Olympics, and after being drafted by Montreal played in the Habs' minor-league system for two years before being traded to Anaheim for Robert Dirk. The Ducks didn't give him much of a shot, so when he had the chance to sign as a free agent with St. Louis, he took it. The Blues gave him a starting role, and Campbell responded with consecutive 20-plus goal seasons.

CAMPBELL, Scott
b. Toronto, Ontario, June 22, 1957
Campbell was a 1st-round draft choice as a teenager, and was out of the game at 25. In between he played just a handful of games, never realizing the potential so many scouts and coaches believed he possessed. Despite being chosen 9th overall by St. Louis in 1977, Campbell opted for a life in the WHA, first with Houston, then with Winnipeg. When the Jets joined the NHL, they could protect only two players. They chose Campbell and Morris Lukowich. But the extreme cold in the 'Peg exacerbated a bad asthma problem, and after a year and a half Campbell asked to be traded. He got his wish, and arrived in St. Louis after all. However, the medication he had been taking for his asthma led to vascular migraine headaches so pronounced he had to sit out most of the '81-'82 season. By the next training camp, he continued to experience painful headaches and retired. Campbell then went into harness racing as an owner, and with a partner bought General D. Brook, a trotter who had excellent success.

CAMPBELL, Wade
b. Grimshaw, Alberta, January 2, 1961
When he stepped on the ice for his first NHL game in 1982, Campbell officially became the biggest hockey player in the league (6'5" and 232 pounds). When he was four and five, he ran across the street to the local rink and asked the caretaker to let him play, which the man did, for hours on end. That was where his NHL dream began, but once realized it didn't endure.

Campbell went into harness racing as an owner.
SCOTT CAMPBELL

Undrafted, he caught on with the Jets in 1982, but despite his physical play became a spare part the following year and spent more time in the minors than with the Jets. He was traded to Boston for Bill Derlago, but again in Boston he saw more action in the minors. Campbell decided to play in France for two years, and then retired after one more year in the AHL.

CAMPEAU, Jean-Guy "Tod"
b. St. Jérôme, Quebec, June 4, 1923
He got into his first two NHL games during the '43-'44 season, then didn't play again for the Habs for four years. Campeau played some more games the next year, but other than that his was a career rooted in minor pro Montreal teams for close to a decade. His only playoff game occurred March 26, 1949, a 3-2 win over Detroit.

CAMPEDELLI, Dom
b. Cohasset, Massachusetts, April 3, 1964
The year was 1982. Dom Campedelli had just been drafted by the Leafs in the seventh round, but his dramatic improvement during the last year at Boston College suggested he had more potential than the average seventh rounder. But Dom wanted big money and he wanted to be paid in U.S. funds, something that just wasn't done at the time. His agent, the third of the 21-year old's pre-NHL career, couldn't come to terms with the Leafs, so Dom was sent to Montreal. After two games, he was sent on to Philadelphia and later to Edmonton, but those two games were the sum total of his NHL bragging rights. Not exactly the basis for negotiating a long-term contract.

CAPRICE, Frank
b. Hamilton, Ontario, May 2, 1962
King Richard's throne was always Frank Caprice's bed of nails. Richard, as in Brodeur, was the number-one goalie in Vancouver for many years, and Caprice was his ever-present backup who could never usurp the King and become number one in net. As a result, Caprice never played a playoff game. Only once was he given a chance to be a number-one son, to start the '84-'85 season when Brodeur was demoted. But that December, Caprice tore his hamstring and the rest of the year was a wipeout. He saw time in Fredricton almost every season he was in Vancouver, and after six years he was excommunicated from the land of the Canucks, spending time first in the minors then for many a year in Europe. His crowning glory came when, as a 19-year-old, he helped Canada win gold at the 1982 World Juniors. After retiring, he returned to Toronto to work for the Ontario Lottery and Gaming Corporation.

Jim Campbell

Wade Campbell

Tod Campeau

Dom Campedelli

Dave Capuano

Leo Carbol

Steve Cardwell

George Carey

CAPUANO, Dave
b. Warwick, Rhode Island, July 27, 1968

His brother, Jack, also played in the NHL and his cousin, Dean, was drafted by Boston in 1990, but Dave managed only one full season in the NHL before moving on. He was traded four times in as many years but spent most of his time in the minors after being drafted right out of high school. Capuano attended the University of Maine and was twice a Hobey Baker finalist, but early promise led only to later disappointment for the NHL teams that acquired him – Pittsburgh, Vancouver, Tampa, San Jose, and Boston. The lone exception to his averageness was the hero's night of February 21, 1991, when he had four assists in a single game.

CAPUANO, Jack
b. Cranston, Rhode Island, July 7, 1966

Here was a case of a player who estimated his worth as being greater than what his team had calculated, asked for and got a trade, but never produced during his second and third chances. After being drafted by Toronto in 1984, he spent a year with Newmarket in the minors, recording a team low -28 in '88-'89. The next fall, he believed he had won a spot on the roster, but after only one game was demoted. Upset, he went home and demanded a trade, which he got, to the Islanders. The Isles sent him to Vancouver before putting him in even one game, and after three starts with the Canucks he was on his way to Boston. Two games later, he had played his last in the NHL. After retiring in 1992, he went into coaching in the East Coast league and later became senior vice-president of operations for the Pee Dee Pride club.

CARBOL, Leo
b. Ottawa, Ontario, June 5, 1910
d. Missouri, November 13, 1991

Six games in the Windy City in '42-'43 was all the reward Carbol received for 14 years in the minors, most of his 500-plus games coming with the St. Louis Flyers of the AHA. He enlisted in the war for two years, and when he was discharged could not make his way back to the Hawks.

CARBONNEAU, Guy ("Carbo")
b. Sept-Iles, Quebec, March 18, 1960

At 40, he was the oldest player in the league in 1999-2000, but he had defined himself years before as the finest two-way player in the game, modelled after teammate and Selke Trophy owner Bob Gainey. Carbonneau came out of the Q and stepped into a Montreal team on the downswing from its four-Cup dynasty in the late 1970s. He established himself as both a 20-goal scorer and the man who played against the other team's best player every night. During his 13 years with Montreal, he won the Cup twice, in '86 and '93, the latter personally more satisfying for his contribution. In that year's finals, the Habs faced Wayne Gretzky and the L.A. Kings, and in game one the Great One had a goal and two assists and L.A. won 4-1. Carbo approached coach Jacques Demers and requested he be allowed to shadow number 99 the rest of the way. Montreal won the next four games straight. Carbonneau was named captain and won three Selke trophies with the team, but was traded for youth in 1994 in the form of Paul Kariya's U of Maine centreman, Jim Montgomery. Although his record in Montreal speaks for itself, there were a couple of off-ice bumps. Early in '86-'87, he and teammate Chris Nilan were benched for a game for missing curfew. In the fall of 1987 he was arrested for drinking and driving and had his licence suspended for a year. Just a couple of months before the trade he gave a news photographer the middle finger while golfing. After one season in St. Louis, he was traded to Dallas, and there he won his third Cup in 1999. He was so old in that final season that his daughter was dating his teammate, the 21-year-old Brenden Morrow. Carbonneau became an assistant coach with the Montreal Canadiens shortly after retiring, and it seems only a matter of time before he assumes head coaching duties.

> **He was so old in that final season that his daughter was dating his teammate.**
> **GUY CARBONNEAU**

CARDIN, Claude
b. Sorel, Quebec, February 17, 1941

A one-game, not-really-that-wonderful wonder, Cardin was Montreal property, played a game during St. Louis's inaugural season after being sold to the Blues, and vanished off the face of the hockey-playing earth after three more seasons in the minors.

CARDWELL, Steve
b. Toronto, Ontario, August 13, 1950

There was plenty of interest in Cardwell once his brief career skimmed off the surface of the NHL and sunk into the waters that were the WHA. He was drafted by Pittsburgh and played only for the Pens for bits and pieces of three seasons (1970-73), but then moved to Minnesota of the WHA in one of four trades in which he was involved in the pirate league. These trips to the airport didn't abet his fortunes much, and he slipped further, playing senior hockey in Ontario a year later.

CAREY, George
b. Scotland
d. unknown

One of hockey's early players, Carey spent most of his

skating life in Quebec, first in senior hockey, then with the Bulldogs of the NHL. He was in the military for a year during the First World War and later played for both Hamilton and the Toronto St. Pats before retiring in 1924.

CAREY, Jim
b. Dorchester, Massachusetts, May 31, 1974
From hero to goat, from good to bad, from puck stopping to lamp lighting, from NHL to minors in the blink of an eye. He's not the Cable Guy or Ace Ventura, and his Mask isn't rubber. This Carey has one "r" and his fame has been as fleeting as the actor's is enduring. His father was an All-American high school football player and his brother was in the Baltimore Orioles system. When Jim was young he played forward, not goal. When he got to the NHL he went undefeated in his first seven games, in '94–'95 with Washington. He played 71 games the following year, won the Vezina Trophy, and set innumerable team records. But when he was traded to Boston, he left his skills behind somewhere on the Boston Common. A year later, he was in the minors pulling in an NHL salary of $2.5 million a season and has yet to resurface in the big time.

CARKNER, Terry ("Carks")
b. Smiths Falls, Ontario, March 7, 1966
A rough-and-tumble bit of business, Carkner has managed to stay in the NHL for some 15 years through defensive ability and toughness. In '96–'97, he went the entire season without scoring a goal, but 8 times he has had more than 100 penalty minutes in a year. Carkner has played for Canada at both the World Juniors and World Championships and was part of the miracle Florida Panthers team that made it to the 1996 Stanley Cup finals in only their third season of play.

CARLETON, Wayne ("Swoop")
b. Sudbury, Ontario, August 4, 1946
He was a talented junior with tremendous size and strength, a blue-chip prospect, one to watch out for. But he suffered two debilitating knee injuries as a teenager, once playing hockey, once playing baseball. Serious surgery was required. He broke his elbow in 1969, followed quickly by a viral infection that sent him to the hospital. He broke his wrist twice and his leg once, but for the first five years of his career his greatest obstacle was coach Punch Imlach, who sent Swoop up and down to the farm with the same windswept ease with which Carleton skated when given the chance. He was traded to Boston midway through the '69–'70 season, was on the bench when Orr flew through the air and won the Stanley Cup, and was just as quickly dispatched to California in the summer of '71, the greatest dive of all. He showed up at camp weighing 245 pounds, unhappy and unfit. Swoop collected his bulk and moved on to the WHA, where he made an impact as a scorer and signed a huge five-year contract. After being traded from Hartford to Edmonton during his WHA days, he claimed that Edmonton owed him $2,300 for moving expenses. A judge agreed, and ordered the Oilers' equipment confiscated just hours before a game. Carleton got his

money. After retiring, he turned to his farm in Stayner, called Springwater Stables. Some of his horses were named Frosty's Bretta, Sly Hal, Minto Don, and Won to Victory. He later worked as a financial planner for an investment syndicate in Kitchener.

CARLIN, Brian
b. Calgary, Alberta, June 13, 1950
He was called up, he was seen, he was demoted. A graduate of the Calgary Centennials and a Los Angeles draft choice, Carlin's career wasn't particularly eventful, though he did score an NHL goal, with the Kings, and not everyone can say that.

CARLSON, Jack ("The Big Bopper")
b. Virginia, Minnesota, August 23, 1954
Yes, he had a big nose. That was his signature physical attribute off the ice, but on the ice he was a tough, physical customer. After playing four years in the WHA he joined Minnesota of the NHL, the team that had acquired his rights from Detroit. He became instantly popular for his physical play, and the organist at the Met Centre would bang out the theme music from *Jaws* when Carlson first appeared on the ice each night. But on April 4, 1979, he suffered a serious back injury that required spinal fusion at the Mayo Clinic. He was out of the league for a year and a half, returning on November 7, 1980. He played two years with the Blues, '82–'84, but his career was not quite done yet. Unhappy as an air freight salesman and playing shinny twice a week in Minnesota, he un-retired in November 1986, some 30 months after having last played. Eight games later, he was done for good. Jack missed his big acting break in 1974-75. While playing for Johnstown, the movie *Slap Shot* was being made. Jack's two brothers, Kent and Steve, were stars of the flick, and Jack was supposed to be the third brother, all of whom were terrorizing the league with their hits and fights. But when he was recalled by the Minnesota Fighting Saints just prior to filming, his part had to be given to Dave Hansen.

CARLSON, Kent
b. Concord, New Hampshire, January 11, 1962
A bad back, a very bad back, did him in. He was drafted by Montreal, but the Habs blueline was chockfull of stars and he only played sparingly except when he was requested to fight. The result was a torrent of injuries: broken hands, a broken nose, damaged tendons and shoulders, slipped discs in his neck. "Every time the phone rang at five in the morning, we knew he was injured again," his mother said. A trade sent Kent to St. Louis, but he had a serious spinal fusion operation that forced him to miss all of '86–'87 and further caused nerve damage in his right arm. He returned for two games in the playoffs almost two years later, and two more with Washington in '88–'89 before packing it in.

CARLSON, Steve
b. Virginia, Minnesota, August 20, 1955
Steve, Jack, and Jeff Carlson, the three brothers who were signed as a hulking forward line for Johnstown in 1974, inspired the hockey action flick *Slap Shot*, starring, more importantly, Paul Newman. Jeff never

Jim Carey

Terry Carkner

Wayne Carleton

Brian Carlin

Kent Carlson

Steve Carlson

made it to the NHL, but Steve played most of one full season with Los Angeles. He swore he fought only because his brothers made it impossible not to, but he did a pretty fair impression of a pugilist in the movie, which became a cult classic and inspired a group of Canadians many years later to try to get the "Hansen brothers" into the Hockey Hall of Fame, such were their contributions to the game's popularity. Steve went on to play a number of years in the WHA, and can even boast to have centred Gordie and Mark Howe in New England in '77-'78. He eventually became a playing assistant coach with Baltimore in the AHL.

CARLSSON, Anders ("Masken")
b. Gavle, Sweden, November 25, 1960
Despite playing only briefly over three years with New Jersey, Carlsson has survived the test of time like few before him. Prior to and after his NHL days, blighted by a sour relationship with coach Doug Carpenter, Carlsson was a standout in Sweden, both in the Elite league and internationally. He started his career in 1978 with Brynas, and continues to play in Sweden to this day. Additionally, he has played for Sweden at six World Championships and the 1987 Canada Cup, proving to himself if no one else that there is plenty of hockey life outside the NHL.

CARLYLE, Randy
b. Sudbury, Ontario, April 19, 1956
The Leafs had their eye on Carlyle while he played junior hockey in Sudbury, and at the 1976 draft they selected him 30th overall. He had already signed a WHA contract, but GM Jim Gregory figured after the three-year deal was up the defenceman would be ready to join the NHL. But Carlyle denied having signed with the Cincinnati Stingers, and Gregory got his signature on a Leafs offer. Then the Stingers entered the fray, saying Carlyle had signed and they were taking him to court for breach of contract. All was eventually sorted out, and the Leafs were winners at the Stingers' expense. Except that after just two years, Toronto gave up on him and traded him to Pittsburgh with George Ferguson for Dave Burrows. And Carlyle's career took off. Two years later, in 1981, he won the Norris Trophy, something no Leaf had ever won. After six seasons in Penguins colours, he was off to Winnipeg for the last nine years of his career. Along the way, he was cut from the 1981 Team Canada for the Canada Cup by coach Scotty Bowman after showing up overweight. In 1989, his one international experience, he was humiliated by the IIHF at the World Championships in Stockholm. Chosen to provide a urine sample after Canada's game with West Germany, he apparently failed the test and

Randy Carlyle

Keith Carney

Prior to and after his NHL days, Carlsson was a standout in Sweden.
ANDERS CARLSSON

withdrew so as not to taint future results of the team. In the wake of the Ben Johnson scandal, Carlyle's case was front-page news across Europe – another Canadian cheat. His name was mud. A day later, the IIHF announced that the B sample was clear as mountain air. No explanations or apologies, only a shamefaced hockey player who had done nothing wrong. After retiring, Carlyle stayed in the Jets organization as a colour commentator for the radio and a staff member of the team's public relations department. His last NHL goal was scored against the team that had given up on him too soon – Toronto. Carlyle was later inducted into the Manitoba Sports Hall of Fame and remained in the 'Peg, where he became the general manager of the Moose in the AHL. In 2002, he was back in the NHL, a coach in Washington.

CARNBACK, Patrik
b. Goteborg, Sweden, February 1, 1968
His first job back home in Sweden was as a truck driver, but hockey was more to his liking. Like many Swedes who made it to the NHL, he began and finished his career in his home and native land, including a brief pit stop in '94-'95 during the owners' lockout. Along the way he played a few games with Montreal before being sent to Anaheim in 1993. Neither a terrific scorer nor a tenacious checker, he played just two and a half seasons in the vaunted green, purple, and white sweater of the Ducks before heading to Germany to play full-time. In 2002-03, he was part of Vastra Frolunda in Sweden where he won the national championship.

CARNEY, Keith
b. Providence, Rhode Island, February 3, 1970
Drafted out of high school by the Buffalo Sabres in 1988, Carney did not provide instant gratification for the Sabres and after three partial seasons was dished off to the Chicago Blackhawks. Three years later, he became a member of the Coyotes, but in between he had his greatest successes, first as a member of the U.S.'s World Cup-winning team and then with the 1998 Olympic team in Nagano. Only once has his team missed the playoffs in his career.

CARON, Alain ("Boom Boom")
b. Dolbeau, Quebec, April 27, 1938
d. Chicoutimi, Quebec, December 16, 1986
His was a life too brief for a player whose career spanned 20 years, if only including one full NHL season. One of the best scorers around, Caron played in an assortment of minor pro leagues. His skating was weak and he was slow, but when he got into the offensive end he could bury the puck like few players.

But it wasn't until the Oakland Seals claimed him in the 1967 Expansion Draft that he made it to the NHL, and after one season he was traded to Montreal, played two games with the Habs, and was out of the NHL for good. Caron made his way to the Nordiques in the WHA in 1972, but by '75 he was down in the North American Hockey League playing for the Beauce Jaros. There he scored 78 goals in 73 games, but that summer, 1978, he suffered a heart attack and had to retire. A decade later, another massive heart attack killed him.

CARON, Jacques
b. Noranda, Quebec, April 21, 1940
The story is as familiar as 1967 is historic to NHL development. Caron was a minor-league goalie, doomed to play for Springfield until he could no longer see a puck. He retired at one point and moved to Toronto to take a job as a machinist, but when news of league expansion made headlines he returned to the game. His decision was wise. The L.A. Kings claimed him, and he got into his first NHL game in '67-'68. Seeing play in just three games later the following year depressed him, and he retired again, only to come back when he had a chance to play for St. Louis. After 10 more games with Vancouver, he moved on again to the minors, leaving Syracuse in early 1977 after a contract disagreement. But for a third time he un-retired after a trade sent him to Binghampton, and in 1980 he retired from play for good to his cattle and horse farm in Noranda. Two years later, he was hired as an assistant coach in Hartford, a job he had to abandon after suffering severe emotional and mental stress that needed hospital treatment. He recovered to join the New Jersey Devils as a goalie coach at the same time a young Martin Brodeur joined the team, and since that time the elder has tutoured the younger into one of the best goalies in the game.

CARPENTER, Bob
b. Beverly, Massachusetts, July 13, 1963
Before Bobby Carpenter, NHL scouts never attended high school games in the United States. After Bobby Carpenter, they all did. He grew up in Peabody, Massachusetts, a stone's throw from the Boston Garden, and his neighbours in town included Gerry Cheevers and Bobby Orr. Number 4 got to know Carpenter's father, Bob, and agreed to advise the youngster. Bobby's grades were good enough to get him into any university he wanted, but by his final year he knew what he really wanted was to play in the NHL. The Hartford Whalers had made public that they would select him with their first pick in the 1981 draft,

Carpenter became the first player to go right from U.S. high school to the NHL.
BOB CARPENTER

4th overall, and Carpenter was looking forward to playing near home. But the night before the draft, Washington made a trade with Colorado, selecting third, and on the big day it was the Capitals, not the Whalers, that selected him. Furious, Carpenter left the Montreal Forum, where the draft was running its course, the first of many public relations gaffes that were to dog his career. Carpenter eventually signed with Washington and became the first player to go right from U.S. high school to the NHL, scoring 32 goals as a rookie and setting a record for American-born players when he scored 53 in his fourth year, '84-'85. The previous record had been 41 by Joe Mullen. He became a staple on America's international teams, though the results were not impressive at the 1981 World Juniors, '84 and '87 Canada Cups, or '87 Worlds. In the summer of '85 he signed a huge four-year contract, but within a year he had a falling out with coach Bryan Murray. He left the team and forced a trade, to the Rangers, but within weeks his welcome had run out and he was sent to Los Angeles in a deal that brought Marcel Dionne to Broadway. It was his third team in one season, and it didn't last long. He played with Boston, Washington again, and New Jersey (where he won his only Stanley Cup) before retiring, never scoring more than 25 goals in any one year after that great first season. A superb career fizzled quickly, and he retired with none of the cockiness he had been known for as a young prospect.

CARPENTER, Everard "Eddie"
b. Hartford, Michigan, June 15, 1890
d. Winnipeg, Manitoba, April 30, 1963
Although born on American soil, his life was Canadian through and through, beginning with a childhood in Lachute, Quebec. Carpenter played senior hockey at age 17 in the Ottawa Valley and turned pro with Moncton of the Maritime League. In 1916-17 he played for Seattle as the Mets won the Stanley Cup, and after serving two years in the First World War saw his only NHL action, with Quebec and then Hamilton. Carpenter retired in 1921 and moved to Port Arthur where he began a successful coaching career, leading that city's senior team to Allan Cup victory in both 1925 and '26 and being elected alderman of Port Arthur in 1941. He moved to Winnipeg two years later and became a railroad engineer, a job he held until retiring in 1953. He died a decade later of liver cancer.

CARR, Al "Red"
b. Winnipeg, Manitoba, December 29, 1916
A wartime skater for Toronto, Carr played five games with the Leafs when many regulars were enlisted in

Alain Caron

Jacques Caron

Eddie Carpenter

"Red" Carr

Lorne Carr

Larry Carriere

Gene Carrigan

Billy Carroll

the armed forces. His nights of glory came on October 30 and 31, and November 4, 7, and 21, 1943. Before and after, he had a long career in the minors in towns and leagues across North America. His son, Gene, went on to play in the NHL in the 1970s.

CARR, Gene
b. Nanaimo, British Columbia, September 17, 1951
The son of Red Carr, Gene had it all, lost it all, and recovered much of it. A talented junior, Carr was drafted 4th overall in 1971 by St. Louis, but bad luck and injuries scuppered his development and brought his career to a resounding halt. After just 15 games with the Blues, Carr was traded to New York, but he missed long stretches over the next couple of years with a broken collarbone and a concussion. Then he suffered a ruptured disc in his back. Although he continued to play for several more years, he never found his scoring touch and he never had perfect health. Carr was forced to retire at age 28 in 1979 because of back pain that simply wouldn't go away. He relaxed for a year in his California home with his family, and then his life went seriously awry. He turned to cocaine and then alcohol for fun, but a second back operation had him on morphine in the hospital with his other drugs in his bedside table. He checked himself into a clinic, got his life in order, and re-established himself as an investment counsellor in Encino, California.

CARR, Lorne
b. Stoughton, Saskatchewan, July 2, 1910
A western boy, Carr signed with the New York Rangers during the 1933-34 season, but after going pointless in 14 games he was sent to crosstown rivals the Americans in the off-season. With the "Amazing Amerks" he starred on a line with Sweeney Schriner and Art Chapman for five years, and in the 1938 playoffs he exacted sweet revenge on his old club. In the deciding game of the best-of-three series, he scored in quadruple overtime to eliminate the Rangers, though the Americans were ousted in turn in the semifinals by Chicago. In 1941 he was sent to Toronto, and that's where he enjoyed his greatest success during his final five years in the NHL. In the 1942 finals, the Leafs rallied from 3-0 down in games to beat the Red Wings and win the Stanley Cup, winning game seven 3-1. Carr assisted on two of those goals, scored by his longtime friend Sweeney Schriner (their linemate was Billy Taylor). In 1945, he again was on the Cup-winning Leafs team. During his time at Maple Leaf Gardens, he led the team in scoring twice and was named to the First All-Star team twice as well. After the war he established a hotel business, pool hall, and minigolf course in Calgary, and it is there he has lived the rest of his life.

CARRIERE, Larry ("Hawk")
b. Montreal, Quebec, January 30, 1952
A rare example of a modern player making it to the NHL out of a Canadian university – in Carriere's case, Loyola. He got his big break while playing on the farm for Buffalo's AHL affiliate in Cincinnati in '72-'73. Jim Schoenfeld and Mike Robitaille both went down with injuries on the Sabres blueline, so Carriere was called up. In his first game, he had a goal and an assist in a

2-2 tie with L.A. When the two regulars returned, he was relegated to spot duty, and soon was on the move to Atlanta, Vancouver, and L.A. At this point, Carriere got a good job offer in Toronto outside of hockey, and asked the Kings to waive him out of the league with the purpose of signing his retirement papers. They waived him, but he didn't get around to signing off when Buffalo's GM Punch Imlach claimed him. Carriere agreed to play with the Sabres, and the Kings filed tampering charges. Nothing came of this, and after nine games he retired, only to return for two games with the Leafs a year and a half later. He later became the assistant general manager of the Sabres.

CARRIGAN, Gene
b. Edmonton, Alberta, July 5, 1907
d. March 15, 1944
He made his way around the continent, hockey stick in hand, hockey bag slung over a well-worn shoulder. Carrigan established himself as a goal scorer in the Can-Am league in 1929-30, but in 33 games with the Rangers the following year he scored just twice and didn't have a single assist. He later played briefly for Detroit and the St. Louis Eagles, but spent most of his time in the minors until retiring during the war.

CARROLL, Billy
b. Toronto, Ontario, January 19, 1959
Here was a man with a keen sense of timing and serendipity. He joined the Islanders as their draft choice in time for the 1980-81 season and won three Stanley Cups with them his first three years in the league. In 1984 he was claimed in the Waiver Draft by none other than the Edmonton Oilers and won another Cup with Gretzky and Co. in the spring of '85. But the following year he was demoted. Refusing to report and threatening retirement, Carroll was traded to Detroit, where he played the final 52 games of his career. He established several businesses in the Toronto area that he continues to operate.

CARROLL, George
b. Sunny Brae, New Brunswick, June 3, 1897
d. Moncton, New Brunswick, August 1, 1939
A lifelong resident of Moncton, Carroll played briefly with the Maroons and Bruins for one year and moved on to coaching after he retired. In his earliest days, Carroll played for the Corncobs Juniors, Moncton Machinists, and Moncton St. Bernards in city leagues. He spent a year in the war before playing with the Moncton Victorias. George was one of seven Carroll brothers who played the game, including Blair, Fred Jr., Harold, Jack, Cecil, and Ken. The family once formed a team and beat the Victorias in an exhibition game in 1922-23. George later coached in Sunny Brae and then in Sunnyside in the PEI Senior league. He guided the Moncton Young Acadiens from 1933 to '35 and was also a referee.

CARROLL, Greg
b. Gimli, Manitoba, November 10, 1956
The line of Don Murdoch, Greg Carroll, and Morris Lukowich was unstoppable in Medicine Hat, yet all three ended up having remarkably different pro careers. Lukowich had a fine career with Winnipeg,

Murdoch had a decent stint with the Rangers, but Carroll simply couldn't find the range in the NHL. Although he was drafted by Washington in 1976, he chose to start his pro hockey life in the WHA (as did Lukowich), and moved on to the Caps two years later. But Carroll played with three teams in two partial seasons. His life was disrupted in 1980 when he was charged with drug possession after a raid by police on a house in Edmonton. Carroll claimed innocence and charges were eventually dropped, but he never played again in the NHL.

CARRUTHERS, Gordon "Dwight"
b. Lashburn, Saskatchewan, November 7, 1944
He got into one game with the Red Wings on March 6, 1966, and another with Philly a couple of years later during their first season. Other than that, he spent a ton of time in Spokane and the WHL before untying the laces for the last time in 1976.

CARSE, Bill
b. Edmonton, Alberta, May 29, 1914
d. Honolulu, Hawaii, October 31, 2000
A western boy through and through, Carse turned pro in Edmonton before making it to the NHL with the Rangers, recording an assist in his first game during the '38-'39 season. He was sold to Chicago, and after three years with the Hawks enlisted in the army, playing for a team in Victoria, British Columbia, that went to the Allan Cup finals against the incredible Ottawa Commandos team. When Carse became a civilian again he moved to Vancouver, playing in 1945-46 before retiring to take a job as a salesman with a nut and chocolate firm in the city. He returned the next season to play, then became a playing coach in '49-'50, a job he reduced to coach only when he ran into Babe Pratt one night and broke some ribs. Carse was strictly a coach in the following season. However, when the Canucks got off to a bad start, he began training for a comeback, one cut short when he was let go as coach.

CARSE, Bob
b. Edmonton, Alberta, July 19, 1919
d. Cleveland, Ohio, July 27, 1999
Younger and slightly more successful than brother Bill, Bob's career was not dissimilar. He played city hockey in Edmonton, graduated to the NHL in 1939 with Chicago and then enlisted. During the war, he was shot and taken prisoner by the Germans and held for six months before being freed. He lost 60 pounds during his incarceration. After the war he signed on with Montreal, but lasted only 22 games before being demoted to Cleveland, where he finished his playing career by

Frank was easily identified by his hair, which had turned grey in his early twenties.
FRANK CARSON

winning three Calder Cups. He remained in Cleveland and became an insurance salesman for Great West Life by day and a linesman for the AHL's Barons at night. He was inducted into four local halls of fame in Ohio.

CARSON, Dr. Bill ("Doc")
b. Bracebridge, Ontario, November 25, 1900
d. Parry Sound, Ontario, May 29, 1967
While playing OHA Intermediate with Grimsby, Carson signed with the Toronto St. Pats after the NHL team gave him a pair of skates as a signing bonus. But on further reflection, he decided not to play for Toronto and instead continue his studies in dentistry at the University of Toronto. Two years later, after graduating, he joined the team, though he was sold to Boston two and a half years later. He became the first Leafs player to score 20 goals in a season, playing on a line with Ace Bailey and Butch Keeling. After the '29-'30 season, he played two more years of minor pro before practicing as a dentist in Parry Sound.

CARSON, Frank ("The Silver Fox"/ "The Grey Eagle"/ "Frosty")
b. Bracebridge, Ontario, January 12, 1902
d. Crumlin, Ontario, April 21, 1957
One of three Carson brothers to skate in the NHL, Frank was easily identified by his hair, which had turned grey in his early twenties. He learned to skate at Woodstock College near his hometown, and went on to play for the strong Stratford midget team that featured a line of Carson, Howie Morenz, and Butch Keltenbourne. He joined the Montreal Maroons and then Americans before settling in Detroit and helped the Wings reach the 1934 Stanley Cup finals. In the summers, he worked for a financial house in western Ontario. A noted backchecker, he retired in 1934 and eventually settled near London, Ontario, where he operated a general store until suffering a fatal heart attack at the age of 65.

CARSON, Gerry ("Stub")
b. Parry Sound, Ontario, October 10, 1905
d. Grimsby, Ontario, November 9, 1956
The last of the hockey-playing brothers, Gerry was the baby on skates. He played most of his career with the Canadiens, though was loaned to the Rangers for half a season in 1928-29. He missed all of '35-'36 after undergoing a serious knee operation, and retired after one final year with the Maroons. The only time the brothers ever played together was briefly in Parry Sound. Gerry settled in Grimsby and became a salesman for a brewing company until his early death.

Greg Carroll

Bob Carse

Dr. Bill Carson

Gerry Carson

Jimmy Carson

Anson Carter

Billy Carter

John Carter

Lyle Carter

CARSON, Jimmy
b. Southfield, Michigan, July 20, 1968
The good news, even before he was born, was that his grandfather changed the family name from Kyriazopoulos to Carson. As a child, his father was a parking lot attendant near the Olympia in Detroit who would occasionally take his son to games, where little Jimmy would sit on the lap of Carol Dionne, wife of Marcel. Marcel was traded to L.A., and Jimmy's favoured lap become but a memory. When Jimmy was 16, he left University-Liggett High School in Grosse Pointe, Michigan, to play in the Q, a transition made easy by his fluency in French. From there he was selected 2nd overall by Los Angeles in the 1986 draft and when he played his first game that fall he was the youngest player in the NHL. Just two years later, he set records for most goals (55) and points (107) in a season by an American-born player, and he was the second-youngest player to hit the 50-goal mark (Gretzky was the youngest). He lived next door to Dionne and they played on a line with another talented scorer, Luc Robitaille. On August 9, 1988, he was the key King involved in the trade that sent Wayne Gretzky out of Edmonton, and the pressure of replacing the Great One on the Oilers was huge. He scored 49 goals in his first season, but just four games into the '89-'90 season he walked out, demanding a trade. A trade it was, back home to Detroit, but Carson was unhappy playing second fiddle to Steve Yzerman, saw his ice time diminish, and forced a trade again, this time right back to LaLaLand, Gretzky, and his only trip to the Cup finals (a loss to Montreal). By this time his stock was worth pennies, not dollars, and his career trickled to an end after curtain calls in Vancouver and Hartford.

CARSON, Lindsay
b. Oxbow, Saskatchewan, November 21, 1960
Carson was a Flyers draft choice who played most of his seven seasons with Philly save for a trade to Hartford for Paul Lawless that saw him dress for the Whalers in his final 27 NHL games. A forward with size and some scoring ability, he made it to the finals twice, in 1985 and '87, only to lose both times to the Edmonton Oilers.

CARTER, Anson ("A.C.")
b. Toronto, Ontario, June 6, 1974
A true feel-good story. Carter was drafted 220th overall by Quebec, a position so low that no player in his right mind would feel confident about making the NHL. And, he was traded even before playing a game, by the Nordiques to Washington. Just 19 games after trying on a Caps sweater, Carter was dealt to Boston with Jim Carey, Jason Allison, and a draft choice for Bill Ranford, Adam Oates, and Rick Tocchet. In Boston he performed credibly for more than three years, but he wound up in Edmonton in a deal that sent Bill Guerin to the Bruins. He developed into a bona fide star and was invited to Team Canada's orientation camp in September 2001 leading up to the 2002 Olympics in Salt Lake City. Though he wasn't chosen for the final team he was near the top of the list in case of injury. In March 2003, he was traded to the Rangers. Carter's international success is impressive. He won gold at the World Juniors in '94 and World Championships in '97 with Team Canada.

CARTER, Billy
b. Cornwall, Ontario, December 2, 1937
Much of Carter's career was spent in the Montreal circuits, first in various city teams, then with the Canadiens. He was claimed by Boston at the 1960 Intra-League Draft, though the Habs purchased him later in the season for peanuts. Carter went down to the Hull-Ottawa affiliate in the EPHL and for 1962-63 team general manager Sam Pollock hired him to act as a playing assistant coach for head coach Scotty Bowman, so respected was his experience. "One of the best hockey players who ever played for me," Pollock said of the man he likened to Ralph Backstrom.

CARTER, John
b. Winchester, Massachusetts, May 3, 1963
Fast, fast, fast! This kid could really fly at RPI. He played with Adam Oates in university and the two tore the ECAC apart with speed and goals. When Oates passed up a final year of eligibility, Carter stuck it out. Undrafted, he signed with the Bruins, but for six seasons he bounced between the farm team in Maine and the main team in Boston. A free agent in 1991, he ventured elsewhere, signing with the newest NHL entry, the San Jose Sharks. The results were all too familiar, though: big team and farm team. During an exhibition game in 1993, he suffered a serious eye injury. He played for two years in the minors, but after eight operations doctors had to remove his injured eye in 1996, thus ending his career.

CARTER, Lyle
b. Truro, Nova Scotia, April 29, 1945
His résumé reads like an atlas of North America, but his time in the NHL can be pinpointed to a few weeks in the 1971-72 season with the hapless California Golden Seals. Carter made it to Californ-I-A based on his great season in goal for Muskegon the previous year in the IHL, when he was named the league's most valuable player.

CARTER, Ron
b. Montreal, Quebec, March 14, 1958
He could light it up in junior, and light it up in the minors, but in between he managed just two unheroic games with the Oilers in the team's first year in the NHL. With Sherbrooke, Carter scored 88 goals and 174 points in his final year, both league bests. But with Gretzky and the boys on the rise, he couldn't hold his own in Edmonton. He was claimed on waivers by Buffalo, but coach Scotty Bowman found no use for him in Sabreland. A few years later, in the ACHL, Carter was again a scoring machine, with back-to-back 50-plus years with an outfit called the Virginia Lancers. He retired in 1986.

CARVETH, Joe ("Dad")
b. Regina, Saskatchewan, March 21, 1918
d. August 15, 1985
Carveth came up through the junior ranks but no sooner had he made Detroit in 1940-41 than he collided with the Leafs' Hank Goldup, broke his leg, and missed the rest of the season. It was his second bad break of the leg, and a few years later this injury

earned him an exemption from the armed forces. A true gentleman and a team man, he was one of the most-liked players wherever he went, including stops in Boston and Montreal before returning to the Red Wings in 1949. He scored the Cup-winning goal for Detroit in 1943, and was with the team again for victory in 1950. Affectionately called "Dad" by his teammates in Detroit, the father of four was crushed when he was demoted to Indianapolis at age 32, his best years clearly behind him, his battle with his weight a losing one. In the summers, he was first employed by Metal Mouldings Corporation of Detroit, but in his second go-round with Detroit he took a softer job as a milkman.

CASEY, Jon

b. Grand Rapids, Minnesota, March 29, 1962

Casey experienced the climax of his career at the same time it was reaching its nadir. Backstopping his team to the '91 Stanley Cup finals against Pittsburgh, his Stars were blown away in the clinching game 8-0, the most lopsided loss for the Cup in league history. He grew up on the Iron Range, in Coleraine, and his father owned a real estate business in Grand Rapids while he attended Greenaway Public School. Casey attended the University of North Dakota, but despite superb results during his four years he was never drafted by an NHL team. His home state North Stars signed him as a free agent, and it was there he played most of his career, first as a sub, then as a starter for five years. At 22 he was invited to the U.S. Olympic camp in September '83 but didn't take the tryout seriously because his wedding day was approaching and he didn't want to play anyway. The Stars traded him to Boston for Andy Moog and Gord Murphy, but after one excellent season he signed with St. Louis, where he finished his career. He returned to school, enrolling at a college in St. Charles, Missouri, to complete his degree.

CASHMAN, Wayne ("Cash")

b. Kingston, Ontario, June 24, 1945

When he retired at the end of the '82-'83 season, Cashman was the last survivor of the Original Six and a man with a huge sense of humour. Once, after a party in Boston, he was pulled over and arrested for drinking and driving. In jail, he exercised his constitutional right to one phone call – and ordered Chinese food. Cashman played junior in Oshawa with Bobby Orr, but he was a winger with not much speed or skill. However, he was the best in the league in the corners, and it was his superb work that got the puck to centre Phil Esposito in the slot time and again so

that Espo could break all goal-scoring records (their linemate was Ken Hodge – part Cash, part Espo). His first game came in '64-'65 as an emergency recall when the Bruins were short of forwards. The team played the Red Wings that night and Cash was assigned the task of covering Gordie Howe, a task he performed admirably. Two years later he earned a full-time job in Beantown, and he became known as a scrapper and a player both. He played on the historic Summit Series Canadian team in '72, but his career was jeopardized in '72-'73 when he slid into a goalpost and hurt his back. Undaunted, he continued to play. In fact, it was easier for him to skate than either walk or sleep. By season's end he could barely move. After a serious operation, he recovered, and in 1977 was named the Bruins' captain. Six years later, he retired.

In 1986 pal Espo, now GM on Broadway, hired Cashman as a scout for New England, the start of a prominent post-skating career in the game. He, Bobby Orr, and retired U.S. Senator Paul Tsongas had tried to buy the Bruins the previous year, and Cashman also worked on a radio sports talk show in Boston. After five years with the Rangers, he acted as an assistant coach for Tampa Bay for four years and moved to San Jose for '96-'97 in the same capacity. On July 7, 1997, he was named coach of the Philadelphia Flyers, and a week later was named an assistant for Canada's entry in the '98 Olympics in Nagano. However, partway through his first year, GM Bobby Clarke removed him from behind the Flyers bench but kept him on as an assistant and adviser. Winner of two Stanley Cups and a Bruins all his playing life (17 years, 1,027 games), Cashman is still one of the most loved B's of the modern era.

CASSELMAN, Mike

b. Morrisburg, Ontario, August 23, 1968

It's too early to write the final chapter on Casselman's NHL career, but it looks pretty clear that the nights of February 24, 25, and 29, 1996, will go down in his autobiography as the only three nights of his pro life, with Florida. A graduate of Clarkson University, he simply never made the grade outside the minors. He was later signed by San Jose, but the Sharks never availed themselves of his services and he went to Europe to continue his career.

CASSELS, Andrew

b. Bramalea, Ontario, July 23, 1969

One of a select group of instant successes, Cassels played his first NHL game on November 19, 1989, and scored a goal on Mike Vernon of Calgary, the team he wound up playing for in 1997. Who would have

Cashman played junior in Oshawa with Bobby Orr.
WAYNE CASHMAN

Joe Carveth

Jon Casey

Andrew Cassels

Bruce Cassidy

known that just a short time later he would receive such honours the ITT Top Gun Award as Hartford's leading scorer in '94-'95, or the Farmington Savings Bank Player of the Month in November 1995? He had been coveted by the Montreal Canadiens while playing junior in Ottawa, but soon after was traded to the Whalers. He also represented Canada at the World Juniors in 1989 and the World Championships in 1996. After Calgary let him go in the summer of 1999, he signed with Vancouver as a free agent and in his first year added to his trophy shelf by winning the Fred J. Hume Award as Vancouver's "Unsung Hero."

CASSIDY, Bruce ("Butch")
b. Ottawa, Ontario, May 20, 1965
Ball hockey can be a dangerous sport. Just ask Butch. Drafted at age 18 by Chicago in '83, the world looked bright for a man the Hawks hoped would boost their offence from the blueline. But the next summer he damaged his anterior cruciate ligament playing hockey on blacktop and was gone for a year of rehab. It just never worked out. A few games here, a few there with Chicago. There were no other takers, so he flew to the less demanding ice lanes of Europe before playing in the "I" in 1994 for a few years. After that, he went into coaching in the East Coast league, and then the AHL, becoming head coach of the Washington Capitals in 2002.

CASSIDY, Tom
b. Blind River, Ontario, March 15, 1952
Beware the ides of March, for players born on that grisly day meet fortunes not in keeping with the NHL. Owned by California and the Kings of Angelinos and then the Bruins before donning that most garish garb of Pittsburgh, young Tom waited five long years from draft to first game in the great league called the NHL. These were the 1970s. And yet his stay was short – too short to merit long romantic tales of glory – and gone. Gone no one knows where, but gone without redemption for a career so brief.

Tom Cassidy

CASSIVI, Frederic
b. Sorel, Quebec, June 12, 1975
From Ottawa to Colorado to Atlanta, Cassivi has bounced around in the systems of various NHL teams, but it wasn't until he was 26 that the Thrashers finally put the goalie into a few games in 2001-02. He has been a minor leaguer before and since.

CASSOLATO, Tony
b. Guelph, Ontario, May 7, 1956
A member of the Canadian team that was invited to the first unofficial World Junior Championships in the Soviet Union in 1974, Cassolato shortly thereafter opted to play in the WHA after no NHL team showed interest in signing him. In 1979, after the league went legit, he signed on with Washington but played only itty-bits of three seasons before going overseas for a brief sojourn of culture and pucks.

Jay Caufield

CAUFIELD, Jay
b. Philadelphia, Pennsylvania, July 17, 1960
He was a two-sport man at U of North Dakota, playing football as a linebacker and hockey as winger before

signing with the Rangers as a free agent. Just 13 games later, he wound up in Minnesota and then settled in Pittsburgh for the final five years of his career. Averaging nearly four penalty minutes a game, Caufield obviously didn't earn his stripes scoring goals and taking spins as the game's first star every night. But he did play on the Penguins Cup-winning team of 1992, and not many can boast of having their name stamped on the glorious old bowl.

CAVALLINI, Gino
b. Toronto, Ontario, November 24, 1962
So he goes to his first NHL training camp, right? In Calgary. Coach Bob Johnson sizes him up, decides the kid's not ready. Sends him to the farm. Moncton. Other side of the country. Tells him to work on his flexibility, strength, the usual. Cavallini enrolls in martial arts classes over the summer, earns his purple belt, and makes the Flames the next fall. It's all good, right? Plays on a line with Carey Wilson and Tim Hunter. People call it the Tank Line because they're all big guys. Then he gets traded. Down to Saint Louis. What's that all about? Turned out to be the best thing for him. Stayed a Blue for six years, but the Blues let him go and Quebec claimed him. Used him as a spare part. No thanks. Took an offer from Milwaukee in the "I," made team captain, had a ball. When his dad died, he grieved. Naturally. He recalled the early-morning practices, the paternal pride of having a boy go on to the NHL. He went to Europe to play. He had fun, and he appreciated what he had. That, *that* is what the game's all about. Once retired, he settled in Milwaukee to pursue business interests that he had cultivated during days with the Admirals.

CAVALLINI, Paul ("Wally")
b. Toronto, Ontario, October 13, 1965
His wife is Tracy Smith, the Canadian who competed in the long jump for Canada at the 1988 Summer Olympics in Seoul. Another plus: He led the NHL in +/- in '89-'90 and was a +116 over a 10-year career. A steady, unspectacular defenceman, he nonetheless had five points in one game, April 12, 1994, versus St. Louis. The younger brother of Gino, he was selected a lowly 205th overall in 1984, so just making it to the big tent was an accomplishment his dad could be proud of. That he lasted 564 games on defence, now that was something he himself could be proud of.

CECHMANEK, Roman
b. Gottwaldov (Zlin), Czechoslovakia (Czech Republic), March 2, 1971
Like countryman Dominik Hasek, Cechmanek was a late draft choice despite a great career back home in the Czech Republic. In Cechmanek's case, he was named top goalie for six successive years (1994-2000) and was backup to Hasek when the Czechs won gold at the 1998 Olympics in Nagano. He also won gold with his country at the 1996, 1999, and 2000 World Championships before the Flyers finally took a chance on him with the 171st selection overall in the summer of 2000. He stepped onto a team with a messy, unresolved goaltending situation, and through his great play cleaned that matter up beautifully. In his

Paul Cavallini

first season he went 35-15-6 and recorded ten shutouts. Midway through the year, the team was so excited by his play that it signed him to a three-year contract extension to the tune of $10.5 million. The next year, he lost the starter's job for part of the year, but emerged in time for the 2002-03 season as strong as ever. He was backup again to Hasek at the 2002 Olympics in Salt Lake City, and when Hasek retired in the summer of '02, Cechmanek quietly celebrated, because finally he could be the number-one man for any international competition for the Czechs in the near future. The Flyers are counting on him, and the Czechs have nowhere else to turn, so now the onus is on Cechmanek to prove his brilliance at the next, and highest, level.

CENTOMO, Sebastien ("Sea Bass")
b. Montreal, Quebec,
March 26, 1981
Buried in the Toronto system, Centomo played all of two periods with the Leafs in 2001-02 but is not likely to see more action given there are at least three goalies ahead of him – Belfour, Kidd, and Tellqvist. Yet, stranger things have happened, and a trade is not out of the question for the prospect who had a fine career in the Q.

CERESINO, Ray
b. Port Arthur, Ontario,
April 24, 1929
The Hockey News of the day called him "the Italian boy" who was "one of the best looking boys in the circuit." This was during Ceresino's long tenure with Cleveland in the AHL after he had played a dozen games with the Leafs, been demoted, been traded, and been shopped around.

CERNIK, Frantisek ("Frank")
b. Novy Jicin, Czechoslovakia (Czech Republic),
June 3, 1953
Cernik arrived in Detroit with Milan Chalupa. The Wings wanted some European talent and went to some lengths to obtain it, convincing the pair to abandon life on the Continent for a chance to play with the big boys. Cernik was a star back home. He had played in five World Championships, two Canada Cups, and the 1984 Olympics in Sarajevo, and happily accepted the challenge. Once in the Motor City, however, he became disillusioned. He didn't score in the exhibition season, so coach Nick Polano reduced his ice time. Five goals in a season was the result, and Cernik returned to Germany to resume his career. After finishing, he returned to the Czech Republic and became general manager for the country's national team for the World Championships and Olympics.

CHABOT, Frederic
b. Hebertville-Station, Quebec, February 12, 1968
He's played 21 games in the NHL but been part of 9 transactions – traded here, claimed there, signed elsewhere, been there and back (to Montreal), owned at some point by 8 different teams, yet he keeps hanging in there and coming back for more when his services are requested. Gotta like that in a kid. But after 10 years at the NHL level and a final send-off to the minors, he moved to Germany to tend the crease of the Nurenberg Ice Tigers, a team not likely to play for the Stanley Cup any time soon, but one in need of a goaler all the same.

CHABOT, John
b. Summerside, Prince Edward Island, May 18, 1962
Part Algonquin, Chabot worked extensively with the National Native Alcohol and Drug Abuse Program in Canada, visiting reserves and trying to help those least fortunate in the country improve their lot in life. He made the most of his, playing eight gentlemanly years in the NHL despite limited skills. Stops in Montreal, Pittsburgh, and Detroit were rewarding but not always quiet. He missed curfew on more than one occasion with the Pens, and was fined and suspended after one late night too many. Nonetheless, he learned, mended his ways, and continued to play. After his NHL time seemed over, in 1991, he moved to Europe to play first in Italy and then in Germany, where he has spent the better part of a decade.

Winner of two Stanley Cups, 73 career shutouts, two Allan Cups.
LORNE CHABOT

CHABOT, Lorne ("Sad Eyes"/ "Chabotsky"/ "Old Bulwarks")
b. Montreal, Quebec, October 5, 1900
d. Montreal, Quebec, October 10, 1946
When he first joined the Rangers at the start of their inaugural season, 1926-27, someone in the PR department had the crazy idea of changing his name to Chabotsky to attract the city's large Jewish population to the games. Someone in Toronto got wind of the hustle, and the name was gone. Chabot is without question the finest goaler not in the Hockey Hall of Fame. Winner of two Stanley Cups (with New York in '28 and the Leafs four years later), 73 career shutouts, two Allan Cups in '24 and '25. Someone, somewhere must not like goalies. He played in two historic games: for Toronto in the 1933 playoff game that went into six overtimes, and three years later in an even longer six-overtimer with the Maroons in a 1-0 loss to Detroit. He said he always shaved before a game because cuts stitched more easily with a smooth face. When he was hit flush in the eye in the '28 playoffs by a Nels Stewart shot, the Rangers

Ray Ceresino

Frantisek Cernik

Frederic Chabot

John Chabot

Ed Chadwick

Milan Chalupa

Murph Chamberlain

Shawn Chambers

thought his career was over. That summer, they happily traded him to Toronto, and would soon see that his career was just beginning. For five years he was numero uno in the Toronto nets, and in his last four years in the NHL he played for four different teams before pursuing a career as a salesman in Toronto and other parts of Ontario for a Winnipeg-based dairy company. Illness overcame him, however, and he retired early. He died of nephritis and osteoarthritis at the Jewish General Hospital in Montreal.

CHAD, John
b. Provost, Alberta, September 16, 1919
d. October 11, 1970
One of the more gentlemanly players of his era, Chad received the Jack Fox Trophy for '49-'50 in the AHL for sportsmanlike conduct. But just as plans were being readied for a formal presentation at the start of the following season, he broke his ankle and missed half a year. These were in the days after the war, when his NHL dreams had been realized but briefly, and he woke up to the fresh smell of AHL arenas. He played with Chicago for two years before the war, enlisted for four years where he was, among other duties, a sapper with the Royal Canadian Engineers, then made a 13-game comeback with the Hawks before going to the AHL.

CHADWICK, Ed ("Chad")
b. Fergus, Ontario, May 8, 1933
His rise to the top was as swift as it was heroic and unpredictable, and his descent was equally so. A product of St. Mike's in Toronto, he grew up dreaming of the day he would play for the Blue and White. Toward the end of the '55-'56 season, Leafs regular Harry Lumley was injured, and coach Howie Meeker called on Chadwick to replace him for five games. He won two by shutout, and recorded three 1-1 ties in the others. Next fall, he was the number-one man, playing every minute of every game for two years. Then Punch Imlach took over and a guy named Bower filled the net. They shared duties for a year, but it was clear that Bower was the man and Chadwick the odd man out. That he ever skated on ice, though, had been a miracle. He was born with a club foot and never even wore a pair of boots until he was 14. His foot became workable only because of the extraordinary devotion of his mother, who massaged it and twisted his toes into shape for thousands of hours, year after year. After retiring, he went into scouting, with Pittsburgh, Oakland, and the Islanders. He was named coach for the Isles affiliate in Fort Worth, and GM Bill Torrey gave him a goalie – Chico Resch – and told him to get Chico ready in two years or else. One year later, Resch was with the Islanders. After leaving the Islanders, Chadwick joined Buffalo and then Edmonton in 1982, where he has been ever since.

CHALMERS, Bill ("Chick")
b. Stratford, Ontario, January 24, 1934
d. December 7, 1994
Playing on a line with Ronnie Spong and Moe Bartoli, Chick Chalmers set a record of 93 assists and 134 points. The year was '59-'60. The league, unfortunately, was the IHL, his league of choice for 14

years after a one-game skate with the Rangers in 1953-54. He was captain of the Toledo Blades for years, including '63-'64 when the team won the Joseph Turner Memorial Trophy as IHL champions. In all, he played 17 years in the minors, and the nickname he had been given as a 17-year-old youngster with Guelph back in junior was long inappropriate.

CHALUPA, Milan
b. Oudolen, Czechoslovakia (Czech Republic), July 4, 1953
He arrived on the Detroit scene with Frantisek Cernik but hurt his groin, didn't make as much of an impression, and didn't last as long before returning whence he came – Europe. Like Cernik, the core of Chalupa's experience was international and included seven World Championships, three Olympics, and two Canada Cups. Other than his 14 games with the Wings in '84-'85, he was a fixture in Czech league and later German league play until 1991.

CHAMBERLAIN, Erwin "Murph" ("Old Hardrock")
b. Shawville, Quebec, February 14, 1915
d. Beachville, Ontario, May 8, 1986
As a kid, young Erwin learned from the best. His hero was Frank Finnigan, and as luck would have it Finnigan spent most of his summers in Shawville and returned occasionally during the snowy months. He'd take the kid out skating, teaching him the finer points of hockey, checking, skating, etc. Finnigan was particularly adept at blocking an opponent, a trick he had learned from his idol, Punch Broadbent. In turn, Chamberlain became one of the best checkers when he got to the NHL. But first he won an Allan Cup with Sudbury Frood Mines in 1937 before joining the Maple Leafs the next year, playing on a line with Nick Metz and Pep Kelly. He went on to play a total of 12 years in the NHL, winning Cups with Montreal in 1944 and '46. During his career he played all forward positions at one time or another. After retiring, he coached for some 20 years, from Sydney to Charlottetown to Vancouver and anywhere else in between, notably Buffalo, Windsor, and Chatham. He ended where he began, in Sudbury for four years, but one day he quit. He became involved in door-to-door distribution of flyers, establishing Paperman Ltd., which thrives to this day. He bought a farm in Pickering for a few years, and with the distribution business thriving he moved to a 375-acre farm in Beachville, Ontario, raising 275 head of cattle and growing corn and grain. But life wasn't all good. He had five operations for cancer, had a grapefruit-sized aneurysm plucked from his stomach, and had a lung removed in 1972. During the lung operation, he suffered a heart attack that would have been fatal had he not been, at that very second, in the hands of a doctor.

CHAMBERS, Shawn
b. Sterling Heights, Michigan, October 11, 1966
This guy is a walking medical report hoping to play hockey someday. He grew up down the road from the brothers Hatcher, teammates with whom he won a Stanley Cup in 1999 with Dallas, but Chambers' career has been a series of hospital visits. On seven separate occasions he hurt his left knee and required surgery or

some lesser form of treatment. But that was early on. In more recent years, his injuries of choice have been manual. He's fractured his hand twice, a thumb once, a finger once. He's sprained his finger joints and bruised his digits enough times to miss games. Despite being in the league for 13 seasons, he's played just 625 games for 5 teams, winning his first Cup in 1995 with the surprising Devils. He was also a fringe member of Team USA's entry in the 1996 World Cup.

CHAMPAGNE, Andre
b. Ottawa, Ontario, September 19, 1943
He was the toast of the town in Toronto for just two nights – February 23 and 27, 1963 – and although the Leafs were to sip bubbly from Lord Stanley's mug that spring, he didn't play enough to get his name on the Cup. Then it was off to the minors for a fruitful career. Champagne had won a Memorial Cup with St. Mike's in 1961 and won again in '64 with the Marlies. It is rare enough to win two such championships, let alone with different teams, and let alone with an NHL appearance sandwiched between them.

CHAMPOUX, Bob
b. St. Hilaire, Quebec, December 2, 1942
March 29, 1964. Hollywood, are you listening? Detroit is playing Chicago. Game two of the Stanley Cup semifinals. Early in the first period Terry Sawchuk, the great goalie, hurts his shoulder. Cut to Bob Champoux, in a suit, sitting nervously behind the Detroit bench. Sawchuk recovers. Champoux sighs with relief. A minute and a half later, Sawchuk is in excruciating pain again. Cut to Champoux, who is told to report to the dressing room. Sawchuk's out – he's in. Champoux skates onto the ice. He's wearing a mask, so the merciless Chicago fans can't see how nervous he is. First NHL game; first time wearing a mask. Norm Ullman scores a pair to give the young goalie a lead and some breathing room. The Wings get another early in the second, but then Chicago strikes for two. Howe scores with three seconds left in the second period: 4-2. Ullman completes the hat trick, but the Hawks strike for two quickies: 5-4 with 15 minutes left in the game. Champoux holds the fort. One year out of Junior B, and he's a hero. Sawchuk returns the next game. Ten years later, Champoux is wearing the sweater of the California Golden Seals. Plays 17 games. Wins twice. Allows an average of five goals each time out. Fade to black.

CHAPDELAINE, Rene
b. Weyburn, Saskatchewan, September 27, 1966
No relation to Marie de Chapdelaine, Rene was

drafted by L.A., played briefly with the Kings for parts of three seasons, and was let go. He drifted off to the "I" to play for Long Beach, and when the IHL merged with the AHL in 2001 and Long Beach joined the WCHL, Chapdelaine followed.

CHAPMAN, Art
b. Winnipeg, Manitoba, May 29, 1906
d. Long Beach, California, December 30, 1962
A dozen years in the NHL in the '30s and early '40s climaxed in 1934-36. Playing on a line with Sweeney Schriner and Lorne Carr, Chapman was the league's leading scorer both years. After retiring, he embarked on one of the most successful coaching careers outside the NHL, starting with a 10-year reign with the Buffalo Bisons that included two Calder Cups. From there he moved to Vancouver to assume coach and general manager duties of the WHL's Canucks for another decade, becoming the most successful coach in Vancouver history. His critics charged him with preaching defensive hockey, to which he replied that if his team stopped goals, eventually they would get one. Chapman then moved down the coast to Long Beach, where he became general manager of the Dunn-Edwards Western Show Corporation, which promoted shows at the Long Beach Arena. It was there he remained until his death at age 56.

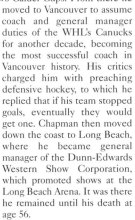

Chapman moved to Long Beach, where he became general manager of the Dunn-Edwards Western Show Corporation.
ART CHAPMAN

CHAPMAN, Blair
b. Lloydminster, Saskatchewan, June 13, 1956
Hot, hot, hot was how he started his career. Playing junior with Bernie Federko in Saskatoon didn't hurt, either. Chapman scored 71 goals in his last year of junior, and the Penguins selected him 2nd overall in 1976. Great expectations, indeed. These were never realized, but the Blues acquired him hoping that reuniting him with Federko would light his bushel. It did, for a time. Chapman had back-to-back 20-goal seasons, but then he suffered a ruptured disc in '81-'82 which cost him most of the year of rehab following surgery. Half a season the following year induced him to call it quits, though he made it to 400 games (402, to be exact), which guaranteed him a nice payday later in life.

CHAPMAN, Brian
b. Brockville, Ontario, February 10, 1968
This guy wasn't out there to score goals. Suspended by both the OHL and the AHL for fighting-related incidents, Chapman racked up penalty minutes like bankers throw strikes. Even during his brief three-bout NHL career he averaged 10 penalty minutes per round. And in the minors, he could be counted on for 200 minutes a season. Nonetheless, he has endured and survived to see another tomorrow

Andre Champagne

Rene Chapdelaine

Blair Chapman

longer than most, and he continues to play in the IHL after some 1,200 games in the minors.

Zdeno Chara

CHARA, Zdeno
b. Trencin, Czechoslovakia (Slovakia), March 18, 1977
Two words: Very. Tall. At 6'9" the tallest player in NHL history, in fact. His father, Zdenek, was a member of the Czech wrestling team at the 1976 Olympics in Montreal, and Zdeno has grappled with his fair share of pros in his day. Young, talented, and tall, the Islanders had hoped his best days were still in the future, with them. Then they traded him to Ottawa in the deal that brought Alexei Yashin to Long Island, and Chara immediately added size and skill to a Sens defence in need of both. During his time with the Islanders, he never appeared in the playoffs. As a result, he was available to Slovakia for the World Championships, appearing in 1999 and 2000 and captaining the 2001 entry.

CHARBONNEAU, Jose "Joe" ("Joltin' Joe")
b. Ferme-Neuve, Quebec, November 21, 1966
The peripatetic life of the guy they call Joe has taken him to the corners of the stick-carrying world. He is one of only two players to skate/blade for both Vancouver hockey teams – the Canucks of the NHL and the VooDoo of the Roller Hockey International league (the other player to do so is Frank Caprice). While with the Doo, he trained with coach Tiger Williams, and it was Tiger who recommended him to Canucks management and became his agent in the process. Joe made the team, but a back injury slowed his progress. Along the way he played for the Canadian National Team (back on ice, now) as well as Rapperswil in Switzerland and an outfit called Meetpoint Eaters Geleen in Holland. His wife possesses the galactic name of Venus, an actress who has graced the small screen in *Street Legal* and *21 Jump Street* and the big screen in *Deadly Vows* and *Hit*. Charbonneau's final NHL game came in 1995, at which point he moved to Germany to play.

Jose Charbonneau

CHARBONNEAU, Stephane
b. Ste-Adele, Quebec, June 27, 1970
No one wanted him during his three years in the Q, but the Nordiques signed him as a free agent in 1991, gave him a couple of games as souvenirs, and threw him to the minors, where he descended ever further, from the AHL to the "I" to the Colonial League to the ECHL. Then home. In the summer, he often played roller hockey before retiring in 1998.

Eric Charron

CHARLEBOIS, Bob
b. Cornwall, Ontario, May 27, 1944
Montreal GM Sam Pollock liked what he saw early on from Charlebois, but after the left winger played a few years in the team's junior system Silent Sam included Charlebois in a package to Minnesota for the Stars' first draft choice in '71, perhaps trying to replicate his theft the following year of Oakland's choice, with which he selected Guy Lafleur. It wasn't to be, for Pollock settled on Chuck Arnason, hardly a memorable find. Charlebois, meanwhile, played just seven games with Minny before going to the WHA

Guy Charron

and then the minors and finishing with the Cape Cod Codders and the Binghampton Dusters of the NAHL. After retiring, he moved to Ottawa and coached the University Gee-Gees for two years, then became the school's coordinator for continuing education.

CHARLESWORTH, Todd
b. Calgary, Alberta, March 22, 1965
An OHL graduate, Charlesworth played briefly with Pittsburgh over five seasons before being signed as a free agent by Edmonton in the summer of '89. The Oilers decided they didn't need him and sent him to the Rangers and after just seven games the Rangers felt the same way. Charlesworth ended up in the Colonial League, first as a player and then as a playing assistant coach in 1992 after missing the previous year because of serious hand surgery.

CHARPENTIER, Sebastien
b. Drummondville, Quebec, April 18, 1977
A goalie drafted in 1995, Charpentier didn't make his NHL debut until midway through the 2001-02 season, with Washington. He graduated from the QMJHL only to end up in the minors for years, though he worked his way into the number-one position with the Caps' farm team in Portland. For the foreseeable future, his chances of usurping Olaf Kolzig in the NHL nets are close to nil.

CHARRON, Eric
b. Verdun, Quebec, January 14, 1970
Things just haven't worked out for Charron as he would have liked. Highly thought of as a teen playing junior in Quebec, he was drafted by Montreal in 1988. After four years in the system and just three games with les habitants, he was traded to Tampa, then to Washington, and then to Calgary in ensuing years. A tough, stay-at-home defenceman, he has spent more time in the minors than in the NHL. His most recent home has been the Minnesota Wild, with whom he signed as a free agent in the summer of 2000.

CHARRON, Guy
b. Verdun, Quebec, January 24, 1949
Night = Charron as player. Day = Charron as coach. As a player, he holds a record no one in his right mind would want: most regular-season games played without participating in the playoffs. His first year, with Montreal in '69-'70, was the rare time the Habs didn't make the playoffs (ah, the past). Midway through the next year he was traded to Detroit. Four years; no playoffs. Kansas City; Washington. Nada. Along the way he had 5 seasons of 25 goals or more. Lots of goals; no luck. All in all, 734 games, none in the playoffs. Not one! But immediately upon retiring in 1983 he was named the GM and coach of the Quebec Remparts. He became an assistant to Dave King under the National program, culminating with three years as assistant at the World Juniors and then coaching the 1990 team to a gold medal. The next year he became an assistant in Calgary for the Flames and four years later, in 1995, moved to the Islanders in the same capacity. He then made head coach down in the IHL with Grand Rapids and in mid-December 2000 became head man with the

Mighty Ducks of Disney, such a long, long way away from Montreal in 1970.

CHARTIER, Dave
b. St. Lazare, Manitoba, February 15, 1961
Perhaps the strangest draft-related story of all time. Most players are drafted into the NHL. Some are not, but still play. Some are drafted twice. Some are drafted high and never make, or drafted low and do make it. Chartier was drafted 191st by Winnipeg in 1980. Big woof. He was called up for one game with the Jets in '80-'81 after spending most of the year in junior with Brandon. But he never signed a contract with the Jets, and re-entered the draft in 1982. This time he was chosen 174th overall by Los Angeles, but never played for the team. Thus, he became the first player to play in an NHL game both after he was drafted and *before!* Now that's a one-game wonder.

CHARTRAND, Brad
b. Winnipeg, Manitoba, December 14, 1974
It wasn't until he was 25 years old that he had any sort of secure NHL contract. Forget about being drafted; he just wanted to play. Chartrand did the typical thing by playing a year of provincial junior hockey in Manitoba before going to the U.S. to play for Cornell. He then joined the Canadian National Team during its final days of existence and played with the St. John's Maple Leafs in the AHL, even though the big Leafs hadn't shown any interest in him. He scored 16 goals that year, and the L.A. Kings decided that was enough to throw him a bone.

He became the first player to play in an NHL game both after he was drafted and before!
DAVE CHARTIER

He played much of the next season on the wing for the Kings, but in 2000-01 played just four times before being farmed out to Lowell.

CHARTRAW, Rick ("Charty")
b. Caracas, Venezuela, July 13, 1954
Needless to say, not too many Venezuelans crack the NHL. Needless to say, there's a story here. Chartraw's father, an engineer, built power stations, and the family was in Caracas for almost four years. They moved to the States – Dayton, Chicago, Orlando – before settling in Erie, Pennsylvania. He played junior in Ontario, but his wayward habits continued to his detriment when he joined the Montreal Canadiens in 1974. Constantly late for team meetings and practices, Chartraw was forever in trouble with coaches, despite his immense talent. He showed up to training camp overweight, stayed out late consuming that which he shouldn't, rented a penthouse in the city while he was spending most of his time with the farm team. Wrong attitude. As a result, his ice time suffered, he was demoted, and he was used sparingly in games he did dress for. Meanwhile, Montreal was

winning the Cup every year, but still Chartraw asked for a trade, which he got, to Los Angeles. Again, limited ice time, and again a trade, to the Rangers and then the Oilers. He later became involved in real estate, operated a marina in California, and became an arena consultant.

CHASE, Kelly ("Chaser")
b. Porcupine Plain, Saskatchewan, October 25, 1967
One of the most penalized players of his era, Chase was as nice off the ice as he was tough on it. He had more than 2,000 penalty minutes during his NHL days, but he won the King Clancy Award in 1998 for his charitable efforts. More than that, though, he made it to the bigs despite never being drafted, proof to himself, if no one else, that he could make the grade. He lasted 11 seasons, finishing where he began, in St. Louis, as one of the most-liked athletes in the city. In between, he played for Hartford and briefly with the Leafs, but after retiring he remained in St. Louis and became a radio announcer for the Blues.

CHASSE, Denis
b. Montreal, Quebec, February 7, 1970
He played for four different teams during his four-year junior career in Quebec, portents of things to come in the NHL, where he again played for four teams in as many years. In 1995-96, Chasse had the distinction of wearing the colours of St. Louis, Washington, and Winnipeg, all in the same season, and after a few games with Ottawa the following year set sail for Europe and action overseas. He began in Germany, then made his way to the Bracknell Bees in Britain before moving on to the Cardiff Devils, where he has most recently plied his blade trade.

CHEBATURKIN, Vladimir
b. Tyumen, Soviet Union (Russia), April 23, 1975
He was just getting bigger and, the Islanders hoped, better, when they drafted him in 1993. A member of Russia's 1995 World Junior team, his development has been slow to date, and a decade later his Islanders days are long gone. St. Louis signed him as a free agent, as did Chicago, and all these years later the word "promise" has slowly faded and been replaced by "not interested."

CHECK, Ludic "Lude"
b. Brandon, Manitoba, May 22, 1919
He played a game with Detroit on March 11, 1944, and a season with Chicago the following year, but Check spent most of his years in the Quebec Senior league with the Aces and then the Senators. He retired in 1951.

Rick Chartraw

Kelly Chase

Vladimir Chebaturkin

Lude Check

Gerry Cheevers

CHEEVERS, Gerry ("Cheesie")
b. St. Catharines, Ontario, December 7, 1940

Never one for practices, Cheevers one day faked injury with Boston after being hit in the mask by a harmless shot. He hurried off to the trainer's room, where he relaxed and had a beverage, until coach Harry Sinden stormed in and demanded that he return to the ice. Cheevers asked the trainer to paint a large "gash" on the mask to show the extent of the mock injury, and thus was born the first and perhaps most famous of all goalie masks of the 1970s. That Cheevers ever got to Boston was due only to good fortune and timing. He went to school at St. Mike's, where he tended goal under the watchful eye of the Leafs. In fact, he played two games for the Blue and White during the '61-'62 season but then was buried in the minors. Toronto, feeling it was strong in goal for the present and future, let the Bruins claim Cheevers in the 1965 Intra-League Draft, and so began the Hall of Fame career of one of the great playoff goalies. He didn't have the traditional goalie's ego, worrying about shutouts and his goals against average. He cared about winning, be it 2-1 or 7-6, and joining an explosive Bruins team that became the highest-scoring team in NHL history, scores tended toward the latter more than the former. After winning Cups in 1970 and '72, Cheevers was at the height of his power and popularity. He cashed those in by signing with the WHA in the summer of 1972, joining Cleveland after signing a seven-year, $1.4 million contract. But after less than four years, he realized there was more to the game than just money and returned to the Bruins fold. He still had some saves left in his glove hand, but his knees were bothering him and he was no longer the dominant player he had been. He retired in 1980 and became the team's coach, one of very few men to go from player to coach over the course of a summer, and one of an even smaller number of goalies to coach at the NHL level. During his career, he never led the league in any statistical category – he was just good and consistent. He was perhaps the first truly wandering goalie, frequently going into the corner to race for pucks and move play up the ice with passes, often leading to success, sometimes leading to empty-net goals for the opposition. Cheevers lasted four and a half years behind the bench, where he had terrific regular-season success but not as much luck in the playoffs. His style was somewhat alienating to the players, and over time played his way out of the picture. In 1985, he was inducted into the Hockey Hall of Fame, though at the time he was in full swing of a second career. In the late 1960s and early 1970s, Cheevers had become interested in the racetrack. He bought horses and raced them for fun and profit, and his silent partner was Bobby Orr.

They started the Four Thirty Stables in 1970. Many of their horses were given hockey-related names such as Wing To Wing, Two On One, In The Crease, At The Net, Around The Boards, and, of course, Number Four, but their most famous nag was called Royal Ski. In 1976, she earned more money than any other two-year-old in North America and Cheevers later planned to syndicate her for more than $2 million until Ski contracted a virus and forced him to withdraw from the deal. After his coaching days, Cheevers became director of Rockingham Park, a track in Salem, New Hampshire.

After his coaching days, Cheevers became director of Rockingham Park, a track in Salem, New Hampshire.
GERRY CHEEVERS

CHELIOS, Chris ("Chelly")
b. Chicago, Illinois, January 25, 1962

A master of the stick, Chelios has managed to survive in the NHL into his forties because of an intensity that is rooted in dirty play but has inspired dozens of teammates who have come and gone during his career. He began his career in an oddly Canadian manner by playing provincial junior hockey before attending college at home. Chelios first rose to prominence at the 1982 World Juniors, and the following year spent the season with the National Team, playing for the U.S. at the 1984 Olympics in Sarajevo. He joined Montreal toward the end of the season and began an NHL tenure that has gone on for more than 1,200 games. During his seven seasons with the Habs, Chelios helped win the surprising Cup of 1986. He also played on the 1984 and '87 Canada Cup teams for the U.S., though neither team performed particularly well. In the summer of 1990, his dream came true when he was traded to Chicago – his home town. He spent the next nine years with the Hawks and had his finest seasons. He won the James Norris Trophy three times ('88-'89, '92-'93, '95-'96) and was named a First Team All-Star four times. His play was never defined by his offence (though he was certainly a capable skater with the puck and sometimes a playmaker) as much as his ability to play half a game or more at top speed. He never worried about dirty play antagonizing opponents and his tactics frequently worked. The Hawks never came particularly close to winning the Cup during his tenure, though he was team captain from 1995 until his trade to Detroit in 1999. During the lockout of '94-'95, Chelios told the media he didn't think NHL Commissioner Gary Bettman's family was safe, a vile remark brandished during the heat of negotiations in words typical of his on-ice demeanour. Chelios was part of the embarrassing U.S. team at the 1998 Olympics in Nagano that finished far from the podium and then trashed various rooms in disrespect, this two years after winning the World Cup over Canada in a thrilling three-game finals. Yet Chelios alone apologized for the incident and paid for the

Chris Chelios

damages. He later played as a 40-year-old on the 2002 U.S. Olympic team that won silver at Salt Lake City. In Detroit, he was supposed to be an experienced part of a team hoping to build on Cup wins in 1997 and '98, and sure enough, in 2001-02, the Wings won their third Cup in six seasons. By virtue of having won only in 1986 and 2002, Chelios set a record for the longest time between Cup wins for a player. A future Hall of Famer three years after he retires, Chelios has led a full and colourful life in hockey. He has never been a record-setter but he has been in the league for two decades, a feat of physical ability that in itself is admirable.

CHERNOFF, Mike
b. Yorkton, Saskatchewan, May 13, 1946
While playing for the Cleveland Barons under coach John Muckler in the AHL, Chernoff scored five goals in the game, three of those coming short-handed. Incredibly, the only other time three short-handed had been scored in a pro game anywhere had occurred just four days earlier when Dave Kryskow of the Dallas Black Hawks turned the trick! Chernoff played a single game with Minnesota with nothing but zeroes on his scorecard, though he later played briefly in the WHA.

CHERNOMAZ, Rich
b. Selkirk, Manitoba, September 1, 1963
Part-time is putting it mildly. Three teams, seven years, 25 games in '86-'87 his longest stint at any one time. Plenty of games in the minors, then he tried his hand at coaching. Chernomaz became playing assistant coach with St. John's in 1993 for two AHL years, but then played for Canada at the Worlds in 1995 and stayed in Europe to play rather than continue to coach. He joined Schwenningen as a player, and after getting the last of his playing out of his system he stayed on and became the team's coach, a position he continues to enjoy.

CHERRY, Dick
b. Kingston, Ontario, March 28, 1937
Don't mess with him: He holds a black belt in karate. Actually, there was a stretch of 12 years between games in the Original Six and the Expansion Era for Cherry. He played six games for the Bruins in '56-'57, but after years in the minors he returned home to Kingston to teach high school. The Flyers not only claimed him in the '67 Expansion Draft, they signed him to a three-year contract. He played two of those three seasons before being claimed right back by the Bruins (hockey types have long memories), though he never played again with the Beantowners. His bro, one Donald S., also made it to the NHL for a game, though he's pretty well known in a suit and tie, as well.

CHERRY, Don ("Grapes")
b. Kingston, Ontario, February 5, 1934
Don Cherry is an institution; a legend; a sartorial king of genius and crassness; a Canadian; a dog lover; a car collector; a lover of Lord Nelson, Trafalgar, and Royal Doulton; a businessman; a team owner; a father; a dedicated member of the community; a superstar TV personality. The NHL career is the easy part. One game, March 31, 1955, he replaced the injured Fern Flaman. Boston was playing at the Montreal Forum in game five of the semifinals, and Cherry was conspicuous in his absence in the team's 5-1 loss. He played a total of 16 years in the minors, a fighter with limited scoring ability, a guy with heart, a man who liked the camaraderie of players, travel, and the game. Early in his career he met a girl named Rose. Their first

One game, March 31, 1955, he replaced the injured Fern Flaman.
DON CHERRY

date was a hockey game; he got into a fight, was ejected, and took her out later. They married, and remained together until her death on June 1, 1997, after 40 years. The son of a Kingston electrician, Cherry retired for the first time in 1969 to work on a construction crew at the Kodak plant in Rochester, but was laid off and became a car salesman before making a comeback for part of the 1971-72 season. He coached the team for the next two years, all the time playing the drums in the Rochester Pipe Band in the summers, and was then hired to coach Bobby Orr and the Boston Bruins, a dream job he held for five successful seasons. He pridefully boasts that it was he who suggested, prior to the overtime of the 1976 Canada Cup finals, that Darryl Sittler fake a shot and skate around the Czech goalie, Vladimir Dzurilla, whom Cherry said came out of his net too far. Sittler did just that, and Canada was victorious. The low point of Cherry's career, though, came the night of May 10, 1979, in a playoff game with Montreal. Late in game seven of the semifinals, Boston was winning 4-3 when the team was called for a too-many-men penalty at 17:26. Guy Lafleur scored on the power play and then Yvon Lambert scored in OT to eliminate Boston, the closest Cherry ever came to the Cup. At the end of the season he left the team and signed with the lowly Colorado Rockies, but after one season he was fired by GM Ray Miron, a decision that did not sit well with Cherry. In retrospect, however, it was the best thing that ever happened to him. He started a sports management planning company with former player agent Gerry Patterson and lawyer Ron Gunning called Gunning, Patterson, and Cherry Inc., which provided advice to athletes. And, in 1980, he accepted a job to do colour commentary for CBC's *Hockey Night in Canada*. Soon he was the centrepiece of Coach's Corner, an intermission feature that allowed him to vent strong opinions on

Rich Chernomaz

Dick Cherry

Don Cherry

subjects about which no one else in the media felt as strongly. It endures to this day, and is as popular for its licentiousness as for its hockey wisdom. He became notorious for derogatory remarks about European players: "Swedes, Finns, Russians, you name it. I don't like them coming over here and taking our jobs. I'm pro-Canadian." He mocked the war in Yugoslavia – "lower Slobovia attacking Slimea," he described – and enraged francophones in Quebec with like-intentioned remarks. He advocated fighting over penalties that discouraged fighting, and his bellicose treatment of sidekick Ron McLean earned him scorn even from his wife one time when Cherry told McLean on air to "shut up." Perhaps, though, the comment that angered the greatest number of people, defined the parameters of his discourse, and created the show's very enduring popularity was the one about Winnipeg Jets assistant coach Alpo Suhonen, whose very name Cherry likened to a dog food. Despite the outcry, he refused to apologize for the remark. In 1987, he co-hosted the World Junior Championships with the CBC's sports director Brian Williams. That year the country was stunned by a bench-clearing brawl in Piestany instigated by the Soviet Union but participated in equally by the Canadians. Both teams were suspended, and Canada lost a sure medal while the Soviets had already been eliminated from the podium. While Williams preached objectivity, Cherry was furious with the Soviets, and the two men almost came to blows on air during their heated discussions. Later, the two became good friends and co-hosted a radio show based in Toronto. Cherry was equally eccentric off the air. He prided himself on his suits, with their high collars, thick cuffs, and Cirque de Soleil hues, and was famous for his love of his bull terrier, Blue, that died in 1987 and was replaced a short time later by Baby Blue. Even the dog inspired a joke. During his Boston days, Blue once nipped Rose and Wayne Cashman told Don he'd have to get rid of her. Don agreed: "It's not going to be the same without Rose," he said. Over the years, the person became the business. Don Cherry restaurants opened across Ontario, *Don Cherry's Grapevine* became a syndicated talk show, his Rock 'Em, Sock 'Em videos have become an annual, best-selling tradition, and he has a long-standing radio show. Coach's Corner has even inspired academic deconstruction. In 1995, professor Rik Knowles of the University of Guelph wrote a paper called *Post 'Grapes,' Nuts and Flakes: Coach's Corner as Post-Colonial Performance*, but despite the criticism, Cherry has remained faithfully Canadian. He vowed to become the coach of the St. Louis Blues in 1983 when it seemed close to certain they would move to Saskatoon, and his support for women's hockey in this country is without parallel. After Rose passed away, in fact, the Canadian national women's team wore a red rose on their sweaters at the 1998 Olympics in Nagano in her honour. In 1997, he was awarded an expansion franchise in the Ontario Hockey League, called the Mississauga Ice Dogs in tribute to Blue. Consistent with his personality, he vowed never to have any Europeans on his team, and even though the first three seasons were unmitigated disasters, he stuck by his beliefs, though he relented in 2001 when he also took over for a year as the team's head coach. The team plays out of the new Hershey Centre, and is located on

Tim Cheveldae

Rose Cherry Boulevard. Rose and Don had two children, Cindy and Tim. While his daughter handles much of the business, Tim almost died of kidney disease; it was Denver's leading research in that field that had prompted Don to go there as a coach in the first place. As a result, Cherry has become a spokesman for Canada's kidney causes as well as numerous other charities. Perhaps at the end of the day, though, what stands out above and beyond the brashness is his hockey acumen. Loud and obnoxious he may be, but his observations are usually bang on and ahead of the time. He railed against the instigator rule for fighting, which in recent years has seen its support wane; he suggested goal crease alterations that were implemented by the NHL; he alerted the league to the use of dangerous equipment, particularly plastic shoulder and elbow pads; and he has used video to instruct kids on hitting from behind, slashing, and other acts detrimental to fair, but tough, play. Cherry is showman and analyst both, and though it might be advisable to ignore his methods, the substance of his diatribes is often right on the money.

CHERVYAKOV, Denis
b. Leningrad (St. Petersburg), Soviet Union (Russia), April 20, 1970
At 256th overall, Chervyakov was one of the lowest draft picks ever to make it to the NHL, though his time was, in accordance with that low selection, suitably brief. After two games with the Bruins in '92-'93, he has played in Europe ever since.

CHEVELDAE, Tim
b. Melville, Saskatchewan, February 15, 1968
The hard-luck kid never got it going with his drafted team, the Red Wings, and Cheveldae never really recovered. In '89-'90 he was a callup from the farm when Detroit's goaltending was both weak and left short-padded by injuries, and he played spectacularly well for a time. In the next three years he became the team's number-one crease son, but each year the Wings fell short in the playoffs, losing to St. Louis and Toronto in seven games in the first round, and being swept by Chicago in the second round of the '92 playoffs. Fans began booing his every play, and he was traded to Winnipeg. In his first game back in Detroit with the Jets, he allowed six goals in a 6-1 loss. This went on for three more years, and although Boston signed him as a free agent, he played just twice with the Bruins before ending up in the "I." He went on to become assistant coach with his former junior team, the Saskatoon Blades, and in 2001 was named goaltending coach for Moose Jaw.

CHEVREFILS, Real ("Chevy")
b. Timmins, Ontario, May 2, 1932
d. Windsor, Ontario, January 8, 1981
Alcohol, plain and simple. Did in his career, then killed him. In Barrie as a junior, Chevy was touted by coach Hap Emms as the best prospect he'd ever seen. His early years in Boston were promising, though his development was stunted by a badly broken leg suffered against Toronto in a game on November 14, 1953, early in his third season. He was traded to Detroit, then back to Boston, and in 1956-57 he scored 31 goals

and appeared finally to have his career on track. All along, however, he consistently "broke training rules," a euphemism for staying out late, drinking, and showing up hungover to practice. Chevy never learned and never controlled his drinking. Two years later, he was out of the league, though in 1959 Jack Adams allowed him to attempt a "comeback," one that lasted five days at training camp in September. Chevrefils retired to Windsor and moved in above a tavern called Lincoln House. Siro Martinello, a friend and manager of the Windsor Arena, was put in charge of his NHL pension money, $200 a month. He portioned it out to Chevy, but more often than not it was used for liquor. One night, after a promise there would be no drinking, the two attended a Detroit-Boston game, and Chevrefils was given a warm welcome by many who still remembered him. He didn't drink, but it was his last night in the Olympia. His wife and six children had left in 1962, but on death's door Chevy wanted only to see his eldest son, John. Martinello tracked him down in British Columbia, and he visited his dad for a week. A few days later, Chevy was dead.

CHEVRIER, Alain
b. Cornwall, Ontario, April 23, 1961
His older brother, Claude, needed a target to practise his road hockey shot so threw his bro in the street net. Alain got to be pretty good at stopping tennis balls and pretty soon moved up to pucks. He tried out for the Cornwall Royals, but coach Doug Carpenter cut him. Chevrier played Tier II with the Ottawa Senators, and he was offered a scholarship to the University of Miami-Ohio. Four years of U.S. college and another in the IHL landed him a contract with the goalie-laden New Jersey Devils. But he persevered and impressed his coach – the very same Doug Carpenter! – to the point that he took over as number-one man from incumbent and Cup champion Chico Resch. But soon he was on the move, to Winnipeg, Chicago, Pittsburgh, and Detroit, never regaining the form that for two years had him playing most nights of the season. He moved to Boca Raton, Florida and worked for a life insurance company.

CHIASSON, Steve ("The Tank")
b. Barrie, Ontario, April 14, 1967
d. Raleigh, North Carolina, May 3, 1999
Chiasson made the love of his life happy for a short while and then made her a widow. Raised in Peterborough, he married a local girl, Susan Turner, in the summer of 1990. He had been named MVP of the Memorial Cup he helped his Guelph Platers win in 1986, and was a bright young star when he joined the Red Wings the following year. But in the summer

of 1989, he pleaded guilty to drunk driving charges. His marriage the next year seemed to help him focus and his career bagan to take shape. He and his wife took part in numerous charitable efforts in Detroit, and he became the team's union rep. After stints in Calgary and Hartford, he ended up with the Carolina Hurricanes after the Whalers relocated. He played on Canada's gold medal team at the 1997 World Championships, and was building his dream home outside Peterborough where he and his family of five would retire to after he finished playing. When the Canes were eliminated from the '99 playoffs, teammate Gary Roberts held a party at his home. When it came time to leave, taxis were hard to come by, so Chiasson drove home despite having had too much to drink. He crashed his car, dying almost instantly and orphaning his children: Michael, 8; Ryan, 3; and Stephanie, 2. He was buried in Peterborough.

CHIBIREV, Igor
b. Penza, Soviet Union (Russia), April 19, 1968
A low, low, low, low draft choice: 266th overall in '93 by Hartford. Nonetheless, for one night he defied the odds. Although he had only 19 NHL points with the Whalers, he recorded 4 of those in 1 game: February 12, 1994, versus Edmonton. Previously he had played in Moscow. Post-NHL he played in Europe, where he became a sharpshooting centreman.

CHICOINE, Dan ("Chico")
b. Sherbrooke, Quebec, November 30, 1957
A bumpy start and a rocky finish bookended this ordinary career pebbled with trades and demotions. Chicoine was drafted by Cleveland, moved to Minnesota in the merger in 1978, and was traded to Quebec in 1981, where he didn't play a single game for the Nords.

CHIMERA, Jason
b. Edmonton, Alberta, May 2, 1979
Still a work in progress, Chimera was drafted by Edmonton out of Medicine Hat. He went on to play a season in the minors, 1999-2000, and saw his first NHL game the following year. A centre with size and speed, his career path is not yet decided – NHL, minors, or Europe.

CHINNICK, Rick
b. Chatham, Ontario, August 15, 1953
A 41st overall selection didn't get a team too much talent back in 1973. Four NHL games, to be exact. Amazingly, Chinnick came out of Peterborough, where he scored 42 goals in his final season of junior, and later, when he skated in the minors, he had 4 straight 20-goal seasons.

Alain Chevrier

Igor Chibirev

Dan Chicoine

Rick Chinnick

Raised in Peterborough, he married a local girl, Susan Turner, in the summer of 1990.
STEVE CHIASSON

Ron Chipperfield

Lex Chisholm

Tom Chorske

Guy Chouinard

CHIPPERFIELD, Ron
("Chipper"/ "Magnificent Seven")
b. Brandon, Manitoba, March 28, 1954

So, who was the first captain of the Edmonton Oilers when they entered the NHL in 1979? Who set a Western league record with 90 goals and 162 points in one season? Whose career was jeopardized by Reiters syndrome, an arthritic condition of the joints? Who had back-to-back 78-goal seasons in Italy after leaving the NHL? What forward was traded to Quebec straight-up for a goalie (Ron Low)? Ron Chipperfield, that's who. The same Ron Chipperfield who went into the Manitoba Sports Hall of Fame in 1995.

CHISHOLM, Alexander "Lex"
b. Galt, Ontario, April 1, 1915
d. August 6, 1981

Given a chance by coach Dick Irvin near the start of the '39-'40 season, Chisholm suffered a broken arm, missed the rest of the season, and never really got back on track. After playing a third of the following season, he was demoted to Pittsburgh, whence he came, after which he joined the armed forces. Once back in civilian clothes, he never played hockey again.

CHISHOLM, Art
b. Arlington, Massachusetts, November 11, 1934

The year was 1961. The team was Boston. The rule was that an amateur could have a three-game tryout with an NHL team. So Chisholm and Tom "Red" Martin were among the first players to go to the NHL from an American university, Northeastern in Chisholm's case, Boston College in Martin's. Chisholm played March 15, 18, and 19, 1961, on a line with Don McKenney and Gerry Toppazzini. Although he was invited to Boston's camp in the fall, marriage and an education took precedence. He finished his degree at NU though he played senior hockey in New England throughout the 1960s. Chisholm was also a goal judge at the Boston Garden for some 18 years, but more significantly he has worked at the MIT Lincoln Laboratory in Massachusetts.

CHISHOLM, Colin
b. Edmonton, Alberta, February 25, 1963

The University of Alberta is responsible for producing this one-game NHLer who signed with Minnesota in 1986, was given the slimmest of chances, and then asked to hand in his North Stars sweater forever.

CHORNEY, Mark
b. Sudbury, Ontario, November 8, 1959

If Chorney had only played every NHL game as if it were his first, he would have averaged a goal a game and the Pittsburgh Penguins would have signed him to a long-term contract. The defensive defenceman scored on his first shot on goal in the league during '80-'81, his only goal of the season. Next year, first game, first shot ... goal. Again, his only score in 60 games. He later played a season with Los Angeles, but after signing with Washington the Caps didn't use him and he had run out of first-game luck.

CHORSKE, Tom
b. Minneapolis, Minnesota, September 18, 1966

A man who knows where he comes from, Chorske took the Stanley Cup home to share with friends, family, and former coaches in Minneapolis when he had his chance in the summer of 1995. He won the right to a day with the Cup as a member of the New Jersey team that won during the lockout-shortened '94-'95 season. Previously, he had played for Montreal and for the U.S. national team in the World Juniors (once) and World Championships (four times), and since then he has played for Ottawa and the Islanders and three other teams in a career that has become more tenuous in the last few years.

CHOUINARD, Eric
b. Atlanta, Georgia, July 7, 1980

Eric was brought into this world in the South while his dad, Guy, was playing with the Atlanta Flames. Of course, he kept his Canadian citizenship, and as Eric got older and the Flames moved to Calgary, he played hockey in his homeland. Young Eric showed tremendous promise as a teen, winning under-17 and under-18 tournaments with Canada, but had a tougher time later. He made Canada's junior team for the 2000 WJC but struggled, and although he got into his first NHL games, with Montreal, the next year, his season ended early because of a shoulder injury. Big and talented, the 1st-round draft choice has yet to live up to his potential, though he is now with Philadelphia.

CHOUINARD, Gene ("Noisy")
b. Ottawa, Ontario, January 5, 1907
d. January 29, 1951

A veteran of just eight games in the NHL with the old Ottawa Senators in '27-'28, Chouinard spent the meat and potatoes of his career in the Can-Am League before turning to coaching.

CHOUINARD, Guy ("Gramps")
b. Quebec City, Quebec, October 20, 1956

The son of a car salesman, Chouinard was the third-youngest player in league history to score 50 goals in a season, in '78-'79 with Atlanta. He had been a scoring sensation in junior with Quebec, and he increased his scoring in each of his first three full seasons. Although he moved north with the Flames when they went from Atlanta to Calgary, he never again scored more than 31 goals and had the ignominious fate of being traded to St. Louis for those dreaded future considerations in 1983. His teammates Bob MacMillan and Eric Vail commented that Chouinard had eyes in the back of his head, but in each of his final four years in the NHL his point totals decreased.

CHOUINARD, Marc
b. Charlesbourg, Quebec, May 6, 1977

He's no longer a kid, and although he was one of the bright prospects involved in the trade that brought Teemu Selanne to Anaheim from Winnipeg, Chouinard has played just half a season with the Ducks after missing most of his first year of pro with a torn Achilles tendon. He has spent most of his time in the minors, and although considered a top face-off man he hasn't augmented this skill with much offence.

CHRISTIAN, Dave
b. Warroad, Minnesota, May 12, 1959

Now this is a hockey family, the finest, in fact, in all of America. Dave's grandfather, Ed, built the city's only hockey arena. His dad, Bill, scored the winning goal in the United States' 3-2 win over the Soviet Union in the 1960 Olympics in Squaw Valley to give the U.S. its first Olympic gold in hockey. Uncle Roger was also on that team, and stuck around to place fifth in the '64 Olympics in Innsbruck. Dave's other uncle, Gord, was on the 1956 team. Bill and Roger went into business after their playing days were over. They established Christian Bros. stick manufacturers. Dave was drafted by Winnipeg in 1979. His younger brother, Eddie, was drafted 170th overall the next year. Before playing a game in the NHL, Dave was already famous, for he was a member of the 1980 Miracle on Ice U.S. team that won gold at the Lake Placid Olympics. Like pappa, like boy. Coach Herb Brooks, needing more offense from his blueline, put Dave on defence for the Olympics, though he reverted to forward when he joined the Jets. After three and a half seasons with Winnipeg, though, he failed to reach agreement on a new contract and the Jets sent him to Washington. There he produced 6 straight 20-goal seasons, including 41 goals and 83 points in '85-'86. Along the way he represented his country again in three Canada Cups, and on the final day of the '92-'93 season he played in his 1,000th game. After retiring, he became the GM and head coach of the Fargo-Moorhead Ice Sharks in the USHL.

Dave's grandfather, Ed, built the city's only hockey arena.
DAVE CHRISTIAN

CHRISTIAN, Jeff
b. Burlington, Ontario, July 30, 1970

No relation to Dave Christian, this Christian also had athletic paternal genes. His dad, Gord, played in the Canadian Football League, but Jeff played only the smallest portions of NHL seasons, being called up from the minors 5 times in the 1990s and never playing more than 11 games in any one year. Since then, he has lived in Germany and continued his career in that country.

CHRISTIE, Mike
b. Big Spring, Texas, December 20, 1949

Texas, maybe, but only in name. His father worked for an oil company based in Big Spring, but when Mike was a boy the family transferred to Calgary and that is where the youngster learned about the beauty of hockey. After earning a business degree from the University of Denver, the undrafted Christie signed with Chicago in the fall of 1972 and struck off to Dallas to play for the team's minor-league affiliate. He was then traded to a series of unfortunate teams –

California, Cleveland, and Colorado – before playing his last nine games with Vancouver. While with the Rockies, coach Don Cherry made Christie captain, but this honour failed to light a fire under either the player or the team. After seven seasons, he had just two playoff games on his resumé.

CHRISTIE, Ryan
b. Beamsville, Ontario, July 3, 1978

He was drafted by Dallas in 1996, a winger with size and scoring ability out of Owen Sound. Christie spent the better part of two years in the IHL and then the Stars called him up for five games in 1999-2000. At the end of that year, Christie became a free agent but opted to re-sign with the club, though he has yet to return to the Dallas lineup since.

CHRISTOFF, Steve
b. Richfield, Minnesota, January 23, 1958

He won the NCAA championship with the University of Minnesota in 1979, won Olympic gold at Lake Placid in February 1980, starred for the North Stars mere days after the Olympics ended, and led the team to a stunning upset of four-time Cup champs Montreal in the quarter-finals of the '80 playoffs. Incredibly, five years and three teams later, he was out of the NHL. A serious shoulder operation in the summer of 1982 didn't help his development, but his was a light that burned bright and faded to black with incendiary speed. He retired and became a pilot for Masaba airlines of Minneapolis.

CHRYSTAL, Bob
b. Winnipeg, Manitoba, April 3, 1930

When he played for Denver in the AHL, Chrystal lost two teeth in a mixup and badly cut his tongue and almost swallowed it. The doctor who stitched him up suggested chewing on gum to prevent a recurrence of the accident, and Chrystal became famous for his sticks – of gum. He learned how to skate from his mother, and when he played minor hockey with Winnipeg's West End Orioles his father encouraged him to think pro even though Bob was only eight or nine years old. By the time he got to the Rangers in 1953, he was thought to be one of the best prospects outside the NHL, a tough, reliable defenceman whom coach Frank Boucher also used periodically on forward as a checker. But near the end of his second year he broke his leg and was never the same. He played for a few years in the minors and then returned to Winnipeg to work as a sales rep for a brewery. He was inducted into the Manitoba Sports Hall of Fame in 1995.

Jeff Christian

Mike Christie

Steve Christoff

Bob Chrystal

Brad Church

Jack Church

Shane Churla

Dave Chyzowski

CHUBAROV, Artem
b. Novogorod, Soviet Union (Russia), December 12, 1979
A tall, thin centreman, Chubarov went to Vancouver in the 1998 draft, though he has played only briefly with the team, spending most of his time in the minors until emerging in the 2001-02 season. The Canucks consider him a developing two-way centre who can score a bit and play well defensively, though he has yet to prove himself entirely. The highlight of his career so far came in early January 1999 when he scored the game-winning goal for the Russians in the gold-medal game against Canada.

CHURCH, Brad
b. Dauphin, Manitoba, November 14, 1976
If a one-game player in the NHL is called a "wonder," why then Church is twice the man, getting his deuce-worth of action in with Washington despite being a 1st-round draft choice. Since then, his has been a career fixed in the minors with seemingly little hope for another shot in the NHL for the foreseeable future.

CHURCH, Jack
b. Kamsack, Saskatchewan, May 24, 1915
d. Toronto, Ontario, January 5, 1996
Church's NHL prayers were answered on December 10, 1938, when owner Conn Smythe promoted him from Syracuse for three games. He witnessed action in parts of the next three years, but was demoted in December '42 and replaced by Bob Goldham. Smythe sold him to Brooklyn, where he played a few games before enlisting with the Canadian Infantry Corps for the better part of three years. He played 1945-46 with Boston before retiring. Church settled in Toronto and became a longtime employee of Labatt Breweries.

CHURLA, Shane
b. Fernie, British Columbia, June 24, 1965
If he only had a dollar for every penalty minute he incurred, Churla would be a rich man. If he could maintain a batting average equal to his yearly total penalty minutes, he'd be an outstanding ballplayer. As it is, he can claim only to be a second cousin to NFL quarterback Mark Rypien. In Churla's second career game he broke his hand in a fight and was out for 13 games. In the minors, he became embroiled with fans and threw a metal pole at the offending patrons. For that he was charged with second-degree reckless endangerment by the Monroe County (New York) district attorney's office. Churla had five successive seasons of more than 275 penalty minutes with Minnesota, the happiest days of his pugilistic life, and in his final season he played on Broadway with Wayne Gretzky as a Blueshirt. In the summer of 1997, he had serious knee surgery and retired, and in February 2000 he was hired by the Phoenix Coyotes as a scout.

CHYCHRUN, Jeff
b. LaSalle, Quebec, May 3, 1966
A man of many moves, Chychrun played for four teams and was traded five times in his eight years. He was a fighter who was included in numerous important deals, including ones involving Jari Kurri and Paul Coffey. In his first full season, '88-'89, he and the Flyers made it to the Stanley Cup semifinals, his only year in the playoffs.

CHYNOWETH, Dean
b. Calgary, Alberta, October 30, 1968
His dad is the longtime president of the WHL. He owns a number of Great Canadian Bagel franchises. He missed much of his rookie season, '88-'89 with first an eye injury and then Osgood-Schlatter disease, which affects growing bones. He was a scrapper who only once played more than 40 games in a season. He was out of the league after nine very part-time years. He became an assistant coach in the IHL and then head coach of Seattle in the WHL.

CHYZOWSKI, Dave ("Chyzer")
b. Edmonton, Alberta, July 11, 1971
At just over 18, he was the youngest Islander ever when he played his first game in October 1989. He arrived on Long Island with expectations weighing on him after being selected 2nd overall in the draft. Coach Al Arbour went so far as to call him "Boss," figuring Chyzowski would be the next Mike Bossy. However, a shoulder injury left him on the sidelines, and he had trouble working himself back into the lineup. By December, GM Bill Torrey decided to loan him to the World Junior team, and there he shone, leading the team in scoring and winning a gold medal. But his return to the NHL lacked a comparable magic. He spent the majority of the next four years on the farm team and in the penalty box, showing a fighting will that belied his NHL performances. He signed with Detroit in 1995, but never saw time at the Joe, then signed with Chicago and played only eight games. His two older brothers had both been drafted but never made the big time at all. Ron was selected 74th by Hartford in 1983, and Barry 156th by the Rangers in '86.

CIAVAGLIA, Pete
b. Albany, New York, July 15, 1969
Belying the hockey player's reputation, Ciavaglia spent four years at Harvard University before becoming the first native New York Stater to play for the Sabres. His tour of duty at "home" lasted but five games over two years before he found his niche in the IHL. He also represented the Stars 'n' Stripes at the World Juniors and the '94 Olympics in Lillehammer, and played a year in Sweden. He became a fixture in the IHL before being forced to retire because of a bad back. The Detroit Vipers retired his number 12. He remained in Detroit and currently helps hockey players invest their money.

CIBAK, Martin
b. Liptovsky Mikulas, Czechoslovakia (Slovakia), May 17, 1980
Tampa Bay is eventually going to be counting on this centre to provide some offence for a team lacking in goal production. He played minor hockey in Slovakia and came to the WHL in 1998 as soon as he was drafted. Cibak made his debut with the Lightning in 2001-02 but has yet to make the team as a regular.

CICCARELLI, Dino
b. Sarnia, Ontario, February 8, 1960
He was charged with indecent exposure when he took the garbage out in, almost, his birthday suit. He scored

50 goals in a season twice. He spent a day in jail after being convicted of assault after a high-sticking incident in Toronto in 1988. He scored 608 career goals in the NHL. He once called a teammate a "gutless little puke" for not playing, even though that player never returned to the NHL because of post-concussion syndrome. He was never drafted, and played 19 years in the NHL. Such were the highs and lows of Ciccarelli's life and career. He was a scorer in junior who remained a scorer with five NHL teams, but he was a nasty bit of business. He made his living in front of the goal, whacking in loose pucks and rebounds while being cross-checked in the back by much bigger players. He played 1,232 regular-season games, but never won a Stanley Cup before retiring because of back problems. Toward the end of his career, he and Shawn Burr (another NHLer) bought the Sarnia Sting of the OHL and Dino became a hands-on owner after ending his career. Twice he scored more than 100 points in a season, and his best goal-scoring year was 1981-82 with Minnesota, his first full year in the league. Despite his ability to put the puck in the net, he never won a major NHL award and played in only four All-Star Games. Defence was never his strength, but the power play was. Of his 608 goals, 232 came with the man advantage.

CICCONE, Enrico
b. Montreal, Quebec, April 10, 1970
He's been traded six times in seven seasons, played for three teams in '96-'97, and survived in the league by fighting. When he retires, he wants to become a professional fisherman. Go figure. Soon enough we'll find out how serious he is. Just three games into the 2001-02 season, he packed it in after playing the previous three years in Germany before heading back to Montreal to play for the Canadiens. A bad back and persistent groin injury did him in. That and the wear and tear of fighting for a living.

CICHOCKI, Chris
b. Detroit, Michigan, September 17, 1963
Cichocki grew up in Detroit, revered the Wings as a kid, and realized a dream when he left university a year early to sign with the same Joe-playing Detroiters. In his rookie season, he suffered a serious injury when the stick of Washington's Bengt Gustafsson was practically shoved down his throat. His second game back, he suffered a bad cut on his lip, and near the end of the season he lost three teeth from a high stick. Still, a dream is a dream. He was traded to New Jersey in March 1987, played just seven games over two seasons with the Devils, and embarked on a lengthy minor-league career in the AHL and IHL.

CIERNIK, Ivan
b. Levice, Czechoslovakia (Slovakia), October 30, 1977
A Slovakian in international play, Ciernik's tour of duty with the Ottawa Senators was brief and uneventful. A 216th overall draft pick in 1996, he lived down to those expectations and has been a solid minor leaguer who got the occasional callup to the Sens for a few games in 1997-98 and 2000-01.

CIERNY, Jozef
b. Zvolen, Czechoslovakia (Slovakia), May 13, 1974
The once-great scorer Craig Simpson knew his time was up when he was traded to Buffalo for Cierny, a guy who had never played a game with the Sabres and who reached the single-game mark just barely with Edmonton and went no further in the NHL. Cierny kicked around in the minors before returning to Europe to skate.

CIESLA, Hank ("Cees")
b. St. Catharines, Ontario, October 15, 1934
d. St. Catharines, Ontario, April 22, 1976
How is it a player can play in almost every game for four years and then be completely unwanted? One day an NHL regular, the next day a career minor-leaguer. Ciesla entered the league with Chicago in '55-'56 and showed great promise with 31 points. Big, though not tough, he was considered a Jean Béliveau-style player, smooth and fast, tall and lean. But a weak second year saw him traded to the Rangers, a team that welcomed him with open arms. He's an "honest workman," GM Muzz Patrick commented, placing him on a line with Gerry Foley and Parker MacDonald, two very competent forwards. Sixty games and two goals later, there was no such encouragement, and by the midway point of the next season coach Phil Watson issued a simple ultimatum: score 10 goals or face a life in the minors. Ciesla had four at the time, finished with six, and sure enough was consigned to the minor-league warehouse that was the AHL.

CIGER, Zdeno
b. Martin, Czechoslovakia (Slovakia), October 19, 1969
Ciger's finest NHL moments came with the Oilers, for whom he scored 22 goals one season and, ironically, 31 in his final year before leaving the NHL while still in his prime to return to Slovakia. The ashes of his NHL life lay during three unproductive seasons with New Jersey, but his international experience was long. This included two World Juniors with the Czech team, three World Championships with Slovakia, and the 1998 Olympics in Nagano. Nashville claimed him in the Expansion Draft in 1998, hoping to woo him

Enrico Ciccone

Jozef Cierny

Hank Ciesla

Zdeno Ciger

Of his 608 goals, 232 came with the man advantage.
DINO CICCARELLI

Rob Cimetta

Joe Cirella

Marian Cisar

Kim Clackson

back to North America from his hockey career in Bratislava, but he would have none of it. It took an offer from the mighty Rangers, three years later, to bring him back to the NHL.

CIMELLARO, Tony
b. Kingston, Ontario, June 14, 1971
Good ol' Kingston boy. Tough guy. Won't back down. Plays hard. Never gives up. Had a rough time with Ottawa there. He'll be back. Good kid. Just needs a chance. Went over, played with Your-peens there for a while. He'll be all right. Come back to Canada, down in the minors there, but not complainin'. Got character. He'll be okay. Small. Doesn't matter. Can't understand why no one gives the guy another shot. Guys like him are the hungry ones.

CIMETTA, Rob
b. Toronto, Ontario, February 15, 1970
Cimetta led the OHL in scoring with 55 goals in his final year of junior, 1988-89, despite missing three weeks to play for Canada at the '89 World Juniors. But when he joined Boston full-time the next year he ended up in coach Mike Milbury's doghouse and was demoted. Sensing the worst, Cimetta's father and agent, Angelo, told him to leave the team and demand a trade, and in November 1990 he was dealt to his dream team, Toronto. He started off in the minors, but when given a chance at Maple Leaf Gardens an abdominal injury prevented him from going full out. Another season split between the Leafs and the minors told him the jig was up, so Cimetta made his way to Germany, where he played until 2000, when a third knee operation forced him to give up his skates. Cimetta then got a job with an investment firm in Florida that required three weeks of seminars as part of his training. The seminars took place on the sixty-first floor of the south tower of the World Trade Center. On the morning of September 11, 2001, he took a short washroom break, during which he heard the fire alarm go off. Everyone took the stairs to the street, and as Cimetta neared the thirty-second floor, the second plane hit, shaking the building and knocking evacuees to the ground. He made it outside safely, but in the ensuing weeks he and his colleagues shared their stories in an effort to raise money for the 9-11 Disaster Relief Fund. All of a sudden, a knee injury and a failed hockey career don't look like much with which to concern oneself.

CIRELLA, Joe
b. Hamilton, Ontario, May 9, 1963
Selected 5th overall by the old Colorado Rockies, Cirella made the team in his first camp as an 18-year-old. By the end of the season, though, he was back in junior, and it was another year still before he was in the NHL for keeps. A tough defenceman, he played with Quebec, the Rangers, Florida, and Ottawa in subsequent years, each time playing for generally weak teams. His 44 points in his second full season, '83-'84 was a career high, and that year he also played in his only All-Star Game. Nonetheless, he survived for 15 years and 828 games, after which he turned to coaching in junior.

CIRONE, Jason
b. Toronto, Ontario, February 21, 1971
It's not whether you win or lose ... it's whether you play the game. Three games does not a Hall of Famer make, but it's better than 99.99 percent of the population. And once the Jets had traded Cirone out of the 'Peg to Florida for Dave Tomlinson in 1993, he kept playing, in Italy and North American minors, for many more years yet.

CISAR, Marian
b. Bratislava, Czechoslovakia (Slovakia), February 25, 1978
Although Los Angeles drafted Cisar in 1996, he was traded to Nashville on June 1, 1998, thus becoming the first acquisition in Predators history. He got into his first NHL game on March 28, 2000, after spending the year in the IHL with Milwaukee and has since become a regular on a weak team desperate for talent. His junior career in Bratislava culminated with his playing in the 1998 World Juniors for his country, Slovakia, a ninth-place finish.

CLACKSON, Kim ("Clacker")
b. Saskatoon, Saskatchewan, February 13, 1955
"My role is that of a tough guy," golden boy Clackson said with a syntactical intelligence that belied his fighting skills. That role was fulfilled initially in the WHA, despite being drafted into the NHL by Pittsburgh in 1975. He finally transferred to the Pens in 1980, but was sent to Quebec the next year, his last season in the pro game. In all, he played 114 career games (regular season and playoffs) without scoring a goal, a dubious non-achievement the record books lay bare for all trivia fans to see.

CLANCY, Frank "King"
b. Ottawa, Ontario, February 25, 1903
d. Toronto, Ontario, November 8, 1986
No player in the long and distinguished history of hockey has made as great a contribution in so many areas of the game over so long a period of time. Clancy started his affiliation with the league in 1921 with Ottawa, and it continued unchecked for 65 years until the day of his passing. Along the way, he was a Hall of Fame player, a coach, general manager, referee, referee-in-chief, Stanley Cup winner, all-star, father of an NHLer, and ambassador for the game. He never had a drop of alcohol in his life, but anyone who came in contact with him was sure he was drunk on life and hockey, such was his ever-heightened state of happiness. His impact with the Senators in 1921 was immediate. Despite being slight even in those days (5'7" and 150 pounds), he was as aggressive a defenceman as there was. He often picked fights with the toughest players in the league, and although (legend has it) he never won a single one he always came back for more. His heart and competitive spirit won him fans across the country. He also a superb defenceman, a rusher with the puck and skilled as a scorer and passer. He also had excellent speed. Clancy acquired his nickname through his father, who was so called because of his outstanding athletic ability in his own youth. King the Younger, though, measured up to the moniker. He played nine years with the Senators,

winning the Cup in 1923 and '27. In the former series, against Vancouver, Clancy made history when he played all six positions in a single game (goalies had to serve their own penalties, and Clancy filled the breach). His life changed forever in the summer of 1930. The Senators were constantly in financial trouble and frequently sold their best players for cash. That year, it was Clancy's turn, and Conn Smythe in Toronto desperately wanted the man he considered the best player in the game. Smythe, a horse man, made a huge bet at a race on a longshot named Rare Jewel. The horse won, and Smythe won half of the $35,000 he eventually paid Ottawa for Clancy. It was an astronomical sum for the day, but King remained in Toronto virtually the rest of his life. He was a marquee name, and when the Leafs moved into Maple Leaf Gardens a year later, he was the drawing card Smythe needed to bring fans to his great new arena. In that first year at MLG, the Leafs won the Cup, and Clancy stayed with the team for seven years. He retired early in the '36-'37 season and was given a special night, an honour for the ages. He was carted to centre ice on a sleigh, and was painted entirely in the Irish green symbolic of his heritage. A year later Clancy began his post-playing career in the league. He coached the Montreal Maroons for part of a dismal season and then turned to refereeing. For almost 15 years he was considered the best the league had to offer, though his adversaries complained that he was too lenient with violence and fighting. He returned to the Leafs fold in 1951 and stayed for good, becoming a coach two years later. That job lasted only two seasons but he stayed on with the team as an adviser of nebulous description. Smythe once asked him what he did around the Gardens, and when Clancy said "absolutely nothing" Smythe nodded and told him to keep right on doing it. Clancy was inducted into the Hockey Hall of Fame in 1958 and is the only man to play in, referee, and coach an All-Star Game. He later filled in for two ailing coaches. During the historic season of '66-'67, coach Punch Imlach was forced to his bed with exhaustion. The Leafs had been playing poorly and the atmosphere around the dressing room had been thick with tension, but in 10 games Clancy guided the team to a 7-1-2 record and imbued it with a much-needed sense of pleasure. The Leafs went on to win the Cup. In '71-'72, Clancy stepped in for John McLellan, whose ulcers had worked him into a frenzy, but again the 69-year-old King took the reins and raised the level of happiness higher than it had ever known. After that, Clancy remained with the Leafs as a constant companion for owner Harold Ballard. He was also in demand by charities and social groups as a guest or

Clancy started his affiliation with the league in 1921 with Ottawa, and it continued unchecked for 65 years, until the day of his passing.
KING CLANCY

speaker, and the media could hardly pass a day without quoting him. It is impossible to quantify what he did all those years save to say that he represented hockey as its finest and most gregarious ambassador. In his later years he, like Ballard, suffered from diabetes, one of the few sicknesses ever to ail him. His passing in 1986 marked perhaps the saddest day in Leafs history, but King lives on in the form of an eponymous trophy awarded annually by the NHL to the player who has made the greatest humanitarian contributions to the game. The first winner was Lanny McDonald, who knew Clancy well from his own days with the Leafs.

CLANCY, Terry ("Whip")
b. Ottawa, Ontario, April 2, 1943
At the time of his birth, Terry's dad, King, was out and about refereeing in the NHL, his second of about a dozen careers in the game that lasted his lifetime. Terry's career, however, in no way replicated that of his great father. He played for Canada's National Team under the auspices of Father David Bauer in the early '60s, then played seven games for the expansion Seals in '67-'68 after being claimed from Toronto. He was purchased by the Leafs, the first in a series of sales, in 1968. Then the cash register opened for his services, though he saw precious little of the money being exchanged. He was sold to Montreal, sold back to Toronto, then sold to Detroit. He retired in 1973 and returned to Wilfrid Laurier University to finish his degree in business administration. He has been a commercial insurance broker for more than a quarter of a century.

Terry Clancy

CLAPPER, Aubrey "Dit"
b. Newmarket, Ontario, February 9, 1907
d. Peterborough, Ontario, January 21, 1978
Born in Newmarket and raised in Hastings, Ontario, Clapper was already playing junior at 13 and by 20 was a regular right winger for the Bruins. In '27-'28, his first season, he had just four goals. The next year he had 9 and the year after 41 in just 44 games, the finest season of his career. Clapper became the first NHLer to play 20 years in the league, a feat he accomplished by remaining with the Bruins the whole time. He starred on the Dynamite Line with Cooney Weiland and Dutch Gainor, winning the Stanley Cup in 1929, the first in franchise history. In '29-'30, he led the team to a remarkable record of 38-5-1, and his 41 goals were second in the league to Weiland's 43. After Clapper was named to an equal to 1932, he remained leader until he retired, with the exception of one year. In 1937, the Bruins needed help on defence so Clapper moved back to the blueline. Partnered with the great Eddie Shore, the pair formed the most

Dit Clapper

Brett Clark

formidable duo in the league, fearless and ruthless. The team won Cups in 1939 and again two years later, and in 1945 Clapper was named the team's coach in addition to maintaining his player's (and captain's) duties. He guided the team for four mediocre seasons and on February 12, 1947, he retired as a player. For the first and only time, he was inducted into the Hockey Hall of Fame at game's end and his number 5 was retired, double testament to his brilliance and assured place in the history of the game. After leaving the game, Clapper settled in Peterborough where he ran a sporting goods store. He was lured back to the game in 1959 when Buffalo made him coach of its AHL team, though his tenure lasted only a single season. He returned again to Peterborough where he worked for a plumbing firm, but in 1964 he suffered a heart attack. In 1973, he suffered a stroke that left him greatly paralyzed and confined to a wheelchair for the rest of his life. His grandson, Greg Theberge, later played in the NHL.

CLARK, Brett ("Clarky")
b. Moosomin, Saskatchewan, December 23, 1976
A youngster who has seen some ice time with Montreal during times of massive injuries to the roster, Clark was a work in progress for the Habs. He played at Paul Kariya's alma mater, the University of Maine, and for a year with Canada's National Team before joining Montreal in 1997. The Thrashers of Atlanta claimed him in the 1999 Expansion Draft and since then he has seen more time with the minor-league affiliate in Orlando than with the parent club in Georgia.

Chris Clark

CLARK, Chris
b. Manchester, Connecticut, March 8, 1976
Clark went to Clarkson for four years honing his skills with the Knights after being drafted by Calgary right out of high school. Although he had a decent college career, he has seen only part-time duty with the Flames since graduating in 1998.

CLARK, Dan
b. Toronto, Ontario, November 3, 1957
Although the lights are always bright on Broadway, Clark saw them shine for but a few days in a career that took place mostly in the dimness of the AHL. A double-draftee, he was chosen first by Philadelphia in 1977 and then by the Rangers in '78 when he couldn't come to terms with the Flyers. In all, he played four games with the Rangers.

CLARK, Dean
b. Edmonton, Alberta, January 10, 1964
The Oilers won their first Stanley Cup in 1983-84.

Gordie Clark

Wayne Gretzky had 205 points on the season and Edmonton had six players at the All-Star Game. There was little ice time for fringe players on the Oilers, so Clark dressed only once, and by the time Gretzky hoisted the Cup in May '84, Clark was nowhere near the trophy. He was in Kamloops competing for the Memorial Cup and then he returned to university, where he could boast of having played with some of the finest skaters the game has ever known.

CLARK, Gordie
b. Glasgow, Scotland, May 31, 1952
A Scotsman by birth, Clark could light up the goal everywhere he played, except for the NHL, where he had just eight games' worth of opportunity with the Bruins (and one more in the playoffs). He had captained the University of New Hampshire team in his final year of college, but he could effect little influence in the big-league dressing room.

CLARK, Patrick "Nobby"
b. Orillia, Ontario, June 18, 1897
d. unknown
In the old days, all leagues traded players with each other, unlike today when NHL teams only trade with other NHL teams. In 1927, Clark was minding his business in Minneapolis, playing for the local Millers in the AHA, when lo and behold he was traded to the Boston Bruins with Dutch Gainor for Red Stuart, cash, and future considerations. After five games, though, he was traded to another league, the Can-Am, with Billy Coutu, who had recently been suspended for life for assaulting an official at the end of the 1927 playoffs.

> It was quite simply one of the hardest, cleanest checks ever delivered.
> **WENDEL CLARK**

CLARK, Wendel
b. Kelvington, Saskatchewan, October 25, 1966
December 29, 1984. It was, quite simply, one of the hardest, cleanest checks ever delivered. Canada was playing the Soviets at the World Junior Championships in Turku, Finland. Defenceman Mikhail Tatrinov was skating around his net with the puck and boom! Canada's Wendel Clark eviscerated him, knocked him unconscious and out of the tournament. In the gold-medal game against the Czechs, Clark scored the tying goal that assured Canada of gold. His was a performance that both anticipated and defined a career. When Toronto finished dead last overall in '84-'85 and had first choice at the Entry Draft, there was no doubt whom the Leafs would select. And from his first skate with the team, it became clear he would become one of the more popular wearers of the Blue and White in team history. In his rookie season he scored 34 goals despite missing 14 games due to injury, a problem that would

plague him for much of his career, particularly in the form of a bad back. Clark played on the Hound Line early on, with Gary Leeman and Russ Courtnall, so-called because all three played midget hockey for the Notre Dame Hounds in Wilcox, Saskatchewan. Although Clark was a defenceman for most of junior, the Leafs moved him to left wing, a fact that rankles his farming father Les to this day. Clark's older brother, Donn, was a coach in Saskatchewan and his younger brother, Kerry, was also in junior, though never made it to the NHL. His cousin, Joey Kocur of Detroit, made a pact with Wendel never to fight each other, one of the few players the rookie didn't take on in that first season. Wendel had 227 penalty minutes, finished a close second to Gary Suter for the Calder Trophy, and played in the All-Star Game his first year, but his stock was only beginning to rise. He led the Leafs to the playoffs and established a new bar for a team that had been miserable for years. If Wendel's Leafs were going to lose, they wouldn't do so without a fight. Clark stayed with the team 9 years, becoming captain and scoring 46 goals in 1993-94. That summer, GM Cliff Fletcher traded him to Quebec in a multiplayer deal that brought Mats Sundin to Toronto. The trade stirred emotions because of Fletcher's cold move and his remarkable success as GM in so quick a time, and also because of Clark's departure. Fans printed bumper stickers that read, "My Canada Includes Wendel," but his time with the Nordiques was short. He suffered an horrific concussion during an exhibition game with his new team, and then the owners' lockout shortened the season. He was traded to the Islanders and it was as a New Yorker that he first played in another sweater at Maple Leaf Gardens. On his first shift, he was accorded an incredible ovation in remembrance of his years with Toronto. Before the season was out, he had been reacquired by Toronto, and although a step slower his impact was still indelible. In his first game back, he had a goal and an assist in a 3-0 win over Minnesota. After the '97-'98 season, after more injuries and reduced production, the Leafs let him go a second time and Tampa Bay signed him as a free agent. Down south, his game went north. He scored 28 goals in 65 games and his popularity alone accounted for his being named to the All-Star Team for the game in Tampa, where he received a thunderous ovation. But the Lightning were going nowhere, and Clark was sent to Detroit at the trading deadline in the hopes of bolstering a Stanley Cup contender. Things didn't work out that way, and he signed with Chicago in the summer. There, things became even worse. His ice time was cut, his production declined to near the zero point, and he was given an outright release. For months he practised on his own, hoping to be claimed by a team. That team was, eventually, Toronto. Coach Pat Quinn played him sporadically, and he responded with brief bursts of important play, culminating in the team's second to last home game of the season, during the playoffs against eventual champions New Jersey. One rush saw him skate through most of the Devils, then ring a shot off the post. It was vintage Wendel and the fans rose to their feet, giving a goalpost shot a standing ovation. New Jersey fans never matched that enthusiasm when their team won the Cup.

CLARKE, Bobby
b. Flin Flon, Manitoba, August 13, 1949

Bobby Clarke

It's impossible to sit on the fence and not formulate a very subjective and pronounced opinion of the captain of Philadelphia's Broad Street Bullies, the dirtiest, most violent teams in NHL history. If you're a Flyers fan, you worship at this man's skates. If you're not, the uncomplimentary words will start flowing. Ditto for the Clarke of today, that same team's GM who has said and done the most extraordinary things during his reign as Flyers boss. Clarke was raised in Flin Flon, a town near nothing, bordering on nowhere and with only one thing to offer – cold. He played junior hockey for the local Bombers and came to notice for a variety of reasons. He was a great scorer, a dogged passer, and had the heart of a pack of lions. He was also diabetic. Thus, when he became available for the 1969 Draft, teams were cautious about his ability to merge his talents and his health problems. Toronto owner Harold Ballard went to great and insulting lengths to point out that no diabetic was going to play for his team, and one Hall of Fame career later, Clarke had proved Ballard wrong for about the millionth time. The Flyers took a chance on Clarke, but sure enough diabetes reared its ugly head on the first day of training camp. Clarke got dizzy and had to stop playing after suffering a serious seizure, and endured another attack just a couple of days later. From that moment on, trainer Frank Lewis monitored him properly and ensured that Clarke was always near a can of Coke or a handful of chocolate bars and, irony of ironies, Clarke proved one of the most resilient men in the game. He centred a line with Bill Barber on the wing, and the two proved magical together. By his third season, it was clear that Clarke was the leader of the team, and when he was given the "C" in 1972 he became, at 23, the youngest captain in league history. He won the Bill Masterton Trophy in 1972 and the year after won his first of three Hart Trophies.

If you're a Flyers fan, you worship at this man's skates.
BOBBY CLARKE

Bobby Clarke

Clarke led the team to back-to-back Cups in 1974 and '75, his goonery and thuggery intimidating factors that had no place in hockey. Furthermore, he was only too happy to shove his stick into an opponent's face – be it Darryl Sittler or Bobby Orr – but he was equally quick to back away from a fight so that his hired thugs – Saleski, Schultz et al. – could do the real work. His first three years had been so impressive that in the summer of 1972 he was chosen to play for Team Canada in the historic Summit Series. He created a controversy that continues to this day when, in game six of that series, he chopped at the ankles of Valeri Kharlamov, CCCP's greatest star, and rendered the player ineffective the rest of the series. In some circles, Clarke was pilloried for his actions, most notably 30 years later by hero Paul Henderson. Yet a few defended Clarke by pointing to the spitting and ankle-kicking of the Soviets, tactics so reprehensible and despicable that a good old chop to the foot in the heat of battle seemed gentlemanly by comparison. Clarke played every NHL game with the Flyers and by the time he retired in 1984 he had produced 1,210 points in 1,144 games – not bad for a diabetic. He won the Lester Patrick Trophy in 1980 and the Frank Selke Trophy three years later, and he played in eight All-Star Games in the 1970s. Everything about his play, about what he brought to the rink every day, can be gleaned from the typical Clarke photograph, a closeup of his face with a gap-toothed smile, blood and sweat pouring down and across his face, his eyes wide and maniacal. To do battle with him means to lose, even in victory. In his first decade away from the ice, Clarke worked with the Flyers, North Stars, and Panthers before returning to Philadelphia in 1994 as GM, a post he continues to hold. An adopted son of owner Ed Snider, he has provided fans with good – but not Stanley Cup – teams, but his methods have been as crazed as in his playing days. He hired the ever-likeable Roger Neilson as coach, then dismissed him when he became ill by saying, simply, that the Flyers didn't go out and ask Roger to get cancer. Paradoxically, Clarke was the first to visit the sickly Neilson in hospital. He became involved in a love-hate relationship with his franchise player that dominated the headlines, for close to a year. Clarke made Lindros team captain, and when the GM was named leader of Canada's team for the 1998 Olympics in Nagano, Clarke responded by naming Lindros captain ahead of the more obvious choice, Wayne Gretzky. Canada finished fourth that year, and soon after a series of health issues left Lindros wanting a trade – specifically to Toronto. For months, Clarke tried to make a deal happen (or so he claims) but on the day a deal was to have been announced, Clarke withdrew the offer and later sent Lindros to the

In 1925, Odie went to the Pittsburgh Pirates as playing coach and even played in goal one night.
ODIE CLEGHORN

Rangers. Life in Flyers land these past 30 years and more has, at the very least, been colourful. Clarke has been a leader and a success story, an incomparable role model for all diabetics who perhaps weren't sure whether they could realize their dreams because of their illness. He has been a successful GM, yet has failed to win anything significant at that level, and the beat marches on for the Hall of Famer as he tries to build a team that will one day win the Stanley Cup.

CLARKE, Dale
b. Belleville, Ontario, March 23, 1978
All through his four years at St. Lawrence University, no team drafted Clarke. But just before convocation, St. Louis signed him as a free agent and assigned him to the farm team in Worcester, calling him up for three games in the 2000-01 season. That's been it so far.

CLASSEN, Greg
b. Aylsham, Saskatchewan, August 24, 1977
The first NHLer to come out of this tiny, tiny town (pop. 150) in this Prairie province, Classen attended Merrimack College before signing with the Nashville Predators on March 27, 2000. He finished the 2000-01 season in the IHL and is one of a precious few players who can claim he made his NHL debut at the Saitama Super Arena in Japan, where the Predators and Pittsburgh Penguins opened the 2000-01 season.

CLEARY, Daniel
b. Carbonear, Newfoundland, December 18, 1978
He got game, he just don't know where he put it. Highly touted as a junior, a teen phenom who didn't play contact hockey until he left the Rock for Belleville, he was a can't-miss kid. He played junior at 15, but in the next three years his stock dropped and he was cut three successive times at camp for Canada's World Junior team. Chicago gave up on him after drafting him 15th overall in '97, and sent him to Edmonton, but so far the Oilers haven't embraced the kid who's not getting any younger and not getting much NHL experience. He played all of the 2000-01 season, getting 14 goals, but his time is now and the clock is ticking.

CLEGHORN, Ogilvie "Odie"
b. Montreal, Quebec, September 19, 1891
d. Montreal, Quebec, July 13, 1956
He died in his sleep peacefully and was found by his sister, with whom he lived, on a Saturday morning. Had Odie wakened, he would have got up early, dressed, and prepared for the funeral of his brother, Sprague, who had died on the Thursday. They were that close. They broke into hockey together, playing for Renfrew in 1910 and joining the Montreal

Daniel Cleary

Wanderers the next year. They played together there for six years and when they returned played in the NHL, though at first for different teams, Odie the Canadiens, Sprague the Senators. (As a condition for exemption from military service, Odie had to agree to sit out the 1917-18 season.) They kept tabs on each other, and any time one was violated the other would assault that opponent next time out. In 1921, Sprague was sold to the Canadiens, and the brothers were reunited for five years. In 1925, Odie went to the Pittsburgh Pirates as playing coach and even played in goal one night when starter Roy Worters had pneumonia. Odie later went on to referee in the NHL after retiring in '28. A superb stickhandler, he was likely the first to introduce the three-line system of hockey to the game. Previously, as in soccer, a player would stay out on the ice for most of the game.

CLEGHORN, Sprague ("Peg")
b. Montreal, Quebec, March 11, 1890
d. Montreal, Quebec, July 11, 1956
One of the toughest, dirtiest, meanest, most violent players of all, Sprague was paradoxically a brilliant rusher for a defenceman and one of the early stars of the game. He won three Stanley Cups with Ottawa and the Canadiens. He missed all of 1917-18 with a broken ankle after slipping on a Montreal sidewalk, but he was known to chase players all over the ice to beat them up. He boasted of having been involved in at least 50 stretcher-case brawls, but equally was a practical joker who once tried to shake hands with the governor-general of Canada with a buzzer in his hand after an introduction at a boxing match. He explained: "The boxing show is poor, the governor looks bored, and deserves some sort of thrill." He retired having scored more goals from defence than anyone with the exception of Harry Cameron. He died in a Montreal hospital as a result of injuries suffered when he was hit by a car two weeks earlier.

CLEMENT, Bill
b. Buckingham, Quebec, December 20, 1950
Hockey is only part of his story. Raised in nearby Thurso, little Bill couldn't find an English hockey team to play on until he was eight. Then, he was stuffed in goal for four years until one coach noticed how well he skated, even with the pads on. Out he came, to centre. His linemate was Guy Lafleur. His speed kept him in the league a long time, 11 years in all with Philly, Washington (where he was named captain), and Atlanta/Calgary. He has the distinction of playing for three different teams in three consecutive games. Game one: the Flyers. Game two: the 1976 All-Star Game. Game three: after being traded, Washington. He married Cissie MacLarty, daughter of CFL star Ted of the Ottawa Roughriders, and after retiring opened a restaurant in Atlanta that ended up a financial disaster. He studied acting in Atlanta at the Alliance Theatre. He got a job as a model, posing nude once for an industrial calendar, and appeared in more than 50 TV ads for, among other products, Deep Woods Off, an insect repellent. He and Cissie once appeared on *All My Children*. He acted in a military training film and became a colour commentator for ESPN to supplement his income.

CLEMMENSEN, Scott
b. Des Moines, Iowa, July 23, 1977
After a sparkling career with Boston College, Clemmensen had the worst drafting experience for a goalie in that he was selected by New Jersey. The chances of him taking over for Martin Brodeur as the number-one man any time in the next decade are nil, so the best-case scenario has him playing backup to the workhorse, and that means no more than 10 games a year. He played briefly in relief for the Devils in 2001-02 to the tune of 20 minutes, and that's the way it will be for him as long as he is in the Devils system.

CLIFFORD, Chris ("Cliffy")
b. Kingston, Ontario, May 26, 1966
On January 7, 1986, Cliffy scored a goal for his Kingston Canadians against the Toronto Marlies, the first goalie to do so in OHL history. He went on to play parts of just 2 games for Chicago (once for 20 minutes, the other, 5 years later, for just 4 minutes) before establishing himself in the IHL and ECHL, becoming that rare combination of goalie and assistant coach for Louisville.

CLINE, Bruce
b. Massawippi, Quebec, November 14, 1931
Even at his heaviest the mighty mouse tipped the Toledos at just 145 pounds, barely moving the needle on the scales at all. But Cline was ferocious and fearless and had a terrific career in the AHL that was punctuated by a 30-game stint with the NHL's Rangers. He broke into the AHL in '55-'56, winning the rookie of the year award in the same season that goalie and teammate with Providence, Johnny Bower, was named the league's MVP. Cline went on to record 8 seasons of 20 goals or more, though with the Blueshirts he managed only a deuce of scores playing on a line with Larry Popein and Dean Prentice. He spent his summers near Sherbrooke, first for pleasure, then as an aspiring restaurateur, and it was there he repaired after hanging up the blades to pursue his food business.

CLIPPINGDALE, Steve
b. Vancouver, British Columbia, April 29, 1956
Abandoning the University of Wisconsin for a career in hockey, Clippingdale moved to the Quebec juniors to prepare for life in the NHL. The life, though, she was a dog. L.A. gave up on him after just 16 games, and a trade to the lowly Caps for Mike Marson didn't make things any better. Within four years of being drafted in 1976 he was out of the game.

CLOUTIER, Dan
b. Mont-Laurier, Quebec, April 22, 1976
A bright prospect when the Rangers drafted him in 1994, Cloutier's star has moved ever more rapidly away from planet NHL. After two chances with New York, he was traded to the lowly Lightning in Tampa in the summer of '99 but showed little spark when given a greater opportunity. He had won the Memorial Cup with the Soo in '93 and a gold medal with Canada's '95 World Juniors, and was on the ice during Wayne Gretzky's final game. He revived his career in Vancouver where he had an outstanding regular season. Cloutier allowed a disastrous goal from centre ice against Detroit in the first round of the playoffs but

Sprague Cleghorn

Bill Clement

Bruce Cline

Dan Cloutier

Real Cloutier

Rejean Cloutier

Ben Clymer

Glen Cochrane

rebounded the next year, 2002-03, to take the Canucks to the top of the standings. His brother, Sylvain, later made it to the NHL.

CLOUTIER, Jacques ("Coco")
b. Noranda, Quebec, January 3, 1960
His NHL initiation got underway in the third period of a Buffalo-Quebec game on December 19, 1981. He allowed one Nordiques goal while showing the Sabres he could be an able backup or even a replacement for starter Don Edwards. But in his whole career, he never got to that next level, remaining pretty much a second-stringer for a dozen years. The Q league graduate from Trois Rivières also played for Canada at the 1986 World Championships and played for Chicago and the Nordiques before retiring. In 1994, he became assistant coach for the Cornwall Aces and the goaltending coach for the parent team, the Nordiques of Quebec. He later became an NHL assistant when the team moved to Colorado.

CLOUTIER, Real ("Buddy")
b. St. Émile, Quebec, July 30, 1956
"I am not Guy Lafleur." Most of his life Cloutier had to defend himself from comparisons to Guy Lafleur, a few years his senior but cut from the same skating and scoring cloth. At 18 Cloutier was playing for the Nordiques in the WHA, setting the league on fire with four consecutive seasons of 56 goals or more. "I am not Guy Lafleur." When Quebec joined the NHL in 1979, he scored 42 goals. "I am not Guy Lafleur." Then he smashed an ankle in the summer playing baseball. His production dipped and he was traded to Buffalo. "I am not Guy Lafleur." Production dipped even more and he was demoted to Flint of the IHL. The only question they ever asked down there was, "Who's Guy Lafleur?"

CLOUTIER, Rejean
b. Windsor, Quebec, February 15, 1960
He played January 26, 27, and 30, 1980, and then two more games the following year. A trade to Edmonton in 1984 didn't get him back in the NHL and he spent a number of years in the minors, becoming property of Montreal in 1986 to no great effect.

CLOUTIER, Roland
b. Rouyn, Quebec, October 6, 1957
His first NHL game came on February 28, 1978, with Detroit, and the next year an injury to Andre St. Laurent forced coach Bobby Kromm to summon Cloutier from the farm in Kansas City. Cloutier played on a line with Errol Thompson and Fern Leblanc, and although he spoke no English, he scored five times in three games and looked like a keeper. But after a few more games with the Wings in Detroit and then the Nordiques the following year, he was out of the NHL for good. Cloutier went to France and played for the next seven years before calling it quits.

CLOUTIER, Sylvain
b. Mont-Laurier, Quebec, February 13, 1974
So far, it doesn't look like it's going to happen. Though he's the bro of Dan the goalie, Sylvain impressed the Hawks only fractionally, spending most of his time in

the minor pros before moving on to lowly Atlanta in the 1999 Expansion Draft. He was later traded to Jersey, but to date his only NHL action was seven games with the Hawks lo those many years ago.

CLUNE, Wally
b. Toronto, Ontario, February 20, 1930
d. Montreal, Quebec, February 3, 1998
A graduate of the St. Michael's Majors in Toronto in the late 1940s, Clune spent most of his hockey life in Montreal, playing mostly Quebec senior before and after his brief trip to the NHL with the Canadiens in '55-'56, one of the years the team won the Cup.

CLYMER, Ben
b. Edina, Minnesota, April 11, 1978
Clymer is one of an amazing threesome of NHLers to come out of the same small high school in Minnesota – Jefferson High. Mark Parrish of the Islanders and Toby Peterson of Pittsburgh not only went to the same school – they were all best friends. Clymer was drafted by Boston in 1997 after two good years with the U.S. national juniors, but he never played for the B's. He signed with Tampa Bay as a free agent, and the Lightning played him most of the 1999-2000 season, less so the year after.

COALTER, Gary
b. Toronto, Ontario, July 8, 1950
Drafted 67th overall by the Rangers in 1970, Coalter never played on Broadway. He was sold to the Seals in Californ-I-A and claimed by K.C. the next year, taking neither team closer to the silver chalice. A career in the minors resulted. He later became involved in the construction business and his son was given a tryout by San Jose.

COATES, Steve
b. Toronto, Ontario, July 2, 1950
Five games and a goal constitute the alpha and omega of his career. Coach Larry Wilson clearly wasn't in Coates's corner, demoting him to the farm in Springfield before giving him much of a chance to fight his way into regular duty. He finished in the minors.

COCHRANE, Glen
b. Cranbrook, British Columbia, January 29, 1958
A tough guy, a policeman, an enforcer, call him what you will, Cochrane ran up a ton of penalty minutes. He joined Philly in '78-'79 and three years later he had a career season, teaming with Mark Howe on the blueline, scoring 24 points, and recording a +42. He played most of the '83-'84 season on left wing with Rich and Ron Sutter, but he encountered his share of setbacks along the way. He suffered a serious back injury that forced him to miss much of '86-'87, and a broken kneecap. When his time was up, he knew it. No final stints in the minors or trips to Europe for him.

COFFEY, Paul ("Coff")
b. Weston, Ontario, June 1, 1961
Like dozens and dozens of juniors, Coffey was supposed to be the next Bobby Orr. He was a defenceman who could skate, shoot, make passes and join the rush, quarterback the power play, and head to

the net as a fourth forward. What separated him from all the other would-be-Bobbys was that he was as close a thing there was to a new Orr – at least, offensively. Edmonton drafted him 6th overall in 1980, but when he got to his first camp Coffey tried to prove his defensive worth. Coach Glen Sather quickly talked him out of that and told him the Oilers wanted him for his rushing ability. That was all the 19-year-old needed to hear. As a rookie, he had just 9 goals and 32 points, but the next year he nearly tripled those numbers. In his fourth year, when the Oilers won their first Stanley Cup, Coffey had an incredible 40 goals and 126 points. The next year, he won his first Norris Trophy, and in '85-'86 he had a year to remember. He scored 48 goals, breaking Orr's record of 46 by a defenceman, and finished with 138 points, 1 shy of Orr's total points mark. His early years, though, fraught with comparisons to number 4, found Coffey wanting in the defensive aspects of his game. It's not often that a single play can diffuse such criticism, but in the 1984 Canada Cup, Coffey managed to do just that. In the semifinals against the Soviet Union, Coffey found himself the lone man on a two-on-one featuring Vladimir Kovin and Mikhail Varnakov. Coffey broke the rush up, controlled the puck, worked a give-and-go passing play with John Tonelli, and then took a shot that was deflected by Mike Bossy into the net for the overtime victory. Coffey won three Cups with Edmonton, but his relations with Sather soured in the summer of 1987 and an odd mix of glory and controversy constituted the 1987 Canada Cup. Coffey helped that team

Wayne Gretzky hired Coffey as a special teams consultant.
PAUL COFFEY

to victory, but right after refused to report to the Oilers training camp until his contract was worked out. About six weeks later, Sather countered by trading the superstar with Dave Hunter and Wayne Van Dorp to Pittsburgh for Craig Simpson, Chris Joseph, Moe Mantha, and Dave Hannan. The Oilers won the Cup again that year, and Coffey had a trade he didn't necessarily want. Nonetheless, he joined a talented Penguins team led by Mario Lemieux and regained his 100-point abilities. He helped the team win the 1991 Cup, but before the next win a year later he was traded to Los Angeles. He went on to Detroit when Scotty Bowman, who had known him from Pittsburgh, arrived in Motown, but Bowman traded him to Hartford so he could acquire Brendan Shanahan, a power forward Bowman thought (correctly) was one of the missing links for the Wings. Coffey finished his career with a string of teams – Hartford, Philadelphia, Chicago, Carolina, and Boston. Health woes, notably his back, had slowed him or caused him to miss much of the year, and he hung on to a career whose best years were a few years in the past. Yet his accomplishments are almost without compare. He won 3 Norris Trophies and played in 14 All-Star Games. He won three Canada Cups and played in the 1996 World Cup. He finished with 1,531 points, second all-time for a defenceman behind only Ray Bourque. In his 21 seasons, he came to epitomize the new rushing defenceman, but he was a better skater than any other. He retired in 2001, and just a year later his longtime teammate, Wayne Gretzky, now owner of Phoenix, hired Coffey as a special teams consultant. In 2004, Coffey will almost surely be inducted into the Hockey Hall of Fame.

COFLIN, Hugh
b. Blaine Lake, Saskatchewan, December 15, 1928
Chicago's chief scout Tiny Thompson was big on him, and so was GM Johnny Gottselig. So when the Hawks blueline was ravaged by injuries early in the '50-'51 season, Coflin was called up to the big time to play alongside Blackjack Stewart. Reputedly a tough and scoring defenceman, he disappointed in his time with Chicago and was demoted, eventually landing in Edmonton of the WHL, where he also set up a drive-in ice cream business. He remained a westerner the rest of his career.

Hugh Coflin

COLE, Danton
b. Pontiac, Michigan, January 10, 1967
He knew the jig was up when he played for four teams in his last two years. The former member of the Michigan State national championship team had his best season with Tampa in '93-'94 when he had 20 goals, was the team's NHLPA rep, and played for the U.S. at the World Championships, his third trip to the Worlds. He finished up in the IHL and turned to coaching with Grand Rapids, the last team for whom he played before a serious stomach muscle injury forced him to retire.

Danton Cole

COLE, Erik
b. Oswego, New York, November 6, 1978
As a rookie with Carolina in 2001-02, Cole quickly developed into one of the most important role players with the Hurricanes. He came out of Clarkson University to score 16 goals and 40 points in his first year, but his season was defined by his playoff performance. He was a key contributor to the 'Canes going to the Cup finals for the first time in franchise history, playing a strong physical game and chipping in with six goals during the dream run. Cole didn't receive many votes for the Calder Trophy but he is a player for the future if he can play with consistency.

COLLEY, Tom
b. Toronto, Ontario, August 21, 1953
Colley had a rough time in the NHL's backyard. He

was let out to play only once, and he committed a foul that earned him a two-minute penalty in that one game. That was 1974-75 with Minnesota. He was then sent away to the farm, in New Haven, where he stayed for a number of years.

COLLINGS, Norm ("Dodger")
b. Bradford, Ontario, May 6, 1910
Collings played just one game, with the Canadiens, but he made the most of it, earning an assist as an emergency replacement during the '34-'35 season.

COLLINS, Bill
b. Ottawa, Ontario, July 13, 1943
Billed as a superb penalty-killing forward, Collins didn't get a chance to show his stuff until after the 1967 expansion when Minnesota drafted him. He was a valuable addition, but he bounced from team to team. Three times he scored more than 20 goals in a season, and for his career he had more short-handed goals (17) than power-play ones (10). After retiring in 1978, Collins variously sold real estate, ran a sporting goods store, and sold advertising for a Michigan newspaper. He later worked in computer sales in Detroit.

Gary Collins

COLLINS, Ranleigh "Gary"
b. Toronto, Ontario, September, 27, 1935
Coming up through the Toronto Marlies, Collins was destined for the Leafs when he turned pro. He stalled at the AHL level, though, and his only career games came during the 1959 playoffs with said Maple Leafs.

Michael Colman

COLLYARD, Bob
b. Hibbing, Minnesota, October 16, 1949
Truly among the most incredible stories. And it happened twice! Collyard worked his way up from college to minor pro to St. Louis in '73-'74, but after 10 games he was demoted and spent the next 10 years in the minors. But go quietly into those minors he did not. In March 1979, he filed a federal lawsuit in United States District Court claiming that he had been disallowed the right to play in the NHL because he was not Canadian. The defendants named included the Washington Capitals, U.S. Secretary of State Cyrus Vance, Attorney General Griffin Bell, and Secretary of Labour Ray Marshall. The government officials were named because it was they, according to Collyard's lawyer James Balmer, who allowed aliens (i.e., Canadians) to be employed in the U.S. in violation of immigration laws. Collyard argued that many less talented Canadians were being employed in the U.S. On September 13, 1983, he was at it again, filing a $540,000 lawsuit against the Milwaukee Admirals for releasing him, allegedly because he was American

and the IHL acquired visas for non-Americans by fraudulently claiming there were no available Americans who could fill the needed positions!

COLMAN, Michael
b. Stoneham, Massachusetts, August 4, 1968
d. Kansas City, Missouri, April 5, 1994
On the night of April 5, 1994, Colman was killed in a car accident, cutting short a life, irrespective of hockey, too incomplete to have ended. Undrafted, he was signed by San Jose and given his only chance to play by the expansion team before going to the minors to play with the Kansas City Blades, where he spent the better part of four years. He died in North Kansas City Hospital at age 25 as a result of injuries he sustained in the crash.

He played with his brother on the Ottawa Commandos that won the 1943 Allan Cup.
NEIL COLVILLE

COLVILLE, Mac
b. Edmonton, Alberta, January 8, 1916
Although he has not ascended the pantheon of greatness as has his older brother, Neil, Mac was a member of the Rangers' famous Bread Line with Alex Shibicky during the years leading up to the war. He and Neil had almost identical careers: starting in 1935, leaving in 1942 to join the army, and returning to the Rangers after the war (Neil played two years longer). After retiring, Mac coached for a year in Vancouver, leading the team to a championship before quitting and moving to New Haven for two seasons. He won his only Cup in 1940 and spent his entire career with the Rangers. He later worked for Imperial Oil in Edmonton and became manager of a plumbing company based in Calgary.

COLVILLE, Neil ("Frosty")
b. Edmonton, Alberta, August 4, 1914
d. Richmond, British Columbia, December 26, 1987
A Ranger through and through, a Ranger wearing blue, a Ranger all his days, a Ranger in his ways. Centre of the Bread Line with brother Mac and Alex Shibicky, he was both a playmaker and a scorer until joining the RCAF in 1942. He played with his brother on the Ottawa Commandos that won the 1943 Allan Cup, and served as a navigator in the war. Upon returning to the NHL near the end of the '44-'45 season, he and his brother, both a step slower, took their place on the blueline, the first ever brother combination to do so. Neil's conversion to defence was seamless, and he became the first player to be named to All-Star teams as both a forward and a defenceman. He retired in 1949 and became coach of the Rangers a year later after serving New Haven in that capacity in the interim. At 36, he was the league's youngest bench boss, but he held the position for just

Mac Colville

a year and a half. Ulcers had forced him to adopt a strictly milk diet and he had half his stomach removed. Out of hockey, he managed a trucking company for a while and then in 1952 he and Jack McGill, another former player, opened the first Dairy Queen in Canada, in Vancouver. Colville then moved to Whitehorse and controlled a closed-circuit TV station there before easing into retirement. At 61, he married for the first time and settled in Vancouver. He was named to the Selection Committee of the Hockey Hall of Fame – himself an inductee in 1967 – but in 1984 he lost a leg to cancer and resigned his position. He passed away three years later from that cancer.

COLVIN, Les
b. Oshawa, Ontario, February 8, 1921
A graduate of the Oshawa Generals, Colvin found himself in the war before he had a chance at the NHL. For four years he offered military service, and for a year after he was on the sidelines with injuries. After regaining his health, he played a few years of senior hockey, but on the night of January 22, 1949, he replaced Frank Brimsek in goal against Montreal (a 4-2 Habs win), his only NHL game.

COLWILL, Les
b. Divide, Saskatchewan, January 1, 1935
Each summer, Colwill returned home to work as a filler in a brewery. Not fancy, not flashy, not a big-city boy, Colwill was born on his father's farm but raised in nearby Lethbridge when the family moved after six months. He played with the local Native Sons team and made his way up through the Rangers system, coached first by Doug Bentley in Saskatoon, then by Don Raleigh in Brandon. He made the Rangers in '58-'59, but in his only full year scored just seven times. GM Muzz Patrick had expected more.

COMEAU, Reynald "Rey"
b. Montreal, Quebec, October 25, 1948
He banged, he hustled, he skated, he killed penalties, he got hurt and never complained, he gave his all and his heart told him to play hockey. Despite his size, he was admired wherever he went and played with an enthusiasm that more than made up for height and weight. But ultimately, he was used as a penalty killer. Montreal had given up on him after just four games in '71-'72, and in Atlanta his ice time varied. One bad outing meant being benched or sitting for long stretches, and a move to Colorado, last stop on the milk run, was all that was left by 1980.

COMMODORE, Mike
b. Fort Saskatchewan, Alberta, November 7, 1979
A ton of size on defence, Commodore was like so many other players of recent years, suffering a serious eye injury in an ever-quickening game. He went to a U.S. college, North Dakota, to get his smarts and hockey skills, and New Jersey drafted him in '99. But while playing for the farm team in Albany, he took a puck in the eye and missed a month recovering from the dangerous shot. Visor time. A year later, he made his NHL debut with the Devils and has yet to make it to the team full-time.

COMRIE, Mike
b. Edmonton, Alberta, September 11, 1980
His father owns the Brick, that chain of stores with the "no interest, no payment until blah blah blah" television ads, but Mike didn't come free or cheap or on any layaway plan. Just the opposite. Comrie was going to the University of Michigan when he saw another teen, Mike Van Ryn, win a court case that allowed him to transfer from U.S. college to Canadian junior and become an unrestricted free agent who could sign with the highest bidder after December 31 of the year he transferred. Comrie did the same, joining the WHL in 2000 the year after being named a Hobie Baker Award finalist. The Edmonton Oilers, the team that drafted him, panicked but managed to sign him to a contract on December 30, 2000, and he played in his first NHL game that very night. Bye bye Kootenay (WHL). Comrie had a decent half-season, but the knock against him was his size. At 5'9" and 175 pounds, he wasn't going to power his way into the blue ice too often. In the off-season, number-one centre Doug Weight went to St. Louis in a trade prompted by contract, and Comrie skated his way onto the first line for the Oilers in 2001-02. He faced the challenge and scored more than 30 goals, quickly establishing himself as a small force of scoring and tenacity and helping the team make the playoffs. A hometown star was born.

COMRIE, Paul
b. Edmonton, Alberta, February 7, 1977
The "C word." In medical terms, it means one thing. In cursing, it means another. In hockey, it means something else all together. It never used to happen; now it's so routine no one reacts anymore.Concussion is the "C" word, and career-ending is what it has become all too often. Like his brother, Mike, Paul lived out a dream when Tampa Bay, the team that drafted him, traded him to his hometown. He played 15 games with the Oilers, then suffered a serious head injury during a game and never played again. He retired living out a post-concussion syndrome nightmare.

CONACHER, Brian
b. Toronto, Ontario, August 31, 1941
His father was Lionel, his uncles were Charlie and Roy, his nephew was Murray Henderson. If this guy didn't have the genes to play, no one did. Despite calling himself nothing more than a journeyman player, Brian's life in hockey has been lifelong, all-encompassing, and as inspiring as the Big Train's or the Bomber's. He played four years with the Marlies while slowly but surely earning his B.A. in history and English from U of Western Ontario in 1968. Although he was given a one-game tryout with the Leafs in '61-'62, he spent two years with Canada's National Team, playing in the '64 Olympics in Innsbruck and the '65 Worlds and joining the team again from 1968 to '71. Out of these experiences came a book, *Hockey in Canada: The Way It Is*, a controversial look at the state of pro hockey, the international game, and Father Bauer's National Team efforts. It was this same Conacher spirit that earlier led him to become involved in the formation of the NHL Players' Association during his time with the Leafs, something that infuriated coach and GM Punch Imlach and

Les Colwill

Rey Comeau

likely cost Conacher some playing time after being a part of the Cup-winning team of '67. The previous year, he had been a candidate for rookie of the year, but in the year-end voting lost to a youngster named Bobby Orr. During his first retirement, from 1968 to '71, he was the property of Detroit, Minnesota, and Toronto before playing 22 games with the Wings and heading to one last year of pro, in the WHA. After retiring, he became sports director for CKLW-TV in Windsor, Ontario, and then became coach of the Mohawk Valley Comets in the newly formed North America Hockey League (NAHL). He held that position for two years before becoming GM in Indianapolis and then Edmonton, and in 1980 he became marketing manager of a holding company in Edmonton. When Hamilton's Copps Coliseum opened in 1984, he became manager there for five years, after which he was named CEO of the Royal Agricultural Winter Fair. In 1992, his life was complete when he became vice-president of Maple Leaf Gardens under the auspices of new GM Cliff Fletcher, a job he left a few years later as the Leafs planned their move to Air Canada Centre. Most recently, Conacher has become the director of the NHL Alumni Association. A journeyman, indeed.

CONACHER, Charlie ("The Big Bomber")

b. Toronto, Ontario, December 20, 1909
d. Toronto, Ontario, December 30, 1967

Many a writer and fan from Conacher's era called Charlie the first superstar of the Maple Leafs. There had been great players before him – Ace Bailey, Happy Day, Lorne Chabot – but none had the skill, speed, and charisma of the man everyone called the Big Bomber. He was one of five boys and five girls in the Conacher clan who grew up near Jesse Ketchum school in downtown Toronto, and although Roy and Lionel also made their way into the Hockey Hall of Fame, few would dispute that Charlie was the best hockey player of the lot. He was inspired by his older brothers to play in ths streets, but although he worked tirelessly on his shot, he rarely skated. When he did get onto the ice, he realized how weak he was and set out to dedicate himself to improving his movements. He started out as a goalie, but one day he moved out of goal and skated until he could no longer stand. The next day, he went out and did it all over again, motivated both by the success of Roy and Lionel and by a sense that hockey could give him a steady job at decent pay. It was this ambition and determination, not to mention pure skill, that helped him become a star in the NHL. Conacher played with the Marlies in 1927, and within two years he and teammate Harvey Jackson led the

He was one of five boys and five girls in the Conacher clan who grew up near Jesse Ketchum school in downtown Toronto.
CHARLIE CONACHER

team to a Memorial Cup. In 1929-30, they both made the leap to the Leafs, and when they were partnered with another youngster, Joe Primeau, to make a forward unit, they were dubbed The Kid Line. It was to become the most famously-named line in all of hockey, a name used to this day for any young line combination, but the original was something special. Conacher became the game's best right winger, an explosive scorer who could use his size (6'1", 200 pounds) to great effect. Five times between 1930 and 1936 he led or tied in league goal scoring. He won the Cup with Toronto in 1932, and from 1933-36 was a First Team All-Star. His style, however effective, also had its drawbacks in the form of injury. In 1931, he had a kidney removed and doctors feared for his career. Conacher, though, was ever resilient, and for every pain there was recovery. He played with tonsilitis for weeks at one stretch. He broke his wrist, and suffered blood poisoning when a skate cut through his glove. He broke his collarbone, dislocated his shoulder and was cut umpteen times, however little could keep him out of the lineup for long. But after nine years, the Leafs traded him to Detroit and from there he closed out his playing days with the New York Americans. He retired in 1941, and in '44 coached the Oshawa Generals to a Memorial Cup. Conacher later led Chicago for three years in the NHL, and then settled into a day job with a brokerage firm back in his native Toronto. He was inducted into the Hockey Hall of Fame in 1961. In later years, he suffered from throat cancer, but in typical manner, he refused to give in to the disease. After one surgery, he promptly left the hospital to go on a fishing trip, but by 1968 he finally lost his toughest battle. He, his family, friends, and admirers set up the Charlie Conacher Research Fund to help find a cure, and his hockey legacy lives on in the form of the Charlie Conacher Memorial Trophy given to a player for outstanding service to the community.

CONACHER, Charles Jr. "Pete"

b. Toronto, Ontario, July 29, 1932

Son of Charlie, Pete got his start in the NHL in circus-like manner. When uncle Roy decided to retire early in the '51-'52 season, the Hawks thought it would be a great idea to pull Pete up from the minors to replace the elder Conacher. No pressure there. And they gave him number 9 as well, just to make the jitters noticeable. Fortunately, the callup was for but two games, and Pete acquitted himself well enough, but in the ensuing years he proved to be a Conacher cut from a cheaper cloth. He played with the Rangers and Leafs, then retired and was reinstated as an amateur so he could join the Belleville McFarlands in their

Pete Conacher

quest for the 1959 World Championships. Mission accomplished, he returned to his employer in Toronto but was coerced into returning to the pros, in his case the Buffalo Bisons, which owned his rights. He played in the AHL another seven years, then retired for good. Conacher played for the NHL Oldtimers for years afterwards and worked as a floor trader for Burgess Graham Securities on the Toronto Stock Exchange.

CONACHER, Jim ("Pencil")
b. Motherwell, Scotland, May 5, 1921

The only child of Robert and Margaret Conacher, Jim was born in Scotland where his father was a football (soccer) star. A few years later the family emigrated to Toronto, and it was there Jim learned to skate. His first team was the Essey bantams in the Toronto playground league, and as he moved up to play for the Oshawa Generals in 1940 he was discovered by Detroit scout Carson Cooper. He attended Detroit's camp the next year and was assigned to Omaha, and it was there, at a local radio station, that he met his wife-to-be, Bonnie Amgwert. Conacher married her, then entered the Canadian army for three years, joining a Scottish infantry group in Cornwall, the well-known Stormont, Dundas, and Glengarry Highlanders. He was made a second lieutenant and training officer at Camp Borden, where he was stationed until being discharged in 1945. After the war he played briefly for the Wings again but was soon traded to Chicago, where he once scored four goals in a game. He finished his career playing briefly for the Rangers after being claimed on waivers.

A boxing champion, he fought Jack Dempsey in a three-round exhibition in aid of the Christie Street hospital for war veterans.
LIONEL CONACHER

CONACHER, Lionel ("Conny"/ "The Big Train")
b. Toronto, Ontario, May 24, 1901
d. Ottawa, Ontario, May 26, 1954

Had Lionel Conacher been alive when he was inducted into the Hockey Hall of Fame in 1994, he would have shrugged his shoulders and said quite simply that hockey was his worst sport! Indeed, he was boxing champion of Canada and one of the country's greatest lacrosse players. He might have been the best football player in the early years of the game, and he was among the best baseball players in Toronto. Yet none of those sports could provide the financial stability of hockey, and he gravitated to that sport as a pro even though he didn't start playing until 16. Conacher was the second of 10 children. He attended Jesse Ketchum School in downtown Toronto and most of his life revolved around the small part of the city near Avenue and Davenport roads. His friends asked him to join their football team, and the Capitals went on to win five city championships from 1912 to '16. He played baseball with the Toronto Hillcrests, winning the amateur championship of Ontario, and went on to play semi-pro hockey with Aura Lee. He was recruited as a decathlete for Canada's Olympic team, and every sport he tried he wasn't just good at – he was the best! A boxing champion, he fought Jack Dempsey in a three-round exhibition in aid of the Christie Street hospital for war veterans. He played football for the Toronto Argonauts and on one memorable day led the Argos to the 1921 Grey Cup and left the field early to play hockey for Aura Lee. By 1923, he had decided to concentrate on hockey, and to that end accepted an offer from Pittsburgh to play pro for the Yellowjackets. Conacher shocked the country when he married 17-year-old Dorothy Kennedy just minutes before going to Pennsylvania. Following a brief ceremony, he took a carriage to Union Station and bid his new bride goodbye, leaving the newspapers in a frenzy to try to report on the wedding of Canada's greatest athlete. Of course, Conacher could not restrict his activities to hockey in Pittsburgh. He also played for the Bellemonte Academy football team, where he became a hero. Conacher played for the 'Jackets for two years, winning the USAHA title both years. In 1925, the team turned fully professional by joining the NHL, as the Pirates, and he scored the first goal in franchise history on November 26, 1925. Just a year and a half later, though, Conacher was traded to the Americans, which almost destroyed his career. The team's owner, Bill Dwyer, was one of New York's biggest bootleggers. He used Madison Square Garden to make much of his bathtub whisky and Conacher became a virtual alcoholic. In '29-'30, he was both player and coach for the Amerks, but by season's end the Big Train was a wreck. Two fortuitous events turned things around for him: one, the birth of his first child, daughter Constance, which compelled him to swear off alcohol forever; two, the Maroons were willing to give him another chance. He made good on both counts and resurrected a grand career. He was renowned for a unique style of shotblocking in which he slid across the ice on one knee to block the puck. As a result, he was called the Travelling Netminder, and his play revived in Montreal. He played six of the next seven seasons with the Maroons, the only exception being '33-'34 when he was in Chicago. He won a Cup that year with the Hawks and another the year after with the Maroons, but by 1937 his body had been ravaged by injuries, particularly to his knees, to the point that he had to retire. During his 12 years in the NHL, Conacher was incredibly active off the ice. He

Jim Conacher

Lionel Conacher

Lionel Conacher

Pat Conacher

coached the Rutgers University football team for two years, was a professional wrestler in Toronto for many years, formed and played for the Wrigley's Aromints pro football team, and prospected for gold in Athabasca with his brother Charlie. Even before he retired, he started a life in politics. Conacher was elected to the Ontario Legislature in 1937, becoming an MP for Bracondale, his family's neighbourhood. He also worked for the Ontario Athletic Commission and during the war was with the RCAF as the director of recreation for soldiers. After the war he went from provincial to federal politics. He was elected to the House of Commons on June 27, 1949, and remained there until his death. Fittingly, he was playing a charity baseball game on Parliament Hill when he collapsed and died while running to first base. In 1950, he had been named Canada's athlete of the half-century and Canada's football player of the half-century. He was a charter member of the Canadian Sports Hall of Fame in 1955 and the Canadian Football Hall of Fame in 1963, and he was elected to the Canadian Lacrosse Hall of Fame in 1966. After his death, flags flew at half-mast to honour a man of extraordinary ability who gave his life to his community and country. Incredibly, his brothers Charlie and Roy also had Hall of Fame careers in the NHL, and his son, Brian, went on to play in the NHL and with Canada's National Team for an extended period of time. Indeed, the name Conacher is synonymous with sporting success in Canada.

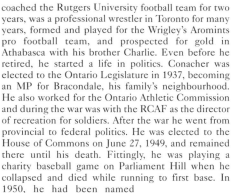

Roy joined the RCAF for the better part of four years, the prime of his hockey life.
ROY CONACHER

CONACHER, Pat
b. Edmonton, Alberta, May 1, 1959
Poor guy. He was a Conacher, but also he wasn't. See, he had the name, but the stud wasn't Lionel or Charlie or Roy. Nope. It was Dad from out west ways. Pat got to the NHL with the Rangers, but snapped his peg during pre-season of '80-'81 and missed the year. Five games with New York the next year was all that was left there, so he signed with Edmonton for 1983-84. Good move, that. A few months later, he won the Stanley Cup. Well, he was there, anyway. Gretzky and Messier and Fuhr and Coffey won it, really. Then there was a series of pit stops for the checking winger – New Jersey, L.A., Calgary, the Islanders. That was all she wrote for this Conacher, who wasn't one of *the* Conachers.

CONACHER, Roy
b. Toronto, Ontario, October 5, 1916
d. Victoria, British Columbia, December 29, 1984
Called the Forgotten Conacher because of both his skill and his anonymity while skating in the shadows of Lionel and Charlie, Roy was every inch the Hall of Famer his two brothers were. There were 10 children in the household, 5 boys and 5 girls. Roy's twin, Bert, was also a fine player as a teen, but he lost an eye in a freak accident playing street hockey with his brothers in front of their Davenport Road house in Toronto. Like the other boys, Roy learned his hockey in the Toronto leagues before making his way to the NHL with Boston. As a rookie, he led the league in goals in 1938-39 with 26, a feat not to be accomplished again until Teemu Selanne in 1992-93. Roy had three more excellent years with the Bruins, helping the Beantowners win Stanley Cups in 1939 and '41. But then, with his Kraut Line teammates (Schmidt, Dumart, and Bauer), he joined the RCAF for the better part of four years, the prime of his hockey life. When he was honourably discharged, Boston GM Art Ross figured those war years had finished Conacher, and it was his comeback as much as anything that made him a legend of sorts. Ross traded Roy to Detroit, a deal he would later call the biggest mistake of his life. Roy not only shone on a line with Ted Lindsay and Jim Conacher, he scored a career-high 30 goals. But after that one season with Detroit, he got into a bitter contract squabble with GM Jack Adams and retired rather than capitulate. Just two weeks later, Jolly Jack sent him to Chicago for cash, and shortly after he signed with the Hawks, Roy's brother Charlie was named the team's head coach. Roy produced four successive seasons of superb hockey, winning the Art Ross Trophy in '48-'49 playing on a line with Bill Mosienko and Doug Bentley. After just 12 games of the '51-'52 season, Roy decided to retire. He moved to Midland, Ontario and became coach of the local OHA Junior C team, winning the championship the next season. He continued to play hockey for the Oldtimers and in NHL charity events and after his retirement moved to British Columbia, where he passed away in 1984. He was inducted into the Hockey Hall of Fame posthumously, as a Veteran Player, in 1998.

CONKLIN, Ty
b. Anchorage, Alaska, March 30, 1976
Yes, of course, you need skill to get to the NHL, but desire and drive are also important qualities. Conklin came from Scott Gomez country to the NHL via the University of New Hampshire and the proverbial Highway of Determination. Despite doing everything a goalie could be expected to do in his final year, Conklin was never drafted. Edmonton signed him as a free agent on April 18, 2002 and the following season he appeared in four games. He had a perfect 2-0-0 record and a 1.62 goals-against average.

CONN, Hugh "Red"
b. Hartney, Manitoba, October 25, 1904
d. Berkeley, California, July 1964
For two years he was a regular on the port side of the Amazing Amerks, but Conn disappeared as quickly as he emerged. His career was spent mostly out west in various leagues in Canada and the States.

CONN, Rob
b. Calgary, Alberta, September 3, 1968
He put up good numbers as a teenager playing at the University of Alaska-Anchorage, but it was hardly a mystery why he went undrafted – scouts didn't usually venture to the remote North. Signed by Chicago in 1991 and then dumped by them after two games, he also played briefly for Buffalo a few years later, but mostly stuck it out in the minors.

CONNELL, Alec (sometimes Alex) ("The Ottawa Fireman")
b. Ottawa, Ontario, February 8, 1899
d. Ottawa, Ontario, May 10, 1958
It was during the war that Alec Connell found out he was a capable goalie. He was working for the Royal Canadian Army Service Corps, stationed in Kingston, when he decided to play hockey. Because he couldn't skate, he played net and found that he liked it and was good at it. Upon his return to Ottawa, he took the game seriously and in 1924 replaced Clint Benedict in net for the Senators. Over his first six seasons, Connell did not miss a single game. He led Ottawa to the Stanley Cup in 1927, and the next year set a record that will never be broken. He recorded 6 consecutive shutouts, not allowing a goal for a period of 446 minutes and 6 seconds. He was easily noticed on ice because he wore a small black cap to keep himself warm. His last few years were marred by changes in uniform and diminished playing time in some instances. He retired in 1935 only to be induced to return a year later with the Maroons. As soon as he retired, he returned to Ottawa and to his job. Connell had joined the Ottawa Fire Department in 1921, where he worked when he wasn't playing hockey. He worked there until ill health forced him to retire in 1950. Throughout his post-playing days he coached, at St. Patrick's College for many years and for the QSHL Senators in '49-'50 before having to give up the position. He worked briefly with Fournier Van and Storage Ltd. but illness forced him to retire. He died in hospital, after several years' illness, just a few weeks after being inducted into the Hockey Hall of Fame. Connell finished his career with 81 shutouts in just 417 games played. His career GAA was a remarkable 1.19.

CONNELLY, Bert
b. Montreal, Quebec, April 22, 1909
d. unknown
He played hockey for more than 15 years in leagues up and down the continent, but Bert played just 87 games in the NHL, with the Rangers and the Hawks. His moment of glory came in his last year, with Chicago. Called up from Springfield, he was part of the Hawks team that beat Toronto for the 1938 Stanley Cup, playing one game in the playoffs and watching the rest of the series from the seats. He had won two Allan Cups with the Moncton Hawks, in 1933 and '34, and he returned to Montreal after the Chicago Cup victory to play senior hockey. His son, Wayne, later played in the NHL, and Bert was inducted into the New Brunswick Sports Hall of Fame in 1970 in recognition of his successful years in Moncton.

CONNELLY, Wayne
b. Rouyn, Quebec, December 16, 1939
Bobby Hull was the most famous name to jump from the NHL to the rival WHA in the summer of 1972. Goalie Terry Sawchuk allowed the first-ever penalty-shot goal in the playoffs. And Bill Masterton died as a result of injuries sustained in a hockey game on January 13, 1968. And Wayne Connelly was there for all of these important events. In fact, Connelly was the first NHLer to sign with the WHA, with the Minnesota Fighting Saints on April 14, 1972. He scored the first-ever playoff goal on a penalty shot, beating the great Sawchuk with a perfect shot. And he played in Minnesota on a line with Masterton and Dave Balon. He was just a few feet away from the horrific hit that took Masterton's life. Along the way, Connelly scored and scored, first in junior with Peterborough, which drew the notice of Sam Pollock of the Canadiens. The Habs called him up for three games when Bernie Geoffrion was injured, but he didn't get a point, the team lost all three games, and he was sold to Boston in the summer. Connelly played mostly part-time with Boston and, as for so many of that era, his break came with expansion in 1967. He played with four teams in four years, then bolted to the WHA for the last few years of his career. After retiring, he moved to Kirkland Lake, Ontario, and with his brother, Cliff, established the Teck News Agency, the largest wholesale distributor of magazines in Ontario's north.

CONNOLLY, Tim
b. Syracuse, New York, May 7, 1981
They give prizes and accolades for everything nowadays. In the 1997-98 season, Connolly was voted the best stickhandler in the OHL Western Conference in a coaches' poll. More substantively, he played for the U.S. at the 1999 World Juniors and burst onto the NHL scene that fall. He has been an NHL regular ever since, starting with the Islanders. So highly regarded a prospect was he that he was traded to Ottawa with Taylor Pyatt for Michael Peca. Young in years, he is an American to watch for in the coming years.

CONNOR, Cam
b. Winnipeg, Manitoba, August 10, 1954
"That's one thing I can't do – " quoth Toronto goalie Mike Palmateer, " – stop someone who doesn't know what he's doing." That someone was Cam Connor, and the night in question was April 21, 1979, game three of the Toronto-Montreal quarter-finals. The game was in double overtime, and Connor had yet to take a shift. Desperate for fresh bodies, coach Scotty Bowman threw the rookie over the boards and he scored a lucky goal to give the Habs a commanding 3-0 lead in the series. Montreal went on to win the Cup, but Connor was claimed by the Oilers in the Expansion Draft of '79. He had got into Bowman's

Rob Conn

Bert Connelly

Tim Connolly

Cam Connor

Harry Connor

Bob Connors

Craig Conroy

Eddie Convey

bad books earlier when he said thanks but no thanks to a Montreal contract offer, opting to play for Phoenix in the WHA instead. Connor was sent to the Rangers, but in four seasons he never established himself. He moved to Edmonton after playing his last and became branch manager for a computer consulting business.

CONNOR, Harry
b. Ottawa, Ontario, December 3, 1904
d. Ottawa, Ontario, March 2, 1947
Three trades in four years, two go-rounds with both Boston and Ottawa, tossed into the NHL in 1927, out by '31. Such was the travelling life of this early hockeyist of slim renown before he hooked up with the Can-Am league for a few years of shinny. He was not a particularly fast skater, but he was known for his consistent and colourful (i.e., rugged) performances. After retiring, he returned home to Ottawa and operated his own business, Harry Connor Washers and Appliances on Bank Street. He was a regular at the Chaudiere Golf Club until he succumbed to illness at just 42 years of age.

CONNORS, Bobby
b. Glasgow, Scotland, October 19, 1904
d. Port Arthur, Ontario, July 27, 1931
Connors, Lewis, and Aurie was one of Detroit's best lines in the late '20s and early '30s. Fleet of foot, though small, little Bobby could more than keep up with his speedy linemates, much to the surprise of his opponents. Tragically, he broke his neck diving into shallow waters near Port Arthur and was paralyzed from the neck down. The next day, he succumbed to his injuries in St. Joseph's Hospital, dying in much the same manner that Hod Stuart had back in 1907.

CONROY, Al
b. Calgary, Alberta, January 17, 1966
So here's the rub. Scouts would come and watch the kid play. They'd nod approval, make note of his number, turn to the program to check the personal numbers. Thirty-forty goals. A hundred-plus points. This could mean something. Five foot six, 155 pounds. Forget it. What else is out there? And so it went for the Conroy kid. Three consecutive seasons of 100 points in major junior, and never drafted by a single team over a 2-year period. Played at the '86 World Juniors and skated like the wind. He knew the knock against him, so he played defensively against the other team's best players. Too small? He fought whenever possible and racked up the pims. Still nothing. On the verge of quitting, he was convinced to continue by his girlfriend. Played in Europe for a while, then Philly gave him a chance for three years

after signing him as a free agent in 1991. But his production dropped off the chart – 9 goals in 114 games – and he was out of the league faster than you can say Mrs. Lilliput. Back to Europe and Japan he went.

CONROY, Craig ("Turbo"/ "CC")
b. Potsdam, New York, September 4, 1971
Four years at Clarkson U got him to Montreal, but not for very long. Short on confidence and lacking experience, Conroy stayed for just 13 games over 2 seasons. He moved to St. Louis in the multiplayer trade that brought Shayne Corson to the Habs, and became a steady if unspectacular regular in the land of the Bluenote until the Blues dished him off to Calgary during the 2000-01 season, one in which he played 83 games, 1 more than the schedule, because of the trade.

CONTINI, Joe ("The Italian Stallion"/ "Broadway Joe"/ "Go Go")
b. Galt, Ontario, January 29, 1957
In 1977-78, Contini was the lowest paid player in the league, hauling in $30,000 a year playing for an outfit called the Colorado Rockies. Fresh off a decent tournament at the World Juniors and drafted a lowly 126th overall, Contini was long on nicknames but short on staying power. Two half-seasons in Denver led to a free agent contract with Minnesota, and this translated to one final game in the Liga Nationala.

CONVERY, Brandon
b. Kingston, Ontario, February 4, 1974
One, two, three, four, each time he was shown the door. Time after time he came into camp, time after time he played like a tramp. The Maple Leafs drafted him 8th overall, but Convery failed to answer the call. He soon got rebellious and wanted a trade; his prayers were answered and it was made. But once in Vancouver the pattern repeated, and given the chance he was always defeated. It was off to the minors, it was down there he went. It was in Syracuse that he paid his rent. Then Los Angeles claimed him on waivers, but soon again he got his walking papers. He won the Swiss championship with Lugano in 2002-03 and won gold with Canada at the 1994 World Championships.

CONVEY, Eddie
b. Toronto, Ontario, December 16, 1910
d. Toronto, Ontario, February 22, 1969
After winning the Memorial Cup with St. Mike's in 1929, Convey was signed by the Leafs and played a year of senior hockey with the Toronto Nationals. After being sold to the New York Americans, he played his only NHL games with that team before

Three consecutive seasons of 100 points in major junior, and never drafted by a single team.
AL CONROY

becoming a star with the Syracuse Stars. Perhaps the nub of his career came one night when the Leafs tried to let him score a goal. He was well liked, and Toronto had a big lead, so the players agreed to let him go right in on goalie Chabot to score. First, Charlie Conacher let him by, then King Clancy let him go in on goal, and finally Chabot himself gave him the net to shoot at. Each time Convey missed the twine, and shortly thereafter he was demoted. After retiring, he became innkeeper of the Noah's Ark Hotel and remained a bachelor all his life.

COOK, Alexander "Bud"

b. Kingston, Ontario, November 20, 1907
d. November 13, 1993
Bud was the youngest of the Cooks, and clearly by the time he came into the world brothers Bill and Bun had taken most of the family's talent. Bud played briefly in the 1930s with Boston, Ottawa, and St. Louis for a total of just 50 games, and he never made it to the Rangers to play on an all-Cook line that would have been a promoter's dream. After these brief stints, he established himself as a regular with the Cleveland Barons for many years leading up to the Second World War.

COOK, Bill

b. Brantford, Ontario, October 6, 1896
d. Kingston, Ontario, May 5, 1986
Until a fella named Howe came along, all who followed hockey swore that Bill Cook was the finest right winger the game had ever known. Amazingly, though, he didn't make the NHL until he was 30 years old, but the First World War had something to do with that late start. Cook joined the war effort in 1915 and served overseas with the Canadian field artillery. He saw action at Ypres, Vimy Rouge, the Somme, and Flanders and later was stationed with other Canadian troops in Siberia during the Russian Revolution. Once home, he pursued comparatively unimportant interests such as chasing a black disc around a confined area of frozen water. He moved from junior to Saskatoon to play for the Sheiks, and when the Rangers formed in 1926, Cook was one of the first players to sign. He was named the first captain and scored its first goal, and that rookie season was one to remember. He led the NHL with 33 goals and soon played on one of the most famous lines of all time. With his brother Bun and Frank Boucher, the Bread Line terrorized enemy goalies with their speed and great passing. The Rangers pulled off a miracle of sorts by winning the Stanley Cup in their second season of operation, and they won again five years later. In the 1928 finals against the Maroons, the Bread Line accounted for all Rangers goals. Cook led the NHL in scoring three times and in points twice. He retired in 1937 having played all of his 11 years with the Blueshirts, and soon after embarked on a successful career as a coach. He led Cleveland to the AHL Calder Cup in 1939 and '41, and also led teams in Minneapolis and Denver before returning to Saskatoon. It was while coaching the Quakers in '51-'52 that he was asked to help boost the sagging fortunes of his NHL alma mater, but after a year and a half with the Rangers he had not done much for the team before retiring. He was inducted into the Hockey Hall of Fame in 1952, shortly after being badly gored by one of his own bulls that he raised on his farm just outside Kingston.

COOK, Bob ("Cookie")

b. Sudbury, Ontario, January 6, 1946
d. unknown
A seasoned minor-leaguer, Cook added a dash of NHL experience to his résumé when the Vancouver Canucks gave him a brief two-game tryout in 1970-71. His next helping of NHL work came with the Wings two years later, and brief forays with the Islanders and North Stars rounded out his light career.

"Bud" Cook

COOK, Fred "Bun"

b. Kingston, Ontario, September 18, 1903
d. Kingston, Ontario, March 19, 1988
Although Bun was eight years younger than his famous brother, Bill, they played almost their entire careers together. They started in the Soo and moved to Saskatoon for the '24-'25 season, their first in the pros. Two years later, they were the cornerstones of the Rangers as that team joined the NHL, and soon after they joined forces with centre Frank Boucher to form the deadly Bread Line. Bun played the left wing, and despite not being quite the scorer Boucher or Bill was, he nevertheless finished in the top 10 in scoring 3 times. Like Bill, he was part of the two Cup teams for New York, in 1928 and '33. He played 10 years with the Blueshirts, the last a shortened year because of an arthritic condition. Sure his career was over, the Rangers sold him to Boston, and Cook played all of '36-'37 with the B's. He then settled into a career in the minors where he played and coached, first in Providence. He led the Reds to a Calder Cup in '37-'38, his first season, and again two years later. In 1943, his playing days done, he coached in Cleveland where he won an incredible five Calder Cups with the Barons before retiring from the AHL in 1956. He then coached in the Soo and Kingston to close out his long and successful career. In 1995, Cook was inducted into the Hockey Hall of Fame as a Veteran Player.

Bill Cook

COOK, Lloyd ("Farmer")

b. Lynden, Ontario, March 21, 1890
d. Taber, Alberta, October 9, 1964
He wasn't born in the city but he knew how far away it was. Although he played just four NHL games, Cook was a star for years with the Vancouver Millionaires, winning the 1915 Cup with the team and then going on to become its playing coach and manager. In one game with Vancouver, he scored five goals. After Boston, he continued his career in California, of all places, retiring in 1931 after 17 years of professional hockey.

"Bun" Cook

COOK, Tommy

b. Fort William, Ontario, May 7, 1907
d. Fort William, Ontario, October 2, 1961
Cook was an original member of the Thundering Herd, the nickname given to the Fort William Forts team that went to the Allan Cup finals in Vancouver, losing to the strong Varsity Grads squad of Toronto. He went on to join Chicago in the NHL in 1929, where he spent eight successful seasons with the team, winning the Stanley Cup in 1934. He played half a season for

Lloyd Cook

Tommy Cook

Matt Cooke

Carson Cooper

Ed Cooper

Harold Cooper

Joe Cooper

the Maroons in '37-'38 and then returned to Fort William, where he worked at the Ontario Department of Highways until retiring in 1960.

COOKE, Matt
b. Belleville, Ontario, September 7, 1978
He's just a kid. Still growing. A decent prospect for Vancouver. Give him a chance. Work him in slowly. See what he can do. Too soon to give up on him. Plays with heart. He could turn into something. Wouldn't be surprised. He's just a kid. Four years and counting, he just gets better. Steady, solid, not big but sturdy. He's here to stay.

COOPER, Carson
("Shovel Shot"/ "Coop"/ "Cars")
b. Cornwall, Ontario,
July 17, 1896
d. Hamilton, Ontario,
April 7, 1955
Cooper had a hockey career on skates to be proud of, but in comparison to what he did off the ice his sweater days were nothing. After playing senior hockey in Hamilton for many years, he played for Boston, Montreal, and Detroit over 8 years, scoring a career-high 28 goals with the Bruins in his second season, '25-'26. After retiring in 1932, he became head scout for the Red Wings, a job he relished and at which he excelled. Virtually every superstar the Wings developed was under the watchful eye of Cooper and at his behest alone. From Red Kelly to Ted Lindsay, to Marty Pavelich, to Harry Lumley, to Bill Quackenbush – all were first seen to have potential by Cooper. GM Jack Adams trusted him with a brother's loyalty, and together they built a team that won back-to-back Cups in '36 and '37. In the summer of 1948, health problems caught up to Cooper. High blood pressure resulted in an operation called a sympathectomy, which involved removing two ribs from each side of his frame, collapsing his lungs, and cutting nerves in his back and stomach to relieve blood pressure. He recovered, and later scouted for the Rangers, though he openly admitted his continuing adoration of the Winged Wheel. The Wings won the '55 Stanley Cup just weeks after his death, and many players dedicated their triumph to Cooper, who had developed so many members of that team.

COOPER, David ("Coops)
b. Ottawa, Ontario, November 2, 1973
Buried, absolutely buried in the minors, Cooper showed some promise and potential with the Leafs, but Toronto gave up on him in 1998, traded him to Calgary, and that's the last that's been heard from him. He had size, a tremendous shot, and terrific acceleration for a defenceman. Buffalo drafted him and let him go without so much as an NHL look-see, and the Leafs later re-signed him as minor-league filler rather than NHL hopeful.

COOPER, Ed
b. Loon Lake, Saskatchewan, August 28, 1960
The Ed-meister played parts of two seasons for the Rockies, but the team couldn't even trade him, try as it might. Colorado sent him to Edmonton for Stan Weir in March '82, but the deal was voided because Cooper showed up in Oil land with a shoulder injury. He was sent to the minors, and there he stayed.

COOPER, Harold "Hal"
b. New Liskeard, Ontario, August 29, 1915
d. unknown
He played a ton of hockey, mostly senior, but during the war Cooper got the call to play with the Rangers for a few games, during which time he made only a marginal impression. Eight games later, he returned to the minors.

COOPER, Joe
b. Winnipeg, Manitoba,
December 14, 1914
d. Tifton, Georgia,
March 30, 1979
One of the biggest men in the league, you can't buy the kind of bad luck Cooper experienced. He lost in the Stanley Cup finals in 1937 as a member of the Rangers, and the next year Chicago won the Cup. Then he was traded to the Hawks, and the Rangers won the Cup. Losers' complex? Perhaps. Cooper was in the league 11 years, and never had his name engraved on the great silver bowl. He retired to Winnipeg and went into partnership with Bill Mosienko, opening a small string of Cooper-Mosienko Bowling Alleys. An avid golfer, he died accidentally on his way home from a Florida vacation.

COPP, Dr. Bobby
b. Port Elgin, New Brunswick, November 15, 1918
Copp was more than just a puck pusher. He came from down east to study dentistry at the University of Toronto and decided to try out for the hockey team, coached by Ace Bailey. Ace liked what he saw, and Copp went on to play two years with the Marlies while finishing his studies. The Leafs offered him a contract for $900 to play the last nine games of the 1941-42 season, but nearing the end of the dentistry program Copp declined. To his regret, the Leafs won the Cup that spring. In the fall of '42 he made the Leafs but at season's end he joined the army and was in the Dental Corps for three years. When he came out, he set up practice in Ottawa, playing all the while for the senior Senators and winning the 1950 Allan

> **The Leafs offered him a contract for $900 to play the last nine games of the 1941-42 season.**
> **DR. BOBBY COPP**

Cup. Conn Smythe lured him back to Toronto for two games, on October 21 and 22, 1950, to replace the injured Bill Barilko, and though he didn't want to give up dentistry to play full-time he did accept Smythe's offer of $25 per skate as a practice player. At year's end, he returned to the nation's capital and has been a teeth man ever since. He continued to play hockey with the senior Senators until they disbanded in '55.

CORBEAU, Bert ("Husky"/ "Con"/ "Pig Iron")
b. Penetanguishene, Ontario, February 9, 1894
d. Georgian Bay, Ontario, September 22, 1942

One of the more respected and the most penalized defencemen of his era, Corbeau won a pre-NHL Stanley Cup with the Montreal Canadiens in 1916 and stayed with the team when the new pro league was formed the next year. During the finals of 1919, postponed because of the flu epidemic, Corbeau alone was not hospitalized. He played a season with the Hamilton Tigers and then joined the Toronto St. Pats, leading the NHL in penalty minutes three times during his career. One day, in the fall of 1942, he was out in his large powerboat with 42 people to celebrate work they had all done on a war contract at a local foundry near Midland. Without warning, the boat listed and sank rapidly. Some 25 souls lost their lives, Corbeau being one of them.

CORBET, Rene
b. Victoriaville, Quebec, June 25, 1973

Despite leading the Quebec juniors with 79 goals in '92–'93, Corbet has settled into a third-line role in the NHL, first with Quebec/Colorado and then with Calgary. He was involved in the front-page trade that sent Theo Fleury to the Avs near the trading deadline in 1999 and later was sent to Pittsburgh with Tyler Moss for Brad Werenka. He was neither scorer nor superb checker, though, and he soon found himself in the IHL. When that league ceased operations, he moved to Germany to continue his career there. In support of his province, he sponsored Olympic judoka team member Luce Baillargeon.

CORBETT, Mike
b. Toronto, Ontario, October 4, 1942
d. Burlington, Ontario, January 9, 2003

He graduated from St. Mike's in Toronto in 1962 and was the last cut at Leafs camp in 1963. In his first game with Rochester of the AHL in '63 '64, he scored a hat trick. But those 3 goals in 1 game turned into just 5 in 50, and his only NHL action came in the 1968 playoffs with the expansion L.A. Kings, on April 11 and 18, both losses to Minnesota. After that, the

itinerant hockeyist took his show on the senior circuit in Ontario and later settled in his native Toronto, where he eventually became a member of the ushering staff at Air Canada Centre. He died of cancer at the age of 60.

CORCORAN, Norm ("Corky")
b. Toronto, Ontario, August 15, 1931

He could fight with the best of them, and brother, there's a reason that goes with it. His uncle Jack was a boxing and wrestling promoter, and taught him everything he knew, so to speak. But Norm gravitated toward the ice game, and while playing at St. Mike's in Toronto was discovered by Baldy Cotton, the Bruins' number-one bird dog. One of three hockey-playing brothers – Raymond and Gordon were the others – Corky grew to prominence in Hershey with linemates Red Sullivan and Jack McIntyre on that club's famed Kid Line. His first real chance with the Bruins came in the '55 playoffs when the team was spoiled by injuries. Corcoran came in and looked real good, as they say, but the next year he played just two games with Boston before being traded to Detroit in the deal that sent Terry Sawchuk the other way. The start to the '55-'56 season was an odd one for Corcoran. He played for the Red Wings in the All-Star Game (the Wings having won the Cup the previous spring while Corcoran was still with Boston) and a couple of days later GM Jack Adams traded him to Chicago for Walt Blaisdell. But Blaisdell didn't report. He had told the Wings he wouldn't play until after his wedding and honeymoon, a month later! Adams cancelled the deal, and Corcoran played two games with the Wings before being demoted to Edmonton. Chicago finally acquired him the following January 21. After 23 uneventful games with Chicago, he spent the next decade in the minors. Have stick, will travel.

Corcoran played two games with the Wings before being demoted to Edmonton.
NORM CORCORAN

CORKUM, Bob ("Cork"/ "Corky")
b. Salisbury, Massachusetts, December 18, 1967

He scored a goal on his first shot in his first NHL game, March 16, 1990, against Toronto, and the travelling faceoff wizard has been on the move ever since Buffalo drafted him in 1986. He had been with the University of Maine for four years, but his hockey life since has been anything but stable. Seven teams in a decade, most recently New Jersey and Atlanta. He also played for the U.S. at the 1987 World Juniors

CORMIER, Roger
b. Montreal, Quebec, March 23, 1905
d. Montreal, Quebec, February 9, 1971

One lousy, stinking game a million years ago with

Bert Corbeau

Rene Corbet

Bob Corkum

Chuck Corrigan

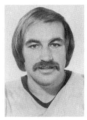

Mike Corrigan

Andre Corriveau

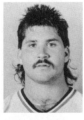

Yvon Corriveau

Montreal during one of the few seasons the Habs didn't make the playoffs (1925-26, to be exact). Then, a perfectly respectable career in the minors for a decade.

CORNFORTH, Mark
b. Montreal, Quebec, November 13, 1972
He played for the Lumberjacks and he don't care, he played for the Cleveland team way down there. The Bruins, they gave him a chance to play, they took six looks and they said no way. He won't be back to the NHL, he's down in the "I" but what the hell. Oh, he's a minor leaguer, he's okay, the AHL's where he gets his pay.

CORRIGAN, Hubert "Chuck"
b. Moosomin, Saskatchewan, May 22, 1916
He had his day, first with Toronto and three years later with the Americans before the war, but by and large Corrigan was one of many talented players who would have made the NHL had it expanded during his era. But it didn't, so he played out his prime days in minor leagues around North America.

CORRIGAN, Mike ("Butch")
b. Ottawa, Ontario, January 11, 1946
It was December 23, 1977, and the Penguins were playing Buffalo in just another game. Pittsburgh's Corrigan got tangled up between checks, fell awkwardly, and broke his ankle. That was his last moment on skates. During the next year he had four casts on the ankle. Plates were inserted, fluid built up, tendons were damaged, and his career was over from an injury that just wouldn't heal. He had been demoted to the minors in Los Angeles after winning a salary arbitration case with Jack Kent Cooke and ultimately traded to the Pens prior to the '76-'77 season. It had been his second go-round with L.A. where he had set a team record with 37 goals in '72-'73. Corrigan is also the only NHLer to score 20 goals from all 3 forward positions. Once his career ended, he stayed in Pittsburgh as an assistant coach until 1984.

CORRINET, Chris
b. Derby, Connecticut, October 29, 1978
The Princeton grad entered the pro ranks of hockey players in 2001 wearing ivy and laurels, but the Washington right winger has been in the minors save for an eight-game stint with the Caps in 2001-02.

CORRIVEAU, Andre ("The Whizzer")
b. Grand-Mère, Quebec, May 15, 1928
b. Ste. Dorothee, Quebec, October 1, 1993
He was a big star with the Whizz Kid line on the

Montreal Nationale with George Bougie and Jean-Paul Bisaillon, and when he got to Valleyfield in Quebec senior play he won the scoring championship three times until a guy named Jean Beliveau started winning it. When Beliveau signed with the Habs, Corriveau was called up to play first right wing, then left wing with Le Gros Bill, and he was so impressive during his brief time that the Habs wanted to sign him to a contract but they couldn't come to terms with Valleyfield. A mere wisp of a player with lightning speed, Corriveau was just too small to prove a surfeit for the NHL team. Toe Blake called him the greatest breakaway player in all of hockey, but how many breakaways can a player create to stay in the game? He retired in 1957 to become manager for all of Quebec for a prosperous fruit juice packager.

CORRIVEAU, Yvon
b. Welland, Ontario, February 8, 1967
His brother Rick was drafted twice, first by St. Louis in 1989, then 168th overall by Washington in 1991 after failing to sign with St. Loo. Rick never made the NHL, but Yvon was the Caps' first pick in '85, 19th overall, and he was expected to be a scoring star for the horrible team. This never happened, despite the requisite responsible grooming by the Caps. He was returned to the minors for more seasoning, played in the farm to learn the trade, then got called up for brief spells in the big time. Nada. He became a pawn in a number of trades down through the years: to Hartford for Mike Liut; to Washington as future considerations to complete a Nick Kypreos deal; back to Hartford as futures again after a stint in San Jose. Then the IHL, Europe, and all that jazz.

CORSI, Jim
b. Montreal, Quebec, June 19, 1954
When Jim Corsi was 17, he turned pro...not with a hockey team, but with the Montreal Olympics of the North American Soccer League (NASL). He saw part-time duty for two years, was a member of the Canadian national team, and toured overseas one summer. He only took hockey, and goaltending, seriously while playing at Concordia University, where he was on his way to an engineering degree summa cum laude. After a year with the Nordiques in the WHA, he hooked up with the Oilers during their first year in the NHL, '79-'80. When he got to camp, though, he had no pads and at first showed off a slapshot that was the envy of many of the players. Once the pads were on and the funny business was over, though, Corsi managed to play just half a season and was clearly not in the team's long-term plans.

> **Taking advantage of dual citizenship offered by his heritage, he moved to Italy and played pro for more than a decade.**
> **JIM CORSI**

Taking advantage of dual citizenship offered by his heritage, he moved to Italy and played pro for more than a decade, becoming in the process one of the more internationally decorated players for Italy in the World Championships, appearing in eight world tournaments from 1981 to '90.

CORSO, Daniel ("Coors")
b. Montreal, Quebec, April 3, 1978
Corso has paid his dues and earned his shot at the big time. Whether he can stay there is a question only time will tell. St. Louis drafted him a distant 169th in 1996 during his junior career in Victoriaville, and from there he played for the Blues farm team before making the Javitts Centre team to start 1999-2000. Since then, he has become a regular … but for how long?

CORSON, Shayne
b. Barrie, Ontario, August 13, 1966
Paul Corson was a big boy. He played Junior B at 14, had a child, Shayne, at 18, and opened two restaurants, one in Barrie called Mom's Pantry, another in Midland shortly thereafter. Son Shayne was as tough as his father, and because of their closeness in age they were as much brothers as father-son. Trouble seemed to seek Shayne out even under innocent circumstances, and at the worst of times trouble out and out flattened him. At 17, Shayne was charged with assault in an incident involving bikers. A year later, 1984, he was drafted by the Montreal Canadiens and on his way to the NHL. But those seven years in the Montreal organization seemed like seven decades. In April 1988 he and teammates Chris Chelios and Petr Svoboda broke curfew and drove into a hydro pole while with two women in the middle of the night. In January 1991, Corson and two others got into a much-celebrated fight outside a Winnipeg bar. Coach Pat Burns had to bail them out of jail in the middle of the night. In February 1992, in a Montreal bar, Corson again became violent and was suspended by the Habs for one game. That same May he got into a fight at another local bar with a football player. But rock-bottom came when father Paul developed cancer of the esophagus in 1992. An operation kept him alive for another year, and Shayne was traded by the Habs, who had had enough of the brawling, to Edmonton. A year later, Shayne was a different man. He had married, his dad had passed away, he was a leader on the Oilers, and he had mellowed. One night at his cottage on Muskoka he got into a late-night boating accident, but he hadn't been drinking and trouble had been averted. Corson later played for St. Louis and Montreal again, and now a veteran he continued to prove his worth as a

scorer, fighter, checker, and team man. His sister married Darcy Tucker, soon to be a Maple Leaf, and the hockey family seemed to develop a bond that defied the drinking and fighting days of yore. When the Leafs signed Corson to a contract to play alongside his brother-in-law, Corson finally seemed at peace for the first time in his career.

CORY, Ross
b. Calgary, Alberta, February 4, 1957
A business administration grad from UBC, Cory walked into the Winnipeg training camp in 1979 and showed such promise that GM John Ferguson signed him on the spot. The spot wasn't so big, however. He played half a season with the Jets and the other half with the farm team, and the next year played just five games in the NHL before becoming a forgotten man in the organization.

COSSETTE, Jacques ("Coco")
b. Rouyn, Quebec, June 20, 1954
The junior numbers were staggering, going from 50 to 127 to 214 points in his three years in the Quebec league. Pittsburgh drafted him, looking for goals, and at his first training camp he weighed in very large and was shipped to the fat farm down in Chocolatetown (a.k.a. Hershey). Cossette was the only player not called up to the Pens in '74-'75, and the year after he was in fighting form. Sadly, he spent most of his time in the minors, scoring well and looking like a sure callup. But whenever he got the chance, he didn't make it.

He was ordained in 1957 after a vigorous seven-year course.
FATHER LES COSTELLO

COSTELLO, Father Les ("Costy")
b. South Porcupine, Ontario, February 16, 1928
d. Toronto, Ontario, December 10, 2002
Here is a story of a truly extraordinary man who honoured the NHL with his presence, albeit briefly. A star on his hometown team, the Holman Pluggers, young Les was hustled off to St. Mike's in Toronto by his father to get an education and play hockey. The Leafs boss, one Constantine Smythe, liked what he saw and signed him to a Leafs contract, and in the 1948 playoffs Costello was called up for a few games. The Leafs won the Cup. Les played only a bit more over two seasons, but though he loved the game he felt unsatisfied playing for Pittsburgh. He quit the game and enrolled in the University of Toronto, earning his B.A. while attending St. Augustine's seminary school for four years starting in 1950. He was ordained in 1957 after a vigorous seven-year course, and though he preferred to be stationed in Ontario's North he never stopped playing hockey. Kirkland Lake, Timmins, Cobalt, Schumacher, wherever he went, wherever he took his collar and Bible and

Shayne Corson

Ross Cory

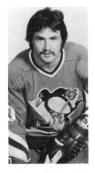

Jacques Cossette

spirits, he also took his skates and stick and gloves. Around 1962 another former athlete, football-playing Reverend Brian McKee, decided to put together a charity team, Costello among that number, to raise funds for a young boy who had lost an eye. The game was a success, and the Flying Fathers were born. They played an increasing number of games and became world renowned for their charitable efforts, travelling around the continent in the name of pucks and donations and in 1970 earning an audience with Pope Paul VI at the Vatican. They gave the pope an autographed hockey stick, which he held upside down until Father Les guided him to the end of righteous wooden holding. For 17 years, Costello never missed a game with the Flying Fathers. Then tragedy struck. Camping with friends near Kukatush, Father Les got lost and was stranded for 28 hours before his friends rescued him. Feet frozen, he wound up losing seven toes, and most skating was denied him evermore. To this day, the Flying Fathers play and pray with equal relish, and their noble efforts have raised millions of dollars for charities, inspired millions of people, and entertained all who have even heard of them. It was during such a game, in Kincardine, that Father Les fell and hit his head on the ice during warmup. He was carried off, in a coma, and died in St. Michael's Hospital a few days later. To recite the "Ballad of the Flying Fathers": "We play the game of hockey and/we prove to everyone/That you can have religion and/still can have some fun./We're playing and we're praying/and we're doing what we should,/And even when we give out checks,/we give out brotherhood." Amen to that.

Rich Costello

COSTELLO, Murray ("Costy"/ "Lou")
b. South Porcupine, Ontario, February 24, 1934
Brother of Father Les, Murray was cut from the same cloth, a fringe player who was to have a greater impact in hockey off skates. He, too, attended St. Mike's, a decade after his brother, but he was called up to the Black Hawks as an emergency replacement, an 18-year old too soon exposed to the ways of the NHL. He floundered and that summer he was traded to Boston. The Bruins gave him a spot on their roster for the year, and although he backchecked with customary zeal, he scored just four times. Midway through the following year he was sent to Detroit, and early in the '56-'57 season he retired. Costello stayed very active in hockey, though. He became publicity director for the Western Professional Hockey League and later became general manager of the Seattle Totems of that league. He was assistant to executive director Gordon Juckes in the renamed WHA and then quit to study

Alain Cote

law at the University of Ottawa before joining a large firm specializing in RRSPs. He became legal counsel for the CRTC and on October 1, 1979, was named president of the CAHA. He later was a member of the Hockey Hall of Fame's induction committee but resigned on April 2, 1993, in light of the fiasco surrounding the ill-founded induction of Gil Stein into the Builders category. He remains an integral part of the International Ice Hockey Federation, sitting on the council that oversees all international tournaments and games. He is also chairman of the IIHF's medical committee.

COSTELLO, Rich
b. Farmington, Massachusetts, June 27, 1963
It's pretty hard for Leafs fans to stomach, but the names Rich Costello and Darryl Sittler are forever linked thanks to a trade on January 20, 1982. That's the day the Leafs sent the future Hall of Famer to Philadelphia for Costello, Ken Strong, and a draft choice (Peter Ihnacak). The 18-year-old Providence College player was highly touted but fizzled quickly when he got to the big time. His agent was Greg Britz, Sr., father of Greg Jr. of the Leafs, but that didn't help much. Costello was sent to the farm in St. Catharines and there he was charged with switching the price tag on a jar of car wax from $16.99 to $5.77, a savings – if the cashier had let the change go unnoticed – that would have amounted to $11.22. As it was, the cashier was the smarter of the two, and Costello pleaded guilty before Judge Harry W. Edmonston,

He remains an integral part of the International Ice Hockey Federation.
MURRAY COSTELLO

who let him off the hook. So, too, did the Leafs, as they bought out his contract two years later. He later found his way to Californ-I-A where he became vice-president of sales for a company called ICU Medical and played pickup on the organization's hockey team.

COTCH, Charlie
b. Toronto, Ontario, January 1, 1898
d. unknown
Did he or didn't he? Until 1998, Cotch never existed in the NHL's official records, but when *Total Hockey* came out, his name was in it. Cotch's name appears in the roster reports for a few games, but there is not a single mention of him in any game report he purportedly took part in for Toronto. Apparently, he played with Hamilton and the St. Pats in '24-'25, scoring a goal with the former. Anything more about him is a mystery.

COTE, Alain
b. Matane, Quebec, May 3, 1957
This Alain Cote holds a unique and unbeatable

record. He was the only player to play in both the WHA and the NHL and play his whole career with the same team – the Quebec Nordiques – a career that began in 1977 and ended in 1989. He became known as one of the premier defensive forwards in the style of Bob Gainey and yet was not without scoring ability when the opportunity presented itself. A proud francophone, Cote was well known for his work off ice with charities. He was president of Maison Partage, an important organization in Quebec, and regional president of the Quebec Games. He has been spokesman for many other causes in Quebec, both as a Nordiques forward and after his retirement as a member of the community.

COTE, Alain G.
b. Montmagny, Quebec,
April 14, 1967

Unlike his Nordiques namesake, this Alain Cote never really established himself in the orange and black of the NHL. He played 32 games in his rookie season with Boston in '85-'86, but besides that was a bit player in a series of casts that included Washington, Montreal, Tampa, and Quebec. He wound up playing for the Sapporo Snow Brand in Japan.

COTE, Patrick ("KO")
b. Lasalle, Quebec,
January 24, 1975

A fighter and proud of it. That's why Nashville claimed him in 1998 – to protect its bevy of superstars – and that's why the Stanley Cup champions let him go. He fought just about every time he played, didn't matter the league, didn't matter the opponent. He trained with Andre Blais, a pro boxer, in the summer, and Cote's stamina was noticeable in longer fights as he wore his opponents down. No worry about goals or points. Just fights. This was hardly enough to keep him employed for long, though, and he was soon in the minors. He all but destroyed his life and career when, on May 17, 2002, the police caught him speeding along a quiet street in New York state. At first, he refused to stop, and when he did, the law discovered 14 kilograms of marijuana in his car. Not good.

COTE, Ray
b. Pincher Creek, Alberta, May 31, 1961

Undrafted and destined for a career in the minors, Cote burst onto the NHL playoff scene with Edmonton during the Oilers' penultimate playoff run in 1983. He was called up from Moncton to sit and watch the world go by and be ready just in case of injury. Injury came in the form of, of all people, Garry Unger. Still, it was Don Nachbaur who got the call. Only after Nachbaur put in a displeasing performance for Glen Sather did Cote earn his

chance, and he made the most of it. He threw his weight around, scored a bit, contributed any which way he could. The summer job he had lined up at a golf course in Pincher Creek had to be put on hold while Lord Stanley's bowl was being contested, and lo, though the Oilers lost, Cote looked ready to establish himself. Training camp. Fall. Different Cote. Lacks speed, grit, enthusiasm, determination. Demoted. Plays just a few games in the next two years, goes to Europe. The heroic beginning gives way to long-term reality.

COTE, Sylvain ("Coco")
b. Quebec City, Quebec, January 19, 1966

When defenceman Cote scored 21 goals for the Washington Capitals in '92-'93, he became an important part of history. Two other Caps d-men also scored 20 or more – Al Iafrate and Kevin Hatcher – the first time a trio of blueliners has reached that plateau. Cote's career seemed stalled in neutral with Hartford, but then the Whalers loaned him to Team Canada for the World Juniors in 1986. He was named to the tournament all-star team, and his confidence soared accordingly. After playing the first 13 years of his career with the two clubs, he was traded to Toronto midway through the '97-'98 season and again to Chicago and then Dallas during 1999-2000. Both moves improved the veteran – Toronto was a solid contender and then the Stars made it to the finals in his first playoffs with the team. He reached the 1,000-game mark that year also, and all that's lacking is a Stanley Cup ring. He signed as a free agent with the Caps again in 2000, though he's unlikely to get a ring there.

The Whalers loaned him to Team Canada for the World Juniors in 1986.
SYLVAIN COTE

COTTON, Harold ("Lucky"/ "Baldy")
b. Nanticoke, Ontario, November 5, 1902
d. Campbellford, Ontario, September 9, 1984

Oh, yes, he could play the game, all right, and play it well for someone his size. The son of a minister, he stuck around a long time, too. Played with Pittsburgh their few years in the league – the old Pirates, that is – then Toronto. Won the Cup the first year at the new Maple Leaf Gardens in '32 and finished off his career with the New York Americans. Then the fun began, a life in hockey unlike any before or since. He coached the Marlies in Toronto for four years, was named the goodwill ambassador of the Gardens for two seasons. Imagine that! Then a new life began, as a scout. He had been working as a sales manager for Acme Farmers Dairy in Toronto, but that was a waste of his talent. Hired by Boston, he scouted for the Bruins for 26 years. He was a regular guest on the Hot Stove League, the great intermission radio feature every

Patrick Cote

Ray Cote

Harold Cotton

Saturday night at the Gardens. Did that for ages as well: radio, then television. Quarter of a century in all. In Boston, he discovered every famous Bruins who went on to play for the team. In 1962, he sat in on a bantam tournament in Unionville, Ontario, liked a kid and asked him his name. Bobby Orr. Baldy made notes that day. In 1967, he retired. Had enough. Two weeks later, the fledgling Minnesota North Stars called about some scouting. He stayed with them for a decade. When he retired for good, he headed up to the cottage on Trent River. Survived three operations for cancer, then his eyesight failed him. One of the greats.

COUGHLIN, Jack ("Jerry")
b. Duro, Ontario, June 6, 1892
d. unknown

Coughlin stayed in Toronto when the Blueshirts of the NHA became the Arenas of the NHL, but didn't last till the end of the season when the team won the new league's first Stanley Cup. He took the next year off, then played briefly with Quebec, Montreal, and Hamilton.

Art Coulter

COULIS, Tim
b. Kenora, Ontario, February 24, 1958

On April 24, 1982, the Dallas Black Hawks were in Salt Lake for a CHL game. Coulis, a Hawk, took a penalty, and on the power play the Golden Eagles scored. Coulis let referee Bob Hall know about his displeasure, resulting in a misconduct. Coulis then cross-checked Hall in the face, rendering him unconscious before he hit the ice. It stands as the most violent assault on a referee in pro hockey. Coulis was suspended for the rest of the year and all the next season. He had played only 19 NHL games to date, with Washington. His only goal came on February 2, 1980, the same night Phil Esposito scored his 700th, against the Caps. Needless to say, Coulis's red light took second place in the history books. But take a look at the penalty records. His actions were hardly new. He arrived in the Soo for a junior hockey career, though he had just been suspended by Kenora, his Manitoba Junior A team. In his first season of OHL play he was suspended eight games for – surprise, surprise – molesting an official, another two games for game misconduct violations, fives games for a hair-pulling incident, and four for butt-ending an opponent. And then the violence began. The victim of the butt-end, Paul Gardner, lost three teeth and suffered severe facial cuts. In Coulis's next game, he brawled again, and the OHL suspended him for 12 games. Clearly, he never learned. A few games after his first NHL goal, a broken wrist ended his season. During the suspension he got a job in a paper mill in northern Ontario, but the tension cost him his marriage. After his

Tommy Coulter

Coulis then cross-checked Hall in the face, rendering the official unconscious.
TIM COULIS

year was up, only Minnesota was willing to sign him, and he played there briefly while working for CP in the summer. He played only 28 games with the Stars over 3 years, and then he retired. None too soon in the eyes of the civilized.

COULSON, D'Arcy
b. Sudbury, Ontario, February 17, 1908
d. unknown

The son of an Ottawa millionaire, D'Arcy was a tough customer in anyone's books. He played only one year, with the briefly seen Philadelphia Quakers. Otherwise, his skating was fleeting and minor league.

COULTER, Art
b. Winnipeg, Manitoba, May 31, 1909

The Hall of Fame career of Coulter began with the St. John's Pro-Cathedral team in Winnipeg, where he won three successive city championships. He then moved to the Pilgrims juvenile team and again won the championship. The Coulter clan moved to Pittsburgh at this point in young Art's life, and as a result he never played any junior hockey. Instead, he requested a tryout with a local team and from there scouts for the Philadelphia Arrows signed him to a contract in the Can-Am league. After two years, he signed with Chicago in the NHL in 1931, teaming with Taffy Abel on the blueline. Three years later, the Hawks won the Stanley Cup. A year and a half later he was traded to the Rangers for Earl Seibert, a star for a star. He became team captain in 1935 and led the team to another Cup, in 1940, but two years later he joined the war as a member of the United States Navy. His hockey career was virtually over. He played for the Coast Guard Cutters and became the first president of the Professional Hockey Players of America. He later got involved in the insurance business in Miami.

COULTER, Neal
b. London, Ontario, January 2, 1963

A minor-leaguer who appeared just briefly in the big top, Coulter was given a chance by the Islanders after the dynasty had ended. His reviews weren't all the rage, so he spent more time with the affiliate in Springfield than on Long Island.

COULTER, Tommy
b. Winnipeg, Manitoba, April 21, 1911

His lone appearance came with Chicago on November 19, 1933 in a 2-1 win over Ottawa. Tommy played with his more accomplished brother, Art, but never made it back to the NHL afterward.

COURNOYER, Yvan ("The Roadrunner")

b. Drummondville, Quebec, November 22, 1943

Every time a coach told Cournoyer he was too small for the NHL, he became more determined to make it. Every time people tried to dissuade him it simply fuelled a fire within that only an NHLer can, by definition, possess. From an early age, Cournoyer built up strength in his legs and practiced his shot with a weighted puck. By the time he made his NHL debut with the Canadiens at the end of the '63-'64 season, he quickly proved to be one of the fastest players with one of the better shots. His first four years with the team were rewarding in that he was now in the NHL, but frustrating in that coach Toe Blake used him almost exclusively on the power play. Blake didn't trust Cournoyer's defensive abilities, but when Claude Ruel took over for the retired Blake in 1968, Cournoyer took a regular shift and produced 43 goals that season. It was the best year of his career for goals, but 1972 was more rewarding in that he was named to Team Canada for the Summit Series. Such was the awe and respect the Soviet fans felt for the Roadrunner that during 30th anniversary celebrations in 2002, he alone was invited to Moscow to join the Soviet players for a few days of recollections and dinner parties. At the end of that '72-'73 season, Cournoyer set an NHL record by scoring 15 goals in the playoffs en route to another Stanley Cup and a Conn Smythe Trophy. He was named team captain in 1975 but a short time later began experiencing back problems that eventually ended his career. He missed the end of the '76-'77 season and all of the playoffs, and in the fall of 1978 he had a career-ending operation. By that time, though, he had made his place in Montreal history. He had won an extraordinary 10 Cups and had recorded 428 goals and 863 points. He had electrified fans with his blazing speed and terrific shot, and he was among the cleanest, most gentlemanly players. Cournoyer settled into a career as a restaurateur, opening a series of Montreal brasseries called Burger 12 (in honour of his number). In 1982, he was inducted into the Hockey Hall of Fame. His back prevented him from playing old-timers hockey, though at the 2000 All-Stars he did make a rare appearance in the Legends game, the Roadrunner come to life for a short while once again.

From an early age, Cournoyer built up strength in his legs and practiced his shot with a weighted puck.
YVAN COURNOYER

COURTEAU, Maurice

b. Quebec City, Quebec, February 18, 1920

Hardly the most famous Maurice in hockey, Courteau was a wartime goaler who stopped a few pucks – just a few – for the Bruins while others were in the army. He did not acquit himself particularly well, and he played only half a dozen games, during which time he allowed a hefty 33 goals.

COURTEAU, Yves

b. Montreal, Quebec, April 25, 1964

It's amazing how many superstar juniors just don't pan out in the NHL. Courteau averaged 33 goals a year with Laval, but couldn't put the puck behind an NHLer to save his career. He was out before he was in, though that's not entirely true. He played in 22 games over 3 years, but his career went off the rails after he suffered a severe stomach muscle injury from which he couldn't fully recover.

Yves Courteau

COURTENAY, Ed ("Courts")

b. Verdun, Quebec, February 2, 1968

An inhabitant of the IHL, Courtenay made two brief pilgrimages to the NHL with San Jose, but his finest days were spent with the South Carolina Stingrays of the ECHL where he won the scoring championship in '96-'97. He later continued his career as a successful scorer in Britain.

COURTNALL, Geoff ("Courts")

b. Duncan, British Columbia, August 18, 1962

On October 16, 1999, Courtnall's career came to a dazed halt after a mid-ice check from Bryan Berard of Toronto sent the recently recovered post-concussion syndrome victim reeling into a semi-comatose spiral that was nauseating to watch. Courtnall had missed much of the '98-'99 season recuperating from a serious blow to the head suffered on November 27, 1998, but with nearly a year off doctors felt he had gained as much strength back as possible. Geoff never wanted to be a hockey player. Soccer and baseball were his first loves, but the more he watched brother Russ play, the more he wanted the same challenge. As a late bloomer, he was never drafted. Instead, the Bruins signed him, gratis, in 1983, but just as he was showing tremendous promise, they traded him to Edmonton. Ditto for the Oilers, who sent him to Washington, and after seasons of 42 and 35 goals, the Caps in turn traded the prolific, yet unwanted, star to St. Louis and Vancouver. He found stability with the Canucks for a while before signing a three-year $6.6 million deal with the Blues, where he sustained his career-ending concussions. Nonetheless, the undrafted player spent 17 years in the NHL and later, along with Russ, was inducted into the B.C. Hockey Hall of Fame.

Ed Courtenay

Geoff Courtnall

Marcel Cousineau

Billy Coutu

Gerry Couture

Rosario Couture

COURTNALL, Russ ("Rusty"/ "Howie")
b. Duncan, British Columbia, June 2, 1965

Archie Courtnall was a prospect in the Detroit Red Wing chains until he broke his leg, took a solid job in the local mill, and raised his family of three boys. Russ, the middle son, possessed blazing speed, though his dad saw him play only until he was 13 before passing away. As a youngster, Courtnall's work ethic lacked equal admiration from scouts as did his skills. Nonetheless, he was drafted 7th overall by Toronto in 1983, but before joining the Leafs he played the rarest double of them all: the World Juniors and Olympics in the same year, just weeks apart, in fact. After Canada finished fourth in both tournaments, Courtnall joined the Leafs, playing the next five years in the Blue and White. He played on the famed Hound Line with Wendel Clark and Gary Leeman but was traded to Montreal early in '88-'89, where he began a career that was rooted in travel, playing for five more teams in the coming years. In all, he scored 20 goals 9 times, yet he never seemed to play to his potential, his speed indicating greater talent, perhaps, than what existed. Nonetheless, he lasted more than 1,000 games in the league, and not many players can boast as much. Archie, wherever he is, has a big smile on his face from watching his boys do him proud. The smile has double meaning, for Russ married Paris Vaughn, daughter of Sarah Vaughn.

COURVILLE, Larry
b. Timmins, Ontario, April 2, 1975

He was once considered one of the top juniors in Canada, and that wasn't too long ago. He helped Canada win gold at the 1995 World Juniors, but that now seems like a lifetime ago. So, too, does the time he felt too good to sign with Winnipeg, the team that drafted him, and re-entered the draft, where he went much much lower to Vancouver, in 1995. Since then he's been bounced around in junior, and then he went from Vancouver of the NHL to the minors with great rapidity. That's the here and now of Courville's career so far.

COUSINEAU, Marcel ("Cousy")
b. Delson, Quebec, April 30, 1973

Can't shake the Cat. Cousineau paid his dues, he worked hard in the minors, he got his break. But while he performed admirably while playing for the Leafs, Cousineau never got a chance to prove his long-term worth while playing backup to Felix Potvin. He was let go and signed with the Islanders at no expense to Toronto, but even there he spent more time in the minors and on the bench than in the blue ice of an NHL rink. He was later traded to Los Angeles, and there, guarding the crease as the number-one goalie, was Potvin again! Bummer.

COUTU, Billy
(sometimes Couture / "Beaver")
b. North Bay, Ontario, March 1, 1892
d. Sault Ste. Marie, Michigan, February 25, 1977

Infamy is his first name, notorious his last. On April 13, 1927, the Ottawa Senators beat the Boston Bruins 3-1 to win the Stanley Cup. So incensed was Bruins defenceman Coutu by a third-period penalty call that after the game he chased the referee Jerry Laflamme down the corridor and attacked him. For that, Coutu became the first and only player to be suspended from the NHL for life. Up to that time he had certainly been a rough-and-tumble character, but many players of that era could outbrutalize him. A career that began a decade earlier in Montreal ended in an arena corridor, but Coutu managed to skate a few more years in the minor pros before turning his hand to coaching in Providence. He retired to Sault Ste. Marie.

COUTURE, Gerry ("Doc")
b. Saskatoon, Saskatchewan, August 6, 1925
d. Saskatoon, Saskatchewan, July 13, 1994

The son of a baker, Couture began his career with Detroit in the 1945 playoffs and earned a regular spot with the team the following year. He helped the Wings win the Stanley Cup in '49–'50, but in the summer of 1951 he was traded to Montreal for Bert Hirschfeld after the Wings felt he had reached a lower potential than what they had expected. After just 10 games with the Habs, he suffered a cut near his ankle. The dye from his sock seeped into the wound and he developed blood poisoning. Montreal sent him to the minors to get himself back into shape, but he never played with the Habs again. Instead, he moved on to Chicago, playing on a defensive line with Jim McFadden and Pete Babando, but by the middle of the '53–'54 season he was back in the minors for good. He had earned his nickname by virtue of two years in medicine at the University of Saskatchewan, but after retiring he lived in Saskatoon and worked as an acoustics expert in construction for some 30 years.

COUTURE, Rosario "Rosie" ("Lolo")
b. St. Boniface, Manitoba, July 24, 1905
d. St. Boniface, Manitoba, March 1, 1986

No decent hockey wife would have approved of her husband going on a road trip and rooming with someone named Rosie, but despite the effeminate moniker, this Couture endured for eight NHL years, all but the last with Chicago. He won the '34 Cup with the Hawks, and for that final '35-'36 season he was sold to Montreal, where he failed to score in 10 games and was dispatched to the Can-Am league. Later in life, he worked for the CNR, based in Winnipeg.

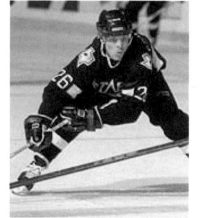

Russ married Paris Vaughn, daughter of Sarah Vaughn.
RUSS COURTNALL

COUTURIER, Sylvain
b. Greenfield Park, Quebec, April 23, 1968
The little bib of high grass around the green is how best to describe the un-par life of Couturier in the NHL-fringe. Snatches of games with the Kings over three seasons, no staying power except for a long life in the "I." Right there … close … but not.

COWAN, Jeff
b. Scarborough, Ontario, September 27, 1976
A graduate of the Ontario Hockey League, Cowan has risen slowly and steadily through the ranks, from minor-leaguer to part-time NHLer to full-time starter with Calgary. The left winger has some size and speed, and is part of a good, young corps that forms the nucleus of the Flames roster. His best years are still ahead of him.

COWICK, Bruce
b. Victoria, British Columbia, August 18, 1951
At one time, this fighter was in high demand. The era was the '70s. The stats were penalty heavy. The team was the Broad Street Bullies. The Flyers traded four young players to get Cowick from San Diego of the WHL, but after a few playoff games he was let loose in the Expansion Draft by Washington. In '74-'75 he was a whopping -42, played a few games with St. Louis, and then disappeared. He resurfaced in Victoria as a police officer, post-playing days.

COWIE, Rob
b. Toronto, Ontario, November 3, 1967
Cowie attended St. Mike's in Toronto in his early teens, then played for Northeastern University on a scholarship. Four years later, in 1991, he signed with Winnipeg after staying draft-free. He signed with Hartford and then L.A., and it was finally the Kings that played him for a couple of seasons before Cowie crossed Davey Jones' locker to skate in Switzerland and Germany.

COWLEY, Bill ("Schoolboy"/ "Cowboy")
b. Bristol, Quebec, June 12, 1912
d. Ottawa, Ontario, December 31, 1993
On the morning of January 6, 1944, Jim Coleman wrote in his regular column in the *Globe and Mail:* "Bill Cowley, a master craftsman from Ottawa and Boston, is engaged busily in re-writing the N.H.L. record book. 'William the Wizard' has amassed a total of 52 points so far this season, and unless he fractures a clavicle in the near future, he will set a new scoring mark." A couple of weeks later, Cowley broke his jaw, missed the rest of the season, and lost the scoring race by a single point. And there's more: During the year, he wrote to NHL president Red Dutton and requested that an assist he had been rewarded be revoked because he felt he hadn't earned it! Cowley began playing hockey in Plouffe Park in Ottawa, as a goalie, but he wanted to handle the puck more so went out of the cage to skate. He moved up to Cambridge Public School and then Glebe Collegiate in the city, then to the Primrose Juniors, playing in the 1931 Memorial Cup. He signed with the St. Louis Eagles, the Ottawa Senators team that transferred to Missouri, and then with Boston, where he played the rest of his career after the Eagles folded. He won two Hart Trophies and two Stanley Cups. Although not known for scoring, his expertise as a passer was so remarkable the standard line was that he made more wings than an airplane manufacturer. Twice he broke the league mark for assists in a season despite suffering serious injuries along the way: the broken jaw in '43-'44, an injured knee in '38-'39, a separated shoulder in '41-'42, and a broken hand in '45-'46. Nonetheless, Cowley's final season of '46-'47 saw him break Syd Howe's record for most career points, regular season and playoffs. On February 12, 1947, he had a goal and an assist, his 572nd and 573rd points, making him number one all-time. At year's end, he retired to coach in Vancouver for a year. This proved a disaster, so he opened the Russell Hotel in Smiths Falls and worked a year with the Department of Lands and Forests in Ontario. He ran the hotel for 15 years, then moved to Ottawa, where he opened the Elmdale House with 2 former football greats, Jake and Frank Dunlap. He was named to the Hockey Hall of Fame in 1968, and after retiring from the hotel business he put the job in the hands of his sons, John and Dan, but continued to live in the city and enjoyed the junior 67's until the day he died.

On February 12, 1947, he had a goal and an assist, making him number one all-time.
BILL COWLEY

COWLEY, Wayne
b. Scarborough, Ontario, December 4, 1964
A life in hockey yielded just 57 minutes guarding the cords of an NHL team's cage, in Cowley's case for the Edmonton Oilers. From there his wandering career continued with worldwide adventures far removed from the gold and black of the NHL when there were a mere 26 teams fighting for the Stanley Cup.

COX, Abbie
b. London, Ontario, July 19, 1903
d. unknown
Despite being a reliable goaler in the minors, Cox saw action only as emergency relief in the NHL. He played on February 1, 1930, when Maroons incumbent Flat Walsh was injured (a 7-2 win); played November 12, 1933, for the injured Roy Worters of the Americans midway through the game; played

Jeff Cowan

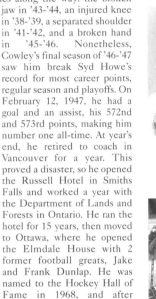

Bruce Cowick

Rob Cowie

Danny Cox

Craig Coxe

Jim Craig

Mike Craig

Bart Crashley

December 10 and 17, 1933, for John Ross Roach; and, finally, played on February 16, 1936, for Wilf Cude in an overtime 1-1 game between the Habs and Rangers.

COX, Danny ("Silent Danny")
b. Little Current, Ontario, October 12, 1903
d. August 8, 1982
From Little Current to Port Arthur to the Arena Gardens on Mutual Street in Toronto came the skates and stick of Danny Cox in 1926. He stayed with the newly minted Leafs for four years before making his way through Ottawa, Detroit, and the Rangers. After his playing days, Cox turned to coaching in 1940 with Seattle in the Pacific Coast league and later returned to Port Arthur, where he became a referee in the amateur ranks.

COXE, Craig
b. Chula Vista, California, January 21, 1964
When Coxe was traded from Vancouver to Calgary, he was smack dab in the middle of playing. Vancouver was in Washington, and during the first intermission he was told of the trade. While the team went out for the second period, he undressed and packed. During the second intermission, he said goodbye to everyone, and the team went on the ice for the third period while he went off to the airport. After four years and countless fights for the Canucks, Coxe left to do his fighting for the Flames, but by and large his ice time was limited wherever he went. Out of the NHL early in the '91-'92 season, he continued to play in the minors long after, and later went into coaching. He scored the first goal in the history of the San Jose Sharks and also played roller hockey for a number of summers.

CRAIG, Jim
b. North Easton, Massachusetts, May 31, 1957
From the highest star to the deepest earth, from the garden to the desert and the mountain to the valley, Craig's brief career represents both the best and the worst of times. He was a hero that day in February 1980 when the U.S. beat the Soviet Union to virtually assure gold at the Lake Placid Olympics, the goalie behind the victory, the man who draped himself in the American flag as he skated around the rink, first looking for his father in the stands, then acknowledging the wild cheers in supreme celebration. Four days after those Olympics ended he made his NHL debut, a victory with Atlanta before a jubilant sold-out home crowd. Two years later, his pro career on the brink, he left a restaurant in Mattapoisett on a rainy night. While driving along Route 6, he saw an oncoming car approach. He swerved, but still sideswiped it, and the other car crashed into the woods, leaving one woman dead. He was charged with vehicular homicide and driving to endanger. Though found innocent by the courts, he was still a nomad, his arrogance having taken him from the Flames to Boston and finally to Minnesota. Refusing to stay in the minors, he retired and became a seller of ad space for a newspaper in Brockton, Massachusetts, his heroism long faded, his waking life having long replaced his Miracle on Ice.

CRAIG, Mike
b. St. Mary's, Ontario, June 6, 1971
Things just didn't work out as they should have. He played on a line with Eric Lindros on the Memorial Cup-winning Oshawa Generals, played again with him while winning gold at the 1991 World Juniors. But when Craig got to Minnesota in the NHL, his size, speed, and intensity didn't keep pace with the league change. He signed as a free agent with Toronto, a dream come true for the Ontarian, but Craig just didn't produce. The Leafs cut him loose in 1997, with a sigh and a shrug and a sad confession that things just hadn't worked out. He went down to the minors, signed with San Jose, and appeared in just one game with the Sharks before returning to the AHL, where he continues to skate.

CRAIGHEAD, John
b. Washington, D.C., November 23, 1971
When a player begins his career with an outfit called the West Palm Beach Blaze, you know his NHL hopes float on melting ice. Such was the fate of the undrafted, though Craighead fought his way into the hearts and minds of fans and opponents alike during his career, in which the only NHL dent was a five-game stint with ye olde Leafs of Maple. But his life was not so simple. His parents divorced when he was three, and he moved with his mother and sister to British Columbia to start fresh. His sister died on the streets of Vancouver, a drug addict, and his best friend died of electrocution in a freak accident. He went to Europe to play, but through his friend and idol, Tiger Williams, he was given another NHL shot, by Vancouver, in the fall of 2002. The Canucks signed him to a two-way contract, and Craighead has been with Manitoba of the AHL trying to forge a renewed pro career.

CRAIGWELL, Dale
b. Toronto, Ontario, April 24, 1971
Craigwell was another member of the early '90s double of Memorial Cup Generals in 1990 and World Junior gold in '91. His career took a major turn for the worse in September '94 when he broke his ankle and missed the entire year recovering. He had just begun developing with the Sharks, and although he returned to play in 1995, he has yet to return to the NHL.

CRASHLEY, Barton "Bart"
b. Toronto, Ontario, June 15, 1946
The Bartman skated for Detroit in the Original Six, then went six years without playing in the big loop. He ended his career after being traded with Marcel Dionne to L.A. for Terry Harper, Dan Maloney, and a draft choice. In between he had a go with the WHA's L.A. Sharks, and after his NHL days he became one of the first players to earn a living, albeit briefly, in Europe, when he signed with the Austrian league in '79-'80. Afterwards, he became an assistant coach with the Guelph Storm in the OHL.

CRAVEN, Murray ("Muzz")
b. Medicine Hat, Alberta, July 20, 1964
He thought he was doing everything by the books. So did his agent. Craven played out his contract with Vancouver in 1993-94, figuring that at age 30, with

more than 10 years' experience and earning less than the league-average salary, he would become an unrestricted free agent. A strange thing happened on the way to the free agent market, though. The NHLPA announced that the average salary was $557,000. The NHL weighed in at $576,000. Craven made $560,000 and was caught in the middle. If unrestricted, he could sell himself to the highest bidder. If restricted, the club signing him would have to provide compensation to the Canucks, thus diminishing his value. Craven wound up sitting at home for more than half a season waiting for an arbitrator to decide the case. By then he had had enough and simply agreed to a trade. The 6-time 20-goal scorer played in more than 1,000 NHL games over a quiet 18-year career, though the closest he came to the Cup was in his third season, with Philly, when the team lost to the Oilers in 1985.

Murray Craven

CRAWFORD, Bob
b. Belleville, Ontario, April 6, 1959

One of four hockey-playing brothers – Peter, Marc, and Lou were the others – Bob played at the World Juniors for the United States in 1978 and '79. Their father, Floyd, was a member of the Belleville McFarlands of 1959, Canada's gold medal-winning entry at the World Championships that year. In three partial seasons with St. Louis, Bob showed little promise and he was left exposed in the Waiver Draft. Hartford claimed him, in 1983, and he proceeded to score 36 goals in what would turn out to be a career year for him. His production dropped, however, and he was traded to New York and then Washington, and his days in the NHL were quickly a thing of the past.

Because of a concussion, he was one of the few players to wear a helmet.
JACK CRAWFORD

CRAWFORD, Bobby
b. Long Island, New York, May 27, 1960

As a young boy, Bobby grew up in Long Island, where his father managed a hockey rink and his mother and sister were professional figure skating teachers. He, naturally, became a rink rat and by the time Crawford was 13 he was playing for the Bronx Shamrocks against 18-year-olds in the Metropolitan Junior Hockey League. At 14 he moved away from home to play for the Austin Mavericks in Minnesota, and the year after moved to Toronto to play Tier II and prepare for a career in the OHL. Three increasingly excellent years with the Generals, however, did not prepare him for the disappointment of not being drafted, his also being adjudged by one and all in the scouting offices to be too great a burden to overcome. Although the hometown Rangers signed him, they traded him to Colorado before giving him a chance, and the Rockies let him go after just 15 games. Detroit

gave him one shot – exactly one shot – and that was it for the speedy small junior superstar from New York.

CRAWFORD, Jack ("Johnny")
b. Dublin, Ontario, October 26, 1916
d. Cape Cod, Massachusetts, January 17, 1979

Sometimes called Jack, sometimes Johnny, sometimes by his middle name Shea, sometimes even the more long-winded Round Squire of Grasmere, Crawford devoted his life to the puck and arena. After graduating from St. Mike's, he took a job at Lakeshore Mines in Kirkland Lake, and that is where his career began and he met the future Mrs. Crawford. From there it was a trip to the Hub – Boston, that is – where he spent his entire 13-year career. Life in the hockey lanes, though, was fraught with injury for Crawford, who played every game of his rookie season and then never again played a full season. Because of a concussion, he was one of the few players to wear a helmet. Typical of the era, Crawford played the game of February 18, 1948, without being told what his coach, Dit Clapper, had known for hours – that his infant daughter, Mary, born four days previous, had passed away. After the game, when informed of the tragedy, he flew home immediately to be with his family. For many years he partnered Eddie Shore on defence, winning Cups in 1939 and '41. In 1949 he became one of a select few Bruins to have a special night in his honour, and his many friends and family members watched with delight as the team presented Crawford with a new car and other gifts of

Bob Crawford

appreciation for his service to club and city. After retiring from the Bruins in 1950, he was named playing coach in Hershey, the Boston farm team, and three years later he put away his whistle and picked up his whistle for keeps. After seven years, he moved on to Providence and then Rochester and later assumed a more prestigious position in a less important loop closer to home. Having made his off-season home in Cape Cod since the late '30s, he happily accepted the dual job of general manager of the Cape Cod Cubs in the Eastern Hockey League and president of the Cape Cod Amateur Hockey League, positions he held until his death.

CRAWFORD, Lou
b. Belleville, Ontario, November 5, 1962

There are the Rockefellers of New York, the Medicis of Florence, and the Crawfords of Belleville, all nine of 'em. A lifelong member of the minors, Lou first signed with Buffalo, then Detroit, and finally Boston before getting into an NHL game in 1989. A couple of years later, a few more games, and that was it for the

Lou Crawford

big time. He followed in his brother Marc's footsteps by becoming coach of the St. John's Maple Leafs.

CRAWFORD, Marc

b. Belleville, Ontario, February 13, 1961

Not to jump right into the fray, but, in a nutshell, he didn't pick Wayne Gretzky as one of five shootout men at the 1998 Olympics in Nagano. Now, back to the beginning. A player of limited ability, Crawford became a student of the game during his time on the benches of the Vancouver Canucks, for whom he played his whole career. However, it was not a 15-year, 1,000-game job full of records, milestones, and First Star twirls after the game. No. It was 176 games played staccato over 6 years. He played junior for Cornwall, became team captain in his final year, and then had that captaincy taken away prior to the Royals representing Canada at the World Juniors that year, 1981. He was reinstated and, ironically, after he retired became the team's coach. His rise through the ranks was meteoric. He became head coach of Toronto's farm team in St. John's in 1991, and three years later became coach of the Nordiques. When the team transferred to Colorado, Crawford guided the team to the Stanley Cup in 1996. The next year, though, things started to sour for him. In game four of the Western Conference final, he got involved in a one-way screaming match with Detroit's Scotty Bowman and was fined $10,000 for conduct "dishonourable" to the game. He immediately apologized, and later in the year was named coach of Canada's NHL entry in the '98 Olympics in Nagano. But in Japan, Canada lost in the semi-finals on a shootout, and that's where Crawford failed to name Wayne Gretzky one of his five shooters. It was a decision for which he was pilloried, and at the end of that season he was fired by the Nordiques. He became a colour commentator for *Hockey Night in Canada*, but at the 1999 All-Star Game he returned to the bench in dramatic fashion when the Canucks fired Mike Keenan and installed Crawford in his place. He hired his younger brother, Eric, to look after video for the team, and although playoff success has eluded the Canucks, Marc Crawford continues to hang in there.

CRAWFORD, Russell "Rusty"

b. Cardinal, Ontario, November 7, 1885

d. Prince Albert, Saskatchewan, December 19, 1971

Crawford played his junior hockey in Vernon, Ontario, before heading out west to Prince Albert in 1909. He moved on to Saskatoon and then to the Quebec Bulldogs of the NHA, precursor to the NHL, winning

Rusty Crawford

Adam Creighton

Dave Creighton

He became a colour commentator for Hockey Night in Canada.
MARC CRAWFORD

the Stanley Cup in 1913. When the NHL was formed in 1917, Crawford joined the Ottawa Senators but was traded to Toronto mid-season. The Arenas won the Cup that spring of 1918, but after one more year in Hogtown he returned to Saskatoon, and played for another decade until he was 45. He retired to his farm and lived there until 1960, when he sold his land to take up residence in nearby Spruce Home, where he lived until his death. Crawford was inducted into the Hockey Hall of Fame in 1962. A versatile player, he is one of a few early greats who proved himself outside the NHL during that league's early years.

CREIGHTON, Adam

b. Burlington, Ontario, June 2, 1965

The guy had size and speed and skill and a nasty streak that made him a dominating presence on the ice when he wanted to be, and after winning a Memorial Cup with the Ottawa 67's and a gold medal with Canada's junior team in 1985, he became a highly coveted project of Buffalo GM Scotty Bowman. Creighton took three years to ease into the league, and in his rookie year of '86-'87 he had 18 goals. Though Bowman had preached patience, he gave up on his giant young charge and shipped him to Chicago a year and a half later, and in '89-'90 Creighton scored 34 goals. It was to be his finest moment. From a prospect with an enormous up side, as the saying goes, he became a big man with little superstar potential and then a fringe player and trade bait for teams hoping they could make him reach that next, heretofore unattained, level. The son of Dave, who ran golf courses in Florida in the winter and Welland in the summer, Adam also became a superb shooter, hoping one day to join the pro tour. That day has not yet arrived.

CREIGHTON, Dave

b. Port Arthur, Ontario, June 24, 1930

When he made his NHL debut with Boston in 1948, Creighton was just 18 years old. After a game or practice, his older mates would all go down the road for a pop; Dave would go somewhere by himself and buy a milkshake. Lonely off the ice, he was a hell of a player on it, scoring 20 goals 3 times over a decade-long career. He eventually made it to Toronto, Chicago, and New York, and while with the Rangers he could see the writing on the wall, and the writing said, "Your NHL days are numbered." He invested in apartment buildings, and continued to make money on the side while playing in the AHL for another decade. He finished out the string with Providence, then became the team's coach and moved to the Hamilton Red Wings midway through the '73-'74 season. For seven years he was an assistant pro at the Burlington Springs Gold Club, and using all the parts of his career to date he, Eddie Shack, and two businessmen built the Vaughan Valley Golf Course, near Toronto. He sold it, and with three new partners purchased the Riverview Club near Fenwick. In 1984, he moved to Tampa full-time and bought the Northdale Golf Club.

CREIGHTON, Jimmy
b. Brandon, Manitoba, November 18, 1903
d. Brandon, Manitoba, May 29, 1990
Creighton played just 11 games for the Detroit Falcons in 1930-31 in a career that was all minor league before and after. He later returned to his hometown and became mayor of Brandon for two terms, one from 1952 to '55 and the other from 1958 to '61. He lived his life in that small city and ran the Creighton Agencies, an insurance company. He later developed Parkinson's and spent his final years in a nursing home. His son, Fred, later coached in the NHL with Atlanta and Boston.

CRESSMAN, Dave
b. Kitchener, Ontario, January 2, 1950
While American universities lure Canadian hockey players to the States on attractive scholarships, Canadian universities offer only the promise of an excellent education that can be used toward building a future. Cressman earned a B.Sc. in physical education from Guelph University in Ontario, writing a paper on skate balance. In it he dispelled the common notion that ankle strength was the key feature of a good skater and noted that boot structure and support were all. "A good pair of skates is the answer," he deduced. As a result of his education, he first turned down and then a year later accepted an invite to Minnesota's training camp. A decent tryout landed him in Saginaw, the workshop to the finished product called the North Stars, and his only real time with the Stars came as a replacement to the injured Rick Kessell. Cressman played the full '75-'76 season with the Stars, then pursued a career in education when it became clear the NHL was not a full-time place for him and his family.

CRESSMAN, Glen
b. Petersburg, Ontario, August 29, 1934
Four games with Montreal during the '56-'57 Cup season that featured 11 future Hall of Famers in the Habs lineup. Not a chance Cressman would crack this lineup at centre ice. Better than Béliveau? Move the Rocket to the bench? More tenacious than Boom Boom or more reliable than Tom Johnson? Nuh-uh. It was the minors for him.

Crisp hit paydirt as a member of the Flyers' two-time Cup-winning teams in '74 and '75.
TERRY CRISP

CRHA, Jiri ("George")
b. Pardubice, Czechoslovakia (Czech Republic), April 13, 1950
A top goalie with the Czech national team for seven years, 1972-79, Crha was among the very first players to defect from behind the Iron Curtain. He, his wife, and two children went for a vacation in West Germany, and it was there he declared asylum with the intention of landing in Canada and playing in the NHL. But when he arrived in Toronto, he got caught in the middle of an NHL-IIHF imbroglio. Any NHL team signing a European was required by contract to pay $50,000 for that player, half upon arrival and half after 40 games in the league. Toronto GM Punch Imlach refused to pay that second installment, and Crha languished with his equipment from November '79 to February '80. Once Imlach caved in, the Czech star could try his luck with the then-hapless Leafs. He won his debut in spectacular fashion, but later in the season faced 61 shots in a loss to Minnesota. While his reflexes were outstanding, he hunched over on the goal line, sometimes seemingly behind it, crouched in the net, and NHL shooters had a field day with the agile, angle-less wonder. If he ever stood up straight, he would have knocked his head on the crossbar. Crha played most of the following season, but clearly he was not up to snuff. He refused to report when the Leafs demoted him to the farm, and then he moved to Germany to rekindle his career and take a turn as a goaltending coach. He also provided advice for teams about other Czech stars and got into the clothing business, as owner of K.C. clothing and as a rep for the Olympia line of German outfits. After retiring, he returned to North America and has become a player agent for NHLers in IMG.

CRISP, Terry ("Crispy")
b. Parry Sound, Ontario, May 28, 1943
A fine checking forward during his years as a player, Crisp hit paydirt as a member of the Flyers' two-time Cup-winning teams in '74 and '75. The following season, while still playing for Philly, he received one of the oddest demotions in league history. The Flyers sent him down to Springfield, not to play but to act as temporary coach for the Indians while incumbent John Hanna recovered from a car accident. Crisp returned shortly after to resume his career, but the coaching itch had been scratched for the first of many times. He retired the next year, but during his playing days he had an amazing record. He had played in game seven of a playoff series six times, and he never lost a one. Crisp then began a 10-year pilgrimage through the pros and minors to understand coaching. This knowledge began as Fred Shero's assistant in Philly for two years, then to

Jimmy Creighton

Dave Cressman

Glen Cressman

Jiri Crha

Ed Cristofoli

Mike Crombeen

Shawn Cronin

Cory Cross

the Soo in the OHL for half a dozen years, then to Moncton to coach the Calgary Flames affiliate. By 1987, Calgary GM Cliff Fletcher deemed him ready for the big time, and with the departure of Bob – "it's a great day for hockey" – Johnson, Crisp moved in behind the Flames bench. Two years later, he was holding the Stanley Cup high, and a year after that he suffered the ignominy of being fired. He turned to broadcasting for a while, but when the Tampa Bay Lightning joined the league in '92, the team hired Crisp as their first coach, an assignment that lasted six long, losing seasons. Since then, he has taken his talkative, effervescent character to television, providing commentary for TSN and Fox, among other networks.

CRISTOFOLI, Ed ("Spags")
b. Trail, British Columbia, May 14, 1967
Ed's dad, Ed, was a member of Canada's 1961 Trail Smoke Eaters that won the World Championship. Ed the Younger played four years at the University of Denver but managed little in the way of a career with the Canadiens after being drafted in 1985. Nine games in '89-'90 was all.

CROGHEN, Maurice ("Moe")
b. Montreal, Quebec, November 19, 1914
d. Montreal, Quebec, February 7, 1979
The coach was Cecil Hart, he of the Hart Trophy. The team captain was Babe Siebert, he of the Siebert Memorial Game after he drowned one summer. And then there was Moe, wearing number 16 and playing a like number of games in '37-'38. He of the one-year career.

CROMBEEN, Mike
b. Sarnia, Ontario, April 16, 1957
Brothers Pat and Brian tried out for the Canadian Olympic team in 1980, but it was Mike who made a name for himself in hockey. Drafted 5th overall by the Cleveland Barons in '77, he played just one season in Jim Brown's city before making a splash with St. Louis and then Hartford. In the 1981 playoffs, it was his double OT goal in the deciding game that eliminated Pittsburgh and gave the Blues one more round of hockey, but for most of his career he had a reputation as a decent checking forward.

CRONIN, Shawn
b. Joliet, Illinois, August 20, 1963
Tough. Defensive minded. Team man. Not afraid to take the body. Doesn't go looking for trouble but won't say no. Good in the dressing room. A real presence. Works hard and earns his ice time. True competitor. Stands up for his teammates. Here and

there in the NHL. Bounced around with half a dozen teams. Lots of pims. Moved to Florida. Went into landscaping. There it is.

CROSS, Cory ("Red"/ "Crosser")
b. Lloydminster, Alberta, January 3, 1971
Cross can play and Cross can talk. He attended U of Alberta, earning a degree in teaching while helping the Golden Bears to a CIAU championship. After being drafted by the Lightning, he joined the team in 1993 and stayed there until a trade during 1999-2000 to Toronto. In 1996 and '97 he represented Team Canada at the World Championships, winning a gold medal the second time, and while playing in the minors for Atlanta, Cross also won a Turner Cup in the IHL. In his first seven seasons he played in the playoffs only once, a difficulty that was eradicated upon joining the Leafs.

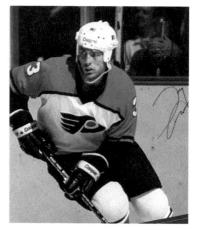

Crossman was the kind of reliable defensive player every coach loved to have on his team.
DOUG CROSSMAN

CROSSETT, Stan
b. Tillsonburg, Ontario, April 18, 1900
d. Port Hope, Ontario, July 26, 1992
Where he came from and where he went to – nobody knows. As obscure an NHLer as they come. A vapour, a ghost, a comet, a mere sighting with Philadelphia when they were Quakers, not Flyers, back in 1930. As far as anyone knows, he never played anywhere else.

CROSSMAN, Doug ("Cross")
b. Peterborough, Ontario, June 13, 1960
A member of the historic 1987 Team Canada that won that year's Canada Cup, Crossman had two distinct parts to his career. The first saw him play eight years with Chicago and Philly, going to the Stanley Cup finals in 1985 and '87, only to lose to the Oilers each time. A plus player and a model of consistency, Crossman was the kind of reliable defensive player every coach loved to have on his team, one who joined the Hawks with junior teammate Doug Wilson and who had offensive talents of his own (his childhood hero was Bobby Orr). But after contract troubles with the Flyers, he was traded to Los Angeles to start the '88-'89 season. This proved to be the start of a six-year stretch that saw him wear the sweaters of as many teams. Trade after trade sent him to ports of call around the league, and finally in 1994 he landed in the minors and out of the loop. In Tampa, he recorded three goals and three assists in a game, the six points being a record for the young franchise.

CROTEAU, Gary ("Crow"/ "Bull")
b. Sudbury, Ontario, June 20, 1946
Talk about being negative for a guy who was in the league for so long, but Croteau was in the playoffs just

one year of his dozen in the NHL. In each and every season he was a minus player; over a 684-game career that amounted to a collective -227. Yet he seemed to get better as he went along, his last four complete seasons being the best of his career. Croteau played with expansion L.A., then Detroit when that team was mired in its worst slump in team history, then the big three of misery – California, Kansas City, Colorado. He graduated from St. Lawrence University with a B.A. in sociology, captaining that school's hockey team. A member of the Fellowship of Christian Athletes, he continued his studies at the University of Missouri at Kansas City for a master's in physical education. But after retiring in 1980, he remained in Denver and became vice-president of marketing for a company that worked with Hartford Insurance Co. to build, among other things, a 1,200-acre office-park in the city.

CROWDER, Bruce
b. Essex, Ontario, March 25, 1957
He earned a teaching certificate from the University of New Hampshire, but the lessons he learned in the NHL were sometimes harder to absorb. Bruce, the older brother of Keith, passed up a junior career with the Kingston Canadians in favour of the education-oriented hockey apprenticeship, but after signing with Boston he spent two years in the minors with nary a phone call to the big time. When he got his chance, in 1981-82, he performed admirably, but in his third season the numbers weren't there and he was released at season's end. Pittsburgh claimed him, but demoted him after 26 games. Crowder refused to report, opting instead for retirement. He resurfaced a year later as an assistant coach at the University of Maine, and liked the experience so much he made it his life's work.

CROWDER, Keith
b. Windsor, Ontario, January 6, 1959
Unlike his golden-boy brother Bruce, Keith opted for hockey over education, and by the time they made it to the NHL the difference had become obvious. Keith played for Peterborough, then jumped to the WHA as an underage junior for the end of the '78-'79 season. He went a respectable 57th in the '79 draft, and played all but his final year with the Bruins. The brothers were teammates from 1981 to '84 in Beantown, the first brothers to play for Boston since the Quackenbush boys in 1950-51. The Crowders hadn't played together since 1975, when they were both members of the Essex 73s, a local team that won the Ontario Junior C title. Keith put together 6 consecutive 20-plus-goal seasons, scoring 30-plus three times, including 38 in '85-'86. He helped the team to the 1988 Stanley Cup finals against the Oilers, playing in the famous blackout game that postponed game four in Boston and gave Edmonton the chance to win the Cup on home ice, which it did. He played in L.A. for his final year. He and his family bought a home in Essex, Ontario, and spent a year fixing it up, trying to ease the post-retirement blues that had plagued his brother and almost every NHLer returning to civilian life. An astute businessman, he once owned four Tim Horton franchises, and on October 16, 1999, he was inducted into the Windsor/Essex County Sports Hall of Fame.

CROWDER, Troy
b. Sudbury, Ontario, May 3, 1968
Junior coach Bill Laforge got Crowder into the fight business, and that's what got the teen into the NHL. But the fighting led to injuries – one of them serious enough to keep him out of the game for two full years – and Crowder was forever being let go and signed as a free agent. When he was healthy and punching, he certainly made his mark. He was once, in fact, considered a boxing prospect for the Canadian Olympic team. Then, when he attended his first training camp, with New Jersey, he quit the game and returned to Sudbury to work in construction for five months before realizing he could do better. He suffered a serious back injury in October 1991 and played just seven games that year and one game in the next two. Los Angeles took a gamble on him when he decided to return in 1994, but during a pre-season game he hit linesman Brad Lazarowich, who was trying to break up a fight, and was suspended for 10 games. He later moved around the minors, signed with Vancouver, played in Europe, and signed with San Jose. The fighting was always the common denominator. He retired to Sudbury and made a go of it as a real estate agent.

CROWE, Philip
b. Nanton, Alberta, April 14, 1970
Undrafted and signed as a free agent four times, Crowe's bread and butter has been in the minors, with only sporadic NHL steak variations along the way. In numbers, that translates to 94 games spread over 4 teams and 6 years.

CROWLEY, Mike
b. Bloomington, Minnesota, July 4, 1975
Crowley's international experience far outstrips the NHL stories he'll tell his grandchildren one day. He has been a member of the U.S. World Junior team and twice played for the Stars 'n' Stripes at the World Championships. A low draft choice by Philly, he was signed by the Mighty Ducks but has played only a handful of games with the quackers over the last few seasons. He came out of the University of Minnesota, where he had been an all-star defenceman. In 2001-02, he suffered a serious Achilles tendon injury and when Minnesota assigned him to the minors, he retired. Crowley settled in Chicago and works as a bond trader for his uncle's security firm.

CROWLEY, Ted
b. Concord, Massachusetts, May 3, 1970
One of only a handful of Americans to play in three World Junior tournaments, Crowley took five years to get to the NHL after being drafted, and another five to play a second season. Toronto made him the 69th selection overall in 1988, but Crowley didn't get into a game until 1993, by which time he was a member of the Hartford Whalers organization. His body was quickly dumped back into the minors, not to be fished out again until 1998, when Colorado signed him, played him, and traded him, all within a span of four months. Chicago later signed him, but ostensibly he has been a minor-leaguer for his whole career.

Gary Croteau

Keith Crowder

Troy Crowder

Mike Crowley

CROZIER, Greg
b. Calgary, Alberta, July 6, 1976

Although he was born in Calgary, his early years easily prepared him for the hockey life. He was raised in Buffalo, went to high school in New England, and went to the University of Michigan as a teen. He helped the Wolverines win a national championship in his first year, 1995-96, and was drafted by Pittsburgh, the team that got him into a single game in 2000-01. The Penguins let him go, but he signed on with Boston after that in the hopes of getting back into the NHL.

CROZIER, Joe ("Crow")
b. Winnipeg, Manitoba, February 19, 1929

His was a life in hockey, no doubt about it, and growing up in the 'Peg, there was but one team to cheer for – the Leafs. When he was seven years old, he already had his own paper route. By 15, he had an ice route, delivering huge chunks of ice to his customers. Three years later, he played junior in Brandon, Manitoba, and by 20 he was a pro with the Quebec Aces. Those were the days when Punch Imlach was the coach and Jean Béliveau the team's star player. By 1956, he and Imlach owned the team, Crozier the player/coach, Imlach the general manager. Once Béliveau turned pro and Imlach signed on with the Leafs, the Aces floundered and the two men sold their shares in the club. Crozier moved on to Spokane as playing coach, beginning a lengthy skein of management positions. His only time in the NHL came when Imlach called him up to play five games – March 12, 13, 17, 19, 20, 1960 – when the Toronto blueline had been hit by injuries. Crozier retired in 1962 and became coach and GM of the Charlotte Checkers of the EHL, but two years later Imlach came a-calling wanting him to coach the Leafs farm team in Rochester. Crozier set off for New York state, and in 1968 he moved on to Vancouver. He was fired a year and a half later, blamed for mismanagement and interference, and wound up suing the Canucks for the balance of his contract. Just weeks later, though, the team wanted him back as it was set to enter the NHL in the fall of 1970. Crow said no. Instead, he stayed on in Vancouver as a radio commentator, but the next year, Punch came a-calling again, this time wanting his best friend to head up operations in Cincinnati for the Sabres farm team. Crozier set off for Ohio, and it was there his sideline in horse racing began. He hooked up with a player on the team, John Gould, and they bought a two-year-old gelding named Teddy Bearcat. Near mid-season Imlach suffered a heart attack while coaching Buffalo. Crozier came up to replace him. He ended up being named full-time coach, but in 1974 he was canned by his best friend. Crozier signed on with Vancouver of the WHA, and then stayed with the team when it transferred to Calgary. When Imlach later became GM in Toronto, he again called on his best friend, and Crow set off for Maple Leaf Gardens. This proved to be a tortuous managerial combination under the inept leadership of incompetent owner Harold Ballard, and both were gone within a year. Joe landed on his feet, as coach and GM of the Kitchener Rangers, and then moved back to Rochester in 1983 to coach the Americans. He later became a special consultant for the Sabres.

CROZIER, Roger
b. Bracebridge, Ontario, March 16, 1942
d. Landenberg, Pennsylvania, January 11, 1996

He burst into the NHL in the 1964–65 season, one of the few goalies to win the Calder Trophy. Detroit acquired him in the summer of '63 when he was nothing more than a minor-leaguer, but the year after he led the NHL with 40 wins and 6 shutouts. Crozier's next year was almost as impressive, and in the playoffs he was brilliant, taking the Red Wings to the finals, where they lost to Montreal. But Crozier's brilliant play earned him the Conn Smythe Trophy, and after two full seasons no goalie in the league looked more certain for a Hall of Fame career. But all his life he had been plagued by stomach troubles, his body's way of making clear the stress it felt from being an Original Six goalie. He suffered increasingly difficult and painful bouts of pancreatitis, missing longer stretches and in the process proving more unreliable. When he did play, his confidence was shot, and, to make matters worse, the Detroit team was on the downswing. He was traded to Buffalo and then on Washington, retiring in 1976 a goalie far greater in possibility than reality. He worked for MBNA, quickly becoming head of construction. In all, he was responsible for some 50 buildings for the company. He died, too young, of prostate cancer.

CRUTCHFIELD, Nels
b. Knowlton, Quebec, July 12, 1911
d. Muskoka, Ontario, July 22, 1985

An up-and-comer, Crutchfield was the centre of a major trade when the Maroons sent him to the Habs for Lionel Conacher and Herb Cain. He played just one season, however, before suffering a career-ending fractured skull in a car crash on September 28, 1935. It was not his first head injury. In a playoff game in 1935, he was shadowing Bill Cook when Cook hit Crutchfield flush on the head with his stick, hurting him badly and starting a donnybrook. As a result of the car accident, the league held a benefit game in his honour in similar fashion to the Ace Bailey game a year previous. Held at the Montreal Forum on January 31, 1936, it was attended by 11,000 fans and raised some $7,000 for the young star. In his heyday, at McGill University in Montreal, he was one of a famous group of football players known as the Four Horsemen that led the Redmen to three championships. He died in a car crash many years later when he entered the intersection of Highways 141 and 11 near Muskoka without yielding and broadsided fast-moving cars.

CUDE, Wilf
b. Barry, Wales, July 4, 1910
d. Montreal, Quebec, May 5, 1968

Welsh by birth but 'Peg by upbringing, Cude was the first spare goaltender hired not by any one team but by the NHL itself! As a result of this unusual arrangement, he played for both Boston and Chicago in '31-'32 without being traded. He wound up in Montreal two years later, and it was there he spent the rest of his career, first as number-one son, then as backup. After retiring, Cude moved to Noranda, Quebec, where he bought rights to distribution in the

Nels Crutchfield

Wilf Cude

Rouyn-Noranda area for British American Oil. He also coached the Noranda Tigers and scouted for the Red Wings. He played in benefit games for both Howie Morenz and Nels Crutchfield, moments he forever considered his fondest memories.

CULHANE, Jim
b. Haileybury, Ontario, March 13, 1965
A graduate of Western Michigan University, Culhane went a lowly 214th in the '84 Entry Draft, played half a dozen games with the Whalers a few years later, and drifted into obscurity before resurfacing with his alma mater as a coach.

CULLEN, Brian ("Frig")
b. Ottawa, Ontario, November 11, 1933
Brian, Barry, Ray, and Bruce all played hockey. Ironically, Bruce was the most talented but he was the least driven, and he was the only of the four not to make the NHL. Brian was, by his own admission, a weak skater, but in a six-team league that wasn't half bad if the desire was there. It was. He hung around for a few years with the Leafs and Rangers, but he had enough horse sense to know he'd be motoring out of the league just as fast as he rode into it. He replaced the arena with the car lot after retiring, working for Hearn Buick Pontiac in Toronto for four years before opening his own GM dealership in St. Kitts. While the business thrived (he opened a leasing company as well), Brian's real passion was the track. Just outside St. Catharines sits Victura Farm, a 71-acre spread where he trains thoroughbreds. Pre Emptive Strike finished third in the '85 Queen's Plate for him, and other prize nags include Crowning Honours, Bishop Bob, Lantana Lady, Friendly Ways, Nice Manners, and Banner Bob. He also became involved in real estate in Florida, and today thrives with his business ventures made possible because of his hockey career oh so many years ago.

CULLEN, Charles "Barry"
b. Ottawa, Ontario, June 16, 1935
As a member of the CBC Line with his brother Brian and Hugh Barlow, Barry helped the St. Catharines Teepees win the Memorial Cup in 1954 on the road to the NHL. Property of the Leafs, he and Brian teamed up to play offensive-minded hockey under leader Billy Reay, combining for 36 goals in '57-'58. Although he was a hard worker, Barry was traded to Detroit and then right out of the NHL. His son, John, made it to the NHL while he followed in the footsteps of his brother and opened a Cullen car dealership for General Motors in Guelph, Ontario.

CULLEN, David
b. St. Catharines, Ontario, December 30, 1976
Yes, he's one of those Cullens. His uncles are Barry, Brian, and Ray, and his cousin is John, former NHLers one and all. David, however, has yet to make his mark in quite the same way as those Cullens who have gone before him. He was never drafted and has spent virtually all his pro career in the minors with the exception of two games he played with Phoenix in 2000-01 season. He played four years with the University of Maine Black Bears, winning the NCAA championship in 1999.

CULLEN, John
b. Fort Erie, Ontario, August 2, 1964
A sad-happy story of skill and courage, determination and success, force of will and force of nature, the life of John Cullen will bring tears to the eyes of any human being. The son of Barry, John followed in his dad's and uncle's footsteps to play for the Maple Leafs as well as three other NHL teams along his hockey journey, but it was not as simple as that penny-biography description. John's brother, Terry, was likely a better player. Terry went to the University of Michigan on full scholarship, and in his fourth game he was cross-checked from behind, snapping his neck and ending his hockey career. John, too, wanted an education, and chose Boston University. No, he didn't get hit from behind. He got his from all sides. Just a few months into his first year, his mother died of cancer. Destroyed, John pursued an NHL career with even greater

The life of John Cullen will bring tears to the eyes of any human being.
JOHN CULLEN

determination. He made it to Pittsburgh, then the personal domain of Mario Lemieux, then Hartford and Toronto, where he donned his dad's old number 19. The Leafs gave up on him, though, and he landed in Tampa in 1995 wearing number 12. At the end of the '96-'97 season, Cullen didn't feel well. He had chest X-rays, and they revealed a cloud in his chest, a cloud that was described as a grapefruit-sized ball of non-Hodgkins lymphoma. A hockey player, in the prime of life, in superior physical condition, had cancer. The next day, the chemo began, and two weeks later not a single hair was left on his head. But the grapefruit had been reduced to a berry. Unfortunately, the cancer wouldn't go away. Cullen needed a bone marrow transplant. Shortly after the operation, he went into cardiac arrest and was clinically dead for a full minute before defibrallators revived him. The marrow eventually took, but his immune system was down to nil and he had to be isolated. No human contact. Determined, the love of his family supporting him every day, Cullen slowly recovered. When his Boston specialist gave him a

Jim Culhane

Brian Cullen

Barry Cullen

Matt Cullen

Ray Cullen

Barry Cummins

Randy Cunneyworth

clean bill of health, he flew home to Tampa where he was greeted by 100 well-wishers. They carried a sign: "Cullen 1, The Big C 0. Final/OT." His teammates put a 12 on the shoulders of their sweaters, and Alexei Selivanov shaved his own head to support his ailing friend. Cleared for training, Cullen prepared to resume his hockey career under the guidance of team trainer John McCortney, a man who pushed Cullen beyond endurance, a man without whom Cullen would not have endured. In the fall of 1998, the Lightning offered Cullen a contract. He made the team, and on opening night he received an ovation so meaningful and moving there wasn't a dry eye in the house. After four games, Cullen was demoted, and a few weeks later, having beaten the Big C, having returned to the NHL, having struggled for himself and for every aspiring hockey player and cancer victim, he retired to assume an assistant coaching position with the club. For his contribution to the game, not in goals and assists or defence or hits, he was awarded the 1999 Bill Masterton Award, symbolic of a man, a life, and a career that had come back from the dead. Soon after, he left the team to join brother Terry in running a car dealership outside Atlanta, adding another Cullen to the long list of NHLers and car dealership owners.

CULLEN, Matt
b. Virginia, Minnesota,
November 2, 1976
His dad was a high school hockey coach, and growing up in Minnesota is the American hockey equivalent to a childhood in Manitoba, so it's no wonder Cullen turned to the skating and shooting game. Drafted by the Ducks, he is considered one of their fine young talents, though he has yet to reach a level or age where the team can determine his full talents. He has also played in two World Championships and one World Juniors for the U.S.

CULLEN, Ray
b. Ottawa, Ontario, September 20, 1941
The baby of the Cullen pack, Ray followed his brothers by quitting the game at age 29 and getting into cars in a big way. He played briefly in '65-'66 in Detroit, centering a couple of guys named Gordie Howe and Alex Delvecchio, but he broke his leg and missed much of the season. Drafted by Minnesota in the expansion selections of 1967, Ray had back-to-back seasons of 28 and 26 goals, then tailed off. He played one final season with Vancouver, then moved his family of five kids to London, where he opened a GM dealership, just like Brian and Barry. Not even a two-year contract with the Minnesota Fighting Saints for $125,000 could convince him to play again.

CULLIMORE, Jassen ("Baby Face")
b. Simcoe, Ontario, December 4, 1972
A giant of a man, even by ever-growing hockey standards, Cullimore is frightful to behold when he catches a player in his headlights. Drafted by Vancouver, both the Canucks and later the Habs gave up on him, allowing him to land in Tampa, where he hopes to develop into a tough, immovable defenceman. His stay with the Lightning has extended to five years, though he has yet to appear in a single playoff game with the team.

CUMMINS, Barry
b. Regina, Saskatchewan, January 25, 1949
Fans of the game who enjoy speed, skating, hitting, beautiful passing, and up-and-down, non-stop excitement will likely revile Cummins and applaud him at the same time. In early December 1973, Cummins, up from the farm to play for the hapless Seals, got into a pushing match with Bobby Clarke of Philadelphia as play moved up the ice. Clarke pulled his stick away, cutting Cummins under the eye, and as both players followed the puck, Cummins took a vicious two-handed swing at the Flyers captain. Clarke fell to the ice in a heap, and Mad Dog Kelly and the rest of the Broad Street Bullies charged on the ice to get Cummins. The Seals bench also emptied. When all was said and done, Cummins was suspended for three games and fined $300, but to any who knew Clarke, it was an assault long deserved and not nearly vicious enough for a man who had meted out much dirtiness

Cummins played the entire '97-'98 season without scoring a goal.
JIM CUMMINS

and paid for so very little during his long career.

CUMMINS, Jim
b. Dearborn, Michigan, May 17, 1970
Think of a tough guy who's had a penalty shot. Not many, though Cummins is one. He missed. Natch. Mike Vernon stopped him. That was April 7, 1996. Cummins played the entire '97-'98 season, 75 games for him, without scoring a goal, and during his more than a decade in the NHL he has been traded 5 times, always as a tough, team player, never for his scoring ability like his boyhood idol, Guy Lafleur. He led his team in penalties virtually everywhere he went, but has hung in there and continued to play, most recently with Anaheim.

CUNNEYWORTH, Randy
b. Etobicoke, Ontario, May 10, 1961
Cunneyworth once scored four goals in a game, but more recently has become a checker of renown. Rarely has a player gone from a 35-goal season (with Pittsburgh) to a 2-goal season (with Ottawa) during his

career, but Cunneyworth has gone from offence to defence as a way to keep playing. That his career lasted some 866 games is remarkable given he was selected a lowly 167th overall in 1980. He went on to coach in the AHL, principally with Rochester.

CUNNINGHAM, Bob
b. Welland, Ontario, February 26, 1941
Four games with the Rangers in the early 1960s didn't give Cunningham much of a chance to walk down Broadway, see a play, listen to some jazz at the Bluenote, or head over to the MoMA for the latest from Pollock or Lichtenstein. Most of his culture came via minor-league teams such as Baltimore, Denver, and Barrie.

CUNNINGHAM, Jim
b. St. Paul, Minnesota, August 15, 1956
One itty-bitty game, one brief fling with NHL glory, one tiny skate on sacred pro ice, one small, quick night sharing dressing room humour with Bobby Clarke and his Flyers mates, one tiny taste test of rarefied NHL spring water, one chance to sing anthems in a big arena with thousands of fans. Just one, but one is better than none.

CUNNINGHAM, Les ("Cunning")
b. Calgary, Alberta, October 4, 1913
d. Calgary, Alberta, April 9, 1993
If the guy's got a trophy named after him, he must have been something special. Indeed, the AHL's MVP prize is called the Les Cunningham Trophy, and that's because during his own 10 years in that league he set every record there was to be set – most goals, most assists, most points, most years with one franchise, most 20-goal seasons, most 30-goal seasons. He played briefly with the New York Americans and the Black Hawks, and even scored an incredible five points in one period. On the night of January 28, 1940, while with Chicago against Montreal, he had two goals and three assists in 10:04 of the third period. It was a record that lasted 38 years until Bryan Trottier of the Islanders bettered the feat in 1978. After leaving Cleveland of the AHL, he took a job as playing coach with San Francisco in 1947, and two years later as coach in Brandon. He became an NHL scout, but the grind of travel got to him so he returned to Calgary, where he retired to enjoy the racetrack and golfing. He had left home at 15 to play for Regina, earning his money as a telegram delivery boy for CPR until his hockey skills were good enough to carry him along.

CUPOLO, Bill
b. Niagara Falls, Ontario, January 8, 1924
Cupolo's dad operated Cupolo's Sports Shop in town, and as a youngster Bill played in Stratford in the early '40s with Howie Meeker. They have been fast friends ever since. He was all set to go off to war, but Cupolo's enlistment was cancelled because doctors spotted a small tubercular spot on his right lung. A year away from hockey and he was healthy, and in the fall of 1944 he made the Boston Bruins. Cupolo played on a line with Frank Maria and Ken Smith, a threesome GM Art Ross dubbed the Typhoon Line. But this was war and the Kraut Line was away on business. After

one year, everything went tabula rasa on Cupolo and he was out of the NHL, playing in a variety of minor leagues, including with Stratford under now-coach Howie Meeker. Because of his heritage, Cupolo was invited to be the playing coach in Milan, Italy, for that country's European Cup entry from 1954 to '56, and as a result of his successes he stayed on to coach the Italian team at the 1956 Olympics in Cortina. He stayed there until '59, marrying a local woman and having his first child, Steve, before returning to the Falls to open an auto body shop with brother Ronny. He also coached the Kerrios in Niagara Falls and then the Canucks, and later acted as supervisor of coaches for the Greater Niagara Minor Hockey Association.

CURRAN, Brian ("The Colonel")
b. Toronto, Ontario, November 5, 1963
They called him the Colonel because he liked to shout orders to his teammates during the heat of the game, a quality he likely got from his rugby-playing, Irish immigrant father. Although the little Colonel arrived in this world in Toronto, he became a big Colonel in Lethbridge, Alberta. where Curran Sr. ran two cattle auction markets. Brian won the Memorial Cup with the Portland Winter Hawks and his whole career has been based on getting to know every penalty timekeeper in the league. He averaged almost five penalty minutes a game, and has one of the lowest goals scored to games played ratios, but his services were always required and as a blueline presence he was an effective player. In February '87, as a member of the Islanders, he and Tomas Jonsson went to a nightclub called Taboo. Unable to find a cab afterwards, they accepted a ride from a stranger and their car was blindsided by a truck. Curran sustained superficial injuries, Jonsson suffered a severely broken jaw, and a 17-year-old girl was knocked unconscious. The incident highlighted a career fraught with injury for Curran, who missed numerous games over the years with a broken wrist and bruised thigh among other hockey-garnered wounds.

CURRIE, Dan
b. Burlington, Ontario, March 15, 1968
Born on the ides of March but unaware of the troubles that would unfold after being drafted by Edmonton in 1986, Currie remained an unhappy minor-league part of the Oilers organization for five years. During that time, with Cape Breton, he improved his goal scoring dramatically each year, going from 29 to 36 to 47 to 50 to 57 goals, but never being given a legitimate shot – in his books – at making the big team. When he became a free agent and signed with L.A., he never excelled and wound up in the minors for the rest of his days, too early thrust from the NHL in his humble opinion.

CURRIE, Glen
b. Montreal, Quebec, July 18, 1958
Uncle Jim to Glen Currie is better known to the rest of the world as Jim Peters, old-timer of the NHL himself. Glen played junior with Mike Bossy in Laval, and himself was a quite a scoring star. However, while Bossy continued to fill the net in the NHL, Currie became a checker and penalty killer, a fourth-line hard worker. It wasn't until '83-'84, his fifth year with

Bob Cunningham

Les Cunningham

Bill Cupolo

Brian Curran

Glen Currie

Hugh Currie

Tony Currie

Paul Curtis

Ian Cushenan

Washington, that he stayed the full season with the team, and two years later he was traded to Los Angeles where he played the last two seasons of his career.

CURRIE, Hugh
b. Saskatoon, Saskatchewan, October 22, 1925
At 15, young Hughie was playing an exhibition game with the great Max and Doug Bentley. At 16, he almost died from injuries sustained in a car accident. He suffered four broken ribs, cut both his arms badly, and bled internally from burst kidneys. Doctors operated, discovered the bleeding kidneys, and saved his life. He was off the ice for a year, but then was signed by Eddie Shore for his team in Buffalo. Currie broke both his kneecaps when hit from behind in '48-'49, but was called up for one game with Montreal. He remained a solid minor-leaguer his whole skating life, playing primarily in the WHL. Currie went into coaching after he retired in 1963.

CURRIE, Tony
b. Sydney Mines, Nova Scotia, November 12, 1957
There was promise, there was hope, there were chances, there was optimism. But soon there were trades and reduced ice time, differences of opinions, and, finally, a demotion to say goodbye to the NHL. Currie scored 73 goals with Portland and continued scoring in Salt Lake City, minor-league home of the St. Louis Blues. When given the opportunity to play in the Bluenote sweater, he acquitted himself well enough, but the team wasn't winning. Traded to Vancouver and then to Hartford, he saw less and less time until finally he was deemed a spare part, a filler in the AHL. Currie stuck around a couple of years, then headed for a new start in Europe.

CURRY, Floyd
("Busher"/ "The Honest Blocker")
b. Chapleau, Ontario, August 11, 1925
Rare are the instances of a life full of events both as coach and as player, but Curry's was just that. He sacrificed his career at an early age, joining the army at 18. A year later, he was back in the Montreal Canadiens organization, and in 1947 he made the team that he would play for his entire career (though in the summers he was a salesman for a fuel oil company). While he had been a scoring star in junior, Curry knew that to make the Habs of his era he would have to convert to being a checker, a change he accepted and perfected. Winner of four Cups and as popular a Habs as there was, Curry was accorded his own special night at the Forum, March 14, 1957, when the hockey team showed its appreciation to his service and commitment to the city and Habs.

Curry was accorded his own special night at the Forum, March 14, 1957.
FLOYD CURRY

Ironically, GM Frank Selke wrote just prior to the night that "Curry is playing so poorly that I wonder whether I can keep him in the line-up until the end of the season... Certainly being a sentimental fellow has its drawbacks in hockey but I am going to do the level best I can for Floyd." And Curry responded, picking up his game and playing one more season. In his entire career, he had only one hat trick, but that was scored in front of Princess (later Queen) Elizabeth. After retiring, he remained with the Montreal organization, coaching the Royals, Quebec Aces, and then the Cleveland Barons, interspersing his bossing duties with time under GM Sam Pollock. By the mid-1980s he had become the team's director of advertising sales.

CURTALE, Tony
b. Detroit, Michigan, January 29, 1962
He played midget hockey in Michigan, junior in Ontario, and NHL in Calgary. He played in the CHL and IHL besides, had a goodly number of penalty minutes, and not many successes beyond that. Still, more should be expected from a player drafted 31st overall in 1980. He was out of the game seven years later and went on to coach the Texas Tornado of the NAHL.

CURTIS, Paul
("Hound Dawg")
b. Peterborough, Ontario, September 29, 1947
The Dawg would go a little wacko sometimes, a feature that kept the other team on its collective toes. Curtis was a slow skater but a fine shotblocker, exposed by Montreal in the 1970 Intra League Draft and claimed by Los Angeles. After a stint with St. Louis, he was traded to Buffalo and then to the Rangers, playing for neither team. Instead, he tried his hand in the WHA, but it was a short-lived career by that point.

CUSHENAN, Ian ("Cush")
b. Hamilton, Ontario, November 29, 1933
He won a Memorial Cup, Calder Cup, and Stanley Cup, a rare triple in the hockey world, and he made a few enemies along the way. Notable on the list of adversaries was Doug Mohns. In a game in December 1957, the two got into a scuffle, but as play moved up the ice, Mohns figured things had settled. Cushenan begged to differ and cold-cocked Mohns from behind, once with each hand, knocking him to the ice and breaking his jaw without Mohns ever having known what had happened. Cushenan was reviled for the incident, and his "toughness" didn't leave a favourable impression on Chicago management. He was sent to Montreal at season's end, then had brief tryouts in New York and Detroit before settling in

with the Bisons in Buffalo, AHL country. He went on to win three Calder Cups before retiring.

CUSSON, Jean
b. Verdun, Quebec, October 5, 1942
Cusson graduated from the University of Montreal and went directly to Father Bauer's National Team in 1965, at the time coached by Jackie McLeod. He played there for three years, including at the 1967 World Championships in Vienna, when Canada won a bronze medal. Cusson signed a tryout contract with Oakland that lasted but two games, and that was the last hockey heard of him.

CUTTA, Jakub
b. Jablonec nad Nisou, Czechoslovakia (Czech Republic), December 29, 1981
Just a pup, he was taken by Washington in the 2000 draft and given a chance to play the first three games of the 2000-01 season before the Caps returned him to junior. That Christmas, he helped the Czech Republic win a gold medal at the World Junior Championships.

CUTTS, Don
b. Edmonton, Alberta, February 24, 1953
His only NHL win came January 30, 1980, an 8-1 victory over L.A. But Cutts was in tough, playing on an emerging Oilers team trying to find its identity in goal. He was one of six goaltenders used that year – Ron Low, Jim Corsi, Bob Dupuis, Ed Mio, and Dave Dryden were the others – while the team awaited the arrival of Grant Fuhr and Andy Moog to take them to the Stanley Cup.

CYR, Claude
b. Montreal, Quebec, March 27, 1939
d. unknown
How was it possible to contemplate playing goal for Montreal in the Original Six when Jacques Plante ruled the cage with an iron grip? Cyr was a fine goaler, raised in Montreal and part of the team's food chain of prospects, but his chances of usurping Plante were anywhere from none to impossibly none. He played one period for the Habs the night of March 19, 1959, the third period of a game against Toronto. He replaced Claude Pronovost in a game that was already 5-3 for the Leafs, and surrendered only one goal, a shot by George Armstrong. Other than that, he watched the Habs like everyone else and played goal for a series of lesser teams in lesser leagues.

CYR, Denis
b. Verdun, Quebec, February 4, 1961
He was one of the "three Denis," or "*les trois Denis*," in Montreal. Three members of the Montreal Junior Canadiens, linemates, all named Denis. There was Denis Savard, Denis Cyr, and Denis Tremblay. And get this: They were all born on February 4, 1961! Denis Savard was selected 3rd overall in 1980, Cyr 13th, and Tremblay, who abandoned his hockey career to take a job in the post office, was not drafted at all. Savard went on to have a Hall of Fame career, and Cyr was in the middle, neither a great star nor another name in the phone book. But after 236 goals with Savard in four years with the Jr. Habs, Cyr's

production certainly dipped. He didn't do much in Calgary, so the Hawks acquired him, hoping that a reunion with Savard might spark him. It did, but not for long. Soon it was on to St. Louis and then to pasture in Peoria as an investment broker. Such was the fate of one of the three Denis.

CYR, Paul
b. Port Alberni, British Columbia, October 31, 1963
Cyr's most noteworthy story occurred far, far away from the madding hockey crowd. On vacation in the Dominican Republic with his girlfriend in 1987, the couple took a taxi to a weightlifting competition. On the way, the driver stopped at the site of an apparent accident, at which time two men and a woman hijacked them and tried to rob the three occupants. Cyr bravely grabbed a gun from one man, and in the ensuing scuffle was shot in the rib cage. The attackers fled, and Cyr was hailed a hero by local police. It took him a few weeks to recover, but he was well enough in time for the new hockey season. Cyr entered the NHL with a reputation for having one of the hardest shots in the game, and this was supposed to translate into goals for the Buffalo Sabres, who drafted him in 1982. While he had some success as a lamplighter – he scored a goal in his first NHL game – it certainly wasn't to the extent the Fire City had hoped for, and Cyr was traded to the Rangers. He hurt his right knee the first game of the '88-'89 season, required surgery, and missed the next two years recovering. Figuring his career was over, the Rangers let him sign with Hartford in 1990, but Cyr produced only another year and a half of middling hockey. He had won gold with Canada's World Junior team in 1982, and after retiring he returned to Port Alberni and became co-owner of a local construction company.

CZERKAWSKI, Mariusz
b. Radomsko, Poland, April 13, 1972
Poland may be a former communist power, an ally of the Soviet Union, a large country, and a cultural and sporting centre, but a hockey nation it is not. The Poles have never won a medal at either the Olympics or the World Championships, and Czerkawski is one of a precious few to play in the NHL (he also played for Poland in the '92 Olympics in Albertville). He married – and divorced – the actress Izabella Scorupco-Czerkawski (try putting that name on the back of a hockey sweater!) and after a bit of a false start with Boston came into his own in Edmonton before being traded to the Islanders for Dan Lacouture on August 25, 1997. On Long Island, he had three successive 20-plus-goal seasons, including a career-high 35 in 1999-2000, but his career took a strange twist when Montreal acquired him in 2002. The Habs sent him to the minors, and he had to play his way back to the NHL.

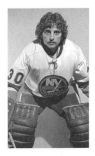

Don Cutts

Denis Cyr

Paul Cyr

Mariusz Czerkawski

DACKELL, Andreas ("Dacks")

b. Gavle, Sweden, December 29, 1972

He may have scored a goal in his first NHL game – on his very first shot! – but to this stage in his career what stands out most occurred the night of October 29, 1998. Going back in his own end to chase down a loose puck, he heard footsteps. Not the ordinary steps of a player forcing the play. Oh, no. These were the giant footsteps of an already ornery giant named Eric Lindros preparing to crush the terrified Senator. Dackell made the mistake of looking down for the puck, and the next moment his cheek and forehead were making a sweat-soaked, indelible impression on the corner Plexiglas. Bleeding and down for the count, he suffered a concussion, though missed only four games. On the brighter side, he was part of Sweden's gold-medal team at the '94 Olympics in Lillehammer that beat Canada in a shootout. Incredibly, he was ignored in the draft until Ottawa took him in 1996 when he was 23, and the Sens later traded him to Montreal for an 8th-round draft choice.

DADSWELL, Doug

b. Scarborough, Ontario, February 7, 1964

His first NHL game in goal was January 22, 1987, one for the record books. His Calgary Flames were in Jersey to play the Devils, but a massive snowstorm delayed the starting time by two hours. When the puck was dropped, there were 320 souls in the building. New Jersey won 7-5. In his only other game that season against the dreaded enemy Edmonton, Dadswell sparkled in a 4-4 tie. The Flames so liked what they saw that they released veteran Reggie Lemelin to make room for him, but one very mediocre season in '87-'88 sent the team scurrying to find another number-two man. Dadswell, they felt, just wasn't it after all.

DAFOE, Byron ("Bysie")

b. Sussex, England, February 25, 1971

Although he lists Sussex as his place of birth, Dafoe (whose middle name is Jaromir) was raised in British Columbia. In '98-'99 he had one of the best seasons in Boston Bruins history and became quick reference to Frank Brimsek. Dafoe had 10 shutouts, the first to register double digits since Brimsek in '38-'39. His 1.99 goals-against average was also the first time under 2.00 since Brimsek that same season. However, in this day and age, superb numbers are not something to build on for the coming year; they're leverage for holding out. To start 1999-2000, Dafoe sat on the sidelines while his agent negotiated a bigger contract, and by the time he rejoined the team, it was too late to salvage much of the season. The team missed the playoffs the following year with him in the crease, but in 2001-02, under the rise of Joe Thornton, the Bruins finally made inroads toward the Stanley Cup. Byron was best man to Olaf Kolzig at the Washington goalie's wedding, and both men are charter members of the Portland Pirates Hall of Fame, having played for that AHL team in their early years. In the summer of 2002, he assumed that his great play with the Bruins would translate to a huge contract as a free agent. He was wrong. Months later, he humbly signed with the Thrashers.

DAGENAIS, Pierre

b. Blainville, Quebec, March 4, 1978

Dagenais scored goals in each of his first two NHL games, with New Jersey in mid-February 2001. He was called up from Albany because of injuries to the Devils, and in his nine games he had three goals and five points. Dagenais was drafted twice by the Devils and signed after the second time in 1998, after just having scored 66 goals for Rouyn-Noranda in the Q. A top scorer with the River Rats, he's one of the young guys the NHL club is looking to for the future.

DAHL, Kevin

b. Regina, Saskatchewan, December 30, 1968

After earning a degree in physical education from Bowling Green, Dahl spent a year in the minors before joining the Canadian National Team in preparation for the '92 Olympics in Albertville. A silver medal later, he moved to Calgary, the NHL team that had drafted him a lowly 230th. He proved to be a reliable but expendable defenceman, and he never caught on with the Flames or the Coyotes, who signed him in 1996. He later played briefly with Toronto and then moved to Europe to play in the German league.

DAHLEN, Ulf ("Ulfie")

b. Ostersund, Sweden, January 12, 1967

When he was drafted 7th overall in '85 by the Rangers, Dahlen became the highest choice ever for a Swede to that point in draft history. Since then he has maintained a dual portfolio, playing in the NHL since 1987 and representing his country at virtually every competition he's been available for, notably the Canada Cup, Olympics, World Championships, and, earlier in his career, the World Juniors. He won gold once, with the men's team at the '98 WC. Dahlen reached his peak with Minnesota, recording seasons of 36 and 35 goals in 1991-93 and helping the team make the Stanley Cup finals in 1991.

DAHLIN, Kjell

b. Timra, Sweden, February 2, 1963

He was welcomed with open arms when he arrived in Montreal from Sweden in 1985, the Euro-skater who would give the Habs some needed offence in the wake of Guy Lafleur's retirement. By the midway point of his rookie season, he had 25 goals and looked a sure winner of the Calder Trophy. Then, the NHL wall hit. Fatigue took Dahlin by storm, and the player used to a 36-game walk in the park schedule back home was in the middle of a gruelling 80-game marathon he couldn't complete. He finished with 32 goals, still a fine total, but there was pessimism in the air as he cleared out his equipment for the summer. Dahlin played two more years in Montreal, scoring just 12 and 13 goals in seasons cut short by injury, and in 1988, at age 25, he abandoned the NHL and returned to Sweden, where the Lord Jim of the ice lanes could look like a much bigger fish in a much smaller pond.

DAHLMAN, Toni

b. Helsinki, Finland, September 3, 1979

Dahlman went from junior and pro in Finland to the Ottawa training camp in 2001. He was assigned to

Andreas Dackell

Doug Dadswell

Byron Dafoe

Ulf Dahlen
(opposite page)

Chris Dahlquist

Cully Dahlstrom

Alain Daigle

J.J. Daigneault

Grand Rapids in the AHL but played 10 games for the Sens during the season. He was recalled midway through the 2002-03 season and scored his first NHL goal on February 12, 2003, against Pittsburgh.

DAHLQUIST, Chris
b. Fridley, Minnesota, December 14, 1962
A defensive defenceman, a checker and shotblocker, Dahlquist lasted 11 years in the NHL through guts and determination. He played for four teams, most notably Minnesota when the Stars reached the 1991 Stanley Cup finals, only to be trashed by Pittsburgh in the final game, 8-0.

DAHLSTROM, Carl "Cully"
b. Minneapolis, Minnesota, July 3, 1912
d. Washington, December 19, 1998
After a solid high school career in hockey, Dahlstrom moved up to the American Hockey Association to apprentice for the big time. He was signed by Chicago, and as fate had it his rookie season was without question his most memorable. He was named winner of the Calder Trophy, scored the series-winning goal in the semifinals against the Rangers, and scored a goal in the Cup-winning game against Toronto. This was Chicago's second Stanley Cup, and so sure was the NHL that the Hawks wouldn't win the championship that the Cup was not taken to Chicago for the deciding game! Dahlstrom played until the end of the war, and later became a real estate appraiser in Escondido, California. He was inducted into the United States Hockey Hall of Fame in 1973.

DAIGLE, Alain
b. Trois-Rivières, Quebec, August 24, 1954
After four years of junior in his hometown, Daigle arrived in Chicago not knowing a word of English. Although he had scored 80 goals in his final year with the Draveurs, *goal* was not a word he got to know quickly in the Windy City, scoring just 56 over the next 5 years. He moved to Europe to continue his career, and that is the brief history of Daigle's hockey life.

DAIGLE, Alexandre
b. Montreal, Quebec, February 7, 1975
The mightier they are, the harder they fall. They don't all fall, mind, but when they do, the crash can be heard for miles around. Daigle was touted as the next Mario Lemieux, the junior player so clearly number one he almost went number zero. He put up big numbers in Victoriaville, was drafted by Ottawa in 1993, and seemed ready to take on the NHL. The Sens signed him to a crazy five-year, $12.25 million

> "I never wanted to be the next Guy Lafleur," he admitted later.
>
> **ALEXANDRE DAIGLE**

contract to make sure he was happy and to put a number on what they expected of him, and like Woody Allen he took the money and ran. Actually, he waltzed. Four and a half years later, he showed no signs of improving, of adjusting to a higher level of play, of making a name for himself in the big league. He came close once, on September 25, 1996, but Daigle would probably like to forget it. While readying to board a flight at Pittsburgh International Airport, he commented that there was a bomb aboard another flight. Customs officials found little humour in the remark and detained Daigle. The Sens shipped him to Philadelphia just a few months later, and after a brief stint of enthusiasm at the end of the '97-'98 season, he packed it in again. He spent that summer dallying with actress Pamela Anderson Lee, whose former husband was serving six months in prison on a spousal abuse conviction, and showed up to training camp fat. Half a season later, GM Bob Clarke had given up on him, shipping Daigle to the last port of call, Tampa Bay. He went on to the Rangers, then disappeared into the California sunshine. He became interested in the entertainment business, played in a pickup league for a team called Priority Records, and counted the millions he had as much as stolen from teams and fans across North America. "I never wanted to be the next Guy Lafleur," he admitted later. He played pro only to make his father proud. "It was my little secret," he said with finality. Imagine how tough it was to explain, then, in the summer of 2002 when he announced his intentions to return to the NHL! Pittsburgh signed him to a low-level contract, but although he tried, the success just wasn't there.

DAIGNEAULT, Jean-Jacques "J.J."
b. Montreal, Quebec, October 12, 1965
When he was six years old, J.J. played for a team called the Montreal Hurricanes, where one of his teammates was named Mario. While little Lemieux knew all along he'd be in the NHL one day, Daigneault was reluctant to commit until he was 15 or 16, all the time playing alongside Lemieux. When he got to Vancouver in the NHL, J.J. began an equally rocky road, full of demotions, trades, injuries, and uncertainties, that has kept him to an average of about 55 games a season. For almost seven years, though, he realized a dream, playing for Montreal and winning the '93 Cup with the Habs. He later played briefly with Lemieux again, in Pittsburgh, but in the last 6 years has played for 7 teams to bring his total to 10 and counting. This ties the all-time record held by Michel Petit who was, naturally, a former teammate

(somewhere, sometime). In all, he has been traded 7 times but has yet to play 1,000 games despite being in the NHL since 1984.

DAILEY, Bob ("Moose"/ "The Count")
b. Kingston, Ontario, May 3, 1953
His dad was a prison guard at the Kingston Pen and young Bob worked for two summers in the jail. Good thing he was six-five in his bare feet. It was this size that also helped him carve out a career in the NHL. Dailey captained the 1972-73 Marlies to Memorial Cup victory, then moved on to Vancouver where, like Team Canada in 1972, he was booed mercilessly. He owned a restaurant and disco in Vancouver, and enjoyed a cherubic nightlife despite the fans' taunts. Philadelphia acquired him for Larry Goodenough and Jack McIlhargey and Dailey became an anchor on the Flyers blueline. Dailey had one of the hardest point shots in the game, but his fearlessness and toughness were equally intimidating for opponents. Along the way, though, his size cost him as many injuries as his reputation earned his team points. Shoulder surgery sidelined him in 1979, a blood infection in '77, and a two-game suspension was imposed after he shoved referee Bruce Hood in 1976. Worst of all, however, was the ankle injury he suffered in November 1981. Going into the corner for a puck, he lost his balance and shattered his ankle as he fell hard into the boards. It was the last game he ever played, though he did try coming back in February 1986 without success. He collected on a $175,000 insurance plan with Lloyd's of London, but his ankle never regained its previous strength. He stayed in Philadelphia and opened the very successful Bob Daily's Sweater Mill.

D'ALESSIO, Corrie
b. Cornwall, Ontario, September 9, 1969
Three shots, three saves. Eleven minutes of perfect hockey in the Hartford cage. Never before. Never again. Not in the NHL, anyway.

DALEY, Frank ("Dapper Dan")
b. Port Arthur, Ontario, August 22, 1909
d. Encinitas, California, October 15, 1968
A long and diverse hockey career rewarded Daley with four NHL games – March 5, 9, 10, and 14, 1929 – in his first year of pro, and two more in the playoffs, March 19 and 21. Unable to make it with the Detroit Cougars, he played for the local Olympics the following season and for the next 15 years travelled with stick and skates to various arenas of call around North America.

DALEY, Joe ("the Holy Goalie")
b. Winnipeg, Manitoba, February 20, 1943
An early life with alcohol led to a later life with God, and in between goalie Joe was mostly a backup in the NHL until he moved on to the WHA. Daley started with lowly Pittsburgh in 1968, but Les Binkley was number one there and Buffalo claimed Daley after two years. A year with the Sabres led to a year with Detroit, parked on the bench behind Roger Crozier, and that summer of '72 he signed with the Winnipeg Jets where he starred with the team, winning the valued Avco Cup in 1977. He settled in Winnipeg

and opened Joe Daley's Sports Collectibles. He was later inducted into the Manitoba Sports Hall of Fame.

DALEY, Pat
b. Maryville, France, March 27, 1959
Wine? Yes. Cheese? Yes. Lights, fashion, film, art, bridges, doggie doo on the sidewalks? Yes. But hockey players? No, that is not typical French fare. Nonetheless, Pat Daley made his way from France to Quebec to the National Hockey League, and after two slight, slight opportunities with the Jets in Winnipeg he got back on a plane and resumed his hockey career for many years, back in France.

DALGARNO, Brad
b. Vancouver, British Columbia, August 11, 1967
A guitar player off the ice, Dalgarno once performed "Friends in Low Places" with Garth Brooks at a concert at the Nassau Coliseum in November 1993. Before that, though, he was billed as the next Bob Nystrom after the Islanders drafted him 6th overall in 1985. Although he spent his entire 10-year NHL career with the team, this translated to just 321 games and only 2 full seasons. In fact, Dalgarno retired in 1989 after a fight with Joey Kocur. In that scrap, Dalgarno fractured his orbital bone, required surgery, and missed the rest of the season. He quit the game and started his own business as a fitness and health consultant, but rejoined the Isles the following year. His best games were spent on the team's Kid Line with Travis Green and Marty McInnis, though he retired for keeps in 1996. He moved to Toronto to beceome managing partner of Starshot Ventures, a marketing, communications, and design agency.

DALLMAN, Marty
b. Niagara Falls, Ontario, February 15, 1963
The bottom fell out of his career before he even had a chance to build a proper floor, but there was a silver lining that kept his career on stable footing. Dallman graduated from Rensselaer Polytechnical Institute (more commonly known as RPI). Although he was drafted by Los Angeles and offered tryouts with New Jersey, Pittsburgh, Calgary, and Vancouver, it was the Leafs that signed him to his first and only contract, in 1986. He played only 2 games with Toronto, but down on the farm in Newmarket he scored 50 goals in '87-'88. This AHL success never got him anywhere on the big team, though, and he moved to Europe and took advantage of his Austrian heritage, playing at the World Championships and the 1994 Olympics in Lillehammer as a member of the Austrian team. He later coached in the WPHL.

DALLMAN, Rod
b. Quesnel, British Columbia, January 26, 1967
Born in B.C. but raised in Saskatchewan, Dallman made a living and established himself as a fighter in a career that was almost exclusive of the NHL save half a dozen games. He had three minor penalties in three games in '87-'88 with the Islanders, incurred a fighting major and misconduct in his one game the following year with same, and fought in one of his two games with Philly in '91-'92. The end.

Bob Dailey

Frank Daley

Joe Daley

Brad Dalgarno

Rod Dallman

Napoleon Dame

DAME, Napoleon ("Bunny")
b. Edmonton, Alberta, December 6, 1913
d. unknown
This Dame burst onto the hockey scene in Kootenay in the 1930s, a decade that culminated with Bunny's appearance in the 1939 World Championships as a member of the Trail Smoke Eaters that claimed gold in Switzerland that winter. Bunny bounced east to Montreal for the '41-'42 season and then enlisted in the army. Upon his discharge in 1944, Dame hustled his hockey skills in Calgary until he retired in 1950.

DAMORE, HANK ("Lou Costello")
b. Niagara Falls, Ontario, July 17, 1918
d. May 12, 1994
A roamer and traveller, Damore played from Niagara to Verdun to Detroit to Fresno and Los Angeles, stopping only briefly in Madison Square Garden with the Rangers in '43-'44 where he scored one goal in four games. He later worked for the U.S. consulate in Canada.

DAMORE, Nick
b. Niagara Falls, Ontario, July 10, 1916
Smack dab in the middle of an eight-year stint with the Hershey Bears came Damore's only NHL twinetending moonlighting, on January 25, 1942. Mister Zero himself, Frank Brimsek, was supposed to start for the Bruins, as was his wont, but on this night he was injured and took to the sidelines. Enter Damore, and his Boston Bears rallied behind the rookie to defeat the Montreal Canadiens 7-3. Older brother of Hank, this was Nick's only wanderings on NHL ice.

Marc D'Amour

D'AMOUR, Marc
b. Sudbury, Ontario, May 29, 1961
It looked pretty good for a while there. The Flames signed him as an undrafted free agent and sent him to the farm in Moncton to play his way up. He split duties with Mike Vernon in '84-'85, and by season's end he had outplayed Vernon as number uno. Unfortunately for D'Amour, his greatest successes were already in the past, and Vernon's were still in the future. D'Amour was mediocre with Calgary the next year, then played a period in relief for the Flyers a couple of years later. That was all she wrote for this life in the NHL.

DAMPHOUSSE, Jean-Francois
b. Alexis-des-monts, Quebec, July 21, 1979
That goalie factory is at it again. Damphousse came out of Quebec hockey to be selected 24th overall by, unfortunately, New Jersey in 1997. The unfortunate part comes in the fact that Jersey has a number-one man. His name is Martin Brodeur, another product of the Q, and he starts about 70 games a year. The chances of Damphousse usurping Brodeur are none. But he did appear in half a dozen games in 2001-02 for the Devils, giving him a taste of NHL pucks for the first time.

DAMPHOUSSE, Vincent ("Vinnie"/ "The Poofer")
b. Montreal, Quebec, December 17, 1967
Son of Yvon, director of equipment for the Jerome Le Royer School Board in Montreal, young Vincent wanted to be a hockey player ever since he was a kid. He went off to play junior for Laval and was drafted at age 18 by the Leafs, stepping into the NHL fires just a few months later and getting an assist in his first game. Damphousse was an effective skater and passer, not the quickest or flashiest, not the strongest or most tenacious. But given the chance, he could move the puck and create scoring opportunities. In his rookie year he scored 21 goals and continued to improve in the coming years, though not always with the Leafs. As a representative of Toronto at the 1991 All-Star Game, Damphousse scored four goals and won the MVP award, but that fall Cliff Fletcher arrived in Toronto as GM and made a huge deal, the principal players being Damphousse to Edmonton and goalie Grant Fuhr to Toronto. He had an excellent year with the Oilers, but this, in turn, led to another trade, home to Montreal. There he reached his peak, scoring 40 goals one year, being made team captain, and helping the team to a surprising Stanley Cup win in 1993. But as his play deteriorated, he became a scapegoat and heard those nefarious boos from the fabulous Forum fans. He wanted out, and got his wish when the Habs shipped him to the quietest team in the league, San Jose. There, he could walk down the street in full uniform and people would think him a homeless maniac before they thought of him as a star player. Damphousse played his 1,000th career game (at one point he had a mini-Iron Man streak of 399) and hit the 1,000-point mark on October 14, 2000. His numbers continue to increase and his chances of another Stanley Cup continue to recede, and although this is a career not likely the stuff of which Hall of Fame induction is made, it is an admirable one all the same.

Mathieu Dandenault

Damphousse hit the 1,000-point mark on October 14, 2000.
VINCENT DAMPHOUSSE

DANDENAULT, Mathieu
b. Sherbrooke, Quebec, February 3, 1976
The youngest player on Detroit's back-to-back Stanley Cup teams in 1997 and '98, Dandenault became a reliable third-line player for Scotty Bowman's Wings. He didn't play in the '97 playoffs after dressing for much of the regular season, and the year after was in just three of the team's Cup games, Bowman choosing to ease the youngster into the

pressure cooker that is the playoffs. Nonetheless, the Detroit draft choice has been a regular for seven years in Motown, and his point production has increased steadily in that time.

DANEYKO, Ken
b. Windsor, Ontario, April 17, 1964

It's official. Ken Daneyko is the worst scorer in the history of the NHL. In March 2002, he set the record by going goalless in his 246th consecutive game, and kept on going and going for another 10 games until October 25, 2002, when he scored after 256 games. And all that time, he played for just one team – New Jersey. He's the only Devil to have played all playoff games in the team's history. He's played more games, more seasons, and has more penalty minutes than any other Devil. He once had a consecutive games-played streak reach 388, then a record among active players. He was part of the team's successful run for the Cup during the lockout-shortened season of '94-'95, the first championship in the team's victory. He played with tenacity, though early in the '97-'98 season his career came crashing down. It had been a long time coming. He had his first drink at age 13, and was a steady tippler by 15 when he left home to play junior. Throughout his NHL days, he continued to drink, but youth allowed him that ability. Then, on November 1, 1997, he entered the NHL/NHLPA's Substance Abuse and Behavioural Health Program for alcoholism, and missed the next three months while he straightened himself out. His decision to enter proved a major victory for both player and system, for he recovered and went on to have a fruitful career, winning the Cup again in the spring of 2000. And for the program, it proved that an open and honest relationship between player and management could lead to solutions, rather than barriers and possible tragedy. He screwed up, he admitted it, and he made good.

DANIELS, Jeff
b. Oshawa, Ontario, June 24, 1968

His dad was the director of operations of the Oshawa Generals, so hockey was in his blood. Jeff himself went on to play four years for the Gens, which led to being drafted by Pittsburgh in 1986. But once in the big time, Daniels had a tough time sticking around. Pittsburgh bounced him up and down, then swapped him to Florida for Greg Hawgood in March '94, and since then he's just continued to bounce, first with Nashville and more recently with Carolina, where he has enjoyed a measure of stability on the 'Canes.

DANIELS, Kimbi
b. Brandon, Manitoba, January 19, 1972

Here we go again. In Swift Current, Daniels scored 30, then 43, then 54 goals in 3 successive years, got to Philadelphia and scored once in 27 games. He played for Canada at the 1992 World Championships but went south to play minor pro in various leagues for the rest of his skating and shooting days.

DANIELS, Scott
b. Mistawasis, Saskatchewan, September 19, 1969

After winning the Calder Cup in 1991 with Springfield, Daniels entered the NHL with Hartford barely able

to keep his gloves on before starting a fight. In his first-ever game, he incurred 19 penalty minutes and over his brief career averaged nearly a fight's worth per game.

DANTON, Mike
(formerly Mike Jefferson)
b. Brampton, Ontario, October 21, 1980

He's still just a pup, but he's being reared in a fine kennel called New Jersey. The small centre came out of St. Mike's and Barrie in the OHL and has made only a brief appearance with the Devils, spending most of his time so far with the farm team in Albany. His most noteworthy move to date has been to change his surname from Jefferson to Danton, which he did in the summer of 2002. His attitude, though, has rankled GM Lou Lamoriello and cost Danton/Jefferson most of the 2002-03 season.

DAOUST, Dan
("Dangerous Dan"/ "Doo")
b. Montreal, Quebec, February 29, 1960

Daoust was never drafted despite being a scorer in the Q as a junior. Instead, Montreal signed him as a free agent, but after just four games decided to try him on waivers. Glen Sather in Edmonton claimed him, so Montreal withdrew Daoust and traded him to the Leafs. At first, the deal was that the Habs would get Toronto's 1st-round draft choice in 1984 if they wished (because they wanted to have Mario Lemieux), but instead settled for a third-rounder. In Toronto, Daoust became a feisty centre with wingers John Anderson and Rick Vaive, playing tougher and heavier than his 160 pounds. A mainstay with the Leafs for nearly eight seasons, Daoust left the team in 1991 when the Leafs refused to offer him a two-year contract (one year was as much as they felt they could commit). As a result, Daoust moved to Switzerland, where he played for many years before returning to the Toronto area to coach junior and make instructional videos.

DARBY, Craig ("Snoop")
b. Oneida, New York, September 26, 1972

He was from New York State, so it was no big dream of his to play for Montreal. Good thing, that, 'cause he played there for only 10 games in '94-'95 before the Habs traded him to a team that mattered, like the Islanders. But the Isles put him on waivers and the Flyers let him go and the Habs re-signed him and Nashville claimed him. Along the way, his great highlight was leading the AHL with 42 goals in '97-'98, the same year the Philly Phantoms won the Calder Cup.

DARCHE, Mathieu
b. St. Laurent, Quebec, November 26, 1976

He didn't get to the NHL the normal way, but then again he was, perhaps, smart enough to know that although he was a great player by society's standards, he wasn't a great player by NHL standards. Darche's older brother, J.P., is a snapper for Seattle in the NFL, and Mathieu went on to Choate down in Connecticut for high school where he played hockey, football, and golf. Recruited all over the place in the U.S., he spurned these offers and registered at McGill

Ken Daneyko

Kimbi Daniels

Scott Daniels

Dan Daoust

Michael Dark

Harry Darragh

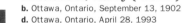

Cleon Daskalakis

Richard David

Bob Davidson

University in Marketing and International Business. During his four years in Montreal, he played hockey and football, and after acquiring his degree signed with Columbus, figuring to ease into the NHL with one of its weak expansion teams. He played nine games in 2000-01 and a few more the year after, and although he will likely not win any awards in the NHL, he has a degree to fall back on and has realized a dream. And, as ol' Blue Eyes crooned, he did it his way.

DARK, Michael
b. Sarnia, Ontario, September 17, 1963
Michael Dark and Mark Hunter were involved in a weird and crazy trade on June 15, 1985, that saw the two Montreal players go to St. Louis along with four draft choices, with five draft choices going the other way. It was the highest draft-choice trade in league history. It was with the Blues that Dark got into his only NHL games between 1986 and '88. From there, he was traded to Calgary but spent the next decade in the minors. In retirement, he returned to Sarnia and became director of a local hockey area owned by Dino Ciccarelli.

DARRAGH, Harry ("Howl")
b. Ottawa, Ontario, September 13, 1902
d. Ottawa, Ontario, April 28, 1993
One of the lightest players ever to skate in the NHL, Darragh won a Stanley Cup with the Leafs in 1932, his first of two seasons with Conn Smythe's team. Smythe had picked him up off waivers after Darragh suffered a serious leg injury the previous year and the Bruins all but gave up on him. He began playing in amateur leagues in his native Ottawa, eventually moving to Pittsburgh in 1923 and remaining with the club when it entered the NHL in '25. In an era of fierce hockey, he was considered the cleanest player in the game. During a 308-game career, Darragh accumulated just 50 penalty in minutes. After 1932-33 with the Leafs, Darragh played briefly in the IAHL before retiring from the game for good. He returned to Ottawa and worked for an agency that serviced refrigerators.

DARRAGH, Jack
b. Ottawa, Ontario, December 4, 1890
d. Ottawa, Ontario, June 25, 1924
Darragh was an oddity in that he played right wing but had a left-handed shot. Noted as one of the speediest players in the game, famous for his rushes from one end to the other, and owner of the best backhand shot of his time, Jack Darragh was one of the finest players of the early NHL. Like his brother, he was considered a clean and gentlemanly player. He refused to sign a pro contract with Ottawa when offered $15 a week in 1910, but when manager Pete Green upped the salary to $20 plus a pair of skates, the temptation was too great for Darragh to resist. From then until 1924, when he died of an appendicitis attack, he played only for the Senators, winning four Stanley Cups and scoring the Cup-winner in 1921, beating Seattle goalie Hap Holmes with – what else? – a high backhand. After the game, Holmes came into the dressing room saying, "I want to shake hands with Jack Darragh. That fellow isn't human." He took a year off, but when he came back the year after it was as though time had stood still. The Sens won the Cup again.

DASKALAKIS, Cleon
b. Boston, Massachusetts, September 29, 1962
After four years in goal for the Boston University Terriers, Daskalakis got a great chance to shine at his rookie training camp with the Bruins after signing as a free agent. Number-one man Pete Petters missed all of camp with an injury, giving the youngster the opportunity to show what he could do. He had won the prestigious Walter Brown Award in his last year of college as the best U.S.-born player in New England Colleges, but he failed to impress coach Gerry Cheevers, himself a former tender of the twine. During the regular season, Cleon played just eight games, and after two more brief stints with the B's was buried in the minors, never to return except as a spare goalie for the U.S. entry in the 1989 World Championships.

DATSYUK, Pavel
b. Sverdlovsk, Soviet Union (Russia), July 20, 1978
The Red Wings might well have the next-generation Sergei Fedorov in their lineup while the original is still in his prime. Datsyuk arrived in Detroit with little fanfare. He played in the Russian leagues but was by no means a star. Detroit, though, drafted him in 1998 and liked his potential, and in 2001-02 he started to show what the Wings had anticipated. Excellent speed and a good skater, he has many a move and goes to the net with confidence. He played the full season with the Wings and had 35 points, getting better and better each game. He also played for Russia at the 2002 Olympics in Salt Lake City, and a few months later was holding the Stanley Cup with the rest of his team. Definitely a player who could one day be a superstar in the NHL.

DAVID, Richard
b. Notre Dame de la Salette, Quebec, April 8, 1958
Three 50-goal seasons in the Quebec junior leagues translated into sweet, not-much-all in the NHL for David. He was drafted by Montreal in the late 1970s when the Habs won the Cup regularly, but instead of trying to make it with an unmakeable team he signed with Quebec in the WHA and stayed with the team when it entered the NHL in 1979. Incredibly, although he couldn't score in the big top, he had 51 goals in the AHL in '81-'82, his finest year of pro.

DAVIDSON, Bob ("Rugged")
b. Toronto, Ontario, February 10, 1912
d. Toronto, Ontario, September 26, 1996
He was born with a Leaf on his heart, lived his whole life under the Maple Leaf flag, and passed away one of the team's immortals. Davidson was the man who replaced Syl Apps as team captain from 1943 to '45 when Apps was at war. A natural, two-way player, Rugged was both a ferocious checker and part-time scorer, though his main job in the playoffs was to stop the other team's big guns. He won two Stanley Cups with Toronto (1942 and '45), and after retiring in 1946 became a coach for the farm team in Pittsburgh for two years. He then began scouting for the team, eventually succeeding Squib Walker in 1951 as the head scout and maintaining that position for the better part of 30 years. It was under his direction that the Leafs recruited Dave Keon, Bob Baun, Bob Pulford, and Frank Mahovlich, and built their 1960s dynasty.

Times changed once Harold Ballard took over. For no reason other than that Davidson represented the past glories of the team, Ballard fired him in 1979. He worked for the Colorado Rockies for two years, then the NHL's Central Scouting services for three more before retiring. In 1995, the new Leafs regime honoured Davidson with the Bickell Cup, the Leafs' team trophy rarely used in recent years to pay thanks for someone's contributions to the team. He died with a Leaf on his heart.

DAVIDSON, Gord
b. Stratford, Ontario, August 5, 1918
d. unknown
A war player for the New York Rangers, Davidson played on Broadway from 1942 to '44 while much of the regular defence was at war. His was a career by definition rooted in the American league, though even there he moved around more than somewhat. After his playing days, he made his summer job as a fireman a full-time job.

DAVIDSON, John ("J.D.")
b. Ottawa, Ontario, February 27, 1953
After a superb junior career in Calgary, Davidson was drafted 5th overall by St. Louis in 1973 and that fall became the first goalie ever to jump from junior to the NHL. A bright start gave way to a serious knee injury and an early end to the season, and the following year he was sent to the minors and the year after was dealt to the Rangers. He started on a team that was on the downturn, but after a few years Fred Shero moved in as coach and Davidson began to play like a number-one goalie while wearing the unique double-oh on the back of his sweater. A recurring back injury grew increasingly serious, and after two operations without much relief Davidson decided to retire. He began working for MSG Network, broadcaster of Rangers games, and it was in the booth that he found his true calling. Today, he is the number-one hockey analyst in the U.S., appears frequently on telecasts in his native Canada, and is a fixture on "Satellite Hot Stove" on *Hockey Night in Canada*.

DAVIDSON, Matt
b. Flin Flon, Manitoba, August 9, 1977
A right winger out of Portland in the WHL, Davidson was drafted by Buffalo in 1995 but never played with the Sabres. Instead, he spent three years with Rochester in the minors before being traded to Columbus. The change of scenery, however, had little impact on his career, though he did play a few games with the team in the coming seasons. Mostly, he was still a minor-league roster player.

DAVIDSSON, Johan
b. Jonkoping, Sweden, January 6, 1976
Brought up in the true tradition of Swedish hockey, Davidsson started in league play back home and represented his country at the 1994, '95, and '96 World Juniors, a fine accomplishment in international circles but a sign he wasn't developing quickly into an NHLer. He was drafted by Anaheim in 1994, but didn't play for the team until four years later. After one full season, he became a part-timer and was sent to the Islanders for another Swede, Jorgen Jonsson. Davidsson later returned home to play for HV71 Jonkoping.

DAVIE, Bob "Pinkie"
b. Beausejour, Manitoba, September 12, 1912
d. Kelowna, British Columbia, October 27, 1990
A life lived does not just consist of some 40 NHL games but also a player's contribution to his community over the years. Davie was a Manitoban all his life, playing hockey in Winnipeg before trying the pro game from 1933 to '36 with the Bruins. His career was cut short, however, by a terrible accident in a sawmill in 1938 on Hecla Island in Manitoba, after which Davie spent the rest of his life in his home province. He lived in Flin Flon from 1941 to '67 and was active in the Elks and Rotary clubs and chairman of the Manitoba Curling Association. He moved to Virden until 1975, working for the Lions Club and the MCA. As a coach, he was responsible for one of the most enduring house league innovations – the three-minute buzzer – to ensure all kids had equal playing time. He ended his professional life in Dauphin as a recreational adviser for the provincial government, and retired in 1978, one of the province's most beloved and loyal sons.

DAVIES, George "Buck"
b. Bowmanville, Ontario, August 10, 1922
April 4, 1948. Detroit 4, Rangers 2. That's the scoreline for Davies' only NHL appearance. He was with the Blueshirts, and that score eliminated them from the playoffs. Other than that, he had a lengthy career in the AHL with Providence, a top centre who had speed rather than size (5'6" and 165 pounds).

DAVIS, Bob ("Friday")
b. Lachine, Quebec, February 2, 1899
d. Vancouver, British Columbia, July 8, 1970
Davis played in the NHL on February 26 and March 3, 1933, for Detroit, two dates he remembered for the rest of his playing days. He had spent much of his time in Fort William, and after retiring he became a master mechanic for the CPR for 48 years, stationed mostly in Moose Jaw.

Gord Davidson

Johan Davidsson

After retiring he became a master mechanic for the CPR for 48 years.
BOB DAVIS

Bob Davie

Lorne Davis

Malcolm Davis

Evgeny Davydov

Jason Dawe

Bob Dawes

DAVIS, Kim
b. Flin Flon, Manitoba, October 31, 1957

Davis had a tough act to follow when he was called up by Pittsburgh in 1978-79. Really tough. He was expected to fill the cement-heavy skates of Dave "The Hammer" Schultz as the team's bad guy enforcer fighter goon animal. And because he proved he could score in the IHL, the Penguins also expected he'd toss in a few goals from his fists. But four callups over four years didn't give the Pens what they wanted, and Toronto acquired him and let him go almost as quickly. He went on to become the commissioner of the Manitoba Junior Hockey League.

DAVIS, Lorne
b. Regina, Saskatchewan, July 20, 1930

He was only 22 when his biggest thrill in hockey occurred, but that didn't stop Davis from loving every minute of his life with sticks and skates. He didn't play at all in the 1952-53 regular season, but he was called up in the playoffs and appeared in seven games with Montreal, winning the Stanley Cup over Detroit, the Habs' great nemesis during this period. Davis then appeared fleetingly in the NHL over the next three seasons before going down to the AHL for a career in the minors. Such was his reputation, though, that when Boston needed a defenceman for its run to the 1960 playoffs, it brought Davis up from Providence, even though he was known primarily as a winger. Sure enough, though, he partnered with captain Fern Flaman for 10 games, though ultimately the B's failed to qualify for the post-season. Davis was then reinstated as an amateur and turned to coaching, most notably with Muskegon. In 1966, he played for Canada's National Team at the World Championships, winning a bronze medal in his last full year as a player. He went on to scout for the Edmonton Oilers, and his name appears on the Cup throughout the 1980s for his bird-dog efforts for that great dynasty.

DAVIS, Malcolm "Mal"
b. Lockport, Nova Scotia, October 10, 1956

Strange career, his. Davis came out of university down east, signed with Detroit, and did the usual minor-league thing by scoring there and not scoring with the Red Wings. Buffalo signed him and it was more of the same until 1984, when he came to camp with an NHL psychology and an I'll-play-so-well-you-can't-demote-me attitude. He was coming off a 55-goal season in the AHL, an MVP year. It worked, and in 47 games he had 17 goals. He tied for the team lead with five game-winners, and everything looked slightly up. The next season, though, more minors and a brief callup. He was mad, left the team, was picked up by Los Angeles, but never played for the Kings. Instead, he went to Europe, and it was there he spent his remaining playing days.

DAVISON, Murray
b. Brantford, Ontario, June 10, 1938
d. Evergreen, Colorado, January 13, 2000

He came out of Kitchener-Waterloo to establish himself in the AHL, a big, burly defenceman who backed down to no one. Davison got his one and only NHL shot with Boston in 1965-66, and the Bruins were so taken with him they asked him to go to the farm in Oklahoma City and both play for and coach the team. He accepted the move, and in six years was near the top of the league five times. He produced such top players as Gerry Cheevers, Bernie Parent, and Wayne Cashman for the NHL, but resigned his position in 1971 when he saw no hope for becoming head coach of the Bruins. He later became coach and general manager again, and in December 1976 he returned to the ice as a player when the Blazers struggled. In one game against the Tulsa Oilers, he promised to let Tulsa coach Orland Kurtenbach shave his head if he lost. The Blazers won. Davison and a group bought the team at season's end, though he sold his stake a few years later to go into the securities business before retiring to Evergreen, Colorado, with his wife.

DAVYDOV, Evgeny
b. Chelyabinsk, Soviet Union (Russia), May 27, 1967

Davydov was a mainstay in Moscow, playing in the Soviet league when he was drafted by Winnipeg in 1989, and he was not able to join the team until after playing for the mother country in the 1992 Olympics in Albertville. In his first full season, he had an impressive 28 goals and the future for the left winger looked rosy, indeed. By early the next season, though, the picture had faded. His scoring stick wasn't working, and two trades in four months couldn't cure his woes. He spent some time in the minors, but without the lure of the NHL he chose to return to Europe to continue playing, which he still does, in Switzerland.

DAW, Jeff
b. Carlisle, Ontario, February 28, 1972

It might turn out that Daw is a one-game wonder, and if that proves to be the case his is a story of perseverance. His life in hockey was perfectly pedestrian – a junior stint at the provincial level leading to four years at the University of Massachusetts-Lowell. But when he graduated in 1996 at age 24, no team wanted him for the NHL. Over the years his rights were owned by Edmonton, Chicago, and Minnesota, but he always played his games in the minors. It wasn't until Colorado signed him that he got into an NHL game, during 2001-02 at the age of 30. To add icing to the cake, he recorded an assist in that game, but Daw has been in the minors again ever since.

DAWE, Jason
b. North York, Ontario, May 29, 1973

He won gold at the 1993 World Juniors for Canada and silver at the 1996 World Championships, but a career that started out so well seemed, in retrospect, so fleeting. Dawe had back-to-back 20-goal seasons with Buffalo, but when the Sabres traded him in 1998 the downward spiral of his fortunes began. He couldn't find the net, his teams were in disarray and losing badly, and he wound up in the minors.

DAWES, Bob
b. Saskatoon, Saskatchewan, November 29, 1924

Dawes was part of the Oshawa Generals team that won the Memorial Cup in 1943, and then he promptly put his career on hold and entered the army. After being discharged, he decided to try the pro game, though most of his immediate post-war playing was in the AHL. The Leafs and Habs called him up for the proverbial cup of coffee in four successive seasons, but his was mostly an itinerant career in the minors. He did play most of the 1949 playoffs, and as a result has his name on Toronto's Cup from that season. A defenceman by training, the Leafs moved him to pivot because of his ability on the faceoffs. A serious leg injury saw Dawes miss the entire 1952-53 season; he spent the year selling tickets at the Forum. He resumed his career, extending it until 1967 with various teams in Saskatchewan, then retired to open a service station that summer. Dawes spent 10 years with the Saskatoon Council for Crippled Children and later worked at a friend's carpet business until it went bankrupt. He retired, but maintained his home in Saskatoon.

DAY, Clarence "Happy"

b. Owen Sound, Ontario, June 14, 1901
d. St. Thomas, Ontario, February 17, 1990

As a kid, Day developed a habit for walking. He grew up in Owen Sound and played much of his league hockey in nearby Port McNicholl, about 8 km away. He routinely walked there and back and as a result developed strong legs that kept him going his whole life. He played senior hockey in Hamilton and then enrolled in the pharmacy program at the University of Toronto. While he played varsity hockey there he was discovered by Charlie Querrie, owner of the St. Pats, who knew right away this player could help his team. Day, though, was reluctant to turn pro until Querrie waved a $5,000 contract in front of him and promised he could still attend classes. Day made his debut on December 10, 1924, playing left wing alongside future Hall of Famers Jack Adams and Babe Dye. After a year he moved back to defence, where he played the rest of his career. He was known unflatteringly as Clarence the Clutch because of his ability to interfere and grab opponents' sticks without being penalized. Occasionally, a foe would let go of his stick, and the referee would see two in Day's hand and know what had happened. In 1926, at the start of just his third season, Day was named team captain, a post he held until 1937. He was a resilient player for his entire career with one exception. On February 2, 1928, a player stepped on the back of his leg and tore his Achilles tendon. It was a painful and debilitating injury that cost Day the rest of the season, though he did make a full recovery. When the Leafs acquired King Clancy in 1930, the two became defence partners and inseparable (and mischievous) friends. On ice, they were a terrific team, but any player finding his fedora cut to bits or the sleeves of his coat cut need look no further than that pair for the culprits. When the team

He retired to St. Thomas, Ontario, where he owned a woodmaking business that specialized in axe handles.
HAPPY DAY

moved into Maple Leaf Gardens, they christened the building by winning a Cup that first season, '31-'32. Amazingly, it was to be the only one of Day's playing career. During these years at the Gardens, he also ran Happy Day's Pharmacy, a store that survived a number of years until being replaced by Dick Dowling's Grill. Day played the final year of his career with the Americans in '37-'38 and then refereed for two years and coached in Toronto. He won the Memorial Cup with West Toronto, and in 1940 was named new coach of the Leafs after Dick Irvin left to try to fortify the crumbling Montreal franchise. Over the next 10 years, Day won 5 Stanley Cups as a coach, but none was more significant than the first, in 1942. The Leafs lost the first three games of the finals to Detroit and Day, realizing drastic action needed to be taken, benched two of his superstar veteran players – Gord Drillon and Bucko McDonald – and inserted two veritable rookies – Gaye Stewart and Bob Goldham. The shakeup worked, and the Leafs rallied to win the series and Cup 4-3, the only time such a comeback has been made in the finals. In the dressing room after game seven, Day dipped his finger into the champagne-filled chalice and sucked on it, his one and only taste of alcohol during his life. He coached the way he played and the players respected him because he skated hard alongside them, led the group in running, and participated in all the drills. He was famous for knowing the rule book verbatim, and when the Leafs won the Cup in 1947, '48, and '49, it marked the first time an NHL team had won three in a row. He became assistant GM to Smythe in 1950 and stayed with the team for seven more years before leaving after a fight with Smythe, who did not name him GM when he decided it was time to let others handle the team. It ended an association that started in 1927 when Smythe ran the team, one that carried from the rink to Smythe's gravel pits, where Day was treasurer and manager. Day was inducted into the Hockey Hall of Fame in 1961. He retired to St. Thomas, Ontario, where he owned a woodmaking business that specialized in axe handles, Elgin Handles. It was a profitable and successful operation that he later passed on to his son, Kerry.

DAY, Joe

b. Chicago, Illinois, May 11, 1968

Oddly, Day played parts of three successive seasons in the NHL in the early 1990s, each time for exactly 24 games. After stints with Hartford and the Islanders, though, he could find no more NHL takers and signed into the IHL, where he has been ever since. He never appeared in the playoffs, and in 72 regular-season games he scored only once.

Happy Day

Happy Day

Joe Day

Eric Daze

Billy Dea

Don Deacon

Barry Dean

DAZE, Eric
b. Montreal, Quebec, July 2, 1975

Time passes quickly, and all of a sudden a top prospect from 1993 has been in the league eight years and counting and has established himself as a solid scorer. In every full season he's played – all with Chicago – Daze has had at least 20 goals. He's not sensational; he's not a superb checker; he can't make the pinpoint pass. But he's a very consistent player whom any team would say yes to acquiring. He made his biggest mark at the 1995 World Juniors with Canada, winning gold, leading the team in goals, and being named the tournament's all-star right winger. On March 15, 1998, he scored four goals against Florida, and in his rookie season he finished second in voting for the Calder Cup behind Daniel Alfredsson.

DEA, Billy ("Hardrock")
b. Edmonton, Alberta, April 3, 1933

After a junior career with Lethbridge that wrapped up in 1953, Dea got into his first games in the NHL, with the Rangers, the next season. He spent the next two years in the minors, then played for Detroit and Chicago before beginning a lengthy drought outside the league. For 9 more seasons and 641 games, he dressed for the Buffalo Bisons until the Hawks gave him another chance in the 1967 playoffs. Along the way, he set an AHL Iron Man mark with his 526th straight game played, and late in the '66-'67 season he incurred his first career fighting penalty (his uncle, Murray Murdoch, was once the NHL's Iron Man). Then expansion came, and he was a free man. Pittsburgh took him, and later Detroit, but despite a long and rich career he played only 11 times in the playoffs. He coached the Junior Red Wings for two seasons and then became an assistant with the big club, though, in truth, he frequently ran the show. Through much of this time, he also ran a ladies' hair salon in Fort Erie, Ontario. A decade later, head man Wayne Maxner was fired and at last Dea was appointed head coach officially, a term that lasted just 11 games and 3 wins. More recently he has became a scout for the Florida Panthers.

DEACON, Don
b. Regina, Saskatchewan, June 2, 1913
d. Vancouver, British Columbia, August 1, 1943

Deacon's amateur career in the 1930s was an impressive dossier of Allan Cup and Memorial Cup appearances, but when he turned pro his claims to fame were mostly related to his time in the International Hockey League. He played 30 games with Detroit that decade, but besides those games was left to fend for himself in the "I" and later in the AHL before his untimely death. He was with the Canadian Army, stationed in Victoria, B.C., when he attended a small party at a friend's apartment. Deacon was leaning on the rail of the balcony when he lost his balance and fell 25 feet to the ground. He died a few hours later of a fractured skull and internal injuries.

DEADMARSH, Adam ("Sheepdog")
b. Trail, British Columbia, May 10, 1975

When Deadmarsh saw the Stanley Cup in the summer of 1996, the one he had spilled his guts for with his Colorado Avalanche teammates all season, he was not amused. He looked for his name on the engraving, and came upon "Deadmarch." He asked to have the error fixed, and the Hockey Hall of Fame complied, though traces of the error are still visible. Like Brett Hull before him, Deadmarsh is officially an American by hockey convenience. Born in B.C., he holds dual citizenship because his mother came from Spokane. Nonetheless, Team USA approached him in 1993 about playing for the Stars 'n' Stripes at the upcoming World Juniors. He preferred Canada, his home and native land, but was told there was no room for him. He sealed his fate and joined the weaker team from the States, with whom he played three WJCs. Later, he represented the U.S. at the 1996 World Cup and 1998 Olympics in Nagano, though he still considers himself Canadian. On the NHL front, the Avs traded him to Los Angeles in the deal that brought Rob Blake the other way, even though Deadmarsh had become a solid member of the community, gastronomically, anyway. He had released his first food product, called Deadmarsh Deli Dills, and later another, Deadmarsh's A-18 Rocky Mountain Steak Sauce, though no word on how his trade west affected Denver sales.

He represented the U.S. at the 1996 World Cup though he still considers himself Canadian.
ADAM DEADMARSH

DEADMARSH, Ernest "Butch"
b. Trail, British Columbia, April 5, 1950

Call him a tough guy, but don't call him a goon. Say he can take care of himself, but don't say he goes looking for trouble. He's no policeman, he only plays the game hard. Call it what you will, Deadmarsh was a physical presence throughout the 1970s in both the WHA and the NHL. In fact, he played in both leagues in 1974-75, first with the Kansas City Scouts and then with the Vancouver Blazers. In his last four years, all in the WHA, he skated for five teams.

DEAN, Barry
b. Maple Creek, Saskatchewan, February 26, 1955

Barry Dean and Bryan Maxwell played junior in Medicine Hat together. They became good friends, and when Maxwell got married, Dean was his best man. They played in the WHA together, Dean with Phoenix and Maxwell with Cleveland. One night, the two went into the corner together, Dean falling. His arm caught another player's skate, and Dean began bleeding profusely until Maxwell put pressure on the arm to staunch the flow. His radial artery was cut 80 percent and Dean required surgery, but it was the fast work of his friend and opponent that saved him a gob of blood. Dean recovered fully after surgery and went on to play in the NHL for much of three years, with Colorado and Philadelphia.

DEAN, Kevin
b. Madison, Wisconsin, April 1, 1969
Drafted in 1987, Dean has survived, hung in there, stuck around, been there and back, and made it here, there, and everywhere in one form or another. After graduating from the University of New Hampshire, he played in the minors for a few years before finally making an impression in New Jersey in the '94-'95 season. It wasn't much of an impression, but over the next four years he became an ever more needed player, and in 1998-99 he played the entire year with the big team and not a second down on the farm in Albany. Since then, he has travelled with his stick in one hand and a suitcase in the other. But he has survived.

DEBENEDET, Nelson
b. Cordeno, Italy, December 31, 1947
Out of the post-war euphoria was born young Nelson in a small Italian town far away from hockey-mad Canada. But Debenedet made his way over at a young age and played the game with Michigan State and then the University of Toronto, where he was doing a doctorate in urban forestry, a paradoxical subject if ever there was one. He turned pro and played a few games with Detroit before a rash of injuries forced Pittsburgh to acquire him, and while with the Pens he moved up from defence to forward and scored a few goals. He was never part of the long-term plans of the team, though, and after a brief time in the minors he returned to his studies.

DEBLOIS, Lucien
b. Joliette, Quebec, June 21, 1957
Deblois was drafted 8th overall by the Rangers in 1977, a shrewd move in the eyes of then-GM John Ferguson. "We took Deblois over [Mike] Bossy," he explained, "because we felt that Bossy didn't check enough for the NHL." True enough, perhaps, but no amount of checking from Deblois could replace the guaranteed 50 goals a season Bossy provided. To be fair, Deblois scored 188 goals in 4 years of junior in the QMJHL, where Bossy also played, so he showed signs of scoring. In his rookie season, Deblois scored a respectable 22 (Bossy had 53), peaking 7 years later with 34 with Winnipeg. But Deblois was a peripatetic player, wearing 7 different sweaters (the Jets' twice) in a 993-game career. He won a Stanley Cup with the surprising Canadiens of 1986 and played for Canada at the World Championships in 1981, but his was a career marked by resilience rather than a burst of greatness. He went to work as a broadcaster for RDS in Quebec and then became a scout and assistant coach with the Nordiques in 1993. He later served as a pro scout for the Mighty Ducks of Anaheim.

DEBOL, Dave
b. St. Claire Shores, Michigan, March 27, 1956
A beautiful skater and clean player, Debol lacked the tenacity and single-minded drive to push himself into a long NHL career. He had two chances with Hartford in its first years (1979-81) but his scoring couldn't compensate for defensive weaknesses and that on-ice laissez faire. He played three times for the U.S. at the World Championships, where his speed and lack of size were advantages rather than disadvantages, though his career ended too soon in the eyes of some of his coaches. He went on to become a sales rep for a sporting goods business.

DeBRUSK, Louie
b. Cambridge, Ontario, March 19, 1971
Big Lou has thrown a few in his day, and he's not a baseball pitcher. Nor are his hockey skills necessarily what got him to the NHL. No, siree. Large and strong, he got to the bigs with his fists, first with Edmonton in 1991 and then with a short series of teams since, fighting all the way.

DECOURCY, Bob
b. Toronto, Ontario, June 12, 1927
In the third period of the Boston-New York game of November 12, 1947, Rangers goaler Charlie Rayner was forced out with an injury and young Decourcy came in to a close game. Sadly, by game's end, the score was no longer close, as he surrendered five goals in his brief outing, the only one of his brief career.

DEFAZIO, Dean
b. Ottawa, Ontario, April 16, 1963
Defazio came and went quickly, spending 22 games with the woeful Penguins in 1983-84 before playing for a few more years in the minors.

DEFELICE, Norman
b. Schumacher, Ontario, January 19, 1933
Imagine this: You're playing goal, no mask, and a shot hits you on the head and knocks you unconscious. A teammate, seeing your predicament, falls on the puck in the crease. Doctors revive you, get you on your feet, and the next thing you know you're facing a penalty shot. That's what happened to Defelice when he played for Washington in the Eastern League in 1955. A career minor-leaguer, he got his brief chance at glory in '56-'57 when Bruins starter Terry Sawchuk went down with exhaustion (goalie's euphemism for shock and depression). His 10-game stint ended January 20, 1957, when Toronto's Jimmy Thomson scored from centre ice to give the Leafs a 3-2 win. Defelice continued to play until 1970, his last team being the Galt Hornets in Senior hockey, a team he coached the next year. His bench bossing career ended, however, when he suffered a heart attack during the Eastern section of the Allan Cup finals. After recovering, he worked in public relations for the Ontario Jockey Club for seven years, then turned to construction. He moved to St. Catharines and became general manager for Transit Mix Concrete and Bass Block and Building Supply based in Beamsville, Ontario.

Kevin Dean

Nelson Debenedet

Lucien Deblois

Bob Decourcy

Norman Defelice

193

Dale DeGray

Denis DeJordy

Matt Delguidice

Xavier Delisle

Andy Delmore

DeGRAY, Dale ("Digger")
b. Oshawa, Ontario, September 1, 1963

Lacrosse was in his blood – his grandfather was Hall of Famer Kelly DeGray – but as a teen Dale switched from the grass and stick game to the ice and stick game. He caught a break in 1980 after being drafted by the Oshawa Generals. He figured he'd be playing Junior B that year, but when the Gens' star defenceman Rick Lanz made Vancouver in his first training camp, a spot opened up and DeGray stepped right in. He himself was drafted by Calgary in 1981 (a remote 162nd overall) but never figured in coach Terry Crisp's plans. A seventh defenceman at best, he was traded to Toronto for a mid-round draft choice, and for a season he looked to catch on in the bigs. Coach John Brophy tried to give him ice time, even moved him up to forward for a while, but again DeGray didn't fit into the team's plans and was left available in the Waiver Draft. Brief stints in L.A. and Buffalo closed out his NHL career, but DeGray would not be so easily defeated. He continued to play for the better part of a decade, mostly in the AHL and "I," until getting into coaching in the United league.

DeJORDY, Denis
b. St. Hyacinthe, Quebec, November 12, 1938

While growing up in Jonquière, Denis played forward and his brother, Roger, was the goalie, but they soon reversed positions and Denis became one of the brightest prospects in all of Quebec. The Habs, with right of first refusal for all French-Canadian players, passed on both brothers DeJordy, and Denis became part of the Hawks system and Roger part of the Detroit chain. Roger became known as a goal scorer in junior and the minor pros but never got a chance to play in the NHL. Denis, meanwhile, became the top goalie prospect, though his career seemed anti-climactic as a result. Over the course of a half-dozen years, he emerged as Chicago's goalie of choice, but when Tony Esposito developed into a superstar, DeJordy became not much more than a reliable backup. He was traded to Los Angeles, then Montreal and Detroit, never to emerge as the star he had looked like as a teen. In his last game, with Detroit in '73-'74, he allowed four goals in one period of play and was promptly returned to the minors. In December '74, though, the Wings hired him as a goalie coach, the first time such a job had been made full-time in the NHL. Smart with his money, he also ran Denis DeJordy Sports Inc. in Dauville and owned two apartment buildings as a further source of income.

DELGUIDICE, Matt
b. West Haven, Connecticut, March 5, 1967

Well, he was given a chance by Boston in the early 1990s, but he didn't make the most of it and as a result played his career in the minors. In the summers, he also played roller hockey for a number of years.

DELISLE, Jonathan
b. Ste. Anne-des-Plaines, Quebec, June 30, 1977

Needless to say, the NHL team most interested in a marginal pro was Montreal, but although the Habs drafted Delisle in 1995, he has played but a game for the team. The right winger is more renowned for his fighting ability than scoring touch, but, hey, every team needs a tough guy, so why shouldn't Montreal's be a home-province boy?

DELISLE, Xavier
b. Quebec City, Quebec, May 24, 1977

X marks the spot for the only NHLer whose first name starts with the 24th letter of the alphabet, born on Victoria Day in Quebec's capital city. Delisle played in the Q and then moved down to Tampa to play twice with his drafted team, though his time in the minors was later punctuated by a brief stint with Montreal, the team that most recently owned his NHL rights.

Del MONTE, Armand ("Dutch")
b. Timmins, Ontario, June 3, 1927
d. unknown

Nicknamed Dutch by his younger brother, Armand always preferred the friendlier, more accessible moniker. He craved hockey from infancy to adulthood, and along the way he had one night's taste of the NHL, in 1945-46, with Boston. Del Monte was just 18 when he made his NHL debut, but thereafter played only in the minors. He was even pressed into service as a referee in the AHL one time, in 1952, when the man who was supposed to have the whistle, Jerry Olinski, missed his flight to an important Pittsburgh-Cleveland game. Del Monte was in town on his way down from Cleveland to Marion of the IHL, and acquitted himself well in his whistle-tooting assignment.

DELMORE, ANDY
b. LaSalle, Ontario, December 26, 1976

Delmore did what no defenceman before or since has ever done – he scored 74 goals in a single game. God's honest truth. Okay, the game took place on Canada Day, 2001, when the Red and White team broke the world record for longest hockey game ever played, but a record's a record and Mr. Guinness will no doubt acknowledge as much. As for the real hockey world: In the early summer of 1995, Delmore did what Don Cherry begs every non-superstar teenager not to do – he attended the NHL's Entry Draft, held that year in Edmonton. There he sat, all afternoon, as 234 names were slowly, slowly called over a long afternoon and evening. Not once was the name Delmore uttered. He went back to junior, in Sarnia, and played superbly, blossoming into a tall, tough, and offensively skilled defenceman. The Flyers signed him as a free agent, and in the 2000 playoffs he scored two goals, including the winner in OT, to get the Flyers back into their series with Pittsburgh, a series they went on to win. Delmore overcame his horrific disappointment, persevered, and has proved himself an NHL-calibre player.

DELORME, Gilbert
b. Boucherville, Quebec, November 25, 1962

He arrived in Montreal in 1981 to a chorus of praise and an orchestra of expectation, but Delorme delivered only a symphony of mid-tones during his two and a half years with the Habs. He later travelled to four other NHL cities and became better known as a reliable, if unspectacular, defenceman, but when he broke his leg in the summer of 1991 his NHL career was effectively over.

DELORME, Ron ("Chief")

b. North Battleford, Saskatchewan, September 3, 1955

A Cree raised on a reserve in Saskatchewan, Delorme almost quit on hockey before ever making it to the big tent. He played junior in Lethbridge with more likely NHL candidates Bryan Trottier and Tiger Williams, but after being drafted by lowly Kansas City, Delorme opted for Denver of the WHA. The year ended in confusion as the franchise moved to Ottawa and then folded, and Delorme retreated to his grandfather's cabin in the bush with no connections to the outside world, convinced he was through with the puck game. But when he came back to civilization, he found that the Colorado Rockies (successors to the Scouts franchise) had been trying to get him. He finished the year with Colorado, and became an effective player. His trademark in his first three years was to fire a bow and arrow at the opposing goalie after scoring a goal, but when Don Cherry became coach in 1979-80 the new boss, who hated such showboating, outlawed the practice. Delorme went on to play another four years with Vancouver, respected as an unselfish team player who was most effective playing left wing, his off side. He later became a scout in the NHL

DELORY, Valentine "Val"

b. Toronto, Ontario, February 14, 1927

Named because of his birthday, Delory knew he wasn't a bona fide NHLer – and he never made a fuss about it. He played a few years in the minors in the northeastern States, getting into one game with the Rangers in 1948-49. He retired from hockey altogether in 1953 and the next year joined the New York Fire Department, where he brought his Toronto roots to bear by starting a firemen's hockey league. He stayed with the NYFD for 30 years, becoming district chief by the time he retired, his NHL days long past.

DELPARTE, Guy

b. Sault Ste. Marie, Ontario, August 30, 1949

Unless you were a Hall of Famer, being drafted by Montreal in 1969 was akin to hockey death. Delparte was not a Hall of Famer. He was drafted in 1969. It was an event akin to hockey death. His only NHL season came seven years later when Colorado signed him. Besides that, it was all minors, all the time.

DELVECCHIO, Alex ("Fats")

b. Fort William, Ontario, December 4, 1932

There is not one player in the long history of the NHL who can boast Delvecchio's record of having played 24 years in the league, all with the same team. His streak of loyalty began on March 25, 1951, when he was called up from Oshawa to play a game for the Red Wings, and ended on November 7, 1973, when he retired as a player to take over as coach for the then-floundering team. He developed with the Generals under former Detroit great Larry Aurie, and after starting the next year, '51-'52, with Indianapolis he was soon recalled and never saw the minors again. At first Delvecchio formed a line with Metro Prystai and Johnny Wilson, and in his first full year the Wings won the Stanley Cup. He became known as a playmaker, someone who could read a game situation and recognize what to do quickly based on what he saw the other team doing. In the fall of 1952, he replaced Sid Abel on the Production Line, centring Gordie Howe and Ted Lindsay. The team went on to win the Cup again in 1954 and '55, but in '56-'57 Delvecchio suffered the one and only injury of his career. He missed 22 games with a serious ankle injury, and during the rest of his career missed only 21 more games, testament to his strength and resilience in a league full of bigger and tougher men. He was also named to the Second All-Star Team for both centre ('52-'53) and left wing ('58-'59), only the third player after Abel and Dit Clapper to make the team at two positions during their careers. Delvecchio became team captain in 1962 and remained so until he retired. He watched the team go from Cup champions in the 1950s to contenders in the '60s to embarrassing misery in the 1970s. He was called Fats because of his round face and warm, gentle smile, though he played with a plumpness in his later years that belied a hockey

Ron Delorme

> **Delvecchio left the game second to Gordie Howe in games played (1,549), assists (825), and points (1,281).**
> **ALEX DELVECCHIO**

player's typical physique. He won three Lady Byng Trophies during his career (1959, '66, '69) in honour of his gentlemanly play. Delvecchio later played on another version of the Production Line with Frank Mahovlich and Howe, and in '68-'69 the threesome combined to score 118 goals, a league record for one forward line. But as the team went into decline, Delvecchio remained one of the few remaining bright spots. His skating and playmaking were counted on more than ever, but so was his leadership. As a result, he decided to retire early in the '73-'74 season to become the team's coach, but during his four off-and-on years the team never performed much better. He was fired in 1977, the same year he was inducted into the Hockey Hall of Fame. Delvecchio left the game second to Gordie Howe in games played (1,549), assists (825), and points (1,281). He formed Alex Delvecchio Enterprises, which manufactured and engraved signs, plaques, and plates for all purposes. On November 10, 1991, his number 10 was hoisted into the rafters of Joe Louis Arena to thunderous applause, as Fats joined the pantheon of Red Wings greats in perpetuity.

Guy Delparte

Tony Demers

Pavol Demitra

Nathan Dempsey

Jean Paul Denis

DeMARCO, Ab ("Deacon of the Deke")
b. North Bay, Ontario, May 10, 1916
d. North Bay, Ontario, May 25, 1989
Like so many small-town NHLers, DeMarco returned whence he came. The North Bay native was a terrific prospect, signing with Chicago in 1938 and playing his first games that season. But after a few more games the following year, DeMarco found himself languishing in the minors until a trade took him first to Toronto and then to Boston toward the end of '42-'43. He played three full years with the Rangers after the Bruins sold him to Broadway for cash, and after that he was back in the minors. He was renowned for positioning his wingers carefully at faceoffs, and then winning the puck cleanly to the exact spot where one was stationed. In 1952, DeMarco returned to the Bay, playing for the local Trappers of the NOHA until he was 41. He then retired and settled into the community as a businessman, working in advertising sales until he retired from the working world, all the while watching his namesake son make a name for himself in the NHL. He also coached for a number of years, mostly in and around North Bay, but in Paisley, Scotland, for '57-'58. He entertained those around him with a superb impression of Groucho Marx, and whenever he could he joined the Flying Fathers, portraying the Flying Nun or Sister Shooter. He had bypass surgery in the early 1980s and made a full recovery, but a few years later he suffered a heart attack just moments after toasting his son and new daughter-in-law at their wedding reception. He died a few days later.

DeMARCO, Ab, Jr.
b. Cleveland, Ohio, February 27, 1949
While li'l Ab was being born, his dad, big Ab, was chasing pucks for the Cleveland Barons in the AHL. His Littleness grew up with hockey in his blood and a commensurate ambition to dad, and Ab Junior went on to play 344 NHL games in the 1970s. He also played for Canada at the 1969 World Championships, and later played briefly in the WHA and in Switzerland.

DEMERS, Tony
b. Chambly Basin, Quebec, July 22, 1917
d. 1997
Extraordinary. The judge wanted to give him 25, then reconsidered and made it 15. The year was 1949. Demers had played parts of six years in the NHL from 1937 to '44, then finished his career in the minors. Three times he scored more than 50 goals in the Quebec Senior league, but nothing – nothing! – could have anticipated the events of September 15, 1949. At a party with his girlfriend, he drank to excess, got into an argument with her, and killed her. On November 21, the judge sentenced him to 15 years in the penitentiary. The previous season, he had been voted the most gentlemanly player in the league.

DEMITRA, Pavol ("Pav")
b. Dubnica, Czechoslovakia (Slovakia), November 29, 1974
Improbably drafted at 227th in 1993, Demitra has proven to be a bona fide NHLer and late-round gem. He has played at all levels of international competition for Slovakia, and after Ottawa traded him to St. Louis he blossomed into an excellent scorer who consistently gives his team 20 goals per year. Additionally, he is a fine two-way player, and his gentlemanly play earned him the Lady Byng Trophy in 1999-2000.

DEMPSEY, Nathan ("Greyhound")
b. Spruce Grove, Alberta, July 14, 1974
He had been the property of the Leafs since 1992, when the team drafted him very low (try 245th on for size), but he's seen only 20 games of NHL play from the Toronto blueline. This has confused Dempsey, because he's talented and has a good shot. He's done what the Leafs have asked; he's paid the price developing on the farm. But the team just won't use him. More than 400 games with St. John's later, he's still barely a spare part with the team, and his time and patience are running out. He knows he can do more and be an NHL regular, but when he got his chance with Chicago in 2002-03, he played well but not superbly.

DENIS, Jean Paul ("Johnny")
b. Montreal, Quebec, February 28, 1924
In a career that began during the war, Denis played until 1962, primarily in Quebec. He had 2 brief stints with the Rangers that totalled 10 games, but he never scored an NHL goal despite lighting the lamp with success and consistency wherever else he played.

DENIS, Louis "Lulu"
b. Vonda, Saskatchewan, June 7, 1928
The guy with the French name didn't come by it honestly, being born a Prairie boy. He made up for this geographic discrepancy by moving to Montreal as a small boy, and it was in that city he learned the puck game. The Canadiens used him for three games from 1949 to '51, but other than that his forte was the Montreal Royals in the Quebec league. He was one of the QHL's leading goalgetters by the time he retired, having tallied more than 160 in his career, which ended in early 1961.

> **He entertained those around him with a superb impression of Groucho Marx.**
> **AB DEMARCO**

DENIS, Marc
b. Montreal, Quebec, August 1, 1977
No goalie could possibly match the junior record of Denis. Two gold medals at the World Juniors (in '96 and '97), goaltender of the year in all of Canadian hockey in 1997, 1st-round draft choice, to Colorado, in 1995. He apprenticed briefly under his hero, Patrick Roy, when he got to the Avs, and then was traded to Columbus where he was fed to the wolves night after night. It was tough, but he got plenty of work at the highest level, and Denis, though still developing, could prove to be one of the stars of the next generation of goalies. He took a favourable step in that direction in 2002-03 when he played a record 4,433 minutes with Columbus, more than any other goalie in a single season.

DENNENY, Corb
(usually "Dennenay"/ "Flash")
b. Cornwall, Ontario, January 25, 1894
d. Toronto, Ontario, January 16, 1963
A superb athlete, Corb excelled at lacrosse as a child, signing a pro contract at age 14 in Cornwall and tying the world track and field record for 100 yards in 1916 during the CNE. He played hockey in the winter, moving to Toronto to play both sports by the early 1910s. When the NHL was formed in 1917, Denneny joined the Toronto Arenas and scored the Stanley Cup-winning goal the next spring. Four years later, the team now called the St. Pats, he again scored the Cup-winner and his speed and grace were acknowledged by all. Corb moved out west to play before returning to Toronto and later moving to Chicago, ending his career in the AHA in 1931. His two years with the Minneapolis Millers were impressive enough that he was later elected to the Minneapolis Sports Hall of Fame. He became playing coach of the Toronto Tecumsehs, a pro team playing out of Maple Leaf Gardens, but that league didn't last long. Denneny remained in Toronto, becoming head masseuse at the YMCA, eventually assuming the position of director of health services. Writers often misspelled his name with an "a" before the "y" but Corb liked it so much he kept it. His brother, Hall of Famer Cy, maintained the Denneny spelling.

DENNENY, Cy
(sometimes "Dennenay")
b. Farran's Point, Ontario, December 23, 1891
d. Ottawa, Ontario, October 12, 1970
In the earliest years of the NHL, there was no finer left winger than Cy Denneny. He was born near Cornwall, Ontario, in a town later flooded by the St. Lawrence Seaway, and he got his first chance as a hockey star in Cornwall. He turned pro with Toronto in 1914 in the NHA but two years later was sent to the Senators, with whom he played when the NHL began operations in 1917. Denneny played on a line with Jack Darragh and Frank Nighbor, and in that first season finished second to Joe Malone with 36 goals, his best year (Malone had 44). He played all but the last of his 12 years in the NHL with Ottawa, helping the team win 4 Stanley Cups through the 1920s. He led the league in goals with 22 in '23-'24 and much of his intimidating shot came from two factors. One, he was the first to experiment with a curved stick. He would soak the blade in water and was able to bend it to whatever degree he wanted. And he was known to be able to curve shots, something no one before or since has been able to do. He finished his career as a playing coach with Boston in '28-'29, winning a final Cup along the way. He later coached Ottawa, in '32-'33, to a dismal 11-27-10 season. In between, he worked as a referee and coached locally in Ottawa. His brother, Corb, was a longtime player, principally with Toronto, and Cy was elected to the Hockey Hall of Fame in 1959.

DENNIS, Norm
b. Aurora, Ontario, December 10, 1942
A team leader, Dennis had his fleeting days in the NHL sun with the St. Louis Blues during the immediate post-expansion years. He had been Montreal property, but the slim chances of him making that team ensured his departure. He later captained teams in the Western and American leagues before retiring.

DENOIRD, Gerry (sometimes "Jerry")
b. Toronto, Ontario, August 4, 1902
d. Toronto, Ontario, October 8, 1989
Denoird came out of Aura Lee in Toronto to play for the St. Pats in the 1922-23 season. He played just 17 games with the NHL team and then returned to amateur play for a short time. He became a referee in the early 1930s, and in one notorious episode he was pushed to the ice by a player. He hit his head and had to be taken to hospital. He later became an employee of Richardson Securities and was active at the Kew Beach Lawn Bowling Club in Toronto.

DePALMA, Larry
b. Trenton, Michigan, October 27, 1965
In 1984-85, DePalma played 65 games for the New Westminster Bruins of the WHL, scoring 14 goals, 16 assists, and 30 points. The next year, with Saskatoon in the same league, he scored 61 goals and 112 points. And he had 232 penalty minutes. He still didn't get drafted. The

Marc Denis

Cy Denneny

Larry DePalma

Denneny remained in Toronto, becoming head masseuse at the YMCA.
CORB DENNENY

Bill Derlago

Philippe DeRouville

Gerry Desaulniers

Matthieu Descoteaux

Joffre Desilets

North Stars signed him as a free agent and in '86-'87 he had but 15 points. It was his 219 penalty minutes that kept him around. But not for long. He played in each of the next five seasons, with the Stars, Sharks, and Penguins, but never for very long and always because of his fighting. More common were his years spent in the "I." He retired in 1996 with 408 penalty minutes in 148 career NHL games.

DERLAGO, Bill ("Billy D.")
b. Birtle, Manitoba, August 25, 1958
Boy, there was a ton of talent in the boy from Birtle. Trouble was, fans didn't always see it. In junior, with Brandon, Derlago scored 234 goals in 192 games. His shot was incredible, his potential unlimited. Vancouver felt lucky to get him 4th overall at the 1978 Amateur Draft. But in his first year with the Canucks, Billy D. blew out a knee, and when he came back there was a tempting trade offer from Punch Imlach in Toronto. Derlago and Rick Vaive, two terrific prospects, were sent to the Leafs for Tiger Williams and Jerry Butler. It was one of the more favourable, lopsided deals in Toronto history, and the only good trade Imlach made during his second tenure as Leafs GM. Derlago flourished in Toronto even while he was slowly destroying himself. His tremendous skills were offset by lethargy in practice, lack of commitment during the year, a smoking habit, and a poor attitude. Nevertheless, he scored 30 goals 4 times and 40 once, but when the Leafs traded him to Boston for Tom Fergus, his will vanished. He played for three teams in two years, went to Europe for a season, and retired at age 29. A waste. He landed a job selling cars in Toronto, and began to drink heavily. His friends and former teammates tried to help him and offer him work, but always with the condition that he go cold turkey. He has spurned all offers.

DeROUVILLE, Philippe
b. Victoriaville, Quebec, August 7, 1974
He was a better goalie than most, but not good enough to be classed among the elite for very long. DeRouville played most of three games with Pittsburgh in the 1990s during his minor-league career. He had come out of the Quebec juniors, and played a game for Canada at the 1993 World Juniors.

DESAULNIERS, Gerry
b. Shawinigan Falls, Quebec, December 31, 1928
d. unknown
A centre who came out of Laval to play senior hockey in Quebec with the Montreal Royals, Desaulniers was given brief tryouts with the Habs on three occasions in

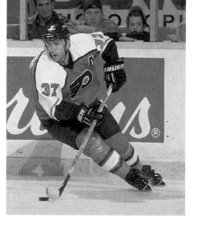

His mother, Gisele, was a hairdresser in Rouyn.
ERIC DESJARDINS

the early 1950s. During the eight total games, he managed but one assist, a far cry from the many goals he had scored in the senior loop. Desaulniers played his whole career in Quebec before retiring in 1960 as a playing coach with Trois-Rivières. The next year he an his wife were in a serious car accident.

DESCOTEAUX, Matthieu
b. Pierreville, Quebec, September 23, 1977
So far, Descoteaux has to be considered a bit of a draft bust, or else Edmonton made a mistake. Either way, the Oilers selected him 19th overall in the first round of the 1996 draft. Yet he spent his first five years in the minors, going to Montreal in a small-player trade, and playing only five games with the Canadiens. Teams hope to do more with a first rounder than five games' worth of NHL play.

DESILETS, Joffre ("Dizzy")
b. Capreol, Ontario, April 6, 1915
d. Renfrew, Ontario, November 30, 1994
Desilets grew up in Toe Blake territory and made his NHL debut with the Habs in '35-'36 a year after Blake joined the Canadiens. However, Joffre failed to impress, as they say, and after three seasons was traded to Chicago for Louis Trudel before the start of '38-'39. Dizzy exacted a measure of revenge in the first Montreal-Chicago meeting, scoring two goals (including the game-winner) for his new team. After two years, he joined the army (the Canadian Fusiliers), playing hockey for the Winnipeg Army team that lost the Allan Cup to the Ottawa Commandos. He later finished his career playing in Renfrew, where he moved after retiring from civilian life.

DESJARDINS, Eric ("Rico")
b. Rouyn, Quebec, June 14, 1969
In the old days, Desjardins would have been a fixture on the Montreal blueline for 20 years. He had a great junior career in Granby, played for Canada in two World Juniors in 1988 and '89, and was drafted by the Habs in 1987. But after six years with Montreal, during which time he established himself as one of the best young blueliners, the Habs traded John LeClair, and Gilbert Dionne to Philadelphia for Mark Recchi and a draft choice. Montreal used that choice to select…Martin Hohenberger. Right. Since then, Desjardins had played in the World Cup and Olympics and become one of the best defensive defencemen in the game. He stops every puck that comes near him, and his strong positional play allows him always to be between the puck and his goalie. He later became captain of the Flyers when Eric Lindros

left the team. His mother, Gisele, was a hairdresser in Rouyn. When Eric was seven, she divorced her husband and raised three children on her own, a fact Eric credits with making him disciplined, tough, and, indirectly, a great defenceman.

DESJARDINS, Gerry ("Bigger"/ "Desi")
b. Sudbury, Ontario, July 22, 1944

One of eight children who grew up with less rather than more, Gerry was a survivor first and foremost. His father worked in the mines in Sudbury, a fate no man wishes on his children and a career he eventually would give up for fresh air, a 400-acre farm near Noelville, and a life away from black lung disease. Gerry played goal from childhood on, eventually becoming property of the Canadiens before the team traded his rights to Los Angeles. With the Kings, he co-wrote a book called *Rookie Goalie* with writer Bill Libby, and the day it was released Desjardins was traded to Chicago. He went from west coast goalie star to, quite simply, "Tony Esposito's backup." Fortunately, the Islanders claimed him in the Expansion Draft, and he began '74-'75 in the WHA until Punch Imlach signed him for his Buffalo Sabres. For two years, Desjardins was the main man, and in 1977 he was the winning goalie in the All-Star Game. A few days later, he was struck in the eye by a deflected puck and was nearly blinded. Crazily, he played once in the playoffs later that year, but off-season surgery for cataracts helped only slightly. After three games the next season, he knew his career was over. He later worked for Pat Stapleton's hockey instruction company called Fundamentals in Action.

DESJARDINS, Martin
b. Ste. Rose, Quebec, January 28, 1967

He came out of junior hockey in Quebec to play eight games with les Canadiens in 1989-90, but Desjardins's career was no NHL walk in the park. He had a tough go of it even in the minors, and it wasn't until he went overseas that he truly found his niche.

DESJARDINS, Vic
b. Sault Ste. Marie, Michigan, July 4, 1898
d. November 1988

He was known as a clever and reliable two-way player in Eveleth during the 1920s, when there was no professional hockey league in the U.S. outside the NHL. He led the USAHA in points in 1927-28. He got two chances to make it in the National league, the first coming with Chicago in 1930-31. The Hawks went to the finals that year before losing to Montreal, and the next year, with the Rangers, he again went to the finals, this time finishing runner-up to Toronto. Despite his scoring fame in the amateur ranks, he scored not once in those 16 playoff games. Desjardins finished his career in the AHA.

DESLAURIERS, Jacques
b. Montreal, Quebec, September 3, 1928

Here was a defenceman who could do anything. His fans, who included opponents and coaches in the Quebec league, said he was the closest thing to Doug Harvey or Red Kelly. He could skate, hit hard, clear the front of the net, move the puck, and create chances on offence. Yet two games with the Canadiens

in '55-'56 was all he ever got out of the NHL. He was a perennial all-star in the minors, and had he been around for expansion in 1967, he no doubt could have proved his big-league worth. He never got the chance.

DesROCHERS, Patrick
b. Penetanguishene, Ontario, October 27, 1979

The goaltending in Phoenix is pretty solid, so the chances of DesRochers playing any more than the odd game are, for now, remote. He appeared in five games for the Coyotes in 2001-02, but has made his mark in Springfield as a fine custodian of the cage. Nonetheless, the team is hoping he will be their goalie of the future, though for now that distinction – goalie of the present, that is – goes to Sean Burke.

DEULING, Jarrett
b. Vernon, British Columbia, March 4, 1974

The career minor-leaguer is not just a thing of the past, an instance from Original Six days of a player who never gets much of an NHL chance. Deuling is active and living proof. He played 15 games with the Islanders in the 1990s, but continues to play in the AHL even though his chances of a callup to the NHL are almost non-existent. It's a living; it's a love; it's a way of life. The NHL is just the added bonus.

DEVEREAUX, Boyd
b. Seaforth, Ontario, April 16, 1978

There was a substantial problem when Devereaux signed with Detroit as a free agent on August 23, 2000. He had worn number 19 during his three years in Edmonton because his favourite player was Steve Yzerman, but when he got to the Wings, well, Yzerman had his own number! Devereaux took 21 and began his career anew with one of the dominant teams of the 1990s. He won a gold medal with Canada at the 1997 World Juniors, scoring two game-winning goals in the elimination round before joining the Oilers. Scoring, though, wasn't his forte as much as strong positional, two-way play, and those are the qualities he has tried to bring to the Winged Wheel of Motown.

DEVINE, Kevin
b. Toronto, Ontario, December 9, 1954

Devine certainly piled up the penalty minutes given that he wasn't very big at all. Despite being drafted by the Leafs in 1974 after an excellent career with the Marlies, he gave sentiment and tradition a pass when the WHA put a contract under his nose, and stayed there until 1979 when that league was absorbed by the NHL. But he wasn't able to join the vintage league at that stage and had to accept playing in the Central league for most of his days. The exception was a two-game callup to the Islanders in '82-'83, the year they won their third of four straight Cups.

de VRIES, Greg ("Devo")
b. Sundridge, Ontario, January 4, 1973

After the Avalanche won the Cup in the spring of 2001, de Vries got to spend a day with the hallowed trophy that summer. He took it home to Sundridge to share with family and friends, then included it in a city parade and helped raise money for the local Sundridge hockey program. He's nobody's superstar, but he is

Gerry Desjardins

Martin Desjardins

Jarrett Deuling

Boyd Devereaux

Tom Dewar

Michel Deziel

Ed Diachuk

Harry Dick

Ernie Dickens

reliable and his name is on the Cup. De Vries was one of the few players to leave U.S. college hockey to play junior in Ontario, and he spent the first part of his career with Edmonton before moving to Nashville and then Colorado.

DEWAR, Tom
b. Frobisher, Saskatchewan, June 10, 1913
d. Calgary, Alberta, July 23, 1982
Most often, the player who appears in the NHL for but the briefest of times does so at the beginning of his career and then goes on to play in the minors forever after. Dewar reversed the process. He came out of Moose Jaw in the early 1930s and kicked around in senior hockey for the longest time leading up to the war. His only NHL games came in 1943-44 with the Rangers when he was already 30 years old. That was his last season of professional hockey. He had settled in Calgary in 1940, and after his playing days returned there, spending his remaining working life with North American Life.

DEWSBURY, Al ("Dews")
b. Goderich, Ontario, April 12, 1926
There were three important junior teams in Toronto during the Original Six years – the Marlies, St. Mike's, and Toronto Young Rangers. The latter was the poor sister of hockey's developmental family, yet it produced players who could overcome adversity and make it to the NHL. Dewsbury was a case in point. The team used to practise at Maple Leaf Gardens ... at four o'clock in the morning, and players had to re-use tape because there was no budget for such a luxury item. Nonetheless, the Red Wings liked what they saw in Dewsbury and put him with the farm team in Omaha, where he played with Gordie Howe. He played parts of three seasons with the Wings, winning the Stanley Cup in 1950 before going to Chicago in a huge nine-player deal that summer. He spent half a dozen years in the Windy City and later was reinstated as an amateur so he could play for the Belleville McFarlands, the team that won gold for Canada at the 1959 World Championships. Dewsbury retired at the end of that season, settled in Toronto, and managed his own company, the Audio Universal Hearing Aid Company, for nearly 30 years.

DEZIEL, Michel
b. Sorel, Quebec, January 31, 1954
It's incredible how a guy like Deziel – long forgotten in the annals of pro hockey – once scored 92 goals and 227 points in one season of junior. Yet, he snuck into one playoff game with Buffalo in the spring of 1975 and that was it. The Sabres went on to the finals that

Dewsbury settled in Toronto, and managed his own company for nearly 30 years.
AL DEWSBURY

year before losing to Philly, and Deziel quickly faded to the AHL and out.

DHEERE, Marcel ("Ching")
b. St. Boniface, Manitoba, December 19, 1920
d. Manitoba, November 2002
After making his NHL start and finish in 1943 with les Canadiens, Dheere played another decade of the pro game in lesser leagues right across the continent.

DIACHUK, Ed
b. Vegreville, Alberta, August 13, 1936
Diachuk played the majority of his career in Edmonton, first in junior, then pro in the WHL, before being given a 12-game shot with Detroit in 1960-61. The left winger was, at best, a third-line player who was tough rather than skilled with the puck offensively, and that was his only time in the NHL.

DICK, Harry
b. Port Colborne, Ontario, November 22, 1920
d. Ottawa, Kansas, December 1, 2002
Considered the best all-round rugby player ever produced by the Owen Sound area, Dick translated his abilities to the hockey rink, where he became known as a hard hitter, a "bad man," and a tough guy that every rink other than his own despised. He learned much of what he knew from Bert Corbeau, former star and friend, on whose yacht he worked as a teenager. His youthful promise, though, gave way to adult disappointment as he turned into a decent player leaning toward fighting as a hockey career. He knocked around in the minors until 1943, when he joined Canada's war efforts, getting his only NHL chance with Chicago after he was discharged from the army. He played minor pro until 1955, at which point he ended up in Kansas City, working with kids' programs, coaching youth teams in the city, and refereeing locally. Later he became a colour commentator for radio broadcasts of Kansas City Blues games in the Central League before settling into a career as a superintendent of a construction company in nearby Overland Park.

DICKENS, Ernie
b. Winnipeg, Manitoba, June 25, 1921
Usually just in the shadows, Dickens was there, just off to the side of fame and glory. He was an important part of Toronto's 1942 Cup win, the one in which the Leafs came back from 3-0 to win game seven against Detroit. After the series, he joined the army and returned to the Leafs for the end of the '45-'46 season when the team failed to make the playoffs after winning the Cup the

year before. And he was part of the massive trade that sent five Toronto players to Chicago for Max Bentley. Dickens finished his career with the Hawks, a team that never made the playoffs in the four years he was there.

DICKENSON, Herb
b. Hamilton, Ontario, June 11, 1931

There are many more eye injuries in NHL history than most people know about. Dickenson is but one such story. During the warmup at Maple Leaf Gardens on November 5, 1952, he was struck in the eye and never played again. Initially, he was taken to a Toronto hospital and remained there for many weeks. Doctors said he couldn't play again that year, but they were hopeful he could resume his career. The eye, however, never regained enough sight to be of use to him, and Dickenson, just 22 and a top Rangers prospect, was done. He had started the previous year in Cincinnati, playing on a formidable line with Buddy O'Connor and Jean Denis. He scored the game winner in his first game with the Mohawks, and so impressed management that he was called up to New York for the last half of the season. He made the team full-time at camp in 1952. In the off-season, he was a cattle exporter, and he returned to the farm after his injury. He helped at his father's farm in Yonkers, New York, where he also rode trotters.

DICKIE, Bill
b. Campbellton, New Brunswick, February 20, 1916
d. Pointe Claire, Quebec, December 23, 1997

His only NHL game came the night of February 5, 1942, when Dickie replaced Sam LoPresti in goal for Chicago and went out and beat Montreal 4-3. Beyond that, however, he was considered the finest goaler ever to come out of the Maritimes. He attended Mount Allison University and led his team to two intercollegiate and Senior B championships, the first time any university completed that double victory. He later won consecutive Senior A titles with different teams and in 1941 took the Sydney Millionaires to the Allan Cup finals. Shortly after that game with the Black Hawks, Dickie retired and took a job with Allied Chemical of Canada, settling in Pointe Claire, Quebec. He was inducted into the New Brunswick Sports Hall of Fame in 1991 and Campbellton Sports Hall of Fame six years later.

DIDUCK, Gerald ("Dids")
b. Edmonton, Alberta, April 6, 1965

Although Diduck has played nearly 1,000 games in the NHL, he never won a Stanley Cup or did something tremendous. As a result, history might remember the Diduck name because of Judy, his Team Canada sister. Over his lengthy career with eight teams, he was a reliable defenceman and tough guy above all else. His sister, meanwhile, won gold at the World Championships with Canada on a number of occasions and helped develop a national program second to none. Gerald retired in 2001 quietly and anonymously, without any gold around his neck or Cup ring around a finger.

DIETRICH, Don
b. Deloraine, Manitoba, April 5, 1961

Sign of the times. In 1984, Dietrich was all set to play for Canada at the Olympics, but he was ruled ineligible because he had played in a handful of NHL games with Chicago. Ironically, he played another handful the next year with New Jersey, and those two handfuls together represented his entire NHL career. He later played in Europe for a few years before retiring.

DILL, Bob ("Shorty"/ "Killer Diller")
b. St. Paul, Minnesota, April 25, 1919
d. St. Paul, Minnesota, April 16, 1981

Dill got his cup of coffee with the Rangers during the war years, a scrapper the team wanted to use so what few stars the Rangers had wouldn't get pushed around so much. One of the few Americans to make it to the league by that time, he played 76 games on Broadway, but one in particular made Killer Diller famous forever. One evening in 1944, against Montreal, Elmer Lach and Joe Scherza got into a tangle. Dill moved in to help Scherza and Rocket Richard made it a foursome. Accounts vary from this point on. Dill's version is that after a short set-to, he and Richard went to the penalty box. He called the Rocket a name, and received a punch and three stitches as a response. Others tell it like this: Richard knocked Dill out cold on the ice. When he got up and went to the box with Richard, they went at it again and the Rocket knocked him unconscious a second time. Dill played in the USHL for a number of years afterwards, and Dill began coaching and later scouting for Chicago once his playing days were over. He and the missus also had a busy home life, rearing nine children in St. Paul, the city of his birth and his USHL team. During his hockey days, he also played AAA baseball in the summer with the Minneapolis Millers (he later became team manager). During the war, he joined the U.S. Coast Guard, though within a year he was discharged because of an asthma condition. After his scouting days were over, he became a wholesale liquor salesman and public relations man for Griggs Cooper Company in St. Paul, and in 1979 he was

Herb Dickenson

He and the missus had a busy home life, rearing nine children in St. Paul.
BOB DILL

Gerald Diduck

Don Dietrich

Bob Dillabough

Cecil Dillon

Gary Dillon

Rob DiMaio

Bill Dineen

inducted into the U.S. Hockey Hall of Fame. He successfully battled his own fight against alcohol and in 1982 ran for office for the post of 4th Ward City Council seat, though he lost the election. Up to his death from liver cancer he had been raising money for the completion of a lodge at Mariucci Camp Confidence, a home in northern Minnesota for developmentally challenged children.

DILLABOUGH, Bob
b. Belleville, Ontario, April 27, 1941
d. Elliot Lake, Ontario, March 1997
He was one of the fastest skaters of his day. His day was the 1960s, his teams a potpourri of ancient (Detroit, Boston) and brand-spanking new (Pittsburgh, Oakland). The speed didn't translate into goals, only trades, and Dillabough moved into the WHA briefly when that league opened in 1972.

DILLON, Cecil ("Ceece")
b. Toledo, Ohio, April 26, 1908
d. Meaford, Ontario, November 13, 1969
Dillon played all of the 1930s with the New York Rangers, and by the end of the decade he had become one of the top scorers in team history. He led the club in goals three times and in points three times, and his pinnacle came in the 1932-33 season as he took the team to a Stanley Cup. In that year's playoffs, he led the league with 8 goals and 10 points. Dillon had five 20-goal seasons and was named the First Team All-Star at right wing in 1937-38. He was also a clean player, being penalized only 105 minutes in his 10 years in the NHL. Although born in Toledo, he moved to Thornbury, Ontario, as a small boy and it was in that part of the world that he learned the game. After retiring, he returned to Thornbury to work for a phone company.

DILLON, Gary
b. Toronto, Ontario, February 28, 1959
The younger brother of Wayne, and a terrific scorer and skater who could not shake the "too small" tag, Gary played for George Armstrong and the Marlies in the mid- to late -1970s. He and John Anderson were one-two in scoring, and when Anderson graduated to the Leafs, Dillon scored 57 goals in his final year. But after a year in the Central League, all he could muster was a 13-game stint with Colorado in 1980-81, his only time in the NHL.

DILLON, Wayne ("Tommy")
b. Toronto, Ontario, May 25, 1955
Wayne was the oldest, Brian was a leading scorer for the Oshawa Generals, and young Gary was almost certainly going to be the best of the hockey-playing Dillon boys.

But Brian never made the big show and Wayne, not Gary, ended up the best. At 18, he signed a contract with the Toronto Toros in the WHA, a three-year, $150,000 contract that stipulated he live at home and attend grade 13 classes in the afternoon at Wexford Collegiate in Toronto. But after two excellent years of hockey, Wayne was lured to the NHL (the opposite of the norm during the WHA days) by a whopping seven-year, $1.4 million offer from the New York Rangers. He arrived on Broadway a 20-year-old superstar on the horizon, the toast of the town, the newest Blueshirt hero. Cut to three years later. Forty-three goals in 216 games. The Rangers, disillusioned, sold Dillon to Birmingham of the WHA (formerly … the Toros). It was a marked step down. The next year, a few games with the Jets, then to Switzerland for a season, and a trip to the AHL to hammer home what Dillon well knew by this time – his glory days were over. Now 26, he retired and entered the phys ed program at York University. High school teaching was his final destination, less glamourous but also less devastating than the NHL.

High school teaching was his final destination.
WAYNE DILLON

DiMAIO, Rob
b. Calgary, Alberta, February 19, 1968
Everything was letter perfect for DiMaio leading up to the NHL. He won a gold medal with Canada at the World Juniors in 1988. A few weeks later he won a Memorial Cup with Medicine Hat and was named tournament MVP. He won a Calder Cup in the AHL during his time starting out with the Islanders, but his time in the NHL has been both long and without event. He's been traded and claimed and exposed and demoted, but mostly he's just hung in there admirably with a succession of teams that need a utility right winger. And that's not so bad.

DINEEN, Bill
b. Arvida, Quebec, September 18, 1932
A terrific high school athlete, Dineen played four years with St. Mike's before turning pro with the Detroit Red Wings in 1953. Ironically, his best season was his rookie year, 17 goals and 25 points, and he won Stanley Cups in both '54 and '55 with the Wings. But by 1958 he had passed out of the NHL and settled in to a lengthy career in the minors, notably in the AHL and WHL. He maintained a place in hockey, though, coaching in the AHL for years, coaching for Houston and New England in the WHA, and from 1991 to '93 taking control of the Philadelphia Flyers. However, his greatest accomplishment is one of siring rather than playing. His five sons were all hockey players of note – Gord, Kevin, Shawn, Peter, and Jerry – and three made it to the NHL – Gord, Kevin, and Peter.

DINEEN, Gary
b. Montreal, Quebec, December 24, 1943

Dineen's days in hockey were counted almost entirely outside the NHL, but that count grew sizable during his many years in the game. He was one of a few players to skate for both St. Mike's and Neil McNeil in the early 1960s when that program changed schools, and from there he joined Canada's National Team, playing in two World Championships and the 1968 Olympics in Grenoble. He played four games with Minnesota in '68-'69 and then went to the minors, where his career took a turn. He retired as a player in 1971 to become coach and general manager of Springfield in the AHL, at 27 the youngest ever to do so, after captaining that team to the Calder Cup that spring. But after a year, he and owner Jack Kent Cooke couldn't get along and Dineen quit. He continued to live in the area, though, and taught hockey to kids for a year. In 1973, he was named coach and general manager of the Springfield Olympics, a team in the New England Junior Amateur Hockey League, and won the Wallace Cup with that team twice. Midway through the '76-'77 season, he was named coach of the Springfield Indians.

DINEEN, Gord
b. Quebec City, Quebec, September 21, 1962

Which one is he? His dad was Bill, and his brothers were Peter and Kevin. Gord started out with the Islanders during their dynasty years, though he was a small player in that glorious organization. In all, he played just 528 games over 13 years in the league because he was often in the minors, but he made his mark wherever he went and he was always wanted somewhere. After bowing out of the NHL in 1995, he continued to play in the IHL for several years.

DINEEN, Kevin
b. Quebec City, Quebec, October 28, 1963

All through his teen years into his two years playing at the University of Denver under coach Ralph Backstrom, Dineen had been a defenceman. But when he was playing for the Canadian Olympic team the coaching staff wanted to use his smaller size but great speed to better effect, so they moved him up to forward, where he spent the rest of his playing days. One of five hockey-playing sons of Bill Dineen, Kevin was drafted by Hartford, where his father had coached and on his father's advice. The son didn't disappoint his father, averaging 33 goals his first 6 years with the Whalers (1984-90) and doing extraordinary amounts of charity work in the city. He became Hartford's most popular athlete and in 1987 after returning home sick from the World Championships, was diagnosed with Crohn's disease. Since then, diet became his first priority in life, yet, amazingly, he has played some 1,200 games in the NHL. He was traded to the Flyers midway through '91-'92, then back to Hartford four years later, and on to a series of teams toward the end of his career. He won silver at the '85 Worlds and was also on one of Canada's all-time great teams, the 1987 Canada Cup-winning squad. Early in the 2002-03 season, he knew the end was near and decided to go out on top rather than as a hanger-on. He ended with Columbus but remained with the team in the front office, a veritable rookie executive after 19 years in the NHL.

DINEEN, Peter
b. Kingston, Ontario, November 19, 1960

His first NHL game was this far away from happening, but in the end it was some seven years in the coming. Drafted in 1980 by Philadelphia, Dineen went to the Flyers camp that fall and looked ready to make the team. But in the final exhibition game against Montreal, he blocked a Serge Savard slapshot, broke a bone in his leg, and spent the rest of the season in the minors after recovering. The next year, the Flyers recalled him, but he sat and sat and never dressed for a game. Then the travelling began, trades, demotions, signings. It wasn't until he went to the Kings in 1986 that Los Angeles put him in 11 games. Three years later, Detroit gave him another opportunity, but he again suffered a bad injury that forced him out for most of the year, a shoulder problem that eventually led to his retirement the year after.

DINGMAN, Chris
b. Edmonton, Alberta, July 6, 1976

How would you like it if this happened to you? You start your career in Calgary, do an okay job as an up-and-comer, a kid, nothing more. The Flames send you on to Colorado, and you couldn't be happier. This is the land of Sakic, Forsberg, Roy, and Foote. This is a Cup team. Sure enough, on June 9, 2001, the team wins the Cup. Then, 15 days later, equipment still wet, bruises still on the leg and soreness still in the bod, the Cup-winning team trades you to Colorado on draft day. Bummer. But at least Dingman was there for the big show, once, and perhaps only once for all time. But once is better than nunce.

DINSMORE, Chuck ("Dinny")
b. Toronto, Ontario, July 23, 1903
d. Toronto, Ontario, December 5, 1982

Dinsmore played for the once-mighty Aura Lee team in Toronto as a teen before joining the Montreal Maroons in 1924. He was a small centre and not much of a scorer, but he formed an effective line with Batt Phillips and Sam Rothschild a year later in helping the team win the Stanley Cup. Dinsmore retired after the next year to coach a city team in Montreal, but he returned to the Maroons fold for a few games in 1929-30 before calling it quits for good.

DION, Connie
b. St. Remi de Rinqwick, Quebec, August 11, 1918

At 5'3-1/2" Dion was the smallest man in hockey. Good thing he was a "pipe and hemp" man ("goalie" to laypersons). All set to embark on a pro career in 1940, Dion joined the army and played hockey in the military ranks for two and a half years when the army took over sponsorship of the Cornwall club. When he came out, he joined Detroit, sharing duties with Normie Smith and Jimmy Franks until December 10, 1945, when he was sent to Indianapolis and a guy named Harry Lumley was called up. He remained in the AHL for most of his career, though in 1949 that almost came to an end when Bobby Frampton of Cincinnati stepped on the back of Dion's net and cut him so deeply doctors feared he would never play again. Dion retired for good in 1951 to assume

Gary Dineen

Gord Dineen

Kevin Dineen

Chuck Dinsmore

Connie Dion

responsibility for the family's lumber business back in Asbestos, the town for which he also wrote a weekly sports column during his playing days (he also wrote an 8,000-word essay on the art of goaltending). He later managed the local arena. One of 13 children, he never drank or smoked and was a paradigm of perseverance.

DION, Michel
b. Granby, Quebec, February 11, 1954

As a teenager, Dion was a better baseball than hockey prospect. In 1971, at age 17, he was signed by the Montreal Expos as a catcher, and played a year for the West Palm Beach Expos in the Florida State League. Ultimately, he returned to hockey, and his successor behind the plate turned out to be Gary Carter. Dion played in the WHA for five years, then signed with the Quebec Nordiques when they joined the NHL in 1979. His career came crashing to a halt the night of December 10, 1980. Midway through the second period of a game against Boston, after giving up a fourth goal, Dion stormed to the bench, threw his catcher and blocker down and said he'd had it. The next day, the Nordiques suspended him, and a week later he was put on waivers. After a brief stint with the Winnipeg Jets, he landed on his feet again with Pittsburgh, thanks to coach and former goalie Eddie Johnston, who liked what he saw in Dion even though he knew Dion couldn't see all he thought he saw. Johnston sent him to an eye doctor, and sure enough Dion needed glasses. After four years with the Penguins, Dion retired. Although he tried a brief comeback with the Edmonton Oilers, he refused to play in the minors and instead moved to Rye, New York, and took up golf, hoping to earn his tour card eventually (he never did).

Michel Dion

DIONNE, Gilbert
b. Drummondville, Quebec, September 19, 1970

Nineteen years younger than his Hall of Fame brother, Marcel, Gilbert inverted the famous Roch Carrier story about the hockey sweater as a kid growing up in Quebec. While all the other boys he played street hockey with wore the famous sweater of the Montreal Canadiens, Gilbert wore what he called the hideous purple and yellow colours of the Los Angeles Kings, the team Marcel had played for so many years en route to becoming the third all-time leading scorer in NHL history. Although taller and faster than his brother, Gilbert simply couldn't match Marcel for skill and hockey sense, yet how cruelly ironic that, in a career that lasted just 223 games, Gilbert won a Stanley Cup with the '93 Habs, a feat Marcel failed to accomplish over 18 years and 1,338 games!

Gilbert Dionne

DIONNE, Marcel ("The Little Beaver")
b. Drummondville, Quebec, August 3, 1951

Almost uncontested, Dionne can lay claim to title of best player never to win a Stanley Cup. In fact, despite his amazing Hall of Fame career, he never came even remotely close to the silverware. He was a scoring sensation in junior with St. Catharines and was drafted 2nd overall by Detroit in 1971. He made the terrible Wings at his first camp and scored 28 goals as a rookie. In all, he played four years with Detroit, years that were both frustrating and rewarding. It was clear pretty quickly that he was the brightest star on a non-playoff team, and he proved his worth as both scorer and playmaker. He eventually became team captain, and in his final year had 121 points, including an NHL-record 10 short-handed goals. A contract fight, though, resulted in his signing with the L.A. Kings in the summer of 1975, and just like that the Wings lost their best player and the Kings gained a superstar. Dionne spent the next 12 years in LaLaLand, exceeding 100 points in 7 of those years and 90 points in 3 others. He had six 50-goal seasons and centred the Triple Crown Line, one of the highest-scoring threesomes in the game. With wingers Charlie Simmer and Dave Taylor, Dionne was the most consistent point producer in the game after Wayne Gretzky and Peter Stastny. In fact, he won the scoring title in '79-'80 despite having 137 points, the same number as Gretzky, because he scored more goals. He also won the Lester Pearson Trophy that season, for the second straight year,

He was, of course, inducted into the Hockey Hall of Fame and soon after began an association with the Hall that came out of Marcel Dionne Enterprises.
MARCEL DIONNE

and played in eight All-Star Games. Dionne had been a rookie invitee to Team Canada's 1972 camp, but his international career began for real in 1976 at the Canada Cup tournament. He also played at the 1981 Canada Cup and at four World Championships, and that last fact irked Dionne the most. To play at the WC was an honour, of course, but it was one accorded players whose teams were not in the playoffs, and Dionne found himself on the outside looking in all too often. In fact, in his 18 years, he played in just 49 post-season games. (By comparison, Gretzky played in 208.) Dionne ended his career with two seasons in New York, retiring in 1989 after accepting a demotion to the IHL at one point. When he was done, his numbers were second all-time only to Gordie Howe: 731 goals, 1,040 assists, 1,771 total points. The numbers were staggering and seemed to add up so quickly, but the truth was that playing in Los Angeles was anonymity personified. He was, of course, inducted into the Hockey Hall of Fame three years later, and soon after began an association with the Hall that came out of Marcel Dionne

Enterprises, a company he set up to sell promotional products. Through the HHOF, Dionne sells authentic Honoured Members merchandise and memorabilia, a noble enterprise in an often nefarious culture. Through this relationship, Dionne ensures that profits of signed pucks, sweaters, etc. go directly to the players, and by buying directly from him through the HHOF Web site fans are guaranteed authentic wares.

Di PIETRO, Paul ("Rocky")
b. Sault Ste. Marie, Ontario, September 8, 1970
He had a great talent for scoring, but at 5'9" and 180 pounds his best chance to show his stick skills was in Europe. Not to say that he didn't give the NHL his all. He did. In fact, he had one great playoffs, in 1993 with Montreal, scoring eight goals and helping the Habs to an improbable Cup that spring. The next year was his only full season in the league, though, and he scored just 13 goals. It wasn't until he got to Switzerland three years later that his goal production picked up. He moved to Milan and helped the Vipers win the national championship in Italy in 2002-03.

DiPIETRO, Rick
b. Winthrop, Massachusetts, September 19, 1981
This is pretty cool. DiPietro is a goalie. He made his NHL debut on January 27, 2001, a 2-1 win over Buffalo, *and* he recorded an assist in the game! Only the seventh goalie ever to earn a point in his first game. He's also the answer to another trivia question: Who was the first goalie ever selected 1st overall in the NHL Entry Draft? Mike Milbury, Islanders GM, put DiPietro in the record books when he chose him first in 2000. It'll be a while yet before we see how visionary or wasteful that selection was for the team.

DIRK, Robert
b. Regina, Saskatchewan, August 20, 1966
Dirk hit the magic 400-game mark in the NHL and then went down to the minors a happy man. A giant of a defenceman, he played from 1987 to '96 with five teams and then took to coaching in the United League, and the WCHL.

DIVIS, Reinhard
b. Vienna, Austria, July 4, 1975
On October 15, 2002, Divis became the first Austrian-born goalie to start in an NHL game, for St. Louis. He had made a brief appearance in relief the previous year, but the start marked an exciting page in Austria's brief hockey history, a rare moment at such a high level of play. During that previous season, Divis also played for his country at the 2002 Olympics in Salt Lake City and he has extensive international experience. Simply being drafted a lowly 261st overall by St. Louis was a big deal back home. Starting an NHL game, though? Historic.

DIVISEK, Tomas
b. Most, Czechoslovakia (Czech Republic), July 19, 1979
The new thing for a European to do is go home if he isn't going to play in the NHL. Divisek played in just two games for the Flyers in 2000-01, and three more the following year. He spent most of his first three years buried in the minors, so rather than continue in that vein, he signed with Pardubice in Czech league play while the Flyers maintained his NHL rights should he ever return.

DJOOS, Per
b. Mora, Sweden, May 11, 1968
The best modern Europeans come to the NHL to star in the premier league, while the second tier come over for a tryout and return whence they came rather than stick it out in the minors. Djoos is of the latter camp. He gave the Detroit Red Wings and New York Rangers a shot in the early 1990s, played for a bit in the AHL hoping to get back to plane travel, and when his air miles remained steady at zero he went home to play Swedish league hockey.

DOAK, Gary
b. Goderich, Ontario, February 26, 1946
Growing up, all Gary Doak wanted to do was play hockey. He began his career in the Detroit organization, then started to move around the league, in large part due to an almost annual serious injury. He began '66-'67 on the shelf with a broken leg, missed most of '68-'69 with mono and a bad back, banged his knee up in '71-'72, broke his other leg the next year, and smashed his collarbone two years later. He smashed his cheekbone in 1978, and had countless other injuries along the way so that despite 16 years in the league he played only 789 games. He won the Stanley Cup with Bobby Orr's 1970 Bruins and was considered a stay-at-home defenceman tougher than nails. Sacrifice was his game, and injuries naturally followed. Doak played 13 of his years with the Bruins, and after retiring in 1981 joined the team as assistant coach to Gerry Cheevers, a position he left after Cheesie was fired. Almost immediately, he was offered the head coaching job at the University of Massachusetts, and he settled there for two years. In 1988 he opened a restaurant, and shortly after focused his attention as director for sports facilities and programs for the Metropolitan District Commission of Massachusetts.

He was offered the head coaching job at the University of Massachusetts.
GARY DOAK

Rick DiPietro

Robert Dirk

Per Djoos

Shane Doan

Brian Dobbin

Jason Doig

Bobby Dollas

Dolly Dolson

DOAN, Shane ("Doaner")
b. Halkirk, Alberta, October 10, 1976

What a close and spiritual group the Doan clan is. They are connected by sports: patriarch, Bernie, was drafted by St. Louis in 1971; Leighann, Shane's sister, played on Canada's national women's basketball team; and Shane made it to the NHL. Although he never made Winnipeg or Phoenix because of his low scoring, his frustration got to him to the point that he started writing scripture on his hockey sticks, hoping a little divine guidance would escort the occasional black biscuit into the net. One such phrase got him going: "In all things, God works together for good. Romans 8:28." With that on his shaft, he went out and scored the overtime winner for the Coyotes in game two of the series versus St. Louis in 1999. And then the goals came and came. In the two seasons that followed he had 26 goals both years, his previous best being a lowly 7. The Bible verses were here to stay, as was Doan in Phoenix. Them that got, shall gain.

DOBBIN, Brian
b. Petrolia, Ontario, August 18, 1966

Dobbin stretched his career out to the last game possible. He played only a few games in the NHL, with Boston and Philly, then went to the AHL, where he scored in gobs. When the goals stopped coming, he went down a notch to the IHL, where the goals started coming again. And when the goals stopped there, he descended to the UHL where, again, the goals came back in goodly numbers. When they stopped there, well, there was no place to go but home. He retired and became an executive in hockey.

DOBSON, Jim
b. Winnipeg, Manitoba, February 29, 1960

None of the teams Dobson played for exist any longer, even though he only played his first game in 1979. That was with Minnesota (now Dallas), and from there he went to Colorado (now New Jersey) and Quebec (now Colorado). All that added up to but a dozen NHL games, though he didn't record a single point in that time and spent most of his prime years in the CHL and AHL.

DOHERTY, Fred
b. unknown
d. unknown

Doherty's career occurred mostly in the NHA prior to the formation of the NHL in 1917. He appeared in one game for the Canadiens during the 1918-19 season.

DOIG, Jason
b. Montreal, Quebec, January 29, 1977

Doig's career hasn't taken off the way a 34th overall

draft choice (1995) should. He won gold with Canada's juniors in 1997 but since then has appeared in fewer than 50 NHL games and a few more in the minors.

DOLLAS, Bobby
b. Montreal, Quebec, January 31, 1965

For one generation of players, expansion in 1967 allowed so many more to play in the NHL. For a later generation, expansion in the 1990s, which saw the league go from 21 to 30 teams, afforded a similar opportunity. Dollas played his first game in 1983-84, but over the next ten seasons he played only 170 games in a career seemingly rooted in the minors. But when Anaheim claimed him in the Expansion Draft in 1993, he played his next 170 games in less than 3 years and for a while, well into his thirties, became an NHL regular, something he never did during his prime.

DOLSON, Clarence "Dolly"
b. Hespeler, Ontario, May 23, 1897
d. 1976

Dolson came to hockey early in life, playing junior with Galt and leading the team to the Northern Hockey League championship in 1914-15 (he also played for the Galt Seniors that year). But put any pro aspirations on hold to fight in the Great War. He served with the 71st Battalion and was awarded the Distinguished Conduct Medal during his three years overseas before playing senior hockey in Stratford, where he worked for the CNR in the daytime. The local Nationals won the Can-Pro title in 1927-28 at a game that was supposed to have been played on natural ice in Kitchener. However, conditions left the ice a mess, so the game was rescheduled for the Detroit Olympia. Dolson was so impressive, Jack Adams signed him to a contract then and there. In his first season, he played all 44 games for the Detroit Cougars, recording 10 shutouts. He played only part of the next year, then another full season, before being relegated to the minors until 1935, when he retired to Stratford. He resumed his work for the CNR, working as a machinist for the next 45 years. His son, Jack, also became a goalie, also nicknamed Dolly, but he never made it to the NHL. Dolson was inducted into the Waterloo County Hall of Fame, one of three NHL goalers so honoured (George Hainsworth and Hugh Lehman are the others).

DOME, Robert
b. Skalica, Czechoslovakia (Slovakia), January 29, 1979

Only time will tell if Dome represents the way of the future, but in October 1995, at 16 years, 8 months, and 8 days, he became the youngest skater to play pro in

At 16 years, 8 months, and 8 days, he became the youngest skater to play pro in North America.
ROBERT DOME

North America. A native of Slovakia, he was advised by his agent, former Leaf goalie and Czech defector Jiri Crha, that if he aspired to play in the NHL, the sooner he got to North America the better. He signed with the Utah Grizzlies of the IHL, the league of preference for a growing number of players, notably Europeans, to use as a developmental source instead of Canadian juniors or U.S. colleges. However, since being drafted by Pittsburgh, Dome has seen only spot duty in the NHL. He made his Penguins debut at age 18, but has yet to earn a full-time spot on the roster. It's too early to write him off, but one has to wonder whether a few years of pro in his native Slovakia might have helped his long-term development.

DOMENICHELLI, Hnat
b. Edmonton, Alberta, February 14, 1976
Not many boys are brought into this world with the name Hnat affixed to their welcome cards, but this Domenichelli could play a little hockey. He has yet to play a full season in the NHL since Hartford drafted him in 1994, but if he's going to do so he'll have his best chance with his current team, the newly minted Atlanta Thrashers.

DOMI, Tahir "Tie"
b. Windsor, Ontario, November 11, 1969
It was October 14, 1995, at Maple Leaf Gardens. The Leafs were down 2-0 to the Rangers late in the game, and New York defenceman Ulf Samuelsson was taunting Domi into fighting even though Samuelsson had a reputation for preferring to run and hide rather than fight. Domi sucker-punched Samuelsson, who fell to the ice unconscious. The crowd cheered. Rumour has it that the entire Vancouver Canucks team, watching the game in their dressing room at the Pacific Coliseum, stood as one and cheered when they saw the play. The reviled Samuelsson had got his own. Domi, though, received an eight-game suspension, but most felt it was a fair trade-off. Domi had been drafted by the Leafs, but after only two games in '89-'90 he was traded to the Rangers and later the Jets. Not a big man, he established a reputation as being utterly fearless and one of the best fighters in the game. He smiled when he was punched, he never fell down, and he took on players much taller and heavier to ensure his teammates were looked after. His fights with the likes of Bob Probert and Sandy McCarthy became legendary, and Don Cherry became a supporter of the tough guy. When the Leafs reacquired him midway through '94-'95, he couldn't have been happier, and in the ensuing years he has become one of the more popular Leafs, on and off the ice. He does terrific charity work, and teammate Wendel Clark was Domi's best man at his

Domi sucker-punched Samuelsson, who fell to the ice unconscious.
TIE DOMI

wedding. He scored 12 goals in 2000-01 and bettered that in '02-'03, though he led the league (unofficially) in diving, trying to draw penalties.

DONALDSON, Gary
b. Trail, British Columbia, July 15, 1952
Add Donaldson's name to the one-game wonder list of NHLers. His fleeting moment of notice came during the '73-'74 season with Chicago, but the rest of his career was strictly minor pro save for the few games he later played in the WHA.

DONATELLI, Clark
b. Providence, Rhode Island, November 22, 1967
An American through and through, Donatelli had many a chance to represent his country internationally. He played at two World Junior Championships, placing sixth in both 1984 and '85. He played at the World Championships in 1985 (fourth), '86 (sixth), and '87 (seventh). And, he was at the 1988 Olympics in Calgary (seventh) and the 1992 Olympics in Albertville (fourth). NHL-wise, he played in 35 games, spending most of his time in the IHL.

DONATO, Ted
b. Boston, Massachusetts, April 28, 1969
Off ice, Donato has certainly led an eclectic existence. He earned a degree in history from Harvard University. He appeared on the television shows *The Price is Right* and *Showcase Showdown*. And, to top it all off, he was arrested during a police raid on a strip joint called Mons Venus in Tampa Bay, reputedly violating a local ban on lap dancing. On ice, life was simpler. He realized a lifelong dream by playing for his hometown Bruins as well as for the U.S. at every level of international competition. He later was moved around after 8 years with Boston, but he scored 20 goals three times during his stay.

DONNELLY, Dave
b. Edmonton, Alberta, February 2, 1962
Here's how he got to play for the Bruins, and not Minnesota, in his first NHL game. The North Stars drafted Donnelly in 1981 because they thought he was an excellent prospect. But the next year, they wanted Brian Bellows in the draft. Problem was, Bellows was slated to go 1st overall, and Boston owned the number-one selection. So Minnesota traded Donnelly and Brad Palmer to the Bruins simply for Boston promising not to choose Bellows with its number-one selection. The Bruins, instead, chose Gord Kluzak, a major blunder, and the Stars took Bellows 2nd in the draft. Donnelly didn't last long with the Bruins or anyone else in the NHL.

Hnat Domenichelli

Gary Donaldson

Clark Donatelli

Ted Donato

Gord Donnelly

Mike Donnelly

Robert Dopson

John Doran

DONNELLY, Gord
b. Montreal, Quebec, April 5, 1962

In the mid-1980s, Gord Donnelly was the resident goon for Quebec and John Kordic was the goon for Montreal. In one two-game set, they fought maniacally during the first game and then again prior to the puck drop of the second game. Both were suspended five games for their conduct, indicative of the kind of skill they possessed away from the penalty box. Nonetheless, Donnelly punched his way through a dozen NHL seasons, averaging almost four penalty minutes a game. What irony that at the end of his NHL rope he ventured to Europe, that bastion of fair play and game misconducts for fisticuffs, for a few more years of the game.

DONNELLY, James "Babe"
b. Sault Ste. Marie, Ontario, December 22, 1896
d. unknown

On March 20, 1916, at the age of 19, Donnelly signed up with the 227th overseas battalion of the Canadian Expeditionary Forces. He made it home safely and took up hockey in the Soo, where he lived with his mother. He played there for years until, out of nowhere, he got the chance to play for the Montreal Maroons in 1926. He stayed the season, but never played in the NHL again. Instead, he kept right on going in minor professional leagues and later coached in Britain before the Second World War.

DONNELLY, Mike
b. Livonia, Michigan, October 10, 1963

Donnelly was a solid player who packed up his bags and moved to nearby Michigan State to play college hockey and complete a business degree. At no point did an NHL team take an interest in him, even though in his final year he set a CCHA record with 59 goals. The Rangers signed him as a free agent, but it was six years and two teams later that he got a chance to play a full season. When he did, he recorded back-to-back 29-goal seasons, with Los Angeles, though his production tailed off thereafter and he started to move from team to team with greater regularity.

DONOVAN, Shean
b. Timmins, Ontario, January 22, 1975

Donovan's only career hat trick came on November 29, 2000, as a member of Atlanta in a game against Detroit. It was slightly out of the ordinary in that one goal was short-handed, one even strength, and one on the power play. Beyond that, his career peaked in junior when he played for Brian Kilrea's Ottawa 67's and won gold with Canada at the 1995 World Juniors, then two years later won gold at the Worlds. Since then, he has made his way to and through the NHL and found his niche with the Thrashers. Donovan's wife, a former Miss Ottawa, raises champion Clydesdales in California.

DOPITA, Jiri
b. Sumperk, Czechoslovakia (Czech Republic), December 2, 1968

That the NHL and European hockey are two different beasts has never been more apparent than in the case of Dopita. For years he was called the best player never to have played in the NHL, and his play justified the appellation. He won a gold medal with the Czechs at the 1998 Olympics in Nagano; he played in seven World Championships, winning three gold and two bronze; he was among the scoring leaders in the Extraleague of the Czech Republic every year he played. Yet he resisted the NHL. Boston drafted him in 1992 and the Islanders in 1998, and his rights went from the Panthers to the Flyers before he finally came to North America. He missed more than a third of the 2001-02 season with injury, scored just 11 times, and played himself off the team. The Oilers acquired him ... and the pattern repeated itself. Great in Europe, a comparative flop in the NHL. The Oilers released him on December 28, 2002, and Dopita returned whence he came.

DOPSON, Robert
b. Smiths Falls, Ontario, August 21, 1967

After just two games, he knew he'd never get back to the NHL, and minor pro held little interest for him. So, when the Ayr Scottish Eagles phoned and offered him a chance to play goal in Britain, he accepted and became something of a hero to the team. In 1997-98, he was named both goalie and player of the year in the league, and helped Ayr win the championship. He later tried his hand in Japan, and continues to play goal a long, long way from little Smiths Falls in eastern Ontario.

DORAN, John "Red"
b. Belleville, Ontario, May 24, 1911
d. Detroit, Michigan, February 11, 1975

Doran played all his youth hockey in Toronto in the late 1920s and early 1930s, but got into the NHL with the old New York Americans, the team that had seen him play in New Haven in '32-'33. In all, he played 98 NHL games up to the war, and afterward settled in Detroit. He coached the Red Wings Oldtimers and died of a heart attack at age 63.

DORAN, Lloyd "Red"
b. South Porcupine, Ontario, January 10, 1921

Red began playing hockey in Timmins, moving up from city and minor hockey to the McIntyre Mines team before turning pro with Omaha in 1941 in the Detroit system. Doran served overseas from 1942 to '45, and upon his return he made the Red Wings for the first and only time, playing half the '46-'47 season. He spent the next several years in the minor pros, but in 1952 he accepted an offer from Belleville to coach the Junior Hawks and act as general "coach-in-chief" of the Belleville Hockey Association while playing Senior hockey in the city. The next summer, he was made recreational director for the city of Belleville.

DORATY, Ken ("Cagie")
b. Stittsville, Ontario, June 23, 1906
d. Moose Jaw, Saskatchewan, May 4, 1981

Doraty led a long and happy hockey life that was punctuated by a moment of glory in one of the greatest hockey games ever played. On the night of April 3, 1933, the Boston Bruins visited Maple Leaf Gardens for the fifth and final game of their semifinals series. After three periods, the score was 0-0. During the first overtime, there was no scoring. Second overtime, ditto. Third, fourth, fifth overtime: nothing. Then, at 4:46 of the *sixth* overtime period, tiny, mighty Doraty scored to give the Leafs an exhausting win in what was then the longest game in history. In all, he played just 103 NHL games, his last 2 with Detroit in 1937-38. Although a native of Ontario, he moved to Saskatchewan at age five and grew up out west. He won a Memorial Cup with the 1924-25 Regina Pats, and after retiring settled in Moose Jaw where he coached the Canucks to the Memorial Cup before losing to the powerful St. Mikes Majors. After his coaching days, he opened a billiard hall and hotel in Moose Jaw, and remained owner until he passed away.

DORÉ, Andre ("Trap")
b. Montreal, Quebec, February 11, 1958

Doré was a defensive defenceman who ended his career as it began – with the New York Rangers. That team drafted him in 1978 and played him for five years off and on before trading him to St. Louis for Glen Hanlon and Vaclav Nedomansky. Doré then moved on to Quebec in '83-'84, but the next year, his last in the NHL, returned to Broadway via the Waiver Draft.

DORÉ, Daniel
b. Ferme-Neuve, Quebec, April 9, 1970

One of the great busts of the 1988 draft, Doré went 5th overall with a selection by the Quebec Nordiques, yet played exactly 17 games in the NHL. He was expected to be a big, strong presence, a talented grinder who could skate well and fight with the best of them in junior. But after graduating from the Q, he never made an impact with the Nordiques, and although he was signed as a free agent by Philadelphia in 1992 he never played again in the NHL.

DOREY, Jim ("Flipper")
b. Kingston, Ontario, August 17, 1947

Jim Dorey was likely the first and only find of a scout named Dodo Imlach, erstwhile wife of Maple Leaf coach Punch and, more importantly, mother of son Brent, skater with the London Knights of the OHA. Mrs. Imlach attended games regularly to watch their boy, but each time she grew more impressed with Brent's teammate, Jim Dorey. She convinced the hubby to come and see Dorey play, and sure enough Imlach eventually found a way to put him in the Leafs lineup. Dorey instantly became a top rookie in the league, a brutally tough defenceman with some offensive abilities. Dorey once got into a fight with teammate Rick Ley during an open practice on Christmas Day 1971. While kids cheered them on,

thinking they were play-fighting, Ley bit Dorey's hand, cutting a tendon. Shortly after, Dorey was traded to the Rangers, but he played only one game after separating his shoulder and missing the rest of the season. That summer, the landmark months in 1972 when the WHA pilfered the NHL at will, Dorey signed with New England and spent the rest of his career in the WHA. He returned to Kingston after retiring and became coach, manager, and part owner of the junior team while doing colour commentator work on the radio for the team as well. By day, he became a broker with Allstate Insurance and raised a son, Jamie, who went on to play in Germany. Dorey's greatest boast was that he never lost a fight, but in the end his was a potential that was never quite realized.

Andre Doré

DORION, Dan
b. Astoria, New York, March 2, 1963

He began with stick and puck on the streets of New York, playing roller hockey, graduating to the ice game only later in his childhood. The prime of Dan Dorion's life took place during his four years playing for the Broncos at Western Michigan University. He set 17 WMU records during his time there and he was a Hobey Baker Award nominee in his final year, 1985-86. He played for the U.S. at the 1985 World Championships and was drafted by New Jersey (albeit a distant 232nd overall in 1982), but his career never took off after graduation. The Devils were impressed enough to give him only four games over two years, and after a few years in the minors he retired. A year later, he surfaced in Europe, playing first in Italy, then in Britain, before finally stowing away his equipment bag in 1994.

Jim Dorey

> When he attended his first hockey team tryout, as an 11-year-old, he was cut within minutes.
> **GARY DORNHOEFER**

DORNHOEFER, Gerhardt "Gary" ("Dorny")
b. Kitchener, Ontario, February 2, 1943

Dornhoefer's father worked for the Smiles and Chuckles Candy Factory in Kitchener, and although young Gary got lots of treats, he developed into a player who was tough as nails, playing on the most reviled, dirtiest, and least talented team – the Broad Street Bullies – to win the Stanley Cup. When he attended his first hockey team tryout, as an 11-year-old, he was cut within minutes, a fate that made him all the more determined to succeed. In junior, his Niagara Falls Flyers made it to the Memorial Cup finals in his final year, 1962-63, before losing to Edmonton, and over the next three years he saw part-time duty with the parent club, the Boston Bruins. But the Bruins were on the upswing, and saw no room for Dornhoefer in their future. They exposed him in the Expansion Draft, the Flyers claimed him, and Dorny

Dan Dorion

Eddie Dorohoy

Jordy Douglas

Kent Douglas

Les Douglas

Jim Dowd

played the rest of his career, another 11 years, with Philly. A tough player who preferred the boards to the slot and a fight to a slug of water, Dornhoefer was also frequently injured. During his career he broke both legs, both cheekbones, both ankles, a wrist, a shoulder, a knee, everything imaginable. Yet amazingly for someone with limited talent, he also had 5 seasons of 20 or more goals, and he won 2 Cups with the Flyers, in '74 and '75, though he was injured the night the team won its first. After retiring in 1978 he became a broadcaster with the Flyers and soon after with *Hockey Night in Canada*, but after five years the travel became too burdensome and he semi-retired to business life. He settled in Conestoga, Ontario, got a job as a representative with Mutual Life of Canada Insurance in nearby Kitchener, and confined himself to only occasional forays in the HNIC booth. An excellent golfer, he opened his own course in Marlton, New Jersey, where he was the club pro.

DOROHOY, Eddie
("The Brat"/ "The Great Gabboo"/
"The Pistol")
b. Medicine Hat, Alberta, March 13, 1929

Rarely has a character come onto the NHL scene with such flair and gregariousness as the rookie in Montreal camp in 1948. A talker, joker, yapper, pepper-mouth yacker, his humour and non-stop banter proved affection-worthy with his teammates, who laughed so much they couldn't hate the cocky conveyances. Murph Chamberlain told him that he had kept his mouth shut about his skills when he entered the league; Rook shot back that perhaps he hadn't been that good. Dorohoy once practiced in nothing but his underwear. In the '47-'48 season his Lethbridge Native Sons made it to the Memorial Cup finals. He broke his leg in one game, but insisted on playing in the next, cast and all! Despite his personality, though, there was little room in Montreal for him. He went pointless in 16 games in '48-'49 and shortly after settled in the PCHL and later in the WHL, where he enjoyed a fine career that endured until 1965. (In 1952, at 23, he was named playing coach of the Victoria Cougars.) He found his way to Winnipeg, where he coached the junior Jets for a number of years.

DOUGLAS, Jordy
b. Winnipeg, Manitoba, January 20, 1958

Winnipeg was always where Douglas wanted to be. He grew up around the corner from the arena watching the junior Jets and dreaming of the NHL himself. He played junior in Flin Flon, and Toronto drafted him in 1978. But Douglas signed with the WHA and was reclaimed by the Leafs prior to his WHA team, the Whalers, joining the NHL. The Leafs then lost him to Hartford in the dispersal of players in the summer of 1979, but Douglas's career was halting. He had an exceptional NHL entry, scoring 33 goals for the Whalers in 1979-80, playing on a team that included Gordie Howe and Dave Keon. Then the injuries came: separated shoulder; broken foot; same shoulder again; surgery. Hartford traded him, to Minnesota, his stock dropped, the Stars traded him to Winnipeg. Happy to be home, he played just 24 games with the Jets before heading off to Finland for

2 years, where he teamed with another native son, Darren Boyko, who also played a game for the Jets and who also had an extensive career in Finland.

DOUGLAS, Kent
b. Cobalt, Ontario, February 6, 1936

A more idiosyncratic player than Mr. Douglas never came to the NHL. In his heyday, he drank 35 glasses of water a day until he was convinced to curb the habit (which he did, and lost 30 pounds in the process!). His coach in the minors, Eddie Shore, also had to talk him into curbing his temper, which is saying something extraordinary in itself, for Shore was always one of the most ferocious men on ice or behind the bench. In 1966, Douglas smeared black charcoal under his eyes to deflect the glare from television lights in arenas, but along the way he was also a fine player. He was the first defenceman to win the Calder Trophy, playing for the Stanley Cup-champion Leafs of '62-'63, and he won three Cups in all with the team during the 1960s. In one game in 1967, he broke his hand in the first period of a game, got the cast put on it in the second, and was back to score a goal in the third. He later became a player coach with the New York Raiders of the WHA and then in the AHL, but a serious eye injury more or less ended his playing days. He settled in Baltimore after retiring from the Clippers, went into real estate, and later worked for the municipal parks department. He also coached the U.S. Naval Academy hockey team at Annapolis.

DOUGLAS, Les
b. Perth, Ontario, December 5, 1918
d. Kingston, Ontario, October 20, 2002

He was Detroit property through and through for many years, but Douglas was happiest when the Red Wings traded him to the Buffalo Bisons of the AHL to play on a line with Tommy Cooper and Joe Bell for the 1947-48 season. Two years later, with Cleveland, he became the first man to register 100 points in a season of pro hockey. Douglas had won a Cup with Detroit back in the spring of '43 and then went off to join the war effort, working as a motorcycle instructor in the Canadian army for two years. He established business as a painting contractor in the summers in Buffalo, and played senior hockey after his AHL days were over.

DOURIS, Peter
b. Toronto, Ontario, February 19, 1966

He was a Leafs fan growing up, of course, but Winnipeg got him in the 1984 Entry Draft, and that is where and how Douris got into his first NHL game. He had his best success with Anaheim a few years later, but in 1998 he moved to Germany to play in the Elite League, where he continues to score goals for Munich.

DOWD, Jim ("J.D.")
b. Brick, New Jersey, December 25, 1968

Dowd grew up in Brick Township and attended Brick High School, where he earned Brick letters in three sports – hockey, soccer, and baseball. Right after finishing high school he was drafted by the local New Jersey Devils, and on that strength Lake Superior State in Michigan offered him a scholarship. The team won the NCAA championship his first year, '87-'88, and during his four years there his confidence and game improved enough that he felt the NHL was not out of sight. Dowd played most of '91-'95 in the minors, given only occasional chances to play with the Devils. He managed to stay with the team through the 1995 playoffs, though, the lockout-shortened season when the Devils won the Stanley Cup. Dowd later went to Hartford, Vancouver, the Islanders, Calgary, and on, never playing a full season until he got to Edmonton and Minnesota.

DOWIE, Bruce
b. Oakville, Ontario, December 9, 1962
Dowie was named OHA rookie of the year for 1979-80, but everything was downhill from there for the one-time Leafs goalie. He missed parts of the next two seasons with injuries, never got drafted, and signed with the Leafs as a free agent as insurance for Ken Wregget and Allan Bester. Dowie played just 72 minutes for Toronto in '83-'84, but spent the rest of his career in the minors, retiring in 1987. His closest moment of glory came the night of January 4, 1985, when he played for Team Canada in an exhibition game against Moscow Dynamo at Maple Leaf Gardens. Canada won 4-3 and Dowie made 38 saves.

DOWNEY, Aaron ("Diesel")
b. Shelburne, Ontario, August 27, 1974
Downey played all over without an NHL contract until Boston decided, what the hey, and signed him to a little something on January 20, 1998. He appeared in a single game for the B's the next season without incurring a single penalty, quite a feat considering his numbers were just about off the charts everywhere else he went, especially in the AHL, where he had back-to-back 400-minute years. That's a ton of fighting and doesn't leave much time for anything else except riding the bike after game misconducts.

DOWNIE, Dave
b. Burke's Falls, Ontario, March 11, 1909
d. Seattle, Washington
His only NHL games – 11 in all – came during February and March of 1933 after an excellent season with Syracuse. Most of Downie's career passed in the PCHL.

DOYON, Mario
b. Quebec City, Quebec, August 27, 1968
At the time, it was a pretty big deal. On March 5, 1990, Chicago traded Doyon, Everett Sanipass, and Dan Vincelette to Quebec for Michel Goulet, Greg Millen, and a draft choice. The package of prospects for older

stars didn't pan out for the Nordiques, as Doyon played just 21 games for the team. He played in the minors for a number of years afterward and then continued his career in Europe.

DRAKE, Dallas ("Dally")
b. Trail, British Columbia, February 4, 1969
It was during his playing career at Northern Michigan University that Drake was drafted into the NHL, by Detroit, in 1989. But he didn't waver from his life plan and earned his degree in economics before joining the Wings in 1992. The previous season he had scored the championship goal – in triple overtime, no less – in the NCAA finals. He has been in the NHL ever since, though the right winger has proved to be a third-liner rather than a superstar. He moved on to Winnipeg and Phoenix before signing as a free agent with St. Louis, his most recent team.

DRAPER, Bruce
b. Toronto, Ontario, October 2, 1940
d. Ottawa, Ontario, January 26, 1968
Leukemia took him from this mortal coil at age 27. Fit and strong and skilled as an athlete, he could not conquer the disease forever. Draper had been a superstar in junior with St. Mike's. He was one of the keys to the team's 1961 Memorial Cup victory. But he played all his career in the minors with the exception of one game – March 3, 1963 – when he dressed for the Leafs.

DRAPER, Kris
b. Toronto, Ontario, May 24, 1971
Gordie Howe helped Detroit win the Stanley Cup in 1950 even though he missed most of the playoffs. In the first game of the semifinals, he took a run at Ted Kennedy, missed, and went flying into the boards, suffering a serious concussion and almost dying. The Red Wings were incensed. They exacted physical revenge the next game and went on to defeat the Leafs and avenge the injury to their young superstar. In the finals, they beat the upstart Rangers in seven games to win the Cup. Such a horrific injury also befell Draper, but the consequences were equally sweet revenge. On May 29, 1996, in game six of the semifinals, Colorado's Claude Lemieux hit Draper from behind right at the players' bench. Draper fell cheek-first into the top of the dasher. He broke his nose and cheekbone, suffered a concussion, damaged his orbital bone, and had five teeth misplaced. He had his jaw wired shut and required plastic surgery, literally to save face. At this point of the playoffs, there could be no retaliation, but no one – no one – on that Detroit bench forgot the dirty hit. Lemieux was issued a slim two-game suspension, and Colorado went on to win the Cup, but the next year the Wings exacted physical

Aaron Downey

Mario Doyon

Dallas Drake

Bruce Draper

On May 29, 1996, in game six of the semifinals, Colorado's Claude Lemieux hit Draper from behind.
KRIS DRAPER

revenge during the regular season and then hammered the Avs in the playoffs en route to their first Stanley Cup since the Howe days of the 1950s. Draper's was an injury that brought the team together, defined the makeup of that era's Wings, and motivated them to play inspired hockey. Lemieux had long been considered a cheap hitter, and Draper was a good, clean kid who deserved to be checked hard and for keeps like anyone else, but not from behind along the boards. He had been acquired from the Winnipeg Jets in 1993 for nothing more than future considerations, and has been with the Wings ever since.

Tom Draper

DRAPER, Tom
b. Outremont, Quebec, November 20, 1966

For a moment, a brief moment, it looked as if Tom Draper had made his mark in the NHL. The year was 1991-92, the team the Buffalo Sabres. He had been drafted by Winnipeg, played eight games with the Jets over two years, and was sent to the Buffalos for a 7th-round draft choice. At any rate, in '91-'92 neither Clint Malarchuk nor Darren Puppa was playing well enough to be number one, so coach John Muckler went with three keepers during the regular season. Draper was the most impressive, and in the playoffs his tending prolonged the first-round matchup against the Bruins to seven games. Unfortunately, Boston won the final game to eliminate Draper and the Sabres. After that, he managed only a few games with Firetown the year after, and although he later played bits and pieces with the Islanders and Jets, he became an IHL man for the rest of his goaling days.

DRILLON, Gord
(sometimes "Drillen"/ "Lefty")
b. Moncton, New Brunswick, October 23, 1913
d. Saint John, New Brunswick, September 23, 1986

It was an incredible testament to his achievements that even though his career lasted just 7 seasons and 311 games, Drillon was inducted into the Hockey Hall of Fame in 1975. He played down east before coming to Toronto, but when he made his NHL debut in 1936 it was as a fill-in for the injured Charlie Conacher. Drillon made such an impression, though, that the Leafs never sent him back to Syracuse. Instead, he found himself on a line with Syl Apps and Bob Davidson, the DAD Line (for the first letters of their last names). In '37-'38, he led the NHL in goals with 26 and in points with 52, a feat not been accomplished by a Leafs player since. He also won the Lady Byng Trophy that year, but perhaps his greatest renown was his pioneering efforts to deflect pucks into the goal. As

a result, he became known for scoring lucky goals, though that dismissive epithet betrayed the hours of practice he put into tipping shots past goalies from the slot. His offensive output was countered by a weakness in the defensive aspects of the game, and the two collided in the 1942 playoffs, both his crowning glory and his worst embarrassment. After losing the first three games of the finals to Detroit, Toronto was desperate for a solution, so coach Hap Day benched Drillon for the rest of the series in favour of Gaye Stewart and the Leafs rallied to win the Cup. It was Drillon's only Cup, and before the following season started he was sold to Montreal. He played on a line with Buddy O'Connor and Ray Getliffe for a year, scoring 28 goals, and added 4 more in the playoffs. His career total of 26 playoff goals was a record that stood for 4 years until being eclipsed by Maurice Richard. In 1943, Drillon joined the Canadian Army and later the RCAF. He returned home to coach and then scouted for the Maple Leafs, recommending Errol Thompson to the team some years later. He worked as a recreational consultant for the New Brunswick Department of Youth, which kept him going for the rest of his life. Drillon was an outstanding softball pitcher, the best in the Maritimes, his contemporaries said. He was also a superb golfer, curler, and tennis player, and in his later years received many honours: New Brunswick Sports Hall of Fame in 1970, Hockey Hall of Fame in 1975, Moncton Hall of Fame in 1983, and Canada Sports Hall of Fame in 1989.

Drillon worked as a recreational consultant for the New Brunswick Department of Youth.
GORD DRILLON

DRISCOLL, Peter ("Grenade")
b. Kingston, Ontario, October 27, 1954

Driscoll turned his nose up at the honour of playing for the Leafs after that team drafted him in 1974 and instead took the path to greater banking by signing with the WHA. He toured many a city in that league before settling in with the Oilers by the time they joined the NHL, but it wasn't just any old deal that got him there. Driscoll was sold to the Oilers by Indianapolis for $700,000 in a deal that also included Eddie Mio and a guy named Gretzky. Driscoll lasted 60 games and 3 goals in Edmonton. Gretzky endured a wee bit longer and few goals more. Driscoll went on to coach and manage the Hobbema Hawks in the Alberta Junior league.

DRIVER, Bruce
b. Toronto, Ontario, April 29, 1962

He was no awful defenceman, that's for sure, but when a bidding war broke out for the free agent's services in the summer of 1995, it was plain to see salaries were spiralling out of control. The Rangers won the day and gave him a three-year deal at almost

Peter Driscoll

$1.5 million a season. Driver was not a scorer, not a rock on defence, not big and strong and tough. He was a good, solid defenceman, and he was coming off a Stanley Cup win with New Jersey. GM Lou Lamoriello had no intention of bidding for Driver's return, even though the player had been in Jersey for the first 12 years of his career.

DROLET, Rene
b. Quebec City, Quebec, November 13, 1944
Although Drolet played close to 1,000 games in his pro hockey career, only 2 came at the NHL level. And although he had 11 straight 20-goal seasons in the minors, he failed to score in either of those 2 big games with Philadelphia and Detroit. And although he scored 52 goals in his final year of junior in Quebec and played 7 years with the AHL Aces, he failed to become a French-Canadian hero in a province famous for its heroes.

DROPPA, Ivan
b. Liptovsky Mikulas, Czechoslovakia (Slovakia), February 1, 1972
A brief pro career in North America neither dampened Droppa's enthusiasm for the game nor compromised his international accomplishments, which were many. He played at two World Junior Championships in 1991 and '92 and later represented Slovakia at the 1996 World Cup. He also played in four Worlds for his new country and in the 1998 Olympics in Nagano. During the majority of these seasons he played first in minor pro and later back home in league competition.

DROUILLARD, Clare
b. Windsor, Ontario, March 2, 1914
Although was owned by a number of NHL teams in the 1930s, Drouillard played only with Detroit, in 1937-38, which was fine by him, a Windsor native who lived across the river from the Olympia.

DROUIN, Jude
b. Mont Louis, Quebec, October 28, 1948
d. unknown
A Montreal draft choice back in 1966, Drouin stirred the pot both on and off the ice on two memorable occasions. In November 1977, he was arrested for spraying a college student with mace after Drouin pulled over a car of students he thought was harassing him. He was charged with possession of a toxic substance and charged with third-degree assault, but that was nothing compared to an altercation with referee Bruce Hood back in 1971 as a member of the Minnesota North Stars. In that game, he became upset with the official's work, and prior to a faceoff said to him, "You're like all the rest." Hood dared Drouin to repeat the remark, which

he did, and the ref gave him a misconduct. Enraged, Drouin came after Hood, but was intercepted by his teammates. He calmed down, but went berserk again as soon as he was free and smashed his stick against the glass near Hood. Hood said the stick struck him on the shoulder, and Drouin subsequently received a three-game suspension. He spent most of his career with the North Stars and New York Islanders before retiring in 1981. He settled in Johnstown, Pennsylvania, to work for an engineering company.

DROUIN, Paul Emile "Polly"
b. Verdun, Quebec, January 16, 1916
d. Ottawa, Ontario, January 1, 1968
When the Ottawa Senators left the NHL in 1934, the team kept its name and played in the Montreal senior ranks for a brief time before joining the Quebec Hockey League. During that time, young Polly played on a line with Rod Lorrain and Tag Millar, the first two signing with the Habs and playing parts of four years there in tandem (though Drouin continued on until '41). During the war, Drouin played briefly with the Commandos, arguably the greatest amateur team in the country, before going overseas to serve with the Royal Canadian Ordnance Corps. He was the son-in-law of Oscar Lepine, another well-known Ottawa sportsman. Drouin spent his final years quite ill before passing away on New Year's Day 1968.

He was the son-in-law of Oscar Lepine, another well-known Ottawa sportsman.
POLLY DROUIN

DROUIN, P.C.
b. St. Lambert, Quebec, April 22, 1974
On two occasions he's played for the B's. Sort of. P.C. stands for Pierre Claude, and Pierre Claude attended Cornell University until graduating in 1996. The B's – as in the Boston Bruins – signed him as a free agent and put him in three games in '96-'97, but shortly thereafter Drouin went off to Britain to play for the Bees – as in the Bracknell Bees – where he's been buzzing about ever since.

DRUCE, John
b. Peterborough, Ontario, February 23, 1966
"Drucemania" may not be flourishing into the 21st century, but for a brief time in the spring of 1990, no player in the NHL was hotter than Druce during the playoffs. A defensive-minded junior who trained with the Petes in his native Peterborough, Druce made a hole for himself in the minors that he seemed destined to live in for all his hockey life. But sometimes strange things happen. As the 1990 playoffs got underway, Washington coach Terry Murray was unhappy with John Tucker's work on the number-one line with Dale Hunter and Geoff Courtnall. He summoned Druce to the big club, and

Rene Drolet

Ivan Droppa

Clarence Drouillard

Jude Drouin

John Druce

Harold Druken

Jim Drummond

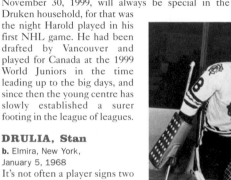

He put on the Gumper's sweater, and finished the game, allowing three goals in a 4-1 Toronto win.
DAVE DRYDEN

Chris Drury

Herb Drury

for reasons only the aligned stars can know, Druce lit up the league, scoring 14 goals in the Caps' 15 playoff games and taking the team to the Conference finals. This earned him a spot with the team for the next year, though it didn't translate into the contract raise he'd been hoping for. He had a decent 22-goal season, but scored only once in the playoffs. His production slipped the following season, and he was traded to Winnipeg, L.A., and Philly in the coming years, scoring just one more playoff goal in 19 games. His reputation as a clutch performer, so remarkable and sure for one season, never returned.

DRUKEN, Harold
b. St. John's, Newfoundland, January 26, 1979
November 30, 1999, will always be special in the Druken household, for that was the night Harold played in his first NHL game. He had been drafted by Vancouver and played for Canada at the 1999 World Juniors in the time leading up to the big days, and since then the young centre has slowly established a surer footing in the league of leagues.

DRULIA, Stan
b. Elmira, New York, January 5, 1968
It's not often a player signs two consecutive NHL contracts as a free agent with the same team, but it can happen if the two signings are seven years apart. Drulia was drafted by Pittsburgh in '86 and signed by Edmonton three years later, but it wasn't until Tampa signed him that he actually played in the NHL. Then, it was all minors from there for seven seasons, during which time Drulia scored a ton of goals in the IHL. After a while, he had no NHL affiliation, so in 1999 the Lightning signed him again and used him for the full season, though he scored only 11 times.

DRUMMOND, Jim
b. Toronto, Ontario, October 20, 1918
d. Peterborough, Ontario, December 12, 1950
He was only 32 when he died in hospital after a long illness, and not far removed from his last professional hockey game in the AHL. Drummond squeezed into two wartime games for the Rangers, and before the war had a lengthy career in the Toronto area. He served with the RCAF and the Canadian Infantry Corps after which he had a brief career in the AHL.

DRURY, Chris
b. Trumbull, Connecticut, August 20, 1976
Chris was the winning pitcher in the 1989 Little League World Series against Taiwan, but he chose to take hockey seriously because it could offer him a full college scholarship. Besides, just months earlier, his

brother Ted had played for the U.S. at the World Juniors and inspired Chris. He attended Boston University, where he set Hockey East on fire, winning the Hobey Baker Award in 1998 and joining the Colorado Avalanche that fall. Life just got better for Drury. He was named the NHL's rookie of the year, and the following year he scored an overtime goal in the playoffs against Detroit. The year after that, he won the Stanley Cup with the Avs, and he has established himself as the kind of fine young star a team builds around.

DRURY, Herb
b. Midland, Ontario, March 2, 1896
d. Pittsburgh, Pennsylvania, July 1965
Although Drury had a fine NHL career in the league's early days, he is perhaps more renowned for competing in the first two Olympics for Team USA in hockey, 1920 and 1924, winning silver to Canada's gold on both occasions. Drury later settled in Pittsburgh, and when the Yellowjackets joined the NHL in 1925, he went along and became a tough forward on the team, renamed the Pirates. He retired in 1931 after playing 213 games in the NHL and remained a Pittsburghian the rest of his life.

DRURY, Ted
b. Boston, Massachusetts, September 13, 1971
While brother Chris is on the verge of NHL stardom, Ted is on the downturn of a career that has been far less rewarding. He has played only two years of seven in the playoffs and is now in the minors looking up. He started out playing everywhere for his country in the early 1990s and broke into the NHL with Calgary in 1993. A checking forward with limited scoring ability, he has suffered the ignominy of playing mostly for Hartford, Anaheim, and the Islanders, teams that never qualify for the post-season.

DRYDEN, Dave
b. Hamilton, Ontario, September 5, 1941
In the olden days of the Original Six, teams carried only one goalie and the home rink always had to have a junior puckstopper in the crowd ready to play in case of an injury to one of the NHL starters. On the night of February 3, 1962, Dave Dryden of the Toronto Marlies was just such a young man, going down to the Gardens to watch the Rangers play the Leafs. But a funny thing happened during play. Gump Worsley was injured and had to leave the game. Dryden was summoned to the Rangers dressing room. He put on the Gumper's sweater, and finished the game, allowing three goals in a 4-1 Toronto win. That was his NHL debut. After that night, he returned to the University of Waterloo to get

his teacher's certificate while playing goal for the Galt Hornets in Senior A. He became part of the Chicago system, but that meant little because Glenn Hall was the starter. He became a teacher and had brief stints with the Hawks and Buffalo Sabres, and in 1971 he and brother Ken became the first goalies to oppose each other in an NHL game. In 1974, Dryden joined the WHA. He ended up with the Gretzky-Messier Oilers, leading the league in GAA, wins, and games played in 1978-79, the last year before the team joined the NHL. He stayed with the Oilers for its first year in the old league, then retired to coach at Peterborough, becoming Detroit's goalie coach two years later. Dryden left the game entirely to pursue teaching full-time, eventually becoming vice-principal at Eden Woods in Mississauga. Later, he returned to the NHL front office, leading a group that reviews injuries and goalie equipment.

DRYDEN, Ken
b. Hamilton, Ontario,
August 8, 1947

Nobody but nobody who was a teen in the 1960s thought the best way to the NHL was Cornell University. Yet young Ken Dryden had made enough of an impression in junior B in Ontario to be drafted by Boston in 1964. Days later, Montreal acquired his rights in a deal of so little consequence that no one paid attention to it for years. He finished his undergrad degree at the Ivy League school and then played for the Canadian National Team, even appearing in the 1969 World Championships. Dryden turned pro in the Montreal system in 1970, and had such a good year that the

Ken played goal the night of December 31, 1975, when the Soviets and Canadiens played to a 3-3 tie.
KEN DRYDEN

Habs called him up for the final half-dozen games of the regular season. No one could have known that he would win all six games and allow just nine pucks into his net. Still, no one could have anticipated that coach Al MacNeil would go with Dryden to start the playoffs, and no one on planet Earth could have predicted that Dryden would almost single-handedly beat the Bruins, the highest-scoring team in NHL history at the height of their powers. The Habs went on to beat Minnesota and Chicago to win the Cup, and Dryden won the Conn Smythe Trophy even before he was eligible to win the Calder Trophy. No matter. He won that a year later after compiling a near-perfect record of 39-8-15 to lead the league, and that fall, with just 96 total NHL games under his belt, he was named one of two goalies for Team Canada at the 1972 Summit Series. What transpired that fall was the stuff of history, and after Paul Henderson's series-winning goal it was Dryden who skated the full length of the ice to join the celebration. He had played in four of the games and Tony Esposito had played the other four. Dryden then returned to the Habs and had a

second outstanding season. He did not acquiesce to his success with the same timourousness as the previous generation of player, though, and Dryden threatened to retire if he did not get a contract offer suitable to his performance. Sure enough, GM Sam Pollock called Dryden's bluff, and the goaler sat out all of '73-'74 while working for a law firm. Montreal lost its leverage when the Rangers eliminated the Habs in the first round of the 1974 playoffs, though, and the next year Dryden was back in the fold. As it turned out, he played only 5 more seasons, but he never won fewer than 30 games and, more amazingly, never lost more than 10 games in a year. He won the Cup four more times and as many Vezina Trophies. In just 8 years in the league, he won 6 Stanley Cups and recorded 46 shutouts in only 397 regular-season games. Along the way, Dryden left his mark on the game the way few modern goalies have managed to do. He and brother Dave became the first goalie-brothers to play against each other in a game, a game that ended in Buffalo with the pair shaking hands at centre ice to a standing ovation. Ken also played goal the night of December 31, 1975, when the Soviets and Canadiens played to a 3-3 tie, one of the most thrilling games ever. He left his mark because of his size, a man tall and gangly and quick and idiosyncratic. When action was in the other end or a whistle delayed the game, the 6'4" goalie would stand with his hands on the top of his stick propped underneath his chin. It was a larger-than-life pose, one that symbolized the poise and calm he exuded during the heat of action. After

Ken Dryden

retiring in 1979, Dryden kept busy with a number of successful projects. He worked as an analyst for U.S. television during the Olympic Winter Games of 1980, '84, and '88, and wrote *The Game*, a best-selling account of his days as a player and the cultural significance of the game to Canadians. It eventually became a TV series, and led him to write other books, including *Home Game* and *In School*, an unrelated examination of the school system. He earned his doctorate from the University of Windsor and was inducted into the Hockey Hall of Fame, and in 1997 he took on a great and long-term challenge when he became president of the Toronto Maple Leafs. Leafs fans of the 1970s could not possibly imagine their greatest adversary now becomimg the team's saviour, but Dryden has brought stability to an often unstable environment. Over the years, his life has bounced in and out of the NHL, to law and publishing and sometimes points elsewhere, but the defining stream has been hockey, that Canadian cultural link between the intellectual and athletic, recondite and common, the sophisticated and the everyday.

Ken Dryden

DUBE, Christian

b. Sherbrooke, Quebec, April 25, 1977

Coaches for Canada's National Junior Team aren't worried about a player's reputation or draft place. They're worried only about how good a player is at the very moment they need him for the Worlds. The result in the long term, though, is that a player's success at the WJC does not necessarily reflect his whole career. Dube played on two World teams for Canada, in 1996 and '97, and although he won gold both times and was a star player, history has proved those were his finest hours. His dad, Norm, had played for Kansas City in the 1970s, and Christian played briefly for the Rangers before going to the minors and then Switzerland, where small, fast players had a better chance of leaving a mark.

DUBE, Gilles

b. Sherbrooke, Quebec, June 2, 1927

Small, quick, and a dynamo on offence, Dube was regarded as one of the best passers outside the NHL for most of his playing days. He played for Montreal in 1949-50 but GM Frank Selke wanted him in Cincinnati, where he was trying to establish a farm team in a new arena and sent Dube to help out. Dube later played briefly in Detroit's Cup-winning season of '53-'54 and then played most of the rest of his career in Quebec, leading the league in scoring in '55-'56.

DUBE, Norm

b. Sherbrooke, Quebec, September 12, 1951

Dube was initially property of Los Angeles in the years shortly after expansion, but the Kings lost him when Kansas City claimed him in 1974. He played 57 games for the Scouts and then accepted an offer from the Nordiques to join the WHA. But when Quebec joined the NHL, Dube was in the minors lighting up the goals of the American league. He led the AHL in points in 1979-80 and was named the league's MVP. With those honours in hand he moved to Switzerland to continue his career and raise his son, Christian, who later darkened the doors of the NHL.

Norm Dube

DUBERMAN, Justin

b. New Haven, Connecticut, March 23, 1970

Anyone who is drafted 230th overall – doesn't matter the year or team – deserves full kudos for playing on and making it to the NHL, even if the stay was as brief as Duberman's four-game stint with Pittsburgh in '93-'94. Beyond that, he played in a variety of leagues and countries in pursuit of hockey and culture. When he retired, he became a player agent.

Justin Duberman

Hockey was a big part of Dudley's childhood, but so, too, was music.
RICK DUDLEY

DUBINSKY, Steve

b. Montreal, Quebec, July 9, 1970

From Chicago to Calgary and back, Dubinsky has hung in there to be a reliable, fourth-line player. He graduated from Clarkson University in 1993 with a B.A. in business and over the next four years split his time between the Hawks and the minors. Just as he was establishing himself as a regular, Chicago traded him to the Flames, but a serious knee injury wrecked his 1999-2000 season there and he re-signed with the Hawks in the off-season.

DUCHESNE, Gaetan

b. Les Saulles, Quebec, July 11, 1962

He came right out of junior as one of the most fluid and fleet skaters in the Quebec league and made Washington in his first camp in 1981. Over the next 14 years he established himself as a consistent scoring defenceman, though playoff success eluded him most of his career. The lone exception came in 1992 when his Minnesota North Stars made it to the finals, only to be wiped out by Pittsburgh. Duchesne scored 24 goals in '87-'88 with Quebec and played a total of 1,028 NHL games.

DUCHESNE, Steve

b. Sept-Iles, Quebec, June 30, 1965

Not many players are traded six times during their career. Not many players play for three different teams on two separate occasions during their career. And certainly not many defencemen play 1,000 NHL games, either. Duchesne has been a moderate winner wherever he has been. His teams invariably make the playoffs, yet they also invariably are eliminated early as well. He has scored 20 goals or more from the blueline on 4 occasions and has played in 3 All-Star Games, but the elusive Stanley Cup remains ever more so as he nears the end of his playing road.

DUDLEY, Rick

b. Toronto, Ontario, January 31, 1949

Yes, hockey was a big part of Dudley's childhood, but so, too, was music. Both his parents were talented pianists, and little Rick began playing piano and guitar in his early teens. All that practice came to fruition years later while he was playing for the Cincinnati Swords in the AHL. He hooked up with the team's organist, Dave Proffit, and went into the studio to record "Natural Man" (A side) and "I Don't Want to Cry" (B side). The platter was produced by Do-Right Records featuring Dudley's own singing, and sold some 10,000 copies. Dudley had been a lacrosse player first and foremost in his later teen years – a superstar lacrosse player, in fact – playing hockey as an afterthought with the Dixie Beehives and making his way up the puck ladder thanks to his fighting abilities. Undrafted, he was signed by Minnesota but ruined his knee in training camp. He wound up in Buffalo, playing with Brian Spencer and Jim Lorentz on a line dubbed the "Kamikaze Kids" because of their bang-and-crash style of play. In the summer of 1975 he signed a lucrative contract with the WHA's Cincinnati Stingers, rejoining the Sabres four years later. A battered body eventually led to his retirement in 1981, at which point he wanted to live the quiet life with his wife, Ja-Hee, on a beach in Florida. Then a friend called, and the second part of his hockey life began. The friend needed help with the Carolina Thunderbirds of the Atlantic Coast Hockey League, a team that was 3-24-0 and going nowhere fast. Dudley surveyed the situation, took up the challenge, and became coach, part owner, and bus driver. The team won the championship that season, and three in the next four years. He moved on to coach in Flint, then to the Sabres, his alma mater. His rise continued unchecked, and in no time he was GM for the Ottawa Senators, moving down to Tampa Bay to take on a greater challenge as GM of the struggling Lightning, a position he holds to this day though his portfolio has expanded to include the verbose title of senior vice-president of hockey operations.

He still holds the record for fastest two goals at the start of a playoff game (68 seconds).
DICK DUFF

DUERDEN, Dave
b. Oshawa, Ontario,
April 11, 1977
He's been a Komet, a Matador, a Thoroughblade, and a Border Cat, but he's been an NHLer only twice, with Florida, in a career that has been the Baedeker equivalent to hockey.

DUFF, Dick ("Duffy")
b. Kirkland Lake, Ontario, February 18, 1936
Dick Duff never seemed to be a superstar. In Toronto or Montreal, on dynasties that did nothing but win, he was overshadowed by Keon and Armstrong or Béliveau and Richard. But Duff never played a game in the minors, won six Stanley Cups, and played 18 years in the NHL. He still holds the record for fastest two goals at the start of a playoff game (68 seconds), a record indicative of his superior play when the Cup was at stake. He began with the Leafs, playing three games at the end of the '54-'55 season on a line with Ted Kennedy and Sid Smith. He never played outside the NHL again, making the Leafs full-time at next year's camp and winning Cups in '62 and '63 with the Blue and White. He was traded to the Rangers and then to the Canadiens, where he won four more Cups. His career in Montreal ended on a controversial note

because of his poor relationship with coach Claude Ruel. Duff skipped practice one day and was soon traded to the lowly L.A. Kings. He became known as the best little man in the game, and he finished his career where he began, under Punch Imlach, though now in Buffalo. After retiring from play in 1972, Duff became a scout and remained in the game until 1993 when he retired to a life of leisure. He coached the Windsor Spitfires of the Southern Ontario Junior Hockey League for half a season in 1974 and later joined Imlach for a third session, this time as an assistant coach with the Leafs, for whom he also scouted. For 10 summers during his playing days he took classes at university, in Toronto and Hamilton, before receiving his B.A. in political science from U of Windsor. His luck as an investor, though, left something to be desired. In the late 1960s he owned stock in a company that made electrical parts for Bell Telephone, but the company took a huge and swift hit on the stock market one day, diving from $43 to $15 to $1 a share in a matter of days. Duff lost some $60,000. One of the most likeable men in hockey, Duff never married – his wife, er, life, was hockey.

DUFFUS, Parris
b. Denver, Colorado,
January 27, 1970
In the spring of 1998, the U.S. finished a pathetic twelfth at the World Championships, forcing the nation to play in a qualifying tournament a few months later to ensure their position in "A" pool. Duffus, out of the NHL, was called on to mind the goal for that team, which won all three games against lesser opponents to right a humiliating wrong. Likely his only NHL time will go in the books as a game in the 1996-97 season with Phoenix when Duffus played all of 29 minutes. Beyond that, he has spent years playing goal in European leagues and later in Russia, more or less pulling himself out of NHL contention in the process.

DUFOUR, Luc
b. Chicoutimi, Quebec, February 13, 1963
He spoke almost no English when he arrived in Boston in 1982 for his first year of pro hockey, but Dufour fell into a depression the night of October 23, 1982, when his best friend, Normand Leveille, suffered a cerebral hemorrhage during a game. Leveille lived, but his career ended the moment he collapsed on the ice, and Dufour, his roommate in Beantown and pal from Chicoutimi in junior, was devastated. He played that year and part of the next with the Bruins, but the year after was traded twice and sent to the minors. That was pretty much the end of the line for Dufour.

Dave Duerden

Luc Dufour

DUFOUR, Marc
b. Trois Rivières, Quebec, September 11, 1941

His brother, Claude, used to tend the goal for Springfield, so the name Dufour was not new to the AHL. But Marc was a bit of a scorer during a lengthy career in the AHL, scoring 30 or more goals 5 times in the 1960s and 1970s. He played 14 games in the NHL over that time, but it was good that he sold beer in the summers, because he wasn't going to get rich playing in the big league.

DUFRESNE, Donald
b. Quebec City, Quebec, April 10, 1967

A low draft choice by Montreal in 1985, Dufresne has his name on the 1993 Stanley Cup because of the good standing he had with coach Jacques Demers. He played only 32 regular-season games and only 1 playoff game before the finals, and after the first 4 games of those finals against the Gretzky-led L.A. Kings he had yet to dress. Demers, knowing the rules, dressed Dufresne who, by playing in the finals, automatically became eligible for Cup-engraving honours. The Habs won the Cup in game five, and Dufresne's place in hockey history was firm. That very summer he was traded to Tampa Bay, and after that he moved from team to team, never catching on full-time with any one club.

Donald Dufresne

DUGGAN, Jack
b. Ottawa, Ontario, December 17, 1898
d. unknown

Rarely has a player been so faithful to one city as Duggan to Ottawa. Regardless what level of play he achieved, it was usually in an Ottawa uniform that he played during the roaring 1920s. Even his only NHL time came with the Senators in 1925-26, when the left winger played on a line with Frank Finnigan and Hec Kilrea, though he registered not a single point.

DUGGAN, Ken
b. Toronto, Ontario, February 21, 1963

A rare free agent signing after a four-year career with the University of Toronto (1982-86), Duggan was dubbed the best defenceman in CIAU hockey by his coach, Paul Titanic. He was big and mobile, and a terrific offensive threat from the blueline, something the Rangers might have used. Duggan's pedigree was sound, having been named to the OUAA 2nd All-Star Team twice and named All-Tournament at the International Cup in Montreal. But he failed to impress and wound up signing with Minnesota as a free agent. He got into one game in January 1988, but that was it. The following year, he joined Canada's National Team, but after a brief stay retired from the game for good.

Ron Duguay

DUGUAY, Ron ("Doogie")
b. Sudbury, Ontario, July 6, 1957

The grace and speed on ice, the curly hair, free-flowing without the restrictions of a helmet, the cocky confidence, the good looks and sex appeal … and, of course, the attendant women. Duguay became friendly with Cher, Bianca Jagger, Cheryl Tiegs, Farrah Fawcett, and models galore. He owned a white Cadillac and a gold boat, appeared in ads for Vidal Sassoon. He owned a restaurant in Manhattan called Sticks, was part owner of a disco in Westchester called 21 North, and scored 40 goals in '81-'82 with the Rangers. But his practice habits were poor, such as not showing up, and Duguay could have cared less about the $50 fines. He was traded, to Detroit, settled down and – ahhh! – got married, but the goals quickly stopped coming. The Red Wings sent him to Pittsburgh, which sent him to the Rangers, which sent him to the Kings. And then he went right out of the country. He played '89-'90 in Germany, then returned to play and coach in the IHL, the cockiness that is mistress to Youth having quietened a bit with the advent of that she-devil Time.

DUGUID, Lorne
b. Bolton, Ontario, April 4, 1910
d. Toronto, Ontario, March 20, 1981

Duguid's hockey career with Montreal, Detroit, and Boston prior to the Second World War was brief and insignificant compared to what he accomplished in the business and sporting worlds after the war. He helped establish the NHL Oldtimers and the Charlie Conacher Research funds, and in 1974 he was part of a group that tried to bring major-league baseball to Toronto. In 1972, he became the first former player to become a member of the Leafs' board of directors, a position he held until his death. His first assignment in this capacity came the night of February 23, 1972, when he and his wife hosted His Royal Highness, Prince Bernhard of the Netherlands, at the Pittsburgh-Leafs game at the Gardens. Duguid's business dealings were of the highest rank. He was president of Daleberry Agency Ltd. and James Barclay Ltd., executive vice-president of Hiram Walker and Sons, and director with Corby Distillery.

DUKOWSKI, Laudas "Duke" (sometimes "Dutkowski")
b. Regina, Saskatchewan, August 30, 1900
d. Vancouver, British Columbia, September 26, 1976

Dukowski is one of the only men to play for both the New York Rangers and the New York Americans, and he did so in the same season, 1933-34. Yet, despite playing in 200 regular-season games, he managed only

Despite playing in 200 regular-season games, he managed only 6 playoff appearances.
DUKE DUKOWSKI

6 playoff appearances. Like a small, but not insignificant, number of other pre-expansion players, he played a few tricks with his name. The Dennenays, for instance, later spelled their name Denneny, and Dutkowski later dropped the "t" from his surname. In later years, he ran an hotel in Vancouver.

DUMART, Woodrow "Woody" ("Porky")
b. Berlin (Kitchener), Ontario, December 23, 1916
d. Needham, Massachusetts, October 19, 2001
Growing up with Milt Schmidt and Bobby Bauer provided Dumart with a lifetime of experience and happiness. The three played at virtually every level of hockey together, culminating with their careers in Boston. While Dumart had started his hockey days as a defenceman, he moved up to the left wing and became a star with his friends on the Kraut Line. The threesome made its collective NHL debut with Boston on the final night of the '35-'36 season, and the year after they were the team's best line. In the years leading up to the war, the Bruins won two Stanley Cups, in 1939 and '41, led by the Kraut Line. In '39-'40, Schmidt, Dumart, and Bauer finished 1-2-3 in NHL scoring, a remarkable testament to their individual and cumulative abilities. The three left as a unit to join the Canadian army, and Dumart returned in 1945 to have nine more productive seasons, all with the Bruins. As the best two-way forward in the game, it was often his job to cover the best players on the other team. By the time he retired in 1954, he was the oldest player in the league and also one of Boston's most popular athletes. Dumart settled in Boston and worked as a sales rep for Bauer Skate Co. well into the 1990s, and for years he was also the official scorer for Bruins home games. He was inducted into the Hockey Hall of Fame in 1992. He suffered a heart attack en route to the FleetCenter where he was planning to attend Ray Bourque Night.

Dumart worked as a sales rep for Bauer Skate Co. well into the 1990s.
WOODY DUMART

DUMAS, Michel
b. St. Antione-de-Pontbriand, Quebec, July 8, 1949
Dumas's career ended on December 26, 1976 as a result of an eye injury. He was scheduled to play that night, but at the morning skate his teammate, John Marks, took an ordinary shot from the blueline. The puck glanced off Dumas's glove and struck the goalie flush in the eye, damaging the macula of the retina of the right eye. Dumas had signed with the Hawks in 1971 as a free agent and bided his time for four years in the minors. He played with the Hawks only briefly because Tony Esposito started virtually every game and the team had a solid backup in Gilles Villemure. But in '76-'77 it appeared Dumas had beat out Villemure as the

backup. He had stayed with the team that year only because he signed with Cincinnati of the WHA but was lured back when Chicago gave him the same signing bonus as the Stingers had offered ($75,000). After only eight regular-season games, his eyesight damaged, Dumas stowed away his pads for the last time. He later became Chicago's chief talent scout.

DUMONT, Jean-Pierre "J-P"
b. Montreal, Quebec, April 1, 1978
A little patience sometimes goes a long way. The Islanders drafted Dumont 3rd overall in 1996, a very preferential position, indeed. But two years later, the Isles traded him to Chicago, and two years more saw him go to Buffalo. At this time, his stock was as low as it could get. He was more or less a throw-in to the Doug Gilmour trade for Michal Grosek, but in his first two years Dumont registered consecutive 20-goal seasons, thus giving rise to the possibility that at only 24 his best years are still ahead of him. The Isles and Hawks might yet rue the deal.

DUNBAR, Dale
b. Winthrop, Massachusetts, October 14, 1961
A Boston-area boy realized his dreams when he played hockey at Boston University and then signed with the Bruins as a free agent. He had played one game with Vancouver previously and played only once with the Bruins in '88-'89. Dunbar later moved to Europe briefly, but his career ended after a serious knee injury in the British league.

DUNCAN, Art ("Dune")
b. Sault Ste. Marie, Ontario, July 4, 1891
d. Aurora, Ontario, April 13, 1975
William James Arthur Duncan began his playing career with the Vancouver Millionaires in the Pacific Coast league in 1915 but on May 12, 1916, he enlisted in the Canadian army, going to France and joining the Royal Flying Corps with future boss Conn Smythe. During his fighting career, he knocked a dozen enemy planes out of the sky, and for one in particular he received the Military Cross: "From the dizzy height of 6,000 feet in the air, Captain Duncan trailed on the tail of a German aeroplane with a wounded Hun aviator at the stick, and forced the enemy to land his machine back of the British lines, where the damaged plane was seized, and the Teuton air warrior made prisoner." He returned to play in the west for a number of years, signing on with Detroit when it joined the NHL in 1926. A year later, he was traded to Toronto, where he played the final four years of his skating career, taking over as the Leafs' coach to start the 1931-32 season. Just four games in, though, Smythe replaced him with

Michel Dumas

J-P Dumont

Dale Dunbar

Art Duncan

Dick Irvin, who took the team to its first Stanley Cup as the Maple Leafs.

DUNCAN, Iain
b. Weston, Ontario, August 4, 1963
Without doubt, his finest hour came at Bowling State University during his four years at the school (1983-87). Duncan was a power forward who could hit and score with equal skill, and when the university selected its all-century team in 2000, Duncan made the second team. He went on to play four part-time years with the Jets before hitting the buses in the minors and then in the minor-minors in places like Toledo and Nashville.

Iain Duncan

DUNCANSON, Craig
b. Sudbury, Ontario, March 17, 1967
When he first went to Los Angeles to test the NHL waters, Duncanson impressed head coach Pat Quinn so much that Quinn was talking about his young left winger as a future captain of the team, a lad who had "leadership" written on his forehead. Two games later, the kid was in the minors. But, in fairness to Quinn, that's the way it would be Duncanson's whole career. His 38 games were lightly sprinkled over 7 seasons, but Quinn's words were prescient to some extent. After retiring, Duncanson became a coach at Laurentian University.

Craig Duncanson

DUNDAS, Rocky
b. Hamilton, Ontario, April 4, 1953
He didn't go looking for trouble, exactly, but trouble had his address, anyway. A hard-nosed player, Rocky was drafted by Montreal but played only five NHL games, all for Toronto. He appeared on October 5, 7, 12, 14, 17, 1989, and at season's end he was out of hockey. Dundas went on to become pastor of Bayview Glen Church in Thornhill, just north of Toronto.

DUNHAM, Mike
b. Johnson City, New York, June 1, 1972
He is as much an international goalie as he is an NHLer, a young man who has worn his U.S. sweater with pride at every opportunity. Dunham, in fact, played most of 1992-94 with the National Team and has played at three Olympics now for his country – 1992, 1994, and 2002. He began his international career at the 1992 WJC, where he was named best goalie, and later played at the World Championships as well. He had the misfortune to break into the NHL as backup to Martin Brodeur in New Jersey, meaning he'd have no chance to be number one for the foreseeable future. When Nashville claimed him in the Expansion Draft, he instantly became the first-string goalie. In four years, his record was just under .500, excellent for a weak and new team in the league.

Judge Frank
Dunlap

DUNLAP, Judge Frank ("Biff")
b. Ottawa, Ontario, August 10, 1924
d. Ottawa, Ontario, October 26, 1993
A university student who could play hockey but aspired to a career in law, Dunlap played 15 home games for the Leafs while doing his undergrad in 1943-44. A couple of years later, he was playing football for the Ottawa Roughriders, winning the 1951

Blake Dunlop

Richie Dunn

Grey Cup, five years after he was named all-Canadian quarterback in the CFL. He enrolled in Osgoode Hall Law School, graduated in 1950 while playing for the Toronto Argonauts, and was named judge for Renfrew County in 1950 under the formal appellation Chief Justice for Killaloe. That same year, he ran as a Liberal in the federal election for the riding of Carleton but was defeated. His brother, Jake, was with him every step of the way, in football and in law, and together they opened a firm in Ottawa. The partnership endured until 1967 when Frank was appointed county court judge for the counties of Ontario, serving in Pembroke until 1982, after which time he became a judge at large.

DUNLOP, Blake
b. Hamilton, Ontario, April 4, 1953
Dunlop quietly put together a string of five consecutive seasons with 18 goals or more (1978-83) playing in Philadelphia and St. Louis. During his time with St. Louis, he also set a record for most games with a point, 14, in the '81-'82 season, but he was never fortunate enough to play on Cup-contending teams. A graduate of the Ottawa 67's, he was released outright by the Blues in late 1983 and signed with Detroit for his final 57 NHL games to finish that season. He went on to work as a stockbroker after retiring from hockey.

DUNN, Dave
b. Moosomin, Saskatchewan, August 19, 1948
Another free agent signing out of a Canadian university, Dunn graduated from U of Saskatchewan before turning pro and joining the AHL. He caught on with Vancouver, but after a season was sent to Toronto for Gary Monahan and John Grisdale. Off ice, he spent his time playing guitar with the Good Brothers – a local band – a natural leap for him given most of his family was musically inclined. But after a year and a half (of hockey, not music) he suffered a pulled stomach muscle and the Leafs called up Claire Alexander, who impressed enough that Toronto felt it could do without Dunn. Dunn refused to report to the minors, but with no other NHL takers that's where he finished the year before signing with Winnipeg in the WHA. He later became an assistant coach with the Canucks under head coach Harry Neale.

DUNN, Richie
b. Boston, Massachusetts, May 12, 1957
While most American kids in the 1960s would have chalked a strike zone on their garage door to practise their pitching, little Richard Dunn asked his father to draft a goal net so he could practise his shooting – as in pucks. Three hundred pucks a day he'd shoot at the garage net, much to his football-loving father's chagrin. Richard wanted to play hockey so much that he moved to Ontario to play junior in the OHL. His dream seemed over, though, when he went undrafted. Desperate, he approached Buddy Kane, Buffalo Sabres scout for the Boston area, and asked for walk-on status at next year's training camp, in 1978. What the hell. Kane made the necessary arrangements, and Dunn was sent to the farm in Hershey with words of encouragement. He was called up for 25 games during

the season when Jim Schoenfeld was hurt, and he was a spare during that spring's playoffs. One game, when Lee Fogolin suffered headaches during warmup, Dunn was called out of the stands to dress. He played about the same number the year after, and in 1979-80 made the team full-time. He played in the 1981 Canada Cup for the U.S., and later bounced around a bit before returning to the Sabres as a spare part until he retired in 1990. That's what achievement is all about.

DUPERE, Denis
b. Jonquière, Quebec, June 21, 1948
In his first NHL season, 1970-71, Dupere scored just 1 goal in 20 games, but that goal is enshrined in his kitchen a photo of it hangs there in perpetuity as one of his crowning moments in life. He scored that goal for the Leafs, his team for four years, though another special time for him came in '74-'75 with Washington. On arguably the worst team in NHL history, Dupere scored 20 goals, though in reference to the Capitals' overall performance, that production contrasted his +/-, which was a whopping -41. After the NHL, Dupere played briefly in France before working in inventory control for a wholesale sporting goods company in Kitchener, Ontario.

Dupont scored 55 goals, but it was over 5 years.
NORM DUPONT

DUPONT, Andre ("Moose")
b. Trois Rivières, Quebec, July 27, 1949
Called up for a look-see with the Rangers toward the end of the '70-'71 season, Dupont incurred a penalty on his first shift and never looked back. He was involved in a multiplayer deal the next year, to St. Louis, but two years later when he was sent to Philadelphia he had found his true home with the Broad Street goons. When he was just a kid, he had been nicknamed Moose because of his resemblance to NHLer Moose Vasko, and he lived up to the billing by playing physically every night. His crowning glory in the mostly empty halls of skill came in game two of the 1974 Stanley Cup finals, when he scored the tying goal in the final minute and then set up Bobby Clarke for the winner in OT. He won two Cups with the Flyers, then was traded to Quebec, where he finished his career in 1983. That fall he became coach of the Trois Rivières Draveurs, and afterwards he remained in that city and opened a sporting goods store.

DUPONT, Jerome ("Jerry")
b. Ottawa, Ontario, February 21, 1962
An all-star in junior with the Marlies during a four-year career in the OHA, Dupont was a 1st-round draft choice by Chicago in 1980. He made the Hawks at his first camp, as a 19-year-old, a move he later felt rushed and hindered his career. The following season he

played in the minors and was again a full-time player in the Windy City for two years until 1986, when he and Ken Yaremchuk were sent to the Leafs as compensation for Chicago signing Gary Nylund. The award infuriated Leaf owner Harold Ballard, who called Dupont and Yaremchuk "spare parts," a crass, unprofessional, and prophetic remark. Dupont played just 13 games for the Leafs before being demoted, and at the end of the season retired from hockey altogether. He and his wife operated a dry cleaning business in Chicago. She also was working toward a degree in exercise physiology and he toward another in accounting. Dupont later relocated to Toronto and became a player agent, then devoted his time to coaching and teaching kids.

DuPONT, Micki
b. Calgary, Alberta, April 15, 1980
His native Flames drafted him near the end of the day in 2000, and DuPont has played just twice for his local team since. He left Kamloops after the draft and has been in the minors ever since.

DUPONT, Norm
b. Montreal, Quebec, February 5, 1957
When Winnipeg Jets GM John Ferguson finally pried coveted prospect Dupont from Montreal for a draft choice in 1982, he truly felt he had got the man he wanted. He felt this Dupont could score 30 goals, and in that respect he was right. Dupont scored 55 goals, but it was over 5 years and those were the only goals he scored. To be fair, Dupont scored 27 times in his first year with the Jets, but that number halved to 13 and halved again to 7 in succeeding years, and Dupont found himself on a plane to Hartford to play for the Whalers. His junior numbers had been staggering and his numbers in Switzerland, where he ended up for many years after the Whalers, were almost as impressive.

DUPRÉ, Yanick
b. Montreal, Quebec, November 20, 1972
d. August 16, 1997
A Philadelphia Flyers draft choice in 1991, Dupré played parts of three seasons with the big team, spending most of his time with the farm team in Hershey. He had played his junior hockey in the Q and had decent speed and scoring ability, but his life was cut short by leukemia. He stopped playing toward the end of the '95-'96 season and underwent chemotherapy in the summer. That seemed to send the cancer into remission, but in April '97 doctors found it had returned. Dupré underwent a bone marrow transplant in June and contracted pneumonia. He never recovered. Dupré also wrote poetry in his spare time:

Denis Dupere

Andre Dupont

Jerome Dupont

Yanick Dupré

Awake
I'm nearly dying
I'm clear, calm, and unafraid
Lost in dreams, bad dreams
I wish to see light, a fresh new light.
I feel no pain
These drugs, drugs of wonders
Do me well
I feel it flow through my water vein well.
It's my heart
My heart of stone and strength
That keeps me alive and rising
Rising to be the man I used to be
All I wish to see is my life
To leave this world unknown to me
This world of morphine and nightmares
I'm unclear, nervous, and afraid
Afraid of what awaits me
Of what has become of me
Of this athlete, this man in me
Will it still feel like me
But worry not, cause I know
I'll be the man I used to be
(February 1997)

Bob Dupuis

DUPUIS, Bob
b. North Bay, Ontario,
August 26, 1952
The Edmonton Oilers used an astounding six goalies during their first NHL season, 1979-80, and Dupuis was one of the lucky sextet. His lone appearance that year, and in his career, was a 5-3 loss to Philadelphia, remarkable only in that Dupuis never seemed to take the NHL seriously as a possibility. He played virtually no semi-pro hockey before or after. The closest thing to anything serious was a spot on the Canadian 1980 Olympic team. But by the time the Oilers signed him in March, they knew they could score at will; they were just searching for someone – anyone – who could stop the biscuit the other way. Dupuis, sadly, wasn't that person.

DUPUIS, Pascal
b. Laval, Quebec, April 7, 1979
On April 2, 2001, Dupuis played in his first NHL game for Minnesota against San Jose and scored a goal. The free agent who graduated from Shawinigan without being drafted, spent most of the year in the minors, but in 2001-02 he made the team full time and chipped in 15 goals from the left wing. Still young, the Wild might well have found in Dupuis a diamond – or, at least a ruby or an emerald – in the rough.

DURBANO, Steve
b. Toronto, Ontario, December 12, 1951
d. Yellowknife, Northwest Territories, November 16, 2002
Look up "trouble" in the dictionary and you'll find a picture of Steve Durbano. At 13, he beat up a friend in an argument. At 17, he quit school to concentrate on

Look up "trouble" in the dictionary and you'll find a picture of Steve Durbano.
STEVE DURBANO

hockey. He hit a policeman over the head in one game, was suspended in junior, and became penalty minutes king. He swept floors at Maple Leaf Gardens, and his dad, Nick, was a former scout for the Rangers and owner of the Hamilton Red Wings of the OHA. Durbano was suspended by the NHL or his club team regularly. He missed most of his rookie year with mono, broke his wrist after an Andre Dupont check and missed much of the following year, yet still piled up the penalty minutes. The wrist had looked like Corn Flakes, according to one doctor, and, as time would tell, it never healed. In seven partial years, Durbano played for five teams and averaged more than five penalty minutes a game. Toward the end, he turned to cocaine to get through his days. On February 7, 1981, he was used as a "patch" and arrested at Toronto airport, charged with importing coke hidden in the soles of his shoes. (A patch is someone who is ratted on by people trying to cut a deal for themselves with the police.) He had wanted to open an Italian restaurant in South America with friends, and while he awaited trial he worked at a restaurant on Avenue Road, inventing a cocktail called Never on Sunday that was runner-up in a bartenders' competition. Durbano was sentenced to seven years in jail. When he got out, nothing had changed. He was arrested in 1991 for stealing T-shirts from a store in the Eaton's Centre; he was arrested again in April 1998 for running an escort service; and then he headed far, far away, to the Northwest Territories, to work for a vacuum company, Electrolux. His dad, now a golf club owner in Florida, refused to speak to him; his mother supported him every step of the way. Durbano entered the hockey world as a bright prospect, a strong skater who was tough. But injuries, lack of self-discipline, and the lure of ecstasy and easy money took its toll. He fought tooth and nail to establish some normalcy in a life that has been anything but normal for half a century, but in late 2002 he died in hospital of liver cancer.

DURIS, Vitezslav "Slava"
b. Pilzen, Czechoslovakia (Slovakia), January 5, 1954
He played hockey back home with Jiri Crha and the Stastny brothers, and like all those men, he defected, leaving his native and communist Czechoslovakia for the West, knowing he'd never be allowed to return. Duris arrived in Toronto and was a walk-on in camp, making the team because of his skating. He played most of '80-'81 with the Leafs, then spent the next year in the minors after adjusting to the language, the smaller ice, the gruelling schedule. He bounced back in '82-'83, rejoining the Leafs, but his world came

Slava Duris

crashing down on November 3, 1982, when John Paul Kelly of L.A. checked him from behind. He suffered numbness in his legs, and a spinal cord injury was not diagnosed for some weeks. His career seemed over, though he and his family got their Canadian citizenship and he qualified for NHL disability insurance. A year and a half later, he had recovered enough to resume playing, which he did, in Germany, for a number of years before retiring in 1990. He settled down to private life in a free country where he could raise his family as he wished and operated 5 Tim Hortons franchises in the Toronto area.

DURNAN, Bill
b. Toronto, Ontario, January 22, 1916
d. Toronto, Ontario, October 31, 1972
But for a knee injury he suffered in 1932, Bill Durnan might well have been a Maple Leafs goalie rather than a stopper for the Canadiens. He took a long time to recover from that injury, though, by which time Toronto had grown impatient and given up on him. Durnan went up to Kirkland Lake to play for the Blue Devils, eventually winning the Allan Cup in 1940. He was convinced to play for the Montreal Royals the next year, and from there his stellar play drew him into the Canadiens fold. He joined the Habs in 1943 as replacement for the very popular Paul Bibeault, and although he had an extraordinary seven seasons with the Habs, he was booed by fans the moment he allowed a goal and shouts of "Bibeault! Bibeault!" rang through the Forum. Durnan was the first rookie ever to win the Vezina Trophy, an award he won six of seven seasons. He led the league in wins four times and in GAA six times, and he won Cups in 1944 and '46. He holds the modern-day record with a shutout streak that lasted 309:21 and included four straight shutouts. But the truth of the matter was that his nerves could not endure the pressure of playing in Montreal, the taunts of the fans, and the need to win every single game. When he retired in 1950, he said only that his nerves were long gone. He was the first proponent of the two-goalie system to help relieve goalies of such stress, but teams didn't relent for many years still. Durnan was the last goalie to captain an NHL team and he was special again for being ambidextrous. In his day, goalies wore two identical gloves, more like large winter mittens than the formal catching glove worn by today's goalies. As a result, he could, and did, shift his stick from hand to hand based on where the puck was, giving him an advantage with angles and positioning that other goalies just didn't have. After retirement, he worked in insurance in Montreal and later as a scout. He coached in several

But for a knee injury he suffered in 1932, Bill Durnan might well have been a Maple Leafs goalie.
BILL DURNAN

leagues, notably for the Kitchener-Waterloo Dutchmen, though he left that team after a fight with management just a short time before the Dutchies represented Canada at the 1960 Olympics in Squaw Valley. He was inducted into the Hockey Hall of Fame in 1964 but in later years was ill for long periods. He died in North York General Hospital just two weeks after his greatest rival, Turk Broda, died a few miles away.

DUSSAULT, Norm
b. Springfield, Massachusetts, September 26, 1925
Talk about first impressions! Dussault was called up by Montreal in December 1947 and in his first game not only played well for Montreal, but was the best player on the ice. He skated on a line with Joe Carveth and Tod Campeau, making a nice play to set up Campeau for the game's opening goal. As a result, the threesome took a regular shift and dominated the Rangers, and Dussault remained with the team most of the rest of the year. Although he was born in Mass. he was brought up in Sherbrooke, Quebec, and learned the game in and around those more hockey-friendly climes. He played for the Canadiens the next three years, but from there he fell back to Chicoutimi and Quebec league hockey for the balance of his career.

Norm Dussault

DUTTON, Norman Alexander "Mervyn" ("Red")
b. Russell, Manitoba, July 4, 1896
d. Calgary, Alberta, March 15, 1987
First, the nicknames. His mother called him Mervyn from a young age and his sporting friends called him Red, so from early on his christened names of Norman and Alexander meant precious little. If it weren't for his remarkable will, it is likely that no one would have called him very much at all, for his life, and hockey career, were almost ended long before he got very far in the world. Dutton joined the army in 1915 and served overseas with the Princess Patricia's Light Infantry. In April 1917 he suffered a shrapnel injury to his leg and doctors considered amputation. Dutton adamantly refused, though, and over the next 18 months he recovered full use of his leg. When he returned home to Winnipeg, he played in seven leagues to ensure that he was on the ice every day for almost the entire day. His strength grew, as did his skills, and in 1920 he turned to professional hockey after a start in business as a subcontractor failed. When the Tigers folded, Dutton signed on with the Montreal Maroons where he played the first four years of his NHL career. He was not the most talented defenceman in the league, but he was determined to make it, and if he didn't star as

Red Dutton

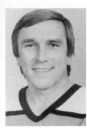

Miroslav Dvorak

Radek Dvorak

Mike Dwyer

Ed Dyck

a scorer, he certainly did as a hitter and fighter. He was traded to the Americans in 1930, and that team was near and dear to his heart for many years. He played his last six years of active duty with the Amerks, but the team never did well in the playoffs and Dutton retired as a player in 1936 without ever having won a Cup. He became coach in his last year and stayed on as coach and manager until 1942, when the franchise folded. Dutton returned to Calgary to continue his business practices, which included building landing strips for aircraft, but in 1943 he was called to Montreal when league president Frank Calder died suddenly. Dutton was asked to became the new president, and said yes for political reasons in the same way that he had been asked to take the position. The owners asked him because Dutton was a strong and respected voice among players, but also because they believed they could control him. Dutton didn't much care. He took the job with the promise that after the war he would be allowed to revive the Americans franchise, a promise the owners had no intention of keeping. By 1946, Dutton could see as much and resigned his position, returning to Calgary where he became a wealthy man as founder and chairman of Standard Gravel and Surfacing Company. He became a trustee of the Stanley Cup in 1952, a position that stirred controversy because of the paradox of Dutton's beliefs. The trusteeship was a lifelong job, but he also had vowed never to enter an NHL building again because of what he considered a decline in the state of the game. Incredibly, he kept his word for 34 years, never entering an arena until October 9, 1980, when he agreed to drop the first puck for the new Calgary Flames franchise. He was inducted into the Hockey Hall of Fame in 1958, won the Lester Patrick Trophy in 1993, and was made a member of the Order of Canada.

DVORAK, Miroslav

b. Hlutobka nad Vltavou, Czechoslovakia (Czech Republic), October 11, 1951

A 10-year veteran of the Czech league, Dvorak was among the second wave of communists to join the NHL. From 1973 to '82 he was part of a system that emphasized international play, and Dvorak represented his country at nine World Championships and two Olympics. He joined the Philadelphia Flyers for 1982-83 and became the first professional to play for the Czech national team at the 1983 Worlds. He was a regular with Philly for three years, playing and rooming with Brad Marsh for most of the time. After being released by the Flyers, he played in Germany for a number of years before retiring, never having played a game in the minors.

DVORAK, Radek

b. Tabor, Czechoslovakia (Czech Republic), March 9, 1977

As a kid, Dvorak was a goalie, but he got sick and tired of being hit by the puck so he discarded the pads, picked up a thin stick, and starting shooting. He got to be pretty good at it, too. Florida drafted him 10th overall in 1995, and he jumped right into the fire that fall, making the team and playing the full season. He played the first four and a half years with the Panthers, but on December 30, 1999, he was traded to San Jose and then to the Rangers in a matter of minutes courtesy of a three-way trade. His point production increased dramatically with the Blueshirts, and he scored 31 goals his first full season with the team, though that number dipped to 17 in 2001-02. He won gold with the Czech Republic at the 2001 World Championships.

He was inducted into the Hockey Hall of Fame in 1958.
RED DUTTON

DWYER, Gord

b. Dalhousie, New Brunswick, January 25, 1978

Three years and counting. Dwyer made his NHL debut on February 12, 2000, and in his first three seasons he has yet to score a goal for Tampa Bay. Granted, his size and pims are his greater strengths, but still one wonders how he held out after being drafted by St. Louis in 1996. That year, he went 67th overall. But the Blues couldn't come to terms with him and two years later Montreal drafted him... 152nd overall. He saw no time with the Habs before being traded to the Lightning, and it is there his goal drought continues.

DWYER, Mike

b. Brampton, Ontario, September 16, 1957

In a brief and part-time career in the NHL, Dwyer had one moment of note to tell the grandkids about. On the night of May 5, 1981, he scored a goal in a playoff game for Calgary against Minnesota. Granted, it came in a 7-4 loss, but it was the only playoff game he ever played. This memorable night came during a four-year career that consisted of just 31 regular-season games.

DYCK, Ed

b. Warman, Saskatchewan, October 29, 1950

The whiz kid with the quick glove hand was a can't-miss NHLer during his two years with the Calgary Centennials, 1969-71. But a year later, the kid missed. A Vancouver draft choice, he appeared in 12 games, had a 1-6-2 record and allowed 35 goals. The year after? Much the same. He transferred to the WHA in '73-'74, but with Indianapolis the following year had a record of 3-21-3, hardly career-establishing numbers.

DYCK, Henry

b. Herbert, Saskatchewan, September 5, 1911
d. unknown

Dyck played in a variety of leagues during a lengthy career that saw him park his carcass in the NHL but once, with the Rangers during the 1943-44 season. A slight forward, he showed some signs of scoring in the American league but never got a real shot to make the New York team before or after the war.

DYE, Cecil "Babe"

b. Hamilton, Ontario, May 13, 1898
d. Chicago, Illinois, January 2, 1962

Not many scoring records from 1922 have stood the test of time, but Dye's has done just that. He won his lone Stanley Cup with the Toronto St. Pats in '21-'22, and in the finals he scored nine goals, a record that has been neither tied nor eclipsed. Dye grew up in Toronto as an all-round athlete. He was a good enough baseball player to have none other than Connie Mack of the Philadelphia Athletics offer him a contract, and he was a halfback with the Toronto Argonauts. But hockey was where his heart was, and from his high school days at De La Salle, Dye wanted to make the game his livelihood. He turned pro with the St. Pats in 1919, and although he weighed in at no more than 150 pounds, he had the hardest shot in the game. Legend has it that in his youth he once scored 12 goals in a game without ever crossing centre ice! Dye quickly became one of the league's top scorers, three times averaging more than a goal a game over the course of a full season. In '20-'21, Dye scored 33 goals in 23 games to lead the NHL, and 2 other times he led the league in goals. One of those times was '24-'25 when he had 38 goals, a team record that lasted 35 years until Frank Mahovlich broke it. He had the pleasure of playing on a forward line with Corb Denneny and Reg Noble, and later Jack Adams replaced Denneny as the line's playmaker. After seven seasons in Toronto, Dye moved on to Chicago and the Americans before returning to the Leafs in '30-'31 at the end of his career. He later coached Port Colborne of the OHA and the Chicago Shamrocks in the American league before turning his energy to refereeing. He held the whistle for five years, most famously in the 1938 Cup finals between Toronto and Chicago, the two cities closest to his heart. He settled in Chicago and worked with a paving contract firm until 1961, when he suffered a stroke. He died a short time later. Dye was inducted into the Hockey Hall of Fame in 1970 and still has one of the highest ratios of goals to games in NHL history, having scored 201 times in just 271 career games.

Legend has it that in his youth he once scored 12 goals in a game without ever crossing centre ice!
BABE DYE

DYKHUIS, Karl

b. Sept Îles, Quebec, July 8, 1972

How's this for a trade? On August 20, 1997, Philadelphia traded Dykhuis and Mikael Renberg to Tampa Bay for four successive 1st-round draft choices in 1998, 1999, 2000, and 2001. Those players turned out to be Simon Gagne, Maxime Ouellet, Justin Williams, and Jeff Woywitka. Wow. Dykhuis wound up playing just 111 games with the Lightning before the Flyers reacquired him, and another 50 games with them before he was sent to Montreal. Early on, he won gold with Canada's juniors in 1991 and played his first NHL games with Chicago the following season.

Karl Dykhuis

DYKSTRA, Steve

b. Edmonton, Alberta, December 1, 1962

Undrafted, Dykstra turned pro in 1982, signing a contract with the Rochester Americans. After just a few games he became property of the Buffalo Sabres, and three years later he had made the team and was in the NHL. In his five years in the league, he played for four teams, though his career nearly ended in the summer of 1986 when he flipped his car in Amherst, New York, in the middle of the night. He was charged with drunk driving, speeding, and failure to use a seat belt, though his injuries didn't cause him to miss too much action. He ended his career in the minors, playing for two years, retiring for two more, then making brief comebacks for four more until calling it quits in 1996.

Steve Dykstra

DYTE, Jack

b. New Liskeard, Ontario, October 13, 1918

A wartime defenceman with Chicago, Dyte patrolled the Hawks blueline for half of the '43-'44 season, though he didn't stick around for the playoffs when the team went to the finals against Montreal. He later became a coach for a number of years back home.

DZIEDZIC, Joe

b. Minneapolis, Minnesota, December 18, 1971

Another tale of optic woe/of stick and puck and poor old Joe. Drafted by Pittsburgh right out of high school, he went on to a fine career at the University of Minnesota and played two full seasons with the Pens in '95-'96 and '96-'97. But after being let go and signing with Phoenix, he played only twice more in the NHL before being demoted to Springfield, where he suffered a career-ending eye injury.

Jack Dyte

EAGLES, Mike
b. Sussex, New Brunswick, March 7, 1963
How can a guy play in the NHL as a regular for 16 years and yet have only 853 games to his credit? Ask the trainers, one after the other. Eagles played for just four NHL teams in that stretch, but he saw the trainer's table as much as the players' bench during his career. A third- or fourth-line forward, he was a minus player in every season but one (in '85-'86 he was +3).

EAKIN, Bruce
b. Winnipeg, Manitoba, September 28, 1962
I scream, you scream, we all scream for Eakin. Well, not quite, but not far off. Eakin was a member of Canada's vaunted gold-medal team at the 1982 World Juniors, though he played only briefly in the NHL (13 games, to be exact). He did, however, become one of the longest-playing Canadians in European hockey history, arriving in Switzerland in 1986 and playing some 14 years in various countries. After retiring, he moved to Orlando, Florida, and opened an ice cream shop, serving iced delights in a cup rather than a rink.

EAKINS, Dallas ("Dally")
b. Dade City, Florida, February 27, 1967
He never played for himself (Dallas, that is), though he has played almost everywhere else in the NHL in the last decade. In fact, only twice has he started consecutive seasons in the same city, Florida in '93 and again in '94, and most recently, Calgary. The atlas of his career reads as follows since entering the league in 1992 (although he was drafted by Washington back in 1985, he never played for the Caps): Winnipeg, Florida, St. Louis, Winnipeg again, Phoenix, Rangers, Florida (again), Toronto, Islanders, Calgary. And all that adds up to just over 100 games played.

EASTWOOD, Mike ("Easty")
b. Ottawa, Ontario, July 1, 1967
The Leafs liked what they saw of Eastwood during his only year with Pembroke in the OJHL, and four years later, after graduating from Western Michigan University, he was ready for the NHL. A feisty, hard-nosed centre, he was a prototypical third-line player from day one, able to win face-offs, rub opponents the wrong way, and kill penalties. He dabbled in stock markets off ice but bounced between the farm and the Gardens for three years before being involved in a series of trades during his tour of the NHL. To this day, he remains the kind forever sought after by teams looking for a role player.

EATON, Mark
b. Wilmington, Delaware, May 6, 1977
Needless to say, when you make the NHL out of Delaware, you're likely making history of some sort. Eaton was the first hockey player to be named that state's athlete of the year by its sportswriters when he copped the award in 1999, and the year after he represented the red, white, and blue in the World Juniors. After a year playing for the Fighting Irish of Notre Dame in '90-'99, he was named CCHA's rookie of the year and on that strength joined the Flyers the next fall as a free agent. He was later sent to Nashville to ply his trade as a defenceman with potential.

EATOUGH, Jeff
b. Toronto, Ontario, June 2, 1963
Buffalo drafted him in 1981, but winger Eatough appeared in only one game for the Sabres and by the end of the decade had made his way through many of the minor leagues and out of the game altogether.

EAVES, Mike
b. Denver, Colorado, June 10, 1956
When little Mike was 12 years old and playing baseball, he chased down a fly ball in centre field. So did the right fielder. They collided, Mike was knocked unconscious, and in the process he suffered his first of a dozen or so concussions that would eventually force him to quit playing hockey in the NHL. He suffered another concussion in high school and two more in college, and as he continued to play the head injuries increased in frequency and were caused by ever-decreasing force. He was born in Denver because his dad, Mike, was studying at the university there, playing college hockey under Murray Armstrong. Mike Sr. got his degree and became a professor of physical education at the University of Ottawa. As a result, Mike Jr. had dual citizenship. He went on to study the same thing as his father, at U of Wisconsin, captaining the hockey team in his last three years and setting up the winning goal to give the Badgers an NCAA title. During a Wisconsin-Duluth game, though, he was hit by Dave Langevin – clean, and not that hard – and remembers only waking up in the hospital. He played for the U.S. at the World Championships and played most of '78-'80 with Oklahoma in the minors, where he suffered two more concussions just two months apart. In '80-'81, he suffered three more while playing with Minnesota in the NHL. The first, a hit from Pat Price, merely prepared him for the worst to come. Barry Beck hit him hard, and then Jean Potvin barely touched him yet sent him off the ice on a stretcher. Incredibly, he kept on playing, but it was only a matter of time before he got the hit that would end it all. He was traded to Calgary in 1983 and played two full, healthy years there. Then, on his first shift in an exhibition game in September 1985, he was hit by Price again, now with Quebec. Doctors told him then and there his career was over, and he agreed. Sort of. He retired to become an assistant coach with the team, but later in the season coach Bob Johnson asked him if he'd be healthy enough to fill in in emergency situations. Eaves began working out just in case, and got the call during the playoffs when Carey Wilson suffered a spleen injury and was gone for the year. Eaves unretired, figuring he'd never been so close to a Stanley Cup. He played in eight games, without incident, but didn't win the Cup and retired for good that summer. He went on to become a development coach for U.S. Hockey and left in 2002 to assume head coaching duties at the University of Wisconsin.

EAVES, Murray
b. Calgary, Alberta, May 10, 1960
The healthy-headed brother of the concussion-prone Mike, Murray had a longer career in the game, though his NHL time was shorter. Murray had two fine years of college hockey with Michigan before turning pro

Mike Eagles

Dallas Eakins

Mike Eastwood

Murray Eaves

Mike Eaves
(opposite page)

Tim Ecclestone

Frank Eddolls

Darryl Edestrand

Duke Edmundson

Tom Edur

with Winnipeg in 1980, but for the next decade he played more in the minors than in the NHL. He moved to Italy and played there for a number of years, then took to coaching in the minors, which is what he continues to do.

ECCLESTONE, Tim
b. Toronto, Ontario, June 24, 1947
Born in Toronto, played in Toronto, found his love in Georgia. Ecclestone was a solid, if unspectacular, forward in the late 1960s and into the 1970s who eventually found himself playing in Atlanta. He had a bit of speed and started with St. Louis after expansion, where he played in three successive Cup finals without winning a game. He was on the ice, though, when Bobby Orr scored his famous goal in 1970, and after finishing with the Flames in 1977 he remained in the city and opened a bar, which has prospered.

EDBERG, Rolf
b. Stockholm, Sweden, September 29, 1950
The broken jaw was the last straw. Edberg had been perfectly happy playing in Sweden, but the lure ($$$) and challenge of the NHL drew him to Washington in 1978. In his first year, he had a decent 14 goals. In his second year, he showed signs of greatness by scoring 23 times. But in his third season, trouble found him. A sore back put him out for most of December 1980, and when he came back to play on a line with Bengt Gustafsson and Dennis Ververgaert things looked better until Calgary's Phil Russell hit him so hard he broke Edberg's jaw. He was gone for the year and then for good, deciding Sweden was preferable for a career in hockey.

EDDOLLS, Frank
b. Lachine, Quebec, July 5, 1921
d. Ridgeway, Ontario, August 13, 1961
It was a life in hockey from start to finish, but a life too short all the same. Eddolls came out of junior hockey in the year leading up to the Second World War and played during his two years in the army. He joined the Canadiens in 1944 and played briefly on the Cup team a year later. He later played for the Rangers, but in 1948 he was involved in an awful car accident just before the start of that season's training camp. Five members of the Rangers were in the car: Buddy O'Connor, Edgar Laprade, Billy Moe, Tony Leswick, and Frank Eddolls. All but Leswick were unconscious and bleeding, and he pulled them all out of the car to safety. Eddolls had the worst injuries. He suffered a badly cut tendon in his right knee and a shoulder and head injury, and missed six weeks recovering. Midway through the '51-'52 season, Eddolls accepted a demotion to Saskatoon so he could both play and coach. He had found his niche. Eddolls coached the Buffalo Bisons for two seasons, then took on the head job for Chicago in '54-'55, his one and only year as an NHL coach. He then returned to Buffalo, and remained there until he died while golfing at the Cherry Hill Country Club.

EDESTRAND, Darryl
b. Strathroy, Ontario, November 6, 1945
That Darryl Edestrand played 455 NHL games is a remarkable achievement. That he scored 34 goals is as

staggering an accomplishment as any Hall of Famer's 50-goal seasons. You see, even before he made the big leagues, Edestrand suffered a badly broken arm, had all the broken pieces removed, and struggled to resume normal life with a left arm that was two inches shorter than his right. That he could lift a hockey puck – let alone a stick – amazed doctors. That he would make the NHL was inconceivable in 1966 after he slid into a goalpost during an AHL game. He missed the better part of a year, and after brief, weak appearances with St. Louis and Philadelphia regained enough strength by '71-'72 to make the Pittsburgh lineup on a regular basis. In '72-'73, he scored 15 goals, from the blueline, and after that became what everyone dreams of becoming – an NHL regular. He focused more on offence than defence to ensure his career had longevity, and by the time he left the NHL in 1979 he had proved that the mind is much, much stronger than the arm.

EDMUNDSON, Garry "Duke"
b. Sexsmith, Alberta, May 6, 1932
He may have been born in Alberta and played his minor hockey there, but it was Edmonton that ended his career years later in adulthood. Edmundson got into one NHL game as an 18-year-old, playing for Montreal in 1951-52. Eight years later, he got into his second game when he played a couple of part-time seasons for Toronto. He wound up playing in San Francisco, liking it so much that when the Seals tried to assign him to Edmonton, he refused to report and retired. He later settled in Corona, California, and became president of Western Homes Corporation a business that builds mobile homes.

EDUR, Tom
b. Toronto, Ontario, November 18, 1954
Edur played for a number of teams during his skating career, but no team was stronger than the Jehovah's Witness who lured him from the ice to the Bible business. Edur played Junior B with Markham under coach Bill White, then moved to the Marlies the next year. That 1972-73 Marlies team, coached by George Armstrong, was likely the finest junior team in history, and the WHA raided it without compunction that summer. Mark and Marty Howe left, and Edur signed a lucrative deal with the Cleveland Crusaders. His NHL rights were sold by Boston, which had drafted him in 1974, to Colorado, and Edur played for the Rockies in 1976 before being traded to Pittsburgh midway through the following season. He was a solid stay-at-home defenceman, but in the summer of 1978 he decided the Jehovah's Witnesses were better suited to his tastes. He admitted he hated the physical and violent qualities of hockey and settled in Evergreen, Colorado, canvassing door to door in the name of Jehovah, never to return to the NHL.

EDWARDS, Don ("The Heart"/ "Dart")
b. Hamilton, Ontario, September 28, 1955
Life, any player will tell you, is far more important than hockey, and any hockey player will add that the most important people in their lives are their parents, the people who drove them to the 6 a.m. practices every Saturday, bought their equipment, and made the many sacrifices necessary to pursue the dream of

the NHL. Don Edwards' world crashed to a halt in March 1991, long after his career was over, when his sister's former boyfriend killed their parents. Since that day, Edwards has spent much of his time trying to toughen Canadian laws for murder. Don's uncle, Roy, played goal in the NHL, which is where he gets his catching hand, perhaps, but during his decade in the NHL Don became one of the league's best goalies. The two are the only players to have come out of the Caledonia area, and at first Don seemed destined to be a backup for either Gerry Desjardins or Bob Sauve. He became the number-one man in his third year of pro, 1977-78, playing in a league-high 72 games and leading the NHL with 38 wins. He earned an invite to the 1981 Canada Cup, though he played only one game behind Mike Liut, and the following year he was sent to Calgary and then on to Toronto. The Leafs gave him plenty of action for one year, but gave up on him to allow Allan Bester and Ken Wregget to mature. Edwards couldn't catch on anywhere in the NHL, so he signed with the Brantford Motts Clamatos, joining former NHLers Rocky Saganiuk, Stan Weir, and Stan Jonathan and winning the Allan Cup in his only season with the team. Edwards later became a goaltending coach for the L.A. Kings and Nashville Predators.

EDWARDS, Gary ("Scoop")
b. Toronto, Ontario, October 5, 1947

It's one of the oddest, most irrelevant, yet curious bits of NHL trivia around. There have been only four men in NHL history with the surname Edwards, yet all of them were goalies! Gary got his first taste of NHL life as a middle man. Middle as in when Jacques Plante of St. Louis was injured and Glenn Hall was hurriedly getting dressed to replace him, Edwards filled in for four shutout minutes of hockey. He played only one more game with the Blues, the next year, before embarking on a long journey with Los Angeles in 1971. After four and a half middling years, he started to move around, and in retrospect his only season of .500 goaltending was in '74-'75, when he had a superb record of 15-3-8. After retiring, Edwards moved to southern California, where he worked for a residential and commercial paint contracting company.

EDWARDS, Marv
b. St. Catharines, Ontario, August 15, 1935

Edwards took the long, long road to the NHL, making his debut in 1969 as the oldest rookie in the history of the NHL. His career to that point looked like a road map, starting in his hometown of St. Catharines as a junior and then spreading out far and wide, his longest time spent in the Eastern League. His early life was marked by success: In 1959, he joined the Belleville McFarlands and won the World Championships for Canada in Czechoslovakia. One of his teammates that trip was Johnny McLellan, future coach of the Leafs who claimed Edwards at the 1969 Intra-League Draft. He played just one year with Toronto, though, went back to the minors, and came up for expansion air with the futile California Seals. In his two years with the Golden boys he had a record of 5-24-3, and in 1974 he retired at age 39. A year later, he began his second calling, as a coach, with the Salt Lake Golden Eagles of the CHL.

EDWARDS, Roy
b. Seneca Township, Ontario, March 12, 1937
d. Hamilton, Ontario, August 16, 1999

He was 19 years old when he won a gold medal with Canada at the 1958 World Championships, but it wasn't until 11 years later that he made his NHL debut, with the Detroit Red Wings. He was playing Senior hockey in Windsor when the Whitby Dunlops asked him to go to Norway for the Worlds, an invite he accepted only reluctantly. After winning, he bounced around in a number of minor pro leagues with teams everywhere from Fort Wayne to Fort Worth to Spokane to Saint Louis. The Wings called him up during the '67-'68 season and he played well enough to stick with the team for the better part of four years. But in 1970, he was hit hard in the head by two oncoming players and knocked unconscious. He suffered a fractured skull and concussion, and lay in hospital for five days. Six weeks later, he was back, wearing a mask for the first time, and becoming the first goalie to attach a piece of helmet for the back of the mask. He retired that summer but was talked back into the net by Pittsburgh. The next season, with Detroit, he had a career year, playing in 52 games and tying Ken Dryden for a league-leading 6 shutouts. A few games the next year was enough, and he retired to Caledon, where he was a hero. He worked in a home renovations business for the next 22 years of his life with his wife, Mary, in their Peeble Street home, until retiring from civilian life. He died of dementia, a condition that plagued him the last few years of his life.

EGAN, Martin Joseph "Pat" ("The Great Eeg"/ "The Skating Boxcar")
b. Blackie, Alberta, April 25, 1918

His house in Calgary had a shamrock on the front door, so his friends started calling him Pat and the name stuck. Only occasionally was he called Marty or Joe, but either way he had an assortment of jobs as a

Gary Edwards

Edwards has spent much of his time trying to toughen Canadian laws for murder.
DON EDWARDS

Marv Edwards

Roy Edwards

Allan Egeland

Jack Egers

Gerry Ehman

Pelle Eklund

Nils Ekman

teen – digging ditches, working in a shipyard – that gave him great strength. Rumour has it that he once lifted a horse back to its feet after it had fallen on an icy street. Egan denied the story, saying it was a team of horses. He was discovered by a New York Americans scout while playing out in Nelson, B.C., in the mid-1930s, working his way up to Eddie Shore's Springfield team, like Shore performing the incredible double duty of playing in both the AHL and the NHL for a brief time in 1939-40. He interrupted his career to join the Canadian army, joining Detroit but being traded mid-season of '43-'44 to Boston for Flash Hollett, one of the greatest defencemen of all time. Hollett was so upset with the trade he almost quit the game, but Egan flourished in Boston. He was both a fighter and an Iron Man, playing in more than 300 consecutive games and twice leading the league in penalty minutes. He was the hardest hitter in the game, and also the most popular Bruin. At every Bruins home game, members of his huge fan club would wear green hats and string green banners wherever they could. He went to the minors after his NHL days, and made quite an impression when he attacked a linesman during a game. He was initially suspended for life, but that was reduced to one year, and he went on to a lengthy career in the minors. He was later playing coach of the Victoria Cougars and then Springfield, and in 1965-66 came out of retirement to play briefly for the Jacksonville Rockets of the EHL at the tender age of 47. Egan later became a security guard at Northeastrn University.

EGELAND, Allan
b. Lethbridge, Alberta, January 31, 1973
Well, he had his day in the NHL sun, but the moon of his career is wide and long and dark. Egeland played 17 games with lowly Tampa Bay in the mid-1990s, but since then has played in the minors and shows no signs of being called up again. He put up big numbers with Tacoma in junior, but not even with the Pensacola Ice Pilots has he managed a modest scoring season.

EGERS, Jack ("Smokey")
b. Sudbury, Ontario, January 28, 1949
A stellar career in junior started the ball rolling, but in the minors Egers suffered a shoulder separation in 1969 that hindered his progress. In his second year in the CHL he led the league in points, but his move up to the Rangers was again short-lived. In 1971-72, in a game against the North Stars, he took a big step backward. He took a slapshot and at the same time absorbed a punishing check from Fred Barrett. Egers hit his head on the ice and swallowed his tongue, but swift-moving trainers saved his life. Nonetheless, he suffered a serious concussion and soon after was

traded to St. Louis. There he was put on a line with Mike Murphy and Garry Unger and had seasons of 21 and 24 goals, using his vaunted slapshot to good effect (he was nicknamed Smokey for that reason). More injuries took their toll, and he was soon forced to retire at age 28. Egers moved to Kitchener, Ontario, and became a firefighter, one of many hockey players to do so after leaving the game (among them the aforementioned Fred Barrett and brother John).

EHMAN, Gerry ("Tex")
b. Cudworth, Saskatchewan, November 3, 1932
There were three pro parts to Ehman's full career. He had a substantial tenure in the AHL, where he scored 30 or more goals 7 times and won a scoring championship. Then there was his time in the Original Six, starting with a goal in his first NHL game, with Boston, and climaxing with four years with the Leafs and a Stanley Cup in 1964. And then there was the expansion career of post-1967 glory, with Oakland at the end of his days, where the players called him Dad and he skated on a line with Ernie Hicke and Tommy Williams. And then, in a suit, came the rest of his hockey career – a lifelong devotion to scouting for a variety of NHL teams.

Egan later became a security guard at Northeastern University.
PAT EGAN

EISENHUT, Neil
b. Osoyoos, British Columbia, February 9, 1967
Osoyoos is south of Penticton, B.C., and north of Washington state by about a foot, and from this tiny, tiny place came Eisenhut, who played ever-so-briefly with Vancouver and Calgary in the mid-1990s. He hung around in the minors for a couple of years and then decided, like 1 of about 650 Canadians a year, to play in Europe. He's been there ever since.

EKLUND, Per-Erik "Pelle"
b. Stockholm, Sweden, March 22, 1963
Eklund interrupted a perfectly successful career in Sweden to try his hand at the North American game, though rarely did he miss a chance to play for Tre Kronor on the international circuit. Prior to joining Philadelphia in 1985, Eklund played in two World Juniors, an Olympics, a World Championships, and a Canada Cup. In the next nine years, he played entirely for the Flyers except for five games, at the end, with Dallas, before returning to Sweden to play. In his second year in Philly, he got to experience Cup finals, against the Gretzky-led Oilers, his closest call to hoisting the prized trophy.

EKMAN, Nils
b. Stockholm, Sweden, March 11, 1976
Ekman was born in Sweden and played for Sweden at

the World Juniors in 1996, but he also played pro in Finland for a number of years before signing with Tampa Bay early in the 1999-2000 season. His 28 games that year is the sum total of his NHL career to date.

ELDEBRINK, Anders
b. Kalix, Sweden, December 11, 1960
Eldebrink played only briefly in the NHL, but from the day he first played internationally for Sweden, in December 1980, he was considered one of the greatest defencemen of all time in his native land. He came to Vancouver in 1981 and a year later played his last game, with Quebec, before returning to Sweden. He won a gold and two silvers at the Worlds and an Olympics bronze, and he played in both the '84 and '87 Canada Cups. He later played in the less-demanding Swiss league before finishing back home at age 38. He was considered a great rushing defenceman with an accurate shot and was an all-star in Swedish league play on five occasions.

ELIAS, Patrik
b. Trebic, Czechoslovakia (Czech Republic), April 13, 1976
One of the new generation of NHL superstars, Elias is in the prime of a tremendous career that has got better and better. He started off playing in the Czech league at age 16, and at 18 was drafted by New Jersey, the team that has held him tight ever since. In his first three years in North America, he developed exactly as an NHLer should, playing more and more games in the NHL and fewer and fewer in the AHL until he played full-time in the big tent. Similarly, his point production has increased, and he is now a bona fide 40-goal scorer who plays superior defence for a left winger. He played in the 2000 All-Star Game in Toronto, and a few weeks later won the Cup with the Devils. In 2001, he was named to the NHL's First All-Star Team and in the following year played for the Czechs at the 2002 Olympics in Salt Lake City.

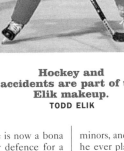

Hockey and accidents are part of the Elik makeup.
TODD ELIK

ELICH, Matt
b. Detroit, Michigan, September 22, 1979
Speed and size are his bread and butter, but youth is the meat that's not yet cooked. He recorded an assist in his first NHL game, with Tampa Bay on February 19, 2000, but since then he has seen little action with the Lightning as he develops in the minors with the IHL's Detroit Vipers.

ELIK, Boris "Bo"
b. Geraldton, Ontario, October 17, 1929
Uncle to Todd Elik, Bo surely believes in fate more than the average Joe. During his teen years, his family moved close to Toronto, but Bo never took to the big city. His parents decided to send him back to Geraldton to continue his hockey playing, and took him to Union Station to catch the train. This was 1949. Unfortunately, they were late and missed the train, so were forced to return the next night. Of course, that night they arrived at the station with time to spare, and another man noticed Bo's Geraldton hockey jacket. His name was Bucko McDonald, former Leaf and current coach of the Sundridge Beavers. Bucko convinced Bo to join him, and the lad learned from the best. He moved on to North Bay a year later, and signed with Cleveland of the AHL a few years after that. Bo was named rookie of the year in 1956-57, helping the Barons win the Calder Cup. Eventually he saw his only NHL action, three games with Detroit in '62-'63. Imagine if he had made that train to Geraldton…!

ELIK, Todd
b. Brampton, Ontario, April 15, 1966
He was lucky just to be alive. When he was a year and a half old, Elik was in a car that smashed into a truck. Todd was thrown through the windshield, and doctors needed 160 stitches to sew his little face together. Hockey and accidents are part of the Elik makeup, though. His father had been a promising junior before breaking his neck in a diving accident and never recovering full use of his legs. He never knew his aunt, who was killed in another traffic accident. Two uncles played serious hockey, one for the Marlies and U of T, the other with Bucko McDonald's Sundridge Beavers. Todd was never drafted, but the Rangers signed him, sent him to the minors, and traded him to the other coast, L.A., before he ever played a game with the Blueshirts. In La La Land, he was a solid centre, scoring 21 goals in 1990-91, his first full season. He went on to Minnesota, Edmonton, and San Jose, having a career year in '93-'94 with the Sharks, where he scored 25 times before simmering down and ending up out of the NHL and in the Swiss League, playing with Langnau in 2002-03.

ELIOT, Darren
b. Hamilton, Ontario, November 26, 1961
Eliot graduated in 1983 from Cornell University with a degree in agricultural economics, but before pursuing his NHL dream he opted to play a year for the Canadian National Team in preparation for the '84 Olympics. He started off in fine form, but as the season went on he felt more and more sluggish, and his performance tailed off. In January '84, just before the Games were to begin, he was diagnosed as being diabetic. He played briefly for Canada at Sarajevo, and by the time he joined Los Angeles the year after he had his diabetes under control. Over the next 5 years

Anders Eldebrink

Patrik Elias

Darren Eliot

he played just 89 games before retiring and getting into broadcast journalism. He worked for the Mighty Ducks and later the even-newer Thrashers, and provided colour commentary for a variety of American television stations. In 1996, Eliot was inducted into the Cornell Athletic Hall of Fame.

ELLACOTT, Ken
b. Paris, Ontario, March 3, 1959

Ellacott may have been one of the goalies Vancouver had hoped would replace Glen Hanlon when the Canucks traded Hanlon the previous season, but when he gave up 41 goals in just a few games, he proved he couldn't be All-Star material. He had had a fine junior career with Peterborough and an equally impressive start to his pro career in the Central league, but after the Canucks sojourn, Ellacott quickly became an also-ran.

Ron Ellis

ELLETT, Dave ("Roy")
b. Cleveland, Ohio, March 30, 1964

The pedigree was certainly a good starting point. His dad was Bob Ellett, who played in the minors for an eternity, never making it to the big dance. Three of Bob's teammates in Cleveland of the AHL were John Ferguson, Les Binkley, and Tom Savage. In 1964, Bob had to leave the team to be by his wife's side as she gave birth to a boy they named Dave. The Elletts went where Bob could find work as a player, and in the summers they returned to Ottawa, where Bob worked in the refrigeration business. At 17, Dave tried out for the Marlies and was cut, forced to return to Ottawa to play Tier II for the year. He was drafted at the end of that season, 1982, by the Winnipeg Jets. Their chief scout was a man named Les Binkley, the team's eastern scout was Tom Savage, and the GM was John Ferguson. Dave accepted a scholarship from Bowling Green, but after two years he had developed so rapidly that he joined the Jets, quickly becoming a top defenceman with size, mobility, and offensive ability. His dad coached in the WHA and then with the Ottawa 67's, and Dave moved up the ranks of the finer NHLers. His entry into this rarified world brought with it some controversy in 1989 when he accepted an invitation to play for Canada at the 1989 World Championships. Team USA coach Bob Johnson was livid, citing Ellett's place of birth and the fact that Ellett had attended Team USA's training camp for the 1987 Canada Cup (to which Ellett retorted that Johnson had never played him, thus keeping his eligibility clean, much like Brett Hull in the other direction). Ellett did, indeed, play for Canada in '89, his first and only international experience. After retiring, he helped his wife, Annie, train for "professional Western shooting" events.

ELLIOT, Fred
b. Clinton, Ontario, February 18, 1903
d. unknown

Elliot played most of the 1928-29 season with the Ottawa Senators, but barely a hockey peep was heard from him before or after that season.

ELLIS, Ron
b. Lindsay, Ontario, January 8, 1945

A lifelong Leaf and one of the more consistent players to wear the Blue and White, Ellis played every one of his 1,034 NHL games with Toronto. He graduated from the Marlies after four years and one Memorial Cup, making his debut with the parent club at the end of the 1963-64 season. He scored 23 goals as a rookie, dipped to 19 the next year, then had 10 successive seasons of

His dad coached
in the WHA and then with the
Ottawa 67's.
DAVE ELLETT

20 goals or more. He was considered the quintessential winger who patrolled the right side as if it were a lane. He won his only Stanley Cup in 1967, scoring his most important goal, the opening score of the Cup-clinching sixth game. Ellis became known as a reliable, clean, and highly effective two-way player. In the summer of 1972, he was invited to training camp for the historic Summit Series, and despite playing with a broken collarbone he was effective in a checking role and played in all eight games. So admired was he that Ace Bailey offered Ellis his retired number six sweater, an honour Ellis accepted accordingly. He became the first man to wear six since Bailey's career had ended in 1933, and as soon as Ellis retired, the number was again taken out of circulation by the Leafs. Ellis quit the game in 1975, finding it increasingly difficult to get motivated night in and night out. He alleviated his depression by rediscovering Christianity. His interest in the game was revived in the spring of '77 when NHLers were allowed to play at the World Championships. He accepted an invitation to play, and his love for the game returned to the point that he attended Leafs training camp in the fall. He played three and a half years, but when his 1960s coach Punch Imlach made a tumultuous return to the Gardens as GM in 1979, his days were numbered. In December 1980, Imlach put Ellis on waivers, a tremendous insult to a classy veteran player, and a few weeks later Ellis was released outright, booted from the team he had considered his family for 16 years. He worked in insurance in Orangeville for three years, then opened a sporting goods store while adjusting to life outside the rink. Ellis later worked for the Hockey Hall of Fame in public relations, but took a year's sabbatical after fighting depression. He returned, stronger than ever, and added president of the Leafs' Alumni Association to his duties.

ELOMO, Miika
b. Turku, Finland, April 21, 1977

Judging by the scouts' notes, by the time he was drafted by Washington in 1995, this Elomo guy was a bona fide up-and-comer. But after just two games in the U.S. capital, he was traded to Calgary and has been in their system ever since.

ELORANTA, Kari
b. Lahti, Finland, February 29, 1956

A life in hockey is not always measured in NHL games. Case in point, Kari Eloranta, born and raised and trained in Finland. He was signed as a free agent in 1981 by Calgary at age 25 after many years of Finnish league play. His first year was fraught with difficulty as he struggled to translate his puck game to the North American style, and he spent most of the year in the minors and partly on loan to St. Louis (though, officially, he was traded to the Blues for futures during the season, and then traded back at season's end for futures). He played three and a half more years of dependable, though never spectacular, hockey and then returned to Europe to play for another decade. Internationally, his resumé is impressive indeed: two World Juniors, four World Championships, and three Olympics. He may not have made an impact in the NHL, but he certainly played many years of high-calibre hockey around the ice world.

ELORANTA, Mikko
b. Turku, Finland, August 24, 1972

A star left wing with Turku in the Finnish league, Eloranta accepted Boston's offer to join the team after playing in the 1999 World Championships. He had been a top scorer back home, but like many others he found the going a little tougher and the schedule more of a grind in the NHL. He had 6 and then 12 goals in his first 2 years, and a trade to L.A. changed his sweater colours but not his numbers. He found his niche as a penalty killer and checker, and that's where he's at in the NHL.

ELYNUIK, Pat
b. Foam Lake, Saskatchewan, October 30, 1967

He played his first game of junior at 16, was a scoring star at 18, and the 8th-overall draft choice of Winnipeg in 1986. The start of Elynuik's career continued on an impressive, if slightly less spectacular road. For his first 5 full seasons he scored 22 goals or more, but then the tank ran dry. By 1993-94, he could score no more than 13 times, and at 26 his career came to an almost dead stop. He continued for a brief time, but his stock went from blue chip to penny in almost the blink of an eye.

EMBERG, Eddie
b. Montreal, Quebec, November 18, 1921

When coach Dick Irvin put Emberg into the lineup for a playoff game against the Leafs on March 29, 1945, little did he know the Habs would win 10-3 or that Emberg would score a goal in this, his first ever NHL game. Naturally, he was back in the lineup for the next game, but the Leafs won that one and Emberg never, ever played in the NHL again! Nonetheless, he went on to a long and happy career with Ottawa in Senior hockey, always able to say he scored a goal in his first NHL game, and in a playoff game to boot.

EMERSON, Nelson
b. Hamilton, Ontario, August 17, 1967

As a result of setting records at Bowling Green University for assists and points (1986-90), Emerson is now a member of that school's Hall of Fame. He went on to win a Turner Cup in the IHL and a gold medal with Canada at the 1994 World Championships. He's had five 20-goal seasons with a long list of teams, but as age has crept into the old bones he's become more of a part-timer and checker, and that is how Los Angeles has used him in the last 3 years. Despite his 700 regular-season games, Emerson has appeared in not much more than 20 playoff games. His career came to a premature end in 2002, when, after sustaining 6 concussions over the previous 3 seasons, he retired to California to try to regain his health.

In the summer of 1972, he was invited to training camp for the historic Summit Series.
RON ELLIS

EMMA, David
b. Cranston, Rhode Island, January 14, 1969

Just as the 1st-overall selection at the NHL Entry Draft is a crapshoot that sometimes comes up sixes, so, too, is the distinction of winning a Hobey Baker Award. Emma won this gem in 1991, but his career has flourished everywhere but the NHL. He has played in every possible international event for the U.S., but rather than slug it out in the minor pros he elected to play in Europe, which he has done since 1997.

EMMONS, Gary
b. Winnipeg, Manitoba, December 30, 1963

Here was a scorer in college, a can't-miss kid who missed at the NHL level despite great hands and superior hockey skills. Emmons played at Northern Michigan University instead of junior in Canada, and set numerous records during his four-year stay there. He became the first player to score 6 goals in a game, had a consecutive goal-scoring streak of 18 games, and set or tied 9 MSU records. After earning a degree in speech communications, he became property of the Rangers, Oilers, North Stars, and San Jose Sharks before finally getting a call from his seemingly

Miika Elomo

Kari Eloranta

Mikko Eloranta

Eddie Emberg

Nelson Emerson

permanent home in the IHL (nine years) to join the Sharks, a rookie at age 30. In three games he scored a goal, but he went right back down whence he came and where he played evermore with the Kansas City Blades. He liked the organization so much, and the feeling was mutual, that when he retired he stayed on as an assistant coach.

EMMONS, John
b. San Jose, California, August 17, 1974

It's perfectly common for a guy to be born in Ottawa and find himself playing for the San Jose Sharks, but a dude born in San Jose playing for the Ottawa Senators? What's that all about? But sure enough, that's the Emmons portfolio. He attended Yale University and was drafted by Calgary, but the Flames said bye-bye and the Sens said hello. So far, the California kid hasn't played very much, but, like, it's a start.

John Emmons

EMMS, Leighton "Hap"
b. Barrie, Ontario, January 12, 1905
d. Niagara Falls, Ontario, October 22, 1988

Hap never was happy; that's why he got the moniker. He spent his life in hockey, from his kid days in a church league in Dalston north of Barrie to 1984, when he suffered a stroke that took away his speech. He played 10 years in the NHL with the Maroons, Americans, and Red Wings, and after he was no longer needed in the NHL (1938) he continued to play until 1943, when he joined the Canadian army. In 1945 he began operations of the Barrie Flyers in the OHA, and remained in junior hockey for most of the next 35 years, with a brief foray as GM with the Bruins. His time in Beantown (1965-67) was highlighted by his historic signing of Bobby Orr. Emms moved the Barrie Flyers to Niagara Falls in 1960, sold the team in 1972, and bought the St. Catharines franchise in 1976, promptly moving it to Barrie. Eight times he went to the Memorial Cup finals, winning half that number, and he sent more than 100 juniors to the NHL. Son, Paul, and nephew, Don, were on the first championship team in 1951. A more upstanding citizen or straighter arrow never graced the hockey world, and Emms tried to change things for what he thought was the better. Players were not allowed to smoke, drink, or swear, and he tried to ban cars and girlfriends for good measure. He was considered thrifty and continued not to smile, but by the time he sold the team in 1978 he was the most successful GM in major junior hockey history.

ENDEAN, Craig
b. Kamloops, British Columbia, April 13, 1968

When Seattle beat Westminster 11-6 early in the WHL's 1986-87 season, it was smack in the middle of an unusual circumstance. The Thunderbirds and Regina Pats had completed a mammoth five-for-five trade a couple of days earlier, but because difficulties in getting all players over the border and to their new teams might prove time-consuming the deal wasn't announced until after this 11-6 game. Trouble was, Endean scored six goals and an assist in the game, and he was one of the traded players! The Pats were mighty happy with what they got, and in the ensuing 59 games Endean scored 49 more goals (in fact, he had 15 points in his final 3 games with Seattle). During this season, he was also called up to Winnipeg to play twice with the Jets, and although he scored another 50 with Regina the following year, he never got another chance in the NHL.

Jerome Engele

Engblom took three years to make it full-time with the Habs.
BRIAN ENGBLOM

ENDICOTT, Shane
b. Saskatoon, Saskatchewan, December 21, 1981

A young centre in Pittsburgh, Endicott has yet to catch on with the Penguins. He graduated from Seattle of the WHL and has played just a few games with Mario Lemieux and the rest of the time with the farm team in Wilkes-Barre.

ENGBLOM, Brian
b. Winnipeg, Manitoba, January 27, 1955

In the 1970s, it was both a blessing and a bane to be coveted by Montreal. A blessing because this was a championship team; a bane because, being a championship team, it was difficult at best to crack the lineup. Engblom took three years to make it full-time with the Habs, but once he did he found himself being called a Stanley Cup champion. He established himself as a good rushing defenceman with size and strength in his own end, but as the Montreal dynasty of that decade petered out, so, too, did his desirability with the team. He wound up changing teams regularly his last five years in the NHL, and his career ended at age 30 after he suffered a serious neck injury that required major surgery. Engblom settled in Los Angeles (where he had played for two and a half years) to work in the import business as well as offer colour commentary for the Kings on ESPN.

ENGELE, Jerome "Jerry"
b. Humboldt, Saskatchewan, November 26, 1950

He knew his time was up before it really was, so that helped ease his transfer from player to coach. Engele was the physical player every team needs, and Minnesota used him in this role from 1975 to '78. But he could see he wasn't going to last a decade in the NHL, and when Saskatoon Blades GM, Jackie McLeod, offered the 28-year-old alumnus a chance to coach, Engele accepted *sans regret*.

ENGLISH, John
b. Toronto, Ontario, May 13, 1966
English is doubly puzzling on the NHL front. First, despite playing in only four games (with L.A. in '87-'88), he had a goal and three assists. Second, these small but impressive totals came from a guy who had made his mark as a tough guy wherever he went. He wasn't a junior scorer or a top prospect or a small, talented kid. But facts are facts. He never played again in the NHL despite averaging 1.33 points a game.

ENIO, James
see **SCLISIZZI, Enio**

ENNIS, Jim
b. Edmonton, Alberta, July 10, 1967
Playing for the Edmonton Oilers' farm team in the 1980s meant drooling for a chance to play with the big team. Imagine getting a callup to play with Gretzky, Messier, Anderson, Kurri, Coffey, and Fuhr! For five games, Ennis lived the dream. The flip side, of course, is that with so much Hall of Fame and Stanley Cup talent on the team, it wasn't likely a kid like Ennis would stick around too long. And he didn't.

ERAT, Martin
b. Trebic, Czechoslovakia (Czech Republic), August 28, 1981
Erat ended his junior career with a bang. He won a gold medal with the Czechs at the 2001 World Junior Championships, and a few months later helped the Red Deer Rebels capture the Memorial Cup. From there, the left winger jumped to Nashville in the NHL, and as a rookie in 2001-02 he scored nine goals and worked his way into the league.

ERICKSON, Autry "Aut"
b. Lethbridge, Alberta, January 25, 1938
Named after Gene Autry, Erickson played a small bunch of games in the NHL, but it was one game in the 1967 playoffs that got him real fame. That game came with the Leafs, the team that went on to win the Cup, and for that small participation, Erickson got his name stamped on the Stanley Cup. After retiring in 1970, he coached the Phoenix Roadrunners for two years and then joined the front office of the newly opened Islanders franchise. He co-coached the team briefly with Earl Ingarfield and then went into private business, first in real estate and later with America West Airlines.

ERICKSON, Bryan
b. Roseau, Minnesota, March 7, 1960
The only season Erickson spent entirely in the NHL was '86-'87 with Los Angeles, when he played in 68 games. In every other year of his decade in the pro ranks he played either part or all in the minors or outside the NHL. Erickson had his share of serious injuries, which further limited his ice time, but wherever he went he was constantly being demoted or called up. He almost never appeared in the playoffs, but he did play for Team USA at two World Juniors and three World Championships. He also played in the 1984 Canada Cup. Erickson managed to record back-to-back 20-goal seasons with the Kings.

ERICKSON, Chad
b. Minneapolis, Minnesota, August 21, 1970
Goalie Erickson played for New Jersey briefly in '91-'92, the same year Martin Brodeur arrived in the Devils' crease. No contest. Erickson never made it back, and Brodeur has never left. Erickson has continued to play in the minors, though, with no NHL contract or affiliation of which to speak.

ERICKSON, Grant
b. Pierceland, Saskatchewan, April 28, 1947
Any trace of Bobby Orr in a player's blood can be only good, so no matter what happened in Erickson's career he can always point to the '68-'69 season and say he played two games with the greatest defenceman of all time. Actually, he got into a few more games the year after with Minnesota, and from there Erickson moved to the WHA, where he spent four moderately successful years.

ERIKSSON, Anders
b. Bollnas, Sweden, January 9, 1975
Eriksson was elevated to hero status by townsfolk in Bollnas in the summer of 1998 when he returned home bearing the Stanley Cup. He had risen gradually but steadily from Swedish hockey to the AHL to Detroit to help the Wings win the Cup for the second straight year, but the following season he was sent to Chicago in a trade that brought ancient defenceman Chris Chelios to the senescent Wings. Eriksson moved quickly down after that, to Florida, then Toronto and soon after into the minors after disastrous play with the Cup-contending Leafs.

Aut Erickson

Bryan Erickson

Eriksson returned home bearing the Stanley Cup.
ANDERS ERIKSSON

ERIKSSON, Peter ("Kessler")
b. Kramfors, Sweden, July 12, 1965
Edmonton drafted him, used him, bid him adieu. In 1989-90, Eriksson played 20 games for the Oil en route to the Stanley Cup, but he didn't see any playoff action. At season's end, he returned to Sweden to continue playing. He had represented Tre Kronor at both the 1987 Canada Cup and 1988 Olympics in Calgary.

ERIKSSON, Roland
b. Tunabro, Sweden, March 1, 1954
Eriksson had some decent NHL memories to take

Roland Eriksson

home with him after he played his last in 1979, but none stood out more than his international accomplishments with Tre Kronor at the 1977 World Championships. On May 8, 1977, he scored all three goals in his team's stunning 3-1 win over the Soviets. Not many NHLers can boast of having scored a hat trick on one Vladislav Tretiak. That win gave Sweden silver, to the Czechs' gold, and made Eriksson a national hero. He played only 193 games in North America before returning home to close out his career with Vasteras. After retiring, he stayed with the club in an administrative capacity and in 1999 became the team's assistant coach.

ERIKSSON, Thomas
b. Stockholm, Sweden, October 16, 1959
Right from the get-go, Eriksson and the NHL just didn't suit each other. Another post-Borje Salming draft choice, Eriksson played the rare double when he represented his country in 1979 at both the World Juniors and the World Championships, winning bronze medals at both tournaments at the ripe old age of 18. On those strengths he was drafted by Philadelphia in the summer, but he played one more year at home before coming to North America and the NHL. Unfortunately, he never fully adjusted to the game, the rinks, the language, the travel, the long schedule, and the physical play. After only a few games, he returned home, though the Flyers convinced him to come back and play out the year with the farm team. The next season, he again went home, this time after only one game, but the next two years he was more committed and stayed the season in Philly. Not so in '85-'86, his last, part-time year with the team. Eriksson returned to the land of Tre Kronor for good in 1986, playing another 10 years, winning a bronze at the 1988 Olympics in Calgary and silver at the 1990 Worlds.

Jan Erixon

ERIXON, Jan ("Mr. X"/ "Exet")
b. Skelleftea, Sweden, July 8, 1962
A child and a bad back brought Mr. X's career to a premature end in the summer of 1993 after 10 NHL seasons fraught with injury. Erixon began playing pro in Sweden at age 17, and in 1981 he was a member of the gold-medal junior team, the first and still only time the Swedes have placed first at the WJC. He was drafted by the Rangers that summer, but apprenticed at home for two more seasons before joining the Broadway Blueshirts in 1983. Erixon became renowned for his checking rather than scoring, shadowing everyone from Mike Gartner to Mario Lemieux and earning a reputation as a tremendously tough player in the corners. However, his third season

Jan Erixon

was a near write-off because of a badly broken leg, and two years later he suffered a back injury from which he never fully recovered. In the ensuing 5 seasons, he never played more than 58 games. In the summer of 1993, his wife gave birth to their second child, and Erixon had had enough of his back problems. He returned to Sweden with the intent of playing, but once home he packed it in and returned to civilian life.

ERREY, Bob
b. Montreal, Quebec, September 21, 1964
A teammate of Steve Yzerman's in Peterborough of the OHL, Errey was drafted by Pittsburgh and played almost 10 seasons with the team, winning two Stanley Cups, in 1991 and '92. Although he scored 53 goals in his last year of junior, he became better known as a two-way player with the Penguins, though linemate Mario Lemieux credited this skill to his own ability to focus on offence and scoring. Although he won the Cup in '91, Errey left the city too early to get his day with the sacred trophy, a mistake he fixed the next year when he made sure to arrange time with Lord Stanley's bowl in his hometown of Peterborough. He took the Cup to The Office, a local restaurant, and made sure all his friends and family had a chance to spend some time with it. This despite the fact that he missed a good portion of the playoffs with an injured shoulder. The year was also difficult because of the coaching change. Bob Johnson had passed away during the summer, and incoming boss

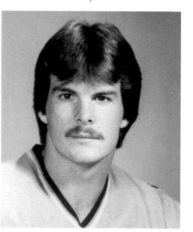

Errey was part of Canada's surprise gold-medal team at the 1997 World Championships.
BOB ERREY

Scotty Bowman didn't play Errey as much. Midway through the next season, he was sent to Buffalo and from there to San Jose. He became the Sharks captain, but internal difficulties with players and management led to another trade, to Detroit. Nevertheless, the Sharks claimed him on waivers a short time later. Errey was part of Canada's surprise gold-medal team at the 1997 World Championships, and his year got even better when he signed a three-year, $2 million contract with Dallas. But when the Stars traded him to the Rangers, he had had enough and retired at season's end. He became an analyst for Pittsburgh radio, and twice made unsuccessful comebacks with the Pens before moving to the broadcast booth once and for all.

ERSKINE, John
b. Kingston, Ontario, June 26, 1980
Dallas is hoping that Erskine fills a Hatcher-like role with the team in years to come. He is a large and forceful defenceman who played half a season with the Stars in 2001-02 and managed to hold his own in this first trial in the NHL.

ESAU, Len
b. Meadow Lake, Saskatchewan, June 3, 1968

In four NHL seasons, Esau moved teams four times, doing the cross-Canada road trip in the dead of winter rather than in the sunny summer. To Toronto, Quebec, Calgary, Edmonton, and back to Calgary he went, playing a few games in the bigs but spending the vast majority of his time in the minors, hoping for a steady job at the top. He was a big, solid defenceman, but even later he never played two full seasons with any one team in the lesser ranks.

ESCHE, Robert ("Chico")
b. Utica, New York, January 22, 1978

A proud American, Esche played for Team USA at both the WJC and the WC. He loved country music, and wore a mask featuring Waylon Jennings and Hank Williams, Jr., personally autographed by the former (in the old days, masks were intended to intimidate and frighten, not promote derision). But after September 11, 2001, Esche turned his mask into a more patriotic statement. His brother, Henry, was a member of the U.S. Marines who went to the Middle East in the weeks after the terrorist attacks, and Esche had a new mask made that featured an American eagle, the Statue of Liberty, and other imagery related to that horrific day. On the hockey front, he has been backup in Phoenix to Nikolai Khabibulin and, more recently, Sean Burke.

ESPOSITO, Phil ("Espo")
b. Sault Ste. Marie, Ontario, February 20, 1942

Too fat, too slow, too bad, Espo was told as he was sent home and told to shape up or stay out. He was a teen, living in the Soo, sure he could make the NHL but unable to convince any coaches of that. In 1962, he finally made a good enough impression with Chicago that the Hawks sent him to St. Louis, but after an excellent season they sent him right back for a second year. During that season, he was called up to the Hawks and scored just 3 goals in 27 games. He knew he had to take his game more seriously, and he did. In 1964, he came to Chicago's camp in good shape, made the team, and scored 23 goals as a rookie. He followed up with seasons of 27 and 21 goals, but never felt that coach Billy Reay had enough confidence in him. He was traded to Boston, and his life changed forever. Arriving in Beantown, he promised that the previously dreadful Bruins would make the playoffs in his first year, compete for the Cup in his second, and win it all in his third. Damn if he wasn't bang-on correct! In his first year with the team, he had 35 goals, then 49 a year later. He also had 126 total points, the first player to reach the

It was a sweat-soaked, impassioned plea from a player to the fans.
PHIL ESPOSITO

100-point mark in the history of the game. The next year, he led the NHL with 43 goals and helped the team win his promised Stanley Cup. He went on to lead the NHL in goals for six seasons, establishing records that were untouchable until Wayne Gretzky came along. Most incredibly, he had 76 goals and 76 assists in '70-'71, records for goals and points (152). The next year, he again led the league in goals (66) and points (133), and in the fall of 1972 he changed the course of hockey history. Esposito was 30 years old and in his prime, the top centreman in the game. He revolutionized the art of scoring by standing in the slot, that precious parcel of ice directly in front of a goalie. Linemates Wayne Cashman and Ken Hodge fed him the puck, and with the fastest release in the game, he fired the puck past surprised goalies. A large, unmovable force, he made scoring look easy even though, of course, there was tremendous skill there. He was named to Team Canada for the 1972 Summit Series, and years later his accomplishments during those eight games were so spectacular that his entire NHL career could be forgotten and he would remain one of the game's greatest players. He and Paul Henderson tied for most goals scored, but it was Espo's leadership, his strength of will, that put him far above everyone else in the world for the 27 days of that series. His speech after game four in Vancouver, a Canadian loss that saw the team booed off the ice, was spontaneous poetry. It was a sweat-soaked, impassioned plea from a player to the fans, and it drew the fans to the team and brought them into the dressing room the way no press conference or news story could. That his teammates never heard the speech was beside the point. Canada's victory was dramatized by Henderson's goal, no doubt, but it was produced by Esposito's power of leadership and his determination not to lose – *at all costs*. He returned to the Bruins a few days later, and over the course of the year led the NHL in goals, assists, and points, the one and only time he completed that triple play in his career. Early in '75-'76 he was involved in another major trade when he was sent to New York with Carol Vadnais for Jean Ratelle, Brad Park, and Joe Zanussi. In his eight years with the Bruins, Espo had had 6 seasons of at least 126 points. He had led the league in goals six times, won five Art Ross Trophies, been named to six First All-Star Teams, and won two Stanley Cups and two Lester B. Pearson Awards. He arrived on Broadway and played five and a half years there, never reaching any of those glorious levels from Boston. He never scored fewer than 29 goals and he took the team to the 1979 Cup finals, but the magic just wasn't there. Neither were Orr, Hodge, Cashman, Sanderson, etc. Espo retired suddenly, midway through

Phil Esposito

Phil Esposito

the '80-'81 season when the passion, he said, was no longer there. Throughout his career, few players were as sporting and sportsmanlike as Espo. Although he was a big man, many remember that he rarely fought. He prayed for the safety of all players prior to every game, and although he used his size for success, he never abused it. He was also a creature of habit and drove to the Boston Garden the same way before every game. One night, early in his career, he caught a cold and wore a black turtleneck sweater to keep him warm. He wore it for the rest of his career. He retired third all-time with 717 goals and 1,590 points, behind only Gordie Howe and Marcel Dionne, and was of course inducted into the Hockey Hall of Fame. He stayed with New York, becoming an assistant coach, and in 1986 he was named vice-president and GM of the team. It was a stormy time, and he became known as Trader Phil because of the frequency of player movement. He even became interim coach on occasion, but ultimately the team's lack of playoff success brought his tenure with the Blueshirts to an end. He later became GM of the expansion Tampa Bay Lightning, but again poor results with a weak team cost him his job. He has remained in Tampa with his brother, Tony, another Hall of Famer, doing work for televised games. Over the years he has worked for Fox Sports and other national stations. From his impassioned speech in 1972 to the present, Esposito has not only witnessed but been party to so many changes in hockey and politics. During his tenure with the Lightning, the greatest irony of all occurred when his daughter married one of the team's players – Russian Alex Selivanov!

Tony Esposito

ESPOSITO, Tony ("Tony O")
b. Sault Ste. Marie, Ontario, April 23, 1943

While growing up with brother Phil, Tony could not have asked for a better shooter to get him ready for goaltending in the NHL. If he stopped Phil, he stopped the best. If Phil scored, hey, Phil could score on anyone (and did). Tony took a much different route to the top, though. He went to Michigan State University, but after four years was never drafted and only Montreal showed an interest in signing him. The Habs assigned him to Vancouver, as far away as a future NHLer could get, but in '68-'69, he got into a few games with the Habs. He played just 13 games but had 2 shutouts, and he made his debut wearing number 29, a number made more famous a short time later by Ken Dryden. And, because the Habs won the Cup that year, Tony O got his name on the Cup even though he was not a major factor in the victory. He never won another Cup. Chicago claimed him in the Intra-League Draft of 1969, and for the next 15 years he became the game's

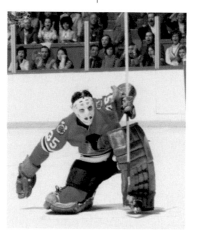

Esposito angered a nation in 1981 when he chose to play for the U.S. in that year's Canada Cup.
TONY ESPOSITO

pre-eminent goalie. In his first full season, '68-'69, Esposito raised the bar higher than he could have anticipated. He led the league with 38 wins, but more amazingly, 15 of those came by shutout, the highest number in the modern era. Needless to say, he won the Calder Trophy for this great rookie performance, as well as the Vezina Trophy, the first rookie to win it since Frank Brimsek in 1939. He had two more outstanding seasons and then, in the summer of 1972, he was named one of the goalies for Team Canada at the Summit Series (with the aforementioned Dryden). He played 4 games in the series of the century, then returned to Chicago and won more than 30 games again. In all, he hit that mark 7 seasons in a row, and throughout his career he proved to be a durable goalie, routinely playing more than 60 games a year. Much of his success came from his pioneering, and unorthodox, style. For starters, he caught with his right hand, which threw off many shooters. And, he used a butterfly style of goaltending. That is, his knees touched but his feet were apart as he crouched in the ready position. The result was that his feet covered more of the lower part of the net, and the open space (the so-called five hole) was so new that players didn't dare shoot at what was, normally, dead centre of a goalie's pads. Espo augmented this stance by falling to his knees quickly and getting back up as fast, again able to cover more net more quickly. By the time he retired in 1984 at age 39, Esposito had won 423 games, third all-time behind Terry Sawchuk and Jacques Plante. His 76 shutouts is a post-1967 record. Esposito angered a nation in 1981 when he chose to play for the U.S. in that year's Canada Cup. In a way, his participation served merely to extend his career, because he never would have been selected to the stronger Team Canada. Tony O wasn't out of hockey long after hanging up the pads. He became director of hockey operations for Pittsburgh and later joined his brother, Phil, with the hapless Tampa Bay organization. He was inducted into the Hockey Hall of Fame in 1988, a truly one-of-a-kind goalie whose contribution is uncontested.

ESSENSA, Bob
b. Toronto, Ontario, January 14, 1965

Essensa was drafted by the Winnipeg Jets out of high school in Toronto, a prescient move by the team. He went on to post an incredible record of 62-13-2 in four years of college hockey with the Michigan State Spartans, leading the team to the NCAA championship in 1986, his junior year. He quickly worked his way into the number-one goalie slot with the Jets, in 1990, and in '91-'92 he led the NHL with five shutouts. Then the bitterness set in. As the

Bob Essensa

'92 playoffs approached, he made it clear that he wanted his contract situation clarified. It was, but not to his satisfaction, the Jets offering $750,000 for the coming season, Essensa seeking $1.26 million. Not surprisingly, the Jets were eliminated in the first round of the playoffs, and in the ensuing summer arbitration battle Essensa won his case in front of Michel Picher, who awarded the goalie $1.25 million, the largest amount ever in NHL history to that point. But the bitterness had set in, and Essensa vowed to play out the year and then become a free agent. Believing him every bit of the way, the Jets traded him at the deadline to Detroit, but, ironically, he played more in the minors than for the big club at the Joe. The Wings shipped him to Edmonton for nothing more than futures, and so began the downward spiral of his career that has since taken him to Phoenix and Vancouver. Despite more than 450 appearances, he has played only 16 times in the playoffs.

EVANS, Chris

b. Toronto, Ontario, September 14, 1946
d. Phoenix, Arizona, May 9, 2000
At a community college in Toronto, Evans studied acting while learning to play hockey with the Marlies, winning the Memorial Cup with the team in 1966-67. He played his first NHL games with the Leafs and then moved around a fair bit in his brief career. He had his best offensive year with St. Louis in 1972–73 when he was moved from defence up to the wing and scored nine goals, but beyond that he didn't have much scoring talent. He later joined the WHA for a number of years, but wherever he played in the winter didn't affect his summers – he returned each year to Arizona, where every night he'd go out and hunt rattlesnakes. His life was turned upside down when he was diagnosed with a brain tumour in 1982. Surgery was successful, but his hockey career was over. He settled in Phoenix, but in 2000 he died from long-term complications of that tumour.

EVANS, Claude

b. Longueuil, Quebec, April 28, 1933
d. unknown
Evans was owned by Montreal during the Original Six days, and that meant he had as much chance of playing as a British subject had a chance to inherit the throne. He got into four games in '54-'55 through the only means possible – a Plante injury – and played another game three years later because of an injury to Boston great Harry Lumley. Besides that, Evans had a lengthy career in the minors.

EVANS, Darryl ("Motorboat"/ "Reggie")

b. Toronto, Ontario, January 12, 1961
He got the nickname Motorboat in junior, because of

his speed down the left wing, but his size – or, rather, lack of it – scared more than one NHL scout away from thinking him NHL material. Los Angeles took a chance on Evans, and in his first year he made believers of the Kings. In the 1982 playoffs, it was his overtime goal that eliminated the Oilers from the Stanley Cup hunt. Although he went on to play for other teams and then in the minors, Evans always felt an affinity for L.A., and when he retired in 1991, that was where he migrated. He became sales manager of a car dealership and also a part-time radio commentator for the Kings, still as much a fan of the game as when he was playing.

EVANS, Doug

b. Peterborough, Ontario, June 2, 1963
Up and down and all around bounced Doug Evans, from the time he was a pre-OHL teen to the day he retired in 1998. An All-Star calibre player in the Peterborough Minor Hockey Council, he was never chosen in the midget draft and was invited to the Petes' junior camp only because he was a local. Coach Dave Dryden cut him from camp and sent him to junior B, but injuries forced him to call Evans up to the OHL. He remained four years, improving his statistics each year. But – what else is new? – by the time he had graduated out of junior, no NHL team had drafted him. He signed with St. Louis as a free agent, and the Blues assigned him to the farm in Peoria, where he spent the entire '84-'85 season. For most of the next five years he was on a string – called up, demoted, called up, demoted, called up, demoted – so much so he gave up on becoming an NHL regular, feeling both obligated to St. Louis for being the only team to give him a chance and frustrated because he felt he never got a true chance to stay in the NHL. He resigned himself to a life in Peoria, and hoped to become an assistant coach and eventually head coach. Just when this plan made sense to him, the Blues traded him to Winnipeg, and his mood improved. After 127 games over 3 years with the Jets, the up-down syndrome occurred again. Then his wife suffered a miscarriage, and he was back in Peoria. Evans played most of 1992-93 with Philadelphia, but then was given his release. He signed with the Rivermen again, and played the rest of his career there, eventually becoming one of the inaugural members of the Peoria Sports Hall of Fame. He returned home to Peterborough where he sold cars for a local dealership.

EVANS, Jack ("Cowboy"/ "Tex")

b. Morriston, South Wales, April 21, 1928
d. Manchester, Connecticut, November 9, 1996
There was a small Welsh community near Drumheller,

Chris Evans

Darryl Evans

Jack Evans

Evans returned home to Peterborough where he sold cars for a local dealership.
DOUG EVANS

Alberta, during the Depression, and it was there that Evans' family migrated upon leaving Morriston when he was but four years old. He grew up neither rich nor unhappy, and his hockey skills led to a life in the game that began with an association with the New York Rangers in 1948. He had always been called Cowboy, but at a house party one night he sang a western song and his Ranger mates changed that to Tex, a moniker that stuck till his dying day. The pipe-smoking Evans was a solid but unspectacular player, extending his limited talents through 14 years in the NHL, a career that climaxed in 1961 while on the blueline of Chicago, winners of the Stanley Cup. After 1963, Evans found himself out of the big time and in the minors, acting as a playing coach for the Buffalo Bisons in '63-'64. The double duty proved too much for him, so he soldiered on as a player, retiring in 1972 at age 44. A career that saw him play for 22 coaches led immediately to his joining the bench-bossing fraternity, coaching the San Diego Gulls in the WHL, the team with which he had spent his last five years as a player. That first season, he was named coach of the year and took the team to a championship, and in 1975 he was named coach of the NHL affiliate, the California Golden Seals. His three years with the Seals and Cleveland Barons produced awful records, and he returned to the minors until Hartford hired him in 1983, a position he held for five years. Only twice did the team make the playoffs, but his tenure was punctuated by an incident in March 1986 when he assaulted a reporter in the dressing room after a game. That the incident ran counter to every bone in Evans' easygoing, fun-loving body probably saved him his job, but his dismissal from the team two years later came in a bizarre moment. He casually suggested that after the following season, 1988-89, he would likely step down as coach, a remark that GM Emile Francis felt sounded like betrayal. Evans was fired the next day, and remained in retirement until he passed away several years later.

EVANS, John Paul
b. Toronto, Ontario, May 2, 1954
If perseverance isn't his middle name, determination is. Evans was drafted out of junior by Los Angeles in 1974 and promptly became IHL fodder for years – despite a 50-goal season with Saginaw – until he was sent to the Flyers as the future considerations of a deal that sent Steve Short to the Kings. But Evans continued to languish in the minors until 1978, when he beat out Blake Dunlop as the team's fourth centre in training camp, a job he later lost to same when Dunlop was recalled and started to score. It was four

more years before Evans got another shot with the team, thanks to head coach Bob McCammon, who knew Evans from their days in the minors with Maine. McCammon put him on a line with Darryl Sittler, gave him time on the penalty-killing unit, and told him to work along the boards, his greatest strength and the one that hid his weak skating the most. His one full season, though, failed to result in long-term stability, and the next season he was back in the minors.

EVANS, Kevin
b. Peterborough, Ontario, July 10, 1965
What could possibly be the record for most penalty minutes in a single season of pro hockey? Guess. Go crazy. A few players have had 300 minutes. So, what could it be: 400, 500, 600? Try 648, set by Kevin Evans in 1986-87 with the Kalamazoo Wings of the IHL in just 73 games, an average of nearly 9 minutes a game. Perhaps being the youngest of six brothers had something to do with his survival-of-the-fittest mentality. Brothers Paul and Doug both played briefly in the NHL, goalie-brother Mark made it to junior, and two other brothers became lacrosse players. Kevin was never drafted by an NHL team after leaving junior in 1985, though he signed as a free agent with Minnesota in 1988 and played 4 games with the team in 1990-91, accumulating 19 penalty minutes. He was then selected by San Jose in the Expansion Draft, but 5 games and 25 pims later he was back in the IHL, spending the rest of his career in the minors, fighting for a living. Even at age 32, playing for an outfit called the Mississippi Sea Wolves in '96-'97, Evans still sat out 505 minutes of fight time. Unbelievable. When he retired, he worked for FedEx and for Oscar Meyer, the weiner people.

When he retired, he worked for FedEx and for Oscar Meyer, the weiner people.
KEVIN EVANS

EVANS, Paul
b. Peterborough, Ontario, February 24, 1955
It's too bad the Toronto Rock didn't exist in the late 1970s. Then, when Evans' slim hockey career ended, he could have taken off his skates, put on his runners, and gone out on the artificial grass of the ACC to play lacrosse for a living. He was likely a better lacrossist than hockeyist, but the pay wasn't there. He played 11 games with the Leafs in '76-'77 and '77-'78, thus making him and brothers Doug and Kevin one of the few three-brother combos to make the NHL. He is also a member of the Ontario Lacrosse Hall of Fame.

EVANS, Shawn
b. Kingston, Ontario, September 7, 1965
The prototypical undertalented defenceman took on a lengthy career as a player, learning every day and

Paul Evans

looking to a job as coach when all was said and done with his skates. Evans played 9 NHL games and some 14 seasons of pro (starting in 1985), going steadily down from the AHL to IHL to UHL. A player can't get much lower than the U without going back to high school, but still the quality was better than shinny, and hockey is hockey no matter where you go. And it was right there in the United league that Evans pulled out his whistle and started his coaching career, in 1999.

EVANS, Stew
b. Ottawa, Ontario, June 19, 1908
d. Palm Beach, Florida, June 2, 1996
An unsung star, Evans was unusual in that almost every game of his pro career took place in the NHL. There were no long stretches in the minors, no callups and demotions, no bad injuries or war duties to obscure his NHL years. He played first for Detroit, until the Wings sent him to the Montreal Maroons on January 2, 1934, for Ted Graham, and in his first full year with the team, '34-'35, they won the Cup. He stayed on with the English-Montreal team and was sold to the dreaded enemy, les Canadiens, to start the '38-'39 season, his last in pro hockey. He established himself in Detroit and became one of the most successful car dealers in the city.

EVASON, Dean
b. Flin Flon, Manitoba, August 22, 1964
Life is funny sometimes. And not just ha-ha funny, but queer, strange funny. Evason was a good prospect when Washington drafted him in 1982. Not great, but good. He grew up in Thompson, Manitoba, a place with one road in and out, a place so small it made Flin Flon look urbane. He scored 71 goals one year with Kamloops, but he was only 5'10". And that's how he played. He wasn't big, wasn't dirty tough, wasn't necessarily strong on the puck, but still, he was a little bit of all those qualities or he never would have made the NHL. His best years came with Hartford playing on the LEG line with Paul Lawless and Stew Gavin, and he had consecutive 20-goal seasons with the Whalers. He stuck around for 803 games with 5 teams, but his size always seemed a detriment, and by 1996 the contract offers ended. He played with the National Team in '96-'97, and that spring he was not only named to the World Championships team for Canada, but named its captain. And lo and behold, the team won gold! No new NHL offers awaited, but some from Europe did, and he accepted. After retiring, he moved back west and started a career as a coach, the WC gold medal still a cherished momento no one can ever take from him.

EWEN, Todd
b. Saskatoon, Saskatchewan, March 22, 1966
Tough guy. Bruiser. Fighter. Policeman. Children's book writer. Huh? As a teenager, he worked in a pit crew for a race car, became a roadie for a band, and worked as a bouncer. He played for the New Westminster Bruins in the early 1980s, likely the toughest, most violent team in junior hockey history. He was drafted by Edmonton in 1986, traded to St. Louis before ever playing a game with Gretzky and Co., and roamed the league for 11 seasons, getting to

know the penalty timekeepers in every NHL rink better than some of his teammates. In his spare time, though, he wrote an illustrated kids book called *A Frog Named Hop*, not much of a stretch for someone who taught himself to play the guitar and piano and learn to draw. He may be a warrior on ice, but off ice he was an aesthete.

EXELBY, Randy
b. Toronto, Ontario, August 13, 1965
Exelby didn't even have time to smell the coffee, his stint in the Montreal goal was so brief. In 1988-89, he played all of three minutes in a game for the Habs, though a year later he played an entire game with the Oilers. Although Edmonton went on to win the Cup that year, his one game wasn't enough to earn an engraving for Exelby.

EZINICKI, Bill ("Wild Bill")
b. Winnipeg, Manitoba, March 11, 1924
After attending a hockey school run by Eddie Shore and winning a Memorial Cup with Oshawa in 1944, Ezinicki was ready for the NHL, though whether the NHL was ready for him was a matter of great debate. He became known as the toughest, hardest checker in the game, ferocious but usually clean. In a game against the Rangers in 1947, he hit Edgar Laprade so hard he knocked him cold and infuriated the Rangers to such an extent that they filed a protest (NHL president Clarence Campbell ruled the check hard and clean). Ezinicki had an insurance policy with the Leafs that paid him $5 for every stitch he needed to close a wound, earning him much additional revenue (the hard way) during his career and many jibes for asking doctors to add a few more stitches whenever possible. But Ezinicki's love of golf superseded his love for the puck game. Mid-career, in 1949, he became pro at the Uplands course in Toronto, and although he played bits and pieces of hockey until 1955, his focus shifted to the green grass. He settled in Boston after his skating days, won all five state golf championships in New England, and finished fourth on the PGA tour one season. In 1966, he was selected Sportsman of the Year by the Press Photographers of Boston, for golf, not hockey. He played senior golf in New England for years, then became pro at the International Golf Club just outside Boston, at 8,325 yards the world's longest course. But he always remained tough. Later in life, an intruder entered the Ezinicki home, and by the time police arrived their first course of action was to call an ambulance for the semi-comatose, would-be burglar.

Dean Evason

Todd Ewen

Bill Ezinicki

FAHEY, Trevor
b. New Waterford, Nova Scotia, January 4, 1944
Fahey did things in reverse. After playing one game in the NHL in 1964-65 with the Rangers, he played in the minors and only then went to university for four years, at St. F-X, after which he went into coaching.

FAIRBAIRN, Bill ("Bulldog")
b. Brandon, Manitoba, January 7, 1947
Fairbairn was scouted in Manitoba by the Rangers' head bird dog, Dennis Ball, back in the early 1960s. Ball recommended the youngster with enthusiasm after watching the line of Bill Fairbairn, Juha Widing, and Erv Zeimer tear up the WHL in Brandon. Fairbairn became known for his great wrist shot and his two-way play, and after making his debut with the New Yorkers in '68-'69, he stayed on Broadway for the next eight years. He later played on the tenacious Bulldog Line with Walt Tkaczuk and Dave Balon in his rookie season, a year in which he scored 23 goals and finished runner-up to Tony Esposito for the Calder Trophy. He went to the finals with New York in 1972 and a year later scored 30 goals. He finished his career with brief stints in Minnesota and St. Louis. After retiring in October 1978, Fairbairn returned to Brandon and worked in real estate and property management. He ran a sporting goods store and continued to play in old-timers' games whenever possible.

FAIRCHILD, Kelly
b. Hibbing, Minnesota, April 9, 1973
Although he was drafted by Los Angeles, Fairchild was traded to Toronto in a grab bag of minor prospects and lesser-knowns, and it was there that he had his real NHL chance. He played in the Leafs system for 4 years and got into 23 games with Toronto in that time, though ultimately he wound up in the IHL, which is not where an NHL aspirant wants to be. He signed as a free agent with Dallas, but after one game with the Stars during what would be their Cup year of '98-'99, he was back in the "I".

FALKENBERG, Bob ("Steady")
b. Stettler, Alberta, January 1, 1946
A stay-at-home defenceman, Falkenberg is part of a rare group of juniors to have won two Memorial Cups, beating Niagara Falls in 1962 and the Bobby Orr-led Oshawa Generals three years later. For the next five years he was a spare part with the Red Wings, playing mostly in the minors and being recalled only occasionally. His sole NHL goal came in Madison Square Garden in his rookie season, and when the WHA began operations in the summer of 1972, Falkenberg took advantage of the instant pay raise and signed with Alberta. He stayed another year, when the team became the Edmonton Oilers, and then was traded to the sunny climes of San Diego. He returned to his home in Edmonton in 1977 to work, but that year the Oilers asked him to play two games on an emergency basis. Falkenberg became a member of the Labatt Breweries team in Edmonton, working his way up to promotions coordinator for northern Alberta.

FALLOON, Pat
b. Foxwarren, Manitoba, September 22, 1972
There is exactly one degree of separation between Pat Falloon and baseball Hall of Famer George Brett. Brett and brother Bobby owned the Spokane Chiefs of the WHL the year Falloon and his mates won the Memorial Cup, in 1991. That summer, Falloon was considered the finest prospect entering the NHL draft, with but one exception: Eric Lindros. Lindros went 1st overall, and the expansion San Jose Sharks made Falloon their first-ever selection, 2nd overall. While he had an excellent rookie season, scoring 25 goals, Falloon felt increasingly stifled under coach Kevin Constantine and early in the '95-'96 season San Jose traded him to Philadelphia. He lasted less than two seasons there, and a career destined for greatness actualized into the great demise. After stints with Ottawa, Edmonton, and Pittsburgh in quick succession, he was out of the NHL in 2000-01, playing only in the Spengler Cup for Canada and then in Davos in Switzerland. He retired soon after and returned to the farm, though he played senior hockey and went to the Allen Cup finals in 2003.

FANKHOUSER, Scott
b. Bismarck, North Dakota, July 1, 1975
Goalie Fankhouser left the University of Massachusetts-Lowell to play junior in Saskatchewan for a year before returning to finish his degree. Being drafted 276th overall will do that to a person. St. Louis had selected him, but the Blues never played him and he signed with Atlanta. In his first year of pro, 1999-2000, he had the distinction of playing in four leagues: NHL, AHL, IHL, and ECHL. The chances of him catching on full-time in the NHL seem remote at best, but, hey, stranger things have happened.

FARKAS, Jeff
b. Amherst, New York, January 24, 1978
Farkas had about as distinguished an amateur career as any American could have at the World Juniors, playing in three successive championships (1996, '97, and '98) and leading the tournament in scoring in the last of those. He also had a fine career at Boston College and made his NHL debut during the playoffs, with Toronto in the spring of 2000. He scored a goal in his second game, but appeared only briefly in the coming seasons. Late in 2002-03, he suffered a serious neck injury in the AHL in Rochester that jeopardized his career.

FARR, Richard "Rocky"
b. Toronto, Ontario, April 7, 1947
It's not a smart career move for a goalie to sign a two-year contract and after one year demand to renegotiate it, especially when the GM to whom the demand is made is Punch Imlach. Farr played junior in the mid-to late 1960s and made his way to Buffalo in 1970 via the Expansion Draft. He appeared in just one game with the Sabres in '72-'73 but played very well for the team's AHL affiliate that season. The next year, he walked out of a contract agreement, and although he played a few more games with the team that year and the next, his career was short and sweet.

Bill Fairbairn

Scott Fankhouser

Jeff Farkas

Rocky Farr

Bob Falkenberg
(opposite page)

Dave Farrish

Rico Fata

Mario Faubert

Alex Faulkner

FARRANT, Walt ("Whitey")
b. Toronto, Ontario, August 12, 1912
Farrant got the call to join Chicago for a single game in 1944 when he was 31 years old. It was a call he had been waiting for during his many hockey years playing minor pro mostly in and around Toronto. He also played with the Minneapolis Millers in the American Association during the 1930s.

FARRELL, Mike
b. Edina, Minnesota, October 20, 1978
In 2000, Farrell cut short his college career at Providence to turn pro in the Washington system. Since that time, though, he has played only a few games with the Caps and the rest of the time with Portland, the team's AHL affiliate.

FARRISH, Dave
b. Wingham, Ontario, August 1, 1956
Steady. Stay at home. Crushing checks. Special teams. Pat and Mario's. Farrish was drafted by the Rangers, made the team during his first camp, and played three full seasons with them. But in his third year, incoming coach Fred Shero was not enamoured with of defenceman's play and left him unprotected in the 1979 Expansion Draft, when four WHA teams joined the NHL. The Nordiques scooped him up but didn't even invite him to training camp. They sent him to Toronto after just four games. Farrish's best years were at Maple Leaf Gardens, though he was in and out of the lineup, up and down from the minors. He spent all of '81-'82 with New Brunswick but was named the league's best defenceman and led the team to the Calder Cup championship. He was back with the Leafs the next year... for a while. During his time there, he went into business with partners to open Pat and Mario's, a bar/restaurant in downtown Toronto that thrived for a number of years. His career was not as enduring, and by 1984 he was out of the NHL for good, though he continued to play in the minors and Europe. After retiring, he became the head coach and vice-president of hockey operations for the Louisiana IceGators in the ECHL.

FASHOWAY, Gord
b. Portage la Prairie, Manitoba, June 16, 1926
In the old days, the important minor leagues featured hockey of such excellent calibre that one could favourably compare a player in, say, the AHL to one in the NHL. So, when Fashoway scored his 545th goal in pro hockey in 1963, it was a big deal because he broke Rocket Richard's record, even though only 3 of those goals came in the NHL (with Chicago in 1950-51). Fashoway had 12 seasons of 29 goals or more in the Pacific and Western leagues, mostly with the New Westminster Royals and later with Portland. After retiring in 1964, he remained in Portland and later coached the junior Winter Hawks. He even had a 10-game stint as head coach with the pitiful Oakland Seals in their first season, '67-'68. After being fired by the Winter Hawks, he was later hired to coach the Dallas Hawks, in 1975.

FATA, Rico
b. Sault Ste. Marie, Ontario, February 12, 1980
Rare, rare, rare are the teens who play junior at 15.

Wayne Gretzky did it, and went on to set a gabillion scoring records. Rico Fata did it, and went on to play exactly 27 NHL games in 3 years. At 15, 16, 17, and 18, he was considered the Next Coming, the Next Big Thing, the New Wayne. His idol had been Gretzky. His agent was Eddie Mio of IMG, whose partner was Mike Barnett, Gretzky's number cruncher. Fata went 6th overall to Calgary at the 1998 draft, and during training camp, held in Japan, he impressed coach Brian Sutter with his tremendous speed. But contract troubles meant last-minute negotiations, and Fata signed on October 9, 1998, just four days before he would have had to return to junior for the year. He became the first player to sign a contract on Japanese soil. But after just 20 games, Fata was demoted. The year after he played just two games, and in 2000-01 he played just five times, still looking for his first career goal. Some junior phenoms make it; some don't.

FAUBERT, Mario ("Tonto")
b. Valleyfield, Quebec, December 2, 1954
Times have changed. The days of calling a part-Indian player Tonto as a friendly nickname have long gone, though the criteria for a good defenceman haven't altered so much. Faubert was an all-star blueliner at St. Louis University and was selected by Pittsburgh in the 1974 Amateur Draft. He spent four seasons splitting time between the Penguins and the farm team, but in camp in 1979, after a full year in the minors, he won a starting job after initially being disappointed he hadn't been taken by an incoming WHA team. Dale Tallon was injured, and Faubert impressed coach Johnny Wilson with a new attitude and a sense of desperation in camp. Faubert added some weight to add strength to his repertoire and began to assert himself physically, playing with a confidence he had never shown before. He improved exponentially the year after, both in points (18 to 52) and in penalty minutes (31 to 188), but in '81-'82 appeared in just 14 games before he suffered a career-ending fracture of his leg on November 18, 1981, when he ran into Mike Crombeen during a game.

FAULKNER, Alex
b. Bishop's Falls, Newfoundland, May 21, 1936
Faulkner's is a story of a small-town, small-province hero who did his roots proud. Former Leafs player and coach Howie Meeker was living in Newfoundland in semi-retirement, and when old pal King Clancy paid a visit they took in a hockey game and discovered Faulkner. The Leafs signed him, and on December 7, 1961, he became the first Newfoundlander to play in the NHL. The Leafs exposed him in the Intra-League Draft that summer and he was claimed by Detroit. The next year he played the full season with the Wings, and in the playoffs he again set the provincial benchmark for first to play and score in a Stanley Cup playoff game. In fact, Faulkner scored five goals that spring, three of them game-winners. In game three of the finals against Toronto, he scored twice on Johnny Bower in a 3-2 Detroit win. *Hockey Night in Canada* guest colour commentator Bobby Hull named Faulkner the first star, and after the game Ward Cornell interviewed him. Premier Joey Smallwood was so impressed that he passed a bill to ensure a school

holiday upon Faulkner's return home. An enormous motorcade formed a parade for their returning hockey hero, though he played just another half-season in the NHL. Faulkner played briefly in Newfoundland with his brothers George and Jack and then enjoyed a stint in the WHL, retiring in 1972 and returning home to work in life insurance (during his playing days, he sold flour for a business owned by Red Wings owner Bruce Norris). He later ran a senior citizens' home and special care facility for the elderly in Bishop's Falls. He was later inducted into the Newfoundland Hall of Fame.

FAUSS, Ted

b. Clinton, New York, June 30, 1961

Baseball or hockey? The Pittsburgh Pirates or the NHL? That was the choice Teddy Two-Sport had to make in high school, and instead of a career languishing in the ball minors for years he accepted a scholarship from Clarkson University, where four years of studying and playing hockey gave him a degree in marketing management. But the hockey part was less promising. He wasn't picked up in the draft, and although the Canadiens signed him to a three-year contract as a free agent in 1983, he did just what he had sought to avoid with baseball – languish in the minors – though he did win a Calder Cup with Sherbrooke. In the summer of 1985, while working out in preparation for another AHL training camp, his back gave out. A broken vertebra was the diagnosis, and Fauss missed an entire season, his tenuous minor-league career in jeopardy. Curses are sometimes blessings. His coach with Nova Scotia (the

He returned to Denver to run **an auto brokerage firm, importing fancy cars from Europe and playing old-timers' hockey.**
DOUG FAVELL

Habs' AHL affiliate) was John Brophy, who soon became coach of the Leafs. The two met at a hockey game a short time later, and the White Ghost invited Fauss to get in shape and report to Leafs camp, which he did. Fauss signed a minor-league contract, but when regular defenceman Chris Kotsopoulos was injured, Fauss was called up, playing parts of both '86-'87 and '87-'88. His time with the team was short, though, and he retired in 1989. He returned four years later to play a few games in the Colonial League with the Utica Bulldogs before leaving the game for good.

FAUST, Andre

b. Joliette, Quebec, October 7, 1969

Like Mark McKay, Faust used Upper Canada College as a springboard to a college career at an Ivy League school, in McKay's case Harvard, in Faust's case Princeton. Faust was drafted by New Jersey but never played with Beezelbub's NHL affiliate, the Devils. Instead, Faust flew like Ariel to Philadelphia, but the Flyers sold his soul to the Jets in Winnipeg. He ended up in the minors and then spiralled down to Goethe's

home country where Faust continued on in the German league.

FAVELL, Doug ("Flaky"/ "The Fav")

b. St. Catharines, Ontario, April 5, 1945

"Did you play?" Favell was asked after one game. Looking down, he responded, "I must have. My underwear is wet." Such was the wit and wisdom of the flaky goaler with the pig's-nose-and-mouth Maple Leafs mask who drove a Bricklin, signed a luxurious contract, injured his body regularly, and made an average stop look spectacular. He attended the training camp of St. Catharines at 17, but was a late cut and managed to get a chance with Niagara Falls in junior. This was 1964, and that year the Flyers won the Memorial Cup. After knocking around in the minors for a couple of seasons, Favell was claimed by the NHL

Ted Fauss

Flyers and made the team in 1967. He stayed six years as the next great goalie, although he was the man in net the night Red Berenson scored six goals. When the Flyers had the chance to retrieve Bernie Parent from the Leafs via the WHA, where Parent had fled and from which he was now fleeing in the other direction, Philly didn't hesitate. But with the Leafs, Favell was one of three goaltenders, with Ed Johnston and Dunc Wilson. He never saw much to cheer about in the way coach Red Kelly handled things, and when the Leafs dealt him to Colorado, both parties seemed happy. Favell kicked off his career with the Rockies to start '76-'77, defeating the Leafs in his first game. Again, though, his stay was short, and after two and a half years he finished out his pro

Doug Favell

career with the Philadelphia Firebirds of the AHL. He stayed in the city and played his other passion – lacrosse – in the National Lacrosse League, then returned to Denver to run an auto brokerage firm, importing fancy cars from Europe and playing old-timers' hockey.

FEAMSTER, Dave

b. Detroit, Michigan, September 10, 1958

Something just wasn't right. Feamster knew it, he could feel it. In his fourth season with Chicago, 1984-85, he was playing poorly. He'd take a few strides, and have no strength or energy. He knew it back in September when he tried out, unsuccessfully, for Team USA's entry in the 1984 Canada Cup. GM Bob Pulford sent him to the minors, but Feamster protested. Skill wasn't the problem, health was. He checked into the Mayo Clinic with exhaustion, but doctors there found something more problematic, a stress fracture in his fifth lumbar vertebra. That was the end of Feamster's career. He moved to Pueblo, Colorado, and became owner of several Little Caesar's Pizza franchises, and coached a local high school team.

Dave Feamster

Glen Featherstone

FEATHERSTONE, Glen
b. Toronto, Ontario, July 8, 1968

The fruits of Featherstone's labour ended where they began, in Toronto. His father had been right-hand man to Steve Stavro during the height of Knob Hill Farms operations, getting up in the middle of the night to inspect the foodstuffs at the various stores in the city. Roy Featherstone managed to get his boy, Glen, a job at Knob Hill during the summers, and Glen once made it to the lofty position of manure manager. Glen went on to play junior for Windsor, during which time he was drafted by St. Louis, in 1986. He earned his stripes as a rugged, stay-at-home defenceman, hockey's euphemism for resident tough guy, and went on to play four other NHL teams. He knew his career was done when, in 1998, after a full year in the minors, he was invited to Stavro's Leafs camp but didn't make the cut. At that time he was reminded of a Boston-Toronto game a number of years previous. After getting into a fight with a Leafs player, Featherstone went to the penalty box. Stavro's seats at the Gardens were directly behind the penalty box, and when he saw Glen he walked right down, shook his hand, and said hello.

FEATHERSTONE, Tony
b. Toronto, Ontario, July 31, 1949

What a difference a year makes. Featherstone scored 5 goals with Nova Scotia in the AHL in 1971-72; the next year, he scored 49 as a member of the highest-scoring line in league history with Yvon Lambert and Moe Stefaniw. Unfortunately,

Tony Featherstone

his successes never translated well to either the NHL or, later, the WHA. Drafted by Oakland in 1969, he was a tentative newcomer and was traded to Montreal just two years later. In the Montreal system, however, only a superstar could have any hopes of making the big club, and Featherstone wound up being sent to Minnesota for futures. A middling year there left his career in limbo, but he got a reprieve in the form of a three-year deal with the Toronto Toros, where he played on a line with Frank Mahovlich, his childhood hero, and Vaclav Nedomansky. Midway through the following year, the Toros wanted to demote him. He refused to report, the team suspended him, and he quit the game. Featherstone remained in Toronto, his lifelong home, and became a senior account agent for an insurance company.

FEDERKO, Bernie
b. Foam Lake, Saskatchewan, May 12, 1956

Quiet superstar. Underrated great player. Silent giant. Those are the words usually used to describe Federko, for although not a household name he surely

accomplished Hall of Fame-type dreams during his 14 years in the NHL. He had four 100-point seasons and seven 30-goal seasons. He played exactly 1,000 NHL games and had 1,130 points, playing every year but his last with St. Louis. Federko was a scorer and superb passer, a team leader who played in two All-Star Games (1980 and '81). Off ice he was as popular an athlete in St. Louis as anyone, and on ice he led the Blues to 10 successive appearances in the playoffs (1980-89). Yet strangely, when he retired, he was not inducted into the Hockey Hall of Fame three years later, the only member, in fact, of the 1,000-point club not so honoured. (He was finally inducted in 2002.) He succeeded Brian Sutter as team captain in 1988, and by the time he retired he was the Blues' career leader in goals, assists, points, games played, and years of service to the team.

In '94 he was granted official pardon for his "defection."
SERGEI FEDOROV

FEDOROV, Sergei
b. Pskov, Soviet Union (Russia), December 13, 1969

From starvation to abundance, from poverty to wealth, from the Soviet Union to America, from boyhood to Anna, Sergei Fedorov's life changed on July 22, 1990, when he failed to show up for a team meal with his Soviet mates at the Goodwill Games in Portland, Oregon. The next day, he was in Michigan, signing a contract with the Detroit Red Wings, the team that had drafted him the previous summer. He had been a superstar back home, a national team member as a 19-year-old and two-time gold medal winner at the World Championships. He had been a World Junior star, the next centrepiece in a new generation of KLM fame and glory. With the Wings, he has been extraordinary, scoring 31 goals his first year and climaxing with 56 goals and 120 points in '93-'94, the year he won the Lester Pearson Award for best player in the league as voted on by the players. In '94 he was granted official pardon for his "defection," given a new passport, and invited to play internationally again for his country, an offer he accepted at the 1996 World Cup and 1998 Olympics in Nagano. Fedorov also quickly established himself as the best two-way player in the game, one with lightning speed and superb offensive talent who also could shut down the other teams' best players. He twice won the Selke Trophy for defensive play, and has appeared in three All-Star Games. The only blip in his 10-year career with Detroit came in 1997-98 when he missed most of the year in a contract dispute, one that ended with Carolina offering him an astronomical $38 million over 6 years ($28 million paid up front) and Detroit matching the offer to get him back in the lineup. Not surprisingly, the Wings repeated as Cup champs that spring, Fedorov scoring 10 playoff goals en route to lifting the sacred trophy. Like his hero, Steve Yzerman, he has played his whole career in Motown, and enlivened the city many a time with his former girlfriend's frequent presence. Anna Kournikova never played much tennis on the weekend, but she sure turned heads when she was in Detroit.

FEDORUK, Todd ("Fridge")
b. Redwater, Alberta, February 13, 1979
A left winger of size, Fedoruk entered the NHL officially on the night of November 1, 2000, when his Flyers faced Jersey. He stayed for 53 games that season, scoring only 5 times but adding that all-important Flyers' quality known as toughness to the lineup. Whether he remains an NHLer, only time will tell.

FEDOTENKO, Ruslan
b. Kiev, Soviet Union (Ukraine), January 18, 1979
Fedotenko sure took an unusual route to the NHL for someone from the Soviet group of countries. At 18, he was in Melfort, Saskatchewan, playing provincial junior A hockey, and the year after he went right to minor pro in the USHL. He moved up to the East Coast league, then to the AHL, and finally to the NHL, with Philadelphia. In his first year, he had a respectable 16 goals and 36 points, and the year after he had 1 more goal but only 9 assists.

FEDOTOV, Anatoli
b. Saratov, Soviet Union (Russia), May 11, 1966
From the Iron Curtain to the Land of the Rising Sun, Fedotov went with stick and skates in search of a game. He was developed by the Soviets in the 1980s in typical fashion, playing on a strong club team (Dynamo) and preparing always for international tournaments. He came to play in Canada with CCCP in the 1987 Canada Cup, but he got into the NHL under odd circumstances. The Jets signed him and used him for one game in 1992-93 (he had two assists), but the league ruled that the contract did not give the Jets the right to bring him up from the farm team in Moncton. He had to be drafted, the league decreed, and that summer Anaheim selected him 238th overall in 1993, thus making him a rare example of a player who played in the NHL prior to being drafted. All the fuss amounted to little. He played just three games for the Ducks, and after some time in the IHL he accepted an offer to play in Japan.

FEDYK, Brent
b. Yorkton, Saskatchewan, March 8, 1967
At the end of the day, this has to have been a disappointing prospect in the minds of Detroit's scouts. Fedyk was drafted 8th overall in 1985, and although he stayed with the Wings for five seasons, his was not a career that bloomed. He had impressed while playing for Regina in the WHL, and with Adirondack in the AHL he played like a leader, scoring goals, winning the Calder Cup in 1989, and showing promise. But in Detroit, he neither scored nor left a mark in any other aspect of his game. His confidence waned, and the Wings sent him to Philadelphia. He had back-to-back 20-goal seasons, and then his production dropped sharply to the point that the NHL no longer saw him as a regular.

FELIX, Chris
b. Bramalea, Ontario, May 27, 1964
Never drafted, Felix nonetheless pursued a hockey career after graduating from the Soo in 1985. He played three full years with the Canadian National Team and continued to the 1988 Olympics in Calgary, after which Washington signed him to a pro contract. Felix played just small, small parts of the next four seasons with the Caps and then accepted an offer to play in Austria. And why not? Income tax free; apartment provided; pace slower and games fewer; culture provided gratis.

Brent Fedyk

FELSNER, Brian
b. Mount Clemens, Michigan, November 11, 1972
Brothers Brian and Denny combined to play just 30 NHL games, one of the lowest totals in league history. Brian went to Lake Superior State before dressing for a dozen games with Chicago in '97-'98, and since then has played in the minors.

FELSNER, Denny
b. Warren, Michigan, April 29, 1970
Older brother to Brian, Denny attended the University of Michigan from 1988 to '92 where he proved to be a first-rate goal scorer on the left wing. He was drafted by St. Louis, but over the next 4 years he played just 18 games and scored only once. Like his bro, he, too, wound up in the minors.

FELTRIN, Tony
b. Ladysmith, British Columbia, December 6, 1961
On December 31, 1985, Feltrin was a perfectly healthy hockey player in the AHL. On January 1, 1986, he was virtually blind in one eye. In a game on New Year's Eve in Halifax, Feltrin, a member of New Haven, rushed the puck up the ice as he had done so many thousands of times before. But this time, a Halifax stick tried to lift his own, and instead carried right up into Feltrin's left eye. He knew at once it was serious. He remained in hospital for two weeks and underwent two operations for a detached retina, but never imagined he wouldn't play hockey again. He rejoined the team for the last month to skate in practice, and the following fall he attended the Rangers training camp. It simply wasn't going to happen. He retired and accepted a job offer from the team to become a scout, a vocation he has practised ever since. He had begun his career playing briefly with Pittsburgh and the Rangers.

FENTON, Paul
b. Springfield, Massachusetts, December 22, 1959
In just eight seasons in the NHL, Fenton was traded six times, signed as a free agent twice, and claimed on waivers once. His was an odd predicament. Undrafted, he nonetheless proved he could score everywhere. But when he asked Hartford GM Emile Francis why he wasn't getting a chance with the Whalers, an argument ensued and he was traded. In his first full season, 1987-00, he had 20 goals with the Rangers, and in '89-'90 he had 32 with Winnipeg. It seemed he could score if given the chance. After that, though, trades, not plays, were the order of the day, and he retired in 1992 without having made the mark he seemed capable of

Paul Fenton

Dave Fenyves

Andrew Ference

Brad Ference

Tom Fergus

in the AHL, where he scored 53 goals in a season, or the IHL, where he had 60 in '82-'83. He went on to become the director of player personnel for Nashville when the Predators joined the league.

FENYVES, Dave
b. Dunnville, Ontario, April 29, 1960
Fenyves was a heavy hitter and stay-at-home d-man rather than a scorer and rusher. He came out of Peterborough and played for Canada at the 1980 WJC, but over a career that lasted more than a dozen years he almost never spent an entire season in the NHL. Demotions and promotions were in the cards for him. Buffalo and Philadelphia were the teams. He won the Eddie Shore Award in the AHL for best defenceman twice, in 1988 and '89, though he never received similar recognition during his 206 games in the NHL.

FERENCE, Andrew
b. Edmonton, Alberta, March 17, 1979
As a kid, he wore a Mario Lemieux sweater when he played street hockey. As a young man, he played alongside Super Mario in the 2001 Stanley Cup playoffs. Ference was too small to play in the NHL. That's what they all said – scouts, GMs, coaches. They were wrong. Ference won a Memorial Cup with Portland in the WHL. He made Team Canada at the 1999 World Juniors. He was named to the WHL all-star team, and he played tough enough to rack up the penalty minutes. The Penguins drafted him 208th overall in 1997, just because. He proved them right. In game two of the playoff series with Buffalo in 2001, he scored the game-winner. His dream had come true.

FERENCE, Brad
b. Calgary, Alberta, April 2, 1979
Looks can be deceiving. Ference seems calm and mild, but on the ice he is a tiger who takes no prisoners and who can go a little wacky sometimes. Although he played in two World Juniors for Canada ('98 and '99), he didn't play regularly until the 2001-02 season, with Florida, thanks in large part to a broken jaw he suffered one camp in a fight with a teammate. He had been drafted by Vancouver but was included in the big deal that sent Pavel Bure to the Panthers, and it was down south that Ference developed into an NHLer. After that great full season, he accepted an invitation to play for his country at the World Championships, a final indication that perhaps, at last, he had arrived.

FERGUS, Tom ("Fergie")
b. Chicago, Illinois, June 16, 1962
Boy, could he shoot the puck... when he chose to.

Fergus developed into a large centre, an excellent face-off man, and a player capable of scoring 50 goals a year just with his wrist shot. Problem was, he couldn't get going for every game, every night, and he didn't use his shot as a weapon. When he was a teen, he had been so small and unimpressive he was cut from a junior B team and wound up in St. George, Ontario, playing junior D. But his father, president of Kidde Corporation in the U.S., was a football-like 6'4" and 285 pounds, so it was just a matter of time before young Tom grew. He played junior in Peterborough and the Bruins drafted him in 1980. A year later, he scored 15 goals with Boston before going down with a serious knee injury, from which he recovered fully. After four years, Fergus was sent to the Leafs for Bill Derlago, and with Toronto his career took off at the same time it was collapsing. He scored 31 times in '85-'86, and the following year he was one of three rotating captains, with Borje Salming and Wendel Clark, until a mysterious mono-like virus ate away at his energy and forced him out of the lineup for the rest of the year. The 1990-91 season was another write-off, this time because of a serious groin injury that required major surgery. In December 1991, the Leafs demoted him to the minors, but he refused to report and instead was claimed off waivers by Vancouver. Two half-seasons later he ended up where all former NHLers seem to find themselves late in their skating life: Europe. Fergus played two years with Zug in the Swiss League, then returned to his home in Oakville, where he coached the local provincial junior entry Blades and started his own sportswear company, Blue Leaf Limited.

FERGUSON, Craig
b. Castro Valley, California, April 8, 1970
There's only so much a guy can take, and for Ferguson, eight years of up and down was his limit. He was smart enough to be accepted into Yale University and skilled enough to be drafted by Montreal, but he wasn't good enough to stick in the NHL. For eight years he played the system, down in the minors, lucky to be called up, same old drill. All that added up to just 27 games between 1992 and 2000, so he packed his bags and headed for Switzerland to continue his career.

FERGUSON, George ("Chief")
b. Trenton, Ontario, August 22, 1952
Ferguson scored his first NHL goal back in 1972 on a shot from outside the blueline that eluded Roger Crozier. In April 1978, he tied an NHL record by scoring three goals in one period of a playoff game.

Ferguson scored his first NHL goal back in 1972 on a shot from outside the blueline.
GEORGE FERGUSON

And in another memorable moment, he broke his hand on road-roommate Tiger Williams's jaw. The Tiger said they were just horsing around. Fergie came out of the Marlies as a very valuable prospect, but in six years with the Leafs he never became what the team had hoped. He and Randy Carlyle were traded to Pittsburgh for Dave Burrows on June 14, 1978, one of many bad trades the Leafs made during those years. Ferguson went on to have 4 successive 20-goal seasons with the Penguins. After retiring, he joined the sales division of the Scole Engineering Company, a manufacturer of medical equipment, and he returned home to Trenton every summer to run a charity golf tournament. He also coached AAA hockey in Toronto.

FERGUSON, John ("Fergie")
b. Vancouver, British Columbia, September 5, 1938

It is the great and entirely consistent paradox of hockey that fighters on the ice are often the most articulate and successful men off it, and there is no greater example of that than John Ferguson. In his 8 NHL seasons he never had fewer than 125 penalty minutes and was, arguably, the league's first bodyguard for his team's star players. He also scored 29 goals one year and 20 another, numbers that attest to his skills over and above fighting. There were also five Stanley Cups during his brief career. Ferguson grew up near Exhibition Park racetrack in Vancouver, where his father was a trainer. He was a goalie in lacrosse and didn't put on skates for the first time until he was 13 years old, by which time he was stick boy for the Canucks of the

Ferguson grew up near Exhibition Park racetrack in Vancouver, where his father was a trainer.
JOHN FERGUSON

WHL. His duty, among others, was to tape the goalie's sticks. That goalie was Johnny Bower. Ferguson's rise on skates was meteoric, though he seemed destined for a career in the AHL, where he signed in 1960, with Cleveland. But the Habs, who had won five successive Cups to close out the 1950s, lost three straight years in the playoffs. They decided changes had to be made, and Ferguson made the team at camp in 1963. Toward the latter part of his career, he suffered two serious injuries, one to his eye, which required two operations to fix, and another to his elbow. In the fall of 1970, he stunned the team by announcing his retirement, and although he changed his mind for one year, he kept his word the following spring, in part because he was a successful businessman away from the rink. He had a clothing interest in Montreal that was going well, and he owned a promising stable of horses. (He combined his two great loves at Blue Bonnet raceway when he put together a hockey team made up of drivers and grooms.) Hockey beckoned in the summer of 1972, when he was named Harry Sinden's assistant coach for the historic eight-game Summit Series, and it was

Fergie who uttered the memorable remark, "He's killing us," that sparked Bobby Clarke to chop down Soviet superstar Valeri Kharlamov. Ferguson became coach and GM of the Rangers in 1976, a stormy two-year reign that yielded limited success. He signed with Winnipeg quickly thereafter, twice winning executive of the year during his 10 years with the team. In 1988 he was fired by the Winnipeg club and accepted a job managing the Windsor Raceway, and in 1992 he became the director of player personnel for the expansion Ottawa Senators. He later scouted for San Jose and became vice-president and director of hockey operations for the St. Louis Blues.

FERGUSON, Lorne ("Fergie")
b. Palmerston, Ontario, May 26, 1930

Although he played for three of the Original Six teams, Ferguson narrowly missed winning the Stanley Cup, arriving either too early or too late to drink the celebratory champagne. After a junior career with Guelph, he played for the New York Rovers and then the Tulsa Oilers before being called up to the Bruins late in the '49-'50 season. A year and a half later, he was back in the minors, but a 45-goal season with Hershey in '53-'54 earned him another shot with the Beantowners. He made good this time, scoring 20 goals, but by the end of the next season the Bruins decided he wasn't in their plans and sent him to Detroit. The Wings, however, had just won four Cups in five years and were on the downswing, and midway through '57-'58 he was traded to Chicago, a team on the upswing. Again, though, he missed out, being relegated to the minors in 1959 just as the team was on its way to winning a Cup in the spring of '61. Ferguson played off and on for the next decade in minor pro and senior hockey, eventually settling in Kingston and becoming a sales representative for a beer company. Both his son and his daughter went on to play serious hockey in junior and university.

FERGUSON, Norm ("Fergie")
b. Sydney, Nova Scotia, October 16, 1945

Impressing even a young Scotty Bowman, a scouting Scotty in his earliest days with Montreal, can never be a bad thing. When Ferguson scored five goals in a single game during a tournament in Halifax, Bowman signed him to a Habs contract and assigned him to Lachine. There he was named rookie of the year and moved up to the Junior Canadiens, eventually moving on in the minor pro circuit before being traded to the lowly Oakland Seals in the summer of 1968. Ferguson not only made the team that fall, he scored 34 goals, an NHL rookie record equalled by Danny Grant that

Norm Ferguson

Scott Ferguson

Manny Fernandez

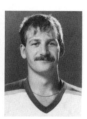

Mark Ferner

Peter Ferraro

same season. Grant edged Ferguson out in Calder Trophy voting, but the Sydney native looked to be on his way to a solid career in the big time. He worked hard on his shot and his skating, though he was primarily a plugger, but over the next three seasons his numbers sank, his effectiveness diminished, and the team kept losing. In 1972, he bolted to the WHA, where the goals came easier, and found himself back in the 30-goal range, where he remained until retiring in 1978 to coach the Edmonton Oil Kings of the WHL. In 1987, Ferguson was inducted into the Cape Breton Sports Hall of Fame for his NHL career.

FERGUSON, Scott
b. Camrose, Alberta, January 6, 1973
He came out of Kamloops after a great junior career, a big, tough defenceman with skill who was never drafted. Edmonton signed him in 1994, but the Oilers played him only once before he moved on to Ottawa and Anaheim. He re-signed with Edmonton after playing almost entirely in the minors, but still he was on the fringes rather than front and centre in the Oilers' team picture.

FERNANDEZ, Emmanuel "Manny"
b. Etobicoke, Ontario, August 27, 1974
As a kid, Manny had trouble skating all out for even a few seconds without becoming short of breath. Once doctors told him the problem was asthma, he had to confine himself to the goal crease to continue playing. From that time on, he dreamed of playing in the NHL, just like uncle Jacques (as in Lemaire). Fernandez developed with Laval in the Quebec league, winning Memorial Cups in 1993 and '94. In '94, he also helped Canada win gold at the World Juniors, and over the next five years he languished in the minor-league system of Dallas. During his brief callups, however, he learned how to play the game, both emotionally and physically, from starter Ed Belfour. His style was atypically Quebec, though, in that he was more of a standup than flopping, butterfly goalie. When he was traded to Minnesota in the summer of 2000, to play under head coach Uncle Jacques, he was ready. In his first season, he had a record of 19-17-4 sharing the goaltending with Jamie McLennan and proving he could play in the NHL.

FERNER, Mark
b. Regina, Saskatchewan, September 5, 1965
Although he played just 91 NHL games, Ferner managed to play for 4 different teams in the late 1980s and into the 1990s, the greatest number coming with Anaheim during its first 2 years of operation. The defenceman was a mainstay in the minors from 1985

right up to the present, and he has not seen the NHL since Detroit in 1995. He has also played in Europe.

FERRARO, Chris
b. Port Jefferson, New York, January 24, 1973
What's the difference between Chris Ferraro and Peter Ferraro? Two minutes. That's how much longer Chris has been in the world, though Peter overcame his youth by playing in the NHL before his twin – though just by a few days. Beyond that, their careers were virtually identical until 1998. Chris was drafted by the Rangers 85th overall in 1992; Peter went 24th. They both played in the USHL for Dubuque and then Waterloo. They attended the University of Maine for two years ('92-'94) and played for Team USA at the World Juniors in '92 and '93. They both played for

What's the difference between Chris Ferraro and Peter Ferraro? Two minutes.
CHRIS FERRARO

Atlanta and were traded to Binghamton in 1994-95. But perhaps their greatest strength as players was their very twinness, for their prospective greatness as a duo far surpassed their achievements. They played everywhere together in the hopes that each would inspire the other or that they played better when on the same team. But when the Rangers recalled the pair, they weren't particularly impressive and both were claimed on waivers by Pittsburgh on October 1, 1997. It was then their careers took separate turns and spelled the end of their double opportunities for a time. Chris was traded back to the Rangers during '97-'98, then bounced around in the minors and the Oilers. Peter went to the Bruins and he, too, bounced around. Their careers remained the same, on the downswing, but with different teams. That is, until the summer of 2001 when Washington signed the pair to contracts and they were together again. Weird.

FERRARO, Peter
b. Port Jefferson, New York, January 24, 1973
Like the Sedins in Vancouver, the Ferraros led indistinguishable lives from a distance. They were buzz saws on the ice, checkers and scrappy forecheckers who made up for lack of scoring touch with a tenacity and competitiveness coaches wished all their players had. Ironically, though Peter is a centre and brother Chris is a winger, they have played on all the same teams together but never on the same line. The one big difference in their careers is that Peter made the 1994 Olympic team for the U.S. while Chris was a late cut. When Peter signed with Boston in the summer of 1998, it marked the first time they had consciously decided to split up, though the move helped neither career, which has been more minor pro and less NHL in the six years since they first played in the NHL. That was remedied in 2001 when

Washington signed them both, to be on the same team again but not on the same line.

FERRARO, Ray

b. Trail, British Columbia, August 23, 1964

The Hartford Whalers drafted Ferraro in 1982 for one reason and one reason only: goals. In his final season of junior, he obliged, setting a Canadian record by scoring 108 times with Brandon. When he got to the NHL, he became a model of inconsistency, scoring 11 goals his first year, soaring to 30 the next, going down to 21 two years later, and back up to 41 in '88–'89. Another downward cycle ensured his departure, to the Islanders, but under coach Al Arbour the trend continued. Ferraro had consecutive seasons of 19, 40, and 14 goals, though the last could be asterisked because he missed 38 games in '92–'93 with a broken leg. Ferraro became a consistent 20-goal shooter in his last few years, mostly with the Rangers and Los Angeles. He played for Canada at three World Championships, winning silver in 1989 and '96 (and also playing in '92). He spent the last of his career in Atlanta, and each playoffs he worked for ESPN. When he retired in 2002, Ferraro moved into the broadcast booth on a full-time basis.

FETISOV, Vyacheslav "Slava"

b. Moscow, Soviet Union (Russia), April 20, 1958

The roles of politics in hockey and hockey in society met full on in the extraordinary life and career of Slava Fetisov. His participation in the game spans the full breadth of Iron Curtain hockey to the freedom of perestroika, yet along the way the one great constant in his life was victory, on and off the ice. His career began in earnest at age 16 when he made the CSKA team in Moscow, a mere boy playing against men. Yet he held his own. He helped the Soviets win three World Junior Championships (1976, '77, '78), and in no time he was considered the best young player the Soviet Union. He was tutored by longtime national star Gennady Tsygankov, but during the '78–'79 season he suffered a serious back injury in a game and had to be carried off on a stretcher. He eventually recovered, but was not fit to play at the 1979 World Championships (he had played in 1977 and 1978). Fetisov took his play to a higher level in 1980 when he was partnered on defence with Alexei Kasatonov. The two played almost a decade together, and got to know each other as both teammates and friends. Throughout the 1980s, there was no greater star than Fetisov. He played at the Olympics in 1980, '84, and '88; he played in the 1981 and '87 Canada Cups; and he played in every World Championships tournament, winning a neckload of gold medals along the way. His life was as good as was possible in the

Ray Ferraro

communist country, though 1985 was not a good year for him. He and his brother, Anatoli, were involved in a car accident that killed Anatoli, an 18-year-old considered to be a superb young player. While Fetisov and Kasatonov led the blueline, the Soviet nationals were dominated on forward by the line of Vladimir Krutov – Igor Larionov – Sergei Makarov (KLM line). As a result, the five were the best of friends, and they all wanted one thing – the NHL. During the 1988 Olympics in Calgary, they were promised a chance at the NHL if they won a gold medal. They did win, but no such chance was forthcoming. The players were furious and outspoken in their anger, all but Kasatonov who was ostracized for his perceived cowardly silence. The rift between the players and coach Viktor Tikhonov worsened the next year, Tikhonov taking the captaincy from Fetisov, and then Fetisov and best friend Larionov handing in their resignations in January 1989. Normally, of course, players who took such actions would be sent to Siberia, but these were the two best players in the country. Their cries could not be ignored nor their screams silenced, and their stand led to their eventual release to North America. Fetisov had been drafted by Montreal in 1978 and later by New Jersey, and although he could have defected he chose to fight democratically for his release. He was loyal to the system and to his country, but he also wanted to help change it. In his homeland, Fetisov was a hero and a giant. He handled the puck beautifully, challenged opponents with physical strength, and captained the team through his every move and word. When he got to the

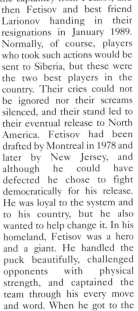

Fetisov had been drafted by Montreal in 1978 and later by New Jersey.
SLAVA FETISOV

NHL with New Jersey in 1989, he had to start again and adjust to a long and arduous schedule. He had to curtail his rushes and get used to not playing most of an entire game. Yet he fit in perfectly, except when the Devils acquired his old friend and more recent foe, Kasatonov. Fetisov refused to speak to his traitorous friend, and the Soviet experiment ended quickly. Fetisov played more than five years with the Devils, but his career took on greater meaning when he was traded to Detroit in 1995. Coach Scotty Bowman was assembling a Russian group of players that could play as a five-man unit (three forwards, two defencemen) just as they had in their formative years. The plan eventually worked, as the Wings won the Cup in '96–'97, an historic victory in that it marked the first true and successful integration of European players into the NHL. Just days after the victory, though, Fetisov was drawn into another horror reminiscent of his brother's death. He, Vladimir Konstantinov, and team masseuse Sergei Mnatsakanov were being driven home by a chauffeur who crashed the car into a tree, seriously injuring Fetisov and paralyzing the other two. Fetisov recovered fully, but to this day

Konstantinov and Mnatsakanov are shadows of their former selves. Later that summer, Fetisov and Larionov took the Cup to Red Square, the first time Lord Stanley's sacred silverware had travelled to Russia, and tens of thousands of fans welcomed the trophy. After winning a second Cup in 1998, Fetisov, now 40, retired. He became an assistant coach with New Jersey – where he won another Cup in 2000 – and was later inducted into the Hockey Hall of Fame. Even in his NHL days, he was revered by NHL Russians for what he had accomplished. He was the guiding light, the unofficial GM of Russia for the 1996 World Cup, and he was in control of the Russian team for the 2002 Olympics at Salt Lake City. He became the secretary of sport for all of Russia in 2001, leaving the NHL temporarily for a greater cause – the redevelopment of Russian hockey and the management of all levels of the sport to produce a new generation of Fetisov-like stars in a democratic system of government.

FICHAUD, Eric
b. Anjou, Quebec, November 4, 1975
His dad was a cop, but so far Eric has been a bust. He was a high draft choice by Toronto in 1994 and he made his reputation in an exhibition game at Maple Leaf Gardens, playing 20 minutes of spectacular hockey against Montreal. From that time, he was considered hot hot hot, but when Toronto traded him to Long Island, his play was decidedly weak in real NHL action. He played with increasing infrequency in the NHL and was owned by six teams during his brief career which seemed to end in October 2001. A year later, though, he re-signed with Montreal to play in the minors.

Mike Fidler

FIDLER, Mike ("Fids")
b. Everett, Massachusetts, August 19, 1956
Drafted by California in 1976, Fidler never played for the Seals because they relocated to Cleveland later in the summer. He thus became one of a few players who, technically, began his career with one team after being drafted by another without being traded. His rookie year with the Barons began well, but a broken leg put an end to that season after just 46 games. In season two, he was charged with felonious assault after he allegedly slashed a man with a broken jar during a barroom fight. Great. In his next year, a broken bone in his knee kept him on the shelf for the first quarter of the schedule. Soon after, he required major shoulder surgery that put the kibosh on that season, and the next year was marred by a dislocated shoulder. The following October the shoulder problems were finally given a name –

Wilf Field

rotator cuff – and the ensuing treatment took him out of the lineup for almost all of '81–'82. Fidler played just a few more games the next season after signing with Chicago, but he wound up playing in Austria and then in the AHL before retiring, a broken and battered shell of the strong youth he once had been.

FIELD, Wilf
b. Winnipeg, Manitoba, April 29, 1915
d. Los Angeles, California, March 17, 1979
Field developed his talents in his native province before signing with the New York Americans in 1936. He stayed with the team for five years before going off to war with the RCAF, and upon his discharge played again briefly in the NHL before being sent to pasture in the AHL. Field took to coaching toward the end of his playing days, doing double duty in Buffalo and Houston before moving to Halifax and the St. Mary's full-time in 1951. He was later inducted into the Manitoba Sports Hall of Fame.

By the time he retired, Fielder was the all-time leading pro point getter, surpassing Howe.
GUYLE FIELDER

FIELDER, Guyle ("Guy"/ "Golden Guyle")
b. Potlach, Idaho, November 21, 1930
If only he hadn't been put on a line with Gordie Howe to replace Sid Abel, everything might have been all right. But Jack Adams was looking for someone to centre Howe, and Howe and Fielder both liked to have the puck. This was the start of the '57–'58 season. The Wings lost six games out of the chute, and Fielder found himself on the fourth line. He went into Adams' office for a talk, and the coach offered him a raise. Fielder said he didn't want a raise – he wanted to play. Adams sent him to Seattle where he spent the next dozen years playing. By the time he retired, Fielder was the all-time leading pro point getter, surpassing Howe, surpassing the 2,000 point mark, accomplishing everything but mastering the NHL game. Although he was born in Idaho, where his father worked, Guyle and family were raised in Nipawin, Saskatchewan, and it was there he learned two skills that cost him much of his reputation later during his hockey career: playing pool and drinking beer. His philosophy rested on two tenets: One, have two beers quickly after a hockey game. Two, when the bus pulls in to town, go to the nearest pool hall until game time to hustle some money, and return right after the game to hustle some more. The Hawks signed him at 15 to his first contract, but after just 3 games in '50–'51, they let him go. He played a few games with Detroit in the '53 playoffs and with Boston the next year, but it wasn't until his second go-round with the Wings that he had a real chance to make it. Before and after, he played minor pro, winning 11 scoring titles in various leagues during his career (9 in the WHL) and

becoming a legend in Seattle during his many successful years there. He retired in 1969, but when a friend became involved in an expansion team in Salt Lake City, he agreed to play and his career continued another five years. The switch of teams had to be formalized with a trade, and Seattle received Bobby Schmautz in the exchange. After retiring, Fielder and his wife settled in Manzanita, Oregon, a small town where he could fish and golf and relax and contemplate his place in history as one of the greatest players never to make an impact in the NHL.

FILIMONOV, Dmitri
b. Perm, USSR, October 14, 1971
The Bre-X of Soviet hockey, Filimonov was a 20-year-old sensation who played in the 1991 Canada Cup and pretty quickly proved to be fool's gold. The hulking defenceman hardly stood out in that event, and after 30 games with Ottawa in '93-'94 during the team's second season, he was in the minors, out of the country, and back in Russia playing in his hometown.

FILLION, Bob
b. Thetford Mines, Quebec, July 12, 1921
He got the "I want to win a Stanley Cup before I retire" thing out of the way pretty quickly. Fillion scored 7 goals for Montreal in '43-'44, the same season Maurice Richard scored 50 in 50 games in an NHL decimated by men going off to war. The Habs won the Cup that year and again two seasons later when Fillion scored four goals in the nine games of that year's playoffs. He was considered a dependable backchecker and two-way left winger. Fillion retired in 1950 having played all of his 327 NHL games with the Habs.

FILLION, Marcel
b. Thetford Mines, Quebec, May 28, 1923
d. unknown
Bob's brother had but a shilling's worth of fun in the NHL, playing a single game, with Boston, in the '44-'45 season. He played for the principal farm team, the Boston Olympics, for a few years and then headed home to Quebec to finish his career.

FILMORE, Tommy
(sometimes Fillmore)
b. Thamesford, Ontario
d. Clearwater, Florida, 1954
Players are loyal employees, and fans are loyal subjects. That's what makes hockey so great. Filmore played 117 NHL games from 1930 to '34 and ended up finishing his career in Springfield in 1940. Almost immediately he became club pro at the Springfield Golf & Country Club until the day he died suddenly, on a golf course in Florida, some 14 years later. To perpetuate his memory, the Indians started a booster club and created a Filmore Trophy to be awarded annually to the series winner between Springfield and Providence (for whom he had played one year).

FINKBEINER, Lloyd
b. Guelph, Ontario, April 12, 1920
d. Goodyear, Arizona, March 30, 1998
No shrinking violet, this Finkbeiner. He played just two

games in the NHL, with the New York Americans in '40-'41, before entering the Royal Canadian Army Service Corps for a year, after which he was everywhere but the NHL for many years to come.

FINLEY, Jeff ("Finner")
b. Edmonton, Alberta, April 14, 1967
Finley was a draft choice of the Islanders in 1985, and despite the fact that he continues to play, he is barely over the 500-game career mark. This is because, quite simply, he did not play a full season without a trip to the minors until he was 29. And only since he hit St. Louis in 1999 has he been what one might call an NHL regular. Finley didn't have the size of Chris Pronger or the offensive skills of Al MacInnis, but he has been an effective fifth or sixth blueliner with the club.

FINN, Steven
b. Laval, Quebec, August 20, 1966
There are few greater ignominies in hockey than being traded for Michel Petit, king of the travelling hockey show and record holder for having played with 10 NHL teams. But that's how Finn closed out his career, going from Tampa to Los Angeles for Petit on November 13, 1995. The defenceman had starred in the Quebec juniors with Laval before joining the Nordiques, though he was traded by the Avalanche before he could play a game with the new team after it transferred in 1995. He played two seasons with L.A. at the end of his NHL career.

FINNEY, Sid
b. Banbridge, Ireland, May 1, 1929
Desire. Ambition. Ferocious determination. Those traits were all that kept Sid Finney from being a superstar in the NHL the way he was for so many years in the Western league. He played with Chicago only parts of three seasons in the early 1950s, preferring the Calgary Stampeders of the lesser league. He routinely scored 30 goals in the WHL, and sometimes 40. Twenty was a given. He starred like no other in the league, winning scoring championships, being named league MVP, being named to all-star teams. Then the Hawks called him up, and nothing. It just wasn't in him.

FINNIGAN, Ed
b. Shawville, Quebec, May 23, 1911
d. unknown
Unlike his more famous brother, Frank, Ed had his finest moments early in life. He won Nugget Shield championships with the CNR Apprentices in 1927 and the T & NO the year after. He played junior in North Bay the year after that, at just 16, and played with Frank for a dozen games with the St. Louis Eagles during that franchise's only season, '34-'35. The next year, he played three times with Boston, and thereafter in lesser leagues.

FINNIGAN, Frank ("The Shawville Express"/ "Fearless Frank")
b. Shawville, Quebec, July 9, 1900
d. Shawville, Quebec, December 25, 1991
The name of the train was the Push, Pull, and Jerk,

Bob Fillion

Tommy Filmore

Jeff Finley

Sid Finney

Ed Finnigan

Jiri Fischer

and it took you from Shawville to Ottawa. That's how Finnigan got his nickname, and that's how he began his career. He played for the Shawville Pets when he was 11, and by the time he could vote he had been recruited to play for the University of Ottawa. The rule was simple: he'd enrol in business administration, but his major would be (being paid to play) hockey. From there he signed with the local NHL entry, the Senators, in 1923, and four years later he won his first Stanley Cup with the team. He played 1931-32 with Toronto when the Senators suspended operations for a season, living at the Royal York Hotel with King Clancy and winning another Cup. He returned to Ottawa when the team restarted the next fall and moved with the team to St. Louis, playing briefly with his brother, Ed. Frank played in the Ace Bailey Benefit Game in February 1934. Finnigan was sold to the Leafs in 1935 and played the last two and a half years of his career with the team, establishing a lifelong passion for the Blue and White. The Senators and Leafs of those years had so many good players that Finnigan's name is often forgotten, though he was considered a star in his own right during his heyday. He skated well and had a good shot, and scored more than his share of goals. After retiring, he hooked up with Mister X, otherwise known as Harry McLean from Merrickville, an eccentric millionaire who threw money out hotel windows during his prime in the 1940s, and the two became good friends. The player owned an hotel in Merrickville briefly and later

Stephane Fiset

returned to Shawville, where he bought the Clarendon Hotel, staying in business until 1980, when he sold it and retired. Still, he was not yet done. When the new Senators were granted a franchise in the early 1990s, Finnigan was front and centre, promoting the new owners and the city, and preparing for opening night festivities when his old number eight would float into the rafters as the team's first retired sweater. Sadly, he suffered a heart attack and passed away just a few months before this night. He has been inducted into three Halls of Fame – the Kingston Hockey Hall of Fame, the Ottawa Sports Hall of Fame, and le pantheon de l'Outaouais.

FIORENTINO, Peter
b. Niagara Falls, Ontario, December 22, 1968
Gargantuan penalty-minute totals got him from Ontario junior to the draft podium in 1988, but fists alone got him only a single NHL game. Fiorentino played with the Rangers in '91-'92 but before and after that he did his fighting in the minors.

Fiorentino played with the Rangers in '91-'92.
PETER FIORENTINO

FISCHER, Jiri
b. Horovice, Czechoslovakia (Czech Republic), July 31, 1980
Detroit's Scotty Bowman, after winning Stanley Cups with the Wings in 1997 and '98, did a good job of working young talent into an experienced, winning lineup. Fischer is one such example. A team draft choice, he made the lineup more or less full-time after two years of junior in Quebec. That was 1999, and he has been steadily improving since, getting more ice time and assuming more responsibility on an ancient blueline.

FISCHER, Ron
b. Merritt, British Columbia, April 12, 1959
He had one of the longest careers in hockey... for a Canadian-born player in Europe. Fischer played briefly with the Buffalo Sabres after leaving the University of Calgary, and after parts of four seasons in the minors he used his dual citizenship to play in Germany starting in 1984. He went on to play at two Olympics and World Championships with the German national team, and the majority of his club play (a total of 12 years) was for Rosenheim.

FISET, Stephane
b. Montreal, Quebec, June 17, 1970
He was one of a long line of excellent goalies to come out of Quebec in the last 15 years, a graduate of Quebec junior who played for the Nordiques for 6 years and moved with the team to Colorado. Fiset played 37 games with Colorado in '95-'96, the year Patrick Roy came to the team and made him redundant. Fiset won the Cup that year with the team and has since established himself in Los Angeles. He twice played at the World Juniors, winning gold in 1990 and being named the Directorate's best goalie. Despite having been in the league a dozen years now, though, he has played only about as many playoff games. His finest moments came in Quebec at the start, when he was number-one goalie for most of two seasons (1993-95).

FISHER, Alvin
b. unknown
d. unknown
One of the players who fell through the cracks. Fisher played nine games with the Toronto St. Pats in '24-'25, that much is certain. He scored a goal. He had played out west. But beyond that, little is known of the man or the player.

FISHER, Craig
b. Oshawa, Ontario, June 30, 1970
Philadelphia drafted him in '88 and gave him two

games the following season. He played two more the year after, and then the bouncing began. Winnipeg and Florida were his other NHL destinations, but Fisher saw a ton of action outside the big league. He was a remarkable scorer everywhere else, scoring as many as 74 goals in an IHL seasson, but he suffered a serious concussion early in the 1999-2000 season in the AHL and that was the end of the line for him. The hit occurred in November. By April, he still couldn't dial his own hone number. He retired.

FISHER, Dunc
b. Regina, Saskatchewan, August 30, 1927

Those who knew him never figured out either why he never stuck in the NHL or why he wasn't given the chance. Fisher retired in 1960 as one of the greatest Hershey Bears of all time. He had four 40-goal seasons, won a scoring championship and a Calder Cup, and was as loved by the fans as any player in team history. With linemates Lorne Ferguson and Red Sullivan, he set team and league records. He had really good runs with both the Rangers and Boston but ultimately he was relegated to the minors. Detroit, looking for scoring, brought him up for eight games in '58–'59, but he didn't register a single point. He was famous for being the only NHLer to play the bagpipes, but when he retired he returned to Regina and became a swimming instructor.

FISHER, Joe
b. Medicine Hat, Alberta, July 4, 1916
d. Medicine Hat, Alberta, April 13, 2002

There aren't too many players who can boast having won three major championships in hockey, but Fisher is one. He won the Cup with Detroit in 1943 (albeit barely), won the Calder Cup with the Indianapolis Capitols the previous year, and won the Allan Cup with the Calgary Stampeders in '46. The Stanley Cup came in his last of four seasons with Detroit, though he played most of those seasons down with the AHL Capitols. After two years in the war, he was reinstated as an amateur. He became head coach of the Regina Caps in 1947, though he continued to play briefly as well for the first season. In the summer, he returned to his native Alberta to run a transport company. In 1970, he and two partners brought a junior team to Medicine Hat, and Fisher kept active with the Tigers until 1979.

FISHER, Mike
b. Peterborough, Ontario, June 5, 1980

An Ottawa draft choice out of the Sudbury Wolves in 1998, Fisher has been an impact player with the Sens ever since. His first season was cut in half by a serious knee injury, but since then he has become one of the team's current stars and potential superstars. He is a centre with size and decent hands who went from 4 to 7 to 15 goals in his first 3 years, and is proud to attribute much of his success to God.

FITCHNER, Bob ("Fitch")
b. Sudbury, Ontario, December 22, 1950

A draft choice out of Brandon, Fitchner paid his dues before making his NHL debut at age 29 with the Quebec Nordiques. He played minor pro for three years after graduating from the Wheat Kings and then signed with Edmonton in the WHA, making it his league of choice. He went to Indianapolis and finally to Quebec, where he remained when the team joined the NHL in 1979. Coach Jacques Demers thought him one of the more valuable guys on the team, the premier face-off man in the game, and a stalwart defensive centre. Fitchner killed penalties and forechecked with the best of them, but early the following season the irreplaceable player was too easily replaced, and his career was over after having played a grand total of 78 NHL games. He and his family moved to Nelson, B.C., where he had grown up.

Dune Fisher

FITZGERALD, Rusty
b. Minneapolis, Minnesota, October 4, 1972

He's still out there playing, though it's been six years and counting since he saw the NHL. Fitzgerald came out of the University of Minnesota-Duluth after 4 years to play for Pittsburgh for 25 games, but soon he was in the minors for good. He suffered a serious knee injury at the start of the '96-'97 season, but after a year and a half off the ice resumed his career in the IHL and United league.

FITZGERALD, Tom
b. Billerica, Massachusetts, August 28, 1968

He's been out there doing some stuff, he's just been kind of quiet. He played for the Islanders during the decade all fans who hate the Islanders love to talk about – the 1990s – because the team was so poor. He went to Florida in the Expansion Draft in 1993, and three years later he played with the Panthers in the Cup finals before being swept by Colorado. He wound up with another new team, Nashville, in 1998, and then in his eleventh season he became the franchise's first captain. Silent Tom has played almost 1,000 NHL games playing on mostly weak teams, but he's been in the spotlight since signing with Toronto in the summer of 2002.

Joe Fisher

FITZPATRICK, Mark ("Fitzy")
b. Toronto, Ontario, November 13, 1968

Rx. Imagine being a top prospect in the NHL. Imagine being big and quick and young and well regarded by your team. Imagine going on a road trip and waking up in your hotel bed to discover your feet had swelled to the size of footballs. That's what happened to Mark Fitzpatrick, through no fault of his own, in the fall of 1990. He was taking a vitamin supplement containing L-Tryptophan and wound up contracting Eosinophilia Myalgia Syndrome (EMS) a disease of the white blood cells that threatens the nerves and muscles. He wasn't the only one. That year, more than 1,500 cases of EMS were discovered to be caused by L-Tryptophan. The U.S. Food and Drug Administration pulled the amino acid from the shelves, and Fitzpatrick's career hung in the balance. He was given Predisone to combat the effects, but the triple dosage doctors had to prescribe had side effects that included weakening of the bones, mood swings, loss of appetite, and cataracts. Fitzpatrick sued the company, Nature's Bounty, for $180 million, and returned to his parents' home in Kitimat, B.C., to recuperate. He missed virtually all of the next two seasons, and when he came back to health and hockey

Mike Fisher

Bob Fitchner

Rory Fitzpatrick

he struggled to re-establish himself. He was traded to Quebec and then claimed by the Panthers in the Expansion Draft in 1993, and has since played with Tampa Bay, Chicago, and Carolina, his once bright and future career now looking like a faint and fading glow.

FITZPATRICK, Rory
b. Rochester, New York, January 11, 1975
Size, of course, counts for so much for scouts in the modern era, especially for defencemen. That's why Montreal drafted Fitzpatrick in 1993, though that alone has hardly kept him in the league. The Habs traded him in a big deal to acquire Shayne Corson, but his three games with the Blues paled in comparison to the three and a half seasons he spent in their minor-league system. Most recently, he landed in Nashville, a great place for a country singer but an awful place for a professional hockey player.

FITZPATRICK, Ross
b. Penticton, British Columbia, October 7, 1960
After graduating from the University of Western Michigan in 1982, Fitzpatrick joined the Philadelphia Flyers and played snippets of the next four seasons there. His true calling, though, was in the AHL, where he proved to be a bona fide scorer. In 1985-86, he scored 50 goals while playing on a line with Tim Tookey, another great AHLer. In 592 career games in that league, he had 308 goals.

FITZPATRICK, Sandy
b. Paisley, Scotland, December 22, 1944
The Rangers considered Fitzpatrick a can't-miss prospect back when he was playing with the team's OHL affiliate in Kitchener from '62 to '64, but they only gave him four NHL games to prove it. Minnesota claimed him in 1967, and a late-season injury to forward Ray Cullen gave Fitzpatrick a chance to prove himself. Skating was the weakest part of his game, but he held his own for 18 games and another 12 in the playoffs. That proved to be his final NHL opportunity, though, and he returned to the minors the following training camp.

Sandy Fitzpatrick

FLAHERTY, Wade
b. Terrace, British Columbia, January 11, 1968
His numbers tell the tale of a backup goalie, so backup, in fact, he turned around and found himself in the minors, where the prospects there have backup written all over them. Flaherty peaked with San Jose in '95-'96 when he played in 24 games, but even during his many years in the minors he wasn't always the first-string man in the blue ice. His win percentage has always been around .333 and his GAA chimes in at about three and a half goals per game. That won't cut it for too long in the NHL.

FLAMAN, Ferdinand "Fern"
b. Dysart, Saskatchewan, January 25, 1927
Half a century in hockey and all Flaman has managed to do is make friends and more friends, even though as a player he was known as a devastating hitter. He came up through the Boston system after the Bruins discovered the 15-year-old playing in Edmonton. He was raised in Regina, where he was also an outstanding

Fern Flaman

ball player, but turned pro with the Boston Olympics at the tender age of 16 and never looked back. He had brief tryouts with the B's during the war years, but it wasn't until 1947, when he was a more mature 20, that he was ready to tackle the NHL full time. He patrolled the Boston blueline for three and a half years but the team sent him to Toronto with Leo Boivin, Phil Maloney, and Ken Smith for Bill Ezinicki and Vic Lynn on November 16, 1950. He won his only Cup later that season with the Leafs, and after Bill Barilko's death in the summer it was Flaman's job to pick up the slack as the heavy hitter on the team. Three years later, though, the Leafs traded him back to Boston, where he played his final seven NHL seasons. During this time he became team captain, and off the ice he was the team's player rep for the ill-fated attempt to form a players' union. Under Flaman's leadership, the Bruins advanced to the Cup finals in 1957 and '58. He played in six All-Star Games before ending his career in the minors in 1961. Flaman took the demotion to Providence so he could start his second career, as a coach. He continued to play, and in '63-'64 added the GM's portfolio to his heavy resumé, though a year later he retired as a player. He later managed the Fort Worth Red Wings in the CHL and out of a scouting assignment he was offered the job of coach for Northeastern University in 1970. So began one of the longest and most successful tenures in college hockey history. Flaman remained 19 years and won 4 Beanpot championships with the team. In 1982, he was named coach of the year. After NU, he joined New Jersey as a special assignments scout, and in 1990 he was inducted into the Hockey Hall of Fame in the Veteran Player category.

FLATLEY, Pat ("Flats")
b. Toronto, Ontario, October 3, 1963
He had the silencer, oh, yes, he had it all right. The smooth, perfect wrist shot was so called by his fellow Islanders because it went to the net with a hum. Those were the fast shots, accurate and true. The Islanders coveted him early on, drafted him, and let him play a year with the Canadian National Team in '83-'84. Flatley wanted to play at the Olympics, and he did. He joined the Islanders at the end of the season, a season that saw the team go to the finals in the hunt for a fifth successive Stanley Cup. Flatley had missed the first four, and this time the Isles were defeated by the surging Oilers. He played his whole career with the Islanders, with one lingering exception, his final year of 1996-97. In that season, he played with the Rangers, thus becoming the first-ever captain of Long Island to turn quisling and play for the execrable Rangers. After retiring, he joined the NHL offices in Toronto and took on important roles with alumni relations.

FLEMING, Gerry
b. Montreal, Quebec, October 16, 1967
It wasn't as if he turned his back on 30 NHL teams or anything quite so dramatic, but Fleming left junior hockey in 1986 to go to university, in Prince Edward Island. His greatest talent in the Q was to drop ye olde gauntlets and bash an armoured combatant, yet after the peaceful life of university hockey he turned pro, went to the AHL, and resumed his bashing. He played briefly with the Canadiens – 11 games, in

1993-95 – but mostly in the minors, and as the millennium came to a close he turned his mind to coaching in the East Coast League.

FLEMING, Reggie

b. Montreal, Quebec, April 21, 1936

His father was Scottish and his mother Polish, which accounts both for his ability to speak perfect Polish and for his nasty bit of a temper. One time, he scalped Gilles Tremblay to the tune of 35 stitches. Another time he speared Eddie Shack. He played for 4 Original Six teams and then the Flyers and Sabres after expansion, and four times scored more than ten goals in a year. He moved on to the WHA when offered $35,000 a year, but soon after he was toiling in the Continental League for the Kenosha Flyers in Wisconsin at $100 a game. His finest moment was likely the 1961 playoffs against Detroit in the finals. In game six, the deciding game, the Hawks were down 1-0 when Fleming scored a pretty goal to tie the game and ignite a Chicago rally that gave the team the Cup. After retiring, he settled in Chicago and established a company called Advertising Specialties, a business that manufactured novelty items other companies used in promotional work.

FLESCH, John

b. Sudbury, Ontario, July 15, 1953

Bit of a wing nut, as they say, a loose screw. One day he had long hair, the next he shaved it all off. Some called him Marine, others Skinhead. He celebrated wildly when he scored, falling over or sometimes hitting his head with his own stick. Sometimes wore a helmet, sometimes not. Absurdly different and unself-conscious, Flesch played on a line with Bill Goldsworthy and Jude Drouin as a rookie ('74-'75), but this was to be his only full season in the NHL. He ended up in the "I" for some eight years.

FLETCHER, Steve

b. Montreal, Quebec, March 31, 1962

If he had a dollar for every penalty minute he accrued, Fletcher would have been a wealthy man. He got into a fight in his first NHL game, a playoff scrap for Montreal in the spring of 1988, and the next year, with Winnipeg, he got into another fight in his only other three games in the league. Beyond that it was the AHL and IHL, but the pims he posted were something to behold. He went on to coach high school hockey in Fort Wayne, Indiana, after retiring.

FLETT, Bill ("Cowboy")

b. Vermillion, Alberta, July 21, 1943
d. Edmonton, Alberta, July 12, 1999

For fans of a certain age, the sight of Flett flying around the ice is a fond memory. He grew up on a ranch in Okotoks, Alberta, and played hockey better than most. He travelled to Melville to play junior, turned pro in the American league, and timed his entrance into the NHL with expansion in 1967. His first five years were in Los Angeles, a remarkable culture shock for the guy who always wore a cowboy hat and drove a pickup. His most notable years, though, were in Philadelphia, vintage Broad Street Bullies. He played wing for Bobby Clarke, and that meant fighting for the captain whenever Clarke stirred up trouble he couldn't answer to himself. Yet Flett scored 43 goals in '72-'73, and he won the Cup with that goon team in '74. But even as his success grew, his decline was in progress because of an ever-increasing drinking problem. He ended his career playing in Edmonton, first in the WHA, then for 20 games in the NHL with Gretzky. He scouted for the Oilers for a season and then created Cowboy Flett Enterprises, a company that specialized in clearing areas of land in preparation for oil drilling. The business did really well, but the good times continued and the alcohol started to take its toll. He dried out at the Betty Ford Clinic, but the damage to his liver had been done. He collapsed one night at an Oilers game, and a liver transplant didn't take. He died of Mickey Mantle Disease at the age of 55. The Cowboy was no more.

Reggie Fleming

He played each game like a gladiator in the Coliseum, playing to live another day.
THEO FLEURY

FLEURY, Theoren "Theo"

b. Oxbow, Saskatchewan, June 29, 1968

An enigma wrapped around a stick of dynamite, Fleury's is a tale of truly miraculous survival, of a character so strong and yet fragile that his very presence, let alone phenomenal success, in the NHL is beyond the stuff of fact. His father was an alcoholic and his mother a Valium addict, and young Theoren was more or less raised by the small community in Russell, Manitoba, where he grew up. Meanwhile, he had a serious internal battle with Crohn's disease just to stay healthy, and a serious blade laceration to his biceps when he was a teen nearly cost him the use of one of his arms. To boot, he grew no higher than 5'6", small even by standards of half a century ago, and he played junior in Moose Jaw where the coach, Graham James, was a sexual predator. Put all that in one package, and what are the chances such a player will make it big in the NHL? Yet within Fleury, buried beneath the Crohn's and unhappiness and anguish, lay a will that has no parallel in the game's history. He played each game like a gladiator in the Coliseum, playing to live another day. He had a drive and tenacity that coaches hadn't seen before and, make no mistake, he was a

Bill Flett

skilled tiger. He played at the 1987 WJC for Canada and was on the ice when the country was disqualified after becoming involved in a brawl. Right after, he swore vengeance, and a year later he had a gold medal wrapped around his neck. The next year, '88-'89, he started with Calgary's farm team in Salt Lake, but after scoring nearly a goal a game for half a season the Flames had no recourse but to call the small star up and see what he was made of. Plenty, it turned out. He averaged a point a game in the last half of the NHL season and helped the Flames win their first Cup, and by the following fall he was on the team for good. Incredibly, he scored 31 goals in his first full season and 51 goals and 104 points in year two. He proved he was no fluke in the coming years, averaging 36 goals a season over the next decade. He became a fan favourite, a leader, and a captain, a player who continued to skate like a hunted animal. He protected himself with a sometimes frightening ferocity, but how else was a 5'6" man supposed to survive in a world half a foot taller and that much heavier and stronger? The Flames never came close to the Cup, though, and Fleury hit a low point in his life during the '97-'98 season. It was then that Graham James was charged and convicted of abusing boys, a conviction that was sealed when one of those boys, Boston's Sheldon Kennedy, bravely came forward and testified. It is unclear how much Fleury knew of the abuse (or refused to know), but it was a time of great pain and anxiety for him and he had the worst season of his career. As his 31st birthday approached (i.e., unrestricted free agency) it became apparent that he could command a top salary in the league and that Calgary couldn't afford to keep him. He was traded to Colorado as a "rent a player" but after an unsuccessful playoff run he signed as a free agent with the Rangers. In his first year on Broadway, Fleury, like the team, played poorly. He vowed a better second season, and delivered in spades. In 2000-01, he came out like gangbusters and led the league in scoring for much of the season – until February 2001. At that point, he checked into the NHL's substance abuse and behavioural health program for what he later admitted was alcoholism. It had been an ongoing problem for him, but he had managed to keep it in check until one night that month when a serious, though private, incident spurred him to take drastic action. It ended his season and jeopardized his possible place on Canada's Olympic team for Salt Lake City. Fleury, though, bounced back. He returned to the game with new energy, vowed a fresh attitude and clean body, and played his way into Wayne Gretzky's heart. Fleury not only made the Canadian team, he was one of its best players. Between that 1988 WJC gold and this Olympics gold, Fleury had been a paragon of virtue for Canada. He played in two World Championships when the Flames were knocked out of the playoffs, and he played in the 1991 Canada Cup. He was arguably Canada's best player at two more recent, unsuccessful tournaments – the 1996 World Cup and 1998 Olympics in Nagano – and he deserved the chance to play in Salt Lake City. In the summer of 2002, though, he was coming off a mediocre season and wanted to get away from the bright lights of New York. During that year, and for the first time, his erratic behaviour spilled onto the ice. He took horrible penalties and went berserk in protest; he stormed into the dressing room and left a game early because he was mad; he played selfishly and could no longer be counted on to control his temper. He signed with Chicago, where life wasn't quite so frantic, but before the start of the season re-entered the league's health program after another setback. Fleury has scored more than 400 goals and 1,000 points. He has accomplished all an NHLer can ask of a career, but still has more to give if he can harness his psychological difficulties. His survival has been a miracle, his success an inspiration, but his endurance in this world will require a daily battle from the greatest little big man the NHL has ever seen.

FLICHEL, Todd
b. Osgoode, Ontario, September 14, 1964
From Osgoode to Bowling Green University, Flichel played hockey and worked his way up to the NHL. He made brief appearances with Winnipeg for three successive seasons, but he was, by and large, a minor-league defenceman.

FLINN, Ryan
b. Halifax, Nova Scotia, April 20, 1980
Not many players can claim to have played for four junior teams, but Flinn did just that during his years in the Q. He was a bit of a lost soul at the NHL level as well, being drafted by New Jersey but signing with L.A. after the Devils never played him. Flinn got into 10 games with the Kings in 2001-02.

FLOCKHART, Rob
b. Sicamous, British Columbia, February 6, 1956
The older, less heralded brother of Ron, Rob preceded his brother into the NHL by playing with Vancouver for five games in early 1977. Unlike Ron, though, Rob's success was fleeting and sporadic during a brief career that had more minor than major league appearances to it. He played just 55 NHL games but spent more than 8 years in the smaller circuits before retiring in 1985.

FLOCKHART, Ron ("Flocky")
b. Smithers, British Columbia, October 10, 1960
They called it Flocky Hockey in Philadelphia when he burst onto the Flyers scene in 1980. It was a style of play marked by skill, flair, offence, and one-man rushes. He didn't pass the puck too often, and his defence wasn't his strong suit, but when he had the puck he lifted the fans off their seats. Flockhart scored 62 goals in his first 2 full seasons, but the bloom was off the rose when he went goalless in the first 8 games of the '83-'84 season. He went to Pittsburgh and then quickly to Montreal, where his selfish, colourful style didn't mesh with the Habs team. His NHL career petered out after brief stops in St. Louis and Boston, so he went to Italy to play until he retired and then went into coaching back in North America.

FLOYD, Larry
b. Peterborough, Ontario, May 1, 1961
As a 16-year-old, Floyd was a member of the

Rob Flockhart

Ron Flockhart

Larry Floyd

Peterborough Oaks, the champion senior (over 21) lacrosse team. The previous year, he had been a member of the city's James Gang juniors, national champions as well. At 17, he went to the training camp of the Fort Wayne Komets of the IHL, but tendonitis forced him home. Once there, he decided to go the more traditional route and play in the OHL for four years before signing as a free agent with New Jersey. Small and fast, he was one of many such players on a team that wasn't particularly good, and he wound up spending most of his career in, ironically, the IHL.

FOCHT, Dan
b. Regina, Saskatchewan, December 31, 1977

Phoenix seems to have made an error in judgment with this defenceman, for the Coyotes drafted him 11th overall in 1996, clear indication that they expected much of him. Yet Focht has wallowed in the minors ever since with the exception of eight games in 2001-02, a tryout that evidently wasn't a huge success because he hasn't become a regular at all.

FOGARTY, Bryan
b. Brantford, Ontario, June 11, 1969
d. Myrtle Beach, South Carolina, March 6, 2002

He had the world in the palm of his hands, but he preferred holding a bottle and the world fell to the floor. Fogarty was one of the greatest junior stars of all time. He broke Bobby Orr's record for goals and Denis Potvin's for points while with Niagara Falls, and Quebec drafted him appropriately high for his achievements, 9th overall in 1987, six places ahead of Joe Sakic. Fifteen years later, at age 32, he was dead. He battled alcohol addiction from his junior days throughout a career marked not by achievement but by disappointment and sadness. He bounced around in the NHL, then the minors and Europe, looking for a sign, for hope, for a way to snap out of his unhappy state. Everywhere he started, he tried to be positive, yet everywhere always turned into someplace else. His skill and name earned him contracts and tryouts, but his demeanour and performance earned him trades and demotions. In the summer of 1999, he reached his nadir. Police were called to Tollgate Technical Skills Centre, a school in Brantford, Ontario, where they found an intoxicated Fogarty standing naked and dazed in the school kitchen with cooking oil on the floor all around him. He tried to improve. He went dry and got married, but on vacation in South Carolina he died of a heart attack, final testament to the abuse he put his body through during his too brief time on the planet.

He had the world in the palm of his hands, but he preferred holding a bottle.
BRYAN FOGARTY

FOGOLIN, Lee, Jr.
b. Chicago, Illinois, February 7, 1955

When the Edmonton Oilers won the Stanley Cup in 1984 with Fogolin on their blueline, history was made in many ways for the team and the players. For Fogolin, the victory ensured his name would go on the Cup, just like his dad's had more than 30 years earlier. The Fogolins became the first father and son team each to achieve the Cup dream. Lee the Younger was highly rated as a junior, not because he was a superstar but because he was a reliable defensive defenceman. He began his career in Buffalo in 1974-75, the year the Sabres went to the finals before losing to Philadelphia. Five years later, the Sabres left him exposed in the Expansion Draft, and Edmonton snapped him up. He won another Cup in '85 with the Oilers, but at the trade deadline in '86-'87 he was sent back to Buffalo, where he ended his career.

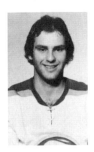

Lee Fogolin, Jr.

FOGOLIN, Lidio "Lee"
b. Fort William, Ontario, February 27, 1926
d. Thunder Bay, Ontario, November 29, 2000

He was no superstar, and no one much bothered him about autographs, but every goalie who called him a teammate revered Fogolin for his trademark ferocious bodychecks and fearless shotblocking. Fogolin split his career nearly equally between Detroit and Chicago over nine years (1947-56), Detroit getting a special smile in his career because the Red Wings won the Stanley Cup in 1950. In 1956, he became a playing coach in Calgary, but the following year he retired and returned home to coach the Port Arthur Bearcats. In 1961, he took that team to Europe on a tour and to compete for the Bunny Ahearne Trophy, which they won. Shortly after, he coached the Thunder Bay Twins until retiring in 1970. He continued his work with a Studebaker car dealership he had been involved in since his playing days, a business that had started out as a small grocery store before expanding. He, his daughter, and his son-in-law bought the Centennial Golf Course in Thunder Bay. He was inducted into the Northwestern Ontario Sports Hall of Fame twice, in 1988 as an athlete and the following year as coach of the Bearcats.

FOLCO, Peter
b. Montreal, Quebec, August 13, 1953

A defenceman, Folco played only two NHL games, with Vancouver in '73-'74. He also played briefly in the WHA, but his pro career was as inconspicuous as it was short.

Peter Folco

Gerry Foley

FOLEY, Gerry
b. Ware, Massachusetts, September 22, 1932
Technically, he was the only American-born player in the NHL during his brief time in the league in the mid-1950s. In reality, he was raised in Garson, Ontario, and it was there he returned after his playing days. He played 142 NHL games, but during a longer and more successful career in the AHL he won three Calder Cups with Springfield and another with Pittsburgh. In the NHL, he was a checker and penalty killer; in the minors, he was a scorer. After retiring, he coached provincial hockey in Garson and ran a nursing home before entering local politics. He was elected councillor four times, and later became deputy mayor and served for the regional municipality known as Nickel Centre. He also ran a real estate office and, with his wife, a group home for girls.

FOLEY, Gilbert "Rick"
b. Niagara Falls, Ontario,
September 22, 1945

Rick Foley

Some called him Father of King Kong; others called him an overweight goon. Regardless, where Foley went, controversy and conversation followed like unwanted brothers. Foley went straight from junior B in Ontario to the EHL, and from there he signed with Chicago. He went on to Philadelphia, but was suspended for being overweight, a problem that plagued him throughout his tenuous pro career. When he played, he took on any and all tough guys in the league, but even that didn't stand him in good stead in Philly because of his off-ice discipline problems. Foley moved briefly to the WHA but was cut, and retired shortly after when he attended a banquet at which Johnny Unitas made a speech. If you no longer enjoy playing, he said, it's time to get out. Foley heard the words, and retired. He was an excellent ball player and golfer, but his post-playing days were not always his best. In October 1982, he was sentenced to 6 months in jail for 11 counts of credit card fraud and defrauding merchants.

FOLIGNO, Mike
b. Sudbury, Ontario, January 29, 1959
One of hockey's very good guys. He played with four teams over a long and distinguished career, and although Foligno never really came close to winning a Stanley Cup, he competed fiercely every night as though it was on the line. In his rookie year, 1979-80, he scored 36 goals for Detroit and established himself as a physical presence by accumulating 109 penalty minutes, a total he nearly doubled the year after. In all, he had 10 seasons of 20 goals or more, and played for Canada at the World Championships on 3 occasions. Two events in his career stand out, both linked to his time with Toronto. On December 21,

Mike Foligno

1991, he suffered a serious broken leg after a check near centre ice at Maple Leaf Gardens, a crack that was heard clearly throughout the building. He missed almost a year, but made his return the following season. Early in 1993, his career was pretty much done after 978 games, but GM Cliff Fletcher traded him to Florida so the classy right winger could get into his 1,000th game. After retiring, Foligno moved straight into coaching, first in the Leafs system, then with the Hershey Bears, and on to Colorado, then back to Chocolatetown.

FOLK, Bill
b. Regina, Saskatchewan, July 11, 1927
It is tragically common for a fortysomething hockey player to have a heart attack during a game of shinny.

He had two brief tryouts with Detroit in the early 1950s.
BILL FOLK

No longer in his prime, he chases down a loose puck with too great a vigour, and he collapses right there on the ice or at the bench. For a pro to experience such a calamity is almost unheard of, yet that is how the playing career (though, happily, not life) of Folk ended. He was captain of the Spokane Comets of the WHL, and near the start of the '61-'62 season he collapsed at the bench. He was rushed to hospital, recovered, but never played pro again. He was just 34 and had been playing since graduating from junior in 1947. He had two brief tryouts with Detroit in the early 1950s, but was better known as a star in the Western league for years. Ironically, he was also known for his strength, having developed his body in the summers while playing lacrosse and working in construction.

FONTAINE, Len
b. Quebec City, Quebec, February 25, 1948
He made quite a ruckus back in his first year as pro, 1968-69. Fontaine signed a registration card with the Port Huron Flags on the IHL, but the newly formed Canadian Hockey League claimed him as its own because he had played the previous year with the Sarnia Legionaires. Court action was threatened both ways, but the IHL won the day and Fontaine went on to become one of the all-time great players in that league. He was named league MVP twice, led the league in '75-'76 with 53 goals and 112 points, and in 13 seasons scored 361 goals. He got his only NHL games in with Detroit from 1972-74, and also played part of a season in the WHA.

FONTAS, Jon
b. Arlington, Massachusetts, April 16, 1958
Fact: There is an award in the IHL for the best U.S.-born rookie in the league. Fact: It was introduced in

Len Fontaine

1978. Fact: Its first winner was Mike Eruzione, who went on to play for the Miracle on Ice team in 1980. Fact: The 1979 recipient was Jon Fontas, who scored 36 goals and 81 points. Fact: The trophy isn't worth a hill of beans in the NHL. Fact: Fontas played two games with Minnesota over the next two years. Fact: Fontas played four years in Finland before retiring.

FONTEYNE, Valere "Val"
b. Wetaskiwin, Alberta, December 2, 1933
He made Dave Keon look like a goon, and Bill Quckenbush like a crazy, penalty-mad policeman! In 820 career NHL games, Fonteyne, a left winger, had 13 minor penalties. No majors, no misconducts, just the occasional trip or hook. He had a streak of 185 games without incurring a single minor penalty, and another that lasted 157 games. He never had more than 4 minutes in any of his 13 NHL seasons. He had a fighting major once with Seattle back in the WHL, but from 1959 to '72 he established himself as the least penalized player in the history of the NHL. In his retired life, he returned to Wetaskiwin and became a delivery truck driver.

FONTINATO, Lou ("Leapin' Lou")
b. Guelph, Ontario, January 20, 1932
He set records for penalties and fought bravely. He was a fan favourite and a solid defenceman, but his two finest moments in the league are ones he might like to forget, for each did him damage. Fontinato got his nickname from a radio announcer in Guelph who watched Lou jump up and down like mad whenever he was given a penalty. His reactions often cost Fontinato a misconduct, but the name stuck. On February 1, 1959, while playing for the Rangers at home, he challenged Gordie Howe to a fight. Actually, he ran straight at Howe, who had no choice but to respond. Howe had not been in a fight in nine years, not since the 1950 playoffs when he nearly died after falling headfirst into the boards. But there was Fontinato, and there he was. Leapin' Lou had facial surgery that night, and pictures of his battered face and the fight ran in *Life* magazine. Lou said the fight was a draw. Howe's unscratched mug suggested differently. On March 9, 1963, while playing for Montreal, Fontinato himself fell headfirst into the boards. He broke his neck and was completely paralyzed for two weeks, but slowly and surely he recovered. He retired to a 265-acre cattle farm in Eden Mills he had smartly invested in, and although his 14-year marriage ended and left him a hurt and sad man, he maintained the farm by himself far away from the glare and screams of NHL rinks.

FOOTE, Adam
b. Toronto, Ontario, July 10, 1971
This guy is a player, as scouts say about a blue-chip, number-one kind of star to be. As a kid, he idolized Darryl Sittler, so, of course, he became a defenceman. Go figure. Foote had the size and foot speed, but not the offensive skill to match Sittler, and he is one of the rare breed of modern player who has been with one team his whole career. Since being drafted by Quebec in 1989, he has been faithful first to the Nordiques and then to the Avalanche when the team moved to Denver in 1995. As a result, he has been on two Stanley Cup winners, in 1996 and 2001, and he played on Canada's gold medal Olympics team at Salt Lake City in 2002. Inside his own blueline, there are few players his equal. He has an intensity and ferocity to his game that few forwards can match, though the downside is that he is susceptible to injuries more than the less physical player might be. He has missed long periods with various ailments, from foot to shoulder, but there are 30 NHL teams that would dearly love to have him. Only one does.

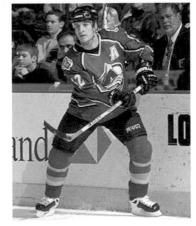

He has an intensity and ferocity to his game that few forwards can match.
ADAM FOOTE

FORBES, Colin
b. New Westminster, British Columbia, February 16, 1976
In his first six years in the league, Forbes played for five different teams, qualifying himself quickly and early for status as journeyman. His first stint was his longest – three partial years with Philadelphia – but since then he has also spent time with Tampa Bay, Ottawa, the Rangers, and Washington. He is a big and strong left winger, but is considered a spare part rather than franchise player.

FORBES, Dave
b. Montreal, Quebec, November 16, 1948
In an era of acute and brutal violence, there was no more pernicious perpetrator of goonery than Dave Forbes. In a game on January 4, 1975, while playing for Boston, he hit Minnesota forward Henry Boucha flush in the eye with the butt end of his stick. The blow led Boucha to numerous eye operations from which he could not recover and that forced him to retire. Forbes, meanwhile, was arraigned in Hennepin District Court in Minneapolis on a charge of aggravated assault. NHL president Clarence Campbell suspended him for 10 games, but the trial ended in a hung jury after some 10 hours of deliberation. Forbes played for five more years before retiring, but he was never able to leave behind an act of violence so mind-numbingly unpardonable. Oddly, perhaps, he settled in California to study to become an ordained minister.

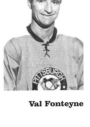

Val Fonteyne

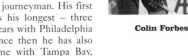

Colin Forbes

Dave Forbes

Mike Forbes

FORBES, Mike
b. Brampton, Ontario, September 20, 1957

On February 25, 1980, Mike Forbes was in the middle of a decent season with the Houston Apollos in the Edmonton organization. He came home that night to find he had left his keys inside, so he tried to crawl through a window to get in. The window broke on his arm, though, cutting arteries and slicing muscles and nerves right to the bone. He lost pints of blood, and doctors originally told him it would be two years before he would have full use of the arm again. Forbes recovered much faster by getting a summer job as a bricklayer, but it was still a debilitating injury. He spent all the next season in the minors, and played just 16 games with the Oilers in 1981-82. He was lucky to be alive, but his career never saw the NHL light of day again.

Jake Forbes

FORBES, Verner "Jake" ("Jumping Jake")
b. Toronto, Ontario, July 4, 1897
d. Hamilton, Ontario, December 30, 1985

There were two distinct parts to Forbes' career in the nets. The first part, 1919-28, consisted of his more or less full-time employment in the NHL. The second part, 1928-33, saw him play only periodically. Forbes started with the Toronto St. Pats but later played for Hamilton in 1924-25, the year the Tigers went on strike and were disqualified from the playoffs as a result. He later joined the New York Americans, the team that evolved out of the Tigers, and during a span of 5 years he played every game in the NHL, 158 in a row. Although he remained with the Amerks, it was as a minor-leaguer more than number-one man. In his last 5 seasons, he played just 11 games. In the off-season, Forbes worked in sales for a fine china wholesaler in Toronto. He had two children, but his son was killed in a car accident when he was only six. Later in life, after being at his daughter's for dinner over the holidays, he went home, got into bed, and died of a heart attack. At 88, he had been one of the oldest living players.

Brian Ford

FORD, Brian
b. Edmonton, Alberta, September 22, 1961

There is only one reason Brian Ford never made it as an NHL goalie: he wasn't good enough. He had a chance – not a great one, perhaps, but a chance all the same – but it's impossible to keep a goalie if he lets in 61 goals in just 11 games. It just won't happen. Quebec and Pittsburgh both tried him out, but despite not making it there he had an excellent career in the AHL during the 1980s.

Connie Forey

FOREY, Conley "Connie"
b. Montreal, Quebec, October 18, 1950

It was the most violent attack on a referee in the history of pro hockey. On February 21, 1974, Forey and his Denver Spurs were playing Seattle in a WHL game. Referee Malcolm Ashford signalled Forey to the penalty box, and the player charged the referee, raining punches on him and breaking Ashford's nose in the process. He was suspended for the rest of that '74-'75 season and all of the next and fined $10,000. That didn't faze Forey much, though. He got busy on the phone, and within days signed a contract with the Chicago Cougars of the WHA. He even played on March 7 against the Quebec Nordiques, but once the league realized who he was, it honoured the WHL ban and suspended him for the same period of time. Forey had started that year by playing four games with St. Louis, his only NHL games in a career cut short by his own act of madness.

FORSBERG, Peter ("Foppa"/ "Peter the Great")
b. Ornskoldsvik, Sweden, July 20, 1973

On February 26, 1994, not many people in Canada had heard of this Forsberg. A day later, everyone knew who he was. In the gold-medal game of the 1994 Olympics in Lillehammer, Canada and Sweden were down to penalty shots to determine a winner. Forsberg, who shoots left, came in on goalie Corey Hirsch and deked left. As Hirsch moved across, Forsberg swept the puck across the crease and with one hand slid the puck into the empty side of the net to give the Swedes gold. It was a risky play, but when it worked, well, it got him on a postage stamp. Forsberg joined the Nordiques that fall. Drafted by Philadelphia, he was part of the massive package used by the Flyers to acquire Eric Lindros, and the Quebec/Colorado franchise has been grateful ever since. Peter the Great, as Swedish newspapers dubbed him, was a unique talent. He wasn't that big, but he had a low centre of gravity and tremendous leg strength. He could not only handle physical play but seemed to invite it on the way to the net, all the while able to control the puck. Puck possession, at all costs, was his game. In '95-'96, his first full year, he had 30 goals and 116 points and helped the Avs win their first Stanley Cup. Over the next five seasons, he was a top point producer and exciting player. He played for Sweden in the 1996 World Cup, and in 1998 he not only won a gold medal with Sweden at the World Championships, but won under head coach Kent Forsberg, his father! Forsberg never duplicated that 116-point season, but he came reasonably close and was always near the top of the scoring leaders –

> **It marked the first time ever a player not from the finals led the playoff race.**
> **PETER FORSBERG**

provided he wasn't hurt. Therein lay the rub. Much as he relished hitting, there were always players ready to hit just a little meaner or harder than he was expecting. Although his puck control was sheer brilliance, Forsberg has paid a substantial price. He missed much of 1999-2000 with a serious leg injury. Then he had off-season shoulder surgery. Ankle surgery followed. The capper came in the 2001 playoffs against Los Angeles. He felt unwell after a game, and the next thing he knew he woke up in hospital with his spleen removed. Recovery lasted months, and when it came time to start the 2001-02 season, there was no life in the bones. He shocked the hockey world by announcing he would take the whole year off, maybe longer. By early in the new year, though, the Olympics looming, he found renewed life and energy and decided he would return. As soon as he stepped on the ice in Colorado to start practising, he hurt his ankle and was gone for the remainder of the regular season! Forsberg missed the 2002 Olympics in Salt Lake City, but did come back in time for the playoffs, and did so with an exclamation mark. Although the Avs didn't make it to the finals, he led the playoffs in scoring with 27 points. It marked the first time ever a player not from the finals led the playoff race, and it was also the first time a player who never appeared in the regular season led the NHL in playoff points. He returned healthy and happy in 2002-03, winning the scoring title on the final day of the season, but Forsberg will face the same problem again and again. The more effectively he plays in a heavy-hitting game, the greater will be the toll exacted on his body. In the meantime, fans can only watch and admire his grace under pressure.

FORSEY, Jack
b. Swift Current, Saskatchewan, November 7, 1914
d. Salmon Arm, British Columbia, January 1, 1998
Forsey had an outstanding junior career that culminated in 1937 when he and his Kimberley Dynamiters went to Europe on a tour and to win the World Championships. He enjoyed the experience so much, and made such an impression, that while most of his teammates returned home after the victory, he accepted an offer to play in London, which he did until the start of the war. Forsey then returned to Canada and turned pro, eventually playing 19 games with the Leafs in '42-'43. He served in the army for a year and later returned to Kimberley to play again for a while prior to retiring.

FORSLUND, Gus
b. Umea, Sweden, April 25, 1908
d. Geraldton, Ontario, August 4, 1962
Although he grew up in and retired to small-town Ontario, Forslund was, in fact, the first man born in Sweden to play in the NHL – long, long before Borje Salming or even Ulf Sterner. Forslund played for the old Ottawa Senators in 1932-33. One full season of 48 games, no more, no less. The tiny right winger weighed in at just 155 pounds, and scored just 4 goals that season.

FORSLUND, Tomas
b. Falun, Sweden, November 24, 1968
The NHL just wasn't his bag, but Forslund had a long career in Europe before and after his 44 games with Calgary (1991-93). He played for Tre Kronor at the 1988 World Juniors and at three World Championships, as well as a number of years in Swedish and German leagues.

FORSYTH, Alex
b. Galt, Ontario, January 6, 1955
Playing for the Washington Capitals in the 1970s was nothing to brag about, but if that's what it takes to get into an NHL game, more power to you. Forsyth was selected 18th overall in the '75 draft by the Caps, and his one game represented one of the worst performances by a first-rounder in NHL draft history. By 1978, he wasn't playing pro anywhere.

FORTIER, Dave
b. Sudbury, Ontario, June 17, 1951
Fortier was very much a part of the Leafs' plans when they took him in the 1971 Amateur Draft, but those plans changed when they had a chance to get Bill Flett from Philadelphia. Toronto unloaded Fortier and Randy Osburn on May 27, 1974, but just two weeks later, in the Expansion Draft, the Islanders took him from the Flyers. In his first season on Long Island, Fortier was fortunate enough to be paired with Denis Potvin on the blueline by coach Al Arbour, but after two seasons the Islanders were improving at a faster rate than Fortier. They sent him to Vancouver, and that was his last NHL stop. He played briefly in the WHA, and by 1979 he was out of hockey. He returned home to Sudbury, joined the city's fire department, and has been there ever since.

FORTIER, Marc
b. Windsor, Quebec, February 26, 1966
In his 4 years with Chicoutimi in Quebec junior, Fortier's numbers increased each season until they reached Mario-like proportions in his final year: 46, 98, 133, 201. The rest of his pro career was altogether banal by comparison, and only justifies the scouts' views he wasn't a talent to be drafted, even though the numbers screamed a different story. Nevertheless, Fortier played 6 years of NHL hockey and 6 in Europe, never coming close to 201 points again.

FORTIN, Jean-François
b. Laval, Quebec, March 15, 1979
He has come up through the ranks on time and according to plan. Fortin left junior in 1999 to play for Portland, and from there he was called up to Washington two and a half years later. The defenceman moved right in and took a regular shift, and in 2002 he earned a spot on the roster right out of training camp.

FORTIN, Ray
b. Drummondville, Quebec, March 11, 1941
He grew up a hockey-loving kid in French-Canadian society, but the NHL was not the be-all and end-all for Fortin. He attended St. Lawrence College and played senior hockey while working in his father's construction business, and it was only after expansion in 1967 that he agreed to join St. Louis, in large part because of a number of connections to home. Jacques Plante was the goalie; Doug Harvey had played there;

Jack Forsey

Tomas Forslund

Dave Fortier

Marc Fortier

Ray Fortin

Jean-Guy Talbot, a player Fortin had admired as a kid, became his blueline partner. He never made the team full-time except for '69-'70, and after a few years in the minors he got out of the game, never having established himself, but having made it all the same.

FOSTER, Corey
b. Ottawa, Ontario, October 27, 1969

That Foster was teammates with John Tucker is no big woof. That they played for the Kokudo Bunnies in Japan is another matter, and that they won three successive championships in the Japanese league is something more. Foster had made Canada's national junior team in 1989, but his 45-game NHL career carried him through 4 teams and right out of the league. He accepted an opportunity to go to the Far East to play, and it was there he had, in some measure, his greatest success. He made his reputation in junior as perhaps having the hardest shot in the world, with the expectation of Al MacInnis.

Corey Foster

FOSTER, Dwight ("Dewey")
b. Toronto, Ontario, April 2, 1957

Foster was a high draft choice of Boston in 1977, a bright prospect who had proved in junior that he could score goals. The same was expected of him in Beantown, but he never played very much with the Bruins and his first two years were compromised by injuries. In his fourth season, he blossomed a bit with a 24-goal season, but rather than be content he became part of a story of bad choices. He signed as a free agent with the Colorado Rockies, but as compensation the Bruins received a second-round draft choice in 1982 and the option to flip first-rounders in the same draft. So what happened? He had a lousy year and an NHL-worst -53, and Colorado finished last overall. This means Boston did, indeed, flip first-round choices and selected first overall! To compound the comedy of errors, though, the Bruins chose Gord Kluzak, ahead of numerous greats including Scott Stevens, Phil Housley, and Dave Andreychuk. Four games into the following season, the New Jersey Devils (formerly Colorado) sold Foster to Detroit for the princely sum of $1. Content, he settled into his role as a solid utility forward who could play the right side or centre and who was defensively responsible, but after four seasons he wound up back in Boston to close out his career. In his post-playing days, Foster worked with an investment firm in Michigan.

FOSTER, Harry "Yip"
b. Guelph, Ontario, November 25, 1907
d. unknown

Foster had bad luck and bad timing choosing his

Harry Foster

Norm Foster

teams. He joined the Rangers in 1929 a year after the team won the Cup, and he played for the Red Wings in '33-'34 and '34-'35 just before they won it. For the most part, though, he played in the American league. Foster settled in Wayne, Michigan, and worked for an aircraft company for many years.

FOSTER, Herb
b. Brockville, Ontario, August 9, 1913

Atlantic City was always good to Foster, and Foster was always good to Atlantic City. He played many years with the local Sea Gulls, affiliated with the Rangers, and played five games on Broadway during the '40-'41 season and a single game after the war. He returned to the Gulls to end his career, and then became part of history in the '50-'51 season with the team. He became the team's coach, and one day early in the new season he got a telegram from the big boys in New York that a player was coming to join him. His name was Art Dorrington, and he was the first black player ever signed to an NHL contract. Dorrington played his first game with the Gulls on November 16, 1950, Foster behind the bench hailing him as a good, skilled, hustle type of player.

FOSTER, Norm
b. Vancouver, British Columbia, February 10, 1965

One of the all-time winningest goalies in U.S. college hockey, Foster won 76 games with Michigan State in the 1980s but was drafted a lowly 231st by Boston. He played just 13 NHL games and spent the majority of his slight career in the minors.

He won a Police Athlete League boxing tournament as a kid, and knew his baseball.
NICK FOTIU

FOTIU, Nick
b. Staten Island, New York, May 25, 1952

He went to a game at Madison Square Garden, and while he was watching he heard God tell him to become a professional hockey player. Fotiu swears that's how it happened. But that's jumping ahead. Growing up in New York, he knew sports, but not hockey. He won a Police Athlete League boxing tournament as a kid, and knew his baseball. He learned hockey, like the Mullens, on roller skates. He bought his first pair of ice skates at 14 and played in a league down in Coney Island, a two-hour subway trip kept interesting by the crowd. He carried a machete in his bag for good luck. His dad died when Nick was 13, and he and his mom moved in with the grandparents. Nick worked at his granddad's construction business but played hockey for the Hyde Park Arrows of the Metropolitan League, which the Rangers sponsored. Emile Francis found him there one night and assigned him to the Cape Cod Cubs. Rather than wait for the Rangers, he signed with the WHA New England entry in 1974, making his Rangers debut two years later after signing as a free agent. He fished lobster in the summers for a while and then opened a bar with Wayne Thomas and Jimmy Troy called the Hunt Club, in Falmouth, Massachusetts. In 1979-80, he had the honour of playing for Hartford, a team that featured Gordie Howe, Dave Keon, and Bobby Hull. After that, he rejoined the Rangers and then moved around. He knew his job – to fight. He couldn't score to save his life, but he could make it easier for others to score by looking out for them. Fotiu retired in 1990 but quickly got into coaching in the East Coast League, working his way up to the point that he became an assistant with the U.S. national team at the 2002 World Championships.

FOUNTAIN, Mike
b. North York, Ontario,
January 26, 1972

A Vancouver draft choice in 1992, Fountain joined an elite group of goalies the night of November 14, 1996, when he played his first NHL game. He shut out the New Jersey Devils, becoming only the eighteenth goalie ever to record a shutout in his first game. Life in the blue ice since then, however, has been less rosy. He played only a few games for three different teams in his first three seasons and has established himself as a minor-leaguer capable of coming up to the NHL for brief stretches.

FOWLER, Jimmy
("The Blonde
Bouncer")
b. Toronto, Ontario, April 6, 1915
d. Toronto, Ontario,
October 17, 1985

He could have been a pro football player, but in Toronto anyone who could play hockey did. Fowler was light and fast, an early rushing defenceman who scored 17 goals with the Leafs in just 2 seasons (1936-38). After the following season he was traded to the New York Americans in a big deal that also sent Busher Jackson, Buzz Boll, Doc Romnes, and Murray Armstrong to New York for Sweeney Schriner. But Fowler was a Toronto boy, through and through. He retired rather than reported and went to work for Glidden as a salesman. During the war, he trained pilots in London, Ontario, for the RCAF, and when peacetime returned he rose quickly in the Glidden company. By the time he retired in 1976, he had been the president for a number of years. He died in 1985 following heart surgery.

FOWLER, Norman "Heck"
b. Peterborough, Ontario, October 14, 1895
d. unknown
Not many goalies can boast of the horrible goals against Fowler posted during his brief NHL career.

In '24-'25, he allowed 42 goals in 7 games with Boston. His 1-6-0 record ensured he wasn't going to see further action any time soon, but a story goes with it. Boston had a horrible team that year, and manager Art Ross had to blame someone in the media so he chose Fowler. Ross had a one-on-one with Fowler and demanded an explanation for Fowler's poor play. The goalie said something about being able to do better if he had better defencemen, but Ross shouted him down with cries of "you're not trying!" Fowler was suspended and fined $1,000. He returned home but shortly after found that the Edmonton Eskimos wanted to use him. Ross, though, had tied up any loose ends by binding Fowler to a contract for $1. He turned around and told Duke Keats, the Eskimos manager, that he could have Fowler if he paid the outstanding $1,000 fine. Keats did so, and Fowler took his $1 and framed it. When he retired, he opened a printing shop in Saskatoon and hung the bill on one of the shop's walls as a reminder of his playing days!

FOWLER, Tom
b. Winnipeg, Manitoba,
May 18, 1924
Fowler played only in 1946-47 with Chicago as far as the NHL goes after rising through the ranks of junior hockey in Winnipeg. He played for a variety of teams after his season with the Hawks.

FOX, Greg
b. Port McNeil, British Columbia,
August 12, 1953
Fox attended the University of Michigan in the fall of 1972 on a hockey scholarship, a good

> **He was the prototypical defensive defenceman who didn't score much.**
> GREG FOX

way, he thought, of getting an education. A funny thing happened at the end of the season, though: Atlanta called his name at the Amateur Draft. Fox's mindset shifted, and he considered a pro career. After graduating, he was determined to give it a try. He made it, first with the Flames and then with Chicago after a trade sent him there toward the end of the '78–'79 season. He was the prototypical defensive defenceman who didn't score much but who could mind his own end of the rink better than most, and he lasted 494 games in the NHL. When he retired, he became owner of a Dominos Pizza franchise in Massachusetts and later a manager of a number of outlets in Georgia.

FOX, Jim
b. Coniston, Ontario, May 18, 1960
How gross is this? Fox's right knee got so bad at the end he had to tape the kneecap before every game because there was almost no cartilage left to hold it in place. That was in the 1989-90 season, his last in the NHL. Fox quietly played all of his 10 years in the

Mike Fountain

Jimmy Fowler

Tom Fowler

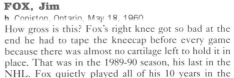

Jim Fox

Frank Foyston

Lou Franceschetti

Bobby Francis

Emile Francis

league with Los Angeles, starting in 1980, but in March 1988 he suffered a serious knee injury against Boston and was gone for a year and a half. During that time he worked for the team's public relations department, but he longed to make a comeback. However, the player who once scored 30 goals a year for 4 straight years no longer had it, and he was nothing but a fourth-liner who was scratched as often as he was played. He retired after just 11 more games with the Kings but stayed on with the team doing PR and television commentary.

FOYSTON, Frank ("The Flash")
b. Minesing, Ontario, February 2, 1891
d. Seattle, Washington, January 19, 1966
Although the majority of his career overlapped with the NHL, Foyston played most of his best years out west, in the PCHL. He played junior hockey in Barrie before moving to Toronto. There he played for Eaton's, the department store, a team that won the '11-'12 OHA senior championship. He then turned pro with the Blueshirts of the NHA and formed a line with Scotty Davidson and Jack Walker that was one of the top-scoring threesomes in the game. In '13-'14, the Blueshirts won the Stanley Cup and Foyston scored the winning goal in a thrilling 2-1 win over Victoria in the deciding game. From there he moved to Seattle to play in the Pacific Coast league. He played for the Metropolitans for nine years, a tenure that culminated in 1917 when they became the first U.S. team to win the Cup (and he their captain). He later played two seasons with Victoria and again won the Cup in '24-'25, the last time a non-NHL team won the great trophy. During his time in the PCHL, Foyston made history by being named to the All-Star Team at three positions – left wing, centre, and rover. He was a top scorer and terrific skater, and when Victoria sold its players to Detroit, he finally made his way to the NHL. He played the first two seasons of Detroit's NHL start, 1926-28, and ended his career with the Olympics a short time later. He later turned to coaching with the Bronx Tigers and Seattle Seahawks of the Northwestern Hockey League for a number of years. He then served as a scout for the Red Wings, and for years operated a turkey ranch in Port Orchard, Washington.

FRAMPTON, Percy ("Bob")
b. Toronto, Ontario, January 20, 1929
Frampton came alive for the Montreal Canadiens for two games in the '49-'50 season in a short career spent entirely in that city and out west in the Pacific Coast league.

FRANCESCHETTI, Lou
b. Toronto, Ontario, March 28, 1958
They're not booing, they're Loooooing. He was popular wherever he played, not because he scored 50 goals or made beautiful plays or went coast to coast with the puck. No, he was popular because he worked hard, skated hard, and tried his best without having all the talent in the world. He played many years with Washington, liked by the fans, under-appreciated by the team, but he had his best season with Toronto in 1989-90. He played the full season, scored 21 goals,

and brought the fans at the Gardens to life with his hustle. The next year, he broke his toe, the team went downhill, and he was traded to Buffalo before ending up in the minors. Not a bad career for a boy who didn't put on a pair of skates until he was nine, played in goal his first two years, and was cut four times in the same season by the Toronto Nats back when a 14-year-old named Gretzky was on the team.

FRANCIS, Bobby
b. North Battleford, Saskatchewan, December 5, 1958
Son of a cat, Emile Francis, Bobby played plenty of hockey but only 14 games in the NHL. Although he was born in Saskatchewan, he was raised in New York while his dad played for and managed the Rangers. Bobby went to the University of New Hampshire and later played most of his pro career in Salt Lake City, but by the time he was 30 his interest in coaching far outstripped his desire to string a minor-league career along any further. Bobby worked his way up the ranks, eventually becoming an assistant in Boston and a head coach with Phoenix where he won the Jack Adams Award for the 2001-02 season.

FRANCIS, Emile ("The Cat")
b. North Battleford, Saskatchewan,
September 13, 1926
Growing up in Saskatchewan, Francis was not only an outstanding goalie, but also a fine baseball player. The two sports influenced him in a way that changed goaltending forever. During the '45-'46 season, while playing junior, Francis experimented by using a stylized first baseman's glove instead of the old-style gloves or gauntlets goalies traditionally used. Thus was born the netminder's catching glove used, and expanded exponentially, by every goalie of the modern era. Francis had an undistinguished NHL career. He turned pro with Chicago in 1946 and a year later was their number-one man. But the Hawks were a weak team, and Francis posted a record of just 18-31-5 after which he was traded to the Rangers. He played just 22 games with the Blueshirts in the coming years, but in the minors he was a solid, small goalie. Called the Cat because of his reflexes, he was the top goalie in the WHL for '52-'53. He kept on playing until 1960 when he retired to coach the Rangers' junior team in Guelph. After two years, he became assistant GM in New York and soon after was made GM and coach, positions he held for a decade. His time as leader of the team climaxed in the spring of 1972 when the Rangers went to the Cup finals, only to lose to Boston. Francis left New York to become executive vice-president, GM, and coach of the Blues. In 1983, he moved on to Hartford where he became president of the team until he retired in 1993. He was given the Lester Patrick Trophy in 1982 and was inducted into the Hockey Hall of Fame that same year. In addition to his great contribution to the game in an executive capacity, Francis also helped minor hockey grow by leaps and bounds wherever he worked. He founded the New York Junior Hockey League and the St. Louis Metro Junior B League, and he helped establish numerous scholarship programs throughout the country to help promote the game in the U.S. and build a foundation for future success.

FRANCIS, Ron
b. Sault Ste. Marie, Ontario, March 1, 1963

Perhaps the case of Ron Francis suggests that it's time the modern player stop taking a back seat to the oldtimers. Francis is an example of a player who has quietly become one of the all-time scorers in league history, yet surely he appears on no fan's top 10 or 20 or even 50 players of all time. He played junior in the Soo and was a fine centre, but he was not expecting to be drafted 4th overall by Hartford in 1981. The Whalers had declared that they would use their choice for Bobby Carpenter, but when Washington beat them to it with the 3rd selection, Hartford weighed-in with Francis. He made the team right away as an 18-year-old, and 22 seasons later he's still in the NHL and still among the game's best passers. He had 25 goals and 68 points as a rookie and has been a model of consistency ever since. He has scored at least 20 goals in every season except two (and one was the lockout year of '94-'95), and only four times has he failed to record 50 assists in a season. In 2002-03, he tied Gordie Howe when he had his 22nd season scoring at least 50 points. Yet there is nothing spectacular about his game, nothing that defines him or separates him from a hundred NHLers except that he does everything exceptionally well whereas the other 99 players do things merely well. He has led the league in assists only twice and has never won an individual offensive award. He has won three Lady Byng Trophies and a Selke Trophy for his defensive play, and in 1999-2000 he won the King Clancy Award for his terrific contributions to the community in Carolina. Francis has played with only the Hartford/Carolina franchise and Pittsburgh, joining the Penguins in time for their Cup wins in 1991 and '92. He has scored more than 100 points three times in his career, but has played in only four All-Star Games. Outside of his Cup wins, his finest playoff performance came in 2002 when he led the Hurricanes to an improbable in the Cup finals where they lost to Detroit. With more than 500 goals and 1,700 points, he is destined to a place in the Hockey Hall of Fame three years after he retires, and although he never lifted fans out of their seats with his great rushes, he certainly has been one of the league's premier playmakers for many, many years.

Francis has quietly become one of the all-time scorers in league history.
RON FRANCIS

FRANKS, Jim
b. Melville, Saskatchewan, November 8, 1914
d. unknown

Franks played his first NHL game on March 27, 1937. Although he played only 30 minutes and lost the game to Montreal 3-1, his Detroit Red Wings came back to win this playoff series and went on to win the Stanley Cup. For that, he got his name on the sacred bowl.

The next year, he played once in the regular season, then was buried in the minors until the war forced the Rangers to use him for part of the '42-'43 season. He played briefly the following year as well, his final stint in the NHL.

FRASER, Archie
b. Souris, Manitoba, February 9, 1914
d. unknown

Brother of Harvey, Archie played only 3 games with the Rangers during the war years in a career that centred around Yorkton, Saskatchewan, for the better art of 15 years.

FRASER, Charles
b. Antigonish, Nova Scotia, July 22, 1897
d. Montreal, Quebec, August 9, 1970

The Bluenose Boy came from down east to try his hand in the professional ranks of the NHL, but managed to get into only one game, with the Hamilton Tigers, back in '23-'24 despite making a favourable impression in workouts with the team.

FRASER, Curt
b. Cincinnati, Ohio, January 12, 1958

He was born in Ohio of Canadian parents, and as a boy Fraser learned the game out west with the Victoria Cougars. Vancouver drafted him in 1978, and in each of his first 4 seasons his goal production improved, to 28. It was around this time that he made a life adjustment when he discovered that he was diabetic during a basic physical in conjunction with earning his pilot's licence. He learned to administer his own insulin, and he developed a diet to maintain a strict blood sugar level. In all, Fraser played 704 NHL games, coming closest to the Cup in 1982 when the Canucks went to the finals against the Islanders. He retired in 1989 and set his dreams on coaching. To that end, he coached the Milwaukee Admirals and then led the Orlando Solar Bears for four years, going to the Turner Cup after leading the team from 3-0 down in a series against Detroit to a 4-3 win. On July 14, 1999, he was named the first head coach of the expansion Atlanta Thrashers, the NHL's newest entrant. Three and a half years later, he was fired, never having taken the team to a level management had hoped for and counted on.

FRASER, Gord
b. Pembroke, Ontario, January 3, 1902
d. London, Ontario, 1966

In five NHL seasons (1926-31), Fraser played for five NHL teams. Although he never won a Cup during

Jim Franks

Curt Fraser

Gord Fraser

these years, he did win one in 1925 with the Victoria Cougars, the last non-NHL team to win the great trophy. That team beat the Canadiens in four games of a best-of-five, and the year after the Cougars again went to the finals, only to lose to the Montreal Maroons. After retiring as a player, Fraser became a coach at the minor pro level.

FRASER, Harvey
b. Souris, Manitoba, October 14, 1915
Like brother Archie, Harvey played for a number of years in Yorkton before seeing his only NHL action during the war. For Harvey, his chance came with the Black Hawks in 1944-45, but he was better known as one of the greatest players in AHL history. Twice he scored hat tricks in successive games in that league to tie a record, and in 3 full seasons with Providence he scored 99 goals.

Harvey Fraser

FRASER, Iain
b. Scarborough, Ontario, August 10, 1969
To think positively, Fraser was certainly wanted by a number of teams in his day. To be negative, playing for six teams in five years can't be a good thing. The breakdown looks a little ugly: Quebec, 60 games; Winnipeg, 12 games; Edmonton, 9 games; the Islanders, 7 games; Dallas, 4 games; and, San Jose 2 games. Ah, the 1990s. Teams were coming, teams were going, and some even remained the same. Fraser? He took his act to Europe.

Scott Fraser

FRASER, Scott
b. Moncton, New Brunswick, May 3, 1972
Not many New Brunswickers make it to the bigs, and those who do become heroes back home. Fraser played minor hockey in Moncton until leaving home for the great Notre Dame College in Wilcox. He was named to the First All-Star team in the Air Canada Cup in the spring of 1990, and that fall attended Dartmouth College on scholarship. He led the team in scoring his last two years, and in '92-'93 was the team's MVP. After being drafted by Montreal, he made his NHL debut with the Habs in '95-'96, but since then his career has been more minors than NHL. Nonetheless, he has fulfilled a dream and continues to play the game in the AHL, waiting and working toward another shot at the big time.

FRAWLEY, Dan
b. Sturgeon Falls, Ontario, June 2, 1962
His hands were made for punching, and that's just what they did, but every now and then Frawley managed a goal or two just to show he could play the game. He didn't play for long in the NHL, but his years with Pittsburgh (1985-89) were particularly rewarding because at every practice and every game he got to

Frank Fredrickson

watch Mario Lemieux perform. When the Pens won the Cup in 1991 and '92, Frawley was in the "I" and then the AHL for good, but when number 66 lifted the Cup, somewhere Frawley watched with a knowing smile of the greatness that went into the victory.

FREADRICH, Kyle
b. Edmonton, Alberta, December 28, 1978
The guy's gig is to fight. At 6'6" and 225 pounds, he's a left winger with virtually no offensive talent who has played very little so far in his NHL career and only slightly more in his minor pro career. When trouble calls, he answers the bell. That's his gig.

FREDERICK, Ray
b. Fort Frances, Ontario, July 31, 1929

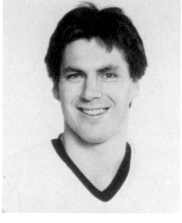

He didn't play for long in the NHL, but his years with Pittsburgh (1985-89) were particularly rewarding.
DAN FRAWLEY

How good was good outside the NHL in the heyday of the Original Six? Pretty good, but any more than that is pure speculation. Frederick was a fine goalie out west, and when he moved to join Ottawa in the Quebec league he more than held his own. In fact, on many nights he was the only reason the Senators stayed competitive. The 1953-54 season started off brimming with controversy because he refused to renew his contract with the team, citing manager T.P. Gorman's insulting offer as the reason. Within a couple of weeks, they agreed to terms, but then Frederick had troubles with the coach, who said Frederick wasn't so hot to start out with. Frederick was upset, but when the coach's name is Turk Broda, an ear has to be given to the words. The next year, the team withdrew from the Quebec league midway through the season, and Frederick was given his chance. Chicago took him as insurance, and he started five games for the Hawks. He allowed 22 goals and never played again. Perhaps the Turk was right after all.

FREDRICKSON, Frank
b. Winnipeg, Manitoba, June 11, 1895
d. Toronto, Ontario, May 28, 1979
In his youth, Fredrickson played with the Winnipeg Falcons, a mostly Icelandic-Canadian team that was virtually unbeatable. He left the team in 1916 to fight in the war, as did most of the players, and worked overseas as a pilot and flight instructor. Upon returning in 1919, he and his mates quickly reformed as a hockey team. Thus was born one of Canada's greatest amateur teams of all time. The Falcons won the Allan Cup in 1920 against the University of Toronto, and left immediately after to go to Antwerp, Belgium, to play in the Summer Olympics, where ice hockey was first played in international competition. The Falcons, representing Canada, demolished the rest of the world

and came home with gold, and Fredrickson immediately turned pro with Victoria in the PCHL. He played there for six years, winning the Stanley Cup with the Cougars in '24-'25. When the Cougars were sold to Detroit of the NHL, Fredrickson moved east and played in the NHL for the first time. Over the next five years, he played for three teams, though the centre didn't display the scoring ability he had with the Falcons or in the PCHL. In '29-'30, he was a playing coach in Pittsburgh, but he suffered a serious leg injury and his career ended as a result. Fredrickson coached at Princeton University and during the Second World War for the RCAF team. After the war he coached at UBC, and in 1958 he was inducted into the Hockey Hall of Fame. He received the Order of the Falcon from the government of Iceland for his studies in charting schools of fish for the commercial fishing industry, though he spent most of his post-playing career in Vancouver as an underwriter. He moved to Toronto, where most of his family lived, in 1978, and passed away in his sleep a year later.

FREER, Mark
b. Toronto, Ontario, July 14, 1968

Every year Don Cherry tells "all you kids out there" not to attend the NHL Entry Draft because it's such a cruel and brutal process for aspiring pros. Freer attended the '86 draft and at day's end went home without hearing his name. He returned to Peterborough, his junior team, and impressed the Flyers enough that they offered him a contract. A loyal player, he remained in the organization for 6 years, even though he played just 59 games with the parent club. He established roots in Hershey and became part of the city's charity efforts, returning to Peterborough every summer to work at hockey schools. Life took a turn when Ottawa claimed him in the Expansion Draft, but a full year with the Senators didn't convince the team to keep him. Freer later wound up in the IHL, playing with Houston for a number of years before re-signing with the Flyers' minor-league affiliate, now also located in Philadelphia.

Freer later wound up in the IHL, playing with Houston.
MARK FREER

FREW, Irv
b. Kilsyth, Scotland, August 16, 1907
d. Calgary, Alberta, April 2, 1995

Wherever he went, winning followed. Frew came to Canada from Scotland when he was two years old. The family settled on a wheat ranch near High River, Alberta, near the ranch owned by the Prince of Wales. He went to high school in Calgary and started his winning ways when he was 19, playing on the Memorial Cup Calgary Canadians of 1926-27. The next year, he turned pro with the Calgary Tigers, and

that team won its title. Then he was off to Stratford, and the Nationals won the IHL championship. He continued to rise until the Maroons signed him, and he played with the St. Louis Eagles and the Canadiens for a season each as well. Although he was only 5'10" and 178 pounds, he was all muscle. He spent the summers on horseback, riding through the foothills and the prairies as a government of Alberta employee of all trades. He was a forest ranger and a fish and game inspector with the Alberta Forestry Service for 38 years. He retired in 1971 and coached kids' hockey for many years.

FRIDAY, Tim
b. Burbank, California, March 5, 1961

Friday had his perspective all backward. He went to RPI to play hockey, but he was never drafted. He went to Detroit's training camp in the fall of 1985, and neither he nor anyone else expected him to make the team. He made the team. He had a few small injuries after starting off strongly, and when he was demoted he went down happily, figuring he'd work out the kinks and be back in due course. He never made it back. A shoulder injury that had hampered him never got fully better, and he retired after one season as a pro.

FRIDGEN, Dan
b. Arnprior, Ontario, May 18, 1959

A car accident ended Fridgen's career but didn't damage his love for hockey. He went to Colgate on scholarship and led the ECAC in scoring his last two years. Hartford signed him as a free agent in 1982 at the end of his senior year, and he played two games with the Whalers at the end of the '81-'82 season, playing on a line with his childhood hero, Dave Keon. He started the next year with the team, but when coach Larry Pleau was fired, his ally was gone and Fridgen was sent to the minors. Two years later, he suffered a depressed skull fracture in a car accident and retired. He worked in radio and marketing for the Binghampton Whalers and then decided to return to school to get his master's degree in business. While trying to organize a hockey tournament, he ended up talking to the head coach at Union College, Charlie Morrison, who hired Fridgen as his assistant. Four years later, he served as assistant at RPI, and when coach Buddy Powers left for Bowling Green five years later, Fridgen was named head coach, a position he has held ever since.

FRIEDMAN, Doug
b. Cape Elizabeth, Maine, September 1, 1971

He's a big, bad bruiser and a thumper of bodies, a workhorse for the penalty box whose time to fight in

Doug Friedman

Jeff Friesen

Karl Friesen

Len Frig

Bob Froese

Miroslav Frycer

the NHL is quickly passing. Friedman made his NHL debut at 26 with Edmonton in 1997-98 and played briefly with Nashville a couple of years later. Now in his thirties, though, his chances of being called up again from the minors are ever diminishing.

FRIESEN, Jeff
b. Meadow Lake, Saskatchewan, August 5, 1976
The talent is all there, always has been. But something was just missing. When he was a bantam, junior teams shied away from him because he was so small. That summer before junior, he grew seven inches, and Regina GM Bill Hicke signed him for the Pats. He put up big numbers and promised to go high in the draft, but many scouts shied away from him. He had the potential to be great, but many just didn't think he would be. San Jose drafted him and gave him nearly seven years, but somehow he just didn't impress even when he was scoring. He had 4 years of 22 goals or more, but when the Sharks had the chance to get Teemu Selanne, they traded Friesen to Anaheim as part of the deal. He has played for Canada twice at the World Juniors and four times at the World Championships (winning gold in '97 and silver in '96), but after 8 years in the league he has played just 34 playoff games and has settled into his role as a decent, but not spectacular, player.

FRIESEN, Karl
b. Winnipeg, Manitoba, June 30, 1958
His parents emigrated to Canada just a month before Karl was born, and his German heritage would come in handy in a big way in due course. Karl was raised a deeply religious man, but he loved to play hockey. He had no real ambitions about the NHL – he was never drafted – and he became an accountant and thought that was that. Wrong. He got married and decided to use his dual citizenship to play in Germany, so he and the missus moved to Rosenheim. When all was said and done, he was a national hero for that country. He played in 6 World Championships and 3 Olympics for Germany, and for 16 years was the star of the league. Four times he was named MVP, unheard of for a goalie. He even had his shot at NHL glory. He played in the AHL for all of '85-'86, and the following year played in four games for the New Jersey Devils, including a game back in Winnipeg against the Jets. He had a couple of bad outings, and rather than fight it out in the minors he returned to Germany, where he played until retiring in 1996.

FRIEST, Ron
b. Windsor, Ontario, November 4, 1958
Friest developed with the local Spitfires before signing a minor-league contract in 1978 with Oklahoma. He was given a brief chance with Minnesota over the next three years, but as a left winger he was faced with having to compete for ice time with the likes of Steve Payne, Tom McCarthy, and Al MacAdam. It was a battle he lost.

FRIG, Len
b. Lethbridge, Alberta, October 30, 1950
Leonard Elroy Frig has to be one of hockey's greatest names. He got into his first games in the 1973 playoffs

when coach Billy Reay in Chicago called him up from Dallas just in case. The next night, regular defenceman Doug Jarrett went down with an injury, and Frig was right there to fill the void. He made the team the next year and played briefly in California, Cleveland, and St. Louis before becoming a staple on the Salt Lake blueline in the minors.

FROESE, Bob ("Frosty")
b. St. Catharines, Ontario, June 30, 1958
St. Louis wasted a draft choice on Froese in 1978. They selected him but never used him, which was a shame because when the Flyers signed him, he entered the NHL and promptly went 13 games without a loss, one shy of the NHL record. In his four and a half seasons with Philly, he had a record of 145–24–12, the best winning percentage for those years (1982–87). The trouble was that in his two playoff appearances, he performed poorly and the Flyers lost confidence in him. When coach Mike Keenan had the chance to make Ron Hextall his number-one man, Froese was on his way to the Rangers. That team, though, was weaker and had a young John Vanbiesbrouck. Froese didn't see much action and retired in 1990. A few years earlier, he was briefly credited with a goal, only the second (after Billy Smith's) given to a tender. In a game against the Islanders, a delayed penalty pulled, ironically, Smith from the nets, but the Islanders put the puck into their own net and Froese was thought to have been the last one to touch it. A day later, though, the call was changed and David Shaw was given credit for having been the last to touch the puck. When he retired in 1990, Froese became an assistant coach with the Rangers, but he also worked with Hockey Ministries International. This gave him a greater satisfaction, and he quit hockey to become a pastor. He currently holds that position at the Faith Fellowship Church in Clarence, New York, saving souls instead of pucks.

FROST, Harry ("Harley")
b. Kerr Lake, Ontario, August 17, 1914
d. Pennsylvania, March 1973
Frost called Chocolatetown home for many of his hockey years, though he got the call to leave Hershey and play for Boston for four games in the '38-'39 season. He stopped playing for two years to enlist in the army, but upon his return he continued a career in the minors for another seven seasons.

FRYCER, Miroslav ("Mirko"/ "Frigo")
b. Ostrava, Czechoslovakia (Czech Republic),
September 27, 1959
He was called Frigo by his Czech friends because that was the Czech name for Buster Keaton, and Frycer was, if nothing else, a man of humour and affability. After starring internationally and in club teams back home, Frycer defected to Quebec for the Stastny brothers and the Nordiques. In his first NHL game he had a hat trick in a 6-3 win over Toronto, the team he was traded to that same season (1981-82). In four healthy and full seasons with the Leafs he never scored fewer than 25 goals, playing on a line with Peter Ihnacak and Walt Poddubny. The freewheeling

threesome were reigned in, though, when John Brophy took over as coach, and combined with a series of injuries Frycer found himself on his way to Detroit. His health never improved, and he wound up in Europe for a brief time, playing in Germany and then establishing himself in Italy, where he turned to coaching in the Italian Ice Hockey Federation.

FRYDAY, Bob
b. Toronto, Ontario, December 5, 1928
Fryday went from the Marlies to the Montreal Royals in the late 1940s, and it was there he played most of his career with the exception of five games with the Canadiens between 1949 and '52.

FTOREK, Robbie
b. Needham, Massachusetts, January 2, 1952
A tragedy occurred and Ftorek became a hockey player. It was destiny, though, for his mom went into labour at a Boston Bruins game and barely made it to the hospital to deliver li'l Robbie. As a boy, he took figure skating. His coach of four years was Marible Vinson Owen, coach of the U.S. Olympic team. This was leading up to 1960, the year Owen and the entire skating team perished in a plane crash. Still in sleepy Needham without a figure skating coach, Ftorek turned to hockey and did quite well, despite his size (or lack thereof). He made the 1972 Olympic team that won a silver medal in Sapporo (Canada did not compete) and joined Detroit later in that '71-'72 season. He later moved on to the WHA where he starred for four years as a scorer, and he joined the Nordiques when the WHA merged with the NHL in 1979. He was not nearly a scorer in the better league, and he retired in 1985 to begin a new career, as a coach. Ftorek moved from AHL to NHL, from assistant to head, from middling success to bona fide success, from Los Angeles to New Jersey and Boston.

FUHR, Grant ("Coco"/ "Fuhrsie")
b. Spruce Grove, Alberta, September 28, 1962
One of the greatest goalies to play the game, Fuhr often never received his due because he played for a team capable of scoring on every shift and allowing a breakaway on every other. To wit, in his first six years with the Edmonton Oilers in the 1980s, he had but two shutouts, hardly a true representation of his play. Wayne Gretzky called him the main reason the team won five Cups in that decade, and Fuhr himself was an offensive star of sorts, retiring with the most assists for a goalie in league history (46, since surpassed by Tom Barrasso) and as record-holder with 14 in 1 season (1983-84). He played junior hockey in Victoria

and was drafted 8th overall by the Oilers in 1981, unusually high for a goalie. He emerged quickly as the number-one man, but after a decade he lost his place to Bill Ranford and was traded to Toronto, the first of several moves in the last few years of his career. In 1995-96 with St. Louis, he played 79 games, the most ever by a goalie in 1 year, and in his final season, 1999-2000 with Calgary, he won his 400th game. He played in six All-Star Games in the 1980s, won the Vezina in '87-'88, and played for Canada at the 1984 and '87 Canada Cups. Away from the rink, he was an avid golfer who often played 18 holes the day of a Stanley Cup game and 36 holes on off-days. He dreamed of being a touring pro, and since retiring has played the celebrity circuit and continues to pursue his tour card. He also became goalie coach for the Flames for a short time.

FULLAN, Larry
b. Toronto, Ontario, August 11, 1949
It was only after graduating from Cornell University that Fullan was able to get some NHL interest, but when Montreal signed him in 1972, it was more to fill their AHL affiliate in Nova Scotia than with an eye to playing him at the Forum. When the Expansion Draft of '74 took place, his name was on the available list, and Washington snapped him up. The Caps played him in four games, but after that he played only briefly in the minors before retiring.

FUSCO, Mark
b. Burlington, Massachusetts, March 12, 1961
Mark and brother Scott both graduated from Harvard with degrees in economics, hardly the training needed for a career in pro hockey. Actually, they also graduated with a Hobey Baker Award, but both also graduated with bodies that measured approximately 5'9" and 175 pounds. Those were not NHL grades, according to most scouts. Mark played at the 1984 Olympics in Sarajevo and the 1985 Worlds, and he was given something of a chance with Hartford in '84-'85. In 63 games, he scored just 3 goals, and the Whalers sent him to the minors hoping he'd develop there. Fusco didn't buy the arrangement and instead retired to work in the family's successful computer business in Boston. Scott went to Europe to play.

He was an avid golfer who often played 18 holes the day of a Stanley Cup game.
GRANT FUHR

Bob Fryday

Robbie Ftorek

Larry Fullan

Mark Fusco

GABORIK, Marian ("Gabby")

b. Trencin, Czechoslovakia (Slovakia), February 14, 1982

The expansion Minnesota Wild selected Gaborik 3rd overall with their first-ever draft choice, in 2000, and he went on to lead the team with 36 points. He scored a goal in his first game, October 6, 2000, against Anaheim, one of 18 on the season for the right winger. He has further connections to the club in that his brother, Brano, is a scout for the team.

GADSBY, Bill ("The Bear")

b. Calgary, Alberta, August 8, 1927

When he was 12 years old, little Bill Gadsby was taken by his family to Lancashire to visit relatives. The trip coincided with the start of the Second World War, and they had a tough time finding a ship headed for Canada. Eventually, they boarded the *Athenia*, one of the last vessels to leave, but soon after departure the craft was torpedoed and its passengers were stranded on lifeboats in the Irish Sea. It was many hours before they were rescued, but the images of fear and death stayed with Gadsby forever. An important face-off or a tough loss never looked as significant by comparison, and Gadsby kept a calm demeanour throughout his NHL career as a result of this early experience. When he returned to terra firma, he made a conscious decision to pursue a life in hockey, and when Chicago, his childhood team of choice, signed him in 1946, he was delighted. He was a big, rangy defenceman who had tremendous offensive ability but who sacrificed his body every shift to play well defensively. He started his '46-'47 season in the minors, but after just a few games the 19-year-old was called up to the Hawks and never went back. In his first game, he was cut for 12 stitches, a portentous accident that repeated itself dozens of times over the years. He played more than eight years with Chicago, and although he developed into a star defenceman he played on the worst team in the league. In all those years, the team made the playoffs exactly once. He had to ease up on his physical style of play after 1950 when he broke his leg and missed most of the season. Gadsby also had to overcome another horrific problem in 1952 when doctors found that he had polio in 58 percent of his body (65 percent would have meant paralysis). He kept his body active and took all the medication required, and after two weeks his body was back to health and a disaster had been averted. He was traded to the Rangers early in the '54-'55, but all that did was move him from sixth to fifth in the standings. The Rangers, too, had a weak team, but they were capable of making the playoffs and Gadsby earned greater respect during his days with the Blueshirts. He was a First Team All-Star 3 times during these years, and in '58-'59 he set an NHL record by recording 46 assists for a defenceman. In 1961 he was traded to the Red Wings, where he played the last 5 of his 20 NHL years. He went to the finals 3 times, yet when he retired in 1966 he had played 1,248 regular-season games without winning a Cup. In his 20 years, he appeared in just 67 playoff games. Gadsby stepped behind the Detroit bench as head coach for '68-'69 but was replaced two games into the following season. He stayed on as scout with the team but later opened Bill Gadsby's Golf Training Centre outside Detroit, where he expended most of his post-NHL energy. He was inducted into the Hockey Hall of Fame in 1970.

GAETZ, Link ("The Missing Link")

b. Vancouver, British Columbia, October 2, 1968

Not your average guy. It all goes back to his birth. He was the last of four kids, and when he was born his mother simply said, well, he's the Missing Link. The name stuck, much to her surprise (but no one else's). Then there was the junior career and time in the minors. One night while his team was travelling by bus, he was hot, so he busted open a window. In a game, he once incurred seven minors and then a major penalty. He tried to take on a number of patrons in a bar one night and wound up with two black eyes the day of the draft. But he likes animals, his mom explained. He plays a physical game, Gaetz explained. He swore he could score and skate and shoot as well as fight, but his numbers reflect a dearth of ability in all categories except the fighting part. He had 326 penalty minutes with San Jose – in just 48 games. His mother knew something when she gave him that nickname, or he felt compelled to live up to the name while growing up. Either way, he was certainly an entertaining figure.

GAGE, Joaquin

b. Vancouver, British Columbia, October 19, 1973

It's tough to get a full-time job in the NHL when you have a record of 2-10-1 in 18 appearances. Doesn't matter how bad the team might be (Edmonton, vintage mid-1990s) or how bad the luck, those numbers just don't cut it. Gage came out of the Western league but spent the majority of his career to date in the minors.

GAGE, Jody

b. Toronto, Ontario, November 29, 1959

His is a great story, and it just so happens it takes place outside the NHL except for 68 games' worth of telling. Gage was drafted by Detroit and played a bunch of games for the Wings and then Sabres, but he left his mark in the AHL and in particular with the city of Rochester. By the time he retired in 1996, his 504 goals placed him third all time behind only Willie Marshall (523) and Fred Glover (520). He started in the league as a kid looking up to teammate Bill Hogaboam, and he finished as a 17-year veteran who was looked up to by youngsters. Eleven of those seasons came with the Americans, and they later raised his number 9 to the rafters of the War Memorial arena and then hired him as the team's assistant general manager. He had seven 40-goal seasons and peaked with 60 in '87-'88, the year he was also named the league's MVP.

GAGNE, Art

b. Ottawa, Ontario, October 11, 1897
d. Kamloops, British Columbia, October 6, 1988

Gagne made the rounds in the late 1920s and early 1930s, being owned by five NHL teams and playing out west for a number of seasons as well. A right winger, he scored 20 goals in '27-'28 with the Canadiens, quite a feat given that the schedule was only 44 games long.

Link Gaetz

Joaquin Gage

Jody Gage

Bill Gadsby
(opposite page)

Paul Gagne

Simon Gagne

Dave Gagne

Garmaine Gagnon

Johnny Gagnon

GAGNE, Paul
b. Iroquois Falls, Ontario, February 6, 1962
It's mind-boggling, actually. Gagne was drafted in 1980 and he could score. He scored in junior, and he scored in the NHL, reaching his peak with seasons of 25 and 24 goals, variously. The rub was, though, that despite playing in the NHL for 10 seasons and 390 games, he never played a single playoff game. Not one. And, he was a minus player every season. That's what playing on bad teams will do to a guy. Gagne missed two and a half years with a serious back injury, and when he returned to action he went almost immediately to Europe to extend his career. The second part of his hockey life took place in Switzerland, and after he retired as a player he remained there to coach.

GAGNE, Pierre
b. North Bay, Ontario, June 5, 1940
Gagne's only NHL action came as a raw 19-year-old in 1959-60 with Boston, pre-Bobby Orr, when the team missed the playoffs annually. Gagne kicked around for a bit in the AHL and IHL, but he never pursued a career in hockey with single-minded determination.

GAGNE, Simon
b. Ste. Foy, Quebec, February 29, 1980
One of the new superstars, Gagne has yet to reach his potential but has still become one of the great players in the game. He was a candidate for the Calder Trophy in 1999-2000 after helping Canada win silver at the previous year's World Juniors, and in each of his first three years his goal production increased, to 33 goals. Gagne shone at the 2001 All-Star Game and the next year was named to Canada's team for the 2002 Olympics in Salt Lake City, where he won gold. Philadelphia drafted him 22nd overall in 1998, and he has turned into one of the team's finest-ever selections.

GAGNER, Dave
b. Chatham, Ontario, December 11, 1964
Before fulfilling his dream of playing in the NHL, Gagner fulfilled another dream that drew a perfect line from that day to this. He played the entire '83-84 season with Canada's National Team, including the 1984 Olympics in Sarajevo. During that time, the team practised outdoors in Germany, a thrill he remembered after retiring. In 1984, though, he joined the Rangers and never looked back. Over the next 15 years, he played nearly 1,000 games with 7 teams and had 6 successive 30-goal seasons with the Minnesota/Dallas franchise. When he retired in 1999, he remembered those outdoor practices and decided that's the spirit he was looking for. He teamed up with a mechanical engineer and formed Custom Ice Rinks Inc., a company that took the backyard rink to new levels. Gagner's were *crème de la crème*, state-of-the-art rinks with piping in the ground to ensure excellent ice even if the weather was too mild for a natural rink. It was expensive for clients, but he rightly figured that for every Canadian who could afford a swimming pool, there was another who would prefer a rink. He's even hoping to build a rink for a maximum-security mental health centre in Penatanguishene, thanks to a strange and wonderful connection. One staff member at that

centre is Paul Henry, a former director of player development for the Florida Panthers and a member of the Rangers' scouting staff back in '83 when Gagner was recommended to the team.

GAGNON, David
b. Windsor, Ontario, October 31, 1967
The goalie graduated from Colgate in 1990, but after two games with Detroit he would never play in the NHL again. He allowed six goals in those two brief appearances and ever since has been in the minors playing his heart out.

GAGNON, Germaine
b. Chicoutimi, Quebec, December 9, 1942
He seemed to be developing into a little bit of something with the Islanders, but then the Flyers' Ed Van Impe cut him down – broke his ankle in December '72 – and he wasn't the same after. A year later he was acquired by Tommy Ivan and Chicago at the trade deadline, at which time Ivan said something to the effect that Gagnon was the best he could do. Fainting with damn praise. By 1976, Gagnon was out of the league, and consensus had it he never got better, psychologically or physically, after the busted ankle.

GAGNON, Johnny
("The Black Cat of Chicoutimi"/ "Black Cat")
b. Chicoutimi, Quebec, June 3, 1905
d. March 22, 1984
He got the nickname for his jet-black hair and the quickness packed into a body just 5'5" and 140 pounds. One of 11 children, he grew up poor and in a non-hockey environment, one might say. That is, when his father caught him playing, he'd break little Johnny's stick! Johnny ran away from home, to Trois Rivières, to pursue his dream of playing for a living. He drew interest from Canadiens boss Leo Dandurand, but when they met face to face the boss told the youngster he was too light to play in the NHL. Gagnon challenged Dandurand to weigh him, filled his pockets with rocks, and tipped the scales at 150. Dandurand, impressed, signed him to a contract. In his first year with the Habs, Gagnon played on a line with Aurel Joliat and Howie Morenz and the team won the Cup that spring, in 1931. He played most of his decade in the league with Montreal, though he ended his career suddenly during the 1940 playoffs while with the New York Americans. Manager Red Dutton told Gagnon he would not receive a full playoff share because he had been acquired during the season, so Gagnon packed his bags and never played in the NHL again. He returned to Providence to play, then coached the team for a season, and then became a scout for the rest of his days, 13 years with those Reds and 14 years with the Rangers.

GAGNON, Sean
b. Sault Ste. Marie, Ontario, September 11, 1973
Gagnon was a large man who played large and intimidated large. He also fought heavy and played defence with his body more than his speed and skill. He had a brief trial with Phoenix, but most of his fighting occurred in the minors.

GAINEY, Bob
b. Peterborough, Ontario, December 13, 1953

It wasn't until after Soviet coach Viktor Tikhonov put into words what most people felt that Gainey started to receive his due. Tikhonov called the left winger the best player in the world from a technical point of view. In other words, he wasn't the best scorer or swiftest skater or hardest hitter, but when you took into account all that he could do and how he played the game, there was no one quite like him. As a kid, he played defence, but he was moved up to the wing when he played in a church league in Peterborough. He played junior with the Petes under coach Roger Neilson, and Sam Pollock, GM in Montreal, became a huge fan of Gainey's. The Habs took him 8th overall at the 1973 Draft, and he made the team as a 19-year-old rookie that fall.

Although Gainey scored but 3 goals that first year, he improved to 17 the next season. More important, he played two-way hockey that had fans and critics recalling the good old days when everyone played that way (and no one did any longer!). Gainey was termed a defensive specialist or a checking forward, even though he was a capable offensive player. Tikhonov made his remarks after the 1976 Canada Cup, and almost because of Gainey's unique style of play the NHL introduced the Frank Selke Trophy, to be given to the best defensive forward. It was Gainey's for the asking in its early years, as he won it the first four years it was available (1977-81). In 1981, he succeeded Serge Savard as team captain, and it was his job to bridge the dynasty of the 1970s and the (hopefully) great teams of the

Tikhonov called the left winger the best player in the world from a technical point of view.
BOB GAINEY

1980s. Gainey had won four Cups with Montreal (1975-79), but as many of the players from those teams left, his job was a huge, if not impossible one. The Habs had a number of disappointing playoff results during the Islanders' great run, though Gainey had one more Cup left in him as the team surprised everyone by winning in '85-'86. He retired 3 years later having played all of his 1,160 regular-season games with Montreal. Gainey moved to France in 1989 to prepare for a career in coaching. He was a playing coach for Epinal for a season and then returned to North America to become Minnesota's head coach. He took the team to the finals in his first season, but after another four and a half years he couldn't repeat his rookie magic. He resigned as coach to focus on his work as the team's GM. It was a fortuitous move, as he built a team that went to the finals in 1990 and won the Cup in 1999. During those years he was inducted into the Hockey Hall of Fame but had to deal with a problem for which no amount of Cups could compensate. His wife, Cathy, passed away following a long battle with cancer, and he had to celebrate that victory in 1999 on his own. His son,

Steve, made it to the NHL, and Gainey himself later resigned as GM, looking for a new challenge.

GAINEY, Steve
b. Montreal, Quebec, January 26, 1979

Were it anyone else, it might smell of nepotism, but Bob Gainey is a fierce competitor and of strong moral fibre. So if Dallas drafted his son, Steve, and even played him in a few games, it was likely to suss out junior rather than do the old man, the team's GM, a favour. That being said, young Gainey has yet to make an NHL impression that would keep him in the lineup for a while.

GAINOR, Norm "Dutch"
b. Calgary, Alberta, April 10, 1904
d. Edmonton, Alberta, January 16, 1962

"Dutch" Gainor

He was considered one of the shiftiest and deceptive players of his era, a man who could saunter up to a defenceman and be by him in a flash. Gainor earned his reputation with the Boston Bruins, helping the team win a Cup in his second season, '28-'29. He later played for the Senators and Rangers, and finished his career with another Cup with the Maroons in '35-'36. It was a short career – Gainor was plagued by varicose veins – but he left behind a legacy as a left winger who came and went too quickly.

GALANOV, Maxim
b. Krasnoyarsk, Soviet Union (Russia), March 13, 1974

Maxim Galanov

Galanov's star did not rise as high in the night sky as the Rangers had hoped when they drafted him in 1993. He developed at home, then moved to the AHL to acclimatize, but when the day was at hand to adjust to the NHL, he floundered. He later ran into injury trouble, and in three years he had played for three different teams.

GALARNEAU, Michel
b. Montreal, Quebec, March 1, 1961

Michel Galarneau

Although he played just 78 games in the NHL with Hartford in the early 1980s, Galarneau is a legend… in France. He did the AHL thing for a short while and then decided to move to France to play in that country's top league. He became a French citizen and played for France at the 1995 World Championships, and although he is but a small name in North America he has been a star overseas for 15 years.

GALBRAITH, Percival "Percy" ("Perk")
b. Toronto, Ontario, December 5, 1898
d. Minneapolis, Minnesota, June 20, 1961

Percy Galbraith

As a teenager, Percy played hockey in Winnipeg and worked at a hardware store, but when he turned 18, he had another priority. He enlisted in the war. This was

John Gallagher

Gerard Gallant

Don Gallinger

Bruce Gamble

August 1917, and it was a full two years before he was discharged and could skate again. He went to the U.S. to play and worked his way up until the Boston Bruins took notice and invited him to camp in 1926. He never looked back. Galbraith played most of seven years with the Bruins. He led the league in playoff points in 1927, and two years later helped the team win the Stanley Cup for the first time. He later returned to Minnesota to end his playing career and begin a new one as coach.

GALLAGHER, John

b. Kenora, Ontario, January 19, 1909
d. unknown

The whole story is not yet known, though it is curious nonetheless. Gallagher came out of the North to play in the NHL for most of the 1930s, starting with the Maroons in 1930-31. Three years later, he missed all but one game in the season after being badly injured in a car accident, and he went on to win the Stanley Cup with Detroit in 1937. The defenceman even scored a goal in that finals series against the Rangers. His career ended with the Americans in 1939 after he was admitted to a mental hospital in Penatanguishene, though he played for the hospital team and even coached a youngster whose father worked at the hospital. This is all that's known about his final days as a player.

GALLANT, Gerard ("Spud")

b. Summerside, Prince Edward Island, September 2, 1963
Very rare are the times a player has a good junior career but an even better NHL career, but Gallant is a case in point. He played like a Sutter from down east, hard, ferocious every night, and this got him to the league, kept him there, and took him out of it a decade later. Gallant played junior in Quebec and joined the Red Wings for the '84-'85 season. He quickly established himself on a line with Steve Yzerman, and in the ensuing years he had four consecutive 30-goal seasons. In addition, the left winger added that all-important "power" element to his game, and it was an incredible feat that in all of those 30-goal seasons he also had 200+ penalty minutes as well. Over time, he suffered some injuries, notably a broken jaw, but after signing with Tampa as a free agent in 1993 he suffered a back injury that forced him to retire. He turned to coaching, first back home in potato country, then in the minor pros and most recently back in the NHL, with Columbus.

GALLEY, Gary ("Gaga")

b. Montreal, Quebec, April 16, 1963
In a 16-year career, Galley came full circle, starting with Los Angeles as a green rookie and finishing with the same team as a grizzled veteran. In between, he played for six other teams and a total of 1,093 games, twice playing for Canada at the World Championships. The closest he came to the Cup was in 1990, when his Bruins lost to Edmonton in the finals, though the defenceman did play in the NHL All-Star Game in both 1991 and '94. He left Bowling Green after three years to join Los Angeles in 1984 and retired in 2001.

GALLIMORE, Jamie

b. Edmonton, Alberta, November 28, 1957
They don't come too much more obscure than this. Gallimore played twice for the North Stars in '77-'78 right out of junior with Kamloops, but his pro career in the minors was short and – poof! – he was gone.

GALLINGER, Don

b. Port Colborne, Ontario, April 16, 1925
d. Burlington, Ontario, February 7, 2000
All people make mistakes when they're young. Some people get caught, others don't. Gallinger made a huge mistake. It continued. He got caught. And he paid a heavy, heavy price. He debuted with Boston as a 17-year-old during the war and played on a line with two other teens, 17-year-old Bep Guidolin and 19-year-old Bill Shill. Together they were the Sprout Line. After two years, Gallinger himself went off to war, working his way to the top of his gunnery class. He led the Bruins in points his first year back, and rejected ball contracts from both the Phillies and Red Sox. On March 9, 1948, the bubble burst. He was barred from the NHL for life for "conduct detrimental to hockey." He and Boston teammate Billy Taylor were found gambling with James Tamer, a Detroit mobster. He had been betting on his team – for and against – in amounts ranging from $250 or $1,000, high even by modern standards. As well, he provided Tamer with information on his team's injury status. Oddly, he once bet a grand on Chicago to win a game and then scored the tying goal in an eventual Boston victory. His life collapsed: His 11-year-old daughter died of cancer, his wife and two other children disappeared, and his resort business on Lake Rousseau fell to ruin. He moved to the United States to start anew, and during this time, on August 28, 1970, his suspension was lifted. All those years, he had not been allowed to engage in any activity connected to hockey, not even act as coach of a bantam team in the remote North if he had wanted. He had tried to have the ban lifted earlier, even going so far as agreeing to a detailed series of interviews for a Toronto newspaper to wipe the slate clean, so to speak. All to no avail. In 1971, Gallinger returned to Canada and got a job as a salesman for Mansfield Shirt Company. A happy moment occurred in 1998 when Gallinger met a son he had had out of wedlock with a rich heiress. The son had been living in California, but didn't know the whereabouts of his father until Don Rasankuski, the radio voice of the San Jose Sharks, helped track him down. The father and son met, with Gallinger's two other sons, in Toronto for the first time. Gallinger died in obscurity in 2000.

GAMBLE, Bruce ("Paladin"/ "Smiley Bates")

b. Port Arthur, Ontario, May 24, 1938
d. Niagara Falls, Ontario, December 29, 1982
Gamble was a particularly curious and odd person, and that he played goal was perhaps a metaphor for his character. He played for four NHL teams and a number more in the minors, his finest moments coming with Toronto during the 1960s. Although he didn't appear in the 1967 playoffs, he did see action in 23 regular-season games during that Cup season. He

was later traded to Philadelphia, but on February 9, 1972, he suffered a heart attack during a game. He didn't check into a hospital, though, until the next morning after an overnight flight. He never played again. He scouted for the Flyers for a year but suffered from depression because of his health. Gamble went into seclusion, moving to the quiet of Niagara Falls, where he operated a catering truck until suffering a fatal heart attack a decade later.

GAMBLE, Dick ("Grumps")
b. Moncton, New Brunswick, November 16, 1928
Gamble played on the 1953 Stanley Cup-winning Montreal Canadiens during a career that was marked "good" in the NHL and "great" in the AHL. He had 1 period in the former ('55-'56) before spending 10 years outside the league until Toronto played him for 3 games over the period 1965-67. All of his AHL time took place in Buffalo and Rochester, but none of his success would have happened had it not been for Gordie Drillon, another Maritimer who had retired from the NHL and returned home to scout. He discovered Gamble and sent him on his way to a lengthy career. Gamble was a scorer: He had 12 successive 20-goal seasons in the AHL and won 3 Calder Cups with the Americans. He coached the team during his last two years as a player (1968-70) and for one more year after hanging up his sweater. From 1963 to '70, he operated a hockey school in Bowmanville, Ontario, assisted variably by Gerry Cheevers and Bobby Orr. He later ran another school in Rochester. After retiring, he was inducted into the New Brunswick Sports Hall of Fame (1984), the Rochester Americas Hall of Fame (1986), and the Moncton Sports Hall of Fame (1987). His number 9 sweater was also retired by Rochester, and after playing he worked first as a travelling salesman and then as an RV salesman. He later became a salesman for a heating firm in Syracuse, New York.

GAMBLE, Troy
b. New Glasgow, Nova Scotia, April 7, 1967
The closest Gamble came to being number one during his time tending the proverbial twine was in 1990-91 with Vancouver, when he appeared in 47 games. He had a 16-16-6 record, but the team was wiped out in the first round of the playoffs and his career petered out from there. In all, he spent the better part of seven years in the "I," which is not where most goalies in the NHL begin. Rather, it's where they end up.

GAMBUCCI, Gary
b. Hibbing, Minnesota, September 27, 1946
Gambucci came from hockey stock. The Boston Bruins expressed interest in his father, but the war changed his life and a career in hockey never happened. His uncle, Andy, played for the U.S. at the 1952 Olympics in Oslo. And Gary carried on the tradition by playing for the U.S. national team for three years (1968-71), during which time he also worked in a management training program for Northwestern Bell in Minneapolis. In all, he played at four World Championships for his country, though he missed out on the 1972 Olympics in Sapporo, playing pro instead in the AHL and making his first NHL appearance, with Minnesota. Gambucci also played briefly in the WHA.

GANCHAR, Perry
b. Saskatoon, Saskatchewan, October 28, 1963
Despite scoring 68 goals in his final year of junior, no NHL team was willing to give Ganchar a true chance to make it big. He played a bit with three teams, but it was the IHL that claimed him as its own, and he returned the favour in kind with a devotion that continues. He played nine years in the "I" with Muskegon and Cleveland, and retired in 1996 at age 33 to become the team's assistant coach, a position that became head coach a year later.

GANS, Dave
b. Brantford, Ontario, June 6, 1964
It's tough to imagine that such a talent would have his only 2 shots at the NHL by the age of 21, but Gans was blessed with and cursed by the early opportunities. He was minding his own business in the OHL playing for Oshawa when the L.A. Kings ran into injury problems, top scorers Dave Taylor and Bernie Nicholls both having been felled. The club called up Gans, leading his team in scoring, and the 18-year-old played in 3 games. After graduating from the Generals, he went to the IHL where he scored 52 goals in his only year there. This led to another three-game look-see and another demotion thereafter. There was no encore, and there is no mention of him on a sign leading to his hometown.

GARDINER, Bert
b. Saskatoon, Saskatchewan, March 25, 1913
d. Los Angeles, California, August 28, 2001
Gardiner played most of his NHL games during the war, having appeared briefly in the 1930s with the Rangers. He was the only goalie to play all 50 games, with Chicago, in '42-'43, but he had a losing record and the Hawks never qualified for the playoffs. His finest days were with the Philadelphia Ramblers, a team in the International league, in the late 1930s. Gardiner was also a first-rate tennis player and was elected to the Alberta Hall of Fame for his racquet skills.

GARDINER, Bruce
b. Barrie, Ontario, February 11, 1972
Gardiner took care of his schooling first and foremost, spending four years at Colgate before going the pro hockey route. St. Louis drafted him, but the Blues never played him and he signed as a free agent with Ottawa. After developing in the Sens system for two years, he made the big team at camp in 1996 and never looked back. He has, however, moved around a bit and been cast as a fourth-liner rather than a star in the making.

GARDINER, Charlie
b. Edinburgh, Scotland, December 31, 1904
d. Winnipeg, Manitoba, June 13, 1934
Born not far from the Royal Mile, Gardiner and his family made their way to Winnipeg in 1911. Because he wasn't an accomplished skater, but loved hockey, he gravitated toward the nets and became one of the greatest goalies in the game. He turned pro in 1927, and with the exception of four games in his rookie season, no man protected the Chicago goal for the next seven years. He played on frequently the worst team in the league, yet he alone was often worth the price of admission. For instance, in his second season,

Dick Gamble

Troy Gamble

Gary Gambucci

Perry Ganchar

Charlie Gardiner

Bill Gardner

Cal Gardner

he had a spectacular GAA of 1.85, which might indicate a superb record. Yet his record was an awful 7-29-8, clear indication of his prowess and of how lost the Hawks would have been without him. Gardiner was a brave goalie, fearless in diving to clear pucks. He also routinely left his net to beat rushing forwards to the disc, earning him the sobriquet of the Wandering Scotsman. He led the NHL in '30-'31 with 12 shutouts and the year after with a GAA of 1.85, but his crowning moment was his final season, '33-'34. That year, he led the league again with 10 shutouts and had a remarkable 1.63 GAA. He played for the All-Stars in the Ace Bailey Benefit Game, and at year's end won his second Vezina Trophy. The Hawks scored fewer goals than any team in the league that year yet managed to win the Stanley Cup, their first, almost entirely because of Gardiner's efforts. Yet two months later, back home in Winnipeg, Gardiner suffered a brain hemorrhage and died three days later. He was just 29 years old.

GARDINER, Herb
b. Winnipeg, Manitoba,
May 10, 1891
d. Philadelphia, Pennsylvania,
January 11, 1972
No one in the annals of the NHL had quite the life and career of Herb Gardiner, and perhaps no one was thinking less of a career in that league than the aforementioned defenceman. He played senior hockey in Winnipeg in 1908, and a year later played for the Northern Crown Bank team that won the banker's league title in that city. A nice prize, yes, but hardly the road to the NHL. Gardiner then was away from hockey for four years. He worked as a surveyor for the Canadian Pacific Railway and in 1915 joined the army, serving overseas for three years before receiving a medical discharge. When he came home, he settled in Calgary and continued to survey, but in the winters he picked up his skates and gloves and played Big Four hockey in that city. He moved up to the Tigers of the WCHL, the highest level yet, competing for the Stanley Cup in 1924 but losing to the Canadiens. The Habs remembered him, and two years later offered him a position with the team, and there he was, at age 35, making his NHL debut! And what a debut it was. Legend has it that he played *every minute of every game* in '26-'27, and although that claim is unsubstantiated, what is known is that he won the Hart Trophy for his outstanding year. He played the following season with the Habs, and the year after joined Chicago as a playing coach. It was a dismal time, as the team won only 7 of 32 games, and he returned to the Canadiens for the final few games of the season. He never played in the NHL again. Gardiner ventured to Philadelphia where he became coach and manager of the Arrows of the Can-

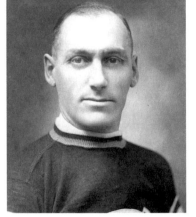

Legend has it that he played every minute of every game in '26-'27.
HERB GARDINER

Am League, a position he held for 20 years. He was inducted into the Hockey Hall of Fame in 1958 even though he played just 3 years and 108 games in the NHL. Gardiner lived the rest of his life in the Philadelphia area.

GARDNER, Bill
b. Toronto, Ontario, March 18, 1960
Here's a story of two teenagers playing for the Toronto Nats, one a 15 – Gardner – the other 14 – Wayne Gretzky. That first season together, it was Gardner, not Gretzky, who was named the team's MVP. After that, Gardner was in junior for four years. During those same years, Gretzky went from the Nats to the OHL to the WHA to being the NHL's best player. Gardner, developing like a normal player, had yet to play in the NHL. Nonetheless, he made the league as a regular in 1981 and stayed on top for much of the decade. He had a career year in '83-'84 with Chicago when he scored 27 goals, but later ended up playing in Europe. In retirement, he returned to Chicago to work as a colour commentator for the Hawks.

GARDNER, Cal ("Ginger")
b. Transcona, Manitoba, October 30, 1924
d. Toronto, Ontario, October 10, 2001
Before Gardner had a chance to play for the Rangers, the team that coveted him, he went off to war, spending most of two years in Scotland with the Royal Canadian Navy after winning the Memorial Cup with Winnipeg. His dream came true, though, because he often played hockey against the RCAF, a team that featured Milt Schmidt, his boyhood idol. Upon discharge, he played for the Rangers farm team, the New York Rovers, on a line with Rene Trudell and Church Russell. The threesome tore up the league and, most unusually, was promoted to the Rangers as a troika toward the end of the '45-'46 season. His finest years came with the Leafs a short time later; he won two Stanley Cups with them (in '49, when he scored the Cup winner, and '51). He met his wife through an act of supreme violence thanks to his lifelong adversary, Montreal's Ken Reardon. Reardon gave Gardner a vicious elbow that forced him to the hospital, and while convalescing Gardner met his wife-to-be. Reardon and Gardner, though, saved their worst for a game a short time later when they engaged in one of the most vicious stick fights in NHL history, both ending up bloodied and dazed and forced by NHL president Clarence Campbell to post peace bonds for the rest of the season. The two developed a hatred for each other that made the Montagues and Capulets look like lifelong pals by comparison, and even 50 years later each swore never to so much as say hello to the other. It

was a rivalry that was born of and epitomized Original Six hockey. Gardner played a season with Chicago and ended his career with Boston, and during his last six seasons he never missed a single game. In 1957, he accepted a job offer to play and coach for Springfield, and after 1961 he was off skates completely and intent on raising his family. Both sons, Dave and Paul, went on to play in the NHL. Gardner remained in Boston and worked as a colour commentator in radio for three years, then settled down in Toronto to do the same for the Leafs on CKFH radio. He worked for a transport company until retiring in 1984.

GARDNER, Dave
b. Toronto, Ontario, August 23, 1952
One of Cal's sons to make it to the NHL, Dave was cherished by just about every hockey team at every level during his development and maturation. He refused to play junior outside Toronto, so the Marlies were able to accommodate him, and Montreal drafted him into the NHL. The Habs in turn traded him in 1974 to St. Louis for a first-round draft choice, but it wasn't until he got to the California Golden Seals that he played regularly. In each of his first 3 seasons he scored 16 goals, and this increased to 19 the next year before things tapered off. Gardner played in the minors for a number of years and then accepted an offer to play and coach with Visp, a third-division team in Switzerland. He remained overseas for two years before returning to Toronto to coach youngsters, including his own son, Ryan.

GARDNER, George ("Bud")
b. Lachine, Quebec, October 8, 1942
By 1970, he was starting to feel frustrated. Gardner had been playing pro for six years with only a few NHL starts to show for his time, and then he came to the Vancouver Canucks in the franchise's first season. Here was a chance to play some goal. But, no. GM Bud Poile wanted to go with three goalies – Charlie Hodge, Dunc Wilson, and Gardner. Guess who was in the press box most nights? Gardner made a fuss and got a few more starts, and he played well on a weak team. But after another year of non-confidence from the Canucks, he jumped at a substantial offer from the L.A. Sharks of the WHA. Unfortunately, he didn't last forever there, either, though he was number one for a year.

GARDNER, Paul
b. Toronto, Ontario, March 5, 1956
Like brother Dave, Paul also refused to play junior away from Toronto, but eventually agreed to go to Windsor, which was within commuting distance. He played his first year of pro right after leaving the Generals, and with the lowly Colorado Rockies he scored 30 goals in each of his first 2 seasons. While with Pittsburgh, he was victim to one of the worst acts of violence of the 1980s. In a game against Winnipeg, he cross-checked Doug Smail, a play deemed bad enough that the league fined him for the blow. In a subsequent game, though, Jets teammate Jimmy Mann enforced his own justice, sucker-punching Gardner from the side and breaking his jaw. Mann was suspended 10 games for the cowardly retribution. Despite three solid years with the Penguins, Gardner found himself

demoted to the minors in '83-'84, and his playing career never got back on track. He set an AHL record with 130 points the following season, but when the opportunity to act as a playing coach in Rochester arose he took it. And so began the next chapter of his life. He worked his way up to head coach of the Leafs farm team in Newmarket in 1986 and stayed in the coaching ranks until he was hired in the same capacity by Nashville toward the end of the 20th century.

GARE, Danny
b. Nelson, British Columbia, May 14, 1954
Toronto's Gus Bodnar scored 15 seconds into his first shift in his first game, the fastest goal by a rookie in NHL history. Every player gets a shot at this record, but you only get one crack at it, and it doesn't take long to slip by. Well, Gare came mighty close. He scored just 18 seconds in, a moment of great satisfaction for the 5'9", 175-pound right winger. Despite scoring 68 goals in 65 games in his final year of junior, that nefarious "too small" tag plagued him at the draft, but Buffalo took him in the second round and he was to reward the team many times over. He scored 31 goals that first season and the team went to the finals before losing to Philadelphia. In his second year, he scored 50 times, and in '79-'80 he led the league with 56. Gare played in consecutive All-Star Games (1980 and '81), but his five seasons in Detroit with a dismal team took their toll on his happiness, and his physical health and stamina weren't at the elite level any more. He announced his retirement, but then in the summer agreed to play with Iserlohn in the German league. After one exhibition game, though, he re-aggravated a bad groin injury and doctors advised him to retire. His decision to leave Germany was made easier because police had raided several teammates' houses in Germany and confiscated goods in a tax crackdown. While Gare was not personally affected, the actions certainly didn't leave him feeling warm and fuzzy about staying on. After returning home, he did colour commentary for Sabres games and entered the restaurant business.

GARIEPY, Ray ("Rockabye Ray")
b. Toronto, Ontario, September 4, 1928
The players were just a little faster in the NHL and played just a little harder than in the AHL. That explains why Gariepy didn't have quite the staying power in the big time. He was considered by many to be the hardest hitter in the game. Any forward coming down his side had better have his head up or he would level him in no uncertain terms. Yet despite an excellent career in the minors with Boston's and Toronto's affiliates, Gariepy played just 36 NHL games in the mid-1950s. His hitting took a toll on his own body – he was not a big man – and in 1958 he retired to work full-time as a salesman with a concrete firm for which he had worked summers during his playing days. He returned to Toronto, played a little Senior hockey, and went on to coach Barrie for a short time.

GARLAND, Scott
b. Regina, Saskatchewan, May 16, 1952
d. Montreal, Quebec, June 9, 1979
Garland was always getting hurt. One time, he fell into

Dave Gardner

George Gardner

Paul Gardner

Denny Gare

Ray Gariepy

Rob Garner

the boards and broke his nose. Another time, a heavy Larry Robinson check broke his wrist. He broke a collarbone in practice. He cut the back of his hand while trying to break up a fight in a Toronto tavern. He had always been injury prone, but his desire to play in the NHL was greater than any dent in his body could curb. He made it, with the Leafs and Los Angeles, but one summer he blew a tire while driving on a Montreal highway, spun out of control, and struck a wall. He died instantly.

GARNER, Rob
b. Weston, Ontario, August 17, 1958
Garner graduated from the Marlies and played only a few years of professional hockey. Pittsburgh thought well enough to draft him in 1978 and well enough to put him in one game four years later, but not well enough to use him even a second time.

GARNER, Tyrone
b. Stoney Creek, Ontario, July 27, 1978
Garner was a bright prospect for Calgary not too long ago, and although he has played only briefly in the league, he is still too young to be dismissed just yet. On the downside, his only NHL games to date, with the Flames, came in the '98-'99 season.

Mathieu Garon

GARON, Mathieu
b. Chandler, Quebec, January 9, 1978
Although Garon has played a few games in goal for Montreal over the last couple of years, his career opportunities with the Habs were severely restricted in the latter half of the 2001-02 season when Jose Theodore emerged as Montreal's goalie of the future. Garon's prospects now seem to be either backup tender in Montreal or, if he wants to be number one, full-time employment elsewhere.

GARPENLOV, Johan
b. Stockholm, Sweden, March 21, 1968
Garpenlov was front and centre in a significant dispute between the NHL and club teams in Europe. The year was 1990, not that long ago, but a time still when Europeans were not commonly drafted and signed to play right away in the NHL. Case in point, Garpenlov, who signed with the Red Wings that summer but almost wasn't allowed to come to camp in September because the Wings had yet to pay his club team, Djurgarden, the appropriate transfer fees. In fact, they had, but the money had to go through the NHL head offices, and that led to a dispute over just how many Swedes could sign with the NHL. President John Ziegler had said a year previous that that number could be as high as the teams wanted, outraging Swedish elite teams that feared, rightly, mass migration to North America. Garpenlov had just helped Sweden win a silver medal at the World Championships, and he later played at the 1991 Canada Cup and 1996 World Cup for Tre Kronor. The Red Wings traded him to San Jose in 1992, and there he got to realize a dream. He had admired the famed KLM line of Krutov-Larionov-Makarov as a boy, and with the Sharks he played on the famed OV line with Larionov and Makarov. He later played for Florida and Atlanta before returning to Sweden at the end of his career.

GARRETT, Dudley "Red"
b. Toronto, Ontario, July 24, 1924
d. At sea, near Newfoundland, November 25, 1944
Garrett was a much-respected defenceman raised in Toronto between the wars. He played hockey locally and was owned by the Leafs. On November 27, 1942, he and Hank Goldup were traded to the Rangers for Babe Pratt, a move that benefited the Leafs immensely insofar as Pratt scored the Cup-winning goal in 1945. Garrett played half the year with the Rangers, spent the other half in the minors, and then enlisted in the navy. His life came to an end during an escort run off the coast of Newfoundland in late 1944. Five years later, the American Hockey League introduced the Dudley "Red" Garrett Memorial Trophy, to be awarded annually to the league's most valuable player. The first winner was Terry Sawchuk.

GARRETT, John ("Chi Chi"/ "Cheech")
b. Trenton, Ontario, June 17, 1951
He had a car and Wayne Gretzky took it away. Garrett was traded from Quebec to Vancouver only days before the 1983 All-Star Game, at which the other Canucks goalie, Richard Brodeur, was set to play. But King Richard got injured and Garrett was named to replace him. He was playing well and looked certain to be the game's MVP, for which the traditional award was a car. Unfortunately, teammate Wayne Gretzky scored four goals in the third period and voters had to re-cast their ballots, scratching out Garrett and writing in number 99. Garrett had played his first six years of pro in the WHA and he remained with Hartford when the team joined the NHL. His first two years with the Whalers, though, were the only two he was an NHL regular. After retiring, he turned to broadcasting, like many of his masked brethren, a job he continues to this day.

GARTNER, Mike ("Garts")
b. Ottawa, Ontario, October 29, 1959
There were a few raised eyebrows, a few whispers, and nuanced words of doubt when Gartner was inducted into the Hockey Hall of Fame in 2001, yet surely his achievements are qualifications beyond reproach. Some pointed to the fact that he played 1,432 regular-season games without coming close to winning a Stanley Cup, yet every generation has had a few Hall of Famers – Marcel Dionne, for instance – who fall into that unfortunate category. Some criticized his 708 career goals, saying they came mostly during an era of tremendous offence that skewed his accomplishments vis-à-vis previous generations. Perhaps that's true, but then why are there not twenty or thirty 700-goal scorers from Gartner's era? Some point to the fact that he never won an individual trophy or led the league in scoring even once. True again, but then he also scored at least 30 goals in a season for 15 consecutive seasons, something players named Gretzky and Howe never managed to do. He also played in the 1984 and '87 Canada Cups, so for at least that 3-year period he was considered among Canada's finest 20 players. The truth is, Gartner, like all other Hall of Famers, was great in his own way. He wasn't perfect, but he made a tremendous contribution to the game that only a few

Dudley Garrett

John Garrett

men can rival. He played for Canada at the 1978 World Juniors and turned pro at age 19 with Cincinnati of the WHA. The next year he joined Washington and scored 36 goals with a weak Caps team. The year after he had 48 goals, and in each of his 10 years with the team he just scored and scored at a high and consistent rate. He peaked in '84–'85 when he came off the Canada Cup win to score 50 goals and 102 points, the only time in his career he reached those milestones. Gartner was traded to Minnesota and then on to the Rangers, but he was traded to Toronto at the deadline in 1994, just before the Rangers won the Cup. He finished his career in Phoenix in 1998, by which time he had joined Gretzky, Howe, Dionne, and Esposito as the only 700-goal scorers. It doesn't matter how you get to that number or in what era, it's a remarkable accomplishment. Gartner was a pure right winger who had a great shot, terrific release, and superb instincts around the net. He was also a clean and gentlemanly player, and was active in the workings of the Players' Association, notably as its president during his playing days. When he retired, he became director of business relations for the NHLPA and became central to the PA's distribution of hockey equipment worldwide to needy kids and organizations. A devout Christian, he went into business with another former Leafs player, Wes Jarvis, forming a company called National Training Rinks. It built rinks that were smaller than normal so kids could play on sheets proportionate to their size. He has also watched his son, Josh, develop into an NHL prospect.

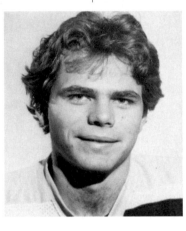

He scored at least 30 goals in a season for 15 consecutive seasons.
MIKE GARTNER

GASSOFF, Bob
b. Quesnel, British Columbia, April 17, 1953
d. Villa Ridge, Missouri, May 29, 1977
The eldest member of the Gassoff Gang died on a motorcycle while climbing a hill when he was hit head-on by a car going the other way. St. Louis teammate Garry Unger had invited some players, wives, and friends to a barbecue at his ranch, and had loaned some of the guys motorcycles he had been given after making a commercial. No alcohol was involved, but Gassoff didn't see the car and died instantly. His number 3 was retired by the team that fall, and the Blues donated a trophy in his name to the CHL to be given to the most improved defenceman each season. Gassoff's widow, though, filed a $3-million suit against Unger, his wife, and the car's driver. Bob was the eldest of four hockey-playing brothers. Brad also made the NHL, Ken played in the Central league, and Gary played junior. Bob had finished his fourth year with St. Louis when he died.

GASSOFF, Brad
b. Quesnel, British Columbia, November 13, 1955
One of the difficulties of being a younger brother is that you frequently have to answer for your older brother's errors. Brad went through junior having to fight guys who were mad at older bro, Bob, but this, in turn, taught him some toughness. Indeed, this Gassoff was scorer and fighter both, though his career was short lived outside the CHL. Four times he was given a chance by Vancouver, and four times he wound up in the Central league. After the first season, he was named rookie of the year, but the bloom was quickly off the rose and he didn't play for long after the Canucks gave up on him.

GATHERUM, Dave
b. Fort William, Ontario, March 28, 1932

It all started on October 10, 1953. Detroit's goalie Terry Sawchuk suffered a nasty gash on his knee in a game against Montreal. He couldn't play the next night, nor could Detroit's number-two man, Glenn Hall, who was playing in Edmonton. Here it was, 11 p.m., and Detroit had no goalie for the game in Toronto the next night. Fortunately, Jake Forbes, coach at Sherbrooke, was at the Detroit-Montreal game. Unfortunately, the man he had to get a message to – Gatherum – had gone to bed for the night and had no telephone in his apartment. Forbes got Tod Campeau and Moe Irving, two of Gatherum's teammates in Sherbrooke, to track the sleeping tender down. They then had to get the trainer to go to the rink to gather Gatherum's equipment, and then had to wait for the Wings' scout to drive from Montreal to Sherbrooke so they could get to Dorval airport in Montreal for a flight to Toronto! Then Gatherum had to play his first-ever NHL game that night. Guess what? He earned a shutout. A few nights later, he had a shutout going into the third period, and ditto for game three of his NHL life. By then, Sawchuk had recovered and Gatherum was back in the minors, never to see the NHL again.

GATZOS, Steve
b. Toronto, Ontario, June 22, 1961
Gatzos injured his ankle in his second season with Pittsburgh in '82-'83, but that was nothing compared to an injury he suffered after a Rick Green check in which his chest collapsed. Doctors couldn't support the chest with pins because they would have been to close to his heart, so his recovery was slow. He never made it back with the Penguins in anything other than a temporary capacity, but he went on to play in Europe and then turned to coaching in the East Coast league.

Bob Gassoff

Brad Gassoff

Steve Gatzos

Armand Gaudreault

GAUDREAU, Rob
b. Lincoln, Rhode Island, January 20, 1970
In only his second career NHL game, with San Jose in '92-'93, Gaudreau registered a hat trick. He went on to score 23 goals, but the team was bad and the next year no better and Gaudreau wanted out. He got his wish when Ottawa claimed him in the Waiver Draft in 1995, but he fared no better in Ottawa. Gaudreau had been an outstanding player at Providence College, a finalist for the Hobey Baker Award, a member of the U.S.'s 1990 World Juniors team, and a two-time All-Star Team member.

GAUDREAULT, Armand
b. Lac St. Jean, Quebec, July 14, 1921
d. St.-Aime-des-Lacs, Quebec, January 18, 2001
A wartime left winger with Boston in '44-'45, Gaudreault was in the minors the year after with Hershey before returning to Quebec to play for the Senior Aces, the team he had been with prior to his NHL plunge, and the team with which he spent virtually his entire professional career.

Leo Gaudreault

GAUDREAULT, Leo
b. Chicoutimi, Quebec, October 19, 1902
d. Montreal, Quebec, March 21, 1950
While Gaudreault played all his NHL games with the Canadiens in the late 1920s and early 1930s, the majority of his pro career came with Providence in the Can-Am League, the precursor to the AHL.

GAUL, Mike
b. Lachine, Quebec, April 22, 1973
Gaul might well have been a one-game wonder, having played for Colorado in '98-'99 after five years of bouncing around minor pro leagues of every stripe and description. His return to the NHL was not imminent, but he continued to ply his trade elsewhere until the expansion Columbus Blue Jackets inserted him in the lineup on two occasions in 2000-01. He played in Switzerland in 2002-03.

Mike Gaul

GAULIN, Jean-Marc
b. Balve, Germany, March 3, 1962
Gaulin may have been born in Germany but he was brought up in Quebec, where he played junior hockey, including with the Canadian National Team at the 1981 World Junior Championships. He scored 50 goals in his final year with Sorel, and this ensured being drafted by the Nordiques. Gaulin played most of the next few years in the minors, and his brief forays to the NHL team weren't enough to keep him there. He wound up playing in France for the better part of a decade before retiring.

Jean-Marc Gaulin

GAUME, Dallas
b. Innisfail, Alberta, August 27, 1963
An excellent student in business management at the University of Denver, Gaume graduated in 1986 before signing as a free agent with Hartford. He played only four games with the Whalers, but rather than toil endlessly in the minors he soon after accepted an offer to play in Norway. He stayed for nine years, with the '92-'93 season an exception because of a serious knee injury, from which he recovered fully.

Fern Gauthier

GAUTHIER, Albert "Art"
b. Espanola, Ontario, October 10, 1904
d. unknown
Over and above his 13 games with the Canadiens in '26-'27, Gauthier played minor pro for a few short years before retiring. Additionally, he appeared in one playoff game for the Habs, on March 29, 1927, a 1-1 tie with the Montreal Maroons.

GAUTHIER, Daniel
b. Charlemagne, Quebec, May 17, 1970
Good hands, good size, weak wheels. That was the Coke-and-popcorn scouting report on Gauthier, drafted 63rd overall in 1988 by Pittsburgh. The Pens abandoned him, though, and it was with Chicago that he played his only NHL games, in '94-'95. Since then, he has played primarily in Europe.

GAUTHIER, Denis
b. Montreal, Quebec, October 1, 1976
Gauthier is a tough, defensive defenceman with Calgary, a first-round draft choice who won a gold medal with Canada at the 1996 World Juniors. His upside is his size and mobility; his downside is his health. Injuries have taken a toll on him every season, but, of course, to play less physically would mean for him to play less effectively. He is a key to Calgary's rebirth, if it is to occur.

GAUTHIER, Fern
b. Chicoutimi, Quebec, August 31, 1919
d. November 7, 1992
Gauthier played for three teams in as many years before settling in with the last of those, Detroit, for a brief time in the 1940s. He played the right wing and had some scoring ability, but anyone not named Howe or Lindsay who played for Jack Adams also played plenty in Indianapolis, and Gauthier was no exception. For every game he played at the Olympia, he played another with the Capitols.

GAUTHIER, Jean
b. Montreal, Quebec, April 29, 1937
In a pro career that lasted some 17 seasons, Gauthier saw it all. He saw the minors, the Original Six, expansion, the Stanley Cup, and the WHA. He went from First Team All-Star in the EPHL in '61-'62 to Cup celebrations with the Habs in '65 to the Flyers in their first year of existence ('67-'68). Most of his NHL games came with the Habs, but during his time with the club he played far more frequently elsewhere in their organization. In 1973, he abandoned the WHA for the AHL to play his final season. He even got to play 11 games with Bobby Orr and the Bruins in '68-'69.

GAUTHIER, Luc
b. Longueuil, Quebec, April 19, 1964
Anyone of a certain vintage who says he played for Sherbrooke or Fredericton can mean only one thing: He was in the Montreal system and never made an NHL impact. Gauthier played three games with the Habs in '90-'91, but he spent the rest of his career happily slugging it out with bruisers in the AHL. When the opportunity to become an assistant coach came up, he

took the chance and learned the trade until 1997, when he took another offer, this time to scout for Nashville.

GAUTHIER, Paul
b. Winnipeg, Manitoba, March 6, 1915
After playing three seasons with the same junior team, the Winnipeg Monarchs, goalie Gauthier embarked on a career that took him to what seemed like every hockey city on the continent. A rough count suggests he played for 15 different teams in a 13-year period, none more frenetic than the '46-'47 season. That year, he played for Houston, Philadelphia, Buffalo, and San Francisco, spanning 3 leagues and only 25 games. His lone NHL stop was with the Habs on January 13, 1938, a 2-2 overtime tie.

GAUTHIER, Sean
b. Sudbury, Ontario, March 28, 1971
He has his own fan club and a split hockey personality, one for summer, one winter. In the winter, he played but a single game with San Jose in '98-'99, a total of three minutes at the end of a game from which Steve Shields had been pulled. Besides that, he has played a decade and more in the minors. In the summer, he tends goal in roller hockey, with Los Angeles and later Sacramento. He also played for Team Canada at the 1997 IIHF championships with Glen Metropolit, another transplanted NHLer.

GAUVREAU, Jocelyn
b. Masham, Quebec, March 4, 1964
On August 30, 1979, Montreal acquired star goalie Denis Herron from Pittsburgh with a second-round draft choice in 1982 for Pat Hughes and Robbie Holland. And with that 1982 draft choice Montreal took 18-year-old Gauvreau 31st overall. Herron had three good years in Montreal, but Gauvreau didn't have even three games with the club.

GAVEY, Aaron ("Gavs")
b. Sudbury, Ontario, February 22, 1974
Gavey has been all over the proverbial map, from Tampa to Calgary to Dallas to Minnesota. He played for Canada in 1994 when the country won gold at the WJC, but it wasn't until he got to the Wild in 2000 that he played a full season in the NHL with no time in the minors. As a rookie, he suffered a 130-stitch cut when Michel Petit accidently stepped on his face.

GAVIN, Stew
b. Ottawa, Ontario, March 15, 1960
First, doctors told him to retire, then a year later they told him he didn't have to. Late in the '92-'93 season, playing with Dallas, he suffered a serious knee injury and retired at age 33. The Stars GM offered Gavin a job as a scout, and he gladly accepted. The following March, though, he had surgery to clean his knee up, and doctors told him everything looked remarkably good. Like a hockey Superman, Gavin tore off his suit and put on his sweater. The Leafs – the team that had drafted him in 1980 and for whom he had played the first five years of his career (before moving on to Hartford and Minnesota) – gave him a tryout at training camp in the fall of 1994. He didn't make it his second time, but he did go to the IHL, where he

played two seasons before packing it in for good. The comeback didn't result in NHL time, but it offered him peace of mind and answered the all-important "what if?" question that has haunted many an athlete.

GEALE, Bob
b. Edmonton, Alberta, April 17, 1962
Geale made the rounds in his day, but every stop was short and sweet, from junior to the AHL and on to Germany, with a single game with Pittsburgh daubed into the '84-'85 season for effect.

GEE, George
b. Stratford, Ontario, June 28, 1922
d. Wyandotte, Michigan, January 14, 1971
Gee put his career on hold to join the navy in 1943, and when he was discharged the excellent prospect found a home in Chicago. A centre, he played on a line with Red Hamill and Alex Kaleta for 3 years, scoring 20 goals in his second year. It was a trade to Detroit, though, that gave Gee his finest moments, notably in the 1950 finals against the Rangers. In overtime of game seven, Gee had a faceoff in the New York end. He motioned winger Pete Babando into position, won the draw, and watched Babando fire the puck past a screened Charlie Rayner in goal to give the Wings the Stanley Cup. Gee ended his career back in Chicago and then accepted an offer as playing manager of the Windsor Bulldogs, a position he held for three years. He passed away after suffering a heart attack while playing in an old-timers' game in rural Michigan.

GELDART, Gary
b. Moncton, New Brunswick, June 14, 1950
His name doesn't cry out with the same importance as Baz Bastien does for one generation or Bryan Berard for another, but Geldart had a fine career in its embryonic stage cut short by an eye injury. In his final year of junior, with London, he was named team MVP over other soon-to-be more prominent teammates Darryl Sittler, Daniel Bouchard, and Dan Maloney. He was drafted by Minnesota and played four games for the Stars in '70-'71, but he spent the next few seasons in the minors before suffering a serious eye injury midway through '73-'74. He came back briefly, but retired at age 27, early in '77-'78.

GELINAS, Martin
b. Shawinigan, Quebec, June 5, 1970
At 18, Gelinas was front and centre in the most significant trade in the history of the NHL. He and Jimmy Corson were the centrepiece in the deal that Los Angeles used to acquire Wayne Gretzky from the Oilers in the summer of 1988, just weeks after the Kings had drafted Gelinas 7th overall. He finished his junior career in Hull that season and played for Canada at the 1989 World Juniors, and the following season he was with the Oilers when they won their fifth Stanley Cup in seven years. Although Gelinas stayed with the team the next three seasons, he failed to become the player Oilers GM Glen Sather had hoped for. He was dealt to Quebec, but the Nordiques put him on waivers after only 31 games. Vancouver claimed him, and with something to prove he had the best stretch of his career. In '95-'96 and '96-'97, he had 30 and 35 goals, respectively, though after that

Sean Gauthier

Aaron Gavey

Stew Gavin

George Gee

Martin Gelinas

Jack Gelineau

the magic wore off and he was traded again, no longer the showcase but rather a more minor figure. Gelinas went to Carolina and, amazingly, played his 900th NHL game during his time there, the once young superstar now a seasoned veteran of middling ability.

GELINEAU, Jack
b. Toronto, Ontario, November 11, 1924
d. Montreal, Quebec, November 12, 1998
At the ripe old age of 20, Gelineau was a hero. He was awarded the British Empire Medal for bravery after he survived a plane crash and helped rescue a crewman. This was 1944. Nothing he would do after that could be so demanding. After his discharge, he attended McGill University, playing goal for the Redmen and earning his degree in commerce. He played a few games with Boston in '48-'49, and the next year played 67 of 70 games for the Bruins and won the Calder Trophy. The year after, he played every minute of every game for the B's, but he tended behind a weak team that decided to make changes that off-season. He ended his career with two games in the Chicago cage in '53-'54 and was later inducted into the McGill Sports Hall of Fame. He spent most of his life in Montreal, and went to work in the insurance business.

GENDRON, Jean-Guy
b. Montreal, Quebec, August 30, 1934

Jean-Guy Gendron

Jean-Guy Gendron and Wilf Homenuik were the first-round leaders of the Manufacturers Life Championship in 1987, an event on the Canadian Professional Golfers' Association seniors tour. Gendron didn't win the event, but he was doing what he wanted. He started off as a hockey player in the 1950s, and although his first three years, with the Rangers, read in the stats sheets 63, 70, and 70 games played, the reality was different. Gendron was one of the self-dubbed "frozen four" along with Harry Howell, Gerry Foley, and Parker MacDonald who sat at the end of the bench much of the time. He bounced around for the next few years, but his big break came with expansion and was delayed by golf. Philadelphia claimed him in 1967, but he showed up 10 days late for training camp because he was competing in a tournament at the Bic Club in Rimouski, where he had been pro 4 years. (Prior to this, he was an assistant at the Montreal Municipal Course.) He made the team full-time the next season, concentrating fully on hockey, and the French Line of Gendron, Simon Nolet, and Andre Lacroix kept the team competitive during those lean years. Gendron had 3 successive years of 20 goals (20, 23, 20), but as his career wound down he returned home and played for Quebec in the WHA for 2 years before coaching the team briefly. Then, it was a life of strictly golf.

GENDRON, Martin
b. Valleyfield, Quebec, February 15, 1974
The height of Gendron's career occurred in 1993 and '94 when he was still a teenager. In those glory years, he won consecutive gold medals with Canada at the WJC after being drafted by Washington in the NHL. A great career beckoned, though the reality was less starry. He did, indeed, play for Washington, but only briefly, and he has played regularly in the AHL ever since, scoring his fair share of goals from the right wing, but never earning a callup to the big time since the Blackhawks gave him two games in '97-'98.

GEOFFRION, Bernie ("Boom Boom")
b. Montreal, Quebec, February 16, 1931
When he was playing junior, Geoffrion was told by one of his coaches that he had no chance of getting to the NHL. It was exactly the kind of remark that spurred him on. He played for Laval and turned pro with Montreal in 1950. Although he was only 19 years old, he brought speed, a great shot, and a fiery, sometimes uncontrollable temper to the team. In his first full season, Geoffrion scored 30 goals and won the Calder Trophy, and for a short time became one of the more popular players. That was before 1955. Toward the end of the '54-'55 season, Maurice Richard was suspended for the rest of the season after assaulting an official. He and Geoffrion were neck-and-neck in the scoring race, and Richard's idleness allowed Geoffrion to win the Art Ross Trophy on the final day of the season by a single point. His hometown fans booed

Geoffrion married Marlene Morenz, the daughter of Howie and a champion figure skater in her own right.
BERNIE GEOFFRION

vociferously when he earned that 75th and deciding point on the year because their hero Richard was denied what would have been his only scoring championship. Geoffrion earned back the love of the fans in the coming years as he continued to be one of the top scorers in the league. Life was also made easier by the fact that Montreal won the Cup every year from 1950 to '60. Geoffrion also started to use the slapshot on a regular basis, the first player to do so. The result was a '60-'61 season in which he became the first player since Richard in '44-'45 to score 50 goals in a season, and when he did so received a standing ovation. In 1958, he nearly lost his life under common circumstances. During a practice, he collided with a teammate and a few seconds later collapsed. He was rushed to hospital and underwent emergency surgery for a ruptured bowel. Given last rites, he nevertheless made a full recovery. After that 50-goal season, Geoffrion had years of 23, 23, and 21 goals and then retired. He coached the Quebec Aces for two seasons, but poor business investments forced him out of retirement to make a few dollars. He signed with the Rangers because he had become upset with the Habs

Martin Gendron

for not hiring him, particularly as coach, the job he truly coveted. He had two mediocre years with the Blueshirts and retired for good, becoming the team's coach for '68-'69. He had to resign after half a season, though, when ulcers forced doctors to remove three-quarters of his stomach. In 1972, he was inducted into the Hockey Hall of Fame and joined Atlanta as coach for the better part of three years. In 1979, he was finally offered the job of head coach of the Habs, but again stomach problems forced his resignation after just 30 games. Geoffrion had married Marlene Morenz, the daughter of Howie and a champion figure skater in her own right. They produced a son, Danny, who played briefly in the NHL, and Bernie created a controversy in 2001 when he took back some 30 items he had donated to the Hockey Hall of Fame and put them up for auction. He justified the cash grab by saying he wanted the money to ensure the education of his eight grandchildren, though the historic loss to the Hall was great and significant nonetheless.

GEOFFRION, Danny
b. Montreal, Quebec, January 24, 1958
Boom Boom Jr. he wasn't. Pocket Boom Boom just didn't sound right. Montreal drafted Boom Boom's son 8th overall in 1978, a fitting tribute to the original, not the next of kin. Danny, in fact, spurned the Habs to sign a lucrative deal with the WHA – Quebec Nordiques, of course – and when he joined Montreal a year later, he went goalless in 32 games under coach papa. He had 20 goals the next season in Winnipeg, to whom he had been sold by the Habs, and although he wore his dad's number 5 there, he was not long for the NHL.

GERAN, Gerry
b. Holyoke, Massachusetts, August, 3 1896
d. September 1981
Geran had two stints in the NHL, separated by a year in the U.S. Army during the First World War. He played for the Montreal Wanderers during the team's only few games at the start of the inaugural NHL season in 1917-18, and eight years later he played for his hometown Boston Bruins.

GERARD, Eddie
b. Ottawa, Ontario, February 22, 1890
d. Ottawa, Ontario, August 7, 1937
In his early years, Gerard played many sports well, including baseball, cricket, and tennis. Primarily, though, he excelled at hockey in the winter and football in the summer and fall. He played in the backfield of the Ottawa Rough Riders from 1909 to '13 during which time he developed his hockey skills as well. He signed with the Senators as a forward in 1913 in the NHA. With the exception of one historic game, he played his entire career with the Sens. When the team joined the NHL in 1917, Gerard moved back to defence where he played with George Boucher. He developed great skill in taking a man off the puck with a solid hit or by steering him into the boards and moving the puck quickly up the ice on a counterattack. His last four years, 1919-23 were his finest. He won the Cup with the Sens in 1920, '21, and '23 with the "Super Six," a term used to describe that mini-dynasty. In '21-'22, the Sens had a rough season in that they finished first overall and then lost to Toronto in the NHL finals. The St. Pats then played the

Vancouver Millionaires for the championship, but when Toronto defenceman Harry Cameron was injured, the St. Pats were allowed to choose any easterner to replace him. They chose Gerard, and he played a pivotal role in their game-four victory, so much so that the Millionaires reused Gerard for game five. No matter, the tide had turned and the St. Pats won the deciding game 5-1. Gerard was honoured by the team at the start of the next season, wearing his Ottawa colours but receiving gifts from the St. Pats for his contributions to the Cup victory. That season, he won his fourth straight Cup. He retired and turned to coaching, working in the NHL from 1924 to '35 non-stop with the exception of the '29-'30 season. He led the Maroons to a Cup in '25-'26, his only great success as bench jockey. He had to resign as coach of the St. Louis Eagles in '34-'35, his asthmatic condition, which had plagued him all his adult life, becoming too restrictive. He retired to Ottawa where he worked as chief clerk of the Department of Geodetic Survey until his death, of throat cancer, in 1937. Gerard was a charter member of the Hockey Hall of Fame in 1945 and later inducted into the Canadian Sports Hall of Fame as well.

GERMAIN, Eric
b. Quebec City, Quebec, June 26, 1966
A minor-league defenceman, Germain graduated from Quebec junior in 1986 and went on to a long career in a variety of leagues and teams in North America, gracing an NHL arena five times, with Los Angeles, in 1987-88.

Danny Geoffrion

GERNANDER, Ken
b. Coleraine, Minnesota, June 30, 1969
The United States National Team was in a heap o' trouble after placing twelfth at the 1998 World Championships. It had to play a qualifying tournament that winter in Austria to be eligible for the "A" pool of the '99 WC, and one player enlisted for that three-game tournament was Gernander, who was playing for Hartford in the AHL. The team won and requalified for "A" pool, but Gernander didn't end up fielding NHL inquiries for his efforts. He was a grad of U of Minnesota and played his only games with the Rangers in the mid-1990s. Apart from those games he was a fixture in the American league. His twin brothers, Jim and Jerry, both played for U of Vermont, and his father, Bob, is the head of scouting for the Dallas Stars and has his name on the Stanley Cup for that team's 2000 victory.

Eddie Gerard

GETLIFFE, Ray ("Gabby")
b. Galt, Ontario, April 3, 1914
Art Ross gave up on Getliffe too soon, no doubt about it. The forward had just helped Boston win the Stanley Cup in 1939 in his third full season with the team, but Ross figured Getliffe's knees were done after both had had torn ligaments. Ross was wrong. In the pre-Maurice Richard days, Getliffe played briefly on a line with Elmer Lach and Joe Benoit and once had five goals and six points in a game against those very Bruins, in 1943. That '43-'44 season he had a career high 28 goals and led the Habs to the Cup. After one more season, he retired, though he continued to ref the odd game for the NHL, often Detroit-Toronto games to keep Jack Adams happy (Jolly Jack didn't like the other zebras available –

Ray Getliffe

Ed Giacomin

Mario Giallonardo

Barry Gibbs

Doug Gibson

Clancy, Chadwick, Gravel). Getliffe was also adept at golf and played in the Canadian Open in 1936. Two years later, he was Ontario amateur champion, and in 1969 was elected president of the RCGA. He settled in Montreal and worked for Leigh Textiles, working his way up to chairman of the board.

GIACOMIN, Ed ("Fort Eddie")
b. Sudbury, Ontario, June 6, 1939

History has shown that often the best way to kill a kid's NHL career is to tell him he's a sure superstar, and the best way to make it happen is to tell him he doesn't stand a chance. Giacomin falls into the latter camp. He played goal in Sudbury as a teen without drawing any notice, yet his desire to make it to the NHL was so great that he turned down scholarship offers for football and baseball from U.S. colleges. It looked for a while as though he had made an imprudent decision. One day, the kitchen stove blew up in front of him and Giacomin suffered serious burns to much of his lower body. He underwent extensive skin grafting and his legs were in bandages for a year. Doctors told him to forget about hockey and worry about living a healthy life; he countered by paying to play with an industrial team to build up his strength and develop his skills. He went to Detroit's training camp in 1958 but was assigned to Washington of the Eastern league as a replacement for his brother. He worked his way up to Providence, and over the next six years became one of the best AHL goalies. In 1965, he finally made the big time, with the Rangers. He and Cesare Maniago split the duties in goal, but after a shaky start he was sent to Baltimore for two weeks. Upon his return, he fell into the team's good graces when Maniago pulled himself from a game. Giacomin moved in – and never left. For the next nine years, he was the number-one man in net, leading the team out of last place and eventually into the Cup finals. In '66-'67, his first full year, he led the league in wins (30) and shutouts (9). In each of the next two years, he was tops in wins again, and each year the team made progress in the playoffs. He became a fan favourite not only for the wins but for his style. He liked to wander from his net, but sometimes didn't just clear the puck, instead skating with it and passing it to his forwards like a third defenceman. He and backup Gilles Villemure won the Vezina Trophy in '70-'71, and the next year Giacomin took the Rangers to the finals where they lost to the mighty Bruins. Early in the '75-'76 season, the Rangers decided they needed a change and put him on waivers. Detroit claimed him, and his first game with the Wings was at Madison Square Garden. In one of the most emotional nights of that rink, fans started chanting his name during the national anthem and didn't let up. When the Rangers scored on him, they skated by and apologized, though by the end of the night Detroit won the game. Early in the '77-'78 season, the Wings decided to go with the younger tandem of Jimmy Rutherford and Ron Low and cut Giacomin loose. He retired with 289 wins, 54 shutouts, and 6 All-Star Game appearances. He remained in Detroit where he ran his own sports bar, though he was upset when Fred Shero was hired as Rangers coach in 1978 after he believed he had been promised the job. Giacomin worked as an assistant with the Islanders and Wings and later as a goaltending coach and scout. He

was inducted into the Hockey Hall of Fame in 1987 when, ironically, the official ceremonies were held for the first and only time in Detroit.

GIALLONARDO, Mario
b. Toronto, Ontario, September 23, 1957

The defenceman's few NHL games came with the lowly Colorado Rockies (1979-81), and his minor-league career was equally brief.

GIBBS, Barry
b. Lloydminster, Saskatchewan, September 28, 1948

For a guy as tough and as frequently hurt as Gibbs, it's amazing he lasted 13 years and 797 games in the NHL. Once, with Minnesota, he broke his jaw and had it wired shut for six weeks. He missed three games. Another time, he played half a season with a broken wrist without even knowing it. Not gifted offensively, the d-man had a career night on New Year's Eve 1975 when he had a hat trick and was a perfect +8 in an 8-1 Atlanta win over the Rangers. That was the season Flames GM Cliff Fletcher called Gibbs one of the 10 best defencemen in the league. Hyperbole, perhaps, but Fletcher was not alone in this belief. Gibbs had been the 1st overall selection at the nascent draft, in 1966 after starring with the Estevan Bruins, and he was named the Central league's best blueliner in '68-'69.

GIBSON, Don
b. Deloraine, Manitoba, December 29, 1967

An oversized defenceman, Gibson had two clear periods of his career broken up neatly by a 14-game stint in the NHL with Vancouver: his 4 years with the Spartans at Michigan State, and his 5 years with the Milwaukee Admirals in the "I." He piled up the penalty minutes and developed a reputation, but he didn't make enough of an impact as a player to hang in there very long.

GIBSON, Doug
b. Peterborough, Ontario, September 28, 1953

He may have been an MVP in the AHL, but he was a Yucker on Boston. Gibson was only the fourth player ever to be named MVP, with Rochester, but on the Bruins, he was one of the Black Aces who practised a bunch but rarely played. They were called Black Aces by Eddie Shore, but the team called those guys Yuckers. Gibson later played in Europe, but he had already made his mark, quickly in the NHL and more substantially in the American league.

GIBSON, John
b. St. Catharines, Ontario, June 2, 1959

There was talent and there was hooliganism, and if a team could have worked the two in together some way, Gibson might have stuck around longer. He played hard enough in junior that the Winnipeg GM signed Gibson to a 10-game tryout contract in '78-'79 with the WHA team. There was the time he got into a fight with Paul Holmgren, Flyers goon, and beat him up so badly the owner of his team, the L.A. Kings, gave him a television set by way of saying good job. There were 3 NHL stints in all, and a 10-game suspension in junior for allegedly kicking a player while he lay prone on the ice. There was the honour of being named best defenceman in the IHL, and there was being cut from

Niagara Falls in junior because his coach, Bert Templeton, said he had a bad attitude. This from a bench boss who advocated fighting and goonery as much as anyone in the game's history.

GIESEBRECHT, Roy "Gus"
b. Petawawa, Ontario, September 16, 1918
Hockey was this family's game. Roy was the oldest of five hockey-playing boys, four of whom played at a high level – Jackie, Bert, and Bruce in the USHL, and Fred. Dick, the other brother, became involved in hockey management. Gus had a son, Donnie, who later played pro, and Donnie's son, Matt, played junior in Ottawa in the 1980s. Gus was the only one, though, to make it to the NHL. He played four seasons with Detroit (1938-42), and his wartime enlistment spelled the end of his pro career. For four years he was overseas, and when he came home he returned to Petawawa, where he worked full-time in the family's paper products wholesale business and the Pepsi-Cola bottling plant.

GIFFIN, Lee
b. Chatham, Ontario, April 1, 1967
He made his NHL debut at 19, and was out of the league forever at 20. It's a cruel world sometimes. Giffin got his chance, of course, because he was a high draft choice by Pittsburgh in 1985. Naturally, the Pens wanted to see him give the pros a shot. Over two years, though, the right winger scored only once. That meant he'd have to go to the minors and earn the rest of his NHL games. The bloom was off the rose. In truth, he never even played in the AHL, only the "I" and leagues lower, where the chances for recall were anywhere from, well, minor to never. In Giffin's case, it turned out to be never.

GIGUERE, Jean-Sebastien ("Jiggy")
b. Montreal, Quebec, May 16, 1977
Giguere has worked his way up through the ranks from junior goalie of promise to NHL regular, from the Quebec league to the Ducks. He started his pro time in 1996 as a 19-year-old, but it wasn't until 2000 when he reached Anaheim that he got a chance to play nightly. When the Ducks failed to make the playoffs in the springs of 2001 and '02, he was invited to join Team Canada at the World Championships. The first time he observed and didn't play; the second time he split goaltending duties with Marty Turco and was outstanding. As a kid, he adored Patrick Roy, and as a pro he had Francois Allaire as a goalie coach, the same man who tutored Roy at a young age.

GILBERT, Ed
b. Hamilton, Ontario, March 12, 1952
After playing junior with his hometown Red Wings, Gilbert was drafted by Montreal in 1972 and assigned to the Canadiens' AHL affiliate in Nova Scotia. In two years, he was never called up by the Habs, and Kansas City claimed him in the Expansion Draft. He was in the lineup for every game of that inaugural '74-'75 season, and although he scored 16 goals he was also a -49 on the year. Midway through the following season, he was traded to Pittsburgh where he played his final NHL games, though he later played in the minors and briefly in the WHA before retiring.

GILBERT, Gilles
b. St. Esprit, Quebec, March 31, 1949
It was called the Gunk, a debilitating and mysterious rash that often covered the entire body, and those who suffered from it couldn't play with it. They had to retire. Tom Reid suffered from it, and so, too, did Gilbert. The Gunk made him retire, which is ironic because as a kid he was a skater, not a goalie. But he idolized the men with the pads, notably Glenn Hall and Terry Sawchuk. Then there was the matter that his dad (one of 24 children!) and brother had played pro as goalies. There was nothing for him but to move into the crease. He started in the NHL with Minnesota in '69-'70, and in one game the following year he surrendered Jean Béliveau's 500th goal. Although Gilbert played well whenever he was given the chance, it was clear that North Stars coach Wren Blair was not going to play him regularly over Gump Worsley and Cesare Maniago. Blair traded him to Boston, home of Bobby Orr. Gilbert had his finest years there, twice winning 30 games and playing upwards of 55 games a season. In the 1974 playoffs, he set a record for goalies by being credited with three assists. Then in 1982, the Gunk hit him hard. Its catalyst was sweat, but no trainer or doctor could figure out any more than that. Tom Reid, Jacques Lemaire, Guy Lapointe, and even Phil Esposito and Gordie Howe suffered from it. With Gilbert, it was a particularly painful strain, and he had to retire. He later worked as a promotions director for the NHL at Rendez-vous '87 in Quebec City. He also worked as a player agent and as a rep for a confection company in Montreal.

GILBERT, Greg
b. Mississauga, Ontario, January 22, 1962
Gilbert's introduction to the NHL could not have been more dreamlike. It came on December 15, 1981, as a member of the New York Islanders. He was playing with the Marlies that season and got a call from the team because he was an available left winger. Two regulars – Anders Kallur and Bob Bourne – were injured, and Gilbert was the replacement. That night, he scored a goal. He returned to the Marlies the next day, but rejoined the Islanders for the playoffs, when they won the Cup again. He made the team the following training camp more or less full-time. After winning his second Cup in 1983, he exploded for 31 goals the year after. Mysteriously, it was a year he never came close to repeating during the rest of his career. Many years later, though, he was on the Rangers when they won the Cup in '94, and two years later he retired. Gilbert became a coach in the AHL, with Worcester, and then an assistant with the NHL Calgary Flames. In the summer of 2001, he was named the team's head coach during a season that started magnificently and ended with the team out of the playoffs again.

GILBERT, Jeannot "Jean"
b. Grande Baie, Quebec, December 29, 1940
No player in his right mind would ever get upset about being called up to the NHL from the farm, but if ever such a thing could happen, Gilbert might be the guy. In '62-'63, he was a rookie in the EPHL with Kingston, and as the season wound down he was leading the league in scoring. Well, he was owned by Boston, and as

Roy Giesebrecht

Lee Giffin

Jean-Sebastien Giguere

Gilles Gilbert

Jeannot Gilbert

the Bruins' season wound down, they were out of the playoffs and decided to give Gilbert a look-see. He came up for five games, and during that time lost the scoring title in the lesser league. Boston took another look a couple of years later, but beyond that Gilbert was in the minors for nearly a decade before signing with Quebec in the WHA for two seasons. He was the MVP in the CPHL and won the scoring title in the AHL '68-'69.

GILBERT, Rodrigue "Rod"
b. Montreal, Quebec, July 1, 1941

Every kid plays junior in the hopes that one day the coach will come over and tell him about the phone call – the big team wants to take a look at you; you leave tomorrow. When this happened to Gilbert at the end of the '59-'60 OHA season, his life changed forever. In the final game in Guelph, he

Stan Gilbertson

slipped on some debris thrown onto the ice and fell awkwardly into the boards. He broke the fifth vertebra in his back, and to repair the damages doctors removed a small bone from his left leg and used it to fuse the fourth, fifth, and sixth vertebrae. Horrible consequences ensued. The leg developed blood clots, and doctors worried they'd have to amputate, but within a couple of weeks the natural healing began and the leg was okay. Time, though, would prove that his back was anything but. Gilbert made his NHL debut on November 27, 1960, assisting on Dean Prentice's goal that gave the Rangers a 3-3 tie with Chicago. He went back to the minors, was called up again briefly at the end of the '61-'62 season, and made the team as a regular that fall. Gilbert earned his stripes as a relentless player with an exceptional shot and a fearless confidence when going into the corners. He had 24 and 25 goals in his second and third seasons and was proving to be one of the team's best young players. But that bone-fusing didn't last long. Prior to '65-'66, that vertebra needed more surgery, so for the year Gilbert wore a special corset to get through the season and endure the pain. But the corset affected his breathing, which affected his play, and midway through the year he couldn't take it any more. He underwent season-ending surgery. He rebounded to have three more strong years, and then in '70-'71 he joined forces with Jean Ratelle and Vic Hadfield on the GAG Line (Goal-A-Game Line). The line peaked in '71-'72 when, for the first time, all 3 members of a line scored 40 goals. Gilbert had 43, and the team went to the Stanley Cup finals before losing to Boston. That fall, Gilbert played for Team Canada at the Summit Series, and in the following five years he had at least 75 points each time out. On March 24, 1974, he became the first Rangers player to score 300 goals, and 2 years later he

On March 24, 1974, he became the first Rangers player to score 300 goals.
ROD GILBERT

won the Bill Masterton Award in recognition of his career-long battle with his back. He also played for Canada at the 1977 World Championships, the first involving the NHL, but before the new season he and GM John Ferguson were locked in a contract fight that delayed the start of his season. When he did get going, he felt flat, and retired just 19 games later. By this time, he had played 1,000 games and scored his 1,000th point, both Rangers records (as was his 406 career goals). He remained with the Rangers for two years, worked in TV, and was known on the Manhattan landscape for his bar/restaurant, Cafe de Sports. He was inducted into the Hockey Hall of Fame in 1982, and in 1991 was given the Lester Patrick Award. Gilbert later served as the Rangers' director of community relations. He also worked as a Wall Street stockbroker.

GILBERTSON, Stan
b. Duluth, Minnesota, October 29, 1944

Gilbertson played in three Memorial Cups in the 1960s, but unlike many a minor pro veteran his big break did not come in 1967 with expansion. He had to wait a little longer to play, with California in 1971, to be precise. A decent left winger and one of the few Americans in the game, he suffered an awful off-ice injury during training camp in 1977 with Pittsburgh. He was driving a friend's jeep when he took a sharp turn only to find a car coming straight at him. He swerved, and the jeep rolled over on a bridge, half hanging over the side upside down. He got free and fell to the ground, but his right leg was mangled. It was amputated below the knee and later had to be cut above the knee. After 10 weeks in the hospital, he was free to go, but he would never play hockey again. He moved to California, became a real estate agent, and coached a seniors team from San Jose. He was, quite simply, happy to be alive.

GILCHRIST, Brent
b. Moose Jaw, Saskatchewan, April 3, 1967

Gilchrist is the prototypical role player, a left winger who can score a bit, hit a bit, and check well. He won't win a game on his own, but without a guy like him no team can win the Stanley Cup. Gilchrist won that trophy with Detroit in 1998, but it was a number of years in the making. He started with Montreal in 1988, but just before the Habs won their surprise Cup of 1993 he was traded to Edmonton and then to Minnesota. He followed the team to Texas, but the Wings signed him in 1997 as a free agent. However, Gilchrist missed much of 1998-2000 when he suffered a serious groin injury and then had hernia surgery and a follow-up procedure, but he came back strong in 2000-01 to reclaim his spot on the roster.

Brent Gilchrist

GILES, Curt

b. The Pas, Manitoba, November 30, 1958

Giles was just 16 years old when he played at the University of Minnesota-Duluth, and over the next 14 years he played most of the time with the North Stars. He had a brief stint with the Rangers after requesting a trade because of lack of playing time, but Minnesota reacquired him and he continued to do what he did best – dole out terrific hip checks. He was slowed down briefly in early 1986 when the tip of his left ring finger was amputated because of a benign tumour near that knuckle. Two weeks later, he was playing again, pain free. Toward the end of his career, he played for Canada at the 1992 Olympics, winning silver in Albertville.

GILHEN, Randy

b. Zweibrucken, West Germany, June 13, 1963

In one stretch, 1990-94, Gilhen played for six teams. Over his career, which lasted some 16 pro seasons, he travelled more than he stayed put, though some team always grabbed him when the opportunity arose. Although he was born overseas, he grew up out west and returned there, to Winnipeg, to close out his career.

GILL, Andre

b. Sorel, Quebec, September 19, 1941

Everywhere he played he was called the tiny goalie, the guy who looked small, like a kid. Then they watched him play – coaches, scouts, fans – and they called him a pro and a star. And yet, he got only five NHL games with Boston in '67-'68, even though he had a shutout in his first game. Then it was back to the minors, filling in, taking over as number one, and playing phenomenal goal. The rap on him was that he was too small, oft heard for a skater, odd for a goaler.

GILL, Harold "Hal" ("Skills")

b. Concord, Massachusetts, April 6, 1975

Here's a sign of the times: Gill is 6'7" and 240 pounds, and he's not the biggest player in the NHL. Close, though. He's a giant of a defenceman renowned for his devastating and clean hit on Eric Lindros that caused one in a series of concussions for the Big E. That's what Gill does best – hit. Hit hard, and hit often. He was an excellent quarterback in high school, but Boston drafted him before he had played a game even at the college level. He has been with the Bruins ever since, not in the tradition of Orr and Bourque, but in a tradition all his own.

GILL, Todd ("Giller")

b. Cardinal, Ontario, November 9, 1965

He was drafted by Toronto in 1984 when the Leafs didn't have much of a scouting team and they were at the height of Ballardian disarray. For many years Gill was an awful defenceman, but, in his own defence, he had no one to show him what to do as a kid entering the league. Then Pat Burns became coach of the Leafs nearly a decade later, and Gill went from being a minus player to a plus player, a solid rock in his own end with some offensive flair on occasion. Then he was traded to San Jose, and the old Gill manifested itself too often. By this time, though, Gill was a veteran, not a rookie, and as such he was a commodity for his years played as much as anything. A string of teams signed him

because of this, and he bounced around and played for past Cup winners or Cup contenders, though he missed the mark ever so slightly each time he came close to the mug. In 2002-03, his career seemingly over, he went to the minors and late in the season was recalled by Chicago, his seventh NHL team. The joy was short-lived, though, as he was demoted after three games, including his 1,000th.

GILLEN, Don

b. Dodsland, Saskatchewan, December 24, 1960

Gillen made his NHL debut in January 1980. One night he was with his junior team in Brandon; the next he was playing on a line with Bobby Clarke in Philadelphia. The Flyers were trailing 3-2 to Edmonton when Gillen scored to ignite a comeback victory, and then he went back to junior to finish the season. As bonus for his NHL performance, the Flyers asked him to play for the farm team in Maine during the playoffs. Fast forward two years: Philly traded Gillen to Hartford, and in 34 games that '81-'82 season he equalled his previous 1-game output with but a single goal.

GILLIE, Farrand

b. Cornwall, Ontario, May 11, 1905
d. unknown

Gillie played a lone game with Detroit in 1928-29 when the team went by the moniker Cougars in their pre-Red Wings days. He spent a number of years in the IHL after that and then returned to Cornwall to play and work outside hockey.

GILLIES, Clark ("Jethro")

b. Moose Jaw, Saskatchewan, April 7, 1954

Gillies had both size and skill. He had 6 seasons of 33 goals or more with the Islanders during their greatest years, but he could also hit and, if need be, fight. He hated the fighting, though, and that's why the mantra of don't wake him up was always good to follow, because he didn't come by mean streak naturally. Rather, it was his means of survival. Gillies became team captain in the mid-1970s, but the pressure proved too great for him to play his best, and the year he resigned his captaincy the team won its first of four Stanley Cups in a row. He made hockey history during the 1977 playoffs when he scored four game-winning goals in as many games, and he was later named MVP of Team NHL at the 1979 Challenge Cup. He also played for Canada in the 1981 Canada Cup. Like any mere mortal, he got old, and in his last 4 full seasons he had no more than 15 goals. The Isles let him go to Buffalo ignominiously, in the Waiver Draft, and Gillies retired early in '87–'88 after injuring a knee that had long given him trouble. He became involved in the securities industry and later opened his own business on Long Island, where fans still remembered the gentle giant. The Hockey Hall of Fame put the crown of achievement on his head when it inducted him in 2002, declaring, in so doing, that he was among the greatest players ever to appear in the NHL.

GILLIS, Jere

b. Bend, Oregon, January 18, 1957

Rena Wuertle came from Montreal. She was a champion skier in the 1950s, and when she married a

Andre Gill

Hal Gill

Todd Gill

Clark Gillies

Jere Gillis

man from out west, they settled just outside Portland, Oregon. She had four children with Gene Gillis, a skier with the U.S. national team, but the couple divorced and Rena took the kids back to Montreal, where she began a ski school in the Laurentians with her sister, Rhoda. Jere, one of the kids, tossed aside his skis (Oregon sports), put on skates (Montreal sports), and developed into an NHL-calibre player. His brother, Chris, and sister Margie, moved to New York to dance, he with the Paul Taylor company, she on her own. The other sister, Nancy, became a freestyle skier. Jere, meanwhile, was drafted 4th overall by Vancouver in 1977 and played pro hockey for the better part of 15 years, mostly with the Canucks, but also with 4 other NHL teams and a selection of teams here and there. By the time he retired, he had played 386 games, though his finest year, '77-'78, was also his first, as he scored 23 goals.

GILLIS, Mike
b. Sudbury, Ontario,
December 1, 1958

Mike Gillis

He was a terrific prospect, but in 4 years he suffered 4 major injuries to hamper his development, all before he was 20 years old. The Colorado Rockies played him when he was healthy (1978-81), but he was convalescing most of the time and they eventually traded him to Boston. He was doing what he could to make the lineup and stay healthy, but late in '83-'84 he suffered a career-ending broken leg. Gillis filed for disability insurance and went back to school to become a lawyer, a fortuitous decision given that his agent was Alan Eagleson. Eagleson told Gillis that the insurance company would not accept his claim, and suggested they take legal action, for which Eagleson would be responsible and be compensated 15 percent for any successful payments from the company. Gillis agreed, and just days later Eagleson had some good news. The company had relented and was willing to pay Gillis $233,750. Eagleson charged his client the appropriate 15 percent, or $41,250. Just one problem, though: The insurance company actually agreed to pay Gillis *before* Eagleson had conned him into taking legal action! Gillis took the Eagle to court – everyone was, after all and the shameful treatment of agent to player was exposed. Gillis himself went on to become a player agent.

GILLIS, Paul
b. Toronto, Ontario, December 31, 1963

Paul Gillis

Gillis arrived in Quebec in 1983 as a draft choice, and he impressed everyone within the organization to the point that within a few years they thought he would turn into another Dale Hunter. So, the Nordiques traded Hunter to Washington, but Gillis didn't develop into very much of anything like Hunter or any

other impact player. Sure, he carried a ton of penalty minutes around, but he didn't score and provide the leadership Quebec had hoped. In the summer of 1987, Gillis had major shoulder surgery that slowed him. He rebounded to have a decent season, but in the summer of 1989 he felt numbness in his hands and feet and went to hospital. Doctors told him he had Guillain-Barre syndrome, which attacks the nervous system, and his recovery took the rest of the summer. Within four years, he had retired, but continued on as a coach in the minors and later, junior in Ontario.

GILMOUR, Doug ("Killer")
b. Kingston, Ontario, June 25, 1963

As a kid, Gilmour revered his older brother, Dave, who went on to play in the Vancouver Canucks system but never in the NHL itself. But Dougie made it on his own. In some ways, the fact that he was small helped him more than it could have defeated him, for he was as tenacious and determined as any player who skated in the big league. He played most of his junior in Cornwall, winning the Memorial Cup in 1981 and then captaining the team the year after. He wasn't drafted at 18, but at 19 St. Louis thought he was worth the gamble of a mid-round selection and Gilmour proved his worth by leading the OHL in scoring with 177 points in '82-'83. He also had a 55-game consecutive-point streak during the year. In St. Louis, he started off as a third-line checker, but his fierce nature earned him more ice time and the moniker Killer from captain Brian Sutter. It was apt, for although he weighed no more

He played a key role in the Flames winning the Cup in 1989, as he scored the winning goal.
DOUG GILMOUR

than 165 pounds, he played with the intensity and ferocity of someone much bigger. In his first 3 years he had point totals of 53, 57, and 53, but in year 4 he exploded by scoring 42 goals and totalling 105 points. A star was born. He played in the 1987 Canada Cup and then had a fine, but not superb season, but all hell broke loose in the summer when he was accused of sexually assaulting his 14-year-old babysitter. The case was set to go to court, then the charges were dropped, but Gilmour's reputation had been damaged in St. Louis. He was traded to Calgary, hoping for a fresh start. In three and a half seasons he never hit the 100-point mark, but he played a key role in the Flames winning the Cup in 1989, as he scored what proved to be the winning goal against Montreal in game six. Midway through the '91-'92 season, Gilmour grew restless and demanded a trade because the team was not prepared to give him the contract he had wanted. He left the team, and on January 2, 1992, the Flames and Leafs orchestrated the biggest trade in NHL history, one involving 10 regulars. Gilmour arrived in Toronto amid the expected hoopla, and over the next five and a half seasons produced some of the most exciting hockey fans had seen in decades. Shifty and quick, he was a superb passer and inspirational figure on a team thin on pure talent. In '92-'93 and '93-'94, he scored 127 and 11 points, the former a team record, and he also won the Selke Trophy. Gilmour took the Leafs to the Cup semifinals both times. He was named captain, and quickly became the top playoff scorer in team history. Off the ice, he was a god. He did TV commercials and worked with kids, and his face was in the newspapers on a daily basis. Toronto traded him to New Jersey for contract reasons and in part because with the arrival of Mats Sundin, there was a conflict over which star would lead the team. Since then, Gilmour has become something of a wanderer. He played in New Jersey, Chicago, and Buffalo, and announced his retirement in the summer of 2001. But as training camp for a new season started, he itched to play. The awful illness of Saku Koivu in Montreal gave Gilmour an opportunity to return, and his inspired play took an awful team in the first half to a great rally in the second half to make the 2002 playoffs. He returned again for the 2002-03 season, his 21st year, by which time he had played in his 1,400th career game and recorded almost as many points, and which ended in a trade to Toronto. A future Hall of Famer, Gilmour has been an inspiration to small, skilled players for more than two decades.

GINGRAS, Gaston ("Gus")
b. Temiscamingue, Quebec, February 13, 1959
Gingras confessed to having accomplished everything he could possibly want by the time he left hockey in the late 1990s. He won a Calder Cup with Sherbrooke, a Stanley Cup with Montreal, and he played and coached in Europe. What more could he want? His greatest regret was how he left Montreal. He arrived in 1979 with so much media hype and so many great expectations that although he was a fine player, the fact he wasn't great upset the Forum fans. He was a solid defenceman and had a great shot, but that wasn't enough. He teamed with partner Larry Robinson for the 1986 Cup win, but that wasn't enough. He was booed out of a Montreal uniform and traded to Toronto, and later moved to Europe with his family to play and coach in Switzerland. However, when he was just 37, he needed a pacemaker, and his career was over. He returned to Montreal, and coached in the Habs system, hoping to be an assistant with the big club one day, a day that hasn't yet arrived.

GIONTA, Brian
b. Rochester, New York, January 18, 1979
During his four years at Boston College (1997-2001), Gionta enjoyed a successful career loaded with accolades and accomplishments. He led Hockey East in goals his last two years, made the All-Star Team three times, and was named HE player of the year in his final season. New Jersey drafted him, but there's just one small problem – he's listed as 5'7" and 175 pounds. Anyone that small you know is actually smaller than the record books show. Generally, small in in for a fight to make the NHL. He doesn't have the nasty streak of a Theo Fleury, though he does have decent skills. Nonetheless, Gionta has yet to establish himself with the Devils as a regular.

GIRARD, Bob
b. Montreal, Quebec, April 12, 1949
Girard was considered an excellent skater, but unlike many a Quebec flower, he was also willing to play physically – hit and be hit, and go into the corners to get the puck. That's why Washington acquired him from the Cleveland Barons in 1977. In his first game with the team, playing with good friend Bob Sirois, Girard scored the winning goal against St. Louis in a 2-1 victory. Unfortunately, he was on a lousy team and scored only one more game winner over the next 51 games. The Caps was the last stop on his five-year NHL tour of duty, one that started with the horrible California franchise in 1975.

GIRARD, Jonathan
b. Joliette, Quebec, May 27, 1980
Girard was a junior oddity in that he played with three different teams in the Quebec league and was named to the All-Star Team in each of those seasons. Drafted by Boston, he is still young and developing, though the Bruins are playing the defenceman more and more each season.

GIRARD, Kenny
b. Toronto, Ontario, December 8, 1936
He was a great hockey player for a golfer, or perhaps it was vice versa. Either way, Girard played both sports with equal skill, though the leisure of a golf career certainly outlasts the physical demands of one in hockey. Girard played parts of three seasons with the Leafs in the 1950s but spent as much time on the golf course in the summer as on ice in the winter. When he hung up his skates, the golf continued, and in 1999 he was champion of the Canadian Seniors PGA Tour.

GIROUX, Art
b. Winnipeg, Manitoba, June 6, 1908
d. Calgary, Alberta, June 5, 1982
Right winger Art Giroux had a long and distinguished career in the American league for some 15 years between the wars. In his only three years in the NHL, he played for as many teams – Montreal, Boston, Detroit. He was sold by the Habs to the Bruins, and the Bruins made him part of a significant trade in which they sent Giroux and Marty Barry to the Red Wings for Cooney Weiland and Walt Buswell. Giroux, though, played only four games with the Winged Wheel before extending his career another decade in the AHL.

GIROUX, Larry
b. Weyburn, Saskatchewan, August 28, 1951
Giroux was a late bloomer if the opinion of others is to be respected. In 1971, his draft year, each NHL team ignored him. St. Louis invited him to its rookie camp, then cut him, and California invited him to its main camp … and cut him. He played a bit in the minors, and two years later the Blues liked his play and signed him to an NHL contract. Giroux had made it. He bounced to Kansas City, Detroit, and St. Louis, playing in the minors and the NHL. St. Louis acquired him and let him go, and in December 1980 the Hartford Whalers signed him. He had, ironically, perhaps the best year of his career with the team, but in the summer he rejected their new contract offer and decided to test free agency.

Gaston Gingras

Bob Girard

Jonathan Girard

Kenny Girard

Art Giroux

Ray Giroux

Paul Gladu

Brian Glennie

Lorry Gloeckner

Fred Glover

The Whalers replaced him by drafting Fred Arthur, and Giroux looked back to the team after receiving no comparable offer elsewhere. Too late, said Hartford, and Giroux never played another game of hockey in his life.

GIROUX, Pierre
b. Brownsburg, Quebec, November 17, 1955
Chicago drafted Giroux in 1975 and kept him in the minors for three years before he moved on as a free agent to the IHL. Giroux played in the "I" for a brief period, and Los Angeles signed him in the summer of '82. He played six games for the Kings and not much more after that.

GIROUX, Ray
b. North Bay, Ontario, July 20, 1976
It just hasn't happened for Giroux so far. He received his share of hockey honours during his four years with Yale's team, but the Flyers traded him to the Islanders after drafting him and the Isles have seen fit to plop him into just a few games to date.

GLADNEY, Bob
b. Come-By-Chance, Newfoundland, August 27, 1957
There is no more poetic hockey town name on the face of the earth than Come-By-Chance, though Gladney grew up in nearby Clarenville where he played midget for the local Caribous. He was drafted by the Leafs out of Oshawa, but Toronto traded him to L.A.. He moved on to Pittsburgh briefly, but in December 1983 he suffered a career-ending eye injury while playing with Baltimore in the AHL. He returned to Newfoundland and settled in Riverview, where he remained in hockey and also worked with Boy Scouts.

GLADU, Jean-Paul "Paul"
b. St. Hyacinthe, Quebec, June 20, 1921
Although Gladu was known for his blazing speed and terrific shot, he claimed his brother, Fernand, was even faster and shot harder. Nonetheless, it was Jean-Paul and not Fernand who made the NHL grade by playing with Boston in the '44-'45 season. After that, he settled into a lengthy and productive career in the AHL, notably with St. Louis, where he arrived at Christmas 1945. There, his biggest obstacle was English – he spoke almost none, but his stick spoke volumes. Playing left wing on a line with Don Grosso and Tony Licari, he scored 51 goals in '48-'49 at the height of his powers (including a league-record 6 hat tricks). He developed his wrist shot in the basement of a grocery store his father ran by shooting pucks along the concrete floor at a small target on the wall. It was such training that kept him in the pro ranks for a decade.

GLENNIE, Brian ("Blunt")
b. Toronto, Ontario, August 29, 1946
He hit like a bus, they said, and doctors attended to him more times than the average family sees a sawbones in a lifetime. Torn knee ligaments, back surgery, shoulder operation, cuts, and a smashed jaw that had to be reconstructed. Glennie was a master of old arts such as shotblocking and hip checks, the kind of open-ice hits no one expects. The summer of 1967 was both great and awful for Glennie. He and the Marlies won the Memorial Cup and the prospects of a pro career were as

good as a kid could hope for. Then, his father died. He had the option to play for the Canadian National Team, and without his dad to advise him – amateur or pro? – he chose the amateur route and ended up in the 1968 Olympics in Grenoble, winning a bronze medal with the team. Then he turned pro, and a year later he was patrolling the Leafs' blueline and hammering any opponents foolish enough to skate in on him head down. He played nine years with Toronto, during which time he was a substitute on the 1972 Team Canada. In 1975, he was victim of a Dan Maloney assault. The Detroit goon didn't like the way Glennie had hit a teammate, so he tackled Glennie from behind and pushed his head into the ice several times. Maloney was charged by police for the attack, though he was later acquitted. Glennie played his final season with L.A. before injuries got the better of him. He retired in late 1978 and worked at his restaurant, Wheels, a 1950s-style diner in Toronto. He later worked as a print salesman, but a heart attack in 1990 forced him to retire, in his case to the quiet of Port Carling and Muskoka.

GLENNON, Matt
b. Hull, Massachusetts, September 20, 1968
He took care of his education, gave pro hockey a shot, and retired to a life of more normal employment. Glennon played for nearby Boston College and was drafted by the Bruins, for whom he played three games in 1991-92. He played only briefly thereafter in the minors before returning to Hull and getting a job as an account executive for Nutrinfo Corporation!

GLOECKNER, Lorry
b. Kindersley, Saskatchewan, January 25, 1956
So much fuss for so little result. Gloeckner was playing for Victoria in the Western league when Boston drafted him in 1976, at the end of his third season. He returned for his final year with the Cougars but rejected the Bruins' contract offer. He sat out all of '77-'78 so he'd become an unrestricted free agent thereafter, and Detroit signed him at the start of the next season. However, Gloeckner played just 13 games with the Red Wings, and a year and a half later he was out of the game altogether.

GLOOR, Dan
b. Stratford, Ontario, December 4, 1952
Gloor played only two games in the NHL, with Vancouver in '73-'74, but there is more to the man than the NHL numbers show. He was rookie of the year in the IHL the previous season, and the subsequent year he was named MVP on his WHL team, Seattle Totems. Although his career was not lengthy, he was a doer of good deeds in that he used the money he made from the game to buy his father a bakery in Stratford.

GLOVER, Fred
b. Toronto, Ontario, January 5, 1928
d. California, August 16, 2001
It's one thing to be called the Wayne Gretzky of the American Hockey League, but imagine the player called the Wayne Gretzky and Tiger Williams! Glover played briefly in the NHL, but he broke records for both goals (522) and penalty minutes (2,402) in the AHL over a 20-year career, the last 16 of which he

spent with the Cleveland Barons. In the NHL, Glover played most of '51-'52 with the Cup-winning Red Wings, scoring nine goals. In the AHL, he had 16 seasons with 20 goals or more. He led the league in scoring twice, was named league MVP three times, and was a First All-Star five times. He retired in 1968 to become coach of the Oakland Seals for the better part of six years, a thankless job if ever there was one. He later worked for the NHL in an executive capacity, and he died just a week after being diagnosed with cancer of the liver, pancreas, and lungs.

GLOVER, Howie
b. Toronto, Ontario, February 14, 1935
Seven years the junior of brother Fred, Howie had a more erratic career than his sibling. He managed to play for 4 Original Six teams, and for 4 years (1964-68) played with Fred in Cleveland, during the last of which he scored a personal-best 41 goals. He had been suspended one year for assaulting a referee back in North Bay, and between 1963 and '65 he missed a year and a half with a pinched nerve in his neck that threatened his career. His only full NHL season was '60-'61 with Detroit, when he scored an impressive 21 times.

GLYNN, Brian
b. Iserlohn, West Germany, November 23, 1967
An army family baby, Glynn was born in Germany while his father was stationed there. The family soon came back to Canada and settled in Saskatchewan, Glynn eventually making his home in Candle Lake. He played in the WHL and went to Calgary in the draft. Little did he know that day he'd wear 7 sweaters in a 10-year NHL career, which began October 8, 1987, with a goal against Glen Hanlon. He twice went to the Cup finals in underdog roles, once with Minnesota in 1991, and again three years later with the Canucks.

GOC, Sascha
b. Calw, West Germany, April 17, 1979
One of the few western Germans to make the NHL, Goc had plenty of experience before joining New Jersey, the team that drafted him in 1997 but didn't play him until October 19, 2000. He played in two World Junior Championships ('97 and '98), and in the latter year had the distinction also of playing in the senior Worlds just a few months later. However, he spent most of his first two years in Albany rather than New Jersey, and in 2001-02 the Devils traded him to Tampa Bay, where he has fared no better in terms of ice time.

GODDEN, Ernie
b. Keswick, Ontario, March 13, 1961
The decline in reputation and performance was remarkable. In '80-'81, Godden was in his last year of junior with the Windsor Spitfires. He set an OHL record with 87 goals and another for 10 short-handed goals, and was named the OHL's outstanding player. Interestingly he broke the goals record by scoring four against Jim Egerton, a right winger put in net after starter Frank Caprice was hurt in warmup and couldn't play. Godden was small, yes, but he accrued enough penalty minutes that no one could have thought him a softie, and yet Toronto took him only 55th overall. And,

in just five games with the Leafs that season, he had a goal and an assist. The Leafs never played him again, and no team stepped up when he was a free agent. He played three years in the minors, a year in Austria, and then was out of the game. Such a long, long way from junior in just four years.

GODFREY, Warren ("Rock")
b. Toronto, Ontario, March 23, 1931
d. February 12, 1998
He was, indeed, a rock on defence, and few forwards got by him without paying the proverbial price. For 11 seasons he was a regular on the blueline of Boston and then Detroit, dependable, resilient, effective. For most of his career he was the only player to wear a helmet on doctor's orders; he had suffered 2 serious concussions early in his career. And then, he was too old, and he was in the minors, unwilling to let go of the thing he loved to do so much. In 1965-66, he was making a bit of a comeback with the Wings when he destroyed his knee and was lost for almost a full season. He was 34, but he wasn't done yet. He worked the knee back into shape, and still the Wings found a place for him, on the farm, with a young team in need of leadership. Godfrey retired in 1969, a well-worn body finally able to relax.

GODIN, Eddy
b. Donnacona, Quebec, March 29, 1957
Right winger Godin was drafted by Washington in 1977 during the height of the team's disastrous start in the NHL. He played just 27 games over the next two years but spent most of six years with the farm team in Hershey.

GODIN, Hogomer "Sam"
b. Rockland, Ontario, September 20, 1909
d. unknown
This guy played everywhere, and he dropped his bags in Ottawa and Montreal long enough to find his equipment and play 83 NHL games between 1927 and '34. Before and after he played the longest with Buffalo in the International league, but his skates also took him to a dozen other cities in a myriad of leagues before he finally said enough in 1941.

GODYNYUK, Alexander
b. Kiev, Soviet Union (Ukraine), January 27, 1970
What an incredible difference just a few years makes. Godynyuk defected from the Soviet Union in 1990, leaving behind his family and girlfriend. He arrived in Vancouver where the Leafs were playing, and immediately told Toronto he wanted to play (the Leafs had drafted him in the summer). The Soviets claimed he was still under contract to his club team, Sokol Kiev, but this was nothing a handsome cheque ($100,000) couldn't overcome, and Godynyuk was in the Leafs lineup soon enough. He spoke little English, and media quoted him verbatim to convey his Tarzan-like capacity to communicate. To wit, on his first game: "I nervous first minutes, later no nervous, later only play." Back home, his country bemoaned the loss of another talent. Godynyuk had won a gold medal at the 1989 World Juniors and the next year was named best defenceman. The older he got, though, the less attractive his prospects

Howie Glover

Brian Glynn

Ernie Godden

Warren Godfrey

Eddy Godin

Pete Goegan

Dave Goertz

Bob Goldham

Bill Goldsworthy

were as he grew into something less in the present than the future had ever held for him. The Leafs included him in the massive 10-player trade with Calgary that brought Doug Gilmour to Toronto, and from there Godynyuk played infrequently until he finally left the NHL and returned to Europe. By then, he could play internationally for his own country at the 1999 World Championships.

GOEGAN, Pete
b. Fort William, Ontario, March 6, 1934
Although Goegan played 11 seasons in the NHL (1957-68), only 3 of those were free of stints in the minors, the nemesis of any player during the Original Six. He was a hard-hitting defenceman whose longest time was with the Red Wings. He played junior in Fort William, and in the summers he built houses and worked in construction as a way of staying in shape. He played his final year in the NHL with Minnesota after being claimed in the Expansion Draft, and after another full season in the minors he retired. Goegan returned to Fort William and worked solidly in construction until a bad back and hip forced him to call it quits in 1990.

GOERTZ, Dave
b. Edmonton, Alberta, March 28, 1965
Any time a player drafted 232nd makes it to the NHL, he can pat himself on the back for having made it to the show. Pittsburgh took Goertz that low in 1983, and four years later he played two games for the Pens when Mario Lemieux was on the team. Not many players can boast of having number 66 as a teammate. Most of Goertz's career, though, took place in the minors.

GOLDHAM, Bob ("Golden Boy")
b. Georgetown, Ontario, May 12, 1922
d. Toronto, Ontario, September 6, 1991
It was a rookie season for the ages. The year was 1941-42, the team the Toronto Maple Leafs. Goldham joined the Leafs for the last half of the season, and in the playoffs he was a key reason the Leafs rallied from 3-0 down in the finals to Detroit to mount the mother of all comebacks and win the Cup 4-3. Goldham scored a goal in game six and assisted on the winner in the deciding game. After the victory, he promptly joined the army and was gone from the game for three years. Upon his discharge, he returned to the Leafs as though no time had passed. Goldham was, however, a defenceman renowned not for goals but for preventing them. More specifically, he was a master shotblocker, the goalie's best friend, and a saint to his own forwards. After two more seasons with Toronto, he was traded to Chicago in the blockbuster deal that brought Max Bentley to Maple Leaf Gardens. From there he went to Detroit, and it was with the Wings that he won three more Cups in the 1950s with one of the greatest teams of all time. He retired in 1956, coached for a time in Toronto, and later he became an insightful and articulate analyst on *Hockey Night in Canada*. He died of a stroke in Toronto General Hospital at age 69.

GOLDMANN, Erich
b. Dingolfing, West Germany, April 7, 1976
Definitely an active one-game wonder in the making, Goldmann appeared for Ottawa in 1999-2000 in his last of three years in North America. He had played extensively for the Germans internationally, most importantly in the Olympics (1998 and 2002) and the World Cup (1996). He returned to Germany to play in DEL in 2001-02, and the likelihood of his returning to the NHL is slim, indeed.

GOLDSWORTHY, Bill ("Goldie")
b. Waterloo, Ontario, August 24, 1944
d. Minneapolis, Minnesota, March 29, 1996
The life of a hockey player is short and the rewards are great, but for some the excesses of fame and money are more than a person can handle. Goldsworthy was a fine hockey player, and he liked the social perks that went along with the gig. He played most of his career with Minnesota, scoring a personal-best 48 goals in '73-'74. He introduced a goal celebration that came to be known as the Goldie Shuffle. He was a member of Team Canada in '72 and 7 times scored 20 or more goals in a season. He spent his last years with Edmonton in the WHA and retired early in '78-'79 after a broken shoulder and collarbone didn't heal properly. Some players handle retirement well; others don't. Goldsworthy fell into the latter category. He drank to excess and was unhappy doing anything outside hockey. Much as he wanted to get into coaching, he went into the air freight business in Minneapolis, the city that retired his number 8 sweater in 1992. Two years later, he was happy again, coaching the San Antonio Iguanas in the CHL. He got sick, and for two months fought pneumonia-like symptoms. When he went to the hospital, though, doctors had a shock for him: He tested positive for HIV. Years of drinking and womanizing were the cause, he admitted, and two years later he was dead.

GOLDSWORTHY, Leroy ("Goldie")
b. Two Harbors, Minnesota, October 18, 1906
d. Edmonton, Alberta, March 16, 1980
Goldsworthy grew up in Edmonton from the age of two, and it was there he played junior hockey until the New York Rangers optioned him to Springfield in 1926. He dressed for the Blueshirts in the 1929 playoffs, made the team that fall, and for most of the next decade was a bona fide NHL right winger. He did play long stretches in the minors, though, and changed teams several times. He played '33-'34 with Chicago, the year the team went on to win the Stanley Cup with a mostly American-born roster. In the summer of 1931, he began to take baseball seriously. He had played most of his life, but this time he made the Winnipeg Maroons in the Class D Northern League. He made an impression on Charley Barrett, a scout for the St. Louis Cardinals, by going 22-6 and leading the league in strikeouts, and Barrett offered him a job in the Cards system – if and only if he gave up hockey. Goldsworthy couldn't do that, and as fate would have it an injury a year later hurt his ball game anyway. After his final years in the minors, he turned to coaching in 1946 with the Buffalo Bisons, the team with which he had ended his playing career. Two years later, he was a GM with the Bisons farm team in the U.S. league, but by season's end he was back coaching the Bisons, a post he maintained for several seasons. Meanwhile, he turned

his summer sport from baseball to golf and became so good he was hired as Jasper Park Lodge pro. The club was frequented by Bing Crosby, and the pair became good friends during the summer months.

GOLDUP, Glenn

b. St. Catharines, Ontario, April 26, 1953

Son of Hank, Glenn played only for Montreal and Los Angeles in the 1970s and on, though his playoff experience was limited to a handful of games. He was a Montreal draft choice, and in this era that meant bad news for all but the superstars. He played some games with the Habs but most years were spent with the farm team in Nova Scotia. When they traded him to L.A. in the summer of '76, it meant going from good team to bad, but it also meant going from not playing to playing. For most of the next five seasons he was a regular winger on the team, though a knee injury early on set him back. After retiring, he worked in public relations for the Toronto Argonauts football team and as an ad salesman for a Toronto radio station. He later transferred his selling abilities to cars in downtown Toronto and radio ads for The Fan.

GOLDUP, Hank

b. Kingston, Ontario, October 29, 1918

Goldup's NHL years bracketed the war almost entirely, his first game coming in the winter of 1939 and his last early in the '45-'46 season. He started with the Leafs and was part of the Cup team that fought back from 3-0 down to beat Detroit 4-3 in 1942. However, the Leafs traded him to the Rangers with Red Garrett to acquire Babe Pratt, the big defenceman who scored the Cup-winner for Toronto in the 1945 finals. Goldup was later traded to Detroit, but he never played with the Wings and wound up in the minors. He broke his leg so severely in a game that he needed a brace for 2 full years, and after retiring moved into sales: 17 years with Molsons, 15 years with Jordan wines, and, more recently, with Victoriaville hockey sticks.

GOLUBOVSKY, Jan

b. Novosibirsk, Soviet Union (Russia), March 9, 1976

He came out of Russia to give the riches of the NHL a whirl, but he ended up back home with less to show than he had hoped. Detroit played him in parts of four seasons at the end of the 20th century, and from there he played a few games in Florida before returning to Russia to play in a richer and revived league. The defenceman simply had too much competition and not enough talent to establish himself with the Wings, and after the Panthers there were no other tangible offers to stay in North America.

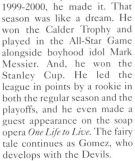

He played '33-'34 with Chicago, the year the team went on to win the Stanley Cup with a mostly American-born roster.
LEROY GOLDSWORTHY

GOMEZ, Scott ("Gomer")

b. Anchorage, Alaska, December 23, 1979

Very few hockey stories have the same positive spin on them that Gomez's does. His father was 1 of 10 kids born in California to a Mexican migrant worker. The father moved to Alaska to work on the pipeline. Scott's mother was born in Colombia and lived in Brooklyn, New York, before moving to Alaska. They met and had a family, and Scott played hockey like a Canadian. He almost accepted an offer to go to Colorado College on scholarship, but changed his mind and played junior in the Western league. From there, his mind was set on the NHL. Even after New Jersey drafted him and cut him, he remained focused. He trained under Vladimir Bure (father of Pavel and Valeri), and when he came to camp the next year, 1999-2000, he made it. That season was like a dream. He won the Calder Trophy and played in the All-Star Game alongside boyhood idol Mark Messier. And, he won the Stanley Cup. He led the league in points by a rookie in both the regular season and the playoffs, and he even made a guest appearance on the soap opera *One Life to Live*. The fairy tale continues as Gomez, who develops with the Devils.

GONCHAR, Sergei

b. Chelyabinsk, Soviet Union (Russia), April 13, 1974

If it hadn't been for Chris Simon, Gonchar might well have been the first Russian goon in the NHL. Gonchar had wanted to play football (soccer) as a kid but his father provided a little tough love by telling him flat out he was too slow. Instead, he handed his son a pair of skates. Sergei loved hockey, but he was a fighter back in his youth. It wasn't until he got to Washington and saw a real fighter – Simon – that he decided he wouldn't do any fighting in North America. Instead, he developed into an offensive-minded defenceman, and since 1998 has scored more goals from the blueline than anyone else in the league. In '98-'99, he became the first Russian d-man to score 20 in a season (21), a year after taking the team to the Cup finals for the first time in franchise history. Gonchar has played his entire career in the U.S. capital and has extensive international experience as well, most recently winning bronze with the Russians at the 2002 Olympics in Salt Lake City.

GONEAU, Daniel

b. Montreal, Quebec, January 16, 1976

Boston drafted him in 1994 during his junior days with Laval, but he said no thanks and carried on playing until 1996 when he re-entered the draft. The Rangers took a shot at him and used him in bits and pieces for three years, but most of his career was in the minors.

Glenn Goldup

Hank Goldup

Scott Gomez

Sergei Gonchar

He ended the 2001-02 season playing for the Bracknell Bees in the European Superleague, a far cry from the young man who figured he'd hold out on Boston and try for more.

GOODEN, Bill
b. Winnipeg, Manitoba, September 8, 1923
d. Naples, Florida, December 17, 1998
Barely 19 years old and wondering where hockey would take him, Gooden was a happy player when he joined the New York Rangers for a special game on October 26, 1942. It was played in his hometown, and the opposition for the Rangers was Winnipeg's Navy team. The exhibition game was for a good cause, and the NHL team cruised to victory before a delighted capacity crowd. The Rangers liked what they saw of Gooden, and a few days later signed him to a contract. He wound up playing only a few games with the team that season and most of next season, but nothing after the war. For 13 years he played in the minors and never received a callup, though he certainly proved a capable winger.

Bill Gooden

GOODENOUGH, Larry ("Izzy")
b. Toronto, Ontario, January 19, 1953
The nickname was a rhetorical question directed at his last name, as in, "Is he good enough to play in the NHL?" Yes, was the answer. Philadelphia drafted him in 1973, and in the '74 playoffs he was called up from the minors in case of injury to a regular. The team went on to win the Cup, but Izzy never appeared in a game, only practices. The team had a convertible with his name on it for the Cup parade, but he was already on a plane home to Thunder Bay. It was a team he didn't feel part of just yet. Not so the next year, when the team repeated as champs but he played a number of games in the regular season and playoffs. Two years later, he was traded to Vancouver, and about 100 games later he was in the minors to stay. Izzy? Yes, but not 4evr.

Larry Goodenough

GOODFELLOW, Ebenezer "Ebbie"
b. Ottawa, Ontario, April 9, 1906
d. Sarasota, Florida, September 10, 1985
From the moment Detroit GM Jack Adams saw Goodfellow play, he knew this was an NHL-calibre player. In 1928, Adams assigned the youngster to the Olympics, and after a stellar season Ebbie made the NHL team. He played centre on a line with Herbie Lewis and Larry Aurie, his skating and long reach and stickhandling his most obvious assets. In his second year, Goodfellow finished second in league scoring with 48 points behind only the great Howie Morenz. He played six seasons as a centre, but his production

Paul Goodman

trailed off and Adams felt a change was necessary. He put Ebbie on defence with Alex Motter, and lo and behold Goodfellow's career came to life. He was an integral part of the team winning consecutive Cups in 1936 and '37, though the year after he fractured his ankle and missed a good portion of the year. He became the team's captain in 1938 but by 1943 his career had trickled to a stop and he joined the army for two years. When he came out, he turned his attention to coaching, first with St. Louis in the AHL. Chicago owner Bill Tobin promised Goodfellow that if he could turn around the Flyers, Chicago's failing farm team, in two years, he would be given the job of coaching the Hawks. He did, and he was. But those two years in the Windy City (1950-52) were unmitigated disasters as the team won just 30 of 140 games. One interesting cultural note, though, was that Goodfellow sat on the players' bench rather than pace up and down in behind it, the last coach to maintain the old method. He was inducted into the Hockey Hall of Fame in 1963 and maintained connections with the Hall by being on their selection committee for many years. In 1952, out of hockey, he became a manufacturers' representative for International Tools, in Windsor, a job he kept in 1974. He retired to Florida where he lived near his old Red Wings roommate, Herbie Lewis. They spent many of their days golfing until Goodfellow succumbed to cancer in 1985.

He played centre on a line with Herbie Lewis and Larry Aurie, his skating and long reach and stickhandling his most obvious assets.
EBBIE GOODFELLOW

GOODMAN, Paul
b. Selkirk, Manitoba, February 25, 1905
d. Seattle, Washington, October 1, 1959
Goodman was minding his own business down Wichita way when the call came for him to play against Toronto in the 1938 Stanley Cup finals. Chicago had won game one of the best-of-five series, 3-1, with Mike Karakas in goal, but Goodman got the call for game two. He allowed five goals and the Leafs won the game, but the Hawks won the next two to win the Cup. Goodman played parts of the next 2 years with the Hawks, and in 52 regular-season games he had an impressive 6 shutouts.

GORDIOUK, Viktor
b. Odintsovo, Soviet Union (Russia), April 11, 1970
He proved he could play in the NHL, but then again, he proved he couldn't. That is, he was good enough to get the chance to play, with Buffalo in the early 1990s, but the left winger never produced or contributed in a way that sold the Sabres on his abilities. Gordiouk played in the minors and then went to Germany, where he proved he could play and where they let him play.

GORDON, Fred

b. Fleming, Saskatchewan, May 6, 1900
d. unknown

Gordon was given consecutive chances to play in the NHL, first with the Detroit Cougars in 1926-27, the team's first NHL season when it played its home games across the river in Windsor, Ontario. Gordon, a right winger, had a decent season, but in the spring he was traded to Boston for Harry Meeking, the great winger who was nearing the end of the line. Gordon played the year with the Bruins but wasn't offered a new contract. He moved down to Minneapolis to play in the American league and shortly after became a coach.

GORDON, Jackie

b. Winnipeg, Manitoba, March 3, 1928

Gordon was successful in hockey for most of his life in an executive way, so this can only mean one thing – his skating career was less so. All great coaches and managers learn their craft from the end of the bench, from playing in the minors and travelling in the buses and observing. Gordon played 36 games for the Rangers (1948-51) but spent 17 years in the minors with Cleveland, as a player, coach, and general manager. He won the Calder Trophy four times, including 1956, the first season he was named playing coach. He was also coach of the year in the AHL four times. He later served as assistant GM for the Rangers but returned to Cleveland in 1968 for two years until Minnesota GM Wren Blair finally convinced him to coach the NHL North Stars. Gordon performed that duty for four seasons but stepped down because of frail nerves from the stress of the job.

GORDON, Robb

b. Murrayville, British Columbia, January 13, 1976

Gordon changed his mind en route to the NHL. He played provincial junior hockey in B.C. in preparation for U.S. college, but after a year at the University of Michigan he returned home and played major junior in the Western league in 1995-96. He scored 51 goals that season and won a gold with Canada's junior team at the WJC, after which he turned pro. A Vancouver draft choice in '94, he played for Syracuse in the AHL and two years later played his only NHL games, four appearances with the Canucks. His contract wasn't renewed and he has been in the minors ever since.

GORDON, Scott

b. Brockton, Massachusetts, February 6, 1963

Most Massachusetts-born players choose an area college as their means to the NHL, and Gordon was no exception. He attended Boston College (1982-86) before turning pro in the American league after never being drafted into the NHL or receiving a contract offer. He played his only major-league games with Quebec 3 years later, appearing in 23 games over 2 seasons, but the goalie had a dismal record of just 2-16-0 in that stretch and allowed 5.60 goals per game. Needless to say, getting back to the NHL proved impossible, though he did play for Team USA at the 1991 World Championships and then at the 1992 Olympics in Albertville the following year. He later coached for the Roanoke Express in the ECHL.

GOREN, Lee

b. Winnipeg, Manitoba, December 26, 1977

His credentials from the University of North Dakota were pretty impressive by the time he graduated in 2000. He led all college players in his final year with 34 goals and was named MVP of the Frozen Four as the Fighting Sioux won the national championship in 2000. A Boston Bruins draft choice, he made his NHL debut on December 2, 2000, and has been trying to work his way into the lineup full-time ever since.

GORENCE, Tom

b. St. Paul, Minnesota, March 11, 1957

One of the better American players during an era when his compatriots didn't fare so well in the NHL, Gorence played six seasons in the late 1970s and early 1980s, mostly with Philadelphia. He had good speed but game in and game out his consistency was too often his downfall. The '80-'81 season was his best – 24 goals – but he never came close to that number again. He played for Team USA in the 1981 Canada Cup and the 1982 World Championships, and he was fortunate enough to play with Edmonton in the '83-'84 season. The Oilers won the Cup that year, but Gorence didn't appear in the playoffs and played only 12 regular-season games. So, although he played with one of the greatest teams of all time, he didn't qualify to have his name on the Cup.

GORING, Robert "Butch"

b. St. Boniface, Manitoba, October 22, 1949

Goring came out of the West after a fine junior career to play for Los Angeles starting in 1969. He immediately had an impact on the team as a fine two-way player, though his sophomore year was shortened by a serious bout of mononucleosis. He then settled in to record 9 successive 20-plus goal seasons with the Kings, though the team underachieved with regrettable consistency each playoff spring. At the trade deadline in '79-'80, he was the beneficiary of a move that saw him go to the New York Islanders, a team poised to challenge for the Cup. The team's GM felt the Isles were a good centreman away from victory, and after failing to acquire Darryl Sittler from Toronto he settled for Goring. Just a few weeks later, the team won its first of four successive Cups, and Goring was there for all of them. He had always been a quirky player insofar as he wore the same helmet he had used since age 12. He liked it; it was comfortable; he saw no reason to use anything else. He also owned a number of racehorses and was considered one of the worst dressers in the league, a fact he neither disputed nor sought to amend at any time. Toward the end of his time on Long Island, Goring was given the added responsibility of being an assistant coach, which meant running the penalty killing during practice. The duties drove him with even greater passion, and he knew that after his playing days he'd pursue a career as coach full-time. That chance came sooner than he had anticipated. He finished his playing career briefly with Boston, and then the Bruins fired head coach Gerry Cheevers. Goring put his name in the hat, and GM Harry Sinden drew it out. Although his term lasted only a year and a half, Goring's ambitions were not sated, and he continued to coach

Fred Gordon

Jackie Gordon

Tom Gorence

Butch Goring

Dave Gorman

Benoit Gosselin

Steve Gotaas

in the IHL, getting his second NHL chance with the retro Islanders in 1999-2000. He later coached Krefeld in Germany.

GORMAN, Dave
b. Oshawa, Ontario, April 8, 1955
By his own admission, Gorman needed an attitude adjustment if he was going to make it in the world of pro hockey. He had it all in junior – the goals, the admiration, the reputation – and when he got the big-ticket contract to play in the WHA at age 19 (1974-75), he had the world in the palm of his hands. Then, things got kind of funny. His pure talent no longer cut it in the pros, and he didn't score as much. He didn't try hard in practice and he quickly acquired a reputation for dogging it. Phoenix sent him and his large contract to the minors, to try to wake him up, but it didn't work. He made it back to the WHA the next year, but he didn't push himself and he didn't excel. He signed with the Atlanta Flames in 1979 after the WHA merged with the NHL, but a determined training camp got him into only three games before he was down in the minors again. He tried hard, but it was too little, too late.

GORMAN, Ed
b. Buckingham, Quebec, September 25, 1892
d. Ottawa, Ontario, March 10, 1963
Gorman played some serious hockey in the Ottawa Valley, but never made an appearance in the NHL until he was 32 years old. That was '24-'25, with the Senators, of course. He played three years with the team, winning the Stanley Cup in 1927, the last time that team ever won. He finished his career with a short stay in Toronto. He died many years later while attending mass at a church in Ottawa, his home most of his adult life.

GOSSELIN, Benoit
b. Montreal, Quebec, July 19, 1957
He wasn't exactly a goon, but when the Rangers called him up in '77-'78 he sat in the penalty box for 33 minutes in just 7 games. The left winger had been a scoring sensation in junior, but the Rangers let him go and although Winnipeg signed him, he never got a chance to play with the Jets. Instead, he was relegated to the minors, where he proved again his ability to score. It was not enough, though, to get him another chance in the NHL.

GOSSELIN, David
b. Levis, Quebec, June 22, 1977
Drafted by New Jersey in 1995, Gosselin proved to be jeans material in a land of silk. The Devils had just won the Stanley Cup and were a team of perfect balance. The chances of Gosselin making it with them any time soon were remote, and he signed with Nashville three years later. It was with the Predators that he got into his first games, though he has played mostly in the minors to date.

GOSSELIN, Guy
b. Rochester, Minnesota, January 6, 1964
A player of limited ability often has many options available to him outside the NHL. Take Gosselin, for instance. He played just five times with Winnipeg in

'87-'88, but he played at two Olympics with the American National Team in Calgary (1988) and Lillehammer (1994). In between, he also played at two World Championships as well as in the minors and Europe. Here, there, and everywhere – the common denominator being skates and stick.

GOSSELIN, Mario ("Goose")
b. Thetford Mines, Quebec, June 15, 1963
Goose, as in loose as a. Goose, as in tiny, thin, eentsy-weentsy. Gosselin was a junior standout who had his coming-out party at the 1984 Olympics in Sarajevo. Team Canada's coach hailed him as the best goalie in that tournament (over a guy named Tretiak), and almost right after the torch had been extinguished he joined the Quebec Nordiques. Gosselin recorded a shutout in his first game – 5-0 over St. Louis on February 26, 1984 – and remained with the team for six years, more often as Daniel Bouchard's backup than as the starter. He retired in 1994 after a knee injury didn't heal properly, but along the way he had moments of glory, notably in 1986 when he played in the All-Star Game.

GOTAAS, Steve
b. Camrose, Alberta, May 10, 1967
Pittsburgh drafted Gotaas in 1985, a year after Mario Lemieux, but although the two played together briefly in 1987-88, their careers were very much on divergent paths. Gotaas went to Minnesota with Ville Siren in a trade that brought Gord Dineen and Scott Bjugstad to the Pens, but Gotaas played only a few games with the North Stars over the remainder of a career carved mostly outside the NHL.

GOTTSELIG, Johnny
b. Odessa, Russia, June 24, 1905
d. Elmhurst, Illinois, May 15, 1986
He was one of Chicago's all-time great players, for 17 years a left winger on a team he helped win 2 Stanley Cups (1934 and '38). And when he retired, he didn't go anywhere. Gottselig's family emigrated to Canada when Johnny was still very young, and they settled out west. Johnny played junior in Regina, joined the Hawks in 1928, and soon after became a longtime roommate of Mush March on road trips. In both his second and his third seasons he scored more than 20 goals, and he led the team in scoring 11 times during his career. In the 1938 playoffs, he led the league with eight points, and he played in both the Babe Seibert and Howie Morenz All-Star games ('37 and '39). During the 1940s, he also coached a ball team in the American Girls' Baseball League. He retired one game into the '44-'45 season to take over as coach, a position he maintained for three and a half years. He later became the team's director of publicity for many years, and when he moved into private life he became an executive with Stone Construction, a manufacturer of concrete pipes.

GOULD, Bobby
b. Petrolia, Ontario, September 2, 1957
Although he could score, Gould had to play well defensively to stay in the NHL. He was one of the early Canadians to play U.S. college hockey as a means to the NHL, with the University of New Hampshire in

the 1970s. Although he got his start in the Atlanta/Calgary organization, he made the league as a player with Washington in the early 1980s. He had three 20-goal seasons but was also tough for his size, and after retiring in 1991 he returned home to Petrolia, near Sarnia, to coach. He landed with the Petrolia Jets of the Western Junior B Hockey League.

Bobby Gould

GOULD, John
b. Beeton, Ontario, April 11, 1949
Gould attended the Leafs training camp in 1969 but wound up playing two years in Charlotte, in the Eastern league, a strange place for a 20-year-old right out of junior. His coach there was Fred Creighton, and later in life this would prove to be a fortuitous connection. Gould signed with the Sabres, but it was after a trade to Vancouver that he had his finest seasons, notably 34 and 32 goals in '74-'75 and '75-'76, respectively. He was traded to Atlanta, where Creighton was the coach, but the Flames left him exposed in the 1979 Expansion Draft and the Oilers claimed him. His time there was a disaster, and he was only too happy to return to Buffalo in a small trade. He retired at year's end, 1980, and attended the Phil Esposito Foundation, a place where newly retired players could try to sort out what they wanted to do with the rest of their lives. Gould returned to Beeton and raced standardbreds. He also joined Fundamentals in Action, a group organized by Pat Stapleton to teach kids across Canada about hockey.

Gould returned to Beeton and raced standardbreds.
JOHN GOULD

GOULD, Larry
b. Alliston, Ontario, August 16, 1952
Brother of John, Larry had a career as brief (2 games) as John's was lengthy (504 games). The 2 games came with John in Vancouver in '73-'74, and although Larry never played in the NHL again he did continue on for a number of years in the "I" as a consistent goal scorer.

Larry Gould

GOULET, Michel
b. Peribonka, Quebec, April 21, 1960
Players get into habits at an early age and are loath to break them. They wear the same equipment, get dressed in a familiar pattern, structure their lives so all their focus and attention can be used for the games themselves. Goulet used a helmet that was as thick as a cardboard box and as safe as paper to protect his head. On March 16, 1994, when he crashed headfirst at top speed into the boards, his life, not goals and assists, was all that mattered. He retired immediately, but although he was only 33 he had accomplished enough to earn him a place in the Hockey Hall of Fame in 1998. Peribonka was so small there were no hockey teams, and when Goulet wanted to play he

had to sneak into an arena in Mistassini, a nearby town. Despite being deprived of ice on a regular basis, and being an average skater as a result, he developed into a player with superb skills and a great shot. He played only one full season of junior, with the Remparts in '77-'78, and ended up scoring 73 goals. The next fall, he turned pro with Birmingham of the WHA as an 18-year-old, and from there he was drafted into the Nordiques when the WHA merged with the NHL. In his first 4 years, he increased his scoring each year from 22 to 32 to 42 to 57 goals. That '82-'83 season was the first of 4 successive 50-goal seasons, and in the 2 years that followed he had 49 and 48 goals. During these years he also played for Canada at the 1984 and '87 Canada Cups. At the start of the '85-'86 season, he was a training camp holdout while he waited for his contract to be renegotiated. He was traded to Chicago for economic reasons at the trade deadline in 1990, but although he scored consistently the numbers were in the 20s now, not the 40s and 50s. Then came the head injury and retirement. A year to the day after the crash, his number 16 was retired by the Nordiques in a moving ceremony at the Colisee. He later became director of player personnel for the Avalanche, a position he continues to hold with the organization that transferred him from Quebec in 1996.

Michel Goulet

GOUPILLE, Clifford "Red"
b. Trois Rivières, Quebec, September 2, 1915
Goupille played his entire career with the Canadiens (1935-43) before heading off to the army and thus more or less ending his pro career. He was a big and strong defenceman who was with the team during its leanest years, when survival in Montreal was by no means certain. After leaving the army, he returned to Quebec and was reinstated as an amateur so he could play senior hockey.

GOVEDARIS, Chris
b. Toronto, Ontario, February 2, 1970
Coming out of junior, there weren't too many players more highly rated in the 1988 draft than Govedaris. Scouts considered him tough and mean and offensively talented. He was one of the few players to start with the Marlies and end with the ill-fated Dukes of Hamilton after the team left Maple Leaf Gardens in 1989. He was drafted by Hartford 11th overall, but Govedaris made little impression with the Whalers and after three years they let him go. Toronto GM Cliff Fletcher decided to give the native son a tryout, and Govedaris hustled and fought his way into the lineup for a dozen games, his last in the NHL. The Leafs demoted him for the rest

Red Goupille

David Goverde

Gerry Goyer

Phil Goyette

of the year, and soon he was in the "I." He accepted an invite to play for Canada at the '95 Worlds (where he won a bronze medal) and stayed overseas to continue his career in Europe.

GOVERDE, David
b. Toronto, Ontario, April 9, 1970

Allowing 29 goals in fewer than 5 full games is not the way to stay in the NHL, particularly if those games are spread out over 3 seasons. Goverde played all his minutes with Los Angeles (1991-94) but spent even more time in the AHL and IHL. He eventually found his home-sweet-home in Phoenix of the WCHL, where he became the star goaltender. He also played goal in roller hockey in the summer.

GOYER, Gerry
b. Belleville, Ontario, October 20, 1936

An almost seamless record of employment in the WHL is broken only by a single season of NHL action, 1967-68 with Chicago. Goyer played 18 years in the Western league and was a terrific scorer, accruing close to 400 goals in that league. The downside was that he was too slow, but when the NHL doubled and the Hawks lost centre Red Hay in the '67 draft, Goyer was given a shot to play on the number-one line with Eric Nesterenko and Dennis Hull. The experiment lasted 40 games, in which time Goyer scored exactly 1 goal, and then it was back to the WHL he went. During his years with Portland, he stayed in the city during the summer and worked in sales, but he moved to San Diego when the Gulls acquired him, and while there he worked in construction as a way of staying in shape in the off-season.

GOYETTE, Phil ("The Professor"/ "The Splendid Splinter"/ "The Thin Man")
b. Lachine, Quebec, October 31, 1933

Goyette wasn't big and physical, but he was renowned for getting out of the way of those who were. He was fleet and shifty and peerless in the faceoff circle, which is why Montreal coveted him, and he had the good fortune to join the Habs at a time when they were the best team on the planet. In his first four seasons (1956-60), he won the Cup every year. Goyette seemed to be constantly in the running for the Lady Byng, averaging about eight minutes in penalties a season, though he won only once, in 1969-70, his only year with St. Louis. Although he was a solid, third-line centre with the Habs, he became number-one man on Broadway when the Habs sent him to New York in a multiplayer deal. He scored as he never had before, registering a career high in points with 78 by the time he got to the Blues. Goyette retired in 1972 and was named the first head coach of the expansion New York Islanders, but this venture lasted only 60 games before he was replaced by Earl Ingarfield. Goyette returned to Montreal and worked as director of sales for a brokerage firm.

GRABOSKI, Tony
b. Timmins, Ontario, May 29, 1916
d. Hidalgo, Texas, September 18, 2000

Tony made it to the NHL, but his brother, Jo-Jo (Joseph), didn't because he had only one good eye. When they were kids, they'd earn money to buy equipment by selling old medicine bottles to drugstores, which would refill them with alcohol. Tony played for Oshawa and Sudbury, and Jo-Jo played for the Wembley Lions, Brockville, and Quebec. They played together in Hershey in 1937-38, but from there Tony went to the NHL and Jo-Jo went to Glace Bay. Tony played parts of three years with the Montreal Canadiens, though he, too, ended up in the minors.

GRACIE, Bob
b. North Bay, Ontario, November 8, 1910
d. Houston, Texas, August 10, 1963

In 1937, there was no doubt that Bob Gracie was the fastest skater in the NHL. He first made headlines as a member of the Leafs, starting in 1930, by which time he had lost both his parents to cancer. He won a Cup with the Leafs in 1932, another Cup with the Montreal Maroons in '35, and by 1939 he was out of the NHL. He had played in the two longest overtime games of all time, Boston-Toronto and Maroons-Detroit, one of only five players who could make such a claim. He played for many years in the American league, setting a record with 95 points in '44-'45. Then, in 1945, he had the opportunity to play and coach a new team in California called the Hollywood Wolves. He accepted the position, and loved the American west coast so much he never came back. He moved his family out and continued to manage the Fresno Falcons after leaving the Wolves, a team that had featured a young Bill Barilko. In the 1930s, Gracie had operated a gas station in Wasaga Beach during the summers. He also worked for a clothing store in Toronto, and earned a reputation for being one of the best dressers in hockey. This helped him out in California, where he became a promoter of the Ice Capades, boxing shows, and anything that might be staged at the Fresno arena. He maintained contacts back east by becoming involved in shipping produce to Canada. One time, as he was preparing to return to Toronto, he felt unwell and saw a specialist in Houston for a throat problem. He required surgery, and died because of a blocked artery at age 52.

In the 1930s, Gracie operated a gas station in Wasaga Beach during the summers.
BOB GRACIE

GRADIN, Thomas

b. Solleftea, Sweden, February 18, 1956

He was a legend in Sweden and part of the second wave of Swedes to come to North America following the success of Borje Salming, Ulf Nilsson, and Anders Hedberg. By the time he played his first NHL game, with Vancouver in 1978, he was already an established young star for Tre Kronor, but he came to Canada and played with incredible determination and skill, forgoing fighting and having to prove himself with the rough stuff. In his first NHL game, he had 2 goals and an assist. Gradin hit 20 goals in each of his first 7 seasons, setting a team record in '81-'82 with 37 goals and 86 points. He played a year in Boston ('86-87) before returning home to play league hockey and coach the national team. Although he played in two Canada Cups – 1981 and '84 – he never played at the Olympics. He has since returned to Sweden and has for many years been the Canucks' top European scout.

GRAHAM, Dirk

b. Regina, Saskatchewan, July 29, 1959

Graham became a national hero in September 1991 during game two of the best-of-three Canada Cup finals against the U.S. With Team Canada up 1-0 in the series and the game tied in the third period, he blocked a Gary Suter slapshot from the point on an American power play. He got control of the puck, and scored a short-handed goal that lifted Canada to victory. It was the crowning moment of his career. Graham had been drafted by Vancouver in 1979 but played the first five years of his career with Minnesota. He was traded to Chicago for Curt Fraser on January 4, 1988, and it was in the Windy City that he enjoyed the finest years of his playing career. He had 33 goals in his first full season with the team and had successful playoff runs with the Hawks in 1989 and '92. He retired in 1995 after the lockout-shortened season and became an assistant coach for one year with the team. He later became a scout, and in 1998-99 became the team's head coach for a brief time before being replaced by Lorne Molleken.

GRAHAM, Edward "Teddy"

b. Owen Sound, Ontario, January 30, 1906
d. Owen Sound, Ontario, December 6, 1978

Graham played for the great Owen Sound Greys for four years, including the 1923-24 team that went to the Memorial Cup, the year he moved from forward to defence. He played Big Six hockey in Ontario with Stratford and London, and then apprenticed in Chicago's system until making the Black Hawks for the 1927-28 season. It was Graham who lined up with Hap Day for one of the most famous photographs of all time – the opening faceoff for the first game at Maple Leaf Gardens. Graham played in the NHL until 1937, when he turned to refereeing. In 1940, he enlisted in the 8th Hussars in London, making captain before venturing overseas to England and Africa. He was returned to Canada and became Officer Commanding Camp Meaford for a year, but he yearned for heavier action and reverted to the rank of lieutenant so he could serve in Belgium and Holland.

GRAHAM, Letham "Leth"

b. Ottawa, Ontario, October 10, 1893
d. Ottawa, Ontario, January 18, 1944

Graham spent the vast majority of his life and playing career in Ottawa, notably with the Senators in the NHA, precursor to the NHL, staying with the team as the NHL came into being. His longest service in any of his 6 years came in 1920-21, when he played 14 games and helped the Sens win the Stanley Cup. After retiring in 1926, Graham settled in the city. He passed away suddenly at age 50.

GRAHAM, Pat ("Paddy")

b. Toronto, Ontario, May 25, 1961

Even back in junior with Toronto and Niagara Falls, Graham had a bad enough back that he had to wear a corset. He used a chiropractor in the Falls, which helped him continue his career, and played briefly with Pittsburgh in '81-'82 before being traded to his hometown Leafs. He lasted only 41 games in T.O. and played a year in Europe before retiring. Graham enrolled at the University of Toronto and earned a B.Sc. in human biology before graduating from chiropractic college himself. He became the chiropractor for the Toronto Blue Jays and opened his own office in the city, where he still practises.

GRAHAM, Rod

b. London, Ontario, August 19, 1946

Fourteen games with Boston in '74-'75 was the apotheosis of this career that had started without an NHL contract two years earlier. Graham signed with the AHL and worked his way up to the Bruins, though most of his six years of pro were with Rochester.

GRAHAME, John ("J.G.")

b. Denver, Colorado, August 31, 1975

As a kid, John played out and in net until he finally settled into the crease for good. His dad had played for the Bruins a generation earlier, and they became the first father-son team to play goal for the B's. John went to Lake Superior State University to study recreation management, and his coach was Jeff Jackson. He was drafted a lowly 229th overall in '94, but he arrived on the scene during a time of flux and made a decent impression when he made his debut in October 1999. Since then, he's had a tougher time of it with Byron Dafoe as the starting goalie, but he remains a man on a mission in the Bruins net.

GRAHAME, Ron ("Rev")

b. Victoria, British Columbia, June 7, 1950

The University of Denver is the most important college in the United States, for it was there that Murray Armstrong presided over the hockey program for decades, nurturing young, mostly Canadian talent in an educational atmosphere at a time when very few players ever considered college as a path to the NHL. Grahame was convinced by his coach back home to take a scholarship at U of D because he wasn't so sensational a goalie that an NHL career was a gimme. Grahame accepted, and how could he have known then that years later he would one day do there what Armstrong did for so long? After graduating, Grahame signed with Houston of the WHA in 1974, playing

Thomas Gradin

Dirk Graham

Pat Graham

John Grahame

Ron Grahame

with Gordie Howe and developing into a fine goaltender. He played 1977-78 with the Bruins and then he was traded to Los Angeles for a first-round draft choice in 1979. Guess who Boston selected with that pick? A guy named Ray Bourque. Grahame played three more years in the NHL to round out a pedestrian NHL career, though he had a fine 50-43-15 record. He moved to California and worked at the May Company for less than a year before returning to Denver as an assistant coach to Ralph Backstrom. He left to coach at St. Cloud State, but then returned to U of D, eventually becoming the associate athletic director in 1993. His son, John, went on to play goal for the Bruins, and his wife worked for the Colorado Avalanche. Ironically, it was she who got her name on the Stanley Cup first, for the Avs' 2001 victory.

operation, he was on a stationary bike in a month and back in the NHL before the end of the calendar year after signing with San Jose, the only team willing to take a risk on him. In his second game back, at home, he scored a hat trick and added an assist. Dr. Martin was in the end seats behind the opponent's end that night and had a perfect view of the performance. At year's end, Granato received the Bill Masterton Trophy, and although he was less effective, he played another three years. He retired to become a member of San Jose's broadcasting department, happy to be alive, victor of life itself. His improbable rise in the NHL's executive ranks reached its zenith midway through the 2002-03 season when he was named head coach of Colorado, replacing the fired, Cup-winning Bob Hartley.

Jean-Luc Grand-Pierre

Benny Grant

Danny Grant

GRANATO, Tony

b. Downers Grove, Illinois, July 25, 1964

It's a story that drove even the hardest men to tears, a story of courage and determination that is the very stuff of hockey legend. And it happened only a few years ago. And it came out of nowhere. Granato had a great career even before he ever played a single NHL game. During his four years at the University of Wisconsin he played in two World Juniors and two World Championships. He then spent a year with Team USA through the 1988 Olympics in Calgary, and only then did he join the NHL with his drafted team, the Rangers. He had 36 goals as a rookie, but the Rangers traded him to L.A. to get Bernie Nicholls. He had 3 successive 30-goal seasons with the Kings, and he was equally successful as an agitator and two-way skater. In February 1994, he perpetrated an awful act on ice when he used his stick like a club and swung fully down on the helmeted head of Chicago's Neil Wilkinson. Although felled by the blow, Wilkinson was not seriously injured. Granato was suspended for his actions, though he claimed not to remember the incident too clearly. On January 25, 1996, Granato was victimized in similar fashion, though to greater effect. That night, he was checked headfirst into the boards. He was hurt, though he played the next game in the hopes his headaches would go away. They got worse, and doctors knew a blood clot was applying deadly pressure on his brain. When they operated, they found a cluster of vessels and removed them, noting that this was likely a condition he was born with but exacerbated by the hard check. The surgeon, Dr. Neil Martin, took into account Granato's occupation and doubled up on the plates and screws he inserted into Granato's head. The final tally: 8 plates and 30 screws. Before the operation, Granato feared for his life and knew he'd never play hockey again. After the

His improbable rise in the NHL's executive ranks reached its zenith midway through the 2002-03 season.
TONY GRANATO

GRAND-PIERRE, Jean-Luc

b. Montreal, Quebec, February 2, 1977

He put up big numbers in the penalty-minutes column but perhaps the biggest thing of all about him is his name. He's the only player in league history to have two hyphenated first and last names. Other than that, the defenceman has yet to distinguish himself in the NHL.

GRANT, Benny

b. Owen Sound, Ontario, July 14, 1908
d. Owen Sound, Ontario, July 30, 1991

An Owen Sounder through and through, Grant grew up there, played there, returned there after his playing days, and passed away there at the ripe old age of 83. In his youth, he played for the Greys, winning the Memorial Cup in 1927 before moving on to play for the Leafs. Unfortunately, he arrived in an era of one goalie, so he played only when regulars Lorne Chabot or George Hainsworth were injured (with a few exceptions along the way). The Leafs loaned him to the New York Americans on a couple of occasions – to replace injured goalers – and by 1934 it looked as if he had played his last NHL game. For the next decade he played in the minors and worked for Imperial Oil in the summers. Then the war came, and while Turk Broda was in the army the Leafs came a-calling, told him to quit Imperial to play goal again. This he could do, because the oil company sponsored the team, and Grant played 21 games in the '43-'44 season. At season's end, he retired for keeps and worked as a stock clerk for Imperial for the next 35 years.

GRANT, Danny

b. Fredericton, New Brunswick, February 21, 1946

Was it really so long ago that he played in the NHL? Grant once had an Iron Man streak stopped at

566 games, and his steady rise to greatness in 1974-75, when he scored 50 goals, was eclipsed only by his meteoric descent. After that great season, he scored just 34 goals over the next 4 years, slowed by injuries. Grant began with Montreal in pre-expansion days. He won a Cup as a part-timer with the team in '67-'68, but his big break came in the summer when he was traded to Minnesota. He scored 34 goals in his first season to win the Calder Trophy, and subsequent years of 29 and 34 goals proved his worth as a bona fide player in the league. Ironically, that 50-goal season, with Detroit, proved the beginning of the end for Grant. The next year he was named captain of the Wings but missed half the season with torn knee ligaments. He never produced impressively again. Grant retired in 1979 and went home, working for Moosehead Breweries and coaching the Fredericton Capitals to the 1980 Hardy Cup. The next year, he became president of the Fredericton Express and came out of retirement to play a few games for the team. He was elected to the New Brunswick Sports Hall of Fame in 1985 and became a board of governor for the Canadian Sports Hall five years later. He went on to coach at UNB in 1994 and joined the Halifax Mooseheads in 1997, first as coach, then as general manager. More recently, he became project coordinator for Enbridge Gas in New Brunswick.

GRANT, Doug
b. Corner Brook, Newfoundland, July 27, 1948
Until he was 10 years old, Grant played out. One night, though, his team was without a goalie, and he volunteered to fill the breach. His team won, and he never left the crease. He played only in Corner Brook until going to Memorial University on a Hockey Canada scholarship, and in the anonymity of that team he was discovered by Larry Jeffrey, who invited him to Detroit's camp the next fall. Grant played the year in the minors ('72-'73), and then early in '73-'74 he caught a break when the Red Wings' number-one man, Roy Edwards, left the team in a contract dispute. Grant got the call and stayed the year, playing in 37 games for a lousy Detroit team. The 7 years of NHL hockey for him, though, were always a case of up and down to the minors. The next 6 seasons saw him play only as many games total as in that first year, and an unlikely career that took shape quickly proved briefer than he would have liked.

GRATTON, Benoit
b. Montreal, Quebec, December 28, 1976
A part-timer to date, Gratton has played for three teams in five NHL seasons and has yet to make his mark in the league. Washington drafted him in 1995 and played him only 22 times, and stints with Calgary and Montreal have been short.

GRATTON, Chris
b. Brantford, Ontario, July 5, 1975
In the months and weeks leading up to the 1993 draft, the two Chrises got most of the publicity – Gratton or Pronger, who would go number one? As it turned out, Alexandre Daigle burst onto the scene to be 1st overall, signing a mammoth contract that was a total waste of

Ottawa's money. Pronger went 2nd to Hartford, and Gratton 3rd to Tampa Bay. He made the Lightning that fall, just 18 and with only 2 years of junior to his credit. Over the next four years, though, the big and tough centre developed to the point where he had 30 goals in '96-'97 and seemed to be blossoming into what Tampa had hoped. That summer, though, he signed with Philadelphia for $16.5 million over five years. That was Daigle-like dough, and Gratton played not much better. A year and a half later, the Flyers traded him back to Tampa and from there he moved on to Buffalo. He remains an NHLer, but a third- or fourth-line, 15-goal man rather than a first-line 40-goal power forward to build a team around, as Jacques Demers once described Gratton during their days of Lightning.

GRATTON, Dan
b. Brantford, Ontario, December 7, 1966
Los Angeles liked this kid so much in 1985 that it drafted him 10th overall. Gratton promptly bolted from his junior team, Oshawa, demanding a trade, but when the Kings told him to get in there and play, he relented. Perhaps the fuss was unwarranted. He played just 10 games before the Generals traded him to Ottawa, and then the 67's traded him to Belleville. That was to be his mark throughout his career, moving like an alley cat from one cul-de-sac to the next. He got his games in with the Kings – seven in all – but he played in most minor pro leagues in the U.S. and did a tour of Europe that would be the envy of any student with a Eurailpass and a hockey bag. Along the way, he also played for Canada's National Team before returning home to finish his career.

GRATTON, Gilles ("Loony Grattoony")
b. LaSalle, Quebec, July 28, 1952
How does a trainer rationally deal with this situation: A goalie crumples to the ice after taking a hard slapshot to the ribs, and the trainer comes running out to help the wounded guardian only to be told the pain is right where an old sword wound is. See, in a previous life, the goalie was a Spanish conquistador. That's why he was called loony. Gratton was a skilled goalie, but quirky doesn't begin to cover the craziness and insanity that pervaded his every thought. He believed that astrology controlled when he would and wouldn't play well. He wore the most amazing goalie mask – of a lion's growling countenance – the NHL has ever seen. He was difficult to play with and for. In 1975-76, St. Louis signed him and he stayed for six games. In two, he took himself out for no apparent reason. In the other four, he went undefeated. He hated coach Garry Young and left the team to rejoin the Toronto Toros of the WHA, and he played the next season with the Rangers. He retired in late 1977, and after his marriage fell apart he travelled Europe and worked in photography. He remarried, settled in Montreal, and found a job in the book department of a Costco.

GRATTON, Norm
b. LaSalle, Quebec, December 22, 1950
Perreault-Martin-Gratton. The French Connection Line. Not exactly, but, yes, for a short time. Actually, Rick Martin and Norm Gratton, the more normal brother of Gilles the Loony, played together for a

Doug Grant

Benoit Gratton

Chris Gratton

Gilles Gratton

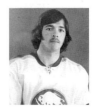

Norm Gratton

subsequent days, doctors had to remove shards of skull from the brain itself, and Green lay in hospital partially paralyzed. A priest had given him last rites, and teammates visited him for what they thought was the last time. But Green was no quitter, not in this life, anyway. He regained consciousness, and over the next year regained most, but not all, of his motor skills and dexterity. Since joining the Bruins at the end of the '60-'61 season, Green had developed a reputation as one of the tough guys. He had also developed into a superb defenceman. He had played in two All-Star Games (1965 and '69) on merit, and was named to the Second All-Star Team in '69 as well. Opponents, though, genuinely feared him, and Maki likely reacted out of self-defence more than animal aggression of his own. Both men were charged by Ottawa police, and NHL president Clarence Campbell suspended Maki for 30 days and Green for 13 games (both were eventually found not guilty by an Ottawa judge). The '69-'70 season ended, of course, with Bobby Orr's flying overtime goal to defeat St. Louis, and the players insisted that Green's name be included on the Cup even though he didn't play a single minute that year. By the fall of 1970, he was ready to play hockey again. His return was a miracle. He wore a helmet and played more tentatively and without the speed, but he played all the same and survived. He stayed with the Bruins through 1972, then they won a second Cup and he moved on to the WHA where things were a little slower. He played for the rest of the WHA's life and then became an assistant coach in Edmonton with the now-NHL Oilers. He never left the bench. He was with Edmonton for the better part of 20 years and all 5 Cups, as an assistant, as a head coach for two and a half years (1991-93), and as an assistant GM. When coach Ron Low moved to New York to be with new Rangers GM Glen Sather, the two took Green with them, and he has remained as faithful to Sather as Slats has been to him. Green might never make it into the Hockey Hall of Fame, but for him being alive is honour and pleasure enough after 1969.

Travis Green

GREEN, Travis ("Vern")
b. Castlegar, British Columbia, December 20, 1970
He's been around for a decade now, and some 700 NHL games, but until he joined Toronto in 2001 he had played in precious few playoff games. Playing for the Islanders and Anaheim throughout the 1990s will do that to a player's post-season stats. The compensation, though, is that he's also played for Canada at three World Championships, notably the gold-medal team of 1997. Green has proved both a capable scorer and an enigmatic centreman, sometimes offensively capable, sometimes a defensive liability.

Jeff Greenlaw

GREEN, Wilfred "Shorty"
b. Sudbury, Ontario, July 17, 1896
d. Sudbury, Ontario, April 19, 1960
In April 1916, Green stopped playing hockey so he could contribute to Canada's war efforts. He served with the 227th Canadian Battalion in France, seeing action at Ypres and suffering a gas attack in Passchendale. When he returned home, he put down his rifle, picked up his stick, and headed for Hamilton where he helped the Tigers win the Allan Cup in 1919. Despite being one of the slightest players in the game, he was no wallflower, and any opponent who tried to trifle with his small frame was quickly hit exponentially harder than he had anticipated. He returned to Sudbury to play senior hockey, but when those Tigers joined the NHL in 1923, Green returned to southern Ontario. He played on a line

Green returned to Sudbury where he operated a men's clothing store.
SHORTY GREEN

with his brother, Red Green, and the great Billy Burch, and the trio was dubbed the Tiger Line. Hamilton didn't have a very good first year, but they made it to the league showdown in their second season, Green acting as their captain. But before their first playoff game against the Canadiens, the players discovered that their bosses had made thousands in profit and they had been paid a pittance. Guided by Green, the players refused to step on the ice against the Habs unless they were guaranteed $200 each per game. The owners refused to capitulate, the Canadiens were awarded the series, and the players, in turn, fined $200. Green ended up with the new New York Americans, and on December 19, 1925, he scored the first-ever goal in the new Madison Square Garden. He played with the team until early 1927 when he suffered a serious kidney injury in a game and was forced to retire. He stayed on the next year with the team as coach, but a year later he took a job in Duluth to coach the Hornets in the American league. Soon after, Green returned to Sudbury where he operated a men's clothing store, and in 1937 he opened the Sudbury Golf Club with two partners. After they died in 1942, he became sole proprietor until 1960 when he succumbed to cancer. He was inducted into the Hockey Hall of Fame two years later. In the 1920s, downtown Hamilton was lined with small green water fountains, some of which remain today. To this day, they are still called by their affectionate appellation, Shorty Greens.

GREENLAW, Jeff
b. Toronto, Ontario, February 28, 1968
His teen years were, quite simply, a mess. Although he was born in Toronto, Greenlaw grew up in the Maritimes and didn't return to Ontario for a number of years, by which time he was one of the finest teen players in the country. He warned all OHL teams

566 games, and his steady rise to greatness in 1974-75, when he scored 50 goals, was eclipsed only by his meteoric descent. After that great season, he scored just 34 goals over the next 4 years, slowed by injuries. Grant began with Montreal in pre-expansion days. He won a Cup as a part-timer with the team in '67-'68, but his big break came in the summer when he was traded to Minnesota. He scored 34 goals in his first season to win the Calder Trophy, and subsequent years of 29 and 34 goals proved his worth as a bona fide player in the league. Ironically, that 50-goal season, with Detroit, proved the beginning of the end for Grant. The next year he was named captain of the Wings but missed half the season with torn knee ligaments. He never produced impressively again. Grant retired in 1979 and went home, working for Moosehead Breweries and coaching the Fredericton Capitals to the 1980 Hardy Cup. The next year, he became president of the Fredericton Express and came out of retirement to play a few games for the team. He was elected to the New Brunswick Sports Hall of Fame in 1985 and became a board of governor for the Canadian Sports Hall five years later. He went on to coach at UNB in 1994 and joined the Halifax Mooseheads in 1997, first as coach, then as general manager. More recently, he became project coordinator for Enbridge Gas in New Brunswick.

GRANT, Doug
b. Corner Brook, Newfoundland, July 27, 1948
Until he was 10 years old, Grant played out. One night, though, his team was without a goalie, and he volunteered to fill the breach. His team won, and he never left the crease. He played only in Corner Brook until going to Memorial University on a Hockey Canada scholarship, and in the anonymity of that team he was discovered by Larry Jeffrey, who invited him to Detroit's camp the next fall. Grant played the year in the minors ('72-'73), and then early in '73-'74 he caught a break when the Red Wings' number-one man, Roy Edwards, left the team in a contract dispute. Grant got the call and stayed the year, playing in 37 games for a lousy Detroit team. The 7 years of NHL hockey for him, though, were always a case of up and down to the minors. The next 6 seasons saw him play only as many games total as in that first year, and an unlikely career that took shape quickly proved briefer than he would have liked.

GRATTON, Benoit
b. Montreal, Quebec, December 28, 1976
A part-timer to date, Gratton has played for three teams in five NHL seasons and has yet to make his mark in the league. Washington drafted him in 1995 and played him only 22 times, and stints with Calgary and Montreal have been short.

GRATTON, Chris
b. Brantford, Ontario, July 5, 1975
In the months and weeks leading up to the 1993 draft, the two Chrises got most of the publicity – Gratton or Pronger, who would go number one? As it turned out, Alexandre Daigle burst onto the scene to be 1st overall, signing a mammoth contract that was a total waste of Ottawa's money. Pronger went 2nd to Hartford, and Gratton 3rd to Tampa Bay. He made the Lightning that fall, just 18 and with only 2 years of junior to his credit. Over the next four years, though, the big and tough centre developed to the point where he had 30 goals in '96-'97 and seemed to be blossoming into what Tampa had hoped. That summer, though, he signed with Philadelphia for $16.5 million over five years. That was Daigle-like dough, and Gratton played not much better. A year and a half later, the Flyers traded him back to Tampa and from there he moved on to Buffalo. He remains an NHLer, but a third- or fourth-line, 15-goal man rather than a first-line 40-goal power forward to build a team around, as Jacques Demers once described Gratton during their days of Lightning.

GRATTON, Dan
b. Brantford, Ontario, December 7, 1966
Los Angeles liked this kid so much in 1985 that it drafted him 10th overall. Gratton promptly bolted from his junior team, Oshawa, demanding a trade, but when the Kings told him to get in there and play, he relented. Perhaps the fuss was unwarranted. He played just 10 games before the Generals traded him to Ottawa, and then the 67's traded him to Belleville. That was to be his mark throughout his career, moving like an alley cat from one cul-de-sac to the next. He got his games in with the Kings – seven in all – but he played in most minor pro leagues in the U.S. and did a tour of Europe that would be the envy of any student with a Eurailpass and a hockey bag. Along the way, he also played for Canada's National Team before returning home to finish his career.

GRATTON, Gilles ("Loony Grattoony")
b. LaSalle, Quebec, July 28, 1952
How does a trainer rationally deal with this situation: A goalie crumples to the ice after taking a hard slapshot to the ribs, and the trainer comes running out to help the wounded guardian only to be told the pain is right where an old sword wound is. See, in a previous life, the goalie was a Spanish conquistador. That's why he was called loony. Gratton was a skilled goalie, but quirky doesn't begin to cover the craziness and insanity that pervaded his every thought. He believed that astrology controlled when he would and wouldn't play well. He wore the most amazing goalie mask – of a lion's growling countenance – the NHL has ever seen. He was difficult to play with and for. In 1975-76, St. Louis signed him and he stayed for six games. In two, he took himself out for no apparent reason. In the other four, he went undefeated. He hated coach Garry Young and left the team to rejoin the Toronto Toros of the WHA, and he played the next season with the Rangers. He retired in late 1977, and after his marriage fell apart he travelled Europe and worked in photography. He remarried, settled in Montreal, and found a job in the book department of a Costco.

GRATTON, Norm
b. LaSalle, Quebec, December 22, 1950
Perreault-Martin-Gratton. The French Connection Line. Not exactly, but, yes, for a short time. Actually, Rick Martin and Norm Gratton, the more normal brother of Gilles the Loony, played together for a

Doug Grant

Benoit Gratton

Chris Gratton

Gilles Gratton

Norm Gratton

Hilliard Graves

Steve Graves

Alex Gray

number of years in their teens. Gratton started with the Rangers in '71-'72 but was claimed by Atlanta in the Expansion Draft, and the Flames sent him to Buffalo on February 14, 1973. Coach Punch Imlach played Gratton briefly with Gil Perreault and Martin, and just about every time he did Gratton scored. The real French Connection, though, was too great to tamper with permanently, and Gratton was soon relegated to a lesser line. He closed out his NHL career with Minnesota.

GRAVELLE, Leo
("The Tiger"/ "The Gazelle"/ "Pluto")
b. Aylmer, Quebec, June 10, 1925
Known for his speed, Gravelle burst into the NHL in 1946-47 by scoring 16 goals from the right wing in Montreal. He played most of five seasons with the Habs before being traded to Detroit for Bert Olmstead. Early in the '49-'50 season, he and teammate Ken Reardon were charged by Chicago police for assault in an incident with fans, though the judge threw the case out of court. Gravelle finished his career playing senior hockey in Ottawa.

GRAVES, Adam
("Gravy")
b. Toronto, Ontario,
April 12, 1968
Graves is a man off the ice and a competitor on it. As a player, he developed with Detroit and Edmonton, winning a Cup with the Oilers in 1990 after being acquired near the trade deadline from the Wings. The Rangers signed him as a free agent in 1991, likely the best free agent signing to that point in NHL history. Graves had consecutive seasons of 26, 36, and 52 goals, that third total coming in '93-'94 when the entire team played beyond its capability to win the first Cup for the Rangers since 1940. Graves was never to have as fine an offensive season, and in 2001 New York sent him to San Jose where he is now a veteran trying to help a young team win. Off ice, particularly in New York, Graves gives much of his time to children's causes, notably Toys for Tots and muscular dystrophy. Sadly, his own family suffered problems. Early in 2000, his wife gave birth to premature twins, one of whom died a month later, the other a short time after that. Graves won the King Clancy Memorial Trophy in 1994 for his humanitarian contributions.

GRAVES, Hilliard ("Hil")
b. Saint John, New Brunswick, October 18, 1950
Graves was born in New Brunswick, raised in Nova Scotia, and played his first serious hockey in PEI. A Maritimer he was. In 1968, he enrolled at U of PEI to study economics and played hockey at the same time.

In New York, Graves gives much of his time to children's causes.
ADAM GRAVES

Cut to the other side of the world, Oakland, where the hockey team had a rookie named Norm Ferguson from Nova Scotia leading the team with 34 goals. The Seals decided to scope Canada's East again, and this time they found Graves. He made his NHL debut in 1970 but played in the minors for most of the next two years. Then things fell into place. He scored 27 goals and 52 points in '72-'73 and developed a reputation as the best hitter in the game, bar none. An asthma problem hurt his play the following year, and although he went on to play 556 NHL games, only once did his team ever make the playoffs, in '74-'75 when the Atlanta Flames were swept by L.A. in a preliminary round. His whole life he had occasionally raced harness horses, and he started a stable during his playing days. His first horse was called Ina Baby Breeze, but when he retired in 1980 he got a job in Dartmouth as the vice-president and general manager of Amca Food Brokers.

GRAVES, Steve
b. Trenton, Ontario, April 7, 1964
This Graves had the misfortune of being drafted by Edmonton in 1982, a time when a young player of average skill had no chance of cracking a lineup that boasted Gretzky, Coffey, Anderson, Messier, Kurri et al. He played 35 games with the Oilers over 5 seasons, but he was forced to go to Europe to find a regular shift.

GRAY, Alex
("Peanuts")
b. Glasgow, Scotland,
June 21, 1899
d. April 10, 1986
Gray moved to Ontario as a young boy and played in Port Arthur for years before the Rangers signed him. He made the team in 1927 and had the good fortune to contribute to a Stanley Cup victory the very next spring. The Leafs acquired him the next year for Butch Keeling, but Gray played only a few games before finding his way down to the IHL to close out his career. He retired to Port Arthur and became a sales rep for a beer company.

GRAY, Gerry
b. Brantford, Ontario, January 28, 1948
He gave pro hockey a shot, but pro hockey didn't give him much of one. Gray played for Hamilton in the Detroit system in the late 1960s, but played only seven games for the Red Wings before being traded in 1972 to the Islanders. Even the expansion team, though, used him only once, and after a couple of part-time seasons he retired and returned to Brantford to work.

GRAY, Harrison
b. Calgary, Alberta, September 5, 1941
The kid was just a kid when he made his lone NHL appearance in a game on November 28, 1963. He was

Gerry Gray

sitting in the stands minding his own business when Detroit's regular – a guy named Terry Sawchuk – got hurt and couldn't come out for the second period with his team trailing 2-1. Gray hurriedly dressed and slowly let in five goals, two in the second, three in the third, in a 7-3 loss. He never watched another NHL game from the crease.

GRAY, Terry
b. Montreal, Quebec, March 21, 1938

So many players are perfectly able to perform in the NHL, but they just don't shine in a way that keeps them there. Gray was such a skater. Skilled, tough, reliable, he played his right wing position responsibly and was never without work during his career. Yet he rarely played anywhere for a long time, and certainly not in the NHL. His junior career climaxed with a Memorial Cup win in 1958 with the Montreal junior team in Hull-Ottawa, though he made his NHL debut with Boston in '61-'62. In all, he played for 4 NHL teams, totalling just 147 games, and spent most of his years with a variety of teams. In 1970, he became a playing coach for the Montreal Voyageurs, but only in a loan arrangement from St. Louis, which owned his rights. The Blues called in their chips at season's end when they used him in the playoffs, though Gray later coached in the IHL.

GREEN, Josh
b. Camrose, Alberta, November 16, 1977

A huge prospect, Green missed more than a year of playing with serious, back-to-back shoulder injuries. He had played for L.A. in '98-'99 before being traded to the Islanders, a team stockpiling young, talented players. Toward the end of the season, he dislocated his left shoulder and missed the final nine games of the year. Over the summer he was traded to Edmonton and recovered, but in training camp he injured the shoulder more seriously and required extensive surgery. He got back into shape and was sent to the minors, when just like that he dislocated his right shoulder. More surgery; gone for the year. He returned to play three times in the playoffs, and is still trying to earn a full-time spot on the roster and stay healthy for a full season.

GREEN, Redvers "Red"
b. Sudbury, Ontario, December 12, 1899
d. Sudbury, Ontario, July 25, 1966

The top line for the Hamilton Tigers in '23-'24 and '24-'25 consisted of captain Red Green on the left side, brother Shorty on the right, and Billy Birch in the middle. On December 5, 1924, Red became just the eighth player to score five goals in a game, all against John Ross Roach of Toronto. The season ended badly

for the team, though, when the Tigers went on strike to protest their playoff salaries and the NHL simply disqualified them automatically. The two Greens and Burch moved as a unit to the New York Americans the next year, and Red played his last game in '28–'29 with Boston and Detroit. He then returned to Sudbury, and when the Elliot Lake townsite opened he operated a commissary there. In 1964, Green moved to Wabush, Labrador, but a year later came back to Sudbury and retired. He died in the Sudbury-Algoma Sanitorium after a long illness.

GREEN, Rick ("Rich"/ "The Green Giant")
b. Belleville, Ontario, February 20, 1956

When Wayne Gretzky first joined the Edmonton Oilers, his teammates called him Brinks because of the long and lucrative contract he signed. Shortly after Washington signed the 1st selection overall at the 1976 Amateur Draft, Rick Green, to a four-year, $4.5-million deal, his teammates started calling him Rich. Green played a ton of hockey for someone who played the way he did. He never played a full season, always injured for at least a few games with an ear infection or a broken wrist or just from blocking one too many shots on a given night. He played the majority of his career with the Capitals and then the Canadiens, winning a Cup with Montreal in 1986. Not surprisingly, he missed half the year with the aforementioned wrist fracture suffered in an exhibition game against the touring Soviet Red Army team.

Green also played in four World Championships for Canada and Rendez-vous '87, and over the course of his career he was regarded as one of the finer defensive defencemen in the game. Tired, he hung up his skates at age 33 in 1989, though he made a bit of a comeback for another couple of years before retiring to his family farm in Lakehurst, Ontario.

GREEN, Ted ("Terrible Ted")
b. Eriksdale, Manitoba, March 23, 1940

He's been in hockey for 40 years, but every day since 1969 has been a bonus he'll have to thank someone at the Pearly Gates for when he finally gets there. It was in an exhibition game, Boston versus St. Louis in Ottawa, that Ted Green and Wayne Maki got involved in the most vicious stick-swinging duel ever. Neither man wore a helmet, and each gave the other's head home-run swings with his club. Maki was stunned and scared and, as Green turned away, delivered one final two-hander that landed on the top of Green's skull and continued inside it. Green lay on the ice convulsing, and later that night required brain surgery. In

> **Green lay on the ice convulsing, and later that night required brain surgery.**
> TED GREEN

Terry Gray

Josh Green

Red Green

Rick Green

subsequent days, doctors had to remove shards of skull from the brain itself, and Green lay in hospital partially paralyzed. A priest had given him last rites, and teammates visited him for what they thought was the last time. But Green was no quitter, not in this life, anyway. He regained consciousness, and over the next year regained most, but not all, of his motor skills and dexterity. Since joining the Bruins at the end of the '60-'61 season, Green had developed a reputation as one of the tough guys. He had also developed into a superb defenceman. He had played in two All-Star Games (1965 and '69) on merit, and was named to the Second All-Star Team in '69 as well. Opponents, though, genuinely feared him, and Maki likely reacted out of self-defence more than animal aggression of his own. Both men were charged by Ottawa police, and NHL president Clarence Campbell suspended Maki for 30 days and Green for 13 games (both were eventually found not guilty by an Ottawa judge). The '69-'70 season ended, of course, with Bobby Orr's flying overtime goal to defeat St. Louis, and the players insisted that Green's name be included on the Cup even though he didn't play a single minute that year. By the fall of 1970, he was ready to play hockey again. His return was a miracle. He wore a helmet and played more tentatively and without the speed, but he played all the same and survived. He stayed with the Bruins through 1972, then they won a second Cup and he moved on to the WHA where things were a little slower. He played for the rest of the WHA's life and then became an assistant coach in Edmonton with the now-NHL Oilers. He never left the bench. He was with Edmonton for the better part of 20 years and all 5 Cups, as an assistant, as a head coach for two and a half years (1991-93), and as an assistant GM. When coach Ron Low moved to New York to be with new Rangers GM Glen Sather, the two took Green with them, and he has remained as faithful to Sather as Slats has been to him. Green might never make it into the Hockey Hall of Fame, but for him being alive is honour and pleasure enough after 1969.

Travis Green

GREEN, Travis ("Vern")

b. Castlegar, British Columbia, December 20, 1970
He's been around for a decade now, and some 700 NHL games, but until he joined Toronto in 2001 he had played in precious few playoff games. Playing for the Islanders and Anaheim throughout the 1990s will do that to a player's post-season stats. The compensation, though, is that he's also played for Canada at three World Championships, notably the gold-medal team of 1997. Green has proved both a capable scorer and an enigmatic centreman, sometimes offensively capable, sometimes a defensive liability.

Green returned to Sudbury where he operated a men's clothing store.
SHORTY GREEN

GREEN, Wilfred "Shorty"

b. Sudbury, Ontario, July 17, 1896
d. Sudbury, Ontario, April 19, 1960
In April 1916, Green stopped playing hockey so he could contribute to Canada's war efforts. He served with the 227th Canadian Battalion in France, seeing action at Ypres and suffering a gas attack in Passchendale. When he returned home, he put down his rifle, picked up his stick, and headed for Hamilton where he helped the Tigers win the Allan Cup in 1919. Despite being one of the slightest players in the game, he was no wallflower, and any opponent who tried to trifle with his small frame was quickly hit exponentially harder than he had anticipated. He returned to Sudbury to play senior hockey, but when those Tigers joined the NHL in 1923, Green returned to southern Ontario. He played on a line with his brother, Red Green, and the great Billy Burch, and the trio was dubbed the Tiger Line. Hamilton didn't have a very good first year, but they made it to the league showdown in their second season, Green acting as the captain. But before their first playoff game against the Canadiens, the players discovered that their bosses had made thousands in profit and they had been paid a pittance. Guided by Green, the players refused to step on the ice against the Habs unless they were guaranteed $200 each per game. The owners refused to capitulate, the Canadiens were awarded the series, and the players, in turn, fined $200. Green ended up with the new New York Americans, and on December 19, 1925, he scored the first-ever goal in the new Madison Square Garden. He played with the team until early 1927 when he suffered a serious kidney injury in a game and was forced to retire. He stayed on the next year with the team as coach, but a year later he took a job in Duluth to coach the Hornets in the American league. Soon after, Green returned to Sudbury where he operated a men's clothing store, and in 1937 he opened the Sudbury Golf Club with two partners. After they died in 1942, he became sole proprietor until 1960 when he succumbed to cancer. He was inducted into the Hockey Hall of Fame two years later. In the 1920s, downtown Hamilton was lined with small green water fountains, some of which remain today. To this day, they are still called by their affectionate appellation, Shorty Greens.

GREENLAW, Jeff

b. Toronto, Ontario, February 28, 1968
His teen years were, quite simply, a mess. Although he was born in Toronto, Greenlaw grew up in the Maritimes and didn't return to Ontario for a number of years, by which time he was one of the finest teen players in the country. He warned all OHL teams

Jeff Greenlaw

other than the Marlies not to draft him, but North Bay did. He refused to play so far from home, and even took the OHL to court, saying that to move so far would compromise his education. North Bay succumbed and traded his rights, but this meant he couldn't play for a year. The long and the short of the mess he made was that he went from junior B in St. Catharines to a year with the Canadian National Team to the Washington Capitals, the team that had drafted him. He had declared his intentions to play until the 1988 Olympics in Calgary, but coach Dave King didn't share the same enthusiasm for his talents as Greenlaw himself did. He played for Washington at age 18 without a day of junior hockey, and over the next 8 years he played a grand total of 57 games in the NHL and a few hundred more in the minors. If only he had reported to North Bay…

GREENLAY, Mike
b. Vitoria, Brazil,
September 15, 1968
Not Brazilian like Pele or the salsa or beach volleyball. Brazilian as in his family lived there and he happened to be born there, but he was really Canadian. That kind of Brazilian. Nonetheless, it's not every day someone from Vitoria grows up to play NHL hockey. Greenlay did it, for two games, with Edmonton in '89-'90, the year the Oilers won the Cup. He was a goalie and appeared only in relief, and he spent several years in the minors before going into broadcasting, most famously with Fox Sports. In 2002, he was named TV analyst for the Minnesota Wild.

GREGG, Randy
b. Edmonton, Alberta,
February 19, 1956
Truly, hockey has produced many, many fine men, but none finer than Dr. Randy Gregg. At 19, he was in the science program at U of Alberta, taking pre-med courses to one day follow in his brother's footsteps. He also played hockey for the Golden Bears, and in four years the team won two CIAU championships and he was named player of the year in 1979, the year he graduated. Being a Canadian university player meant, of course, not being drafted, but no matter. Gregg accepted Father David Bauer's offer to play for the National Team and go to Lake Placid for the 1980 Olympics. From there, he headed to Japan, hardly a career move for a 24-year-old hoping to play in the NHL. Gregg played for and coached the Kokudo Bunnies for two seasons, and then signed with his hometown Oilers. It was there he spent the next nine years on the blueline of one of the greatest teams of all time, winning five Stanley Cups and ensuring his place in hockey history. But even during those years, his mind wandered and his spirit grew restless. In 1986, he retired, though relented six weeks later and

returned to the fold. In 1987, he left again for most of the season, this time to live in residence and do his orthopaedic surgery requirements. In 1990, he retired a third time, for the whole year, and after 21 games the year after he hung up his blades for good. He opened a clinic in Edmonton for sports medicine, and has worked as a doctor ever since.

GREIG, Bruce
b. High River, Alberta, May 9, 1953
While other players might have watched video to see how they skated or looked for the opening or backchecked, Greig taped his fights to see how he could improve his technique. For he unabashedly knew he had no talent in hockey save the ability to throw his fists at opponents. That's the only reason California drafted him in 1973. He made the team in the fall, but was unimpressive and soon learned he had mono. That laid him low for the rest of the season. Next year, he came back to camp and tore his knee ligaments after just eight games, and that cost him another season. The year after, he came to camp weighing 240 pounds, good enough to get him to the minors, whence he never returned.

GREIG, Mark
b. High River, Alberta,
January 25, 1970
Here is one of the oddest family facts in all of hockey. His brother, Bruce, was out of the NHL 16 years before Greig got into his first NHL game! Now that has to be a record. Mark has pottered around for more than a decade on the fringe of the NHL, playing for Hartford in 1990-91 and on to other teams while playing mostly in the minors. The right winger had some ability as a scorer and certainly didn't rely on fighting to the extent his brother did, though Mark wasn't exactly a wallflower.

GRENIER, Lucien
b. Malartic, Quebec, November 3, 1946
He is the poster boy for the movable nets the NHL switched to in the 1980s. He's the "before" picture, an image of a player lying in pain on the ice, his career threatened, his leg shattered, his every breath filled with agony and shot through with pain. Grenier joined the new Atlanta Flames in the fall of 1972, and coach Bernie Geoffrion had called him the team's best forward. In the final game of the exhibition schedule, against California, he was tripped by Dick Redmond while going in on a breakaway. He fell hard into the goalpost – the unmovable goalpost – and broke his leg in two places. Players and trainers from both teams came out to look at him and see what they could do. That's how bad it was. He took a year to recover, and

Mike Greenlay

He is the poster boy for the moveable nets the NHL switched to in the 1980s.
LUCIEN GRENIER

Randy Gregg

Bruce Greig

Mark Greig

never played again in the NHL. He had played with Montreal and Los Angeles, winning a Cup with the Habs in '68-'69 by virtue of appearing in two playoff games with the team.

GRENIER, Martin
b. Laval, Quebec, November 2, 1980

Goon would not be quite so accurate a word to describe Grenier. In his four years in the Q he brutalized opponents, but although he was owned by Colorado and Boston, it wasn't until Phoenix signed him as a free agent that he got into the NHL. In the minors, he has continued his fighting ways.

GRENIER, Richard
b. Montreal, Quebec, September 18, 1952

He got his NHL games in early, so that dream was taken care of in 1972 when he was barely 20. Then, the speedy centre with the smooth hands and quick shot played everywhere else on the planet, just about, his longest stint coming in Austria. After a while, he qualified to play nationally for his adopted country, and Grenier competed for Austria at the 1987 World Championships, "B" pool, finishing in third place.

Richard Grenier

GRESCHNER, Ron
b. Goodsoil, Saskatchewan, December 22, 1954

Sometimes the player gets played. He married actress Carol Alt, but after a number of years they divorced and now Alt is with another player, next generation, named Alexei Yashin. Greschner came from a small town in which his dad ran the local hotel. He played junior in B.C. and then joined the Rangers in 1974, the team to which he was faithful his entire 16 years in the NHL. He became the highest-scoring defenceman in team history. Four times he scored 20 or more goals, and 5 times he had more than 50 points. Over time, though, injuries took their toll, mostly in the form of a bad back, which reduced him to just 10 games in '82-'83, and a bad shoulder, which hurt him off and on for the rest of his career. He had been captain of the team, but his poor relationship with coach Michel Bergeron induced him to resign that duty, though he stayed with the team. When GM Neil Smith released Greschner outright in 1990, it was a crushing blow. He had wanted to stay another year and play in his 1,000th game with the Blueshirts, but no other team wanted him, either, and he retired having played in 982 games. He worked for a time with MSG Broadcasting afterwards.

Ron Greschner

GRETZKY, Brent
b. Brantford, Ontario, February 20, 1972

The pressure of being Wayne's brother was probably greater than that of being Wayne himself, for the greater player would know instinctively how to handle that pressure while the lesser, by virtue of his being not as skilled, would not be as adept. The jokes were always there, some hurtful, some playful, some funny. He was called "The Good One" by some. Others noted that he and Wayne are the highest-scoring brother combination in NHL history (even though Brent contributed all of 4 points in 13 games). Regardless, Brent loved to play. He had 121 points with Belleville in junior, which only served to fuel

Brent Gretzky

expectations, and although he didn't make the NHL in a big way, he certainly had his moments in the minors and even, for a brief time, played for the other Gretzky, Keith, who turned his hockey passion into coaching.

GRETZKY, Wayne
("Brinks"/ "The Great One")
b. Brantford, Ontario, January 26, 1961

What Bobby Orr was to one generation of hockey folk, Wayne Gretzky was to another, though Gretzky had much greater on- and off-ice responsibilities in that by the time he was playing the league was fast becoming an international arena in a cable world and the game was much bigger than just the NHL. But despite the scope of Gretzky's career and that of the NHL during his career, it all began as it did for almost any Canadian kid – on a backyard rink. His dad, Walter, built a small rink so that he could watch his boy play from the warmth of the kitchen, and although there was Keith and Brent and a sister and another brother, it was almost always Wayne who was out back on his own, skating circles around pylons and shooting puck after puck into a small net. By the time he was six, he was a vastly superior skater and puckhandler to any other kid in his age group, so he played with 10-year-olds and grew up with the older boys. In his first year, he scored a single goal, but by his fourth year, when he was 10, playing with boys his own age, he scored 378 goals. This was no fluke or aberration, merely a sign of things to come. He was interviewed for a local radio station and the *Hockey News* made mention of his feats, and he earned the nickname "the White Tornado" because he wore white gloves. He continued to improve, but as he did so the jealousy from other families in Brantford was too much for him and he decided to transfer to Toronto where he could be anonymous and where great achievements were a bit more common and accepted. He played for the Toronto Young Nats, and at 15 got a three-game callup from Peterborough of the OHA. The next year, 1977-78, he played his only full season of junior hockey, with Sault Ste. Marie. He got there only to discover that number 9 which he had always worn in honour of his hero Gordie Howe, was taken by a veteran on the team, Brian Gualazzi. It was suggested that he double the 9 and wear 99, and from then on the number was his. In January of that season he played for Canada at the World Junior Championships, the first of a series of successful appearances he made for Team Canada over the years. The team finished a disappointing third, but the 16-year-old Gretzky led the WJC in scoring. Ironically, the only reason the scrawny teen was invited to camp for Team Canada was because he was leading the OHL in scoring. After missing almost a month of the junior year because of the tournament, he returned to the Soo and was still leading the league in scoring. In the summer of 1978, it was clear another year of junior would do Gretzky no good. Yet he was only 17 and three years away from draft eligibility to the NHL. Nelson Skalbania, owner of the Indianapolis Racers of the WHA, signed him to a personal-services contract, and Gretzky turned pro at 17. Skalbania, however, was in financial turmoil, and just eight games into the '78-'79 season he traded

Gretzky to Edmonton. Under coach Glen Sather, Gretzky set records that might never be broken, and if they are those days are at least 20 years away. Sather used Gretzky as the cornerstone of a young team that was chock-full of emerging talent, from Mark Messier to Glenn Anderson to Paul Coffey and Grant Fuhr. But Gretzky was Sather's target in particular. The coach made sure that the player never felt satisfied, that one achievement did not mean Gretzky could relax but that it was simply a new, higher measuring stick to gauge another achievement. And Gretzky did not wither; he shone. In his first NHL season, he led the league in assists (86) and tied for the overall scoring race with 137 points. Marcel Dionne, though, was declared winner of the Art Ross Trophy because he had more goals. The next year, there was no tie.

Wayne Gretzky

Gretzky set an all-time assists record of 109 to better Bobby Orr's mark, and he scored 152 points to better Phil Esposito's single-season point total. Gretzky was only 20, but he had already hammered into the ground two of the most prestigious scoring records of all time. He began '81–'82 playing for Canada at the 1981 Canada Cup, a poor showing in the finals coached by Scotty Bowman. Gretzky led all scorers in the tournament, and in the regular season, well, he set new records that defied believability. First, he scored 50 goals in just 39 games, humbling the 50-in-50 that had previously been the threshold of all scoring endeavours. At season's end, he had 92 goals, 120 assists, and 212 points, records that should have stood the test of time except that number 99

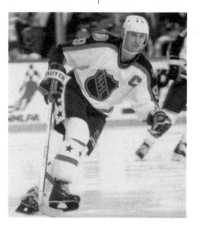

Gretzky scored his 802nd goal to pass Gordie Howe for goals and then his 1,852nd point to become the all-time leading scorer.
WAYNE GRETZKY

was still only 21. The next year, he again led in all three offensive categories, but as important: the Oilers went to the Stanley Cup finals. They had been inching ever closer to the great day of holding the trophy but had been scuppered by over confidence and a lack of experience, but the 1983 finals were the final lesson. They lost to the Islanders, but learned once and for all what winning was all about. The next year, the Oilers won their first Stanley Cup. They won again the next year and Gretzky was named winner of the Conn Smythe Trophy, and in '85–'86 reached his peak by setting a record for assists (163) and points (215) that survive to this day. Whoever can beat those records is likely not yet born. Gretzky spent the first nine years of his career with the Oilers. He led the league in assists each and every one of those years, and in points every year but one. He helped Canada win the 1984 Canada Cup, and in 1987 he teamed with Mario Lemieux to make history, setting up Lemieux on the Cup-winning goal with a minute and a half left in the deciding game. The Oilers won two more Cups, in '87 and '88, but soon

after that latter victory Peter Pocklington started to talk to Bruce McNall about trading Gretzky to Los Angeles. It was a preposterous idea to break up the heart of a team that could still win another five or six Cups together, but Pocklington was under financial duress. Although the trade, consummated on August 9, 1988, included top prospects, it also saw "Peter Puck" receive a lump sum payment of $15 million. Gretzky's trade and subsequent arrival in Los Angeles resulted in nationalistic fervour in Canada, but the Kings knew they were getting the best hockey player around. Gretzky not only transformed the team, he changed the geography of hockey. The game became cool in a city where cool was common and hockey long considered dull. He attracted Hollywood stars to games and the Fabulous Forum

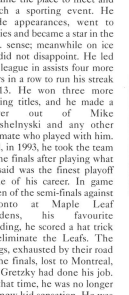

Wayne Gretzky

became the place to meet and watch a sporting event. He made appearances, went to parties and became a star in the L.A. sense; meanwhile on ice he did not disappoint. He led the league in assists four more years in a row to run his streak to 13. He won three more scoring titles, and he made a scorer out of Mike Krushelnyski and any other linemate who played with him. And, in 1993, he took the team to the finals after playing what he said was the finest playoff game of his career. In game seven of the semi-finals against Toronto at Maple Leaf Gardens, his favourite building, he scored a hat trick to eliminate the Leafs. The Kings, exhausted by their road to the finals, lost to Montreal, but Gretzky had done his job. By that time, he was no longer the new kid sensation. He was a mature man at the height of his powers. He had scored at least 50 goals for eight successive years, and up until 1992 his worst year was when he had 121 points. He became close friends with McNall off ice, and together with actor John Candy bought the Toronto Argonauts, eventually building a team that won the Grey Cup. Gretzky was also working on career records by now, and while he was in L.A. scored his 802nd goal to pass Gordie Howe for goals and then his 1,852nd point to become the all-time leading scorer. But it was proved that McNall acquired his fortune through illegal means and he was soon on his way to prison. While Gretzky always remained faithful to him, he felt no particular allegiance to the Kings and as a result he was traded to St. Louis in February 1996 shortly before he was to become a free agent. By the time he left, the NHL was on its way to a radically different look. Because of Gretzky, new leagues were established in the western U.S. The NHL itself expanded to Anaheim, San Jose, and Phoenix thanks to his immense popularity. Gretzky's time with the Blues was short, though, and the

Wayne Gretzky

Wayne Gretzky

anticipated Gretzky-to-Brett Hull tandem didn't quite measure up under the coaching of Mike Keenan. That summer, Gretzky signed with New York, hoping to finish his career with longtime friend, Mark Messier. Throughout his career, Gretzky had combined two disparate offensive skills – passing and scoring. As a scorer, he never went end-to-end with the puck but had as hard a shot as any in the league. That shot came from a somewhat slender player and not a hulking, Bobby Hull-like player gave him an advantage in that he never looked menacing coming in on the goalie. And in close, there was no one who knew a goalie's abilities better that Gretzky. He never aimed for corners but cracks where the goalie had a tough time reaching, over his collarbone, for instance. As a passer, he was without compare. Linemates routinely flubbed scoring chances because they got a pass from him that they didn't think was possible to make. Coming in over the blueline, he used defenceman Paul Coffey as the trailer on the play, rather than looking directly for the man in front of the goal. And then there was Gretzky's Office, the small piece of ice directly behind the goalie. From there, he confounded defencemen who waited for him to make a play, but Gretzky was happy to wait back there with the puck for five or ten seconds if need be. The problem with his three years in New York was a decided lack of talent around him. Gretzky's passing ability had not diminished a bit, but he made perfect passes to open ice and no one was there. He made plays to teammates who were out of position, and he moved the puck along Madison Square Garden ice, a surface so bereft of smooth ice that making any pass was a miracle. Nonetheless, he led the league in assists in his first two seasons on Broadway. However, the team made the playoffs the first year and failed to qualify his second and third years. He also took part in his final two international competitions, the 1996 World Cup and the 1998 Olympics. In the former, he was still a top player on the team, and in the latter he was the best player. Coach Marc Crawford was too clever by half in the semi-finals at Nagano when he did not list Gretzky as a shooter in the shootout, and the image of a dejected Gretzky on the player's bench was the last the world saw of him in that context – as a player. It wasn't until the very end of the '98-'99 season that Gretzky made his retirement known, and it was in Ottawa that his unofficial yet emotional farewell took place. On the final Sunday afternoon of the regular season, his team a long way from the playoffs, Gretzky played his final game. During pre-game ceremonies, NHL commissioner Gary Bettman announced that his number 99 was to be given league-wide retirement, the first time such an honour had been conferred upon a player. Gretzky completed the game and then skated a few farewell laps before heading off to a press conference. After 20 years in the NHL, his playing days were over. He had set some 60 NHL records by that time, but most untouchable was his 2,857 total points. In real terms, a player would have to have 29 consecutive 100-point seasons to better his record or 15 consecutive 200-point years. Over a 20-year career, he averaged nearly two points a game. Considering he is the only man to have a 200-point

Mike Grier

season (four, to be exact), the likelihood of that happening any time soon is remote in the extreme. Other notable records include his 51-game consecutive point-scoring streak, his 50 career hat tricks, and, of course, his 50 goals in 39 games. Gretzky left the game with promises that after a year off he wanted very much to get back into the scheme of things, and he was true to his word. In the summer of 2000, he had the opportunity to become GM and part owner of the Phoenix Coyotes, and he took it, and just a short time later accepted an even greater challenge when Bob Nicholson named him the GM of Team Canada for the 2002 Olympics in Salt Lake City. It was a challenge that brought out his best. He assembled a team of coaches and players who went and won gold for Canada, the first Olympic gold since the Edmonton Mercurys in 1952. Gretzky made up for the gold he hadn't won in Nagano, and also established himself as a savvy GM. Soon after, he said he would accept the same position for Canada at the 2004 World Cup, if asked. Gretzky arrived in the NHL at a time when international hockey was expanding, yet at every step of the way he led Canada and the NHL with distinction and pride. Not once did he say *no* to his country, and each time he was the tournament's top performer. Playing best against best was a challenge he lived for and a thrill to be part of, and he realized the personal and cultural value of tournaments such as the Canada Cup, World Cup, and NHL Olympics. He has been an ambassador for the game on ice through his conduct and exemplary play and off ice through his incredible relationship with media worldwide. He was inducted into the Hockey Hall of Fame in 1999 and since then a stream of honours has celebrated his career. Books have been written about him, videos compiled, and still, every day Gretzky lives the game with a passion that is first and foremost his trademark. That, above all, is what has kept him in the game. That was what inspired him to set records, win Stanley Cups, establish hockey in the west, and play for Canada whenever possible. Passion.

GRIER, Mike
b. Detroit, Michigan, January 5, 1975
Grier might not be the superstar on the Oilers, but the right winger is certainly an important part of the team's exciting combination of speed and size. He is a powerful skater who came out of Boston College drafted a lowly 219th overall by St. Louis in 1993. He never played for the Blues, though, because the team traded him to Edmonton with Curtis Joseph for consecutive first-round draft choices in 1996 and '97. To date, Grier peaked with 20 goals in '98-'99 and he has one international appearance to his credit, at the WJC for the U.S. in 1995.

GRIEVE, Brent
b. Oshawa, Ontario, May 9, 1969
Grieve was a decent prospect out of the Oshawa Generals in 1990 after winning the Memorial Cup, but knee injuries were his undoing. He wound up playing for four teams in as many years. A series of stints in the minors studded his NHL armour, and by 1997 he was out of the game and back in Oshawa.

GRIGOR, George "Shorty"
b. Edinburgh, Scotland, September 3, 1916
Grigor's family moved to Canada between the wars, and young George developed his talents as a hockeyist in Toronto. He played only two NHL games, in '43-'44 with Chicago, and scored once as a wartime replacement.

GRIMSON, Stu ("The Grim Reaper")
b. Kamloops, British Columbia, May 20, 1965
They don't make too many God-fearing goons in the NHL factory, but somehow Grimson slipped through the cracks and came to believe in God and fighting both. During his junior career in Regina, his GM dubbed him the Grim Reaper and the name stuck, but Grimson didn't think a pro career was in the works. Yes, Detroit drafted him back in 1983, but he didn't sign. Two years later, Calgary drafted him a little higher, but he enrolled at U of Manitoba rather than the Flames training camp. It was only two years later he turned pro, and so began an NHL odyssey that lasted much longer than he could have anticipated. Yes, he was a Christian, but he believed the fighting was about protecting his smaller, skilled teammates. He himself scored irregularly at best, though his shining moment came in the 1995 playoffs when he scored the tying goal against Chicago in the conference finals for Detroit. The Wings went on to the finals, though they were swept by New Jersey that year. His career came to an end as a result of a concussion from which it took more than a year to recover. Grimson's religious side was never far away from his tough side. He worked closely with Hockey Ministries International (HMI) and took part in clinics and camps in the summer, preaching God and hockey in the same breath and with the same enthusiasm.

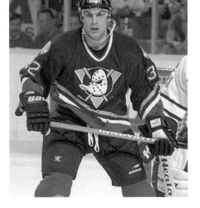

His career came to an end as a result of a concussion.
STU GRIMSON

GRISDALE, John ("Grizzy")
b. Geraldton, Ontario, August 23, 1948
What was he thinking? If he wanted to be a professional hockey player, why did he go to the University of Michigan Tech to earn a degree in mechanical engineering? Sure, he went on scholarship and played hockey, but a player just didn't develop there as he would have in Canadian junior. Or, at least, that was the conventional wisdom. Grisdale graduated, and then attended Toronto's 1971 training camp. The defenceman was impressive, but the Leafs sent him to Tulsa for a year of seasoning, and the year after he made the big team full-time. He was traded to Vancouver the following year, though, and lasted five more years, never playing a full season. A debilitating back injury forced him to miss the last half of '77-'78 when he was the team's best on the blueline, and he wasn't the same the year after, his last in pro hockey.

GROLEAU, François
b. Longueuil, Quebec, January 23, 1973
Owned earlier by Calgary and Quebec, Groleau played only with Montreal in the NHL, eight games in the mid-1990s. Beyond that, he has been able to maintain a steady position in the AHL.

GRON, Stanislav
b. Bratislava, Czechoslovakia (Slovakia), October 28, 1978
His NHL chances get shakier and shakier with every passing day since making his only-game debut with New Jersey in 2000-01. The big right winger has languished in the minors ever since.

GRONMAN, Tuomas
b. Viitasaari, Finland, March 22, 1974
Quebec drafted him in 1992, but it was four years before Gronman saw the NHL light of day. En route, he tied a Finnish record by playing in three World Juniors (1992, '93, '94), although he never won a medal with those teams. He played briefly for Chicago and Pittsburgh, then made the Suomi national team in Nagano, winning a bronze medal. Early in the '98-'99 season, though, he suffered a serious knee injury while playing in the "I." He returned home to recuperate, and when healthy he decided not to leave, signing with Jokerit, a Finnish league team. He ended his career in France in 1997 and then took the unlikely job as head coach of the Australian national team, going to a country known for many things – but not hockey!

GRONSDAHL, Lloyd
b. Norquay, Saskatchewan, May 10, 1921
Perhaps it would have been a great career, perhaps not more than what it was, but Gronsdahl joined the army just as he was getting a chance to play for Boston, in '41-'42. He played 10 games at the end of the season as a 19-year-old, but after being in the war for 3 years, he came out to find the NHL was no longer accessible to him.

GRONSTRAND, Jari
b. Tampere, Finland, November 14, 1962
Passed over in the draft until he was 23, Gronstrand was a late bloomer according to Hexi Riihiranta, the North Stars scout of Finnish talent who suggested in 1986 that Minnesota select him. Gronstrand came to North America to realize his dream of playing in the NHL, but he played in the minors a lot more than in his

John Grisdale

François Groleau

Tuomas Gronman

Lloyd Gronsdahl

Jari Gronstrand

Michal Grosek

Lloyd Gross

Don Grosso

Wayne Groulx

John Gruden

dream league during his five years with four different teams. He spoke little English, and although he was a fine skater and good shooter, coaches questioned his ability to handle the physical strength needed for the league and the long schedule. In 1991, he returned home to continue to play, though he eventually made his way to France as player and later coach.

GROSEK, Michal
b. Vyskov, Czechoslovakia (Czech Republic), June 1, 1975

Grosek started his career in Winnipeg in 1993, but in three years with the Jets he made only sporadic appearances with the team. Apparently not in the team's plans, he and Darryl Shannon were traded to Buffalo for Craig Muni, and it was with the Sabres that Grosek established himself. He became an excellent two-way player, scoring 20 goals in '98-'99, the year the Sabres went to the finals. But if the name of the city is Buffalo and the name of the game is the finals, then the destiny of the team must be bridesmaid. Buffalo lost to Dallas, and Grosek's regular-season magic lost its lustre in the post-season, for he scored nary a single goal all playoffs. Over the next two years, he played for three teams, settling down with the Rangers as the team failed to make the playoffs at all.

GROSS, Lloyd
b. Berlin (Kitchener), Ontario, September 5, 1905
d. unknown

A star between the wars, Gross played locally in Kitchener before joining the Leafs in '26-'27, the year the team changed names from the St. Pats. He played for many years in the minors, making periodic NHL forays over the next decade though skating mostly in the minors. Although he proved to be something of a scorer, his time in the NHL was without many scores – 11 to be precise, in 62 career games.

GROSSO, Don ("Count")
b. Sault Ste. Marie, Ontario, April 12, 1915
d. Detroit, Michigan, May 14, 1985

Grosso played the majority of his career in Detroit, though he did make brief pilgrimages toward the end with the Hawks and the Bruins. His finest moments came during the early 1940s. In '42-'43, he played on the Medicine Line with Sid Abel and Eddie Wares and scored 23 goals. In the playoffs, he led the league with eight goals. The next year, the Wings won the Cup. After retiring, Grosso returned to the Soo, where he coached the junior Greyhounds from 1950 to '54 until a falling-out with management led to his firing. In those four years, he had won three NOHA titles. However, time rewarded him, for he was re-hired in 1958. He later worked as a salesman.

GROSVENOR, Len
b. Ottawa, Ontario, July 21, 1905
d. Ottawa, Ontario, March 15, 1981

A forward, Grosvenor played from 1927 to '33 with three teams, most notably with Ottawa in the years right after the dynasty ended and just before the team was on its last legs. He ended his career with the Canadiens and went to work for the civil service in Ottawa.

GROULX, Wayne
b. Welland, Ontario, February 2, 1965

After winning a bronze medal with Canada at the world junior baseball championships, the star shortstop rejected overtures from the Los Angeles Dodgers and declared his sole intention was to make a career in hockey, the other sport at which he was pro-level skilled. During his four years with the Soo in junior, it looked as if he had made the right choice. Scouts compared him to Steve Yzerman, and he put up the requisite numbers on the scoresheet. Then, he played exactly one NHL game, with Quebec in '84-'85. After that, he went to Europe, played for the Canadian National Team, and then used his heritage to play for Austria at the 1992 World Championships. He helped the team win "B" pool and a promotion to "A" pool for '93, and he returned the next year to play. All the while, he made Austria his home, and the NHL and major league baseball never looked so far away.

GRUDEN, John
b. Virginia, Minnesota, June 4, 1970

It's not every day that a graduate of the Ferris State University Bulldogs goes on to play in the NHL, but Gruden was one such beast. Drafted by Boston, he played first for the Bruins before being signed by Ottawa as a free agent. A defenceman with offensive skill, he has yet to make it full-time in the big show – and time may have run out already for him to prove he belongs as a regular.

GRUEN, Danny
b. Thunder Bay, Ontario, June 26, 1952

The WHA lured many a big ticket to its league from NHL rosters, but although Gruen also made the move, his name was not writ Hollywood large across the vast expanse of hockey sky. He made his pro debut with Detroit, but after two middling years of mostly minor-league work he signed with the Michigan Stags. Over the next three years, he played for five WHA teams before returning to the NHL with Colorado. He scored a mildly impressive 8 goals in 29 games, but he never made it back after that season.

GRUHL, Scott
b. Port Colborne, Ontario, September 13, 1959

Gruhl went from high school in Ontario to Northeastern University in the States, but after two years he returned home to play junior hockey. From there he turned pro, in 1979, and embarked on a lengthy career that started in the minors and finished in the minors. In between, there were 20 NHL games, with L.A. and Pittsburgh. Gruhl played the left wing and scored bundles of goals in the IHL, but his callups to the big time were far less successful. He had 16 straight seasons of more than 20 goals in the minors, topping out at 59 with Muskegon in '85-'86. He later managed a bowling alley.

GRYP, Bob
b. Chatham, Ontario, May 6, 1950

After four years with the Boston University Terriers, Gryp struck out for the big time, signing with the Braves in Boston. He had been drafted by Toronto in 1970, but the Leafs never signed him to an NHL contract and exposed him in the Reverse Draft. The Bruins jumped in, and sent him to the Braves. He played only a single game for the B's in '73-'74 before they, too, left him unprotected in the Expansion Draft. Washington stepped in and claimed him, but even the Caps used him on only a part-time basis for two years.

GUAY, François
b. Gatineau, Quebec, June 8, 1968
Guay took his act to Europe almost immediately after leaving junior in Quebec. He played a single game with Buffalo in '89-'90 and a bit more in the minors but accepted an offer in Austria and hasn't looked back. The centreman has averaged nearly 30 goals a year overseas, despite the much shorter schedules of club teams.

GUAY, Paul
b. Providence, Rhode Island, September 2, 1963
When Minnesota GM Lou Nanne traded Guay to Philadelphia late in the '83-'84 season for Paul Holmgren, he knew he was sending the Flyers a second-level prospect. Guay had played that season with the U.S. National Team and on into the 1984 Olympics in Sarajevo, and Nanne's assessment was bang on. Guay could skate a bit, but he wasn't going to change the sagging fortunes of the Flyers. In fact, he never got much of a chance there and soon was on a plane to L.A., and then to Boston, and then to Long Island. Guay never played a full season in the NHL, and retired in 1993 after a long stretch in the minors.

During his high school years, he was as good at lacrosse as hockey.
BILL GUERIN

GUENETTE, Steve
b. Gloucester, Ontario, November 13, 1965
Guenette didn't distinguish himself much until his last year of junior, but he made up for the late blooming by having a great season. He won the Memorial Cup with Guelph in 1986, was named best goalie of the tournament, and made the OHL's Second All-Star Team. Pittsburgh signed him as a free agent, and in his second year he had excellent numbers both in the minors and during his callup with the Pens, when he went 12-7-0. He was never going to usurp Tom Barrasso, though, and the Pens had a Cup-contending team. They traded Guenette to Calgary, also at the height of its power, and by that time he was pegged as a minor-leaguer and not an up-and-comer. His NHL days were behind him and his minor pro days not far behind.

GUERARD, Daniel
b. LaSalle, Quebec, April 9, 1974
Call it burnout or indecision or lack of interest. Whatever you call it, it caused Guerard to "retire" at age 16 after being drafted high in the Quebec midget

draft. He took a year off and then played provincial junior hockey in LaSalle, moving into Victoriaville before the year was out. He played well enough to be drafted 98th overall by Ottawa in 1992, but he played only 2 games with the Sens a couple of years later. He soon decided to play overseas, though he later returned home without the juice (or skill?) needed to pursue a career in the game.

GUERARD, Stephane
b. Ste. Elizabeth, Quebec, April 12, 1968
Guerard injured his right knee for the first time in November 1987 while playing for the Nordiques. He injured it again the year after, and then the year after that. He injured it for the last time in September 1990 and underwent surgery in December to try to salvage something from the pin. He never played again.

GUERIN, Bill
b. Worcester, Massachusetts, November 9, 1970
Make no mistake. Although his birth certificate places him in Worcester, Wilbraham claims him as its own, for that's where the Guerins moved when Bill was just a year old. By the time he was three, he was skating on Bruuer Pond in town, and he just kept getting better and better and having more and more fun. During his high school years, he was as good at lacrosse as hockey, but by the time he headed off to Boston College his focus was the NHL after New Jersey took him 5th overall in the 1989 draft. Guerin played twice for the U.S. at the World Juniors and then quickly played himself onto the Devils. In his third full year, he won the Cup with the team during the lockout year, and somehow managed to score more than 20 goals with a team that used Jacques Lemaire's stifling defensive style of play. He took the Cup back to Wilbraham in the summer, where Bill Guerin Day was celebrated by the entire little city. From a personal perspective, Guerin couldn't have been happier the day he was traded to the skatingest team in the league, Edmonton, in early 1998. Although he played well there, the Oilers traded him to Boston, his dream team, and he continued to prove his worth as a top scorer, although his first experience with Bruins management proved to be distasteful. He went to arbitration over his contract – and won – forcing the Bruins to pay him $5.1 million for 2001-02 and making him an unrestricted free agent at year's end. He played for the U.S. on the winning World Cup team in 1996 and the dreadful 1998 Olympics team in Nagano, but he didn't record his first Pro Classics goal until the 2002 Olympics in Salt Lake City, where he scored four times and won a silver medal. That summer, he signed with Dallas in the hope of winning another Cup.

Paul Guay

Steve Guenette

Stephane Guerard

Jocelyn Guevremont

Aldo Guidolin

Bobby Guindon

Stephen Guolla

Miloslav Guren

GUEVREMONT, Jocelyn

b. Montreal, Quebec, March 1, 1951

He was a big, strong defenceman with offensive ability, and Vancouver drafted him 3rd overall in 1971 as a result. He had been playing for the Montreal Jr. Canadiens, where he was named top defenceman in the league. A few years earlier, prior to the draft and expansion, his affiliation with the Jr. Habs would have meant a life with the Habs. Guevremont joined the Canucks and brought the team some goals from the blueline, but his +/- in his first three years was a cumulative -107. Nonetheless, he was a spare with Canada's '72 team, and he went on to play for Buffalo and the Rangers before retiring in 1980. He became coach of the expansion Drummondville franchise in the Quebec juniors, but after just 19 games was fired. He later was hired in a similar capacity with Cornwall.

GUIDOLIN, Aldo

b. Forks of the Credit, Ontario, June 6, 1932

He didn't make it for too long as an NHLer, but his life was hockey and hockey welcomed him with open arms wherever he went. Guidolin played with the Rangers in the early 1950s and then established himself in the American league first as a player, then as a playing coach, and finally as a coach only. His first year as playing coach came with Baltimore in '62-'63, a season cut short, ironically, because he broke an ankle during a fight and missed the rest of the season. But he stood behind the bench with cast and crutches and guided the team into the playoffs anyway, and he spent most of his career with the Clippers until he retired in 1969. He is a second cousin to Bep of Boston fame, and became a scout for California and Atlanta before landing in Colorado with the Rockies. He started there as a scout, moved up to director of player personnel, and then got a demotion – to head coach. The team, of course, was no good, and Guidolin's tenure lasted until the end of the season, when he returned to the player personnel post and the team found a new coach.

GUIDOLIN, Armand "Bep"

b. Thorold, Ontario, December 9, 1925

It's one thing to start skating only at age 13; it's quite another to be playing in the NHL three years later as the youngest player the league has ever known. And it's still another to survive the ordeal and become a regular, a star even, in the six-team league. That, in a nutshell, is the early life of Guidolin. He played all of '42-'44 with the Bruins because of a war-depleted lineup, and then Guidolin himself enlisted and left the game for two years. He returned to Boston and moved on to Detroit and Chicago, and the small left

Guildolin was an early advocate of a player's union, the likely cause of his early exit from the NHL, in 1952.
BEP GUIDOLIN

winger averaged more than 10 goals a season. Incredibly, his best year was his second – he was still just 17! – when he had 17 goals. Guidolin was an early advocate of a players' union, the likely cause of his early exit from the NHL, in 1952. He continued to play for many years in the minors, and in 1961 stopped skating and took up coaching. He led the Belleville Mcfarlands to an Allan Cup, coached Bobby Orr in Oshawa, and coached him again with the Bruins. In fact, Guidolin witnessed Orr's first knee injury, with the Generals, and years later was behind the bench with Orr and his ravaged knee in the 1974 finals. Guidolin left the Bruins – stupidly, he admitted later – because of a large financial offer to coach the new and dreadful Kansas City Scouts, a term that ended prematurely and with him owed most of the money previously offered. He coached for a number of teams in the OHA and then settled in Barrie with his wife to work at Molson Breweries as a sales rep in the area. He later worked in the parts department of Douglas Lincoln Mercury.

GUINDON, Bobby

b. Labelle, Quebec, November 19, 1950

Guindon had the right pedigree and earned plenty of respect outside the NHL, though he played only six games, for Winnipeg, in '79-'80. He played every WHA season, going to the Avco Cup finals five times and winning three. This after a career with the Montreal Jr. Canadiens in which he won two Memorial Cups. Guindon spent most of that '79-'80 season in the minors as an assistant playing coach with the Jets farm team in Tulsa, helping out head coach Mike Smith.

GUOLLA, Stephen

b. Scarborough, Ontario, March 15, 1973

Expansion was the name of his game, as Guolla played for three new teams in the late 1990s before being released by Atlanta and signing with Albany in the AHL for 2001-02. He started off with San Jose and Tampa after a season in Ottawa's system, and because of his club choices he never made it to the playoffs in his five NHL seasons.

GUREN, Miloslav

b. Uherske Hradiste, Czechoslovakia (Czech Republic), September 24, 1976

Guren played for the Czechs at the '95 and '96 World Junior Championships after being drafted by Montreal in 1995. Whereas the fate of a Montreal draft choice a generation earlier was promise and glory, a contemporary selection by the once-great club was more likely to be a bad omen than good.

The large defenceman has played a few games with the Habs but did little to ensure his long-term place with the team, and has been in the minors for most of his career so far.

GUSAROV, Alexei
b. Leningrad, Soviet Union (Russia), July 8, 1964
By the time Gusarov made his NHL debut in 1990, he was 26 and already had a great career to be proud of back home in the Soviet Union. He had played in the 1984 and '87 Canada Cups and '87 Rendez-vous. He had won a gold medal at the 1988 Olympics in Calgary. He had played in five World Championships (winning three golds, a silver, and a bronze) and one WJC. The next decade, in the NHL, was a second career that only augmented his greatness to those who knew him back home. He played in the 1991 Canada Cup and '98 Olympics in Nagano, and he played on Colorado's Cup-winning team of '95-'96. Up to 2000, his entire North American career had been with the Quebec/Colorado franchise, but in his final year, 2000-01, he played for the Rangers and Blues in addition to the Avs. A season-ending knee injury in February 2000 contributed to his travels during that final year, though his accomplishments still rank him high in contemporary Russian hockey.

GUSEV, Sergei
b. Nizhny Tagil, Soviet Union (Russia), July 31, 1975
A modern Russian primed for the NHL, Gusev proved to be a short-lived model. He played for Dallas and Tampa, but on December 19, 1999, he suffered a knee injury that cost him the rest of the season. He trained hard to come back, but just a few games into the next season re-injured the wonky knee and was gone again.

GUSMANOV, Ravil
b. Naberezhnyye Chelny, Soviet Union (Russia), July 25, 1972
After winning a silver medal with the Soviets at the 1991 WJC, Gusmanov went on to play for Russia at the 1994 Olympics in Lillehammer before making his only NHL appearances with Winnipeg in the following season. He played his first game on November 21, 1995, but after only three more was in the minors to stay. He returned to Russia in 1997, and in the summer of 2001 he signed with the Minnesota Wild, a desperate move by the expansion team to try to lure him back to North America. He never played with the team, though, content to skate for his club team back home, Metallurg Magnitogorsk.

GUSTAFSON, Derek
b. Gresham, Oregon, June 21, 1979
Goalie Gustafson signed with Minnesota as a free agent in the summer of 2000 but has played only in emergency situations for the team, four games that first year and a mere one period the year after. He moved to British Columbia to play provincial hockey in 1996 and had a spectacular 39-3-0 record in his final year before going to St. Lawrence for a season.

GUSTAFSSON, Bengt-Ake
b. Karlskoga, Sweden, March 23, 1958
The four stages of Gustafsson's career encompass the full and possible range of hockey activity. One: He grew up in Sweden and played in league hockey and internationally for Tre Kronor. Two: His play at the 1978 World Championships impressed the talented Edmonton Oilers, and that fall he was in the Edmonton lineup. He was claimed by Washington in '79 and played seven seasons with the Capitals. A knee injury forced him home to play in the less demanding Swedish league for a year, but he returned to the Capitals for two more seasons. Three: He ended his career playing in Europe, for another decade, mostly in Austria. Four: He became a coach in the Swiss league. He had been a defenceman before Washington converted him to a winger, and in his 9 NHL seasons he averaged more than 20 goals a year. In addition to two Canada Cups and 6 World Championships, Gustafsson played in the 1992 Olympics in Albertville, and when he retired he was considered one of the greatest players Tre Kronor had ever produced. In 2003, he was inducted into the IIHF Hockey Hall of Fame.

Alexei Gusarov

GUSTAFSSON, Per ("Gus")
b. Osterham, Sweden, June 6, 1970
Jonkoping is a small town with its own hockey team in the Swedish league. It's where Gustafsson played for 8 years, starting in 1988 as an 18-year-old, before he finally came to the NHL. At 261st overall in 1994, he is one of the lowest draft choices ever to play, so the fact that he lasted 89 games over 2 seasons is impressive enough. After stints in Florida, Toronto, and Ottawa failed to work out, he returned to Junkoping to continue his career.

GUSTAVSSON, Peter
b. Bollebygd, Sweden, March 30, 1958
Another Swede faithful to his native league, at age 23 Gustavsson decided to try North America for a year. He had been playing for Frolunda, and spent most of '81-'82 with Fort Worth. The Colorado Rockies, with nothing to lose except more games, called him up for two games at the end of the year, but he returned to Frolunda for the rest of his career.

Bengt-Ake Gustafsson

GUY, Kevan
b. Edmonton, Alberta, July 16, 1965
Once a westerner, always a westerner, Guy had the pleasure of spending most of his career in Canada's left-hand side of the map. He played junior in Medicine Hat and joined Calgary in 1986. The Flames traded him to Vancouver, and three years almost to the day he went back to Calgary, where he finished his NHL time. He continued to play in the minors for a few years, though the big defenceman never got the call to return to the big tent.

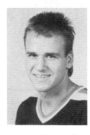

Kevan Guy

HAANPAA, Ari
b. Nokla, Finland, November 28, 1965

Haanpaa celebrated being drafted by the Islanders in 1984 by going out and tearing his knee early in the '84-'85 season in Finland. He recovered enough to play for Suomi at the Worlds later that year, and averaged almost a goal a game. He joined the Isles the following fall, along with countryman Mikko Makela. He came in as a versatile player who could skate on either wing and who was physical enough to handle the NHL, and the team hoped he would be new blood to keep alive the dynasty that had won four Cups in that decade (1980-83). He also acted as interpreter for Makela, but not for long. Haanpaa played just 18 games that year and not many more in the succeeding 2 years, and soon found himself back home playing like a star outside the big league. Makela, meanwhile, endured for longer stretches with the team.

HAAS, David
b. Toronto, Ontario, June 23, 1968

If he plays in Toronto, he's going to get noticed – and he did. Haas had the typical start to his career, playing in the MTHL, then Ontario junior, then the minors, and on to the NHL. He played just five games with Edmonton in '90-'91 and two more with Calgary a few years later, but for the most part he was destined for the smalls. After a while, he took his bag to Europe, where the culture was enlightening, the food wonderful, the schedule lighter, and the practices less frequent. And why not?

HABSCHEID, Marc
b. Swift Current, Saskatchewan, March 1, 1963

Nicholas Habscheid arrived in Canada from Luxembourg in 1949 and worked on his uncle's farm until 1954, when the uncle passed away and Nicholas took over the 2,000-acre property. It was there that young Marc came into the world, and by the time he was three his dad was building a rink out back for him to twirl and fall on to his heart's content. Those were the days that instilled a love of the game in the boy, and those were the ways he developed a skill for the game. He played long stretches with the Canadian National Team and played with four different NHL teams. He started with Edmonton in 1981, a dream because he so doted on Wayne Gretzky's every move. Of course, he didn't have the skill that number 99 had, but he did have a surety and cockiness that Gretzky never had. The minors were the solution, but Habscheid got more and more bitter every time he was demoted, year after year he thought he should be on the team. The Oilers traded him to Minnesota, and he peaked there in '88-'89 with a 23-goal season. Soon, though, he was out of the league and playing in Europe. He returned home in 1997 and coached in the WHL, first for Kamloops and later for Kelowna, and in the spring of 2002 he was named head coach of the National Team for the 2003 World Juniors in Halifax. They won a silver medal. Although his NHL career wasn't as star-studded as he may have hoped, he did win gold with Canada at the 1982 World Juniors, a superb collection of underrated talent. He also represented Canada at the 1988 Olympics in Calgary.

HACHBORN, Len
b. Brantford, Ontario, September 4, 1961

The NHL numbers begin in 1983 and end in 1986, and after that his rap sheet reads like a man on the run. Hachborn came to Philadelphia camp in 1983 as an unknown quantity, but although he was slowed by injuries he made enough of an impression that the Flyers thought him a real prospect. He ended up playing half a season at the Spectrum, but the year after he made little progress and Philly sold him to L.A. From there, he toured the States and Europe, playing for a seemingly endless string of teams before rooting himself in the WCHL as the century came to a close.

HACKETT, Jeff
b. London, Ontario, June 1, 1968

Hackett's career got off to a fluttering start in goal for the Islanders and San Jose from 1988 onward as the young netminder learned the ropes and coped with harder, faster shots. He was traded to Chicago by the Sharks in the summer of 1993, and from that day on he became a true NHL goalie. He started as Ed Belfour's backup, but as he got better he gave the Hawks some leverage to trade the Eagle. In 1997-98, Hackett might have set some sort of record. In 58 starts he went 21-25-11, but of those 21 wins, 8 were by shutout. The Hawks traded him to Montreal early the next year, but as Hackett always seemed to be filling in, he again played well on a team that didn't make the playoffs. In fact, in his dozen NHL seasons, he has played just nine times in the post-season. In Montreal, he proved to be the pin that held the team together between the Patrick Roy years and the Jose Theodore years, though 2000-01 was a writeoff because of a broken hand that kept him out for two-thirds of the season. By the time he returned the next year, Theodore was the number-one man and Hackett was fighting for his career but in 2002-03 he made a great recovery. While Theodore struggled, Hackett reasserted himself as a top goalie, and was traded to Boston where he became the Bruins' starter.

HADDON, Lloyd
b. Sarnia, Ontario, August 10, 1938

He was supposed to be an excellent defenceman – he certainly was well talked about coming out of junior in Hamilton – but Haddon had only a short tryout with Detroit in February and March 1960 during a mostly WHL career.

HADFIELD, Vic
b. Oakville, Ontario, October 4, 1940

It's amazing that Hadfield got 1,000 games in the NHL. Always hurt or coming back from injury, it was his knee that finally did him in in 1976, though it was the last in a long line of wounds that began near his first career game in 1961, when he broke his hand. Along the way he broke his foot and severed an Achilles tendon, but in 1971-72 he stayed healthy the whole year and scored 50 goals and 106 points for the Rangers, the year they lost in the Stanley Cup finals to Bobby Orr's Bruins. It was his first year as Rangers captain, and he played on one of that team's greatest lines, the GAG (goal-a-game) Line featuring Jean

Ari Haanpaa

Marc Habscheid

Jeff Hackett

Lloyd Haddon

Vic Hadfield
(opposite page)

Jim Haggarty

Sean Haggarty

Roger Hagglund

Ratelle and Rod Gilbert. Ironically, it was also the first year the banana blades were banned by the NHL, and Hadfield had been one of its biggest supporters after borrowing a Bobby Hull stick once and scoring two goals with it. That fall, he became part of a controversy during the Summit Series. He was used sparingly in the first half of the series, in Canada, and upon arriving in Moscow was told he wouldn't be playing at all. He flew home with Richard Martin, Gil Perreault, and Jocelyn Guevrement with promises that Alan Eagleson would explain things to the media, but the Eagle never did and Hadfield was excoriated during the season, notably in Toronto and Montreal. He never came close to either the Cup or 50 goals again, and retired when his knee couldn't take the battering any longer. Hadfield did some scouting for the Rangers and colour commentary for U.S. television. He later settled in Toronto and became a sales rep for Pacific Rim Containers. He and a friend also opened a sports restaurant in downtown Toronto, and he bought the Indian Wells golf club in Burlington, Ontario.

HAGGARTY, Jim
b. Port Arthur, Ontario, April 14, 1914
d. Montreal, Quebec, March 8, 1998

It was inconceivable, but a boy from Port Arthur, a hot kid scouted by the Toronto Maple Leafs, turned down a scholarship offer from Conn Smythe. Instead, he accepted an offer to play hockey in England. That same year, Canada was putting together its 1936 Olympic team and asked Haggarty if he'd like to play in Garmisch. He accepted, but the team lost the gold medal after losing a game to Great Britain 2-1. It was the first time Canada had failed to win gold. Haggarty remained in England until the war, winning the first Curtis Bennett bowl for gentlemanly play, but when the guns started blazing, he returned to Canada. En route to Port Arthur, he was convinced by the manager of the Montreal Royals, Gus Ogilvie, to play senior hockey in Montreal. He relented, and a short time later he met his future wife at a party hosted by the legendary Bill Durnan, a friend of Haggarty. He went on to play just a few games with the Canadiens before enlisting in the army, and when he came out he returned to the senior loop with the Royals. He later refereed in the city and went into private business, though one day much later he discovered that his 1936 silver medal had been stolen. However, his memories of representing his country at the Olympics could never be taken from him until he shed this mortal coil.

HAGGARTY, Sean
b. Rye, New York, February 11, 1976
Truth or fiction, who's to say, but what apparently happened was this: Coach Jack Parker at Boston University tried unsuccessfully to recruit Sean's older brother, Ryan. Then he tried to get Sean to play for him, but Haggarty opted to play in the OHL. He went on to play at the World Juniors for the U.S. during the '95-'96 season, but the next year Parker, the national coach, didn't invite him. Was it payback or did Sean not deserve the invite? It's tough to think he didn't deserve it, because he was scoring a goal a game and led the OHL with 60 by year's end. However, he played only once for the Maple Leafs, the team that drafted him, and just 10 more games with the Islanders, the team that traded for him, before he landed, on his way down, with Nashville.

HAGGLUND, Roger
b. Umea, Sweden, July 2, 1961
d. Sormjole, Sweden, June 6, 1992
Umea is pretty far north in Sweden, not quite the land of reindeer, but close. Hagglund played almost his entire career there, save for a season in North America that culminated in two games with Quebec in 1984-85. He had played for his country at the World Juniors and the WC prior to his pro sojourn, but Hagglund was killed in a car accident in the summer of 1992 at age 30.

HAGMAN, Matti
b. Helsinki, Finland, September 21, 1955
The first time Canadians saw Hagman play was in the '76 Canada Cup. Canada vs. Finland. Early in the game, the Finns trying to forecheck, Hagman flew at Bobby Orr and sent him flying. Orr got up, of course, but Hagman swore he didn't know who he had hit until after the play. Nonetheless, Harry Sinden was impressed. He had drafted Hagman in 1975, only the third Finn to be claimed by an NHL team, and shortly after the Canada Cup Hagman joined the Bruins, becoming the first Finn to play in the NHL. He had a decent season, but early the following year it was obvious he wasn't developing at the speed Boston had hoped. Sinden upset the NHL when he loaned Hagman to Quebec of the WHA for the balance of the season, a move designed to avoid waivers, for Hagman surely would have been claimed by another NHL team. Hagman returned to Finland for two years, though, and it was only after much persuasion that he agreed to try the NHL again. He signed with Edmonton, and playing second-line centre behind Wayne Gretzky he had a pair of 20-goal seasons. This time, he returned to Finland for good. He continued to play for IFK Helsinki, and because he was that team's leading scorer every year he played, he became known as Mr. IFK. He played at four World Championships and countless other international

He signed with Edmonton, and had a pair of 20-goal seasons.
MATTI HAGMAN

games, and he became the first 100-point man in Finnish league play (regular season and playoffs). By the time he retired, he was second all-time on the scoring list for his country, a legend who excelled at home and made it in the NHL. His sister, Riitta, was a world-class middle-distance runner.

HAGMAN, Niklas
b. Espoo, Finland, December 5, 1979
After working his way up to the Florida Panthers during the 2001-02 season, Hagman realized a dream when he was named to the 2002 Finnish Olympic team for Salt Lake City. He was not supposed to be part of the team, but when Ville Peltonen suffered a season-ending shoulder injury, Hagman, who was having a fine season with the Panthers, was named as his replacement. Hagman had been playing in Finland until the start of that year, but the left winger seems close to being able to call himself a bona fide NHLer.

HAHL, Riku
b. Hameenlinna, Finland, November 1, 1980
He established himself with a good showing at the 1999 World Juniors, but when Colorado drafted the centre in the summer he knew it would be tough going to make the NHL. In 2001, Hahl came to North America to try his luck, and was assigned to the minors. He was called up in January 2002 and stayed with the team the rest of the year and through the playoffs, essentially replacing Peter Forsberg. When Forsberg came to camp in 2002 fresh and rarin' to go, Hahl was back in the minors.

HAIDY, Gord ("Adam")
b. Winnipeg, Manitoba, April 11, 1928
When Gord Haidy was playing pre-NHL hockey, it was in the International Amateur Hockey League, a post-war version of the old Michigan-Ontario Hockey League. There were four teams, two in Windsor – the Junior Spitfires and the Gotfredsons – and two in Detroit – the Auto Club and Bright's Goodyears. Haidy skated for the Jr. Spits and from there he went to the Red Wings system. He was called up for one game in the 1950 playoffs, the year the Wings won the Cup, though his name never appeared on the Cup because of the malicious effort of Jack Adams to make Haidy pay for the ultimate indiscretion – refusing to sign the contract Adams had offered him. That refusal more or less blackballed Haidy from the NHL, though he played several more years outside the league. In 1960-61 he became playing coach of the Milwaukee Falcons of the IHL, though three years later he had to retire from playing because of bad knees. He spent the very last part of his life suffering from Parkinson's disease.

HAINSWORTH, George
b. Toronto, Ontario, June 26, 1895
d. Gravenhurst, Ontario, October 9, 1950
It wasn't until he was 29 that Hainsworth made it to the NHL, but his career up to that time had been long and successful nonetheless. He played amateur hockey in Berlin (Kitchener) and then senior hockey in the same city, winning the Allan Cup in '17-'18. He didn't turn professional until 1923, but his spectacular play in Saskatoon over three seasons impressed Leo Dandurand, who signed Hainsworth to replace Georges Vézina. Over the next seven seasons with the Canadiens, Hainsworth was so dominating that the NHL had to change its rules. He won the Vezina Trophy in each of his first three seasons, but the third and last of those was record setting. He allowed just 43 goals in 44 games, and recorded an improbable 22 shutouts. Amazingly, the low-scoring Habs won only 22 games! The NHL, seeing that defence ruled supreme, initiated a rule whereby forward passing was permitted, thereby ensuring neither Hainsworth nor anyone else would ever record a shutout in every other game. Hainsworth won two Stanley Cups with Montreal, in '29-'30 and '30-'31, but in October 1933, he was traded to Toronto for Lorne Chabot. He played three more spectacular seasons for the Leafs, but after a few games to start the '36-'37 season behind new number-one man Turk Broda, he retired. The Habs talked him back into goal for four games, and then he called it quits for good at age 41. Hainsworth finished with an unheard of GAA of 1.93, and his 94 shutouts was tops for decades until Terry Sawchuk bettered it in the late 1960s. Hainsworth died tragically on a highway near Gravenhurst when his car collided with a small truck. He was inducted posthumously into the Hockey Hall of Fame for a career that has few equals.

HAJDU, Richard
b. Victoria, British Columbia, May 10, 1965
Hajdu graduated from the Western league to play five games for Buffalo in the mid-1980s. He also played in the minors and for the Canadian National Team. After retiring in 1993, he returned to B.C. and became a real estate agent.

HAJT, Bill
b. Borden, Saskatchewan, November 18, 1951
Perhaps no player epitomizes the term *ordinary superstar* so much as Hajt. A defensive specialist, he never scored much, never dazzled with the moves or went end to end for the highlight goal, and played his entire 14-year career with the Sabres keeping the puck out of the net. He joined the team briefly in '73-'74 and made the Sabres the next year. The next spring, the team went to the Stanley Cup finals, and it was, ironically, Hajt's goal that tied game three, the "fog game," and sent it into overtime. It was 10 years before he scored his only other career playoff goal. Hajt hit hard and blocked shots, and for this he paid a price. Injuries kept him out of the lineup regularly, sometimes for a game or two, sometimes longer, and by 1983 he had had enough (twice he was named to play in the All-Star Game, and twice he had to pull out because of injury). Or so he thought for 10 days, and then he showed up at camp to play again. In truth, it was the '86-'87 season that was his last. He was slowed for weeks by a groin injury, and then he was a healthy scratch some nights. A prideful man, he hung them up rather than hang on. He returned to the farm where he became a successful grain merchant

HAJT, Chris
b. Saskatoon, Saskatchewan, July 5, 1978
The son of Bill, Hajt played a single game with the

George
Hainsworth

Bill Hajt

Anders Hakansson

Slim Halderson

Larry Hale

Bob Halkidis

Steven Halko

Oilers in 2000-01 and is still a young prospect in the organization. Like papa, he's big and strong and defensive minded.

HAKANSSON, Anders
b. Munkfors, Sweden, April 27, 1956
While he played hockey in Minnesota, Hakansson's parents were in Bai Bang in the depths of Vietnam helping the villagers build a factory that converted wood to paper products. Back on ice, Anders was feeling despondent and homesick because the team wasn't winning and he wasn't playing much. He had come to North America in 1981 after a successful time in the Canada Cup, but by the next year he had been traded to Pittsburgh. He played again in the '84 Canada Cup, when Sweden faced Canada in the finals, and by now he was with the Kings. Two and a half seasons later, the Kings demoted him and he simply refused to report to the minors. Instead, he packed up and went home.

HALDERSON, Haldor "Slim"
b. Winnipeg, Manitoba, January 6, 1900
d. Winnipeg, Manitoba, August 1, 1965
What a long career had Halderson! His first great achievement came when the Winnipeg Falcons played in the 1920 Olympics in Antwerp, the first time hockey had been played at the Olympics. He and his teammates easily won gold, and the mostly Icelandic-Canadian players returned to Winnipeg to go their separate ways. Halderson moved to B.C. to play in the Pacific Coast league, where he was a member of the Cup-winning Victoria Cougars of 1925. He got into his only NHL games in 1926-27 with Detroit and Toronto and continued to play in the minors for years afterwards. After hanging up his skates, he returned to the 'Peg and settled into the less hectic job of accountant with the Manitoba Liquor Control Commission, a position he held for 21 years.

HALE, Larry
b. Summerland, British Columbia, October 9, 1941
When Dick Cherry got hurt early in the '68-'69 season and the Flyers needed to find a defenceman, they put Hale into the lineup. He remained there for the rest of the season. On a new team, he was solid in his own end, and at 27 he had 6 years of minor pro experience to help him out. He played with the team until '71-'72 when he was relegated to the minors again, and in the summer he signed with Houston in the WHA to play alongside the Howe family.

HALEY, Len ("Comet")
b. Edmonton, Alberta, September 15, 1931
He had great speed (ergo the cosmic nickname), good strength on the puck despite his size, and one glaring fault – a desire, too often, to do it all himself. Haley had the hands to score, and he did so wherever he went, but he didn't get a chance to do a lot of it at the NHL level. Between 1959 and '61, in fact, his chance amounted to 30 games with Detroit. Beyond that, he was a mainstay in the WHL and could be counted on for 25 goals per annum. Oddly, he never lost a tooth playing hockey, but he had his nose broken 13 times. That has to hurt.

HALKIDIS, Bob ("Hawk")
b. Toronto, Ontario, March 5, 1966
Halkidis and Gretzky went to training camp the same year, and Halkidis was not only more impressive, he lasted much longer and made a greater contribution to his team. That's Bob Halkidis and Keith Gretzky, Buffalo's training camp, 1984. Both players were returned to junior, but Halkidis was called up at the end of the season and continued to be called up during a lengthy career that never saw him establish himself. He played for 6 NHL teams during his 15-year career but usually as a spare part, an injury replacement, something along those lines. Never as, Bob, you're on the team for good now. That would have been too easy. All those years added up to just 256 games, but that's 256 more than most NHL aspirants ever play.

HALKO, Steven
b. Etobicoke, Ontario, March 8, 1974
Halko ended his college career by captaining Michigan to a national championship, although he didn't join his drafted team, Carolina (née Hartford), right away. After a year in the minors, he worked himself slowly into the Canes lineup. Needless to say, he's a defenceman not acquired for offence, because in his first 153 NHL games, he failed to score even once, not on a deflection or a bad bounce or a shot off his butt. Nothing.

HALL, Adam
b. Kalamazoo, Michigan, August 14, 1980
Hall averaged better than a point a game in his four years with Michigan State. When he graduated in 2001, he finished that 2000-01 season with Nashville, playing a game with the Predators and a few more in the AHL. Considered a smart player, his best success has come on the Predators power play.

HALL, Bob ("Red")
b. Oak Park, Illinois, October 13, 1899
d. September 8, 1987
Little of Hall's life is known save that he played for the New York Americans in early 1926 and also played professional baseball. All of his hockey occurred in the U.S.

HALL, Del
b. Peterborough, Ontario, May 7, 1949
Strange but true, Hall went from Canadian university to the IHL in one year, then signed with the California Golden Seals in 1971. He played just nine games with the Seals before embarking on a career in the WHA, where he proved a worthy scorer for a short time with the Phoenix Roadrunners. He played on the Dynamite line with Robbie Ftorek and John Gray, and for most of '75-'76 it was the top scoring line in the league.

HALL, Glenn ("Mister Goalie")
b. Humboldt, Saskatchewan, October 3, 1931
Virtually every goalie that endured in the six-team NHL was a Hall of Famer; it was a prerequisite, it seemed. But among the Bowers and Sawchuks and Henrys and Rayners there towered Glenn Hall, almost without argument the greatest goalie of them all. There are great

records in hockey and great accomplishments by many of his padded colleagues, but no record is more unbreakable, more sealed-behind-glass than Hall's of playing in every minute of 502 consecutive regular-season games and 50 more in the playoffs. The number of skaters who have played 500 games in a row can be counted on two hands, but for a goalie to achieve such a streak is super-human – a record that will *never* be broken. Of course, the reason he played all those games without substitution is that he was the best. The reason he played so many consecutively, though, was not because he wanted to. No goalie hated his "job" more than Hall. No goalie hated to practice more than Hall. The fact that he threw up before every game reflected his disdain for the task of having to go out in front of 15,000 screaming fans and not allow a single goal. Later in his career, he was known to kick a leg out to make a save while he was sleeping on planes, to which his teammates would say, "nice save." Hall turned professional in the Detroit system, starting with Indianapolis in 1951. He played a few games with the Wings a year later, but at the end of the '54-'55 season he played in two games and earned shutouts in both. That was enough for Jack Adams, who traded the immortal Terry Sawchuk to Boston because he felt he had someone better in Hall. As a rookie, Hall won 30 games, recorded a league-high 12 shutouts, and began his string of 502 complete games played. He won the Calder Trophy for his spectacular start and was named to the Second All-Star Team. He was late for virtually every training camp, using the same excuse over and over – had to paint the barn – that it became the stuff of humour. But when the referee dropped the puck to start play, no one was more competitive or more effective. After two seasons in Detroit, Hall was traded to Chicago, where he spent the next 10 years. Despite his nightly heroics, and the great talent on the team, the Hawks won only one Stanley Cup, in '60-'61, the only one of his career. He didn't miss a game until November 8, 1963, when he had to leave the ice with a bad back. He was claimed by St. Louis in 1967 and played the last four years of his career with the Blues, sharing the goaltending with Jacques Plante. The pair won the Vezina Trophy together in '68-'69, the oldest duo to be the best goalies in the league. In 1968, the Blues were swept by Montreal in the finals in four games, but the losing goalie, Hall, was so remarkable that he won the Conn Smythe Trophy. He was a First Team All-Star 7 times and played in a record 13 All-Star Games. When he finally retired for good in 1971, he went back to his farm in Stony Plain, Alberta, and lived the quiet life he had always craved. Yet, paradoxically, he also missed the game and later became a goalie coach in the WHA with

No record is more unbreakable, more sealed-behind-glass than Hall's of playing in every minute of 502 consecutive regular-season games.
GLENN HALL

Alberta and the NHL with St. Louis and Calgary. Hall wasn't just good – he was also pioneering. Lost in Jacques Plante's introduction of the facemask was Hall's use of "V" formation to block more of the lower part of the net and help goalies go down and up more quickly. He was lightning fast with his glove and pads, and as adept as Plante at clearing the puck. He once said, though, that he'd rather go to a hanging than become a coach. He was inducted into the Hockey Hall of Fame in 1975, but it wasn't until 20 years later that he finally settled down on the farm and kept away from the rink altogether. It was a loathsome job, but he had to do it.

Joe Hall

HALL, Joe ("Mean Joe"/ "Bad Joe")
b. Staffordshire, England, May 3, 1882
d. Seattle, Washington, April 5, 1919

Few players were blessed with the skill and cursed with the temper of Hall. He was a defenceman of the first rank in the early days of the game, and a good man off the ice, but he was an animal at times on it. He had a long battle with Newsy Lalonde when that star was with the Canadiens and Hall was with Quebec in the NHA, but they later became teammates and friends on the Habs. Hall played six years with the Bulldogs, winning the Stanley Cup in 1912 and '13. He joined the Canadiens in 1917 when the NHL began operations, and in one game he and Toronto's Ken Randall became involved in such a gruesome stick battle that police had to be called in. Both men were charged, though the case was later dropped. Hall had moved to Winnipeg at age two and soon after to Brandon. He worked the railway in Winnipeg during the summers and the two salaries allowed him to buy a substantial property for his family just outside Brandon. In the spring of 1919, the Canadiens travelled to Seattle to play the Metropolitans for the Stanley Cup, but with the series tied at two wins each (and one tie) the championship was stopped by the Department of Health because of a serious outbreak of influenza. It was the only year the Cup has never been presented. Many players were hospitalized, but recovered, with the exception of Hall, who at 36 was the old man of pro hockey. He contracted pneumonia and died a few days later in the Columbus sanitarium. He was buried in Brandon before his wife and three children.

HALL, Murray
b. Kirkland Lake, Ontario, November 24, 1940
For whatever reason, fans liked to boo Hall whenever he wasn't scoring, regardless of where he was playing. This, in part, came from his reputation as a scorer, and by and large he didn't disappoint. He had his slumps, but over the course of a season he usually turned the

Murray Hall

Taylor Hall

Wayne Hall

Kevin Haller

Milt Halliday

Jeff Halpern

boos to cheers. He grew up in the days of sponsorship, and that meant that playing for St. Catharines in junior ensured he'd play for the Hawks if he ever made the NHL. He did, and he did. He also played for Detroit during the pre-expansion years of the 1960s, but he later joined Minnesota and Vancouver. In 1970-71, he played his only full NHL season, with the Canucks, and after getting off to a slow, boo-filled start, he finished the year with 21 goals. The year after he was back in the minors, and then he signed with Gordie Howe's Houston Aeros, where he kept on scoring for four seasons.

HALL, Taylor ("City")
b. Regina, Saskatchewan, February 20, 1964

Who knows exactly the long-term effects from that game early in the '84-'85 season when Gerald Diduck rammed Hall into the unmovable goalposts and tore the ligaments in Hall's knee. Hall had been a terrific prospect, and a left winger to boot, the weak side of the Vancouver offence. In his first seven games of that year, Hall had five points, but after the injury he required surgery and missed the entire season. The next year, he had 5 goals in his first 19 games, but management sent him to the minors, ostensibly never to return. He played many years in the minors and scored plenty of goals, but had he kept on going that rookie season, who knows… ? After retiring, Hall turned to coaching in the Western Pro league, a gig he has continued for a number of years.

HALL, Wayne
b. Melita, Manitoba, May 22, 1939

Hall played four games for the Rangers in 1960-61, a kid just out of junior with Flin Flon. He never got a second look, and the left winger skated in the minors until retiring in 1969.

HALLER, Kevin
b. Trochu, Alberta, December 5, 1970

He came out of junior in 1989–90 as the WHL's best defenceman, a season accented by a gold medal at the World Juniors over the Christmas break and a two-game trial with the Sabres at the end of the year. He had been a first-round draft choice by Buffalo the previous season, but it was after he was traded to Montreal that he had his finest moment. In '92–'93, he scored 11 goals, an astounding number for a defenceman who averaged about 3 a year, but like so much else about that season, everything was perfect. Montreal won the Stanley Cup on the strength of 10 consecutive overtime wins during those playoffs, and Haller had his name in history. In July 2000, he signed a three-year, $4.8 million contract with the Islanders

but soon after suffered a debilitating groin injury that will likely end his career.

HALLIDAY, Milt ("The Blonde Flash")
b. Ottawa, Ontario, September 21, 1906
d. Ottawa, Ontario, August 16, 1989

Halliday played all of his early hockey in Ottawa, so it was no surprise that the Senators signed him in 1926. He played his rookie year on a line with Hec Kilrea and Jack Duggan, and the Senators went on to win the Stanley Cup, the team's ninth and last. Halliday played parts of two more years with the team and moved on to the minors, establishing himself as a regular left winger for many years. After retiring, he settled in Ottawa, his city of birth and, 82 years later, death.

HALLIN, Mats
b. Esklistuna, Sweden, March 9, 1958

Unfortunately, Esklistuna will never claim Hallin as its own, not because he wasn't a fine hockey player but rather because it has a greater claim – home of Bjorn Borg, likely the most popular Swede of all time. Hallin was not the typical Swede to play in the NHL. He was 24 when he played his first game for the Islanders, but he didn't come straight from home to the NHL. He played a year and a half in the minors and got to know the North American game. He was also more physical than most Europeans, and more adaptable. Coach Al Arbour used him on right wing as much as left, for instance. The Isles won a Cup during his first year, '82-'83, but midway through his second season he ran into troubles. He suffered a concussion, and then as he was skating his way back into shape, he was cut near the jugular vein during a practice, and it was only the quick work of the trainers that prevented a dangerous situation from possibly occurring. Hallin played just five seasons in the NHL before returning home to play, but that first Cup ensured his place in NHL history.

Hallin played just five seasons in the NHL before returning home to play.
MATS HALLIN

HALPERN, Jeff
b. Potomac, Maryland, May 3, 1976

How the game is changing. No longer does every boy dream of playing for the Leafs or the Canadiens. No longer is every player from Canada. Halpern grew up in Maryland dreaming of playing for … the Washington Capitals. He played for the Little Capitals in his early teens, and went on to play at Princeton University. He became one of only five Tigers to go on to the NHL after an outstanding career, and although he wasn't drafted he was delighted to sign with his beloved Caps as a free agent. Halpern made his debut with the team in 1999-2000 and has been with the

Caps through the early part of his pro development. He has also represented the U.S. at the 2000 and 2001 World Championships.

HALVERSON, Trevor
b. White River, Ontario, April 6, 1971
Myth number one: You don't get hurt in a fight. Myth number two: Concussions are not a serious problem in hockey. Myth number three: The league and players are doing their best to deal with myths number one and two. Fact number one: Halverson suffered a career-ending concussion after fighting three times during an exhibition came at Washington's camp in September 1999. Fact number two: Two years later, he was finally off medication. Fact number three: He filed his retirement papers and enrolled at Algoma College to study psychology and computers. Fact number four: Facts number one through three occurred before his thirtieth birthday.

HALWARD, Doug ("The Hawk")
b. Toronto, Ontario, November 1, 1955
Halward was all over the map. He played most of his first three seasons in the minors, with Boston, and when he was traded he refused to endure the same fate. When he was promoted, he suffered acute tonsilitis and was gone for three weeks. In Vancouver, he broke curfew and ended up demanding a trade. He contracted phlebitis in his leg and missed the end of the '86-'87 season. In 14 NHL seasons, he played only 653 games, but when he did play he was a tough, skilled defenceman who was the envy of most teams. The closest he came to the Cup was with the Canucks in 1982, but for the most part he played on teams that didn't get too deep into the post-season. After retiring in 1989, he settled in Vancouver and joined a waste management firm.

HAMEL, Denis
b. Lachute, Quebec, May 10, 1977
It's not every day that a draft choice still playing in junior is traded, but that was Hamel's fate. St. Louis chose him in the 1995 Entry Draft while he was still with Chicoutimi, and the next year the Blues traded him with Charlie Huddy for a draft choice to Buffalo. After two years in the minors, he joined the Sabres and has remained with the team ever since, though his 2000-01 season was cut short by a knee injury. The left winger is counted on more for physical play than for putting the puck in the net, but since every team needs a guy like him, he's the guy in Buffalo.

HAMEL, Gilles
b. Asbestos, Quebec, March 18, 1960
For a year, anyway, Hamel made Scotty Bowman look bad. The left winger had been playing with the Sabres since 1980 but had developed a reputation as a coward who didn't work hard, check hard, or score enough to warrant suffering the first two characteristics. In 1985-86, he had a team-low -27 to his credit, symbolic of his weak defensive play. Bowman dished Hamel off to Winnipeg for Scott Arniel in the summer of 1986, and Hamel came out with guns blazin' in '86-'87. He scored 27 goals and was a plus player, but the year after his production tapered off as his defensive play

slipped badly. He was on his way to California, his final resting place in a 519-game tour of NHL duty.

HAMEL, Herb "Hap"
b. New Hamburg, Ontario, June 8, 1904
d. unknown
Hamel came out of the Can-Pro league to play four NHL games, all with the Leafs, on December 9, 13, 18, and 20, 1930.

HAMEL, Jean
b. Asbestos, Quebec, June 6, 1952
Add another name to the list of players with career-ending eye injuries. Hamel was hit in the left eye by a Ken Linseman shot in an exhibition game on October 4, 1984. Hamel had just finished his first year with the Habs and had had his longest playoff success, but after the injury he couldn't see out of the eye. He tried to play in December, but when he realized his vision was poor, he retired. The team immediately hired him as an assistant coach for the team's AHL affiliate in Sherbrooke. Hamel, brother of Gilles, had played in the NHL since 1972 for St. Louis, Detroit, and Quebec. His longest stay was with the Red Wings, but it came during a time the team was at its all-time weakest.

HAMEL, Pierre
b. Montreal, Quebec, September 16, 1952
Teams dress 18 skaters and just 2 goalies for every game, so there just aren't as many goalie jobs in hockey as goalies would probably like. For Hamel, this meant trying to remain upbeat and positive in the face of downbeat and negative, situations he too often encountered. Although he was signed by the Leafs, he attended five training camps with the Leafs and never made it. Twice he was called up – for four games in '74-'75 and one game four years later – but the minors were his comfort zone and the NHL his dream vacation. Winnipeg claimed him in the Expansion Draft of 1979, but that didn't change the course of his career, only his team name.

HAMILL, Robert "Red"
b. Toronto, Ontario, January 11, 1917
d. Sudbury, Ontario, January 1986
Nails aren't tough compared to Hamill – they're more like sponge. As a player, he hit hard and punched harder. He started in Boston in 1937, but over the next five years he just couldn't make it as a regular. The B's sold him to Chicago, and that's where he finished his career, in style. He scored 28 goals in '42-'43 and then left the team for two years' active service in the army. He returned to the Hawks when world peace returned, and became team captain for '46-'47. He patrolled the left wing, and although he could score his reputation was for hitting and fighting when the need arose. He later coached the team briefly, and when he retired in 1951 he pursued that full-time, mostly in junior hockey. Then life hit him hard. Poor circulation forced doctors to amputate his left leg, but he would not go down fighting. He learned to skate with an artificial limb so he could continue to coach and teach kids, but then doctors told him the right leg had to come

Trevor Halverson

Denis Hamel

Jean Hamel

Red Hamill

Al Hamilton

Jim Hamilton

Jackie Hamilton

**Inge
Hammarstrom**

off, too, after four operations failed to clear up the problems that had plagued his left. He vowed to continue on, but passed away before he fully recovered from the second amputation.

HAMILTON, Al
b. Flin Flon, Manitoba, August 20, 1946

You got injuries or a banged-up body? Talk to Hamilton and you'll feel much better. He played a bunch of games with the Rangers, but Buffalo claimed him when the Sabres joined the NHL in 1970. Two years later, he fled to Alberta/Edmonton of the WHA, and that is where he had both the best of times and worst of times. In '74-'75, he fell into the goalpost and broke his knee. That's an excruciating injury. As he was getting better, he fell going down the stairs in his house and re-broke the same knee. He played the '75-'76 season, all right, but on one leg. Then, he took a shot to the eye and was almost blinded, but he came back, sans shield. Then he suffered a separated shoulder that was so bad he couldn't lift two pounds. Through it all, though, he remained the Oilers' best and most reliable defenceman. He stayed with the team for its first season in the NHL, and later became coach of the Sherwood Park Crusaders of the Alberta Junior league. All good trivia experts will call out his name when someone asks, "Who was the first Edmonton Oilers to have his sweater retired?" Al Hamilton's number 3.

HAMILTON, Chuck
b. Kirkland Lake, Ontario, January 18, 1939

Hockey people usually protect and support their own, and Hamilton's life in the puck game started with his devotion and loyalty and came full circle after he retired. Although his first NHL game came with Montreal in '61-'62, he played the vast majority of his career with the Hershey Bears, eight years, in fact, under coach Frank Mathers (1963-71). Along the way, he missed the entire 1970-71 season after severely breaking his leg in an exhibition game during training camp. He later played three games with the St. Louis Blues, and shortly after retiring he heard news that Mathers was finally going to retire. Hamilton dropped by to see if this was true, it was, and he applied for the job. A few days later, he was the new coach of the Bears.

HAMILTON, Jim
b. Barrie, Ontario, January 18, 1957

In the old days, he could have blamed the dictatorial coaches or the lack of opportunity with just six teams. But in the post-expansion era, the way Hamilton's career went was insane. He played in the NHL for eight years, 1977-85, and in each and every one of

those seasons he was up and down to the minors with the Pittsburgh farm team. His callups lasted anywhere from 2 to 25 games. They came early in the season, mid-season, late in the season. They continued into the playoffs to the tune of six games. He never signed anywhere else, but he never made it in Pittsburgh. Up and down. Up and down. Down.

HAMILTON, John "Jackie" ("Gabby")
b. Trenton, Ontario, June 2, 1925
d. Toronto, Ontario, March 23, 1994

His time with the Leafs came during the war years, though he himself took 1944-45 off to join the army. Hamilton played for years after the war, principally in the AHL, though he later played senior hockey before retiring.

Hamilton played most of his career with the Leafs before and after the war.
REG HAMILTON

HAMILTON, Reg
b. Toronto, Ontario, April 29, 1914
d. Mississauga, Ontario, June 12, 1991

It was such a career / from year to year / loving friendships were made / the great Cup parades / the cheers were so good to hear. Hamilton played most of his career with the Leafs before and after the war. He won two Cups with Toronto, in 1942 and '45, before being sold to Chicago. He partnered with Hap Day on the blueline until Day retired, and he had played literally every minute of his kid hockey in his hometown. He hit hard and was a rock on the blueline, and midway through his final season with the Hawks they asked him to go to the minors, in Kansas City, to play and coach. He took the team from last place to first, though it didn't hurt that the players included Leo Reise, Bert Olmstead, and Vic Stasiuk. He returned home to coach the Marlies, and then retired to take a position in the purchasing department for Carlton Cards.

HAMMARSTROM, Inge
b. Sundsvall, Sweden, January 20, 1948

"He could go into the corner with six eggs in his pocket and come out without any broken." Or something like that. That was how Hammarstrom played according to his boss, the rusty crusty lusty Harold Ballard in Toronto. Hammarstrom and Borje Salming came to the Leafs in 1973 in a signing that changed the very nature of the game. They were the first two professional Swedes to make it to the NHL, though Hammarstrom didn't play as long or as beautifully as Salming. He did have three 20-goal seasons, but his timorous play was not what NHL teams were looking for during the dark days when the Philadelphia goons walked the earth hunting dinosaurs and listening to head clubmaster, Fred

Shero. Hammarstrom returned to Sweden in 1979 to play a little longer and then went into real estate. He was later hired by Jim Gregory of the NHL – and his GM from those Leafs days – to do scouting in Europe. And how's this for irony so thick you can't hear the laughter: In the late 1980s, none other than Bobby Clarke phoned Hammarstrom and asked him to be the Flyers scout for all of Europe. And guess what? Hammarstrom said yes!

HAMMOND, Ken
b. Port Credit, Ontario, August 22, 1963

Good size. Handles the puck well. Tough kid. If anyone makes it, he'll be the one. Those were the compliments thrown Hammond's way during his college days at RPI in the early 1980s, when he took the school to the NCAA championships for the first time in its history. He was named to the First All-Star Team, and Los Angeles looked forward to seeing what its draft choice could do at the next level. But during a seven-year NHL career, Hammond played for eight teams. Only once, in his last year with the dreadful expansion Ottawa Senators, did he play close to a full year, and he was a -42 over that '92-'93 season. He returned to RPI to finish his studies, and after graduating became an engineer in Kansas City.

HAMPSON, Gord
b. Vancouver, British Columbia, February 13, 1959

Gordie Howe managed to hang in there long enough to play with his sons, an incomparable achievement in pro sports. Young and old Hampson, though, also came pretty close. Father Ted retired in 1976 from the WHA, and son Gord played at the University of Michigan in 1977. As far as the NHL goes, a bit more distance stands in the way, but not that much. Ted's last game was in 1972, while Gord's first was in 1982. In fact, the two could have played together, for Ted came out of retirement to play briefly for Oklahoma through to 1981, and Ted played for that same team the very next year. Gord ended up playing only four NHL games, with Calgary the year after, but this father-son story is certainly a close second to the Howes' own family success.

HAMPSON, Ted
b. Togo, Saskatchewan, December 11, 1936

Hampson won the Memorial Cup with Flin Flon, his adopted town, in 1957, and went on to play some 20 years of pro hockey, including 676 NHL games. A utility centre, he went from Original Six to expansion teams until the WHA opened shop in 1972, and it was there he played the last of his big-time career. He settled down in Minnesota because he had played for the North Stars before moving to the Fighting Saints in the same city, and worked for a hockey equipment business and coached at the junior level in the city. In 1978, he accepted an offer to coach Oklahoma of the CHL, the Stars farm team, and over the next three seasons he also played occasionally for the team. When Minnesota shut down the team, Hampson worked for central scouting at the NHL and two years later became director of scouting for St. Louis. All three of his sons attended U.S. colleges on scholarship, and Gord went on to play in the NHL.

HAMPTON, Rick
b. Toronto, Ontario, June 14, 1956

His dad and mom both skated. His sister was a figure skater and teacher, and both of his younger brothers showed promise with a puck. Rick played forward all his life until California drafted him in 1974 and tossed him into the mix that fall. Then, they moved him back to the blueline. He didn't score as much as he would have liked, and his first four years were complicated by the fact that the team was in financial ruin from day one. He moved with the team to Cleveland, and nothing changed except the Seals became the Barons. The highlight of this period was his play in the World Championships for Canada in 1977 and '78, the first times Canada played internationally since leaving in 1970 because of the pro-amateur conflict with the IIHF. Hampton finished in Los Angeles and then played in Europe, but a serious knee injury midway through his '82-'83 season in Switzerland more or less ended his career. He later became manager of a rink in King City, Ontario and played oldtimers hockey on the side.

HAMR, Radek
b. Ústí nad Labem, Czechoslovakia (Czech Republic), June 15, 1974

Hamr played a few games with the new Ottawa Senators during their darkest days in the early 1990s, but for the most part his career has centred in Europe, notably Sweden and the Czech Republic, the two countries he has bounced between for much of the last decade. He is a solid defenceman with a hard shot and good mobility, but he was not, it seems, physical enough to last in the NHL or ambitious enough to play in the AHL and work his way back up.

HAMRLIK, Roman
b. Gottwaldov, Czechoslovakia (Czech Republic), April 12, 1974

He's been in the NHL for more than a decade now, the big defenceman who was the first Czech player to go 1st overall in the Entry Draft back in 1992. Hamrlik made an enormous impression at the '92 World Juniors and joined Tampa Bay that very fall to help the expansion team break into the NHL. After five and a half seasons, he was part of a blockbuster trade: Edmonton acquired him and Paul Comrie for Bryan Marchment, Steve Kelly, and Jason Bonsignore. Two and a half years later, his stock still high, the Oilers sent him to the Islanders in a three-for-one deal that saw Edmonton get Eric Brewer, Josh Green, and a draft choice. Hamrlik played for the Czechs at the '96 World Cup and two years later was part of his country's historic gold-medal win at the Olympics in Nagano.

HAMWAY, Mark
b. Detroit, Michigan, August 9, 1961

After graduating from Michigan State in 1983, Hamway turned pro and played a total of four seasons, three of which included stints with the Islanders. His longest stretch came in '85-'86 when he played 49 games for the team, but beyond that he played in the minors. He returned to Michigan, where he started coaching young players in the state's minor leagues.

Ken Hammond

Ted Hampson

Rick Hampton

Radek Hamr

Roman Hamrlik

Ron Handy

Michal Handzus

Al Hangsleben

Red Hanlon

John Hanna

HANDY, Ron
b. Toronto, Ontario, January 15, 1963

It was no fun being an Islanders prospect in the early 1980s, going into the dressing room and seeing all the Cup winners and future Hall of Famers. That's how the 21-year-old Handy made his NHL entrance in the '84-'85 season, and after an unimpressive showing he was sent to the minors and released a short time later. He was small and he could score, which meant Europe beckoned, but he signed with Indianapolis because his wife came from there. In '86-'87, he led the IHL with 55 goals, leading to interest from the St. Louis Blues. He had an excellent year with their farm team, and even got the call for four games when Doug Gilmour was injured, but that was his last NHL chance. Handy played the next decade in the minors, and as the century came to a close he opted to go into coaching rather than extend his career into the 21st century.

HANDZUS, Michal ("Zeus")
b. Banska Bystrica, Czechoslovakia (Slovakia), March 11, 1977

A Slovak first, an NHLer second. Handzus played on the historic team that won the gold medal at the 2002 World Championships, a remarkable rise to power that signalled the beginning of a new era with a new team among the elite. A decade earlier, Slovakia had been competing in "C" pool; now they were world champions! Handzus joined the team quickly after his Phoenix Coyotes were eliminated from the playoffs. He had played in St. Louis until being acquired late in the 2000-01 season, and it was with the Blues that he played on the great Slovak line of Michal Handzus-Lubos Bartecko-Pavol Demitra, the two others also contributing to the WC victory in Sweden. Handzus had also played at two World Junior tournaments for his country, though to lesser success. He was also runner-up to Steve Yzerman for the 1999-2000 Selke Trophy.

HANGSLEBEN, Al ("Hank")
b. Warroad, Minnesota, February 22, 1953

From the heart of Hockey Country, USA, came Hangsleben, a big and versatile player who developed at the University of North Dakota in the early 1970s before playing five years in the WHA. His NHL draft team was Montreal, but the Habs lost him in 1979 when the four WHA teams joined the NHL and the Whalers claimed him in the draft. He played only half a season with Hartford, though, before a trade sent him to Washington. There he proved his worth to coach Gary Green, who played him as much on the left wing as on defence. Ironically, he was more physical as a forward, but he was effective and reliable from the blueline. He later played briefly for L.A. before ending his career in the minors.

HANKINSON, Ben
b. Edina, Minnesota, May 1, 1969

Perhaps his was a marginal career in the NHL, but Hankinson used his all-round experience to great success after he retired. During his four years at the University of Minnesota (1987-91) he set records for penalty minutes, and like most fighters he was smart off the ice. He earned a degree in business management, speech communication, and psychology and then played parts of three years with New Jersey and Tampa Bay. He was traded to Detroit, but he never made it to the Red Wings' NHL team. After three years in the minors, he retired and became part of SPS, a group designed to help pros in a number of ways. Hankinson is a certified player agent, but he also runs camps to help NHLers train and get in shape.

HANKINSON, Casey
b. Edina, Minnesota, May 8, 1976

Brothers Peter, Ben, and Casey grew up in Edina with a friend, Randy Skarda. Casey, the youngest, was always tossed in goal, but one day a rubber puck slapped by Skarda hit Casey flush in the head. That was the last time he played goal! Ben went on to play in the NHL, as did Skarda, though Peter's career ended prematurely because of a shoulder injury. Their dad had been an all-star quarterback in his college days, and Casey has had a brief career so far in the NHL. He has played briefly in the league, with Chicago, but has become more of a minor-leaguer and seems destined not to be a player in the big show.

HANLON, Glen ("Red")
b. Brandon, Manitoba, February 20, 1957

There are not many goalies who go on to be coaches in the NHL, but Hanlon is determined to be among that number. He had a lengthy but ordinary career between the pipes, playing for four teams from 1977 to '91, and has been in the game in some capacity of coaching ever since. He served as an assistant coach with Vancouver for a number of years, and then in his first year as head coach with Portland of the AHL he was named coach of the year. His is one of those names that pops up more often than not when a vacancy becomes available, but in the meantime he's slowly building an impressive portfolio. He was inducted into the Manitoba Sports Hall of Fame in 1997 for his playing career, which included 477 games and 167 wins. His best year came with the Rangers in '83-'84 when he was 28-14-4, though he had some decent years with Detroit toward the end of his career. He began with such promise, but in his first full year he suffered a serious knee injury with Vancouver, a team that thought it had the best young goalie in the league. He went on to a coaching career in the AHL, notably with Portland.

HANNA, John ("Junior")
b. Sydney, Nova Scotia, April 5, 1935

Hanna took a back seat to no man in the toughness department, a fact most directly hammered home the night of February 28, 1959, when his Rangers faced the Canadiens at the Forum. He claimed that Ralph Backstrom kicked his skates out from under him – slew-footed him, in the modern parlance – and that precipitated a full-scale brawl that saw Hanna fight three Habs at various points during the free-for-all. He played three seasons with the Rangers, a few games with Montreal three years later, and a few more with Philly four years later. His career in the minors, though, was extensive, mostly in the AHL and WHL. Toward the end of the '72-'73 season, though, he broke his right leg, effectively ending his playing days. That summer, he signed with the Cleveland Crusaders to be both player and coach for the WHA team, but his wonky leg forced him to the bench. Nonetheless, emergency situations forced him into a few games, but he went on to coach Syracuse and Tidewater in later years. He was supposed to coach Springfield in '76-'77, but something truly bizarre happened. He couldn't find his way to the rink, so spotting a police car he pulled in behind it. He got out of his car to ask for directions, but stepped into the path of a truck and was hit, suffering a broken hip that sidelined him for most of the year.

HANNAN, Dave
b. Sudbury, Ontario, November 26, 1961

Hannan was always the kind of player every team needed but few went out and acquired. Not big but fast, he was a perfect utility forward who could kill penalties, win faceoffs, and get a team going with a big hit. He started in the Pittsburgh organization in 1982, playing six and a half years with a team that soon was to be built around Mario Lemieux. Fortune smiled on him, though, when the Pens sent him to Edmonton early in the 1987-88 season, one in which the Oilers won the Cup. No sooner had he contributed to that victory, though, than the team exposed him in the Waiver Draft, and Pittsburgh reclaimed him. From there he went to the tempestuous Leafs, and Toronto, not needing him, suggested he play for Dave King and the National Team in the hopes of playing in the 1992 Olympics in Albertville. Hannan agreed, won a silver medal, but then returned to the same troubles in Toronto. After a number of years in Buffalo, he had one more shot at playoff glory when Colorado acquired him at the '96 deadline. He was the perfect role player, and the Avs won the Cup in the year the team had moved from Quebec. Hannan retired a year later and moved back to Pittsburgh, where he became a financial adviser.

HANNAN, Scott
b. Richmond, British Columbia, January 23, 1979

Nothing but good things can be said about Hannan at this stage of his career. San Jose liked him in 1997 during his junior career with Kelowna, and he has quickly worked himself into the lineup on a regular basis. He is sound defensively, with an ability to create offence, and he has size and toughness to boot. If the Sharks develop into a winning team, Hannan will be one of the reasons.

HANNIGAN, Gord ("Hopalong")
b. Schumacher, Ontario, January 19, 1929
d. Edmonton, Alberta, November 16, 1966

The Hannigans were famous at St. Mike's in Toronto during the post-war years. The three boys – Gord, Pat,

and Ray – came from Ontario's North to the big city to pursue careers with the Maple Leafs, and they all made it. Gord lasted four years in the 1950s before landing in the minors. After he retired he settled in Edmonton and he and brother Ray opened that city's first ice cream drive-through, a business that expanded to include five franchises at its height.

HANNIGAN, Pat
b. Timmins, Ontario, March 5, 1936

The youngest Hannigan brother is better remembered to most as the commentator with Rick Azar on Buffalo Sabres broadcasts in the 1970s, inveighing Danny Gare and the boys to great accomplishments through boosterism not well regarded in hockey. Nonetheless, he came to the NHL as a player, making his first appearance on December 17, 1959, with Toronto. It was to be his only game with the Leafs, for less than a year later Punch Imlach traded him and Johnny Wilson to the Rangers to get Eddie Shack. Hannigan played most of the next decade in the minors, though he did stay two years in New York and another in Philadelphia after expansion. After retiring, he joined WKBW-TV in Buffalo and was later honoured by the Hockey Hall of Fame for his contributions to that part of the game. Sadly, he has been beset by Alzheimer's in his later years.

HANNIGAN, Ray
b. Schumacher, Ontario, July 14, 1927

The Hammerin' Hannigans played like brothers hell-bent on making an impression, and that's just what Gord and Ray did during their NHL careers.

He was left to raise seven children, more or less alone.
RAY HANNIGAN

Ray's was the briefest, just three games with the Leafs in '48-'49, but he had a lengthy career in the minors with Pittsburgh and Edmonton before retiring. He scored the game winner of the 1952 Calder Cup for the Hornets and later settled in Edmonton. For a while he could do no wrong. The ice cream business was booming and he was well off with a wonderful family. Then brother Gord died, his dad died, and his wife died of multiple sclerosis. He was left to raise seven children, more or less alone. He sold the ice cream shops and invested the money in a venture that proved imprudent, and with a life in chaos he turned to God. He became a priest, and to this day has improved his life and those of many others through his Catholic guidance. The man who once accrued fighting majors to survive in pro hockey now preaches peacefulness as a way to happiness.

HANSEN, Richie
b. Bronx, New York, October 30, 1955

Baseball. Foot-longs. Boxing. The zoo. Those are a few associations with the Bronx. Hockey? Way down

Dave Hannan

Gord Hannigan

Pat Hannigan

Richie Hansen

Oscar Hanson

Keith Hanson

Nick Harbaruk

Jeff Harding

Joe Hardy

the list. Hansen, though, was raised in Northport, just down the slender road that is the centre of Long Island. He grew up a Rangers fan (when the Islanders didn't exist), and he used to travel with his dad, Max, who was a referee in the Eastern league. He played in the Metropolitan Junior Hockey Association in Brooklyn, and the only thing better than June 1975, when the Islanders drafted him, was February 1977, when they played him. In the end, he played just 20 NHL games, but his scoring in the CHL was legendary. In just a few years, he became the league's all-time scorer in 1983–84 when he had his 498th point. He also held the record for most assists and was close to many other records when he decided to retire at that season's conclusion. He settled in Long Island, where he grew up, and worked in the building management department of the local school system, and at night coached kids hockey.

HANSEN, Tavis
b. Prince Albert, Saskatchewan, June 17, 1975
Years of patience just didn't pay off for Hansen. He was drafted by Winnipeg in 1994, but over the next 8 years he remained faithful to the team and was rewarded with just 34 games. He spent virtually all that time in the minors, though he missed much of 2000-01 with a serious arm injury. The following year, he was out of the NHL altogether.

HANSON, Dave ("Killer")
b. Cumberland, Wisconsin, April 12, 1954
The Hanson brothers in the movie were based on this one Hanson and his three cousins – Jeff, Steve, and Jack Carlson. *Slap Shot* is the movie, of course, voted the best hockey movie ever made. Hanson played two full seasons with the Johnstown Jets, the team mimicked in the movie. And, yes, his real-life penalty minutes were pretty absurd. Yet somewhere in the mayhem, Hanson got his chance to play pro. He was in the WHA in '76-'77, the year he played for five different teams in four leagues. He played in the WHA for two more years, and in '78-'79 made his NHL debut, with Detroit. He later played for Minnesota, and in 2001 he reprieved his role in *Slap Shot 2*, a movie so bad it went direct-to-video despite enormous hype during production and leading up to its release.

HANSON, Emil
b. Camrose, Alberta, November 18, 1907
d. Minneapolis, Minnesota, 1955
Brother of Oscar, Emil's NHL career was equally short and equally centred around St. Paul and Minneapolis. In fact, the brothers played for a number of years together on those teams. Emil's only NHL time came with Detroit, seven games in '32-'33.

HANSON, Oscar ("King Oscar")
b. Camrose, Alberta, December 27, 1909
d. Minneapolis, Minnesota, February 17, 1998
King Oscar came down from Alberta to establish himself in Minnesota and make a substantial contribution to the state in which he played much of his hockey. He played primarily for St. Paul and Minneapolis in the 1930s, but his career ended early the next decade when he crashed into a goalpost and

hurt his hip. He required surgery and never played again. He was one of Minnesota's early hockey heroes, and he settled in Minneapolis to raise a family. He was inducted into the Minnesota Hockey Hall of Fame and the Augsburg College Hall of Fame, though his later years were anything but joyous. In 1980, muscular dystrophy forced him into a wheelchair, and that is how he spent the final 18 years of his life.

HANSON, Keith
b. Ada, Minnesota, April 26, 1957
As a member of the Northern Michigan University Wildcats, Hanson established himself as a bona fide NHL prospect. He had been drafted out of high school by Minnesota, but after graduating and playing two years in the minors he was no closer to playing with the North Stars. They traded him to Calgary, and the Flames played the large defenceman in 25 games in '83-'84, his only time in the NHL during a very brief pro career.

HARBARUK, Nick
b. Drohiczyn, Poland, August 16, 1943
Born in the thick of the Second World War, Harbaruk and his family moved to Toronto in 1948 to start a new life. Nick turned into a good hockey player, played junior with the local Marlies, and turned pro with Rochester in 1964. The Leafs owned his rights and sent him on Tulsa, a perfect fit for him to play and earn a B.Sc. in economics from U of Tulsa. The Leafs had wanted to move him to their AHL team, but he refused to go because of his education and his wife, a Tulsa native. Pittsburgh claimed him, and he played four of his five NHL years with the Pens (1969-73), but after a year in St. Louis he accepted a lucrative offer to play with Indianapolis in the WHA. After retiring, he returned to Toronto and coached the men's hockey team at Seneca College for seven years, during which time he was charged with assault when a fan was hit by a stick behind the Seneca bench. Harbaruk won three Ontario college championships with the team but resigned in 1986 to go into business with his brother, who was running their dad's business, John Harbaruk Ltd., a company that grew sod for area landscapers.

HARDING, Jeff
b. Toronto, Ontario, April 6, 1969
Ah, the lure of the NHL. Harding was drafted in 1987 at the tender age of 18 shortly after accepting a scholarship to Michigan State. After one decent season, though, he decided to turn pro and join the Flyers, but he played just six games before earning a three-game suspension for pushing linesman Pat Dapuzzo in a scuffle. The rest of his very short career was interrupted regularly by injuries.

HARDY, Joe ("Gypsy Joe")
b. Kenogami, Quebec, December 5, 1945
Hardy who? Hardy who beat Wayne Gretzky to the punch by almost 20 years, that's who. Hardy who scored 208 points in a single season, 1975-76, with Beauce of the North American Hockey League (NAHL). Hardy who played only briefly with

Oakland/California in the NHL and who played the better part of three years in the WHA afterwards. Hardy who went on to lead the Binghamton Dusters in scoring in his final year, '77-'78. Hardy who took over as coach of those same Dustmen the next year, that's who.

HARDY, Mark
b. Semaden, Switzerland, February 1, 1959

Mark's dad, Lea, played pro hockey in Switzerland and later Quebec when he moved the family to Montreal. His mom finished in seventh place in figure skating at the 1952 Olympics in Oslo. And Mark, not surprisingly, was on skates by age two. His brother also played junior, and Mark played for Montreal in the Quebec league in the winter and worked at his dad's furniture store in the summer.

Then, Mark was drafted and had to face the NHL music. He had his coming out in 1979 with Los Angeles, and played pro hockey for almost 20 years. California was his lynchpin. He played some nine years with the L.A. Kings, and went from top prospect to young, learning defenceman to solid performer to NHL regular – all in the space of a year. He later had a long stint with the Rangers, but even in the minors, toward the end of his playing days, he gravitated toward the west coast. He got his first job as an assistant coach with Long Beach, and in 1999 he was promoted to a similar position with the Kings.

HARGREAVES, Jim
b. Winnipeg, Manitoba, May 2, 1950

The 1969-70 season was a banner one for Hargreaves: He was named best defenceman in the west in junior hockey, he made the all-star team, and Vancouver drafted him into the NHL. However, when a team keeps a player in the lineup because of injuries to a regular, the vital signs are not strong. Hargreaves played most of his three years in the system and little on the parent team, so when the WHA opened shop and gave him another option, he took it, finishing his career in the pirate league.

HARKINS, Brett ("Harks")
b. North Ridgeville, Ohio, July 2, 1970

Just as expansion gave one generation of players a chance in the NHL back in 1967, so, too, did future expansion give another generation hope for life outside the minors. A graduate of Bowling Green, Harkins never played for the Islanders, the team that drafted him. In fact, he signed as a free agent three times as a means of getting into games in the mid-1990s, with Boston twice and also with Florida. Then, he was in the minors for almost five years before

Columbus signed him and gave him some minutes in 2001-02, rescuing him from the oblivion of the "I."

HARKINS, Todd
b. Cleveland, Ohio, October 8, 1968

Brother of Brett and just as big, Todd left a place called Miami University in Oxford, Ohio (go figure) in 1990. He played for Calgary and Hartford, but like Brett was more minor league than NHL prospect. He played twice for the U.S. in the World Championships (1992 and '95), but after a few years in the minors he opted for a career in Europe, playing in the DEL (German league) as the 1990s drew to a close.

HARLOCK, David
b. Toronto, Ontario, March 16, 1971

Everything up to his first NHL game was roses; everything since then has been more thorn than petal. At the University of Michigan, he was only the second player to captain the team for three years. He won gold with Canada's National Team at the 1991 WJC, and after graduating he spent a season with the national program again, playing through the 1994 Olympics in Lillehammer. New Jersey drafted him but chose to ignore him, so he couldn't have been happier to start his pro career by signing with his beloved, hometown Leafs. During the ensuing three seasons, however, he saw minors and more minors, save eight games at Maple Leaf Gardens. The Leafs cut him loose and he wound up with Washington and the Islanders before finding his niche with the Atlanta Thrashers, where the now-veteran has had plenty of ice time and a commensurate amount of responsibility.

Jim Hargreaves

Brett Harkins

Scott Harlow

He won gold with Canada's National Team at the 1991 WJC.
DAVID HARLOCK

HARLOW, Scott
b. East Bridgewater, Massachusetts, October 11, 1963

Harlow played pro hockey for six seasons, though he never had the success in later years that he had at the college level. He went to Boston College and studied economics, and in his final year was team captain and a finalist for the Hobey Baker Award. Although he was drafted by Montreal in 1982, the Habs traded him to St. Louis for lowly "futures" six years later, and it was with the Blues that he got in his one and only NHL game late in the '87-'88 season. Harlow retired a few years later, and like most who love the game, he stayed associated with it as a coach in the amateur levels.

HARMON, Glen
b. Holland, Manitoba, January 2, 1921

Harmon was likely the quietest superstar for Montreal

Glen Harmon

during the war and immediate post-war period. He was not a big man, and neither was his usual partner, Frank Eddolls. Yet the two once played 34 consecutive games without being scored on! Harmon was a decent scorer, and by 1957, six years after retired, he was still the fourth-leading goal getter in the history of Montreal defencemen. He played in two All-Star Games and was twice named to the NHL's Second All-Star Team. Harmon won Cups with the Habs in 1944 and '46, and after finishing his career he stayed in Montreal and sold cars for GM for 31 years.

HARMS, John

b. Saskatoon, Saskatchewan, April 29, 1925
d. Vernon, British Columbia, January 5, 2003

Opponents tried to keep out of Harms' way, but he didn't try to keep out of theirs. Just the opposite, in fact. The "mighty mite," as he was sometimes called, was a fan favourite for his checks and aggressive play despite his small stature. He saw NHL time at the end of the war, with Chicago, and was out of the league by the time he was 20. From there, Harms had a long and prosperous minor-league career, notably in Kansas City and British Columbia, where he played senior hockey for a number of years, winning the Allan Cup with Vernon in 1956. Part Cree by birth, he was adopted by Mennonite farmers. He retired to Vernon in 1984 after working many years with BC Hydro and is a member of the B.C. Hockey Hall of Fame.

John Harms

HARNOTT, Walter ("Happy")

b. Montreal, Quebec, September 24, 1909
d. Montreal, Quebec, January 8, 1977

Harnott's only NHL games came with Boston in 1933-34 while he was playing for the affiliate Cubs. In all, Harnott played parts of four years with the Cubs before moving to the AHA and returning to Montreal to enlist in the army, effectively ending his playing career.

HARPER, Terry

b. Regina, Saskatchewan, January 27, 1940

There's a happy childhood story and an unhappy one. Happy: As a kid growing up in the West, Harper loved to ride his bike to the airport and watch planes take off and land. The first thing he did when he could afford it – thanks to hockey – was take flying lessons, and with time he became a certified pilot. Unhappy: At age 11, he was burning garbage when a can of oil exploded and set him on fire. He suffered burns to his whole body and was bedridden for three months, but a Polish doctor, a refugee from the Second World War, healed him and allowed him to live a full and normal life. Harper played the first 10 years of his NHL

Terry Harper

career with Montreal (1962-72), winning five Cups in that time. He was a prototypical defensive defenceman who scored only 14 goals in that decade with the Habs. With the arrival of coach Scotty Bowman, though, he grew less content and was pleased when GM Sam Pollock traded him to Los Angeles after Harper himself engineered the deal with Jack Kent Cooke. L.A. wasn't a winning team, but it was an environment in which he was happier. In the summer of 1975, however, L.A. signed Marcel Dionne, and Harper was named as part of the compensation package that had to be surrendered to Detroit. Harper refused to go, and he took the NHL to court over the matter. The case was eventually resolved when the two teams worked out a deal that Harper reluctantly agreed to. He retired in 1980 to act as an assistant coach in Colorado, but injuries to the team forced him out of retirement for 15 games. When the Rockies moved to New Jersey, Harper remained in Colorado to go into the real estate business.

HARPER, Tim

b. Bloomington, Minnesota, May 10, 1957

Harper had a very convincing college career at the University of Minnesota, where his scoring increased every year, from a freshman 14 goals in '76-'77 to a senior 53 in '79-'80. His first three years of pro offered the same hope for glory in the Central league, but squeezed into those years were three games with Calgary, the only NHL chance he ever had in a career that burned bright but not for long.

Harris was an avid photographer, and during his days with the Leafs carried his camera into the dressing room.
BILLY "HINKY" HARRIS

HARRINGTON, Leland "Hago"

b. Melrose, Massachusetts, August 13, 1904
d. Melrose, Massachusetts, July 1959

If there were such a thing as the Melrose Hockey Hall of Fame, Harrington would be its charter member. He lived his whole life there and was associated with hockey in Boston for much of that time, first as a player and later as a coach. He played for the Bruins in 1925-26 and again two years later, and then briefly with the Canadiens toward the end of his career. He played almost exclusively for Providence in the minors, and after retiring in 1936 he became part of the management of the Boston Garden. He also coached the Boston Olympics for some 13 years.

HARRIS, Billy ("Hinky")

b. Toronto, Ontario, July 29, 1935
d. Toronto, Ontario, September 20, 2001

Over the years there were greater Leafs, Leafs who scored more goals or won more Cups or who were more popular. But never was there a more devoted man to the team and the game, a man whose passion for hockey kept him in Toronto for much of his career and also shot him around the world. Harris played for the Marlies in the mid-1950s, that team's glory years, and after winning the Memorial Cup in 1955 he made the Leafs full-time. For the next decade he played nowhere else, and won three Stanley Cups with the team during their dynastic run (1962-64). The Leafs traded him to Detroit in 1965, and he closed out his pro career with stops in Oakland and Pittsburgh. Harris was nowhere near finished with hockey, though. His passion merely moved from the Leafs and the NHL and playing to the international game and coaching. He played briefly with the Canadian National Team in '69-'70, and after a short time behind the Hamilton bench in the OHL he became coach of Tre Kronor, Sweden's national team, guiding them through the 1972 Olympics in Sapporo. It was he as much as anyone who convinced Sweden's finest players – Nilsson, Hedberg, Sjoberg – that they could compete with the rest of the world. Harris returned to Canada to coach in the WHA and then went back to Europe, this time to coach the Italian team. In 1977, he helped that nation win the "C" pool tournament, and settled in Toronto after a series of shorter coaching stints, including as an assistant with the Edmonton Oilers. Harris was an avid photographer, and during his days with the Leafs carried his camera everywhere, including into the dressing room. He captured the team's greatest moments on film, and years later released a book called *The Glory Days* that captured the nostalgia of the pre-expansion Leafs. He later toured with the images, calling his project "The Leafs Before Ballard," a reference to the post-Conn Smythe regime that Harris viewed as a disaster and an embarrassment to the franchise. A loyal Leafs player and a devoted man of the game, Harris had no enemies. He spent the last six years of his life fighting leukemia and cancer before passing away in 2001, not long after former teammate Carl Brewer.

HARRIS, Billy
b. Toronto, Ontario, January 29, 1952
First, the trivial stuff: He was born in Toronto. His name was Billy. His middle name was Edward. He played for the Leafs. And, no, he wasn't *that* Billy Harris! This Billy Harris played a generation later, and was, in fact, the most highly regarded junior in 1972. He had just finished a year in which he led the OHL in scoring with the Marlies. He was drafted 1st overall by the Islanders in June. His agent, Alan Eagleson, negotiated the highest rookie contract in the history of the NHL after Harris rejected an even higher offer from the WHA. And, he was going to Maple Leaf Gardens in August to participate in Team Canada's 1972 Summit Series training camp. In his first 6 years with the Islanders, Harris averaged almost 26 goals a season, solid numbers but below what was expected of a number-one selection. He was a fine two-way player and used his size well, but he didn't have that extra gear that Lafleur or Perreault had coming out of junior. He was traded to L.A. and on to Toronto, but he never regained that Marlies magic that had made him the toast of the town back when. Harris relocated to California and opened a nightclub called Harry O's.

HARRIS, Fred "Smokey"
b. Port Arthur, Ontario, October 11, 1890
d. Portland, Oregon, June 6, 1974
Harris played most of his hockey in the Pacific Coast league before and after the formation of the NHL in 1917. His finest moments came with the Vancouver Millionaires in 1921 and '23 when his team went to the finals, though both times they were beaten by the Ottawa Senators. He made his only NHL appearances with Boston in '24-'25, the team's first year in the league, and after that he played in California.

HARRIS, George "Duke"
b. Sarnia, Ontario, February 25, 1942
No matter how hard he tried – and he did try hard – Harris just couldn't do enough in the minors to catch the attention of NHL scouts and GMs. He played in the great league only in '67-'68, and in just part of the season at that, spending most of his time in the AHL until the WHA opened its doors. Then, he signed with the Houston Aeros (pre-Gordie Howe) and finished with Chicago.

HARRIS, Henry
b. Kenora, Ontario, April 28, 1906
d. March 6, 1993
In the old days, before the more-recent old days, player movement was much more common than during the sponsorship era of the Original Six. This allowed Harris to play one year in the Pacific Coast league, the next in the NHL, and the one after in another league. It was 1930-31 that he played for the Bruins, and his career landed him in Calgary at the end, playing for the once-mighty Tigers.

HARRIS, Hugh
b. Toronto, Ontario, June 7, 1948
In an era when sponsorship was ending and the universal amateur draft was establishing itself as the way for players to join the NHL, Harris broke all the rules and still managed to play in the league. He never played for a sponsored team, never signed a C-form binding him to an NHL team, and never was drafted, either. Instead, at 19, he signed with Muskegon in the IHL in 1967 and apprenticed in the minor pros! From there, he graduated to the AHL, and then in '72-'73 he played for the Buffalo Sabres. After that, he spent the last five years of his career in the WHA, playing for a total of seven teams, notably Indianapolis where he was team captain.

HARRIS, Ron
b. Verdun, Quebec, June 30, 1942
Harris played the same way every night, provided he was healthy. He hit everything in sight, which made his goalies happy, but the long-term effects had as damaging results to his own body cumulatively as to his opponents' individually. Harris played in minor-league obscurity before expansion in '67, making quick appearances with Detroit before being claimed by Oakland. Ironically, once he played a full year in the NHL and the Wings saw what he could do, they reacquired him. It was a trade to the Rangers, though, in November 1972 that led to his finest hours, on the Blueshirts blueline. It was in large measure due to his fantastic hitting that the Rangers eliminated the

Billy Harris (b. 1952)

George Harris

Hugh Harris

powerful Bruins from the '73 playoffs, but this style of play soon cost him his livelihood. The next year, he suffered a painful break of his hip socket, and just three games into the '75-'76 season he suffered a knee injury that ended his career. He ended up taking Lloyd's of London to court over his insurance policy, claiming he was owed $200,000 for the damage that prevented him from playing.

HARRIS, Ted
b. Winnipeg, Manitoba, July 18, 1936

Ted Harris

It isn't very often a player's biggest break comes when he's discovered by someone in the AHL, but when that someone happens to be a guy named Eddie Shore, the entire hockey world pricks up its ears and listens. Shore, like everyone before and since, defied common sense in taking a liking to a player he admitted didn't skate very well. That is, after all, the first tenet of the game. But Harris made up for this lack of basic skill by doing everything in his power to keep enemy forwards at bay, and Shore gave him ample credit for ability on this part of the scorecard. And so Harris left the WHL to join Shore's Springfield Indians in 1959, and played there for four years until Montreal decided he was ready. Good thing, too, because Harris was on four Cup-winning teams with Montreal in the 1960s, doing what he did best: hitting, fighting, defending at all costs. Toward the end of the decade, though, he and new coach Claude Ruel didn't see eye to eye, so Harris was happy to move on to Minnesota, where he was named captain and helped bring the new team to respectability. He retired in 1974, but Philly coach Fred Shero convinced him to play one more season, which brought Harris his fifth Stanley Cup. He immediately returned to Minnesota to become the team's head coach, but after two poor years the welcome home ended just 19 games into his third season.

HARRISON, Ed ("Little Ed")
b. Mimico, Ontario, July 25, 1927

He was called Little Ed by teammates to differentiate him from Big Ed, his teammate and cousin, Ed Sandford. The cousins had played together in school at St. Mike's, but while Sandford basked in the warmth of the star's lights, Harrison grew chilly in the shadows of obscurity. Yet Harrison was just as important as cousin Ed in helping the Majors win the 1947 Memorial Cup, and, in fact, it was Harrison who signed with the Bruins before Sandford. Yet Sandford was the better prospect, the larger-than-life figure, the one who was destined for a long career in the NHL. Harrison did make it, for three years and a bit, anyway. He used his speed to great advantage and played on the top line sometimes,

Paul Harrison

but ultimately was traded to the Rangers and then relegated to the minors while Sandford kept on in the NHL. It was a great run for Harrison, just not as long as he might have hoped.

HARRISON, Jim ("Max")
b. Bonnyville, Alberta, July 9, 1947

A life in hockey so shocking and horrifying, one wonders how the game and the events ever met. Harrison was like any other player, coming out of junior in the 1960s and making his NHL debut with the great Bruins in '68-'69. He played 23 regular-season games the following year, when Bobby Orr won the B's the Cup, and then was traded to Toronto. He moved to the WHA, and returned to the NHL to play with Chicago for three years, beginning in 1976. Two

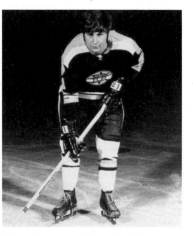

The Hawks refused to forward his medical files to the clinic, thus denying Harrison means to file for insurance.
JIM HARRISON

years later is when it all really began. He was cross-checked by Steve Vickers during a game and suffered what would be a serious back injury. GM Bob Pulford, though, didn't believe him. He thought Harrison was faking the injury (ever met an NHLer who faked an injury?). Pulford sent him to the minors, but Harrison, in pain, refused to go. He called his agent, Alan Eagleson, to help him out. Problem, though: Eagleson also represented Pulford! Guess what happened? Harrison was suspended without pay until he reported to the farm in New Brunswick. He reported, played two games, then went to the Mayo Clinic, such was the pain. Doctors there told him not to play again. The Hawks refused to forward his medical files to the clinic, thus denying Harrison means to file for insurance. Harrison moved to Toronto and after lengthy acupuncture treatments recovered to the point that he considered coming back. Glen Sather signed him in Edmonton, but after just three games he knew he couldn't play. When he filed his retirement papers, Eagleson wanted him to sign a form releasing everyone of all medical liability, hardly the advice a conscientious agent would consider for a client. For years, Harrison was not capable of working and had to rely on his wife for support. They lost their house and virtually all his earnings, and to this day he has yet to receive any compensation for his injury. His wife died in 1999 after a long battle with cancer, and Harrison wasn't even able to afford funeral payments. Today, he receives $580 in pension money, his pride, dignity, and income all but gone. Hockey has done so much good for so many, but Harrison has not benefitted.

HARRISON, Paul
b. Timmins, Ontario, February 11, 1955

Minnesota may have drafted him, but Lou Nanne quickly decided he had made a mistake and didn't hesitate to trade the young goalie to Toronto when the opportunity presented itself. In his three partial seasons with the North Stars (1975-78), Harrison had a record of 6-22-3 and a GAA most figure skaters would love as scores for artistic merit. When he got to the Leafs, the door was open for him to be the backup to Mike Palmateer and perhaps take over as the starter, but Harrison's play warranted nothing short of a ticket to the minors. In his post-career days, he became a police officer in Timmins.

HART, Gerry
b. Flin Flon, Manitoba, January 1, 1948
No one in his right mind would work in the mines if he could skate on the ponds. Hart knew this firsthand because his father laboured for Hudson Bay Copper & Zinc Company for 35 years down below, and he himself worked there in the summers. If hockey was his way out of the mines, he'd fight tooth and nail to succeed on ice. Hart played junior in Flin Flon with teammates Bobby Clarke and Reg Leach, and although he played his first four years of pro with Detroit he made his mark with the Islanders, an original selection in the '72 Expansion Draft. He was as unglamorous a defenceman as Denis Potvin was smiles and spotlight. He scored as few goals as Mike Bossy scored many. But he rarely missed a game and went into the corners to fish the puck out with the same enthusiasm night after night. He was part of the famous team that, in the '75 playoffs against Pittsburgh, rallied from 3-0 down in games to eliminate the Penguins in game seven, though he was claimed by Quebec just before the Isles were to win four Cups in a row. He finished his career in St. Louis, where serious knee and clavicle injuries forced him into retirement at 33. He returned to Long Island and went into two business ventures, one in real estate, the other in the development of a sports complex management system called "The Rinx."

Hart played junior in Flin Flon with teammates Bobby Clarke and Reg Leach.
GERRY HART

HART, Wilfred "Gizzy"
b. Weyburn, Saskatchewan, June 1, 1902
d. Weyburn, Saskatchewan, June 22, 1964
Hart was part of the Victoria Cougars in the mid-1920s when the team was the last non-NHL club to win the Stanley Cup. That was 1925, and the next year the Cougars went to the finals, only to lose to the Montreal Maroons. The year after that, he played briefly with Detroit and later with the Canadiens, though he spent most of these years in Providence. Hart was known primarily for his speed, and after retiring in 1933 he returned to Weyburn, where he spent the rest of his life in the retail card business and as a restaurant owner. He coached senior hockey for a

number of years and was also an excellent ballplayer and runner.

HARTIGAN, Mark
b. Fort St. John, British Columbia, October 15, 1977
Hartigan finished his college career at St. Cloud State on a high note, leading the CCHA in scoring, being named the division's MVP, and being named to the First All-Star Team. At season's end, he signed with Atlanta as a free agent and played two games for the Thrashers, joining a young and dynamic team.

HARTMAN, Mike
b. Detroit, Michigan, February 7, 1967
Hartman never realized a dream by playing with his hometown Red Wings, which is too bad because he would have looked great in a Detroit sweater. His dad, the team photographer, would have made sure of that. Instead, Hartman was drafted by Buffalo in 1986, where his tenacity and physical play likened him to Danny Gare. Unfortunately, Hartman didn't manage to score in his entire career what Gare scored in '75-'76: 50 goals. No, indeed. His best season was eleven goals and by 1994, with 43 career scores to his credit and the Rangers no longer interested in him, he was out of the NHL and in the minors.

HARTNELL, Scott ("Bird Dog"/ "Harts")
b. Regina, Saskatchewan, April 18, 1982
Watch out for this guy in the coming years. He's big and strong, has great hands, and is still learning. A high draft choice by Nashville in 2000, he is still a long way from reaching his full potential, In his rookie season, he was the youngest player in the league. In his second season, he nearly tripled his points. In 1999, he scored the OT winner for Canada at the U-18 Four Nations Tournament. And since arriving in Nashville he has become a leader off the ice as well, doing community and charity work with the same enthusiasm as his idol, Wayne Gretzky.

HARTSBURG, Craig
b. Stratford, Ontario, June 29, 1959
Hartsburg came out of junior with the Soo to play for Minnesota, and he remained with the Stars until the day he retired. Over the 10 years and 570 games he played for the team, he established himself as a leader and defenceman whose presence could help make the team better. In the summer of 1982, after his third year, he signed a seven-year deal with the team, the longest in North Stars history, and he honoured each and every year of it. The road wasn't entirely smooth, though. He missed much of '83-'85 with knee injuries

Gizzy Hart

Mike Hartman

Craig Hartsburg

in successive seasons, and, similarly, in his last two years injuries caused him to miss more games than he played. The team had only moderate playoff success during his tenure, and this freed him to play for Canada at the World Championships, which he gladly did on three occasions. He was named best defenceman in the 1987 tournament, and he also played in the World Juniors (a bronze in '78) and the 1987 Canada Cup. Hartsburg wasted no time in making the transition from playing to not playing. He became an assistant with the team the fall he retired and became head coach of the Guelph Storm in the OHL for '94-'95, after which he was named coach of the year. He got his shot at coaching in the NHL the next year, with Chicago, but after three increasingly poorer years the team let him go. In 1998, Anaheim hired him, but again poor results ensured his dismissal.

Buster Harvey

Hugh Harvey

Todd Harvey

HARVEY, Doug
b. Montreal, Quebec, December 19, 1924
d. Montreal, Quebec, December 26, 1989

As heavyweight boxing champion of the Canadian Navy during the Second World War, Harvey brought a reputation to the rink from the get-go. He played junior and senior hockey with the Montreal Royals for a number of years, a time that climaxed with an Allan Cup victory in 1947. From there, it was on to the NHL and conquering the best league in the world. Harvey was considered a precursor to Bobby Orr, but to say that both were rushing defencemen is to minimize their individuality. Harvey was not nearly as explosive or fast as Orr, but he was able to control the play and make the game flow to his pace like Orr. He was a rushing defenceman in that he moved the puck, but he didn't go straight for the goal with the puck or go end to end. In fact, he had only 88 goals in more than 1,100 career games, and it took him more than 70 games and 8 years to get his first playoff goal. Harvey played the first 14 years of his career with the Canadiens, winning 6 Stanley Cups and establishing himself as the best defenceman in the world. From 1955 to '62, he won the Norris Trophy every year but one, and he was a member of the First All-Star Team a record 10 times. When Maurice Richard retired in 1960, Harvey was named the team's captain, though his involvement in trying to form the first players' association meant he was traded to the Rangers just a year later. His first year with the Rangers was one for the record books. He not only played defence but coached the team, and he won the Norris Trophy as best defenceman as well. He is the only man to win the trophy in successive years with different teams. The rest of the 1960s was a tumultuous time for Harvey. He went on to play for Detroit and

He ended up as a security guard for the Connaught Racetrack in Ottawa.
DOUG HARVEY

St. Louis, and this Hall of Famer played in the minors for the better part of five seasons. Once he retired in 1970, he had extreme difficulty in coping with life without ice. His glorious reputation earned him chances as a scout and assistant coach, but he suffered from alcoholism and couldn't hold a job, even when the Canadiens hired him as an Ottawa-area scout. He had always been enormously popular in the dressing room, a figure who was calm when everyone else was all nerves, and wherever he went, regardless of his condition, he was greeted with grand hellos and good cheer. But, the drinking never stopped, and life didn't get better when his once-popular restaurant, Chez Harvey, went bankrupt. In 1973, he was elected to the Hockey Hall of Fame but refused to attend the ceremonies because he believed the delayed induction was due to his drinking problem. He ended up as a security guard for the Connaught Racetrack in Ottawa, but in late 1989 succumbed to cirrhosis of the liver in a Montreal hospital. One of the greats ended his days looking nothing like the charismatic, strong man hockey fans around the country had worshipped. In that respect, too, he and Orr were different.

HARVEY, Fred
"Buster"
b. Fredericton, New Brunswick, April 2, 1950

He was an Islander, all right, but not one from New York. No, he came from down east, New Brunswick way, a place that produced lobster and unemployment in greater numbers than hockey players. When he made the Minnesota North Stars in 1970, that was big news back home. Sure, he didn't last past 1977, but those 407 games were quite well and good, thank you. Harvey returned to New Brunswick after his playing days and coached the Fredericton Jr. Red Wings. He also worked radio for the Fredericton Express, and to earn a living he owned a business called Saunders Equipment. He was even inducted into the New Brunswick Sports Hall of Fame for his life in hockey.

HARVEY, Hugh
b. Kingston, Ontario, June 25, 1949

The Kansas City Scouts existed for only two years – '74-'75 and '75-'76 – and Harvey was right there to document both seasons, though not for very long. His 18 NHL games were encircled by long loops in the minors from which he could never entirely disentangle during his short career.

HARVEY, Todd
b. Hamilton, Ontario, February 17, 1975

In his rookie season, 1994-95, with Dallas, Harvey

realized a dream when he scored a hat trick at Maple Leaf Gardens during a *Hockey Night in Canada* game. He finished with 11 on the year, and this more or less typified his annual contribution to teams in the goals department. His role, though, was much more important. He was a hitting forward, the kind who could check the other team's best player onto the ice, kill penalties, and chip in with good offensive play. He played four years with Dallas, a year and a half with the Rangers, and more recently has been with San Jose, one of the best young teams in the league.

HASEK, Dominik ("The Dominator")

b. Pardubice, Czechoslovakia (Czech Republic), January 25, 1965

On January 1, 1983, Hasek made his first significant appearance at the WJC, against Canada. He allowed all seven goals in a 7-7 shootout, and at tournament's end went back to the Czech league where he developed into a star who would not give up seven goals on a regular basis. Players from Iron Curtain countries can be neatly divided into those who were loyal to communism and those who wanted to leave it. Hasek lived in the former camp, so although he knew of the NHL and knew that Chicago drafted him in 1983, he was not going to defect. Instead, he played for Pardubice and became the country's number-one goalie for international tournaments. These included five World Championships, the 1987 Canada Cup, and the 1988 Olympics in Calgary. It wasn't until 1990, when he was 25, that Czech authorities allowed him to play in the NHL. When he got to Chicago, the superstar of the Czech league hardly took North America by storm. In his first 2 years, he played only 25 games for the Hawks and spent much of his time in the minors. No one was particularly impressed by his unique style of play, which to the unknowing eye looked only like so much flopping and gambling that some nights he looked great, others not so great. Chicago had the more reliable Eddie Belfour in goal, so the team had no problem trading Hasek to Buffalo for nothing more than a backup goalie (Stephane Beauregard) and a draft choice (Eric Daze). The Sabres, though, gave him the chance to be their starter, and he proved worthy of the opportunity. In his second season, he led the league with a GAA of 1.95, though his enigmatic play befuddled most. Hasek didn't just go down; he flopped and stayed down. He played happily without his goal stick and shot his arms and legs out looking for pucks he couldn't see. He relied on instinct, but his unpredictability intimidated shooters. An open net was soon blocked by the stab of a leg while Hasek was

In 2005 he will return to Toronto to be inducted into the Hockey Hall of Fame.
DOMINIK HASEK

on the ice and facing his goal. A deke that forced the goalie to sprawl created an opening that was closed by a sliding blocker. He was orchestrated chaos in the crease, and players couldn't adapt after seeing hundreds of goalies who played a disciplined – and, therefore, predictable – game. The downside was that he handled the puck poorly behind his net, and he was oddly susceptible to letting in routine, long shots. But game in, game out, Hasek was spectacular. He had his best two years in '96-'98. In '96-'97, he became the first goalie since Jacques Plante more than 35 years earlier to win the Hart Trophy, and the year after he repeated the feat. In '97-'98, he also recorded 13 shutouts and played for the Czechs at the 1998 Olympics in Nagano. Hasek became a hero on two counts. In the semifinals against Canada, he stopped all five shootout penalty shots to give his team a victory, and in the finals he shutout Russia 1-0 to give the Czechs their first-ever Olympic gold. The celebrations in Prague a couple of days later attracted hundreds of thousands of fans, and Hasek had realized a dream. His '98-'99 season was shortened by a serious groin injury, the bane of all goalies, and he declared the coming season was to be his last. The injury resurfaced, though, and he recanted on his decision and kept on playing. In the summer of 2001, he became a free agent and signed with Detroit, abandoning the dream of bringing a Stanley Cup to Buffalo. A year later, he was in a Red Wings sweater, hoisting the Cup, and a few days later he announced his retirement. Hasek has won the Vezina Trophy six times. He has

Dominik Hasek

accomplished what any goalie could dream of, and he took his family back to the Czech Republic knowing that in 2005 he will return to Toronto to be inducted into the Hockey Hall of Fame. Of that there can be no doubt.

HASSARD, Bob

b. Lloydminster, Saskatchewan, March 26, 1929

There aren't too many players who can boast about having won three championships in consecutive years with three different teams in three different leagues. So, try this: Hassard won the Allan Cup with the Marlies in 1950, the Stanley Cup with Toronto in 1951, and the Calder Cup with Pittsburgh, the Leafs' farm team, in 1952. All because at age 18 he had spurned an offer by the Brooklyn Dodgers to play ball in their system. Hassard played four of his five years with the Leafs, the last, '54-'55, coming with Chicago. Although he played for a while in the minors, he retired in 1958 and went into the insurance business, eventually settling in Stouffville, Ontario, and running the Hassard-Birkett Agency with a partner.

Bob Hassard

Kevin Hatcher

Ed Hatoum

Brett Hauer

Niclas Havelid

HATCHER, Derian
b. Sterling Heights, Michigan, June 4, 1972

If Hatcher were to retire any day soon, he could do so knowing he had pretty much accomplished it all. No, he never won the Hart Trophy or broke Bobby Orr's records, but the extra large, defensive defenceman has done what could be reasonably expected of anyone. He won a Stanley Cup with Dallas in 1999. He won the World Cup with Team USA in 1996. He's played at the World Championships (twice) and the Olympics (in 1998) and the All-Star Game (in 1997). He has played his entire career with the Minnesota/Dallas franchise and become team captain, and even had the pleasure for two years of playing with his older brother, Kevin, in Dallas. His other brother, Mark, played pro but never made it to the NHL, but Derian's career is pretty much a complete package all ready to go.

HATCHER, Kevin
b. Detroit, Michigan, September 9, 1966

Like his younger brother, Derian, Kevin can retire almost a happy man, knowing he's done everything he set out to do, with the exception of win a Stanley Cup. He spent the first 10 years in Washington (1984-94) where he was fortunate enough at first to be paired on the blueline with Rod Langway, a perfect way for the 18-year-old to learn his position. He slowly emerged from Langway's shadow into his own man, a ferocious checker who could rush the puck and anchor a power play. In '92-'93, he had 34 goals, one of a small number of defencemen to reach that mark. Midway through the next season he was traded to Dallas, where he played with Derian, but his stay lasted only two years, not long enough to win the Cup with the team in '99. He has played in five All-Star Games as well as the '87 and '91 Canada Cups. With Derian, he also played at the World Cup in '96 and the Olympics in Nagano two years later, and is well past the 1,100-game mark for his NHL career.

HATOUM, Ed
b. Beirut, Lebanon, December 7, 1947

The incredible part about Hatoum's birthplace is that there is no asterisk to the story, nothing to dilute its purity. Hatoum's dad wasn't a native Canadian digging for oil or working with the army or vacationing with his pregnant wife. The Hatoums were genuine Lebanese living in a small village outside Beirut. It was a family of 10, and in 1954 his father moved to Canada to live with his uncle in Ottawa. Dad took one son and one daughter with him, but it took three years before they had earned enough money to bring the rest of the family over.

Young Ed saw his first rink at age 10, and played in a league for the first time two years later. By 17, he was playing junior and being scouted by the Red Wings. In 1968, he played in his first NHL game, though the Red Wings used him only sparingly the next season before letting him go in the Expansion Draft. Hatoum had a new start with Vancouver, but the day he played his best game, toward the end of training camp, was also the day he destroyed his shoulder. Its separation had to be helped by a pin, and he missed several weeks. When he did come back, it was slowly and without that confidence he had developed in his first weeks with the team. That was to be his final NHL year, but Hatoum did play in the WHA afterward, a remarkable career for a boy born so far removed from the game.

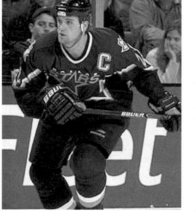

He has played his entire career with the Minnesota/Dallas franchise.
DERIAN HATCHER

HAUER, Brett
b. Richfield, Minnesota, July 11, 1971

Hauer had an outstanding career with the University of Minnesota-Duluth Bulldogs (1989-93) that culminated with an appearance at the '93 Worlds and led to the next season, when he played the year for the U.S. National Team. Hauer finished the year by playing at the Olympics in Lillehammer and then joined Las Vegas of the IHL. He played the next year in Sweden, of all places, and made his NHL debut with Edmonton the year after. It would be four years later that the Oilers used him again, and he later joined Nashville, the last outpost of NHL hockey, though he still played mostly in the minors.

HAVELID, Niclas
b. Stockholm, Sweden, April 12, 1973

When Niclas Havelid played in his first NHL game, on October 2, 1999, he was 26 years old and freshly drafted by Anaheim. One of the oldest players to be selected in the 1990s, he was an established star in the Swedish Elite League before coming to North America to play. Despite good performances with the Ducks, each of his first two years was marred by serious injuries, the first a broken finger and the second a season-ending torn ACL. Interestingly, he had played for Tre Kronor at the 1993 World Juniors, and his teammates that year included Peter Forsberg, Markus Naslund, and Kenny Jonsson. More important, he also played on the gold-medal team that beat Finland at the 1998 World Championships in Zurich.

HAVLAT, Martin
b. Mlada Boleslav, Czechoslovakia (Czech Republic), April 19, 1981

By the time Havlat made his NHL debut, with Ottawa on October 5, 2000, he had already pulled off one of the rarest doubles in international hockey history: gold at the World Juniors and WC in the same year. For Havlat, that came in the early part of 2000 with the Czech Republic while he was still just 19 (18, actually, when the WC began!). He got an assist in his first NHL game, and since then he has improved by increments, still young, experienced for his age, with nothing but upside to him, as the scouts *parler* about such matters.

HAWERCHUK, Dale ("Ducky")
b. Toronto, Ontario, April 4, 1963

To be a great centre in the 1980s was to go virtually unrecognized because two guys – Gretzky and Lemieux – were so dominating and so superior that extraordinary players like Yzerman, Stastny, and Hawerchuk didn't get their due credit. Hawerchuk won Memorial Cups with Cornwall in 1980 and '81, the latter season one in which he scored more than a goal a game. That summer, the Jets drafted him 1st overall, and during his outstanding career he lived up to that selection every day. As a rookie, he scored 45 goals and 103 points to win the Calder Trophy, his first of six 100-point years in 7 seasons. In all, he spent 9 years with the Jets, averaging 42 goals a season over that stretch. The only mitigating factor to his success was the team's playoff performance. Slotted in the Smythe Division with, notably, Calgary and Edmonton, the Jets were fodder in the first round virtually every year. Great as he was and solid as the team was, they were no match for Gretzky, Messier, Anderson, Coffey, et al. Hawerchuk was traded to Buffalo in 1990 where his play slipped a notch, though not much, but again the Sabres were not a strong playoff team, even with Dominik Hasek in net. He finished his career in St. Louis (where he scored his 500th career goal) and Philadelphia, and in that last year with the Flyers, '96-'97, he made his first and only appearance in the Stanley Cup finals, though they lost to Detroit. He was forced to retire because of a bad hip that was becoming degenerative, but by that time he had reached all the great milestones: 1,188 games played, 518 goals, 1,409 career points. Because of Lemieux and Gretzky, he never won an individual award after the Calder, and only once did he make it to an All-Star Team (the Second Team, in '84-'85). He played for Canada three times at the World Championships (as a result of early playoff exits), and was on the 1987 and '91 teams for the Canada Cup. Controversy ensued in 2000 when Joey Mullen was inducted into the Hockey Hall of Fame but Hawerchuk – by consensus a vastly superior talent – was not. A year later, all was righted when it was Hawerchuk's turn. He and his wife retired to north of

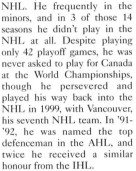

Because of Lemieux and Gretzky, he never won an individual award after the Calder.
DALE HAWERCHUK

Toronto where they raise and breed show-jumping horses, an anonymous labour of love far from the screams and cheers of the rink.

HAWGOOD, Greg
b. Edmonton, Alberta, August 10, 1968

Few players had the junior career that Hawgood had, yet it led to both a long career and an unsure one. In Kamloops, Hawgood won two Memorial Cups, one in 1984, the second two years later. In his last of five years with the Blazers, he also won gold with Canada at the WJC, and in '87-'88 he was named the best defenceman in all of junior hockey in Canada. He made his debut with Boston at the end of the '87-'88 season, and so began a journey that saw him play 14 years of pro, though only 4 of those years were exclusively NHL. He frequently in the minors, and in 3 of those 14 seasons he didn't play in the NHL at all. Despite playing only 42 playoff games, he was never asked to play for Canada at the World Championships, though he persevered and played his way back into the NHL in 1999, with Vancouver, his seventh NHL team. In '91-'92, he was named the top defenceman in the AHL, and twice he received a similar honour from the IHL.

Greg Hawgood

HAWKINS, Todd
b. Kingston, Ontario, August 2, 1966

Drafted a distant 217th overall in 1986, Hawkins did himself proud by making the NHL for 10 games, with Vancouver and Toronto (1988-92). Beyond those games, he has been a fixture and a staple in the AHL and "I." Although he doesn't put up the giant penalty-minute numbers he did in his prove-it youth, he still manages to get into more tussles than goal-scoring celebrations.

Todd Hawkins

HAWORTH, Alan
b. Drummondville, Quebec, September 1, 1960

In some respects, Haworth had a lightning-quick career. In other respects, it was quite sensational. In his 8 NHL seasons, he never failed to score at least 20 goals except in his first, when he had 16 in just 49 games. He had excellent skating skills and had his most productive years with Washington in the 1980s, but in 1988 he left the NHL to play for SC (Skating Club) Bern, where he again was equally productive. His father, Gord, played briefly for the Rangers.

Alan Haworth

HAWORTH, Gord ("Red")
b. Drummondville, Quebec, February 20, 1932

Most summers, Haworth returned to Drummondville regardless of where he played his winter hockey. Just before leaving for Portland in 1960, he was given a bouncing baby boy he and his wife named Alan. One

Gord Haworth

day, Alan would go on to play in the NHL, but at the time, Gord had to get ready for another season himself. He started and finished his career in Drummondville, and in between he played mostly in the WHL and Quebec league. He played two games with the Rangers in '52-'53, but beyond that the centreman did his scoring in the minors before returning home to coach.

HAWRYLIW, Neil
b. Fielding, Saskatchewan, November 9, 1955

The only "1" on Hawryliw's NHL scorecard is for games played. Other than that, the most prominent feature is the "I" of the IHL, where he spent his formative years. The "1" came with the Islanders in '81-'82; most of the "I" came with Muskegon before and after. When he retired, Hawryliw gravitated toward what he knew: He returned to Muskegon and became manager of the renovated Walker Arena.

Dwayne Hay

HAY, Bill ("Red")
b. Lumsden, Saskatchewan, December 9, 1935

Hay was perhaps the first graduate of a U.S. college to go on to play in the NHL, and not just in a marginal capacity. In 1958, he completed a B.Sc. in geology from Colorado College, where he also played for the hockey team, winning the NCAA championship in 1957. He had come from an athletic family that included his father (an amateur goalie of note), mother (track and field star), and uncle (Earl Miller, a former NHLer). After a year in the Western league, he signed with Chicago in 1959 and played the next eight years with the Hawks, his entire NHL career. He won the Calder Trophy that first season. Hay centred the famed Million Dollar Line with Bobby Hull and Murray Balfour and was the playmaker of the trio. He led the Hawks to the Stanley Cup in 1961, the team's first since 1938. He retired in 1966 but was coaxed out of retirement for half a season before settling in Calgary to pursue business interests in the oil industry. Over the next 23 years, he established himself as a leader in the industry, but at age 55 he joined Hockey Canada as its president and COO. He later worked for the Calgary Flames in a similar capacity, and after a few years with the Hockey Hall of Fame's Selection Committee he was named the Hall's new leader, succeeding the retired Scotty Morrison. He was later inducted into the Colorado Springs Sports Hall of Fame for his outstanding career with the Tigers.

George Hay

HAY, Dwayne
b. London, Ontario, February 11, 1977

Hay came up through junior in Guelph and won gold with Canada at the 1997 World Juniors. After turning

pro, though, he played for four different NHL teams in as many years and was quickly pegged as a minor-leaguer.

HAY, George ("The Western Wizard")
b. Listowel, Ontario, December 31, 1885
d. Stratford, Ontario, July 13, 1975

Although he was born in Listowel, Hay grew up in Winnipeg where one of his early friends was Dick Irvin. The played together on the Monarchs, but Hay went off to war and served with the Canadian Forestry Corps until 1919. He played senior hockey in Regina and turned pro with the Capitals in 1921. The left winger was an outstanding scorer with the team, and he moved to Portland when the Caps transferred there in 1925. He joined the NHL with Chicago, and on November 17, 1926, Hay scored the first goal in Hawks history. A year later, he was sold to Detroit where he scored 22 goals in his first season. He spent seven seasons in all with the team, though increasingly in the minors as the years passed. He retired one game into the '33-'34 season so he could coach their farm team in London, during which time he also began a career in the insurance business. Hay retired from coaching in 1936 to devote himself full-time to insurance, but during the Second World War he worked with the RCAF as a flight-lieutenant and instructor. He returned to insurance and worked happily until 1965 when he retired. Hay was inducted into the Hockey Hall of Fame in 1958, noted for being one of the great little men of the game and among the finest stickhandlers the NHL had ever seen.

Hay centred the famed Million Dollar Line with Bobby Hull and Murray Balfour.
BILL HAY

HAY, Jim ("Red Eye")
b. Saskatoon, Saskatchewan, May 15, 1931

Hay was quite a remarkable player in hockey's golden years. Although he didn't play in the NHL for very long, he had a lengthy career nonetheless. This in itself is nothing special, but he was a heavy-hitting defenceman who was also, paradoxically, as durable as any. He was built like a brick somethingorother and chalked up 100 annual penalty minutes wherever he played, but rare were the times he got hurt and missed more than a game here or there. Hay got 3 callups from Detroit in the early 1950s, sticking around the longest in '54-'55 when the Wings won their last Cup for more than 40 years. He played forever in the WHL with a variety of teams, eventually becoming the all-time leader in penalty minutes before a trade sent him to Jersey in the EHL. He became playing coach in February 1971, and after retiring a year and a half later stayed on as the team's coach sans playing gear. His uncle was another NHLer, Earl Miller.

HAYEK, Peter
b. Minneapolis, Minnesota, November 16, 1957
No American state has greater hockey presence than Minnesota, and Hayek was one of many players developed in an area of the country that has the same cultural feel for the game as does Canada. Hayek went to the University of Minnesota, and out of that experience he turned pro, though his career was short-lived. He played one game for the North Stars, which ensured he'd get the alumni newsletter for the rest of his days, but he left the game in 1982.

HAYES, Chris
b. Rouyn, Quebec, August 24, 1946
Life is pretty good if you cut right to the chase. Some players spend their best years trying to win the Stanley Cup, and they must cringe when they read a story such as Hayes'. Played only one NHL game, he did, but it came in the 1972 playoffs and it came with the Bruins, the team that won the Cup. Yup. One game, and he could boast he was on a Cup-winning team!

HAYNES, Paul
b. Montreal, Quebec, March 1, 1910
d. Montreal, Quebec, May 12, 1989
Haynes' was a life rooted in Montreal, but not necessarily in hockey. He was a junior boxing champion in the early 1920s and was an outstanding quarterback for Loyola College, so much so that he later became an inaugural inductee into its Sports Hall of Fame. He won the Allan Cup with the Montreal AAA in 1929, and then embarked on an 11-year pro career in the NHL, first with the Maroons. He played a year with Boston and then the final half-dozen seasons with Montreal, notably on a high-scoring line with Toe Blake and Johnny Gagnon. After retiring, he remained close to the Habs, first as a coach and later as a scout and play-by-play man for radio. His claim to fame from this period was that while coaching the Montreal Amateurs, he converted a left winger into a right winger, a move that proved historic to the game. The player in question was Maurice Richard. Haynes also established International Surveys Limited, a marketing appraisal company, retiring in 1974 as its president and chairman of the board. Haynes was not so easily sated, though. He registered at NYU, where he earned his master's degree in cinema studies, and subsequently worked on a movie about Montreal.

HAYWARD, Brian
b. Toronto, Ontario, June 25, 1960
For a TV commentator, Hayward was a great goalie. He had a perfectly pedestrian college career at Cornell before signing with the Jets as a free agent in 1982. He established a solid reputation, and when Montreal traded Steve Penney to John Ferguson's team to get Hayward, he seemed well on his way. In his four years in Montreal, he won three William Jennings trophies with Patrick Roy, but Roy got the lion's share of the work. At training camp in 1990, he left the team and asked for a trade so he could be number one. Play, not pay, was what mattered to him. He wound up in Minnesota and then San Jose through the Expansion Draft, winning the first game in Sharks history. He suffered a back injury, though, and during his convalescence worked for Sharks TV and radio, an experience he enjoyed so much he took it up full-time a year later when he re-injured his back and retired. Back in the summer of 1990 Hayward also brought a popular innovation to the game when he introduced Montreal and Toronto fans to three-on-three hockey, an idea that came out of Doug Jarvis's brainstorm for three-on-three roundball.

HAYWARD, Rick
b. Toledo, Ohio, February 25, 1966
He piled up the pims the way millionaires pile up dollar bills. Yet despite being owned by four NHL teams, Hayward played only four games with L.A., in '90-'91 in a career that had "I" written all over it for a decade. He later moved to Germany, and though his circumstances changed, his game didn't.

HAZLETT, Steve ("Stumpy")
b. Sarnia, Ontario, December 12, 1957
Hazlett was a star for Canada at the first WJC in 1977, but the left winger just never got his chance to play in the NHL. There was a single game for Vancouver a couple of years later, but only a brief career in the minors.

HEAD, Don
b. Mt. Dennis, Ontario, June 30, 1933
A doctor once looked at X-rays of Head's knees, and without knowing the goalie's profession the doctor observed that this person definitely wasn't walking. Head was as brilliant in the WHL as he was sub-ordinary in his short NHL stay, with Boston in '61-'62. He began with little hope of playing for pay, and his early highlight came in 1960 when he played for Canada at the Olympics in Squaw Valley. It was only then that he turned pro, and in '67-'68 he set a league mark with a 2.52 GAA, the lowest in the league's history. He was rookie of the year in the WHL, the best goalie twice, and a First All-Star three times. Most of all, though, he pre-dated Ron Hextall by a quarter-century. Head was a notorious fighter, and on delayed penalties, rather than come to the bench for the extra attacker, he used to dash up the ice to join the play. He did this with such frequency that after a while his team expected no less. When penalty killing, he'd smack his stick on the ice looking for a pass. And most prescient, he would practise firing the puck off the boards and into the empty net at the other end. It seemed only a matter of time before he scored a goal that way, though he never did. He was Jacques Plante, Billy Smith, and Martin Brodeur rolled into one!

HEAD, Galen
b. Grande Prairie, Alberta, April 16, 1947
Head climaxed a great junior career with a Memorial Cup win with the Edmonton Oil Kings in 1966. The next year, he gave the pro ranks a try and appeared in one game with Detroit as a 19-year-old. It was his only NHL game, but he went to Johnstown of the EHL and had a productive career there. Those were the Johnstown days of *Slap Shot* fame with the Carlson and Hanson characters. Head became the team's playing coach in 1973, and he saw first-hand much of the mayhem that appeared in Paul Newman's slapstick hockey flick.

Chris Hayes

Paul Haynes

Brian Hayward

Fern Headley

Rich Healey

Mark Heaslip

HEADLEY, Fern ("Curly")

b. Crystal, North Dakota, March 2, 1901
d. Omaha, Nebraska, 1950
Headley played his teen hockey in Saskatchewan before playing the '24-'25 season with Boston and Montreal. He appeared for the Habs in the Cup finals that year in a losing cause against Victoria, and later played in the AHA for many years leading up to the war.

HEALEY, Paul

b. Edmonton, Alberta, March 20, 1975
Healey did plenty of scoring in the minors, although there were four years between NHL appearances with Philadelphia (1997) and Toronto (2001). In between, Nashville and Edmonton owned his rights, but they kept him out of sight and he had his biggest impact after signing with the Leafs, where he played excellent hockey in 2001-02 when the team was depleted due to injuries.

HEALEY, Rich

b. Vancouver, British Columbia, March 12, 1938
Healey's career was all over the map, though his name is part of the wonderful history of one-game wonders. His dash to the bigs came with Detroit on January 4, 1961.

HEALY, Glenn ("Heals")

b. Pickering, Ontario, August 23, 1962
When Healy traipsed off to Western Michigan University to pursue a degree in business, he wasn't necessarily expecting a whole lot of hockey to come out of the experience. Yet in his four years there, his record got better and his GAA decreased each season each year. Still, no NHL team drafted him, and it wasn't until just before his 23rd birthday that he was offered a contract, by Los Angeles. He allowed six goals in his first game with the Kings, and didn't see the NHL for another two years. He later signed with the Islanders, and when he moved on to the Rangers in 1993 he became one of a small list of goalies to play for both New York teams. That first year on Broadway was special. He was backup to Mike Richter during the team's winning Stanley Cup season, and he tended four seasons in all for the Blueshirts. Healy ended his career in his home, Toronto, and although he never won a Cup with the team he did take part in the historic parade from Maple Leaf Gardens to the new Air Canada Centre. And he did so in style, playing the bagpipes and dressed in full regalia (Healy was a member of both the Peel Police and the Highland Creek bagpiping bands). After retiring, he remained in Toronto and worked in television, both for the Leafs and as a colour commentator on networks across North America.

Healy was a member of both the Peel Police and the Highland Creek bagpiping bands.
GLENN HEALY

HEAPHY, Shawn

b. Sudbury, Ontario, November 27, 1968
Heaphy was a one-game wonder who scored buckets everywhere, but he never collected even one puck from his lone NHL appearance, with Calgary in '92-'93. He graduated from Michigan State and played in the minors as well as Europe, but try as he might he never got into a second NHL game.

HEASLIP, Mark

b. Duluth, Minnesota, December 26, 1951
The only reason he enrolled at the University of Minnesota-Duluth in 1971 to study political science, Heaslip admitted, was to play hockey and stay out of Vietnam. He managed both of those feats, but he also managed to smoke the doobie-doo and drink more than his fair share. When he discovered he could smoke and drink and play all at the same time, well, life couldn't get any better. For seven years he played professional hockey like this, but his skills deteriorated each year and by 1980 he had no contract offers. He spent the summer doing coke and drinking heavily, and hockey was no longer a possibility for him. When he was convicted by a Minnesota judge of conspiring to sell cocaine in January 1984, he knew he had hit rock-bottom. Through the Phil Esposito Foundation, he checked into a rehab centre and got clean. He lived with his dad outside Duluth, and eventually got a job with a TV station selling ads. Then Esposito called and asked him to do some speaking in New York. Heaslip agreed, of course, also tended to some unfinished business – he talked Espo into giving him a tryout with the Rangers. This forced Heaslip to get back into prime shape, and although he didn't quite make it, he was one of the last players cut by the team. Years ago, he had captained Springfield to a Calder Cup, and his last pro outing, an exhibition game, took place for New Haven against the Indians, in the same building.

HEATH, Randy

b. Vancouver, British Columbia, November 11, 1964
Heath put up monster numbers in junior with Portland, but the "small" tag affixed to the foreheads of so many teen stars was indelibly stamped on his. He won a Memorial Cup in '83 with the Winter Hawks and played for Team Canada at the WJC the year after, but the Rangers gave him only 13 games over 2 seasons to show his stuff before sending him packing. He eventually found a place in Sweden.

HEATLEY, Dany

b. Freiburg, West Germany, January 21, 1981
There are hundreds of Murray Heatleys in Europe

right now, players who were never quite good enough to make the NHL but plenty skilled enough to have a decent career overseas. During that time, Murray started a family before returning home to Calgary, and his son and future star was born. Dany was clearly a great player from even his earliest years. He had tremendous size and quickness, strength, and good skating ability. Atlanta drafted him 2nd overall in 2000, and after another year at the University of Wisconsin he made the team in 2001. Usually paired with another teen phenom, Ilya Kovalchuk, Heatley became one of the most exciting players in the league. The duo combined on almost all of each other's goals and represented the future of the team and the league. Heatley finished that first season with 26 goals and 67 points and won the Calder Trophy for his outstanding year. He also played for Canada at the 2002 World Championships, and should the NHL participate in the 2006 Olympics in Turin, Heatley will be there for Canada. No question about it. At the 2003 All-Star Game, MVP Heatley scored 4 goals and an assist to further enhance his reputation.

HEBENTON, Andy ("Spud")
b. Winnipeg, Manitoba, October 3, 1929

There are two qualities needed to hold a record for Iron Man in the NHL. One: an ability to play in the league for a long period. Two: the ability to remain injury free. Hebenton has the distinction of holding an unbelievable record: In his nine NHL seasons, he missed not a single game. And if you also include his AHL games played, he went 1,062 games in a row without missing one! His secret? Potatoes (ergo his nickname). He loved potatoes. Hebenton played pro for a quarter of a century (1949-75, 26 years, in fact). His NHL time came in the middle of that and consisted of eight years with the Rangers and a final season with Boston before returning to the WHL for another dozen years. He won the Lady Byng in the NHL in '56-'57, and won the WHL equivalent six times. He came close to pulling a Howe at the end of his career when his son, Clay, made the WHA as a goalie, but as much as he wanted to play, no team offered him a contract. Hebenton settled in Portland (his longtime WHL home) and went into the cement business until retiring to private life in 1994.

HEBERT, Guy
b. Troy, New York, January 7, 1967

Quebec, more than any other place on earth, is known for producing great goalies. Hebert, from New York, knew this, so when he was young he put an accent on the first "e" of his last name so people would think he

was French! Once he became established, he removed the accent and proceeded to have a number of fine seasons with Anaheim. He won 20 games 5 times and was Mike Richter's backup in the 1996 World Cup, but a move to the Rangers in 2000-01 did him no good. They already had Richter, and soon the phenomenal young Dan Blackburn, so there was no room for Hebert. Time to re-add the accent and reboot the old career.

HEBERT, Sammy
b. Ottawa, Ontario, March 31, 1893
d. Ottawa, Ontario, July 23, 1965

Standing less than 5'4" tall, little Samuel James Hebert played goal mostly in the Ottawa area before and during the First World War. He played just two games for the Toronto Arenas – December 19, 1917, and January 2, 1918 – during the NHL's inaugural season, but that summer he joined the army and never returned to the pro loop. During his years in Ottawa, he also worked as a piano tuner.

HECHT, Jochen
b. Mannheim, West Germany, June 21, 1977

Because he is German and a good hockey player, Hecht has an outstanding international resumé that includes a record four appearances at the World Juniors (1994-97), his first coming as a 16-year-old. Twice he has played at the WC in the same year as the WJC, and he has also played for his country at the World Cup and Olympics. On the NHL front, he is a little thin on experience, but he's making up for that on an almost daily basis. He made his debut, with St. Louis, near the end of the '98-'99 season, but the Blues traded him to Edmonton in the deal that brought Doug Weight to St. Louis. He threatened to return to his new bride and old home in Mannheim for the 2001-02 season because of contract troubles with the Oilers, but the teams settled and Hecht has relaxed into his role with a team challenging to make the playoffs.

HEDBERG, Anders
b. Ornskoldsvik Grandsunda, Sweden, February 25, 1951

Quite simply, one of the greatest Swedish players of all time. Hedberg turned pro as a 16-year-old in 1967, and within three years he was on the national team as one of the top players on Tre Kronor. He was nicknamed "The New Tumba" in reference to Tumba Johansson, star of the 1950s, and Hedberg didn't disappoint fans or coaches. He played in four World Championships in the early 1970s, and then he and countryman Ulf Nilsson came to Canada to play for the Winnipeg Jets. They skated on a line with Bobby Hull to form the highest-scoring line in hockey

Guy Hebert

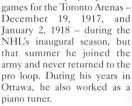

Jochen Hecht

Anders Hedberg

In his nine NHL seasons, he missed not a single game.
ANDY HEBENTON

Bret Hedican

Gerry Heffernan

Michael Heidt

Bill Heindl

Lionel Heinrich

history. In his four years with the Jets, Hedberg had seasons of 53, 50, 70, and 63 goals, but in 1978 he and Nilsson signed as a free agents with the Rangers to try their hand in the NHL. Hedberg had four 30-goal seasons with New York, and had decided to make '84-'85 his final year when he was hit in the eye by a wayward stick. He recovered to finish the season, and after retiring became a scout for the Leafs for many years, eventually moving up to the position of assistant general manager. He had wanted desperately to be an NHL GM, and believed the Leafs were grooming him for the position, but when he learned this wasn't the case he resigned his post and returned to Sweden. He became GM for the Tre Kronor entry at the 2002 Olympics in Salt Lake City, a tournament that ended disastrously for Sweden with a 4-3 loss to lowly Belarus in the quarter-finals. He later became director of player personnel for Ottawa.

HEDBERG, Johan ("Moose")
b. Leksand, Sweden, May 3, 1973
A little slice of Manitoba down in the Igloo never hurt anyone. Hedberg's is a simple, feel-good story of dedication and perseverance. He was drafted by Philadelphia in 1994 while playing in the Swedish league, but the Flyers never even invited him to camp. No problem – Hedberg came to North America anyway in 1997 and signed with Baton Rouge. He bounced around in the minors, returned to Sweden for a year, and eventually was back in Winnipeg, playing for the IHL's Moose in 2000-01. The Penguins acquired his rights from San Jose and called him up at the end of the season. Well, he went 7-1-1 down the stretch and had an excellent playoffs. For luck, he continued to wear his Moose helmet and pads – thus the nickname – and was the number-one man for 2001-02. Despite not making the playoffs in 2002, he established himself as one of the bright "young" goalies in the league.

HEDICAN, Bret
b. St. Paul, Minnesota, August 10, 1970
His wife's name is Kristi Yamaguchi. There, that's out of the way. The tough defenceman and the lovely ice ballerina met in 1992 when both were representing the U.S. at the Olympics in Albertville. They said a mutual "I do" in the summer of 2000 on the island of Mauna Lani. Hedican made it to the Cup finals in 1994 with Vancouver, but no one could have thought that eight years later, when Carolina acquired him from Florida, he would be making his second finals appearance. His play has always been marked by work in his own end, rather than as a scoring defenceman, and his ability to play Paul Maurice's system with the Hurricanes was one reason the team did so well that season. Hedican began in the NHL in '91-'92 with St. Louis and has also played twice for his country at the World Championships.

HEFFERNAN, Frank ("Moose")
b. Peterborough, Ontario, January 22, 1891
d. New York, New York, December 21, 1938
After playing in and around Toronto, Heffernan joined the army in 1916 and was out of hockey for a time. When he returned, he played most of the 1919-20

season with the Toronto St. Pats, partly as a playing coach, partly as just a player. That was his last season of pro hockey.

HEFFERNAN, Gerry
b. Montreal, Quebec, July 24, 1916
A lifelong resident of Montreal, Heffernan played virtually every game of pro hockey in his hometown, mostly with the Royals in the senior league. For 3 years, though, he played parts of seasons for the Canadiens, winning a Cup with the team in 1944 when he had an outstanding season with 28 goals.

HEIDT, Michael
b. Calgary, Alberta, November 4, 1963
A two-step with the passport transformed this healthy western Canadian into a German national team member. Heidt performed the old citizenship switcheroo after a few games in L.A. in '83-'84 and two years in the minors. He packed his duffle bag, used his parents' place of origin, and voila! – he was playing for Germany at the World Championships and Olympics and World Cup. He also moved to Germany and settled into a perfectly respectable career in that country's premier league.

HEINDL, Bill
b. Sherbrooke, Quebec, May 13, 1946
d. Richmond, British Columbia, March 1, 1992
Most pro hockey players will admit that the hardest part about the game is walking away. Heindl's retirement damn near killed him. He played only 18 NHL games in the early 1970s and kicked around the minors a bit longer. When he retired in 1977, he turned to coaching, guiding the Steinback Huskies to an appearance in the Allan Cup finals in his first season. Then he hurt his back badly in a car accident, and the coaching career ended. He slumped into an awful depression. His marriage ended badly, his father had passed away, and Heindl became alcoholic. He was selling insurance in Winnipeg, a job that didn't fulfil him in the same way hockey had. One day in 1980, he jumped off a bridge over a highway. He didn't die, but he was paralyzed from the waist down. When Bobby Orr heard of the near tragedy, he organized a charity game (they had been junior teammates in Oshawa). Heindl seemed to rally, and he became an administrative assistant with the Canadian Paraplegic Association, finding a purpose in life, all right, but doing it the hard way.

HEINRICH, Lionel
b. Churchbridge, Saskatchewan, April 4, 1934
As a boy, Lionel never played indoors. Nonetheless, he played junior in his home province and was noticed by the Bruins, who sent him to Hershey in 1954 for a year of development and then brought him to the Garden the following season. It was to be his only NHL time, though, and he was out of the game altogether a shortly thereafter.

HEINS, Shawn
b. Eganville, Ontario, December 24, 1973
A true success story, Heins was playing junior B

hockey at age 21. Four years later, he was in the NHL. The defenceman showed nothing but promise with Renfrew, and after two years in minor pro he signed with San Jose in 1997. To date, his only games have been with the Sharks, though he has been scratched more than he has played. He made his reputation as a fighter, though he has tried to establish himself as a defenceman who can score as well.

HEINZ, Rick
b. Essex, Ontario, May 30, 1955

It was only after his first season of pro, in the minors, that Heinz was offered an NHL contract, but signing with the Blues in 1979 was both good and bad. It was good because the contract had the NHL shield at the top of the page, but bad because the starting goalie in St. Louis was Mike Liut, who gladly would have played every game of the season if the coach wanted it so. As a result, Heinz played very little in his five NHL seasons, including three games with Vancouver. Of course, he didn't help his cause by allowing no more than four goals a game, but when he was sent to the minors he acquitted himself nicely. In all, he played seven seasons for the Salt Lake Golden Eagles, and in his final year, '86-'87, backstopped the team to the Turner Cup. He later became a player agent and ran hockey camps. (To develop his own future clients?)

HEINZE, Steve
b. Lawrence, Massachusetts, January 30, 1970

When Columbus selected Heinze in the Expansion Draft in the summer of 2000, he just couldn't resist. He changed his sweater number to 57, and ever since he's been Heinze 57, a saucy play on words, if you will. It wasn't meant to be, though. A Mass boy through and through, he earned a degree in marketing from Boston College in 1991, three years after his native Bruins drafted him. He spent a year with the National Team and played in the 1992 Olympics in Albertville, and the day after he was in a Bruins sweater. He played nine uninterrupted seasons with the B's, but after that wore three different sweaters in two years – Columbus, Buffalo, and Los Angeles.

HEISKALA, Earl
b. Kirkland Lake, Ontario, November 30, 1942

By his own admission, he was a policeman, a guy who kept the other teams honest with his own stars, a guy who made the other tough guys around the league take notice or pay the price. Surprise, surprise, he played for Philadelphia, from 1968 to '71, the nascent days of the Broad Street Bullies. He didn't last long because he wasn't exactly a smooth skater with soft hands who played two-way hockey. He fought in the

minors, he was brought up to fight, and he later moved on to the WHA, where he fought.

HEISTEN, Barrett
b. Anchorage, Alaska, March 19, 1980

Heisten is the kind of problem the NHL is going to have to deal with sooner or later. He went to the University of Maine in 1998, and after his first year he was drafted by Buffalo. But after his second year he transferred to Seattle of the WHL, going from college hockey to Canadian major junior hockey and declaring himself a free agent. The Rangers signed him, and Buffalo lost a selection because of a U.S. court ruling that any such transfer negated a player's obligation to a drafted team and rendered him a free agent. He played briefly with the Rangers before being traded to Dallas.

HEJDUK, Milan
b. Ústí nad Labem, Czechoslovakia (Czech Republic), February 14, 1976

Hejduk slipped under the radar, a much better player than everyone knew he was. As a teen, he played in Pardubice, but just as the team was on the road to the playoffs he tore ligaments in his shoulder. He played in two World Juniors (1995 and '96) but was ineffective, and in the 1998 World Championships he broke his jaw in the Czechs' first game. Colorado, which had drafted him 87th in 1994 (when the team was still in Quebec), was reluctant to bring him over, but the 1998 Olympics in Nagano changed the team's mind. He played a more important role as the tournament wore on, and was key to Petr Svoboda's winning goal that gave the Czechs gold. Hejduk made the Avs that fall, and accented his arrival by scoring a goal and an assist in his first NHL game. Since then, he has become an ever more important part of the team. In 2000-01, he scored 41 goals en route to the Stanley Cup, and that summer he took the sacred bowl home, where thousands of fans greeted him. In 2002-03, he scored 50 goals to win the Rocket Richard Trophy, the only player in the league to hit that mark for the season.

HELANDER, Peter
b. Stockholm, Sweden, December 4, 1951

Back in the summer of 1982, Los Angeles GM George Maguire was ecstatic. He had drafted Helander a distant 153rd overall, and with the selection described his new defenceman as a "much better" skater than Borje Salming. You okay, George? Whatever he was smoking lasted a while, but in hockey terms not long at all. Helander had partnered with Salming at the Worlds in the spring of '82 and done just fine, and his

In 2000-01, he scored 41 goals en route to the Stanley Cup.
MILAN HEJDUK

Shawn Heins

Rick Heinz

Steve Heinze

Earl Heiskala

play created an interesting irony. Because Maguire thought Helander would be around a long time, he bought out the contract of Ian Turnbull, Salming's partner from their best days with Toronto a few years earlier. Helander was 31 when the Kings chose him. He had been a star back home in the Swedish league, but when he joined the NHL in September '82, he lasted just seven games. Demoted, he trudged to the minors for a few more games and then decided to go home.

HELENIUS, Sami
b. Helsinki, Finland, January 22, 1974

Always on the fringes, Helenius is the kind of d-man a coach likes because he'll give you the minutes at little risk. He won't score or work the power play point, but he's reliable and handles the puck well. Yet, since joining the NHL in 1996 with Calgary, he has played for four teams and never had a complete season in the big tent. Twice he has been traded for future considerations, hockey's term for "nothing," yet he has managed to play his way onto the Dallas Stars, the team that signed him as a free agent in the summer of 2001.

HELLER, Eberhardt "Ott"
b. Berlin (Kitchener), Ontario, June 2, 1910
d. Kitchener, Ontario, June 15, 1980

Even at 45 years of age, Heller was playing hockey and skating circles around players half his age. He turned pro in 1929 with Springfield, and two years later he made his NHL debut with the Rangers, the team with which he played his entire 15-year career in the big league. In those early days he played with either Ching Johnson or Babe Siebert on the blueline. The team lost in the finals his first year but won in 1933, Heller scoring three important goals in the playoffs. He was one of the first defencemen to carry the puck up the ice on a regular basis, though by no means did he attack the net the way Bobby Orr did many years later. In 1935, Heller played alongside rookie Babe Pratt, a future Hall of Famer, and together they led the Rangers to its other Cup victory of this era, in the spring of 1940. Heller captained the Rangers for the last three years of his NHL career. Although he left the NHL in 1946, his playing days were still nearly a decade away from completion. He went down to New Haven for one year as a player, and in 1947 became the team's playing coach, a position he enjoyed with several teams over the next few years, mostly in the AHL but also going down to the New Haven Nutmegs in '52-'53 and on to Valleyfield in '54-'55.

Ott Heller

Bryan Helmer

HELMAN, Harry
b. Ottawa, Ontario, August 28, 1894
d. unknown

Helman's affiliation was as much to the city of Ottawa as to hockey. He fought in the First World War and went on to play in the nation's capital after the war, his career culminating in 1923 when the Senators won the Stanley Cup. He played only a year and a bit more before retiring to Ottawa.

HELMER, Bryan
b. Sault Ste. Marie, Ontario, July 15, 1972

Success stories are always encouraging, particularly at the NHL level, where success seems to require a regimented approach to the game. Helmer didn't even play major junior in Ontario (well, six games) and had to make his way to the AHL via provincial hockey. He signed with Albany, which was a good sign because the River Rats were New Jersey's farm team of, and in 1994-95 he helped that franchise pull off a surprise double: the Devils won the Stanley Cup, and the Rats won the Calder Cup. Helmer's cause wasn't helped, though. He remained in the minors for five years in Albany, so when he had the chance to sign with Phoenix in 1998, he took it. The Coyotes gave him his first NHL games, and he has since moved on to St. Louis and Vancouver, where he has become at least a semi-regular. Not bad for someone with only six games of junior under his belt.

HELMINEN, Raimo
b. Tampere, Finland, March 11, 1964

No one on planet Earth has played more international hockey games than Raimo Helminen. He played for his country at the World Juniors in 1982, and at the Worlds in 2002 – and at virtually everything in between. In Olympics history, the Finns have won a silver and two bronze. Helminen was on board for all of these medals. In fact, he has played in a record six Olympics for Suomi. In WC history, the Finns have won a gold, four silver, and a bronze. Helminen won all but one silver. In league play, he has been with Malmo and Tampere, for the most part. He rose to prominence in North American eyes at the 1984 WJC, when he led the tournament with a total of 22 points in just seven games. The Rangers pounced in the draft that summer, and a year later Helminen made his NHL debut with the team. He went on to play just 117 games, hardly a noteworthy fact beside his 327 and counting international appearances. His career was in jeopardy during his last season with the Islanders, 1988-89, when his back was so painful he couldn't walk. It was at that point he returned home and found a specialist who managed to work out the kinks and prolong Helminen's career.

HEMMERLING, Tony
b. Landis, Saskatchewan, May 15, 1911
d. unknown

A career minor-leaguer, Hemmerling was nonetheless a long-standing member of the hockey fraternity, from his days as a teen in his home province in the 1930s to his coaching career into the 1950s. He played briefly for the New York Americans (1935-37) before moving to the International-American league, where he established himself as a decent offensive player. He later coached in the PCHL and moved to the Seattle Ironmen in '51-'52, but they didn't last the full season.

HENDERSON, Archie
b. Calgary, Alberta, February 17, 1957

So much fighting, so little playing. A tough guy of the first order, Henderson heaved his fists at opponents in a wild variety of leagues, dropping the gloves in the NHL with 3 teams in just 23 games over three years, 1980-83. He ended his career in the minors and then the Washington Capitals, one of the teams he had toughed it out for, hired him to be their pro scout, a job he held for many years as the team developed into a top contender.

Archie Henderson

HENDERSON, Jay ("Hendy")

b. Edmonton, Alberta, September 17, 1978

He still has the last blush of youth on his side, but time is running out for Henderson to make it in the NHL as a regular. Boston drafted him about a millionth overall in 1997, but since then his AHL seasons have been punctuated by only the shortest callups to the FleetCenter. He combines size with scoring in the minors, though he hasn't shown – or had the chance to show – much of either with the Bruins so far. He missed all of 2001-02 with a serious knee injury and has been struggling to get back to form ever since.

HENDERSON, John ("Long John")

b. Toronto, Ontario, March 25, 1933

Sugar Jim Henry had nothing to worry about, the coach assured. Henderson was going to start a few games in '54-'55 to rest the 34-year-old veteran. Best thing for him. Not! Henderson came in, stole the show, and removed Henry from the pipes for most of the year. Henderson was just 22, and seemed the Boston goalie of the future. Not! That summer, instead of being happy to have the young star who had had such a great rookie season, the Bruins went out and acquired Terry Sawchuk. Can't blame them for that, but it meant the end of Henderson. He played another year of serious hockey and then more or less retired. He settled in Toronto and established himself as a salesman, and did such good business he expanded to San Francisco. Then he got a call to play again. The time off had been good for him, but he certainly missed the game.

Turin may have its shroud. Canada has Paul Henderson.
PAUL HENDERSON

With expansion in 1967, opportunities were greater at all levels. He accepted, and joined Hershey, where he played the better part of three years. Ironically, the best season of his career came in '68-'69, when the 35-year-old was playing so well it seemed inevitable an NHL team would sign him. This never happened, but he closed his career on a high note rather than the sour one on which he had left the game years earlier.

HENDERSON, Matt

b. White Bear Lake, Minnesota, June 22, 1974

Henderson had the time of his life with the University of North Dakota Fighting Sioux in 1996-97. He took the team to the NCAA championship round and was named MVP. A year later, Nashville signed the undrafted right winger, but he played only two games with the Predators before moving on to Chicago by way of Philly, where he got into his only other games.

HENDERSON, Murray ("Moe")

b. Toronto, Ontario, September 5, 1921

Henderson's mother was a Conacher – sister of Lionel,

Charlie, and Roy, Hall of Famers all – so it's no wonder he took hockey seriously from the day he was born. He worked his way up through the Marlies, but then war broke out and he became a pilot in the RCAF for two years. Henderson accepted an invitation to practise with the Boston Olympics, and this led to a few games with the Bruins at the end of the '44-'45 season. He made the team that fall, and for seven seasons proved to be an enduring, rushing defenceman with the team. In 1952, he accepted an offer from Hershey to play and coach, but after 4 seasons he returned to Toronto and worked for Seagram's and later William Mara in the liquor and wine trade, becoming Ontario sales manager until he retired some 30 years later.

Jay Henderson

HENDERSON, Paul

b. Kincardine, Ontario, January 28, 1943

Turin may have its shroud. Assisi may have its weeping painting of Mary. Canada has Paul Henderson. He played 12 seasons in the NHL. Doesn't matter. He had seven 20-goal seasons. Doesn't matter. He was part of the mammoth deal that sent Frank Mahovlich to Detroit. Doesn't matter. Only one thing matters: September 24, 26, and 28, 1972. Those are the dates that will live on forever in hockey history, Henderson scoring the game-winning goals in games six, seven, and eight of the '72 Summit Series against the USSR. Late in game eight, the score tied 5-5, Henderson screamed at Pete Mahovlich to come off the ice. Mahovlich complied, and Henderson skated into the Soviet end to beat Vladislav Tretiak at 19:34 of the third period to give Canada a 6-5 game win and a 4-3-1 series win. It was the most important goal ever scored. It changed Henderson's life. It changed Canada. It changed hockey. It defined all of those things. Henderson later became a Christian, and from the day he returned to Canada until the day he dies, he will be congratulated on that goal. It has been put on stamps and posters. Team Canada '72 was named the greatest team of the 21st century by Canadian Press. Some feel that goal has earned Henderson the right to be inducted into the Hockey Hall of Fame. In the modern era, with players from around the world playing in the NHL, the importance of that goal cannot be replicated, its political and cultural importance cannot be overstated. The most famous words ever broadcast in hockey, by Foster Hewitt, were also the most succinct: "Henderson has scored for Canada!"

Murray Henderson

HENDRICKSON, Darby

b. Richfield, Minnesota, August 28, 1972

It's not every member of the Richfield High School

Darby Hendrickson

John Hendrickson

Hall of Fame who goes on to play in the NHL, but then try to find a player who, after being drafted, still attended high school for a year. Because of his birthdate, Hendrickson was actually drafted in 1990 at age 17, and after finishing high school went on to the University of Minnesota. He left after two years to play for the USA National Team and on into the 1994 Olympics in Lillehammer. At season's end, he joined the Leafs in the playoffs in a series against Chicago, the last games ever played at the grand old Stadium. Hendrickson bounced to the Islanders and back and has since moved on to other teams, always as a third- or fourth-line checker, a guy who can kill penalties, win important faceoffs, and contribute in ways other than 30 goals a season. Incredibly, those two playoff games for the Leafs to start his career are still the only ones he's ever played, but as a result, he has managed to play for the U.S. in four World Championships. He missed all of 2001-02 with a badly broken arm, but midway through the following season returned to action.

HENDRICKSON, John ("Jake")
b. Kingston, Ontario, December 5, 1936
Another good old Kingston boy who played for Detroit on three separate occasions, one game in '57-'58, three more the next year, and a single game in '61-'62. He had an extensive career in the minors, never staying put for too long in any one spot.

HENNING, Lorne
b. Melfort, Saskatchewan, February 22, 1952
He was there from day one with the Islanders, the 17th choice overall by the expansion

Lorne Henning

team in 1972 at the Amateur Draft, and he was a faithful team man for 12 years, 9 as a player. He was neither big nor offensively talented, but he was an essential component of the team as it evolved, first as a competitive team, then as a challenging team, and finally as a Stanley Cup team. He was playing in 1980 and '81, when the team won the championship, and acting as assistant coach the next two years, when they kept going. In 1984, he left Long Island to become head coach in Springfield, and a year later he was in the NHL again, as head man with Minnesota. Since then he has been either an assistant or a head coach somewhere, most recently back on Long Island with a team trying desperately to make the playoffs, a pale shadow of its glory days when Henning was a player.

HENRY, Camille ("Camille the Eel")
b. Quebec City, Quebec, January 31, 1933
d. Quebec City, Quebec, September 11, 1997
The happy is, tragically, followed by the sad, the glory mere deceptive prelude to the reality of life after hockey. His first year was '53-'54, one to remember. He

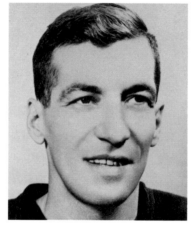

In 1982, he worked as a security guard for $245 a week.
CAMILLE HENRY

scored 4 power-play goals in a single game, an NHL record, and 24 on the year for the Rangers, good enough to win the Calder Trophy. The following year, though, he sputtered, and in the Original Six the bosses let you sputter in the minors. After a couple of years spent working out the kinks, he was back with the Rangers to stay, playing steadily until 1969 (with the exception of '66-'67, when he retired). He won the Lady Byng Trophy in '57-'58, though the league could have chosen just about any year to honour him – in 727 career games, he had all of 88 penalty minutes, due in large part to the fact that he never weighed more than 137 pounds during his pro career! Henry exploded for 37 goals in '62-'63, but the closest he came to the Stanley Cup was '64-'65, when his Hawks made it to the finals against Montreal, only to lose game seven at the Forum. Then came the bad. For the first eight years of his life off-ice, he was severely incapacitated by a bad back that required two major surgeries. He had a steel pin inserted his left arm, wrist to elbow, courtesy of the vagaries of play. In 1982, he worked as a security guard for $245 a week, one of the few jobs he could manage given his health. Shortly after retiring, he was told by doctors that he was diabetic, a condition he ignored steadfastly until his weight was down to 116 pounds and his wife had to take him to the hospital in a near coma. He worked in New Jersey with Fundamentals in Action, an organization that stressed skills to kids, but his $4,800 pension hardly covered his annual rent. He was one of the first players to benefit from a court decision that gave the old-timers millions of dollars in owed pension money. In Henry's case, that amounted to $85,000. He died one year after getting the cheque after living in near poverty for a quarter-century.

HENRY, Dale
b. Prince Albert, Saskatchewan, September 24, 1964
Henry's career with the Islanders in the 1980s was strictly a part-time affair, but it was enough to teach him about the game and give him the chance to play and learn. In each of his six years with the team he was sent to the minors – or promoted to the Islanders, whichever way you look at it – but starting in 1990 it was all minor leagues from there on in. He ended his career in the WPHL and went on to coach the Corpus Christi IceRays, more than a step away from the NHL, but still the same stick-and-puck game, nonetheless.

HENRY, Gord ("Red")
b. Owen Sound, Ontario, August 17, 1926
d. Owen Sound, Ontario, October 3, 1972
January 18, 1955 was a date that marked Henry for the

Dale Henry

rest of his life. That night, he was driving a car when he was involved in an horrific head-on collision that killed his wife, injured three others, and ended his playing career. He was playing for Hershey that season, but spent the rest of the schedule in hospital recovering from various broken bones. He was also charged with involuntary manslaughter in his wife's death. Henry had been considered by many to be the best goalie not in the NHL, although he played eight games with Boston over a five-year span (1948-53). He spent most of his years with the Bears, usually playing the whole season in goal, and won two Calder Cups. After the accident, he returned to Owen Sound and played some senior and intermediate hockey with the Meaford Knights.

HENRY, Jim "Sugar Jim" ("Sam")

b. Winnipeg, Manitoba, October 23, 1920

Nicknames are funny tags. Some players get them when they join a particular team; others when they come up to the NHL. Occasionally, a player will get stuck with one from his junior days that seems never to go away, but Henry got Sugar Jim when he was just a baby! He had a habit of going to his neighbour's house and dipping his pacifier in a bowl of sugar they had, and from that day to this no one has called him anything but Sugar Jim. He won the Allan Cup with Regina in 1941 and played the entire '41-'42 season with the Rangers before working for both the army and the navy during the war. He won another Allan Cup with the incredible Ottawa Commandos team in 1943. Upon his return, he shared the duties with Charlie Rayner, but a trade to Chicago nearly ended his career. Despite playing all 60 games of the '48-'49 schedule, he fought with coach Charlie Conacher and the Big Bomber tossed him to the minors. He was traded to Detroit and on to Boston, where he helped revive an awful Bruins team in 1951 after making a miraculous recovery from an accident in which he suffered severe burns from a fire at his fishing lodge. In the next 3 years, he played in 210 straight games for the Bruins, but midway through '54-'55 he lost his job to Long John Henderson and didn't play much the rest of the regular season. His career ended in the playoffs, on March 31, 1955, when he was hit by a Calum MacKay shot just under the eye. It was during this time that he was party to one of Maurice Richard's most memorable nights, when Richard came back from being knocked unconscious to score the winning goal in the playoffs. A priceless photo shows a bloodied Richard shaking Henry's hand, the goalie semi-bowed in what looks to be reverence. After retiring, Henry operated a tourist

His career ended in the playoffs, on March 31, 1955, when he was hit by a Calum MacKay shot just under the eye.
JIM HENRY

lodge in Kenora with Charlie Rayner for 22 years. He also worked as an assistant service manager at a Winnipeg car dealership until 1985 and also had a cattle farm in Plums, Manitoba

HENTUNEN, Jukka

b. Joroinen, Finland, May 3, 1974

No one in North America took much notice of Hentunen until his career in Finland was well underway. Calgary drafted him when he was 26, and he didn't make his NHL debut until a year later. The Flames traded him to Nashville after a few games and Hentunen has been trying to establish himself with the Predators ever since. He played for his country at both the 2000 and 2001 World Championships.

HEPPLE, Alan

b. Blaydon-on-Tyne, England, August 16, 1963

When the Ottawa 67's drafted Hepple in 1980, it was as a centre, but almost from the moment he got to the team the 67's needed more help on the blueline than up the middle and Hepple made the conversion. That's how the New Jersey Devils saw him when they drafted him two years later, and although he was in the lineup on opening night in October 1983, that was the only game he played with the team all year. The next season, one game, and the season after … one game. The rest of Hepple's career as a "little Devil" (because of his size) was spent in the minors. He went on to coach the Utica Blizzard in the CHL and then became scout of the OHL for the Nashville Predators.

Alan Hepple

HERBERS, Ian

b. Jasper, Alberta, July 18, 1967

Despite playing just 65 NHL games, Herbers played for 3 teams over a 7-year period. He made his debut with Edmonton in 1993, and for the better part of the next six years he toiled in the minors, hoping for another shot at the big time. That chance came in 1999-2000 when he played for both Tampa and the Islanders, but after another year in the minors he flew the coop and accepted an offer to play for the Ayr Scottish Eagles.

Ian Herbers

HERBERTS, Jim "Sailor"

b. Cayuga, Ontario, October 31, 1897
d. Buffalo, New York, December 5, 1968

Herberts got his nickname due to his many summers spent working as a deckhand on steamers in the Great Lakes. He was a later arrival to pro hockey, making his NHL debut with the Bruins during their inaugural season, '24-'25. He wasted no time, though, in leaving his mark. He led the team in scoring his rookie year

Jim Herberts

and the following season placed third overall with 26 goals and 31 points. Herberts later played for Toronto and Detroit and finished his career in the IHL. He retired to Buffalo, where he lived until passing away after a long battle with throat cancer.

HERCHENRATTER, Art

b. Berlin (Kitchener), Ontario, November 24, 1917
A slim left winger, Herchenratter played 10 games with Detroit during the war years and spent the majority of his time in the Kitchener area, finishing in senior hockey before retiring in late 1949.

Art Herchenratter

HERGERTS, Fred

b. Calgary, Alberta, January 29, 1913
Hergerts came out of Calgary and turned pro in Syracuse in 1933. The next year he played for the New York Americans, but soon after he was in the IHL. He spent a number of years in the AHL, where he became a first-rate scorer, culminating in the '39-'40 season when he led the league in scoring and was named to the All-Star Team. The year after, his St. Louis Flyers won the championship. He later moved to B.C. to become a player coach, and when his legs were gone he remained simply a coach. After coaching, he worked for the CPR in Calgary.

Fred Hergerts

HERGESHEIMER, Phil ("Hergy"/ "Hergy the Elder"/ "Phantom")

b. Winnipeg, Manitoba, July 9, 1914
There was never a time when Philip and brother Wally played together. Thirteen years older than Wally, Philip was in the NHL long before his brother and out long before Wally was in. Philip's only NHL time came with Chicago, during the war (1939-43), before and after which he was in the American league for a goodly chunk of his career. Philip was the first American league player to score 250 goals, 48 of which came in '46-'47 with Philadelphia. He moved to Kelowna to coach, and retired there years later.

Phil Hergesheimer

HERGESHEIMER, Wally ("Fingers"/ "Garbage Collector"/ "Hergy")

b. Winnipeg, Manitoba, January 8, 1927
He was always "little Wally," and if the odds weren't stacked enough against him making the NHL, the Fates tried to ensure his failure by lopping off his index and middle fingers to the knuckles in a punch press accident (thus the black-humoured nickname of Fingers). Nevertheless, with his older brother as inspiration, Wally fought tooth and nail to make it, which he did with the Rangers in 1951. He scored 26 goals as a rookie, good enough to win the Calder Trophy most years except that one, when Bernie Geoffrion scored 30 (he had won AHL rookie honours the previous year). Wally followed up with seasons of 30 and 27 goals playing with centreman Paul Ronty, but Hergesheimer was forever underappreciated because of two other right wingers named Howe and Richard. Late in the '53-'54 season, Hergesheimer broke his leg, the first of three serious injuries to plague him in coming seasons. The year after, he played only 14 games after breaking it again, and two years after that he fractured his shoulder, ostensibly ending his career. He played in two All-Star Games

Wally Hergesheimer

('53 and '56), the first being particularly memorable because he scored two goals and played on a line with Ronty and Ted Lindsay. Coach Lynn Patrick referred to that tremendous troika as the Garbage Line. In 1962, Hergesheimer settled in Winnipeg, where he worked for the Manitoba Liquor Commission for the next 23 years.

HERON, Robert "Red"

b. Toronto, Ontario, December 31, 1917
d. Toronto, Ontario, December 14, 1990
A Toronto boy through and through, Heron started and finished his career in the City of Churches, coming up through the ranks in junior and senior hockey to play for the Leafs in 1938. He played much of three seasons for Conn Smythe before being traded to Brooklyn, the last year of the Americans' franchise. Brooklyn, in turn, sent him to the Canadiens toward the end of the year, and afterward Heron returned to Toronto to enlist in the Canadian war efforts.

HEROUX, Yves

b. Terrebonne, Quebec, April 27, 1965
In NHL circles, Heroux is a pretty fair example of a "draft mistake," though he had an extensive career outside the big show. The Nordiques drafted him in 1983, but he played just a single game for Quebec three years later. After that, he spent many years in the minors before heading to Europe, the retirement home for hockey players. He later became involved in developmental programs for young players.

HERPERGER, Chris

b. Esterhazy, Saskatchewan, February 24, 1974
It's not a good sign when you're owned by four teams in your first three years in the NHL, but Herperger, who was raised in Stockholm, Sweden, has both struggled and endured. Drafted in 1992 like any 18-year-old prospect, he didn't make his NHL debut until 7 years later, with Chicago. It was a long time coming, but by 2001 he was in Ottawa and earned a spot in the lineup on a nightly basis, contributing on left wing to a playoff team. He later became Vancouver property, but perhaps most amazing of all was that he could walk. At 16, he was hit from behind into the boards, broke his neck, and was out of the game for a year. Draft shmaft.

HERR, Matt

b. Hackensack, New Jersey, May 26, 1976
Herr was drafted by Washington prior to starting at the University of Michigan. He went on to play for the U.S. at the 1996 WJC and made his debut with the Caps in 1998. The Caps released him in 2001, but although Florida signed him he played only three games with the Panthers and now, no longer a prospect, he seems more likely destined to a career in the minors.

HERRON, Dennis

b. Chambly, Quebec, June 18, 1952
If Guy Lafleur had played against Herron every night, Gretzky would have had to play until he was 60 to beat the Flower's goal-scoring records. On three separate occasions, Herron was in net when Lafleur

Chris Herperger

scored his fiftieth goal of the season. He couldn't have been happier – or Lafleur unhappier – when the Habs acquired him in 1979 when his reputation was at its peak. He changed the pronunciation of his name from "HAIR-en" to "ehr-ONH," but the peak quickly became a quagmire, as he didn't win the starter's job and neither did his competition. The result was a three-goalie system in the years after the Habs dynasty, something that didn't sit well with Herron, although he, Richard Sevigny, and Michel Larocque did win the Vézina Trophy in 1980-81. Herron played 10 seasons with Pittsburgh, those years broken into 3 stints with the team. The first consisted of his early, developmental years until a trade cruelly took him to Kansas City, home of the goal against and capital of the loss. It was when the Pens rescued him from that hockey hell in 1976 that he had his best years, though his GAA was at its lowest in Montreal.

HERTER, Jason
b. Hafford, Saskatchewan, October 2, 1970
Herter was skating for the University of North Dakota Fighting Sioux as the 1989 draft approached. Some commented on his fluid skating, others on his skill level. He had played for the Hounds in Notre Dame back home, so his pedigree couldn't have been better, and Vancouver chose him 8th overall. But they were wrong. Vancouver let him walk before he ever played a game with them, and the Islanders played him in only one game in '95-'96, a game in which, ironically, Herter registered an assist. He has since gone on to a career in the "I" and then Germany, and doesn't look likely to re-join the NHL any time soon. Herter might be one of the rarest one-game wonders of all, the kind who has a point in his only NHL appearance.

HERVEY, Matt
b. Whittier, California, May 16, 1968
It's not much of a record to brag about, but Hervey ranks near the top of a list for most career NHL games and most career NHL points without a goal. He played 35 games and recorded 5 points with 3 teams from '88 to '93, but the defenceman, whose attributes at best were related to toughness, never scored. The bulk of his short career passed in the minors.

HESS, Bob
b. Middleton, Nova Scotia, May 19, 1955
Just as a great player from one era would be a great player in any era, so, too, would a great player on one team or under one coach be a great player with another team or coach. Or not. Hess was a high draft choice in 1974 by St. Louis on the merit that the

Hess was a high draft choice in 1974 by St. Louis.
BOB HESS

defenceman was a good skater who lacked defensive skills (which could be taught) but was effective rushing the puck (a skill that can't be taught). In '74-'75, he felt stifled under coach Garry Young, who wanted him to focus on defence, and ended the year with nine goals. The next season, under new coach Leo Boivin, he was told to use his wheels to take off and join the rush. By season's end, he had scored … nine goals. Slowly but surely, he played less and less with the Blues, to the point that in '80-'81 he played just four games before being traded to Buffalo. He played his last in Hartford before spreading the last of his goals among a number of minor-league teams.

HEWARD, Jamie
b. Regina, Saskatchewan, March 30, 1971
In hockey parlance, he has a rocket from the point. To laypeople the world over, he has a great slapshot. Whether that was enough for Heward to leave his mark in the NHL was debatable, though. Pittsburgh drafted him in 1989, but the Pens didn't use him and were happy when he played all of 1994-95 with the Canadian National Team, including at the World Championships. The Leafs signed him as a free agent after that, but his delight turned to disappointment as the team used him only infrequently. After that, Heward moved around until landing a full-time gig with Columbus, and, indeed, his rocket did come in handy. He scored 11 goals for the Jackets in 2000-01, 9 of which came on the power play in Al MacInnis-like fashion.

Jason Herter

Jamie Heward

HEXIMER, Orville ("Obs")
b. Niagara Falls, Ontario, February 16, 1910
d. Niagara Falls, Ontario, July 16, 1988
The youngest Niagara Falls-er ever to play in the NHL, at 19, Heximer joined the Rangers in 1929 and later played for the Bruins and New York Americans. He spent several years in the Can-Am league and then the American league before retiring in 1939 and returning to the Falls. He got a job with Niagara Power Co. and worked there for 37 years as a rigger-mechanic until retiring in 1975. During these years, he also coached minor hockey and baseball and was an outstanding member of the community.

HEXTALL, Bryan ("Hex")
b. Grenfell, Saskatchewan, July 31, 1913
d. Portage La Prairie, Manitoba, July 25, 1984
Manitoba can take the greater claim as Hextall's home because he grew up in Poplar Point and played his first hockey there. He played junior in Portage and turned pro with Vancouver out west, making his NHL debut with the Rangers in '36-'37. A remarkably gentlemanly

player, the right winger made the team full time at training camp in 1937 and spent his entire 11-year career with the Blueshirts. He played on their top line with Phil Watson and Lynn Patrick, and Hextall scored 20 or more goals seven times. He led the NHL in that department twice, and in '41-'42 led the league in points with 56, the last time a Rangers player did so. He was also a First Team All-Star for three successive seasons (1939-42). Hextall's crowning moment came in the 1940 Stanley Cup finals. In game six, he scored at 2:07 of overtime against the Leafs' Turk Broda to give the Rangers the win. It was their last Cup for 54 years. Hextall proved a tough player as well. From 1937 until '44, a span of 340 games, he didn't miss a single start. He did, though, have to play senior hockey in Canada in '44-'45 as he was refused entry into the U.S. After just three games of the next season, he had to go to hospital for a serious liver problem and missed the remainder of the season. His recovery to return to the NHL the year after was a miracle to doctors, and after another year split between the Rangers and the AHL, Hextall retired. He returned to Manitoba to work on his two wheat farms and coached minor hockey. He also proved to be the start of one of the greatest hockey families the NHL has ever known. His sons, Bryan Jr. and Dennis, both played in the NHL and his grandson Ron, son of Bryan Jr., also had a long and distinguished career in the league. Bryan Sr. was elected to the Hockey Hall of Fame in 1969, though the last years of his life were marred by the greatest misfortune that could befall such an athletic and active man. Poor circulation forced doctors to amputate both of his legs below the knees in 1978, though artificial legs enabled him to walk short distances and pursue his favourite hobby, hunting. He died, at home, of a heart attack.

Bryan Hextall, Jr.

Dennis Hextall

HEXTALL, Bryan, Jr.
b. Winnipeg, Manitoba, May 23, 1941
One of hockey's great families, the Hextalls have been a near continuous presence in the NHL for much of the league's existence. Bryan's father enjoyed a Hall of Fame career in the NHL, and Bryan Jr. made the Rangers in 1962. However, he played only half a season with the team before being demoted, and it was another six and a half years before he saw the bigs again. Expansion brought forth a team in Pittsburgh, and the Pens acquired his services in 1969. He played for five years there. He later bounced around a bit, finishing his days with Minnesota playing with his brother, Dennis, for the first time. Hextall stayed with the North Stars as a scout for two years and then headed back to the comfort of home. He raised a family, which included a son, Ron, who went on to play

On December 8, 1987, he became the first goalie to shoot the puck into the other team's net.
RON HEXTALL

goal for many years in the NHL as the most penalized netminder in league history. The Hextalls became the first family to send three generations of players to the NHL. Bryan worked for 10 years with Molson Breweries in Brandon and later moved to Victoria, B.C., where, clearly more relaxed than in his tough NHL days, he opened a teahouse called Adrienne's.

HEXTALL, Dennis
b. Poplar Point, Manitoba, April 17, 1943
As a boy, Dennis was surrounded by sports. First, there was dad, a Hall of Famer. Then, there were two uncles who played in the NHL, Ron Lyons and Lin Bend. Then, there was an aunt who played in the All-American Girls League during WWII and pitched that league's first no-hitter. Yet despite those influences and his own obvious skill, Dennis Hextall didn't gravitate to hockey with the same passion early on in life. He played junior in Brandon and college at the University of North Dakota, always the tamest of the Hextall clan. He finally took his hockey seriously and turned pro, and then he started to fight. He wasn't big, and he didn't want to play tough, but he knew he'd have to defend himself if he was going to last. He did, and he did. He made his NHL debut with the Rangers in the 1968 playoffs, and over the next 13 years played for 6 teams. His finest seasons came with Minnesota, 1972-74, when he had consecutive 82-point seasons. He also represented the North Stars at the 1974 and '75 All-Star Games. After retiring, Hextall settled in suburban Detroit and became part owner of Maybee Associates, a manufacturers representative for the major auto makers and the military in the United States.

HEXTALL, Ron
b. Brandon, Manitoba, May 3, 1964
When Ron Hextall stepped onto the ice in a Philadelphia Flyers sweater to start the '86-'87 season, he became the first grandson of an NHLer ever to play in the league. He was also the family's first goalie, but that did not prevent him from playing with the same fistic roughness his ancestors had become famous for in the NHL. Indeed, by the time Ron retired, he was the single-season and all-time leader in penalty minutes by goalies. His rookie season was a remarkable introduction: He led the league in games played and wins, and although he didn't win the Calder Trophy he did win the Conn Smythe for his heroics in the Cup finals against eventual winners Edmonton. This despite his actions in game four, when he slashed Kent Nilsson and was suspended for the first eight games of the next season. Hextall was

just beginning. On December 8, 1987, he became the first goalie in the NHL to shoot the puck into the other team's net (the only other NHL goal being credited to Billy Smith for being the last player to touch the puck before an own goal was scored). A year and a half later, Hextall replicated the feat in the playoffs, the first tender to score in the post-season. The goals were symbols for his amazing puck-handling skills, and he was referred to as a third defenceman so skilled was he with the puck. He was also a fearless battler in the style of the aforementioned Smith, and was suspended numerous times for taking the warrior definition too far. He dropped his blocker without compunction to enter fights, and in that rookie season he was assessed 104 penalty minutes, a record he himself broke the next year. In the final game of the '89 playoffs against Montreal, Hextall ran into the corner to hunt down Chris Chelios, a worthy act to many a Chelios hater, but an act that cost him 12 games at the start of the next season all the same. In an exhibition game in 1991, he slashed Jim Cummins and was suspended for another six-pack, and even in the Team Canada 1987 training camp for the Canada Cup he hacked Sylvain Turgeon and broke his forearm. Despite these colourful qualities, Hextall did not turn into the superstar that first year promised. His behaviour was erratic, and he never took the team further into the playoffs than during that misty rookie season. He was with Philly again in 1997 when the Flyers went to the finals against Detroit, but he wasn't the number-one goalie and the team still lost. Shortly after retiring, he joined father Bryan and uncle Dennis as an inductee into the Manitoba Sports Hall of Fame.

He returned to Regina and opened his own store, Kyles Sporting Goods, which thrived for years.
BILL HICKE

HEYLIGER, Vic
b. Boston, Massachusetts, September 26, 1919
The shiny NHL numbers are small and tell only a shard of the glitzy life in hockey that is Heyliger's story. Heyliger played a few games for Chicago in '37-'38, the year the team won its second Cup in four years. Six years later, he played again for half a season with the team when war shortages created a dire situation for the Hawks, but during and after he was coaching most of the time. In 1944 he joined the University of Michigan, and after getting that program in order he led the Wolverines to a record 10 successive NCAA championships. He left the college to accept a position in promotions in Broadmoor World Arena for the 1962 World Championships in Colorado Springs, and then he took on an even greater challenge, coach of the West German National Team, a job that involved not only preparing the Germans for the next two World

Championships but also organizing the entire hockey program, adult to youth, in Germany. Thirty-three games in the NHL hardly tells his story.

HICKE, Bill
b. Regina, Saskatchewan, March 31, 1938
The worst thing Hicke could have done in junior was to score 54 goals in his final year. That was 1958. The second-worst thing he could have done was to score another 41 with Rochester in the AHL. That was 1959. When he joined the Montreal Canadiens a year later, he was being called the next Maurice Richard. No kid needs that label while playing his first year in the NHL. Of course, he wasn't the next Richard. He was a solid player, a decent scorer, but not a Rocket man. He played less and less, got mad and asked for a trade, and was given his wish. The Rangers acquired him, but in his first camp he suffered a serious illness. An overpowering series of allergies put him in a coma for two weeks. When he came out of it, doctors found he tested positive to 140 of 180 allergy tests. Oh, and he had asthma. Later, when he got to Oakland, another asthma attack almost killed him again, but he bounced back and had some decent years. In 1972, he went to the WHA and became president of the league's players association, but the asthma problems recurred and he retired. He returned to Regina and opened his own store, Kyles Sporting Goods, which thrived for years.

Vic Heyliger

HICKE, Ernie
b. Regina, Saskatchewan, November 7, 1947
Okay, time for a bit of double trivia. Those smart hockey people all know about the great Sam Pollock trade made with Los Angeles to preserve the 1st overall draft choice in 1971 that turned out to be Guy Lafleur. But "preserve" is the important verb, for the Habs already owned the number-one pick. How did they acquire that, pray tell? They traded their first-round draft choice and Ernie Hicke to Oakland for Oakland's first-rounder (Lafleur) and Francois Lacombe! Ernie hadn't played a game for Montreal, and when he got to the coast he joined brother Bill. Ernie wasn't long for the Seals, though, or anywhere else for that matter. In 8 years, he played for 5 teams, including Minnesota in '76-'77 when he had 30 goals. He played a while in the minors and then retired to Rocklin, California, where he opened a small restaurant in Auburn, not far away.

Ernie Hicke

HICKEY, Greg
b. Toronto, Ontario, March 8, 1955
Yes, the more or less unknown, or forgotten, brother of Pat played one game with his older sibling in New

Alex Hicks

Doug Hicks

Glenn Hicks

Harold Hicks

York in '77-'78, his only NHL appearance. He played minor pro for a while and after retiring settled in Toronto and coached at the kids' level. More materially, he became head pro at the Nobleton Golf Club, a position he has enjoyed since 1986. The seasons may have changed and the surface may be a different colour, but sticks are sticks.

HICKEY, Pat ("Hitch")
b. Brantford, Ontario, May 15, 1953
He was one of the darlings to start his career in the WHA. In 1973, Hickey came out of the OHL and joined the Toronto Toros. Young, with long blond hair, and a sleek skater, he was a darling to fans and media both. He signed with the Rangers 2 years later, and in each of his 3 seasons he improved dramatically, scoring 40 goals in '77-'78. He went to Colorado, and then had the misfortune of being traded to Toronto in the deal that sent Lanny McDonald to the Rockies, perhaps the most controversial trade the Leafs ever made. Hickey never had the same impact with another team as he had with the Rangers, but when his time was up he retired without regret or apprehension. During his days on Broadway, he also got involved on Wall Street during the summers, and it was there he gravitated after hanging up the blades. He became an institutional sales rep with L.F. Rothchild of New York and later moved to Hamilton to work for CIBC Wood Gundy.

HICKS, Alex
b. Calgary, Alberta, September 4, 1969
It's not every day that a Division III U.S. college tosses a player into the NHL circus, but that's exactly what the University of Wisconsin-Eau Claire did once Hicks had finished his four years with the Bluegolds in 1992. He worked his way up from the East Coast league until Anaheim signed him in 1995, but he was traded around like a playing card until he suffered a serious knee injury that ended his 1999-2000 season. He recovered, but went to Europe to continue his career.

HICKS, Doug
b. Cold Lake, Alberta, May 28, 1955
In the short term, he got his wish. In the long term, what he wanted could not be stopped from happening. Hicks had played for Minnesota and Chicago in the late 1970s when out of the blue he became one of Glen Sather's reclamation projects in 1979. Hicks couldn't have been happier. The organization was great, and the players – Gretzky, Messier, Fuhr, Anderson – were Stanley Cup bound. On March 9, 1982, that same Sather traded Hicks to Washington for Todd Bidner. Hicks was crushed. He knew he had lost out on a Cup,

and so every day in Washington, he looked at the standings and prayed for an Oilers loss, a sign that they had made the wrong move in dealing him. In the short term, Edmonton did lose that year and the next. In the long term, they won four Cups in five years. If it made Hicks feel any better, Bidner wasn't around for any of those Cups, either. A short time later, Hicks accepted an offer to play in Austria, and the defenceman was converted to centre. He found himself playing between two Soviet legends, Victor Shalimov and Sergei Kapustin, and for a while he was happy.

HICKS, Glenn
b. Red Deer, Alberta, August 28, 1958
Brother of Doug, but not cut from the same cloth, Glenn was the spark plug on the Detroit Red Wings in 1979-80, that catch-all euphemism for fighter. In his first game, he got into two fights, and sat in the penalty box feeling like a fool and wondering if this is what he had to do to stay in the league. He calmed down after that, but chipped in only one goal. The next season wasn't much more impressive, and soon he found himself in the minors trying to prove he was more than just a fighter. He may have thought he had done that in 1983 when the North Stars signed him, but they never called him up and he wound up skating in Switzerland.

In 1973, Hickey came out of the OHL and joined the Toronto Toros.
PAT HICKEY

HICKS, Harold "Henry"
b. Sillery, Quebec, December 10, 1900
d. Ottawa, Ontario, August 14, 1965
Hicks was an Ottawa boy in upbringing, playing with a variety of teams until turning pro with Stratford in 1926. He signed with the Maroons two years later, and in the summer of 1929 they sold him to Detroit. He finished his career playing in London, Ontario, and then returned to Ottawa to work for Canadian National Railways. He was chemical superintendent of motor power equipment in Ottawa, a post he held until 1963 when he retired.

HICKS, Wayne
b. Aberdeen, Washington, April 9, 1937
Numbers don't lie? Sure they do. They conceal greater truths at the cost of reductive hypotheses. Take the case of Wayne Hicks. He had been a consistent 30-goal scorer in the AHL, rifling off 5 such seasons in the 1960s before dipping to 14 goals in '69-'70. The numbers suggested he was done. The truth was that toward the end of the previous season, in which he had scored 33 times, he smashed his right femur and needed a steel plate put in his leg and a nail in his hip to get back on his feet again. He followed this off-year with four more slightly subpar seasons in the WHL, but

the truth was that while he could score in the American league, he couldn't in the National. He played with 3 Original Six teams in the early 1960s and then with Philly and Pittsburgh in the first year of expansion, but with the Flyers, he went 25 straight games without a goal during one particularly bad stretch.

HIDI, Andre ("Muscles")
b. Toronto, Ontario, June 5, 1960

Hidi made his way to the NHL via the path less beaten, although his first season with Peterborough in the OHL suggested the opposite. In '79-'80, he starred with the Petes and played for Canada at the World Juniors, but he then left junior to enrol at the University of Toronto and made his way toward a doctorate in economics and political theory. He was too good to ignore, though, and the NHL was too big a lure for *him* to ignore. Washington signed him, and at the end of the '83-'84 season the Caps put him in a game. He acquitted himself well, for they gave him a summer program of strengthening and conditioning, which he followed with scholastic aptitude. But although he arrived at camp in great shape and had an excellent exhibition season, he played only six games for the Caps. Two years in the minors pushed him back to school and out of the pro game.

HIEMER, Uli
b. Fussen, West Germany, September 21, 1962

Hiemer had the right attitude. He knew early on he was blessed with talent, and certainly in Germany there were few players who had his skill. So rather than remain a star back home forever, he tried the NHL. By the time he arrived in New Jersey in 1984, though, he had already amassed a fantastic international portfolio. He had played in two WJC and three WC. He had played in the 1984 Olympics in Sarajevo and the 1984 Canada Cup (a tournament that ended early for him due to a badly broken nose). So when he arrived in North America, his only fears were the usual ones for a European of that generation: the 80-game grind, the travel, the fierce play every night. Hiemer scored a hat trick in just his eighth game, one of the fastest rookie hat tricks for a defenceman in league history, but on the season he had only two more goals all year. He played three seasons with the Devils, but each one saw less and less time in the NHL and more and more in the AHL. By the spring of '87 he was ready to come home. He enjoyed a lengthy career again, playing in two more Olympics and five more World Championships, a man who had proved himself on both sides of the ocean.

HIGGINS, Matt
b. Calgary, Alberta, October 29, 1977

Pickings have been slim for Higgins down at the Molson Centre. Montreal, a team once so adept at drafting, chose Higgins 18th overall in '96, perhaps a tad optimistic for the Moose Jaw junior who is working toward scoring his second career goal in his fifth career season with the Habs.

HIGGINS, Paul
b. Saint John, New Brunswick, January 13, 1962

Higgins might well be Toronto's NHL nominee for the worst player ever to appear in the NHL. Thoroughly, unequivocally without hockey talent, the horrific Leafs of the early 1980s brought this 19-year-old kid up from junior to fight. He gooned his way into a suspension for a vicious high stick, and he tried to fight during every shift on the ice because he couldn't skate or pass or shoot like anyone else in the league. He was out of the league by 1983 after 25 games and 152 penalty minutes, but he wasn't out of the news. There was the high-speed chase that got him 30 days in jail. There was the charge of criminal negligence causing bodily harm and possession of a weapon. A fight with baseball bats and sticks cost him 60 days in the slammer. He had been drafted from the Leafs right out of high school, the first such player in league history, and he proved too immature to handle the life of a pro. It took him years to settle down, but he eventually did. Higgins married his high school sweetheart and raised a family of three while working in property maintenance in Mississauga. A bad guy gone good.

HIGGINS, Tim
b. Ottawa, Ontario, February 7, 1958

For a time there, New Jersey's Tom McVie looked like a genius. On January 11, 1984, he acquired Higgins from Chicago for Jeff Larmer, a proven commodity. Higgins had twice scored 20 goals in a season with the Hawks, but McVie still thought Higgins' talents weren't appreciated by the Hawks. To finish the '83-'84 season, Higgins had 18 goals in just 37 games. McVie looked so very smart. Trouble was, the year after Higgins had just 19 goals in 71 games and Larmer had his first of four 40-goal seasons with Chicago. The next year was even worse for Higgins, and he was dispatched to Detroit that summer. He later became the assistant general manager of Nationwide Arena in Columbus.

HIGHTON, Hec
b. Medicine Hat, Alberta, October 10, 1923

When Highton announced his retirement from the game at the age of 27, he meant it. His wife had seen Hec take enough rubber to make an 18-wheeler out of the tiny goalie, and enough was enough. He returned home to California, and never played again. Highton grew up in Alberta during the years between the wars. He'd get up at 4 a.m. to ride his bike to the rink for practice, and he got his break one night in the PCHL championship game when the goalie went on strike and the coach summoned Highton to fill in. The team lost 5-4 in overtime, but Highton had impressed enough that his pro career officially began. He played 24 games for Chicago in '43-'44 during a stretch in which the Hawks tried their hardest to prove themselves the worst team of all time, and after the war Highton played for a few years in the AHL until he got married and settled into the California state of mind. He had spent his summers there for years, but once he lived there year-round there was no stopping him. He retired at 27 and never looked back. He got his own TV show in Hollywood and became both producer and director of Los Angeles Blades telecasts in the 1960s for KTLA, Channel 5.

Uli Hiemer

Matt Higgins

Tim Higgins

Ike Hildebrand

Al Hill

Brian Hill

Sean Hill

HILBERT, Andy
b. Howell, Michigan, February 6, 1981

After leaving the University of Michigan in 2001 to play for the Bruins, Hilbert has found himself in Providence, not Boston. He played a few games for Boston in that rookie season but has been pegged as a minor-league centre for the time being.

HILDEBRAND, Isaac "Ike"
b. Winnipeg, Manitoba, May 27, 1927

Not only was Hildebrand one of the finest lacrosse players ever to come out of Canada, he also played a bit of serious hockey in his day, too. On the hockey front, his finest moment came at the end of his career. He was playing coach with the Belleville McFarlands in 1958 when the team rallied from 3-1 down to win the Allan Cup 4-3 in games. This meant an invite to represent Canada at the '59 World Championships in Czechoslovakia. There, Hildebrand scored the winning goal in Canada's 3-1 victory over the Soviet Union, a gold-medal victory. He had started playing with Oshawa and the Marlies, but when Conn Smythe asked him to sign with the Leafs, Oshawa coach Lionel Conacher told him to ask for more money. Hildebrand never played with the Leafs, but in 1953 he joined the Rangers and then Chicago for parts of two seasons. His NHL career ended, more or less, because of a broken leg in 1954, but he played and coached senior hockey for years after. More than hockey, though, Hildebrand was a lacrossist. That is why he is in the Canadian Sports Hall of Fame and Lacrosse Hall of Fame. He was a national champion in 1944 at age 15, and the year after he was MVP in the Mann Cup victory for his New Westminster Salmonbellies. He played in 13 Canadian championships, winning 9 times, during his 20 years in the sport. When all was said and done, he settled in Toronto and opened Hildebrand Sports Sales, a manufacturer's representative, though later in life he retired to British Columbia to fish and golf and relax.

HILL, Al
b. Nanaimo, British Columbia, April 22, 1955

February 14, 1977, was the most famous debut in the history of the game. That night, Al Hill scored a goal just 36 seconds into his first game; pretty good, but not a record. By the end of the night, though, he had two goals and three assists – now that's remarkable! Five points in his first NHL game! For the record, the St. Louis goalie he scored on went by the name of Yves Belanger. In his next eight games, Hill had one point. The next year, oh for three games. He settled into a career that was more minors than NHL, though all of his 221 career games came with the

Flyers. After retiring, he stayed in the game as a coach in the AHL.

HILL, Brian
b. Regina, Saskatchewan, January 12, 1957

Hill scored 53 times in junior with Medicine Hat in '76-'77, and this prompted Atlanta to draft him that summer. Hartford took him from the Flames when the team joined the NHL in 1979, but he played just 19 games before moving over to Europe. He loved it so much in Austria he got his citizenship and played twice for his adoptive country in the World Championships during the years when the nation was in "B" pool.

HILL, Mel ("Sudden Death")
b. Glenboro, Manitoba, February 15, 1914

d. Fort Qu' Appelle, Saskatchewan, April 11, 1996

It is, without doubt, one of the all-time nicknames, a diminutive that was earned not because of hair colour or personality or character, but because of accomplishment. In the semifinals of 1939, Hill and the Bruins were playing the Rangers. In that seven-game series, Hill scored three overtime goals, a record. For those heroics, he earned the nickname Sudden Death, but perhaps the greatest irony is that he never scored another OT goal. He did win two more Stanley Cups, though, one with the B's two years later and another with the Leafs in 1945. In Boston, Hill played on a line with Bill Cowley and Roy Conacher. He was never known as a scorer, and again the irony is that following his best season for goals – '42-'43, when he had 17 for Toronto – he broke his ankle and missed much of the year. He finished his career in Regina, and after retiring he settled there and owned and operated a Pepsi-Cola and Canada Dry bottling plant, which he ran for a quarter-century. He then retired to a farm near Fort Qu'Appelle, Saskatchewan. Hill is a member of the Manitoba Sports Hall of Fame.

In that seven-game series, Hill scored three overtime goals, a record.
MEL HILL

HILL, Sean ("Hilly")
b. Duluth, Minnesota, February 14, 1970

Hill got his Cup glory out of the way early, though it was more Cup than glory. He played for Montreal during the '92-'93 season, the last Cup thread woven into the fading history of Montreal's fabric, and from there he went to Anaheim in the Expansion Draft. He has spent most of his recent years with Carolina, including 2001-02 when the team went to the finals. Earlier in his career, Hill also had international success with Team USA at all levels, notably the 1992 Olympics in Albertville. He also won an NCAA Championships with his University of Wisconsin Badgers in 1989.

HILLER, Jim
b. Port Alberni, British Columbia, May 15, 1969

Port Alberni will claim Steve Yzerman before Hiller any day of the week, but that's no slight to Hiller, only a compliment to Stevie Y. Hiller played provincial junior to prepare for Northern Michigan, and he moved on to Los Angeles in 1992. He can proudly claim association to another Hall of Famer because on January 29, 1993, he, Sylvain Couturier, and Paul Coffey were traded to Detroit for Jimmy Carson, Marc Potvin, and Gary Shuchuk. Nothing worked out quite right, though, and he wound up going to Europe, where he continues to hustle his skating and shooting in Germany.

HILLER, Wilbert "Dutch"
b. Berlin (Kitchener), Ontario, May 11, 1915

Hiller grew up in Kitchener during a fecund time in that city's history. He counts Schmidt, Dumart, and Bauer among his childhood friends, though Hiller began his pro career while the others became famous in Boston. Hiller played with Phil Watson and Bryan Hextall in the late 1930s on the Roughneck Line, though the Rangers' PR department didn't much like that name and instead called Hiller "Dutch" because he was always in dutch (i.e., in trouble) on the ice. Hiller played left wing on the team that won the 1940 Cup, but a couple of years later he was traded because he got into Lester Patrick's bad books. Hiller later won a Cup with Montreal in 1946, his last NHL season, and after a year in the minors his career was over, not because of failing skill but rather failing eyesight. He tried an early form of contact lenses that didn't quite work, and in 1948 he and his wife moved to California because of her ill health. Hiller settled down to work as a salesman for a drug company based out west, though years later he moved back near Toronto to be closer to the hockey environment that had so consumed him for most of his life.

Hiller settled down to work as a salesman for a drug company based out west.
"DUTCH" HILLER

HILLIER, Randy
b. Toronto, Ontario, March 30, 1960

Eleven seasons in the NHL is nothing to sniff at, and for a defenceman with limited talent and limitless heart, it's a fair representation of a fine career. Hillier never went end to end or quarterbacked the power play, but he was solid and reliable for the four teams he dressed for during his career. He was around for parts of Pittsburgh's Cup win in 1991, its first ever, but soon after that he was out of the league. He played seven seasons with the Pens, and it was in Pittsburgh he established some friends and roots for his retirement. He settled there and became a financial adviser.

HILLMAN, Floyd
b. Ruthven, Ontario, November 19, 1933

Brother Larry played 790 NHL games. Brother Wayne played 691 NHL games. Brother Floyd played just six. His small pack came with Boston in '56-'57, and he went on to play several years in the minors before retiring.

HILLMAN, Larry ("Morley")
b. Kirkland Lake, Ontario, February 5, 1937

Friends often called Hillman by his middle name, Morley, and he had many friends. In a career that spanned 20 years and umpteen teams, Hillman was a loved defenceman wherever he went. He got his big break early on, being called up to Detroit in 1955 as an 18-year-old and winning the Stanley Cup just a few weeks later. In the pre-expansion years, he played for Detroit, Boston, and Toronto, his longest stint coming with the Leafs (1960-67), during which time he won two more Cups. Every year but his first in Toronto saw him spend significant parts of the schedule in the minors, a frustration that was solved with expansion. He won his last Cup with Montreal in 1969, and in 1973 he jumped to the WHA. Ironically, he retired after '75-'76 with Winnipeg because of a nasty contract dispute, but once that issue was settled the Jets hired him as their head coach. Because so many of the Jets were European, the team held training camp overseas, and over New Year's 1978 he coached against Viktor Tikhonov in a three-game exhibition (Winnipeg vs. CCCP) in Tokyo, Japan. Hillman later ran a tourist camp in Charlton, Ontario, but in 1984 he was stricken by Guillian-Barre syndrome, a condition that brought about near-total paralysis. He had to re-learn to walk, which he did with the same determination and focus that kept him in hockey for so many years.

HILLMAN, Wayne ("Mooner")
b. Kirkland Lake, Ontario, November 13, 1938
d. Cleveland, Ohio, November 24, 1990

You don't get any luckier than this Hillman, so lucky, in fact, he might as well have packed it in after one game. Hillman's first NHL game came the night of April 16, 1961. No, he didn't score a goal or get into a fight or do anything like that. His team, Chicago, won the Stanley Cup. One game, his name on the Cup. The rest is all denouement. In truth, Hillman lasted another decade in the NHL – and never came remotely close to another Cup. In 1973, he left to play with his brother Larry for Cleveland in the WHA, and he retired two years later. He settled in Cleveland but, like his brother, ran into health troubles. His were much more serious, and in 1990 he died in a local hospital after a fight with cancer.

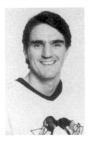

Randy Hillier

Floyd Hillman

Larry Hillman

Wayne Hillman

John Hilworth

Dan Hinote

Andre Hinse

Dan Hinton

HILWORTH, John
("Too Tall"/ "Jasper")
b. Jasper, Alberta, May 23, 1957

It was a too-short career in the NHL for Hilworth, a large and imposing defenceman who played for Detroit from 1977 to '80. Most of his career during those years and after was carried out in the minors, though, in leagues not likely to help him get another shot at the big time.

HIMES, Normie
b. Galt, Ontario, April 13, 1903
d. Kitchener, Ontario, September 14, 1958

His durability came in handy and his versatility earned him some time as a goalie way back when when tenders weren't always in plentiful supply. In the game's early days, most players who went in goal did so for two minutes while a goalie had to serve his own penalty. Himes, though, was called upon for greater feats. On December 5, 1927, New York Americans goalie Joe Miller was hurt early in the third period of the game against Pittsburgh, and Himes was asked to fill the breach. He played 19 minutes of shutout hockey. Almost a year to the day later – December 1, 1928 – Jake Forbes was too ill to play and Himes donned the equipment for the full 60 minutes. He performed admirably in a 3-0 loss to Toronto. In real life, though, he was a centreman famous for wearing a black cap while playing, a tiny man who weighed as much as a bag of dry feathers. He played his entire career with the Amerks (1926-35), and played more than 360 consecutive games at one stretch. In 1929-30, he scored 28 goals, though in all his years with the team he appeared in only 2 playoff games. He later became club pro at Westmount Golf Club in Kitchener, and he was both a fine player and teacher of the game. He died at the clubhouse in 1958 after suffering a heart attack. He had just finished a round of golf with an old hockey teammate, Al Murray.

HINDMARCH, Dave
b. Vancouver, British Columbia, October 15, 1958

What a difference a year makes. For the 1984-85 season, the NHL adopted a leaguewide rule for use of movable nets that collapse on heavy contact. Had these been in place the previous season, Hindmarch could have played a decade longer than he did. The truth is, though, that on the night of December 16, 1983, he drove to the net when Vancouver's Rick Lanz tripped him up. Hindmarch fell into the post with both legs, damaging cartilage in both knees in a way doctors described as more a car accident than a hockey

injury. Hindmarch required major reconstructive surgery on both knees and then underwent what turned out to be a year and a half of intense rehab. He built the strength up, but when he skated with his Calgary teammates, he could feel that extra gear missing. Doctors cautioned him against returning, saying further damage could have permanent implications, so Hindmarch went to the University of British Columbia, where his dad was director of phys ed, and finished his own degree in phys ed. If only those nets had been in place a year earlier …

HINOTE, Dan
b. Leesburg, Florida, January 30, 1977

Scoring your first NHL goal is always so special. You make a nice play, you deflect the puck, it goes in off

He played more than 360 consecutive games at one stretch.
NORMIE HIMES

your butt, whatever. You know you've scored, you scoop the puck up and toss it to the trainer. You feel like you've arrived. Not for Hinote. On March 4, 2000, his teammate Adam Deadmarsh scored a goal against Tampa Bay. The game ended, the players showered, did interviews, left the building. Only then did officials review the goal and decide that credit should have gone to Hinote, not Deadmarsh. Hinote would have to be satisfied with a day-old celebration. Nevertheless, it gave him satisfaction because he had actually attended the United States Military Academy at High Point for a year, training to become an FBI agent. It was only after some hockey that he realized he might be able to play as a career, and in his first full season he won the Stanley Cup, thus ensuring that if he ever did go on to become an FBI type, he sure wouldn't be undercover.

HINSE, Andre
b. Trois Rivières, Quebec, April 19, 1945

Rumour had it that Hinse preferred the easygoing lifestyle of playing in the minors in Phoenix to the tougher, more wintry endeavours of the NHL in, say, Toronto, the team that signed him. Hinse played his only four NHL games with the Leafs in '67-'68, but the team kept him in the minors besides. Hinse thought he had made Vancouver in camp in 1971, but he pulled his groin and wound up playing the season … in Phoenix. He joined the Houston Aeros of the WHA in '73 and had the pleasure of playing with the Howe boys before retiring.

HINTON, Dan
b. Toronto, Ontario, May 24, 1953

After just a year of junior with the Soo in '72-'73, Hinton turned pro with the Dallas Black Hawks, minor affiliate of Chicago, the team that had drafted him. The left winger developed into a decent scorer, but when the Hawks called him up for 14 games a few years later, he registered not a point and didn't merit, in the Hawks' eyes, a return invite at a later date.

HIRSCH, Corey
b. Medicine Hat, Alberta, August 10, 1972
Yes, Hirsch was the goalie for the gold-medal shootout in 1994, the famous one where Peter Forsberg made the deke and went in the same direction as the goalie, only to pass the puck to the opposite side and one-hand it into the net for the victory. Years later, Sweden contacted him because the nation was making a commemorative issue stamp of the play and wanted to use Hirsch's likeness. He demurred, and later acknowledged that was a mistake. Hirsch came to the NHL with a glowing c.v. featuring a Memorial Cup and four outstanding seasons with Kamloops. He made his debut with the Rangers in January 1993, but never got going with New York and they dished him off to Vancouver. He earned his first shutout with the Canucks in a game using the experimental puck that the NHL was allowing Fox TV to play with, but he never made a lasting impression with the Canucks beyond a couple of years. Hirsch had been goalie of the year in Canadian junior hockey in 1992 and AHL rookie of the year a season later, but his stock just wasn't NHL calibre. In 2002, he signed with the Utah Grizzlies as a third goalie, to help tutor and develop the next generation of Hirsches in the crease.

He earned his first shutout with the Canucks in a game using the experimental puck that the NHL was allowing Fox TV to play with.
COREY HIRSCH

HIRSCH, Tom
b. Minneapolis, Minnesota, January 27, 1963
The smile coming out of high school was as wide as a country night is black. Hirsch was an outstanding teen player, recruited by dozens of colleges with terrific scholarship offers. He accepted U of Minnesota's because that was where he had watched so much hockey, and even before he played a game with the Gophers the North Stars drafted him. In addition to his college career, he played for the U.S. National Team and at the 1984 Olympics in Sarajevo, an unsuccessful follow-up to the Miracle on Ice. His first two years of pro, though, saw demotions to the minors, and then in October 1985 he separated his shoulder near the end of training camp. He required surgery, and then more surgery, and he missed two full years recovering. He came back for one game in '87-'88, but he just didn't have it. The smile had been replaced with pain and disappointment.

HIRSCHFELD, Bert
b. Halifax, Nova Scotia, March 1, 1929
d. Halifax, Nova Scotia, July 3, 1996
An early Haligonian star of the ice, Hirschfeld learned the game with St. Mary's before moving to the Montreal Royals for further development. In 1948-49, he captained that team to the Memorial Cup, and the year after he joined the Habs for 13 games. He played 20 games for the team the next year but ended his career in the minors before playing senior hockey at home in Halifax. He became a member of the city's fire department and retired years later as captain. Hirschfeld was inducted into the Nova Scotia Sports Hall of Fame.

HISLOP, Jamie
b. Sarnia, Ontario, January 20, 1954
This is why U.S. college is a smart route for players to take, and why Canadian universities should adopt scholarships if they are to compete with their neighbours. Hislop attended the University of New Hampshire for four years (1972-76) during which time he played serious hockey and earned his teacher's certificate. He then played for Quebec and Calgary and developed into a perfectly solid NHLer. December 1, 1983, changed all that. The Islanders' Anders Kallur accidentally hit Hislop in the eye with his stick, and Hislop's career was all but over. Twice he tried coming back, but even corrective surgery couldn't ensure proper vision. He decided to return to Sarnia, where he started a family and taught at a variety of high schools. But he couldn't find a full-time job in the classroom, so he returned to coaching, first for the Flames' farm team in Salt Lake City, later with the big club.

HITCHMAN, Lionel ("Hitch")
b. Toronto, Ontario, November 3, 1901
d. Glen Falls, New York, December 19, 1968
The RCMP can't boast of having brought too many NHLers into the game, but Hitchman is certainly one. He played in Toronto before moving to Ottawa with the RCMP, where he played senior hockey with the New Edinburghs as well as in the Civil Service League. It was out of this play that Tommy Gorman signed Hitchman to play for the Senators in the team's successful quest for the Cup against Vancouver, but midway through the '24-'25 season he was sold to Boston. It was there that he enjoyed his greatest years, being paired on the blueline with Eddie Shore. Shore rushed the puck while Hitchman stayed back, and together they were the best tandem in the NHL. Their only Cup, however, came in 1929, though they were serious challengers in each year's playoffs. Hitchman finished his career with the Bruins in 1934 but continued to scout for the team for a number of years after coaching the Cubs for a brief time.

Tom Hirsch

Bert Hirschfeld

Jamie Hislop

Lionel Hitchman

Jan Hlavac

HLAVAC, Jan
b. Prague, Czechoslovakia (Czech Republic), September 20, 1976

Nineteen ninety-nine was a very good year for Hlavac. He scored the game-winning, gold medal-winning goal for the Czechs at the World Championships, and that fall he joined the Rangers for his first NHL season. The year after, he played on the Czechmate line with Petr Nedved and Radek Dvorak, scoring 28 goals and looking like a player of the future on Broadway. The Rangers included him in part of the package to acquire Eric Lindros from Philly, though, and the Flyers sent him on to Vancouver, where he remains a scoring threat.

HLINKA, Ivan
b. Most, Czechoslovakia (Czech Republic), January 26, 1950

If only he had made the effort to learn English, he might have made history over and above what he accomplished during his career. Hlinka was a superstar in Czech league play from the late 1960s into the early 1980s. In today's NHL, he would have been a first-round draft choice. Then, he lived in a communist country and was not allowed to leave. By the time he joined the NHL with Vancouver in 1981, he had played in 11 World Championships and 2 Olympics and had 2 knee operations that reduced his speed and power significantly. In his first year, though, he scored 23 goals and helped the Canucks reach the Cup finals. He played only one more season before returning to Europe to finish his career in the comfort of the Swiss league, and then he re-joined Litvinov, the team, for which he had given so much

Mario Lemieux then hired him as an assistant with Pittsburgh in 1999-2000.
IVAN HLINKA

during his life. He became the team's coach, as well as the national coach, a time that peaked with a gold medal at the 1998 Olympics in Nagano. Mario Lemieux then hired him as an assistant with Pittsburgh in 1999-2000, and the understanding was that he would be the first European head coach in the NHL the next year, on a Pittsburgh team with a number of Czech stars. Sure enough, Penguins GM Craig Patrick made the announcement (though Chicago nipped in and hired Alpo Suhonen days earlier), and Hlinka joined the team that fall. But his English was poor and, even worse, he used a defensive system that even the Czechs – Jagr, Straka et al. – hated. The team missed the playoffs, and Lemieux told Hlinka his communication needed to be better. Learn English, make the effort, and we'll keep you. He didn't, and they didn't. He didn't coach the Czechs at Salt Lake City, but he did accept a lucrative offer to coach in the Russian league for 2002-03, keeping his name in the game in another part of the ever-expanding hockey world.

Milan Hnilicka

Justin Hocking

HLUSHKO, Todd
b. Toronto, Ontario, February 7, 1970

Hlushko's dream of playing for Canada at the Olympics was clouded by the death of his father just a few months before he made the National Team and played for Canada in Lillehammer in 1994. He had devoted two years of his life to the team, and although he was nothing more than a fourth-liner, he scored two goals against France in one of the tournament's games. Not many players were drafted after Hlushko went 240th overall in 1990 (a dozen, in fact), yet he went on to join the Flyers after Lillehammer. After six seasons of part-time work, he headed off to Europe to play, though he still represented Canada at the occasional international tournament during the year.

HNIDY, Shayne
b. Neepawa, Manitoba, November 8, 1975

Buffalo drafted him, Detroit signed him, but only Ottawa played him. By the time he made his NHL debut, on October 5, 2000, he was almost 25, yet over the next 2 seasons, he was frequently a healthy scratch. He played a tough, conservative defence from the blueline but has yet to establish himself with the Sens.

HNILICKA, Milan
b. Litomerice, Czechoslovakia (Czech Republic), June 25, 1973

There was a hiccup in Hnilicka's early career, like that between the first two letters of his last name, yet there he is, in the NHL. Hnilicka was drafted in 1991, and after another year of goaling back home, he decided to play junior in the WHL to learn the North American game. He had an incredible 46-12-2 record, but after two years in the minors, he went home, figuring he'd play more and enjoy himself more. The NHL never seemed so far away. Back home, Hnilicka played internationally, winning gold with the Czech Republic at the 1999 and 2001 Worlds. It was only after the '99 tournament that the Rangers decided to sign him, but he played only twice for the team before spending the rest of the year in the minors. His big break came that summer when Atlanta signed the free agent, and since then he has been an important part of the expansion team's success.

HOCKING, Justin
b. Stettler, Alberta, January 9, 1974

A huge defenceman, Hocking was owned by four NHL teams but used by only one, Los Angeles, in a single game back in '93-'94. He has remained in the minors ever since, but a decade later the chances of him returning to the NHL seem remote, even though he's by no means old and has lots of hockey left in his skates.

HODGE, Charlie
b. Lachine, Quebec, July 28, 1933

Hodge likely set a record for being a backup goalie longer than any man. On the positive side, though, he is also one of a small number of players to be part of two distinct dynasties – in his case, Montreal of the 1950s and Montreal of the 1960s. He played his first game for the Habs in '54-'55, but with a guy named Plante in the cage every night, he wasn't likely to play much in any given season. Hodge spent far more time in the minors over the next decade, but he was around long enough to win Cups with the team in '58, '59, and '60. His finest year was '63-'64 when he played 62 games, led the league with 8 shutouts, and won the Vezina Trophy with a GAA of 2.26. Five of those shutouts came against Toronto, but the Habs lost in the opening round of the playoffs. The next year, his appearances diminished slightly, and by the following year he had serious difficulties because another great, this one named Worsley, was number one for the team. Hodge received a slight extension of his career when Oakland claimed him in 1967, and after playing his last, with Vancouver in '70-'71, he became involved in real estate in British Columbia. Later, he was hired as a scout by the Winnipeg Jets, focusing on west coast talent for the team.

HODGE, Ken
b. Birmingham, England, June 25, 1944

It was one of the most lopsided trades of all time. Ken Hodge, Fred Stanfield, and Phil Esposito were sent by Chicago to Boston for Gilles Marotte, Pit Martin, and Jack Norris on May 15, 1967. It was a deal that sealed Boston's fate as a Stanley Cup champion and ensured Chicago would never win one of its own during this generation of play. Hodge had played three seasons with Chicago, a talented prospect whose greatest weakness was his skating. It was also something he worked at relentlessly, and in his first year with the Bruins he had 25 goals. In his second season, he had 45. He won two Cups with the team, in 1970 and '72, and had his best years with Tom Johnson as coach. At one end of his career, he didn't see eye to eye with Harry Sinden, and at the other end Don Cherry disdained his attitude. In between, though, Hodge had two 100-point seasons playing on the greatest line in league history to date with Phil Esposito and Wayne Cashman. His scoring also came to life when he moved away from the banana blade he had adopted under the influence of Bobby Hull and Stan Mikita to an almost straight blade in 1970. Yet, he was always confused in Boston. The more he scored, the more fans booed him because they wanted him to be more aggressive, fight more. He finished his career in New York when Cherry came along, and like most Bruins he settled in Boston after retiring. He went into the printing supplies business.

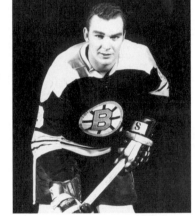

He won two Cups with the team, in 1970 and '72, and had his best years with Tom Johnson as coach.
KEN HODGE

HODGE, Ken, Jr.
b. Windsor, Ontario, April 13, 1966

Like father, like son. Sort of. Almost. Kind of. Okay, not really. Ken Jr. went to Boston College, of course, but from the day he was drafted by Minnesota in 1984 he admitted to having an attitude problem. Maybe he expected everything to come easily to him because of his old man. Maybe he took the NHL too lightly. Maybe he just wasn't good enough and was afraid to admit as much. The Stars traded him to Boston, of course, and in 1990-91 he had 30 goals. That's more like pops. Hodge, though, scored only 6 more NHL goals, one of the worst all-time follow-ups to a 30-goal season.

HODGSON, Dan
b. Fort Vermillion, Alberta, August 29, 1965

Everyone and his uncle knocked Hodgson without cessation during the kid's junior career in Prince Albert, even when he was tearing the league apart, even when he captained Canada to a gold at the 1985 WJC or was named Canada's outstanding junior at the end of that year. When he got to the Leafs for his first big chance that fall, he suffered a series of small injuries, but once healthy he just wasn't the same package he had been in junior. The Leafs traded him to Vancouver, but he performed no better, and by 1989 he was so far out of the NHL he couldn't hope to return. But, like all small, skilled players, a secondary career awaited him in Europe, and so Hodgson packed his things and went to the land of the small schedule and tax-free paydays to continue playing.

HODGSON, Rick
b. Medicine Hat, Alberta, May 23, 1956

Hodgson was a sturdy defenceman for Calgary in the Western league in the 1970s and was drafted by Atlanta. After finishing junior with the Centennials, he was shipped to Tulsa of the Central league, but it wasn't until Hartford joined the NHL in 1979 that he got his only NHL chance, with the Whalers.

HODGSON, Ted
b. Hobbema, Alberta, June 30, 1945

Anyone who can boast of having played with Bobby Orr is a million miles ahead of the rest of the hockey world. For Hodgson, four games in '66-'67 with Boston was all it took to make that claim, but the claim still stands. Hodgson, a full-blooded Indian, was truly a minor-leaguer, and even expansion in '67 didn't help him get

Charlie Hodge

Ken Hodge, Jr.

Dan Hodgson

Rick Hodgson

Ted Hodgson

Kevin Hodson

Cec Hoekstra

Ed Hoekstra

Phil Hoene

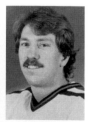

Bob Hoffmeyer

a full-time spot in the NHL. The startup of the WHA, though, was another matter, and in '72 he got into the pirate league for two years with Cleveland, though from there he was soon back in minor pro again.

HODSON, Kevin
b. Winnipeg, Manitoba, March 27, 1972
He had had enough. He was frustrated with the politics of the sport, upset no team seemed to want to give him a chance, down on himself. He wasn't having fun any more. He retired. He was 20 years old. Hodson had had a great junior career with the Soo, yet he was never drafted. Chicago signed him and wanted him to play in the minors, but he didn't want to. He returned to the Soo as an overager but quit and decided to work in a sporting goods store and with the mentally handicapped. He wanted to go to the University of Western Ontario and take business courses as part of a pre-law program. Then he changed his mind. He gave the Greyhounds another chance, and the team won the Memorial Cup. He was named the best goalie in the tournament. Detroit signed him, and this time he was prepared to work his game through the minors. He joined the team in 1995, and during his four years with the Wings he got his name on the 1998 Stanley Cup. Then, he was traded to Tampa and on to Montreal. He retired again, but after two years as an assistant coach in the OHL, returned to the NHL with Tampa in 2002, but only in a small role. Always a prospect, never a starter.

HOEKSTRA, Cec
b. Winnipeg, Manitoba, April 2, 1935
What's worse, to play for a last-place team every night, or to be part of an organization so good it always wants you in reserve and never plays you? Ask a man with pride, and he'll say the first option is always the preferable one. Hoekstra, though, was chained in perpetuity to the second option. Hoekstra won the Memorial Cup in 1954 with St. Catharines and turned pro in the Montreal system the next year. From 1956 to '60 the Habs won the Cup each spring, and Hoekstra was called up to the team four times. He didn't play a single game. He did get into four regular-season games in '59-'60, against four different teams, but beyond that he was in the minors his longest stay coming with Cleveland. Throughout his lengthy career, Hoekstra returned faithfully to St. Catharines every summer to work at the Golf and Country Club, and after hangin' up the blades he gravitated to the course. His first stop was the Windsor Park Country Club, then a club in Buffalo, and for more than a decade he was at Cherry Hill in Ontario.

HOEKSTRA, Ed
b. Winnipeg, Manitoba, November 4, 1937
The younger brother of Cec suffered a similar hockey fate, being buried in the minors for most of his pro life. Ed, though, did play a full season with Philadelphia during the first year of expansion. Like Cec, he played junior in St. Catharines, where the family moved with the help of Rudy Pilous just as the boys were ready to play serious teen hockey. For Ed, it was the Quebec Aces that gave him his experience throughout the 1960s, and after his season with the Flyers he ended

up in Denver, where he captained the team for a season. He was always among the least penalized players in whatever league he played in. Hoekstra retired early in the '69-'70 schedule, feeling he was no longer contributing, but Buffalo talked him out of retirement later in the year. Less than a minute into his return he broke his wrist and missed the rest of the year, but he did continue to play. After retiring for good in 1974, Hoekstra returned to St. Kitts, where he became a carpenter.

HOENE, Phil
b. Duluth, Minnesota, March 15, 1949
A small left winger who came out of the University of Minnesota-Duluth, Hoene played parts of three years with Los Angeles (1972–75). His claim to fame is almost unique. He scored his first goal on a penalty shot, a feat performed only once before, by Ralph Bowman back in 1934.

HOFFINGER, Dr. Val ("Doc")
b. Seltz, Russia, January 1, 1903
d. unknown
Without doubt, the least interesting part of this fascinating life was his two years in the NHL, 1927-29 with Chicago. Hoffinger grew up in Salvador, Saskatchewan, and bounced around in the pro game for a few years. He was recruited by the Germans to coach their 1936 Olympics team, and to that end he enlisted the services of some Saskatchewaners of German ancestry to tour Europe in preparation. Although he was well paid for his efforts, he was not allowed to leave the country with the money, so he remained and invested in an education. He studied chiropody in Berlin, and at one time was even introduced to Hitler. Hoffinger returned to Canada in 1939 and opened an office in Toronto. He was the personal foot doctor to a number of luminaries, including the terpsichorean Danny Kaye. Keeping his work his pleasure, he married Bernice Scholls, daughter of *the* Dr. Scholls, and they inherited the mega-company when the patriarch passed away.

HOFFMAN, Mike
b. Barrie, Ontario, February 26, 1963
Hoffman's NHL days were frustratingly brief in number and short on quality. He played nine games with Hartford in the 1980s and most of five years with the farm team in Binghamton before moving to Germany for a short time. Having had enough, he returned to Ontario and enrolled in Georgian College to complete his education, and he continued to play hockey for the team on a record-setting line with Mike Kappell and Craig Cullen, younger brother of John.

HOFFMEYER, Bob
b. Dodsland, Saskatchewan, July 27, 1955
Hoffmeyer came out of the West to play for Chicago, Philadelphia, and New Jersey (1977-85), though most of those years saw him spend in some time with the minor-league affiliates, mostly in Maine. As soon as he retired, the Devils kept him on as a special assignment scout, and after that he became an assistant coach under Doug Carpenter.

HOFFORD, Jim
b. Sudbury, Ontario, October 4, 1964

No goals, no assists, no points, 47 penalty minutes. Those were his NHL stats with Buffalo and L.A., but his contribution to the Rochester Americans is what Hofford would like to be remembered by. He played six years with the Amerks, three as captain, and helped the team win the Calder Cup in 1987. He was leader in penalty minutes when he retired in 1990, but he was also one of the most popular players the franchise ever had on its roster. As a result, he was later inducted into the Rochester Americans Hall of Fame.

HOFFORT, Bruce
b. North Battleford, Saskatchewan, July 30, 1966

Odd. Hoffort had two phenomenal seasons with Lake Superior State, but at age 23 he still hadn't been drafted. Philadelphia signed him as a free agent, and then an incredible thing happened in his short NHL career. Over 2 seasons, he played only 9 games, yet he was undefeated – 4-0-3. His GAA of 3.59 was not outstanding, but he remains the undefeated goalie with the most games played in a career.

HOGABOAM, Bill
b. Swift Current, Saskatchewan, September 5, 1949

Despite eight years in the NHL, Hogaboam played in just two playoff games. Nonetheless, he was a fleet skater who had a number of good years with Detroit and Minnesota in the 1970s, notably '76-'77 when he captained Minnesota and played 73 games, a season high for him. He ended his career in the minors, and then moved to Kelowna, B.C., where he got into the insurance business. He also ran practices for the Kelowna Wings of the Western league, and midway through the '84-'85 season he took over as head coach, despite a lack of experience.

HOGANSON, Dale ("Red")
b. North Battleford, Saskatchewan, July 8, 1949

After an outstanding junior career in Estevan, Hoganson spent most of his pro career dealing with a series of painful and debilitating injuries that would have forced the average man to pack it in. Yet, despite the physical setbacks and the bruising nature of being a defensive defenceman, Hoganson relished the competition and the challenge. In his first year with L.A. in '69-'70, he broke his ankle. The next year, it was his shoulder, and in the coming few seasons he had two operations on the right one and one on the left. Then it was his back, a seemingly mysterious pain that different doctors gave different names without a successful remedy. Hoganson went to

Montreal in the multiplayer deal that took Rogie Vachon to the coast, but then he went to the WHA in 1973 and didn't come out until the Nordiques joined the NHL in 1979. After two and a half more seasons, though, he called it a day and moved back to his ranch, raising quarter horses and purehead cattle, his summer job for all his playing days now his quiet, full-time job.

HOGANSON, Paul
b. Toronto, Ontario, November 12, 1949

His cousin was Dale, but Paul was a goalie. He started out in peewee playing left wing, but as these things happen, his coach needed a goalie for a game and stuck Paul in the nets. He never came out. He worked his way through junior in Ontario, but Pittsburgh played him only twice in '70-'71 and, unfortunately, he didn't play very well, allowing seven goals in less than a full game's worth of work. Hoganson joined L.A. in the WHA in 1973 and played much of the next five years in that league as his career wound down before it ever got going.

HOGLUND, Jonas ("Hogie")
b. Hammaro, Sweden, August 29, 1972

Rumour has it that the Swedes more or less booed Hoglund out of their league and that is why he ended up in the NHL in 1996 at age 24. He had played a number of years for Farjestad, but from day one in Canada he has given the modern Swede a bad name. Hoglund has size and skill, but not much grit and determination, qualities that go unnoticed in the regular season, perhaps, but are salient to any player's success in the playoffs. He had a decent first year with Calgary, but the Flames traded him to Montreal, where he had a less than enjoyable year and a half stay. He signed with the Leafs in the summer of 1999 and for two years was a boon to the team in games against the Habs, averaging a goal a game against his former team. The rest of the league was another story, and the post-season a relative nightmare. The Leafs traded Hoglund to Boston in the summer of 2001 for Kyle Wanvig, but a jammed fax machine caused the deal to be nullified by the NHL and Hoglund was back on the number-one line with Mats Sundin for a third year. And for the third year, he was Stanley Cup invisible, though slightly less so than in the first 2 seasons when he scored 2 goals in 22 games. Internationally, he has won a silver medal for Sweden at both the World Juniors (1992) and the WC (1997).

HOGOSTA, Goran
b. Tunabro, Sweden, April 15, 1954

The question is, really, why did the Islanders sign Hogosta in the summer of 1977? Yes, they had seen him

Bill Hogaboam

Internationally, he has won a silver medal for Sweden at both the World Juniors (1992) and the WC (1997).
JONAS HOGLUND

Dale Hoganson

Paul Hoganson

Goran Hogosta

Benoit Hogue

Terry Holbrook

Mark Holden

Bobby Holik

play well for Tre Kronor at the recent World Championships, his third WC tournament, but they had Billy Smith and Chico Resch back home, one of the top tandems in the game. Where and when would Hogosta play? In fact, he got into his only game with the team during a romp over the Flames. Coach Arbour gave Billy Smith a breather midway through the third period of a 9-0 game, and Hogosta did the rest. Sure, it's a cool trivia question (what goalie shared a shutout in his NHL debut?) but Hogosta was all minors until the Isles traded him to Quebec. He got into 21 games with the Nordiques but at season's end, returned to Sweden where he could continue his career more productively.

HOGUE, Benoit ("Benny")
b. Repentigny, Quebec, October 28, 1966
Hogue had 3 terrific 30-goal seasons with the Islanders (1991-94) that established him as a scoring centre, but once he had the rep he never lived up to the billing. He danced from team to team, each time hoping to find the spark from the Islanders days, and each team finally cut bait and let him go elsewhere. Dallas acquired him at the deadline in 1999, as insurance, and he gave the Stars a little depth down the middle during their successful playoff run. After that, it took him months to find work, but Phoenix signed him in January 2000. Ditto the next year and the year after as his career crawled to a close and Hogue looked to any team wanting to sign an experienced centre.

HOLAN, Milos
b. Bilovec, Czechoslovakia (Czech Republic), April 22, 1971
Pierre Gauthier was the creepy sleeze who released Holan from Anaheim's training camp in 1998. Sure, thousands of players have been dumped by thousands of coaches and GMs over the years, but Holan's situation was unique. His dad had played pro in Czechoslovakia, and Milos had started skating by age five. He was exceedingly talented, and in 1993 was named his country's player of the year. Philadelphia drafted him that year, but after eight games with the Flyers Holan was traded to the Ducks. At training camp in 1995, though, Holan's life changed. Doctors discovered he had chronic granulocytic leukemia. In layperson's terms, drugs would help in the short-term, but in the near future he would need a bone marrow transplant or he would die. His wife was pregnant and he continued to play for a few weeks, but then stopped playing and looked for a donor. A Maryland man who had registered with the national program tested a perfect match and was happy to help. On February 1, 1996, the transplant was made at the City of Hope Cancer Center, but after chemotherapy the 6', 200 pound defenceman weighed only 130 pounds. Holan, though, like any hockey player, was in superb physical condition, and within a year and a half he did, indeed, feel strong enough to play. He went to camp in Anaheim hoping to play one exhibition game, not for himself but to show the world that diseases can be beaten and perseverance can overcome illness. Gauthier said no. The Ducks, meanwhile, failed to make the playoffs that year, and attendance was on its

way south fast. Holan returned to the Czech Republic and resumed his career. Perhaps one day he will, in fact, play again in the NHL. Not with Anaheim, though.

HOLBROOK, Terry
b. Petrolia, Ontario, July 11, 1950
Holbrook wasn't long for the NHL. Drafted in 1970 by L.A., he debuted with Minnesota two years later after a trade sent him to the Stars. The right winger failed to stay on past two stints and in 1974 went to the WHA, where he ended his career.

HOLDEN, Josh
b. Calgary, Alberta, January 18, 1978
He came out of junior as a hot prospect, a kid who could skate, shoot hard, hit, and play a team game. Vancouver chose him 12th overall in '96, but his first four years of pro have been marked by misses more than hits. The Canucks traded him to Carolina, but soon got him back. They later traded him to Toronto. His career had taken a serious turn for the worse in 1998 when a skate severed ten tendons on the back of one of his hands. Since then, he's been surviving more than thriving.

HOLDEN, Mark
b. Weymouth, Massachusetts, June 12, 1957
Holden came to the attention of the Montreal Canadiens at the right time, but they just didn't feel he was the right goalie. In the immediate post-Ken Dryden years, the team was looking for a number-one man. Holden came out of Brown University, and after a few years in the minors his timing was bang on. In '83-'84, he was ranked ahead of Steve Penney in Nova Scotia, but in his one NHL game he was injured in a goalmouth scramble and had to leave the ice. Penney later rose to fame and locked up the starter's job for the next year, but with the departures of Richard Sevigny and Rick Wamsley, the backup job was still up for grabs. Holden didn't impress at camp, and the Habs traded him to Winnipeg, where he played his final few NHL games. He later became involved in coaching in the new Maritime Junior Hockey League.

HOLIK, Bobby
b. Jihlava, Czechoslovakia (Czech Republic), January 1, 1971
Back home, he was always Robert. In North America, he is the friendlier Bobby. Opponents call him much worse. His hockey stock can't get much better. His father, Jaroslav, was a great player and later coached the Czechs to gold at the 2001 World Championships. His sister was a world-ranked tennis player. His uncle, Jiri, was also one of the greatest Czech players of all time. And his brother-in-law is Frantisek Musil, also of the NHL. Bobby might have been the most complete player ever to come out of his country. He began his rise to prominence at the 1990 World Championships, playing on a line with Jaromir Jagr and Robert Reichel, and that fall he came to North America. He was a mammoth 6'4" and 230 pounds. He had phenomenal quickness and used his body to purpose. He could score as well as anyone, and he could check the best players in the league onto the ice. Bobby started with Hartford in 1990, but two years later the Whalers gave

him to New Jersey with a draft choice for Sean Burke and Eric Weinrich. In Jersey, he just got better and better. During the regular season he contributed offensively, and during the playoffs he shut down the best the other team had to offer. The result was two Stanley Cups – in 1995 and 2000 – and an outstanding career to date. A teetotaler, he swears to drink only champagne, and only out of the Cup. He became an American citizen in 1996 and more than most players frequented museums and other places of culture during the team's downtime. In the summer of 2002, a free agent, he signed a massive contract with the Rangers and promptly had the worst year of his career.

HOLLAND, Jason
b. Morinville, Alberta, April 30, 1976
Holland has some of the parts to be an NHLer, but all of them? Time is quickly suggesting no. He came out of Kamloops after winning consecutive Memorial Cups with the Blazers in '94 and '95, and in 1996 he won gold with Canada's junior team. Since starting for the Islanders in '96-'97, though, he has been humbled by the experience of not making it for the first time in his life. Stints in Buffalo and L.A. haven't improved his fortunes, and the big defenceman is still trying to make it happen in the big tent.

HOLLAND, Jerry
b. Beaverlodge, Alberta, August 25, 1954
If only every game were like his first, minors or NHL, take your pick. The Rangers drafted Holland in 1974 and sent him to the minors for the proverbial seasoning. In his first game with the Reds, he scored four goals. And he didn't lose his touch over the course of the season. He finished with 44, tops in the league, and was named rookie of the year. The Rangers called him up for a game, and he scored in that, too. Next year, though, the bloom was off the rose, and he scored a more average seven goals in half a season. He never saw the NHL again, though he did skate briefly with Edmonton in the WHA a few years later.

HOLLAND, Ken
b. Vernon, British Columbia, November 10, 1955
Way back when, when dinosaurs roamed the earth and water was blue, Holland aspired to be an NHL goalie. The Leafs drafted him and he played all of four games for Hartford and Detroit, but it was after he tossed aside his pads that his career really began. Holland started as a western scout for the Wings in 1985, working his way up to assistant general manager and working closely with Scotty Bowman to put together the two Cup teams in the 1990s. He became GM outright in 1997 and put together his own championship team in 2002 with a

blend of talented newcomers and mostly veterans, notably Dominik Hasek, Brett Hull, and Chris Chelios to go with longtime Wings Steve Yzerman and Brendan Shanahan. Holland played only 206 minutes as a goalie, but his life as a GM seems to have many years left in it.

HOLLAND, Robbie
b. Montreal, Quebec, September 10, 1957
Holland's dream went sour pretty quickly. The Montreal native was drafted by the hometown Habs in 1977, but after two years with Nova Scotia the Habs decided they didn't need him and traded him to Pittsburgh to get Denis Herron. He allowed a lot of goals (177) in not a lot of games (44) during his 2 years in the Igloo, and Holland wound up playing in the Central league for a good number of years. The Islanders acquired his rights for the ever-nebulous "futures" but never put him into another NHL game.

HOLLETT, William "Flash" ("Busher")
b. North Sydney, Nova Scotia, April 13, 1912
d. Oakville, Ontario, April 20, 1999
Hollett might well be the greatest defenceman not in the Hockey Hall of Fame. He played more than 30 years B.O. (before Orr), yet he was to the between-the-wars generation what Orr was to the generation following expansion. He started with Toronto in 1933 and carried on to Ottawa over the first few years of his career, but it was with Boston that he established himself as the first and finest rushing defenceman. He played on the blueline with partner Dit Clapper, and the two were instrumental in the Bruins' run to the Cup in 1939 and again two years later. In '41-'42 he set an NHL record with 19 goals for a defenceman, a mark he equalled the year after and improved by 1 in '44-'45 with Detroit, the year he was named to the First All-Star Team. By the time he was done with the NHL in 1946, his 132 goals was second all time to King Clancy (136). He retired from the NHL after a contract dispute with Jack Adams and due to his desire to please his wife and stay in southern Ontario. He played senior hockey and won the Allan Cup in his final year before settling into a career with a brokerage house in Toronto. In his later years he struggled with heart problems and cancer and died of a heart attack in a nursing home just outside Toronto.

HOLLINGER, Terry
b. Regina, Saskatchewan, February 24, 1971
You're born out west in the heart of the Canadian Prairies, you play junior for Regina and St. Louis drafts you. You work hard in the minors, you try your damnedest, you think you can make it. You're just not

His 132 goals was second all time to King Clancy (136).
FLASH HOLLETT

Jason Holland

Jerry Holland

Ken Holland

Robbie Holland

Terry Hollinger

Gord Hollingworth

Bill Holmes

Charlie Holmes

Lou Holmes

dreaming of playing for the Iserlohner Roosters. Yet, that's what happened. The Blues played him only five times in '93-'94 and '94-'95, and after many years in the "I" Hollinger decided to accept an offer to play in the DEL in Germany. It wasn't the NHL, but it was hockey.

HOLLINGWORTH, Gord ("Bucky")
b. Montreal, Quebec, July 24, 1933
d. Hampton Beach, New Jersey, February 2, 1974
Hockey rules. Life sucks. Hollingworth is proof. Here's a guy who was a rock, a strong, physical player in top shape, a fine hockey player, a well-liked person. Then, in a game in Rochester on February 23, 1962, while captaining his Hershey Bears, he fell ill. He was taken to hospital, and doctors diagnosed him as having chronic leukemia. Adopting a proper lifestyle would ensure his life, and step number one in that regard demanded no strenuous activity. He put on his equipment that night like any other; he took it off in the hospital for the last time. Hollingworth had come up through the Montreal system but played in the NHL with Chicago and Detroit in the mid-1950s. He went down to Hershey, where he became an experienced leader, but after that night he retired to Hampton Beach, New Jersey, where he ran a hotel and acted as executive director for the Chamber of Commerce in that city. After a few years, he built his strength up to the point that he scouted for St. Louis. He later became a referee for amateurs and high school players until his death in 1974 at age 40.

HOLLOWAY, Bruce
b. Revelstoke, British Columbia, June 27, 1963
Despite playing pro hockey for only three seasons, Holloway managed to play for five different teams in three leagues, including a two-game stopover in '84-'85 with the Canucks, the team that had drafted him three years earlier after a junior career in the WHL.

HOLMES, Bill
b. Portage la Prairie, Manitoba, March 9, 1899
d. Ridgeway, Ontario, March 14, 1961
The 1920s didn't roar for Holmes so much as whisper a few NHL thoughts in a quiet decade of pro play. He played with the Canadiens and Americans, so his North American content was covered, but even in the semi-pro and minor pro ranks his position was always somewhat tenuous.

HOLMES, Charlie
b. Edmonton, Alberta, September 21, 1934
A perfect 17-year career in the Western league was

broken only by 2 brief appearances for the Detroit Red Wings, the first a 15-game callup in '58-'59, the second an 8-game stint 3 years later. Holmes retired from the WHL having played almost exclusively for Edmonton and Seattle. His 926 total games played in that league was among the all-time leaders, and in 1971 he became head coach of the Totems, the team he had ended his playing days with the previous spring. He later coached in Europe.

HOLMES, Harry "Hap"
b. Aurora, Ontario, February 21, 1892
d. Fort Lauderdale, Florida, June 28, 1941
One of the greatest, longest-serving, and most successful goalies in hockey's early years of pro play, Holmes was considered a fearless netminder who could, on a given day, outperform anyone. He started with the Toronto Blueshirts of the NHA in 1912, winning a Cup with them in his second year. He went out west to play in the Pacific Coast league with Seattle, and won a second Cup with the Metropolitans in '16-'17. Toronto lured him back when the NHL began in 1917, and he won his third Cup with the Arenas in the league's first year. Holmes then went back to the west and stayed in Seattle for a number of years, moving up the coast to Victoria for the '24-'25 season. Not surprisingly, he won a Cup with the Cougars, and to this day is part of a small group of men to win the trophy with four different teams. He closed out his career in the NHL when the Cougars players were brought east to form the new Detroit entry. After 2

He moved to Florida for the weather and operated a fruit farm until his sudden death.
HAP HOLMES

seasons and 17 shutouts in 85 games, he retired in 1928. The next year, Holmes became associated with the Cleveland entry of the AHL, helping bring hockey to that city. He was coach, manager, and part owner for a number of years, but ill health forced him out of the day-to-day management of the team. He remained stockholder and assistant manager of the Cleveland Arena, but he moved to Florida for the weather and operated a fruit farm until his sudden death. In 1941, the AHL introduced the Harry Holmes Memorial Trophy, presented annually to the league's best goalie. Holmes was inducted into the Hockey Hall of Fame in 1972.

HOLMES, Lou
b. Rushall, England, January 29, 1911
Holmes had his only NHL action in 1931 to '33 with Chicago, his days over by the time he was 22. He settled into a career out west, mostly in Edmonton and Portland, and after the war he returned to Edmonton to settle down. He became coach of the Edmonton Mercurys and took the team to Oslo,

Norway, where the Mercs won a gold medal at the 1952 Olympics, the last Canadian team to place first for fully a half-century.

HOLMES, Warren
b. Beeton, Ontario, February 18, 1957

Holmes always had a special spot in his heart for Saginaw. It was with the IHL Gears that he first played pro back in 1977-78, and it seemed whenever he had no place to play he could always count on that city to welcome him. The Kings gave him his only NHL games, but it wasn't a legit chance to be a player on the team. He wound up in their farm system, and then back in Saginaw, and after he retired he stayed there in an administrative capacity, eventually becoming assistant coach in 1997, the team now in the United Hockey League.

HOLMGREN, Paul
b. St. Paul, Minnesota, December 2, 1955

Animal is just about the only appropriate word to describe Holmgren, a goon who was brought in by Philadelphia during their brawling days in the 1970s to continue the fighting, maniacal ways of a team that seemed to pride itself on not having too much talent. His career almost ended in 1976 when he hurt his right eye in a fight. He needed two surgeries, and although he never regained anywhere near full vision, it was still good enough to club Carol Vadnais over the head with his stick and to club Torrie Robertson over the eye with a stick and to kick another player and to give referee Andy Van Hellemond a punch. Holmgren actually scored 30 goals with the Flyers in '79-'80, proof that even on a goon team someone has to score. Hockey was done a greater service when his career eventually ended due to a series of injuries, the most serious of which were – surprise, surprise – to his shoulders. Hockey, however, was not spared his absence for long, as he went on to coach those same Flyers for four years and then coach and manage in Hartford. In his eight years behind the bench, his team made the playoffs only once, and even during this time he could not stay out of trouble. He was convicted of drunk driving and admitted to having a problem with alcohol, one he strove to tackle in the only admirable and worthy fight he ever had during his ugly, ugly career.

His career almost ended in 1976 when he hurt his right eye in a fight.
PAUL HOLMGREN

HOLMQVIST, Johan
b. Tofta, Sweden, May 24, 1978

Between a rock and a hard place is not where a young goalie wants to be, but as a hopeful with the Rangers that's just where Holmqvist finds himself. The starter there has been Mike Richter, and during the 2001-02 season 18-year-old Dan Blackburn emerged as the clear backup and, toward the end of the year, a possible threat to Richter as the go-to guy. This means Holmqvist has to sit in the minors and wait for Richter to retire or move on, and even then he doesn't seem likely to usurp young Blackburn. Only time will tell, of course, but Holmqvist came to the team with fine credentials in the Swedish league and WJC play.

HOLMSTROM, Tomas
b. Pitea, Sweden, January 23, 1973

There aren't many long-shot stories to outdo Holmstrom's, who in 1994 was drafted at age 21 a cosmic 257th overall by Detroit. Yet there he was two years later, making the team and winning the Stanley Cup, though he made only one playoff appearance. To prove that this was no fluke, his contribution the year after to Cup number two was all-encompassing, and for Cup number three in 2002 he was again a valuable member of the team. He gave Scotty Bowman some versatility from the left wing – a few goals, disciplined play within the system – and 400 games into his NHL career, he is one of the all-time great low low low draft choices.

HOLOTA, John
b. Hamilton, Ontario, February 25, 1921
d. Denver, Colorado, March 10, 1951

It was a mystery, but the tragedy was the greater upset the night of March 7, 1951. Holota was in a car driven by Bill Warwick. With them were Denver Falcons teammates Bruce Giesebrecht and Motto McLean, and George Homenuke, trainer of Omaha. They said they were driving home, but they were going in the opposite direction. Apparently no alcohol was involved because police pulled Warwick over and gave him a ticket for running a red light. An officer said later that had Warwick been drinking, the ticketing constable would have detected as much and not let them continue. Continue they did, though, and the story was that the men got lost. What is known without argument is that Warwick hit a construction barrier, smashed into a concrete bridge, and flipped the car into a ditch 10 metres below the road. All the men were hurt, but only Holota seriously. He was taken to hospital, where he lost consciousness and died three days later. Doctors said the injuries in the crash didn't kill him – a weak heart did. Holota had played during the war with the Red Wings, then found his niche in the AHL, where he became one of the league's top scorers.

HOLST, Greg
b. Montreal, Quebec, February 21, 1954

Holst was small and skilled, but he was never going to

Johan Holmqvist

Tomas Holmstrom

John Holota

Gary Holt

Randy Holt

Toots Holway

Ron Homenuke

be a force in the NHL in the 1970s. He played a while for the Rangers and very quickly decided to pursue a career in Europe, where his speed and quickness were more suitable for success. Holst settled in Austria in 1978 – and has never left. He played in leagues there for 15 years, got his citizenship and represented Austria at 4 World Championships ("B" pool), and then stayed on as a coach, eventually helping the national team reach "A" pool. He was assistant to Ron Kennedy at the 2002 Olympics in Salt Lake City and has made an enormous impact on Austria's small hockey program.

HOLT, Gary
b. Sarnia, Ontario, January 1, 1952
Only a year older than brother Randy, Gary played 101 NHL games in a career devoted more to Salt Lake City in the CHL. In all, he played six years for the Golden Eagles during their developmental years in the 1970s, when he racked up some impressive penalty-minute numbers in front of what must have been confused and shocked Mormon eyes.

HOLT, Randy
b. Pembroke, Ontario, January 15, 1953
Four goals in 395 games gives a hint as to why Holt is in the record books, and it ain't for playin' pretty. On March 11, 1979, Holt accrued a minor, 3 majors, two 10-minute misconducts, and 3 game misconducts. His 67 penalty minutes is a record for 1 game and it typified the contribution he made to the game and his teams. Of course, the standard excuse is that somebody had to do it, and Holt was the guy, the policeman, the protector. Whatever. He started with Chicago in 1974 and ended with the Flyers a decade later, and along the way he was suspended many times, once a 10-game sentence for clubbing Billy MacMillan over the head, another for pushing a linesman. He was a minus player every season he was in the league, and he played for seven teams during his NHL years. In his spare time, Holt had a passion for, of all things, growing flowers.

HOLWAY, Albert "Toots" (sometimes Holloway)
b. Belleville, Ontario, September 24, 1902
d. Belleville, Ontario, November 20, 1968
Toots and brother Bouncer (a.k.a. Howard) were top prospects in the 1920s. Toots got his big break when the Toronto St. Pats signed him in 1924, and after two seasons he joined the Maroons, who went on to win the Cup that spring of '26. He went down to Stratford for two years before getting one final NHL chance with the short-lived Pittsburgh Pirates. He then settled in London, playing and later managing with

He started out as a figure skater, but it didn't take him long to convert to the art of shooting and hitting.
BRIAN HOLZINGER

the Tecumsehs, a very reputable outfit of the day. He and Bouncer bought a gas station in Belleville in 1930 and another in Trenton a short time later. It was good insurance for him, because a few years later he suffered a serious tendon injury that, in effect, ended his playing career. He settled in Belleville and coached junior in the city. After selling the businesses, he worked as a salesman for O'Keefe Breweries and died of bowel cancer in 1968. In 1987, he was among the inaugural inductees into the Belleville Sports Hall of Fame.

HOLZINGER, Brian
b. Parma, Ohio, October 10, 1972
The Hobey Baker Award is presented annually by the Decathlon Athletic Club of Bloomington, Minnesota, to honour the best player in U.S. college hockey. Sometimes it goes to a player who becomes great (e.g., Paul Kariya), sometimes to someone who never makes it to the NHL (e.g., Lowell Macdonald's son, Lane). Holzinger fits somewhere in between. He went on to play in the NHL, but he certainly didn't have a Kariya-like presence when he joined Buffalo in 1995, the same year he won the Hobey after an outstanding career with Bowling Green. He started out as a figure skater, but it didn't take him long to convert to the more manly art of shooting and hitting. He was cut from the 1994 U.S. Olympic team but went on to have a great senior year with the Falcons. After six seasons with Buffalo, Holzinger was traded to Tampa Bay, and it is there that the centre has tried to continue making progress in the meat of his career.

HOMENUKE, Ron
b. Hazelton, British Columbia, January 5, 1952
Yes, he's a one-game wonder, but with Homenuke, the accent is on the "wonder" not the "one-game" for very, very good reason. In October 1976 he went climbing on a glacier off the coast of British Columbia. He lost his footing, fell more than 650 metres, and had to learn to walk all over again. His career was over, his marriage ended, but he came to be a believer. From that time on, he devoted himself not just to God but to children, primarily in Manila. He became a missionary, but that had serious drawbacks at first. He contracted hepatitis and typhoid fever, and later dengue fever, a far more serious strain. In 1994, though, he moved from Manila to the more remote and sedate Olongapo City to the north, and ever since he has been working with impoverished children, trying to make their lives better, their circumstances more conducive to happiness and success. His one game with Vancouver in '72-'73 was a long time ago, indeed.

HOOVER, Ron
b. Oakville, Ontario, October 28, 1966

Hoover's slice of NHL life consisted of a thin wedge of playing time with Boston and St. Louis to the tune of 18 games. He was better known for his career in the "I" with Peoria in the 1990s, where he had four 20-goal seasons. After retiring in 1998, he became a medical representative for a supplier of orthopaedic parts.

HOPKINS, Dean
b. Cobourg, Ontario, June 6, 1959

The son of a construction company owner, Hopkins had the requisite winter backyard rink to play and play and play on as a kid with his brother. He turned in a fine junior career with London and then went to L.A. in the '79 draft. He surprised himself by making the team that first year – he admitted his skating was weak – but four middling seasons saw him in the minors for as lengthy a stay. Edmonton and Quebec each gave him a chance, but by and large the last eight years of his career came in the AHL.

HOPKINS, Larry ("Hoppy")
b. Oshawa, Ontario, March 17, 1954

Hopkins not only made the NHL out of a Canadian university, he did so after turning down a chance to attend Atlanta's training camp in 1974, the year the Flames drafted him. Instead, he opted to attend the University of Toronto, where he earned a degree in business and commerce and captained the varsity team in his final two years under coach Tom Watt. After graduating, he got into his first pro games with his dream team Maple Leafs, but that was all the chance he got there. He attended the Detroit camp the year after to no avail, and later the following season he was signed by the Winnipeg Jets. This was no surprise, because the coach was that same Tom Watt who regarded him so highly. Hopkins went on to play 41 games in '81-'82, scoring 10 goals in his only semi-regular duty in the NHL.

HORACEK, Tony
b. Vancouver, British Columbia, February 3, 1967

Horacek came out of the Western league in 1989 to join Philadelphia, the team for whom he played 116 games over the next 3 years. The left winger scored just nine goals, though he didn't see much ice time, and the Flyers traded him to Chicago for Ryan McGill on February 7, 1992. A briefer stint with the Hawks led to a few years in the minors, and when he retired he stayed down below as a coach, eventually winding up with the Hershey-Metro Falcons in Junior B.

HORAVA, Miloslav
b. Kladno, Czechoslovakia (Czech Republic), August 14, 1961

A career that stretched into 4 decades touched down for just 80 NHL games, but Horava was greater as a Czech hero than as a North American pro. He was drafted by the Rangers at age 19 in 1981, but he didn't join the team – wasn't allowed to – for another 7 years. For more than 20 years before and after that brief time with the Blueshirts, Horava played in the Czech league, and this, in turn, prepared him for a long list of international appearances: 2 World Juniors, 5 WC, 3 Canada Cups, and 4 Olympics. He was never considered a spectacular defenceman, but he was there for every major tournament for many, many years.

HORBUL, Doug
b. Nokomis, Saskatchewan, July 27, 1952

He wasn't real Horbul, but he didn't last long in the NHL, either. Horbul was originally drafted by the Rangers in 1972 and developed in the AHL, where he had a fine season with Providence before being claimed by Kansas City in the Expansion Draft. He lasted just four games, but did get to keep a puck from his one and only NHL goal, and after that he had a career in the AHL.

HORCOFF, Shawn
b. Trail, British Columbia, September 17, 1978

If he's with Edmonton, he must be able to skate. He can. Horcoff's dad was a university player, and Shawn went to Michigan State to develop his skills. He was a finalist for the Hobey Baker Award in 1999-2000, the same season he was named CCHA player of the year. He joined the Oilers that fall and is slowly working his way into a roster spot on the club, though his best years are still ahead of him and his future is by no means determined.

HORDICHUK, Darcy ("Hordy")
b. Kamsack, Saskatchewan, August 10, 1980

One of a growing number of players with a Web site, Hordichuk has no problem talking about fighting and his role as an enforcer. It's the new model, though, one in which he shows respect for other sincere tough guys, not the model cut from the Ted Lindsay cloth of an eye for an eye. Hordichuk did win a Turner Cup championship with Orlando in the "I" and he is by no means an NHL regular yet despite his pride in "team." which, to date, has meant Atlanta and Phoenix for brief stays.

HORDY, Mike
b. Thunder Bay, Ontario, October 10, 1956

Hordy's NHL career lasted 11 games with the Islanders (1978-80), but he made his best contributions in the CHL, where he helped his Fort Worth Texans win the championship in '78. He proved a capable offensive defenceman, though he didn't register a single point during his time with the Isles.

HORECK, Pete ("Pistol")
b. Massey, Ontario, June 15, 1923

The Michael Peca of his day, Horeck packed a ton of meanness and physical punishment into his 145-pound body. He signed his first pro contract with Atlantic City in 1941 and wound up in Chicago three years later, establishing a reputation as a ferocious checker who was both fearless and reckless. His first 2 NHL seasons came with 20 goals apiece, but midway through his third year he was traded to the Red Wings. In Detroit, it was more of the same and he became a fan favourite, the little guy who could. Again, though, he was sent on, this time to Boston, and in the first round of the '51 playoffs he had his most controversial moment when he chased after a loose puck, racing

Dean Hopkins

Larry Hopkins

Miloslav Horava

Doug Horbul

Pete Horeck

Toronto goalie Al Rollins. They collided, and Rollins was lost for the series with ligament damage to his knee. The Leafs, though, were incensed and suitably inspired to victory. Horeck announced his retirement almost immediately, citing an excellent business opportunity with a jewellery store in Chicago, but once he got there he quickly unretired and continued to play for another season in the NHL and then several more in northern Ontario. He settled in Sudbury and started Pete Horeck Enterprises, a business for marketing chocolate bars and like products in northeastern Ontario. Although he once suffered a serious cut to his foot during his playing days, his worst hockey injury, ironically, came in 1975 during an old-timers' game when he broke his leg. He never skated again after that.

Shorty Horne

HORNE, George "Shorty"
b. Sudbury, Ontario, June 27, 1904
d. Lake Gogoma, Ontario, August 1, 1929
Horne came out of Sudbury, where he played with the Cub Wolves before embarking on a pro career that took him first to the Maroons in 1925. The very next spring, the team won the Cup, though Horne didn't skate in the playoffs. He was ill for part of the next season but made a full recovery and played a fine role on the Maple Leafs in '28-'29. Tragedy occurred that summer, though, when he embarked on a prospecting trip with three friends. They went out canoeing one day, and Horne dove into the water and never surfaced. He was considered a fine swimmer, and the cause of death was never ascertained beyond being called a drowning.

HORNER, Reginald "Red"
b. Lynden, Ontario, May 28, 1909
Dainty little flyweights like Dave Schultz and Tiger Williams each led the NHL in penalty minutes four times during their NHL careers. Horner led the league in minutes in the sin bin for *eight successive years!* He was the champion of bad men, a man so feared and strong he once appeared on the cover of *Maclean's* magazine. Horner grew up in Toronto and played in a church league and with the Marlies at the same time. Conn Smythe saw him and knew this was an NHLer. Despite playing Friday night and Saturday afternoon, Horner was called on by Smythe to play that Saturday night, December 22, 1928, at the Arena Gardens on Mutual Street. The defenceman didn't impress with his skating, but he could move the puck, and every time he hit his man the wind went out of the building. From that day forward, he never played anywhere or for anyone other than the Leafs. Horner was on hand

Horner led the league in minutes in the sin bin for eight successive years!
RED HORNER

the night of November 12, 1931, when the Leafs moved into their new building, Maple Leaf Gardens. He was on hand at season's end when the team won the Cup, a victory that would prove to be his only one. While the Leafs went to the finals most years in the 1930s, they always lost, with the exception of '32. Horner quickly established himself as a great hitter and even greater fighter who was at first challenged by all and later feared. In December 1933, after Eddie Shore ended Ace Bailey's career with a vicious check, Horner knocked Shore, one of the toughest men of all, unconscious with one punch. He was booed wherever he went, a sure sign of his popularity as the Bad Man of the NHL. In 1938, he became team captain for the final two years of his career, and after retiring in 1940 he never stayed close to the team the way many players do. Horner was an astute businessman. He worked for 15 years with Elias Rogers Fuels Ltd. and then moved to Canada Coal Corporation Ltd. where he became president until retiring from the business world. He was inducted into the Hockey Hall of Fame in 1965, and on February 13, 1999, he helped say goodbye to the great arena he had said hello to some 68 years ago. Horner dropped the opening puck at the final game in the Gardens, and then was part of the opening of the Air Canada Centre a week later. He is the oldest surviving Leafs player, the oldest member of the Hall of Fame, and the only player still left from that historic Cup champion team of 1932. He spends half his year in Toronto and then goes to Florida for the winter, where he still strokes a pretty fair golf ball.

HORNUNG, Larry
b. Weyburn, Saskatchewan, November 10, 1945
d. Regina, Saskatchewan, May 8, 2001
Good people don't deserve bad fates, so it's completely without reason why Hornung had to watch his son play for Regina one night in 1987. Young Brad was a good NHL prospect, but on this night he was hit from behind and never got up. He fell headfirst into the boards and wound up paralyzed for the rest of his life. Every dad wants to see his son play hockey, but this was an unwarranted affront on any man's dreams for his kids. Larry had a brief NHL career in the early 1970s and spent some time in the minors before closing out his career in the WHA, where he played every season but the last. After retiring, he became a scout for the Jets and later the Coyotes, and in 1998 the Leafs lured him away as their scout. It was in that capacity he was serving when he found out in 2000 that he had cancer, a disease that took his life a year later.

Larry Hornung

HORTON, Miles "Tim"

b. Cochrane, Ontario, January 12, 1930
d. St. Catharines, Ontario, February 21, 1974

Cochrane, Ontario, was no heaven on earth, no northern paradise to draw unhappy city dwellers. It's a place to be born in and then leave, especially if you are born into the poverty Horton was in 1930. Hockey was his refuge and his salvation, and when he was recruited by the Leafs and sent to St. Mike's, he couldn't have been happier. From the first day to the last, he made a name for himself as a strong man, strong as in there is no one stronger. No one. Between 1949 and '52 he worked his way into the Leafs, playing in the minors and earning two brief callups to get his feet wet. He made the team in 1952 and was forced to wear contact lenses because of his weak eyesight, the first NHLer to do so. Horton spent the next 22 years in the NHL, playing more games on defence than anyone in the history of the game. Fortunately for opponents, Horton was a peaceable man rather than fighter. He used his strength to control players bent on starting a fight, and his bear hug was known as a preventative measure to which there was no countermeasure. He could hug a player around the ribs and break them, but he did so only when necessary. The early part of his career was dominated by one check that Horton received rather than dished out. Late in the '54-'55 season, he collided with Bill Gadsby of the Rangers and broke his leg so badly he was in a cast all summer and missed half of the following year. It took a while for him to get back on track, but when he did he was better than ever. Horton was paired with Allan Stanley when he got to the team in 1958, and together they formed the team's foundation. Horton was a fast skater and good puckhandler capable of creating offence, and with Stanley the team won three successive Cups in 1962, '63, and '64. After one more win in 1967, though, the team went into decline and Horton was the last great defenceman left standing. As a result, he demanded an exorbitant salary – $80,000 a year – and got it, and for '69-'70 he was the oldest blueliner on the team by some 16 years. Nonetheless, few players have remained as effective into their forties as Horton. He was later traded to the Rangers, Pittsburgh, and Buffalo, and with the Sabres his life came to a tragic end. After playing a game against Toronto at the Gardens, Horton drove back to Buffalo. Alcohol was involved in the car crash, and the hockey world mourned the loss of one of its greatest players. During his days with the Leafs, Horton had tried numerous business ventures and failed, but in 1964 he and partner Ron Joyce opened a Tim Hortons

During his days with the Leafs, Horton had tried numerous business ventures and failed.
TIM HORTON

doughnut store. It was a success, and they expanded with franchises throughout Canada. But Horton's great play and business acumen had a price. He drank too much and became dependent on painkillers (also found in his blood during the autopsy) and was not a picture-perfect husband for wife, Lori, and their four daughters. After Tim's death, Lori became a pill-popping alcoholic and sold her interest in the business to Joyce for a paltry $1-million. She claimed later that she didn't know what she had done and tried to regain ownership, but after several intense and nasty lawsuits, Joyce won the day. When Horton died, there were 39 Tim Hortons stores (the apostrophe was ditched at some point). In 2001, there were more than 2,000 stores across the country, generating more than $1-billion in business. Yes, that's *billion*. Horton was inducted into the Hockey Hall of Fame in 1977 and his number 7 was later retired by the Sabres and honoured by the Leafs.

HORVATH, Bronco

b. Port Colborne, Ontario, March 12, 1930

His career was as long as his schnozz was big, but for Horvath nothing was bigger than the '59-'60 season. That year, he was at the height of his powers. He centred Boston's famous Uke Line with Johnny Bucyk and Vic Stasiuk. He played in the All-Star Game on the one-game famous H line with Gordie Howe and Bobby Hull. And he placed second in league scoring, though he lost the title in his own building to his nemesis. Both he and Bobby Hull had 80 points heading into the last game of the season, but that night Hull got an assist and Horvath was blanked. He led the league with 39 goals, though he never scored more than 30 in any other season. During the pre-expansion days, he played for five of the six teams (all but Detroit), and after a six-year hiatus in the minors he closed his career with a few games in Minnesota in '67-'68. He went on to coach junior in Cape Breton and London, then retired to his home in South Yarmouth, Massachusetts, where he opened a dry cleaning business.

Bronco Horvath

HOSPODAR, Ed ("Boxcar")

b. Bowling Green, Ohio, February 9, 1959

Some called him the best open-ice hitter in the game; others called him a goon; others called him much worse. Regardless, it was his job to hit and disturb and keep the other team distracted, and throughout the 1980s he was one of the best at those skills in the game. He was suspended for brawling and broke his hand while fighting. The best goons from around the league were after him and some accused him of acting. He frequently changed teams and retired at the ripe old age of 29. And like many a fighter before him, as soon

Ed Hospodar

as he left the game he became a pacifist. In his case, this change in philosophy manifested itself in a serious and successful business organizing and overseeing year-round clinics to help young players master every art and skill needed to turn pro – except, of course, fighting.

HOSSA, Marcel
b. Ilava, Czechoslovakia (Slovakia), October 12, 1981
The younger brother of Marian, Marcel is having a bit more trouble establishing himself in the NHL. Like Marian, he played junior in Portland, but Marcel has been in the Montreal system with only a short foray into the Bell Centre (née Molson Centre). He was called up for a few games in 2001-02 but started the next season in the minors.

HOSSA, Marian
b. Stara Lubovna, Czechoslovakia (Slovakia), January 12, 1979
The Hossa clan sure knew how to play hockey. Papa Frantisek played for Dukla Trencin for many years and produced two pros as sons, Marian and Marcel. Marian immediately came to North America after being drafted by Ottawa in 1997, spending the next season with Portland and helping the team win the Memorial Cup. He also made his debut with the Sens, and the year after he was one of the starting left wingers on the team. Since then, he has developed from being a good prospect into a young star, and he seems perfectly capable of taking the next step as a spectacular and consistent NHLer, a regular 30-goal man. What he has still to learn is to take his game to another level during the playoffs, something he started to do in the spring of 2002 when he had 4 goals in the Ottawa's 12 games.

Greg Hotham

Doug Houda

Claude Houde

> **Papa Frantisek played for Dukla Trencin for many years and produced two pros as sons, Marian and Marcel.**
> **MARIAN HOSSA**

HOSTAK, Martin
b. Hradec Kralove, Czechoslovakia (Czech Republic), November 11, 1967
A big prospect for Philadelphia in 1987 yielded surprisingly few results for the team when it brought Hostak into the fold in 1990. He brought little to the team despite his wealth of experience and success in Czechoslovakia, and after a year and a half Hostak repaired to Sweden to continue his career. He still was considered desirable by his own national team and played at the 1994 Olympics in Lillehammer and the Worlds in 1995, his third WC appearance.

HOTHAM, Greg
b. London, Ontario, March 7, 1956
At first, it looked like it just wasn't going to happen. Although the Leafs drafted Hotham in 1976, they stuck him in the IHL for two years. Hotham played hard and persevered, and in 1979 he made the team

as a regular part-timer, not exactly a main man on the blueline but a guy the team would call up from the minors without hesitation. The next two years just got worse, though, and Hotham wound up skating on wood with a team called the Cincinnati Tigers – remember them, Leafs' trivia buffs? – until Pittsburgh acquired him. Coach Eddie Johnston made Hotham a reclamation project of sorts, and for more than two years he was a steady and experienced defenceman on the team. Of course, all good things must pass, and Hotham passed out of the NHL and into the "A," where he finished his career. He moved back to Simcoe County in southern Ontario and raised a son who himself has gone on to play a bit of hockey.

HOUCK, Paul
b. Vancouver, British Columbia, August 12, 1963
After an exceptional sophomore year with the University of Wisconsin in '82-'83 in which he scored 38 goals, Houck had increasingly poor seasons in his junior and senior years and crawled rather than flew into the pros. As a result, Edmonton traded their draft choice before playing him, and Minnesota used him for only a few games over three seasons. Houck wound up going to Holland, where he put up U of W numbers.

HOUDA, Doug
b. Blairmore, Alberta, June 3, 1966
Houda first played hockey as a five-year-old with Darcy Wakaluk in the Crowsnest Pass minor hockey system, and both would go on to the NHL. The two remained friends, and were best man at each other's wedding later in life. Houda played junior in Calgary and was drafted by Detroit. He got into his first game with the Wings at the end of the '85-'86 season, though he had been to two training camps. It was the start of a 15-year career that had minor-league spasms and included 2 stints with both Buffalo and Detroit. Houda was a rugged defenceman who always seemed to be in the wrong place at the wrong time. In all his NHL years, his teams made the playoffs just three times, and he never won a round. In all, he played more than 1,000 games of pro, more than half of which came in the NHL.

HOUDE, Claude
b. Drummondville, Quebec, November 8, 1947
Oddly, Houde got his NHL games in at almost the very end of his career, playing for Kansas City in parts of two seasons (1974-76) shortly before retiring. His first year ended early after he separated his shoulder, and his second year just didn't impress management, as the saying goes.

HOUDE, Eric
b. Montreal, Quebec, December 19, 1976

Local boy drafted by local team plays locally in the NHL, then heads so far south the NHL looks as if it's at the North Pole. Houde was a decent prospect in junior, but the Habs always jump on anyone with a French name in the hopes he can revive the old glory of the team. For most of the last 20 years, they have been disappointed, and Houde is but one case in point. He was called up for parts of three seasons, but it was clear Montreal wasn't going to play him and he walked away a free agent. Although he later signed with Edmonton and Phoenix, neither has seen him as anything more than stock for the minors.

HOUGH, Mike
b. Montreal, Quebec, February 6, 1963

There was a time not so long ago that this guy was a real player. He came out of junior in 1982, winning a Memorial Cup with teammates named Al MacInnis and Scott Stevens. Unlike those two, though, Hough struggled a bit to make the NHL. He spent three years in the minors, and each year the points increased as did his work ethic, and by 1986 he was with the Nordiques for most of the season. Hough spent the first seven years of his career with Quebec, assuming the team captaincy in 1991-92, the year he played on a line with Joe Sakic and Owen Nolan. In the summer of '93, his rights were tossed twice in a matter of days, first to Washington and then to Florida, and after four years with the Panthers he ended his NHL days with the Islanders.

HOULDER, Bill
b. Thunder Bay, Ontario, March 11, 1967

Houlder took a little longer to develop than most, and NHL teams took a little longer to decide he was pro material. He joined Washington in 1987, but although he saw NHL action in each of his first six years, he was really a callup and minor-leaguer. But in '92-'93, he had a breakthrough season in the "I" with San Diego. He was named the best defenceman in the league and named to the First All-Star Team, and as a result Anaheim claimed him that summer in the Expansion Draft. Ironically, although he was now a bona fide NHLer, he was also being batted around pretty regularly. Over the next seven seasons, he didn't play a single game in the minors, but he did change teams five times. Always wanted, never needed. His most recent stop took him to another new team, Nashville, where the veteran was expected to bring experience and stability to a young and only marginally talented team.

HOULE, Rejean ("Reggie")
b. Rouyn, Quebec, October 25, 1949

The chances of Houle being hired in an executive capacity outside Montreal are exactly nil. Always were, always will be. He played his entire career with the Habs, though his value as trivia goes back a bit further, to the Amateur Draft of 1969. Montreal was awarded the first two draft choices for French Canadians – as biased a rule as ever existed in the league – and it chose Houle 1st overall and Marc Tardif 2nd. Houle joined the Habs that fall and had continuous service to the team except for the 1973-76

period, when he played for the Nordiques in the WHA. His early years with the Habs had been frustrating, and both fans and media were harsh critics of his play. In the more relaxed environs of the WHA, he peaked with 51 goals in his final season, though when he returned to the Canadiens his numbers halved. In all, he won five Cups with the team, though he was more passenger than hero each time. After retiring in 1983, Houle worked for Molson for a dozen years, but in 1995 the Habs hired him as general manager even though his resumé for the job was as blank as his stare would become from the press box. He saw Montreal through some of its worst days and made a number of awful trades, though the one he'll be most remembered for – Patrick Roy – was the one the player forced. Nonetheless, he didn't exactly win the deal. He sent Roy and captain Mike Keane to Colorado for Jocelyn Thibault, Andrei Kovalenko, and Martin Rucinsky. Houle was fired in 2000 and replaced by Andre Savard.

HOUSLEY, Phil
b. St. Paul, Minnesota, March 9, 1964

Before he had played a single NHL game, Housley said he'd be greater than Bobby Orr. When a reporter politely suggested those were pretty big skates to fill, Housley noted in that way that is particularly American that he had pretty big feet. Twenty years later, it's safe to say not one part of Housley's play came remotely close to Orr's, with the exception of the "games played" column of his stats. For starters, his teams have missed the playoffs more often than they've made it, and the closest he came to the Cup was in 1998 when his Washington was swept by Detroit in the finals. Other than that year, his teams have won exactly one playoff round. Housley certainly lasted a long time, though. Amazingly, he played his first NHL game the same year he finished high school, making the jump to the NHL the way few before him had done. He played more than 1,300 games and averaged nearly a point a game. He scored 20 goals 7 times, peaking with 31 in his second season, and 5 times he had more than 50 assists in a season. He played for seven teams, his longest stay being his first, Buffalo, which lasted eight years until he was traded to the Jets in the summer of 1990. Always a classy and gentlemanly performer, he appeared in seven All-Star Games but only once, in 1992, was he ever elected to the end-of-year All-Star teams. Housley has also been faithful to the U.S. national program, four times playing at the WC, as well as the Canada Cup in '84 and '87 and winning the World Cup in 1996. His first World Championships came, incredibly, before he ever played in the NHL, in 1982, the same year he also played for the U.S. at the WJC. Brash remarks of the 18-year-old, pre-NHLer aside, Housley has, indeed, had a career to be proud of – just not Orr-like proud.

HOUSTON, Ken
b. Dresden, Ontario, September 15, 1953

Ken Houston played in the NHL from 1975 to '84, but one season in particular stands out above the rest: 1980-81. The year couldn't have started more horribly for the big right winger as he was felled by a case of

Eric Houde

Mike Hough

Bill Houlder

Rejean Houle

Phil Housley

Ken Houston

Frank Howard

Garry Howatt

chronic hepatitis. He missed half the season and spent as much time at the Mayo Clinic as with his family or teammates. Still, he managed 15 goals for Calgary during the regular season, but his best was yet to come. In the quarter-finals of that year's playoffs, he was key to one of the great upsets of the decade as the Flames eliminated Philadelphia, winning game seven on Spectrum ice by a score of 4-1. In that series, Houston tied an NHL record by scoring five power-play goals, and although the team lost to Minnesota in the next round, Houston had hammered home his importance to the team. He had six 20-goal seasons during his career, and while by no means a household name he seemed able to lift those around him to play better as a team. It was widely acknowledged, for instance, that Houston was the reason Kent Nilsson played his best hockey when the two played together. Houston hit hard and skated with every ounce of energy. He proved time and again that if you try your best at all times, good things will happen.

HOWARD, Frank ("Jack")
b. London, Ontario, October 15, 1911

His only NHL games with Toronto came on November 26 and 28, 1936, in an AHL career that lasted exactly 10 years. Howard, who was often and erroneously referred to as Jack, was a typical defenceman of the day, a solid hitter and stay-at-home type.

HOWATT, Garry ("Toy Tiger")
b. Grand Centre, Alberta, September 26, 1952

When Howatt was 14 years old, everything seemed great. He played hockey, lived on a beautiful farm in the middle of nowhere, went to school with friends, and had a great family. One day, he didn't feel well, went home, and had what was later diagnosed as an epileptic seizure. From that day forward, Howatt has had to take a strict regimen of pills to minimize the risks of further attacks, but he was able to control things to the point that he made it to the NHL and had a tremendous impact with the New York Islanders. He was nicknamed Toy Tiger because he was small and ferocious. He fought one and all, never backed down, and seldom came out on the wrong end of a fight. Incredibly, the only seizures he had during his career came right after the season, the comedown, as it were, after a year-long high of playing. Howatt was an original Islander from 1972, so it was sweet and just reward that his last two years with the team, '80-'81 and '81-'82, were Cup-winning seasons. He was most effective with Bob Nystrom and Dave Lewis as a crashing and banging third or fourth line. During his career, he had three agents: the first, the fraudulent Dick Sorkin, cost Howatt a good deal

of money. As a result, Howatt became an agent in 1986 shortly after he retired, hoping to serve players in ways he hadn't been during his most fruitful years. He joined Harvey Lakind of International Artists and Athletes Management and later developed a golf facility in Mount Freedom, New Jersey.

HOWE, Gordie ("Elbows"/ "Power"/ "Mr. Hockey")
b. Floral, Saskatchewan, March 31, 1928

His first pair of skates were so big that he had to wear street shoes to make them fit properly. This didn't deter Gordie Howe from playing at every opportunity, and as he grew older he worked as a ditch digger and labourer, developing muscles that would one day make him the strongest player in the NHL. At 15, he was

At 15, he was invited to the New York Rangers training camp.
GORDIE HOWE

invited to the New York Rangers training camp, but the youngster had never been away from home before and grew so homesick that he left early to return to the farm. The next year, he attended Detroit's camp, and from the first time Detroit GM Jack Adams saw Howe play, he knew he was watching someone special. Adams sent Howe to junior for a year, in Galt, and the year after, Howe turned pro at age 17 with Omaha, the Red Wings' USHL affiliate. In 1946, Howe made the NHL with Detroit and began a career that has no parallel. In his rookie season he had only seven goals, but he established himself one night by knocking out Maurice Richard with a single punch. At 6', 200 pounds, he was one of the bigger players in the league, and he was extraordinarily strong. He liked to use his elbows to make a little room for himself on the ice, but he was still shy and quiet. Soon enough, Howe was on a line with his best friend, another young player named Ted Lindsay, and Sid Abel, a veteran centreman who helped develop the young stars. Called the Production Line, they became the highest-scoring threesome in the game. In 1949-50, the three players finished 1-2-3 in the scoring race, Howe scoring 35 goals. It was clear he was now the best young player in the league, and he was now playing with a poise and confidence that belied his age. At 22, he had already played four full seasons in the NHL, but in the 1950 playoffs that seemed to be what his career totals would be. In game one of the semi-finals, he took a run at Ted Kennedy of Toronto. Kennedy got out of the way and Howe stumbled head-first into the boards at full speed. The injury was not just horrific, it was life threatening. He broke his nose and cheekbone, lost some teeth, and suffered a serious concussion and fractured skull. His condition worsened overnight at hospital, and doctors feared for his life. They performed an operation to relieve pressure on his brain, and Howe's strength was

Gordie Howe

pushed to the limit. He recovered slowly, but as his team rallied behind him and went on to the finals, he followed them on the radio. When the Wings won the Cup at home in game seven, fans chanted, "Gordie! Gordie!" until he came out of the stands in a suit and appeared on ice with his teammates. He started the next year wearing a helmet, and in the coming years he picked his fights more carefully. His ferocity to compete, however, had not diminished. In that '50-'51 season, Howe led the league in goals (43), assists (43), and points (86), testament to his rise to the top of the league. He powered his way to the net and usually played 45 minutes a game, and he was the only truly ambidextrous player in the game, a man who could skate down the left wing and shoot left on one shift and then do the same from the right wing on the next. He was also an economical skater. He always kept his legs moving but accelerated and used his full energy only when he needed to. The next year, he again led the NHL in goals and points and took the Wings to their second Cup in three years. He helped the Wings win two more Cups, in 1954, and '55, but then the team slowly fell into the middle of the pack as Montreal, Boston, and Toronto surged into the contenders' role for the Cup. Howe was not to fall back, though. In all, he led the league in goals five times and points six times. He also won the Hart Trophy six times, and he played in the All-Star Game every year from 1948 to 1971, with one exception when he was injured. He scored at least 23 goals for 22 consecutive seasons, and 17 times he played the complete schedule of games in a season. His longevity has no compare, and his ability to play at the highest level for so long defies genetics. He was among the top-ten scorers in the league for 21 consecutive seasons, but by 1971 he had arthritis in his wrists that made it too painful to play effectively any longer. After 25 seasons in the game, Howe retired as the all-time leader in games played, goals, assists, and points. He had surgery on his wrists and then took a desk job with the Red Wings, a job he ultimately felt was unimportant. Bored, he was pulled in the opposite direction by an offer so dreamlike he had to pinch himself. In February 1971, he had played a charity game in Detroit with his sons, Marty and Mark. Then, in 1973, the Houston Aeros wanted to sign the two boys and have the old man come out of retirement to play on a line with them. Father playing with son had never been accomplished at such a high level of the game, but Gordie and the boys said yes and history was made. For six amazing years, the three Howes played together, and then in 1979 another chance came to fruition. The WHA was merging with the NHL, and the Whalers (to whom the Howes had migrated after four years in Houston) was one of the

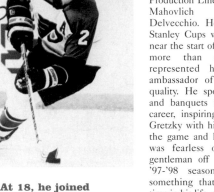

At 18, he joined the WHA in a move that was historic and controversial.
MARK HOWE

merging teams. Gordie agreed to play one final NHL season, with Mark and Marty, at age 52. Amazingly, Gordie was no embarrassment. He scored 15 goals and had a +/- rating of +9, but the highlight of the season came during the All-Star Game in Detroit. Coach Scotty Bowman named Howe to the team, and when the old man skated out during the introductions, a reverential applause shook the new Joe Louis Arena unlike anything before in hockey. Howe's first All-Star Game came in 1948, and his last was some 32 years later. His linemate, playing in his first NHL season, was Wayne Gretzky. Howe retired at season's end with incomparable numbers: 26 seasons, 801 goals, 1,049 assists, 1850 total points. Amazingly, he never scored four goals in a game, never scored an overtime goal, and never had a 50-goal season. Nevertheless, he won four Stanley Cups and did have 103 points in '68-'69 at age 41, a record that almost certainly won't be broken. That record came while playing on the Production Line II with Frank Mahovlich and Alex Delvecchio. Howe won four Stanley Cups with the Wings near the start of his career, but more than anything, he represented hockey as an ambassador of incomparable quality. He spoke at dinners and banquets throughout his career, inspiring a 10-year-old Gretzky with his dedication to the game and his fans. Howe was fearless on ice and a gentleman off it. During the '97-'98 season, Howe did something that, for the first time in his life, created as much criticism as praise. He had played hockey in every decade from the 1940s to the 1980s, and he decided to play a single shift with the Detroit Vipers of the IHL so that he could say that he had played pro hockey in six decades. Some viewed this as an unnecessary and unworthy publicity stunt, while others, notably Gretzky, defended Howe and talked about the importance of the unofficial record to Howe. Either way, the arena was sold out, and a 69-year-old Howe skated for one shift to give himself this distinction. Howe was inducted into the Hockey Hall of Fame in 1972. Despite the 30-team NHL of the 21st century, no player has appeared in more games than Howe (1,767) and only Gretzky has bettered his various scoring records. Howe remains in a class by himself, a man who owes his life to hockey but who is owed as much by the game he helped fortify and develop.

HOWE, Mark

b. Detroit, Michigan, May 28, 1955
Six weeks to the day after watching her husband, Gordie, win the 1955 Stanley Cup with Detroit, Colleen Howe gave birth to Mark, a strapping lad who grew up to be an excellent hockey player in his own

Gordie Howe

Mark Howe

right. How good, though, we'll never fully know for sure, as a serious injury prevented him from reaching his full potential. Because of his dad, Mark had dual citizenship, and at the tender age of 16 he played for the U.S. at the 1972 Olympics in Sapporo (Canada didn't compete that year). From there he went on to play for the Marlies, and in 1973, at 18, he joined the WHA in a move that was historic and controversial. It was controversial because Howe was violating the NHL's agreement of drafting that dictated a player had to be 20 before he could play professionally. It was historic because he made the move so he could play for the Houston Aeros with his brother Marty and his dad, the very Gordon himself. It was – and remains – the only time father and sons have played together on a sheet of pro ice. It was a sensational spectacle, but Mark and Gordie were of a calibre that made the occurrence remarkable rather than preposterous. Mark was a rushing defenceman of the first order, and he played with his old man right through '79-'80 when the three Howes joined Hartford of the NHL. But on December 27, 1980, Mark's life changed forever when he slid hard into the middle of an old-style net. The sharp base plate lifted in the collision and stabbed him in the buttock, almost paralyzing him. He lost pints of blood, and although he recovered, he was never going to be a rushing defenceman again. He became a superb defenceman nonetheless and soon moved on to Philadelphia, where he played for 10 years. He was named to the First All-Star Team three times and played in four All-Star Games, and in 1992 he realized a dream by signing with Detroit, the team his dad had made so famous. As he got older, he began to experience back problems, which caused him to miss much of '90-'91. By the time he got to Detroit, he knew the end was nigh. After retiring in 1995, Howe stayed on with the Wings in an administrative capacity and worked with the team's young defencemen in the minors.

HOWE, Marty
b. Detroit, Michigan, February 18, 1954

Murray Howe never had a problem with his dad's fame and wanted no part of trying to be an NHLer himself. Mark was a bona fide star in the pros, and Marty was comfortably in between. By no means did he have Mark's skill, but he was not handed a career nicely gift-wrapped simply because of his surname. Like Mark, Marty played for the Marlies before joining bro and dad in the WHA in 1973. He joined the two in Hartford for '79-'80 in the NHL, but played only six games before breaking his arm and missing most of the rest of the year. He later played briefly for Boston before returning to the Whalers, where he retired in 1985. One summer

Marty Howe

in the 1980s he suffered a serious burn to his leg when the generator belt on his powerboat engine caught his pant leg and burned a hole in his skin. He required several skin grafts and was laid up for two months. Howe established himself in Hartford as a real estate agent after his playing days were done, though he also had business connections through an investment firm in Detroit. After this hiatus, he got the hockey bug again and started to coach, first in the Colonial League and later in the IHL.

HOWE, Syd
b. Ottawa, Ontario, September 28, 1911
d. Ottawa, Ontario, May 20, 1976

As a kid, Howe skated on Patterson's Creek and the Rideau Canal. He was an outstanding athlete in high school, but hockey was always nearest to his heart. In 1926, he played for the Lansdowne Park Juveniles, and a year later he moved up to the Ottawa Gunners in the new city league. In the spring of 1928, the Gunners met the Regina Monarchs for the Memorial Cup, and although they lost, they were the first Ottawa team to compete for the top junior trophy in Canada. Howe moved up to the NHL's Senators for a dozen games the following season. He was loaned to Philadelphia the next year, and then continued on to Toronto, Ottawa, and St. Louis before finally landing in Detroit in February 1935. He spent the next 12 years of his life there, developing into one of the top forwards on the team. Howe was on the ice at 2:25 a.m. on March 25, 1936, when teammate Mud

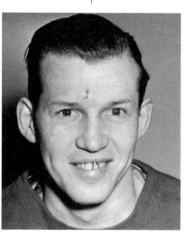

By the time he retired in 1946, he was the all-time scorer in the NHL with 528 points.
SYD HOWE

Bruneteau scored in the sixth overtime period to give the Wings a 1-0 win over the Canadiens in the longest game in NHL history. Amazingly, the Wings mustered enough energy to win the series and the Cup, and they won again the next year. Howe's most important individual contribution to the Wings came on March 19, 1940, when he scored in overtime to give the team a 2-1 win over the Americans in a quarter-finals game. It stood as the fastest OT goal for 29 years, though Detroit failed to win the Cup that year. On February 3, 1944, he scored six goals in a game, a modern-day record that has been equalled twice since but never surpassed. Although he never led the league in any one offensive category, he was a consistent scorer and playmaker. By the time he retired in 1946, he was the all-time scorer in the NHL with 528 points, though that record has been surpassed many times. He lived in Detroit year-round and worked for the Ford Motor Company in the summers. After retiring, he was convinced by Tommy Gorman to return to Ottawa and play senior hockey, which he did for a season. When his brother passed away, Howe took over the daily running of Howe Sporting Goods Store. He entered the civil service two years later with the Department of Supply and Services, working as a purchasing agent. He was inducted into the Hockey Hall of Fame in 1965.

HOWE, Vic
b. Saskatoon, Saskatchewan, November 2, 1929

Wayne Gretzky has his Brent. Mario Lemieux has his Alain. Larry Robinson has his Moe. And Gordie Howe has his Vic, the obscure, minor figure of a brother lurking in the shadow of the great man. Vic never had Gordie's drive and ambition, and obviously never had his skill, but the boys played together as kids with their older brothers, Vern and Norm. Gordie moved away to pursue the NHL, and Vic didn't, yet he was still talented enough that teams took notice. His first NHL game for the Rangers was against Gordie and Detroit in 1951, and after that he played 1 game in '53-'54 and 29 more the year after, during which time he scored his last 2 NHL goals. Vic went on to play senior hockey in Regina and Nelson and came to know Percy Nicklin, who later became manager of the Harringay Arena in England. Howe wrote him and got an invite to play for the Racers in 1956 for two seasons, including a number of exhibition games on the Continent. He played his last six years of serious hockey in Moncton, and it was there he got a job with CNR as a constable, one he kept for more than 30 years.

He went to the Rangers camp in 1952 and for the next 21 years played in the NHL.
HARRY HOWELL

HOWELL, Harry
b. Hamilton, Ontario, December 28, 1932

In 1949 the University of Michigan offered Howell a scholarship in hockey, an unheard of gesture for a future NHLer of that era. Howell, of course, rejected the offer so he could play junior with Guelph, and it was there, with the Biltmores, that he developed into a superb defenceman. He went to the Rangers camp in 1952, made the team, and for the next 21 years played in the NHL. Unfortunately, although he played an incredible 1,411 regular-season games, he played only 38 times in the playoffs. He never made it to the finals, and despite his greatness as a player he holds records for most seasons and games played without a Stanley Cup. Howell played 17 of those 21 years with the Blueshirts, missing only 37 games during that time. At the start of his fourth season, '55-'56, he was named team captain, and at 22 he became the youngest "C" man in league history. Most of the 1950s and '60s, though, were lean years for the team as a whole, and Howell was merely a bright spot in a dark hole that was the Rangers. His career peaked in '66-'67, the year he was named to

the First All-Star Team and won the Norris Trophy. For the succeeding eight years, it was won by Bobby Orr. That year was also highlighted by January 25, 1967, Harry Howell Night at Madison Square Garden. He was showered with gifts and cheers, and it was a rare honour, indeed, for a Rangers player to be accorded such attention by the team. In the summer of '69, Howell was sold to Oakland and had renewed inspiration to play well. In that off-season, he had had serious spinal fusion surgery and the Rangers figured his career was over. He played four more years with the Seals and then the L.A. Kings, retiring and returning almost every season. From 1973 to '76, the pattern repeated itself in the WHA as he couldn't quite leave the game. When he finished with the Calgary Cowboys in 1976, at age 44, he knew every ounce of energy had been squeezed out of him. Howell began a long and fruitful career as a scout, with Minnesota, and in '78-'79 he was appointed interim coach for 11 games. He later became director of player personnel for the team until retiring. Ironically, he was inducted into the Hockey Hall of Fame in 1979, the same year as Orr, the man who took possession of Howell's Norris Trophy.

HOWELL, Ron
b. Hamilton, Ontario, December 4, 1935
d. Hamilton, Ontario, March 16, 1992

To the hockey world, he was the brother of Hall of Famer Harry Howell, the lesser-known, less skilled player who appeared with the Rangers for three games in '54-'55 and one

Ron Howell

more the year after. Pro hockey, though, was just one side of him. Howell played 12 years in the CFL for Hamilton, B.C., Toronto, and Montreal. His specialty was punt returning, during an era when blocking punts was illegal and returning them all the more hazardous. Howell returned five for touchdowns, a record. In 1958, he was named the outstanding Canadian in the East, and after he retired from both sports he remained more faithful to his hometown Tiger Cats than any other of his former teams. He died too young, of cancer, after losing part of his stomach and esophagus in the battle, though not before getting in a final round of golf with his friends.

HOWSE, Don
b. Grand Falls, Newfoundland, July 28, 1952

Howse made everyone in Newfoundland proud in 1979 when he got into his first NHL games, adding his name to the small list of players to come from that province. He played some junior in Ottawa, and although Montreal signed him in 1973, the Habs were at the height of their powers and never used him.

Don Howse

Dave Hoyda

Jiri Hrdina

Jim Hrivnak

Instead, he played for the farm team in Nova Scotia for six seasons until the Kings signed him. Howse wasn't spectacular in any one facet of his game, but he did play 33 times for the Kings that year. He retired shortly after and went into minor league coaching.

HOWSON, Scott
b. Toronto, Ontario, April 9, 1960

Here's one for the history books. Before hitting the NHL, Howson played in the CHL for Indianapolis. In 1982-83, he helped the team win two Adams Cups (CHL's version of the Stanley Cup), and in the second of those he scored two overtime goals, both coming at the exact same time: 6:08! That's odd. Howson wasn't, though. His dad, Rich, had once captained the U of T Blues in Toronto, and Howson did something pretty incredible when the Islanders called him up in early 1985: He scored four goals in his first four games. These were his only four goals, though, and he was sent back to Springfield after only eight games. The year after, he lasted 10 games in what proved to be his final season of pro. Howson returned to Toronto and graduated from Osgoode Law School in 1990. Four years later, he was hired as GM of the Oilers farm team in Cape Breton, and he remained with that team for several years until Kevin Lowe hired him as an assistant in Edmonton, a position he still holds.

HOYDA, Dave
b. Edmonton, Alberta, May 20, 1957

Quiz time. He played in the 1970s. He was drafted by Philadelphia. He was big. Was he (a) a skilled player (b) a scoring star through junior, or (c) a thug? The correct answer is neither (a) nor (b). Hoyda was part of the Broad Street Bullies during their waning, desperate years when Montreal's skill had long conquered the barbarian antics of the Spectrum "assassins" and he lasted even fewer games when Winnipeg claimed him in 1979.

HRDINA, Jan
b. Hradec Kralove, Czechoslovakia (Czech Republic), February 5, 1976

Hrdina is a perfect example of the modern Euro player. He played teen hockey in Czechoslovakia and once he decided to take hockey to the next level, he came to Canada and played in the WHL, where Pittsburgh drafted him in 1995. He worked his way up through the minor pros and since 1998 has been a fixture at centre for the Penguins, assuming an ever more important role with the team and responding with ever greater statistics since the departure of Jaromir Jagr. Hrdina is the core of the future of the team as Mario Lemieux enters the twilight of his return and new blood will be needed to keep the team successful.

HRDINA, Jiri
b. Mlada Boleslav, Czechoslovakia (Czech Republic), January 5, 1958

The literal translation of his name is George Hero, and hero he was back home for a number of years. Hrdina played on the cusp of international freedom, and although he wasn't permitted to join Calgary in 1984 when the team drafted him, he was allowed to go four years later after the 1988 Olympics. The next year, he helped the Flames win their first Stanley Cup, and midway through '90-'91 he was traded to Pittsburgh. It was a unique trade. It was certainly based in part on Hrdina's skills, but it was also based simply on his being Czech. The Pens wanted a protective friend for their young teen star, Jaromir Jagr, who was new to the country and league and spoke very little English. Hrdina made his contributions both ways, and the Pens won Cups in the two years he was with the team. He was never the most talented player, but he played extremely well within his means and this had endless value for his reputation. After retiring following that '92 Cup with Pittsburgh, Hrdina became a scout for Calgary and later Dallas.

Hrdina is a perfect example of the modern Euro player.
JAN HRDINA

HRECHKOSY, Dave
b. Winnipeg, Manitoba, November 1, 1951

Hrechkosy came out of the 'Peg to play minor pro in the early 1970s until California acquired his rights from the Rangers. In his first full season, '74-'75, he had an incredible 29 goals on an awful team, and sported a haircut so peculiar his team mates called him Flintstone for a time. Although he didn't win the Calder Trophy, he was voted northern California's athlete of the month for February '75 by the Citizens Savings Athletic Foundation, and that's no joke. Hrechkosy struggled through another half-year before being traded to St. Louis, and 28 games later he was back in the minors.

HRIVNAK, Jim
b. Montreal, Quebec, May 28, 1968

It's been more than a decade since Hrivnak last saw NHL rubber hurled his way, but in recent years he's kept his pads in the game in Europe, where the shots are just as hard. Hrivnak had an outstanding career with Merrimack College and joined the Washington Capitals in 1990. Over the next 5 years, though, he played for 3 teams and never appeared in more than 27 games in a season. Nonetheless, his career record is nicely above .500.

HRKAC, Tony
b. Thunder Bay, Ontario, July 7, 1966

It was Hrkac's ninth life that proved his best, at least for goals. Hrkac came out of the University of North Dakota flying. He won the Hobey Baker Award that year, the first UND player to do so, after a season in which he had a record 125 points in a 48-game schedule. St. Louis had dibs on him, the first but not the last team to give him a chance to make it big in the NHL. Over the next six years, though, Hrkac failed to make a dent in any of the four team lineups he appeared in at various times. Yet amazingly, among those NHL ruins was the '92-'93 season spent in the IHL, when he won the scoring championship. St. Louis gave him another half-chance, and then Hrkac went back to the minors. He was 27, he'd had his chance, and it looked like sayonara. For three and a half years he played in the IHL, affirming his reputation as a great passer, and in 1997 he made it back to the NHL, this time with Dallas. The Stars let him go and then signed him again for '98-'99, a propitious time for Hrkac, who lasted a full season in the NHL for the first time in eight years and won a Stanley Cup as a result. Since then, he's remained on top, most recently with Nashville, his ninth team, just one shy of Michel Petit's cross-country journey with 10 NHL teams. Ironically, it was with the Predators, a woeful team lacking talent, that Hrkac had a career-high 18 goals in 2001-02. The previous season, with Anaheim, he was involved in a fight with mild-mannered Pierre Turgeon. It was his first fight in all his years in the league.

He took the Kings to their only appearance in the Cup finals, in 1993.
KELLY HRUDEY

HRUDEY, Kelly
b. Edmonton, Alberta, January 13, 1961

The personable and insightful commentator on *Hockey Night in Canada* began his life in hockey as a goalie, the one with the headband. He came out of Medicine Hat to play for the Islanders in '83-'84, a team hoping he'd become the next Billy Smith. Unfortunately, he was joining the team as its dynasty was ending, and he didn't have the same team in front of him as Smith had during the great years. Hrudey played parts of six years with the Isles, and only once, during his last, had a sub-.500 record. He appeared in the famous playoff game against Washington that the Islanders won in the fourth overtime, one of the longest games ever played. The Islanders traded him to L.A. on February 22, 1989, and it was with the Kings he had his finest years, playing behind the likes of Wayne Gretzky and Rob Blake. He took the Kings to their only appearance in the Cup finals, in 1993, though the team lost to Montreal in five games. He rounded out his career with 2 years in San Jose, a

career that, in some ways, false-started in 1984 when he was on the Canadian Olympic team roster until the Americans complained that he was a professional (having played 10 games for the Islanders at that point). He was eventually left off the team, though he did play for Canada later at the World Championships. Toward the end of his career, his teams routinely out of the playoffs, Hrudey joined *Hockey Night in Canada* as a colour commentator on Don Cherry's off nights. Articulate and insightful, Hrudey became a full-time member of the HNIC team when he retired, a position he continues to hold.

Tony Hrkac

HRYCUIK, Jim
b. Rosthern, Saskatchewan, October 7, 1949

Hrycuik won the Calder Cup with Hershey in 1973-74 during a year in which he scored 26 goals. His play impressed the expansion Washington Capitals, which claimed him in the Intra-League Draft, and Hrycuik made the Caps at training camp that fall. Or did he? He has the distinction of scoring the first goal in franchise history, October 9 against the Rangers, but although he had six points in his first nine games, he didn't feel secure with the team. He was scratched for some games, sat on the bench for stretches of others, and wasn't supported by the coaching staff. Soon enough, he was demoted, and a year later he was out of the game for good.

Jim Hrycuik

HRYMNAK, Steve
b. Port Arthur, Ontario, March 3, 1926

Back with Port Arthur before the war, Hrymnak developed into a solid player capable of filling any position except goalie. He joined the military as a member of the armoured corps for a year, and when he came out he was ready to turn pro. He started off in the Rangers system, though Chicago was so impressed by his play in New Haven that the Hawks bought his rights and dressed him in St. Louis. Hrymnak became team captain, and as he went, so went the team. The Hawks called him up for much of December '51 to January '52, using him mostly on defence. He captained the team in St. Louis for two years, playing every position but goal, and then on September 23, 1952, the Hawks sold him with Red Almas and Guyle Fielder to Detroit. Outside of two playoff games with the Wings, Hrymnak remained in the minors, eventually returning to Port Arthur to play senior hockey and begin a career in coaching.

Steve Hrymnak

HRYNEWICH, Tim
b. Leamington, Ontario, October 2, 1963

Hrynewich did the dumbest thing a guy can do when

Tim Hrynewich

Bill Huard

Willie Huber

Greg Hubick

he joins the NHL. He made the Pittsburgh Penguins in 1982 out of junior in Sudbury, and came to the team with long, flowing hair. Dumb. One initiation later, his head looked more army than Goldilocks, but he was now a player. Not for long, though. He played regularly at first, then sat on the bench for long stretches, and finally he was sent back to the Wolves. The year after, it was the same story, though it was the AHL, not the OHL, that benefitted from his demotion. He spent the next five years in the "I," and after retiring became a coach in the Muskegon amateur hockey association.

HUARD, Bill
b. Welland, Ontario, June 24, 1967
Huard had to do a ton of fighting to get to the NHL, and once he got there he fought for six teams over eight years in the 1990s. He was owned by a seventh, Atlanta, but the Thrashers never used him and he went to Britain to try his luck there. Huard's only full NHL season came with Ottawa in '93-'94, but apart from his policing duties he scored only twice in 63 games.

HUARD, Rolly
b. Ottawa, Ontario, September 6, 1902
d. unknown
Huard's only NHL game came the night of December 13, 1930, and he scored a goal. Only Dean Morton can also say he's accomplished this unique feat for one-game wonders. Huard was called up from Buffalo of the International league as an injury replacement, and as a result had to be sent back after the one-game recall. He never acquitted himself well enough in all his other years to warrant interest from another team, and he retired after a few more years and returned to his native Ottawa.

HUBACEK, Petr
b. Brno, Czechoslovakia (Czech Republic), September 2, 1979
Still a pup, Hubacek was a low and distant draft choice by Philly in 1998. He played a few games for the team a couple of years later but since then has been in the minors trying to work his way into being considered for a callup to the big team.

HUBER, Wilhelm "Willie"
b. Strasskirchen, Germany, January 15, 1958
Huber's problem was not his size. At 6'5" and 230 pounds, he was a giant of a man. The problem was that he wasn't as aggressive as he should have been – he didn't use his size. Big mistake for a defenceman. In his 10 years in the NHL (1978-88), he was a minus player each and every season. The cumulative number was exactly -203. Not good. He had some offensive ability, but his years in Detroit were hampered by an ever-stressful relationship with GM Jimmy Devellano, which eventually led to his trade to the Rangers. In New York, management advised the party-lovin' Huber to find a place outside of town, lead a quiet life, and focus on hockey. In his final NHL season, he was traded twice. He had represented Canada at two World Juniors (silver in '77 and bronze in '78) and one World Championship (fourth place in 1981).

HUBICK, Greg
b. Strasbourg, Saskatchewan, November 12, 1951
Poor Greg Hubick. He has become a small part of Toronto's more recent bad history rather than its better history of earlier days. On June 26, 1975, the Leafs felt they were so strong up the middle that they traded their 1st-round draft choice, Doug Jarvis, to Montreal for Hubick. Jarvis went on to be a great role player for the Cup-winning Habs; Hubick played one full season with the Leafs before being dished off to the minors. He had been drafted by the Habs in 1971 and promptly spent three years with Nova Scotia waiting for a chance with Montreal. It never came. He was all set to retire and return to his farming life in Strasbourg when the Leafs acquired him, and he played a perfectly small but decent role with the team as a checker and penalty killer. Nothing fancy, just effective. For the next five years, though, he played down in Dallas in the CHL, with the exception of five games with Vancouver. He retired soon after and worked for the municipality of McKillop, Saskatchewan.

HUCK, Fran
b. Regina, Saskatchewan, December 4, 1945
Ha! Huck set a record that even Wayne Gretzky never came close to breaking, though the leagues were of different scale. In '64-'65 with Regina, Huck scored an incredible 50 goals in just 29 games en route to a 77-goal season. That was down from his previous year's record of 88. Indeed, not many juniors headed for the pros with the notice and anticipation that greeted Huck, but instead of shooting for the NHL, he veered off and landed with the Canadian National Team and Father Bauer. For five years he stayed there, playing at the Worlds and at the 1968 Olympics Grenoble. He probably would have kept on going except that Canada withdrew from international competition, leaving Huck no meaningful reason to stay with the program. He finished the '69-'70 season with the University of Manitoba, where he finished his law degree, and then accepted a tryout offer from Montreal, which got him into his first NHL games at age 25. Huck, though, played just parts of four seasons with the Habs and St. Louis before signing with the WHA. He scored points in 28 straight games in the WHL in '71-'72, another record, and at year's end he was named league MVP. Once retired from hockey, Huck settled in Calgary to practise law. His most notorious case was to represent an unnamed plaintiff who, along with Sheldon Kennedy, had been a victim of sexual abuse at the hands of former junior coach Graham James.

HUCUL, Fred
b. Tubrose, Saskatchewan, December 4, 1931
By his own admission, Hucul's first chance in the NHL came too soon. He was too green, too young, and too much lacking in experience when he came up with Chicago late in the '50-'51 season at the age of 19. He played parts of four years with the Hawks, but when he was sent to the minors, he thought he was there for good. For 14 seasons he played mostly in the WHL, dreaming of another chance now that he was older and more experienced, but it never came until

Fran Huck

the good old '67 expansion. St. Louis acquired his rights, but by that time he was at the other end of his career – too old, too slow – to be as effective as he was in his prime. Most of that prime came with the Calgary Stampeders, and part of it came with his brother, Alex "Sandy" Hucul. The two played defence together, Sandy the more defensive of the two, Fred the playmaker, rusher, and passer. Fred set a WHL record with 21 goals in '55-'56, and at various times he was playing coach or team captain. After his season in St. Louis, he turned to coaching full-time in Kansas City, and Sandy also became a coach after his playing days.

HUDDY, Charlie ("Chuckles")
b. Oshawa, Ontario, June 2, 1959
His might not have been a Hall of Fame career, but if not, it was second best. Although Huddy was born in the "Shwa," he grew up in Toronto and played minor hockey there against Wayne Gretzky at one point. Incredibly, he was never drafted, testament to the fact that scouts don't know everything and that players should never give up on their dreams. Huddy joined the Oilers for the '80-'81 season, and over the course of the next 11 seasons he was part of the most exciting team the world of hockey has ever known, winning 5 Stanley Cups. Although he had one 20-goal season – an aberration, really – he was one of the defencemen who kept the puck out of his net. While Gretzky, Messier, Coffey et al. were scoring at record levels, he was earning fame for his +/- numbers,

Incredibly, he was never drafted.
CHARLIE HUDDY

notably a league-high +62 in '82-'83, which won him the disgustingly named Emery Edge Plus/Minus Award (later renamed the Bud Light Plus/Minus Award). Huddy later wound up in Los Angeles with Gretzky again, and at the end of '95-'96 was reunited with him a third time in St. Louis for the final few games of the season. After retiring, he went into coaching, and was teamed again with number 99 in New York, Gretzky playing out the last of his career, Huddy starting his first gig as an assistant coach.

HUDSON, Dave
b. St. Thomas, Ontario, December 28, 1949
Hudson left St. Thomas far behind and wound up living in a place called Mount Pleasant, Texas, the home of his wife, whom he met in the early 1970s while playing for the Dallas Black Hawks. He had just come out of the University of North Dakota and joined the expansion New York Islanders in 1972. Over the next six years he played for teams that never qualified for the playoffs until the Rockies made a brief appearance in '78.

HUDSON, Lex
b. Winnipeg, Manitoba, December 31, 1955
Hudson was a low Pittsburgh draft choice in 1975 and played just two games for the Penguins after graduating from the University of Denver. He played pro for only two years.

HUDSON, Mike
b. Guelph, Ontario, February 6, 1967
For no reason whatsoever, Hudson's career went from one of perfect stability to flux in the matter of moments. He played his first five years in the NHL with one team, Chicago, and then in his last five years he played with six teams. Fortunately for him, one of the spots he touched down in was New York in '93-'94. Although he didn't play in the playoffs, he appeared in 48 regular-season games, enough to have his name on the Cup. He later played in Germany at the end of his career, but almost from the moment he came out of junior he was slotted as a third- or fourth-line player, a forward who could serve a number of different roles, none of which involved high offence.

HUDSON, Ron
b. Calgary, Alberta, July 14, 1911
Hudson's pro career more or less ended with his enlistment in the Canadian army in 1942. He had played 33 games for the Red Wings in earlier years but more recently had been confined to the minors. He later became a referee in the IHL.

HUFFMAN, Kerry
b. Peterborough, Ontario, January 3, 1968
The irony of circumstance. In the 1986 Memorial Cup, Huffman was named the most gentlemanly player. Just a few months later, at the World Juniors in Piestany, he was involved in a full-scale brawl that was instigated by the Russians but left the Canadians disqualified and without a medal. Huffman joined Philadelphia later that year and for the next six seasons patrolled the Flyers blueline with efficiency. In the summer of '92, though, he was part of the massive package the Flyers used to acquire Eric Lindros from Quebec, and Huffman was later moved to Ottawa when the Nordiques put him on waivers. He ended his career back in Philly and after retiring he settled in New Jersey with his wife and became an executive with a mortgage banking firm. He also became president of firstpromortgage.com.

HUGGINS, Al ("Chink")
b. Toronto, Ontario, December 21, 1910
The three Huggins boys all played hockey. Frank played for Newmarket when they won the Memorial Cup in 1933, Lyn played for the National Seafleas,

Dave Hudson

Lex Hudson

Mike Hudson

Ron Hudson

Kerry Huffman

Al Huggins

**Brent Hughes
(b. 1943)**

Frank Hughes

Howie Hughes

and Al played 20 games for the Montreal Maroons in 1930-31 before a knee injury ended his season and soon after forced him to retire. He moved to Timmins to coach hockey in the winters and baseball in the summers, and by day he sold air time for radio station CKGB. He later returned to Toronto and got into the steel business, becoming so successful he was able to retire at 52.

HUGHES, Al

b. Guelph, Ontario, May 13, 1901
d. unknown
Hughes played two seasons with the New York Americans (1930-32) during a brief career centred around that city. By 1934, he was out of hockey altogether.

HUGHES, Brent

b. Bowmanville, Ontario,
June 17, 1943
Hughes played junior like everyone else, but he was owned by both Boston and Detroit in the days before the draft, and neither club had any use for him. In 1967, the new Kings in Los Angeles claimed him and put the defenceman in the lineup almost right away; he remained with the Kings for the better part of three years. Hughes played almost as long in Philadelphia and ended his NHL days with lowly Kansas City in '74-'75 where he was a -51, fair indication of where the Scouts were, defensively, in the league. In the summer of '75 he signed with the WHA's team in San Diego, playing in that league for four years before ending in the minors.

HUGHES, Brent

b. New Westminster, British Columbia, April 5, 1966
The Brent Hughes of New Westminster who played in the 1990s shouldn't be confused with the Brent Hughes of Bowmanville who played in the 1970s. This Brent Hughes played junior for his hometown Bruins and, undrafted, signed with Winnipeg in 1988. In a pro career that lasted a dozen years, Hughes played more in the minors than in the NHL. The left winger was a decent scorer in the AHL, less so in the NHL, and after retiring in 1999 he became head coach and director of hockey operations for the Austin Ice Bats of the WCHL, positions he has held with some success for three years.

HUGHES, Frank

b. Fernie, British Columbia, October 1, 1949
In golf, the expression is "drive for show; putt for dough." To translate that to the Houston Aeros during its years with the WHA, the three Howes were the "drive for show" part of the equation, and the Go Go Line was the "putt for dough" part. That line had

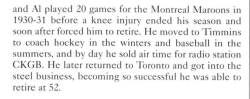

He went to prep school to improve his grades, and in 1976 Harvard accepted him into its economics program.
JACK HUGHES

played together in Phoenix in '71-'72, setting scoring records. It featured Frank Hughes, Larry Lund, and Andre Hinse, and each had a role. Hinse dug the puck out of the corners, Lund made the passes, and Hughes did the scoring. So, while the Howes got all the ink, Hughes was quietly leading the league in scoring through much of the '73-'74 season. In fact, although he went goalless in his only five NHL games, with California, Hughes routinely scored 30 goals elsewhere, including 42 and 48 goals with the Aeros. His dad had played hockey in the air force and had put young Frank on skates by the age of four, so it was no surprise he turned into a fine player. After retiring, he became a PGA golf pro for five years and settled back home in Fernie, where he became a very successful real estate agent.

HUGHES, Howie
("Howard Hughes")

b. St. Boniface, Manitoba,
April 4, 1939
Rich in talent and experience more than money-rich like his nickname namesake, Hughes played right wing as a left-hand shot, *à la* Maurice Richard, to get a better angle coming in on goal. Throughout his career he was considered an honest player who could score at one end and backcheck at the other. He played two and a half seasons under Jack Kent Cooke in Los Angeles in the middle of a 15-year pro career that saw him move all over the place. He settled in Seattle during the off-season, working as an electrician's helper. For his long and successful pro career, he was inducted into the Manitoba Sports Hall of Fame in 1992.

HUGHES, Jack

b. Somerville, Massachusetts, July 20, 1957
Somerville is just a stone's throw from Harvard, which is why Hughes wanted to go there later in his teens, but it was such a small place that the only two players who could skate backward on his hockey team were automatically made to play defence. He was one of those two. As he got older and better, he chose hockey over baseball and football, two other sports he excelled at, but when it came time to choose schools, he was rebuffed by Harvard because of low marks (or, rather, not high enough Harvard-type marks). He went to prep school to improve his grades, and in 1976 Harvard accepted him into its economics program. After three years, Hughes left the school to play for the U.S. National Team in the hopes of making the Olympics. He was the last player cut, and as a result missed out on the Miracle on Ice gold medal. He went on to play two years for Colorado, but retired in 1982 after those two seasons. He entered the brokerage business in Boston – with a defenceman from that

1980 Olympics team, Jack O'Callahan – with a company called Beanpot Financial Services.

HUGHES, James ("Rusty")
b. Webbwood, Ontario, May 12, 1906
d. unknown
Hughes played a full season with Detroit in 1929-30 when the team was still called the Cougars. He later played a number of years in the IHL before retiring in 1936.

HUGHES, John
b. Charlottetown, Prince Edward Island, March 18, 1954
A tough guy from down east, Hughes moved to Toronto and played for the Marlies in the early 1970s, a period that climaxed with the great team of '73 that won the Memorial Cup. Like a number of others from that team, he signed with the WHA, spurning the NHL draft in which Vancouver had claimed his rights. Hughes stayed in the WHA for five years, the last including half a season with Gretzky and the pre-NHL Oilers. Ironically, when the WHA joined the NHL, Vancouver reclaimed him and he made his NHL debut with the Canucks in '79-'80. Doubly ironic, they put him on waivers after a season, and the Oilers re-claimed him. After retiring in 1982, Hughes moved back to PEI, where he played a pretty serious game of golf and became involved in high school athletics at the administrative level.

HUGHES, Pat
b. Calgary, Alberta, March 25, 1955
Hughes holds a pretty difficult NHL record to break. While with the Oilers, he once scored 2 short-handed goals 25 seconds apart. That's amazing. Hughes won two Cups with the Oilers, in '84 and '85, after having won one with Montreal in 1979 at the end of that dynasty. During his 4 years in Edmonton, Hughes had 3 seasons of 24 goals or more, making a decent contribution to an incredible team. After retiring, he and his wife settled in Ann Arbor, Michigan. At first, he was transportation manager for Little Caesar's, and then he quit to realize a dream by becoming a police officer while his wife ran a small publishing company called Sleeping Bear Press.

HUGHES, Ryan
b. Montreal, Quebec, January 17, 1972
The one-time captain of Cornell's hockey team later played for Canada at the World Juniors before turning pro in 1993. His only NHL games were with Boston two years later, and they totalled only three.

HULBIG, Joe
b. Norwood, Massachusetts, September 29, 1973
Hulbig seems to be losing the battle of becoming a full-blown NHLer, but he's giving it the good old college try. Like most kids in hockey-mad Massachusetts, he went from prep school in Needham to a state college, in his case Providence. In his senior year, '95-'96, the Friars were champions of Hockey East, and from there he went to Edmonton, the team that had drafted him a very ambitious 13th overall in 1992. Since then, he signed with Boston as a free agent, but he wasn't able to play his way onto the roster in either city. In 2001-02, he played the entire season outside the NHL, the first time in his career he had slipped so much.

HULL, Bobby ("The Golden Jet")
b. Pointe Anne, Ontario, January 3, 1939
A Hall of Fame player is a special beast, a man who does more than just record a certain number of goals and assists. A Hall of Famer lifts fans from their seats and turns a casual fan into a fanatic. That was the effect Hull had on the Chicago Black Hawks and the NHL. He played just two years of junior, in St. Catharines, but it was so obvious that he was going to be a star that at 18 Chicago invited him to its 1957 training camp. Hull never saw he minors. Instead, he became the shining left winger on a mediocre Chicago team that was getting better day by day. He scored 13 goals as a rookie, and 18 the year after, and in his third year he led the league with 39. It was just a small sign of what he was capable of, but it wasn't just the getting of the goals that mattered – it was how he got them. Hull was the fastest skater in the league. It was said that after just one stride from a stationary position he was in full flight, and he used his extraordinary acceleration to burst down the left wing with fearsome abandon. Then there was the shot. Not only did he patent the slapshot, as it were, but he, along with teammate Stan Mikita, favoured the banana blade for a curve on his stick, rendering his shot not only hard but also unpredictable. He could shoot at a goalie's head early in the game and then score along the ice later because his shot was so intimidating that goalies were on their heels as soon as they saw him wind up for a shot. And, of course, he had all the puck skills needed to get into the open to unleash the big shot. When Hull was on his game there was no one in the league in the 1960s who could excite the fans and terrify the goalies quite like him. People said that his shot was so hard it knocked the glove from a goalie's hand. Hull slumped to 31 goals in '60-'61, but the Hawks won the Stanley Cup, their first since 1938. The following year, he tied Maurice Richard and Bernie Geoffrion by scoring 50 goals, and in '65-'66 he set an NHL record by scoring 54, the most goals in any single season. It was also the first

> He could shoot at a goalie's head early in the game and then score along the ice later.
> **BOBBY HULL**

James Hughes

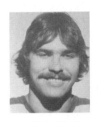

John Hughes

Pat Hughes

Ryan Hughes

Bobby Hull

Bobby Hull

time one player had ever had more than one 50-goal season, and it was the first of four successive years that he led the league in goals. In '68-'69, he scored 58, and everyone thought he had set a standard that would last for years (though Phil Esposito scored 76 just two years later). By 1972, Hull had scored 604 NHL goals, second only to Gordie Howe on the all-time list. In his 15 NHL seasons, he was named an amazing 10 times to the First All-Star Team, and had won two Hart Trophies, in '64-'65 and '65-'66. But during the '71-'72 season, Hull's life changed forever. In February 1972, the new WHA announced its intentions to start playing in the fall, and the Winnipeg Jets later made Hull the first pick of the new league. The Hawks scoffed at their ridiculous $1-million offer, but didn't offer Hull a contract themselves. In the summer, Hull stunned the hockey world by signing with Winnipeg, in one fell swoop establishing the new league and paving the way for every other player to choose to leave the NHL in favour of a league that provided much more generous salaries. He was, in a very real sense, the main reason salaries escalated at all through the 1970s. His signing caused a tremendous furor on another count. It was assumed – a certainty, in truth – that he would play for Team Canada in the upcoming '72 Summit Series, but the NHL decreed that, in order to punish the renegades who fled the league to abet the cause of a rival, the players would be selected only from NHL club teams. During the summer, even Prime Minister Pierre Trudeau became involved in the controversy, asking the organizers to forget about league affiliation in the name of patriotic duty and name Hull to the team. No amount of reasoning or pleading worked, and Hull was left off the team. Within the hockey world, there was no greater political statement than when Hull was in the stands in Winnipeg for game three of the series, in a suit rather than in a Team Canada sweater. He scored more than 50 goals in each of his first two seasons with the Jets and then played on a line with Anders Hedberg and Ulf Nilsson, two "super-Swedes" who worked wonders with Hull. In '74-'75, he scored 77 goals, one better than Esposito's, but the NHL refused to acknowledge any record. Hull's line was the most dominant in the WHA, and he swore the magic that he felt with the two Swedes helped extend his career by years. He got his best chance at international stardom in 1976 when he was allowed to play for Team Canada at the inaugural Canada Cup, in many ways his swan song to top flight hockey. Hull was one of the few men to play every season of the WHA, and when that league joined the NHL in 1979, he decided to play another season. In the end, he appeared in just 18 games with the Jets before being traded to Hartford where he teamed with Gordie Howe, one of the great pairings in hockey history. Because of his star status, Hull's every move off ice was also closely followed. When he decided to wear a hair piece and then try a transplant, it made the front page of the sports sections. When he got a divorce, everyone knew about it. At one point, he asked for all his donations to the Hockey Hall of Fame to be returned to him because the Hall wanted to charge a dollar admission, a policy that went against Hull's perception of the Hall, which had always had free admission and was, therefore, accessible to any hockey fan regardless of social status. He even sat out one game to protest what he saw as a dramatic increase in violence in the game. When he retired in 1980, he went back to his cattle farm in Demoretsville, Ontario, but he was still in the public eye through advertisements. He made frequent public appearances and worked with the Hawks' alumni, and became involved in the Northern Algonquin Brewing Company. Later, he became embroiled in a disturbing controversy when a Toronto newspaper accused him of making racist remarks during a trip to Russia, a story that resulted in him launching a defamation suit against the paper. Hull was inducted into the Hockey Hall of Fame in 1983. He was a man who set records and created a stir whenever he played, a tough competitor and a gentlemanly player. He helped bring hockey into the modern day by signing with the WHA, and he stood out as a leader, not a follower. His brother Dennis also played in the NHL for years, but these days Bobby is more proud to say that he is the father of Brett than to boast of his own accomplishments.

> **He repeatedly admitted that he preferred golf to hockey any day of the year.**
> **BRETT HULL**

HULL, Brett
("Hullie"/ "The Golden Brett")
b. Belleville, Ontario, August 9, 1964

In 1963-64, Bobby Hull led the NHL in goals with 43, the third time he had managed the feat. His Hawks were eliminated by Detroit in the semifinals of the playoffs, and Bobby returned to Belleville for the summer, where his wife gave birth to a boy they named Brett. Well, who'da thunk that the boy would outscore the old man one day, given that the Golden Jet was one of the greatest scorers of all time. Brett grew up out west with his mother, and played provincial hockey in British Columbia before playing at the University of Minnesota-Duluth. He could always score, but in the early days he lacked ambition and discipline, and he ate like a pig. The nickname Pickle was given to him because, as he admitted, there was no food he didn't like. His weight was why he was never given a chance to play for Canada at the World Juniors, and in 1986 he accepted an offer to play for the U.S. at the World Championships (the team finished sixth that year), a decision that branded him American for the rest of his career in the eyes of the IIHF Hull's reputation followed him to Calgary, and the Flames were a Cup-contending team that had no interest in trying to baby a player along. They traded him to St. Louis with Steve Bozek for Rob Ramage and Rick Wamsley on March 7, 1988, a move that helped Calgary win the Cup a year later. In St. Louis, Hull blossomed. In his first 3 seasons, his goal totals went from 41 to 72 to 86, and when he scored 70 the year after it marked the third year in a row he led the NHL in goals. He had 2 more 50-goal seasons to make it 5 in a row, but hasn't reached that plateau since. He scored 50 goals in 49 games one season to become the third fastest to do so, and along with Gretzky, Lemieux, and Yzerman he was among the premier scorers in the game. Unlike those others, though, his detestation of backchecking and team play looked bad on his resumé. In his 72-goal season, for instance, he was a -1, an embarrassing figure that is made good only when compared to his 54-goal season in '92-'93 when he was a -27. Hull's greatest skill as a scorer was the quick release, often from the left side and often on the power play. Yet in his 11 seasons in St. Louis, the team never advanced very far in the playoffs and Hull seemed destined to be both a scorer and a loser, someone who never lifted his teammates and who played his best at big times. He was aloof and caustic, critical of the NHL and often disinterested in the game. He repeatedly admitted that he preferred golf to hockey any day of the year. In the summer of 1998, Hull received a free agent offer from Dallas that was too financially rewarding to pass up, even though it meant joining a defence-oriented team. His goal production dropped and he bought into coach Ken Hitchcock's stress on defence, and lo and behold the Stars won the Cup in 1999, Hull scoring the winning goal in overtime on a controversial play because his foot was definitely in the crease (a no-no at the time). Not surprisingly, he was also a personal-best +19 on the year. Three years earlier, he had eradicated all doubts about big-game play when he helped the U.S. beat Canada in the 1996 World Cup, Hull again scoring the winning goal on a deflection that was clearly above the crossbar (and thus illegal). Hull also played for the U.S. at the 1998 Olympics in Nagano and the 2002 Olympics in Salt Lake City, and he made several appearances at All-Star Games. The only individual trophies he ever won were the Lady Byng in 1990 and the Hart and Pearson the year after. After signing with Detroit in 2001 he won a Cup with that

He became athletic director at the Illinois Institute of Technology.
DENNIS HULL

veteran team the following spring. When Hull scored his 1,000th career point, he became part of the only father-son combo to reach that milestone and in 2002-03 he scored his 700th career goal.

HULL, Dennis
b. Pointe Anne, Ontario, November 19, 1944

Dennis never got full credit for his skills because he played with and behind his more-superstar brother, Bobby. Yet Dennis had the same dynamite shot and ability to score; his was just a degree less than Bobby's. Dennis had seven 20-goal seasons with Chicago, playing mostly on a line with Pit Martin and Jim Pappin. Hull played his entire career with the Hawks save his last season, '77-'78, when he was traded to Detroit. He was also part of the famous Team Canada '72, an odd circumstance because Bobby was excommunicated from the team after signing with the WHA. Dennis twice took the Hawks to the Cup finals, and in '72-'73 he led the league with 15 playoff assists. He played in five All-Star Games, and was known for his fantastic sense of humour. This served him well after retiring, for he became one of the more popular and hilarious speakers at banquets, golf tournaments, and the like. He became athletic director at the Illinois Institute of Technology and later settled into a job with a car dealership in southern Ontario.

Dennis Hull

HULL, Jody
b. Petrolia, Ontario, February 2, 1969

Imagine a pro hockey player named Jimmy Orr from Quebec or Dave Gretzky from B.C. or Zach Mahovlich from New Brunswick. That's the problem for Jody Hull, a decent enough player but, no, not one of *the* Hulls. This average Hull played junior in Peterborough and won a gold medal with Canada at the '88 WJC before starting his NHL career with Hartford. A gentlemanly player, he's been traded around like a non-Hull and scored only a handful of goals each season, like a non-Hull. Nonetheless, he continues to survive in the league, playing most recently with Philadelphia, and in that respect he is every bit a Hull, a career NHLer.

Jody Hull

HULSE, Cale ("Chopper")
b. Edmonton, Alberta, November 10, 1973

Hulse will never be given a speeding ticket if he goes through life on skates, but he knows as much and has made a place for himself in the NHL regardless. New Jersey drafted him, and before he played a game with the Devils he helped the farm team in Albany win the Calder Cup in 1995. He won't score very much, but his is a physical game from the blueline, first with

New Jersey, then Calgary, and finally Nashville, where he has become a veteran on an expansion roster.

HUML, Ivan
b. Kladno, Czechoslovakia (Czech Republic), September 6, 1981

It's still early, but Huml has played his way into the hearts of the Bruins pretty quickly. He was drafted in 2000 and spent a year in the minors, and in 2001-02 he played in a single game for the team. Coming out of training camp to start the 2002-03 season, though, he made the NHL team to get a chance to prove himself on a nightly basis.

HUNT, Fred
b. Brantford, Ontario, January 17, 1918
d. Buffalo, New York, October 4, 1977

Fred Hunt

If it hadn't been for Hunt, the NHL might never have opened the door to a franchise in Buffalo, for it was his love of and longtime association with that city that spurred on the Knox family bid to bring the Sabres to life. Hunt had a long career in the AHL, which saw him play briefly for the Rangers and Americans during the war years. Mostly, though, he skated for the Buffalo Bisons, helping them win a Calder Cup in 1946. After retiring as a player in '49, Hunt went into private business for three years, but he discovered he missed hockey too much. He became GM of the Bisons in 1952, and remained there for 18 years. When he learned of the NHL's bold and ambitious expansion plans, he convinced the Knox family that Buffalo could support the NHL. In return, the Knoxes hired

Dave Hunter

him in 1970 once they had a team in place, and Hunt remained there until 1977, when he suffered a heart attack and died a few weeks later.

HUNTER, Dale
b. Petrolia, Ontario, July 31, 1960

Perhaps the polite way to put it is to say that players hated playing against him and wanted him on their team rather than on the other side. Or, more directly, most players hated him. More bluntly: He was a disturber of fecal matter, or words to that effect. Hunter jabbed and pushed and sticked and punched and hacked every player on every shift. To his coaches, that meant he competed. He did that for 19 years and some 1,407 regular-season games, all but 12 of which came with Washington or Quebec. Amazingly, although there were a few close calls, he never won a Cup, despite appearing 186 playoff games. He holds a unique record in that his 323 career goals are the most in league history by a player who never had a 30-goal season. The importance of

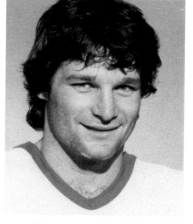

His 323 careers goals are the most in league history by a player who never had a 30-goal season.
DALE HUNTER

that number merely highlights his consistency, longevity, tenacity, and dogged play every night. He also retired in 1999 as one of the all-time penalty minutes leaders, the highlight from that part of his business coming in 1993. In those playoffs, against the Islanders, Hunter delivered a vicious cross-check to the back of Pierre Turgeon after the player had raised his arms to celebrate a goal. It was unspeakably cowardly and dirty, and Hunter was suspended 21 games, the most ever for such a foul. Hunter's two brothers, Dave and Mark, also made it to the NHL. After he retired, Dale became a scout for the Capitals, who retired his number 32 sweater, though a short time later he became closely involved with Mark, who had become GM of the OHL's London Knights. Dale was named the team's president and governor, and later its head coach.

HUNTER, Dave
b. Petrolia, Ontario, January 1, 1958

The late 1970s were strange time for Dave Hunter. In the summer of 1978, he was drafted by Montreal in the NHL and Edmonton in the WHA. He chose Edmonton, and played the '78-'79 season with the Oilers. But the next summer, the WHA joined the NHL, so Hunter's rights reverted to Montreal, the NHL team that had drafted him. Then Montreal exposed him in the Expansion Draft and Edmonton claimed him, so he kept right on playing with the Oilers! Good thing, too, because over the next nine years he won three Cups with the high-flyin' team. He also played briefly with Pittsburgh and Winnipeg, and he competed with a family ferocity matched only by the Sutters. Dave wasn't as skilled offensively as Dale, but he was as tenacious and was fortunate to land with a great team. Dave's time in Edmonton was all glory, with the ugly exception of a drunk driving conviction that forced him to spend a month in jail.

HUNTER, Mark
b. Petrolia, Ontario, November 12, 1962

Oil Springs is a small farming community outside Petrolia, near Sarnia, and that is where the six Hunter children – four boys, two girls – were reared. Mark was the baby of the boys, and to many he was the most skilled of the hockey players. He was no daisy, though, and like Dale and Dave had no problems throwing his weight around. But he could also score. With St. Louis in '85-'86 he had 44 goals, and the year after 36, and then 32. Interestingly, the only time any of the brothers played together in the NHL was when Mark played with Dale in Washington for just seven games in '92-'93, the last of his career. After retiring, he immediately became head coach of Sarnia in the

Mark Hunter

OHL, and he moved up to the AHL a few years later. He and Dale were later involved in an executive capacity in London (Mark as GM, Dave as coach), and it's clear the Hunters intend to make Ontario junior hockey their home just as the NHL was for so many years.

HUNTER, Tim
b. Calgary, Alberta, September 10, 1960

If he could have turned penalty minutes into dollars, Hunter would have been a rich man. Well, actually, since he made his living as a tough guy, penalty minutes *were* dollars! Hunter was fortunate enough to play 11 years with his hometown Flames, going to the finals in 1986 and winning the Stanley Cup 3 years later. He was always a team man and knew how to be more disciplined in the playoffs, rarely taking penalties unless he took an opponent with him to the box. Hunter watched the game from the bench more than most, and has translated this experience into a post-playing career as a coach. In 1997, after retiring, he was hired as an assistant coach to Ron Wilson in Washington, and it's only a matter of time before he gets a head coaching offer from some team.

HUNTER, Trent
b. Red Deer, Alberta, July 5, 1980

Drafted by Anaheim and traded to the Islanders using a Columbus draft choice the Ducks had acquired, Hunter made his NHL debut in the 2002 playoffs for the Islanders in their first-round series against Toronto. He came out of the WHL and played two full seasons in the AHL before getting this chance, though he didn't make the Islanders at camp in 2002 and, in the team's opinion, still has some work to do before qualifying as an NHL regular.

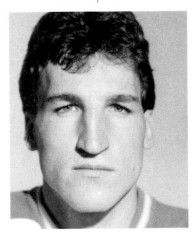

In 1997 he was hired as an assistant coach to Ron Wilson in Washington.
TIM HUNTER

HURAS, Larry
b. Listowel, Ontario, July 8, 1955

The fact that the Rangers had no use for Huras beyond a two-game look in '76-'77 didn't affect him at all. After a few years in the minors, he packed his bags, picked up his wife, and flew to Europe. That was 1980. They have yet to return. Huras continued to play for 14 years in France, and then embarked on a coaching career that keeps getting better and better. He landed jobs in Switzerland, most recently with Lugano, and also served as an assistant coach for Canada's Spengler Cup entries in the early part of the 21st century. In addition to his work as player and coach, Huras quickly established a presence on Eurosport, the Continental sports television station. He did commentary for many international events, notably the last three Olympics, providing both play-by-play and colour commentary. Most recently, he has coached for Lugano in the Swiss league.

HURLBURT, Bob
b. Toronto, Ontario, May 1, 1950

A one-gamer with Vancouver in '74-'75, Hurlburt played just five years of pro after leaving the OHA in 1970.

Bob Hurlburt

HURLBUT, Mike
b. Massena, New York, October 7, 1966

Hurlbut has been a pro since 1988 and has been in the NHL since 1992, yet he has played just 29 games in the big show. A big defenceman, he has not scored since that first season, but it seems that he is more minor-league than NHL material.

HURLEY, Paul
b. Melrose, Massachusetts, July 12, 1946

Hurley's claim to fame lies in a dubious place in hockey history is where. On February 21, 1971, Hurley and his Oklahoma City Blazers were playing Kansas City in a game attended by fewer than a thousand people because of a massive snowstorm in K.C. Late in the game, the Blazers were trailing 2-1 and they pulled their goalie on a late rush. Hurley dumped the puck into the Kansas City end, but goalie Michel Plasse got to the puck first and whipped it down the ice into the net, becoming the first goalie to score a goal. Despite this gaffe, Hurley went on to a decent career in the WHA. He had played his only NHL game with Boston a few years earlier, and even that is of note because he had an assist in the game, one of a small number of players to register a point in his one and only NHL appearance.

Mike Hurlbut

HURME, Jani
b. Turku, Finland, January 7, 1975

Hurme might well have reached his peak in '96-'97 in Finland when he was named the league's MVP. That summer, the goalie was chosen by Ottawa in the second round of the draft with praise that he was the Sens' goalie of the future. Then, he struggled. He was sent down to Detroit in the "I," but a lack of playing time forced a trade to Indianapolis, where he had problems adjusting to the smaller rinks and different angles. He stuck with it, though, and made his inaugural NHL appearance in 1999-2000, and over the next two seasons established himself as the backup. He's not there yet, but he might be the team's starter soon.

Paul Hurley

HURST, Ron
b. Toronto, Ontario, May 18, 1931

Growing up in Toronto in the 1940s meant that Hurst would play for either the Marlies or St. Mike's if he

Jani Hurme

Ron Hurst

Jamie Huscroft

were going to go on to the NHL, and indeed it was the former he played for in the years after the war. Hurst, however, was no superstar; he was a fringe player with limited ability who went to the Maritimes, to Ottawa, and to northern Ontario to play after leaving junior because the Leafs weren't calling and no other NHL team was trying to sign him. But Hurst persevered, and for the '55-'56 season he wound up in Pittsburgh, the Leafs farm team. Leafs coach Howie Meeker called him up early in the year, though, and he stayed with the team through the playoffs. Those 50 games played became just 14 the next season, and Hurst spent most of the season with the Rochester Americans. He played the next three full years in the minors, and in 1960, just 29, he quit hockey because he knew it wasn't likely he'd ever get called up again. Instead, he became a stockbroker, first in Toronto, then in Oshawa, a job he continued to practise until 1991 when he underwent quadruple bypass surgery. Hurst then retired to private life, though remained active in NHL Oldtimers' and alumni relations.

HUSCROFT, Jamie
b. Creston, British Columbia, January 9, 1967
It was his determination and persistence, rather than just his talent, that got Huscroft into 352 NHL games. And it was a serious concussion that took him out of the game altogether early in the 2000-01 while playing for the Portland Pirates. He was a strong defenceman whose work ethic carried the day wherever he went, from seven NHL teams to a host of AHL cities. Sometimes he spent a full year in the big league; other times he saw only minor-league arenas. His career lasted 14 years, though, but after an injury that left him unable to play with his children without supervision – for *his* health, not theirs – he knew it was time to move on. He promised to be back in the game as a scout one day, once the headaches go away.

HUSELIUS, Kristian
b. Osterhaninge, Sweden, November 10, 1978
One of the outstanding rookies of 2001-02, Huselius had the advantage of experience when he got to the NHL. He had played in the Swedish Elite League previously, and he stepped right into the Florida lineup and scored 23 goals on a weak team. Huselius capped off this great season by winning a bronze medal with Sweden at the World Championships, finishing second among scorers.

HUSKA, Ryan
b. Cranbrook, British Columbia, July 2, 1975
Huska made history long before he ever played in the NHL. He is one of a small number of players to have

Ron Huston

Dave Hutchison

won three Memorial Cups, a phenomenal junior career accomplishment. He did it with Kamloops in 1992, '94, and '95. A Chicago draft choice, he played his only NHL game on January 5, 1998. Before and since, his career has been all minor leagues, but that's okay – he made it to the show, if only for a day.

HUSTON, Ron
b. Manitou, Manitoba, April 8, 1945
Huston graduated from Brandon in 1965, but no NHL team was interested in his services and he spent a number of years playing senior hockey. Three times his Spokane Jets went to the Allan Cup finals, finally winning in 1970. Huston later turned pro with Salt Lake City in 1972, where he scored 42 goals and was named rookie of the year in the CHL. This gave the struggling California Golden Seals some hope. They signed him, and for the better part of a year and a half he played out west in the NHL. In 1975, Huston signed with Phoenix of the WHA and wound up in the minors.

Hutchinson embarked on a lengthy career that saw him play just nine games.
RON HUTCHINSON

HUTCHINSON, Ron
b. Flin Flon, Manitoba, October 24, 1936
After winning the Memorial Cup with Flin Flon in 1957, Hutchinson embarked on a lengthy career in the WHL that saw him play just nine games with the Rangers in '60-'61. A centre, he was the prototypical small and fast forward who didn't get much of a chance in the days of the six-team NHL.

HUTCHISON, Dave ("Hutch")
b. London, Ontario, May 2, 1952
He had no problem with his role. He was an enforcer, a protector of talent, a stirrer-upper of the first order, a fighter. Drafted by L.A., he was mired in west coast anonymity for four years before the Leafs acquired him. Unfortunately, he arrived in Toronto in the middle of the horrific Imlach II regime. When he learned of his trade from Toronto to Chicago, he and some teammates were throwing darts at a board with Imlach's picture on it. Hutchison wound up in New Jersey, but he fell awkwardly into the boards one game and hurt his back. He took this to be a signal that, after nine NHL seasons, it was time to pack it in. He returned home to London, but early in the '83-'84 season the Leafs, post-Imlach, came calling and he answered the bell for one final season of hard work and glove-dropping. He settled back in London and started a softer career in real estate.

HUTTON, Bill
b. Calgary, Alberta, January 28, 1910
d. Vancouver, British Columbia, March 1, 1974
He got his start as a teenager with Boston in 1929-30, the year after the team won its first Stanley Cup. Yet

before the season was over, he was sent to Ottawa for Harry Connor, and then in an unusual move the two players were traded back to their original teams prior to the next season. Hutton played briefly for the Philadelphia Quakers and then spent much of the next dozen years in the Pacific Coast league before retiring.

HYLAND, Harry

b. Montreal, Quebec, January 2, 1889
d. Montreal, Quebec, August 8, 1969

There have been a small number of two-sport athletes, but Hyland is perhaps the only double champion. He played all of his kid hockey in Montreal, and the right winger turned pro with the Shamrocks in 1908. The next year, the team joined the NHA and became the Wanderers, and Hyland scored more than two goals a game to help lead the team to the Stanley Cup. In 1911, he was lured out west to the Pacific Coast league to play for New Westminster. But he didn't limit himself to hockey. He also played for the local lacrosse team, and it went on to win the Minto Cup, symbolic of national supremacy in that sport. Hyland returned to the Wanderers a year later, and in addition to playing he also coached the team at Loyola College for the next four years. On January 27, 1913, he scored 8 goals in a 10-6 victory over Quebec, his best single game. He stayed with the Wanderers when they joined the NHL in 1917, but when the arena burned down after just a few games, he went to Ottawa to finish out the year. He later coached Columbus in the Quebec Amateur Hockey Association for four years. Hyland was inducted into the Hockey Hall of Fame in 1962. In the early winter of 1967, he suffered a broken hip when he was hit by a car while crossing a street. He made a full recovery but died in his sleep two years later of natural causes.

On January 27, 1913, he scored 8 goals in a 10-6 victory over Quebec.
HARRY HYLAND

HYNES, Dave

b. Cambridge, Massachusetts, April 17, 1951

Not many players come out of Harvard to play in the NHL, and even fewer in the early 1970s when U.S. college was not the general route to the NHL. Hynes did, though. And, after three years of college and a chance to play for the local Bruins, he took off for the big time and turned pro. His play for the Boston Braves (AHL) in '73-'74 earned him a short tryout with the Bruins, and the year after he made an even better mark for himself by becoming the first member of Rochester to score five goals in a game. He ended the season with 42, a remarkable total given that he also played 19 games with the Bruins. At season's end, though, Boston didn't re-sign him and he accepted an offer from New

England of the WHA. He ended his career with another Massachusetts destination, playing for Springfield in the AHL.

HYNES, Gord

b. Montreal, Quebec, July 22, 1966

The Olympic dream lived within Hynes more than any other, so although it was nice that Boston chose him in 1985, he preferred to put an NHL career on hold until he got a chance to play for his country. Hynes played in the AHL for two years before joining the Canadian National Team in 1988, and for four full seasons he toured with the team until playing at the 1992 Olympics in Albertville. Only then did he join Boston, but the Bruins let him go at season's end and he signed with the Flyers. They, too, dispatched him to the minors after just 37 games, and from there Hynes went overseas, settling into a long and fruitful career in Germany.

HYVONEN, Hannes

b. Oulu, Finland, August 29, 1975

He wasn't drafted until he was 24 and didn't play in North America until 26, and since 2001 Hyvonen has been a minor leaguer. He was called up by San Jose for a few games in the 2001-02 season. In 2002-03, he played with Farjestad in the Swedish league, helping the team reach the finals.

Dave Hynes

IAFRATE, Al ("Skis")
b. Dearborn, Michigan, March 21, 1966

Few players entered the NHL in the 1980s with expectations for stardom as high as Iafrate's. A giant defenceman who had terrific acceleration and strength, scouts saw him as a Paul Coffey-type player with size. Mario Lemieux went 1st overall in that '84 draft, but the Leafs chose Iafrate 4th and put him into the lineup that fall as an 18-year-old. It took him three years to find his form, but then in '87-'88 he scored 22 goals for Toronto and looked to be on his way. He played in the All-Star Game that year and began to assert himself physically and move the puck up the ice on his own. Teammates called him Skis because of his enormous feet, and he called himself the Human Highlight Film because his dashes often ended in spectacular collisions. It looked good, and Iafrate seemed to have fun even when being hit, but soon these blows would have a lasting impact on his career and body. Iafrate never developed off-ice or learned from his mistakes, and the defensive lapses that can be forgiven a rookie persisted through his mature years. The Leafs traded him, and he had some good times with Washington, but soon enough injuries took their toll on his battered body. Iafrate was traded to Boston for Joé Juneau on March 21, 1994, but hurt his knee soon after and missed the next two years recovering his strength. He returned to play with San Jose after the Bruins figured he was done, only to hurt his back and miss much of the next two seasons. His career was virtually over, but since he insisted on trying to play again Carolina signed him and let him prove his value. He couldn't, and he retired for good, ending a career that was over before it reached its full potential.

IGINLA, Jarome
b. Edmonton, Alberta, July 1, 1977

This here's the real deal. Iginla is a Nigerian name, meaning "big tree," and he is one of the biggest in the NHL forest. His rise to superstardom has been consistent and impressive, right from his days in Kamloops when he won two Memorial Cups in '94 and '95. Internationally, he is part of a rare group of gold-medal hat trickers, having placed first at the World Juniors (1996), the World Championships ('97), and the Olympics (2002). After his final year in junior, he joined the Flames for the '96 playoffs and was with the team full-time from the following training camp. But what few fans remember is that he wasn't drafted by the Flames; Dallas took him in 1995 and soon after traded him to Calgary with Corey Millen for Joe Nieuwendyk. It was a trade that eventually helped the Stars win the Cup (in 1999), but it gave Calgary one of the game's finest prospects. Iginla scored 21 goals as a rookie, and although he dipped a bit the year after, his next four seasons each saw significant improvements. His coming-of-age season was the Olympic year of 2001-02. He started the season as a Team Canada hopeful, but by the time Wayne Gretzky chose his men on December 15, Iginla had played himself onto the team unquestionably. Once the team got to Salt Lake City, he proved to be one of the best among the best, scoring twice in Canada's decisive 5-2 gold-medal win over the U.S. He returned to the NHL leading the league in scoring,

and finished with 52 goals and 96 points, tops in both categories. Iginla has the size and speed to be a power forward, and the hands and skill to be a scoring forward. He is also one of the league's gentlemen. Although he also possesses great poise, that attribute was put to the test one night in Calgary when he stood at his blueline and listened to Susan Schuchard – his mother – sing the national anthems!

IGNATJEV, Victor
b. Riga, Soviet Union (Latvia), April 26, 1970

Way back when, scouts wondered whether Ignatjev had the physical endurance to play in the NHL. They knew he had the skill and the size to be a defenceman, but he hadn't shown much in the way of hard play in Riga. Some of these concerns were alleviated by his play in the minors (1992-98), where he played with an NHL determination and ambition for which few Europeans had the patience. Pittsburgh signed him in the summer of 1998, but 11 games into the season he suffered a season-ending shoulder injury. The year after, fully recovered, he moved to Germany to continue playing. He was named to the Latvian team for the 2002 Olympics in Salt Lake City, the highlight of his career to date.

IHNACAK, Miroslav ("Miro")
b. Poprad, Czechoslovakia (Slovakia), November 19, 1962

The intrepid ingenuity that brought Ihnacak from Czechoslovakia to Toronto was worthy of a spy thriller. The stage had been set for his defection for quite some time. His brother, Peter, had defected in 1982, the same year the Leafs selected both young men in the NHL draft. Once Peter was in Canada, it seemed only a matter of time before Miro joined him. As a result, Czech officials refused to let Miro play outside the country. Thus, word of his talent was unreliable, yet what word was out there suggested he was more talented than Peter, who was doing quite nicely with the Leafs. Toronto, though, had excellent underground connections inside Czechoslovakia (that's how Peter was spirited out of the country), and in early 1986 Miro finally made his way to Canada via Austria under the most surreptitious of circumstances. He was given a hero's welcome, and in his first game he scored a goal while playing on a Czech line with his brother and Mirco Frycer. That was his one and only NHL moment of glory. He struggled with the Leafs and spent most of the next three years in the minors, and signing with Detroit did nothing to help his cause. He tried to re-establish his game by playing in Halifax, but in 1992 he gave up and returned to Europe, playing in Germany. When the Czechs and Slovaks parted ways politically, Ihnacak was finally able to return home to play for Slovakia. He played in the historic '95 Worlds that saw the young nation win "B" pool and advance to "A," where they won gold in 2002 (without him) to confirm their place among the great hockey-playing nations.

IHNACAK, Peter
b. Poprad, Czechoslovakia (Slovakia), May 3, 1957

Finland, the site of the 1982 World Championships, was also the site of Ihnacak's defection from the Czech team to a life of freedom. He made his way to

Al Iafrate

Victor Ignatjev

Peter Ihnacak

Brent Imlach
(opposite page)

Peter Ing

Earl Ingarfield

Bill Inglis

Jack Ingoldsby

Toronto in the summer, and it was there he played his entire NHL career. Interestingly, the Leafs drafted Ihnacak using a choice they had acquired from Philadelphia when they traded Darryl Sittler. Since the other player in the deal, Rich Costello, turned out poorly for the team, the trade consisted of, in reality, Sittler for Ihnacak, and as a result the Czech player's career is a bit tarnished. In truth, he had 28 goals as a rookie, and this was to be his best season. Ihnacak turned into an excellent all-purpose centre, though, capable of scoring and checking. He spent his last year in North America mostly in the minors and then moved his family to Germany, where he has been ever since. Starting in 1990, he picked up where he left off as a player, and in 1997 he retired and became a coach. He maintained a presence in Toronto through much of this time, and on the few occasions when an opening for an assistant coach's position has come up he has applied for the job. His son, Brian, is also an NHL prospect.

IMLACH, Brent
b. Quebec City, Quebec, November 16, 1946
Coach's boy makes the NHL – yeah, right. Hardly. Nepotism is not a word coach Punch Imlach knows as well as despotism, and although Brent played for his dad on the Leafs in the 1960s, there was no currying of favour or advantage given to the boy. Just the opposite. Brent got a call to play in January 1966 when Wally Boyer was hurt, and he played another game a year later. He never turned pro, because his dad offered him such a poor salary, and instead earned his master's degree in business administration at York University. He was one of the first player agents not named Eagleson, and his prize client was Charlie Simmer. Imlach was integral in setting up a sort of players' union for juniors to help them reach the NHL. He later became the director of advertising for Molson Breweries, one of the top jobs in the company. Events under this aegis included the 1986 Molson Indy and the 1988 Olympics in Calgary. In 1989, Imlach became vice-president and GM of the Vancouver Canadians, a Triple A baseball team in the Pacific Coast League.

ING, Peter
b. Toronto, Ontario, April 28, 1969
The Leafs had hoped that by calling Ing direct from junior to the parent club, he could develop into their goalie of the future. He had size and quickness – duh – but what the team really needed was stability and consistency. Ing was given a chance in 1990-91, when he played in 56 games, but he was traded to Edmonton in the deal that saw the Leafs obtain the great Grant Fuhr. He played a few games for the Oilers and then Detroit, but most of his time came in the minors. His career was cut short in 1996 by a serious hernia, but by then his NHL days had ended. Ing decided to settle in Las Vegas, where he had played briefly for the Thunder in '93-'94. He became a casino manager trainee, and for the next five years learned the ropes in the magical world of cards and slots. Wanting to raise his kids in Canada, he quickly accepted an offer to become executive director of slot operations at Casino Niagara, and he has earned his living there ever since.

INGARFIELD, Earl
b. Lethbridge, Alberta, October 25, 1934
It's one thing to be traded, but it's another to be unwanted by the team that acquires you. And it's just plain weird for the team that traded you to want you back immediately. Such was the fate that befell Ingarfield in the heart of his career. He had been sailing along quite nicely with the Rangers since 1958 when they lumped him together with three others in a trade with Montreal. The Habs, though, had no intention of using Ingarfield, so the day after the trade they exposed him in the Intra-League Draft and the Rangers scooped him up. Two years later, Pittsburgh claimed him, and Ingarfield wound up in California playing for the dreadful Seals. Ingarfield retired in 1971 to coach in Regina, but he missed Lethbridge so much he resigned after a year and became a scout for the Islanders. Halfway through its first season, though, the team fired coach Phil Goyette and convinced Ingarfield to fill the breach for the rest of the year. He did such a good job the position was his for the asking, but he begged off to return to scouting for the team. He returned home, and it was he who suggested that the team should draft a young prospect named Bryan Trottier. Ingarfield left the Islanders after buying the Lethbridge Broncos and becoming the team's coach and GM. After two years, he left hockey altogether and became sales manager for a local radio station, but in 1982 he returned to scouting for the Islanders.

INGARFIELD, Earl, Jr.
b. New York, New York, January 30, 1959
By his own admission, Earl was just like his dad, the kind of player who never did anything spectacular or showy. But he did like to think he did things well in a quiet sort of way. Regardless, he didn't do things for as long as the old man, who lasted 746 games. Earl Junior lasted just 39 games between 1979 and '81 and spent most of his short pro career in the minors.

INGLIS, Bill
b. Ottawa, Ontario, May 11, 1943
Had expansion not occurred in 1967, Inglis would have been buried eye-high in the minors while he read about one Habs Cup win after another. Thankfully for him and so many others, his career came to life, in his case with the L.A. Kings. Truth be told, Inglis was a minor-leaguer, but the Kings did give him some games in the NHL to tell the grandkids about. Down below, he scored more than his fair share – in the AHL, WHL, etc. – and he scored exactly once in the NHL. After retiring, he became a scout for the Sabres, and then midway through '78-'79 he caught a break when the team fired coach Marcel Pronovost and GM Punch Imlach. Inglis was brought in as coach and did an excellent job with the club down the stretch with a record of 28-18-10. He would have been offered the job full-time, but the Sabres were able to hire Scotty Bowman in the summer to act as coach and GM. Inglis later coached in the minors, notably Toledo and Kalamazoo.

INGOLDSBY, Johnny "Jack" ("Ding")
b. Toronto, Ontario, June 21, 1924
d. Oakville, Ontario, August 10, 1982
Strictly a wartime replacement in his hometown,

Ingoldsby played 29 games with the Leafs over a 2-year period and played a number of years in senior hockey and minor pro. He won the Allan Cup with the Owen Sound Mercurys in 1951.

INGRAM, Frank
b. Craven, Saskatchewan, September 17, 1905
d. unknown

Right wing Ingram played three years with Chicago during the team's early years (1929-32), helping the team go to the finals in 1931, where they lost to Montreal. That season, he had a very respectable 17 goals, one of the most productive years of his pro career, which took place mostly in the American league.

INGRAM, John "Jack"
b. Halifax, Nova Scotia, 1894
d. December 14, 1957

A one-game wonder from way back when, Ingram came and went with Boston in '24-'25, the team's inaugural NHL season. He spent most of his career down east, playing in Halifax and Moncton between the wars.

INGRAM, Ron ("Bim Bim")
b. Toronto, Ontario, July 5, 1933

Coming out of the Marlies in 1953, Ingram slipped into a career in senior hockey before Chicago signed him in 1956. Although the numbers didn't necessarily support it, he brought a reputation as an offensively able player to the team along with another rookie, Moose Vasko. Ingram lasted only this one year, though, and was relegated to the minors for six years in Buffalo before Chicago gave him another chance. On June 5, 1963, he and Roger Crozier were traded to Detroit for Howie Young, and although Ingram was having an excellent year with the Wings he was traded before the end of the season to the Rangers for Junior Langlois. Ingram finished his career in the minors, and later coached the Syracuse Blazers and San Diego Mariners. His most noteworthy hour, though, came after these stints when he coached in Indianapolis for Nelson Skalbania's WHA team, the one that traded a kid named Gretzky to Edmonton.

INNESS, Gary ("The Man with the Golden Glove")
b. Toronto, Ontario, May 28, 1949

Inness might well have been the only goalie to come straight out of a Canadian university to play goal in the NHL. He played at McMaster in Hamilton and then at U of Toronto, during which time he earned a degree in physical education and history intended to take him to a career in teaching. In 1973, though, Pittsburgh signed him, so he decided to put the classroom on

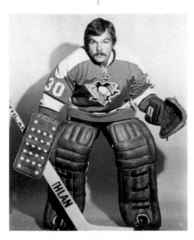

He played at
McMaster in Hamilton and
then at U of Toronto.
GARY INNESS

hold and take his stick and pads to the highest level. His entry into the league was rough, and when the Penguins went bankrupt they traded him to Philadelphia, where he played little behind Bernie Parent. Washington signed him in 1978, and it was with the Caps that he had his finest hour and earned his nickname. No sooner had he made a favourable impression one year than he started poorly for the team the next. He wound up in Hershey, first as a goalie and then as an assistant coach to Bryan Murray. When Murray moved up to the Caps after they fired Gary Green, Inness became the head coach with the Bears. In 1985, he retired to Barrie, where he took up his initial vocation, teaching phys ed and history in high school.

INTRANUOVO, Ralph
b. Toronto, Ontario,
December 11, 1973

There was a time, and it wasn't that long ago, when Intranuovo was pretty top drawer. He scored 50 goals one year in junior, and he was important to Canada's 1993 World Junior gold medal, playing on a line with Rob Niedermayer and Tyler Wright. A few weeks later, his Soo Greyhounds won the Memorial Cup. The year after, he made his NHL debut, registering an assist with Edmonton and later winning a bronze at the WC with Canada after a 46-goal season in the minors. He played briefly with the Leafs and wound up in the minors until deciding to give Europe a try, an option he has exercised since 1999.

IRBE, Arturs ("Archie")
b. Riga, Soviet Union (Latvia), February 2, 1967

If dogs are a man's best friend, then Irbe is no man. Or, he's the unluckiest of men, for it was his dog, Rambo, that jeopardized his career in the summer of 1994. Irbe had just completed his third year in the NHL. He led the league in games played (74) and minutes played (4,412) and had established himself as San Jose's goalie of the present and future. But that summer, he was doing sit-ups beside a sleeping Rambo. He accidentally nudged the dog at one point, and Rambo awoke with ferocity, tearing into the arteries and nerves of Irbe's hands. Irbe had to put his much-loved dog to sleep, and the injuries caused him much physical grief as well. It was months before he was ready to play, and when he did he showed little confidence. He had trouble gripping the stick, and he let in long shots and weak goals that had never been characteristic of his play. The next year, confidence all but shot, he made just 22 appearances for the Sharks. Brief and unimpressive stops in Dallas and Vancouver left him happy to sign with Carolina, just about the only team in the league

Frank Ingram

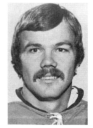

Gary Inness

Robbie Irons

that would take him. By this point, though, he was fully recovered. He had restored some confidence with his play for Latvia in the 1996 World Championships "B" pool, which took the team to "A" pool for the following season, and coach Paul Maurice gave Irbe all the minutes possible with the Canes. Irbe again was near the top in games played, and his performance culminated in 2002 when the team stunned hockey fans and experts by advancing to the Cup finals. Irbe had joined San Jose in 1991 after a number of years of pro in Riga. He was as quirky as any goalie, a man who relaxed before games by doing jigsaw puzzles and who left his mask and gloves on the player's bench during intermissions. He patched his own pads and glove with needle and thread, the same equipment he had used all his pro life. But, of course, whatever worked for him was not about to change, and no one around him messed with his habits and superstitions. He has played in five World Championships for his country, and he also appeared for Latvia in the 2002 Olympics in Salt Lake City.

IRELAND, Randy

b. Rosetown, Saskatchewan, April 5, 1957

During Ireland's career as a goalie, he virtually never played for the same team two seasons in a row until the last part of his career. Although he appeared in parts of two games for the Sabres in '78-'79 he roamed from team to team and league to league and back again without ever really establishing himself as a consistently good goaler.

IRONS, Robbie

b. Toronto, Ontario, November 19, 1946

Generally speaking, one-game wonders can hide behind that number and say, simply, that they played in the NHL. For goalies, however, where ice time is always calculated, hiding isn't as possible. So, Irons is not only a one-game wonder but also the goalie whose stay in the NHL was briefer than any other's – three minutes. He replaced Glenn Hall during a game on November 13, 1968, and never played in the NHL again. The irony, though, is that he had a hall of fame career in the IHL with the Fort Wayne Komets. He played there for 12 years, and when he retired in 1981 the team retired his number 30! He remained in his adopted town to work in radio for the team at night, and in the daytime he was a Pepsi brands manager.

IRONSTONE, Joe ("Kelly")

b. Montreal, Quebec, June 28, 1898
d. Sudbury, Ontario, December 12, 1972

The Jewish Star, as newspapers of the 1920s and '30s called goaltender Ironstone, was one of six children in the Ironstone family, which started in Montreal but moved to the nickel-rich north of Ontario late in the

Joe Ironstone

19th century. Joe was the most athletic in the family, and also the most strong-willed and temperamental, qualities that helped get him to the NHL and qualities that kept him out after a two-game career. Ironstone played junior in Sudbury from 1921 to '24 and played his first NHL game for the New York Americans in '25-'26, replacing the starter in one game and allowing three goals over two periods of hockey. After that, he played minor pro until March 3, 1928, when he replaced the injured John Ross Roach in a Toronto-Boston game at the Arena Gardens. Conn Smythe, desperate for a goalie, called Ironstone on the day of the game. Ironstone accepted the invitation, but at his price, not Smythe's. The Leafs GM was forced to accede to Ironstone's demands, and the goalie shut out the Bruins for 70 minutes in a scoreless overtime tie.

But Smythe was no man to be trifled with, and he made sure Ironstone never, ever played in the NHL again. It wasn't until 1936 that the goalie retired altogether, at which time he returned to Sudbury to work in the family's clothing store with his brother Moe. Ironstone remained there until the early 1960s, when the store burned to the ground. Ironstone was a man's man. He hunted and fished as much as possible at his cottage near Lake Penage, and he was a longtime member of the Granite Club in Sudbury. He died in 1972 of congestive heart failure and was buried in a Jewish cemetery in Toronto.

He raised more than 300 birds on his farm outside Regina and showed many in exhibtions.
DICK IRVIN

IRVIN, James Dickinson "Dick"

b. Limestone Ridge, Ontario, July 19, 1892
d. Montreal, Quebec, May 16, 1957

Because his family moved to Winnipeg in 1899, Irvin qualifies more as a Prairie boy than a native of southern Ontario. He played all of his minor and junior hockey in that city, eventually playing well enough to earn a spot on the Monarchs team that won the Allan Cup in 1915. He interrupted his playing career to join the 1st Depot Battalion of the Manitoba Regiment, serving with the Fort Garry Horse. When he was discharged he picked up where he left off, playing senior hockey in Regina. He played there for six years and then joined Portland, and in 1926 he was recruited by the fledgling Hawks. Irvin was the team's first captain, and in his first NHL season at age 34 he led the league with 18 assists and finished second in scoring behind only Bill Cook. The next season was damaging for Irvin. He was checked hard by Red Dutton of the Americans, and the fall to the ice fractured his skull. He missed the rest of the year and was named coach of the team for '28-'29, though he returned to play as well. He was ineffective and retired as a player, though he stayed on to coach the Hawks a second season as well. He left Chicago to coach Toronto, and over the next decade he had a remarkable record.

The team made it to the playoffs every year, and in 7 of those seasons the Leafs advanced to the Cup finals. They won just once, though, in 1932. Irvin was given permission by owner Conn Smythe to go to Montreal to coach. The Canadiens were a floundering franchise, and all concerned believed Irvin could save the team. He did. For the next 15 years he coached the Canadiens, missing the playoffs only once. He went to the finals eight more times, and won in 1944, '46, and '53. Like most coaches of the day, he was a colourful figure. He forbade his players to drink, and he could rant and rave with the best of them when occasion called. He sometimes ran out onto the ice to pursue a referee, and verbal matches in hotel lobbies were not uncommon. To stay calm and sane, Irvin had an unusual hobby away from the rink. He was a chicken and pigeon fancier. He raised more than 300 birds on his farm outside Regina and showed many in exhibitions. Over the years, he won many prizes at the Royal Winter Fair in Toronto. In 1955, Irvin decided to leave Montreal to coach Chicago, but after one season his health was bad and he had to retire permanently. He had bone cancer in one leg, and spent much of the next year in hospital before succumbing to the disease. A year later, he was inducted into the Hockey Hall of Fame for his playing career, though he qualified equally as a builder for his coaching. Irvin retired having coached 1,449 games, winning 692, both records until Al Arbour and Scotty Bowman came along some 20 years later. Irvin left behind a young son, Dick Jr., who would go on to his own exemplary career in hockey, though off the ice. Dick Jr. was a broadcaster with *Hockey Night in Canada* for decades, and with Danny Gallivan formed arguably the best duo in the business.

IRVINE, Ted
b. Winnipeg, Manitoba, December 8, 1944
Irvine was initially the property of the Bruins in the early 1960s, and got into his first NHL game with the team in '63-'64. He languished in the minors for the better part of four years until L.A. claimed him in 1967, and then began a 10-year career. Late in his third season, the Kings traded him to the Rangers, and he had his finest moments with the Blueshirts. He played with Pete Stemkowski and Bruce MacGregor to form one of the better two-way lines, and in '71-'72 Bobby Rousseau replaced Stemkowski during the team's march to the finals, where they lost to Bobby Orr and the Bruins. Irvine ended his career in St. Louis and then returned to the 'Peg, where he acted as a scout for the Blues. After leaving hockey altogether, he and his wife, Loretta, formed their own life insurance company called T.L.C. Irvine Insurance Services.

IRWIN, Ivan ("The Terrible")
b. Chicago, Illinois, March 13, 1927
He may have been terrible during his playing days, but the latter-day Irwin is a puddy-tat by comparison. Those halcyon days of skates and sticks took place with Montreal and New York in the 1950s. Irwin had a reputation for devastating hip checks, though much of his career took place in the minors. He was, at the time, the only American player in the NHL, and almost the second he retired he started to work for the players. He helped found the NHL Oldtimers with Wally Stanowski, Harry Watson, Danny Lewicki, and Bob Goldham, and over the next 23 years he helped raise some $2-million for retired NHLers, many of whom were impoverished or nearly destitute despite a life in the game. He later became part owner and president of Ballycliffe Lodge in Ajax, Ontario, and remained supportive in all old-timers' activities in southern Ontario and, when possible, beyond.

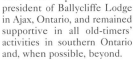

Over the next 23 years he helped raise some $2 million for retired NHLers.
IVAN IRWIN

ISAKSSON, Ulf
b. Norrsunda, Sweden, March 19, 1954
Isaksson and friend Peter Helander joined Los Angeles together in 1982 as NHL rookies after a decade of Swedish league play, but Helander lasted only 7 games and Isaksson 50 before the experiment ended. Isaksson spent the rest of the year in the minors and then hightailed it back to the life he knew, playing in Stockholm, the city to which he had given his finest hours. He twice represented Tre Kronor at the World Championships, in 1981 and '82.

ISBISTER, Brad
b. Edmonton, Alberta, May 7, 1977
A gold-medal graduate of the '97 World Juniors team, Isbister went on to play for Canada at both the 2000 and the 2001 World Championships because his NHL team, the Islanders, didn't qualify for the playoffs. He had a partial breakout year in 1999-2000 with 22 goals, though the season was tarnished because he missed 16 games with a badly sprained ankle. The next year, he missed 15 games with a fractured jaw. Only now approaching his prime, he might become a force or he might slip back, though the Islanders are now a playoff-strong team, which should help, not hinder, his development.

ISSEL, Kim
b. Calgary, Alberta, September 25, 1967
Trying to crack the Edmonton lineup in the 1980s was a task only Hall of Famers could reasonably expect to accomplish, so it's no surprise that Issel played four games with the Oilers and a number of years in the minors. By 1991, he had had enough of the farm team and headed to Europe, where he played in a number of countries for the rest of the decade.

Ted Irvine

Ulf Isaksson

Brad Isbister

Kim Issel

Art Jackson

JABLONSKI, Pat ("Jabber")
b. Toledo, Ohio, June 20, 1967

Funny thing, but not many goalies choose to play their final good years of hockey in Europe. For whatever reason, once they've stretched for their final save in North America, they retire, most often, it seems, to the broadcast booth. Not Jablonski. He turned pro in 1987, but he continues to block shots in Sweden since being shipped out of the NHL to the "I." In his 8 years in the big league, Jablonski played for 5 teams but appeared in just 128 games. He had an unimpressive 28-62-18 record and appeared in the playoffs only as a substitute. Most of his time was spent in the minors, and even there he wasn't a number-one goaler. He did play for the U.S. at the 1995 World Championships, and when the chance to play in the Swedish league with Vastra Frolunda presented itself in 1999, he jumped at it.

JACKMAN, Barret
b. Trail, British Columbia, March 5, 1981

Jackman's reward for being the best player with Worcester in 2001-02 was to be called up to the parent team, St. Louis, for a game on April 14, 2002, his first in the NHL. He was a solid and rough defenceman in junior in Regina, which is why the Blues drafted him 17th overall in 1999. He made the team in 2002-03, and paired with Al MacInnis, has played well beyond his years so far.

JACKMAN, Richard
b. Toronto, Ontario, June 28, 1978

A kid to admire, a career yet to be summarized in full, Jackman made a stink in 1996 when he passed up the chance to play at the CHL's Prospects Game in order to play a critical game with his club team in the Soo. It was a decision based on conviction and team loyalty, and he went on to win gold for Canada at the 1997 WJC. However, after being drafted 5th overall by Dallas in '96, he has yet to make an NHL impression with either the Stars or Boston, the team that acquired him in 2001.

JACKSON, Art
b. Toronto, Ontario, December 15, 1915
d. St. Catharines, Ontario, May 15, 1971

Younger brother of the great Harvey "Busher" Jackson, Art had a respectable career of his own in a decade of play that finished when the time the war ended. He won a Memorial Cup with St. Mike's in 1934, and when he joined the Leafs the next year with Nick Metz and Pep Kelly, the three were named "war babies" because they were all born during WWI. Known more as a checker in Toronto, Jackson had his greatest years with Boston from 1939 to '45, winning the Cup with the Bruins in 1941. Playing on a line with Bill Cowley and Herbie Cain, he had consecutive seasons of 22 and 28 goals, and he closed out his career in Toronto after the Leafs acquired him down the stretch toward their own Cup victory in 1945. Jackson soon settled in St. Catharines and became the first coach of that city's new OHA team in 1947. He left that position after a short time to become the personnel manager of Port Weller Dry Docks Ltd.. His untimely death came one weekend when he suffered a heart attack while playing in the Opening Day tournament at the St. Catharines Golf Club.

JACKSON, Dane
b. Castlegar, British Columbia, May 17, 1970

Coming out of the University of North Dakota in 1992, Jackson was tabbed as a legitimate dark horse to make it. Tall and gangly, he had to improve his skating and fill out if he were to have any impact. Vancouver had drafted him in 1988, but he played only a few games for the Canucks and two other teams before finding his niche in the AHL. He captained the Rochester Americans to the 1996 Calder Cup, and more recently signed to captain the new Manchester (New Hampshire) Monarchs, though his chances of returning to the NHL seem slim now.

JACKSON, Don
b. Minneapolis, Minnesota, September 2, 1956

The great thing about being an athlete is that you can have two lives, your pro career and then your working life. Never say no to the pros – the rest can always wait. Jackson came out of the University of Notre Dame, and it was evident pretty early on that he was no superstar. What ice time he got, he earned, and that didn't guarantee anything the next night. And so it was that while he played sporadically with Minnesota and more often in the minors, he developed a small but successful real estate business in Minneapolis. This worked out well for four years, but when the North Stars traded him to Edmonton in 1981, he almost didn't go. In the end, he relented, more because the early 1980s was a bad time for real estate than because he wanted to continue playing. Of course, the story has a great ending. He was partnered with Randy Gregg on the blueline, and after losing in the '83 finals, he won consecutive Cups with the Oilers in '84 and '85. He was later traded to the Rangers, but that wasn't a great chance and he returned to Minneapolis to resume his real estate business until fate grabbed him by the skates again. He realized how much he missed the game, and when the chance to coach came his way, he accepted. For several years, he kicked around the minors as an assistant coach and then head coach, and he had a couple of NHL chances as an assistant coach to boot, most recently with Chicago. There will always be real estate, but hockey has a more finite life.

JACKSON, Doug
b. Winnipeg, Manitoba, December 12, 1924

The Chicago Black Hawks of '47-'48 finished dead last in the NHL with a record of 20-34-6 and Jackson was on goal for 6 of those games (2-3-1). Unfortunately, he allowed a whopping 42 goals during a season in which he was starring in the U.S. league with Kansas City. He never made it back to the NHL and retired from the game soon after.

JACKSON, Harold ("Hal")
b. Cedar Springs, Ontario, August 1, 1918
d. unknown

Jackson played four full years in the NHL and parts of three others. Ironically, he won two Cups during the part-time years and none while a regular. The wins

Pat Jablonski

Richard Jackman

Dane Jackson

Don Jackman

Harold Jackman

Art Jackson
(opposite page)

came with Chicago in '38 and Detroit five years later, and those were the two teams with which he played his entire NHL career. After retiring, he became a linesman in the league and was one of the first men to advocate players promoting the game off-ice through community involvement.

JACKSON, Harvey ("Busher")
b. Toronto, Ontario, January 19, 1911
d. Toronto, Ontario, June 25, 1966

This is the saddest story in hockey. Jackson was so much more than just a good soldier doing battle on ice. He was a poet, a dancer, a blade artist, as they used to say. He started, appropriately enough, skating on Poverty Pond in the west end of Toronto, and eventually made it to the Ravina Rink. Frank Selke couldn't take his eyes off him, and signed him to a contract with the Leafs. Jackson rose up through the Marlies and made the Leafs in 1929, a left winger with great speed and a shift in his stride that could fool any defenceman. At 18, he was the youngest player in the league and was soon put on a line with two other babes, Joe Primeau and Charlie Conacher. The Kid Line was born. Until Primeau's retirement in 1936, this threesome dominated the NHL. They were stars and scored seemingly at will. Jackson had five 20-goal seasons with the Leafs, and in '31-'32 he led the NHL in scoring with 53 points, only the second Leafs player, after Ace Bailey, to do so. That year, he was also named to the First All-Star Team and, more important, the Leafs won the Cup. He once scored four goals in a period to set an NHL record, and the Kid Line routinely was the highest-scoring troika in the league. Jackson was a Hollywood star. He drove fancy cars, spent money freely, showed up at swishy parties, and smiled at every camera pointed his way. Leafs GM Conn Smythe smelled trouble and urged Jackson to save some of his earnings, going so far as to match him dollar for dollar to help build the kitty. Jackson ignored the pleas. He was traded to the New York Americans after an injury and then on to Boston, where he finished his career in 1944, and upon returning to Toronto, the cameras pointed elsewhere, the money not coming in as freely, the troubles became more noticeable. He fought with both of his wives, whom he eventually divorced, and he drank to excess. The fun turned into alcoholism, and no matter how hard his friends helped him get a job, he would lose it through poor conduct and lax attitude. He suffered from jaundice, and once, in 1958, broke his neck falling down stairs in his house (he swore he was sober). Legend has it that he could be found outside the Gardens selling broken hockey sticks of

John Jackson

Jeff Jackson

Jim Jackson

He once scored four goals in a period to set an NHL record.
HARVEY JACKSON

Leafs players to anyone who would pay him a bit of cash. Smythe was so appalled that he blocked Jackson's admission into the Hall of Fame with Primeau and Conacher, saying his personal life was so reprehensible it did not become an honoured member. Jackson died of liver failure in 1966, and in 1971 the Hall of Fame finally admitted him. Smythe resigned from his position on the selection committee in protest.

JACKSON, John "Jack"
b. Windsor, Ontario, May 3, 1925

If you call 'em as you see 'em, you're gonna have to pay the price, and for Jackson the price was his career. In 1946, he came up from Kansas City to make the Chicago team as a regular defenceman. It was his only NHL season, and after a few more years with K.C. he wound up in the PCHL with an outfit called the Seattle Ironmen. Late in the season, the team had a meeting to see what it could do to prepare for the playoffs, and Jackson suggested it would be better for the fifth-place team to finish sixth, a spot that would assure a weaker opponent. Though he spoke the truth, any taint on the team's play for the rest of the season could not be tolerated, and management suspended him there and then. He was told to leave the meeting, and he never played hockey again.

JACKSON, Jeff ("Jesse")
b. Dresden, Ontario, April 24, 1965

After winning a gold medal with Canada's juniors in 1985, Jackson joined the Leafs for the final few games of the season and seemed poised to crack the lineup full-time in the fall. Toronto, however, was going through its roughest years, and before giving Jackson a chance to develop slowly and learn the game the team traded him to the Rangers. That summer, he was traded again, to Quebec, and it was with the Nordiques that Jackson had his finest years. He was with the team for three and a half years, and although he wound up in the minors, he couldn't complain about not being given a chance. After retiring in 1992, Jackson attended the University of Western Ontario in London and earned a law degree. He moved to Toronto, where he became an entertainment specialist for the firm of Heenan Blaikie.

JACKSON, Jim
b. Oshawa, Ontario, February 1, 1960

Ain't got nuthin' to lose when no one wants you and you singin' da blues. Jackson was playing provincial junior hockey (pejoratively referred to too often as Tier II) when he signed with Richmond in the EHL in 1980. He scratched and clawed and fought his way up the ladder, moving to the "I" the next year and the NHL, with Calgary, the year after that. It was an improbable achievement, and his cause was aided by Flames scout Gerry Blair, who was Jackson's neighbour in Oshawa. Blair begged the team to give Jackson a tryout and sign him to a contract, and although Jackson started the '82-'83 season in the minors (this time, the CHL), he got a call when Kevin Lavallee and Carl Mokosak of the Flames were both injured. Jackson stepped in and scored eight goals in half a season playing on a line with Kent Nilsson and Eddy Beers. The year after was much the same, and after that his career trickled to a stop until he was back in the minors. But for a guy who started out with nothing, Jackson wrote a pretty fine tale of joy for himself.

JACKSON, Lloyd
b. Ottawa, Ontario,
January 7, 1912
d. Ottawa, Ontario,
February 15, 1999
Jackson's is a name connected in a small way to one of the great Stanley Cup stories. He was playing for the New York Americans in 1936-37 when the Amerks traded the centreman to New Haven of the American league for the well-travelled goalie Alfie Moore. The next season, Moore was loaned to Chicago for game one of the Cup finals against Toronto – pulled out of a tavern according to lore – which he won and which sent the Hawks on the road to victory. Jackson, meanwhile, never returned from the minors. He went off to war, then settled in Ottawa.

JACKSON, Percy
b. Canmore, Alberta, September 21, 1907
d. unknown
When Jackson was called up in the '31-'32 season from the Boston Cubs to play a few games for the Bruins, he acquitted himself handsomely, allowing just eight goals in about four games of work. The same could not be said for his next two callups. One came on March 18, 1934, when he allowed nine goals in a New York Americans loss to Boston. The other came on November 1, 1934 when he watched eight pucks go by in another loss. He played once more a year later with Boston, then settled in Vancouver and played in the PCHL.

JACKSON, Stanton "Stan"
b. Amherst, Nova Scotia, August 27, 1898
d. Ridgeway, Ontario, November 28, 1956
As a teenager, Jackson halted his developing hockey career to serve in the Royal Air Force during WWI. Upon his discharge in 1920, he made his way up through the ranks and signed with the Toronto St. Pats, where he played parts of three seasons. He

later played two years for Boston and a final eight games with the Ottawa Senators in '26-'27. He went down to London to help the Panthers win the CanPro championship, and after retiring in 1934 he worked as an immigration officer at the Peace Bridge in Fort Erie, Ontario. He held this position until two years before his death, with the exception of 1941-45 when he enlisted again and was put in charge of the control tower at the RCAF base in Trenton, Ontario.

JACKSON, Walter ("Red")
b. Ibstock, England, June 3, 1908
Jackson grew up in Winnipeg and graduated to the AHA in the early 1930s before joining the New York Americans in 1932. He played for the Amerks for just over two years and finished his career in Boston before returning to the AHA. He retired in 1938.

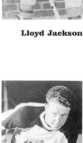

Lloyd Jackson

JACOBS, Paul
b. unknown
d. unknown
Perhaps the most obscure player ever to appear in the NHL, Jacobs was a North American Indian who appeared in five games for the Toronto Arenas in 1918-19 – January 7, 14, 21, 31, and February 4, 1919. He was also an excellent lacrosse player.

JACOBS, Tim
b. Espanola, Ontario,
March 28, 1952
Jacobs is one of the all-time leaders in the dubious category of most career NHL games played without scoring a goal. He played 46 games with California in '75-'76, and although he registered 10 assists, he scored nary once.

Walter Jackson

His first moment of fame came during the lockout year of '94-'95 when he won the Art Ross Trophy for the first time.
JAROMIR JAGR

The defenceman didn't score much in any league he played in and spent most of his minor-league career with Salt Lake City.

JAGR, Jaromir
b. Kladno, Czechoslovakia (Czech Republic),
February 15, 1972
Wayne Gretzky's last hockey game took place at Madison Square Garden, the Penguins in town to visit. Perhaps the ending was perfect symbolism on that historic day, for it was Jagr who scored the game-winning goal in overtime. The torch was passed from one superstar to the next in that afternoon, and after Gretzky closed his equipment bag for the last time, Jagr became the game's most dominant player. He was a tremendous prospect in the late 1980s, but few NHL teams were optimistic about their chances of getting him. He was not the kind of man to defect, and he still had military duty to complete before the Czechs would even consider letting him play outside the country. When Pittsburgh chose him 5th overall in 1990, it was a more prescient move than they could have known, for later

Tim Jacobs

that summer the country split and Jagr was free to leave. He arrived in Pittsburgh shy and timorous, knowing only a few words of English. He chose to wear number 68 to commemorate his country's uprising against Soviet rule in 1968. In his first year, he scored 27 goals and behind captain Mario Lemieux won the Stanley Cup, and the next year he was even more of a force for a repeat victory. Key to his success was the team's acquisition of Jiri Hrdina, a skilled Czech who kept an eye on Jagr and talked to him constantly about the game in a language with which he felt comfortable. One writer ingeniously discovered that scrambling the letters in Jaromir results in Mario Jr., a perfect way to illustrate Jagr's role on the team and his place in Penguins history. His first moment of fame came during the lockout year of '94-'95 when he won the Art Ross Trophy for the first time. The next year, he had a staggering 62 goals and 149 points. He went on to win the Art Ross four times in succession (1998-2001), and as Lemieux retired he became the league's premier player. Like all great players, he has a style all his own. He isn't lightning fast. He doesn't park himself in the slot or score on slapshots. He is without equal in tight and when being checked. Along the boards, back to the net, he can fight off two or three players to make a perfect pass or move out front. He is disarmingly strong and plays with one hand on the stick with the same strength as most players with two, and just when he seems trapped is often when he is, in truth, most dangerous. Jagr helped the Czechs win a historic gold at the 1998 Olympics in Nagano, and was team captain on the less successful team in Salt Lake City four years later. He won two Lester Pearson Awards (league MVP as selected by the players), but just as all good things must pass his time with the Penguins ended just as, ironically, owner, hero, and captain Mario Lemieux came out of retirement. Despite a successful season together again in 2000-01, Jagr was traded to Washington for the next season, a result that ensured both the Pens and the Caps missed the playoffs. In February 2003, he joined that most elite group of NHLers when he scored his 500th goal. Jagr has been a quiet superstar by NHL standards, uncomfortable in inheriting Gretzky's throne as league ambassador because of his lack of confidence with English. He is, though, a devout believer in the Bible, and if Heaven is like hockey, Jagr may have some problems in the next life: If the first will be last and the last first, he'll be at the back of the line, because in this life he is among the first as far as hockey is concerned.

JAKOPIN, John
b. Toronto, Ontario, May 16, 1975
Jakopin's parents are Slovenian and taught their boy to

John Jakopin

He was inducted into the Canadian Football Hall of Fame and still holds a record for most rushing touchdowns in a season (18, with Winnipeg, in 1957).
GERRY JAMES

speak their native tongue. One day, he hopes to get dual citizenship and perhaps represent Slovenia internationally. In the meantime, the hulking defenceman is trying to make a go of it in the NHL, and so far he's having a tough time. Drafted by Detroit, the Wings let him go without a fuss in 1997, at which time he signed with Florida. The Panthers gave him a few games over four years but not enough to make him feel as if he had made the team. His last move took him to Pittsburgh, but it's only been more frustration for Jakopin so far.

JAKS, Pauli
b. Schaffhausen, Switzerland, January 25, 1972
Fitting tribute to Jaks' qualities as a goalie can be seen in his being named best goalie at the 1991 WJC despite his country's seventh-place finish. More important, Jaks was drafted by Los Angeles into the NHL and played a game for the Kings a year and a half later. He made the road to the big league a little easier for David Aebischer, and now other Swiss players are more likely to be drafted than ever before. Jaks played two years of minor pro in North America and since that time has returned home to play in the Swiss league.

JALO, Risto
b. Tampere, Finland, July 18, 1962
No matter how successful a European player is in his native country, his competitive fire will eventually get the better of him and push him to try his hand in the NHL. For Jalo, that time came in 1985 when he joined the Oilers toward the end of his Finnish league season. In three games he had as many assists, but he returned home and never went to North America again. In Finland, he was a star, appearing internationally for Suomi on many occasions. He won silver and bronze with the Junior team and also played at the 1984 Olympics in Sarajevo and in four World Championships in a career that didn't end until 1998. His finest year might well have been '83-'84 when he was named to the First All-Star Team, won the Raimo Kilpio Trophy as most gentlemanly player, and was one of the league's leaders in points with 45.

JALONEN, Kari
b. Oulu, Finland, January 6, 1960
The careers of Risto Jalo and Kiri Jalonen are remarkably similar. Jalonen, too, had a long and distinguished career in Finland, and he, too, tried for a brief time to make it in the NHL. He was only slightly more successful than Jalo, lasting 37 games with Calgary and Edmonton, the 2 best skating teams in the league willing to try European talent in the mid-1980s. Funnily enough, although he was considered a passer rather than

Kari Jalonen

scorer back home, he had nine goals and three assists with the Flames and also appeared briefly in the '83 playoffs for the team. He played some 17 years in the Finnish league and in six World Championships for his country. He also played long stretches for the national team and at the 1981 Canada Cup. After retiring in 1996, he later became head coach of TPS Turku, the team for whom he had played five seasons.

JAMES, Gerry
b. Regina, Saskatchewan, October 22, 1934

Why play one sport if you can play two? So rationalized James, who was as good a football player as a hockeyist. Throughout the 1950s, he alternated sports or went from one to the other with the ease of a driver shifting gears. He played junior for the Marlies, yet after winning the Memorial Cup in 1956 he decided the CFL was his thing. He played for the Winnipeg Blue Bombers, but at the end of that season the NHL sked was only just getting into full swing. He packed up his cleats, unpacked his skates, and ventured to Maple Leaf Gardens. James played nothing but hockey the year after, but in '57-'58 it was again two-sport Gerry. He was about to do this for a third season, but, inevitably, a football injury caused him to miss the entire hockey season. He helped the Leafs advance to the finals in 1960, playing with Duke Edmundson and Johnny Wilson on the self-dubbed Puke Line, a spoof on the highly skilled Uke Line (the Pukes were strictly checkers and disturbers, not goal scorers). After retiring, James settled in Yorkton, Saskatchewan, where he ended his playing days in senior hockey. He ran a motel and also coached the junior team for two years (1972-'74). He was inducted into the Canadian Football Hall of Fame and still holds a record for most rushing touchdowns in a season (18, with Winnipeg, in 1957).

JAMES, Valmore "Val"
b. Ocala, Florida, February 14, 1957

His name alone has a story. His aunt named him after Valmore Gore, a pro football player, but those around him shortened it to Val. Later in life, he, more often than not, shortened others. At first he was a bouncer, and then he tried to do the same job on skates. Voila, an enforcer! Better pay, greater fame, meet new people. He played only 11 NHL games with Buffalo and the Leafs, but earned his stripes down in the minors, primarily the AHL, where he piled up the penalty minutes and bodies in equal number.

JAMIESON, Jim
b. Brantford, Ontario, March 21, 1922

Even those outside the NHL, Jamieson's was a short and incomplete career. Inside the NHL, his name can be added to the list of one-gamers who get an assist in their only appearance. For Jamieson, that night came during the '43-'44 season with the Rangers. After retiring, he returned to Brantford to coach.

JANASZAK, Steve
b. St. Paul, Minnesota, January 7, 1957

He doesn't mind being famous for something he didn't do, and he doesn't mind being in the middle of a famous photo he had nothing to do with, really. In 1980, Janaszak was the spare goalie for the U.S.'s Miracle on Ice team. He played regularly throughout the exhibition and pre-season schedule, but during those Olympics goalie Jim Craig stood out and rightfully got the call each night. But at the final horn to end the team's great win over the USSR, Janaszak's sweater with his name on it is clearly in the famous celebration picture! Immediately after the win, he signed a contract with Minnesota and just a few days later was in goal for a 2-2 tie with Buffalo. He didn't play in the NHL again for two years, and only two more games with Colorado at that. He wound up in the CHL and decided that was not the level of play for him. He used his four years of education at the University of Minnesota to good effect and later worked for an investment banking firm that had offices on the 85th floor of the World Trade Center until the terrorist attacks on September 11, 2001.

JANECYK, Bob ("Janny")
b. Chicago, Illinois, May 18, 1957

It's one thing to play in goal in front of fans among which you used to number yourself, but Janecyk's path to the NHL and the Black Hawks was hardly paved and straight. He played for Chicago State University, not exactly the future-NHLer capital of the world. But the man who ran the Southwest Ice Arena in Crestwood, just outside Chicago where the team used to practise, thought he was a good goalie. That man, Frank Cristina, notified Lou Angotti, former Hawk and current broadcaster. Angotti agreed and told Hawks GM Bob Pulford so, and Pully signed Janecyk as a free agent. That was just the beginning. Then, there were four years in the minors. In March 1984, though, Chicago regular Murray Bannerman was hurt, and Janecyk got the call. He tied his first game and stopped 48 shots in a victory in his second game. The native son had returned a hero, though only for a short time. He was traded to Los Angeles in a multiplayer deal in large part so the Hawks could draft another local boy, Ed Olczyk. In L.A., he played fewer and fewer games and soon found himself more of a minor-leaguer than an NHLer. After retiring, he later became a scout with the Ottawa Senators.

JANKOWSKI, Lou
b. Regina, Saskatchewan, June 27, 1931

Jankowski was one of the all-time great minor-league scorers from the time he turned pro in 1950 to the time he retired to try coaching in 1969. His first NHL games couldn't have been more poorly timed, coming with Detroit in '50-'51 and '52-'53, the only years in the 1950-55 era that the Wings didn't win the Cup. He ended up in Chicago a few years later at the nadir in team history, but it was with Buffalo (AHL) and Calgary (WHL) that he left his mark. He had five 40-goal seasons in the ensuing years with those teams, including a league-leading 57 in '60-'61, the year he was named WHL MVP. That summer, at a banquet, he stunned the crowd by announcing his retirement so he could return to Simcoe, Ontario, and relax on his tobacco farm. By fall, however, Calgary management had convinced him to return, and Jankowski just kept on scoring. Upon retiring in 1969, he was hired to coach the Jersey Devils of the Eastern league, but he quit just four months later citing stress.

Jim Jamieson

Steve Janaszak

Bob Janecyk

Lou Jankowski

Mark Janssens

Marko Jantunen

Doug Jarrett

Gary Jarrett

Pierre Jarry

JANNEY, Craig ("C.J.")

b. Hartford, Connecticut, September 26, 1967

There are two sides to most coins, and Janney's qualities as a player are based on what he did and did not do with the puck. He drove many people crazy with his reluctance verging on refusal to shoot the puck, yet he was one of the finer passers in the game during his prime (the 1990s). He developed into a great playmaker in Boston, but after four and a half seasons the Bruins traded him to his mirror image, Adam Oates. Something brown and soft hit the fan in March 1994 when St. Louis signed Petr Nedved as a free agent and Janney was awarded to Vancouver as compensation. He refused to report, and the two teams had to work out a deal to keep Janney with the Blues and give the Canucks equal value. His career petered out as he played for four teams in his final four seasons, retiring in 1999 as one of the most heralded American-born players.

JANSSENS, Mark

b. Surrey, British Columbia, May 19, 1968

On the morning of September 11, 2001, Janssens was preparing to start a new job in the World Trade Center. He took the subway downtown, and when he got outside he saw one of the planes hit the building. It was that close. He had recently retired from 13 years in the NHL, years of defensive play as a centre and playing tough to survive. He had been a scorer in junior with Regina, but he had also been a fighter, and when he got to the NHL the latter attributes were more easily attainable than the former. He played for seven teams and struggled to survive, but no one appreciated life more than he did when he woke up on September 12, 2001, his new job on hold.

JANTUNEN, Marko

b. Lahti, Finland, February 14, 1971

He didn't last long in the NHL, but that's okay because Jantunen was drafted 239th overall in 1991 and can't have expected more. He played three games for Calgary in '96-'97, yet despite a lack of glory in North America, Jantunen has had a perfectly reputable career in Europe. He has played in both the Finnish and the Swedish leagues since 1990, and as recently as 1997 represented his country at the World Championships.

JARDINE, Ryan

b. Ottawa, Ontario, March 15, 1980

Drafted by Florida in 1998, Jardine's career has been anything but a walk in the park to date. He played a few games with the Panthers late in the 2001-02 season but before and after has been in the minors. He is a left winger who is a scoring prospect for the team.

JARRETT, Doug

b. London, Ontario, April 22, 1944

All slapshots are definitely not the same. Jarrett is living proof of that, for his career ended after taking a Bobby Orr shot off the ankle in a game at Madison Square Garden in early 1977. The pain shot up his back to the point that he couldn't undo his skates in the dressing room. He hired a lawyer who initiated Jarrett's insurance policy, and he was paid for the rest of the year. His back, however, wasn't right for the next five years, until finally doctors injected papaya juice into the area. He has been pain-free ever since. Jarrett was the first Londoner to make it to the Original Six as a defensive defenceman. His first contract was actually a three-way deal that paid him $5,500 for the CHL, $6,500 for the AHL, and $9,500 for the NHL. He got his first chance in December 1964 after the Hawks had a miserable start. Jarrett was tossed into the lineup, the team went on a lengthy winning streak, and he never played in the minors again. Keith Magnuson quickly gave him the nickname Chairman of the Boards because of his penchant for nailing rushing forwards along the wall, which is how he survived in the league for so long. After regaining his health, he coached kids in Niagara Falls and then became a steel salesman based in Windsor.

JARRETT, Gary

b. Toronto, Ontario, September 3, 1942

Down in Cleveland during the WHA's days the arena was in an area where buildings were being torn down and people mugged with seeming equal regularity. It was also there that Jarrett ended his career making $100,000 a year and where he fell in love and got married. By all rights, Jarrett should have been a Leafs player for many years, but when he first joined the team in 1961 he lacked the temperament and maturity to make it. The Leafs buried him in the minors and the Wings exhumed him when they acquired Billy Harris from the team, and Jarrett established himself as an effective if unspectacular forward. He played his last four years in Oakland and decided to retire, but then the Crusaders lured him out of a lifelong vacation with an offer he couldn't – and didn't – refuse. When his days in Cleveland were done, he and his wife moved to Evergreen, a suburb of Denver, where established his own real estate company and did colour commentary on radio for the CHL's Colorado Flames.

JARRY, Pierre ("Pete")

b. Montreal, Quebec, March 30, 1949

Jarry made the transition from junior to minor pro with ease, scoring 46 goals in the CHL in his second season, 1970-71. The next stage, though, to the NHL, was slower. The Rangers tried him on for size and found him too small, so they traded him to Jim Dorey in a trade of irony. Dorey was one of the tougher players in the league, and Jarry brought with him a reputation for being a "featherduster," that is, a player who checks an opponent with his stick way out in front of him so as not to get hurt. He later played for Detroit and Minnesota, but only once, in '75-'76, did he score more than 20 goals. He missed much of the next season after a serious knee injury, and that was the beginning of the end for Jarry who retired at the finish of the following year. He returned to Montreal and went into business, starting Pierre Jarry Productions.

JARVENPAA, Hannu

b. Iives, Finland, May 19, 1963

North America was just not the place for Jarvenpaa. Montreal had drafted him in 1982 but didn't bring him over, so four years later the Jets drafted him and did use him. It was Jarvenpaa's dream to play in the NHL, but his three years in Canada were a nightmare. In his first exhibition game he scored 4 goals and thought, this is easy. In his first 10 regular season games he scored no goals and realized, this is hard. He started to play a little tougher and hungrier, but then made a pass and kept his head down and crunch! Torn knee ligaments and reconstructive surgery put an end to his season and part of the next. The year after, things weren't going that well to start out with and then in January 1988 his mother was seriously injured in a car crash that killed his father. He went home for the funeral, and although he came back his heart wasn't in it. At season's end, he returned to Finland to resume what had been a fine career. He played in the 1991 Canada Cup for Finland as well as 5 WC and 2 WJC and the 1992 Olympics in Albertville. He retired in 1995 at peace for having tried the NHL but harrowed by its results.

JARVENTIE, Martti
b. Tampere, Finland,
April 4, 1976
A longtime player in his native Tampere, Jarventie came to North America in 2001 and played the season in the minors. He played a single game with the Canadiens that year, but the defenceman was not able to make it back for a longer stay.

JARVI, Iiro
b. Helsinki, Finland,
March 23, 1965
He was drafted into the NHL as an 18-year-old in 1983 but Jarvi didn't play until he was 23, preferring to stay in Finland. When he did join the Nordiques for 1988-89, he scored only eleven goals in 75 games and the year after he was in the minors half the year. Like most Europeans of his vintage, it was the NHL or nothing as far as North American hockey goes, so in 1990 he packed his bags and returned home. Back in Europe, he had an outstanding career, and internationally he played at every level, notably the '87 and '91 Canada Cups and the '88 Olympics.

JARVIS, James "Bud"
b. Fort William, Ontario, December 7, 1907
d. Thunder Bay, Ontario, May 7, 1983
Jarvis developed his skills in Port Arthur where he helped bring the Allan Cup home in 1929. As a result, the Pittsburgh Pirates signed him, and he scored eleven goals as a rookie. He moved down to Philadelphia when the team transferred there but after that he spent most of the rest of his career in the minors. The lone exception was a half a season's play with the Leafs in '36-'37. After retiring in 1944, Jarvis coached in Fort Frances and took the team to the Allan Cup in 1951. He worked in private business the rest of his life with Great West Timber, Northern Wood Preserves, the Department of Lands and Forests,

Iiro Jarvi

Great Lakes Shipping, and the Hammermill Paper Company. He was posthumously inducted into the Northwestern Ontario Sports Hall of Fame in 1998.

JARVIS, Doug
b. Brantford, Ontario, March 24, 1955
One of the worst trades Toronto ever made was to send Jarvis to Montreal for Greg Hubick just days after drafting the young centre out of Peterborough in 1975. Hubick went on to have little impact with the Leafs, while Jarvis started his career by playing in a record 964 straight games and winning Stanley Cups in each of his first four years with the Canadiens. He was the definitive answer to two-way hockey, a player who inherited Bob Gainey's title as best defensive forward and penalty killer supreme. It was soon after he missed his first game, on October 11, 1987, that his career ended. He was sent to Hartford's minor-league team in Binghamton, and began helping out as an informal assistant coach. From there, he retired from playing, assumed a more formal title with the club, and worked his way up to the NHL, first with Minnesota and then with Dallas when the franchise moved south and won the Cup in 1999.

James Jarvis

JARVIS, Wes
b. Toronto, Ontario,
May 30, 1958
There was nothing particularly innovative about Jarvis the player, but Jarvis the retired player was another story. His career was perfectly pedestrian coming out of the OHL in the late 1970s. He was the rookie of the year in the "I" in '78-'79 and then signed with Washington and played for

Doug Jarvis

three other teams in his nine years in the NHL. After he retired, he opened a unique hockey rink in Newmarket, Ontario, one designed especially for kids and adult three-on-three hockey. It was a mini version of the standard rink, giving kids more end-to-end skating during games and giving adults an intense workout. It was hugely popular, though has yet to catch on as a revolutionary concept for house leagues. Jarvis was also an assistant coach for the Barrie Colts.

Wes Jarvis

JASPERS, Jason
b. Thunder Bay, Ontario, April 8, 1981
Forward Jason Jaspers played three years in Sudbury before joining the Phoenix organization in 2001. He played just four games with the Coyotes in his first year of pro, spending most of the season in the minors.

JAVANAINEN, Arto
b. Pori, Finland, April 8, 1959
A scoring sensation in Finland does not necessarily come to North America and continue his goal-getting ways. Javanainen is living proof of that. He was a whiz

Arto Javanainen

He retired in 1995 at peace for having tried the NHL but harrowed by its results.
HANNU JARVENPAA

Bob Jay

Dean Jenkins

Roger Jenkins

Bill Jennings

in Finland, routinely scoring 30 goals in the short 36- or 44-game season and almost as routinely leading his league in goals. Yet when he came to Pittsburgh, he did not have the complete game needed to play in the NHL. He saw action with Pittsburgh for 14 games in '84-'85, but he spent most of that year in the minors and returned home at season's end. Needless to say, his international resumé was chockfull of appearances for the Finnish National Team.

JAY, Bob
b. Burlington, Massachusetts, November 18, 1965

One of the shortest names in the NHL had one of the shortest careers as well. Three games for L.A. in '93-'94 was all the defenceman could muster in a career dominated by time in the IHL. He spent the last five years with the Detroit Vipers, and can boast Gordie Howe – for a few seconds, anyway! – as one of his teammates. After retiring in 1999, Jay stayed on as an assistant coach and later moved up to Manchester of the AHL.

JEFFERSON, Mike
see **DANTON, Mike**

JEFFREY, Larry
b. Goderich, Ontario, October 12, 1940

It was truly amazing that Jeffrey played even one NHL game, and quite extraordinary that he lasted as long as he did. In junior, he suffered such a severe charley horse that calcium deposits so large formed on his leg that it took a painful procedure to remove them. Any higher, doctors had warned, and he might not have been able to walk. He had a fine start with Detroit in '61-'62 but the year after, Ted Green hit him and Jeffrey tore ligaments in his knee. It was an injury that never really went away, and although he played until 1969, he had nine operations on the knee during that time. His crowning glory came in '66-'67 when he played on the Cup-winning Leafs team. In camp in '69, he broke his kneecap in an exhibition game, and that ended his career. Jeffrey returned to Goderich to run a tugboat and later scouted for the Wings for eight years. He slowly built up a stable of horses and later ran a company called Sales Creators that specialized in advertising.

JELINEK, Tomas
b. Prague, Czechoslovakia (Czech Republic), April 29, 1962

At 30 years of age, Jelinek was one of the oldest players ever drafted into the NHL when Ottawa selected him a lowly 242nd in 1992. The lowness, however, was no reflection on his abilities, but rather his origin. The Sens weren't necessarily sure that Jelinek would play for the team, but that fall he did, indeed, play 49 games for Ottawa. He returned home the year after to resume

his European career, onethat started with the World Junior Championships in 1980 and finished in Czech league play in 1999. He went on to become a European scout for the Calgary Flames.

JENKINS, Dean
b. Billerica, Massachusetts, November 21, 1959

Merrimack and Lowell were two Massachusetts universities that had intense and mighty games during their heyday, but none more maniacal than one in which Jenkins played during his four years at Lowell (1977-81). A fight that involved Jenkins' family broke out in the stands. The player looked up to see what was going on and charged into the stands to his family's rescue, only to be hit in the face by a beer bottle. That's how Jenkins was on the ice as well, a tough guy who played four years of pro, including five games with the L.A. Kings in '83-'84. Although he later signed as a free agent with Boston, he never got to play with his hometown team.

JENKINS, Roger ("Broadway")
b. Appleton, Wisconsin, November 18, 1911
d. unknown

Roger Jenkins took part in one of the strangest Stanley Cup celebrations in both 1934 and '38. After the Black Hawks won the NHL title, he popped goalie Chuck Gardiner in a wheelbarrow and pushed him around downtown Chicago during the festivities. Jenkins played for the Hawks on 3 separate occasions and made 9 team changes in his 325-game career. During his time with the New York Americans he made one desperate appearance in goal when starter Earl Robertson was injured midway through the game. Jenkins played fully half a game and allowed 7 goals in an unheroic 11-5 loss. He later played in the minors for several years before retiring. He migrated to Seattle and became very successful in the tire business. Although he was born in Wisconsin, he grew up in the Port Arthur area and was later inducted into the Northwestern Ontario Sports Hall of Fame.

JENNINGS, Bill
b. Toronto, Ontario, June 28, 1917

Not to be confused with William Jennings of the eponymous goaltending award, this more casual Bill played with Detroit and Boston strictly as a wartime replacement. He had been one of a number of Canadians to play in England for Earls Court in the years leading up to the war, and in his final NHL year, with the Bruins in '44-'45, he scored 20 goals in just 39 games. Even this, though, wasn't enough to earn him a job when the number-one players were discharged after the war.

His crowning glory came in '66-'67 when he played on the Cup-winning Leafs team.
LARRY JEFFREY

JENNINGS, Grant
b. Hudson Bay, Saskatchewan, May 5, 1965

His was definitely not a skill game, and as a defenceman he was never going to see time on the power play. Jennings was the working man's player, a guy who punched the clock (or an opponent, if need be) and did his job dutifully and without much fanfare. He began in the minors and ended in the minors, but in between were nine seasons of NHL hockey and two Stanley Cups with Pittsburgh in 1991 and '92. He cleared the front of his net, tended to goings-on in his own end, and left the scoring to players named Mario and Jaromir. And for his efforts, he got his name on the Cup. Not a bad deal at all.

JENSEN, Al
b. Hamilton, Ontario, November 27, 1958

Jensen didn't play an NHL game outside the 1980s, but during that decade he was often one of the better goaltenders around. In 1983-84, he and Pat Riggin won the William Jennings Trophy, and during his six years with the Caps he had a fine record of 94-48-18. In all his years, though, the team had a woeful time in the playoffs, never winning a single round. Strangely, the two trades he was involved in were for non-goalies, and after retiring he began work for the NHL's Central Scouting Service. He also represented Canada at the '77 and '78 World Junior Championships.

JENSEN, Chris
b. Fort St. John, British Columbia, October 28, 1963

Jensen came out of the University of North Dakota with a degree in recreation and a reputation for his shot and speed. During his pro days, though, his scoring came mostly in the AHL, during and after six very part-time years in the NHL. He failed to establish a presence with either the Rangers or the Flyers, although 30 goals was the norm in the lesser leagues for the right winger. After retiring, he went into coaching.

JENSEN, Darren
b. Creston, British Columbia, May 27, 1960

Jensen played 30 NHL games, and although the first was rough, the next 29 were even more difficult. The first came on February 5, 1985, a 7-5 Philadelphia loss to the Islanders. Jensen was in net for all seven goals, not an auspicious beginning. His second career NHL game came in November 1985 again with the Flyers. He played in net after the death of Pelle Lindbergh, and it was his job both to play well and earn a spot on the team and to help his teammates, whom he didn't really know, stabilize as a hockey team and focus on the season. Jensen did his part, and by season's end he and Bob Froese won the Jennings Trophy. As reward, Jensen was demoted the year after and never played in the NHL again.

JENSEN, David A.
b. Newton, Massachusetts, August 19, 1965

To be saddled with a middle initial in your name is not the way to go through life, but the names and careers of the two David Jensens – A and H – are too close to distinguish otherwise. Both played for the U.S. National Team. Both played in the NHL and AHL. Both played in the 1980s. And both played in Italy toward the end of their careers. The biggest difference is that David A played at the 1984 Olympics in Sarajevo and played slightly longer in the NHL (69 games to David H's 18). But for two years, 1984-86, they both played in the big league – A for Hartford and Washington, H for Minnesota – confusing fans and broadcasters to no end.

JENSEN, David H.
b. Minneapolis, Minnesota, May 3, 1961

David H didn't quite do what David A did – play at the 1984 Olympics in Sarajevo. Both had played '83-84 with the U.S. National Team, but obviously the coaches couldn't be fooled and were able to differentiate their on-ice abilities enough to decree that A was worthy of the team and H was a substitute. Nonetheless, David H went on to play three years in the NHL, joining Minnesota right after the Olympics but seeing only spot duty during his time with the North Stars. Like David A, David H later played in the Italian league before retiring.

JENSEN, Steve ("Bomber")
b. Minneapolis, Minnesota, April 14, 1955

Jensen scored 22 goals in his first full season, in Minnesota in '76-'77, and it was then he got his nickname. Playing on a line with Alex Pirus on the right side and Roland Eriksson in the middle, he was the blond winger who would streak down the left side and take a pass at full speed while heading over the enemy blueline. That was how he scored most of his goals in the second half of the season, although his second year wasn't nearly as productive. The Stars lost him to Los Angeles as compensation when they signed Gary Sargent, and Jensen resurrected his scoring touch somewhat, though his goals were offset by woeful numbers in the (perhaps meaningless) +/- stat. Jensen played at all international levels for the U.S. including four World Championships, one Olympics (1976), and one Canada Cup (1976). He ended his career as a playing coach in Switzerland and then became a full-time coach in Austria for two years before settling in Michigan. He opened the Heartland Hockey Camp, of which he was executive director, and for the last 15 years and counting that has been his full-time occupation.

JEREMIAH, Eddie
b. Worcester, Massachusetts, November 4, 1905
d. Hanover, New Hampshire, June 7, 1967

Jeremiah's is no household name, but his contributions to hockey in the U.S., and in particular at Dartmouth College, will never be forgotten. In high school in Somerville, Jeremiah earned nine letters in sports, three each for hockey, football, and baseball, the sports he continued to play right through his college days at Dartmouth. His hockey career was reasonably brief, occurring mostly in the Can-Am league with 15 games in the NHL in 1931-32. He is best remembered for his contributions after he retired from playing. He coached the famed Boston Olympics to an NCAA championship in '35-'36, and from '37 to '43 he did as a coach what he had done as a player: guided Dartmouth's hockey, football, and baseball teams. He then enlisted in the war effort as a lieutenant commander of Harbour Entrance Control for the navy. Upon discharge, he

Grant Jennings

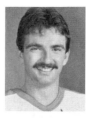

Al Jensen

Chris Jensen

Darren Jensen

Steve Jensen

resumed his triple coaching duties. Under his guidance, Dartmouth's hockey team set a record of 46 games without a loss. In 1951, he was college coach of the year, and the year after he served on the Olympic committee for player selection. He also wrote four books on hockey and edited the entry on ice hockey for *Encyclopaedia Brittanica*. He remained coach at Dartmouth until his death in 1967, shortly before he was to retire. In 1969, he was posthumously awarded the Lester Patrick Trophy for his contributions to the game in the U.S., and he was also inducted into the U.S. Hockey Hall of Fame.

JERRARD, Paul
b. Winnipeg, Manitoba, April 20, 1965
Lake Superior State University claims Jerrard as an alumnus after his four there in the mid-1980s. He graduated with a degree in recreation management, went on to play just five games with Minnesota in the NHL, and established himself as a hard-working tough guy in the "I," notably with Kalamazoo. His last pro season was in Hershey in '96-'97 when the Bears won the Calder Cup, and then the hard-working Jerrard threw his hat into the coaching ring. He spent a year in the AHL but soon returned as assistant coach where it all began, at LSSU with the Lakers, under head man Mike Anzalone, a former Miracle on Icer.

JERWA, Frank
b. Bankhead, Alberta, March 15, 1909
d. unknown
Frank and brother Joe played together with Boston during two seasons, '31-'32 and '33-'34, though Frank's career was shorter. They also skated on the same teams extensively in the minors, where they had more control over their fate, although Frank finished out west and Joe in Cleveland.

Frank Jerwa

JERWA, Joe
b. Bankhead, Alberta, January 20, 1907
d. unknown
Defenceman Joe Jerwa was the tallest player around during the height of his career in the 1930s. He played for Boston and the two New York teams but spent an equal amount of time in the minors. He had his best season with the Boston Cubs in '34-'35 and followed up with nine goals for the Amerks the year after, an impressive total for a blueliner in this era. He later settled in Vancouver.

Jaroslav Jirik

JILLSON, Jeff
b. North Smithfield, Rhode Island, July 24, 1980
A big and mobile defenceman, Jillson had an excellent college career at Michigan before turning pro with San Jose. He had been drafted 14th overall by the Sharks and graduated from U of M with a degree in sports management and communications. On the day of a playoff game in the spring of 2002, he flew to Ann Arbor to receive his degree and got back to the team in time to play that night.

JIRIK, Jaroslav ("Brambor")
b. Vonjuv Mestec, Czechoslovakia (Czech Republic), December 10, 1939
Jirik made history when he became the first player

Rosario Joanette

trained in Czechoslovakia to play in the NHL. He was permitted to leave the country because at the time, '69-'70, he was 30 years old and considered expendable but not useless. He played most of that season for the St. Louis farm club in Kansas City, but coach Scotty Bowman called him up after injuries left him short a left winger. Jirik acquitted himself well for three games, but at season's end he returned home. He was considered one of the fiercest competitors to come out of Czechoslovakia at this time, a man who hated to lose in practice and who once played a whole tournament with a broken arm. He appeared in six World Championships and three Olympics with his country, winning plenty of silver to Soviet gold. He led his club team, Kladno, to six league titles, and after retiring in 1975 he coached extensively, first at home and later in Switzerland. He later became a player agent, using his fame and experience to help young players make the right decisions in their own careers. Jirik is a licensed pilot, and once survived a plane crash in his own craft.

JOANETTE, Rosario ("Kitoute")
b. Valleyfield, Quebec, July 27, 1919
d. October 9, 1998
Jean Béliveau called him the toughest centre to play against. Sam Pollock brought him along with Valleyfield. But try as he might, Joanette never got a second call after playing two games for Montreal in '44-'45, the year he led the Quebec league in virtually every offensive category, including 45 goals, 56 assists, and 101 points. He played more than a decade with the Braves, notably the '49-'50 season when he played with his boyhood idol, the legendary Toe Blake. Joanette got his nickname while a boy at school, and he became known for his great speed, tricky shot, and almost inhuman resilience.

JODZIO, Rick
b. Edmonton, Alberta, June 3, 1954
Hockey has seen its fair share of barbarity, but even by its lowest standards Jodzio's attack on Marc Tardif in a playoff game on April 11, 1976, ranks as one of the worst. Playing for the Calgary Cowboys, Jodzio attacked Tardif, a talented scorer for the Quebec Nordiques, from behind, knocking him unconscious. While Tardif lay prone on the ice, Jodzio continued the attack with either his stick or his skate, no one could determine which. This precipitated a bench-clearing brawl and Jodzio was later charged with assault causing bodily harm. Tardif took months to recover from a serious concussion, but Jodzio was suspended only for the balance of the playoffs and fined $3,000 by the court. Ironically, during the time between trial and conviction, Jodzio was involved in a fight in the lobby of the Erie County Fieldhouse and filed charges of his own against two of his opponents. He later dropped those charges. Incredibly, it was after this that he got his only shot in the NHL, with Colorado and Cleveland in '77-'78.

JOHANNESEN, Glenn
b. Lac La Ronge, Saskatchewan, February 15, 1962
Two games with the Islanders in '85-'86 punctuated a brief pro career that started at Western Michigan University. Johannesen was drafted by the Islanders

even before playing for WMU, but his biggest asset, physical strength, was something in plentiful supply and not irreplaceable in the eyes of the NHL.

JOHANNSON, John
b. Rochester, Minnesota, October 18, 1961
Jim and John Johannson is a mouthful, but both brothers attended the University of Wisconsin for two years in the early 1980s. Jim didn't make it to the NHL, but John did for five games, with New Jersey, in '83-'84. John didn't stay around long as a pro, but he did convert his knowledge and experience into a career as a television analyst for U of W and other college games in the States.

JOHANSEN, Bill "Red" (sometimes Johnson)
b. Oslo, Norway, July 27, 1928
d. Thunder Bay, Ontario, March 21, 2001
The son of Trygve and Hjordis, the Johansen clan moved to Fort William when Bill was six years old. His love for hockey grew into a career that climaxed when he won the Allan Cup in 1949 with the Toronto Marlies, and the year after played his one and only NHL game, with the Leafs. Early on, Johansen changed his name to Johnson to make it more familiar to Canadian hockey fans, though his son, Trevor, kept the family spelling during his own career a generation later. Bill played many years in the minors, and when he retired he settled in Thunder Bay, where he worked for Merriman's Sheet Metal for more than 30 years until retiring in 1996.

JOHANSEN, Trevor
b. Thunder Bay, Ontario, March 30, 1957
His father was Bill "Red" Johnson, a man who changed the spelling of his name so it sounded more Canadian. In Trevor's generation, it was beneficial to have the more Swedish spelling! Nonetheless, like his papa, Trevor played for the Leafs at first, though the team gave up on him after a year and a half when he was still only 22. Too bad, because his heart was there: While playing for the Marlies, he worked as a janitor at the Gardens. Johansen settled down a bit in Colorado, but the Rockies were hardly a winning outfit capable of playing solid defence and he moved on to L.A. and then back to the Leafs. One highlight came when Johansen was a last-minute addition to Team Canada for the 1979 World Championships in Moscow. In a game against Finland, he scored in the final minute to eliminate that team and was named Team Canada's best defenceman. After retiring, Johansen settled in Denver, where he started his own commercial real estate company.

His father was Bill "Red" Johnson, a man who changed the spelling of his name so it sounded more Canadian.
TREVOR JOHANSEN

JOHANSSON, Andreas
b. Hofors, Sweden, May 19, 1973
The medical report that has been Johansson's career has gone a long way toward determining his contributions to the NHL so far. He was drafted in 1991 by the Islanders but waited four years before coming overseas. In '95-'96, he felt confident and ready for the NHL, but after just a few games he broke a bone under one eye in a fight, and when he returned to the lineup he broke a finger. The next season, he was traded to Pittsburgh and promptly injured his shoulder. The year after that, he played on the Penguins' top line with Ron Francis and Jaromir Jagr until he broke two ribs, but when Ottawa signed him in 1998 he settled in to play a full season. After a 21-goal year, though, the Sens traded him, and the year after saw another trade and a serious back injury that wiped out his season. Johansson played a year in Switzerland, but returned to the NHL with the Rangers in 2001-02 where he again appeared in only a fraction of the schedule. He returned to the NHL for the 2002-03 season to play with Nashville.

JOHANSSON, Bjorn
b. Orebro, Sweden, January 15, 1956
It was supposed to herald a new era, and although it did, in some ways, Johansson was not a beneficiary. In 1976, California selected him 5th overall, the first time a European had been drafted in the first round. The 20-year-old Swede was modelled on Borje Salming – good size and speed, good vision and puck skills – but Johansson played only 15 games over 2 years with the franchise, and moved to Cleveland shortly after the draft. By 1978, he was back in Sweden to resume his career, and although the European invasion was just beginning, Johansson was not much a part of it.

JOHANSSON, Calle
b. Goteborg, Sweden, February 14, 1967
Toward the end of the 2000-01 season, Johansson became one of the few Europeans to play 1,000 NHL games, a fitting plateau for a durable, if unspectacular, defenceman. He came out of Sweden to join Buffalo as an 18-year-old in 1987, and never played a single game in the minors. Midway through his second season, he was traded to Washington, the team he was with for the next 14 seasons. He routinely logged more ice time than any other player on the team and quarterbacked the Caps' power play. In 1998, he helped the team reach the finals for the first time in franchise history, and over the course of his career has set numerous team records including most games and most seasons. Internationally, he has played for Tre Kronor whenever possible. He played in his first WJC at age 16 and went

Bill Johansen

Andreas Johansson

Bjorn Johansson

Calle Johansson

Roger Johansson

Don Johns

Bob Johnson

Brent Johnson

Brian Johnson

on to play in all other major tournaments, notably the 1991 and '92 World Championships when Sweden won consecutive gold medals.

JOHANSSON, Roger
b. Ljungby, Sweden, April 17, 1967
Despite being drafted a decent 80th overall by Calgary in 1985, Johnsson didn't join the Flames for four years and then didn't make much of an impact while he was there. As always during these years, a European player didn't play in the minors to try to win a spot with the team. He was either good enough to be an NHLer or he wasn't. Calgary deemed him not worthy, and he went home to play for a year between stints with the Flames and then another try with Chicago in '94-'95, none of which worked out particularly well. Johansson returned to Sweden for good in 1995, though he returned with Tre Kronor to play in the '96 World Cup, one of many international tournaments he played in for his country.

JOHNS, Don
b. St. George, Ontario, December 13, 1937
There's nothing like an Eddie Shore story. He was the toughest, meanest hombre around, both as player and later as owner of Springfield, where Johns played during the '61-'62 season. In the middle of a slump, Johns was called into Shore's office. The owner/GM told Johns he could improve his play if he parted his hair on the other side. Hmm. Whether Johns did or not is not common knowledge, but Johns did play himself out of his slump and get into some games with the Rangers. He had played most of the previous season with the Blueshirts, but for every word of praise about his quickness in moving the puck out of his end there was a word of criticism for his lack of physical play.

JOHNSON, Al
b. Winnipeg, Manitoba, March 30, 1935
It was a long time coming, that first stay in the NHL, one that Johnson hoped for but never anticipated during his years of apprenticeship. Coming out of Manitoba, he played for St. Boniface and was, prima facie, Montreal property. The Habs wanted him to play for Chicoutimi to work his way up, but he didn't want to. He was going to school in the 'Peg, and when his dad was laid off the family ran into financial troubles for a time. Johnson then did something taboo for the time, akin to crossing a picket line in today's world. He played for the Dominion-States League, an outlaw league that played in and around Winnipeg five nights a week. The pay wasn't great, but in the short term the circumstances were to his benefit. A year later, Johnson asked Montreal to take him back, which it did, on their terms.

The Habs played him in a couple of games in '56-'57 to get his feet wet, and then he started travelling through the minors. Nothing could have been better for him than to be claimed by Detroit, because the right winger had no chance of beating Maurice Richard, Bernie Geoffrion, and Claude Provost out of the first three right wing jobs in Montreal. Johnson played a year and a half with the Wings, and then began roaming the minors throughout the U.S., playing for teams in Huntington, Toledo, and Fort Wayne, among others, in the International league. Once his pro days were over, he played for Canada at the 1965 World Championships, helping the team win a bronze medal. During his earlier playing days, he held a number of interesting summer jobs, including lumberjack, CPR yard switchman, and rock driller on the Trans-Canada pipeline.

During his earlier playing days, he held a number of interesting summer jobs.
AL JOHNSON

JOHNSON, Bob
b. Farmingham, Michigan, November 12, 1948
It wasn't always a great day for hockey for this Bob Johnson, a goalie who played just 24 games in the NHL during the early 1970s. He played briefly in the WHA and sired a son, Brent, who is currently active as a goalie. Together, they are one of the very few father-son netminding tandems in NHL history.

JOHNSON, Brent ("Johnny")
b. Farmingham, Michigan, March 12, 1977
Colorado drafted Johnson in 1995 in the hopes that he might be a backup or heir apparent to Patrick Roy, but neither turned out to be the case. The Avs traded him to St. Louis before he ever played a game for them, and with the Blues Johnson developed into a possible number one. He played good portions of two seasons after a slow start, and he's still young enough that the team might have found a big and solid goalie. One thing is certain: His lineage is pretty good. His grandfather is Sid Abel and his dad, Bob, played in the NHL as well.

JOHNSON, Brian
b. Montreal, Quebec, April 1, 1960
Johnson got into the official NHL books by playing with Detroit on October 9, 15, and 19, 1983, during his short career. He was called on to goon things up for the team, though he incurred but one fighting major in those games.

JOHNSON, Craig
b. St. Paul, Minnesota, March 8, 1972
Johnson was a sort-of prospect with St. Louis who became famous when the Blues packaged him with four other players in a trade to Los Angeles that sent Wayne Gretzky to St. Loo. With the Kings, Johnson

stepped up, played more, and developed into a decent player, though by no means was he a superstar find. His reputation reached its peak in 1994 when he made the U.S. Olympic team, and during the years the Kings didn't make the playoffs he made two appearances at the World Championships.

JOHNSON, Danny

b. Winnipegosis, Manitoba, October 1, 1944
d. March 6, 1993

The Leafs claimed Johnson as their own in the 1960s under the sponsorship system of the day, but they played him only once before losing him to Vancouver in the Expansion Draft of 1970. In his only full season, he scored 15 goals, but he spent his last 3 years of pro at home, playing for the Jets in the WHA. After captaining the team in '74-'75, he retired at the tender age of 30.

JOHNSON, Earl ("Ching")

b. Fort Frances, Ontario, June 28, 1931

Who could possibly have known that March 20, 1954, would have been Johnson's first, last, and only NHL game? He was only two years out of junior, and in that first year he had scored 37 goals and missed rookie of the year by a nose to Guyle Fielder. Yet after that single game with Detroit, Johnson bounced all over the place for years, never playing two seasons in the same city until he got to Spokane in 1958. There he played on a line with two former teammates – Al Johnson and Del Topoll – from his days in Quebec, and the threesome ran wild. Ching scored 40 goals and followed with seasons of 31 and 32, and then he was on the road again until he retired in 1964.

JOHNSON, Greg

b. Thunder Bay, Ontario, March 16, 1971

Johnson was a class act. He won medals for Canada at the 1994 Olympics in Lillehammer and the '91 WJC, and while playing in U.S. college hockey he was a three-time finalist for the Hobey Baker Award (1991, '92, and '93), though he never won it during his time at the University of North Dakota. He played three and a half seasons with Detroit before a series of moves gave him a look at a few other NHL teams. His brother, Ryan, is also an NHLer, and for years Greg has run his own successful hockey school in Thunder Bay during the summer.

JOHNSON, Ivan "Ching" ("Ivan the Terrible")

b. Winnipeg, Manitoba, December 7, 1897
d. Silver Spring, Maryland, June 16, 1979

Growing up in Winnipeg, Johnson played on nothing but outdoor rinks and never particularly serious hockey. That didn't matter much in 1916 when he went off to war, where for three years he served with a Canadian Army mortar trench outfit in France. In 1919, he returned home and worked for an electric light company in Winnipeg while playing for the Monarchs. This led to a three-year stint in Eveleth, and from there he was discovered by the Rangers. He was close to 30 by this time but said he was 28 and demanded a three-year contract, figuring it would be his only one. He got the contract, but he lasted 11 seasons in the NHL. At 6' and 210 pounds, Johnson

was one of the tallest and heaviest players in the league. Unfortunately for opposing forwards, the huge defenceman also relished physical contact and when he was partnered on the blueline with the 250-pound Taffy Abel, well, they formed a wall of flesh along the Rangers blueline that was not easily penetrated. Johnson helped bring the Rangers their first Stanley Cup, in 1928, and he won his only other championship with the team five years later. He was a crowd favourite for his hard but clean hitting, and as a result helped establish professional hockey in that city. In his early days he was called Ivan the Terrible, simply because of his name, but he became more familiarly known as Ching. It had started as Chinaman and shortened to Chink, because of his Asian face, and over time Chink was softened to Ching. His style of play was not without risks and consequences. He missed most of '28-'29 after breaking his collarbone, and in the 1930 playoffs he was forced to wear a steel mask because of a broken jaw. The Rangers released him in 1937 thinking he was now too slow. Their rivals, the New York Americans, thought differently, and offered him a contract, and Johnson took up the challenge for a year. He later played in Minneapolis and Washington, where he played and coached and even officiated in the Eastern Hockey League. He settled there and worked for a construction business as a contractor and retired to Maryland a number of years later. He was inducted into the Hockey Hall of Fame in 1958.

JOHNSON, Jim

b. New Hope, Minnesota, August 9, 1962

After 13 years in the league, Johnson may not have accomplished all he set out to do, but he sure didn't have anything left to prove, either. He played 829 games and made it to the Cup finals with Minnesota in 1991. He played at four World Championships and at the 1991 Canada Cup for the U.S. He played tough hockey and survived. So, when he suffered a concussion early in the '97-'98 season and doctors told him to retire, it was an easy decision. Johnson got right back into the game when his head was clear. He became an analyst for Phoenix Coyotes television and he was named assistant coach to the U.S. World Junior teams, a post he has held for three years and counting.

JOHNSON, Jimmy

b. Winnipeg, Manitoba, November 7, 1942

Every player who has appeared in the NHL has left his mark on the game in some small or great way. For Johnson, it was during a game his Flyers were playing against California in December 1970. Yes, he got a hat trick in the game, a memorable feat for any player, let alone at the NHL level. What was truly amazing, though, was that his second goal of the game came at 19:59 of the first period and his hat-trick goal came at 19:59 of the second period! Any goal at 19:59 is rare. Two in the same game has likely never been accomplished. But two *by the same player* is unheard of. Those 3 goals represented almost one-fifth his season's total of 16, and in 8 seasons he had just 75 goals all told before jumping to the WHA when it opened shop in 1972.

Danny Johnson

Greg Johnson

Ching Johnson

Jim Johnson

Mark Johnson

Matt Johnson

Norm Johnson

Ryan Johnson

Terry Johnson

JOHNSON, Mark

b. Madison, Wisconsin, September 22, 1957

Movies are great because the improbable happens with casual regularity and heroes are not only made but they fade only to return to glory in the twilight of their lives. Johnson's hockey life was the stuff of cinematic legend, starting with his two goals to help beat the USSR during the Miracle on Ice in 1980. He immediately joined Pittsburgh to begin an 11-year NHL career that was not blemished by even 1 game in the minors. Johnson had four 20-goal seasons during his career, and although he was never a superstar and never won a Stanley Cup, he contributed wherever he went. He was also active during a time of flourishing international hockey, testament to which is his resumé, which includes three Canada Cups and eight World Championships. Then there was the heroic (mini)return. The U.S. tanked at the 1998 Worlds, finishing twelfth, and were forced to play a qualifying tournament that November to avoid the humiliation of being relegated to "B" pool. Johnson, an assistant coach at his alma mater, the University of Wisconsin, phoned his old buddies – the three Brotens – and came out of retirement to play in the qualifier and assure the U.S. of continued presence in the "A" pool. They won that tournament, and Johnson's hockey life came to a happy ending, even though most people in his homeland could have cared less about the prestige of the Worlds. Johnson had retired in 1992 and immediately began coaching, first in high school and then at UW, where he soldiers on to this day.

JOHNSON, Matt

b. Welland, Ontario, November 23, 1975

Some willful acts of violence are cowardly, unforgivable, and violent beyond what is acceptable in any society, and Johnson's actions on November 19, 1998, were all three. Playing for Los Angeles in a game against the Rangers, he sucker-punched Jeff Beukeboom from behind, knocking the player unconscious the moment the blow struck. Johnson, at 6'5" and 230 pounds, is no lightweight, and the blow, not to mince words, ended Beukeboom's career. He suffered a serious concussion and never recovered his faculties to the point of being able to perform any physical activity. Johnson was suspended a paltry 12 games for his horrific actions and kept right on playing, with L.A., Atlanta, and Nashville. If there is such a thing as comeuppance, he himself missed a total of 25 games in 2000-01 because of three separate, though cumulative, head injuries. What goes around, comes around.

JOHNSON, Mike

b. Scarborough, Ontario, October 3, 1974

There he was, at Bowling Green University playing hockey and playing well, even though as a kid he gave up the game for a number of years because he was too small. When he grew, he turned to basketball and tennis, but at BGU he developed into an excellent hockey player. By the time he was finishing his degree in business and finance, NHL teams were offering him competing bids. Hometown Toronto won the day, and Johnson stepped right into the lineup at the end of the '96-'97 season and proved himself an NHL-calibre player. He had an assist in his first game and played the next two and a half years with the team, most effectively on the MAD line with Alyn McCauley and Derek King. However, when the Leafs had a chance to get Darcy Tucker from Tampa Bay, they parted with Johnson. At the end of that season, he played for Canada at the 2000 World Championships, and was later traded to Phoenix, where his unlikely success continues its course.

JOHNSON, Norm

b. Moose Jaw, Saskatchewan, November 27, 1932

The RCMP's slogan states that they always get their man. In Johnson's case, one must append an "almost" to that motto. Johnson played hockey as a kid out west, of course, but he was thrilled whenever a contingent of Royal Canadian Northwest Mounted Police rode through his tiny hometown. At 17, he left home one day to sign up, but just before he got to the RCMP offices he encountered a parade of horses and officers. For the first time, he noticed not the colourful uniforms or the beautiful horses, but the shiny weapons, the swords and guns. He turned around and went home. Johnson played junior hockey that year and for the next four, and turned pro in the Western league before Boston claimed him in 1957. He played part of the regular season and then stayed with the Bruins during their run to the finals, but the year after he was traded to Chicago. His time with the Hawks was short-lived, but Johnson went on to have many fine seasons in the WHL, retiring near the top of the all-time scoring list. He scored at least 22 goals in each season he played and won a championship in his last year, '70-'71, before going into coaching and later, into the lumber business.

JOHNSON, Ryan

b. Thunder Bay, Ontario, June 14, 1976

Johnson played with his brother Corey at the University of North Dakota, and then played against another brother, Greg, in the NHL. He left UND to play for the Canadian National Team for half a year, then moved up to the NHL. Ryan was drafted by Florida but traded to Tampa only to be reacquired by the Panthers.

JOHNSON, Terry

b. Calgary, Alberta, November 28, 1958

Takin' care of business in his own end is what Johnson's game was all about. He did what it took to take the other team's best out of the play and away from the front of the net, and he was pretty good at it or he wouldn't have lasted nine years in the NHL. He scored only 3 goals in his 285-game career but he was always one of the most reliable defenceman a team could have in the lineup. He came out of the University of Calgary in 1979 to play for Quebec, and he retired in 1988 to begin a career in coaching. This eventually led back to U of Calgary, where he was hired as an assistant to head coach Tim Bothwell.

JOHNSON, Tom

b. Baldur, Manitoba, February 18, 1928

Until the time he was 18 and playing junior for the Winnipeg Monarchs, Johnson had never played in an indoor arena. Once he started, though, he didn't impress Toronto management with his skating. The Canadiens begged to differ and signed him in 1947, but GM Frank Selke had trouble obtaining his transfer from the CAHA and Johnson spent most of the next season in limbo. In 1948, Johnson was assigned to Buffalo, and for two years developed into an outstanding blueliner. He made the Habs in 1950, but with Doug Harvey around he didn't see much ice time and certainly not on the power play. Johnson became a fine penalty killer, though, and he developed his own sneaky form of stripping a man of the puck without heavy body contact, and moving the puck up the ice all the more quickly. He was on the team that won the Cup in 1953, and as the decade progressed, so did his play. Every summer he returned to Winnipeg, where he raised racehorses, and he later opened an electrical appliance store in town with a former great, Baldy Northcott. Johnson became an important part of the Canadiens as they won five successive Cups (1956-60), and coach Toe Blake would sometimes play him at centre if the team needed a late goal. Johnson played in eight All-Star Games, but '58-'59 was likely his finest season. He was named to the First All-Star Team and won the Norris Trophy, the only major individual award he won. After the dynasty, Johnson formed a partnership with newcomer Jacques Laperriere on the blueline, but midway through the '62-'63 season he suffered a frightening facial injury that damaged his eyes. The Habs thought his career was over, but Boston signed him for the next season. It was the beginning of a new relationship that has lasted some 40 years. He played the better part of two seasons with the Bruins until he suffered severed tendons in his leg and was forced to retire. He became assistant to the president and GM for Boston and in 1970 took over as coach when Harry Sinden resigned. That fall, he was also inducted into the Hockey Hall of Fame. Johnson led the team to the 1972 Stanley Cup, but after another season he was let go. He has remained with the club ever since as assistant GM, later working with the alumni.

Every summer he returned to Winnipeg, where he raised racehorses.
TOM JOHNSON

JOHNSON, Virgil

b. Minneapolis, Minnesota, March 14, 1912
d. Eden Prairie, Minnesota, September 9, 1993
He was tiny, tiny, tiny for a defenceman, but he could sneak his stick in anywhere and fish the puck away before anyone had a chance to react. That quickness was both his trademark and his saving grace. Johnson played most of his pro hockey in Minnesota and out of the NHL, but in '37-'38 he joined a mostly American team to win an improbable Stanley Cup after the Black Hawks had recorded a sub-.500 regular season. It was dubbed the Cinderella team. He had written

the team in 1930, asking for a tryout, and the response he received was, simply, thanks, but no thanks. It wasn't until 1943 that he made it back to the NHL, and in between and after he played mostly in St. Paul and Minneapolis. After retiring in 1952, Johnson became a salesman for a tool company for a short time and then took a job as a carpenter for Insulation Sales in Minneapolis, a job he held until retiring in 1974. He was later inducted into the United States Hockey Hall of Fame. He suffered a stroke in June 1993 and moved in with his son in Eden Prairie, and it was there he passed away at age 81.

JOHNSSON, Kim

b. Malmo, Sweden, March 16, 1976
What's better, not to be drafted at all or to be drafted so near the end that you can still hear the echo of your name being called as the teams pack up and leave the arena? Johnsson was an echo-guy, selected 286th in 1994, one of the lowest draft choices of all time to make it to the NHL, and dead-last that year. He went on to win a bronze medal with Sweden at the 1999 World Championships and joined the Rangers that fall. He has been in the NHL ever since, though he is best remembered so far for being named top defenceman at the 2001 World Championships and playing for Sweden at the 2002 Olympics in Salt Lake City.

JOHNSTON, Bernie ("B.J.")

b. Toronto, Ontario, September 15, 1956
Both of Johnston's parents were deaf and mute, but that didn't stop Mr. Johnston from taking his eldest son, Barry, to the skating rink, which, in turn, only encouraged Bernie to go as well. Bernie became a fine hockey player as the years passed and he developed. He played on the 1974-75 Marlies team that won the Memorial Cup, and after turning pro he wound up playing for Hartford when the Whalers claimed him from the Philadelphia roster during the 1979 Expansion Draft. Johnston played parts of two seasons for Hartford and then moved to Switzerland to continue his career.

JOHNSTON, Eddie ("E.J.")

b. Montreal, Quebec, November 24, 1935
It is altogether common for a retired player to stay in the game as a coach or in some administrative capacity, but it is far less common among the goaltending fraternity to remain in the game in that way. Johnston was one of the exceptions, and arguably the most successful of that number. He began in the six-team era of the NHL, making his debut with Boston in 1962 at age 27. Those were the dark, pre-Bobby Orr days, but

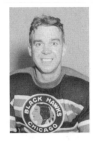

Virgil Johnson

Kim Johnsson

Bernie Johnston

by his second season Johnston was playing the entire 70-game schedule. He stayed with the Bruins for 11 years, witnessing the transformation of the team from league doormat to league superpower. As the team got better, though, he saw reduced activity, for part of that betterment involved the development of Gerry Cheevers in goal. No matter. Johnston played second fiddle with perfect pitch, and whenever he came in he did a great job. He won two Cups with the Bruins (1970 and '72) and finished with three other teams. After retiring in 1978 he immediately became a coach, in the AHL at first. After only one year, he was head coach in Chicago, and then in 1980 he began an affiliation with Pittsburgh that continues to this day. He started there as coach, moved up to GM, went back to coaching, and then became assistant GM to Craig Patrick. It was Johnston who called the name Mario Lemieux at the 1984 Entry Draft, and he was part of the team for the Penguins' only two Cups, in '91 and '92.

JOHNSTON, George
b. St. Charles, Manitoba, July 30, 1920
The war afforded many fringe players the chance to play a few NHL games during a minor-league career, and Johnston was one such beneficiary. Most of his games came during the war years, all with Chicago, and although they added up to 58 games and 20 goals, he never played in the league after 1947, even though he was only beginning his prime years. These he spent mostly with Tacoma in the Pacific Coast league, and although he was part of the Rangers system later, they never called him up for a tryout.

JOHNSTON, Greg
b. Barrie, Ontario, January 14, 1965
For seven years he did what he was told. For seven years he toed the line and worked in the Boston system under the assumption that he would get a fair chance. For seven years he was a Bruin. Then, in the fall of 1989, he had had enough. He came to camp, played well, figured he had made the team. They scratched him, tried to send him to the minors, and he said enough is enough. He went home until he was traded, and the Leafs acquired him. Once in Toronto, he was down in the minors. Two straight years, just like Boston. Enough. He packed his equipment and moved to Europe, and for the last decade he has been a regular in Germany, playing every day.

JOHNSTON, Jay
b. Hamilton, Ontario, February 28, 1958
Johnston's only eight games came with Washington during their dark, early years. He was brought up as a

fighter, performed his duty briefly, and went back to the minors where he racked up some pretty frightening penalty minutes.

JOHNSTON, Joey
b. Peterborough, Ontario, March 3, 1949
In the summer of 1975, for reasons unknown to all but the Great Maker, Fate looked down at Johnston and decreed that misfortune should befall him. That summer, he was involved in a car crash that left him with a broken wrist and serious head injuries. He was transferred to Toronto, where doctors weren't sure at first whether he would survive. Johnston had been playing hockey the previous four years with the awful California Seals, the dregs of the NHL ever since entering the league in 1967. Nonetheless, the left winger managed to score and play as one of the best on the team. For three years – 1973, '74, and '75 – he was the lone Seals representative at the All-Star Game. In the summer, he asked for a trade because he could no longer stomach losing. A month later, after a deal took him to Chicago, the car accident occurred. Johnston tried to come back. He played 32 games with the Hawks, but he was not well. He went to the minors for a conditioning spell, but it wasn't his shape that was the problem, it was the headaches, the imbalance, the double vision. At 27, he retired and returned to Peterborough. He received the $250,000 disability premiums, and began working for his brother in the heating business. Then he tried construction, but nothing came close to giving him the buzz that the NHL had. He started drinking. His marriage ended. He drank more. In three consecutive summers he was arrested for impaired driving three times. He was sentenced to 90 days in a local halfway house, and slowly got his life back on track. All that pain because of a car crash. Pain, thy name is Fate.

JOHNSTON, Larry
b. Kitchener, Ontario, July 20, 1943
Oh, he was one of the bad ones, all right, one of the baddest of them all. He set records for penalties in the EHL, CPHL, and AHL in the span of a few years in the late 1960s. He had calmed down a bit by the time he got to the NHL, but only a bit. An eye injury gave him a scare in the '72-'73 season, and he missed the end of the next year in a salary dispute with the Red Wings. He sat out, then signed with the WHA, and when he returned to the NHL a year later, he joined Kansas City. Late in the '76-'77 season he accepted a post as coach with the Maine Nordiques of the NAHL, and he later became a scout.

Greg Johnston

Joey Johnston

Larry Johnston

It was Johnston who called the name Mario Lemieux at the 1984 Entry Draft.
EDDIE JOHNSTON

JOHNSTON, Marshall

b. Birch Hills, Saskatchewan, June 6, 1941

Few people have been around the game in as many capacities for as long as Johnston, a man whose humble beginnings on frozen ponds took him to the Olympics and the NHL for years to come. In 1959, though, the teenager didn't take the usual route to hockey glory. He enrolled at the University of Denver, where he earned a four-year business degree, after which he shunned the NHL in favour of a five-year career with Canada's National Team under the aegis of Father David Bauer. Johnston played at the 1964 Olympics in Innsbruck (fourth place) and again in '68 in Grenoble (a bronze), and only then did he join Minnesota, the team who had acquired his rights from the Rangers after the Blueshirts got fed up waiting for him to turn pro. Johnston played parts of seven seasons in the NHL but retired midway through another awful season with California to become the team's head coach. This misery lasted 69 games over 2 seasons during which time he produced a record of 13-45-11. Johnston returned to the happier confines of Denver to coach college hockey for a few years, and in 1981 he assumed the role of GM for Colorado. For the next 20 years he served a number of roles in the NHL, most notably as director of player personnel for New Jersey (1985-93) and later as GM of the Ottawa Senators. For his international career, Johnston was inducted into the IIHF Hockey Hall of Fame in 1998. In 2002 he stepped down as Senators GM.

For his international career, Johnston was inducted into the IIHF Hockey Hall of Fame in 1998.
MARSHALL JOHNSTON

JOHNSTON, Randy ("R.J.")

b. Brampton, Ontario, June 2, 1958

Johnston was no superstar, but he was a solid defenceman who managed to play only four games with the Islanders in the '79-'80 season. He played five years in the minors, but that wasn't the life for him and he knew he wasn't going back to the big time. He retired and went into the consulting business, first as a stockbroker, then as an investment management consultant. He worked his way up to senior vice-president, investments for SSB Consulting Group in Birmingham, Alabama.

JOHNSTONE, Eddie

b. Brandon, Manitoba, March 2, 1954

Although Johnstone was drafted by the Rangers in 1974, he decided to sign with Michigan of the WHA. He was smart enough to get out partway through his first year, though, and by year's end the Stags had moved and then folded. He joined the Rangers and

improved slowly until he had 2 career 30-goal seasons. After an off year in '82-'83, he was traded to Detroit in a deal that was the endgame to his career. He played poorly, lost confidence, and played less. His career petered out, but his interest in the game never waned. When his playing days were done, he went into coaching and has been at it ever since. From a stint in junior to the Slapshot Johnstown Jets, Johnstone has made his way up to the AHL in recent years, his quest to coach at the NHL level not yet ended.

JOHNSTONE, Ross ("Blondie")

b. Montreal, Quebec, April 7, 1926

Johnstone drew praise from Leafs scouts during the 1942-43 season when he played first for the Marlies during the regular season and then helped the Oshawa Generals win the '43 Memorial Cup. He came to Maple Leaf Gardens that fall and played 18 games with the team and another handful in Providence. The next year he played 24 games, but by the fall of 1945 most of the regulars had returned from war and Johnstone could not crack a star-studded lineup. He was sent to the farm in Pittsburgh and traded to Eddie Shore's Springfield Americans the year after. Johnstone retired in 1952 and settled in Toronto, deciding to make his summer job a full-time effort. During his playing days he worked in office construction, easily matching in earnings the $4,000 he made playing hockey. He learned the ropes thoroughly, and in 1966 started his own company, general contracting, which lasted 20 years until he retired in 1987. Johnstone continued to play hockey at a lower level, and Bob Davidson, who oversaw the Leafs minor-league system, hired him to coach the Toronto Marlies Junior B team. Since '87, Johnstone has divided his time between Toronto and Florida.

Eddie Johnstone

JOKINEN, Olli

b. Kuopio, Finland, December 5, 1978

The old change-of-scenery trick has revived Jokinen's career. In 1997, Los Angeles drafted the Peter Forsberg-like centre 3rd overall, an ambitious but not unexpected placing then, a major disappointment in the years that followed. He was impressive as a junior at the WJC, but his NHL play left plenty to be desired. The Kings gave up on him in the summer of 1999 when they traded him to the Islanders, and after one season on Long Island, 1999-2000, he was traded to Florida, where his play shot through the roof under coach Mike Keenan. In 2002-03, for no other apparent reason, Jokinen became the team's top scorer and one of the best in the league. A star is born.

Olli Jokinen

JOLIAT, Aurel
("Mighty Atom"/ "Little Giant")
b. Ottawa, Ontario, August 29, 1901
d. Ottawa, Ontario, June 2, 1986

Emile Joliat came to North America from Bern, Switzerland, at age 17 and travelled the continent working a number of jobs before landing with the Ottawa Police Department. He was such an outstanding member of the force that in 1931 he was named chief of police, but by that time his son, Aurel, was vastly more famous as a left winger for the famed Montreal Canadiens. He was small (5'6") and light (135 pounds), but he was fast as electricity and could spin away from a check faster than anyone. He joined the Canadiens in 1922 and a year later was playing alongside Howie Morenz. For the next 11 years, the pair was inseparable on ice and as they scored the Habs won. Joliat also had a temper, never more apparent than when someone knocked his little black toque from his head. Prematurely bald, he was self-conscious of his shiny dome, and opponents would often rile him with a purposeful swipe at the knitted headgear. Joliat and Morenz were first teamed with Billy Boucher on the right wing and in '23-'24 the Habs won the Cup because of this deadly trio. The year after, Joliat scored a personal best of 30 goals, the same year his brother, Rene, was given a one-game callup by the Canadiens. Joliat helped the team win Cups again in 1930 and '31, and in '33-'34 he won the Hart Trophy, but when Morenz died in 1937, Joliat was not the same. He played one more season, scoring a dismal six goals, and retired. He left having played 16 NHL seasons, all with Montreal, and his 460 total points was a record for left wingers that remained for many years. He coached senior hockey in Verdun and Valleyfield and even worked as a linesman until doctors told him he had arthritis and had to give up serious skating. He never gave up skating, though, and played in old-timers games almost until his death. He returned to Montreal for a while, running his own grocery store and working for the provincial liquor board. He then moved back to Ottawa where he worked for the Canadian National Railway. His number 4 was co-retired with Jean Béliveau's, and Joliat was inducted into three Halls of Fame – the Hockey Hall, the Canadian Sports Hall, and the Ottawa Sports Hall. He died at home of a heart attack while getting ready to go to a doctor's appointment.

JOLIAT, Rene
b. Ottawa, Ontario, April 25, 1898
d. Ottawa, Ontario, August 10, 1953

Yes, Aurel had an older brother, a one-hit wonder who made only a fractional contribution to the game vis-à-vis the great one. Other than one appearance with the Canadiens with his brother in '24-'25, Rene played for a short time in and around Ottawa.

JOLY, Greg
b. Calgary, Alberta, May 30, 1954

Without intending to be too harsh on Joly, he was Washington's fool's gold in 1974. The defenceman capped off an excellent junior career in Regina by being named MVP of the Memorial Cup that spring, and for the Caps that was good enough. They selected him 1st overall in the Amateur Draft, one of the worst 1st-overall selections in the history of the game. In his first two years with the worst hockey team of all time, Joly was -68 and -46, staggering numbers that reflected badly on him despite the team's lowly quality. His cause wasn't helped by many injuries, notably one he suffered in Detroit a few years later during the 1978 playoffs. He broke his wrist and had it placed in a cast for the entire summer. When doctors removed the cast, they discovered the bone hadn't healed correctly and had to re-cast the joint for four more months. Despite playing 365 regular-season games, Joly made just 5 playoff appearances with Detroit.

His number 4 was co-retired with Jean Béliveau's and Joliat was inducted into three Halls of Fame.
AUREL JOLIAT

JOLY, Yvan
b. Hawkesbury, Ontario, February 6, 1960

If Joly had been better prepared for the NHL, he might have made it. But he came into his first camp out of shape, and that put him in Montreal's bad books right off the bat. Not good when the year is 1979 and the team has been winning the Cup every season. He played once in the 1980 playoffs and once more the following year, but try as he might in the minors, he wasn't going to get a callback. He scored 43 goals in Nova Scotia, but sealed his fate when he reacted angrily to comments made by Guy Lafleur, who said that one of Montreal's problems was not having any talent in the system. Joly spewed venom publicly over the remark, and coincidental or not his last NHL game occurred that season.

JOMPHE, Jean-Francois
b. Harve St. Pierre, Quebec, December 28, 1972

In 1995, he was still young and at the top. Jomphe played for Canada's junior team and played the following year with the Ducks in Anaheim. When the team didn't make the playoffs, he was invited to join Team Canada at the Worlds. One more unimpressive year with Anaheim, though, and the bloom was off the rose. No more long NHL seasons, no more international invites. Only the minors beckoned, but after answering the call for a while, Jomphe decided to

Greg Joly

Yvan Joly

go to Germany and play a little DEL hockey, which he's still doing, happily.

JONATHAN, Stan
b. Ohsweken, Ontario, September 5, 1955

Of native ancestry, Jonathan was 1 of 14 children and had to fight for everything in his life, including his job in the NHL. He was a Bruins left winger through-and-through, one of Don Cherry's boys in the good old days, a guy who would go through a wall to help his team win. Jonathan scored 20 goals twice but was more legendary for his incredible fights involving the best from around the league, and on occasion the best in the stands as well. He appeared in the memorable playoffs in 1978 when the Bruins were so close to knocking out Montreal until a delay-of-game penalty killed their chances. During that series, Jonathan's grandfather, a chief of the Tuscarora, concocted a secret potion using herbs and shrubs to help the Bruins win. It almost worked, but the Habs beat the B's and the potion in game seven. After retiring in 1983, Jonathan returned to his reserve to continue a life among his people.

JONES, Alvin "Buck"
b. Owen Sound, Ontario, August 16, 1917

His pursuits gained him admission to the Owen Sound Sports Hall of Fame, but his American wife refuses to move to his hometown now that they are in their later years. Jones was one of many Canadians to play in England in the years leading up to the Second World War, but after hearing Hitler's speeches broadcast on the streets of Berlin he returned to Canada in 1938 to turn pro with Detroit. He met his future wife at his first training camp. Jones played parts of three seasons with the Wings and another with Toronto before enlisting in the army, and for three more years he was back in Europe, this time wearing fatigues and sans hockey stick. Upon returning home, the Leafs saw Jones had slowed a bit and assigned him to the minors. Jones played until 1954 and settled in Tampa, raising two sons who went on to earn scholarships to U.S. colleges for their football skills. Jones worked in the retail business for 32 years with Maas Brothers until retiring to domestic life in 1987 and continues to volunteer at the city's main hospital.

JONES, Bob
b. Espanola, Ontario, November 27, 1945

His NHL rap sheet might be just 2 games long, but his involvement in hockey has extended to 30 years and counting. Jones came up through Kitchener in the late 1960s and played his two games with the Rangers, though he played most of his first pro years with the

Buffalo Bisons under coach Fred Shero, who used him both on defence and as a forward. Jones went on to play in the WHA for parts of four years.

JONES, Brad
b. Sterling Heights, Michigan, June 26, 1965

Neither more nor less than a diligent left winger, Jones played 6 years in the NHL, though never more than 53 games in any season. He graduated from the University of Michigan to join Winnipeg late in the '86-'87 season, and later played with Los Angeles and Philadelphia before winding up in the minors and then Europe. After retiring in 1998, he turned to coaching and worked his way up to head coach and director of hockey operations for the BC Icemen of the United Hockey League.

JONES, Jim
b. Espanola, Ontario, July 27, 1949

Neither Jim nor Bob owns bragging rights over the other brother. Bob played in two NHL games, and, coincidentally, so did Jim. His pair came with California in '71-'72, and like Bob he had a minor-league career besides. Jim also moved on to the WHA, though for a shorter time, and retired in 1975.

JONES, Jimmy
b. Woodbridge, Ontario, January 2, 1953

To steal and adapt a Rodney Dangerfield joke, if you look up the word "checker" in the dictionary, you'll see a picture of Jones. He came up through Peterborough and signed with Vancouver in the WHA in 1973. After two years in the AHL he signed with the Leafs. For two years he was the team's thorn in the opposition's side, driving players to distraction with his tenacity. Once the Leafs gave up on him, he returned to the minors for a brief time and then became coach of the Marlies. This job lasted all of two seasons, and after middling results he was fired. Jones then realized a dream by becoming a police officer for York region, a position he has held ever since.

JONES, Keith
b. Brantford, Ontario, November 8, 1968

For Jones to be drafted in 1988 at age 20 was a slap in the face in one sense, but for a guy who never thought he'd be good enough to play, it was a miracle that four years later Washington played him on a regular basis. In the interim, Jones got an education at Western Michigan University, but once with the Caps he stayed in the NHL for most of a decade. He was considered a checker who could score a bit, and a digger who could muck in the corners and dig the puck out to the front of the net. He was also known for

Jones was one of many Canadians to play in England in the years leading up to the Second World War.
ALVIN JONES

Stan Jonathan

Bob Jones

Brad Jones

Jimmy Jones

Keith Jones

Ron Jones

Hans Jonsson

Jorgen Jonsson

Tomas Jonsson

Chris Joseph

his trash-talkin', rapier-like wit. Jones went on to play for Colorado and Philadelphia, but by 1998 he began to experience serious knee troubles. These continued to the point that in 2000-01 he played in only eight games, and at year's end doctors told him there was no cartilage left in the knee. The pain was almost unendurable, and he was forced to retire.

JONES, Ron
b. Vermillion, Alberta, April 11, 1951
He was considered the best defenceman in the WHL in 1970-71, and this was followed by necessary but unfair comparisons to Bobby Orr. Jones had a good shot and good speed, and he could play both sides of the blueline. But he, like everyone else, was no Orr. Boston drafted Jones 6th overall in '71 and he played with Orr for a few games over the next two years, but even when he moved on briefly to other teams, he failed to establish himself. He spent most of his six pro years in the minors.

JONES, Ty
b. Richland, Washington, February 22, 1979
A right winger with size, strength, and speed. What more could a team want? No wonder Chicago took Jones 16th overall in 1997. What a disappointment that after eight games – with zeroes across the board – Jones was sent to the minors whence he has yet to return.

JONSSON, Hans
b. Jarved, Sweden, August 2, 1973
It was six years between Jonsson's draft year and the first year he appeared in the NHL, with Pittsburgh, in 1999. He had starred on defence in Sweden and had also appeared internationally for Tre Kronor on four occasions, one WJC and three World Championships. Since coming to the Penguins, he has been a fixture on the blueline as a solid checker rather than a rusher or power-play specialist.

JONSSON, Jorgen
b. Angelholm, Sweden, September 29, 1972
Jorgen wasn't the prospect his brother, Kenny, was, but both did play for Sweden at the gold-medal 1994 Olympics in Lillehammer. While Team Canada and Sweden were battling hammer and tongs during two exhibition games between the Canada and Moscow legs of the '72 Summit Series, mom Jonsson was very preggers, and the day after Paul Henderson scored his famous goal, out came Jorgen. Yet he played at home until he was 27, and came to North America only after his younger brother had paved the way with his play. Jorgen's stay lasted just one season, a year he split between Anaheim and the Islanders before heading home to continue playing with Farjestad.

JONSSON, Kenny
b. Angelholm, Sweden, October 6, 1974
Never before in the country's history did Sweden have a year like 1994, and never before or since did a player have the season Kenny Jonsson had. He became a member of one of the rarest groups of players in history when he played at all three international tournaments within a span of weeks, winning medals at each. He won a silver at the World Juniors, a gold at the Olympics, and a bronze at the World Championships, completing the rarest triple of them all in hockey. The year after, he made his NHL debut, with Toronto, but it was as a member of the Islanders that he matured into a top defenceman. His move to Long Island was precipitated by a trade in which the Leafs reacquired Wendel Clark, but just as he was establishing himself he was also experiencing serious injuries. He suffered concussions in consecutive years as well as assorted minor wounds that took their toll and kept him out of the lineup, and he was named captain of the team and later replaced. When healthy, he logs more ice time than any other Islanders defenceman, and his ability to play in all situations and at both ends of the ice have made him an important part of the team.

He won a silver at the World Juniors, a gold at the Olympics, and a bronze at the World Championships.
KENNY JONSSON

JONSSON, Tomas
b. Falun, Sweden, April 12, 1960
Mats Naslund, Hakan Loob, Peter Forsberg, and Tomas Jonsson hold a unique distinction among their countrymen as the only players to have won gold at the World Juniors, World Championships, and Olympics as well as the Stanley Cup. Jonsson's two Cups came for the Islanders during the first two NHL seasons (1981-83) of a career he spent almost entirely on Long Island. Jonsson's international resumé is as long as his arm, starting with the WJC in 1978 and ending with the '95 WC. After his NHL days, which comprised the 1980s, he returned home to Leksand and played until 1999, when he retired.

JOSEPH, Anthony
b. Cornwall, Ontario, March 1, 1969
Joseph's only NHL games came and went by the time he was 20 years old, after which the large right winger was relegated to the minors during an injury-riddled career that began after graduating from Oshawa in 1989 and ended six years later.

JOSEPH, Chris ("Chewy")
b. Burnaby, British Columbia, September 10, 1969
Few players in the past 15 years have travelled and changed teams as often as Joseph, even though he started his career with both a solid reputation and a streak of 7 seasons with Edmonton. He won gold with

Canada at the '88 World Juniors and the following month played for his country at the Olympics in Calgary. He had started his NHL career with Pittsburgh at the beginning of the season, but in November '87 he was involved in the huge trade that sent Paul Coffey to Pittsburgh. Once in Edmonton, the pressure was on for the highly rated draft choice to develop, yet during most of his time with the Oilers he played frequently in the minors for long stretches. When he was traded to Tampa in late 1993, it marked the first of seven team changes he would make in the next eight years. After the 1999-2000 season, Joseph was awarded the King Clancy Trophy for humanitarian accomplishments, the only individual honour to come his way during his pro career.

JOSEPH, Curtis ("Cujo")
b. Keswick, Ontario, April 29, 1967

An adopted child, Joseph had more trouble than just about any other NHLer getting respect as a young player. He never played major junior hockey in Canada and he was never drafted into the NHL. He played provincially with the great Notre Dame Hounds before going to the University of Wisconsin on a scholarship. After a phenomenal year in '88-'89, St. Louis signed him and put him to work the next season. For six years he developed and then maintained a reputation for superior play, his style as unorthodox as it was unclassifiable. What he did, in simple terms, was keep the puck out of the net. How he did it was of little concern to his coaches. In the summer of 1995, Joseph was traded to Edmonton, and in the next three years he took his game to another level, marking his domain as one of the top playoff goalies of his generation. This was attributed largely to the annual Dallas-Edmonton confrontation, which the Oilers won often because of Joseph's incredible play. In 1998, Joseph became an unrestricted free agent and signed with the Leafs, in part because of the money, in part because of the proximity to his home. He continued his fine play, yet proved not to be a Stanley Cup goaltender. In truth, Joseph has more than 100 playoff wins to his credit and is the winningest goalie in NHL playoff history not to win a Cup. Although his teams have invariably qualified for the post season, they have never gone to the finals, both facts in large measure due to his play. Joseph was the main goalie in the 1996 World Cup, a finals loss to the U.S., and in 2002 he was given the chance to be the number-one goalie for Canada at the Olympics in Salt Lake City, but his weak performance in the first game convinced coach Pat Quinn to go with Martin Brodeur, a decision that helped give

> **Joseph signed a contract with Detroit in the summer of 2002 in the hopes of joining a Stanley Cup team for the first time.**
> CURTIS JOSEPH

Canada the gold. Ironically, Joseph signed a contract with Detroit in the summer of 2002 in the hopes of joining a Stanley Cup team for the first time, a move that ended in disaster when Detroit was swept by lowly Anaheim in the first round of the 2003 playoffs. Away from the crease, Joseph is famous for his horses, notably Millennium Allstar, and wherever he has played his work with underprivileged children has been a remarkable success.

JOVANOVSKI, Ed
b. Windsor, Ontario, June 26, 1976

Sometimes you have to take a step back to be able to go ahead two. Sometimes you have to play poorly to learn how to play well. Sometimes only failure will create success. Jovanovski's father, Kostadin, was a professional soccer player in Yugoslavia, and when he and his wife moved to Canada and had two sons, he wanted his boys to follow suit. Yet no matter how many times he turned the TV off when hockey was on, the kids wanted nothing to do with the ball and everything to do with the puck. Ed matured into a hulking 18-year-old who was selected 1st overall in the 1994 draft. Things couldn't have gone better, which might have been where the problems began. At his first training camp with Florida, the Panthers sent him down to junior. He made the team his second year, and for three and a half seasons played with the team but without being overly impressive. The accolades of his teenage years gave way to derisive calls of "Special Ed" because he was slow to learn

Ed Jovanovski

the game. In 1999 the Panthers traded him with Dave Gagner, Kevin Weekes, Mike Brown, and a first-round draft choice in 2000 to Vancouver for Pavel Bure, Bret Hedican, and a 3rd-round draft choice in 2000. The move awakened Jovanovski, and he developed into their best defenceman and one of the hardest hitting in the league. In short, Vancouver reaped the benefits of Ed having apprenticed with Florida, so by the time they got him he was ready to assume a big role with an emerging team. Now in his prime, Jovanovski is coveted and considered one of the best in the league.

JOYAL, Ed ("Jet")
b. St. Albert, Alberta, May 8, 1940

Early in his career they called him the Jet because of his explosive speed – give him a step, and he's gone. Yet early on, all that speed earned him was time in the minors. Joyal made his NHL debut with Detroit in '62-'63, but after three part-time years he was traded to Toronto, where things went from bad to worse. In Detroit, he began with plenty of ice time and slowly moved to the bench and into the press box. With the

Ed Joyal

Leafs, he was never anything more than an add-on. His career proper began only in 1967 when L.A. claimed him, and it was there that he blossomed, both on and off the ice. His teammates called him the Detective or the Spy because of the hat and glasses he wore off the ice. He was the best-dressed player on the team, and style oozed out of him, often via his playboy lifestyle. Joyal had three 20-goal seasons with the Kings and played the last 4 years of his career with the Oilers, once the WHA got going in 1972. Like many a former player, he became a real estate agent after leaving the game.

JOYCE, Bob
b. Saint John, New Brunswick, July 11, 1966

Bob Joyce

His birth certificate might say Saint John, but Joyce grew up in Winnipeg. His next-door neighbour was a guy named James Patrick, and the elder Patrick had a great influence on the younger Joyce. Joyce played for the Hounds in Notre Dame and from there went on scholarship to the University of North Dakota in 1984 soon after watching Patrick play for Canada at that year's Olympics in Sarajevo. In his final year, Joyce played on a line with Tony Hrkac and led the NCAA with 52 goals. The next year, Joyce played exclusively with the National Team in preparation for the Olympics, and under the tutelage of coach Dave King the high scorer was turned into a defensive-minded forward. Come the Olympics, though, he was bumped from the lineup when Jim Peplinski arrived, and played only half the games. He joined the Bruins right after and scored two goals in his first NHL game, the first coming on his first NHL shot. He never got on track as a scorer, though, and trades sent him to Washington and Winnipeg before he ended up in the minors and Europe, where he continues to skate.

JOYCE, Duane
b. Pembroke, Massachusetts, May 5, 1965

He got his three games in, with Dallas in '93-'94, but Joyce was a staple in the "I" for more than a decade before going into coaching in Boston with kids' teams. He won the Turner Cup with Kansas City in '91-'92 and made it to the finals on three other occasions.

JUCKES, Winston "Bing"
b. Hamiota, Manitoba, June 14, 1926
d. West Point, Mississippi, December 31, 1990

Juckes' first cousin was Gordon, longtime president of the CAHA, and Bing learned the game against his kitchen walls, according to his mother. He played only a few games with the Rangers after the war and never

He achieved his master's degree in aeronautical engineering.
JOÉ JUNEAU

settled with one team during his career, which ended in 1954. Juckes continued his nomadic ways while coaching in both Canada and the U.S. for a number of years, and he eventually settled in Mississippi, where he owned and operated the Limeco Lime Plant until his death.

JUHLIN, Patrik
b. Huddinge, Sweden, April 24, 1970

In the first half of the 1990s, Juhlin was everywhere, playing in Sweden, playing internationally at every level, and finally making the trek to the NHL to join Philadelphia. He was a member of the gold-medal team at the 1994 Olympics in Lillehammer and won medals at the '93 and '94 World Championships, but his stay with the Flyers lasted only two half-seasons before he returned to Europe to continue his career in Switzerland.

JULIEN, Claude
b. Blind River, Ontario, April 23, 1960

Like many men who spend a life in hockey, Julien played only briefly but has coached extensively since retiring. He got into a few games with the Nordiques in the 1980s and played extensively in the minors until he retired in 1992. He had signed with St. Louis, but in an unusual trade the Blues sent him to Quebec along with Gord Donnelly when St. Louis signed coach Jacques Demers in the fall of 1983, one of the rare times a coach has been "acquired" for players. Julien then became an assistant coach with Hull in the Quebec league, and in 1997 he concluded his first year as head man by winning the Memorial Cup. He was later named head coach of Canada's under-18 team and moved on to coach at the AHL level until his big break came: In January 2003, he was named head coach of the Montreal Canadiens.

JUNEAU, Joé
b. Pont-Rouge, Quebec, January 5, 1968

When Juneau bought a piece of property in Quebec's remote north, he had a problem in that it was only accessible by plane. So, he built himself a plane. From scratch. Because he could. When he first started to attend classes at RPI in 1987, he couldn't speak English. He achieved his master's degree in aeronautical engineering within a few years, speaking only English. He was, in short, a rocket scientist. And then there was hockey. He spent parts of three years with the National Team leading up to the 1992 Olympics in Albertville, and after contributing to Canada's silver medal he joined Boston of the end of the season and established himself as a solid scorer and phenomenal passer. In his first full season, 1992-

93, Juneau had a career-best 102 points. Although his numbers subsequently decreased, he was a valuable commodity who had his longest stay with Washington after being traded there for Al Iafrate in early 1994. Juneau helped get the Caps to the '98 finals, and after brief stops in Buffalo, Ottawa, and Phoenix, he signed with his home team, Montreal, and added an accent to the "e" at the end of his first name for that authentic French touch.

JUNKER, Steve
b. Castlegar, British Columbia, June 26, 1972
After winning a Memorial Cup with Spokane in 1991, Junker played in the Islanders organization for a year before joining the Long Island team for just a few games. He wound up playing in the minors and moved to Germany to revive his career in the DEL.

JUNKIN, Joe
b. Lindsay, Ontario, September 8, 1946
Many hockey players, certainly in the old days, ran or helped out at hockey schools in the summer. It was a way of staying on skates and perhaps establishing a post-career business, and it certainly was a way to stay popular and share their love of the game. Junkin lived in Oklahoma City for a few years, and he helped out at a hockey school in the summer of 1970. It was the worst thing he could have done, for a shot hit him flush in the left eye and more or less ended his career. He tried to come back in the fall but doctors would not clear him, and although he went on to play parts of two seasons in the WHA he just wasn't the same. He made his NHL claim to fame in '68-'69 when he guarded the Boston cage for all of eight minutes, one of the shortest stints for any goaler. Overall, his specialty was penalty shots. He stopped all 14 he faced at various levels during his career.

JUTILA, Timo
b. Turku, Finland, December 24, 1963
Jutila played all of 10 NHL games, with Buffalo in '84-'85, but he was one of the most decorated and famous Finns of all time. He was known as a small and speedy defenceman, not a hard hitter but a shifty player who could move the puck quickly. He made his international entrance at the 1981 World Juniors, a tournament he played in for three successive years, winning silver and bronze the first two times out. He played in eight World Championships for Suomi, including in 1995 when the country won its first and only gold medal. Jutila played at three Olympics – 1984, '92, '94 – and two Canada Cups – 1987 and '91. In league play, he skated for Tampere at home and Lulea in Sweden, and by the time he retired in the

late 1990s he was one of the crowning jewels in Finland's pantheon of great players. He was inducted into the IIHF Hockey Hall of Fame in 2003.

JUZDA, Bill ("The Beast")
b. Winnipeg, Manitoba, October 29, 1920
In the years immediately before the war, Juzda played defence with Kenora with such passion the Rangers called him up for a few games in 1940. He made the team full-time the next year, but then put his career on hold for three seasons while he played his part in the war. Juzda was with the Coastal Command as a pilot of Cansos, which were Catalina Flying boats with wheels. He escorted convoys leaving Yarmouth, Nova Scotia, en route to the Atlantic in search of German U-boats. After being discharged he rejoined the Blueshirts, but in 1948 the Leafs acquired him. He won two Stanley Cups with Toronto, the first in 1949, the second two years later. As Bill Barilko's defence partner, he was on the point when Bashin' Bill scored the dramatic overtime winner in 1951. The pair were regarded as the hardest hitters in the game, and proof for Juzda comes in the form of a famous photograph from the Gardens that shows Maurice Richard breaking the "unbreakable" Herculite glass, the result of a thundering Juzda check. By 1952, Juzda was in the minors, and he continued to play for 10 years. Each summer throughout his career, he returned to Winnipeg, where he worked for the Canadian Pacific Railway. He started as a fireman shovelling coal as a kid and worked his way up to engineer. After retiring from hockey, he worked for CPR full-time for 28 years until retiring in 1980 to a life of golf and relaxation at his cottage on Lake Winnipeg.

As Bill Barilko's defence partner, he was on the point when Bashin' Bill scored the dramatic overtime winner in 1951.
BILL JUZDA (LEFT)

Joe Junkin

KAARELA, Jari

b. Tampere, Finland, August 8, 1958

If you give up a goal for every 10 minutes of game you play, you won't last long in the NHL. Kaarela's career was brief all over, from five games in the NHL to just a few seasons in domestic league play back home. He took the basic tools of the trade, though, and parlayed his knowledge into a coaching career back home, working extensively in international competition for the Finnish national teams.

KABEL, Bob

b. Dauphin, Manitoba, November 11, 1934

Kabel performed his duties to perfection when the Rangers recalled him early in the '59-'60 season, but that didn't mean he was going to stick around any longer than necessary. He found himself centring a line with Dean Prentice and Andy Bathgate, and the trio clicked right away. Yet he played only half a season and a few more games the year after in a career that lasted some 15 years of pro. In the summers, he returned to Dauphin, where he had a reputation as one of the city's best baseball players.

KABERLE, Frantisek ("Frank")

b. Kladno, Czechoslovakia (Czech Republic), November 8, 1973

His dad was a pro back home for many years, and his younger brother took after him and played hockey well enough to beat him to the NHL by a year, even though Frantisek is five years older than Tomas. He was drafted later than Tomas but much higher, a result of Tomas's great rookie season with the Leafs. Frantisek had been playing club hockey for years in Czechoslovakia and won three successive gold medals with the National Team at the World Championships in 1999, 2000, and 2001. Yet Frantisek was not as gifted a puck carrier as Tomas, and in his first season played only 37 games with Los Angeles before being traded to Atlanta. Nonetheless, he has established himself with the Thrashers as a reliable defenceman.

KABERLE, Tomas ("Kabby")

b. Rakovnik, Czechoslovakia (Czech Republic), March 2, 1978

Being raised by a hockey player is certainly apt preparation for a life in the sport. Kaberle's dad, Frantisek, played pro in Czechoslovakia and was a member of the National Team. He later moved the family to Japan for two years where he ended his career, and they spent time in Germany right after when he accepted a coaching position in Duisburg. When the family settled in Velka Dobra outside Kladno, Tomas started to develop his own hockey skills. As he got older, NHL scouts were unimpressed by Kaberle's skills, and only Anders Hedberg, a Leafs scout, held out any hope for the teen. The Leafs drafted Kaberle a lowly 204th overall in 1996, and at his first training camp a year later the Leafs sent him home to play some more. The following season, though, Kaberle returned to Toronto a different player – bigger, faster, more poised. He made the team and has been there ever since, with the exception of the start of the 2001-02 season, when a contract dispute kept him out of the lineup. His puck movement and skating ability set him apart, and he has

become one of the team's top defencemen, though his refusal to shoot the puck during power plays has frustrated coaches and fans alike. His reputation grew around the league as well, and Kaberle was named to Czech's Olympic team for Salt Lake City in 2002, though the team failed to repeat as gold-medal winners.

KACHOWSKI, Mark

b. Edmonton, Alberta, February 20, 1965

A tough guy who came out of Kamloops, Kachowski signed with Pittsburgh as a free agent in 1987 after no NHL team drafted him. He played parts of three seasons with the team without making much of a dent in the lineup and soon ended up in the minors. His connections to the Pens, though, later helped get him a small part in the action movie *Sudden Death*, shot mostly at the Arena and starring Claude Van Damme.

KACHUR, Ed

b. Fort William, Ontario, April 22, 1934

Something magical and mysterious happened to Kachur when he was traded to Providence early in 1965 from Los Angeles in a seemingly innocuous minor-league trade. Coach Fern Flaman put the right winger on a line with Willie Marshall and Len Ronson, and the trio played dynamite hockey for the rest of the year. Kachur's performance improved to the point that three years later he led the AHL in scoring, even though at no previous point in his career had he been noted for his offence. He got his only NHL chance much earlier with Chicago and failed to distinguish himself, and although he played for nearly 20 years he never lit the lamp the way he did when he got to the Reds toward the end of his career.

KAESE, Trent

b. Nanaimo, British Columbia, September 9, 1967

Small-town players invariably return to their roots after their playing days. That's where they're well known, and that's where they're most comfortable. Kaese took his one-game career with the Sabres to the minors for a career that stretched overseas to Europe, but when he retired from playing he returned to Nanaimo to coach the local Clippers, a provincial junior team, and to pursue a leisurely business opportunity. He became owner and manager of the nearby Cottonwood Golf Course.

KAISER, Vern

b. Preston, Ontario, September 28, 1926

In his first game with Montreal at the start of the '50-'51 season, Kaiser found himself on a breakaway. He missed, and coach Dick Irvin worried that the gaffe might scar the young lad for the rest of his days. Kaiser proved Irvin wrong by scoring in his next game and earning player-of-the-week honours in his first seven days of NHL hockey, but he didn't make it to the end of the season before being demoted, and he didn't make it back at any future date, either. In fact, Kaiser was out of hockey altogether by 1954.

KALBFLEISH, Walter ("Jake")

b. New Hamburg, Ontario, December 18, 1911
d. unknown

Kalbfleish had the distinction of playing for three

Tomas Kaberle

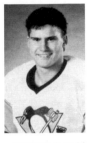

Mark Kachowski

Walter Kalbfleish

Bob Kabel
(opposite page)

defunct teams prior to the Original Six era and between the wars. He turned pro right out of junior and joined the Ottawa Senators in '33-'34, and the year after he moved to St. Louis when the Sens transferred to Missouri in the hopes of resuscitating a dying franchise. He later played for the New York Americans before playing one game with the Bruins in '36-'37, and he finished his career in the minors.

KALETA, Alex ("Sea Biscuit"/ "Killer")
b. Canmore, Alberta, November 2, 1919
d. Medicine Hat, Alberta, July 9, 1987
The son of a coal miner, Kaleta rose through the ranks as a junior and played for Chicago in 1941-42. He halted his career just as it was getting going, though, and for three years he was in the army. Upon discharge, he rejoined the Hawks and played on a line with Clint Smith and Red Hamill, scoring 19 goals. That number increased to 24 the following year, but a weak follow-up season earned him a trade to the Rangers, where he played his last NHL games. Once Kaleta had been demoted, he started to focus on a career in coaching, and midway through the '54-'55 season an opportunity presented itself. He quit playing and took the reins of the Moose Jaw Canucks, and later settled in Medicine Hat where he led the Tigers for a year. Kaleta became recreation director for Medicine Hat in 1955 and held that position until 1974, when he took over as manager of the arena and convention centre. He retired in 1984 and lived out his final days in Medicine Hat.

Alex Kaleta

KALININ, Dmitri
b. Chelyabinsk, Soviet Union (Russia), July 22, 1980
The first time Kalinin played serious hockey in North America was at the 1999 World Junior Championships in Manitoba, the year Russia won gold. That fall, he returned, this time to Buffalo, where the defenceman played the year in the minors. He got into four games with the Sabres that season, and in 2000 he made the team as a regular, a position he has held ever since. He won't win a game with his scoring, but he can play the body well and blocks his fair share of shots.

Dmitri Kalinin

KALLIO, Tomi
b. Turku, Finland, January 27, 1977
Colorado drafted Kallio in 1995, but four years later he was still playing for Turku in the Finnish league when Atlanta claimed him in the Expansion Draft. Still, he played another year at home before finally joining the Thrashers for 2000-01, setting modest team records for goals (14) and points (27). His follow-up season was not as impressive, but on a team with so little talent, whatever he brought to the table was considered a contribution of some sort. Now in his prime, it is up to

Anders Kallur

Kallio to prove whether his fine Finnish career can be translated to the NHL. Back home, he was a league star and was key to Finland's bronze medal at the 2000 WC. He joined Vastra Frolunda in January 2003 and in the decisive game of the Swedish championship he scored in the sixth overtime period to give his team a championship for the first time in 38 years.

KALLUR, Anders
b. Ludvika, Sweden, July 6, 1952
Kallur was overlooked in the 1970s European drafts, and after having an outstanding season in Sweden and being named player of the year, the New York Islanders signed him in the summer of 1979. He joined the team that fall as a 27-year-old rookie and became one of the reasons the Islanders won four straight Stanley Cups. Kallur gave the team speed from the right wing and scoring ability, even though he missed most of training camp and the start of the year with a bad groin injury. In his second season he contributed 36 goals, though injuries slowed him down in his last years with the team. After the Islanders released him late in the '84-'85 season, he found no other takers and retired. By then, he was the all-time leader on the team with 19 short-handed goals, a testament to his offensive abilities and defensive reliability.

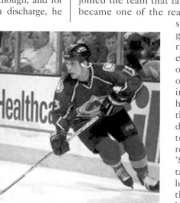

North Americans first saw him at Rendez-vous '87, where he and Wayne Gretzky were named the respective MVPs of the Soviet and NHL teams.
VALERI KAMENSKY

KAMENSKY, Valeri
b. Voskresensk, Soviet Union (Russia), April 18, 1966
By the time Kamensky made it to the NHL in 1991 at age 25, with the blessing of Soviet officials, he was already considered one of the top players in the world. He had been playing in the Soviet league for eight years, but he had also made a name for himself with his exceptional play in the toughest competitions. North Americans first saw him at Rendez-vous '87, where he and Wayne Gretzky were named the respective MVPs of the Soviet and NHL teams, and Kamensky only augmented his reputation through his play in that fall's Canada Cup. In the 1990-91, he was named player of the year back home as well as MVP at the World Championships, but during training camp for the '91 Canada Cup he broke his leg. Soviet authorities negotiated an agreement with Quebec for his release – perhaps in part because he acted as spokesman in Canada for Lada cars – and the Nordiques got him into 23 games toward the end of the season in one of the more anticipated NHL debuts. Injuries befell the gifted star the next season, though. First he broke his thumb, and then days after returning he broke his ankle and was again lost for months. It wasn't until '93-'94 that he played a full season, and he came through with 28 goals. His best years came after the lockout-shortened '94-'95 season after the team

relocated to Colorado. He won the Stanley Cup with the Avalanche and won a silver medal with Russia at the 1998 Olympics in Nagano, but as the decade came to a close he was traded three times in as many years. His goal production dipped dramatically, and from 1999 to 2002 he scored just 20 times.

KAMINSKI, Kevin ("Killer")
b. Churchbridge, Saskatchewan, March 13, 1969
Kaminski came out of Saskatoon with a fighter's spirit and reputation, a young man determined to make the NHL at all costs. He paid the price. He fought opponents to make an impression; he had his face stitched with frightening regularity; he paid his dues in the minors to earn a shot at the big time. He played many more games in the minors than the NHL, and after being drafted in 1987 it was eight years before he played a full season in the top league without a trip to the minors. All along he had huge penalty-minute totals, and his game caught up to him in late 1999 when he suffered a career-ending concussion. The next fall, he was back in the game, but as an assistant coach for the Cincinnati Mighty Ducks, AHL affiliate to Anaheim. In 2002-03, he had his first head coaching job, with Long Beach.

KAMINSKY, Jan
b. Penza, Soviet Union (Russia), July 28, 1971
After winning a gold medal with Russia at the 1993 Worlds, Kaminsky came to Canada to play for Winnipeg, the team that had drafted him two years previous. He played just once with the Jets before being traded to the Islanders, where he lasted only a little longer before being relegated to the minors. Kaminsky won the Turner Cup in 1996 with Utah in the IHL, and he retired in 1999 and became affiliated briefly with the Atlanta Thrashers organization.

KAMINSKY, Max
b. Niagara Falls, Ontario, April 19, 1912
d. New York, New York, May 5, 1961
When Kaminsky joined the NHL with Ottawa in 1933, he was touted as the best – and only – Jewish forward in the NHL. His only religious colleague was Alex Levinsky, a Toronto defenceman. He was considered one of the finest players to come out of the Falls, highly regarded for his smooth skating and excellent passing abilities. In his four years in the NHL, he changed teams a like number of times, but he went on to have a superb career in the AHL once he passed out of the big loop. He was a playing coach for Pittsburgh the last three years of his career and then became GM of the Philadelphia Rockets for three seasons. Kaminsky settled in Niagara Falls, New York, where he opened a bar and restaurant, but he did not forsake hockey. He coached the St. Catharines Tee Pees to a Memorial Cup in 1960, but soon resigned his position due to illness. For a year he battled cancer before succumbing in Mount Sinai Hospital in New York City.

KAMPMAN, Rudolph "Bingo"
b. Berlin (Kitchener), Ontario, March 12, 1914
d. Kitchener, Ontario, December 22, 1987
They called him Bingo for the sound he made when he hit opponents, and although he didn't play very long in the NHL, he was part of the miracle 1942 Leafs team that won the last four games of the finals after falling behind 3-0 in the series. He played his whole career with the Leafs, starting in 1937 when the team traded an aging Hap Day to the New York Americans and were in need of a defenceman. They found Kampman, who had won the Allan Cup with the Sudbury Tigers the previous spring, but his career ended after that '42 Cup triumph when he marched off to war. He was posted to Ottawa, achieved the rank of corporal, and played for the powerful Ottawa Commandos team, one of the finest amateur teams ever assembled. It featured the likes of Sugar Jim Henry in goal as well as the Colville brothers – Neil and Mac – Ken Kilrea, and Kenny Reardon, and won the '43 Allan Cup. But after the war Kampman could do no better than senior hockey, finishing with the Kitchener Dutchmen in '50-'51. After retiring he became a sales representative for the two big breweries, Labatt and Carling, but his later years were spent in misery. A man famous in his prime for being able to lift a table with his teeth (and noted for his belief in conditioning) was confined to a nursing home from 1967 to '87 as a result of poor health and near blindness. In July '87 he was moved to St. Mary's Hospital, where he died a few months later.

KAMPPURI, Hannu
b. Helsinki, Finland, June 1, 1957
Perhaps the odd spelling of Kamppuri's name represents the oddness of his career. He signed with Edmonton in 1978 and allowed 10 goals in a game and a half. A year later, he returned home until the Devils coerced him back to North America. By the time he arrived on the smelly shores of New Jersey in 1984, he had been a perennial all-star in Finland. At camp with the Devils, he performed well enough to earn the backup role on the team, yet in just 645 minutes of play he allowed a staggering 54 goals. This added up to a lousy 1-10-1 record and earned him a trip out of the NHL forever. By season's end, he returned to Finland to continue his career.

KANE, Francis "Red"
b. Stratford, Ontario, January 19, 1923
Jack Adams put Kane into two games during the war for Detroit and then kept the young defenceman in Indianapolis until trading him. Kane played a few more years in the minors before retiring, never having made it back to the NHL.

KANNEGIESSER, Gord
b. North Bay, Ontario, December 21, 1945
The older brother of Sheldon, Gord had a shorter NHL career but an eventful one all the same. He played briefly with St. Louis during its first year in the league and was a regular on the farm teams blueline. He was called up for four games in '71-'72 but with the advent of the WHA and in eight of his ever-impending demotion, he signed with the Houston Aeros in 1972. He played there for two years, including the season when Gordie, Marty, and Mark Howe helped the team win the Avco Cup.

Kevin Kaminski

Max Kaminsky

Hannu Kamppuri

Red Kane

Sheldon Kannegiesser

KANNEGIESSER, Sheldon
b. North Bay, Ontario, August 15, 1947
Like his brother, Gord, Sheldon knew he was not the next Bobby Orr, or even the one after that. No, he was a plumber, a journeyman who had to appreciate every shift because it could be his last. He managed to survive for 366 NHL games, but he admitted that even at the best of times, his heart wasn't in the game with the same passion as, say, Orr. As a result, he looked past his playing days even during his early years in the game. When he retired in 1978, he snapped into action and learned the business world. He established himself in Los Angeles, changed his name to the more accessible Kane, and set up Kane-Runner, a business that acted as a marketing company and limousine service and expanded to other principal U.S. cities. He set up an Arabian horse business, marketed investment products, and became top-notch in the business world as he never had been in the hockey world.

Sami Kapanen

KAPANEN, Niko
b. Hattula, Finland, April 29, 1978
No relation to Sami of Carolina, Niko is also a small, skilled forward. He played all of his career in Finland until joining Dallas in 2001. He played only a few games for the Stars that first year but made the team full-time to start 2002-03 playing on a line with Rob DiMaio and Jere Lehtinen, the team's best. At 5'9", he is not the biggest player around, but he has the skills to stay in the NHL.

KAPANEN, Sami
b. Vantaa, Finland, June 14, 1973
Hannu Kapanen played professionally in Finland for many years, and after retiring he raised his two children – Sami and Jari – and turned his devotion to coaching. Both boys went on to become fine players, though Sami was the best of the clan. He was small in stature, but he had great moves and superior speed to survive despite the toughness of the game. Sami had tremendous international success early on, most notably with the Finnish team that won gold at the 1995 World Championships, its first such honour. That summer, Hartford drafted him into the NHL and Kapanen came right over. His career almost ended before it officially began, however, when he collided with Gerald Diduck in training camp. Kapanen suffered a serious concussion and back injury and spent half the season in the minors getting back into shape. Once he established himself, he became a successful player in the NHL, and since 1997 has never failed to score 20 goals a season. He moved with the Whalers when they transferred to Carolina, and it was in large measure due to his play that the team made it to the finals in 2002, even though he didn't score a goal. Midway through the 2002-03 season he was traded to Philadelphia. He played at the 1998 and 2002 Olympics, and at the 2000 All-Star Game he won the fastest-skater competition.

Mike Karakas

KARABIN, Ladislav ("Laco")
b. Spisska Nova Ves, Czechoslovakia (Slovakia), February 16, 1970
It was only in Europe that Karabin was able to hold down a steady job before and after a three-year hiatus in North America that was a moderate success at best.

Jere Karalahti

In 1993, he joined Pittsburgh for just nine games and spent most of his North American time in the minors before returning to his native Slovakia to play. He had won a bronze medal with the Czechs at the 1990 WJC in the days before his country divided.

KARAKAS, Mike ("Iron Mike")
b. Aurora, Minnesota, November 13, 1910
d. Wakefield, Minnesota, May 2, 1992
Few goalies make as quick a positive impression in the NHL as Karakas did in 1935 when he joined Chicago and went on to become the first American-born superstar of the nets. He played every game that year and had 9 shutouts in just 48 games. In fact, in his first four seasons with the Hawks he didn't miss a single game – ergo his nickname – though he played on a not-very-good team. In spring of 1938, he saved his best for the playoffs, taking a weak team to the Stanley Cup in a historic win for the team because of its mostly American lineup. He was sent to Montreal at the end of the '39-'40 season and then spent the better part of three years in the minors until Chicago recalled him in 1944. For the second time, Karakas won the starting position with the team and took the Hawks to the 1944 finals before losing to Montreal. After retiring, Karakas settled in Boston and became a successful sales executive. He was later inducted into the Providence Reds Hall of Fame for his seven seasons of excellent service to that team, and was also honoured by the United States Hockey Hall of Fame.

KARALAHTI, Jere ("Chief")
b. Helsinki, Finland, March 25, 1975
The son of a police officer who became a heroin addict, Karalahti is trying to cling to the slim thread of hope that is hockey. As a kid, he was privileged, and with that came parties and social opportunities unavailable to most. Some can handle it, some can't. As a superb 18-year-old player, he travelled with the Finnish team to play in the World Juniors in Red Deer. Almost as soon as the team's plane landed in Alberta, he went off on a drinking and smoking binge that had his coaches worried. He returned, explained, apologized, and was allowed to play. Yet he did not learn from his mistakes and the lure of drugs became stronger. The low point came a short time later when he was arrested in Finland and charged with possession of heroin. Yet the team that had drafted him in 1993, Los Angeles, stuck by him. The Kings finally brought him over in 1999 after persuading U.S. immigration officials he could be trusted, but a relapse sent him to the NHL's substance abuse program. The Kings finally let him go to Nashville, but Karalahti has spent most of his pro years in the minors. The once-talented defenceman battled through his drug addiction for a time, but after violating the NHL's substance-abuse policy a third time, he was suspended for six months. Rather than change his ways, he vowed never to stop drinking and never to play in the NHL again.

KARAMNOV, Vitali
b. Moscow, Soviet Union (Russia), July 6, 1968
The big bucks and fast times couldn't be passed up, but Karamnov didn't last long with St. Louis in the high-paced world of the NHL. He came out of the Soviet

league and went back to the European leagues, and in between played three years in North America, mostly in the minors. He played for Russia at the 1996 World Championships, when the team finished in fourth place.

KARIYA, Paul
b. Vancouver, British Columbia, October 16, 1974

Family, school, hockey, in that order, represented the world of Paul Kariya. His father was a fine rugby player, his mother a teacher, his brothers and sisters the most trusted people in his life. He started figure skating at age three but quickly turned to hockey and learned to skate better than kids much older. Like his idol, Wayne Gretzky, Kariya developed by playing in leagues with much older boys, and by the time he was 16 he was playing provincial junior hockey with an eye to a U.S. scholarship, which would allow him to play serious hockey and acquire an education. He went to the University of Maine in 1992 and in two years developed so quickly that it was impossible not to see him in the NHL, sooner rather than later. He won an NCAA title with the Black Bears and was awarded the Hobey Baker Award in 1993, but during his two years in college his focus was on Canada's National Team as much as on Maine. He played at two WJC tournaments and left Maine to play with Canada leading up to the 1994 Olympics in Lillehammer. It was there that Canada and Sweden went to a shootout to decide the gold medal, and it was there that in sudden-death penalty shots the gold medal came down to one shot, Kariya's against goalie Tommy Salo. Salo

> **His father was a fine rugby player, his mother a teacher, his brothers and sisters the most trusted people in his life.**
> PAUL KARIYA

made the save, and Kariya was crushed, though he would get a chance to exonerate himself later. He turned pro with Anaheim in 1994, the year of the lockout, and in his first full season he scored 50 goals and 108 points. His explosive stride and unparalleled speed made him the most exciting young player in the world, but he played in a city not serious about winning and without a supporting cast to help him and the team. The only exception came when the Ducks acquired Teemu Selanne, and for a brief time the two played brilliantly together. Kariya had a chance to play for Canada again at the 1998 Olympics in Nagano, a time that would have been extra special for him because of his Japanese ancestry. However, just a month before the Games he was viciously cross-checked by Chicago's Gary Suter and sat out the rest of the year with post-concussion syndrome. When he returned the next fall, he had a stronger helmet, a mouthguard, and a new attitude that dismissed his previously gentlemanly play, which had earned him the Lady Byng trophies in 1996 and '97. Loyal to a fault, he continued to play for Anaheim and resisted the desire to change teams, yet in

nine seasons in the league the Ducks have made the playoffs just three times. His skilled partner Selanne is long gone, and teams know that if they check Kariya, they have a great chance to win the game. Kariya's supreme skill was best demonstrated at the 2002 Olympics in Salt Lake City, playing alongside Mario Lemieux. The pair were a perfect combination, and Canada's gold-medal win can be attributed largely to their synchronized play. Still in his prime, Kariya continues to be one of the most exciting players in the game, though his dominance is less visible at the club level with the weak Ducks than at higher levels among his true peers. An intensely focused player, he refuses to do interviews on game day. He stretches for 90 minutes before each game, and his sister is his business assistant who declines most offers on Paul's behalf because of his desire to concentrate on the game rather than its ancillary elements.

Steve Kariya

KARIYA, Steve
b. North Vancouver, British Columbia, December 22, 1977

The family rivalry is as intense as it is unequal. Paul is no giant or heavyweight, but Steve is even smaller. Paul is one of the most talented players in the game; Steve is not. Following his brother, Steve also attended U of Maine, but he was never drafted and signed with his local Canucks as a free agent. He wore number 18 when he made the team in the fall of 1999, vowing to be twice as good as his brother. Yet he was demoted before the season was done and has yet to establish himself to anywhere near the degree Paul has. Steve Kariya is a very skilled hockey player, but he is a marginal NHLer.

KARJALAINEN, Kyosti
b. Gavle, Sweden, June 19, 1967

Despite the Finnish name, Karjalainen is a Swede by birth and by hockey experience. Even by his own league's standards, though, he is no superstar, a fact confirmed when the right winger played 28 games for Los Angeles in the early 1990s. Once his days in Sweden were done, he took a step down and played in Germany.

KARLANDER, Al ("Olle")
b. Lac la Hache, British Columbia, November 5, 1946

In 1967, Karlander became the first college player to be selected in the NHL Amateur Draft, a distinction he earned while playing for Michigan Tech, the school that sent Tony Esposito and Lou Angotti on to the NHL. Karlander earned three letters during his years at Michigan while studying business. After graduating, he joined Detroit and had four decent years with the team, but when New England offered him a once-in-a-lifetime contract to skip over to the

Al Karlander

Andreas Karlsson

David Karpa

WHA, he couldn't refuse. He ended his career with Indianapolis and settled in the city after retiring, going into the mortgage business and coaching kids' teams in the city for 20 years. He later became head coach of Carmel High School in Carmel, Indiana. He was also inducted into the Michigan Tech Hall of Fame for his college accomplishments.

KARLSSON, Andreas ("Andy")
b. Ludvika, Sweden, August 19, 1975
Thanks to expansion and a bloated 30-team NHL, Karlsson made it to North America in 1999 to play with the humble Atlanta Thrashers. He had played with Leksand at home for seven years, but although Calgary had drafted him in '93 the Flames couldn't find a home for him on their roster. They traded him to Atlanta for nothing more than futures. Karlsson's greatest thrill came in 1995 with Tre Kronor when he played in the World Juniors.

KARPA, David
b. Regina, Saskatchewan, May 7, 1971
In 1991, hard-hitting David Karpa aborted a college career with Ferris State, where his major was recreation leadership management, in order to join Quebec and play in the NHL. He was the first player to leave the Bulldogs for the big time, though he was noted for his fighting as much as anything else. His 13:1,070 goals-to-penalty minutes ratio attests to as much. Despite his defensive and team efforts, he has only been to the playoffs in four years, and only once made it past the first round. As a teen, he played for Notre Dame and captained the Hounds in his final season, '89-'90.

KARPOV, Valeri
b. Chelyabinsk, Soviet Union (Russia), August 5, 1971
In the old days, Soviets had no choice. Then, they had the choice of going to the NHL. Now, they have the choice of staying at home or going to the NHL and returning home to a good career. Karpov experienced all of the above. He began as a junior under the Soviet regime, and after playing for Russia at the 1994 Olympics in Lillehammer he joined Anaheim in the NHL. After three part-time years, it was clear his North American status had been imprinted with "minor league," so he returned home to play in the new Russian league, a league that paid players very well, pampered them, and put together competitive teams.

KARPOVTSEV, Alexander ("Potsie")
b. Moscow, Soviet Union (Russia), April 7, 1970
In boxing, a glass jaw pretty much predetermines a fighter's chance of victory. In hockey, Karpovtsev has the body equivalent – a glass skeleton, perhaps? Make

no mistake – he is a fine and talented defenceman. It's just that for every blocked shot, there seems to be a broken bone. For every jarring hit, a torn this or pulled that. He joined the Rangers in 1993 shortly after winning gold for Russia at the World Championships. As a rookie he helped the team win its first Cup in 54 years. He was traded to Toronto near the start of the '98-'99 season, but the Leafs were frustrated by the combination of his injuries and his salary demands. Off he went to Chicago, where he again missed games to injury. When he played, he helped the Hawks become a playoff team for a year, at least.

KASATONOV, Alexei
b. Leningrad, Soviet Union (Russia), October 14, 1959
Soviet hockey produced many stories of intrigue and subterfuge, and out of this came friendships and animosities. Kasatonov came from Leningrad, a large Soviet city not known for its hockey players. But national coach Viktor Tikhonov took to the youngster because of his positioning and strength. He thought there was hope for Kasatonov, and to this end he paired him with the more talented Slava Fetisov. Kasatonov roomed at Fetisov's house and the two became great friends as well as the best defensive pair in the land. The trouble began when Fetisov started petitioning to be allowed to play in the NHL. His friend and partner remained silent on the matter, and this not only outraged Fetisov but cost the pair their friendship. Between 1977 and 1989, Kasatonov played in every important tournament for the Soviets, and New Jersey thought it had been smart to draft both players in the hopes of reuniting the pair in North America. Sadly, by the time that day came, in 1989, the two players were no longer talking. What a paradox to see the two greatest defencemen of the Soviet era playing in the NHL as a pair, the one unwilling to utter a word to the other! Kasatonov was traded to Anaheim and then to two other teams before retiring.

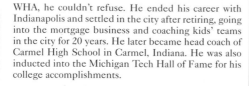

The Islanders drafted him 5th overall in 1992 and in his first year he made a tremendous impression.
DARIUS KASPARAITIS

KASPARAITIS, Darius
b. Elektrenai, Soviet Union (Lithuania), October 16, 1972
When he was 16 years old, Kasparaitis became the first player born in Lithuania to be asked to play for a Soviet league team. That's how good he was, and that was only the beginning. The Islanders drafted him 5th overall in 1992 and in his first year in the NHL, coming off a WC gold with Russia, he made a tremendous impression. Not only did he have a great regular season, but in the playoffs he was assigned to neutralize Mario Lemieux, who had won the two previous Cups with Pittsburgh. Kasparaitis did just

Alexander Karpovtsev

Alexei Kasatonov

that, and his reputation was solidified: he was a tough disturber who got under a player's skin and hit hard despite being under six feet tall. When the Islanders traded him and Andreas Johansson to Pittsburgh for Bryan Smolinski, there was an outcry on Long Island, such was Kasparaitis's popularity. In Pittsburgh, of course, he was coming to his most notorious den, but fans loved him for the same reasons they had hated him years earlier. On the verge of free agency in early 2002, he found himself traded to Colorado, though the team failed to win the Cup and he moved on to the Rangers. Perhaps no better indication of both his competitiveness and his slight lunacy was his behaviour at the 1992 World Juniors. After a loss to the Czechs, the Russian players gathered around their goalie, Ildar Muhametov, to console him, but Kasparaitis stepped in and decked him with one punch. That's just the kind of guy Darius is.

KASPER, Steve ("The Friendly Ghost")
b. Montreal, Quebec, September 28, 1961

In a later incarnation as a coach with Boston, the team with which he played much of his career, Kasper benched Cam Neely in a game at Maple Leaf Gardens. That is, he dressed him, and then let him sit on the bench for the entire 60 minutes. It was a cruel and vicious act against one of the most competitive players of the modern era. It was also perplexing given that Kasper entered the league in 1980 and earned a spot on the team ahead of star prospect Barry Pederson because of his own tenacity. Indeed, Kasper was a checker before being a scorer, a hard worker and not a purely talented star. He earned every shift and fought and clawed his way into the lineup every night, and he hated to lose. He won the Selke Trophy in 1982 because of his two-way play, and it was because of contributions like his that the Bruins made it to the '88 finals against the Oilers. A serious knee injury ended his year early in '91-'92 with Philadelphia, and after retiring a year later he went into coaching. After his two years as head of the Bruins, he went into a hockey line far more enduring – he became a player agent.

KASTELIC, Ed
b. Toronto, Ontario, January 29, 1964

At age 18, Kastelic was drafted into the NHL, but by age 21 he was in and out of the league after 15 games and he was having a rough time. He quit the game and enrolled at York University in Toronto, figuring he'd take some time off and get an education. He got a job as a car jockey in a downtown condo building, where one of the tenants was the Leafs' Russ Courtnall. Kastelic snapped out of his funk and returned to the team, but for most of seven seasons his was a part-time role. During one of his stints in the AHL, Kastelic was suspended by the league for 20 games for biting the hand of a linesman during a fight, and retribution, being sweet and nasty, had its day soon after when Kevin Kerr was suspended 9 games for biting Kastelic's hand during another set-to! Kastelic went on to play several years in Europe and even played a World Championships qualifying tournament for Slovenia in 1999, a passport trick he could manage after that country declared independence.

KASZYCKI, Mike ("Kaz")
b. Milton, Ontario, February 27, 1956

There's nothing poetic about Milton, Ontario, unless you're an aviation freak, for that is where Toronto's international airport is located. It's also where Kaszycki got his start in life, and it's appropriate he lived near an airport because one day he flew away and never came back. In his final year of junior, Kaszycki led the league in assists and points, but he also accomplished something else rather special. In a game for the Soo in 1976, he had 2 goals and 9 assists, and those 11 points stand as an OHL record for most points in a game. With that under his belt, he turned pro and joined the Islanders a year later, in 1977. He never came near his junior feats, though, and he was soon on the move, first to Washington and then Toronto. Back home, he joined a team in disarray and bounced up and down to the minors more often than he would care to remember. By 1984, he had had enough. He packed his bags, moved to Switzerland, and had such a great experience that he became a Swiss citizen just a year later.

KAVANAGH, Pat
b. Ottawa, Ontario, March 14, 1979

All's quiet so far. Since being drafted in 1997, Kavanagh has played just three times, in the playoffs, with Vancouver, the team that acquired him from Philly for a sixth-round draft choice in 1999 (Konstantin Rudenko). Kavanagh plays the right wing and came out of Peterborough, but he has yet to make coach Marc Crawford take too much notice to date.

KEA, Ed
b. Weesp, Holland, January 19, 1948
d. Six Mile Lake, Ontario, August 31, 1999

What a strange, upsetting story was the life and career of Ed Kea who had the shortest name in NHL history. He was the thirteenth of 14 children, and when he was 3 his family moved from Holland to Collingwood. He made do as a big and solid defenceman, though half his career ran its course in the minors, where it also ended prematurely. He had been sent to the minors in '82-'83 to skate through a groin injury, and March 7, 1983, turned out to be his final game, even though he had been scheduled to rejoin St. Louis the next day. In that game, while playing for Salt Lake City, he collided with George McPhee (later GM of the Washington Capitals). Kea careered into a teammate of McPhee and then hit his head on the top of the boards, falling to the ice face first. He required immediate brain surgery to release pressure, and was in a coma for two weeks. Once he came to, he remained in hospital another two months. His playing days were over, but this story has no happy ending. The brain damage was irreversible. He couldn't drive, he became depressed, and his short-term memory was affected for the rest of his life. Because the game took place in the minors he didn't qualify for NHL disability insurance. He took the team to court and reached a settlement, but the toll on him and his family was great. His nephew was Jeff Beukeboom, whose own career ended because of a serious concussion. Kea's life ended early, in 1999, when he drowned in Six Mile Lake, just south of Parry Sound.

Steve Kasper

Ed Kastelic

Mike Kaszycki

Ed Kea

Mike Keane

Doug Keans

Dennis Kearns

Duke Keats

KEANE, Mike
b. Winnipeg, Manitoba, May 29, 1967
It's amazing what determination will do for a person – that and turning a deaf ear to all the critics who said Keane was too small and not skilled enough to make the NHL. Every scout agreed, because Keane was never drafted. Yet Montreal signed him, and he developed to the point that he was named captain late in his career with the Habs. He proved a tenacious checker and a hard worker, a team man and a leader. He grew up admiring the Boston Bruins, and he was cut from the same cloth as Terry O'Reilly and Bobby Schmautz. Keane won a Cup in 1993 with Montreal, but he caused a furor when he said that French was not an essential language in the team's dressing room. Keane was part of the trade that sent Patrick Roy to Colorado, and like all Montreal trades in the 1990s, it was a stinker. Roy, Keane, et al. won the Cup their first year with the team, and Keane later became part of history when he won a third Cup in 1999 with Dallas, his third team. He didn't score many goals, but GMs realized he was exactly the kind of player every Cup champion needed. Not bad for a guy nobody wanted as a teenager.

KEANS, Doug
b. Pembroke, Ontario, January 7, 1958
Keans was a tiny goalie who came into the NHL sooner than even he had expected, and though his trial by fire was difficult, it enabled him to become a solid goalie for a short period. L.A. had intended to develop him in the minors for a couple of seasons, but when they weren't happy with the play of either Mario Lessard or Ron Grahame, they brought Keans up midway through the '79-'80 season. He stayed only 10 games, but helped bring the team out of a funk. His big break came in 1983 when he was claimed by Boston, and for five years he was the second-string goalie for the Bruins. He had an excellent record during this time (83-46-13), but when the team acquired Andy Moog in 1988, Keans became redundant. He spent the rest of his career in the minors.

KEARNS, Dennis
b. Kingston, Ontario, September 27, 1945
Kearns embraced Vancouver, and the city gave him a great big hug right back. He played his entire NHL career with the Canucks (1971-81) as a skating and rushing defenceman. Physical strength and intimidation were not his fortes – puck movement was. He was small and never made his reputation as a hitter, but he certainly was a playmaker on a team that lacked both offence and defence to various degrees. After retiring, Kearns settled on the North Shore of the city and opened his own business, Dennis Kearns and Associates, which specialized in personal insurance and money management. He continued to run an annual golf tournament that bore his name, all proceeds of which went to charity. He also sat on boards in the city and became an outstanding member of the community.

KEATING, Jack ("Red")
b. Kitchener, Ontario, October 9, 1916
d. Indianapolis, Indiana, December 29, 1951
During his short life, Keating made a lasting impression. He played only 11 NHL games, with Detroit before the war, but his was the key contribution to Indianapolis's Calder Cup win in '41-'42. Keating led the AHL playoffs with 9 goals and 18 points, and soon after the win he served as a physical training instructor for the U.S. Army Air Corps for 3 years. After the fighting ended, he played two more years in California and then enrolled at the Los Angeles College of Optometry, graduating in 1951. He returned to Indianapolis to start a practice there but died just a few months later.

KEATING, John ("Jackie"/ "The Miramichi Flash")
b. Newcastle, New Brunswick, February 12, 1908
d. Saint John, New Brunswick, June 5, 1985
One of the lightest players ever to skate in the NHL, the 136-pound, Keating rose from the ranks of Harkins Academy in his hometown to go on to Saint John at age 17 to play for the Fusiliers. He turned pro in 1930 and the year after played with the Americans in the NHL. After 35 games over 2 years, he continued his career in the minors until 1941, when he retired as a player and returned to Saint John. It was there his second life started, a life of coaching that made him as famous in the Maritimes as his playing ever did. He coached the local Beavers for nine years, taking the team to the Maritime Senior Championship in 1946. One of his players, Gus Kyle, went on to a career in the NHL. After retiring from coaching, Keating became the director of minor hockey for Saint John and managed baseball teams in the summer. He also worked as a surveyor for the city, and in 1958 he was lured out of retirement to coach the Beavers/Oilers team for two years. Keating was also a superb ball player, and in his youth he won the batting championship in the New Brunswick Senior Baseball League. He was inducted into that province's Sports Hall of Fame in 1973.

KEATING, Mike
b. Toronto, Ontario, January 21, 1957
A draft choice of the Rangers in 1977, Keating played one game with the New Yorkers the very next year and was out of the loop almost right away. He won only three years of pro and then retired. He won a silver medal with Canada at the inaugural World Junior Championships in 1977.

KEATS, Gordon "Duke" ("Iron Duke")
b. Montreal, Quebec, March 21, 1895
d. Victoria, British Columbia, January 16, 1972
It was in North Bay that Keats grew up and learned how to skate and stickhandle with breathtaking brilliance. By the time he was 17, he was in Cobalt making $75 a week playing the game he loved, and by 1915, experienced at age 20, he was in the NHA with Toronto. He joined the Canadian army in 1916 and didn't return for three years, but the time off had done nothing to diminish or rob him of his skills. Keats played for the Edmonton Eskimos for the next seven years. Legend and truth blurred with time, but as the story goes he once collected the puck in his own end and skated the length of the ice to score – all the while skating backward! Regardless, he routinely led the league in goals and was its greatest superstar performer. That team reached its peak in 1923 when it went to the Cup finals before losing to the Senators. He finally joined the NHL in 1926, but played only a little more than two seasons.

Nevertheless, he saw action with Boston, Detroit (where he was playing coach briefly), and Chicago during his brief career in that league. He was not in good shape, though, and he had slowed a step, so the NHL did not see him at his best. He wound up playing most of '28-'29 in Tulsa where he led the AHA in scoring and was instrumental in the very organization of the Oilers. The team won the league title in '30-'31, and then Keats issued a challenge to the NHL, demanding to play the winners of the Stanley Cup. Nice try, but the request was denied. He returned to Edmonton to close out his career, retiring in 1934 but staying on to coach and manage the team. He went on to coach a number of teams in the west – Saskatoon, Lusgar, Coleman – and worked briefly for the Black Hawks before settling in Victoria permanently in 1947. In 1958, he was inducted into the Hockey Hall of Fame. He worked for the government in Victoria and became president of the Victoria Commercial Hockey League in his off-hours. He suffered from ulcers later in life and died at Veterans' Hospital in Victoria after a long illness.

KECZMER, Dan
b. Mt. Clemens, Michigan, May 25, 1968
Rarely has a player been such a consistent part-time fixture in the NHL as Keczmer. Only once, in '93-'94, did he play a full season in the league, and even then it was split between two teams. In every other year of his 10, he played long stretches in the minors or was a healthy scratch. Even before he made it to the big time, he played for the U.S. at the 1990 WC, and a year and a half later he devoted himself to the National Team in the hopes of playing at the 1992 Olympics in Albertville. These hopes were not realized, so he tried to make a go of it with Hartford after San Jose acquired his rights from Minnesota and traded him to the Whalers before ever using him. Over the years, he changed teams periodically, only to find his role with the new team the same as the old: steady, reliable, fill-in. He retired in 2000.

KEEFE, Sheldon
b. Brampton, Ontario, September 17, 1980
When he was at St. Mike's, Keefe established himself as a top prospect for the NHL draft, but he was on a weak team and demanded a trade to a contender. It was a selfish move, yet when he got to Barrie he led the OHL in points for 1999-2000 and took the team to the Memorial Cup. Keefe's bravura evaporated when he hit the mean streets of the NHL, though, and despite playing for the lowly Lightning he has by no means proved himself a star in the toughest league of them all. Time is still on his side … but for how much longer?

KEELING, Melville "Butch"
b. Owen Sound, Ontario, August 10, 1905
d. Toronto, Ontario, November 12, 1984
In game four of the best-of-five 1933 Stanley Cup finals, the Rangers had a chance to win the Cup in their series against Toronto. That game went into overtime after a scoreless 60 minutes, and Keeling's pass to Bill Cook allowed Cook to score the Cup-winning goal. Keeling had played the first two years of his career with Toronto, but the Leafs traded him for Alex Gray in 1928. Keeling spent the rest of his career with the Rangers, though he

never won another Cup. He was a fine, scoring winger for the Blueshirts, and after he passed out of the NHL in 1938 he moved into coaching. He later became a referee in the NHL for three seasons.

KEENAN, Don
b. Toronto, Ontario, August 8, 1938
The NHL was not the point for Keenan. He played for St. Mike's in his early teens, but knew he wasn't going to be beating out Hall or Plante for a job any time soon, so he enrolled in mechanical engineering at St. Francis-Xavier University. For his third year, in 1958, he decided to return home and complete his schooling at St. Mike's through U of Toronto. To keep his mind and body sharp, he agreed to be the spare goalie for the Majors, but this meant little playing time, which was fine with him. On March 7, 1959, Boston was in town to play the Leafs, but their star goalie, Harry Lumley, was ailing. Keenan got a call at 5:25 p.m. and was told to report to the Bruins – he might be needed. Once he got to Maple Leaf Gardens, he discovered that Lumley was, indeed, too ill to play, and he would have to don the pads. After two periods, the score was 1-1, and it was only a final-period attack that gave the Leafs a scary 4-1 win, beating a rusty engineering student to get the two points. Keenan continued with his education and never saw the NHL again from the confines of a crease.

KEENAN, Larry
b. North Bay, Ontario, October 1, 1940
In 1961, praise couldn't have come on a grander scale than to have Punch Imlach call you the greatest junior player in all of Canada. Those are the terms under which Keenan signed with the Leafs following an outstanding junior career with St. Mike's. Fortunately for Imlach, he extolled Keenan's virtues in the summer so that by the fall, when his star junior played only two games, his words were history. Keenan was consigned to the minors until expansion, when St. Louis gave him plenty of ice time, and his career was extended another five years. After retiring, Keenan returned to North Bay and ran a fitness centre for four years. He then worked for Pepsi-Cola as a sales rep and later started his own coffee supply business. He coached local house-league teams and developed the skills of his son, Corey, who went on to play in the 1990 Memorial Cup with Kitchener.

KEHOE, Rick
b. Windsor, Ontario, July 15, 1951
It was a hit like any other, nothing special, but by the time Kehoe fully recovered, his career was long over. Late in the '83-'84 season, he started to experience pain in his neck and numbness in his arm. Doctors discovered a problem with his vertebrae, but no amount of therapy or exercise could control the pain. Surgery was an option, but doctors promised nothing. Kehoe decided to retire. He had begun his career in Toronto in 1971 and quickly developed into the scorer the Leafs had hoped. In his second season, he had 33 goals, but he became very unhappy the next year playing under coach Red Kelly. He asked for, and got, a trade, to Pittsburgh, and it was there he spent the rest of his playing career. In '80-'81, he scored 55 goals, and on 4 other occasions he had 30 or more. A gentlemanly

Dan Keczmer

Butch Keeling

Larry Keenan

Rick Kehoe

Ralph Keller

player from start to finish, Kehoe was awarded the Lady Byng Trophy in 1981, and after retiring became the director of the Pens' pro scouting department. He has been with the team ever since, first as an assistant coach, and then replacing Ivan Hlinka as head coach in the 2001-02 season. He was fired in April 2003 after the team missed the playoffs again.

KEKALAINEN, Jarmo
b. Tampere, Finland, July 3, 1966
The U.S. college route is often taken by Canadians as an alternative to junior, and Canadian junior is often used by NHL-aspiring Americans and Europeans. But a rare hybrid occurs when a European player gets to the NHL via a U.S. college. That's how Kekalainen made it to the Boston Bruins in 1989, after three years at Clarkson University. Nothing about Kekalainen screamed the beaten track. After two seasons with the Bruins, he returned to Finland to play, then accepted an offer from Ottawa. He closed out his career in Sweden, then returned to Canada and became director of player personnel for the Senators, a rare senior executive position for a European in the NHL.

KELLEHER, Chris
b. Cambridge, Massachusetts, March 23, 1975
Like almost every good Massachusetts boy, Kelleher went to a local college, in his case Boston University, where he refined his hockey. He had been drafted by Pittsburgh in 1993 but it wasn't until eight years later that his local Bruins signed him as a free agent and he was given an NHL chance. He had spent the intervening years in the minors, but the Bruins called him up for a single game in the big time.

KELLER, Ralph
b. Wilkie, Saskatchewan, February 6, 1936
The life and times of Ralph Keller can be neatly divided into two sections. The first was his time in the WHL. The second, following a three-game trial with the Rangers in '62-'63, was his dozen years in the AHL. Keller played 11 of those seasons with Hershey, where he became a popular athlete in the city. He was a rugged defenceman who won two Calder Cups with the Bears, and on February 21, 1971, he set an AHL record when he scored his 81st career goal to surpass Hy Buller. After retiring, he coached for a short time but settled in Hershey and made it his home.

KELLGREN, Christer
b. Goteborg, Sweden, August 15, 1958
The Rockies thought they had a gem when they scooped Kellgren from the Swedish league, but they dumped him in the minors after only five games. End of tryout. Kellgren finished the year with Fort Worth of the Central league and then returned to the land of Tre Kronor, where he enjoyed a number of decent seasons in second-division league play and eventually led Vastra Frolunda back to the top division in 1989.

KELLY, Bob ("Mad Dog"/ "The Hound"/ "Hound Dog"/ "Kamikaze Kelly")
b. Oakville, Ontario, November 25, 1950
Coming out of Oshawa in 1970, Kelly was considered one of the toughest men to play junior, and in those

Bob Kelly ("Mad Dog")

Bob Kelly

days that was saying a lot. He joined the goon show in Philadelphia, and for 10 years hit and fought and brawled his way to 2 Stanley Cups. Kelly's series of nicknames began with Joe Watson, who called him Mad Dog because of the reckless abandon with which he skated. Coach Fred Shero knew how to handle his animals from behind the bench, and with Kelly the plan was "less is more." Kelly didn't see many shifts, but when he was out there he was hell-bent on leaving his mark in every corner and on every player. This zealousness produced many scoring chances and a like number of fights, most notably in 1976 when the Leafs and Flyers played one of the most violent playoff series of the modern era. Kelly and three other teammates were charged by Ontario police with assault for their part in a brawl that spilled into the stands. Kelly pleaded guilty and was fined $750. Toward the end of his career he was traded to Washington, but after a year and a bit he agreed to have his contract bought out and he retired.

KELLY, Dave
b. Chatham, Ontario, September 20, 1952
By the time he graduated from Providence College in 1975 at age 22, Kelly had received no offers to play in the NHL. Desirous to play pro regardless, he signed with the Flyers at the end of the summer and agreed to join their farm team in Richmond. He had a decent enough season that Detroit acquired his rights and played him in 16 games the year after, but Kelly was back in the minors the following season, his last.

KELLY, J. Bob ("Battleship")
b. Fort William, Ontario, June 6, 1946
This Bob Kelly used his first initial to separate him from the other Bob Kelly of his day, though often that wasn't enough. The only reason this Bob K. got any work in the NHL was to combat goons like his namesake. This Bob was hired by St. Louis in 1973 at the age of 27, and during his six years he played for three NHL teams. He had seasons of 27 and 25 goals with Pittsburgh, though his scoring dropped dramatically in the following 3 years and he finished his career in the minors.

KELLY, John Paul "J.P." ("Jeep")
b. Edmonton, Alberta, November 15, 1959
Kelly came off the farm to play junior in New Westminster and made it to the NHL in large part because of his physical strength (ergo the nickname Jeep). He was drafted by L.A. in 1979 and made the team at his first camp, surprising even himself. For the next seven years he skated down the left wing, created havoc, and chipped in the occasional goal. But when the Kings, a last-place team, didn't offer him a new contract in the summer of '86, he knew his time was up. He returned to the family farm northwest of Lloydminster and took on the responsibility of managing the land with his wife, a love of soil that continues to this day.

KELLY, Pete
b. St. Vital, Manitoba, May 22, 1912
Not many players can boast that their first playoff goal won the Stanley Cup, but Kelly is one such lucky man.

Although he came from out west, he played his junior years in Montreal and turned pro in PEI, where he not only developed into a fine player but met his future wife. Kelly played either wing with equal proficiency, and the St. Louis Eagles signed him in '34-'35. The year after, he was traded to Detroit, and in the 1936 playoffs he had a year to remember. First, he appeared in the game of March 24, 1936, the longest one ever played (six overtime periods), and then, in the finals, it was his goal that gave the Wings a 3-2 win over Toronto for the Stanley Cup. Kelly won another Cup with Detroit the year after, but then his NHL time decreased and his time in the minors increased. He ended his career in Springfield in '41-'42 under the aegis of the difficult Eddie Shore, and despite leading the league in scoring Kelly preferred retirement to playing another year under Shore. Kelly joined the YMCA War Services, serving down east and then in England. While playing overseas, he suffered a serious break of his leg that ruined any future chances he might have had to play serious hockey. In 1947, he became head coach of the University of New Brunswick, a post he held for 20 years. He later served as athletic director, until retiring in 1977. He was inducted into the New Brunswick Sports Hall of Fame.

KELLY, Leonard "Red"

b. Simcoe, Ontario, July 9, 1927

Although Red Kelly was duly inducted into the Hockey Hall of Fame in 1969, the five-year waiting period cut to two, he is almost without a doubt the most underrated member of hockey's most elite group. He attended St. Mike's in Toronto from 1943 to '47, but the Red Wings stole him from under the nose of the Maple Leafs. He finished junior by winning a Memorial Cup with the great team of '47 and then joined Detroit in the fall. In his 20-year career, he never spent a shift in the minors, and from the start he proved a star in the world's toughest league. Kelly was a defenceman, though he played every position but goal during his 13 seasons in the Motor City. What was remarkable about him was that he could rush the puck and play exceptionally well in his own zone as well. This provided the team with a tremendous threat because Kelly could not only check a man off the puck, he could collect it and move up the ice without a moments hesitation. He was the defence and counterattack both. He had 9 seasons with more than 10 goals from the blueline, a record, and he was the first defenceman to score 100 career goals. He was key to Detroit's dynasty of the 1950s when the Wings won four Cups in six years, and Kelly was a fair and gentlemanly player besides. He won the Norris Trophy in '53-'54 and was a First Team All-Star six times

during the decade. He also won 4 Lady Byng Trophies and over the course of his career he played in 13 All-Star Games. Nonetheless, in the '59-'60 season, management publicly criticized Kelly for poor play, even though it knew confidentially that he had been playing with a broken foot. On February 5, 1960, the Wings traded him to the Rangers with Billy McNeil for Eddie Shack and Bill Gadsby, but both Kelly and McNeil refused to report. Kelly announced his retirement and started working for a business in Toronto. NHL president Clarence Campbell stepped in, as did Leafs management, and a deal was worked out a few days later that sent Kelly to Toronto for Marc Rheaume. It was, quite simply, the most favourably lopsided deal in Leafs history. Rheaume made little impact with Detroit; Kelly helped turn the Leafs into a 1960s dynasty. One of the first things coach Punch Imlach did was move Kelly permanently to centre. In his first three full seasons, this resulted in Kelly's only three 20-goal years. Frank Mahovlich, playing on Red's left side, scored a club-record 48 goals, and the Leafs won the Cup in 1962, '63, and '64. Kelly had another itch to scratch, though. He had considered a career in politics during his Detroit days but eventually decided against it. Now, he felt the urge to try for real. In 1962, he ran for the Liberals in the York West riding and won, maintaining his position as Member of Parliament until 1965. Those were busy years for Kelly. He travelled between Toronto and Ottawa every week, spending his free time in Ottawa practicing by himself on a rink he rented in Hull. For

Red Kelly

In 1947, he became head coach of the University of New Brunswick, a post he held for 20 years.
PETE KELLY

Wednesday-night games he had to hustle home and then back to Ottawa right after the game, and ditto for games in the U.S. on Sunday nights. It was a frenetic pace, but he shirked neither his MP nor his hockey duties, but after three years the grind was too much and he returned to hockey full-time. Kelly's last playing season was '66-'67, and it ended in spectacular fashion. He was 39 years old, and he knew he was retiring, so the '67 playoffs were a time to give every ounce of effort he had. He was one of five men from the Leafs Over-the-Hill Gang that Imlach had on the ice in the final minute to preserve a 2-1 win over Montreal in game six at the Gardens, and George Armstrong's empty-net goal assured the team of this historic, centennial Stanley Cup. Kelly retired and became coach of the expansion L.A. Kings (though not before Imlach demanded a player – Ken Block – in return for Kelly's rights!). He led the Kings for two years and then moved to Pittsburgh for four more, but it was back in Toronto that he had his greatest impact as a coach. He guided the Leafs for four seasons as they moved from poor team to solid playoff team, but

Pep Kelly

Steve Kelly

Stan Kemp

Bill Kendall

Dean Kennedy

there no was more famous a series than the Toronto-Philadelphia one of 1976 when Kelly invoked Pyramid Power to help his team. Pyramids, he argued, were a source of energy and strength, and to that end he placed small pyramids everywhere that would be beneficial, notably in the dressing room and under the players' bench. The Leafs lost the series, but it was an entertaining one. The next year, Kelly tried positive ions, but they didn't have the same cachet or allure, and just as the pyramids had failed, so, too, did the ions. Kelly was fired by the Leafs in 1977 and then established a company that served airline computers. His career is virtually without parallel. Check that, his two careers. His first saw him lead a Detroit dynasty from defence to four Stanley Cups; his second came as a centre that led his team to four more Cups. His 10 years as coach was merely icing on a huge cake, and his induction into the Hall of Fame was to be expected.

KELLY, Regis "Pep" ("Pepperpot")
b. North Bay, Ontario, January 9, 1914
d. North Bay, Ontario, 1990
It's cold and snowy in North Bay and the winters are long, conditions that are ideal for playing endless hours of hockey on outdoor rinks day after day, as Pep Kelly did as a kid. He was a tireless skater, which accounted for his moniker, and he moved quickly from Newmarket to St. Mike's after Leafs scouts liked what they saw of him as a teen. Kelly graduated to the NHL team at Maple Leaf Gardens in 1934, and his first 2 seasons he scored a respectable 11 goals each time, earning additional praise for his efforts as a penalty killer. But in '36-'37 he floundered, and the Leafs loaned him to Chicago for Bill Kendall for the remainder of the season. He had a strong finish, scoring 13 times in just 29 games, and rejoined the Leafs to start '37-'38. After three more seasons, and good but not spectacular performances in the playoffs, Conn Smythe sold Kelly outright to the Hawks. He finished his career playing a few games with Red Dutton's Brooklyn Americans in '41-'42, but continued to play at a lower level for a number of years after he realized how much he missed the game. After retiring, he joined the Canadian Pacific Railway, first as a fireman and then as an engineer. A train collision in 1952 caused serious injury to his hip, which took him off skates forever and even prevented him from playing golf ever again. Nevertheless, he turned his energies to coaching in North Bay. He was elected to that city's Hall of Fame in 1991.

KELLY, Steve
b. Vancouver, British Columbia, October 26, 1976
After going 6th overall to Edmonton in the 1995 Draft, Kelly had every right to feel comfortable if not altogether confident that his career would have some degree of stability and sensible direction. Yet after playing his first year of pro with the Oilers and the farm team, he dressed for five different teams in 1997-98, two in the NHL, two in the "I," and one in the AHL. He later played for Tampa, New Jersey, and Los Angeles, as well as a long list of IHL teams, and his career has been anything but stable. His lone accomplishment was playing for the Devils in 1999-2000 when they won the Cup.

KEMP, Kevin
b. Ottawa, Ontario, May 3, 1954
d. August 25, 1999
It would have been a miracle had Kemp scored in any of his three NHL games with Hartford in 1980-81, because at the time the Whalers recalled him from the minors he was in the midst of setting a dubious record in the AHL. Between 1978 and 1981, Kemp went 174 games without scoring a goal, a feat not worth bragging about but a fact nonetheless. In fact, that streak likely would have been extended had Kemp not retired after that season.

KEMP, Stan
b. Hamilton, Ontario, March 2, 1924
d. unknown
Kemp was a regular in the AHL by the time he was 19, but he never made the leap to the big tent with the same success. His one night with the Leafs came on January 23, 1949, and after that it was back to the minors. After retiring, he returned to Hamilton, where his roots showed through for all to see. He established Stan Kemp Construction, a profitable business he operated until his death.

KENADY, Chris
b. Mound, Minnesota, April 10, 1973
He's played for the IceCats and Grizzlies, and Ice Dogs and Wolf Pack, a veritable hockey zoo of teams along the road to brief stops in the NHL with St. Louis and the Rangers. The pride of Mound has spent most of his career in the minors, where he's known more for his toughness than his scoring.

KENDALL, Bill ("Cowboy")
b. Winnipeg, Manitoba, April 1, 1910
d. unknown
Kendall played almost all of his NHL hockey with Chicago and almost all of his AHL hockey with St. Louis. As a rookie with the Hawks, he contributed to the team's first-ever Stanley Cup in 1933-34 and stayed with the team for about four and a half years. His only other NHL stint came when he was loaned to the Leafs for 15 games. Before and after his NHL days, Kendall was a staple on the right wing with the St. Louis Flyers, where he was quite a scorer. The team won two league championships during his years in St. Louis, a career that was interrupted by two years of service in the Canadian army.

KENNEDY, Dean
b. Redvers, Saskatchewan, January 18, 1963
To explain how small Redvers was, Kennedy liked to place the city by saying it was near Antler, Saskatchewan. Like that helps. He was one of those innocuous, anonymous players of the modern era who appeared in 717 games and left fans wondering how he could have played for so long without leaving more of an impression. He played for five teams over his dozen years, but as a hitting and checking defenceman it was never his job to do the spectacular or make people take notice of his presence, except through a hard hit. His first coach was his dad, Ed, and when Dean left home at 16 to play provincial hockey, his parents warned him that if his school grades suffered, so, too, would he (in

a manner of speaking). It was that ethic that kept Kennedy in the game for so long, and while nobody else might have taken notice, his parents surely did.

KENNEDY, Forbes
b. Dorchester, New Brunswick, August 18, 1935

Kennedy was born in New Brunswick but the family moved to Charlottetown, PEI, when he was still an infant. His dad worked as a prison guard in Dorchester and his mother feared an inmate might escape and cause some harm, so dad got a job as a salesman on PEI. Forbes didn't put on skates until he was 11, and as he got older he rose in the ranks of Montreal teams before Chicago acquired his rights. He played 1956-57 with the Hawks but was traded to Detroit the next year in the deal that saw a vengeful Jack Adams trade Ted Lindsay and Glenn Hall to the Hawks – the worst team in the league – after Lindsay had tried to start a players union. Kennedy went on to play a number of years in the NHL, his role as a fighter clearly defined from the outset. That fighting reached its climax in his last NHL game ever on April 2, 1969. Boston beat Toronto 10-0, and during the game Leafs defenceman Pat Quinn knocked Bobby Orr cold with a hard check along the boards. Later in the game, a brawl erupted and Kennedy fought several Bruins and punched a linesman in a dustup that lasted about 45 minutes. When all was said and done, Kennedy was assessed a minor, two majors, a misconduct, and a game misconduct. These were in addition to three earlier minor penalties, and the 48 penalty minutes in a game still

Kennedy went on to play a number of years in the NHL, his role as a fighter clearly defined from the outset.
FORBES KENNEDY

stands as a record. That summer, doctors removed cartilage from one of Kennedy's wonky knees and his playing days were all but over. He could barely walk let alone skate. Kennedy returned to PEI and became a coach, a job he loves and swears he'll keep until the day he dies. He bought a piece of the Charlottetown Jr. Abbies and worked the city's baseball diamonds in the summer. The hard-drinking ways of his playing days gave way to a teetotalling retirement, and he has become an icon in Charlottetown, both for his past successes in the NHL and his present meritorious contributions to the city.

KENNEDY, Mike
b. Vancouver, British Columbia, April 13, 1972

Almost from the word go, Kennedy was slotted as a third- and fourth-line centre rather than a prospective top shooter. In his five years in the NHL he fit the bill perfectly, but his eventual demotion to the minors in 1998 signalled his departure from the league. The next year, he accepted an attractive offer to play in Germany, and has been in the DEL ever since.

KENNEDY, Sheldon
b. Elkhorn, Manitoba, June 15, 1969

If only hockey were simply a game. If only life were so simple. Kennedy was 13 when he attended a hockey school near Winnipeg. One of the coaches there was Graham James, a man who took an immediate liking to Kennedy. James arranged to have Kennedy traded to his club team, the Winnipeg Warriors, and Kennedy, whose relationship with his father was bad at best, welcomed the chance to leave home. James, though, began sexually abusing Kennedy, took advantage of the boy's fears and hockey ambitions, and controlled Kennedy for many, many years. In 1984, James joined the Swift Current Broncos, and a short time later the team acquired Kennedy and the abuse continued. On ice, Kennedy's performance in the face of his private

Sheldon Kennedy

horror was extraordinary. He scored 53 and 58 goals in his final 2 years of junior, and he won a gold medal with Canada at the 1988 World Juniors. As the abuse and manipulation continued, Kennedy became an alcoholic in his private life and a top draft choice by Detroit in his hockey life. Kennedy's two sides collided during his early days with the Wings when he was arrested for reckless driving in 1992 and a short time later jailed for violating the terms of his probation. After being traded to Calgary, Kennedy confided in coach Pierre Page about the drinking and abuse, but did not name James. In 1996, however, James was arrested in connection with several sexual assaults, and Kennedy stepped forward and admitted he had been one of the victims. It was the bravest decision any player ever had to make, and far more complicated than enduring a Gordie Howe elbow or a Bobby Orr undressing with the puck. James was convicted and sent to prison, and Kennedy tried to get on with his life by playing and going to therapy. By season's end he had had enough, though a serious bike accident forced him to take a year away from the game anyway. He wanted to open a ranch out west for boys who experienced similar troubles, but his fundraising efforts fell short and were fraught with controversy. While he raised money for the Sheldon Kennedy Foundation, the press learned he was being paid a monthly stipend for his work. He also had a relapse involving alcohol, and tried to make a hockey comeback with Manitoba of the IHL, one that ended after just 24 games. Graham James was released after serving his sentence and found work coaching a junior team in Spain. During his incarceration, he continually tried to phone Kennedy, and the player quietly slipped out of the limelight to get his life in order with the help of his wife and family. Playing the game was both his release and his bane, but his life would go on long after he scored his final goal.

KENNEDY, Ted ("Teeder")

b. Humberstone, Ontario, December 12, 1925

When Pete Langelle left the NHL after scoring the Cup-winning goal, there was a void at Maple Leaf Gardens, one filled by Kennedy a year later. It wasn't a void in terms of the roster or goal scoring or personality; it was a void in terms of John Arnott. Arnott was the world's first and most famous vocal NHL fan, and every night he would scream, "Come on, Peter!" during stoppages in play to cheer on Langelle. Those screams were replaced by shouts of, "Come on, Teeder!" a cry so famous that years later when Arnott passed away, Kennedy was one of the pallbearers. Kennedy got the nickname from his kid sister, who pronounced his full name, Theodore, with all the glitches any kid might produce. Theodore became Teeder, and Teeder stuck for all time. Teeder never knew his father, who had been killed in a hunting mishap while his mother was pregnant, but he grew up loving hockey. Ted was such an outstanding hockey player that at 16 the Canadiens invited him to training camp. But, as would happen with Gordie Howe a short time later, he was so homesick he left camp early and returned to the safety of home. Montreal, fearing it might never get Kennedy to leave, traded his rights to Toronto for another great prospect, Frankie Eddolls. The deal was made by Frank Selke, who was acting as Toronto's GM while Conn Smythe was at war. When Smythe found out about the deal, he was furious, not because of the exchange of players but because he hadn't been consulted. Selke explained how urgent the timing of the deal was, and things smoothed over when Eddolls proved to be a minor leaguer and Kennedy a Hall of Famer. From the day he entered the NHL until the day he left, no one ever accused Kennedy of being a great skater. But to this day, many will argue he was the greatest faceoff man the league has ever seen, and even more will swear he was the best captain, a natural-born leader, the league has ever known. He was a tenacious centre who had no problem going into the corner to get the puck or getting on the other team's defence to pressure a turnover. He scored 26 goals as a rookie and 29 the next year, '44-'45, when the Leafs won the Cup. In 1946, he centred a line with wingers Howie Meeker and Vic Lynn, called the KLM line (for the first letters of their last names), that helped bring home three consecutive Cups, 1946-49. In 1948, Kennedy replaced the retiring Syl Apps as team captain and his position as team deity was secure. In game one of the 1950 semifinals against Detroit, Kennedy was involved in a near-

tragic incident. He was carrying the puck up the ice when he heard a player coming up on him and saw the image of Gordie Howe in the Plexiglas moving fast and furious toward him. Kennedy stopped in the nick of time, and Howe fell and barrelled headfirst into the boards. The great Gordie nearly lost his life on that play. He required brain surgery and was lost to the team for months, but the Red Wings believed that Kennedy had tripped Howe and was to blame for the horrific injury. In game two of that series, a brawling, violent game, they went after Kennedy, and although Teeder stood his ground, the Leafs lost that playoff series in seven games. The next year, Kennedy captured his fifth and last Cup. He announced his retirement in 1954 right after the playoffs, but decided to come to training camp and play a final year. He retired in 1955 and this time his rest lasted a year and a half, but midway through the '56-'57 season, the Leafs off to a poor start and beset by injuries, he returned for the last half of that year, one in which the team missed the playoffs. Despite his value to the team and his leadership abilities, Kennedy never was named to the First All-Star Team. He made the Second Team three times, and ironically won his only individual trophy – the Hart Trophy – in '54-'55, the year he came back after retiring. During his playing days, he dabbled in horses. His first two nags were called Winter Rules and Outboard, and after leaving hockey he made a quick and clean break from the game. He became more involved in horse racing, and later operated a racetrack in southern Ontario near his home in Fort Erie. Kennedy was inducted into the Hockey Hall of Fame in 1966, and his number 9 was honoured by the Leafs at the start of the '93-'94 season. In large measure because Kennedy had never won an NHL trophy to that time, Conn Smythe inaugurated the J.P. Bickell Trophy, a Leafs trophy, in 1953, and made Kennedy the first winner for his contributions to the team. Kennedy started out as Montreal property, but played his every game with the Leafs and has become synonymous with everything great about that team.

Ted Kennedy

Kennedy started out as Montreal property, but played his every game with the Leafs.
TED KENNEDY

KENNY, Ernest "Eddie"

b. Vermillion, Alberta, August 20, 1907

d. June 2, 1970

Kenny played just 10 NHL games way back when, 6 with the Rangers in '30-'31 and 4 with Chicago 4 years later. He spent most of his career out west in the minors, and his play was marked by both his hard-checking defensive style and his ability to move the puck up the ice.

KEON, Dave

b. Noranda, Quebec, March 22, 1940

Many will posit – and few will argue – that Dave Keon was the greatest player in the history of the Toronto Maple Leafs. Yet over time, he has distanced himself so far from the club he once revered that perhaps it has done his reputation more harm than good. Keon grew up in an odd family in which his mother was a schoolteacher and his father was illiterate. Dave and brother Jimmy grew up playing hockey as a way out of the mines to which his dad had been consigned, and they were inspired by their uncle, Tod Sloan, a lifelong Leafs forward. Jimmy, though, never quite made it the way Dave did. Keon went to high school at St. Mike's in Toronto, a sure sign the Leafs were hoping he would develop into an NHL player. Keon's time there was perfect: He learned about teamwork and camaraderie; he learned discipline and technique on the ice; he learned to leap out of his child's skin and run free in a man's body. The Leafs did, indeed, cherish the youngster, and it was to no one's surprise that he made the team at training camp in 1960. He scored 20 goals and won the Calder Trophy that year, but more important than the numbers was his style of play. Foster Hewitt called him Mister Perpetual Motion because his legs were always working like mad. Keon was a uniquely gentlemanly player, taking just three minor penalties all year as a rookie, a pattern that continued until he retired. Most important, he was relentless every second he was on the ice. He skated as hard as he could going into the offensive end, and then backchecked with unmatched fervour. He hit hard every time, not hard enough to hurt but hard enough to make an impression. He had a low centre of gravity and was hard to knock off the puck. Technically, at the age of 20, he was a perfect NHL player. In each of the next three years, the Leafs won the Cup, and in the first two of those seasons Keon won the Lady Byng Trophy because he accrued only one penalty in each season. When fans recall the great Cup triumph of 1967, they remember George Armstrong's empty-net goal, or the heroic goaltending of Sawchuk and Bower, or the great play of Imlach's Over-the-Hill Gang. But it was Keon who won the Conn Smythe Trophy. In the ensuing years, he was named team captain to replace Armstrong once the Chief retired. And, as the team floundered, Keon had his best scoring years and more than pulled his weight. He was not big and strong, but he was tough as nails and his methods of captaining didn't always suit everyone. He thought complaining was for the press box or trainer's table, not for the ice or the players' bench. He was durable and never suffered a serious injury during his career, and he was among the most popular and

Dave Keon

respected men in Toronto. The Dave Keon-Billy Harris hockey schools, which the pair ran in the summer months for years, were successful means of inculcating the next generation of fans into the Blue and White fold. In 1975, that meant nothing to Leafs owner Harold Ballard. Keon had been with the Leafs for 15 years. He was the leader, the prime connection between the glory years and the Ballard years, and the owner simply didn't offer Keon a contract that summer. Keon walked away in silence, and he has, more or less, maintained that silence ever since, long after the owner was dead and buried. Keon signed with Minnesota of the WHA and moved on to New England where he played for four years until the new league merged with the NHL. He stayed with Hartford in 1979, and for three years played with the Whalers. One of the most special moments at the hallowed Gardens was the night Keon returned to play the Leafs. He received a tremendous ovation from the fans, and after the game Conn Smythe paid him a visit. It was the first time in his life that Smythe had ever entered the visitors' dressing room at Maple Leaf Gardens. Keon retired from the NHL in 1982 at age 42. He left having played 1,296 games and having incurred just 117 penalty minutes. The odd number of minutes (117 as opposed to, say, 116) betrays Keon's one transgression. On April 7, 1974, he got into a fight with Boston's Gregg Sheppard after Sheppard high-sticked him. It was the one and only fighting major of Keon's career. The low penalty-minutes total was a symbol; it showed that a small player could be tough and successful without fighting, and it showed that clean play could

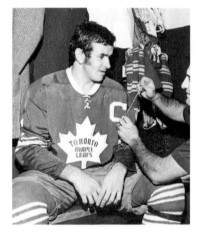

Keon retired having played 1,296 games and having incurred just 117 penalty minutes.
DAVE KEON

lead to victory as much as dirty play could intimidate a path to victory. He also proved that a player who was obsessed with defensive detail could also become a goal scorer and playmaker if he simply put his mind to it. Keon's departure left the NHL a lesser league. He moved to Florida to be away from the game, and worked in real estate. He harboured enormous animosity toward Ballard and the entire Leafs organization, an almost palpable hatred that fans understood and supported. But Ballard died and new owners sought to bring the alumni into the fold. The Gardens closed and Air Canada Centre opened, but still Keon would not return. He refused to take part in the closing ceremonies of the Gardens, the palace in which virtually his every hockey memory was ensconced, and even in the ACC he has remained aloof in Florida, though he returns quietly to the city to visit his son, David Jr., who has worked at the NHL offices in Toronto for years. Keon did attend the Hockey Hall of Fame induction ceremonies in 2000 (himself an inductee in 1986), but that has proved to be a unique appearance rather than a sign of softening his position. However, his absence from the hockey world

Dave Keon

does not diminish the great accomplishments he made on the ice over a 22-year professional career. With or without his continued presence, Keon remains one of the greatest players the NHL has ever known.

KERCH, Alexander
b. Arkhangelsk, Soviet Union (Russia), March 16, 1967
Despite a career in the NHL that lasted just five games, Kerch's contribution to hockey can be measured more meaningfully by his time with the national team of Latvia. He played for years in Riga when his country was under the authority of the USSR, but after perestroika he played at the 1993 World Championships for Latvia in "C" pool. Latvia rose to "B" pool three years later, and the year after it had ascended to its place among the elite countries in "A" pool. Kerch was there every step of the way, and he continued to play in the Worlds for a number of years while forging a league-play career in Germany.

KERR, Alan
b. Hazelton, British Columbia, March 28, 1964
Kerr came along with the Islanders at the right time for the team and the wrong time for him. He played his first games with the team in '84–'85, the year after the Islanders finished a run of four straight Stanley Cups. He missed out on the championships, but the Isles saw him as part of the team's next wave, and after two part-time years he became a regular right winger with the team in 1986. He went on to have two 20-goal seasons while the likes of Clark Gillies and Mike Bossy were on their way out, but because the new team wasn't improving much he also found himself being traded, to Detroit and then to Winnipeg. After retiring in 1993, he settled in Kelowna, B.C., where he was assistant and then head coach of the Rockets in successive years. He went into private business and then joined Chain Reaction Sports products, an enterprise that combined business and sports in the B.C. area.

KERR, Dave
b. Toronto, Ontario, January 10, 1910
d. Belleville, Ontario, May 11, 1978
There aren't many players who can boast of having made the cover of *Time* magazine, but Dave Kerr is one of them, having graced the outside of the issue of March 14, 1938, issue. From his humble beginnings with the Toronto Canoe Club to his years with the Abitibi Paper Company in Iroquois Falls, Kerr was a standout goalie with a lightning-fast right hand and extraordinary eyesight. He always wore sunglasses off the ice to protect his eyes and he never looked directly at snow. During his time in Iroquois Falls (1927-29), he worked

Alan Kerr

Dave Kerr

as a CPR railway detective, met his future wife, and pursued goaling as a career. He moved to Montreal, and won the Allan Cup in 1930 while guarding the AAA net. He signed with the Maroons later that year, but in 1934, after bouncing between the NHL and the farm team, he was sold to the Americans to replace Andy Aitkenhead. It was there he played his last seven years and achieved his greatest glory. While he came close to personal and team success, it wasn't until 1939-40 that everything fell into place. He won the Vezina Trophy, was selected to the First All-Star Team, took his team on a 19-game unbeaten streak, played all 48 games for the Blueshirts, and led them to a Stanley Cup victory over Toronto. After retiring the year after, he invested in numerous hotels in Ontario, including one in Belleville that he later leased to the Ontario Ministry of Health for a pilot self-care test. By the mid-1960s, he had sold his interests and gone into advertising in Toronto. Kerr is not in the Hockey Hall of Fame despite efforts to have him inducted. His successes and numbers suggest that, if nothing else, he is among the finest goalies not in the Hall's pantheon of greats.

Kerr was a late bloomer to be sure, and Philadelphia was the beneficiary.
TIM KERR

KERR, Reg
b. Oxbow, Saskatchewan, October 16, 1957
Kerr had a career year with Chicago in 1980-81 playing on a line with Denis Savard and Tim Higgins. He scored 30 goals and had as many assists, the highlight of his time with the Hawks. He made his way to the NHL via the Cleveland Barons, but that sad team traded him straight up to Chicago in 1977 for Randy Holt. Kerr ended his career with a brief week in Edmonton, then returned to the Chicago area for a life outside the game. He settled in Highfield Park, Illinois, where he worked in a business that sold office furniture.

KERR, Tim ("The Sultan of Slot")
b. Windsor, Ontario, January 5, 1960
There are so many parts to Kerr it's tough to know which ranks where in importance. He was never drafted into the NHL, in part because he didn't have a particularly take-notice junior career, in part because his draft year, 1979, had only six rounds to it, in part because the scouts collectively goofed – big time. Kerr was a late bloomer to be sure, and Philadelphia was the beneficiary. One of their scouts, Eric Colville, gave Kerr a tryout in 1980, but he made the team only because Ken Linseman had suffered a broken leg and the Flyers needed a last-minute replacement. Little did they know what they were getting. Kerr started with seasons of 22 and 21 goals, but his third year was cut short by a knee injury. In 1983, he was healthy and played the full season, and the result was 54 goals. It was his first of four successive 50-goal seasons, and '85-

'86 was notable because he set an NHL record with 34 power-play scores. Kerr's forte was the quick shot from in close, the new Phil Esposito who used the slot to perfection. The downside was his soft hands and tremendous strength was the physical punishment he absorbed, and in his case the brunt of the abuse was taken by his shoulders. Over his career he had numerous operations on those blades, but shoulder injuries forced his early retirement in 1993 nonetheless. Of his 370 career goals, 150 of them came on the power play. Kerr's time in Philadelphia was punctuated in October 1990 by a devastating loss. Just 10 days after the birth of their baby, Kerr's wife died at the age of 30. Kerr never played another full season. He left the game as a player in January 1993 and became an assistant coach with Hartford's farm team in Springfield. He left after a short time and settled in Avalon, New Jersey, where he earned a real estate licence and opened his own office, Power Play Realty. He remarried, had more kids, and has been very active in many charities, raising large sums of money for those less fortunate.

Dan Kesa

KESA, Dan
b. Vancouver, British Columbia, November 23, 1971
Kesa's four NHL seasons have been spread thin over a decade of pro play, and each passed with a different team. His finest scoring years occurred in the minors, and after playing in 1999-2000 with Tampa he has yet to return to the big time. He went down to the IHL, but when that league merged with the AHL, Kesa signed to play in the Russian league, many miles from home.

KESSELL, Rick
b. Toronto, Ontario, July 27, 1949
On March 21, 1970, Kessell scored a goal just a minute and a half into his first NHL shift while playing for Pittsburgh. Unfortunately, his second goal didn't come until his fourth NHL season, and his third and fourth goals the year after turned out to be his last. After a brief callup as a rookie, he looked like a good bet to make the team the next year, but just before training camp he suffered a double fracture of an ankle in a water-skiing accident. He was later claimed by California, but even the Seals gave him only one season before sending him to the minors.

KETOLA, Veli-Pekka
b. Pori, Finland, March 28, 1948
A player of Ketola's skill and from his generation should have had a long and distinguished international career, but a turn of events at the 1974 World Championships changed everything for the Finnish star. That year, the Finns beat the Czechs 5-0 in a key game, only to have the decision nullified

Rick Kessell

when their goalie, Stig Wetzell, tested positive for doping. Rumour has it Wetzell was set up by his own teammates, though, and in protest both Wetzell and Ketola vowed never to play for the National Team again. Ketola was an outstanding centre in league play, averaging nearly a goal a game. He had played in two previous Olympics and five Worlds, but after '74 the only tournaments he played in for Suomi were the 1976 and '81 Canada Cups. Two years earlier he had joined the multinational Winnipeg Jets of the WHA, and in his second season he helped the team win the Avco Cup. He returned home in 1977 but went back to North America to play in the NHL with Colorado, a stint that lasted 44 games. Ketola played mostly for his hometown Pori team and became a hero in Finland, so much so that the league introduced the Veli-Pekka Ketola Trophy and made its namesake its first winner. After retiring in the early 1980s he became a coach and then GM with Pori, a run that ended in the summer of 2000 when the team failed to qualify for the playoffs.

KETTER, Kerry ("Cowley")
b. Prince George, British Columbia, September 20, 1947
Hockey players have a sick sense of humour, and that's why Kerry Kenneth Ketter (KKK) was affectionately nicknamed Cowley. (Cowley County in Kansas was where the Klu Klux Klan had its early, violent origins.) He was, however, in no way affiliated with anything but Kanadian hocKey, starting in the late 1960s with Edmonton. Ketter earned a reputation for being a fierce and hard-hitting defenceman, but although he was the property of several NHL and WHA teams he didn't make a mark until Atlanta used him in '72-'73. He played for Edmonton in the WHA three years later, his last season of pro.

KHABIBULIN, Nikolai ("Habby"/ "The Bulin Wall")
b. Sverdlovsk, Soviet Union (Russia), January 13, 1973
Khabibulin's ascent to the rank of top goalie was as swift as it was progressive. He won a gold medal with Russia at the 1992 World Juniors and was the number-three goalie for the team at the Olympics a few weeks later when the Russians won gold. But at the medal ceremony, the 23 medals allocated for the players were reallocated by the coach, Viktor Tikhonov. The 22 players who actually played received medals, and Khabibulin was denied the last medal by his coach, who scooped it for himself. Khabibulin joined Winnipeg in the NHL two years later and split goaltending duties with Tim Cheveldae. The year after, Khabibulin assumed the starter's role, and the year after, the team now in Phoenix, he played 72

Veli-Pekka Ketola

Kerry Ketter

Khabibulin's ascent to the rank of top goalie was as swift as it was progressive.
NIKOLAI KHABIBULIN

Sergei Kharin

Alexander Khavanov

Dmitri Khristich

Ian Kidd

games for the Coyotes. Two more strong seasons took him to restricted free agency, and when negotiations turned ugly he refused to play for the team ever again. He played all of 1999-2000 in the IHL, and the year after Phoenix finally traded him to Tampa Bay, though he played only twice at season's end. Although he played for Russia at the 1996 World Cup, Khabibulin refused to join his teammates for the 1998 Olympics in Nagano, going so far as to refuse to discuss his feelings with his boyhood idol, Tretiak, who had been sent to talk him into playing. The 2001-02 season marked the goalie's first full year of play since '98-'99, and he performed as though time had stood still. He was one of the top goalies in all statistical categories, and his shutout in the third period of the All-Star Game made him the hottest netminder in the world heading into the 2002 Olympics in Salt Lake City. He struggled early in that tournament, though, and by the time he played well, it was too late. Russia lost to the U.S. and had to settle for a bronze-medal win over Belarus.

KHARIN, Sergei
b. Odintsovo, Soviet Union (Russia), February 20, 1963
Freedom cannot be quantified or assigned a number. Freedom is a state of mind, a place where happiness and success are real possibilities. For Kharin, who grew up just outside Moscow in the days before freedom, the chance to go to North America was one that could not be comprehended by those who took freedom for granted. Kharin was good enough to play in Moscow, where one of his teammates was Sergei Priakin, the first Soviet player to be allowed by the government to move to Canada to play in the NHL. Once in Canada, Priakin had his agent contact Kharin, who gladly went to Winnipeg in 1990. He played only seven games with the Jets in a season rooted in the minors, but he neither complained nor sought a return home after perestroika. He was happy to be in a free land, and chose to play in the minors in the hopes of making it back to the NHL. He never did, but for more than a decade he did what no European had done – he stuck it out in the minors, in the various leagues that countless less-talented Canadians called home, and he enjoyed it. The leagues had names like Colonial or United or East Coast, but to Kharin they all translated as freedom.

KHARITONOV, Alex
b. Moscow, Soviet Union (Russia), March 30, 1976
This up-and-comer is running out of time to prove his NHL worth. He came to Tampa with fine credentials from his native Russia, but after one season the Lightning included him in a big trade with the Islanders to acquire Mathieu Biron. He played only a few games with the Isles in his first season there, and as he heads into his late twenties he has yet to establish himself as anything but a part-timer.

KHAVANOV, Alexander ("Khavy")
b. Ryazan, Soviet Union (Russia), January 30, 1972
It seems that everything has happened to Khavanov a decade later than it happened to everyone else, with one curious exception. He was drafted in 1999 at the advanced age of 27 and came to North America a year

later to earn a full-time spot with St. Louis. The curious part is that when he was 20 and undrafted, he came to the East Coast league to play for a year. Rather than stay, he returned home, and for the following seven seasons played in the Russian league, neither receiving offers nor trying the minors again until the Blues offered him an invite.

KHMYLEV, Yuri
b. Moscow, Soviet Union (Russia), August 9, 1964
Another old draft choice because of his uncertain status in newly formed Russia, Khmylev came to the Buffalo Sabres in 1992 as one of the more successful players of the previous decade back home. He won a gold medal at the 1984 World Juniors, and won two more gold and a silver at the World Championships. He played in the 1987 Canada Cup and the 1992 Olympics in Albertville, where the Russians won gold. He scored 20 and 27 goals in his first 2 years in the NHL, but his production dropped off during the year of the lockout and he never recovered his scoring touch.

KHRISTICH, Dmitri ("Deem")
b. Kiev, Soviet Union (Ukraine), July 23, 1969
Harry Sinden, like any man, is only human, and as such that means he makes mistakes and is not always right. But he's been around long enough and he knows what good looks like, so when he says he sees bad, his opinion should at least be respected. Khristich joined Washington in 1990 after a decent start to his career back home. In years 2, 3, and 4 he scored 36, 31, and 29 goals, and he developed a reasonable reputation as a scorer. In the playoffs, though, the goals were few and far between. Strangely, he and Byron Dafoe were traded to L.A. in a multiplayer deal in 1995, and then the pair were traded again, to Boston, two years later. It was with the Bruins that Khristich incurred the wrath of GM Harry Sinden. For 2 years, he turned 29-goal regular seasons into 2 and 3-goal playoff performances, and at the end of the second season he took Boston to arbitration over his salary. Sinden lost his argument and had either to pay Khristich the awarded amount or had to let him become a free agent. He let Dmitri walk. Toronto signed him, and Khristich tanked. The Leafs traded him to the Caps and, like the Invisible Man, he continued to disappear during the heat of the playoffs.

KIDD, Ian
b. Gresham, Oregon, May 11, 1964
The first year of the NHL's Supplemental Draft was 1986. The rules were new to everyone, the guidelines for selecting nebulous and untried. Detroit picked first and took Kidd, finding out only after the fact that their choice was nullified because Kidd hadn't played his first game at a U.C. college until he was 21 (rules stipulated players had to have first played between ages 18 and 20). So Kidd returned to school, and the next summer Vancouver signed him as a free agent. He played 20 games over 2 seasons with the Canucks and then enjoyed a lengthy career in the IHL. His finest moment, though, came at the University of North Dakota in a game against Minnesota-Duluth. His team was trailing 7-3 with 2:56 left to play, but the

Fighting Sioux scored 4 goals to tie and then Kidd scored the winner in overtime. It was one of the greatest comebacks in hockey history, one Kidd had hoped might repeat itself somewhere in the NHL.

KIDD, Trevor
b. Dugald, Manitoba, March 29, 1972

Kidd's career looks like the graph of a company that starts out fresh, rises to greatness, and then free falls. His starting point was in 1988, when he joined Brandon to begin a career in Canadian junior. His peak was the period of 1990-92. And his free fall began shortly after he started in the NHL. Kidd won gold medals at the 1990 and '91 World Juniors and then was part of the silver-medal team at the 1992 Olympics in Albertville. This was the end of his junior career, and Calgary drafted him a very high 11th overall in 1990 after he was named the best goalie in junior hockey. His stock was at its highest, and when he joined Calgary he became the backup almost immediately. In 1994-95, he ascended the throne and played 43 of the team's 48 games during the lockout season, but in the playoffs the Flames lost in the first round. This seemed to signal a downward trend. He never took the Flames past the first round of the playoffs, and as he was traded to Carolina and on to Florida he was pegged as a solid number-two man. The high hopes associated with his status as a prospect gave way to a more established reputation as a backup, confirmed finally when he signed with Toronto in 2002 to back up starter Eddie Belfour.

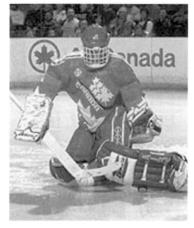

Kidd won gold medals at the 1990 and '91 World Juniors.
TREVOR KIDD

KIESSLING, Udo
b. Crimmitschau, Germany, May 21, 1955

To Canadians, he might be a one-game wonder, but to Germans, he is the greatest player ever to come out of that country. Kiessling only played in the NHL, with Minnesota in 1981-82, because of Lou Nanne. Nanne captained the U.S. entry in the '77 Worlds and saw a young Kiessling play. Nanne tried to convince him to come to the NHL, but Kiessling demured. A few years later, Nanne tried again, and with his team out of the German league playoffs early, Kiessling agreed. He played one game and returned home with no ambitions to return. Kiessling had been born in East Germany, where his father, Gerhard, coached the National Team, but the family snuck into West Germany and settled in Frankfurt. Gerhard coached the Germans at the 1968 and '72 Olympics, and Udo became adept at the game from an early age. His international career is staggering: 15 World Championships, 5 Olympics, and the '84 Canada Cup. In league play, he performed almost exclusively for Kolner and was named player of the year three times. At the '87 Worlds, he was named to the First All-Star Team defence with Slava Fetisov, though many players over the years called him the dirtiest opponent they had ever faced.

KILGER, Chad
b. Cornwall, Ontario, November 27, 1976

If humongous were a real word, it would most appropriately be attached to the expectations Anaheim had for their hulking 4th-overall selection in the 1995 draft. Gargantuan is a real word, and it surely can be most appropriately tagged to the disappointment those same Ducks felt after watching Kilger play for half a season. Anaheim traded him as part of a deal to land Teemu Selanne, but in the ensuing years Kilger changed teams four times with ever-diminishing hopes. By the time he got to Montreal, nothing was expected of him, so much so that he relaxed and settled into a decent few seasons. Yet, despite his size, he never played tough. And, despite his quick hands, he never scored much. Kilger's dad, Bob, was a referee in the NHL for a decade, and led the Cornwall Royals to the 1981 Memorial Cup, and was later elected to the House of Commons representing Stormont-Dundas.

Chad Kilger

KILREA, Brian
b. Ottawa, Ontario, October 21, 1934

His NHL playing days might have been limited to just 26 games, but Kilrea has been in hockey longer than almost anyone else, and at the junior coaching level in Canada he has no peers. Kilrea came from a hockey family. His uncles include Ken, Wally, and Hec, NHLers all, and it was due to their influence that he took hockey so seriously at a young age. He graduated from junior to play in the IHL for many years, earning a one-game callup to Detroit (he was the seventh player to wear number 7 that year) during the 1957-58 season before returning to the minors. He played there in obscurity for the next 10 years. Kilrea's only real chance in the NHL came in the first year of expansion, '67-'68, when he played a third of a season with Los Angeles. The centre scored only 3 goals despite being an annual 20-goal man in the AHL, and quickly found himself back in the minors until he retired in 1970. Almost without missing a beat, he became coach of the Ottawa 67's. From day one the job seemed to be his natural calling. He ran intense practices, provided support and loyalty to his players, and built his team year by year through the draft. He won his first Memorial Cup in 1984, and that summer accepted a job as assistant coach with the New York Islanders. After two years, it was clear to him he wasn't going to be offered the head coaching job there, so he returned to the 67's and the team kept

Brian Kilrea

on winning for him. In the mid-1990s, Kilrea stepped down as coach and became a scout when his health was in question, but as soon as he felt better he moved back behind the bench. On January 17, 1997, he set a Canadian junior record with his 742nd career win to better the mark held by Ken Hodge in Portland. Two years later, the 67's won the Memorial Cup again, and Kilrea's career-win mark topped 1,000 games toward the end of the 2002-03 season. He has been named coach of the year four times, has won three league titles, and has sent countless young men to the NHL, from Doug Wilson (Chicago) and Denis Potvin (Islanders) to Alyn McCauley (Toronto) and Brian Campbell (Buffalo).

Ken Kilrea

KILREA, Hec ("Hurricane Hec")

b. Blackburn, Ontario, June 11, 1907
d. Detroit, Michigan, September 6, 1969

As a kid, Kilrea was a great baseball and football player, but when he skated, everyone took notice: the speed, the stride, the strength of his movement drew oohs and ahs from scouts, notably in Ottawa. The Senators signed him in 1925, and a year and a half later he helped them win the Stanley Cup. He went on to play for Toronto and Detroit, and one of his most glorious moments took place in the 1936 playoffs when his pass to Mud Bruneteau helped end the longest game in the history of the NHL. The Wings went on to win the Cup that year and the next. In 1929-30, Kilrea scored an astounding 36 goals in the 44-game schedule, a total he never reached even half of for the rest of his days. Kilrea ended his playing career with Detroit's farm team in Indianapolis, and while there set a pro record by scoring just two seconds after the start of a game! He enlisted in the army after taking out a U.S. citizenship. Kilrea served in France, Belgium, Germany, and Italy and was awarded the Distinguished Service medal after being wounded in France. (He received shrapnel wounds.) He was also honoured with the Croix de Guerre for gallantry in action and the Purple Heart. After returning to Detroit, Kilrea worked for the Ford Motor Company until he retired. He died on a Saturday afternoon while preparing to go to a Tigers ball game, and was buried in Ottawa.

Wally Kilrea

KILREA, Ken

b. Ottawa, Ontario, January 16, 1919
d. Destin, Florida, January 14, 1990

Ken was the youngest and perhaps the least successful of the Kilrea brothers as far as an NHL career goes, but just growing up and making it to the NHL was half the battle for Kenny. As a child, he was taken to all the

Kilrea served in France, Belgium, Germany, and Italy and was awarded the Distinguished Service medal after being wounded in France.
HEC KILREA

Darin Kimble

Ottawa home games by brother Hec, a young star on the team, usually sitting with the son of George Boucher, himself to become a pro later. In 1931, the boys' mother died and Ken was overcome. For three months he lay in the Ottawa Civic Hospital being cared for by a nerve specialist, though over time he made a full and healthy recovery. He began a career in hockey as soon as he was well, and though he never had the skill of his brothers he did have a terrific shot that they didn't. He played a modest 91 NHL games, all with Detroit, a number that pales in comparison to brothers Hec and Wally and nephew Brian. Ken played just about everywhere in hockey before and after his pro years of 1938-44. He was bounced up and down from the minors by GM Jack Adams, taking the rough treatment in stride. Once, Adams brought him up specifically to shadow Rocket Richard, but after two periods Maurice had two goals and three assists, and Ken had two penalties. Down he went to Indianapolis. Ken enlisted in the army in 1942 and was stationed in Ottawa, where he played on the Commandos hockey team, winners of the Allan Cup the following spring and one of the most talented amateur teams ever assembled. He also saw action in England and Germany. After the war he played minor pro before retiring in 1951. He passed away after suffering an aneurysm in Florida while on vacation.

KILREA, Wally

b. Ottawa, Ontario, February 18, 1909
d. London, Ontario, July 3, 1992

Wally's NHL career ended almost in perfect sync with brother Hec's and in spectacular fashion. Hec and Wally played together with Detroit in the mid-1930s and were part of the double Cup champion teams of 1936 and '37. Hec was the bigger scorer of the pair and Wally the less dominant, yet Wally played nine years in the big league before being farmed out, like Hec, to the AHL. Wally had an extended stay in Hershey before retiring in 1944.

KIMBLE, Darin

b. Lucky Lake, Saskatchewan, November 22, 1968

Despite not having played in the NHL since 1994, Kimble continues to play the puck game. Since leaving junior in 1988, he has amassed an impressive resumé that includes stops with 15 teams in 6 leagues. The size of the puck hasn't changed, the nets are all the same size, and fights are fights and goals are goals. In his NHL prime, he was a puncher more than a sniper but just as those types of guys are always needed, they are also the easiest to replace. Kimble wasn't drafted until 1988, after his final year with Prince Albert, and Quebec was interested in him because he scored 35 goals in a year during which he also amassed 307 penalty minutes. Unfortunately, Kimble never made that combination work in the NHL.

KINDRACHUK, Orest ("O"/ "The Big O"/ "The Little O"/ "Bo-Bo")
b. Nanton, Alberta, September 14, 1950

Kindrachuk had so many nicknames he knew that if he heard someone on the ice calling for a pass using "Orest" it had to be an opponent. For more than half his career, he played in Philadelphia, the team that couldn't believe how lucky it was to sign him in 1971. Kindrachuk quickly developed into a strong third centre behind Bobby Clarke (to whom he was sometimes compared) and Rick MacLeish. He was part of the brawling teams that won Cups in 1974 and '75, and when he was traded to Pittsburgh he became team captain. He finished his career with a few games in Washington, and when he retired in 1981 he settled in Cherry Hill, New Jersey, where he became an executive with the Equitable Life Insurance Company.

KING, Derek ("Yoda")
b. Hamilton, Ontario, February 11, 1967

In '84-'85, King made a fine entrance onto the junior stage with the Soo when he was named rookie of the year, beating out Darren Turcotte and Sean Burke in the voting. Oddly, he was never named to a World Junior team for Canada, but the Islanders drafted him high and he went on to play for the team for 11 years. Those were the lean years, though, the years when the playoffs were nowhere in sight and the Trottiers and Bossys of Cup glory were gone. King filled the breach partially, scoring 40 goals in '91-'92, a year in which the team again failed to qualify for the post-season. He signed with Toronto as a free agent in 1997, but his performance with the Leafs was inconsistent and, come playoff time, disappointing. Despite being a decent scorer in the regular season, King had just 4 goals in 47 playoff games, and it was this proverbial disappearing act that caused the Leafs to trade him. King played his last with St. Louis before retiring in 2000.

KING, Frank
b. Toronto, Ontario, March 7, 1929

Leroy Brown might well have been the baddest man in his town, but he obviously never lived in the same city as Frank King during King's hockey-playing days. King played a few games for the Canadiens in '50-'51 and the next year he distinguished himself with the Quebec Aces, winning the Alexander Cup as league champions. It was the year after, in Halifax, that Leroy Brown was glad he was nowhere near Nova Scotia's beautiful port city, for it was there that King incurred two match penalties that season, the first man twice banished in the Maritime League's history. His first sentence was augmented by a six-game suspension, again the longest in league history, for swinging his stick at Lou Kiley. He continued his career as both a feared scorer and swift skater and, more temperamentally, a ferocious wild man.

KING, Kristopher "Kris"
b. Bracebridge, Ontario, February 18, 1966

No one ever accused King of being too skilled or scoring too much, but no one had a bad word to say about the tough guy with the big heart and the team attitude that kept him in the game for 13 years. King stood up for his teammates and played a fourth-line role wherever he went, and although he never went too far in the playoffs, he was always a presence in whatever city he played. His involvement in charities and his work with children were the pride of the league, and he won the King Clancy Trophy in 1996 for those accomplishments. He had a chance to close out his career playing for Toronto, his childhood dream team, and in December 2001 he joined Colin Campbell in the NHL's hockey operations department. For more than 15 years he has operated a summer hockey camp in Gravenhurst with his father, Dave.

Orest Kindrachuk

KING, Scott
b. Thunder Bay, Ontario, June 25, 1967

After compiling a 55-20-3 record at the University of Maine, King looked to be a goalie with a promising future. He left the Black Bears in 1990, but in the following two years saw only bits of action with Detroit. Unfortunately, he was competing for playing time with Tim Cheveldae and never managed to make it as the team's backup. He finished his brief career in the minors.

KING, Steven
b. Greenwich, Rhode Island, July 22, 1969

Coming out of Brown University, King was a double achiever. On the academic front, he earned a bachelor of science in economics and organizational behaviour and management. On the hockey front, he played well enough to gain the interest of the New York Rangers, who assigned him to Binghamton in 1991. King earned a callup the following year, and in the summer of 1993 Anaheim made him a top selection in the Expansion Draft. King's career was seriously jeopardized by a series of shoulder injuries that had an adverse effect on his ability to stick with the Ducks during their emerging years. He wound up playing in the minors for the last few years of his career, then retired in the summer of 2000 to accept a position as assistant coach back at Brown.

Derek King

KING, Wayne
b. Midland, Ontario, September 4, 1951

King came out of Niagara Falls to sign with the Golden Seals, but the centreman just didn't stick with the team for any length of time. His career was one long waltz between California in the NHL and Salt Lake City in the minors, but after five years he'd had his fill of the dance and returned home to southern Ontario, where he went into coaching at the kid level.

Scott King

KINNEAR, Geordie
b. Simcoe, Ontario, July 9, 1973

Once a rat, always a rat, though in the un-Cagney case of Kinnear, he was never dirty. Kinnear was, in fact, a Jersey prospect, but from the time he left junior in 1993 to the time he retired in December 2000, he played almost exclusively with the Devils farm team, the Albany River Rats. In 1999-2000 he had a brief four-game stay with Atlanta, with whom he had signed as a free agent, but Jersey soon re-acquired him and sent

Wayne King

Brian Kinsella

Bobby Kirk

Bob Kirkpatrick

Mark Kirton

him back to Albany. He was the team captain there for three seasons and played more games for the Rats (406) than anyone else. A serious neck condition forced him to retire on the advice of doctors, who told him he risked paralysis if he continued to play. In the summer of 2001, he was hired as an assistant coach with the Rats, continuing his long associaton with the AHL team.

KINSELLA, Brian
b. Barrie, Ontario, February 11, 1954
Kinsella played a few games with the hopeless Capitals when the team first started, but it wasn't until a little later in the IHL that he found his form and turned into a scoring star outside the glare of the NHL. He retired with 252 "I" goals to his credit.

KINSELLA, Ray
b. Ottawa, Ontario, January 27, 1911
d. Ottawa, Ontario, April 29, 1996
Ray Kinsella was the central figure in W.P. Kinsella's novel *Shoeless Joe*, later made into the film *Field of Dreams*, starring Kevin Costner as Ray. Is there a connection between W.P., a Canadian, and Ray Kinsella the hockey player? Only W.P. would know the answer. The hockeyist saw his glory with Ottawa in 1930-31 during a brief career.

KIPRUSOFF, Marko
b. Turku, Finland, June 6, 1972
Like any talented European, Kiprusoff had some fine moments on the international stage, starting at the World Juniors in 1991 and continuing through the decade. He helped the Finns win silver at the 1994 Worlds and the year after made history with the team that won the first-ever World Championship gold for Finland. On the strength of these performances, Montreal drafted him in '94 and he played part of '95-'96 with the team, but he wasn't prepared to carve out a minor-league career and opted to return to Finland rather than play in the AHL. He played in Switzerland in 2002-03. Kiprusoff also played at the 1994 Olympics in Lillehammer and the 1996 World Cup.

KIPRUSOFF, Mikka ("The Finnisher")
b. Turku, Finland, October 26, 1976
If Finland becomes a goalie hotbed in the early part of the 21st century, Kiprusoff might be one of the starting points. He was named Finnish league player of the year in 1998-99 and played for the National Team at the WC that spring in Norway. He had been drafted by San Jose a few years earlier and joined the team in 2000, when he appeared in five games, a figure he increased fourfold the year after. Young, big, and quick, he might well be the goalie of the future for the Sharks.

KIRK, Bobby
b. Doughgrange, New Ireland, August 8, 1909
d. Leeds, Ontario, July 11, 1970
He was dubbed the Smilin' Irishman was what by those who knew him because he never seemed in an adverse mood. Whether as player or coach, Kirk had an even temperament that stood him in good stead during his lifetime in the game. Born on the Emerald Isle, he and his family moved to Canada and settled in Winnipeg in the early 1920s. He played for championship teams in

Elmwood in '28-'29, when the Millionaires lost the Memorial Cup to Toronto, and Philadelphia in '35-'36, the year he led the league in scoring with 62 points. It was during his years with the Ramblers that he got the call to play for the Rangers, in '37-'38, and after a brief spell with Hershey he ended his playing career in Philly in 1942, the year he enlisted with the Royal Canadian Air Force. Kirk rose to the rank of corporal, and after his discharge went into a lengthy career as coach, first in New Westminster in the Pacific Coast league and later in Saskatoon. He bossed the Buffalo bench a decade later, the year after winning the Memorial Cup with Flin Flon in 1957.

KIRKPATRICK, Bob
b. Regina, Saskatchewan, December 1, 1915
Kirkpatrick began his pro career playing in England in 1936, just months after a Canadian-stacked English team beat Canada for Olympic gold. In the years leading up to the war, many Canadians flocked to Britain to play, and with the outbreak of war, most of them returned home. Kirkpatrick got into the NHL in 1942-43 with the Rangers, but although he acquitted himself well it was to be his only season in the league. He finished his career in Lethbridge, and like many a retired pro he opened an hotel in town as a constant meeting place of sorts.

KIRTON, Mark ("Kirt")
b. Regina, Saskatchewan, February 3, 1958
His birth certificate says he's a westerner, but Kirton spent most of his youth in and around Toronto developing the speed that would become his trademark a little later on. His other trademark was size – or lack of it – and that's what the Leafs thought was his biggest problem. As a result, Kirton played just 13 games with Toronto in 1979-81 before being tradedto Detroit. In his first game at Maple Leaf Gardens for the Wings, he had 2 goals and an assist, and on the year he had 18 goals in just 50 games. It was to be his best season, and he ended up going to Vancouver early in 1983. After a stint in the minors, Kirton re-signed with the Leafs, but this time his role was clear: He was going to the farm in Newmarket to provide leadership and experience. After retiring, Kirton returned to the Toronto area and settled in Oakville, where he went into the real estate business.

KISIO, Kelly
b. Peace River, Alberta, September 18, 1959
A funny thing happened on Kisio's ascent to the NHL: He made it. Coming out of junior, he was a phenomenal scorer, but he the junior tag "small" attached to him. No team drafted him, so he signed with Dallas in the CHL in 1981 and promptly scored 62 goals to lead the league. Still no takers. He went to Switzerland the way all small Canadians do, and his career looked to be European in theme until, finally, Detroit signed him for the rest of that '82-'83 season. In his next three seasons with the Wings he hit the 20-goal mark each time. Not great, but not small-shabby, either. Detroit traded Kisio to the Rangers in the summer of '86, and it was with that team he had his best years. He continued to score, and was team captain for almost four years. He moved on to play for San Jose and Calgary, and after retiring he

remained in the Flames organization as a scout and later an assistant coach.

KITCHEN, Bill
b. Schomberg, Ontario, October 2, 1960

Bill was just that much younger than his brother, Mike, that the two never played together or opposed each other during their junior days, though this changed once both young men made it to the NHL. Bill made it 5 years later than Mike, in 1981, and played only 41 games for Toronto and Montreal over a 4-year span. He spent the vast majority of those years in the minors. He settled in Ottawa, where he got a job with Mutual Life Insurance, and that, happily, was a position that did last.

KITCHEN, Hobart "Hobie"
b. Newmarket, Ontario, February 8, 1901
d. unknown

Kitchen made the most of a short career. He joined the Montreal Maroons in 1925-26, the year the team won the Stanley Cup, but the next year he signed with Detroit and played half a season for the Cougars, his last season of pro. Oddly, he soon after seemed to disappear from the face of the earth.

KITCHEN, Mike
b. Newmarket, Ontario, February 1, 1956

It's not quite a record, but because Kitchen played exclusively for the Colorado/New Jersey franchise he had to suffer a playoff fate made in hell. Despite his 474 regular-season games, he played only 2 in the playoffs, both losses to Philadelphia in 1978 during the best-of-three days. This was a shocking turn of fortune for the defenceman who won the Memorial Cup with the Marlies in 1975. After retiring in 1984, Kitchen worked for Kwik Kopy in Toronto in sales, but he quickly realized how much he missed the game. He became an assistant coach for the Leafs farm team and made it back to the NHL with Toronto in 1989. But after a decade with the Leafs he came to another realization – Toronto didn't consider him head-coach material. So he went to St. Louis to join another ex-Leaf, Blues coach Joel Quenneville, who was in need of an assistant.

KJELLBERG, Patrik
b. Falun, Sweden, June 7, 1969

How is it that a decent-scoring left winger takes six years to score his first NHL goal? Well, if your name is Kjellberg, there's a perfectly good explanation. He was drafted by Montreal in 1988. Over the next decade, he loaded his neck with medals, notably gold from the 1992 and '98 World Championships and 1994 Olympics. The Canadiens played him only seven times in the early part of the '92-'93 season, so he figured his career was going to pass quietly back in Sweden. He played primarily for Sweden, and in summers he had a most interesting job: He was a police officer for the Stockholm force. In 1998, Nashville signed Kjellberg as a free agent, and he secured a two-year leave of absence from the police force to try his hand at the NHL once again. He had a couple of decent years with the Predators, and then he had a decision to make: Go back to Sweden and resume his dual life, or stay in North America and give up the police gig. In the old days of sane salaries, it might have been a tough choice, but not any longer. Kjellberg chose

the latter, and he has been in the NHL ever since making gobs more money than even the top cops of the Swedish force!

KLASSEN, Ralph
b. Humboldt, Saskatchewan, September 15, 1955

Even though Klassen missed almost half of his final junior season with mono, California was not about to give up on him in the draft. The Seals selected him 3rd overall in 1975 and he joined the team that fall. He always considered himself more of a passer than a scorer, but such a trait assumes the presence of a scorer to whom he could pass. During most of his time in the NHL, Klassen had no such skilled object to receive his passes and his own production suffered. He finished his career in St. Louis in 1983 and then went into coaching, most recently with the Saskatoon Blazers in 2000-01.

KLATT, Trent
b. Robbinsdale, Minnesota, January 30, 1971

Klatt's is a career that has been petering out for more than a decade now – he just doesn't seem to give up or go away. He came out of U of Minnesota, winning the WCHA championship in 1992 before joining Minnesota at year's end. He played briefly on a line with the young phenom, Mike Modano, and in 1996 he was again in privileged company when the Stars sent him to Philadelphia. There, Klatt scored 24 goals playing with Eric Lindros and John LeClair on a pre–Legion of Doom line. After he was traded to Vancouver in 1998, he played on a line with the Sedin twins when they joined the team two years later. He missed much of 2001-02 with a serious abdominal injury, but came back the next year to excellent form. At every step of the way he has been a quiet performer, a man who can skate and score and hit and play with the best, yet a man who gets almost none of the credit.

KLEE, Ken
b. Indianapolis, Indiana, April 24, 1971

Defensive defencemen are the toughest players to define or pin down because their efficiency relies on nightly, tedious labour. They do not excel under the bright lights but rather prevent those who do excel from, well, excelling. Klee has played the first 500-games of his career with the same team, Washington, over an 8-year period, a mutual devotion not often found in the modern NHL. Perhaps part of the reason is his role on the team, and his reasonable salary in comparison to those of the millionaire stars he checks every night. In addition to his NHL life, Klee has played for the U.S. at three international events: the 1991 WJC and the 1992 and '97 World Championships.

KLEIN, Lloyd "Dede"
b. Saskatoon, Saskatchewan, January 13, 1910
d. Saskatoon, Saskatchewan, December 9, 1966

A Saskatoon boy through and through, Klein turned pro with the local Sheiks at the start of his career before joining Boston in 1928. He played just eight games with the B's that year, but the team went on to win the Stanley Cup. Over the next 20 years, Klein played for a great many teams in the minors, appearing sporadically in the NHL. He played with Boston again in '31-'32 and had steady work with the Americans

Bill Kitchen

Mike Kitchen

Patrik Kjellberg

Trent Klatt

Lloyd Klein

through much of the 1930s before playing most of the next decade in the AHL. After retiring as a player in 1948, Klein returned to Saskatoon, where he coached the Elks in the Western Senior League for a year. He remained in his hometown the rest of his life.

Scott Kleinendorst

KLEINENDORST, Scott
b. Grand Rapids, Minnesota, January 16, 1960

Hockey is part of the DNA of many a Minnesota kid, and certainly that of Scott Kleinendorst. He started skating at age four, and by his late teens colleges from the various hockey powers were requesting his skills. He accepted a scholarship from Providence College, where coach Lou Lamoriello was building a terrific team, and after his second year the Rangers drafted Scott and his brother, Kurt. Kurt never made it, but Scott certainly did. He joined the Rangers in '82, and the big defenceman went on to Hartford in a one-for-one deal that sent Blaine Stoughton to New York. In his eight NHL seasons, though, he spent as much time in rehab as on the ice. Injuries to his back, knees, and hand all took their toll, and he retired an old 30 in 1990. He returned to his home state and became involved in coaching at the kid level.

KLEISINGER, Terry
b. Regina, Saskatchewan, October 10, 1960

Bad luck hounded the goalie almost from the get-go. Kleisinger had a tremendous college career at U of Wisconsin, winning two NCAA championships and setting a school record with nine career shutouts. The year he should have turned pro, though, 1984-85, turned out to be the year he lost altogether due to a serious bout of mononucleosis. Even the next year, after winning a spot with the Rangers, he grew tired toward the end of games. New York sent him to the minors to regain his strength, confidence, and skills. A year later, though, he was badly hurt in a car accident and forced to retire. Once he recovered, he began coaching young players. He started with a AAA team in Madison, Wisconsin, and later moved to Vail, Colorado, for a similar job. He also acted as a volunteer assistant coach at Colorado College, working primarily with the goalies.

Jon Klemm

KLEMM, Jon
b. Cranbrook, British Columbia, January 8, 1970

He's the kind of player you don't pay special attention to or notice because of his star presence, but no team can win without a Klemm dimension on its team. A graduate of Spokane in 1991, he was never drafted despite winning the Memorial Cup that year. He signed as a free agent with the Nordiques and spent most of the next four years in Quebec's system, developing slowly and learning how to play defence. In 1995, the team now in Colorado, he was ready to assume a full-time position, and, not coincidentally, the Avs won a Stanley Cup that season. He remained with the team through 2001, but after winning a second Cup that spring he bolted to Chicago, where a lucrative contract awaited him.

KLESLA, Rostislav
b. Novy Jicin, Czechoslovakia (Czech Republic), March 21, 1982

If the Columbus Blue Jackets have a future, Klesla is it. Known for big hits and a big shot in equal measure, he was the team's first pick, 4th overall, in 2000. He stepped right into the lineup in the fall, but spent most of the season back in junior. In 2001, he was with the team for keeps. As he improves, so do the Jackets.

He spent the summer of 1989 in two spots: 35 days in jail, and 45 days in rehab.
PETR KLIMA

KLIMA, Petr
b. Chomutov, Czechoslovakia (Czech Republic), December 23, 1964

Freedom is both a blessing and a curse. Blessing because, of course, it provides choice and opportunity. Curse because it provides… choice and opportunity. Klima came out of nowhere, defecting from his country via West Germany and joining the Red Wings immediately. He wore number 85 in tribute to the year of his freedom, and in each of his first 3 seasons he scored at least 30 goals. That freedom, though, also gave him plenty of American money to spend, and a drinking problem that he had had back in Czechoslovakia translated only too easily to the bars in a city where he was extremely popular. Three times he was arrested for drinking and driving, and he spent the summer of 1989 in two spots: 35 days in jail, and 45 days in rehab. During his time with the Wings, he was forever complaining about the team's defensive system and how he hated to backcheck. Things came to a head early in the '89-'90 season, and he demanded, and got, a trade, to Edmonton. Luckily, he joined the right team, for the Oilers were about to win their fifth Cup in 7 years, and Klima scored 25 goals to help them get there. He had a career-high 40 goals the next year, but much of the 1990s was spent moving around and trying to regain top form. He played for three other teams, and then both Detroit and Edmonton gave him a second chance. Klima retired in 1999 and returned to the Czech Republic, but after two and a half years he missed the game and glory so much he began playing again. He signed with Litvinov, where he was made team captain, and immediately brought experience and maturity to the team, his best years far behind him, his wisdom the meat of his contributions. Finally, he seemed to understand freedom.

KLIMOVICH, Sergei

b. Novosibirsk, Soviet Union (Russia), March 8, 1974

In the late 1980s and early 1990s, so many great stars from communist Europe were selected late in the draft because no one knew whether they'd ever be allowed to play in North America. Klimovich was the opposite. He was selected a high 41st overall by Chicago in 1992, yet he played only 1 NHL game with the team some 4 years later. He stuck around in the minors for a few years, though he returned to Europe in 1998 and has prospered there since.

KLINGBEIL, Ernest "Ike"

b. Hancock, Michigan, November 3, 1908
d. Colorado Springs, Colorado, June 17, 1995

Ike's NHL career lasted just five games with Chicago in '36-'37, but he made enough of an impact in his home state that in 2001 he was inducted into the Upper Peninsula (Michigan) Sports Hall of Fame. Accepting the posthumous honour on his behalf was his grandson, Chuck, who a year later was also inducted because of his many years as a pro football player in both the CFL and the NFL.

KLOUCEK, Tomas

b. Prague, Czechoslovakia (Czech Republic), March 7, 1980

A true modern European, Kloucek came up from Czech league play as a teen to spend a season in junior in Quebec before apprenticing in the AHL and then joining the Rangers. He has been with the team ever since, and has developed into a solid defenceman with a mean streak. His best years, if they are there, are still ahead of him.

KLUKAY, Joe ("The Duke of Paducah")

b. Sault Ste. Marie, Ontario, November 6, 1922

Klukay got into his first NHL game in the 1943 playoffs and then didn't play with the Leafs again for three and a half years. He spent most of the interim with the Royal Canadian Navy, and in 1945 resumed his hockey career with the farm team in Pittsburgh. By the fall of '46, Klukay was in the NHL for good. In four of his first five years he won a Cup with some of the greatest Leafs teams of all time, and his contributions were salient to those wins. On offence, he played right wing (as a left-handed shot) on a line with Max Bentley and Ray Timgren. Defensively, he and Nick Metz might well have been the finest penalty killers to that point in NHL history, and Klukay was as fine a defensive forward as there was in the game. The Leafs sold him to Boston in 1952 and reacquired him two years later, and he settled in Windsor where he played senior hockey and worked at his second vocation. He worked as a tool and die maker for 25 years, eventually relocating to Southfield, Michigan, where he now lives in retirement.

KLUZAK, Gord

b. Climax, Saskatchewan, March 4, 1964

Bees knees can be such a silly expression, but in Kluzak's case it was painful, for he and a bee seemed to have that much in common – neither had any knees. He started out with knees, two perfectly good, strong pins, but over the years the cartilage and muscle around each got smaller and smaller until he couldn't stand the pain any more. Kluzak played just two years of junior and was clearly one of the best players available in the 1982 draft. Boston selected him 1st overall after he helped Canada win gold at the '82 WJC, and he made the B's that first training camp in September. For two seasons, he developed into a large and commanding presence on the Boston blueline. Then, a knee injury cost him the entire '84-'85 season. He played another full season, then missed the following year again with knee woes. He came back the year after, again went down, and this time it was the beginning of the end. Over the next three seasons, he played three and eight and two games, finally retiring after seeing more of the team doctors than the team coach. In 1990, he was awarded the Masterton Trophy for his perseverance, but fortunately for him he had one strong part of his body to fall back on – his brain. He enrolled at Harvard in economics, and after graduating in 1998 became a financial manager with Goldman-Sachs in Boston.

KLYMKIW, Julian

b. Winnipeg, Manitoba, July 16, 1933

It's not every goalie who can boast of having given up just two NHL goals, one to Claude Provost, the other to Gordie Howe. On October 12, 1958, Howe was tripped up while charging toward the goal. He slid into Rangers goaltender Gump Worsley, who had to leave the game on a stretcher with a severely pulled groin. Detroit's assistant trainer and substitute goalie, Klymkiw, came to the rescue. He played the last 19 minutes of the game and surrendered those 2 goals as his Wings defeated "his" Rangers 3-0. Klymkiw was a prominent Winnipegger most of his life, and when the Manitoba Moose began operations after the Jets moved, the team inaugurated the Julian Klymkiw Community Service Award for the player whose contributions to the city were noteworthy.

KNIBBS, Billy

b. Toronto, Ontario, January 24, 1942

He wasn't a natural and graceful skater, but he was an aggressive and dogged checker, and that's how Knibbs built his reputation. He got his only NHL games in during the '64-'65 season and beyond that was a productive and consistent player in the AHL. His time with the Bruins came while centring a line with Reg Fleming and Wayne Rivers, and he later led Omaha to an Adams Cup in 1971. Some time after retiring, Knibbs wound up in Penetang, where he worked as an accountant.

KNICKLE, Rick

b. Chatham, New Brunswick, February 26, 1960

Being an Air Force baby meant that Knickle's place of birth was almost irrelevant to, though not entirely so in that he spent most of his early years in Greenwood, Nova Scotia. The goalie played junior with Brandon, and Buffalo drafted him in 1979. Over the next 18 years, he played in every league imaginable and came close to holding the unique distinction of having won a championship in each of those leagues. His Wheat Kings narrowly missed winning the Memorial Cup in 1979, and Los Angeles lost in the 1993 NHL finals.

Joe Klukay

Gord Kluzak

Billy Knibbs

Rick Knickle

Fred Knipscheer

Nick Knott

Paul Knox

Espen Knutsen

However, Knickle won titles in the AHL, IHL, and ECHL. He didn't make his NHL debut until late in the '92-'93 season when he was 33 years old. He retired in 1997 and was immediately hired as a western scout for the nascent Nashville Predators, scouting U.S. colleges, Canadian junior, and the NHL out west.

KNIPSCHEER, Fred
b. Fort Wayne, Indiana, September 3, 1969
Knipscheer established a few records in his college career at St. Cloud, but he played only a few games in the NHL with Boston and St. Louis in the early 1990s. He played in the minors until 2000, and then settled in Carmel, Indiana, where he went into real estate and did some pro scouting. He also became an assistant coach for the Carmel Icehounds at that city's high school.

KNOTT, William Earl "Nick"
b. Kingston, Ontario, July 23, 1920
d. Tulsa, Oklahoma, April 12, 1987
Knott was a big, tough customer, and it's not known exactly what sort of success he might have had had he not been of age and therefore played during the war years. As a kid, he saw action for the Brooklyn Americans in 1941-42, the last year of that franchise's existence, but then he enlisted. For the better part of three years he was a member of the Royal Canadian Electrical and Mechanical Engineers, reaching the rank of lieutenant before being discharged. After the war, Knott made it no higher than the United States league, playing with Tulsa until he retired.

KNOX, Paul ("Bill")
b. Toronto, Ontario, November 23, 1933
As a teen, Knox attended St. Mike's in Toronto, the first step en route to a career with the Leafs. He was no great star or prospect of the first order, so he enrolled at the University of Toronto. During his year at U of T, Conn Smythe hauled him out of the classroom to play one game for the Leafs, the night of March 12, 1955. It was his only NHL game, but he went on to play for Kitchener the year after. The Dutchmen were chosen to represent Canada at the 1956 Olympics in Cortina, and Knox performed admirably in that competition, helping Canada win a bronze medal.

KNUBLE, Mike
b. Toronto, Ontario, July 4, 1972
Toronto was his place of birth, but Grand Rapids, Michigan, was Knuble's place of childhood. It was there he went to East Kentwood High School and set scoring records that led to a scholarship offer from Red Berenson at the University of Michigan. Again, his scoring prowess stood him in good stead, and, oddly, he played at the World Championships (for the U.S.) before either the WJC or the NHL. He joined Detroit in '96-'97 and was a part of the '98 Cup win, though coach Scotty Bowman didn't dress him too often in the playoffs. Knuble moved on to the Rangers and the Bruins, where he established himself as a big and dependable, though unspectacular, right winger.

KNUTSEN, Espen ("Shampoo")
b. Oslo, Norway, January 12, 1972
Yes, the land that produces all those bearded men with frost hanging off their faces from marathon, cross-country skiing sessions also produces the occasional hockey export. Knutsen was the third Norwegian to play in the NHL after Bjorn Skaare and Anders Myrvold, and he left his homeland with great expectations from his fans. Known for his Ron Duguay locks back home, he got a decent haircut before arriving in Anaheim in 1997 as a way of declaring the seriousness of his NHL intentions. His father was also a pro in Norway and a part-time hairdresser, and his slick stickhandling coupled with his job led to the nickname Soap. As a result, the son of Soap became Shampoo in the dressing room. Knutsen was not big or fleet of foot, but he knew what to do with the puck. He had played pro in Sweden before his NHL debut and had appeared with the Norwegian National Team as its outstanding player. His first NHL stint lasted just 19 games, and in 1998 he returned to play in Sweden, figuring he'd had his chance and that was that. Wrong. Expansion allowed Columbus to bring him back, and perhaps it was a trip he wished he'd never taken. In March 2002, he took a slapshot that was deflected by Calgary's Derek Morris into the crowd. The puck struck 13-year-old Brittanie Cecil in the head, and she died in hospital a short time later. Knutsen, by no means at fault, was devastated but carried on, playing with the tenacity needed to stay in the NHL, but thinking all the while of a sweet girl taken from life for no good reason. As a result of the accident, all NHL rinks were fitted with netting behind both goals in time for the 2002-03 season.

KOCHAN, Dieter
b. Saskatoon, Saskatchewan, May 11, 1974
Desperate for something, anything to help his team win, Tampa Bay's GM recalled Kochan from Binghamton of the UHL and put him in goal against Stanley Cup champions Dallas on March 28, 2000. Kochan allowed three goals on six shots. Over his first three seasons, he played just a few games and allowed just a few too many goals to raise eyebrows. Kochan has spent most of his time on a variety of minor-league teams and has yet to show the brilliance needed to make a mark in the NHL.

KOCUR, Joey
b. Calgary, Alberta, December 21, 1964
There aren't too many players who won three Stanley Cups in the 1990s, but Kocur is one of them, courtesy of one win with the Rangers in 1994 and two with the Wings in '97 and '98. Kocur had hands of cement, hands meant for fighting, not scoring. He fought everything that moved during his years in the league, everything, that is, except his cousin and best friend Wendel Clark. Kocur led the league in penalty minutes in '85-'86 with 377, and over the next 5 years racked up 200 or more each season. Off the ice, he was one of the most popular athletes in Detroit, and he lived in the city year-round. His career seemed over after 1996 when no team wanted him, but the Wings re-signed him and for two more years he was back in the fold. His career more or less ended after a serious abdominal injury that required surgery. For a year and a half he tried to come back, but when he knew the end was nigh he retired and became the team's video coordinator.

KOEHLER, Greg
b. Scarborough, Ontario, February 27, 1975
It was in 1998 that Koehler first played pro, but since then he has done more than his fair share of travelling. He has been owned by three NHL teams and has played in the AHL, IHL, and ECHL, his lone NHL game coming with Carolina on December 29, 2000. Entering his late twenties, he is running out of chances to prove his worth at the NHL level.

KOHN, Ladislav
b. Uherske Hradiste, Czechoslovakia (Czech Republic), March 4, 1975
Kohn spent the first two years of his junior career in the Western league in Swift Current before turning pro with Calgary in 1995. Although he has proved his worth as a perfectly consistent 25-goal scorer in the AHL, he has yet to prove as much during his time in the big tent. Five teams have owned him in his young career, and none has kept him around for too long, save Anaheim in 1999-2000, when Kohn responded with just five goals.

KOIVU, Saku
b. Turku, Finland, November 23, 1974
There was nothing out of the ordinary on the day in September 2001 when Koivu boarded a plane in Finland to travel to Montreal for another training camp and another season of NHL hockey. Within a day of touchdown, though, his life seemed imperilled, his world was thrown upside down, and a season of extraordinary difficult and heroism was about to begin. He told doctors he didn't feel well, and they told him he had cancer. They quickly discovered it was non-Hodgkin's lymphoma. He would begin chemotherapy immediately, and his future health – forget about his career – was uncertain at best. Because of his great physical condition, he was able to endure much higher doses of chemo than the average patient and, miraculously, within seven months he was on skates again. He returned to the team at the end of the regular season, and with seemingly supernatural powers proved to be the team's best player in the post-season. An inspiration, yes, but a performer also. His tale of woe, while horrible, was in some ways only one in a series of misfortunes for Koivu. Small and rugged, he suffered numerous injuries during his career with the Habs and never played a full season. Despite his skill, his best season was his first, when he scored 20 goals. In Finland, he began as a superstar almost from his first day on the ice. He played at three World Juniors and was named his country's best player in '94-'95. He also played in the '94 and '98 Olympics, as well as the '96 World Cup, and his reputation is

His remarkable battle with cancer was acknowledged by the league when he was awarded the Masterton Trophy in 2002.
SAKU KOIVU

arguably that of the finest player ever to come out of Finland. His remarkable battle with cancer was acknowledged by the league when he was awarded the Masterton Trophy in 2002, and he returned to Montreal that fall both a hero and a leader, the indefatigable captain unwilling to give in to disease.

KOLANOS, Krys
b. Calgary, Alberta, July 27, 1981
Two years into his studies at Boston College, Kolanos bolted the school to join the Coyotes in 2001. He had had two excellent years with BC and stepped right into the Phoenix lineup to start the 2001-02 season, though he wasn't sure where he was by season's end. On January 19, 2002, he was knocked unconscious by a hit and for the better part of a year suffered from post-concussion syndrome. His career has been in jeopardy ever since.

KOLARIK, Pavel
b. Vyskov, Czechoslovakia (Czech Republic), October 24, 1972
At the ripe old age of 27, his career in the Czech Republic well established, Kolarik was drafted 268th overall by Boston in 2000. Why not give the big show a try? He played most of the next year in Providence, but the team thought enough of him to recall him on 5 different occasions and dress him in 10 games. A solid defenceman, his fate still hasn't changed, the recalls coming, and the demotions following.

KOLESAR, Mark
b. Brampton, Ontario, January 23, 1973
Kolesar was raised on a farm in Neepawa and made his way back east to the Big Smoke after the Leafs signed him as a free agent in 1994. Four times he attended training camp, and four times he didn't quite make it. The Blue and White played him in 28 games during this time, but when his contract elapsed neither Toronto nor another NHL team offered him a contract. So he went overseas, ending up with the London Knights of the Super League in 2000.

KOLNIK, Juraj
b. Nitra, Czechoslovakia (Slovakia), November 13, 1980
Still a pup, Kolnik has yet to show the flashes of offensive brilliance that characterized his time in junior in Quebec. The Islanders have played him only sporadically, and he has yet to make a serious impression.

KOLSTAD, Dean
b. Edmonton, Alberta, June 16, 1968
In a 10-year career as a professional hockey player, Kolstad played 40 games in the NHL with Minnesota

Ladislav Kohn

Pavel Kolarik

Dean Kolstad

Neil Komadoski

George Konik

**Steve
Konowalchuk**

Steve Konroyd

and San Jose. The large defenceman never stuck in the big show and made the IHL his home until he went down to the Western Pro league. After retiring in 1998, Kolstad returned to Canada and became club pro at the Bedford Valley Golf Course in Saskatchewan. He also earned a Class A PGA teaching card and turned his attention full-time to the game of summer sticks.

KOLZIG, Olaf
("Ollie the Goalie"/ "Godzilla")
b. Johannesburg, South Africa, April 9, 1970
There is nothing German about Kolzig except his name and parents, yet that's about all it took for him to be named that Germany's goalie for the 1996 World Cup. He was born in South Africa to German parents, but Kolzig grew up mostly in Toronto and Halifax during a childhood that saw him move around regularly. His rise to fame and stardom was most peculiar. Washington drafted him in 1989 and put him in the net for two games the following year. He spent the next two full seasons in the minors, during which time he scored a goal. In all, he spent eight years in the minors and it didn't look like he would ever get a chance to make an impact with the Caps. But Washington kept signing him and Kolzig persevered, and by 1996 he was the team's backup. The year after, he started off well and kept on going, playing in 64 games and registering a fantastic 2.20 goals-against average at the age of 28. Since then, he's been the Caps' starter and has proved as resilient as he has been consistent. And although he only lived in Germany for a few months as a kid, that country has pinned its international hopes on the big goalie from… the world.

KOMADOSKI, Neil
b. Winnipeg, Manitoba, November 5, 1951
This defenceman played with Los Angeles on a regular basis for five and a half years in the 1970s, and then a trade to St. Louis saw his playing time halved over three more seasons. He was always the tough guy, though, no matter where he played or how often, and his career had a great effect on at least one person – his son, Neil Jr. Little Neil was drafted by Ottawa in 2001 and promises to follow his dad to the NHL one day.

KOMARNISKI, Zenith
b. Vegreville, Alberta, August 13, 1978
Perhaps the World Junior Championships of 1998 were portentous for Komarniski, or perhaps they were misleading. Early signs point to the former. Canada's entry that year finished a worst-ever eighth and since then the defenceman has played only 18 NHL games, with Vancouver in 1999-2000. He has moved from the AHL down to Manitoba of the IHL, not the place a young NHL hopeful should be playing.

KONIK, George
b. Flin Flon, Manitoba, May 4, 1937
Konik seemed to have a good many separate careers during his time in hockey, starting, typically, with a stint in junior in his hometown. The Flin Flon Bombers won the 1957 Memorial Cup, but Konik didn't head to the NHL and he wasn't assigned to the minors. Instead, he headed to the University of

Denver to get an education and continue playing. He won a national championship there in 1961 and only then did he begin a pro career that was entirely located in the minors until expansion in 1967. At that point, Konik had his NHL glory, a year with Pittsburgh during which he scored seven goals. Soon after, he began another career as an American international star. He played for the U.S. in "B" pool of the 1970 World Championships, which the team won, and then in "A" pool the following year. He finished his career in the WHA and later became the chairman of the voting committee for the Hobey Baker Award.

KONOWALCHUK, Steve
b. Salt Lake City, Utah, November 11, 1972
Only three U.S. entries have ever won a medal at the World Juniors, and Konowalchuk was on the '92 team that came away with a bronze. He made his NHL debut with Washington toward the end of that '91-'92 season, and quickly became a steady centre who has played every game of his career (600 and counting) with the Caps over the last decade and more. He will neither score a bunch of goals nor harm his team defensively, and that has always suited his coaches perfectly. Unfortunately, the Caps have never gone too deep in the playoffs, and the one year they did, 1998, was the year Konowalchuk missed the entire post-season with a bad wrist injury.

KONROYD, Steve
b. Scarborough, Ontario, February 10, 1961
For 15 years Konroyd played in the NHL, the consummate unsung hero, the man no one noticed or paid attention to except when he was checking the opposing team's top players. He played for six teams and came closest to the Cup in 1989 and '90, when Chicago made it to the semifinals in successive years. He retired early in the '94-'95 season and began a career in broadcasting that continues to this day, providing TV colour commentary for San Jose and Columbus.

KONSTANTINOV, Evgeny
b. Kazan, Soviet Union (Russia), March 29, 1981
If Konstantinov never makes it back to the NHL, he will have had the shortest career of any goalie in NHL history. He's a great prospect in the hearts and minds of Tampa Bay management, but to date he has played just 24 seconds in a game against Colorado on December 18, 2000. Youth is still very much on his side, though, and the Lightning will surely give him a decent chance to prove his worth.

KONSTANTINOV, Vladimir
("Vlad the Impaler")
b. Murmansk, Soviet Union (Russia), March 19, 1967
When Konstantinov was in his prime, no one would have believed that he would be given ovations by opponents and be regarded highly as a human being. But, then again, no one could have anticipated the horrific events of June 17, 1997. The Red Wings had just won their first Cup since 1955 and were having a team golf tournament and dinner. Konstantinov, teammate Slava Fetisov, and team masseuse Sergei

Mnatsakanov were on their way home in a limousine. The driver, Richard Gnida, fell asleep at the wheel, and the limo crashed into a tree. Fetisov was hurt, but he made a full recovery. Mnatsakanov was badly hurt, but Konstantinov was seriously injured. He lapsed into a coma, and when he came out of it five weeks later, he couldn't walk or talk. His life had been transformed to a series of baby steps as he relearned everything, and in the coming months his physical strength helped him regain some abilities. By the following post-season, when the Wings won the Cup again, he was still in a wheelchair, though the players brought him onto the ice and captain Steve Yzerman gave the Cup to him first after the victory. The team never took anything out of his dressing room stall, and his memory lives on as he continues to improve, slowly and gradually. He was captain of the Soviet National Team after Fetisov left for North America, and he followed Fetisov under conniving plans. He declared he had a rare form of cancer that could be treated only in the United States, and had Detroit doctors confirm the falsehood. He joined the Wings for the '91-'92 season and made an immediate impact as an unpleasant foe who would stick and jab at opponents to throw them off and frustrate them with small but illegal tactics. Konstantinov went to North America to play hockey, and instead he wound up fighting for his life, the greatest joy in the sport – the Stanley Cup – quickly overshadowed by an horrific injury.

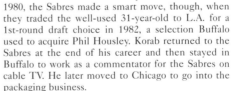

Konstantinov went to North America to play hockey, and instead he wound up fighting for his life.
VLADIMIR KONSTANTINOV

KONTOS, Chris
b. Toronto, Ontario,
December 10, 1963

It's one of those inexplicable things, but Kontos had a playoffs in 1989 that defied anything he had ever done before. In just 11 games, he scored 9 goals, a burst that seemed to come out of nowhere. In his previous 49 NHL games over 3 years, he had scored 5 times. In junior and the minors, he had scored a bit, but never at a goal-per-game pace. Then, in '92-'93 with Tampa, he had another goal outburst, scoring 27 times in 66 games. He started with the Rangers in 1982 and truly did not display a knack for scoring. In fact, when the Blueshirts demoted the 20-year-old, he went home to enrol at U of T until being talked into reporting to Tulsa. He moved around from team to team, and later won silver for Canada at the 1994 Olympics in Lillehammer, mostly because he had no NHL takers. He credited his Tampa turnaround to one thing – a book. Written by the esteemed Maxwell Maltz and titled *Psycho Cybernetics*, it coached Kontos on the art of staying relaxed. It obviously worked. In 1993, he was named North America's Greek athlete of the year. After retiring, he settled in Barrie, Ontario, and worked as a sportscaster at a local television station.

He also started his own business, which produced multimedia CDs for companies.

KOPAK, Russ
b. Edmonton, Alberta, April 26, 1924
d. Kirkland, Washington, November 25, 1998

Kopak played with the Bruins in '43-'44, the same year he began his pro career with the Olympics in the same city. His best year came the next season, when he averaged a goal a game and led the Olympics to the Boardwalk Trophy and the Walker Cup. Kopak retired from the game in 1950.

KORAB, Jerry ("King Kong")
b. Sault Ste. Marie, Ontario, September 15, 1948

Hockey, like life, can be a metaphor for so many things, and Korab lived the metaphor. He liked to say hockey was always a gamble, both in the attempt to make it to the NHL and the decisions a player makes during every shift. Korab lived this metaphor in that he loved to go to Las Vegas with his wife every chance they got. He was good at poker, and his metaphor also helped build a successful hockey career. He hated his nickname but earned it because he was a big and heavy-hitting defenceman. He survived 15 years in the league despite a series of injuries that might have felled a lesser man. Korab began in the Chicago system in the last days of sponsorship in the 1960s, but he was likely best known as a Sabre, especially as part of the '74-'75 team that went to the Cup finals against Philadelphia. On March 10, 1980, the Sabres made a smart move, though, when they traded the well-used 31-year-old to L.A. for a 1st-round draft choice in 1982, a selection Buffalo used to acquire Phil Housley. Korab returned to Sabres at the end of his career and then stayed in Buffalo to work as a commentator for the Sabres on cable TV. He later moved to Chicago to go into the packaging business.

KORDIC, Dan
b. Edmonton, Alberta, April 18, 1971

Dan was the younger brother of John, and both boys knew only one way to play – tough. Dan played all of his 197 NHL games with Philadelphia during the 1990s after graduating from Medicine Hat, but he spent considerable time in the minors. When he was with the Flyers, he was fighting, of course. After a while, he came to the Beckettian realization that the nothingness of his role was stultifying. To make amends, he became a referee in the Ontario Hockey Association, and there is every chance that one day he'll be tooting his whistle in the NHL.

Chris Kontos

Russ Kopak

Jerry Korab

Dan Kordic

John Kordic

Jim Korn

Mike Korney

Evgeny Korolev

KORDIC, John

b. Edmonton, Alberta, March 22, 1965
d. L'Ancienne-Lorette, Quebec, August 8, 1992

Does a man choose what he does with his life, or does Destiny choose for him? For a man who wastes his life and his gifts, the answer doesn't much matter if he's in a coffin by the age of 27. Like his brother, Dan, John grew up a hard-nosed player, but no matter how much he fought he still had the hockey skills necessary to make it to the NHL. Kordic was lucky enough to play his rookie year in Montreal in 1985-86, the year the Habs unexpectedly won the Cup. His play so impressed Toronto that the Leafs traded Russ Courtnall to get him, but in the next two years Kordic wasted his talent on drinking, partying, and a bad attitude. He wound up in Washington and then Quebec, where the final scene of his tragic life played out. The Nordiques signed him, but only on the condition that he submit to random drug testing. They released him in January 1992, but the Oilers farm team took him on for a few games. On the night of August 8, 1992, he died after a violent, drunken fight with a dozen police officers. He was in town to appear in court on charges of assaulting his fiancée in July. Steroids and needles were in his hotel room when police arrived, and he died in an ambulance en route to the hospital. The cause of death was given as lung failure related to a malfunctioning heart.

KORN, Jim

b. Hopkins, Minnesota, July 28, 1957

Single-minded devotion and ambition can take a player from the local arena to the NHL, but it's a curious ambition for someone who lacked on-ice talent and who also possessed the cerebral talent that gave him an alternative. Korn graduated from Providence College in 1979 magna cum laude with a degree in economics. He didn't ever have to play hockey to be successful in life or feel worthy, yet he went to Detroit's training camp that fall after appearing in the World Championships shortly after rearranging the tassel on his mortar block. He went on to play for 10 seasons, often missing action for long periods because of his style of play. He was a fighter, a man who understood the business of life and translated that to the business of hockey, irrespective of the damage done to his opponents' jaws. For every NHL goal he scored, Korn accrued 27 penalty minutes. Yet he played until his body eventually gave out. Only then did he settle down to a good job, ending up in Minneapolis as a sports attorney for the firm of Fredrikson and Byron.

KORNEY, Mike ("Kornball")

b. Dauphin, Manitoba, September 15, 1953

Korney played pro for seven years during which time he must have set records for the number of teams played for. In 1973-74, he started in London, England, playing for Detroit's European farm team experiment, the Lions, and ended up with the Wings for two games. The next year, he played for the Wings again as well as four other clubs in the minors, and the year after he played for three more teams. By the time he retired in 1982, he had played for 16 pro teams. He won the Allan Cup in 1982 with the Cranbrook Royals and later became a helicopter pilot, even flying in the Persian Gulf!

KOROLEV, Evgeny

b. Moscow, Soviet Union (Russia), July 24, 1978

Despite playing parts of three seasons with the Islanders, Korolev has yet to make his mark in the NHL, perhaps because he's a defensive defenceman who's not particularly comfortable with the physical aspects of the game. He's still learning, but whether New York continues to give him chances to prove himself is what will determine his fate with that team.

KOROLEV, Igor ("Iggy")

b. Moscow, Soviet Union (Russia), September 6, 1970

Growing up an hour outside Moscow, Korolev was happy to play for the top teams in his country as a means of a better life, and he took his childhood sweetheart with him. He played for the USSR at the 1991 Canada Cup, and a year later joined St. Louis, the team that had drafted him. It took him a while to get going, and by the time he scored 22 goals he had been claimed by Winnipeg. He became a free agent in 1997 and signed with Toronto, and it was there his life took on special importance amid its greatest frustrations. He became the team's all-purpose centre who could score, take important faceoffs, and kill penalties. He suffered a fractured thumb late in '98-'99 and when he returned, he broke his ankle. The thumb never fully healed but he played through the problem, and soon after becoming a Canadian citizen he was traded to Chicago, where he has continued on with a number of former Leafs acquired by former GM Mike Smith.

Soon after becoming a Canadian citizen he was traded to Chicago.
IGOR KOROLEV

KOROLL, Cliff

b. Canora, Saskatchewan, October 1, 1946

No one, not then, not now, has been more important to U.S. college hockey than Murray Armstrong. The number of Canadians he recruited to his University of Denver program ranks in the hundreds, and the number he sent to the NHL is in the dozens. Count Cliff Koroll among those converts. Koroll finished Armstrong's program in 1968 and immediately checked in with the Chicago farm team, making the Hawks in 1969. Keith Magnuson had been a high school opponent, and now the two were teammates in the Windy City. Koroll was an abrasive right winger, not as skilled as some of the other Hawks, but capable of scoring 20 goals a year while checking the other team's best players. He was part of a team that came so close to the Cup every year but never won, and because of his style of play he was done by the time he was 34. In 1980-81, he became assistant coach to head man Magnuson, and though his friend was fired the following year Koroll survived until the end of the decade in one capacity or another. After leaving the game, he remained in Chicago and worked for the McClement Sales Company, a food supplier for McDonald's restaurants. Five years later, he moved on to Cargill Inc., a company similar to McClement but one that operated worldwide.

KOROLYUK, Alexander ("Korky")
b. Moscow, Soviet Union (Russia), January 15, 1976
Even before he played a game in the NHL, Korolyuk had been in two World Juniors and one WC. At the 1995 WJC, he led Russia in scoring en route to a silver medal, but he continued to play at home rather than come to North America to develop. That changed in 1996 when he played for Manitoba in the IHL. He made the Sharks the following year and to date has been good for about a dozen goals a year as a playmaking right winger.

KORTKO, Roger
b. Hafford, Saskatchewan, February 1, 1963
He definitely had some skill, but trying to crack the Islanders lineup in the early 1980s was not a task for anyone but a superstar – and Kortko wasn't that. He ran into bad luck in '84-'85 when the Islanders brought him up and after a short time he broke his ankle. The next year, he played 52 games but scored only 5 goals, a long way from the 62 he managed in his last year of junior. Soon enough, Kortko was back in the minors and then on his way to Holland to close out his career.

KOSTOPOULOS, Tom
b. Mississauga, Ontario, January 24, 1979
The right winger was drafted low by Pittsburgh in 1999 and has played only a few games with the Penguins. He has played primarily in Wilkes-Barre for the team after a junior career in London.

KOSTYNSKI, Doug
b. Castlegar, British Columbia, February 23, 1963
Kostynski moved to Port Coquitlam when he was two and grew up in those parts. After junior, he joined the Bruins in 1983, but in two seasons he failed to make enough of a scene to stay. He wound up playing in Moncton in the AHL, and although he played in Finland for a while after that, he returned to Moncton to settle down after retiring. He worked in that city and continued to play in commercial leagues for several years.

KOTALIK, Ales
b. Jindrichuv Hradec, Czechoslovakia (Czech Republic), December 23, 1978
After playing pro in the Czech Republic for 4 years, Kotalik came to Buffalo's camp in 2001 and was

assigned to Rochester during a year in which he played 132 times for the Sabres.

KOTANEN, Dick
b. Port Arthur, Ontario, November 18, 1925
In a long and varied career, Kotanen made it to the NHL for a single game in 1950-51 with the Rangers during a four-year term with the local Rovers. He moved on to play in a series of leagues of minor repute before winding up whence he came – or close to it – in North Bay.

KOTSOPOULOS, Chris ("Kotsy")
b. Scarborough, Ontario, November 27, 1958
He wasn't really a goon, but he wasn't a smooth-skating, fleet-footed member of the skating fraternity, either. Rather, he was a tough defenceman who relied on his effectiveness at taking the man and taking responsibility for whatever else might happen on the ice. Although he was the kind of player who needed a solid work ethic and great attitude to play regularly, he was dogged by weight problems and poor fitness during his career. Nonetheless, he played a decade (1980-90) in the NHL, notably with his hometown Leafs. After retiring, he moved to rural Pennsylvania.

KOVALCHUK, Ilya
b. Tver, Soviet Union (Russia), April 15, 1983
In the round-robin series of the 2001 World Junior Championships, Russia was leading Canada 2-1 late in the game. With the Canadian goalie on the bench and the team pushing to tie the score, Kovalchuk got a loose puck and waltzed in on the empty Canadian net. As he did so, he pumped one arm in the air to celebrate the win, and this showmanship upset the Canadians more than the loss. Just a few months later, he and Canadian opponent Dany Heatley were linemates and formed the most exciting rookie duo in the league. In between, Kovalchuk was the 1st-overall selection by Atlanta in the draft, and he made the team as a 19-year-old. Like Heatley, he was strong on the puck and liked to go to the net, though he was more of a scorer and Heatley a passer. The race for the Calder Trophy might well have been the closest ever except that Kovalchuk broke his leg and missed the last quarter of the season. Nonetheless, he had 29 goals and 51 points. He played for Russia at the 2002 Olympics in mid-season, winning a bronze medal, and the duo continue to show promise of becoming mature superstars in the league who might well meet at the 2006 Olympics in Turin.

KOVALENKO, Andrei ("Tank")
b. Balakovo, Soviet Union (Russia), June 7, 1970
They called him Tank because he was reasonably short (5'10") and incredibly squat and strong (215 pounds). They also called him Tank because he moved when he felt like it. When he did, he was a tremendous player. When he didn't, well, "tank" took on a more aquatic connotation. Kovalenko was a rarity in the Soviet Union in that he came from a reasonably wealthy family. He both went into the army and played hockey during his teens. He joined the Quebec Nordiques in 1992 and in three and a half seasons started to play like a decent prospect. The team, now in Colorado, included him in a package to get Patrick Roy from Montreal, and once

Alexander
Korolyuk

Roger Kortko

Chris Kotsopoulos

Andrei Kovalenko

Joe Kowal

Don Kozak

Les Kozak

Viktor Kozlov

with the Habs Kovalenko went into the aquatic tank. He was soon on his way to Edmonton and then to other NHL ports of call, losing chunks of reputation with every move and every game. The gold medal he had won in 1992 with Russia seemed very far away as his career came to a close, but he returned to Russia and found new life playing in the Superleague with Lokomotiv Yaroslavl.

KOVALEV, Alexei
b. Togliatti, Soviet Union (Russia), February 24, 1973
By the time he was 14, it was clear to everyone who saw him play that Kovalev would be a star. He made the Moscow Dynamo team at 16 and by 19 he was in the NHL with the Rangers. As a rookie, he was suspended three times, two for stick fouls and one for slew-footing Dale Hunter. He was not going to be pushed around. In his second year, he scored 23 goals and was one of the best players during the team's playoff run. In every full season he played, he kicked in at least 20 goals, and while playing with Wayne Gretzky upon the Great One's arrival, the Rangers waited for Kovalev to assume even greater heights. This just never happened, though, and on November 25, 1998, he was involved in a big trade, going to Pittsburgh with Harry York for Petr Nedved, Chris Tamer, and Sean Pronger. In his first three years under Mario Lemieux's eyes, Kovalev had 46, 66, and 95 points and looked to be close to breaking into the upper echelons of superstardom. The loss of Jaromir Jagr hurt his output, but Kovalev remains one of the finer players in the game, combining size, stickhandling, and speed to generate offence. Sadly, his contract was bigger than Lemieux, as Pittsburgh owner, could afford, and he was traded to the Rangers during the 2002-03 season. If he has that final gear, the motivational *je ne sais quoi* that will allow him to go from great to truly amazing, he has yet to show it.

In his first three years under Mario Lemieux's eyes, Kovalev had 46, 66, and 95 points.
ALEXEI KOVALEV

KOWAL, Joe
b. Toronto, Ontario, February 3, 1956
If you think of this story as being set in 1920s Los Angeles – big old cars, top hats, cigars, and champagne – you might capture the flavour of Joe Kowal's life. It has humble beginnings, in Toronto in the 1950s, and continues in that city as Young Joe develops a passion and skill for hockey. He grows to a towering 6'5" and is a decent skater, and Buffalo drafts him in 1976 just a few weeks after his Hamilton Fincups capture the Memorial Cup. He plays just 22 games with the Sabres over the next 2 years before settling into a career in the minors, but his passion for horses gets the better of him. Kowal retires from the puck game in 1981 and soon after moves to California. He becomes a banker and a horse owner, and his reputation grows hundredfold when he spends $400,000 on a private purchase of the filly Rings a Chime, which goes on to win several Grade 1 stakes races. That, friends, is a long way from the Memorial Cup in Hamilton.

KOZAK, Don
b. Saskatoon, Saskatchewan, February 2, 1952
Anyone who holds an NHL record is worthy of special mention, and Kozak is one such player. On April 17, 1977, in a playoff game against Boston, the L.A. right winger scored just six seconds into the game, the fastest playoff goal ever from the start of a game. Kozak holds no other distinctions or records, though he did score a bundle of goals with the Edmonton Oil Kings in junior. He played most of his NHL career with L.A., though the Kings traded him to Vancouver, which is where he finished in the NHL before moving on to the minors.

KOZAK, Les
b. Dauphin, Manitoba, October 28, 1940
Kozak's is so not a hockey life it's amazing he can call himself an alumnus of the same game as Wayne Gretzky and Bobby Orr. Kozak went to St. Mike's in the late 1950s, where he played on a line with Dave Keon and Larry Keenan. After graduating, he attended U of T and planned a life in the priesthood. Just before his second year, he decided to enrol at St. John Fisher College in Rochester, where he could study under the Basilian fathers and play hockey for the Leafs farm team. During that '61-'62 season, he was called up by Toronto for 12 games, and he scored his only NHL goal against Detroit. When he was sent back down to the Americans, he suffered a fractured skull and his hockey career was over. Kozak then finished his education. He earned a degree in chemistry, of all things, and enrolled in a biochemistry program at Notre Dame. He finished his Ph.D. there and then did post-graduate work at Michigan State, where he developed a keen interest in genetics. Kozak moved to Bar Harbor, Maine, and became the senior staff scientist and deputy director of Jackson Laboratory, where he worked on the origins of genetic diseases. He later continued his work at Louisiana State University, where not a soul would have a clue if Kozak ever told them he once scored something called a goal on a player named Terry Sawchuk!

KOZLOV, Viktor
b. Togliatti, Soviet Union (Russia), February 14, 1975
Leading up to the 1993 draft, the rhetoric was over the top, even for general managers. Kozlov was one of the top choices. Many scouts would have selected him 1st overall. He had all the skills to be a superstar. When

San Jose got him 6th overall, analysts were stunned. Might be the biggest steal in draft history, they said. This guy will be better than the others in three years (better, that is, than Alexandre Daigle, Chris Pronger, Chris Gratton, Paul Kariya, and Rob Niedermayer). Well, as it turned out, Wayne Gretzky's grandmother, who used to play goal for little Wayne, could have been better than Daigle. Gratton and Niedermayer? On the bubble. Pronger and Kariya? Not even close. Kozlov came to the NHL in 1994, the year of the lockout, and when he returned home to play he broke his ankle after just three games. He returned to San Jose and convalesced at Arturs Irbe's house, but over his four partial years with the Sharks, Kozlov showed little grit and not much skill. He wound up being traded to Florida, where nothing changed, and at every step he was dogged by untimely injuries. He was set to play for Russia at the 1998 Olympics in Nagano when he hurt his shoulder. He was set to play at the 1999 All-Star Game when he reinjured the same shoulder, and when he played a full season he just didn't play as the drooling scouts had anticipated or as his coaches back home had envisioned when they fought over the 17-year-old phenom. Steal of all time at the draft? More like just another semi-bust.

KOZLOV, Vyacheslav "Slava"

b. Voskresensk, Soviet Union (Russia), May 3, 1972

When Kozlov arrived in Detroit hoping to play for the Red Wings toward the end of the '91-'92 season, he was a mess. He had suffered a number of serious injuries in a car accident in Moscow the previous November, and his first stop was the hospital, not Joe Louis Arena. While the Wings figured he would soon be healthy enough to play, authorities suggested differently. It seemed that Kozlov had recently signed a five-year contract with his Central Red Army team, so when he came to Detroit to sign an NHL deal, his previous contract was still in effect and binding. Kozlov acknowledged the first signing, but revealed he had been more or less forced to agree to the deal. Once the legalities were worked out to Moscow's satisfaction, Kozlov joined the Wings on the ice. He had two assists in his first game, and soon, like his former junior teammate Pavel Bure, he was the toast of the league. Kozlov played with the Wings for nine years, winning Cups in '97 and '98. He twice had more than 30 goals, and 3 other times had more than 20, but Detroit gave him to Buffalo to acquire Dominik Hasek in the summer of 2000. Hasek went on to win the Cup with the Wings, while Kozlov fought with coach Lindy Ruff for ice time. It was not how he envisioned his new start, but that is the way of the new NHL, which stresses finances first and foremost.

Kozlov played with the Wings for nine years, winning Cups in '97 and '98.
VYACHESLAV KOZLOV

KRAFT, Milan

b. Plzen, Czechoslovakia (Czech Republic), January 17, 1980

Kraft capped a terrific junior career by taking the Czech juniors to a gold medal in 2000 and being named the best forward of the tournament. Since then, he has spent as much time in the minors as with Pittsburgh, trying to turn his great teen skills into mature NHL ability for Mario Lemieux's team.

KRAFTCHECK, Steve

b. Tinturn, Ontario, March 3, 1929
d. Providence, Rhode Island, August 10, 1997

Wherever he played, Kraftcheck impressed because of his unrelenting determination and desire. As with many a defenceman, he was neither the most talented player nor the smoothest skater, but he played every night as if it was the last of his life. He played parts of four seasons in the NHL during the 1950s, but made his real mark in the AHL, notably with Cleveland and Rochester. By the time he retired in 1964, he was second on the all-time list of assist leaders, and much of his last six years was spent as a playing coach. He was a First All-Star in the AHL in four successive years, and in 1959 he was named the league's best blueliner.

Steve Kraftcheck

KRAJICEK, Lukas

b. Prostejov, Czechoslovakia (Czech Republic), March 11, 1983

Only time will tell if Krajicek can fit into Mike Keenan's scheme of things, but it's a good thing he got into a few games with the Panthers at the start of 2001-02, just in case. That turned out to be a busy season for the young defenceman. In addition to the five games he had with the Panthers, he was returned to junior in Peterborough for the year. He also played for the Czech Republic at the 2002 WJC, but to start 2002-03 he was returned again to junior.

KRAKE, Philip "Skip"

b. Rabbit Lake, Saskatchewan, October 14, 1943

It's just a hop, skip, and a jump from Rabbit Lake (birthplace) to North Battleford (growing-up territory), but from there it's a real hike to the NHL. By virtue of playing for Estevan in the early 1960s, Krake was Bruins property from the get-go, but in his four seasons with the B's he was used almost exclusively as a penalty killer. A trade to Los Angeles seemed to be the best thing for him, but although he played more he didn't produce more. After a short stay in Buffalo, Krake signed into the WHA, where he had four decent seasons before having to retire because of an injury during the '75-'76 season. He

Philip Krake

Igor Kravchuk

settled in Lloydminster, Saskatchewan, where he ran Lloydminster Sporting Goods and later became the Edmonton Oilers corporation manager of retail outlets for the region.

KRAVCHUK, Igor
b. Ufa, Soviet Union (Russia), September 13, 1966
The staggering success of Kravchuk in international hockey renders his NHL career somewhat trivial by comparison, though it consisted of a perfectly meritorious decade. To wit, the Olympics: gold, 1988; captain and gold, 1992; silver, 1998; bronze, 2002. Canada Cup: 1987 and '91. World Championships: gold, 1990; bronze, 1991; and (a disappointing) ninth, 2000. Kravchuk made his NHL debut on February 27, 1992, scoring a goal for Chicago. It was, ironically, the only goal of the season for him, but goals were never the defenceman's forte. He tried to lead by example and play within his means, and for him this constituted smart, defensive hockey. He moved on to Edmonton and St. Louis, and when the Blues traded him to Ottawa for Steve Duchesne, he thought he had found his niche. He was paired with Chris Phillips and was counted on to help develop the youngster, but as all good things must pass, so, too, did Kravchuk, on to Calgary. He has rarely played for excellent teams in the NHL, a contrast to his play for his country, where he has been one of the best among the best.

Mikhail Kravets

KRAVETS, Mikhail
b. Leningrad (St. Petersburg), Soviet Union (Russia), November 12, 1963
Some Russians gravitate toward home at the first sign of failure in North America; others can never go back. Kravets, who played just two NHL games with San Jose, would much rather slug out a career in the depths of the minors than go home to play. He appeared once for the Sharks in '91-'92 and again the next season, but since then Kravets has gone from the "I" to the East Coast league, where nary an NHL up-and-comer can be found but many tire-at-the-bottom-of-the-ocean players subsist.

KRENTZ, Dale
b. Steinbach, Manitoba, December 19, 1961
A good, honest player, Krentz went from Michigan State to Detroit and the farm team to Germany in three simple steps. The Red Wings signed him as a free agent in 1985, but his 5 years in the organization yielded only 30 games and he moved overseas to continue playing.

Sergei Krivokrasov

KRESTANOVICH, Jordan
b. Langley, British Columbia, June 14, 1981
Although he got better and better during his junior career in Calgary, Krestanovich has a ways to go before he'll be playing in Colorado night in, night out. The Avs drafted him in 1999 and gave him a taste of the NHL two years later, but for now he's mostly a prospect hoping to make it.

KRIVOKRASOV, Sergei
b. Angarsk, Soviet Union (Russia), April 15, 1974
The sure sign of a player whose stock is dropping is the number of teams he plays for over a short period

Robert Kron

of time. Krivokrasov is no exception. He came to the NHL in 1992 as an 18-year-old star in the making, and for 6 years he played right wing for the Hawks without contributing a whole lot to the offence. He spent ever-decreasing parts of his first four years in the IHL, being named MVP at that league's All-Star Game in 1993. But after winning a silver with Russia at the 1998 Olympics in Nagano, Krivokrasov played for four teams in as many years, his experience, more than his skill, his number-one commodity.

KROG, Jason
b. Fernie, British Columbia, October 9, 1975
During his four years at the University of New Hampshire, Krog set scoring records and led the team offensively in his last three years and won the Hobey Baker Award in his final year. Nevertheless, he was never drafted, and although the Islanders signed him in 1999 he played fewer and fewer games with the team. If confidence plus opportunity equals results, then Krog's numbers are perilously close to zero, despite his skill.

KROL, Joe
b. Winnipeg, Manitoba, August 13, 1915
d. Calgary, Alberta, October 26, 1993
Not to be confused with the great CFLer of the same name, this Joe Krol was the same vintage as the running back. He played briefly for the Rangers and Americans in the years leading up to the war, but in 1942 he stopped playing to join the RCAF. He achieved the rank of leading aircraftman, but upon being discharged he never played hockey again. In peacetime, he worked for Air Canada in Winnipeg and Montreal for 31 years.

KROMM, Rich
b. Trail, British Columbia, March 29, 1964
Kromm's timing wasn't exactly impeccable. He started with the Flames in 1983 when the team was building a Cup contender, but he was traded to the Islanders with Steve Konroyd for John Tonelli on March 11, 1986. The trade was part of New York's post-Cup dynasty purge, so Kromm missed out on that run as well. Of course, during his time on Long Island, Calgary went to the '86 finals and won the Cup three years later. Kromm followed in his father's footsteps after retiring. He started coaching in 1993-94 in the IHL and has been at it ever since throughout the minors.

KRON, Robert
b. Brno, Czechoslovakia (Czech Republic), February 27, 1967
Kron came to the NHL with Vancouver in 1990 as a mature and experienced player. He had appeared in numerous international tournaments, most impressively the '87 World Juniors where he was named best forward. His best years were with Hartford a short time later, where he had seasons of 24 and 22 goals during a career that carried over to Carolina when the Whalers moved south. Kron's usefulness to the Hurricanes maxed out by the summer of 2000, when the team let him go to Columbus in the Expansion Draft. He has played out the final moments of his NHL life there.

KROOK, Kevin
b. Cold Lake, Alberta, April 5, 1958
Despite making a reputation for himself as a fighter, Krook played only one season of pro. He got into a few games with Colorado in '78-'79, played some in the minors, and retired at season's end.

KROUPA, Vlastimil
b. Most, Czechoslovakia (Czech Republic), April 27, 1975
In the end, Kroupa was just one more draft pick that didn't pan out. The fledgling San Jose Sharks drafted him in 1993 and used him right away, but over the first four seasons his status was always part-time and callup rather than full-time and part of the building of a winning team. The Sharks traded him to New Jersey soon after he won a bronze medal with the Czechs at the 1997 World Championships, but his career has run its course in the minors.

KRULICKI, Jim
b. Kitchener, Ontario, March 9, 1948
Krulicki is near the top of that dubious list for most career NHL games without a goal. The left winger played 41 games in 1970-71 with the Rangers and Detroit, recording 3 assists but no goals. It was his last season in pro hockey, after which he returned to Kitchener to go into private business.

KRUPP, Uwe
b. Cologne, West Germany (Germany), June 24, 1965
The many sides of Uwe Krupp have added up to a great story in his homeland and a not-so-great story in Detroit. He was named after the great German footballer Uwe Seeler, but Krupp was much more of a winter than a summer person. In his spare time, his passion, his obsession, became dogsledding. He began his NHL career with Buffalo in 1986 as a huge defensive defenceman, and established his reputation on this premise for the better part of a decade before he achieved his crowning moment. In 1995-96, he blew out his knee and missed all but the final six games of the regular season, and as the playoffs arrived, he was just returning to form. Doctors had predicted he'd miss a full calendar year, but Krupp regained strength by entering several sledding competitions, a luxury he never usually had during the busy hockey season. It was his simple point shot that gave the Avs the Stanley Cup a few weeks later, scoring in triple overtime of their game-four sweep of Florida. Krupp was instantly a hero in Germany, the first European to score a Cup winner. Detroit was delighted to sign him as a free agent in 1998, but that delight turned to anger shortly after he suffered a herniated disc that December. He missed the rest of the season, but in the summer the Wings learned that he had been sledding, a no-no

given the seriousness of his injury. The Wings demanded to see his medical charts, he refused, and the team suspended him. They've been at loggerheads ever since, and it seems clear Krupp is now, if not at the end of his career, at the very least damaged goods.

KRUPPKE, Gord
b. Slave Lake, Alberta, April 2, 1969
He was a rough and tough defenceman, and although he played only 23 games with Detroit, Kruppke survived in the minors throughout the 1990s with pride. He didn't register a single point with the Red Wings, but even down below he wasn't a scorer or point-getter. He received most of his cheers through fighting and heavy hits.

KRUSE, Paul
b. Merritt, British Columbia, March 15, 1970
Left winger Kruse made it to the NHL mostly because of his fists. Calgary drafted him, and slowly but surely he saw more time with the Flames and less time in the minors, to the point that by his fourth year, 1993-94, he was on the team's roster. In all, he was with the Flames for seven years before being traded to the Islanders and on to Buffalo. His full seasons once again trickled to partial years, diminishing to the point that he played just a single game, with San Jose, in 2001-02.

KRUSHELNYSKI, Mike ("Krusher")
b. Montreal, Quebec, April 27, 1960
Probably Krushelnyski was in a room with high ceilings on the day of June 21, 1984. That was the day he was traded from Boston to Edmonton straight up for Ken Linseman, and chances are, if he had been in a room with regular ceilings, he would have hit his head and hurt himself badly during celebration. Funny how in his first year with the Oilers, playing on a line with Wayne Gretzky, he scored 43 goals. Like that was going to happen again. Krushelnyski was in the right place at the right time, and he had the perfect blend of speed and size to go with Gretzky. He won three Cups with Edmonton, and then was included in the deal that sent Wayne to L.A. in the trade of the century. There he lived in the land of twentysomething goals playing on a non-99 line, and by the time he got to Toronto, the cougar was scoring in the teens. After his career ended, he went into coaching, eventually making it back to the NHL as an assistant with the Red Wings.

KRUTOV, Vladimir ("The Tank")
b. Moscow, Soviet Union (Russia), June 1, 1960
That poetry gets lost in translation is simply a perfect way of saying that beauty in one place or language or

He was named after the great German footballer Uwe Seeler.
UWE KRUPP

Kevin Krook

Jim Krulicki

Paul Kruse

Mike Krushelnyski

Vladimir Krutov

time is not necessarily beauty in another place or language or time. Krutov-Larionov-Makarov was without question the most successful and skilled line ever to play outside the NHL. While Larionov excelled when he got to the big league, Krutov did not. He arrived with his linemate in Vancouver in 1989, but Krutov struggled with language and culture, and took to pizza more than his body permitted. The result was a single, unspectacular season from a man who had won umpteen medals internationally and was clearly one of the finest skaters and scorers of his generation. He returned to Europe after the Canucks released him at his second training camp with the team, and the transference of the great KLM line was a failure. That does not diminish its greatness, however, it only places it more specifically. After retiring, Krutov became an assistant coach to his longtime boss, Viktor Tikhonov, with the Red Army team in Soviet league play.

KRYGIER, Todd
b. Chicago Heights, Illinois, October 12, 1965
Not many players graduate from the University of Connecticut Huskies and go on to the NHL, but Krygier did so in 1988. The left winger played in Hartford's system for three years before spending most of his NHL career in Washington, often playing on a line with Adam Oates. Krygier was never good for more than a dozen goals in a season, but he was a useful utility player. He played for the U.S. three times at the World Championships, though he spent the last two years of his career in the minors.

Todd Krygier

KRYSKOW, Dave
b. Edmonton, Alberta, December 25, 1957
Kryskow's basic measurements are not much different from Bobby Hull's, and it was as a potential Hull replacement that Kryskow made the Hawks in 1972-73, the first year of the Golden Jet's takeoff to the WHA. Needless to say, Kryskow was no Hull, though during his season in the minors he set a pro hockey record by scoring three short-handed goals in a single game. He was claimed by Washington in the '74 Expansion Draft, and went out and score the Caps' first-ever short-handed goal. That's it as far as the distinctions went. After a quick stop in Detroit, he passed out of the NHL in 1976 when Atlanta gave him his outright release and moved on to, ironically, Hull's Winnipeg Jets for two years.

Dave Kryskow

KRYZANOWSKI, Ed ("Krizzie")
b. Fort Frances, Ontario, November 14, 1925
The first player to come out of Fort Frances made it to the NHL via a most circuitous route. Hockey was not much on his mind when he joined the navy in 1944 and was stationed at Cornwallis, Nova Scotia. While there, he played intermediate hockey and was spotted by Ace Bailey, former Leafs great and then coach of the University of Toronto Blues. Bailey convinced Kryzanowski to enrol at U of T and play for him, and then Boston's chief scout, Baldy Cotton, took a liking to the kid. In 1948, Kryzanowski attended Bruins training camp but hurt his groin and wound up in Hershey. When he was called up, though, he acquitted himself well, scoring on his first shift on a

Ed Kryzanowski

long shot that beat Sugar Jim Henry. Over the next four years, he played every position but goal for the team. In the summers, he worked as a greenskeeper at the Idle Hour Golf Club, where Bill Ezinicki had once been the club pro. He was renowned for his wicked slapshot (yes, even in the pre-Boom Boom Geoffrion days the slapshot flourished), and finished his NHL career with Chicago in 1953.

KUBA, Filip ("Kubs")
b. Ostrava, Czechoslovakia (Czech Republic), December 29, 1976
Not a top prospect even as a late teen, Kuba started with Florida and was claimed by Minnesota in the Expansion Draft. He's seen regular duty with the Wild, a weak team, but he has yet to make an impact in the league. Although he was one of the Czechs' initial selections to their 2002 Olympics team, he didn't see any action in Salt Lake City.

KUBINA, Pavel
b. Celadna, Czechoslovakia (Czech Republic), April 15, 1977
One of the perks of playing with Tampa Bay is that, for a European like Kubina, you also get to play in the World Championships. The downside is that the only way he'll ever see the Stanley Cup is by going to the Hockey Hall of Fame in Toronto. Be that as it may, Kubina won two gold medals with the Czechs, at the 1999 and 2001 WC, and the large defenceman is in the process of establishing himself as one of Tampa's top young players.

KUCERA, Frantisek
b. Prague, Czechoslovakia (Czech Republic), February 3, 1968
While brother Vojtech contents himself as a scout for Washington, Frantisek returned to the NHL in 2000 after an absence of three years when he returned to Europe. He made his first trip to North America in 1990 to play for Chicago, but after the Hawks never established himself for any length of time anywhere else. Most of his accolades and accomplishments come from international play, starting with the gold medal he helped the Czechs win at the 1998 Olympics in Nagano. The year after, he was named best defenceman at the Worlds, where he won another gold. Since 1987, when he made his first appearance in his country's sweater at the WJC, Kucera has appeared frequently for the Czechs. Ironically, he was acquired by Washington in 2001 in the deal that sent Jaromir Jagr to the Caps, and no doubt a good word from his brother helped Frantisek's inclusion in the trade!

KUDASHOV, Alexei
b. Elektrostai, Soviet Union (Russia), July 21, 1971
He gave North America about two and a half years, and North America gave him an experience to take home. Kudashov arrived in Toronto with a reputation as one of the speedier playmakers in Russian hockey, but in 25 games with the Leafs he scored exactly 1 point, a goal. He returned to Europe to continue his career and played in three successive World Championships for his country (1998-2000).

KUDELSKI, Bob

b. Springfield, Massachusetts, March 3, 1964

Where a player starts out and where he ends up are often so completely different you can't imagine it's the same person from start to finish. Kudelski went to Yale University and was drafted by Los Angeles in the college Supplemental Draft in 1986. He went on to have a perfectly respectable career, scoring 20 goals 5 times with L.A. and Ottawa. The downside was that his teams never made it far into the playoffs. When he retired in 1995, Yale, the NHL, the goals and connections in the game meant nothing to Kudelski. He wound up in Wyoming selling fishing permits. Go figure.

KUDROC, Kristian

b. Michalovce, Czechoslovakia (Slovakia), May 21, 1981

If the size of NHL players has gotten silly and out of hand, Kudroc is item number one. He stands 6'7" and weighs in at 240 pounds, numbers that suggest a sparring partner for *Rocky XII* or wide receiver for some NFL team. Put this guy on skates and allow him to hit whatever moves – Tampa Bay felt it had a potential great. So far, he's seen limited action, and Kudroc had better develop as a player or his time will lessen, not increase.

KUHN, Gordon

b. Truro, Nova Scotia, November 19, 1905
d. Halifax, Nova Scotia, July 29, 1978

Kuhn grew up in Windsor, Nova Scotia, and played for the Truro Bearcats when they won the Maritime Senior championships. He went on to play in the American league for many years, his only NHL stop coming in 1932-33 with the New York Americans. After retiring in 1940, Kuhn settled in Halifax, where he passed away many years later.

KUKULOWICZ, Adolph "Aggie"

b. Winnipeg, Manitoba, April 2, 1933

A most curious personality, Kukulowicz knew he wasn't going to make it big in the NHL, but he had a love for languages that extended his career from then until now. He played with the Rangers from '52 to '54 and with a myriad teams elsewhere, and wherever he hung his hat he took courses in various languages. He came to learn English, Russian, French, German, Polish, and Ukrainian. Meanwhile, he wound up back in Winnipeg playing senior hockey and working in the cargo department for Air Canada at the Winnipeg International Airport. When that city started flights to Moscow, Air Canada needed baggage handlers who spoke Russian. The job description fit Kukulowicz to a T. He lived in Russia for five years, and in his spare time he played and watched hockey and got to know everyone who was important in the game. He

returned home, but when negotiations for the '72 Summit Series started, both the Soviets and the Canadians requested Kukulowicz's presence as an open and trusted interpreter. So began his long career translating Russian for Canadian hockey people and vice versa. For years he worked with Alan Eagleson in this capacity, through the various Canada Cups and World Championships discussions. He later became the liaison officer for the Canadian Olympic Association at the 1980 Spartakiade in Moscow. Along the way, he had three children, each born in a different country. There was Shayne, born in the U.S., who went on to play hockey at Harvard; Jeffrey, born in Canada and who followed his dad's other career, working his way up within Air Canada; and Susan, who was born in the Soviet Union.

When negotiations for the '72 Summit Series started, both the Soviets and the Canadians requested Kukulowicz's presence as an interpreter.
AGGIE KUKULOWICZ

KULAK, Stu

b. Edmonton, Alberta, March 10, 1963

Kulak's career was jeopardized in 1984 when he suffered a torn abdominal muscle that required surgery and a layoff of almost a year and a half. He had played a few games with Vancouver by that time, but he managed to recover and play for another 15 years and more. He played for five teams in four NHL years but found greater stability in the minors, where he made the rounds with almost as many teams as existed.

Stu Kulak

KULLMAN, Arnie

b. Winnipeg, Manitoba, October 9, 1927
d. Hershey, Pennsylvania, June 11, 1999

The sweets-est man in hockey began his career in the 'Peg until signing with the Boston Olympics in 1947. The Bruins called him up for a game that year and a few more a couple of seasons later, but it was for his 12 years in Hershey that he is remembered in hockey circles. The centreman was a fine scorer and penalty killer, and by the time he retired in 1960 he was also one of the top point getters in AHL history. He settled in Hershey and worked for Hershey Chocolate World. He also owned and operated two ice cream trucks that were so popular and well known that Kullman was called "the ice cream man." He was inducted into both the Pennsylvania Sports Hall of Fame and the Manitoba Hockey Hall of Fame. His cousin, Eddie, also played in the NHL.

KULLMAN, Eddie

b. Winnipeg, Manitoba, December 12, 1923
d. Winnipeg, Manitoba, 1997

Older than cousin Arnie by four years, Eddie followed a similar life path in a slightly different way. For starters, after captaining the Winnipeg Rangers to the Memorial Cup in 1943, he joined the RCAF, achieving the rank of leading aircraftman. After

Eddie Kullman

discharge, he joined the Rangers in 1947 and played six of the next seven years on Broadway. He didn't have a lengthy post-NHL career in the minors and retired soon after his days with the Rangers were done. He played primarily with Buddy O'Connor and Reg Sinclair on the third or fourth line.

KULTANEN, Jarno
b. Luumaki, Finland, January 8, 1973
Drafted at age 27 in the summer of 2000, Kultanen came out of the Finnish league, where he had played all his adult life in relative obscurity. And for good reason. His time with the Bruins so far has been sporadic at best, and he's not likely to have an impact with the team as a 30-year-old newcomer to the NHL.

KUMPEL, Mark
b. Wakefield, Massachusetts, March 7, 1961
How many players in the minors would say, thanks, but no thanks when the coach tells them to report to the NHL? That's what Kumpel did during the '84-'85 season with the Nordiques, because he was coming off an injury and didn't want to go up and look out of place. He got his chance later in the year, though, and had a decent – not spectacular – debut. He was one year out of a season with the U.S. National Team that took him through the 1984 Olympics in Sarajevo. In '85-'86, he started off like a madman, scoring six goals in the team's first seven games. He had just 4 more in the next 40, and was back in those minors he had so loved the year previous. That's the way it was for much of Kumpel's career until he retired in late 1992. Up and down. He turned to coaching, and has been gainfully employed in the minors ever since, both as an assistant and as a head coach.

Mark Kumpel

Alan Kuntz

Murray Kuntz

KUNTAR, Les
b. Elma, New York, July 28, 1969
Despite an outstanding college career in goal with St. Lawrence University, Kuntar was never given a serious chance to make the NHL. Montreal played him six times in '93-'94, and although he later signed with Philadelphia, the Flyers never found a use for him, either. Undaunted, he operated the popular Les Kuntar Goalie School.

KUNTZ, Alan
b. Toronto, Ontario, June 4, 1919
d. March 7, 1987
A short-term, wartime player, Kuntz was training in Brockville and awaiting assignment with the Canadian army when the Rangers wanted him to play, in December '42. He received permission to go to New York, and almost immediately teamed successfully with Grant Warwick on the right wing and Clint Smith at centre to form the team's top-scoring line. He scored 11 goals in just 31 games that season, but returned to the army the following year and never got his playing career back on track. The Rangers called him up for 14 games in '45-'46, but Kuntz spent the next decade in the minor pros, notably in Vancouver and Ottawa in the PCHL and QMHL, respectively. Kuntz had earned his first chance with New York based on his superb display of skill in Washington and Philadelphia, where he proved to be a scorer and passer both. He retired in 1956.

KUNTZ, Murray
b. Ottawa, Ontario, December 19, 1945
Don Cherry, GM and coach of the Rochester Americans, made some great moves at the start and finish of the '73-'74 season. He bought Kuntz for $15,000, watched him score 51 goals for the team, and then sold him to St. Louis of the NHL for $40,000. Murray the K had scored gobs of goals wherever he had played, but after seven games with the Blues he was back in the minors and never scored prolifically again. He had won the Calder Cup in the spring of '73, which was what prompted Cherry to buy the left winger in the first place.

In 2001, he became the first Finn inducted into the Hockey Hall of Fame.
JARI KURRI

KURRI, Jari
b. Helsinki, Finland, May 18, 1960
It was at the European Junior Championships in 1978 that Kurri first rose to a prominence that would one day lead to the NHL and then the Hockey Hall of Fame. In the gold-medal game, he scored early in overtime to give Finland a 4-3 win over the virtually unbeatable Soviets. He returned to his club team in Jokerit, and in the coming seasons stood out in the World Junior Championships and the 1980 Olympics in Lake Placid. That summer, on the advice of European scout Matti Vaisanen, Edmonton drafted Kurri 69th overall. He joined the Oilers that fall and never looked back. Kurri arrived in Edmonton not knowing a word of English. Fortunately, he had two Finnish teammates in Matti Hagman and Risto Siltanen who helped ease his transition, and on the ice his adaptation to the NHL game couldn't have gone any easier when, 19 games into the season, he was put on a line with Wayne Gretzky. He scored a hat trick in their first game together – all goals assisted by Gretzky – and then went into a 17-game tailspin. Still, by season's end he had 32 goals as a 20-year-old rookie, a figure he repeated the next season. Year three saw him produce 45 goals and 104 points, and in '83-'84 he had 52 goals and 113 points, the first of 4 successive 50-goal seasons and the second of five 100-point years. Not surprisingly, the Oilers won the Cup in '84 and '85, and

again in '87 and '88. Kurri and Gretzky were among the league's top combinations, and the '87 victory was especially sweet because Kurri's second-period goal in game seven proved to be the game winner. He stayed with the Oilers until 1990, two years after number 99 had been traded to L.A. He demanded a trade to the Kings, and when GM Glen Sather refused to grant him this wish, Kurri packed up and headed to Italy to play for a year. Realizing a trade was better than losing Kurri's talents altogether, Sather traded him the next year, and the great pair was reunited in L.A. Kurri's scoring power had diminished, but he was still capable of some magic on Gretzky's right wing and was part of the team that went to the finals in 1993. He ended his career with a string of cameos with the Rangers, Anaheim, and Colorado, never replicating the special feeling with another centre that he had with the Great One. Nevertheless, Kurri retired in 1998 as the top-scoring European of all time. He finished with an incredible 601 goals and 1,398 points and played in an incredible 200 playoff games. At every stage of his career, he played for his country whenever occasion permitted. These appearances included the 1981, '87, and '91 Canada Cups, three World Championships (including a silver in 1994), the 1996 World Cup, and the 1998 Olympics in Nagano at which the Finns beat Canada for the bronze medal. Although he won only one individual trophy – the Lady Byng in '84-'85 – Kurri played in eight All-Star Games. He returned to Finland where he worked as a TV commentator, and he was an assistant coach for Suomi at the 2002 Olympics in Salt Lake City. In 2001, he became the first Finn inducted into the Hockey Hall of Fame, ensuring this national hero even greater fame in a land where many of today's NHL stars are born.

KURT, Gary
b. Kitchener, Ontario, March 9, 1947
You can't give up 60 goals in about 14 full games (16 appearances) and expect to earn a full-time goaler's job in the NHL – even if your team is the California Golden Seals. And a 1-7-5 record just doesn't look good on a resumé. Kurt had three outstanding seasons in the AHL and moved on to the WHA, his career coming to a close in 1977.

KURTENBACH, Orland
("The Enforcer")
b. Cudworth, Saskatchewan, September 7, 1936
He was considered one tough hombre in his playing days, a large, two-way player who was a leader on and off the ice. He played with three Original Six teams during the 1960s but when the Rangers left him exposed in the 1970 Expansion Draft, Vancouver pounced. The Canucks made him their inaugural captain, and he responded with his only two 20-goal seasons in his first 2 years with the team. He retired in 1974 after a bad knee injury and started coaching, first in Seattle and then winning the Adams Cup with Tulsa of the CHL. In 1976, Vancouver brought him back as head coach, but after two poor seasons he was shown the door. Kurtenbach moved to Richmond, B.C., where he ran a general insurance business and developed a driving range in nearby Surrey. He later made his way to White Rock, B.C., where he became a stockbroker.

KURTZ, Justin
b. Winnipeg, Manitoba, January 14, 1977
Even though he has only recently played in his first NHL game, Kurtz was drafted by Winnipeg, that pre-Phoenix dinosaur of a team classified as "small market." Ironically, he later played for the Moose in that city, the IHL team that replaced the Jets. In 2001, Vancouver signed him and Kurtz stuck around for 27 games, though he was back in the minors to start 2002-03.

KURVERS, Tom
b. Minneapolis, Minnesota, September 14, 1962
When Tom Kurvers graduated from the University of Minnesota-Duluth in 1984, the NHL was expecting a triumphal entrance for the young American. He had good size and a great shot; he could move the puck and act as a fourth forward when the occasion called for it. Montreal drafted him and roomed him with Chris Chelios on the road, and the two were integral to the team's surprise run to the 1986 Stanley Cup. In short order, though, the Habs traded Kurvers to Buffalo and the Sabres sent him on to New Jersey. In his two years with the Devils, he developed into a first-rate defenceman, but the Devils traded him to Toronto for a 1st-round draft choice in 1991. Kurvers initially refused to join a Canadian team, but in the end agreed to go to the Leafs. Early in the new season, though, he tore his knee and the Leafs traded the now-less-mobile blueliner. Meanwhile, at the draft, Jersey used the Leafs selection to take Scott Niedermayer. Kurvers moved around again during his final 3 seasons, oddly playing for 7 teams in an 11-year career despite his excellent reputation. After retiring, he became a scout for the Phoenix Coyotes.

KURYLUK, Merv
b. Yorkton, Saskatchewan, August 10, 1937
Chicago coach Billy Reay brought Kuryluk up for the start of the 1962 playoffs, but the plan backfired. In Kuryluk's first game, March 27, 1962, the Hawks lost to Montreal 2-1. In his second game, they lost 4-3. Kuryluk never played in the NHL again. He continued to play in the minors, though, where he scored goals and contributed to his team's successes until his retirement in 1965.

KUSHNER, Dale
b. Terrace, British Columbia, June 13, 1966
Kushner was a right winger on the 1989 Memorial Cup-winning Medicine Hat Tigers but it wasn't until after that win, at age 21, that the Islanders signed him as a free agent. They gave him a couple of games a short time later but let him sign with Philadelphia in the summer of 1990. The Flyers made him part of the team for '90-'91 and a bit of the following year, and then it was down to the minors for Kushner.

KUTLAK, Zdenek
b. Ceske Budejovice, Czechoslovakia (Czech Republic), February 13, 1980
A big but mild defenceman, Kutlak is still getting his feet wet in pro hockey, struggling to make it with the Bruins while playing in the system with Providence. He was a low selection in the 2000 draft (237th overall) and so far Kutlak has played to that draft position.

Gary Kurt

Orland Kurtenbach

Tom Kurvers

Merv Kuryluk

KUZNETSOV, Maxim

b. Pavlodar, Soviet Union (Kazakhstan), March 24, 1977

Over the last decade, Detroit has been able to incorporate Russian players into the NHL more successfully than just about any other team, a fact that bodes well for young Kuznetsov. He is part of the next generation of Russians on the team, learning from and hopefully replacing the likes of Igor Larionov, Slava Fetisov, and Vyacheslav Kozlov. Scotty Bowman worked the defenceman into the lineup in the player's first two seasons (2000-02), and now it is up to Kuznetsov himself to earn a place on the team through his play rather than his potential.

KUZNIK, Greg

b. Prince George, British Columbia, June 12, 1978

One game with Carolina in 2000-01 qualifies Kuznik for active membership of the one-game wonder club, but in a career that has passed in the minors it is tenuous at best if he will make a second or longer appearance in the NHL. He graduated from Seattle of the WHL in 1998 after being drafted by Hartford two years earlier.

Dmitri Kvartalnov

KUZYK, Ken

b. Toronto, Ontario, August 11, 1953

The Toronto boy went to Boston University for hockey and school and never came back. He played two years with the woeful Cleveland Barons (1976-78) in a minor-league career rooted in the Central league, and when his playing days were done he turned to coaching. He settled in New Hampshire and has become a fixture with the St. Anselm Hawks in one capacity or another since 1985.

Oleg Kvasha

KVARTALNOV, Dmitri

b. Voskresensk, Soviet Union (Russia), March 25, 1966

His was truly a swift rise and a perplexingly swift demise in the NHL. Kvartalnov joined the Bruins in 1992 as a mature 26-year-old left winger, fresh off a season in the IHL in which he led the league in goals and points and was named the league's best rookie. During one stretch in the early part of the season with the B's, he scored eight goals in as many games playing on a line with Joé Juneau. On the year, he scored 30 goals and 72 points, numbers suggesting stardom. The year after, though, he played half the season in the minors, and the year after that he was back in Europe, where he has been ever since, playing in the obscure shadows of leagues in Switzerland, Germany, and Austria, far away from the brilliance of his NHL debut.

Bill Kyle

KVASHA, Oleg

b. Moscow, Soviet Union (Russia), July 26, 1978

The big left winger hit the NHL after a year in the AHL as a 19-year-old, but after 2 years with Florida he was part of a big deal involving primarily young players. The Panthers sent Oleg Kvasha and Mark Parrish to the Islanders for Roberto Luongo and Olli Jokinen. On Long Island, Kvasha has been given plenty of ice time and a chance to develop, but he still has yet to reach his full potential according to coaches' expectations.

KWIATKOWSKI, Joel

b. Kindersley, Saskatchewan, March 22, 1977

Drafted by Dallas in 1996, Kwiatkowski signed as a free agent with Anaheim two years later. The Ducks, though, kept him in Cincinnati until trading him to Ottawa in the summer of 2000 for Patrick Traverse. Since then, Kwiatkowski has made a few appearances with the Senators, but not enough to make him feel like a member of the team. A big defenceman, he's trying to crack the lineup of a team that is fairly solid on the blueline.

Kwong intended to stay in Europe for a year – he wound up staying for 15.
LARRY KWONG

KWONG, Larry ("King Kwong")

b. Vernon, British Columbia, June 17, 1923

A unique life that crossed through the NHL, Kwong, was the first Chinese Canadian to make it to the big show. He played in and around Vernon in his youth and then spent two years in the army, reaching the rank of corporal while stationed in Red Deer and Wetaskiwin. After being discharged, he joined the New York Rovers when he attended the Rangers camp and was assigned to the minors. He played in the last game of the '47-'48 season with the Rangers and then moved on to Valleyfield and the Quebec league, where he stayed for many years. He started a restaurant, Larry Kwong's, but when he left for Europe in 1957 his brother ran it. Kwong intended to stay in Europe for a year – he wound up staying for 15. He played in Switzerland, and Britain, and then retired to Switzerland where he worked in a sporting goods store. He earned a diploma to teach tennis in the summers, and in 1969 his brother joined him for three years. They both returned to Canada in 1972 to run Food-Vale supermarkets in Calgary, a job that kept Kwong busy until he retired in 1995.

KYLE, Bill

b. Dysart, Saskatchewan, December 23, 1923
d. Regina, Saskatchewan, April 16, 1968

Kyle joined the Canadian Infantry Corps right after junior hockey, and when he resumed his skating career he did so out west. He led the league in scoring one season with Portland and in 1948 he moved back to Regina, where he had a fruitful dual career. On ice, he was a speedy scoring sensation. Off ice, he and brother, Walter, formed Kyle Brothers Sporting Goods that specialized in making crests and uniforms for sports teams in the city. In fact, they spent all their non-hockey time at the store, cutting the crests, balancing the books, and taking the orders. In the summer, the pair played for the Regina Caps of the Southern Saskatchewan Baseball League. Kyle had his chance with the New York Rangers for two games in '49-'50 and another game the following year, after which he returned to Regina and became playing coach for the Capitals. He remained in Regina to continue at his store after his coaching days were over. He suffered a heart attack in March 1968 and never came out of hospital.

KYLE, Walter "Gus"
b. Dysart, Saskatchewan, September 11, 1921
d. Afton, Missouri, November 17, 1996

Trivia is an endless trove of interesting and useless information. Did you know, for instance, that in the 1930s a patrolman with the Northwest Mounties could not get married until he had served seven years? Kyle found that out the hard way. He was stationed just above the Maine border, fell in love with a local girl, and had to secure his release from the Mounties so he could marry her. And he did. He also played hockey. Most of his career took place in the minors, but he played 1949-51 with the Rangers when his brother, Bill, was there. The difference was that Bill's was a brief appearance and Gus stayed the year. He also played the following season with the Rangers. He was a Chatty Cathy with a great sense of humour and a practical joker, and on the ice he ensured that opponents kept their heads up. He retired in 1956 to coach in Calgary and later in Saint John, and he moved on to lead Chicago's farm team in St. Louis for five seasons (1961-66). When the league doubled to 12 teams in '67, the Blues hired him as sales director and he later became a colour commentator for the radio broadcasts. He was fired in 1983, and a short time later he suffered what friends say was a related heart attack. Hockey had been his life, and now he was out of the game. For 18 years, Kyle worked in the insurance business in St. Louis by day. Although he was brought back to the radio a while later, he suffered another heart attack in 1991, and his weakening heart eventually led to a fatal attack five years later.

KYLLONEN, Markku
b. Joensuu, Finland, February 15, 1962
That Kyllonen made it to the NHL at all is pretty

Kypreos sat out the year with post-concussion syndrome.
NICK KYPREOS

amazing, because he played only one season of first division hockey in Finland. The rest of his career passed in divisions two and three, and in countries with even poorer quality of play. Nonetheless, the experimenting Winnipeg Jets played him for nine games in 1988-89 and Kyllonen finished the season in the minors, his only North American experience.

KYPREOS, Nick ("Kipper")
b. Toronto, Ontario, June 4, 1966
No, fighting doesn't *usually* cause injury to the combatants, but that's information that mean precious little to Kypreos, or any fan who remembers seeing a closeup of his bloodied and unconscious face on the ice at Madison Square Garden after being punched out by Ryan VandenBussche. The fight occurred in an exhibition game prior to the '97-'98 season, and Kypreos sat out the year with post-concussion syndrome. A year later, though, he wasn't exactly a new man, except that he was smart enough to call it quits while he could still walk and talk. He fought VandenBussche in the first place because that was his role during his career. He never scored much, never got his share of minutes, but always fought when the occasion called for it. A team guy, as they say. He remained in Toronto and started working as a commentator for the fledgling Sportsnet cable station.

KYTE, Jim
b. Ottawa, Ontario, March 21, 1964
In some respects, skill is the least important ingredient for success. Determination and perseverance and ambition can overcome lack of skill, and Kyte had a will so powerful that being nearly completely deaf didn't dissuade him in the least from playing in the NHL. His father, after all, had a serious hearing impairment yet was named athlete of the half-century at St. Francis Xavier University in Nova Scotia and a substitute for Canada's high jump team at the Olympics one year. Jim's four brothers also suffered hereditary impairment. For Kyte, lack of hearing was as normal as wanting to be an NHL player. When Winnipeg drafted him 12th overall in 1982, no one in the organization knew that he played with two hearing aids. He was a physical and combative defenceman, large and imposing, and that's all they cared about. Nearly 600 games and 13 years later, Kyte finally played his last in the league, but his successes provided no end of inspiration to deaf kids all over. He coached and held clinics and worked with deaf people of all kinds, showing them how unimportant hearing is if you really want to succeed. He didn't win a Stanley Cup or an individual award, but his career was, in many ways, so much more important than those familiar symbols of hockey success.

Gus Kyle

Markku Kyllonen

Jim Kyte

LAAKSONEN, Antti ("Laakso")
b. Tammela, Finland, October 3, 1973

Laaksonen achieved the greater part of his reputation as a checker on a line with Wes Walz and Cam Stewart with the Wild, though he was the first player in (young) franchise history to score a hat trick. He had signed as a free agent after Boston had let him go. The left winger realized a dream in the spring of 2001 when he won a silver medal with Finland at the World Championships.

LABADIE, Michel "Mike"
b. St. Francis D'Assisi, Quebec, August 17, 1932

One sure way to draw attention to yourself is to break a record held by a couple of guys named Béliveau and Geoffrion. So, when a speedy 20-year-old named Michel Labadie scored 8 goals in a single game while playing for Quebec in junior, everyone took notice and decided to watch him a little more closely. And the Rangers decided to try his magic in the NHL for three games. Labadie didn't score and, amazingly, he was never given another chance to play. He became a staple with the Quebec Aces under coach Punch Imlach and later travelled around the AHL, but he never captured the imagination of fans or scouts the way he did that one night back in January 1953.

LaBARBERA, Jason
b. Burnaby, British Columbia, January 18, 1980

Surely he'll get another chance in the nets with someone, at some time, but for now a 10-minute stint with the Rangers on October 14, 2001, stands as his only NHL time. The goalie didn't allow a goal, but he was dispatched to the minors and hasn't seen Madison Square Garden since. He's part of the new breed of goalie – large and quick and a standup stopper who covers his own rebounds.

LABATTE, Neil
b. Toronto, Ontario, April 24, 1957

Labatte's five-year pro career was mostly a Salt Lake City affair in the Central league, spackled by two brief appearances with St. Louis in '78-'79 and '81-'82. He later wound up in Texas, where he coached kids teams in Dallas.

LABBE, Jean-Francois
b. Sherbrooke, Quebec, June 15, 1972

By the time Labbe played his first NHL game at age 27 in 1999 he had been owned by 4 NHL teams and won just about every honour possible outside the league. He was a star in junior in the Quebec league. He was the top goalie and rookie of the year in the Colonial League in 1993-94. He was top goalie and MVP in the AHL in 1996-97. Yet no team that acquired his rights ever wanted to use him until the Rangers called him up for one game in which he allowed only three goals. After that, he was on the move again, and two years later played three times for Columbus just before his thirtieth birthday.

L'ABBE, Maurice "Moe"
b. Montreal, Quebec, August 12, 1947

He can boast forever and a day that one night in the Central league, while playing for Dallas, he scored five goals in a game. That was the same number of games Chicago dressed him for in '72-'73 – five. The right winger spent most of his time in Texas before retiring in 1976.

LABELLE, Marc
b. Maniwaki, Quebec, December 20, 1969

Growing up in Quebec, playing junior for Victoriaville – les Tigres – and signing as a free agent with the Habs, you just don't think that one day you'll be getting a paycheque from the El Paso Buzzards. But, yes, that's the fate that befell Labelle, a fighter who ran his way through a variety of leagues while punching with the Dallas Stars in the late 1990s for nine games. He was also owned by Ottawa and Florida, but no one else gave him time outside leagues that made the "I" look like the best.

LaBINE, Leo ("The Lion"/ "The Haileybury Hurricane"/ "The Magnificent Screwball")
b. Haileybury, Ontario, July 22, 1931

One of the all-time great hockey photographs shows a bowed Sugar Jim Henry shaking hands with a bleeding Maurice Richard after the Montreal star scored to eliminate Boston from the 1953 semifinals. As the story goes, Richard was knocked unconscious, came back undaunted, and took the Habs to the finals. What no one remembers is that it was LaBine, Richard's career nemesis, who had knocked the Rocket out. LaBine wasn't big, but he was as ferocious and brutal on ice as any forward of the Original Six. He also had a sense of humour on the ice and might be the grandfather of all trash talkers, such was his rep for trying to throw players off their game with a few sharp words. He started in Montreal's training camp as a youngster, but caused so much trouble the Habs simply told him to get lost. Boston signed him and felt the same way, but the B's also saw the value of such a disturber. He stayed with the Bruins for a decade, finished with Detroit, and then played in Los Angeles in the WHL for five seasons. He returned to Ontario and settled in North Bay, where he worked for Carling O'Keefe Breweries for 12 years. He then moved to Husband Trans as a sales rep for the CN transportation company, retiring in 1995.

LABOSSIERE, Gord
b. St. Boniface, Manitoba, January 2, 1940

Critics of expansion pointed directly at players like Labossiere and said, "See, the league is diluted now." Prior to 1967, he had two brief flings in the NHL and didn't score a goal despite being a prolific scorer in the minors. After expansion he had semi-full-time work for a few years and scored only a few goals, proof that what he had accomplished in the minors was worthless in the NHL. In fact, he won the scoring championship in the AHL in '66-'67 with the Quebec Aces, but the 40 goals he scored that year translated to just 13 with L.A. the following season. He earned a reputation for being a so-so skater who was good at getting the puck out of the corners. Labossiere wound up as an assistant coach for half a season before jumping to the WHA in 1972 to join the Houston Aeros. He stayed there four years and played with the Howes but was released at camp in 1976.

Antti Laaksonen

Marc Labelle

Gord Labossiere

Leo LaBine
(opposite page)

Eric Lacroix

Pierre Lacroix

Randy Ladouceur

Nathan Lafayette

**Christian
Laflamme**

LACROIX, Eric

b. Montreal, Quebec, July 15, 1971

While his dad was GM of Quebec, Eric hoped and prayed that he wouldn't have to play there – and he didn't. But later, when the team moved to Colorado, Pierre Lacroix did, indeed, acquire his son, from Los Angeles, in 1996. And after retiring, Eric had a job waiting for him, as video coach in Colorado. Eric had been a fine prospect in the Toronto system until the Leafs sent him to the Kings in a package of minor names that amounted to little. He played for the Avs between the Cups, missing the '96 celebration and departing before the 2001 victory. He retired young and worked for his dad as the video coach for the Avs.

LACROIX, Pierre

b. Quebec City, Quebec,
April 11, 1959

More often than not, great juniors don't become great NHLers. Equally, most great GMs in the NHL had pedestrian careers as players. Lacroix fits both these descriptions. In 1978-79, the defenceman had an amazing 137 points and was named Canada's best junior player. Yet his four years in the NHL were highlighted only by their sheer banality and lack of follow-up to the great junior years. Lacroix's NHL time more or less ended in the summer of 1983 when he was seriously injured in a car crash. He needed a five-hour operation on a perforated aorta and he missed an entire year recovering. During this time, he studied insurance, but when he felt better he decided to play again, in Europe, where he could forge a career as coach as well. He returned to Canada in 1994 and became GM of the Nordiques, taking the team to Colorado in 1995 and winning the Cup at the end of the year. Since then, he has won another Cup and established the team as one of the more consistently successful in the game. Under his guidance, the team acquired Patrick Roy and signed a host of stars to long-term contracts, notably Joe Sakic, Rob Blake, and Peter Forsberg. The team's on-ice success also ensured the success of a new building for the team, the Pepsi Centre.

LADOUCEUR, Randy

b. Brockville, Ontario, June 30, 1960

He didn't quite make it to 1,000 games, but for an undrafted defenceman who never made the spotlight, 14 years and 930 games isn't too shabby. Ladouceur was a formidable presence in his own end, though in all those year with Detroit, Hartford, and Anaheim he never made it past the first round of the playoffs. He captained his last two teams, and after retiring in 1996 joined the staff of Carolina as an assistant coach, a position he has held ever since.

LAFAYETTE, Nathan

b. New Westminster, British Columbia, February 17, 1973

After a decent junior career in Ontario, Lafayette joined St. Louis in 1993, where he began a roller-coaster career that had him move to four NHL teams and as many AHL teams before settling down with Los Angeles. He never played a full season in the NHL and suffered a setback in March '98 when a concussion caused him to miss the last quarter of the year. He retired in 2000 after almost a full year in the minors. In 1993, Lafayette played on Canada's gold-medal WJC team.

LAFERRIERE, Rick

b. Hawkesbury, Ontario, January 3, 1961

Yes, he had a good junior career, and, yes, he was drafted, but it became clear pretty quickly to Laferriere that he wasn't going to be the next great goalie to stop NHL shooters night in, night out. He played exactly one period with Colorado on February 23, 1982, and after a brief time in the minors retired to start a successful career in real estate. For the last 16 years and more, he has sold property in Barrie and the surrounding cottage country.

LAFLAMME, Christian

b. St. Charles, Quebec,
November 24, 1976

A once-promising defenceman, Laflamme's stock has dropped considerably recently. He has moved around and been hampered by injuries and is no longer a mainstay on any team's blueline. Chicago drafted him in 1995 and made him a regular for two seasons, but since then Laflamme has had trouble staying with one team.

**He was the youngest player
to reach 1,000 career points.**
GUY LAFLEUR

LAFLEUR, Guy ("The Flower")

b. Thurso, Quebec, September 20, 1951

The effort that Montreal GM Sam Pollock took to ensure Lafleur started his career in a Montreal sweater is without compare. Pollock had acquired Oakland's first draft choice for 1971 because he was certain that the Seals would finish dead last in the NHL, thus ensuring first selection in the Amateur Draft. With that selection, Pollock planned on taking Lafleur because, for one, the kid was averaging two goals a game in junior with the Quebec Remparts. But as the '70-'71 season unfolded, the Seals played decent hockey and the L.A. Kings were playing themselves into last place. On January 26, 1971, Pollock took action. He traded star forward Ralph Backstrom to Los Angeles for Ray Fortin and Gord Labossiere. Pollock had no interest in either player he acquired. What he was interested in was giving the Kings a good player to help prop up the team, improve its record, and lift it above Oakland to ensure that the

LAAKSONEN, Antti ("Laakso")
b. Tammela, Finland, October 3, 1973
Laaksonen achieved the greater part of his reputation as a checker on a line with Wes Walz and Cam Stewart with the Wild, though he was the first player in (young) franchise history to score a hat trick. He had signed as a free agent after Boston had let him go. The left winger realized a dream in the spring of 2001 when he won a silver medal with Finland at the World Championships.

LABADIE, Michel "Mike"
b. St. Francis D'Assisi, Quebec, August 17, 1932
One sure way to draw attention to yourself is to break a record held by a couple of guys named Béliveau and Geoffrion. So, when a speedy 20-year-old named Michel Labadie scored 8 goals in a single game while playing for Quebec in junior, everyone took notice and decided to watch him a little more closely. And the Rangers decided to try his magic in the NHL for three games. Labadie didn't score and, amazingly, he was never given another chance to play. He became a staple with the Quebec Aces under coach Punch Imlach and later travelled around the AHL, but he never captured the imagination of fans or scouts the way he did that one night back in January 1953.

LaBARBERA, Jason
b. Burnaby, British Columbia, January 18, 1980
Surely he'll get another chance in the nets with someone, at some time, but for now a 10-minute stint with the Rangers on October 14, 2001, stands as his only NHL time. The goalie didn't allow a goal, but he was dispatched to the minors and hasn't seen Madison Square Garden since. He's part of the new breed of goalie – large and quick and a standup stopper who covers his own rebounds.

LABATTE, Neil
b. Toronto, Ontario, April 24, 1957
Labatte's five-year pro career was mostly a Salt Lake City affair in the Central league, spackled by two brief appearances with St. Louis in '78-'79 and '81-'82. He later wound up in Texas, where he coached kids teams in Dallas.

LABBE, Jean-Francois
b. Sherbrooke, Quebec, June 15, 1972
By the time Labbe played his first NHL game at age 27 in 1999 he had been owned by 4 NHL teams and won just about every honour possible outside the league. He was a star in junior in the Quebec league. He was the top goalie and rookie of the year in the Colonial League in 1993-94. He was top goalie and MVP in the AHL in 1996-97. Yet no team that acquired his rights ever wanted to use him until the Rangers called him up for one game in which he allowed only three goals. After that, he was on the move again, and two years later played three times for Columbus just before his thirtieth birthday.

L'ABBE, Maurice "Moe"
b. Montreal, Quebec, August 12, 1947
He can boast forever and a day that one night in the Central league, while playing for Dallas, he scored five goals in a game. That was the same number of games Chicago dressed him for in '72-'73 – five. The right winger spent most of his time in Texas before retiring in 1976.

LABELLE, Marc
b. Maniwaki, Quebec, December 20, 1969
Growing up in Quebec, playing junior for Victoriaville – les Tigres – and signing as a free agent with the Habs, you just don't think that one day you'll be getting a paycheque from the El Paso Buzzards. But, yes, that's the fate that befell Labelle, a fighter who ran his way through a variety of leagues while punching with the Dallas Stars in the late 1990s for nine games. He was also owned by Ottawa and Florida, but no one else gave him time outside leagues that made the "I" look like the best.

LaBINE, Leo ("The Lion"/ "The Haileybury Hurricane"/ "The Magnificent Screwball")
b. Haileybury, Ontario, July 22, 1931
One of the all-time great hockey photographs shows a bowed Sugar Jim Henry shaking hands with a bleeding Maurice Richard after the Montreal star scored to eliminate Boston from the 1953 semifinals. As the story goes, Richard was knocked unconscious, came back undaunted, and took the Habs to the finals. What no one remembers is that it was LaBine, Richard's career nemesis, who had knocked the Rocket out. LaBine wasn't big, but he was as ferocious and brutal on ice as any forward of the Original Six. He also had a sense of humour on the ice and might be the grandfather of all trash talkers, such was his rep for trying to throw players off their game with a few sharp words. He started in Montreal's training camp as a youngster, but caused so much trouble the Habs simply told him to get lost. Boston signed him and felt the same way, but the B's also saw the value of such a disturber. He stayed with the Bruins for a decade, finished with Detroit, and then played in Los Angeles in the WHL for five seasons. He returned to Ontario and settled in North Bay, where he worked for Carling O'Keefe Breweries for 12 years. He then moved to Husband Trans as a sales rep for the CN transportation company, retiring in 1995.

LABOSSIERE, Gord
b. St. Boniface, Manitoba, January 2, 1940
Critics of expansion pointed directly at players like Labossiere and said, "See, the league is diluted now." Prior to 1967, he had two brief flings in the NHL and didn't score a goal despite being a prolific scorer in the minors. After expansion he had semi-full-time work for a few years and scored only a few goals, proof that what he had accomplished in the minors was worthless in the NHL. In fact, he won the scoring championship in the AHL in '66-'67 with the Quebec Aces, but the 40 goals he scored that year translated to just 13 with L.A. the following season. He earned a reputation for being a so-so skater who was good at getting the puck out of the corners. Labossiere wound up as an assistant coach for half a season before jumping to the WHA in 1972 to join the Houston Aeros. He stayed there four years and played with the Howes but was released at camp in 1976.

Antti Laaksonen

Marc Labelle

Gord Labossiere

Leo LaBine
(opposite page)

Max Labovitch

Dan Labraaten

Yvon Labre

Patrick Labrecque

Elmer Lach

LABOVITCH, Max
b. Winnipeg, Manitoba, January 18, 1924

Whenever a Jew made it to the NHL, it was news, especially to the locals. So, when Jewish Winnipeggers learned that their Max had been called up to the Rangers, they were proud. It was for only five games, but that was five more than most players got. He went on to play a little bit in the IHL, and his achievements, small though they were, got him into the Manitoba Hockey Hall of Fame.

LABRAATEN, Dan ("Rusty")
b. Grums, Sweden, June 9, 1951

Labraaten turned pro with the Winnipeg Jets in 1976 when Detroit was hoping to sign him. Then, Detroit took him in 1978 when the Jets were hoping to re-sign him. He was so popular because the winger could streak down the left side like few others in the game. He had been a top international player for Tre Kronor in the previous decade and Canadians first saw him in the '76 Canada Cup. In Detroit, he played on the top line with Dale McCourt and Vaclav Nedomansky, scoring 19 goals his first year and 30 the next. His output trailed well off after that, though, and he returned to Sweden to play out his last years. After retiring, he became a scout, working his way up to head of European scouting for the New Jersey Devils.

LABRE, Yvon
b. Sudbury, Ontario, November 29, 1949

Hard work and relentlessness earned Labre every shift he ever played at every level. He had little talent and big arms with which to fight, but most of all he had miles and miles of heart. He made his debut with Pittsburgh in 1970, but he made history after Washington claimed him in the 1974 Expansion Draft. He was the most popular player in the city and the key to the team's defence, even though he played on an awful team that allowed more goals than any other in NHL history. In 1976, he was named team captain, but in the next few years he suffered two serious knee injuries that forced his early retirement in late 1980. He became the first, and still only, Caps player to have his sweater retired, and his number 7 still floats high above the team when they play at home. Labre settled in Washington and served as the director of community relations for the team and operated hockey schools and clinics in the city as well.

LABRECQUE, Patrick
b. Laval, Quebec, March 6, 1971

If he's French and he skates, the Habs will give him a chance. And if he's a goalie, they'll tell him he's the next Jacques Plante before tossing him behind their 1990s defence. Labrecque didn't have a particularly special junior career, and his time in the minors was not marked by special successes or achievements. Nonetheless, the Habs put him in two games during the '95-'96 season, his only NHL time, of course.

LABRIE, Guy
b. St. Charles Bellechasse, Quebec, August 11, 1920

You can count on one hand the number of NHL players who can ask their grandfathers, "What was it like to play in the NHL in your day?" Sure enough,

though, P.C. Drouin of the modern Bruins could ask that of his grandpa, Guy Labrie, who played with the Bruins and Rangers during the war. He played most of his career in Quebec, and he can always boast of having scored four times in the best league of all.

LACH, Elmer
b. Nokomis, Saskatchewan, January 22, 1918

Had there been a Bill Masterton Trophy in Lach's day, he likely would have won the award for dedication and perseverance on at least three occasions. His ability, his strength of character, to continue playing despite serious injury was a marvel to teammates and opponents alike. Lach played minor hockey in Saskatchewan before joining Montreal in 1940. He showed tremendous skating ability, determination in the heat of battle, and creativity with the puck. No sooner had his rookie season ended than he hurt his elbow in the first game of the next season and was gone for the year. He returned hale and hearty for '42-'43 and scored 18 goals, and the year after coach Dick Irvin put him on a line with Toe Blake and Maurice Richard. The Punch Line was born, and it scored goals at will for the Canadiens. Lach accounted for 24, but he had double that number in assists and the team marched on to win the Stanley Cup. The next year, he led the league in assists and points and the year after the team won another championship. Lach's year in '46-'47 was cut in half after a near tragedy. In February 1947, he was checked and fell to the ice, hitting his head and suffering a serious skull fracture. Doctors told him his career was over, but he not only came back to play, he led the league in scoring. The next year, he suffered a broken jaw and missed half the year again, but again he returned the following season to reclaim his spot on the Punch Line. By the time he retired in 1954, he had scored 215 goals and had 623 points to his credit, number one on the all-time list for both assists and total points. His large assists total was due to his superior passing and, of course, passing to future Hall of Famers who could score didn't hurt his cause. He won a final Cup in 1953, and he won it in style. It was his goal at 1:22 of overtime that gave the Habs a 1-0 win over Boston in game five of the series and earned the team the Cup. Lach went on to coach the Junior Canadiens and then the Montreal Royals before settling into a business career in public relations with a large trucking company based in Montreal. He was inducted into the Hockey Hall of Fame in 1966.

LACHANCE, Michel
b. Quebec City, Quebec, April 11, 1955

Michel's only chance of making it to the NHL was with the Colorado Rockies, where, for 21 games, he got the opportunity to wear major-league togs. The defenceman graduated from the Remparts in Quebec without being drafted, and he retired in 1981 after a season in France.

LACHANCE, Scott
b. Charlottesville, Virginia, October 22, 1972

Right from the start, Lachance forged a reputation and career as a defensive defenceman who could move the puck up the ice quickly and efficiently. Still, it was surprising to see such a player drafted 4th overall in 1991, by the Islanders. He had just finished his freshman season at Boston University, and '91-'92 proved to be a busy and rewarding season for him. He played for the U.S. at both the World Juniors and the Olympics, and at season's end joined the Isles for a few games. He never played a game in the minors. In eight seasons with the team, he provided depth on the blueline, but in that time the team played exactly three playoff games. He was later acquired by Montreal and Vancouver, but wherever he went, a playoff drought followed, until the spring of 2002 when the Canucks finally made it back to the post-season.

LACHER, Blaine
b. Medicine Hat, Alberta, September 5, 1970
It's easy to play well in your first NHL game – how can it not be? But can a player be as good in his 100th game and 500th and 1,000th? Most often, the answer is, simply, no. Lacher was a goalie out of Lake Superior State with two notes on his report card: one, he set a record with a shutout streak of more than five games; two, discipline problems almost had him cut from the team. The Bruins signed him as a free agent in 1994, and in his first 3 games with the team to start the new season he was 3-0-0 and gave up just 2 goals. He was called the Lack Net Monster by media and fans hoped he was the new saviour in goal, but his cockiness drove shotgun to his skills and eventually took control. By year's end, he proved entirely fallible and ordinary, and the year after he was a spare part who was out of the league and gone. He could not sustain the great start that he rode on emotion.

LACOMBE, Francois
b. Montreal, Quebec, February 24, 1948
Here is what expansion really meant. In '67-'68, Lacombe was sitting on the bench with the Montreal Jr. Canadiens, unable to play himself into a regular shift. The next year, the Oakland Seals acquired him and he became a regular. The honeymoon was over after a season, though, and Lacombe was in the minors for most of the next three years until the Nordiques lured him to the WHA. He played with the team for the next seven years, and for a few games in '79-'80 when the team joined the NHL. After retiring, he turned to coaching in the AAA league in Quebec (known as QJAAAHL) where he stayed for many years, most notably with Kahnawake.

LACOMBE, Normand
b. Pierrefonds, Quebec, October 18, 1964
Another in a series of reclamation projects by Edmonton GM Glen Sather, Lacombe was given up by Buffalo after four years in the system with what the team felt were mediocre results. With the Oilers, he became a solid third- and fourth-line player, winning a Cup with the team in 1988, his first full season with the club. After two and a half seasons he was sent to the Flyers, but was forced to retire in 1991 because of chronic exertional compartment syndrome, an affliction that causes extreme pain and irritation in the shins after playing or practising.

LACOUTURE, Dan
b. Hyannis, Massachusetts, April 18, 1977
In the old days, trades always made sense: a superstar for a superstar, a goalie for a goalie, a fighter for a fighter. Today, it's all about payroll and salary structure. That's one of the reasons Edmonton traded Mariusz Czerkawski to the Islanders for Lacouture in 1997. It wasn't a good trade, as Czerkawski went on to become a terrific scorer and Lacouture became a solid, but unremarkable checker and role player. The Oilers later moved him to Pittsburgh, and he had a career year in goals with eight in 2001-02.

LACROIX, Alphonse "Frenchy"
b. Newton, Massachusetts, October 21, 1897
d. Lewiston, Maine, April 12, 1973
Lacroix played amateur hockey as a goalie for years in his home state, coming to prominence in 1924 as the starter for the U.S. Olympic team in Champoux, France. He recorded 4 successive shutouts until losing 6-1 to Canada in the gold-medal game, but on the strength of his performance he gained a greater reputation and a chance to replace a legend. In 1925, he was the Canadiens' backup goalie, a sinecure if ever there was one because incumbent Georges Vézina had played literally every game for the Habs since 1918. But on opening night of the '25-'26 season, Vézina spat up blood during the first period and Lacroix had to go into the net. Vézina died tragically a few days later, and Lacroix played five games for the team. He went on to play with the Lewiston-Auburn team, and after retiring scouted professionally for a number of years. Two of his nephews – Dick and Jean Malo – also turned out to be fine players. Lacroix followed the game closely for years and remained in Lewiston the rest of his life.

LACROIX, Andre
b. Lauzon, Quebec, June 5, 1945
Gordie Howe always said that WHA points should be included in NHL totals because scoring there was just as difficult. Time and again, though, stats suggested just the opposite was true. Case in point: Andre Lacroix. In Philadelphia's early years, he proved a 20-goal man for exactly 3 seasons. In the WHA, he had a 50-goal season, a 40-goal year, and three 30-goal efforts. The youngest of 14 children, he led the WHA in points twice, including 147 in '74-'75, almost triple his NHL best. Six times he had more than 100 points, a plateau he never came close to in the NHL. He later played with Howe in the NHL in '79-'80, when the small centre scored 3 times in 29 games. It was his last year of pro, after which he went on to become the director of hockey operations at the Oakland Ice Centre.

LACROIX, Daniel
b. Montreal, Quebec, March 11, 1969
It was six years from draft day to first NHL game, and nine years to first full NHL season for Lacroix, a skating gangster who fought all comers to get to where he went. The Rangers drafted him in 1987 during his junior fighting days, and then he fought in the AHL for a number of years before finally earning a full-time stint as a boxer with the Flyers in '96-'97. He later wound up playing in Britain after 188 NHL games spread thin over 5 teams.

Blaine Lacher

Francois Lacombe

Normand Lacombe

Andre Lacroix

Daniel Lacroix

Eric Lacroix

Pierre Lacroix

Randy Ladouceur

Nathan Lafayette

**Christian
Laflamme**

LACROIX, Eric
b. Montreal, Quebec, July 15, 1971
While his dad was GM of Quebec, Eric hoped and prayed that he wouldn't have to play there – and he didn't. But later, when the team moved to Colorado, Pierre Lacroix did, indeed, acquire his son, from Los Angeles, in 1996. And after retiring, Eric had a job waiting for him, as video coach in Colorado. Eric had been a fine prospect in the Toronto system until the Leafs sent him to the Kings in a package of minor names that amounted to little. He played for the Avs between the Cups, missing the '96 celebration and departing before the 2001 victory. He retired young and worked for his dad as the video coach for the Avs.

LACROIX, Pierre
b. Quebec City, Quebec,
April 11, 1959
More often than not, great juniors don't become great NHLers. Equally, most great GMs in the NHL had pedestrian careers as players. Lacroix fits both these descriptions. In 1978-79, the defenceman had an amazing 137 points and was named Canada's best junior player. Yet his four years in the NHL were highlighted only by their sheer banality and lack of follow-up to the great junior years. Lacroix's NHL time more or less ended in the summer of 1983 when he was seriously injured in a car crash. He needed a five-hour operation on a perforated aorta and he missed an entire year recovering. During this time, he studied insurance, but when he felt better he decided to play again, in Europe, where he could forge a career as coach as well. He returned to Canada in 1994 and became GM of the Nordiques, taking the team to Colorado in 1995 and winning the Cup at the end of the year. Since then, he has won another Cup and established the team as one of the more consistently successful in the game. Under his guidance, the team acquired Patrick Roy and signed a host of stars to long-term contracts, notably Joe Sakic, Rob Blake, and Peter Forsberg. The team's on-ice success also ensured the success of a new building for the team, the Pepsi Centre.

LADOUCEUR, Randy
b. Brockville, Ontario, June 30, 1960
He didn't quite make it to 1,000 games, but for an undrafted defenceman who never made the spotlight, 14 years and 930 games isn't too shabby. Ladouceur was a formidable presence in his own end, though in all those year with Detroit, Hartford, and Anaheim he never made it past the first round of the playoffs. He captained his last two teams, and after retiring in 1996 joined the staff of Carolina as an assistant coach, a position he has held ever since.

LAFAYETTE, Nathan
b. New Westminster, British Columbia, February 17, 1973
After a decent junior career in Ontario, Lafayette joined St. Louis in 1993, where he began a roller-coaster career that had him move to four NHL teams and as many AHL teams before settling down with Los Angeles. He never played a full season in the NHL and suffered a setback in March '98 when a concussion caused him to miss the last quarter of the year. He retired in 2000 after almost a full year in the minors. In 1993, Lafayette played on Canada's gold-medal WJC team.

LAFERRIERE, Rick
b. Hawkesbury, Ontario, January 3, 1961
Yes, he had a good junior career, and, yes, he was drafted, but it became clear pretty quickly to Laferriere that he wasn't going to be the next great goalie to stop NHL shooters night in, night out. He played exactly one period with Colorado on February 23, 1982, and after a brief time in the minors retired to start a successful career in real estate. For the last 16 years and more, he has sold property in Barrie and the surrounding cottage country.

LAFLAMME, Christian
b. St. Charles, Quebec, November 24, 1976
A once-promising defenceman, Laflamme's stock has dropped considerably recently. He has moved around and been hampered by injuries and is no longer a mainstay on any team's blueline. Chicago drafted him in 1995 and made him a regular for two seasons, but since then Laflamme has had trouble staying with one team.

**He was the youngest player
to reach 1,000 career points.**
GUY LAFLEUR

LAFLEUR, Guy ("The Flower")
b. Thurso, Quebec, September 20, 1951
The effort that Montreal GM Sam Pollock took to ensure Lafleur started his career in a Montreal sweater is without compare. Pollock had acquired Oakland's first draft choice for 1971 because he was certain that the Seals would finish dead last in the NHL, thus ensuring first selection in the Amateur Draft. With that selection, Pollock planned on taking Lafleur because, for one, the kid was averaging two goals a game in junior with the Quebec Remparts. But as the '70-'71 season unfolded, the Seals played decent hockey and the L.A. Kings were playing themselves into last place. On January 26, 1971, Pollock took action. He traded star forward Ralph Backstrom to Los Angeles for Ray Fortin and Gord Labossiere. Pollock had no interest in either player he acquired. What he was interested in was giving the Kings a good player to help prop up the team, improve its record, and lift it above Oakland to ensure that the

Seals finished last. It worked to perfection, and in the summer Pollock chose Lafleur 1st overall. Such was Lafleur's reputation that the team offered him Jean Beliveau's number 4, but Lafleur declined, in part so as not to offend Le Gros Bill, in part so as not to put even more pressure on him to live up to his pre-NHL billing. In '71-'72, hockey's most famous chain-smoker scored 29 goals, and in the next 2 years he had 28 and 21. He had his rough moments, but he was clearly a star in the making. More than that, though, he brought a charisma to the team that spoke of the long Canadiens tradition. He had long, blond hair and a fluid, fast stride down the right wing, and when he got control of the puck he literally brought the fans out of their seats. He had that intangible quality of a star, a player that symbolized a team and represented its successes. He was a hero. The '74-'75 season was the start of something great for him. He scored 53 goals and had 119 points to start a streak of 6 successive seasons of more than 50 goals and 100 points, the first player in NHL history to achieve so consistently hockey's greatest single-season milestones. He won the Art Ross Trophy 3 successive years and led the league in scoring with 60 goals in '77-'78. Not surprisingly, the team was also winning Stanley Cups along the way. He won five in all during the 1970s, and in the '77 playoffs he won the Conn Smythe Trophy. The next year, he made himself notorious after the Cup win when he borrowed the trophy without telling anyone and took it to his house in Thurso. There, he displayed it on the front lawn for any and all passers-by to see. Perhaps more amazing, though, was what Lafleur *didn't* win during his career – the Lady Byng Trophy. As the premier right winger in the league, he was forever being shadowed or being given extra "attention," as the euphemism goes for being roughed up and hacked and slashed. Yet he never retaliated, never fought, never lost control of his temper. In his 1,126 career games, he had just 399 penalty minutes. He was the youngest player to reach 1,000 career points, and he holds the record for most assists and points by a Canadiens player. In 1981, his life changed forever. He had been a carefree and popular man about town. He did many TV commercials and his face was plastered on billboards everywhere, and when someone wanted to buy him a drink he had no problem saying, yes, thanks. But in 1981, he was involved in a serious car accident and came close to losing his life. He settled down, appreciated the importance of his family, and became a more docile figure. He retired just 19 games into the '84-'85 season, feeling that he had lost some of his magic and not wanting to be a second-rate player hanging on to a position based on his reputation. He worked in public relations with the team, and in 1988 was inducted

Guy Lafleur

into the Hockey Hall of Fame. His number 10 was retired by the Canadiens, and he left the game at the top, just as he had wanted. He was just 33 when he retired, however, and the intervening three years had given him pause to appreciate his skills and good fortune. No sooner was he in the Hall than he was back on the ice, with the Rangers, and a year later he signed with the Nordiques, where he played two more years. He became only the second player, after Gordie Howe, to play in the NHL as an Honoured Member of the Hall of Fame, and he went out in style, appearing in the 1991 All-Star Game. He took another front office job with the Habs, but this time he had left all his hockey on the ice and he could go in peace. Yes, he had all the requisite stats to get into the Hall of Fame, but he also had that intangible *je ne sais quoi* that separates the greats from the merely productive, the stars from the bright lights. When Lafleur retired, there was a little less twinkle in the NHL.

LAFLEUR, Roland
b. Ottawa, Ontario, 1899
d. unknown
A lifelong Ottawan during his playing days, Lafleur made it to the NHL with the Canadiens for a single game in '24-'25.

LAFONTAINE, Pat
b. St. Louis, Missouri, February 22, 1965
One would hope that when a Hall of Fame-calibre player like Lafontaine loses his career to a concussion, the league would actively try to cut down on head injuries, but years after the player's career-ending collision nothing has been done to prevent a similar fate befalling an equally talented young star.

Pat Lafontaine

Nothing prepared him for the concussion he suffered on October 17, 1996, the result of a vicious elbow.
PAT LAFONTAINE

Lafontaine's career was nothing short of fantastic; the only thing missing was the Cup. He played teen hockey in Quebec junior rather than U.S. college, setting scoring records in the process. The Islanders drafted him 3rd overall in '83, and he more than lived up to the hype. He scored 50 goals twice, 40 goals 5 times, and 30 goals twice with the Islanders and later the Sabres. He played for the U.S. at the '87 and '91 Canada Cups, the '96 World Cup, and the 1998 Olympics in Nagano. His career was upset a few times by injury, though, notably a broken jaw in '91-'92 and a serious ACL injury in '93-'94, for which he won the Masterton Trophy after a year and a half of rehab. Nothing prepared him for the concussion he suffered on October 17, 1996, the result of a vicious elbow. It was the fifth of his career, and by far the most serious. He suffered from headaches and loss of coordination for months afterwards, and Buffalo refused to play him again, instead trading him to the Rangers in September 1997 to allow him to continue his career. He was having a decent season, played in the Olympics and scored his 1,000th NHL point, but

Bob Laforest

Mark Laforest

Claude Laforge

Pete Laframboise

Leo Lafrance

on March 16, 1998, he collided with a teammate at centre ice. He never played another game.

LAFORCE, Ernie
b. Montreal, Quebec, June 23, 1916
A big, rangy defenceman, Laforce got into one game with the Habs in '42-'43 during a lengthy career with the local Montreal Royals in senior hockey.

LAFOREST, Bob
b. Sault Ste. Marie, Ontario, May 19, 1963
The smoke and mirrors of a junior career was no more evident than in the case of Bob Laforest versus the NHL. At 18, he wasn't drafted because the scouts didn't like what they saw. But in his final year of junior, with the North Bay Trappers, he scored 58 goals playing on a line with Paul Gillis and Rick Morocco. All of a sudden those same scouts took notice. Los Angeles drafted him 89th overall and put him in 5 games, but he was relegated to the minors pretty quickly, and forever. The scouts, it seemed, had been right with their first prognosis, though brother, Mark, lasted much longer in the NHL.

LAFOREST, Mark ("Trees"/ "Bush")
b. Welland, Ontario, July 10, 1962
Goalies aren't as likely to travel from team to team with the same longevity that players do, but Laforest certainly wore his share of sweaters, from the NHL right down to an outfit called the Mohawk Valley Comets. In his first year of pro, with Detroit, he had a pitiful record of 4-21-0 playing on an equally pitiful team, and he never really improved on that in the NHL. He spent his best years in the AHL, winning top goalie honours on two occasions ('86-'87 and '90-'91). But by the time he retired in 1996, he was down in the Colonial League and had no hope of returning to the NHL, his last games coming three years previous with the fledgling Ottawa Senators.

LAFORGE, Claude
b. Sorel, Quebec, July 1, 1936
Laforge scored his first goal in 1958 and immediately sent the puck home for mantel privileges. Norm Ullman and Red Kelly assisted on the score, but the left winger didn't light the lamp too often in the NHL. He played pro for 17 seasons but appeared in just 193 NHL games, mostly with the Wings and ending with the Flyers during their first 2 seasons. The AHL was a different story for Laforge, who routinely had 20 goals in a season there and was a top scorer for his team with reliable consistency.

LAFORGE, Marc
b. Sudbury, Ontario, January 3, 1968
One would think a lifetime suspension from a league would have an adverse effect on a player's career. Apparently, not so. On November 6, 1987, Laforge went ballistic during a brawl in junior with Sudbury, punching eight players as they were held in true roller-derby fashion and then knocking the goalie's head onto the ice repeatedly. OHL commissioner Dave Branch banned the animal from the league for the next two years, but Hartford, the team that had drafted him, still ended up signing him and using him

in nine games. He played a few games with Edmonton four years later, and since then has been fighting his way through the minors, trying to beat people up with little regard for the puck or the goal.

LAFRAMBOISE, Pete
b. Ottawa, Ontario, January 18, 1950
In some ways, his timing couldn't have been better. Laframboise graduated from the Ottawa 67's in 1970 and worked his way up through the California system. After a year in the minors, he made his Seals debut in '71-'72, and that fall the team was torn apart by defections to the WHA. As a result, he was able to make the Seals full-time in the fall, and he responded with 16 goals in his first full season. The next year, though, his production halved and he wound up being sent to Washington and on to Pittsburgh before making his way through the minors.

LAFRANCE, Adelard "Adie"
b. Chapleau, Ontario, January 13, 1912
Lafrance ended his pro career when the war began, but previously he had played three games for the Canadiens in the early 1930s in an uneventful decade in the game.

LAFRANCE, Leo
b. Allomette, Quebec, November 3, 1902
d. Duluth, Minnesota, January 10, 1993
Two partial years in the NHL in the mid-1920s was all the fuss Lafrance made at the highest level of the game. He played pro in the American league for much of his career.

LAFRENIERE, Jason ("Hawk")
b. St. Catharines, Ontario, December 6, 1966
In junior, Lafreniere tied a record for most points in a game with eight. This was in '85-'86, when he finished fourth in scoring in the OHL and was named the league's nominee for player of the year. In the ensuing years he played briefly for the Nordiques and the Rangers but never came close to providing explosive offence for those teams. He was buried in the minors, but four years later his career was resuscitated by expansion when Tampa Bay played him a few times. Since 1994, Lafreniere has been in the minors and in Europe, all over, really, playing the game for as long as he can.

LAFRENIERE, Roger
b. Montreal, Quebec, July 24, 1942
In '66-'67, while Roger was in Buffalo playing for the American league Bisons, the missus was at home in St. Catharines, giving birth to a boy the couple named Jason. While Roger didn't play much in the NHL, Jason would go on to a longer career. Roger played briefly with Detroit before expansion and with St. Louis after, and in the minors he earned a reputation for his hustle and aggressive play. He could play up or back on the blueline, kill penalties, and shoot the puck with some success. His temper got the better of him more than once, but in particular toward the end of the '69-'70 season when he swung his stick at an opponent and was suspended for the remainder of the season.

LAGACE, Jean-Guy
b. L'Abord a Plouffe, Quebec, February 5, 1945

Lagace was always trying to pick and choose his spots for getting into the lineup, but most frequently had to rely on a coach's decision or an injury to get him a semi-regular place. He was initially owned by Montreal and was traded to Pittsburgh in 1968, and it was with the Pens that he saw his first NHL action. Ironically, he never played a full season until his last, '75-'76 with Kansas City, at which point he bolted to the WHA for one final year of pro. Not big, he was a scrappy defenceman who played like a tiger, sometimes to his detriment, against much bigger opponents.

LAIDLAW, Tom
b. Brampton, Ontario, April 15, 1958

Laidlaw was smart enough to get an education at Northern Michigan University before joining the Rangers in 1980 and beginning an NHL career. He was a big and reliable defenceman who had limited ability, but he survived 705 games in the NHL and played only 5 games in the minors. His teams never made it deep into the playoffs, though he did play with Wayne Gretzky in L.A. after the great trade of 1988. Laidlaw retired in 1990 and formed his own business as a player agent, going on to represent stars such as Brian Boucher and Bryan Berard. He later joined forces with IMG, one of the biggest agencies in North America.

LAIRD, Robbie
b. Regina, Saskatchewan, December 29, 1954

When Laird heard that Pittsburgh had drafted him in 1974, little did he know it would take five years to get into an NHL game and that the chance would not come with the Penguins or that that one game would be his only one. He made his name as a fighter, but he was also a scorer and more complete player than his penalty minutes might suggest. Laird spent most of his career with the Fort Wayne Komets, helping the team win the Huber Cup as regular-season champs in '77-'78. The year after, he played on the famous Western Union Line with Al Dumba and Terry McDougall. Laird scored 45 goals, and out of that season came a contract from Minnesota. He played two years in the North Stars system and got into his one NHL game, but in 1982 he retired. A year later, he missed the game too much and returned to the Komets, and after retiring again in 1986 he coached the team. He went on to guide Phoenix in the IHL, and then scouted for the L.A. Kings.

LAJEUNESSE, Serge
b. Montreal, Quebec, June 11, 1950

Detroit thought highly of Lajeunesse after he played on the double Memorial Cup Montreal Jr. Canadiens (1969 and '70), but the Wings were less enamoured after watching him play in their organization. From 1970 to '73, he played 97 games with the team before being traded to Philadelphia, but the change of venue didn't alter his circumstances. Lajeunesse was a minor-leaguer according to NHL teams.

LAJEUNESSE, Simon
b. Quebec City, Quebec, January 22, 1981

Any time that Lajeunesse wants to mature and step into the Ottawa net, he's free to do so – the position is wide open. He was drafted by the Sens in 1999 and has played only a few minutes in goal for the team, but his play in the minors indicates he might be the excellent goalie the Sens are looking for. He played junior in Moncton, and in his first year of pro helped Grand Rapids to the lowest goals against in the AHL for 2001-02.

LAKOVIC, Sasha ("The Pit Bull")
b. Vancouver, British Columbia, September 7, 1971

Oh, sure, you could probably justify the frenetic rampage he went on during the '96-'97 season when a spectator in Calgary tossed beer on his coach and Lakovic went after the fan. Not exactly a class act, but it was a spontaneous moment of insanity. But the time in the IHL when he sucker-punched Alan May and knocked him unconscious? That was barbaric and more typical of Lakovic's style of goon hockey. It would be nice to think that's why he never stayed long in the NHL, where the fighters have to have some skill and the barbarity is kept to a minimum.

LALANDE, Hec
b. North Bay, Ontario, November 24, 1934

It was awfully hard for some players to handle the minors after playing in the NHL, knowing they were good enough to make the grade. Lalande to played two games with Chicago midway through the '53-'54 season and looked terrific. He was only 19 and still in junior. He went on to play two full seasons for the Hawks, but they sent him to Detroit in December '57. GM Jack Adams called him up for a dozen games, then sent him to Hershey forever. But when the Bears sent him down to the EPHL in 1962, he had trouble accepting such a demotion. After less than half a season, he retired. Almost a year passed and then Wren Blair, GM in Clinton, called and convinced Lalande to come out of retirement to help the team. In two-thirds of a season, he passed the 100-point mark and regained his love of the game. He played a few more years before calling it quits for good.

LALIME, Patrick
b. St. Bonaventure, Quebec, July 7, 1974

Records are generally set by one of two kinds of player: the superstar, whose records highlight his greatness, or the complete unknown who, for a game or a week or a year, played beyond his wildest dreams. Time has yet to determine which fate will claim Lalime, but one thing is certain: By going undefeated in his first 16 games, he made the most successful NHL entrance ever for a goalie. It was a lucky break to get the call, but everywhere Pittsburgh looked they had injured goalies. Lalime was in the IHL and playing well, and when he came up to replace Tom Barrasso he was exceptional. When all returned to normal, though, he was demoted, much to his dissatisfaction. The Pens, unwilling to sign him to a big contract because of his start, traded him to Anaheim, and although he didn't play for the Ducks he set more records in the "I" until they traded him to

Tom Laidlaw

Serge Lajeunesse

Sasha Lakovic

Hec Lalande

Patrick Lalime

Bobby Lalonde

Ron Lalonde

Mike Lalor

Joe Lamb

Ottawa. The Sens, desperate for a star goalie, were happy to give Lalime a chance, and so far he has risen to the occasion. In 1999-2000, he played 38 games, but that number increased dramatically over the next 2 seasons to the point that Lalime was clearly their goalie of choice. The minor-league goalie who made the most of his chance seems to be proving that even in the IHL there is the occasional player who belongs in the NHL.

LALONDE, Bobby
b. Montreal, Quebec, March 27, 1951
At every stage of his career, there were two clear and unequivocal facts about Lalonde: He was highly skilled, and he was very small. He won two Memorial Cups with the Jr. Canadiens in '69 and '70 and joined Vancouver in 1971. In his second season, he scored 20 goals, but the year after he was slowed by a serious knee injury, the skill of the previous year giving way to the size problem. He was a tenacious player who held on to the puck well and wasn't afraid of rough play, but that kind of game didn't suit his skills and he never had the impact in the NHL that he had had in junior. His best year was '78-'79, when he had 24 goals with Atlanta, but his teams never had any success in the playoffs. Lalonde retired in 1982 to become a representative for All-State Insurance in the Toronto area.

LALONDE, Edouard "Newsy"
b. Cornwall, Ontario, October 31, 1887
d. Montreal, Quebec, November 21, 1970
As a kid, Lalonde worked as a reporter and then a printer for the *Cornwall Freeholder*, so when he became a hockey player, everyone called him Newsy and no one stopped. He started organized hockey in Cornwall with a team nicknamed the Sweepers because instead of paying for their ice they shovelled it. After another year in Woodstock, he was offered a job with the Soo in the IHL in 1906, the first all-pro league in North America. From there, the legend of Lalonde grew and grew. He was a scorer without compare and he could skate faster than anyone and played rougher than anyone when when occasion called. He moved to Toronto to play, and in 1909 joined the new Montreal Canadiens in the NHA, leading the league in goals his first season. After a year out west, he returned to the Habs in 1912, thus beginning an uninterrupted 10-year association with the team. He led the league in scoring again in '15-'16 as the team captured its first Stanley Cup, and the team was part of the NHL when the new league formed in 1917. Lalonde led the league in scoring the year after, and on January 19, 1920, he scored six goals in a single game. In 1922, after an argument with owner Leo Dandurand,

he was traded to Saskatoon for another remarkable prospect named Aurel Joliat. He returned to the NHL in 1926 to coach the New York Americans, though he did play a game for the team. Incredibly, in his 99 career NHL games, Lalonde scored 124 goals. He went on to coach the Ottawa Senators for two years (1929-31) and then the Canadiens for two and a half years before leaving the game altogether in 1935. He was usually the highest-paid player wherever he went, but Lalonde was also such a great lacrosse player that in 1950 he was named Canada's player of the half-century in that sport. That year, he was also elected to the Hockey Hall of Fame. He moved back to Montreal where he was manager of a liquor store for a number of years, but in 1970 he suffered a hip injury and had to be hospitalized. He died a few weeks later in a convalescent home from complications related to that injury.

LALONDE, Ron ("Newsy")
b. Toronto, Ontario, October 30, 1952
Lalonde is right up there among the leaders in the dubious category of most regular-season games played without appearing in the playoffs. His career, in the 1970s, covered only Pittsburgh – often in a defensive role – and Washington, both horrible teams at the time. As a result, Lalonde got in the playing time but never played on a winner. He made up for this, though, by winning a Calder Cup in his final season in the AHL, with Hershey in '79-'80.

LALOR, Mike
b. Buffalo, New York, March 8, 1963
For the first 10 seasons of his career, Lalor's teams made it into the playoffs, starting with Montreal in 1986, his rookie year in which the Habs won the Cup. That was to be Lalor's only championship, though the stay-at-home defenceman played a dozen years in the NHL despite never being drafted. His last year was '96-'97 with Dallas, after which he coached kids hockey in the Boston area.

LAMB, J.G. "Joe"
b. Sussex, New Brunswick, June 18, 1906
d. Ottawa, Ontario, August 21, 1982
Lamb was one of eight children born to the mayor of Sussex and as a late teen he worked in a bank. He was transferred to Ottawa to a similar institution, and that's where he played his first serious hockey, quickly moving up the ranks on ice and leaving the counting of money to others. Lamb turned pro in 1927, and over the next 11 years he played for 7 teams, more than any other NHLer to date with the exception of Carl Voss. Lamb was a fast skater with a blistering shot and he was, at the very least, an extremely rough player,

He started organized hockey in Cornwall with a team nicknamed the Sweepers.
NEWSY LALONDE

"robust" in the words of Lady Byng recipient Frank Boucher. J.G. finished his career in Springfield before entering the war. He went overseas with the RCASC as a captain and in the ensuing years was promoted to major and awarded the MBE for meritorious service. He was one of the very few men who didn't seek discharge after the war. In fact, he loved the military and stayed closely involved in Ottawa until 1959, by which time he had achieved the rank of lieutenant colonel. Throughout his life, golf was a close second in passion. In 1936, he won the Maritime Amateur Golf Championship. He won the Ottawa Hunt Club championship in three decades and was the honorary secretary-treasurer of the Ottawa District Golf Association from 1965 to '76. He was inducted into the New Brunswick Sports Hall of Fame in 1972.

LAMB, Mark
b. Ponteix, Saskatchewan, August 3, 1964
Despite being drafted by Calgary in 1982, Lamb played exactly one game with the Flames, three years later, before moving on to Edmonton. It was there that the small but tenacious centre had his best year with 12 goals in 1989-90, the year the Oilers won their fifth Cup in 7 years. He later played for Ottawa, Montreal, and Philadelphia before winding up in the IHL at the end of his career. After retiring, he returned to the Oilers as an assistant coach, but after two years Dallas lured him to the Lone Star state to perform a similar function.

LAMBERT, Dan
b. St. Boniface, Manitoba, January 12, 1970
Well, Lambert wasn't quite the Bobby Orr of the IHL. Go down a few notches – he was the Ray Bourque of the IHL, an offensively skilled player, though unlike Bourque he had a bit of a mean streak. Lambert was the MVP at the 1989 Memorial Cup when his Swift Current team won it all, and after 29 games with the Nordiques (1990-92) he spent most of his career in the "I," where he won a host of honours.

LAMBERT, Denny
b. Wawa, Ontario, January 7, 1970
Undrafted but by no means unwanted, Lambert has punched out an NHL career based on his smart toughness and his ability to be a tough guy without being a mindless goon, a fighter who doesn't take too many "stoopid" penalties. Since joining the NHL in 1994, he has played exclusively for expansion teams looking to "beef up" their lineup, and the stocky left winger has done his job without much fanfare.

LAMBERT, Lane
b. Melfort, Saskatchewan, November 18, 1964
He had his day on the ice, and although it wasn't always NHL ice, it was a long day. Lambert played six years with Detroit, the Rangers, and Quebec in the 1980s, over which time he went from scorer to set-up man. But his time was tenuous and he always had to fight to make the team and impress management, more so, anyway, than when he went to Europe and was a star. He returned in 1996 to close out his career in the IHL, taking Houston to the Turner Cup in 1999 and captaining the team during his last season. Lambert returned to Moose Jaw, felt his way around

the game, and landed a job as assistant to the WHL's Warriors, hoping to start a new career in hockey with a whistle and chalkboard.

LAMBERT, Yvon
b. Drummondville, Quebec, May 20, 1950
It was a combination of skills and factors that enabled Lambert to make the Canadiens in the fall of 1973. For starters, he was big and strong and ready to fight. Second, he had just come off a season in the AHL in which he led the league in goals and points. Third, the Habs, like most teams, felt the loss of players to the WHA. And fourth, when he was given the chance to play, he performed well. He could be counted on for 20 goals a year and he was a force on the power play that was at or near the top of the league in efficiency throughout the 1970s. Lambert won four Cups with the Habs, and after a season in Buffalo he went down to Rochester of the AHL to coach and play. He then became head coach with Verdun, but after a short time he decided to return to the Montreal organization. He became manager of the restaurant at the Forum, and when the team moved to the Molson Centre he moved also, to run the restaurant.

LAMBY, Dick
b. Auburn, Massachusetts, May 3, 1955
Lamby was only 20 years old when he played for the U.S. at the 1976 Olympics in Innsbruck, a solid fifth-place showing for his country. He went on to play for Boston University the next fall and joined St. Louis briefly in 1978. In his three seasons with the Blues, Lamby played most of his hockey with Salt Lake City in the Central league, and after another year in the minors with little chance for another chance at the NHL, he retired.

LAMIRANDE, Jean-Paul
b. Shawinigan Falls, Quebec, August 21, 1924
d. Belleville, Ontario, January 30, 1976
Unlike most hockey players who joined the army, Lamirande didn't play a single game during the three years he was with the Canadian Infantry Corps, so when he got out, the NHL was not first on his mind. Nonetheless, he played his first games with the Rangers in '46-'47, but over the next four years he could never manage to stick around. His game was more defensive, yet '49-'50 was particularly frustrating because he was called up to Broadway from New Haven on five separate occasions. In each of the first three stints, he scored a goal his first game up, but had no effect on management and he was sent back down each time. Lamirande coached and played for Trois Rivières in '55-'56, and two years later was reinstated as an amateur so he could represent Canada at the World Championships. He completed a rare double by playing for the Whitby Dunlops in 1958, the year they won a gold for Canada, and the next year joining the Belleville McFarlands, with which he won a second gold and was named the tournament's best defenceman.

LAMMENS, Hank
b. Brockville, Ontario, February 21, 1966
Lammens is one of the few NHLers to have competed

Mark Lamb

Dan Lambert

Denny Lambert

Jean-Paul Lamirande

Hank Lammens

Leo Lamoureux

Mitch Lamoureux

Mike Lampman

Jack Lancien

Eric Landry

in the Summer Olympics, a feat he accomplished in 1992 in Barcelona when he represented Canada in sailing. During his university career at St. Lawrence, sailing was as important to him as hockey, and although he graduated in 1988 to go on to play in the AHL, he still sailed seriously. Lammens won the Finn World Championships in 1990 and '91 and missed the entire '91-'92 hockey season to prepare for Barcelona. Once done, he played for Canada's National Team (as captain), and then in 1993 he joined the Ottawa Senators shortly after signing as a free agent. It was his only season in the NHL.

LAMOTHE, Marc
b. New Liskeard, Ontario, February 27, 1974
Growing up, Lamothe's favourite team was Montreal, so when the Habs drafted him in 1992, it was a dream come true for the goalie. Despite having had a strong career in junior, though, he didn't stand on his head in the Canadiens system and ended up signing with Chicago. The Hawks put him in two games in 1999-2000, but he wound up signing with Edmonton two years later and the Oilers have yet to use him. Nevertheless, he has continued to play with the hope of getting back to the NHL some day, and for a longer time.

LAMOUREUX, Leo
b. Espanola, Ontario, October 1, 1916
d. Indianapolis, Indiana, January 11, 1961
A tough and impregnable force on the blueline for Montreal, Lamoureux won Stanley Cups in Montreal in 1944 and '46 during a brief but successful NHL career. He passed out of the NHL in 1947 but continued to play and coach as well. From the AHL as a player, he moved to Shawinigan, Charlottetown, and North Bay as a coach, and in 1956 he was named bench boss of Indianapolis in the IHL. He stayed for two years, and after a two-year retirement he returned in 1960 for a short stint. Lamoureux became ill with an acute case of hepatitis and had to resign his position. He died in hospital a short time later at age 44.

LAMOUREUX, Mitch
b. Ottawa, Ontario, August 22, 1962
When Lamoureux came to Pittsburgh's camp in 1982 after a terrific junior year, goals were what the coaching staff expected of him. He didn't make the team, but in the minors he scored 57 times and earned a quick shot in the NHL the year after. He scored but once, and the year after he was given another chance, but this time he made a new role for himself. The new guy in town – a guy named Mario – was going to score, and Lamoureux was now expected to be a checker. He stayed the year and was effective in that role, but with the exception of a few games with the Flyers he spent the next decade in the minors. After retiring, he became the director of media relations for the United Hockey League and soon after was promoted to vice-president of hockey operations for the UHL.

LAMPMAN, Mike
b. Lakewood, California, April 20, 1950
We'll never know whether the '76-'77 season was going to be a breakthrough year for Lampman. In his previous four seasons, he was a part-time player in the NHL and

a solid winger down in the minors. He switched teams in each of his first three seasons, but in that last year he played a career-high 27 games with Washington. He seemed to make the team that fall of 1976, but in his 22nd game of the year, his career came to an end. While playing against the Flyers on December 3, 1976, he collided with Andre Dupont and suffered what doctors called an abnormal slippage of the fifth and sixth vertebrae in his neck. The initial prognosis was that he would miss several weeks of action, but the reality was that he never regained enough strength in his neck to risk the physical demands of a return to the game. He had been known for his booming shot and great ability in close, and for having being born in California, but was done at age 26. He settled in Denver.

LANCIEN, Jack
b. Regina, Saskatchewan, June 14, 1923
Lancien had a lengthy but anonymous career that touched down for a short time in the NHL with the Rangers (1946-51). A defenceman, he played mostly out west, though he did play in the 1950 playoffs for the Rangers, the year they lost the first-ever finals to be won in overtime of game seven (by Detroit).

LANDON, Larry
b. Niagara Falls, Ontario, May 4, 1958
Landon cut his teeth in the minors during his short pro career that saw him play a few games with both Montreal ('83-'84) and Toronto ('84-'85). After retiring, though, he stayed in the game and became the Bob Goodenow for minor-leaguers, that is, the executive director of the Professional Hockey Players' Association, the group that represents all non-NHLers in North American pro hockey.

LANDRY, Eric
b. Gatineau, Quebec, January 20, 1975
At his best, he is a small power forward, a nasty bit of business who can score and fight with the same set of hands. Trouble is, the AHL has been home to his skills plenty more often than the NHL, where Landry has played just a few times with Calgary and, most recently, Montreal.

LANE, Gord
b. Brandon, Manitoba, March 31, 1953
Night and day. Black and white. Pleasure and poison. No matter how contrasts are drawn, none is more clear-cut than the two halves of Lane's playing career. From 1975 to '79, he played for Washington, the horrible Capitals that never went to the playoffs and couldn't win even if the other team didn't show up. Lane was despised by Caps fans, who even had a "We Hate Gordie Lane" club, a rare show of enthusiasm from fans who knew embarrassingly little about the game. Early in the '79-'80 season Lane left the team in a contract dispute, and the Caps settled the matter when the Islanders, in need of a tough, stay-at-home defenceman, acquired him for Mike Kaszycki. For the next five and a half years, Lane's career was pure gold. He played regularly for four Stanley Cup teams with one of the great dynasties, and fans loved him. He retired in 1985 to coach Brandon in the WHL and later coached Springfield in the AHL. He left the

rink altogether soon after, though, to start his own financial advising firm, in Maryland, specializing in investments for pro athletes.

LANE, Myles

b. Melrose, Massachusetts, October 2, 1902
d. New York, New York, August 6, 1987

He helped hunt down criminals. He exposed corruption in all facets of government. He brought to trial members of the underworld. And he supported the small citizen in fights to live a decent life. Hardly the attributes of most hockey players, but Myles J. Lane was a unique and extraordinary human being. He began life in sports, as an All-American halfback at Dartmouth College, where he led the nation in scoring one year. He also played on the school's hockey team, and after graduating in 1928 it was to hockey he gravitated. The Rangers signed him but traded him to the Bruins during that '28-'29 season, and Lane was fortunate enough to play on that year's Cup-winning team. He played sporadically with the Bruins over the next few years because in both 1932 and '33 he was head football coach at Boston University and the year after he was backfield coach at Harvard. The income from these jobs helped finance his years of study at Boston College Law School, from which he graduated in 1934. He joined the firm of O'Connor and Faber in Manhattan, and just three years later he was named assistant attorney for the Southern District. During the war, Lane served in the navy for four years, leaving as a commander. He was named chief assistant of the attorney's office and became United States attorney in 1951, a position he held for two years until returning to private practice. In 1968, he was elected to the Supreme Court in Manhattan and six years later he was appointed to the Appellate Division of the Supreme Court, First Department, a position he held until his retirement in 1979. During his time in power, he chaired a committee to look into drug problems, investigated underworld activities, and probed bid rigging within municipal governments. For most NHL players, life is never so good as on ice. For Judge Lane, hockey was only the beginning of a valuable career serving the public.

In 1968, he was elected to the Supreme Court in Manhattan.
MYLES LANE

LANG, Robert

b. Teplice, Czechoslovakia (Czech Republic), December 19, 1970

The NHL isn't in trouble? Robert Lang scored 18 goals and 50 points in 2001-02, and this led to a free agent offer from Washington for $25 million over 5 years. Think he could sign that contract quickly enough? Lang has been a good player, decent, skilled, a fine contributor. He has never been a superstar, and the Caps hoped that playing with former Penguins teammate Jaromir Jagr might light a fire under both players. Internationally, he has had fine success as well, including a bronze medal at the 1992 Olympics in Albertville and gold in 1998 with the Czechs at Nagano. He's big and skilled and plays centre, but his best season was 23 goals. That's what five mil' gets an NHL owner these days? Yikes.

LANGDON, Darren

b. Deer Lake, Newfoundland, January 8, 1971

Langdon came late to hockey and didn't play in one of the three premier junior leagues in Canada. Instead, he played in the Maritimes and snuck up on the NHL after a few years as a heavyweight in the minors, scoring his first goal in 1994 against Patrick Roy. The Rangers signed him as a free agent in 1993, and he quickly worked his way into the lineup full-time, where he calmed down a bit from his barbaric days in the AHL. Early in the 1999-2000 season, though, he suffered a herniated disc and missed the rest of the year. The Rangers gave up on him and traded him to Carolina, and it has been with the 'Canes and later Vancouver that Langdon has tried to kick-start his career.

LANGDON, Steve

b. Toronto, Ontario, December 23, 1953

A left winger, not very big, Langdon skated hard in the minors, mainly in Rochester. He was drafted by the Bruins and played all of his seven NHL games with the team during a short career, but it was in the AHL that he left his mark. After retiring, he went on to coach the team, including his son, Mark, who was on the roster in the late 1990s.

LANGELLE, Pete ("Snake Hips")

b. Winnipeg, Manitoba, November 4, 1917

Much is made of Bill Barilko's goal that won the 1951 Stanley Cup because, as the song goes, "the last goal he ever scored/won the Leafs the Cup." But nine years earlier, without the tragic end, a similar fate befell Pete Langelle, who scored the Cup-winner in the most remarkable comeback of all time. The Leafs lost the first three games of the '42 finals to Detroit, then stormed back and won the next four, the last on Langelle's marker midway through the third period. He never played again in the NHL. Born in Winnipeg as Pete Landiak to Polish-Ukranian parents, Langelle grew up with another player of similar heritage, Wally Stanowski. Stanowski went on to play with the Monarchs, but Landiak had to play in St. Boniface, a French-Canadian part of town. While club officials liked the way he played, they asked him to change his name to attract the local fans, and so Landiak became a

Robert Lang

Darren Langdon

Jamie Langenbrunner

Chris Langevin

Dave Langevin

Daymond Langkow

Alain Langlais

Langelle sensation overnight. He developed into an effective two-way player: a set-up man in the offensive zone, a tenacious checker in his own end. His three years with the Monarchs culminated with a visit to Maple Leaf Gardens for the Memorial Cup, and after winning the national championship Langelle was signed by Conn Smythe then and there. Langelle was assigned to Syracuse for two years, making his NHL debut at the end of the '38-'39 season and making the club for keeps at camp in 1939. For three years he was a star with the team, but after the '42 Cup win he entered the army and remained in active duty for five years. When he was discharged, the Leafs were a dynastic powerhouse and there was simply no room for a rusty, pre-war player, even one of Langelle's calibre. He played for a number of years in the minors, with Pittsburgh, and after being reinstated as an amateur in '52 won the Allan Cup in 1954 with the Winnipeg Maroons. Satisfied, he retired from the game, settled in his hometown, and worked for Labatt Breweries for the next 29 years.

LANGENBRUNNER, Jamie
b. Duluth, Minnesota, July 24, 1975
One of the longest surnames in the history of the game, Langenbrunner brought a fierce intensity to the rink every night. That's why Dallas drafted him in 1993 and didn't hesitate to put him into the lineup when he was still just 19. He quickly developed into exactly the kind of player the team was expecting, bringing hard hits and goals and single-minded will to the game every night. He played on the U.S.'s 1998 Olympic team and in 1999 was a huge factor in Dallas's first-ever Stanley Cup, scoring 10 goals in the playoffs, including 3 game winners. Incredibly, 6 of his first 15 career playoff goals were winners, and when he went to New Jersey he continued his scoring success in the 2003 playoffs.

LANGEVIN, Chris
b. Montreal, Quebec, November 27, 1959
November 22, 1985, was the last time Langevin skated properly. He was playing for Buffalo. The opposition was Quebec. It was just the 22nd game in his young and developing NHL career, but after injuring his knee in a collision that night, he was never the same. He recovered, but not enough to play the game at a high level again, and the tough guy out of Chicoutimi in junior was out of a job.

LANGEVIN, Dave
("Bam Bam"/ "Moose")
b. St. Paul, Minnesota, May 15, 1954
Langevin stayed the full four years at the University of Minnesota-Duluth (1972-76) to ensure he walked away with at least a teaching degree. From there, he signed with the Edmonton Oilers in the WHA – because of the money – but the Islanders, the NHL team that had drafted him during his university days and had wanted him ever since, took him in 1979 when the WHA merged with the NHL. It was a tough loss for the Oilers. They could protect only two players before the draft. One, obviously, was Wayne Gretzky, and the other was a tossup between Langevin and Bengt Gustafsson. Glen Sather chose the wrong guy. Langevin earned his nicknames because he hit to hurt every time, even

though he played on one knee for much of his career. The ligaments in his right knee had been eviscerated by operations but he kept playing hard and was key to the Islanders' four Stanley Cups. He retired in 1986 and moved back home to be an assistant coach for the Apple Valley High School team, but he eventually returned to the minors with New Haven for a few games and then the parent club, Los Angeles, called him up for a few more. By this time, Langevin's knee had nothing left to give and he retired. He stayed at home in Minnesota and coached the Idaho Steelheads in the WCHL until 1998, at which time he moved to the South Suburban Steers of the Minnesota Junior Hockey League. He has been inducted by both the University of Minnesota-Duluth and the U.S. Hockey Halls of Fame.

LANGFELD, Josh
b. Fridley, Minnesota, July 17, 1977
The 2001 graduate of the University of Minnesota played in a game for Ottawa the next year at age 24 and has been developing in the minors. A right winger, Langfeld has never scored many goals at any level, and if he makes the Sens he will have to do so on the strength of a more complete game. His first game was a rough one – he left with a concussion.

LANGKOW, Daymond
b. Edmonton, Alberta, September 27, 1976
Despite not living up to the hype of being a 5th overall draft choice (in 1995), Langkow has blossomed into a fine centre since coming to Phoenix. He had an outstanding junior career in the WHL, leading the league in goals and points in '94-'95 and winning gold with Canada at the World Juniors the next year. Langkow played his first four years with Tampa, a team that never made the playoffs, yet he held his own and used the time to develop and mature. He was traded to the Flyers with Mikael Renberg for Chris Gratton and Mike Sillinger on December 12, 1998, and it was with Philadelphia that he started to take his game to another level. When the Coyotes acquired him for 2 draft choices about 3 years later, he delivered his first 20-goal season and became one of the team's fine, unsung players.

LANGKOW, Scott
b. Sherwood Park, Alberta, April 21, 1975
Soon after the Coyotes traded Scott to Atlanta, they acquired brother Daymond. Scott, a goalie, turned pro with Winnipeg in 1995 but didn't played much with the Jets. And with the arrival of Nikolai Khabibulin, Langkow's chances for more time were thin, indeed. With the Thrashers, Scott played behind Damian Rhodes, and although he got into a few more games, his 3-11-0 record didn't help him any. Atlanta sent him to Anaheim, and from there he signed with Kalamazoo, the NHL looking ever further away. Most of his years have been in the AHL, and he has had admirable success in that league, including being named the best goalie in '97-'98.

LANGLAIS, Alain
b. Chicoutimi, Quebec, October 9, 1950
It was truly a strange series of events that finally got Langlais into a Minnesota uniform and the NHL. He

was a great scorer in junior but no team drafted him. California invited him to camp in 1970 but cut him, and he spent the next two years in the minors with virtually no hope of an NHL offer, let alone a callup. He signed with the Nordiques in 1972, but they, too, wanted to send him to Greensboro, their farm team, and Langlais retired. He considered taking a job as a ditch digger – banal as a symbol of desperation, but true – and then he got an offer to try out for Minnesota because one of their scouts recalled having seen him play well in Baie Comeau. The North Stars signed him and assigned him to Saginaw in the IHL and New Haven in the AHL, and then late in the '73-'74 season, Langlais caught a break. Tony Featherstone broke his hand, and Langlais was called in to take the NHL spot. He scored 3 goals in 14 games, but the year after he again played only a few games and then was down in the minors for the rest of his career.

LANGLOIS, Albert "Junior" ("Whitey")
b. Clairmont, New Hampshire, November 6, 1934
Named junior because he had the same name as his dad, Langlois joined Montreal at the end of the '57-'58 season and had such an impact that he stayed through the playoffs and won a Stanley Cup. He won Cups the next two years as well, playing regularly on the blueline with Doug Harvey in both Montreal and later New York. Langlois has another connection to another immortal defenceman. He played his final season in the NHL with Boston in '65-'66 – and he wore number 4. The next year another guy took the number since Langlois was down in the minors in another organization, and no one since Bobby Orr has ever donned that digit. Upon retiring, Langlois settled in Montreal, where he worked in the sales department of Canadian Hockey Equipment. During his playing days he had studied to become a real estate broker, but he soon packed up and moved to Beverly Hills, where he worked for Merrill Lynch.

LANGLOIS, Charlie
b. Lotbinière, Quebec, August 25, 1894
d. Sudbury, Ontario, August 31, 1965
Four years, four teams, three now defunct. In the pre-Original Six days, there were as many as a dozen teams in the NHL, and Langlois played for entries in Hamilton, Pittsburgh, and New York (the Americans). He also played half a season in Montreal in '27-'28, his last in the league, though he played parts of a number of years in lesser leagues before and after his NHL stint.

LANGWAY, Rod
b. Maag, Formosa, May 3, 1957
Being the son of a serviceman in the U.S. Air Force accounts for Langway's foreign entrance into this world, but he grew up in the more familiar environs of Randolph, Massachusetts. In high school he was a three-sport athlete, and he attended the University of New Hampshire on a football scholarship. Yet hockey was in his bones. Montreal drafted him in 1977, but he signed with the WHA because he couldn't agree on a contract with the Habs. A year later, they agreed, and Langway was part of another Montreal Cup in the 1970s. He was a physical, defensive defenceman who knew he would never make the great rushes or the amazing passes. He

simply took his man, covered his own end, and did his all to prevent goals. The Habs traded him to Washington in 1982, and he played the last 11 years of his career with the Caps. Of course, he never came close to winning another Cup, but he brought to the Caps the same sense of poise and leadership on the blueline. By the time he retired in 1993, the team captain earned retirement of his number 5. Langway won two Norris Trophies ('82-'83 and '83-'84) and played in six All-Star Games. He also played for the U.S. at three Canada Cups and for the NHL at Rendez-vous '87. He went into coaching for a number of years, in the minors, after which he settled in Maryland to work in his family's business, Richmond Heat Treating in Richmond, Virginia. In the fall of 2002 he was inducted into the Hockey Hall of Fame, three years after receiving a similar honour from the U.S. Hockey Hall of Fame.

LANK, Jeff
b. Indian Head, Saskatchewan, March 1, 1975
It's always a gamble to re-enter the draft, and invariably it's an agent-driven strategy that backfires. Lank was drafted a respectable 113th overall by Montreal in 1993, just weeks after the team had won the Cup. Yet he decided not to sign. He continued his junior career in Prince Albert, and in 1995 Philadelphia selected him … 230th overall. It was another four years before he saw an NHL game (two, in fact), and within a year he was coaching boys in Little Caesar's Detroit-area AAA league.

LANTHIER, Jean-Marc
b. Montreal, Quebec, March 27, 1963
His was a simple career. Vancouver drafted Lanthier in 1981 and used him for parts of five seasons. Boston and Jersey later acquired his rights but gave him time only in the minors. He came out of the Q and was back home in Montreal inside a decade, but he had realized a dream by making it to the NHL.

LANYON, Ted
b. Winnipeg, Manitoba, June 11, 1939
A career that came full circle passed only fleetingly through the NHL for Lanyon in the 1960s. He came out of St. Boniface to turn pro with the Johnstown Jets in 1959, and from there began a tour of every conceivable team and league from Greensboro to Amarillo. He played five games for the Penguins during their inaugural NHL season, and in 1972 he wound up back in Johnstown, this time as a playing coach.

LANZ, Rick ("Rico"/ "Lanzer")
b. Karlovy Vary, Czechoslovakia (Czech Republic), September 16, 1961
Forget about hockey – Lanz was lucky to be a free man. The year was 1968 and he was just a boy living in Czechoslovakia. He had a brother named Robert, and the family was vacationing in Bulgaria when a local saw the licence plate on their car. He asked if they had heard about the Soviet invasion of Czechoslovakia, and they had not. Bohuslav and Zdena Lanz decided then and there never to return. They sold the car and bought plane tickets to Canada, arrived at the house of a Czech priest in London,

Albert Langlois

Rod Langway

Jean-Marc Lanthier

Ted Lanyon

Rick Lanz

Ontario, and started a new life. Bohuslav, an engineer back home, found work in construction, and the boys, like any other Canadian kids, started to play hockey. Robert went on to sell cars in Vancouver, and Rick settled there, too, after the Canucks drafted him in 1980. He developed into a fine defenceman, a terrific rusher who could quarterback the power play, who had size and speed both. After six and a half years with the team, he left and demanded a trade because he could no longer get along with the team's management. The Canucks obliged, sending him to Toronto on December 2, 1986, for Jim Benning and Dan Hodgson. The move did nothing to help Lanz's career, and he played only two seasons before moving around and playing out the last of his skating days. He returned to British Columbia and started to coach, first in provincial junior hockey and later in the WHL. He had played for Canada at the 1980 World Juniors and the 1983 World Championships, and he owed his entire career to a vacation his family took so many years ago. What a happy accident that was!

LAPERRIERE, Daniel
b. Laval, Quebec,
March 28, 1969
Jacques Laperriere not only produced Stanley Cups during his career in Montreal but also a son who went on to the NHL as well. Daniel never won a Cup, though, and in fact had a tough go of it in the league, but he still had a decent career that included some games with St. Louis and Ottawa before going down to the minors and continuing his career in Europe.

LAPERRIERE, Ian
b. Montreal, Quebec, January 19, 1974
Laperriere made the transition from junior to the NHL by making a change in his game. In Drummondville, he was a scorer and top offensive player, but he couldn't continue those ways in the NHL. He had a decision to make, and his coaches in St. Louis and Los Angeles helped him along: either he became a defensive player in the NHL or stayed a scorer – in the minors. He chose the former, and since that time has had a regular spot in the lineup, helping the Kings become one of the better young teams in the league. He no longer scores more than seven or eight goals a year, but he fights and checks and hits his way into the minds of opponents night after night.

LAPERRIERE, Jacques ("Lappy")
b. Rouyn, Quebec, November 22, 1941
At 6'2" Laperriere was one of the tallest defencemen in the league, but at 180 pounds he was by no means feared for his bodychecks or physical play. Instead, Laperriere was quick and shifty. He could strip an opponent off the puck using his long reach and move the puck quickly up the ice to counterattack. Like most players in the Montreal system, he was given time to develop so that, at age 22, when he made the team, he was ready to contribute without making the proverbial rookie mistakes. He played junior and minor pro with Hull-Ottawa and got into a few games with the Habs in '62-'63, though it wasn't until a year later that he became a regular. Laperriere fit into the Canadiens so smoothly that he was counted on in all important situations. At the end of the year, he won the Calder Trophy, and for 12 years he was the team's most underappreciated superstar. He didn't have much offensive capability but he was always near the top of the league's +/- leaders because of his defensive talents. He was part of the team's silent dynasty of the 1960s, winning four Stanley Cups, and in the early part of the next decade he won in 1971 and '73. Laperriere won the Norris Trophy in '65-'66 and played in five All-Star Games. He might well have carried on winning Cups into the late 1970s but for a serious knee injury midway through the '73-'74 season that forced him to retire. He coached junior in the Montreal system a year later but after just one season resigned in protest of what he felt was excessive violence in hockey at the youth and amateur level. In 1980, he returned to the fold by joining the staff of the Canadiens as an assistant coach. For some 16 years his was a constant presence, and despite the often spotty quality of those Montreal teams, they were frequently among the best defensively in the league, thanks to Laperriere's experience and knowledge. In 1997, he joined the Bruins in the same capacity for a short term of duty. He was inducted into the Hockey Hall of Fame in 1987, some 13 years after he played his last NHL game. In his case, better late than never.

Ian Laperriere

Darryl Laplante

Laperriere won the Norris Trophy in '65-'66 and played in five All-Star Games.
JACQUES LAPERRIERE

LAPLANTE, Darryl
b. Calgary, Alberta, March 28, 1977
Just when it seemed Laplante got going, he got lost. And then when it seemed he had a great chance to play, he didn't. Laplante started with Detroit in the late 1990s when the team was a yearly Cup favourite, and coach Scotty Bowman worked him into the lineup slowly. In 1999-2000, though, he played in 30 games and seemed to be turning a corner. And when Minnesota claimed him in 2000, his lot seemed better if for no other reason than he was going to a bad team that would play him. Wrong. He was sent to the minors, later traded to Boston, and stayed in the minors. Now he has to fight to get back into the NHL, a fight he hasn't given up, but one he hasn't won, either.

LAPOINTE, Claude
b. Lachine, Quebec, October 11, 1968

Despite being a late late late draft choice in 1988, Lapointe has played for more than a decade, proving the scouts wrong – starting with his first NHL game, as a Nordiques, in which he scored a goal. Scoring was never his forte, but he did develop into a great team player, someone who was great on faceoffs, could block shots, and could kill penalties. He moved to Colorado when the team left Quebec, but early in that relocation season (1995-96) he was traded and missed out on a Stanley Cup. He ended up with the Islanders, and that is where he seems destined to finish his career, the team eager to keep a leader and contributor in the lineup.

LAPOINTE, Guy
b. Montreal, Quebec,
March 18, 1948

His father was a fireman and his brother worked for the police, and it was toward the latter that Lapointe gravitated until his dad suggested he give hockey a try for a while, the police force would always be there. And so Guy took his hockey seriously, working his way up from the Junior Canadiens to Houston to the Voyageurs before finally making the Habs in 1970. He asserted himself as a defenceman capable of offensive ability but big and tough enough to play defence with the best on the team. In his rookie season, the Canadiens won the Cup, and he was soon one of the Big Three on defence that also featured Larry Robinson and Serge Savard. As a group, they

Claude Lapointe

were the best blueliners in the game and such was Lapointe's development that after only two seasons he was named to Team Canada for the 1972 Summit Series. He had been drafted into the WHA by Quebec but spurned offers from the lesser league at all times. Although he never won an individual award, he was runner-up to Bobby Orr for the Norris Trophy in '72-'73, a year in which he scored 19 goals. He later had 3 successive seasons of at least 20 goals, topping out at 28 in '74-'75. Many of his goals came on his patented low, hard slapshots from the point during power plays. He played 14 seasons with Montreal, and while he was a terror to opponents on the ice, he was equally a terror to his teammates off it. He was not allowed to be the last one out of the dressing room or the first one in, such was the reputation he built up for shenanigans and hijinx. Once, during a time when all players dressed formally, he cut a hole in everyone's hat, including his own, and then watched the players' shocked reactions as they doffed their doughnut-like headwear. After six Stanley Cups with Montreal, he was traded to St. Louis at the deadline in 1982 and

finished his career in Boston, a stretch shortened by serious injuries to an eye and cheekbone. He retired in 1984, but hardly slowed down. He joined the Nordiques as an assistant coach, and in 1985 was named GM and coach of Longueuil in junior, a team that won the Memorial Cup in 1987 under his tutelage. He returned to the Nordiques again until 1990, when he went out west to play a similar role with Calgary. He was inducted into the Hockey Hall of Fame in 1993 and later joined Jacques Lemaire's staff with the new Minnesota Wild, where he continues to work as the coordinator of amateur scouting.

LAPOINTE, Martin
b. Ville Ste. Pierre, Quebec, September 12, 1973

It isn't possible to hold Lapointe accountable, yet his name was dragged through the mud in the summer of 2001 when Boston offered him a four-year contract worth $20 million. He couldn't find a pen quickly enough, and the offer came after a career year in which he had scored 27 goals with Detroit as a power forward. It was impossible for him to live up to the hype, but the deal made clear the financial problems that are rife in the NHL. Of course, in his first season with the Bruins, he had 14 goals. That's what $5 million gets you these days. With the Wings, he was a valuable role player who chipped in a few goals and played in-your-face hockey every night. He won Cups with the Wings in '97 and '98 but he was no Steve Yzerman superstar. He had won two gold medals with Canada at the WJC... but

Martin Lapointe

$20 million? Wow.

LAPOINTE, Rick ("Jumbo")
b. Victoria, British Columbia, August 2, 1955
d. October 17, 1999

It was rare, indeed, for an NHL club to outbid a WHA team for a player's services in the 1970s, but that's exactly why Lapointe started his pro career in 1975 with Detroit and not the Toronto Toros. The Wings wanted a defenceman who could play right away rather than one who needed a few years to develop, and as such they made him a regular in the fall of '75, the same year they drafted him. He proved right off the bat that he belonged, showing a patience and poise with the puck that belied his age. Over the next 11 seasons he played for 5 teams, never winning a Cup but always providing stability on ye olde blueline. After he retired, he returned home and coached at the Victoria Racquet Club, which also boasted a series of fine kids hockey teams. Lapointe's son played there, and Rick coached for years until his sudden death from a heart attack in 1999.

Rick Lapointe

He was runner-up to Bobby Orr for the Norris Trophy in '72-'73, a year in which he scored 19 goals.
GUY LAPOINTE

LAPPIN, Peter
b. St. Charles, Illinois, December 31, 1965
Despite an excellent college career, Lappin didn't make it to the NHL save for seven games over two years. His finest hour came at St. Lawrence University, where he was a Hobey Baker Award finalist and scored all 3 goals in the team's 3-2 semifinals win over Minnesota en route to the NCAA finals in 1987. Most of his five years of pro after that were in the IHL, and he never had a chance to make an impact in the NHL.

LAPRADE, Edgar ("Beaver")
b. Mine Centre, Ontario, October 10, 1919
At age 4, Laprade moved from Mine Centre, a tiny town some 400 kilometres west of North Bay, to Port Arthur where he and his brothers played their kid hockey. Edgar reached prominence with brother Bert in 1939 when the Bearcats won the Allan Cup, and the team was all set to represent Canada in the 1940 Olympics until the war broke out and forced the cancellation of the Games. Edgar joined the army in 1943 – with brothers Bert, Raymond, and Albert – and worked as an army instructor in Kingston for the balance of his service. He had been named MVP of the Thunder Bay Senior Hockey league twice (in 1939 and '41), and in 1945 he was the only one of the family to make a pro career of hockey. He joined the Rangers that fall and spent 10 years with the Blueshirts, though he and goalie Charlie Rayner were frequently the only bright lights on a dimly talented team. As a rookie, Laprade won the Calder Trophy but, as would happen in 8 of his 10 years, the team failed to qualify for the playoffs. He didn't incur a single penalty all season, the first of three times this would happen to an extremely clean player. Laprade was known for his skating and his great defensive play. He was a master of the pokecheck and a playmaking centre as much as a scorer, and his hard work earned him the nickname Beaver. Laprade played in 4 successive All-Star Games (1947-50), and in '49-'50 had a career-high 22 goals while also being named winner of the Lady Byng Trophy. He retired with 500 regular-season games to his credit, during which time he was assessed all of 42 penalty minutes, an average of 2 minors a season. Despite his talents, though, he appeared in just 18 playoff games, 12 of those coming in 1950 when the Rangers lost to the Red Wings in a thrilling 7-game finals. After leaving the Rangers in 1955, he returned to Thunder Bay where he played senior hockey for several seasons. He tried coaching, but hated it, and opted to open a sporting goods store in town, which he operated until 1975. Since then, he has lived mostly at a small summer camp near Thunder Bay. He was inducted into the Hockey Hall of Fame as a Veteran Player in 1993.

LAPRAIRIE, Ben ("Bun")
b. Sault Ste. Marie, Michigan, October 20, 1911
d. April 1986
Little is known of Laprairie except that he played seven games for Chicago in 1936-37 under owner Major Frederic McLaughlin, an American who espoused the use of players from his own country for his team. He later became manager of the Marigold Gardens in Chicago.

LARAQUE, Georges
b. Montreal, Quebec, December 7, 1976
He's fearless and tough and a good team man, which all goes to say he's a fighter and checker and fourth-line player. Laraque came out of junior after winning the Memorial Cup with the Granby Predateurs in 1996, and in each of his first three seasons he played more and more with Edmonton until 1999 when he became a full-fledged member of the team. The days of demotions were over, but, of course, the threat remains.

LARIONOV, Igor ("The Professor")
b. Voskresensk, Soviet Union (Russia), December 3, 1960
In Detroit, they called him the Professor because he was old and wore glasses. But when he was young, his teammates could have awarded him the same appellation because of his studious approach to the game. He was a thinking man's player, one who did things on the ice for a reason, a player who took into account the spontaneity of the game and crafted a strategy in the quiet of his mind, away from the ice. In every on-ice situation, he knew what to do because he had thought about it already. It was a philosophy that stood him well during a career that is, by definition, what the Hockey Hall of Fame is all about. Larionov centred the KLM line with Vladimir Krutov and Sergei Makarov on the wings, one of the greatest lines of all time. He played at the 1984 Olympics in Sarajevo, and 18 years later he was in Salt Lake City. He played on the three Canada Cups in the 1980s and won gold after gold with the CCCP teams that used to dominate the World Championships. He was a superstar in Soviet league play and didn't make it to the NHL until 1989, when he was 29 years old. Yet he still played more than 800 NHL games, winning Stanley Cups with Detroit in 1997, 1998, and 2002. Larionov was not a big man, but a beautiful skater and a perfect passer, an interpreter of the game no matter where he played. It was these qualities that made him so successful for so long, these and the two glasses of wine he swore by

Georges Laraque

Igor Larionov

> **He was a master of the pokecheck and a playmaking centre as much as a scorer, and his hard work earned him the nickname Beaver.**
> **EDGAR LAPRADE**

every night before bed. Two of his children have already made it to the NHL in a non-playing capacity. Daughters Alyonka and Diana have sung the U.S. national anthem at some of Detroit's home games.

LARIVIERE, Gary
b. St. Catharines, Ontario, December 6, 1954
His special talents lay more in what he did outside playing the game, though Lariviere certainly had four decent seasons in the NHL. He started his career with the WHA in 1974, playing with Phoenix and later moving to Quebec, the team he stayed with when the league merged with the NHL in 1979. The Nordiques traded him in 1981 to Edmonton, where he began an informal career as a coach, for Paul Coffey credited Lariviere with crafting him into a star defenceman. Lariviere was out of the NHL by 1983 and played three years in the AHL in St. Catharines, where he also ran horses, namely Twin B Playboy. In his AHL first season, he was named the league's best defenceman. Lariviere also coached the local Falcons and then began a lengthy career as a coach at all levels, becoming an assistant with the Maple Leafs under head man John Brophy in 1986.

LARMER, Jeff
b. Peterborough, Ontario, November 10, 1962
Despite being a super sniper in junior, Jeff couldn't put NHL pucks in the net the way his brother, Steve, could. He started with Colorado in 1981 and moved with the team to New Jersey, where he had 21 goals the following season. It was his only truly successful year in the league. The Devils traded him to Chicago, the Hawks hoping that by playing with Steve, Jeff would get things going, but it didn't work out that way. The brother act played fewer than 100 games together and Jeff ended up in the minors where he once again turned into a decent scorer.

LARMER, Steve
b. Peterborough, Ontario, June 16, 1961
Larmer scored in junior and scored just as much in the NHL. A right winger, he had a terrific shot and played on a line with Denis Savard and Al Secord, one of the top lines in the league. Larmer won his only individual award, the Calder Trophy, after his first year, one in which he scored 43 goals. It was the first of five 40-goal seasons in a 441-goal career spent almost entirely with Chicago. Ironically, he was traded to the Rangers in 1993 and won his only Stanley Cup with that team at season's end. With the Hawks, he had made it to the finals but had never held the great Cup high. Larmer also set an Iron Man record for the Hawks, appearing in an incredible 884 consecutive games. He won a silver medal with Canada at the 1991 World Championships and appeared in the '91 Canada Cup and '96 World Cup as well. After retiring in 1995, Larmer returned home to coach a team of eight-year-olds and studied business at Sir Sandford Fleming College. He later joined the staff of the NHLPA.

LAROCHELLE, Wildor
b. Sorel, Quebec, September 23, 1905
d. Montreal, Quebec, March 21, 1964
Never the player to grab all the attention in Montreal

during the 1920s and 1930s, Larochelle quietly played on the team's second line with Pit Lepine and Georges Mantha and helped the Habs win Stanley Cups in 1930 and '31. The aggressive right winger spent 11 seasons in Montreal before he was sold to Chicago. He played his last two seasons in the NHL with the Hawks and ended his playing days in New Haven. After retiring, he worked in the hotel business with his father, but in 1951 he contracted tuberculosis and was confined to a convalescent home for the last 13 years of his life.

LAROCQUE, Denis
b. Hawkesbury, Ontario, October 5,, 1967
A Los Angeles draft choice in 1986, Larocque played just eight games with the Kings a year later. He played six years of pro altogether, going down down down until finally he was with a team called St. Thomas in the Colonial League, whence no NHLer returns.

LAROCQUE, Mario
b. Montreal, Quebec, April 24, 1978
He was a top prospect once, but that seems like a long time ago – 1996. He was a tough guy playing in the Q and Tampa drafted him, but he played just five games with the Lightning before finding himself on the move. He went down to the IHL and signed with Buffalo in 2001 as a free agent, but the Sabres assigned him to the minors and he hasn't made it back to the show.

LAROCQUE, Michel "Bunny"
b. Hull, Quebec, April 6, 1952
d. Hull, Quebec, July 29, 1992
When you read about a goalie who won four Stanley Cups in his career, you think, Wow, this guy must have been something. But if you read on, you won't – because he wasn't. Larocque was not famous for a save or a moment or a team so much as for a teammate: He was the nightly, monthly, yearly backup goalie behind Ken Dryden, but that wasn't Dryden's fault. In fact, the starting job was Larocque's for the taking. In fact, Dryden's career might have turned out quite differently had Larocque been a first-rate NHL goalie. Dryden left the Habs in 1973 in a contract dispute disguised as a law career, and that year's training camp happened to be Larocque's second with the team. He had spent all of the previous season in the minors, so the chance was his. He played well, but not spectacularly, and when Dryden returned after a year's absence, the law degree taking a back seat to a fine, new contract, Larocque was condemned to the end of the bench in seeming perpetuity. Yes, he was on the team that won 4 Cups in a row, but in those years he played exactly 20 minutes of playoff hockey. Here's how bad Larocque's situation was: Those 20 minutes constituted the final period of a 4-1 loss in game one of the 1979 finals against the Rangers. Coach Scotty Bowman called on Larocque to start game two, his first start after watching Dryden take the previous 64 playoff games! In the warmup, though, Larocque took a shot off his helmet, and when the game began he was at the hospital having X-rays taken while Dryden was in the net. Larocque eventually got a much needed trade but he never made an impact anywhere else. In his one season as the starter, '81-'82 in Toronto, he played on a weak

Gary Lariviere

Jeff Larmer

Steve Larmer

Wildor Larochelle

Michel "Bunny" Larocque

team and allowed almost five goals a game. After retiring, he became vice-president of the QMJHL but in May 1992 doctors discovered he had brain cancer. After three weeks of radiation therapy, he died of the disease in a Hull hospital. He was 40 years old.

LAROCQUE, Michel
b. Lahr, West Germany, October 3, 1976
He may be a goalie, but he's unrelated to the perennial backup in Montreal from a previous generation. This Larocque was drafted by San Jose in 1996 and traded to Chicago three years later. He played at Boston University, and after graduating was sent to the minors until 2000-01 when he played three games for the Hawks in January 2001, after which he was out of the NHL, seemingly for good.

LAROSE, Charles "Bonner" ("Bonny")
b. Ottawa, Ontario, February 14, 1901
d. Ottawa, Ontario, January 19, 1963
Larose's life revolved around Ottawa, starting in his youth when he played minor hockey with St. Joseph's and later St. Brigid's before turning pro with New Haven in 1924. The following year, he played for the Pittsburgh Fort Pitt Hornets on a high-scoring line with Joe Sills and Paddy Sullivan. He moved up and played six games with Boston the year after, but he soon had to give up the game because of injuries. Larose returned to Ottawa where he spent the rest of his life in the civil service, working for the federal government until he suffered a fatal heart attack in early 1963. Among his duties, Larose acted as the Usher of the Black Rod, a position of prestige during the procession from the Hall of Honour to the office of the Speaker of the House during the opening of Parliament each session.

Claude Larose

LAROSE, Claude ("Rosey")
b. Hearst, Ontario, March 2, 1942
It's every Canadian boy's dream to win the Stanley Cup, of course, but what's implied in that dream is to be part of the celebration, hugging the goalie at the end of the game, drinking champagne from the bowl in the dressing room, that sort of thing. Well, when Montreal won the Cup in 1973, Larose, who had started the game, was nowhere near the silverware. He had slid hard into the immovable goal during play and broke his leg. By game's end, the cast was already on, and Larose was waiting impatiently for an ambulance to take him back to the arena so he could celebrate. He got on the plane that night with the boys, cast and all, and he flew home a champion. It was the fifth Cup of his career with the Habs, a career that began in 1962 when he was called up from the minors to play a few games. Within two years he was a force on the right wing, but in 1968 the Habs traded him to Minnesota. He captained the North Stars for two seasons, but when they had a chance to get Bobby Rousseau from Montreal, they sent him home. Larose closed out his career with four years in St. Louis and then became a scout with the team based out of Ottawa right away. From that day to this, Larose has continued scouting, most recently for Carolina. He also acted as assistant coach with the Blues for a short time. As the first NHLer to come out of Hearst, that

Guy Larose

Pierre Larouche

town named its arena in his honour. He also sent his son, Guy, on to the NHL, though the son didn't have a five-Cup career like his old man.

LAROSE, Claude
b. St. Jean, Quebec, May 17, 1955
Life did this Claude Larose no favours by giving him the name of a Cup-winning star who retired just a year before this unheralded Larose entered the Rangers lineup in 1979. Actually, that's not entirely true. This Larose began in 1975 in the WHA before signing with the NHL team that had drafted him. He played only a few games with the Rangers, but his career in the AHL was more successful. Larose led the league in scoring in 1983-84 and had five 30-goal seasons before retiring in 1986.

LAROSE, Guy ("Rosie")
b. Hull, Quebec, August 31, 1967
Shortly after Guy entered this world, his father, Claude, left home to go to another Montreal training camp. At season's end, the Habs won the Stanley Cup, and when Guy became a fine young player his father gave him that '68 Cup ring as a good luck charm and memento. Although Larose was a fine junior, Buffalo drafted him almost at the end of the 1985 draft and didn't play him. He signed with the Jets, who put him in a few games in three years, but nothing to write home about. Larose got his big break hen he was traded to Toronto. He brought incredible energy and speed to the lineup, and the fans responded by shouting "Guy!" every time he was on the ice. Nevertheless, he was only a part-timer with the Leafs, and that's how his career went. His best chance for stability came in 1995 when Boston offered him a great contract, but his agent advised him to accept a deal from the Detroit Vipers. Larose made more money on the deal, but it ended his NHL dreams. Since then, he has continued to play – more than 1,000 pro games now – most recently with an outfit called the Augusta Lynx.

LAROUCHE, Pierre ("Lucky")
b. Taschereau, Quebec, November 16, 1955
Not too many players came out of junior on the heels of a 251-point season the way Larouche did in 1974, but exactly 10 years before Pittsburgh drafted Mario Lemieux, the team selected Larouche. He scored 31 goals as a rookie, and the next year he exploded the sophomore jinx by scoring 53 goals and 111 points, becoming the youngest player ever to reach the 50 and 100 plateaus (until Wayne Gretzky came along, anyway). He was young, good looking, the toast of Pittsburgh, and a superstar in the making. The year after, he led Canada in scoring at the World Championships, and on November 29, 1977, he got his dream trade, going to Montreal to play alongside many of his childhood heroes. Despite winning two Cups with the Habs in '78 and '79, he was on the outs with coach Scotty Bowman, who wanted him to be more attentive to the defensive aspects of the game. After Bowman left, Larouche had another 50-goal season and became the first player to reach that mark with two different teams. He later played for Hartford and the Rangers, scoring 48 goals one season

with the Whalers. In '85-'86, though, he suffered the humiliation of being demoted, but he kept on scoring and was eventually recalled. That season, he added his name to an exclusive list of players who scored 20 goals in both the NHL and the minors in the same year. In all, Larouche averaged more than a point a game despite missing significant chunks of time with a back and knee injuries. After retiring, he focused on his second love, golf, and became one of the winningest players on the Celebrity Players Tour. He came close to qualifying for the U.S. Open in 1993 and has established himself in New York, where he also does extensive charity work.

LAROUCHE, Steve
b. Rouyn, Quebec, April 14, 1971
Larouche got his NHL time in quickly and quietly, playing 26 games spread thin over 3 teams in a 2-year period (1994-96). He has spent most of his career scoring piles of goals in the IHL, but in 2001 he signed with the Berlin Polar Bears to begin a career in the German league.

LARSEN, Brad
b. Nakusp, British Columbia, January 28, 1977
As usual, the drafted player who refuses to sign and re-enters the draft does more harm than good, though in Larsen's case it was odd indeed that that happened. Ottawa took him in 1995, and in the next two years he won two gold medals with Canada's juniors, captaining the '97 team. Colorado redrafted him, but in the years since Larsen has barely made a dent in the lineup, spending almost every waking hour in Hershey with the other farm team aspirants.

LARSON, Norm
b. Moose Jaw, Saskatchewan, October 13, 1920
d. Shell Beach, California, December 2001
From the time he was 11, Larson knew he wanted to be a professional hockey player. Hockey was all he cared about, and hockey was all he wanted to do. He played in Moose Jaw until he was 20, when the New York Americans signed the youngster to a contract. He played all of '40-'41 and '41-'42 with the team and then enlisted in the army. Larson never served overseas and was able to play hockey with army teams, and when he came out in 1945 he set the AHL on fire, missing the scoring championship that first season by a single point. He started the next year playing a single game with the Rangers, but when he was sent down to New Haven the injuries began. In his first game with the Ramblers, he broke his leg and shattered his kneecap in three places, and the year after he missed almost the whole season again with another serious knee injury. The next year, he managed to play, even though the muscles in his left leg were an inch and a half thinner than in his right. He continued to play for several more seasons, but his NHL days were long over by this point and he spent most of his time in the Western league.

LARSON, Reed
b. Minneapolis, Minnesota, July 30, 1956
There is no doubt that Larson was a fine defenceman, and as his career slowly came to an end, he set records every time he scored a goal or collected an assist.

He was, in his day, the highest-scoring American-born defenceman in NHL history. He had 5 consecutive 20-goal seasons with Detroit and finished with 222 total, yet the Wings were perennial playoff also-rans and castoffs. Larson controlled the power play, provided offence from the blueline, and captained the team, yet the team itself was never any good during his 10 years with the Wings (1976-85). Detroit traded him to Boston, but in the summer of 1987 his career almost came to an end in a freak car accident. A car collided into the side of his while he had his arm out the window, and he required extensive surgery to make his left arm right again. Although he returned that November, he was never the same player again, and the last two years of his NHL career elapsed in short spells with four teams. Larson played and coached in Italy for a few years and then returned to Minneapolis, where he worked as an insurance executive.

LARTER, Tyler
b. Charlottetown, Prince Edward Island, March 12, 1968
Spud country hasn't produced too many NHLers, but it's proud of each and every one of them, even if, as in the Larter's case, they played just a single game. Larter's pro career lasted six years ('88-'94), mostly in the minors, partly in Europe, and one game with Washington in '89-'90.

LASAK, Jan
b. Zvolen, Czechoslovakia (Slovakia), April 10, 1979
He might have been rookie of the year for 1999-2000 in the ECHL, and he might have played a few games in goal for Nashville two years later, but his professional North American accomplishments pale beside what he has done for Slovakia. Lasak played in the 2002 Olympics in Salt Lake City, and more important backstopped the emerging hockey power to a gold medal at the 2002 World Championships in Sweden. What he does in the NHL is secondary for the foreseeable future.

LASKOWSKI, Gary
b. Ottawa, Ontario, June 6, 1959
After playing four years at St. Lawrence University in New York, goalie Gary Laskowski had nowhere to go. No offers, no drafted team, no hopes. So he took a plane to Victoria, British Columbia, where Los Angeles was holding its 1982 training camp, and attempted to win a spot in the organization. He had a good camp, but no one was more surprised than Laskowski himself when coach Don Perry tagged him as the number-one man, ahead of incumbent and star Mario Lessard. The team was caught as off-guard as the goalie, for by opening night Laskowski still hadn't signed a contract. In fact, he made just $200 per game his the first few appearances, but once he proved himself a contract appeared and he stayed the year. His biggest game came in L.A. against Edmonton when he stopped Wayne Gretzky on a breakaway and made two other great stops on 99, halting the Great One's consecutive-game scoring streak at 30. He had a 15-20-4 record with the Kings that year, and the next season he played just 13 times. The NHL dream was over, but for Laskowski it had lasted a year and a half, and that's not a bad run for a walk-on.

Steve Larouche

Brad Larsen

Reed Larson

Gary Laskowski

Jiri Latal

David Latta

Brad Lauer

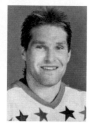

Craig Laughlin

Mike Laughton

LATAL, Jiri
b. Olomouc, Czechoslovakia (Czech Republic), February 2, 1967
Okay, trivia time: What do Jiri Latal, Joel Otto, and Gary Lupul have in common? They are the only players whose last names are palindromes! Latal came out of Czechoslovakia in 1989 after three appearances at the World Juniors to play for Philadelphia, the team that had acquired his rights from Toronto. The Flyers used the defenceman for three seasons but then continued his career in Europe. After retiring, Latal became a successful coach, most recently in his homeland.

LATOS, James
b. Wakaw, Saskatchewan, January 4, 1966
Latos's career is a veritable road map of small-town hockey in the US of A, marked by time in places like St. Thomas and Lee Valley, not to mention Louisiana and Wichita. He played once for the Rangers in the late 1980s, his only NHL stop.

LATREILLE, Phil
b. Montreal, Quebec, April 22, 1938
It's easy to see why Latreille was the first player ever to leave a U.S. college and join the NHL directly. This was back late in the 1960-61 season, with the Rangers. In his 4 seasons with Middlebury College in Vermont, he scored 250 goals, staggering totals in any league anywhere. The NHL was much different than college, though, and Original Six hockey was even more different. Latreille was held pointless and he returned to Montreal without ever getting another shot at the big time.

LATTA, David
b. Thunder Bay, Ontario, January 3, 1967
When Quebec grabbed Latta 15th overall at the 1985 Entry Draft, the team thought it had a true scoring prospect, even though he hadn't filled the net in the OHL. The Nordiques were patient and tried to develop Latta in the minors, but he didn't progress as they had hoped. In 36 games with the Nords over 4 years, he had 4 goals, but by 1991 he was out of the NHL. He moved to Europe to play second-division hockey in Germany, and it was there he had his most productive seasons.

LAUDER, Martin
b. Durham, Ontario, January 26, 1907
d. unknown
Lauder played with the Owen Sound Greys team in 1926-27, and won the Memorial Cup with teammates Benny Grant, Red Beattie, and Jack Markle. He went on to play three games for Boston the following season, and spent the rest of his brief career in the International league. After retiring, he became a car salesman.

LAUEN, Mike
b. Edina, Minnesota, February 9, 1961
Before graduating from Michigan Tech in 1983, Lauen had the privilege of representing the U.S. at the World Juniors as an 18-year-old. The team placed seventh, but Lauen was drafted by Winnipeg and went on to play four games for the Jets in '83-'84. He played only briefly in the minors and then returned to Minnesota, where he became a high school hockey coach.

LAUER, Brad
b. Humboldt, Saskatchewan, October 27, 1966
A good old Western boy, Lauer went to the Islanders in 1986 out of the Regina Pats, and the Sutter boys, Brent in particular, took the youngster under their wings and taught him the ropes. Lauer played parts of six seasons on Long Island and later moved on to Chicago, Ottawa, and Pittsburgh, always playing in the minors throughout his NHL years save the first two on Long Island. He then found a niche in the IHL until the summer of 2000, when that league ceased operations and Lauer was at a crossroads. He decided to go into coaching and was shortlisted for a job in Regina, but when he wasn't hired he decided to play for Mike Blaisdell with the Sheffield Steelers, realizing that his playing days were numbered and his coaching days, by comparison, were in plentiful supply.

LAUGHLIN, Craig
b. Toronto, Ontario, September 14, 1957
For years, Laughlin's birthday has been incorrectly published as September 19 when, in fact, he was born on the 14th. There was one simple reason, he explained, for never clarifying this erroneous information: Training camp never started by September 14, so he would have missed out on all the presents he got when players thought he was born on the 19th! Such was the easygoing nature of Laughlin, a solid, two-way player who could score 20 goals and give a team plenty of toughness and defensive play. He started in Montreal in 1981 and was traded to Washington the year after, and his love for that city was so great he made it clear he wanted to retire and get a job there. True to his word, he did. He played a bit for Toronto and L.A., but after retiring in 1990 he returned to Washington and became an analyst for Caps games, a position he held for 14 years.

LAUGHTON, Mike
b. Nelson, British Columbia, February 21, 1944
At age two, Laughton was already taking figure skating lessons. His father saw the shortage of ice time for boys' hockey teams and remedied that by building a backyard rink that became the hub of the neighbourhood. Mike became a fine skater, and as he got older he realized he could play professionally. He attended Notre Dame University in Nelson on scholarship for two years (studying phys ed) and turned pro with California in 1967. He scored 20 goals in his second season, but in 1970 he suffered a serious knee injury that ended his year and, for all intents and purposes, finished his NHL career. He wound up in Nova Scotia the year after, where he captained the Voyageurs to a Calder Cup, and he went on to play briefly in the WHA before returning to Nelson. Laughton settled down with his wife and family and coached many local teams while running a hockey school in Calgary with his brother.

LAUKKANEN, Janne
b. Lahti, Finland, March 19, 1970
As a kid, Laukkanen was too good a player not be noticed by many people who wanted him. At the under-18 tournament in 1988, he helped Finland win a silver medal at the prestigious European event, and

HPK Hameenlinna signed him soon after his hometown team ran into financial troubles (HPK is short for Hockey Playing Knights). Drafted by Quebec in 1991, Laukkanen remained at home for three years, playing at all the important world tournaments before joining the Nordiques in 1994. By the time the relocated Avalanche won the 1996 Cup, Laukkanen was in Ottawa with his new team. He had some productive years there until serious abdominal surgery in September 1998 cut into his development. The Senators traded him to Pittsburgh with Ron Tugnutt to acquire Tom Barrasso, and it is with the Pens that Laukkanen has most recently toiled.

LAURENCE, Don "Red"
b. Galt, Ontario, June 27, 1957

Times have changed. If Bobby Orr were playing today, all his knee injuries could have been solved by arthroscopic surgery and a couple of weeks of rehab. And if Don Laurence were playing today, his fate also would be different. While playing for Kitchener in the OHL, on December 12, 1976, he was tripped on a breakaway and crashed into the goalpost. Today, the net would fall off, and Laurence would skate to the bench for some water. Instead, he suffered a broken leg that required a temporary steel rod from his kneecap to his ankle. He was scoring more than a goal a game, but the sure first-round draft choice all of a sudden felt lucky to be selected at all. Atlanta GM Cliff Fletcher believed in the kid and chose him in the second round. After a year of hard work, Laurence was ready to play, so the Flames assigned him to Tulsa, where he reinjured the knee after a few games. He returned later in the year, though, and next season played 59 games for Atlanta. Clearly, he was not the same player. Fletcher traded him to St. Louis, but soon Laurence was in Salt Lake City playing in the CHL. That, as it turned out, was where he had phenomenal success. He became the first player to win 4 successive Adams Cups (the Stanley Cup of the Central league), and in each of those 4 seasons he scored no fewer than 39 goals. He later moved to Switzerland to continue his career, and right up until the end he scored in bunches.

LAUS, Paul
b. Beamsville, Ontario, September 26, 1970

Growing up in Ontario's wine country, Laus likely didn't dream about becoming a lifelong Florida Panther, yet life, in its inimitable way, has so far made his non-dream come true. He was drafted by Pittsburgh and developed in its farm system, but when the Cats entered the league in 1993, Laus moved south to Florida. Since then, he has been their

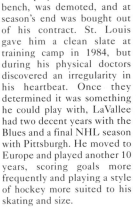

He became the
first player to win 4 successive Adams Cups.
DON LAURENCE

resident goon, their fighter. He's been good for the team, and the team has been faithful to him, and that's all a player can ask for. Perhaps not a dream team, then, but certainly a dream situation.

LaVALLEE, Kevin
b. Sudbury, Ontario, September 16, 1961

Talent isn't everything. Timing, circumstance, good fortune or bad – all can contribute to a player's career. LaVallee experienced all of these. He joined Calgary as a rookie in 1980 and scored 15 goals his first year and 32 his second. An off third year did nothing to help his reputation, and he was criticized for his defensive play (or lack thereof). That summer, Bob Johnson became the coach and decided to trade him to Los Angeles, a team that had a number of smaller, skilled players. He sat on the bench, was demoted, and at season's end was bought out of his contract. St. Louis gave him a clean slate at training camp in 1984, but during his physical doctors discovered an irregularity in his heartbeat. Once they determined it was something he could play with, LaVallee had two decent years with the Blues and a final NHL season with Pittsburgh. He moved to Europe and played another 10 years, scoring goals more frequently and playing a style of hockey more suited to his skating and size.

LaVARRE, Mark
b. Evanston, Illinois, February 21, 1965

In the *veni-vidi-vici* tradition of hockey players, LaVarre worked his way up, made it, and, as a postscript, worked his way right back down. He opted to play Ontario junior hockey rather than U.S. college hockey, and after two seasons in the OHL made his debut with Chicago in '85-'86 for two games. He stayed with the team most of the following year, and the season after that he was back down in the ILL for the better part of the year. A year and a half later, he was out of hockey altogether.

LAVENDER, Brian
b. Edmonton, Alberta, April 20, 1947

Lavender made the rounds quickly and quietly in the early 1970s, playing for four awful teams – three expansion teams and the then-woeful Red Wings – before landing in the WHA for his final season of pro in 1975-76.

LAVIGNE, Eric
b. Victoriaville, Quebec, November 4, 1972

From Hull, Quebec, to Hull, England, Lavigne has played all over the world, but his most prized possession is his memory of that one NHL game in

Paul Laus

Kevin LaVallee

Mark LaVarre

Brian Lavender

Jack Laviolette

Dominic Lavoie

Paul Lawless

Mark Lawrence

Danny Lawson

Los Angeles with Wayne Gretzky as a teammate. He played junior in Hull, Quebec, and after years in the AHL and IHL he ended up signing with the Hull Thunder in the British League in 2001, a long way from Quebec, perhaps, but a puck is a puck.

LAVIOLETTE, Jean Baptiste "Jack" ("Speed Merchant")
b. Belleville, Ontario, July 27, 1879
d. Montreal, Quebec, January 10, 1960
Laviolette grew up in Valleyfield, Quebec, where he was an outstanding two-sport athlete in hockey and lacrosse. He played organized hockey in the Montreal City League and then the Federal League in 1903. The year after he played for the Michigan Soo, after which he returned to Montreal and played out the rest of his career. The fight for players between the Eastern Canadian league and the National Hockey Association reached its peak in 1909 when the NHA won out. Laviolette was named captain of the newest team in the league, the Montreal Canadiens, for the 1909-10 season, and for the next five seasons he was a stalwart on defence. In 1914, he moved up to forward and played on a line with Newsy Lalonde and Didier Pitre, the greatest line of the era. Laviolette was more the playmaker than the finisher on the combination, and in 1916 the team won its first Stanley Cup. He stayed with the team in 1917 when it joined the NHL, and this turned out to be his only NHL season. Laviolette liked to race cars in the summer just as Art Ross and Sprague Cleghorn spent their free time racing motorcycles. In the summer of 1918, Laviolette was tuning a car when he got into a serious accident and lost his right foot. The Speed Merchant's hockey career was over. In 1921, Leo Dandurand arranged a benefit game in honour of the great player, and Laviolette not only attended, but had an artificial foot made and went out onto the ice and refereed the game! He was later inducted into the Canadian Sports Hall of Fame for his career as a lacrosse player, and in 1962 he entered the Hockey Hall of Fame as one of the great early players.

LAVIOLETTE, Peter
b. Norwood, Massachusetts, December 7, 1964
He was only 33 when he retired as a player in 1997, but he had done all he could to extend a career that was destined for NHL brevity. Despite his brief fling in the big league with the Rangers, Laviolette played on the 1988 and 1994 Olympic teams for the U.S. and had a decent career in the minors. An undrafted defenceman, he learned the game the hard way, and he learned it well. He went into coaching as soon as he was done, leading Providence to the Calder Cup in his second year (1999-2000) and being hired as an assistant for the NHL Bruins that summer. In 2001, he took over as head coach of the New York Islanders.

LAVOIE, Dominic
b. Montreal, Quebec, November 21, 1967
For six long years Lavoie did his best to make the NHL. He signed with St. Louis in 1986 after no one else drafted him, and played in the minors while waiting for a chance. That chance came two years later, but it was for just one game. It was a pattern that repeated itself each year as he played most of the

season in the minors and was recalled for the quickest of NHL appearances. He won a Turner Cup in 1990-91 with Peoria in the IHL, a nice footnote to a pro career but not necessarily a highlight. In 1994, Lavoie opted to play in Austria, and has been there ever since. Not only has the defenceman been a mainstay in the Alpenliga, but he has also acquired his Austrian citizenship. Since 1999, he has played for that country at the World Championships and Olympics, something he never could have done with Canada.

LAW, Kirby
b. McCreary, Manitoba, March 11, 1977
The NHL has not been on Law's side, and the chances for him to make it in the league are slipping away. He came out of junior without an offer and decided to play in the IHL. Atlanta signed him a year later but the Thrashers never used him before trading him to Philadelphia. He played in his first and only NHL game on March 5, 2001, and has been part of the farm team ever since.

LAWLESS, Paul
b. Scarborough, Ontario, July 2, 1964
In 1980, Lawless was playing in the Metropolitan Toronto Hockey League, a league for talented teens. Two years later, he was 18 and in the NHL, ahead of his time in ways both good and bad. He was playing for Hartford, a terrible team looking for some punch, but he was a kid, unable to handle the responsibilities that went with the career. He stayed out late and partied too hard, as they say, and his play suffered. The next year, the Whalers sent him to the minors to mature after he reported to camp overweight, and he responded with 49 goals in the IHL. That summer of 1985, he devoted himself to preparing for the coming NHL season, and the work paid off. He spent the next 2 years with the team, scoring 17 and 22 goals, but he was soon to start the trade circuit that took him to 3 more teams in a 2-year period. When the Leafs released him early in the '89-'90 season, the frustrated Lawless packed his bags and headed for Europe. He returned four years later to play for the Cincinnati Cyclones of the IHL, and retired in 1997 so he could become that team's coach and co-owner.

LAWRENCE, Mark
b. Burlington, Ontario, January 27, 1972
Much of Lawrence's career has been centred in Michigan, from his junior days in the OHL with Detroit to his IHL days with Kalamazoo to his coaching days with the same. En route, he played briefly with Dallas and the Islanders, his last year coming in 1999-2000 when he played 29 games for the Isles.

LAWSON, Danny
b. Toronto, Ontario, October 30, 1947
Because his dad was a house builder, the Lawson family moved out west when Danny was a baby. Danny played a little hockey, but he didn't play in a league until he was 12 and back in Toronto. A natural, he was scouted right away by Herb Carnegie, who wanted to sign him to a contract. Lawson refused, and even when he accepted offers from Detroit he signed only one year at a time. In his final year of junior he scored 52 goals

and made his NHL debut with the Red Wings. Detroit traded him to Minnesota, though, because it had too many right wingers, and he was used as a checker and penalty killer with the North Stars. After a full season with Buffalo, he decided to accept a fantastic offer from Philadelphia in the WHA. He led the league in scoring that first year with 61 goals and he, not Bobby Hull, was the first man to reach 50 goals in that league. During his five years in the WHA he established solid financial footing. He formed the Danny Lawson Holding Company (which subdivided land in Orangeville, Ontario) and Dan-Law Sports Enterprises (to handle endorsements), and by the time he retired in 1977 he was well on his way to becoming a wealthy man.

LAWTON, Brian
b. New Brunswick, New Jersey, June 29, 1965
On ice, there is nothing as pure and fast and exciting as hockey. Off it, the game can be twisted and cruel and create surreal contradictions. Lawton was selected 1st overall by Minnesota in the 1983 Entry Draft, the first American taken in this position of ultimate prominence. On the one hand, he was delighted by his meteoric rise; on the other, he and his agent almost refused to sign with the Stars because of money. On the one hand, he was the best prospect in the world; on the other, many prospects have done diddly-squat in the NHL. As time would tell, Lawton was a solid and decent player – he just wasn't Wayne Gretzky or Mario Lemieux. He passed up a chance to play for his country at the 1984 Olympics to sign a big contract with the Stars in '83, but in that first season he had exactly 10 goals. Five a year later. Then 18, and 21. After 17 goals the year after, Lawton started to field phone calls: you've been traded. New York. Hartford. Quebec. Boston. Wherever he went, teams were willing to give him a chance, hoping he could find that magic, pre-NHL touch. He never did. By 1990, he was in the minors, a washed-up non-superstar. He had a decent '90-'91 season with Phoenix in the IHL, but toward the end of the year, his wife committed suicide. No one deserves that kind of break. San Jose signed him as a free agent, and he played another two seasons, though he ended up in the minors again. He retired, got his life together, and tried to start over. He formed Lawton Sport & Financial, and with his new wife he started a career as a players' agent, hoping to guide young stars through the NHL waters, which are both beautiful and dangerous at their best.

LAXDAL, Derek
b. St. Boniface, Manitoba, February 21, 1966
Not exactly blessed with oodles of talent, Laxdal played with Toronto for small parts of four years in the 1980s and two more years with the Islanders in a similar capacity. He wound up going to Europe for a number of years, starring in Britain before returning to North America in 1999. He joined the Odessa Jackalopes as a player but went on to become an assistant coach and director of youth hockey for the team. In early 2003, he was named head coach of the Wichita Thunder.

LAXTON, Gord
b. Montreal, Quebec, March 16, 1955
In his second, and final, year of junior with New Westminster, Laxton was called Iron Horse by his teammates because he started virtually every game for the team that went on to the Memorial Cup. But when Pittsburgh called him up for his NHL debut in October '75, he won his first game but let in an average of 4.5 goals per game in his short time with the team. By the time he was out of the NHL, his average had ballooned to 5.5 per game, and Laxton spent the next few years in the minors.

LAYCOE, Harold "Hal"
b. Sutherland, Saskatchewan, June 23, 1922
d. Langley, British Columbia, April 28, 1998
Odd were the results of Montreal trading Laycoe to Boston on Valentine's Day 1951. He had been with the Habs for parts of four seasons, but left his mark on the game with events that followed the game on March 13, 1955, when Montreal was playing in Boston. Laycoe was a hard-hitting defenceman for Boston, the only player of his era to wear glasses while playing, and in the third period he hammered Maurice Richard. The Rocket proceeded to swing his stick at Laycoe's head, and when linesman Cliff Thompson tried to restrain Richard, Montreal's number 9 punched him. That led to Richard's suspension, and to the Richard Riot at the Montreal Forum a few days later. After retiring as a player a year later, Laycoe became coach of Portland, leading the team to seven league titles in nine years. His success earned him the head coaching job with L.A. in 1969, and Laycoe moved on to Vancouver the following year for a two-year stint. Despite missing the playoffs both years with his new team, he was GM. In 1976, he coached the Dutch National Team and later became a special assignment scout for the Islanders, specializing in Vancouver and Europe.

LAZARO, Jeff
b. Waltham, Massachusetts, March 21, 1968
By the time Lazaro retired from hockey in the spring of 2002, he was the all-time leading scorer of the New Orleans Brass, his last stop on a 12-year hockey junket that saw him play 102 NHL games at the start of his career. He came out of the University of New Hampshire to sign with Boston, but spent most of his time in the AHL. Along the way, Lazaro had the distinction of playing for Team USA at the 1994 Olympics in Lillehammer and two World Championships and playing for a while in Europe before returning home.

LEACH, Jamie
b. Winnipeg, Manitoba, August 25, 1969
You know time is passing when the children of players from the 1970s have had a long career in the game, have retired, and have started a management career after their playing days! Leach's dad was a scorer for Philadelphia during the goon days of the 1970s, and Jamie made it to the NHL in 1989 with Pittsburgh, though to lesser effect. Jamie played parts of four seasons with the Pens, including the Cup years of '91 and '92, but he didn't appear in the playoffs at all in those seasons. He later played for Hartford and Florida, and after some time in the minors he closed his career with a number of years in Britain. He never had the shot his old man had, but he could skate, and

Brian Lawton

Derek Laxdal

Gord Laxton

Hal Laycoe

Jeff Lazaro

he had the desire to play. After retiring, he returned to Manitoba to take over the dual position of head coach and GM of the Southeast Blades in provincial hockey.

LEACH, Larry
b. Lloydminster, Saskatchewan, June 18, 1936

Coming up through Boston-sponsored teams, Leach impressed scouts and coaches with his skating, his intensity, his ambition. The only thing they didn't like was his lack of scoring, but they felt this would develop with time. On that one point, they were wrong, and that was Leach's undoing. The B's sent him first to Humboldt, because it was near home and the team was among the best in the league. But over four seasons (1958-62) Leach made little impression when the Bruins called him up from Providence, and it was soon clear he was all out of chances. By 1964 he was no longer in the plans of the NHL team, so management asked him where he would like to play. Leach chose Portland because it was close to Lloydminster, and so for the next decade he played with the Buckaroos. After retiring, he settled back onto the farm at home, coaching junior and intermediate teams for many years and playing for the famous Neversweats, an old-timers' outfit.

Reggie Leach

LEACH, Reggie ("The Rifle")
b. Riverton, Manitoba, April 23, 1950

They called him the Rifle because of the slapshot – deadly accurate and quickly released – he let go while racing down the right wing. The booming shot fooled goalies more times than not. Strangely, Leach began his career in the Boston system and played with Bobby Orr in '70-'71 and part of the next year, but before the Bruins won the Cup he was traded to California in a multiplayer deal that brought Carol Vadnais the other way. Leach had consecutive 20-goal seasons with the Seals, playing on the worst team in the league, and the Flyers acquired him in a steal of a deal in 1974. He was one of the missing links to a Flyers team that won two Cups, in 1974 and '75, notably because he was one of the only skilled players on a band of thugs and animals that terrorized the league. In '75-'76, Leach led the league with 61 regular-season goals and 19 more in the playoffs, the first player to hit 80 for the complete season. He also had the rare distinction of winning the Conn Smythe Trophy while playing for a losing team to Montreal's Cup team that year. He had one more 50-goal season in his career, but despite his incredible talents he was sometimes a difficult player to motivate. By the time he left the NHL in 1983, he had 381 goals in 934 games, but somehow it seemed as though he could

Stephen Leach

Leach began his career in the Boston system and played with Bobby Orr in '70-'71.
REGGIE LEACH

have reached greater heights had he pushed himself more. In junior, with Flin Flon, he averaged well over a goal a game, but the Riverton Rifle didn't maintain the same intensity over his entire NHL career. After retiring, Leach became an alcoholic, dealing with a battle he had fought during his playing days. He eventually won the good fight and started a lawn care business that made him as successful off the ice as he had been on it.

LEACH, Stephen
b. Cambridge, Massachusetts, January 16, 1966

There are certain injuries you can overcome and others you just can't. Leach hurt a knee and broke a foot and came back to play, no problem. He didn't have his scoring touch, but he could still contribute. But midway through the '97-'98 season in Carolina he injured a disc in his back and he was gone for the year. He recovered, passed the medicals, signed a new contract with Ottawa, but there's no kidding the body – he was no longer the player he once was. He played the first six years of his career in Washington, but life improved immeasurably for the Massachusetts native when he was traded to the Bruins. He scored 31 and 26 goals with his dream team, and then the injuries took him out of the lineup. He was traded to St. Louis and on to the Hurricanes, but his Ottawa contract had two parts to it. The first called for a salary through nine games; the second called for bigger money once he played that tenth game (and made the team, in other words). Well, guess what? After nine games, the leery Sens bought him out. He wound up playing a bit in Phoenix and a year in Pittsburgh, but the 31-goal player was now reduced to banging home 2 pucks in the entire 1999-2000 season with the Pens.

LEAVINS, Jim
b. Dinsmore, Saskatchewan, July 28, 1960

It was a good thing that Leavins played with Kevin and Shawn Dineen at the University of Denver – that's the only reason he made it to the NHL. After graduating from U of D in 1984, Leavins signed with the Fort Wayne Komets of the IHL because there were no other takers. He played the year and then went home to Dinsmore, unofficially retiring because he couldn't see his way to mucking about in the minors with no chance at the NHL. That October, though, Kevin and Shawn's dad, Bill, who had watched many a U of D game, offered Leavins a tryout with the Wings. Invite accepted, Leavins signed with the Wings and started the year with Adirondack in the minors. He was called up for the last half of the season by coach Brad Park, and made a decent impression. In the off-season, though, he was traded to the Rangers, and with no safety net he played just four games before going down to the minors. He closed out his career in Europe.

LEBEAU, Patrick
b. St. Jerome, Quebec, March 17, 1970
The younger brother of Stephan, Patrick was of like stature (small) and a great scorer, though he didn't adjust nearly as well to the NHL as Stephan did. Ironically, Patrick was drafted, by Montreal, while Stephan never was. Patrick played junior in Quebec and made his Canadiens debut in '90-'91. He scored bunches in the minors that year to earn rookie of the year in the AHL and left the team in early 1992 to play for the Canadian National Team and the Olympics team. Over the next decade, he played just a few games with three other NHL teams while earning plenty of ice time in the minors and Europe, notably Switzerland and France.

LEBEAU, Stephan
b. St. Jerome, Quebec, February 28, 1968
Just as Stephan is two years older than his brother, Patrick, he won the AHL rookie of the year honours in 1989, two years before Patrick did. But whereas Patrick was a fine goal scorer, Stephan was exceptional. In junior, he scored 281 goals in 270 games, and in that first AHL year he fired 70 more to lead the league. In the NHL, he had 3 successive seasons of at least 22 goals with Montreal, and when he had a career high of 31 in '92-'93 the Habs won the Stanley Cup. The brothers played together on the same line with the Habs for two games in '90-'91, but Patrick was quickly sent down and Stephan stayed and made an impact. Like his brother, his career petered out in the NHL and he made his way to Europe for a number of successful seasons in Switzerland before retiring in 2001.

LEBLANC, Fern
b. Gaspesie, Quebec, January 12, 1956
Another smallish French-Canadian, Leblanc played three partial seasons with Detroit during the horrible 1970s and then made his way to Europe for a more successful career on the bigger ice with less hitting and a shorter schedule.

LEBLANC, Jean-Paul "J.P."
b. South Durham, Quebec, October 20, 1946
Despite not playing for years and years in the NHL, Leblanc still carved out a reputation as a quality player, and despite his size it was for qualities other than the speed and scoring one normally associates with the smaller set. Leblanc was known as a set-up man, a guy who could hang on to the puck, make a perfect late pass, and happily absorb the punishment that went with said hanging on. He played for Detroit and Chicago in the NHL, but it was in the lesser leagues that he racked up assists and became a sort of early version of Adam Oates. In his four years in the WHA, he centred scorers including Gary Veneruzzo and Marc Tardif. In the CHL, he led the league in assists one year, and everywhere he went his assists far outnumbered his goals.

LeBLANC, John
b. Campbellton, New Brunswick, January 21, 1964
LeBlanc's is a feel-good story for two reasons. One, he came out of a Canadian university to make it to the NHL. Two, he came out of tiny, perfect New Brunswick to do same. In 1982 he attended Mount Allison University, but after a year decided to switch to UNB. That cost him a year of playing, so he spent the season playing junior in Quebec. At UNB he had an exceptional year and was offered a tryout at Calgary's camp. The Flames didn't offer him a contract, so he returned to UNB, where he was named player of the year for all of Canada in '85-'86. Vancouver then extended him a tryout and contract, and he made the leap to the pro ranks then and there. LeBlanc had an impressive 12-year career as a pro, but played only sporadically in the NHL. His specialty was western Canadian teams, notably Vancouver, Edmonton, and Winnipeg, but he never played a full season in any of those cities. After retiring, he returned to New Brunswick and became a coach in provincial junior leagues.

LeBLANC, Ray
b. Fitchburg, Massachusetts, October 24, 1964
Getting to play in the NHL, even for one game, is a privilege and an honour, for LeBlanc the occasion was tinged with a hint of unhappiness. Like any goalie, he came up through the ranks, opting to play in the OHL. Despite his success, he was never drafted and after leaving Kitchener he began a career in the minors in 1984. It wasn't until five years later that Chicago signed him to a minor-league contract, and he was more or less resigned to a life beneath the NHL. In 1992, he played a number of games for the U.S. National Team and then performed admirably in the Olympics, helping his country to an impressive fourth-place finish in Albertville. About a month later, the Hawks called him up to play a game, a 5-1 win over San Jose. He made some fine stops, the crowd chanted his name, and he was sent to the minors the next day. The reason for the callup? Chicago had to play him once in order to expose him in the Expansion Draft so they could protect their top three goalers – Ed Belfour, Dominik Hasek, and Jimmy Waite. Sadly, no team claimed LeBlanc, and he spent the rest of his days in the familiar confines of the minors.

LeBOUTILLIER, Peter
b. Minnedosa, Manitoba, January 11, 1975
Drafted by the Islanders and redrafted by Anaheim two years later in 1995, LeBoutillier came out of junior in Red Deer to play two partial seasons with the Ducks and more time with the farm team in Cincinnati. He went to Britain in 2001 to play for the Sheffield Steelers.

LeBRUN, Al
b. Timmins, Ontario, December 1, 1940
In the old days, bird dogs discovered the talent, signed them to contracts, and put them in a system designed to develop them for the big time. Players, that is. LeBrun was discovered as an early teen skating for the Timmins Juvenile Lions. The scout was Jack Humphreys, a Rangers bird dog, who put LeBrun in Guelph, junior team for the Rangers. LeBrun came up to the big team

Patrick Lebeau

Stephan Lebeau

Jean-Paul Leblanc

Ray LeBlanc

Peter LeBoutillier

Bill Lecaine

Vincent Lecavalier

Jackie Leclair

Mike Leclerc

Rene LeClerc

for four games in '60-'61 and played solid defence with partner Harry Howell. All he needed was time, everyone felt, but a serious spinal injury forced LeBrun to miss the entire '63-'64 season. He came back and had another short stint with the New Yorkers, but spent most of the rest of his career in the WHL.

LECAINE, Bill
b. Moose Jaw, Saskatchewan, March 11, 1940
After a fine junior career with Regina in the 1950s, Lecaine embarked on a long, long career in the IHL that briefly segued into the NHL for four games with Pittsburgh in '68-'69. Beyond that, he played some 652 games in the "I," almost exclusively with Port Huron, before retiring in 1974.

LECAVALIER, Vincent
b. Île Bizard, Quebec, April 21, 1980
On the day of the 1998 Entry Draft, when Lecavalier was selected by Tampa Bay 1st overall, team owner Art Williams called the 18-year-old the Michael Jordan of hockey. True, Lecavalier skated as well as Jordan jumped – maybe better – but Williams certainly expected too much of the kid too soon. He had two good years of junior, but Lecavalier entered the NHL standing 6'4" and weighing a skeletal 180 pounds, not enough to tough it out in the world's premier hockey league. He filled in a bit and developed into a fine centre, but when he was named team captain at 20, the youngest captain in the NHL's history, it only added burden to the already daunting task of becoming a star. He signed a big contract, and at one time wanted a trade, and so Lecavalier has run into as many snakepits as he has hugs of celebration. He might turn out to be a Joe Thornton who takes five or six years to develop, or he may go the way of the dodo bird. Time will tell – and his time may not be far off.

LECLAIR, Jackie
b. Quebec City, Quebec, May 30, 1929
He was once the property of Toronto, but Leclair joined Montreal in the summer of 1954 and made the Habs at training camp. Coach Dick Irvin used him at centre between Maurice Richard and Bert Olmstead, though Leclair suffered a frightening injury and missed a number of games. In a collision with Larry Cahan, Leclair fell to the ice as Cahan lost his balance. Cahan's skate sliced across the throat of the falling Leclair, and he was rushed to hospital. He lost a pint and a half of blood but recovered and finished out the season with the team. Leclair helped the Habs win the Cup in each of the next two seasons, but after that he was out of the NHL and touring the minors. In 1965, he wound up in

New Haven as playing coach, a position he held for two years until being fired in the spring of 1967.

LeCLAIR, John
b. St. Albans, Vermont, July 5, 1969
With size comes strength and with strength skill, but with both come injuries. The best hockey player ever to come out of Vermont, LeClair developed into one of the best scorers of the modern game, a power forward who was plagued by serious ailments. He was drafted by Montreal during his college days at U of Vermont and joined the Habs at the end of the '90-'91 season. He stayed with the team for parts of five seasons, winning the 1993 Cup in fine fashion – he became the first man to score consecutive overtime goals in the Cup finals. But the Montreal of the 1990s did not draft and trade as it had in the past. Just the opposite. They traded LeClair, Eric Desjardins, and Gilbert Dionne for Mark Recchi and a draft choice. In Philly, LeClair blossomed. He had 3 consecutive 50-goal seasons, and while playing on a line with Eric Lindros and Mikael Renberg, the Legion of Doom became the highest-scoring and most feared threesome in the NHL. But LeClair's style also pained him. He missed much of two seasons early in his career with a serious knee injury, and later had back troubles that caused him to miss a number of games and then undergo major surgery in the summer of 2002. He played for the U.S. on the winning 1996 World Cup team and also played at the Olympics in Nagano in 1998 and Salt Lake City in 2002, where he was one of the top scorers. Off the ice, he

He was awarded a $7-million contract through arbitration, the highest amount ever awarded.
JOHN LeCLAIR

was awarded a $7-million contract through arbitration, the highest amount ever awarded, and like his former teammate Lindros presents the best and worst of being big and playing physically – it can be both intimidating and painful.

LECLERC, Mike
b. Winnipeg, Manitoba, November 10, 1976
Right on schedule, Leclerc has made slow but sure progress in the formative stages of his career with Anaheim. He came out of junior hockey in the WHL and he's been a textbook example of development, playing three years with the farm team while earning callups each year, then making the team as a roster player in 1999. In his first 3 seasons, he went from 8 to 15 to 20 goals and kept the gritty, mucking side of his game intact. If Anaheim becomes a playoff team, Leclerc will be one of the reasons.

LeCLERC, Renald "Rene"
b. Ville de Vanier, Quebec, November 12, 1947
Like many a fringe player in the NHL of the day,

LeClerc decided to chuck a part-time career in the big league in favour of a full-time gig in the WHA. He had played parts of two seasons with Detroit, but when he got to the WHA he became one of only a few men to play each and every season, 1972-79. He spent all of his time with Quebec and Indianapolis and numbered Wayne Gretzky among his teammates with the Racers.

LECUYER, Doug
b. Wainwright, Alberta, March 10, 1958
He had all the talent in the world, but his temper kept scouts and coaches leery of the youngster as a junior. Lecuyer could score and had great potential, but his penchant for going ballistic overshadowed his skills. Cheap shots, brawls, headhunting, and hooliganism. Those were the words that described Lecuyer who made a name for himself by fighting Wayne Gretzky on March 14, 1980. Nonetheless, he was given chances by NHL teams during his brief pro career (1978-83), but perhaps Lecuyer lacked discipline because he knew he had an alternative – golf. By 19, he was already a 3-time junior champion in Alberta, a provincial senior champion, and a sixth-place finisher in the national championships. He retired from hockey in 1983 to become an assistant pro, and by virtue of winning a championship that year he qualified to play in the 1984 Canadian Open.

LEDINGHAM, Walt
b. Weyburn, Saskatchewan, October 26, 1950
In 1995, Ledingham was inducted into the University of Minnesota-Duluth Sports Hall of Fame in recognition of his outstanding college career there (1968-72). After graduation, he went on to play for Chicago and the Islanders, but spent most of his time in the minors before retiring in 1977.

LEDUC, Albert ("Battleship")
b. Valleyfield, Quebec, November 22, 1902
d. Montreal, Quebec, July 31, 1990
In his day, he was everything one could hope for in a defenceman. Big, strong, and unstoppable (hence the nickname), he was one of the top-scoring blueliners when he retired. Fierce and pugnacious (hence the nickname), he took care of business on ice when the business was there for the taking. Fast and fierce (hence the nickname), he helped the Canadiens win Cups in 1930 and '31. He spent most of his 10 years with the Habs, and upon retiring coached Quebec for two years and Providence for same, during which time he was credited with discovering Toe Blake. He returned home to Valleyfield to build an arena for a hockey team he financed, and he hired the now-retired Blake as the team's coach. He helped build a hockey factory in that town, and quietly became known as a philanthropist to ailing players, notably Hooley Smith and Dunc Munro. Later, Leduc became the Quebec representative for Alberta Distillers and Château-Gai Wines, working in Montreal, and he became a wealthy man. He retired to Miami, which is where he spent nine months of each year toward the end of his life.

LEDUC, Rich
b. Île Perrot, Quebec, August 24, 1951
Squeezing into the history books is okay. It's not perfect, but, hey, if you can do it, do it. So, October 18, 1978, saw Leduc snuggle into the soft parts of trivia experts' minds because on that night he scored a goal playing for Indianapolis in the WHA. What made it special was that Wayne Gretzky drew an assist, his first pro career helper. That's it – that's the trivia. And here's another one. Leduc played for Boston briefly a few years earlier (1972-74), making him one of a very few players who can claim to have been teammates of both Bobby Orr and Wayne Gretzky.

LEDYARD, Grant
b. Winnipeg, Manitoba, November 19, 1961
Hal Ledyard was a quarterback whose finest moment came in the 1962 Fog Bowl when he came off the bench to win the Grey Cup for the Winnipeg Blue Bombers. He had a wife and six kids, but in those days he never made enough to get rich throwing the pigskin. When he retired, he sold beer and liquor dispensers, and during one road trip he went for a swim in a dangerous area and drowned. One of his kids, Grant, went on to become an NHL hockey player, and though he never recalled vividly his dad's exploits on the gridiron, he took inspiration from his life. Grant was a scoring defenceman in junior, but it was evident pretty quickly he wasn't going to be as successful in the NHL. He had to adjust his game, and he had a hard time adjusting his mentality. While playing in New York and L.A., he got caught up in the off-ice activities of the cities and came close to blowing his NHL chances. Then he settled down and became a reliable defensive defenceman, and throughout the years his conditioning ensured his survival. The quiet kid from the 'Peg has now played in more than 1,000 NHL games with 9 teams, and although he's never gone too far in the playoffs, he has endured.

LEE, Bobby
b. Montreal, Quebec, December 28, 1911
d. Worthing, England, December 31, 1974
In England, the names Richard, Howe, and Broda meant nothing. The name Bobby Lee stood large above all others, and upon his death he was called the greatest athlete of the post-war era in Brighton. Lee studied at Queen's University in Kingston, Ontario, and in 1932 he was chosen to do a year of post-graduate work at the University of Switzerland, which gave him a chance to study and play hockey around the Continent. He returned to Canada and then played in Baltimore for two seasons, but in 1936 he received a call that changed his life. Don Penniston, an old teammate from the Montreal Royals, asked him to come to England and play in Brighton. He played there for a year, then in Earl's Court, London, for two more. He met his future wife there, but in 1939 the couple returned to Canada so Lee could join the Canadian army (he became a corporal in the RCAF). After the war, Lee returned to play for the Brighton Tigers, and in '46-'47 the team won every championship in sight. Lee was the team's top scorer and its manager, and for the next eight years he set records of Gretzky-like proportion. He was the first to score 300 goals in a British career, the first to score 400, and by the time he retired in 1954 he was closing in on 500. After he retired, he became a manager of another sort – of the Mile Oak Inn and then of the Windmill Inn

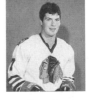

Doug Lecuyer

Walt Ledingham

Albert Leduc

Rich Leduc

Grant Ledyard

in Southwick until the time of his death of pneumonia on New Year's Eve 1974.

LEE, Edward
b. Rochester, New York, December 17, 1961
Princeton University graduates plenty of scholars and academics, but it surely does not specialize in producing quality hockey players. Lee, then, was the exception rather than the rule. Perhaps not surprisingly, though, he was not an exceptional hockey player. After graduating in 1984, he played two games for the Nordiques and only a couple of years of pro hockey.

Edward Lee

LEE, Peter
b. Ellesmere, England, January 2, 1956
Hot, hot, hot. In junior, no one could touch this guy. In his four years with the Ottawa 67's, Lee set records for goals in a career (213) and in a season (81), and when he went on to the NHL in 1977 the 67's were the first OHL team to retire a player's number – Lee's number 14. Montreal drafted him only 12th overall, though, which clearly indicated teams' reluctance to rely on a small player to have an impact. Records and all, the NHL was a different league altogether. Peter's father, Eric, was a pro soccer player in England and a star performer at the 1948 Olympics, but when Peter was just three the family emigrated to Canada and settled in Ottawa. Eric became a vice-principal at a high school in Hull, and Peter grew up loving sports. He never did play with Montreal, because the Habs traded him to Pittsburgh with Pete Mahovlich for Pierre Larouche. Lee had two 30-goal seasons with the Pens, but his last 2 of 6 seasons were poor and he ended up in the minors. In 1983, he moved to Germany where he had a lengthy career, first as a player and then as a playing coach.

Peter Lee

LEEB, Brad
b. Red Deer, Alberta, July 27, 1979
Well, if nothing else happens, he'll at least get the alumni newsletter. Leeb was never drafted after playing in Red Deer, but he did play four games for Vancouver in a career that has been lodged in the minors so far. The small right winger will, inevitably, wind up in Europe, but until then he maintains a hold on the NHL dream.

Brad Leeb

LEEB, Greg
b. Red Deer, Alberta, May 31, 1977
Smaller and a bit older than brother Brad, Greg has had an equally tough time getting into the NHL. So far, Dallas has obliged with a couple of games, but besides that Leeb has played in the IHL and then the AHL with Edmonton's affiliate in Hamilton.

LEEMAN, Gary
b. Toronto, Ontario, February 19, 1964
So much negativity and controversy surrounded Leeman's 50-goal season he might have wished he never had such a great year. A local boy, he couldn't have been happier when the Leafs drafted him in 1982 and worked him into the lineup. He had been a defenceman in junior, but the Carlton St. brain trust decided to put him on the right wing, and he slowly developed into one of the best young players at that position. In '86-'87, he scored 21 goals, and then had years of 30 and 32. All looked quite fine, indeed. It was in '89-'90, though, that he made a name for himself by scoring 51 goals, only the second Leaf to do so (Rick Vaive had been the first). His success came from the formation of the Hound Line, featuring Leeman with Wendel Clark and Russ Courtnall (all of whom played for the Notre Dame Hounds in Saskatchewan). The next season he separated his shoulder, missed a bunch of games and wound up with only 17 goals. The year after, Cliff Fletcher wanted to make his mark as the team's new GM and made the largest trade in NHL history: five Leafs went to Calgary, and five Flames came to Toronto, the most prominent part of the deal being Leeman for Doug Gilmour. Gilmour went on to have the finest years of his career in Toronto, while Leeman utterly evaporated 59 games and 11 goals later, claiming he had trouble adjusting to the higher altitude in Alberta. He was traded to Montreal where he won a Stanley Cup after scoring just six goals (and one more in the playoffs), and from there things went from bad to worse. He was chased out of the NHL and signed a rich deal with an Italian club, but even there he could no longer score and his contract wasn't renewed. Leeman blamed injuries for his demise. Critics just blamed him, period, for a total lack of production after his one big season.

It was in '89-'90 that he made a name for himself by scoring 51 goals.
GARY LEEMAN

LEETCH, Brian
b. Corpus Christi, Texas, March 3, 1968
He came out of Texas high school a fireball pitcher and skated his way into hockey annals as arguably the best American-born defenceman to play the game. Even before he played his first game with the Rangers at the end of the '87-'88 season Leetch had played at two World Junior tournaments, a World Championships, and an Olympics. He was 19. He had played a season at Boston College, where his father had also played a generation earlier and where he was a Hobey Baker Award finalist. In his first full year with the Rangers, he won the Calder Trophy, had his first of four 20-goal seasons, and anchored the defence of a team that was in

the process of becoming a Cup contender. In '91-'92, he had 102 points, joining the exclusive company of defenceman at the century mark. He had the year of a lifetime, though, in '93-'94 when the Rangers brought the Cup to Broadway for the first time since 1940, and Leetch led the playoffs with 23 assists and 34 points and was named winner of the Conn Smythe Trophy. He won the Norris Trophy twice (1992 and '97), and when Mark Messier left the team to sign with Vancouver, Leetch was named team captain. He played in the 1996 World Cup and the 1998 and 2002 Olympics and has now played more than 1,000 games, all with the Rangers. He holds virtually every Rangers defenceman record and is a sure Hall of Famer after his playing days are done.

LEFEBVRE, Guillaume
b. Amos, Quebec, May 7, 1981
One of a small number of juniors who played for four teams in the Q, Lefebvre turned pro in 2001 and has since played a scant three games with the Flyers. He was a low draft choice in 2000 and has plenty of work to do on the left wing in the minors before he will become a regular in the Philadelphia lineup.

LEFEBVRE, Patrice
b. Montreal, Quebec,
June 28, 1967
Just a little, wee, tiny guy, Lefebvre was one of the oldest rookies to make it to the NHL. He went straight from junior to Europe in 1988 because he attracted no NHL interest, but after several seasons overseas he decided to accept an offer from Las Vegas to play in the IHL. Not only did he play, he excelled, both as a fine scorer and as one of the best playmakers in the league. After another five years of play in the "I," Washington finally offered him a contract, and at age 31 he finally played in the NHL! The gig lasted but three games and he was soon back in Europe, but Lefebvre made it to the league that counts most.

LEFEBVRE, Sylvain ("Sly")
b. Richmond, Quebec, October 14, 1967
It's difficult to quantify a defensive defenceman's work. There are no numbers or points for taking your man or making solid contact or clearing the puck. The only thing these warriors have to go on is reputation and a chance to play and compete. That's all Lefebvre ever asked for, but in 1986 Montreal was the only team willing to give the undrafted, unheroic superstar a chance. He never scored many goals or anchored the power play, but he was the best penalty killer and played against the top players in the league. The Habs traded him to Toronto for a song, and under Pat Burns Lefebvre had a chance to show he was among the best at his job. He was later traded to Quebec in the deal

He had the year of a lifetime in '93-'94 when the Rangers brought the Cup to Broadway.
BRIAN LEETCH

that brought Mats Sundin to Toronto, and he won a Cup with the team in Colorado. He signed as a free agent with the Rangers in 1999, and he has been with that non-contending team ever since. In photographs, he's always the player standing up a star at the blueline, playing the body and not looking at the puck, tying up an opponent along the boards or in the corner. He performs those chores as well as anyone.

LEFLEY, Bryan
b. Grosse Isle, Manitoba, October 18, 1948
d. Bolzano, Italy, October 29, 1997
If you are a good hockey player, there are many options and possibilities outside the NHL. Hockey is a sport that crosses borders and one based on a common language that has sticks and pucks as its nouns and verbs. Lefley made it to the NHL in the 1970s with a series of bad teams, but he was no superstar and he didn't have the intensity to try to make it every single night. He played much of the decade in the minors, but in 1978 he moved to Germany and changed the course of his life. He played for a few years, then became a coach with Zurich, making his way to Italy shortly thereafter. He coached that country's National Team until the fall of 1997 when he was killed in a car accident, his hopes of guiding the team to the Olympics lost.

LEFLEY, Chuck
b. Winnipeg, Manitoba, January 20, 1950
Brother Bryan went one way, to a career in hockey that led to Europe. Chuck went another, to a career that led to Europe and then back to the family farm. He played for Father Bauer's National Team in the late 1960s, culminating with an appearance at the 1969 World Championships, and made his NHL debut with Montreal at the end of the '70-'71 season, the year the team won the Cup. Over the next three years, he worked his way into a star-studded lineup, sometimes playing on a line with Jacques Lemaire and Yvan Cournoyer, sometimes relying on his great shot to score and generate offence. He was traded to St. Louis, but after two and a half years he retired, fed up and longing for the farm, almost immediately after signing a new three-year contract. Late in the summer, though, he was lured to Finland, and Blues GM Emile Francis was furious. This was the era when compensation to European teams was all the rage for NHL teams pillaging the Continent for players, but Francis demanded that the reverse be true: Teams in Europe that steal North American players should also have to pay. Lefley played the following season in Germany and then returned to the Blues to honour his contract. But during his first year back he suffered a

Patrice Lefebvre

Sylvain Lefebvre

Bryan Lefley

Chuck Lefley

Manny Legace

Roger Leger

Barry Legge

David Legwand

Hugh Lehman

separated shoulder, and after two games in his second season he found that ambition just wasn't there. He returned to the 900-acre farm in Manitoba and got out of the game for good.

LEGACE, Manny
b. Toronto, Ontario, February 4, 1973

Legace is a two-Cup goalie, one of the rarest breed of players. And like any skilled player, he learned from experience. Near the end of his junior career, he joined Canada's National Team in the hopes of playing at the 1994 Olympics. During one practice he was hit square in the crown jewels by a shot and has worn two cups instead of the usual one ever since. He didn't play at Lillehammer and it was four long years in the minors before he got into an NHL game, with L.A. Since 1999 he has been with Detroit, trying to be the number-one man but having to settle for backup to the likes of Chris Osgood and Dominik Hasek. Although he was part of the team that won the Cup in 2002, he played just 11 minutes in the playoffs and watched the rest of the games from the bench as the Dominator dominated the post-season. His finest moment came in 1993 at the World Juniors when he recorded a perfect 6-0-0 tournament, won gold for Canada, and was named outstanding goalie of the championships.

LEGER, Roger
b. L'Annonciation, Quebec, March 26, 1919
d. L'Annonciation, Quebec, April 7, 1965

Leger got into his first NHL games during the war, with the Rangers in 1944. He went on to play several years in the minors, mostly in Buffalo, though he did appear for most of three full seasons with Montreal soon after. He ended up in Victoria in 1950 and had an outstanding season with the Cougars, being named league MVP. He returned to Quebec after another year, and in 1954 became a playing coach for the Shawinigan Cataracts. Midway through his second season, his playing days ended when he suffered cracked ribs and was forced to stand behind the bench. At season's end, he remained as coach only, and the year after he moved on to the Montreal Royals. Leger later returned home to L'Annonciation, a resort town in the Laurentians, where he ran a resort and bar. He died suddenly of a heart attack at age 46.

LEGGE, Barry
b. Winnipeg, Manitoba, October 22, 1954

Legge made the leap from junior in Winnipeg to the WHA in 1974 when he signed with the short-lived Michigan Stags. Thus began a journey through that league until 1979, when he remained with WHA teams in an NHL environment, namely Quebec and Winnipeg. He retired in 1982.

LEGGE, Randy
b. Newmarket, Ontario, December 16, 1945

Legge went from junior to the minors to the NHL, but after just a dozen games with the Rangers in '72-'73 he was handed around again in the minors and WHA until 1977, when he said enough is enough. And it was.

LEGRIS, Claude
b. Verdun, Quebec, November 6, 1956

Legris's pedigree in junior couldn't have been purer. In 1973-74, he set a QMJHL record by going undefeated in 17 straight games, but by the time he joined Detroit in 1980 he never got the chance to prove his worth at the NHL level. He played only 91 minutes of hockey over 2 years and was out of the game altogether by 1983.

LEGWAND, David ("Leggy")
b. Detroit, Michigan, August 17, 1980

Coming out of junior in Ontario, Legwand was one of the top American-born prospects in recent years. Nashville selected him 2nd overall in 1998 and he got into a single game with the Predators that year while continuing in junior. In 1999, the team felt he was ready for the NHL, and at age 19 he was a regular centre on an expansion team. In his first three seasons, though, he hasn't scored more than 13 goals and the checking, pace, and hitting of the pro game has been too much for him many nights. He's had a chance to play for Team USA at the Worlds because the Preds haven't made the playoffs, but he hasn't yet taken his game to the next level.

LEHMAN, Hugh ("Old Eagle Eye")
b. Pembroke, Ontario, October 27, 1885
d. Toronto, Ontario, April 8, 1961

It is worth arguing that for the era he played in, there was no finer goaler than Hugh Lehman. He first came to heroic recognition by playing for Pembroke in 1906 when the team went undefeated and won the Citizen Shield. He then went to Sault Ste. Marie in the old IHL, afterwards moving back to Pembroke before heading to Berlin (now Kitchener) to play in the Trolley League. In the 1909-10 season, he played for both Galt and Berlin when those teams challenged, unsuccessfully, for the Stanley Cup. In 1911, when the Patricks organized the Pacific Coast league, they recruited Lehman and he happily obliged, playing the next 15 years out west. He routinely led the league in goals against and wins and made frequent appearances in the Stanley Cup finals, though he won only once, in 1915 (for which his name is inscribed inside the original bowl of the trophy). In 1926, he finally agreed to play in the NHL, with Chicago, and the now 41-year-old played in every game for the Hawks and led the league in minutes played. He coached the team the following year, playing only a few games in goal, but it was a dismal season and he was replaced. Lehman was a pioneer in his day. Legend has it that he once scored a goal by skating through the entire opposition and beating the goalie with a shot. Although there is no solid documentation of this, it is irrefutable that he frequently carried the puck as far as the opponent's blueline before making a pass. In 1928, once fully retired, Lehman returned to a job he had maintained on a part-time basis during his career. In all, he worked for the Warren Bituminous Paving Company for some 50 years before retiring as president in 1956, though he stayed on with the board of directors until his death. He was a shy man, but there was no hiding his hockey accomplishments, and in 1958 he was inducted into the Hockey Hall of Fame. He died in hospital three years later.

LEHMANN, Tommy
b. Stockholm, Sweden, February 3, 1964
Boston skeptically drafted Lehmann 228th overall in 1982 and saw neither hide nor hair of him until five years later. Lehmann stuck around only two and a half years, playing his last game with Edmonton before returning to Sweden to resume his career in that country's national league.

LEHTINEN, Jere
b. Espoo, Finland, June 24, 1973
Lehtinen ranks among the first class of modern Finnish players. He had an outstanding pre-NHL career in international hockey, appearing in three World Juniors, three World Championships, and the 1994 Olympics in Lillehammer before joining Dallas in 1995. Since then, he has been a consistent 20-goal scorer and excellent two-way player for the Stars, and his 10 goals in the 1999 playoffs was an important part of the team's Stanley Cup victory. Lehtinen is a two-time winner of the Selke Trophy as the league's best defensive forward, in '97-'98 and '98-'99, but he missed most of the following season because of a badly broken ankle that he reinjured after returning for just a few games. He has played in the last three Olympics for Suomi, and the right winger is entering the prime of his life as an established NHL star.

LEHTO, Petteri
b. Turku, Finland, March 13, 1961
Lehto made his longest-lasting mark in his hometown, where he played professionally for more than a decade. He also represented Finland at the 1984 Olympics in Sarajevo and played half a dozen games for Pittsburgh in '84-'85. After retiring in 1990, he became a player agent specializing in Finns. Among his most noteworthy clients is Ville Nieminen.

LEHTONEN, Antero
b. Tampere, Finland, April 12, 1954
Washington took a chance on Lehtonen, and he on them, but after one season it was obvious things just weren't going to work out. He came to camp in 1979 and quickly broke a finger and missed training camp. Then the team went on a long road trip and played a ton of games in a short period, something the Finn wasn't used to. He burned out, and went down to the minors, where he played really well and earned a promotion. Coach Gary Green put him on a fourth line with Wes Jarvis and Mark Lofthouse, and the trio played sporadically but effectively. At year's end, Lehtonen had just nine goals to his credit and returned to Finland, where he continued a perfectly productive career that included trips to three World Championships.

LEHVONEN, Henri ("Hank")
b. Sarnia, Ontario, August 26, 1950
His Finnish extraction eventually took him to Europe, but before then Lehvonen graduated from Ontario junior to played in the "I" for a number of years, his time punctuated by a four-game stint with Kansas City in '74-'75. He had his best years with Port Huron but in 1978 accepted a contract offer from Finland and played there for the better part of four seasons.

LEIER, Edward
b. Poland, November 3, 1927
Leier played 16 games with Chicago over a 2-year period (1949-51) during a brief career spent mostly in the minors. He finished in 1956 playing for Eddie Shore and the Springfield Indians.

LEINONEN, Mikko
b. Tampere, Finland, July 15, 1955
On April 8, 1982, Leinonen put his name in the record books with a performance that has since been equalled only once, by a guy named Gretzky. On April 8, 1982, Leinonen recorded six assists in a playoff game, a Rangers 7-3 win over Philadelphia. It was a nice finish to a decent first NHL season for the Finnish veteran, but it was not portentous. Leinonen scored 17 goals the next year and after that he was mostly in the minors. To start '84-'85, he returned home, only to be signed by Washington and lured back to North America toward the end of the season. Leinonen appeared in all the prestigious international tournaments for his country prior to his NHL time. After retiring, he stayed in the game and later became the GM of the Tappara club in Tampere, Finland.

LEITER, Bob ("Knobby")
b. Winnipeg, Manitoba, March 22, 1941
It was the hairpiece that got everyone laughing, the toupée, the rug, call it what you will, Leiter decided to cover his baldness one day and scored three goals in his first game wearing it. A hat trick. Things weren't always that way. He had a full head of hair when the Winnipeg Braves won the 1959 Memorial Cup with him and teammates Ted Green and Gary Bergman in the lineup. Starting in 1962, he played with the Bruins for two seasons, but early in the third year he broke his arm and missed the rest of the season. The year after, he contracted tuberculosis and was again sidelined for the season. By that time, the team had Orr and Esposito to build around, and Leiter spent five seasons in Hershey waiting for another chance. That came first with Pittsburgh in 1971, and the year after with Atlanta. As a Flames centre, he had consecutive 26-goal seasons before his production tailed off badly. During his early

Leiter played pro for 15 years and then settled in Gimli, Manitoba, where he opened an insurance office.
BOB LEITER

Tommy Lehmann

Jere Lehtinen

Antero Lehtonen

Henri Lehvonen

Mikko Leinonen

Jacques Lemaire

Moe Lemay

Reggie Lemelin

Roger Lemelin

Alain Lemieux

years, he worked summers in Winnipeg for a dry cell manufacturer based in Madison, Wisconsin, that had a large plant in Manitoba. Although he always felt he could fall back on this job if hockey didn't pan out, Leiter played pro for 15 years and then settled in Gimli, Manitoba, where he opened an insurance office.

LEITER, Ken
b. Detroit, Michigan, April 19, 1961
After graduating from Michigan State University in 1982, Leiter joined the Islanders system, slowly working his way into the lineup. At training camp in 1986, he beat out veterans Randy Boyd and Gerald Diduck for a spot on the blueline, and during that year he played his way onto the power play. The year after, though, he was felled by a number of injuries, and in 1988 he retired to start a home renovation business. Minnesota signed him in 1989, but after four games Leiter retired permanently.

LEMAIRE, Jacques
b. LaSalle, Quebec, September 7, 1945
One of nine children, Jacques left school to work at age 14 when his father died of polio. Fortunately, he was also blessed with great hockey ability, and this was enhanced by an ambition and perseverance that took him to the NHL. From the moment he entered the league in 1967 with the Canadiens, he was renowned for his slapshot, which most people rated second only to Bobby Hull for speed. He played exactly 12 seasons in the NHL, and it was a remarkable career at that. He never scored fewer than 20 goals a season, and he won 8 Stanley Cups, including 2 to start his career. In '72-'73, he had a career high of 44 goals, but it was a little later that he produced even more gratifying results. His overtime goal on May 14, 1977, gave the Habs a 2-1 win and a four-game sweep of Boston to win the Cup. Two years later, he scored the game winner in game five to give the team a 4-1 win against the Rangers, thus making him one of only five men to score two Cup-winning goals during a career. Like most of Montreal's centres, he was an excellent skater and playmaker, but was as sound as the dollar defensively as well. He retired in 1979 as he had begun, a Cup winner, and left to play and coach in Switzerland to prepare for a career behind the bench in the NHL. After two seasons, he became coach of Plattsburgh State University in New York and then coached in Quebec junior for a year. Lemaire replaced Bob Berry as coach of the Habs with 17 games to go in the '83-'84 season, and the year after won the Jack Adams Trophy for his first full season in the NHL, one in which he was inducted into the Hockey Hall of Fame for his playing career. The pressure of the job, however, forced him to resign and he took a softer position in the organization as assistant to the managing director. During his eight years there, he won the Cup in 1986 and '93 with the Habs, and felt ready to try coaching again. He accepted the job in New Jersey, and during his five years there he was both loved and hated. The love part came about because he crafted the Devils into a winner, notably in 1995 when the team won its first Cup in franchise history. He was reviled, though, by players and fans around the league, because he coached his team to play the trap, a boring, defensive system of play that is the antithesis, ironically, of the firewagon hockey he had played with Montreal in the 1970s. He

was let go after the '97-'98 season and returned to Montreal as assistant GM, a position he held until 2000 when he was named first head coach of the expansion Minnesota Wild. Since then, he has quickly taken the team out of the lower depths of the league and formed a solid – and defensive-minded – team.

LEMAY, Maurice "Moe"
b. Saskatoon, Saskatchewan, February 18, 1962
Most Canadians who end their careers in Europe return home to find work. Not Lemay. He left the NHL in 1989 and has yet to return home. He had a great junior career in Ottawa and was crushed when Vancouver sent him down after his first camp in 1981, but before the season was over he got a callup for a few games with the Canucks. Lemay played parts of six years with Vancouver, playing mostly left wing but also some games on the right side. On March 10, 1987, he got the treat of his life when he was traded to Edmonton and won the Cup with the great Oilers just a few weeks later. The next year, though, Edmonton sent him to the farm after just four games and at mid-season he was traded to Boston and soon after to Winnipeg. Lemay then entered phase two of his career. He moved to Europe and played in Germany for a decade, and when he hung up the blades he stayed there and got a job in Dortmund as a house builder.

LEMELIN, Rejean "Reggie"
b. Quebec City, Quebec, November 19, 1954
The many phases of goalie Lemelin's life highlight the pros and cons of hockey as a career. Lemelin was drafted by Philadelphia in 1974 (good), but the Flyers kept him in the minors and never used him (bad). Atlanta signed him (good) and over the next five years he worked himself into the number-one position (good). But as the Flames were building a Stanley Cup team (good), Lemelin found himself on the bench each playoff year (bad). And although the Flames went to the finals in 1986 (good), he played just 109 playoff minutes that year (bad). He signed as a free agent with Boston in 1987 (good) and took the team to the Cup finals before losing to Edmonton (bad). Two years of declining success led to his losing the starting job to Andy Moog (bad), and early in '92-'93 the Bruins placed him on waivers for the purpose of demoting him (bad). He retired in stead and became a goalie coach, first with St. Louis and now, for nearly a decade, with the Flyers. Good.

LEMELIN, Roger
b. Iroquois Falls, Ontario, February 6, 1954
Outside the minors, Lemelin's career featured time with the Kansas City/Colorado franchise during the unpleasant 1970s, when the team never made it to the playoffs. At that, his time in the NHL was sporadic at best. He won the Calder Cup with Hershey in 1980.

LEMIEUX, Alain
b. Montreal, Quebec, May 24, 1961
There can be nothing more difficult than being the older brother of one of the greatest hockey players of all time. Alain was a perfectly fine skater in his own right and scored more than his share of goals in the Q, but he had to work his butt off to get into each of his NHL games. He came into the league in 1981, three

years before Mario, but he was a part-timer at best. While Mario scored a goal on his first shift and never looked back, Alain struggled with the minors and tried Europe for a while. He ended his career in the IHL and then went into management, eventually coaching in the East Coast league for Mario's Penguins. The hiring might have been nepotistic, but Alain's firing just a short time later was all business.

LEMIEUX, Bob
b. Montreal, Quebec, December 16, 1944
Lemieux played junior in the final days of sponsorship, but before he could play for Montreal he was claimed by Oakland in the Expansion Draft of 1967. He played just a few games for the Seals, and after a brief career in the minors he retired to become GM of the Fort Worth Wings.

LEMIEUX, Claude ("Pepe")
b. Buckingham, Quebec, July 16, 1965
One of the most important playoff performers of the modern era, Lemieux is also one of the league's most vilified characters, simultaneously a skilled clutch performer and a dirty, vicious, cheap-shot winger. He won Stanley Cups with three different teams (including two wins with New Jersey at different times), one of only five players to do so, and he ranks among the top in career playoff game-winning goals. Lemieux was called up to the Habs as an 18-year-old while playing junior in Verdun, and his entrance into the NHL was a classic metaphor for his on-ice character. He was called up on a holiday, and the Verdun

> **At his best he has been a "disturber," but at his worst, flagrantly dirty.**
> CLAUDE LEMIEUX

arena was locked. To get his equipment, he had to break in, and he made the plane only in the nick of time. He scored a goal in that first game, and after 3 partial seasons with the team he established his reputation in the 1986 playoffs, when he scored ten goals. He has had five 30-goal seasons playing for Montreal, New Jersey, and Colorado, and every time he has changed teams he has won a Cup. But along with the glory has come his fair share of infamy, notably with the Avs during their run to the 1996 championship. In the conference finals, he hit Kris Draper from behind at the boards, knocking the Red Wings forward into the top of the dasher and resulting in serious facial injury. Lemieux was suspended for just two games, and the hit inspired the Wings to defeat the Avs the following year. At his best he has been a "disturber," but at his worst, flagrantly dirty. His play has never resulted in much international fanfare, though Lemieux did make the 1987 Canada Cup team and the '96 World Cup squad for Canada. After winning his second Cup with the Devils in 2000, his career seemed over until his friend Wayne Gretzky signed him for his Phoenix Coyotes.

Lemieux was subsequently traded to Dallas at the deadline in March 2003.

LEMIEUX, Jacques
b. Matane, Quebec, April 8, 1943
A Montreal prospect in the days of sponsorship, Lemieux was scooped up by L.A. in 1967, but he made only the smallest of inroads into the Kings roster during his time in the game. He was traded to Toronto in 1970 but retired rather than accept an assignment to the minors.

LEMIEUX, Jean
b. Noranda, Quebec, May 31, 1952
A defenceman with Atlanta in 1973, Lemieux played parts of three seasons with the Flames before being involved in a blockbuster trade on January 22, 1976. He, Gerry Meehan, and a first-round draft choice went to Washington for Bill Clement. Clement stayed six and a half seasons with the Flames, but Lemieux lasted just 64 games with the Caps. He wound up in the minors before retiring.

LEMIEUX, Jocelyn
b. Mont Laurier, Quebec, November 18, 1967
Brother of Claude, he didn't have the same, lengthy career or the same success, but he did play in 598 NHL games over 12 seasons. Jocelyn wasn't a scorer and he did more travelling, playing for seven different teams in the NHL. He started with St. Louis in 1986, but after suffering a broken leg he fell back in his development and the Blues traded him to Montreal. He had his best success in Chicago when the team went to the Cup finals in 1992. He ended his playing days first with Phoenix and then in the minors, but he returned to the Coyotes after retiring, joining the team's community relations department.

LEMIEUX, Mario ("Super Mario")
b. Montreal, Quebec, October 5, 1965
Not that his junior career in Laval needed any sort of exclamation mark, but in his final game at the end of the '83–'84 season, Lemieux had 12 points (six goals, six assists) in a 16-4 win to finish the year with a record 282 points. In the summer, he was drafted 1st overall by last-place Pittsburgh, though his relations with the Penguins to that point had been so acrimonious that he refused to take the podium when his name was announced. That was a long time ago. Lemieux entered the NHL in 1984 as the most heralded player since Wayne Gretzky, but there was trepidation to go with the excitement. For one, his points came in the Quebec league, a junior circuit known for scoring. Also, it was as though the hockey world could not believe that even while Gretzky

Bob Lemieux

Jacques Lemieux

Jean Lemieux

Jocelyn Lemieux

Mario Lemieux

was in his prime his successor was already making his way into the league. The expression was always that a player like Gretzky comes along once every 20 years, or something to that effect, and here was Mario coming along just five years after Gretzky first played in the NHL. There was no mistaking Lemieux's talent, though. On his first shift, he stripped Ray Bourque of the puck and scored on Pete Peeters, a play made with an ease that was to become one of Lemieux's trademarks. He was 18 years old. At the All-Star Game that year, not only was the rookie chosen to play, he also stole the spotlight and was named MVP, the best of the best. By season's end, he had scored 43 goals and became only the third rookie after Dale Hawerchuk and Peter Stastny to score 100 points in his first year (Gretzky, because of his WHA season, was never considered a rookie). Of course, he won the Calder Trophy, and his point total set a precedent that is unmatched – Lemieux has never played a full season of hockey and had fewer than 100 points. He had 141 in his second season and fell back to 107 the year after, and in the fall of 1987 he made the first of his historic impacts on the game, the stuff of legend that fans talk about for decades. Lemieux was named to Team Canada's 1987 Canada Cup team, and it was his breathtaking play with Wayne Gretzky that kept the Canada Cup trophy in its homeland. He led the tournament with 11 goals, nine of which were assisted by Gretzky, and in the dying moments of game three of the best-of-three finals he scored the most memorable goal since Darryl Sittler's Canada Cup winner in 1976 and perhaps the most dramatic goal in Canadian international history with the obvious exception of Paul Henderson's 1972 score. Coming down the left wing, Lemieux took a simple and perfect drop pass from Gretzky and then placed the puck in the top corner with a great wrist shot to give Canada a 6-5 lead with a minute and a half to go. He jumped into Gretzky's arms, and history was made. It was during the training camp for that tournament that Lemieux developed as a man and a player. Gretzky lashed out at him for taking his skills for granted and not pushing himself, for coasting instead of going hard, for making do instead of making great. Lemieux responded to the challenge, and after the Canada Cup had the best two years of his career, scoring 168 and 199 points and winning his first two Art Ross Trophies. As Lemieux became 1A in the league to Gretzky's 1, the Penguins were also evolving into a playoff team and a Cup-contending team that was selling out home games and establishing itself financially in a way it had never enjoyed since entering the NHL in 1967. Yet as he was reaching his zenith, he was also physically near his nadir. In 1989-90, he suffered back problems that kept him out

Mario Lemieux

of the lineup for 23 games, and the following year played only 26 regular season games. He returned healthy and, given the long NHL season, rested, and in the playoffs was again his dominating self. He led all playoff scorers in assists (28) and points (44), but more important he led the team to the Stanley Cup, a preposterous thought seven years previous when he had yet to play for the team. In one game against New Jersey, he also made history by scoring five goals in five different ways, the first and only player to date to accomplish this (regular strength, power play, short handed, penalty shot, empty net). Lemieux led the team to another Cup in 1991-92 and won another scoring championship, but his back continued to plague him. The year after, he led all players in points with 160, but more remarkable was that he did this while playing only 60 games. The two year period 1993-95 was a disastrous one for Lemieux, whose back was so bad that the trainer had to do his skates up before every game and undo the laces after. His problems were compounded when he learned that he had Hodgkin's disease, and the ensuing radiation treatments knocked him out of the game for so long many wondered whether he would ever return. In 1995, he not only returned, he led the league in scoring the next two seasons, a feat that even left opponents dazed by his skills and determination. But by 1997, Lemieux was tired. His body had been beaten into submission, and the game had changed to the point that vicious slashes, centre-ice hooks, and interference away from the puck were so

Had he been healthy his whole career, he might well have challenged Gretzky's points record.
MARIO LEMIEUX

commonplace that he had lost all interest in playing. He left the game leaving the public confused by this superstar talent. Whereas Gretzky was an ambassador and diplomat, an outgoing, media-friendly player, Lemieux felt no such obligation. He didn't mind saying *no* when Canada asked him to play at the World Championships, and he positively infuriated fans when he refused to play in the World Cup in 1996. He retired just before the NHL was getting involved in the 1998 Olympics in Nagano, another blow to Canada's international hopes. His retirement precipitated a decision by the Hockey Hall of Fame to waive the usual three-year waiting period and induct him immediately, and the Penguins retired his number 66. Over the next three years, Lemieux took on another challenge – save the Penguins. The team became less secure through the 1990s as salaries escalated many times faster than revenues, and Pittsburgh one day looked like a small market team that couldn't afford to sign star players. Lemieux had deferred much of his salary for after his playing days, but now it looked like he might never see those millions of dollars owed him. Eventually, he bought the team and tried to bring fiscal responsibility back to the franchise. He sought to build a new arena but was met with skepticism or rejection at every point, but the team continued to perform well, in large part because of the play of his friend and mentor, Jaromir Jagr. By early in the 2000-01 season, though, a combination of forces led Lemieux to come out of retirement. Certainly the financial problems would be better served with Lemieux in the lineup, but also the league had started to clean up the game and make skill the preferred means of playing. In December 2000, he made his debut against Toronto at home, and set up a goal on his first shift. He later scored and had another assist on the night. Mario was back. Over the course of the rest of the year, he played near his career average of two points a game, and the team went all the way to the conference finals. More important, Lemieux was enjoying the game and promptly served notice that he planned to be around a few more years. When Team Canada GM Wayne Gretzky announced the first eight players for the 2002 Olympics at Salt Lake City, he called Lemieux's name first and made him the team captain. To start the 2001-02 season, Lemieux announced plans to not play games on consecutive days (to help his back), but he played only sporadically because of a sore hip. When he got to Salt Lake City, though, he put on a performance reminiscent of his play at the 1987 Canada Cup. He scored two goals against Dominik Hasek in Canada's game against the Czechs, a huge psychological lift as it was Hasek who had foiled all shooters in the 1998 Olympics in Nagano. In the gold-medal game against the U.S., he made the play of the tournament by faking a shot on a pass from the point and freezing goalie Mike Richter. Lemieux let the puck slip past him to teammate Paul Kariya who had an open side of the net to score. When he held a bunch of yellow roses in his hand and wore a gold medal around his neck after the victory, Lemieux spoke of realizing a dream for Canada, and for the first time in 15 years he had represented his country with extraordinary skill. But Lemieux did not return to the Pittsburgh lineup. His hip became too painful to play, and he missed the rest of the season recovering from yet another debilitating injury. To start the 2002-03 season, though, he was healthy again and the NHL's further crackdown on obstruction opened the game even more for Lemieux. He averaged two points a game again, played with an enthusiasm that had been lacking in his later years before retirement, and inspired another generation who watched in awe as he played with incomparable skill. Lemieux was only the third Hall of Fame member to play in the NHL after being inducted (Gordie Howe and Guy Lafleur were the others). His accomplishments are many and of the highest quality, and his perseverance in playing despite major injuries to his back and hip, and his battle with Hodgkin's is inspiring and truly amazing. Despite being in the league for 16 years, he still has not played 1,000 career games yet is in the top seven of career-scoring leaders. No one in the game's history is as natural a scorer, as skilled with the puck when going in goal. His calmness under pressure is paralleled by few in the game, and his ability to raise the level of his teammates through his own play is Gretzky-like in its brilliance. Had he been healthy his whole career, he might well have challenged Gretzky's points record. Even as he is, Lemieux remains one of the game's greatest players.

LEMIEUX, Real
b. Victoriaville, Quebec, January 3, 1945
d. Montreal, Quebec, October 25, 1975
Thirty is too young to die. Lemieux was a regular with four teams from the time he entered the NHL in 1966 to the time he had to retire in 1974. He was a durable and reliable left winger who lacked the offensive magic of some players but who was a solid contributor and occasional spark plug. Soon after leaving the game, he developed a fatal blood clot in his brain and died in a Montreal hospital.

Real Lemieux

LEMIEUX, Richard
b. Temiscamingue, Ontario, April 19, 1951
The Montreal Jr. Canadiens were blessed with an abundance of talent in 1969 and '70, when the team won back-to-back Memorial Cups, and Lemieux was blessed to be a part of that great double victory. He was drafted by Vancouver and went on to centre the team's big line, dubbed the Pony Express Line and featuring Lemieux at centre with Andre Boudrias and Bobby Lalonde on the wings. The expansion team never made it to the playoffs in the three years Lemieux was there, and he later played for Kansas City and Atlanta before retiring.

Richard Lemieux

LENARDON, Tim
b. Trail, British Columbia, May 11, 1962
The Maine Mariners' 1986 training camp was kind of odd. The coach was Tom McVie, and he agreed to take in a kid named Tim Lenardon for good reason. As a kid himself, McVie had played with Norm Lenardon, Tim's dad. McVie went on to a pro career, and Norm went on to play for the Trail Smoke Eaters during their gold-medal win at the 1961 World Championships. Any son of Norm's was worth a chance, McVie thought. Tim had shown tremendous scoring ability, and he did fine with Maine, scoring 28 goals and earning a callup to the Devils for 7 games. In succeeding years, he scored well in the minors but earned only one other promotion, to Vancouver three years later. After retiring, he became a regional scout for the Canucks and became involved in hockey operations for Chain Reaction Sports.

LENARDUZZI, Mike
b. London, Ontario, September 14, 1972
It doesn't matter how good or bad you are, someone always needs a goalie. Although Lenarduzzi played only 189 minutes of NHL hockey, he has moved around – from Springfield to Salt Lake City to Mobile and to Baton Rouge – taking shots from players in every league imaginable since leaving junior in 1992. If there are pucks to be stopped, Lenarduzzi is your man.

Mike Lenarduzzi

LEPINE, Alfred "Pit" ("Pete")
b. St. Anne de Bellevue, Quebec, July 30, 1901
d. Au-Bon-Aire, Quebec, August 2, 1955
Arguably the finest player not in the Hockey Hall of Fame, Lepine had both the fortune and the misfortune of playing second fiddle to Howie Morenz during the heyday of the Canadiens in the 1920s and 1930s. He

Pit Lepine

Hec Lepine

Francois Leroux

Jean-Yves Leroux

Curtis Leschyshyn

Art Lesieur

was a brilliant player, a smooth skater noted for his sweep check, and a fine stickhandler to boot, and it was usually Lepine who played late in the game to protect a lead or to shadow the other team's best player. He was first discovered by Leo Dandurand while playing with Hochelaga in the old Bankers' League in Montreal (later called the Banque Canadienne Nationale). Lepine made his debut with the Habs in '25-'26, played on a line with Armand Mondou and Wildor Larochelle, and quickly established himself as both a checker and a scorer. On December 18, 1929, he recorded five goals and an assist against Ottawa. Lepine was on two Stanley Cups teams, in 1930 and '31, and no one in Montreal liked him more than Detroit GM Jack Adams, who tried many-a-time to acquire Lepine. Pit came into his own after Morenz was traded out of the city in 1933. He was also noted as an outstanding faceoff man and one of the cleanest players in the game, though he never won the Lady Byng Trophy. Lepine retired in 1938 and coached in New Haven for a year before becoming coach of the Habs in 1939. But the team failed to qualify for the playoffs and that ended his career as an NHL bench boss. Lepine became ill in 1952 and moved into a retirement home, where he passed away three years later.

LEPINE, Hec
b. Ste. Anne de Bellevue, Quebec, December 7, 1897
d. Ste. Anne de Bellevue, Quebec, March 29, 1951
Less accomplished than his brother, Pit, Hec had a memorable year in the NHL, 1925-26 with Montreal. That season, he played on a line with his brother and Wildor Larochelle. It was his only full season of pro hockey, and while he retired he watched his brother go on to terrific things in the game.

LEROUX, Francois
b. Ste. Adele, Quebec, April 18, 1970
The knock on him as a teen was simple: He has the size – he should use it or get lost. Scouts like size, but in their opinion without a physical quality, big players are worthless. So Leroux worked on this aspect of his game, though it only got him full-time work with one team – Pittsburgh. He was drafted by the Oilers in 1988 but for five seasons was more or less confined to the minors, with only fleeting callups. Ottawa tried him, and then the Pens played him for two and a half years. After a final season with Colorado, Leroux was dispatched to the minors again, and after three seasons he knew he wasn't going back to the show. He signed with Germany in 2001 to continue his career overseas.

LEROUX, Gaston "Gus"
b. Montreal, Quebec, January 9, 1913
One Gaston Leroux wrote *Phantom of the Opera* while another played for the Montreal Canadiens. One Gaston's work became a world-famous success, while the other's two games with the Habs in '35-'36 were quickly forgotten. So much, as it turns out, is in a name.

LEROUX, Jean-Yves
b. Montreal, Quebec, June 24, 1976
It's appropriate that Leroux's hero as a kid was Cam Neely, though the connection has to do with injuries and style of play rather than prolific scoring. Leroux

recorded an assist in his first NHL game, with Chicago on April 13, 1997, but since then he has missed substantial parts of each season with injury. Various small hurts cost him 11 games in '97-'98, a torn abdominal muscle cost him 42 games the year after, and he also missed 25 games with a groin and finger injury and 17 games with a sprained knee. Leroux played hard but wasn't a scorer, and in 2001 he found himself in the minors, unable to crack the Hawks' NHL roster.

LESCHYSHYN, Curtis ("Kid")
b. Thompson, Manitoba, September 21, 1969
Being drafted 3rd overall in 1988 was not necessarily the best thing that could have happened to Leschyshyn, because his was not a spectacular game. He was a rock solid, defensive defenceman who looked good only when the other team didn't. Quebec selected him and put him in its weak lineup right away, and it took him a few years to come around. He remained with the team for nine years, including for the Cup win after the Nordiques moved to Colorado, but since then he has been on the move a fair bit. Wanted by all and loved by none, he played the better part of four seasons with Hartford/Carolina and then parts of other seasons with Washington, Minnesota, and Ottawa. Ironically, outside the Cup year of 1996, he has had little playoff success, but his experience and strength has kept him in the game a long time.

LESIEUR, Art
b. Fall River, Massachusetts, September 13, 1907
A stalwart on defence for the pre-war Canadiens, Lesieur helped the team win the 1931 Stanley Cup. He played three other seasons in the NHL, though he had a more successful career in the minors with Providence. He played in the minors for many years in Providence and after his days remained there, becoming a parking lot attendant at two local race tracks, Lincoln Downs and Narragansett.

LESSARD, Francis
b. Montreal, Quebec, May 30, 1979
Fighting is the name of his game, plain and simple. In the Q league he fought to get himself drafted by Carolina, and after the Flyers acquired him it took Lessard just three seasons to accrue almost 1,000 penalty minutes and become the team's all-time leader in that dubious statistic. He moved on to Atlanta in 2001-02 where he played five games for the Thrashers, but he has been fighting in the minors most of his career.

LESSARD, Mario
b. East Broughton, Quebec, June 25, 1954
Funnily enough, Lessard's mother's maiden name was Vachon, and when Mario made it to the NHL, he was in L.A. taking over for another Vachon – Rogie. Mario was 1 of 12 children and he developed into a good goalie quickly. In Saginaw, he was tutored by Wren Blair, and by 1978 he was ready for the NHL. For four years (1978-82), Lessard was the toast of L.A., as popular as Magic Johnson, fans chanting his name. He earned a shutout in his first NHL game, and in his third year he led the league in wins with 35. Then, according to GM Vachon, Lessard lost his confidence.

He wound up in the minors, and despite sounding confident about his career, when the Kings bought him out in 1983 he couldn't find another NHL home.

LESSARD, Rick
b. Timmins, Ontario, January 9, 1968
A large, strong, fight-based defenceman, Lessard played 15 NHL games in a 6-year pro career (1988-94). He played junior with Ottawa, joining the 67's in 1984 just after the team won the Memorial Cup. He played for Calgary and San Jose as well as a number of teams in the minors.

LESUK, Bill
b. Moose Jaw, Saskatchewan, November 1, 1946
After playing just 11 games over 2 seasons, Bill Lesuk won a Stanley Cup. That's because he played with Bobby Orr and the Bruins in 1970, and he got the call in the first place because in many respects he was the finest two-way player in the minors. That summer, the B's lost Lesuk to the Flyers, and midway through the season the famous LBJ line was tossed together by coach Vic Stasiuk. It featured Lesuk, Serge Bernier, and Jimmy Johnson, and for a while it was the hottest threesome in the league. Lesuk scored 17 goals that season, by far his best offensive year, and after bouncing around for a while his life took on new meaning when he went to Winnipeg in 1975 to finish out his career with the WHA's Jets. He played 5 years with the team, the last back in the NHL, but only 49 games in that final year. A healthy scratch too often, he realized that the end of his career was at hand so he retired to become a scout with the team. Nine years later, he was named the team's director of scouting, a position he held for a further 11 years, discovering Keith Tkachuk, Teemu Selanne, and Nikolai Khabibulin, among others. It was a full life in hockey, and Lesuk has left his mark on what is now the Phoenix Coyotes.

LESWICK, Jack ("Newsy")
b. Saskatoon, Saskatchewan, January 1, 1910
d. Winnipeg, Manitoba, August 7, 1934
Murther on the Assiniboine, a murther most foul. Jack and his brothers Pete and Tony all played in the NHL. Jack worked his way up from the Duluth Hornets to play for Chicago in '33-'34, and he had a fine season, indeed. Before returning home, he signed a contract for the next year, and then made his way to Winnipeg to spend some time with his brothers at a house he had rented. One night, he went for a walk. Four days later, his body was found in the Assiniboine. Police called it a suicide, even though Jack was a happy-go-lucky character. Further evidence to the contrary was found in that his gold pocket watch was not on his body and his car could not be located. It was, perhaps, the most mysterious death in NHL history.

LESWICK, Pete
b. Saskatoon, Saskatchewan, July 12, 1918
It's very odd, indeed, that three brothers would all play in the NHL and yet their careers followed each other in perfect sequence with no overlap or playing with or against each other. Jack played in '33-'34, Tony from 1945 to '58, and dead in the middle was Pete, who played for the New York Americans in '36-'37 (scoring a goal in his first NHL game) and Boston in '44-'45. In between and after, Pete played primarily in the American league, where he routinely scored 25 goals. For six straight seasons in the league he made the All-Star Team, and by the time he retired he was one of the top scorers of all time. In retirement, he bought a tavern in Glendale, California, and called it Sports Haven.

LESWICK, Tony ("Mighty Mouse")
b. Humboldt, Saskatchewan, March 17, 1923
d. New Westminster, British Columbia, July 8, 2001
He was called Mighty Mouse for a variety of reasons: Despite being just 5'6" and 160 pounds, he was a tough customer who had lengthy and frequent battles with, among others, Maurice Richard. Despite his size and style of play, he missed exactly 2 games in his 11 full seasons in the NHL. He hit hard and took penalties, but he was also expert as a penalty killer. He was a goal scorer, passer, and hero, all rolled into one. Leswick won three Stanley Cups with Detroit in the first half of the 1950s, none more satisfying than the 1954 victory because it was his goal that gave the team the Cup. The night was April 16, 1954, game seven of overtime, Detroit versus Montreal. Early in the fourth period, Leswick took a long shot at goalie Gerry McNeil, but Hall of Fame defenceman Doug Harvey tried to bat the puck down. It hit his glove changed direction, and slipped by the unsuspecting McNeil to give Detroit the dramatic – and lucky – win. Leswick began his career with New York. The Rangers bought his rights at the end of the '42-'43 season, but had to wait two years to get Leswick into a Blueshirts uniform because he enlisted for military service. He divided his time more or less equally between the Rangers and the Wings, and also played with Chicago for a year. Part of his fighting evolved from his job as agitator and star checker. After retiring, Leswick held several jobs – bar manager, car salesman, and owner of a fruit and vegetable stand. He settled in New Westminster to manage a hotel, and died of cancer in that city many years later.

LETANG, Alan
b. Renfrew, Ontario, September 4, 1975
It's not very often that a Canadian kid plays junior in Ontario and pro in Europe before seeing his first NHL game, but that's the route Letang took to get to the show. He finished in the OHL in 1995, and although Montreal had drafted him the Habs didn't use him. After two years in the minors, he hightailed it to Germany. It was only in 1999 that Dallas signed him as a free agent, and later Calgary played him twice in his only NHL action to date.

LETOWSKI, Trevor ("Lootie")
b. Thunder Bay, Ontario, April 5, 1977
After helping Canada win gold at the 1997 World Juniors, Letowski looked good as, well, first place. He was a low draft choice by Phoenix the previous year, but he blossomed as a playmaker in Sarnia and played with confidence. In his first full year he had 19 goals, but since then he has fallen back rather than taken his game to the next level. Phoenix traded him to Vancouver midway through the 2001-02 season, but Letowski has developed a reputation for defence rather than scoring.

Bill Lesuk

Pete Leswick

Tony Leswick

Trevor Letowski

Joe Levandoski

Jean-Louis Levasseur

Normand Leveille

Scott Levins

Alex Levinsky

LEVANDOSKI, Joe

b. Cobalt, Ontario, March 17, 1921
d. Kingston, Ontario, December 20, 2001

The war prevented Levandoski from getting to the NHL any faster. After turning pro in 1941, he joined the Royal Canadian Engineers and made it to the Rangers in 1946-47 for eight games. He had a lengthy career in the minors, finishing in Kingston and settling in the city after retiring to work for the Corrections Services.

LEVASSEUR, Jean-Louis

b. Noranda, Quebec, June 16, 1949

At the very time Levasseur was being named the starting goalie for the East Division in the WHA's 1977 All-Star Game, his team, the Minnesota Fighting Saints, was all but dead and the goalie was looking for work. He caught on with the Oilers and then moved about until he landed with the North Stars in the more stable NHL for '79-'80. Levasseur spent most of the season in the minors, but on February 24, 1980, he got into his one and only big-league game. Unfortunately, it was a 7-5 loss to Detroit, and a year later Levasseur was out of hockey altogether.

LEVEILLE, Normand

b. Montreal, Quebec, January 10, 1963

It could have happened in bed or in a park or at the family dinner table. Instead, it happened in the dressing room during a game on October 23, 1982, probably a blessing in disguise. That night, the 19-year-old Leveille suffered a brain aneurysm and had to be rushed to hospital. He needed six hours of surgery, and he remained paralyzed for a long time afterwards. In one moment, the promising career of a teen in superb physical condition ended, and the reality of having to live life in a wheelchair and dependent on others took hold. Leveille was a shy kid who came to Boston in 1981 not speaking any English. He hurt his knee early in that first season, only 18 years old but impressive in his play, and took a while to rebound from the inactivity. In his first nine games of his second season, he had nine points, and then disaster struck. Yet over the years those Boston teammates have never forgotten him, and have played charity games to help finance his recovery. Two decades later, he remains paralyzed, but he lives alone and is independent. He walks with the aid of a cane and still has trouble talking, but he has established the Normand Leveille Foundation in the hopes of building a summer camp for the disabled. At the closing of the Boston Garden, the team brought Leveille to Boston, and he even skated a bit with Ray Bourque. Leveille's NHL career ended prematurely, but he has fought a tougher battle and is winning big time. The cup of life is his forever.

LEVEQUE, Guy

b. Kingston, Ontario, December 28, 1972

Leveque is still young enough to play, so perhaps it's not right to append the "R" word (as in, retired) on him quite yet, but serious back surgery in the summer of 1998 has left him unable to play since. He played for Los Angeles in the early 1990s to the tune of 17 games, and for several years afterwards found skating

work in the minors. He is a cousin of Mike Murray, who played a game for Philadelphia in '87-'88.

LEVER, Don

b. South Porcupine, Ontario, November 14, 1952

Teammates in Vancouver called him Crazy Legs because of his awkward, almost funny way of skating, but during a career that lasted more than 1,000 games, Lever managed to get from here to there in pretty fair time. He had nine 20-goal seasons to his credit, including a career-high 38 in his third year with the Canucks (1974-75), and became known as one of the best penalty killers around. Lever captained both Vancouver and New Jersey, and he usually played on weak teams that didn't make the playoffs. Despite all those regular-season games over 15 seasons, he played only 30 playoff games, 16 coming in 1981 with Calgary. He played his final two seasons with Buffalo, the city to which he became closely attached after retiring in 1987. That fall, he became Ted Sator's assistant, and for the past 15 years he has worked in that capacity save for 3 years when he acted as head coach for the farm team in Rochester.

LEVIE, Craig

b. Calgary, Alberta, August 17, 1959

Depending on outlook, Levie was frequently in the right place at the right time or the wrong place at the wrong time. Dubbed "King of the Waiver Draft," he switched teams three times via this don't-need-him route and another time was claimed off waivers. Yet for every team that exposed him in the draft, another was there to claim him. He was the guy teams acquired to "shore up the blueline" or "add depth on defence" or "bring some insurance to the team." After doing this for five years, though (1981-86), Levie headed to Europe and played for Davos in the Swiss league. Just six games into the season, he suffered a serious groin injury and returned home. He signed with Vancouver later in the year, but when he saw he wasn't in their plans he went back overseas, this time to Italy.

LEVINS, Scott

b. Spokane, Washington, January 30, 1970

Naughty Scotty had his moment of infamy in Germany in March 2002. During a heated moment in a game featuring his Berlin Polar Bears and a team from Iserholm, Levins called opponent Lars Muller a Nazi. He was fined and suspended, though charges of making the Nazi salute (illegal under German law) were dropped. Levins went to Germany after five part-time seasons in the NHL gave the big forward little hope he could establish himself as a regular. He played mostly in the minors until 1999, when he thought he'd give Europe a shot. All went well until March 2002 when he was fired by the German Ice Hockey League for calling an opponent a "Nazi" during a game.

LEVINSKY, Alex ("Mine Boy")

b. Syracuse, New York, February 2, 1910
d. Toronto, Ontario, September 1, 1990

"That's mine boy!" his father used to scream as he watched his son at practice. The nickname stuck, as did his father's enthusiasm, and Alex went on to become one of the first Jewish stars of the NHL. Conn Smythe signed him to the Leafs toward the end of the '30-'31 season, and for three years after that Levinsky developed into one of the best defencemen in the game. He won a Cup with the Leafs the next year and later played for the Rangers and the Black Hawks. After retiring, he returned to his home in Toronto and became a successful businessman. He ran a bowling alley and was co-owner, vice-president, and general manager of University Avenue Motors Ltd. until his retirement.

LEVO, Tapio
b. Pori, Finland, September 24, 1955
Like most Finns who came to North America, Levo had an outstanding international record before playing in the NHL. He played in the invitational WJC in 1975, and the year after played in both the World Championships and the inaugural Canada Cup. He went on to play in four more WC, and the 1980 Olympics and the '81 Canada Cup. Pittsburgh, who had drafted him in 1975, no longer could lay claim to him when he decided to try the NHL in 1981. Colorado signed him as a free agent, but after just 34 games he broke his arm and returned home. He decided to try again with the team, now playing out of New Jersey, the following season, and he epitomized all that was good and bad about the team. Levo had an excellent shot and was superb on the power play. His 47 points ranked fourth in the NHL for defencemen. On the flip side, he played for an horrific team and his -41 highlighted his weak defensive play. At season's end, he returned to Finland and continued his career with his hometown Pori team, for whom he played 18 seasons in all.

LEWICKI, Danny ("Dashin' Danny")
b. Fort William, Ontario, March 12, 1931
By the time Danny Lewicki was 20 years old, he had accomplished, quite literally, all that could be done in hockey. At 17, he won a Memorial Cup with Port Arthur. At 19, he won an Allan Cup with the Marlboros. And at 20, in 1951, he won a Stanley Cup with the Leafs, capping off a triple victory that few players can boast. He was a competitor and a sportsman both, a consistent scorer and a runner-up for the Lady Byng one year, and in 1955, while with the Rangers, he was named U.S. Ukrainian pro athlete of the year. Lewicki lasted nine years in the NHL and finished his pro career with the Quebec Aces. He settled in Toronto and coached the Hamilton Red Wings for a season, then worked in ad sales for CHUM radio for the next 13 years. From there he worked for Monroe shock absorbers as its Ontario sales manager, and seven years later he became sales manager for an auto warehousing company. In 1990, he taught himself photography and then became an entrepreneur at the SkyDome, taking fantasy pictures of fans in Blue Jays regalia. His novel job was run out of town five years later when Kodak bought all photo rights to the Dome.

LEWIS, Dale
b. Edmonton, Alberta, July 28, 1952
Despite never playing major junior hockey, Lewis turned pro in 1972 in the EIIL and forged a small career out of his talents. He never played in the WHA, which might have been a natural line of development,

but he did play eight games with the Rangers in '75-'76. The rest of his years passed peacefully in the American and Central leagues.

LEWIS, Dave ("Big Lewie")
b. Kindersley, Saskatchewan, July 3, 1953
He began as an Islanders defenceman when the team was just entering the league, and it was Lewis's misfortune to be traded to L.A. just weeks before the team began its run of four consecutive Cups. Lewis was a stay-at-home type who didn't score much or look pretty. He was a take-your-man kind of guy for more than 1,000 NHL games, and he made a solid living doing just that. Actually, he lost a good part of that solid living in the early 1980s when he switched agents. He ditched Arthur Kaminsky and hired Peter Spencer in an effort to save money, and in the process Spencer wound up losing $100,000 of Lewis's money in bad investments. The case scandalized the league and called into question the very nature of player-agent relationships, but the money was gone and in the end Lewis had only himself to blame. His career ended early in the '87-'88 season when he was scratched from as many games as he played. Detroit GM Jim Devellano, who first scouted Lewis while he was working for the Islanders, told him he could continue to play about half the games or he could help coach the defence. Lewis retired, took the assistant coach job, and has been with the team ever since. For the better part of 15 years he worked in that capacity, but in the summer of 2002, when head coach Scotty Bowman retired, the Wings selected Lewis as the new head coach, a great opportunity and a daunting challenge both.

LEWIS, Doug
b. Winnipeg, Manitoba, March 3, 1921
d. Winnipeg, Manitoba, August 10, 1994
Plain and simple, he loved the game. Born in East Kildonan, a suburb of the 'Peg, Lewis played with the EK Bisons as a kid and moved steadily up to turn pro in the AHL. He played much of his career in Buffalo, and in 1946-47 he got into three games with Montreal. He returned to Winnipeg later and coached at the Sturgeon Creek Community Club before moving out of hockey altogether. He became an estimator in heating and ventilation, working with Air-Master Sales and later with General Equipment. He passed away after a lengthy fight with cancer.

LEWIS, Herbie ("The Duke of Duluth")
b. Calgary, Alberta, April 17, 1906
d. Indianapolis, Indiana, January 20, 1991
After developing his playing skills with the Calgary Canadians, Lewis, the son of a railway conductor, moved to Duluth and helped put Hornets hockey on the map. He was the team's best player, the league's highest-paid player, and the star of the show wherever he went. He dominated the league for four years until 1928 when he accepted an offer to join Detroit in the NHL. Lewis holds the distinction of playing with that city under all three nicknames – Cougars, Falcons, and Red Wings. He played primarily on a line with Cooney Weiland and Larry Aurie and never played for another NHL team. Lewis played in the longest game

Tapio Levo

Danny Lewicki

Dave Lewis

Dale Lewis

Herbie Lewis

Rick Ley

Tony Licari

Bob Liddington

Doug Lidster

Nicklas Lidstrom

of all time at the start of the 1936 playoffs, against the Maroons, a series in which the Wings won en route to the Stanley Cup. Pete Kelly scored the winning goal against Toronto in the finals, on a pass from Lewis. They won the Cup again the next year by which time Lewis was on a line with Marty Barry and Hec Kilrea. Lewis left the NHL in 1939 to act as GM, coach, and player for the fledgling Indianapolis Capitals. He restricted his activities to GM and coach the next year, and in '41-'42 the team won the Calder Cup. He retired a year later. Lewis and his family had lived year-round in Duluth for a number of years. He operated an oil company that serviced gas stations in the city but moved to Pompano Beach, Florida, to enjoy his retirement. He lived near Ebbie Goodfellow, road roommate and longtime friend from the glory days with the Red Wings. In 1986, though, Lewis suffered a stroke and was plagued by emphysema. He was forced to move to Indianapolis. Although he was inducted into the Hockey Hall of Fame in 1989, poor health prevented him from attending the ceremonies. He died two years later from heart failure.

LEY, Rick
b. Orillia, Ontario, November 2, 1948
The Hartford Whalers retired only three numbers in their history: Gordie Howe's 9, Johnny McKenzie's 18, and Rick Ley's 2. Ley began his career with the Leafs, but like so many wearers of the blue and white he left the team and its owner in 1972 when the WHA began operations. Ley was one of a handful of players who remained with a single WHA team for the full run of the league's history, and he stayed another year and a half after the Whalers joined the NHL. Recurring knee injuries forced him to retire early in the '80-'81 season, and he immediately became an assistant coach under Larry Pleau. He then coached in the minors, and in '83-'84 he was GM and coach of the Mohawk Valley Stars of the Atlantic Coast league. He worked his way up the ranks, paid his dues, and in 1989 was named Hartford's head coach. After two disappointing seasons he became an assistant in Vancouver and later became the head coach of the Canucks, after which he joined Pat Quinn in Toronto as an assistant for his former team.

LIBA, Igor
b. Kosice, Czechoslovakia (Slovakia), November 4, 1960
Among that first wave of Iron Curtain players to head to the NHL, Liba played for the Rangers and Los Angeles in 1988-89 at age 29 after a successful international career. He helped the Czechs win gold at the 1985 World Championships, one of six he played in. He also appeared in three Olympics, winning bronze in 1992, and he played for many years in the Czech leagues. His success in the NHL was marginal, and he returned to Europe after one season to continue playing in a number of countries.

LIBBY, Jeff
b. Waterville, Maine, March 1, 1974
In an unrelated but connected set of twin horrors, Libby lost an eye while playing for the Lowell Lock Monsters. On November 7, 1998, he was cut in the right eye by Mark Deyell's skate and had to have it

removed. His career was over. Just a short time later, Deyell lost the use of an eye in another on-ice incident. Libby had played one game with the Islanders in '97-'98 and was being developed by the team in the minors at the time of the accident.

LIBETT, Nick
b. Stratford, Ontario, December 9, 1945
Developed in the Detroit system, Libett got better and better as a teen until, at age 23, he proved himself a bona fide NHLer and never looked back. He stayed with the Wings for 12 of his 14 seasons and once had a streak of 389 consecutive games until a knee injury forced him to miss a game in 1979. Six times he scored 20 goals, and although he played for the team during its worst period, he was a loyal and faithful winger. He played in the 1977 All-Star Game and two years later played for Canada at the World Championships. He was traded to Pittsburgh for Pete Mahovlich on August 3, 1979, but after two years he retired and returned to Detroit to make a living off the ice. He formed Gibbons Libett Sales, a company that represented manufacturers from the Far East.

LICARI, Tony
b. Ottawa, Ontario, April 9, 1921
After a lengthy four-year stay in the army, Licari played nine games for Detroit in '46-'47 before embarking on a career in Britain. The right winger became a scoring star with the Harringay Racers before retiring.

LIDDINGTON, Bob
b. Calgary, Alberta, September 15, 1948
For a while, it seemed as if Liddington couldn't find a WHA team to play for. After a few games with the Leafs in '70-'71, he signed with the Chicago Cougars in 1972 and played with them for three years. Then, in a span of two seasons, he played for four teams in the league.

LIDSTER, Doug
b. Kamloops, British Columbia, October 18, 1960
Lidster played more than half his career in Vancouver, where he was a steady defenceman on an often weak team. His +/- numbers usually looked bad, but it was generally a case of getting a ton of ice time with a team that wasn't very good and, as a result, being on the ice for many goals against. Teams around the league knew his worth, though, and when the Rangers acquired him in the summer of '93, he helped take the team to the Stanley Cup. Ditto a few years later when the Rangers let him go and his career seemed done. Dallas signed him in February 1999, and the Stars won the Cup just a few months later. Lidster retired after that victory and hoped to go into coaching, but instead returned to Kamloops to take care of his sick parents. A year later, he coached in Syracuse and later joined the Canucks staff in Vancouver.

LIDSTROM, Nicklas
b. Vasteras, Sweden, April 28, 1970
It took Lidstrom a few years longer to get the respect he deserved, but he is arguably the best defenceman playing today. He made his debut in the NHL with Detroit – with whom he has played his entire career –

in 1991-92 and was runner-up to Pavel Bure for the Calder Trophy. Since then, other great defencemen have had their final days in the limelight (Paul Coffey, Al MacInnis, Ray Bourque) and Lidstrom has patiently performed incredibly well outside the limelight. He was runner-up for the Norris Trophy in three successive seasons (1998, 1999, 2000) until 2001, when he was finally given overdue acknowledgement for being the best. Technically, he is a perfect defenceman. He is a powerful skater, has a great shot, moves the puck well, anticipates, and reads the flow of the game as well as anyone. He has won three Cups with the Wings, and since 1991 has represented Tre Kronor at every important international tournament for which he has been available. Right now, he might well be the king of the blueline.

LILJA, Andreas
b. Landskrona, Sweden, July 13, 1975
Lilja wasn't drafted into the NHL until 2000, when he was already 24 years old and had been playing pro at home for a number of years. He came to the Kings right away, and has been slowly working his way into the lineup on an ever more regular basis, though to date he is still more a hopeful than a should-be player.

LILLEY, John
b. Wakefield, Massachusetts, August 3, 1972
While attending Boston University, Lilley had the chance to play for the U.S. at the 1992 World Juniors, an experience he improved upon a couple of seasons later when he spent most of the year with the National Team and played at the 1994 Olympics in Lillehammer. At the end of that '93-'94 season he made his NHL entrance, with Anaheim, but played just 23 games with the Ducks because he was considered too small. After spending some years in the minors, Lilley went to play in Germany, and shortly after retiring he became an assistant coach with the National Team Development Program in Ann Arbor, Michigan.

LIND, Juha
b. Helsinki, Finland, January 2, 1974
Like most aspiring NHLers, Lind was drafted as an 18-year-old, in 1992. Unlike most, it took him five years to make his NHL debut and his career in North America was wracked by unease. He played half a season for Dallas in '97-'98 and won a bronze medal with the Finns at the 1998 Olympics in Nagano. He returned to Finland, but in 1999 he played with Dallas and later Montreal, who acquired him for Scott Thornton. After another half-season with the Habs, Lind signed with Sodertalje in Sweden, and it now seems his career will continue outside the NHL.

LINDBERG, Chris
b. Fort Frances, Ontario, April 16, 1967
It's the old "have puck, will travel" phenomenon with Lindberg, whose 116 NHL games represent the smallest part of his career. He has played for Canada's National Team on a number of occasions, notably at the 1992 Olympics in Albertville, at which Canada won silver. He also played in the minors and in Europe.

LINDBERGH, Pelle
b. Stockholm, Sweden, May 24, 1959
d. Stratford, New Jersey, November 12, 1985
The irony of this short life taken too early because of alcohol is that hockey players have long been known to eschew flashy cars in favour of beat-up jalopies. Being small-town family-oriented boys, they don't like the flash and glitz of expensive cars. Lindbergh did, however, and on November 10, 1985, he went bar hopping in his turbo-charged Porsche. Late in the evening, legally well past the limit, he slammed his car into a concrete barrier. He was pronounced brain-dead, and two days later the family allowed doctors to disconnect his life-support system. Two passengers suffered serious injuries and later sued the Lindbergh estate for damages. The story had a happy ending, though, in some respects. In the summer of 1985, Lindbergh was at the height of his fame and popularity, while New Jersey resident John Keeler was waiting to die. A few months later, Lindbergh was dead, and Keeler received Lindbergh's heart and found a second life with his wife and children. Lindbergh was likely the finest goalie Sweden has ever produced, making his way to Philadelphia in 1981 and quickly proving his worth as a star. In his second year, he was the team's starter and was named to the '83 All-Star Game. There, he suffered his worst psychological setback. In the third period of that game, he surrendered four goals to Wayne Gretzky and took almost a full year to regain his confidence. In '84-'85, he had a career year, leading the NHL in wins with 40, being named to the All-Star Team, and winning the Vezina Trophy. He was off to another excellent start in '85-'86 when he threw his privileged life away for the most common of tragedies – drinking and driving.

LINDBOM, Johan
b. Alvesta, Sweden, July 8, 1971
Lindbom didn't give the NHL much of a chance, and the feeling was mutual. The Rangers draft choice played on Broadway for half of the '97-'98 season, but like many Europeans he wasn't willing to put in the years in the minors to work his way back up. He returned whence he came and has continued his career in Sweden.

LINDEN, Jamie
b. Medicine Hat, Alberta, July 19, 1972
The brother of Trevor, Jamie wasn't nearly as talented, but one day soon he may be in the position to thumb his bro to the penalty box. Jamie had a four-game stint with Florida in '94-'95 but was strictly a minor-leaguer the rest of the way. He retired early and quickly entered the officiating world, currently working as a linesman in the WHL and on his way up. He might one day make it to the NHL, and Trevor still has some time left as a player. Imagine: Linden calling Linden for two minutes!

LINDEN, Trevor
b. Medicine Hat, Alberta, April 11, 1970
Linden won two Memorial Cups with the Medicine Hat Tigers and was drafted 2nd overall in 1988. Big and skilled, time was the only thing he needed to become a superstar, and for a number of years he

Juha Lind

Pelle Lindbergh

Trevor Linden

delivered the goods. He scored 30 goals as a rookie and had six 30-goal seasons with the Canucks in the coming years. Linden became team captain and took Vancouver to the Cup finals in 1994, but when he was traded to the Islanders in 1998 his career changed. The Isles dished him off to Montreal, then he was on to Washington, and finally in 2001-02 he wound up back in Vancouver, where he had played the first decade of his career. The only difference was he was older, slower, and not the same player. His crowning moment came at the 1998 Olympics in Nagano. In the semifinals, he scored in the final two minutes to tie the game for Canada 1-1 with the Czechs.

LINDGREN, Lars
b. Pitea, Sweden, October 12, 1952

He wasn't the first NHLer to come out of Pitea. That honour goes to Stefan Persson. But he was the first defenceman and the first great blueline prospect since Borje Salming to arrive from Sweden, and that drew inevitable – and unfair and inaccurate – comparisons. Lindgren was far more a defensive specialist and not nearly as fluid a skater. He also wasn't as resilient as Salming and missed his share of games with injuries. He joined Vancouver in 1978 and stayed with the Canucks for five and a half years until being traded to Minnesota. In 1984, he returned home and played a number of years with Pitea, a local hero coming back to the fold. After retiring, he became Pitea's coach and took them to a championship.

Lars Lindgren

LINDGREN, Mats
b. Skelleftea, Sweden, October 1, 1974

Of course, starting in the 1990s, players from Europe can't get to the NHL quickly enough after being drafted. Lindgren went in the 1993 draft and two years later he attended Edmonton's training camp. He was sent to the minors, but early in the season he took a vicious slash, suffered nerve damage in his left leg, and missed the rest of the season. The next season was a little better. In his first NHL game, on November 3, 1996, he scored a goal on his first shot on his first shift. He never scored enough goals to suggest offence was his strength but he was a solid, two-way player. He appeared for Tre Kronor at the 1998 Olympics in Nagano, and the Oilers traded him to the Islanders with a draft choice to obtain goalie Tommy Salo, a deal that has swung wildly in Edmonton's favour in the years since. Lindgren has continued to be reliable, but Salo has become the backbone of the Oilers.

Mats Lindgren

LINDHOLM, Mikael
b. Gavle, Sweden, December 19, 1964

Drafted 237th overall in 1987, it was a miracle Lindholm made it to the NHL at all, yet for 18 games he skated for the L.A. Kings. He scored two goals – hopefully the first puck is on his mantel back home – and then was sent to the minors for the following year. At that point, mission accomplished and the dream over, he returned to Sweden, where he has continued to play ever since.

LINDQUIST, Fredrik
b. Stockholm, Sweden, June 21, 1973

Eight years after New Jersey drafted him, Lindquist

Brett Lindros

made his NHL debut with Edmonton in 1998, the team that acquired his rights in a deal involving numerous draft choices. The tough, physical play of the league didn't suit his style very well, though, and half a season in the minors convinced him that Swedish hockey was better for him. He later played for Tre Kronor at the 2000 WC.

LINDROS, Brett
b. London, Ontario, December 2, 1975

For every right, there has been a wrong in Brett Lindros's life to this point, just past the quarter-century mark. The bigger, stronger brother of Eric, he was highly thought of, coming out of junior, despite being cut from Canada's junior team that went on to win gold in 1995. The Islanders chose him 9th overall in 1994 and played him for half a season. He showed plenty of promise but was returned to junior, and early the next year suffered a concussion in a game on November 2, 1995, that ended his career. Months later, he still had headaches and memory troubles, and the very nature of head injuries took centre stage in the NHL because he was so young. Lindros had suffered numerous head injuries in junior, and clearly it was the cumulative effect that ended his career. Lindros became active in head injury research and helped raise funds to that effect. He went on to become a television personality for "Be A Player" but didn't do anything for his reputation when he crashed his snowmobile into Crane Lake, north of Toronto, in the middle of the night.

LINDROS, Eric ("The Big E")
b. London, Ontario, February 28, 1973

The extraordinary series of events that make up the life of number 88 render his achievements pale by comparison (not that there have been few). More than any other player before or since, he believed it was his right alone to control his hockey career, and he went to great lengths to prove the point. As a kid, he played for St. Mike's, but when it came time to play junior, he steadfastly refused to play outside the Toronto area. This was at odds with OHL rules, which prohibited a team from trading its 1st overall draft pick, but because the league didn't want to have its marquee player go elsewhere it invoked the so-called Lindros rule and allowed just that to happen. Thus, Sault Ste. Marie traded his rights to Oshawa for five players, and Lindros got his way. In his first year there, '89-'90, the Generals won the Memorial Cup, but a greater kerfuffle lay ahead. Lindros announced that he would not play in the NHL with Quebec, and the Nordiques, clearly the worst team in the league and destined to have the 1st overall selection, were equally adamant that they would select him. Lindros countered by saying he would happily play elsewhere for two years and re-enter the draft, and his actions proved he wasn't bluffing. L'affaire Lindros, as the scandal was dubbed by French-Canadian press, carried on for more than a year. Lindros played in the 1991 Canada Cup – the only non-NHLer there – and looked impressive in a limited role given to him by coach Mike Keenan. He played at the World Juniors, returned to junior, and played at the 1992 Olympics in Albertville, anywhere but Quebec. At the 1992 Entry

Draft, Quebec capitulated, trading him to Philadelphia for six players, notably Peter Forsberg, Steve Duchesne, Mike Ricci, Kerry Huffman, and Ron Hextall. It turned out to be a trade that brought the Nordiques franchise (as the Avalanche) two Stanley Cups, and Lindros joined the Flyers with incredible expectation and pressure. He responded. In three of his first four seasons he scored 40 goals, and in '94-'95 he led the league in points and won both the Hart and Pearson trophies. His eight years with the team were marked mostly by highs, from an appearance in the 1997 Cup finals to the formation of the Legion of Doom line with John LeClair and Mikael Renberg, the top-scoring line in the league. Toward the close of the century, though, things started to go wrong. His GM, Bobby Clarke, was also GM of Team Canada for the 1998 Olympics and selected Lindros as captain. The team didn't win gold. Then Lindros suffered a punctured lung after a game, and would have died had he travelled with the team. He and his family criticized Flyers doctors for not diagnosing so serious and obvious an injury; the team shot back that he hid his pain. The upshot of the furor was that Clarke stripped Lindros of his captaincy. Like his brother, Lindros played a game of skill on offence while delivering punishing and clean checks. The old sporting adage of the bigger they are, the harder they fall might never have seemed as true as with this clan. Although Lindros intimidated many an opponent, hurt others, and broke bones along the way, he also suffered his share of injuries, namely concussions.

Eric Lindros

for this unprecedented deal, Lindros more or less ensured that he wouldn't be dealt to his hometown. Months of negotiations finally resulted in a deal that sent Lindros to the Rangers, and it was there he started the 2001-02 season. He had a new team, he'd had a year and more to recover from the series of career-threatening head injuries, he had something to prove, and he was still young. Lindros came up with a 37-goal season, but he again suffered a small concussion that forced him out of the lineup briefly. He also played on Canada's gold-medal 2002 Olympic team, though not as captain, under the successful management of Wayne Gretzky. Lindros entered the NHL as the man to take the Flyers to the Stanley Cup. He has proved his worth as an individual talent, and he has played on some great teams, but the silver chalice has proved elusive for the big star who is one hit away from permanent retirement.

Bert Lindsay

LINDSAY, Bert
b. Garafraxa County, Ontario, July 23, 1881
d. Sarnia, Ontario, November 11, 1960

Of course, every Hall of Famer has a father, but only a very few have a father who himself played in the NHL. Ted Lindsay is one such case, one of the greatest players of the Original Six, whose father had a less memorable career, as a goalie, in the NHL's first years of existence. Bert played for McGill at the turn of the 20th century and in 1908 played goal for the Edmonton team that challenged for the Stanley Cup. He played out west in the Patricks' Pacific Coast league and returned to Montreal to play for the

L'affaire Lindros, as the scandal was dubbed by French-Canadian press, carried on for more than a year.
ERIC LINDROS

On March 7, 1998, a clean but ferocious open-ice hit by Darius Kasparaitis crumpled the Big E. Two years later, Hal Gill of the Bruins gave him similar pain. The accumulation of concussions, from junior through the NHL, was catching up to him. Any doubts on this count were confirmed on May 4, 2000, when he collided lightly with a teammate during practice. He suffered a concussion from a hit he wouldn't even have felt a decade earlier. The *coup de grâce* came in the 2000 playoffs when Scott Stevens of New Jersey levelled Lindros coming across the blueline with his head down. It was a premeditated but clean hit, and left Lindros almost legless. Again his family lashed out at the Flyers doctors for giving Eric medical clearance in light of earlier concussions during the year, and again Clarke talked about Eric being dishonest with the medical men. In the end, two events occurred simultaneously. One, Lindros missed a year with the injury; two, he demanded a trade to Toronto. Clarke, though, was neither the OHL nor the Nordiques, and he had no intention of trading Lindros to a team of the player's choosing. In fact, by asking

Wanderers in 1915. Lindsay stayed with that team until a fire destroyed their arena five games into the inaugural NHL season, 1917-18, and played the next season with the Toronto Arenas. That summer, he broke both his legs in a construction accident and had to retire from the game. Bert moved to Renfrew, where he ran a car dealership for a number of years, and then to Kirkland Lake, where he began a long tenure with the Toburn Gold Mines while raising his family. He produced five sons, and while Ted proved to be one of the toughest players in the game his siblings took their fighting to Europe during the Second World War: Jimmy with the Tank Corps in Italy, Bill with the Algonquins, Jerome with the Ordnance Corps in Holland, and Otto with the RCAF in England. Bert invented the collapsible goal net long before the NHL finally replaced immovable nets in the early 1980s. The Lindsay Miracle Goal Net made its way into the world in the late 1940s, and NHL president Clarence Campbell liked it so much he tested it in the Eastern Hockey League with the New York Rovers at Madison Square Garden. The net featured hydraulic pumps inside the base of each post, so when a player rammed into the crossbar the goal moved back and then returned to place. Like a prospect that doesn't pan out, though, the net never made it to the NHL because goalies simply moved the goal back and forth whenever they wanted to avoid scoring chances. Although the idea was brilliant and prescient, it was soon forgotten. In 1956, Bert moved to Sarnia, where he spent the last four years of his life.

LINDSAY, Bill

b. Big Fork, Montana, May 17, 1971

In the old days, he'd have been called a utility forward, but today he's a fourth-liner, a guy who can give the coach minutes without being a liability on the ice. Lindsay is heading steadily and inexorably to 1,000 games played, though he has never scored more than a dozen goals in a year. The left winger developed in the WHL and played internationally for the U.S., though he holds dual citizenship (Canada). He established his reputation in Florida, where he played six seasons and scored the first goal in franchise history. Since 1999 he has bounced around, employment looking less secure or, at least, less stable, but a player with his skills and teamwork will likely always find work as long as he's seeking it.

Bill Lindsay

LINDSAY, Ted ("Tonto"/ "Terrible Ted")

b. Renfrew, Ontario, July 29, 1925

If Lindsay's contributions on the ice are considered on their own merit, he is among the top 10 players of all time. If his off-ice performance is also considered, he is top three – no ifs, ands, or buts. The son of NHL goalie Bert Lindsay, Ted played a year of junior at St. Mike's and was whisked off to the Red Wings in 1944 at age 19. He stood 5'8" and weighed no more than 160 pounds, so to look at him was to smile the smile of the ignorant. Players who challenged him or tried to intimidate him left the scene of the accident with blood streaming down their faces or only with the help of trainers and teammates. Lindsay was the meanest, most vicious and competitive left winger who ever lived. He could also play the game with the best of them, and by the time he retired he was not only the all-time leader in penalty minutes, he was the highest-scoring left winger in the history of the game. As a rookie in '44-'45, he scored 17 goals, and after an off-season he improved to 27 and 33 goals to lead the NHL in '48-'49. He joined forces with veteran Sid Abel at centre and another youngster, Gordon Howe, on the right wing, and together the Production Line was the best in the league. In '49-'50, the threesome finished 1-2-3 in the scoring race,

Ted Lindsay

Lindsay finishing on top with 78 points, the only time he led the league. While the line worked magic on the ice, Lindsay and Howe were inseparable off it. They lived together, roomed on the road together, went everywhere and did everything together. They were the reason the Wings won the Stanley Cup four times in six years and finished first in the regular-season standings a record seven straight years. Lindsay was a First Team All-Star 8 times and played in 11 All-Star Games (he was the first player to score a hat trick in an All-Star Game). He led the league in penalty minutes only once, toward the end of his career, but was near the top every year. He was revered in Detroit and reviled everywhere else, no more so than in 1956 when he received death threats during the Toronto-Detroit semifinals. Lindsay's response was famous. He ignored the threats and went out and scored three goals to win the game for Detroit, after which he turned his stick around and, holding it like a gun, pretended to fire shots into the Gardens crowd, rat-a-tat-tat! No one ever intimidated Terrible Ted. His ferocity on the ice was real, but it also served to camouflage an ambition of his – to form the players into an association so that their lesser members would be better paid and more fairly treated. He enlisted the help of Toronto's Jim Thomson, a man with whom he had perhaps the longest-lasting, most violent on-ice feud in the history of the game. There they were, enemies meeting secretly after a game trying to get their teammates on board. The owners eventually crushed the attempt, and Detroit GM traded Lindsay to Chicago, the worst team in the league, with

The Hockey Hall of Fame waived the five-year waiting period and inducted Lindsay in 1966.

TED LINDSAY

Glenn Hall in 1957. It was a debasement and embarrassment for such a great player, but he reacted defiantly in accepting the trade. He played three seasons with the team and then retired. For the next three years he hosted his own radio show in Windsor while living in Detroit, but in 1964 he decided to return to the Wings for a final season, such was his undying loyalty to the team. Amazingly, the Wings finished first overall again, and then Lindsay retired in peace after 1,068 regular-season games and 851 points. The Hockey Hall of Fame waived the five-year waiting period and inducted Lindsay in 1966, but when he found out it was a stag affair (no women, please), he refused to attend. He sent a blistering letter asking that women be permitted, believing that after so many years of being a hockey husband he owed it to his wife to share in the tribute. The Hall refused, and true to his word, he did not attend. The next year, the induction ceremonies were open to one and all, and since then the mixed evening has become the showcase of the Hall's season. By this time, the players had rallied around a young Toronto lawyer named Alan Eagleson to form a proper union to ensure fair treatment. Lindsay became Red Wings GM in 1977 and in the coming few years acted as interim coach on two occasions. However, the team was at its lowest point and not even his inspiration and presence could rally the inferior troops to greater success. By 1981 he was no longer affiliated with the team. The story of how he tried to form a players' association was later turned into a book and made-for-TV movie. It celebrated an attempt so brave and independent that it represents a kind of *On the Waterfront* heroism in the hockey world. Lindsay dared to take on the NHL owners, the 6 most powerful men in the game who controlled the lives of the 120 players who could only appreciate being permitted to play in the league. Lindsay changed those sentiments. He gave the players a new language that included words such as minimum salary, waiver protection, and respect. He forced change – although not on his terms nor according to his timetable – and ensured that the players of tomorrow would have greater strength as a group to know they were the show, they were the reason fans came to the games, and they were the talent the owners needed to earn their living. Not the other way around. Ted Lindsay scored a bunch of goals and won some Stanley Cups and bopped a few opponents on the head, but what he did off the ice showed far greater heroism.

LINDSTROM, Willy ("Willy the Wisp")
b. Grums, Sweden, May 5, 1951
Lindstrom is the only man on the planet who can boast of having been a linemate of both Bobby Hull and Wayne Gretzky. He played with Hull during the final years of the WHA on a Jets team loaded with European talent, and then on March 7, 1983, he was traded from the Jets, now in the NHL, to the Oilers. He was called the Wisp because of his great speed. Even fellow Swedes say he was the fastest skater that country produced. He came to Winnipeg in 1975, and made a name for himself in the trivia world by winning an Avco Cup with that team and then two Stanley Cups with the Oilers ('84 and '85). He was a solid 20-goal man in the NHL, and after playing his final 2 years with Pittsburgh he returned home to play some more with Brynas. After retiring, he remained involved with the NHL by becoming Hartford's European scout, and since 1991 has held that position, which now comes with Carolina.

LING, David
b. Halifax, Nova Scotia, January 9, 1975
Being tutored by Forbes Kennedy in Charlottetown can mean only one thing for a player – if you're tough, you'd better get tougher; if you're not, you don't belong here. Ling was a prodigy at 14, and at 18 he led the OHL in penalty minutes with Kingston in '93-94. That summer, though, his coaches suggested he use his skills more and his fists less, and in one season he went from penalty king to leading goal scorer and Canadian junior player of the year. Ling's adjustment to the pros has been prolonged and not as successful as his teen years predicted. He played three games with Montreal and the rest of the time in the minors, making a small ripple in the IHL until Columbus signed him as a free agent in 2001. This move yielded just a few more NHL games, and served only to add to his career totals in the minors.

LINSEMAN, Ken ("The Rat")
b. Kingston, Ontario, August 11, 1958
No one liked him, though, funnily enough, he got his nickname not because he was a pest (which he was), an agitator (yes), or a vermin-like player every opponent wanted to wipe out (definitely). Instead, he got the moniker from Bobby Clarke because the former captain of the Flyers thought that's what Linseman looked like when he hunched forward and skated. The name, though, was a brilliant summation of Linseman's style. In junior with Kingston, he was convicted of common assault for kicking an opponent in the head with his skate. He took the entire Canadian junior hockey system to court so he could play in the WHA in 1977 as an underage 19-year-old, and when he got to the NHL – Philadelphia, of course – he established his trademark dirty play and frustratingly effective offensive ability. While players tried to hunt him down for a secret spear or unnoticed slash, he was on the move, scoring a goal or setting one up. He goaded more players into retaliation penalties than likely any other in the game's history, and though universally despised he was, admittedly, effective. By the time he retired in 1992 to work in commercial real estate in New Hampshire, Linseman had scored the Cup-winning goal for Edmonton in 1984 and had seven 20-goal seasons to his credit. His finest years came with the Flyers centring the Rat Patrol line with Paul Holmgren and Brian Propp, and he also played with Boston and Toronto, going to the Cup finals with the B's in 1988. After retiring, Linseman became a commercial real estate broker in New Hampshire.

LINTNER, Richard
b. Trencin, Czechoslovakia (Slovakia), November 15, 1977
He has made some inroads during his NHL career, but Lintner's far greater accomplishments came with the Slovakian National Team. Twice he has represented the new hockey nation at the World Juniors (1996 and '97), but more important, Lintner was an integral part of the team during the watershed year of 2002. He played for the Slovaks at the Olympics in Salt Lake City, the Games at which not all Slovaks were allowed to compete, and he followed that up with an appearance at the World Championships, which the Slovaks won. It was a gold medal that confirmed to the world that this was hockey's newest powerful nation, joining the Big Six and deserving of equal respect. Lintner's NHL time came with Nashville, but his international experiences have been far greater.

LIPUMA, Chris
b. Bridgeview, Illinois, March 23, 1971
While playing high school hockey at St. Lawrence in Chicago, Lipuma worked as a vendor at Comiskey Park and Wrigley Field before heading to Kitchener to play junior. Never drafted, he signed with Tampa Bay and later San Jose and played five years as the resident tough guy, taking on the league's heavyweights and being delighted to be in the league at all. When he was demoted in 1996, he continued to hope for a recall, but that has yet to happen and now likely never will. He suffered an extremely serious knee injury in 1998, but almost a year later returned to the IHL to continue his career, for the love of the game.

Willy Lindstrom

Ken Linseman

Richard Lintner

Chris Lipuma

LISCOMBE, Harold Carlyle "Carl" ("Lefty")
b. Perth, Ontario, May 17, 1915

Although Liscombe was born in Perth, he moved at a young age to Huntsville and then Galt as a result of his father's job. A cornetist, Harry Liscombe found work with the Galt Kiltie Band and so took his wife, daughter, and four sons to Galt, where they lived for many years. All the boys played hockey and baseball, and three of the four took their sports seriously. George went on to become a minister, but Carl and Frank both played for the Hamilton Tigers in '34-'35, the year the team won the Allan Cup. Jack later played semi-pro with the Detroit Pontiacs in the Michigan-Ontario League. Carl was, without doubt, the best hockey player in the family. He led the Tigers in scoring that season, and when Jack Adams came calling with a contract, Carl signed and started in the Red Wings organization. He made his NHL debut in '37-'38 as a replacement for Herbie Lewis, setting a record that season by scoring three goals in a span of just 1:52. On November 5, 1941, he set a league mark with seven points in a game and quickly became one of the NHL's top scorers. Liscombe led the league in goals and points in the 1943 playoffs, leading the Wings to the Stanley Cup. It was his one and only Cup celebration, playing on a line with Syd Howe and Mud Bruneteau. The '45-'46 season was Liscombe's last in the NHL, but he gladly continued to play in the AHL, with Providence, for four more years and in senior hockey after that. He tied a record in '47-'48 with 118 points and was twice named the league's MVP. After retiring, Liscombe returned to Detroit and operated a carpet business with another former Galtonian, Zory Sarkasian, and later moved into insurance. When the Wings won the Cup next, in 1997, Liscombe was at the Joe Louis Arena cheering the team on.

LITTLE, Neil
b. Medicine Hat, Alberta, December 18, 1971

It wasn't until after his 30th birthday that Little finally made the big leap to the NHL, and it was a leap that lasted all of one night. He was a low Philadelphia draft choice in 1991 after his first year guarding the goal for the RPI Engineers, but after graduating Little was a minor leaguer for nearly nine years. He got the call to the Flyers for the game against Carolina on March 28, 2002, but after losing 4-1 was back in the minors. Little's finest hour came in 1997-98 when he led the AHL Phantoms to the Calder Cup.

LITTMAN, David ("Litty")
b. Cranston, Rhode Island, June 13, 1967

As a kid, Littman played at the Islanders' practice rink and he had the pleasure of meeting Chico Resch one day. When Resch learned that Littman played goal, he had one word of advice for the youngster – don't. Well, like Resch, he did, and he even managed to go places. He played at Boston College and then got into three NHL games between 1990 and '93, but for the most part he was a minor-leaguer. He divided his time between the AHL and IHL, and after 1997 he retired briefly before being talked back into the game with Orlando in the "I." He retired for good early in the 1999-2000 season because of recurring knee injuries, but

David Littman

Ed Litzenberger

Lonnie Loach

remained in Orlando to work as a colour commentator for the Bears' television and radio broadcasts.

LITZENBERGER, Ed ("Litz")
b. Neudorf, Saskatchewan, July 15, 1932

Litzenberger began his NHL career in the '54-'55 season in a trivia kind of way. He became the only rookie to win the Calder Trophy during a season he was traded. He had played a few games with Montreal in the 2 previous years, and started the '54-'55 season with the Habs, but they sold him to Chicago after 29 games and Litz went on to score 23 goals and win the top honour for first-year players. He had some fine years in the Windy City as a forward, gangly and deceptively shifty. He had 3 consecutive 30-goal seasons. In '60-'61, as team captain, he helped the Hawks win the Cup for the first time since 1938, but his relations with management were never very good and he was traded to Detroit in the off-season. He never endeared himself to GM Jack Adams in the Motor City, either, so the Wings sent him to the Leafs midway through the year and Litz won another Cup with a different team in successive years, another rarity. In fact, he stuck around to win Cups with Toronto in '63 and '64 as well, and after a couple of years in the minors he moved to New York to work on Wall Street and learn the stock markets. Once he mastered that trade, he moved back to Toronto and worked in stocks until he retired. He stayed in close contact with the old-timers from his generation through charity games and monthly lunches.

LIUT, Mike
b. Weston, Ontario, January 7, 1956

During a long career in goal, Liut had his finest years early on and struggled to play to expectations as the years wore on and his body broke down. He graduated from Bowling Green and played two years in the WHA leading up to the 1979 merger, at which time he signed with his NHL team, St. Louis. His first 3 years were his finest as he played more than 60 games in each and was among the top goalies in the league. In '80-'81, he was a First All-Star Team goalie and won the Lester Pearson Award. As a result of his play he was named starter for Canada at the 1981 Canada Cup by Scotty Bowman, who overlooked other notables, including Glen Hanlon. The tournament ended disastrously for Bowman and Liut, Canada losing to the Soviets 8-1 in the finals, but Hanlon rebounded and had another fine season. Liut later played with Hartford and Washington, and in later years he led the league in average while playing a reduced load. Early in '91-'92, recurring back injuries forced him to retire. Liut graduated from the Detroit College of Law while working at the NHLPA, and soon after became a player agent based in Detroit, later working with Brian Lawton and Larry Kelly.

LOACH, Lonnie
b. New Liskeard, Ontario, April 14, 1968

He wasn't very big, so right off the bat this meant minors and Europe rather than long-term NHL. Loach played junior in Guelph and was drafted by Chicago in 1986, but Detroit signed him five years later when the Hawks let him walk. From there, he was claimed by Ottawa, and it was with the expansion Sens that he saw his first NHL action, in 1992-93. Three games later, though, the Sens put him on waivers and L.A. claimed him and used him for half a season. After a few games with Anaheim the next year, Loach headed for the minors – the "I" – and then on to Switzerland.

LOCAS, Jacques

b. Pointe aux Trembles, Quebec, February 12, 1926
d. Île Bizard, Quebec, September 26, 1995

Locas first came to notice during the 1947-48 season playing for the Montreal Royals, the team that won the Allan Cup. He joined the Canadiens in the fall, but in a year and a bit showed none of the scoring ability he had or would show in future years. Back in the Quebec league, he was a consistent and top scorer, and he only got better as he got older. The two years he led the league in scoring were at the end of his career.

LOCHEAD, Bill ("Whip")

b. Forest, Ontario, October 13, 1954

In junior, with Oshawa, Lochead was a natural scorer, but he was also a well-grounded young man who worked full-time for an auto supply firm while playing. Detroit took him 9th overall in 1974 and he signed with the Wings a year after he had rejected offers to play in the WHA. The 50-goal seasons with Oshawa translated to about 15 in the NHL. After his second year he hurt his neck badly in a car accident in the summer, which didn't help his development. He played a few games with Colorado and the Rangers and then took off to Europe, where he has been ever since. He settled in Germany as a player, and turned to coaching when his skating days were done. For the past 15 years he has been employed in this capacity with a variety of teams overseas, his reputation and resumé fine credentials for as long as he wants to stay there.

LOCKETT, Ken

b. Toronto, Ontario, August 30, 1947

There aren't many goalies who come out of Ontario universities to make the NHL, but Lockett came out of U of Guelph to play for Vancouver. He holds two small distinctions in the annals of Canucks history: He was the first goalie for the franchise to record back-to-back shutouts, and he was the first to surrender a penalty-shot goal. Lockett was backup for two seasons (1974-76) and played a year in the WHA before retiring.

LOCKHART, Howie ("Holes"/ "Gutty")

b. Toronto, Ontario, April 22, 1897
d. unknown

After playing locally in and around North Bay as a boy,

Liut graduated from the Detroit College of Law while working at the NHLPA.
MIKE LIUT

Lockhart interrupted his career in 1916 to join the army. In his first year, he managed to play goal for the 228th Battalion in Toronto, after which he served overseas. Upon returning, he was active in the NHL for a number of years, most significantly with Hamilton in 1920-21 and the year after when he played every game of the Tigers schedule.

LOCKING, Norm

b. Owen Sound, Ontario, May 24, 1911
d. Southampton, Ontario, May 15, 1995

He almost died before he had a chance to play pro, but Locking rallied and honoured his contract with Chicago. In 1930, he attended the Hawks training camp. One night, a number of the players went to see the Army-Navy football game at Soldier's Field, during which Locking contracted a serious case of pneumonia. He was rushed to hospital and given up for dead, but a month later he rallied and slowly recovered. He returned to Owen Sound to play with the Greys, the team he had started with in 1927 as a sub with a club that won the Memorial Cup. Recovered, he moved up to Pittsburgh in 1931 and made it to the Hawks three years later. After a year and a half, though, he had contributed just two goals and was sold to the minors, where he played his remaining days.

LOEWEN, Darcy

b. Calgary, Alberta, February 26, 1969

Buffalo didn't give Loewen much of a chance, but Ottawa played the left winger for a year and a half before letting him walk. Without offers from other NHL teams, he signed with Las Vegas in the IHL and played there for four years before ending his career with brief stops in Britain and Idaho. He retired in 2000 after 11 years in pro hockey.

LOFTHOUSE, Mark

b. New Westminster, British Columbia, April 21, 1957

His hometown Bruins had a terrific run in the 1970s, winning two Memorial Cups and going to the finals on two other occasions. Lofthouse was part of three of those (including a win in 1977) and moved on to play for Washington. He was a scoring forward in junior, but when he got to the NHL … he wasn't. He spent parts of six years in the league, but his finest was surely '80-'81 down in Hershey, when he led the AHL in goals (48) and points (103). He finished his career in that league in 1989.

LOGAN, Dave

b. Montreal, Quebec, July 2, 1954

Probably the toughest part of the enforcer's role is, simply, to accept it for what it is and not try to stretch its

Jacques Locas

Bill Lochead

Norm Locking

Darcy Loewen

Dave Logan

made his own contribution to the game in a more light-hearted vein some years later while playing for Buffalo. In the 1975 playoffs against the Flyers, he swatted a bat out of the air and killed it. The animal had been flying around above the ice for some time, but players couldn't get it and arena staff couldn't corral it until Lorentz's mighty swat left the animal dead on the ice for all to see. From that day forward, Lorentz was known as Batman. He had some fine years in Buffalo, and after retiring in 1978 decided to give coaching a try with the Buffalo Junior Sabres. He found the travel too much, so he became the team's colour commentator for television broadcasts. Away from the ice, he was also an accomplished fly fisherman who regularly wrote articles and conducted workshops on the sport.

LORENZ, Danny
b. Murrayville, British Columbia, December 12, 1969
Well travelled, near and far, and devoted to the game, Lorenz won one game in eight NHL appearances in the early 1990s before moving around like a rental goalie. He was a star with a dreadful Seattle team in the Western league as a teen, but after brief stints with the Islanders he made his way through North America before moving on to Britain and conquering the crease there, with Nottingham and, most recently, Guildford.

LORIMER, Bob
b. Toronto, Ontario, August 25, 1953
In one fell swoop, Lorimer went from the penthouse of the hockey world to the basement – without using an elevator. The defenceman played at Michigan Tech for four years and came along steadily in the Islanders system to earn a full-time spot on the team in 1978. The next two years, the Islanders were Cup champions, and Lorimer's steady play in his end contributed in its own way while Denis Potvin led the offence from the blueline. But days before the start of the '81-'82 season, another Cup year for the Isles, Lorimer was traded to Colorado, the lowest of the low, the worst of the worst. Sayonara playoffs. He accompanied the team to New Jersey and played four more years, retiring in 1986. He moved to Toronto and became an account executive with Prudential Corporation.

LORRAIN, Rod
b. Buckingham, Quebec, July 26, 1915
d. October 22, 1980
In hockey's pre-expansion years there were some men who, toward the end of their playing careers, left the NHL and became reinstated as amateurs. But the number of players who, after being reinstated, subsequently rejoined the NHL is very small indeed. Rod Lorrain is one such specimen. As a child he played in Buckingham in the River Side League before joining the Lasalle Juniors. Among his teammates was Paul Drouin, whom he would meet again at the Montreal Forum. Lorrain graduated to the Ottawa Senators in senior play and, despite being only 20, so impressed the Canadiens that he was offered a contract. The speedy but chunky winger played one game for Montreal in '35-'36 and played regularly for the next four years, but in 1940 he left the team and

became an amateur again, playing in St. Jerome, an intermediate team. Just a year later, the Habs were lacking in right wing experience and re-signed Lorrain, who played four games with the team in '41-'42 before continuing the pro game in the AHL and then with senior teams in Quebec. He retired for keeps in 1945.

LOUGHLIN, Clement "Clem"
b. Carroll, Manitoba, November 15, 1894
d. Alberta, February 8, 1977
A long, long time ago, when the NHA and NHL were in their earliest years, players actually had another option – the Pacific Coast league. The pay was great and the skill level high, and players routinely left the Eastern leagues to play out west. Loughlin was one of them. He played for just three years in the NHL, but for a decade in Portland and Victoria, winning a Stanley Cup with the Cougars in 1925. After NHL time with Detroit and Chicago, Loughlin finished his career in the International league in 1933. A year later, he returned to the Hawks as their head coach, a position he held for three decreasingly successful seasons.

LOUGHLIN, Wilf
b. Carroll, Manitoba, February 28, 1897
d. June 25, 1966
Like brother Clem, Wilf spent most of his years out west, though his career wasn't nearly as long or successful. His only NHL time came with the Toronto St. Pats, precursors to the Maple Leafs, in 1923-24.

LOUSTEL, Ron
b. Winnipeg, Manitoba, March 7, 1962
Rare, indeed, is the time a goalie gives up 10 goals in a game, and rarer even that he stays in net for the full 60 minutes. Yet on March 27, 1981, Loustel was tossed in the cage and wasn't pulled despite clearly having an off night against Vancouver. Thus, he has the distinction of having given up the most goals in his one and only NHL start.

LOVSIN, Ken
b. Peace River, Alberta, December 3, 1966
The dream of the Olympics was of far greater inspirational value to Lovsin than pro hockey or the NHL, perhaps because the skill wasn't there, perhaps because he cherished the purity of purpose behind the competition. Either way, he played at U of Saskatchewan in 1988 and played four full years with the Canadian National Team afterward, culminating in a silver-medal victory at the 1994 Olympics in Lillehammer. Along the way, he played a single game for Washington. After retiring, he settled in Barrhead, Alberta, and bought an IGA store. In addition to managing it, he coached his son's and daughter's hockey teams and spoke at the occasional banquet.

LOW, Reed ("Sweets")
b. Moose Jaw, Saskatchewan, June 21, 1976
He's there to fight, plain and simple. He does it well and he's well paid for it, and he fills a role St. Louis needs him to fill. Coming out of Moose Jaw in the WHL, Low paid his dues – three years in the minors – before making the team full-time in 2000.

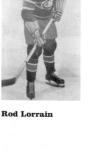

Bob Lorimer

Rod Lorrain

Clem Loughlin

LOW, Ron ("Lowtide")
b. Birtle, Manitoba, June 21, 1950

For a coach, he was a great goalie, and as a former NHL goalie, he went on to become the most successful coach in league history. As a player, Low filled the role of backup more than starter during his career, and he had a rather unimpressive record of 102-203-38 over his dozen or so years in pro. Perhaps as telling was the fact that he went to the playoffs only twice, more an indication of the poor teams he played for than his own performance. When he retired in 1985, he did something very few goalies do – went into the coaching business. He went down to the minors and worked his way up from assistant to head coach with the Oilers farm team in Nova Scotia, and then did same for the Oilers in Alberta. He stayed four and a half years, and after being fired he joined Houston of the IHL as GM and coach. When Glen Sather moved to New York in 2000, he brought Low along and in so doing Low became the first-ever former goalie to coach two different NHL teams. For a former player, that doesn't sound like much, but for a 'tender, it was history making. Two non-playoff seasons later, though, Slats had to fire him. Still, Low has coached more NHL games than any other former goalie.

LOWDERMILK, Dwayne
b. Burnaby, British Columbia, January 9, 1958

Anyone who ever made it to the NHL had to have some skill (okay, almost anyone), and Lowdermilk was no exception. He played only two games, for Washington in 1980-81 after the Caps acquired his rights from the Islanders, but what he did after retiring was even more important. The minors just didn't do it for him, so he set up shop in Langley, B.C., and established National Training Rinks, a year-round facility that teaches all levels of hockey to boys and girls.

LOWE, Darren
b. Toronto, Ontario, October 13, 1960

A Toronto boy through and through, Lowe attended university in the City of Churches, where he graduated in 1983. He had the chance of a lifetime to play for the National Team and carry on to the Olympics – which he took – and immediately after he signed with Pittsburgh. Lowe played just eight games with the pre-Mario Pens and then played all over for a few years before retiring and returning to Hogtown. He became an assistant coach at Ryerson University in 1991 and a year later moved to U of T, becoming head coach there in 1995 and assuming a position held by such greats as Ace Bailey, Tom Watt, and Mike Keenan. The NHL cannot be far off for him.

He went from assistant coach to head coach to GM in consecutive years.
KEVIN LOWE

LOWE, Kevin
b. Lachute, Quebec, April 15, 1959

If he's not a Hall of Famer, he's pretty damn close. Lowe came to the Oilers in 1979, the year the franchise joined the NHL, and for the next 19 years he was one of the steadiest and most successful defencemen in the game. While Paul Coffey was flying Orr-like up the ice, Lowe was watching from behind, protecting his own end as much as possible on the highest-scoring team in NHL history. He won six Cups in all, five with the Oilers and then a sixth with the "New York Oilers" of '94, which featured so many of the greats from the 1980s Edmonton dynasty. Those were the only teams he played for, and when he retired he returned to Alberta to begin what has been a meteoric rise through the executive ranks. He went from assistant coach to head coach to GM in consecutive years, and because he had the trust of Wayne Gretzky he was named an assistant to Canada's 2002 Olympic team, which won gold. Lowe played in seven All-Star Games and in 1990 won the King Clancy Trophy, but he was never named to an All-Star Team.

LOWE, Norm "Odie"
b. Winnipeg, Manitoba, April 15, 1928

In a life of senior hockey, Lowe played just four games with the Rangers, though he did score a goal. That was the '49-'50 season, near the start of his career. Lowe went on to play another dozen years, after which he coached the Flin Flon Bombers.

LOWE, Ross
b. Oshawa, Ontario, September 21, 1928
d. Lake Haliburton, Ontario, August 8, 1955

Lowe was one of those players who would have been in the NHL instantly if there had been seven Original Six teams. He was that good. He was a speedy skater, a fine scorer, an aggressive competitor, and a desired asset whom Montreal acquired from Boston for Hal Laycoe in 1951. He abruptly retired in early 1953 because he was sick of the minors and wanted to return home to Whitby to explore business opportunities outside hockey. The next year, he was persuaded to return, and in '54-'55, he had his finest season as a pro with Springfield when he scored 32 goals and was named the AHL's MVP. In the summer, though, tragedy struck. He and a friend were diving off a boat on Lake Haliburton when a gust of wind pushed the boat away. Lowe swam after it, collapsed from exhaustion, and drowned. He had been vacationing with his wife and two children.

Ron Low

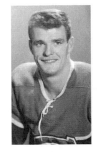

Ross Lowe

Ed Lowrey

LOWREY, Ed
b. Manotick, Ontario, August 13, 1891
d. Ann Arbour, Michigan, November 27, 1973
One of the game's early stars, Lowrey played during the crossover years when the NHA gave way to the NHL in 1917. In NHA days he skated in Toronto, Ottawa, and Montreal. In the NHL, he saw action with the Senators and the Hamilton Bulldogs, scoring a total of 2 goals in 27 games.

LOWREY, Fred ("Frock")
b. Ottawa, Ontario, October 12, 1899
d. Ottawa, Ontario, January 24, 1968
Long before the amazing Sutter family ever hit an NHL sheet of ice, there was the seven-member Lowrey family. Now, all seven didn't make it to the NHL, but they all did play hockey and collectively are part of Ottawa history in a significant way. Brothers Ed and Gerry went on to the NHL. The Reverend Robert was a fine hockey and football player. Tommy played with Fred in the City League and later edited the *Ottawa Journal*. He also took the Ottawa Shamrocks on a European tour in the 1930s featuring younger brother Frank. Billy, the baby, was a fine player in junior and senior hockey in the city. Once, the entire septet played the Shams in an exhibition game. Fred joined the army in 1918 before turning pro. An auto mechanic by trade, he joined the 2nd Depot Battalion and served for a number of years. In the NHL, he played for the Maroons and the Pittsburgh Pirates (1924-26) and later played in assorted leagues before returning to Ottawa.

Dave Lowry

LOWREY, Gerry
b. Ottawa, Ontario, February 14, 1906
d. Ottawa, Ontario, October 17, 1979
Lowrey was one of four members of the 1923-24 North Bay Trappers, NOHA junior champions, to go on to the NHL (Art Gauthier, Bud Maracle, and Shorty Horne were the others). The previous year, Lowrey had won the Copeland Cup with the Iroquois Falls Eskimos, and by 1927 he had developed into NHL material. In six years, he played for five teams, starting with Toronto, but the light left winger who weighed in at 150 pounds had his best seasons with two defunct teams, Pittsburgh and Philadelphia. Like all members of the Lowrey clan, he retired to Ottawa and formed Gerry Lowrey Ltd., which he ran until his death.

LOWRY, Dave
b. Sudbury, Ontario, February 14, 1965
From the time he picked up a stick, Lowry was not a scorer. As a kid, he played in Nepean on the same line as Steve Yzerman. Stevie Y scored about a million goals,

of course, and Lowry, well, didn't. In St. Louis, he played on a line with Brett Hull when the Golden Brett was scoring 70 and 80 goals a year and Lowry was, well, not. In fact, when St. Louis sent him to the minors in 1988, Lowry almost retired to become a police officer. He hung in there and has played more than 1,000 NHL games. A checker all his pro life, he had his best time in the 1996 playoffs when the upstart Florida Panthers raced to the Cup finals. Lowrey scored 10 goals in 22 games that playoff year, equalling his regular-season output over 63 games. He was hot, a scorer, a star, and the Panthers were defeated by Colorado in four straight games. Lowry went back to his checking ways, ways that have kept him in the league for 17 years and more. Back home, he bought a share of the Coquitlam entry in the BCJHL with former players Bill Ranford and Darcy Rota.

> **As a first-rounder,**
> **he was a bust, but as a person**
> **he was accomplished.**
> **DANNY LUCAS**

LOZINSKI, Larry
b. Hudson Bay, Saskatchewan, March 11, 1958
A late draft choice by Detroit in 1978, Lozinski went on to play just half a season with the Wings a couple of years later. The rest of his short career took place in the minors, but by the time he was 25 he was out of the game altogether.

LUCAS, Danny
b. Powell River, British Columbia, February 28, 1958
Philadelphia had 3 selections in the first 14 of the 1978 Amateur Draft. The Flyers took Behn Wilson 6th overall, Ken Linseman 7th, and Danny Lucas 14th. It was a natural progression of events for Lucas, who played junior in Victoria with Mel Bridgman as his centre. He then played at UBC for a year and decided to finish his junior eligibility by playing 1977-78 with the Soo Greyhounds. A right winger who shot left, his centreman was Wayne Gretzky. Lucas scored 50 goals that year (hell, anyone could score 50 playing alongside 99), so his high selection was no surprise. He worked that summer at a pulp and paper mill in Powell River and then went to Philly for training camp. They played him in six games and then sent him to the minors, and he played there for two and a half years before retiring. He went to the University of Southern Maine to finish his education (most of his time in the AHL was with the Maine Mariners) and after graduating he became a real estate agent in Portland. As a first-rounder, he was a bust, but as a person he was accomplished.

LUCAS, Dave
b. Downeyville, Ontario, March 22, 1932
Lucas got into his only NHL game on February 24, 1963, after nine years in the minors, mostly in the EHL, mostly with Johnstown. In fact, he was one of the greatest and longest-serving Jets of all time, playing 11

Larry Lozinski

years with the team and coaching wherever he played from 1964 on. He won three EHL championships with the team, in 1960, '61, and '62. In 1967 he left the Jets to play and coach for the Salem Rebels, but he left that team in 1969 to become a scout.

LUCE, Don
b. London, Ontario, October 2, 1948

When Luce was called up to join the Rangers in 1970, he knew his role would be different than it had been in junior, where he had scored his fair share of goals. New York was deep at centre, and the only way he was going to play was if he became a defensive-minded, two-way player. That style defined his 13-year career and earned him a reputation as the best of his kind. Luce made his mark with Buffalo, where he played most of those years. He killed penalties with best friend Craig Ramsay and in '74-'75, the year the Sabres made it to the Cup finals, Luce had eight short-handed goals and was also named winner of the Bill Masterton Trophy. Midway through that season, Luce also made his only appearance in an All-Star Game. In addition to checking the best players on opposing teams, he also had 6 consecutive seasons of 20 goals or more. After retiring, he became a scout for the Sabres and then director of scouting for the U.S. He later expanded his portfolio to include director of all Sabres scouting.

LUDVIG, Jan
b. Liberec, Czechoslovakia (Czech Republic), September 17, 1961

Ah, the fortunate Canadian who gets to the NHL via junior hockey, one of the privileges of living in a free society. Ludvig was a Czech kid in the late 1970s who wanted to go to Canada but couldn't simply go to the airport and buy a one-way ticket to Toronto. He defected from his homeland in May 1981 using a tourist visa for Yugoslavia, but he had to spend five months in an Austrian refugee camp before being allowed to seek asylum in Canada. Once in North America, he signed a contract with New Jersey and stayed with the Devils for four seasons. His best was his second, when he scored 22 goals, but by his fourth year he was in the minors and soon after was traded to Buffalo for Jim Korn. His two years in Buffalo constituted 26 games and 3 serious knee injuries, forcing him to retire on February 24, 1989.

LUDWIG, Craig
b. Rhinelander, Wisconsin, March 15, 1961

When he first got to the University of North Dakota in 1979, Ludwig was given an old pair of shin pads by the team's trainer, Dave Cameron. When he retired in 1999, Ludwig was still using them and the Hockey Hall of Fame was interested in acquiring them.

Ludwig said the only way they would get in the Hall of Fame was if he did, and fine a player though he may have been, the chances of that happening are exactly nil. Ludwig's greatest skill was blocking shots with those pads, playing stifling defence, and minding his end of the ice. He divided his lengthy career about equally between Montreal and Minnesota/Dallas, winning a Cup early in his career with the Habs in '86 and finishing his career with a Cup with the Stars in 1999. He became a scout with the team and then an assistant coach in the minors, and he plans to put the pads up in his bar in Wausau, Wisconsin.

LUDZIK, Steve
b. Toronto, Ontario, April 3, 1962

Circumstance and happenstance are bastard brothers if ever there were a more unnaturally related pair. Steve Ludzik and Steve Larmer are the human personification of those brothers. They were linemates in Niagara Falls when the two tore up the OHL, often with linemate Pat Graham, and both made it to Chicago in the fall of 1982. Larmer lucked out and wound up on the number-one line with Denis Savard; Ludzik got the call to the fourth line and was moved from centre to the right side. Of course, the scoring wasn't there, and although he played with the Hawks for eight years he was a role player more than a guy who made a difference each night or any night. He ended his career in the Buffalo system and then went into coaching, first in the lesser leagues for seven years and then with the hapless Lightning in Tampa Bay in 1999.

He ended his career in the Buffalo system and then went into coaching.
STEVE LUDZIK

LUHNING, Warren
b. Edmonton, Alberta, July 3, 1975

"He got his bell rung" is no longer an acceptable diagnosis in hockey, not from a player or a coach, and Lord knows not from a doctor. Luhning was drafted by the Islanders in 1993 before starting four years at the University of Michigan that earned him a B.A. in economics. After graduating, he played just a few games with New York over two years while spending most of his time in the minors. When Dallas acquired him in the summer of 1999, he looked forward to a new beginning with a new team at a time when he was starting to mature as a player. But in the last shift of his fourth game with the team, on October 22, 1999, he was cross-checked by Randy McKay of New Jersey. He felt awful, but at that precarious time in his career he felt it too risky to go to the team doctors and reveal the extent of the blow. He played six more games, and looked weaker each time out. Dallas demoted him, and in Kalamazoo his injury affected him to the point

Don Luce

Jan Ludvig

Craig Ludwig

Brad Lukowich

Morris Lukowich

Chuck Luksa

Dave Lumley

that he couldn't remember whether or not he had washed his hair in the shower. He sought the advice of Dr. James Kelly in Chicago, the foremost expert on concussions, who told him that had he been diagnosed with a concussion after the initial hit, he might have made a full recovery. Now, Dr. Kelly warned, retirement was the only safe option. Luhning, of course, took that route, but Dallas refused to pay him the rest of his NHL contract, saying the injury took place in the minors, which meant a payout of $75,000. Luhning countered that the injury occurred in the NHL and entitled him to $375,000 for the NHL part of his contract. He filed a grievance with the Stars, and in the meantime moved to Calgary and started working for a software company. That $300,000 isn't much for active players, but for those who are retired, it's a small fortune.

LUKOWICH, Bernie
b. North Battleford, Saskatchewan, March 18, 1952
Before sending a son, Brad, on to the NHL in the 1990s, Bernie himself had a bit of an NHL career of his own a quarter of a century earlier with Pittsburgh and St. Louis. He also played briefly in the WHA, but for the most part he was a minor-leaguer who settled in Cranbrook, B.C., after retiring.

LUKOWICH, Brad
b. Cranbrook, British Columbia, August 12, 1976
Father Bernie and cousin Morris made it to the NHL first, and so far Brad's career is in between the two forebears in terms of quality and content. Brad played on the double Memorial Cup Kamloops Blazers teams in '94 and '95 before joining Dallas in 1997. He managed what no other Lukowich had done, though – to win a Stanley Cup, with the Stars in 1999 in a part-time capacity. He was later traded to Minnesota in 2000 and then traded right back to the Stars a few days later.

LUKOWICH, Morris
b. Speers, Saskatchewan, June 1, 1956
His brother, Ed, couldn't skate, but he was instrumental in Morris's enthusiasm for hockey. Ed was no ice loser, though. He was a champion curler, and Morris went on to play eight years in the NHL in the 1980s. Despite the "too small" tag that followed him everywhere, Lukowich averaged 33 goals in his first 5 years in the league. He was a fantastic offensive threat on weak Winnipeg teams, and he lasted longer and was far more effective than anyone expected. He finished in Boston and L.A. and then joined the Canadian National Team in 1987, a stint that lasted only a month when he accepted an offer to play in Italy. He later coached in Japan and back home in roller hockey, and after leaving the hockey world

altogether Lukowich settled in Calgary and worked as a stock trader and financial consultant.

LUKSA, Chuck
b. Toronto, Ontario, February 19, 1954
Defenceman Charlie Luksa appeared in eight games for Hartford during the Whalers' first NHL year after a season with Cincinnati in the WHA. He retired in 1982 after a career spent primarily in the AHL.

LUMLEY, Dave ("Lummer")
b. Toronto, Ontario, September 1, 1954
One Christmas when Lumley was at the University of New Hampshire, he planned to drive home to Toronto with some friends. His mother told him to save time and fly, and his friends opted to drive. They ran out of gas on the highway and a truck plowed into the car, killing one and badly burning the other two passengers. Death took a pass on Lumley that time, but claimed both his parents in quick succession. His mom died of cancer during his senior year and his dad died of a heart attack two years later, never having seen Dave play at Maple Leaf Gardens. Lumley started with Montreal in the late 1970s when the Habs were Cup champions, and he was traded to Edmonton in June 1979, the best thing that could have happened to him. He played all but 48 games of his career with the Oilers and was a checking, fourth-line player with one remarkable exception. In 1981-82, he was put on a line with Wayne Gretzky and scored a goal in 12 consecutive games, almost an NHL record. He ended the year with 32, a total he never came close to repeating the rest of his career. He retired in 1986 and went on to do community relations for the Texarkana Border City Bandits, happy just to be alive.

He made his debut with the Red Wings in the '43-'44 season, at 17 becoming the youngest goalie ever to play.
HARRY LUMLEY

LUMLEY, Harry
("Apple Cheeks"/ "Lum")
b. Owen Sound, Ontario, November 11, 1926
d. London, Ontario, September 13, 1998
One of the greatest goalies of all time, Lumley can lay claim to being the only netminder to play for five of the Original Six teams, dressing for every club except Montreal during his lengthy career as a maskless puckstopper. He made his debut with the Red Wings in the '43-'44 season, at 17 becoming the youngest goalie ever to play in the league (a record that still stands). He also made an emergency appearance for the Rangers that season, but the next year he was the starting netminder for Detroit. The year after, at 19, he played every game and every minute of the season, and earned his nickname because of his ruddy complexion. Lumley's career peaked in '49-'50 when

he led the Red Wings to the Stanley Cup. He was sensational in both the regular season and the playoffs, but his reward was a trade to the worst team in the league, Chicago, so the Wings could bring Terry Sawchuk into the fold. He lasted just two years in the Windy City before Conn Smythe rescued him and brought him to Toronto, but the Leafs were in between dynasties and Lumley was often the only player on the team worth cheering for. In his four seasons with the Blue and White (1952-56), he led the league in shutouts twice and goals-against average twice, but Smythe sent him back to Chicago. Lumley refused to go there but was content to play in the AHL with Buffalo, and the Bruins temporarily rescued him from the minors for parts of three seasons. He was out of the NHL in 1960 but played another year in the minors and then got his amateur card back so he could play with the Collingwood Shipbuilders. From 1950 on, Lumley was part owner of Dominion Motors in Owen Sound, a business that had a second arm as operator of a horse racing stable. Lumley sold cars in the summers during his playing days, but once he retired he became more active in the horses, sometimes even riding a mount in races! He was inducted into the Hockey Hall of Fame in 1980, his 330 wins and 71 career shutouts among the leaders in those categories. On September 6, 1996, he suffered a heart attack at home and was taken to Victoria Hospital in London where he died a week later. Lumley is called by most people in Owen Sound the finest athlete that small city has ever produced.

LUMME, Jyrki
b. Tampere, Finland, July 16, 1966

Lumme was drafted by Montreal in 1986, but it was only after the 1988 Olympics in Calgary, when he helped Finland win a silver medal, that he was prepared to join the NHL. He was the first Finn ever to play for the Habs, but he didn't last long in Montreal, a defensive team not looking to give an offensive player too much ice time. A trade to Vancouver was the best thing for the young Lumme. He got the ice time, saw time on the power play, and became one of the team's top blueliners. For nine years he remained a Canuck, but in 1998 the free agent took his services to Phoenix for two seasons before joining Dallas. He had a miserable time under the stifling coaching of Ken Hitchcock, and a trade to Toronto liberated Lumme's spirit and brought some pep back into his step. Throughout his career, Lumme played for Finland whenever the chance occurred: World Juniors, World Championships, Canada Cup, World Cup, and Olympics.

LUND, Pentti
b. Karijoki, Finland, December 6, 1925

The Lund family emigrated to Port Arthur, Ontario, when Pentti was just six. It was there that he first started playing hockey, but his career came to a sudden stop when he enlisted in the navy. Immediately after being discharged in 1947 he joined the Bruins, but played only three games with them, all in the playoffs, in two seasons (1946-48). The B's traded him to the Rangers, and he had a terrific rookie season there. Playing on the "L" line with Edgar

Laprade and Tony Leswick, Lund scored 14 goals and won the Calder Trophy. The next year, he led the playoffs in scoring as the Rangers lost to Detroit in game seven of the finals. After one more season on Broadway, Lund played two final years with Boston. His career more or less ended on November 13, 1951, when Clare Martin's stick poked him in the eye. Lund was out of action for three months and lost most of the use of the eye, but he returned to play a full season for the Bruins the next year. He was traded out west, but rather than uproot his family he was reinstated as an amateur and played in the Soo for two final seasons. After retiring, he returned to Port Hope and became a journalist there and later sports editor for the *Fort William Times Journal*.

LUNDBERG, Brian
b. Burnaby, British Columbia, June 5, 1960

A single game with Pittsburgh in '82-'83 marked Lundberg's ascent to the hockey heavens. A U of Michigan graduate, he played just three years of pro before retiring.

LUNDE, Len
b. Campbell River, British Columbia, November 13, 1936

Of course, any player who makes the NHL deserves bragging rights in hockey over everyone else, but among those elite some can brag more than others. Any man who can say he centred a line with Gordie Howe on one wing and Alex Delvecchio on the other gets special, lifetime dispensation to smile at the thought of his NHL days. That was in the '58-'59 season, with Detroit, when the rookie Lunde scored a career-high 14 goals. Generally speaking, he was more of a playmaker, but he did have his innings as a scorer. In '64-'65 with Buffalo, he became one of the few men to hit the 50-goal mark for a season, and 5 years later, in the WHL, he scored all five of his team's goals in a game, a rarity for any league. Lunde also played with Chicago during the Original Six and then with Minnesota and Vancouver in the expanded NHL. In 1971, he went to Finland for a two-year stay, first as a player, then as a coach. He later worked for two years as the director of a hockey program on a Native reserve near Edmonton and afterwards scouted for the Oilers in Sweden and Finland, where his job included, among other things, monitoring the progress of Esa Tikkanen and Jari Kurri.

LUNDHOLM, Bengt
("Swift"/ "Silly Putty")
b. Falun, Sweden, August 4, 1955

It wasn't until he was 26 years old that the NHL took a serious interest in Lundholm, who was playing hockey at night while working as a kindergarten teacher in the daytime. St. Louis and Winnipeg both indicated a liking for the slender left winger, and Lundholm opted for the 'Peg because the Jets teams of the 1970s featured countrymen Ulf Nilsson and Anders Hedberg, among other Europeans. For four and a half years he defied critics who thought he'd get wasted by NHL d-men, feinting and shifting while darting in and around opponents with skill. Prior to his Canadian arrival, he had been a star in league play in Sweden and a regular at the World Championships.

Jyrki Lumme

Pentti Lund

Len Lunde

Bengt Lundholm

He also represented Tre Kronor at the 1980 Olympics in Lake Placid and the Canada Cup a year later.

LUNDRIGAN, Joe
b. Corner Brook, Newfoundland, September 12, 1948
St. Francis Xavier University, down Antigonish way, is affectionately called St. F-X by those who know about things down east, and a lovely campus it is, even if it couldn't claim Lundrigan as an alumnus (but it can). He left St. F-X in '71 to play in the minors for Tulsa, in the Leafs system, and the year after he caught a break when most of the Leafs defence abandoned ship. Rick Ley and Brad Selwood jumped to the WHA, Bobby Baun retired, and John Grisdale and Brian Glennie were injured. Enter Lundrigan, stage right. He filled in admirably for much of that season, but the year after he was back in the minors. He played three more games with Washington but soon returned to Corner Brook and left the pro ice game behind.

Tord Lundstrom

LUNDSTROM, Tord
b. Kiruna, Sweden, March 4, 1945
Kiruna is a small place north of the Arctic Circle, which is about as far north as you can get. Lundstrom became one of that town's most famous sons, primarily for his career with Brynas, which, by the time it was done, had fans voting him the greatest Brynas player of all time. The team retired his number 6 in honour of his 15 years of service, which was interrupted only by a short pro stint with Detroit in 1973-74. In fact, Lundstrom played only 11 games with the Wings and half the season in London, England, with Detroit's European farm team. Besides that, his life was Brynas, Brynas, and more Brynas. He also played a number of major international tournaments. He later coached Brynas after retiring, but two short stints confirmed his disinterest and lack of success in this field altogether different from playing.

Roberto Luongo

LUNDY, Pat
b. Saskatoon, Saskatchewan, May 31, 1924
d. Surrey, British Columbia, November 23, 1991
Military duty as a teen stalled Lundy's ascent to the major leagues for two seasons, but by 1945 he was ready to pursue the NHL dream. Of his first four years with Detroit, only his second, in '46-'47, was a full year with the big team. The centre scored a respectable 17 goals, but most of his years passed with the farm team in Indianapolis. The Wings sold him to Chicago at the start of the '50-'51 season, and Lundy stayed with the team most of the year before passing into the minors for good. He later moved west, to B.C., to train and race standardbreds.

Gary Lupul

LUONGO, Chris
b. Detroit, Michigan, March 17, 1967
After captaining Michigan State in his final year of college in '88-'89, Luongo turned pro in the Detroit system. He played four games with the Wings before joining Ottawa for a full season, but really it was the Islanders that gave him his best chance to prove himself. He worked his way into the lineup, yet just after playing his first full season with the team, in '95-'96, he was back in the minors. Enough of that, said Luongo, and he headed to Germany to play. The schedule and

Roman Lyashenko

circumstances of those years enabled him to play for the U.S. at the World Championships on a few occasions.

LUONGO, Roberto
b. Montreal, Quebec, April 4, 1979
It's the big and tall goalies who usually take the longest to develop and adjust to the NHL, so it's still early in Luongo's career. When the Islanders chose him 4th overall in 1997, it marked the highest selection ever used to acquire a goalie, and his rise has been steady without being successful. The Isles traded him to Florida after one season because GM Mike Milbury had his eyes on Rick DiPietro, and Luongo played increasingly well in goal for the Panthers to the point that in 2001-02 he appeared in 58 games and was clearly the team's number-one man. Trouble was, the team was horrible, but that meant great experience for him.

LUPIEN, Gilles
b. Lachute, Quebec, April 20, 1954
He never thought much about a pro career because he knew he didn't have the skill. In his pre-NHL days, Lupien ran a lumber supply company in Lachute, but when Montreal expressed an interest in him, he expressed right back. He played in the Montreal system for six years, winning Cups in '78 and '79, but he was never happy. He sat on the bench for long stretches, and coaches and fans alike wanted the 6'6" defenceman to do one thing – clobber an opponent. Lupien wanted to play and he wanted respect, but after trades to Pittsburgh and Hartford he realized he had been painted by the same brush. Fight or don't play was the unspoken dictum, so he retired. Lupien later became a player agent, and one of his first big clients was Felix Potvin during the goalie's meteoric rise with Toronto in the early 1990s.

LUPUL, Gary ("Loop")
b. Powell River, British Columbia, April 4, 1959
He didn't have a particularly long career, but Lupul spent all of it with Vancouver in the 1980s. Coming out of Victoria in junior, hew as never drafted but signed as a free agent with his home-province Canucks. Over the years he played mostly with the Canucks, though also saw what the minors looked like. He was a fourth-liner who had to work hard to stay in the lineup, and when he didn't, he didn't, simple as that. In 1985 he went to Europe to play for a few years, but when he retired he returned to Vancouver. Lupul remained active in the game at a number of levels: He worked as Vancouver's video replay coordinator and taught at clinics and hockey schools.

LYASHENKO, Roman
b. Murmansk, Soviet Union (Russia), May 2, 1979
A mere child, Lyashenko started his career with Dallas before being traded to the Rangers during the 2001-02 season. He played on three World Junior teams for Russia (1997, '98, and '99), but so far he has yet to make a significant mark on the NHL.

LYDMAN, Toni
b. Lahti, Finland, September 25, 1977
A young Finn who has yet to realize his full potential,

Lydman is strong and tenacious and part of a fine corps for the Calgary blueline. Over the last couple of years he has established himself as a regular, though he isn't blessed with offensive ability or a nasty streak that never hurts in the NHL. Lydman played twice for Finland at the World Juniors.

LYLE, George ("Sparky")
b. North Vancouver, British Columbia, November 24, 1953
Ah, the early years are always the best. Lyle had a great college career with Michigan Tech, winning the NCAA championship in 1975 as a sophomore and going to the finals the next year before turning pro with New England in the WHA. As a rookie, he scored on his first shot and had 39 goals on the season. He was named the league's best rookie, yet never scored as many goals in the next seven years of hockey. He transferred to the NHL in 1979, first with Detroit and then with Hartford. In those final four seasons, he never played more than 31 games and his superb wrist shot just didn't cut it in the big league as it had in college and the WHA.

LYNCH, Jack
b. Toronto, Ontario, May 25, 1952
Some guys have all the luck, and those hogs never share it with the likes of Lynch, who had none of it in his career. He grew up in Barrie, north of Toronto, and played junior in Oshawa. From the time he joined Pittsburgh in 1972 to the time he retired in 1979, he appeared in 382 regular-season games and not one in the playoffs. Brutal, brutal teams. A defenceman, his cumulative +/- rating was -197. In Detroit, the team was awful. In Washington, the team had one year with a road record of 1-39-0. In December 1977, Lynch tore his knee and never fully recovered. After retiring, he stayed in Washington for a few years doing colour commentary – no rest for the wicked – and returned to Barrie in 1982. He became a promotions officer for the Ontario Ministry of Tourism and Recreation, which operated a broadcast studio for information on local attractions.

LYNN, Vic
b. Saskatoon, Saskatchewan, January 26, 1925
In the long and glorious history of the Original Six one player – and only one – played for each and every one of those six teams. Vic Lynn. He joined the Rangers in 1942 and from there moved on to Detroit (in '43), Montreal ('45), Toronto ('46), Boston ('50), and Chicago ('53). Interspersed were stints in the minors, but his best years were with the Leafs, where he won three successive Cups (1947, '48, and '49). Lynn played with Howie Meeker and Ted Kennedy on the famed KLM line, and he killed penalties with Joe Klukay or Johnny McCormack on that Leafs team that was the first in NHL history to win three in a row. As a kid, he was called the Saskatoon Streak or Saskatoon Speedboy because of his pure and brilliant skating, and it was his legs that kept him in the game so long. After the Black Hawks demoted him in 1953, he played another decade in the minors, often coaching as well. During his playing days, he spent most of his summers putting up billboard advertising, but once he retired from hockey in 1964 he opened a

small hotel outside Saskatoon and spent his days playing golf on two artificial knees and chewing the fat with visitors.

LYON, Steve
b. Toronto, Ontario, May 16, 1952
A Minnesota draft choice in 1972, Lyon played his only NHL games with Pittsburgh four years later in a short pro career. He played senior hockey after 1977 for a number of years and retired in 1984 after a final season in the Atlantic Coast Hockey League.

LYONS, Ron ("Peaches")
b. Portage la Prairie, Manitoba, February 15, 1909
d. unknown
Lyons played for Boston and the Philadelphia Quakers in 1930-31, his only NHL season. It was an odd season, though, because he started with the Bruins, went to the Quakers, and was traded back to the B's before the end of the year. Beyond that, he played mostly out west.

LYSIAK, Tom
b. High Prairie, Alberta, April 22, 1953
The 1980s were a time of change in the NHL. The league successfully ended bench-clearing brawls, it invoked the instigator rule to diminish fighting, and it cracked down on stick violations and misconduct against officials. It was the latter that embroiled Lysiak the night of October 30, 1983. Off a faceoff outside the Chicago blueline, Lysiak moved toward the puck and, as he did so, tripped linesman Ron Foyt, who had just dropped the disc and was backing out of the way. To most observers, the trip was a deliberate act, an act of frustration that came out of events of the game. But a deliberate assault of an official carried an automatic 20-game suspension, which the league duly levied. Lysiak was upset, and challenged the suspension, obtaining a restraining order so he could keep playing until given a fair hearing. In the end, the ban remained, but he did succeed in altering the way hearings are carried out and suspensions levied. Ironically, this, the longest suspension of its kind in league history, came in a season in which Lysiak accrued only 35 penalty minutes. He was not a fighter or a vicious player, and the act was uncharacteristic. Coming out of junior, he was drafted 2nd overall by Atlanta in 1973, behind only Denis Potvin. Lysiak led the Western league in scoring his last 2 years in junior, and during his NHL career he had nine 20-goal seasons. During his six years with the Flames, he played mostly with Jacques Richard and Larry Romanchych. His trade to Chicago was difficult because he was replacing three of the team's most popular players – Ivan Boldirev, Phil Russell, and Darcy Rota – but he scored and led his way into fans' hearts. He retired in 1986 on his own terms and settled on his horse farm outside Atlanta. For the first part of his career he lived on a farm outside Medicine Hat, but his farm in Georgia allowed him to set up his own landscaping company as well.

George Lyle

Jack Lynch

Vic Lynn

Ron Lyons

Tom Lysiak

MacADAM, Al
b. Charlottetown, Prince Edward Island, March 16, 1952
The wee island of PEI has sent a few players to the NHL, but none with the longevity and success MacAdam has experienced from 1973, when he first made the Philadelphia Flyers, to his ongoing and continuous involvement in the pro game. He played just a few games with the Flyers, not enough to get his name on their '73-'74 Cup, and was traded to California in the summer, where he got a chance to play plenty and develop his talents. He became a consistent NHL scorer, reaching his apex in '79-'80 when he had 42 goals with Minnesota. In all, he had 240 goals and represented Canada at the World Championships in 1977 and '79. He played at the All-Star Game in '76 and '77, and in 1980 he was awarded the Bill Masterton Trophy. Each summer during his career, MacAdam returned home to work on his B.A. in history at UPEI. After retiring, he became assistant athletic director and hockey coach at St. Thomas University in Fredericton, a position he held for 10 years. He moved on to become head coach for the Leafs farm team in St. John's, and in the summer of 2000 Chicago hired him as an NHL assistant for the Hawks.

MacDERMID, Paul
b. Chesley, Ontario, April 14, 1963
In the lingo of Don Cherry, MacDermid was a lunchpail player, a guy who came to the rink every night and gave you an honest game. His 14-year career began with Hartford in 1981 and after 4 years of working his way into the lineup he became a regular right winger in '85. He went on to play for Winnipeg, Washington, and Quebec but the durable and tough forward succumbed to injuries over his last two years. He hurt his back in a game early in the '93-'94 season, tried to return later that year and again at the start of the new season, and realized he was, as they say, done.

MacDONALD, Blair ("B.J.")
b. Cornwall, Ontario, November 17, 1953
Why did a guy named Blair MacDonald score 46 goals in '79-'80 and never come close to that total again? Simple: He played right wing to Wayne Gretzky. That was MacDonald's rookie season, and coach Glen Sather put him on a line with the Wayner and Brett Callighen. The year after, Jari Kurri arrived on the scene to bump MacDonald from the number-one line. He was traded later in the year to Vancouver, and within two years was in the minors. MacDonald went to Austria to play, first in Vienna and then in Innsbruck, taking advantage of the wide ice surface. He stayed on as a coach for a number of years before returning to the pro game in North America to carry on in a similar capacity.

MacDONALD, Brett
b. Bothwell, Ontario, January 5, 1966
After 1999, no one who played for the Flint Generals was allowed to wear MacDonald's number 77, which was given an official retirement in March 2002. In his eight years with the team, known earlier as the Spirits and later as the Bulldogs, MacDonald distinguished himself on the blueline in a way he couldn't boast about from his NHL days – or, more accurately, *day*.

He played only once, with Vancouver in '87-'88 in a career based in the minors.

MacDONALD, Craig
b. Antigonish, Nova Scotia, April 7, 1977
It doesn't look like he's going to be a regular NHLer. MacDonald came out of Harvard University in 1997 but has appeared in just a handful of games for Carolina since. He played all of 1997-98 with the Canadian National Team, which included winning the Spengler Cup at Christmas. Other than that, it's been the minors all the way.

Paul MacDermid

MacDONALD, Doug
b. Assiniboia, Saskatchewan, February 8, 1969
MacDonald has been loyal to the teams he's played for, and most of the time that loyalty has been reciprocated. After four years of university hockey at Wisconsin, he played for Buffalo in the NHL and Rochester in the AHL (the Sabres affiliate). Buffalo used him only 11 times in 3 years, though, so when he had a chance to move, he took it, signing with Cincinnati in the IHL. After four and a half years there, another opportunity arose, this time to play in Germany, and he's been there ever since.

MacDONALD, Kevin
b. Prescott, Ontario, February 24, 1966
A one-game wonder with the Ottawa Senators in '93-'94, MacDonald piled up a mountain of penalty minutes in a long career in the minors. Tired of punching, he retired at 32 and started coaching. His first major gig was as head man of the Bakersfield Condors, a reign that ended in 2002 after three years with the WCHL team.

Craig MacDonald

MacDONALD, Kilby ("Kibby")
b. Ottawa, Ontario, September 6, 1914
d. Seminole, Florida, May 11, 1986
MacDonald's career stats sheet has a curious element to it. He played all his kid hockey in Ottawa, his birthplace, but developed away up in Kirkland Lake. It's a curiosity easily answered once you know that he had no eye to a professional hockey career. MacDonald needed work, and he found it in Kirkland Lake as a miner. Every summer he'd be down in the mines, but winters were easier because he played hockey. After a while, he had a better job but one more dangerous, as a safety man who would inspect areas of the mines. The hazards of the job go without saying. While playing in these parts, he was discovered by Bill Brydge, a former NHLer who was bird-dogging for the Rangers. MacDonald joined their system, going from the Rovers, where he played with his brother, Ab, on up until he played on Broadway for two years, 1939-41. In his first season, he helped the team with the Stanley Cup and won the Calder Trophy, but after another year he left New York to join the army. He was a private in the Canadian Military Staff Clerks for two years, after which time he rejoined the Rangers. Illness slowed him down during his final two seasons and he returned to Ottawa, where he worked for Labatt Breweries for many years, promoting sports in the area with tireless energy and enthusiasm.

Doug MacDonald

Kilby MacDonald

Al MacAdam
(opposite page)

Lowell MacDonald

Parker MacDonald

Hub Macey

Bruce MacGregor

MacDONALD, Lowell
b. New Glasgow, Nova Scotia, August 30, 1941

Lowell MacDonald began his career with the Detroit Red Wings organization during the Original Six era. First getting into an NHL game in '61-'62, he played but 46 games over 4 seasons with the Wings before he was traded to Toronto in a blockbuster deal. On May 20, 1965, MacDonald was sent to the Leafs along with Marcel Pronovost, Larry Jeffrey, Eddie Joyal, and Aut Erickson in return for Andy Bathgate, Billy Harris, and Gary Jarrett. MacDonald never saw the ice at Maple Leaf Gardens and was drafted by the L.A. Kings in the 1967 expansion. Playing regularly, he showed the scoring touch he had exhibited in junior. But during the Kings training camp in Barrie, Ontario, prior to the '69-'70 season, MacDonald packed his suitcase and retired, citing his fear of flying. After much of the season had expired, the Kings were able to convince him to report to Springfield of the AHL. That summer, Pittsburgh claimed him from the Kings, but early into the '70-'71 season, he damaged his knee badly and was sidelined for two full seasons. The surgeries and rest did MacDonald's knee a world of good, and he joined the Penguins for '72-'73 and had an outstanding season, winning the Masterton Trophy for his perseverance in returning to the game. After four strong seasons, he injured his shoulder and struggled through the final two seasons of his career, retiring after '77-'78. During summers, he had earned a B.A. from St. Mary's College in Halifax, and upon his retirement, followed an academic course, he accepted the athletic director position at University School in Milwaukee, a prep school he was loyal to for 19 years. He also acted as a scout for the Penguins and ran a hockey school with Dennis Hull in the summers. In 2002, he was named lead producer for NHL telecasts on ESPN and NBC. He had a son, Lane, who went on to win the Hobey Baker Award at Harvard but whose NHL aspirations were cut short by serious, concussion-like head injuries incurred on the ice.

MacDONALD, Parker ("Park")
b. Sydney, Nova Scotia, June 14, 1933

The year 1960 changed MacDonald's life. Not because he became a great player or was traded to a better team or developed confidence. No, that would be too obvious. It was important because that was the year his doctor discovered part of a drill bit in his shoulder that had broken off during an operation years earlier! Pain free, he went on to a fine career with Detroit after the Rangers had given up on him, bad shoulder and all. In '62-'63, he scored 33 goals playing on a line with Gordie Howe and Alex Delvecchio, and he later had brief stints with Boston and Minnesota, where he ended his career in 1969 after some 676 games. He went into coaching, and early in the '73-'74 season replaced Jackie Gordon as coach of the North Stars, a position he then yielded at season's end. He had just one more NHL coaching assignment, eight years later with L.A. MacDonald was elected to the Cape Breton Sports Hall of Fame in 1987.

MacDONNELL, Moylan
b. Stony Mountain, Manitoba, August 27, 1889
d. unknown

McDonnell played some hockey before the Great War, but his last season was also his only one in the NHL. He played the 1920-21 campaign with the Hamilton Tigers, a team that finished last in the standings of the four-team NHL.

MacDOUGALL, Kim
b. Regina, Saskatchewan, August 29, 1954

The 20-year-old grad of Regina in the Western league in 1974 played a single game for the North Stars the next year and then two years in the minors in a short pro career. The defenceman had been a draft choice by the team.

MacEACHERN, Shane
b. Charlottetown, Prince Edward Island, December 14, 1967

Undrafted, MacEachern played one game for St. Louis in '87-'88 in a peripatetic career that took him through the minors and to Europe over an eight-year period.

MACEY, Hubert "Hub"
b. Big River, Saskatchewan, April 13, 1921

By the time he was 20 and just starting out with the Rangers on February 23, 1942, Macey had a medical report that would frighten any boy aspiring to play hockey for a living: 14 teeth gone from a high stick; both thumbs broken; nose broken 5 times; 8 ribs cracked; and, of course, umpteen stitches. Macey grew up in The Pas, Manitoba, playing juvenile hockey there before moving to Portage la Prairie for junior. In the 1941 Memorial Cup, a member of the Winnipeg Rangers was injured and Macey took his place. Hub helped the team capture the championship, and the year after he turned pro with the New York Rovers until the Rangers called him up. That year and the next, he played just nine games each before leaving hockey to join the army. During his absence, he was traded to Montreal, and played his final 12 NHL games with the Habs before going to the minors for a number of years.

MacGREGOR, Bruce
b. Edmonton, Alberta, April 26, 1941

After advancing to two Memorial Cup finals with the Edmonton Oil Kings in 1959 and '60, MacGregor was called up to the Red Wings with a dozen games to go in the '60-'61 regular season for the final playoff drive. The Wings made it to the post-season, and MacGregor's first career goal came in the finals at just the right time. He scored the winner in game four of that series, to even it 2-2 with Chicago. Although the Hawks won the next two games to win the Cup, MacGregor had built a solid foundation for next year's training camp, where he started a nice run of 13 complete seasons in the NHL. The centre flourished in Detroit, first playing alongside Ted Lindsay in his final season, and then playing with Paul Henderson and Norm Ullman on the HUM line, behind only the Production line as the highest-scoring trio in team history. Midway through the '70-'71 season, he was traded to New York, and after hemming and hawing about retiring, he decided to report. MacGregor had three and a half productive seasons with the Blueshirts before signing with his native Edmonton in the WHA. It was there he finished one career (as a player) and started another (as an executive), becoming the assistant GM of the franchise for many years.

MacGREGOR, Randy
b. Cobourg, Ontario, July 9, 1953

Despite playing just two NHL games, MacGregor has both a goal and an assist to show for his brief foray into the world of big-time hockey. He signed with Hartford midway through the '80-'81 season but really made a name for himself in Binghamton, where he played the better part of nine years. In 1998, he was part of the inaugural group of players inducted into the Binghamton Hockey Hall of Fame.

MacGUIGAN, Garth
b. Charlottetown, Prince Edward Island, February 16, 1956

If you stay in one place long enough, you're bound to set some records. MacGuigan hoped to set those records with the Islanders, but he was playing during their halcyon days as the 1980s began and he was privilege to just two quick callups. Most of his career passed in the CHL and with Indianapolis, where he set Checkers records for points (406). En route, he helped Fort Worth win the Adams Cup in 1978 as CHL champs, and the previous season he had been named IHL rookie of the year with Muskegon.

MacINNIS, Al
b. Inverness, Nova Scotia, July 11, 1963

Yes, he's won a Stanley Cup. Yes, he's won Olympic gold. Yes, he's one of the all-time leading scorers among defenceman. But what people will remember about MacInnis long after he has retired is the Shot, almost without question the hardest, most dangerous the game has ever seen. The Shot has accounted for more than 150 goals on the power play alone. The Shot has won "hardest" at virtually every All-Star Game skills competition he's entered. The Shot is why forwards close their eyes when they try to block it. The Shot is, quite simply, deadly. MacInnis has played for just two teams in his career, Calgary (1981-94) and St. Louis (since '94). He won his Cup with the Flames in 1989, the year he was also given the Conn Smythe, and he has received all the requisite accolades along the way. His All-Star Game count is at 12 and climbing. He won the Norris Trophy in 1999, more for a career of close calls than anything remarkable about that season in particular. He played in the successful 1991 Canada Cup, and in both the 1998 and 2002 Olympics. He is one of a small number of blueliners to have 300 goals and 1,100 points, and 7 times he's scored more than 20 goals in a season. He's not a great skater or a deadly hitter, but he does everything very well and is solid positionally. Above all, though, MacInnis has the Shot.

What people will remember about MacInnis long after he has retired is the Shot.
AL MacINNIS

MacINTOSH, Ian ("Mickey")
b. Selkirk, Manitoba, June 10, 1927

When MacIntosh finally broke into the Rangers in '52-'53, it represented the culmination of a number of years' worth of playing in the minors and also the last moment of glory in his career. At year's end, he returned to Winnipeg and played locally but never again in the pros.

MacIVER, Don
b. Montreal, Quebec, May 3, 1955

A rugged defenceman, MacIver left St. Mary's University to play with the Winnipeg Jets in 1979, their first year in the NHL. He played just six games, though, and spent the next four years in the minors before retiring.

Don MacIver

MACIVER, Norm
b. Thunder Bay, Ontario, September 8, 1964

As a kid, he was a forward, just like his idol, Guy Lafleur. Then, he realized defencemen got more ice time, so he changed positions and became a star. He went to the University of Minnesota-Duluth on scholarship, and graduated in 1986 with a degree in communications. He was a Hoby Baker Award finalist, and the all-time assists leader for the Bulldogs. Undrafted, he signed his first contract, with the Rangers, on his 22nd birthday, but every day it seemed someone questioned his size (or, decided lack of it). Maciver proved to be a late bloomer. For five years he played some NHL games and almost as many in the minors, but in 1992 Ottawa was delighted to see his name in the Waiver Draft and he immediately found full-time work with the expansion team. Maciver scored 17 goals and 63 points in '92-'93, a career year, yet continued to be on the move. In all, he changed teams six times, but he was always reasonably injury-free with one exception. In 1993, he played for Canada at the World Championships, where he took a hard hit that doctors diagnosed as a bruised heart. He made a full recovery and continued on as a small, playmaking defenceman who survived despite not being able to clear the big boys from the front of his net.

Norm MacIver

MacKASEY, Blair
b. Hamilton, Ontario, December 13, 1955

MacKasey grew up in Montreal, where he aspired to play for a team called the Expos. In fact, he played two seasons of minor-league ball in hopes of catching on with that team, but it was in hockey that he was more blessed. He was drafted by Washington in 1975 but traded to the Leafs, and it was with the blue and white that he got into his only NHL game, on October 5, 1976. He took a cross-checking penalty on his first shift, and

Blair MacKasey

Calum MacKay

Dave MacKay

Mickey MacKay

Fleming Mackell

his NHL career was over. The Leafs sent him to their CHL affiliate in Dallas. Down south, he hurt his back but continued to play until the pain started shooting through his right leg. Doctors discovered a vertebra was out of place, and the ensuing surgery ended his playing days. While his uncle, Bryce MacKasey, was a member of Parliament, Blair went on to scout for the Phoenix Coyotes. He later coached in the QMJHL, and in 2002 he was named the director of scouting for the CHA.

MacKAY, Calum ("Baldy")
b. Toronto, Ontario, January 1, 1927
d. Hamilton, Ontario, August 21, 2001

Ironically, MacKay's best years were his last. He was born in Toronto but grew up in the north, in the Port Arthur/Fort William area, where he played his kid hockey during the war years. He got his feet wet at the end of the '46-'47 season when Detroit called him up for a few games, but he spent most of the next three years in the minors until Montreal acquired him for Joe Carveth on November 11, 1949. He scored 18 goals in '50-'51, the year the Habs lost to Toronto in the all-overtime finals, and although he spent most of the next 2 years in the minors, the Habs called him up for the 1953 playoffs when he helped the team win the Cup. He also excelled in the 1955 playoffs as replacement for Maurice Richard, who had been suspended. Playing on a line with Ken Mosdell and Floyd Curry, he scored 11 points that spring. After retiring, MacKay settled in the small town of Marathon, Ontario, where he worked for many years for the Liquor Control Board of Ontario. Rarely has a player inherited so inappropriate a nickname – he was called Baldy after his bare-headed father yet was as full-headed as a bear himself.

MacKAY, Dave ("Red")
b. Edmonton, Alberta, January 14, 1919

While playing football and hockey for the University of Alberta Polar Bears in the late 1930s, MacKay was called the greatest amateur prospect since Eddie Shore and Ching Johnson. Those in the know were awed by his size and strength, but university looks, apparently, were deceiving, and he left U of A with a degree in mining engineering as his best prospect. MacKay played just 29 games with the Hawks in '40-'41 before doing military duty, and when he returned to civilian life he could find no better skating employment than the Pacific Coast league. After retiring, he coached extensively on the west coast, mostly in British Columbia.

MacKAY, Duncan McMillan "Mickey" ("The Wee Scot")
b. Chesley, Ontario, May 21, 1894
d. Ymir, British Columbia, May 21, 1940

In a career spent largely on the west coast, MacKay earned such accolades that many felt he was the best player ever to perform in the Pacific Coast league. He had great speed and was without peer one-on-one with the goalie, and his stickhandling was something to marvel at. His hook check, said Frank Patrick, was as good as Frank Nighbor's. MacKay learned to skate on the Saugeen River near Chesley. He dreamed of playing in the PCHL, and in 1914 Patrick brought him to Vancouver. MacKay had been stationed at Valcartier

Camp in Quebec until it was learned he was too young to be in the army. He went out to B.C., scored a hat trick in his first game, and led the league in goals with 33 that year. He also helped the Millionaires to the Stanley Cup. In all, he played 12 years out west, almost all with Vancouver. He took the team to the Cup finals in 1918, losing to Toronto, and in 1924 Vancouver lost to the Canadiens for the Cup. In 1926, the league folded and all players were sold to clubs in the east (i.e., the NHL). MacKay played in Chicago for two years alongside Dick Irvin, and in '28-'29 he played for Boston, winning the second Cup of his career. He played a final year and then settled in Grand Forks, B.C., his wife's hometown. MacKay went into the mining business and helped coach local hockey teams. One day in 1940, on his way to a meeting, he crashed his car into a telephone pole and was killed instantly. Twelve years later, he was inducted into the Hockey Hall of Fame.

MacKAY, John "Murdo"
b. Fort William, Ontario, August 8, 1917
d. unknown

For a while – a long while – it looked as if MacKay might never see the NHL. After the traditional junior career in the Fort, he played for the New York Rovers without ever getting a callup to the Rangers. Then the war came and MacKay did his part for about 3 years, but it was only after the fighting ended, when Montreal acquired his rights and he was 28 years old, that he played his first game. In all, he played just 34 regular-season and playoff games over 4 years, but that was enough to show him where he stood on the skill line. In the AHL, MacKay was a noted scorer, recording 8 successive 20-goal seasons, 5 of them being 30-or-more years. He ended his career playing senior hockey with Punch Imlach and the Quebec Aces and then settled in Head of the Lakes, Ontario, where he sold real estate.

MACKELL, Fleming ("Flem"/ "Mac"/ "Suki")
b. Montreal, Quebec, April 30, 1929

Today, the Entry Draft is the most important to an aspiring teenage hockey player. Way back when, it was a kid's 16th birthday that was utterly sacred, for that was the day one of the six NHL teams could pay a kid $100, put his name on its negotiation list, and get him to sign a C-form binding him to that team. On the morning of Flem's 16th birthday, the Canadiens came a-calling to the Mackell household, only to learn that at 12:01 a.m. the Leafs had already placed him on their list. That was fine with Flem, who cherished playing for the Leafs because he revered Foster Hewitt. His family name had gone from McKell to MacKell to Mackell, but Flem was more constant in his love for the Leafs. He wanted dearly to go to St. Mike's – and he did. He then went to the Leafs farm in Pittsburgh as an underage player because he wanted to get to the big team as soon as possible. Mackell played parts of five seasons with the Leafs, winning Cups in 1949 and '51, but he played the majority of his career in Boston after the Leafs sent him there to acquire Jim Morrison. By this time, he hadn't a tooth of his own left in his mouth (a football injury at St. Mike's accounted for about half the loss), and by the time he was 27 he already had 5 kids. His dad, Jack, was also an NHLer, and they are one of the few father-son tandems to both win Cups. After retiring, Mackell became an insurance salesman in Montreal, where he also operated a gas station. He later worked out in the suburb of Dorval, selling cars for a Pontiac-Buick dealership.

MacKELL, Jack
b. Ottawa, Ontario, December 4, 1894
d. Hudson, Quebec, November 25, 1961

Military duty in the Great War took precedent over a puck and a stick, but though his career was short, MacKell certainly left his mark. A rover, he played only two seasons in the NHL, both with Ottawa, in '19-'20 and '20-'21, and both Cup champion years. He moved to Montreal after retiring where he practiced his trade (lithography) and raised his son, Fleming, who went on to a fine NHL career of his own. Jack died of a heart attack while watching a football game on television at his home in Hudson, just outside Montreal.

MacKENZIE, Barry
b. Toronto, Ontario, August 16, 1941

Few men have given as much to the game with the anonymity that has accompanied MacKenzie, a man who has been in hockey for more than 40 years. He won a Memorial Cup with St. Mike's in 1961, the year Father David Bauer pulled the Majors out of junior hockey. Bauer had a tremendous influence on MacKenzie, who joined the National Team in 1963 and stayed with the program for five years. During that time, MacKenzie played at two Olympics and three World Championships, winning a total of three bronze medals. He learned all he knew about the game under Father Bauer, and although he went on to play six games with the North Stars in '68-'69, his life had little else to do with the NHL. MacKenzie coached in Japan for three years (1975-78) and then accepted the most prestigious position in high school hockey when he became a coach, and later principal and president of Pere Athol Murray's Notre Dame College in Wilcox, Saskatchewan. MacKenzie stayed there for 22 years, sending players such as Wendel Clark, Curtis Joseph, and James Patrick on to the NHL. In 2000, MacKenzie made a commitment to the NHL, joining the expansion Minnesota Wild as its coordinator of player development.

MacKENZIE, Bill
b. Winnipeg, Manitoba, December 12, 1911
d. Winnipeg, Manitoba, May 29, 1990

A defenceman with four teams in the 1930s, MacKenzie won a Cup with Chicago in 1938 during his second term as a Black Hawk. He began his career in that city before moving around, but midway through this '37-'38 championship season the Habs traded him back to the Windy City. Two years later, the Hawks sent him to the AHL where he finished his career, winning a Calder Cup in '40-'41. He later served as a rifleman in the 2nd Battalion Royal Winnipeg Rifles, and after the war he returned to Winnipeg where he worked for the Manitoba Liquor Control Commission for a quarter of a century, retiring in 1976. MacKenzie was later inducted into the Manitoba Sports Hall of Fame for his contributions to hockey.

MacKENZIE, Derek
b. Sudbury, Ontario, June 11, 1981

Drafted by Atlanta in 1999, MacKenzie played a solitary game for the Thrashers in 2001-02, his first year of pro, which he spent mostly with the Chicago Wolves of the AHL.

MacKENZIE, Shawn
b. Bedford, Nova Scotia, August 22, 1962

Goaltender MacKenzie didn't tend the goal so much as fish the puck out of the net during his brief NHL time, but his pro career prepared him for a second life as a coach. He played for New Jersey, four games in '82-'83, and after retiring in 1986 he migrated to Ontario where he was an assistant in Belleville and head coach in Newmarket. He then returned home where he continued coaching, becoming an assistant GM with the Halifax Mooseheads and then head coach in 2000.

MACKEY, David
b. Richmond, British Columbia, July 24, 1966

A lowwwww draft choice by Chicago in 1984, Mackey played parts of two seasons with the Hawks a short time later before seeing time with Minnesota and St. Louis. Before, during, and after he became a fixture in the IHL, playing some 13 years in that league as a fighter.

MACKEY, Reg
b. Ottawa, Ontario, May 7, 1900
d. unknown

Mackey is right up there near the top of the wacky and completely trivial list of most career games played without a goal. He played 34 times for the Rangers in '26-'27 without bulging ye olde twine even once. It was the defenceman's only NHL time in a short minor-league career.

MACKIE, Howie
b. Berlin (Kitchener), Ontario, August 30, 1913
d. Pittsburgh, Pennsylvania, March 9, 1952

Mackie was a small part of the 1937 Red Wings that won the Stanley Cup, appearing in a few regular-season games and eight more in the playoffs. He played briefly with the team the following year but spent the better part of the next decade in the minors. Mackie played mostly in the AHL with Pittsburgh and lived there until suffering a fatal heart attack at age 38.

MacKINNON, Paul
b. Brantford, Ontario, November 6, 1958

Early in the '79-'80 season, defenceman MacKinnon was taking his man in front of the goal when a slapshot nailed him in the face. He didn't go down, he skated off the ice on his own, and team doctors told him nothing bad had happened. The Caps were a dreadful team, and so were their doctors. That night, MacKinnon couldn't sleep and became nauseous from swallowing so much blood. The next day, he had a face-saving operation. His jaw was wired shut, and the inside, right part of his nose was wired to keep the many broken orbital bones set properly. His face was such a mess any layman could have guessed he was in serious trouble. He was gone for six weeks, and when he came back he did what he did best – play solid, positional defence. After a fine junior career under Gary Green in

Barry MacKenzie

Bill MacKenzie

David Mackey

Howie Mackie

Paul MacKinnon

Don MacLean

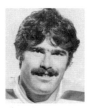

Paul MacLean

Brian MacLellan

Billy MacMillan

Peterborough, MacKinnon played a year with the Winnipeg Jets in the WHA (where they won the Avco Cup) before joining the Caps in 1979. The year after his facial problems, he tore his knee and missed almost the entire season, and his last three seasons in pro were divided between the NHL and the minors.

MacLEAN, Don ("Mac")
b. Sydney, Nova Scotia, January 14, 1977
Every day he was demoted – rarely did he get promoted – he'd get upset and cry, "this'll be the day that I die." MacLean was one fine prospect in Quebec before he was selected by the Kings in '95, but after just a few NHL games he was sent to the minors and never got a call back to the team. In 2000, he signed with Toronto, but there again he was sent down and had a tough time getting his head around the fact he didn't make it with the team on a regular basis. That's where things stand for now, for this frustrated slice of Maritime pie.

MacLEAN, John
b. Oshawa, Ontario, November 20, 1964
In the coming years, there will be any number of John MacLeans retiring, players who had fine, long, unspectacular careers. He played 15 of his 19 years with New Jersey, a rewarding journey that saw him play on an awful team that slowly built until it won the Stanley Cup in 1995. He knew no hockey outside Oshawa until he joined the Devils in 1984, and his style of play was marked by tenacity along the boards and an enthusiasm to play every night. MacLean had three 40-goal seasons (1988-91), but that summer he had reconstructive knee surgery, missed the entire new season, and was never quite the same. He won a silver medal with Canada at the 1989 World Championships and scored 413 goals in a career that ended in the summer of 2002 after two years with Dallas. That fall he was hired by the Devils as an assistant coach.

MacLEAN, Paul
b. Grostenquin, France, March 9, 1958
MacLean might well be one of the more incredible goal scorers of the non-superstar set. He'll never be ranked up there with Gretzky, Lemieux, Yzerman, and Sakic, but in the clutch of stars one rung below, he is certainly a quiet presence. He was born in France while his father was in the Canadian Armed Forces, and once back in Canada he grew up in a Baedeker world that included Coldwater, Alberta; Chatham, New Brunswick; and Antigonish, Nova Scotia. Although he was drafted by St. Louis in 1978, he wasn't entirely sure what he wanted to do. He played at Dalhousie University for a year, then spent '79-'80 with the Canadian National Team through the Olympics at Lake Placid. After playing a single game with the Blues the year after, he was traded to Winnipeg, and blossomed during the greatest scoring era in NHL history. Over the next 9 years, MacLean never scored fewer than 27 goals in a season. Three times he hit the 40 mark, and 5 times 30. His career ended midway through '90-'91 when he tore cartilage in his ribcage and then retired at the end of the year to accept a scouting position with St. Louis. Since then, he has remained in the game as a coach and assistant at various levels, notably in the IHL and with the Coyotes in Phoenix.

MacLEISH, Rick
b. Lindsay, Ontario, January 3, 1950
How's this for improvement? In '71-'72, MacLeish, playing for Philadelphia, scored one goal, added two assists, and finished the year with three points. The next year, he scored 50 goals, added 50 assists, and finished with 100 points! Scoring was nothing new for the kid. In '61-'62, *The Hockey News* noted that he was the best peewee player in Ontario after having scored 270 goals in the season. Now, to temper matters slightly, that 100-point season was his best, but he did win two Cups with the Flyers – scoring the winner in '74 – as one of the only skilled players on the team. He played centre for half his career before being moved to left wing for a while, and his Flyers days ended in 1981 when he was traded to Hartford and then Pittsburgh. MacLeish played part of '82-'83 in Zurich before returning to the Pens for a few games and retiring in 1984. He moved to the Flyers front office that fall as a part-time salesman of season's tickets for the team.

MacLELLAN, Brian
b. Guelph, Ontario, October 27, 1958
Hockey was the last thing on Brian's mind when he was a boy, his legs in braces because of Legg Perthes disease, which affects the hip joints. Doctors recommended he try skating, though, because the combination of exercise and cold might do him good. In truth, it did him great. His condition went away, and he turned into an excellent hockey player by his teens, so much so that many a U.S. college recruited him. MacLellan attended Bowling Green starting in 1978, and although he had four fine years there and won two NCAA titles, he was never drafted. No matter. He signed with L.A. and, playing on a line with Marcel Dionne, had seasons of 25 and 31 goals. A trade to the Rangers did nothing for either party, but a subsequent deal to Minnesota allowed MacLellan the offensive freedom to score a career-high 32 goals. He later was traded to Calgary near the deadline in 1989, and a few weeks later was drinking champers from the Cup. After retiring, he stayed in the game as a scout, most recently with Washington, and returned to Bowling Green to finish his masters degree in business administration.

MacLEOD, Pat
b. Melfort, Saskatchewan, June 15, 1969
MacLeod did little to distinguish himself during his short stints in the NHL, but his time in the IHL is another matter altogether. In his 10-plus years in the league, the defenceman became not only a leader but a model citizen, culminating in 1999-2000 when he was named IHL's man of the year. He and his wife had two sets of twins during those years, and as he raised them he decided the kids' books available weren't very good. One night, after a game, he wrote his own, and a short time later he wrote another. Now, all he needs is a publisher. Most people in the hockey world, though, feel he'll make a great coach, books and all besides.

MacMILLAN, Billy ("Yacky")
b. Charlottetown, Prince Edward Island, March 7, 1943
Best known for his years with the expansion Islanders starting in 1973, MacMillan had a whole career in hockey before joining the new New Yorkers. He came

west to play at St. Mike's in Toronto but after what he felt was a lowball offer from the Leafs he returned to PEI to study phys ed at university. The following year, the pattern repeated itself, so MacMillan joined the Canadian National Team, where he played for five years. He also finished his degree through U of Manitoba, and in 1970 he finally agreed to join Toronto when the national program disbanded. He scored 22 goals as a rookie and moved on to Atlanta and New York before ending up in the minors. He stayed with the organization and coached the CHL affiliate in Fort Worth to an Adams Cup in 1978, the same season he was named coach of the year. He became an assistant to Al Arbour with the parent club, but after winning the Cup in 1980 he took a job as head coach of the lowly Colorado Rockies. He later coached New Jersey before returning to Long Island. Since 1986, MacMillan has worked in his most pleasurable position – he is the manager of a liquor store in Charlottetown.

MacMILLAN, Bob ("Bobby Mac"/ "Mac the Knife")

b. Charlottetown, Prince Edward Island, December 3, 1952
The brother of Billy, Bob was one of five kids raised mostly by their mom after their father died of a heart attack at 37. Each child went to university, much to the mother's delight, and for Bob that meant taking courses in history over time with UPEI while playing. He was a fine prospect, and the first first-round draft choice in 1972 to forgo the NHL in favour of the WHA. He signed with the Rangers two years later, and began a career that lasted 11 years in the NHL. MacMillan was noted for his speed and streaky scoring. Twice he scored 30 goals and 3 other times he had more than 20, though he generally played on weaker teams. He won the Lady Byng Trophy in '78-'79, a rare individual award for a player from the tiny province that also gave the NHL Hilliard Graves, Al MacAdam, and Kevin Devine. His career ended on January 16, 1985, when he suffered a serious shoulder separation. He had a farm with about 600 head of sheep, but when he returned home he set up shop in the city as a coach in senior hockey. He also opened a bar called Sport Page Club and ran a lawn care business before becoming involved in local politics. On April 17, 2000, he was elected an MLA to Charlottetown representing District 12.

MacMILLAN, John

b. Lethbridge, Alberta, October 25, 1935
If a Canadian took his hockey and education seriously, as a package, in the 1960s there was only one place he would have wanted to go: University of Denver and legendary coach Murray Armstrong. MacMillan went to U of D, graduating in 1960 with a

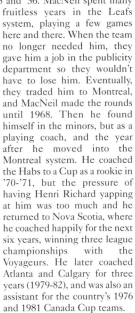

Macoun missed an entire year of play, but he returned as good as ever.
JAMIE MACOUN

degree in civil engineering. Despite never making the NHL full-time, he spent much of the next five years with Toronto and Detroit, winning Cups with the Leafs in '62 and '63. MacMillan wound up in the minors in 1964 and spent the next seven years in the lesser league, finishing his career with a five-year stay in San Diego and captaining the Gulls the last three of those seasons.

MacNEIL, Al

b. Sydney, Nova Scotia, September 27, 1935
As a defenceman, Allister Wences MacNeil was as ordinary as any NHLer. He didn't stick out, but he was playing in the world's best hockey league. After winning Memorial Cups with the tremendous Marlboros teams of '55 and '56. MacNeil spent many fruitless years in the Leafs system, playing a few games here and there. When the team no longer needed him, they gave him a job in the publicity department so they wouldn't have to lose him. Eventually, they traded him to Montreal, and MacNeil made the rounds until 1968. Then he found himself in the minors, but as a playing coach, and the year after he moved into the Montreal system. He coached the Habs to a Cup as a rookie in '70-'71, but the pressure of having Henri Richard yapping at him was too much and he returned to Nova Scotia, where he coached happily for the next six years, winning three league championships with the Voyageurs. He later coached Atlanta and Calgary for three years (1979-82), and was also an assistant for the country's 1976 and 1981 Canada Cup teams.

MacNEIL, Bernie

b. Sudbury, Ontario, March 7, 1950
Branded an animal by some WHA opponents, MacNeil enjoyed a brief career in the minors and a four-game stay in the NHL with St. Louis in '73-'74. He played two years in the WHA before retiring in 1976.

MACOUN, Jamie ("Cooner")

b. Newmarket, Ontario, August 17, 1961
There are precious few players who have passed through the NHL who were as special as Macoun. For starters, he was never drafted. No team wanted him, and yet from the time he made the NHL in 1983 until the time he retired in 1999, all teams would have liked to have had him for free back when they had the chance. Calgary got there first, though, and he spent ten seasons with the Flames, spending not one minute in the minors. Paired with Ric Nattress on defence, he helped win the Cup in 1989, a remarkable achievement because by rights he shouldn't have even been alive in 1989. In the 1987 playoffs, he suffered a bruised spleen

Bob MacMillan

John MacMillan

Al MacNeil

Bernie MacNeil

and kidney, but after a two-week stay in hospital he was released. A couple of weeks later, he was back. One night, driving home, he lost control of his car. It spun across the highway and flipped, and Macoun's arm was pinned between metal and asphalt. Half his ear had to be sewn back on, and the elbow was so badly cut doctors had to wait two weeks just to determine where it had been broken. Macoun missed an entire year of play, but he returned as good as ever. He and Nattress were a trademark pair of defencemen who formed an impenetrable tandem. For years, they were the league's best. Macoun went on to play in seven seasons with Toronto, but he won a second Cup with Detroit in 1998 after the Leafs traded him at the deadline that March. He retired a year later having played 1,128 regular-seasons games, not a bad total for someone no team had wanted to draft.

MacPHERSON, Jim "Bud"
b. Edmonton, Alberta, March 31, 1927
d. Edmonton, Alberta, 1988
At 6'4" MacPherson was the tallest player in the league for a number of years. He had a tough time breaking into the top ranks, though, starting in '48-'49 with Montreal. He played his entire NHL career with the Habs, but he also spent plenty of time outside the big league. He helped the team win the Stanley Cup in 1953, but the year after knee woes limited both his playing time and his effectiveness. The next year, he reinjured the knee at training camp and had to start the season in the Quebec league. He made it back to Montreal for a few games the year after, but ostensibly his NHL days were over. He ended up in the WHL as a playing coach with Edmonton.

MacSWEYN, Ralph ("Big Mac")
b. Hawkesbury, Ontario, September 8, 1942
Because he always played hockey with kids much older than him, young Ralph was relegated to the nets for the first 17 years of his life. His grandfather built the requisite outdoor rink on their dairy farmland each winter in Dalkeith, and finally, at age 17, MacSweyn moved to defence. His early grooming in goal is likely what made him one of the best shotblockers around. He made his way up through the Eastern league with Johnstown and signed with Philadelphia in 1967. Over the next five years, he played mostly in the minors, but wherever he went his reputation as a ferocious hitter preceded him. He moved on to the WHA and finished his skating days with the Vancouver Blazers. He returned to the family farm, which he continues to run, and for years coached his daughter's hockey team. In 1993, MacSweyn was inducted into the Glengarry (Ontario) Sports Hall of Fame.

MacTAVISH, Craig
b. London, Ontario, August 15, 1958
It's a spectacular clash of morals and ethics and reason, of fair and unfair, right and wrong, crime and punishment. On the night of January 25, 1984, MacTavish rear-ended another car while driving intoxicated. The woman in the other car died of her injuries, and MacTavish pleaded guilty to vehicular homicide. He was sentenced to a year in jail. A year for a life. The friends and relatives of the victim, 26-year-old Kim Radley, could not have believed the punishment fit the crime. A year in correction centres and MacTavish was a free man. He had played five years with Boston, but when he was released he wanted a fresh start and Glen Sather in Edmonton complied. For the next nine years, MacTavish was an upstanding citizen and fine hockey player once again. He was around for three Oilers Cup wins, and a fourth with the "New York Oilers" in 1994. He paid the price for his crime, and resumed his career a new man, wiser and forever aware of his wrongdoings. After retiring in 1997, he started life as an assistant in New York, then returned to Edmonton where he became head coach when former boss Kevin Lowe moved up to GM.

MacTavish pleaded guilty to vehicular homicide. He was sentenced to a year in jail.
CRAIG MacTAVISH

MacWILLIAM, Mike
b. Burnaby, British Columbia, February 14, 1967
It's almost too disgusting to ingest, this career of MacWilliams, so wrecked by self-inflicted injuries. Ever since he was 16, desperate to play pro hockey, he's been a fighter, taken on the heavyweights, proved himself wherever he played, that sort of thing. Yet over the years, the destruction of his body has been staggering. He had nine shoulder operations, four of which were major reconstructions. He broke his hands seven times. Once, after a titanium rod had been inserted, he bent it during a subsequent fight. He broke his thumb, he suffered a hernia, he tore his hamstring, all in the name of fighting. Somewhere in that mayhem, from the IHL to the Cardiff Devils, he played six games with the Islanders in '95-'96. After retiring, he fell back on his second love, music, and became a sound engineer for Martyn Joseph, both on extensive tours and in the studio.

MADDEN, John ("Mad Dog")
b. Barrie, Ontario, May 4, 1975
Growing up in Toronto, Madden played with a ton of teams, impressing almost no one along the way. He played junior B before heading off to the University of Michigan, where he studied kinesiology and set an all-time NCAA record with 23 short-handed goals in his 4 years. No one drafted him, but he had one thing going for him: his teammate was Brenden Morrison, a New

Ralph MacSweyn

Mike MacWilliam

John Madden

Jersey draft choice. Every time Devils GM Lou Lamoriello went to watch Morrison play, he came away thinking about Madden. In 1997, he signed the U of M graduate as a free agent and sent him to Albany. Three years later, Madden scored a short-handed goal, the winning goal, in game four of the Stanley Cup finals to give the Devils a 3-1 lead in the series. A few nights later, he was drinking from the Cup, and a year later he was awarded the Selke Trophy as the best defensive forward in the NHL. The moral of the story? Never lose the dream.

MADELEY, Darrin ("Mades")
b. Holland Landing, Ontario, February 25, 1968
Unfortunately, someone always has to play goal for expansion teams, even in the first years when the teams are horrible. Such was the fate that befell Madeley, who played parts of the first three seasons with the new Senators (1992-95). His cumulative record of 4-23-5 allowed him to see the minors, where he was slightly better, but his finest days had been in college. In three years with Lake Superior State, he was an all-star with a record of 73-16-8, Hall of Fame numbers if he had kept it going in the NHL. But, he didn't.

MADIGAN, Connie ("Mad Dog")
b. Port Arthur, Ontario, October 4, 1934
It's a record that likely won't ever be broken, a record that speaks to a love of the game and a dedication to playing that belies common sense. Madigan played in his first NHL game on February 6, 1973, with St. Louis. At 38, he was the oldest rookie ever. By the mid-1950s, playing in Penticton, Madigan had a decent idea the NHL was a long shot. By 1972, he had been in the minors for 14 years, yet the aging, defence-strapped Blues needed a tough, stay-at-home defenceman. At 38, not only was Madigan happy to stay at home, he was likely to be asleep. He played 20 games for the Blues, and 5 more in the playoffs, and then the tough guy went right back to the minors, where he played until 1974. He retired to Portland and later appeared in the movie *Slap Shot* as Mad Dog Madison. He wasn't a one-game wonder – he was a wonder, plain and simple.

MADILL, Jeff ("Mad Dog")
b. Oshawa, Ontario, June 21, 1965
Madill was a scorer in the IHL and even, in his small way, in the NHL. In 14 games with New Jersey in '90-'91, he scored 4 times, but he never had much of a chance to stick around besides. He appeared in 7 playoff games that spring (no goals), but in the minors he had six 30-goal seasons. He won back-to-back Turner Cups in '94 and '95 with Atlanta and Denver, and after retiring he went into coaching, most recently with the Penticton Rage.

MAGEAU, Fern
b. Verdun, Quebec, May 3, 1916
d. Ville St. Pierre, Quebec, June 17, 1966
When he made his debut with Montreal at training camp in 1943, Mageau was 27 and in the prime of his career. He scored 20 goals that season and helped the team win the Stanley Cup, but the next year he lasted only a few games before being demoted. Mageau

spent most of his playing career in Quebec, but that season and a half was all his NHL time.

MAGEE, Dean
b. Rocky Mountain House, Alberta, April 29, 1955
After graduating from Colorado College in 1978, Magee stepped right into the Minnesota lineup for seven games. The big, tough left winger didn't make much of a mark, and didn't get a chance to leave another. He played briefly in the WHA and lesser leagues in the minors, and 2 years later, at 25, he was out of the game altogether.

MAGGS, Daryl
b. Victoria, British Columbia, April 6, 1949
Maggs was drafted in 1969 but decided to go to the University of Alberta before trying to crack the Hawks lineup. After a year, he opted for the minors over U of A, and the year after he made the NHL team. A rough defenceman who let others create scoring chances, Maggs played just two seasons before jumping to the WHA, where he remained until 1979. He played five games with the Leafs after the leagues merged, but when Toronto released him his playing days were over.

MAGNAN, Marc
b. Beaumont, Alberta, February 17, 1962
When Mike Tyson bit a chunk of Evander Holyfield's ear off to earn a disqualification in their heavyweight fight a few years ago, there were at least two hockey people who were, like, "whatever, already been there." In April 1985, Magnan, toiling for Indianapolis in the IHL, got into a fight with Chris McSorley, brother of fighter and NHLer Marty. On this night, in this fight, Chris bit a piece of Magnan's nose off in the fight, and also bit him on the lips in a putative attempt to do same to that part of his face. McSorley was known for this sort of thing, and Magnan filed suit against his opponent as well as the IHL for not having banned the biter previously. Magnan had played a few games for the Leafs earlier and spent the rest of his days in the IHL before going into coaching.

MAGNUSON, Keith
b. Saskatoon, Saskatchewan, April 27, 1947
It might well be there was a tougher hockey player than Magnuson, and if that player lands his spaceship on earth and tries his hand at the NHL, we'll all see exactly what that means. Magnuson, meanwhile, played his whole career in Chicago after graduating, undrafted, from U of Denver with a business degree. He played just 10 years and 3 NHL games, but when you play them as hard as he did, you can double that number to get a sense of the price he paid to play. Everyone of a certain age will remember him blocking a Brad Park slapshot with his jaw, then skating off the ice on his own steam, refusing to take the stretcher that was waiting for him. He hurt his knees and his back, and sacrificed his body to prevent goals. A fierce competitor on the ice, he was no fool off it. From his rookie year in '69-'70, he worked part-time for 7-Up, experience that would help him later. He retired early in the '79-'80 season and became the team's assistant coach, and the year after he replaced Ed Johnston as head coach. The team didn't play particularly well

Darrin Madeley

Connie Madigan

Jeff Madill

Dean Magee

Keith Magnuson

Kevin Maguire

under Magnuson, and after a year and a half he was out. He started to work full-time for Coca-Cola, and today he is the director of chain sales in the Chicago area.

MAGUIRE, Kevin
b. Toronto, Ontario, January 5, 1963

He didn't play organized hockey until he was in his late teens, but Maguire made up for it with a will to succeed and an ability to fight. He went from provincial hockey to the AHL in 1984 and two years later he was in the NHL playing for the Leafs. As a rookie, he played 17 games without registering a single point but incurring 74 penalty minutes. That was the way of his career. He endured until 1992 when the opportunity to referee came up and he took it. Since then, the violator has become an adjudicator, working his way up from the minors until he got his first NHL assignment in 1999. Like King Clancy and Paul Stewart, Maguire is one in a line of players who has made good as a zebra.

MAHAFFY, John
b. Montreal, Quebec, July 18, 1919

The theory was that players who did well during the war would never do well after it, when the best would be back in the game. Mahaffy played his 38 NHL games during the war, with Montreal and the Rangers, and after 1945 he was consigned to the AHL and had 5 successive 20-goal seasons. He ended in the Quebec league and then settled in Montreal, where he went into insurance.

MAHOVLICH, Frank
("Gutch"/ "The Big M")
b. Timmins, Ontario, January 10, 1938

There likely wasn't an NHL player – a Hall of Famer, no less – who was talked about as much for what he did not do as for what he did. Despite being one of the highest scorers in the league for many years, fans and coaches truly believed that Mahovlich didn't come to play every night – if he did, they said, he could establish scoring records no one would break. The way Mahovlich came to the Leafs was the same for many kids – through St. Mike's College. His parents in small-town Ontario were nervous about their son going to the big city, but when they knew he'd be placed in a school where religion was important and education did not take a back seat to hockey, they were relieved. At St. Mike's, Mahovlich developed into such a good player it was patently obvious he was made for the NHL. He made a brief appearance with the Leafs at the end of the '56-'57 season and after the following training camp the 19-year-old had a place on left wing at Maple Leaf Gardens. As a rookie, he scored 20 goals and won the Calder Trophy, and in the next 2 years he had 22 and 18 goals. But in '60-'61, the Big M had a year everyone had been waiting for

Frank Mahovlich

– almost. For much of the season he averaged nearly a goal a game, and after 56 games he had 48 goals. That left him 14 games to get 2 goals and become the first person since Maurice Richard to get 50 in a season. It was obvious he was going to match the record; when, was the only question. Goals number 49 and 50 never came, and in Montreal, Bernie Geoffrion ended the season by scoring his 50th. In some ways, the non-record was a turning point in Mahovlich's career. His coach, Punch Imlach, and fans, too, believed he was a talented player who had no killer instinct, no drive to do better and better and better. They might have been right. After all, in the year in which he had his highest goals total, he also had by far the most penalty minutes of his career (131). Further, he had a long and effective stride that looked kind of lazy and slow. He seemed to be skating beautifully, but not with purpose or determination. He had such skills, he could do well without really trying. Of course, he swore that he tried, but Imlach didn't always believe him. Mahovlich was the only player in Leafs history who was booed after scoring a goal or playing a good game. Imlach tortured him publicly and privately to try to get him going, often calling him "Maholovich" to reporters. The Leafs won the Cup in 1962 and again in each of the next two years. As a result, they hosted the All-Star Game each year. In 1962, Chicago offered the Leafs a cool $1-million for Mahovlich, a deal Toronto turned down but one in which the player's value on the open market was established. After the 48-goal year, he averaged 30 goals a year for the next 5 years, good numbers, but not the kind Imlach knew Frank could make with more tenacity. In '64-'65, Mahovlich was hospitalized for what later was acknowledged to be tension and depression as a result of his relationship with Imlach. This happened again near the start of the '67-'68 season, during which time he was gone more than a month. His goal production had dropped significantly, and the Leafs decided a trade was mutually beneficial. On March 3, 1968, he was traded to Detroit with Pete Stemkowski, Garry Unger, and Carl Brewer for Norm Ullman, Paul Henderson, Doug Barrie, and Floyd Smith. The deal was greeted with protest outside the Gardens, but in Mahovlich's heart it was one that afforded him some peace. Playing on a line with Gordie Howe and Alex Delvecchio, he scored 49 goals the year after – another good season, another just short of spectacular – but he was traded to Montreal. He had three solid years with the Habs, won two more Cups (in '71 and '73), and was also named to Team Canada for the Summit Series. Typically, the cynic might say, he had a good series, not great. His one goal was hardly the contribution he had been expected to make, but the team won and, in the end, that was all that mattered. At 36, Mahovlich

Playing on a line with Gordie Howe and Alex Delvecchio, he scored 49 goals.
FRANK MAHOVLICH

decided to finish his career in the WHA with the Toronto/Birmingham franchise. After four years, he still received offers from Montreal and Pittsburgh to return to the NHL, but time and a sore back dissuaded him. Funnily enough, he never scored 50 goals in a season and never had 100 points in a year, but he did pass the all-important career milestones of 500 goals and 1,000 points. He won six Stanley Cups, but after that Calder Trophy for his rookie season he never won another individual award. He played in 15 All-Star Games, and in 1981 was inducted into the Hockey Hall of Fame. Mahovlich returned to Toronto where he ran a travel agency for years. His brother, Pete, also played in the NHL for years, and their father frequently sharpened skates at Leaside Arena where the next generation of Mahovliches were learning the game. In 1998, out of the blue, Mahovlich was appointed to the Canadian Senate by Prime Minister Jean Chrétien. It was an affirmation of Mahovlich's place in society, as a hockey player and hero, as a sportsmanlike individual, as a model for success. Since then he has devoted himself almost exclusively to politics, taking on the responsibilities of a Senator with atypical relish. He can't go back and try to score those 49th and 50th goals or try to score 60 or 70 as Imlach had hoped, and he can't dwell on what he didn't do the way some fans might. He can, though, look back on what he did accomplish and realize that since not many players did as much, it wasn't a half-bad career in the end.

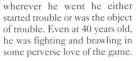

MAHOVLICH, Pete ("The Little M")
b. Timmins, Ontario, October 10, 1946

Imagine how different Canadian culture would be if Mahovlich had ignored Paul Henderson's cries to come off the ice late in the game of September 28, 1972! Fortunately, he heeded the call, came to the bench, and watched Henderson score the most important goal in the history of the game. Mahovlich was no slouch, though. In fact, he holds the Montreal record for most points by a centreman, with 117 in '74-'75. He wasn't the superhero that brother Frank was, but he had his day in the sun, nonetheless. He began his career in Detroit and moved to Montreal in a trade in the summer of 1969. He spent nine years with the Habs, winning four Cups in the 1970s through times that weren't always sweet. He had his differences with coach Scotty Bowman, who took no joy in Mahovlich's easygoing, game-playing nature, his late nights and clowning around that were, in Bowman's eyes, a distraction. When the coach had the chance to trade him to Pittsburgh in 1977, he took it, and the Little M lost out on two more Cups with the dynastic Habs. He finished his career in Detroit, went into coaching for a while, and then became a colour commentator for New Jersey Devils

He holds the Montreal record for most points by a centreman, with 117 in '74-'75.
PETE MAHOVLICH

broadcasts. Most recently, he has been a scout in the NHL for Atlanta. His 773 career points combined with Frank's 1,103 make them one of the all-time scoring brother combinations in the game.

MAILHOT, Jacques
b. Shawinigan, Quebec, December 5, 1961

What's amazing is not that he was a fighter – that's all too common. What is amazing is how long he lasted. In fact, Mailhot was 27 before he played a game of pro hockey anywhere, and 28 when he made his brief appearance in the NHL. Since then, he's played in all those obscure leagues that string together small towns in the States, from Johnstown to Utica to Fresno to a team called the Central Texas Stampede. Technically, he was a left winger, but the position had little importance because wherever he went he either started trouble or was the object of trouble. Even at 40 years old, he was fighting and brawling in some perverse love of the game.

Jacques Mailhot

MAILLEY, Frank
b. Lachine, Quebec, August 1, 1916
d. February 1976

There is some debate about whether Mailley ever played in the NHL, but he is officially credited for one game for Montreal in 1942-43 during a short pro career. The game has not been authenticated, though, but what is known is that he ended up in Alexandria, Virginia selling commercial real estate.

MAIR, Adam ("Bomber")
b. Hamilton, Ontario, February 15, 1979

The Ad-Man had a fine junior career that culminated in Winnipeg with a silver medal at the 1999 World Juniors, and in the playoffs later that year he became just the second Maple Leaf in team history to score a goal in an NHL debut that was also a playoff game. The next year, though, he made only a brief pilgrimage to Toronto, and the Leafs traded him to L.A. to get Aki Berg. With the Kings, Mair has yet to play more than a few games, and the bright prospect now has his work cut out to make it in the NHL. He didn't help his cause in December 2001 when he left the bench during an on-ice fight and was suspended by the league for 10 games.

Adam Mair

MAIR, Jim
b. Schumacher, Ontario, May 15, 1946

Mair played for Johnstown in the late 1960s, the pre-*Slap Shot* days for the team that that movie made famous, but he was every bit the ruffian the movie made its players out to be. Yet in his five brief showings in the NHL he was more pacifist than fighter and did his best to play defence on some pretty bad expansion teams. He retired in 1975 and settled in Timmins where he became, appropriately, a police officer.

Jim Mair

Mark Major

Sergei Makarov

Chico Maki

MAJEAU, Fern
see **MAGEAU, Fern**

MAJOR, Bruce
b. Vernon, British Columbia, January 3, 1967
Major just wasn't going to be a player, and he knew early on he'd have to do something else with his hockey skills beyond relying on the NHL. He came out of U of Maine in 1989, the school Paul Kariya would make famous just a couple of years later, but after three years of pro (including four games with Quebec), he retired and went back to B.C. Major and became involved with Mid Island Hockey Schools of Canada, centred in Vernon but offering camps and courses all over North America. Along with Bob Beers and others, he taught power skating and a variety of hockey-based courses year-round.

MAJOR, Mark
b. Toronto, Ontario, March 20, 1970
A big fighter, he came up to Detroit in 1996 to play his first NHL game at Maple Leaf Gardens. Tie Domi wanted to help him out, and he obliged him with a fight – isn't that nice? – so Major could show the Wings what he could do. He played only twice in the NHL, no points and one major, and before and after he's been fighting in the minors, most recently with the Wheeling Nailers.

MAKAROV, Sergei
b. Chelyabinsk, Soviet Union (Russia), June 19, 1958
Each member of the KLM line of Krutov-Larionov-Makarov made it to the NHL in disparate manner. Krutov didn't play much at all, Larionov had a lengthy and successful career, and Makarov was somewhere in between. Like his Soviet linemates, he made his name in Soviet league play and an international career of remarkable success. He won a neckful of gold at the Worlds and Olympics and was on the 1981 Canada Cup-winning team. Makarov was the playmaker of the three, small but lightning fast. He could hang on to the puck as long as he wanted, do with it what he wanted, and waited until his linemates got into scoring position. He was also perfectly capable of scoring. Makarov made it to the NHL in 1989 at age 31, playing with Calgary the year after the team had won the Cup. In his first 5 seasons in the league he averaged 25 goals, and when he went to San Jose he was united with Larionov. The pair played with Johan Garpenlov on what was dubbed the OV line and the Sharks came within one game of the semifinals in the 1994 playoffs. Makarov played briefly with Dallas before returning to Russia in 1997 where he played with Red Army under political conditions radically different from when he started out as an 18-year-old. His career in the NHL was fine, but his previous incarnation as a Soviet star ranks him as one of the greatest players that nation has ever produced.

MAKELA, Mikko
b. Tampere, Finland, February 28, 1965
Makela was one of the first highly successful Finns to come to North America at a young age and adapt to the NHL. After an outstanding junior career, he joined the Islanders in 1985 with countryman Ari Haanpaa. The two looked so similar many players had a tough time telling them apart. Makela stayed in the NHL for 6 years, improving each of the first 3 until '87-'88 when he scored 36 goals for the Isles. He returned home for three seasons and helped Suomi win silver at the '92 WC and bronze at the 1994 Olympics in Lillehammer, but in 1994 he decided to give the NHL another chance and signed with Boston toward the end of the season. The move was a mistake, and after 11 games he returned to play in Europe. After retiring, he became head coach of Ilves Tampere, the team for which he once played as a junior, and in 2002 he was hired as an assistant coach for the Lethbridge Hurricanes of the WHL, and in December 2000 he became the first European-born player to become head coach of a junior team in Canada.

MAKI, Ronald "Chico"
b. Sault Ste. Marie, Ontario, August 17, 1939
Long before he ever played hockey, Ronald was nicknamed Chico by his mother, who loved the Marx brothers, the quiet Chico reminding her of her son. Technically, Chico played on the Cup team in Chicago in '60-'61, even though he appeared in only one game – in the playoffs – all year long. That victory made up for the ensuing 14 years, when he was a regular but never won the Cup with some very good Chicago teams, teams that lost heartbreakers to Toronto in 1967 and Montreal in 1971. Maki's best years were '64-'67 when he played right wing on a line with Phil Esposito and Bobby Hull. He was never a star scorer, merely a reliable performer every night. He played in three All-Star Games and later watched his brother, Wayne, make the grade, albeit briefly. Maki decided to retire in 1974 after two awful events. In May, Wayne died, and then as training camp for the '74-'75 season opened, his son suffered a bad farm accident in which he lost four toes from his left foot. Maki returned to the 300-acre property near Tillsonburg, but a year later decided to return to the Hawks. Just 22 games into a new season, Maki realized how emotionally removed he now was from the game and left for good. He sold the farm and livestock and opened a hotel/restaurant in Tillsonburg.

MAKI, Wayne
b. Sault Ste. Marie, Ontario, November 10, 1944
d. Vancouver, British Columbia, May 12, 1974
"He almost kilt a man dead," is how Yogi Berra might have said it, except for the fact there was no humour in the game of September 20, 1969. Wayne Maki of St. Louis and Ted Green of Boston collided in an exhibition game in Ottawa, and Maki came up swinging his stick at Green's head until the player fell to the ice semi-conscious. Green missed a year of play, during which time he overcame paralysis and a delicate operation to remove shards of skull that had fallen onto his brain. Both men were charged and acquitted of criminal action, though Maki was suspended 30 days and Green 13 games. Maki was never a fighter, and one theory around the sinister act was that he was terrified of Green, a known fighter, and thought it better to hit first and ask questions later. The duel remained in Maki's psyche the rest of his life, a life that was, ironically, short. He played with the expansion Canucks in Vancouver starting in 1970, but after two fine scoring seasons he slumped badly to start the

third. The team finally sent him home during a road trip, and doctors discovered he had a brain tumour. He never played again but remained in Vancouver where he apprenticed as an electrician. Less than two years later, he died, and even years later his wife swore the problems with Maki's brain were the result of Green's blows during that altercation years earlier.

MAKKONEN, Kari

b. Harjavalta, Finland, January 20, 1955
A mere speck in the NHL cosmos, Makkonen was a star in his own right back home, especially in Pori where he played for some 16 seasons. His NHL time came with the great Oilers in their infancy, '79-'80, but most of his career passed in Finland. He also played in seven World Championships and in the '76 and '81 Canada Cups. After retiring, he went into coaching in Finland, eventually becoming an assistant for the National Junior Team in 1998.

MALAKHOV, Vladimir ("Vlad")

b. Ekaterinburg, Soviet Union (Russia), August 30, 1968
An enigma wrapped in a roll of hockey tape, Malakhov has always looked better or seemed better than he actually played. He began not on a frozen lake or in a neighbour's yard but at the Physical Culture Institute in Moscow, where he was admitted to the hockey department. He made his way up through the ranks quickly, and by 1990 he was with CCCP for the World Championships. He embarked on an NHL career after winning gold with the Commonwealth of Independent States (CIS) at the 1992 Olympics in Albertville. First with the Islanders and then with Montreal, Malakhov showed great promise and ability but he never seemed to be a star of the blueline and never looked to be a player who could, or would, take charge. At training camp in 1999 he suffered a serious knee injury and missed much of the year. His time with the Canadiens expired when he was discovered skiing during a supposed rehab and convalescence, and soon after he returned to the lineup he was traded to New Jersey. It was a move full of vindication for him, for the Devils went on to win the Cup a few weeks later and the Habs failed to qualify for the playoffs. In the summer, he signed as a free agent with the Rangers, and his career resumed as per usual, a superstar-looking player without the superstar performances.

MALARCHUK, Clint

b. Grande Prairie, Alberta, May 1, 1961
On March 22, 1989, the NHL narrowly avoided tragedy after Malarchuk's jugular was cut by a skate during a scramble in his crease. Quick action by the Buffalo trainers staunched the flow of blood, and he was rushed to hospital where his life was saved. Amazingly, Malarchuk returned later that season, his first with the Sabres. He had developed over the previous seven years with Quebec and Washington, but by 1992 he was out of the NHL and in the IHL, where he ended his career. He played his last with the Las Vegas Thunder, and remained there in an executive capacity. He became assistant GM and later coach, though a shortage of goalies twice forced him back into the nets in the coming years. The Thunder retired his number

30, but in 1998 he took a coaching job with the Idaho Steelheads. In 2002, he returned to the NHL as goalie coach in Florida.

MALEY, David

b. Beaver Dam, Wisconsin, April 24, 1963
A Wisconsin boy in his early years, David and the family moved to Minnesota during his teens and that's where he developed into a bona fide player. After graduating from the University of Wisconsin in 1986, he joined Montreal at season's end and played on the team that won an improbable Cup that spring. He later played for New Jersey for five years before travelling around the league as his career wound down. Maley retired and settled in California, where he started a business venture called Rollin' Ice Roller Hockey in the hopes of bringing the game to the west coast and converting sports fans to hockey through a summer sport. His dream was to develop at least a couple of players who would go on to play in the NHL, though this hasn't happened yet.

MALGUNAS, Stewart

b. Prince George, British Columbia, April 21, 1970
An itinerant hockeyist, Malgunas has been in the pro game since 1990 although that has translated into just 129 NHL games. The defenceman started out in the Detroit system before being traded to Philadelphia, and since then he's been on the go from team to league and back. He has played more in the minors than the NHL, most recently in the top league with Calgary, though he missed much of the 1999-2000 season with an inner ear injury. After recovering, he returned to the minors and then tried his hand at hockey in Germany.

MALHOTRA, Manny

b. Mississauga, Ontario, May 18, 1980
If this kid turns into a player, it won't be because of the Rangers, the team that drafted him 7th overall in 1998 and did more to destroy his chances than promote them. They thought he was capable of great things, so that meant throwing him into the NHL at 18 – that's the way they think in New York. He wasn't dominant, so instead of letting him develop in peace and quiet, the team sat him on the bench for most of the games. In his second year, he earned enough Air Miles to take his family to China and back, but mercifully the team traded him to Dallas. Malhotra has shown speed and skill with the puck and away from it, and if given time he might yet turn into a player. If he does, the Blueshirts won't be the reason.

MALIK, Marek

b. Ostrava, Czechoslovakia (Czech Republic),
June 24, 1975
At 6'5" and 235 pounds, Malik is filling out quite nicely to be one of the biggest players in the league. Ferocious, though, he is not. He has been in the Hartford/Carolina system his whole career, starting with his first game on January 22, 1995, when he recorded an assist. Since then he's been a solid defenceman and one of the reasons the Hurricanes advanced to the Cup finals in the spring of 2002. In 1997, Malik left the team to spend a year in Europe playing in Sweden for Malmo, but a year later he returned to the NHL.

Vladimir Malakhov

Clint Malarchuk

David Maley

Manny Malhotra

Marek Malik

Merlin Malinowski

Dean Malkoc

Troy Mallette

Greg Malone

Dan Maloney

MALINOWSKI, Merlin ("The Magician")

b. North Battleford, Saskatchewan, September 27, 1958

Technically, the nickname comes from his tricky stickhandling and fast skating, but with a name like Merlin his friends would have found any excuse to call him the Magician. He played 5 years in the NHL starting in 1978, scoring a career-high 25 times in '80-'81 with the woeful Rockies. He later moved to Switzerland, where he played for a number of years, and he represented Canada at the 1988 Olympics in Calgary.

MALKOC, Dean

b. Vancouver, British Columbia, January 26, 1970

Being born on the same day as Wayne Gretzky does not, sadly, guarantee greatness, and Malkoc is living proof. He has but 1 career goal to Wayne's 894, but for a short time they were, at least, colleagues. Malkoc fought his way to the NHL but played only parts of four seasons (1995-99) in a career full of minor-league scraps.

MALLETTE, Troy

b. Sudbury, Ontario, February 25, 1970

Mallette was the kind of tough guy who wouldn't hurt a team too much and who could protect his players as befits a man of the fist. In nine years he played for seven teams, but each season his stock dropped a bit. He began as a late first-round draft choice continued as a reliable pro and ended as an expansion pickup before a back injury forced him to retire just three games into the '97-'98 season.

MALONE, Cliff

b. Quebec City, Quebec, September 4, 1925

A lengthy career in post-war Montreal with the Royals resulted in a three-game callup for Malone in '51-'52 with the Canadiens. The winger regularly scored 20 goals in the Quebec senior league, but he didn't tally a one with the Habs and never played again in the NHL.

MALONE, Greg ("The Grinder")

b. Fredericton, New Brunswick, March 8, 1956

It's not very often this happens: Malone was a solid checker in junior, but when he came to a weak Pittsburgh team in 1976 he was asked to score! For the most part, he was up to the task. In 9 full seasons, he averaged about 20 goals a year, though the Pens, and later Hartford and Quebec, rarely made the playoffs. He became a top gun on the Pittsburgh power play and one of the leading point getters on the team. He once set a team record with six assists in a game. Soon after retiring, Malone returned to Pittsburgh, where he had played 7 of his 11 seasons, and became scout for Ontario and the CCHA. He was later inducted into the New Brunswick Sports Hall of Fame.

MALONE, Joe ("Phantom")

b. Quebec City, Quebec, February 28, 1890
d. Montreal, Quebec, May 15, 1969

No one scored goals at the pace Malone did, not before him and not since. By 17, he was already playing with the Quebec Crescents and a year later he started his career with the Bulldogs. Malone captained the team to two Stanley Cup wins in 1912 and '13. In the latter, he scored nine goals in a game against Sydney, and during his nine years with the team he averaged well over a goal a game. In 1917, he joined the Canadiens when the NHL was formed, his Bulldogs electing not to compete that season. He scored 44 goals in the 20-game schedule, an average that will never be matched and a total that wasn't eclipsed until '44-'45 when Maurice Richard scored 50 times in a 50-game season. He played that year on a line with Newsy Lalonde and Didier Pitre and in one stretch scored in 14 successive games. He suffered a broken arm the next year that limited him to just eight games, but in 1919-20 he was back, with Quebec, and again scored at will. He led the NHL with 39 goals, including 7 in one game, still a league record. He later played for Hamilton before ending his career with the Cup-winning Canadiens of '23-'24, after which he went into business. He worked as a tool designer but his fame allowed him to explore other business ventures as well. A gentlemanly player in a day when violence was rampant, Malone was a great skater with plenty of moves (thus the nickname Phantom – now you see him, now you don't). He was inducted into the Hockey Hall of Fame in 1950 and died at his home peacefully in 1969.

He scored 44 goals in the 20-game schedule, an average that will never be matched.
JOE MALONE

MALONEY, Dan ("Satch")

b. Barrie, Ontario, September 24, 1950

He once jumped Leafs defenceman Brian Glennie and repeatedly drove the player's head into the ice (he was later acquitted of assault charges). Later, he coached the team to the worst record in franchise history, 20-52-8, in '84-'85. As a player, Maloney was a thug, but for a short time he was viewed as a cross between a goon and a power forward, more skilled as the former, not as skilled as the latter. In the mid-1970s, Maloney had consecutive 27-goal seasons with Detroit, and that was enough for the Leafs to break their high-scoring line of Sittler-McDonald-Thompson, trading Errol Thompson in a deal to land Maloney. As a Leafs left winger, he continued to fight and didn't have nearly the offensive effectiveness the team had hoped he would, and midway through the '81-'82 season he retired to join the team's coaching staff. Maloney became head coach in 1984 and after two horrific seasons bolted the team because he was unhappy with their new contract offer.

He signed with Winnipeg where, after three increasingly poor seasons, he was fired. He never made it back as coach. Instead, he got into the hockey equipment business and sold real estate in Barrie.

MALONEY, Dave
b. Kitchener, Ontario, July 31, 1956

Dave the defenceman contrasted nicely with brother Don, the forward, though their careers took them to the same spot, New York, for many years. In fact, Dave spent nearly his entire career with the Rangers, starting in early 1975 when he was called up from Providence to play in a few games for the team. After one more partial season, he became a mainstay on the defence in 1976, and in 1978 he succeeded Phil Esposito as team captain, taking the team to the finals. Maloney was a decent playmaker and valuable addition to the power play, and from the start of the '78-'79 season until December 1984 he had his brother as a teammate. Dave was traded to Buffalo, played the final 52 games of his career with the Sabres, and then returned to New York where he worked with a brokerage firm. He later did colour commentary for Fox TV.

MALONEY, Don
b. Lindsay, Ontario, September 5, 1958

Few team men have been as popular in recent years as Don Maloney was with the Rangers. He came to the team the same year his brother was named team captain, and in the ensuing 11 years he left his mark on the ice and off. On, he was a scorer and hard worker who was effective on the power play. Off, he did work in the community and lived in the city in the off-season, working on Wall Street. Maloney had 5 successive seasons of 22 goals or more, but in December 1988 he was traded to Hartford and then on to the Islanders. After he retired, it was the Isles and not the Rangers that wanted to keep him in the loop. They made him assistant GM and then GM, but his tenure ended in December 1995 when he acquired Kirk Muller but then failed to convince the player to report and couldn't trade him, either. Maloney bounced back, though, and after a year scouting for San Jose he became assistant GM with the Rangers, a post to which he was also named for Canada's entry in the 2003 World Championships.

MALONEY, Phil ("The Fox")
b. Ottawa, Ontario, October 6, 1927

He had a small impact in the NHL, but he was one of the finest players ever to skate in the WHL. Maloney played his entire career in that league with the Vancouver Canucks, 14 years in all, before retiring in 1970. Along the way, he also played parts of five seasons in the NHL – with Boston, Toronto, and Chicago – and parts of five seasons in the AHL. He was the WHL's most valuable player three times, and the Canucks gave him a special night in honour of his contributions to the team. He was a playing coach for a brief time, and after retiring he coached in the WHL until 1973 when he was named coach of the Canucks, now an NHL team. Later in the '73-'74 season he added GM to his portfolio and for three and a half seasons he was the toast of the town again until he lost his job first as coach, and then as GM. Back in '49-'50, he had finished

second in Calder Trophy voting to Boston teammate Jack Gelineau. Maloney was later inducted into the British Columbia Hockey Hall of Fame.

MALTAIS, Steve
b. Arvida, Quebec, January 25, 1969

Funny how a player at one level doesn't amount to a hill of beans, but at another level is as noble as anyone around. Maltais scored a piddly 9 goals in a 94-game NHL career, but in his years in the IHL he has averaged 50 a season. He's led the IHL in goals five times, won the Turner Cup, and been named Chicago Wolves captain, and has a long and distinguished career outside the NHL.

MALTBY, Kirk
b. Guelph, Ontario, December 22, 1972

He likes the heavy going, he kills penalties and plays hard, he plays a defensive-minded game as a right wing on Detroit's Grind Line, and he can chip in with the occasional goal, too. Maltby has played with the Wings since being traded by Edmonton for Dan McGillis on March 20, 1996, and that means he's won three Stanley Cups. He came out of junior in Owen Sound as the team's captain and the year after helped Cape Breton win the Calder Cup in 1993. He suffered a scratched cornea during the '95-'96 season and a hernia in 1999-2000, the only significant injuries of his career despite his abrasive play. In his prime, he's one of the core players who will see the Wings from the current era to the next one.

MALUTA, Ray
b. Flin Flon, Manitoba, July 24, 1954

After four years in Flin Flon as a junior, Maluta made brief appearances with the Bruins in '75-'76 and '76-'77 in a short career that had him in Rochester most of the time. He later returned to Flin Flon to work for the Bombers and then became involved in in-line hockey. He managed the state-of-the-art ESL Center in Rochester, New York, which became the host site for the U.S. in-line championships, and he conducted clinics and coaching seminars throughout the year at the Center.

MANASTERSKY, Timothy "Tommy"
b. Montreal, Quebec, March 7, 1929

He was christened Timothy but his mother always called him Tommy, but whatever the moniker there wasn't a whole lot this kid couldn't do sports-wise. He was a great hockey player and a better football player. In high school he was a champion diver, and breast stroke was his specialty as a swimmer. He was also a fine water polo player. In hockey, he started as a forward but moved back to the blueline while he was still young. In football, he went to Holy Cross and made the team, but became homesick and moved home. When he was 16, his father died, and his mother moved to Drummondville to live with her daughter. Tommy lived on his own in Montreal from that day forward. He preferred football, and in 1949 he won the Memorial Cup with the Montreal Royals and also played in the backfield of the Montreal Alouettes, winning the Grey Cup (he had also played with the Als in 1946 and '47). He played in the NHL with the

Dave Maloney

Don Maloney

Phil Maloney

Steve Maltais

Kirk Maltby

Kent Manderville

Dan Mandich

Kris Manery

Randy Manery

Cesare Maniago

Habs for six games in '50-'51, but continued to play pro football until 1953, one of the few two-sport NHLers. He also worked in Montreal in the sporting goods department of a major store.

MANCUSO, Felix "Gus"

b. Niagara Falls, Ontario, April 11, 1914

Not to be confused with the Giants catcher, this Gus Mancuso played three partial seasons with the Habs before the war but spent most of his time down in New Haven. The Habs sold him to the Rangers at the start of the '42-'43 season, and he got another chance on Broadway for half a season before being sent back to the Eagles in the American league. Mancuso joined the army in 1943, and when he was discharged he finished his career in California. He settled in Los Angeles and worked as a parking lot attendant at the Pan Pacific Auditorium.

MANDERVILLE, Kent ("Mandy")

b. Edmonton, Alberta, April 12, 1971

Like many film festival movies, the biopic that is Manderville's life starts off full of promise but has a weak ending. A high Calgary draft choice in 1989, he left Cornell early to play for the Canadian National Team, culminating with a silver medal at the 1992 Olympics in Albertville. However, before he could get into a game with the Flames, they included him in the massive, 10-player trade with Toronto that saw Doug Gilmour join the Leafs and Gary Leeman skedaddle to Calgary. Manderville started as a fourth-liner and never played himself into a promotion, and over the years penalty killing and defensive play have been his various fortes. He's moved around a fair bit, and once went through a skein of 122 games without a goal.

MANDICH, Dan

b. Brantford, Ontario, June 12, 1960

Imagine missing a year and a half of playing time because of an injury you did nothing to incur. Mandich was a tough defenceman who started with Minnesota in 1982 and earned a regular turn in the lineup. On January 16, 1984, though, he went into the hospital for an arthrogram, a test on his right knee. All was fine, and cortisone revealed no damage. That night, he developed a staph infection and spent the next month in the hospital, where he lost 35 pounds. Scar tissue formed around the knee and when doctors tried to clean it up they cut a ligament. He missed a year, and didn't return until the final 10 games of '84-'85. He got into a fight, suffered an infection to his hand, and missed the playoffs. When he returned the year after, it just wasn't there and he had to retire. All because of a simple trip to the hospital.

MANELUK, George

b. Winnipeg, Manitoba, July 25, 1967

Maneluk was never destined to stardom, but he did play in four games for the Islanders in '90-'91 in a short, minor-league career that took him to nearly every league on the continent.

MANELUK, Mike

b. Winnipeg, Manitoba, October 1, 1973

A great '97-'98 season in the AHL got Maneluk into the NHL. That year, he had 27 goals in the regular season and then led the league in playoff goals, assists, and points while guiding the Philadelphia Phantoms to the Calder Cup. The year after, he started with the Flyers but ended up playing for three teams that season, and soon after he was back dominating the AHL. He later moved to Switzerland to play.

MANERY, Kris

b. Leamington, Ontario, September 24, 1954

A different breed of player, Manery graduated from the University of Michigan in 1977 with a mortar block on his head and a hockey stick in his hand. The stick helped him become the Wolverines' all-time leading scorer. The block represented his Bachelor of Science in zoology. He roared into the NHL that fall and promptly scored 22 goals with the weak Cleveland Barons, but over the next 4 years he had a hard time staying put and was soon in the minors. Kris, younger brother of Randy, later signed with Chur in Switzerland, where he continued his career away from the frenzy of the NHL.

MANERY, Randy

b. Leamington, Ontario, January 10, 1949

The first hockey lines for Manery note his junior years in Hamilton, but they fail to acknowledge the fact that during those years he studied at McMaster University, eventually earning a degree in English and geography. He turned pro with Detroit in 1970, but it wasn't until Atlanta claimed him two years later that he truly made the NHL grade. In his five seasons with the Flames, Manery became a consistent and reliable defenceman who could move the puck well and lead by example. He was later traded to L.A. where he was the Kings' number-one man on the blueline, but in his third year out west something happened to him. He became lethargic and error prone, and it wasn't immediately discovered that he had an iron deficiency. He recovered to finish out the year but then retired. Manery tried his hand at several small business ventures (an ice cream store, a construction company, a dry cleaning shop) before settling in Atlanta and working as a fundraiser for the Haggai Institute, a Christian organization.

MANIAGO, Cesare ("Hail Caesar")

b. Trail, British Columbia, January 13, 1939

The world is a small place. Maniago's dad worked for a man at Cominco mines in B.C. who was close friends with Conn Smythe, lord of the rinks in Toronto. That's the connection that got a boy from out west into a school uniform at St. Mike's and into the Leafs system in 1957. But during the pre-expansion days, no matter how well Maniago played he was never going to be a regular. Toronto had Johnny Bower, Montreal had Jacques Plante, and the Rangers had Eddie Giacomin. Maniago's real goaltending life began in 1967 when Minnesota claimed him, and for nine years he was the starter and the aging Gump Worsley his backup on a struggling team. Maniago played his final two years in Vancouver, a perfect end to his career. During his playing days he had acquired his stockbroker's licence, worked in real estate, and dabbled in construction. He knew from experience that contacts were important, and that's how he eventually set up his own sporting goods store in Burnaby called Maniago Sports Ltd. He also kept his pads in the game by acting as the Canucks goaltending consultant.

MANLOW, Eric ("Manny")

b. Stirling, Ontario, April 7, 1975

Drafted by Chicago in 1993. Sounds good. That's the easy part. "Excuse me, could you tell me how to get to the NHL?" "Play, play, play," comes the answer. Seven and a half years later, after playing in every league around, Manlow caught a break. Boston had signed him and assigned him to the farm – where else? – but he led the team in scoring early on. Coach Mike Keenan was trying to make his own point, so he recalled Manlow, and on December 19, 2000, Manny made his NHL debut. He got an assist in his second game, and ended up being recalled three times for a total of eight games. Then three games the next year. In 2002, he ended up with the Islanders and made the team, finally, as a regular.

MANN, Cameron

b. Thompson, Manitoba, April 20, 1977

Chris Pronger might be a terrific scout for an all-star NHL defenceman. Back in junior, with Peterborough, the Petes asked him to scout a midget tournament. He recommended Mann as a potential up-and-comer, and the Petes took Mann in the '93 Midget Draft. He went on to have a great, four-year career in Peterborough and was drafted by Boston along the way. Unfortunately, in his four partial years with the Bruins, Mann played mostly in the minors. He has since been traded to Dallas and Nashville but has yet to return to the NHL, his great teen potential still unrealized in the manly NHL.

MANN, Jimmy

b. Montreal, Quebec, April 17, 1959

As a noun, "Mann" might be defined as "animal, barbarian, goon without elemental skills with which to practice hockey." The definition might be based on the events of January 13, 1982, when, in the words of hockey scribes, the game received one of its worst black eyes. Mann and Winnipeg were at home playing Pittsburgh when Pens forward Paul Gardner gave Doug Smail a vicious cross-check to the face that referee Dave Newell missed. Smail appeared to be seriously injured, and during the next shift Jets coach Tom Watt sent his madman onto the ice. Gardner was yapping with Dave Babych when, from out of nowhere, Mann sucker-punched Gardner with all his might (an eye for an eye, a face for a face, perhaps). Gardner fell to the ice and suffered a badly broken jaw. Mann was suspended 10 games by the NHL and

charged with assault causing bodily harm and fined $500 by a Manitoba court. It crystallized his career more than it was an aberration thereof. Mann fought wherever he went, completely without care what a puck looked like or where it skitted. Punching other people was how he earned his living, a living that came to an end in 1989. He later owned and operated several apartment buildings in Trois Rivières, Quebec, and has been closely involved with old-timers' hockey and the Legends of Hockey tours.

MANN, John "Jack"

b. Winnipeg, Manitoba, July 27, 1919

Mann's road to the NHL was one well-trodden: He came up from the New York Rovers to play for the Rangers during the war, stuck around for a few games, and went back down to the minors, never to return to the big league again. In his case, he managed three goals and seven points in nine games with the Blueshirts. He was later inducted into the Manitoba Sports Hall of Fame.

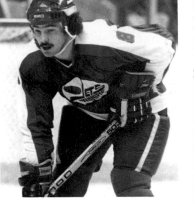

Punching other people was how he earned his living.
JIMMY MANN

MANN, Ken

b. Hamilton, Ontario, September 5, 1953

Believe it or not, there was a day – and it was a long day – that the Allan Cup was far more prestigious a trophy than the Stanley Cup. Parades were held, players were heroes and gods, winning towns across the country were abuzz with celebration. Today, the Allan Cup is a small footnote in hockey's annual history, though Mann is a part of that more recent, less glorious, day. He coached the Brantford Motts Clamatos to victory in 1987 and later coached another senior team, the Dundas Real McCoys. His only NHL playing time came on February 25, 1976, when he appeared for Detroit.

MANN, Norm

b. Bradford, England, March 3, 1913
d. Mattawa, Ontario, February 9, 1994

The common misperception is that Mann was born in Paris, Ontario, the town where he grew up. But he came to Paris via England as a boy and made his first impact as a hockey player in Newmarket, helping the Redmen win the 1933 Memorial Cup. The next year, he and the Marlies won the senior championship and the year after he won the Mercantile championship with the British Consuls in Toronto. Mann made a quick NHL debut in the 1936 playoffs for one game and then had a more important callup in 1939 when he filled in for an injured Syl Apps. That's how he saw Maple Leafs action while in Toronto, his last NHL stint. He served in the Royal Canadian Navy during the war, and after retiring from hockey settled in Mattawa, his home for the rest of his life.

Eric Manlow

Cameron Mann

Jack Mann

Ken Mann

Norm Mann

Ren Manners

Bob Manno

Georges Mantha

MANNERS, Rennison "Ren"

b. Ottawa, Ontario, February 5, 1904
d. Ottawa, Ontario, December 26, 1944

As a boy growing up in Ottawa, Manners was a star baseball pitcher with the Senators as well as a fleet skater with the Montagnards. He turned pro with Pittsburgh in the NHL in 1929 and played a few games with Philadelphia the following year, but his career was short and he returned to Ottawa where he had a lengthy career working as a brakeman for Canadian National Railways. He died suddenly of a heart attack one night while waiting for a streetcar, the same day his uncle, by coincidence, also died.

MANNO, Bob

b. Niagara Falls, Ontario, October 31, 1956

For a number of years, Bob Manno was the highest-paid player in the league. No, it's not a Halloween joke – it's the Italian league, is all. He did all the traditional, NHL-type things first – got drafted, played in the minors, made his debut with Vancouver in 1977, got traded to Toronto. There were some fine moments. In '81-'82, he scored 50 points, an excellent year for a defenceman. He subbed for Borje Salming at the All-Star Game. But at season's end, he played for Italy at the World Championships and he loved the experience. The next year, he played full-time in the big boot of a country, but he was arrogant. He fought, acted like a prima donna, but didn't sign like one. He returned to play two years in Detroit, and then with a new attitude he moved to Italy. He played incredibly well, and became famous and well paid. In all, he played in seven World Championships for Italy and then in the 1992 Olympics in Albertville, something he had no hope of doing for Canada. After retiring, he stayed in Europe and coached, both in Italy and in Germany, his name ingrained as one of the finest players the Continent has seen.

MANSON, Dave ("Charlie")

b. Prince Albert, Saskatchewan, January 27, 1967

In his early days, he was a real fighter, a guy who'd take on anyone. But, he was also a fine defenceman, nasty, defensive minded, tenacious. One time, during a set-to with Sergio Momesso, he took a punch to the throat, and since then his voice has been a raspy, weak shadow of its former self. He'll have a corrective operation when his playing days are done, but the timeless warrior might not be ready to settle down for a while. He has passed the 1,000-game mark and has shown determination and resilience that have been his trademarks throughout his career. After winning the Memorial Cup in 1985 with Prince Albert, he's been to two Cup finals (Chicago in 1990 and Dallas in 2000), and he has always been that defenceman a coach can count on for solid minutes without mistakes. During his early years with Chicago and Edmonton, he also had some scoring ability and worked well on the power play point. As he aged, he played more conservatively and within his limits, and in recent years he was a healthy scratch more times than he'd like. He took the hint and retired, becoming an assistant coach in Prince Albert, where he first learned the game.

MANSON, Ray

b. St. Boniface, Manitoba, December 3, 1926

Mason was a one-game wonder twice, first with Boston, then with the Rangers, in the years immediately after the war. He was a fine scorer in the minors, and as a junior he won the scoring title in '46-'47 with Brandon. He was later inducted into the Manitoba Sports Hall of Fame.

He has passed the 1,000-game mark and has shown determination and resilience.
DAVE MANSON

MANTHA, Georges

b. Lachine, Quebec, November 29, 1907
d. Montreal, Quebec, January 25, 1990

He played all 13 of his NHL seasons with the Canadiens, and although neither as aggressive nor as successful as brother Sylvio, Georges was still one of the finer players on the Habs from this era. He won a Cup with the team in 1930 and scored five playoff goals the following year to return the Cup to Montreal. In his early years, he played on a second line with Pit Lepine and Armand Mondou, and in 1936-37 he moved to the top line with Lepine and rookie Toe Blake. He scored 13 goals that year, and the next year led the team with 23 goals and 42 points, good enough for fourth overall. When he retired from hockey, he made Montreal his lifelong home. For 30 years he was the director of parks and playgrounds for the city. In his last years, Mantha fought a losing battle with Alzheimer's.

MANTHA, Moe

b. Lakewood, Ohio, January 21, 1961

Mantha was a capable defenceman in the NHL for 12 years (1980-92) though he was more a steady player than a spectacular one. Despite his contributions, his teams never made a serious run through the playoffs, and in all those seasons Mantha played only 17 post-season games. More important to his career was his participation with Team USA in international competition. He played on three World Championships teams as well as the 1992 Olympics team, and after retiring he started coaching in the minors for several years while going back to the U.S. National Team. He was an assistant at the 1998 WC, and in 2002 was named coach of the U.S. National Development Program.

MANTHA, Sylvio
b. Montreal, Quebec, April 14, 1902
d. Montreal, Quebec, August 7, 1974

With the exception of four games with Boston at the end of his career, Mantha played virtually every minute of his hockey career for a variety of teams in Montreal. In 1918-19 he played junior for Notre Dame de Grâce. In the city's Industrial League, he skated for Montreal Imperial Tobacco and Montreal Northern Electric, and then a short stint with the Nationales led the Canadiens to sign him. He had been a right winger all this time, but when he got to the NHL the Canadiens needed a defenceman to replace Sprague Cleghorn so they moved him back to the blueline. He was no wallflower, but he certainly was not the violent player that Cleghorn was during his colourful career. Mantha and the Habs won the Cup in '23-'24 and he established himself immediately as a superb player. He could rush the puck and hurry back to make defensive plays when necessary. He had a good shot and was a fine playmaker. His brother, Georges, joined the team in 1928 and the two played together for the next eight years, winning the Cup in 1930 and again in '31. Mantha captained the team from 1926 to '32 and 1933 to '36. In '35-'36, he was also playing coach, but when the Habs had an awful record of 11-26-11 and missed the playoffs he was let go. He signed on with Boston for the next year but after only a few games retired. He then worked as a linesman and referee in both the NHL and the AHL, but the travel schedule was too much for him and he stopped altogether. He lived in Montreal the rest of his life, working as a coach for much of the 1940s. He started with the Concordias until 1943, then was with the Laval Nationales ('43-'45), the Verdun Maple Leafs ('45-'47) and the St. Jerome Eagles ('47-'48). He was inducted into the Hockey Hall of Fame in 1960, his role as Montreal's finest defenceman of his era already well ensconced in the team's annals.

MARA, Paul
b. Ridgewood, New Jersey, September 7, 1979

His brother, Rob, didn't quite make it after being drafted by Chicago in 1994, but Paul has made it, though not to the extent his 7th-overall selection in 1997 might indicate. A big and strong defenceman, he had his best career in 2001-02 after being acquired by Phoenix, so the upside is his youth and the downside is his lack of quick development to date. He played in three WJC tournaments for the U.S. during his junior days with Plymouth in the OHL.

MARACLE, Elmer "Bud" ("Chief")
b. Ayr, Ontario, September 8, 1904
d. unknown

It was in Tulsa in the mid-1930s that Maracle made a name for himself as the sensation who would take the pre-game skate wearing a traditional Indian headdress to get the crowd going. He was one of the first Natives to play in the NHL, in '30-'31 with the Rangers based on his fine play with Springfield in the AHL. He had been a player on the great North Bay Trappers team of '23-'24 before moving to, appropriately, the Indians, and it was in Tulsa that Chief finished his career.

MARACLE, Norm
b. Belleville, Ontario, October 2, 1974

Despite winning the 2001 Turner Cup and being named playoff MVP with Orlando in the IHL, Maracle got into only one game the year after with Atlanta. That's the way it's been for the young goalie who has shone in the minors and not been given much of a chance in the NHL. Detroit played him for parts of two years, but in 1999-2000, his first with the Thrashers, he played well yet had a dismal record of 4-19-2.

MARCETTA, Milan ("Millie")
b. Cadomin, Alberta, September 19, 1936

Milan Marcetta and Aut Erickson are obscure and trivial names in the annals of Toronto Maple Leafs history. They were the two players called up in the 1967 playoffs by coach and GM Punch Imlach as insurance, and both played only long enough to get their names on the Cup. Marcetta was 30 years old at the time, a seasoned veteran of the minors with no possible hope of seeing the NHL. Yet his first NHL game was a critical playoff game for the Leafs. The next year, he was traded to Minnesota, where he played parts of two years, and then it was back to the minors. When he retired, he went about as far away from the game as possible, running a minor hockey association in Anchorage, Alaska. He later settled in Vancouver, where he opened a building maintenance business and became a loyal Canucks supporter.

MARCH, Harold "Mush" ("The Musher")
b. Silton, Saskatchewan, October 18, 1908
d. Paxton, Illinois, January 9, 2002

Only superfans of Dick Tracy would know that the nickname Mush comes from Mush Mouth from that great comic strip. Yet March had more in common with King Clancy, another flyweight who played like an undefeated heavyweight throughout his career. From the time he entered the NHL in 1928 to the time he retired 17 seasons later, March wore only Chicago's colours. The right winger had an excellent career and missed few games because of his size, but he will always be remembered for three historic goals. One: On November 21, 1929, he scored the first goal in the history of the old Chicago Stadium, though the team lost the game 6-5 to Ottawa. Two: He scored the first goal in the history of Maple Leaf Gardens on November 12, 1931, a 2-1 Toronto loss to the Hawks: Three: On April 10, 1934, at 10:05 of the second OT, he scored against Detroit to give the Hawks the team's first Stanley Cup. He won the Cup again four years later, and a knee injury finally forced him to retire in 1945. March remained in the NHL as a referee for 11 years and then settled in Chicago where he reffed college hockey – same game and pay, but no travel. He later worked for General Bearings, a local company and had his own small businesses on the side. He was also a scratch golfer who for years was club pro in the summer, notably at Mesaba Country Club in Minnesota and Valparaiso in Indiana. Before he passed away at age 93, March had one more glorious hockey moment. On February 13, 1999, he returned to the scene of his greatest crime, Maple Leaf Gardens, for that building's final game. He brought with him the simple, black

Sylvio Mantha

Bud Maracle

Milan Marcetta

Milan Marcetta

Mush March

Todd Marchant

Brian Marchinko

Bryan Marchment

Lou Marcon

Hector Marini

puck with which he had scored the first goal in MLG history, and used it during the opening ceremonies attended by an opponent, Red Horner, who had also played that opening night in 1931. For 68 years he had kept the puck in his home, and both he and it outlived the glorious building that helped made hockey famous.

MARCHANT, Todd ("Speed Marchant")
b. Buffalo, New York, August 12, 1973
Perhaps the NHL has seen no finer display of pure speed in recent times than on April 19, 1997, when Marchant blew down the right side, cut in on goal, and scored to the far side in overtime of game seven to give his Oilers a first-round playoff victory over conference nemesis Dallas. It was a beautiful display of what the game can be, yet as has been the case with Marchant as well, it isn't on display often enough. He played for the U.S. at the 1994 Olympics in Lillehammer and joined the Rangers soon after, but he had to wonder what he did wrong. Three days later, he was traded to Edmonton, and it was with the speedy Oilers that he developed into a player. Despite his tremendous skills, though, he has yet to have a 20-goal season, a modest plateau for offensive success in the league, but he remains capable of producing the occasional highlight reel rush, and for that the NHL should be grateful.

MARCHINKO, Brian
b. Weyburn, Saskatchewan, August 2, 1948
Just his luck. Marchinko was claimed by the Islanders in the Expansion Draft of '72 after playing a few games with the Leafs in previous seasons. In his first full NHL season, he hurt his knee and missed half a year. It was his only chance to be a regular, and the year after he was back in the minors for most of the season and the rest of his career.

MARCHMENT, Bryan
b. Scarborough, Ontario, May 1, 1969
There are a number of levels for hated players. There are those you hate to play against but love to have on your own team. The Sutters, for instance. Then there are those you hate, plain and simple, but they are effective. Ken Linseman or Claude Lemieux. Then there are the dirty guys with skill. Chris Chelios. Then, way way down and below all of these types is a guy named Bryan Marchment. A career ender. A knee hunter. The kind of player, when he gets to your team, you demand a trade or refuse to talk to him. The kind of guy who starts trouble and is so deserving of payback his teammates don't even come to his defence. Marchment has been suspended 10 times (and counting), more than any other player in league history, for a total of just 35 games. His specialty is the knee. He calls it old-time hockey, but in the old days there were no knee hunters, only hip checkers, open-ice hitters, and shoulder-to-shoulder rough checkers. He's also been suspended for head butting, hitting from behind, spearing, and elbowing. His excuse is that he likes to play physically and throw the other team off its game. The only thing more appalling than his track record for truly violent behaviour during play is the NHL's unwillingness to punish him properly. One day, if and when he gets his own, no one will bat an eye. In the meantime, he has played 14 seasons in the league and

only once made it past the second round of the playoffs. Perhaps his methods aren't as purposeful as he makes them out to be?

MARCINYSHYN, Dave
b. Edmonton, Alberta, February 4, 1967
Marcinyshyn played nine, five, and two games with three different teams in successive seasons in the early 1990s in a career spent almost entirely in the AHL and IHL. The defenceman did more than his fair share of fighting wherever he went.

MARCON, Lou
b. Fort William, Ontario, May 28, 1935
The reports from the minors were glowing. When Marcon was called up to Detroit in 1958, players and coaches didn't think they'd see him again. Marcon reminded Wings GM of Jack Stewart. Others pointed to his phenomenal shotblocking and called him a second goalie or another Bob Goldham. Nonetheless, Marcon spent even his Red Wings years more in the minors than at the Olympia, and when the Wings gave up on him, there were no other NHL takers and he spent the rest of his skating days in the AHL and leagues below.

MARCOTTE, Don
b. Asbestos, Quebec, April 15, 1947
"Club" can mean many things. It can mean a team. It can mean to hit hard. It can mean a place to socialize and drink. In the case of Marcotte, all three are applicable. In the first sense, he was a team player with Boston, spending his entire 15-year career with the team. He was a 2-way player, tremendous defensively yet a 20-goal scorer on 6 occasions. He hit hard, was one of the best penalty killers in the league, and was a two-time winner of the Cup in 1970 and '72. When he retired, he tried coaching for a year and didn't like it. He returned to Boston and with Milt Schmidt ran the famous Madison Square Garden Club at the Boston Garden. He later became the Club's director, and when the team moved to the Fleet Center, he moved there to run the private club at the new digs.

MARHA, Josef
b. Havlickuv Brod, Czechoslovakia (Czech Republic), June 2, 1976
Sometimes the allure of a European is greater than his mettle, and sometimes all that glitters is not gold. Marha was a high draft choice by Quebec in 1994, but he made little impact with the Avs (after the Nordiques moved to Colorado) before being traded to Anaheim for nothing more than Warren Rychel and a 4th-round draft choice. A year later, he was traded to Chicago, this time for just a 4th-rounder, sans the Rychel-type player, and soon after Marha was in Switzerland playing for Davos.

MARINI, Hector
b. Timmins, Ontario, January 27, 1957
By 1985, Marini had been abandoned in the minors and there seemed little hope he'd ever return to the NHL. He played for Maine in the American league because he loved the game and it was a great way to make a living, but his employment came to a sudden and horrible end on December 4, 1985, when a slapshot

deflected off a stick and the puck hit him flush in the left eye. Doctors had no choice but to remove it, and Marini had no choice but to retire. He had started his career with the Islanders, playing part of '80-'81, when the team won the Cup. He was all set to win again the following year, but midway through the season he broke his hand in a fight with Jack McIlhargey and missed the rest of the season. At training camp the following year, he was traded – to New Jersey, the "Mickey Mouse" Devils in the words of Wayne Gretzky at the time. Marini was named to play at the All-Star Game because he was the best of a bad lot and each team had to have one representative, and after half a season more he was consigned to the minors, where he remained until the eye injury. He later studied to become an official with Canada Customs.

MARINUCCI, Chris
b. Grand Rapids, Minnesota, December 29, 1971
Awards are given for meritorious achievement over a specific period of time, and what is given today certainly does not guarantee anything for tomorrow. Marinucci won the Hobey Baker Award in 1994, capping off a fine four-year career at the University of Minnesota-Duluth, from which he graduated with a degree in biology. Yet he played only a dozen games with the Islanders the next season before a trade to Los Angeles got him into one more, final game. He spent the rest of his years scoring goals aplenty in the IHL, and when that league disbanded he headed to Germany to play in the DEL.

MARIO, Frank
b. Esterhazy, Saskatchewan, February 25, 1921
d. Cornwall, Ontario, June 18, 1995
A few cities played an important part in Mario's life. Regina: This is where he grew up and where he won an Allan Cup in 1941 with the Rangers. After retiring, it's where he returned for six years to coach the junior Pats. Hershey: Mario played seven years of pro with the AHL Bears, having his finest season as a centreman, scorer, and Calder Cup winner. Boston: Mario's two pro seasons were spent here, interrupted by a two-year hiatus with the Canadian Infantry Corps as a provisional 2nd lieutenant. In Boston, he helped set an NHL record for the four fastest goals by a team – 1:20 – by scoring the second and third of those goals. Finally, Cornwall: His home for most of his life after hockey, Mario coached here and retired here. He lived in Cornwall while he scouted for St. Louis and Colorado/New Jersey before retiring altogether in 1985.

MARIUCCI, John ("Maroosh")
b. Eveleth, Minnesota, May 8, 1916
d. Minneapolis, Minnesota, March 23, 1987
Because his parents wanted him to become a musician, Mariucci wasn't allowed to wear skates until he was 15 years old. That he was skating in the NHL nine years later was a miracle of sorts in itself, but it was his lifelong devotion to hockey in his home state that earned him the moniker "godfather of Minnesota hockey." Mariucci attended the University of Minnesota, and it was there he played football and developed his hockey skills with remarkable swiftness. He made such an impression that Chicago signed him and used him for half the '40-'41 season, and he did so well that the next year he was a

full-time member of the Black Hawks. Abruptly, though, he enlisted in the army and was out of the NHL for three years. He returned to play three more seasons for the Hawks, establishing himself as a fearless defenceman who backed down from no man. Mariucci ended his playing days in the minors, and after retiring in 1952, took the head coaching job at his alma mater. For 14 years he led the U of M, and he was revered for using mostly American-born players for his team at a time when Canadian kids packed college teams in the U. S. He also coached the U.S. National Team to a stunning silver medal at the 1956 Olympics in Cortina. In 1967, Mariucci left the school to become an assistant general manager for the new state franchise in the NHL, the Minnesota North Stars, the team for which he worked until his untimely demise from prostate cancer in 1987. He was an inaugural inductee into the new United States Hockey Hall of Fame in 1973, and four years later received the Lester Patrick Trophy for his contribution to the game in the U.S. In 1985, he received his crowning honour when the Hockey Hall of Fame inducted him as a Builder.

MARK, Gordie
b. Edmonton, Alberta, September 10, 1964
The early signs were good, New Jersey felt, after drafting Mark in 1983. He progressed nicely in his final year of junior with Kamloops, and he was the most improved player in his first year of pro, with Maine of the AHL in 1985-86. In his first NHL game with the Devils the year after, Mark learned a lesson. He suffered a separated shoulder, and knew then and there if he were to make it he would have to initiate contact, not sit back and wait for it. He did, but it got him into only 55 games over the next 2 years. He wound up in the minors, and it wasn't until six years later that the local Oilers agreed to sign him. Mark played 30 games over 2 more seasons, and though he played a while longer the NHL was no longer an option.

MARKELL, John
b. Cornwall, Ontario, March 10, 1956
Yes, he made it to the NHL. That looks good on the resumé and sounds nice to tell the grandkids, but Markell has made his mark elsewhere. At Bowling Green University (1975-79) he became one of only five players to be named to the CCHA First All-Star Team three times. After his brief NHL career (55 games over 4 years with 3 teams), he moved to Germany where he became a top scorer with Nauheim for 2 years. He then moved to Wolfsburg where he became a playing coach, never finishing lower than fifth in scoring as a player, and never lower than fifth with the team as a coach. When the chance to return to the CCHA came up, he accepted an assistant coach's position at Ohio State, and two years later became the head man. Under Markell, the team has gone from a sad sack loser to a perennially strong team, and his coaching style has had a tremendous influence on the school's hockey program.

MARKER, August "Gus"
b. Wetaskiwin, Alberta, August 1, 1905
d. Kingston, Ontario, October 7, 1997
Marker was a small but durable piece of business who came from small-town Alberta to take the NHL by

Chris Marinucci

Frank Mario

John Mariucci

John Markell

Gus Marker

storm. He made his NHL entry with Detroit in 1932 and two years later was traded to the Maroons where he had four fine years playing on a line with Bob Gracie and Dutch Cain. The team won the Cup in Marker's first year, 1934-35, and he later played for the Leafs on a line with Billy Taylor and Red Heron for three seasons. After a brief stop with the Brooklyn Americans, Marker played for and coached the Tulsa Oilers and then settled in Kingston. He established several successful businesses, including Marker Ready-Mix Concrete, Marker Block and Tile, and Marker Building Materials. He also briefly went into politics and was an alderman for the City of Kingston.

Danny Markov

MARKHAM, Ray
b. Windsor, Ontario, January 23, 1958
The Ray Markham Case had widespread implications for hockey. He had been playing in the Rangers system for a year and a half when the team called him up toward the end of the '79-'80 season. He continued to play with the Rangers through their playoff exit, and at training camp the following year he was injured in a game. Meanwhile, he cleared waivers and the Rangers sent him back to New Haven, but he didn't recover from the injury until December. Markham appealed to NHL president John Ziegler that he should have been paid his NHL salary during his convalescence since his injury occurred in the NHL. Ziegler agreed, and contracts have never been the same since. Neither, really, was Markham, who played four years more in the minors without ever seeing the NHL again.

MARKKANEN, Jussi
b. Imatra, Finland, May 8, 1975
Known more for play in Finland and on international ice, Markkanen is hoping to make inroads with Edmonton in the NHL, the team that drafted him, belatedly, in 2001. He had played in two World Junior Championships (1994 and '95) and had a lengthy career with SaiPa in Finnish league play, but it wasn't until November 28, 2001 that he finally got into an NHL game. Markkanen joined the most elite of goaltending fraternities when he recorded a shutout in his first game, and in 14 games with the Oilers he had a fantastic goals-against average of just 1.84. He was also used as the third goalie for Finland at the 2002 Olympics in Salt Lake City, and later that season played for Suomi at the World Championships.

MARKLE, John "Jack"
b. Thessalon, Ontario, May 15, 1907
d. Pulaski, New York, June 25, 1956
Although Markle made it into only eight NHL games, with Toronto in '35-'36, he was a top scorer in the IHL and American league during their formative years. The right winger led the league in scoring 3 times and was named league MVP once, scoring 20 goals in a season 5 times during a career in which he played almost exclusively with Syracuse.

MARKOV, Andrei
b. Voskresensk, Soviet Union (Russia), December 12, 1978
Coming out of Russia, the young defenceman arrived in Montreal with a reputation as an offensively gifted

John Marks

player, capable of playing well in his own end and moving the puck quickly and with authority. He was also good on the power play and is an important part of a weak Montreal defence. Still young, he's already competed in two World Championships for his country.

MARKOV, Daniil "Danny" ("Elvis"/ "Sputnik")
b. Moscow, Soviet Union (Russia), July 11, 1976
According to his teammates, he's way out there (ergo the otherworldly nicknames). Markov is perhaps the finest late draft of the last decade, the Leafs claiming him 223rd overall in 1995. After just 10 games in the minors, he was called up to the Leafs in '97-'98 and played his way into a starring role with the team. Utterly fearless on the ice, he'll block shots, play through inordinate pain, and hit anything on his radar screen. The Leafs traded him to Phoenix in the summer of 2001, and Markov helped the Coyotes make a surprise appearance in the playoffs at the end of his first season with Wayne Gretzky's team.

MARKS, Jack
b. Brantford, Ontario, June 11, 1885
d. Toronto, Ontario, August 19, 1945
Marks played during a turning point in the history of the game, when the NHA gave way to the NHL. In truth, he was an NHA star who played the last part of his career in the newly created league. He won consecutive Cups with the Quebec Bulldogs in 1912 and '13 and remained with the team until joining the Montreal Wanderers during the inaugural days of the NHL. When the Wanderers' building was razed by fire, Marks joined the Toronto Arenas, winning the first NHL Stanley Cup. He later returned to the Bulldogs for a game in 1919.

MARKS, John
b. Hamiota, Manitoba, March 22, 1948
The transition from defence to left wing was a great one for Marks, who played on the blueline his entire career until the playoffs of his first NHL season in 1973. He spent the rest of his career on the port side, though he longed to return to the defence because he thought it would be better to be a scoring defenceman rather than a second- or third-line forward. Marks was one of the league's Ironmen, playing more than 500 games in a row at one stretch. He also worked at a bank part-time throughout his career, figuring this was a line of business that would interest him after hockey. Wrong. Almost as soon as he retired in 1982, he got into the coaching game, and for some 20 years now that's how he's earned his living. From college hockey to the minors, he's been behind the bench since 1983, most recently with the expansion Grenville Grrowl of the ECHL.

MARKWART, Nevin
b. Toronto, Ontario, December 9, 1964
It is almost without doubt the oddest name in the NHL directory of names, the Markwart unusual, the Nevin born of an obstetrical tale. When Mrs. M. was in the hospital, she was watching the Leafs play and at the very moment she went into labour, Bob Nevin scored. Why it wasn't Bob Markwart is a question that will remain unanswered for now, but hockey fans

should be thankful it wasn't Pete Stemkowski who did the scoring. (For the record, Montreal beat the Leafs 3-2 that night.) Young Nevin grew up to be a fine hockey player, and after a career in junior with Regina he passed up a chance to attend Princeton University so he could play for the Bruins. For the better part of eight seasons he split his time between the B's and their farm team, though his last seasons were marred by a stomach injury that required surgery. He finished his career by playing 10 games with Calgary, and in 1993 decided to do what he had passed up a decade earlier – he enrolled in the MBA program at Princeton. Markwart graduated a year later and worked in the city for Standish Ayer & Wood, eventually becoming a director and partner in the company.

MARLEAU, Patrick ("Patty")
b. Aneroid, Saskatchewan, September 15, 1979

You don't go to Aneroid to visit the movie house or buy your groceries or fill your prescriptions. In fact, you leave Aneroid to do anything but farm. By virtue of his birthdate, Marleau was actually drafted at age 17, and he went 2nd overall, to San Jose, in 1997. In the succeeding years, he hasn't lived up to that high number, but amazingly he had 5 NHL years under his belt before he turned 23. In the off-season, he returns to Swift Current where he and friend Trent McCleary work at a hockey school and help children less fortunate. The big centre has much to improve on before becoming a star, but his experience is far greater than his age, so there's hope yet.

It is almost without doubt the oddest name in the NHL directory of names.
NEVIN MARKWART

MAROIS, Daniel
b. Montreal, Quebec, October 3, 1968

There was a time, albeit brief, when Marois first came to the NHL, that he was a great scorer. He starred with the Leafs for almost 4 full years, scoring 31 and 39 goals in his first 2 seasons. He had the quick shot, the determination to get the puck, that defines a scorer, but he tailed off his last two years and was traded to the Islanders. Then the back troubles began. He missed much of the next two years with back pain and all of '94-'95 after an operation, and soon after he began his recovery he moved to Europe where the going was easier. He returned to North America to play in 2001, but by then, of course, his ace scoring days were long gone.

MAROIS, Jean
b. Quebec City, Quebec, May 11, 1924
d. Quebec City, Quebec, 1996

He was known as the millionaire who played goal because he loved hockey, and he must have loved it a bunch because he played the game for more than a decade and made only three NHL appearances. He was 18 when he first entered the NHL on an emergency basis. He was a student at St. Mike's when Benny Grant, Toronto's starter, couldn't play on November 18, 1943. Marois was called in and gave up 5 goals in a 5-2 loss to Montreal. He then spent the better part of the next 10 years in the Quebec league, but on November 22, 1953, he was summoned to Chicago because Hawks regular Al Rollins came down with chicken pox and couldn't play. Again he gave up a bunch of goals – 11 in 2 games – and at the end of the next year he retired, winless in 3 NHL games, but a veteran of the great league all the same.

MAROIS, Mario
b. Quebec City, Quebec, December 15, 1957

Although Marois played for five NHL teams, his most cherished time was with his native Nordiques in Quebec City, where he was captain for three years and played for eight. He was a rock of a defenceman who played every shift as if it were his last, but he frequently played for weaker teams and never had a great deal of playoff success. His Rangers went to the finals in 1978-79 (his first full season) and the Nordiques to the semis in '85, but beyond that he never made it past the second round in his 15 years in the league. He finished his career in the minors and then in Switzerland, after which he became an amateur scout for Vancouver.

MAROTTE, Gilles ("Captain Crunch")
b. Montreal, Quebec, June 7, 1945

A fine catcher in Quebec league baseball, Marotte gave up the diamond game to focus on hockey. He broke into the NHL with Boston in 1965 and a year later his defence partner was 18-year-old Bobby Orr. The next year, Marotte was part of the package in the disastrous trade that brought Phil Esposito and Ken Hodge to Boston, and in his three seasons as a Hawk he never quite fit in. He was given the moniker Captain Crunch when he got to Los Angeles, and while fans appreciated his hard bodychecks the team never once made the playoffs and he was traded again, to the Rangers, in 1973. He later played with St. Louis before moving to the WHA to close out his career.

MARQUESS, Mark
b. Bassano, Alberta, March 26, 1924

Despite an enduring and impressive career in the minors, Marquess played with Boston in 1946-47 in just his second year as a pro and then never again in the NHL. The right winger became a reliable scorer in the AHL and WHL but never got a second chance after the Bruins were eliminated by Montreal in the semifinals of the '47 playoffs.

Patrick Marleau

Daniel Marois

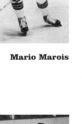

Mario Marois

Gilles Marotte

Brad Marsh

Gary Marsh

Peter Marsh

Bert Marshall

Don Marshall

MARSH, Brad
b. London, Ontario, March 31, 1958

In his final NHL season, '92-'93, Marsh not only played in his one and only All-Star Game, he scored a goal. This doesn't sound like too heroic an event, but for Marsh it was the symbolism more than the occurrence: The other team let him score, and did so because Marsh was one of the best-loved players around the league who also has the dubious honour of being the lowest-scoring player in NHL history over 1,000 games. In his 1,086 games, he scored just 23 times. That All-Star Game goal was no fluke – it was a gift! Marsh had been a high draft selection by Atlanta in 1978 and he moved with the team to Calgary two years later when the Flames relocated. He had his longest stay in Philadelphia (seven seasons), where he went to the finals in 1987. He also played with Toronto and Detroit before finishing with Ottawa, but wherever he went the fans loved him. He was all heart and effort, and almost no skill. He skated as if he were wearing snowshoes and his shot couldn't break wind. Yet every night the perspiration was there, the determination overcame the deficiency of natural ability, and Marsh survived 15 seasons. After retiring, he opened Marshy's, a bar/restaurant in the Corel Centre, home of the Senators. It became so popular he eventually was hired by the team to act as director of community relations, and he'll work there, perpetual smile on his face, until he chooses to retire.

MARSH, Gary
b. Toronto, Ontario, March 9, 1946

Marsh developed in the Red Wings system in the 1960s, but he played only six games with the Wings and one more with Toronto before being relegated to minor-league play.

MARSH, Peter
b. Halifax, Nova Scotia, December 21, 1956

Marsh was a fine skater and a terrific scorer, that wasn't the problem. The problem was his +/- statistic, which always showed that he was on the ice for more goals allowed than scored. A lot more. He played to score, but he didn't score so much that he could ignore defence, which he did anyway, and that got him into trouble with the coach. In the WHA, he was a defensive liability, and when he joined the NHL in 1979 with Winnipeg, the trend to awful minus figures continued. He was traded to Chicago where his defence improved, but his scoring also came to a near standstill.

MARSHALL, Bert
b. Kamloops, British Columbia, November 22, 1943

When Marshall made the NHL with Detroit in 1965, he couldn't have been happier. He was in the best league, playing for a great franchise, and his Wings went to the finals before losing to Montreal. When he was traded to Oakland in January 1968, he briefly thought it was a good opportunity, but as each game passed and players left town and the team kept losing – games, fans, money – Marshall grew despondent. He endured 6 seasons of hockey with that terrible franchise, a total of 313 games with no hope of playoff success. When he was traded to the Rangers, he knew

he wouldn't be staying long, but he was still playing and he was *not* in Oakland. The Islanders claimed him, and he enjoyed a rejuvenation, staying on the blueline for six more seasons and watching the team develop into a Cup contender. After retiring in 1979, he became an assistant coach to Al Arbour and then a head coach for the farm team in Indianapolis before returning to the NHL as a head coach with the woeful Rockies in 1981. It was a tenure that lasted all of 24 games, during which time Marshall's team had a record of 3-17-4.

MARSHALL, Don
b. Montreal, Quebec, March 23, 1932

For some NHL players, there is always a tradeoff with success. Take Marshall. He was a gifted centre and a great skater, and all through junior and the minors he proved he could score more than his share of goals. But when Montreal called him up in 1954, he was asked to be a defensive centre, a checker and penalty killer and harasser of the other team's top players. Marshall acquiesced to the change in style even though it was a less glorious assignment, and the payback was five successive Cups with the Habs from 1956 to '60. When he was traded to the Rangers in 1963, his scoring numbers increased. The Rangers knew what he could do offensively, and they asked him to do just that. In Montreal, he had 1 season of 20 goals or more (22 in '57-'58); in New York, he had 4 – but he didn't win another Stanley Cup. He finished his career with Buffalo and Toronto and returned to Montreal, where he worked in sales for a power transmission company. He also worked in a brokerage firm, and at 51 he retired to Florida to enjoy a life of leisure.

MARSHALL, Grant
b. Mississauga, Ontario, June 9, 1973

If any boy or girl needs a story of inspiration, this is it. If any boy or girl thinks life is tough, stop feeling self-pity and discover what Marshall plowed through to get to the NHL. As a boy, he had a learning disability and was hearing impaired in his right ear. In December 1990, he was hit from behind in junior, broke his neck, and wore a halo for months afterwards, only to recover and earn an invitation to Canada's camp for the '92 World Juniors a year later. The Leafs drafted him but sent him to Dallas as compensation for signing Peter Zezel, and even with the Stars, Marshall had problems understanding practice drills and breakout plays. The Stars helped him, and he responded, and in the spring of 1999 he held the Stanley Cup above his head. Life dealt Marshall no great hand, but he took what he was given and turned it into a royal flush. Nothing is impossible unless you say it is. So says Marshall.

MARSHALL, Jason
b. Cranbrook, British Columbia, February 22, 1971

Even expansion teams need tough guys, though Marshall is more than just a goon or fighter. In junior, back in 1990-91, he was not only among the leaders in penalty minutes in the WHL but also a gold-medal winner with Canada's junior team. After a short audition with St. Louis, Marshall spent most of the 1990s with Anaheim, playing his tough game with one of the new teams. Most recently, he ended up in

Minnesota performing a similar function with another expansion team.

MARSHALL, Paul
b. Toronto, Ontario, September 7, 1960

Every step of the way, they said this kid could play. Pittsburgh drafted him in 1979 and he decided to turn pro after just two years of junior, but no sooner had he made that decision than he became involved in a contract dispute. When that was resolved, he made the team and played rookie-well. He began poorly the next year, and Pens GM Baz Bastien traded him to Toronto with the salvo that he would never make the grade. Something to prove, Marshall returned home and didn't prove much more than Bastien's wisdom. Most of his time came in the minors, and in 1983 he retired at 23 to take over his father's business. Mr. Marshall had been an entrepreneur in the city, starting a service called Dial-a-Bottle, an alcohol home delivery service that Paul took over in 1984.

MARSHALL, Willie ("Willie the Whip")
b. Kirkland Lake, Ontario, December 1, 1931

Marshall can't quite be called the greatest player never to make the NHL because he did play 33 games for the Leafs as an emergency callup in the 1950s. But he is likely the greatest AHL player of all time, NHL appearances or not. From the time he started with Pittsburgh in 1952 till the time he retired in 1972, Marshall established Gretzky-like records in the American league for most goals (523), assists (852), points (1,375), games played (1,205), playoff assists (71), and playoff points (119). He shares the record for playoff goals with Fred Glover – 48. Yet despite this incredible longevity and success, Marshall has exactly one NHL goal and six points to his name. After retiring, he became the president of a small mining company that traded on the Alberta Stock Exchange, but settled in North Tonawanda, New York, after suffering a heart attack in 1985.

MARSON, Mike
b. Scarborough, Ontario, July 24, 1955

Is it important to know that Marson was just the second black NHLer ever after Willie O'Ree in 1960-61? Yes, because it points to an important racial fact about hockey. But, then again, no, because a player is a player. On that note, it must be pointed out that when the 19-year-old showed up to camp in Washington in 1974, he was a blimp. He worked himself into shape and ate properly, eventually reducing 22 pounds to his playing weight of 200. He scored 16 goals that year on the worst team in league history, and his -65 is clear indication of that. The next year he struggled, and the year after and the year after that, too. In six pro seasons he spent more time in the minors, but at least he made some inroads for blacks to play the modern game.

MARTIN, Clare ("Square")
b. Waterloo, Ontario, February 25, 1922
d. unknown

Martin began in the Boston system, playing for the Olympics before getting called up to the B's in 1941-42. It was five years before he saw the NHL again, and over the next five years he played for four Original Six

teams, winning a Cup with Detroit in 1950. He later returned to Kitchener and played amateur hockey with the Dutchmen, winning the Allan Cup in both '53 and '55 and retiring after being signed as an emergency replacement for the 1956 playoffs.

MARTIN, Craig
b. Amherst, Nova Scotia, January 21, 1971

Primarily a fighter, Martin played pro for a decade including, 21 NHL games. He played here and there and everywhere, dropping the gloves in the name of his team time and time again until packing his bags in 2001 and going home for keeps.

MARTIN, Frank
b. Cayuga, Ontario, May 1, 1933

In the spring of 1953, Martin rejected a contract offer from the Brooklyn Dodgers so he could continue his burgeoning career in the ice game. He had played briefly with Boston the previous year, and at camp in the fall of '53 he made the team full-time. He was traded straight up to Chicago the next year for Murray Costello, and he played his last four seasons with the Hawks. Martin then continued in the AHL for a number of seasons, and throughout his career he was known for being the only ambidextrous shooter besides Gordie Howe. Depending on where he found himself or where the puck came to him, he was equally adept at shooting left or right.

MARTIN, Grant
b. Smooth Rock Falls, Ontario, March 13, 1962

Martin played on the 1982 Kitchener Rangers team that won the Memorial Cup, and after a year in the minors he saw some NHL time with Vancouver. Whether it was the Canucks or, subsequently, the Capitals, he saw only spot duty as a left winger, spending the greatest part of his career in the minors. In 1987 he moved to Europe, where he extended his career another decade, eventually settling in Germany where he played for nine seasons.

MARTIN, Hubert "Pit"
b. Noranda, Quebec, December 9, 1943

Like Mush March and Gump Worsley, Pit Martin got his nickname from a comic strip character in a newspaper. He was always one of the smaller players in the league and one of the first to wear a helmet for safety reasons. Martin began his career with Detroit in 1962 before a trade sent him to Boston in 1965. He played with the Bruins for a year and a half and then had the misfortune to be included in the bad trade that sent him, Jack Norris, and Gilles Marotte to Chicago for Phil Esposito, Ken Hodge, and Fred Stanfield in one of the more lopsided deals in league history. Happily, Martin flourished in Chicago. He had seven 20-goal seasons and was a part of the core of the team that went to the Cup finals in 1971 and '73. Martin won the Bill Masterton Trophy in 1970 and played in four All-Star Games. He was always a gentlemanly player and a scholar, having earned a degree in French and history from Windsor College. After retiring, he settled in St. Clair Beach, Ontario, where he opened a restaurant. He later sold it and started a business specializing in swimming pool servicing.

Paul Marshall

Mike Marson

Clare Martin

Frank Martin

Pit Martin

Rick Martin

Ron Martin

Seth Martin

Terry Martin

Tom Martin
(b. 1947)

MARTIN, John "Jack"
b. St. Catharines, Ontario, November 29, 1940
Martin will always remember the night of November 27, 1960, because it was his one and only NHL game, playing for the Leafs. He'll also remember it because Gordie Howe scored his 1,000th point that night, the first player in NHL history to reach that mark. Terry Sawchuk also got the shutout in Detroit's 2-0 win, and after the game Martin was on his way back to the minors. He later had two great seasons in the EHL, recording consecutive 100-point seasons before retiring in 1965.

MARTIN, Matt ("Marty")
b. Hamden, Connecticut, April 30, 1971
It seemed like a great choice when the Leafs drafted Martin right out of high school. He went on to play for the Black Bears at U of Maine at the same time Paul Kariya was there, and they won the NCAA championship in 1993. Martin spent the next year with the U.S. National Team and played at the 1994 Olympics in Lillehammer, after which he joined the Leafs. He was a terrific prospect in every way. He had size and quickness and was skilled at taking the man and moving the puck. But every time the Leafs promoted him, they quickly demoted him, and when he got a chance to play regularly, he broke his ankle and missed weeks of action. Nothing changed in 1998 when he signed with Dallas – the Stars kept him in the system but never recalled him. A once-mighty defenceman is now just looking for a chance.

MARTIN, Rick ("Rico")
b. Verdun, Quebec, July 26, 1951
Scotty Bowman may have hung around the game a long time and attached himself to great teams for many years, but there are a few people scattered about the hockey world who have choice words to say about him, and Martin is one of them. The fantastic left winger came out of the Montreal Jr. Canadiens, winning two Memorial Cups and then leading the league in goals with 71 in '70-'71. He played for the Sabres for nine years on one of the great lines of the modern era, the French Connection Line, with Gilbert Perreault and Rene Robert. Martin never scored fewer than 28 goals, 3 times scored more than 40, and twice scored 52 in a season. He played in seven All-Star Games. But on November 9, 1980, his career came to an end. Coming down the left wing, he ran into goalie Mike Palmateer and injured his knee. Coach Scotty Bowman insisted Martin was fine and kept playing him. Martin played another seven games until he could barely walk. To save face, Bowman traded him to L.A., convincing the Kings the injury wasn't so bad. Over the next two years, though, Martin played just four games until doctors told him he risked permanent and debilitating injury if he continued. He was 30 years old. Martin then filed a $10-million lawsuit against the Sabres, Bowman, and the team doctor, alleging they had forced him to play while he was seriously injured. Martin settled in Niagara Falls, New York, and opened a restaurant. He also opened an automotive shop and operated a trucking firm. He later invested in a gold mining project in Côte d'Ivoire that proved successful, and he bought a 120-acre farm in New York State.

MARTIN, Ron
b. Calgary, Alberta, August 22, 1909
d. Los Angeles, California, February 8, 1971
He was no star at any level, but Martin had a long and fruitful career, at least until the war broke out. He started out third time lucky, going to the Memorial Cup three times with the Calgary Canadiens before finally winning it in 1926. From there he turned pro, and until 1941 had a regular job skating and shooting, notably with Buffalo in the International league and Portland out west. His NHL time came with the New York Americans (1932-34) after the Red Wings traded him there, but his two full seasons on Broadway yielded no further interest or takers elsewhere in the NHL.

MARTIN, Seth
b. Rossland, British Columbia, May 4, 1933
To the modern North American fan, the name might not mean a whole lot, but in the 1960s he was far and away the most popular Canadian in Europe. He would walk down the streets of Rome or Prague and people would call out his name in admiration; "Seeeth! Seeeth!" they would cry. At home, Martin was Trail's goalie for many years, but internationally he played in more tournaments for Canada than any other 'tender. He played at the World Championships in 1961, '63, '66, and '67. He played at the 1964 Olympics in Innsbruck, and he played most of those years with Father Bauer's National Team. Martin didn't play in the NHL until he joined St. Louis in 1967 at age 34, sharing the duties with Glenn Hall. But more important than those few games with the Blues was his induction into the IIHF Hall of Fame to honour his years with Canada's teams. After retiring, Martin returned to Trail, where he opened a sporting goods store. He later worked as a fireman for Cominco Mines and became the manager of the very Smoke Eaters for whom he had played so long.

MARTIN, Terry
b. Barrie, Ontario, October 25, 1955
The problem with the NHL draft is that it's surrounded by so much hype fans and executives alike expect instant results from their choices. Truth is, though, 18-year-olds take 5 to 7 years to mature and develop. Martin was drafted by Buffalo in 1975, but by the time he had his best years the Sabres had long given up on him. In '80-'81 and '81-'82, with Toronto, he had seasons of 23 and 25 goals and was a terrific all-round player for the team. Having gotten the most out of him, Toronto traded him to Edmonton, and he finished in the minors after a brief stop in Minnesota. Martin turned to coaching, first in the AHL with Newmarket, then with the Marlies in Toronto, and finally in the Buffalo system with Rochester. He ended up as a scout for the Sabres.

MARTIN, Tom
b. Toronto, Ontario, October 16, 1947
d. Ottawa, Ontario, August 24, 2002
It was pretty clear to Martin early on that he wasn't going to be scooping up any 200th goal puck or be honoured for 1,000 NHL games. That didn't limit his options, merely directed them. He won a Memorial Cup with the Marlies in 1967 and played his only three NHL games, with the Leafs, the following season. He later played in the minors and signed with the WHA

when the chance arose, but in 1975 he accepted an offer to play for and coach a team in Sweden. He stayed there for four years, then returned home to coach the Bramalea Blues in Metro junior B and the year after in Milton. In 1983, he was hired to coach the Marlies, but his term lasted only two seasons before he was fired. From 1964 to 1992, Martin served with the RCEME Corps of the Canadian forces, and another decade as a civilian consultant. He was with the Canadian Airborne Regiment for five years (1976-81) and passed away after a short fight with brain cancer.

MARTIN, Tom
b. Kelowna, British Columbia, May 11, 1965

There's never been a trade like it – never. On January 19, 1983, the Seattle Breakers of the WHL traded the rights to Tom Martin to the Victoria Cougars – for a used bus. The Breakers' old bus had recently broken down and they had a player, Martin, they weren't using, so the deal was a natural fit for owner John Hamilton. It was, of course, embarrassing for the player. One night, Martin wasn't having a very good game, so a fan screamed out, "Hey! Put in the bus!" Martin made it to the NHL in a more traditional manner, via the draft, but in six seasons he was always up and down between the big club and the farm. He retired in late 1990. No word is available as to how long the bus lasted.

MARTINEAU, Don
b. Kimberley, British Columbia, April 25, 1952

In a six-year pro career, Martineau played for as many teams, three in the NHL in the 1970s. He was drafted by Atlanta in 1972 and moved on to play for Minnesota and Detroit before retiring in 1978.

MARTINEK, Radek
b. Halickuv Brod, Czechoslovakia (Czech Republic), August 31, 1976

After the Islanders drafted him in 1999, Martinek stayed in the Czech Republic and played two more years before venturing to the New York training camp. He looked so good that he made the team, but his fine first year was cut short by a serious knee injury. He had helped the Czechs win gold at the 2001 World Championships, and in 2002-03 he rejoined the Isles to continue his NHL career.

MARTINI, Darcy
b. Castlegar, British Columbia, January 30, 1969

A graduate of Michigan Tech, Martini has been sampling hockey around the world since leaving the Huskies in 1992. His only NHL stop was a two-game stint with the Oilers in '93-'94, and beyond that he has

played in the "I" and throughout Europe, from Austria to Germany to, most recently, Italy.

MARTINS, Steve
b. Gatineau, Quebec, April 13, 1972

After scoring a goal in his first NHL game, Martins hasn't had a long streak of luck or good fortune. He spent most of his first three years in the Hartford/Carolina system and played himself onto Ottawa at his first camp with the Sens in 1998. He missed part of that season with injury, though, and since then has been on the move, returning to the Senators during the 2001-02 season.

MARTINSON, Steve
b. Minnetonka, Minnesota, June 21, 1959

He turned pro in 1981 at age 22, even though he had no hope of going anywhere. He hadn't played junior, hadn't been drafted, and hadn't made an impact on anyone. Yet Toledo signed him to an IHL contract, and the left winger played his way through time until Detroit called him up for a few games some six years later. He later played with Montreal and Minnesota, but Martinson found his true calling in San Diego. He finished his playing career there and then became the team's coach, winning four league titles and becoming the winningest coach in WCHL history.

Maruk is the most anonymous 60-goal scorer in NHL history.
DENNIS MARUK

MARUK, Dennis ("Pee Wee")
b. Toronto, Ontario, November 17, 1955

Maruk is, without a shadow of a doubt, the most anonymous 60-goal scorer in NHL history. Like any Toronto kid worth his hockey salt, Maruk played junior with the Marlies – that is, until the team traded him to London so the Howe brothers could play together. Maruk was so upset he almost gave up hockey to play lacrosse (he was a great goalie) but he reported to the Knights and became one of their greatest scorers. He continued to score when he got to the NHL, and his achievements were amazing for a number of reasons: one, junior scorers seldom became NHL scorers; two, he was small; three, he played on awful, awful teams. In fact, Maruk's California, Cleveland, Minnesota, and Washington teams didn't make the playoffs his first 9 years in the league, yet he had seasons of 50 and 60 goals, the latter including 76 assists for 136 points with the Capitals, a team that finished 15th out of 21 overall and scored only 319 total goals. As a result, Maruk was usually available for the World Championships and represented Canada four times. He retired in 1989 with 356 goals to his credit. Maruk worked for a marketing firm in Minneapolis and later became the director of hockey operations for the Baton Rouge Kingfish of the ECHL.

Tom Martin (b. 1965)

Don Martineau

Steve Martins

Steve Martinson

Paul Masnick

Bob Mason

Charley Mason

Jamie Masters

MASNICK, Paul
b. Regina, Saskatchewan, April 14, 1931

Because Masnick wasn't quite in the star class of many of the other Montreal players of the 1950s, his time with the Habs was forever tenuous. There were some years, such as '52-'53, when he took a regular shift all year and won the Stanley Cup, and there were others when he played just a handful of games. He was more of a checker in the NHL, but in the minors he proved his worth as a scorer.

MASON, Bob
b. International Falls, Minnesota, April 22, 1961

Imagine an hyperbolic curve. The line leading to the top of it represents Mason's early career, his four frustrating years in Washington during which time he had to fight for every game in goal and every starting assignment. The peak is the '87-'88 season, when he played 41 games for Chicago and was the Hawks' starter. The line back down is the time after that season, starting with the summer of '88 when a double whammy knocked him out of the Chicago cage. One, he became embroiled in a contract dispute with the team; two, the Hawks signed a young NCAA winner named Ed Belfour (a.k.a. Eddie the Eagle). Mason was traded to Quebec for, ironically, Mike Eagles, and played fewer and fewer games as his career came to a quick close. Mason can claim two other notable facts on his resumé: He played for the U.S. at the 1984 Olympics in Sarajevo, and he was in goal the night Washington and the Islanders played a four-OT playoff game in 1987, ended by a Pat LaFontaine goal on Mason. He later became goalie consultant for the Atlanta Thrashers.

MASON, Charley ("Dutch")
b. Seaforth, Ontario, February 1, 1912
d. Saskatoon, Saskatchewan, May 17, 1971

In the early days of the NHL, it was not uncommon for a player to come out of a Canadian university, and Mason was a case in point from U of Saskatchewan. He made his NHL debut with the Rangers in 1934, and over the next five years played for a variety of teams in the league. He played the majority of his career, though, in the minors, and after he retired he settled in his adopted province, opening an hotel in Saskatoon. He also had local business interests in real estate and with radio station CKOM.

MASON, Chris
b. Red Deer, Alberta, April 20, 1976

In the days after Ron Hextall and Martin Brodeur started scoring goals with accurate long shots, we forget the good old days when someone like Billy Smith was credited with scoring because he was the last opponent to touch the puck when a team scored on its own goal. Well, Mason recalls that simpler era. While playing for Milwaukee, he made a shoulder save on a delayed penalty, and his opponent shot the puck down the ice errantly into his own empty net. Goal to Mason. His career with the Admirals has been fine, but the parent team in Nashville hasn't been as kind to him, giving him but a few games' worth of action to date.

MASSECAR, George
b. Waterford, Ontario, July 10, 1904
d. Niagara Falls, Ontario, July 14, 1957

Left winger Massecar played all of his 100 NHL games with the New York Americans, but the team didn't qualify for the playoffs during his 3 years with them (1929-32) and he was traded before the start of the '32-'33 season. He ended his career in 1936 in the minors.

If Masterton played today, he wouldn't have even flinched at that fatal check.
BILL MASTERTON

MASTERS, Jamie
b. Toronto, Ontario, April 14, 1955

He had everything going for him but his career, so he packed his goodies and headed for Europe. Masters did it all according to the textbook. He had a good junior career. He was drafted, by St. Louis in 1975. He got his callups and developed in the minors. But that breakthrough training camp never happened. That injury to the regular to give him a chance never materialized. That great game that raised the coach's eyebrows never occurred. So, he left, went to Germany and made a perfectly good living playing defence on the Continent.

MASTERTON, Bill
b. Winnipeg, Manitoba, August 13, 1938
d. Minneapolis, Minnesota, January 15, 1968

While the great expansion of 1967 gave so many players a chance to prove their NHL skills, it also led to Masterton's tragic and untimely death. He grew up in Winnipeg, but in 1957 he decided to attend the University of Denver where he could study and play. He earned a degree in engineering but in his final year he was also named MVP at the 1961 NCAA tournament. He earned a master's degree in finance and played pro in the minors for two years. He retired to work for Honeywell Corporation in Minneapolis and also played for the U.S. National Team when the opportunity arose. In the summer of '67, Montreal sold his rights to Minnesota, and the opportunity to give the NHL a chance, without having to move, was too great a rabbit not to chase. He tossed aside the helmet he had worn throughout his college days and joined the Stars, proving to be a fast skater capable of scoring. But on January 13, 1968, in a game against California, he was checked hard and fell backward, hitting his head on the ice. It was the kind of play that had happened a million times in the game, but on this occasion Masterton couldn't protect his head or react quickly enough. He lapsed into a coma, and two days later died in hospital with his wife, children, parents, and brother by his side. The accident occurred just two days before the All-Star Game, a celebration that had a pall cast over it by the tragedy. Players still refused to wear a helmet despite the senselessness of his death, but the NHL introduced the Masterton Trophy, to be given annually to a player who exemplifies perseverance and dedication to the game. That first season, Claude Provost of Montreal won the award and Masteron's memory lived on. Today, every NHLer wears a helmet. If Masterton played today, he wouldn't have even flinched at that fatal check.

MATHERS, Frank
b. Winnipeg, Manitoba, March 29, 1924

Oh, but the best laid plans took Mathers out of the classroom and onto the ice almost without him knowing it. He played hockey and football in his youth but what he really wanted was an education. He was good friends with Bobby Copp, who played a little hockey and then left the NHL to become a dentist. Mathers wanted the same thing. He took two years of sciences at Ottawa University and played senior hockey with the Senators, and in 1946 he also played for the Rough Riders in the CFL before he was told to quit (because of the injury risk). Conn Smythe then tempted him with an offer, one he had already rejected from the Rangers. For Mathers, though, five years of dentistry in school and five more to start a practice was difficult to justify given Smythe's offer. He signed with the Leafs, and figured if it didn't work out dentistry was still an option. As it turned out, there was another road in his life. The Leafs used him only a few times over the years, and he spent most of 1948-56 in the AHL with their affiliate in Pittsburgh. Then, he was traded to the Hershey Bears, and his life changed. That first year, he was a playing coach, and over the next six years he guided the team to three Calder Cups. When he retired as a player in '62, he was the AHL's all-time leader in assists and points for a defenceman. He remained coach for the next 11 years, and in 1973 was named president and GM. Over the next 18 years, the Bears won 3 more AHL championships and Mathers established himself as the single most important man in that franchise's history. He retired in 1991 and was given his own special night in Hershey in tribute to his contributions to the team. He was awarded the Lester Patrick Trophy in 1987 and five years later was inducted into the Hockey Hall of Fame as a Builder. He started his career reluctantly in 1948 as a Leafs defenceman, and ended it 43 years later far away from the world of dentistry but far and away one of the most important executives the game has ever known.

MATHIASEN, Dwight
b. Brandon, Manitoba, May 12, 1963

The hullabaloo that surrounded the signing of Mathiasen was as cacophonic as was the complaining after he started his NHL career. While at the University of Denver, Mathiasen looked to be another innocuous player until his third year ('85-'86) when he started to score in bunches and attract every scout's eye. Everyone shuffled around bemoaning the fact that the right winger hadn't been drafted, and some 10 teams bid for his services. Pittsburgh gave him a $1-million contract in the hopes he'd play right side to Mario Lemieux's centre. The Penguins brain trust saw goals and more goals from this deadly duo. As it turned out, Mathiasen was deadly because of the stink, not the shot. Over 3 seasons he scored 1 goal in 33 games, and all other teams and scouts heaved a sigh of relief that they had lost the now-preposterous bidding war. Mathiasen soon retired and changed his life's course. He returned to U of Denver to finish his degree in finance and then became a consultant and estate planner with Lincoln Financial Advisors. From there he went to Plumpjack Wines, and in September 2001 he was hired by Signorello Wines of Napa Valley, California, as their national sales director.

MATHIESON, Jim
b. Kindersley, Saskatchewan, January 24, 1970

Just because the NHL couldn't use him, didn't mean he had to pack it in. No, Mathieson played two games for Washington in 1989-90 and then plied his trade in the AHL for years before he accepted an offer to play in Britain in 1996. Since then, he played for Newcastle and Nottingham before joining the Ayr Smelly Eagles, as opponents mockingly call the Ayr Scottish Eagles.

MATHIEU, Marquis
b. Hartford, Connecticut, May 31, 1973

It's not only that he played a ton in the minors before getting into his first NHL game; it's that, even down there, he was traded and demoted and shifted from team to team! After graduating from the Q, Mathieu played five years of minor hockey for a total of eight teams before the Bruins signed him. His first game was a satisfying 9-2 drubbing over Boston's worst enemy, Montreal, but Mathieu didn't crack the lineup for long before being demoted. The year after, he suffered a bad hip injury that took almost a full year to heal, and he then lapsed into his minor-league ways again.

MATTE, Christian
b. Hull, Quebec, January 20, 1975

One of the better discrepancies between the NHL and AHL is this Matte fella. In the NHL, he's barely been able to find the net. In the AHL, with Hershey in 1999-2000, he led the league in points. He's small and a proven asset at the under-NHL level, and in the summer of 2002 he signed to play in Switzerland where the salary is fine, the schedule half that in North America, and the living a whole lot better than in Chocolatetown, USA.

MATTE, Joe
b. Bourget, Ontario, March 6, 1893
d. Montreal, Quebec, June 13, 1961

What everyone knows about the Toronto St. Pats, precursors to the Maple Leafs, is that they were given that nickname to capitalize on the large Irish population in the city. What few people know is that part of that marketing called for local players of "English" extraction to prevail in the lineup. Matte, a

Frank Mathers

Dwight Mathiasen

Christian Matte

Stephane Matteau

Dick Mattiussi

Markus Mattson

**Richard
Matvichuk**

French-Canadian, was one of the few who broke the mould when he played for the Pats in '19-'20. He later played for Hamilton, Boston, and the Canadiens in the NHL, and out west he played for the Vancouver Maroons in '23-'24, the team that lost to the Canadiens in the Stanley Cup playdowns.

MATTE, Joe
b. Bourget, Ontario, March 15, 1908
d. unknown
Matte has the distinction of making his first NHL appearance in 1929 (with Detroit) and his next one in 1942 (with Chicago), a 13-year gap that is among the longest between appearances in NHL history. In between, he played mostly with the St. Louis Flyers of the American league. His son, Tom, played for the Baltimore Colts of the NFL from 1961 to '72.

MATTEAU, Stephane
b. Rouyn Noranda, Quebec, September 2, 1969
Stephane Matteau and Pierre Turgeon played baseball together, and in 1982 they were in the Little League World Series together. Both, of course, went on to become fine hockey players. Matteau played junior in Hull, Quebec, on a line with Jeremy Roenick and Martin Gelinas. Drafted by Calgary, Matteau made his NHL debut with the Flames to start the '90-'91 season, and he's been in the league ever since. Matteau established a reputation as a defensive forward, a skill that came in handy a few years later when the Rangers acquired him at the deadline in 1994. A few weeks later, the Blueshirts won the Cup, and Matteau was an integral part of that victory. He scored the series-winning goal in game 7 of the semifinals against New Jersey, a goal that was later ranked as the 31st most important in the Top 100 moments in New York City's sports history. He later moved on to St. Louis and San Jose, and has been with the Sharks continuously since 1997.

MATTEUCCI, Mike
b. Trail, British Columbia, December 27, 1971
An odd transition is for a player to go from college hockey – where fighting is more or less banned – to the pros, where he becomes a tough guy. Such is the life of Matteucci, who played on Lake Superior State's 1994 NCAA championship team. He went on to play briefly for Minnesota, but his years in the IHL were marked by fighting majors and rough play, something he didn't hone in college hockey. He has yet to make a name for himself in the NHL, though.

MATTIUSSI, Dick
b. Smooth Rock Falls, Ontario, May 1, 1938
Recruited by Toronto in the mid-1950s, Mattiussi was sent to St. Mike's by the Leafs, but they traded him to the AHL in a multiplayer deal to get Kent Douglas before he ever appeared for Toronto. Before turning pro, he played a season in Kitchener with the Dutchmen under coach Bill Durnan. Mattiussi played only with expansion teams in the early years of the 12-team NHL. He was much more highly regarded for his AHL career, which constituted 12 years, mostly with Rochester and Cleveland, where his reputation was impeccable. The defenceman retired in 1974 to coach the Amerks, and

later returned to Smooth Rock Falls where he became safety coordinator for Mallette Kraft-SRF.

MATTSSON, Markus
b. Suoniemi, Finland, July 30, 1957
A career's worth of headlines tells a story of great promise and diminishing returns. Mattsson was Finland's national goalie in '76-'77, first at the '76 Canada Cup, then at the '77 Worlds. He came to North America to play in the WHA and made a favourable impression. Winnipeg signed him to a long-term contract when the Jets joined the NHL in 1979, and the team heralded him as the goalie of the future. Two part-time seasons later, he was released outright. Then, after signing with Minnesota, he was traded. In all, his record of 21-46-14 gave little proof of those early accolades and press conferences trumpeting his future. Mattsson returned to Finland to finish his career.

MATVICHUK, Richard
b. Edmonton, Alberta, February 5, 1973
One of the last survivors from the North Stars days, Matvichuk has played his whole career with the Minnesota/Dallas franchise. He started as a North Stars draft choice in 1991 and worked his way up through the minors to become a regular in 1995. Matvichuk is a perfect combination of a great defensive defenceman who can block shots and an offensive player who can quarterback the power play and move the puck quickly. His maturity came in sync with the maturity of the team and franchise, and it was in large part due to his play that the Stars won the Cup in 1999 and went back to the finals the year after. He was named the WHL's best defenceman in '91-'92, the same year he represented Canada at the World Juniors.

MATZ, Johnny
b. Caspar, Wyoming, June 1, 1892
d. White Rock, British Columbia, December 21, 1969
Matz played most of his career out west in the formative days of hockey, when the NHL wasn't the only game in town. In 1924-25, he became one of the first American-born players to start for the Canadiens, at centre, but his career with the Habs lasted just that one year.

MAXNER, Wayne
b. Halifax, Nova Scotia, September 27, 1942
As a junior in Niagara Falls, Maxner was a dynamite prospect who was sure to explode when he hit the NHL. Unfortunately, he imploded instead. He indulged in a number of damaging off-ice habits, most importantly drinking, and he lost his skill and edge. He had one decent season with Boston in '64-'65 but the left winger sunk into the AHL and leagues below until there was almost nowhere left for him to play. A broken leg in 1968 didn't help his career, either. Around 1973, he got a coaching job with the Spits in Windsor and straightened himself out. In succeeding years, he had a number of junior jobs and he coached the Red Wings for parts of two horrid seasons during their lean years. In all, he was fired no fewer than five times in junior. In between the successes and debris of his coaching life he returned home to Halifax and operated a Pizza Delight franchise. He was only the second Haligonian, after Bert Hirschfield, to make the NHL.

MAXWELL, Brad
b. Brandon, Manitoba, July 8, 1957

Like many a kid, Maxwell was influenced by his dad at an early age, and although Mr. Maxwell was a semi-pro hockey player, he was also a superb golfer. Thus, Brad, learned golf before hockey, perhaps an explanation for his excellent slapshot years later when he took the puck game more seriously. In junior, in the 1970s, he played on the New Westminster teams that routinely went to the Memorial Cup with their goon tactics, and Maxwell's moment of turning pro was likely the most bizarre in the annals of the sport. He agreed to a contract with Birmingham of the WHA in 1977, and but for a connecting flight he would have started his career there rather than with Minnesota in the NHL. However, en route to Alabama, he had to change planes in Chicago. He was met (or, in Birmingham parlance, ambushed) at O'Hare by the North Stars, who prettied up their contract offer, got him to accept, and flew him to the Twin Cities. Meanwhile, down in Birmingham, owner John Bassett, a band, a group of luminaries, and even Miss Alabama awaited the arrival of Maxwell – an arrival that never came! Maxwell remained in Minnesota for eight years, helping the team get to the Cup finals in 1981 for the first time. He was among the top defencemen in the league for a few years and played at the World Championships for Canada on three occasions. Injuries slowed him down and with time he became expendable. In his last three seasons, he played for five teams, including the North Stars twice, and by this time he knew his career was done.

> **Like many a kid, Maxwell was influenced by his dad at an early age.**
> **BRAD MAXWELL**

MAXWELL, Bryan ("Jaws")
b. North Bay, Ontario, September 7, 1955

It's a common situation that happens to at least a few players every year. They become embroiled in a contract dispute, so they stay at home and skate with the local junior team to stay in shape and wait for the finances of their game to be resolved. That's what happened to Maxwell in September 1984. The only unusual thing was that he returned to the junior team the first chance he got. During his stop-and-start NHL career, Maxwell was a protector of talent rather than a purveyor of fine qualities, but he was forever missing time because of injury. Then, in the fall of '84, he and Pittsburgh couldn't come to terms, so he skated with Medicine Hat. Coach Doug Sauter suggested he stay as an assistant coach, and a year later he did. Since then, that's been Maxwell's line of work, mostly in junior though for a season with L.A. in the NHL under two coaches, Mike Murphy and Robbie Ftorek.

MAXWELL, Kevin
b. Edmonton, Alberta, March 30, 1960

During his playing days, Maxwell was likely the most unabashed stick collector in the league. With a kid-like joy, he'd ask opponents for their twig so he could add it to his collection. He had to work quickly, too, because his career started with Minnesota in 1981 and finished 3 years later after 66 games. He had won a national championship with U of North Dakota in 1979 and played for Canada at the 1980 Olympics in Lake Placid, and after a number of years in the minors Maxwell found his true calling as a scout. He filled that position for Philadelphia (four years), Hartford (four years, two as director of scouting), and then the Islanders, where he has been since 1996.

Kevin Maxwell

MAXWELL, Wally
b. Ottawa, Ontario, August 24, 1933

Most every player in the Leafs system – the Marlies or St. Mike's – got at least a quick tryout with the big club at Maple Leaf Gardens, and Maxwell was no exception. He played on January 10 and 14, 1953, at the ripe old age of 19, his first, last, and only NHL games.

Wally Maxwell

MAY, Alan
b. Swan Hills, Alberta, January 14, 1965

When his teammates called *"m'aidez"* May jumped right in and helped out. That was his job during his NHL career, and he did it well and admirably. He was never drafted but turned pro in the AHL in 1986 before signing with Boston a year later. May spent the longest stretch of time in Washington, but by 1995 he had been relegated to the IHL, where he stayed until getting into the coaching business. In 1999, he was hired as the first boss for the Lubbock Cotton Kings in the WPHL, and after a very respectable season, he resigned. May also coached the Dallas Stallions in roller hockey.

Alan May

MAY, Brad
b. Toronto, Ontario, November 29, 1971

A paradox within a conundrum in a puzzle, May was many things as a person and a player. On the surface, he is a fighter who made a living as an enforcer, from the time he entered the league in 1991 to the present with Phoenix. Yet on April 24, 1993, he scored one of the most important goals in Buffalo history when his overtime shot eliminated the Bruins from the playoffs, the first time in a decade the Sabres had won a post-season series. Recently, he got into a fight with the law outside an Arizona nightclub, but May has also been active in charity work with children throughout his career. Not blessed with much hockey savvy and

Brad May

talent, he has also been taking courses in golf course architecture to ready himself for a post-NHL career.

Darrell May

MAY, Darrell
b. Edmonton, Alberta, March 6, 1962
It's hard to believe, but after a spectacular career with Portland in junior, and a terrific start to the pros in the minors, May flopped during his chance in the NHL. Vancouver drafted him in 1980, but it wasn't until St. Louis signed him five years later that he had any chance at all after taking Peoria to a Turner Cup in 1985. He played just six games with the Blues but made a more favourable impression with the Rivermen before retiring in 1989. Since then, May has stayed in the game. He acted as either a scout or a goaltending consultant for a number of teams before settling down with Kootenay in 1996, and in 2001 he was named to both positions with the Tri-City Americans. For his career in Peoria, May was inducted into the Central Illinois Sports Hall of Fame, the first hockey player so honoured.

Derek Mayer

MAYER, Derek
b. Rossland, British Columbia, May 21, 1967
Canadians who play a good deal of international hockey usually end up playing in Europe, both because of the style of play and because of their availability. Mayer appeared in just 17 games with Ottawa in '93-'94, but played three and a half seasons with the National Team as well as two World Championships and the 1994 Olympics in Lillehammer. After leaving the University of Denver, he gave the minors a try, but the Senators experience told him he wasn't likely to get called up again soon. He moved the Europe and has been playing in Germany since 1996.

Shep Mayer

MAYER, Edwin "Shep"
b. Sturgeon Falls, Ontario, September 11, 1923
As a teen, Mayer won numerous hockey and rugby titles in Sturgeon Falls, but he was particularly noted in hockey circles for his great solo dashes that involved speeding in on the goalie and then stopping suddenly to pick an opening the falling or sliding goalie had left. He impressed Leafs GM Frank Selke, who played Mayer in a dozen games in '42-'43, but Mayer enlisted in the Royal Canadian Air Force and that spelled the end of his NHL career. He remained in the military for many years after the war and eventually moved to North Bay.

MAYER, Gilles "Gil" ("The Needle")
b. Ottawa, Ontario, August 24, 1930
Didn't matter how good he was, Mayer just wasn't going to beat out Turk Broda or Harry Lumley as the Leafs goalie. And Mayer was good. If he had played in 1967, he likely would have been the first man taken in the Expansion Draft. Instead, he had to settle for a Hall of Fame career in the AHL, where he played nearly 700 games and retired second in career shutouts with 42, behind only a guy named Johnny Bower. He replaced Broda for a game in 1949, and in subsequent years replaced Lumley for eight games. In the AHL, he won five Calder Cups and had the best goals-against average on five

Jamal Mayers

occasions despite standing in the crease at 5'7" and 128 pounds. After retiring, he settled in Lincoln, Rhode Island (he finished his career in Providence), and for more than 20 years worked for the state's building department.

MAYER, Jim
b. Capreol, Ontario, October 30, 1954
NHL teams drafted 247 players in 1974, and Mayer was the 239th selection that season. He played just four games, with the Rangers five years later, but that alone is an accomplishment. The winger graduated from Michigan Tech and played in the WHA for three seasons, though even there most of his time came in the minors. He retired in 1982 despite a trade to the hopeless Rockies two years previous that yielded no further NHL time. In '78-'79, Mayer scored a CHL record: six goals in a game with Dallas, farm team of the Edmonton Oilers.

MAYER, Pat
b. Royal Oak, Michigan, July 24, 1961
The key to being a quality goon is to get into fights that end up in equal penalty minutes for the two teams. A fighter can't take the proverbial dumb penalty to leave his team short-handed – that defeats the purpose. Mayer got his call for a single game with Pittsburgh in '87-'88 during a season in which he was accumulating a league-leading 450 minutes in the IHL. He accrued two minors in his one game with the Pens and never played another game with that team or any other in the NHL.

MAYERS, Jamal ("Jammer")
b. Toronto, Ontario, October 24, 1974
Graduating from Western Michigan, Mayers made his NHL debut, with St. Louis, in 1996, though he spent most of that season in the minors. He played himself into the lineup within two seasons and has been a solid, third-line player ever since, though he has been part of a Blues team that has had disappointing playoff results after superb play in the regular season. He is a decent combination of skating, scoring, and defence, though he'll never become a force so much as part of a winning team.

MAZUR, Eddie ("Spider")
b. Winnipeg, Manitoba, July 25, 1929
d. Winnipeg, Manitoba, July 3, 1995
Mazur spent 6 of his 18 professional years in the NHL, mostly with Montreal, in the 1950s. He had two quick callups in '50-'51 and '51-'52, but the following year he had an impact in the playoffs, scoring two goals and helping the Habs win the Stanley Cup. The next year, he stayed the full season, frequently playing on a line with Jean Béliveau and Bernie Geoffrion and again going to the finals before losing to Detroit. He finished with Chicago, but once he was demoted to the AHL for good, Mazur had a long and distinguished career. He had 6 consecutive 20-goal seasons in the AHL. After retiring, he returned to Winnipeg and worked with Molson Brewery for 15 years in sales. He also co-owned the Brooklands Inn and performed a great deal of volunteer work in the city before succumbing to cancer.

MAZUR, Jay
b. Hamilton, Ontario, January 22, 1965

When you're 35 or 36 and you're signing contracts with teams like the Alexandria Warthogs or the New Haven Knights you know the NHL is a long-distant memory. Mazur's four partial years with Vancouver in the late 1980s and early 1990s represent that shift of priorities. Yet being a 240th-overall draft choice never promised much hope in the first place. Mazur has been an excellent scorer whose skill has always been in demand – it just never happened in the NHL.

McADAM, Gary
b. Smiths Falls, Ontario, December 31, 1955

McAdam played junior in Ottawa and St. Catharines, but his big break came in 1975 when he was drafted by Buffalo and had a chance to play with Gilbert Perreault. No sooner was he tabbed as a scorer than he was put on a checking line, and then the trading started. It's a unique player who can be traded in one deal straight up for Dave Schultz and in another deal for Errol Thompson. In all, McAdam played for 7 teams in his 11-year career. When he retired, he took a job working for UPS and then settled in Portland, where he became a bus driver. McAdam later studied at a Maine college to become a surgical technologist.

McADAM, Sam
b. Sterling, Scotland, May 31, 1908
d. unknown

McAdam spent most of his playing life in the Canadian west, especially Vancouver in the Pacific Coast league. He played five games with the Rangers in '30-'31 and after retiring he stayed in B.C. and opened an hotel in Vancouver.

McALLISTER, Chris ("Mac"/ "Cally")
b. Saskatoon, Saskatchewan, June 16, 1975

At 6'8" in his bare feet, McAllister is an imposing figure, to say the least. But his size also produces a slowness that he has not altogether overcome, and his intimidating presence is mitigated by an inability to use his size to his advantage. Nonetheless, he has worked his way into the NHL as a semi-regular, first with Vancouver in '97-'98, and more recently with Toronto and then Philadelphia.

McALPINE, Chris
b. Roseville, Minnesota, December 1, 1971

It's not a particularly rare double to win the Calder Cup and Stanley Cup during a career, but it's rare, indeed, to win both championships in the same season and even rarer not to play a single playoff game with either team! In '94-'95, McAlpine split the season between Albany and New Jersey coming out of the University of Minnesota. But despite playing for both teams in the regular season, he saw action with neither in the playoffs. He later made Albany his home until the Devils traded him to St. Louis, and since then McAlpine has been on the move regularly, going to Tampa Bay, Atlanta, and Chicago in quick succession.

McAMMOND, Dean
b. Grand Cache, Alberta, June 15, 1973

A sturdy, speedy centre, McAmmond had a career year with Calgary in 2001-02, scoring 21 goals for a team that didn't even make the playoffs. He had been a 1st-round draft choice in 1991 by Chicago but a couple of years later he helped Canada win gold at the World Juniors. The Hawks traded him to Edmonton with Igor Kravchuk for Joe Murphy on February 24, 1993, and he developed into a reliable player with the Oilers. McAmmond suffered a serious Achilles tendon injury early in the '94-'95 season and bounced around before being acquired by the Flames from Philadelphia. He was later sent to Colorado and back to Calgary at the trade deadline in March 2003, but the transaction violated a strange rule in the CBA and he was ruled ineligible to play the rest of the season. He also played in two World Championships for Canada, winning silver in 1996.

McANDREW, Hazen
b. Mayo, Yukon, August 7, 1917
d. Niagara Falls, Ontario, August 27, 1993

One of a sizable number of Canadians to play in Britain leading up to the Second World War, McAndrew returned to Canada and ended up playing a few games with the Brooklyn Americans before joining the Royal Canadian Naval Volunteer Reserve as a stoker. By the time he was given his discharge, his NHL days were done and he played just a short time longer before retiring.

McANEELEY, Edward "Ted" ("Dude")
b. Cranbrook, British Columbia, November 7, 1950

The good life is there to be had, and for McAneeley that meant sunshine and beauty and relaxation after the final game. He and his brother, Bob, were reared by father, Ed, who had been a star goalie in the WHL in the 1940s. Bob and Ted played together everywhere until 1970, when Ted was drafted by California. Bob never made the NHL, but Ted played two and a half seasons with the awful Golden Seals. He made it to the top by sheer will of force, determination, and a knowledge of his strengths and weaknesses. Everyone thought he was too small for a defenceman (5'9"), so he made up for this shortcoming by becoming a superior shotblocker and quick skater. The team was too bad to establish a good reputation, though, and he wound up in the minors and WHA. After retiring, McAneeley ended up as the hotel manager for the Waikiki Prince. He also acted as an adviser to NHL Commissioner Gary Bettman at the 1998 Olympics in Nagano and his hotel in Hawaii hosted the U.S. women's team after their stunning gold-medal triumph over favoured Canadians.

McATEE, Jerome "Jud"
b. Stratford, Ontario, February 5, 1920

After winning the Memorial Cup with Oshawa in both 1939 and '40, McAtee became a wartime player for one full season, '44-'45, with Detroit. He had made two, one-game appearances previously with the Wings, but in his complete season he scored a respectable 15 goals playing mostly with Mud Bruneteau and Syd Howe. Once the regular stars got back from their military service, McAtee spent the last five years of his career in the minors.

Gary McAdam

Chris McAllister

Chris McAlpine

Dean McAmmond

Ted McAneeley

brain surgery soon after and was slowly recovering when he returned to hospital for further treatments and passed away. He was inducted posthumously into the Manitoba Sports Hall of Fame in 1995.

McCALMON, Eddie
b. Varney, Ontario, May 30, 1902
d. unknown
A graduate of the University of Saskatchewan in 1927, McCalmon went on to play two seasons in the NHL, one with Chicago a year later, the other with the Philadelphia Quakers in '30-'31, his last season of pro.

McCANN, Rick
b. Hamilton, Ontario, May 27, 1944
It was a strange symbiosis, indeed, that kept McCann and the Red Wings together for so long. From 1966 to '75, he played in the Detroit system, and the Wings called him up unfailingly nearly every year and just as unfailingly sent him back down. In all those years, he played just 43 NHL games, all with Detroit. The team didn't want him, but it also didn't want to give him up. And McCann didn't want to go even though staying meant playing mostly in the minors. The centreman was a reliable scorer below the NHL, but he recorded only one goal in his big-league career.

Rick McCann

McCARTAN, Jack
b. St. Paul, Minnesota, August 5, 1935
Before Jim Craig, the hero-goalie for Team USA's Miracle on Ice gold medal at the 1980 Olympics in Lake Placid, there was Jack McCartan, the 1960 hero at Squaw Valley. The goalie backstopped the U.S. to victories over Canada, Czechoslovakia, and the Soviet Union to give his country a stunning win at that year's Olympics, without question the highlight of his career. He graduated from the University of Minnesota with a degree in education and then joined the army in 1959. During that season, he played with the American team at the World Championships in Prague, which turned out to be his audition for Squaw Valley. Right after the victory he signed a 5-game tryout with the Rangers, but his stay lasted only 4 games because his 30-day military leave ran out. McCartan beat Detroit 3-1 in his NHL debut and followed with two ties and a loss. He attended training camp that fall, but his luck ran dry after a shutout in his first game. He allowed six goals in each of his next seven games and was sent to the minors, where he stayed until 1972 when he played in the WHA. He had some fine years along the way, but he never made it back to the NHL before retiring in 1974. He later ran a summer hockey camp and in the winter scouted for the Vancouver Canucks. He also coached the U.S. entry at the 1977 World

Kevin McCarthy

Championships. He was inducted into the U.S. Hockey Hall of Fame in 1983.

McCARTHY, Alexander "Sandy"
b. Toronto, Ontario, June 15, 1972
The difference between a goon and a fighter might be slim by most people's accounts, but McCarthy is more the latter in that he doesn't necessarily go brawling or look for a fight at every opportunity. Or, at least, not any more. In junior, he was a wild man with Laval, and in the NHL, first with Calgary in 1993, he had to prove his worth and earn his stripes and all that fun, fightin' jargon. But he's an agitator as much as a barbarian, a lippy fecal disturber as much as a drop-the-gloves-every-night kind of right winger. He's always there to defend his teammates, though, and he's certainly one of the top penalty-minutes men in the league most seasons. When he's disciplined, he's effective, and when he's not, he's not.

In junior, he was a wild man with Laval.
SANDY McCARTHY

McCARTHY, Dan
b. St. Marys, Ontario, April 7, 1958
What a strange, brief, successful time he had of it in the NHL! McCarthy played only five NHL games, with the Rangers in '80-'81, but scored four goals in that callup and never made it back. Everyone in the business complained about his size, but dunking nearly a goal a game should have netted him a second look somewhere along the way. Instead, he played in the minors for six years and then got on with life. He established the Do It Right Foundation and he became the GM and coach of the Connecticut Wolves, a junior hockey team. He resigned as coach early in the 2000-01 season, though remained as GM.

McCARTHY, Kevin
b. Winnipeg, Manitoba, July 14, 1957
On December 29, 1978, Philadelphia made a significant mistake when it traded its 1st-round draft choice, McCarthy, to Vancouver after he had played just 84 games with the team. He had been a highly regarded junior after scoring 127 points with Winnipeg in '76-'77, and went on to have some fine years with the Canucks. He also played in the 1981 All-Star Game. The defensive aspect of the game was his greatest challenge, but he mustered a good portion of the Canucks' offence from the blueline. He retired in 1988 after winning the Calder Cup with Hershey, back in the Flyers system, and stayed in the organization to act as a pro scout for two years. McCarthy then joined Hartford as an assistant before becoming Carolina's minor-league coach. He joined the Hurricanes as an assistant in 1997. McCarthy was inducted into the Manitoba Sports Hall of Fame in 1999.

McCARTHY, Steve
b. Trail, British Columbia, February 3, 1981
Still a work in progress, the McCarthy rap sheet is pretty impressive to date. He won gold with Canada at the Under-18 championships, bronze at the 2000 WJC, and captained the 2001 bronze-medal team. He recorded an assist on his first NHL shift, with Chicago, but is still developing and hasn't made the team full-time.

McCARTHY, Tom
b. Hamilton, Ontario
d. unknown
An early star of the NHL, McCarthy played just two years soon after the league was formed in 1917. He played for Quebec in 1919-20 and Hamilton the following year and retired soon after. The right winger averaged better than half a goal a game.

McCARTHY, Tom
b. Toronto, Ontario, September 15, 1934
A graduate of the Toronto Marlies in the 1950s, this Tom McCarthy was a callup for Detroit and Boston during a lengthy career outside the NHL. He was a replacement and short-term player in the big loop, but in the lower ranks he was a tremendous scorer who was incredibly well travelled. Despite his skills, it was rare he played in the same city for consecutive seasons, an odd feature of a career that lasted some 20 years. Thirty goals was an average season for McCarthy until injuries slowed him down with Rochester in '69–'70, and he twice led his league in scoring, once in the Eastern Pro league, another time in the Central league.

McCARTHY, Tom
b. Toronto, Ontario, July 31, 1960
McCarthy played junior hockey in Oshawa and was such a prolific scorer that John Bassett offered him a contract to turn pro with the WHA's Birmingham Bulls. McCarthy's agent, and grandfather, suggested Tom keep playing, which he did until joining Minnesota of the NHL in 1979. McCarthy spent seven seasons with the North Stars. In '83-'84, he scored 39 goals in just 66 games, but that turned out to be his best season in the league. Two years later he was traded to Boston after having a season from hell. That year, his list of injuries could have represented a career's worth: knee injury, bruised hand, separated shoulder, influenza, broken thumb, and Bells palsy. With something to prove, he went out and scored 30 goals with the Bruins the year after, but that performance turned out to be his last

hurrah, but his new, awful life was just beginning. He became a drinker and drug addict, and in 1994 the FBI stormed his house in Minnesota. He was charged, and pleaded guilty to, conspiracy to traffic drugs and transporting drugs. He was sentenced to 70 months in prison, and it was during his time at Leavenworth that the new man emerged. He arranged to bring hockey to the prison, teaching criminals of all races and backgrounds a game they had never played! The experiment was an unqualified success, and when he was released in 1998 he settled in Mississauga and coached the local Rebels, a AAA kids team. From the NHL to prison to minor hockey, McCarthy has seen all sides of life.

Steve McCarthy

McCARTNEY, Walt
b. Regina, Saskatchewan, April 26, 1911
d. unknown
After developing in the provincial junior ranks, McCartney played two games with the Canadiens in '32-'33 before moving out west to continue his pro career. The left winger never made it back to the NHL, or the east, before retiring.

McCARTY, Darren
b. Burnaby, British Columbia, April 1, 1972
He might well be the best of his style of player in the NHL. Around Detroit, where he has played his entire career, he is equally well known for beating up Colorado's Claude Lemieux and for scoring the Cup-winning goal in 1997. McCarty led the OHL with 55 goals in '91-'92, but the big knock

Tom McCarthy (b. 1960)

McCarty is also the lead singer of a band called Grinder.
DARREN McCARTY

against him was his skating. Determined to make it, he proved everyone wrong and became a capable scorer, a fine fighter, and a tremendously reliable player who has never had a minus season in the +/- statistics. He never takes stupid penalties and knows how to shoot the puck, a fact he proved by scoring a hat trick on Patrick Roy during the 2002 playoffs. McCarty's career came unhinged in 1995 when he dealt with an alcohol problem, but he fought the good fight successfully and walked around Janne Niinimaa to score the winning goal for the team in the 1997 finals. He also had to deal with his father's myeloma cancer and set up a foundation to support charity efforts for victims of this cancer. McCarty is also the lead singer of a band called Grinder that put out a CD in support of Vladimir Konstantinov and Sergei Mnatsakanov after their horrific car accident in 1997 following the Cup win.

Tom McCarthy (b. 1934)

McCASKILL, Ted
b. Kapuskasing, Ontario, October 29, 1936
Yes, it was toughest of all to make the NHL during the Original Six days, but anyone playing for the Nashville

Ted McCaskill

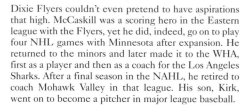

Alyn McCauley

Trent McCleary

Kevin McClelland

Dixie Flyers couldn't even pretend to have aspirations that high. McCaskill was a scoring hero in the Eastern league with the Flyers, yet he did, indeed, go on to play four NHL games with Minnesota after expansion. He returned to the minors and later made it to the WHA, first as a player and then as a coach for the Los Angeles Sharks. After a final season in the NAHL, he retired to coach Mohawk Valley in that league. His son, Kirk, went on to become a pitcher in major league baseball.

McCAULEY, Alyn ("Mac"/ "Shooter")
b. Brockville, Ontario, May 29, 1977

This is a career story whose final chapters have yet to be written, a career so far that has been studded by success and pockmarked by the worst luck any player can experience. In junior, with the Ottawa 67's, McCauley was nothing short of sensational. He was named the best junior in the country for '96-'97, he played in two WJCs for Canada, and he led the OHL in goals. New Jersey had wisely drafted him in 1995, and Toronto wisely acquired him two years later in a big deal that involved Doug Gilmour going to the Devils. McCauley's first year and a half in Toronto were marked by incredible optimism. He was a player who could score, yet the sure future winner of the Selke Trophy, so good was he defensively as a centre. He came to play every night; he was a leader. He was a perfect representation of what a future should look like. Then, March 3, 1999 came along. McCauley was hit hard into the new glass at Air Canada Centre, lost consciousness, and suffered a serious concussion and post-concussion syndrome. Worse, his confidence was shot and he played scared, something no player can do effectively. He appeared jinxed when he got back, suffering assorted injuries from a knee problem to a broken ankle to food poisoning. He ended up in the minors to skate back into an NHLer, and slowly but surely he re-established himself with the team in 2001-02 only to be traded to San Jose at the deadline in March 2003.

McCLANAHAN, Rob
b. St. Paul, Minnesota, January 9, 1958

As with everyone on that Miracle on Ice team, the gold medal at Lake Placid was the crowning moment of McClanahan's career. It was the main reason he got a chance to play in the NHL. He joined Buffalo right after the win, but his was an unimpressive season and a half and the Sabres let him go to Hartford in the Waiver Draft. He had his best season in '82-'83 with the Rangers when he scored 22 goals, but in the summer of '84 he was traded first to Detroit and then to Vancouver. When the Canucks tried to send him to the minors to start the new

year, he simply quit. McClenahan later became an investment broker in Minnesota.

McCLEARY, Trent
b. Swift Current, Saskatchewan, September 8, 1972

As far as on-ice accidents go, this ranks up there among the worst the NHL has ever seen outside the fatal check on Bill Masterton. On January 29, 2000, McCleary dove awkwardly to block a shot from Philadelphia's Chris Therien. It hit him flush in the throat, and doctors had to perform surgery in the hallway behind the Montreal bench. He needed a tracheotomy, he fractured his larynx, and he suffered a collapsed lung. It was months before he could speak again, and the tissue that accrued from the tracheotomy caused a partial blockage of his windpipe thus restricting air flow to and from his lungs. McCleary was forced to retire. This was not the first horrible accident to befall the young player – in fact, it was the third. The first occurred in the minors with the PEI Senators when he took a stick in the right eye, causing retinal damage and forcing him out for three months. He came back wearing a visor, but that didn't prevent another serious injury to the same eye. He fell heavily with another player whose skate got under the shield and cut the eye open. Still, he recovered and played his first NHL game at the start of the '95-'96 season. He played the following year with Boston before signing with Montreal as a free agent. His brave comeback attempt with the Habs over, he retired and became a scout in the WHL for the Canadiens.

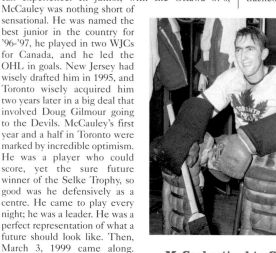

McCool retired to Calgary where he became a nightwatchman for the Albertan.
FRANK McCOOL

McCLELLAND, Kevin ("Mac")
b. Oshawa, Ontario, July 4, 1962

Yes, those great Oilers teams of the 1980s had more offensive firepower than any other in the game's history, but they were a fighting team as well. They had Dave Semenko and Marty McSorley, and Kevin McClelland was no shrinking violet, either, during his seven years with the team. He routinely had more than 200 penalty minutes, but he also won 4 Cups with the Oilers during that decade, his finest years in pro. He scored one of the biggest goals in team history in game one of the 1984 finals, the only goal of the game. Coming against Cup champions and nemesis the Islanders, it gave Edmonton a 1-0 lead in the series and proved to the team that they could win. Once the lustre of Cup glory faded, though, he was bounced around and even sent to the minors. That's when he knew enough was enough, so he retired to start anew as a coach. He worked his way up from junior to the AHL, becoming an assistant with St. John's, the Leafs farm team in Newfoundland.

McCOOL, Frank ("Ulcers")

b. Calgary, Alberta, October 27, 1918
d. Calgary, Alberta, May 20, 1973

McCool had no ambitions to play in the NHL. In fact, he literally couldn't stomach the idea. A Calgary boy, he attended Gonzaga University in Spokane, Washington, before returning to Alberta where he played goal for the Knights of Columbus and worked as a copy boy in the sports department of the *Calgary Albertan*. He later played for a Calgary team in the Canadian army but he was released from military duty because of a stomach condition. He joined the Maple Leafs for the '44-'45 season because Turk Broda was enlisted and Montreal refused to allow Paul Bibeault play for the Leafs for a second season. McCool was both brilliant and living on the edge. He played every minute of that year and led the NHL with four shutouts, earning the Calder Trophy as a result. In the playoffs, he recorded another four shutouts, including three in the finals against Detroit. His stomach got so bad in that last series that he had to take frequent breaks to drink milk, and the Wings charged that these usually occurred when the Leafs were being pressured. McCool refused to play the year after because he and owner Conn Smythe were $500 apart in agreeing on a contract, but he came back only as long as Broda was away. McCool happily retired to Calgary where he became a nightwatchman for the newspaper, but the publisher, Max Bell, asked him to start writing stories for the *Albertan*. McCool became assistant sports editor and then editor in 1949, general manager in 1957, and finally publisher in 1969. He was also deeply involved in community events, and his death in 1974 was the result of those stomach problems that had plagued him much of his life.

McCORD, Bob

b. Matheson, Ontario, March 20, 1934

He played much of his career with a bad back, yet McCord endured the sometimes overpowering pain until he was 41 years old. Never blessed with great speed, a blistering shot, or finesse moves, he relied on solid defensive play to survive, mostly in the minors, for 21 years of pro hockey. From the time he turned pro in 1954 to his NHL debut a decade later with Boston, McCord played mostly with Springfield, his adopted home where he worked as a carpenter in the summer. Two seasons with Boston only led to the minors with Detroit after a trade, but expansion gave him more options. He returned to the WHL after two seasons with Minnesota, first as a player, then as coach, then as GM, and then a return to player. Another stint, this time with St. Louis, seemed to be his last, and he retired, only to come back in the WHL with Denver. McCord retired for good in 1975 and later worked for the Ontario Forestry Commission.

McCORD, Dennis

b. Chatham, Ontario, July 28, 1951

Vancouver drafted him (1972), used him thrice ('73-'74), and sent him to the minors for good. McCord never played in the WHA, never fought for long in the lower echelons to try to make it back, and never made a grand impression during his short career. He retired in 1976.

McCORMACK, John ("Goose")

b. Edmonton, Alberta, August 2, 1925

Despite registering an assist on his first NHL shift, with the Maple Leafs, Goose McCormack's stays in Toronto were brief and, ultimately, tumultuous. He had unnaturally long arms, and early on in his junior career he was called Goose for that reason (and for his long, thin body). McCormack initially wanted to go into the priesthood, and played hockey at St. Mike's with that calling in mind, but when the Leafs didn't invite him to camp in the fall of '47 he worried about his future and entered pre-law studies and played for the Marlboro Seniors. Late in the season, the Leafs called him up, and his hockey aspirations were revived, although he had earned a B.A. while continuing to play. Between 1947 and '51 he played just 84 games, though he became a noted penalty killer and, with those arms, a master poke checker. During the '50-'51 season he angered GM Conn Smythe by getting married (the suggestion being that one can't focus on hockey while preparing for such a big event), and was summarily sent to the minors, never to resurface with the Blue and White. The Leafs sold him outright to Montreal in 1951 and he played most of four years with the club, winning a Stanley Cup in 1953 and proving his worth as an NHL-calibre player. After one final year with Chicago ('54-'55) and another in Edmonton in the Western league, McCormack settled in Alberta and worked in the steel industry. He established his own business, then became part of Lake Ontario Steel out of Whitby where he worked for 17 years until retiring.

McCOSH, Shawn

b. Oshawa, Ontario, June 5, 1969

He was owned by five teams during his career, yet he played just nine games with two of them, Los Angeles and New York. McCosh was drafted by Detroit in 1989 but the Wings sent him to L.A. before he ever played in the Motor City. He spent the better part of 9 years in the AHL, a tough centre who could be counted on for 20 goals per annum, but he moved to Germany for a final season in 1999. He scored his only NHL goal with the Rangers in '94-'95.

McCOURT, Dale ("Chief")

b. Falconbridge, Ontario, January 26, 1957

In 1977, there was no bigger player in hockey than Dale McCourt. He was a big scorer in junior. He had led the WJC in scoring, he was the 1st-overall draft choice, by Detroit, and he was named the best junior in Canada. He was only 20 years old and ready to take on the NHL. Little did anyone know at the time that "take on" would have a more legal interpretation than a hockey one. After his rookie season, in which he scored 33 goals, he was awarded to L.A. as compensation for the Wings signing Rogie Vachon as a free agent. The only problem was, McCourt refused to go. He didn't want to play in L.A., and he argued that he had a binding contract with Detroit. He took the case to court, and during this time he was allowed to continue to play for the Wings (as did Vachon). More than a year later, L.A. knew it wasn't going to get McCourt so it engineered a trade, on paper, than sent McCourt back to Detroit and gave the Kings some new talent. Ironically, two years later, McCourt was traded to

Bob McCord

John McCormack

Dale McCourt

Bill McCreary

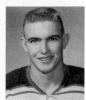

Bill McCreary, Jr.

Johnny McCreedy

Brad McCrimmon

Jim McCrimmon

Buffalo, but because he felt this was a valid deal, he accepted the move. He recorded his fourth 30-goal season in 5 years, but his production dropped in his last 3 NHL years to exactly 20 each time. McCourt played his last in Toronto, where his uncle George Armstrong had played his whole career, and then he went to Switzerland to play with Ambri for eight years before becoming a coach in Germany. He was the most talked about player when he entered the NHL, but more than anything, he exposed a crucial flaw in the way the league and players had set up free agency and compensation, a system that underwent radical changes in the ensuing years.

McCREARY, Bill
b. Sundridge, Ontario, December 2, 1934
It's a good thing Sam Pollock acquired the rights to McCreary in 1962 or else the player would never have had his finest years in hockey. He had had only three brief callups with the Rangers and Detroit and played all of the rest of his time in the minors. His four years in Springfield under Eddie Shore were not unpleasant, but when the Hall of Fame owner refused to give McCreary what he wanted for the '62-'63 season, he quit. Pollock acquired him, talked him into returning, and gave him a few games with the Canadiens. In 1964, back in the minors, McCreary became a playing coach with Omaha, but he resuscitated his career when the Blues acquired him from Montreal in 1967. For four years he played in St. Louis, retiring for good in 1971 to coach at Denver. In subsequent years he had three NHL coaching jobs – St. Louis, Vancouver, California – all disastrous outings that ended in his dismissal.

McCREARY, Bill, Jr.
b. Springfield, Massachusetts, April 15, 1960
On January 3, 1981, Edmonton beat Toronto 4-1 at home. That was not the big deal. The moment that made that night special came when a punk named Bill McCreary caught a star named Wayne Gretzky with his head down at the Leafs blueline, and *whack!* McCreary nailed Gretzky with a clean and devastating open-ice hit, the hardest the Great One ever absorbed in his career. Other than that, McCreary's importance in NHL annals have to do with lineage. His dad, Bill, played in the NHL, as did two uncles (Keith McCreary and Ron Atwell) and a cousin (Bobby Atwell). This Bill lasted just a dozen games with the Leafs and then played for a number of years in the "I" before retiring.

McCREARY, Keith
b. Sundridge, Ontario, June 19, 1940
Despite graduating from junior in 1960, McCreary played all of 10 games with the Habs until 1967 and then oodles more after expansion when he was claimed by Pittsburgh. He was a decent skater and solid positional player who had three 20-goal seasons during his career, though playing with the Pens and later Atlanta meant he had no chance of playoff success. He was both captain and player rep with Pittsburgh. After retiring in 1975, he settled in Bolton and opened an insurance brokerage firm. He also served as a counsellor for Peel Region in Ontario.

McCREEDY, Johnny
b. Winnipeg, Manitoba, March 23, 1911
d. Toronto, Ontario, December 7, 1979
In all likelihood, McCreedy accomplished something no other hockey player will ever duplicate: he won the Stanley Cup, the Allan Cup, the Memorial Cup, and a World Championship gold medal. The Memorial Cup came in 1937 with his hometown Winnipeg Monarchs. His Allan Cups came with the Trail Smoke Eaters in 1938 and the Kirkland Lake Blue Devils in 1940. His World Championship gold came with those same Smoke Eaters in 1939, and his Stanley Cups came with the Leafs in 1942 and '45. Between those last victories, McCreedy served as a flying officer in the RCAF. The 1942 win was likely the sweetest because the Leafs came back from 3-0 down in the finals to beat Detroit four games to three. McCreedy assisted on Pete Langelle's winning goal. After hockey, McCreedy joined Inco at the Copper Cliff plant in 1949 and worked his way up the ranks, becoming the chairman and CEO of the company. He died in a Toronto hospital from complications following surgery.

McCRIMMON, Byron "Brad" ("Sarge")
b. Dodsland, Saskatchewan, March 29, 1959
Over the course of his 18-year NHL career, McCrimmon had a cumulative +/- record of +444, a true indication of his abilities as a defenceman. He won one Stanley Cup, with Calgary in 1989 in the middle of his career, and he had been to the finals two years earlier with Philadelphia. He was a stocky and strong player, especially resilient for a defenceman, and logged a ton of minutes every game. He played the power play and penalty kill and his team made the playoffs every one of the first 13 seasons he was in the league. McCrimmon was drafted in 1979, perhaps the greatest draft year ever, and never played a minute in the minors. He also played in the World Juniors in '78 and '79 as well as the 1988 All-Star Game. After retiring in 1997, he became an assistant coach with the Islanders and two years later a head coach with Saskatoon in the WHL.

McCRIMMON, Jim
b. Ponoka, Alberta, May 29, 1953
Here was a defenceman with size who went to the Memorial Cup in 1973 with Medicine Hat, but who didn't last long in the pros. He played in the WHA for parts of three years and just two games in the NHL with St. Louis. McCrimmon ended his career after the 1977-78 season in which he won an Allan Cup with the Kimberley Dynamiters, by this time a trophy and team that paled in importance to 40 years earlier when that team last won the once-prestigious championship.

McCULLEY, Bob
b. Stratford, Ontario, February 8, 1914
Despite playing in the minors for years in the pre-war era, McCulley is one of the more obscure NHL entries, having made a single appearance with the Habs in '34-'35. He was a big man for his era, but he was neither a scorer nor a champion.

McCURRY, Dr. Francis "Duke"

b. Toronto, Ontario, June 13, 1900
d. Toronto, Ontario, November 8, 1965

By the time McCurry went down to Pittsburgh in 1923 he was already a legend in Toronto, a sort of mini-Lionel Conacher, and not by much. While playing hockey at De La Salle school, he was on the Canadian junior champion teams of 1917 and '18 and then the champion Canoe Club the following two seasons. He also captained the baseball and football teams in Toronto, and in 1916 he was the amateur welterweight champion of Canada. For three years, 1920-22, he was also on Canada's all-star lacrosse team. He moved to Pittsburgh to study dentistry and play for the Yellowjackets, an endeavour that became more serious in 1925 when the team joined the NHL as the Pirates. He played on that team for four years and continued to play for the team after it left the NHL and became the Yellowjackets once again.

McCUTCHEON, Brian ("Boom Boom")

b. Toronto, Ontario, August 3, 1949

His first year at Cornell was Ken Dryden's last, but although both would go on to the NHL, one would to have a Hall of Fame career while the other would have, well, a career. All of McCutcheon's games came with Detroit in the mid-1970s, but it was pretty clear pretty quickly that he wasn't going to star in the big time. When the chance to play and coach in Austria in 1978 fell into his lap, he took it and has been coaching ever since. He returned to North America and coached for years at U.S. colleges before moving back into pro and working his way methodically from the IHL to the AHL and most recently to the NHL as an assistant in Buffalo.

McCUTCHEON, Darwin

b. Listowel, Ontario, April 19, 1962

December 31, 1981, was a night to remember for the gargantuan defenceman McCutcheon, for that was his one and only NHL game, for Toronto. It came during his final year of junior and the rest of his pro years were all in the minors. After retiring, he ended up in Avon, Colorado, working for the Forbes Group, a real estate company, and running his own ski shop, Aalta Sports.

McDILL, Jeff

b. Thunder Bay, Ontario, March 16, 1956

After leaving the Western league in 1976 to turn pro, McDill played a single game with Chicago during a four-year career that passed quickly and harmlessly in the AHL and IHL.

McDONAGH, Bill

b. Rouyn, Quebec, April 30, 1928

The left winger played only four games with the Rangers in 1949-50 during a season spent mostly in the AHL. He played most of his career down east, primarily in New Brunswick.

McDONALD, Alvin "Ab"

b. Winnipeg, Manitoba, February 18, 1936

It's one thing to dream of playing for the Montreal Canadiens, especially during the glorious 1950s. It's another to get what you want and see what that dream is made of. McDonald joined the Habs for the '58 playoffs after two years in the AHL, and over the next four years he won Cups each time with the dynastic team. So what's the problem? Simple. He arrived a rookie as Bert Olmstead was playing his last, and McDonald was expected to replace the Hall of Famer. Instead, he became a great fourth-liner, which caused Forum fans to boo, even though McDonald had done no wrong. When he was traded to Chicago in the summer of 1960, he was delighted, and a year later he was vindicated, for the Hawks won the Cup at Montreal's expense. McDonald had his best years in Chicago, playing with Stan Mikita and Ken Wharram on the famed Scooter Line. They scored bundles, but were also a fine defensive trio. McDonald was traded again in 1964 and began the second phase of his career, one that involved packing his belongings and moving about. In all, he played in five All-Star Games before finishing his career in Winnipeg in the WHA. He settled in St. James, Manitoba, started an equipment rental business, and did some scouting for St. Louis. He may never have replaced Bert Olmstead, but McDonald did win 4 Stanley Cups and play 15 years in the best hockey league on the planet.

McDonald was traded again in 1964 and began the second phase of his career.
AB McDONALD

McDONALD, Andy

b. Strathroy, Ontario, August 25, 1977

Only time will tell, but the 2001-02 season might be the turning point in young McDonald's career. Coming out of Colgate where he had been a Hobey Baker Award finalist, he split the 2000-01 season between the Ducks of Anaheim and the Ducks of Cincinnati. The next year, though, he played mostly in Anaheim, and at season's end he accepted an offer to play for Canada at the World Championships in Sweden. There, he was one of the team's top scorers and skated with a confidence he had yet to develop in NHL. Undrafted, he might well be a Ducks surprise in the years to come.

Brian McCutcheon

Jeff McDill

Bill McDonagh

McDONALD, Bob
b. Toronto, Ontario, January 4, 1923
Like many a Rangers player of the era, McDonald was called up because of his play with the New York Rovers. In his case, the call was for just one game in 1943-44, and he played the balance of his short career in the Windsor-Detroit area in the formative days of the IHL.

McDONALD, Brian
b. Toronto, Ontario, March 23, 1945
McDonald was given 2 chances in the NHL in the days immediately after expansion, but in 20 career games he never recorded so much as a point. He signed with Houston of the WHA in 1972 and played in the pirate league for five years before retiring.

Brian McDonald

McDONALD, Byron "Butch"
b. Moose Jaw, Saskatchewan, November 21, 1916
When he was called up from Indianapolis midway through the '39-'40 season, McDonald was touted as the great blond youngster who could do no wrong. That reputation didn't carry him far. He and two other star prospects – Connie Brown and Joe Fisher – played on a youthful line together, but it was five years before McDonald got another chance with the Wings and only then because of the war. He was traded to Chicago on January 2, 1945, where he managed 6 goals in 26 games and then was sent to the minors where his production increased dramatically playing alongside lesser lights.

McDONALD, Gerry
b. Weymouth, Massachusetts, March 18, 1958
Making it to the NHL after playing Division III for North Adams State College is like being able to afford a room at the Ritz with a dollar in your pocket – not flippin' likely. Yet McDonald turned the trick. Not for long, but long enough to say he had been there, with Hartford, for eight games in the early 1980s. His pro career lasted just four seasons, but he classifies as a former NHLer nonetheless.

McDONALD, John "Jack"
b. 1888
d. Montreal, Quebec, January 24, 1958
McDonald was one of a small number of players to have a lengthy career in the NHA and then stick around to do some damage in the NHL after 1917. In the former, he was a mainstay with the Quebec Bulldogs, winning the Cup with them in 1912. In 1917, he was claimed by the Montreal Wanderers in the Dispersal Draft of NHA players to form the new league, but after their arena burned down he joined the city's other team, the Canadiens. He also

John McDonald (b. 1888)

played briefly with the Toronto St. Pats before retiring in 1921.

McDONALD, John "Jack"
b. Swan River, Manitoba, November 24, 1921
d. unknown
The classic war player, McDonald appeared for the Rangers in the '43-'44 season and never anywhere else before or after. He played junior in Portage, but this was hardly an enduring career. He did manage 10 goals that year, though, not a bad NHL total by any stretch.

McDONALD, Lanny
b. Hanna, Alberta, February 16, 1953
Any hockey player will tell you that family got him to whatever level of success he attained, and there's no more obvious example of that than McDonald. Growing up on a farm in Craigmyle, he was taught the importance of hard work by his father. His mother was a teacher in a three-room schoolhouse that counted Lanny among its students. He had been playing hockey since age five, but saw little in the way of serious hockey until he tried out for the Lethbridge Sugar Kings, a provincial team. In his first year, he scored 2 goals, but the next season he had 37. From there he went to the WHL with Medicine Hat and developed into a superstar scorer known for his great shot down the right wing and his physical, no-nonsense style of play. Toronto drafted him 4th overall in 1973 and he made the team right away. McDonald stayed six and a half years with the Leafs, experiencing the highs and lows of the NHL and

He played with linemate and best friend Darryl Sittler in the 1976 Canada Cup.
LANNY McDONALD

hockey's most intense city. He had just 14 and 17 goals in his first 2 years and fans grew a little restless during his slow start. In his third year, though, he scored 37 times, and this was only prelude to 4 consecutive 40-goal seasons. He played with linemate and best friend Darryl Sittler in the 1976 Canada Cup, assisting on Sittler's Cup winner, and had a moment of glory all his own when his overtime goal eliminated the Islanders from the 1978 playoffs and put the Leafs in the semifinals. His friendship with Sittler was a major reason why he was traded to the lowly Colorado Rockies on December 29, 1979. Owner Harold Ballard had hired Punch Imlach as GM at the start of the '79-'80 season, and Imlach detested Sittler's prominence in the city and with the team. He sought to hack away at what, in part by trading the captain's best friend, in what was an awful trade for the team. Fan protest was extraordinary, and raged outside Maple Leaf Gardens on the day of the trade. What was done was done, though, and McDonald went to the Rockies and continued to play the only way he knew. He was traded to Calgary early in the '81-'82 season, and it was with the Flames that he spent the next seven and a half years and experienced his finest career moments. In his first full year with Calgary, '82-'83, he scored 66 goals, though the year after his total was exactly half and continued downward from there. He also won the Bill Masterton Trophy, played in the All-Star Game, and was named to the Second All-Star Team to close out that career year. Toward the end of his career, he was one of the team's captains, but '88-'89 was simply an unforgettable year for one of hockey's good guys. He scored his 500th goal and his 1,000th point, and in the last game of the year, game six of the Stanley Cup finals in Montreal, he scored a goal to help the Flames defeat Montreal 4-2 and win their first Stanley Cup. Throughout his career, McDonald worked extensively with underprivileged children, primarily through the Special Olympics. He gave unstintingly of his time and was awarded the King Clancy Trophy for '87-'88 in acknowledgement of his generosity of spirit. He retired a champion. Never was a player more deserving of Cup glory than McDonald. Three years later, he was inducted into the Hockey Hall of Fame, but his affiliation with the game continued. He worked as an executive with the Flames for years, although he resigned when he was passed over for the GM position. He later returned to the team as the executive adviser to hockey operations but again left, in April 2003. He was named GM by Wayne Gretzky for Canada's entry in the 2001 World Championships, and McDonald will no doubt remain an integral part of the game for many years to come. Hockey is better for having him in the loop.

McDONALD, Terry

b. Coquitlam, British Columbia, January 1, 1956
There's not much meat on the NHL body that is McDonald's career. He played eight games with the horrible Kansas City Scouts but spent the rest of the 1970s in the minors and then retired. He left junior out west a year early to play in the NHL after being drafted by the Scouts in 1975.

McDONALD, Wilfred "Bucko"

b. Fergus, Ontario, October 31, 1914
d. Burks Falls, Ontario, July 27, 1991
The many sides of McDonald all enclosed a hockey personality who was involved the game for some 40 years. He started out, though, in lacrosse, helping the Brampton Excelsiors win the Mann Cup and turning pro soon after. He became a prolific scorer at that game but he played hockey in Sundridge and developed a keen interest in the ice game. He earned a tryout with the Leafs but Detroit signed him in 1934 and he made his debut with the Wings later that year. At 205 pounds, he was one of the heaviest players in the game, and the defenceman had no reluctance to use every pound to his advantage. He became known as a fierce hitter, and in the playoffs of 1936 and '37 a rabid Red Wings fan, Harry Jacobsen, promised McDonald $10 for every opponent he knocked off his feet. The Wings won the Cup both years, but Conn Smythe finally got him into a Leafs sweater the year after when he parted with Bill Thomson and $10,000. Bucko helped the Leafs win a Cup in 1942, and finished his career in 1945 with the Rangers. McDonald returned to Sundridge and went into politics, serving as Liberal MP for Parry Sound-Muskoka from 1949 to '57. He then went into coaching,

first in the AHL and later in minor hockey in his neck of the woods. His finest discovery was a 12-year-old from Parry Sound named Bobby Orr.

McDONNELL, Joe

b. Kitchener, Ontario, May 11, 1961
Much as he might have liked to stay in junior, after five years his eligibility was up and he had to leave the safety of teen hockey to try the pros. McDonnell left Kitchener in 1981 and signed with Vancouver for the next season, but his only long stretch of play came with Pittsburgh three years later when he stayed half a season. He packed it in in 1986 and later became the eastern scout for Detroit.

McDONNELL, Moylan

see **MacDONNELL, Moylan**

McDONOUGH, Al ("Gunner")

b. Hamilton, Ontario, June 6, 1950
Even though L.A. drafted him high in 1970, it became clear to McDonough pretty quickly that he wasn't going to be given a chance to prove his worth with the Kings. When he was traded to Pittsburgh, a struggling team in need of scoring, he couldn't have been happier, and when he was put on a line with Syl Apps and Lowell MacDonald, he was happier still. In his first full year with the Pens, he scored 35 goals and looked to be one of the stars of the future. But in the summer, he and the team couldn't come to terms on a new contract, so when the Pens had a chance to trade him midway through '73-'74, they did, to Atlanta. McDonough had an immediate conflict with his new team because the next game fell on his wedding day, which he had scheduled around the Pittsburgh season. The Flames let him off for the night, but at season's end he bolted to the WHA. He returned four years later for a short stay with the Red Wings, and after retiring worked for many years at a skating school.

McDONOUGH, Hubie

b. Manchester, New Hampshire, July 8, 1963
The small college Hobey Baker Award was started by Princeton University and didn't last very long. It was intended to honour hockey players in U.S. colleges outside the prestigious Division I schools, and in 1985 McDonough of St. Anselm College was awarded it despite playing on a losing team. He became that school's all-time points leader and went on to a five-year career in the NHL, spending as much time in the minors until 1993 when he went down to the IHL for keeps. The "I" was good for McDonough. He played there seven years and was a regular scorer in the league, and when he retired in 1999 he started an executive career as an assistant coach with Orlando. A year later, he became the director of hockey operations for the team, and the next year he moved to the Manchester Monarchs in a similar capacity.

McDOUGAL, Mike

b. Port Huron, Michigan, April 30, 1958
The varied career of Mike McDougal began in earnest when he moved up to Montreal to play junior hockey in 1974. He later represented the U.S. at the World Juniors and turned pro in the IHL, at the time an unusual route to the NHL. Odd, yes, but successful, too. He signed

Terry McDonald

Bucko McDonald

Joe McDonnell

Al McDonough

Pete McDuffe

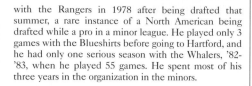

Shawn McEachern

Jim McElmury

Jim McFadden

with the Rangers in 1978 after being drafted that summer, a rare instance of a North American being drafted while a pro in a minor league. He played only 3 games with the Blueshirts before going to Hartford, and he had only one serious season with the Whalers, '82-'83, when he played 55 games. He spent most of his three years in the organization in the minors.

McDOUGALL, Bill

b. Mississauga, Ontario, August 10, 1966

It's one thing not to be drafted or not to get a fair chance in the NHL, but when a player brings the kinds of numbers to the table that McDougall brought, it is difficult to understand why he wasn't given more of a break. He never played a day of major junior hockey, but McDougall scored gobs of goals in other leagues, notably '89-'90 when he led the ECHL in goals, assists, and points while spending a ton of time in the penalty box. Detroit and Edmonton used him for two and four games, respectively, but in the AHL he again proved very capable. In the 1993 playoffs with Cape Breton, he tore the league apart, leading all scorers with 26 goals and 52 points in just 16 games. Tampa was the only team that gave him any chance, but 22 games hardly constituted enough of one in McDougall's mind and he soon moved to Europe to play, which he has been doing steadily since 1994.

McDUFFE, Pete

b. Milton, Ontario, February 16, 1948

He had the stomach to play for the Kansas City Scouts during their inaugural year, but he didn't have the backbone to carry on much after that. McDuffe came out of junior in the 1960s undrafted, and after two outstanding seasons in the Central league he signed with St. Louis in 1971. His was an inauspicious beginning, though, as he appeared in 10 games that year without winning one. He moved on to the Rangers and then the Scouts, where he compiled a record of 7-25-4. McDuffe's career ended after '75-'76 when he had serious back surgery. Although he tried to come back, his few games in the minors and WHA convinced him to retire, and he returned to Milton to run a sporting equipment business.

McEACHERN, Shawn

b. Waltham, Massachusetts, February 28, 1969

Strange as it seems, McEachern never played at the World Juniors though he played at the World Championships in 1991 and at the 1992 Olympics in Albertville before ever playing an NHL game. He joined Pittsburgh after Albertville and just a few weeks later won the Stanley Cup with the Mario Lemieux-led team. It was a grand way to start a career and it has been

his highlight to date. McEachern moved around for a few years until 1996 when he was traded to Ottawa. He has been a Senators winger ever since, and in 2000-01 he had a career year with 32 goals, his sixth 20-plus-goal season. Not big, he has been a versatile player capable of killing penalties and scoring on the power play.

McELMURY, Jim

b. St. Paul, Minnesota, October 3, 1949

McElmury attended Bemidji State University (1967-71) for one reason only – it was the only school that offered him a hockey scholarship. That he began skating only at age 12 was likely the biggest factor, but he made up for lost time and in his final year he was asked to play for the national team at the World Championships. The next year, he helped the U.S. win

After retiring, he became a coach for Oklahoma in the CHL.
MIKE McEWEN

silver at the Olympics and by then he was confident he could play at the highest level. Never mind that he wasn't drafted. He signed with Minnesota in 1972 and two years later with Kansas City, where he played alongside Tracy Pratt on the awful Scouts blueline. He finished his career in 1978 after tearing ligaments in his right knee, though he played one more WC with the U.S. in 1977 on the sixth-place team.

McEWEN, Mike

b. Hornepayne, Ontario, August 10, 1956

Even when he was playing for the Rangers, McEwen was one of baseball's top Canadian prospects, but as one ball scout noted, he can't be a prospect if he's not interested in playing. And he wasn't. Hockey was McEwen's game, and from the time he moved from tiny Hornepayne to Toronto to play for the Marlies, that's what he wanted to do. The Rangers drafted him in 1976, but just before training camp Birmingham lured him away with a big contract. New York upped its deal, and McEwen made the team right away, contributing 14 goals as a rookie. His luck went from bad to great when first he was traded to Colorado so the Rangers could get Barry Beck and then he was sent to the Islanders at the 1981 trade deadline. He won three Stanley Cups on Long Island, but after seven full NHL seasons he was sent to the minors for a brief stay. That's when the trades 'n' travel began in earnest, and by 1987 McEwen opted for the safety of Europe to close out his career. After retiring, he became a coach for Oklahoma in the CHL.

McFADDEN, Jim ("Torp"/ "Scotty")

b. Belfast, Ireland, April 16, 1918
d. Carman, Manitoba, August 28, 2002

Born in Belfast but reared on a 100-acre wheat farm in Darlingford, Manitoba, McFadden became the oldest player to win the Calder Trophy when, at 27, he was named rookie of the year with Detroit for '46-'47.

Funnily enough, some executives around the NHL initially argued that he was not a rookie at all, that he had played for the Montreal Canadiens before the war. Well, yes and no. He did play for a team so called, but it was a senior team and not the NHL Habs. It was, though, McFadden's extended stay in the military that delayed his entrance into the NHL. He scored 24 goals that year, including 2 in 8 seconds, and he had 24 assists, including 5 in 1 game. Ironically, it was his finest season in the league from a points point of view, though the 1950 playoffs were more rewarding, for that was the year the Wings won the Cup in overtime of game seven. McFadden was later traded to Chicago, and after the Hawks demoted him in late 1953 he retired rather than report. He later joined Calgary of the Western league, though, and played his last with the Stampeders before ending things once and for all. McFadden lived in Oklahoma City where he went into business after his playing days.

McFADYEN, Donnie
b. Crossfield, Alberta, March 24, 1907
d. unknown
A remarkable life that touched down in the land of hockey for a number of successful years, McFadyen made every day count. He grew up in Calgary, helped the Canadians with the Memorial Cup in 1926, and then attended Marquette University in Milwaukee for four years on scholarship. When he graduated, he had the choice of playing for the Chicago Black Hawks or the Shamrocks. The latter offered a better salary, so that's where he played. Two years later, he joined the Hawks and in his second year helped the team win its first-ever Cup, scoring two important goals in the semifinals against the Maroons. Each year, McFadyen attended law school at U of Chicago, and when he finally graduated from that program in 1936, he quit the NHL. He practiced and reffed for four years and then served in the military. When he got out, he continued with law until he decided to move his practise to Pompano Beach, Florida, where he continued for another 25 years. He became active in politics and was elected an associate judge in the municipal court of that city for three years, at which point he retired and practiced a little law on the side.

McFALL, Dan
b. Kenmore, New York, April 8, 1963
For most people who play hockey, it remains a game, a passion that stays in the blood for all time. McFall was never going to be a Stanley Cup overtime hero, but he played at Michigan State on a scholarship and from 1984 to '86 played a few games with the Winnipeg Jets. He represented the U.S. at two WJC tournaments, but in 1986 he retired at age 23 to go into business. He started the Dan McFall Full Stride Hockey Training Programs, a powerskating school for kids and adults that eventually became a national concern in the United States.

McFARLANE, Gord
b. Snowflake, Manitoba, July 18, 1901
d. unknown
McFarlane played his only two NHL games during the inaugural season with Chicago, in 1926-27. Beyond that, his career extended only as far as the minors.

McGEOUGH, Jim
b. Regina, Saskatchewan, April 13, 1963
Would he have done it all again, would he have done it at all, had he known what was to befall him after leaving Billings of the WHL in 1982? He had 4 stints in the NHL in subsequent years, with Washington and Pittsburgh, but the *Oxford Atlas of North America* has nothing on the next 20 years of McGeough's life. He played in the AHL, IHL, Colonial league and Central league. He played in the WCHL and ECHL and Sunshine league, not to mention in Europe. He played for Hershey and Muskegon and Springfield, Richmond and Nashville and Bracknell. He played for the Freeze, the Rage, the Thunder, the Choppers, and the Renegades. And when he signed with the Lubbock Cotton Kings in the summer of 2000, he added to his history that encapsulates the modern game. Would he do it all again? In a heartbeat.

McGIBBON, John Irving "Irv"
b. Antigonish, Nova Scotia, October 11, 1914
d. Antigonish, Nova Scotia, February 1, 1981
McGibbon lived virtually his entire life in Nova Scotia and played almost all his hockey there, too, but for one game in the 1942-43 season when he dressed for the Montreal Canadiens. He never played in the minors or returned to the NHL, but headed straight back to the east coast, playing out his career and retiring in Antigonish. He did see time in the army, though, as a private with the Royal Canadian Regiment.

McGILL, Bob ("Big Daddy")
b. Edmonton, Alberta, April 27, 1962
In the class of 1980, McGill was a solid prospect, a defenceman who, as the coach tells you, ignores the puck and takes the man. Sometimes he kept on taking the man until the man had to be carried off the ice. Yes, McGill could also fight, and all his skills together was something that appealed to Toronto. The Leafs drafted three defencemen that year with high choices – Jim Benning, Fred Boimistruck, and Bob McGill. They were supposed to be the anchors of the re-emerging Leafs, but, of course, anything with Harold Ballard attached to it was more likely to sink than swim. So, McGill toiled admirably for the Leafs, fighting whenever possible and trying to take his man with some reliability. He wound up playing for 6 teams in his 13-year career, but he never came particularly close to the Stanley Cup. After retiring, he became a coach, first an assistant with Hershey, then a head coach in the United Hockey League, and later with Baton Rouge in the ECHL. He also coached kids' teams along the way and continues to hope for an NHL shot at some point.

McGILL, Jack
b. Ottawa, Ontario, November 3, 1910
d. unknown
McGill played his most serious pre-NHL hockey with McGill, where he earned a degree in commerce. It was there that he was discovered by the Canadiens, and for three years (1934-37) donned the Montreal livery. He later lived in Toronto and became the advertising manager for Tuckett Tobacco Co.

Donnie McFadyen

Jim McGeough

Bob McGill

Jack McGill (b. 1910)

Ryan McGill

Dan McGillis

Jack McIlhargey

Bert McInenly

McGILL, John "Jack"
b. Edmonton, Alberta, September 19, 1921
d. Vancouver, British Columbia, January 13, 1994
McGill's parents came from Ireland to settle in Edmonton, and it was there that son Jack grew up and developed into a fine hockey player. He played junior in Nanaimo, and his performance earned him a tryout with Hershey in 1941. The Bears sent him to the Boston Olympics to develop, and he was tearing the league apart when his big break came. Bill Cowley suffered an injury, and McGill was called up to centre the Bruins' top line between Roy Conacher and Eddie Wiseman. In just 13 games, McGill recorded 19 points (including 8 goals), but when Cowley was better, McGill, of course, was demoted. He later had three more chances with the B's, playing all of the '45-'46 season in his longest stretch before being sent to the minors for good the next year. He settled permanently in Vancouver and ran the Georgian Towers, a popular hotel. McGill died after a lengthy battle with cancer.

McGILL, Ryan
b. Prince Albert, Saskatchewan, February 28, 1969
Nothing was ever the same after April 5, 1995, but McGill had the fortitude of character and peace of mind not only to recover but to thrive. That night, the big, strong defenceman for Edmonton went to the front of the net to take his man, an Anaheim player. Before he knew it, he had been struck in the left eye by the puck. Three weeks later, doctors confirmed that he was legally blind in that eye, and after 4 years and 151 games, his NHL career was over. McGill took a year off to feel sorry for himself and regain his strength, and then the past was the past and he looked forward. He got a job as assistant coach with the Edmonton Ice in 1996, and a year later he was named head man. He transferred with the team to Kootenay in 1998, and three years took them to the Memorial Cup finals, a tournament he had won as a player in 1988 with Medicine Hat. Blind in one eye, his focus remains hockey, a focus that comes from a wealth of inner strength and resolve. In 2002, McGill was named head coach of the AHL's Hartford Wolf Pack.

McGILLIS, Dan
b. Hawkesbury, Ontario, July 1, 1972
The draft is such a crapshoot, and no greater illustration of that is needed than McGillis. He was selected 238th overall by Detroit in 1992, but after four years at Northeastern University he was traded to Edmonton for Kirk Maltby, who had been chosen by the Oilers 65th overall. Yet, in their own way, each has made the deal seem valid and fair. Maltby has been an important part of Detroit's mini-dynasty, and McGillis, after a subsequent trade to Philadelphia, is one of the cornerstones on the Flyers defence, thanks to his hard hitting and defensive play.

McGRATTAN, Tom
b. Brantford, Ontario, October 19, 1927
His was one of the shortest appearances by a goalie in NHL history. On November 9, 1947, McGrattan replaced Harry Lumley in goal with about eight minutes

to go in the game. He surrendered a goal, but it made little difference to the score that night – Toronto 6, Detroit 0. A year later, he was out of the game.

McGREGOR, Alexander "Sandy"
b. Toronto, Ontario, March 30, 1939
A two-game appearance with the Rangers in '63-'64 interrupted a seven-year career with Baltimore in the AHL for McGregor, who has the distinction of having his best season as his last. In '68-'69, he scored 44 goals and 63 points, his top numbers, and then he retired.

McGUIRE, Frank "Mickey"
b. Gravenhurst, Ontario, July 7, 1898
d. unknown
He played pro for much of the 1920s and into the next decade, mostly in the International league, but for two years (1926-28) McGuire also played in the NHL, with the Pittsburgh Pirates.

McHUGH, Mike
b. Bowdoin, Massachusetts, August 16, 1965
McHugh's stock was never higher than in 1988 when he was a Hobey Baker Award finalist and was taken 1st overall in the NHL's Supplemental Draft of U.S. college players. Yet over the next four years, he made only brief appearances in the NHL with Minnesota and then San Jose in a career spent almost entirely in the IHL. McHugh later moved on to the AHL, where he spent seven seasons before retiring in 1998.

McILHARGEY, John "Jack" ("Wolfman")
b. Edmonton, Alberta, March 7, 1952
It's tough not to look at goons of the past with a touch of sentiment, but the truth is fighters were fighters, just like today, though that fact doesn't justify their place in the game prima facie. In 1974-75, McIlhargey tied an AHL record by accumulating 51 penalty minutes in a single game. When he got to the NHL, with the animal Flyers later that same season, he started his punching ways that led to brawls, stick-swinging incidents, and suspensions. McIlhargey never scored more than three goals or eight points in a season, so his value as a player was nil, unless you asked his teammates or coaches, who praised him for his attitude and team-centred focus. Assorted injuries added up, and in 1982 he retired to take on more civil posts in the coaching world, most determinedly with Vancouver as an assistant but also in the minors for a number of years.

McINENLY, Bertram "Bert"
b. Quebec City, Quebec, May 6, 1906
d. Ottawa, Ontario, October 15, 1993
He played six years in the NHL in the 1930s, but McInenly was much more than just a skater. He paddled for the Rideau Aquatic Club in Ottawa, played semi-pro baseball, and was an excellent football and basketball player. In hockey, he got his start with Detroit in 1930 but soon moved on to see time with the Americans, Senators, and Bruins. He later played in the minors before settling in Ottawa, where he entered private business.

McINNIS, Marty
b. Weymouth, Massachusetts, June 2, 1970
After three years at Boston College, McInnis took most of the next year off to play for the U.S. National Team and carry on to the 1992 Olympics in Albertville. He led the team in scoring en route to a fourth-place finish, and soon after joined the Islanders, the team that had drafted him in 1988. His finest season came 2 years later when he scored 25 goals and was a +31, but although he has had 2 subsequent 20-goal seasons his teams – Calgary and Anaheim – almost never went to the playoffs. He's a defensively reliable left winger who can also perform on the power play. McInnis also appeared at the World Championships in 1996 and '97.

McINTOSH, Bruce
b. Minneapolis, Minnesota, March 17, 1949
McIntosh attended the University of Minnesota on scholarship (1967-71), going to the NCAA finals in his last year. Never drafted, he signed with the local North Stars after a good training camp in September '72 and played just two games with the team. By season's end, he was out of hockey entirely.

McINTOSH, Paul
b. Listowel, Ontario, March 13, 1954
In 48 games with Buffalo over 2 seasons (1974-76), McIntosh made only a slight impression on defence, enough to get him work in the AHL but not enough to earn further callups. He retired in 1980, but his career has come to life since then. He coached the London Knights for three years (1980-83) before joining the scouting staff in Vancouver and then Calgary, and he later returned to the Knights as GM. Since the summer of 2000, he has been scouting for the Dallas Stars, rising to the position of head of pro scouting.

McINTYRE, John "Jack" ("Jake")
b. Brussels, Ontario, September 8, 1930
d. Ipperwash, Ontario, March 15, 1998
Born in Brussels and raised in Listowel, McIntyre called London home for most of his life. He played for three Original Six teams in the 1950s, his best years coming with Chicago and Detroit, though he went to the finals for the one and only time with Boston, in 1953. After retiring, McIntyre became the first coach of London's junior A entry, called the Nationals. He later coached the Johnstown Jets and several senior teams in Guelph before leaving the game to work in sales for General Motors. He played charity hockey every chance he could until a knee injury curtailed his skating, but right up until his last he had a passion for the game that inspired his friends to call him Smilin' Jack. He died at home of prostate cancer.

McINTYRE, John
b. Ravenswood, Ontario, April 29, 1969
In some respects, it was a miracle he ever made it back on skates after a serious accident in junior in which a player's blade tore deep into his calf and severed a muscle. He needed a brace just to walk, and leading up to the 1987 draft scouts asked him if he'd ever play again. He vowed he would, but could offer no medical proof to corroborate his optimism. Nonetheless, the Leafs took him 49th overall, and when he came up to the Gardens in 1989, he looked like he would be a player. He had size and defensive commitment to offset a lack of offensive flair. He had dedication and enthusiasm, and he did what he was told. But when the Leafs had the chance to scoop Mike Krushelnyski from L.A., they traded the prospect to the Kings. McIntyre later moved on to the Rangers and Vancouver and retired in 1996 to return to his farm and the quiet life, never quite having made the impact that had been expected.

McINTYRE, Larry
b. Moose Jaw, Saskatchewan, July 13, 1949
It just wasn't meant to be. After making his NHL debut with Toronto in 1970, McIntyre worked in the system to make it back to the Leafs for good. Then, he separated his shoulder and ended in the minors, and the year after he didn't make enough of an impression during his half-season opportunity. Back in the minors. He retired in 1976 and went into coaching in the minor pros, leading a wide range of teams in leagues well below the NHL.

McKAY, Alvin "Doug"
b. Hamilton, Ontario, May 28, 1929
That McKay played a single NHL game is nothing special – the league is full of one-game wonders. What puts McKay above the others, though, is that his lone appearance, on April 15, 1950, was a playoff date, a 4-0 Detroit win over the Rangers in game three of the Stanley Cup finals. The Wings went on to win the series, so despite playing only once, McKay has his name on the Cup. That is amazing. He later coached in the AHL, and his son went on to become a coach himself, though Doug Jr. never played in the NHL.

McKAY, Randy
b. Montreal, Quebec, January 25, 1967
McKay knows his job and knows it well, and even more to the point he does it better than almost anyone else in the game. He started out with Detroit in 1988-89 but didn't establish himself at all until three years

He and teammate John Madden both scored four goals in a game.
RANDY McKAY

Marty McInnis

Jack McIntyre

John McIntyre

Larry McIntyre

Doug McKay

Ray McKay

Walt McKechnie

Jay McKee

Tony McKegney

later when he was sent to New Jersey as compensation for the Wings signing Troy Crowder. With the Devils he became a gritty right winger who could score a bit, play disciplined hockey within the Devils' defensive system, and contribute offensively as well. He, Bobby Holik, and Mike Peluso formed the vaunted Crash Line, a successful unit that helped the team win the Cup in 1995. McKay was around for the team's second championship in 2000, but midway through 2001-02 he was traded to Dallas. Before departing, he and teammate John Madden made a bit of history when both scored four goals in a game. It marked the first time this had been done since the Cleghorn brothers had each scored four times in 1922.

McKAY, Ray
b. Edmonton, Alberta, August 22, 1946
In a 13-year pro career, McKay played a total of 140 NHL games with 3 teams in the 1970s. At 6'4" he was the tallest player in the league and he established himself as a defensive type not too concerned about what happened in the offensive zone. He played most of his games in the minors, though he also played parts of four years in the WHA. After retiring, he established the Elite Defenseman's Training Camp, a school designed especially for aspiring blueliners.

McKAY, Ross
b. Edmonton, Alberta, March 3, 1964
A goalie, McKay didn't spend too much time in the crease before he knew what he wanted to do. He attended the University of Saskatchewan, and after four years he signed with Hartford as a free agent on May 2, 1988. He played in the system for two years and got into a Whalers game in 1990-91, allowing three goals in just over half a game. At season's end, he retired to pursue a career as a chiropractic physician. He graduated from the National College of Chiropractics in 1994 and set up a practice in Illinois, where he also teaches goaltending.

McKAY, Scott
b. Burlington, Ontario, January 26, 1972
Fresh out of junior, McKay got his one NHL game in with Anaheim in 1993-94 but spent the rest of his five pro years in the depths of the minors. Young and enthusiastic, he retired in 1998 and settled in San Diego, where he taught roller hockey. He also became involved with the World Youth Inline Hockey Challenge, an IIHF sanctioned event intended to spread the gospel of the rollerblade version of the ice game.

McKECHNIE, Walt ("McKech")
b. London, Ontario, June 19, 1947
He of the long, long stick, McKechnie did more travelling in his career than most commercial pilots. In his 16 years in the NHL, he played for 8 teams, his longest stint with California (197 games) and his shortest with Washington (16 games). He was a reliable scorer wherever he went, but McKechnie had the unlucky lot in the NHL to be traded from one bad team to another. Despite playing 955 regular-season games, he made the playoffs only twice (15 total games). He scored at least 23 goals in a season 4 times, and he played for Canada at the 1977 World Championships. After retiring, he

moved to Haliburton, Ontario, where he ran a sports bar/restaurant called McKech's.

McKEE, Jay
b. Kingston, Ontario, September 8, 1977
By no means the most talented player in the world, McKee has developed and progressed to the point where he is one of Buffalo's quiet superstars on defence. He doesn't get the recognition and praise of the big-ticket names, but he is as effective in his own end as anyone in the league. Since being drafted by the Sabres in 1995 (with a pick acquired in the deal that sent Alexander Mogilny to Vancouver), McKee has remained in the organization and helped the team go to the finals in 1999 for the first time. Ironically, though he's not a scorer, he recorded an assist in his first-ever game.

McKEE, Mike
b. Toronto, Ontario, June 18, 1969
His name is by no means household and his accomplishments are not the stuff of legend, but McKee made it to the NHL and his career ended because of a series of head injuries that threatened permanent damage if he continued playing. He was an outstanding high school student whose number 5 hangs in the rafters of Upper Canada College in Toronto, and he attended Princeton University after being recruited by that Ivy League school. He was the 1st-overall pick by Quebec in the 1990 draft of U.S. college players, but almost as soon as he played for Halifax in the AHL the head injuries started. Fortunately, he played with the Nordiques for 48 games in '93-'94, so by the time the final blow came back in the minors – a routine check behind the net that left him dizzy getting to the bench – he could retire knowing he had made it. Luckily for him, he had brains to fall back on. He enrolled at Harvard Business School to pursue a career that was rewarding, challenging – and safe.

McKEGNEY, Ian
b. Sarnia, Ontario, May 7, 1947
Chicago was the only team that expressed an interest in signing McKegney, which it did in 1972, though he spent all of the next five years playing for the farm team in Dallas with the exception of three games with the parent Hawks. During those years in the CHL, McKegney was twice named best defenceman ('74-'75 and '75-'76) and league MVP once ('75-'76). He retired soon after but kept skating for the Kincardine Oldstars, one of the oldest, regularly competing teams of former pro players.

McKEGNEY, Tony
b. Montreal, Quebec, February 15, 1958
While it is certainly interesting to know that when he broke into the league in 1978 McKegney was the only black player around, his family and background are even more intriguing. McKegney was born in Montreal but was given up for adoption. He grew up in Sarnia under unusual circumstances in that the McKegneys, a white couple with three children of their own, adopted three more children, all black boys. Young Tony had the good fortune to be blessed with natural athletic ability. When he got to the NHL, he did everything he could to shift the media's glare away

from his skin colour and toward his performance. McKegney was a player. He had nine 20-goal seasons and had a career-best 40 goals with St. Louis in '87-'88. The left winger had a great shot and was a force on the power play, but like many a mid-range superstar he was also well travelled. In his 13 seasons, he played for 7 teams and scored 320 goals. His race may have been important to him personally, but professionally it was his accomplishments of which he was most proud. He settled in Michigan and worked as a sales rep for a local business.

McKENDRY, Alex
b. Midland, Ontario, November 21, 1956

In just seven seasons of pro hockey, McKendry played for five different CHL teams and two more in the NHL. Despite being a high draft choice by the Islanders in 1976, he played just 10 games on Long Island before a trade sent him to Calgary. The Flames used him for half a season, but the hulking forward did not make enough of an impression to earn a return engagement. He retired in 1983.

McKENNA, Sean
b. Asbestos, Quebec,
March 7, 1962

By the time he got to Toronto, the damage had been done and he had lost his scoring touch. McKenna started his career with Buffalo in '81-'82 and in his first 2 full seasons he scored 20 goals in each. When he was traded to L.A., though, he was transmogrified into a strictly defensive player and his production dropped. More important, his instincts around the enemy net left him, and by the time the Leafs acquired him he couldn't bury his chances. The Leafs ended up sending him to the minors, and he retired soon after. McKenna later worked as a sales representative for Inglasco, the company that produces most of the pucks used in North American pro hockey.

McKENNA, Steve ("Mac")
b. Toronto, Ontario, August 21, 1973

Okay, Zdeno Chara inches Steve McKenna out as the game's tallest player (6'9" versus 6'8"), but where Chara is a defenceman McKenna is a fighting left winger who has shown little skill in the scoring department and great skill in the going-to-the-penalty-box department. He was drafted by L.A. but has also played with the expansion Wild in Minnesota and Pittsburgh. His most recent stop has been New York, where he does his ice-boxing on Broadway.

McKENNEY, Don ("Slip")
b. Smiths Falls, Ontario, April 30, 1934

For a guy who never aspired to the NHL, the boy did okay. While playing kid hockey at home, McKenney was scouted by Baldy Cotton, one of the best in the business. He invited Don and brother Glen to try out for the Barrie Flyers, the top junior club for Boston, and Don passed with flying colours. In his second season there, he was key to the team winning the Memorial Cup, and that meant another promotion, to the top farm team in Hershey. Another great season, a callup to the Bruins of the NHL, and McKenney scored 22 goals as a rookie, becoming runner-up in Calder Trophy voting. He played 9 seasons in all with the Bruins, scoring at least 20 goals in each, except '55-'56, and going to the Cup finals twice. He was traded to the Rangers and then to Toronto, where he won his only Cup in 1964, although he suffered a bad knee injury in the finals and missing the deciding game. He continued to play for a brief time, but his knee never fully recovered and in 1970 he retired. He joined his old Boston teammate Fern Flaman as an assistant coach at Northeastern University, a position he held for 19 years until Flaman retired. McKenney then assumed the head coaching job for two years before semi-retiring. He scouted for the Colorado Avalanche (New England prep schools) for six years and then retired to a life of relaxation for good.

Sean McKenna

While playing kid hockey at home, McKenney was scouted by Baldy Cotton.
DON McKENNEY

McKENNY, Jim ("Howie")
b. Ottawa, Ontario,
December 1, 1946

Back in the mid-1960s, when he was skating like a dream on the blueline of the Marlies, McKenny was touted as the best prospect in the country with one exception – Bobby Orr. The comparisons lasted but a brief time, in part because Orr was obviously so much better than everyone else put together, in part because by age 16 McKenny was, by his own admission, more or less an alcoholic (which is, in part, why he was nicknamed Howie, after Young, another great but alcoholic player). He led the good life, played for Canada's team, and had nothing but smiles to look forward to every day. But his first four years turned into a laborious effort to make the team at all. He spent most of the time in the minors, because of attitude, not skill problems, and when he made the Leafs for good in 1969 he was a solid player, not another Orr. At various points during his career he dried out, and at various others he fell off that ever-precarious wagon. In all, he played 13 seasons for the Leafs, though his days were almost over before the team ever flourished. He played a few games with Minnesota and then went to Switzerland for a year, where he had fun but his family didn't. He returned the year after for a couple of weeks alone, and at that

Jim McKenny

Kirk McLean

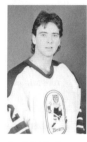

Scott McLellan

Dave McLelland

McLEAN, Jeff
b. Port Moody, British Columbia, October 6, 1969
For his eight years of professional hockey, McLean has one NHL puck to show for his efforts, a goal he scored with San Jose in '93-'94. Besides that, the U of North Dakota grad played almost exclusively in the minors.

McLEAN, Kirk
b. Willowdale, Ontario, June 26, 1966
Forget about hockey – McLean owned a Queen's Plate winner! In 1995, Regal Discovery, racing out of No. 1 Stables, which McLean owned with his wife and partners, won Canada's most prestigious race after starting at 9-1 odds (Discovery beat out, among others, Ice Agent, a horse owned by Gary Leeman and named after his NHL agent, Don Meehan). The No. 1 comes from McLean's sweater number as an NHL goalie, but McLean never had such a brush with greatness during his long and successful hockey career. The closest he came was in 1994, when he took the Canucks to game seven of the Cup finals the year the Rangers won it all. McLean played 11 seasons in Vancouver and he was the team's number-one goalie most of that time. He started in New Jersey, but the Devils had a plethora of blue-ice talent and sent him out west in a multiplayer deal in 1987. The beginning of the end came in '97-'98 when he was traded twice and his star status quickly petered out. He played in two All-Star Games, but with horses like Regal Discovery, the most important stats might be those quadrupeds he trains in his post-NHL life.

McLELLAN, John
b. South Porcupine, Ontario, August 6, 1928
d. Toronto, Ontario, October 27, 1979
Hockey wasn't quite his wife – he had a lovely wife named Sheila – but it certainly was his life. Literally. As a player, McLellan was highly successful. He won the Memorial Cup in 1947 with St. Mike's (Red Kelly was his roommate), and two years later won the Allan Cup with the Marlies. He played two games for the Leafs soon after but spent most of the next few years in the minors until he played for Belleville in '58-'59 as an amateur. He travelled with the McFarlands to the World Championships, winning a gold medal, and then became interested in coaching. McLellan won two EHL titles with Nashville and coached Tulsa in the CHL for two seasons before being named head coach of the Leafs in 1969 to replace Punch Imlach, who was fired the night the Leafs were eliminated from the playoffs. McLellan's four years as coach were a mixed bag. The team played well, but not Stanley Cup-contending well, and the stress of the job took a heavy toll on him. Twice during the '71-'72 season he had to

step away from the game to have ulcers treated, and a year later he resigned as coach because of his health. He remained with the team as director of scouting, but one fall day in 1979 he collapsed in his yard while raking leaves. He died a short time later in hospital.

McLELLAN, Scott
b. Toronto, Ontario, February 10, 1963
Imagine the excitement when, at age 20 and playing junior in Peterborough, your coach tells you the Boston Bruins have called you up to the NHL! The year was 1983 and McLellan was on his way to a 100-point season with the Petes. He played in two games for the Bruins on right wing and then over the next two years heard terrific silence from the NHL. He retired, became a Toronto-based scout for Boston, and also became active in girls hockey.

He travelled with the McFarlands to the World Championships, winning a gold medal.
JOHN McLELLAN

McLELLAN, Todd
b. Melville, Saskatchewan, October 3, 1967
Gary Green and Paul Maurice were among the youngest men ever to coach in the NHL, but they ain't got squat on McLellan, who retired as a player at the ripe old age of 21 to pursue a coaching career. McLellan's career is worth a simple sentence: junior in Saskatoon, a few games with the Islanders, a year and a half of pro in the AHL. From there, he coached in Holland for three years before returning to the WHL, where he worked with Swift Current. He coached there for six years before moving to Cleveland of the IHL for a year, a move that backfired when the league folded at season's end. Undaunted, McLellan landed the head coaching job of the Houston Aeros and continues on his way to an eventual NHL opportunity.

McLELLAND, Dave
b. Penticton, British Columbia, November 20, 1952
It really wasn't a career to write home about, though something is better than nothing, of course. McLelland appeared in two games for Vancouver during his short pro career. In his first outing, March 25, 1973, he beat the Leafs 7-4 and earned a start six nights later. Los Angeles blew six goals by him, though, in a 6-3 win, and he never made it back to the big tent after that.

McLENAHAN, Roland "Roly"
b. Fredericton, New Brunswick, October 26, 1921
d. Fredericton, New Brunswick, April 23, 1984
Quite simply, he was the most important person New Brunswick has ever produced from a sports perspective, regardless of only nine games played with Detroit in '45-'46. He had a lengthy career in the AHL, and in 1953 he started coaching, first with Cincinnati of

the IHL. He returned to the AHL in '57-'58 to lead Rochester to a Calder Cup, and then he went home to New Brunswick. He was a scout for Montreal for eight years (1960-68) and later sent Danny Grant and Buster Harvey on to the NHL for Detroit. It was as an administrator that he had his greatest and longest-lasting influence, though. In 1961, he was appointed the province's first sports director for the Department of Youth, a position he held for 20 years. During his tenure he expanded the province's recreation department exponentially. He was a founding father of the N.B. Sports Hall of Fame, the New Brunswick Amateur Hockey Association, and more than 200 recreational councils throughout the province. He served on the Canada Games Council twice and was a director with the CAHA and Hockey Canada. In 1981, doctors discovered he had lung cancer, and three years later the disease fatally moved to his brain.

McLENNAN, Jamie ("Noodles")
b. Edmonton, Alberta, June 30, 1971
McLennan's career ground to a halt after a year with Minnesota in 2000-01. It began in 1991 when the Islanders drafted him, but in the summer of 1996 he became a free agent and signed with St. Louis rather than hope for a full-time chance on Long Island. With the Bluenotes, he partnered with Grant Fuhr, learning from the best every night he didn't play, and gaining valuable experience when he did. Things changed when Fuhr departed and Roman Turek arrived, and McLennan was claimed by the Wild in the Expansion Draft. He had an awful 5-23-9 record with the new team, and that was the end of the NHL line for him. In 1998, he won the Bill Masterton Award.

McLEOD, Al ("Moose")
b. Medicine Hat, Alberta, June 17, 1949
Defenceman Al McLeod graduated from Michigan Tech in 1971 and turned pro in the Detroit system. He played his few NHL games with the Wings but spent most of three seasons in the minors. When he had the chance to jump to the WHA in 1974, he took it, and played his final five seasons of hockey there. After retiring, he settled in Calgary, where he became a director for the Calgary Buffaloes Hockey Association, a junior team with which he had played in his teens.

McLEOD, Don ("Smokey")
b. Trail, British Columbia, August 24, 1946
From the land of the Smoke Eaters came a goalie named Don McLeod who had his share of highs and lows in his career. The highs included a Memorial Cup with Edmonton in 1966 and turning pro a year later. The highs included replacing Roy Edwards in January 1971 with Detroit and winning his first game. The highs carried over to the WHA, where he played six years, twice leading the league in wins. The lows included not sticking around in the NHL longer. The lows finished with a comeback with Toronto in the NHL in 1979 after he had been retired for a year and selling novelty items in a shop. But surely the oddest fact about McLeod is that he must be the only player to be drafted into the NHL – 104th overall by Pittsburgh in 1973 – after already having played 2 seasons in the league!

McLEOD, Jim
b. Port Arthur, Ontario, April 7, 1937
You never know, you just never know. After 11 years in the minors, almost all in the WHL, McLeod had no idea he would get into the NHL as a 34-year-old rookie. But to start the '71-'72 season, the St. Louis Blues were in a state of flux. Ernie Wakely and Pete McDuffe were the goalies, but the team was playing poorly and coach Bill McCreary tried to shake things up. He recalled McLeod from Portland but didn't play him right away, but the team kept losing so he threw McLeod in against California and the team won 5-1. McLeod played 16 games in all with a 6-6-4 record, and although he went back to the minors he had made enough of an impression that the WHA was a viable alternative for the new season. McLeod played three seasons in that league before retiring.

McLEOD, John "Jackie"
b. Regina, Saskatchewan, April 30, 1930
Like most Canadian boys, McLeod grew up playing hockey. Unlike most, he was very, very good. He played junior hockey in Moose Jaw but surprised everyone when he decided to leave the team at 19 to try his hand at the pro ranks, with the Rangers. He further surprised everyone when he made the team (despite suffering a broken nose in his first practise!). The right winger was a good skater and shooter, but after two full seasons with the team he found himself in the minors more often than not. Most of those years were spent in the WHL, and it was with Saskatoon in '55-'56 that McLeod found his truer calling, as a coach. Midway through the season, he replaced Doug Bentley as coach of the Quakers, though he continued to play and later returned to his amateur status to continue his playing days. He represented Canada with the Trail Smoke Eaters at the 1961 World Championships, winning a gold medal, and in '62 and '63 he joined other teams – Moose Jaw and Saskatoon – to compete at the Worlds. In 1965, he formalized his relationship with Canada's international hockey by becoming GM and coach of the National Team. Under McLeod, the country won bronze at the 1968 Olympics in Grenoble. Once the national program stopped in 1970, when Canada withdrew from international hockey, McLeod became coach and GM of the Saskatoon Blades in the WHL, a post that lasted a decade. He retired in 1980 and four years later was inducted into the Saskatchewan Sports Hall of Fame. In 1999 he was inducted into the IIHF Hockey Hall of Fame for his international career.

McLLWAIN, Dave
b. Seaforth, Ontario, January 9, 1967
Really, how bad can it get, as long as you're in the NHL? For McLlwain, the '91-'92 season couldn't have been much worse. He had played the previous two years with Winnipeg, so he knew he'd be reporting to that city for training camp in September of 1991. Three games into the season, he was traded to Buffalo. Okay. No sweat. Get it out of the way early. Settle in and make a contribution to the new team, get to know the players, blah blah blah. Five games later – another trade. The Islanders. Crazy but true, he headed off to Long Island, settled in, got to know his

Al McLeod

Don McLeod

Jim McLeod

Jackie McLeod

Dave McLlwain

Mike McMahon

Sammy McManus

Bob McManama

Tom McMurchy

teammates, the weeks passed, all looked good. Then, the phone rings. You gotta be joking. Nope. Toronto. Four teams in one year. He was a versatile player with excellent speed, and teams were always looking for such a player. That's what each GM said to him coming in, and going out. In all, he played for 7 teams in 10 seasons, and then moved to Europe to continue playing. Wherever he was during the season, though, he always returned to Seaforth in the summers to run his hockey school. *That* was his constant.

McMAHON, Mike
b. Brockville, Ontario, February 1, 1915
d. Fort Erie, Ontario, December 3, 1974
Whether he would have had a longer or shorter career had he not played around the time of the Second World War, we'll never know. But the truth is, his entrance into the NHL was delayed by his time in the militia with the Stormont, Dundas, and Glengarry Highlanders. He came out in time to play for Montreal in the 1943 playoffs, and the year after was his only full season. What a year it was, though! He led the league in penalty minutes with 98 and the Habs won the Stanley Cup. He played one more partial year before going down to the minors, and after retiring as a player he became a linesman in the AHL. This second career was cut short in 1958 when he suffered a heart attack immediately after working a game in Buffalo. His son, Mike Jr., also played in the NHL.

McMAHON, Mike, Jr.
b. Quebec City, Quebec, August 30, 1941
Mike Junior was born in Quebec City because that's where his old man was playing, with the Aces. Like father, like son, young Mike also turned into a defenceman, but played a good deal longer than dad because of expansion. His best year was with Minnesota in '67-'68 when he scored 14 goals and 47 points, an incredible difference from the rest of his career. In his other 150 games outside this season, McMahon scored exactly once. He toured the NHL, playing with six teams, and in 1972 moved to the WHA, back in Minnesota. He retired five years later.

McMANAMA, Bob
b. Belmont, Massachusetts, October 7, 1951
As a student, McManama could pahk the cah in Hahvahd yahd anytime he wanted, for it was at that Ivy league school he earned his degree in history. He was also a great scorer, centring the Local Line with David Hynes and Bill Corkery on his wings. When he joined the Pittsburgh Penguins in 1973, he became the second person (after George Owen in the 1920s) to go from Harvard to the NHL. He played on a line with

Greg Polis and Jean Pronovost, but in each of his three seasons his NHL time decreased and his AHL time increased. Not desiring a career in the minors or a fight to make it back, he retired in 1976 at age 24.

McMANUS, Sammy
b. Belfast, Northern Ireland, October 22, 1910
d. Toronto, Ontario, July 1, 1976
The McManus family moved to Toronto in 1912 and young Sammy took an immediate interest in hockey when he was old enough to skate. After playing junior with the Canoe Club and senior with the Goodyears, McManus moved down east to begin a long and rewarding career in those parts. He won the Allan Cup with Moncton in 1933 and again the next year, and the Hawks beat the Detroit White Stars to win the Willis Cup as senior champs of North America. He got his NHL chance with the Maroons the year after, a season in which the English Montrealers won the Stanley Cup. He later played a game for Boston but spent several more years in the lower ranks, mostly in the Maritimes. After retiring, McManus worked for the New Brunswick Electric Power Commission. His grandson, Scott Pellerin, later played in the NHL.

McMURCHY, Tom
b. New Westminster, British Columbia, December 2, 1963
Five feet ten inches tall, 170 pounds. Say no more, say no more. The writing is on the wall, the bio writ in stone. Scorer in junior, not given much of a shot in the NHL, winds up in Europe. That's how it reads. His NHL games all came in the 1980s, and he

He acted as GM for Team Canada at the 1982 World Championships.
MAX McNAB

did manage to play in nine games with the Oilers in '87-'88, the team's last Cup year with Gretzky.

McNAB, Max
b. Watson, Saskatchewan, June 21, 1924
Max McNab played his only NHL hockey with Detroit from 1947 to '51. This had two advantages: one, he got to play alongside the likes of Gordie Howe and Ted Lindsay; two, he learned about the game from Jack Adams, the brilliant and demonic GM of the Wings. McNab got his NHL glory in '49-'50 when he won the Stanley Cup, but his NHL career ended early because of a serious back injury. He played on in the minors for another seven seasons, finishing his career as a playing coach with New Westminster in the WHL. He coached out west for a number of years, and in 1966 he was named coach and GM of San Diego in the Western league. In 1974, he became president of the CHL, a position he held for just a year because he wanted to be GM with the expansion Capitals in Washington. He acted as GM for Team Canada at the 1982 World Championships, and a year later he held the same post

for the New Jersey Devils, where he spent the rest of his working days. His son, Peter, also played in the NHL.

McNAB, Peter

b. Vancouver, British Columbia, May 8, 1952

What a great way to end a fine career, for a player to walk into the GM's office and say, "Dad, I'm retiring." After 954 games and 813 points, McNab called it a career in the summer of 1987. He had played most of his years in Boston where he scored 35 goals or more in 6 consecutive seasons. He never won a Cup – never came close, really – but the big centreman was a force on the power play and for 10 seasons in a row he appeared in the playoffs. Late in his career, his dad, GM of New Jersey, signed him as a free agent, perceived by some as an act of nepotism, but given Peter's production and the fact that Max lost no players in the deal, it was hardly a move loaded with controversy. After hangin' 'em up, Peter stayed in New Jersey and worked for the Devils' expanded television coverage for eight years before moving to Colorado in a similar capacity. His brother, David, meanwhile was on the coast acting as assistant GM for Anaheim.

Peter McNab

McNABNEY, Sid

b. Toronto, Ontario, January 15, 1929
d. Toronto, Ontario, February 7, 1957

Sidney William McNabney lived not long enough, just 28 years, in fact. He played junior hockey with the Barrie Flyers and spent four years in the AHL, squeezing five playoff games out of the Montreal Canadiens in 1951. He retired a year later and returned to Toronto, where he got a job in a post office. Late in 1956, though, he was stricken by cancer and had to quit his job. Six months later, he was dead.

McNAMARA, Gerry

b. Sturgeon Falls, Ontario, September 22, 1934

At what point does respect – regardless how hollow – control truth, or should it always? McNamara was human, like anyone, and he was a special hockey player, like anyone who makes the NHL, if even for a Beckett-breath of time. His active career was typical of the time: a career minor-league goalie had no chance of usurping Johnny Bower and Terry Sawchuk from the Leafs net. He made seven appearances as an emergency replacement with the team, but he could do, and expect, no more. When he retired, he made a name for himself by going to Sweden to scout Borje Salming and Inge Hammartsrom, and when he brought them both under contract and into Leafs sweaters, he made hockey history and changed scouting. The problems began when he was named Leafs GM in 1982, a mouthpiece for owner Harold Ballard, a yes-man, and a man who

He retired and opened a gas station near Montreal.
GERRY McNEIL

quickly proved he was in so far over his head he couldn't see the top. Ballard gave McNamara a dog named Puck, and McNamara in turn made some bad trades and even worse decisions. Highlights? There was the time he made a colossal ass of himself on television, ranting at reporters instead of talking about the team. There was the time he fired coach John Brophy, only to be told by Ballard that Broph was still employed. But worst of all, and perhaps fittingly symbolic, was his successful court case. McNamara had been in a car accident and had sued the other driver, claiming he had incurred brain injuries. The worst part? He won his case. This was while he was GM of the Leafs. Behind the scenes, he was nicknamed B.D. (for brain dead), and by the time Ballard fired him in 1988, the team had plummeted to its nadir in 70 years of operations.

McNAMARA, Howard

b. Penetang, Ontario, November 22, 1890
d. September 4, 1940

At 240 pounds, he was one of the heaviest players ever. In the 1910s, he was a giant. Howard and brother, George, played defence together as kids, and were called the Dynamite Twins for good reason. They played in the Soo and turned pro in Halifax, and Howard quickly became known for his heavy hits, fine puck carrying, and gentlemanly play. The brothers settled in Toronto around 1912 and played hockey locally until serving overseas. Upon discharge, Howard played with the Montreal Canadiens in the newly formed NHL, but his best years would come after he retired. He and George went into the road contracting business in Toronto and became millionaires, such was their success.

Peter McNab

McNAUGHTON, George

b. Gaspé, Quebec, April 4, 1897
d. unknown

McNaughton played a single game with the Quebec Bulldogs during the 1919-20 season, most likely because he played locally and might have been well known to the team. He didn't distinguish himself in any other league at any other time, and his career was a short one.

McNEIL, Gerry

b. Quebec City, Quebec, April 17, 1926

As a teen, McNeil idolized Boston's Frank Brimsek, and when McNeil was 17, at his first Canadiens training camp, he played his first exhibition game in Quebec City against Boston and that same Brimsek! But he didn't make the team that year. Instead, he spent most of the next six years with the Montreal Royals, appearing in two games in '47-'48 before joining King Clancy's Cincinnati Mohawks for

Gerry McNamara

Billy McNeill

George McPhee

Mike McPhee

'49-'50. It was at this point that McNeil caught the biggest break of his career. Bill Durnan had just retired, and Jacques Plante was still a few years away from claiming the Habs' job for a generation, so there was an opening for starting goalie in Montreal – McNeil earned the job. In his first two years, he played every regular season and playoff game for the team, and he staked his claim to immortality when he was in net the night Bill Barilko scored his diving, heroic, Cup-winning goal in 1951, the year all five finals games between Toronto and Montreal went into overtime. For McNeil, though, his great triumph had come in the '51 semi-finals as he led the team to an upset win over Cup champs of a year before, Detroit. In 1952, McNeil lost again in the finals, but in '53 everything went perfectly and he won his first Cup. Prelude to the victory was the last game of the regular season against Detroit. Gordie Howe entered the game with 49 goals on the year, but try as he might he couldn't beat McNeil for number fifty. After McNeil had played one more year, Plante assumed the throne and McNeil was on the outs. The low point of his career came in the '54 semifinals when he shut the Bruins out 2-0. In the dressing room, the happiness subsided when coach Dick Irvin looked at McNeil and complained that the goalie had stopped all the shots the wrong way! In the finals, it was McNeil's misfortune to be in goal for the last game, won 2-1 by Detroit in overtime to capture the Cup. Tony Leswick skated in over the blueline and directed a routine shot on goal, but defenceman Doug Harvey tried to catch the puck and clear it. However, he didn't play the puck cleanly; it hit his glove, changed direction, and skittered past an out-of-position McNeil. To this day it is one of the flukier Cup-winning goals of all time. McNeil's passion for the game had been sapped by Irvin's comment. He retired and opened a gas station near Montreal, but when Irvin left the team and Toe Blake, a former teammate of McNeil's, became the new coach, things changed. Blake approached McNeil and offered him a contract to be the spare goalie – same salary as a starter would make. He took the job, played in nine games in '56-'57, and was part of another Cup team. Rejuvenated, he played four more years, albeit in the minors, and retired permanently in 1961. He went to work for Seagram Distilleries, a job he had for some 20 years, before retiring altogether.

McNEILL, Billy
b. Edmonton, Alberta, January 26, 1936
The common wisdom about the Original Six era is that there were so many good players in the minors. What a shame. They were ready to take an NHLer's job if he slacked off. Not much was usually made of a guy like McNeill, though, who played for years in the minors and did not do so happily and was not in awe of the NHL and did not think he had been given a fair chance. In fact, he played 17 years in the minors (1954-71) and sprinkled throughout those years were 5 trips to the Red Wings, four of which lasted the better part of a season. But McNeill was a right winger who could score, and complain though he might, the truth is it took him more than 240 NHL games to hit the 20-goal

mark. What separated the NHLers was their ability to perform – instantly, on command, under pressure, *now!* McNeill retired in 1960, only to return, and he did the same again the year after. He had two outstanding seasons in the WHL to earn MVP honours in '64-'65 and '65-'66. He spent many of his last years playing in Vancouver and working as a sales rep for Carling Breweries, and when he finally did retire for good he worked for the beer company full-time.

McNEILL, Mike
b. Winona, Minnesota, July 22, 1966
Not only did McNeill graduate from the University of Notre Dame in 1988, he also participated in the Goodwill Games two years later. As a hockey player, he spent most of his time in the "I," though he did get into a number of games with Chicago and Quebec in the early 1990s. After a brief stint in Germany, McNeill retired as a player to assume the job of athletic director, youth council for USA Hockey.

McNEILL, Stewart
b. Port Arthur, Ontario, September 25, 1938
How did the Red Wings like Stewart McNeill? So much that they invested $5,000 in his education at medical school to keep him happy. This was in the late 1950s, when five grand was almost as good as a year's salary. He had been given a two-game amateur trial in '57-'58 and had performed well, and the next year, during a three-game trial, he impressed the Wings to such a degree they finally persuaded him to sign a pro contract. Ironically, he played five games without a point and retired at season's end to pursue his true love, medicine.

McPHEE, George
b. Guelph, Ontario, July 2, 1958
Most every hockey player starts out in the same way – he has to – but most every one finishes differently. For McPhee, hockey began while he was earning a business degree from Bowling Green University (1978-82), a tenure that ended with his being named Hobey Baker Award winner. He joined the Rangers for a few games the year after, playing on a utility line with Ron Duguay and Mike Backman, but early on in his career injuries to his shoulder and back almost immediately cast a pall over his ability to last. By 1989, he was forced to retire, but he still wanted to take part in the game. McPhee earned a law degree from Rutgers and then became the assistant GM in Vancouver before assuming the GM position outright in Washington. Under his leadership, the Caps went to the finals for the first time and later acquired Jaromir Jagr, one of the great stars of the modern game.

McPHEE, Mike
b. Sydney, Nova Scotia, July 14, 1960
A sort of poor man's Bob Gainey – which is a compliment, not a putdown – McPhee impressed Gainey both when they played together in Montreal and when Gainey went into management. McPhee was a durable, hard-working winger capable of scoring 20 goals but equally capable of checking and playing solid defence. He first joined the team in '83-'84 and made the Habs full-time the year after. His tenure of nine

years included the Cup season of '85-'86, and he played for coach Gainey in Minnesota in 1992, going to Dallas with the team the year after. Since retiring, McPhee has become active in developing kids sports in Nova Scotia.

McRAE, Basil
b. Beaverton, Ontario, January 5, 1961
In Philadelphia in the 1970s, Bill Barber was the master innovator of the odious move called the dive, the faked foul designed to draw a penalty out of thin air. A generation later, Basil McRae was master craftsman of another unsportsmanlike gesture, the fake fight. He'd jostle with an opponent, who would then drop his gloves, and McRae would skate away looking at the ref as if to say, Look at that guy starting a fight. The reason he was so good at it was that he often did fight – that was his job. He threw the fakes in as a bonus. McRae was the designated fighter for seven teams, but near the end of the line he broke the same leg in successive seasons. He was a fan favourite in Minnesota and St. Louis, where he had his longest stays, and after retiring he returned to the land of the Arch to work as a financial adviser.

McRAE, Chris
b. Beaverton, Ontario, August 26, 1965
Cut from the same cloth as his brother, Basil, Chris was also a scrapper, though he lasted considerably fewer years in pro, in large part because of a serious eye injury he suffered during the '89-'90 season. He signed with the Leafs as a free agent in 1985, though it was 2 years before he played with the team and his career with Toronto lasted just 14 games over 2 seasons. He played his only other NHL games with Detroit before retiring in 1992 at the ripe old age of 26.

McRAE, Gord ("Bird")
b. Sherbrooke, Quebec, April 12, 1948
It is fair and accurate to state that McRae spent his entire career with Toronto, but that fact should not conjure up the oohs and ahs reserved for the likes of Alex Delvecchio (24 years with Detroit) and George Armstrong (21 seasons with the Leafs). No. For McRae that career represents some 71 games over 6 seasons (1972-78), during which time he was never able to become the number-one man. He had some fine years in the minors in the 1970s as well, in the CHL, but his performance there never translated well to the NHL when he was given the opportunity to play with the Leafs.

McRAE, Ken
b. Winchester, Ontario, April 23, 1968
A battler and a hustler, McRae had to fight for every minute of ice time, sometimes with that competitive spirit that kept him in the game, sometimes more literally with his fists. Despite being a high draft choice for Quebec in 1986, he played only one full season for the Nordiques, three years later, before being traded to Toronto. His time with the Leafs was even more tenuous, and soon he was in the minors for good. McRae finished up in the IHL and then stayed on with Houston, his last team, as an assistant coach. He later filled the same role with the Austin Ice Bats.

McREAVY, Pat
b. Owen Sound, Ontario, January 16, 1918
d. Owen Sound, Ontario, November 13, 2001
McReavy, a centre, played for the Sudbury Wolves in 1937-38, the season the Wolves represented Canada at the World Championships in Czechoslovakia and came home with gold. On this strength, he joined the Bruins the following year, though he spent most of the next few years in the minors. His finest moments came in the '41 playoffs when he helped the Bruins win the Cup, scoring once in the finals despite playing only seven games during the regular season. The year after, he was sent to Detroit for Dutch Hiller – a big deal at the time – but by season's end his NHL career finished when he joined the army. He never made it back, instead returning to Owen Sound and playing senior hockey. McReavy retired in 1951 after winning the Allan Cup with the Mercurys and later became a wholesale distributor in North Bay.

McREYNOLDS, Brian
b. Penetanguishene, Ontario, January 5, 1965
Brian and his twin brother, Blair, were quite the pair of hockey players as kids, though it was Brian only who persevered and played pro. He went to Michigan State in 1985 on scholarship, and at the end of his first season the Spartans won the NCAA championship. Although he had been drafted by the Rangers, McReynolds played all of '88-'89 with the Canadian National Team and signed with Winnipeg before making his NHL debut. Ironically, he was traded to the Rangers for Simon Wheeldon, a player whose career mirrored McReynolds' in that they both spent some of their happiest years in Europe. McReynolds played in the minors until 1995 and then moved to Germany, where he played for four years.

McSHEFFREY, Bryan
b. Ottawa, Ontario, September 25, 1952
McSheffrey was lucky enough to play junior in his hometown before being drafted by Vancouver in 1972. He played just parts of two seasons with the Canucks and a few games more with Buffalo before finishing in the minors. He ended his career in Holland, one of the

He was a fan favourite in Minnesota and St. Louis.
BASIL McRAE

Chris McRae

Gord McRae

Ken McRae

Brian McReynolds

Bryan McSheffrey

Don McSween

Dale McTavish

Gord McTavish

Charlie McVeigh

lesser hockey-playing countries in Europe but a beautiful nation regardless, and after retiring settled back in Ottawa. He later coached the Senators alumni teams that played charity games across Canada.

McSORLEY, Marty
b. Hamilton, Ontario, May 18, 1963

Particular moments in history define a player's contribution to the game and symbolize a career that is often consistent with that moment. McSorley's fans might disagree that the night of February 21, 2000, was an aberration and not fair criteria to judge his 17 years in the game; his detractors would argue vehemently the opposite. While playing for Boston, McSorley had a running feud all night with Donald Brashear of Vancouver, a feud that ended with McSorley hitting Brashear along the side of the head, knocking him unconscious. The police charged McSorley, and at trail later that year he was convicted of assault with a weapon but given a conditional discharge. The NHL, meanwhile, suspended him for the rest of the season (23 games) and later extended the suspension to last exactly 1 year. It was a vicious and cowardly act and by no means McSorley's first. He had been suspended at least 4 times in the NHL and once in the AHL for 10 games for a deliberate attempt to injure. The assault on Brashear ended McSorley's playing days in the NHL, though he played briefly in the IHL the year after in hopes of returning. Yet during his career he was not without skill of one kind or another. He was a large and intimidating defenceman who usually did

It was a vicious and cowardly act and by no means McSorley's first.
MARTY McSORLEY

his dirty work ethically by simply dropping his gloves and fighting. He won two Cups with Edmonton while protecting Wayne Gretzky in the post-Dave Semenko days, and he was traded with Gretzky to L.A., where he performed a similar function. Yet McSorley's violence of the against a player – Brashear – who was clearly prepared to fight and play the game with an enforcer's code, will always be regarded as the defining moment for the goon gone bad. He played in Britain with his brother, Chris, for a short time, but Gretzky, a man loyal to a fault, hired McSorley as an assistant coach for the Phoenix farm team in Springfield in 2002.

McSWEEN, Don
b. Detroit, Michigan, June 9, 1964

A career that started in 1987 with promise ended in 2000 with a minor-league bang. McSween had played with Michigan State before making the Sabres in '87, though in his five years with the team he played just nine games outside the AHL team in Rochester. Ditto for his career with Anaheim, the team with which he signed as a free agent. He ended in the IHL and then in the United

league playing for Muskegon, winning the Colonial Cup in 1999 and retiring a year later. McSween also played at the 1994 World Championships for the U.S.

McTAGGART, Jim
b. Weyburn, Saskatchewan, March 31, 1960

By his own admission, he was not a finesse defenceman who could feather those beautiful passes and move the puck up the ice *à la* Orr. He hit hard, and for that he often had to answer with a fight, and he was solid in his own end. Undrafted, he signed with Washington in 1979 and made the team the following year. The year after, though, he was relegated to the minors for most of the year, and the year after that he was out of the league altogether. By 1984, he retired rather than continue in the lower reaches. He became an assistant coach for the Seattle Thunderbirds in the WHL, and later became a full-time instructor for Hockey Education Systems (HES) based in Mountlake Terrace, Washington.

McTAVISH, Dale
b. Eganville, Ontario, February 28, 1972

He played in the NHL and scored a goal. The rest was gravy. McTavish was never drafted after his four years of junior in Peterborough. He went to the Memorial Cup in his final year, '92-'93, and then went to university at St. F-X in Nova Scotia. His nine NHL games came with Calgary in '96-'97, and after that he played mostly in Europe, joining the touring Canadian National Team whenever occasion permitted.

McTAVISH, Gord
b. Guelph, Ontario, June 3, 1954

Not one of Montreal's better draft choices, McTavish went 15th overall to the Habs in 1974 but never played a game for the team. In fact, he was traded to St. Louis for Mike Korney on October 7, 1978, and Korney was exposed by Montreal in the Waiver Draft. Thus, McTavish was given away. He played a single game with St. Louis and 10 more with Winnipeg a year later, and his short career came to a quick end.

McVEIGH, Charlie ("Rabbit")
b. Kenora, Ontario, March 29, 1897
d. May 7, 1984

What an honour it was for hockey to be able to call McVeigh a participant for so many years! Just days before his 19th birthday, the boy enlisted in the army and saw heavy fighting at Vimy Ridge in 1917. He lost much of his hearing from his time in the war, but that did not deter him from pursuing hockey when he came home. He set out to play in Regina and then Portland,

and it was with Pete Muldoon's Rosebuds that McVeigh earned his nickname. He was charged wildly by an opponent, but the little forward hopped over the enemy and moved in on goal. Muldoon declared then and there that McVeigh was going to be called Rabbit. McVeigh joined the NHL with Chicago the next year, '26-'27, and stayed two years. He played the rest of his NHL days with the New York Americans and finished his career in the IHL for a final season, '35-'36. He became a referee in that league and the newly formed AHL, eventually becoming the AHL's referee-in-chief. All this time he was living in Detroit and working for the Ford Motor Company, and in truth it wasn't strictly his love of the game that kept him involved. Yes, he became the most respected official in the league, but he had a daughter afflicted with an incurable disease and a wife who was nearly as ill, and he needed every penny to pay for their medical expenses. He retired from the AHL in 1950 only because Ford refused to continue granting him the necessary leaves of absence. McVeigh was a treasure not only to the game but also to humanity, a great player but an even greater man.

McVICAR, Jack
b. Renfrew, Ontario, June 4, 1904
d. unknown
McVicar played two full seasons with the Montreal Maroons (1930-32) but his other pro activities were pretty much confined to the Can-Am league, precursor to the AHL. The defenceman also played for the team in the playoffs, though in both seasons the team was eliminated in the early going.

MEAGHER, Rick
b. Belleville, Ontario, November 2, 1953
Meagher had an outstanding college career with Boston University, but this didn't earn him any points come draft day. He signed with Montreal as a free agent, but despite having 24 goals with Hartford in '81-'82, it was with St. Louis a few years later that he played to his potential. With the Blues he was allowed to play a skating, free-flowing game that helped him both on the power play and on killing penalties. He played six years in St. Louis and won the Selke Trophy in '89-'90, his last full season. After retiring, he coached Peoria in the IHL and later returned to St. Louis, where he became an integral part of the scouting department.

MEEHAN, Gerry
b. Toronto, Ontario, September 3, 1946
Much as he wanted things to work out with Toronto, it just wasn't meant to be. Meehan won the Memorial Cup with the Marlies in 1967 and played part of the year after with the Leafs, but soon was traded to Philadelphia. Two years later, Meehan landed in Buffalo, where he had his finest hour. He averaged 25 goals a year over 4 seasons and was made team captain by Punch Imlach. More important, the centre helped give the team some depth beyond the French Connection line. Meehan later moved around the league for a few years after leaving Buffalo in 1974, but soon after retiring he made his way back to the city to complete his law degree at the State University of New York. He worked on Sabres' broadcasts and then became the team's assistant GM to Scotty Bowman. When Bowman was fired on December 2, 1986, Meehan became the GM, a post he held for seven years. He later became involved in the St. Mike's Majors when the team returned to the OHL, but principally Meehan has most recently worked for the law firm of Hodgson Russ Andrews Woods in Toronto.

MEEKE, Brent
b. Toronto, Ontario, April 10, 1952
Needless to say, by playing all his NHL games with California and Cleveland, Meeke's only playoff exposure came via the television. The defenceman made a small impact with the Seals and spent most of his career in the minors playing out of Salt Lake City. He later moved to Germany where he finished his career playing in that country's league.

MEEKER, Howie
b. Kitchener, Ontario, November 4, 1924
Strange but true, the war ended Meeker's career, though he didn't begin that career until after the war. Here are the hows and whys. After playing kid hockey, Meeker enlisted in the army in May 1942 and didn't come out until '46. He was based in England as a machinist's apprentice in the Royal Canadian Engineers. During basic training, a stupid soldier inadvertently tossed a live grenade between Meeker's legs, blowing him high in the air and injuring him badly. He recovered, though, and went on to build bridges in the Rhine. When he was discharged, he joined the Leafs, and in his first season accomplished three incredible feats: one, he scored five goals in a game, a rookie record that stands to this day; two, he won the Stanley Cup; three, he won the Calder Trophy over another rookie, a guy named Gordie Howe. He never achieved another season as personally rewarding as that. Meeker played his entire career with the Leafs, winning four Cups in his first five years. In 1951, he entered the political arena, winning a by-election for Waterloo South, his first of four years as an MP. He retired from playing in 1954 because of a bad back, a lingering reminder of his accident during the war. He coached the farm team in Pittsburgh for a year and was promoted to Toronto coach in 1956, but the team failed to make the playoffs and he was given a chance to be Leafs GM the

Jack McVicar

Rick Meagher

Gerry Meehan

Brent Meeke

He was based in England as a machinist's apprentice in the Royal Canadian Engineers.
HOWIE MEEKER

Mike Meeker

Harry Meeking

Paul Meger

Ron Meighan

Barrie Meissner

following summer. Incredibly, he was fired later in the fall before ever having done much, and he moved out east where he signed a contract with the St. John's Newfoundland Stadium Commission as a player, coach, and manager (though he didn't play much). In the early 1970s he began another career – as intermission analyst for *Hockey Night in Canada*. For a new generation of fans, Meeker became an icon. His enthusiasm for the game was as infectious as his sermonizing on the importance of the fundamentals. He preached practice and skills and prophesied the advent of Europeans because of their skating, passing, and shooting, not their rough play. Meeker became the first hockey analyst to look at video replays to dissect a game's plays and important moments, and by the time he left HNIC his mark had been entrenched in the mind of every Canadian who loved the game. He retired to Vancouver and published his autobiography in 1999 entitled *Golly Gee, It's Me*, a reference to his trademark phrase from his HNIC days.

MEEKER, Mike
b. Kingston, Ontario, February 23, 1958
Well, the strategy worked, but the result was nothing to write home about, at least, not to uncle Howie, who had been a star in the NHL in the 1940s. Meeker went to U of Wisconsin on scholarship in 1975, but after scoring five goals in a game near the start of his third year he returned to Canada to play junior in Peterborough, in the hopes that strong play would be better noticed by scouts and push him into the first round of the draft. That's the part that worked. He averaged nearly a goal a game with the Petes and went early in the second round of the 1978 draft to Pittsburgh, and the year after he played four games with the Pens during a season in which he was named AHL rookie of the year. That was the last pro hockey saw of Meeker.

MEEKING, Harry ("Meek")
b. Berlin (Kitchener), Ontario, November 4, 1894
d. Toronto, Ontario, December 13, 1971
Meeking played most of his early hockey in Toronto, and that's how he became familiar to fans in 1915 playing in the NHA with the Blueshirts and again two years later with the Arenas. He won a Cup with the team in that first NHL season, but spent the greatest part of his career in the Pacific Coast league where he won a second Cup with the Victoria Cougars in '24-'25. He returned to the NHL for a final season in '26-'27 and retired after a few more years in the minors. The left winger was known for his fine skating more than his goal scoring, though he certainly was capable of that skill as well.

MEGER, Paul
b. Watrous, Saskatchewan, February 17, 1929
The Meger family moved to Selkirk, Manitoba, when Paul was still a young boy and it was there he learned his hockey, on the frozen Red River. Amazingly, he never played organized hockey until junior. He made the Barrie Flyers at training camp in 1946, and he impressed coach Hap Emms that Emms also gave Meger a job in his hardware store. After three years with the Flyers, Meger moved on to the AHL where he was named rookie of the year in '49-'50 with Buffalo. He moved up

to the Canadiens a year later, and in 1951 he made the team on a full-time basis. In that first full season, the left winger scored 24 goals, and the year after he helped the Habs win the Stanley Cup. Meger's career ended in near tragedy on November 7, 1954, at the Boston Garden. Playing on a line with Bernie Geoffrion and Jean Beliveau, Meger was hit on the side of the head by the skate of Leo LaBine in a freak accident. He required four brain operations and spent a year in hospital, and though doctors initially gave up on him, Meger fought the good fight and slowly but surely made a full recovery. He returned to Barrie to work again in Emms' hardware store and earned his licence as an electrician. Meger worked for Sears as a technician for 20 years before retiring in 1988. He was later inducted into the Manitoba Sports Hall of Fame, lucky just to be alive.

MEIGHAN, Ron
b. Montreal, Quebec, May 26, 1963
There's nothing more frustrating than playing well and not getting ice time, or earning a chance to prove yourself but not getting said chance. Meighan felt a little bit of both. He was drafted 13th overall by Minnesota in 1981, ahead of Al MacInnis, Steve Smith, and Chris Chelios. Meighan justified this high selection in his next year of junior in Niagara Falls by scoring 27 goals, being named best defenceman in the OHL, and having an impressive few games with the North Stars. The next year, though, he was involved in an important trade with Pittsburgh, but the Pens sent him right back down to junior without so much as a quick trial. When they did bring him up, they didn't play him much. The next year, he was buried in the minors and at season's end he retired at age 21.

MEISSNER, Barrie
b. Kindersley, Saskatchewan, July 26, 1946
Here is another example of a fine junior who doesn't crack through to the NHL elite. After playing junior with Regina in the mid-1960s, Meissner timed his entry perfectly, debuting with Minnesota in 1967. The winger scored when he was sent to the minors but didn't make an impression when given an opportunity with the Stars, and ended his career in the American league just a few years later. His older brother, Dick, also played in the NHL for several years during the Original Six era.

MEISSNER, Dick
b. Kindersley, Saskatchewan, January 6, 1940
Meissner was recommended to the Bruins by his junior team's coach, Scotty Munro, back when Meissner was living in Delisle at the age of 16. That's how he came to play junior in Estevan and go on to a career with the Bruins. In fact, his first taste of NHL action came in a unique way, when the Bruins and Rangers played a barnstorming tour of Europe. Meissner made the B's at camp in '59, but he played with the team only three years and then played a handful of games with the Rangers soon after. His downfall was his knees, which were operated on five times, and then his wrist, which he broke in the '63-'64 season. He managed to recover enough to play in the minors for a number of years, and when he retired he settled in Portland (one of his AHL stops) and worked as a building contractor.

MELAMETSA, Anssi

b. Jyvaskyla, Finland, June 21, 1961

Too much too soon? A wrong decision? Not up to the task? Who knows, exactly, but in 1978 Europeans traditionally did not come to Canada to play junior as preparation for the NHL. Melametsa, at 17, came to Peterborough, but after just one season he returned home to continue developing in more familiar surroundings. He also played at two WJC tournaments and two World Championships, and also represented Suomi at the 1984 Olympics in Sarajevo before coming to the NHL. His career with the Jets lasted all of 27 games, though, before he headed home to finish his career.

MELANSON, Dean

b. Antigonish, Nova Scotia, November 19, 1973

Melanson seems destined for a career in the minors, though he continues to hope and play. He's had a few games with Buffalo and Washington, but since 1993 he has been confined mostly to the minors.

MELANSON, Rollie

b. Moncton, New Brunswick, June 28, 1960

Timing is everything, especially in comedy and hockey. Melanson wasn't very funny, but he did graduate from junior in time to join the Islanders in 1981, just as the team was on a four-Cup roll. He played backup goaler to Billy Smith, winning three of the dynastic four championships, though his later career wasn't nearly as successful. He and Smith shared the William Jennings Trophy in '82-'83, but he later played increasingly long stretches in the minors as the NHL gave up on him as being too old. Melanson returned to Moncton after retiring and became an assistant coach with the Wildcats of the Quebec league. He kept his popular Rollie the Goalie hockey school going each summer. In 1997, he was hired as an assistant with the Canadiens.

MELICHAR, Josef

b. Ceske Budjovice, Czechoslovakia (Czech Republic), January 20, 1979

If he were going to fail or succeed, he wanted to make sure he gave it his best chance. To that end, Melichar left his homeland at 18 to play junior for two seasons after being drafted by Pittsburgh. So far, so good. The defenceman spent two additional years in the minors, making his NHL debut on October 8, 2000, but in 2001-02 he spent the full year with the Pens, giving him hope that he has established himself on a Pittsburgh blueline in need of some skill.

MELIN, Roger

b. Enkoping, Sweden, April 25, 1956

In the years immediately after the arrival of Borje Salming in Toronto, many a Swede tried to emulate the King's success, but precious few succeeded. Melin was a Division 2 player in Sweden, but when he signed with Minnesota at the end of the '80-'81 season and played a single game, he had little idea his stay would be as short as it was. He played just two games the next year and the rest of his season in the minors, after which he returned home to play out his career in friendly arenas. After retiring, he turned to coaching, most recently with the Brynas Tigers and Rogle.

MELLANBY, Scott ("Mel")

b. Montreal, Quebec, June 11, 1966

It happened pretty early on in his career with Florida. Mellanby had been a great prospect, a Tim Kerr-like player with great hands and a quick release. However, a serious injury took his pure scoring away, and the Panthers were able to claim him in the Expansion Draft. One day, he looked around the dingy dressing room that was home base in Florida when he saw a rat. Bang! He killed it. His teammates chuckled, the press got hold of the story, and pretty soon every time the Panthers scored a goal the fans threw plastic rats on the ice. Not a few of them, not like octopi in Detroit. Thousands of them! It got to be so enjoyable that the NHL had to curtail the practice by introducing a law that gave the referee the power to penalize the home team for delay of game while the rats were shovelled off the ice. Party poopers. It made Mellanby a hero in town, though, and he played all of the team's first seven seasons, including the great run to the finals in 1996. His scoring had been taken away from him in 1989 during a barroom brawl in which he came to a friend's aid and wound up with an horrific cut from a broken beer bottle that severed four tendons, a nerve, and an artery in his left arm. Surgery repaired the arm, but doctors held little hope for him – they were simply glad not to have had to amputate. Nonetheless, he has managed to produce eight 30-goal seasons and play 1,000 NHL games. The son of longtime *Hockey Night in Canada* producer Ralph Mellanby, Scott naturally grew up a hockey nut and rink rat.

> **He has managed to produce eight 30-goal seasons and play 1,000 NHL games.**
> SCOTT MELLANBY

MELLOR, Tom

b. Cranston, Rhode Island, January 27, 1950

By the time he left Boston College for keeps in 1973, Mellor was the all-time scorer for defencemen in that school's history. Along the way, he took some time off to play for the U.S. at the 1972 Olympics in Sapporo, and when he joined the Red Wings in 1973 he was a

Dean Melanson

Rollie Melanson

Tom Mellor

top prospect. Time would refute this scouting report, though he did go on to win top defenceman honours in the IHL in '76-'77, his last year of pro. Mellor settled in Marlboro, Massachusetts, and became a broker for Wyndham Capital in Boston.

Gerry Melnyk

MELNYK, Gerry
b. Edmonton, Alberta, September 16, 1934
d. Edmonton, Alberta, June 14, 2001
Edmonton was his home and life, his place of perfect certainty. Melnyk played junior in his hometown and turned pro with the WHL Flyers, but his best break occurred when the team was eliminated from the '56 playoffs. The big boss, Jack Adams in Detroit, called him up for the NHL playoffs, and he got his chance in game four of the semifinals against Toronto, playing on a line with guys named Lindsay and Howe. Melnyk was back in the minors for three years after this dream callup and spent three more years in the NHL full-time, first with Detroit, then with Chicago. His career ended at training camp with St. Louis in '68-'69 when he suffered a heart attack, and soon after he was hired by Philadelphia as a scout. It was Melnyk alone who pleaded and begged his bosses at the 1969 draft to select a kid named Bobby Clarke, and a generation later he was the man who touted Mike Ricci and Peter Forsberg. In 2000, he was diagnosed with leukemia and a year later he passed away, scouting for the Flyers to the end.

Larry Melnyk

MELNYK, Larry
b. Saskatoon, Saskatchewan, February 21, 1960
If you're a fringe player, you'll take your fame and fortune in whatever form and dose it's given. For Mellor, that meant two Stanley Cups with Edmonton (in '84 and '85) despite playing only parts of the seasons with the Oilers. He later played on the blueline for the Rangers and Vancouver where he got more playing time but experienced far less success than with the great Edmonton team. Nonetheless, he retired in 1990 having played some 432 regular-season games.

MELOCHE, Eric
b. Montreal, Quebec, May 1, 1976
A new crop of NHL sons is just now arriving on the scene, and Meloche is one of that ever-expanding number. His father, Gilles, was a goalie for years in the league, and currently scouts for Pittsburgh, the team (coincidentally or not) that drafted Eric in 1996. Eric went to Ohio State University for four years (1996-2000), studying management, and during that time he proved to be a dangerous offensive player with good speed and intense presence in the offensive end of the

Gilles Meloche

ice. He played about a third of 2001-02 with the Penguins, without scoring a goal, and has played in the minors besides hoping to find his form.

MELOCHE, Gilles
b. Montreal, Quebec, July 12, 1950
Almost without question, Meloche is the greatest goalie to have a sub-.500 record over such a lengthy career. He played 18 seasons, yet his numbers initially look weak: 270 wins, 351 losses, 131 ties. These numbers speak not to Meloche but to the teams he played with – California and Cleveland, where even Terry Sawchuk would have had a hard time winning; Minnesota, which had a decent though not spectacular team; and Pittsburgh, another weak team in the early stages of Mario Lemieux's career. Thirteen times did Meloche played at least 40 games in a season, yet in those 18 years his team made the playoffs in just 6 and made it past the first round only half that number. Year after year, game after game, he was the only reason his team had even a slight chance of winning, and his two appearances in the All-Star Game attest to his greater reputation around the league. For years he owned or shared the NHL record for assists in a game by a goalie – two. After retiring, he became a scout for those Penguins he ended his puck-stopping days with, and he had a son who went on to play college hockey – but not as a goalie.

Melrose got by on a minimum of skill and a maximum of desire.
BARRY MELROSE

MELROSE, Barry
b. Kelvington, Saskatchewan, July 15, 1956
Never the most talented defenceman wherever he played, Melrose got by on a minimum of skill and a maximum of desire and fighting. He played exactly 300 NHL games in the 1980s after a starter series of years in the WHA, but he ended up in the minors and soon got involved in coaching. He was named head coach for L.A. in 1992, and due to his enthusiastic style and the presence of Wayne Gretzky, the Kings made it to the Stanley Cup finals in Melrose's first year. In both of the next two years, though, the team failed to make the playoffs at all, and Melrose and his style, passé, were gone. The cousin of Wendel Clark then got into television as a colour commentator for ESPN.

MENARD, Hilary ("Minnie")
b. Timmins, Ontario, January 15, 1934
Brother of Howie, and 1 of 10 children (9 boys), Hilary managed just 1 game in the NHL, with Chicago during the '53-'54 season at the end of his final season of junior. He had a lengthy playing career, though his greatest highlight came in senior play when he was with the Allan Cup-winning Belleville McFarlands in '57-'58. His career ended in

1967 when he was struck by a puck and lost an eye. He was a salesman at the time, playing senior hockey for the fun of it.

MENARD, Howie ("Minnie")
b. Timmins, Ontario, April 28, 1942

Howie and brother Hilary shared two things, one fun, the other awful. Fun: Both, because of their diminutiveness, were nicknamed Minnie. Awful: Both suffered serious eye injuries. Howie's eye injury didn't cause too much lost time in the '64-'65 season. His game was always classified by its pep. He hustled every shift, worked harder than anyone, chased every loose puck, and played aggressively to compensate for his 5'6", 160-pound body. He played but four semi-full seasons in the NHL during the 1960s, three after expansion, though from 1970 on he was strictly a minor-leaguer. He ended his career in senior hockey, playing with the Whitby Warriors in the mid-1970s, a team that featured Mike Keenan and Eddie Shack.

MERCREDI, Vic
b. Yellowknife, Northwest Territories, March 31, 1953

Gold and cold and polar bears, Pierre Berton and saloons. Those are the things the Canadian North is made of, not NHL hockey players. Yet from the snowy pre-Nunavut wilderness came Mercredi, who played two games with Atlanta in '74-'75 during a short professional career. He later played in the WHA and other minor leagues, but when he retired in 1979 he returned to Yellowknife to work with the Department of Municipal and Community Affairs as a special adviser. He was also an advocate for improved education and development of recreational programs for the Aboriginal peoples of the NWT.

MEREDITH, Greg
b. Toronto, Ontario, February 23, 1958

A "chance" in hockey terms can last a shift or a season, depending on the circumstances. Fair or not, a player must do something special with his chance or risk not getting another. Meredith's chance was briefer than it was lengthy, and he did well to keep going, but not for long. He graduated from Notre Dame in 1980 with a degree in finance and received as many academic as sporting honours. He was the all-time leading scorer at right wing and he had a three-game trial with Calgary the year after. Meredith spent most of the next three years in the minors, though he spent about half the '82-'83 regular season with the Flames. In the playoffs, he was put into the lineup for the final game of the first-round series against Vancouver, replacing Lanny McDonald. It was his overtime goal that eliminated the Canucks, and that was good enough for

another chance later in the playoffs. Of course, no one can score an OT goal every time out, and this was pretty much Meredith's last chance. He played one more year in the minors, then retired to pursue a law degree and career in that discipline.

MERKOSKY, Glenn
b. Edmonton, Alberta, April 8, 1959

Life changed for the better that summer day in 1985 when Merkosky signed with Detroit. He had been a pro for five years and had seen a little NHL time with Hartford and New Jersey, but although his opportunity with the Red Wings was no great shakes, he developed a link with the team that remained through the end of the century. He played six seasons in Adirondack, the Detroit farm team, scoring goals and becoming the most popular player in franchise history. After he retired, the team hung his number 15 sweater in the rafters, and he stayed with Detroit first as a scout and later in the coaching ranks in Adirondack. Since 1996 he has been the head coach of the team, and although the minor Wings have encountered some tough times, Merkosky has endured.

MERONEK, Bill ("Smiley")
b. Stony Mountain, Manitoba, April 5, 1917
d. Winnipeg, Manitoba, May 25, 1999

The turning point in Meronek's career came in 1938 when he played for Verdun, a team in the Canadiens system coached by Aurel Joliat. Joliat taught Meronek the art of stickhandling and evading checks, for both had one thing in common – a lack of size and physical strength. And so, that was Meronek's trademark, a player who was shifty and could handle the rough going by cleverly avoiding it altogether. He played just 19 games for the Habs during the war and spent the rest of his career in Quebec senior leagues. During the war, he was classified as essential to Canada's war efforts as a supervisor of airframe mechanics on the Harvard Trainers at Nordyne Aviation. In 1946, out of hockey for the most part, Meronek worked for Curtis Publishing and 11 years later he returned home to Winnipeg to join Western Engine Works Ltd. A fiddler in his youth, he was a superb golfer in old age, winning the Manitoba Seniors championships in 1981 and 1984. He was later inducted into the Manitoba Sports Hall of Fame.

MERRICK, Wayne
b. Sarnia, Ontario, April 23, 1952

There was the early part of his career, with bumbling teams like St. Louis and California and Cleveland. And there was the late part of his career, with the Islanders, Lord Stanley, and a permanent smile of satisfaction.

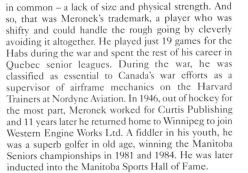

By the time he retired in 1984, Merrick had his name on the Cup four times.
WAYNE MERRICK

Howie Menard

Vic Mercredi

Greg Meredith

Glenn Merkosky

The one could not possibly have anticipated the other, although one certainly led to the other. Merrick was a top prospect and when he got to the NHL he played as well as he had in junior. This established his reputation with the lesser teams and created a desire by the Islanders to make him a piece of their Cup puzzle. When he joined the Isles in early 1978, he played on a third line with John Tonelli and Bob Nystrom, becoming the top checking line in the league. Come playoffs, though, they also contributed on offence. By the time he retired in 1984, Merrick had his name on the Cup four times. He then started his own air filtration company and later sold life insurance.

MERRILL, Horace
b. Ottawa, Ontario, November 30, 1884
d. Ottawa, Ontario,
December 24, 1958
Merrill played his entire career in Ottawa, indeed spent his whole life in the capital city. He rose to prominence in the NHA with the Senators and closed his career with two brief appearances for that team after the formation of the NHL in 1917. He was a small part of the Stanley Cup team of 1919-20.

MERTZIG, Jan
b. Huddinge, Sweden,
July 18, 1970
Size isn't everything, as Mertzig found out when he got to the NHL from Sweden. He was a low draft choice of the Rangers in 1998, but after only 23 games the 6'4", 235-pound defenceman was sent to the minors, where he decided not to continue his playing days. He returned to Europe, played in Austria for three years and then went back to Sweden to play with Linkoping of the Swedish Elite League.

Jan Mertzig

MESSIER, Eric ("Mess")
b. Drummondville, Quebec, October 29, 1973
Hollywood is full of stories about dishy young actresses who are discovered at a pizza parlour or on some club's dance floor. Messier was discovered not in a hockey rink, but at a roller hockey game in 1995 by the coach of Colorado's minor-league team, one Bob Hartley. Hartley liked what he saw of the Montreal Roadrunners defenceman (the team was owned by the NHL's Roadrunner, Yvan Cournoyer) and told Messier to give him a call. Ironically, both men eventually made it to the Avs and won the Cup together in 2001. Messier started as a defenceman only, but Hartley has also used him as a forward. His career, now more than 300 games old, has been all Avs to date.

Eric Messier

MESSIER, Joby
b. Regina, Saskatchewan, March 2, 1970
Perhaps never before has a fine and promising career

been so annihilated by serious injuries as Messier's was. While playing for Michigan State, he was called the best defensive defenceman that school had ever seen. For four years he developed his game in the same way his brother Mitch had at the same college (Mark was a cousin). The Rangers drafted him and first gave him some NHL time in '92-'93, but three years later he missed the entire season recovering from a serious knee injury he incurred during training camp. He missed most of the following year because of a serious car accident that killed two people and ended Mitch's career because of serious neck and head injuries. And then, the *coup de grâce:* On November 8, 1997, Joby suffered a serious head injury of his own in an IHL game and never played again.

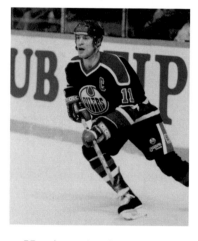

Messier not only promised a win in game six but also scored three goals in the third period.
MARK MESSIER

MESSIER, Mark ("Moose")
b. Edmonton, Alberta,
January 18, 1961
The closest thing to Gordie Howe the modern generation of hockey fans has seen, Messier will be inducted into the Hockey Hall of Fame three years after he retires. That means he might never get in, for he shows no signs of retiring. Since turning pro in 1978 in the WHA, and entering the NHL a year later, Messier has accomplished more than just about any player not named Mario or Wayne. In his rookie season, he scored just one goal, on a shot from centre ice, but that was enough to catch the eye of Edmonton coach and GM Glen Sather. Hard to believe, but Messier wasn't drafted by the Oilers until 48th overall in 1979, but he joined a team destined to rewrite the history and record books. In his first four seasons, he had point totals of 33, 63, 88, and 106, increases that mirrored the successes of the team. He scored 50 goals one season and 100 points 6 times, but from day one his greatest asset was his leadership. While teammate Wayne Gretzky scored at a phenomenal pace, Messier ensured that the team played like a team and that each player was accountable to him for his play. When Gretzky was traded to L.A. in 1988, Messier became team captain and led the Oilers to a less-probable fifth Stanley Cup, in 1990, to ensure his place in history outside the Gretzky spectre. When he was traded to the Rangers in 1991, he became the most popular player that city has ever seen thanks to his heroics two years later in leading the Blueshirts to their first Cup since 1940. It was a victory defined by Messier's promise of a win in the conference finals against New Jersey. Trailing 3-2 in the series, Messier not only promised a win in game six but also scored three goals in the third period to make that promise a reality. From that moment, he was a hero to the 18,200 fans that attend every home game.

When the Rangers beat Vancouver in game seven to win the Cup, a celebration of unprecedented glory began, and New Yorkers spent the summer revelling in Messier's accomplishments. Messier left the team in the summer of 1997 to sign with Vancouver as a free agent, a move that slightly sullied his reputation. Out west, his Canucks failed to make the playoffs in each of the three seasons he was there, and he returned to the New York fold to play with his pal Gretzky as number 99 closed out his career. Messier's list of achievements are enough to fill a book. He won the Conn Smythe Trophy for his incredible playoffs in 1984 to give the Oilers its first Cup. Twice he won the Hart Trophy and Lester Pearson Award (1990 and '92) as league MVP, and he has played in 14 All-Star Games. He never won the Art Ross because either Gretzky or Lemieux won it every year for nigh on two decades, but he captained three teams and was the first man to captain two different teams to the Cup. He is among the all-time leaders in games played (regular season and playoffs), goals, assists, and points. Although he missed much of 2001-02 with a shoulder injury, he seems destined to became only the second player after Gordie Howe to play for a quarter-century. Internationally, he represented Canada at the 1984, '87, and '91 Canada Cups (all victories). He captained the '96 World Cup team, and the only snub of his career came in 1998 when he was left off the Olympics team. Messier has few equals in the history of hockey, and those men are all the greatest who have ever played.

MESSIER, Mitch
b. Regina, Saskatchewan, August 21, 1965
During his college career with Michigan State, Messier helped the Spartans win the 1986 NCAA championship. He later played parts of four seasons with Minnesota, but spent most of the next eight seasons in the minors. On August 23, 1996, his life changed when he and his brother Joby were involved in a serious car accident that ended Mitch's career. He survived the crash, slowly recovered, and made his way to Canmore, Alberta, where he worked as a real estate agent for Re-Max.

MESSIER, Paul
b. Nottingham, England, January 27, 1958
Moe Robinson, Alain Lemieux, Keith Gretzky, Jean Potvin, Paul Messier. They all have one thing in common: They were incredibly fine hockey players (or they wouldn't have made it to the NHL), but they played in the microscopic fringes of the shadows of their more famous brothers. In Paul's case, that was Eric Messier. Paul played all of nine games with Colorado in '78-'79, then hung around in the minors for a few years before moving to Germany where he put up Eric-type numbers in an Eric-type (not!) league.

METCALFE, Scott
b. Toronto, Ontario, January 6, 1967
Maybe it was appropriate that his first big event came at the 1987 World Junior Championships, because that was where the Soviets instigated a brawl with Canada that resulted in disqualification of the Canadian team destined for either gold or silver. Metcalfe was a fighter, plain and simple. In the NHL, he lasted just 19 games, but since he last played in the big show

(1990) he has alternated the venue for his punching between the minors and Germany, though geography never altered his style of play: Punch first, score goals later.

METROPOLIT, Glen
b. Toronto, Ontario, June 25, 1974
There were three children. The girl, Nicole, was an honour student. The two boys were fathered by different men but the same woman, Linda Hachey. One son came to no good and wound up in Toronto court after a vicious and violent abduction of a wealthy couple. That was Troy. The other son loved hockey and made it to the NHL. That was Glen. Glen's dad left his mom before Glen was born, and when Hachey took up with another man, Bruce Metropolit, the couple named Glen after the paternal, not biological, father. Bruce, as it turned out, was no great role model. For years he was in and out of jail, and never exactly became a family man. Troy had no interests that were conducive to a productive life, but Glen was saved from a like fate because of his love for the puck game. He's played only briefly with Washington since signing as a free agent in 1999, but he's a pro in the minors and an established right winger.

METZ, Don
b. Wilcox, Saskatchewan, January 10, 1916
There are only three Leafs who have won five Stanley Cups: Turk Broda, Ted Kennedy, and Don Metz. Ironically, Metz never played a full season with the team, but he timed his contributions perfectly and when he was given a chance he made the most of it. The crowning glory of his ability to perform gracefully under pressure came in the spring of 1942. Trailing 3-0 in the best-of-seven finals, coach Happy Day benched veterans Hank Goldup and Gord Drillon and inserted Metz and Gaye Stewart. Metz scored four goals in the next four games and helped the Leafs complete the most remarkable comeback in the history of the game. He was primarily a defensive player whose career was much shorter than brother Nick's, but the two played for Toronto for their entire careers, much of that time overlapping. Don quit a year after Nick to return to their farm in Wilcox, 500 acres of largely wheat and barley that he worked until 1991 when he finally retired.

METZ, Nick ("Handy Andy"/ "Red")
b. Wilcox, Saskatchewan, February 16, 1914
d. Regina, Saskatchewan, August 24, 1990
Along with brother Don, Nick was a pre-eminent penalty killer of his day. He played his entire career with Toronto (1934-48), though he missed the better part of two years after the 1942 Cup win when he joined the army. Metz was a gunner with the Royal Canadian Artillery, and after receiving his discharge he returned home in time to win his second Cup, in 1945. Unlike his brother, Metz was a fine scorer. He played junior hockey with St. Mike's in Toronto after being discovered by a Leafs bird dog out west, and he retired a healthy 34 years old to return to the family farm.

MEZEI, Branislav
b. Nitra, Czechoslovakia (Slovakia), October 8, 1980
The large, Slovakian defenceman came to Belleville

Paul Messier

Scott Metcalfe

Glen Metropolit

Don Metz

Nick Metz

played mostly in the 1950s when the team was at a low point and never went past the first round of the playoffs. After retiring early in the '59-'60 season, he worked at Head of the Lakes but soon turned to coaching for his hockey fix. He led the Tulsa team for a couple of years, and when Pittsburgh entered the NHL he was named a scout for the team. From there he moved to Buffalo in a similar capacity, and for more than 20 years he tracked talent for the Sabres, most notably encouraging the team to draft a high school student named Phil Housley.

MIKA, Petr
b. Prague, Czechoslovakia (Czech Republic), February 12, 1979

He looks to be on the road to the minors, but Mika is still young and has miles to go before he can be counted out entirely. The defenceman played briefly with Ottawa in the OHL but returned home for a final year of junior before playing with the Islanders for a few games in 1999-2000, his only NHL appearances so far.

MIKITA, Stan ("Stosh")
b. Sokolnice, Czechoslovakia, May 20, 1940

He played in 4 decades in the NHL, 22 seasons with the same team, and never spent a day in the minors. Mikita came into the world on the other side of the planet, born Stan Guoth. But when he was eight, he came to Canada with his uncle, Joe Mikita, and aunt, and took the Mikita name. They settled in St. Catharines, Ontario, and Stan didn't speak a word of English at first. He learned the language, though, just as he learned to play road hockey with the neighbourhood kids, and when he was on the ice, everyone paid attention to him. He wasn't the most fluid skater, but he was effective, a player who could see the ice well and create scoring chances out of how he saw the play unfold. At 16, Chicago assigned him to the Teepees in junior, and by his third season he was the top scorer in the OHL. He had a brief callup toward the end of the '58-'59 season, and the next year he was on the team. In each of his first five seasons his goal scoring increased and in both '63-'64 and '64-'65 he led the NHL in points. He won the Stanley Cup with the Hawks in '60-'61 at the end of his third season, leading the league with six goals in the playoffs. It was to be his only Cup in an illustrious career. In '66-'67, Mikita made history. He won the Art Ross Trophy (for a third time), the Hart Trophy, and the Lady Byng Trophy, the first time a player won all three in the same season. The Byng was particularly noteworthy because it marked a complete turnaround in style of play. In his early years, Mikita was feisty and had no problem getting into a fight and standing up for himself. But coach Billy Reay had tried to emphasize that he was too talented to waste

Petr Mika

away in the penalty box. Mikita listened and learned, and almost overnight the once semi-tough guy was now the league's most gentlemanly player! Incredibly, he won all three trophies again the year after. By the mid-1960s, he was a bona fide 30-goal scorer, a fact attributable to both his skill and a pioneering invention of his – the curved stick. Mikita once played with a slightly broken blade that had a small curve in the middle, and he noticed the puck moved differently coming off this curved blade than it normally did. That night, he propped a number of sticks under a doorframe, and in the morning he had a wicked, "banana" blade. In practice and games, he saw the puck dip and curve and wobble in ways confusing to goalies, but in an era of maskless men in the nets this presented an element of danger. The league abolished the big hook, and the experiment was over – but not before Mikita had bagged dozens of goals. The other key element to his great success was his linemates. For years he played with Ken Wharram and Ab McDonald on the Scooter Line, the highest-scoring threesome in team history. The line played together for most of the 1960s, until Wharram suffered a heart attack in 1969 and had to retire. In 1972, Mikita was named to Team Canada's roster for the Summit Series. He didn't play much against the Soviets, but in his case that was almost beside the point. What mattered more was the exhibition game the team had promised to play against a Czech team in Prague on September 29. Mikita was front and centre, given an enormous ovation as a national hero in the NHL. Soon after, Mikita suffered a concussion during a

Mikita suffered a concussion during a game and became a strong and vocal advocate for mandatory helmet use.
STAN MIKITA

game and became a strong and vocal advocate for mandatory helmet use. He designed his own Mikita-style headgear, which was used by many players in the coming years, both NHL and amateur. Toward the middle and end of the decade, he became less productive and the team went into something of a tailspin. A serious back injury early in the '79-'80 season forced him to retire, but by this time he had had a remarkable career. He played all of his 1,394 games with Chicago and had scored 541 goals and 1,467 total points. He won the Lester Patrick Trophy in 1976, and in 1983, exactly three years after calling it quits, he was inducted into the Hockey Hall of Fame with teammate Bobby Hull. He settled in Chicago, of course, and embarked on a long and successful career in business. A superb golfer, he became director of the Kemper Country Club just outside Chicago. He also founded the American Hearing Impaired Hockey Association, helping deaf people play the game with the same enjoyment he always had. He went into business with Glen Skov as manufacturers of plastics, which continues to occupy him. Mikita sat on the selection committee of the Hall of Fame for several years, though it would be hard to choose many players as deserving as he to be included among the greatest of the greats.

MIKKELSON, Bill
b. Neepawa, Ontario, May 21, 1948

Go big or go home, Mikkelson set a record not likely to be broken and equally not likely to be envied. In 1974-75, he played for the pitiful Capitals, the team that went 8-67-5 over the year, the worst record in NHL history. The Caps went with four defencemen that year, and Mikkelson was one of them. He had a plus-minus that year of -82, a number that would frighten polar bears. He had played briefly with L.A. and the Islanders, where his rating was pretty awful as well, -11 with the Kings and -54 with New York. Washington got him gratis in the Expansion Draft. He played just one more game with the team a couple of years later and retired in 1977 to become a big plus. Today, Mikkelson is a senior executive for IBM in Edmonton.

MIKOL, John "Jim"
b. Kitchener, Ontario, June 11, 1938

Mikol was an American leaguer primarily in the AHL in the 1960s, but he did play four games with the Leafs and another half-season with the Rangers. Not a spectacular player to watch, he forged a career through effective play and hard work. Ironically, he was traded out of the NHL by New York as part of a package to Providence so the Rangers could acquire Ed Giacomin, who quickly became a longtime member of the team.

MIKULCHIK, Oleg
b. Minsk, Soviet Union (Belarus), June 27, 1964

The true irony of the new world order in hockey can be appreciated by the start and finish of Mikulchik's career. Before perestroika, the Belarussian could play only for the Soviet Union, whether he liked it or not, and he developed into a fine defenceman. He played in the 1980s with Dynamo for years, but in 1992 came freedom and for Mikulchik that meant hockey in North America. In all, he played five years in the AHL and IHL, touching down in the NHL with Winnipeg and Anaheim. At the first opportunity he represented Belarus at the World Championships and then, of his own volition, played the last years of his career in Russia! He was part of the 2002 Belarus Olympic team that stunned the world by defeating Sweden and advancing to the bronze-medal game, where it lost to Russia and finished an astounding fourth.

MILBURY, Mike
b. Brighton, Massachusetts, June 17, 1952

There aren't too many players who can be defined by an incident off the ice rather than on it, but in Milbury's case, it really wasn't *far* off the ice. In one game against New York at Madison Square Garden, things got a bit out of hand and a number of Bruins players went into the stands to fight with the paying customers. Of course, this is a precarious situation at best, for starters because those steps aren't made for skates and players can slip easily. Also, players are stronger than most fans, so although they may want to beat up the patrons, they have to try do to so gently. Milbury went into the crowd and started to scuffle with a fan. He got the man's shoe

off his foot and started beating him with it, a fairly tame method of violence that all these years later is as *Slap Shot*-ish as the NHL could possibly get. (Life imitates art?) Milbury was a rugged defenceman besides. He played his entire career with the Bruins (1975-87) and retired in 1985 hoping to get into coaching. His rest was short-lived, though, when three Boston defencemen were hurt and he had to get back into the game. Once he retired with finality a year and a half later, Milbury did, indeed, get into the coaching game, first in the minors and then with the Bruins. He had two successful playoff runs in 1990 and '91 and later coached the Islanders for four years starting in 1995, the team with which he remains affiliated. He later became the team's GM, and under his regime the team continued to flounder, missing the playoffs every year when he was a coach, and making the post-season for the first time only in 2002 during his GM years. Along the way, he made a number of poor trades, many in the name of finances, but in the summer of 2001 he was given a bigger budget and acquired both Michael Peca and Alexei Yashin, a double coup that took the team to the playoffs and suggested that Mad Mike – as he had been dubbed over the years – wasn't so. Although he was a brawler as a player, he was no dummy. He attended Colgate in the early 1970s and tried in vain to alert his Boston teammates to what he considered the shady practices of lawyer/agent Alan Eagleson. Milbury is plenty young enough that his final hockey chapter has yet to be lived or written, but to date he has been a colourful figure whose career, while not entirely successful, has certainly been eventful.

MILKS, Hibbert "Hib"
b. Eardley, Quebec, April 1, 1902
d. Shawville, Quebec, January 22, 1949

Here was a talented athlete whose skills rested inside an unhappy body that fled this earth too soon. Milks played is junior in Ottawa and joined the NHL with Pittsburgh in 1925. Over the next 8 years, he established himself as a very capable, skilled forward who scored 87 goals in his career. He played his last few games with Ottawa, but his playing days ended as a result of a bizarre incident in the team's dressing room in which Milks hurt his knee badly. That was December 29, 1932, and although he played a few more games, the pain was too great and he retired. Milks moved back to Ottawa, where he got a job as a ticket agent for CPR, and two years later he moved to Hamilton where he was a tank inspector for the British army until the end of the war. He moved to Shawville when his health problems mounted, and then turned to alcohol. Those who knew him in later life knew him as a drinker first, a former NHLer second.

MILLAR, Al
b. Winnipeg, Manitoba, September 18, 1929
d. unknown

He played exactly 6 games in the NHL, but also played pro for some 20 years, guarding the goal of every conceivable team in a peripatetic crease career. Millar started in the AHL in 1950 and changed teams or leagues on a seemingly annual basis. One time, in 1953, he was charged with common assault when a woman along the rails spit on him and he swung his

Bill Mikkelson

John Mikol

Oleg Mikulchik

Mike Milbury

Al Millar

Craig Millar

Mike Millar

Cory Millen

Greg Millen

Aaron Miller

stick at her, glancing a blow off her shoulder and swiping her face. He was found innocent of the charges and kept on playing, his best year coming soon after with the Quebec Aces when he was named the league's best goalie. After that season, he worked in Cambridge, Massachusetts, managing a drive-in restaurant, and the next year the B's called him up for a few games. He won only once and surrendered 25 goals, and never made it back to the NHL. Millar's last season was '69-'70 with Rochester, a year in which he filled many roles. He was the backup goalie who took some shots in the warmup and played a few games; when he sat on the bench he recorded statistics for the coach; and when the Amerks weren't playing he was driving all over the continent scouting games for the team. When he retired, he scouted for the Buffalo Sabres, but in the summer of 1971 he was seriously injured in a car crash in Quebec and was forced to retire.

MILLAR, Craig
b. Winnipeg, Manitoba, July 12, 1976
You certainly don't grow up in Winnipeg and play four years of junior with Swift Current longing and hoping to play in Slovakia one day, but that was the path Millar skated down in the ice lanes of life. He played a few games here and there after graduating from the Broncos in 1995, most impressively with Nashville for most of 1999-2000, but ultimately he chose to accept an offer in Bratislava for 2001-02 rather than hang around in the minors waiting for another – not guaranteed – recall.

MILLAR, Hugh
b. Edmonton, Alberta, April 3, 1921
d. unknown
If there was one man in hockey a player never wanted to rub the wrong way, his name was Jack Adams, GM of Detroit. Millar won the Memorial Cup with the Winnipeg Rangers in 1941 and after leaving hockey to join the army he returned to the Detroit organization and played a few games for Jolly Jack in '46-'47. Adams wanted Millar as stock for the farm team in Indianapolis, but in 1948 Millar decided to quit the team so he could run an hotel and coach junior. Furious, Adams prevented Millar from coaching the Canadiens junior team in Manitoba, but a year later another Winnipegger convinced Adams to let Millar coach the Winnipeg Black Hawks, which he did.

MILLAR, Mike
b. St. Catharines, Ontario, April 28, 1965
The Dundas Real McCoys, one of the great modern, unknown teams to win the Allan Cup, can add Millar to its impressive list of alumni after he joined the team for the 2001-02 season. Millar was a draft choice of Hartford in 1984 and played 78 games for 4 NHL teams in the ensuing years, but he was primarily a minor-leaguer who decided to take his act on the road. For the better part of a decade he played in Europe, principally in Germany for teams in Kassel (the Huskies) and Hamburg (the Crocodiles) before returning to Canada as his career dwindled.

MILLEN, Corey
b. Cloquet, Minnesota, March 30, 1964
Millen had tons of what every man would love, except that when he found he had so much, he really didn't want it all. Huh? At the 1989 World Championships he was fingered for doping following the U.S.'s 8-2 loss to Canada. Tests revealed he had abnormal amounts of testosterone in his system, more than the body naturally produces, the IIHF argued. He fought the decision, but was suspended from international competition for 18 months. He had played for his country at the 1984 and '88 Olympics and the '87 Canada Cup, but it was another decade before he ever played for the U.S. Millen came out of the University of Minnesota in 1987 and played eight years in the NHL. He was a small but feisty forward, perfectly capable of scoring. His name is particularly noteworthy because of a trade between Dallas and Calgary on December 19, 1995. The Stars sent him and Jarome Iginla to the Flames for Joe Nieuwendyk, a trade that was beneficial to both teams. After a year and a half in Calgary, though, Millen moved to Europe to play out the last of his career.

MILLEN, Greg
b. Toronto, Ontario, June 25, 1957
He always wanted just one shot at the Cup – geez, who doesn't? – and although he never got it, Millen still played in 604 more NHL games than most people. The goalie started with Pittsburgh in 1978 but really matured and starred with Hartford three years later. A tireless competitor, he appeared in at least 55 games for 4 consecutive years, though the team never made the playoffs. When he was traded to St. Louis, he played nearly as much on a team that qualified for the post-season with regularity, but the Blues never went deep into the playoffs and Millen's dream went unfulfilled. He closed out his career with brief stops in Chicago and Detroit, and soon after went into broadcasting, where his humour and casual camera style suited *Hockey Night in Canada*. Millen has moved around a bit over the last decade, but today he is one of a large number of goalies-cum-analysts that populate the hockey airwaves in Canada.

MILLER, Aaron
b. Buffalo, New York, August 11, 1971
What rotten luck! Drafted in 1989 by the Rangers, Miller was traded to Quebec in 1991 and slowly became part of one of the emerging powers in the NHL. He graduated from the University of Vermont in 1993 and over the next three years played a few games with the Nordiques while learning to play defence in the AHL. Trouble was, in 1995-96, when the team moved to Colorado and won the Cup, Miller played just five games. The year after, he made the team full-time and for the next four years was a solid player in his own end. Then he was traded to L.A. at the deadline in 2001, and a few weeks later the Avs won their second Cup. Miller's career fits snugly between the two victories, and now that he's in L.A., the chance for another chase for the bowl is nowhere in sight.

MILLER, Bill
b. Campbellton, New Brunswick, August 1, 1911
d. Campbellton, New Brunswick, June 12, 1986
Back home, Miller wasn't just a hockey player – he was a hero. This was the 1930s, and players from pokey places like Campbellton didn't just skate their way into the NHL the way Miller did. He played on two Allan Cup-winning teams with the Moncton Hawks, playing both forward and defence (in 1933 and '34) and the next year he won a Stanley Cup with the Maroons. No New Brunswicker had ever done anything like that! What's even more amazing about his first NHL season was that although he scored just 3 goals in 22 games, he scored all 3 in his *first* game. He played two more years in the league, with the Maroons and then the Canadiens, and after retiring in 1937 he returned to Campbellton to take an active role in local golf and make his way in the business world.

MILLER, Bob
b. Billerica, Massachusetts, September 28, 1956
In hockey, as in life, there are good surprises and bad surprises. Miller was a bit of both. He came out of the University of New Hampshire in 1977 to make the Bruins at his first training camp, and playing only part-time he scored 20 goals. The Bruins traded Gregg Sheppard to get a defenceman, figuring Miller was the new Sheppard and the trade made sense. But in his second year, playing regularly, Miller slumped to just 15 goals. The year after wasn't much better, and soon he was on his way out of town, to Colorado. Not a good career move. Even the Rockies bought him out and it wasn't until three years later he got a last chance with L.A. Miller also played in three World Championships for the U.S. as well as the 1981 Canada Cup, and ended his career in Switzerland.

MILLER, Brad
b. Edmonton, Alberta, July 23, 1969
The rough-and-tumble play of Miller landed him an NHL job periodically over his years in the game, though he spent the vast majority of his time in the minors, first in the AHL, then even lower, in the "I." He was a large defenceman who specialized in play in his own end and play with his gloves off, but he never lived up to his 22nd-overall selection by Buffalo at the 1987 draft.

MILLER, Earl
b. Lumsden, Saskatchewan, September 12, 1905
d. Regina, Saskatchewan, June 20, 1936
Over the years a number of players have died early in life or during the height of their playing days, but Miller's sudden death might be the most mysterious. He started in the NHL with Chicago in 1927 and after five years was sold to Toronto during the '31-'32 season. He helped the Leafs win their first Cup at the new Maple Leaf Gardens and went on to play in the minors for a few years. One summer day in 1936, his body was found in a field in Regina. Foul play was not suspected, but no natural cause of death was ever publicly revealed.

MILLER, Jason
b. Edmonton, Alberta, March 1, 1971
Odd. How does a player who averages 51 goals over his last 3 years of junior and is drafted 18th overall decline so quickly in his team's eyes that he plays only 6 times in the NHL? Ask Miller. New Jersey loved the kid in 1989, but by 1993 they wanted nothing to do with him. He played well in the minors, and signed with Detroit, but there was no second chance for him, only Europe. Miller has been playing overseas for close to a decade, mostly in Germany, and is an established scorer in a less intense game.

Bill Miller

Bob Miller

One summer day in 1936, his body was found in a field in Regina.
EARL MILLER

MILLER, Jay
b. Wellesley, Massachusetts, July 16, 1960
Ah, the osmotic influences of advertising! Catch-all phrases used to sell a product become a part of everyday language, and the lexicon of the sell is woven into the formal use of descriptive words. Miller was a fighter who played for his dream team, Boston, in the 1980s and L.A. soon after, and when another team's goon came on the ice Miller often followed soon after. His very appearance came to be known as "Miller time," which in itself was a euphemism for "here comes a fight." He averaged 4 penalty minutes a game over his career, and in the 1988 playoffs he accrued 124 in just a dozen games.

MILLER, Joe
b. Morrisburg, Ontario, October 6, 1900
d. Toronto, Ontario, August 12, 1963
How about that!? You start your NHL career with a team that doesn't make the playoffs, yet you end up winning the Stanley Cup that year. Yes, Miller started the '27-'28 season with the New York Americans, where he made an excellent impression on a not-very-good team. In that year's playoffs, the Rangers' Lorne Chabot was injured, and the Blueshirts got Miller on loan from the Amerks for the balance of the post-season. He proved his worth again, allowing just three goals in as many games and giving the Rangers their first Cup. That fall, he was traded to Pittsburgh for Roy Worters, and he had 11 shutouts in the 44-game schedule. For the next three years he continued to play well on bad teams. His career record was an awful 24-87-16, yet his goals-against average was a sparkling 2.92.

Brad Miller

Jay Miller

Kelly Miller

Kevin Miller

Kip Miller

Perry Miller

MILLER, John "Jack"
b. Delisle, Saskatchewan, September 16, 1925
Like his neighbours, the Bentley brothers, Miller was a wheat farmer in the summer and a hockey player in the winter. Unlike the Hall of Famers, though, Miller played just a few NHL games, with Chicago in 1949-51, in a brief pro career. He was a terrific goal scorer in the minors, but in his 17 games with the Hawks he failed to register a single point.

MILLER, Kelly
b. Lansing, Michigan, March 3, 1963
Only those closest to the NHL could possibly know that Miller played more than 1,000 games in the league. He was a low draft choice with the Rangers in 1982, and for 15 years was one of the quietest, steadiest players around. Not blessed with a great shot or blazing speed or a quick release, Miller was hard working, a captain in deed if not in name. The Rangers traded him to Washington in 1987, and he spent the last 13 years of his career with the Caps. He was the team's player rep with the NHLPA, he did enormous amounts of charity work in the city, and in the summers he and his wife ran a real estate business. He retired to become an assistant coach for Anaheim, but after two years he signed with Grand Rapids to be a playing assistant and led the team to the Turner Cup finals. In the summer of 2001, Miller signed on as an assistant with the Islanders.

MILLER, Kevin
b. Lansing, Michigan, September 2, 1965
The Miller family was connected with Michigan State University the way few families can boast. Kevin and both his NHL brothers, Kelly and Kip, were Michigan, as did father, Lyle, uncle Butch, and cousin Dean. Like Kelly, Kevin was a low draft choice by the Rangers, in 1984, but he played a dozen years in the NHL with nine teams. Pack lightly, travel often, was his mode of conduct. Miller was by no means a dirty player, and he scored 20 goals 4 times. Toward the end of his career, he saw time in the minors, and then decided to finish his playing days in Switzerland, where he became involved in an unfortunate incident. In a game on October 31, 2000, he elbowed Andrew McKim viciously, a blow that ended McKim's career and drove him to launch legal action. Miller had led the Swiss league in scoring in 1999-2000 with 29 goals and was suspended just 8 games for the blow.

MILLER, Kip
b. Lansing, Michigan, June 11, 1969
It's rare, but every now and then a bona fide NHLer slips through the cracks these days. Fortunately for Miller, he persevered and finally earned his dues. Drafted in 1987, he attended Michigan State like the rest of the Miller clan, but uniquely he won the Hobey Baker Award in 1990. Still, between 1990 and 1998 he was a minor-leaguer who got called up to the NHL for a few games here and there. He moved from team to team, signed as a free agent to stock various farm teams, but then just like that he made the Pittsburgh team at training camp in 1998 at age 29. He's been an NHL regular pretty much since then. In the AHL and IHL he was a proven 30-goal scorer,

and although his numbers have been smaller with the Penguins, Anaheim, and the Islanders, he's contributed in other ways and established himself a decade later than most.

MILLER, Paul
b. Billerica, Massachusetts, August 21, 1959
Bob's brother played three games with Colorado in 1981-82 and recorded three points, all assists, yet he never got a longer look from this weak team or any other. In all, he played just five seasons of pro in the minors, though he did represent the U.S. at the 1982 World Championships, an eighth-place finish for the country.

MILLER, Perry
b. Winnipeg, Manitoba, June 24, 1952
It was a big deal in the summer of 1977 when Detroit signed Miller to an NHL contract. He had been playing with Winnipeg in the WHA for 3 seasons, where he established records for most goals (4) and points (6) by a defenceman in a game. But in three and a half seasons with the Wings, his play wasn't so magical and the team wasn't so good, and after some time in the minors he retired. Miller returned to his hometown and opened two bars, Wise Guys Bar & Grill and Wise Guys on Campus.

MILLER, Tom
b. Kitchener, Ontario, March 31, 1947
Even though Miller attended the University of Denver for four years (earning a degree in engineering) he was still Rangers property because he had played with the Kitchener Rangers in the early 1960s. A trade sent him to Detroit, where he played his first NHL games, in 1970-71. His only full year came two seasons later with the Islanders, and by 1975 he was out of hockey and back on his farm outside Kitchener.

MILLER, Warren
b. South St. Paul, Minnesota, January 1, 1954
Miller came out of the University of Minnesota to play in the WHA starting in 1975. After two decent seasons, he signed with Edmonton only to hold out for a better contract. The Oilers traded him soon after, and by the time the new league joined the NHL in 1979, Miller was claimed by the Rangers. He had his best season with Hartford the year after, scoring 22 goals, but by 1983 he decided to retire. He also played for the U.S. in the 1981 World Championships and then the Canada Cup.

MILLEY, Norm
b. Toronto, Ontario, February 14, 1980
A Buffalo draft choice in 1998, young Milley saw the NHL in January 2002 when he was called up from Rochester to replace the injured Erik Rasmussen. He was sent back to the minors when Rasmussen recovered. In junior, Milley was a top-flight scorer, leading the OHL in goals for 1999-2000.

MILLS, Craig
b. Toronto, Ontario, August 27, 1976
Mills didn't play very many games in the NHL, but he realized a dream by making it to the big show. And

while he was developing as a player, his father was also realizing a dream. Dennis Mills was a Toronto MP who sent his son to St. Mike's, the high school he himself had attended and that had produced more NHLers (160 and counting) than any other single establishment on the face of the earth. While Craig was playing junior in Belleville, dad was working with the OHL to bring back the Majors, and by the time Craig was in the NHL, dad had succeeded. Craig, as it turns out, has been a minor-leaguer, but the Majors have reasserted themselves as a fine hockey team with an almost unparallelled tradition.

MINARD, Mike
b. Owen Sound, Ontario, November 1, 1976
One of the few undefeated goalies in NHL history, Minard would actually like a chance to lose a game. You see, he's only played once, for the Oilers, but he's been a pro since 1996. He'd love the chance to get back into the NHL to wreck that perfect record – or keep it going a while longer – but he seems destined to remain confined to minor league creases across the continent. Even in the minors he's been more backup than starter, but he plays and waits for the call. Although he most recently signed with St. John's, the Leafs' AHL affiliate, he did so for the league minimum of $37,500, a wee bit below the $7 million Curtis Joseph was hauling in at the ACC at the same time.

MINER, John
b. Moose Jaw, Saskatchewan, August 28, 1965
If he's trying to set a record, he might look back and rue his early years in the minors, for Miner has been playing in Europe since 1988 and shows no signs of stopping. The graduate from the Regina Pats played three years in the minors before Edmonton called him up for a few games in '87-'88, but he quickly decided that a small, speedy defenceman would be better off in Europe than taking an AHL pounding game after game while waiting for another chance in the NHL. He started in Austria, moved to Switzerland, and most recently has established himself in Germany.

MINOR, Gerry
b. Regina, Saskatchewan, October 27, 1958
Minor saw no hope, and in 1979 he almost quit the game. But he returned to the minors and hoped Vancouver would call him up. The Canucks used him for all of five games, but his big break came the next year when he beat out Chris Oddleifson in camp to win the job as eleventh forward. Then, when Ivan Boldirev broke his cheekbone, Minor was promoted to the top line. The year after, he broke his ankle and

Mironov joined the Winnipeg Jets in 1993.
BORIS MIRONOV

missed much of the year, though he returned in time to help the team make an improbable run to the finals. He never got back on track, though, and spent almost all of the rest of his career in the minors before retiring in 1987.

MIO, Ed
b. Windsor, Ontario, January 31, 1954
He's called Eddie as much as Ed, so he can't qualify with Ed (always called Ed) Kea as having the shortest name in league history. But he can claim to be of trivial value on another point. It was he and Peter Driscoll who were sold with Wayne Gretzky from the floundering Indianapolis Racers to the Edmonton Oilers at the start of the WHA's '78-'79 season. Mio then stayed with the Oilers for two NHL years in the pre-Grant Fuhr days and later made his way to the Rangers and Detroit. After retiring in 1986, he settled in Detroit – being from Windsor, it was his home away from home – and started as a sales rep in the car industry. He later joined IMG Hockey as a player agent, until being hired in 2002 by the ever-faithful Gretzky as director of player development in Phoenix.

MIRONOV, Boris
b. Moscow, Soviet Union (Russia), March 21, 1972
Boris and brother Dmitri were among the first pair of Soviet brothers to play in the NHL, the result of their father's desire to see his children become athletes. Mironov senior was a cyclist and initially took the kids to water, but when he moved to a new home, there was no pool nearby, only a skating rink. That's how the boys became involved in hockey, but they stayed involved because they were good. Boris played in Moscow, winning a silver medal with the National Team at the 1991 WJC. The next year, he won gold at the WJC and soon after won another gold with the Commonwealth of Independent States (CIS), the team that was formed after the dissolution of the Soviet Union and prior to the stabilization of Russia and the various independent countries that had been part of the USSR for all those decades. Mironov joined the Winnipeg Jets in 1993, but before the end of the season he was traded to Edmonton. He developed into a tremendous defenceman with the Oilers, strong on the man, skilled with the puck, and aggressive at both ends of the ice. He was with the team for six seasons, and the only reason he isn't still there is money. GM Glen Sather couldn't afford him, so Mironov was sent to Chicago where he sat out part of 1999-2000 in a contract dispute. For all the glowing reviews he has given himself, though, Mironov has never scored more than 46 points in a season and his team has made the playoffs exactly thrice in 9 years of play.

Mike Minard

John Miner

Gerry Minor

Ed Mio

MIRONOV, Dmitri ("Tree")

b. Moscow, Soviet Union (Russia), December 25, 1965

Unlike brother Boris, Dmitri was a late bloomer, in part because he didn't much like playing hockey through his teens, in part because in his homeland he didn't play for either the Red Army or the Soviet Wings, the best two teams in the country. He made his international debut at the 1991 Izvestia tournament and later played at the World Championships, where Toronto scouts first considered him a prospect. Within a year, Mironov had played at the 1991 Canada Cup and the '92 Worlds, and that convinced the Leafs to bring him to Toronto right away. He played seven games at the end of the '91-'92 season, scoring a goal and breaking his nose. Welcome to Canada. He played three more years with Toronto and was an NHLer until 2000 for five teams in all, having the fortune to play with many of the greatest players of his generation: Doug Gilmour in Toronto, Mario Lemieux in Pittsburgh, Paul Kariya in Anaheim, Steve Yzerman in Detroit, and Adam Oates in Washington. The only time he played defence with his brother was at the 1998 Olympics in Nagano, a silver-medal win. His time with the Red Wings resulted in a Stanley Cup, which he took to his house in Toronto for a party with his closest friends.

MISZUK, John

b. Naliboki, Poland, September 29, 1940

This is a truly Canadian experience, so it's only fitting that hockey is involved. Miszuk grew up in Poland with his parents and two sisters on a farm, but during the war the Germans confiscated the Miszuk's land and the family lived an itinerant existence for years. After the war John's three uncles emigrated to Hamilton and saved money to bring the family over, which they did, in 1949. John didn't start skating for another two or three years, but he developed quickly while playing in the Hamilton police minor league. That he made it to the NHL within 10 years of first skating is amazing, though the knock on him was that he was gangly and awkward on skates (which is one reason he moved from forward to defence). Nonetheless, he played three seasons on a part-time basis, and with expansion in 1967 he made it full-time with Philadelphia and then Minnesota. He later played in the minors for a few years before finishing his career in the WHL.

MITCHELL, Bill "Red"

b. Toronto, Ontario, September 6, 1912

Like virtually every player nicknamed Red, Mitchell acquired the moniker as a boy because of his hair colour. He grew up in Toronto and played for the Marlies before turning pro with the Detroit Olympics

in 1933. It was eight years yet before he got into an NHL game, with Chicago, and it wasn't until 1942-43 that he played an entire year in the league. He played a third and final season toward the end of the war and then was sent to the minors. After he retired, Mitchell went into coaching, notably with Springfield in 1954 and then with the Washington Lions. He was also a graduate of the University of Toronto and a golf pro in the summers.

MITCHELL, Bill ("Willie")

b. Port Dalhousie, Ontario, February 22, 1930

A day after his 34th birthday, Mitchell played his only NHL game, with Detroit, after being called up from Windsor, having won the Allan Cup with the Bulldogs the previous spring. He played hockey for more than 20 years, his longest stint coming with Toledo in the IHL in the 1950s. As his career wound down, he took on duties as playing coach in Ohio, though the Mercurys were now called the Blades. He played for Canada at the 1962 World Championships and later became strictly a coach.

MITCHELL, Herb

b. Meaford, Ontario, January 4, 1896

d. Trenton, Ontario, January 12, 1969

Mitchell played senior hockey in Hamilton before joining the Bruins for their first NHL season, '24-'25. He played part of this season and most of the next with the team, though he quickly learned that coaching, not playing, was his true calling. He finished his skating in Windsor, and by 1934 had assumed head coaching responsibilities with Hershey of the Eastern Amateur League. He took the team to three titles, and when it turned pro in the new International-American league, Mitchell stayed on until 1942. In 1956 he became the team's chief scout in charge of player development. He later retired to Toronto, where he became a druggist.

MITCHELL, Ivan "Mike"

b. Toronto

d. unknown

Mitchell's only NHL games came with the St. Pats in the early days of the NHL. He started in 1919 but within 2 years his body was ravaged by poisoning of an undisclosed form and he was forced to retire having played just 22 games in goal for the team.

MITCHELL, Jeff

b. Wayne, Michigan, May 16, 1975

Known more for his physical play than his goals or skating, Mitchell played briefly with the Dallas Stars in a minor-league career in which even the AHL looked pretty good. He hovered in the IHL and other

Amazingly, he has never won an individual award.
MIKE MODANO

John Miszuk

Willie Mitchell

lesser leagues before retiring to get into media and communications, eventually becoming involved in both sales and broadcasting for the Topeka Scarecrows of the USHL.

MITCHELL, Roy
b. Edmonton, Alberta, March 14, 1969

A low draft choice by Montreal in 1988, Mitchell signed with Minnesota before he got a chance, albeit quick, to play in the NHL. He spent the majority of his career in the minors, floating on to Dallas and New Jersey on paper but never getting a callup to play defence with the NHL teams.

MITCHELL, Willie
b. Port McNeill, British Columbia, April 23, 1977

Way back when, Les Mitchell, Willie's grandfather, played in the West Coast league and had a tryout with the Rangers. In his day, there was no thought of a time when the NHL would have 30 teams, let alone entries in places like New Jersey or with names like Wild. Yet Willie has made good in just that era. He left Clarkson University early to play for the Devils, and played his first NHL game in Toronto on a *Hockey Night in Canada* broadcast on March 25, 2000. He was traded to Minnesota a year later, where he has had a chance to show what he can do.

MODANO, Mike ("Modo")
b. Livonia, Michigan, June 7, 1970

When Modano was 10 years old, the U.S. Olympic team was performing its Miracle on Ice at Lake Placid. Eight years later, Modano became only the second American-born player to be drafted 1st overall (Brian Lawton, in 1983, was the first). Modano did a reverse-Canadian move by playing junior hockey in Prince Albert, and in the fall of 1989 he made Minnesota in camp and has never looked back. A likely Hall of Famer when he retires, there is little he hasn't accomplished save the large numbers that only a full career can produce. He has nine 30-goal seasons to his credit, and in '93-'94 he scored 50 times. In 2002-03, he earned his 1,000th career point, and goal 500 won't be far behind. Like Steve Yzerman, he is one of a rare species who has played his entire career with one franchise. He has displayed tremendous speed for a man his size, and his wrist shot and backhand are among the hardest in the game. He has represented the U.S. at every major tournament, from the World Juniors as a teen to the World Championships on two occasions. He played on the 1991 Canada Cup team, and led the U.S. to a victory in the 1996 World Cup of Hockey. Modano played at both the 1998 and 2002

Olympics, winning silver in the latter, and in 1999 he led the Stars to the first Stanley Cup in franchise history. Amazingly, he has never won an individual award, though he has played in a number of All-Star Games. Even if he never plays another game, Modano has established his place in the game's history and has helped develop the U.S. into a genuine world hockey power.

MODIN, Fredrik "Freddy"
b. Sundsvall, Sweden, October 8, 1974

To read the scouting report without knowing his birthplace, one wouldn't think Modin was Swedish. He was not known for his skating, his passing skills, or his stickhandling. Instead, he was known for his booming shot, a shot that would scare the bejesus out of anyone. Yet after he joined the Leafs in 1996, he displayed a puzzling reluctance to use that shot, cannon though it was. He scored just 6 goals his first season, and turned that into 16 in his second and third, but still he left the coaches wanting. The Leafs gave up on him perhaps a bit too soon, for in year 4 he scored 32 times, finally reaching expectations with a weak Tampa team that gave him plenty of ice time. Internationally, Modin achieved gold in 1998 with Tre Kronor at the Worlds, overcoming an eye injury and playing on a line with Mats Sundin and Peter Forsberg, the top Swedes in the country.

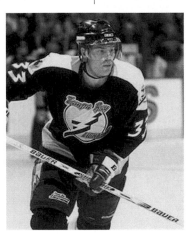

Modin achieved gold in 1998 with Tre Kronor at the Worlds.
FREDDY MODIN

MODRY, Jaroslav
b. Ceske Budejovice, Czechoslovakia (Czech Republic), February 27, 1971

It's taken a few years, but Modry has settled into a nice career with Los Angeles, his team since 1996. Loaded with offensive skills, he's played an increasingly important role on the team since Rob Blake was traded to Colorado, and his ice time has increased appropriately. Modry was a low draft choice of New Jersey, but the Devils sent him to Ottawa for a draft choice with which they selected Alyn McCauley in 1995. Modry played as much in the minors as in the NHL until the Blake trade but has proved his ability to make a greater contribution as the team has needed it.

MOE, Billy
b. Danvers, Massachusetts, October 2, 1916
d. Long Beach, California, July 13, 1996

Hockeyist, jockey, Disneyland driver, Moe led a full and vigorous life from start to finish. He grew up in Minnesota and took a liking to hockey at a young age. He worked his way up to the pros and established himself in the AHL, where he introduced a novel method of checking. While most defencemen hit with their hips or shoulders, Moe, a small man to begin

Mike Modano

Jaroslav Modry

Billy Moe

with, crouched low and "blocked" oncoming forwards in a football manner. It was a unique kind of hit, and NHL bosses took notice. Moe signed with the Rangers in 1944 and played most of five seasons with the Blueshirts. The team wasn't particularly strong in this post-war era, but Moe did his part. The only year the team made the playoffs, 1948, was bittersweet for Moe because he cracked a vertebra in his first game and missed the rest of the post-season. He finished his career with a couple of years in the minors, but in the early 1950s his life changed when he went to California on vacation. He went on a blind date, fell in love, and married Effie. It was the second marriage for both, and Moe settled in Long Beach, where he lived the rest of his life. He became a harness-racing driver at the Los Alamitos Race Course for the next 20 years, then drove horses with the Horsedrawn Streetcars at Disneyland, a less demanding position. Later in life, he was ravaged by Parkinson's disease and then lung cancer, to which he succumbed at age 79.

Lyle Moffat

MOFFAT, Lyle
b. Calgary, Alberta, March 19, 1948
Even though Moffat graduated from Michigan Tech with a degree in business administration in 1971, he missed his last season of hockey with the Huskies because of a bad knee and ankle injury. Nonetheless, the Leafs invited him to training camp, and after a year in the minors he got into his first NHL game. For the most part, though, Moffat spent his three years with the team in the CHL, so when he had the chance to jump to the WHA, he took it. He spent most of his career with Winnipeg, staying with the team for a final NHL season when the Jets joined the big league in 1979. Moffat wanted to remain in hockey, but he wasn't exactly sure how. He coached Kamloops for a year, then returned to the Jets as director of community and media relations. After five years, he moved back west to be the director of marketing for the Victoria Cougars, but when the franchise relocated to Prince George, he remained in Victoria. He was hired by Seacoast Communications Group as a marketing consultant, and it is there he remains.

Mike Moffat

MOFFAT, Mike
b. Galt, Ontario, February 4, 1962
Glenn Hall threw up before every game. Everyone knows that – it was the stuff of legend. The reality, though, was that his upchucking was not a superstition like taping your stick one way or putting on your equipment another. It was about nerves, pressure, the ordeal of having to stop every shot hammered your way by the best players in the world while 16,000 maniacs watched. Hall was perhaps the greatest goalie ever, so he learned to deal with the psychological aspects of goaltending. Lyle Moffat never did. He helped Canada win a gold medal at the 1982 WJC (named best goalie in the process) and at the end of the year the Bruins called him up for the final two games of the year just to see what he was like. Well, he played so well in those games he became the starter for the playoffs! Again, he played incredibly, and in a couple of weeks went from being a kid in junior trying his best to a pro in the NHL expected to be the next Gerry Cheevers. Coming out of the chute

Sandy Moger

the next season he played poorly and was sent to the minors to collect himself. But the pressure he put on himself gave him severe headaches and insomnia. In one AHL game, he allowed nine goals. The next morning, he flew to Toronto and enrolled in correspondence school to prepare for university, then retired. At Wilfrid Laurier he studied business and slowly got back into the nets, for fun, no strings attached. Dave King convinced him to play with the National Team, but after a few games he walked away for good. He settled in Unionville, Ontario, north of Toronto, and became district salesman for a building supply company, far from the roar of the crowd.

MOFFAT, Ron ("Atlas")
b. West Hope, North Dakota, August 21, 1905
d. Seattle, Washington, August 19, 1960
If timing is everything, then Moffat had nothing, for although he made it to the NHL, he arrived just a few years too early. He played for Detroit for parts of three seasons in the early 1930s, but if he had hung around just a few more years he would have been part of the two Cup teams the Wings produced in 1936 and '37. Instead, he was in the Pacific Coast league, playing out the last of his career.

MOGER, Sandy
b. 100 Mile House, British Columbia, March 21, 1969
Not only has Canada produced most of the great players in hockey's history, it has produced, without a shadow of a doubt, the best place names on the planet. Where else could you find Head-Smashed-In, Newton Robinson, Rocky Mountain House, and Moger's hometown of 100 Mile House? Moger was a large and imposing player who attended the pedestrianly named Lake Superior State University, graduating in 1992 and turning pro in the Vancouver system. He had a decent run with Boston and L.A. after the Canucks let him walk, but since 1999 has been in the minors trying to work his way back into the NHL.

MOGILNY, Alexander
b. Khabarovsk, Soviet Union (Russia), February 18, 1969
Here is a player who looks aloof off the ice and sometimes on it, but perhaps that's because at age 14 Moscow put him in an army barracks 300 days a year to train with men old enough to be his father. Mogilny wasn't just good and talented – he was great and without peer. Nobody in the Soviet Union skated as fast as he did, and when he had the puck, not his opponents, decided when it would leave his stick. His wrist shot looked harmless until the moment the puck left his stick, at which point it travelled faster than a car on a highway. In 1989, Mogilny played at the WJC and later, in Sweden, at the World Championships where he won gold. He then defected, flying to Buffalo in the hope of starting an NHL career. He was the first Soviet player to defect (which is why he wears number 89), and within 4 years he became the first to score 76 goals in a season. Barring catastrophe, he will also be the first Soviet to hit the 500-goal and 1,000-point marks for a career. While his skill and stickhandling have never been questioned, his desire has been. His play has been erratic from game to game

and season to season. When he is on, there is no one more exciting to watch; when he is off, you don't even know he's playing. He left Buffalo for Vancouver, and for five years seemed to be unhappy and ever desirous of a trade, one that finally came at the 2000 deadline to New Jersey. He won a Cup with the Devils, but when he became a free agent he signed with Toronto, a team he admitted wasn't his first choice. Mogilny lacked the drive to win an individual trophy and his days of 50 goals are over, but he remains one of the most talented players his country has ever produced.

MOHER, Mike
b. Manitouwadge, Ontario, March 26, 1962
If Mike Moher ever got wind of the fact that Leroy Brown was the baddest man in the whole damn town, he would have done serious damage to one Mr. Brown. That's what Moher did, most infamously in junior where he fought so much that commissioner Dave Branch instigated a special rule just for him. In '81-'82, the right winger had been suspended a total of nine games for various infractions when he went into the stands to start yet another fight. Branch suspended him for another 10 games and told him he'd be suspended for every fight he started for the rest of the year, the sentence doubling with each infraction. Moher led the OHL in penalty minutes in each of his three seasons, though he finished his teen career by winning the Memorial Cup with the Rangers. He played just nine games with New Jersey the year after and fought for another year in the minors before packing it in. Moher went into coaching, eventually becoming an assistant with the Penticton Rage.

Mike Moher

His wrist shot looked harmless until the moment the puck left his stick.
ALEXANDER MOGILNY

MOHNS, Doug ("Diesel")
b. Capreol, Ontario, December 13, 1933
Talk about cautious. Not only did he wear a hairpiece, he also wore a helmet! Diesel Doug got his name because Capreol had two things to boast about – hockey and the railway. He played junior in Barrie, winning Memorial Cups in 1951 and '53, and although he was slated to develop in the minors, the Bruins had no time for that. Jack McIntyre went down with an injury before the start of the '53-'54 season, and Mohns took his place. Twenty-two years later, Mohns still hadn't played a game in the minors. His career was long and successful as both a defenceman and a winger, though he went into the history books as having played a staggering 1,390 NHL games without winning a Cup. His decade with Boston ended just before the arrival of Bobby Orr, and his years with Chicago came after the Hawks had won the Cup in 1961. Mohns became most famous for his role on the Scooter Line in Chicago with Kenny Wharram and Stan

Mikita, one of the highest-scoring troikas in the league. With this combination, he scored 22 goals or more in 4 successive seasons, though he played his final year with the hopeless Capitals in '74-'75. He worked as an insurance agent and real estate agent in the summers, but when he retired Mohns helped found the New England Rehabilitation Hospital, where he also served as an administrator. He also helped found a child abuse prevention centre in Boston.

MOHNS, Lloyd
b. Petawawa, Ontario, July 31, 1921
He got into his only NHL game, with the Rangers during the war, as a callup from the Rovers, but Mohns had an anonymous career until it was almost over and he was back in senior hockey. In a game during the '47-'48 season, he struck referee Frank Elliot while disputing a call and was suspended from the league for life. It was a dramatic way to end a pale career.

MOKOSAK, Carl
b. Fort Saskatchewan, Alberta, September 22, 1962
Mokosak may have been big and mobile in the eyes of most scouts, but he could fight and that's what gave him market value. In just 83 games, he managed to play for 5 teams in a career that passed mostly in the minors until he retired in 1991. Brother, John, was cut from pretty much the same cloth.

MOKOSAK, John
b. Edmonton, Alberta, September 7, 1963
Rough and tough like his brother, John didn't last as long in the pro ranks, though he made an impression with his fists wherever he went. He played 41 games with Detroit (1988-90) during a 10-year career in the minors, and although he was also property of Boston and the Rangers he never made it back to the NHL.

MOLIN, Lars ("Molla")
b. Ornskoldsvik, Sweden, May 7, 1956
Molin loved hockey and wanted the challenge of the NHL, but for him it was not the be-all and end-all to make it as a star in the North American league. From the time he started playing with Modo in 1975 to the time he retired in 1991, Molin played at every level for his country. He made his living in the Swedish Elite League, but from 1981 to '84 he played for the Vancouver Canucks. His time in the NHL was not a bust, nor was it a tremendous success. By the end of his three-year contract, he was ready to return home and the Canucks weren't pleading with him to stay. After retiring, Molin became involved in coaching, moving up to national junior coach in 1999 and also guiding teams in the national league of his homeland.

Doug Mohns

Carl Mokosak

Lars Molin

MOLLER, Mike
b. Calgary, Alberta, June 16, 1962

Moller and brother, Randy, were gold medal winners with Canada at the 1982 WJC. Mike was on loan from Buffalo, the team with which he had made his NHL debut the previous season. He played five years in the Sabres system before being traded to Edmonton, but again his time passed mostly in the minors. When he retired in 1989, he settled in Red Deer and worked in the insurance business by day and on Rebels radio broadcasts at night. He also sat on the Red Deer Minor Hockey Commission, a board that oversaw kids leagues in that city.

MOLLER, Randy
b. Red Deer, Alberta, August 23, 1963

Randy Moller

Randy and brother, Mike, won gold with Canada as juniors in 1982, a particularly special tournament for Randy, who scored the championship goal. He then began a lengthy career with Quebec during the team's heyday. He was a physical defenceman, a trait that came in handy with the Nordiques during their heated rivalry with the Canadiens in the 1980s. He later played for New York and Buffalo, and ended with Florida. Throughout his career, Moller suffered a series of injuries, from back spasms to broken bones to knee problems to shoulder pains. He retired in 1995 after a final knee injury and stayed with the Panthers as their analyst on radio broadcasts.

MOLLOY, Mitch
b. Red Lake, Ontario, October 10, 1966

A big left winger who came out of nowhere, Molloy played two games with Buffalo despite never having played junior or establishing himself in any league as a teen. The Sabres scouted him in Johnstown and then assigned him to Rochester after his brief tryout in 1990, but he never made it back. Molloy retired in 1993.

MOLYNEAUX, Larry
b. Sutton West, Ontario, July 9, 1912
d. unknown

Here was a defenceman who played 45 games with the Rangers in the late 1930s without scoring a goal. Molyneaux came out of the Can-Am league and finished in the American league in 1941, and in addition to his regular-season shutout you can add another 10 goalless games in the playoffs! He later settled in Newmarket and became a sales manager.

MOMESSO, Sergio ("Mo")
b. Montreal, Quebec, September 4, 1965

As knee injuries go, they don't get much worse. On December 5, 1985, Momesso collided with Michael

Thelvin. He tore a ligament and cartilage and fractured his kneecap. Doctors had to use a synthetic fibre to help rebuild the knee, but Momesso had two factors in his favour – he was 20 years old and he was in great physical condition. The injury ended his first full season with Montreal, but during his time with his hometown team he was chased by coach Pat Burns, who pushed him to do better. Momesso had great size and strength and a nasty streak, but he seldom put all together into a one-game package to become a dominating forward. As a result, a cycle began whereby he'd be traded, try to assert himself and turn that corner to stardom, fall back, and be traded again. He had two 20-goal seasons but never developed a consistency of play. He skated for 6 teams in his 13 seasons and finished his career in Germany. After retiring, Momesso returned to Montreal, where he became an assistant coach at Concordia University.

He skated for 6 teams in his 13 seasons and finished his career in Germany.
SERGIO MOMESSO

MONAHAN, Garry ("Mondo")
b. Barrie, Ontario, October 20, 1946

When Montreal selected Monahan 1st overall in the draft, no one cared, no one knew who Monahan was, and no one raised an eyebrow at his NHL prospects. That's because Monahan was drafted in 1963, not only 1st overall but the first player ever drafted – period. He was 17 and playing at St. Mike's, and the only players who could be drafted back then were those not already signed to a C-form or committed to an NHL team. So Monahan felt none of the pressure that goes with a number-one choice in the modern world of 30 teams and million-dollar contracts. Nonetheless, he went on to have a decent 12 years in the NHL, mostly as a checking left winger who can also score a bit. Interestingly, he played for all three Canadian teams at the time – Toronto, Vancouver, Montreal – six years with the Leafs. Toward the end of his career, he was recruited by the Japanese and played for Seibu for three years under coaches Terry O'Malley and Barry MacKenzie, two Canadian Olympians. After three years, Monahan returned to Toronto to finish his degree in education, but rather than pursue a teaching career he moved to Vancouver and became a stockbroker by day and a Canucks analyst by night.

MONAHAN, Hartland
b. Montreal, Quebec, March 29, 1951

Ah, the mother of all hockey family trees produced a funny result. The great Howie Morenz had a daughter. She married Bernie Geoffrion. Bernie's daughter then married Hartland Monahan, and they had a son named Shane. So, Shane looks up and sees his dad (an NHLer), his grandad (Geoffrion, a Hall of Famer), and his great-grandad (Morenz, a Hall of Famer). And what

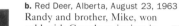

Larry Molyneaux

Hartland Monahan

does he do? Becomes a major league baseball player! The nerve. After winning the Memorial Cup with the Jr. Canadiens in 1970, Hartland went on to play seven NHL seasons. He had years of 17 and 23 goals with the hopeless Capitals and retired in 1981 after playing for St. Louis, his sixth team.

MONDOU, Armand
b. Yamaska, Quebec, June 27, 1905
d. Montreal, Quebec, September 13, 1976

He spent his entire 12 years in the NHL with Montreal, but Mondou was always second fiddle to the great puck conductors of the Canadiens during the 1930s. The left winger was not a great scorer, but he did have a reputation for having a great shot. He won the Cup with the Habs in 1930 and again the next year, his first full years in the league, but he never won after that. Toward the end of his career he spent some time in the minors and, knowing the end was nigh, retired in 1940. Mondou later became president of the Quebec Veterans Hockey Association.

MONDOU, Pierre
b. Sorel, Quebec, November 27, 1955

He was centring Montreal's best line with Mats Naslund and Mario Tremblay. He was having a fine season, and he had scored the winning goal on March 9, 1985, against Hartford. But with the flick of a stick it was all over. Ulf Samuelsson's blade caught Mondou in the eye, and he could no longer play. Desperate, he returned after 11 games to try, but 2 games later he knew it was over. The Canadiens hired him as an assistant in Verdun, and Mondou later moved into the team's NHL front office, but it was no way to channel his ability. After a rookie-of-the-year season in the AHL, Mondou joined the Habs for the '77 playoffs in which the team won the Stanley Cup, and he made the roster full-time in the fall. Montreal won two more Cups, and Mondou contributed both on offence (three 30-goal seasons) and on defence.

> **Ulf Samuelsson's blade caught Mondou in the eye, and he could no longer play.**
> PIERRE MONDOU

MONGEAU, Michel
b. Montreal, Quebec, February 9, 1965

You just can't convince the scouts that size doesn't matter. Mongeau should know. Not big, he scored 324 points in his final 2 years of junior in Laval, but not a single team used a draft choice to secure his rights. Not one. So he went to the minors, again put up big numbers, and three years later St. Louis signed him in 1989. In 3 years with Peoria he averaged 33 goals a year, but in 50 games with the Blues, he had just 5 goals. Same old, same old. Mongeau had a lengthy career in the minors, though his life changed on February 27, 1994, when he was cross-checked from behind by Chris Tamer. Mongeau hit the goalpost face first, breaking his

face in seven places. He needed three metal plates inserted, his jaw was wired shut for a month, and he was out of action for a year. He took Tamer to court, but the first action ended in a mistrial. At the second trial, few witnesses made themselves available and Mongeau lost the case, the opinion of the court being that the incident was an accident. He lived in Montreal as part-owner of a golf course and as a real estate agent.

MONGRAIN, Bob
b. La Sarre, Quebec, August 31, 1959

Another small player to come out of Quebec junior without an NHL team, Mongrain made a slight impact with Buffalo for six years starting in 1979, but made an even greater showing in Rochester. Down on the farm, he scored bundles of goals and helped the Amerks win the 1983 Calder Cup, and his career accomplishments got him into the Americans' Hall of Fame. Mongrain later played for several years in Switzerland, and when he returned to Canada he went into coaching, notably with Hull and Halifax of the Quebec league.

MONTADOR, Steve
b. Vancouver, British Columbia, December 21, 1979

It wasn't until the summer of 2000, when he was 20, that Montador signed a pro contract with Calgary. He had played his four years of junior without any NHL interest, but has been developing in the Flames system ever since. In December 2001 he played for Canada at the Spengler Cup, and he played his first few games with the Flames as well.

MONTEITH, Henry "Hank"
b. Stratford, Ontario, October 2, 1945

Hank and Stephen Monteith left an indelible and lasting impression on the University of Toronto Blues hockey team. They won CIAU championships with the Blues in 1966 and '67 and were both inducted into U of T's Sports Hall of Fame, Stephen in 1991, Hank six years later. Hank graduated after that second championship with a degree in commerce and signed with Detroit. He played parts of three seasons with the Wings, but his time in the minors was enough of a pro hockey experience and he retired. He and Stephen later donated a trophy bearing their name to U of T, to be presented annually to the Blues' leading scorer.

MONTGOMERY, Jim
b. Montreal, Quebec, June 30, 1969

Montgomery not only played on a line with Paul Kariya at U of Maine, he was the NCAA tournament MVP as the Black Bears earned their first-ever national championship. Unfortunately, his NHL

Armand Mondou

Michel Mongeau

Bob Mongrain

Hank Monteith

career was not as star-studded as Kariya's. Montgomery played '93-'94 with St. Louis, but since then he's played almost entirely in the minors with the exception of a few games with Montreal and the Flyers and then a few more with San Jose and Dallas after four more years in the lesser ranks.

MOOG, Andy
b. Penticton, British Columbia, February 18, 1960

Be most wary of getting what you want. Moog wanted to be the number-one goalie in Edmonton during the Grant Fuhr years, and he was willing to wait and apprentice and be patient. He joined the Oilers in 1980, but by the time the Cups started coming in '84 he was the backup, and in the playoffs this translated to little game action. In 1987 he forced the issue – make me number one, or trade me. And he gave his team plenty of time to think about it, joining the National Team and playing in the 1988 Olympics in Calgary. GM Glen Sather traded Moog to Boston, and lo and behold the two teams met in the Stanley Cup finals! Edmonton versus Boston became Fuhr versus Moog, and Moog lost convincingly. He did get his big honcho status, though, and continued playing for another decade. In all, Moog had an impressive career. He won 372 games and appeared in 132 playoff matches. He won 3 Cups with the Oilers and had eleven 20-win seasons. After retiring, he became an owner of the Forth Worth Brahmas of the WPHL and served as a goalie consultant for Vancouver. In 2000, he became the first goalie coach for the Canadian junior team.

He won 372 games and appeared in 132 playoff matches.
ANDY MOOG

MOORE, Alfie
b. Toronto, Ontario, December 1, 1905
d. unknown

It's awful to have to dispel a myth, especially one as good as this, but truth is often the better story, anyway. April 5, 1938, made Moore famous the hockey world over. It was game one of the Stanley Cup finals, and Chicago was in Toronto to face the Leafs. The Hawks' star goalie, Mike Karakas, had broken his toe and couldn't play, so the team was scrambling to find a replacement. They asked for Dave Kerr of the Rangers, but Leafs GM Conn Smythe adamantly refused. Chicago manager Bill Stewart knew for a fact that Alfie Moore lived in Toronto and might be available, for earlier in the day he had sold Alfie a pair of tickets to the game. The myth is that Moore was hauled out of a tavern (half-drunk, depending on who is telling the tale), but that was not the case. He was at home, and was called by Leafs assistant GM Frank Selke, who told Moore to be at the

Gardens by 6 p.m. with his equipment. It was only then that he learned he'd be playing – for Chicago! Moore was thrilled, but his brother, Freddy, wasn't. Freddy had been housebound for seven years, ever since being kicked in the head during a football game, and he loved the Leafs. Alfie played the game of his life and beat the Leafs 3-1 in a series Chicago won in 4 games. Needless to say, he was *persona non grata* at MLG the rest of his playing days. In all, Moore played 18 years of pro hockey, only 24 games of which were at the NHL level. He was a top goalie in the minors, and later became a coach of a senior team in Belleville in the early '50s. But for the rest of his life he was known as the man who came out of a bar to beat the Leafs in the playoffs.

MOORE, Barrie
b. London, Ontario, May 22, 1975

You know your fortunes have dropped when Columbus selects you in the Expansion Draft and then doesn't play you once. Moore had been a low Buffalo draft choice in 1993, but he played just a few games in the ensuing years while bouncing from team to team. He eventually moved to England to play for a year, and when he returned in 2001 he went straight to Portland of the AHL.

MOORE, Dickie ("Digging Dickie")
b. Montreal, Quebec, January 6, 1931

Of all the players to win a scoring title in the NHL, none accomplished the feat with quite the same resolve and under more debilitating circumstances than Moore when he led the league in scoring for 1957-58. Midway through the year he suffered a broken wrist and had doctors fit him with a cast that permitted him to grip his stick. By season's end, his 36 goals and 84 points were tops in the league. The next year, fully healthy, he set a league record by recording 96 points, one better than Gordie Howe's previous best for a season. Moore was beset by injuries his whole life. He was born with weak knees, and as a child he broke his leg twice. Yet he persevered and never took injuries sitting down, as it were. In junior, he won Memorial Cups with the Montreal Junior Royals in '48-'49 and with the Jr. Canadiens the following year. His tenacity, skill, and toughness earned him the admiration of Montreal GM Frank Selke who worked him into the lineup slowly over the course of three years. He was a part-timer in '52-'53 when the team won the Cup, but the next year he established himself as a bona fide NHLer. He played just a few games in the regular season of '53-'54, but in the playoffs led the league in assists and points. Despite playing with a chronic shoulder problem (which led to three separations over the years), Moore scored 20 goals

Alfie Moore

Barrie Moore

six out of his seven full seasons. He was part of the dynasty that won five Cups in a row (1955-60) and during that time he was a combination of Maurice Richard and Jean Béliveau. He was ferocious inside the blueline, and his skills were second to none. He retired in 1963 at age 32, in large measure because of his health. Moore had always been smart off the ice. He worked for the CPR during the early years of his career, and later invested in a golf course and a Dairy Queen. The lure of the game was too great, though, and the Leafs were able to talk him out of retirement a year and a half later. Again he retired, but two years later, St. Louis brought him back to the ice where he was their best player during the 1968 playoffs. Moore then retired for good and established a very successful heavy machinery rental business. He was inducted into the Hockey Hall of Fame in 1979 despite playing only nine full seasons, his contributions firmly entrenched in the minds and memories of those who saw the great left winger play.

MOORE, Robbie
b. Sarnia, Ontario, May 3, 1954
Tiny Robbie Moore couldn't do much more, especially on his gimpy knees, but try as he might to make the NHL, the NHL wouldn't have him. He had an outstanding career in goal for the University of Michigan (1972-76), and in his NHL debut, with Philadelphia, he recorded a shutout. He had a small but perfect record that year of 3-0-1 with a 1.77 GAA, and over the next three years he accomplished something strange. In the AHL, he shared the Hap Holmes Award for fewest goals allowed with three different goalies – Pete Peeters, Rick St. Croix, Pelle Lindbergh – all of whom went on to have careers of varying length with the Flyers. Not Moore, though. He retired in 1984 after getting into only one more NHL period, with Washington.

MOORE, Steve
b. Windsor, Ontario, September 22, 1978
A Harvard graduate, Moore had an excellent college career during which time Colorado drafted him. So far, he's been playing in the minors with Hershey, with the exception of a few games in 2001-02 to replace injured Avs, notably Stephane Yelle for a few games.

MORAN, Ambrose "Amby"
b. Winnipeg, Manitoba, April 3, 1894
d. Vancouver, British Columbia, April 8, 1958
There was only one Amby Moran, and for that the world was a better place but also thankful. As a teen, he was reputed to be the finest athlete Winnipeg had ever produced. A dazzling soccer player and top-notch baseballer as well, Moran chose hockey as his sport, even though Babe Ruth himself had tried to woo him to join the Yankees. Moran chose hockey because it paid the best, and money was important to him as he had an enormous thirst to slake on a daily basis. He was a large defenceman, and he could score well from that position and hit as hard as any man in the game. As the story goes, one night he went for a check and missed, slamming into the boards. The game had to be held up while arena attendants removed three broken boards to free Moran! His drinking led to *avoirdupois*, not a good term for a

hockey player. That's why he lasted just a few games with the Canadiens in 1926 and again a year later with Chicago. Moran also liked to fight police, a habit that landed him in jail on more than one occasion, and when he quit playing hockey he didn't alter his ways. He umpired ball and refereed hockey, still as drunk as ever. When he moved to Vancouver to play the last of his hockey, though, he joined AA and straightened out. He worked in a shipbuilding yard during the war, and was as enthusiastic and determined a non-drinker as he had been a boozer during his glory days.

MORAN, Brad
b. Abbotsford, British Columbia, March 20, 1979
A death in the family forced Serge Aubin to leave Columbus for a few days in April 2002 and Moran was called up from Syracuse as his replacement. Moran had been having a superb season with the Crunch, but after three games he was sent back down. He had played five years of junior, and as an over-age player in 1999-2000 he led the WHL in assists and points. He was drafted by Buffalo but never signed and the Blue Jackets offered him a contract as a free agent in the summer of 2000.

Robbie Moore

MORAN, Ian
b. Cleveland, Ohio, August 24, 1972
He's not shy about physical play, but he's no tough guy, heavy-hitting, looking-for-trouble kind of player. Yet trouble has routinely found him and slammed him through the infirmary door. Moran started with Pittsburgh in 1995 and has been with the team ever since. Along the way, he's missed large swaths of the schedule with, among other things, shoulder surgery, a serious knee injury, a broken ankle, another knee injury, a broken hand, and a broken thumb. When healthy, Moran has been an effective right winger, not flashy but reliable.

MORAVEC, David
b. Vitkovice, Czechoslovakia (Czech Republic), March 24, 1973
Looks like we can chalk up another one-game wonder. Buffalo drafted him in 1998 but the Sabres used him only once. He had been playing all year in his hometown, and ever since he has been back in Vitkovice, a long, long way away from the NHL. His career highlight came at the 2001 Worlds when he scored the game winner in overtime against Finland to give the Czechs a gold medal, their third in a row.

Ian Moran

MORE, Jayson
b. Souris, Manitoba, January 12, 1969
A tough defenceman, More suffered a career-ending concussion on December 10, 1998, early in his 11th NHL season. He had been traded several times during his career, having his longest stay in San Jose (five years). More was drafted 10th overall by the Rangers in 1987 but it wasn't until '91, with the Sharks, that he established himself in the league. He signed with Nashville as a free agent, which is where he was playing when he incurred his injury. He came back to play on December 12, but another hard hit did him in for good.

Jayson More

Ethan Moreau

MOREAU, Ethan
b. Huntsville, Ontario, September 22, 1975

Moreau was a high Chicago draft choice in 1994 but the Hawks gave up on him and included him in a big trade of top prospects. They sent him with Daniel Cleary, Chad Kilger, and Christian Laflamme to Edmonton for Boris Mironov, Dean McAmmond, and Jonas Elofsson on March 20, 1999. Moreau has been with the Oilers ever since but has yet to turn into the power forward scouts thought he might become while watching him in Niagara Falls in junior.

MORENZ, Howarth "Howie"
("The Mitchell Meteor"/
"The Stratford Streak")
b. Mitchell, Ontario,
June 21, 1902
d. Montreal, Quebec,
March 8, 1937

The reason it's impossible to compare today's star players with the greats from, say, the 1920s and 1930s is that there is no game-action footage of those old stars to show us what they were truly like. Their reputations survive by oral history, which can't offer the same objectivity as videotape. Nonetheless, many people swear that Morenz was the greatest of them all, greater even than Orr, Gretzky, or Howe. He didn't score at will – though he scored plenty – and he didn't fight. What he did do was skate like no one else. Every time he touched the puck, fans in Montreal came out of their seats to see what he would do with it. He played junior hockey in Stratford, where he first burned lines in the ice, and Montreal signed him in 1923 to replace Newsy Lalonde. He also worked for the Canadian National Railways during his time in that city, which he called home since leaving Mitchell at age 14. Morenz played on a line with Aurel Joliat and Billy Boucher, and in his first year he won the Cup with the Habs. He scored 28 goals in his second year and in '27-'28 led the league with 33 goals and 51 points, the first of 2 scoring crowns. In his first 10 years in the league, he was among the top 10 scorers every year. He won Cups again in 1930 and '31, and in October 1934 was traded to Chicago with Marty Burke and Lorne Chabot for Lionel Conacher, Leroy Goldsworthy, and Roger Jenkins. It was a trade that shocked fans and stunned teammates, so much so that his number 7 sweater remained in its stall for the next three years until his eventual return. In Chicago and later New York, Morenz was like a fish out of water. The streak was no longer in him, the goals didn't come, and the teams didn't win. When Cecil Hart agreed to become Montreal's manager in 1936, he vowed to bring Morenz back to the fold. Fans were ecstatic, and although he was not the great skater he had

Angelo Moretto

been, lesser Morenz is much better than vintage for most players. On January 28, 1937, everything ended. While going around the back of the net, Morenz was checked by Chicago's Earl Seibert. In those days, the boards were literally that, slats of wood nailed together to form an enclosure. Seibert took his man, and as Morenz fell his skate got caught in a small gap between two sections of the boards. His leg was pinned, the rest of him moved on, and the result was a severely broken leg. Everyone knew instantly that his career was over, though he put on a brave face and talked about coming back the following fall. As he lay in hospital, though, his room became something out of a Noel Coward play. Montreal's famous came and went, saluting their hero and wishing him the best. Teammates and friends literally camped in the room to keep him company and attend to him, and all of this did not go on with the seriousness befitting a hospital room. Cigarettes and alcohol were prevalent, and Morenz was not convalescing so much as being the centre of a continuous party. A month later, he died of a heart attack, but to everyone who knew him, his death was a symbol, a metaphor for what they know really happened – he died of a broken heart. Just as later generations could not imagine Marilyn Monroe as anything but young and beautiful, so too could Morenz not imagine himself alive on this earth without being able to play hockey. The Forum was turned into a giant theatre to commemorate his departure, and as his body lay in state at centre ice three days later, thousands of fans streamed by to pay their last respects. In 1945, he was an inaugural inductee into the Hockey Hall of Fame, and 5 years later, some 13 years after his passing, his reputation was still so powerful that he was named Canada's hockey player of the first half-century. Oddly, he became a hero to the French population of Montreal, even though he was of German heritage. His daughter later married Bernie Geoffrion, who went on to a Hall of Fame career, and Geoffrion's son, Danny, also played in the NHL. No, there are no tapes of Morenz in action for any longer than a few seconds, but through the power of words, and the consistently praiseworthy reports that survive of his play, we can regret not having seen him play and we can rest assured he was a player of incomparable talent.

He became a hero to the French population of Montreal, even though he was of German heritage.
HOWIE MORENZ

MORETTO, Angelo
b. Toronto, Ontario, September 18, 1953

Of course, Wayne Gretzky's three goals with Indianapolis of the WHA in 1978 are among the least important of the Great One's accomplishments, but pardon Moretto if he vehemently disagrees. Moretto was Gretzky's linemate for those goals (along with Kevin Nugent), and those were Moretto's last pro games before retiring to let Gretzky move on to bigger and better things. Moretto graduated from the University of Michigan in 1976 and played his only NHL games with Cleveland the following year. He later moved to Texas to coach senior high school hockey.

MORGAN, Jason
b. St. John's, Newfoundland, October 9, 1976

An L.A. draft choice in 1995 out of the OHL, Morgan just never got it going in the NHL. He played but a few games with the Kings and has disappeared into the lowest depths of the minors. Now in his mid-twenties, there appears to be little hope he can add to his 14 NHL games played.

MORIN, Pierre "Pete"
b. Lachine, Quebec, December 8, 1915
d. January 5, 2000

Joseph Pierre Morin went by many names. He was considered the finest stickhandler around – inside or outside the NHL – and many likened him to the second coming of Aurel Joliat. At 5'8" and 135 pounds, he had the same physique as Joliat and the same ability to squeeze around the bigger men in the game. The French who worshipped him called him Petit Pete and fans in Montreal called him the Alderman because he was usually the member of the Royals (for whom he played most of his 14 years of pro) who was asked to be an after-dinner speaker. Other players called him Pistol Pete for his speed, and the masses called him simply Pete. He began with the Royals in 1936 and soon formed one of the most entertaining lines in the game. The Razzle Dazzle Line featured Morin, Buddy O'Connor, and Gerry Heffernan, and they could score like nobody's business. The line played as a whole for the Canadiens during the '41–'42 season, and Morin had a respectable 10 goals and 22 points. It was to be his only NHL action. He was a leading aircraftsman for the RCAF during the war, and upon discharge he returned to the Royals. In 1947 he captained the team to the Allan Cup, which led to an offer from the Rangers to attend their training camp in Lake Placid in the fall. Just as he was set to sign a contract, the Canadiens jumped in and notified all parties that Morin was still their property, and the team forced him back to Montreal to rejoin the Royals. He retired in 1950 as one of the city's most popular athletes of all time, despite his too-brief NHL career. He lived in the city, played industrial hockey in the Depression League, and went into the insurance business for more than 40 years. Morin also holds several rowing titles achieved with the Lachine Racing Canoe Club.

MORIN, Stephane
b. Montreal, Quebec, March 27, 1969
d. Oberhausen, Germany, October 6, 1998

It's a story whose beginning and middle are so frequently told but whose ending is more tragic than any other. Drafted in 1989, Morin was given a chance to play over a few years but mostly was kept in the minors. The centre had a fine career in the IHL and in the summer of 1998 he decided to sign with Berlin and play in Germany. Just a few games into the season, though, he collapsed on the ice. He was taken to the dressing room where he died of a heart attack. He was just 29.

MORISSET, Dave
b. Langley, British Columbia, April 6, 1981

When Morisset was traded from St. Louis to Florida on February 9, 2001, he had big shoes to fill. Going the other way was Scott Mellanby, the most popular player in Panthers history. The Panthers argued, though, that they were getting a first-rate prospect. He has yet to prove as much, but is still an emerging and developing talent. Morisset played four times for his new team late in the 2001-02 season.

MORISSETTE, Dave ("Moose")
b. Baie Comeau, Quebec, December 24, 1971

It's only when you see how many wannabe fighters have passed through the NHL that you can appreciate the ability to survive that has characterized the careers of Bob Probert, Tie Domi, and other fighters. Morissette started his punching in 1988 in junior, but it wasn't until a decade later that he got into an NHL game, with Montreal. In his 11 NHL matches, he averaged a fighting major each time out, but he was soon out of the league and back in the minors.

MORISSETTE, Jean-Guy
b. Causapscal, New Brunswick, December 16, 1937

On October 30, 1963, Morissette went to the Forum to watch the Leafs play Montreal, just as he did for every Canadiens home game as the spare goaltender. On this night, though, Gump Worsley suffered a hamstring injury four minutes into the second period with Toronto ahead 2-0, and Morissette was summoned to Montreal's dressing room to replace the Gumper. Untried and nervous, he allowed four goals and the Leafs coasted to a 6-3 win. The next day in practice, he was hit by a shot and suffered a broken cheekbone that put him out for the year and erased any hopes he had of replacing Worsley for the three weeks he was sidelined. Morissette went on to play a few more years in the minors, but his one night in an NHL goal was the highlight of his career.

MORO, Marc ("Mad Dog")
b. Toronto, Ontario, July 17, 1977

Moro went from sad to happy early in the 2001-02 season when first Nashville gave him his outright release and then his hometown Leafs claimed him. Moro not only was born in the city of Blue and White, his father, Tony, played for the Toronto Argonauts way back when. Moro was assigned to the farm team in St. John's, where the Baby Leafs wanted him to use his trademark toughness and defensive strengths. He played in three games for the big boys at Air Canada Centre, realizing a dream, and continues to work in the minors hoping for another, longer, stay with the Leafs on Bay Street.

MOROZOV, Aleksey
b. Moscow, Soviet Union (Russia), February 16, 1977

On October 1, 1997, Morozov realized a dream by scoring a goal on his first shot on his first shift. Playing for Pittsburgh, for whom he has played the life of his career so far, he has produced erratically over the years, scoring in bunches and going long stretches without the sort of inspirational play needed on a nightly basis in the NHL. Morozov was named

Jason Morgan

Pete Morin

Stephane Morin

Marc Moro

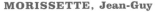

Aleksey Morozov

Derek Morris

Jon Morris

Brendan Morrison

Dave Morrison

Don Morrison

winner of the Directorate Award as best forward of the 1997 WJC, and he also played in two World Championships. He played for Russia at the 1998 Olympics in Nagano, winning silver.

MORRIS, Bernie
b. Regina, Saskatchewan, 1895
d. unknown
It was not because of his NHL career that Morris was a legend by the time he retired. He played just six games with Boston in 1924. Previously, though, he was one of the great players of the Pacific Coast league, winning a Stanley Cup with Seattle in 1917 and establishing himself as one of the great scorers of the game. In the 1917 finals, he scored 14 goals in the series against Montreal with the great Georges Vézina in the nets. He is not in the Hockey Hall of Fame, but some consider his exploits comparable to other PCHL stars such as Cyclone Taylor, Tommy Dunderdale, Mickey MacKay, and Frank Foyston, who are in the Hall. Perhaps his exclusion is because of the 1919-20 season, which he spent in prison after some trouble with U.S. Immigration.

MORRIS, Derek
b. Edmonton, Alberta, August 24, 1978
Imagine being a kid in the 1980s in Edmonton, loving your Oilers and watching them win Stanley Cups, and then when you get old enough to be a serious player Calgary – Calgary, the arch enemy! – drafts you. Such was the start Morris experienced, but he has handled the "adversity" well and has become one of the best young defencemen in the game. He will, without question, be on Canada's 2006 Olympic team should NHLers participate. He is strong and a superb skater, capable of offence but physical in his own end. He admired Paul Coffey as a kid, and he's become his own mini-Paul in an era when 100-point defencemen don't exist. The only question was whether the small-market Flames could afford to keep Morris, a question they quickly answered when they traded him to Colorado.

MORRIS, Elwin ("Moe")
b. Toronto, Ontario, January 3, 1921
d. Toronto, Ontario, February 6, 2000
A two-sport athlete in the 1940s, Morris was doubly amazing given the fact that he was virtually blind in one eye. He grew up in Toronto and played football in the summers and hockey, with the Marlies, in the winter. He played two seasons with the Toronto Argonauts (1940 and '41) and then joined the Royal Canadian Naval Volunteer Reserve, from which he was discharged because of poor eyesight. Morris, who was cross-eyed, was one of the first six patients of Dr. Bochner to have surgery to repair this disorder. The procedure corrected the condition but weakened one of Morris's eyes virtually to the point of blindness, yet it was at this point he began his NHL career. He played three years with the Leafs, winning a Cup in 1945 paired with big Babe Pratt on defence. He later played briefly with the Rangers and closed out his career in the minors. In 1954, he moved to Stratford where he sold cars and coached the city's senior team. He later moved to Kitchener for the same reason, but returned to Stratford to retire. Morris was part of the

closing ceremonies at Maple Leaf Gardens on February 13, 1999, and less than a year later he passed away in Toronto of a heart attack.

MORRIS, Jon
b. Lowell, Massachusetts, May 6, 1966
Drafted right out of high school, Morris went on to play university hockey for four years at Massachusetts-Lowell before making his NHL debut, with the Devils, in 1989. But over the next six years he never firmly established his place in the league. He later played briefly in Europe and represented the U.S. at the 1995 World Championships, where the team placed sixth.

MORRISON, Brendan
b. Pitt Meadows, British Columbia, August 15, 1975
Here's how good New Jersey thought Morrison was destined to become: He played 11 games at the end of the '97-'98 season and 3 more in the playoffs, and so impressed the Devils that they didn't try to re-sign Doug Gilmour, figuring Morrison would be able to replace the future Hall of Famer. That same year, Morrison led Albany in scoring, and the year after he was with the Devils full-time. They continued to think highly enough of him that they traded him with Denis Pederson to Vancouver to get Alexander Mogilny. In the next three seasons, Morrison's goals went from 7 to 16 to 23, and the 1997 Hobey Baker Award winner does indeed seem mere minutes away from superstardom.

MORRISON, Dave
b. Toronto, Ontario, June 12, 1962
It could have been bad for Los Angeles, but in the end, it wasn't. The Kings drafted Morrison in 1980 and signed him to a three-year contract. During that time, he played a few games with the team and helped Canada win gold at the 1982 World Juniors. After his third year in the system, the Kings had to offer him a new contract or he would become a free agent. They sent him a letter, not a contract, and he declared free agency. The league wanted to go to court, arguing that a letter was as good as a contract, but the Kings demurred, thinking he wasn't worth the bother. They let him walk and got nothing in return. Morrison played just eight more NHL games, with Vancouver. He moved to Europe, and for the next 14 years played overseas before retiring in 1999 to become a scout for the Canucks. He even played for Holland at the World Championships, in "B" pool. His dad, Jim, had a long and distinguished career with the Leafs through the 1950s.

MORRISON, Don
b. Saskatoon, Saskatchewan, July 14, 1923
Why put your body through the rigours of a hockey season if you can fly around in a private plane and operate a massive and successful business building houses? That was the question the Morrison brothers, Don and Rod, answered pretty quickly for themselves, and they retired from the game at an early age. Don played pro in the immediate post-war years, playing two and a half seasons with Detroit and Chicago but spending most of the time in the minors. When the boys were sent to Omaha they saw the chance to get into the house-building business, and hockey was abandoned.

MORRISON, Doug
b. Vancouver, British Columbia, February 1, 1960
Morrison's scoring exploits in junior and in the minors never carried over to the NHL, where the smallish forward had more trouble manoeuvring. All of his 23 games came with Boston after the Bruins drafted him in 1979, though his years in the minors were filled with goals. He finished his career in Europe and then returned to B.C. to coach junior. His brother, Mark, also played in the NHL.

MORRISON, Gary
b. Detroit, Michigan, November 8, 1955
If Philadelphia drafts you in 1975, you'd better show how tough you are or forget about playing with the Bullies. Morrison couldn't do much of that fighting stuff at the University of Michigan, but as soon as he got to the minors he wasted no time in dropping the gloves. He played very little for the Flyers over a three-year period (1979-82) and retired at age 26.

MORRISON, George
b. Toronto, Ontario, December 24, 1948
While playing under coach Murray Armstrong at the University of Denver, Morrison played with Cliff Korroll and Keith Magnuson before signing with St. Louis in 1970. He came highly recommended, and it was thought that his blazing speed and quick shot would result in 20 goals or more on a yearly basis. Such was not the case, at leas, not in the NHL. He scored 15 times as a rookie and only twice in half a year in '71-'72, and then he went to Minnesota of the WHA. Morrison didn't exactly tear the league open, but he did score with consistency for the better part of five years. He and his wife – a former Miss Colorado – settled in Toronto and Morrison went into business there. He donated his stick from the game of April 3, 1974, to the Hockey Hall of Fame because on that night he scored 3 goals in just 43 seconds.

MORRISON, Jim ("Mo")
b. Montreal, Quebec, October 11, 1931
It was a paradox of Morrison's play that he was widely regarded as one of the fastest defencemen in the league, but he was not a rushing type who would use his speed to attack. Nonetheless, his skills served him well during a 22-year career that started with Boston in 1951 and ended as a playing coach in the AHL with Baltimore in 1973. Morrison's longest stint was a seven-year stay with Toronto where he was known as a great shotblocker and a strong presence in his own end. He was also very durable, but when the Rangers sent him to the minors in 1961 he spent nearly nine years in the AHL before getting another chance in the post-expansion NHL. After two seasons with Pittsburgh, he joined Baltimore and was promoted to coach during '72-'73, his last year as a player. He remained bench boss for two years and then moved into the OHL with Kitchener and Kingston, where he stayed eight seasons. Morrison moved to Mississauga and then spent several years as a scout for the Bruins.

MORRISON, John "Crutchy"
b. Selkirk, Manitoba, March 4, 1896
d. Selkirk, Manitoba, March 14, 1956
On the cusp of full military service, Morrison won the 1916 Allan Cup with the Winnipeg 61st Battalion. After the war, he played out west, notably for Edmonton in its run to the Cup finals of 1923, and he played his only NHL games with the Americans in '25-'26. He finished his career in the AHA and then returned to Selkirk and farming for a living. He later operated J.W. Morrison Hardware in his hometown. He had learned to skate on the Red River with his father, Dave, who coached the Selkirk Fishermen. Later in life, he organized a golf school for youngsters, and he himself was a fine player at the Pine Ridge Golf Club. Morrison was inducted into the Manitoba Sports Hall of Fame in 1999.

MORRISON, Kevin
b. Sydney, Nova Scotia, October 28, 1949
Morrison had 4 goals, 11 assists, and 15 points in 41 NHL games with the Colorado Rockies, but, amazingly, 5 of those points came in one game, against Philadelphia. The outburst was nothing new for him. Morrison stepped into the WHA in 1973 and in his first year set a record for defencemen by scoring 24 goals. It was the first of 3 successive seasons reaching the 20-goal mark, but outside that half-season with the Rockies he never returned to the NHL. In 2000, he was inducted into the Nova Scotia Sports Hall of Fame.

MORRISON, Lewis "Lew"
b. Gainsborough, Saskatchewan, February 11, 1948
For a right winger, his statistics were lousy, but chances are, if they were any better he wouldn't have been doing his job. Right from the word go, Morrison was a defensive specialist, a checker, a penalty killer, a hanger-on to the other team's top players. He teamed in Philadelphia with Garry Peters and later filled the same job description with Atlanta, Washington, and Pittsburgh, weak teams in the 1970s that never made the playoffs or were dispensed with quickly in the first round. He retired in 1978.

Doug Morrison

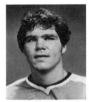
Gary Morrison

George Morrison

Kevin Morrison

Lew Morrison

Morrison's longest stint was a seven-year stay with Toronto.
JIM MORRISON

Mark Morrison

MORRISON, Mark

b. Prince George, British Columbia, March 11, 1963

The kid plays junior in Victoria, B.C., but winds up being a hero half a world away! Morrison won gold with Canada at the 1982 World Juniors and played 10 games with the Rangers over the next couple of years. After a brief time in the minors, he decided Europe was the way to go, and he went all the way. He started in Italy and Switzerland, but for the better part of a decade he has made the Fife Flyers his home, scoring oodles of goals and playing like a big fish in a small pond.

MORRISON, Rod

b. Saskatoon, Saskatchewan, October 7, 1925
d. October 10, 1998

Roderick Finley Morrison turned pro in 1943 as an 18-year-old and was sent by Detroit to Indianapolis to develop. He played on the Diaper Line with Jack O'Hara and Roy Glover, two other promising teens, and the trio performed well for the club. Morrison spent a year in the army and then moved to Omaha where he played with his brother and developed a business building houses. Rod hurt his knee and missed much of the season, and the same thing happened the year after. He made it to the Wings in '47-'48, but after three more years in the AHL he retired to go into the house-building business full-time.

MORROW, Brenden

b. Carlyle, Saskatchewan, January 16, 1979

It's not as sick as it sounds, but it sure made the dressing room a lively place when word got out that Morrow was dating a

Brenden Morrow

teammate's daughter. The mathematical reality, though, is that Morrow was 21 at the time, and the daughter was the 18-year-old offspring of 40-year-old mate Guy Carbonneau, the oldest player in the league. After winning silver with Canada at the '98 WJC, Morrow joined Dallas a year later and is one of the team's top prospects. Carbonneau is no longer playing, and whether the relationship is still in bloom isn't public fodder, but Morrow is turning into a reliable scorer and playmaker.

MORROW, Ken

b. Flint, Michigan, October 17, 1956

It was undoubtedly luck and good fortune that brought Morrow his unique success in 1980, but those qualities are usually born of talent and determination. He came out of Bowling Green and made the 1980 U.S. Olympic team, winning the gold medal with the Miracle on Ice team. Immediately after the celebrations ended, he joined his drafted team, the Islanders, and weeks later he was holding the Stanley Cup, a remarkable double accomplished in the same year. Morrow was not a flashy

defenceman but he was entirely reliable and he chipped in with timely offence. In the '84 playoffs, for instance, he scored in overtime to eliminate the Rangers, and in the semifinals he earned an assist on Mike Bossy's game winner against Montreal. He played all of his 10 years in the league with the Islanders, a career that was cut short by knee problems. After retiring in 1989, Morrow coached with Flint and Kansas City in the IHL and then returned to Long Island as an assistant. He later served as the director of pro scouting. In 1996, Morrow was inducted into the U.S. Hockey Hall of Fame, the same year he was given the Lester Patrick Trophy.

MORROW, Scott

b. Chicago, Illinois, June 18, 1969

A graduate of the University of New Hampshire in 1992, Morrow played three years in the minors before getting his one and only callup to the NHL, with Calgary. Since then, he's been back in the minors bouncing from team to team, restless and wandering and showing few signs of wanting to settle into a career with any particular team.

MORTON, Dean

b. Peterborough, Ontario, February 27, 1968

Why is it that the guys who had the most quibbles with referees during their playing days become one themselves the first chance they get? In Morton's case, it's a bit more understandable because he had a perfect hockey career, so why not quit while ahead? Morton played in only one NHL game – October 5, 1989 – but he scored a goal. He played in the minors until 1993 and then quit as a player to start as an official. Working his way up through the minors, he made his NHL debut on November 11, 2000, and with the two-referee system still in vogue, he's likely to be around the NHL even more in the coming years.

He joined the army and was discharged because of a bad leg.
GUS MORTSON

MORTSON, Angus "Gus"
("Old Hardrock"/ "The Gold Nugget Kid"/
"The Gold Dust Twins" with
Jimmy Thomson)

b. New Liskeard, Ontario, January 24, 1925

From the silver of Lord Stanley's Cup to the gold of the Canadian north, Mortson mined his way through life's prospects and came out a winner every which way. As a player, he made a name for himself with the St. Mike's team that won the 1945 Memorial Cup, one of the greatest junior teams of all time. He joined the army and was discharged because of a bad leg, but that didn't stop Conn Smythe from signing him for the Leafs. He was teamed on defence with Jim Thomson and together they were called the Gold Dust Twins, in part because they were from the north, in part because they were that good. Thomson was the defensive player, Morton the rusher with a mean streak. He led the NHL in penalty minutes four times, and in the 1950s no one was penalized more often. The Gold Dust Twins allowed less than a goal a game during their years, and they won four Cups with the great Leafs teams of the late 1940s. Mortson later played a number of years with Chicago, and over his career he played in six All-Star Games. During the summers, he headed north to prospect gold and silver, and he was quite successful in this regard. He also worked for a frozen food company in Toronto, and when he retired in 1960, it was Mortson, of all people, who introduced frozen pizzas to Canada. He worked at this for about eight years and then became a stockbroker, but finally the mining business got too good and busy to ignore. He became president of Pelangio Larder Mines Ltd. and worked as a technical representative for Haak Properties. Of course, Mortson played as much old-timers' hockey as possible.

MOSDELL, Ken ("Big Mo")
b. Montreal, Quebec, July 13, 1922

Unofficially, Mosdell ranks second on a unique list: He had his nose broken 10 times during his career, trailing only the incredible Hall of Famer Eddie Shore, who had his beak shattered 14 times. Mosdell played most of his career with Montreal as an underappreciated centre on a team laden with talent. He was the second-line forward, the defensive pivot, the silent hero from the time he joined the Canadiens in 1944 (he made his debut with Brooklyn in 1941 and then served with the Air Force until '44). Over the next 11 years, Mosdell won 3 Cups with the Habs and twice scored 20 goals despite his role. He was named to the First All-Star Team in '53-'54 and the Second Team a year later. He played a year with Chicago, and when Montreal reacquired him he was nothing more than a minor-leaguer to the team. He made his final NHL appearance in the 1959 playoffs, replacing the injured Jean Béliveau, but that was enough to win another Cup. For many summers during his career he ran a service station in Montreal, and when he retired in 1960 he went there for full-time work until retiring at age 63 and moving to Vermont.

MOSIENKO, Bill ("Mosie")
b. Winnipeg, Manitoba, November 2, 1921
d. Winnipeg, Manitoba, July 9, 1994

Discovered by Joe Cooper on the outdoor rinks in Winnipeg, Mosienko's rise to stardom in the NHL was improbable. He was 1 of 13 children born to a boilermaker for the CPR, but he wanted more than anything to play professional hockey. Cooper recommended him to Chicago, and the Hawks assigned him to Kansas City to develop in the minors. Mosienko made the Hawks in 1943 and, playing on a line with Clint Smith and Doug Bentley, the threesome registered an NHL-record 219 points on the year, Mosienko accounting for 32 goals and 70 points in his first full year. Two years later, he became part of an even more productive combination. The Pony Line consisted of Mosienko and Max and Doug Bentley. All three were small and could skate like lightning. More than anything, though, Mosienko was famous for a few seconds of remarkable play. On March 23, 1952, he scored 3

goals in 21 seconds, a record that stands today (linemate Gus Bodnar assisted on all 3). By the time he retired in 1955, Mosienko had scored 258 goals and given fans in Chicago much to cheer about. He won the Lady Byng Trophy in '44-'45, a season in which he did not incur a single penalty all year. He was involved in only one fight his whole career and had just 121 total penalty minutes. Mosienko returned to Winnipeg and helped bring pro hockey to his hometown. He established the Warriors and played for the team for four seasons, winning a championship in their first year. He coached the team for '59-'60 and then devoted himself full-time to running a string of bowling alleys in the city with the man who gave him his start, Joe Cooper. Mosienko was inducted into the Hockey Hall of Fame in 1965 and the Manitoba Sports Hall of Fame in 1980.

MOSS, Tyler
b. Ottawa, Ontario, June 29, 1975

If nothing else, Moss can claim to have faced two of the best, one on one. He stopped Mike Modano on a penalty shot, but was beaten by Joe Sakic on another. Not many goalies can tell the grandkids that. However, Moss should have been able to tell them so much more. He was a top goaler with Kingston in the early 1990s but never had that big game in the NHL to prove he could step in and do the job. It's not a league for training, it's a league for performing, and Moss has spent most of the past seven years up and counting in the minors, trying to find his rhythm and form, hoping for another chance of goaltending glory at the NHL level.

MOTT, Morris
b. Creelman, Saskatchewan, May 25, 1946

Mott was just a student when he started out in hockey, but by the time he finished playing he had a Ph.D. Instead of major junior hockey or the pros, Mott joined Canada's National Team in 1965 and played for Father Bauer's team for five years. He played in three World Championships and the 1968 Olympics in Grenoble, and also earned his master's degree from U of Manitoba. In 1970, Mott enrolled at Queen's University and did most of his work on a doctorate in history. In 1972 he finally made his NHL debut, with California. The right winger played three seasons with the hopeless Seals and then moved to Sweden to play for a year. In late 1974 he was featured in *Time* magazine for his achievements as an athlete and scholar. Soon after, he received his Ph.D. and taught at U of M for a number of years. Dr. Mott then became a professor of history at Brandon University, where his exploits in the classroom superseded his past life as a pro hockey player.

MOTTAU, Mike
b. Quincy, Massachusetts, March 19, 1978

It hasn't been easy for Mottau to get into the NHL, but he certainly had the credentials to justify being given a chance. In his four years at Boston College he set a school record for assists and became only the third defenceman ever to win the Hobey Baker Award. In 2000, he played for the U.S. at both the WJC and World

Ken Mosdell

Bill Mosienko

Morris Mott

Mike Mottau

Alex Motter

Mark Mowers

Jim Moxey

Bill Muckalt

Championships, and the year after he made his NHL debut, with the Rangers. Since then, though, he's played just a few games and has had to bide his time in the minors, waiting for another chance, trying to play himself into the position of earning it.

MOTTER, Alex
b. Melville, Saskatchewan, June 20, 1913
d. Livonia, Michigan, October 18, 1996
From his days playing kid hockey right through to his start in the NHL, Motter was a centre. He played junior with Regina and then joined the Bruins in 1934, playing in the system for almost four seasons. But when GM Jack Adams acquired Motter for his Detroit club, the first thing he did was move him back to defence. Motter hated the move but adapted quickly and spent most of the next six seasons on the Red Wings blueline, winning a Cup with the team in 1943, his last year in the NHL. Motter enlisted in the army, but after being discharged he couldn't regain his position with the Wings and had to be content playing out his career in the minors. The boy who aspired to be an electrical engineer ended up in professional hockey in the world's toughest league.

MOWERS, Johnny
b. St. David's, Ontario, October 29, 1916
d. Farmington Hills, Michigan, December 7, 1995
When Detroit scout Carson Cooper spotted Mowers tending goal in Niagara Falls, he knew the kid was a winner. He signed him to a pro contract in 1939, and a year later Mowers began a meteoric rise that saw him become the best goalie in the NHL for about three years. Mowers played all but five games for Detroit from 1940 to '43, and in that final season he led the Wings to a Stanley Cup victory with a league-leading 2.47 goals-against average. But just as he was at his prime, he enlisted in the Royal Canadian Air Force, and by the time Corporal Mowers was discharged a chap by the name of Harry Lumley was in goal. Say goodbye, Johnny. He played a year in the minors, but was overcome by back problems and retired and moved back to Niagara Falls, his home since he was a year old. Mowers became a successful insurance broker there but later moved to Detroit, where he became a sales representative for the Automobile Club of Michigan.

MOWERS, Mark
b. Whitesboro, New York, February 16, 1974
Mowers was a Hobey Baker Award finalist with the University of New Hampshire (1994-98) but he was never drafted and had to sign with Nashville in 1998, not an auspicious way to enter the league. So far, he's seen only limited action for the Predators as a utility forward. His finest moment to date came in the spring

Mowers played all but five games for Detroit from 1940 to '43.
JOHNNY MOWERS

of 2002 when he played for the U.S. at the World Championships in Sweden.

MOXEY, Jim
b. Toronto, Ontario, May 28, 1953
No one who played for California or Cleveland knew anything about the playoffs first-hand, and Moxey was no exception. He was drafted by the Seals in 1973 and was sent to Salt Lake City, much to his annoyance because he thought he had a good training camp. Moxey wasted no time in making his point: He set a WHL record by scoring 4 goals in his first pro game and finished the year with 26. For the next three years he spent long stretches with the Seals, but it was never enough to avoid the ever-unsettling demotion. He retired in 1978 after playing another full season in the minors.

MRAZEK, Jerome ("Jerry")
b. Prince Albert, Saskatchewan, October 15, 1951
A goalie, Mrazek played just six minutes in the NHL, with Philadelphia. He allowed a goal, which rendered his lifetime average an unflattering 10.00. He had a decent career at the University of Minnesota-Duluth, and he played in the minors until 1978, but he never had the chance to improve upon his NHL total.

MUCKALT, Bill
b. Surrey, British Columbia, July 15, 1974
There was nothing to suggest the embarrassment of 2001-02 was just around the corner. Muckalt was runner-up to Chris Drury for the 1998 Hobey Baker Award. In his four years at U of Michigan, the team had won two NCAA titles. He averaged nearly 26 goals a season with the Wolverines, and as a rookie with Vancouver in 1998-99 he scored 16 times. He was traded to the Islanders, missed some time with an injury, and came back healthy as ever, but in 2001-02 Muckalt didn't score a single goal. Not one. Sure, he was more of a checker or two-way player, and, yes, he didn't get the ice time he had in the past. But not one goal? Then, the strangest thing happened: At the start of the 2002-03 season, he scored five goals in four games! Then, worse: He suffered a separated shoulder and lost all his scoring momentum.

MUIR, Bryan
b. Winnipeg, Manitoba, June 8, 1973
He's been playing in the NHL on a part-time basis since 1995, but already Muir has been on five different teams. Luckily, his last and most current has been Colorado, for whom he played a bit in the 2001 post-season to get his name on the Stanley Cup. A large but not intimidating defenceman, Muir has

spent long periods in the minors since being signed as a free agent by Edmonton to start his career.

MULHERN, Richard
b. Edmonton, Alberta, March 1, 1955

Things started off great but became incrementally worse during Mulhern's six years in the NHL. In 1975-76 he played mostly in the minors but got a brief callup with Atlanta. The next year, the defenceman not only made the team, he scored 44 points. Everyone and his uncle noted that when Bobby Orr was a rookie, he had 41 points. Uh-oh. The Orr-comparison blues. In each of his seasons thereafter, his point totals diminished and he was traded to L.A., Toronto, and Winnipeg, ending in the minors and retiring with disappointing numbers. He didn't get along with the coaches in Atlanta and L.A., he suffered a few small injuries, the trades hurt his confidence – and he was gone.

MULHERN, Ryan
b. Philadelphia, Pennsylvania, January 11, 1973

Philadelphia is a great hockey town, but it isn't known for producing players, just fans. Mulhern is a rare exception, though his career lasted only a brief time. Calgary drafted him in 1992 out of high school, but after four years at Brown University he hadn't signed with the Flames. He turned pro in the East Coast league, not a good sign, and a year and a half later Washington signed him and gave him three games to show his stuff. Unimpressed, the Caps let him go to the minors, and three years later, at 27, Mulhern retired. He returned to St. George's Academy, where he had played some high school hockey, and became the team's head coach.

MULLEN, Brian
b. New York, New York, March 16, 1962

Ah, Manhattan, a world unto itself. The building-high neon signs, taxis racing down Fifth Avenue, the Guggenheim, and irascible street noise – all part of the asphalt garden of the city. It's a city you associate with basketball at the south end and baseball at the north end, but there are no hockey rinks. Yet from the mayhem of Manhattan came the Mullen brothers, who lived in Hell's Kitchen and played hockey at Skyrink (a 16th-floor arena downtown) or on the streets in rollerskates (in the pre-blade days). Brian was the less talented of the boys, but then Joe made it to the Hall of Fame so that's hardly an insult. Ironically, Brian was drafted and Joe was not, the former tied to Winnipeg in 1980. In his 11 NHL years, he never scored fewer than 18 goals a season. His dream came true in 1987 when the Jets traded him to the Rangers

and he got to play before his friends night in, night out. Mullen also played for the U.S. at the 1984 Canada Cup and at two World Championships, but his career came to a sudden end on August 9, 1993, when he suffered a small stroke. Doctors determined the cause was a tiny hole in his heart, which in turn created a blood clot in his brain. He had open-heart surgery, and within two months he was back on skates thinking of a return. In March 1994, the Islanders said they'd give him a chance to play himself into shape in the minors. Mullen accepted the offer, but just a few minutes later suffered a seizure that laid to rest any plans of a comeback. He later became the director of off-ice programs for the NHL, and in 1995 he was awarded the Lester Patrick Trophy.

MULLEN, Joe
b. New York, New York, February 26, 1957

Being born in New York is a generic starting point that can refer to an exclusive, private-care hospital or, in Mullen's case, the mean streets of an area called Hell's Kitchen. The Kitchen was controlled by a mob that future mayor Rudy Giuliani called the most vicious in that city's history. Many of Mullen's friends never made it out alive and many more strayed to a life of guns and drugs. Mullen had his family, though, which included three brothers and a father who worked as a member of the ice crew at Madison Square Garden. Mullen learned his hockey on cement, not skates. He played in the yard of the New York School of Printing, which had a nice stretch of blacktop, and didn't put skates on until he was 10 years old. One day while Mullen was playing roller hockey, Emile Francis, coach and GM of the Rangers, wandered by and saw the kids playing. That partly inspired Francis to create the Metropolitan Junior Hockey League of New York, in which Joe and brother Brian later played. Joe was good enough to get a scholarship to Boston College to play, but after four years he was not drafted by an NHL team and signed with St. Louis as a free agent. He was assigned to Salt Lake City in 1979 and spent the next two years in the minors. He caught a break the year after when the Blues called him up midway through the year after a great start with the Eagles. He never went back. By the end of that '81-'82 season, Mullen had made history by becoming the first player to score at least 20 goals in the minors and NHL in the same year. He recorded consecutive 40-goal seasons with the Blues, and when he was traded to Calgary midway through the '85-'86 season, he kept right on scoring. He reached his peak in '88-'89 when he had 51 goals and 110 points, and the Flames won their first Stanley Cup. He also led

Richard Mulhern

Mullen had made history by becoming the first player to score at least 20 goals in the minors and NHL in the same year.
JOE MULLEN

Ryan Mulhern

Brian Mullen

Wayne Muloin

the playoffs with 16 goals. Despite his unflinching play, he also won his second Lady Byng Trophy that year. He was traded to Pittsburgh in the summer of 1990, and the timing could not have been better. The Penguins won the Cup in each of the next two years. Mullen retired in 1997 as the highest-scoring American-born player in NHL history. His 502 goals and 1,063 points were incredible accomplishments for a player no one deemed worthy of so much as a draft selection. He also had a fine international career. He played at the 1979 World Championships and at three Canada Cups, in 1984, '87, and '91. In the 1998 World Championships, the U.S. team finished an appalling twelfth-place and had to play a qualifying tournament the following year. Mullen came out of retirement to ensure U.S. victory and continued participation in "A" pool play at the WC. He was inducted into the Hockey Hall of Fame in 2001, a fitting end to a career so fairy-tale and Hollywood that it really isn't to be believed. Now in the real world, Mullen has been an assistant coach for Pittsburgh since retiring in 1997.

MULLER, Kirk ("Captain Kirk")
b. Kingston, Ontario, February 8, 1966
Mario Lemieux was the first name called at the 1984 Entry Draft. Muller's was the second. His junior career featured plenty of goals, tremendous intensity, two-way play, and inspiring leadership. He made New Jersey that fall at age 18 and for 7 years played exactly as he had in junior, but at a higher level. In his years with the Devils, Muller averaged 26 goals, but the team rarely made it to the playoffs and as a result he also played at four World Championships. When he was traded to Montreal in 1991, Muller was at his peak. He soon became team captain, and scored 36 and 37 goals in his first 2 seasons. His leadership and play were salient to Montreal's stunning Cup win in 1993, and his departure was greeted with a chorus of boos. The Canadiens traded him to the lowly Islanders, and Muller didn't try to hide his upset over the deal. He lasted just 27 games with the team before moving on to Toronto, and by then he was a lesser player but valuable nonetheless. He ended up in Florida, seemingly the last of the line for his career, and all seemed hopeless when the free agent had no takers to start the 1999-2000 season. Dallas, defending Cup champions, signed him in December, though, and Muller became an effective role player, a flattering euphemism for fourth-liner. His experience and continued intensity helped the Stars reach the finals again, and he re-signed with them in 2002 to ensure his continued survival, in a lesser role, with one of the league's premier teams.

Glenn Mulvenna

Grant Mulvey

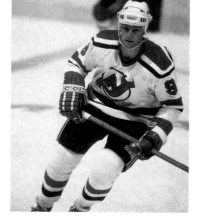
Mario Lemieux was the first name called at the 1984 Entry Draft. Muller's was the second.
KIRK MULLER

MULOIN, Wayne
b. Dryden, Ontario, December 24, 1941
At 5'7" it wasn't just that Muloin was small; it's that he was a ferocious hitter, launching his body wilfully and wholly each time an opponent came at him. His slapshot was awful (though he once knocked out six of Ed Van Impe's teeth with a blast) and his NHL career reasonably uneventful, but he had a couple of fine years with California. Muloin played in three games for Detroit in the pre-1967 days – where his brother-in-law, Detroit Tigers pitcher Bill Monbouquette, could watch him play – but his real break came with expansion. After six years in the minors, he made the Seals as a result of a determined effort to go into training camp and prove himself a hard-hitting defenceman. He left the NHL to join the WHA in 1972, where he closed out his career. Muloin later settled in the Cleveland suburb of Avon, Ohio, where he worked as a construction foreman.

MULVENNA, Glenn
b. Calgary, Alberta, February 18, 1967
The refrain is sung in this endless tune of too-small players who never get a chance to make it in the NHL. Mulvenna was a perfectly good, quality player with loads of skills, but he played in only two games, one with Philly, the other with Pittsburgh. He skated in the minors for a few years and in 1996 he headed to Europe. In 2000, he became an assistant coach with the Newcastle Jesters, but the team folded after a year. Mulvenna lucked out when he came home to accept the post of head coach with the Peterborough Pirates in 2001-02.

MULVEY, Grant
b. Sudbury, Ontario, September 17, 1956
Mulvey was only 17 when he was drafted by Chicago in 1974, though he was 18 by the time he made his NHL debut later that year after making the Hawks at training camp. He arrived at a time when the great Chicago teams of the 1960s and early 1970s were a thing of the past, and he quickly made an impact. He was a hitter and banger and checker, the kind of guy who wasn't squeamish about going into the corner to dig a puck free. He never claimed to be a scorer, but it was him – not Bobby Hull or Stan Mikita – who set the club record by scoring five goals in a game and equalling the NHL record of four in a period. Indeed, Mulvey did score 39 goals in '79-'80, though he missed half the next year with a broken arm. He suffered what turned out to be a career-ending knee injury early in the '82-'83 season, missing all that year and making an unimpressive return the following year. After retiring, Mulvey worked as a graphic artist, a restaurateur, and a coach and then co-owner of the new Chicago Wolves of the IHL.

MULVEY, Paul
b. Sudbury, Ontario, September 27, 1958

Make no mistake, hockey is a world. It has its leaders and its hewers of water, its laws and creeds and beliefs. Mulvey was its outlaw, and he was excommunicated in no uncertain terms. On January 24, 1982, Mulvey and his L.A. Kings played a home game against Vancouver. In the second period, a brawl erupted and Kings coach Don Perry tapped Mulvey on the shoulder and said, "Go out there – and don't dance." The hulking Mulvey didn't move, nor did he react after a second and third exhortation from the coach. When it was clear both benches were emptying, only then did Mulvey join the fray. In the dressing room, the coach publicly humiliated Mulvey and after the game put him on waivers and sent him to the minors. Mulvey never played another game in the NHL and retired a year later, thoroughly convinced he had been blacklisted by every NHL team for his inaction that night. Perry was suspended 15 days and fined $5,000 and Mulvey later launched a lawsuit against the Kings that was settled out of court. Mulvey woved to Washington, where he became credit manager for a department store and for more than 20 years has been a full-time instructor for kids in the area. He also coached a bantam team in north Virginia called the Reston Raiders.

Paul Mulvey

MUMMERY, Harry ("Big Mum")
b. Chicago, Illinois, August 26, 1889
d. Brandon, Manitoba, December 9, 1945

He was the stuff of legend, a man larger than life and larger than large, period. At 245 pounds, he was the biggest player ever to appear on the NHL stage, and his appetite was legend. He was known to cook two steaks in the boiler room of the Mutual Street Arena before game time and then head down the hall to get dressed. He was so big, special pants had to be made for him, and trainers claimed they could fit the underwear, socks, and sweaters of the whole team inside those pants. On ice, Mummery was a docile figure who was likely the first truly rushing defenceman. He began with Quebec in the NHA in 1912, winning the Stanley Cup his first year. He joined Toronto when the NHL formed in 1917 (winning another Cup that season), and in '20-'21 he scored an unheard of 15 goals from the blueline. During these years, he also worked as an engineer or fireman on the CPR. Mummery also played goal more than any other skater in the history of the game. In the early days, it was common for a defenceman to fill in while a goalie served a 2- or 3-minute penalty, but in his career Mummery played a total of 192 minutes in goal, including 3 full games, a feat no other player has

matched. After retiring in 1922, Mummery continued his eating ways and although he played in charity games his weight ballooned to 315 pounds.

MUNI, Craig
b. Toronto, Ontario, July 19, 1962

The problem with drafting players at age 18 is that they usually take at least 5 or 6 years to reach their full potential. To judge them at 19 is folly, to trade them at 24 premature. Yet, to play them full-time in the NHL for 6 years is also counterproductive. Muni joined his hometown Leafs in 1981, a dream come true for the local boy. But he was a big defenceman, and by and large needed strong coaching and patience. The Leafs gave him almost no opportunity to make the team and kept him in the minors until trading him to Edmonton. Toronto, a non-playoffs team at the time, had no use for him, while Oilers GM Glen Sather found a spot for him on arguably the most talented team of all time. Go figure. Muni anchored the defence out west and won three Cups with Edmonton. He later made the rounds for short periods with other teams, but he had made his legacy by that time. After retiring in 1998, he became a scout for Tampa Bay.

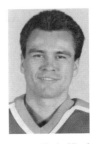

Craig Muni

Mummery played goal more than any other skater in the history of the game.
HARRY MUMMERY

MUNRO, Dunc
b. Moray, Scotland, January 19, 1901
d. Montreal, Quebec, January 3, 1958

In his early days, Munro was better known as a halfback for the Toronto Argonauts of Big Four football, from 1920 to '22. He played hockey in the winters and got his big chance when the Toronto Granites won the Allan Cup in 1923, thus ensuring that team's participation in the following year's Olympics. As captain, Munro led the club to a lopsided gold-medal victory, and then became the first in a long line of respected amateur players to turn pro with large salaries. He joined the Maroons in the fall of 1924 and won a Cup with the team at the end of his second season. In all, Munro played seven years with the English-Montreal team and a final year with the Canadiens. He was known as a gentleman and as generous to one and all. Part of his contract with the Maroons called for him to receive royalties on the sales of game-night programs, and this combined with his ventures into the stock market made him the wealthiest player of his era. Munro missed almost all of the '28-'29 season after suffering a heart attack, but he returned the next year not only to play but also to coach. The year after, he played just a bit while continuing to boss the bench. Once retired, he settled in Montreal to go into business, but several heart attacks over the years weakened him until he suffered a fatal attack in 1958.

Dunc Munro

Gerry Munro

MUNRO, Gerry
b. Sault Ste. Marie, Ontario, November 28, 1897
d. unknown
After playing in the Soo for several years, Munro signed with the Maroons for the '24-'25 season as a defenceman. He played a few games in Toronto the year after, and spent the rest of his career in the American league before retiring in 1931.

MURDOCH, Bob
b. Kirkland Lake, Ontario, November 20, 1946
This Bob Murdoch was a defenceman who started his career much differently from the other one. He earned a degree in math and phys ed from the University of Waterloo and played his first hockey with the Canadian National Team, 1968-70, including the 1969 World Championships. Montreal signed him in 1970, and for the next two years he played just a few games with a powerful team. In his third year, he took a regular turn on the blueline and helped the team win the Cup. He was traded to Los Angeles and then Atlanta, playing the remaining nine years with these two organizations. Following his playing days, Murdoch began an even lengthier career as coach. He led Chicago and then Winnipeg, where he was coach of the year in 1989-90, and then took his whistle and chalkboard overseas, working with a variety of teams over the next decade. He was an assistant for the Italian team at the 1998 Olympics in Nagano and later established himself in Germany.

**Bob Murdoch
(b. 1946)**

MURDOCH, Bob
b. Cranbrook, British Columbia, January 29, 1954
The lesser known of the NHL's two Bob Murdochs, this one is brother to Don. He was never drafted but signed with California in 1974, and after a year in the minors with Salt Lake City he made the team at camp in 1975. Murdoch had a perfectly respectable 22 goals as a rookie and 23 the year after, but after 2 lesser years he was back in the minors. He later went into coaching in Cranbrook.

MURDOCH, Don ("Murder")
b. Cranbrook, British Columbia, October 25, 1956
It's not the game that gets to some players – it's the glory. It's not doing the razzle-dazzle with the puck that's tough – it's doing it before 18,000 screaming fans and still going home the same person. Murdoch had all the skill in the world. As a junior, he ended with seasons of 82 and 88 goals with Medicine Hat, tops in the Western league. The Rangers drafted him, and his first year was like a dream. He scored twice in his first game. In another, he tied Howie Meeker's record for goals in a game by a rookie when he scored five against Minnesota. In 15 games, he had 15 goals. He was well

Murray Murdoch

on his way to winning the Calder Trophy when he caught his skate in the boards and tore tendons in his ankle, putting him out for the rest of the year. He already had 32 goals. His production dipped in each of the next two years, and his career virtually ended in August 1977 when authorities at Toronto's airport found 4.5 grams of cocaine hidden in a sock in his luggage. The law let him off easy – a fine, and nothing more – but NHL president John Ziegler suspended Murdoch for one year. After an appeal, the sentence was halved, but Murdoch was traded to Edmonton and couldn't find his confidence. He played half a year for Detroit and then wound up in the minors, far from the glory and goals of Broadway. The Rangers later hired him as a scout and he then became director of player personnel for Tampa Bay until he went into coaching. Murdoch became bench boss for the Louisiana IceGators of the East Coast league, his problems behind him, his career wrecked years earlier because he couldn't handle the fame as well as he handled a puck.

MURDOCH, Murray
b. Lucknow, Ontario, May 19, 1904
d. Pawleys Island, South Carolina, May 17, 2001
When he died at age 96, Murdoch was one of the oldest NHLers, a man who had lived a full life and dedicated his every hour to hockey. He attended the University of Manitoba (1921-24), playing for the team and earning a B.A. in mathematics. He played in the minors until 1926 when he joined the Rangers, and he played 11 uninterrupted seasons with the Blueshirts, winning Cups in 1928 and '33. He was a left winger who could score, though he played on the second line. The team made the playoffs every year he was there with but one exception. After he retired, Murdoch became the coach at Yale University, a position he held for 27 years. He was Ivy League champion twice with Yale, and after retiring as coach he became the school's athletics administrator for seven years. He later teamed with Lynn Patrick start and develop a peewee hockey league in the Hamden, Connecticut, area, where he continued to live. He moved to Pawleys Island just six months before his death to live with his daughter, his only living relative.

MURPHY, Brian
b. Toronto, Ontario, August 20, 1947
November 28 and December 18, 1974, were the only games Murphy ever played in the NHL, and those came after six years in the AHL. He had been the property of both Los Angeles and Toronto, but neither team used him at the NHL level and he wound up in Detroit. He played the rest of that season and all of the next in the American league before retiring.

As a junior, he ended up with seasons of 82 and 88 goals with Medicine Hat.
DON MURDOCH

MURPHY, Gord

b. Toronto, Ontario, March 23, 1967

As Murphy closes in on 1,000 games played, he can look back on a career that has been marked by consistent defensive play for, primarily, Philadelphia and Boston. More recently he has been in Florida and Atlanta, though the Bruins reacquired the 34-year-old in 2001. Murphy played his entire junior career in Oshawa and also played for Canada at the 1998 World Championships.

MURPHY, Hal

b. Montreal, Quebec, July 6, 1927

d. unknown

On November 8, 1952, Murphy played his one game in goal for Montreal when starter Gerry McNeil was injured and couldn't play. The Habs helped him out after falling behind 3-0, and despite allowing 4 goals he won the game 6-4 over Chicago at the Forum. Murphy left the game to attend Sir George Williams University and never played serious hockey again, leaving the NHLer with a perfect 1-0-0 record.

MURPHY, Joe

b. London, Ontario, October 16, 1967

It's tough to knock a player who has earned more than 500 career points in the NHL, but when he was a teen there was just so much more to Murphy than a few goals and a few assists. He played only one year of college hockey, with Michigan State in '85-'86 before the Red Wings had seen enough to draft him 1st overall the next summer. He made the weak team as an 18-year-old and spent the next 4 years between the Wings and Edmonton, his point totals improving to the level managers and scouts had expected. That fourth year saw Murphy collect 35 goals and 82 points, but the next year he sat waiting for a big contract from the Oilers. They traded him to Chicago, where he was a problem, and although he had 3 successive 20-goal seasons, his scoring dropped each year, he became sullen and idiosyncratic in the dressing room, and he simply wasn't worth the bother. St. Louis signed him to a huge contract – a huge mistake – and then Murphy travelled on to San Jose, Boston, Washington, and, finally, Ottawa, where he didn't play a single game in 2001-02. As a 1st-overall selection, he was more Wickenheiser than Lemieux.

MURPHY, Larry

b. Scarborough, Ontario, March 8, 1961

Over the course of 20 years in the NHL, Murphy accrued statistics that will virtually guarantee his induction into the Hockey Hall of Fame. He played more games than any other defenceman in the history of the game – 1,558 – and was only the fourth d-man to

record 1,000 points. He won 4 Stanley Cups, 2 with Pittsburgh (1991 and '92) and 2 with Detroit (1997 and '98), and appeared in 209 playoff games. He had five 20-goal seasons and 11 years scoring more than 60 points, including his first when he set a rookie defenceman record with 76 points. There were mitigating factors to his achievements. He never won an individual trophy and was never named to the First All-Star Team. There was nothing singular that defined his on-ice persona. He was not tough; he was painfully slow; he didn't have a booming shot; he didn't have the ability to go end to end with the puck. He simply played and played and played. He obviously made an impression with coaches and opponents, though, for he played on three Team Canada entries in the Canada Cup – 1984, '87, and '91. In fact, after the '87 victory, his Washington teammates started quacking when they saw him because he was the most famous decoy in hockey. It was Murphy who charged to the net on the game-winning play in which Wayne Gretzky dropped the puck to Mario Lemieux, who fired the winning goal. The chances of Lemieux passing to Murphy on that play were, of course, nil! Enigmatic and confounding, Murphy found a way to play his game for two full decades, and there aren't more than a dozen defencemen in the history of the game who can make that claim.

Gord Murphy

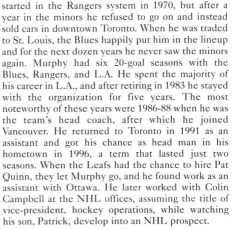

When the Leafs had the chance to hire Pat Quinn, they let Murphy go.
MIKE MURPHY

MURPHY, Mike ("Murph")

b. Toronto, Ontario, September 12, 1950

Still very much a part of hockey, Murphy is one of the best loved, affable men around, but those who know him today might not know

Joe Murphy

that he once scored 30 goals in the NHL. Once. Coming out of the Marlies in the late 1960s, he started in the Rangers system in 1970, but after a year in the minors he refused to go on and instead sold cars in downtown Toronto. When he was traded to St. Louis, the Blues happily put him in the lineup and for the next dozen years he never saw the minors again. Murphy had six 20-goal seasons with the Blues, Rangers, and L.A. He spent the majority of his career in L.A., and after retiring in 1983 he stayed with the organization for five years. The most noteworthy of these years were 1986-88 when he was the team's head coach, after which he joined Vancouver. He returned to Toronto in 1991 as an assistant and got his chance as head man in his hometown in 1996, a term that lasted just two seasons. When the Leafs had the chance to hire Pat Quinn, they let Murphy go, and he found work as an assistant with Ottawa. He later worked with Colin Campbell at the NHL offices, assuming the title of vice-president, hockey operations, while watching his son, Patrick, develop into an NHL prospect.

Larry Murphy

Rob Murphy

Ron Murphy

Al Murray

Bob Murray

Jim Murray

MURPHY, Rob
b. Hull, Quebec, April 7, 1969
Maybe numbers do tell the whole story, but that story is often deceiving. Murphy was drafted high in 1987 after a decent year in the high-scoring Q league, but in his five years in Vancouver he never played anywhere close to a full season. The hulking centreman, in fact, scored only 6 goals in 73 games, and his performance or ice time didn't improve in Ottawa or L.A., his last two stops. Murphy wound up buried in the "I," and in 1997 he moved to Germany to continue playing.

MURPHY, Ron
b. Hamilton, Ontario, April 10, 1933
An Original Six man through and through, Murphy played for the four American teams during a long and eventful career. It all started in '52-'53 in his final year of junior, when he was called up to play for the Rangers. Things het up the next year when he was involved in the stick-swinging duel of the year with Bernie Geoffrion, a brutal double assault that left Murphy in hospital for a week with his jaw wired shut and the season more or less over. He was traded to Chicago for Hank Ciesla in the summer of 1957 and spent seven fine years with the Hawks, winning the Cup in the spring of 1961. After a brief stop in Detroit, Murphy retired, only to be coaxed back by Boston. After a second retirement and coaxing, Murphy played on a line with Ken Hodge and Phil Esposito in '68-'69 and had his best offensive year with 54 points. He retired for good after only a part of the next year and tried his hand, briefly, at coaching. Once he knew that was not for him, Murphy bought a farm and hotel in Hagersville, Ontario before retiring altogether.

MURRAY, Al ("Little Man of Iron")
b. Stratford, Ontario, November 10, 1908
d. Stratford, Ontario
He was such a hero in Stratford that when his New York Americans played, the city stood still. A defenceman, he was, they say, the heaviest hitter in the NHL, at least on a pound-for-pound basis. He teamed on the blueline with Joe Jerwa and for seven years dished out the hits for the Amerks. He didn't get many points, but then neither did the forwards coming in on his goal. After retiring in 1940, he became a coach in junior, first for Guelph and later for Brantford and Galt.

MURRAY, Bob
b. Peterborough, Ontario, July 16, 1948
There were actually three Bob Murrays. One didn't make it to the NHL but played for the German National Team as a Canadian ex-pat, another played 1,000 games with Chicago, and the third played four years with Atlanta and Vancouver. The last of these played college hockey at Michigan Tech and then signed with the AHL team in Nova Scotia without an NHL contract, although he became Montreal property. A defenceman, he joined Atlanta in 1973, and by 1977 he was back in the minors, retiring at year's end.

MURRAY, Bob
b. Kingston, Ontario, November 26, 1954
Every player likes the Original Six notion of playing his entire career with one team, but the truth is that even in the early days few managed to achieve this dream. Murray did, however. Drafted by Chicago in 1974, he made the team full-time a year later and didn't leave the organization for 15 years. He was a solid defenceman with strong offensive skills, and he played in two All-Star Games (1981 and '83). By the time he retired in 1990 he had been to the semifinals with the Hawks five times and was their career leader in games played for a defenceman. He remained in the organization, became the director of player personnel, and later was the GM for two seasons (1997-99).

MURRAY, Chris
b. Port Hardy, British Columbia, October 25, 1974
It was an innocuous injury at the time, but it turned into a career-ending one for Murray, who severely dislocated his wrist on December 26, 2000, in a minor-league game with Worcester, the St. Louis farm team. He had surgery, and Toronto signed him in the hopes he could replace Tie Domi for his suspension to start the 2001-02 season. But Murray never played with the Leafs, either. The wrist never healed. He had won a Memorial Cup with Kamloops in 1994 before joining Montreal for three seasons of part-time hockey, and he later played for four other teams during his few years in the pros. He retired on October 24, 2001.

MURRAY, Glen
b. Halifax, Nova Scotia, November 1, 1972
A power forward when he is on his game, Murray started with Boston, but after four years the Bruins sent him to Pittsburgh after he showed little of the promise that had made him a first-round draft choice. He went on to have two 29-goal seasons with Los Angeles, and Boston benefitted from his development when they reacquired him in the Jason Allison trade during the 2001-02 season and he scored 35 with the Bruins.

MURRAY, Jim
b. Virden, Manitoba, November 25, 1943
In 1962, Murray and the Brandon Wheat Kings went to the Memorial Cup, and lost. In 1963, same thing. Ditto for '64. He turned pro in the Eastern league until L.A. acquired him when the Kings became a franchise in 1967, but after 30 games he was sent to the minors and never returned. He was told to put weight on his 158-pound body, which he did, and he was told to hit more, which he also did. He also gave up smoking, but none of this helped his NHL chances. He spent most of his time in Phoenix, but he did play a few games with Johnstown, the team on which the movie *Slap Shot* was based.

MURRAY, Ken
b. Toronto, Ontario, January 22, 1948
After registering an assist in his first NHL game, with the Leafs in 1970, Murray produced just 10 more points in the remaining 105 games of his career. The defenceman was renowned for his hitting and physical play, but that didn't keep him around for too long with any one team. He retired in 1978.

MURRAY, Leo
b. Portage la Prairie, Manitoba, February 15, 1906
d. unknown
In the 1920s and 1930s Murray was a longtime regular in

the Can-Am League, the league that preceded the AHL. He saw his only NHL action with Montreal, playing six games in '32-'33, and retired three years later.

MURRAY, Marty
b. Deloraine, Manitoba, February 16, 1975

It took a bunch of years before he made it happen, but in 2001 Murray finally made an NHL team – the Flyers – and played the full year with them. He had played in the 1994 WJC and again the year after, leading the tournament in scoring and being named best forward in '95. He then turned pro with Calgary, but the Flames showed little confidence in him because of his size. After three years mostly in the minors, Murray played in Europe, but the Flyers signed him as a free agent in the summer of 2001 and promised to give him a fair chance. He responded with a decent 27 points in his first full year at age 27.

MURRAY, Mickey
b. Peterborough, Ontario, October 14, 1898
d. unknown

A career minor-leaguer, Murray got the call of his life when he was asked to fill in for the injured George Hainsworth for a game on February 25, 1930. There was no fairy-tale ending, though, as the visiting Americans beat Montreal 4-2, spoiling Murray's sole venture into NHL nets.

MURRAY, Mike
b. Kingston, Ontario, August 29, 1966

It's never a good sign to be traded after being drafted and before being given a chance to make the team. Murray was picked by the Islanders in 1984, but after two more years in junior he had made little enough of an impression that the Isles traded him to Philly for a fifth-round choice in 1986. The Flyers put him in exactly one game, and he has been in the minors ever since. Murray varied the pace a bit by going to Europe for a few seasons, and in 1996 he retired for three years before returning to the game with Knoxville in the United League and then Louisiana in the East Coast league.

MURRAY, Pat
b. Stratford, Ontario, August 20, 1969

By the time he was 23, Murray had played his last NHL game, but that didn't stop him from having a fulfilling career. He came out of Michigan State in 1990 to play for the Flyers, but after two brief stints in consecutive seasons he was down in the minors for four years. Murray moved to Germany to finish his playing days, and when he returned to North America he became head coach of Lansing Catholic High School in Michigan. He earned his MBA in finance from Michigan Tech and then settled with his family

in Indianapolis and working as an assistant coach with nearby Carmel High School in Indiana.

MURRAY, Randy
b. Chatham, Ontario, August 24, 1945

In a short career, Murray played four NHL games, all with Toronto – November 9, 12, 15, 1969, and April 5, 1970. He played in the minors briefly but retired in 1973. He later became an owner of Bow West Realty in Alberta.

MURRAY, Raymond "Rem"
b. Stratford, Ontario, October 9, 1972

Even though L.A. drafted him in 1992, Murray never played a game for the Kings. Instead, he finished his college play, graduating from Michigan State in '95 without a contract. It was only at training camp with Edmonton that fall that the Oilers signed him and sent him to the minors, and after a strong season in Cape Breton he joined Edmonton the following year. He played with the Oilers for five and a half years before being traded to the Rangers, the Blueshirts wanting a skilled, skating forward who can do many things well.

Marty Murray

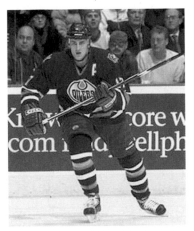

He played with the Oilers for five and a half years before being traded to the Rangers.
REM MURRAY

Randy Murray

MURRAY, Rob
b. Toronto, Ontario, April 4, 1967

His mammoth penalty-minute total and minuscule goal total tell the tale of Murray, a centre who made his pro debut in 1987 and his NHL entrance two years later. He continues to play, though his last NHL appearance was in 1998 with Phoenix, the franchise he has been affiliated with for more than a decade going back to its days in Winnipeg. Murray has played the vast majority of his time in the minors, getting only the occasional callup for a dozen games or so periodically.

MURRAY, Terry
b. Shawville, Quebec, July 20, 1950

Ever since 1967 when he started his junior career with the Ottawa 67's, Murray has been involved in hockey in a career way. He was a big, sturdy defenceman in his playing days, though he spent a fair bit of time with not very good teams, starting with California. Murray likely holds the record for the longest time from the start of a career to score a goal. Although he played his first game in 1972, he scored his first goal on March 14, 1981, a span of some 220 games! The next season, his last, he exploded for three more goals, with Washington, at which time he retired. He stayed with the team as an assistant coach and then moved to the AHL as head coach. In the last 20 years, he has rarely been out of work in this capacity, holding down head coaching jobs with 3 NHL teams. His most recent was as

Rob Murray

coach of Florida under GM Bryan Murray, his brother. Both were fired after a poor start by the Panthers in the 2000-01 season.

MURRAY, Troy
b. Calgary, Alberta, July 31, 1962

In 1982, Murray had so much success he almost couldn't handle it. He won gold with Canada at the World Juniors, he won an NCAA title with University of North Dakota, and he played in his first NHL game, with Chicago. The next year, as a full-time rookie with the Hawks, he became better known as a nightlife player than for hockey until goalie Tony Esposito told him where his focus should be. Murray then developed into a bona fide star with the team, improving in goals, assists, and points in each of his first four seasons, culminating with a 45-goal, 99-point year in '85-'86. From there, it was almost as steady and consistent a decline until he wound up as a utility man with Colorado. The upside was that the season was '95-'96, when the team won the Cup. The year after, Murray was in the "I" the entire season without being called up, and at that point he retired. He settled in Chicago, where he worked as an analyst on Hawks broadcasts and as a commodities trader.

Dana Murzyn

MURZYN, Dana ("Hank")
b. Calgary, Alberta, December 9, 1966

A classic stay-at-home defenceman, Murzyn got into the NHL with Hartford, had his glory years with Calgary, and played his longest stretch with Vancouver as an experienced leader. The Flames acquired him midway through the '87-'88 season when the team was developing into a real contender. The next year, they won their first and still-only Stanley Cup, and Murzyn stayed with the team another year and a half. He was sent to Vancouver for Ron Stern and Kevan Guy and for the next eight and a half years was the defensive lynchpin on the Canucks blueline. He suffered a serious knee injury early in '97-'98, but after a brief comeback the following year Murzyn retired and returned to Calgary where he became involved in the meat business.

Jason Muzzatti

MUSIL, Frantisek ("Frank")
b. Pardubice, Czechoslovakia (Czech Republic), December 17, 1964

In hockey terms, Musil and Dominik Hasek were like brothers – until they went their separate ways. They grew up together, played on the same kid teams together, were good friends. They played in the World Juniors and World Championships together, and both knew they were top-level players in their country. Both wanted to play in the NHL, but they took dramatically different roads to get there. In the summer of 1986, Musil became convinced the only way he would ever play for Minnesota, the team that had drafted him, was to defect. He called a player agent, Rich Winter, who helped the process along, and Musil boarded a plane without telling his parents or friends. Hasek would never have defected and could not accept Musil's decision, and it was years before the two had a pleasant conversation again. Musil played some 13 years in the NHL, a big and surprisingly physical defenceman who played for 4 teams, none of which ever made it past the first round of the playoffs. His career came to an abrupt end in Edmonton at training camp in 1999 when he fell and damaged two vertebrae. He retired and became a European scout and development coach for the Oilers, though he returned to play again in the less demanding Czech league. Late in the 2001-02 season, he was involved in an ugly incident when he slashed Robert Pospisil's hand twice so hard that he severed the player's pinky finger. Musil faced criminal charges for the incident.

His career came to an abrupt end in Edmonton when he fell and damaged two vertebrae.
FRANTISEK MUSIL

MUZZATTI, Jason
b. Toronto, Ontario, February 3, 1970

A long scar runs from his throat to his sternum, the result of a greater fight than making any hockey team. At birth, doctors discovered that Muzzatti suffered from aortic stenosis, a narrowing of the aortic valve that allows blood to flow through the body. He had an operation at age 13 to expand the valve, and 5 years later had it replaced shortly after being drafted in 1988 by Calgary. Ten years later, the valve had to be replaced and he missed most of the '98-'99 season recovering. It was, in some sense, an operation that ended his NHL days, for no team wanted to sign him after that last surgery. Muzzatti had played 5 seasons in the big league, his best chance coming with Hartford when he played 53 games over 2 seasons. Whether he was stigmatized because of his heart or he just never performed at the NHL level when given a chance is a matter only Muzzatti can possibly know, but since his most recent operation he has been playing full-time in Europe, mostly in Finland and Germany.

MYERS, Harold "Hap"
b. Edmonton, Alberta, July 28, 1947

Myers won two important championships during his career, one at the start, one at the end. In 1966 he and his Edmonton Oil Kings won the Memorial Cup, and in 1973 he and his Cincinnati Swords won the Calder Cup. In between, he played 13 games with the expansion Buffalo Sabres. The year after the Calder Cup win, the Swords folded with the arrival in town of the WHA Stingers, and Myres never played pro again.

Hap Myers

MYHRES, Brantt
b. Edmonton, Alberta, March 18, 1974
A well-travelled fighter, Myhres began his NHL life with Tampa Bay in 1995 and has been fighting in the minors most of the time since, hoping to get a callup to whatever team he is the property of. Philadelphia and San Jose have also put him to use for a few games, but Myhres hasn't been up since 2000 and his prospects for such a call dim with each passing day.

MYLES, Vic
b. Fairlight, Saskatchewan, November 12, 1914
When Myles was playing for the Moose Jaw Millers, he was noticed by a New York Rangers scout who promptly got Myles into the Rangers Hockey School that operated in Winnipeg. This was in 1939, and by that fall the team had assigned him to the farm, with Philadelphia. After this season, the Rangers decided not to operate the Ramblers team, so Myles was put on the market. New Haven grabbed him, and he played there for two years before the Blueshirts finally called him up. At 208 pounds, he became one of the biggest men ever to play in the NHL, but after just one season he was returned to the minors and never came back. He wound up back in the Canadian west with a number of teams, becoming coach of those same Millers in '52-'53.

MYLLYS, Jarmo
b. Savonlinna, Finland, May 29, 1965
The three lives of Finnish goalie Myllys add up to the greatest accomplishments in net his country has ever produced. First, there was the international glory. He helped Finland win its first-ever Olympic medal, a silver in 1988 in Calgary. He was in net for the first gold at the World Championships, in Stockholm in 1995. And he beat Canada at Nagano in 1998 to give the Finns a bronze medal. He also has a bronze from Lillehammer in '94, and two other WC medals. Second, he played in the NHL for four years, one of the first Finns to do so, with Minnesota and San Jose (1988-92). His play was by no means remarkable, but just making it was an act of hockey heroism for his Suomi admirers back home. Third, after leaving the NHL, he moved to Sweden, where he has become the greatest goalie in Lulea history. He already holds the all-time record for shutouts, and on January 16, 1999, he became the first goalie in Swedish league history to score a goal. Toronto and Ottawa both tried to bring him back to the NHL at various times over the last decade, but Myllys has been content playing the role of crease god to an adoring public in Sweden.

MYLNIKOV, Sergei
b. Chelyabinsk, Soviet Union (Russia), October 6, 1958
Someone had to be the one, and Mylnikov was it. In the final moments of the 1987 Canada Cup, when Gretzky passed to Lemieux and Mario fired a perfect shot into the top corner of the net for the win, Mylnikov was in the goal. From his point of view, he atoned just a few months later by leading the USSR to gold at the 1988 Olympics in Calgary, a fair tradeoff, no doubt, in the minds and hearts of every Canadian fan. Mylnikov was groomed to take over for Tretiak as far back as the late 1970s, when he won two golds

with his country at the WJC in '77 and '78. It wasn't until that Canada Cup, though, that he got a chance to prove himself, because in between Evgeny Belosheikin became the country's successor to Tretiak. Mylnikov played only a few games with Quebec in '89-'90, his only NHL season, and then returned home. European hockey history is somewhat fuzzier and not as well documented as North American hockey, but apparently Mylnikov closed out his career playing third division hockey in Sweden as late as 1996 as backup to his son, Dmitri!

MYRE, Phil
b. Ste. Anne de Bellevue, Quebec, November 1, 1948
Few people remember that Phil Myre and Rogie Vachon shared the goaltending for Montreal in 1970-71, the year the Habs won the Cup. Perhaps that's because when Ken Dryden came in at the end of the regular season and stayed for the playoffs, the other two never got to play. After another year of limited action, Myre knew Dryden was the Habs' future. He was left open for Atlanta at the Expansion Draft, and for five and a half years he was the starter for the Flames. He later played for 4 other teams, and although he was around for a while he never won 20 games in any one season. His most notable year of pro was his first, with Houston in the CHL, when he won the Terry Sawchuk trophy for fewest goals allowed. It was a fitting connection because he patterned himself after Sawchuk, relying on quickness and speed rather than coming out and playing the angles. After retiring, he became a coach and has been associated with L.A., Detroit, Chicago, and, most recently, Ottawa.

MYRVOLD, Anders
b. Lorenskog, Norway, August 12, 1975
From the land of Henrik Ibsen and 3 p.m. sunsets, from the streets that inspired Edvard Munch's great painting "The Scream" comes a man almost never before seen – NHL hockey player. Myrvold was drafted by Quebec in 1993 while he was playing internationally for Norway. He played in three World Junior Championships, all in "B" pool, and an "A" pool WC to prove that he could play among the elite, but he played only 13 NHL games thereafter. His time with Colorado and Boston was vital to the Norwegian hockey program, though, because it proved it could produce an NHLer of some sort. The defenceman went on to play in the minors and then returned to Europe to continue playing, most recently in Germany.

Vic Myles

Jarmo Myllys

Sergei Mylnikov

Phil Myre

Anders Myrvold

NABOKOV, Dmitri
b. Novosibirsk, Soviet Union (Russia), January 4, 1977
There was great promise when Nabokov turned 18 and became draft eligible. He was a kid who had size and speed and skill, nothing but upside and a future to turn promise into performance. Chicago took him 18th overall in 1995, yet after just 25 games 2 years later they gave up on him. He was traded to the Islanders, and exactly the same thing happened. The upside turned down, and by 2000 Nabokov was out of the game altogether.

NABOKOV, Evgeni
b. Ust-Kamenogorsk (Oskemen), Soviet Union (Kazakhstan), July 25, 1975
In the post-perestroika age, Nabokov's part of the Soviet Union became Kazakhstan, and thankfully the name of Ust-Kamenogorsk was changed to Oskemen. Either way, it was a small town where hockey was the difference between pleasure and pain for any boy. Nabokov's dad was a goalie in town, and Evgeni took after dad. He was a low draft choice by San Jose in 1994 and after two years in the minors he joined the Sharks in 1999-2000 for a few games, proving his worth almost instantly. In the following two seasons, he established himself not only as an NHLer but as one of the best young goaltenders in the game. He won 32 and 37 games in those years, and is part of a dynamic, young team that has great promise. Nabokov also made history on March 10, 2002, when he became the first European goalie to score a goal, against Vancouver.

NACHBAUR, Don
b. Kitimat, British Columbia, January 30, 1959
Nachbaur went from the penthouse to the outhouse, as the saying goes, pretty quickly. Coming out of junior and a year in the minors, he made Hartford in 1980 and played two full seasons with the team. He was an all-purpose centre who was reliable and could score a bit, but whose first role was as a protector of talent. The next year, when he was traded, he was lucky to see the NHL at all, and that's how it was the rest of his career. He spent his last 5 seasons in the Philadelphia organization, mostly in the minors, and at one time he played 23 games as a result of 6 separate callups from the minors. He moved to Austria in 1990 at the close of his career and afterward went into coaching. He was head man in Seattle in the WHL, was an assistant with Canada's under-18 team, and later moved up to the AHL with the Phantoms in Philly as an assistant.

NAGY, Ladislav
b. Saca, Czechoslovakia (Slovakia), June 1, 1979
Nothing Nagy did before May 2002 could compare in honour and joy to what he and his Slovak teammates accomplished at the World Championships in Sweden. The tiny nation with a small collection of the world's best players beat all comers to win gold for the first time in Slovakia's brief history, thus heralding the arrival of a seventh hockey power to the Big Six that had long dominated the sport. Nagy had finished his best season in the NHL, scoring 23 goals with Phoenix, in what is still a blossoming career.

NAHRGANG, Jim
b. Millbank, Ontario, April 17, 1951
A Husky from Michigan State through and through, Nahrgang started his career there and finished it there some 15 years later. He began in 1970, earned a four-year degree in business administration, and became one of the all-time great defencemen for that college. He played parts of three seasons with the Red Wings in the NHL, but by 1978 it was clear he was going to see much more ice time in the minors than the big league, so he retired to accept a position as assistant coach at Michigan. After a four-year apprenticeship, he became head coach of the team, a position he held for three years after which he resigned because he felt the team was doing too poorly under his guidance. Nahrgang became involved in construction, moving up to the position of vice-president of human resources for Ryan Companies of Minneapolis. His brother-in-law, Bob Lorimer, also played in the NHL, and his daughter, Andrea, was a biathlete on the 2002 U.S. Olympic team. Nahrgang was later inducted into the Michigan Tech Sports Hall of Fame for his playing career.

NAMESTNIKOV, Yevgeny "John"
b. Arzamis Ig, Soviet Union (Russia), October 9, 1971
The brother-in-law of Slava Kozlov, Namestnikov never had the skills or career to match his wife's brother's. Namestnikov played 43 games with 3 teams, not scoring a single goal throughout the 1990s. He spent most of his time in the minors, and then in 2001 the defenceman returned to Russia to continue his career in his country's burgeoning pro league.

NANNE, Lou
("Sweet Lou from the Soo")
b. Sault Ste. Marie, Ontario, June 2, 1941
The stories told of players having to leave the game not of their own volition are many. Some risk permanent injury if they keep playing, while others are not offered contracts despite their skill. Nanne had to quit the game because it was, quite literally, killing him. Although he was born in Ontario, he went to the University of Minnesota in 1960 and within a few years decided that he wanted to become an American. He played pro in Rochester and in 1968 captained the U.S. Olympic hockey team. After those Olympics, he signed with Minnesota, and began an intense, 20-year relationship with that team and city. He played for the North Stars for 11 years, a solid performer who rose to glory in '71-'72 when he scored 21 goals. He played at two World Championships for the U.S. and appeared at the inaugural Canada Cup in 1976. When he retired in 1977, he did so only so he could coach the team, which he did until season's end. He became the GM for the next decade – as well as GM of the next three U.S. entries in the Canada Cup – but he put more work and worry into the job than was good for him. Long hours, ceaseless anxiety, and self-tormenting moments affected his health, and doctors told him to retire or risk fatal results from the job. He did just that, settling in to a more relaxing position as vice-president and president of the club until he felt it better to leave altogether. He stayed in the city and worked for Piper Capital Management, a money managing firm, travelling across the continent, taking in the occasional

Evgeni Nabokov

Don Nachbaur

Ladislav Nagy

John Namestnikov

Lou Nanne

Jim Nahrgang
(opposite page)

Richard Nantais

Mark Napier

Tyson Nash

Markus Naslund

Alain Nasreddine

game, but never hyperventilating about a possible bad trade the way he had as GM.

NANTAIS, Richard
b. Repentigny, Quebec, October 27, 1954
After an explosive final season of junior in which he recorded 194 points in the Q league, Nantais played only sporadically with Minnesota over the next 4 years. He was relegated to the minors for most of his years, and retired in 1978 having played just 63 NHL games.

NAPIER, Mark
b. Toronto, Ontario, January 28, 1957
Not many players could skate and shoot like Napier, and even fewer could do it at age 18 the way he could. The Toronto boy played locally with the Marlies, winning the Memorial Cup in 1975 and then turning pro in the WHA. He was that league's rookie of the year, followed up with 60 goals in year 2, and after a third season felt ready for the NHL. Napier joined Montreal in 1978 and won a Stanley Cup that year. In his 5 full seasons with the Habs, he scored 11, 16, 35, 40, and 40 goals, but the team traded him to Minnesota in a deal that brought Bobby Smith to Montreal. Napier joined Edmonton about a year later, and won another Cup with another great dynasty. In his later years he never reached the scoring levels he had earlier, but he played in the NHL until 1989 and moved to Italy to close out his career. After four seasons, he returned to Toronto and worked at Elite Cresting in Markham, Ontario, and in May 1997 he got the chance of a lifetime when he was named head coach of the St. Mike's Majors, a team recently returning to the OHL. His one year was less successful than hoped for, and he moved into business in downtown Toronto. His teenage son later published a best-selling children's book, *Z is for Zamboni*.

NASH, Tyson ("Nasher")
b. Edmonton, Alberta, March 11, 1975
Feisty and nasty, Nash has established himself in St. Louis, where he has played all of his NHL games, starting in 1999. But his greater accomplishment was winning three Memorial Cups with Kamloops – 1992, '94, and '95 – one of only four players to do so since the trophy's beginnings in 1919.

NASLUND, Markus
b. Ornskoldsvik, Sweden, July 30, 1973
Few trades of the modern era were as lopsided as the one made on March 20, 1996. Pittsburgh sent Markus Naslund to Vancouver for Alek Stojanov. Stojanov played just 45 games with the Penguins over the next

year. Naslund, in his first game for the Canucks, scored a hat trick and hasn't looked back. Pittsburgh, though, is not entirely to blame. Naslund looked at first like so many Canadian kids coming out of junior. He set a WJC record by scoring 13 goals at the 1993 tournament in which Sweden won silver and he looked to have all the skills needed to be a star. But in three years in the Penguins system he did little scoring and little else to impress management. Vancouver seemed to be Naslund's wakeup tonic, though. He had a couple of decent seasons, and then in '98-'99 he scored 36 goals and started to realize his full potential. He was named team captain, signed a long-term contract, and came back with years of 41 and 40 goals while cracking the top 10 of scoring leaders. Now maturing as he enters his thirties, Naslund looks to be a late-blooming superstar of the first order, and the Canucks got him for virtually nothing.

After retiring, he became a TV sports commentator in Sweden.
MATS NASLUND

NASLUND, Mats ("Le Petit Viking")
b. Timra, Sweden, October 31, 1959
There is virtually nothing Mats Naslund didn't accomplish during his brilliant hockey career, at home in Sweden and in the NHL with Montreal. He won gold medals at the Olympics (1994) and the World Championships (1991), and won the Stanley Cup (with Montreal in '85-'86). He won 3 Swedish national championships, and when he joined the Habs in 1982 he was the first European to play for the mighty team. In his 8 seasons, he never scored fewer than 21 goals and he peaked with consecutive 40-goal seasons. He won the Lady Byng Trophy in '87-'88 and played in three All-Star Games, and by the time he returned to Sweden in 1990 he had made his impact on Montrealers. Although he returned to the NHL four years later to play briefly for Boston, his post-Montreal career passed quickly and brilliantly in Swedish and Swiss league play, where he spent four seasons. After retiring, he became a TV sports commentator in Sweden.

NASREDDINE, Alain
b. Montreal, Quebec, July 10, 1975
Florida, Chicago, Montreal, Edmonton. Such is the Greyhound route that Nasreddine's career has taken so far, though it has amounted to precious few NHL games for all his troubles. He has yet to register a point, but that's because he's supposed to be fighting people, not playing Waltzing Matilda on the power play. Braun is his game, but none of the aforementioned teams have needed to rely on him to any great extent.

NATTRASS, Ralph
b. Gainsboro, Saskatchewan, May 26, 1925
Coming out of Moose Jaw in 1945, Nattrass stepped

into the pro fray with Kansas City, farm team to Chicago. Johnny Gottselig had tagged him as a can't-miss kid, and with the Pla-Mors he helped Doc Romnes' team win the championship that first season. That earned Nattrass a callup for much of the following year, and he remained a steady performer for another three seasons. Nattrass's play was marked by heavy hitting and taking the man. The defenceman never scored much, which was fine by the Hawks, but the team also failed to make the playoffs during his years. After retiring, he settled in Chicago and became an NHL linesman for a short time, and then he went into business. He had married a woman from Kansas City and taken out American citizenship, and he sold insurance and later worked as a sales manager at a car dealership selling Cadillacs.

NATTRESS, Eric "Ric" ("Stash")
b. Hamilton, Ontario, May 25, 1962

Before the glory came the ignominy. In the summer of 1983, Nattrass was found to have 3 grams of marijuana and 1 gram of hashish in his car. He was fined $150 after being convicted of possession, and NHL president suspended the second-year player for a year, the same sentence given to Don Murdoch in '78-'79. Like Murdoch, Nattrass had his suspension reduced, in his case to 30 games, and he tried to get his game back on track with Montreal. He wound up going to St. Louis and on to Calgary, and it was with the Flames he had his finest years teamed with Jamie Macoun as the premier defensive pairing in the league. He helped the Flames win the Cup in 1989, and later played briefly with Toronto and Philadelphia before retiring in 1993. He became an assistant with Hamilton of the AHL for two years and then with the London Knights. He also did some consulting out of Hamilton, and has continued to play with the Legends group of old-timers that tours the country.

NATYSHAK, Mike
b. Belle River, Ontario, November 29, 1963

The Belle River Minor Hockey Association produced two NHLers – Tie Domi and Mike Natyshak. The former continues to punch his way through a career in the game; the latter had to retire after just four games with Quebec in '87-'88 because of injury. He had been a graduate of Bowling Green University.

NAUMENKO, Gregg
b. Chicago, Illinois, March 30, 1977

First, Naumenko turned pro right out of high school, playing in the USHL. Then, he went back to college for a year, and went pro again thereafter. His NHL time has amounted to just 70 minutes in goal over 2 games with Anaheim, and he's been buried so deep in the minors that Anaheim isn't even an option if he gets any sort of phone call. Too anxious to turn pro at 18, he's paying the price now through a lack of big-league opportunity.

NAZAROV, Andrei
b. Chelyabinsk, Soviet Union (Russia), May 22, 1974

Sure, the Europeans come to North America with all their speed and skills and their hours of practice, and then they send someone like Nazarov into the mix, a huge and powerful fighting machine who possesses no flashes of quickness, no pinpoint passing, and no end-to-end capability. He spent his first five seasons in the league starting in 1993-94, but since then he's been traded a fair bit. He's had 200 penalty minutes in a season 3 times and is one of the few enforcer-type players the Russians have produced for the NHL.

NDUR, Rumun
b. Zaria, Nigeria, July 7, 1975

Ndur was, of course, the first player ever born in Nigeria to skate in the NHL, though he was raised in Ontario and played his junior hockey with Guelph. He developed a skill for fighting, which is why Buffalo drafted him in 1994 and why other teams have had a marginal interest in him over the years since. He's spent the greater part of his career in the minors, which is likely where he'll finish before making another NHL team, not having played since Atlanta used him briefly in 1999-2000.

NEATON, Pat
b. Redford, Michigan, May 21, 1971

It hasn't been all sunshine and roses, but a guy can do many worse things in his life than play pro hockey outside the NHL. Neaton came out of the University of Michigan in 1993, and in November that year played his only nine games, with Pittsburgh. He was a fixture in the IHL for years, but when that league folded he moved to Europe and played in Vienna. Neaton also played for the U.S. at the World Championships and WJC.

NECHAEV, Viktor
b. Vostochnaya, Soviet Union (Russia), January 28, 1955

It's an obscure question and an obscure answer, but that's what trivia is, by definition. Who was the first Soviet-trained player to score a goal in the NHL? Why, Viktor Nechaev, of course. Until 1982 he played all his hockey in the Soviet Union, but those in the know knew he skated well and had a great shot. L.A. drafted him on a whim, and Soviet officials, for the first time, actually let one of their own join the NHL. Nechaev began the year in the minors, and when he was called up for three games, he scored a goal. He balked at returning to the AHL, but when he did he played so poorly that New Haven farmed him out to the IHL, in Saginaw. Again, he played so poorly the Gears released him when no other team was willing to take him for free, and Nechaev went to Germany the year after to continue his modest career.

NECKAR, Stanislav "Stan" ("Basa")
b. Ceske Budejovice, Czechoslovakia (Czech Republic), December 22, 1975

The bad blood caused by agents between players and teams accounts for much of the loss of that old-time feeling of players staying an entire year with a team. One good season, it seems, and a player's agent wants his client to be paid *crème de la crème* wages. Neckar joined Ottawa in 1994 just in time to experience a players' strike, but he played his first 130 games in a row without injury. A big, young defenceman, he held his own and looked solid, but five games into his third year he tore his knee apart and missed the season. After one

Ric Nattress

Rumun Ndur

Pat Neaton

Stanislav Neckar

Vaclav
Nedomansky

Vaclav Nedorost

Petr Nedved

Zdenek Nedved

more year, he did the holdout thing, asking for huge dollars because he considered himself one of the top defencemen after 195 career games. The two sides agreed to a deal, and three games into the new season Ottawa traded him to the Rangers, which then passed him on to Phoenix, and from there it was down to Tampa. So now, almost a decade into his career, no one, not even his wife, would rank him as one of the best defencemen in the NHL. He did win a gold with the Czechs at the 1996 World Championships, though the sum total of his career hardly represents a contract worth millions a year. His agent, though, would disagree.

NEDOMANSKY, Vaclav ("Big Ned")
b. Hodonin, Czechoslovakia (Czech Republic),
March 14, 1944

It's a lawsuit that, at the time, was controversial and sensational. It's a lawsuit that, today, makes perfect sense. While we might have sided with one party in 1984, we would unflinchingly side with the other today. Nedomansky sued his agent, Alan Eagleson, for $1-million for breach of contract in 1979. Detroit had offered the megastar a $2-million deal that was to last 15 years, 5 as a player, 10 as a scout. Big Ned never signed the deal because of Eagleson's negligence and eventually had to settle for a five-year deal with a buy-out clause, which the Wings enacted two years later for just $510,000. Sadly, not only did the courts side with the Eagle, they forced Nedomansky to pay his adversary's legal bills. This was gross humiliation given the revelations that would be forthcoming about Eagleson's practices. Nedomansky was the first great defector from Czechoslovakia (with teammate Richard Farda). He signed with the Toronto Toros of the WHA because he knew the coach, Billy Harris, and he was awed by two recent signings – Paul Henderson and Frank Mahovlich, two players he knew well from the recent Summit Series. Back home, there was no bigger star than Nedomansky. He led his league in scoring almost every year he played, and he had played in nine World Championships and two Olympics for the Czechs, including gold at the '72 WC, one of the most stunning victories in international competition over the vaunted Soviets. He had just graduated from university with degrees in physical education and biology and army duty was up next for him. He had been promised to be allowed to join the Rangers after the '68 Olympics, but when that didn't happen he knew he would never be free unless he forced the issue. He couldn't have defected at a better time. After three and a half years in the WHA, he signed with Detroit and had seasons of 38 and 35 goals, proof that he was of NHL calibre. After being bought out by the Wings, he ended his playing days with the Rangers and St. Louis but returned to Detroit for his post-playing career as a promoter for Pripps, an athletes' drink cut from the same cloth as, say, Gatorade. Although his six years in the NHL hardly make him a candidate for the Hockey Hall of Fame, he is in the IIHF Hall in recognition of his outstanding international career.

NEDOROST, Andrej
b. Trencin, Czechoslovakia (Slovakia), April 30, 1980
Out of 293 players drafted in 2000, Nedorost was selected 286th, by Columbus. He had played junior in

the Czech Republic and pro in Germany, but in 2001 he came to North America to play, spending most of his time in the minors. He played seven games for the Blue Jackets that year but has been returned to Syracuse since.

NEDOROST, Vaclav
b. Budejovice, Czechoslovakia (Czech Republic),
March 16, 1982
In his first NHL game, on October 3, 2001, Nedorost scored a goal and had an assist for Colorado. He went on to play a third of a season with the Avs and the rest of the time in the minors, though he made the team out of training camp to start 2002-03. He won consecutive gold medals with the Czech juniors in 2000 and 2001 and is one of Colorado's most coveted prospects.

NEDVED, Petr
b. Liberec, Czechoslovakia (Czech Republic),
December 9, 1971
One wintry day in Calgary, in January 1988, a 17-year-old Nedved was touring with a group of juniors from Litvinov. He didn't speak a word of English, but he decided not to get on that plane bound for Czechoslovakia. He defected, and the next year played junior in Seattle where he had a sensational year. This led to being drafted 2nd overall in 1990 by Vancouver, and his rise with the Canucks was nothing short of meteoric. Such was his development that he learned the ways of the West off the ice as well, and after a season in which he had 38 goals and 71 points he demanded large sums of money to stay in B.C. Vancouver refused, and Nedved, who had acquired a Canadian citizenship, fled to the National Team and played at the 1994 Olympics in Lillehammer. He signed with St. Louis, but the Canucks had the sweet revenge of going to the finals while the Blues were swept in the first round by Dallas. The Rangers acquired him, but he didn't get along well with the coach or star Mark Messier, and off he went again, to Pittsburgh. He scored 78 goals with the Pens over 2 seasons and played for the new Czech Republic at the '96 World Cup, and then, as was his way, he sat out a full season looking for a big contract. The Rangers reacquired him and gave him the large *dineros*, and the comfortable Nedved responded with a succession of mediocre seasons.

NEDVED, Zdenek ("Zed")
b. Lany, Czechoslovakia (Czech Republic), March 3, 1975
A dazzling teenager, Nedved played almost poetic hockey at two World Juniors in '94 and '95 before joining the Leafs at the end of the latter season. He had been playing junior in Sudbury, and although he had the skills, he suffered a serious shoulder injury with the Leafs soon after scoring his first goal and missed much of the '95-'96 season. He played 2 more years of pro but the Leafs used him only 23 more times, after which he returned to Europe to continue his career.

NEEDHAM, Mike
b. Calgary, Alberta, April 4, 1970
Although he retired at 26, Needham accomplished a very great deal in a short time. He won a Memorial Cup with Kamloops in 1990, just weeks after winning gold with Canada at the World Juniors, and in his first

year in Pittsburgh the next season he won the Stanley Cup. Needham didn't play much for the Pens in that championship season, but he did play on a fourth line during the playoffs with Jock Callander and Mike Michayluk. He spent three part-time years with Pittsburgh in Mario Lemieux's prime and played a few games with Dallas before going to the minors.

NEELY, Bob ("Waldo")
b. Sarnia, Ontario, November 9, 1953
No one ever had to tell Neely to slow down or to ease up on the slappers, he's going to hurt someone with that shot. Nonetheless he was a fine player who earned everything he got in the NHL. He played five years with the Leafs on left wing, but while he wanted to use his skills the Leafs wanted him to be a tough guy. The result was he did neither particularly effectively, pleasing neither himself nor the club. He played a few games with Colorado, wound up in the minors, and retired in 1980. Neely went into business and became the district sales manager for Snap-On Tools in Ontario.

NEELY, Cam
b. Comox, British Columbia, June 6, 1965
A power forward is a player who can score because of his skill and size, a guy who is strong enough to muscle his way to the net, to go through, rather than around, defencemen, a player who hits as well as dekes. The term was introduced with Neely in mind, for no player in the game has ever been such a physical presence and such a prolific scorer, and been ravaged by injuries as a result of his style of play. He played 13 years in the league, but when he retired in 1996 at age 31, it was not because of old age. He spent his first three seasons in Vancouver, but defined his career in Boston, where he played his remaining games. He scored 50 goals 3 times, including '93-'94 when he hit 50 in just 49 games. His last five years were all shortened by serious injury, all to his lower body from heavy contact. He ruined his knee and missed an entire year; he suffered a serious thigh injury and a hip injury that was his final undoing, yet he always came back and scored as if he had never missed a game. Most famously, he hurt his knee as the result of a dirty hit by Ulf Samuelsson, master of the cheap shot, in the 1991 playoffs. Neely won the Masterton Trophy in 1994 for one of his comebacks and played in five All-Star Games. After two years of retirement, he tried to make a comeback at Boston's training camp but quickly realized his body simply couldn't endure the demands of the NHL game.

NEIL, Chris
b. Markdale, Ontario, June 18, 1979
Even young enforcers have an advantage over their older colleagues, and it was in part for that reason that Neil made Ottawa for 2001-02. He had been pro for two seasons, racking up the penalty minutes in the minors before impressing the Sens with his fighting. Despite seeing limited ice time, Neil also chipped in with 10 goals during his rookie season in the NHL. Unfortunately, he also fought off the ice, most notably in June 2001. He was charged with assault, pleaded guilty a year later to a lesser charge of common assault, and tried to resume his career a wiser man.

NEILSON, Jim ("Chief")
b. Big River, Saskatchewan, November 28, 1940
Hockey is a reasonably equal opportunity sport. Players come from the city and the country, from wealthy families and poor, from Canada and abroad. Few, though, came out of the nothing that was Neilson's childhood. Part Danish, part Cree, he grew up in St. Patrick's Catholic orphanage, getting an education and playing hockey with kids who had little hope of going making a mark in the world. His father was a mink rancher and his mother lived on a reserve, and when they separated Olaf Neilson thought an orphanage was the best place for his kids. Neilson was blessed with skill and an inner fight, and that's what got him into junior hockey with Prince Albert and then into the Rangers system. He played for the Blueshirts for a dozen years starting in 1962. He was a perfect blend of offensive ability and defensive grit, but a serious knee injury in February 1970 prevented him from making sharp turns for the rest of his days. He was with the team as it became a Cup contender in the early 1970s, but he was claimed by California in 1974 and played his final four years in that lowly organization. He had one final go of it in the WHA with Wayne Gretzky and the Oilers, but chronic back pain forced him to retire. He initially worked as an Oilers scout out west for a year and a half, then he moved to California as part owner of a golf course. Three years later, he returned to Canada to join the federal Native Economic Development Program. He even played with Sagkeeng, a native team based in Manitoba that raised money for the development of native players. His son, David, made it as far as the AHL.

NELSON, Gord
b. Kinistino, Saskatchewan, May 10, 1947
At the age of 20, Nelson turned pro with Tulsa and for two years the defenceman plied his trade on the Oilers' blueline. The Leafs signed him to a tryout contract on December 10, 1969, and put him in that night's game as well as the games on December 11 and 13. They sent him back to Tulsa and from there

He scored 50 goals 3 times, including '93-'94 when he hit 50 in just 49 games.
CAM NEELY

Mike Needham

Bob Neely

Jim Neilson

Gord Nelson

he went to Phoenix for two years before retiring, his three NHL games a thing of the record books already.

Jeff Nelson

NELSON, Jeff
b. Prince Albert, Saskatchewan, December 18, 1972
The Nelson boys of Prince Albert – Jeff and Todd – both played a little in the NHL during lengthy pro careers. Jeff played with his brother with the local Raiders in the WHL before getting some time with Washington in 1994-95 and again the year after. The centreman was a decent scorer in the minors but had major trouble finding the net in the big league. He wound up a staple in the AHL and then in 2001 headed to Germany to play in the DEL.

NELSON, Todd
b. Prince Albert, Saskatchewan, May 11, 1969
The older of the Nelson boys got to the NHL first, but stayed a shorter period of time. Todd also came out of his hometown Raiders system to play for Pittsburgh and then Washington, but his minor-league career was where it all happened for him. He played for years in the IHL and AHL, spending most of his time in Grand Rapids after being the first player the expansion team signed in 1996. When he retired in 2002, he stayed with the team as an assistant coach.

Sergei Nemchinov

NEMCHINOV, Sergei ("Chimo")
b. Moscow, Soviet Union (Russia), January 14, 1964
For those who believe that New York is the centre of the universe, Nemchinov is half of the full answer to the following trivia question: Who are the only players to have played for all three New York-area teams (Devils, Rangers, Islanders)? Pat Conacher is the other half. Nemchinov was the 244th of 252 players drafted in 1990, his talent unquestioned but his place of origin a concern – would he ever be allowed to leave the Soviet Union? A year later, the answer was yes, and the Rangers were the beneficiaries. He had been a star back home, winning gold at the WC and WJC tournaments. When he joined the Blueshirts at age 27, he immediately established himself as a goal scorer and helped the team win the Cup in 1994. But after his first three seasons, in which he scored fewer and fewer goals, he was sent to Vancouver and from there to the Islanders and the Devils. Once a flashy skater, he is now a veteran at the end of his career. He won his second Cup with the Devils in 2000, and is now a two-way player rather than a sharpshooter with Lokomotiv Yaroslavl in the Russian league.

David Nemirovsky

NEMECEK, Jan
b. Pisek, Czechoslovakia (Czech Republic), February 14, 1976
Nemecek is a Czech from Pisek who moved to Quebec as a teen to play junior in Hull. He was a late L.A. draft choice in 1994 but played only seven games with the Kings before becoming a full-fledged minor-leaguer. He later gave up on the North American pro game to play in Germany.

Eric Nesterenko

NEMETH, Steve ("Stormin'")
b. Calgary, Alberta, February 11, 1967
As a kid playing junior in Lethbridge, Nemeth had big things to look forward to. He figured he'd finish his

Lance Nethery

junior career, join the National Team, and play for Canada at the Olympics right in his own backyard. He had the skill, and when he made the junior team in 1987 to play in Czechoslovakia, he felt sure he was that much closer to his dream. But something bad happened. At a crucial moment in a game in Piestany during the WJC, the Soviets started a brawl and the game went into the books as a disqualification. All players were suspended from international hockey for 18 months. The edict was handed down despite the fact that Nemeth never dropped his gloves and was the only player on either side who tried to restore order and stop the fighting. Of all players, he was the only one who was likely to make the '88 Olympics team for his country, so the injustice of the peacekeeper being given such a stiff penalty rankled him for years. He turned pro with the Rangers and spent much of the next three years in the minors and with the National Team after the Olympics, and afterwards embarked on a decade-long career in Britain. The one exception was the '97-'98 season, when he was a playing assistant coach in Tacoma. After retiring, he returned to Calgary and became involved in grassroots hockey.

NEMIROVSKY, David
b. Toronto, Ontario, August 1, 1976
Florida drafted Nemirovsky in 1994 and used him for four seasons, but when the Panthers had the chance to acquire prospect Jeff Ware, they sent Nemirovsky home to Toronto. Since then, his dream of playing at the ACC was never realized. After some time in St. John's, he left to play in Sweden in 2001-02 and later in Finland.

NESTERENKO, Eric ("Nester"/ "Elbows")
b. Flin Flon, Manitoba, October 31, 1933
In his early days, Nesterenko was a jack of all trades. He worked for Foster Hewitt one summer as a DJ for CKFH, he worked in construction, and he studied philosophy at the University of Western Ontario while playing for the Hawks at the same time. Later, when he moved to Chicago, he worked for a brokerage firm in Evanston, and when he retired from hockey he became a ski instructor at Vail, Colorado. But first, there was his start with the Leafs, where the right winger began in 1952 with teams that couldn't compete with the powerful clubs in Detroit and Montreal. He was sold to Chicago in 1956 and spent the next 16 years there, including the great season of 1960-61 when the team won the Stanley Cup. He was a player who could do everything well. He scored, played physically, stickhandled nicely, and backchecked. When his NHL days ended in 1972 after some 1,219 regular-season games, he headed to Switzerland to coach. In addition to his skiing pursuits, he also took up acting in a small way, taking a part in a 1979 CBC movie called *Cement Head* about hockey violence. He also coached at Trail, home to the World Champion Smoke Eaters.

NETHERY, Lance
b. Toronto, Ontario, June 28, 1957
After setting scoring records at Cornell, being named to NCAA all-star teams, and leading the ECAC in points, Nethery couldn't land much of a job in the NHL. He played for the Rangers in '80-'81, but 11 goals in 33

games wasn't good enough and he was sent to the minors. He accepted this lot for only a couple of years before going to Europe – and he hasn't come back! Nethery was a scoring sensation in Switzerland for years, and since retiring he has been a coach, starting with his former club, Davos. From there he became coach and GM with Kolner in the DEL in Germany, and in 2001-02 he ceded his coaching position to focus on being a manager.

NEUFELD, Ray ("Neufy")
b. St. Boniface, Manitoba, April 15, 1959

Neufeld played his first games in the NHL for Hartford the year the Whalers joined the NHL. In his first three seasons, he did little to impress coaches and by his own admission he wasn't ready for the big time. Then, his attitude changed and he became determined not to be a minor-leaguer. He started to hit, to use his hard shot, to play with confidence. He made the team, his ice time increased, and he scored. He had 3 seasons of 26 goals or more, and when his stock was at a high, the Whalers traded him to Winnipeg for Dave Babych. Neufeld's scoring declined, and then he was sent to Boston for Moe Lemay. He finished his career in the AHL in 1990.

NEVILLE, Mike
b. Toronto, Ontario
d. unknown

Neville played for Toronto in the NHL's earliest days, starting with the Toronto Arenas in 1917-18. He later played for the St. Pats and New York Americans, though most of his playing time came in the minors.

NEVIN, Bob ("Nevvy")
b. South Porcupine, Ontario, March 18, 1938

In the early years, Toronto was his life, but when he was traded, he felt betrayed, and when he was traded again he felt angered. Nevin won the Memorial Cup with the great Marlies team of the mid-1950s, in his case the '56 edition, and for the next three years apprenticed in the minors. He rose to prominence in game six of the 1962 finals when he scored the tying goal and assisted on the Cup winner, and he was part of a second Cup with Punch Imlach's team a year later. Imlach then traded Nevin, Rod Seiling, Dick Duff, Arnie Brown, and Bill Collins to the Rangers for Andy Bathgate and Don McKenney, a trade that some say helped the team win a third Cup in a row but left others feeling it prevented the team from winning every Cup of the 1960s. On Broadway, Nevin came into his own. He was named team captain and routinely scored more than 20 goals a season. He took the team deep into the playoffs, and when he was traded to

He rose to prominence in game six of the 1962 finals.
BOB NEVIN

Minnesota in 1971 he was upset. This was the reward for all he had given the team? He later had a 31-goal season for L.A. and after retiring he happily admitted that all he did was marry a wealthy woman and lead a life of leisure. He golfed, played in the odd old-timers' game, and enjoyed life. No hockey job, no business venture, no worries.

NEWBERRY, John
b. Port Alberni, British Columbia, April 8, 1962

After having two high-scoring years with the University of Wisconsin, Newberry played only briefly with Montreal (1982-86) before going to the minors and then on to Europe. He retired in 1993, returned to Canada, and became a firefighter in Victoria, B.C.

NEWELL, Rick
b. Winnipeg, Manitoba, February 18, 1948

An anonymous pro career in the 1970s brought Newell to Detroit for six games, but the defenceman played the rest of his years in the minors. He went to London, England, to dress for the Lions, Detroit's European farm team, but was rooted in the North American game besides. Newell was a 1970 grad of the University of Minnesota-Duluth.

NEWMAN, Dan
b. Windsor, Ontario, January 26, 1952

Few players make it out of Division III college hockey to the NHL, but Newman landed with the Rangers circuitously after leaving St. Clair College. He turned pro with Port Huron in the "I," and when the Rangers took possession of the club, it called Newman up for half a season in '76-'77. He wound up playing in Montreal and Edmonton as well before retiring in 1980.

NEWMAN, Johnny
b. Ottawa, Ontario, April 24, 1910
d. Hollywood, Florida, April 17, 1967

He played a few games with the Detroit Falcons in 1930 when he was still a kid and had no idea he'd never be back after being demoted to the Olympics. Newman played a decade of pro hockey, but the forward failed to impress GM Jack Adams to the point of seeing further action with the Wings or attracting interest from another NHL team.

NEWTON, Cam
b. Peterborough, Ontario, February 25, 1950

As a teen, Newton came out of nowhere to join the Marlies for their run to the 1967 Memorial Cup. After the usual 4 years of junior, he was drafted by Pittsburgh but appeared in just 16 games for the Pens. Dismayed by this lack of opportunity, Newton didn't

Ray Neufeld

Rick Newell

Dan Newman

Cam Newton

ignore the advances of the WHA, and in 1973 he signed with the Chicago Cougars. He had a fine first year with the team, building a record of 25-18-2, but he played less and less in the succeeding three seasons before he retired.

NICHOL, Scott
b. Edmonton, Alberta, December 31, 1974

All he ever wanted to do was play in the NHL, and all he continues to do is pursue that dream every day. Nichol was too small to make it, and his selection 272nd overall at the 1993 draft confirmed as much. Trouble was, Nichol wasn't prepared to accept the verdict, so he went to the minors and worked like crazy. He skated like a buzz saw, brought nothing but positive attitude to the dressing room, fought when he had to, and scored a few goals. At the end of '95-'96, the Sabres out of the playoffs, he got a call for the final two games. A couple of years later, three more games. He later signed with Calgary and played even more in 2001-02 on a team hoping to go to the post-season. He's been there and back and knows how far it is, and that's okay by him, as long as he gets to go there again.

Bernie Nicholls

NICHOLLS, Bernie
b. Haliburton, Ontario, June 24, 1961

He was a great scorer with quick hands and a dynamite shot, but like anyone else he was a different player when he was on a line with Wayne Gretzky. Nicholls started with L.A. in 1981, a city that was good for his character. He liked odd clothes, he liked a relaxed attitude as game time approached, he wasn't cut from the common cloth. Playing with Charlie Simmer, he had five 30-goal seasons, culminating with a 100-point year in '84-'85. Even that season, though, paled in comparison to his year with Gretzky. Nicholls scored a preposterous 70 goals and 150 points, numbers he had started to replicate the year after when he was traded to the Rangers. Down, down, down went his numbers, and soon he was packaged to the Oilers in the deal that sent Mark Messier to Broadway. In Edmonton, Nicholls got into a dispute with Glen Sather over money, and spent his last few years bouncing around and scoring in dribbles. He was as flamboyant on the ice as off, and his fist-pumping celebrations after scoring came to be known as Pumper Nicholls. He was known throughout the league to have a body fat count of about 5 percent, almost inhumanly low and testament to his fitness. By the time he retired in 1999, Nicholls had amassed 1,209 points, though he never came particularly close to winning a Cup.

Neil Nicholson

NICHOLSON, Al
b. Estevan, Saskatchewan, April 26, 1936
d. 1979

This is not something too many players can lay claim to: The first time Nicholson ever saw an NHL game in person was when he suited up for the Boston Bruins in 1955! The 19-year-old grew up in Estevan (his father was a concessionaire at the local auditorium) and played junior in Humboldt until the start of '55-'56, when he was farmed out to Hershey. He never had occasion or opportunity to see a big-league game, and then the B's called him up to play left wing. Little did he know that just 19 games later, he'd never play in the NHL again.

Paul Nicholson

Nonetheless, he played another 15 years of pro hockey, almost all in the WHL. He starred with San Francisco until 1966 when he became an original Gull in San Diego, and for all his years he was a remarkably consistent 25-goal scorer. He was released by the Gulls at training camp in '72-'73, his bum leg not healed after surgery. Nicholson stayed with the team as a salesman of program ads and season's tickets, a job he had held the previous three summers. He died of cancer.

NICHOLSON, Eddie ("Nick")
b. Portsmouth, Ontario, September 9, 1922
d. Kingston, Ontario, January 15, 1987

While most players of a certain generation lost part of their careers to the war, Nicholson actually gained from his enlistment, which lasted more than three years. While still a teen he was sent to Borden, England, where he worked in truck repair shops as a vulcanizer, but he also got to play hockey. The war being what it was, he played with and against some of the best in the game, name skaters such as Tony Licari, Sid Abel, Red Hamill, and Jackie Giesebrecht. By the time he returned to Canada in 1945, he was a better player than when he left, and while he waited to be discharged he played senior hockey in Kingston. He played the next two years with Detroit's farm team, Indianapolis, and was called up for one game. He travelled with the team for the '48 playoffs, though he never saw action, and the next year he was demoted for what turned out to be the rest of his career.

NICHOLSON, John "Hickey"
b. Charlottetown, Prince Edward Island,
September 9, 1911
d. November 22, 1956

Outside his two games with Chicago in '37-'38, Nicholson made a name for himself primarily in his hometown, though he did play for a short time in the American league before retiring in 1940.

NICHOLSON, Neil
b. Saint John, New Brunswick, September 12, 1949

At almost the exact instance Detroit was set to call Nicholson up to the Red Wings from Providence in January 1970 he suffered a season-ending injury in the AHL. He came back to play twice in the playoffs for the Wings but stagnated in the minors until the Islanders acquired him two years later. Over the next six years, he played a few games on Long Island and the rest in the minors, and soon after he decided to give Europe a go. He finished his playing days in Switzerland and then coached in Zurich for two years (1988-90) before coming upon a unique job. Realizing that only more and more Canadians would be playing overseas at the close of their careers or as an alternate to the minors, he became a player agent for Europe-bound stars.

NICHOLSON, Paul
b. London, Ontario, February 16, 1954

London is in his bones. It's where he played junior hockey until 1974, when he joined the Washington Capitals. And it's where he returned after his brief career ended in 1978 after four years spent mostly in the minors. Nicholson started his own business and ran power and skating schools, and he was an innovator for his work in youth hockey in London. He not only coached, he also constructed programs with Larry Riggin for coaches, to help them do their job better.

NICKULAS, Eric
b. Hyannis, Massachusetts, March 25, 1975
Not much has happened in the NHL life of Nickulas, who has been with Boston for a number of years but has played only a few games. He left the University of New Hampshire early to pursue a pro career in 1997, but has yet to make the team in anything more than a cursory capacity since.

NICOLSON, Graeme
b. North Bay, Ontario, January 13, 1958
After playing just one game with Boston in '78-'79, Nicolson was discouraged. After playing another full season without being recalled at all, he quit hockey to go back to school. A year later, he signed with Colorado, a team he likely would have a better chance with because it wasn't of the same quality as the Bruins. Yet after a decent half-season, he was left exposed in the Waiver Draft and the Rangers claimed him, only to use him a sparse 10 times on the season. Nicolson retired in 1985 after two more years in the minors.

NIECKAR, Barry
b. Rama, Saskatchewan, December 16, 1967
In the 1990s in the AHL, Nieckar amassed 491 penalty minutes in 65 games, testament to his work as an enforcer. Everywhere he has been he has been a fighter, even in lowly England where he beat people up for London and Nottingham. He played 8 NHL games without registering a shot on goal, let alone a point, but he did collect 21 NHL penalty minutes, which are not as easy to scrape off the ice and frame above the mantel.

NIEDERMAYER, Rob
b. Cassiar, British Columbia, December 28, 1974
Here was a top prospect in junior in every sense of the word. Niedermayer was a big, strong centre for Medicine Hat who won a gold medal with Canada's juniors in 1993. In that year's draft, he went to Florida 5th overall behind only Alexandre Daigle, Chris Pronger, Chris Gratton, and Paul Kariya. Yet his eight years with the Panthers produced mixed results. He helped the team go to the finals in 1996, the year he broke out with 26 goals. But, he has yet to come close to that number again and many around the league consider him damaged goods. He has suffered a series of concussions that forced him to miss almost half a year, and when he was traded to Calgary in 2001-02 his play remained average. Blessed with talent, the head

injuries seem to have gotten the better of him for now – though hopefully not for the rest of his career.

NIEDERMAYER, Scott
b. Edmonton, Alberta, August 31, 1973
Whether he is more or less talented than his brother, Rob, is a moot point. What does count is that Scott, another high draft choice, has lived up to his billing and performed like a 3rd-overall selection should play. He won a gold with Canada at the 1991 WJC and made his debut with the Devils at the end of the following season. Since 1992 he has spent his every hockey day with New Jersey, leading the team to two Stanley Cups and, with Scott Stevens, anchoring the blueline. Niedermayer has great offensive ability with an explosive stride and excellent passing and he has proved resilient during his decade with the team. More recently, he has been involved in two high-profile cases of violence. In March 2000, he swung his stick at Florida goon Peter Worrell's head and was suspended 10 games. Then, during the Toronto-New Jersey playoff series in 2001, he was knocked unconscious by a cowardly elbow from Leafs goon Tie Domi, who was suspended the rest of the series and the first eight games of the next season. Niedermayer played for Canada at the 2002 Olympics in Salt Lake City, helping bring gold back to his country.

Niedermayer played for Canada at the 2002 Olympics in Salt Lake City.
SCOTT NIEDERMAYER

NIEKAMP, Jim
b. Detroit, Michigan, March 11, 1946
Niekamp spent five years in the minors trying to break into the NHL, but his only chances came with Detroit in '70-'71 and the year after. The tough-minded defenceman didn't make a strong enough impression with the Wings, but he did with the Los Angeles Sharks of the WHA, which offered him a contract. He spent the next five years in that league and retired in 1977.

NIELSEN, Chris
b. Moshi, Tanzania, February 16, 1980
Sure, the modern NHL is international, but this is ridiculous! Nielsen's father, Jim, was in Tanzania working for the Canadian International Development Agency, teaching the people how to farm. When Chris was a year old, the family returned to Canada and settled in Goodlands, Manitoba, a more likely place for a future NHLer to grow up. He was a scholar and an athlete as a teen and also won a humanitarian award while playing for Calgary in the WHL. He was drafted by the Islanders but traded to Columbus, making his NHL debut on December 14, 2000. Nielsen is blessed with speed, but is still developing, his best years well in the future.

Barry Nieckar

Rob Niedermayer

Jim Niekamp

Jeff Nielsen

Ville Nieminen

Kraig Nienhuis

Frank Nighbor

NIELSEN, Jeff
b. Grand Rapids, Minnesota, September 20, 1971
A graduate of the University of Minnesota, Nielsen was drafted by the Rangers but had his best years with Anaheim as a digger and checker who could chip in with a few goals. He played for the U.S. at the 2000 World Championships, but then signed with Minnesota and suffered a concussion in November. He was released at season's end, and although Carolina showed interest in the right winger, he has yet to play for the 'Canes or any other team since 2001.

NIELSEN, Kirk
b. Grand Rapids, Michigan, October 19, 1973
Named Harvard's athlete scholar during his four years at the Ivy League school (1992-96), Nielsen was an outstanding defenceman and prospect and the brother of Jeff from U of Minnesota. Kirk didn't last nearly as long in the NHL. He got a quick chance with Boston in '97-'98, but after spending the year in the minors he opted to sign with an IHL team, Cincinnati, rather than stay in a Bruins system that offered little hope. After just a year with the Cyclones, though, Nielsen retired.

NIEMI, Antti-Jussi
b. Vantaa, Finland, September 22, 1977
He hasn't yet made an impact in the NHL, but Niemi has twice played for his country internationally, at the 2000 and 2001 World Championships. He was drafted by Ottawa and later traded to Anaheim, for which he has played his few NHL games. He has been trying to make a favourable impression in the minors, though to little effect so far. He began his career as a pro for Jokerit in Finland.

NIEMINEN, Ville ("Nemo")
b. Tampere, Finland, April 6, 1977
A junior in Finland, Nieminen is the perfect example of the modern European. After being drafted in 1997, he made his way to Colorado where the Avs assigned him to the minors. He made his NHL debut on January 29, 2000, and the next year was recalled four times. The first three were brief visits during which time he impressed management. During the fourth callup, the team decided he couldn't be sent back and he helped the Avs win the Cup in the spring of 2001. He was later traded to Pittsburgh as part of the deal to bring Darius Kasparaitis to the Avs for what proved to be an unsuccessful playoff run in 2002.

NIENHUIS, Kraig
b. Sarnia, Ontario, May 9, 1961
The son of Dutch immigrants who settled in Ontario in the 1950s, Nienhuis grew up in Sarnia and attended RPI on a scholarship. The understated left winger helped the Engineers win an NCAA championship in '84-'85, and then signed with the Bruins as a free agent. He was given a full year's apprenticeship with the B's as a rookie, but in his second and third years his time dwindled to close to nothing. He then moved to Europe and had a successful career, primarily in Austria where he played long enough to gain citizenship for the World Championships in 1996. He finished his career in 2001 in the United league with Port Huron, a stone's throw across the river from his hometown.

NIEUWENDYK, Joe
b. Oshawa, Ontario, September 10, 1966
It all makes sense when you look at the whole package. His brother, Gil, is a fine official. His cousin is Jeff Beukeboom and his uncle is Ed Kea. He grew up with Gary Roberts, and Nieuwendyk was considered the finest lacrosse player in the country, winner of the Minto Cup, the über-championship in that sport. Nieuwendyk was drafted by Calgary in 1985 and was a Flames star for the first nine years of his career. He won the Calder Trophy by scoring 51 goals in his first full season, and shook off any talk of a sophomore jinx by scoring 51 in his second season, a year in which he scored 10 more times in the drive to the Stanley Cup. Nieuwendyk used his lacrosse-carved body to become a dominant power forward. He had remarkable speed and physical strength, the combination of which intimidated many an opponent. The only reason the Flames traded him, in 1995, was to acquire Jarome Iginla, a next-generation Nieuwendyk. In Dallas, he combined with Mike Modano to form a great one-two punch up the middle, and he won his second Cup, with the Stars, in 1999 when he also was named winner of the Conn Smythe Trophy. In recent years, he has been ravaged by serious knee injuries, but his tremendous conditioning has kept him at the top of the heap. He was named to Canada's Olympic team for 2002, a move for which GM Wayne Gretzky received some criticism, but that dissipated when Nieuwendyk et al. won gold in the tournament. Nieuwendyk was traded again, in early 2002, to the Devils, and it is with that team he scored his 500th goal and recorded his 1,000th career point during what is shaping up to be a Hall of Fame career.

His brother, Gil, is a fine official. His cousin is Jeff Beukeboom and his uncle is Ed Kea.
JOE NIEUWENDYK

NIGHBOR, Frank ("The Pembroke Peach")
b. Pembroke, Ontario, January 26, 1893
d. Pembroke, Ontario, April 13, 1966
By the age of four, Nighbor was skating on the Muskrat and Ottawa rivers, learning the fundamentals of hockey. He became a sensation in leagues as he grew

up, but was considered too small and fragile for the professional ranks. In 1911, he was benefactor to a fine gesture by a friend, Harry Cameron. Cameron was invited to play for Port Arthur, but he refused to go unless the team also took Nighbor. It agreed, but Nighbor sat on the bench game after game until finally an injury precipitated his use. He scored six goals in his first game, and by the following year was being recruited by the Toronto Blueshirts for play in the NHA. He moved to Vancouver a year later and soon helped the Millionaires capture the Stanley Cup in 1915. Nighbor then returned to Ottawa to play in the NHA again, and he stayed with the Senators for the next 15 years. He was master of the sweep check, a method of taking the puck off an opponent's stick that had never been seen before and confounded all attackers who tried to get around him. But he was a centreman and was equally skilled and crafty when he had the puck. He helped the Sens win four Cups in the 1920s with the first semi-dynasty in the NHL, and in '23–'24 he was the first winner of the new Hart Trophy. A year later, he was again the inaugural winner of the Lady Byng Trophy, an honour he received again the following season. He closed out his career in Toronto in '29–'30 and was offered a chance to coach the team, but had to return home to care for his wife, who was dying of tuberculosis. He later coached in Buffalo and London in the International league but in 1935 he left hockey to run an insurance business he had started with a partner many years earlier. He did so until stricken by serious illness. In 1947 he was inducted into the Hockey Hall of Fame, and he succumbed to cancer in 1966.

NIGRO, Frank
b. Richmond Hill, Ontario, February 11, 1960
Where you were born and what country you play for are two different things. Just ask Nigro, who played for Italy at three World Championships ("B" pool) and the 1992 Olympics in Albertville. He has no affiliation with Italy, but any player who plays for three years in Italy becomes an "Italo" and can represent Italy at an international competition (provided he hasn't played for another country previously). It wasn't supposed to be that way for Nigro. He was drafted by the Leafs in 1979, and that's when his troubles began. He went back to junior for '79–'80 and broke his wrist. The injury required the insertion of a pin, and he missed the year. He attended Leafs training camp in 1980, but in an exhibition game his back was broken by a vicious cross-check and he missed another year. The year after, he tore knee ligaments and missed half a season, and now his body looked more like something from an anatomy lesson than one ready for serious hockey action. The Leafs played him for about a year and a half and then gave up on him, and that's when he moved to Italy to pursue a second-tier career – a very successful one, too. After retiring in 1992, Nigro returned to Richmond Hill and started a landscaping business.

NIINIMAA, Janne
b. Raahe, Finland, May 22, 1975
Needless to say, any time a 16-year-old plays at the World Juniors it seems like a good bet he's going to be considered a great prospect. Niinimaa played at three

WJCs, two World Championships, and the 1996 World Cup – all by the time he was 19. When he joined the Flyers in '96 right after the World Cup, he was a teen with a man's experience and ready for the NHL. In two seasons, he established himself as one of the great young defencemen in the league, and won a bronze medal with Finland at the 1998 Olympics in Nagano. The Flyers traded him to Edmonton for Dan McGillis and a draft choice in early 1998, and he became part of a talented Oilers blueline corps, capable of generating offence and moving the puck quickly and reliably. None of that chip-it-off-the-glass stuff from Niinimaa, who was later traded to the Rangers in March 2003.

Frank Nigro

NIKOLISHIN, Andrei
b. Vorkuta, Soviet Union (Russia), March 25, 1973
He's one of the first players any coach for Russia chooses for an international tournament, and Nikolishin is a strong and tenacious player with excellent hands. He won't score a pile of goals, but he will make the big play to generate scoring chances. Nikolishin won a gold medal with Russia at the 1994 Olympics in Lillehammer and joined Hartford near the start of the following season. He was traded to Washington about two years later, and he's been a Caps forward ever since, notably in 1997-98 when the team went to the finals for the first time.

NIKULIN, Igor
b. Cherepovets, Soviet Union (Russia), August 26, 1972
A one-game wonder with a twist, insofar as his only NHL appearance, with Anaheim, came during the 1997 playoffs. After three years in the minors in North America he returned to Russia to play in the league there, never having been given a second chance with the Ducks.

NILAN, Chris
b. Boston, Massachusetts, February 9, 1958
Let's see. There was the two-game suspension for throwing a puck at Paul Baxter. Two games for a fight with Curt Fraser that spilled into the corridors after both had been tossed from the game. There was an eight-game sentence for butt-ending Rick Middleton in the mouth. There was the time at an exhibition game prior to the 1984 Canada Cup that sucker-punched Rick Vaive in a parking lot outside the Forum. There were the five games he was suspended as a coach for coming to the aid of one of his players, but that was with Chesapeake in the East Coast league, so that hardly counts. Nilan survived in the NHL for 13 years as a tough, competitive player, but he was a goon, first and foremost. His job was to beat players up, intimidate them, scare them, hurt them. He was very good at his job, and by the time a final run-in with Montreal coach Jean Perron got him a trade to the Rangers, he was the Canadiens' all-time penalty minutes leader. No mean feat, that. Twice he led the league in penalties, later in his career he got to play for his hometown Bruins, and he won a Cup with Montreal in 1986, the playoff season he amassed 141 penalty minutes in just 18 games. He was no dumdum, though. He had studied, appropriately, criminal law at Northeastern University, and after retiring in 1992 he became a successful coach in the ECHL.

Janne Niinimaa

Chris Nilan

Jim Nill

Marcus Nilson

Kent Nilsson

Lou Nistico

Reg Noble

NILL, Jim
b. Hanna, Alberta, April 11, 1958
How would you like to come from an itty-bitty town, make a great NHL career for yourself, and still be the *second* most famous person around? That was Nill's fate, but, of course, he'll happily take second billing when the number-one son is a guy named Lanny McDonald. Nill was a stable, travelling winger in his day. He never scored much but, as coaches would say, he did many small things well. From the day he joined St. Louis in 1981 to the day he retired in 1991, he was a strong player whose teams almost always made the playoffs. Toward the end, he suffered two serious injuries, to a knee and a shoulder, and after retiring he stayed in the game. He first did some scouting for Ottawa, and then moved into the Detroit organization as assistant GM, helping the team win three Cups, in 1997, 1998, and 2002. Nill was also named director of player personnel for Team Canada at the 2003 World Championships.

NILSON, Marcus
b. Balsta, Sweden, March 1, 1978
A young pup, Nilson is developing according to plan with Florida. He's made slow but steady progress since joining the team from Sweden in 1998, and after two years mostly spent in the minors he has been a full-time Panthers forward since 2000.

NILSSON, Kent ("Magic Man"/ "Kenta")
b. Nynashamn, Sweden, August 31, 1956
Hockey Night in Canada is the best, most important hockey show in the world because of moments like this. To start a profile on Nilsson one time, an interviewer talked with him in a corner of the ice. The broadcaster pointed to the goal 65 metres away and asked Nilsson how many shots it would take for him to hit its crossbar. One shot later, the hockey world had its answer. Moments like that earned him the nickname Magic Man, trick skills like that gave Wayne Gretzky reason to call Nilsson the best, most purely skilled player he had ever seen. Perhaps nothing typifies the compliment more than the "Nilsson feint" a move in which he dekes a goalie to one side, shifts hands, and puts the puck in the empty side of the net. Peter Forsberg perfected the move to give Sweden a gold at the 1994 Olympics in a shootout with Canada, but it was a Nilsson patent. He came to the WHA in 1977 at age 21 and joined Atlanta in the NHL 2 years later. He had three 40-goal seasons and two 30-goal years, twice hitting the magic 100-point mark. He averaged better than a point a game in his pro career, which finished, more or less, with Edmonton in 1987, winning a Cup. He returned to Europe and then went on a magical tour of the Continent, playing everywhere from Austria and Spain to the bigger hockey-playing nations such as Switzerland and, of course, Sweden. He returned to the Oilers for a few games in 1995, and when he retired, his place as one of the greats was firm and secure in the minds of hockey fans around the world. He settled in Stockholm and became the Oilers' European scout.

NILSSON, Ulf (Lil-Projsarn)
b. Nynashamn, Sweden, May 11, 1950
From the time he made his grand international entrance at the 1972 Izvestia tournament, Nilsson played like a star. The year after, he appeared at the World Championships playing with Ulf Sterner and Stig-Goran Johansson, and in the 1976 Canada Cup, Canadian fans got to see what the fuss was about. After that tournament, he joined the WHA with Winnipeg, forming the first international line in the history of the game, playing alongside Bobby Hull and Anders Hedberg. The threesome broke all scoring records in the league and proved the most exciting line in that league. When he joined the Rangers in 1978 with Hedberg, though, Nilsson suffered a rash of injuries that limited his effectiveness. His passing was still evident, but his scoring diminished. After retiring, Nilsson worked for a Swedish beverage company and in real estate. Most recently, he has been employed by Bredbandsbolaget, an IT company.

NISTICO, Lou
b. Thunder Bay, Ontario, January 25, 1953
A colourful character, Nistico played his best hockey in the WHA with the Toronto/Birmingham entry. Bulls coach Pat Kelly later moved to Colorado of the NHL and brought Nistico in for three games, but he hurt his leg and had to retire. He played in the Allan Cup with Brantford in 1978 and also for the Welland Sunys of the Canadian International League, a team that toured Austria and Yugoslavia. Nistico coached intermediate hockey in Flamboro for four years by night and worked for Carling O'Keefe by day. He later moved to Ottawa to become the brewery's eastern region sales manager.

NOBLE, Reg
b. Collingwood, Ontario, June 23, 1896
d. Alliston, Ontario, January 25, 1962
One of 10 children raised in a small house in Collingwood, Noble rose to fame and prominence as a hockey star in the NHL's formative years. Even in childhood and his early teens he displayed a skill for skating and puckhandling that earned him a reputation well beyond his waterfront home. In 1915, he was invited to attend St. Michael's College in Toronto, but was found on the rink more often than in a classroom and was quietly asked to leave. This proved to be an ironic "career" with St. Mike's insofar as the school later boasted that Noble was the first of dozens of alumni to go on to play in the NHL! He ended the year with the Toronto Humbersides and turned pro the next year with the Blueshirts of the NHA. When the NHL was formed another year later, Noble stayed in Toronto and played on a line with Babe Dye and Corb Denneny, the best combination in the league. The Arenas won the Cup that first season and again in 1922 when the team had changed names to the St. Pats. He was sold to the Maroons early in the '24-'25 season, and by the following year was moved from forward to defence. It proved a fortuitous decision. He was paired with Dunc Munro, and the team won the Cup in 1926. After another year, though, Montreal believed Noble was at the end of the line. Detroit GM Jack Adams disagreed and brought him to the Cougars and Noble, indeed, played on and on. He ended his playing days in '33-'34 with Cleveland in the IHL and then went into refereeing. In 1939, at the start of the war, he worked

for the federal government in the military. He was stationed at Camp Borden, in construction engineering, and he also coached an airforce team there. He later flew missions over Europe in 1944, and remained in the military the rest of his life. He died of a massive heart attack early in 1962, just a few months before he was inducted into the Hockey Hall of Fame.

NOEL, Claude
b. Kirkland Lake, Ontario, October 31, 1955
Nothing but zeroes follow Noel's seven games in the NHL, given to him by Washington after the Caps signed him as a free agent in 1979. He played many years in the AHL and IHL, and then got into the coaching game in those leagues. He moved up to Milwaukee, farm team of the NHL's Nashville entry, and after being let go he was named coach and director of personnel for the Toledo Storm of the ECHL in 2002.

NOLAN, Owen ("Buster")
b. Belfast, Ireland, February 12, 1972
It's been a bit of a strange ride for Nolan, the 1st-overall draft pick in 1990, by Quebec. He had an awful rookie season, scoring just three goals and looking like a 1st-overall bust à la Doug Wickenheiser. Then he scored 42 goals and added 183 penalty minutes to look like the best young power forward in the game. He became feared for his blistering wrist shot and tremendous strength, but the team, now in Colorado, traded him near the start of what would be a Stanley Cup season in 1995-96. He wound up in San Jose and seemed to get his second wind, becoming not just a scorer and hitter but an experienced leader with one of the youngest, most talented teams in the NHL. He became Sharks captain in 1998, and his career hit a high note in February 2002 when he helped Canada win Olympic gold. In March 2003, he was traded to Toronto in the hopes of leading the team to a Stanley Cup.

NOLAN, Pat "Paddy"
b. Charlottetown, Prince Edward Island, December 1, 1897
d. New Glasgow, Nova Scotia, April 12, 1957
Nolan spent most of his career in the Maritimes but he did play twice for the Toronto St. Pats in December 1921.

NOLAN, Theodore "Ted"
b. Sault Ste. Marie, Ontario, April 7, 1958
In one respect, Nolan's playing career is insignificant in the broader context of his life. He played briefly for Detroit and Pittsburgh in the mid-1980s and had to retire after rupturing two discs in his lower back.

His career hit a high note in February 2002 when he helped Canada win Olympic gold.
OWEN NOLAN

Like so many before him, he wanted to stay in the game as a coach, and like so many, he paid his dues. He joined the Soo Greyhounds in 1988. Three years later he was coach of the year, and further two years after that he brought the team its first Memorial Cup. These accomplishments rightly earned him an assistant's job with Hartford in 1994, and a year later he was named head coach of Buffalo. In his first season with the Sabres, he started to turn the team around; in his second year, he brought the team into the playoffs with a record of 40-30-12 and won the Jack Adams Award. The numbers tell only part of the story, though, for Nolan accomplished this with a bad team full of non-stars. His coaching, motivation, and abilities to lead, explain, and motivate were all widely hailed as the reasons the Sabres won even once all year. That summer, he became involved in a contract dispute and was replaced by Lindy Ruff. From that day to this, he hasn't worked in the NHL. Pro-Nolan supporters claim that racism is behind his blacklisting. An Ojibwa, he is a hero to the First Nations community, and no one can figure out why he hasn't been hired. Some say his temper and personality are not worth the bother, and Nolan did spurn two offers. One, to coach in Tampa, he rejected because of an awful ownership question, and the other, as an assistant with the Islanders, he felt was too much of a gamble on his part. Other difficult coaches have routinely found work (Mike Keenan, Pat Burns), but Nolan remains unemployed, spending his time with Native kids and developing players and programs to help them learn the game.

Ted Nolan

NOLET, Simon
b. St. Odilon, Quebec, November 23, 1941
As much as anyone of his era, Nolet came to life in 1967 with expansion. Prior to that year, he didn't get a single chance in the NHL, but when he joined the new Flyers he embarked on a 10-year career in the league. Nolet became a decent scorer and a smart and team-oriented player. He won a Cup with the team in 1974, and just a few days later was claimed by Kansas City in the Expansion Draft, going from the best team to the worst in one fell swoop. After ending his career in 1977, Nolet returned to Quebec City to work for a brewery but soon got back into the game as a scout and then assistant coach for the local Nordiques. He then joined the Flyers as a scout, convincing them to select Simon Gagne in 1998, one of their best moves of the last decade. The Nolet-Gagne connection was more than fleeting. Nolet had gone to Flyers camp with Gagne's father, who didn't make the team and went on to become a police officer. Nolet watched the young Gagne grow up, and knew well he was a "player" in the NHL sense.

Simon Nolet

Brian Noonan

NOONAN, Brian
b. Boston, Massachusetts, May 29, 1965

For some players, it's the NHL or nothing. Wayne Gretzky does not wind down his career playing in the "I," for instance, but Noonan has no problem with that. After a dozen years and more than 600 games in the big show, he went down to the IHL and played another 3 years before retiring in 2001. Along the way, he spent most of his career with Chicago and the Rangers, winning the Cup on Broadway in 1994. The Hawks had drafted him in 1983 while he was still in high school, and he made the team four years later after some time in the minors.

Robert Nordmark

NORDMARK, Robert
b. Lulea, Sweden, August 20, 1962

Nordmark was drafted by St. Louis and joined the team in the fall of 1987 for a number of reasons. One, he had won silver with the Swedes at the '86 World Championships and gold at the '87 tournament. Two, he had size and strength, making him, in the eyes of NHL types, an atypical European of that vintage. Three, Ric Nattress was on his way out of town and the Blues needed a top-flight defender to fill his skates. Nordmark lasted one season in St. Louis before being traded to Vancouver, where he played the better part of three years. He then returned to Europe to keep playing in Sweden and elsewhere, winning another silver at the '95 WC. Most recently, he played in Britain with Nottingham.

Peter Nordstrom

NORDSTROM, Peter
b. Munkfors, Sweden, July 26, 1974

He wasn't drafted until he was 24 years old, and Boston's gamble didn't reap much more than token rewards. Nordstrom played twice for the B's in '98-'99 but afterwards, as before, he played in the Swedish league. He also represented Tre Kronor at the 2000 World Championships, a fifth-place showing for the Swedes.

Dwayne Norris

NORIS, Joe
b. Denver, Colorado, October 26, 1951

There's a one-eyed Jack and a one-horse town, a one-way street and a one-hit wonder. And then there's a one-R'd Noris. He played parts of three seasons in the NHL in the 1970s, but made San Diego his life. As a player, he was the only man to be a part of all three San Diego teams – the Gulls of the WHL, the Mariners of the WHA, and the Hawks of the PHL. When he retired in 1979, he settled in San Diego and became involved in a number of hockey-related businesses. He coached kids hockey, and in 1990 became president of the San Diego Barracudas of the roller hockey league. In 1996, he played on the national-champion San Diego Hosers, and he also hosts a sports radio program devoted to hockey both on ice and on blades.

Mattias Norstrom

NORONEN, Mika
b. Tampere, Finland, June 17, 1979

It's way too early to make sweeping statements about the kid, but he brings with him words that suggest he might be the best goalie Finland has ever produced. He hasn't played much with Buffalo yet, but in the post-Hasek age he'll be given plenty of chance to prove his worth. In the 2000 Calder Cup playoffs in the AHL, he set a record with six shutouts. He has also played for his country at both the World Juniors and the World Championships.

NORRIS, Dwayne ("Newf")
b. St. John's, Newfoundland, January 8, 1970

It's one thing to play for Canada at the World Juniors, but in 1990 Norris scored the gold medal-winning goal in the final game of the tournament, a 2-1 win over the Czechs. He was on leave from Michigan State, where he was playing on scholarship while working toward a degree in construction. He was drafted by Quebec, and after graduating played for the National Team and on into the 1994 Olympics in Lillehammer. He joined Quebec soon after, but over the next three years played mostly in the minors. In 1996, he accepted an offer to play in Germany, and he's been there ever since, skating for Kolner.

NORRIS, Jack
b. Saskatoon, Saskatchewan, August 5, 1942

It's something he'll never be able to shake, even though he's not at fault. Norris was one of the players Boston sent to Chicago to get Phil Esposito, Ken Hodge, and Fred Stanfield in 1967, one of the worst deals the Hawks, or any team, ever made. Norris hadn't seen much action with Boston, didn't see much more with Chicago, and still didn't play much in L.A. after he was traded there. He wound up going to the WHA for the last four years of his career.

NORRISH, Rod
b. Saskatoon, Saskatchewan, November 27, 1951

Coming out of junior with Regina in 1971, Norrish joined Cleveland in the AHL and promptly broke his leg. He missed half a year, and over the next 3 seasons he played just 21 games with the North Stars, the team that had drafted him. He retired in 1975.

NORSTROM, Mattias
b. Stockholm, Sweden, January 2, 1972

Norstrom has been a marquee defenceman for Sweden and in the NHL for the last decade. He had his beginnings of greatness at the 1992 World Juniors, winning a silver medal, and joined the Rangers in '93. He slowly but surely established himself as a heavy hitter and superior shotblocker. He was traded to L.A. in 1996 in a huge, multiplayer deal, and because those teams made the playoffs so infrequently he also had the chance to play for his country at the World Championships four times over the years. He has also played at the World Cup and Olympics, and although he never puts many points up on the board he is one of the best at keeping the other team's best at bay.

NORTHCOTT, Lawrence "Baldy"
b. Calgary, Alberta, September 7, 1908
d. Winnipeg, Manitoba, November 7, 1986

A less heralded star in the NHL for 11 seasons, Northcott was a fine player with the Montreal Maroons for 10 of those seasons. The pinnacle of his years came in 1934-35 when he led the playoffs in goals (4) and scored the Cup-winning goal against the

Leafs to give the M's a 3-0 sweep of Toronto. On defence, he was credited with checking Charlie Conacher onto the ice. Northcott twice scored 20 goals in a season, a benchmark of offensive ability in the old days, and he played a final season with Chicago before retiring in 1939. He settled in Winnipeg and later opened an electrical appliance store with Tom Johnson of the Canadiens.

NORTON, Brad
b. Cambridge, Massachusetts, February 13, 1975
It's a long time between that magical draft day and the even more magical first NHL game, and the months and years in between present an emotional challenge not for everyone. Norton was chosen by Edmonton in 1993, but it wasn't until after four years of college and five years in the minors that he made his NHL debut, with Florida. The big, tough defenceman played 22 games for the Panthers, but in 2002 was acquired by the Kings and became a more consistent presence on the Los Angeles blueline.

NORTON, Jeff
b. Acton, Massachusetts, November 25, 1965
One of the NHL's passport kings, Norton has been here, there, and everywhere since entering the league in 1987. He's been a Sharks player three times, a Panthers twice. He's played for the Islanders, Blues, Oilers, Lightning, Penguins, and Bruins – and he's still going strong as he approaches 1,000 games. His longest stint was his first, a 6-year stay with the Islanders, but since then he's been lucky to play 100 games with any given team before being traded.

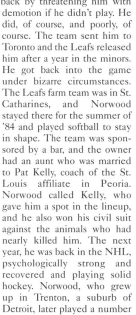

He wound up going to the WHA for the last four years of his career.
JACK NORRIS

NORWICH, Craig
b. Edina, Minnesota, December 15, 1955
Norwich played but two seasons in the NHL, 1979-80 with Winnipeg and the year after with St. Louis and Colorado. His experience in the game, though, started well before this and continues to this day. He earned a B.A. from the University of Wisconsin and went on to play in Europe for eight years. After retiring, he became the director of hockey and the head coach for Shattuck St. Mary's in Faribault, Minnesota, a dual position he held for six years. In 1996, Norwich moved to Vail and became the director of the AAA program, and in 1999 he was named head coach of the Rochester Mustangs of the UHL. In 1998, he received his Elite Level Coaching Certificate, which he completed through the Latvian Ice Hockey Federation. He also played for the U.S. at four World Championships.

NORWOOD, Leonard "Lee"
b. Oakland, California, February 2, 1960
After what happened to him at training camp in 1982, Norwood was happy just to be alive. He started his career with Quebec in 1979 but was traded to Washington midway through the '81-'82 season. Prior to training camp in '82, he attended a Save the Caps rally and then went to a bar with friends. On his way out, he was attacked by three underage kids who had been thrown out of the bar and who mistook Norwood for the bouncer. They beat him long past the point of consciousness, and when he awoke in hospital the damage was considerable: a shattered face, a cracked skull, a broken jaw, eight lost teeth, a severe concussion. He spent 10 days in intensive care. Unbelievably, the Caps forced him back by threatening him with demotion if he didn't play. He did, of course, and poorly, of course. The team sent him to Toronto and the Leafs released him after a year in the minors. He got back into the game under bizarre circumstances. The Leafs farm team was in St. Catharines, and Norwood stayed there for the summer of '84 and played softball to stay in shape. The team was sponsored by a bar, and the owner had an aunt who was married to Pat Kelly, coach of the St. Louis affiliate in Peoria. Norwood called Kelly, who gave him a spot in the lineup, and he also won his civil suit against the animals who had nearly killed him. The next year, he was back in the NHL, psychologically strong and recovered and playing solid hockey. Norwood, who grew up in Trenton, a suburb of Detroit, later played a number of years for the Wings, and after retiring in 1994 returned to Detroit to work as a strength and conditioning coach for the team. He also owned a golf course in the area, but worked primarily as a senior loans officer for a Michigan-based mortgage company.

NOVOSELTSEV, Ivan
b. Golitsyno, Soviet Union (Russia), January 23, 1979
Young and developing, Novoseltsev is an able left winger who has the size and shot to do well. He joined Florida in 1999 and has been with the team ever since, but is still learning how to play at the top level and his final contribution to the NHL game is years away from being evaluated.

NOVY, Milan ("Balik")
b. Kladno, Czechoslovakia (Czech Republic), September 23, 1951
His nickname translates to country bumpkin and refers to his humble childhood in a small town. By the time he retired, they were calling him hero. Novy was one of the greats to come out of Czechoslovakia. In his

Baldy Northcott

Jeff Norton

Craig Norwich

Lee Norwood

Ivan Novoseltsev

Milan Novy

Hank Nowak

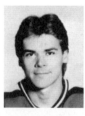

Teppo Numminen

Mike Nykoluk

Michael Nylander

first year of pro at home, in 1972-73, he led the league in scoring, and he never let up for almost 20 years, becoming the all-time scoring leader in Czech league history. He played in seven World Championships, was named player of the year at home three times, and scored one of the most important goals in the country's history. At the 1976 Canada Cup, he was the lone scorer in the Czechs' 1-0 win over Canada, the first time Czechoslovakia beat the great Canada. Novy joined Washington in 1982 at age 31. It was his only year in the NHL and he scored a respectable 18 goals before returning home. After retiring, he worked as the team secretary for Kladno and then got out of the game altogether – working in the cosmetic business.

NOWAK, Hank
b. Oshawa, Ontario, November 24, 1950
Nowak took a circuitous route to the NHL. He was drafted by Philadelphia in 1970, claimed by Hershey in the Reverse Draft (which consigned him to the AHL), and sold to Pittsburgh, which then played him in 1973. The Penguins traded him quickly to Detroit, and the Wings traded him to Boston because they wanted him to be more physical. The Bruins used him 105 times over 3 seasons, and then he was in the minors for good, though that proved to be for only a little more than 3 years.

NUMMELIN, Petteri
b. Turku, Finland, November 25, 1972
Son of Finnish legend Timo, Petteri has had a fine career of his own in Europe, though it touched the NHL only briefly. The defenceman played most of his early pro hockey in his homeland before joining Frolunda in Sweden in 1995. Two years later he went to Switzerland to play, and it was while with Davos that the Columbus Blue Jackets took notice of him and made him a selection in the 2000 Entry Draft. He played one full season in the NHL with Columbus and then returned to Switzerland to continue his career, neither defeated by the NHL nor enamoured by its qualities as many of his countrymen have been. Nummelin has had his greatest impact at the international level. He played in his first World Championships in 1995 when Finland won its first gold medal, and played in seven successive tournaments. He later won a silver and a bronze, and at the 2001 WC he captained the team. During the 2001-02 season, though, he played at neither the 2002 Olympics at Salt Lake City nor the later WC, though for the new season he remained in Europe to continue his career. In 2002-03, he became only the second defenceman in Swiss league history to lead the league in scoring, a feat he accomplished with HC Lugano.

NUMMINEN, Teppo ("Repo")
b. Tampere, Finland, July 3, 1968
He is the Steve Yzerman of Winnipeg and Phoenix, and by the time he retires he will be called one of the greatest Finns of all time. By the time he joined Winnipeg at age 20 in 1988, he had already played in all major international tournaments. Since that time, he has played for only the Jets and Phoenix, and in 2001 he became the team's captain during a season in which he played his 1,000th game. With more than

500 career points and counting, he is one of the top-scoring European defencemen of all time, and his durability is confirmed by his 360-game Iron Man streak that ended in early 2000. He has played in three Olympics, something that made his father proud because the old man coached the Finnish National Team at Lake Placid in 1980.

NURMINEN, Kai
b. Turku, Finland, March 29, 1969
After joining Los Angeles for the 1996-97 season, Nurminen had a decent 16 goals on the left wing. The team didn't make the playoffs, he returned home to play for Finland, and it was three years before he came back. That happened when Minnesota signed him. The Wild threw him to the minors but did call him up for two games, and that's the last the NHL has seen of him so far.

NURMINEN, Pasi
b. Lahti, Finland, December 17, 1975
The 2001-02 season was a busy and successful one for Nurminen. He made his NHL debut with Atlanta. He played for Finland at the 2002 Olympics in Salt Lake City. In the minors, he led Chicago to the Calder Cup. And, he was named AHL playoff MVP for his efforts with the Wolves. He had been a star in the Finnish league, and in 2002-03 he made the Thrashers as a regular.

NYKOLUK, Mike
b. Toronto, Ontario, December 11, 1934
Most people of a certain generation remember Nykoluk as the not very successful coach of the Leafs in the early 1980s, while people from another time will remember him as – believe it or not – one of the best players in the history of the Hershey Bears. He started his career full of promise as a winger for the Marlies that won back-to-back Memorial Cups in '55 and '56, but played only 32 games with the Leafs the following year. These proved to be his only NHL games, and when he was demoted to Rochester he played a year and a half before being traded to the Bears. Nykoluk played 14 years in Chocolatetown, and when he retired in 1972 he ranked fourth on the list of all-time scorers in the AHL. He was named league MVP for '66-'67, and the team retired his number 8 at the end of his playing days. That summer, Nykoluk was hired as an assistant coach to Fred Shero in Philadelphia, only the third time such a position had been created by a team (after Al MacNeil with the Canadiens and Doug Harvey in Los Angeles). He won two Cups with the goons on Broad Street and then turned to colour commentary for radio until Harold Ballard convinced him to coach the Leafs in January 1981. In two and a half seasons the Leafs won all of one playoff game and he was fired. Nykoluk eased his way into retirement in Toronto.

NYLANDER, Michael
b. Stockholm, Sweden, October 3, 1972
There have been a few rocky days in Nylander's NHL life, but his international career is virtually a template of success. He helped Sweden win gold at the 1992 World Championships one of six he has competed in,

and he has won medals at the WJC, and played at the Olympics in both 1998 and 2002. A fluid skater and beautiful stickhandler, he is better suited to the European game, and while he has shown scoring ability on the European ice surface, he has been less effective in the more intense NHL. His career in North America began in 1992 with Hartford, but a year later he was demoted by coach Pierre Maguire for indifferent play without the puck. He missed most of the lockout season of '94-'95 with a wrist injury, and two years later he played the year in Switzerland. He has also played for Calgary, Tampa Bay, and Chicago, but in a decade of NHL action he has appeared in only 13 playoff games.

NYLUND, Gary ("Beaker")
b. Surrey, British Columbia,
October 28, 1963

This wasn't necessarily a case of bad drafting so much as bad luck. The Leafs took the hulking defenceman 3rd overall in 1982 after a junior career in Portland in which Nylund was physically dominating, a good old-fashioned rock on the blueline. Unfortunately, in his first two seasons he suffered two serious knee injuries, and when he finally played a full season, in 1984-85, he had trouble adjusting to the NHL. The Leafs let him go to Chicago, and he was given ice time with the Hawks and developed into a solid defenceman. He later played on the Islanders, but throughout his 11 NHL years he played for weak, non-playoff teams. After retiring in 1992, Nylund returned to B.C. and became a firefighter in Delta. In 2001, he was credited with saving a colleague's life.

He tried real estate and sporting goods, but settled for the Islanders marketing department.
BOB NYSTROM

NYROP, Bill
b. Washington, D.C., July 23, 1952
d. December 31, 1995

The irony could not have been more tragic, nor the fate more undeserving for a man of his physical health. Nyrop never smoked and was in top condition his whole life, yet by the time he was 43 he had succumbed to inoperable cancer that consumed his colon, liver, and lungs. He was born into money – his father owned Northwest Orient Airlines (which became Northwest) – and he attended the University of Notre Dame. After graduating, he joined Montreal and was part of three successive Cup teams in his first three years (1975-78). But Nyrop was never comfortable in Montreal and never felt fulfilled by the game. He went into the insurance business but returned to the NHL in 1981 to play with Minnesota. A year later, he retired again and entered law school and then returned to the game one final time as coach and owner of the West Palm Beach Blaze of the Sunshine

Hockey League. After winning three league championships, he sold his interest because of poor health. He had a law practice in Coeur d'Alene, Idaho, but when he experienced shortness of breath he visited his doctor and discovered he had cancer. He passed away a short time later.

NYSTROM, Bob
b. Stockholm, Sweden, October 10, 1952

The Nystrom family moved to Canada when Bob was four, and he played hockey out west until being drafted into the NHL by the expansion Islanders in 1972. He spent most of his first pro year in the minors and then became a key member of a team that was destined for greatness. He played his entire 900-game career with the Isles and won four Cups there, and he was nobody's passenger. He could score goals, but he and linemates Bob Bourne and Wayne Merrick were the hardest-working and most effective checking threesome in the league. It was his overtime winner in 1980 that gave the team its first Cup – and the first of four in a row – and he continued to score timely playoff goals throughout his career. In all, he had four OT playoff goals. His last two seasons were marred by first a serious wrist injury and then an eye injury suffered during practice that eventually rendered him less effective than he thought was acceptable for playing. For two years he was the team's assistant coach, and he also dabbled in other interests, trying to find a job that consumed him as much as hockey had. He tried real estate and sporting goods, but settled for the Islanders marketing department and his own consulting firm. In August 2002 he helped neither job by assaulting two gas station attendants. He did some radio commentary for the team and trained relentlessly for triathlons and marathons.

Gary Nylund

Bill Nyrop

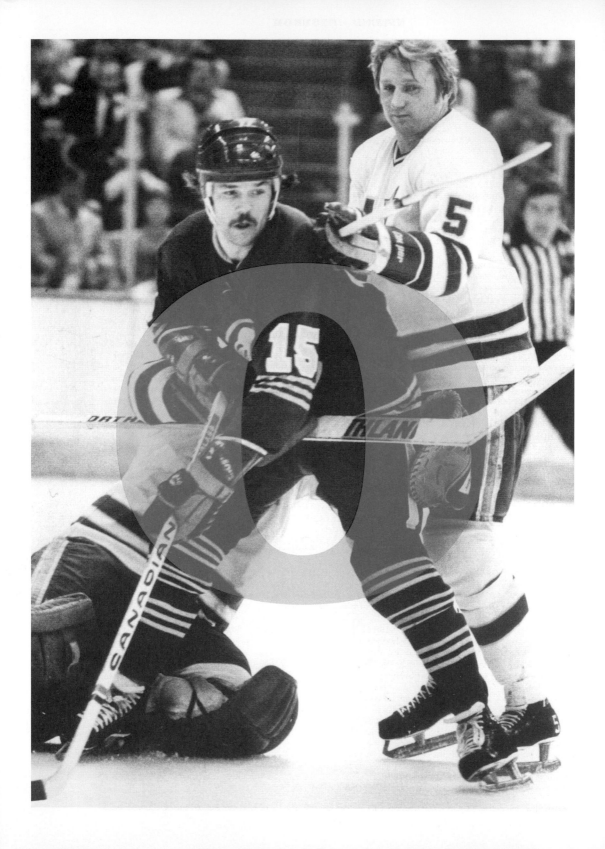

OATES, Adam
b. Weston, Ontario, August 27, 1962

The undrafted players who make an impact in the NHL are true testament to the crapshoot that is the annual Entry Draft. Oates played three years with RPI, helping the team win the NCAA in '84-'85, yet no team drafted him. Detroit signed him, and so began what is certainly a Hall of Fame career for one of the greatest passers in the history of hockey. Oates has played more than 1,200 games and recorded more than 1,000 assists. He's reached 100 points in a season 4 times and for most of his career played comfortably in the shadows of Wayne Gretzky as the second-best passer in the game. Oates made his greatest name in St. Louis, where he was set-up man for Brett Hull, but wherever he has gone that has been his role: centre the number-one line and pass to the scorers. Oates has played in five All-Star Games but has never won a Cup (he came closest with Washington in '97-'98). Despite his great skills he has never won an individual trophy or been named to the First All-Star Team. He lacks the flash of Steve Yzerman or the speed of Joe Sakic, but year after year Oates shows up to camp and goes about his business, marching irrevocably toward the record books as a passer of great renown.

OATMAN, Russell
b. Tillsonburg, Ontario, February 19, 1905
d. Keswick, Ontario, October 25, 1964

Oatman grew up skating on the Otter River at the edge of town, but at 14 he moved to Victoria with his older brother, Eddie, to play senior hockey. He turned pro in 1925-26, joining the Cougars team that went all the way to the Stanley Cup before losing to the Maroons. When the team was sold to Detroit, he moved east and played in the NHL, but he was sold to the Maroons in mid-season. It was there that Oatman scored the biggest goal of his career, the lone score in a 1-0 win over the Canadiens in the first round of the playoffs to give the Maroons a victory in the series. He later played briefly for the Rangers but suffered a leg injury in a car accident that ended his career. He was reinstated as an amateur and played with the Simcoe intermediate team for a number of years. He also coached and worked as a referee.

O'BRIEN, Dennis
b. Port Hope, Ontario, June 10, 1949

Personal loss always outweighs professional accomplishments. O'Brien had a 10-year NHL career but he'd trade it all if he could have his daughter back. He played the entire 1970s, mostly with Minnesota, where he became feared for his hitting and capable as a playmaker of some skill. After he retired in 1980 at age 31, he lost his daughter to a kidney ailment. He moved his family back to Port Hope, and O'Brien worked at the Brookside Youth Centre with troubled teens. He later became a corrections officer for kids over 16.

O'BRIEN, Ellard ("Obie")
b. St. Catharines, Ontario, May 27, 1930

O'Brien made his pro debut with Tulsa in 1950 and for the next 12 years played almost exclusively in the AHL. He had two games with the Bruins in '55-'56, but that was the only NHL sniff he had. Early in his career he shuffled between defence and forward, but with time he became a left winger who could score about as well as anyone on Hershey, his team of choice for eight years. He retired in 1962.

OBSUT, Jaroslav
b. Presov, Czechoslovakia (Slovakia), September 3, 1976

It doesn't look like it's going to happen for Obsut. Signed by Winnipeg, he never played for the team and went on to St. Louis in April 1999. Just a few months later, though, he suffered a season-ending knee injury and played just four games with the Blues before they gave up on him. In 2001-02, Obsut played just three more times with Colorado, and the defenceman had little hope of cracking that team's lineup.

O'CALLAHAN, Jack
b. Charleston, Massachusetts, July 24, 1957

Talk about a smart move! O'Callahan was drafted by Chicago in 1977 while he was playing at Boston University, but decided to focus on the U.S. National Team first and the NHL second. He played at the 1979 Worlds, and then spent the next full season with the team, winning a gold medal at the 1980 Olympics in Lake Placid. Only then did he begin his pro career, in which he became a tough hombre on the Black Hawks blueline. After seven years of pro he finished his career at the 1989 Worlds, and then settled in Chicago. O'Callahan managed Beanpot Financial Services at the Chicago Mercantile Exchange.

O'CONNELL, Mike
b. Chicago, Illinois, November 25, 1955

It's tough growing up the son of a famous athlete. Tommy O'Connell was the star quarterback for the University of Illinois and later played in the NFL. He had two sons, Tim and Mike, who both went on to play pro hockey – Tim in the WHA, Mike in the NHL. Mike moved to Ontario to play junior and started his pro career with Chicago in 1977. Although he was born in the Windy City, Boston had been his home for many years, so it wasn't special for him to be with the Hawks over and above making the NHL (though he was the first Chicago-born player to play for the Hawks). He missed his first training camp after suffering injuries in a car accident, but went on to play 13 industrious seasons in the NHL with Boston and Detroit after Chicago. He was a checker and a scrapper, and after retiring in 1990 he stayed in the game, first as coach of San Diego in the IHL. He later became an assistant with Boston and a head coach with the Bruins affiliate, and in 1994 he was named assistant GM to Harry Sinden. For six years O'Connell apprenticed under the great man who had built a Cup team in 1970 and led Canada to victory in the historic Summit Series two years later, and when Sinden was ready to step down, O'Connell became the new GM in 2000, a post he continues to hold along with coach, a title he picked up toward the end of the '02-'03 season after firing Robbie Ftorek and stepping behind the bench himself.

O'CONNOR, Herbert "Buddy"
b. Montreal, Quebec, June 21, 1916
d. Montreal, Quebec, August 24, 1977

By comparison, Bill Quackenbush was an animal and

Adam Oates

Jaroslav Obsut

Jack O'Callahan

Mike O'Connell

Buddy O'Connor

Dennis O'Brien
(opposite page)

Myles O'Connor

Chris Oddleifson

Selmar Odelein

Jeff Odgers

Dave Keon was a goon. In 10 NHL seasons, O'Connor was penalized for exactly 34 minutes of infractions, an unprecedented testimony to his good cheer. As a kid, he learned to skate not in his backyard and not on frozen rivers. No. In Verdun, the sewers overflowed at the start of each winter and the very roads themselves froze to perfection! He rose up through the ranks of city teams to play for the Royals in junior and then senior, making the Allan Cup finals on a regular basis and becoming a celebrity playing on a line with Pete Morin and Gerry Heffernan. Known as the Razzle Dazzle Line, the threesome made such an impression that in 1941 they were signed by the Canadiens and brought up to the NHL. An injury to Morin near the end of that first season put an end to the Razzle Dazzle, but O'Connor was only just beginning. That he survived in the NHL, let alone flourished, was a miracle in itself. He weighed no more than 145 pounds, but made up for his feathery physique by skating quickly, eluding checks magically, and mastering the art of passing. He won two Cups with Montreal, in 1944 and '46, but in 1947 the team traded him to the Rangers. In '47-'48, he showed just what a mistake the Canadiens had made. He had career bests with 24 goals and 60 points, and won the Hart and Lady Byng trophies, the first player to win both in the same season. He was also named Canada's best athlete for 1948. O'Connor was out of the NHL by 1951, but he went to Cincinnati to act as playing coach for the AHL team. He was forced to retire after suffering a nervous breakdown, so he returned to Montreal and helped start the NHL Oldtimers' association. He turned to politics and ran for a place in the Quebec government on the National Union ticket, but was not elected. In later years he was ill for long stretches, and he died in a Montreal hospital. It wasn't until 1988 that he was inducted into the Hockey Hall of Fame as a Veteran Player.

O'CONNOR, Myles
b. Calgary, Alberta, April 2, 1967
As a teen, O'Connor couldn't have played under better circumstances. In high school, he skated for the great Notre Dame team in Wilcox, Saskatchewan, under Barry MacKenzie, former longtime member of the Canadian National Team under Father Bauer in the 1960s. And then, he forsook the NHL and Canadian junior after he was hand-picked by Red Berenson in 1985 for his new program at the University of Michigan trying to rebuild an awful team. O'Connor was once touted as a top prospect in high school, but New Jersey drafted him 45th overall in '85 and after four years with the Wolverines his stock had dropped. O'Connor began in the minors, and over four years saw increasingly less

action in the NHL until 1994 when he was in the IHL to stay. All along, he was smart enough to get an education first, and for that he should be commended.

ODDLEIFSON, Chris ("Oddy")
b. Brandon, Manitoba, September 7, 1950
His was not an especially long career, but Oddleifson left his mark in Vancouver where he continues to live. He was drafted by California in 1970 but traded by the Seals a year later before he had a chance to suit up in the colourful uniforms of the west coast club, and after 55 games with the Bruins he was on the move again to Vancouver, where he played the rest of his career. A tall and all-purpose centre, he was sound defensively and great on face-offs, and he could chip in offensively as well. He was named team captain in 1976 and after retiring he stayed in the city and worked as a real estate agent. Oddleifson also became active in alumni games for the Canucks.

ODELEIN, Lyle
b. Quill Lake, Saskatchewan, July 21, 1968
In his heyday, Odelein was with Montreal, taking a regular turn on defence, fighting the good fight when opponents required a lesson, and even winning a Cup in 1993. For seven years he was a Habs blueliner, and for another four he played with New Jersey. Then the trades started and he moved around, his best days behind him and retirement looming. He was named team captain when he got to lowly Columbus in 2000, but the Jackets traded him to Chicago after a year and half.

He was named team captain when he got to lowly Columbus in 2000.
LYLE ODELEIN

ODELEIN, Selmar
b. Quill Lake, Saskatchewan, April 11, 1966
The oldest of three brothers of Norwegian extraction, Selmar was drafted by Edmonton in 1984 two years before brother Lyle went to Montreal. Selmar's career, though, was the shorter of the two. In 3 years with the Oilers he played just 18 games and wound up playing out the rest of his career in Europe, principally Austria and Britain, before retiring.

ODGERS, Jeff ("Odgie")
b. Spy Hill, Saskatchewan, May 31, 1969
After three years with Colorado (1997-2000), Odgers had the misfortune of going to Minnesota in the Expansion Draft and on to Atlanta a few weeks later. The next year, the Thrashers watched the playoffs on television and the Avs won the Cup. Odgers started his career with San Jose coming out of Brandon in 1991 and became the team's leader and tough guy. He played a season with Boston before joining the Thrashers and he continues to rack up penalty minutes in the name of teamwork.

ODJICK, Gino
b. Maniwaki, Quebec, September 7, 1970

His father was a lumberjack who also ran the hockey program for the River Desert band, and young Gino tried to follow in the footsteps of another Native, Stan Jonathan. Taunted for his heritage, Odjick kept fighting, literally and figuratively, until he reached the NHL. Once there, he did more of the same with redoubled effort. He's been in the league since 1990, spending the first eight years of his career with Vancouver where he became one of the most popular players on the team. Fans chanted his name, and they practically brought down the house on October 19, 1991, when he scored a goal on a penalty shot against Mike Vernon and the hated Flames from Calgary. Odjick led the league in penalty minutes in '96-'97 and has continued to fight to play (a paradox since fighting means not playing!). His career took a turn for the worse, though, when he suffered a concussion in the summer of 2002 and had a fallout with Montreal management over his health. The result was that he didn't play at all in '02-'03.

O'DONNELL, Fred
b. Kingston, Ontario, December 6, 1949

They'll play Sinatra singing "My Way" at O'Donnell's funeral because no one told him how to do what he had to do. Minnesota drafted him in 1969, and he refused to go to the Stars, preferring to play senior hockey in Kingston and attend Queen's University to work on his business degree. Fine, so the Stars traded him to Boston and he reported to the Bruins, playing in the minors and joining the NHL team in 1972. For a year and a half he was a right winger on the great Orr-Esposito team, but when the Bruins traded him to Vancouver, he refused to report. The Canucks even put an ad in the Boston newspaper trying to coerce him: "Fred O'Donnell – Try us . . . you might like us." He didn't. At the start of the next year he signed with New England of the WHA, and after two years he retired. In 1977, he became coach of Queen's and also sold real estate, and after a number of successful seasons he became head coach of the OHL Canadians.

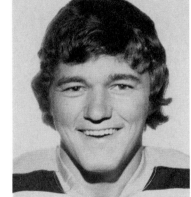

In 1977, he became coach of Queen's and also sold real estate.
FRED O'DONNELL

O'DONNELL, Sean
b. Ottawa, Ontario, October 13, 1971

It took the better part of four seasons in the minors before O'Donnell made the NHL, but once he did he never looked back. Although Buffalo drafted him in 1991, the Sabres traded him three years later to get Doug Houda, and it was with Los Angeles that he became an aggressive and physical defenceman. He stayed with the team six seasons, but Minnesota grabbed him in the 2000 expansion and made him the first captain in team history. It was a short-lived honour, as the Wild traded him before the end of the season and he signed with Boston the following summer.

O'DONOGHUE, Don
b. Kingston, Ontario, August 27, 1949

His only NHL games came with the Oakland/California franchise when the team, well, wasn't very good. O'Donoghue joined the Seals in 1969, but after one full year he became a part-timer the next year and a fringe forward the year after. He was traded to Boston but never got a chance to play with the great and mighty Bruins, so in the summer of 1972 he signed with the WHA, where he played four years. O'Donoghue finished his career in Hampton, playing for the Gulls in the Southern league until the team folded and then the year after in the American league until it folded again.

ODROWSKI, Gerry ("Snowy"/ "The Hook")
b. Trout Creek, Ontario, October 4, 1938

It kind of worked in reverse for Odrowski. When he was about nine, he lost all his hair for reasons that mystified doctors, but by his late teens it started to grow back. He quipped that by the time he was 65 he'd have a full head of hair! As a youngster, he was championed by Bucko McDonald, resident of nearby Sundridge and former Leafs great. Odrowski played junior at St. Mike's and senior in the Soo, and in 1960 he was named the Eastern league's best defenceman. He played two years with the Red Wings, but contract troubles led him back to the minors and he didn't resurface until expansion, when Oakland acquired him. He later became one of the first players to jump to the WHA, and he became the first president of that league's player association. Wherever he went, he was always one of the more popular players, and he even had his own fan club for a number of years. After retiring in 1976 he sold car parts for his brother's business in North Bay and then became involved in politics. Odrowski was a councillor for four years in South Himsworth township and more recently was Reeve for the area.

O'DWYER, Bill
b. Boston, Massachusetts, January 25, 1960

After four decent seasons at Boston College (1978-82), O'Dwyer suffered a series of injuries that hampered his progress and wreaked havoc on his body. He started out playing a few games with Los Angeles, but the Kings buried him in the minors and he suffered one pain after another. He broke his jaw, pulled his groin, and tore ligaments in his thumb over the course of two years, and by the time the Bruins signed him in

Gino Odjick

Sean O'Donnell

Don O'Donoghue

Gerry Odrowski

Bill O'Dwyer

1987 he was happy just to get a shot at playing. After a fine first year with the B's, though, he hurt his knee, missed the season, and was never quite the same again. O'Dwyer retired in 1992 and settled in Braintree, outside Boston, where he started his own business.

**Peanuts
O'Flaherty**

O'FLAHERTY, Gerry ("Flapper")
b. Pittsburgh, Pennsylvania, August 31, 1950

Born in Pittsburgh because his dad was playing for the Leafs farm team at the time, Gerry went on to have a career similar to his father's. He started with Toronto, playing just two games in '71-'72, but was claimed by Vancouver in the summer's Intra-League Draft. This surprised no one because by this time Gerry's old man was scouting for the Canucks. Nothing was easier – or, perhaps, more difficult – than selecting his own son for the team! Gerry played six solid years with Vancouver. He was a fine 2-way player, but his 3 successive 20-goal seasons point to an offensive ability as well. After retiring in 1979, Gerry worked in the car muffler business, and like his father also became a western scout for the Montreal Canadiens, work he continues to this day. He also became active in Canucks alumni activities.

Brian Ogilvie

O'FLAHERTY, John "Peanuts"
b. Toronto, Ontario,
April 10, 1918

Although he played just 21 games in the NHL, O'Flaherty had a long and impressive career in hockey, starting in 1933 when he played for St. Mike's and sold peanuts at the Gardens. A local scribe spied him at work, and the nickname stuck for the rest of his days. O'Flaherty won the Memorial Cup in 1936 with the West Toronto Nationals, coached by Hap Day and starring Punch Imlach. Imlach and O'Flaherty were teammates again with the Toronto Goodyears, and Peanuts got into his only NHL games with the Americans during the war. He himself was a tail-gunner for three years in the RCAF, and when he came out he had a distinguished career in the AHL. He then coached for many years, with Rochester, the Saint John Beavers, and numerous minor pro and amateur teams. He scouted out west for Vancouver for seven years and then returned to Toronto to retire and sell the occasional car, a job he had toward the end of his Vancouver stay.

John Ogrodnick

OGILVIE, Brian
b. Stettler, Alberta, January 30, 1952

Nothing but part-time work in the NHL could Ogilvie find. From 1972, when he joined Chicago, through 1980, when he retired, he was mostly a minor-league centreman who earned the occasional callup. Outside that first season, Ogilvie spent his entire career in the St. Louis organization, but he rarely

Mattias Ohlund

stayed in a Blues uniform for too long before going back down to his regular job in the Central or American league.

O'GRADY, George
b. Montreal, Quebec
d. unknown

O'Grady played with the Montreal Wanderers during their days with the NHA, and when the team joined the NHL he stayed with the club. It was a short stay, though, and when the team's arena burned down no other club acquired his services and there is no record of him playing pro anywhere thereafter.

OGRODNICK, John
b. Ottawa, Ontario, June 20, 1959

Nothing was easier – or, perhaps, more difficult – than selecting his own son for the team!
GERRY O'FLAHERTY

He may have played for three teams in his NHL days, but make no mistake – Ogrodnick was a Red Wings player through and through. He began his career in 1979 as a Wings and ended it in 1993 as same, and in between his finest years were with the Winged Wheel. He played in 5 All-Star Games, was named to the First All-Star Team in 1984-85, and in 1985 became only the third Red Wings player to score 50 goals in a season (he finished with 55). He finished that year with 105 points, but he rarely went far in the playoffs. Detroit traded him in January 1987 to Quebec, but he played only 32 games with the team before forcing a trade. His wife, an American, didn't like the city, and the family went to beautiful New York the next year. One of the most natural goal scorers of his era, Ogrodnick retired with 402 goals to his credit.

OHLUND, Mattias
b. Pitea, Sweden, September 9, 1976

It was an exhibition game in September 1999. Ohlund threw the puck up the middle and it was picked off. An Ottawa player took a quick shot but one of Ohlund's teammates deflected the puck, and it sailed directly into Ohlund's right eye. He collapsed in a pool of blood. After half a season, doctors determined he had 70 percent eyesight left in that eye. Then – as is the way with all NHLers in this scenario – he put on a shield. A year later he needed surgery on the eye, but before, during, and after he has remained Vancouver's best defenceman, the core of the blue-line, and the team's key offensive threat from the point. He was a star back home in Lulea before coming to the Canucks in 1997, and he had played in all international tournaments for Tre Kronor. He can block shots and hit, move the puck up the ice, and quarterback a power play. Despite reduced vision, he is still a star in the NHL.

OJANEN, Janne

b. Tampere, Finland, April 9, 1968

Three Olympics, six World Championships, two Canada Cups, a World Cup, and two World Juniors. Since making his debut in 1986, Ojanen has done it all. He also played parts of four seasons with New Jersey and played pro for years in Sweden and Finland. Ojanen likely could have played much longer in the NHL, but in 1993 he chose to return home where he can continue playing for several years yet, if he chooses.

OKERLUND, Todd

b. Burnsville, Minnesota, September 6, 1964

With the success of *The Osbournes* we now have proof that even the most maniacal performers go home to some form of domestic environment. This knowledge is further confirmed by Todd Okerlund, son of Mean Gene Okerlund of wrestling fame (not the Olympic sport, but rather the faked form of violent entertainment). Todd went to the University of Minnesota on scholarship, but early in his third year, 1986-87, he tore his knee and spent a year recovering from a serious ACL injury. He recovered just in time to play for the U.S. National Team and a few games in the 1988 Olympics in Calgary, and after that he played four games with the Islanders. Okerlund's knee, though, was shot, and he retired before the year ended. He was just 24.

OKSIUTA, Roman

b. Murmansk, Soviet Union (Russia), August 21, 1970

When you have the 209th selection in the draft, you can afford to waste the choice on a what-the-hell pick and see what happens. That's what the Rangers did in 1989 to obtain Oksiuta, and the league probably got a little more than its money's worth – but not much. At the height of his reputation, he was traded with a draft choice to Edmonton for Kevin Lowe, but the large right winger never did much with the Oilers to impress GM Glen Sather. Oksiuta was traded three more times in swift succession, never having a lasting impact, even with Vancouver where he scored 21 goals over 78 games. In 1997, he returned to Europe to play and retired two years later after a stint in Finland.

OLAUSSON, Fredrik

b. Vaxjo, Sweden, October 5, 1966

There's no better way to go out than on top, figured Olausson, so soon after he won his first Stanley Cup, in 2002 with Detroit, he announced he was returning to Sweden to finish his career. Fifteen years in the NHL was enough, he declared. Although he failed to play in his 1,000th game before going home, he was only the second European defenceman to reach 500 career points (the first was Borje Salming), so he made his

name in North America. He spent his first eight seasons with Winnipeg and prior to his year with Detroit had won only one playoff round, back in his rookie season of '86-'87. He scored 15 or more goals on 5 occasions, though he never played in an All-Star Game. Although he played some international hockey early in his career, the last time he wore the Tre Kronor sweater was in 1989 at the World Championships.

OLCZYK, Ed ("Eddie O")

b. Chicago, Illinois, August 16, 1966

One of the first true American superstars, Olczyk was drafted 3rd overall in 1984 by his hometown Hawks and played his career up to his billing. He had size but more finesse than a power forward, and he could beat any goalie with his shot. He was, first and foremost, a scorer and playmaker, an offensively creative centreman who played mostly on weak teams but who managed to find his way to that all-important one Stanley Cup. Olczyk had nine 20-goals seasons, including a career-high 42 with Toronto in '87-'88 during the team's darkest hours. He was on the Rangers in '93-'94 but missed most of the season with a broken thumb, though he did return briefly in the playoffs. Over and above his 1,031-game NHL career, he also represented the U.S. frequently during his peak years. He played at the 1984 Olympics in Sarajevo, the '87 and '91 Canada Cups, and four World Championships. After retiring, Olczyk became a respected and hard-working member of the broadcasting fraternity, primarily for Fox Sports out of Pittsburgh.

Olczyk had nine 20-goals seasons, including a career-high 42 with Toronto.
ED OLCZYK

OLESCHUK, Bill

b. Edmonton, Alberta, July 20, 1955

"Rocky Hockey" was nothing to aspire to. It referred to the play of the hopeless Colorado Rockies during their brief and pitiful existence, and unfortunately Oleschuk was privy to the inner machinations of said sport. Once, he allowed a goal on a slapshot from outside the blueline, the first shot of the game, and coach Don Cherry pulled him. During Oleschuk's time with the team in the mid- to late 1970s, he had a record of 7-28-10, not numbers with which to start a goaltending school after retirement. In '77-'78, Oleschuk played for five different teams in four different leagues. The year after, he shared net duties with Doug Favell but managed only 6 wins in 40 games. Oleshuk's was a short NHL career, but every night was long.

OLESEVICH, Dan ("Ole")

b. Port Colborne, Ontario, September 16, 1937
d. Tilbury, Ontario, July 15, 1983

Some stories seem so absurd or bizarre they have to be

Roman Oksiuta

Fredrik Olausson

Bill Oleschuk

David Oliver

Harry Oliver

Murray Oliver

Krzysztof Oliwa

made up. Except they're not, which is why Ole's tale is merely ordinarily amazing. From 1952 to '59 he played goal in the Detroit system, and his last year was a tough one. Playing for the Windsor Bulldogs, he took a puck in the eye and remained in hospital for three weeks. He finished the year down in Charlotte, and with 10 seconds to go in the final game he was clipped on the lip to the tune of 21 stitches. He was getting married that summer and had to decide what to do. Retirement seemed like a good option. Fate had other ideas. Detroit's practice goalie and assistant equipment manager, Julian Klymkiw, broke his leg while playing soccer, and by the time training camp rolled around he wasn't fit for work of any sort. Jack Adams asked Olesevich if he wanted the job, and the goalie said sure. But on October 21, 1961, the Rangers were in Detroit to play the Wings. In the second period, New York goalie Gump Worsley fell and hit his head on the ice. He had to leave the game, and Olesevich went to the dressing room to take over in goal – for the Rangers. New York was winning 3-2, but Olesevich allowed 2 goals to give his employers a 4-3 lead. In the third period, he played extremely well, and the Rangers scored to tie the game. After the 4-4 tie, Olesevich returned to the Detroit dressing room, where none of the players were exactly greeting him warmly. He returned to his job picking up towels and sorting sweaters. He never played in goal again. He died in a car accident at age 45.

OLIVER, David
b. Sechelt, British Columbia, April 17, 1971
Oliver was a goal scorer at the University of Michigan in the early 1990s, which is why Edmonton drafted him. He scored 36 goals in his first 2 seasons, and then a bad start to his third year caused the Oilers to put him on waivers. The Rangers grabbed him and Ottawa and Phoenix later signed him, but the goals never came. They stayed far away from Oliver's stick, and he played in the minors where, evidently, his goals had been waiting for him. He later played in the DEL for a year in Germany, then signed with Dallas in 2002, hoping he still had some NHL goals left.

OLIVER, Harry ("Pee Wee")
b. Selkirk, Manitoba, October 26, 1898
d. Selkirk, Manitoba, June 16, 1985
Anyone who grew up in Selkirk either watched the Fishermen play or played for the Fishermen if they were good enough. Oliver was good enough to play for the junior and senior teams until 1920, when he left for Calgary to begin a professional career. The right winger played in that city for six years until joining the new Boston Bruins in the NHL in 1926. Playing on a line with Bill Carson and Percy Galbraith, Oliver led the

team in scoring in each of his first three seasons, the last of which brought the Stanley Cup to Beantown in the spring of 1929. He was a gentlemanly and consistent performer during his eight years with the Bruins, but on November 2, 1934, he was sold to the New York Americans with whom he closed out his career in 1937. He returned to Selkirk and worked as an electrician, but a few years later moved to Winnipeg where he worked for the Weights and Measures Department of the federal government. He was inducted into the Hockey Hall of Fame in 1967 on the basis of his sportsmanship and the speed and grace with which he had played.

OLIVER, Murray
b. Hamilton, Ontario, November 14, 1937
In his teen years, Oliver took a greater fancy to baseball

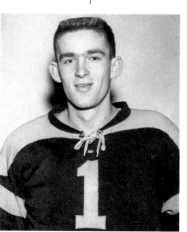
Playing for the Windsor Bulldogs, he took a puck in the eye and remained in hospital for three weeks.
DAN OLESEVICH

than hockey, and he was scouted by the Cleveland Indians. After he suffered a broken arm, though, he changed his focus to hockey and played for Hamilton, in the Detroit system. He played parts of three years with the Wings starting in 1958, but the team was solid at centre and traded him to Boston in January 1961. In his first 5 seasons he averaged 20 goals with the Bruins on a team that missed the playoffs every year he was there, and he was traded to Toronto and later to Minnesota. He retired in 1975 after a bitter contract dispute with the team, having played 1,127 career games. Oliver worked in sales for Northland sticks and then former North Stars teammate Lou Nanne hired him as an assistant coach. Oliver became head coach for parts of two years and stayed with the organization until 1988. He later returned to hockey with Vancouver, working his way up to become the director of pro scouting.

OLIWA, Krzysztof
b. Tychy, Poland, April 12, 1973
As a teen in Tychy, Oliwa had the pleasure of working in the hellhole that is the centre of this mining town, and when his hockey skills got him a chance to play in Welland, Ontario, when he was 19, he took it as fast as he could. A year later, New Jersey drafted him, and although it was another three years before he saw the NHL light of day, the minors was considerably better than his homeland alternative. That's also why he took to his job as an enforcer with a certain philosophical shrug. Fight in an environment of freedom and excellent wages, or return to Tychy. He solved that problem for good in 1998 when he became a U.S. citizen, but his role in the NHL has been the same. At 6'4" and 230 pounds, he's an intimidating presence, and has recorded goon penalty minutes during his short career to date. He's not a goal scorer at the best

of times, but in 2001-02 he scored not once with Pittsburgh during the entire season. He made up for it, though, in the spring of 2002 when he was chosen to play for Poland at the World Championships. He scored a goal but could not keep the nation in the top pool of 16 countries for the 2003 WC.

OLMSTEAD, Bert
b. Sceptre, Saskatchewan, September 4, 1926

Why every player couldn't be like Olmstead was a mystery. Talented but by no means overflowing with skill, he was simple, direct, honest, a player who worked hard, coached himself, tried his best every night, played his position, and played for the team first and foremost. He played junior hockey in Moose Jaw and then in Kansas City, Chicago's minor-league team.

Olmstead made his NHL debut with the Hawks in '48-'49 and soon was playing alongside his Moose Jaw teammate Metro Prystai on the Boilermaker Line with Bep Guidolin. The year after, his first full season in the league, Olmstead counted 20 goals, but the following season was traded to Montreal for Leo Gravelle. He played eight years in Montreal, mostly on a line with Bernie Geoffrion and Jean Béliveau, and those two superstars credited the under-appreciated Olmstead for their success. Olmstead "coached" that line, told the others what their jobs were and where they should play. He was never given his due because he was a western English player on a line with two native francophones, but got his dues in '55-'56 when he set an NHL record with 56 assists, a record that lasted 5 years until Béliveau broke it. Olmstead won four Cups with the Canadiens but by 1958 the team felt that his tender knees were failing. They left him exposed in the Intra-League Draft, and the Leafs happily claimed him. Even though he played just four seasons with the Leafs, he was revered in Toronto and given all the credit he deserved. The first thing Punch Imlach did when he took over as coach early in the '58-'59 season was make Olmstead a playing assistant coach. The dual role took its toll over the course of a few months, but it was in large measure due to Olmstead's experience and steadying influence that the team became a Cup contender once again. After winning the Cup in 1962, Imlach gambled and left Olmstead exposed in the draft, just as the Canadiens had done. This time, the Rangers pounced, but Olmstead had no interest in reporting to Broadway and retired. He settled in Calgary, though every summer he returned to the farm in Sceptre to help bring home the crop. In 1967, he was offered a choice of coaching Oakland or L.A. He chose the Seals, but after less than a year the stress was too much and he

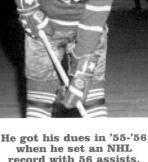

He got his dues in '55-'56 when he set an NHL record with 56 assists.
BERT OLMSTEAD

left the game for good. It wasn't until 1985 that Olmstead was inducted into the Hockey Hall of Fame, a delay he felt was attributable to having made enemies with certain members of the selection committee over the years. Nonetheless, in a 14-year career, he went to the Cup finals 11 times and won 5. Not a bad career at all.

OLSEN, Darryl
b. Calgary, Alberta, October 7, 1966

After attending Northern Michigan University in 1985 for four years, Olsen embarked on a lengthy career in hockey that has flourished away from the pro rinks as much as in them. He was a one-game man with Calgary in '91-'92, but his years with Salt Lake City in the IHL were where he started a second line of work.

He established Olsen Sports Management, a skating school he ran part-time during his playing days but full-time since he retired in 2000. Along the way, Olsen played a number of years in Europe, but he settled in Salt Lake City to give his school his undivided attention.

OLSON, Dennis ("Ollie")
b. Kenora, Ontario, November 9, 1934

He may have been only good enough to play 4 games with Detroit (in '57-'58), but in February 2002 Olson was inducted into the Springfield Indians Hall of Fame for his seven years of service with that great AHL club. Olson played junior in Port Arthur and graduated to the IHL with Troy, where he became one of the league's top scorers. At 6'3" he was one of the tallest men in hockey and he used his reach to good advantage.

OLSSON, Christer
b. Arboga, Sweden, July 24, 1970

The St. Louis Blues didn't think much of him, then they did, then they didn't. They drafted him a lowly 275th overall in 1993 when he was 22 and past his status as a prospect, thinking he might be filler on the farm team or a part-timer with the parent club. Their thinking changed, though, when Olsson had an outstanding World Championships in 1995 and was named the tournament's best defenceman, and they brought him to St. Louis that fall hoping he could step in and have an impact. When they gave him a chance, they went back to their position on draft day and traded him to Ottawa. Olsson returned to Sweden to play and has participated in three more WCs since then.

OLVESTAD, Jimmie
b. Stockholm, Sweden, February 16, 1980

In his first game, opening night of the 2001-02 season with Tampa Bay, Olvestad scored a goal. It was one of

Bert Olmstead

Darryl Olsen

ORLANDO, Gaetano "Gates"
b. Montreal, Quebec, November 13, 1962

He may not have left much of a mark with Buffalo, but in Italy the great Gates became one of the best all-time players to appear nationally and internationally. Orlando earned a business management degree from Providence College (1980-84) before turning pro with Rochester, the Sabres affiliate in the AHL. Over the next three years he was called up numerous times but never earned a spot on the roster. By 1987, he knew how he had been slotted by the team and decided to play in Europe, and for the next 12 years he divided his time between Italy and Switzerland. He was a top scorer and playmaker, and he qualified to play for the Azzurri internationally. Orlando played in 10 World Championships and 2 Olympics for Italy before retiring in 1999 a national hero. He returned to Canada and became a coach in Rochester in the North American league that December, though the team folded at season's end. That summer, Orlando was named head coach of the Adirondack IceHawks of the UHL, and his hockey career continues.

ORLANDO, Jimmy
b. Montreal, Quebec, February 27, 1915
d. Montreal, Quebec, October 24, 1992

November 7, 1942, was quite likely the darkest day in NHL history, not so much because of the stick-swinging that occurred at Maple Leaf Gardens during the Detroit-Toronto game as because it was caught by photographer Nat Turofsky and immortalized as the most violent fight of all time. That night, Orlando and Gaye Stewart had a running feud that culminated in the two swinging sticks at each other's heads. The blows left both men semi-conscious, and the famous photograph shows referee King Clancy helping Orlando off the ice, blood streaming down his face, his eyes clearly not those of a functioning player. The photo was the first-ever hockey image to appear on the cover of *Life* magazine. The '42-'43 season was Orlando's last in the league, and it ended well when the Wings won the Cup. He had played all of his six NHL seasons with the Wings, partnered on defence with Jack Stewart. From day one, Orlando had a reputation as a "bad boy" in the NHL, one of its meanest competitors. After leaving the NHL, he played senior hockey for a few years and then settled in Montreal. He operated a nightclub called the Champ Snowbar for years and also refereed wrestling matches. His hockey connection didn't disappear, either, as he scouted locally for Detroit for more than a quarter-century.

Bobby Orr

ORLESKI, Dave
b. Edmonton, Alberta, December 26, 1959

It didn't take long for Orleski to move into and then out of a pro career. He won a Memorial Cup with New Westminster in 1977 and played for Canada at the World Juniors a year later, and in 1979 the large left winger stepped into the Montreal system with Nova Scotia. Orleski played just two games with the Habs and six in the minors before retiring in 1984.

ORR, Bobby ("Number Four")
b. Parry Sound, Ontario, March 20, 1948

Perhaps on one of the cold planets out there in the vast universe there exists a player who was as good as Bobby Orr, but on this planet no man who ever put on a pair of skates can even pretend to be equal to

From day one, Orlando had a reputation as a "bad boy" in the NHL.
JIMMY ORLANDO

Bobby Orr. From the time he was 12 years old playing in Parry Sound he was hailed as the next great player, and by the time he retired at age 30, knees ravaged, he had proved everyone right. At 14, he was playing provincial junior hockey. At 15, he was playing major junior with Oshawa, and the only thing that he needed during the ensuing three years was time while the young boy grew into a man and filled out a body that would become as strong as any in the league. Oshawa was affiliated with the Boston Bruins, and fans in that city waited impatiently for Orr's arrival as their team missed the playoffs year after year. When he got to Boston in 1966 at age 18, he was offered Dit Clapper's number 5 sweater, an honour he turned down in respect to one of the greatest Bruins of all time. Instead, he immortalized his own number, the poetic number 4 of Bobby Orr, though it wasn't quite so simple a start to a great career. He had retained a lawyer, an agent named Alan Eagleson, who demanded that Orr be paid $40,000 a season, the highest amount ever for a rookie and one of the top five salaries in the league. The Bruins balked, but Eagleson threatened that Orr would happily go and play for Canada's National Team. Having missed the playoffs the last eight successive seasons, the Bruins didn't have much leverage and caved in. Orr became the richest rookie ever, though it still turned out to be a bargain of a deal for Boston. His first NHL game came against Detroit, after which Gordie Howe gave the kid rave reviews for his skating, passing, shot blocking, and hitting. Orr wasn't like other defenceman. He had a skating stride that was more powerful than any forward, and he didn't just move the puck up ice, he charged to the goal after making a pass. He was the master of the give-and-go, the originator of the rushing defenceman who joins the offence by going to the net. As a rookie, he scored 13 goals and was named Calder Trophy winner, but in his second year his one weakness started to rear its ugly head. He missed almost half the season with a knee injury, though he returned for the playoffs. Orr combined puckhandling skill with speed that no player could match. He had many different gears and could control play with speed or by slowing play down. He loved skating through open ice, and was reckless in slinking along the boards, the result was that he left his knees vulnerable to checks. The first injury in '67-'68 came as his knee was pinned and stretched along the boards during a rush, but the subsequent time off did nothing to deter him. His strength was skating fast and moving the puck, and that's the only way he knew how to play the game. Yet, despite playing just 46 games that year, Orr was so easily the best defenceman in the league that he won his first Norris Trophy. He came back the next year to score 21 goals, a record for a defenceman, and the Bruins made it to the semi-finals in the playoffs. The next year, Orr established himself as the greatest defenceman ever to play the game. He set another record with 33 goals. He led the league with 87 assists (another record for blueliners). He won the scoring championship with 120 points, still the only defenceman to achieve this incomparable feat. And then there were the playoffs. The Bruins marched to the finals to face an inferior St. Louis team, they won the first two games in Missouri and came home for what all fans expected to be a sweep. The Bruins had not won the Cup since 1941, but with Orr, this was their hoped-for moment. They won game three, but the fourth went into overtime. On May 10, 1970, at the forty-second mark of OT, Orr took a pass from Derek Sanderson and scored on Glenn Hall. As he started to celebrate, Orr was hooked at the ankle by Noel Picard and flew into the air, an image that was captured by a number of photographers that day and remains the greatest Cup image of all time, a defining moment for what the Stanley Cup means, and a defining image of Orr's ability to, literally, fly. To add to his trophy case, he was named Hart Trophy winner for the regular season and Conn Smythe Trophy winner for the playoffs. His four individual trophies that year were also a record, yet he was by no means finished. In '70-'71, he kept going, scoring 139 points and finishing the year with a +124, a record that seems unlikely ever to be broken. In 1971-72, he signed a five-year contract worth $1 million, the first million-dollar deal in league history. He again eclipsed 100 points and took the team to its second Stanley Cup, once more scoring the winning goal (though in less dramatic fashion) against the Rangers

No man who ever put on a pair of skates can even pretend to be equal to Bobby Orr.
BOBBY ORR

Bobby Orr

and winning a second Conn Smythe Trophy. Another knee injury, though, forced him to miss the 1972 Summit Series. Although he trained with the team and travelled with the players to Moscow, doctors would not give him a clean bill of health and he had to watch the victory from the stands. Over the next three years, Orr continued to be the dominant player in the game. In '74-'75 he set a record with 46 goals, and his 135 points gave him his second scoring title. He also won his eighth successive Norris Trophy. But the team faltered in the playoffs after '72, coming close but never winning a third Cup with this corps of talented players. In the off seasons, Orr repeatedly had surgery on his knees. In '75-'76, he missed almost the entire year with another serious knee injury, and made what turned out to be his last stand at the 1976 Canada Cup. He led all scorers with nine points and was named tournament MVP, playing better on one knee than anyone else on two. That summer was a tumultuous one for Orr. He became a free agent, and Eagleson lied to him about contract offers from the Bruins in order that he might sway Orr to sign with Chicago. On June 24, 1976, Orr stunned the Bruins and the hockey world by doing just that, signing a huge deal with the Hawks that made him far-and-away the highest-paid player in the NHL. But after that performance in the Canada Cup, Orr played just 20 games with Chicago before realizing his knee was in bad shape. He decided to take the rest of the year off, and then again in 1977 decided to rest for a full year, hoping to work the knee

Bobby Orr

back into top shape and give it one final chance for recovery. He came back with Chicago to start '78-'79, but after just six games announced his retirement, his knees simply lacking in cartilage to endure the physical play and to allow him to play as he demanded of himself. He was 30 years old. In 1979, he was immediately inducted into the Hockey Hall of Fame and he was also awarded the Lester Pearson Trophy. It was a sad moment, indeed, when he dropped the puck to start the 1979 Challenge Cup in New York, when he well could have been playing in it, but saddest of all were the knees. With today's medicine, those major operations he endured would have been nothing more than routine arthroscopic procedures, costing him two weeks of play not four months. Orr fundamentally changed the game during his career. His speed was such that other players looked to be standing still even as they were chasing him. His offence from the blueline frustrated opposing coaches, many of whom tried to put a shadow on him, to no good effect. Orr pinched in at the blueline so frequently because he knew that if he made a

Bobby Orr

Vladimir Orszagh

Keith Osborne

Mark Osborne

Randy Osburn

mistake he had the speed to cover up for it. But he was also a superb defenceman. He was extremely strong and blocked shots with the best of them, and he played in the days of the Big Bad Bruins, and that meant he could fight. He defended himself and his teammates, and he made his own room on the ice. He was also in impeccable condition and routinely played 40 minutes a game, and legend has it that once with Oshawa he played the full 60 minutes. He was, in a sense, his own mini-team: he could score and prevent goals; he could play offence and defence. After retiring, it took Orr many years to work himself into a comfortable setting. He worked as an assistant to NHL president John Ziegler but was bored by the lack of challenge. He tried colour commentary on *Hockey Night in Canada*, and he had his own intermission feature as well. He was involved in several businesses in Boston, the city to which he returned, and he has continued to give endless hours of his time and energy to the Bruins' alumni, particularly those players from his teams in the early 1970s. His relationship with Alan Eagleson deteriorated quickly after Orr discovered Boston's generous contract offer back in 1976, and the two men who were once best friends never spoke again. It wasn't until a few years ago, though, when Orr started to work as a player agent, that he discovered his post-playing place in the hockey world. He recruits and scouts youngsters from around the continent, and continues to stay involved in the game through appearances, endorsements, and charity efforts of all kinds. Almost from the day he started playing in the NHL, he has inspired future players to emulate his style. There will never, ever, be another Bobby Orr.

ORSZAGH, Vladimir
b. Banska Bystrica, Czechoslovakia (Slovakia), May 24, 1977
Only time will tell if 2002 was a breakthrough season for Orszagh, but it had all the makings of such good possibilities. Drafted by the Islanders in 1995, he went on to play just 34 games over the next few seasons with the team, spending most of his time in the minors. By 2000, he had left the NHL to play in Sweden, but when Nashville signed him as a free agent he came back for another go. The Predators gave him a regular shift for the year, and the winger responded with 15 goals. More important, he played for Slovakia at the 2002 World Championships, becoming a part of that historic gold-medal team. A career that stumbled out of the gate may have found its form.

OSBORNE, Keith
b. Toronto, Ontario, April 2, 1969
No sooner had Osborne been drafted 12th overall in 1987 than he went out and suffered serious injuries to his wrist and foot at training camp in North Bay that fall. He ended up crawling into the NHL rather than flying, and the Blues used him in only five games before trading him to Toronto. The Leafs assigned him to the minors until Tampa took him in the Expansion Draft, but even the Lightning gave him only 11 NHL games. The rest of Osborne's career, which ended in 2001, was spent in the minors, with teams like the San Antonio Dragons, Zurich Grasshoppers, Augsburger Panthers, and Macon Whoopee.

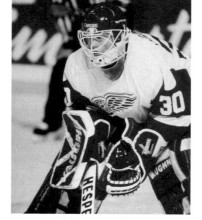

In 1996-97, Bowman made Chris Osgood the starting goalie for Detroit and aging veteran Mike Vernon his backup.
CHRIS OSGOOD

OSBORNE, Mark ("Ozzie")
b. Toronto, Ontario, August 13, 1961
When he was in his prime and at the top of his game, Osborne was as good as they came. His best situation was as a third-line player, a guy who could hit hard and clean, check an opponent to the point of frustration, and score his share of goals to put an exclamation point on his feistiness. That's why Detroit put him to work in 1981, and that's why the Leafs had him for eight years and two stints with the team. He was used on the power play, but for a while he also could kill penalties with the best of them. After leaving the NHL in 1995, Osborne played a short time in the IHL and went into coaching with Cleveland, his only team in the "I," and from there he ended up coaching back home with St. Mike's in the OHL in Toronto.

OSBURN, Randoulf "Randy"
b. Collingwood, Ontario, November 26, 1952
After playing part of the '72-'73 season with the Leafs, Osburn was consigned to the minors until Philadelphia acquired him in the summer of 1974. Osburn played just one game with the Flyers the next year, a Cup-winning season for the Bullies. It wasn't enough to get his name on the Cup. He finished his career in that city in 1978, playing for the local Firebirds.

OSGOOD, Chris
b. Peace River, Alberta, November 26, 1972
Scotty Bowman might have been the winningest coach of all time, but no one ever accused him of being compassionate. Perhaps that's why he won so much. At any rate, in 1996-97, Bowman made Chris Osgood the starting goalie for Detroit and aging veteran Mike Vernon his backup. This was as it should

have been in the Detroit scheme of things. Osgood had been in the Red Wings system since 1992 and had made steady and impressive progress through his early years. The previous season he played 50 games and led the league with 39 wins while taking the team to the conference finals, and he even scored a goal in the process. Vernon's addition to the team was to strengthen the goaltending, not alter it. Yet come the playoffs, Bowman pulled a reversal and made the veteran Vernon the starter and Osgood the backup. That meant virtual relegation to the bench, and sure enough Osgood played only 47 minutes in the post-season as Detroit won its first Cup since 1955. The next year, Bowman felt Osgood was ready to handle the pressure of a drive to the Cup, and the goalie stood tall in leading the team to a second successive victory. He continued to be the number-one man until the summer of 2001, when the Wings signed Dominik Hasek. Osgood's $4-million salary became unneeded baggage, and he was traded to the Islanders. He promptly played the team into the post-season for the first time in years, and established himself as a solid, top-flight goalie still very much in his prime. A sub-par '02-'03 season, though, combined with a $4-million-a-year contract, saw him traded to St. Louis, a more legitimate Cup contender.

O'SHEA, Danny
b. Toronto, Ontario, June 15, 1945

When St. Louis acquired O'Shea from Chicago in February 1972, it seemed to be the start of something good for both parties. O'Shea had a strong finish to the season, and in the summer the Blues signed him to a five-year contract. They even got his brother, Danny, to play with him. One year later, after an average season, the Blues cut O'Shea from training camp for the '73-'74 season. They offered him a demotion or outright release. He refused the demotion and went home to Beaverton – disappeared, actually. His agent, Alan Eagleson, went to the league seeking money for his client because at the time of his release – which was not a contractual possibility, anyway – O'Shea was "injured," or, in ill health. He suffered from ulcers, and he was depressed, in part because his wife had just had a miscarriage, in part because a team that a year ago wanted to make him the cornerstone of the franchise no longer wanted him around. The matter was resolved, but O'Shea missed the entire season. He played for Minnesota in the WHA the next year and then retired, his five-year NHL career mysteriously aborted. He had begun his career with the Canadian National Team, playing with the squad for two years while earning his B.A. and competing in the 1968 Olympics in Grenoble.

O'SHEA, Kevin
b. Toronto, Ontario, May 28, 1947

One man's passion is another man's poison, which is why O'Shea's time with the National Team ended in controversy and he became the object of Punch Imlach's hockey desires. Like brother Danny, Kevin spent some time playing international hockey, and he made the team that played at the 1969 World Championships in Stockholm. During a game against the home side, he nailed an opponent behind his own goal, earning a five-minute penalty. On the way to the box, he hit another player and earned a misconduct as well as the wrath of local fans and media. Those were, however, exactly the qualities that Buffalo GM and coach Imlach wanted for his expansion team, and in 1970 O'Shea joined the Sabres in a tough-guy capacity. He was traded to St. Louis a year later when the Blues wanted to unite the brothers, and in the playoffs Kevin scored the most important goal of his life, an overtime score over Minnesota in game six to send the Blues into the semifinals. The next year, though, he was demoted, and in 1974 he played in the WHA. He closed out his professional career by playing in Sweden, going over with Morris Mott, another former member of the National Team.

OSIECKI, Mark
b. St. Paul, Minnesota, July 23, 1968

In his two NHL seasons (1991-93), Osiecki played for four NHL teams, not a welcoming sign for the 23-year-old graduate of the University of Wisconsin. He spent the bulk of his brief career in the IHL, though he did play for the U.S. at the 1992 World Championships. He retired in 1995 to get into coaching. He started in high school, worked his way up to college, and then in 1997 was named head coach for the Green Bay Gamblers of the USHL.

O'SULLIVAN, Chris
b. Dorchester, Massachusetts, May 15, 1974

Nothing has been given to this young man in his life. One of 11 children, they raised themselves after both parents died of cancer. Chris grew up to be a fine hockey player and attended Boston University on scholarship. Five games into his career at BU he suffered a serious neck injury, missed the season, required an operation, and came close to paralysis. He bounced back, though, and played for the U.S. at the World Juniors and World Championships. Calgary drafted him, and for three years he tried to work his way into the lineup. Once this failed, he traded to the Rangers but signed with Vancouver as a free agent in 1999. That summer, his best friend was murdered. Needless to say, he didn't have the best

Danny O'Shea

He made the team that played at the 1969 World Championships in Stockholm.
KEVIN O'SHEA

Mark Osiecki

Jaroslav Otevrel

Gerry Ouellette

Ted Ouimet

Dennis Owchar

season. He moved on to Philadelphia, an emotional nomad looking for strength. That didn't work, so he tried playing overseas, moving to Kloten and playing in Germany. O'Sullivan is still young in years and experience on the ice, but inside, off the ice, he's an old man. Hockey has never seemed so trivial, or important.

OTEVREL, Jaroslav
b. Gottwaldow, Czechoslovakia (Czech Republic), September 16, 1968
Just because it happened far away from the NHL doesn't mean it can't happen here. In a Finnish league game late in the '95-'96 season, Otevrel suffered a neck injury that left him paralyzed below the waist. The injury ended his career, of course, at age 27, but it just as easily could have happened while he played for San Jose in previous seasons in the NHL. He had been a decent prospect in the Czech Republic, but after two partial years with the Sharks he decided to go to Finland in 1994 to continue his career with Pori.

OTTO, Joel
b. Elk River, Minnesota, October 29, 1961
One of the great undrafted stories of the modern game, Otto had size and strength enough to entice any scout to toss away a draft choice on him – yet none did. Instead, he graduated from Bemidji State and signed with Calgary, and during his 11 seasons with the Flames he developed into a forceful and important element of the team's drive to their 1989 Stanley Cup. Otto could do it all. He was a physical presence when he had to be, he was a first-rate, 2-way player, he was good for 15 goals most seasons; he put the team first. He ended his career with the Flyers, and his international resumé is almost unrivalled by his compatriots of the era. Otto played at two Canada Cups, two World Championships, a World Cup, and an Olympics. After retiring, he became a professional player consultant for MacLeod Dixon, a law firm specializing in athlete representation and advice, and later worked for a company that manufactures custom-made golf clubs.

OUELLET, Maxime
b. Beauport, Quebec, June 17, 1981
The Flyers think they have one of the best young goalies in the world, and although they put him into two games in 2000-01, they have no desire to rush him. He played for Canada at the World Juniors and is now in the minors, learning the game at a proper pace in the right place. He will be heard from in the NHL for years to come – just not yet.

OUELLETTE, Eddie
b. Ottawa, Ontario, March 9, 1911
d. unknown
A career that began in 1929 in the IHL was stopped suddenly in 1935 when Chicago decided it needed Ouellette to play centre. Three goals in a full season convinced the Hawks they were mistaken, and Ouellette wound up in Portland to play most of the rest of his career.

OUELLETTE, Gerry "Red"
b. Grand Falls, New Brunswick, November 1, 1938
Ouellette was invited to try out in the Montreal system by Sam Pollock in 1957, but he suffered the flu and had to return home. He was invited again the next year, provided he pay his own way and with the proviso that if he made the team he would be reimbursed. He made a favourable impression the second time around and Pollock sent him to the Waterloo Siskins, where Ouellette averaged nearly a goal a game. During that year, he also impressed Boston scout Baldy Cotton – and Cotton managed to sign him right under Pollock's nose. He joined the Bruins in December 1960, but in 34 games scored only 5 goals. It was his one and only NHL opportunity. Ouellette played another decade in the minors and when he retired he made Cambellton his lifelong address. He led the Tigers to three Hardy Cups during his 10 years as head coach, and coached several other teams as well, including the Junior B North Stars and Juvenile North Stars. He also the director of the Memorial Gardens Minor Hockey Association and Cambellton Minor Baseball Association, and sports director for the City of Campbellton until he retired in 1993.

OUIMET, Ted
b. Noranda, Quebec, July 6, 1947
Goalie Ouimet got into only one NHL game, and he allowed just two goals but lost the game. On March 22, 1969, he got the call to start but the Pittsburgh Penguins won 2-1. Ouimet then spent the better part of seven seasons in the minors before retiring. He later settled in Strathroy, Ontario.

OWCHAR, Dennis
b. Dryden, Ontario, March 28, 1953
During his six years in the NHL, Owchar, more than almost any other defencemen, inspired fear in opposing forwards who cut over the blueline without knowing where he was. By the time they figured it out, they were likely butt on the ice and out of it. Owchar never set any scoring records, but he hit

After retiring, he became a professional player consultant for MacLeod Dixon.
JOEL OTTO

like a wall and struck like thunder. He played only for lowly Pittsburgh and Colorado, but once he was in the lineup he was not easily moved out of it. In 1977, though, he was on the receiving end of a vicious Tiger Williams high stick that cut him badly and the broke Tiger's stick. Williams was charged with assault, and in the ensuing trial a famous incident occurred in which the prosecutors heaped stick after stick on the courtroom floor after trying to smash them against a steel cylinder (in an attempt to exhibit the force needed to break a stick). Williams was exonerated, but the case once again brought hockey violence into Ontario's courts, a theme of the 1970s under Attorney General Roy McMurtry. Owchar finished his career in the minors and later relocated to Toronto, where he worked in computer sales.

OWEN, George

b. Hamilton, Ontario, February 12, 1901
d. Milton, Massachusetts, March 4, 1986

One of the greatest athletes and men of honour to be associated with the NHL, Owen began his adult life in full stride. He graduated from Harvard in 1923 – where he had been All-American in football, baseball, and hockey – but rather than go directly to the big league he played amateur hockey and didn't make good on his wonderful start. He finally joined the Bruins in 1928, and as a rookie he anchored a defence that led the team to its first Stanley Cup. Wearing number 4, he became captain in 1931 but retired in 1933 after an appendectomy and subsequent phlebitis. He had been the highest-paid player on the team, but he entered politics and experienced the same level of success. He became a special assistant within the Republican ranks and later an assistant to the Republican state committees of three states. He was an investment broker and journalist for the *Boston Globe*, and in the Second World War he managed a tool company that made machine gun parts. Owen scouted for the Phillies in hockey and the Pirates in baseball, and in 1952 he became administrative assistant at Vermont Academy. A year later, he began teaching at Milton Academy and also coached baseball, football, and hockey. He retired to private life in 1965, his hockey years well behind him, his contributions great, his zest for life never fully sated.

He was an investment broker and journalist for the Boston Globe.
GEORGE OWEN

OZOLINSH, Sandis ("Ozo")

b. Riga, Soviet Union (Latvia), August 3, 1972

San Jose knew something most other teams didn't when it drafted Ozolinsh 30th overall in 1991. The next year, he was on the blueline helping Russia win gold at the '92 World Juniors, and that fall he was in the NHL. He was a star in the making, a surefire hit, one of the finest young rushing defencemen in the game. His three-and-a-bit years in San Jose were marked by two events. In the 1994 playoffs against Toronto, he had a great opportunity to score but chose to pass into the corner. It was overtime of game six, and the Leafs came back to win the series. For a long time, whenever anyone saw him, all that was asked was, "why didn't you shoot?" The second defining moment came on October 26, 1995, when he was traded to Colorado for Owen Nolan, a blockbuster deal that worked well for both teams but really well for Ozolinsh. At season's end, the Avs won the Cup. Ozolinsh had scored an incredible 26 goals in his second season with San Jose, and his creativity from the blueline was his greatest asset. For five years he anchored the team, but in the summer of 2000 free agency reared its monetary head and Ozolinsh was on the move. Carolina signed him to a five-year, $25 million contract no one could have turned down, but a year later he was sent to Florida, and then on to Anaheim in 2002-03. This allowed him to play for his mother country, Latvia, in the 2002 World Championships in Sweden, the first chance he had to do so. Earlier that year, he played for Latvia at the Olympics in Salt Lake City.

Sandis Ozolinsh

PACHAL, Clayton
b. Yorkton, Saskatchewan, April 21, 1956
Pachal came out of New Westminster in 1976 just before the Bruins became a junior powerhouse and started winning Memorial Cups like they were ping-pong tournaments. He played a few games with Boston and Colorado but spent most of his pro career in the minors.

PADDOCK, John
b. Brandon, Manitoba, June 9, 1954
Being called up to the Washington Capitals in the middle of the '75-'76 season to help the team was like asking a newborn to disprove the Theory of Relativity – not likely. Fortunately for Paddock, the callup lasted just eight games and he was traded to Philadelphia in the summer. In all, the right winger played 87 games in the NHL, but remained active in the game from almost the moment he retired in 1983. Primarily he has coached, his big chance coming with Winnipeg in 1991. He later became the team's GM as well, though in his last season he was coach only and then assistant GM only. He has also coached extensively in the minors, most recently with Hartford, so although his playing days were short, his executive days have now stretched to two decades' worth of time in the game.

PAEK, Chison "Jim"
b. Seoul, South Korea, April 7, 1967
It's not surprising that Paek's career has taken him around the world, given that he was born on the other side of the planet. When his parents came to Canada, they changed his Eastern name of Chison to the Western Jim, but unlike many Asians he played hockey rather than follow a path toward higher education. He played at St. Mike's and Oshawa and turned pro in 1987 with Muskegon, Pittsburgh's IHL affiliate. Paek was called up toward the end of the '90-'91 season and stayed with the Pens through the playoffs, a most fortuitous time as the team won its first Stanley Cup. He played most of the next year as well, winning another championship, and became the first South Korean to have his name stamped on Lord Stanley's sacred hockey bowl. After one more season with the Pens, though, his address changed with great frequency. He was traded to L.A. and Ottawa, and then wound up in the minors for good. He played in the "I" for five years and later wound up in Anchorage in the WCHL where he had a second role of being the team's defence coach. In 2001-02 he played in Nottingham, where he remains.

PAGEAU, Paul
b. Montreal, Quebec, October 1, 1959
He made it to the NHL, was shelled, and never made it back. Pageau was a star goalie in Quebec junior and played for Canada at the 1980 Olympics in Lake Placid. That summer Los Angeles signed him as a free agent. On February 3, 1981, he got his chance, a road game against the Cup-champion Islanders – and he paid the price. Final score, 8-1 for New York. Pageau played the entire game. He spent five years in the minors and retired in 1985 with an unfortunate GAA of 8.00.

PAHLSSON, Samuel "Sami"
b. Ornskoldsvik, Sweden, December 17, 1977
After almost five years playing in Sweden's premier league, Pahlsson came to the NHL in 2000 to try his luck with Boston. The young centre played just 17 games with the Bruins before he was traded to Anaheim, and then played his first year and a half with the Ducks. Still an emerging talent, Anaheim isn't sure how much better he will get, though he's getting a fair chance to prove himself and that's all any player can ask for.

Clayton Pachal

PAIEMENT, Rosaire "Rosie"
b. Earlton, Ontario, August 12, 1945
Rosie and Wilf Paiement made it to the NHL, but they had 14 brothers and sisters who didn't! Their father, Wilf Sr., was a Canadian arm wrestling champion, and many of the boys in the family took after their old man and were known for appearing at various tournaments with brazen biceps. Rosie played in the NHL for 5 years with Philadelphia and Vancouver, scoring 34 goals with the Canucks in '70-'71. In 1972, he signed with the WHA's Chicago Cougars, and played six years in that league until he was elbowed and sucker-punched in the left eye by Dave Semenko. The damage was so severe that Paiement had to retire, but his outlook on life remained sunny. He settled in Fort Lauderdale and bought the Coral Ridge Motel. He opened a bar named the Penalty Box, and for years every French-Canadian passing through those parts have paid Rosie a visit.

Jim Paek

PAIEMENT, Wilf
b. Earlton, Ontario, October 16, 1955
When you're the youngest of 16 children – and the next youngest is your tough 10-year-old brother, Rosie – you learn to fight early in life. Wilf took after Rosie in the toughness and hockey aspects of life, making his way to the NHL. Because of their age differences, though, Rosie was out of the NHL before Wilf entered it. Wilf joined Kansas City in 1974, and for five and a half years played for the horrible franchise that only had two playoff games. It was a blessing and a curse when the Leafs acquired him, a blessing because he was going to a decent team in the hockey capital, a curse because he was traded for Lanny McDonald, one of the most popular players in team history. He never failed to score fewer than 21 goals in a season, and in his first full year with the Leafs he had a career-high 40. The Leafs soon traded him to Quebec, where he had his finest years, and then his career petered out with a series of short stops. Paiement played in 3 successive All-Star Games – 1976-78 – and scored 356 NHL goals. He also had more than 100 penalty minutes in 13 of his 14 seasons, though a series of injuries and resultant body fatigue told him to retire in 1988. Paiement settled in Mississauga, Ontario, where he had acquired numerous properties during his playing days, and managing those lands kept him busy in his post-playing years.

Rosie Paiement

PAILLE, Marcel
b. Shawinigan Falls, Quebec, December 8, 1932
Little did Marcel Paille know that when he joined the Citadelle as a junior rookie in 1949 he would play his last game of pro hockey in 1974. He spent the better

Marcel Paille
(opposite page)

part of that quarter-century in the AHL, mostly in Providence, but for parts of seven years he dressed for the New York Rangers. Fewer than 20 goalies have recorded a shutout in their NHL debut, and Paille is among that tiny number. On November 2, 1957, he beat Boston 5-0, his only shutout in 33 games that year. The shutout also marked the first on CBS's broadcasts, then in just its second season, with Bud Palmer and Fred Cusick doing the work for American hockey fans. Paille's next four stints were all short, but he led the AHL in wins on a regular basis, played the full complement of 70 games, and won numerous awards and honours. Without question, though, his most commanding presence in the NHL came during the '64-'65 season when he shared duties with the elder Jacques Plante. Paille not only played well, he beat Plante for starting goalie honours and watched as the future Hall of Famer was sent to the minors. His last nine years were all in the minors, save a short stay in the WHA.

PALANGIO, Pete
b. North Bay, Ontario, September 10, 1908
One of the oldest living players and the oldest Habs star from the 1920s, Pete was 1 of 11 children, 8 of whom were boys. He grew up playing in North Bay, and as a kid he was spotted by referee Mike Rodden, who contacted the Canadiens. They sent someone to look Palangio over and offered him a contract right away. He demurred and kept on playing with the Trappers, and by year's end he led the league in goals and received a much better offer from the Habs. At 18, he signed on the dotted line, and a few months later was playing the game with Joliat and Morenz. Brother Carl attended training camp with Pete, but Carl was farmed out and Pete got to stay with the big boys. For two and a half years he was an NHLer, but then spent the better part of nine years in the IHL and AHL. In '36-'37, Palangio finished the season in remarkable fashion. First, he helped the St. Louis Flyers win the AHA championship (with brother Tom), and then, just a few weeks later, Chicago called him up and he won the Stanley Cup! From then on, it was the minors all the way for Palangio, but as the years went on his knees became wonkier and wonkier. After retiring, he returned to North Bay in 1944 and took over the family's Chrysler dealership for 15 years until he found another project. He bought a small vending machine business, transformed it into Palangio Vending, and expanded it to include jukeboxes and catering. He also stayed in hockey, sponsoring the Palangio Blackhawks, which won the NOHA senior title in 1949. He later owned and managed the Trappers for many years at the junior and senior level, producing many champions.

When the Canadiens closed the Forum in 1996, they invited Palangio to the ceremonies.
PETE PALANGIO

When the Canadiens closed the Forum in 1996, they invited Palangio to the ceremonies, and the oldest living player stepped onto the ice to join Lafleur, Richard et al. for a final farewell to the building.

PALAZZARI, Aldo
b. Eveleth, Minnesota, July 25, 1918
The worst part about suffering an injury that ends your career is not knowing how good you could have become. Palazzari was just starting out in 1943 when he played for Boston. He was traded to the Rangers toward the end of the season and in October '44 went to the Rangers camp looking to build on a decent rookie year in which he had scored 8 goals in 35 games. He lost an eye in a freak accident and never played again. He was just 26. He returned to Eveleth to raise a family of six, and one of his boys, Doug, had a fine pro career a generation later.

PALAZZARI, Doug ("Pizza")
b. Eveleth, Minnesota, November 3, 1952
Following in his father's footsteps, Doug wanted to play hockey during every free moment as a kid. And, also following in his footsteps, Doug had some nasty injuries during his pro career. He played for the U.S. at the World Championships in the early 1970s before joining St. Louis in 1974, but '74-'75 was to be his only full season in the NHL. He did see action in three other years, though he suffered a serious injury while in Kansas City that almost ended his career. In a practice, he chased teammate Joe Zanussi on a breakaway, but as he dove to catch him, Zanussi's skate hit Palazzari in the face. The blow knocked out 11 teeth and shattered his jaw in 6 places, and he decided it was time to retire. St. Louis talked him out of it, and though his time with the Blues was short, he went to Salt Lake City and forged a sensational CHL career. Twice in three years he led the league in goals, assists, and points, also winning MVP honours both years. After that, he missed most of '80-'81 after an injured shoulder required surgery, and when he reinjured the blade the next year he knew it was time to quit. He remained with the team in the PR department and later moved to his alma mater, Colorado College, as an assistant coach. The time at CC spurred his interest in the game, and in 1991 he moved on to USA Hockey where he became the director of the Youth and Education Program. He remains there today. In 2000, Palazzari was inducted into the U.S. Hockey Hall of Fame.

PALFFY, Zigmund "Ziggy"
b. Skalica, Czechoslovakia (Slovakia), May 5, 1972
Back home, Palffy goes by the nickname Zigo (Baron)

Doug Palazzari

Ziggy Palffy

because he shares a last name with a famous noble family in Slovakia. Hockey's Palffy is possessed with wealth of talent and success as he enters the prime of his career. Even before arriving in North America in 1993, Palffy had great success. He played for Czechoslovakia at the World Juniors and in the 1991 Canada Cup, and he was slated to play at the 1992 Olympics until he injured his shoulder. His greater dream came true two years later, though, when he represented his homeland, Slovakia, at the 1994 Olympics in Lillehammer. After 2 part-time seasons with the Islanders, he made an enormous impact with the team in '95-'96, scoring 43 goals in his first full season. Since then, the right winger has not let up, becoming one of the top and most consistent scorers in the NHL. In the summer of 1999, he was traded to L.A. in a major deal that gave the Kings a star player on offence, and since then the Kings have made the playoffs each year. Palffy's career reached its first great climax in 2002, though, after the Kings were eliminated from the playoffs and he travelled to Sweden to play for Slovakia in the World Championships. His play was key to the team winning its first gold medal, and Palffy became not just a national hero, but a national treasure.

PALMATEER, Mike ("The Popcorn Kid")
b. Toronto, Ontario, January 13, 1954

Knees ravaged by goaltending activity, Palmateer was forced to retire in 1984 at 30 years of age. In his day, he was one of the most exciting and popular goalies in the league, his southpaw, flop-around style both magical and confounding. He played six of his eight seasons with Toronto, at first part of a team so close to being a real contender and then traded by the maniacal Punch Imlach in his second go-round as GM. Palmateer was quirky and fun – he once claimed to have cut himself while hanging drapes in the middle of the night – and his style fit his personality. When Palmateer returned to the Leafs fold, sanity no longer prevailed and his knees just couldn't take the grind of games and practices. Once in Washington, he was in hospital prepping for knee surgery when the Caps phoned him in desperation after their other goalie, Wayne Stephenson, was injured. Palmateer took an ambulance to the game, played, and had the operation a few days later. In his first years after retiring, he opened a restaurant north of the city and worked in real estate, though he eventually got back into the game. First, he worked with the NHL's Central Scouting service, and then, in the summer of 2002, the Leafs hired him as an amateur scout.

Palmateer was quirky and fun and his style fit his personality.
MIKE PALMATEER

PALMER, Brad
b. Duncan, British Columbia, September 14, 1961

He had the shot, the great shot, the shot that goalies couldn't see, the shot that the net was hard pressed to contain within its mesh. He was drafted high by Minnesota in 1980 as a result of that shot, and when he made the North Stars he scored on long shots goalies whiffed at. That lasted a season, when he scored 22 goals in '81-'82. Then, opponents figured him out. He took too big of a windup. They got to him before he had a chance to let go the slapper. He didn't fight in close for the puck and he didn't go to the net with physical determination. He was traded to Boston and from there was in the minors and off to Europe with slapshot speed. After retiring, he settled in Victoria, B.C., and coached kids hockey.

Brad Palmer

PALMER, Rob
b. Detroit, Michigan, October 2, 1952

In the years leading up to his NHL initiation with Chicago in 1973, Palmer had a pretty spoiled hockey upbringing. He played kid hockey with a couple of guys named Marty and Mark who had a dad named Gordie. In university, at Denver, he had a coach named Murray Armstrong, the most influential coach in U.S. college history. Unfortunately for Palmer, none of this translated to more than a cursory career in the big time. Over three years he played a few games with the Hawks, but in 1976 he retired, never having established himself.

PALMER, Rob
b. Sarnia, Ontario, September 10, 1956

A defenceman out of the University of Michigan, Palmer played seven NHL seasons as a diligent offensive player. He played all but two of his years with Los Angeles, the last seasons spent with New Jersey after the Kings failed to offer him a contract. He retired in 1986 after the Devils sent him to the minors and failed to recall him over his final two seasons of pro hockey.

PANAGABKO, Ed ("Can of Tobacco")
b. Norquay, Saskatchewan, May 17, 1934
d. January 18, 1979

When this son of a Polish shoemaker first played junior hockey in Humboldt in 1951, it marked the first time he had ever played indoors. Norquay had an outdoor NHL-sized rink where Ed and his brother played as kids and Ed developed his skating and his tenacious style of play. The NHL, though, being what it was, didn't much like variations from Smith or Johnson or Campbell, so when Panagabko made the Bruins in 1955 he underwent a transformation. Teammates asked him how to pronounce that jumble of letters, and after repeated attempts to get it right

Rob Palmer

Jay Pandolfo

Darren Pang

Greg Pankewicz

Joe Papike

Leo LaBine said, more or less, "the hell with it – I'm calling you can of tobacco," and the nickname stuck. Can of Tobacco wasn't supposed to play for Boston in '55-'56, but at camp the team experienced a series of injuries to starters, including Flem Mackell, Vic Stasiuk, and Lorne Davis. Over two partial seasons, though, the left winger cum centre didn't score a single goal, and when he was sent down he never came back. Instead, he played for a decade in the AHL and WHL, becoming team captain of the San Francisco Seals. He was just 44 when he died of liver disease.

PANDOLFO, Jay ("Pando")
b. Winchester, Massachusetts, December 27, 1974
The scoring side of Pandolfo's brain, which had been so active during his college days at Boston University, was lobotomized when he got to New Jersey, a team that stresses defence until all scoring brain cells are dead. In his final year at BU, he led the NCAA with 38 goals, a total he failed to equal in his first 5 years in the NHL. The tradeoff was worth it to the Selke Trophy aspirant, though, because he won the Cup with New Jersey in 2000 and got to take the sacred grail home for a day. He's been with the team since entering the NHL in 1996 and is now an established player in the team's system.

PANG, Darren
b. Meaford, Ontario, February 17, 1964
After winning a Memorial Cup in 1984 with the Ottawa 67's, Pang played a single game with Chicago the following year before finding himself buried in the minors. Given that he was only 5'5" it made it even tougher for him to find his way out of those small-town bushes, but he played so well at training camp with the Hawks in 1987 that he became the team's number-one man. Over 2 seasons he had 76 starts, but at camp in 1990 he injured his knee and was forced to retire (he had won a Turner Cup in Indianapolis the previous spring). Like any former goalie worth his salt, he wound up in television as a colour commentator, with ESPN in the U.S., where he put his trademark wit to good work.

PANKEWICZ, Greg
b. Drayton Valley, Alberta, November 6, 1970
Active in the game but inactive in NHL circles, it looks as if Pankewicz will go down in history as having played 21 games in the big time. Undrafted, he signed with the expansion Ottawans after two fine years in the minors, but after just three games he was consigned to the eternity that was the minors. He didn't resurface until 5 years later with Calgary, but there, too, he went goalless in an 18-game stint. Since then he's been back in the lower echelons of the game, most recently with Pensacola in the East Coast league.

PANTELEEV, Grigori
b. Gastello, Soviet Union (Russia), November 13, 1972
A Latvian by birthright, Panteleev has only recently been able to play for his country in international competition, but he has made up for lost time. He has played in the last three World Championships for Lettland during his now European-based career. He began in 1992 with Boston, but after four years with the Bruins and then Islanders he was in the minors. Most of his seven years in North America passed in the AHL and IHL, so in 1998 he moved to Germany and then to Russia and Sweden to play.

PAPIKE, Joe
b. Eveleth, Minnesota, March 28, 1914
d. Eveleth, Minnesota, May 28, 1967
Papike spent most of his time in the AHA, precursor to the AHL, in the years before and during the war. While he also served in the military, the conflict gave him his only NHL chance, with Chicago. The Hawks brought him up from Kansas City for parts of three seasons, but once the war ended, so, too, had Papike's career.

PAPINEAU, Justin
b. Ottawa, Ontario, January 15, 1980
Drafted 46th overall in 1998. Drafted 75th overall in 2000. His stock went down because of his numbers in junior with Belleville, so he had less leverage, not more, when the Blues signed him. Papineau played a single game with the Blues in 2001-02, and played the rest of the season with Worcester in the AHL. In 2002-03, he made the Blues because of his offensive ability and despite his defensive weaknesses.

He made his debut with Toronto in 1963 after three years in the minors.
JIM PAPPIN

PAPPIN, Jim ("Pappy")
b. Sudbury, Ontario, September 10, 1939
One of Punch Imlach's whipping boys during the 1960s, Pappin made the most of his time with the Leafs until he was traded to Chicago in 1968. He made his debut with Toronto in 1963 after three years in the minors, and over the next five years Imlach made sure Pappin spent at least part of every season down in Rochester. But the Leafs won the Cup in his rookie season, and in the 1967 playoffs Pappin scored the Cup-winning goal in game six against Montreal. In fact, he led the playoffs that year with 7 goals and 15 points. By the time he got to the Hawks, he credited Imlach with teaching him about two-way play, and formed a terrific line with Pit Martin and Dennis Hull. He had 5 seasons of 27 goals or more and played in 2 Cup finals with Chicago, but his career came to a crawl and then a stop in California and Cleveland. He missed part of one season with Bell's palsy, a rare eye

disease, and the next with a bad back that forced him to retire. Pappin returned to Sudbury where he ran a tennis complex, but a strike by Inco, the company that drives everything in this mining town, forced him out of business. He got right back into hockey by scouting for a number of teams and settled in as the director of U.S. scouting for Chicago.

PARADISE, Bob
b. St. Paul, Minnesota, April 22, 1944

Before 1980's Miracle on Ice team, there weren't that many Americans who went on to play in the NHL after appearing in the global tournament. Paradise was one. He played in 1968 in Grenoble and in the Worlds the following year before making his NHL entrance with Minnesota in 1971. He was traded to Atlanta and on to Pittsburgh and Washington, always counted on for being a defensive defenceman rather than a Bobby Orr type. His play resembled that of his father-in-law, Bob Dill, who played with the Rangers, but it also gave him cause for concern with a series of nagging and painful injuries, particularly groin and stomach problems. After retiring in 1979, Paradise settled in Minneapolis where he set up a property management business and a construction consulting firm. In 1989, he was inducted into the U.S. Hockey Hall of Fame.

PARENT, Bernie
b. Montreal, Quebec, April 3, 1945

It is almost a universally accepted fact within the hockey world that the most talentless teams to win the Stanley Cup were Philadelphia's in 1974 and '75. It also is an even greater surety that the Flyers never, ever would have won had it not been for the mind-boggling goaltending of Bernie Parent. He grew up in Montreal idolizing Jacques Plante, a good choice of hero. Plante's sister lived next door to the Parent family, so whenever Jacques visited, young Bernie hovered nearby waiting to talk about goaltending. Parent didn't start skating until he was 11, but he loved stopping shots. He developed into a great prospect and played junior with Niagara Falls. He and Doug Favell led the Flyers to the Memorial Cup in 1965, and this was not the last time their paths would cross. At the time, the Niagara Falls Flyers were the sponsored team of Boston, and Parent got his start with the Bruins. The Flyers claimed him in the Expansion Draft of 1967, but although he became the starter for the team for the next three and a half years, he wasn't set forever. The Flyers were not a good club at that point, and they believed that his backup, the same Doug Favell, was the better of the two. They traded Parent to Toronto, and for a year and a half he was in heaven, sharing goaltending duties with his hero,

Parent didn't start skating until he was 11, but he loved stopping shots.
BERNIE PARENT

Plante, whose career was winding down. Parent was a replica of Plante. He wore the same style mask; he played his angles to perfection and kept his legs tight together; he worked on handling the puck and communicating with his defencemen. But as the '71-'72 season wound down, Parent fielded offers from the WHA as it prepared to launch its first season. Team owner Harold Ballard unwisely mocked Parent and the offers, telling Parent he could sign wherever he wanted. Ballard believed the league would never get off the ground and that Parent was easily replaced, and Parent, incensed, signed with the Philadelphia Blazers. He made history by wearing number 00, but after a year he wanted to return to the NHL – provided it wasn't with the Leafs. The Flyers acquired Parent's rights by sending Toronto a draft choice and Doug Favell (!) and Parent returned to the Flyers in 1973 at age 28 and in the prime of his career. The team was now brawling its way to victory on a regular basis, and good goaltending was the one element that coach Fred Shero knew a team needed to win, no matter how much intimidation it faced elsewhere on the ice. In the next two years, 1974-76, Parent was the best goalie in the world. He led the league in wins (47 and 44) and shutouts (12 and 12) both years. He led the league for lowest GAA both seasons (1.89 and 2.03), and in the playoffs he was even better. He alone stopped Bobby Orr and the Bruins in 1974, and Parent went on to win the Conn Smythe Trophy for both playoffs. Fans in Philadelphia adored him, and bumper stickers appeared everywhere that read, "Only the Lord Saves More than Bernie Parent." He missed most of the next year, though, with a serious eye injury, and the two years after that were more difficult as skill replaced goonery around the league. Parent's career ended in February 1979 when he was inadvertently poked in the eye by a stick during a scramble in front of the goal. His depth perception was badly damaged, but in the years that followed so, too, was his psychological makeup. He found it difficult going from Cup winner and player to goalie coach with the team, and developed a serious drinking problem. Time and AA cured that, and he learned to appreciate what he had and what he could still give to the game. He was inducted into the Hockey Hall of Fame in 1984.

PARENT, Bob
b. Windsor, Ontario, February 19, 1958

All he ever wanted was a chance, but in that flick of a switch of time, Parent failed to deliver a remarkable performance and he paid for it. He left Ontario junior in 1978 only to find himself firmly ensconced in the "I" for much of four years. The Leafs played him in 2 games, and Parent did himself no favours by allowing

Bob Paradise

Bob Parent

Rich Parent

13 goals. The Leafs gave him another brief shot and that was it. It wasn't much, but you have to stop the puck, as they say.

PARENT, Rich
b. Montreal, Quebec, January 12, 1973
Another Parent who turned into a goalie, Rich appears to have played his last in the NHL. He was never drafted, and it was only after three fine seasons in the minors that St. Louis signed him in 1997. He was named the Colonial League's best goalie, but in his first season he made only a brief appearance as a fill-in. The year after, he played 10 games with the Blues, but during his time in the minors suffered a ghastly injury – a scrotal contusion and ruptured testicle, the words alone conveying a level of pain that makes one wince. Parent later went to Tampa and then to Pittsburgh, but in 2001 he played in the DEL in Germany, dissatisfied by how few games he was playing.

PARGETER, George
b. Calgary, Alberta, February 24, 1923
His long career in the American league through the 1940s and into the 1950s was highlighted by four games with Montreal in '46-'47, though his goallessness in that time didn't speak to the numbers he put up in the minors. Pargeter was a healthy scorer, notably with the Bisons, though he finished his career in Calgary in 1955.

Michel Parizeau

PARISE, Jean-Paul "J.P." ("Jeep")
b. Smooth Rock Falls, Ontario, December 11, 1941
It was a moment of frustration and violence, of temper and scorn and disgust. It was a gesture that crystallized what was happening in the Summit Series, and it was both cheered and loathed by Canadian supporters. Early in game seven, in Moscow, Parise nailed Alexander Maltsev with a devastating hit and was called for a penalty. He objected vehemently and was given a 10-minute misconduct, and in that moment he raised his stick above his head and swung it at the referee's head. As the ref flinched, Parise stopped the stick just short of contact, and for that he received, of course, a game misconduct. That last penalty was one of the few Team Canada truly earned in the entire series, but it demonstrated an overwhelming frustration with the biased officiating. Nonetheless, Parise's very inclusion on this superb roster was the culmination of years of hard playing. He was put on a line with Phil Esposito and Wayne Cashman, and the pluggers were supposed to dig the puck out and get it to Espo in the slot. It worked, because he led the Series in goals (tied with Paul Henderson). Parise was in the middle of an eight-year stay with Minnesota, representing about half his time in the NHL. He was an

Early in game seven, in Moscow, Parise nailed Alexander Maltsev with a devastating hit.
J.P. PARISE

honest worker, not blessed with gobs of natural ability but sincerely blessed with an ability to persevere and outhustle his superior opponent. Yet he scored 20 goals 5 times and played in 2 All-Star Games on his own merit. He retired in 1979 after 890 games, his last year a return to Minnesota. He remained with the team, became an assistant to coach Glen Sonmor, and left soon after to work in the insurance industry for a while. Parise missed hockey, though, and came back to coach prep schools in the Minnesota area. In 2002, the Parise name was back in the news as his son, Zack, developed into a fine player at the World Junior Championships – playing for the U.S.!

PARIZEAU, Michel
b. Montreal, Quebec, April 9, 1948
In '71-'72, Parizeau played for both St. Louis and Philadelphia in his only NHL season. He signed with Quebec in the WHA in the summer and played seven years in that league before retiring. He went into coaching, where things got interesting. After a stint with Syracuse in the AHL, he became an assistant with Canada's juniors in 1986 while he was head coach in Drummondville. In the Q league playoffs later that year, all hell broke loose. His Voltigeurs were playing Chicoutimi in a best-of-nine series (yes, the Quebec league had to be different), and in game seven a series of calls went against his team and rendered Parizeau apoplectic. He ran onto the ice and went after the referee – and his entire team followed suit. They attacked the official until order was restored, and Parizeau was suspended for a full year for his outburst.

PARK, Bradford "Brad"
b. Toronto, Ontario, July 6, 1948
For his entire career, Park was known as the second-best this and the second-highest that, the most talented defenceman in the game with one exception – Bobby Orr. But unlike Orr, who was considered a future NHL superstar from the age of 12, Park took a bit longer to develop and emerged from the shadows rather than the limelight to earn his place in hockey history. As a kid, he was small and not that fast, but as he grew, he put on some weight and strength, and developed skills that had his hometown Leafs plenty interested. They got him into the Marlies lineup in 1965, and over the next three years it became ever clearer that he was going to play in the NHL. The only trouble was that these were the years of the emerging Amateur Draft. In 1966, the Rangers selected him with the 2nd overall, and Park's initial disappointment gave way to excite-

ment when he realized that the Blueshirts needed defencemen and he'd be given a great opportunity to play. He made the Rangers in 1968 and for the next seven and a half seasons developed into – you guessed it – the best defenceman in the game after Orr. Park could do most of the same things, but without that special Orr sparkle or magic that separated him from mere mortals. In '71-'72, Park scored 24 goals, had 73 points, and took his Rangers to the finals to face Orr's Bruins. It was a galactic battle between thetwo great blueliners, and Orr won out, scoring the Cup-winning goal and being named winner of the Conn Smythe Trophy. Park, though, was named to Team Canada's roster for the '72 Summit Series, and he contributed strong, though not breathtaking, play in helping Canada win. Back in the NHL, Park continued to define himself as a rushing defenceman. He skated beautifully, fluidly. He made hard, pinpoint passes and quarterbacked a strong New York power play. He logged much of the ice time and made the Rangers into a winner. But, just like Orr, his style of play contributed to knee problems that started early and plagued him his whole career. Over the course of his years in the league, he endured five major operations on his knees and four arthroscopic surgeries, and by the end, like Orr, he was skating better on one leg than most players did on two. Park and Orr were related in another sense. On November 7, 1975, Park, Jean Ratelle, and Joe Zanussi were traded to Boston for Phil Esposito and Carol Vadnais. The move was made by Bruins GM Harry

In his 17 NHL seasons, his teams made the playoffs every year.
BRAD PARK

Sinden in part to guard against Orr's loss to injury. In November 1975, the two best defencemen in the game were teammates. They played together for only 10 games before Orr was felled by another knee injury, but during those games the team was 6-1-3 and with Orr and Park on the power play point, the team might have kept winning for years if both had remained healthy. Park played seven and a half years with the Bruins, taking the team to the playoffs every year but never winning the Cup. Although he never won an individual trophy, his record was astounding: He finished runner-up in the Norris Trophy voting six times, four to Orr and twice to emerging star Dennis Potvin. Park finished his career with two seasons in Detroit with not very good teams, but in the end he had compiled a remarkable 896 points in 1,113 career games. In his 17 NHL seasons, his teams made the playoffs every year. He coached the Wings the next year, '85-'86, but his term was not successful. The Wings had a record of just 9-34-2 under Park, and he was fired. He was inducted into the Hockey Hall of Fame in 1988 and later opened a

theme park called Amesbury Sports Park in Massachusetts. More recently, he became a pro scout for the Rangers, the team that gave him his first chance to star way back when.

PARK, Richard
b. Seoul, South Korea, May 27, 1976

Like great music or food, Park is a mix of a few things. He was born in South Korea, so is oriented by his cultural heritage. He has lived in California since age three, so he is part modern American. And he learned all of his hockey in Canada, so he is steeped in the finest puck culture there is. As a kid, Park was invited to play hockey and fell in love with the sport. He eschewed baseball and basketball for the winter cool of the ice, and one time played a rep team from Toronto. That was when he knew he wanted to move there and play in the Metropolitan Toronto Hockey League, the world's largest hockey organization and the place any young teen could develop. He made the move, found a billet, and did, indeed, develop. He played junior in Ontario, but when the time came he represented the U.S. at the World Juniors in 1994 and '95. Although he was drafted into the NHL by Pittsburgh, his coming years were fraught with minor-league work studded with only brief appearances in the NHL. He moved around from team to team, but it wasn't until 2001 when Minnesota coach Jacques Lemaire took him under his wing, gave him playing time, and assured him mistakes would not be punished by demotion. Park played with greater confidence, and years from now his big break might be the culmination of that 2001-02 season when he was asked to play for the U.S. at the World Championships in Sweden. He was the team's best player, and showed a creativity and skill perhaps even he didn't know he possessed.

Richard Park

PARKER, Jeff
b. St. Paul, Minnesota, September 7, 1964

After leaving Michigan State in 1986, Parker turned pro with Buffalo only to find that life with the Sabres was no bowl of cherries. In four years, he played almost as much in the minors as in the NHL, and then was included in a large deal that helped the Sabres acquire Dale Hawerchuk from Winnipeg. He played only four more games, with Hartford a year later, and then retired.

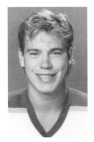
Jeff Parker

PARKER, Scott ("Parks")
b. Hanford, California, January 29, 1978

If I'm going to take this hockey thing seriously, Parker concluded during his teens, I'm going to Canada to play junior. So he did, in Kelowna, where he quickly

Scott Parker

Mark Parrish

Dave Parro

George Parsons

became the most feared player around. Big, mean, and talented, he could score and fight both. He was drafted in 1996 by New Jersey, but Parker decided to try his luck again and, unlike most teen gamblers, he won his roll of the dice. Colorado took him in the first round two years later, and Parker quickly made his mark with the Avs as a replacement for another tough guy, Chris Simon. Parker was part of the team that won the 2001 Stanley Cup, and is now an established member of the team and the designated fighter on a highly talented lineup. In his first 96 career games, though, he scored exactly 3 goals.

PARKES, Ernie
b. Dunnville, Ontario, November 4, 1894
d. July 9, 1948
It was only at the end of his career that Parkes got a chance to play in the NHL, with the Maroons in '24-'25. He had played in the Pacific Coast league for a number of years in Vancouver, coming close but never winning a Cup with the team in the playoffs.

PARKS, Greg ("Parksy")
b. Edmonton, Alberta, March 25, 1967
After an outstanding career at Bowling Green, Parks was unable to continue his playing ways in the NHL. He played a handful of games with the Islanders in the early 1990s, moved to Europe in 1993, and has been there ever since, playing in a variety of countries for a paycheque and cultural benefit both. Ironically, he has 1 goal in 23 NHL games, that 1 score coming in his first game!

PARRISH, Mark
b. Edina, Minnesota, February 2, 1977
Jefferson High School in Bloomington has its own significant place in hockey history, for it produced three NHLers who grew up together as best friends – Ben Clymer, Toby Petersen, and Mark Parrish. Parrish won silver with the U.S. at the 1997 WJC before joining Florida in 1998, and as a rookie he scored an impressive 24 goals. He was later traded to the Islanders, and in 2001-02 he had a career year with 30 goals. He has fit in nicely on Long Island on an emerging team, though he has proved to be a streaky player for goals. Nonetheless, his inspirational tattoo is proving valuable – on his shoulder is etched the phrase "Dreams never die, only dreamers." So far, Parrish is very much alive.

PARRO, Dave
b. Saskatoon, Saskatchewan, April 30, 1957
Boston drafted Parro coming out of Saskatoon but the Bruins let him go to Quebec in the 1979 draft before he ever played in Beantown. Even the Nordiques traded

him before he played a game, but the acquiring team, Washington, started him in a few games in 1980-81. The next year, Parro had played his way into the starter's role, and over 52 games he had a decent 16-26-7 record with a not very good team. That was to be his only full season, though, and his most satisfying years came with Hershey in the AHL. When he retired in 1987, Parro relocated to that city and became involved in coaching.

PARSONS, George ("Bubs"/ "Cannonball")
b. Toronto, Ontario, June 28, 1914
d. Toronto, Ontario, June 30, 1998
It was March 4, 1939. The Leafs were hosting Chicago, and Parsons was lined up for the home side. In a fight for the puck with Earl Robinson, Robinson

He was found in his office, dead from a gunshot wound to the head.
DUSAN PASEK

tried to lift Parsons' stick and missed. The blade struck Parsons' eye, and he never played again. He played all his youth hockey in Toronto and Conn Smythe felt he was a skilled prospect, tough as nails and capable of playing any position well. He was in his first full season with the Leafs after having worked his way into the lineup over the past two years, but all that hope ended in a hospital later that March night. Parsons worked for CCM for many years, using his hockey connections to good business effect and acting as a sales rep in Toronto and then in the Maritimes. He returned to Toronto in 1954, became a popular dinner speaker, and also worked with the NHL. Parsons later devised the first stick measurement gauge used by the league after it instituted a rule limiting a stick's curve. He passed away three weeks after suffering a stroke.

PARSSINEN, Timo
b. Lohja district, Finland, January 19, 1977
As soon as Parssinen was drafted, in 2001 by Anaheim, he came to North America to play pro. He spent most of that year in the AHL, though, and in 17 games with the Ducks he didn't score a single goal.

PASEK, Dusan
b. Bratislava, Czechoslovakia (Slovakia), September 7, 1960
d. Bratislava, Slovakia, March 15, 1998
The ending was as tragic as the beginning was bright, and when Pasek left this world he left both a legacy and a conundrum for those who knew him or admired him. He was found in his office, dead from a gunshot wound to the head. He was president of the Slovak Hockey Federation and had just watched his new country perform at the 1998 Olympics in Nagano. Yet, he gambled and accrued debts, and six (!) suicide notes were found

in his briefcase. Flash back to 1977. The teenage sensation joined Bratislava, a team dominated by the Stastny brothers. Pasek was the next generation of superstar, a great scorer and, off the ice, a man with flair, colour, and character. Over the years, he played in five World Championships, three Canada Cups, and two Olympics. His reward for loyalty and lifelong contributions to the sport back home was that he was allowed to play in the NHL in '88-'89. For two seasons he played in North America – the first with Minnesota, where he did not score like a superstar, and the second in the IHL. He returned to Europe and continued to play until 1993, and after retiring was salient to the development of the Slovakian hockey program and its meteoric rise from "C" pool to "B" pool to "A" pool. If only he had lived to see his nation win gold at the 2002 World Championships, defeating all the world's top countries!

PASIN, Dave

b. Edmonton, Alberta,
July 8, 1966

A first-round draft choice by Boston in 1984, Pasin did not live up to his billing as far as the Bruins were concerned. After 2 high-scoring seasons with Prince Albert in junior, he joined the Bruins and scored 18 goals as a rookie and then went to the minors the year after. Los Angeles acquired him a year later, but for the next decade he played outside the NHL after the Kings played him in five games and then let him go. He spent many of those years in Europe, though he made Moncton his home and lived there for a number of years.

PASLAWSKI, Greg

b. Kindersley, Saskatchewan,
August 25, 1961

For someone who claimed to be not much of a scorer, Paslawski was quite a scorer. He played from 1983 to '94, primarily with St. Louis where he once scored 29 goals. In all, he had five 20-goal seasons, though perhaps more satisfying was '85-'86 when his team went to the Stanley Cup semifinals. He played for five teams in his last four years before being demoted to Peoria in the "I," where he played another two and a half years. When he retired, Paslawski went where he knew – St. Louis. He became an independent contractor in the city for which he had played some six seasons.

PASSMORE, Steve

b. Thunder Bay, Ontario, January 29, 1973

Ever since he turned pro in 1994 in the Edmonton system, Passmore suffered from severe cramping. He didn't know why, but it got so bad he missed almost the entire '95-'96 season. Doctors told him to retire, but further tests revealed a chemical imbalance of metals in his body. Since then, he's been taking chelation therapy once a month and his goaltending has

From the time he started in the NHL in 1980 with Detroit, nothing was handed to him.
JOE PATERSON

improved. He worked his way into a few games with the Oilers in '98-'99 and then signed with Chicago, an excellent situation for him because the team was looking for either a number-one man or a reliable backup to Jocelyn Thibault. Passmore has proved able in the second duty while challenging for the first, and finally seems relaxed in goal without any health concerns to distract him.

PATERA, Pavel

b. Kladno, Czechoslovakia (Czech Republic),
September 6, 1971

The name Patera hardly strikes fear or awe in the minds of any NHLers, but on the world stage few players his age have had his incredible success. Patera won gold with the Czechs at the 1998 Olympics in Nagano. He then captained the team to gold at the World Championships in 1999 and won gold again in 2000 and 2001. Four years, four tournaments, four gold medals. Yet his NHL time is limited to just a few games with Dallas and Minnesota. Such are the vagaries of NHL teams and their lack of respect for international achievement.

PATERSON, Joe

b. Toronto, Ontario,
June 25, 1960

There are few players who had to sweat and grunt for every second of ice time the way Paterson did during his NHL tour of duty, but he did so with ambition in every breath and pride in every drop of perspiration. He played junior in London, but from the time he started in the NHL in 1980 with Detroit, nothing was handed to him. For almost all of his 9 seasons in the league he played in the minors as much as in the NHL, never playing more than 47 games with the big guys. The result was a young man who appreciated what he had and learned about the game every day, and these qualities stood him in good stead when he retired in 1992. He turned his hockey mind to coaching and for the last decade has been a fixture behind the bench of numerous AHL teams, most recently Louisville, before becoming a pro scout for the Florida Panthers.

PATERSON, Mark

b. Ottawa, Ontario, February 22, 1964

Orwell's signature year of 1984 certainly changed Paterson's life. In that year, he played for Canada at the World Juniors, won the Memorial Cup with the 67's, and played in his first NHL games, with Hartford. It was to be his signature year as well. He missed much of the next year with mono, ran into conflict with the Whalers after refusing to report to the minors, and ended his short career in the IHL. He later became CEO of www.puckchat.com.

Dave Pasin

Greg Paslawski

Steve Passmore

Mark Paterson

Rick Paterson

Doug Patey

Larry Patey

Glenn Patrick

PATERSON, Rick

b. Kingston, Ontario, February 10, 1958

He played his entire career in Chicago, and although it wasn't Bucyk-like in length it still represented 430 games over 9 years, starting in 1978. Paterson took some time before he made the team as a regular, and he combined with Bill Gardner and Peter Marsh to form one of the league's better checking lines. Paterson became expert as a penalty killer, and of his 50 career goals, 14 came short-handed. He holds the Hawks record for fastest two short-handed goals, just 2:30 apart. He finished his career in the IHL in '87-'88, a season Paterson knew would be his last and one he used as a transition. To that end, he actually refereed some exhibition games in that league under the auspices of the NHL, but at season's end he gave up a career as an official to become assistant coach with Pittsburgh. He later joined Tampa in that capacity, and for eight games in '97-'98 was their head coach. The team failed to earn a single point during this stretch.

PATEY, Doug

b. Toronto, Ontario, December 28, 1956

Larry's younger brother didn't have the same NHL lifespan. In his five years of pro (1976-81) he played with Washington only sporadically, spending the vast majority of his time in the minors.

PATEY, Larry

b. Toronto, Ontario, March 19, 1953

Ineligibility was the NHL's gain and Boston University's loss. Patey accepted an invite to go to BU on scholarship in 1972, but wasn't eligible to play for the team as a freshman and so played for a local team called the Braintree Bruins. Scouts discovered his talents in an exhibition game against the U.S. National Team, and Patey joined California instead of BU the next year. He scored 25 goals in his first full season, but it was only after being traded to St. Louis a couple of years later that he reached his peak. Patey became a superb two-way player and defensive specialist, and in '80-'81 he scored a team-record eight goals and finished runner-up in Selke Trophy voting. Although he finished his career with the Rangers, it was his nine years in a Bluenote sweater that defined his play. When he retired, he returned to St. Louis and worked as a real estate agent.

PATRICK, Craig

b. Detroit, Michigan, May 20, 1946

There wasn't much about Patrick's playing career to impress the selection committee of the Hockey Hall of Fame, but his contributions to the game as a general manager were impressive enough that in 2001 he was inducted into the Hall as a Builder. Patrick was born into one of hockey's noble families. His grandfather, Lester, father, Lynn, uncle, Muzz, and great uncle, Frank were all lifetime members of hockey's fraternity, and Lester, Lynn, and Frank were all previous inductees. Craig played his early hockey in Montreal where his parents sent him to develop his skills. From there he went to the Univeristy of Denver, winning two NCAA championships (1968 and '69) and earning a degree in business administration. After captaining the 1971 U.S. entry in the World Championships, Patrick joined California in the NHL to begin a pedestrian, nine-year pro career. He played for the U.S. at the 1976 Canada Cup, and four years later was an assistant coach to Herb Brooks for the Miracle on Ice. In June 1981, the Rangers hired him as GM, and at 35 he was the youngest man in league history to hold that title. He stayed on Broadway for five years, and in 1989 Pittsburgh hired him for a like role. Under his guidance – and the play of Mario Lemieux, of course – the Penguins won their only two Stanley Cups, in 1991 and 1992. In 1996, Patrick was inducted into the U.S. Hockey Hall of Fame, and four years later received the Lester Patrick Trophy. He remains the longest-serving general manager in team history.

Under his guidance the Penguins won their only two Stanley Cups.
CRAIG PATRICK

PATRICK, Glenn

b. New York, New York, April 26, 1950

How is it possible to establish your identity as a player when your last name is Patrick? To forge a career independent of the greatest name in hockey? To be content with a good career when almost everyone else in your clan has had a Hall of Fame career? These were the psychological obstacles Glenn had to deal with. The son of Lynn (Hall of Famer), brother of Craig (Hall of Famer), nephew of Muzz (a mere mortal), grandson of Lester (Hall of Famer), and grand-nephew of Frank (Hall of Famer), it was all Glenn could do to breathe hockey in the museum of greatness that was his family tree. He played only 38 games in the NHL in the 1970s but since 1982 has coached extensively and with success at all levels of the minors. Most recently, he has been with Wilkes-Barre, the Penguins affiliate in the AHL, since 1998.

PATRICK, James ("Jeeper")

b. Winnipeg, Manitoba, June 14, 1963

He can't boast of being part of *the* Patrick clan, but his brother Steve made the NHL and his dad was no slouch, either. Steve Sr. was a quarterback with the Winnipeg Blue Bombers for 13 seasons and later entered politics as an MP in Manitoba, so there was something noble in Patrick's veins growing up. He started in New York as a fresh-faced kid with the Rangers, and is now an ageless wonder on the Buffalo blueline, more than two decades after his NHL debut. As a freshman at the University of North Dakota, he helped the team win an NCAA championship in 1982, just weeks after winning gold with Canada at the World Juniors. In the next year, he played at another WJC, a World Championships, and the 1984 Olympics in Sarajevo before joining the Rangers at the end of the '83-'84 season. He never played a game in the minors. Patrick combined speed and skill with defensive maturity beyond his years. He moved the puck extremely well and was durable year to year. Patrick played 11 years with the Rangers, part of 1 season with Hartford, 4 and a half years with Calgary, and since 1998 has been with Buffalo. He has played in more World Championships games than any other Canadian player, a record he established in 2002, and has played 1,100 regular-season games in the NHL. The closest he got to the Cup was in 1999 with the Sabres, and amazingly he has never won a major trophy or been named to an All-Star Team. Nonetheless, Patrick's longevity and consistent performance has left an indelible impression on the game and the Canadian national program.

James Patrick

PATRICK, Lester ("The Silver Fox")

b. Drummondville, Quebec, December 30, 1883
d. Victoria, British Columbia, June 1, 1960

Co-patriarch, as it were, of hockey's royal family, Lester and his brother, Frank, were among the most important men in hockey in the early 20th century. Lester was the oldest of nine children, and almost from the day he was born hockey was on his mind and in his heart. He grew up in Montreal, played for the MAAA juniors in 1901-02, and two years later was on his way west. His intended destination was British Columbia, but he was in no hurry to get there. In Brandon, Manitoba, he was guaranteed a good job in a laundry store if he played hockey with the local team, and it not only won the provincial championships but challenged the Ottawa Silver Seven for the Stanley Cup. He returned to Montreal and captained the Wanderers who won the Cup in 1906 and '07 after which he moved to Nelson, B.C., to work for his father, Joseph, in the lumber business. He continued to play hockey, and in 1909 he and brother Frank sold their services to the highest bidder, Renfrew. Not only did they play together, they realized that hockey could be approached as a business, not just a sport. To that end, they moved to B.C. in 1911 and convinced their father to help finance the building of two artificial rinks, in Victoria and Vancouver. Then, they set about starting a league that would surpass the NHA, and later the NHL, in quality and success. They had players put numbers on their sweaters so fans could easily identify

He captained the
Wanderers who won the
Cup in 1906 and '07.
LESTER PATRICK

everyone on the ice. They instituted a formal playoff system that generated much-needed income. They lured the best players from the east with generous salaries and a league, the Pacific Coast Hockey League, that was the most exciting in the world. Lester played with Victoria for many years, and after retiring as a player in 1922 he continued to coach the Cougars. In 1926, the brothers agreed to sell the league to the NHL, in essence so the NHL could get all the players back east and simply shut down the PCHL, which was, in many ways, an early, more successful incarnation of the WHA. Lester moved east at that time to manage and coach the Rangers, a position he held from 1926 to '39. During that time, he made history. In the 1928 playoffs, his Rangers were playing the Montreal Maroons in game two of the Cup finals. Their goalie, Lorne Chabot, was hurt in the second period, but the Maroons refused to allow a substitute goalie from the crowd. Patrick, then 45 years old and never having played goal, donned Chabot's equipment and went the rest of the way for the team. The score was 1-1 in regulation time, but the Rangers scored in overtime and Patrick was hailed a hero. He retired on the spot, signed Joe Miller to fill in for Chabot, and the Blueshirts won the Cup. Patrick left the Rangers in 1946 and settled in Victoria. He soon became coach and GM of the Cougars, now a WHL team, continuing on until 1956. In 1946, he was named to the Hockey Hall of Fame. Since 1966, the Lester Patrick Award has been given annually to the person or people who have made an outstanding contribution to hockey in the United States. Patrick himself watched two of his sons, Muzz and Lynn, go on to careers in the NHL, Lynn and brother Frank also joining him as members of the Hockey Hall of Fame.

PATRICK, Lynn

b. Victoria, British Columbia, February 3, 1912
d. St. Louis, Missouri, January 26, 1980

Lynn and brother Muzz grew up out west while their father, Lester, was playing in and running the PCHL. However, because of the balmy weather in Victoria, there was little natural ice and the kids gravitated toward other sports. Lynn played on a B.C. all-star rugby team and a Canadian champion basketball team, and was a superb football player as well. His hockey was curtailed completely in 1925 when the Patricks' arena burned down, and it wasn't until four years later when Lester sent the boys to Montreal that they were back on skates. They attended McGill University for a year and played for the Montreal Royals, and Lynn developed into a fine left wing and

Lynn Patrick

centre. Skating had always been the bane of his hockey skills, but he worked tirelessly on improving and gradually impressed many of Lester's colleagues with the Rangers. Lester was loath to bring his son to New York for fear of charges of nepotism, but those around him convinced him that Lynn was a genuine prospect. Lynn joined the Blueshirts in 1934, but after a slow start, sure enough, the criticisms came fast and furious. In time, though, Lynn proved his worth and when the Rangers won the Cup in 1940 the tide began to turn in the family's favour. Lynn played on a line with Phil Watson and Bryan Hextall, and led the team in scoring four times. In '41-'42, his 32 goals were tops in the NHL, and the year after he had 61 points, the best total of his career. Lynn joined the U.S. Army in 1943 and sacrificed two years of his playing career. He returned to play one more season with the Rangers and then went down to the farm team in New Haven to start a career in coaching. The Rangers hired him as their bench boss in 1948, and he coached a year and a half before joining Boston, where he remained for five years. He became the team's GM until 1965 and two years later was named first coach and GM of the new St. Louis Blues, though he quickly gave way to Scotty Bowman. Patrick moved up to vice-president, but when the team was sold in 1977, he and most other front-office staff were replaced. Early in 1980, he left a Blues home game early after not feeling well, and on the way home suffered a fatal heart attack. Just as he was the son of an NHLer, so, too, did he father two boys – Craig and Glenn – who became involved in the NHL. Lynn was inducted into the Hockey Hall of Fame a few months after his death, and in 1989 he was posthumously awarded the Lester Patrick Trophy, named after his father, for contributions to hockey in the U.S.

Steve Patrick

Colin Patterson

Dennis Patterson

PATRICK, Murray "Muzz"
b. Victoria, British Columbia, June 28, 1915
d. Riverside, Connecticut, July 23, 1998
Needless to say, when your father and uncle literally introduced hockey to the west, started the PCHL, and brought artificial ice to B.C., hockey is in your blood. As a boy, Murray earned his nickname from a friend who described his curly, full head of hair as Fuzzy Muzzy. Muzz grew up to be a strapping lad, becoming the amateur heavyweight champion of Canada. He gravitated toward hockey, though, and turned pro in 1938 with the Rangers, the team closely associated with the Patricks since the NHL began. A year later, he was briefly involved in one of the great fights in Rangers history, brief because he knocked out Eddie Shore with one punch. A legend was born. Muzz helped bring the Cup to Broadway in 1940 and a year

Muzz helped bring the Cup to Broadway in 1940.
MURRAY PATRICK

later served in the U.S. Army as an officer in North Africa, in the battle for Anzio in Italy, and during the invasion in the south of France. He returned to play one more year for the Blueshirts and turned to coaching. On January 6, 1954, he became coach of the Rangers, a job held variously by both his father and his brother. At season's end, he became GM, a post he held for a decade. One more year of coaching, in '62-'63, was followed by another decade in the administration of the team, and Patrick retired in 1973. He died at home of a heart attack.

PATRICK, Steve
b. Winnipeg, Manitoba, February 4, 1961
Buffalo made Patrick a first-round draft choice in 1980, largely because of his size and potential. He never lived up to the promise the Sabres had foisted on him, and in six years he played for three teams. In the fall of 1986, he was supposed to attend Quebec's training camp after finishing the previous season with the Nordiques, but he phoned in his retirement to the team, saying his love for the game just wasn't where it should be to play at the highest level. Patrick returned to Winnipeg to help run his father's business, Patrick Realty Ltd., which has been in operation since 1955. Steve eventually became the company's president, and the small office thrives as one of the city's more successful independent real estate offices.

PATTERSON, Colin
b. Rexdale, Ontario, May 11, 1960
It's a good thing for peripheral vision. Patterson was happily playing hockey at Clarkson College, working away at a degree in marketing and management, when a scout from the Calgary Flames came to look at one of Patterson's teammates, Jim Laing. Lo and behold, the scout came away wanting to know more about this Patterson kid, and by the spring of 1983 Patterson had signed a contract with the Flames. He worked on his degree part-time, but on the ice he developed into a full-fledged NHLer. Patterson spent 8 of his 10 years in the league with the Flames, helping the team go to the finals in 1986 and win the whole shebang 3 years later. After finishing his playing days with Buffalo, he settled in Calgary where he worked for Montreal Trust as the assistant vice-president of corporate development. He later became VP of Shaw Cablesystems in the city.

PATTERSON, Dennis
b. Peterborough, Ontario, January 9, 1950
Although he didn't make much of a mark on the NHL as a player, Patterson has had his hand and mind in the game for more than 30 years. He played junior in his

hometown before turning pro in the AHL, and his first two seasons came with the hopeless Kansas City entry in 1974. He later played three games for Philadelphia, but more important he became a key part of the franchise, first in the minors with Maine. He captained the team for 6 years, and when he retired in 1983 the team retired his number 26. He remained with the team as its OHL scout, and in 1990 moved to Minnesota only because he was offered the job of chief scout. The Flyers later gave him the same position, and he remains with the team in that capacity.

PATTERSON, Ed
b. Delta, British Columbia, November 14, 1972
The IHL was where Patterson spent his early years in the pro game, though in 2001 he took his act to Germany to play with the Berlin Solar Bears. He came out of the WHL to play parts of 3 seasons with Pittsburgh, but his tough guy play didn't earn him more than 68 games' worth of action over that time.

PATTERSON, George "Paddy"
b. Kingston, Ontario, May 22, 1906
d. Kingston, Ontario, January 16, 1977
Although Patterson scored 51 goals in his NHL career, there was one in particular that made history. On February 17, 1927, he scored the first goal for the team that had changed its name from the St. Pats to the Maple Leafs, the dawning of a new era in NHL history. Toward the end of the '30-'31 season, he was part of a funny, though unfortunate, incident. Playing for the Americans, the team seemed destined to make an amazing run to the playoffs, passing the Maroons. Team owner, Bill Big Dwyer, a bootlegger, had a premature celebration at his farm in which the players drank to excess and started to race horses around the track. Patterson, not the most equine-oriented of the lot, fell off his horse and broke his right arm. The team collapsed down the stretch, the Maroons rallied to make the playoffs, and the premature celebration turned into a disaster. Patterson recovered and went on to play in the NHL until 1935, then played another decade in the American league.

PAUL, Art "Butch"
b. Rocky Mountain House, Alberta, September 11, 1943
d. Memphis, Tennessee, March 25, 1966
The kid had no luck at all, no luck. He came to training camp with Detroit in 1964 with a broken wrist, and broke his leg in a game after a big defenceman fell on him. He broke it again after just three games with the Wings. The next year, playing in Memphis, he was driving home from a game when another driver, a 19-year-old woman, sideswiped a car, caromed off the

median, and struck Paul's car head-on. She and Paul were killed instantly. He was just 22 years old, and only 2 blocks from home.

PAULHUS, Rollie ("Tubby")
b. Montreal, Quebec, September 1, 1902
d. Alma, Quebec, December 1964
After starting his career with the Canadiens in 1925-26, Paulhus played mostly in the Can-Am league, precursor to the AHL, until 1932. He later worked for Leo Dandurand as a cashier at various racetracks owned and operated by the Canadiens executive.

PAVELICH, Mark
b. Eveleth, Minnesota, February 28, 1958
The on-again, off-again career of Pavelich took him near and far during his years in the game. He began a career in the limelight by playing on the 1980 U.S. Olympics team that won gold at Lake Placid, but unlike many of his teammates he didn't run to the NHL right away for a quick shot at the big time. Instead, he played in Switzerland for a year before signing with the Rangers. In his first 3 years, he had impressive totals of 33, 37, and 29 goals, but after a mediocre year he became unhappy when new coach Ted Sator preached a tedious dump-and-chase game. That signalled Pavelich's first retirement, but then his Olympic coach, Herb Brooks, coaxed him back for part of the next year. Pavelich then headed for Italy, and after two seasons retired again. Two years later, he again scratched the itch to play by signing with San Jose, but after two games he quit for a third and final time. Pavelich returned to Minnesota and established himself in Lake Superior, where he worked as a home builder and fishing and hunting guide.

PAVELICH, Marty ("Sabu")
b. Sault Ste. Marie, Ontario, November 6, 1927
While his brother had a Hall of Fame career as a linesman, Marty had a splendid skating career with Detroit. He played all of his 10 years in the league with Detroit and earned a reputation as one of the top checkers around. While the top line of Lindsay, Abel, and Howe scored the goals, the threesome of Pavelich, Leswick, and Skov were charged with keeping the top players opponents at bay. It worked, and Detroit developed a dynasty of its own, winning Cups in 1950, '52, '54, and '55, Pavelich a key element in all. He retired in 1957 while still young and in his prime because he was business partners with Ted Lindsay. Lindsay had tried to form a players' union, and was punished by being traded to lowly Jack Adams. Once the prickly GM discovered the players' business

George Patterson

Marty played all of his 10 years in the league with Detroit.
MARTY PAVELICH

Butch Paul

Mark Pavelich

collaborations, Pavelich figured that he, too, would be banished, so he beat Adams to the punch by calling it quits. Pavelich and Lindsay ran a very successful manufacturer's rep business in the Detroit car industry, and Pavelich eventually retired to Montana.

Jim Pavese

PAVESE, Jim
b. New York, New York, May 8, 1962

Maybe the OHL just didn't know what to make of an American kid who had come to Canada to make it into the NHL, but it certainly was unusual for a teen to play for three teams in a junior career. He started in Peterborough, where he watched and learned more than he played, and then Kitchener not only drafted him but made the rookie team captain. Too much too soon for the big defenceman, and it wasn't until he was traded to the Soo that he settled down and just played hockey. Drafted by St. Louis, he joined the Blues in early 1982 and stayed on the blueline there for seven years. He later played for three other teams before retiring in 1989. Pavese eventually moved to Long Island where he became a sales rep for a pharmaceutical company.

PAYER, Evariste
b. Rockland, Ontario, December 12, 1887
d. 1963

Payer played for the Canadiens when the team was in the NHA, and he stuck around long enough to play a single game for the team in its NHL incarnation.

Davis Payne

PAYER, Serge
b. Rockland, Ontario, May 7, 1979

There was a scary time in Payer's life during the '98–'99 season while he was playing junior in Kitchener. He suffered from Guillain-Barre syndrome and at one point was so weak he could barely get out of bed. Over the months that he was affected he lost 50 pounds, but he made a remarkable recovery and within 2 years was playing in the NHL. He made his NHL entrance, with Florida, on November 13, 2000, and over the year scored the first 5 goals of his career. Still young, he has spent most of his time in the minors to date.

PAYNE, Davis
b. Port Alberni, British Columbia, September 24, 1970

The signs were there – no denying that – so Davis followed his instincts and cut his playing days short to get into coaching. He was drafted by Edmonton in 1989, but it wasn't until six years later with Boston that he got into an NHL game. In 2 seasons with the Bruins he played 22 games, but beyond that his career passed in the minors. In 2000, he retired to become an assistant coach with the Greenville Grrrowl of the ECHL and by Christmas he became head coach for the Pee Dee

Mel Pearson

Pride, a position he continues to maintain thanks to the club's excellent performance.

PAYNE, Steve ("Rooster")
b. Toronto, Ontario, August 16, 1958

Payne was an unbelievably talented player whose career was cut short by a serious neck injury. He developed under Brian Kilrea with the Ottawa 67's, developed in the sense that he really never thought he'd have made the NHL without Kilrea. He did, though, and in his 7 full seasons he averaged better than 30 goals a year. As a rookie in '78-'79, he scored 23 times, a number that peaked at 42 the year after. In his third season, the Stars went to the finals for the first time, and Payne had an incredible 17 goals in 19 post-season games, earning the nickname Mr. April for a short while. His career unravelled in the '85 playoffs, though, when he suffered a neck injury. Over the next three seasons, he tried comebacks of various lengths and degrees of success, but the bottom line was that he was no longer the player he had been and with every game he risked more serious, permanent damage. He retired in 1987 and a short time later started working in the hockey industry as a U.S. sales rep, earning a reputation as one of the best in the business.

His career unravelled in the '85 playoffs when he suffered a neck injury.
STEVE PAYNE

PAYNTER, Kent
b. Summerside, Prince Edward Island, April 17, 1965

Being a low draft choice in 1983, Paynter wasn't given much hope for a grand career in the NHL, but he made do with a lengthy stay in the minors. He played just 37 NHL games over 7 seasons and scored just once, but the defenceman spent parts of 13 years in the AHL and IHL before retiring in 1998.

PEAKE, Pat
b. Rochester, Michigan, May 28, 1973

In 1993, Peake was the first American to be named player of the year in Canadian junior hockey. He did so despite missing a third of the season with a broken ankle in a year that would typify the problems of this glass superstar. He retired in 1997, just four years after that prestigious and historic award, felled by a series of debilitating injuries. He suffered mono, a shattered thyroid, a bad shoulder, a kidney ailment, and finally a shattered heel that impeded his walking, let alone skating. He played all his NHL games with Washington over those four years (plus one game to start the '97-'98 season), leaving the game in less than one piece, as it were.

PEARSON, Mel
b. Flin Flon, Manitoba, April 29, 1938
d. January 9, 1999

In a long and wandering career, Pearson played a few

games with the Rangers in the years immediately before expansion and then two games with Pittsburgh during its inaugural year in the NHL. He played mostly in the minors, and after the Penguins demoted him Portland became home for five years. A winger, he went to Minnesota in the WHA in 1972, but early in '73-'74 went to the Phoenix Roadrunners. After just four games, though, he accepted the head coaching position with the Flin Flon Bombers, though he was fired two years later. His son, Mel Jr., has coached for many years under Red Berenson at the University of Michigan.

PEARSON, Rob
b. Oshawa, Ontario, March 8, 1971
It looked as if Pearson's career moved to a higher level when he moved from Belleville to Oshawa in junior early in the '90-'91 season. Playing with Eric Lindros, he upped his intensity and tempo of play and scored 57 goals for the Generals. He joined the Leafs a year later, but most of his intensity in the NHL came in the form of fighting. He did score 23 goals in his second season but he never built on that fine year and the Leafs wound up trading him. He played himself deep into the minors until 2001 when he accepted an offer to play in Germany, that Lindros-inspired enthusiasm for the game a thing of the past.

PEARSON, Scott
b. Cornwall, Ontario, December 19, 1969
It wasn't Pearson's fault that the Leafs drafted him 6th overall in 1988 and that he didn't live up to their expectations. Their drafting was splotchy at best during this era, and by the time he was 20 the Leafs had traded him. He began a tour of duty that covered much ground in the NHL and a number of teams in the minors. Most recently he played in the DEL in Germany in 2001-02.

PEAT, Stephen
b. Princeton, British Columbia, March 10, 1980
His physical presence for Washington has led him into a number of fights, and that's fine with Peat because that's his role with the Caps. He graduated from the WHL and joined the Washington blueline corps as a tough guy, but missed much of his rookie season, 2001-02, because of a groin injury. He was right back out there for the next season, though, relishing his role and the support he gets from fans who shout his name when he gets a shift.

PECA, Michael
b. Toronto, Ontario, March 26, 1974
When the Canucks drafted Peca in 1992, they didn't know what they had. If they had, they surely wouldn't

have traded him to Buffalo in a deal that sent unhappy Alexander Mogilny to Vancouver while Peca developed into hockey's version of nitroglycerin. At 5'11" and 180 pounds, he was nowhere near what anyone would call a big man, but any scout, coach, or GM who ever watched him would quickly call him the hardest hitter in the league, hands down. Peca was a remarkable package. He was as sound defensively as any centre in the league (winning the Selke Trophy in '96-'97). He was a fine scorer and playmaker, and Buffalo likely had never had such a leader before. In 1998, he was named team captain, and at the end of that season he led his Sabres in their first Cup finals. In the summer of 2000, though, he and the team became embroiled in nasty contract talks, insults flying both ways, and Peca sat out the entire 2000-01 season waiting for a trade, vowing never to play for Buffalo again. True to his word, he didn't play, except for Team Canada at the World Championships, which he had to leave early after hurting his leg. He got his trade wish – and a large contract – when the Islanders acquired him, and he played as though he hadn't missed a day. He led the team to the playoffs, and in the middle of the season helped Canada win gold at the 2002 Olympics in Salt Lake City. One of the finest players in the league, Peca is in the prime of his career.

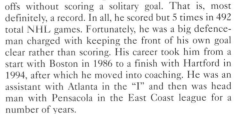

Peca sat out the entire 2000-01 season waiting for a trade, vowing never to play for Buffalo again.
MICHAEL PECA

PEDERSEN, Allen ("Beach")
b. Fort Saskatchewan, Alberta, January 13, 1965
Between November 1986 and February 1990, Pedersen played 238 regular-season games and 35 more in the playoffs without scoring a solitary goal. That is, most definitely, a record. In all, he scored but 5 times in 492 total NHL games. Fortunately, he was a big defenceman charged with keeping the front of his own goal clear rather than scoring. His career took him from a start with Boston in 1986 to a finish with Hartford in 1994, after which he moved into coaching. He was an assistant with Atlanta in the "I" and then was head man with Pensacola in the East Coast league for a number of years.

PEDERSON, Barry
b. Big River, Saskatchewan, March 13, 1961
He may have been born in Big River, but he grew up in B.C. and Boston has become his post-career city of choice. Pederson's great junior career with Victoria meant a first-round draft selection, by the Bruins in 1980, and in his first 2 seasons he scored 44 and 46 goals. Welcome to the NHL. He "slumped" to 39 the year after, and missed much of the following year with an injury to his shoulder as doctors removed a large tumour from the area. The injury caused him to miss

Rob Pearson

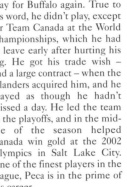

Scott Pearson

Allen Pedersen

Barry Pederson

Denis Pederson

Mark Pederson

Tom Pederson

Pete Peeters

his chance to play for Canada at the 1984 Canada Cup. The year after, Pederson slumped even more, despite making a remarkable comeback from the surgery. With their too-frequent penchant for making a bad trade, the Canucks acquired him for Cam Neely *and* a first-round draft choice in 1986, and Pederson settled in to a second-tier career with the Canucks while Neely became the top power forward in the game. Pederson played for Pittsburgh in '90-'91 to earn an engraving on the Cup with the Pens, and by 1991, when he finished in Boston, he was a pale shadow of his former self. He stayed in the Hub, worked for Bruins television, and later moved into the investment business.

PEDERSON, Denis
b. Prince Albert, Saskatchewan, September 10, 1975
New Jersey liked Pederson so much it drafted him 13th overall in 1993 after his second year of junior with Prince Albert. And Vancouver liked him so much it parted with Alexander Mogilny for Pederson and Brendan Morrison, two top prospects. In his five years with the Devils – developmental years, really – he became a solid player but not a star. Ditto for his years with the Canucks, which ended when he was traded to Phoenix. He plays with an edge, though, and has strong leadership skills, so perhaps Wayne Gretzky will be able to make more of him with the Coyotes than did the Devils or the Canucks.

PEDERSON, Mark
b. Prelate, Saskatchewan, January 14, 1968
A member of the back-to-back Memorial Cup-winning Medicine Hat Tigers in 1987 and '88, Pederson had nothing but up looking at him when he hit the NHL with Montreal. Yet, despite two great seasons with the farm team in Sherbrooke, the Habs traded him after watching him play at the Forum only nine times. In his five scattered seasons of play, he didn't land in any one place for too long, and by 1993 was out of the big league for good. Pederson quickly moved on to play in Europe, and in 2003 he played in the WCHL in the hopes of pursuing a coaching career.

PEDERSON, Tom
b. Bloomington, Minnesota, January 14, 1970
Everything started out letter-perfect for Pederson. He went to the University of Minnesota, enrolling in 1988. He played for the U.S. at both the World Juniors and the World Championships. He was drafted by his hometown North Stars. The Stars let him go to San Jose, and the Sharks used him more often than not. Although small for a defenceman, he was a good skater with offensive flair. After four years, though, he accepted an offer to play in Japan, returning later in the year to try to restart his NHL life, with Toronto. This didn't work, and he soon went to Germany, preferring culture and a lesser quality of play to bussing around Nowheresville, USA, playing in the minors.

PEER, Bert
b. Port Credit, Ontario, November 12, 1910
d. unknown
He may have been a one-game wonder with Detroit in '39-'40, but Peer as a legend in Britain for his three

years playing principally with Harringay (1935-38). He was considered a great scorer and leader. He wound up returning to Toronto to play, but in 1955 was inducted into the British Ice Hockey Hall of Fame for his pre-war feats with the Racers.

PEETERS, Pete
b. Edmonton, Alberta, August 17, 1957
For a while, there, Peeters was the best, most unbeatable goalie in the NHL. He joined Philadelphia in '78-'79 but spent most of that rookie season in the minors, where he and Robbie Moore led the AHL by allowing the fewest goals. The next year, he had a 29-5-5 record with the Flyers and his play guided the team to a remarkable 35-game unbeaten streak, the longest in NHL history. That club went on to the Cup finals, only to lose in six games to the powerful Islanders. It was the closest Peeters would get to the Cup. Philadelphia traded him to Boston for Brad McCrimmon and Peeters promptly led the league with 40 wins and won the Vezina Trophy with a 2.36 GAA and 8 shutouts. He was second in voting for the Hart Trophy behind annual winner Wayne Gretzky, and at one time during the year had an unbeaten streak of 31 games. Peeters helped Canada win the Canada Cup in 1984, playing perhaps the best game of his life in a 3-2 Canada win in overtime over the Soviet Union in the semifinals. He had a sub-par NHL season, though, and was traded to the Capitals early in the next season. He continued to play well, but he was no longer the guaranteed number-one goalie and his team was not always strong. He returned to Philly for two final years as backup goalie and retired in 1991. Since then, he has worked part-time as a goalie coach and with his wife runs their cattle farm in Alberta.

PEIRSON, Johnny
b. Winnipeg, Manitoba, July 21, 1925
When Don Gallinger and Billy Taylor of Boston were suspended for life in March 1948 for gambling, two roster spots on the Bruins opened and Peirson, who had had a quick callup the previous year, was given a better look. He never returned to the minors, playing the next nine and a half seasons with the Bruins (he was in retirement from 1954 until Christmas '55 when he was lured back to the team). He had been recruited from the McGill champion team in '45-'46 and became a top goal scorer with Boston. In the summers, he stayed in the city to learn the furniture business under the watchful eye of his father-in-law, and when he retired in 1958 it was there he directed his energies until retiring in 1996. He also worked in local television in Boston and developed a reputation as a fine interviewer.

PELENSKY, Perry
b. Edmonton, Alberta, May 22, 1962
Pelensky was brought up to Chicago to fight, and in four games he did just that. In his three-year minor-league career, he demonstrated an ability to score a bit as well as scrap, but that '83-'84 season was his only NHL opportunity.

PELLERIN, Scott
b. Shediac, New Brunswick, January 9, 1970
You know a kid from New Brunswick takes his

hockey seriously when he ventures halfway across the country at 16 to play for the great Notre Dame Hounds in Saskatchewan. That team won the Centennial Cup with Pellerin, Rob Brind'Amour, and Curtis Joseph on the team. Pellerin then went to the University of Maine, where he had an outstanding college career. He was captain his last two seasons, he won the Hobey Baker Award in 1992, and his number 8 was retired by the Black Bears in honour of his contributions. He was ready for the NHL, but it took him five years to develop to the point where he played a full season in the league. He started with New Jersey and went to St. Louis in 1996, but since 2000 he has played for four teams in quick succession and the stability most players hope for is not in the cards for him. His grandfather was Sam McManus, who won a Stanley Cup with the Maroons in 1935.

PELLETIER, Jean-Marc
b. Atlanta, Georgia, March 4, 1978

To date, young Pelletier has played just one game in goal in the NHL. On March 4, 1999, he stood in the Philadelphia cage at home and allowed 5 goals in a 5-0 loss to the visiting Senators. He spent the rest of the year in the minors and was traded a year later to Carolina. The 'Canes, in turn, have kept him out of the NHL, hoping he'll develop and earn a callup to the big club.

PELLETIER, Marcel
b. Drummondville, Quebec, December 6, 1927

Few goalies in the history of hockey played for as many teams in as many leagues as Pelletier. And even fewer had to wait as long between NHL chances – 12 years – as did Pelletier. He began his pro career toward the end of the '49-'50 season and played six games with Chicago a year later when regular Harry Lumley was injured. Pelletier was no hero, putting together a record of 1-5-0 before being returned to the minors. For the next 12 years he played in a variety of places, most notably Victoria for half that time where he had his finest years. In '62-'63 he filled in twice for the Rangers, his second and last NHL opportunity. He finished in the minors and in 1968 became coach of the New Jersey Devils. Pelletier then became a scout with Philadelphia and in 1970 he was named the team's director of player personnel and served in that capacity for many years.

PELLETIER, Roger
b. Montreal, Quebec, June 22, 1945

In a nine-year career in the American league (1965-74), Pelletier played a single game with the Flyers the year they joined the NHL.

PELOFFY, Andre ("Pelo")
b. Sete, France, February 25, 1951

He played nine games with Washington in the team's inaugural season of '74-'75, but Peloffy's finest days came later in leagues and countries removed from the NHL. He captained Springfield in '76-'77 and won the scoring championship in the most dramatic way imaginable, on an empty-net goal with 10 seconds to go in the final game of the season! Peloffy moved to Europe in 1979 and played for the next decade in France and Austria. He represented France in six World Championships and at the 1988 Olympics in Calgary, and when he retired in 1990 he turned to coaching. He started in Paris, but after a number of seasons with the Volants he moved to Zug, Switzerland, where he assumed a similar position.

PELTONEN, Ville
b. Vantaa, Finland, March 24, 1973

Is he an NHLer or isn't he? Yes and no. Peltonen has certainly played in the NHL, starting with San Jose in 1995, but he has also played extensively in Finland and even a year in Sweden. His international career is the most impressive part of his hockey portfolio. He played at the World Juniors in 1993 and has barely missed a tournament for Finland since then. He played at the 1994 and '98 Olympics, winning bronze in the latter, and played in the Worlds from 1994 to 2000. He also played in the 1996 World Cup. When all this time is totalled, it makes his 200 or so NHL games pale by comparison. In truth, only in 1999-2000, when he was with Nashville, did he play a full season in the big league. In 2002-03, he captained Jokerit Helsinki to victory in the Continental Cup.

PELUSO, Mike
b. Pengilly, Minnesota, November 8, 1965

Peluso played hockey at the University of Alaska in Anchorage, and became the finest defenceman that college ever produced. He set records for career points and was renowned for his offensive skills and quick thinking. It was no surprise that Chicago signed him in 1989 as a free agent (New Jersey let him walk after drafting him five years previous), but as soon as he joined the Hawks he was told to fight if he wanted to stay with the team. Fight he did, to the tune of 728 penalty minutes in his first 2 full seasons. The transformation was perplexing, but he was a big man and the Hawks did their thinking the simple way. Peluso was happy when Ottawa claimed him in the Expansion Draft and told him to go on the offence a bit more, but after a successful year in which he scored 15 goals he was on the move again – to New Jersey. He was with the Devils for four years, includ-

Jean-Marc Pelletier

Marcel Pelletier

Andre Peloffy

Ville Peltonen

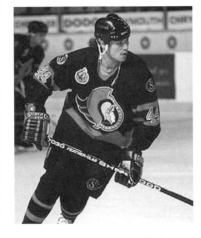

As soon as he joined the Hawks he was told to fight if he wanted to stay with the team.
MIKE PELUSO (b. 1965)

Mike Pelyk

Chad Penney

Steve Penney

Jim Peplinski

ing the successful run to the Cup in '94-'95, but his career came to a sudden end at Christmas 1997 when he suffered a spinal cord injury and was forced to retire.

PELUSO, Mike
b. Bismarck, North Dakota, September 2, 1974
It truly was a long and twisting path to the NHL, but in the end Peluso realized a dream. During his college days with the University of Minnesota-Duluth, he was drafted by Calgary. His agent wanted to get him to a U.S. team, so he didn't sign with the Flames. When he became a free agent, he signed with Washington, but the team had plenty of forwards and the Caps never used him. Ditto for St. Louis. Finally, Chicago showed an interest and Peluso thought he was a good fit for the team. In November 2001 he made his first appearance for the Hawks, and scored a goal on his first shift. Peluso also runs a hockey school back home, and in the summers he is a pro walleye fisherman of some note. How long he stays in the NHL remains to be seen, but he knows there will always be fish in the Bismarck River, at least for a while, anyway.

PELYK, Mike ("Mike Mikita"/ "Kita")
b. Toronto, Ontario, September 29, 1947
Few people remember that just a few weeks before the Leafs won the Cup in 1967 the hometown Marlies won the Memorial Cup as well. Pelyk was on that team and went on to spend his entire nine-year career with the Leafs, though that time wasn't always sparkled with gold. The defenceman joined a team on the downswing, and though the Leafs had some fine moments in the late 1960s and 1970s they fell back as often as they rose. Pelyk was frequently booed because he didn't bring the Cup home, and in 1974 he left to play in the WHA for two years. He returned to the Blue and White fold for two partial seasons and then stayed in the city. Pelyk worked in commercial real estate, rising to manager for Wendy's in that capacity as well as for Burger King and the Hudson's Bay Company.

PENNEY, Chad
b. Labrador City, Newfoundland, September 18, 1973
Penney grew up in Riverview before moving to North Bay, Ontario, to play junior. He played for Canada at the WJC in 1992 and two years later played his only three NHL games, with Ottawa, before beginning his tour of duty in the minors. In the AHL he played for PEI and Charlottetown and then played in Britain before finishing his career, in 1999, in the West Coast league.

PENNEY, Steve
b. Ste. Foy, Quebec, February 2, 1961
Ever since Ken Dryden's meteoric rise, the Montreal media have loved to celebrate and then annihilate every new goalie who dons the putatively sacrosanct bleu, blanc, et rouge. Penney is merely one man, one name, on that list. Montreal head coach Jacques Lemaire was frustrated with his goalies as the '83-'84 season was drawing to a close, so he recalled Penney from the minors to inject a little je ne sais quoi into the lineup. Penney, like Dryden, quickly took the team by storm and was the main man in goal for the playoffs, recording three shutouts and winning nine games. The media, of course, considered him a hero. The next year, Penney rode his confidence to a great season and was named to the All Rookie Team. The playoffs were less successful, though, and by the following year he was the backup. A trade to Winnipeg didn't help, and Penney quickly faded to black. He retired in 1988, settled in Quebec City, and became a sales rep for an eyeglass company. From saviour to spectacles in five quick years.

PENNINGTON, Cliff
b. Winnipeg, Manitoba, April 18, 1940
In a career strewn with appearances in leagues and with teams all over the hockey map, Pennington played parts of three seasons in the NHL with Montreal and Boston. Prior to his Habs debut in 1960, though, he had a distinguished junior career out west, culminating with a spot on the Canadian team that won a silver medal at the 1960 Olympics in Squaw Valley,

He later became a timer and ID chief at Assiniboia Downs, a Winnipeg racetrack.
CLIFF PENNINGTON

California. The next season, when he was called up to the NHL, he won the scoring championship with the Montreal affiliate in Hull-Ottawa. He spent the next two seasons with Boston where he became a utility player, seeing time on the power play and penalty killing unit, and spotting the top two lines with occasional shifts. Pennington made a tour of the minors before packing it in in 1973. His one blip during that decade was the '64-'65 season, when he moved to Montreal to coach at a boys school and assume the role of athletic director. He later became a timer and ID chief at Assiniboia Downs, a Winnipeg racetrack.

PEPLINSKI, Jim ("Pepper")
b. Renfrew, Ontario, October 24, 1960
He was born in Renfrew and grew up in Toronto, but from the moment he touched down in Calgary, he knew he had found a home. Peplinski played for the Marlies until he joined the Flames in 1980, the team's first year after transferring from Atlanta in the summer. Big, tough, and skilled, he became one of the most popular athletes the city had ever known, both

for his play and character on ice and his indefatigable efforts for kids and charities off it. He won the Conacher Trophy in 1984 for his contributions to the community. Peplinski stayed with the Flames his entire career and watched through the 1980s as they developed into a Cup team. They came close in 1986, losing to Montreal in the finals, but when they won in '89 the moment was tinged by sadness. Peplinski, who was by now team captain, was also toward the end of his career, and coach Terry Crisp scratched him from the lineup for the deciding game. It was bizarre, indeed, when the captain was not in uniform for the presentation of the Cup. Six games into the new season, he retired. Coaches had told him he wouldn't last, so after 10 years he had nothing to regret. He moved upstairs to work as a colour commentator for *Hockey Night in Canada*, and four years later made a brief comeback before retiring to private life. Peplinski has been running a successful car leasing business in Calgary for years and continues his charitable work.

PERLINI, Fred
b. Sault Ste. Marie, Ontario, April 12, 1962
On February 20, 1982, Perlini had the time of his life. In the afternoon, he played for the Marlies, scoring a goal in a 6-1 win. In the evening, he filled in for the injured Don Luce and helped the Leafs beat St. Louis 8-5. Now that's a doubleheader that would kill any baseball player. Perlini was a good prospect with the Marlies. He had rejected a contract offer from the Leafs a few months ago, and prior to this double duty he signed a lucrative, four-year deal that, with all due respect, proved to be a large waste of Maple Leafs greenback. Perlini played seven games that season and one more the year after. In 1986, he moved to Britain and over the course of the next 11 years became a hero of untold proportions. On 3 occasions he scored 100 goals in a season (seasons being about 30 games), and in '92-'93 he set an unofficial pro record when he had 135 goals and 226 points for Streatham in just 31 games. The Lord Jim of hockey retired in 1997 having scored 958 goals in just 341 games.

PERREAULT, Bob
("Michie"/ "The Glove")
b. Trois Rivières, Quebec, January 28, 1931
d. Lawrence, Massachusetts, August 1996
In his youth, Perreault was a boxer in the 147-pound class who fought under the name Kid Flamingo. The flamingo kid had a big problem, though. He hated the cold, but did most of his boxing in big, cold arenas throughout Quebec. Frequently, he wore long underwear under his trunks, but one night the referee told him he couldn't fight like that. Perreault's boxing

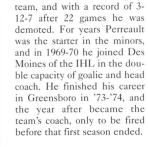

He centred the great French Connection Line which also featured Rick Martin and Rene Robert, the best line the Sabres ever produced.
GILBERT PERREAULT

career was *fini*. He turned his attention to hockey, but as he got older he didn't get any taller than 5'5" and became rather roly-poly. He was lightning fast, though, quick on his feet, and, as is easy to understand, he had quick hands. He played in the minors for more than 20 years, but along the way he had 3 NHL experiences. In '55-'56, he took over in the Montreal net for six games while Jacques Plante tended to an injury, and earned a shutout in his first-ever game. Three years later, he played thrice for the Red Wings, this time because of injury to Terry Sawchuk. Finally, four years later, he was named the number-one goalie for the Bruins. At 31, he was the oldest rookie regular in team history. Perreault earned a shutout in his first game, went undefeated in his first three, and then the roof fell in. Boston was not a good team, and with a record of 3-12-7 after 22 games he was demoted. For years Perreault was the starter in the minors, and in 1969-70 he joined Des Moines of the IHL in the double capacity of goalie and head coach. He finished his career in Greensboro in '73-'74, and the year after became the team's coach, only to be fired before that first season ended.

PERREAULT, Fern
b. Chambly Bassin, Quebec, March 31, 1927
Perreault started playing serious hockey in the post-war years, drawing interest from the Rangers, who sent him to the Rovers for developing. They recalled him for a total of three games in the late 1940s, but beyond that he played out his days in the minors, principally in Quebec.

PERREAULT, Gilbert
b. Victoriaville, Quebec, November 13, 1950
If Guy Lafleur was that one special player of the 1970s who lifted fans from their seats because of his rushes, Perreault was a close second for much the same reason. A powerful and graceful skater, he had a stride and puckhandling skill that were breathtaking when he was in full flight. He played junior hockey in Montreal and helped the Jr. Canadiens win consecutive Memorial Cups in 1969 and '70. That summer, Buffalo and Vancouver, the two newest teams, spun a wheel to see who would select first in the draft, and the Sabres won honours. They chose Perreault, and from that moment to this he has been associated with the Sabres and no other team. As a rookie, he scored 38 goals and won the Calder Trophy, and there was little let-up throughout his career. He centred the great French Connection Line which also featured Rick Martin and Rene Robert, the best line the Sabres ever produced. After just two seasons in the league, Perreault was selected to Team Canada for the '72 Summit Series, but he saw limited action in the games in Canada and, although he

Fred Perlini

Bob Perreault

Fern Perreault

Yanic Perreault

Brian Perry

Stefan Persson

travelled with the team to Moscow, left when told he wasn't going to play again. Many players were angered by his perceived betrayal of their cause, but Perreault argued that if he wasn't playing he wanted to get back to Buffalo's training camp. In the coming years he had three 40-goal seasons and twice hit the 100-point mark in a year. He took the team to the Cup finals in 1975, but they lost to the Flyers and never came close again during his career. Perreault played in the 1976 Canada Cup and in '81 played on a line with Wayne Gretzky. He was playing the best hockey of his life when he broke his ankle and missed the start of the NHL season. Although he had a couple of chances to leave the Sabres and sign with other teams, Perreault chose the safety and comfort of the only team he had known in the NHL and remained with Buffalo for all of his 17 seasons. He retired early in the '86-'87 season when he no longer had the drive to compete or the skating ability to make those rink-long dashes he was famous for, but by that time he had accomplished a great deal. Although he never won a Stanley Cup, he did score more than 500 goals and 1,000 points, sure barometers for entry into the Hockey Hall of Fame, to which he was elected in 1990. He has stayed with the Sabres ever since, working with the alumni and in community relations.

PERREAULT, Yanic ("Yan")
b. Sherbrooke, Quebec, April 4, 1971
If statistics make the man, then Perreault is a modern man of the NHL, a player whose reputation has been created largely by the new era of tracking everything from hits to blocked shots to – Perreault's specialty – face-off percentage. He is an excellent third-line centre and a stretch as a second-line player, but he is master supreme of the face-off, leading the league in this category with stealth-like regularity. The Leafs drafted him but decided early on he wouldn't develop – too small, not physical enough, yadda, yadda – and sent him to L.A. Perreault responded with a 25-goal season in '95-'96 and 28 goals a couple of years later. When the Leafs reacquired him, he filled a role nicely with a strong playoff team, but they again decided he was not worth the bother and let him sign as a free agent with Montreal, his current team. Perreault got a contract that paid him $8.4 million over 3 years, which is terrifying to think in terms of a 20-goal scoring, face-off specialist.

PERROTT, Nathan
b. Owen Sound, Ontario, December 8, 1976
The old "resident tough guy" epithet applies to Perrott, who has paid the price to get to the NHL with years of service in the minors. He was once drafted by New

Jersey, though that seems like a million years and teams ago because as soon as he turned pro in 1997 he was in the "I" and then the East Coast league. It wasn't until more than four years later, his rights having gone to Chicago and then Nashville, that he made it to the NHL, with the Predators. He fought as hard and often as he could given his limited playing time, and is trying to make it as an enforcer with the expansion team.

PERRY, Brian
b. Aldershot, England, April 6, 1944
Nestled between Kirkland Lake and Timmins is the small town of Swastika, Ontario, where Perry lived during his playing days. In the winters, he was a hockey player, and in the summers he worked for the Ontario Department of Lands and Forests. Those winters were long. He played in the minors, but was given a chance by Oakland in 1968 and for a year and a half was a regular centreman. As a rookie, he scored 10 goals, including a hat trick in a game against Chicago. He played one game with Buffalo after being claimed in the Expansion Draft, and then went to the WHA to finish his career.

He had begun his career with Montreal in 1964 and moved to Philadelphia after expansion.
GARRY PETERS

PERSSON, Ricard
b. Ostersund, Sweden, August 24, 1969
At first, Persson saw no reason to interrupt a good thing. New Jersey drafted him in 1987 but he was just starting a career in the Swedish league with Leksand. Eight years passed before the Devils could coax him to come to the NHL, and when they did, they hardly played him before trading him to St. Louis. The Blues also had him in the minors for parts of the next three seasons, and Persson didn't help his own cause by being injured. When he came to Ottawa in 2000, he provided the Sens with maturity on the blueline, but missed half of each of his first two years with bad injuries, most notably a concussion. He ended up playing in Germany. Had he known what his fortune would be in North America, perhaps he never would have come over at all?

PERSSON, Stefan
b. Pitea, Sweden, December 22, 1954
Little did Persson know when he joined the Islanders in 1977 just what kind of sweet hockey history he would soon be making. Yes, Salming and Hammarstrom were the first Swedes to truly break the NHL barrier, and yes, Hedberg and Nilsson played with Bobby Hull as the highest-scoring, most exciting line in the WHA, but Persson won four Stanley Cups with the Islanders as a rock-steady defenceman. In fact, he played his entire career on Long Island, a career that ended on March 11, 1986. On that day, he was traded to Winnipeg for an eighth-round draft

choice. Rather than make the move, he retired and returned to Sweden. He ended his playing days with Boras, and when he retired he stayed with the team in an administrative capacity. He later became GM of the country's national junior team, and also owned and operated a factory in Boras.

PESUT, George
b. Saskatoon, Saskatchewan, June 17, 1953

Drafted by St. Louis, traded to Philadelphia, and sent to California to complete the Reggie Leach trade, Pesut finally made his NHL debut with the Seals in '74-'75. He played parts of two seasons with the team, and after a brief trial in the WHA went to Europe to continue playing. For some 14 years he played defence, mostly in Germany where he was frequently a playing coach in the second division. He returned to Canada and settled in B.C., where he tried to start a "where are they now?" Web site of former NHLers.

PETERS, Frank
b. Rouses Point, New York, June 5, 1905
d. unknown

For one season, Peters was a full-time NHL defenceman. The year was 1930-31. The team, the New York Rangers. He didn't register a single point in 43 games, and the Blueshirts lost in the semifinals of the playoffs. Peters returned to the minors where he continued his short pro career.

PETERS, Garry
b. Regina, Saskatchewan, October 9, 1942

His was one of the first cases, and Peters didn't cave in to the giant NHL in his fight to play in the WHA. Peters had played most of '71-'72 in the minors, though he had played two regular-season and one playoff game with the Bruins during their Stanley Cup season. That summer, the Islanders claimed him in the Expansion Draft, but the New York Raiders of the WHA lived up to their name by trying to poach him from the Isles. The case went to court, which ruled that he was contractually obliged to play for only the Islanders during the coming season. Peters, though, upset that his movement had been restricted, refused to play for the Islanders, forcing them to reach an agreement with the Raiders for his release. He retired after a second year in the league, and later settled in Saskatoon where he worked with kids and a variety of hockey-driven programs and charities and more formally for Saskatchewan Lotteries. He had begun his career with Montreal in 1964 and moved to Philadelphia after expansion. In his first year with the Flyers, he suffered a serious eye injury on Christmas night (those were the days!), but he made a full recovery and resumed his career at training camp in 1968.

PETERS, Jimmy ("Shaky")
b. Montreal, Quebec, October 2, 1922

Before he could think about becoming a pro hockey player, Peters had more important things on his mind – like the war. In 1944, he put down his stick and took up his gun and worked for the 3rd Canadian Heavy Recovery Corps in Normandy. His task was to clean up heavy equipment left behind after the invasion, and during a tank accident he lost the tips of two fingers on his left hand. The accident did not prevent him from holding a stick, and when he returned home in 1945 he was able to play for Montreal. In his first season, he played principally on a defensive line with Murph Chamberlain and Ken Mosdell, a threesome that was integral to stopping Boston's Kraut Line during the '46 Cup finals, which the Habs won in five games. Peters later played for those Bruins and moved on to Detroit to help the Wings win the Cup in 1950, and he finished his career with Chicago, sort of. He retired in 1953 but was lured back for another year only to have the Hawks sell him to Detroit. That was a blessing in disguise, for the Wings won the Cup again and this time Peters retired for keeps. He stayed in Detroit and became a valuable member of the community. He worked for Motor City Tool Company and coached the Detroit Junior Red Wings, whose star player was none other than Jimmy Peters, Jr., his son, who would go on to play in the NHL himself. Peters the elder became commissioner of the Metropolitan Detroit Junior Hockey League.

In 1944, he worked for the 3rd Canadian Heavy Recovery Corps in Normandy.
JIMMY PETERS

PETERS, Jimmy, Jr.
b. Montreal, Quebec, June 20, 1944

Peters was born in Montreal, where his father was playing, but from age 11 he grew up in Detroit, where dad finished his career and settled. Jimmy was not the player his dad was, a journeyman rather than an established star, a fourth-liner more than a Cup winner. He won the Memorial Cup in 1962 with Hamilton, and joined the sponsoring NHL Red Wings two years later. Over his 12 pro years, he played 309 games in the NHL, and when he retired he obtained a unique scholarship offer from Northern Arizona University. He got a free education, and in return he coached intramural hockey. Peters earned a B.A. in education and an M.A. in physical education and then was hired by RPI as an assistant coach and recruiter. One player he brought to the campus, his cousin, Glen Currie, went on to play in the NHL as well. He later became a teacher and athletic director at a prep school in Vermont.

PETERS, Steve
b. Peterborough, Ontario, January 23, 1960

A smallish centre, Peters played twice with the old and lowly Colorado Rockies in '79-'80 at the start of

George Pesut

Garry Peters

Jimmy Peters, Jr.

Steve Peters

Brent Peterson

Michel Petit

Sergei Petrenko

his career, but after two years in the minors he headed for the wide open ice lanes of Europe. He retired in 1990, and a number of years later became video coach for the Phoenix Coyotes.

PETERSEN, Toby
b. Minneapolis, Minnesota, October 27, 1978
A graduate of Colorado College, Petersen has quickly made the Penguins. He made his NHL debut on December 5, 2000, in a season spent mostly in the minors, but in 2001 he became a regular. He, Mark Parrish, and Ben Clymer attended the same Bloomington high school together as kids.

PETERSON, Brent
b. Calgary, Alberta, February 15, 1958
Big things looked possible when Detroit drafted Peterson 12th overall in 1978. He made the team that fall, but on October 13, just five games into the season, he suffered a serious leg break and missed the rest of the year. In fact, it was five months before he could even put on skates. The next year, the Wings brought him up from the minors and told him he'd be staying a while – and two days later they demoted him. He hung in there until December 1981 when he was traded to Buffalo, and it was with the Sabres he got his career underway. He was with the team for four years, but his was the kind of game coaches both loved and thought replaceable. Peterson was a two-way player, a hitter and banger who worked for every loose puck and every shift. When Vancouver claimed him, the team used him as a penalty-killing specialist, and he finished his career in Hartford. Peterson moved into coaching right away and over the last decade and more has established himself as the kind of man destined to be back in the NHL one day. He was an assistant with the Whalers, and in 1991 took on the head coaching job with Portland of the WHL. His tenure peaked in 1998 when his Winter Hawks won the Memorial Cup, and his reputation was such that Nashville hired him as an assistant. In the spring of 2001, Peterson was also an assistant with Canada's entry in the World Championships.

PETERSON, Brent
b. Calgary, Alberta, July 20, 1972
Coming out of Michigan Tech in 1995, Peterson was welcomed with open arms by Tampa Bay. The Lightning placed him in the minors for a season before giving him a taste of NHL life, but in three seasons it became clear to both parties he wasn't going to stay with the parent club. After a few more years in the "I" he moved to Germany to continue his career.

PETIT, Michel
b. St. Malo, Quebec, February 12, 1964
Vancouver, Rangers, Quebec, Toronto, Calgary, Los Angeles, Tampa Bay, Edmonton, Philadelphia, Phoenix. Ten teams, one player. The all-time record. He was no stay-at-home defenceman. No. He moved and moved and moved. He was offensive-minded in his youth, but as he got older he clung to his career like Linus clings to his blanket. He contemplated retirement in 1998 after he not only was sent to the minors but suffered his sixth, perhaps seventh, concussion. But Petit just couldn't stay down. He played in Europe for a couple of years, felt better, and attended Pittsburgh's training camp in 2001. The Pens declined to be team number 11, and finally Petit dragged his equipment home and stored it in the garage.

Peterson was a two-way player, a hitter and banger who worked for every loose puck.
BRENT PETERSON (b. 1958)

PETRENKO, Sergei
b. Kharkov, Soviet Union (Ukraine), September 10, 1968
He was a longtime star with Dynamo, from the days of Iron Curtain hockey in Moscow through the lean but free perestroika days until 1999. Petrenko skated on the left wing in league play and internationally for more than a decade. He played for his country first at the 1992 Olympics in Albertville, and over the years played at five World Championships. Most recently, Petrenko played in the Czech Republic. His only NHL games came in '93-'94 with Buffalo.

PETROV, Oleg
b. Moscow, Soviet Union (Russia), April 18, 1971
It took Petrov 156 NHL games spread over 8 seasons of pro hockey to score 22 goals. He once went for four years without scoring, yet he scored 24 times in the 2001-02 season alone! Is he a late bloomer or was that a career year that will never be replicated? Time will tell. Petrov came up from the minors to join the Habs at the end of the '92-'93 season, the year the team won a surprising Cup. Over four seasons, his time with the Habs was sporadic at best and his stays in the minors prolonged, so in 1996 he opted to play in Switzerland. He stayed for four years, but the Canadiens lured him back in 1999 and he's quickly become an important scorer on a team sadly lacking in punch.

PETROVICKY, Robert
b. Kosice, Czechoslovakia (Slovakia), October 26, 1973
He may be small, but he's a world-class player who has done as much for his country as anyone. Petrovicky's NHL career has been sporadic at best, a few games with Hartford near the start of the 1990s, plenty of time in the minors, and stops in Buffalo and St. Louis, a longer stay with Tampa to close out the decade, and a brief go with the Islanders. But Petrovicky's

obsession has been to get Slovakia to the top of the international heap, to get the Big Six of hockey to move over and allow a seventh nation to squeeze in. He played for Slovakia at the 1995 Worlds when they were in "B" pool. They won the tournament and advanced to "A" for the following year, and each season has seen some development. Just being at the 1998 Olympics in Nagano was a giant step, and although the team wasn't allowed to put their best team on the ice at Salt Lake City four years later, they did a few weeks later at the 2002 Worlds. And they won. Petrovicky captained that team, just as he had at Salt Lake City, and when he held the WC trophy high above his head, he ushered in the era of the Big Seven.

PETROVICKY, Ronald
b. Zilina, Czechoslovakia
(Slovakia), February 15, 1977
Nothing is guaranteed if you are drafted 228th overall, as Petrovicky was by Calgary in 1996. But that didn't deter him. He played junior in Canada to get to know the game, and he apprenticed in the minors until the Flames gave him a chance in 2000-01. He played more in 2001-02, but has yet to burst onto the NHL scene with a consistent effort over a long period.

PETTERSSON, Jorgen
b. Goteborg, Sweden, July 11, 1956
Emile Francis loved Pettersson from the moment he saw the Swede play in Stockholm. He signed him to a nice contract and brought him to St. Louis in 1980, and in his first 3 seasons Pettersson scored 37, 38, and 35 goals. A tremendous start fell off a bit over the next two years, but by then Francis was GM in Hartford and traded to get Pettersson, figuring he could revive the sagging fortunes of the skilled winger with the soft hands and sizable body. But Pettersson had nothing left in the NHL tank and even Francis traded him away, to Washington. At the end of the '85-'86 season, he returned to Sweden and to Frolunda, his club team from his pre-Francis days.

PETTIE, Jim ("Seaweed")
b. Toronto, Ontario, October 24, 1953
Pettie was as off the wall as any goalie – and that's saying something – but he's a valuable member of the trivia fraternity on two counts. One, he was George Plimpton's roommate when the *Paris Review* editor was with the Bruins during training camp, writing his book *Open Net*, and played part of an exhibition game for the team. Two, Pettie was the starting goalie on December 1, 1976. It was his first NHL game, but more important he was the first Boston goalie to play against Bobby Orr. Boston won that game 5-3, and Orr got an assist for the Hawks. Pettie appeared in a total

of 21 NHL games during his career that, beyond these 2 events, was uneventful.

PETTINGER, Eric "Cowboy"
b. North Bierley, England, December 14, 1904
d. Wallaceburg, Ontario, December 24, 1968
An accomplished player despite his somewhat short NHL career, Pettinger played amateur and senior hockey for a number of years before turning pro with Boston in 1928. He was traded to the Leafs and finished his NHL days with Ottawa in 1931, but continued in the International league for a number of years. In 1937, he was named head coach at the University of Western Ontario, by which time his brother, Gord, was an established star in the NHL. From UWO he went to Wallaceburg in 1952 to coach the junior "B" team. Pettinger also worked at Dominion Glass Company.

In 1937, he was named head coach at the University of Western Ontario.
ERIC PETTINGER

PETTINGER, Gord
b. Harrogate, England, November 11, 1911
d. April 12, 1986
He was no superstar of the old days, and people didn't talk about him years later the way they might have a more colourful character, but Pettinger did manage something few players in the history of the game did: He won the Cup with three different teams. So, he must have done something right because nobody is that lucky that often, especially in an eight-year career. Pettinger got started quickly, joining the Rangers for 1932-33 and winning the championship in the spring. He was sold to Detroit after that season and played four and a half seasons with the Wings. They won back-to-back Cups in 1936 and '37, and a year after being traded to Boston, well, he did it again. He ended his career in the minors and didn't live long enough to see his great-nephew Matt make it to the NHL himself in November 2000.

PETTINGER, Matt
b. Edmonton, Alberta, October 22, 1980
Like many a Canadian looking to combine hockey and school, Pettinger played provincial junior in B.C. and then attended the University of Denver before turning pro with Washington. He played his first games with the Caps in 2000-01 and a year later established himself as a regular. He won silver with Canada's 2000 World Junior team.

PHAIR, Lyle
b. Pilot Mound, Manitoba, August 31, 1961
He was right to think about education first, and in some ways he was lucky he was never drafted. Phair went to Michigan State, and when he graduated in 1985 he was a free agent because no NHL team had scooped him in

Jorgen Pettersson

Jim Pettie

Gord Pettinger

Lyle Phair

Harold Phillipoff

Chris Phillips

Michel Picard

Noel Picard

the Entry Draft. However, he had developed so nicely over his years with the Spartans that he was in demand, and his agent, one Bob Goodenow, attracted a bidding war for his student player. L.A. won the derby, but in the coming three years the young left winger didn't mature into a top-flight NHLer. He retired in 1989 and coached at the University of Illinois in Chicago, and in 1993 went to work for Suburban Hockey, a management business that operates out of Farmington Hills, Michigan. Phair is responsible for much arena programming in the state, organizing clinics and schools for hockey players of every stripe.

PHILLIPOFF, Harold
b. Kamsack, Saskatchewan, July 14, 1956
The Atlanta Flames really felt they had a player when they took Phillipoff 10th overall in 1976 and weren't concerned when he had a lousy year with Nova Scotia after turning pro. After all, the Voyageurs were Montreal's farm team, so Phillipoff wasn't going to be hogging the ice time. In 1977-78, he made the Flames and looked to be an unbelievable player. He had 17 goals and 53 points and was a feared fighter. He seemed to be the complete package. In successive seasons, though, he damaged first his right, then his left knee, and the package grew less and less complete. Phillipoff retired in 1982 and settled in Vancouver where he went into business.

PHILLIPS, Bill "Batt"
b. Carleton Place, Ontario, September 23, 1902
d. Thessalon, Ontario, January 10, 1978
A wandering forward who didn't stay in one place for any length of time, Phillips touched down in the NHL with the Maroons in 1929-30 for much of the season and wound up in the International league soon after.

PHILLIPS, Charlie
b. Toronto, Ontario, May 10, 1917
Although he grew up in Toronto, Phillips called the Maritimes home for much of his life. He moved to Moncton to start his pro career, and over the years he was scouted by the Canadiens. Phillips was called up for half a season in '42-'43, and then entered the war. He served overseas for three years, playing hockey in England and throughout Europe during that time. When he returned, he settled in Moncton.

PHILLIPS, Chris
b. Fort McMurray, Alberta, March 9, 1978
It's taken longer than Ottawa had anticipated, but slowly and surely Phillips has developed into one of the top defencemen in the league. Large, physical, and a powerful skater, he grew up way too soon. When he

was just 10, his dad became legally blind because of diabetes. Two years later, his mom went shopping one day and by the evening was paralyzed from the waist down, felled by a virus called transverse malaitis. As a result, Chris stayed at home a while longer than most teen hockey aspirants, ensuring the proper care of his parents. He won gold with Canada's juniors in both 1996 and '97 and was drafted 1st overall by the Senators in 1996. He missed much of his second year with an injured back and ankle, but recovered to develop into a true force on the Ottawa blueline as the team became a playoff contender.

PHILLIPS, Merlyn "Bill"
b. Toronto, Ontario, May 24, 1895
d. Thessalon, Ontario, January 10, 1978

After retiring in 1933, he ran a tourist resort called Bill Phillips Camp.
BILL PHILLIPS

At 5' 5-1/2" Merlyn Joseph Phillips was just a wee centreman for the Montreal Maroons, but an effective one nonetheless. He entered the war in 1916 with the 63rd Depot Battery, and upon discharge went to Sault Ste. Marie where he played happily for a number of years. The Maroons discovered him and brought him to Montreal near the close of the '25-'26 season, one in which the team won the Stanley Cup. The 30-year-old rookie went on to play 8 seasons with the Maroons and finished his career with the New York Americans. After retiring in 1933, he returned to Thessalon, where his parents lived and where he grew up, and ran a tourist resort called Bill Phillips Camp, on Basswood Lake. He also coached the local Thessalon Eagles and was a popular and well-respected figure in the area.

PICARD, Michel
b. Beauport, Quebec, November 7, 1969
Maybe because of his size, maybe because of ice time or line combinations, Picard has not proved to be nearly the star in the NHL that he has been at every other level. He was drafted by Hartford in 1989, but since then has played fewer than 200 games in the big time. He has, however, been regularly employed elsewhere – and everywhere – during that time, most recently in Germany. He has been owned by seven NHL teams and played for five of them, but never more than half a season with any one team.

PICARD, Noel
b. Montreal, Quebec, December 25, 1938
He got his name from his date of birth, though he was front and centre in a great moment of celebration for someone else later in life. Picard was consigned to the minors in the Montreal system until expansion in 1967, though he did play a few games in '64-'65 to

earn his name on the Cup that spring. In 1967, though, St. Louis claimed him, and Picard proved to be a solid, mobile, and experienced defenceman for a team half of which seemed on its last legs, the other half being so young the NHL was too much. But because of the playoff structure, the Blues made it to the Cup finals in three successive years, never winning a game. It was during the third of that run that Picard found himself in front of the net watching an overtime give-and-go between Boston's Derek Sanderson behind the Blues net and Bobby Orr cutting in front. Just as Orr scored the Cup-winning goal, Picard hooked his stick around Orr's ankle, sending him into the air to be caught by numerous photographers in hockey's immortal image of Cup celebration. Picard's life changed during a hunting trip in November 1971.

Robert Picard

He went horseback riding, but in an accident his mount fell on his ankle, crushing it so severely that three bones stuck out. It was hours before he got to a hospital in St. Louis, by which time doctors contemplated amputation. Eventually, Picard's foot was saved and he vowed to defy doctors and all who said his career was done. He returned to start the '72-'73 season, but he was a lesser player. Gone was his speed and mobility. The Blues put him on waivers and Atlanta claimed him, and at season's end, his point made, Picard retired. He returned to St. Louis and became a colour commentator for Dan Kelly on broadcasts. He also trained Clydesdale horses for Anheuser-Busch, the city's beer giant.

Pierce was a fine centre in junior: quick hands, good skater, decent prospect.
RANDY PIERCE

PICARD, Robert
b. Montreal, Quebec, May 25, 1957

In Washington they called him Moses, in Toronto they called him … bad names, and in Montreal they wanted to call him another in a series of great defencemen. Picard was none of the above, though. The Capitals generated hype initially by drafting him 3rd overall in 1977, and in his three years with an horrific team he was the best they had – by far. When he got to Toronto, though, fans booed him because he didn't play like any Moses, and in Montreal too much was expected of him, of course. Yet Picard played on and on, his longest stay coming with Quebec after a stint with Winnipeg, and he ended in Detroit. He was offensively gifted, but rarely played on a quality team. However, Picard did play in the All-Star Games of 1980 and '81. After his career, he moved to Jacksonville, Florida, and became regional manager for a car wash equipment company.

PICARD, Roger
b. Montreal, Quebec, January 13, 1935

The less-heralded brother of Noel, Roger played with the Blues during their first year, though he was a forward

to Noel's defence. Roger played most of his hockey in Quebec, and after a season and a half in the minors he returned to Montreal. He won the Allan Cup with Drummondville in 1967.

PICHETTE, Dave
b. Grand Falls, Newfoundland, February 4, 1960

Although no team drafted him, it was a no-brainer for Quebec to sign Pichette in 1980. After all, he had just finished an outstanding career in town with the Remparts, and the fans loved him. As he found out, the NHL was different. He hurt himself in training camp, and after a convalescence in the minors he started slowly with the Nordiques. The fans turned on him, booing him and making him nervous to the point of forcing mistakes. He was traded to St. Louis, where his situation worsened, but he thought he hit his stride in New Jersey. In '84-'85 he scored 17 goals as a defenceman, but the year after was back in the minors where he finished his career. There was one short stint with the Rangers in between. After retiring, he continued to be very active in the Oldtimers Hockey league, playing across the country and raising money for charities.

Roger Picard

PICKETTS, Harold "Hal"
b. Asquith, Saskatchewan, April 22, 1909

Picketts played a full season with the Americans in 1933-34 after a year in the Can-Am league, but the Amazing Amerks weren't so great that season and missed the playoffs. He ended up in the IHL and later returned to Saskatchewan to finish his career.

PIDHIRNY, Harry
b. Toronto, Ontario, May 5, 1928

Pidhirny played just two NHL games, with Boston, in '57-'58. In the AHL, he was one of the league's great gods. He played 18 seasons in that league and became the first player to appear in 1,000 games. He once scored 6 goals in a game to tie a league record, and he scored 400 career goals. The team he was best known for was Springfield, working miracles at centre ice under the dominating gaze of owner and GM Eddie Shore. The tribe eventually retired Pidhirny's number 8, and in 1966 Shore made him the team's coach. It was a role Pidhirny had played into, acting as an assistant with the San Francisco Seals five years earlier, but Shore became too intolerable and Pidhirny resigned after just half a season.

PIERCE, Randy
b. Arnprior, Ontario, November 23, 1957

Sometimes, you'd like to be able to choke all the scouts and coaches in the world who don't know what

Dave Pichette

they're doing. Pierce was a fine centre in junior: quick hands, good skater, decent prospect. Then, he was told to be a fighter. The coach moved him to the right wing and he tried to play a game that wasn't his. He ended up being neither a good scorer nor an intimidating presence. Then, one game, he was hit from behind and fell straight into the boards, dislocating his shoulder. Forced back too quickly time and again, he'd play, get hurt, play, get hurt. Then he got hit by a puck in the eye socket, smashing his nose and cheekbone. Meanwhile, the shoulder kept going out on him, and being good friends with Barry Beck he saw the devastation such an injury can cause. In 1985, Pierce retired. He ran a hockey school in the U.S. for a while, worked as an assistant coach in the IHL, and scouted for Ottawa. He settled in Pakenham, Ontario, near his childhood home, and coached the Junior B Packers while he watched his son, Matt, become a prospect in his own right.

PIETRANGELO, Frank
b. Niagara Falls, Ontario, December 17, 1964

Everyone in Pittsburgh called it, simply, "the save," the key moment of the 1991 playoffs in which the Penguins won their first Stanley Cup. It was game six of the division semifinals, Pittsburgh playing New Jersey and trailing 3-2 in the series and 3-2 in that game. Pietrangelo dove across the net to rob Peter Stastny of a sure goal, and the Pens game back to win the game 4-3. In game seven, Pietrangelo earned a shutout. He was in goal only because starter Tom Barrasso was injured, and after three more starts Pietrangelo was back on the bench. But when the team was celebrating, players spoke of that moment as a save of destiny. It was his fourth year as backup, but he was on his way to Hartford a year later and after two and a half uneventful years with the Whalers, Pietrangelo was out of the NHL. He retired for two years and then went to Europe to play, becoming a hero in goal for Manchester until retiring in 2001 because of a recurring and serious knee injury. Wherever he goes or whatever he does, Pietrangelo will always have the memory of that save with Pittsburgh as a Stanley Cup memento no one can ever take from him.

PIKE, Alf
b. Winnipeg, Manitoba, September 15, 1917

By virtue of his junior affiliation with the Winnipeg Monarchs in the 1930s, Pike was destined to play for the Rangers if he ever made the NHL, and from early on it was clear he would. In 1936-37, he played on a feared line with Johnny McCreedy and Dick Kowcinak that took the team to the Memorial Cup, but the year after, when he turned pro, he had two seasons mired by injury to a knee and collarbone. Pike made the Rangers at camp in 1939, and in his rookie season the team won the Stanley Cup. Pike was known for his shot and passing, and also his versatility, able to play every position but goal in a pinch. He was a regular with the team excepting two seasons spent in the army, and after being sent out of the league he started a lengthy and successful tenure as coach, beginning with Winnipeg. He was the man assistant GM Punch Imlach had wanted to hire for the Leafs after Billy Reay was fired, and think how Toronto history might have played out had the hiring gone through! Instead, Pike's NHL coaching experience was limited to two seasons with the Rangers. He also coached at Calgary and assorted minor-league cities before packing it in. Pike moved to Guelph to work for a sporting goods business.

Alf Pike

Rich Pilon

Pietrangelo dove across the net to rob Peter Stastny of a sure goal.
FRANK PIETRANGELO

PILAR, Karel
b. Prague, Czechoslovakia (Czech Republic), December 23, 1977

It's fortuitous for the Leafs that as a teen Pilar played in the Czech Republic without so much as a glance from scouts. Yet, by the time he was 22 and drafted by Toronto, he had won a gold medal at the 2001 World Championships and was playing like an NHLer in the minors. When the Leafs brought him up during the 2001-02 season, they had such a tough time returning him that the last callup was for good. His play on the blueline was stellar. He was strong, fearless, and good with the puck. The only downside was that during the playoffs he broke his hand, but Toronto counted on him to become a regular and he proved worthy of the assignment until a bad start in 2002-03 forced his demotion to the AHL. Things went from bad to worse when he contracted a virus that weakened his heart and ended his career after just 17 AHL games.

PILON, Rich ("Chief")
b. Saskatoon, Saskatchewan, April 30, 1968

When defenceman Rich Pilon scored 2 goals for the Rangers during the 2000-01 season, it was a staggering total that doubled his output from any season of his previous 13 and represented 25 percent of his career total of 8. He once went 245 games without scoring, testament to his skills in other areas or else he never would have lasted as long as he did. Pilon played all of his career with the Islanders before the Rangers acquired him on December 1, 1999. He was a tough and solid defenceman beset by serious injuries for much of his career. He missed most of one season from an eye injury, most of another because of a shoulder problem, and most of two others because of a serious wrist wound. After his brief stint with the Blueshirts, he signed with the Blues – only to miss much of the year with an injury. The wrist might well force his premature retirement.

PILOTE, Pierre ("Pete")
b. Kenogami, Quebec, December 11, 1931

It was an odd paradox that, although Pilote was skating soon after he was walking, he didn't play organized hockey until he was 17. In fact, when the local arena in Fort Erie burned down when he was 14, he didn't skate at all for three years! When he did, he impressed Rudy Pilous enough that Pilote was invited to the training camp of the St. Catharines Teepees. Although he was not a graceful skater or slick stickhandler, Pilote was determined and his spirit never faltered. Toward the end of his second season with the Teepees he was given a tryout by Buffalo of the AHL, and three years later, in 1955, he was with the Hawks in the NHL. Pilote's first ambition was to establish himself as a physical presence in the league. He did this by hitting hard and often, and when he had to fight, well, fight he would. One night, he knocked both Maurice and Henri Richard out cold, and life got easier for him from then on! He played in 376 consecutive games, from his first through more than 5 full seasons until he dislocated his shoulder late in '61-'62. His defence partner was Moose Vasko, and Pilote was never afraid to rush with the puck. Pilous, in fact, said that Pilote was the team's best defenceman both up the ice and back. He helped the team win the Cup in 1961, and that fall was named captain. He was named to the Second All-Star Team for three straight years (1959-62) and then to the First Team for five in a row (1962-67). He also won three consecutive Norris Trophies (1962-65) and played in eight straight All-Star Games. Pilote was traded to Toronto in 1968, though he played only one season for the Blue and White before retiring. Buffalo selected him in the 1970 Expansion Draft, but he didn't want to keep playing. He had run a number of laundromats throughout southern Ontario, but settled in Toronto and became successful in the luggage business. Pilote was inducted into the Hockey Hall of Fame in 1975, one of the best rushing defencemen of his era, and also one of the best in his own end of the ice.

One night, he knocked both Maurice and Henri Richard out cold.
PIERRE PILOTE

PINDER, Gerry
b. Saskatoon, Saskatchewan, September 15, 1948

Pinder had a plan, but it didn't work out. He wanted to play for the National Team and go to university at the same time, play in the 1970 World Championships in Winnipeg and get a degree in commerce. He played for Canada at the 1968 Olympics in Grenoble and the 1969 WC, but he left the team because of a dispute with manager Buck Houle. He joined Chicago in 1969, but his ice time dwindled over his two years and he left the team because of another dispute, this time with Hawks coach Billy Reay. After a year with California, Pinder moved to the WHA, but his career took a turn for the worse in the 1974 playoffs when he took a stick in the eye and lost partial use of it. He donned a helmet, but not a visor, and played less effectively for another three years. He settled in Denver, but in 1988 moved to Calgary to run a real estate development company called Gerly Holdings.

PIROS, Kamil
b. Most, Czechoslovakia (Czech Republic), November 20, 1978

After playing a number of years with Litvinov in the Czech league, Piros came to the NHL to try his hand with Atlanta in the fall of 2001. He started the season with the Thrashers but was soon assigned to Chicago, where he helped the Wolves win the Turner Cup. He started the next season back in the AHL.

PIRUS, Alex
b. Toronto, Ontario, January 12, 1955

It was an odd transformation, to say the least. Pirus began his life as a hockey player, renowned as being one of the hardest hitters in the game. He came out of the University of Notre Dame with a business degree in 1976, but in each of his four NHL years he played fewer games and scored fewer goals until he was out of the league by 1981. A born-again Christian, he became involved in the Living Light Ministries, serving God and teaching hockey and proving that one does not preclude the other.

PISA, Ales
b. Pardubice, Czechoslovakia (Czech Republic), January 2, 1977

Pisa was a veteran of Pardubice in club play in the Czech Republic, but after Edmonton drafted him in 2001 he naturally decided to reap the rewards of play in the NHL. He spent most of his first year in the minors, but by 2002 Pisa was a regular on the Oilers blueline.

PITLICK, Lance
b. Minneapolis, Minnesota, November 5, 1967

His university career started in 1986 in Minnesota when the homestate North Stars drafted him; it ended four years later when Philadelphia signed him. Four more years went by and he still hadn't seen the NHL, so Ottawa signed him and put him to good use. Pitlick proved to be a natural leader and solid defenceman, and for five years led a blueline corps out of the wilderness and into the playoffs. He left the team in

Gerry Pinder

Alex Pirus

Lance Pitlick

Domenic Pittis

Michal Pivonka

Barclay Plager

Bill Plager

1999 when he signed a better contract with Florida, but his role has been the same wherever he has played: go hard, play smart, lead by example.

PITRE, Didier ("Cannonball")
b. Valleyfield, Quebec, September 1, 1883
d. Sault Ste. Marie, Michigan, July 29, 1934

They say he had the hardest shot in hockey, so hard, in fact, that sometimes when the puck hit the end boards they moved back from the sheer force of his drive. He was also a dazzling skater and could move backward as quickly as most players could forward. In an era when boards were low and patrons sat right at the ice in their dinner attire, Pitre also had the mischievous habit of stopping quickly and sending showers of snow onto the fans as they were eating dinner or enjoying a drink! Pitre played in Michigan during the early years of the International league and joined the fledgling Montreal Canadiens in the NHA in 1909. With the exception of 1 year in Vancouver, he spent the rest of his career – 13 years – with the Habs, winning a Stanley Cup in 1916. He was one of the game's early superstars, a player who commanded a salary of $3,000 when everyone else was making between $300 and $1,000. He was a terrific scorer, and a shifty skater for one so big and strong. His nephew, Vic Desjardins, later played in the NHL, and Pitre retired immediately after his final game, against Ottawa in 1923. His friends took him out for a special dinner after that game, and the next day he handed in his skates and thanked Canadiens management for their support. Pitre returned to Sault Ste. Marie, Michigan, where he had played in the IHL and worked as a truck driver. He died of acute indigestion at age 50 and was inducted into the Hockey Hall of Fame in 1962.

PITTIS, Domenic
b. Calgary, Alberta, October 1, 1974

Time and again players have proved that the NHL is simply much, much more difficult than the AHL or any other league. Take Pittis, for instance. Neither Pittsburgh nor Buffalo gave him much time to prove himself, yet he won the American league scoring championship in '98-'99. Edmonton then gave him a healthy chance, but in 47 games he scored only 4 times. A star in the AHL, a survivor, at best, in the NHL. Not big, but skilled, if he were going to make it anywhere it would be with the high-flying Oilers on their smooth sheet of ice.

PIVONKA, Michal
b. Kladno, Czechoslovakia (Czech Republic), January 28, 1966

In the space of two and a half years, Pivonka played at three World Juniors and two World Championships for Czechoslovakia. He fulfilled his army duty, and then, at age 20, fled the country with his girlfriend, defecting to Washington in July 1986 to start a new life as an NHL player. He arrived a star, a kid with huge potential and unlimited future, and although that promise was tempered by his performance, he remained a faithful Capitals centre for the full 13 seasons of his career. At the height of his powers, he scored 20 goals 4 years in a row. He adjusted quickly to life in the West, the pace on the streets and the ferocity of the game. His last years with the Caps were halved by injuries, including 1998 when the team went to the finals for the first time. Pivonka ended by playing two final seasons in the IHL after no other NHL teams showed an interest in him.

He was one of the game's early superstars, a player who commanded a salary of $3,000.
DIDIER PITRE

PLAGER, Barclay ("Barc the Spark")
b. Kirkland Lake, Ontario, March 26, 1941
d. Creve Coeur, Missouri, February 6, 1988

Everyone who was close to him was the better for it. Everyone who met him walked away a better person. Everyone who had the honour of shaking his hand was the stronger for the experience. Plager had that effect on people. It is fair to say that on the talent level, he might well have been dead last in the NHL, but in terms of effort, heart, passion, and resolve, the whole league put together didn't match him. He came out of northern Ontario to play pro in the minors for seven years. Only expansion in 1967 got him into the NHL, yet once there no one was going to take his achievement away from him. He was a leader in St. Louis with brothers Bill and Bob, and for 10 years he helped forge the team's identity and helped it evolve and grow into a lasting franchise. When he retired, he turned to coaching the team, and later he was an assistant with the Blues. Yet his life was meant to be short. In 1985, he was diagnosed with cancer, and after doctors thought the tumours had gone into remission, a new one, inoperable, was found on his brain. He took treatments, but remained the team's assistant, right up until near the end when he told doctors to stop the medication and disconnect the life support system. He was only 46.

PLAGER, Bill
b. Kirkland Lake, Ontario, July 6, 1945

On the one hand, yes, he was one of the Plagers. On the other hand, he was by far the nicest of the three, and this was not necessarily a good thing. Both Barclay and Bob also played defence, so when the Blues acquired Bill, the team thought it was getting a third solid blueliner and, as a brother-threesome on defence, a headliner as well. The problem was that

Bill couldn't crack the lineup – the team was too strong on defence! After four very part-time years with the Blues, he moved on to Atlanta and Minnesota, never having quite the same impact as his brothers before he retired in 1977.

PLAGER, Bob
b. Kirkland Lake, Ontario, March 11, 1943

Barclay held the OHA record for penalty minutes until Bob came along and broke it. In fact, they once fought each other in junior. Cut from the same cloth, Bob was the only Plager to see some Original Six action before expansion, playing a few games here and there with the Rangers. Like Barclay, his break came in 1967 when St. Louis acquired him. For the next 11 seasons, he established the franchise on the blueline with his hard hits and big fights, helping the team get to three successive Stanley Cup finals. Like his brothers, he was immensely popular. Bob opened a restaurant in the city and was once named the team's best groomed player. More important, he was always a great practical joker and no player – rookie, his brothers, or even the team owner – was immune from his antics. In the summers, he had the enviable job of being a beer taster in Kapuskasing, but St. Louis was really his life. He coached the team briefly in '92–'93 on an emergency basis and performed extensive scouting for the Blues. Most recently, Plager has been the Blues' vice-president of player development.

He knit his own toques and sweaters well into his twenties.
JACQUES PLANTE

PLAMONDON, Gerry
b. Sherbrooke, Quebec, January 5, 1925

Plamondon joined the Canadiens for a few games right after the war and thus became a member of the '45-'46 Cup team. In his five years with the organization, he was a part-timer who scored buckets in the minors but had trouble finding the net in the NHL. He finished his career in the minors and later returned to Quebec to work.

PLANTE, Cam
b. Brandon, Manitoba, March 12, 1964

In his final season of junior, 1983-84 with Brandon, Plante set records in the WHL for most assists in a season by a defenceman (118) and most points (140), yet these heroics translated into exactly 2 NHL games, with Toronto the year after. Plante spent the better part of four years in the minors and then set off for Europe, settling into a great career in Britain before retiring in 1998. He returned home to Brandon and opened his own business called Total Eye Care Centre.

PLANTE, Dan
b. Hayward, Wisconsin, October 5, 1971

He left the University of Wisconsin a year early to play for the Islanders, but just as he was making headway he tore his ACL in training camp in 1994. Plante recovered to play two full seasons with the Isles, but the futile team never came close to the playoffs and he's been in the minors ever since. His Islanders days did yield two nice chances to play for the U.S. at the World Championships, but all of his recent pro time has been with the Chicago Wolves, which he helped win the Turner Cup in 1999-2000.

PLANTE, Derek
b. Cloquet, Minnesota, January 17, 1971

Plante's career has had a little bit of everything. He went the university route to get to the NHL (four years at the University of Minnesota-Duluth) and represented the U.S. at the WJC and WC. He became a solid player with Buffalo when he joined the team in 1993 and had three 20-goal seasons there. And he became an expendable veteran, though perhaps a little earlier than he would have liked. Dallas acquired him at the trading deadline in March 1999, and he played the role of utility man to perfection and was rewarded with a Stanley Cup. He got to be unwanted by any team in the league, and he dropped to the minors and more recently went to Europe, where he played in Germany and then Switzerland.

PLANTE, Jacques ("Jake the Snake")
b. Shawinigan Falls, Quebec, January 17, 1929
d. Geneva, Switzerland, February 26, 1986

If Glenn Hall gets the nod as the greatest goalie the world has ever known, then with equal conviction one can say that Plante was the most important and influential puckstopper of all time. He grew up not well off, and as a result the practical kid learned how to knit so he could keep himself warm even if his parents couldn't afford to buy him the necessary winter clothes. He knit his own toques and sweaters well into his twenties, and, of course, by the time he hit serious hockey leagues this idiosyncrasy was ridiculed by his teammates. Plante played for the Montreal Royals and then replaced Gerry McNeil as the top goalie for the Canadiens. He made his debut toward the end of the '52-'53 season and by 1954 there was only one goalie in town worth talking about – Plante. In '54-'55, his first full season, Plante won 31 games, and the year after he started a streak of success that has never been replicated. In the five-year period of 1955-60, he won the Vézina Trophy every year and won five successive Cups. He had an off-season in '60-'61, but the year after he combined another Vézina with the Hart

Bob Plager

Gerry Plamondon

Dan Plante

Jacques Plante

Mark Plantery

Trophy, the last goalie to win the award until Dominik Hasek in 1997. But beyond the numbers and silverware was his style of play, and there is no date more important to goalies than November 2, 1959. That night, Plante was hit in the face by an Andy Bathgate shot and had to leave the ice to get stitches. The game was delayed, and Plante refused to return to the ice unless he could wear a mask. Coach Toe Blake was furious. A lesser goalie would never have dared to make such a demand, and if he had he would have been exiled to the minors in perpetuity. But this was Plante, a game was at stake, and Blake had no alternative. He capitulated, and for the first time in an NHL game a goalie wore a mask for protection. His cause was further helped because the team won the game and went on an extended unbeaten streak, and the team lost the one game later in the season when Plante didn't wear the mask. The game had changed forever, though it took time. Many fans were physically disturbed by Plante's first mask, a green, kabuki-like covering that forced some spectators to leave the game. Over the years, he experimented with colour (eventually settling on flesh tone and then plain white) and design, trying to ensure protection while allowing the skin to breathe and the goalie to see pucks at his feet. Along with this innovation, Plante became the most active cage guardian the league had seen. He skated behind the goal to stop the puck for defencemen and prevented success on shoot-ins. On an icing call, he held his arm up in the air to alert his teammates. He passed the puck up to them and worked on coming out of his net to cut down the angle. In short, he became the most studious goalie of all time, a man who knew there was more to playing his position well than simply quick reflexes. Later, he wrote a book called *The Art of Goaltending*, the first book that considered all facets of play for a goalie. It was another masterful and pioneering effort to understand why things were done and how they could be done more effectively. He was traded to the Rangers in 1963 but after two years retired. He was lured back in 1968 by the chance to play for St. Louis and to share the goaltending with Glenn Hall. Plante had just had a knee operation, but he finished the year with an astounding 1.96 GAA at the tender age of 40, and the pair shared another Vezina Trophy! In the playoffs, he led the league with eight wins and three shutouts, but his 1.43 GAA wasn't enough to beat his old team, the Canadiens. The next year, the ancient pair again took the Blues to the finals before losing to Boston. Plante continued on. He was sold to Toronto and for nearly three seasons played half the time and coached Bernie Parent for part of that time. Few people will recall, though, that his final NHL games came

with Boston toward the end of the '72-'73 season. Still, he was not done. He went to work for Quebec in the WHA, and then in '74-'75 was back in goal for the Edmonton Oilers before finally calling it quits at age 46. He worked as a goalie coach for St. Louis, but he and his wife moved to Switzerland where they lived permanently. Theirs was a true love story, for while Plante played and coached, he spent his evenings alone in a variety of hotel rooms writing love poems to her. Plante was diagnosed with stomach cancer. Doctors found that it was inoperable, and he died a short time later. He was inducted into the Hockey Hall of Fame in 1978, but his contributions to the game live on. The masks, the puckhandling, the discipline of style and technique that every goalie lives by today are all parts of the game invented by the great pioneer puckstopper, Jacques Plante.

He worked well on the power play and was one of the team's top scorers.
PIERRE PLANTE

PLANTE, Pierre
b. Valleyfield, Quebec,
May 14, 1951
Although Philadelphia drafted Plante in 1971 and used him for a few games, when the opportunity to acquire Andre Dupont from St. Louis arose the team had no problem in parting with Plante. Yet the right winger had some fine moments with the Blues. He worked well on the power play and was one of the team's top scorers, but the Blues never went far in the playoffs. In quick succession he went from Chicago to New York to Quebec, and although he made it to the finals with the Rangers in 1979, he made it to the outhouse with the Nordiques after slamming head coach Jacques Demers and assistant Andre Boudrias at season's end, claiming they both were inept. Plante retired soon after those remarks.

PLANTERY, Mark
b. St. Catharines, Ontario, August 14, 1959
Life never looked better to Mark Plantery than when he was 16 years old. He was a baseball catcher as well as a hockey player, so good with the ball that the New York Yankees signed him to a pro contract, the youngest player they had ever signed. Ever! The Yankees! Plantery even had a clause put in his contract that allowed him to continue with hockey, but at 18 he would have to make a decision. He chose hockey, but by the time he was 20 he hadn't been drafted. Winnipeg signed him as a free agent but put him in only 25 games, and Plantery spent the next 5 years in the minors before retiring. If he had taken the baseball route… ?

PLASSE, Michel
b. Montreal, Quebec, June 1, 1948
On February 21, 1971, Plasse was tending goal for the

Kansas City Blues of the CHL when he scored a goal into an empty Oklahoma City net late in a game the Blazers were trying to tie. He became the first goalie to score, and in the same season he made his NHL debut with the senior Blues in St. Louis. It was his only game with the team, as they sold him to Montreal, and for a year Plasse sat on the bench most nights and watched Ken Dryden take the Habs to another Stanley Cup. He didn't become a starter until he got to Pittsburgh and then Colorado, but despite playing 11 seasons in the NHL he appeared in only 4 playoff games, such were the quality of his destinations. No matter – that first goal will always be what people remember.

PLAVSIC, Adrien

b. Montreal, Quebec,
January 13, 1970

Plavsic's dream was to play in the Olympics, and he structured the early part of his career to that end. He played 1988-89 with the National Team to gain experience and establish himself within the program, and a year later represented Canada at the World Juniors. He played a few games with St. Louis and half the next season with Vancouver after the Canucks acquired him in a trade, and then his pro career came to a standstill. Plavsic rejoined the National Team for the start of the 1991-92 season and stayed right through the Olympics in Albertville, and only then did he rejoin the Canucks, with a silver medal hanging around his neck, no less. Yet, once he was ready to dig in to a fruitful NHL career, the NHL was not so eager to welcome the defenceman with open arms. He bounced around a bit, and when Anaheim used him in the minors for almost the entire '96-'97 season, he decided to head to Europe to play. He has been in Switzerland since 1998.

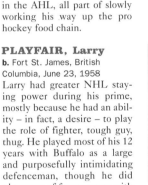

Plavsic rejoined the National Team for the start of the 1991-92 season.
ADRIEN PLAVSIC

PLAXTON, Hugh

b. Barrie, Ontario, May 16, 1904
d. unknown

Hugh, Bert, and Roger Plaxton all played for Canada at the 1928 Olympics in St. Moritz, though only Hugh went on to a pro career in the NHL. Hugh helped the University of Toronto Grads win the Allan Cup the previous year, led by coach Conn Smythe, and after winning an easy gold medal for Canada Plaxton returned to Toronto to start a law practice with another brother, Herb. They later teamed with another Plaxton, James, who was in an office with John Wright and James Hall. Hugh's NHL time came with the Maroons in 1932-33 when he played half a season, including one game in goal, but he retired at year's end to resume his law career. He was later a member of parliament.

PLAYFAIR, Jim

b. Fort St. James, British Columbia, May 22, 1964

There were six Playfair kids, and five of them were boys. Jim and Larry went on to play in the NHL, but at one time Dennis was the best prospect. Jim was drafted by Edmonton in June 1982, the highlight of his life, and two weeks later the low point came when another brother, Jeff, was killed in a car accident. The Playfairs were devout Catholics, but it was a blow to the family not easily overcome. Jim won the Memorial Cup with Portland the following year, but in the ensuing seasons played only 21 NHL games with the Oilers and later Chicago. He spent the vast majority of his time in the minors until retiring in 1992, but immediately went into coaching. He start in the "I," moved to Dayton in the East Coast league, and worked his way up to head coach in Michigan back in the IHL. In 2000, he became head coach of the Saint John Flames in the AHL, all part of slowly working his way up the pro hockey food chain.

Jim Playfair

PLAYFAIR, Larry

b. Fort St. James, British Columbia, June 23, 1958

Larry had greater NHL staying power during his prime, mostly because he had an ability – in fact, a desire – to play the role of fighter, tough guy, thug. He played most of his 12 years with Buffalo as a large and purposefully intimidating defenceman, though he did play parts of four seasons with Los Angeles. He was durable in body throughout his career, with one notable exception – he incurred major damage to his left knee over the years. When he suffered a ruptured disc in the 1989-90 season, he decided it was time to retire. He settled in Buffalo and worked on Sabres broadcasts. He also opened two tool rental shops in town.

Larry Playfair

PLEAU, Larry

b. Lynn, Massachusetts, January 29, 1947

He didn't get the press that some of the other NHL defectors got, but Pleau certainly made a statement when he left Montreal and signed a lucrative contract with New England. He was an American who came to Montreal to play for the Jr. Canadiens, but before he joined the big Habs he played for the U.S. at the 1968 Olympics in Grenoble and the '69 WC. He played parts of three seasons with the Habs, but rather than be a spare part at centre with a team that had future Hall of Famers waiting to play that position (or, so it seemed to him), Pleau returned to the U.S. and played for the Whalers. He was one of the few players who stayed with the WHA for every year of its operation, but in 1979, when Hartford joined the NHL, he decided to retire and become the team's assistant coach. For the next 10 years he remained faithful to the organization as coach, assistant GM, and finally GM. He then moved to the Rangers, where over eight years he moved up to the position of vice-president of player personnel. Most recently, he has built a Cup-contending team as GM in St. Louis, where he continues to work toward putting together that city's first championship team.

PLETKA, Vaclav
b. Mlada Boleslav, Czechoslovakia (Czech Republic), June 8, 1979
In the fall of 2000, Pletka decided to leave the Czech league and attend Flyers training camp. He was assigned to the Phantoms in the AHL, and over two seasons appeared in a single game for the NHL team. He then returned home to continue his career, his connection to the NHL as remote as it had been before coming to North America.

PLETSCH, Charles
b. Chesley, Ontario, July 22, 1892
d. unknown
Pletsch's brief career reportedly took him to the Hamilton Tigers in the NHL for one game during the 1920-21 season, though confirmation of that game is sketchy at best. Almost nothing else is known of his life or career.

PLETT, Willi
b. Asuncion, Paraguay, June 7, 1955
The Plett family travelled near and far before coming to Canada when Willi was three. His parents lived in Russia, moved to Germany, and then fled to Paraguay to escape the Second World War. Eventually, they found sponsors in Canada, and in 1958 moved to Niagara-on-the-Lake, Ontario. Plett didn't start in organized hockey until he was 12, but he developed quickly into an excellent player. He moved his way up through the ranks as an early power forward, by modern terms, able to score with one hand and fight with the other. Atlanta drafted him in 1975, and after a year in the minors he joined the Flames to score 33 goals and win the Calder Trophy. In his six years with the organization, he became a feared forward for the two aforementioned reasons. He moved with the team to Calgary, and scored a career-high 38 goals in the team's first season in Alberta. When he was traded to Minnesota, though, his role changed dramatically as the North Stars wanted him to forget about skill and focus on fighting. For five years, his scoring dropped significantly and his penalty minutes rose, but he was not a happy camper. He ended his career in Boston and then returned to Atlanta where the memories were all happy ones. He developed a sports theme park in Marietta, Georgia, just outside Atlanta, that continues to thrive.

PLUMB, Rob
b. Kingston, Ontario, August 29, 1957
Rob and Ron, the Plumb brothers, both had long hockey careers, though together they combined for just 40 games in the NHL. No matter. Rob played for Detroit in the late 1970s when the team was awful, but later moved to Switzerland and had a fruitful career before retiring in 1988.

PLUMB, Ron
b. Kingston, Ontario, July 17, 1950
While brother Rob went to Switzerland after his few games in the NHL, Ron took another route during his career. He was drafted by Boston in 1970 after being named the OHL's best defenceman, but ended up in the minors for two seasons and then spent seven years in the WHA. His last year and a half came with New England, and when the team became Hartford and joined the NHL, Plumb made 26 big-league appearances. He later played and coached in England and in '84-'85 was named coach of the year while leading Fife.

POAPST, Steve
b. Cornwall, Ontario, January 3, 1969
Life is funny, life is strange, and for Poapst it was also rewarding at a surprising time. He graduated from Colgate in 1991 at age 22, but no NHL team wanted him so he ended up playing in the minors. Washington signed him in 1995 and he played three games for the Caps that season, and three years later played a few more games, but his career was going nowhere and he was, as they say, not getting any younger. Then Chicago signed him in 2000, and all of a sudden he was a regular with the Hawks, breaking into the NHL for the first time at age 31. He wasn't outstanding and he didn't scale tall buildings in a single bound, but he was a reliable defenceman and every team needs some of those. At least, Chicago does.

POCZA, Harvie
b. Lethbridge, Alberta, September 22, 1959
When he was nine years old, Pocza was one of the best kid bowlers in Canada, but, of course, he played the more manly game of hockey and that became his greater passion. He played provincial junior hockey and later a season in the WHL before playing a single game with Washington in 1979-80 and two more games two years later. He retired in 1983, but by 1991 the bowling itch needed to be scratched so he pulled the ball out of his cupboard and went to work. He appeared in a number of tournaments, finishing second in the Chinook Autumn Open, one of the bigger tour events in that sport.

Rob Plumb

Ron Plumb

Plett didn't start in organized hockey until he was 12.
WILLI PLETT

Steve Poapst

PODDUBNY, Walt ("Sarge")
b. Thunder Bay, Ontario, February 14, 1960

In the end, Poddubny recorded some decent seasons in the NHL, but at every step of the way it seemed he was underachieving rather than pushing himself and reaching his potential. Poddubny had a great shot, but he was an awkward skater and, at times, lazy. He started with Edmonton, but a trade sent him to Toronto where he had 28 goals and showed signs of greater possibilities. Knee injuries slowed him significantly over the next three years, but when the Leafs traded him to the Rangers he started to show what he might do. In the next 3 years, he had 40, 38, and 38 goals, numbers to support that great shot. Amazingly, he never scored more than four goals in another year after that. He did extensive damage to his right knee and simply couldn't play at top pace again. He stayed in the game as a coach, first with Daytona and later in other minor leagues. He led the Anchorage Aces for a number of years but retired to run a restaurant because he was, simply, burned out. But midway through 2001-02, he returned to the bench after coach Butch Goring was fired.

PODEIN, Shjon ("Podes")
b. Rochester, Minnesota, March 5, 1968

Big, fast, strong, and determined, Podein very quickly made his way out of the University of Minnesota-Duluth and into the NHL. He started with Edmonton, but the Oilers didn't see much potential there and let him become a free agent in 1994. Philadelphia signed him, and for five years the winger had a significant impact, culminating with a trip to the finals in 1997. He was later traded to Colorado, where he won the Cup in 2001, but the year after he was traded to St. Louis. Podein is one of the better penalty killers in the league and an active presence in charity efforts. He won the King Clancy Memorial Trophy in 2001. Internationally, Podein has also played in three World Championships for the U.S.

PODKONICKY, Andrej
b. Zvolen, Czechoslovakia (Slovakia), May 9, 1978

When St. Louis traded Podkonicky to Florida for Eric Boguniecki on December 17, 2000, it looked like a nothing deal. But Boguniecki started off like a house on fire with the Blues in '02-'03 while Podkonicky wasn't even in North America. He played just a few games with the Panthers after the trade, spent most of his time in the minors, and at season's end decided to play in Europe again. He had played in the WHL and the minors, but the centre didn't make the right impression with either of his NHL teams and moved on to Finland and then Slovakia in 2001.

PODLOSKI, Ray
b. Edmonton, Alberta, January 5, 1966

Podloski played as a rookie with Portland during the team's 1983 run to the Memorial Cup, and after graduating from the Winter Hawks three years later he turned pro. He played a few games with Boston a couple of years later, but since 1990 he has happily made a living playing in Europe.

PODOLLAN, Jason ("Pods")
b. Vernon, British Columbia, February 18, 1976

Life was never sweeter than 1996 when he and the rest of Team Canada won gold at the World Juniors, but Podollan, a fine prospect, has neither been consigned forever to the minors nor developed into an established NHL star. Since turning pro in 1996, he has played most of his time in the AHL, but played well enough to rate callups on a regular basis. He has made appearances with four NHL teams, but has yet to play well enough to stick around. He can't stay, but he won't go away.

PODOLSKY, Nelson "Nels" ("Nellie")
b. Winnipeg, Manitoba, December 19, 1925

There is no closer connection in all of hockey than that of Podolsky to Ted Lindsay. They both grew up in Kirkland Lake and were great friends. Both of Podolsky's parents died suddenly and Ted brought Nelson home like a stray dog and asked his parents if he could live with the family. The Lindsays said yes, and the two became as close as brothers. That was only the beginning. Podolsky was in the army in 1944-45, and when he got out he entered the Detroit system, playing in Indianapolis. His first year of pro ended badly when he slid hard into the goal and tore thigh muscles in both legs. To get in shape in the summer, he convinced Lindsay and Gus Mortson to go on an extended prospecting trip in the bush, and the three amigos walked 12 to 15 miles a day. Still, it was three months before Podolsky could walk without a limp. He had been the most popular player in Indianapolis because of his hustle and constant effort, and in his second year he was the team's most improved player. During his third season, he received a call to the Red Wings. It was only for a game – to replace the injured Lindsay! – but it made Podolsky's career. He played another decade in the minors and never got another chance, but his adopted brother made it all possible in more ways than one.

POESCHEK, Rudy
b. Kamloops, British Columbia, September 29, 1966

He was lucky enough to play for his local Winter Hawks during the 1980s when the team was a powerhouse, but

> There is no closer connection in all of hockey than that of Podolsky to Ted Lindsay.
> **NELS PODOLSKY**

Walt Poddubny

Shjon Podein

Andrej Podkonicky

Rudy Poeschek

Don Poile

his NHL career seems over after more than a decade of fighting for a living with a variety of teams. In 12 years, though, he was always the player who punched out the other team's tough guys and come playoff time would sit in the press box. He last played in the NHL with St. Louis in 1999-2000, and with a new generation of tough guys rolling into the game he isn't likely to get another crack at the big game.

POETA, Tony
b. North Bay, Ontario, March 4, 1933
Playing with the Galt Black Hawks meant a trip to Chicago or not at all in the NHL, and for Poeta his trip lasted one game while he was still a teen in junior in 1952. It was all minor and senior hockey after that for him, and once his days were done he returned to North Bay, the town he has called home most of his life.

POILE, Don
b. Fort William, Ontario, June 1, 1932
The younger brother of Hall of Famer Bud, Don had but a brief career in the NHL, though he left a greater mark in the Western league where he played for many years. He was that league's rookie of the year in 1953-54, with Edmonton, and on that merit he got a short callup to Detroit the following season for four games. It was three years before he got another train ticket to Detroit, but he stayed the full season that time. Beyond those games, Poile played almost his entire career in Edmonton before retiring in 1962.

POILE, Norman "Bud"
b. Fort William, Ontario, February 10, 1924
He was a mere child of 18 when he signed with Toronto in November 1942, and as a rookie Poile scored 16 goals. In the playoffs, he led the team in scoring, but curtailed his career early the next season to enlist in the army. Poile returned to Toronto near the end of the '45-'46 season and the year after helped the Leafs win the Cup. Poile played on the famous Flying Forts Line with Gaye Stewart and Gus Bodnar, so-named because they all hailed from Fort William. Poile was then one of the players traded to Chicago for Max Bentley, and Poile ended up playing for five of six teams in the league befor leaving the NHL (the exception being Montreal). After closing out his playing days with Edmonton in the WHL, he remained out west as a coach and began his second, more prosperous career as an executive. Poile served as GM for Philadelphia and Vancouver in the NHL, and was later named commissioner of the CHL and IHL. It was in large part due to his work that the "I" developed such a close association with the NHL, operating sevens teams as affiliates. He was inducted into the Hockey Hall of Fame in 1990 as a Builder after a lifetime devoted to the development and betterment of the game he started playing as a boy.

POIRIER, Gordie
b. Maple Creek, Saskatchewan, October 27, 1914
d. Montreal, Quebec, May 25, 1972
There are many in Britain who will say that Poirier was the best defenceman that nation has ever seen play on a regular basis. He made his first European trek in 1933-34 to coach and play for the Diavolo Rosso Neri team in Milan, taking them to victory in the Spengler Cup the next year. After a year of touring in North America, he returned to Milan for '35-'36 as player and coach and then joined Brighton where he had a long run as a player before the Second World War. His first season almost ended tragically when a serious chin injury became septic and doctors gave him just five years to live. He made a full recovery and returned to Canada to serve in the army, attaining, appropriately, the rank of captain. He also scored the winning goal as the Ottawa Commandos won the 1943 Allan Cup, and after playing in Ottawa for another season he accepted an offer to return to Brighton in 1946. He finished his career in Harringay in '50-'51 and then returned to Canada to open a restaurant and run an import business. He was also a scratch golfer and a champion canoeist in his youth.

Tom Polanic

John Polich

Poile played on the famous Flying Forts Line with Gaye Stewart and Gus Bodnar.
BUD POILE

POLANIC, Tom
b. Toronto, Ontario, April 2, 1943
An early proponent of U.S. college hockey, Polanic graduated from St. Mike's high school in Toronto and went south to play at the University of Michigan. He had been Leafs property but wound up with Minnesota, where he played his only NHL games. The bulk of his playing career came in the WHL and senior hockey in the Toronto area.

POLICH, John
b. Hibbing, Minnesota, July 8, 1916
d. Alhambra, California, May 27, 2001
Polich was 100 percent American, 100 percent original, and 100 percent an innovator – the hockey was a bonus. He grew up in the east, playing not only hockey but football and track and field. In 1935, he was given a scholarship to Loyola University in L.A. to play both hockey and football, and he became the star at the school, leading the team to the Pacific Coast championship all four years. He accepted the chance to play for the Rangers in 1939, and for two seasons he was the highest-profile American the league had seen in years. In 1942, though, he returned to the west coast to play for and coach the new Los Angeles

Monarchs, named after his high school team and featuring the Rangers colours. In 1946-47, the team won the PCHL title. After one more successful season, Polich changed the course of his life. He was friends with Klaus Landsberg of television station KTLA (originally called W6XYZ in true experimental fashion), and as a result Polich got to direct the first live coverage of the Tournament of Roses Parade, in 1947, to about 300 TV sets in the L.A. area. He remained with the station for 32 years, directing any and every sporting event possible, from boxing to baseball to UCLA and Lakers basketball games. He died of liver cancer at his home.

POLICH, Mike ("The Shadow")
b. Hibbing, Minnesota, December 19, 1952

By the time Polich joined Montreal for the 1977 playoffs, he was ready. The University of Minnesota graduate had played at two World Championships for the U.S. and the '76 Canada Cup, and he had had a fine year in the minors in Nova Scotia. The Habs won the Cup that spring, and although his career was but five games old, he already had his name on hockey's greatest trophy. He played virtually all of the next season with the Voyageurs, and then signed with his homestate North Stars where he played the last three years of his career. He earned his nickname because during his short career he was among the best checkers and defensive forwards, and it was he before anyone else on the team who was called upon to shut down the other teams' best players when the situation called for it.

> **He fought and brawled his way into the NHL, and when he got to Detroit he fought more to stay.**
> **DENNIS POLONICH**

POLIS, Greg ("Pole Cat"/ "Pole Eye")
b. Westlock, Alberta, August 8, 1950

Polis learned to play hockey in the farmland of Dapp, Alberta, and in his last two years of junior he finished second in scoring behind first Bobby Clarke and then Reggie Leach. He joined Pittsburgh in 1970, a perfect situation for him because it wasn't a good team and he would get plenty of ice time. He missed the last part of his rookie year with mono, yet before he took ill he had already scored 18 goals. He had 30 and 26 in succeeding years, and in each of his first 3 seasons he also played at the All-Star Game. In the third of these, he scored two goals and was named MVP. He played the second big chunk of his career with the Rangers, a less successful time because he was expected to play with Jean Ratelle and Rod Gilbert on the GAG line, but the three just didn't dovetail nicely. He ended his career first in Washington and then in the AHL with Hershey. The Bears won the Calder Cup his two years there, but his contribution was so slim it can't be said accurately that he was part of the team.

POLIZIANI, Dan
b. Sydney, Nova Scotia, January 8, 1935

A speedy skater, Poliziani was not big and had trouble with injuries over the years as the physical aspects of the game took their toll on his body. Nevertheless, he starred in the AHL from 1954 to '65, playing a single game with Boston in the middle of that stretch. He ended up coaching at Yale University for many years after retiring.

POLONICH, Dennis ("Polo")
b. Foam Lake, Saskatchewan, December 4, 1953

On October 25, 1978, Polonich was clubbed in the face by Wilf Paiement during a game. Paiement was suspended by the league for 15 games, and Polonich had a fractured nose and other facial bones. Two years later, his career also broken by the incident, Polonich sued Paiement and won his case. He was awarded $850,000 after claiming his career had been damaged by the attack. He was only 5'6" but at every level he was one of the most ferocious players around. He fought and brawled his way into the NHL, and when he got to Detroit he fought more to stay. He began in 1974-75, and midway through the season two years later was named team captain. Although he experienced no playoff success with the Wings, he won a Calder Cup with Adirondack and a Turner Cup with Muskegon at the close of his career. He went on to become a GM in junior with Medicine Hat and Prince George, and won a championship with Yorkton in Saskatchewan junior hockey. He later became a player agent for NHLers and aspiring pros.

PONIKAROVSKY, Alexei
b. Kiev, Soviet Union (Ukraine), April 9, 1980

For people in the west, perestroika was the best thing that ever happened to the Soviet Union, but in a strange way it was not such a godsend for young Ponikarovsky. He was a great skater almost from infancy, and at age six was scouted by the Soviets' hockey machine and treated like a little king who was on the road to development à la Kharlamov and Larionov. Then, the Ukraine declared independence, and Ponikarovsky was back in Kiev, part of a poor family that couldn't afford hockey equipment. He wore skates sent home by NHLer Alexei Zhitnik, but he also went to Moscow at 15 and played his way onto the Dynamo club for a number of years. He was too good to ignore. The Leafs drafted him and have used him only sparingly over the last two seasons, but Ponikarovsky is in the NHL and learning the game on the farm in St. John's. He has size and a willingness to use it – now it's just a matter of consistent play and taking advantage of his chances to dress for the Leafs.

Mike Polich

Greg Polis

Dan Poliziani

Larry Popein

Jack Portland

Jukka Porvari

Mike Posavad

POOLEY, Paul
b. Exeter, Ontario, August 2, 1960
Fifteen games was the full extent of Pooley's NHL career, with Winnipeg from 1984 to '86, but on the college scene few men have been as busy and successful over the last 20 years. As a student, he played at Ohio State with his twin brother, Perry, on some of that school's finest hockey teams. By the time he graduated in 1984, he was the Buckeyes' all-time leader in goals, assists, and points. After retiring, he returned to Ohio as an assistant coach and then went to Lake Superior State where, under head coach Jeff Jackson, the team won NCAA championships in 1992 and '94. That summer, Pooley became the head man at Providence College, and he has been there ever since, taking a weak school and turning it into a perennial winner and competitive college with a good reputation.

POPEIN, Larry ("Pope")
b. Yorkton, Saskatchewan, August 11, 1930
Most of his professional life, Popein was affiliated with either New York or Vancouver. He played junior out west with Moose Jaw and turned pro with the Canucks of the PCHL, but in 1954 he made the Rangers as a centreman and for seven years was a versatile player on a team that wasn't very good. He could score a bit and hit like thunder, but in 1960 he was sent down to the Canucks to play out his career. In 1964, he was named the team's playing assistant, and in 1967 he left the team to give the NHL one more crack with the expansion Oakland Seals. After retiring in 1969, Popein returned to the Rangers fold to coach the new minor-league affiliate in Seattle and moved to Omaha a year later. In 1973, he replaced coach Emile Francis as Rangers coach, but after half a season of what GM Francis saw as mediocre play he fired Popein and took over behind the bench. He later became a scout for Vancouver, now an NHL team, and worked his way up to director of player personnel.

POPIEL, Poul "Paul"
b. Sollested, Denmark, February 28, 1943
The family moved to Canada when Poul was still young, and he ended up a fine hockey player in junior in the early 1960s. Popiel made his NHL debut with Boston in 1965-66 but played mostly in the minors for three years until Detroit acquired him in November 1968. Not big, he was still a strong and solid defenceman who left the NHL to sign with Houston in the WHA in 1972. He stayed with the Aeros through the Howe family years, but when the team folded in 1978 he signed a contract to play in Innsbruck with the dual responsibility of coaching. He averaged 50 to 55 minutes of playing time a night, and the team won the league championship. Popiel returned to Houston in the summer content to resume his career in the Central league so as not to have to uproot his family, but when Edmonton lost Al Hamilton to injury, Glen Sather called Popiel. For 10 games, he filled in, playing with Wayne Gretzky and the gang in Alberta before returning to Houston to play out the last of his career.

POPOVIC, Peter
b. Koping, Sweden, February 10, 1968
He was 20 when he was drafted, 25 when he made his NHL debut, and 33 when he bowed out of the league to return home. Popovic was a giant defenceman (6'6" and 235 pounds) who played 5 years in Montreal before a contract dispute put the Habs in the frame of mind to trade him. They did, to the Rangers, and in successive seasons he moved on to Pittsburgh and Boston. In 2001, he decided to return to Sweden to continue his career, with Sodertalje.

PORTLAND, John "Jack"
b. Waubaushene, Ontario, July 30, 1912
d. Brockville, Ontario, August 22, 1996
Before turning his large body to hockey, Portland was as talented an athlete as existed in Canada. He competed in the high jump at the 1932 Olympics in Los Angeles, clearing 6'4-1/2" and finishing just out of the medals behind winner Duncan McNaughton, also of Canada, who cleared the bar in 6'5-1/2". He was also accomplished at the javelin and broad jump and was a noted boxer who might have done damage in that sport. Instead, he joined the Montreal Canadiens, largely because Bert Corbeau spotted him and recommended Portland to the Habs. It was with Boston, though, that he had his greatest success. Teamed with Eddie Shore on the blueline, the pair formed a fearsome line of defence and helped the Bruins win the Cup in 1939. At 6'2" he was the tallest player in the league, and his long stride and broad shoulders cut an imposing swath across the ice lanes during his prime. He ended his career in Montreal, joining the army in 1943 as part of the Canadian Provost Corps and rising to the rank of lance corporal. He never made it back to the NHL after being discharged, and retired to Maitland, Ontario. He opened the Little Denmark Motel on the Toronto-Montreal highway and for years welcomed hockey people of all stripes who knew of Portland's roadside rendezvous. He also coached the nearby Brockville Braves, an eastern Ontario junior team.

PORVARI, Jukka
b. Tampere, Finland, January 19, 1954
Colorado took a chance on Porvari, and Porvari took a chance on the Rockies, and by mutual agreement it was not a great fit. Porvari was having a perfectly fine career with Tappara in his hometown when he decided to give the NHL a try in 1981. But over 2 seasons he played just 39 games with the franchise and returned to Europe to close out his career.

POSA, Victor
b. Bari, Italy, November 5, 1966
Posa was all over the map as far as a career in hockey went. He never stayed any one place for too long, though his longest stretch came in the IHL in the 1980s. He played in two games for Chicago in '85-'86 and retired in the mid-1990s never having created any further NHL interest for his slapshots and passes.

POSAVAD, Mike
b. Brantford, Ontario, January 3, 1964
Eight games with St. Louis in the mid-1980s was the sum total of Posavad's NHL experience, though he played four years in the Blues system with Peoria in the IHL. After retiring in 1988, he returned to

Peterborough, where he played junior hockey and became a real estate agent. He also coached minor hockey for various teams, notably in Cobourg and Bowmanville, while working in real estate in Peterborough.

POSMYK, Marek
b. Jihlava, Czechoslovakia (Czech Republic), September 15, 1978

When the Leafs drafted Posmyk in 1996, he had had a good tournament at the World Juniors and was a huge defenceman (6'5") with great potential. Then he broke his wrist and didn't develop during his time in the minors, and Toronto traded him to Tampa Bay as a throw-in in a larger deal. Even the Lightning used him only briefly, and in 2001 Posmyk returned to his native Czech Republic to continue his career, still plenty young enough to return at any time, still unproven enough to warrant a full-time NHL roster spot.

POTHIER, Brian
b. New Bedford, Massachusetts, April 15, 1977

Not everyone is named MVP at the Chowder Cup, but such was Pothier's performance at that 1995 tournament in his home state that he won the award. He went on to play college at RPI, where he captained the team as a senior, and slowly but surely he has made inroads with the Atlanta Thrashers. Still young, he has a ways to go to prove he is NHL class, or not.

POTI, Tom
b. Worcester, Massachusetts, March 22, 1977

At 6'3" Poti is no longer considered a huge defenceman, but he is developing into a first-rate blueliner with Edmonton. He helped the U.S. win a rare medal, at the 1996 WJC, and joined the Oilers in 1998 where he has been ever since. He's fast, moves the puck well, and has great stamina, all attributes that got him on Team USA for the 2002 Olympics in Salt Lake City. In 2002-03, he led the Rangers in scoring for much of the season.

POTOMSKI, Barry
b. Windsor, Ontario, November 24, 1972

After playing junior in the OHL with London, Potomski turned pro in the East Coast league when no NHL team drafted him or expressed an interest in signing him. In his first year, 1992-93, he ended the season with Toledo and won the league championship. In 1995, he got an offer from L.A. and played two half-seasons with the Kings before going to San Jose for what turned out to be his final nine games. He returned to the minors and played in a variety of towns, finishing in 2001 with Idaho. He had played briefly with the Las Vegas Thunder, and it was in that town he settled after retiring to begin a quixotic career as a landscaper.

POTVIN, Denis
b. Ottawa, Ontario, October 29, 1953

As a teen, Potvin was as good at football as hockey, but when push came to shove he put down the pigskin, took up the stick, and focused on the ice game. He played junior with the local 67's, during which time he developed into a surefire NHLer. Teamed with Ian Turnbull on the blueline, the pair became one of the most offensively-gifted duos junior hockey has ever seen. In his final year, '72-'73, Potvin set a record with 123 points, and that summer the Islanders drafted him 1st overall. Potvin stepped into the lineup that fall and delivered a Calder Trophy season. He had 17 goals and 54 points and played like a defenceman who was going to be around a while. The year after he had 21 goals and 76 points, and in his third season he had 31 goals and 98 points

and won the Norris Trophy, the first player not named Orr to win it since Harry Howell a generation earlier in 1967. And therein lay Potvin's Achilles heel. He played with Orr at the 1976 Canada Cup, and Orr, on one leg, was sensational. Orr was named tournament MVP, but afterwards Potvin wrote in a magazine article that he himself should have been named MVP. It was a pompous and unfounded statement that made him no new friends or admirers. Nonetheless, the coming years saw Potvin mature into a defenceman influenced by Orr. He rushed the puck well, quarterbacked the power play, and joined in the offence. From 1973 to '78, he also had the pleasure of playing with his brother, Jean, another defenceman though a lesser light who was on the

From 1973 to '78, he also had the pleasure of playing with his brother, Jean.
DENIS POTVIN

move for two years but returned to the Islanders in 1979 for another year and a half. In '78-'79, Potvin had his only 100-point season and won his third and last Norris Trophy, but the Isles were upset by Toronto in the quarter-finals. That summer, he was named team captain, a position he held until 1987. He missed half of that '79-'80 season with a broken thumb but came back for the playoffs as the expansion team won the Cup for the first of four consecutive times. Ironically, he had some of his poorest points years during the Cup-winning dynasty, though the team had so much talent that goal scoring was never a problem. The thumb was his only significant injury, and on this front he and Orr were also very different. Potvin didn't rush the puck with the same hell-bent determination as Orr. That meant he was not nearly as exciting, but it also was a style of play that helped extend his career. He played in the 1981 Canada Cup, the only time Canada lost, but by the time he retired in 1988 he had made an impact statistically that no defenceman had. He was the all-time leader in goals (310), assists (742), and points (1,052), the first blueliner to pass the 1,000 mark. Potvin played in nine

Barry Potomski

Jean Potvin

All-Star Games and had his number 5 retired by the Islanders in a special ceremony on March 31, 1988. In 1991, he took his rightful place in the Hockey Hall of Fame when, for the first time, the ceremonies were held in Ottawa. His number was also retired by the 67's, and he was named to the all-time OHL team in a special poll at the end of the 20th century. He settled in New York and worked in television while forging a career with F.C. Financial Services in Manhattan. Potvin was no Orr, but in that second tier of great defencemen he was among the finest and most talented to play in the NHL.

POTVIN, Felix ("The Cat")
b. Anjou, Quebec, June 23, 1971

It's not as if he put Grant Fuhr out of work, but certainly Fuhr's injury midway through the '91-'92 season gave the Leafs a chance to call Potvin up from the Rock and see what he could do. Wow! He didn't win a game in his four starts, but he made it quite clear he was ready for the NHL. He returned to St. John's and won AHL rookie-of-the-year honours. A year later, the Leafs traded Fuhr knowing Potvin was a capable starter, and for the next six years he was one of the league's top goalies. In that first full season, he led the NHL with a 2.50 GAA and won 25 or more games in 5 of his years with the Leafs. He backstopped the team to consecutive semifinals appearances. The dream job turned bad when the Leafs signed Curtis Joseph in the summer of 1998, clearly paving the way for a Potvin trade. The Leafs sent him to the Islanders and then he moved on to Vancouver, and his post-Leafs time was awkward at best. His career seemed stalled until Los Angeles acquired him for nothing more than future considerations during the 2000-01 season, and with something to prove the Cat went out and proved it. He played superbly in that half season with the Kings, and in 2001-02 Potvin started in 71 games and re-established himself as a bona fide number-one man. The fresh-faced, lightning-quick goalie who entered the league with a bang is now a 12-year veteran of the NHL.

POTVIN, Jean
b. Ottawa, Ontario, March 25, 1949

The older brother of Denis, Jean began his career with Los Angeles in 1970, but it was a trade in March 1973 that had everyone talking. That month, the Islanders acquired him, and rumour had it the move was made to entice Denis to Long Island at the summer's draft. If that was the plan, it worked, and the two were paired on the blueline for a number of years. Unheralded Jean even recorded 72 points in '75-'76,

His career seemed stalled until Los Angeles acquired him.
FELIX POTVIN

Daniel Poudrier

Dave Poulin

impressive by any standards, but more so given the anonymity of skating in his brother's shadow. He was upset when the team traded him to Cleveland, but the Isles acquired Wayne Merrick because it needed a centreman. In 1979, he rejoined the Islanders but he was near the end of his career. Fortunately, he was able to combine careers by working as a colour commentator on game nights he didn't play. Frequently, he would take the warmup, find out he was scratched, and head to the broadcast booth to join Jiggs McDonald. After he retired, he remained in New York and became a financial adviser.

POTVIN, Marc
b. Ottawa, Ontario, January 29, 1967

Like many an enforcer or fourth-liner, Potvin didn't play much, observed well, and retired to go into coaching. He played sporadically in the 1990s with four teams, punching his way into the lineup but never playing well enough to stay out of the minors for too long. In his last year, '97-'98 with Chicago in the IHL, he also acted as assistant coach on that championship team, and went on to coach with Mississippi in the East Coast league and then Springfield of the AHL.

POUDRIER, Daniel
b. Thetford Mines, Quebec, February 15, 1964

Poudrier never let the lack of success in the NHL in his youth deter him from playing hockey elsewhere and for a long time. He played 25 games with the Nordiques over 3 seasons (1985-88) but soon went to Europe to have a long career centred in Germany. In 2000, he returned home and continued to play senior hockey for Thetford Mines.

POULIN, Dan
b. Robertsville, Quebec, September 19, 1957

Although Montreal drafted him in 1977, there was no way a kid named Poulin was about to usurp the blueline corps of Robinson, Savard, and Lapointe. As a result, he played in the minors for four years, earning a number of honours along the way for his great offensive prowess. He played just three NHL games, with Minnesota, and then went to Switzerland to play out the rest of his career.

POULIN, Dave
b. Timmins, Ontario, December 17, 1958

The scouts let this one get away – big time. Poulin played four years at the University of Notre Dame (1978-82) where he graduated with a degree in business marketing and played hockey the way no one on the Fighting Irish had ever played before. He was powerful and intense, played to win, and then went out and won. Yet not only did no NHL team draft him, no team wanted him when he graduated. So, he went to Sweden to play for a season, and his coach turned out to be Ted Sator, who did some European scouting for the Flyers. Needless to say, he phoned the NHL team and told them to sign him, and before the year was out Poulin was playing at the Spectrum. In his rookie year he scored 31 goals, and when captain Bobby Clarke retired that summer of 1984, Poulin was named team captain because everyone in the organization, from players to upper management, felt the two were cut from the same cloth. Poulin proved to be the bulb that lit the building, and for five and a half seasons he wore the "C" with pride. Then, one day, GM Clarke stripped him of the captaincy on the ridiculous pretext that the team needed a younger leader. Poulin was traded to Boston, yet remained classy amid the turmoil. He later ended his career in Washington, and retired in 1995 to return to his alma mater to coach, where he has been ever since. As in his playing days, he took the UND team to greater heights, and the Fighting Irish went to the CCHA championships in both 1999-2000 and 2001-02.

POULIN, Patrick
b. Vanier, Quebec, April 23, 1973
After an outstanding final year with Ste. Hyacinthe, Poulin was named Canada's best junior for 1991-92 and went on to play for Hartford. He scored 20 goals as a rookie, but since then has come nowhere near replicating that offensive achievement. Instead, he has become a defensive specialist, now with Montreal, a third-line forward who can give the coach some minutes without being a liability. He got to the Habs via Chicago and Tampa Bay and has proved to be a useful penalty killer as well.

POUZAR, Jaroslav
b. Cakovec, Czechoslovakia (Croatia), January 23, 1952
In the 1980s, there were two kinds of Czechs: those who defected, and those who waited for government permission to play in the NHL. Pouzar was of the latter mindset, and so didn't join Edmonton until 1982 when he was 30. He had already won gold, silver, and bronze at the World Championships, and played in two Olympics and two Canada Cups. He adjusted to the NHL slowly, but proved to be one of the strongest men in the game. Although he played only four years in the league, they all came with Edmonton and three were Cup-winning seasons. Thus, he became one of a small group of players to win both the Cup and WC gold. He finished his career in Germany, retiring at age 39.

POWELL, Ray
b. Timmins, Ontario, November 16, 1925
d. Kelowna, British Columbia, October 1999
A superb player and dominating scorer in the minors, Powell played in the prime of the Original Six when he simply wasn't going to be given much of an NHL chance. He was the MVP in the USHL in 1950, and the MVP in the AHL two years later, and both years he led those respective leagues in scoring. His only NHL time came with Chicago in 1950-51 when he played half a season for an injured Doug Bentley, and

Powell managed 22 points in 31 games. After retiring, he went into coaching briefly, but his tenure was disastrous. In 1960, he took on the head post with Kelowna in the Okanagan Valley league, but injuries forced him into the lineup for a few games and then a lack of fan support, among other unpleasant conditions, grew intolerable and he quit after just two months on the job.

POWIS, Geoff
b. Winnipeg, Manitoba, June 14, 1945
Powis played just two NHL games, with Chicago, in 1967-68 at the start of his career. He played another nine years in the minors but never got another chance to make it back to the big show. A centre, he played junior hockey in Moose Jaw.

POWIS, Lynn
b. Maryfield, Saskatchewan, July 7, 1949
The brother of Geoff, Lynn Powis played at the University of Denver at the same time as Keith Magnuson and wound up playing with him in Chicago in 1973, a few years after turning pro. He started in the Montreal system but neither liked it there nor believed he had a chance of ever making the team. Although Powis played just two seasons in the NHL (the other with Kansas City), success followed him wherever else he went. He won the Calder Cup with Nova Scotia in '71-'72, the Adams Cup with Omaha the year after, and the Avco Cup in the WHA with Winnipeg in '77-'78. He later played in Germany, but after retiring returned to Denver where he became a real estate agent and coached kids hockey teams.

PRAJSLER, Petr
b. Hradec Kralove, Czechoslovakia (Czech Republic), September 21, 1965
After watching teams from Canada and the U.S. play at the 1987 World Championships, Prajsler decided the adjustment to the NHL wouldn't be so hard. He took his wife to Yugoslavia, and with clandestine assistance made it to Austria where he asked for, and received, refugee status from the U.S. He then flew to L.A. to be with the team that had drafted him two years earlier. A big, defensive defenceman, Prajsler never did make that purportedly easy adjustment, and in 5 years in North America he played only 46 NHL games with the Kings and Boston. He returned to the new and free Czech Republic to continue playing, eventually winding up in the fourth division with HC Chotebor as a playing coach.

PRATT, Jack
b. Edinburgh, Scotland, April 13, 1906
d. unknown
As a hockey player, Jack Pratt could eat no fat if he intended to stay in fighting trim, but he played just 37 games with Boston from 1930 to '32.

PRATT, Kelly
b. High Prairie, Alberta, February 8, 1953
After two seasons with Swift Current Pratt signed with the WHA in 1973, but before the year was out Winnipeg had sent him to the minors. The next fall, he attended Pittsburgh's training camp and was the

Patrick Poulin

Ray Powell

Geoff Powis

Lynn Powis

Petr Prajsler

Kelly Pratt

Nolan Pratt

Tracy Pratt

only rookie to make the team. But as with the previous season, he was demoted partway through and never made it back. He played a few more years in the minors before retiring.

PRATT, Nolan

b. Fort McMurray, Alberta, August 14, 1975

A big and strong defenceman, Pratt came out of Portland in the WHL to play with Hartford in 1996, the franchise's last year in that city before relocating to Carolina. Although not much of a scorer, his first goal in the league proved to be a game winner against Anaheim. He remained with the team for four years and had the good fortune to move to Colorado that summer, and the Avs went on to win the Cup. Pratt played much of the year with the team though didn't appear in the playoffs. He was traded again in the summer to Tampa Bay. His brother, Harlan, was drafted by Pittsburgh in 1997 but has yet to play in the NHL.

PRATT, Tracy

b. New York, New York, March 8, 1943

Pratt was a perfect example of the expansion player, being chosen by Oakland after four years in the minors. In his 10 years in the league, he moved around a fair bit, teams always in need of a defenceman who could move bodies from in front of their own goal. The son of legendary Babe Pratt, Tracy was, in this regard, just the opposite of his dad, who was a fine rusher and puckhandler. After retiring, he returned to Vancouver, where he had grown up (he was born in New York only because Babe was with the Rangers at the time), and coached and managed junior. He later opened his own bar, T.R.'s Cabaret.

PRATT, Walter "Babe" ("Baz")

b. Stony Mountain, Manitoba, January 7, 1916
d. Vancouver, British Columbia, December 16, 1988

He was one of a kind, a man whose charisma outlasted his reputation to allow him to enter the Hockey Hall of Fame in 1966, a year before his son, Tracy, embarked on an NHL career of his own. He got his nickname as a kid, a fine ballplayer who was, they said, a regular Babe Ruth. The purloined moniker stuck, though some called him Baz as a shortened form of his middle name. Either way, he was a great hockey player, a champion at every level he played from the time he was 10 to the time he left the NHL. He won in Winnipeg and Elmwood and then Kenora as a 17-year-old junior, when he led the league in scoring despite being a defenceman. He impressed Rangers' scout Al Ritchie so much that Ritchie called him the best prospect he had ever seen play. Pratt was signed and sent to the

Rangers farm team in Philadelphia in 1935, but halfway through the year he was called up to Broadway and never left the NHL for a dozen years. In 1939, he was teamed on the blueline with Ott Heller, and they proved to be a magnificent match. The Rangers won the Cup in large part because when they were on the ice, the opposition almost never scored. But Pratt was traded to Toronto early in the '42-'43 season for reasons that had nothing to do with puck chasing. At 6'3" he was the tallest man in the NHL. He was also good-looking, young, energetic, and most definitely a man about town. As they said, he knew the emergency exit to every hotel in New York. He had Hollywood looks and the braggadocio of Jack Johnson. He liked women and drink in that order, and sometimes not. By November 1942, Rangers management had, quite simply, become tired of looking for him. The Leafs felt if they could discipline the great star they would have the best defenceman in the game playing for them. For a good while, they were right. In '43-'44, Pratt had a phenomenal 57 points and was named the Hart Trophy winner. The year after, he took the team to the playoffs and scored the Cup-winning goal. That playoffs was unique in that the Leafs, not wanting to take any chances with their hulking hero, had Pratt room with coach Hap Day on the road! That was the only way to ensure he kept curfew, and for a few weeks the strategy worked and paid off. The next year, though, Pratt was suspended by NHL president Red Dutton for life after he admitted to betting on hockey games. He qualified his admission by saying that he never bet on his own games, and besides, he was so bad at it that he lost money. The league's governors, not Dutton, rescinded the lifetime ban and turned it into only a few games, but the Leafs missed the playoffs and Pratt was traded to Boston. After half a year, he was sent to the minors, and the once-sensational NHLer was now a humble player in the AHL and then the PCHL. Pratt retired in 1952 and got out of hockey altogether for a long time. He moved to the interior of B.C. and worked in the lumber industry, becoming a foreman in a sawmill and a log-buyer for some 17 years. After retiring, he settled in Vancouver and became a public relations man for the Canucks, doing TV commentary and going to dinners and banquets telling hilarious stories of the good old days. He died while attending a Canucks game and was remembered as a free spirit with a great sense of humour, the betting scandal a thing of the past and barely worth mentioning in the minds of his fans and admirers.

In '43-'44, Pratt had a phenomenal 57 points and was named the Hart Trophy winner.
BABE PRATT

PRENTICE, Dean
b. Schumacher, Ontario, October 5, 1932

Being born in a mining town provides plenty of motivation for any kid to stay out of the mines and get out of the city as fast as possible. Not everyone can just put on the skates and do that with quite the same success that Prentice did, but then again he might well have been the most underrated star of his era. After all, he played 22 years in the NHL, though his great regret was never winning a Cup, or even coming close, over the course of 1,378 regular-season games. Prentice played 11 years with the Rangers starting in 1952 and eventually got on a line with Andy Bathgate and Larry Popein. It was among the top-scoring lines in the league, but playoff success never followed. He later played for 4 other teams and had ten, 20-goal seasons in all. In 1961-62, he hurt his back and was forced to wear a corset for the rest of the season to ease the pain. His teammates in New York called him Mrs. Prentice, but the pain of a slipped disc is no laughing matter. Two years later, he missed half a season with recurring pain, but eventually learned to live with the problem and soldiered on. A Christian, he promoted Bible studies during his last years, with Minnesota, and after he retired he became involved in Hockey Ministries International, a group that promotes both the Bible and the puck. He worked there with Laurie Boschman and was the Toronto rep for some 15 years. Prentice also coached in the AHL and managed an arena in Michigan and later a community centre in Ayr, Ontario. (He was director of parks and recreation in Ayr.) His brother, Eric, also played in the NHL.

After he retired he became involved in Hockey Ministries International.
DEAN PRENTICE

PRENTICE, Eric ("Doc")
b. Schumacher, Ontario, August 22, 1926
d. Coleman, Alberta, December 8, 2002

When Prentice skated onto the ice on October 30, 1943, he was just 17 years old, the youngest player (still) ever to appear for the Leafs. His mini-career lasted just five games, but how he got to the Leafs was a story in itself. Prentice had been espied by Detroit GM Jack Adams, but as soon as Toronto coach Happy Day caught wind of the Red Wings' interest, he signed Prentice to a contract. Furious, Adams stole a player, Tommy Love, out from under Day's eyes and then telegrammed Day to suggest a trade of the two prospects. Day responded, "Sorry, not interested in that kind of Love." Prentice ended his playing days in California and then returned to Schumacher with his wife and five children. In 1970, they moved to Alberta where Prentice became actively involved in curling and hockey in Grande Cache and Coleman. He spent the last 20 years of his life fighting emphysema and Lou Gehrig's Disease.

PRESLEY, Wayne ("Elvis")
b. Dearborn, Michigan, March 23, 1965

Almost any Michigan kid who had pro potential played for Little Caesar's, Mike Ilitch's team for pre-junior age players. From Al Iafrate to Derian Hatcher to Pat LaFontaine, Presley became an alumnus of a prestigious club, after which he moved to Ontario to play for Kitchener in the OHL. He was drafted by Chicago in 1983 and for seven years went this way and that with the team. He was a rookie, then a scorer, then a defensive liability, and, finally, he became a solid, two-way player. He spent his last few years with four other teams refining his play as a penalty killer, defensive specialist, and checker. After retiring in 1997 he settled in Troy, Michigan, and worked for Synova Corporation, a technology company.

PRESTON, Rich
b. Regina, Saskatchewan, May 22, 1952

Preston came from a sports background insofar as his father was the longtime GM of the Saskatchewan Roughriders of the CFL. Rich went on to play at the University of Denver where his teammates included Cliff Korroll and Keith Magnuson, but when he graduated he was told by Chicago that he'd begin in the minors. Preston accepted a more attractive offer to play for Houston in the WHA, and for five years he developed into a fine two-way forward in that league. He finally joined Chicago in 1979, scored 31 goals as an NHL rookie, and went on to play 8 seasons as a checker and capable scorer. He retired in 1987 and got back into hockey soon after, starting as an assistant with the Hawks before becoming head coach for Regina in the WHL. He later returned to the NHL as an assistant in Calgary, and in 2000 joined San Jose in a like capacity.

PRESTON, Yves
b. Montreal, Quebec, June 14, 1956

Preston played his 28 games with Philadelphia, scoring his first goal on a pass from goalie Bernie Parent in a December 1978 game. He returned to the AHL after nine games and helped Maine win the Calder Cup, scoring the overtime winner in game one of the finals and a hat trick in game two. His only other Flyers stint came two years later, and he played the rest of his eight-year career in the lower leagues.

PRIAKIN, Sergei
b. Moscow, Soviet Union (Russia), December 7, 1963

It wasn't how well he did in the NHL that mattered, it's that he made it at all that counted. Priakin was the first Soviet player to come to North America with approval from the Soviet Ice Hockey Federation, so

Wayne Presley

Eric Prentice

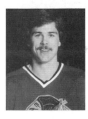

Rich Preston

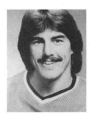

Yves Preston

Sergei Priakin

Jack Price

Noel Price

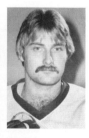

Pat Price

Tom Price

Ken Priestlay

when he played for Calgary on March 31, 1989, he paved the way for future players to make the sanctioned trip. He played just three games that year with the Flames on a team that won the Cup, and he played only parts of the next two seasons. Priakin finished his career playing in Europe after having scored just three goals in the NHL, but he made his reputation much earlier with the Soviet national teams in international competition. He was never good enough to play in the Olympics, but he did play in the 1987 Canada Cup and two World Championships.

PRICE, Jack
b. Goderich, Ontario, May 8, 1932
Toward the end of the 1951-52 season, another in a dismal series for Chicago, the team called up some of its youngsters to let them see what the NHL was like. That's how Price got into his first game, on February 17, 1952. He played 10 games the next year and 46 the year after, but that was it for his NHL experience and he played the next decade in the minors. He did, however, win three Calder Cups in the AHL, one with Pittsburgh and two with Hershey, before retiring in 1963.

PRICE, Noel ("Tubby"/ "Shiny"/ "Baldy"/ "Grumpy")
b. Brockville, Ontario, December 9, 1935
Rare, indeed, is the player who has a significant impact in two leagues. Almost always, it's the NHL hanger-on who has a great career in the minors or the NHL great who never sees the lower leagues. Price was truly a star in both the NHL and the AHL. In the NHL, he played 14 years with 7 teams, beginning with Toronto in 1957. He won the Cup with Montreal in 1966, albeit as a part-time player, and he played in the 1967 All-Star Game. Price was an offensive-minded player, a good skater and puckhandler. He graduated from St. Mike's, and in addition to his 499 NHL games he played in the AHL for parts of 13 years, mostly with Springfield. He was the only player to win the Eddie Shore plaque three times (1970, '72, and '76), emblematic as the league's best defenceman, and in 1996 he was the first inductee into the new Springfield Hall of Fame (he is also enshrined in the Brockville Sports Hall of Fame). After retiring in 1976, Price coached the Sudbury Wolves for two years and then moved to Ottawa where he sold insurance, mutual funds, and real estate. He worked for Vancouver for eight years (1991-99), scouting junior teams in Canada and college teams in the U.S. before retiring and staying in Ottawa.

PRICE, Pat
b. Nelson, British Columbia, March 24, 1955
Price was a first-round draft choice in the WHA in 1974 and a first-rounder for the Islanders the next year, and he began his career in that order in consecutive seasons. He started with the WHA because Vancouver offered the rookie a $1.3 million contract, and only a fool would turn that down. He was a bust in the team's eyes, though, and joined the Islanders the year after, and for four years he developed into a fine defenceman. Then, in the 1979 playoffs, coach Al Arbour scratched Price who, incensed, demanded a trade. Arbour happily obliged, and Edmonton was the

beneficiary. Price later moved on to Pittsburgh and Quebec, and soon after his arrival with the Nordiques hockey took a back seat to life. He was stricken with a rare form of viral encephalitis that left him paralyzed for a brief time. He was in the hospital for a month and out of hockey for three, but he was happy just to have survived this often-fatal disease. He eventually returned to lead a normal NHL life, though his best years were behind him. He retired in 1988 and later worked at Jim Harrison's Hockey in the Rockies camps and clinics in B.C.

PRICE, Tom
b. Toronto, Ontario, July 12, 1954
For 10 years, Price played pro hockey, getting into 29 NHL games along the way. He signed with California in 1974 and moved on to Cleveland and Pittsburgh, but the defenceman didn't score a single goal in his NHL career. He moved around in the minors as well, but his last shot at the big time came in 1979 with the Pens and it didn't work out.

PRIESTLAY, Ken
b. Richmond, British Columbia, August 24, 1967
He began his pro career in the Buffalo system but a contract dispute led to a Stanley Cup for Priestlay. In 1986, he was with the Sabres, but over a four-year period he played more in the minors with Rochester than in the bowels of Buffalo itself. The contract troubles led to a year with the Canadian National Team in '90-'91, and a forced trade, to Pittsburgh, was the result. He played much of the '91-'92 season with the Pens, though he was in the IHL for that league's play-offs when Mario Lemieux hoisted the Cup in Penguinland. After that, he never made it back to the NHL, and two seasons later he went to Britain to play. His stay lasted six years, the last three of which he acted as a playing coach. Priestlay returned to B.C. and coached the peewee rep team in South Delta, and in the summer of 2001 he was hired as an assistant for the WHL's new franchise, the Vancouver Giants.

PRIMEAU, Joe ("Gentleman Joe")
b. Lindsay, Ontario, January 29, 1906
d. Toronto, Ontario, May 14, 1989
When Conn Smythe saw Joe Primeau play as a teen, he knew the kid would turn into something special, and sooner rather than later. Primeau played junior for Toronto St. Mary's in the mid-1920s, the team that became the more famous Marlies. When Smythe was made GM in 1926 with the Rangers, he wanted to take Primeau with him, but Smythe was fired and came back to Toronto. Wisely, he had signed Primeau to a personal contract, so when Smythe took over the St. Pats he was able to keep his young star in the fold. For the next two seasons (1927-29) Primeau played mostly in the minors and in 1929 he made the Leafs. Around Christmas, Smythe put Primeau, a centre, out with Charlie Conacher and Harvey Jackson. The Kid Line was born. While Conacher and Jackson did most of the scoring and got the lion's share of the glory, it was Primeau who was, so to speak, the brains of the operation. He made the passes. He orchestrated the rushes. He knew where his wingmen would be. Not surprisingly, Primeau led the NHL in assists three times over the next five seasons.

The line took the Leafs to the Cup in 1932, but Primeau retired in 1936, just 30 years old. It was a different era then. During his brief career, he had worked in the summers for a concrete firm and invested in a concrete-block company. Business opportunities were peaking for him in 1936, and hockey salaries did not offer a lifetime of financial salvation the way they do now. He quit to establish Joe Primeau Block and later amalgamated with another company to form Primeau-Argo Block. Once he had these interests under control, Primeau returned to the game as a coach. He was every bit as successful as he had been as a player. He started with St. Mike's, winning the Memorial Cup with them in 1945 and '47, and losing to the Winnipeg Monarchs in game seven in '46. In '49-'50, he took the Marlboro seniors to the Allan Cup and then took over as coach for the Leafs. He won a Cup his first year, '50-'51, to complete the great championship hat trick, but after two more years the business started to take off again. By 1953, he was overseeing production at five plants in southern Ontario, and it became his full-time occupation until he retired to private life. He also taught a course at the University of Toronto preparing men to coach physical fitness, and later NHL president Clarence Campbell asked him to tour the west and conduct clinics for amateur coaches. He was inducted into the Hockey Hall of Fame in 1963 and was the last surviving member of the Kid Line before his death.

PRIMEAU, Keith

b. Toronto, Ontario, November 24, 1971

When Detroit drafted Primeau 3rd overall in 1990 the team expected mondo years of primo service from the behemoth centre with the soft hands, hard shoulders, and strong heart. He led the OHL in scoring the previous year and made the team at his first training camp, yet all the Wings got was frustrated. Six years of patience and waiting and hoping, and Primeau delivered mediocrity and unsuperstar results hardly befitting a 3rd overall selection. When the Wings had a chance to acquire Brendan Shanahan for Primeau in 1996, they took it. Shanahan has proved to be one of the pieces that brought Detroit three Cups in the ensuing years, while Primeau has continued to be a mixed bag of great player somehow not quite great enough. He's had his share of goals, but never more than 31 in any year, and he's never been really close to a Cup chance. He was ineffective at the 1996 World Cup for Canada, and although he played well at the 1998 Olympics in Nagano he, again, did not dominate. Despite his underachieving, he refused to report to Carolina (Hartford had relocated) in 1999 and demanded a large contract. Hurricanes GM, Jim Rutherford, refused and ended up trading Primeau to Philadelphia, but the move has been anything but spectacular for the Flyers. A hugely talented player, Primeau has never proved to be a game breaker, the kind of star who can win a game on his own or produce a five-point night at any given time.

PRIMEAU, Kevin

b. Edmonton, Alberta, January 3, 1956

During his four years at the University of Alberta in the 1970s, Primeau's team won two CIAU championships and his play caught the eye of the local Oilers, for whom he played a few WHA games in '77-'78. But at season's end, Primeau couldn't refuse an offer to play and coach in Switzerland, the first of many such opportunities he accepted. He played some games with Canada's touring National Team and eventually returned to North America to play for his country at the 1980 Olympics in Lake Placid. He scored in each of Canada's first four games before being shut out the rest of the way and later in the year played his only NHL games, with Vancouver. He was sent to the minors where he suffered a career-ending neck injury, but he returned to Europe to coach again. Primeau has more recently returned to Canada to launch an x-treme sports park in western Canada.

PRIMEAU, Wayne

b. Scarborough, Ontario, June 4, 1976

Brother Keith scored more goals in any of his six best seasons than Wayne has in his entire career, which is not a bad thing as long as teams don't expect him to score like Keith. He's just as large as his older brother but is more of a fourth-line centre, a penalty killer who can hit and check and play solid defence. He started with Buffalo at the end of the '94-'95 season and has since moved on to Tampa Bay and Pittsburgh, where, if nothing else, he can watch Mario Lemieux play most nights.

PRINGLE, Ellis "Ellie" ("Moose")

b. Toronto, Ontario, August 31, 1911
d. Sutton, Ontario

Pringle made a good enough impression on New York Americans coach Eddie Gerard at training camp in 1930 that he stayed with the team for the first part of the season as an alternate on defence. But after six games, Gerard had a reversal and sent Pringle to the farm in New Haven. That was to be his only NHL chance, and although he played another dozen years of pro, he never saw the NHL again as a player.

PROBERT, Bob

b. Windsor, Ontario, June 5, 1965

Unless some wonderful miracle occurs, Probert will be able to brag about one thing for the rest of his life: He

When Conn Smythe saw Joe Primeau play as a teen, he knew the kid would turn into something special.
JOE PRIMEAU

Keith Primeau

Wayne Primeau

Martin Prochazka

Goldie Prodgers

scored the final goal in the history of Maple Leaf Gardens. At 11:05 of the third period on February 13, 1999, he scored on Curtis Joseph and promptly scooped the historic puck for his collection. But perhaps the thing he should boast most about is simply being around to score that Gardens goal and accrue so many penalty minutes, because during the prime of his career it looked like he might go the way of John Kordic. Probert played the first nine years of his career in Detroit, and quickly became one of the most feared fighters of his era. To go with his intimidating fists, he also played with a smooth set of hands. To wit, in his third year, 1987-88, he scored 29 goals and led the league with 398 penalty minutes, a combination of totals that was singularly impressive. The very next year, though, he self-destructed. On March 2, 1989, he was arrested at the Detroit-Windsor border for possession of cocaine. He was suspended for life by NHL president John Ziegler, who pointed out Probert had been to rehab five times, but that ban was later reduced to a year and Probert seemed to have learned a scary and very real lesson. In the summer of 1994, he signed with the Chicago Blackhawks, in part for a change of scenery, in part because the Hawks gave him $6 million for four years of play. Not long after the ink was dry on that contract he got drunk, did cocaine, and crashed his motorcycle. Charged again, he was suspended indefinitely this time, commissioner Gary Bettman putting the onus fully on Probert to prove he was clean before he could play again. He went into a six-month rehab program in California, and a year later Bettman let him back in the league. Years after, he managed to confine his maniacal behaviour to the ice and has been a model citizen. Married with a child, he continued to fight, and although his goal production was down, he was still a solid role player until early in the 2002-03 season when he was eased into retirement by the Hawks. He hadn't had a drink since that fateful day in 1994, and was a walking example of determination, a hockey Beowulf who has slayed his inner dragons. But when he moved from the ice to the broadcast booth, he had a relapse and in January 2003 re-entered the NHL's substance abuse program.

PROCHAZKA, Martin
b. Slany, Czechoslovakia (Czech Republic), March 3, 1972
By no means a household name in North America, Prochazka is one of the most decorated players in the modern Czech Republic. The Toronto Maple Leafs drafted him in 1991 and used him for just 29 games 6 years later, and Atlanta played him 3 times in 1999-2000, before he left to play in Russia. Beyond those insignificant NHL numbers, though, Prochazka won four consecutive gold medals with his country, starting

with the 1998 Olympics in Nagano and continuing with three successive first-place finishes at the World Championships in 1999, 2000, and 2001. In all, he played in six Worlds, three WJCs, and the World Cup. He's not big, which might explain his lack of NHL success, but his international results are almost without compare in modern times.

PRODGERS, George "Goldie" (sometimes Prodger)
b. London, Ontario, February 18, 1892
d. London, Ontario, October 25, 1935
A veteran of the NHA, Prodgers won the Stanley Cup with Quebec in 1911-12 and the Canadiens in the '15-'16 before he joined the army while he was in North Bay and served with the 228th Battalion in Toronto. Upon discharge, he signed with the Toronto St. Pats and began a six-year NHL career, the last five of which passed with Hamilton. Prodgers retired in 1925 and returned to London, where he managed the Arena and coached the Panthers in their first year in the Canadian Pro league in '25-'26. The team won the title that first season, and Prodgers later managed the Tecumsehs in London. He died suddenly, at home, of a heart attack in his sleep.

PROKHOROV, Vitali ("Little V")
b. Moscow, Soviet Union (Russia), December 25, 1966
He may have escaped notice playing in Moscow, but he was too good at the 1991 Canada Cup and 1992 Olympics in Albertville to be ignored forever. St. Louis signed him and experimented with a Moscow Express Line of Prokhorov, Vitali Karamnov, and Igor Korolev, but the troika just didn't work well together. On Halloween 1992, Prokhorov made a big impact by scoring a hat trick, but his play was hampered for two months by a bad shoulder and then his season was wrecked after he was checked from behind into the boards. The year after, he broke his toe and ended in the minors, and the year after that he ran into a new coach named Mike Keenan. Iron Mike would have none of the speedy little Soviet and dumped him in the minors, and Prokhorov returned to Russia to continue his career.

PROKOPEC, Mike
b. Toronto, Ontario, May 17, 1974
By virtue of being drafted by Chicago in 1992, Prokopec played his only NHL games with the Hawks 3 years later, totalling 15 over 2 seasons. He didn't register a point and spent the rest of his six-year career in the minors. His final stop was with Manitoba in the IHL, but he separated his shoulder just before the start of the playoffs in 2000 and never played again.

Probert played the first nine years of his career in Detroit.
BOB PROBERT

PRONGER, Chris ("Prongs")

b. Dryden, Ontario, October 10, 1974

A giant of a man, it took Pronger many years of development to reach the stage where at the 2000 NHL Awards he received the Hart Trophy and Norris Trophy, a twin prize of excellence last won by Bobby Orr. Pronger went 2nd overall in the 1993 draft to Hartford, after Ottawa erred by picking Alexandre Daigle 1st overall. Pronger had had an outstanding junior career, culminating in the spring of '93 with a Memorial Cup with Peterborough after winning gold with Canada's juniors in January. But in his two years with the Whalers, he neither moved mountains nor brought home the Cup, and the fans booed him mercilessly. St. Louis traded Brendan Shanahan to get Pronger in a one-for-one deal, and promised that Pronger would become the best defenceman in the league with time. He was correct. Pronger learned to use his size, improved his footwork, and even developed an offensive element. He combined with Al MacInnis to form the best pair of blueliners in the league, playing together on the power play and rarely together besides. Each played 30 minutes a game, and it was a struggle for any team to win playing against either of those two all night long. Pronger played for Canada at the disappointing 1998 Olympics in Nagano but was also on the gold-medal team four years later in Salt Lake City. In 1997, he became the youngest captain in team history, and today, in his prime, he is the one defenceman any team would love to have. All that has eluded him so far is the Stanley Cup, and only time will tell whether the Blues are a team worthy of hoisting the great trophy. Pronger certainly was, until the 2002 playoffs when he suffered a serious wrist injury that required complex surgery, forced him to miss almost the entire 2002-03 season, and threatened to jeopardize his career.

He combined with Al MacInnis to form the best pair of blueliners in the league.
CHRIS PRONGER

PRONGER, Sean ("Prongs")

b. Dryden, Ontario, November 30, 1972

The older brother of Chris, Sean wasn't nearly the prospect and as a result took a different route to the NHL. First, he went to Bowling Green on a scholarship and earned a business degree while playing hockey. Although Vancouver drafted him in 1991, the Canucks never signed him and it wasn't until 1995 that he signed with Anaheim. Since then, it's been a life of trades and travel. Six NHL teams and counting, and almost as many in the minors. He has his brother's size (almost), but he's a forward who is not, by style, a scorer. Still, he played 2001-02 with Columbus after a two-year hiatus in the "I" with Manitoba, and he has made a hockey career out of a university education, which is better than just all right.

PRONOVOST, Andre

b. Shawinigan Falls, Quebec, July 9, 1936

When Pronovost graduated from the Montreal Jr. Canadiens in 1956, his timing couldn't have been better. He was a fine left winger who made the team that fall, and in each of his first four seasons he won the Cup with the greatest dynasty in league history. Early the next season, though, he got the shock of his life when the Habs traded him to Boston, the lowest of the low. Reluctant to report, he eventually saw no alternative, and almost two years to the day later he was traded to Detroit, a Cup contender. Pronovost played most of the next seven years in the minors, with only an eight-game stint with expansion Minnesota as his final NHL dance. After retiring, he settled in Longueuil and opened a restaurant.

PRONOVOST, Claude

b. Shawinigan Falls, Quebec, July 22, 1935

It's an amazing thing to get a shutout in your NHL debut, but it's even more amazing to get that shutout against the team that employs you! On January 14, 1956, Boston came to Montreal to play the Habs at the Forum. The Bruins were without starter Terry Sawchuk, who was injured, but they had Long John Henderson, his capable backup. Only problem was, Henderson's size 13 skates didn't make the trip, so he couldn't play. That left Pronovost, Canadiens practice goalie, to play for the Bruins against his own team. He did too good a job, shutting down a team that would win the Cup at season's end while Leo Boivin and Lorne Ferguson scored to give the B's a 2-0 road win. It was three years before Pronovost played again – two appearances in relief. He played the rest of his career in the minors, tracking the more successful careers of his brothers, Marcel and Jean.

PRONOVOST, Jean

b. Shawinigan Falls, Quebec, December 18, 1945

Jean was the 11th of 12 children and the last of 9 boys in the Pronovost household, and it was curious that his older brother, Marcel, was his idol because of the 15-year age difference. Jean was no Hall of Famer like Marcel, but he was a remarkable player in his own right and made a name for himself during his 14 years in the NHL. Jean was part of the Boston system prior to expansion, but in 1967 the Bruins traded him to Pittsburgh for John Arbour. It was a steal of a deal. He was a right winger who had 12 consecutive 20-goal seasons, and his best years saw him score 40, 43, and 52 goals with a Pens team that wasn't very good. That 52-goal year also saw Pronovost total 104 points, and during his prime he played in four successive All-Star Games (1975-78). He played on a line with Syl Apps and Lowell

Sean Pronger

Andre Pronovost

Claude Pronovost

Jean Pronovost

McDonald, but was traded to Atlanta in 1978 and finished his career with Washington. Pronovost went into coaching in Quebec, both with McGill University and junior and pro, and he also worked with Hockey Ministries International, the group that combines religion and hockey as a way of life.

PRONOVOST, Marcel
b. Lac la Tortue, Quebec, June 15, 1930

It has been an incredible ride for Pronovost, and no one says it's quite over yet. He got his name on the Stanley Cup for the first time in 1950, and again in 2000 with New Jersey. That 50-year span is without compare in the annals of hockey. Pronovost was one of 12 children who grew up in Shawinigan Falls. He was a high-scoring centreman in high school, but the Canadiens passed him over and Detroit signed him after a tournament in Quebec City. The Wings were there to look at the Wilson brothers – Larry and John – and Larry told scout Marcel Cote to take a look at Pronovost. He looked, he saw, he signed, and Pronovost was shuttled into the Detroit system, first with Windsor in junior and then on to Omaha and Indianapolis. In the 1950 playoffs, Gordie Howe was seriously injured in the first game of the semifinals against Toronto. As a result, Red Kelly was moved up to forward, and Pronovost was called up from the Knights to play defence. The team won the Cup, and Pronovost started the next year in the AHL, again proving so superior that the Wings called him up again and he never left. He was a hard-hitting defenceman and although he suffered very few serious injuries, he suffered countless minor ones. For years he had a clause in his insurance policy that paid him $5 for every stitch he required from a hockey injury, and over time he claimed to have broken his nose 14 times. When he started with the Wings, his English was awful, but he read as many as three books a week to master the language. Pronovost played 16 seasons with Detroit. He was part of all four Cup teams in the first half of the 1950s, and he remained through the revivifying 1960s when the team reached a small peak before going into a long period of horrible play. He was traded to Toronto in 1965 and played the final four and a half years of his NHL career with the Leafs, notably with the Over-the-Hill Gang of '66-'67 that won the Cup. In all his years he never won an individual trophy, though he did play in 11 All-Star Games and was named to either the First or Second All-Star Team a total of 4 times. He finished his career playing in the AHL with Tulsa for a year and a half, retiring at age 41. He coached the Oilers for a few years and then took the same job with the Buffalo Sabres in 1977. But when Punch Imlach was fired early the year after, so, too, was coach Pronovost. He was

inducted into the Hockey Hall of Fame in 1978, coached Windsor of the OHL briefly, and then landed a scouting job with the NHL's Central Scouting Bureau. From there he joined New Jersey, winning Cups in 1995 and 2000. His brothers, Jean and Claude, also made it to the NHL, though neither had the long and outstanding association with the game that Marcel has had.

PROPP, Brian
b. Lanigan, Saskatchewan, February 15, 1959

The son of a Lutheran minister, Propp grew up believing in himself, and by the time he retired he had everyone else believing in him, too. He led the Western league in points in his last two seasons, first playing with Bill Derlago and accumulating 182 points, then with Laurie Boschman and collecting 194. He was so good at his first camp in 1979 with Philadelphia that coach Pat Quinn couldn't leave him off the opening-night roster. He clicked with whomever coach Quinn played him, and his two-way play was exemplary. He scored 34 goals as a rookie, had four 40-goal seasons with the Flyers, and led the team to the finals in '85 and '87, losing both times to Edmonton. After nearly ten and a half years, he was traded to Boston and on to Minnesota, where the Stars went to the 1991 finals, and he finished his NHL career with Hartford in '93-'94. Propp played in five All-Star Games, was a catalyst on the power play for the Flyers, and was known for his timely goals. After retiring, he returned to Philadelphia to work on Flyers radio broadcasts and he operated a golf business in the summer.

In all his years he never won an individual trophy, though he did play in 11 All-Star Games.
MARCEL PRONOVOST

PROSPAL, Vaclav
b. Ceske Budejovice, Czechoslovakia (Czech Republic), February 17, 1975

After being drafted by Philadelphia in 1993, Prospal couldn't get to the airport quickly enough to come to North America. He played most of his first four years with Hershey, but in the last of these he played his first 18 NHL games with the Flyers, and by the next year he was a full-time member of the team. Philly traded him to Ottawa in the disastrous deal that netted the Flyers the wayward Alexandre Daigle, and Prospal has since been on the move to Florida and Tampa Bay. Named to the Czechs' 1998 Olympic team, he missed the Nagano showcase because of a broken leg, and although he won a gold medal with his country at the 2000 WC, his stock had dropped by the next year and he didn't play at Salt Lake City in 2002.

PROULX, Christian
b. Sherbrooke, Quebec, December 10, 1973

Montreal's plan for Proulx was to draft him (which it did in 1992) and then let the defenceman develop in

Brian Propp

Christian Proulx

the minors. Those plans were scuppered when the Habs were beset by injuries in December 1993, and he was called up for seven games. He played well and coach Jacques Demers promised he'd get another shot. He never did. Proulx was buried in the minors until 1998 when he moved to Europe to play. He's been there ever since, most recently in Germany.

PROVOST, Claude ("Joe")
b. Montreal, Quebec, September 17, 1933
d. Hallandale, Florida, April 17, 1984

Awkward to look at as a skater, Provost became one of the game's pre-eminent players, though he is in no Hall of Fame and does not elicit gasps of admiration or cries of celebration when his name is mentioned. Toe Blake put him on a line with Andre Pronovost and Phil Goyette, and this trio became the league's best third line. Provost in particular was the nightly nemesis of Bobby Hull, the über-shadow who could skate a scorer into the boards and make him wonder how he ever got a single score. Provost, in turn, developed into a shooter of note himself, and in '61-'62 he led Montreal with 33 goals. He started with the Habs in 1955 and finished with them in 1970, one of a select few to be part of two separate and distinct Montreal dynasties. He won five consecutive Cups in the 1950s and four more with the "silent dynasty" of the next decade. He played in 11 All-Star Games and won the inaugural Bill Masterton Trophy in 1968, yet despite his remarkable career no one points to him as one of the best Habs ever. After retiring, Provost ran a small hotel north of the city and operated a health and fitness centre in town, the Centre Paul Sauve Health Centre. He also had a home in Florida, and suffered a fatal heart attack near there while playing tennis.

PRPIC, Joel
b. Sudbury, Ontario, September 25, 1974

At 6'6" and 225 pounds, Prpic isn't going to sneak up on anyone but, then again, in the NHL no one will ever ask him to do as much. The behemoth centre graduated from St. Lawrence University in 1997 and started in the Boston system, though he played just 15 games over 2 seasons. In the minors, he was part of the Calder Cup win by Providence in 1999, scoring the Cup-winning goal against Rochester. He moved on to play briefly with Colorado and has most recently been part of the San Jose organization.

PRUSEK, Martin
b. Ostrava, Czechoslovakia (Czech Republic), December 11, 1975

He made his NHL debut in goal for Ottawa in 2001-02, a single game during a season in the minors. But in Grand Rapids, Prusek had an outstanding year and was named the AHL's best goalie. At camp in the fall of 2002, his play got even better and he was named backup to Patrick Lalime with the Sens. His style is reminiscent of Dominik Hasek.

PRYOR, Chris
b. St. Paul, Minnesota, January 23, 1961

A large and physical defencemen out of the University of New Hampshire, Pryor played 6 years in the NHL,

culminating in '86-'87 when he appeared in 50 games with Minnesota. Beyond that, his stays with the Stars and Islanders were brief and sporadic. He retired in 1992 after 10 years of pro hockey.

PRYSTAI, Metro ("Meatball")
b. Yorkton, Saskatchewan, November 7, 1927

Prystai and Bert Olmstead were the stuff of legend in Moose Jaw, for when they played together the Canucks went to three straight Memorial Cup tournaments (1945-47). They were reunited just a short time later in Chicago, where they formed two-thirds of the Boilermaker Line (along with Bep Guidolin). In '49-'50, Prystai scored 29 goals with this unit, but the next year he was traded to Detroit. Initial disappointment turned to glory as he played alongside Gordie Howe and Ted Lindsay and won two Cups with the Wings. In 1952, the team went undefeated in the playoffs, and in the clinching game against Montreal, Prystai had two goals and an assist. He rounded out his career in the same way it began, going to Detroit (again) and then Chicago (again). In the summers, he worked variously at a golf course and a gas station, but when he retired in 1958 he had greater opportunities. He turned down a chance to coach in Poland and instead became manager and coach of his alma mater in Moose Jaw. He also scouted for Detroit but then got out of hockey to work for O'Keefe Breweries. He later sold insurance, real estate, and cars in Saskatchewan.

PUDAS, Al ("Puddy")
b. Siikajoki, Finland, February 17, 1899
d. Thunder Bay, Ontario, October 28, 1976

Pudas arrived in Port Arthur, Ontario, when he was just three years old, and the region would be home for the rest of his life. He played hockey like any young boy in town, and graduated to the junior ranks with the local Bearcats, winning the Allan Cup in '24-'25 and '25-'26. As a result of these successes, he attracted NHL interest, and the Toronto St. Pats signed him on November 10, 1926. Although he played only four games with the team – his only NHL games – his hockey career was lengthy and he was the first Finnish-born player to make it to the big league. He played pro until 1928 and then became a coach in Port Arthur, guiding the ladies team to a western Canadian championship and having great success with local senior teams. His career reached its climax when he coached Canada to a silver medal at the 1936 Olympics in Garmisch, after which he retired. Since 1924 he had worked for CNR as an office supervisor, and he maintained this full-time job for 40 years until 1964 when he retired. He was also a fine golfer and a longtime treasurer of the Thunder Bay Fish & Game Association, and was inducted into the Northwestern Ontario Sports Hall of Fame on two occasions, in 1982 for his feats with the Allan Cup Bearcats, and five years later for his coaching of the Canadian Olympic team.

PULFORD, Bob ("Pully")
b. Newton Robinson, Ontario, March 31, 1936

Pulford grew up in Toronto and much of his playing career centred on the hockey capital. He played junior with the Marlies under coach Turk Broda, winning Memorial Cups in 1955 and '56. He made the Leafs

Joel Prpic

Metro Prystai

Bob Pulford

Dave Pulkkinen

Dale Purinton

Clifford Purpur

that fall, and never played a game in the minors during his 16-year career. A left winger, he proved a valuable addition to the team on many fronts. He was durable and missed only a handful of games because of injury. He was a great leader who inspired his teammates with his play. He was a hard-working, two-way player who could score goals and check well. And he was one of the best forecheckers in the game, a man who took that skill to an art form. He knew just when to take the man or poke the puck away, and he used quickness and strength to get the puck before opposing defencemen knew what had happened. He scored 20 goals 4 times during his career, though goals were not his greatest asset. Nonetheless, he played on four Cup winners with the Leafs in the 1960s, and although he scored only once in the '67 playoffs, it was a biggy. In game three of the finals, his overtime score gave the Leafs a 3-2 win over Montreal and put them in control of that series. Off the ice, he was also important. In 1964, after seven years of night school, he earned a B.A. from McMaster University in Hamilton, and went on to become the first president of the NHL Players' Association. Pulford was traded to L.A. in 1970 after 14 years with the Leafs, one of the longest-serving players in the history of the Blue and White. He played two years with the Kings and then became one of the few men to move directly into coaching. He led the Kings from '72-'73 until 1977, peaking in '74-'75 when the team had 105 points and he was named coach of the year. He left L.A. to assume a similar role in Chicago, a better hockey city, and from that day to this has been affiliated, for better or worse, with the Hawks. He became both GM and coach for two years and occasionally went behind the bench on an interim basis after firing a coach. He became senior vice-president of the team, but in 1999-2000 found himself behind the bench after firing Lorne Molleken during a dismal season. During his more than quarter-century with the team, the Hawks have never won the Cup, though they did go to the finals in 1992. Perhaps Pulford could have been inducted into the Hockey Hall of Fame as a Builder for his long executive career with the Hawks, but the fact was that in 1991 he was inducted as a player.

PULKKINEN, Dave
b. Kapuskasing, Ontario, May 18, 1949
Grinding out a career in the minors and struggling like mad to get to the NHL just didn't have the appeal to Pulkkinen that it did to others. He played two games with the Islanders in their first season – in December 1972 and in March '73 – but retired as a player in 1974.

He returned home to his wife and children, and later coached the kids in their minor hockey league. He also became involved with the OHL's Sudbury Wolves, but when he refused the head coaching job that association ended. Pulkkinen joined the Ontario Public Service and worked as a corrections officer. He also worked on his golf game whenever he could. In 2001, he finished fifteenth at the Northern Amateur Championship.

PUPPA, Daren ("Poops")
b. Kirkland Lake, Ontario, March 23, 1965
Puppa's luck couldn't have been better when early in 1983 he spurned an offer to play for the University of Denver and opted for RPI instead. The U of D coach, Ralph Backstrom, was Puppa's father's cousin, and while talking to Buffalo coach Scotty Bowman about another player, he bemoaned the loss of Puppa for his university program. Bowman put down the phone, got to work, and drafted Puppa in the summer of '83. In his eight years with the Sabres, Puppa saw the highest highs and the lowest lows. He recorded a shutout in his first game, and in '89-'90 he led the league in wins with 31, but for much of this time he was backup to Tom Barrasso. He played eight games with Toronto, but the Leafs had acquired him only to expose him in the 1993 Expansion Draft. Puppa ended up in Tampa Bay where he had another mini-career similar to what he had with Buffalo, being the number-one man for three years. Serious back injuries started to take their toll, though, and Puppa was eventually forced to retire as a result.

In his eight years with the Sabres, Puppa saw the highest highs and the lowest lows.
DAREN PUPPA

PURINTON, Dale
b. Fort Wayne, Indiana, October 11, 1976
Cal Purinton never made the NHL, but he did play for many years with Fort Wayne in the IHL and later was inducted into the Komets Hall of Fame. When he retired, he settled in that city and started a family, and son Dale was born. Dale went on to play junior in western Canada, and was drafted by the Rangers in 1995. Since then he's been only a part-time player, though his specialty has always been fighting and it is as an enforcer that he hopes to get to the NHL on a regular basis.

PURPUR, Clifford ("Fido")
b. Grand Forks, North Dakota, September 26, 1912
d. Grand Forks, North Dakota, February 21, 2001
Purpur was just a little fellow who stood but 5'5" and tipped the scales at about 157 pounds. But he was tenacious and determined, as any kid from North Dakota would have to be about playing in the NHL. He played half a season with the St. Louis Eagles in

1934-35 and seven years later made Chicago, where he played for four years. It was around this time, 1941, that he suffered from an illness doctors couldn't identify, but its effects included a high temperature and loss of strength. Purpur struggled on, though, and played until 1947. While his younger brother, Ken, went on to play for the U.S. at the Olympics, Fido set out to promote and enhance hockey programs in North Dakota. He tried to improve minor hockey programs, and he also coached the UND team from 1949 to '56. His day job was in construction, and he continued to play with his brother for a while with the Grand Forks Amerks in the States-Dominion League where, in 1950, he scored 4 goals in 25 seconds. He was inducted into the U.S. Hockey Hall of Fame in 1974, and in 1981 he received the Theodore Roosevelt Rough Rider Award, the highest honour in North Dakota. In May 2000, he was forced to move into a retirement home, and he passed away after suffering a seizure.

PURVES, John

b. Toronto, Ontario, February 12, 1968
He got into the NHL and he scored a goal, two accomplishments Purves will have forever. Drafted by Washington in 1986, he played seven games with Washington four years later, but since then has been a career minor-leaguer, almost exclusively in the "I."

PUSEY, Chris

b. Brantford, Ontario, June 30, 1965
Pusey appeared in his only NHL game on October 19, 1985, when he took over for starter Corrado Micalef to begin the second period. He allowed three goals the rest of the way and was returned to the minors, where he played in obscurity until 1992. He then focused his attention on triathlons. In 2001, he came out of hockey retirement to play for the Dundas Real McCoys, a senior team that went to the Allan Cup finals before losing. What made this doubly interesting was that Pusey did not play goal for the team – he played as a defenceman.

PUSHOR, Jamie ("Push")

b. Lethbridge, Alberta, February 11, 1973
Detroit coach Scotty Bowman had such a surplus of talent during the 1990s that he didn't have to rush any young players into the lineup. Let them develop in the minors, give them a sampling of the NHL, and see where to go from there. That was his philosophy, and Pushor was an example of it. Drafted by the Wings in 1991 after becoming the main defenceman with Lethbridge during his junior days, it was four years before he played for the Wings. By 1996, he was a regular, and in that first full season he won the Cup. Unfortunately, Bowman traded him to Anaheim for experience in Dmitri Mironov, and since then Pushor has travelled more than he would have liked. In 2001-02 he found himself Columbus-bound, and although a lousy team the move affords him the chance to become the mainstay of the Blue Jackets blueline.

PUSIE, Jean

b. Montreal, Quebec, October 15, 1912
d. Montreal, Quebec, April 21, 1956
In the grand and complete history of the game, there was never a player of so little ability who became so popular with fans, who was doted on by the media, and who made such a bizarre ass of himself on the ice that he is as much myth as man, as much comic as player. He scored one of his first goals in pro hockey in 1930 with a great slapshot that knocked the goalie's glove and puck into the net. Pusie skated up to the beaten netminder and counted his fingers before heading back to centre ice. He was known to stop and talk to railside fans during play, and one time, by the boards, four opponents converged on him as he was on a rush. He dropped his stick and gloves, fell to his knees, and clasped his hands, but they just took the puck and waltzed in on goal and scored. He played 61 NHL games in the 1930s with Montreal, Boston, and New York, winning a Cup as a rookie with the Canadiens in 1931. His antics, though, while crowd pleasing, were hard for players, even teammates, to endure and he was forever being traded in the minors as well. He once got so upset he destroyed 15 box seats in a Kansas City arena and had to be taken away by police. In his last game out west, he slugged a referee, left the ice, and headed straight for the dressing room. One of the reasons he could do these things was that he was so big. At 6' and 200 pounds, he was considered (and called) a giant. When he left hockey, he became a boxer and wrestler until suffering a fatal heart attack.

PYATT, Nelson ("Nels"/ "Nelly")

b. Port Arthur, Ontario, September 9, 1953
Pyatt could have gone to a U.S. college to play hockey and get an education, but his dad knew Gus Bodnar, coach of Oshawa in the OHL, so he took the junior route. He was drafted by Detroit in 1973, but the Wings barely gave him a look in the NHL before trading him to Washington. Despite scoring 26 goals in his first season with the Caps, the team let him go to Colorado rather than give him a generous contract and he came up with a 23-goal season. That was his last fine year, and he petered out quickly into the minors before retiring. He returned home to Thunder Bay (which ate up Port Arthur in an amalgamation) and became a fireman. He also had the privilege of raising a son, Taylor, who made his NHL debut with the Islanders in the 2000-01 season.

PYATT, Taylor

b. Thunder Bay, Ontario, August 19, 1981
Son of Nelson, Taylor is a huge young prospect. Drafted 8th overall in 1999 by the Islanders, he played the 2000-01 season with the team before being traded in a truly complimentary fashion. He and Tim Connolly were sent to Buffalo for Michael Peca, the Sabres' great star who became embroiled in a contract dispute with that team and promised never to play for them again. No greater show of Pyatt's prospective worth can be made than through such a deal, but now, of course, he has to live up to all the advanced billing.

John Purves

Jean Pusie

Nelson Pyatt

Max Zuacken

QUACKENBUSH, Hubert "Bill" ("Quack")

b. Toronto, Ontario, March 2, 1922
d. Lawrenceville, New Jersey, September 12, 1999

His father was a police officer but his aunt got her way. She liked neither Hubert nor his middle name, George, so decided to call the baby Bill, and no one called him anything but that for the rest of his life. He played hockey like any boy in Toronto before going to Brantford where Tommy Ivan coached. Ivan made sure Quackenbush went to the Red Wings, but when he was called up in '42-'43 Quack lasted only 10 games before he broke his wrist. The next year he made the team and developed into one of the best defencemen in the league. Quackenbush was skilled on many levels. He was a superb rusher and playmaker in the offensive end, but in his own end he mastered the art of checking without making the devastating hit intended to injure. Rather, he played tactically clever defence and manoeuvred players off the puck with a minimum of effort. This allowed him to play upwards of 40 minutes a game and, even more rarely for a blueliner, it kept him out of the penalty box. Quackenbush was usually partnered with Red Kelly, and in '48-'49 Quack became the first defenceman to win the Lady Byng Trophy. (Only one other defenceman has ever won the award – Kelly.) That season, Quackenbush did not incur a single penalty, and in fact he once went 132 games between minor penalties. In his 14-year career, he had but one fighting major, in '47-'48, and witnesses say this was a dubious call for a quick wrestling match with Gaye Stewart. In the summer of 1949, Quackenbush and Pete Horeck were traded to Boston for Jimmy Peters, Pete Babando, Clare Martin, and Lloyd Durham. The move gave Bill the chance to play with his brother Max, but it was also made because the Bruins were thin on blueline talent. Quackenbush spent the last seven years of his career in Boston, but he never won a Cup. In his 774 career games, he had just 95 penalty minutes. He also played in eight consecutive All-Star Games (1947-54). After retiring in 1956, Quackenbush remained in Boston and by day worked for a construction supply firm selling steel joists. By night, he attended Northeastern University until he earned his degree in civil engineering in 1962. While at Northeastern, he assisted the hockey coach but after graduating kept on with the construction company. In 1967, he began a career with Princeton University that consumed him for the rest of his working days. He coached the men's hockey team from 1967 to '85, the women's team from '78 on, and the golf team from '71 till his retirement. He also coached a peewee hockey team in Lawrenceville. Quackenbush was highly successful in all facets of coaching life at Princeton but when he retired he spent much of the year in Orlando, Florida, golfing. He recorded six holes-in-one during his life. He returned to New Jersey permanently in 1997 and died in hospital there two years later. Three of his sons later graduated from Princeton, and Quackenbush was inducted into the Hockey Hall of Fame in 1976.

QUACKENBUSH, Max

b. Toronto, Ontario, August 29, 1928

Sergeant John Quackenbush of the Toronto police department and his wife produced four boys, three of whom played serious hockey. Ted lost an eye and had his pro aspirations quashed, Bill had a Hall of Fame career, and, in the middle, Max played a few games but never made a lasting impact in the NHL (the other son, Jack, became a lieutenant in the Canadian army). Max played most of the 1950-51 season with Boston, but his dream came true the next year when Chicago acquired him. For 14 glorious games, he played with his brother before being sent down to the minors. He finished his career out west and then returned to Toronto where he, too, joined the police force and became responsible for the Coroner's Building.

Bill Quackenbush

QUENNEVILLE, Joel ("Herbie")

b. Windsor, Ontario, September 15, 1958

For a guy who almost quit hockey to study medicine, Quenneville was a helluva defenceman. He didn't think much of his play in junior at the start, but each year he got better and then the Leafs drafted him in 1978. That's when hockey became his priority. He established himself pretty quickly on the blueline in Toronto, nothing fancy or overwhelming, just a solid and positional player. He got caught up in the Punch Imlach insanity the next year, though, when the senescent GM traded him and Lanny McDonald to Colorado, and from there Quenneville went on to Hartford. He played well on a fairly bad team, though the Whalers were playoff fodder for Montreal with the same annual consistency in the east that Winnipeg was for Edmonton in the west. When his career was nearing its end, Quenneville knew he wanted to go into coaching, so his final year of playing came in the AHL with Toronto's affiliate in St. John's. He moved into coaching the team under head boss Marc Crawford and later became an assistant to Crawford in Colorado, winning the Cup with the Avs in 1996. A year later, he took his first head coaching job in the NHL, with St. Louis, a team on the cusp of greatness but in need of guidance. So far, Quenneville has fallen short in the post-season, but he has all the talent in the world to take the Blues deep into the playoffs.

Joel Quenneville

QUENNEVILLE, Leo

b. St. Anicet, Quebec, June 15, 1900
d. unknown

He played most of his hockey in Quebec, but Quenneville moved into the Can-Am League and IHL in the mid-1920s and was eventually thought worthy of the NHL by the Rangers. They played him in '29-'30 for half a season, but he was soon back playing in Quebec. After retiring, he settled in Chicoutimi and became involved in a garage business.

QUILTY, Johnny

b. Ottawa, Ontario, January 21, 1921
d. Ottawa, Ontario, September 12, 1969

The son of Sylvester "Silver" Quilty, a great football player in his day, Johnny started skating on rivers when he was six. All through his youth he played on championship teams, notably with the Glebe and St. Patricks teams in Ottawa. He was invited to try out for Montreal in 1940, and to his surprise he made the

Max Quackenbush
(opposite page)

team, debuting in the NHL at 19. He won the Calder Trophy that rookie season, and the year after had another fine run with the Canadiens before joining the army. Quilty achieved the rank of sergeant with the RCAF, and when he was discharged he rejoined the Habs, though the times had changed. Montreal traded him to Boston the following year and then midway through the '47-'48 season his pro career ended. He collided with Bob Goldham of Chicago – a hard rock if ever there was one – and suffered a compound fracture of his left leg. Weeks and months passed, but Quilty couldn't regain the needed strength in his leg and was forced to retire at age 27. He returned to Ottawa and rejoined the RCAF, but died suddenly in his apartment at age 48.

Dan Quinn

QUINN, Dan
b. Ottawa, Ontario, June 1, 1965

Rightly or wrongly, Quinn's life changed on November 10, 1992, when he and a group of friends, Mario Lemieux among them, attended a party. The fun continued in his hotel room and, depending on the twists and turns of the story, connubial bliss was had with or without the woman's consent and (possibly) with Mario in the room. The woman alleged rape and police eventually decided not to press charges, but the damage had been done. Minnesota released Quinn and he had to go to Europe to continue playing. Up to that point, Quinn was a fast and skilled forward who once had seasons of 40 and 34 goals with Lemieux and the Penguins. Once in Switzerland, he was contacted by the expansion Ottawa Senators, and was able to get his career back on track, sort of. He moved around his last few years, never came close to scoring as he formerly had, and retired in late 1996 after a brief comeback with Pittsburgh. He devoted all his time to golf and became a dominant player on the Celebrity Tour, winning numerous events and hoping to earn his PGA card in due course. In 2000, he caddied for John Daly at the U.S. Open. On the 18th hole of the first round, Daly went *Tin Cup*-crazy and took a 14 on that hole.

QUINN, Pat
b. Hamilton, Ontario, January 29, 1943

The life and times of Pat Quinn are extensive enough to fill a book and renowned enough to get him into the Hockey Hall of Fame one day. For now, he must content himself with coaching Toronto and taking satisfaction in a hockey career that began in Hamilton in the late 1950s. Quinn is of Irish stock and grew up in rough Hamilton. Taking care of himself was a prerequisite, and he passed with flying colours. He played junior in Edmonton but no NHL

Pat Quinn

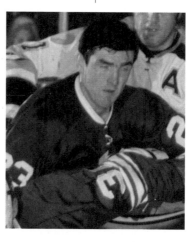

Quinn earned a law degree from Widener University at the Delaware School of Law.
PAT QUINN

team cared a whit for him at that point, so he turned pro in the minors and played and waited. The Leafs acquired him in 1968 and used him on their blueline for two seasons. Burly and rough, no one moved around him with ease and he established a physical presence that reached a crescendo during the 1969 playoffs. In the first round, the Leafs played the up-and-coming Bruins, and Boston swept the series in four humiliating games, the first two being 10-0 and 7-0 whitewashes for the home team. During that first pasting, Quinn caught Bobby Orr coming out of his own end along the boards in full flight – with his head down. He stepped in front of Orr and hit him hard, knocking Orr unconscious. The rest of the game was brawl-filled, and charges of a vicious elbow were levelled at Quinn from that day to this. He was claimed by Vancouver (1970) and Atlanta (1972) in successive Expansion Drafts, and closed out his playing days with the Flames having played precious few playoff games in his nine-year career. Almost without missing a beat, he turned his mind to coaching, joining Philadelphia for the last half of the '78-'79 season. The next year, he took the Flyers on the greatest winning streak ever, 35 games without a loss from near the start of the season until January 1979. The team lost to the Islanders in the finals, and Quinn won his first Jack Adams Trophy at season's end. Over the last 20 years, Quinn has coached and managed almost nonstop. After four years with the Flyers he went to L.A., and three years later he went to Vancouver under controversial, illegal circumstances. In December 1986, he signed an agreement to become coach and GM of Vancouver the following year, even though he still had a contract with Los Angeles. He was barred from coaching the Canucks for three and a half years, though he left the Kings in the summer and worked for the team after the '87 draft. When he did begin coaching Vancouver, in 1990-91, he built a team that came within a game of winning the Cup: In 1994, the Canucks met the Rangers in game seven of the finals, only to lose. In 1998, Quinn became coach in Toronto and a short time later assumed GM duties as well. He has become the longest-serving coach of the team since Punch Imlach in the glory days of the 1960s, and his influence has been as profound as Imlach's, in some ways. Quinn came to Toronto and vowed to build a team based on speed and attack, scoring goals rather than preventing them, beating the trap, not practising it. He proved true to his word, and the Leafs became a top-scoring team every year. Quinn's style also caught the fancy of Wayne Gretzky, who was charged with putting together

Canada's 2002 Olympic team. One of his first moves was to name Quinn as coach, believing that speed and skill were the means of winning gold for the first time since 1952. He was right. Quinn did lead Canada to gold, but his life changed during that 2001-02 season. As coach and GM of the Leafs and coach of Team Canada, the 300-pound Quinn was physically taxed to the maximum. By the time the NHL playoffs rolled around, his body could no longer keep up, and during the Conference finals against Carolina he collapsed and had to be hospitalized. The drama surrounding his health usurped the more dramatic possibility of the Leafs getting to the finals, and the team lost in six games. Over the summer, Quinn went on a strict dietary regimen and returned to the Leafs some 50 pounds lighter and healthier. A journeyman player with limited ability, Quinn earned a law degree from Widener University at the Delaware School of Law. His coaching and managing career has been lengthy and successful, but it lacks the one credential that will raise him to a new level of admiration – a Stanley Cup victory.

QUINNEY, Ken
b. New Westminster, British Columbia, May 23, 1965
When you go from small-town B.C. to Las Vegas, the culture shock is palpable. Quinney was a westerner who played parts of three seasons with the Nordiques in the 1980s and into the '90-'91 season, but most of his career was spent in the minors and most of that was with the Thunder in Vegas. He ended his career in Germany in 2001, but once retired he returned to the city of slots and became a coach in the minor hockey system of the Las Vegas Outlaws.

QUINT, Deron
b. Durham, New Hampshire, May 12, 1976
As a rookie in 1995-96, Quint played for Winnipeg and scored just five goals all year, but two of those established an incredible record. He scored two goals just four seconds apart to tie a speedy mark set by Nels Stewart in 1931 – and Quint was a defenceman! He moved to Phoenix with the team and after the most recent expansion ended up in Columbus, and there he set another, albeit lesser, record. He scored three goals in a period (he had just seven on the season) for his first career hat trick. What will his next scoring feat be? Only time will tell.

QUINTAL, Stephane
b. Boucherville, Quebec, October 22, 1968
After playing three partial seasons with the Bruins from 1988 to '91, Quintal got his big break when Garry

Galley was injured and the team needed someone for a longer stretch. Quintal stepped in and performed admirably, but soon after he was traded to St. Louis with Craig Janney for Adam Oates. He has moved several times since, though Montreal has been his city of choice. In 2001, he wound up with the Habs a second time, a nod to his heritage as much as his defensive abilities. Incredibly, he has played some 900 NHL games, and also represented Canada at the 1999 World Championships.

QUINTIN, Jean-Francois
b. St. Jean, Quebec, May 28, 1969
At training camp with San Jose in 1991, Quintin was the team's leading scorer when he suffered a serious knee injury in an exhibition game and missed much of the season. He recovered to play a few games with the Sharks, scoring three goals in just eight games, but the next year he played only a few games more before being sent to the minors. He became a regular with the Kansas City Blades in the IHL but it became clearer and clearer that he likely wasn't going back to the NHL, so he headed to Europe. Quintin landed in Germany and has been playing there ever since.

Deron Quint

He ended his career in Germany in 2001.
KEN QUINNEY

RACHUNEK, Karel
b. Gottwaldov (Zlin), Czechoslovakia (Czech Republic), August 27, 1979
The modern Czech, like the modern Canadian, is drafted at 18 if he is considered a player, and Ottawa thought as much of Rachunek when they took him in 1997. He continued to develop in the Czech league rather than play in Canada, but starting in 1999 he has worked himself into the lineup as a regular defenceman on a promising team.

RACICOT, Andre
b. Rouyn Noranda, Quebec, June 9, 1969
From the time Racicot made his debut with Montreal in the '89-'90 season to the time the Habs cut him loose in the summer of 1994, two things were clear. One, the Habs desperately hoped he would be the backup and heir to Patrick Roy. Two, he let in a ton of goals. Obviously, one and two don't make happy playmates, and everyone but Racicot's family called him by the cynical nickname of Red Light. He did, however, get his name on the Cup because he was around during the Montreal improbable run in 1993, but since then Racicot has been buried in the minors so deep he can't see the sky for the soil.

RACINE, Bruce ("Racer")
b. Cornwall, Ontario, August 9, 1966
Records are made to be broken? Not Racine's, that's for sure. Here is a guy who played at Northeastern University and backstopped his team to two Beanpot tournament victories, a prestigious Boston-area showdown. He played for years in the minors until he earned the right to be backup in St. Louis for the '95-'96 season. The only problem was that Mike Keenan was the coach and Grant Fuhr the starter, which meant that as long as Fuhr was breathing he'd get the nod in net. It also meant that because of the whimsical coach, Racine'd see some action in relief as was Keenan's penchant for pulling or switching goalies without compunction. As a result, Racine played in 11 games for the Blues that year but didn't start a single one – an NHL record for most career games without a start. The next year, he was back in the minors and he later moved to Europe.

RACINE, Yves
b. Matane, Quebec, February 7, 1969
A solid defenceman with offensive capability, Racine had a fine junior career in Quebec that culminated with a spot on Canada's 1989 WJC team. He joined Detroit the next year, but after four seasons the Wings shipped him to Philadelphia and so began a series of moves that wore him out by 1998. Racine packed his bags and headed for Europe to play in Finland and, more recently, Germany.

RADIVOJEVIC, Branko ("Raddy")
b. Piestany, Czechoslovakia (Slovakia), November 24, 1980
During his fine junior career with Belleville Radivojevic was drafted by Colorado, but although the Avs never played him he went on to make the Coyotes. He played half of 2001-02 with Wayne Gretzky's team and then made the team out of camp

in 2002 as a right winger who can create offence and keep the other team off balance.

RADLEY, Henry "Yip"
b. Ottawa, Ontario, June 27, 1908
d. Ottawa, Ontario, April 19, 1963
Like a small but important number of hockey players, Radley played pro football before he embarked on a career in the puck game. He was a powerful lineman with the Ottawa Rough Riders for three years in the late 1920s during his winter hockey career with the Montagnards. He played the opening game of the '30-'31 season for the New York Americans and then spent six seasons in the minors. The Maroons signed him in 1936, and coach Tommy Gorman put him in the lineup when defenceman Gerry Carson was injured. He got his only career NHL point, an assist, on a Bob Gracie goal, and then it was back to the minors for the rest of his days. After retiring, Radley coached the hockey team at Royal Military College in Kingston and for 23 years worked as recreational director for the Aluminum Company of Canada in that city.

RAFALSKI, Brian
b. Dearborn, Michigan, September 28, 1973
Are all great hockey players discovered eventually because as long as they keep playing they are great by definition, or do some great players never get their due and wind up playing forever in anonymity and obscurity? There's the rub the undiscovered feel more strongly than the ones who make it after a time. Rafalski got his break, to be sure, but it wasn't as an 18-year-old coming out of college. He earned an agricultural economics degree from the University of Wisconsin in 1995, but no team wanted him. He spent the summer as an intern with the Philip Morris Company, one of the tobacco giants, and then got a call from a team in Sweden, Brynas. With not a single option to rival it, he accepted the offer and for four years he played there and then in Finland with IFK Helsinki. The problem? He was a 5'9" defenceman and no amount of talent could convince anyone he could play the position as well as a 6'3", 220-pound giant. Then, New Jersey GM Lou Lamoriello wanted some speed on his blueline, and his European scout, Dan Labraaten, touted Rafalski as the best defenceman on that continent. Bingo! Rafalski was offered a contract, and he made the team at training camp in 1999. The next spring, he was holding the Stanley Cup aloft and had established himself as an asset. He could read plays, move the puck, and skate well. He just couldn't hammer large opponents in front of his own net. A fair tradeoff. That's how careers are made.

RAGLAN, Clare "Rags"
b. Pembroke, Ontario, September 4, 1927
Hockey enthusiasts might think he got his nickname because he could rag the puck, but, in truth, he was called Rags Raglan after a comedian popular at the time. He grew up in Toronto and played for the Marlies while attending Runnymede Collegiate Institute. He was signed by the Quebec Aces in 1947 to play under coach Punch Imlach, and in 1949 moved to Detroit. The Wings assigned him to Indianapolis, and the team won the Calder Cup by winning eight in

Karel Rachunek

Bruce Racine

Brian Rafalski

Yves Racine
(opposite page)

a row in the playoffs. Raglan made his debut with the Wings the following year and was traded to Chicago the year after. He was back in the minors for the rest of his career after playing half of the '52-'53 season with the Hawks, and although he played for a number of years, his career changed forever on November 20, 1956, when he broke his right leg in two places while playing for Vancouver. He was never the same player again. Raglan later played for and coached the Washington Presidents for a year. He settled in Peterborough and for years ran his own renovating company. His son, Herb, later played in the NHL.

RAGLAN, Herb
b. Peterborough, Ontario, August 5, 1967

Herb Raglan

Son took after father in making it to the NHL, though Herb, playing in a bloated league, had more staying power than his Original Six dad. Herb played mostly with St. Louis, starting in 1986 but out of the NHL altogether by 1994. He played until '98 in the minors, and throughout his career he was a quality role player, someone who could do a little bit of everything. He later returned to Peterborough to go into business.

RAGNARSSON, Marcus ("Rags")
b. Ostervala, Sweden, August 13, 1971

Marcus Ragnarsson

Another feel-good story from the world of hockey, Ragnarsson played for six years in Sweden before joining San Jose in 1995 at age 24. He has played his whole career to date with the Sharks and is a key player on the team's defence. Internationally, his experience has been a mixed blessing. He won a gold medal with Sweden at the 1990 World Championships, but was injured at the '95 WC and missed the '96 World Cup because of injury. He was named to his country's 1998 Olympic team but played only three games. In 2001, Ragnarsson played in his first NHL All-Star Game.

RALEIGH, Don ("Bones")
b. Kenora, Ontario, June 27, 1926

He came by the nickname honestly, for although he was 5'11" he weighed a scant 150 pounds. He was also one of the few players to sport a moustache, and he was the only one whose poetry was reviewed in the *New York Times*. Raleigh played part of the '43-'44 season with the Rangers before joining the Canadian Army. He returned to the Blueshirts in 1947 and was a mainstay on the team for the next nine years. Raleigh was a master playmaker, and when he left the NHL in 1956 he was only the third Rangers player ever to record more than 200 assists (after Frank Boucher and Phil Watson). He was also remembered for two famous goals. In the 1950 finals, the Rangers met Detroit for the Stanley Cup. In games

four and five, Raleigh scored in overtime to win both games, though the Rangers ultimately lost game seven in Detroit. He retired in 1958 after a few years in the minors and settled in Winnipeg where he ran the J.D. Raleigh insurance company.

RALPH, Brad
b. Ottawa, Ontario, October 17, 1980

A one-game wonder with an asterisk beside his name denoting "still active," Ralph played for Phoenix on October 5, 2000, the team's opening game, and has been in the minors ever since. He's still plenty young enough to see many more NHL games, but for now the Oshawa Generals graduate is in the East Coast league trying to play himself up.

RAM, Jamie
b. Scarborough, Ontario, January 18, 1971

His older brother also played hockey and needed a target, so he stuck his kid brother in the net. Little did he know that the kid would turn out to be a great puck stopper. He went to Michigan Tech on scholarship, and in addition to earning a degree in business management he was drafted by the Rangers in 1991. He played only half a game with the team four years later, on February 3, 1996, when he stopped all nine shots he faced. That looks to be the only action he'll get in the NHL. He played in the minors for years, and in 2001-02 had a great season in Finland, posting a league-best 1.71 GAA with Jokerit.

Ramage was traded to the Leafs right after winning the Cup.
ROB RAMAGE

RAMAGE, Rob ("Rammer")
b. Byron, Ontario, January 11, 1959

The various stages of Ramage's career took him to the highest highs and the lowest lows, in no particular order. He came out of junior in London as the best prospect around, and Colorado chose him 1st overall in the 1979 Entry Draft. With the Rockies he was an offensive star from the blueline, but he was weak defensively and a teenager expected to save a franchise. He breathed a great sigh when he was traded to St. Louis, and under the guidance of Barclay Plager he turned into a complete player. On March 7, 1988, he and goalie Rick Wamsley were traded to Calgary for Steve Bozek and Brett Hull, a move that benefitted both teams. Ramage proved to be one of the links needed to bring the Cup to Calgary, in 1989, and Hull became a perennial scoring star in St. Louis. Ramage was traded to the Leafs right after winning the Cup and was immediately named captain on a team rebuilding after the death of Harold Ballard. His career wound down with a series of moves, though he did wind up with Montreal in 1992-93 when the Habs won the Cup. After retiring in 1994, he returned to the scene of his longest stay, St. Louis,

Jamie Ram

where he worked as a stockbroker by day and as a colour analyst for Blues TV by night.

RAMSAY, Craig ("Rammer")

b. Weston, Ontario, March 17, 1951

Games, goals, wins, these are the things hockey fans love, cherish, and follow. The mundane stuff of any man's life – the stuff we all know and endure as common facts of life – are not as colourful or interesting. Ramsay satisfies the former in a number of ways. He played more than 1,000 games in the NHL, all with Buffalo. He won the Selke Trophy in 1985 and played in a Cup finals and an All-Star Game. What few people know is that he did this all with a stomach that just wasn't right. He played junior in Peterborough under Roger Neilson, the man who would be Ramsay's greatest influence. But by the time he got to the NHL in 1971, his stomach, not the other team, was his greatest adversary. He suffered from a congenital digestive-tract ailment that, in a nutshell, didn't get food through his system properly. He had an operation at age 20 that was unsuccessful, and another at 31 in which doctors rearranged his stomach around the esophagus. So far, so good. Ramsay retired in 1985 and immediately went into coaching, working his way up to assistant GM with the Sabres in 1993. Then, he had the chance to be an assistant coach to Neilson in Florida, an offer he couldn't refuse. Just as he was getting ready to travel south, an undetected ulcer in his stomach exploded and he had to have emergency surgery. That night, doctors told his wife they didn't think he would live to see the sun rise. He did, only because of two further operations and the complete removal of his stomach. Ramsay lost 40 pounds but recovered and joined the Panthers under Neilson, and the 2 teamed up again in Philadelphia. In February 2000, Neilson had to leave the team for his own treatment for bone marrow cancer, and Ramsay stepped in as interim coach. Ramsay had a fine career and his devotion to the game continues, but his life story is the more admirable and compelling, despite its lack of hockey-style flair.

He played junior in Peterborough under Roger Neilson, the man who would be Ramsay's greatest influence.
CRAIG RAMSAY

RAMSAY, Les

b. Verdun, Quebec, July 1, 1920

After being discharged from the army in November 1944, Ramsay had his NHL debut delayed while a legal matter was resolved. He was playing for the Ottawa Commandos, but signed with Cleveland of the AHL after January 15, 1945, a no-no in each hockey season. A player can only sign after this date with the consent of his amateur team, but since the Commandos never gave the okay, Ramsay was suspended from all hockey for two weeks while an agreement was worked out. He made his NHL debut with Chicago (Cleveland's

sponsor) on February 18, 1945, and played 11 games with the Hawks before being demoted. He played most of the next five years in Quebec before retiring.

RAMSAY, William "Beattie"

b. Lumsden, Northwest Territories (Saskatchewan), December 12, 1895

d. Regina, Saskatchewan, September 30, 1952

Ramsay attended the University of Toronto in 1914 but a year later joined the Royal Flying Corps, serving in Italy as a lieutenant for four years before resuming his studies at U of T. He earned a B.A. in applied science and played for the school's hockey team, losing the Allan Cup in 1920. He then joined the Toronto Granites, and captained the team to Allan Cup victory in 1921 and again in '23. As a result, the Granites were chosen to represent Canada at the 1924 Olympics in Chamonix, winning gold with the greatest of ease. Upon returning home, he accepted a position as coach of the team at Princeton University, but in 1927 he turned pro and played with the Maple Leafs in the NHL. After just one year, he returned to Saskatchewan and coached the Prince Albert Mintos and Regina Aces, and in 1946 he became president of the Pats, a position he held until shortly before his untimely death. For many years he had a contracting business, Beattie Ramsay Construction Co. Ltd., in Regina.

Beattie Ramsay

RAMSEY, Mike

b. Minneapolis, Minnesota, December 3, 1960

In 1979, Ramsey became the first American player to be drafted in the first round when Buffalo selected him 11th overall. A year later, he played defence on the Miracle on Ice team at the 1980 Olympics in Lake Placid, and soon after joined Buffalo to start a 1,000-game NHL career. Not an offensive star, Ramsey nonetheless was a fine skater and playmaker. He also represented the U.S. at the 1984 and '87 Canada Cups, and spent 14 seasons with Buffalo before Pittsburgh acquired him in early 1993. He finished his career in Detroit, though he missed winning Cups in both instances. He also played in four All-Star Games. In 1997, he opened his own sporting goods store and became an assistant coach with the Sabres. Three years later, he assumed a similar position with the new Minnesota Wild. In 2001, Ramsey was inducted into the U.S. Hockey Hall of Fame.

Mike Ramsey

RAMSEY, Wayne

b. Hamiota, Manitoba, January 31, 1957

Once a farmer, always a farmer. Ramsey came off the land to play for Brandon in junior and then in his first year of pro he played his only NHL games, on February 4 and 5, 1978. He spent the rest of his four years in the minors, but his summer farming took more and more of his time until he quit hockey to make it his full-time occupation. He played some senior hockey and coached kids teams nearby.

RANDALL, Ken

b. Watertown, New York, December 14, 1888
d. Toronto, Ontario, June 17, 1947

If accounts of his career on ice are even half true, the Bob Proberts and Tie Domis of the modern world wouldn't have survived a shift against Randall, a no-nonsense defenceman who used his stick with surgical ability and neanderthal viciousness. He started playing in the old NHA and joined Toronto in 1917 when the NHL formed. He slammed Sprague Cleghorn into the boards, breaking his leg; he poked his blade in the mouth of then-rookie Hooley Smith to damaging dental effect; he knifed his blade across the forehead of a too-aggressive Buck Boucher; he took a high stick from Joe Hall, the baddest man of all, and responded with a more vicious whack of his own. In a land where survival of the fittest ruled hard and fast, Randall survived and was among the fittest. He played with Toronto for six seasons, winning Cups in 1918 and '22, and became the playing coach in Hamilton the year after. He later played for the Americans and closed his career in the minors before settling in Toronto. Most people believe Randall was born in Kingston, but he moved there at a young age because he couldn't get along with his stepdad. One of his brothers was a prizefighter, and the other was Doug Gilmour's grandfather. From Kingston, Ken moved with his sister to Lindsay, where she managed a pharmacy, and that's where he played his first serious hockey. By trade, he was a plumber and steam fitter.

Paul Ranheim

George Ranieri

Erik Rasmussen

RANFORD, Bill

b. Brandon, Manitoba, December 14, 1966

Edmonton was blessed with three great goalies in the 1980s, and each time the end of one segued beautifully into the start of the next. Andy Moog gave way to Grant Fuhr, and when GM Glen Sather knew Fuhr was the best he traded Moog to Boston for a young Bill Ranford. Over time, Ranford became number one, and Fuhr was traded to Toronto. And when the Oilers signed Curtis Joseph, Ranford was on his way to Boston. Ranford showed potential in Boston when he made his NHL debut in 1986, but it was in Edmonton that he became, for a short time, the best goalie in the world. He usurped Fuhr slowly through the '88-'89 season, took over the starter's job the next year, and got better and better as the season went along. Backed by Ranford, the team won its fifth Cup, in 1990, and he was named winner of the Conn Smythe Trophy for his

He backstopped Canada to victory at the 1991 Canada Cup.
BILL RANFORD

playoff perfection. A year later, he backstopped Canada to victory at the 1991 Canada Cup, and in 1994 he was again spectacular as Canada won gold at the World Championships for the first time since 1961. He was named best goalie in that tournament, but was never again the cut-and-dried number-one goalie. After he was traded back to Boston in 1996, he played for a series of teams and his career closed in 2000 with a whimper. He moved to New Westminster, B.C., and taught hockey to "at-risk" kids at an alternative school.

RANHEIM, Paul

b. St. Louis, Missouri, January 25, 1966

Ranheim turned natural skill into experience to stay in the NHL as long as he had. He came out of the University of Wisconsin in 1988 to play in the Calgary organization, and in his first six seasons he developed a reputation for a good wrist shot on offence and solid two-way play at the other end of the ice. But with each successive trade – to Hartford and then on to Philadelphia – his role became more and more defensive, more third or fourth line, more checker and penalty killer. He has adapted, changed his game, and endured. He has also played in three World Championships for the U.S..

RANIERI, George

b. Toronto, Ontario, January 14, 1936

Some things never change; others always do. Yesterday's problems are today's jokes, and Ranieri's predicament on February 10, 1957, was one example. He was playing in Victoria in the WHL, his first year of pro, when Boston told him to be in the lineup the next night. He was ecstatic, but it was a 19-hour journey from Victoria to Boston. He made it, but was exhausted. He played again the next night, and then had to make the 19-hour trip in reverse. It was worth it, though, because those were his only two NHL games. He spent the rest of his career in the minors, but the '58-'59 season stands out as a special one. He set the IHL single-season record by recording 124 points on the year with the Louisville Rebels, and then led his team to the Turner Cup in the playoffs.

RASMUSSEN, Erik

b. Minneapolis, Minnesota, March 28, 1977

In his two years at the University of Minnesota (1995-97), Rasmussen was touted as a player of the future, a kid who was going to go far, a big boy who would grow into a sizable star. In his two World Junior appearances with the U.S. he played well in the same way, like someone who was going to play so much better with time and experience and maturity. Well, those past predictions are now present pressures. Rasmussen has been with the Sabres since '97, and although he has become a full-time member of the Sabres, he hasn't shown much of that hope and promise. It might not be quite yet time to give up on him, but he certainly doesn't look like a superstar power forward ready and able to break out any time soon.

RATCHUK, Peter

b. Buffalo, New York, September 10, 1977

Despite being drafted by Colorado in 1996, the team that had just won the Stanley Cup, Ratchuk decided he didn't want to play with the Avs. He returned to Bowling Green and then played a year in the Quebec league, and when he left a free agent he signed with Florida. Since making his debut with the Panthers in '98-'99, he's had only two stints in the NHL and hasn't given the team enough reason to keep him around. It's been the minors ever since.

RATELLE, Jean

b. Lac Ste. Jean, Quebec, October 3, 1940

The lives, careers, and fortunes of Jean Ratelle and Rod Gilbert were intertwined for much of their hockey-playing days right from junior. Lac Ste. Jean is some 500 kilometres north of Montreal, but from an early age Ratelle demonstrated a superior ability to play the game. He went to Guelph to play in the OHA in 1958, yet it wasn't until six years later that he was a regular with the Rangers in the NHL. Ratelle became a top-scoring centre with the Biltmores playing alongside Gilbert and in '60-'61, his last year, he was given a three-game tryout by the Blueshirts. Using his great wrist shot and puckhandling skills, he had two goals and an assist in his brief look-see, but still the next four years were trying ones. In '63-'64, he required spinal fusion to mend a badly injured back (Gilbert also had to overcome a back injury early in his career), and the year after he re-injured it and spent much of the year playing below his abilities. Ratelle started the '65-'66 season on the third line, but Gilbert lobbied for the two to play together. He scored 21 goals, but again missed much of the next season with injury. The '67-'68 season was pivotal for Ratelle. He was healthy and playing on the GAG Line (goal-a-game line) with Gilbert and Vic Hadfield, and Ratelle had 3 successive seasons of 32 goals and at least 74 points. In '70-'71, he had an off year points-wise, but he won the Bill Masterton Trophy in honour of his dedication to the game. Ratelle was supremely gentlemanly and never got into a single fight in his career. He never swore and was a paradigm of hard work and determination. In '71-'72, he had his best year, even though he missed the end of the regular season and much of the playoffs with a broken ankle. He scored 46 times and compiled 109 total points. He won the Lester Pearson Award and the Lady Byng

He never swore and was a paradigm of hard work and determination.
JEAN RATELLE

Trophy, and his brilliant play earned him an invite to play for Team Canada at the '72 Summit Series. Ratelle played all eight games and happily resigned himself to a checking role with the team, though he did record two important assists in game eight. On November 7, 1975, he was involved in the biggest trade of the decade, going to Boston with Brad Park and Joe Zanussi for Phil Esposito and Carol Vadnais. In Boston, he continued to produce offensively, though in his 21 seasons of play he never won the Stanley Cup. He went to the finals with the Rangers in 1972, and with Boston in '77 and '78, usually playing on a line with Rick Middleton and Stan Jonathan. By the time he retired in 1981, Ratelle was just short of the magic 500-goal mark (finishing with 491) and had 1,267 points, sixth among the all-time leaders. He was inducted into the Hockey Hall of Fame and has been a longtime amateur scout for the Bruins. Tall, elegant, and a true leader, he was cut from the same cloth as Jean Béliveau and ranks among the greatest centres ever to play the game.

Peter Ratchuk

RATHJE, Mike

b. Mannville, Alberta, May 11, 1974

At 6'5" and 230 pounds, they don't make defencemen much bigger in the hockey factory where Rathje came from. He was drafted 3rd overall by San Jose in 1992, but trying to assess the value of a defensive defenceman is much harder than with a scorer or goalie. He has been paired much of his time with Marcus Ragnarsson, another big boy, and together they get the lion's share of the ice time for the Sharks. He won a gold medal with Canada at the 1993 World Juniors, but his playoff success in San Jose has been limited so far, despite the young, talented roster.

Mike Rathje

RATHWELL, John "Jack"/ "Jake"

b. Temiscamingue, Quebec, August 12, 1947

The name John is frequently supplanted by its owners in favour of the more refined-sounding Jack, but Jack does not normally become Jake without good reason. It changed in Rathwell's case because of circumstances that arose when he turned pro with the Clinton Comets in 1968. The captain was Jack Kane, so to avoid confusion the rookie had his name undergo phonic manipulation to come out Jake for the sake of clarity. In his first two seasons, the team won the Walker Cup. He was named rookie of the year in year one, and led the league with 56 goals in year two. He then moved around in various organizations, always in the minors, until Boston acquired his rights. Coach Don Cherry needed some help, and when he called down to Rochester, Rathwell was promoted. He played his one and only NHL game on January 27, 1975, a game noteworthy because three Temiscamingue-born

Joe Reekie

REEKIE, Joe
b. Victoria, British Columbia, February 22, 1965
It took Reekie a long time to establish himself in the league. He made his first NHL appearance with Buffalo midway through the '85-'86 season, but in each of his first seven seasons he spent time in the minors (excepting '87-'88 when he missed most of the year with a serious knee injury). Since 1992, though, he hasn't played a single minute outside the NHL and he has become a defensive defenceman of the most reliable order. Big and strong, of course, he did set a dubious personal record when he went 198 games without scoring a goal. He had his longest stay with Washington (8 years), and has quietly become an 18-year NHL man without so much as a peep. Reekie retired in January 2003 after 902 NHL games.

REESE, Jeff ("Reeser")
b. Brantford, Ontario, March 24, 1966
Yes, most records are meant to be broken, but some just happen, and once they've happened they seem impossible to break. On February 10, 1993, goalie Reese set a record in Calgary's 13-1 shellacking of San Jose: He recorded 3 assists. The chances of another puck stopper coming along and getting four assists surely makes winning the lottery look like a sure thing, but there it is. Reese had an unspectacular career besides, playing with 5 teams in his 174 games' worth of NHL play. He retired in 1999 after a short and poor second time round with Toronto, becoming Tampa Bay's goalie coach that fall. He has also scouted for the team.

REGAN, Bill
b. Creighton Mines, Ontario, December 11, 1908
d. unknown
As a teen, Regan was so big that opposing teams frequently questioned his age. By the time he got to the majors, when size didn't matter, he wasn't quite the gargantuan presence he had been. The Rangers were so enamoured of his play they sent Yip Foster and $15,000 to Boston to get him, in 1930, but within two years they had lost interest. He played with the Americans for a few games, ended his career in the minors, and then was out of the game for good.

Larry Regan

REGAN, Larry
b. North Bay, Ontario, August 9, 1930
At every stage of his life and career, Regan was a bit here, there, and everywhere. As a kid playing with the Marlies in the late 1940s, he also worked in the Leafs' publicity department. Subsequently, as a pro in Ottawa, he also worked selling real estate and building cottages in the summer. He didn't make his NHL debut until 1956, with Boston, and then he made such a great debut that at age 26 he won the Calder Trophy. Regan played just five full NHL seasons until 1961 when he accepted the role of playing coach for Toronto's farm team, in Pittsburgh. Not content to settle down, he moved to Austria to coach. He was so successful that he wanted to bring Gordie Howe and Terry Sawchuk and others overseas to run clinics, but the IIHF stood in his way and he returned to Canada. He played a final season in the AHL and then new L.A. owner Jack Kent Cooke hired Regan as Kings GM. It was a time of adjustment, and in October 1968

Earl Reibel

Regan punched referee Bruce Hood in the face after a game in which Regan, obviously, didn't like the officiating (he was fined $1,000 and Cooke, disgusted, sent him on a scouting trip to Czechoslovakia to cool his jets). Regan became the team's coach for a little more than a year and later became a special assignment scout for Vancouver. He then became managing director for the Canadian Oldtimers' Hockey Association.

REGEHR, Robyn
b. Recife, Brazil, April 19, 1980
It wasn't so much that he played for Canada at the 1999 and 2000 World Junior Championships that was amazing to Regehr. It was that, in the interim, he was not lying in a coffin six feet under. On July 4, 1999, he was driving with some friends on a stretch of highway when a car coming in the other direction drifted into Regehr's lane. The cars collided, and none of his friends were hurt, but he broke both his legs. Two of the four passengers in the other car were killed. His career in danger of being over before it began, Regehr amazed everyone when he was playing pro just four months later, first with Saint John in the AHL and then with Calgary in the NHL. The defenceman became the youngest Masterton nominee in 1999-2000 and has since been able to focus on his talents more than his health with an up-and-coming Flames team.

REGIER, Darcy
b. Swift Current, Saskatchewan, November 27, 1956
Yes, the Darcy Regier who is the GM of the Buffalo Sabres once played the game. It was a long time ago, and he's a better GM than player, but that's what experience is all about. He got his NHL games in with Cleveland (1977-78) and the Islanders (1982-84), but he also played eight years in the minors. Regier's most important time came in Indianapolis, where then-GM of the Checkers, Jim Devellano, taught him much of what he would later apply to his own job with the Sabres. After retiring in 1984, he stayed in the Islanders organization and worked for years in the administration of the team, moving from assistant coach to assistant GM to developing an amateur system. He later became Buffalo's GM at a time of flux, one that has only gotten worse. He's had to trade goalie star Dominik Hasek, deal with the arrest and indictment of team owner John Rigas, and live with an interim owner – the NHL itself – which meant restrictions on budget and personnel moves.

REIBEL, Earl "Dutch"
b. Kitchener, Ontario, July 21, 1930
Milt Schmidt is still kicking himself. There he was in Kitchener, his family living next door to the Reibel family, yet the teenage Earl was signed by Detroit and not Schmidt's Bruins. It was almost a moot point. In 1952, Reibel was thrown through the windshield in a bad car crash and was nearly blinded in his right eye when the optic nerve was damaged. He not only recovered, he led the WHL in scoring that same year and joined Detroit at camp in 1953. Reibel played on a line with Gordie Howe and Ted Lindsay, winning the Cup in both of his first two seasons. He led all Wings in points with 66 in '54-'55 as the team's

marquee playmaker between the two great stars, and the year after he won the Lady Byng Trophy for his sportsmanlike play. When he was traded to Chicago, though, in December 1957, his love and passion for the game dissipated. A final year with the Bruins gave way to two years in the AHL with Providence, and then Reibel retired in 1961 rather than move with the franchise to San Francisco. He returned to Kitchener where he worked for many years with Brewer's Retail.

REICHEL, Robert
b. Litvinov, Czechoslovakia (Czech Republic), June 25, 1971

It wasn't as important as Paul Henderson's goal in 1972, nor was it as great an upset as Team USA's Miracle on Ice. It wasn't as magical as Slovakia's 2002 WC win, either, but Reichel's penalty-shot goal off the post to beat Patrick Roy in the shootout in Nagano pushed the Czechs toward their first Olympic gold, the most important moment in that country's hockey history. It was fitting that Reichel scored that shootout-winning goal, because from his first WJC in 1988 he was for years the best prospect his country had ever known, better even than Jaromir Jagr. He played again in the 1989 and 1990 WJC, leading the tournament that third time with 21 points. He played in seven World Championships for his country (winning gold in 1996, 2000, and 2001), the 1991 Canada Cup, and the 1996 World Cup. He was an international star, but his pro career was more checkered, more controversial, and more of a disappointment. He joined Calgary in 1990 and in his third and fourth years scored 40 goals each. Soon, he was asking for a huge pay raise, and in disgust he fled to Germany to play a season. He returned to Calgary and later played for the Islanders and the Coyotes, where he was nowhere near the 40-goal mark. He left Phoenix in 1999 after scoring 26 goals and demanding $3 million a season, a figure too rich for the smart blood of the Coyotes. Reichel returned to the NHL for a third time in 2001 only when he was traded to Toronto and agreed to a new contract, but he promptly checked in with a 20-goal season, another in a series of disappointments.

REICHERT, Craig
b. Winnipeg, Manitoba, May 11, 1974

It's not over 'till it's over, of course, but Reichert isn't getting any younger and it looks as if the three games he played for Anaheim in February 1997 will go into the books as his only three NHL appearances. He has been a mainstay in the AHL, though, where the right

Craig Reichert

winger has been good for 20 goals a season, though he did play in Germany in 2000-01.

REID, Dave
b. Toronto, Ontario, January 11, 1934
d. 1978

Reid had only three quick stints in the NHL, all with his hometown Leafs. The first time, December 10, 1952, he was in the lineup because of injuries to Leafs stars Max Bentley and Rudy Migay. He was playing with the Marlies at the time. Ditto for his one game the next year. The year after, just as he seemed poised to make the team, he hurt his knee and played only four times before the end of the year. In his last two appearances, Reid was at the University of Toronto studying engineering. He never pursued a minor-league career and never made it in the NHL with the Leafs or anyone else, so he retired in 1957.

REID, Dave
b. Toronto, Ontario, May 15, 1964

Although Reid had size and speed, it seemed from day one he was destined to become a checking forward, a third-liner, a penalty killer, a banger and crasher. He started out with Boston in 1983, but the Bruins had him in the minors most of the time and five years later they bought him out. A free agent, he signed with his hometown Leafs and satisfied his passion for collecting cards by opening his own store, All-Pro Sports Collectibles. He played on a line with Lou Franceschetti and Dave Hannan, and the threesome became effective in its boring, checking style. Like all players of his type, they are needed by every team and discarded too easily. He moved back to Boston and then to Dallas, winning his first Cup with the Stars in 1998-99. The next year, he signed with Colorado, and in 2001 he won his second Cup before retiring. Amazingly, Reid played for 4 teams over 18 years and was never traded once. He became an on-air analyst with the NHL Network.

REID, Gerry
b. Owen Sound, Ontario, October 13, 1928

It wasn't the NHL, but it was a helluva way to start a career. Reid turned pro in 1948 with Indianapolis, farm team of Detroit, and in his first game he scored three goals. He played the year on a line with Fred Glover and Calum MacKay, scoring 31 goals. For the NHL playoffs, Red Wings GM called up Reid and Glover as insurance, and they got the call on two occasions. Unfortunately Detroit was swept aside by the Canadiens, and Reid never got another NHL chance. He returned to Owen Sound to play senior hockey and work in town.

Dave Reid

Gerry Reid

He was an international star, but his pro career was more checkered.
ROBERT REICHEL

Reg Reid

Tom Reid

Ed Reigle

Paul Reinhart

REID, Gord
b. Mount Albert, Ontario, February 19, 1912
d. unknown
In a career spent entirely in the American league, Reid had one night of NHL glory. On December 29, 1936, he joined the New York Americans in a bitter game against crosstown rivals the Rangers. In a fight-filled game, Reid incurred one third-period minor penalty, the only statistic he left behind before returning to the minors to play out his career.

REID, Reg ("Rusty")
b. Seaforth, Ontario, February 17, 1899
d. St. Thomas, Ontario, January 14, 1986
Reid played all of his pre-NHL hockey in Seaforth before signing with the Toronto St. Pats in 1924. He played a year and a half with the team before closing out his career in the minors. He finished his career in Stratford, and settled there to work as a salesman. In his later years he lived in a nursing home in St. Thomas to be near his daughter, and it was there he passed away.

REID, Tom
b. Fort Erie, Ontario, June 24, 1946
Imagine developing a rash on your body so severe that to have your skin touch any material is painful. Imagine having to sleep in a straight-back wood chair because bedsheets would tear the skin off your body. Imagine putting on something as ordinary as hockey equipment and feeling such itching, burning pain that you had to take it off and never, ever put it back on. That is how Tom Reid's career ended. In the fall of 1974, he was attending his eighth training camp in the NHL, playing now for Minnesota after starting his career in Chicago. He was a rock-solid defenceman, but that year he got a small rash on his arm. It got worse and worse. The trainers looked into the chemicals in the equipment, what the sweaters and socks were made of. The sweating made the rash act up, the friction between equipment and skin became painful. Everyone started calling it the Gunk. Reid changed his clothes between periods. He covered his body in special ointments before each game. There were times it got so bad he had to spend two weeks in hospital swathed in a solution day and night. Nothing, absolutely nothing could be found to root out the problem or to cure it. Crazy as it sounds, he had to retire, in 1978, and from that moment he never had another rash. He stayed in Minnesota and worked as a colour analyst for North Stars home games and Gophers college hockey, and as a sales manager for a printing company.

REIERSON, Dave
b. Bashaw, Alberta, August 30, 1964
Most people have tasted a little slice of Bashaw without necessarily knowing it, for that tiny prairie community is the cheese capital of western Canada. It was there that Reierson first skated on the new rink, built in 1974, and developed into a fine young player of national quality. He was drafted by Calgary in 1982, but didn't play his first NHL game until February 18, 1989. In the interim, he played for Michigan Tech and Canada's National Team, and also in the minors to give his career a pro start. His only other NHL games came four nights later, and then Reierson spent the next decade playing in Europe, retiring in 1999.

REIGLE, Ed
b. Winnipeg, Manitoba, June 19, 1924
It's often the players with the harmless-looking NHL stats who have done the most for the game as a whole. Reigle's NHL claim to fame is a 17-game stint with Boston in 1950-51, a stay surrounded by 12 years in the minors. He was known for his great shot, and many of the defencemen's shots resulted in goals. Reigle closed out his playing days by doubling as coach for the North Bay Trappers, and then in 1957 he accepted the position of coach for the Swedish National Team. From there he carried on to Switzerland to coach league teams and then led the West German National Team into the 1968 Olympics in Grenoble. A year later, he returned home to coach the Oshawa Generals and then scouted for the California Golden Seals. Reigle's last stop was with the Canadian Major Hockey League operating out of Toronto.

REINHART, Paul
b. Kitchener, Ontario, January 6, 1960
In a way, it was brutally unfair; in another way, it showed how hockey works. Reinhart was traded from Calgary to Vancouver on September 6, 1988. He had been with the Flames organization for nine years, since the team's last year in Atlanta. He was drafted as a defenceman but was so offensively gifted that he played forward sometimes. From the blueline, he scored, passed, orchestrated rushes, and quarterbacked the power play. He could do it all. Then, one day, he couldn't do anything. He turned back one way while looking the other, and something in his back gave. Just like that, he was in pain and couldn't do anything. He missed most of '83-'84 with what doctors called a herniated disc, and the '87-'88 season was also shot because of pain. A new treatment worked – doctors injected papaya juice into the affected area of his back. The trade, though, was difficult. He played effectively with the Canucks for two years, but the Flames won the Cup – with a team he had helped build – the same season he was sent west. After retiring, Reinhart became part of an investment group that produced, among other things, hyperbaric chambers for athletes to help them recover more speedily from injury. He later became part owner of the Vancouver Ravens of the National Lacrosse League.

REINIKKA, Oliver "Ollie"
b. Shuswap, British Columbia, August 2, 1901
d. 1962
Born to Finnish immigrants, Reinikka played kid hockey in Alberta before joining Vancouver in the Pacific Coast league in 1924. His only NHL time came with the Rangers in 1926-27 thanks to the Patrick connection between the PCHL (which Frank Patrick had run) and the Blueshirts (run by brother Lester). He spent the rest of his career in the minors, out west most of the time.

REINPRECHT, Steve
b. Edmonton, Alberta, May 7, 1976

Although Reinprecht played a single game for L.A. during the 1999-2000 season, it was during the next year that he came into his own and realized a dream. He started that season with the Kings, but moved on to Colorado with Rob Blake and won a Cup with the Avs. He took the Cup home to Edmonton in the summer and posed with it beside the great Wayne Gretzky sculpture outside the arena. In 2001-02, Reinprecht followed up with an even better season, and he is going to be counted on to bridge the transition from the older generation of players who won with the Avs in 1996 and the newer players who will be expected to continue winning.

REIRDEN, Todd ("Reirds")
b. Arlington Heights, Illinois, June 25, 1971

He paid his dues, all right, and he doesn't even have to thank expansion for his big break. Patience, hope, tenacity – those were the qualities he showed during his years in the minors when no one expressed an interest in him. New Jersey drafted him in 1990, but by the time he signed as a free agent with Edmonton eight years later, the Devils contract was dusty and unused. Reirden played at Bowling Green and for four years played so far down in the minors that the AHL looked like a gold mine by comparison. Eventually, the Oilers played him, and he moved on to St. Louis and Atlanta, a defenceman who does yeoman's work in his own end without worrying about offence.

REISE, Leo
b. Pembroke, Ontario, June 1, 1892
d. Brantford, Ontario, July 8, 1975

While playing hockey as a young lad in Pembroke, Reise lost the use of an eye and was more or less told to give up the game. He refused and instead ventured to Hamilton to play junior and then senior hockey, winning the Allan Cup with the Tigers in 1919. That team was allowed to turn pro and join the NHL for the following campaign, and Reise stayed with it to test his fortunes in the league. In his second season, he tied Punch Broadbent for the league lead in assists with 14. He played out west for three years before returning to the Americans, the team that had replaced the Tigers. He was 39 years old when he quit playing. He coached in Grimsby and Chatham but settled in Brantford, raising a son, Leo, who also went into the NHL. They were the first father-son combination in NHL history.

He spent six profitable years with the Wings, winning the Cup in 1950 and '52.
LEO REISE, JR.

REISE, Leo, Jr. ("Radar")
b. Stoney Creek, Ontario, June 7, 1922

Leo junior didn't have the same confidence as his father. In the years leading up to the war, he thought about a pro career but instead enrolled at Hamilton College and studied for two years to become a chartered accountant. He enlisted in the army and played some serious hockey with a number of teams across the country, including one outfit that boasted Charlie Rayner as a goalie. Reise had developed to the point that Rayner insisted he try out for the NHL after the war, and buoyed by this show of confidence, Reise tried out for Chicago in 1945. He played a few games for the Hawks over the next two seasons, but his career took off when he was traded to Detroit. He spent six profitable years with the Wings, winning the Cup in 1950 and '52. In that first playoffs, he scored two overtime goals in the semifinals victory over Toronto. Reise closed out his career with the Rangers, but throughout his playing days he was an astute businessman as well. When he retired, he was ready for the next stage of his life. He finished a degree in science at McMaster University, became a chartered accountant, and started working in the steel business with Trevor Steel Company in Brantford. He later settled in Hamilton, where he owned a plumbing business and operated a fruit farm.

RENAUD, Mark
b. Windsor, Ontario, February 21, 1959

Not a particularly big defenceman, Renaud dreamed of playing hockey for as long as he remembered. He played junior in Niagara Falls and was drafted by Hartford in 1979, and for six years he played a bit in the NHL and more in the minors. Nevertheless, he made it, even if he was a -42 in '82-'83, his only full NHL season. He ended his career in 1985 in the Buffalo system and returned to Windsor, where he coached minor hockey and wrote articles for www.ska8ters.com.

RENBERG, Mikael
b. Pitea, Sweden, May 5, 1972

Before making his NHL debut with Philadelphia in 1993, Renberg played in Lulea for three seasons and developed into a formidable player. By the time he got to the Flyers, he was ready for NHL action, and he didn't disappoint. He scored 38 goals as a rookie, losing the Calder Trophy to Martin Brodeur, but played on a line with Eric Lindros and John LeClair. A modern line of go to the net, dig the puck out, and cycle the opposition into dizziness, this threesome came to be called the Legion of Doom Line and it took the Flyers to the Cup finals in 1997, where they lost to Detroit. Renberg was then traded to Tampa,

Steve Reinprecht

Todd Reirden

Leo Reise

Mark Renaud

Mikael Renberg

then back to the Flyers, and then to Phoenix, but in the summer of 2000 he shocked the Coyotes by returning home to continue his career. In the middle of a divorce, he wanted to live with his daughter rather than make more millions in the NHL. A year later, though, his private life sorted out, he agreed to return to North America, with Toronto, the team that had acquired his rights. Playing on the number-one line much of the season, he scored just 14 goals. He also played for Tre Kronor at the 2002 Olympics in Salt Lake City (he had played in 1998 as well), and his international portfolio features two medals, a gold from the 1998 Worlds and a silver from the '93 WC.

RESCH, Glenn "Chico"
b. Moose Jaw, Saskatchewan, July 10, 1948

After earning a degree in education from the University of Minnesota-Duluth in 1971, Resch soon started his career with the Islanders. He rose quickly to become the number-one goalie, having his first great season in '74-'75 in which he became the starter for the playoffs. In the post-season, the small, quirky goalie became famous for kissing his goalposts, and the year after he was the undisputed main man in goal. His rise and decline met head-on in '79-'80, the first of four Stanley Cups the team would win. He was still number one, but in the playoffs Billy Smith stole the spotlight and made Resch's presence redundant. He was shipped off to Colorado the next year, a pernicious fate for a Cup winner. So bad was the team that he won the Masterton Trophy in '81-'82 simply for his dedication to the game by standing in the Rockies crease night after night. He stayed with the team as it went on to New Jersey and after six seasons he finished his career with the Flyers as backup to Ron Hextall. Not a big man, he relied on his reflexes for his success. He played in three All-Star Games and because of his dual citizenship played for the U.S. in the 1982 World Championships and the 1984 Canada Cup and for Canada as a spare goalie at the earlier Canada Cup in 1976. After retiring, the chatty and personable goalie moved easily into a career in broadcasting. He also spent more time working on his collection of goalie memorabilia and became active with the Tri-City Americans of the WHL, working variously as scout, coach, and GM for the junior team.

REYNOLDS, Bobby
b. Flint, Michigan, July 14, 1967

The Leafs took a chance on Reynolds, drafting him out of high school while he was still a kid. They hoped he would grow, fill out, develop physically. He didn't. They hoped he would mature as a player. He didn't, at least not to their liking. The Leafs gave him seven games in '89-'90, his first season of pro after graduating from Michigan State. He stayed in the minors for a few years and then went to Europe to play, settling for the most part in Germany. Reynolds returned to the minors in 1999 and most recently has been playing for his hometown Flint Generals in the UHL.

RHEAUME, Herb
b. Mason, Quebec, January 12, 1899
d. Vancouver, British Columbia, January 1, 1953

Tragedy helped Rheaume get into the NHL, but his brief stay was not the stuff of legend fans in Montreal had hoped for. Rheaume played for the Habs in 1925-26, signing with the team after the sudden death of Georges Vezina. Rheaume played the rest of the year but the Habs didn't make the playoffs and at season's end he returned to minor pro. He ended up playing out west, and settled there after retiring.

RHEAUME, Pascal
b. Quebec City, Quebec, June 21, 1973

There is only one man in the world who can make this most extraordinary claim, but Pascal Rheaume made his NHL debut *after his sister!* Manon Rheaume played in an exhibition game for Tampa Bay on September 23, 1992, and Pascal, who was never drafted, didn't turn pro until the following year when New Jersey signed him. He played with Albany for three years until the Devils called him up on February 20, 1997, and he has worked his way into the league ever since with St. Louis, Chicago, and Atlanta.

RHODES, Damian ("Dusty")
b. St. Paul, Minnesota, May 28, 1969

During his college career at Michigan Tech, Rhodes was best known for scoring a goal for the Huskies on January 21, 1989. Drafted by Toronto, he made his Leafs debut a year later and worked his way into the organization by becoming Felix Potvin's backup. Rhodes developed into a number-one goalie while playing second fiddle, so when the Leafs sent him to Ottawa he had his chance to shine. He led Ottawa into the playoffs but couldn't take the team far, and the Sens exposed him in the 1999 Expansion Draft. As a result, Rhodes became the first member of the Atlanta Thrashers, and tended goal for that lowly team until 2002. He maintained a respectable goals-against average and, best of all, he gave the new club a chance to win every night.

After retiring, the chatty and personable goalie moved easily into a career in broadcasting.
GLENN RESCH

Pascal Rheaume

Damian Rhodes

RIBBLE, Pat
b. Leamington, Ontario, April 26, 1954

A large and reliable defenceman, Ribble started his career with Atlanta and finished it with the Flames in Calgary eight years later. In between, he shifted from team to team, trying to find his niche, his city of comfort, without total success. His time in Chicago was shortened by injury. In Toronto, the team was at its Imlachian nadir, and in Washington the team was just plain awful. Ribble closed out his career in the minors and then returned to Leamington where he worked for a natural gas company. He also played alumni hockey with Detroit.

RIBEIRO, Mike
b. Montreal, Quebec, February 10, 1980

In his final year of junior in the Q, Ribeiro led the league in goals, assists, and points. That and a dime would get him a cup of coffee – in the NHL. He made his debut, with Montreal, the following year but since then has been a part-timer with the club. The goals that flew off his stick in junior have evidently been caught in the blade in his NHL time so far, but he's still very much a work in progress.

RICCI, Mike
b. Scarborough, Ontario, October 27, 1971

Look at Ricci at the end of a shift, wet hair shooting out from underneath his helmet, teeth missing, face maniacal from effort. Then take a look at Hannibal Lecter. It's a toss-up who looks more intimidating. Ricci is the wild man of hockey, not a big man but a centre who plays every shift as if his life depends on it. He captained Peterborough in junior, and captained Canada to gold at the 1990 World Juniors. Philadelphia drafted him 4th overall that summer, and since then he's taken his Sutter-like intensity to a new level. The Flyers included him in their massive package to Quebec to acquire Eric Lindros, and Ricci won the Cup with that franchise in 1996 in Colorado. He was later traded to San Jose, and there he has been a leader on one of the most talented young teams in the league. If the Sharks go deep into the playoffs any time soon, it will be largely due to the contributions of Ricci, a goal scorer, a checker, a born leader.

RICCI, Nick ("Tricky Nicky")
b. Niagara Falls, Ontario, June 3, 1959

Who would have thought that a part-time goalie a generation ago would become a millionaire in the hotel industry in his honeymoon hometown and parlay that into the purchase of the hapless Mississauga Ice Dogs? Life is never a straight line. Ricci was a goalie who played 19 games with

Pittsburgh over 4 years (1979-83). He retired in 1984 when it became clear he wasn't going to be a star, and he returned home to go into business. He made his fortune, but over time he dreamed of bringing junior hockey back to the Falls. In 2002, he abandoned that dream in favour of buying the Ice Dogs from Don Cherry et al. and moving to Mississauga, though many fear he will, indeed, move the team "home" one day.

RICE, Steven
b. Kitchener, Ontario, May 26, 1971

As a junior, Rice won consecutive gold medals with Canada's National Team at the 1990 and '91 tournaments, captaining the latter victory. He joined the Rangers at the start of the '90-'91 season but was traded to Edmonton a year later in the deal that sent Mark Messier to Broadway. Rice played the last five years of his career in the Hartford/ Carolina organization. He retired in 1998 following a swift decline in play. In that final season, he scored just twice in 47 games and was a healthy scratch 29 times. The Hurricanes bought him out and he agreed it was time to move on. That fall, he attended Leafs training camp, but Toronto released him and Rice retired. He returned to Kitchener and set up his own business, Steve Rice Sports, which specializes in clothing. He also runs the Steve Rice Hockey Academy out of Waterloo and has coached the Kitchener Dutchmen.

Henri played more years, won more Cups, and had more points, yet was never considered the player Maurice was.
HENRI RICHARD

RICHARD, Henri ("The Pocket Rocket")
b. Montreal, Quebec, February 29, 1936

What an odd coincidence that a man who got to celebrate his birthday only every four years was also one who got to celebrate Stanley Cup victory every other year he played! For, in his 20 NHL seasons, Richard won 11 Cups, more than any other player in the history of Lord Stanley's prized bowl. His career also held a paradoxical relationship to his brother's. Henri played more years, won more Cups, and had more points, yet was never considered the player Maurice was. He was smaller (5'7" and 160 pounds) and less explosive, and he didn't score the number of goals in the exhilarating way that Maurice did. Nonetheless, when he was inducted into the Hockey Hall of Fame in 1979, it was an honour worthy of his career. He was brother to Maurice in some ways, but not in others. The two didn't play hockey in the basement or on the street together. They didn't lie awake at night in the same small bedroom and talk about NHL dreams. No, by the time Henri was playing a little hockey and learning to handle a puck, Maurice, 15 years older, was already a superstar in the NHL. Henri learned from his brother not as equals, but while watching Maurice from the stands at the Forum. Henri developed into a superb

Pat Ribble

Mike Ribeiro

Mike Ricci

Nick Ricci

Steven Rice

Henri Richard

Henri Richard

player, though, playing two years for the Jr. Canadiens (1953-55) and leading the league in scoring both years. He joined the NHL in 1955, and the brothers made a remarkable record. They played together only five years before Maurice retired, but the Habs won the Cup each and every year! Early on, there was a truly fraternal element to their play. Players went after Henri because he was smaller, and taunted him for being Maurice's brother. Maurice defended him, but Henri also made a point of standing up for himself to show Maurice and the rest of the team and league that he needed help from no man to survive in the NHL. While Maurice always had many more goals than assists, Henri was the opposite. He had nine 20-goal seasons, but led the league in assists twice ('57-'58 and '62-'63) and always had more assists than goals by season's end. He was a playmaker to Maurice's finisher, a quick and shifty centre to Maurice's driving right winger style. Henri won five Cups with Maurice (1956-60), and then in the 1960s was part of the quiet dynasty that won another four championships during a decade dominated more by the Leafs four victories. The pinnacle of his career came in 1966 when he scored the Cup-winning goal in overtime, a controversial goal to beat Detroit. He took a shot on goalie Roger Crozier, but as he did so fell forward and crashed into the goalie, pushing himself and Crozier into the goal. The referee awarded the goal, and the Wings were furious. The 1971 playoffs were less contentious. Against Chicago, Richard again scored the Cup winner, and that summer was named captain of the team, replacing the retiring Jean Béliveau. When he won the Cup in 1973, it marked his eleventh championship as a player, an all-time NHL record. Richard retired after the '74-'75 season, one in which he was slowed by injury. Amazingly, the only individual award he ever won was the Masterton in '73-'74, and he was a First Team All-Star only once ('57-'58). He was spectacularly consistent throughout his career, never the best centre in the league but always in the top tier. He was a leader and a constant source of inspiration and he retired with 1,046 points. During his playing days he operated a tavern in the city, and he easily fell into this job full-time after he hung up the blades. He also worked for Carling O'Keefe brewery in promotions and made numerous appearances in Montreal, his lifelong home.

RICHARD, Jacques
b. Quebec City, Quebec, October 7, 1952
d. Issoudun, Quebec, October 8, 2002
The highs and lows of hockey are apt metaphor for the highs and lows of life, and both on and off the ice Richard's experiences ran the gamut. He played junior with the Quebec Remparts with Guy Lafleur, and

scouts who drooled over the talented Flower also predicted that Richard might eventually be the better player. In 1971, the team won the Memorial Cup, and the year after Richard led the league with 71 goals and 160 points. He was now being hailed as the next Richard, as in Maurice or Henri. Of course, no one could enter the NHL with this advanced billing and live up to those expectations. He played well in Atlanta, but away from the rink he drank, gambled, and became enamoured of white powder. He was traded to Buffalo, where he sank into a deeper abyss and was arrested for drunk driving. The Sabres sent him to Quebec, and Richard figured this was it – if he couldn't shine in his hometown, where he had such great junior moments, he was done. Well, for one season he did shine. In 1980-81, he scored 52 goals and 103 points, superstar numbers that proved his skill. The next year? Fifteen goals. He never tried to improve his off-ice habits, and by 1983 he was in the minors and then retired. His dependency on drugs grew, and of all the things he could have done, he decided to open a bar. He lost $150,000 in a year just from playing cards and, broke, he did something even the most desperate addict would call folly. He flew to Columbia, filled his golf bag with cocaine, and came home. Of course, authorities caught him – 2.8 kilos with a street value of $1.8-million – and he was sentenced to seven years in prison. He served only 14 months before being released to a halfway house where he tried to get his life in order. Once out, he settled in Montreal and spoke at schools, looking for work, hoping for a helping hand. Fifty goals in an NHL season never seemed so far away – at least on the outside. The day after he celebrated his 50th birthday, he crashed his car into a culvert and died. Police discovered five grams of cocaine in the car.

The day after he celebrated his 50th birthday, he crashed his car into a culvert and died.
JACQUES RICHARD

RICHARD, Jean-Marc
b. St. Raymond, Quebec, October 8, 1966
A small defenceman out of junior in Chicoutimi, Richard played just a few games with the Nordiques in '87-'88 and '89-'90 before being relegated to a life outside the NHL. Nonetheless, he was named the IHL's best defenceman in '91-'92, but after 10 years in the minors he moved to Europe to play, first in Germany and then more recently with the Vipiteno Broncos in Italy.

RICHARD, Maurice ("The Rocket")
b. Montreal, Quebec, August 4, 1921
d. Montreal, Quebec, May 27, 2000
Certain players conjure certain images. Gordie Howe – a rock. Bobby Orr – a plane. Wayne Gretzky – a magician with a stick for a wand. Maurice Richard –

fire. He was the first-born of eight children, and his father brought the family from Gaspé to Montreal so he could work for the CPR. In his youth, Maurice was a good baseball player and boxer, but hockey was his passion. He once played for two teams, assuming the pseudonym Maurice Rochon so he wouldn't be forced to quit one. He played senior hockey with the Canadiens and then in the NHL starting in 1942, but his early years were anything but portentous. He broke an arm one year and a leg the next, and everyone wondered whether the talented Richard might, after all, be too fragile for the rigours of professional hockey. In 1943, he was healthy and strong. Playing on a line with Elmer Lach and Toe Blake, the Punch Line took the Habs to the Stanley Cup. The next year, Richard took his achievements to another level by scoring 50 goals in 50 games. Granted, this was '44-'45, a war year when the NHL was littered with less than top goalies, but Richard hit a magic number that stands today as the pinnacle for any player's season. In fact, he never scored 50 again. Nevertheless, he became a hero of untold scale to Quebecers. By 1945, the Canadiens had many great French players and heroes, but Richard touched the people in a special way. He came from a big and not wealthy family. He did not have the skill of Lalonde or the speed of Morenz or the style of many other legends. What he had was that fire, a determination that fans, coaches, opponents, and everyone who saw him play swore was visible in his eyes. When he hit the blueline, he was going to the net regardless of what stood in his way. He would club the puck into the goal if that's what it took. He would fight for position, fight to defend himself, do whatever it took to score. He was no passer, no finesse player, no dainty deker. He was a goal scorer. He led the league in goals five times and won eight Stanley Cups. Midway through his career, on November 8, 1952, he scored his 325th goal to pass Nels Stewart as the league's all-time leading scorer, and that puck was sent to Queen Elizabeth! In his 18 seasons, all with Montreal, he missed the playoffs just twice, and if he had fire in his eyes in the regular season he had a veritable inferno during the playoffs. On March 23, 1944, he scored all five goals in a 5-1 semifinals win against Toronto and was named all three stars by the Forum announcer. In 1951, he tied Mel Hill's record with three overtime goals in one year, and his six career OT goals remains a record to this day. In 1952, against Boston, he was knocked unconscious during the game, only to return to score the winning goal in overtime. Roger St. Jean's photo of a bloodied Richard shaking hands with tiny Sugar Jim Henry, the Boston

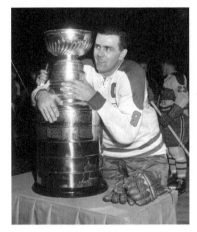

He was no passer, no finesse player, no dainty deker. He was a goal scorer.
MAURICE RICHARD

goalie with head bowed in near-humility, is one of the most revealing and important hockey images ever made. But without doubt, the defining event of Richard's life, let alone career, came in March 1955. He had never won a scoring championship but was on the way to doing just that. On March 13, in Boston, he and Hal Laycoe became involved in a fight that saw Richard hack viciously at Laycoe's head with his stick. Referee Cliff Thompson intervened, and Richard responded by hitting the referee. Two days later, NHL president Clarence Campbell suspended Richard for the final three games of the regular season and all of the playoffs. It was a fair but stunning punishment that left the entire province of Quebec apoplectic. Campbell attended the Detroit-Montreal game on March 17, and soon after the game began a riot erupted. Campbell was pelted with tomatoes, but soon homemade tear gas and explosives were thrown toward him. He left the building, but the Forum turned into an ugly mob scene that quickly spilled into the surrounding streets. Stores were looted, fires set, cars vandalized; the city looked lost in a civil war. To the casual fan, this was a ridiculous response to a suspension. To Richard and his supporters, it was an act of malice by an English-Montrealer (Campbell) against a French-Montrealer (Richard). In no other city and for no other player would such a reaction have occurred. Richard had to go on radio to appeal to the people to stop the violence, but in hockey terms the damage had been done. Bernie Geoffrion passed Richard to win the scoring title (fans booed his every point), and Montreal did not win the Cup. The event had galvanized the city, and Richard never forgave Campbell for the suspension. The Habs then reeled off five successive Cup wins after this, the last coming in Richard's final season, '59-'60. Just as satisfying was that all these Cup wins came while he played with his younger brother, Henri. On October 19, 1957, Richard became the first player to score 500 goals, and on April 12, 1960, he scored his final playoff goal, scooping the puck up as soon as it went in, knowing the end was nigh. He finished with 544 career goals, and a year later was inducted into the Hockey Hall of Fame, the 5-year waiting period waived for so obvious a choice. After such a life on ice, it was all but impossible to live a satisfying life off it. He made umpteen special appearances, of course, and did promotional work for Molson Brewery. He always wanted to work with the Habs in a serious way – managing or the like – but was only ever given superficial tasks such as representing the team corporately. He coached the Quebec Nordiques for a brief and unsuccessful period, and made many

Maurice Richard

Maurice Richard

Todd Richards

Travis Richards

Dave Richardson

Glen Richardson

Luke Richardson

commercials and endorsed many products, but the truth was the present Richard could never outstrip the past legend. When the Forum closed, he was given the longest ovation of the night. In 1998, the NHL inaugurated the Rocket Richard Trophy for the player who scored the most goals each year. When his family later tried to sell off his possessions, the provincial government stepped in and declared certain ones to be national treasures. They were purchased by the government and will be housed in the Canadian Museum of Civilization in Hull, Quebec in February 2004. Whenever the club looked back, Richard was front and centre, fans admiring him even if they never saw him play. When he died in the summer of 2000, his body lay in state at the Molson Centre in a tribute similar to that given by the team for Howie Morenz in 1937. He died a great hockey player, but to the people of Quebec he was a cultural hero, an icon who represented the best of French culture, a man who earned everything on his own and who, like the song says, did things his way.

RICHARD, Mike
b. Scarborough, Ontario, July 9, 1966
Although he was born in Toronto and played junior there with the Marlies, Richard grew up in Moncton. He was a scoring whiz in the OHL, and when Washington signed him as a free agent, it felt the team had a late-blooming NHL-calibre centreman. His first full pro season was '87-'88 when he played for Baltimore in the AHL. He went on a league-record streak, scoring points in 31 straight games and winning rookie of the year. On that note, the Caps called him up to the big time, and his debut came at home, in Maple Leaf Gardens. He was sent down after four games and looked to be a player still, but he wasn't recalled for another two years. Those were his last NHL games, and since then he has played in Europe continuously, almost exclusively in Switzerland.

RICHARDS, Brad
b. Montague, Prince Edward Island, May 2, 1980
Tampa Bay expects big things from its 1998 draft. He proved he could score in the minors in goal-crazy Quebec, but can he do same at the elite level? So far, the answer is yes. In his rookie season, he led all first-year players in goals (21) and points (62), and in his second year he had the same number of points. Tenacious and durable, he is one of the key players if Tampa is ever going to make the playoffs. He also played twice for Canada's juniors, in 2000 and 2001.

RICHARDS, Todd
b. Robindale, Minnesota, October 20, 1966
It was a small incident, but whether it triggered his trade from Montreal to Hartford only those who made the deal know. In the fall of 1990, the Canadiens went on a mini-tour of Europe during camp, and they brought the young Richards along for a look. But during a practice in Stockholm, he suffered a tachycardia attack (an unusually high heart rate) and the team doctor had to treat him on the spot. Soon after, Richards was traded to the Whalers but played only eight games over two seasons. He spent 11 years in the minors, mostly with Orlando in the IHL, but

when that league folded, he moved to Switzerland to play. That odd heart attack never affected his play at any time in the future, but it certainly didn't seem to help his cause with the Habs all those years ago.

RICHARDS, Travis
b. Crystal, Minnesota, March 22, 1970
They call him Mr. Griffin because since the franchise was born in 1996 he has played in more regular-season games than any other player and in all the team's playoff games. Grand Rapids was in the IHL and transferred to the AHL in 2001, and although it's a ways away from the NHL, Richards has still made his mark. He studied child psychology at the University of Minnesota, his first year '89-'90 coming right after his brother, Todd, had played his last year. Travis spent most of '93-'94 with the U.S. National Team, including the 1994 Olympics in Albertville, and he played his only NHL games, three in all, with Dallas a short time later.

RICHARDSON, Dave
b. St. Boniface, Manitoba, December 11, 1940
Richardson grew up playing in the Rangers system, so it was natural that the team would give him his first NHL chance, which it did in 1963. He had long ago established a reputation as a hustler and disturber, and he had that exact effect on NHL opponents when he came up. His play over and above that was thought to be wanting, though, and he remained a bit player with 3 teams to the tune of just 45 games. He played most of his games in the minors and in the '65 playoffs with Baltimore he came close to losing an eye when he was struck by a puck in practice. He returned the next year and played into the early 1970s.

RICHARDSON, Glen
b. Barrie, Ontario, September 20, 1955
He played junior in Ontario and made it to Vancouver in the 1975-76 season, but Richardson spent most of his three years in pro in the minors with Tulsa in the Central league.

RICHARDSON, Ken
b. North Bay, Ontario, April 12, 1951
One of the few Canadian university students to make it to the NHL, Richardson's road to the big time was hardly black top all the way. After leaving Laurentian in 1973, he signed to play in the IHL and it was there that St. Louis became interested in the forward. Over the next few years, he played some 49 games with the Blues but mostly he was a minor-leaguer.

RICHARDSON, Luke
b. Ottawa, Ontario, March 26, 1969
If anyone watching rookie Richardson play for the Leafs in 1987 had suggested that the young, big defenceman would play in the NHL for 15 years and 1,100 games, said person would have been carted off to a padded institution with the greatest of rapidity. Although he was tough and worked hard, he made error after error for a not very good team. Edmonton turned him into a solid defenceman, and in Philadelphia he positively shone. Imagine the irony

when in the summer of 2000 he became a free agent. Not only did Toronto seek his services, it was prepared to offer him $2 million a year! As it was, he re-signed with the Flyers, and although his has not been a spectacular career, Richardson has made himself at home in the NHL with his physical play and his play inside his own blueline.

RICHARDSON, Terry
b. Powell River, British Columbia, May 7, 1953
Sadly, Richardson has been pegged as one of the worst draft choices ever made, by Detroit in 1973, because he was selected 11th overall and played only 20 NHL games. The goalie started with the Wings in 1973-74, but in just over five games he allowed a whopping 28 goals. The next year, in just over 3 games he allowed 23 goals, and the year after he allowed 7 goals in his only start. The Wings eventually sent him to St. Louis, and in his last career game he allowed nine goals. His career record in the NHL was 3-11-0, yet in the minors he was just fine. He won trophies for allowing the fewest goals in both the IHL and the CHL and had a fine record and reputation – just not in the NHL.

RICHER, Bob
b. Cowansville, Quebec, March 5, 1951
Very few careers were as short and concise as Richer's. He turned pro in 1971 and was out of the game by '74, and in between his only NHL games came with Buffalo. Three of them, to be exact.

RICHER, Stephane
b. Hull, Quebec, April 28, 1966
There were two Stephane Richers whose careers overlapped for a few years, making things confusing except for the fact that one was a scorer and one was not, one was a forward and one was a defenceman, one was a career NHLer and one was not. This Stephane played only 27 games in the NHL despite having a career as long. He came out of the Q league undrafted and played in the minors for five years. Montreal, L.A., and Montreal again signed him during these years but never called him up. It wasn't until the expansion Tampa Bay Lightning started operations that he saw action in the big time, but soon he was traded to Boston and then on to Florida. In 1995, his NHL chances getting forever slimmer, Richer flew to Germany to continue his career, and from then until now he has been a mainstay in Mannheim.

RICHER, Stephane
b. Ripon, Quebec, June 7, 1966
As a teen, Richer had no confidence in his abilities. A police officer who doubled as a coach saw him play and invited him to try out for his Granby team. The cop was Pat Burns, future coach of the Habs. In his first and only full season with the Bisons, Richer was named rookie of the year and rose quickly in the ranks, making his NHL entrance the following year with the Canadiens. The year after, he scored 21 times as a rookie with the Habs, and the team won the Stanley Cup. Richer went on to record two 50-goal seasons with the team, but beneath the surface of success was a tempestuous dressing-room situation. Richer was not the most loved player. He didn't "give it his all" every night, and as a result found his way into the very crease of Burns' scowl. He was traded to New Jersey, where he won another Cup in 1995, but in succeeding years he never came close to those two great seasons. He wound up back in Montreal, then Tampa and St. Louis, and in the fall of 2000 he was at Washington's training camp. Fed up, he retired, but signed with Pittsburgh the year after. His scoring touch all but gone, the Pens used him as a penalty killer and he passed the 1,000-game mark. During his year off, he finally confronted a demon that explained his state of mind even as a teen when he didn't think he could make it. He suffered from chronic depression, and admitted that after winning the Cup in 1995 he cried all the way home from Jersey to Montreal. His suicidal thoughts led him to intensive therapy and helped him restart his career with the Pens.

He was traded to New Jersey, where he won another Cup in 1995.
STEPHANE RICHER (b. Ripon)

Terry Richardson

RICHMOND, Steve
b. Chicago, Illinois, December 11, 1959
There was no doubt in his mind what he wanted to do with his life. At 16, Richmond left Chicago and moved to Pickering, Ontario, to play junior B. His play over 2 seasons was so impressive he earned a scholarship to the University of Michigan, and once there he set several records for defencemen, notably 22 goals in a year. Despite fine years with the Wolverines, he wasn't drafted into the NHL but he did sign with the Rangers. He was assigned to the farm team in Tulsa, and the next year got into his first games, scoring a goal on a great slapshot in his debut. Over the next few years, though, he was consigned to the role of callup and part-timer, never playing a full season. He retired in 1990 as a minor-leaguer and returned to Chicago, where he coached all levels of kids hockey. He was named hockey director for the Glenview Stars and won the Illinois state championship three times. Richmond then scouted for the Hawks for five years, becoming responsible for all amateur hockey. In 2001, he was named GM and head coach of the UHL's Chicago Steel, and happy as he was to be a pro coach, he was even happier to have as one of his players a lad by the name of Danny Richmond, who more commonly answered to "son" when Steve spoke.

Steve Richmond

Dave Richter

Curt Ridley

Mike Ridley

RICHTER, Barry
b. Madison, Wisconsin, September 11, 1970

The pedigree is good. Barry's father, Pat, was an All-American wide receiver for Wisconsin when it went to the Rose Bowl, and was later drafted by the Washington Redskins. Barry went to the same school for hockey, and he, too, was a great prospect who didn't quite make it. Before he joined the Rangers in 1995-96, he built an extensive international portfolio, culminating in an appearance at the 1994 Olympics in Lillehammer. He played a few games with four different teams. In the minors, he was a star; in the NHL, he didn't have staying power. In 2001, he moved to Sweden and played for Linkopings, and was one of the league's top players. He played with league champions HC Lugano in Switzerland in 2002-03

RICHTER, Dave
b. St. Boniface, Manitoba, April 8, 1960

At the University of Michigan, Richter studied phys ed until leaving the program to turn pro with Minnesota in 1982. At 6'5" and 225 pounds, the defenceman was expected to play in his own end and do the dirty work when necessary. He survived nine NHL years doing as much for the four teams he represented, and wound up in the minors doing much the same thing. He scored all of 9 goals but accumulated 1,030 penalty minutes in just 365 career games.

RICHTER, Mike
b. Abington, Pennsylvania, September 22, 1966

Arguably the greatest American-born goalie ever to play hockey, Richter can retire whenever he wants with full knowledge that he has done almost everything possible for someone at his position. He joined the Rangers for the 1989 playoffs, but even before then was an accomplished puck stopper. He had played in two World Juniors and World Championships as well as the 1988 Olympics in Calgary, and when he got to New York he made an impact almost immediately. In fact, the ever-prescient *New Yorker* magazine ran a 12-page profile of him in its November 23, 1992 issue. Richter started as backup to John Vanbiesbrouck, and for a number of years the pair developed into the best tandem in the NHL. But it was clear that Richter was too good to be a backup, and he assumed the starter's role with natural ascension. His career peaked twice in the coming years, timing that will ensure his place in American hockey history long after he has made his last save. In 1993-94, he led the league with 42 wins and took the Rangers to the Stanley Cup. A year and a half later, he played as well as any goalie ever has by almost single-handedly defeating Canada at the 1996 World Cup. He was named MVP of the tournament, and at that moment, no goalie in the world could claim to be his equal. As the Rangers struggled in the next few years, so, too, did he. The team missed the playoffs for four successive years, and Richter did not play well at the 1998 Olympics in Nagano. He bounced back in 2001-02 with the Salt Lake City Olympics on the horizon, and led Team USA to the finals against Canada, where he had to settle for silver. Early in the 2002-03 season, he won his 300th game to move into the uppermost chamber of goalie greatness, and he seems destined to play his entire career with the Rangers.

The ever-prescient New Yorker magazine ran a 12-page profile of him in its November 23, 1992 issue.
MIKE RICHTER

RIDLEY, Curt
b. Minnedosa, Manitoba, September 24, 1951

Early on, and later, he couldn't buy good luck. Ridley started out in Boston, when the team had Gerry Cheevers and Eddie Johnston. That meant the minors. He went to the Rangers, but they had Ed Giacomin and Gilles Villemure. Atlanta? Dan Bouchard and Phil Myre. Finally, in Vancouver, there was an opening, and for two seasons he took it. The only problem was that the team was lousy, so when Glen Hanlon came in and performed miracles, that meant Ridley was sent to the minors. This time, though, he refused to go, and the Canucks traded him to Toronto, a team in a bad way that was using the unorthodox five-goalie system. Soon after getting his chance, Ridley broke his hand and went down to the minors. In 1983, he settled in Winnipeg and was the playing coach of the Morden Bombers of the Central Amateur Senior Hockey League. After retiring, he scouted briefly for the Leafs and ended up in Mesquite, Texas, as a sales rep for an engine re-manufacturing company.

RIDLEY, Mike
b. Winnipeg, Manitoba, July 8, 1963

No one expected Ridley to make the NHL ever, let alone as quickly as he did – and that includes Ridley himself. At 15, he broke his leg and didn't play hockey for a year. At 16, he was cut from the St. Boniface team. He decided to go to the University of Manitoba to earn a degree and play, but he was named Canadian university player of the year in 1984, which brought a bit of interest. In the fall of 1985 the Rangers invited him to their training camp. Sure, he thought, it will be a great experience, and then I'll be back at U of M. Wrong-o. He was outstanding at camp, made the team, and scored 22 goals as a rookie. After another half-season he was traded to Washington, and during his eight years with the Caps he developed into a bona fide player. He never scored fewer than 26 goals and peaked with 41 in 1988-89, the year he also played in the All-Star Game. Ridley was traded to Toronto, but after just one season was moved to Vancouver because coach Pat Burns thought him too soft. Ridley suffered a back injury and missed half a year, and after one more season he retired. Over that summer of 1997, though, he felt better and signed with his hometown Manitoba Moose. Four games later, he called it a career.

RIENDEAU, Vincent
b. St. Hyacinthe, Quebec, April 20, 1966
In early 1999, Riendeau became the first Canadian to go to Russia to play in that country's elite league. How he got there is a terpsichorean tale appropriate to the life of a goalie. Undrafted, he signed in 1985 with Montreal and a year later allowed fewer goals than any other stopper in the AHL. In his one and only game with the Habs, though, he allowed 5 goals in just 36 minutes and soon after was traded to St. Louis. The Blues loved him. They loved him so much they wanted to send his backup, Curtis Joseph, to New Jersey as compensation for signing Brendan Shanahan. Ironically, Scott Stevens wound up going, and Joseph wound up usurping Riendeau from the number-one role. From there Riendeau went to Detroit and Boston without making a great impression. Soon, he was in the minors with no NHL interest, so he played in Europe and finally accepted an offer from Togliatti becoming the first Canadian goalie to play in Russia. Even there, though, competition limited his game time, so he came home, settled in Toronto, and worked as a goalie coach in the Leafs system and for the North American Hockey Academy.

RIESEN, Michel
b. Oberbalm, Switzerland, April 11, 1979
It may be something of a baby step to the hockey world, but to Swiss hockey Riesen's presence in the NHL is monumental. He played with the Swiss junior team that won a historic bronze medal at the 1998 WJC, the first time the country had won a significant medal since its bronze at the 1953 World Championships. Riesen played 12 games with Edmonton in 2000-01, and was traded to St. Louis with Doug Weight in the summer of 2001. Riesen didn't play with the Blues that year – he returned home, instead – but even those dozen games for a Swiss player has enormous impact on the national program back home.

RIGGIN, Dennis
b. Kincardine, Ontario, April 11, 1936
Dennis and son, Pat, became the second-ever father-son goalie combination in NHL history (after the LoPrestis). Dennis was a career minor-leaguer, almost exclusively in the WHL, starting in 1955, but his career was cut short by two serious eye injuries. He made nine appearances with Detroit in both the '59-'60 and '62-'63 seasons, but was hit in each eye by a puck in separate incidents. The first injury forced him to hospital for 18 weeks, the second for 16 weeks, and in each case he suffered a detached retina. Not only did Pat go on to the NHL, but his daughter Colleen (named after Gordie Howe's wife) also played goal for her women's team. After retiring in 1963, Dennis worked for Molson Breweries for more than 25 years, eventually becoming the district sales manager for Ontario.

RIGGIN, Pat
b. Kincardine, Ontario, May 26, 1959
Son of Dennis, Pat had a career that bounced quickly between great and poor, stable and unstable, minors and NHL. One minute it looked as if he couldn't stop a beach ball; the next he was putting together a 200-minute shutout streak. He started with Atlanta in 1979 and moved with the Flames to Calgary the next year, but it was after he was traded to Washington in the summer of 1982 that he had his finest moments. He and Al Jensen won the Jennings Trophy in '83-'84, Riggin leading the goal-crazy NHL with four shutouts at a time when one was a near miracle. He later played for Boston and Pittsburgh but wasn't the starter in either situation and didn't hide his displeasure. He ended up in the minors, and in 1988 he retired altogether. Riggin settled in London, Ontario, and worked as a harness racer.

RILEY, Bill
b. Amherst, Nova Scotia, September 20, 1950
As a kid growing up in Nova Scotia, Riley had no NHL aspirations whatsoever. He played in Halifax and Amherst, but when he got a job in a factory in British Columbia he played for the Kitimat team in senior hockey, figuring that was about as far as he would ever get. But Tom McVie, coach of the Dayton Gems, discovered Riley as the player led the league in scoring for three successive years. He offered Riley a tryout with Dayton, and the player made the team. The story gets better. McVie went on to become coach of the Washington Capitals. Knowing full well Riley's abilities as a scorer, scrapper, and disciplined team player, and wanting to put his own fingerprints on the team, he called Riley up to the NHL. From 1974 to '79, Riley played 125 games with the Caps, scoring a few goals, settling a few scores, and making a contribution. Then, he was traded to Winnipeg. Unfamiliar territory, new coach, different rules, he was out of town after 14 games. Riley was determined to

Vincent Riendeau

As a kid growing up in Nova Scotia, Riley had no NHL aspirations whatsoever.
BILL RILEY

Dennis Riggin

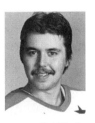

Pat Riggin

keep going, though. He returned to the Maritimes thinking about coaching, and played only with that end in mind. He was a playing assistant with Moncton in the AHL, then a playing coach with the St. John's Sr. Capitals. In 1989, he made history, becoming head coach and GM of the Amherst Ramblers, the first time a black pro had become a head coach. Riley remained for eight years, and in 1996 was coach and later director of player personnel for the Moncton Wildcats.

RILEY, Jack ("Shovel Shot")
b. Berckenla, Ireland, December 29, 1910

Although Irish by birth, Riley grew up in Vancouver where his peculiar style of shooting the puck earned him his nickname. He turned pro in 1929 and bounced around for a number of years before Detroit used him in the 1932-33 season. From there, the centre moved on to Montreal and Boston, though he was out of the NHL by 1936. Nevertheless, Riley played mostly in the American league for another nine years, and after retiring became a coach at West Point Academy for many years. He settled on Cape Cod and his two sons took over as coaches at West Point.

Jack Riley

RILEY, Jim
b. Bayfield, New Brunswick, May 25, 1895
d. Seguin, Texas, May 25, 1969

Despite playing most of his pro hockey career in the Pacific Coast league, Riley is a distinguished alumnus of the sport for a number of reasons. He played for Seattle on the 1916-17 Stanley Cup team. He missed 1918-19 while serving in the army. He played nine games in the NHL with Chicago and Detroit during the 1926-27 season. He is the only New Brunswicker to win a Cup. And, he is the only NHLer period who also played major league baseball. He played for the St. Louis Browns in 1921 and for the Washington Senators in 1924. Not bad for someone trained to be a tinsmith!

RING, Bob
b. Winchester, Massachusetts, October 6, 1946

Goalie Ring got into the Bruins cycle of goaltenders only once, on October 30, 1965. He replaced Eddie Johnston midway through an 8-2 romp by the Rangers, and although he wasn't credited with the loss, he allowed 4 goals all the same. He never made it back into an NHL crease.

RIOPELLE, Howard "Rip"
b. Ottawa, Ontario, January 30, 1922

It was no sure thing that Riopelle would ever see the inside of an NHL dressing room. He was at the age when going to war was preferable to a pro puck career, but beyond that he was more of a checker and digger than superstar scorer. He went overseas for three years and then returned and turned pro with the Montreal Royals, where he played as expected – worked hard, contributed, didn't make mistakes. But he was a star in the '47 Allan Cup with the winning Royals, and that earned him a stint with the Canadiens. For three years, Riopelle was a true-blue NHLer, but a bad back that had plagued him since his teen years finally forced him to retire in 1950. He returned to Ottawa and opened a store called Riopelle Fabric Shop, reputed to be cutting edge for fashion design in the city. After a year off, though, he was convinced by Tommy Gorman of the local Senators to return to the game. For three and a half more years Riopelle not only played well, but played the best hockey of his career. He played on a line with Dusty Blair and Leo Gravelle, and the threesome scored goals by the bushel. (Riopelle even employed Gravelle at the fabric store!) He retired in 1955 and remained in the city with his store.

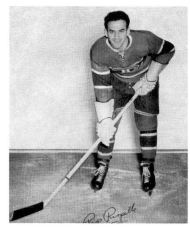

He opened a store called Riopelle Fabric Shop, reputed to be cutting edge for fashion design in the city.
RIP RIOPELLE

RIOUX, Gerry
b. Iroquois Falls, Ontario, February 17, 1959

The Jets signed the right winger to play during their inaugural NHL season, but Rioux played only eight games in 1979-80. He spent most of two years in the minors before retiring.

RIOUX, Pierre
b. Quebec City, Quebec, February 1, 1962

Imagine being 40 years old, looking back at your hockey career, and seeing that its finest hour came when you were 19! For Rioux, that was the truth. He won a gold medal with Canada's junior team at the 1982 WJC and played just 14 games with the Calgary Flames the next year. Three years in the minors was enough proof for him that he wasn't going to get called up – too small, not tough enough, blah, blah – so he took his skating skills to Europe. For 15 years he played, mostly in Germany, and when he returned home he coached the Saint-Georges Garaga of the Quebec Senior Professional Hockey League. He moved to the Quebec Remparts to coach in 2002.

RIPLEY, Vic
b. Elgin, Ontario, May 30, 1906
d. unknown

It's hard to fathom the early years of the NHL when today's league is so big and today's players are as productive as they are. Ripley made his NHL entrance with Chicago in 1928-29 and led the Hawks in scoring – with 13 points! During his 7 seasons in the league, he recorded a total of 100 points, perfectly fine totals for a left winger of his era. He later played in the Pacific Coast league to close out his career.

Vic Ripley

RISEBROUGH, Doug
b. Guelph, Ontario, January 29, 1954

During his 13 seasons in the NHL, Risebrough was a successful role player with Montreal and Calgary. He started with the Habs in 1974 and soon played on a line with Yvon Lambert and Mario Tremblay. This so-called Kid Line was charged with checking the opposing team's top unit into the ice. Risebrough was effective as a chippy "pest" but he played his role to a T and the Habs won four successive Cups in the late 1970s with just such players. He was traded to Calgary at training camp in 1982 and played the last five years of his career with the Flames. After retiring in 1987, he became an assistant coach with the team and then its coach, but he later worked under GM Cliff Fletcher to learn the managerial ropes. In 1991, Risebrough was made GM when Fletcher left to join Toronto, and the two hooked up on January 2, 1992, to make the biggest trade in league history and, for Toronto, the most favourably lopsided deal of all time. The key players exchanged were Doug Gilmour to the Leafs and Gary Leeman to the Flames, and while Gilmour went on to play remarkable hockey for Toronto, Leeman was booed out of Calgary in short order. Risebrough never recovered from the effects of that trade, and the Flames never made the playoffs. He was fired in 1995 and ended up as an assistant GM in Edmonton before returning as a GM with the expansion Minnesota Wild. Ironically, he had been short-listed by Toronto president Ken Dryden for the once-vacant GM job with the Leafs.

He started with the Habs in 1974 and soon played on a line with Yvon Lambert and Mario Tremblay.
DOUG RISEBROUGH

RISSLING, Gary
b. Saskatoon, Saskatchewan, August 8, 1956

"Talented" was a moniker never attached too firmly to the name Rissling, but he was a good team man with a sense of humour, and he'd fight all night if that's what it took to stay in the league (and it often did). In the CHL, he set a record by accruing 49 penalty minutes in a single game. With Washington and Pittsburgh (1979-85), he was at times maniacal but he wasn't going to win too many games with his scoring. In all, he averaged nearly five penalty minutes a game and finished his career fighting in the minors.

RITA, Jani
b. Helsinki, Finland, July 25, 1981

He made his debut with Edmonton, on March 2, 2002, and although that was the only NHL game of the year for Rita, it will likely be the first of many. He starred for Finland at two World Junior Championships and played all of his other pre-NHL hockey with Jokerit until coming to North America in 2001. Rita spent his first year of pro with Hamilton in the AHL, but the Oilers drafted him 13th overall in 1999 because they thought of him as a top prospect.

RITCHIE, Bob
b. Laverlochere, Quebec, February 20, 1955

Small and fast, Ritchie played his first NHL game in, of all places, Philadelphia during the height of the Broad Street Bullies' reign of terror. Perhaps that's why he didn't last longer. The Flyers traded him to Detroit, and he endured another 28 games before retiring.

RITCHIE, Byron
b. Burnaby, British Columbia, April 24, 1977

The goals came much easier and faster in the WHL for Ritchie than they have in the NHL. Of course, he was a regular with Lethbridge and hasn't enjoyed the same ice time since joining Carolina and later Florida. The small centre scored his first goal only during the 2001-02 season, his fourth part-time year, and looks more like a regular callup than an NHL starter.

RITCHIE, Dave
b. Montreal, Quebec, January 12, 1892
d. unknown

He began his career in the NHA but started the NHL with the Montreal Wanderers, playing in the team's four games before its arena burned down and the franchise withdrew from the league. He later played for 3 other teams during his 58-game career.

RITSON, Alex
b. Peace River, Alberta, March 7, 1922

The war gave Ritson a chance to make a single NHL appearance that he might not have had at another time when the best 120 players in the world had exclusive rights to that league. He played for the Rangers in '44-'45 near the start of his career and went on to play mostly senior hockey for the balance of his career.

RITTINGER, Alan
b. Regina, Saskatchewan, January 28, 1925

Another in a series of wartime replacements, Rittinger was playing locally for the Olympics when the Bruins called him up for part of the '43-'44 season. He played another year with the minor-league team and spent most of the last years of his career out west.

RIVARD, Bob
b. Sherbrooke, Quebec, August 1, 1939

It was odd that Rivard was named AHL rookie of the year for '66-'67. Yes, he had a fine season, but he was 27 years old and had been pro for 6 seasons. Those years, though, passed in the IHL, where in the year previous to his AHL award he won the scoring

Gary Rissling

Bob Ritchie

Bob Rivard

Fern Rivard

Jamie Rivers

Shawn Rivers

Craig Rivet

Garth Rizzuto

championship. Yet the AHL didn't consider his time in the "I" worthy enough of "pro" status, thus qualifying him for the rookie honours the next year. After expansion, Rivard played part of the '67-'68 year with Pittsburgh and then returned to the AHL, where he had many a productive year.

RIVARD, Fern
b. Grand'Mere, Quebec, January 18, 1946
One faction suggested he wasn't really an NHL goalie; another said he was a good goalie on a bad team. Either way, Rivard played for Minnesota sporadically in its first few years of existence, but he gave up four goals a game and compiled a dubious record of 9-26-11. He never played for another team or for the North Stars when they got competitive, so perhaps only Rivard knows which hypothesis is more accurate.

RIVERS, Gus
b. Winnipeg, Manitoba, November 19, 1909
d. Providence, Rhode Island, October 15, 1985
He scored only two goals in the playoffs, but one came after 68:52 of overtime to give Montreal a 2-1 win over the Rangers en route to the Stanley Cup. It is the sixth-longest playoff game in NHL history and the crowning glory of Rivers' career. He won a Cup the next year with Montreal as well, and after one more year he went to Providence where he played his final years.

RIVERS, Jamie ("Sugar"/ "Boom Boom")
b. Ottawa, Ontario, March 16, 1975
A top prospect coming out of Sudbury, Rivers won a gold medal with Canada at the 1995 WJC and then began a pro career with St. Louis that lasted four seasons. The defenceman worked his way into the lineup and then, in the eyes of Blues management, worked his way out. He was left unprotected in the 1999 Waiver Draft and the Islanders claimed him. He quickly moved on to join Ottawa and Boston, but the defenceman can take heart in the fact that he learned enough from his older brother, Shawn, to last longer in the league.

RIVERS, Shawn
b. Ottawa, Ontario, January 30, 1971
The older brother of Jamie, Shawn played just four games with Tampa Bay during the team's first season and then spent the rest of his career outside the NHL. Most of his time came in the "I," but he also played in Europe. He retired in 1999, returned home to Ottawa, and started his own company called Promografix, a distributor of promotional products such as pens and trophies.

RIVERS, Wayne
b. Hamilton, Ontario, February 1, 1942
The elemental parts of his career made up a successful whole that individually might not seem that rich in achievement. Rivers played most of his NHL games during the Original Six, though his time spilled over post-1967 with St. Louis and the Rangers. All of these years, though, saw him play mostly in the minors, where he proved worthy of the epithet goal scorer. From 1968, he was out of the NHL but played five full seasons in the WHA. The unsurpassed highlight of these later years was the '74-'75 season when he scored 54 goals with San Diego, and he stayed out west to close out his career a few years later.

In his first 12 seasons of play, he missed exactly 4 games!
JOHN ROSS ROACH

RIVET, Craig
b. North Bay, Ontario, September 13, 1974
Having played his whole career in Montreal, Rivet enjoyed 2001-02 the most when the injury-plagued team rallied at season's end to make it into the playoffs. Since joining the team in 1995, he has been part of a struggling Canadiens franchise for which the post-season is a luxury, not the norm. The previous year, he was one of the badly hurt players who have, over the last several years, seemed to outnumber healthy bodies in Montreal. Rivet missed much of 2001-02 with an injured shoulder, but the defenceman rebounded to take his place on the blueline thereafter.

RIZZUTO, Garth
b. Trail, British Columbia, September 11, 1947
After playing minor pro hockey with Dallas in the Chicago organization, Rizzuto became an original member of Vancouver when the Canucks chose him in the 1970 Expansion Draft. He played 37 games with the team that year but after another year and a half in the minors jumped to the WHA, where he closed out his pro career. He returned to B.C. and continued to play with Canucks old-timers.

ROACH, John Ross ("Port Perry Woodpecker")
b. Port Perry, Ontario, June 23, 1900
d. Windsor, Ontario, July 9, 1973
One of the great goalies of the early days, Roach was extraordinarily durable even during an era when a goalie routinely played every game of the season for his team. In fact, in his first 12 seasons of play, he missed exactly 4 games! As a rookie in '21-'22, he led the Toronto St. Pats to the Stanley Cup. He was the first great stopper the Toronto franchise had, and he later played for the Rangers and Detroit. In New York, he had 13 shutouts in '28-'29, a 44-game season,

and in 1932 he was the first goalie for the Red Wings after the franchise changed names from the Cougars. The beginning of the end came prior to the '33-'34 season that for Roach. He suffered a badly broken jaw in an off-season car accident and missed a good part of the year, and the year after he suffered two serious cuts to his face that told him it was time to retire. He remained in Detroit and worked for many years as a car salesman for Hettche Ford dealership, and later in life moved across the river to Windsor. Roach suffered from emphysema and succumbed to carcinoma at age 73. His body was sent to Port Perry, where he was interred.

ROACH, Michael "Mickey"
b. Glace Bay, Nova Scotia, May 1, 1894
d. Oshawa, Ontario, April 1, 1977
In his prime, Roach could skate faster than anyone. His rise to stardom began in the 1918-19 season when he came up to Hamilton and captained the Tigers to an Allan Cup victory. The next year, he signed with the St. Pats and began an NHL career that lasted eight years. As a rookie, he scored five goals in one game, but the team later sold him to Hamilton. Roach finished his career with the New York Americans and later settled in Windsor. He coached teams in Buffalo, Rochester, and Syracuse in ensuing years, and his son, Cliff, also played in the minors for many years. Roach was later inducted into the Nova Scotia Sports Hall of Fame.

He was invited to Team Canada's camp for the 1976 Canada Cup, though he didn't play.
RENE ROBERT

ROBERGE, Mario
b. Quebec City, Quebec, January 25, 1964
Only 14 months older than his brother, Serge, Mario had his little phobia just like elephants hate mice. He was one of the toughest hombres around, but he hated having his toupée knocked around his pate for all to see. That didn't happen too often, but he didn't need to get any angrier to perform his job, which was to fight. All of his five NHL years were with Montreal, including the surprising 1992-93 Cup season, and he ended up in the minors as a playing assistant coach.

ROBERGE, Serge
b. Quebec City, Quebec, March 31, 1965
The younger brother often feels a competitive need to outdo the older, and in the Roberge household that meant beating up more people to get to and stay in the NHL. Roberge recorded staggering penalty minutes wherever he played, from junior to the minors to his nine games in the NHL with his hometown Nordiques. He continues to smack people around, now in the senior hockey in Quebec, but his heyday was in the AHL, where he frequently spent more than 300 minutes in the penalty box each season.

ROBERT, Claude
b. Montreal, Quebec, August 10, 1928
The Canadiens liked what they saw of Roberge and assigned him to play with their new farm team in Cincinnati in 1950, but before the season was out the Habs had called him up for a total of 23 games. Roberge scored but one goal and never made it back to the NHL, though he continued his career in the province for several years. When he retired, he returned to Montreal and became a police officer. He made the news once in the early 1960s when he ran after a bank robber, overpowered him, and made the arrest.

ROBERT, Rene
b. Trois Rivières, Quebec, December 31, 1948
As the right winger on Buffalo's famed French Connection Line (initially called, simply, the French Line), with centre Gil Perreault and left winger Richard Martin, Robert helped the Sabres reach the Stanley Cup finals in 1975 during the team's fifth year in operation. Buffalo lost to the Philadelphia Flyers, but the team's meteoric rise to the top of the league was due largely to this line's scoring ability. Although the mustachioed Robert began his career in the Toronto organization and spent a brief time with Pittsburgh, it was in Sabres colours that he distinguished himself, peaking in '74-'75. That season, Robert scored 40 goals and 100 points, played in the All-Star Game, and at season's end was named the team's MVP. A shooter first and passer second, Robert saw time on the point during power plays, making Buffalo's special team one of the league's deadliest. He attributed part of his success to coach and general manager Punch Imlach. Once Imlach was replaced by Scotty Bowman, Robert found himself traded to Colorado, but he was named captain and became loyal to another coach, Don Cherry. When Cherry was summarily dismissed by Ray Miron, team captain Robert and teammates Lanny McDonald and Bobby Schmautz publicly protested. This led to one last trade, back to Toronto, where he was the only player on the team to not wear a helmet. Ironically, Miron had coveted Robert for years. Despite missing many games due to injury over the years, Robert scored 30 goals 4 times during his career. He was invited to Team Canada's camp for the 1976 Canada Cup, though he didn't play. After retiring in 1982, he worked in Toronto as a sales rep for Molson Brewery and later became president of the NHL Alumni Association, making great strides in getting that organization respect and regard from the NHL and NHLPA.

Mario Roberge

Phil Roberto

Dave Roberts

Doug Roberts

Gordie Roberts

ROBERTO, Phil ("The Enforcer")
b. Niagara Falls, Ontario, January 1, 1949

It was a monumental task to make the Habs in 1969, when Roberto first tried to make an impression in Montreal. In his three part-time years, he played a few games and contributed in the 1971 playoffs, when the team won the Cup. But in the summer of 1973, after a year and a half with St. Louis, he suffered a serious cut to his arm while preventing a sheet of glass from hitting him in the face. He severed a nerve, and doctors told him to forget about hockey, advice that is, of course, pure motivation for a player. Roberto came back a year later, but he wasn't quite the same player. He bounced around from poor team to poor team, and ended his career in the WHA with Birmingham. Roberto later became head coach and GM of the Birmingham Bulls when the team joined the East Coast league, and from there he moved on to become president and GM of the Columbus Cottonmouths of the same league, a post he has held since 1996.

ROBERTS, Dave
b. Alameda, California, May 28, 1970

A graduate of U of Michigan, Roberts played for the U.S. at the 1994 Olympics in Lillehammer before making his NHL debut with St. Louis. He spent most of the next year with the farm team in Peoria, and when he was called up in March 1995 he made a fine impression, scoring 6 goals and 11 points in 19 games. He also played with Edmonton and Vancouver and finished his career in Europe.

ROBERTS, Doug
b. Detroit, Michigan, October 28, 1942

As kids, Gordie and Doug Roberts were stick boys at the Detroit Olympia, so it was no surprise hockey was in their blood or that both would go on to play in the NHL. Doug took the college route, attending Michigan State for both football and hockey. He turned pro with Detroit in 1965, and in coming years bounced to Oakland and Boston. Roberts played only three games in the '71-'72 season, when the Bruins won the Cup, so he didn't qualify for name-engraving honours. He played much of the next year with the team, though, but the year after he was traded back to Detroit when Boston reacquired Derek Sanderson. He finished his career in the WHA and minors, and in 1979 was hired to coach at Connecticut College. Some 23 years later, he's still there, and his son, David, went on to play in the NHL in the 1990s.

ROBERTS, Gary
b. North York, Ontario, May 23, 1966

Some injuries don't faze a hockey player at all. Cuts, sores, small broken bones – no big deal. Others can't be ignored, like a torn ligament. And then there are the two or three that scare a player and force him to re-evaluate his night job – a concussion or, in Roberts' case, a neck injury that worked its way down his spine and caused tingling in his arms. Not good. His parents came from Twillingate, Newfoundland, and moved to Toronto before Gary was born. He started skating as soon as he could and quickly developed into the kind of kid who looks like a player even as a 10-year-old. He won a Memorial Cup with Ottawa in 1984, played with Canada's juniors at the WJC in '86, and stepped into the Flames lineup in Calgary a year later. He was a natural. Intense as the sun is bright, he brought a winning attitude to a team on the rise, and became part of its improvement. He helped the team win the Cup in 1989 and 3 years later he scored 53 goals in the season. By 1994, the wear and tear of the game – of his style of play – was catching up to him. He missed most of the next two years with neck injuries, and came back too soon each time. When he couldn't hold a knife and fork at the dinner table, he knew something was wrong. In 1996, fearful of permanent spinal damage, he retired and underwent serious surgery on his neck. During his rehabilitation, though, he did more than the ordinary citizen would do. He trained and worked out, then put himself under the guidance of a chiropractor in Phoenix. A year later, in perfect shape and feeling better, he was cleared to play. Carolina was the only team willing to give him a chance – or, take the risk – and he rewarded the 'Canes with three strong seasons. In the summer of 2000, though, when he took the chance to sign with Toronto. He brought to the Leafs a professionalism unparalleled, a single-minded approach to fitness and performance that verged on the delusional, and a winning attitude. The Leafs made it to the Conference finals in his second year, only to lose to those same 'Canes. His dedication, however, made it clear to teammates and fans that his focus reached a new level in the playoffs, but came with a price. In the off-season, he had surgery on both shoulders, the result of further wear and tear on a body made to play hockey and driven to perform beyond reasonable ability. His successful return to the Leafs toward the end of the 2002-03 regular season elevated his status to cult hero in the city.

His successful return to the Leafs toward the end of the 2002-03 regular season elevated his status to cult hero in the city.
GARY ROBERTS

ROBERTS, Gordie
b. Detroit, Michigan, October 2, 1957

Most players who make it to the NHL say they were born with an ability to play the game better than most. They were blessed with talent. Roberts was blessed with the name Gordie because his dad named him in tribute to his idol, Gordie Howe. Roberts also had the skills, because he grew up not only to play in the NHL but to play with Howe! After just two years of junior, Roberts signed with New England of the WHA in 1975 and stayed with the team for six years, the final two in the NHL. He played not only with Howe but also with Dave Keon, Bobby Hull, and his brother, Doug. Roberts had offensive ability but he was also slow. Thus, he was more playmaker than attacking defenceman, and his quick passes rather than his quick feet kept him in the league. He played eight years with Minnesota and toward the end of his career came to Pittsburgh in time to be that ingredient called experience on a team that won the Cup in 1991 and '92. He ended his 15-year stay in the NHL with Boston, though continued to skate in the IHL for 2 more seasons, the last in Manitoba as a playing coach. In the end, longevity was his greatest skill. He never won an award or was named to an All-Star Team, never played in an All-Star Game. He did play in two World Championships for the U.S. (1982 and '87) and in the 1984 Canada Cup. Roberts later worked as director of player personnel and assistant coach with Phoenix of the NHL.

ROBERTS, Jim
b. Toronto, Ontario, June 8, 1956
The younger and less accomplished of the NHL's two Jim Roberts, this Jim played parts of three seasons with Minnesota in the 1970s at the same time the other Jim was winning Stanley Cups with Montreal. He played only four seasons of pro before retiring in 1980.

ROBERTS, Jimmy
b. Toronto, Ontario, April 9, 1940
There was no better way for Roberts to start his career than with Peterborough in junior in '58-'59, for his coach was Scotty Bowman, with whom he would have a long hockey relationship. Roberts turned pro two years later and made his Canadiens debut in '63-'64. A steady but thoroughly unspectacular player, he could do what was asked of him with a fiery temperament that hated to lose. Roberts helped the Habs win Cups in 1965 and '66, and he rejoined Bowman in St. Louis when the Blues made him its first player chosen in the 1967 Expansion Draft. To maximize his usefulness, Bowman used Roberts on defence as well as wing, and for five years he was one of the team's veteran leaders. He rejoined Montreal in the 1970s and won three more Cups with the Habs, and after a final season with St. Louis he retired in 1978. For the next 24 years, Roberts stayed in the game. He was assistant coach with Buffalo for six seasons (again, part of that time with Bowman) and was the head coach for half the '81-'82 season. He then joined Pittsburgh and moved on to Hartford, then returned to St. Louis where he remained an assistant coach until retiring in 2002.

Roberts helped the Habs win Cups in 1965 and '66.
JIMMY ROBERTS

ROBERTS, Moe
b. Waterbury, Connecticut, December 13, 1905
d. Cleveland, Ohio, February 7, 1975
It would take a true trivia expert to know that Roberts, to this day, holds a unique place in goaltending history. He holds the record for the longest time between his first and last NHL games – 26 years! He played 2 games for Boston in the '25-26 season, and then spent most of the next 15 years in the minors. He had two brief stints with the Americans in the 1930s, but in 1942 joined the army and when he got out he was more or less retired. He got a job as Chicago's assistant trainer, a position in the old days that usually meant he was also the team's practice goalie. Well, on November 25, 1951, Harry Lumley was injured and the 45-year-old was called upon to play the final period of the game. To that point, he was the oldest goalie ever to play in the NHL. He continued to be the team's trainer, though he wasn't forced between the pipes again.

ROBERTSON, Earle
b. Bengough, Saskatchewan, November 24, 1910
d. January 19, 1979
Long before Ken Dryden came in and stole the Cup for Montreal in 1971, Earl Robertson was putting on a great pinch-hitting show of his own in goal. He had been playing pro for a number of seasons and had worked his way into Detroit's system. In the 1937 playoffs, he was called in to replace an injured Normie Smith and promptly took the Wings past Montreal and the Rangers to win the Cup. He was then traded to the Americans, who were looking to fill the void left by Roy Worters, and Robertson came in and did it again. He was their starter for four and a half years and played incredibly well with a weak team, but in 1942 he went off to war. He served as a trooper with the 19th Alberta Dragoons, and when he came out his career was over. Robertson worked in the car business in Wetaskiwin, Saskatchewan, and later relocated to Toronto where he continued to do well for himself.

ROBERTSON, Fred
b. Carlisle, England, October 22, 1911
d. September 20, 1997
By the time he passed away, Robertson and Red Horner were the only surviving members of Toronto's 1932 Stanley Cup team, the first at Maple Leaf Gardens. Robertson was a rookie that year, coming directly from the Toronto Marlies, and after another year in the NHL he played many more seasons with Cleveland in the American league. He later became a truck driver for Canada Packers.

Jim Roberts

Earle Robertson

Fred Robertson

Torrie Robertson

ROBERTSON, Geordie

b. Victoria, British Columbia, August 1, 1959

To the NHL, he is a footnote, an asterisk, a trivia answer or something as marginal. To the city of Rochester, Robertson is so very much more. After leaving Victoria of the WHL in 1979, he was assigned by the Sabres to Rochester, and played 7 of his 10 seasons of pro there. His 119 points in '82-'83 is still a team record, and in 1986 he led the team to a Calder Cup victory. He was the first player to be called "Mr. Amerk," such was his popularity. He played his final year in Switzerland and then returned to Rochester, where he worked for a company called Financial Partners. He also was head coach at Monroe Community College in Rochester, a position he continues to hold. In 1993, Robertson was inducted into the Americans Hockey Hall of Fame.

Bert Robertsson

ROBERTSON, George

b. Winnipeg, Manitoba, May 11, 1928

As a teen playing for the Winnipeg Monarchs, Robertson became a hero in 1946 in the Memorial Cup finals against St. Mike's. The Toronto school had beaten the Monarchs in '45 to take home the great amateur prize, and this '46 showdown went to seven games. In the third period, with the score tied 2-2, Robertson scored twice to give the Winnipeggers their title. It was sweet satisfaction for George who, along with brother Dave, formed a perfect pair for a Clifford Odets play. Dave the scholar went on to become a professor at Columbia University in New York; George, who was a rabble-rouser and undisciplined student, went on to a pro career in hockey. He was owned by the Rangers but they made a huge deal on August 19, 1947, that caused a furor in Montreal. The Habs sent Buddy O'Connor and Frank Eddolls to New York, and the Rangers sent Hal Laycoe, Joe Bell, and a player to be named later to Montreal. Laycoe and Bell never even made the team, and fans in Montreal screamed at GM Frank Selke, wondering why he had given up two players for nothing. The player to be named later turned out to be Robertson, and for a fleeting moment at the start of the '48-'49 season he created a stir. On opening night, he scored a goal just three minutes into the game, and all of a sudden the deal looked sweet for the Habs. Unfortunately, he scored only 1 more goal in the next 29 games. He was sent to the minors and never returned, and hindsight – and history – has proven this was, indeed, one of the master Selke's poorer deals.

Stephane Robidas

ROBERTSON, Torrie

b. Victoria, British Columbia, August 2, 1961

Just when he was trying to do good, trying to change for the better, his world came crashing down. Until he was traded to Hartford in 1983, Robertson was seen as

Florent Robidoux

Robertson became a hero in 1946 in the Memorial Cup finals against St. Mike's.
GEORGE ROBERTSON

a one-dimensional goon, largely because he played like a one-dimensional goon. In junior, he fought everything that moved, which got him drafted. In the minors and with Washington, then, he kept fighting whomever challenged him or looked at him sideways. With the Whalers, he skated on a line with Greg Malone and Bobby Crawford, and in his first year he scored something called a hat trick, a heretofore unknown troika of goals not accumulated in a year but in a single season. The next two years, he kept going, but in December 1986, in a fight with Shayne Corson of Montreal, he fell awkwardly, broke his leg in two places, and was never the same. Of course, he came back and played another three years. But, he just wasn't the same player.

ROBERTSSON, Bert

b. Sodertalje, Sweden, June 30, 1974

It just doesn't look like he's going to make it in the NHL. Since being drafted by Vancouver in 1993 long after most players' families had gone home, he's played with three teams but never a full season. Even Nashville, who acquired him in 2001, kept him in the minors without recalling him. He played in Finland for Iives Tampere during the 2002-03 season.

ROBIDAS, Stephane ("Robie")

b. Sherbrooke, Quebec, March 3, 1977

Montreal hopes that after years of development Robidas is ready to be a top-six defenceman with the team. He played junior in Shawinigan and then most of three seasons in the AHL, but although he's been a mainstay the last couple of seasons with the Habs his size (5'10" and 180 pounds) is not typical for an NHL blueliner. Yet, he does have offensive ability and at every level has proved resilient.

ROBIDOUX, Florent

b. Treherne, Manitoba, May 5, 1960

It was a career that more or less ended before it began. Robidoux played in the WHL before signing with Chicago in 1979, and after another year with Portland the left winger turned pro. He played a number of games with the Hawks but more in the AHL with New Brunswick, and in the spring of 1982 the team won the Calder Cup. A few weeks later, he married, and three days after that the happy couple was driving along a Florida highway when a runaway trailer came right at them. Robidoux got partially out of the way, but the trailer slammed into the driver's door, breaking his leg badly. It was six months before the last of the casts came off, and he missed an entire year convalescing. Although he played the following season, he started the year in the minors and was ineffective when Chicago gave him a chance for nine games. He played two and a half more years, in the lesser leagues, and retired at age 26.

ROBINSON, Doug

b. St. Catharines, Ontario, August 27, 1940

The tenacity and will to succeed that is ingrained in every hockey player carries over to life as well. Throughout his playing days, Robinson took courses at McMaster University in Hamilton, Ontario. It took him seven years, but in 1968 he finally earned a B.A. in history. Robinson played junior and minor pro before being called up by Chicago for the 1964 playoffs, his first NHL appearance, and the succeeding fall he made the team as a winger. Although he played pro until 1972, his NHL years were carved around a minor-league career in the AHL. He was named that league's rookie of the year in '62-'63 and was a fine goal scorer. In '69-'70, he scored 45 times for Springfield, but his career came to a crashing halt in early 1972 when he was hit in the eye by a stick while playing for Nova Scotia. He lost sight in the eye, retired, and became a scout for the Montreal Canadiens. Thirty years later, he soldiers on in this capacity.

ROBINSON, Earl

b. Montreal, Quebec,
March 11, 1907
d. Toronto, Ontario,
September 8, 1986

After making his NHL entrance at age 21 in 1928, Robinson settled into a very respectable 11-year career that ended prematurely because of injury. He played all but one season in Montreal, mostly with the Maroons. He helped the English Montrealers win the Cup in three straight games over Toronto in 1935, but three years later when the M's folded he was sold to Chicago. A year later, he was sent back to Montreal, the Canadiens happy to have him on their side, but after suffering a broken jaw during practice he retired from the NHL. He was a sergeant in the Royal Canadian Ordnance Corps, and after the war he owned Haliburton Lodge north of Toronto. Robinson also played in both the Babe Siebert and the Howie Morenz All-Star Games in 1937 and '39, respectively.

ROBINSON, Larry ("Big Bird")

b. Winchester, Ontario, June 2, 1951

Robinson looked gangly and awkward when he skated, but if you watched him long enough gangly turned into dominant and awkward into quick. He was a big man who didn't appear to carry his size well, but then he knocked opponents down, always stayed on his feet, and was a force from the blueline in the other team's end. He grew up on a dairy farm in eastern Ontario and

Doug Robinson

played junior hockey in Brockville and then Kitchener. With the Braves in provincial hockey he had to commute three times a week to games and practices, but he never complained and he never missed one. With the Rangers, he learned to play defence in his singular style. Montreal drafted him in 1971 and placed him with Nova Scotia, but after a year and a half he was too good to keep on the farm and the Habs recalled him for good during the '72-'73 season. He was part of the Cup-winning team that year, and within two seasons had become one of the most dominant young defencemen in the game. Robinson, Guy Lapointe, and Serge Savard formed the Big Three, as they were known, of the Canadiens blueline. Robinson was physically the strongest and a great puck rusher. He had a great low shot from the point that always seemed to find its way to the net, and as a result he was the point man who made the power play work. He never scored 20 goals in a season, but he did have at least 40 assists 8 times. The numbers, though, only tell a partial tale of his success. He played 20 seasons in the NHL and never missed the playoffs, a record that will surely be tough to match. The Big Three anchored the great Montreal teams of the 1970s that won four Cups in a row ('75-'79), and Robinson won the Norris Trophy twice in and around these glory years ('76-'77 and '79-'80) and in 1978 was named winner of the Conn Smythe Trophy. But it was his last Cup that was his greatest memory. In the early 1980s he felt he was on the downward slope of his career, but in 1984 Team Canada coach and GM Glen Sather invited him to camp for

He grew up on a dairy farm in eastern Ontario and played junior hockey in Brockville and then Kitchener.
LARRY ROBINSON

the upcoming Canada Cup tournament. It was an invitation that Robinson truly didn't expect, yet he played some of the best hockey of his career and put aside any thoughts of retiring. When the Habs won the Cup in 1986, with almost all of the great players from the 1970s long gone, Robinson felt immense satisfaction. In 1989, he decided it was time to move on. Montreal was not keen on having the 37-year-old on the team any longer, and he didn't feel any sentimental need to play his entire career with the team, especially if he still wanted to play. He signed with Los Angeles and played three more seasons before retiring in 1992. Three years later, he was inducted into the Hockey Hall of Fame. Robinson had also played in the first two Canada Cups in 1976 and '81 and as soon as he retired he went into coaching. He started as an assistant with New Jersey, and after three years became head coach in L.A. He never quite liked it enough out west to feel dedicated to the job for a long period, and after four years he returned to the Devils as assistant in 1999. With just a few games to go in the 1999-2000 season, head coach Robbie Ftorek was fired and

Earl Robinson

Robinson had the daunting task of filling in with the playoffs just two weeks away. He knew what he was doing, though, because when all was said and done he held the Stanley Cup, his first as a coach. But what goes up must come down, and Robinson was fired midway through the next season. He stayed with the team, however, as a special coach, and a new generation of players got to know him as a coach, not a Hall of Fame, all-star defenceman. In 2002, he semi-retired to Florida to work on his polo, though he stills acted as a consultant for the team.

ROBINSON, Moe
b. Winchester, Ontario, May 29, 1957

Moe Robinson

As Brent is to Keith (as in Gretzky) and Rene is to Aurel (as in Joliat), so, too, is Moe to Larry (as in Robinson). While Larry had a Hall of Fame career with L.A. and Montreal, Moe played a single game with his brother on the Canadiens blueline. He was clearly not on a par with his brother, and he retired soon after his NHL appearance.

ROBINSON, Rob
b. St. Catharines, Ontario, April 19, 1967

Rob Robinson

The son of Doug, Rob was drafted by St. Louis and not Montreal, the team for whom the old man scouted. Rob went to the University of Miami-Ohio and played in the IHL for three years before the Blues gave him a chance in 1991-92. Just 22 games later, though, he was back in the minors and, more recently, in Europe.

ROBINSON, Scott
b. 100 Mile House, British Columbia, March 29, 1964

Coming out of the University of Calgary in 1988, Robinson went on to play a single game with Minnesota a short time later, though he spent the rest of his five years in the "I."

ROBITAILLE, Luc ("Lucky Luc")
b. Montreal, Quebec, February 17, 1966

Trying to place Robitaille in the history of the game is difficult at best. He is the highest-scoring left winger of all time, having recently surpassed Bobby Hull. So, any assessment of him is awkward. On the one hand, there's no way Robitaille is half the player Hull was – that's an opinion that rolls off the tongue easily and can only produce nods from aficionados. On the other hand, there are so many great stars today that perhaps they are underrated – if not altogether maligned – unfairly. After all, Robitaille has as hard a shot as Hull, but so do many players of the 21st century. In his day, there was only one Bobby Hull slapshot. Robitaille can't do anything about these comparisons, and his facts speak for themselves: one 60-goal, two 50-plus, and five 40-plus seasons add up to 600 goals and counting. He won the

Lucky Luc has proven that there is much more to scoring goals than luck.
LUC ROBITAILLE

Calder Trophy in 1987 and has played in seven All-Star Games. In 2001-02, he signed with Detroit, scored 30 goals, and won his first Stanley Cup though the year after his scoring deserted him and he was sometimes a healthy scratch. Nonetheless, it was quite a career considering he was hard-pressed for praise as a junior in Hull. Scouts said he couldn't skate and wouldn't last in the NHL, and the fact that L.A. drafted him 171st overall attested to the universality of that belief. Yet all these years later, Lucky Luc has proven that there is much more to scoring goals than luck.

ROBITAILLE, Mike
b. Midland, Ontario, February 12, 1948

Leaving the game on your own terms is painful enough, but leaving on terms over which you have no control is even worse. Robitaille entered the NHL as one of the bright hopes for the game. He had a fine junior career in Kitchener, and played well in Omaha as prelude to joining the Rangers, but from almost the minute he made the NHL to the moment he left, nothing went right for him. At training camp in 1970 he broke his ankle, and in his absence Brad Park stepped up, played well, and made Robitaille's presence redundant. In Detroit, things didn't work out and he was traded to Buffalo, where he was paired with Tim Horton on defence. When Horton was killed in a car crash, Robitaille was devastated and never got back on track with the Sabres. In Vancouver, he played well for a year and a half and seemed to have found a home. Then, he started feeling pain in his back, pain that got considerably worse. The Canucks pressured him into continuing on, and gave him Valium for the pain. As the pain became more intense, he became addicted to the Valium. To combat the addiction, he went to a psychiatrist, a move that, in Vancouver's eye, made him a head case. In a game against Pittsburgh, he was blindsided after stepping out of the penalty box and injured his neck. Still, he played on. At training camp the following year he didn't show up and the Canucks sued him for breach of contract. He countersued, citing negligence on the team's part in cutting his career short. Robitaille was awarded $355,000 and was absolved. He regained his strength, and eventually returned to Buffalo to work with the team in broadcasting and community relations.

ROBITAILLE, Randy
b. Ottawa, Ontario, October 12, 1975

Despite having fine offensive skills and terrific speed, Robitaille has been slagged for his defensive efforts and his lack of killer instincts needed to survive in the NHL. The Bruins signed him in 1997 and used him for a game after his season at the University of Miami-

Randy Robitaille

Ohio ended, but he injured his shoulder and missed the rest of the year. He spent most of the next two years in the minors, but helped Providence win the Calder Cup in 1999. This attracted Atlanta, but the Thrashers just traded him to Nashville, where he played a full season and scored just 11 goals. Since then, he's been to L.A. and Pittsburgh, but has yet to settle into a steady career in a stable environment.

ROCHE, Dave
b. Lindsay, Ontario, June 13, 1975
A designated fighter, Roche has yet to really land with one team. He started his fighting with Pittsburgh in 1995 but has been on the move regularly ever since, spending increasing time in the minors, to boot.

ROCHE, Earl
b. Prescott, Ontario, February 22, 1910
d. Montreal, Quebec, August 15, 1965
Like brother Des, Earl won the Allan Cup with Montreal AAA in 1930 and then turned pro with the Montreal Maroons. He played all his NHL games during the next four years with a total of five teams, and then embarked on a lengthy career in the minors. After the war he settled in Montreal and years later died of a heart attack after playing tennis with friends.

ROCHE, Ernie
b. Montreal, Quebec, February 4, 1930
Known for his long stride, Roche was a star in Quebec and out west in the 1950s, playing four games with the Canadiens in '50-'51. He won the Memorial Cup with the Jr. Canadiens in the spring of '50, but the defenceman spent the bulk of his career in the minors.

ROCHE, Michel "Des"
b. Kemptville, Ontario, February 1, 1907
d. unknown
Not only were Des and Earl brothers, they also played long stretches of their careers together. They rose to prominence in the '29-'30 season, winning the Allan Cup with Montreal AAA and joining the Maroons the following year. They even skated on the same line with Paul Haynes. Des spent much of the next three years in Windsor, and when he returned to the NHL he bounced from team to team. He had a career year in '33-'34 with Ottawa when he scored 14 goals, but after another year in which he played for 3 NHL teams, Roche ended in the minors before retiring in 1939.

ROCHE, Travis
b. Grand Cache, Alberta, June 17, 1978
Although Roche has yet to make an impact in the NHL, he is still young enough that it is not out of the question that he might still do so. The defenceman was part of the NCAA champion North Dakota Fighting Sioux in 1999-2000, and at the end of the following year he played in his first NHL game, on April 8, 2001, with Minnesota. Since then he has been in the Wild system but has played only a few additional games.

ROCHEFORT, Dave
b. Red Deer, Alberta, July 22, 1946
Rochefort had the good fortune to play for the Edmonton Oil Kings in the early 1960s when the team was the finest junior outfit in Canada. He won two Memorial Cups, in 1963 and again three years later, before embarking on a pro career. That journey took him to the NHL for one game, on March 28, 1967. He spent the rest of his few years in the minors before retiring and settling in Edmonton.

ROCHEFORT, Leon ("Cheesey")
b. Cap de la Madeleine, Quebec, May 4, 1939
Andy Bathgate hung the nickname on Rochefort during the '62-'63 season, one in which Rochefort made an impact on the team with his goals and energy. All of his years prior to expansion, though, were nothing more than tryouts and half-seasons, replacement chances that didn't pan out. Technically, he was on Montreal's Cup team in '65-'66, though he played just once all season and four times in the playoffs. In 1967, Philadelphia claimed him in the draft, and he had an immediate impact. On November 4, 1967, he scored the first hat trick in team history, and by season's end he led the Flyers in goals with 21. He ended up back in Montreal in '70-'71, but this time he was a bona fide contributor. By the time he retired in 1976, Rochefort had played 15 NHL seasons with 7 teams.

ROCHEFORT, Normand
b. Trois Rivières, Quebec, January 28, 1961
In the modern game, statistics and numbers define a player in most eyes, and the "value" of a defensive defenceman becomes that much harder to nail down because for such a beast numbers are insignificant to his play. Rochefort manned the Quebec blueline for years, if not in obscurity then certainly without fanfare or great appreciation. He joined the Nordiques in 1980, and after seven fine seasons earned his due in two ways: one, he was named to the NHL's team for Rendez-vous '87; two, he was invited to Canada's training camp for the 1987 Canada Cup. In both tournaments, he was one of the best players on any team. He later played for the Rangers and Tampa, and ended his career in the IHL in 1998. Rochefort later became an assistant coach for Acadie in the Q, but in the summer of 2002 he wanted

Dave Roche

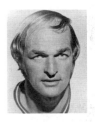
Leon Rochefort

Normand Rochefort

Robitaille entered the NHL as one of the bright hopes for the game.
MIKE ROBITAILLE

Marc Rodgers

Stacy Roest

John Rogers

Mike Rogers

to make history. He came out of retirement at age 41 and signed with Promutuel, a senior team, so he could play with his son, Billy. Now if only the pair could somehow get into the NHL…

ROCKBURN, Harvey "Rocky"
b. Ottawa, Ontario, August 20, 1905
d. Concord, New Hampshire, June 9, 1977
Playing between the wars, Rockburn was recruited by Detroit in the team's earliest NHL days and was assigned to the Olympics in 1927. Two years later, he made the Cougars and established himself as one of the toughest, roughest players in the NHL. He led the league in penalty minutes in his second season, but his only other games came with Ottawa a few years later. He closed out his career in the minors.

RODDEN, Edmund "Ed"
b. Mattawa, Ontario, March 22, 1901
d. Toronto, Ontario, September 10, 1986
Rodden went down to Toronto in his youth and played with some of the finest teams in the city, notably De LaSalle, Aura Lee, and Granites. He made the NHL in 1926 with Chicago and played for four teams during his short career, though he finished in the minors. He settled in Toronto after retiring and was a longtime employee of the Ontario Jockey Club.

RODGERS, Marc
b. Shawville, Quebec, March 16, 1972
His dream came true and his bubble burst – both for the same reason. Rodgers played junior in the Q but was never drafted. In 1992, he signed with Wheeling and began a career that has taken him all over the minor-league map, with but one NHL exception. In the fall of 1999, Detroit signed him. The Wings had a few injuries to worry about and some contract troubles, so Rodgers provided a little insurance for the team up front. He scored a goal in his 21 games, but the injuries and contracts were resolved and he became expendable as easily as he had been available. Since then, he's continued in the minors.

ROENICK, Jeremy ("J.R.")
b. Boston, Massachusetts, January 17, 1970
Well on his way to 500 goals for his career, Roenick is one of the generation of star American players to evolve in the 1990s as a result of the Miracle on Ice in 1980. He led the WJC in points in 1989 with 16 even though the U.S. finished fifth, and when he joined Chicago toward the end of the season he would start a career that has never taken him to the minors. In his first 3 seasons he vaulted from 26 to 41 to 53 goals, and the third of those saw him begin another streak of 3 successive 100-point seasons. He played for his country at the 1991 World

In the summer of 2000, he and several other NHLers made an appearance on the soap opera One Life to Live.
JEREMY ROENICK

Cup and the two NHL Olympics – 1998 in Nagano and 2002 in Salt Lake City – but he has yet to win a Stanley Cup. Not huge, he is a fiery competitor, and off the ice he has been part of his share of contract negotiations, always seeking market value for his play. In the summer of 2000, he and several other NHLers made an appearance on the soap opera *One Life to Live*, and a year later he signed a five-year contract with Philadelphia for $37 million. He then went out and scored just 21 goals, and the Flyers were humiliated by Ottawa in the first round of the playoffs.

ROEST, Stacy ("Rudy")
b. Lethbridge, Alberta, March 15, 1974
As a kid, he was a goalie, but as he grew up he got smarter and decided it was more fun shooting at a target than being one. Roest played junior in Medicine Hat, and although never drafted he joined the Detroit system by signing with Adirondack. He played well enough in the AHL that the Red Wings signed him, and he spent most of the '98-'99 season with the NHL club. After another year, Detroit lost him to Minnesota through free agency, but reacquired him via the same route in 2002 as a versatile, all purpose-player.

ROGERS, John
b. Paradise Hills, Saskatchewan, April 10, 1953
The news and reviews were all good for Rogers in the early going. He ended a good junior career in Edmonton in '72-'73 by scoring 63 goals, and when Minnesota called him up briefly the next year he scored twice in 10 games. Within three years, he was out of the game for good, his young promise unrealized.

ROGERS, Mike
b. Calgary, Alberta, October 24, 1954
Without a shadow of a doubt, Rogers is by far the last name any trivia expert would invoke if asked to name a player who had 3 consecutive 100-point seasons in the NHL. At 5'9" and 170 pounds, he was small even in junior, and not many people thought he stood a chance in rough-and-tumble 1970s NHL hockey. Indeed, Rogers started his pro career in the WHA, first with Edmonton and then New England, staying with the Whalers in 1979 when they joined the NHL. Amazingly, his numbers didn't go down in the better league, as occurred with most WHA stars – instead, they increased! In 3 years, 2 with the Whalers and 1 more with the Rangers, Rogers reached 100 points, and though his production decreased after that, he had had 3 magnificent years that no one could have predicted. After retiring, he returned to Calgary where he became executive vice-president of Follgard Group, a software company.

ROHLICEK, Jeff
b. Park Ridge, Illinois, January 27, 1966

In a 12-year career, Rohlicek managed to play just 9 NHL games, with Vancouver, in the late 1980s. The centre played in most of the minor leagues with a plethora of teams, and although he racked up more than his share of points, he failed to garner a one with the Canucks.

ROHLIN, Leif
b. Vasteras, Sweden, February 26, 1968

A long and prosperous career in Europe was punctuated by two years in the NHL with a patient Vancouver team. The Canucks drafted him in 1988, but he ignored them and kept right on playing in Vasteras. He won Olympic gold with Tre Kronor in 1994 in Lillehammer, and in 1995 finally played in the NHL. Rohlin was a solid defenceman with some offensive skills, but in 1997 he returned to Europe and played in Switzerland before going home to Sweden. He also played for his country in the 2001 World Championships.

ROHLOFF, Jon
b. Mankato, Minnesota, October 3, 1969

In a game in December 1996, the Bruins decided to play Rohloff, a born defenceman, on the wing. The team lost 4-2, but he scored both goals. Evidently, the team considered this a fluke because it didn't try to convert him. Nor did they keep him on the blueline. In his third season, and fourth with the organization, Rohloff slipped down to the minors and hasn't been seen on NHL ice since. The University of Minnesota-Duluth graduate played for the U.S. at the 1997 World Championships, but beyond that has stayed out of the top echelons of the game.

ROHLOFF, Todd
b. Grand Rapids, Illinois, January 16, 1974

After graduating from the University of Miami-Ohio in 1998, Rohloff did not step smartly into the NHL. Instead, the undrafted defenceman played three years in the minors before impressing Washington at camp in 2001. He had a good stint with the Caps but was slowed by an ankle injury and found himself back in the minors to start the 2002-03 season.

ROLFE, Dale ("Goat")
b. Timmins, Ontario, April 30, 1940

A defenceman with tremendous strength, when Rolfe put his mind to taking his man and keeping him away from the puck, there was little the opponent could do. Scouted by Boston, he played junior in Barrie and earned a three-game trial with the Bruins at the end of the '59-'60 season. From then until expansion, he was a

minor-leaguer and spent much of his time in the asylum of hockey cities, Springfield. Under the insane methods of Eddie Shore, Rolfe both came to loathe the game and learned enormous amounts about playing his position from one of the greatest. He nearly retired from hockey because of Shore, but was rescued by L.A. in 1967. For the next eight years, he was a star blueliner in the NHL, but toward the end of his career he was a party to two serious injuries, one on the giving end, one on the receiving end. He inadvertently hit Barry Ashbee in the eye with a shot during the 1974 playoffs that ended Ashbee's career, and then less than a year later he broke his ankle at Madison Square Garden, which ended his own career. He blamed poor ice at MSG for the accident and took legal action against the Rangers, but dropped his suit when New York hired him as a special assignments scout. Rolfe later moved to Gravenhurst, Ontario, where he started his own plumbing and electric company.

In the spring of 1966, at 39, he backstopped Drumheller to an Allan Cup and then retired.
AL ROLLINS

ROLLINS, Elwin "Al"
b. Vanguard, Saskatchewan, October 9, 1926
d. Calgary, Alberta, July 27, 1996

Conn Smythe was a smart cookie if ever there was one. Even while his great goaler Turk Broda was winning Cups and flashing his affectionate smile, Smythe knew he'd have to find a replacement one day. He found his man in Rollins, and in 1949 Rollins joined the Leafs as a backup, discussing the position daily with coach Happy Day. Midway through the next year, Rollins took over full-time for Broda and was nothing short of brilliant. He had a near-perfect record of 27-5-8 and won the Vezina Trophy with a 1.77 GAA. He capped that '50-'51 season with a Stanley Cup, and the year after played all 70 games for the Leafs. In 1952, Smythe traded him to Chicago because he liked Harry Lumley of the Hawks. With Chicago, Rollins was asked to stop more pucks in a game than he had in a season with Toronto (or so it felt). The team was awful, but he was heroic in goal. In '53-'54, he won the Hart Trophy on an awful team and despite giving up 213 goals. Chicago, though, won only 12 games all year, and 5 of those were courtesy of Rollins shutouts. His last full season was '56-'57, and he played a few games for the Rangers a few years later. In the spring of 1966, at 39, he backstopped Drumheller to an Allan Cup and then retired. The fact that he was a number-one goalie in the six-team NHL for almost seven years leaves no doubt he was one of the greats. He went on to a long career as a coach, in the minors and with the University of Alberta. One son, Jerry, was later drafted by Detroit, and Al settled in Tempe, Arizona, where he became a hockey consultant and player agent. He later retired to Calgary, where he passed away.

Jon Rohloff

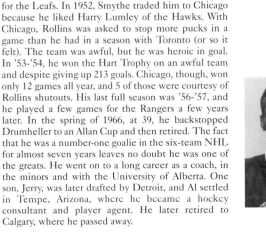

Dale Rolfe

Dwayne Roloson

Brian Rolston

Larry Romanchych

Roberto Romano

Dale Rominski

ROLOSON, Dwayne ("Rolie")
b. Simcoe, Ontario, October 12, 1969
The road from Calgary to Minnesota is not that far if you know the right people. Roloson was signed by Calgary GM Doug Risebrough in 1994 and then years later the two hooked up again with the Wild. Roloson, though, came late to hockey. He didn't start at University of Massachusetts-Lowell until he was 21, and he didn't play for the Flames until 6 years later. But with the Flames and subsequently Buffalo, he was backup, and it wasn't until Risebrough brought him to the expansion team that Roloson became a true number-one starter.

ROLSTON, Brian
b. Flint, Michigan, February 21, 1973
A big man who's scored some big goals, Rolston is in the prime of his career now. He scored the game-winning goal for Lake Superior State in the NCAA championship game in 1992, and four years later scored the overtime winner against Russia to give the U.S. a bronze medal at the World Championships. In between, he was the top scorer on Team USA at the 1994 Olympics in Lillehammer, and he started his career with New Jersey in '94-'95, winning a Cup with the Devils in his rookie season. Nevertheless, his best season with the team came in '98-'99 when he scored 24 goals, and it proved to be his last full year with the team. The next season, he played for three teams, landing in Boston where he developed into a true star. His 31 goals in 2001-02 was a career high, and he finally found ways to use his size, speed, and tremendous shot to full advantage. He also played for the U.S. at the 2002 Olympics in Salt Lake City, winning a silver medal.

ROMANCHYCH, Larry ("Swoop")
b. Vancouver, British Columbia, September 7, 1949
Like the majority of players who pass through the NHL, Romanchych's career had a progression, peak, and then regression. He got a taste of the NHL in 1970-71, made it full-time two years later with Atlanta, and four years later fell back into the minors where he ended his career. A right winger, he had a terrific shot, but he just didn't learn how to use it to become a true scorer.

ROMANIUK, Russ
b. Winnipeg, Manitoba, June 9, 1970
The local boy was drafted by the Jets and played most of his NHL games with them, so he realized a dream just by stepping onto the ice in 1991 to play best against best. Romaniuk played most of his games in the IHL and AHL until 1999, when he decided to

step out and see the world. He has since played in Germany and Italy, and most recently for the Manchester Storm.

ROMANO, Roberto
b. Montreal, Quebec, October 10, 1962
At the ripe old age of 22, Romano had had enough. He was through. He was sick of the travel, the lifestyle of a pro, he wasn't happy with his play, wasn't even happy with his Pittsburgh mates in front of the goalie. Over the summer, he reconsidered, showed up to training camp in September 1985, and had his best year in the NHL, winning 21 games. The year after, more frustration led to a trade and finally a trip to Italy to finish the season. He ended up staying a few years, and even played for Italy at the 1992 World Championships (the Azzurri finished ninth that year). When he returned home, he retired, though he did play a few more games with the Penguins on an emergency basis.

ROMBOUGH, Doug
b. Fergus, Ontario, July 8, 1950
While brother Lorne played in the WHA, Doug was having a go of hockey in the NHL, starting with Buffalo in 1972, the year the WHA began operations. Doug was a big centre but not a gifted or natural scorer. He went from the Sabres to the Islanders in a trade that sent Brian Spencer the other way, and after two partial seasons he was on his way to Minnesota with Ernie Hicke while J.P. Parise came to Long Island. He retired three years later after the Stars demoted him and then never recalled him.

He coached kids and held clinics as best he could until very late in life.
ELWYN ROMNES

ROMINSKI, Dale
b. Farmington Hills, Michigan, October 1, 1975
Time ran out on Rominski pretty quickly. He played four years with the University of Michigan, but after graduating there were no pro takers for his services. It wasn't until late in the summer that Tampa Bay signed him, and he appeared in just three games with the Lightning that year. Over and above that tryout, he's been in the minors.

ROMNES, Elwyn "Doc"
b. White Bear Lake, Minnesota, January 1, 1907
d. Colorado Springs, Colorado, July 21, 1984
Although Romnes won the Lady Byng Trophy for the 1935-36 season, he is more famous for a violent incident two years later in the playoffs when his Black Hawks played the Leafs in the finals. In game one, his nose was smashed in five places by a punch from Red Horner, the toughest man in the league and penalty-minutes leader for a record eight successive seasons. Romnes vowed to get even. Early in the next game, he took a swing at Horner with his stick, missing but

enraging Horner again and fainting dead away from the prospects of another beating. Toronto's trainer, Tim Daly, had to revive the fallen Hawks forward with smelling salts before the game could continue. Chicago went on to win the Cup, but early the next season Romnes was told he had been traded . . . to Toronto. The thought of being teammates with the dreaded Horner so daunted Romnes that he retired then and there, until he was persuaded to go to Toronto by manager Bill Tobin, who guaranteed Romnes a $1,500 bonus for reporting (a bonus he had in his contract for scoring a certain number of goals). Off Romnes went to Union Station, and the first person to greet him was Horner. Romnes retired in 1940 and coached at Michigan Tech for five years. He went to Kansas City of the USHL, led the team to the championship the next year, and then accepted a coaching job at the University of Minnesota, staying on until 1952. Romnes was plagued by severe arthritis. He moved to Colorado Springs because the weather seemed more favourable to his joints, particularly his knees, but in later years he was a virtual cripple. Nonetheless, he coached kids and held clinics as best he could until very late in life.

RONAN, Ed
b. Quincy, Massachusetts, March 21, 1968
Growing up in a suburb of Boston, Ronan developed his hockey skills in the American city that most hated the Montreal Canadiens. Yet it was those hated Habs that drafted him in 1987 on the eve of his college career at Boston University. After graduating, he started his career with Montreal, and in his first full season (1992-93) the team won the Cup. One more full season turned out to be his last, and he quickly moved on to Winnipeg and Buffalo, where he couldn't crack the lineup and ended up in the minors. He retired in 1998.

RONAN, Erskine "Skene"
b. Ottawa, Ontario, February 9, 1889
d. Ottawa, Ontario, June 25, 1937
Ronan grew up in Ottawa and lived most of his life there until his sudden passing. He started his pro career in 1908 with Pittsburgh and moved up to Haileybury before returning to the Ottawa area. He was a first-rate scoring star with the Senators in the days of the NHA and played for the Canadiens when they won the Cup in 1916. He played his only NHL games with the Senators early in the 1918-19 season, and then joined the 74th Battalion for overseas duty. He was shipped to Europe but the armistice was reached before he got to the front, and he returned to Canada safely. His career over, he became manager of

Despite his lack of size, he's strong, durable, and has no fear.
CLIFF RONNING

Carleton Motor Sales and then joined Paquin Motors, where he worked until the day he died. He woke one morning, felt ill, and returned to bed, and by evening he was in hospital, where he passed away in the night.

RONNING, Cliff ("Rat")
b. Burnaby, British Columbia, October 1, 1965
It was a nice story at the time, but it has become better and better with age. When he played midget hockey with the Burnaby Winter Club, Ronning scored the winning goal in the Air Canada championship, the national tournament for that age group. The game was played at Victoria Memorial Arena, and the goalie he beat was Patrick Roy. Roy grew into a Hall of Fame goalie, but Ronning never grew, period. When it came draft time for him, no one wanted to gamble on a 5'8", 170-pound shrimp who'd get creamed in the NHL. Only St. Louis did, in 1984, and more than 16 years and 1,000 games later, the Blues look pretty savvy for making the selection. He's scored 20 goals 8 times, but his most satisfying years came with Vancouver when he took the Canucks to the 1994 Cup finals. Despite his lack of size, he's strong, durable, and has no fear, and the resulting personality makes him a natural leader. He has spent his most recent years with the expansion Nashville team, and as his career winds down he can smile with each passing game, knowing that back in 1984, no one expected him to play even once in the NHL.

RONNQVIST, Jonas
b. Kalix, Sweden, August 22, 1973
Another late draft choice from Sweden, Ronnqvist was 26 when Anaheim selected him in 2000. He had played second-division hockey in Sweden before moving up to Lulea, but in his two pro seasons in North America he played just half a season with the Ducks. Ronnqvist, a right winger, failed to score a single goal and has been in the minors ever since, skating for Cincinnati.

RONSON, Len
b. Brantford, Ontario, July 8, 1936
For one night, he was a hero. On October 5, 1960, Ronson made his NHL debut, with the Rangers, and scored the winning goal, much to the delight of coach Muzz Patrick. Ronson's very place in the lineup was a miracle, and his performance all the more remarkable. He attended his first Rangers camp in 1957 and failed to make a favourable impression before being dished off to the minors. Ditto for 1958 and '59. But in 1960, he was hellbent on making the team, and Patrick was in a bind because he had no other left wingers. His three regulars – Dean Prentice, Eddie Shack, and Camille Henry – were all injured. So, it was Ronson or

Ed Ronan

Len Ronson

bust. Thirteen games later, bust won out over Ronson, who headed back to the AHL. He had his NHL moment in the sun, but he was by no means done. He played another 12 years of hockey, and his scoring prowess lasted many of those years in the Western league, where he became the all-time leader in goals, assists, and points for the San Diego Gulls.

RONTY, Paul
b. Toronto, Ontario, June 12, 1928
He made his reputation as a playmaker, but Ronty could also score. In his first full season, '48-'49, he led Boston with 49 points, including 20 goals. He played four years with the Bruins, four more with the Rangers, and finished his career in '55-'56. Toward the end of the season, the Blueshirts put him on waivers and Montreal claimed him to take the place of Maurice Richard, who had just been suspended for the balance of the year for punching a linesman. Ronty closed out the season with the Habs, but had established his own business, Paul Ronty Insurance, in Boston and didn't want to uproot his family. At 27, he retired, returned to Boston, and ran his company for years afterward.

ROONEY, Steve
b. Canton, Massachusetts, June 28, 1962
During his final year at Providence College, Rooney had about as busy a year as a student/player can have. He led his Friars to the NCAA championships and then was called up to Montreal for the last few games of the season and the playoffs. He scored a goal for the Habs against Boston on his wedding day (April 13, 1985), and throughout the playoffs went back to Providence to write final exams to complete his degree in business administration. The next year, the tough winger made the Habs full-time, but he missed half a season with an injury. He was a healthy scratch for the entire post-season until the last game, when coach Jean Perron put him into the lineup so he could have his name on the Cup. That surprise run to the Cup was followed by uncertainty for Rooney, who was traded to Winnipeg and New Jersey in successive seasons. He finished in the minors and made his home in Boston, where he saw his son, Joe, go on to play for Boston College and hope to make it to the NHL one day himself.

Steve Rooney

ROOT, Bill ("Rooter")
b. Toronto, Ontario, September 6, 1959
It's toughest of all for a stay-at-home defenceman to make a noticeable impression because his role, by definition, is to be spectacularly unspectacular, to shine by being dull, to perform by negative force. Root left junior in 1979 to sign with Montreal, but spent three years in the minors without a hope of making a star-studded Habs defence. When he finally did get his chance, in 1982, he was impressive, and the team kept him for a year and a half before trading him to Toronto as a new wave of super-defencemen joined Montreal. His three years with the Leafs were marked by injury, demotions to the minors, and fluctuating degrees of happiness and unhappiness, and after a season with St. Louis and the Flyers, Root returned to the Leafs fold for the farm team in Newmarket, where he played the final three years of his career.

Bill Root

ROSA, Pavel
b. Most, Czechoslovakia (Czech Republic), June 7, 1977
On the surface, Rosa's short NHL career seems to have been a bust, but mitigating circumstances go a long way to explain his inability to make an impact in the league. He moved to Quebec in 1995 to play after being drafted by Los Angeles that summer, hoping to adapt to the Q and prepare for the NHL by immersion. He led Hull to a Memorial Cup in 1997, and attended the Kings training camp full of hope. That hope was crushed by a serious concussion, and it took Rosa a year and a half to make a full recovery from post-concussion syndrome. He played some games with L.A. that year and just three more the next, but after playing mostly in the minors returned to Europe to continue his career on the larger ice where head injuries are fewer and farther between.

ROSATI, Mike
b. Toronto, Ontario, January 7, 1968
He never allowed a goal in his entire NHL career, which is good, but he played only 28 minutes, for Washington, which is less good. Rosati played at St. Mike's and then moved to Hamilton to play junior, but although he was drafted by the Rangers in 1988 he played his first year of pro in the East Coast league, not a positive sign for the goalie. As a result, he accepted an offer to play in Italy, and he has been there, more or less, ever since. The only exception was '88-'89 when he played for the Caps and in the minors. Rosati has also used his status in the Italian league to play for the national team, notably at the World Championships four times.

ROSS, Art ("Dour Scot")
b. Naughton, Ontario, January 13, 1886
d. Boston, Massachusetts, August 5, 1964
Almost from the day he was born until the day he died Ross was involved in hockey. He gave everything he had to the sport and made as fine a contribution to the game as any man who walked the earth. His father worked as a factor, or storekeeper, in the Thousand Islands, and a group of Ojibway made Ross his first pair of skates. He learned to glide on Whitefish Bay and when he was old enough he left home to live in Montreal and play hockey. By the time he was 20 the Kenora Thistles brought him in as a ringer for their Stanley Cup challenge and they thought so much of him that they paid him $1,000 a game for the two-game series they won. The next year, Ross won the Cup again with the Montreal Wanderers, the team for which he played most of his career. The one exception was 1909-10 when he played in Cobalt, mining country, again after being lured there for a fantastic salary. Ross played in the NHA with the Wanderers and Ottawa Senators until 1917 when the league became the NHL. He played just three games with the Wanderers in the new league before their arena burned down and then he retired as a player. He immediately became a referee and later coached the Hamilton Tigers in senior hockey. In 1924, Charles Adams was intent on bringing NHL hockey to Boston, and he recruited Ross to help him. Theirs was a fortuitous match, and Ross quite literally lived the rest of his life in the Hotel Kenmore in downtown Boston.

He coached or managed the team from 1924 to '54, winning 10 league championships and 3 Stanley Cups. He discovered almost every great star of the era for the team, from Eddie Shore to the Kitchener Kids (i.e., the Kraut Line) to the Dynamite Line. In 1945, he was among the inaugural group to be given the official scroll of admittance to the International Hockey Hall of Fame, located in Kingston, Ontario (later to become the Hockey Hall of Fame relocated in Toronto) during a presentation at the Boston Garden prior to a game. Ross also was a pioneer on two other fronts. One, he convinced the league's board of governors to adopt pucks made of synthetic rubber, not natural rubber, for a more consistent puck. This became known as the Art Ross puck (sometimes the Ross-Tyer puck) and is more or less the same weight, size, and design as the standard NHL puck of the 21st century. Two, Ross persuaded the league to use a B-style goal net, square in front with a double-round back to ensure that pucks stay in the net. In 1947, to honour Ross, the league instituted the Art Ross Trophy, to be given annually to the league's leading point-getter in the regular season, a trophy, of course, that continues to be handed out every year in recognition of one of the game's greatest men.

Ross persuaded the league to use a B-style goal net, square in front with a double-round back.
ART ROSS

ROSS, Jim
b. Edinburgh, Scotland, May 20, 1926
Ross grew up in Toronto during the years leading up to the Second World War and then embarked on a pro career that took him to the NHL by 1951 with the New York Rangers. He played defence with the Blueshirts for a season and a half and wound up in the WHL with Saskatoon at the close of his career.

ROSSIGNOL, Roland "Rosie"
b. Edmunston, New Brunswick, October 18, 1921
It's a good thing he got his NHL games in before October 26, 1947. That night, in an AHL game, he collided with Les Costello and broke his leg. It wasn't just any break, though. Rossignol was in hospital for a year, never able to walk without the aid of crutches. When the last cast was finally removed, his progress was painfully slow and it was another year before he could skate full out and play with contact. By that time, though, it was patently clear to him that the NHL was not an option and he played senior hockey the rest of his days. He had been in the NHL during the war, playing for Detroit and Montreal after establishing himself in the Quebec senior league.

ROSSITER, Kyle
b. Edmonton, Alberta, June 9, 1980
Large, tough, fast, and mobile, Rossiter might develop into a formidable defenceman. He played for Canada at the 2000 World Juniors during his WHL career and turned pro with Florida in 2001. He made his NHL debut at the end of the 2001-02 season but found himself back in the minors to start the next year.

ROTA, Darcy
b. Vancouver, British Columbia, February 16, 1953
When doctors tell you you need stitches, you hurry to the medical room. When they tell you you need to rehab an injury, you do so without blinking. When he tells you you might wind up in a wheelchair if you reinjure yourself, you listen long and hard. Rota was a high Chicago draft in 1973 after scoring a ton of goals in junior, but when he joined the Hawks that fall he lived up to his billing as both a scorer and a weak defensive player. He scored 20 goals in each of his first four seasons with Chicago, but a slump sent him to Atlanta and Vancouver. He had his best years with his hometown, including a 42-goal season in '82-'83, his last full season. In February 1984, he injured his neck when hit by Jay Wells of L.A. in front of the net, and then reinjured it in a fight a short time later. He missed a few games, didn't feel right, and saw doctors. That's when he had surgery on his neck and was told another injury could land him in a wheelchair. On December 4, 1984, Rota retired, sore but healthy. He worked with the Canucks in public relations and then as director of player personnel. He also coached and managed the Burnaby Bulldogs of the BCJHL and hosted his own TV talk show on the CBC. Most recently, Rota has become co-owner of the Coquitlam entry in the B.C. junior league with Bill Ranford and Dave Lowry.

ROTA, Randy
b. Creston, British Columbia, August 16, 1950
It was not a monster trade by any means, but strangely it helped Rota break into the NHL. At the start of the '71-'72 season, California traded him to Montreal for John French and Lyle Carter and a year later he made his NHL debut with the cream of the crop rather than the dregs of the league. Playing on a line with Frank and Peter Mahovlich, he scored his first goal in his first game, but played only once more with the Habs before being traded to L.A. and then Kansas City. He played his last two seasons in the WHA before settling in Kamloops, where he became an underwriter for Mutual Life of Canada. His cousin, Darcy Rota, also made it to the NHL.

Jim Ross

Darcy Rota

Randy Rota

ROTHSCHILD, Sam

b. Sudbury, Ontario, October 16, 1899
d. Sudbury, Ontario, April 15, 1987

The first Jewish player in the NHL, Rothschild played for the Montreal Maroons in each of the team's first three years of existence, 1924-27. At 125 pounds, he was one of the lightest players the pro game has even known. Rothschild played on a line with Bill Phillips and Frank Carson and helped the team win the Stanley Cup in 1926. He closed out his career in '27-'28 with Pittsburgh and the Americans and then returned to Sudbury. Rothschild became a prominent citizen and highly successful clothier in the city, serving as city alderman and losing a mayoral election in 1963. He was also a sales executive with Seagrams and the president of the Dominion Curling Association in 1957-58. From 1979 until near his death he was in a nursing home in Falconbridge.

ROULSTON, Orville "Rolly"

b. Toronto, Ontario, April 12, 1911
d. April 24, 1983

It was the best and worst of times for Roulston because he played for Detroit for three important seasons, 1936-38, when the team won consecutive Cups in the first two years. Unfortunately, the team was so strong that Roulston appeared in only a handful of games during the regular season and none in the playoffs. He finished his career in the American league.

ROULSTON, Tom

b. Winnipeg, Manitoba, November 20, 1957

You can't get much closer to winning a Cup than Roulston got. He played for Edmonton from 1980 to late '83, increasing his contributions each year as the team became a champion capable of defeating the reigning New York Islanders. But in December '83, he was traded to Pittsburgh for Kevin McClelland and a draft choice, and it was McClelland who won four Cups and not Roulston. After the Penguins, he gravitated to Europe, and once his playing days were over he retired to Wichita, where he had played parts of two years in Edmonton's system. In fact, in '80-'81, when he appeared in just a few games for the Oilers, Roulston led the CHL with 63 goals. He was out of the game for five years and then was coerced to play in the CHL for the renamed Wichita Thunder, and the team went on to win the championship. At season's end, he retired for good and continued to work in the city.

ROUPÉ, Magnus

b. Jonkoping, Sweden, March 23, 1963

In an almost 20-year career in Sweden, Roupé used

Tom Roulston

Magnus Roupé

Bob Rouse

his play at the 1987 Canada Cup as a springboard to the NHL, joining Philadelphia right after that series ended. He stayed for just a little more than a year, and when he realized he was bound for a career in the minors, he packed his bags and went home. He helped Sweden win a silver medal at the 1990 World Championships and continued to play for close to another decade.

ROUSE, Bob

b. Surrey, British Columbia, June 18, 1964

They don't make defensive defencemen more perfect than Rouse, who couldn't break a sheet of glass with his shot but who also couldn't be got around without the greatest of efforts. He turned pro with Minnesota toward the end of the '83-'84 season, and it wasn't until 17 years and 1,061 games later that his career was done. Along the way, he helped Toronto become a force once again in the early 1990s, and like a number of Leafs defencemen – Larry Murphy, Todd Gill, Dmitri Mironov – he wound up playing for Detroit. In Rouse's case, that meant winning Cups with the Wings in 1997 and '98, and he closed out his career with San Jose. He never won an individual honour and was never named to an All-Star Team, but Rouse went about his business in a quiet and successful manner throughout his years.

Rousseau was known for his great speed and terrific shot.
BOBBY ROUSSEAU

ROUSSEAU, Bobby

b. Montreal, Quebec, July 26, 1940

While playing junior for the Hull-Ottawa Canadiens in the late 1950s, Rousseau earned a reputation as perhaps the most promising teen in all of Canada. One of 12 children, he felt familial pressure to succeed because 2 of his older brothers had unsuccessfully tried to crack the NHL (Roland and Guy played just a few games each). He got further inspiration when the Leafs refused to loan Dave Keon to Canada's 1960 Olympics team and the Canadiens gave Rousseau up. He played well, helped Canada win a silver medal, and played a few games with Montreal the next year. He won the Calder Trophy for '60-'61 and stayed with the Habs for 10 years, winning 4 Cups along the way. Rousseau was known for his great speed and terrific shot, though some criticized him for a lack of physical play, attributable to his size (5'10" and 175 pounds). He was also perhaps the first diver in the league, known to go for a long dive to try to draw a penalty whenever an opponent came near him. He was traded to Minnesota in 1970 for Claude Larose, a move that stunned both him and Montreal fans, and a year later he moved on to the Rangers where he closed out his career. Rousseau was a superb golfer, acting as an assistant pro in the summers and even playing in the 1962

Canadian Open. Once he retired, he bought the Louiseville Golf Club and turned his occupation and obsession from winter sport to summer.

ROUSSEAU, Guy
b. Montreal, Quebec, December 21, 1934

The older brother of Bobby and the younger brother of Roland, Guy recorded only one NHL point, an assist, but is one he'll remember forever. He was called up to the Habs in December 1954 because of injuries, but in 1 of only 2 games he assisted on Maurice Richard's 400th career goal. Two years later, he was up for two more games, but beyond that he played mostly in the AHL and later Quebec senior.

ROUSSEAU, Roland
b. Montreal, Quebec, December 1, 1929

The oldest of five brothers in the large Rousseau clan, Roland was marked as a prospect from the time he played in the 1949 Memorial Cup and threw his weight around with a veteran's authority. His development, though, didn't impress the Canadiens and he played just twice with the Habs a few years later. Rousseau spent most of the rest of his career playing in the Quebec league and in senior hockey, never getting another callback despite the great teen promise he had shown those many years ago.

ROUSSEL, Dominic
b. Hull, Quebec, February 22, 1970

The domineering father might be a leitmotif in women's tennis, but to see it in hockey is strange, to say the least. After a fine junior career in Quebec, Roussel was intent on making the Flyers lineup in 1991 when he went to camp with the team. He hired his father, Andre, to act as his agent and financial adviser, and all started smoothly when Dominic played as well as starter Ron Hextall when given the chance. By his third season, he was the number-one man and had a record of 29-20-5. This sent his father to the bargaining table, demanding huge sums for his son, but the Flyers balked and countered by signing Garth Snow, a proven goalie who could adequately fill the role as backup. Roussel's father told his son to sit out, but this resulted only in a demotion when he finally caved in. His reputation beaten down, Dominic fired his father and had to take him to court to reclaim his money. When the dust settled, he had a new agent, had reacquired all his earnings, and had signed with Anaheim looking for a fresh start. He settled into the backup role behind Guy Hebert, but soon was traded to Edmonton. In 2001, Roussel could find no takers over and above Quebec senior hockey, and a once-

By his third season, he was the number-one man and had a record of 29-20-5.
DOMINIC ROUSSEL

promising career had dimmed to the point of near oblivion because of an overzealous father.

ROUTHIER, Jean-Marc
b. Quebec City, Quebec, February 2, 1968

There really wasn't a whole lot to get excited about even in junior. Routhier was drafted by his local Nordiques in 1986 and played eight pointless (literally) games for the team. All told, he played just a season and a half of pro hockey before quitting in December 1989 to return to school.

ROWE, Bobby
b. Heathcote, Ontario, 1886
d. unknown

Rowe made it to the NHL only toward the very end of his career, but it wasn't lack of skill or opportunity that took him so long. He played in the pre-NHL days of the NHA, and had the option of playing in the Pacific Coast league where salaries and competition were comparable to the east. He won a Stanley Cup with Seattle in 1917, the team he spent much of his career with, and in 1924 he played a few games with Boston in the NHL.

Bobby Rowe

ROWE, Mike
b. Kingston, Ontario, March 8, 1965

Here was a defenceman who provided his teams with the euphemistic physical presence. From his days with the Marlies in the early 1980s to his only games in the NHL, with Pittsburgh, he fought his way into the hearts of coaches. Rowe quickly realized he wasn't going to be a Probert or a Domi, though, and accepted an offer to play in Britain, an offer he continued to accept for seven years. All the while, he kept right on fighting and fighting.

ROWE, Ron
b. Toronto, Ontario, November 30, 1923

In a lengthy minor pro career, Lowe was called up from the New York Rovers to play for the Rangers for all of five games in the '47-'48 season. A forward, he was a capable scorer but all of his years in the Pacific Coast league never earned him another NHL chance.

ROWE, Tom
b. Lynn, Massachusetts, May 23, 1956

Hockey clearly on his mind from an early age, Rowe moved to Ontario to play junior rather than go to a college at home. He worked his way into the Washington lineup in '76-'77, and within 2 years had scored 31 goals, the first-ever American to reach 30. He was traded to Hartford and then started to move around, and his career trickled to a close with more and more time in the minors. Rowe retired in 1984 and returned

Tom Rowe

Andre Roy

Patrick Roy

to the Whalers, working as a scout and then assistant GM. When the team moved to Carolina, he assumed a number of roles with the farm team in Lowell, from GM to assistant coach.

ROY, Andre
b. Port Chester, New York, February 8, 1975
A fighter, plain and simple, Roy, paradoxically, once won Ottawa's hardest shot competition – slapshot, that is. He began his career with Boston in 1995 and carried on with the Senators, reaching the nadir of his career toward the end of the 2001-02 season when he left the penalty box to get at an opponent. In the process, he struggled with a linesman, and that combination earned him a 13-game suspension.

ROY, Jean-Yves
b. Rosemere, Quebec, February 17, 1969
Roy has played long stretches with Canada's National Team, notably in the years leading up to the 1994 Olympics in Lillehammer where the Canadians won a silver medal. In the immediate years afterwards he played for three NHL teams, having his biggest impact with Boston. Nonetheless, in 1998, Roy accepted an offer to play overseas rather than fight for NHL time by playing in the minors, and he's been in Germany and Switzerland ever since.

ROY, Patrick
b. Quebec City, Quebec, October 5, 1965
Great goalies of the past have been associated with a number of epithets. They were crazy for playing without a mask, fearless, idiosyncratic, loners. But before Patrick Roy, there wasn't a top goalie whom you could have called egomaniacal, a goalie who played with a confidence and acted off ice with an arrogance heretofore not befitting the position. He brought another dimension to the game and, love him or hate him, he has succeeded with it on his own terms. As a kid, he idolized Nordiques goalie Daniel Bouchard, and when Bouchard gave young Patrick a goalie stick, the boy slept with it every night. When he got old enough to play junior, Roy was in Granby, the worst team in the Q. This suited him just fine, because it meant getting 50 shots a game and developing his skills faster than the goalie on the best team who only got 20 shots. By his third year, he earned a callup to the Habs and recorded his first win in his first game by playing just one period while the team raffled for a victory. He spent the end of that '84-'85 season with the team's AHL affiliate in Sherbrooke and improbably became the starting goalie and led the team to the Calder Cup. The next training camp, he was the number-one goalie for the Habs, and by year's end his play alone gave the

His equipment got **to be so large that the NHL recently imposed stricter limits on size.**
PATRICK ROY

team a Stanley Cup it had no right to win otherwise. He was named the Conn Smythe Trophy winner, and everyone in Montreal called him Saint Patrick. In his 12 years with the team, Roy won 30 games 5 times, replicating in 1993 his Cup heroics of seven years previous. He won three Vezina Trophies and was a hero to the city, but everything changed on December 2, 1995. He had never gotten along well with coach Mario Tremblay, but on this night Detroit came to the Forum and beat the Habs 12-1. Roy was in net for the first nine goals before being pulled, and was so incensed that on his way off the ice he told team president Ronald Corey that he had played his last game for the Habs. Corey traded him to Colorado, and that very spring he helped the Avs win the Cup, his third. He won another championship in 2001 and has piled up statistics that have surpassed all of the greats. He is the first goalie to play in 1,000 regular-season games and the only goalie to win 500. He holds playoff records for most games played and most victories. In his early years, he was the first goalie to wear oversized equipment as a way of stopping the puck. He wore webbed sweaters to trap pucks between his arms and body, and his catching glove grew to be much larger than anything Sawchuk or Hall ever used. His equipment got to be so large that the NHL recently imposed stricter limits on size, but Roy has continued his winning ways regardless. Internationally, he has played only once in his entire career, at the 1998 Olympics in Nagano when he lost a goaltender's battle with Dominik Hasek in the semifinals. He was a contender for one of three goalie positions for Team Canada at the 2002 Olympics in Salt Lake City, but publicly announced he would not play in that tournament in order to rest for the NHL playoffs. The extra rest apparently did him little good because in game seven of the conference finals against his old nemesis Detroit, the Wings hammered the Avalanche 7-0. Wings forwards Steve Yzerman and Brendan Shanahan, gold medallists at Salt Lake City, went on to win the Cup as well. In all, Roy has played in eight All-Star Games and is the only goalie to win three Conn Smythe trophies. He is a certain member of the Hockey Hall of Fame after he retires, and has established records that will take years to break.

ROY, Stephane
b. Ste. Foy, Quebec, June 29, 1967
Unlike his brother, Patrick, Stephane never made it in the NHL beyond the 12 games he played for Minnesota in the 1980s. The brothers played together in Granby, but from there their paths diverged. Stephane played for Canada's juniors in 1987, the year

the team was disqualified following a Soviets-instigated brawl, and after he passed through the NHL he returned to the National Team for three years. Roy then moved to Europe, and then back to the minors in North America. He retired for a year but missed the game too much, and he continues to play senior hockey now that the top minor pro leagues are out of the question for him.

ROYER, Gaetan
b. Donnacona, Quebec, March 13, 1976

Evidently, Royer did not have a good season in 2000-01 in the Calgary system. He had been playing in the minors for four years without any NHL affiliation, but after one season in Saint John with the AHL Flames he was let go. Tampa Bay signed him and moved him around in the minors, but at least the Lightning also called him up for three games.

ROYER, Remi
b. Donnacona, Quebec, February 12, 1978

Considering he was drafted in the second round by Chicago in 1996, Royer has done precious little in the NHL. The tough guy stuck around for only 18 games with the Hawks and since then has played for a number of minor pro teams. He's now a staple in the East Coast league, and a callup means going to the AHL. Despite his toughness, it's not likely he'll make it back to the NHL.

ROZSIVAL, Michal
b. Vlasim, Czechoslovakia (Czech Republic), September 3, 1978

It didn't take Rozsival long to go from the draft in 1996 to the WHL to finish his junior career and adapt to the NHL style of play. He played a year in the minors, and when he joined Pittsburgh in 1999 he made a significant contribution to the blueline. Rozsival is a solid hitter and defensively capable player who has given the Pens some decent offence from the blueline as well. Young and solid, he is likely to be part of this resurgent team if it goes into the playoffs any time soon.

ROZZINI, Gino
b. Shawinigan Falls, Quebec, October 24, 1916
d. April 18, 1996

It was very simple. Boston needed as many able-bodied players as it could find during the war, so it went to the Quebec Aces in 1944, the team that had just won the Allan Cup, and signed Rozzini, a scoring centre. The B's used him for half of the '44-'45 season, and he played the rest of the year with the Olympics in the American league. He even played through the '45 playoffs when Boston lost to Detroit in the semifinals, but thereafter Rozzini played for many years in Spokane.

RUCCHIN, Steve
b. Thunder Bay, Ontario, July 4, 1971

A rare bird on two counts. Rucchin came out of the University of Western Ontario with a B.Sc. in biology in 1994. Not only did he make it to the NHL, he had an impact. And since joining Anaheim that fall, he has played his entire career with the Ducks, the second-longest service to the team after Paul Kariya, leader of the quack. Rucchin has been a godsend to Kariya, one of the few skilled players the team has had who can put the puck in the net and take some pressure off him to do all the scoring. Rucchin's abilities on the power play are also key to the team's modest success in that area. Rucchin's career took a serious turn downward in mid-December when he was hit in the face by a puck. He missed the rest of the season with post-concussion syndrome and the Ducks missed the playoffs. He also represented Canada at the 1998 World Championships.

Rucchin came out of the University of Western Ontario with a B.Sc. in biology in 1994.
STEVE RUCCHIN

RUCINSKI, Mike
b. Wheeling, Illinois, December 12, 1963

After attending the local University of Illinois-Chicago, Rucinski signed with Calgary and then his own Hawks after the Flames never used him other than in the minors. He could score goals, but when Chicago brought him up for the 1988 playoffs he didn't do much in his two games played. He appeared only once more for the team the next year and retired soon after, his NHL dream being attained but not sustained.

RUCINSKI, Mike
b. Trenton, Michigan, March 30, 1975

This Mike Rucinski of the next generation grew up in the more serious hockey clime of the OHL, playing for Detroit. Drafted by Hartford, he played his only games with Carolina after the franchise shifted south. Most of his career, though, he's been in the minors playing defence outside the glare of the NHL.

RUCINSKY, Martin
b. Most, Czechoslovakia (Czech Republic), March 11, 1971

A medallist at all levels of international hockey, Rucinsky had the misfortune of being traded from Colorado to Montreal after Patrick Roy threw a tantrum and refused to play for the Habs again after letting in 9 Detroit goals one night. The Avs went on to win the Cup, and Rucinsky went on to become one of the top scorers on a team that was touch-and-go to make the playoffs. In 2001-02, he played for the Habs, Stars, and Rangers during a season full of flux, but is still a reliable scorer. He started his career in Edmonton, though he also played four seasons with Quebec before moving down to Colorado. Rucinsky

Remi Royer

Michal Rozsival

Martin Rucinsky

Jason Ruff

also won gold with the Czechs at the 1998 Olympics in Nagano and the '99 World Championships. In 1991, he won bronze with the WJC team.

RUELLE, Bernie
b. Houghton, Michigan, November 23, 1919
d. Houghton, Michigan, August 4, 1995
Houghton was a university town, home to Michigan Tech, and although Ruelle didn't attend the school, it did become a prominent part of his life later on. During the war, he played two games for the Red Wings before he himself enlisted. After the conflict ended, his very short career was more or less over so he returned to Houghton, where he became a bartender. He later bought his own joint, the Hillside Bar, which he ran for a number of prosperous years.

RUFF, Jason
b. Kelowna, British Columbia, January 27, 1970
A superstar in the IHL, Ruff made a name for himself in the 1994 playoffs, leading Atlanta to the championship. He had played briefly with St. Louis and Tampa Bay, but after 11 years in the "I" he went to Europe to play, first in Germany and more recently with the Belfast Giants.

RUFF, Lindy
b. Warburg, Alberta, February 17, 1960
Never the most talented player in the world, Ruff got by on determination and a modicum of skill in a career that passed mostly with Buffalo. He began in 1979 as a defenceman when 2 regulars, Jerry Korab and Jim Schoenfeld, were injured, and for the next 10 years he was a mainstay with the team. In 1983, he moved up to play left wing for three years, a rare example of a player who seemed perfectly comfortable at forward and defence. Ruff became Sabres captain but was traded to the Rangers. Injuries slowed him down, and he finished his career in a place he had never visited before – the minors. As soon as he retired, Ruff became an assistant coach with Florida and then head coach with the Sabres in 1997. He remains with Buffalo and is now one of the longest-serving coaches in the NHL. Under his leadership, the team went to the finals for the first time, in 1999, before losing to Dallas.

Kent Ruhnke

Darren Rumble

As soon as he retired, Ruff became an assistant coach with Florida.
LINDY RUFF

RUHNKE, Kent
b. Toronto, Ontario, September 18, 1952
With a c.v. like his, not many people would have discarded NHL and pro hockey with the apparent ease Ruhnke did. He was a star for the University of Toronto Blues in the early 1970s under coaching legend Tom Watt, and he had a two-game tryout with Boston. He played two years in the WHA and another in Germany, but really wanted to teach. And so he did. In 1979, he

gave up hockey altogether to become the assistant athletic director of Sheridan College in Toronto, but he eventually missed hockey, though not as a player. He moved to Switzerland to coach, and remains there to this day. In 2000, he coached the ZSC Lions to a championship in the Swiss league, where he was for 14 years before moving to Bern in 2001.

RUMBLE, Darren
b. Barrie, Ontario, January 23, 1969
The Flyers really liked what they saw of Rumble in the OHL with Kitchener and drafted him 20th overall in 1987. For a first-round choice, though, Rumble was something of a disappointment. The Flyers nursed him in Hershey for three years and gave him a quick look-see, but they exposed him in the 1992 Expansion Draft and Ottawa scooped him up. Philadelphia later signed him as a free agent, but Rumble was, more or less, a full-time minor-leaguer. That didn't make him chopped liver by any stretch, though. He was named the AHL's best defenceman for '96-'97 and played pro for a dozen years. Not everyone can boast as much.

RUNDQVIST, Thomas
b. Vimmerby, Sweden, May 4, 1960
The two NHL games he played with Montreal in '84-'85 got him acknowledgement in North America, but the truth is he had a superb international career that carried far more weight. In league play, he made Sweden his home for 14 years and ended with a 5-year stay in Austria, all with Feldkirch. But wearing the blue and yellow sweater of Tre Kronor, Rundqvist was exceptional. He won gold in 1987 and again in 1991 at the World Championships, and in 1993 he scored an overtime goal to put Sweden in the finals where they won silver after losing to Russia. In all, he played in eight WC, as well as the 1988 and '92 Olympics in Calgary and Lillehammer, respectively. He also played at the 1987 and '91 Canada Cups, and by the time he retired in 1998 he was one of the top performers in his country's history. He settled near Karlstad and worked for Farjestad of the Swedish league, and he was part of the organizing committee that hosted the 2002 World Championships in his home country.

RUNGE, Paul
b. Edmonton, Alberta, September 10, 1908
d. Vancouver, British Columbia, April 27, 1972
Paul August Runge had a stop-and-start career in the NHL through the 1930s with Boston and Montreal. A forward, he was never quite skilled enough to stick around permanently, yet he proved he was worthy of callups whenever a team needed a fresh body. He played in the minors during this period, and ended his

days with the Portland Buckeroos. Runge settled in Vancouver and became coach of Kerrisdale in the Okanagan-Mainline league. He was also a charter member of the B.C. Benevolent Hockey Association. He suffered a fatal heart attack while playing golf at the Peace Portals course.

RUOTSALAINEN, Reijo ("Rexy"/ "Rental Rexy")
b. Oulu, Finland, April 1, 1960

A small defenceman, Ruotsalainen was heralded as the best Finnish player ever to go on to the NHL. He had speed to burn and a wicked slapshot, making him an ideal player for a skating team geared toward offence – the Edmonton Oilers, for instance. He started his career in New York in 1981 because Lars-Erik Sjoberg, former player and scout of the Rangers, recommended Rexy summa cum laude. Four years later, he moved to Switzerland to play because of a contract dispute, and was traded to the Oilers to join Gretzky, Messier et al. before the season's end. That's when the fun began. They won the Cup that year, '86-'87, and again in '89-'90, but Ruotsalainen had no qualms about playing outside the NHL. Before joining the Rangers, he was a star in Finland and tied a WJC record by playing in the pre-eminent junior tournament four times. Between stints with the Oilers, he also played in Switzerland where crowds of 14,000 jammed the arena in Bern to watch him perform. after 1990, he returned to Europe to play his final years, winning league championships with Bern in 1991 and '92 and then playing for his home club in Oulu. He later became an assistant coach with the Miami Matadors of the ECHL after which he returned to Oulu Karpat in a similar capacity.

RUPP, Duane
b. MacNutt, Saskatchewan, March 29, 1938

During the last years of the Original Six, Rupp played mostly here and there with Toronto, coach Punch Imlach preferring to see him stay in the AHL. In '67-'68, Rupp played the season with the Leafs before moving on to Minnesota and Pittsburgh. He had his greatest successes as a Penguins defenceman. Given the gift of large hands, he brought stability to the blueline for nearly five years during the team's hopeless, early years. He ended up bolting to the WHA and finishing his career in the AHL, with Rochester. Rupp won two Calder Cups with the Americans as a player, and another as a playing coach before being fired in December 1978. In 1991, he was inducted into that team's Hall of Fame. Rupp settled in Pittsburgh, established Rupp's Sporting Goods, and became involved in rink management in Delmont, Pennsylvania.

RUPP, Pat
b. Detroit, Michigan, August 12, 1942

It was the thrill of a lifetime for the 21-year-old, and time would prove it to be a singular thrill. On March 22, 1964, local boy Rupp was called in to replace the great Terry Sawchuk in goal for a game. Rupp acquitted himself well in a 4-1 loss to Toronto and then began a lengthy career in the IHL, predominantly with the Dayton Gems. He was later inducted into the Gems Hall of Fame and also played in two Olympics for the U.S., in 1964 and '68.

RUSKOWSKI, Terry ("Roscoe")
b. Prince Albert, Saskatchewan, December 31, 1954

He had the heart and ferocity of a lion inside his small body, but no one ever entered a battle with Ruskowski and came out looking pretty. He defined the word gritty as used in hockey, though he began his career with the Howe family in Houston of the WHA in 1974. Ruskowski stayed in that league for five seasons, joining Chicago in 1979 only when the two leagues combined forces. After spending much of two seasons in the penalty box, he toned down his roughhousing and developed into a decent playmaker. He captained the Hawks and Kings, to whom he was traded in 1982, and closed out his career in Minnesota, where he was also team captain, a few years later, definitely the worse for wear. Ruskowski quickly made the change from player to coach, going first to the WHL and later to minor pro. Most recently, he has coached Knoxville in the UHL and Laredo in the CHL.

RUSSELL, Cam
b. Halifax, Nova Scotia, January 12, 1969

Big, tough players have been the rage in the NHL the last 20 years or more, but in hockey, perhaps more than any other sport, the bigger they are, the harder they fall. Case in point, Russell. A large defenceman adept at hitting, he was a feared opponent at the start of his career, but the impact of such physical play was as much self-felt as any that oncoming forwards had to deal with. Russell played all but the last of his 10 years with Chicago, finishing with Colorado in '98-'99 following a series of injuries that battered his body to the point of retiring. He finished that season in his hometown, acting as an assistant coach with the Halifax Mooseheads, a job he liked so much he kept right at it.

RUSSELL, Churchill "Church"
b. Winnipeg, Manitoba, March 16, 1923
d. March 31, 1999

Winnipeg is certainly the city with the closest old-time connections to the Rangers, and Russell is but

He suffered a fatal heart attack while playing golf at the Peace Portals course.
PAUL RUNGE

Duane Rupp

Terry Ruskowski

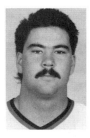
Cam Russell

Church Russell

one of many players to come out of the 'Peg and play on Broadway. He played three seasons with the team in the years immediately after the Second World War, the great year being '46-'47. Playing with Cal Gardner and Rene Trudel, this troika was known as the Atomic Line, so named for the era because of its explosive ability. Russell played the rest of his career in the minors, finishing in Winnipeg. He had postponed his NHL entrance to join the war effort, and for the better part of two years he was a stoker in the Royal Canadian Naval Volunteer Reserve. He was later inducted into the Manitoba Sports Hall of Fame.

Phil Russell

RUSSELL, Phil
b. Edmonton, Alberta, July 21, 1952
Not only was Russell a big and strong defensive defenceman, he was also durable and a survivor. He played more than 1,000 games in the NHL, starting with Chicago in 1972 after being drafted 13th overall. Russell established himself right away on the Hawks blueline, but this was a team in decline, its best years just now over and not a Cup to show for its efforts since 1961. Russell was traded to Atlanta and moved to Calgary with the team, but despite playing his best hockey there he couldn't help the team go very far in the playoffs. He played in three All-Star Games (1976, '77, and '85), and at the end of his career played briefly in Europe, a short but important time for him. Chicago hired him as a scout, and more recently he hooked up with another former player, Blair MacDonald, in an odd partnership. The two became co-coaches in Cleveland, with the Lumberjacks, and then were hired as a tandem to coach the Frankfurt Lions in Germany.

Wayne Rutledge

Rutherford had the dire misfortune to play for teams that almost never made the playoffs.
JIM RUTHERFORD

RUTHERFORD, Jim ("Roach"/ "Rut")
b. Beeton, Ontario, February 17, 1949
A quick, tiny, sharp goalie, Rutherford had the dire misfortune to play for teams that almost never made the playoffs. Throughout his career, he was never thought of as a starter but ended up as such when the putative number one demonstrated an inability to perform the leader's duties. In his decade in Detroit, management was always finding someone to bring in to be the go-to goalie – Ed Giacomin, Ron Low, Rogie Vachon were all brought in, yet none succeeded in pushing Rutherford to the bench for very long. The highlight of his time with the Wings was a three-consecutive-shutout performance, and the low point was falling victim to Ian Turnbull the night the Toronto defenceman scored a record five goals. After retiring, Rutherford became manager for Compuware Sports Corporation and later coached and managed Windsor in the OHL. This eventually led to his hiring

Christian Ruuttu

Jarkko Ruutu

in 1994 as GM of Carolina when the team was still in Hartford, a term that climaxed in the spring of 2002 when the Hurricanes reached the Cup finals for the first time in franchise history.

RUTLEDGE, Wayne
b. Barrie, Ontario, January 5, 1942
The only goalie of his era to wear contact lenses, Rutledge couldn't help but rub his eyes when he saw Terry Sawchuk, his idol, walk into training camp with Los Angeles with a cast on his arm. That meant Rutledge would be the starting goalie for the expansion Kings, a blessing for any kid, but a job tinged with curse because of the team's owner, Jack Kent Cooke. Cooke didn't fancy Rutledge's play too much, and let the media know it. Rutledge's playing time decreased until he was in the minors, but he knew he was a better goalie than an Eastern league puckstopper so he signed with Houston in the WHA in 1972. After all, he had won an Allan Cup with Windsor in 1963 and went on a European tour with that team, performing well enough to give him confidence to make a pro career out of goaltending. In the WHA, Rutledge enjoyed six successful seasons before retiring and moving to Huntsville, Ontario, where he raises horses on his farm and works as a glazier for Dawson Glass and Mirror.

RUUTTU, Christian
b. Lappeenranta, Finland, February 20, 1964
Like many a European, whatever Ruuttu did in the NHL was gravy on the career, not the meat of it. Although he played nine seasons in North America (1986-95), his international accomplishments are more important. He never played in any Olympics for Suomi, but he did play in eight World Championships, though not the 1995 WC when his country won gold for the first time. He also played in two Canada Cups and the 1996 World Cup. In the NHL, he began with two 20-goal seasons and an appearance in the 1998 All-Star Game while playing in Buffalo, the city where he spent six of his NHL seasons.

RUUTU, Jarkko
b. Vantaa, Finland, August 23, 1975
One day – and not too far in the future – there could be three Ruutus skating through the NHL. Brother Mikko has been drafted by Ottawa and brother Tuomo by Chicago, and if it does happen this would be the first Finnish threesome to play in the big league. Jarkko himself is only just starting out, with Vancouver. He has worked his way into the lineup with consistent, physical play after a number of years in pro hockey in Finland. He has no significant

international experience, which means, at least back home, he isn't considered a top player.

RUZICKA, Vladimir ("Rosie")

b. Most, Czechoslovakia (Czech Republic), June 6, 1963

A hero of mythic proportions in the Czech Republic, Ruzicka came to the NHL at the height of his hockey powers after a brilliant career with Litvinov in the Czech league. He had led the league in scoring four times and twice won the Golden Hockey Stick Trophy as the league's MVP. He had played in six World Championships, winning gold in 1985, and when he joined Edmonton he was sure to bring the team goals and speed. It wasn't until two years later, though, with Boston, that he demonstrated his full abilities. That season, he scored 39 times, by far his most productive season. He returned to the Czech Republic in 1994 and played out his career in 2000 after suffering groin and back injuries that reminded him of his age. In 1998, he played in his third and final Olympics, winning gold for the first time. He went on to become GM for Praha, his final team, and worked as an assistant for the team's 2002 entry at the Olympics in Salt Lake City.

RYAN, Terry

b. St. John's, Newfoundland, January 14, 1977

Ryan had a paradoxical relationship with Montreal. On the one hand, he was the first Newfoundlander to play for the Habs (only in 1996), yet he was shafted by the team in a way that has made him resolute in his desire never to play for them again. In his WHL days with Tri-City, Ryan suffered a concussion and serious post-concussion syndrome effects that went undetected. It wasn't until after he played three games with the Habs, when he was feeling ill, that doctors told him to take the rest of the year off. Not good news for a young player who has made a reputation as a fighter. He came back and played just a few games over the next two years, but Montreal GM Rejean Houle told Ryan he had no chance of making the team. Nonetheless, the Habs gave him a qualifying contract offer to ensure that they kept his rights until he turned 31 in 2008, then put him in the minors. Ryan eventually wound up in the West Coast league, playing well below his skill level but unable to get back to the NHL. He got plenty of ice time with Colorado, but when he moved on to Idaho he suffered a bad ankle injury that cost him another half-year of play. His dream of being drafted by the Habs has now turned into a nightmare.

RYCHEL, Warren

b. Tecumseh, Ontario, May 12, 1967

Rychel had the good fortune to make it to the NHL,

but he was even more fortunate to be alive. As a kid, he was best friends with Mike Stapleton, son of Pat Stapleton of NHL fame and glory. The boys were playing on the farm near Strathroy when Warren fell into a funnel used to move grain into storage. He got lodged at the bottom and was trapped, screaming for help. Pat and friends formed a human chain to pull Warren free from the accumulating grain. From then on, everything else was gravy. Rychel was a journeyman fighter of limited skill but resourceful heart and ambition. In his dozen years in the pro ranks, he played for five NHL teams, notably with Colorado during the Cup year of '95-'96. He ended his career with the Avs late in 1998 when he hurt his hand and the Avs let him go, but there were no other takers for a 31-year-old fighter with serious hand troubles. Rychel later became a scout for Phoenix.

RYCROFT, Mark

b. Nanaimo, British Columbia, July 12, 1978

Even though he was never drafted, Rycroft nonetheless left the University of Denver in 2000 after three years to play pro in the minors in the St. Louis system. More than a year later he was recalled by the Blues for a few games, but has remained with Worcester the rest of his career so far.

RYMSHA, Andy

b. St. Catharines, Ontario, December 10, 1968

The six games he played for the Nordiques in '91-'92 might have been his only NHL action, but it was just the tip of a hockey iceberg that has kept Rymsha going in the sport for more than a decade. He has played throughout North America and Europe and has been particularly active in roller hockey, helping Canada win the in-line world championship in 1998. Wherever he has gone, the large defenceman has also made a name for himself as a fighter, becoming popular with the hometown folks and an arch-enemy to opponents.

Vladimir Ruzicka

Terry Ryan

In his dozen years in the pro ranks, he played for five NHL teams, notably with Colorado.
WARREN RYCHEL

SAARINEN, Simo
b. Helsinki, Finland, February 14, 1963

The karma wasn't good, nor were the results. The name Saarinen translates to "islander" yet he was drafted by the Rangers. He started the '84-'85 season with the Blueshirts, but in his eighth game he went to retrieve a puck behind his own goal, lost his footing, and crashed into the (then-unmovable) net. He damaged his knee and missed the rest of the year after surgery. Year 2, he started in the AHL, but after just 13 games, the knee swelled and he was forced out for the rest of another year. The joint didn't get better, so he received a $175,000 disability payment, returned to Finland, and figured his career was over. But Frank Moberg, GM of the Helsinki team of the Finnish league, asked him to come back. Saarinen underwent another surgery, and a few months later found he could still play the game. He was forced to return the diability payment, but went on to play another decade back home. He also played in-line hockey for Finland at the 1996 World Championships, where he was named best defenceman.

SABOL, Shaun
b. Minneapolis, Minnesota, July 13, 1966

Despite being drafted a lowly 209th overall by Philadelphia in 1986, Sabol left the University of Wisconsin after a year and a few games to turn pro, starting with Hershey in the American league. In five seasons, though, he appeared only twice with the Flyers and retired in 1992 never having made a breakthrough in the NHL.

SABOURIN, Bob
b. Sudbury, Ontario, March 17, 1933

Not the brother of Gary, Bob played one NHL game, with Toronto, while he was an 18-year-old at St. Mike's. He turned pro the following year and had a lengthy career, notably with Pittsburgh in the AHL, but he never made it back to the Leafs. At the end of his playing days he wound up in the Eastern league as a playing coach with the Rockets in Jacksonville, Florida.

SABOURIN, Gary
b. Parry Sound, Ontario, December 4, 1943

Few players of such limited talent had the same burning desire to play in the NHL as Sabourin had while growing up. In the years leading up to expansion in 1967, he played in the Central league, where his hard work earned him notice from the Rangers, who signed him and later traded him to St. Louis when the Blues officially started operations. Sabourin flourished in St. Louis, playing seven years with the new team and going to three successive Stanley Cup finals with them. He scored 4 times, but when he fought with coach Lou Angotti he was traded to Toronto and a year later to California. Sabourin suffered from weakened knees in his last years and retired midway through '76-'77 after giving it his all. Even after his days were done, he played oldtimers hockey for the love of it until more surgeries required him to stop skating altogether. He settled in Chatham, Ontario, bought a Buns Master franchise, and operated his bakery with the help of his family.

SABOURIN, Ken
b. Scarborough, Ontario, April 28, 1966

He didn't exactly score the winning goal or anything, but Sabourin did play a few games with Calgary in '88-'89 and once in the playoffs to stake a claim as part of the Flames' run to their first Stanley Cup. He played just a few more games with the team in the next two years and faced a similar problem with Washington after being traded to the Caps in 1991. A tough defenceman who accrued much more than his fair share of penalty minutes, Sabourin ended his playing and fighting days in the "I," where he played for years. He later became an insurance salesman.

SACCO, David
b. Malden, Massachusetts, July 31, 1970

The Leafs drafted Saccos back to back, selecting Joe in 1987 and David in 1988, and although both played for Toronto during their careers, they weren't teammates there as they were almost everywhere else. They played together at Boston University, but while Joe turned pro early David continued on at BU and played internationally as well. David played at the 1993 World Championships and then spent the next year with the U.S. National Team, through the 1994 Olympics in Lillehammer. He joined the Leafs for a few games and the next year was traded to Anaheim to play with Joe. After just a few games over two years, David was in the minors and then went to Europe to close out his career in Germany.

SACCO, Joe
b. Medford, Massachusetts, February 4, 1969

Joe's hockey prospects were better than brother David's, and as a result he left Boston University early to play some games with Toronto in '90-'91. Once he realized he was not in the Leafs' plans, though, he joined the U.S. National Team and played at the World Championships and then the 1992 Olympics in Albertville. He saw some more action with the Leafs, but it wasn't until Anaheim claimed him in the Expansion Draft that his career really got on track. Not particularly big or flashy, Sacco did many other things well. He could check and kill penalties, play defensively, and chip in the odd goal. He's hung around long enough to play 700 games, and shows no signs of slowing down. Additionally, he has played in six World Championships for his country, most recently in 2002 in Sweden.

SACHARUK, Larry
b. Saskatoon, Saskatchewan, September 16, 1952

Who knows how high high could have been had Sacharuk not been hit in the eye by a puck during practice with the Rangers in the '75-'76 season. To that point, he had shown tremendous promise, though he was by no means perfect. In junior with Saskatoon, he scored 50 goals in his final year, a common total for a forward but an exceptional one for a defenceman. To this day, no one has broken that record. He played most of his career with the Rangers, though in '74-'75 he was with St. Louis and scored 20 goals that year, becoming just the seventh defenceman ever to reach that plateau in the NHL. Then came the eye injury, a detached retina, that caused him to miss half a year and more or less ended his NHL days.

Simo Saarinen

Gary Sabourin

Ken Sabourin

Joe Sacco

Larry Sacharuk

Bob Sabourin
(opposite page)

SAFRONOV, Kirill

b. Leningrad, Soviet Union (Russia), February 26, 1981

Phoenix made Safronov a high draft choice in 1999 and he came to Canada to play junior in the Quebec league that very fall. A year and a half of pro followed before the Coyotes called him up for a single game on December 23, 2001, and before the end of the year they had traded him to Atlanta. He played two games with the Thrashers to end the season and then made the team's starting defence corps for 2002-03. He played his way back to the minors, though, and, in the opinion of the Thrashers, still has some developing to do. During his first year in the AHL, 2000-01, he helped his team win the Calder Cup.

SAGANIUK, Rocky

b. Mymam, Alberta, October 15, 1957

Rocky Saganiuk

Rocky Ray Saganiuk was named after Rocky Marciano and Sugar Ray Robinson, but Saganiuk was too small to become a fighter, either in the ring or at the rink. Drafted by Toronto in 1977, he almost lost his career before it ever started. In an AHL game, he was viciously cross-checked and broke two vertebrae in his neck. He recovered, but the injury never fully went away before it got worse. After another season in the minors in which he was named AHL MVP and got a chance with the Leafs, he made the team permanently in '79-'80 and played on the Kid Line with John Anderson and Laurie Boschman. The 24 goals he scored with that threesome was never repeated, though, and soon he was back in the minors and on his way to Pittsburgh. Saganiuk hurt his back with the Pens and needed surgery, and the Leafs re-signed him in the hopes he might recover again. He didn't. He did manage to play senior hockey in Ontario, winning the Allan Cup with the famous Brantford Motts Clamatos team of '87-'88. He moved to England to play and coach, and upon returning, became coach of the Lethbridge Hurricanes in the WHL. He was fired early in the '95-'96 season and later found a job in Woodbridge, Illinois, working for the Seven Bridge Ice Arena.

SAKIC, Joe

b. Burnaby, British Columbia, July 7, 1969

One of the greatest players in the history of hockey, Sakic can be classed in that most remarkable of groups that includes Orr, Gretzky, Howe, Yzerman, Messier, and Lemieux. His accomplishments are extraordinary, his abilities almost without compare, and his rise to the top progressive but successful. While most players who have incredible skill are aware they have a gift, Sakic was perhaps made more aware by the tragedy of December 30, 1986. Playing for Swift Current in the WHL, he and his mates were on a bus trip when an accident claimed the lives of four players. Sakic drew strength from the horror and brought his team closer together, and the year after he was the uncontested star of the league. Drafted by Quebec, a terrible team at the time, he joined the Nordiques in 1988 as a 19-year-old. In both his second and third years he eclipsed 100 points on the year, though the team was far from playoff contention. He not only accumulated points, but also became the leader of the team, forcing players to compete at higher levels and making them more competitive. The team quickly made it to the playoffs, and after moving to Colorado they won the Stanley Cup in 1996, his eighth year with them. He scored a record eight game-winning goals in those playoffs, including two in overtime. He was the Conn Smythe Trophy winner, and during the span of half his career he had taken the worst team in the league to the greatest hockey championship around. Two years earlier, he had played for Canada at the World Championships, and there he led the nation to a gold in that tournament for the first time since 1961. Sakic has gone on to score his 500th goal and 1,000th point. He played for Canada at the 1996 World Cup and the two NHL Olympics in 1998 and 2002, and he has captained the team longer than any current NHLer with the exception of his counterpart in Detroit, Steve Yzerman. In 2000-01, he had another exceptional year, leading the team to its second Cup and

Drafted by Quebec, a terrible team at the time, he joined the Nordiques in 1988 as a 19-year-old.
JOE SAKIC

winning three individual awards – Hart, Lady Byng, and Pearson. Sakic has exceptional acceleration, the best quick wrist shot in the game, and about a dozen eyes in his head used for passing and finding open areas of ice. He is both big enough to play a physical game and yet sportsmanlike enough not to make it a part of his game. He is as sure a Hall of Famer as is playing in the NHL now, and when he retires, the game will be the lesser for his loss.

SALEI, Ruslan

b. Minsk, Soviet Union (Belarus), November 2, 1974

Salei has been an NHLer since 1996, playing all his games and years with Anaheim on the Ducks defence. But nothing – nothing – comes close to what he helped accomplish at the 2002 Olympics in Salt Lake City. In the quarter-finals, his Belarus team made history by beating Sweden 4-3 in one of the greatest upsets in international hockey. Salei was on the blue-line for the team, and although it went on to lose to Canada and Russia to place fourth, it was a staggeringly high finish for the tiny, young nation.

Ruslan Salei

SALESKI, Don ("Big Bird")
b. Moose Jaw, Saskatchewan, November 10, 1949

Like every other member of the Flyers' two Cup teams in 1974 and '75, Saleski did little outside his days with the most violent team in NHL history. Euphemistically called a role player, he was, more directly, a fighter and intimidator, a slow, plodding forward whose job it was to hook and clutch and punch the league's skilled players. He managed three 20-goal seasons with the Broad Street Bullies with his limited skills, but take him outside Fred Shero's goon system and there wasn't much on the talent scale. Sometimes popular with fans, other times reviled for poor play, he lasted eight seasons with the team and at one point had his own disco, Bird's Nest, in town. After retiring, he returned to Philadelphia, of course, and did some television work for the Flyers. He later became director of business development for the Spectacor Corporation in that city.

Don Saleski

SALMING, Borje ("B.J."/ "King")
b. Kiruna, Sweden, April 17, 1951

The word *pioneer* evokes images of the old men of the game, men such as Lord Stanley or Art Ross or Georges Vezina or Cyclone Taylor. But Salming was a modern-day pioneer, a trailblazer, a Swedish hockey player who became the first superstar from that country and who made it possible for other Europeans to follow. It was no mean feat and it was not easily accomplished, though. Salming played league hockey first in his hometown of Kiruna, near the Arctic Circle, and then with Brynas. Toronto scout Gerry McNamara made a trip to Sweden to scout Inge Hammarstrom, a trip that in itself was pioneering because the NHL had, previously, no interest in Europeans. McNamara liked Hammarstrom, but loved Salming, and quickly endeavoured to get the pair to Toronto as quickly as possible. If it sounds like a fairy tale, it wasn't. They came to Toronto in 1973, and the rest of the league set about testing the mettle of these "chicken Swedes," as they were known, by treating them to the roughest form of North American hockey. In Salming's first game, he was the first star. In his second, he was attacked by Philadelphia goon Dave Schultz and managed to hang on and not get beat up by this almost talentless thug. In coming games, Salming withstood challenges from all teams, and over time he earned a respect that could only come by enduring the rites of NHL passage. His was a bravery that allowed him to survive and permitted him to go home in the summer proud of having made the NHL. Another man might have cowered and given up, but by fighting back Salming showed his country that the NHL was a possibility, as long as you wanted badly enough to play there. Meanwhile, during the games, Salming proved to be

remarkably skilled. In his own end, he was tough as nails and blocked shots fearlessly and with perfect technique. Once he had the puck, he was a fleet and graceful skater who could make pinpoint passes, the European kind in which the puck flies three or four inches off the ice, over enemy sticks, to land softly on a teammate's stick. He had the moves of a forward and a great shot and he became an important part of Toronto's offence as well as its blueline corps. As well, Salming was one of the best-conditioned athletes in the game and routinely played 30 minutes for the team. Personally, Salming believed he had finally fit into the team and league during the 1976 Canada Cup. In a Sweden-USSR game at Maple Leaf Gardens, he worried about the reception he would get when local fans saw him in a sweater other than the blue and white of the Leafs. A resounding standing ovation confirmed his place in the city's heart. Salming and Ian Turnbull represented much of the team's offence. Salming had 7 seasons in which he scored at least 10 goals and another 7 with at least 40 assists. One of his low points came in the 1978 playoffs against the Islanders when he was accidentally hit in the eye by a high stick. He came perilously close to losing his sight, but Turnbull stepped up and played the best hockey of his life to take the Leafs to victory in the series. Salming was back at training camp the next year, as healthy as ever. He suffered from sinus problems for much of his career, but an injury in 1986 was one of the most horrific ever suffered in a game. In a game against Detroit, he was on the ice near the crease when a Red Wings player stepped on his face. Salming raced off the ice, and it wasn't until pictures

Borje Salming

> **Salming was a modern-day pioneer, a trailblazer who made it possible for other Europeans to follow.**
> **BORJE SALMING**

the next day revealed a gash that ran the full length of his face and required nearly 300 stitches that people saw how serious the cut was. Later that year, he admitted to having tried cocaine, a confession that earned him an eight-game suspension, but one the fans forgave him. In all, Salming played 16 seasons with the Leafs and 1,099 games. Only George Armstrong and Tim Horton have played more in a Toronto sweater. His time was sweet and bitter both because he played on teams in the 1970s that were close to serious contenders for the Cup and others in the 1980s that were the worst in team history. He never won the Norris Trophy, appeared in only three All-Star Games, and finished his NHL career with a year in Detroit in '89-'90. His career, though, was not quite done. He played three years at home for AIK Solna and competed in both the 1991 Canada Cup and the 1992 Olympics in Lillehammer. He retired for good in 1993, and three years later became the first European NHLer to be inducted into the Hockey Hall of Fame. Swedes of the current NHL all acknowledge his influence, the one hero back home who helped deliver the message that the NHL dream was possible. Once out of the

Sami Salo

Barry Salovaara

Dave Salvian

Phil Samis

game, Salming settled in Stockholm and started a successful clothing company. He also imports Canadian beer to Sweden! Salming returned to Toronto for the closing of Maple Leaf Gardens in 1999 – when he received one of the loudest ovations – and has returned occasionally since to play in oldtimers games, still skating with the same grace he did when he first came to Toronto in 1973.

SALO, Sami
b. Turku, Finland, September 2, 1974
After joining Ottawa in 1998, Salo had a strong rookie season followed by two more that were severely shortened by injury. He won a silver medal with Finland at the 2001 World Championships and played at the Olympics in Salt Lake City a year later. He has developed into a fine playmaking blueliner on a young Ottawa team that has played exceptionally well in the regular season and poorly in the playoffs.

SALO, Tommy
b. Surahammar, Sweden, February 1, 1971
History is, by definition, written looking backward, so it was inconceivable at any time in Salo's life to think he would be the focal point of the most glorious day in Tre Kronor Olympic history and later its most infamous day. The best came first. He was in goal for Sweden at the 1994 tournament in Lillehammer when his country beat Canada in a shootout to win Olympic gold for the first time. At one end, Peter Forsberg scored the winning goal; at the other, Salo's great pad save on Paul Kariya ensured that Forsberg's goal held up as the winner. Salo then pursued a pro career in North America. He was the top rookie in the IHL a year later, and then quickly took over as number-one goalie with the Islanders. The Oilers stole him away in 1999, and since then he has been their goalie of choice. In the interim, he played internationally whenever he had the chance. He played at the 1996 World Cup, won gold with the Swedes at the 1998 WC after a disappointing run at the Nagano Olympics, and played at the WC in 1999 and 2000. Then came 2002, the second NHL Olympics. Salo, of course, was Sweden's goalie, and the country couldn't have asked for a better start to the tournament. They beat Canada 5-2 in the first game and waltzed through the preliminary round to set up a quarter-final match with lowly Belarus. A team party was planned, and Belarus already had bus transportation ready to go to the airport after the game. But with 2:24 left in the third period, Vladimir Kopat took a long shot from centre ice that hit Salo awkwardly on the mask and shoulder and trickled over the goal line. The Swedes were out after the 4-3 loss, and Salo was pilloried by Swedish media. Incredibly, at season's end, the

He was in goal for Sweden at the 1994 tournament in Lillehammer when his country beat Canada in a shootout to win Olympic gold.
TOMMY SALO

Oilers failed to make the playoffs and Salo accepted an invitation to play at the World Championships on his native soil. He played extremely well and exonerated himself by leading the team to a bronze medal. It was a great show of spirit and dedication in light of his Olympic experience, and his play with Edmonton demonstrated further that he is a world-class goalie.

SALOMONSSON, Andreas
b. Ornskoldsvik, Sweden, December 19, 1973
Drafted at the ripe old age of 27, Salomonsson made his way to the Devils in 2001 as soon as he could. He played half a season with the Devils and the rest of the time in the minors. He had been a pro in Sweden for years and impressed the Devils with his play at the 2001 World Championships, where he was one of Tre Kronor's better players.

SALOVAARA, Barry
b. Cooksville, Ontario, January 7, 1948
Salovaara wasn't given an NHL chance until his mid-twenties. That came with Detroit for two years (1974-76) though it was a short-lived career with a bad team at the time. He had been playing in the minors since 1968 but retired soon after playing in Finland for a brief time.

SALVADOR, Bryce ("Salvy")
b. Brandon, Manitoba, February 11, 1976
Tampa Bay got first crack at him in the 1994 draft while Salvador was playing junior in Lethbridge, but the Lightning let him become a free agent and he signed with St. Louis. Another case of a bad team making an apparently bad decision, Salvador has become a regular on the Blues blueline since 2000 with a team close to challenging for the Stanley Cup.

SALVIAN, Dave
b. Toronto, Ontario, September 9, 1955
He has two bits of trivia connected to his name, but not much else. Salvian was one of a few Islanders to make his NHL debut in the playoffs when he appeared in 1977. He is also one of a very small number of one-game wonders whose only appearance is a playoff game and who also recorded a point in that game! He had an assist on April 7, 1977, in the team's 2-1 win over Chicago. Besides that, he passed five quiet and mostly uneventful years in the minors before retiring in 1980.

SAMIS, Phil
b. Edmonton, Alberta, December 28, 1927
There was good reason why the career of Samis was short and to the point: Academics were as important to him as pucks and gloves. He went to high school at St.

Mike's to get an education and a chance to play for the Leafs, and he got both. He made the 1948 playoffs, which qualified him for his name on the Cup, and he played a couple more games with the team a while later. When he ended up with Cleveland in the AHL, he attended Western Reserve University and studied dentistry. When he graduated he moved to Montreal, played a few games with the Royals, and set up his practice there. Now retired, he still lives in that city, his hockey dreams and academic ambitions both having been realized.

SAMPSON, Gary
b. Atikokan, Ontario, August 24, 1959
Born in Ontario, Sampson was an American who attended Boston College on scholarship in 1978.
After graduating four years later, he spent two years playing for the U.S. National Team, including at the 1984 Olympics in Sarajevo. At that point, he had his first NHL interest, and Washington signed him to a contract. He played parts of four years with the Caps, but they thought they were getting a goal scorer, and when he didn't produce, they didn't play him. He was sent to the minors for good in 1987 and retired at season's end. Sampson went into coaching, his longest stint coming with the Rochester Mustangs of the USHL, but he resigned his post to move to Alaska and operate a hunting lodge.

Gary Sampson

SAMSONOV, Sergei ("Sammy")
b. Moscow, Soviet Union (Russia), October 27, 1978
Fast, skilled, powerful, hard to knock off the puck, able to make plays at top speed. These are some of the abilities scouts liked about Samsonov – when he was 16. Drafted by Boston, he moved to Detroit and played for the Vipers of the IHL at 18 because Russian hockey and junior hockey would provide him no test, he felt. That year, he was named the IHL's rookie of the year and the team won the Turner Cup.
The next year, he joined the Bruins and won the Calder Trophy, just as his idol Sergei Makarov had done. His career was off to a flying start, and he is part of the young nucleus of a Boston team that might go far in the playoffs. He's averaged close to 25 goals a season and is left wing on the team's top line, though he hasn't played internationally save for his one WJC appearance in 1997.

SAMUELSSON, Kjell
b. Tingsryd, Sweden, October 18, 1958
At 6'6" and 235 pounds, he was a behemoth defenceman who obviously used his size to full advantage. In his 14 NHL seasons, Samuelsson had his best days

After retiring, Samuelsson ran a car dealership in Pittsburgh and did television work for Sweden.
ULF SAMUELSSON

with Philadelphia and Pittsburgh, going to the 1987 finals with the former and winning the Cup in 1992 with the latter. He wasn't blessed with great hands and smooth puckhandling skills, but he was difficult to get around and a tyrant in clearing the front of his own goal. After retiring in 1999, he didn't return home. Rather, he became an assistant coach with Trenton of the ECHL and a year later with the Flyers farm club, the Phantoms, hoping one day to work his way up to the NHL.

SAMUELSSON, Mikael
b. Mariefred, Sweden, December 23, 1976
For a modern European, Samuelsson has come to North America a little later than most, but after a season spent mostly in the minors (2000-01) he landed with the Rangers and made the team after being traded from Tampa Bay.

Sergei Samsonov

SAMUELSSON, Ulf ("Ulfie")
b. Fagersta, Sweden, March 26, 1964
Without doubt, Samuelsson was the most-hated player in the NHL during his day, and also the dirtiest. Less than that, though, he was spectacularly cowardly for someone who went looking for trouble and he refused to stand up for himself after dishing the dirt, as it were. After establishing himself over the course of three WJC tournaments, Samuelsson made his way to Hartford in 1984. Seven years later, he moved on to Pittsburgh where he was lucky enough to be a part of two Stanley Cup teams with the Pens in 1991 and '92. From there he went to the Rangers, and his career petered out with brief stops in Detroit and Philadelphia, where he suffered a shoulder injury that, in effect, forced him to retire. Along the way, he was infamous for his dirty hit on Cam Neely that ended Neely's season, but the hockey world celebrated a moment at Maple Leaf Gardens early in the '95-'96 season. Late in a Rangers-Toronto game, Samuelsson, doing his usual best to play outside the rule book, was suckerpunched by Tie Domi and fell to the ice unconscious. The next day, reports had it that the entire Vancouver Canucks dressing room jumped for joy as one. Although the NHL suspended Domi eight games for the punch, most fans thought it fair comeuppance for Samuelsson's career of vicious hits and dirty plays. After retiring, Samuelsson ran a car dealership in Pittsburgh and did television work for Sweden at the 2002 Olympics in Salt Lake City.

Kjell Samuelsson

SANDELIN, Scott
b. Hibbing, Minnesota, August 8, 1964
During his career at the University of North Dakota,

Scott Sandelin

Sandelin was considered the best defenceman prospect in the U.S. When he graduated in 1986 with a degree in marketing, the world was nothing but rose-scented for him. The Canadiens had drafted him, the U.S. Olympic Team wanted him, and he was 21 years old. Time, though, was less kind to him. The Habs kept him in the minors for most of his three years in the organization, as did Philadelphia and Minnesota when they acquired him later on. It didn't help that he suffered a series of injuries to his back, and by 1992 the combination of minor-league play and a bad back forced him to retire. Sandelin immediately turned to coaching, joining Fargo and returning to his alma mater as an assistant in 1994. During his six years there, UND experienced tremendous success, and in the summer of 2000 Sandelin was offered a chance to control his own team when the University of Minnesota-Duluth offered him the head coaching job. He's been there ever since, putting his stamp on another successful program.

SANDERSON, Derek ("Turk")

b. Niagara Falls, Ontario, June 16, 1946

There were long stretches – years, in fact – when there was no hope at all that the Sanderson story would have anything but a tragic ending. He had his first beer at age 7, could handle 3 by the age of 12, and by the time his hockey career was taking off he was a full-time alcoholic doing speed, cocaine, Valium, and whatever else was being passed around or near at hand. On the ice, Sanderson was almost without compare, and for a short time was the highest-paid player in the world. He played junior in his hometown and joined the Boston Bruins at a time when Orr, Esposito, and Cheevers were helping to shape a Stanley Cup winner. Sanderson was no less important an ingredient. Coach Harry Sinden used him as a third-line centre, asking him to score but also to check the top players onto the ice. Sanderson was a master at everything. He was the best faceoff man in the league, he had a great shot, and he had speed to burn. He could backcheck his opponent into the boards behind his own goal and score at the other end a few seconds later. He won the Calder Trophy in '67-'68 and for five years was the best two-way player in the NHL. It was his lovely slip of a pass in overtime in 1970 that put Bobby Orr in front of Glenn Hall to score the memorable flying goal that won the Cup that year, and Sanderson was front and centre two years later for the Bruins' second victory. Off the ice, he lived up to his nickname and then some. He was the most eligible bachelor in Boston, a true ladies' man who was always available. He was on the town nightly, drove expensive cars, and lived the life of a white, hockey-playing

Geoff Sanderson

Jack Johnson. More than any other player of his era, Sanderson had everything. Everything, though, changed quickly for Turk. In 1972, he was lured to the WHA by a multi-million-dollar offer from the Philadelphia Blazers, an awful move that had him pleading to leave after just eight games. He returned to Boston, but the booze and drugs had finally won the race. He was traded to the Rangers for Walt McKechnie, and later played for St. Louis, Vancouver, and Pittsburgh, with a few humbling games in the minors along the way. He retired, but poor investments and the continuing drinking problem took him lower than anyone could have imagined. He wound up on the streets of New York stealing bottles from semi-comatose bums in the park, but finally his friends helped him off the street and into a new world.

Over the years, he had been through detox 13 times, but matters improved when he needed double surgery on his weak hips to help him to walk. He got back on his feet – literally and figuratively – and stayed clean. He spoke to kids and did community work to teach others of the horrors of his life, and he found meaningful work. At night, he was a colour analyst for the Bruins, and in the daytime he became an investment specialist for State Street Research Company in Boston, helping athletes invest their money with greater wisdom than he had in his prime. Sanderson scored 24 goals in a season 6 times. He has his name on the Stanley Cup and he is revered in Boston for his glory years. But what might have been is a sadder tale of a talent not fully realized, of a player who gave up maximum effort in the name of common fun. He had the ability to be a Hall of Famer – but coulda, woulda, shoulda, and $10 will gain you admission to the Hall.

> **He was the best faceoff man in the league, he had a great shot, and he had speed to burn.**
> DEREK SANDERSON

SANDERSON, Geoff

b. Hay River, Northwest Territories, February 1, 1972

In the obscurity of Hartford, on a not-very-good Whalers team, Sanderson was a remarkable scorer, the finest unsung player in the league, perhaps. He had two 40-goal seasons and two 30-goal seasons, but when Vancouver and then Buffalo acquired him for his goals, they stopped coming. The year the Sabres went to the finals, '98-'99, he accounted for only a dozen goals in the regular season and four more in the playoffs. Only when he got to Columbus did he hit the 30-goal mark again. Internationally, he played for Canada at the 1994 and '97 World Championships, winning gold on teams that broke a dry streak dating back to 1961. He has one of the oddest regimens in the game in that he uses a shorter and shorter stick for each period of a game, feeling that the shorter stick reminds him to hunker down and not get fatigued and lazy.

SANDFORD, Ed ("Sandy")

b. Mimico, Ontario, August 20, 1928

As a teen at St. Mike's in the mid-1940s, Sandford was fought over by Boston and Toronto for his NHL rights, and for a rare time the Leafs lost out. From the moment he hit the ice as a Bruins forward in 1947, he was the future of the team, the kid who couldn't miss being a star. For the most part, he didn't disappoint except for the fact that injuries were forever slowing him down or preventing him from reaching his full potential. Most serious of these was a torn Achilles tendon he suffered in 1949 in an awkward collision with Bill Barilko. He missed most of the year, but at first doctors feared he would never play again. The Bruins flipped him from centre to left wing with regularity, but he had his best success playing on a line with Dave Creighton and Zellio Toppazzii, the youngest threesome in the league. He played in five All-Star Games and ended his career at training camp with Chicago in the fall of 1956 in St. Catharines. He found he no longer had the legs, and rather than go to the minors, he returned to Boston and started a new life. He became a goal judge at the Garden, played in numerous alumni games, and also became a successful broker in the city.

SANDLAK, Jim ("House")

b. Kitchener, Ontario, December 12, 1966

A 4th-overall draft choice should turn out to be a superstar if the drafting team has chosen wisely, so in this sense Sandlak was a disappointment to Vancouver fans. He played with the Canucks for 8 years but had 20 goals only once, in '88-'89. He was large and physical, and coupled with his enormous appetite he earned his nickname early in his career. Despite his size – or because of it – he sustained a never-ending series of injuries that cut short his final three seasons and eventually convinced him to pack it in. He later returned to Kitchener and became involved in the grocery business.

SANDS, Charlie

b. Fort William, Ontario, March 23, 1911
d. Hollywood, California, April 6, 1953

The life of Sands was a long trip, to say the least. Like any Fort William kid, he grew up playing hockey and hoping to play for the Leafs, a dream he realized in 1932. He played in the NHL for the next 12 years, though the Leafs sold him to Boston just two years after his debut. He won the Cup with Boston in 1939 and later played for the Canadiens and the Rangers, but in 1944 he accepted a unique offer to go to California and coach the Hollywood Wolves. The next year, he was playing for the Los Angeles Monarchs when he had the chance to be an extra in a movie called *Gay Blades* that featured several hockey sequences. After retiring, Sands worked at the Hollywood Bowl and died young because of complications from an ulcer.

SANDS, Mike

b. Mississauga, Ontario, April 6, 1963

A goalie has a mental "book" on all his opponents – they are all potential shooters in his eyes. Perhaps that was how Sands made the jump from the crease to the scouting department in one easy step. He played for Minnesota in the mid-1980s and had a small but sorry record of 0-5-0 and a GAA over 5.00. He retired before the calendar hit 1990 and became a scout for the Central Scouting Bureau. His lengthy term there led to the post of director of amateur scouting, which the Calgary Flames bestowed on Sands in the summer of 2001.

SANDSTROM, Tomas

b. Jakobstad Pietarsaari, Finland, September 4, 1964

Most people around the league called him Endangered Species. This came about for one reason only – while most Swedes were considered passive and not adept at physical play, Sandstrom was universally reviled as the most "sneaky dirty" player in the league. Every team in the NHL could boast at least one player who wanted to hurt Sandstrom badly in fitting retribution for a high stick or slash, but few got their way. Sandstrom was a real European oddity in the NHL in that he was born in Finland but raised in Fagersta, Sweden. His 15 NHL years is second only to Borje Salming among Swedish players, and he was a capable goal scorer as well as a dirty right winger. He came close to winning a Cup with Los Angeles in 1993 and won four years later with Detroit. Internationally, he scored an important goal with 1:21 left to give Tre Kronor a 2-2 tie with the Soviets at the 1987 World Championships en route to a gold medal, one of three WC he played in. He also played in two Olympics and Canada Cups, and at the end of his career he returned to play in Sweden before finally retiring in 2000.

SANDWITH, Terran

b. Edmonton, Alberta, April 17, 1972

Philadelphia liked him for his size when it drafted him in 1990, but it wasn't until seven years later that Sandwith played in the NHL, with Edmonton. He was a mainstay in the minors for nine years until 2001, when he signed to pay with the Belfast Giants, taking with him one of the best-sounding names to make it to the NHL, albeit for just eight games.

Every team in the NHL could boast at least one player who wanted to hurt Sandstrom.
TOMAS SANDSTROM

Ed Sandford

Jim Sandlak

Charlie Sands

Mike Sands

Terran Sandwith

Everett Sanipass

Oleg Saprykin

Gary Sargent

Geoff Sarjeant

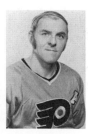

Dick Sarrazin

SANIPASS, Everett

b. Big Cove, New Brunswick, February 13, 1968

Why would a kid from New Brunswick be thrilled to be drafted by Chicago? Because of the crest on the sweater. Sanipass was a Mi'kmaq who grew up on Big Cove Reserve, the first Native Canadian from New Brunswick to make the NHL. He made his Hawks debut soon after the bench-clearing brawl at the 1987 WJC in Piestany, his first of five NHL seasons with the Hawks and later the Nordiques. He didn't score many goals, but he sure knew how to fight, and after retiring he found even more rewarding work. His home province hired him as its Aboriginal Projects Officer for the Aboriginal Affairs Department, where he could share his experiences and pass on his successes to Native kids.

SAPRYKIN, Oleg

b. Moscow, Soviet Union (Russia), February 12, 1981

Unlike most Europeans who come to North America after being drafted, Saprykin couldn't wait. At 17, he joined the WHL to play junior and impress scouts, a strategy that worked just fine since Calgary drafted him in 1999. Since then, he's played mostly in the minors, though he did get an assist in his first NHL game on October 2, 1999, before being sent down for development. He played most of 2000-01 with Calgary, but when teammate and countryman Valeri Bure was traded to Florida, Saprykin's play suffered. In October 2002, he walked out on the Saint John Flames, Calgary's AHL affiliate, jeopardizing both his season and career.

SARAULT, Yves

b. Valleyfield, Quebec, December 23, 1972

It's amazing how consistent and persistent Sarault has been since making the pro grade in 1992. Not since two years later has a season gone by when he hasn't played in the NHL, but he's never played more than 28 games in any one year. He has found his strange niche as a regular callup who can fill in adequately in a pinch yet who has obviously developed a reputation as someone who cannot play in the NHL full-time. The minors are his home, and the NHL his part-time residence, though he has also played in Switzerland.

SARGENT, Gary

b. Red Lake, Minnesota, February 8, 1954

A full-blooded Chippewa, Sargent turned down an offer from the Minnesota Twins to pursue a hockey career. He turned pro in 1974 in the AHL with Springfield after being drafted by Los Angeles, but from the next year when he joined the Kings to the end of his career eight years later, he was hindered by painful back and knee injuries that eventually forced him to retire. The nadir of his injuries came in March 1980 when he agreed to undergo a risky spinal fusion operation at the Mayo Clinic. Doctors warned him there was only a 40 percent chance he'd ever walk again, but such was his desire to play hockey that he took the chance. He did play again, but the pain never fully went away and then he had three knee operations for good measure. After retiring, he opened a marine shop in Rosemere, outside Minneapolis, and did some scouting for Los Angeles.

SARICH, Cory

b. Saskatoon, Saskatchewan, August 16, 1978

In his first 208 NHL games, Sarich had a grand total of one goal. Naturally, he was a defenceman. He had a stellar apprenticeship as a junior, playing for Canada at consecutive WJC tournaments and winning gold in 1997. He started his pro career with Buffalo but has been the property of Tampa Bay since March 2000.

SARJEANT, Geoff

b. Newmarket, Ontario, November 30, 1969

There was just no room in goal in St. Louis for Sarjeant after he graduated from Michigan Tech in 1992. He was immediately sent to the IHL by the Blues and it wasn't until three years later that he played a few games for the team. He was a fixture in the "I" until 1999 when he accepted an offer to play for Ayr, where his good college friend, Jamie Steer, played. A year later, Sarjeant played in the DEL, his last season of pro.

SARNER, Craig

b. St. Paul, Minnesota, June 20, 1949

Sarner was part of an odd international combination in 1972 with the U.S. The team won a silver medal at the Olympics in Sapporo, but at the World Championships they finished second in "B" pool play! Saner was on both teams and then left the University of Minnesota to play pro in the minors. He appeared in only seven games for the Bruins and then moved to Europe where he played several more years. After retiring in 1981, he stayed on as a coach, first in Switzerland, then in Germany. He returned home, coached extensively at a number of Minnesota high schools, and later joined the staff of the Minnesota Hockey Camp as a coach and instructor.

SARRAZIN, Dick

b. St. Gabriel de Brandon, Quebec, January 22, 1946

There were promising moments for Sarrazin when he joined Philadelphia in 1968. For each of his first two years, he made the team and started off strong. In year 1, he played most of the season with the Flyers and scored 16 goals, and year two started out as well. He played on the French Connection Line featuring Andre Lacroix and Jean-Guy Gendron, but his pro-

There are two sides to Satan's hockey life, the NHL side and the Slovakian side.
MIROSLAV SATAN

duction fell off the map and he ended up the minors. Ditto for year three, the last of his NHL chances. He played briefly in the WHA but finished his career in the minors.

SASAKAMOOSE, Fred ("Chief Thunder Stick"/ "Chief Running Deer")

b. Sandy Lake Reserve, Saskatchewan, December 25, 1933

His name has been spelled every which way, from Sacamoos to Saskamoose, and he was the first full-blooded Native to play in the NHL. He made the difficult decision to leave home and play junior in Moose Jaw in 1950, but four years later he was considered the best player in the WHL. At the end of that fourth year, he played 11 games for the Hawks, and the organist, Al Melgard, welcomed him by playing a sampling of Indian-themed music. Those were his only NHL games, and Sasakamoose was desperately unhappy in the minors, away from the reserve and his wife and friends. Two games into the '55-'56 season in Calgary, he left hockey altogether, hopping in a cab and travelling 1,000 kilometres back home. The Hawks suspended him and refused to reinstate him as an amateur for a year. He played senior hockey where he became almost a freak-show attraction – the Indian who made the NHL. He became a band chief in 1980 and in 1994 was inducted into the Saskatchewan Indian Hall of Fame.

SASSER, Grant

b. Portland, Oregon, February 13, 1964

Not many players come out of Portland to play in the NHL, but Sasser had the benefit of playing in his hometown in the WHL. He won the Memorial Cup with the Winter Hawks in 1983, the first American-based team to win Canada's top amateur trophy, and the year after he played his only three NHL games, with Pittsburgh. After only one year of pro, in the minors, he retired.

SATAN, Miroslav "Miro"

b. Topolcany, Czechoslovakia (Slovakia), October 22, 1974

There are two sides to Satan's hockey life, the NHL side and the Slovakian side. The latter is by far the richer, despite his successes in the former. Satan first played for Slovakia in 1994 at the Olympics and World Championships. The young nation finished sixth at Lillehammer and then finished first in "C" pool at the WC. The next year, they finished first in "B" pool, and the year after the first part of their meteoric rise was done when then played in "A" pool. Satan was named best forward at the 2000 WC, but the best was yet to come. Satan played only briefly at the 2002 Olympics in

Salt Lake City because of time restrictions placed on NHLers by the league, but Satan and his teammates made up for this difficulty at the 2002 WC. Slovakia won gold, and Satan led the way. He was named tournament MVP, and the central figure in putting his country on the hockey map with the elite six nations. In the NHL, Satan has been a high and consistent scorer with Buffalo. The Sabres acquired him on March 18, 1997, in a steal of a deal, sending Barrie Moore and Craig Millar to Edmonton to acquire him. He helped the Sabres reach the '99 finals, but he will be remembered as an international hero at home for many years to come.

SATHER, Glen ("Slats")

b. High River, Alberta, September 2, 1943

This was the kind of shrewd man Sather was as a player. After a junior career with the Edmonton Oil Kings in which he helped the team win the 1963 Memorial Cup, he became property of the Red Wings. A clause in his contract stipulated that as long as he was in the NHL the Wings would pay for his entire university education. Sather went on to become a Boston Bruins forward and was later traded to the Rangers. He had always run a hockey school in the summer but by 1972 he was free of those obligations and wanted to take some university classes. He informed the Wings, but they refused to pay his bills based on a clause in a contract a decade and two teams ago. NHL president Clarence Campbell, a lawyer in his own right, heard Sather's argument and agreed with the player. The Red Wings had to pay his tuition!

> He studied child psychology and physical education, hoping these would help him in his post-playing life.
> **GLEN SATHER**

He studied child psychology and physical education, hoping these would help him in his post-playing life. It was a wise decision on his part because although he played 10 years in the NHL, he was no star. Sather was a journeyman, a survivor who did what he could to avoid the minors. To his credit, he never was demoted during his career. He played for six teams as a fourth-liner, a checker and penalty killer. His closest brush with success came in 1972 when he went to the Cup finals with the Rangers. By 1976, he knew his time was almost up, so went to Edmonton of the WHA. Midway through the year he became the playing coach and at year's end retired as a player and concentrated on coaching. His timing was impeccable. The Oilers had many young stars and were about to enter the NHL, and once they got their feet wet they became the most successful and dominant team of the 1980s. Sather and his staff drafted wisely, and then it was up to him to develop his great young stars, notably Wayne Gretzky, Mark Messier, and Paul Coffey. Sather successfully integrated European players and changed the way the

Fred Sasakamoose

Grant Sasser

Bernie Saunders

Bob Sauve

Jean-Francois Sauve

Andre Savage

game was played. His motto was simple: goals, goals, goals. He wanted to score and score more, and it was he who first put out his superstars to kill penalties, realizing that open ice was advantageous for his own great skaters as much as for the team with the man advantage. From 1984 to '90, the team won five Cups and scored more goals than any other in league history. Sather was often the coach, though he increasingly left that job to others such as Ted Green, John Muckler, and Ron Low. The success of the 1980s, though, gave way to a dismal financial picture in the following decade. Fans spoiled by success didn't support a middling team as much, and skyrocketing payrolls put the Oilers in the have-nots rather than the haves class. Sather was bound by economy more than player availability, and the team was sold to what turned into a group of 37 investors who saved the Oilers from being relocated. As a competitive manager, Sather was feeling more and more frustrated, and in the summer of 2000 he resigned from the Oilers and signed with the Rangers to be their GM. He found an open chequebook at Madison Square Garden, though his many expensive free agent signings have yet to yield a playoff-strong team. Critics charged that he was only as good as the players he inherited (i.e., in Edmonton), though much the same can be said for Scotty Bowman, who had excellent teams in Montreal and Detroit but failed miserably in Buffalo when given a chance to do whatever he wanted to the team. Sather was a pioneer in Edmonton, a man who brought excitement to the game and put together what might be the last team that could hold so many superstars at any one time. A very average player, he was inducted into the Hockey Hall of Fame as a Builder in 1997, an honour befitting a man who pushed Wayne Gretzky to take more and do even more with it.

SAUNDERS, Bernie
b. Montreal, Quebec, June 21, 1956
The fact that he was just the fifth black player to make it to the NHL might not mean a great deal anymore, but to Saunders it was a huge accomplishment and he felt that by making it he was helping the next generation make it with, perhaps, greater ease. During his three years at Western Michigan University (1976-79), race didn't matter because Saunders was too good a player to be treated unfairly. Far from it – he became a WMU Hall of Famer for his college career. He went on to play just 10 NHL games, with the Nordiques over 2 seasons, but that was enough. Saunders played two more years in the minors and then became a coach in Michigan while raising a son, Jon, who played in the NAHL in a multiracial environment that was, indeed, a more open hockey society than the one Bernie knew as a player.

SAUNDERS, David
b. Ottawa, Ontario, May 20, 1966
After a four-year career at St. Lawrence University (1983-87), Saunders played a year with Vancouver with only middling results. He played for only a short time in the minors before retiring. His brother, Matthew, was drafted by Chicago in 1989, though he never made it to the NHL.

SAUNDERS, Teddy
b. Ottawa, Ontario, August 29, 1911
d. Aurora, Ontario, May 21, 2002
By the time he passed away peacefully at age 90, Saunders was the last surviving old Ottawa Senators player and the last of nine children. He played hockey for many years before the war, but his pride and glory was the half-season he played for the old Senators in '33-'34. He scored just one goal that season, but he had a tremendous wrist shot that helped put many more pucks past goalies in the minor leagues. In 1941, he joined the army, and a year later helped the powerful Commandos team win the Allan Cup. He was sent overseas and trained to be a dental technician, though he never saw active combat. When he returned home, his playing career was done, but he used his training to good effect. He set up a dental laboratory in Ottawa where he made crowns and dentures. For the 1999-2000 season, the new version of the Senators put him on their media guide and honoured him at a game as the oldest player from the original team.

SAUVE, Bob
b. Ste. Genevieuve, Quebec, June 17, 1955
In 1975, Buffalo drafted three goalies, two of whom – Sauve and Don Edwards – later played together and triumphed together. Sauve came out of the Quebec league and worked his way into the Sabres lineup over the course of four years. By 1979-80, the Sauve-Edwards tandem was the best in the NHL, the pair winning the Vezina Trophy and Sauve leading the league with a 2.36 goals-against average. The next year, Sauve's high-flying brother, Jean-Francois, joined Buffalo, but Bob was quickly traded to Detroit. He later returned to Buffalo and in '84-'85 Sauve won the Jennings Trophy. He ended his career with two seasons each in Chicago and New Jersey, but by the time he retired in 1989 he had never come close to winning a Stanley Cup. Sauve invested with Mike Bossy in a Montreal-area golf course, and then became a successful player agent. In 2000, he watched his son, Phillipe, play for the U.S. at the World Junior Championships.

SAUVE, Jean-Francois
b. Ste. Genevieve, Quebec, January 23, 1960
Bob's tiny brother had a tough time scoring goals in the NHL, but all 5'6" of him was an outstanding sniper in leagues outside the biggest. In junior, he scored more than 60 goals twice, but when he played with his brother in Buffalo, he scored just 24 goals in 98 games over 3 seasons. In Quebec, it was much the same, though the Nordiques used him extensively on the power play where he had more room. The result was that in '85-'86, Sauve scored 13 of his 16 goals on the year with the extra man. He later played in Europe for a number of years, scoring easily on the bigger ice while skating through smaller opponents.

SAVAGE, Andre
b. Ottawa, Ontario, May 27, 1975
A four-year career at Michigan Tech didn't get Savage drafted, but it did get him a contract with Boston in 1998. He played only a few games and a half-season

with the Bruins over the next couple of years, and although Vancouver signed him as a free agent, he has been a minor-leaguer ever since.

SAVAGE, Brian
b. Sudbury, Ontario, February 24, 1971
If only the entire NHL schedule could be squeezed into October and November, Savage might well lead the league in points every year. Unfortunately for him, there are many months after those two when games must be played, and during those times Savage is hard pressed to register any points. He's facetiously called Mr. October, and although he has 5 career 20-goal seasons, Savage typically scores more than half of those in the first few weeks of the season. As a result, Montreal had no qualms about trading him to Phoenix in 2001-02 when he demanded ludicrous millions for his scoring. Puzzlingly, Phoenix happily signed him to a lucrative contract, which he followed by scoring exactly six times with the Coyotes. Savage did make two scoring impressions in the Montreal ledgers. He recorded the first Montreal hat trick at the new Molson Centre (in October, of course, 1996), and he had six points in a road game against the Islanders early in 1998, the first Hab to have such a night since Joe Malone in 1918.

SAVAGE, Joel
b. Surrey, British Columbia, December 25, 1969
The knock on him in junior with Victoria was that he was a good skater with lots of grit and determination who had little hope of making the NHL. The scouts were partly right in that he played three times for Buffalo in '90-'91 and that was it for the NHL, but he played many years in the AHL and has been going strong in Europe – on the bigger ice surface – since 1995. The only downside was that the Sabres used a 1st-round pick to claim him in the 1988 draft.

SAVAGE, Reggie
b. Montreal, Quebec, May 1, 1970
You can teach defence, but offence is something a player either has or doesn't. Savage had it, so Washington drafted him high in 1988. He never scored fewer than 50 goals in junior, and for a while he scored well in the minors. But in the NHL? Nothing doing. His speed and instinct couldn't overcome his lack of size or the faster environment and he played just 34 games in the big time. He played a year in Italy, '98-'99, but then came back and had two fine seasons in the AHL, playing his way into an NIIL contract with Columbus, though he has yet to play with the expansion team.

SAVAGE, Gordon "Tony"
b. Calgary, Alberta, July 18, 1906
d. Covina, California, February 28, 1974
The only chance Savage had to play in the NHL came in '34-'35. He started the year with Boston but was traded to the Canadiens for Jack Portland and played the rest of the year in Montreal. He had been in the minors before, and that is exactly where he reported the next year, in his hometown. He later became coach and GM for Providence of the AHL.

SAVARD, Andre
b. Temiscamingue, Quebec, February 9, 1953
In the early 1970s, the Quebec Remparts were the best junior team in the country. They won the Memorial Cup in 1971, made 3 appearances in the tournament in quick succession, and boasted the league's top scorer, Savard. He played for only 3 teams in his 12 NHL seasons – Boston, Buffalo, and Quebec – and although he never scored as he had in junior, he was certainly a productive centre wherever he went. He retired in 1985 after hurting his knee badly midway through the previous season. He held out hopes of returning, but when doctors dissuaded him, he took their advice. He stayed with the Nordiques organization and became coach and GM of their farm team in Fredericton, and in 1987 he was hired as head coach for the NHL team. This lasted a disastrous 24 games, after which he became a scout and eased his way back into coaching with the Nordiques and then the Senators. In the summer of 2000, Savard was named director of hockey personnel for the Canadiens, and that November he became the team's GM.

SAVARD, Denis
b. Pointe Gatineau, Quebec, February 4, 1961
The story of the three Denis is an incredible one. Three boys – Denis Cyr, Denis Savard, and Denis Tremblay – were all born on the same day, February 4, 1961, within a few miles of each other. All three grew up together and played hockey on a line together as teens with the Montreal Juniors. All three were drafted into the NHL. Tremblay didn't make it, Cyr made it in a small way, and Savard made it in a Hall of Fame way. Savard was selected 3rd overall by Chicago in 1980. He made the team as a 19-year-old and brought his own style of excitement to the NHL. As a rookie, he had 28 goals and 75 points, and Hawks fans were dazzled by his play. He liked to carry the puck on rink-long rushes. He had speed to burn and could stop on a dime. His "spin-o-rama" move saw him come right at a defenceman, stop and turn quickly, and accelerate past the confused defender. In his second year he had 119 points and was destined for stardom, though the one thing that was

As a rookie, he had 28 goals and 75 points, and Hawks fans were dazzled by his play.
DENIS SAVARD

Brian Savage

Joel Savage

Reggie Savage

Andre Savard

always missing was extended playoff success. In his 10 years with Chicago, Savard hit the 100-point mark 5 times, and on March 11, 1990, he scored his 1,000th point in the league and with the team. He was traded to Montreal in 1990, a hugely unpopular deal even if the Hawks were getting Chris Chelios, a local boy. Savard, meanwhile, was coming home, in a sense, and in his three years, a step slower, he still made a contribution. He won a Cup with Montreal in 1993, even though he didn't dress for the Cup-winning game. He later played for Tampa and in 1995 was traded back to where it all began, Chicago. Diminished by time, Savard became that experienced player who becomes smart rather than flashy. He was not always on the power play anymore and he wasn't being double-shifted, but the fans appreciated his every effort. He retired in 1997 and immediately assumed a coaching position with the team, one he maintains to this day. His popularity in the city and within the organization is such that it is only a matter of time before he becomes head coach. His number 18 was retired by the team and in 2000 he was inducted into the Hockey Hall of Fame. Amazingly, Savard never led the league in any offensive category and never won an individual award. He played in 7 All-Star Games and finished with 1,338 points, but more than that he will be remembered for his style of play, his skating ability that allowed him to do so much more than the average player. He played hockey as a kid with his brothers, and he played with his friends, the other Denis for years, yet it was Savard who emerged from Verdun a hero to his family, his neighbourhood and the fans of Chicago.

Jean Savard

Marc Savard

Ryan Savoia

SAVARD, Jean
b. Verdun, Quebec, April 26, 1957
Here's a player who led the Quebec league in scoring in '76-'77 with 84 goals and 180 points, yet when he joined Chicago the next year he managed only 7 goals. The next year, he had not one in an 11-game callup, and he was soon in the minors for good. Savard played briefly in Switzerland and retired into the quietude of professional life without having made the NHL impact he once had hoped for.

SAVARD, Marc
b. Ottawa, Ontario, July 17, 1977
While playing junior with Oshawa, Savard twice led the league in scoring, a feat that had been accomplished only twice previously – once by Billy Taylor, once by Marcel Dionne. Not bad company. Since entering the NHL in 1997 with the Rangers, Savard hasn't shown quite the same proficiency, but he has developed into a fine passing centre for Calgary, the team that acquired him in 1999. The comparisons with Taylor and Dionne

He worked as an organizer for the Union Nationale party at the provincial level and for the Liberals federally.
SERGE SAVARD

end in junior, but he is trying to turn a weak team into a playoff team, and that is task enough.

SAVARD, Serge ("The Senator")
b. Montreal, Quebec, January 22, 1946
Savard was first spotted by the Canadiens at age 15 while playing in a school league. They put him on their reserve list and sent him to the Jr. Canadiens, but he balked when they tried to turn him pro. He wanted to finish high school, but the Habs convinced him to go to Houston of the Central league in 1966. Before the end of the season he had been given a brief tryout with the Habs, and by the start of the next year he was in the NHL for good. He was not the puckhandler that Larry Robinson was but he was a big man who could check with the best of them. The team won the Cup in each of his first two full seasons, and in the second, '68-'69, he won the Conn Smythe Trophy. Savard had two debilitating injuries in '70-'71 and '71-'72. In the first, he dove trying to stop a breakaway and ended up fracturing his left leg in five places. He needed three operations to have it set properly, but partway through the next year he broke the same leg again. Nevertheless, that summer he was invited to play for Team Canada in the upcoming Summit Series. Savard can boast of being the only player on either team who never played in a losing game. He played in five of the eight games, winning four and tying one. He returned to the Canadiens and had nine mostly healthy seasons, winning five more Cups (eight in all). Perhaps the most rewarding of all came in 1976 when the team ousted the violent Broad Street Bullies, a win Savard hailed for all of hockey over mere intimidation. He was awarded the Bill Masterton Trophy for '78-'79 to acknowledge his dedication and perseverance. Savard retired in 1981, but over the course of the summer the Winnipeg Jets talked him into playing for them. He signed a three-year contract, and for two seasons helped improve the awful team to one of the better teams in the league, but then Montreal bought his rights for the third year so he could come home and become the managing director of the Canadiens. Savard earned his nickname because of his involvement in politics. He worked as an organizer for the Union Nationale party at the provincial level and for the Liberals federally. He was also an extremely successful businessman who owned some of Montreal's most valuable real estate, and it is in this business he continues to work. In 1986, Savard was inducted into the Hockey Hall of Fame.

SAVOIA, Ryan
b. Thorold, Ontario, May 6, 1973
According to how players make it to the NHL, Savoia

never should have been there. He never played junior hockey, and after one outstanding year at Brock University he turned pro in the "I" in 1995 after signing with Pittsburgh. Still, it was four more years before he ever played with the Pens, and then for just three games. He played the 1999-2000 season with the Canadian National Team, and was supposed to play at the 2000 World Championships until he had to have an emergency appendectomy overseas and was lost to the team for the balance of the tournament.

SAWCHUK, Terry ("Uke"/ "Ukey")

b. Winnipeg, Manitoba, December 28, 1929
d. Long Beach, New York, May 31, 1970

If you were to take aside a 10-year-old boy and tell him that one day he was going to set every NHL record a goalie could possibly set, that he would be inducted into the Hockey Hall of Fame and be considered one of the greatest goalies ever to play the game, that boy would smile and look forward to his life. His friends would be both admiring and envious, and marvel at the life that awaited their pal. Yet by the time Terry Sawchuk died in a Long Island hospital at age 40, he had lived a life so rife with unhappiness and so riddled with injury and depression that that 10-year-old would cringe at the suffering that would go with the greatness he would attain. On the surface, Sawchuk was an extraordinary goalie. Surely no man will begin a career with the flourish he did, winning rookie of the year in three different leagues on his way to NHL stardom. He won first with Omaha in the USHL in '47-'48, then with Indianapolis the next year in the AHL, and finally with Detroit in the NHL in '50-'51. The previous season he played seven games for the Wings to fill in for the injured Harry Lumley, but he had made such a favourable impression that GM Jack Adams happily traded the future Hall of Famer Lumley to make the 20-year-old Sawchuk his starting goalie. As a rookie, he played all 70 games, won 44 to lead the league, recorded 11 shutouts to lead the league, and had a GAA of 1.99. The next year, he was even better, and in the '52 playoffs he performed like no man before or since. He was a perfect 8-0 (the first time that had happened), and in those eight games he had four shutouts and allowed just five goals. In the first five years of his career, Sawchuk led the NHL in wins each season and never had a GAA over 1.99. He won three Cups, but no sooner had he won in 1955 than he was traded to Boston. Two years later, he was back with the Wings, where he stayed for seven years, and then moved on to Toronto (winning a Cup in '66-'67) before winding down his career with L.A., Detroit, and New York. By the time he was done, he had played in more games than any other goalie (972, a record broken by Patrick Roy only in October 2002), and had more wins (446), more minutes (57,254), and more shutouts (103). His was without a doubt a Hall of Fame career, and his play would put him in the top three goalies of all time on any hockey fan's list. Yet there were the seemingly infinite horrors that accompanied his career, a retelling of which renders the professional achievements in a completely different light. Terry was coached by his older brother Mike, but when Terry was 10, Mike died of a heart murmur and Terry inherited his brother's goalie equipment. He had another brother, Roger, who later died of pneumonia. When Terry was 12 he broke his right arm badly while playing rugby, but he told no one. The arm healed horribly and ended up being two inches shorter than his left. He suffered terrible pain for years, and 3 subsequent operations saw some 60 bone chips removed, easing the pain but never giving him full mobility of the arm. Nevertheless, he was an outstanding ballplayer and the St. Louis Cardinals offered him a tryout. He declined, citing hockey ambitions, and when he made the Red Wings in 1950, he thought he had made the right decision. At 18, he was hit in the eye by a stick in Omaha, and it was only by fate that one of the country's top eye specialists was in that city on that day to save his sight. After the 1952 playoffs, he was in a serious car accident and suffered a punctured lung. He recovered, of course, to continue his brilliant play, but psychologically he was baffled and destroyed by his trade to Boston after having won the Cup in 1955. What more was he supposed to do? In Boston, he suffered a bout of mononucleosis and then a blood infection, and he left the team soon after, announcing his retirement and revealing he had had a nervous breakdown. He came back, but on one occasion was hit in the face by a Bobby Hull slapshot. He put on a mask, but in another game Bob Pulford of Toronto skated over his left (catching) hand, severing tendons and requiring 79 stitches to close the horrible cut. He could never close that hand again, and doctors told him he'd never regain its full use. During the 1964 playoffs, he was in hospital for pinched nerves in his shoulders, but doctors released him to play. After every game, he returned to the hospital. In 1966, he had spinal surgery and doctors discovered two ruptured vertebrae that had become so because of his hunched-over style of play. The operation was a success and Sawchuk no longer had the headaches that had plagued him most of his adult life. And, he could sleep. He had never slept at night for more than two hours at a time because of pain. His wife filed for divorce in 1958, but they patched things up and tried to continue to raise their six children together. She left him for good in 1969. Those major injuries were forever augmented by "minor"

Terry Sawchuk

> **When Terry was 12 he broke his right arm badly while playing rugby, but he told no one.**
> **TERRY SAWCHUK**

Terry Sawchuk

Kevin Sawyer

Peter Scamurra

Dave Scatchard

Peter Schaefer

ones such as facial cuts (which required some 400 stitches over his career), concussions, arthritis, and charley horses. Off the ice, he drank, sometimes a little, sometimes much more than a little. His mind and body were ravaged, and he was unfriendly to reporters, teammates, and even small children looking for an autograph. He played his last season, '69-'70, with the Rangers, and that summer rented a cottage with teammate Ron Stewart. Accounts vary as to what happened one night at the E & J Pub in Long Beach. Both men drank, that's for sure, and an argument ensued. They were told to leave, so returned to their cottage. The argument continued (one version), or they reconciled and started play fighting (another version), and Sawchuk fell and had to be rushed to hospital. His gallbladder was removed and then a few days later another operation was required after he was transferred to a hospital in New York. Complications arose from major intestinal surgery, and Sawchuk died on the operating room table. Police considered charging Stewart with manslaughter, though they never did. Sawchuk was buried as both a goalie of incomparable skill and as a man wrecked and ravaged by 40 years of experience that would have killed most men much earlier. Unhappy, misunderstood, anti-social, bitter, and brilliant, he was immediately inducted into the Hockey Hall of Fame, his legend living on long after his wartorn body had given up for the peace and solace of death.

SAWYER, Kevin
b. Christina Lake, British Columbia, February 21, 1974
Every team wants him enough to try him, but no team wants him enough to keep him. In his first five NHL seasons, Sawyer played for four teams, and at that only the occasional game until the Ducks played him for most of 2001-02. His assets are his left hand and his right hand, preferably with his gloves on the ice, for Sawyer fights and piles up penalty minutes

SCAMURRA, Peter
b. Buffalo, New York, February 23, 1955
In the history of the NHL, there was never a worse place for a rookie to play than Washington starting in 1974, the team's first year of existence. Scamurra joined the team the next year and played parts of four seasons with the Caps. The last two years were compromised by two serious knee injuries from which he never recovered, and after a few games in the minors he retired.

SCATCHARD, Dave
b. Hinton, Alberta, February 20, 1976
Hockey players know about family and sacrifice and how fortunate they are to have the skills they've been blessed with. They are members of their community and are aware that no superstar is an island. The last time Scatchard scored two goals in a game, it was with purpose. While playing with Vancouver starting in 1997, he gave his time to a local Ronald McDonald House and got to be fast friends with Nicholas Beresford, a 12-year-old with leukemia. They spent time together, but the relationship ended suddenly when Scatchard was traded to the Islanders in December 1999. Just a short time later, Nicholas died. Scatchard promised to score a hat trick in a game that night in the boy's memory, and although he fell a goal short, the emotion and feeling

seemed to be appropriate and right. It was a life event that took place on the ice during an NHL game, and Scatchard, and the community, were the better for it.

SCEVIOUR, Darin
b. Lacombe, Alberta, November 30, 1965
Drafted by Chicago in 1984, Sceviour played his one and only game with the Hawks after graduating from Lethbridge of the WHL. He played overseas for a few years after two seasons in the minors in North America.

SCHAEFER, Joe
b. Long Island, New York, December 21, 1924
d. Ladson, South Carolina, January 2001
They don't make games like they used to, that's for sure. Joe Schaefer was just a guy. In his youth, he was a goalie in New York for the Sands Point Tigers, an amateur team in the Metropolitan Hockey League of New York. He played a bit in the minors, but he knew he had to get a real job, and he did. He worked in an office equipment company, but since the early 1950s he had been the Rangers' statistician at home games. Out of this job came the chance to earn a little money as the team's practice goalie, and on two occasions that got him into a heap of NHL excitement. On February 17, 1960, with the Hawks in town, Gump Worsley suffered torn tendons in his stick hand and had to go to hospital. Joe was called in, and he turned a 1-0 into a 5-1 loss. On March 8, 1961, again against Chicago, the Gumper stretched to make a save on Bobby Hull and tore a muscle in his thigh. Schaefer came into a 1-1 game, and the Rangers lost again, this time 4-3. He never had to come into a game again, though he did remain the team's stats man until 1986, when he retired to South Carolina.

SCHAEFER, Peter
b. Yellow Grass, Saskatchewan, July 12, 1977
It didn't take Schaefer long to take control of his future. Vancouver drafted him in 1995, and over a three-year period he seemed to establish himself with the Canucks, starting in 1998 and playing full-time the next two seasons. But in the summer of 2001, he signed to play in Finland and turned his back on the Canucks, playing for TPS Turku. He won gold with Canada at the 1997 World Juniors, and played for his country again at the 2000 World Championships. His year in Finland ended with a call from GM Lanny McDonald, who asked him to play again at the 2002 WC in Sweden. Schaefer gladly accepted.

SCHAEFFER, Paul "Butch"
b. Hinkley, Minnesota, November 7, 1911
d. unknown
He was one of Major McLaughlin's Americans. The Chicago owner was determined to build a team made up of primarily U.S.-born players, and for five games in '36-'37 Schaeffer counted himself among that number. He played little professional hockey besides. Schaeffer later lived in Eveleth, Minnesota, and worked as a cabinet maker.

SCHAFER, Paxton
b. Medicine Hat, Alberta, February 26, 1976
He's a star with the Baton Rouge Kingfish, but those

in the NHL have long forgotten the name Paxton. He played three games in goal for Boston in '96-'97 but was soon farmed out to Providence and then farmed out further to the East Coast league. That is where he has made his mark, and a promotion, which seems less and less likely, would be to the AHL. The NHL is unattainable for now.

SCHAMEHORN, Kevin
b. Calgary, Alberta, July 28, 1956
A member of the brawling New Westminster Bruins of the mid-1970s, Schamehorn continued his fighting ways to earn three quick chances in the NHL. Neither Detroit nor Los Angeles kept him for more than 5 games, and he made his living in the IHL where he skated for 12 years. During the last half of his career, he cut down on the penalty minutes and demonstrated a real talent for scoring, but by then NHL teams had moved on and Schamehorn had to content himself with goal celebrations in the "I" for the rest of his days.

SCHASTLIVY, Petr
b. Angarsk, Soviet Union (Russia), April 18, 1979
After helping Russia win gold at the 1999 World Junior Championships in Winnipeg, Schastlivy came to Ottawa in the fall to start a career in the NHL. Since then, he has played more for Grand Rapids, in the minors, than with the big team, and his progress was slowed in 2001-02 by a knee injury that kept him out for half a season.

SCHELLA, John
b. Port Arthur, Ontario, May 9, 1947
One of the tough guys of the game, Schella was strong in a way few men were. He played a year and a half with expansion Vancouver when the Canucks first joined the NHL, but rose to greater prominence with Houston in the WHA where he played for six years, from the team's inception in 1972 until '78.

SCHERZA, Chuck
b. Brandon, Manitoba, February 15, 1923
During his long and lively career, Scherza played every position, including goalie. He had his NHL shot during the war when he played for Boston and the Rangers, but he was without compare in Providence in the AHL. He played an even decade for the Reds and was loved by fans for his hard skating, heavy hitting, and gentlemanly play. Once, he fell heavily into a goalpost and punctured his lung, and although he lay in hospital near death, he battled back to resume his career. Scherza had an Iron Man streak of 302 games that was stopped not by injury or ailment but because he had to return to Brandon to examine the scarred land that was left after his house burned down. He was later inducted into the Manitoba Sports Hall of Fame.

SCHINKEL, Ken ("Schink")
b. Jansen, Saskatchewan, November 27, 1932
Schinkel's career can be perfectly cut into two pieces, the years leading up to expansion and the years after it. Pre-expansion was a bit of a mixed bag for him. He played five years for the Rangers, but that healthy chunk of Original Six time was bookended by four years in the minors at the start of his career and another three at the apparent end of his playing days. Pittsburgh, though,

resuscitated his legs and for six years he had his most offensively successful seasons. He played in two All-Star Games. The team never fared too well in the standings or playoffs, but at age 40 Schinkel was still scoring goals and contributing. When Red Kelly was fired as coach, Schinkel stepped in and guided the team for parts of four years with moderate success. He was fired and replaced by Marc Boileau and later re-hired for two seasons. He stepped down for health reasons but stayed with the team, first as an assistant GM and later as a scout.

SCHLEGEL, Brad
b. Kitchener, Ontario, July 22, 1968
Schlegel never let a little thing like the NHL stop him from enjoying a long and successful career in hockey. He was, first and foremost, a dedicated member of Canada's international teams for years, from 1988 when he played three full years in the program right up to 2002 when he played for his country at the 2002 World Championships in Sweden. After playing at the 1992 Olympics in Albertville, Schlegel turned pro with Washington, but over the next three years he played mostly in the minors. He again played at the 1994 Olympics in Lillehammer and then embarked on a lengthy European career in Austria, though most recently he has transferred to the DEL in Germany.

SCHLIEBENER, Andy
b. Ottawa, Ontario, August 16, 1962
He was drafted in 1980 and out of the game by 1986, and in between there was more action in the minors than in the NHL. Nonetheless, Schliebener played 84 games with Vancouver during this period.

SCHMAUTZ, Bobby
b. Saskatoon, Saskatchewan, March 28, 1945
Success came slowly to the right winger, but once it came it wouldn't go away for the longest time. After playing junior in his hometown, he went to the WHL until Chicago called him up for a few games in '67-'68. Over the next 5 years, he made only a small impression but with Vancouver in '72-'73 he exploded for 38 goals and became an instant star. Although he never scored that many goals again, he truly hit his stride in Boston, where he played for more than six years. He was a solid 2-way player on a talented team, and in the 1977 playoffs he led the league with 11 goals. For much of his career he lived in Portland in the summer and worked as a roofer. When he retired in 1981, he settled there permanently and joined his brother, Arnie, full-time in the business, building roofs and importing supplies from Canada. His other brother, Cliff, who played for years in Portland and had a brief stint in the NHL, was the other main partner in the business.

SCHMAUTZ, Cliff
b. Saskatoon, Saskatchewan, March 17, 1939
d. Portland, Oregon, February 11, 2002
Playing on a line with Art Jones and Dick Van Impe, Schmautz was among the finest and most talented players in the WHL. He played 10 years with the Portland Buckaroos, leading the team to 8 regular-season first-place finishes and 3 Lester Patrick Cups as league champions. He led the league in scoring in '65-'66 and when he retired in 1975 he was the third all-time scorer

Petr Schastlivy

John Schella

Ken Schinkel

Bobby Schmautz

Cliff Schmautz

in team history. Schmautz was the stuff of legend who, according to everyone outside the NHL, could do it all. Yet he played just one season – with Buffalo and Philadelphia – in the NHL. During the summers of his career and year-round after he retired, he worked with his brothers, Arnie and Bobby, at Buckaroo Roofing in Portland. Cliff passed away in a Portland hospital because of complications following heart surgery.

SCHMIDT, Clarence
b. Williams, Minnesota, September 17, 1925
d. January 2, 1997

Hopefully, somewhere in a relative's home is the puck that Schmidt fired into the net for Boston during the '43-'44 season, for it was his only NHL goal in his seven-game career with the Bruins. He got his chance because of the war and a depletion of players in the league, but he spent the rest of his very short career with the farm team in the city, the Olympics.

SCHMIDT, Joe (sometimes Otto Schmidt)
b. Odessa, Saskatchewan, November 5, 1926

Like brother Jackie, Joe played junior in Regina and had a chance with the Bruins during the war. He never enlisted, though, and instead played many years in the minors. After retiring, he returned to Regina where he became a car salesman.

SCHMIDT, John "Jackie"
b. Odessa, Saskatchewan, November 11, 1924

Milt Schmidt

Odessa was a farm community about 100 souls strong, but Schmidt grew up in Regina. He played for a team called the Abbotts, and there were so many players named John on the team that he acquired the nickname Jackie pretty quickly. He joined the Bruins in 1942 and played on a line with Bep Guidolin and Don Gallinger. All teenagers, they were known as the Sprout Line. At season's end, Schmidt joined the army and served overseas for three years where he found a war bride but didn't play much hockey. When he returned to Canada, out of shape, he spurned an offer from the Canadiens and signed with Valleyfield, a senior team in Quebec. The team won the first Alexander Trophy, in 1951, and in the summers he studied at U of Toronto. After retiring, he settled in Toronto and became the national sales manager of the Qualitrol division for the Canadian Pneumatic Tool Company. His brother, Joe, also played briefly in the NHL, and Jackie was credited with discovering Fern Flaman in his Regina days.

SCHMIDT, Milt ("Uncle Milty")
b. Kitchener, Ontario, March 5, 1918

The lives of three people do add up to a hill of beans if

Milt Schmidt

their names are Schmidt, Dumart, and Bauer, for the Kraut Line was the best combination in all of hockey during its heyday. The three grew up together in Kitchener and played junior together. When Bauer attended Boston's training camp, he brought his friends along and the three were signed and sent to Providence as a unit. It didn't take long for Schmidt to be recalled. He played half the '36-'37 season with the Bruins, but it wasn't until the final day that all three played together in a game for Boston. They scored soon after and remained Bruins the rest of their lives. They were a remarkable troika in that they lived together and developed a special friendship. As a result, they became better players. Schmidt was the most physical of the three, and although he played centre he was not always barrelling through the middle of the ice. His habit was to carry the puck along the boards and use his size to get into the opponent's end, but the result was both an intimidating player and an oft-injured one. A broken jaw, broken ribs, torn cartilage in both knees, all slowed him down over the years, but, like Bobby Orr a generation later, this was the only way he knew to play. The line brought 2 Cups to Boston before the war, in 1939 and '41, and in the season in between, '39-'40, Schmidt led the league in scoring with 52 points. It was also an amazing year for his linemates because for the first time an entire forward line finished 1-2-3 in the scoring race. One of the most poignant nights in hockey history occurred on January 10, 1942, a game in which Montreal was in Boston. It was the Kraut Line's last game in the NHL for a while, as the three were off to join Canada's war effort. Boston won, and after the game players from both teams carried the famed threesome around the ice on their shoulders to receive the fans' farewell. Schmidt did not return to the Bruins until the start of the '45-'46 season, but he and Bauer and Dumart picked up right where they had left off. Schmidt won the Hart Trophy in '50-'51, his first year as team captain, and on March 18, 1952, the line had another final, special moment. Bauer had retired in 1947, but on that night in 1952 the team wanted to honour all three players so he came out of retirement for the game. Bauer scored a goal, and Schmidt scored his 200th career goal to make the night all the more memorable. He finished his career on defence, the hope being that he would handle the puck less, gamble less frequently with his body, and extend his career. Schmidt retired midway through the '54-'55 season to become the Bruins coach. He led the team until 1966 with the exception of 1 year ('60-'61), thus completing 30 years of service to the team. The Bruins retired his number 15, but he wanted it back in circulation and in 1957 Larry Regan was given it (though the Bruins later retired it again permanently).

Schmidt won the Hart Trophy in '50-'51, his first year as team captain.
MILT SCHMIDT

In 1974, Schmidt became GM and sometimes interim coach of the new Washington Capitals franchise. It was the lowest point of his career, and the team was the worst ever to play in the league. Two years later, he was back in Boston, working as a salesman. When he retired to private life, he remained just outside the city, and today is one of the oldest living members of the Hockey Hall of Fame, having been inducted in 1961.

SCHMIDT, Norm
b. Sault Ste. Marie, Ontario, January 24, 1963
A mobile defenceman out of Oshawa, Schmidt was drafted by Pittsburgh in 1981 and went on to play all of his 125 games with the Penguins. His only full season was '85-'86 when he had 15 goals and 14 assists, a particularly odd statistic in that defencemen almost never have more goals and assists. His career was stalled twice because of serious knee injuries and then ended altogether after a serious back injury in October 1987 required surgery.

SCHNABEL, Robert
b. Prague, Czechoslovakia (Czech Republic), November 10, 1978
At 6'6" and 234 pounds, all Schnabel had to do was skate and he'd draw interest from the NHL. The defenceman was chosen by the Islanders in the 1997 Draft but opted to turn pro in the AHL and try his luck again. He was drafted much lower by Phoenix and wound up in Nashville before making his entrance in the NHL. Schnabel played a single game for the Predators in 2001-02.

SCHNARR, Werner
b. Berlin (Kitchener), Ontario, March 23, 1903
d. unknown
An original Bruins forward, Schnarr played much of 1924-25 without registering a single point. It was his only serious year of pro hockey after coming out of Kitchener where he had developed as a junior.

SCHNEIDER, Andy
b. Edmonton, Alberta, March 29, 1972
After playing for Canada at the 1992 World Juniors and finishing his junior career in the WHL, Schneider played just 10 games with Ottawa in the team's first season. He played for a short time in the minors and has since made an excellent career for himself in Europe, most recently in the DEL in Germany.

SCHNEIDER, Mathieu
b. New York, New York, June 12, 1969
The best thing for Schneider was to be out of Montreal and Toronto and in New York and Los Angeles where hockey is not the all-consuming way of life it is in the two hockey capitals of Canada. When Schneider broke in with the Canadiens in 1987, the defenceman showed plenty of skill but little else. He was not a team man, on or off the ice, and his dressing room attitude left something to be desired. He fought with goalie Patrick Roy and captain Kirk Muller, and when he was traded to Toronto things got worse, if possible. His social life was a mess, and he suffered a serious lower stomach injury that kept him out for almost a full year. Unliked by his teammates, the pattern continued until he was traded

to the Rangers and on to Los Angeles, where he found peace. In March 2003, he was traded to Detroit for a group of young players and draft choices, a steep price to pay. On the ice, he was part of Montreal's Cup team in 1993 and played the best hockey of his career at the 1996 World Cup for the U.S. He was part of the American debacle at the 1998 Olympics in Nagano and was never considered for the 2002 Olympic team, his best years now behind him.

SCHOCK, Danny
b. Terrace Bay, Ontario, December 30, 1948
By playing a single game in the 1970 playoffs, the first game of his career, Schock got his name on the Cup thanks to Bobby Orr and the rest of the Bruins who had slugged it out all year long. The next year, he played just a few games with the B's before being traded to Philadelphia with Rick MacLeish for Mike Walton, but he lasted just 14 more games on Broad Street. Schock finished his career in the minors, though his brother, Ron, had a lengthy NHL stay.

SCHOCK, Ron
b. Chapleau, Ontario, December 19, 1943
In the pre-expansion days, Schock didn't see much playing time with Boston. That changed in 1967 when St. Louis claimed him, but his career reached its peak in Pittsburgh two years later. Schock, now a veteran, was a leader on a young team full of promise. The Penguins reached their peak – and demise – in almost the same breath. In '74-'75, Schock scored a career-high 23 goals and was named team MYP, and the Penguins entered the playoffs full of hope. They swept St. Louis in the best-of-three preliminary round, and against the Islanders they won the first three games of the series before collapsing the way only one other team had ever done, the 1942 Detroit Red Wings. Yes, the Islanders stormed back to win the series four games to three, and all the momentum from the franchise seemed to have been sucked out. Schock did not have a single goal in the '75 playoffs. After retiring in 1980, Schock and his wife settled in Rochester, where he had played his final year, in the AHL, and he sold real estate in the area.

SCHOENFELD, Jim
b. Galt, Ontario, September 4, 1952
The words will never leave Schoenfeld's side no matter what he accomplishes. After his playing days, he coached New Jersey, and in a 1988 playoff game he became upset by the refereeing of Don Koharski. After the game, Schoenfeld chased after the ref and screamed at him to "go eat another doughnut." The epithet "you fat pig" was also part of the verbal assault that cost the coach a thousand bucks and a one-game suspension. As a player, Schoenfeld was as intense. A big, solid defenceman, he played the majority of his career on the Buffalo blueline, although his games and years were forever being imperiled by injury. He was part of the team that went to the 1975 finals, and such was his popularity in town that he actually cut two records, the first called *Schoenie* and the second *The Key Is Love*. Today, those are sacred and rare keepsakes! A final and serious shoulder operation forced him to retire in 1984, and he became Buffalo's coach for Rochester the following year. Yearning to play, though, Schoenfeld

Norm Schmidt

Andy Schneider

Mathieu Schneider

Ron Schock

Jim Schoenfeld

Dwight Schofield

Wally Schreiber

Paxton Schulte

Dave Schultz

came out of retirement for a number of games in that '84-'85 season, and then turned to bossing the bench full-time. He coached the Sabres the year after, then New Jersey, Washington, and Phoenix, most recently returning to the Devils for a short stint. He also worked for ABC Sports as a colour analyst.

SCHOFIELD, Dwight ("Sconan")
b. Waltham, Massachusetts, March 25, 1956
He wanted to be considered a barbarian on ice, so he gave himself a nickname to make his point clear. Schofield was a fighter who played for six NHL teams in seven years, always wanted as tough-guy insurance for a team looking to bulk up, as they say. He played mostly in the minors, and since retiring in 1988 he has started Schofield Ice and In-Line Hockey, a business devoted to providing innovative and quality equipment for players.

SCHREIBER, Wally
b. Edmonton, Alberta, April 15, 1962
One of the longest-serving Canadians in Europe, Schreiber has played exclusively in Germany since 1989. He came out of junior and stepped right into the IHL, and later played parts of two seasons with Minnesota. He has also contributed significantly to the Canadian National Team program over the years, culminating with his participation at the 1988 Olympics in Calgary.

SCHRINER, Dave "Sweeney"
b. Saratov, Russia, November 30, 1911
d. Calgary, Alberta, July 4, 1990
Technically, Schriner was the first Russian-born player to make it to the NHL, but since his parents moved to Calgary when he was a month old, he was not even potty-trained in that country let alone trained in the arts of skating, shooting, and passing. He learned those skills on the outdoor rinks near his home, though he skated so much his mother worried for him and tried, unsuccessfully, to restrict his skating time. He was a skilled athlete in whatever he tried, notably baseball, and one of his heroes was a player named Bill Sweeney. Schriner emulated his style of play and soon became known as Li'l Sweeney, and the Li'l was eventually dropped. Schriner liked his nickname so much he refused to speak to anyone who greeted him as David. He was invited to the training camp of the New York Americans in 1933, and although he lacked some skills, his skating impressed the team enough that they signed him and assigned him to Syracuse of the IHL. The next year, Schriner was in the NHL. He scored 18 goals as a rookie, and in his second and third years led the league in points. After five successful seasons with the Amerks, he was traded to Toronto in

an unprecedented deal. On May 18, 1939, Conn Smythe sent Busher Jackson, Doc Romnes, Buzz Boll, Murray Armstrong, and Jimmy Fowler to the Americans for Schriner, true testament to his value and reputation at the height of his career. In his four years with the Leafs before the war, he gave the team much-needed scoring. His play proved critical in the 1942 finals when the Leafs rallied from 3-0 down in the series to win the Cup. He scored two goals in game seven, a 3-1 win that brought Toronto its most remarkable Cup. Schriner played out west in '43-'44 because he wasn't satisfied with Smythe's contract offer, but returned to the team the year after and played two more seasons with the Leafs, winning a second Cup in 1945. He then went out west to coach the Lethbridge Maple Leafs and Regina Capitals, and after leaving the game altogether in 1949 he settled in Calgary. Schriner became extremely successful in the oil and gas industry, working with Canadian Fina until retiring in 1977. He had been inducted into the Hockey Hall of Fame in 1962, and during his years in Calgary remained in hockey through the Calgary Oldtimers Hockey Association.

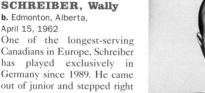

He scored 18 goals as a rookie, and in his second and third years led the league in points.
SWEENEY SCHRINER

SCHULTE, Paxton
b. Onaway, Alberta, July 16, 1972
An NHL alumnus on the strength of two games – one with Quebec and one with Calgary – Schulte has enjoyed greater success in the minors and Britain, where he continues to play. He's known as a clean but heavy hitter who has skill and scoring ability, though it's the physical side of his game that gets the most attention and respect (not to mention, notice).

SCHULTZ, Dave ("Sergeant Schultz"/ "The Hammer")
b. Waldheim, Saskatchewan, October 14, 1949
Only a few players are truly an embarrassment to the game, and Schultz surely is at the top of this list. There was virtually no talent attached to this animal who came out on the ice for brief periods with the single-minded purpose of beating up as many players as possible. Of course, under Fred Shero in Philadelphia's Cup-winning days, hockey was a distant second on the team's list of priorities. Nowhere outside that city were the players admired or respected, but within Flyers-land they were revered. Schultz set an NHL record in '74-'75 when he punched his way to 472 penalty minutes, the third of four times he led the league in that dishonourable statistic. He put out a record called *The Penalty Box*, and got into a fight with his publisher over the title of his autobiography. The editor wanted to go with *King Goon*, but Schultz won the day with *Hammer: Confessions of a Hockey Enforcer*. After retiring, he worked in cable television, operated a limousine service in New Jersey,

and managed an arena called Skatium, in Pennsylvania. He also went into coaching in the lowest depths of the minors with teams such as Baton Rouge, Virginia, and most recently, the Mohawk Valley Prowlers based near his home in Utica, New York.

SCHULTZ, Nick
b. Regina, Saskatchewan, August 25, 1982
It was a busy 2001-02 schedule for Schultz. He left Prince Albert of the WHL the previous spring at age 19 to turn pro, and made Minnesota at his first camp. He played the year with the Wild, except for five weeks in December and early January when he was loaned to Team Canada for the World Junior Championships. After the NHL's regular season, he went to the team's minor-league affiliate in Houston to play in the AHL playoffs. He was back full-time with the Wild for 2001-02.

SCHULTZ, Ray
b. Red Deer, Alberta, November 14, 1976
Schultz has been trying to establish himself as a tough guy in the modern NHL, though he has been only a bit player for the Islanders since making his debut in 1997. He came out of the WHL, but the defenceman doesn't seem to be in the club's long-term plans.

SCHURMAN, Maynard
b. Summerdale, Prince Edward Island, July 16, 1957
After leaving Mount Allison University, Schurman signed with Philadelphia but soon was claimed by Hartford in the Expansion Draft in 1979. He played just seven games with the Whalers and only a few short seasons of pro before retiring.

SCHUTT, Rod
b. Bancroft, Ontario, October 13, 1956
For a short time, the Habs couldn't make up their mind whether they wanted Schutt or not. They played the winger in a couple of games in '77-'78, and then the shenanigans began. The Canadiens traded him to Washington, but the NHL vetoed the deal. They told him not to return to training camp in Montreal, then changed their mind and told him, yes, report. But before he arrived, they had already traded him to Pittsburgh. Things settled down for the first three years as he became a capable offensive player on a line with Peter Lee and Greg Malone. Schutt developed back problems, though, and spent the rest of his career between the NHL and the minors, trying to make it back to the NHL, trying also to stay healthy and play without pain. In 1986, he gave up trying and retired. Since then, he has coached in the Sudbury Wolves junior organization and also developed a career in construction.

SCHWAB, Corey
b. North Battleford, Saskatchewan, November 4, 1970
Those who don't believe in fate, read on. The son of an auto technician from a small prairie town, Schwab went to a junior game with his father, Ken, and spent his last dollar on a program. Inside, his lucky number was drawn and he had a chance to win a car if he shot a puck from centre ice into a small hole in a board in front of the goal. He did, and as a result he was able to afford to commute from Seattle, where he went to play junior. Ironically, though, Schwab wasn't a shooter – he was a stopper of pucks. The goalie had an excellent junior career, although he was drafted only 200th by New Jersey in 1990. He had little chance of usurping Martin Brodeur in goal, and a trade to Tampa Bay gave him just the opposite treatment – many games, many shots, bad losses. His career was on the downturn until he signed with Toronto, and it took a major turn forward when starter Curtis Joseph broke his hand soon after returning from the 2002 Olympics in Salt Lake City. Schwab filled in for the rest of the season and performed, if not brilliantly, then certainly very competently. In the summer he earned a new contract with New Jersey, ending up right where he began – as Martin Brodeur's backup! It was a long way to go a short distance, indeed.

SCISSONS, Scott
b. Saskatoon, Saskatchewan, October 29, 1971
The 5th-overall draft choice in 1990 was Jaromir Jagr. The 7th was Darryl Sydor. The 6th was Scott Scissons. The centre had it all – size, speed, skill. But he played just three games with the Islanders in the coming few years, spending most of his three years of pro in the minors and recuperating from a series of back injuries. Unable to recover fully, he retired at age 22 while still in good health. He returned to Saskatoon and joined his family's recreational-vehicle business.

SCLISIZZI, Enio ("Sils") (sometimes James Enio)
b. Milton, Ontario, August 1, 1925
James Enio Sclisizzi was his full name, and he was thankful there were three parts to it. He played for Detroit and Chicago in the years after the war, and during those radio days the most influential and popular man in hockey was a raspy-voiced genius named Foster Hewitt. Well, the name Sclisizzi never rolled off Hewitt's tongue as easily as Howe, Kennedy, and Ree-chard, so the master of play-by-play changed the player's name from Enio Sclisizzi to James Enio. Voila! There was a hockey name that radio folk could understand and make sense of. No matter, though, because he was only a regular for one season, '48-'49. Besides that, he was a frequent callup during a long and productive minor-league career.

SCOTT, Ganton
b. Preston, Ontario, March 23, 1903
d. unknown
One of the more obscure players of hockey's early days, Scott played for three teams from 1922 to '25. He was also one of the early players to go from the NHL to California to finish his career in the early 1930s when professional hockey was a new sport to the area.

SCOTT, Laurie
b. South River, Ontario, June 19, 1896
d. San Jose, California, February 15, 1977
Around 1920, the Scott family moved from Ontario to Tofield, Alberta, where Scott became not only a great hockey player but also a pro baseball prospect. He played two seasons in the NHL, one with the New York Americans, the other with the Rangers a year later when they won the 1928 Stanley Cup. As soon as he was out of the NHL, he coached and managed in the AHA with Duluth and soon after in the California

Ray Schultz

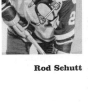

Rod Schutt

Corey Schwab

Laurie Scott

Ron Scott

Travis Scott

Darrel Scoville

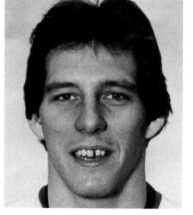

Claudio Scremin

Pro Hockey League. After the war, Scott settled in San Jose and owned a trailer park, which he ran for more than 20 years. In the summers of his hockey career, he was playing manager for the Selkirks and a noted catcher with a strong arm.

SCOTT, Richard
b. Orillia, Ontario, August 1, 1978
Like many a thug in the pros, Scott is a fighter on the ice and a gentleman off it. He beats up opponents in the name of his team, then goes out into the community to do charity work longer than all the superstars put together. He played just a few games with the Rangers in 2001-02 and has spent most of the last three years with their farm team in Hartford, where he is one of the most popular players on the team.

SCOTT, Ron
b. Guelph, Ontario, July 21, 1960
The great beginning didn't have a fairy-tale ending, but Scott still went to places few are able to go. He won a Memorial Cup with Cornwall in 1980 and then had a superb college career at Michigan State, but his stay with the Rangers was not as successful. Over a 4-year period, he had a record of 3-7-4 in 16 games, and when he signed with Los Angeles he played just 12 more games. Even in the minors he was a backup, and he retired in 1991.

SCOTT, Travis
b. Kanata, Ontario, September 14, 1975
On November 28, 2000, Scott made his NHL debut in net for Los Angeles, coming in midway through the game against the Rangers and giving up 3 goals in 25 minutes of play. So far, that is his only NHL appearance, and his minor-league career suggests it might be a lucky day if Scott ever makes it back to the big time.

SCOVILLE, Darrel
b. Swift Current, Saskatchewan, October 13, 1975
When Calgary signed Scoville out of Merrimack College, it got a big, strong defenceman who had never been drafted. Since then, the Flames have used him only six times, and he's not getting any younger. Scoville is fast becoming a career AHLer.

SCREMIN, Claudio
b. Burnaby, British Columbia, May 28, 1968
After graduating from the University of Maine with a degree in economics, Scremin signed with San Jose and turned pro in the IHL. He won a Turner Cup with Kansas City in '91-'92, the same year he made his inaugural appearance with the Sharks. After a few games the year after, though, he has been out of the NHL altogether and for years was a star with K.C. He

later gave Europe a try and most recently has been playing in the DEL. He is also a certified pilot.

SCRUTON, Howard
b. Toronto, Ontario, October 6, 1962
Four assists in four games is something to be proud of, even if those were all the NHL games he played. Scruton signed with L.A. in 1981 after there were no takers at the draft, and he played four years in the Kings system before retiring.

SEABROOKE, Glen
b. Peterborough, Ontario, September 11, 1967
For those who think the Lindros family was out of line in questioning the medical practices of the Philadelphia Flyers, or that Dave Babych is not justified in taking legal action against said team for medical reasons, read on. Seabrooke was a very talented junior. The Flyers drafted him 21st overall in 1985 and kept him in junior, but two serious injuries ended his career before it ever began. The first was a tumour in his pelvis that needed removal, but the second was the real deal-sealer. In a game with Hershey in the AHL, he flew over the goalie on a rush and crashed into the net. It didn't move, but Seabrooke's shoulder did. Philly doctors called it torn cartilage and recommended aggressive physiotherapy, but this only made it worse. Three serious operations later, Seabrooke couldn't hold a book in front of him for even a few minutes before the shoulder gave him extreme pain. He retired in 1989 after just three seasons because he couldn't move properly, let alone play hockey, and after scouting for the team for a year he was summarily dumped. Seabrooke took the Flyers doctor to court, and in the summer of 1995 he was awarded $5.5-million in the malpractice suit.

As a teen, he fought forest fires in northern Ontario from planes, and during the summers he took flying lessons.
AL SECORD

SECORD, Al
b. Sudbury, Ontario, March 3, 1958
In his heyday, there were few players like Secord. He was one of the league's top goal scorers and heavyweights. His best years came with Chicago in the 1980s when he had more than 40 goals 3 times (54 in '82-'83) and he routinely had close to 200 penalty minutes a season as well. His career started to peter out in 1987 when the Leafs acquired him, and he retired in 1990 after a short return to the Hawks. As a teen, he fought forest fires in northern Ontario from planes, and during the summers he took flying lessons and logged the necessary hours to get his licence. When he retired, he got a job flying for United Express, and most recently has been a Texas-based pilot for American Airlines.

SEDIN, Daniel
b. Ornskoldsvisk, Sweden, September 26, 1980

It's impossible to consider Daniel without Henrik, and vice versa, but that's likely the way with any set of identical twins. These are the first such pair to make it to the NHL, and from their birth to their last game they have done everything together. They were top prospects playing together in Sweden, and in 1999 Brian Burke of Vancouver engineered a trade to draft Daniel 2nd overall and Henrik 3rd overall. In '98-'99, they were co-winners of the Swedish league's MVP honours, and with the Canucks they have played mostly on the same line. Time is starting to separate them a bit, though. Daniel scored 20 goals as a rookie but dropped to 9 in his second year. He is slightly smaller and more the playmaker, and he seems to be having just a bit more difficulty adjusting to NHL-style hockey. The twins are very young still, however, and their best years are likely in the future.

SEDIN, Henrik
b. Ornskoldsvisk, Sweden, September 26, 1980

A centre to Daniel's left wing, Henrik is the bigger and more aggressive of the Sedin twins. He has also improved over the early part of his career at a slightly better pace. They both played for Sweden at the 2000 and 2001 World Championships after twice playing in the WJC, where Henrik was again more impressive. Like Daniel, though, the Sedins have much to learn about the NHL before the verdict can be handed down as to their success or failure in the NHL.

SEDLBAUER, Ron
b. Burlington, Ontario, October 22, 1954

Sedlbauer's strange career passed mostly in Vancouver, where the fans didn't much appreciate the work of the 6'3", 200-pound winger. From his beginnings with the team in 1974, he showed promise but didn't deliver – until '78-'79 when he scored 40 goals. The next year, he was back to his middling ways and was traded to Chicago and then on to Toronto. He retired in 1982 and had no worries about a postplaying career. His father had started a business called Susan Shoe Company (named after his wife), which makes Cougar boots and shoes. Sedlbauer moved in and over time became the company's vice-president. He also became president of the Burlington Cougars of the OHA.

SEFTEL, Steve
b. Kitchener, Ontario, May 14, 1968

A decent prospect according to Washington when he was drafted in 1986, Seftel played just four games with the Caps. In all, his pro career lasted just three and a half years.

SEGUIN, Dan
b. Sudbury, Ontario, June 7, 1948

Not big, Seguin was given a few games to prove himself but was found wanting. As a junior, he was Rangers property by virtue of his playing for Kitchener, but the Blueshirts traded him to Minnesota in 1968 and it was with the North Stars that he got into his first NHL games. Seguin later played briefly for Vancouver but spent most of his seven years in the minors, where he was a prolific goal scorer.

SEGUIN, Steve
b. Cornwall, Ontario, April 10, 1964

His five games of pro all came with Los Angeles during the '84-'85 season, his first year of pro. Seguin had graduated from the OHL, where he was a 55-goal scorer in his final year, but his few years of pro, in the AHL, betrayed little of that teen ability to put the puck in the net.

Ron Sedlbauer

SEIBERT, Earl ("The Flying Dutchman")
b. Berlin (Kitchener), Ontario, December 7, 1910
d. Agawam, Massachusetts, May 20, 1990

When Earl Seibert was inducted into the Hockey Hall of Fame in 1963, he joined his father, who had been enshrined two years earlier. They were the first father-son combination to have such spectacular careers, though much happened between Earl's first serious hockey game and Hall induction to leave him indifferent to the honour. Earl played junior in his hometown and then went to Springfield of the Can-Am league in 1929. During his two

Dan Seguin

years there he suffered a serious concussion and thereafter wore a helmet, the first player to do so. He joined the Rangers in 1931 and for the next four and a half years learned the NHL game and how to handle his defenceman's responsibilities. He was a big man yet he had tremendous speed; he was a great shotblocker but could move the puck as quickly as anyone. Midway through the '35-'36 season he was traded to Chicago for Art Coulter, and then his career took off. He spent nine seasons with the Hawks and was generally regarded as the second-best blueliner in the game after the great Eddie Shore. And it was this fact that stuck in Seibert's craw. Shore was a great player but also a great promoter. He was a crowd favourite who played up to the fans and shone even more brightly in the spotlight. Seibert was more reserved; he let his playing do the talking. As a result, he was, he felt, underappreciated. From 1935 to 1944 Seibert was a selection to either the First or Second All-Star Team, but only four of those were to the First, almost the reverse of Shore. Seibert lived in Shore's shadow, even though Shore once confessed that Seibert was the only man he was afraid to fight. Yet, everyone

Steve Seguin

From 1935 to 1944 Seibert was a selection to either the First or Second All-Star Team.
EARL SEIBERT

from that day always said that the only thing that held Seibert back was Seibert himself. Shore gave 100 percent every night; Seibert didn't. Seibert gave the team what they paid him for, and not a penny's worth of play more. Therein lay the real difference, for Shore would go through a brick wall for free, just to prove he could do what everyone else feared doing. Seibert won two Stanley Cups, with the Rangers in 1933 and the Hawks in 1938, the latter for which owner McLaughlin gave full credit to Seibert. He finished his career in Detroit where he took a substantial pay cut because GM Jack Adams felt he was well past his prime. Then, ironically, Seibert hooked up with Shore. They bought the Springfield Indians of the AHL and played with the team for a while before managing it. As expected, Shore was the man who took charge, made decisions, and led by example. Seibert endured being second fiddle again for five years and then packed up and went home, as it were. He owned and managed his own grocery store in Springfield for years, then retired to Agawam where he passed away in virtual obscurity. He refused to go to his Hall of Fame induction in 1963, feeling it was too late and that he had never been given his due as a player. There was another moment that perhaps damaged Seibert's glossy view of the game. On March 28, 1937, he checked Howie Morenz into the end boards, causing Morenz to break his leg and end his career. The great Canadiens star died in hospital a month later, ostensibly of a broken heart, and Seibert unfairly blamed himself for Morenz's death for the rest of his life. It was a legacy he wished upon himself, and completely undeserved given that he was the second-best defenceman of his generation.

SEILING, Ric

b. Elmira, Ontario, December 15, 1957

He comes from a family steeped in sports, but hockey is only one of them – harness racing is the other. Ric's older brother, Rod, had a long NHL career before moving to the track, and a third Seiling, Don, had a decent AHL career before training standardbreds. Ric played 10 years in the NHL, all but one with Buffalo, from 1977 to '87. During his best years, he played on a line with Gilbert Perreault and Rick Martin, and 4 times he scored at least 20 goals in a season. His career changed dramatically, though, on January 30, 1982, when he was poked in the eye by a stick. He wore a visor the rest of his days, but never fully recovered his vision. Before he retired he got his driver's licence for harness racing, and as soon as he hung up his skates he went to the track and started riding, eventually gravitating toward the Ontario Jockey Club.

Ric Seiling

SEILING, Rod ("Sod")

b. Kitchener, Ontario, November 14, 1944

For years, many in the know considered Seiling the most underrated defenceman in the game. Coming out of St. Mike's in the late 1950s, he played his first NHL game with the Leafs, of course, but also won the Memorial Cup with the Marlies and played for Canada in the 1964 Olympics in Innsbruck. Seiling was best known as a Rangers blueliner, though. He played a dozen seasons with the Blueshirts and took them close to the Cup in 1972, the same year he played at the All-Star Game and played for Canada in the historic Summit Series. He retired in 1979 not because of old age or injuries or lack of drive, but simply because he had another love, another job to go to – harness racing. He became the general manager of the Elmira Raceway and owner of Seiling Farms Inc. with his brother Don (other brother and NHLer, Ric, joined them after his career on ice), though funnily enough the fourth Seiling brother, Ken, became a politician and was voted mayor of Woolwich Township. Rod continued his success in the racing business and later became the executive vice-president for Race Tracks of Canada.

Rod later became the executive vice-president for Race Tracks of Canada.
ROD SEILING (RIGHT)

SEJBA, Jiri

b. Pardubice, Czechoslovakia (Czech Republic), July 22, 1962

Prior to joining Buffalo in 1990 at age 28, Sejba had a fine career in his homeland. He appeared in four World Championships, winning gold in 1985, and played in both the 1987 Canada Cup and the 1988 Olympics in Calgary. His trial with the Sabres was brief, though, and he spent most of his two North American years in the minors, after which he returned to Europe to continue his career.

SEKERAS, Lubomir ("Seko")

b. Trencin, Czechoslovakia (Slovakia), November 18, 1968

One of the good things about Sekeras not being invited to play for Slovakia at the 2002 World Championships, as he had been the previous year, was that the country had enough good young players that it didn't have to rely on a 34-year-old to bolster its lineup. That team won its first-ever gold medal at such a high level, and Sekeras had been part of the nation's developing quality. He had previously played in 2000 and 1998, winning silver at the former tournament. On the NHL front, he wasn't drafted until 2000, by Minnesota, and has been a regular on the team's blueline ever since.

SELANNE, Teemu ("The Finnish Flash")

b. Helsinki, Finland, July 3, 1970

Hockey is the lesser because Teemu's twin brother,

Paavo, never had a like passion for the game. As a junior in Finland, Teemu played with a speed and skill that prompted most fans to hail him as the greatest player Finland had ever produced. He was a star for Jokerit, and by age 21 he had played in every international tournament possible. Winnipeg drafted him in 1988 and he made his debut with the Jets four years later. It was the finest rookie season in the history of the game, Selanne scoring 76 goals to lead the league. That mark was not only a rookie record – it obliterated the previous record of 50 set by Mike Bossy. Selanne was named Calder Trophy winner by the NHL, and named the Finnish Flash by everyone who watched him play. Selanne settled into a tremendous career that reached a new level of excitement when he was traded to Anaheim. Teamed with Paul Kariya, the pair were the most explosive and exciting skaters in the world, but with no supporting cast they often had to go it alone. As they went, so went the Ducks. He was later traded to San Jose, a team with greater overall talent, and although 76-goal seasons are a thing of the past, he continues to be one of the game's top players. In 1998-99, he won the inaugural Rocket Richard Trophy, and he has passed the 400-goal mark in just 10 seasons of play. Internationally, Selanne is accomplished yet wanting. He has been named to every Finnish team for which he qualifies, but despite winning a number of bronze and silver medals he has yet to hang gold around his neck. At home, he has long been a hero and treasure, for both his hockey and his charitable work with children. His love of fast cars is the stuff of legend, and he has raced in three World Championship rallies in Finland. Once, though, his career was almost jeopardized when he got into an accident. Police charged him with endangering public safety, and a conviction could have landed him in jail for two years. Instead, the courts fined him for a traffic offence, but in Finland the fine is determined according to a person's monthly wage. Selanne's fine worked out to $62,500, a rather expensive transgression even for a hockey millionaire.

His love of fast cars is the stuff of legend, and he has raced in three World Championship rallies in Finland.
TEEMU SELANNE

SELBY, Briton "Brit"
b. Kingston, Ontario, March 27, 1945
After winning the Memorial Cup with the Marlies in 1964, Selby made his Leafs debut a year later, and the year after that made the team as a regular on the left wing. He won the Calder Trophy for '65-'66, and lo these many years later he remains the last Leafs player to win the league's award for best rookie. Unfortunately for him, the honour did not portend greater feats in the future, as it is meant to. Selby became a regular but by no means spectacular player with three teams, and like so many others he left for the WHA in the summer of 1972. After retiring, he returned to Toronto and became a history teacher at North Toronto Collegiate, where he stayed for many years.

SELF, Steve
b. Peterborough, Ontario, May 9, 1950
Self signed with the IHL in 1973 but played only four years of pro, all with Dayton. His only time outside the "I" was a three-game stint with Washington. He also acted as playing coach for the Gems for part of his tenure with the team.

SELIVANOV, Alexander "Alex"
b. Moscow, Soviet Union (Russia), March 23, 1971
How times have changed. In 1972, the only chance that Phil Esposito would ever hug a Russian would be with his stick at eye level. But toward the end of the century, while he was GM of Tampa Bay, he watched his own flesh and blood – daughter, Carrie – marry Russian player Alex Selivanov. Selivanov had a 31-goal year with the Lightning and faded fast after that, recovering a bit of steam in Edmonton in 1999-2000. But the Oilers let him walk, and after a year in Columbus he and Carrie moved to Germany, where he continued his career in the DEL.

SELLARS, Luke
b. Toronto, Ontario, May 21, 1981
On March 23, 2002, Sellars played in his first, and so far only, NHL game. He came out of junior with Brian Kilrea's Ottawa 67's and went into the Atlanta system to start 2001-02, spending the rest of his time to date in the minors.

SELMSER, Sean
b. Calgary, Alberta, November 10, 1974
The process of getting from junior to the NHL was an exercise in patience for Selmser. He was drafted in 1993 by Pittsburgh while playing for Red Deer, but two years later he heard nothing from the Penguins and started his career in the depths of the minors. Five years later, he played a single game with the Columbus Blue Jackets, and he hasn't been heard from since at the elite level. Selmser continues to play in the AHL, though, and is ready and waiting for another callup.

SELWOOD, Brad
b. Leamington, Ontario, March 18, 1948
A defenceman who played here, there, and everywhere, Selwood was born to coach as much as play. In the NHL, he started with the Leafs in 1970, but two years later migrated to the WHA and played his prime years in that league. He came back to play a season with Los Angeles and later was an assistant coach for the team,

Brit Selby

Alexander Selivanov

Brad Selwood

Alexander Semak

Anatoli Semenov

George Senick

but he gave up playing to return to Toronto to coach in the Metropolitan Toronto Hockey League. By day, he worked at a car leasing business in Leaside, in Toronto, and in the summers he managed a baseball team there. Although he has craved to return to the pros as a coach, his dream has not yet been realized.

SEMAK, Alexander
b. Ufa, Soviet Union (Russia), February 11, 1966
For years before he made his NHL start with New Jersey in 1991, Semak was a star with Dynamo in the Soviet league and a constant presence on the national team. His finest moment in international play came in the 1987 Canada Cup. He scored only one goal in the tournament, but it was the overtime winner in game one of the best-of-three finals that Canada eventually won. Despite his successes and experience, though, he never played at the Olympics for his country. In his first full year with the Devils, he scored 37 goals and looked to be a superstar scorer the team desperately needed. Such was not the case, and he travelled a fair bit over the next few years, ending in the minors with little hope of returning to the NHL. At that point, he returned to Europe and continues to play in the Russian league.

SEMCHUK, Brandy
b. Calgary, Alberta, September 22, 1971
He took to the west coast and made it his home, though in NHL terms Semchuk played only a single game. He played for the Canadian National Team for two seasons (1988-90) before turning pro, and after his lone appearance with Los Angeles he rooted around in the minors until retiring in 1999. Semchuk then became heavily involved in coaching minor hockey teams and conducting clinics year-round in California.

SEMENKO, Dave ("Sammy"/ "Semenk")
b. Winnipeg, Manitoba, July 12, 1957
Compare Dave Semenko to Dave Schultz. Schultz accumulated penalty minutes for their own sake. He fought because he wanted mayhem and universal intimidation. He fought because he couldn't do anything else, and he fought to create a frenzy that was maniacal and utterly beyond anything to do with hockey. Semenko was Wayne Gretzky's bodyguard. His job was to fight players who hit the Wayner and convince players not to do that again. He, too, lacked skill, but through fighting he was trying to create skill – by allowing Gretzky to play a skating, offensive, goal-oriented game. Semenko was very good at what he did, and despite his "job" he never had more than 194 penalty minutes in any season. He won two Cups with the Oilers, and night in and night out he could go to bed saying mission accom-

plished because Gretzky set virtually every scoring record that ever existed. Yet it was not a glorious job or a job that was truly fun. It was a *job*. When he was traded to Hartford and then Toronto, he had no Gretzky-like star to protect, and to fight for the Schultzian sake of mayhem and purposeless intimidation was of little interest to him. Toward the end of the '87-'88 season, he walked out on the Leafs and retired. He had done his work and deserved a rest. Time has only improved the reputation of those high-flying Oilers, and though Semenko might appear in the record books to be nothing more than a goon, his contribution to the game was something worthier than perhaps any other fighters. When the Oilers retired Gretzky's 99 sweater, the great Hall of Famer wanted Semenko on the ice with him, a fitting tribute and reminder of their partnership.

Semenko went on to scout for the Oilers, further affirmation within the Edmonton family of his value to those great teams of the 1980s.

When the Oilers retired Gretzky's 99 sweater, the great Hall of Famer wanted Semenko on the ice with him.
DAVE SEMENKO

SEMENOV, Anatoli ("Tony")
b. Moscow, Soviet Union (Russia), March 5, 1962
It was only after the Soviets had used him up that he moved to the NHL, at age 28 an 11-year veteran of the Dynamo team back home. Semenov was an important forward with the Soviet national teams over the years leading up to 1990, playing in two World Juniors, two Canada Cups, an Olympics, and a World Championship. He joined Edmonton for two games in the 1990 playoffs and promptly got his name on the Cup, though the next seven seasons weren't as successful. He played for 6 teams in a short period of time and scored 20 goals only once, with the Oilers. After retiring, he settled in Anaheim, where he had played for three years, and operated a hockey school.

SENICK, George ("Rocket")
b. Saskatoon, Saskatchewan, September 16, 1929
d. Saskatoon, Saskatchewan, January 13, 2003
Unfortunately, Senick didn't get his nickname because of his speed or scoring ability, though he had a bit of both. No, he got it simply because he looked like Maurice Richard. Senick was a pro through the 1950s, playing with the Rangers for a few games in '52-'53 when he was at the height of his powers. He was a strong skater and had a temper, and played much of his career in Saskatoon. Later, in senior hockey, he was suspended from the league for a good part of a season for two serious infractions. In one, he threw his stick into the crowd, a no-no anywhere, any time. As soon as he came back from that suspension he threw a tantrum, assaulted an official and a fan, started a melee, and went berserk. For that, he was gone for the year. That was

senior hockey, after all. He returned the year after, though, and continued playing well into the 1960s.

SEPPA, Jyrki
b. Tampere, Finland, November 14, 1961
He hoped for a career in the NHL, and after Winnipeg drafted him in 1981 his career was pointed in the right direction. Seppa came to North America in 1982 and played in the AHL for a year, but in his few games with the Jets the year after he didn't make a sufficient impression to warrant a long stay or another callup. At season's end, he returned to Finland to continue playing for a short time.

SERAFINI, Ron
b. Highland Park, Michigan, October 31, 1953
The plan was to move to Ontario to play junior and go on to a career in the NHL. It worked, but only in the most superficial sense in that Serafini played two games with California. In his short pro career, he was well travelled, playing for eight pro teams in just four seasons during the 1970s.

SEROWIK, Jeff
b. Manchester, New Hampshire, January 10, 1967
An itinerant defenceman, Serowik graduated from Providence College in 1990 to make a go of it with the Leafs. Three years later, he had played but one NHL game, and the pattern repeated itself in Boston. Serowik played in the "I" for four years and then got a real chance in the league when Pittsburgh signed him. The Penguins planned on using him for the year, but that changed the night of December 30, 1998, when Florida's giant animal of a forward, Peter Worrell, hit Serowik from behind, smashing his head into the boards. Serowik suffered a serious strain of post-concussion syndrome for more than two years and was forced to retire. The only good news was that he already knew what he would do after his playing days ended. Years earlier, he had established a summer hockey camp called Pro Ambitions in Massachusetts, and he made this his full-time job.

SERVINIS, George
b. Toronto, Ontario, April 29, 1962
Although he was never drafted during his college career at RPI, Servinis closed out his hockey days there by scoring the winning goal at the 1985 NCAA championships. That was all the impetus Minnesota needed to sign him, but he played only five games with the team a couple of years later. He retired soon after.

SEVCIK, Jaroslav
b. Brno, Czechoslovakia (Czech Republic), May 15, 1965
Sevcik played hockey all over the world, throughout Europe and in the minors in North America. He played 13 games with Quebec in 1989-90 in the middle of his playing days, and after retiring he became an instructor at the Top Gun hockey program in Dartmouth, Nova Scotia.

SEVERYN, Brent
b. Vegreville, Alberta, February 22, 1966
A left winger of size, Severyn played for five teams in his six years in the NHL. He was a fighter who wasn't

going to get too much time on the power play. He had played at the University of Alberta and spent a good portion of time in the minors as well. His last NHL team was Dallas, and he settled there after retiring. He became vice-president of Hockey Tuff, an instructional company. He also worked for the Stars' radio coverage.

SEVIGNY, Pierre
b. Trois Rivières, Quebec, September 8, 1971
Even though he has played in a number of leagues at a number of levels, Sevigny has managed to play most of his hockey in Quebec. He played junior in St. Hyacinthe and most of his brief NHL days with the Canadiens in the early 1990s, but he went long stretches without producing and has spent most of his career in the minors. The Rangers played him three times, but Sevigny has more recently become a fixture with the Quebec Citadelles.

SEVIGNY, Richard
b. Montreal, Quebec, April 11, 1957
Like many a goalie, Sevigny put the pads on at age eight because he wasn't a very good skater. At first, he wasn't a very good goaler, either, but he was determined to improve and made a career out of stopping a puck from passing a red goal line. Like all post-Ken Dryden goalies, he was given a chance to be a hometown saviour, and like all but Patrick Roy he didn't make it. He was with the Montreal Canadiens for five years and then was given a similar chance with the Nordiques for two years, but his first full season was by far his best. In '80-'81, he split the goaltending with Michel Larocque and Denis Herron. Sevigny played 33 games, had a spectacular record of 20-4-3, and led the league with a 2.40 GAA. He never came close to replicating that season. After retiring in 1987, he became a coach in France, a position he held for four years until the team folded. He returned to Montreal and became a special education teacher at Montreal College, but the stress of dealing with the kids' lives was too much and he quit. He later became coach and GM for the Montreal Roadrunners of the Roller Hockey league, but when that team folded he found himself unemployed again.

SHACK, Eddie ("The Entertainer"/ "Nuts and Bolts"/ "The Horn")
b. Sudbury, Ontario, February 11, 1937
Hockey cannot have enough players like Eddie Shack, but if there were even one more like him that would be too many. He was, without a shadow of a doubt, one of the most energetic, entertaining, combustible, wacky skaters ever to grace an NHL sheet of ice, but what few might remember was that he was also a hell of a hockey player. In addition to winning 4 Stanley Cups with the Leafs in the 1960s, Shack can proudly boast of being part of a small club of players who have scored 20 goals in a year with 5 different teams. Ordinary Joes don't do that. Couple his skill with his life, and Shack is truly a unique member of the NHL alumni. He could neither read nor write, and he couldn't find a school that would keep him very long, but he was one of the most acute businessmen around, even in his early teens. He worked as a butcher and truck driver, and it was the solidity of

Jyrki Seppa

Ron Serafini

Jeff Serowik

Pierre Sevigny

Richard Sevigny

Joe Shack

Konstantin Shafranov

Paul Shakes

Yevgeny Shaldybin

those two jobs that gave him confidence to try out for the Guelph Biltmores in 1952. He made the team and became instantly recognizable for his skating, legs and arms akimbo, hellbent on moving in a direct line from A to B and pity anyone who got in the way. He played with the Rangers in 1958 but his three seasons there were not productive and he was traded to Toronto. It was there he had his best years and there he played disciplined hockey with a maniacal edge every now and then. He could skate fast and punch hard, and teammates and fans loved him. In later years he moved around a bit, but he carried his personality everywhere. Once, with Boston, he got into a vicious stick swinging duel with Larry Zeidel. Another time, in Toronto, he had the entire St. Louis team trying to chase him down on the ice. When he was named one of the stars following a Leafs game, his exuberant dash to centre and spin was worth the price of admission. In all, he played more than 1,000 games and endured 17 seasons, no mean feat. Away from the rink, he was one of the most success-ful and recognizable faces in the game. He earned fortunes from television commercials for garbage bags, tires, soft drinks, golf courses, and sundry other products. The song "Clear the Track, Here Comes Shack" defined his status in Toronto, and produced ancillary items that also paid him well. Shack was famous for years for selling Christmas trees in Toronto, the proceeds going to charity, and to this day he is as popular as ever. The ovation he received the night Maple Leaf Gardens hosted its final NHL game was among the loudest, and occa-sionally he gets in the news for being charged with, for instance, drinking and driving. As old age creeps up on him, he also made public his prostate problems in the hopes of helping others reach early diagnosis. Shack has lived a long life, a full life of fun and success and happiness. He has made more money than he would have as a butcher or truck driver, but more important, he has made more friends than 100 prime ministers.

SHACK, Joe ("Smokin' Joe Shack")
b. Winnipeg, Manitoba, December 8, 1915
d. London, England, May 5, 1987
He may have played a season and a half with the Rangers during the war, but Shack was a much greater hero to the small but strong supporters in England during what was called the Golden Era of British hockey. He first went to England in 1936, playing for Harringay for three years. He led the league in scoring in '38-'39 and then returned to Canada when war broke out. During this period he played in the NHL, but in 1948, when all was clear, he returned to England and played for Harringay for another six years. After retiring, he was appointed coach of

Sweden's national team for the '55-'56 season. He then went to work for a television station in London and spent his last years in Hornsey, North London.

SHAFRANOV, Konstantin
b. Kamennogorsk, Soviet Union (Russia), September 11, 1968
Even though he played most of his early pro years in Russia, Shafranov was instrumental in getting his homeland of Kazakhstan on the hockey map. He played with the team at the World Championships in "C" pool and later played at the 1998 Olympics in Nagano when they finished a surprising and healthy fifth. His NHL time has been less successful, being limited to five games with St. Louis in '96-'97.

SHAKES, Paul
b. Collingwood, Ontario, September 4, 1952
His success was modest, but he was only starting out when he had to stop. Shakes played for Salt Lake City in 1972-73 and joined the parent team, in California, the next year, for 21 games. He was a small defenceman but capable offen-sively, but after two more years in the minors he suffered a her-niated disc. Shakes required surgery and retired, fearing fur-ther damage to his back.

SHALDYBIN, Yevgeny
b. Novosibirsk, Soviet Union (Russia), July 29, 1975
Life is better in North America for most former Soviets, so when Shaldybin had a chance to play hockey in the Boston Bruins organization, he was only too happy to make the most of his chance. He played three games for the Bruins in '96-'97 and has been in the minors ever since, and there is little to suggest that great play in the United Hockey League will earn him a callup any time soon.

SHANAHAN, Brendan ("Shanny")
b. Mimico, Ontario, January 23, 1969
For the last 15 years, Shanahan has been one of the league's most dominant power forwards. His accom-plishments will one day put him in the Hall of Fame, and even though he likely won't win any individual awards in the NHL, he is one of its prime assets. Shanahan has scored more than 500 goals and 1,000 points. He has played in more than 1,100 games. He has won three Stanley Cups with Detroit (1997, 1998, 2002), an Olympic gold (with Canada at Salt Lake City in 2002), a World Championship gold (1994), and a Canada Cup championship (1991). He has averaged nearly 40 goals a season and has never had fewer than 100 penalty minutes in any year. Drafted 2nd overall by New Jersey in 1987, he had a rough rookie season because he played the whole year on a badly sprained

> **He earned fortunes from television commercials for garbage bags, tires, soft drinks, golf courses, and sundry other products.**
> **EDDIE SHACK**

ankle. He was signed by St. Louis in a move that saw the Blues give up Scott Stevens as fair compensation to the Devils. With the Blues, Shanahan scored 50 goals twice and became one of the most popular athletes in the city. His trade four years later caused a furor in town, but the Whalers acquired a franchise player. Early in the 1996-97 season, though, Detroit coach Scotty Bowman craved Shanahan and gave up Paul Coffey and Keith Primeau to get him. It was a move that put the Wings over the top, and the team won its first of three Cups in the next six seasons. Shanahan is most effective on the power play and on his "wrong" wing, using his quick release and superb shot to greatest effect. He combines strength and skill, finesse and intimidation, to get into position and create scoring chances. He is, in short, a truly dominating player when he's at the top of his game.

SHANAHAN, Sean
b. Toronto, Ontario, February 8, 1951

Montreal, Colorado, and Boston all gave Shanahan a chance in the NHL, but none kept the forward very long. He came out of Providence College in 1973 to turn pro before graduating, and he ended up where he began, in the minors, at the end of his career. He retired in 1978 after a short stay in the WHA.

SHAND, Dave
b. Cold Lake, Alberta, August 11, 1956

More a tough presence on the blueline than a fancy dancer with the puck, Shand impressed Atlanta during his junior years at Peterborough. At the 1976 draft, the Flames chose him 8th overall, but during his four seasons in Georgia the team never got by the preliminary round of the playoffs. Shand was traded to Toronto and Washington, where much the same situation prevailed, and he wound up spending as much time in the minors as with the NHL team. He ended his career by playing four years in Austria and then went back to the University of Michigan. He had studied there for two years before going to the Petes in the OHL, and now he returned to act as an assistant coach to Red Berenson and finish his law degree. That done, he left U of M altogether but remained in Michigan and opened his own practice.

SHANK, Daniel
b. Montreal, Quebec, May 12, 1967

For one season, he led the high life. He was playing NHL hockey in Detroit, in 1989-90, and he had more money than he knew what to do with. But when coach Jacques Demers was replaced by Bryan Murray, the good times ended and Shank was in the minors, traded to Hartford, and then in the minors for good. His signature celebration of kissing the blade of his stick after a goal no longer had quite the magic feeling

With the Blues, Shanahan scored 50 goals twice and became one of the most popular athletes in the city.
BRENDAN SHANAHAN

to it, and he played in the "I" for the next six years. Since then, he's been to Germany and back, and although Shank keeps on playing his days of NHL glory have long given way to the West Coast league.

SHANNON, Chuck ("Specs")
b. Campbellford, Ontario, March 22, 1916
d. unknown

The call to play in the NHL was what Shannon had been waiting for for more than four years. But, the timing couldn't have been worse. He had played most of his career for Syracuse in Toronto's system in the 1930s until the Americans acquired him in 1939. They sent him to Springfield but recalled him when they needed a defenceman. The difficulty was that he was suffering from a bad groin injury and could barely walk, let alone skate and compete at the highest level. After four games of suffering, he was returned to the minors and, as he had feared, never made it back. The brother of Gerry, Chuck was only the second NHLer to wear glasses while playing (after Russ Blinco). They were shatterproof and tied to his ears with tape!

SHANNON, Darrin
b. Barrie, Ontario, December 8, 1969

The Shannon brothers were close in age and similar in look, but Darrin was the winger and Darryl the defenceman. Darrin came out of junior smelling like a rose. He captained his Windsor team in the OHL and played for Canada at the 1989 World Juniors. Pittsburgh drafted him 4th overall and then traded him to Buffalo with Doug Bodger for Tom Barrasso and a draft choice, to give a sense of what his pre-NHL value was. As such, his career fell short of its projections. Scouts said he could do it all, but at the NHL level he didn't demonstrate as much. When he was traded to Winnipeg in a multiplayer deal, there wasn't a big name in the deal, though he played seven years with the Jets/Coyotes and not a day in the minors. He suffered a bad knee injury, though, during the '97-'98 season and kept on playing, and off-season surgery kept him away from the game almost the entire year. Although he played a few games in the minors and was given a shot by Toronto to make the team, that knee injury really was the end of the line for Shannon.

SHANNON, Darryl
b. Barrie, Ontario, June 21, 1968

Darryl and Darrin played parts of three years in Windsor together, Darryl being named the OHL's top defenceman for 1987-88, and parts of three more seasons in Winnipeg. Darryl was drafted by Toronto but never really caught on with the Leafs, in large part because of a serious car accident he was involved in in the summer

Sean Shanahan

Dave Shand

Daniel Shank

Darrin Shannon

Darryl Shannon

Gerry Shannon

Jeff Shantz

Vadim
Sharifijanov

Jeff Sharples

Glen Sharpley

of 1990. He and his girlfriend were hit head-on on the highway near Toronto, and Shannon suffered a broken leg and arm and a deep chest bruise. It was Christmas before he was playing again, and he never played a full season with the team before he was let go. Shannon signed with the Jets and played with his brother but later was traded to Buffalo, where he played three and a half full seasons as a top-six defenceman for the Sabres. Since then, he has become more expendable in the eyes of team GMs, and played with three teams before being released outright by Colorado when he attended Avs training camp in September 2001. Shannon then signed to play in the DEL and has been in Germany since.

SHANNON, Gerry
b. Campbellford, Ontario, October 25, 1910
d. Ottawa, Ontario, May 1, 1983
He broke into the NHL in 1933 with Ottawa and played five years as a left winger in the world's best league, but it was who he was later in life that was more important. Shannon retired near the start of the war and settled in Britannia, a suburb of Ottawa. He organized the first house-league teams in the area, coaching teams on the outdoor rinks. There was no pecking order, and tryouts were based on who showed up, not on who hoped to be the next pro player. Shannon lived in Ottawa the rest of his life, trying to inspire those around him to play for fun, and within his own family he had success. Gerry Jr. played hockey, and his sons, in turn, donned the blades – just for the fun of it.

SHANTZ, Jeff
b. Duchess, Alberta, October 10, 1973
The son of the town's mayor, Shantz has played much of his hockey for a Sutter. In Indianapolis, he played for Duane. In Chicago, it was Darryl. In Calgary, it was Brian. In each case, the Sutters liked him because he was a foot soldier, a competitor who didn't have all the talent in the world but who did have heart. He turned pro with the Hawks in 1993, and a trade in 1998 marked the only movement he has experienced in the league. More serious, though, was the knee injury he suffered in March 2001, so bad that doctors had to wait months before they could perform two operations on it. He missed almost a year, but rejoined the Flames in the hopes of being part of the team when it finally returned to the playoffs.

SHARIFIJANOV, Vadim
b. Ufa, Soviet Union (Russia), December 23, 1975
When New Jersey drafted him in 1994, Sharifijanov was still a teenager of unknown quality. He came to North America after another year playing in Russia, but in four seasons he played more in Albany than with the Devils. He was traded to Vancouver but didn't fare any better, and in the summer of 2000 he decided to return home to play in the Russian league.

SHARPLES, Jeff
b. Terrace, British Columbia, July 28, 1967
When Sharples joined the Red Wings in 1987, the intention was to ease him into the lineup. He played much of the regular season but watched most of the playoffs from the press box. Ditto for the year after, but in 1989 he was traded to Edmonton in the monster deal

that included Joe Murphy, Petr Klima, and Adam Graves for Jimmy Carson, Kevin McClelland, and a draft choice. Sharples never played a game with the Oilers but did spend the next 11 years in the minors. He spent most of his time in Utah, but retired after suffering a concussion in early 2000. Sharples later owned and operated a Little Caesar's franchise.

SHARPLES, Warren Scott
b. Montreal, Quebec, March 1, 1968
Sharples was the all-time leader in games played (137) when the goaltender graduated from the University of Michigan in 1990, though Steve Shields broke the record later. Sharples was drafted by Calgary and played for Salt Lake City in the minors, and one day Warren decided he wanted to go by his middle name of Scott. Scott Sharples played a single game for the Flames on April 2, 1992, a 4-4 overtime tie against Vancouver. When he was sent back down to Salt Lake City the next year, fans thought Warren had a goalie-brother named Scott. It was quite confusing, but Warren and Scott played only one more year before retiring.

SHARPLEY, Glen
b. York, Ontario, September 6, 1956
On December 19, 1981, Sharpley's career and eyesight changed forever. While playing for Chicago, he skated into the Washington end on the forecheck when an errant stick caught him in the eye. He suffered retinal damage that eventually finished his active duty, though not without a fight. He spent months recovering and finally doctors found a fluid that helped his vision in the weak eye. He returned to the Hawks for the 1982 playoffs and, ironically, played some of the best hockey of his career. Once the drug wore off, though, his vision was weak again and the Hawks let him go. Sharpley retired, and found work with Northwest Orient Airlines, and received a disability claim from Lloyd's of London. His career seemed over, but he later returned to play with the Hawks' farm team in Baltimore and later in the minors. He had always been a great skater and a fine scorer, but those abilities were hampered by the injury and he retired without getting another chance in the NHL. He later moved to Haliburton and ran a sporting goods store across the street from Walt McKechnie's restaurant.

SHAUNESSY, Scott ("The Truck")
b. Newport, Rhode Island, January 22, 1964
He was a boxer whose tale of the tape revealed a 6'4" frame covered by 220 pounds of muscle. He was an amateur boxer, and the package as a whole earned him his moniker. Coming out of Boston University in 1987, he drew interest from the Nordiques for his physical qualities but didn't stay long before beginning a lengthy career in the minors where he piled up the penalty minutes. His father, Robert, was an offensive tackle with the Pack in Green Bay and the Patriots in New England. After retiring, Shaunessy became involved with the WPHL's Austin Ice Bats, moving up to executive director after a number of years with the team.

SHAW, Brad
b. Cambridge, Ontario, April 28, 1964
In junior, Shaw won the Memorial Cup with Ottawa in

1984 after a bronze with Canada the previous year, but it took him a while to latch on in the NHL with the same success. In fact, it wasn't until 1989 that he played a full season in the league, with Hartford, the team that had used him sparingly in the previous years. In five full seasons with the Whalers and then the Senators, Shaw provided stable defensive play, captaining the Senators in their inaugural season. He then became a playing assistant coach for the Vipers in the IHL, and after a few games back in the NHL he retired to go into coaching full-time. He has been an assistant with Tampa Bay, and in the summer of 2002 he was named head coach of the Cincinnati Mighty Ducks, Anaheim's AHL affiliate.

SHAW, David
b. St. Thomas, Ontario,
May 25, 1964
In the modem world of the NHL and pro hockey, there are so many Shaws who play for 15 or 20 years and seem to pass through without a ripple. Amazingly, Shaw began with Quebec in 1982 and didn't retire until 2001, about 1,000 pro games later. He played for six NHL teams as a defensive defenceman, his career punctuated by the occasional injury but besides that going game by game. When he went down to the IHL in 1998, he retired for a short time but returned to play a few years yet. He finished with Chicago in the IHL in 2000-01.

David Shaw

In the summer of 2002 he was named head coach of the Cincinnati Mighty Ducks, Anaheim's AHL affiliate.
BRAD SHAW

SHAY, Norm
b. Huntsville, Ontario,
February 3, 1899
d. Hamden, Connecticut,
November 28, 1968
Most hockey players either return to their hometown after their retirement or settle in the city they played in last or longest. In Shay's case, the latter decision prevailed. He grew up in southern Ontario and played with Boston and the Toronto St. Pats in the mid-1920s, after which he was manager for the Philadelphia Arrows of the Can-Am league. Shay finished hockey in New Haven and stayed in that city to open the New Haven Sporting Goods Company, which he managed for 40 years until his retirement in 1959.

SHEA, Pat
b. Potlach, Idaho, October 29, 1912
d. unknown
Shea's few and only NHL games came with Chicago while he was a teen. From 1932 on, he was a minor-leaguer who played principally for Minneapolis and Kansas City.

SHEARER, Rob
b. Kitchener, Ontario, October 19, 1976
The kiss of death for a player's career is a trip to Europe. It's a sign he doesn't feel he'll make it in the NHL or receive due chance in the big time. Shearer played junior in Windsor, but appeared only twice for the Avalanche since turning pro. He spent the rest of his time in Hershey, and in 2001 decided to play in Finland, where his chances of being recalled were exactly nil.

SHEDDEN, Doug
b. Wallaceburg, Ontario, April 29, 1961
Not surprisingly, Shedden's goal scoring increased significantly when he played on a line with a rookie in Pittsburgh named Lemieux. He had two 20-goal seasons prior to Mario's arrival, but playing alongside 66 gave Shedden 35- and 32-goal seasons. He later bounced around for a number of years, playing as much in the minors as the NHL, trying to get back on track. This became impossible after 1991, when he suffered a serious knee injury that left him Europe-capable but not NHL-viable. Since retiring, Shedden has become a coach in the minor leagues with great success. He has won four championships, including three President's Cups as CHL champions, most recently with the Memphis RiverKings.

Doug Shedden

SHEEHAN, Bobby
b. Weymouth, Massachusetts,
January 11, 1949
Without a shadow of a doubt, there was a ton more skill inside Sheehan than the 48 goals in 310 NHL games he gave teams and fans. Known for his speed and skill in a small package, he was, however, also known for his wit and late-night repartee, his breaking of curfews, and his almost complete inability to take the game seriously when occasion called for it. He played for seven NHL teams, each one hoping it would hold the key to unlocking his discipline. He roamed the minors, was even knocked off the U.S. National Team for late hours, but nowhere could he hunker down to a solid attitude of professional hockey. By the time he retired in 1983, no one was shaking his hand for a job well done – everyone who knew him was shaking his head at what could have, and should have, been a great career.

Bobby Sheehan

SHEEHY, Neil
b. Fort Frances, Ontario, February 9, 1960
From the day he was born, Sheehy held dual citizenship as a result of his birthplace and his home on the other side of the Rainy River, in International Falls, Minnesota. He graduated from Harvard University in 1983 with a degree in economics and a successful college hockey resumé as well, and played much of his career with Calgary. These were his best years, and he helped fuel the great Battle of Alberta. Sheehy was a fighter but also a tenacious checker, and it was his responsibility to shadow Wayne Gretzky whenever the two teams met, which was often. He played for the

Neil Sheehy

Doug Shelton

U.S. at the World Championships, and in 1992 went to Slovenia where he was a player and coach. When he returned home, he attended the William Mitchell College of Law, graduating in 1996. Since then, he has been a player agent for aspiring hockey professionals with his brother, Tim, also a former NHLer.

SHEEHY, Tim
b. Fort Frances, Ontario, September 3, 1948
Like brother Neil, Tim was born in Ontario but grew up in Minnesota. He was wooed by OHL teams but opted to play college hockey at Boston College starting in 1966. Until the 1972 Olympics and the formation of the WHA, Sheehy played extensively for the U.S. National Team, winning silver at the 1992 Olympics in Sapporo and then signing with New England for the fall '72. He later joined the Oilers and played just 27 NHL games, with Detroit and Hartford, spending much of the rest of the time in the minors. He later went into business with his brother as a Minnesota-based player agent. He was inducted into the U.S. Hockey Hall of Fame in 1997.

Gregg Sheppard

SHELLEY, Jody
b. Yarmouth, Nova Scotia, February 7, 1976
One of the first Mooseheads to go on to the NHL, Shelley had to wait a few years in the minors to get his chance. Strictly a fighter, he was called up by Columbus in February 2001, and he knew why – to fight. He had been on the ice for 15 seconds when he found his man, Krzysztof Oliwa, and Shelley earned 10 minutes in penalties during that first shift! He made the team as a regular fighter the next year and has proven his willingness to do whatever is necessary to stay in the NHL, albeit with the Blue Jackets.

Johnny Sheppard

SHELTON, Doug
b. Woodstock, Ontario, June 27, 1945
When he made the Hawks coming out of training camp in 1967, Shelton looked to have a future with the team and in the NHL. He had a terrific shot, great attitude, and enough skill to carry him by as a fourth-liner. That was the inside scoop on him, but after five games he was sent to the minors and never came back, not with Chicago, not with another team.

SHEPPARD, Frank
b. Montreal, Quebec, October 19, 1907
d. unknown
He played eight games with Detroit in '27-'28 when the team was called the Cougars, but Sheppard never played in the NHL after this callup. He played in the American league for a few years before ending his career out west.

Ray Sheppard

Like brother Neil, Tim was born in Ontario but grew up in Minnesota.
TIM SHEEHY

SHEPPARD, Gregg
b. North Battleford, Saskatchewan, April 23, 1949
One of the most underrated Bruins in an era dominated by Boston superstars, Sheppard was a terrific player with determination and ambition. He was near the top in Calder Trophy voting for '72-'73 and went on to have three 30-goal seasons with the team. A superb penalty killer to boot, he filled his role on the team as well as any other player. Sheppard was upset when he was traded to Pittsburgh in 1978 and refused to report because of what he felt was an insubstantial contract offer. He eventually relented but the scoring he had shown in Beantown was completely lost. Near the end of the '81-'82 season he was released by the Pens and decided to retire to the farm rather than look for work with another team.

SHEPPARD, Johnny ("Jake")
b. Montreal, Quebec, July 27, 1902
d. August 28, 1969
When Johnny was a small boy, both his parents perished in a house fire and he and his brother were sent to Selkirk to be raised by their uncle. Thus, he played junior in Selkirk and turned pro in Edmonton before being sold to Detroit in the NHL in 1926. The deal started an eight-year NHL career for Sheppard, who won a Stanley Cup in his final season, with Chicago in '33-'34.

SHEPPARD, Ray
b. Pembroke, Ontario, May 27, 1966
He wasn't pleased with Buffalo's contract offer after being drafted in 1984, so Sheppard returned to junior to see if he could work his way into a better deal. After leading the OHL in goals (81) and points (142), he most certainly could. He played a year in the minors, and in his first season with Buffalo, '87-'88, he produced 38 goals. In the coming years, he was traded almost as much as he scored. Overall, he scored 24 goals or more with 6 NHL teams, highlighted by a 52-goal season with Detroit in '93-'94. Yet for all his shooting ability, he went to the Cup finals only once, with Florida during the improbable run of 1996. He retired in 2001 after playing a season in Switzerland, and Sheppard's NHL totals include some 357 goals.

SHERF, John
b. Calumet, Michigan, April 8, 1913
d. August 19, 1991
After Vic Heyliger and Jack Tompkins, Sherf was only the third player to leave the University of Michigan to go on to the NHL, which he did in 1935. Over the course of many years, he played in only 19 games for Detroit – a game here, another there – but in '36-'37 it was enough to claim to be a part of the Cup-winning Wings. He played mostly in the minors, though in

1981 he was inducted into the Michigan Athletic Hall of Honour for his college achievements.

SHERO, Fred ("The Fog")
b. Winnipeg, Manitoba, October 23, 1925
d. Camden, New Jersey, November 24, 1990

Who could have known in the post-war years that such a banal and pedestrian defenceman named Shero would later become the most evil and nefarious coach ever to appear in the NHL? Back then, he wore glasses and struggled to make it in the big league. Shero had been a stoker in the Royal Canadian Volunteer Reserve before getting a chance with the Rangers, and after two and a half seasons he was a minor-leaguer for another eight years. He turned to coaching in 1958 with Moose Jaw and was in the Rangers system for a dozen years. He was hired in 1971 by Philadelphia, where he quickly damaged the reputation of the game to the point that most Americans considered it on par with Roller Derby for its apparent violence. Shero preached brawling as a means to intimidate. He looked for fighters instead of players as a way to win hockey games. His first credo was that referees couldn't call everything, so the more rule violations, the better. He coached the Broad Street Bullies to two gruesome and ferocious Stanley Cups, in 1974 and '75, victories that nearly sounded the death knell for speed and skill and hockey values far above blood and bench-clearing brawls. He infuriated captain Bobby Clarke and many other players in 1978 when he betrayed the team by signing with the Rangers, but after one season of going to the finals he had another mediocre year and a half and then resigned. Shero coached in Holland for a year and then returned to the Flyers as a special consultant. He also worked as a radio analyst for the Devils. In hockey circles, Shero was considered an oddball. He gave up a career in boxing to try his hand at hockey; he played the violin and studied law through correspondence courses; he attended seminars on coaching in Europe and studied the habits of the great coaches as a way to learning more about the game. Yet when all is said and done, all Shero really did was propagate violence as a way to nullify the speed and skill of a game physical enough in its beauty without his senseless brawling. Inside Philadelphia, he is a legend. Outside it, he is a pariah.

SHERRITT, Gordon ("Moose")
b. Oakville, Manitoba, April 8, 1922

It is not every hockey player who can claim to have skated before the king and queen and Winston Churchill, but Sherritt can make that boast because he won the championship with Harringay in '39-'40. Those worthy dignitaries were in attendance for the final game,

Fred Shero

and because of the war Sherritt returned home to continue his career before non-royal fans in Canada. He played eight games for Detroit during the war years and played for a number of years in the minors, where he used his imposing size (6'1" and 200 pounds) to live up to his nickname and intimidate opponents.

SHERVEN, Gord
b. Gravelbourg, Saskatchewan, August 21, 1963

Everything started off according to plan. Sherven played college hockey at the University of North Dakota, but his second season was one of transition. A top prospect, he played for Canada at the World Juniors, and at the end of the season also played at the World Championships. He then left UND to join the Canadian National Team so he could play for the year through the 1984 Olympics in Sarajevo. A month before the Games were to begin, though, he hurt his knee and ended up watching the Olympics on television. Sherven recovered and turned pro with Edmonton, but in 1986 he restarted the dream and joined the National Team again. This time, all went well, and in 1988 he played for Canada at the Olympics in Calgary. Ironically, it ended his NHL career, for he never made it back. Instead, he went to Europe and played anther 12 years, almost exclusively in Germany.

SHEVALIER, Jeff
b. Mississauga, Ontario, March 14, 1974

Despite putting up big numbers in junior, and despite scoring a goal in his first NHL game, with Los Angeles, Shevalier has been a long-time minor-leaguer whose last NHL stint was in 1999-2000 with Tampa Bay. The left winger has spent the last two years with Idaho, and his chances of getting back to the big league get slimmer with each passing day.

SHEWCHUCK, John "Jack"
b. Brantford, Ontario, June 19, 1917
d. May 15, 1989

In the years leading up to the war, Shewchuck played for the Copper Cliff Redmen, a team scouted closely by Boston and with good results for the Bruins. They signed Shewchuck, his defence partner, Johnny Crawford, and two forwards, Red Hamill and Mel Hill. Yet Shewchuck's luck couldn't have been any worse. In '38-'39 and '40-'41, when the team won the Cup, he played just a few regular-season games and none in the playoffs. In the year in between, he was a regular. Shewchuck interrupted his on-and-off career to join the army, where he attained the rank of corporal with the Canadian Infantry Corps, and when he returned he played a full season with the Bruins before being farmed out for good.

A top prospect, he played for Canada at the World Juniors.
GORD SHERVEN

Jack Shewchuck

Alex Shibicky

SHIBICKY, Alex

b. Winnipeg, Manitoba, May 19, 1914

He played all his years in the NHL with the Rangers, and was a key player on the 1940 team that won the Stanley Cup. He skated on the left wing with the Colville brothers – Mac and Neil – and although all three shot right, they worked well in combination and were among the league's top scorers. Shibicky joined the Blueshirts in 1935, and in 1942 he left the team with 13 others from that year's roster, to join the army. After he was discharged, he played one more season, but as his career wound down he played in the minors. Shibicky later coached at New Westminster and Flin Flon, and after leaving the game he pursued a number of business opportunities. He farmed near Winnipeg, operated a drive-in theatre near Red Deer, and owned a restaurant in Vancouver.

SHIELDS, Allan ("The Big A"/"Pete")

b. Ottawa, Ontario, May 10, 1906
d. Ottawa, Ontario, September 24, 1975

On the ice, he was a heavy-hitting defenceman, but off it he was an easygoing and social man. Shields was big enough to handle himself, and lore had it he once waxed none other than Eddie Shore. Shields began with the old Ottawa Senators right after the local Montagnards lost in the Allan Cup. That was his first of 11 NHL seasons with 5 teams and many moves along the way. He won the Cup with the Maroons in 1935 and didn't come close any other year. After finishing his career in the minors, as a playing coach in Washington, Shields joined the army and was stationed in Amprior where he again played and coached the hockey team. He was stationed in PEI until 1946 and upon discharge became a referee in the AHL for three years.

Allan Shields

SHIELDS, Steve

b. Toronto, Ontario, July 19, 1972

It looked good for a year, and then it looked bad. Shields was acquired by San Jose in 1998 after playing parts of three seasons in Buffalo where his chances of becoming number one over Dominik Hasek were exactly zero. Shields started out with the Sharks as Mike Vernon's backup, and then in 1999-2000 became the team's starter. However, just as he was getting comfortable, Evgeny Nabokov was developing into a great goalie, and he and Jeff Friesen were traded to Anaheim for Teemu Selanne. Shields is backup again with the Ducks, though he is a solid and reliable number two goalie despite his unorthodox style. At the University of Michigan, he had a record of 121-25-8 and in '95-'96 he led Rochester to the Calder Cup with great performance in the AHL playoffs.

Steve Shields

SHILL, Bill

b. Toronto, Ontario, March 6, 1923

The brother of Jack, Bill didn't have quite the distinguished career, though he did play in one memorable World Championships. That came at the end of his career when he played with the East York Lyndhursts, the team that represented Canada in 1954. It was a historic WC because the Soviet Union competed for the first time, and it was made more historic because Canada lost the gold medal to its

Bill Shill

Communist adversary. Previously, Shill had played parts of three seasons with Boston during and right after the war. His best season was '45-'46, when he played on a line with Don Gallinger and Bep Guidolin. Dubbed the Sprout Line because its members were all young, it was an exciting scoring line, and Shill contributed with 15 goals.

SHILL, John "Jack" ("Porky")

b. Toronto, Ontario, January 12, 1913
d. Toronto, Ontario, October 25, 1976

Before Bill Mosienko, there was Jack Shill. While playing for the Marlies in 1932, Shill scored 3 goals in 26 seconds, a record until Mosienko turned the hat trick in 21 seconds with Chicago on March 23, 1952. Shill went on to play for his local Maple Leafs, though he was Toronto's great nemesis toward the end of his career. In 1938, as a member of Chicago, he scored the Cup-winning goal when the upstart Hawks defeated the Leafs in one of the great finals upsets. After a short time in the minors to close out his playing days, Shill returned home to Toronto and became a long-time employee of the City of Toronto.

SHINSKE, Rick

b. Weyburn, Saskatchewan, May 31, 1955

A solid skater and a centre prospect when California drafted him in 1975, Shinske squeezed in a few games with Cleveland, where the lowly Seals moved, and later St. Louis. In the minors, he was a reliable player, but at the NHL level his size and lack of production did him in.

SHIRES, Jim

b. Edmonton, Alberta, November 15, 1945

Another graduate of the University of Denver from the 1960s under the coaching leadership of Murray Armstrong, Shires moved on to the Detroit organization for his start as a pro. The left winger, though, played just a few games with the Wings, St. Louis, and Pittsburgh during a brief career that ended in 1975.

SHMYR, Paul

b. Cudworth, Saskatchewan, January 18, 1946

After a so-so start to his NHL career in the years between expansion and the WHA, Shmyr opted to join the new league in 1972 to see how he would fare. He did just fine, and in '75-'76 was awarded the Dennis A. Murphy Trophy as the league's best defenceman. On the strength of that season, he was one of only two WHA players invited to Canada's training camp for the 1976 Canada Cup. The other was Bobby Hull. Although Shmyr was cut, he continued on in the WHA until 1979, when the leagues merged. He signed with Minnesota and became the team's captain, leading the North Stars to the Cup finals in 1981. Unfortunately, the joyous run to the playoffs was dampened first by a knee injury and then by the fact that he was a healthy scratch. The Stars lost the Cup to Pittsburgh, and Shmyr retired a year later. He moved to Vancouver and became involved in his family's construction business.

SHOEBOTTOM, Bruce

b. Windsor, Ontario, August 20, 1965

Goons are a fairly predictable lot. They fight. They like

to fight, they're told to fight, they look for fights. Fighting is how they make their reputation and living. But wild men of the game are less predictable, and don't necessarily just drop their gloves and punch a guy for hitting a star player. Shoebottom was more wild man than goon, more sideshow than NHL, and more *Slap Shot* than Stanley Cup finals. In 1991, he was arrested and held overnight for attacking a fan. In 1994, he got into such a brawl that police had to pepper spray him and apply a choke hold (which rendered him unconscious) to prevent him from attacking an officer to get at an opponent. Shoebottom played mostly in the minors where the wild stuff is more likely to happen, and although he played a few games with Boston from 1987 to '91, it was as a wild man he had some appeal. As his career wore on, his knees got bad, but even still he played in Austin in the Western Professional league, causing disturbances until retiring in 1998.

SHORE, Eddie ("The Edmonton Express")

b. Fort Qu'Appelle, Saskatchewan, November 25, 1902
d. Springfield, Massachusetts, March 16, 1985

Violent, colourful, skilled, and flashy, Eddie Shore was everything that Boston needed to help sell hockey at the box office and produce a winner on the ice. His career spanned half a century and was marked by controversy and success, fame and infamy. He lived on a horse ranch near Cupar on the North Dakota border, and his years of hauling grain, breaking in horses, and herding stock gave him a physique that made him a rock of a man even by the toughest standards. He studied with his brother at the Manitoba Agricultural College in Winnipeg, but in 1923 left to play senior hockey in Melville. He immediately established himself as a fearlessly tough and skilled skater, and he moved up to Regina and Edmonton in successive years. When the WHL folded in 1926, Shore joined the fledgling Boston Bruins on defence and, partnered with Lionel Hitchman, made himself the talk of the league. He scored 12 goals, an unheard of number for a defenceman, and sat in the penalty box for 130 minutes, another staggering number for the era. More important, he proved that when he was on the ice, he controlled the game. In his third season, he took the team to their first Stanley Cup. During the 1930s, Shore won the Hart Trophy an extraordinary four times, a feat never duplicated by a defenceman. He was also named to the First All-Star Team seven times, but in '33–'34 he won no such accolades. On December 12, 1933, he was hit hard by Toronto's Red Horner on a rush, and as the Leafs brought the puck into Boston territory he went after Horner to give him his comeuppance. The only problem was that he hit Ace Bailey by mistake, and Bailey hit his head hard on the ice and lost consciousness. Horner then knocked Shore out, and in the aftermath it was discovered that Bailey was near death. Shore recovered, but the injury ended Bailey's career. Shore was suspended for 16 games, and the league held a special All-Star Game in Toronto on February 14, 1934, at which Shore and Bailey shook hands. It was an emotional moment, and the violent Shore regretted the incident for the rest of his life. Shore was a combination of greatness. He could rush the puck like no other player, and he helped the Bruins become a winner right off the mark. But he was also a showman who knew the theatrical value of the game and how to exploit it. When he played, the Boston Garden was always sold out. When, for instance, he was suspended,

During the 1930s, Shore won the Hart Trophy an extraordinary four times, a feat never duplicated by a defenceman.
EDDIE SHORE

attendance dropped to half. He skated in the warmup with a black cape to get the fans going, and frequently looked to be hollering at the referees much to the delight of fans (who didn't know he was really just asking after their families!). Shore took the team to another Cup in 1939, but realized he was slowing down and his career nearing its end. He bought the Springfield Indians of the AHL in the summer of '39 and owned the team until retiring from hockey for good in 1976. In '39–'40, he did what no other player has even done – he played in the NHL and AHL simultaneously. One night he was in the lineup for the Indians, the next for the New York Americans, to where he had been traded for geographic convenience. In the playoffs, he once played six consecutive nights! When he retired, he devoted himself full-time to managing and coaching the team, and did so in a way that was so unorthodox people still talk about his methods. Some considered him a master teacher; others hated him with their every fibre. Shore was notoriously cheap. He had his players work the box office, sweep the arena floors, change the light bulbs, do everything to maintain the building. Players who wanted a raise were often given it, but Shore fined those men and bled the money back over the course of a year. If the team played poorly, he would often hold a practice right after the game, much to the amazement of departing fans. Yet, some players credit him with teaching them everything they know of the game. During the war, the U.S. Army took over the Coliseum so he moved the team to Buffalo and won two Calder Cups. He returned to Springfield in 1946 and continued his bizarre, austere ways. The low point for the players came during the '66–'67 season when the entire team went on strike, fed up with carrying boards outside the arena to promote the evening's game or having to buy their own sticks. The players brought in Alan Eagleson from

Steve Short

Mikhail Shtalenkov

Gary Shuchuk

Ron Shudra

Toronto, and Shore agreed to sell the team, only to buy it back at season's end. He was elected to the International Hockey Hall of Fame in 1945, the first year of its inception (it later became simply the Hockey Hall of Fame), and his number 2 was retired by the Bruins. The Eddie Shore plaque is handed out annually by the team for their best defenceman, and in 1970 Shore was given the Lester Patrick Trophy for his tremendous contribution to hockey in the U.S. Shore was hated and revered. He could club a player over the head with his stick on one shift and score a beautiful goal on the next. He was intense and ferocious, brilliant and unfair, cruel and understanding. Above all, he gave his life to the game, providing a lifetime of experience and understanding the likes of which the league has never seen before or since. Martyr or devil, he was nothing if not flamboyant, colourful, and the epitome of what the game is all about.

SHORE, Hamilton "Hamby"
b. Ottawa, Ontario, February 12, 1886
d. Ottawa, Ontario, October 13, 1918
Had he been playing today, Shore never would have been cut down in the prime of his life. He had completed the 1917-18 season with his hometown Ottawa Senators, a season he left early because of a bad cold and assorted other ailments. It wasn't likely he would have played in the upcoming '18-'19 season because his throat still bothered him, but matters became grave when his wife contracted pneumonia. Shore attended to her night and day, and he, too, fell ill. He never recovered as she did, and passed away in an Ottawa hospital. Shore had been a star for many years before the formation of the NHL. He played in 1904 and '05 when Ottawa defeated the Dawson City team in the historic challenge for the Stanley Cup, and he won the Cup again in 1911 with the Sens, for whom he played the rest of his days. Shore also worked in the distribution branch of the interior department of the government during his last 10 years.

SHORT, Steve
b. Roseville, Minnesota, April 6, 1954
In six NHL games, Short collected not one point, but he was never expected to. In the vernacular, he's what might be called a loose cannon. To wit, the final night of the '77-'78 AHL season. His Springfield team was in New Haven, and Short, well, kind of lost it. Most straight-ahead fighters duke it out on the ice. The occasional wild men go at it in the penalty box. A rare nutbar continues things in the hallways, but in a singular act of looniness, Short scampered into the opponent's dressing room and attacked a player who was naked and being stitched up after a fight. Both teams piled into the New Haven room, and after order was restored, Short was ejected from the game. He retired in 1981.

SHTALENKOV, Mikhail
b. Moscow, Soviet Union (Russia), October 20, 1965
After winning a gold medal with Russia at the 1992 Olympics in Albertville, Shtalenkov decided he was ready for North America. He had played in the Soviet league for a number of years, and his '91-'92 season started with the Canada Cup and finished with the World Championships. He signed with Milwaukee in the IHL and was named rookie of the year, and on these strengths Anaheim drafted him in 1993. For the next seven years, Shtalenkov was a mainstay in the NHL, though more as a backup than a starter. He later played for Edmonton, Phoenix, and Florida, and finished his career with a year in Moscow with Dynamo, the team he had started his career with in 1986.

SHUCHUK, Gary
b. Edmonton, Alberta, February 17, 1967
After 4 standout seasons at the University of Wisconsin (1986-90), Shuchuk had a less than outstanding stay in the NHL, playing 142 games with Detroit and Los Angeles. The goals that came freely with the Badgers and in the AHL barely came at all with the big boys, and Shuchuk moved to Europe to continue his career, which now passes in Germany.

SHUDRA, Ron ("Rocket Ron")
b. Winnipeg, Manitoba, November 28, 1967
From junior in Kamloops to Edmonton in the NHL, Shudra made the transition to pro that saw him end quickly in the minors. Three years of almost constant time without a shot at the NHL told him his days were done after just 10 games with the Oilers, so he moved to England and became a legend. He played for 10 seasons in the British league, mostly with Sheffield where the fans dubbed him Rocket Ron. He led the Steelers to their first championship and ended his career after 1999-2000, a season in which he was player-coach for the Hull Thunder. After just a few games, though, he left this post to assume the position of promotions manager in Sheffield, but on December 15, 2001, he was forced out of retirement when injuries depleted the club. Not only did he play forward instead of his usual defence position, he scored a goal and earned a standing ovation for his efforts.

SHULMISTRA, Richard
b. Sudbury, Ontario, April 1, 1971
Even though Shulmistra isn't likely to make it any further in the NHL, he has played twice and played well.

He was traded to Los Angeles early in the '84-'85 season, but at year's end he decided to retire rather than forge another career on the west coast.
STEVE SHUTT

The goalie played once for New Jersey in '97-'98 and once with Florida two years later, but the University of Miami-Ohio grad was a mainstay in the minors before and since.

SHUTT, Steve

b. Toronto, Ontario, July 1, 1952

Shutt was a natural left winger who was not a particularly graceful skater or magical stickhandler, but he always managed to read the game well and was in the right place at the right time. The Marlies recruited one of their own in 1969, and over the next three years he developed into one of the OHL's top scorers. He played on a line with Dave Gardner and Billy Harris, and in his final two seasons of junior Shutt had 235 points. Montreal drafted him 4th overall in 1972, and he passed up a scholarship to play college football (he was a kicker) to pursue a hockey career. After just six games with Nova Scotia the next year he was in the NHL for good. After scoring 8 goals as a rookie, Shutt increased his scoring in increments of 15. He had 15 in '73-'74, 30 the year after, 45 the year after that, and in '76-'77 he set an NHL record for left wingers with 60 goals to lead the league. He played on a line with Pete Mahovlich and Guy Lafleur, and though not as flashy as either he earned more than his fair share of points and also earned a solid reputation with coach Scotty Bowman. By '76-'77, he was with Lafleur and Jacques Lemaire. Shutt was blessed with a very accurate wrist shot and slapshot, and a quick delivery that caught goalies by surprise. In the ensuing years he never reached 50 again, but he did contribute to 5 Stanley Cups during the 1970s. He was traded to Los Angeles early in the '84-'85 season, but at year's end he decided to retire rather than forge another career on the west coast. Shutt never won an individual trophy and played in only three All-Star Games, but did play in the 1976 Canada Cup. He retired with 424 goals to his name and went to work as a TV commentator until 1993 when the Habs hired him as an assistant coach. He did that for four years and later went into business with Cimco Lewis Refrigeration, a company that provides cooling systems and floors for arenas. He was inducted into the Hockey Hall of Fame in 1993.

SHVIDKI, Denis

b. Kharkov, Soviet Union (Ukraine), November 21, 1980

Florida expects this young Ukraine player to develop into an NHL star. After finishing his junior career in the OHL, he turned pro with the Panthers in 2000, splitting the season between the NHL and AHL. In 2001-02, he was mostly a minor-leaguer thanks to a concussion and torn ligaments in one ankle, but Shvidki is still a kid by pro terms. He won a gold medal with Russia at the '99 WJC in Winnipeg, but so far has proved only minor-league worthy.

SIDORKIEWICZ, Peter

b. Dabrowa Bialostocka, Poland, June 29, 1963

Getting his name and birthplace right is a chore in itself, but the man dubbed Peter Alphabet had a lengthy career in both the NHL and the minors. He played junior in Oshawa, where his family had emigrated to, and turned pro in the Hartford system in 1985. Unfortunately for Sidorkiewicz, most of his NHL time came with weak teams, notably the expansion Senators in '92-'93 when he had a sad record of 8-46-3. His dedication to the team, though, earned him a spot in that year's All-Star Game. His best years of pro came with Binghamton in the AHL, and in 2002 he was inducted into that city's Hockey Hall of Fame for his accomplishments with the Whalers. After hanging up the pads in 1998, Sidorkiewicz became the assistant coach of the Erie Otters in the OHL, a position he continues to hold.

Peter Sidorkiewicz

SIEBERT, Albert "Babe"

b. Plattsville, Ontario, January 14, 1904

d. Lake Huron, Ontario, August 25, 1939

In the summer of 1939, Siebert retired from hockey and became the new coach of the Montreal Canadiens. He was vacationing at his cottage when, one day, his children were out on the water playing with a tire. It drifted from them, and Babe went in to swim after it. The tire continued to drift, and Siebert quickly got tired and then disappeared from sight. He drowned before his children's eyes. Everyone in the hockey world was shocked by what was called a double tragedy, because he was indispensable to his wife. She was an invalid, and anyone who ever went to a game at the Forum could recall seeing Babe carry his wife into the arena before every game and then out of the arena afterward. She had been paralyzed while giving birth to their second child, and Babe was faithful and loyal to her until the moment he died. Most of his income went to a nurse who tended for her, but he neither complained nor compromised the attention she received. Siebert was a star of the game. He grew up in Zurich, Ontario, not far from Plattsville, and played hockey every day of his childhood, indoors on rainy days. Siebert impressed Frank Selke while playing in Kitchener, but it was the Montreal Maroons who obtained his rights in 1925. Almost immediately he played on a line with Hooley Smith and Nels Stewart, and the S Line became one of the most lethal

Siebert impressed Frank Selke while playing in Kitchener, but it was the Montreal Maroons who obtained his rights in 1925.
BABE SIEBERT

Mike Sillinger

Risto Siltanen

Jon Sim

combinations in the game. The Maroons won the Cup in Siebert's first year, in large part due to the work of this line. Stewart was the scorer and Smith the passer, but Siebert was the man who got the puck over the blueline and who used his body to create space and time for the others. He was traded to the Rangers in 1932, and again in his first season with the Blueshirts they won the Cup. He moved on to Boston and then in 1936 was traded to the Canadiens. To get the most out of him, the Habs moved him from left wing to defence. He won the Hart Trophy in '36-'37 as a defenceman and retired two years later as one of the most complete players of his era. After his tragic demise, the NHL organized a memorial All-Star Game in the fall of 1939 for his family (as they had for Ace Bailey and Howie Morenz). Despite a poor attendance in Montreal of only 6,000, the game raised some $15,000 for his widow and children. Siebert was inducted into the Hockey Hall of Fame in 1964.

SILK, Dave
b. Scituate, Massachusetts, January 1, 1958

The exodus from amateur to pro was never as fervent as in the days after the Miracle on Ice. Some 22 American university students were the most sought after players on the planet following their stunning gold medal at the 1980 Olympics in Lake Placid, and Silk was among that number. Yet like almost all of his teammates, the glory of gold never came close to being replicated in the NHL. Silk signed with the Rangers on March 3, 1980, but after two full seasons and bits of two others it was clear he wasn't going to be an impact player. He had modest success for a short time when his local Bruins signed him, but in 1986 his NHL days were at an end and he went to Germany to play. After retiring, Silk settled in Boston (where he had gone to university) and started working for Putnam Investments.

SILLINGER, Mike ("Silly")
b. Regina, Saskatchewan, June 29, 1971

It was only in his tenth NHL season, playing with 2 of the worst teams in the league, that Sillinger had his first 20-goal season. In 1999-2000, he played for Tampa Bay and Florida and combined for 23 goals. Two years later, with the equally horrid Columbus team, he scored 20 again. Scoring had never been his forte since junior, when he had three 50-goal seasons. Since entering the NHL in 1991 after winning gold with Canada at the 1991 WJC, Sillinger was more of a role player, a utility forward who could do a little bit of everything. To cap off that first scoring season, he captained Canada at the 2000 World Championships.

SILTALA, Mike
b. Toronto, Ontario, August 5, 1963

Washington called Siltala up to the NHL when he was just 18, to give him a taste of the big time, and it was just about the only taste he had. The rest of his career passed in the minors with the exception of two brief callups with the Rangers a number of years later, and although L.A. signed him in 1988, the Kings never used his services.

SILTANEN, Risto ("The Littlest Hulk")
b. Mantta, Finland, October 31, 1958

At 5'8" he wasn't the tallest player in the league, but at 185 pounds he was stocky and strong with a low centre of gravity that made it hard to knock him off the puck. Siltanen was a great Finnish prospect in the 1970s when Finns didn't typically come to North America, but he joined Edmonton in 1978 while the team was still in the WHA and stayed with the team as it moved to the NHL. In his eight years he also played for Hartford and Quebec, and in 1987, when it was clear that his NHL days were nearing an end, he returned to Europe to play for many years yet. Siltanen retired in 1997 and was inducted into the Finnish Ice Hockey Hall of Fame a year later. He had also played in two WJCs, three World Championships, and the 1981 Canada Cup.

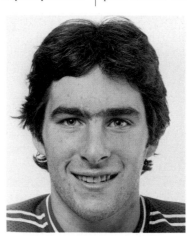

After retiring, Silk settled in Boston and started working for Putnam Investments.

DAVE SILK

SIM, Jon
b. New Glasgow, Nova Scotia, September 29, 1977

It's not the biggest hockey-producing area of the country, but it's pretty amazing that playing on the same AAA midget team in Pictou County in the early 1990s were Colin White and Jon Sim, both of whom won the Stanley Cup. Sim got his break when he was cut by Laval in the Quebec league and picked up by Sarnia. He went on to become the second-highest scorer in team history behind Doug Gilmour, and since being drafted by Dallas has slowly worked his way into the lineup on a part-time basis.

SIM, Trevor
b. Calgary, Alberta, June 9, 1970

After winning a Memorial Cup with Swift Current in 1989, Sim embarked on a 10-year pro career that had him travelling as much as playing for most of those years. He was still a teenager when he played three games with Edmonton, but the rest of his career came with teams called the Crunch, the Brass, the Bears, the Checkers, and the like.

SIMARD, Martin
b. Montreal, Quebec, June 25, 1966

Undrafted, Simard made the most of his limited

talents – in large measure, with his physical play. After leaving junior in 1987, he was signed by Calgary and assigned to Salt Lake City, playing in the system for 6 years and getting into 16 games with the Flames. He later played a few games with Tampa, but for the most part Simard patrolled the right wing in the IHL and AHL for the rest of his career, which ended in 1998 with Springfield.

SIMICEK, Roman
b. Ostrava, Czechoslovakia (Czech Republic), November 4, 1971
Because every European player who enters the NHL has to be drafted first, Simicek had the distinction not only of being chosen 273rd overall by Pittsburgh but of being selected in 2000 at the age of 28. And, he made his NHL debut in Japan! He was acquired by Minnesota during the 2000-01 season and has been with the Wild since, though at 30-plus he doesn't seem as much a late bloomer as a player getting a chance because of the thinning of NHL talent due to expansion.

SIMMER, Charlie
b. Terrace Bay, Ontario, March 20, 1954
How does a kid from a town served only by a highway and railway wind up marrying a Playboy Playmate? Hockey, of course. In Los Angeles, natch. Simmer played only one season of major junior hockey in Ontario before being drafted by California. He later signed with the Kings, but the first five seasons of his career were all brief tryouts and minor-league disappointments. Then, one night in Detroit, coach Bob Berry put Simmer on a line with Marcel Dionne and Dave Taylor and Dionne scored four goals. The Triple Crown Line was born, and Simmer became the league's top scorer. As such, he became a popular figure in the city, and managed to meet Teri Welles, a Playmate, and the two were later married. In '79-'80 and '80-'81, Simmer scored 56 goals each year, but just as he was reaching his peak, he shattered his right leg in a game at Maple Leaf Gardens and missed almost a full year. He had 2 weak seasons as he slowly recovered, but the Triple Crown Line had one more explosive season, '83-'84, in which Simmer scored 44 times. He was later traded to Boston, where his production dipped into the 30s, but for his strong recovery and comeback he won the Bill Masterton Trophy in '85-'86. By the time he retired, he had 342 goals to his credit and could boast of having played on one of the highest-scoring lines of all time. He later coached the San Diego Gulls in the IHL and became involved in commercial real estate. More recently he has become involved in broadcasting as an analyst for Anaheim and Phoenix.

SIMMONS, Al
b. Winnipeg, Manitoba, September 25, 1951
It wasn't a long career in the NHL, but it was represented entirely with prime numbers. Simmons played one game with California in '71-'72, three games with Boston two years later, and seven games with Boston again the year after. In his 11 total NHL games, he had 1 point. Simmons' short pro career ended in 1976.

SIMMONS, Don ("Dippy")
b. Port Colborne, Ontario, September 13, 1931
Ask a million people to describe fortune and no doubt a million distinct answers would be provided. Here's what Simmons' might sound like. On January 18, 1964, the Toronto goalie played in net against Boston, the worst team in the league. The Bruins, though,

The Bruins handed the Leafs an 11-0 drubbing, and Simmons was in goal for the entire game.
DON SIMMONS

handed the Leafs an 11-0 drubbing, and Simmons was in goal for the entire game. Furious, Toronto coach Punch Imlach promised that Simmons would never play for the Leafs again. He recalled Al Millar from the minors and told him to be in Chicago for a game the next night. Millar suffered a series of delays, though, and with Johnny Bower injured Imlach had no choice but to play Simmons again. He shut out the Hawks 2-0 and regained his spot on the team – all because of a flight delay in Victoria, B.C. Simmons had been Boston's goalie in the late 1950s before the Leafs acquired him, and he was with Toronto for the three Cups in 1962, '63, and '64. He later played in the Rangers system for a few years, and after retiring became a coach for the Welland Sabres of the Southern Ontario Hockey Association, a provincial junior A team. He also opened the Don Simmons Sporting Goods Store in Fort Erie, Ontario, which he ran for many years.

SIMMONS, Gary ("Cobra")
b. Charlottetown, Prince Edward Island, July 19, 1944
Goalies are, by definition, oddballs, but even by their standards Simmons was from another planet. He played junior with Edmonton in the mid-1960s but saw no future in goaltending professionally. There were six NHL teams, and those nets were guarded by six Hall of Famers. Nobody named Simmons was going to step in and win a job. So, when he was offered a position with the Lethbridge police, he took it. By the end of his first day, though, he had an offer to play in Newfoundland, one too good to pass up. His days of keeping the peace were over before they began. Simmons played through expansion in 1967 and '70 and '72 before he finally drew interest from California, and when he joined the Seals in 1974, he was giving the team something they never had before. He wore western clothes and had 10 tattoos on his body.

Charlie Simmer

Al Simmons

Gary Simmons

They called him Cobra because of his quickness, so he had a large and imposing snake painted on his mask. He spoke his mind and did his own thing, but he was also pretty fair at stopping the puck. Although his NHL career lasted just over five years, he was well respected around the league for his play, despite the quality of his own team. After retiring, Simmons settled in Concord, California, and started a chain of seven Roundtable pizzerias.

SIMON, Ben
b. Shaker Heights, Ohio, June 14, 1978
Simon played for the U.S. at the 1997 and '98 WJC, winning a rare silver medal at the former. After graduating from the University of Notre Dame in 2000, he joined Orlando of the IHL and captained the team to the Turner Cup. The next year, he played a few games with Atlanta, his first in the NHL, though he continues to be mostly a minor leaguer so far.

SIMON, Chris
b. Wawa, Ontario,
January 2, 1972
He didn't grow up on a reserve, but Simon was half Native in blood and all Native in soul. He was a member of Wikmemikon, a subgroup of the Ojibway. His father was a Native who also played junior and minor pro, and his mother was a dietitian. Simon left home at 14 to play hockey in Ottawa, and during his teen years grew into a large young man capable of drinking plenty of beer. Simon had that edge, but once in a game in 1997 he used a racial slur against Mike Grier, a black member of Edmonton, and was suspended by the NHL for three games. Simon was a fighter, but he also looked like someone who might lose it at any time. It was an intimidating persona on ice, but off the ice it got him into barroom brawls and unsavoury social situations. Eventually, he knew he had to stop drinking or become just another alcoholic, and with the help of junior coach and mentor Ted Nolan, Simon chose the former. He was part of the deal that Quebec landed when it traded Eric Lindros to Philadelphia, and Simon won a Cup with the Avalanche in 1996. He was later traded to Washington, and just as he was developing he suffered serious shoulder injuries that ended two successive seasons with surgery. When he came back, in 1999-2000 with a greater devotion to fitness, he scored an amazing 29 goals. Of course, as often happens, he then demanded a huge salary based on that one season, and he was a holdout to start the new season until the Caps gave him a two-year, $4.5-million contract. Simon then produced just 24 goals over those 2 years, his problems with alcohol seemingly licked, his problems with the puck as a so-called scorer just beginning.

Cully Simon

Simon left home at 14 to play hockey in Ottawa.
CHRIS SIMON

Thain Simon

SIMON, Cullen "Cully"
b. Brockville, Ontario, May 8, 1918
d. Brockville, Ontario, August 2, 1980
It's not often that a woman helps a man get into the NHL through her contacts, but such was definitely the case with Simon's appearance in the NHL. He married Dorothy Giesebrecht, whose brother, Gus, was an NHLer. Gus appealed to Jack Adams in Detroit to give Cully a tryout, and over the course of three training camps Simon finally made it into the Red Wings lineup during the '42-'43 season. He distinguished himself on defence for his hard hits and tenacity, and teamed with Alex Motter they formed a very efficient tandem. When Simon was traded to Chicago in January 1945, he paired effectively with Black Jack Stewart, and the year after Simon began a lengthy career in and association with Pembroke. He played with his brother, Thain, on the Lumber Kings, and later coached the team to the 1952 Allan Cup finals. The brothers also operated the Pepsi-Cola franchise in the city until Cully bought a ladies' clothing store. He later ran an hotel in Renfrew until it burned down, after which time he worked in PR for the Ontario Hotel Association. In his later years, he spent a good deal of time in Florida, where he also had businesses.

SIMON, Jason
b. Sarnia, Ontario,
March 21, 1969
In 5 career NHL games, Simon had 34 penalty minutes, a true indication of the kind of game he brought to the rink. Fighting was his style, and he did it well and long, from junior, where he started as a novice, where he honed his pugilistic craft. New Jersey drafted him in 1989, and he was also owned by the Islanders, Winnipeg, and Colorado.

SIMON, Thain
b. Brockville, Ontario, April 24, 1922
The careers and lives of the brothers Simon overlapped and connected much of the time. Thain also played for Detroit, though in '46-'47, two years after Cully. He soon returned to Pembroke, where he had been playing, to join coach Cully, who was just arriving, and together they formed a successful combination. Thain coached the Lumber Kings in '52-'53, the year after Cully, and the pair entered business together as operators of the local Pepsi-Cola franchise.

SIMON, Todd
b. Toronto, Ontario, April 21, 1972
It seems everyone coming out of junior set a record of some sort or led the league at some time, and Simon was no exception. He led the OHL in scoring in

'91-'92 with Niagara Falls, but he played just 15 games with his drafting team, Buffalo, before beginning a lengthy career in the minors. For 8 seasons he was a solid 25-goal scorer, but in the summer of 2000 he accepted an offer to play in Germany, where he's been since.

SIMONETTI, Frank
b. Melrose, Massachusetts, September 11, 1962
While attending Norwich University, Simonetti captained both the hockey and the soccer teams and became the highest-scoring defenceman in school history. He left his engineering studies after two years to sign with Boston in 1984, but through his four NHL years he was wrecked by injury. He retired in 1986, returned to engineering, and rose to president of Data Engineering, a manufacturers rep firm based in Windham, New Hampshire.

SIMPSON, Bobby
b. Caughnawaga, Ontario, November 17, 1956
A Mohawk who grew up just outside of Montreal, Simpson broke in with Atlanta in 1976 but played in the NHL only sporadically over the next few years. He established a side business with a friend, opening a hairstyling salon just outside Atlanta, but spent much of his career on the move before retiring in 1987. Much of his time was complicated by injury. Simpson pulled a groin in his first camp, hurt his groin and shoulder the following year, and hurt his knee after slamming into the boards a year later.

SIMPSON, Cliff
b. Toronto, Ontario, April 4, 1923
d. Toronto, Ontario, May 30, 1987
As a teen, Simpson played with the Toronto Young Rangers and the Brantford Lions before turning pro in 1942. He played in the AHL with Indianapolis but interrupted his career to join the army. Simpson was a craftsman with the Royal Canadian Electrical and Mechanical Engineers, serving in England, Holland, Belgium, and Germany. He returned to play briefly with the Red Wings, but made history in the AHL with the Capitols. In the '46-'47 season, he scored 48 goals and 110 points to break the record held by Wally Kilrea, and when he scored his 100th goal with the team in February 1948 he was given a trophy in recognition of the achievement. After retiring in 1952, Simpson worked in Aylmer, Ontario, as the town's recreation director and coached the minor hockey team. He died after a two-year fight with cancer.

SIMPSON, Craig ("Simmer")
b. London, Ontario, February 15, 1967
On paper, there was nothing out of the ordinary in Simpson going to Michigan State to play college hockey. But, do the math, and you see that when he went, in 1983, he was 16, the youngest player in NCAA history. While his brother Dave played minor pro but never had the desire to make it to the NHL, Craig had the drive and the skill to make it and be successful. He was drafted 2nd overall by Pittsburgh in 1985 and immediately hit it off with the previous year's number-one choice, Mario Lemieux. Simpson had the privilege of being traded to Edmonton at the perfect time, early

in the '87-'88 season when the Oilers were on track for another Stanley Cup. Simpson scored a combined 56 goals in what was to be his career year. His goal production slowly declined, but he never scored fewer than 24 goals in 7 full seasons before back troubles affected his health. Simpson retired in October 1995 after two partial years in Buffalo, after which time his back simply wasn't strong enough to withstand the rigours of the NHL game. He became a successful analyst and commentator for Sportsnet in Canada, and with his brother formed Sonar Investment Corporation, a London, Ontario-area business that invested heavily in many local golf courses.

SIMPSON, Joe ("Bullet Joe")
b. Selkirk, Manitoba, August 13, 1893
d. Coral Gables, Florida, December 25, 1973
Growing up in Selkirk, Simpson and his friends thought about little else other than the first snowfall that would freeze the ground and water and allow for skating. He played junior with the local Fishermen and then senior with the Winnipeg Victorias in 1914-15. He joined the Canadian army, but before going overseas was able to play a season with the Winnipeg 61st Battalion, which won the Allan Cup in 1916. Overseas, Lieutenant Simpson served with the 43rd Cameron Highlanders and was wounded twice in action, at the Somme and Amiens. He was awarded the Military Medal for valour before being sent home in February 1919, and again played for the Fishermen before joining Edmonton of the Big 4. When the league folded in 1925 he was bought by the NHL's New York Americans and the 32-year-old began a new career. Fans saw why he was called Bullet Joe. His end-to-end rushes were the stuff of legend, his skating without compare. Newsy Lalonde called him the best player alive, a great compliment from one many considered the best player alive himself! Simpson was a player with the Amerks for six years and then coached the team for another three. He also managed at New Haven and Minneapolis and then moved to Florida in 1938 to promote hockey. He suffered a heart attack that kept him inactive for two years, and then another retired hockey player and Floridian came to his aid. Art Coulter hired Simpson to work at the Coulter-White Hardware Store in Coral Gables, a position he held until 1965. Simpson was inducted into the Hockey Hall of Fame in 1962.

SIMPSON, Reid
b. Flin Flon, Manitoba, May 21, 1969
The strapping, scrappy winger from Manitoba has certainly been making the rounds. To date, he has played for eight NHL teams and counting, accumulating penalty minutes along the way in defence and support of his mates. He left the WHL in 1990 to break into the AHL, making his NHL debut a year and a half later with Philadelphia. His longest stint was with the Devils organization, for whom he played parts of five seasons.

SIMPSON, Todd
b. North Vancouver, British Columbia, May 28, 1973
He makes his living as a big and tough defenceman, most recently with Phoenix. While Simpson's brother, Kent, never made it to the NHL (he has played for

Frank Simonetti

Craig Simpson

Joe Simpson

Reid Simpson

Todd Simpson

Al Sims

Alex Singbush

Ilkka Sinisalo

Ville Siren

years in Europe), Todd signed as a free agent with Calgary in 1994 and spent four years with the Flames after a season in the minors. He later played for Florida, but the Panthers traded him to the Coyotes in 2001 for a second-round draft choice.

SIMS, Al
b. Toronto, Ontario, April 18, 1953

You can count on one hand the number of players who were as fortunate as Sims was when he joined the league in 1973. Playing as a rookie with Boston, he was paired on the blueline with Bobby Orr. Not surprisingly, Sims was a +64 on the year, but the Bruins were upset by Philadelphia in the Cup finals. Sims played six years with the B's, much of the last four in the minors, though. He then moved around in the NHL before heading to Europe, and when he retired he became a coach, first with Fort Wayne. He won the Turner Cup with the team in '92-'93 and that fall joined Anaheim as an assistant. His one and only head coaching job so far was with San Jose in '96-'97, but a 27-47-8 record scuppered any chances of his returning. Most recently, he was head man for Reading in 2001, the team's first season in the ECHL.

SINCLAIR, Reg
b. Lachine, Quebec, March 6, 1925

Told he had no future in the game, Sinclair proved skeptics wrong. He was a rare graduate of McGill University to play in the NHL, but when he made the Rangers in 1950 he proved he could play. Then he scored 18 goals over the year, proving he could play well, and the year after he had 20. That summer, he worked as a disc jockey in Sherbrooke, but after one more year of hockey he retired to work for Pepsi-Cola, becoming successful in the promotions side of the company in Montreal.

SINGBUSH, Alex
b. Winnipeg, Manitoba, January 13, 1914
d. March 8, 1969

During the war, Singbush played much of the '40-'41 season with the Canadiens after being called up from New Haven. He played a number of seasons in the minors, mostly in the AHL, before retiring in 1945.

SINISALO, Ilkka ("Ile")
b. Valkeakoski, Finland, July 10, 1958

Signed as a free agent at age 22 by Philadelphia early in 1981, Sinisalo was a skilled player who made an impression in the 1981 World Championships and then later at the Canada Cup. In his 9 years with the Flyers he became one of the team's better scorers, hitting the 20-goal mark 6 times and peaking with 39 in '85-'86. Injuries, particularly to his knees, slowed him down in

> He never won a Stanley Cup and fell just shy of the magic 500-goal club but he did have 1,121 career points.
> **DARRYL SITTLER**

his later years, and he closed out his career in the Finnish league. After retiring in 1996 he became a scout for San Jose, and in 2000 was GM of the Espoo Blues for a season. In 2001, he rejoined the Sharks as a scout.

SIREN, Ville
b. Tampere, Finland, February 11, 1964

When Hartford drafted Siren in 1983, the Whalers had no idea whether he would agree to come to North America. A year later, there was still no hope, so they traded him to Pittsburgh for Pat Boutette, and the Pens were now stuck with a player they, too, weren't sure would ever play for them. In both instances, the teams felt the gamble was worth it. In 1985, Siren did, indeed, agree to join the Pens, but just as he started to get used to the game, he blocked a shot and broke his ankle. Nonetheless, he came back strong and played well for Pittsburgh, but each year brought with it fresh injury. A sprained knee, a broken foot, a sore back – all put Siren out of the lineup for extended periods. In 1990, he returned to the more placid confines of the Finnish league and played healthily until 1999. Along the way, he played in all the important international tournaments, notably the 1984 Olympics in Sarajevo where he won a silver medal. He later became the European scout for Washington, responsible for both amateur and pro players on the continent.

SIROIS, Bob
b. Montreal, Quebec, February 6, 1954

That Sirois could play the '76-'77 season with Washington and end a +1 was a miracle, in part because the team wasn't very good, in part because he missed half the season with injuries and played hurt the other half. He hurt his knee; he broke his thumb; he injured his shoulder; he had a bad back. All in one season, yet the right winger was still on the ice for more scored than allowed. He played the last five years of his career with the Caps after being traded from the Flyers for future considerations, which turned out to be John Paddock. As a kid, he grew up in a part of Montreal called Ahuntsic, an area where he regularly saw Maurice Richard. In his only two complete and injury-free years in the NHL, Sirois scored 24 and 29 goals.

SITTLER, Darryl ("Sitt")
b. St. Jacobs, Ontario, September 18, 1950

February 7, 1976, represented the apogee of Sittler's hockey career, one full of event during its 15 years. Playing a home game for the Leafs, he scored 6 goals and 4 assists – 10 points – against Boston and goalie Dave Reece, the best night ever in NHL history. It turned out to be Reece's last game in the league, as he was demoted and never recalled, but for Sittler it was a magical night in an 11-4 win. In fact, it was the first of three tremendous Sittler feats in the calendar year of 1976. The second came in the playoffs against Philadelphia that year when he tied a record with five goals in a game, but the third was even more significant. In game two of the best-of-three finals against Czechoslovakia in the inaugural Canada Cup, Sittler scored the overtime Cup-winning goal by faking a shot against goalie Vladimir Dzurilla and scoring into the vacated net. This was a year that saw the Leafs captain at the height of his powers. He was drafted by Toronto in 1970 after a solid junior career in London, but did not blossom into an NHL star right away. He learned the pro game gradually but consistently, improving until '75-'76 when he had 41 goals and 100 points. He played on a high-scoring line with Errol Thompson and Lanny McDonald, and the team developed into a contender as other young stars such as goalie Mike Palmateer and defencemen Borje Salming and Ian Turnbull emerged. Sittler inherited the captaincy from Dave Keon in 1975 and wore the "C" proudly. He was a fan favourite for his determined, classy play, and he and his wife, Wendy, were popular in the city for their community work. In '77-'78, Sittler set a team record with 117 points on the year, but life in Leafland took a decided turn for the worse when owner Harold Ballard hired Punch Imlach as GM in 1979. A team that was on the verge of great things in the playoffs was dismantled by the autocratic Imlach, and Sittler's best friend, McDonald, was traded

He was the first Swedish captain in North American professional hockey, and led the Jets to the Avco Cup.
LARS-ERIK SJOBERG

to Colorado. Imlach knew he couldn't trade the popular captain, so he traded the players he knew were close to him. The result was that one night Sittler came out on the ice with the "C" torn off his sweater. Ballard called him a cancer on the team, and a trade seemed inevitable. Over the summer, though, differences were resolved and Sittler assumed team leadership again, but it seemed just a matter of time before things went awry. Midway through '81-'82, he left the team, citing depression and exhaustion (just as Frank Mahovlich had done under Imlach a generation earlier), and finally was traded to Philadelphia, Toronto's archenemy. He had two and a half productive seasons with the Flyers before being traded to Detroit, at first balking at the move but eventually agreeing to go. After one year, Sittler retired in 1985. He never won a Stanley Cup and fell just shy of the magic 500-goal club (finishing with 484) but he did have 1,121 career points, 15th on the all-time list at that time. A consummate leader and fiery competitor, he was inducted into the Hockey Hall of Fame in 1989, and two years later returned to work for the Leafs in the public rela-

tions and marketing departments, acting as a goodwill ambassador and representative for the team throughout the year. He and Frank Mahovlich were going to share an evening at Air Canada Centre near the start of the 2001-02 season when their mutual number 27 was to be honoured, but Wendy Sittler passed away and Darryl had to postpone the honour until later in the season. He lives in Buffalo. His son, Ryan, has played in the World Junior Championships for the U.S., and his daughter attends college while playing hockey as well. He remains the all-time points leader for the Leafs, though his single-season mark was bettered by Doug Gilmour, and over the last quarter-century some of the game's greatest stars have come and gone and not been able to come near his 10-point night, which might well be a record that is never equalled.

SJOBERG, Lars-Erik ("The Little General")

b. Falun, Sweden, April 5, 1944
d. Uppsala, Sweden, October 30, 1987

How a man conducts himself in this life is how he will be remembered forever, and although Sjoberg lived only 43 years in this world, he will always be highly regarded as a player and a human being. In Sweden, he was one of the great players, catapulting to stardom in 1974 when he was named best defenceman at the World Championships. He came to Canada with the WHA, the Jets, and countrymen Ulf Nilsson and Anders Hedberg, and the common belief on the team was that Hull, Nilsson, and Hedberg made the headlines, but Sjoberg was the team's backbone. He was a defenceman who saw the ice well and moved the puck efficiently, and in his own end he wasn't going to be beat one on one. He was the first Swedish captain in North American professional hockey, and led the Jets to the Avco Cup. He starred for Sweden at the 1976 Canada Cup, and stayed with the Jets in '79-'80, their first year in the NHL and his only season there. He retired after that year and returned to Sweden, where he became the Rangers' chief European scout, tipping them to players including Tomas Sandstrom, Ulf Dahlen, and Reijo Ruotsalainen. At the 1987 draft, friends noted that he didn't look well, and he explained it was a case of shingles. He talked to the Rangers about his son, Magnus, and hoped that the club would hire him. In truth, Sjoberg was planning. He had been undergoing chemotherapy for cancer of the stomach and esophagus. He died before training camp – and the Rangers did, indeed, hire Magnus.

SJODIN, Tommy

b. Timra, Sweden, August 13, 1965
Sjodin's year and a half in the NHL came at his peak

Tommy Sjodin

and interrupted a fine career rooted in his home country. Sjodin was drafted in 1985 as a 20-year-old, but it was 7 years before he joined Minnesota and gave the big league a try. He returned to Sweden in 1994, and never came back. Internationally, he played in four World Championships as well as the 1992 Olympics in Albertville, when Tre Kronor finished fifth.

SKAARE, Bjorn
b. Oslo, Norway, October 29, 1958
d. Karlskoga, Sweden, June 21, 1989
He grew up in Oslo as a young boy, but he knew he took hockey more seriously than anyone he encountered in Norway. So, Skaare moved to Sweden to play junior, and during one tournament in Ottawa asked coach Brian Kilrea if he could practise with the 67's. Skaare looked so good that the next year Kilrea brought the youngster over to play in the OHL. From there, he was drafted by Detroit, and on November 29, 1978, he became the first Norwegian to play in the NHL. It was his only game, and he soon returned to Norway to play in his home league, where he was the best player in the country. He died in a car accident not far from the Norwegian border, leaving behind a fiancée and their son. Skaare had been planning a return to hockey.

He died in a car accident not far from the Norwegian border.
BJORN SKAARE

SKALDE, Jarrod
b. Niagara Falls, Ontario, February 26, 1971
There might not have been another player like him, and he's by no means done yet. Since being drafted in 1989 by New Jersey, Skalde has played for 8 teams totalling just a little more than 100 games. Between January 8 and March 6, 1998, he was claimed off waivers five times. During that '97-'98 season he went from San Jose to Chicago to Dallas and back to Chicago. In the minors, he's played with more teams than he can count, yet has been a terrific scorer in the AHL and IHL. By the time he retires, he might well play for an eleventh NHL team to set a new record. It's something to aim for, anyway.

SKARDA, Randy
b. St. Paul, Minnesota, May 5, 1968
His home state was where his life was, and Skarda attended the University of Minnesota to be close to home. Drafted by St. Louis in 1986, he played a few games for the Blues but spent most of his career in the minors. He also played roller hockey with the Minnesota Arctic Blast, and later became involved in a Web site devoted to training programs for aspiring players.

SKIDMORE, Paul
b. Smithtown, New York, July 22, 1956
Two men set records on the same play. One would happily talk about it; the other wants to forget it. On December 20, 1981, Paul Smail of Winnipeg scored five seconds into the game against St. Louis, the fastest goal from the opening faceoff in NHL history. In net was Skidmore – playing in his first NHL game. No goalie has ever allowed a faster score to start his career. Worse, he allowed another goal a minute later, and the Blues went on to lose 5-4. Skidmore got his second start a week and a half later and won 6-1, but he was sent down to Salt Lake City and never came back.

SKILTON, Raymond "Raymie"
b. Cambridge, Massachusetts, September 26, 1889
d. Ossipee, New Hampshire, July 1, 1961
He played most of his career in Boston, but the war and the formation of the NHL overlapped serendipitously for Skilton. A munitions expert, he was stationed in Montreal by the U.S. government, but played hockey locally. The Wanderers called him up for one game on December 21, 1917, at a cost of just $1. He resumed his career in Boston after the war.

SKINNER, Alf ("Dutch")
b. Toronto, Ontario, January 26, 1896
d. Toronto, Ontario, April 23, 1961
In a long and successful career, Skinner accomplished most of what a hockey player hoped to do. He was just a teenager when he was a pro with the Toronto Shamrocks, staying with the franchise as it became Blueshirts and then Arenas and moved from the NHA to the NHL. In the first season as the Arenas, Skinner helped win the first NHL Stanley Cup for Toronto, and after one more season he fled to the Pacific Coast league. He played in Vancouver for five years, coming close but never winning a second Cup. Once the PCHA joined the WCHL, Skinner returned to the NHL with Boston, Montreal, and Pittsburgh. After retiring, he turned to coaching in Ontario and scouting for the Red Wings. He worked full-time for the City of Toronto and became president of the Spadina Men's Progressive Conservative Association.

SKINNER, Larry
b. Vancouver, British Columbia, April 21, 1956
No matter what happens in hockey history, Skinner's place was etched in time when he scored the first goal for the Colorado Rockies in 1976. Over the next four years, he played just a few games for the team and spent most of his time in the minors before heading to Europe. After retiring, he settled in Ottawa, played with the local alumni in many charity games, and became involved in minor hockey in the city. He also worked for the *Ottawa Sun* in the circulation department.

Larry Skinner

SKOPINTSEV, Andrei
b. Elektrostal, Soviet Union (Russia), September 28, 1971

Drafted at age 26, Skopintsev's NHL experiment didn't last long. Before coming to North America, he played pro in Russia and Finland for years and played for Russia at three World Championships. But after a handful of games with Tampa and Atlanta, he returned home to continue his career in more familiar confines, his time on this side of the Atlantic marked by minor-league duty more than NHL glory.

SKORODENSKI, Warren ("Skoro")
b. Winnipeg, Manitoba, March 22, 1960

It was likely the longest suspension ever handed to a goalie, and it occurred in an overtime game in the minors on November 20, 1983. Skorodenski was scored on to lose the game and went after referee Dave Lynch, incensed by the penalty call that gave New Haven a power play it converted. For the assault, Skorodenski was suspended 20 games, and felt sure the lost time would hurt his chances of making it in the NHL. Not so. He played backup the following year in Chicago, but in the coming years his time dwindled and he was used more as a minor-leaguer and callup than regular second-string goalie. He ended his career playing for Canada's National Team, though he never played in any of the major IIHF tournaments.

SKOULA, Martin
b. Litomerice, Czechoslovakia (Czech Republic), October 28, 1979

With singular dedication to making the NHL, Skoula played in the OHL for two years starting in 1997 even before he was drafted. After that first year, Colorado selected him, he joined the Avs at training camp in 1999, and hasn't spent a day in the minors since. Skoula has the ability to be a complete defenceman with the Avs for years to come. He is poised and a good puck carrier, can create chances on offence and play positionally in his own end. Most important of all, through his two years in junior and early years in the NHL, the Avs have noticed a gradual improvement, meaning his best is yet to come and his peak is not in the past. He helped the team win the Cup in 2001, and in the summer took the trophy to Litomerice to share with family and friends.

SKOV, Glen
b. Wheatley, Ontario, January 26, 1931

His brother, Elmer, was owned by the Leafs but never made it to the NHL, and his cousin Art did make it to the big time as a linesman, but when Glen made it he became one of the most durable men in the league. In his 9 full seasons, he missed all of 4 games, once extending an Iron Man streak to 422 before missing the game of February 7, 1957. Skov divided his time fairly evenly between Detroit and Chicago. He began with the Wings in 1950, but the forward was in an awkward situation in that he was a quality player on a team laden with offensive talent. As such, he was asked to become a checking centre, a job at which he excelled, and a penalty killer. Some said he was the best two-way player in the NHL. He wore fingerless white gloves under his hockey gloves because he was allergic to the leather and his hands frequently broke out in a rash. The Wings loved the way he played and he helped the team win three Cups in the first half of the 1950s. He was traded to Chicago in the summer of 1955 and finished his career in Montreal. The Habs wanted him to coach their minor-league team in Hull-Ottawa, but they couldn't meet his salary demands and he retired after one season. Skov settled in Chicago and formed a company with Stan Mikita that specialized in manufacturing plastics.

SKRASTINS, Karlis
b. Riga, Soviet Union (Latvia), July 9, 1974

More than his NHL career, which has passed in the ignominious shadows of Nashville since 1998, Skrastins can be proud of helping build an international program in Latvia, having played in three World Championships (1999, 2000, and 2001) for the young and emerging hockey nation. The team remains in the lower half of the top nations but seems on the cusp of better things, and this defenceman's play will be a contributing factor if Latvia is able to make a breakthrough in the next few years.

SKRBEK, Pavel
b. Kladno, Czechoslovakia (Czech Republic), August 9, 1978

Time is running out on Skrbek if he hopes to make a dent in the NHL annals. To date, he has played just a few games with Pittsburgh and Nashville. It's not a good sign when the Predators send him back to Kiadno for the season, as they did in 2001-02, and it doesn't help matters when Skrbek suffers a concussion, as he did in that season as well.

SKRIKO, Petri
b. Lappeenranta, Finland, March 12, 1962

He may have played for four teams in the NHL, but three were at the end of his career and meaningless compared to the seven years he spent in Vancouver. Skriko was a small, fast winger for the Canucks, one of their top goal getters, and a fan favourite through much of the 1980s. He had 4 successive 30-goal seasons with the team, and in one 8-day stretch in November 1986 he had 2 hat tricks and a 4-goal game. Skriko also played extensively for the Finnish national team, and in 1993, when his NHL days were done, he moved to Denmark to play. He spent six years with the Herning club, and when he retired in 1999 he stayed on with the team as its successful coach.

SKRUDLAND, Brian
b. Peace River, Alberta, July 31, 1963

The epithets tied to Skrudland's name are not pretty, but they are admirable: gritty, grinder, relentless, playoff performer, never-say-die attitude. Despite these qualities, he was never drafted after finishing junior in Saskatoon. Desperate, he joined Dave King's National Team in the fall of 1983, hoping to stay through the Olympics. Instead, he was the last cut at camp, and months later, after a fourth-place finish in Sarajevo, King admitted that releasing Skrudland was his biggest mistake. Skrudland signed with Montreal, and the Habs assigned him to Nova Scotia, where for two years he worked his tail off. He made the big team in 1985, and at the end of his rookie season he was holding the Stanley Cup. He was later claimed by Florida

Warren Skorodenski

Martin Skoula

Glen Skov

Karlis Skrastins

Petri Skriko

Peter Skudra

John Slaney

John Sleaver

in the 1993 Expansion Draft and was the first captain in Panthers history. Skrudland put his mark on the team and led by example, and they surprised everyone by making it to the finals in 1996. He won his second Cup in Dallas in 1999, and after retiring a year later joined Calgary as an assistant coach. In 2002, his number 10 was retired by the Blades in honour of his outstanding junior career.

SKUDRA, Peter
b. Riga, Soviet Union (Latvia), April 24, 1973
Finding a team to play goal for has as much to do with timing as skill. After spending three years in the minors, Skudra signed with Pittsburgh but never solidified his position with the team because there was always a number-two goalie breathing down his back. The emergence of Jean-Sebastien Aubin allowed the Penguins to let Skruda go, and when he signed with Buffalo in 2000 he couldn't beat Martin Biron as Dominik Hasek's backup. Boston claimed him and he had a solid chance to play, but had only 6 wins in 26 games and that was the end of the line there. With the Rangers in 2001, he hoped to be Mike Richter's backup, but the incredible play of 18-year-old Dan Blackburn meant his release. He signed with Vancouver after Martin Brochu had a weak start, and finally played himself onto the Canucks as a fine backup to starter Daniel Cloutier.

SLANEY, John
b. St. John's, Newfoundland, February 7, 1972
Resilient is the word that best describes Slaney. Since turning pro in 1992, he has yet to play a full season in the NHL, but he keeps on playing and playing. Teams sign him and let him go, give him ice time and send him to the minors. He plays a solid defence, nothing flashy, but he has yet to find the team or situation where he can be a top-six blueliner. Most recently, he has been in Philadelphia, which has the bonus of having both an NHL and AHL team. Slaney won gold with Canada at the 1991 World Juniors and played again the following year before starting his pro career.

SLEAVER, John ("Long John")
b. Copper Cliff, Ontario, August 18, 1934
Tall and slim, Sleaver had a long career with a plethora of teams, making two quick stops in the NHL with Chicago in the 1950s. His best opportunity came around Christmas 1956, when he played for the Hawks on a three-game tryout. He made such a good impression that the team offered him a contract, but just 9 games later he was demoted. A lover of cigars, he was frequently seen enjoying a stogie with little more than a towel around his waist, sitting in his stall

He played on the 1998 Czech Olympic team that won gold in Nagano.
JIRI SLEGR

after a game, relaxing. He played in the minors for 17 years after his junior days in Galt, retiring in 1970 with but 13 NHL games to his credit.

SLEGR, Jiri (née Bubla)
b. Jihlava, Czechoslovakia (Czech Republic), May 30, 1971
Jiri Bubla might well have been the best defenceman to come out of Czechoslovakia. Late in his career, he played for Vancouver in the NHL, but off the ice life was not so simple. He and his wife had a son, Jiri, but Bubla left the family when Jiri Jr. was still young and he never came back. Mrs. Bubla remarried, and Jiri Jr. took the name of his stepfather, Josef Slegr. The genes were good, obviously, for Jiri Slegr turned out to be a great defenceman. He was a star in his home country, and when he got to the NHL, he was drafted by – you guessed it – Vancouver. In the interim, after retiring, Jiri Bubla fell on hard times. In 1987, he was arrested in Vienna for trafficking cocaine, and served four years in an Austrian prison. When he was released, he found a job – as a janitor at the Pacific Coliseum in Vancouver, where his talented young son was just starting out. They crossed paths, the father hoping for reconciliation, the son not at all interested. Over time, Bubla found another job, as a truck driver, and Slegr slowly developed into an NHL-calibre player. The two started talking a little, always about hockey, and Slegr moved on, to Edmonton, Pittsburgh, and Atlanta. He played on the 1998 Czech Olympic team that won gold in Nagano, and he has played in numerous international tournaments, just like his dad.

SLEIGHER, Louis
b. Nouvelle, Quebec, October 23, 1958
There have been many, many bench-clearing brawls over the years, and all of them have been, by definition, violent. But since the advent of television, there has probably been nothing like the Quebec-Montreal brawl in the 1984 playoffs that started toward the end of the second period, when Sleigher viciously blindsided Jean Hamel with a punch that knocked the Montreal player unconscious. A full-scale brawl ensued, the teams went to the dressing rooms, and all was done. The officials, however, didn't notify the players who had been ejected from the game not to return for the third period, and when the teams returned to the ice, there was Sleigher and the others who had received game misconducts. Another, equally violent brawl ensued as a number of Montreal players went after Sleigher. He played the last part of his career in Boston but was forced to retire in 1987 after a serious groin muscle injury he had suffered two years previous did not heal properly.

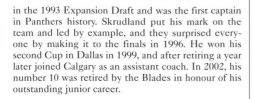

Louis Sleigher

SLOAN, Blake

b. Park Ridge, Illinois, July 27, 1975

The penthouse to the outhouse might not be the best move but if it keeps the career going, well, a player has to do what a player has to do. Sloan came out of the University of Michigan in 1997 with a degree in English and an eye for the NHL. Undrafted, he was signed by Dallas, of all teams. A few weeks later, he was holding the Stanley Cup after he put in a gritty performance in the playoffs as a checking and banging right winger (he had played defence in the minors). He continued on with the Stars for another two years, but in March 2001 he was put on waivers and claimed by Columbus. Within a year he was on the move again, to Calgary, a team with a slew of young players on the rise. Anything but the Jackets.

Blake Sloan

SLOAN, Tod ("Slinker")

b. Pontiac, Quebec, November 30, 1927

When Leafs coach Hap Day went to St. Mike's to watch his future stars play, he saw in Sloan a player with what he considered the hardest, most accurate shot he had ever seen. Sloan led the OHL in scoring in '45-'46, the year after he had helped the Majors win the Memorial Cup, and after a couple of years of seasoning in Pittsburgh he made the jump to the NHL. Sloan was an adept stickhandler and capable of giving and receiving hard checks. His first full year was '50-'51, and he was salient to the team's winning the Cup. In those finals, Toronto and Montreal played five successive overtime games, and but for Sloan it might have been only four. In game five,

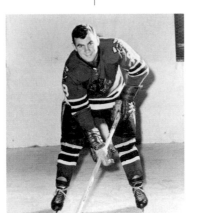

Sloan later operated a taxi business north of Toronto and worked as a sales executive in Keswick for a realtor.
TOD SLOAN

the Leafs trailed 2-1 in the final minute, but with the goalie on the bench, Sloan tied the score to force a record fifth overtime that ended on Bill Barilko's diving, monumental goal. Sloan played all but the last three years of his career in Toronto, but when he helped try to form a players' association he was sent to Chicago, the worst team in the league. In 1961, he was reinstated as an amateur and played for Canada at the 1962 World Championships in Colorado Springs, a tournament made famous because it was the first time the Swedes, en route to gold, had ever beaten Canada in international competition. Sloan later operated a taxi business north of Toronto and worked as a sales executive in Keswick for a realtor. He also owned an hotel in Jackson's Point, and when he sold it he moved across the street to be near a golf course. Recently, he won a gold medal in a GTA senior division tournament.

SLOBODIAN, Pete

b. Dauphin, Manitoba, April 24, 1918
d. November 17, 1986

If you're going to spend only a year in the NHL, it might as well be with the best. Slobodian played '40-'41 with the New York Americans, but his partner on the blueline was none other than Charlie Conacher, converted scoring sensation from the Kid Line in Toronto a few years earlier. Slobodian interrupted his career to join the RCAF, and when he returned to hockey he was sent to the AHL. That he made the pros at all was due in large measure to his sneaky determination. One of eight children, his father was a religious man and believed that hockey was frivolous. Young Pete, therefore, had to sneak out of the house to play hockey, though years later when he became successful his father eased his strict stance on the sport.

SLOWINSKI, Eddie

b. Winnipeg, Manitoba, November 18, 1922
d. Tonawanda, New York, August 21, 1999

Pete Slobodian

Even before he could pursue a pro career, Slowinski entered the war effort, first with the army and then with the navy. During his years in service, he played with the famous Ottawa Commandos that won the 1943 Allan Cup, and then he was all set to make it big with the Rangers in 1947 after leading the Quebec league in scoring the previous season. At camp, though, he hurt his leg, and displayed a bad habit of not training hard. He was sent to the minors to shed some weight before being given a chance with the Rangers, and the next year the pattern repeated itself: weight problems, leg injury, minors. Slowinski got the point and made a determined effort in 1949. He played full-time with the team for four years

Eddie Slowinski

before being farmed out to the AHL for the rest of his playing days. He was never as good as he had been in 1949 with St. Paul, when he led the team to the championship.

SLY, Darryl

b. Collingwood, Ontario, April 3, 1939

While starring in kids hockey in Collingwood, Sly played centre, but when he arrived at St. Michael's College in Toronto, coach Bob Goldham put him on defence. Sly rejected Leafs offers to turn pro in 1958 and instead pursued his dream of teaching. He played for Kitchener-Waterloo and went to teachers' college, and during these years he played for Canada at the 1960 Olympics in Squaw Valley and on the gold-medal team at the 1961 World Championships. It was only then that Sly turned pro. He played for years in Rochester and only a few games with Toronto, Minnesota, and Vancouver. Each year with the Americans he started on defence and was moved up to right wing. They won three Calder Cups in the 1960s with Sly leading the way, and most scouts agreed that that Rochester team could

Darryl Sly

Doug Smail

Richard Smehlik

Al Smith

Alex Smith

have played in the NHL. After his pro days, Sly returned to senior hockey in Barrie, where he played and coached the team. He won the Allan Cup in 1975 and later became a teacher. More recently, he has lived in Collingwood and managed Blue Mountain Chrysler, a car dealership in town.

SMAIL, Doug
b. Moose Jaw, Saskatchewan, September 2, 1957
This might well be the toughest record to break. On December 20, 1981, Smail scored five seconds after the opening faceoff. Two players have since tied the record, but to do it in four seconds would take a hockey miracle. His feat came early in his second season with the Jets, his first badly shortened by two serious injuries (a broken jaw and then thrombosis in his right arm). In all, he spent 11 seasons with the team, becoming a fine scorer and a first-rate penalty killer. Unfortunately, he played in an era when the team was knocked out of the playoffs by Edmonton on an almost annual basis. He finished his career in Britain, and after retiring moved to Arvada, Colorado, where he became president of Hot Hockey Academy, an instructional camp that operates year-round.

SMART, Alex
b. Brandon, Manitoba, May 29, 1918
He started his career with a bang and ended his time in hockey with a flourish, enough to ensure that Smart had an important place in the game he devoted his life to. On January 14, 1943, he made his NHL debut and became the first player to score a hat trick in his first game. Over the next seven games, he registered four more points, yet these turned out to be his only NHL games. He played senior hockey in Montreal and Ottawa, winning the Allan Cup with the Senators in '48-'49, and after retiring he settled in the nation's capital and coached both junior and senior hockey for years. Later, he became a scout for the Los Angeles Kings, and as draft day in 1984 approached he begged management to select a player he had been following and watching. Finally, the day came, and late in the draft, Smart still pleading, the Kings relented. They selected Luc Robitaille in the ninth round.

SMEDSMO, Dale
b. Roseau, Minnesota, April 23, 1951
In February 1973, Smedsmo played in four games for the Leafs, his only NHL games. He went on to play in the WHA and ended his career in the obscurity of the Pacific Hockey League in 1979. He then returned to Minnesota to pursue business interests.

SMEHLIK, Richard
b. Ostrava, Czechoslovakia (Czech Republic), January 23, 1970
A decade with one team is a big deal in the current NHL, so Smehlik's devotion to Buffalo is to be admired. The defenceman came to the Sabres in 1992 as a skating, offensively capable player. Before his arrival, he played at the World Juniors, the World Championships, the 1991 Canada Cup, and the 1992 Olympics in Albertville. He later won gold with the Czechs at the 1998 Olympics in Nagano, and he played on the 2002 team as well. Although he has been a durable player, he missed all of '95-'96 after suffering a serious knee injury in camp that required ACL surgery.

SMILLIE, Don
b. Toronto, Ontario, September 13, 1910
d. unknown
Even though he played at the University of Toronto, Smillie was not highly coveted by Leafs owner Conn Smythe. Instead, Boston signed him and called him up in '33-'34 for a dozen games, and Smillie played just two more years of pro before calling it quits.

SMITH, Al ("The Bear")
b. Toronto, Ontario, November 10, 1945
d. Toronto, Ontario, August 7, 2002
Life promises nothing and delivers less. Live by that motto and you'll never be disappointed. Smith, then, was never disappointed. One summer in the mid-1970s, in the middle of his career, he left his family to live in a motel and write a play. He was hooked, and over the next quarter-century that's all he did with whatever time and money he had. Smith was a goalie going back to 1965 with Toronto and up to 1981 with Colorado. In between, he hit a number of teams in the NHL and WHA, and in 1983 he tried to start an athletic club that cost him most of his savings. He turned to plays and the theatre, and sent scripts out to everyone. Everyone sent them back. When he got a large pension cheque, he invested all of it in the production of *Confessions of Anne Sexton*, a play that bombed. To support himself, he drove a cab for more than 13 years. When he died, no one remembered his plays and few remembered his saves, but he was here and he tried to make his mark.

SMITH, Alex ("Boots")
b. Liverpool, England, April 2, 1902
d. Ottawa, Ontario, November 29, 1963
One of Ottawa's finest athletes of the 1920s and 1930s, Smith played most of his hockey career in that city with the Senators on defence. In '26-'27, his third

Because Smith was the last New York player to touch the puck, he was credited with the goal, the first time an NHL goalie had made the scoresheet as a scorer.
BILLY SMITH

season, he won what was to be his only Stanley Cup, and when the Senators disbanded he signed with Boston, pairing on the blueline with Lionel Hitchman. He finished his career with the Americans and then turned to coaching, leading the great Ottawa Commandos team of '42-'43 to the Allan Cup. He later coached the senior Senators in the Quebec league. He was also a noted curler and golfer and played for the Rideaus football club in his youth.

SMITH, Art
b. Toronto, Ontario, November 29, 1906
d. Toronto, Ontario, May 15, 1962
There was a good reason why Smith was in training camp with Ottawa in 1930 and not in Toronto, where he had played the previous three seasons. He and Eric Pettinger and $35,000 were transferred to the Senators, and in return Toronto acquired King Clancy. It was the richest, greatest deal in hockey history to that point. Smith played just one season with the Sens and returned to Toronto. He started Art Smith Construction Supply Co., a very successful interest that ran until the day he died.

SMITH, Barry
b. Surrey, British Columbia, April 25, 1955
Not to be confused with the Detroit assistant coach, this Barry Smith played briefly with Boston and Colorado, the common denominator being coach Don Cherry. Smith spent most of his years in the AHL, primarily with Rochester, and after retiring in 1981 he became a coach in the lowest levels of the pros. More recently, he has worked his way up to the American league.

SMITH, Billy
("Battlin' Billy"/ "Hatchet Man")
b. Perth, Ontario, December 12, 1950
On November 28, 1979, Smith made history without really doing very much. He was in goal for the Islanders, as he was so very often during his career, and the team was playing Colorado. There was a delayed penalty against the Isles, so the Colorado goalie left the net for the extra man as play moved into the Islanders zone. The Rockies got a shot on Smith, who made the save but did not control the puck. Rob Ramage got to it and fired a pass back to his defence partner, who wasn't there. The puck slid into the net, and because Smith was the last New York player to touch the puck, he was credited with the goal, the first time an NHL goalie had made the scoresheet as scorer. Over and above this trivial achievement, Smith was one of the finest playoff goalies of the modern age. Few will remember that he began his career with Los Angeles, winning the Calder Cup in Springfield

in '70-'71 and then playing a few games for the Kings the following year. His time out west was short, though, because the Islanders claimed him in the 1972 Expansion Draft and he spent the rest of his career on Long Island. He had two poor seasons with a weak Islanders team, and then for a dozen years had a record better than .500. More important, he was the goalie of choice for coach Al Arbour in the playoffs. He shared duties in the regular season with Chico Resch, but when winning was on the line, Smith was in the net. He won four straight Cups with the team, and took home the Vezina Trophy in '81-'82 and the Conn Smythe Trophy the following year. Smith led the league in playoff appearances and victories for five straight seasons, but his forte wasn't really his goals-against average or shutouts – it was, simply, allowing fewer goals than the guy at the other end. He also controlled the area in front of his net with greater vigour than anyone previously. An opponent who tried to screen him or get in the way to deflect a puck was greeted by a thundering slash across the ankles. Despite being the player who was supposed to be untouchable, Smith also got into fights almost as often as his forwards, mixing it up with the tough players to make his point that he was not a target subject to abuse – he would dish it out, too. He was much admired by his teammates and loved by fans, but elsewhere he was, of course, vilified for his stick swinging. In the end, he had a playoff record of 88-36, one of the best win percentages since expansion in 1967. Smith retired in 1989 and stayed with the team as goalie coach. On February 20, 1993, his number 31 was retired by the team, and later that year he was inducted into the Hockey Hall of Fame. That fall, he moved to Florida to work with the Panthers as their goaltending coach, a position he held until 2000.

SMITH, Bobby
b. North Sydney, Nova Scotia, February 12, 1958
Big and tall but not at all tough, Smith would happily go into corners to stir up trouble and then skate backward away from the fray, content to talk the talk but unwilling to walk the walk. He had a superb junior career in the 1970s, setting the mark of 192 points in a season with Ottawa before being drafted 1st overall by Minnesota in 1978. He delivered on his high selection immediately, scoring 30 goals as a rookie and winning the Calder Trophy. He helped the North Stars get to the 1981 finals before they were hammered by the New York Islanders, and the year after Smith had his best statistical season, scoring 43 goals and totalling 114 points. He was later traded to Montreal, where the Habs won the Cup in 1986 thanks to the goaltending of

Art Smith

Barry Smith

He helped the North Stars get to the 1981 finals before they were hammered by the New York Islanders.
BOBBY SMITH

Patrick Roy, and he ended his career in Minnesota by scoring just 5 goals at age 35 in '92-'93. Smith played more than 1,000 games and recorded more than 1,000 points. He scored more than one-third of his goals on the power play and while he was no defensive specialist, he was a talented scorer. He played in four All-Star Games, and after retiring worked his way through the managerial ranks to become GM of Phoenix from 1997 to 2000, when Wayne Gretzky took control of the team and fired him on day two of the new regime. In 1998 the Ottawa 67's retired Smith's number 15. He had moved to that city as a baby, and later attended U of O to study chemistry and psychology before going into medicine. Hockey, though, became too great a lure. Although he has now been retired for a decade he looks to be the only 1,000-point player who might never be inducted into the Hockey Hall of Fame.

SMITH, Brad ("Motor City Smitty")

Brian Smith (b. 1937)

b. Windsor, Ontario, April 13, 1958

Nobody who skated in the NHL for even a game – or for 1,000 – worked as hard or with so little natural talent as Smith. No one persevered, fought in the face of defeat, and gave that proverbial 110 percent more than Smitty. Tall, tough, and determined, he bowled his body through nine seasons of NHL hockey, his finest two years his last, with Toronto, where fans cheered him because of his bare-bones effort. He started in 1978 with Vancouver, and wherever he went the minors were sure to follow. Through 5 years in the Detroit system, he played a scant 63 games with the Wings, and even with Toronto he wasn't a regular. But Toronto fans appreciated his honest effort, his fighting, checking style, and even his occasional goal. One fan was Fred Fisher, a racer of horses who owned Wendelmania and King of the Wing (for Wendel Clark). He named a two-year-old colt Motor City Smitty in the player's honour. When he retired, Smith was respected and appreciated. He coached at Windsor, his stomping ground in junior, and later became a scout with Colorado, winning the Cup in 2001. Imagine: Motor City Smitty with his name on the Stanley Cup! If that can happen, hockey is capable of fairy-tale endings and miracle finishes.

SMITH, Brandon

b. Hazelton, British Columbia, February 25, 1973

Smith can definitely be called a career minor-leaguer now that he has hit the big three-oh. He has made three guest appearances with Boston since 1998, but since signing with San Jose he has been right back where he started – the AHL. Undrafted, he signed into the East Coast league in 1994 and then signed with Detroit, where he played four years in the AHL without a single callup to the Wings.

Imagine:
Motor City Smitty with his name
on the Stanley Cup!
BRAD SMITH

SMITH, Brian

b. Creighton Mine, Ontario, December 6, 1937

Of the more than 60 Smiths in the NHL's past and present, more than a few are related. Brian came from father Stu, but he played only parts of three seasons with Detroit between 1957 and '61. Beyond that, he had a decade-long career in the minors, though it was almost cut short in 1962 when he suffered a fractured skull after being checked hard during a game in the AHL.

SMITH, Brian

b. Ottawa, Ontario, September 6, 1940
d. Ottawa, Ontario, August 2, 1995

The whims of a sick and demented individual stole Smith's life for no good reason whatsoever. He came from a hockey family of the first order. His dad, Des, played in the NHL, as did his brother, Gary, and nephew, Roger. Brian played mostly in the minors but made it to the NHL in 1967 with Los Angeles and Minnesota a year later. He retired in 1973 and immediately joined CJOH, an Ottawa TV station. He was efficient, popular, pleasant, married to a reporter, and an outstanding member of the community. On August 2, 1995, he left the station as he had for 22 years and while walking through a parking lot was shot in the head by a man with a .22-calibre rifle who was angry with the media and wanted to hurt someone.

SMITH, Carl "Winky"

b. Cache Bay, Ontario, September 18, 1917
d. Omaha, Nebraska, January 9, 1967

Like more than 150 other players, Smith got his start at St. Mike's in Toronto. He embarked on a pro career that took him to Detroit for a few games during the war, but it was in Omaha that he left his longest-lasting mark. He played for the Knights for four seasons, and after retiring in 1949 he lived in the city the rest of his life. His brother, Nakina, also played in the NHL.

SMITH, Clinton "Clint" ("Snuffy")

b. Assiniboia, Saskatchewan, December 12, 1913

Playing junior in Saskatchewan, Smith was quickly recognized as a superior playmaking centreman. He was not small and he played the game as cleanly as anyone ever did, but the Rangers were impressed with him and at age 18 he was at their training camp in Lake Placid. The Blueshirts assigned him to Springfield, and at the time he was the youngest player in the pro ranks. He moved to Vancouver a year later, in 1933, to play for the Lions, and immediately fell in love with the city. He stayed three years, but in 1936 the Rangers wanted him move east to monitor his progress more closely. They put him into two games that year – he scored a goal – and the next year

Brian Smith (b. 1940)

he centred a line featuring Cecil Dillon and Lynn Patrick. He scored 14 goals as a rookie and did not incur a single penalty. The year after, he had 21 goals and won the Lady Byng Trophy for his gentlemanly play, and in '39-'40 he helped the Rangers win the Stanley Cup. Smith was traded to Chicago in 1943 and in his first year with the Hawks set a new NHL record with 49 assists playing on a line with Bill Mosienko and Doug Bentley. On November 11, 1943, Smith made history. With Boston trailing Chicago 5-4 late in the game, Bruins coach Art Ross pulled goaler Bert Gardiner for an extra attacker. This strategy had been tried only a handful of times, but when Smith scored into the empty net, he became the first NHLer to do so. He also won the Lady Byng again this year, becoming the first player to win the trophy with two teams.

A year later, he scored four goals in a period, an NHL record that has been tied a number of times since, but never bettered. Smith played three more years with Chicago, but ailing knees forced him to retire – sort of. He coached in the USHL, but feeling better, he also played. Years later, he rued his decision to leave the NHL, feeling that his knees had more to give. After retiring for good in 1952, Smith moved to Vancouver, the city that had so impressed him. He first worked at a gas station and then became involved in the import business. Despite great success over 16 years, he left to become a sales rep for Guardian Chemical, the job he held until retiring in 1965. During his years in Vancouver, Smith also stayed involved in hockey in an important way. For six years he served as president of the British Columbia Benevolent Hockey Association, an organization that helped former players who were down on their luck and in need of assistance. In 1991, he was inducted into the Hockey Hall of Fame as a Veteran Player, his contributions long ago but not forgotten.

When Smith scored into the empty net, he became the first NHLer to do so.
CLINT SMITH

SMITH, Dallas
b. Hamiota, Manitoba, October 10, 1941
The paradox of Smith's career is that when the Bruins were a lousy team in the early 1960s, he couldn't make the grade, but when they became a Cup team, he was one of their stars. Of course, *star* is a relative term because on Boston's defence there was Bobby Orr and everyone else. Smith was not Orr but he was a capable puckhandler, strong as a bull and rock-solid in his own end. On another team, he would have been a superstar. In Boston, all he did was win two Stanley Cups. His career +/- was +355, including a league-leading +94 in '70-'71. He retired in 1977 after playing for Canada at the World Championships, but his old buddy Phil Esposito, now with the Rangers, talked him out of

retirement for half a season. Once done, Smith settled in Portland to work in construction, and also helped his brother back on the family farm in Hamiota.

SMITH, Dalton "Nakina"
b. Cache Bay, Ontario, July 26, 1913
d. San Diego, California, March 1982
There has been a small number of players who finished their careers in California during the old days of hockey and who lived there the rest of their lives. Smith is one. He played junior in Ontario in the early 1930s and moved on to pro in the American league, and his only NHL games came during the war with Detroit. He moved to L.A. to play for the Monarchs in the PCHL, and after retiring in 1950 he made his home there. He stayed active in the game by working as a minor official at L.A. Blades home games in the WHL and later moved to Hermosa Beach, California.

SMITH, Dan
b. Fernie, British Columbia, October 19, 1976
It looks as if the minors are where Smith will play much of his career. Colorado drafted him 181st overall in 1995, but cracking a Cup-contending team is no easy feat, particularly for a defenceman. Smith has played in a few games for the Avs, but in 2001-02 he played in the anonymity of the West Coast league.

SMITH, Dennis
b. Detroit, Michigan, July 27, 1964
Although he played 13 years of pro hockey, Smith saw the NHL for just 8 games with Washington and L.A. before retiring in 1997. He was a long-time resident of the AHL and then IHL, winning a Calder Cup with Adirondack in '88-'89. He was owned at various times by four NHL teams.

SMITH, Derek
b. Quebec City, Quebec, July 31, 1954
During most of his career in Buffalo, Smith was by turns an exciting player and an injured one. Twice he reached the 20-goal mark ('79-'80 and '80-'81) but three seasons were shortened by bad health. He broke his jaw, pulled stomach muscles, and then damaged his right shoulder, injuries that slowed him down. He finished his career in the Detroit organization, first with the Wings and then with Adirondack in the minors.

SMITH, Derrick
b. Scarborough, Ontario, January 22, 1965
No one ever came home after a game raving about having seen Smith play, but he was a genuine, NHL player. He lacked skill but had the tenacity and ambition to succeed in the big league, and this desire overcame the

Dallas Smith

Dan Smith

Dennis Smith

Derek Smith

Derrick Smith

D.J. Smith

Don Smith

Doug Smith

Floyd Smith

skill issue without doubt. He joined Philadelphia in 1984 and contributed as a checker and hitter, using his size and quickness to good effect. He was invited to Team Canada's training camp in 1987, and although he was cut the invite alone spoke volumes about his reputation. He had three great playoff runs in the 1980s, going to the finals in '87, when the Flyers lost to the Oilers. After joining the Minnesota/Dallas franchise, Smith finished his playing days in the minors.

SMITH, Des
b. Ottawa, Ontario, February 22, 1914
d. Ottawa, Ontario, September 26, 1981
Playing in the 1930s in Ottawa meant playing for the Montagnards if you were anybody, and Smith most certainly was. He turned pro down east and then went to England for a number of years as the hockey craze first made its way to the U.K. When Smith returned home, in 1937, he turned pro with the Maroons, but a year later the team folded and the Canadiens claimed him. He was sent to the minors midway through the season and played for Chicago and Boston, joining the Bruins in time to contribute to their 1941 Stanley Cup. Like many, Smith cut his career short to join the war, which meant serving as a lieutenant in the Canadian Infantry Corps. After retiring from the game, Smith became a referee in the AHL for a number of seasons before returning to Ottawa. He started frequenting the Rideau Carleton Raceway in 1962, and because the PA system was so poor he would call the race in one corner of the stands for kids who couldn't hear the announcer. This got the attention of the general manager, and Smith began a 21-year tenure as caller for the track as he watched his sons Gary and Brian go on to play in the NHL.

SMITH, D.J.
b. Windsor, Ontario, May 13, 1977
The former captain of the Windsor Spitfires has been playing pro since 1997 but has seen precious little NHL ice. A big, heavy-hitting defenceman, he came to Toronto with Wendel Clark from the Islanders, but neither Toronto nor any other club has played him for any stretch of time. The Leafs called him up twice because of injuries and demoted him a like number of times when said injuries had healed.

SMITH, Don
b. Cornwall, Ontario, June 3, 1888
d. unknown
A star in the NHA in Montreal, Smith played his only NHL games with the Canadiens in 1919-20 after being discharged from the army. It was his final year of pro hockey.

SMITH, Don
b. Regina, Saskatchewan, May 4, 1929
As a halfback playing high-school football with Scott Collegiate in Regina, Smith was besieged with scholarship offers from U.S. colleges to play the pigskin game, but he rejected one and all so he might do as his older brother, Ken, did – play in the NHL. He so desperately wanted to make it, he actually cried and begged the New York Rovers coach, Phil Watson, to give him a chance to play. The result helped get him to the Rangers for 11 games, but the rest of Smith's long career passed in the minors. He scored a goal in his first game, on February 26, 1950, his only career NHL goal.

SMITH, Doug
b. Ottawa, Ontario, May 17, 1963

Like many, Smith cut his career short to join the war.
DES SMITH

From a personal point of view, Smith made it to the NHL and played in 535 games. From an organizational point of view, Los Angeles blew it big time when the Kings drafted Smith 2nd overall in 1981. Second overall is a spot for superstars and Hall of Famers, and Smith definitely did not fit that bill. He had a good junior career with the 67's in Ottawa, but the Kings were expecting much more than just good. They traded him to Buffalo early in 1986, but soon he was on the road again to three other teams in the next three seasons. Smith finished his career playing in Austria.

SMITH, Floyd ("Smitty")
b. Perth, Ontario, May 16, 1935
When he was just a boy, Smith was blind for 10 months after a homemade arrow struck him in the eye. He got better and went on to play hockey, devoting himself to a game he has loved all his life. Smith started in the pro ranks nearly half a century ago, joining Boston for a few games in '54-'55. Over the next decade, he played in the minors more than the NHL, his best times coming with Detroit in the years leading to expansion. Smith was later traded to Toronto and Buffalo, and in both cities he got to know Punch Imlach. He retired early in the '71-'72 season after being the first captain of the Sabres in order to go to the farm team in Cincinnati and become a coach, and in 1974 he moved up to Buffalo as the head man. In 1979, he followed Imlach to Toronto, and after the demise of the ill-fated second coming of Punch, Smith worked for the Leafs as a scout. During that time, he was under further personal duress. On March 14, 1980, while still coach, he was charged with drunk driving after an accident that caused the death of two people in the other car. He was later cleared of those charges and stayed with the Leafs, rising to the unsavoury position of GM in 1989, a post he held for two tumultuous seasons. Smith stayed on to become the team's head of scouting.

SMITH, Gary ("Ax"/ "Suitcase")
b. Ottawa, Ontario, February 4, 1944

He came up from Ottawa to play goal at St. Mike's in 1961 and ended up playing for the Marlies and winning the Memorial Cup in 1964. Smith got his nickname, Suitcase, because he moved around the NHL and minors, and got his other – Ax – because of the way he brandished his stick. He was a big man and very capable, and after expansion he had some very fine years. In '74-'75, with Vancouver, he played 72 games and had 6 shutouts in helping the Canucks to the division title. He played in that year's All-Star Game, the only one of his career, and three years earlier shared the Vezina Trophy with Tony Esposito, though Tony was the main man in goal that year. In all, Smith appeared in 532 games, though he rarely played for Cup-contending teams. He played briefly in the WHA, with Winnipeg, though long enough to win the Avco Cup in 1979. Smith finished his career in the minors with Tulsa, and in one game he actually played as a forward. In his first year of retirement, he scouted for the Jets and then worked at a racetrack in Phoenix. After a nasty divorce, he returned to Ottawa to work in the sheriff's office, though he later relocated to Vancouver and renewed his interest in thoroughbred racing. His father, Des, was also an NHLer and a noted track enthusiast, and brother Brian also made it to the NHL.

SMITH, Geoff
b. Edmonton, Alberta, March 7, 1969

As a rookie, Smith made the Oilers for the '89-'90 season, a fortuitous time to start an NHL career. At season's end, he was holding the Stanley Cup, and as so often happens, he never came close to winning again. He was part of Florida in '95-'96 when the team went to the finals, but he missed much of the year with injury. Smith was a strong defenceman in his own end and let his teammates worry about scoring and creating offence. He played for Canada at the WJC in his final year of junior before joining Edmonton, and he also played for his country at the 1993 World Championships. He retired in 1999 after spending most of that last season in the minors.

SMITH, Glen
b. Lucky Lake, Saskatchewan, March 19, 1931

A mere blip on the NHL screen, playing twice with Chicago in '50-'51, Smith was a legend in Moose Jaw, where he played senior hockey for a number of years between the war and expansion.

SMITH, Glenarvon Grafton "Glenn"
b. Woodstock, Ontario, April 25, 1895
d. unknown

After spending his childhood in Woodstock, Smith moved to Toronto where he played hockey until joining the Canadian Army Dental Corps. After being discharged, he returned to Toronto and played 9 games with the St. Pats, the last pro games of his career.

SMITH, Gord
b. Perth, Ontario, November 17, 1949

Gord, Jack, and Billy were three hockey-playing brothers who aspired to play in the NHL. Jack made it as far as the minors; Billy made it to the Hockey Hall of Fame, slashing and hacking his way to fame and infamy both; Gord made it, but to a lesser degree than Billy. Gord was an original Washington Capitals defenceman. He had played in the L.A. system, winning the AHL's best defenceman honours in '73-'74, but didn't make it to the NHL until the Caps claimed him. He survived the rigours and battles of that team's blueline for an incredible five years. He then played for Winnipeg in its first NHL season, '79-'80, and ended up in the minors having never made it to the NHL playoffs.

SMITH, Greg
b. Ponoka, Alberta, July 8, 1955

Quietly and with little fanfare, Smith played in the NHL for 13 years, though had a shot of his been 2 inches to one side of the post, he would have been a hero rather than just another defenceman. Smith played for Washington in the 1987 playoffs when the Caps took the Islanders to game seven. The game was tied 2-2 and went into overtime, and Smith hit the post in the first OT. Things then went from bad to worse. He broke his kneecap in the second OT, and in the fourth OT, the Islanders prevailed and the Caps were eliminated in one of the longest games ever played. Smith's finest previous playoff experience came in 1981 with Minnesota when the North Stars reached the finals against the Islanders. He also played for Canada at two World Championships, in 1977 and '79.

SMITH, Jason
b. Calgary, Alberta, November 2, 1973

Seeing Smith on the Edmonton blueline today makes you wonder why neither New Jersey nor Toronto wanted to make this guy the core of their bluelines. Tough as nails, big and composed, he is an old-time defenceman in the modern game. He'll be lucky to score a goal a year and even luckier to see the power play, but he'll play half the game and the other team won't score while he's on the ice. After winning gold with Canada at the 1993 World Juniors, he played four seasons with the Devils before they sent him to the Leafs in a big deal to acquire Doug Gilmour. He developed into a first-rate player with the Leafs, but they gave up on him and sent him to Edmonton for two draft choices. Out west, he became a leader of a

Geoff Smith

Gord Smith

Greg Smith

Jason Smith

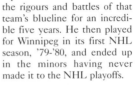

He played briefly in the WHA, with Winnipeg, though long enough to win the Avco Cup in 1979.
GARY SMITH

Kenny Smith

young and evolving team, and in 2001 he became team captain. As Smith goes, so go the Oilers.

SMITH, Kenny ("Danny")
b. Moose Jaw, Saskatchewan, May 8, 1924
d. Lancaster, Pennsylvania, September 23, 2000
At 5'7" and 155 pounds, Smith was forever tagged with the epithet "little" before his name. Despite his size, he was tough as nails and particularly resilient, once, in fact, playing 237 consecutive games. He had a brother, Don, who made the NHL, and another, Bunny, who played in leagues below the NHL, but from almost the day he joined the Bruins in 1944 he was called Danny because of his resemblance to Danny Kaye. He played on Boston's first line with Paul Ronty and Johnny Peirson and scored 20 goals on 2 occasions during his 7 seasons in the Hub. After he passed out of the NHL, he played another seven seasons in the American league, finishing with Hershey in 1956. He settled in Mount Joy, Pennsylvania, near Hershey, and opened a sporting goods store that flourished for years.

SMITH, Mark
b. Edmonton, Alberta, October 24, 1977
Eyebrow, Saskatchewan, was where Smith grew up and where his family lives, a village of 150 souls with one of Canada's great names. Smith played junior in Lethbridge, was drafted by San Jose, and has been with the Sharks since playing his first game at the start of the 2000-01 season. In his free time, he's axeman for the Epic Latitudes, a band that performs regularly in the off-season.

He settled in Detroit and worked for Ford in the personnel department.
NORMIE SMITH

SMITH, Nick
b. Hamilton, Ontario, March 23, 1979
Who knows where Smith will end up playing at any given time? Since turning pro in 1999, he has played for no fewer than six teams, one of those being Florida of the NHL. He stayed with the Panthers for 15 games, but the centre did not register a single point and was returned to the AHL.

SMITH, Normie
b. Toronto, Ontario, March 18, 1908
d. Stuart, Florida, February 2, 1988
At 16, Smith stopped playing hockey when he got the chance to move out west and work. He toiled on fishing fleets going up and down the Pacific from Vancouver to Alaska, but at 20 he got back into the game when the Maroons wanted him in their organization. Within two years he was playing in the NHL, in 1931, with the Maroons, but three years later when he was traded to Detroit his career took off. His greatest claim to fame was his first playoffs with the Wings in 1936, when he was the goalie for the team's historic 1-0 win over the Maroons after six overtime periods. He recorded a

Hooley Smith

shutout in game two, and when Montreal finally scored in the third game Smith had run his record streak to 248:32 without allowing a goal. Smith won the Cup with Detroit that season and next, when he also won the Vezina Trophy. He retired early in the '38-'39 season, though he returned in an emergency during the war for a few games. He settled in Detroit and worked for Ford in the personnel department. After retiring from the labour force, he moved to Stuart, Florida, where he spent the final 20 or so years of his life.

SMITH, Randy
b. Saskatoon, Saskatchewan, July 7, 1965
The NHL is the be-all and end-all for some players, and it's completely insignificant to the careers of others. On the one hand, Smith played just three NHL games, with Minnesota, which doesn't sound very good. On the other hand, he played pro for 15 years. Impressive. He split those years fairly evenly between the minors in North America and British league hockey until retiring in 2000. He also played for Canada on three occasions, twice at the World Championships (1991 and '92) and at the 1992 Olympics in Albertville.

SMITH, Reginald "Hooley"
b. Toronto, Ontario, January 7, 1903
d. Montreal, Quebec, August 24, 1963
One of 13 children born in the Beach, an east-end part of Toronto on Lake Ontario, Smith excelled at any number of sports growing up. He was a first-rate paddler, a star football player, an amateur lacrosse star, and, of course, a fine hockey player. He earned his nickname from Happy Hooligan, a popular cartoon of the day, and happily accepted the shortened Hooley over Reginald. Smith played hockey in the Beach before moving up to the Toronto Granites, a superb amateur team that included the likes of Beattie Ramsay, Dunc Munro, Harry Watson, and Bert McCaffery. The team won the Allan Cup in 1923 and went on to represent Canada at the 1924 Olympics, the first official Olympic Winter Games, held at Chamonix. This team steamrolled the competition and won a gold medal uncontested, and upon their return the players were showered with offers to turn professional. Some accepted, others demurred. Smith joined the Ottawa Senators that fall and began a 17-year career in the NHL, retiring in 1941 as the longest-serving player in the league to date. In his third year with the Sens, he led the team to the Cup, but not without a price. He was a talented player who combined with Frank Nighbor and Cy Denneny as the best two-way line the league had ever seen. All were highly capable scorers, but Nighbor and Smith particularly were good at the

sweep check and poke check to gain possession of the puck. Smith, though, also had a temper, and in the finals against Boston it got the better of him. He attacked Harry Oliver with such ferocity that league president Frank Calder banned Smith for the first month of the following season. It was a year that took place in Montreal, as the Maroons purchased Smith from the Bruins for the astronomical price of $22,500. Smith reached his peak with the Maroons, playing on the S Line with Babe Siebert and Nels Stewart to form the most potent threesome in the game. They took the team to the 1935 Stanley Cup (with Smith as captain), but after another season the line was split up. Siebert went to the Canadiens while Stewart and Smith were sold to Boston. Smith played just one year with the Bruins and finished his career with the Americans, where he played for four seasons. He ended his career with exactly 200 goals, a magic plateau for the day akin to the modern 500-goal mark, and was one of only a few players to have 1,000 penalty minutes. He returned to Montreal where he found it difficult to adjust to life after hockey. He owned his own business, manufacturing soaps and assorted cleaning products, and later worked in a brokerage house and ran his own pool hall. His daughter, Barbara, was a nurse at St. Mary's Hospital, and was shocked one Saturday afternoon in 1963 when ambulance attendants brought in her father, Hooley, who had suffered a heart attack while watching a baseball game. He died just a couple of hours later, never having made it into the Hockey Hall of Fame, an honour that was finally conferred upon him nine years later.

SMITH, Rick
b. Kingston, Ontario, June 29, 1948
For Smith, education came first, pucks second. He could do both, and managed to combine school and hockey into one successful life. A superb defenceman, he had the fortune to play with the Bruins in their prime, winning a Cup in 1970 before being traded to Charlie Finley's sad-sack team out west. Smith bolted to the WHA in 1973 and returned to the NHL only when St. Louis acquired his rights (or, more properly, when he was no longer obligated to the Seals). He had a great reputation for his defensive ability, and when he rejoined the Bruins they again achieved great things, doing everything but win another Cup toward the end of the 1970s. Smith had always wanted to become a doctor or a dentist, and by the time he retired he had finished his B.A. at McMaster University in Hamilton. He lived on a marina in Buck Lake, north of Kingston, while he finished his master's degree in computer science, and then stayed on at Queen's University as a professor, teaching that very subject.

SMITH, Rodger
b. Ottawa, Ontario, July 26, 1897
d. Ottawa, Ontario, January 30, 1935
A longtime referee, Smith was coming home from a game in Cardinal, Ontario, when his car stalled. He contracted a chill while servicing it and the chill turned into pneumonia. A week later, he was dead. Smith started out in Ottawa before joining the Pittsburgh Yellowjackets in 1923. When the team joined the NHL two years later, he did, too. In fact, he was one of only five players to play for the Pirates in all five years they were in the National league. He finished his career with another defunct team, the Philadelphia Quakers, and then retired to his home in Ottawa, where he died suddenly just three years later.

In game two of the finals against Detroit, he scored all three goals in a 3-1 win.
SID SMITH

SMITH, Ron
b. Port Hope, Ontario, November 19, 1952
After winning the Memorial Cup with Cornwall in 1972, Smith played in the Islanders organization, appearing in 11 games with the team the next year. He coached in Guelph after retiring, taking the Platers to a league championship in '77-'78. It was the start of a coaching career that continues to this day. Smith worked his way up in New York to coach the Rangers in '92-'93 as Roger Neilson's replacement. He then coached Cincinnati in the IHL for six years and most recently has been the boss of Lowell in the AHL.

SMITH, Sid ("Muff")
b. Toronto, Ontario, July 11, 1925
If ever there were a case for belated inclusion into the Hockey Hall of Fame, Smith would be it. By the time he retired in December 1957, only 3 active players had scored more goals than his total of 186 – Gordie Howe, Maurice Richard, and Ted Lindsay. He was one of a select few to score 20 or more goals in 6 successive seasons, and in 7 of 8 full years he played in the All-Star Game. He came up to Toronto for a short stay in '46-'47, and over the next two years proved himself a superb left winger. He had great speed, a terrific shot, and was counted among the best rebounders and getters of loose pucks the game had ever seen. He was also durable, putting together an Iron Man streak of more than 400 games. He made his first significant impression in the 1949 playoffs after a year in the minors in which he set a record for goals (55) and led the league in goals and points (112). In game two of the finals against Detroit, he scored all three goals (all on the power play) in a 3-1 win and prompted Gordie Howe to ask the now-famous question to a reporter afterwards, "Who's Sid Smith?" Playing on a line with Ted Kennedy and Bill Ezinicki, he continued to score, helping the Leafs to three Cups. When Kennedy

Rick Smith

Ron Smith

retired, Smith was named team captain. He retired to go back to senior amateur hockey in Whitby, becoming playing coach of the Dunlops. He led the team, as Canada's representatives, to a gold medal at the 1958 World Championships, and retired after one more season. Smith went on to work for a paper mill in Quebec and then in the photography industry before returning to Toronto to retire to private life.

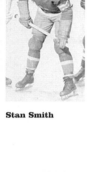

SMITH, Stan
b. Coal Creek, British Columbia, August 13, 1917
A standout scorer as a teen in Rossland, Smith was recruited by the Rangers in 1938 and assigned to the Rovers. After a fine year in the minors, he received a one-game callup to the NHL team when Clint Smith was injured, but after eight more games the following year he was out of the NHL. He ended his career with San Francisco in the PCHL.

Stan Smith

SMITH, Steve
b. Trenton, Ontario, April 4, 1963
The Philadelphia Flyers could not believe that Smith was available when it came time for their selection at the 1981 Entry Draft. They snapped him up and declared themselves the official winners of the draft right there and then. They called him a fireplug, and at 5'9" and 214 pounds Smith was just that. They called the son of a fireman a killer, a force, and other things having to do with strength and intimidation. And, after seven years in the Flyers system, they called him to say that Buffalo had claimed him in the Waiver Draft. In the interim, he played but 15 games with the team, and with the Sabres he played just 3 more times. He later played in the minors and Europe for several years.

SMITH, Steve
b. Glasgow, Scotland, April 30, 1963
Greatness sometimes seems banal compared to infamy, the former something to envy, the latter something that can be perversely rapturous. No matter how great Smith's career and how successful his accomplishments, most fans will think of him first and foremost for game seven against Calgary in the 1986 playoffs. Midway through the third period of a tie game, he made a huge error, putting the puck in his own net and eliminating the Oilers from the playoffs. What made the goal doubly horrible was that Edmonton had won the previous two Cups and would go on to win the next two. The Oilers would have matched Montreal's unprecedented five in a row of the 1950s, establishing their reputation as the greatest among the greats. The Oilers were a team, though, and when they won the Cup in 1987, captain Wayne Gretzky accepted it and immediately put it in the arms of Smith, a tremendous gesture of absolution for the previous year's sin. Over and above that, though, Smith was one of the best defencemen in the game. He was enormous and powerful, a tremendous hitter and fighter when need be, a good skater and passer. He played his finest years with Edmonton, but later played for Chicago and then did the unthinkable by signing with Calgary, the arch-enemy of his once-sacred Oilers. He retired in 1997 and became an assistant coach with the Flames, only to return after a

Stu Smith

Tommy Smith

year's absence, but in January 2000 he suffered a serious neck injury in a game against Los Angeles. Determined, he came back from the injury, but only for a few games before retiring for good.

SMITH, Stu
b. Basswood, Manitoba, September 25, 1918
In a long and successful career, Smith played five games with the Canadiens during the war. Beyond that, he was active in small Ontario towns for many years, starting with Kenora with Babe Pratt and moving up to Kirkland Lake where he helped the Blue Devils win the Allan Cup in 1940. He won another Allan Cup with Ottawa in 1949 and continued to play senior hockey in Smiths Fall, where he was named league MVP in '52-'53. He set up shop as a plumber in that city and worked at that job during the day. Smith also had the pleasure of watching his son, Brian, go on to play in the NHL.

SMITH, Stu
b. Toronto, Ontario, March 17, 1960
Hartford thought it had a gem of a draft in Smith in 1979 after he helped Peterborough win the Memorial Cup just weeks earlier, but over five seasons the big defenceman didn't develop into the force the Whalers had hoped. Instead, he became a solid minor-leaguer worthy of a few callups, in their eyes, and retired in 1985 after just 77 games with the team.

SMITH, Tommy "Tom" ("Bulldog")
b. Ottawa, Ontario, September 27, 1885
d. Ottawa, Ontario, August 1, 1966
One of 13 children, young Tom was educated at St. Patrick's Lyceum in Ottawa until the age of 15. At that point, he left school to apprentice as a machinist in the shop of James Enright, who also coached a team called the Enright Pets. Tom became the star of that team, and his reputation carried far and wide. His brothers, Alfred and Harry, won the Cup with the famous Ottawa Silver Seven, and Tom joined the lesser Vics of the Federal league, though the Senators played him for a few games toward the end of that '05-'06 season. Rather than stay in Ottawa, though, Tom accepted a lucrative offer to play pro in Pittsburgh, where he became the leading scorer. He moved around a fair bit in those days, going where the money was best, but in 1912 he landed with the Quebec Bulldogs after four seasons in Ontario. He played on a line with Jack Marks and Joe Malone, led the team to his only Stanley Cup, and finished second in league scoring behind the great Malone. He later played in Toronto and Montreal, and his only NHL time came with the Bulldogs in 1919-20. Smith was known for his deadly accurate shot. Although he was small and never looked for rough play, he certainly surprised opponents who tried to intimidate him. In the summers, he always returned home to work as a machinist, and during the war years, he and Malone worked as such at a Quebec munitions plant. Smith married, and although his wife died, he settled in Ottawa where he worked for the National Research Council after retiring from hockey for good in 1920. He passed away in hospital after a severe bout of pneumonia. He was inducted into the Hockey Hall of Fame in 1973, where he joined brother Alf who had been inducted in 1962.

SMITH, Vern
b. Winnipeg, Manitoba, May 30, 1964
Coaching in minor hockey is what Smith has done with a career that took him to the Islanders for one game. That was in '84-'85, after which he played in the AHL and IHL for a number of years before a knee injury slowly ended his career. He settled in New England in 1992 and coached in the state's junior Coyotes system with kids in their early teens.

SMITH, Wayne
b. Kamsack, Saskatchewan, February 12, 1943
One of the finest defencemen to graduate from the University of Denver, in 1966, Smith started his pro career the following season with Chicago. He had a goal and an assist in his two games with the Hawks, but after two seasons in the minors, Smith retired.

SMITH, Wyatt
b. Thief River Falls, Minnesota, February 13, 1977
After leading the University of Minnesota Gophers in scoring in his final two years of college, Smith attended Phoenix's training camp in the fall of 1999. To date, he's seen action primarily in the minors, with Springfield, though he has been called up in each of his first three seasons in a bid to stay with the team. For now, he remains a prospect.

SMOLINSKI, Bryan
b. Toledo, Ohio, December 27, 1971
Good skills and excellent instinct were the two qualities most coaches liked about Smolinski, and for a number of years these helped him produce fine NHL seasons. He graduated from Michigan State in 1993 and joined Boston right away. In his first full season, he scored 31 goals, but time would tell this was beginner's luck more than portent of things to come. Although he has scored 20 goals 3 other times since then, each of those seasons came with a different team. In 2001-02, he scored just 13 goals with Los Angeles, and compliments such as "useful" and "versatile" replaced "skilled" and "great instinct." He was traded to Ottawa during the frenzy that was the deadline in March 2003. The highlight of his career came in the fall of 1996 when he played for Team USA and won the World Cup. Smolinski has also played at two World Championships for the U.S. and at one WJC.

SMREK, Peter
b. Martin, Czechoslovakia (Slovakia), February 16, 1979
Determined to play in the NHL, Smrek did the unusual by playing in the USHL in '98-'99 to showcase his talents and prove himself worthy. In the middle of that season, he went to Winnipeg to play for Slovakia at the World Juniors, winning an historic gold

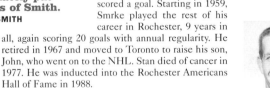
When they won the Cup in 1987, captain Wayne Gretzky accepted it and immediately put it in the arms of Smith.
STEVE SMITH

with the young nation. Since being drafted, though, he has played just a few games with St. Louis and the Rangers, though he is still young enough to make his way to the NHL full time.

SMRKE, John
b. Chicoutimi, Quebec, February 25, 1956
During his NHL days, Smrke was more proud of his Memorial Cup with the Marlies from 1975 than he was excited about ever winning a Stanley Cup one day. Good thing, because he never got much of a chance at Lord Stanley's bowl, playing parts of two seasons with St. Louis and a third with Quebec. Most of his years were spent in the minors, though he did move to Italy to play briefly in the early 1980s. The son of Stan, he grew up in Toronto and started to develop into a true player only after his dad retired and spent hours coaching him on the basics of the game. In the summers, Smrke changed sports and played inter-county baseball with the Toronto Maple Leafs for a number of years.

SMRKE, Stan
b. Belgrade, Yugoslavia, September 2, 1928
d. Toronto, Ontario, April 13, 1977
He was a legend in Chicoutimi and Rochester, and when he played a few games with the Canadiens in the mid-1950s, Smrke became the first Yugoslav-born player to make it to the NHL. The left winger was a fine scorer, and as part of his callup he played in the 1957 All-Star Game – and scored a goal. Starting in 1959, Smrke played the rest of his career in Rochester, 9 years in all, again scoring 20 goals with annual regularity. He retired in 1967 and moved to Toronto to raise his son, John, who went on to the NHL. Stan died of cancer in 1977. He was inducted into the Rochester Americans Hall of Fame in 1988.

SMYL, Stan ("The Steamer")
b. Glendon, Alberta, January 28, 1958
He might not be in the Hockey Hall of Fame in Toronto, but he is number one in the unofficial Vancouver Canucks Hall of Fame. His number 12 hangs in the rafters of GM Place, and for good reason. By the time he retired in 1991, Smyl had played all of his 13 NHL seasons with the team and finished as its all-time leader in games played (896), goals (262), assists (411), and points (673). He played junior in New Westminster, winning Memorial Cups in 1977 and '78 and learning to play a tough and nasty game, characteristics essential for someone of his size (5'8"). At the start of his fifth season with the team he was named captain, a position he held with honour for nine seasons, another team record. The highlight of

Wyatt Smith

Peter Smrek

John Smrke

Stan Smrke

Stan Smyl

Brad Smyth

Greg Smyth

Kevin Smyth

his career was the 1982 playoffs as the Canucks marched to the Cup finals, only to lose to the powerful Islanders. As soon as he retired, he stayed with the team as an assistant coach, and in 1999 he was named head man for their farm team in Syracuse. Since then, he's moved on to Kansas City and most recently to the Manitoba Moose.

SMYLIE, Roderick "Rod"
b. Toronto, Ontario, September 28, 1895
d. Toronto, Ontario, March 3, 1985

For some players, hockey is everything, the thing that keeps them happy and gives them a reason to live. For others, it's a means to an end. Smylie hardly thought about hockey in his youth. He grew up in New Liskeard and played the game, of course, but at 14 he travelled to western Canada and became an itinerant salesman of encyclopedias. He considered hockey seriously only while he was back in Toronto going to university and studying medicine. He captained U of T's Dentals team from 1916 to '20 and was also an exceptional runner, captaining the track and field team as well. Smylie qualified for the 1920 Olympics in Antwerp, but because he was a one-sport athlete he couldn't go. Economics of the day permitted only multi-discipline track stars to travel to Belgium. Instead, Smylie turned professional in hockey, joining the local St. Pats and winning the Cup in his second season, '21-'22. He played until midway through the '25-'26 season, by which time he had become a doctor and could start to practise. For more than 50 years he worked as a GP at St. Michael's Hospital in Toronto, and he reared two sons – Rod Jr. and Doug – who played CFL football for the Toronto Argonauts. In later years he suffered from heart troubles, though he didn't retire from medicine until he was 77. He died in his sleep at home.

SMYTH, Brad
b. Ottawa, Ontario, March 13, 1973

In a decade of pro hockey, there are few players who can match the discrepancy between the minors and the NHL as can Smyth. In the big league, he has played 72 games for 5 teams, signing, being traded, moving around like a castoff. In the AHL, he has been one of the league's top scorers. In '95-'96, he led the league in goals (68) and points (126), and 5 years later he scored 50 goals. He's never scored fewer than 26 goals at any level of the minors, yet he just can't make it in the NHL.

SMYTH, Greg
b. Oakville, Ontario, April 23, 1966

He could fight with the best of them, and he often

did. That's how he survived 14 years of pro hockey, many of those in the NHL. Smyth counted only four goals in his NHL days, never scoring even two in any season. He played more in the minors than in the NHL, but when given the chance he tried to prove himself worthy. He signed with Toronto in 1996 at the end of his career, and again spent most of his time in the minors, with St. John's, though this time with a purpose. He worked his way into a job as assistant coach, and also acted as coach for the Royal Newfoundland Constabulary hockey team after retiring in 1999.

SMYTH, Kevin
b. Banff, Alberta, November 22, 1973

On December 28, 1996, Smyth was playing for Orlando in the IHL when a deflected puck hit him flush in the right eye. The horrifying injury required five operations, but his sight could not be saved and Smyth's hopes of returning to the NHL were virtually over. He had played parts of three seasons with Hartford after being drafted by the Whalers in 1992, two years before his brother was selected by Edmonton. The first thing Kevin did after the injury was to call Ryan and tell him to wear a shield, advice that did not go unheeded. Amazingly, Kevin regained his general health, and, determined to play, made a comeback in the IHL the following year.

Not particularly big, he hit hard, blocked shots, and sacrificed his body.
RYAN SMYTH

SMYTH, Ryan
b. Banff, Alberta, February 21, 1976

Smyth's affiliation with international hockey could not have got off to a worse start. The 11-year-old was a stick boy when Team Canada came to Banff to prepare for the 1987 Canada Cup. After one practice, he was in the parking lot when Glenn Anderson got in his car and, not seeing the kid, backed over his foot. On his way to a golf tournament, Anderson dropped the kid off at the hospital, and doctors discovered only a sore ankle. An ankle, ironically, almost kept Smyth from playing at the 2002 Olympics in Salt Lake City, but much happened between the two injuries. Young Ryan developed into a junior star in Moose Jaw. Yes, he had the numbers, the goals and points and all, but there was more to him than that. Not particularly big, he hit hard, blocked shots, and sacrificed his body. He led by example. He was a team player who would do anything to win. In 1995, he helped Canada capture gold at the World Juniors, and the Oilers drafted him a lofty 6th overall in 1994. From that day to this, he has been the team's best player. In his first full season, he scored 39 goals, but he brought an attitude to the rink that was worth more than just points. He's been an Oilers forward his whole career, and the only blemish on his record is a lack of playoff success. The fallout of this, though, has been remarkable contributions to Canada's international teams. He played in four successive World Championships (1999-2002), the last one with screws in his ankle that were due to come out with surgery he had postponed in order to play. His payoff came at Salt Lake City when he helped Canada win gold at the Olympics.

SNEDDON, Bob
b. Montreal, Quebec, May 31, 1944
There were signs in the early years that Sneddon was a goalie of note. In '65-'66, for instance, in his second year of pro, he finished tops in the IHL for goals against. When California landed him in 1970, he had a good camp and won the backup role on the team behind Gary Smith, but he allowed 21 goals in less than 4 full games and was sent to the minors. Sneddon spent the rest of his time in the minors, though he was recruited as a ringer in the '76-'77 season by the Brantford Alexanders and helped the senior team win the Allan Cup.

SNELL, Chris
b. Regina, Saskatchewan, May 12, 1971
After helping Canada win gold at the 1991 WJC, Snell turned pro in the Buffalo organization. Two years in the minors and an outright release later, he signed with Toronto and got into his first NHL games. The Leafs, too, had little long-term use for him, as did Los Angeles, so in 1997, sick of the AHL and IHL, he signed to play in Germany. Snell has been in the DEL ever since.

Bob Sneddon

Chris Snell

It was at the very end of his career that he played in the NHL.
TED SNELL

SNELL, Ron
b. Regina, Saskatchewan, August 11, 1948
Snell was drafted by Pittsburgh into the NHL in 1968 and by Winnipeg into the WHA in 1972, and he took both offers at various stages of his career. Coming out of Regina, he joined the Penguins as a 20-year-old and scored 3 goals in 4 games during his first callup. He had just one more callup, though, and spent most of the next five years in the minors before joining the Jets in 1973. After two years, he was sent to the WHA minors and retired soon after.

SNELL, Ted
b. Ottawa, Ontario, May 28, 1946
Rare is the hockey player so dedicated that he asks for a trade out of the sun and into the snow. But Snell, who played in the minors for years, was happy in Hershey, one of minor hockey's all-time great cities. He was not thrilled to be traded to Phoenix and asked for a trade back east. The Roadrunners

complied, and Snell helped the Bears win the 1969 Calder Cup. He won a Memorial Cup with a hugely talented Niagara Falls team in 1965 before turning pro, but oddly it was at the very end of his career that he played in the NHL. His chance came in 1973 with Pittsburgh, by which time he was 27, though he was a regular for just two seasons. His second year was split between Kansas City and Detroit, and he ended up back in the minors.

SNEPSTS, Harold
b. Edmonton, Alberta, October 24, 1954
He didn't play his entire career in Vancouver, but his 781 Canucks games is second only to Stan Smyl, a teammate. Snepsts began with the Canucks in 1974 and wasn't traded until a decade later, to Minnesota. He was a popular player who never wore a helmet and who suffered more than his share of cuts and bruises and breaks, and even plastic surgery to his ear. He played in two All-Star Games (1977 and '82) and is the only Vancouver defenceman to take a penalty shot. By the time he retired in 1991, he had played more than 1,000 NHL games. He became a coach in the IHL and then an assistant with the Blues in St. Louis. He became a head coach in Portland with the WHL but more recently joined the NHL's Central Scouting Bureau.

SNOW, Alexander "Sandy"
b. Glace Bay, Nova Scotia, November 11, 1946
If you played for Hamilton in the days of sponsorship, you were going to play for the Red Wings first and foremost. Snow played three times with Detroit – November 16, 20, and 23, 1968 – but spent the rest of his time in the minors, notably with Flint in the IHL.

SNOW, Garth
b. Wrentham, Massachusetts, July 28, 1969
Patrick Roy may have introduced oversized equipment to the NHL, but Snow certainly took it to an egregious level in the mid-1990s with Philadelphia when he attached blocks of wood to the top of his shoulder pads. He hadn't needed that advantage at the University of Maine when he played with Paul Kariya and won the NCAA championship in 1992-93, the year he had a perfect record of 21-0-1 in goal for the Black Bears. He played for the U.S. at the 1994 Olympics in Lillehammer and debuted in the NHL with Quebec, but never had a chance to be the starter until he got to Vancouver, after being traded by the Flyers for Sean Burke. Since then, he has continued to move around, to Pittsburgh and the Islanders, but his role is slated as second-stringer.

Ron Snell

Harold Snepsts

Garth Snow

Dave Snuggerud

Dennis Sobchuk

Gene Sobchuk

Tommy Soderstrom

Doug Soetaert

SNUGGERUD, Dave
b. Minnetonka, Minnesota, June 20, 1966
Minnesota was his life. He played university there in the 1980s and was taken by Buffalo first overall in the Supplemental Draft of U.S. collegians. His best year was his first, when he scored 14 goals, and then he became earmarked as a checker and penalty killer. After retiring, he became head coach of the Chaska Hawks, a high school team in Chaska, Minnesota.

SNYDER, Dan
b. Elmira, Ontario, February 23, 1978
He came out of junior from Owen Sound without being drafted, but the new Atlanta franchise signed him as a free agent. Since then, though, Snyder has played mostly in the minors. He made his NHL debut on April 3, 2001.

SOBCHUK, Dennis
b. Lang, Saskatchewan, January 12, 1954
When he was scoring goals at will in Regina in junior, Sobchuk was hands down the most promising teenager in the country. In an effort to keep the momentum of the league going, the WHA was pursuing him through several teams, but in the end Cincinnati won out with a massive contract that called for Sobchuk to receive $2-million spread out over 10 years. He was still in junior at the time, and the contract kicked in in 1974 when he turned pro. Sobchuk had some good years in the WHA, but nothing like what the hype had prepared for. He was traded to the Oilers when the Stingers became cash-strapped, but Edmonton invoked a clause in the deal that said he could be bought out after five years, and after a serious shoulder injury, he was. He played part of 1979-80 with Detroit in the NHL, but his season was hacked to bits by injuries, and the next year started out just as poorly when he hurt his knee in training camp. Sobchuk went to Switzerland to finish the season, and then retired. He farmed his land, south of Regina, and figured his career was over. Then, in November 1982, Edmonton GM Glen Sather offered him a minor-league chance, which he took. He ended up playing two games for the Nordiques later in the season, then retired for good. In 1986, he became coach of his junior alma mater, the Regina Pats.

SOBCHUK, Gene
b. Lang, Saskatchewan, February 19, 1951
The older brother of the much-heralded Dennis, Gene played only one NHL game, with Vancouver. He later played with Dennis in the WHA, but by 1978 he was retired and back on the family farm in Lang.

SODERSTROM, Tommy
b. Stockholm, Sweden, July 17, 1969
As a teenager in Sweden, Soderstrom grew up knowing one thing – everyone in the country considered him the next Pelle Lindbergh. In other words, he was the best goalie the nation had produced. It was with him in net that Sweden won its first-ever European Championships, and it was with him that Tre Kronor subsequently won gold at the 1991 and '92 World Championships and silver at the 1993 WC. The team didn't fare so well at the 1992 Olympics in Lillehammer (finishing fifth), but when Soderstrom joined Philadelphia, Lindbergh's old team, in 1992, great things were expected of him. He played well when he played, but he had a monumental hurdle to overcome. He suffered from Wolff-Parkinson-White syndrome, a rare affliction that sets the heart rate abnormally high. In the space of a few short years, Soderstrom had five operations to try to cure the condition, but none was perfectly successful. After a few partial seasons with the Flyers and then the Islanders, he ended up returning to Sweden to continue playing, but retired in 2000 after losing interest in the game.

SOETAERT, Doug
b. Edmonton, Alberta, April 21, 1955
In many ways, Soetaert was an ideal backup goalie. Skilled and reliable, he could do a good job while the number one got a night off. In his dozen NHL seasons (1975-87), he was numero uno for two, with the Jets. He spent the first half of his career in New York, very much a part-timer with the Rangers as they played him in the minors much more than in Madison Square Garden. Soetaert was given the chance to be starter in Montreal in the fall of 1985, but he didn't measure up in the eyes of head coach Jean Perron and by year's end rookie Patrick Roy was the main man. Roy led the team to the Cup, but Soetaert was part of the team. Through all his years, he played just five times in the playoffs, the time of year when the backup rarely plays. After retiring in 1987, he stayed in the game at the administrative level, starting as coach in 1990 and working his way up to the position of vice-president and GM of Kansas City. When that IHL franchise folded in 2001, Soetaert soon was named to a similar position for the WHL's new franchise in Everett, Washington, slated to begin operations in 2003-04.

SOLHEIM, Ken
b. Hythe, Alberta, March 27, 1961
From 68 goals in Medicine Hat as a junior to 4 goals in 29 games with Minnesota the next year, Solheim just couldn't muster the same firepower in the NHL that he had as a superstar junior. During his six pro seasons he played for four teams, and five more in the minors, and he retired in 1986.

SOLINGER, Bob ("Solly")
b. Star City, Saskatchewan, December 23, 1925
He never quite made it with the Leafs, though in the AHL he had a great career and an unusual reputation. It seemed that Solinger perfected a kind of slapshot that dipped as it approached the goal. Real or unreal, it certainly gave him a bit of a psychological edge, which Solinger never complained about. He was part of a small group of players to score 200 goals in the American league, with Pittsburgh and Hershey, and he was the all-time playoff point getter when he recorded his 90th in 1959. He spent the last few years of his pro life in the WHL, retiring in 1964, though he later returned to play senior hockey in Alberta, where he settled at the end of his playing days.

SOMERS, Art
b. Winnipeg, Manitoba, January 19, 1902
d. Winnipeg, Manitoba, January 29, 1992
After a brief start with the Selkirk Fishermen, Somers

made a great name for himself in '20-'21 when he played on the Winnipeg Falcons juniors and beat Howie Morenz and his Stratford team to win the Memorial Cup. He moved his way up through the ranks out west until Chicago recruited him in 1929 for the upcoming season. He played for two years and then was traded to the Rangers, where he helped win the Cup in 1933 after losing to Toronto in the finals the previous season. In all, Somers played four years with the Blueshirts until the spring of 1935, when he suffered a serious head injury in a game and was forced to retire. He turned to coaching, and in successive years guided junior teams in Prince Albert and Moose Jaw, where his players included the Bentley brothers and Elmer Lach. He coached for years, including a stint in Houston, where Montreal set up a farm team, and a Canadian Army team in the Service League during the war. After retiring, he spent many a winter in California with his nephew, Bobby Summers, a jockey, and this love of horses led him to raise his own thoroughbreds on his farm outside Winnipeg. In the summer, he worked for many years with Lathing Contractor, a construction business. He was later inducted into the Manitoba Sports Hall of Fame.

SOMMER, Roy
b. Oakland, California, April 5, 1957

If you live in California and you want to play serious hockey, there's only one place to go – Canada. Sommer finished high school in Calgary while developing into a topflight player. He was drafted by Toronto in 1977 but played his only three NHL games in Edmonton. Throughout his 10-year career he played in a number of leagues, garnering a reputation for toughness that was seconded by his fists. He won a Calder Cup in 1984 and a Turner Cup two years later, and he also both played and coached roller hockey. Since retiring in 1987, Sommer has not stopped working as a coach. He coached at Richmond in the ECHL for five years, moved up to San Jose as an assistant in 1996, and two years later became head coach of the Sharks farm team in Kentucky.

SONGIN, Tom
b. Norwood, Massachusetts, December 20, 1953

A graduate of Boston College in 1977, Songin was never drafted, which meant his most likely destination was his home team, Boston. The Bruins signed him as a free agent, but he played just 43 games with the team over a 3-year period. He retired in 1982 and started a power washing business called Bombs Away. In 1999, he was hired by the Bruins as a pro scout.

He moved his way up through the ranks out west until Chicago recruited him in 1929.
ART SOMERS

SONMOR, Glen ("Rocky")
b. Moose Jaw, Saskatchewan, April 22, 1929

Way back when, before Sonmor became more famous as a coach, he played the game at the highest level. Not a flashy player or a gifted skater, he got by on hard work and determination. He played a few games with the Rangers in the mid-1950s, but his career ended in an AHL game when he was hit in the left eye by a puck. His career over, he enrolled at the University of Minnesota to take a degree in physical education. He also coached the freshman team and assisted Johnny Mariucci with the varsity team. In ensuing years, he coached at Springfield and Cleveland in the AHL and made a name for himself as an excellent after-dinner speaker. Sonmor was the son-in-law of longtime head scout of Detroit, Johnny Mitchell, who had coached Springfield at one time. Sonmor took over for Mariucci as head coach at U of M, and later coached at the NHL level with the North Stars. He had three stints with that team, the first culminating with a trip to the Stanley Cup finals in 1981 during five years of service. He later coached in '84-'85 and then on an interim basis for two games a couple of years later. After 30 years in the game, stress and health concerns pushed Sonmor out the door.

Glen Sonmor

SONNENBERG, Martin
b. Wetaskiwin, Alberta, January 23, 1978

Young with potential, Sonnenberg has been in the Pittsburgh system since 1998 when he left junior and signed as a free agent. He has spent most of his time in the minors, though he did play half of '98-'99 with the Pens, scoring just one goal as a left winger.

SOPEL, Brent
b. Calgary, Alberta, January 7, 1977

A textbook case of player development, Sopel will hopefully develop for Vancouver into a front-line defenceman. He played his junior in Saskatoon and eased his way into the AHL, and as he was establishing himself in that league the Canucks were giving him a few NHL games. This turned into a good chance in 1999-2000 and most of the next season, leading to a full year in 2001-02, which should get Sopel nicely on his way. What he does with his opportunity remains to be seen.

SOROCHAN, Lee
b. Edmonton, Alberta, September 9, 1975

A powerful defenceman who didn't develop as his drafted team, the Rangers, had hoped, Sorochan went from the NHL to Europe faster than he would have liked. The Rangers drafted him in 1993 but six years

Brent Sopel

John Sorrell

Sheldon Souray

Emory Sparrow

Fred Speck

Bill Speer

later, unused, he was traded to Calgary. The Flames played him three times, but in the summer of 2000 Sopel signed with the London Knights in Britain and moved to Germany a year later.

SORRELL, John ("Long John")
b. Chesterville, Ontario, January 16, 1906
d. November 30, 1984
After playing kid hockey in Chesterville, Sorrell moved to Saskatchewan to play in Rosetown before turning pro in 1927 in the Can-Am league. He led the IHL in scoring with the London Tecumsehs in '29-'30 and that season earned him a chance to make the Detroit team, then called the Falcons. That opportunity began his 11-year NHL career. He was a fine left winger who played on 2 Cup teams, in 1936 and '37, and he twice scored 20 goals in a year for Detroit, impressive figures in his day. During the summers, Sorrell played semi-pro baseball in Manitowic, Wisconsin. He finished his career in the minors, first with Hershey and then Indianapolis, where he settled. He coached the AHL team in that city, and with also worked as a linesman for AHL games.

SOUCY, Christian
b. Gatineau, Quebec, September 14, 1970
Without question, there are a few skaters who have had shorter NHL careers, but his ice time has not been tracked since 1917 the way goalies' time has been. Thus, Soucy and Robbie Irons have the distinction of having the shortest careers in league history. On March 31, 1994, Soucy played just three minutes of a game for Chicago, a mere blink in NHL annals. In addition to this record, Soucy holds another: He has played in every pro league possible for someone of his era. Since turning pro in 1993, Soucy has played in the NHL, IHL, CHL, ECHL, AHL, WPHL, WCHL, and UHL. There's no league in North America in which he hasn't played!

SOURAY, Sheldon ("Hammer")
b. Elk Point, Alberta, July 13, 1976
Another large, brick wall of a defenceman, Souray started his career with New Jersey in 1997, three years after being drafted by the team. Montreal acquired him in March 2000 near the trade deadline, his great misfortune because the Devils went on to win the Cup that spring. In Montreal, he has been beset by injury, though he remains one of their top blueliners.

SPACEK, Jaroslav
b. Rokycany, Czechoslovakia (Czech Republic), February 11, 1974
It's a paradox of hockey. Internationally, Spacek has been steady as a rock. In the NHL, he is fast turning into a vagabond. He played at the 1998 Olympics in Nagano for the Czechs, winning gold, as well as at the 2002 Games in Salt Lake City. In between, Spacek has won gold at the 1999 and 2001 World Championships. In NHL terms, though, he has started his career since 1998 by playing with three teams in his first four years. Worse, the third of those was Columbus, the bottom of the NHL barrel and a place where, if he doesn't make it there, he likely won't make it anywhere in the Show.

SPANHEL, Martin
b. Zlin, Czechoslovakia (Czech Republic), July 1, 1977
Before he had played a single NHL game, Spanhel had been traded twice and owned by four teams. Philly drafted him and dished him off to San Jose. The Sharks handed him over to Buffalo and the Sabres never offered him a new contract so Columbus signed him in 2000. Since then, he's played just a few games for the Blue Jackets and doesn't appear to be a part of their building plans, either.

SPARROW, Emory ("Spunk")
b. Hartney, Manitoba, September 15, 1897
d. Lancaster, Pennsylvania, February 2, 1965
In 1915, Sparrow stopped playing hockey so he might join the army, and when he was discharged he resumed his career playing out west. He spent most of his career with one team or another in that part of Canada but he did play eight games for the Bruins in '24-'25.

SPECK, Fred
b. Thorold, Ontario, July 22, 1947
Such were the vagaries of the various leagues that Speck made history in the AHL in his fourth year of pro. He had played in the CHL, NHL, and WHL, but '70-'71 was his first year in the American league. He led the league in scoring and was named rookie of the year, only the third player in league history to claim that mighty double prize. He had played a few games with Detroit, and as a result of that season he was picked up by Vancouver and played another 18 games with the Canucks in '71-'72. Speck later played in the WHA and at the end of his career he won an Allan Cup with the Brantford Alexanders in senior hockey in '76-'77.

SPEER, Bill
b. Lindsay, Ontario, March 20, 1942
d. Fenelon Falls, Ontario, February 12, 1989
The only barber in post-NHL history, Speer died tragically when his snowmobile sank near Fenelon Falls. He had had a long playing career in the minors, beginning in 1962 in the Eastern league, and the defenceman had the privilege to play with the Bruins in '69-'70 when they won the Cup. Speer saw his first NHL action with Pittsburgh in 1967 after expansion and after his time with the Bruins he played two years in the WHA before retiring. He returned to Lindsay and opened his own barbershop, where he worked until his untimely death.

SPEERS, Ted
b. Ann Arbor, Michigan, January 28, 1961
After graduating from the University of Michigan in 1983, Speers passed through the NHL draft untouched and unclaimed. He managed to latch on with his local Red Wings in Detroit, and his short and uneventful four years in the minors were interrupted by only four NHL games. He later returned to the organization in an administrative capacity, moving up to the position of director of marketing, which he currently holds.

SPENCE, Gord

b. Haileybury, Ontario, July 25, 1898
d. unknown

Did he or didn't he play in the NHL? That is the question. He was listed as being in the lineup for games on March 6, 11, and 13, 1926, wearing number 12 for Toronto, yet there are no accounts in newspapers of his performance, his being called up, or his being demoted. Yet, the official NHL stats say he was there.

SPENCER, Brian ("Spinner")

b. Fort St. James, British Columbia, September 3, 1949
d. Riviera Beach, Florida, June 3, 1988

From literally the time he played his first NHL game until a man put a long-barrelled revolver to Spencer's chest and pulled the trigger, he led a life of frantic tragedy and diurnal unrest. He grew up not well off – born on a dirt floor in a log cabin – but his father Roy did everything he could to see that his boy could play hockey. He scraped together enough money to get Brian into a hockey school, and the boy responded by developing into an exceptional player. He played junior out west and when the mighty Toronto Maple Leafs drafted him in 1969, well, the Spencers were delirious. While playing for Tulsa, Brian got the call to go to Toronto. He called his dad, who had *Hockey Night in Canada* on his television. Then, all hell broke loose. *Hockey Night* out west showed the Vancouver game, and Roy went berserk. He packed a gun, got in his car, and drove 135 kilometres to the CBC's Prince George station to demand that the Leafs game be put on. It was, but at game's conclusion Roy was met outside by the RCMP. Shots were fired both ways, and Roy was killed. Stunned beyond words, Brian continued to play because he knew his father would have wanted as much. The next Saturday night, the game being televised in Fort St. James, he scored a hat trick. Spencer played 10 years in the NHL. A rugged and frenetic left winger, he could score a bit and check a bit, and he moved through four teams during his career. He had two marriages fail, and even during his playing days he was prone to violent outbursts. After retiring, he moved to Florida. Riviera Beach, though, was Harlem to the Fifth Avenue of the nearby Palm Beach. It was the most impoverished area, where crime and drugs were rampant, and where Spencer never should have gravitated. He went from job to job, blew his money, and wound up destitute. In 1987, he was charged with kidnapping and murder and faced the death penalty if convicted, but his friends testified vigorously in his defence and he was acquitted. He never changed his life, though. Three months later, he was in the worst part of Riviera Beach with another

Irv Spencer

man buying cocaine. They were robbed at gunpoint, and Spencer was shot in the chest. By the time his friend arrived at the hospital, Spencer was dead.

SPENCER, Irv

b. Sudbury, Ontario, December 4, 1937

From the time he turned pro with the Rangers in 1959, Spencer was an asset to every team he played on – and that meant a good deal because he travelled as much as any player of his day. He could play any position except goal, but defence was where he was most often found. His longest NHL stints came with the Rangers and Boston, though he also played a bit with Detroit and lingered in the Wings system for a while. In the minors, it seemed each season brought with it a change of teams. He finished his career in the WHA in Vancouver, and afterwards became the head of the savings and loans department of a bank.

SPEYER, Chris

b. Toronto, Ontario, February 6, 1907
d. Toronto, Ontario, December 26, 1966

After playing junior with the local Granites in 1921-22, Speyer turned pro and joined the St. Pats two seasons later. In his 13 seasons, he played just a few games with Toronto and the Americans, spending most of his time in the Can-Am league. He was also a fine baseball player and after retiring in 1936 went into coaching for a while. By day, though, Speyer managed a number of Toronto hotels and was a wine salesman for many years. One of his three sons played hockey for U of T in the 1960s and went on to become a member of Parliament for Cambridge, Ontario.

SPOONER, Andrew "Red"

b. Port Arthur, Ontario, August 24, 1910
d. May 7, 1984

Goaltender Spooner played most of his career in Ontario's north, but for one game – January 18, 1930 – he made a special guest appearance in the NHL, for Pittsburgh, to replace Joe Miller, who couldn't play because of injury. Spooner allowed 6 goals in a 6-5 loss to the Rangers and never made it back to the big time.

SPRING, Corey

b. Cranbrook, British Columbia, May 31, 1971

A dream came true for the Nanook Spring when he scored an NHL goal in his second game, in March 1998, but the Tampa Bay prospect has since spent most of his career outside the top league. In 1999-2000, he was released by both Detroit and Manitoba in the IHL and has been playing in Germany since. A lover of body art, he sports a super-stylized tattoo of Canada's international sweater.

In 1987, he was charged with kidnapping and murder and faced the death penalty if convicted.
BRIAN SPENCER

Corey Spring

Don Spring

SPRING, Don

b. Maracaibo, Venezuela, June 15, 1959

His dad worked for an oil company and was transferred to Venezuela, where Spring spent the first four years of his life. The family moved back to Canada and settled in Edson, Alberta, and Spring went on to play hockey at the University of Alberta, where he won two national championships and a berth on Canada's 1980 Olympic team. From there he made it to the NHL as a defenceman who took care of things in his own end and moved the puck up to his forwards without any fanfare. In 259 career games, he had all of 1 goal. He played all his games with Winnipeg.

SPRING, Frank ("Gentle Giant")

b. Cranbrook, British Columbia, October 19, 1949

A great game can always be explained by circumstance, a fluke that comes without notice and leaves with no promise of ever returning. A great season is a bit more mysterious because it carries on for many weeks and months, but it, too, comes from ethereal matter and leaves whence it came. For Spring, that great season was 1975-76 in the minors with Salt Lake City. He led the league by scoring 44 goals even though he had never scored as many as 18 in any other pro season. He had been a high draft choice by Boston in 1969, but he played just once with the Bruins and a few more times with St. Louis before ending up with California and, by extension, the farm team in Utah. The great year meant a longer look with Cleveland when the franchise moved the next year, but he was back in the minors and off to the WHA before too long. He had two hockey-playing brothers as well. Danny played in the WHA while Derek eschewed the pro game to get an education and play senior in Spokane. After retiring, Frank returned to Cranbrook where he sold cars and managed a car leasing business.

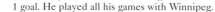

After retiring, Frank returned to Cranbrook where he sold cars and managed a car leasing business.
FRANK SPRING

SPRING, Jesse ("Jess")

b. Alba, Pennsylvania, January 18, 1899
d. Toronto, Ontario, March 25, 1942

The end shouldn't come on a downtown street. For a great athlete, a more dignified exit is deserved But one day in Toronto, Spring collapsed and was rushed to hospital where he died just a few hours later at age 43. He was easily and uniformly recalled as a superb all-round athlete. He played pro hockey in the NHL from 1923 to '30, with Toronto and three other teams. He was a middle wing with the Toronto Argonauts football club and at one time was reigning amateur heavyweight boxing champion of Canada. Spring was also a great lacrosse and baseball player, and after retiring from active play he coached. In baseball and hockey, he guided teams in

Ron Stackhouse

Brockville and Oshawa. He was an early coach of the great Kirkland Lake Blue Devils teams and he was sports director for Wright-Hargreaves Mines in Kirkland. In 1941 he was named coach of the River Vale Skeeters in the Eastern United States Amateur Hockey League, but ill health forced him to resign.

SPRUCE, Andy

b. London, Ontario, April 17, 1954

Eyesight is, perhaps, the most precious gift of life. Take it away and life is altered. Spruce found out the scary way when he was high-sticked in the right eye by teammate Dennis Owchar during a scramble in front of the net in a game in January 1978. Doctors feared the worst, but just two weeks later Spruce was back on the ice scoring a goal – assisted by Owchar. Spruce ended up with 19 goals that season, though his production dropped dramatically the year after and he was soon in the minors for the rest of his career. He had played junior in London, and in January 1984 he took over as coach in Sudbury, a position he held for a year and a half.

SRSEN, Tomas

b. Olomouc, Czechoslovakia (Czech Republic), August 25, 1966

He continues his career in Europe, a veteran, a grizzled and experienced pro since 1986. Yet there was a time back in 1990 when he wanted to give the NHL a try. Srsen played two games for the Oilers and most of two seasons in the minors, but his preference was Euro-hockey to a life on buses with no guarantees of planes. He played for the Czechs at the 1994 Olympics in Lillehammer, and also in two World Championships, and spent most of his years in the Czech and German leagues.

STACKHOUSE, Ron ("Stack")

b. Haliburton, Ontario, August 26, 1949

Growing up in Haliburton and Guilford, Stackhouse dreamed of playing in the NHL, but en route he certainly never expected to face a penalty shot! He played junior in Peterborough, though, under the whacky, inventive, and envelope-pushing guidance of coach Roger Neilson. So, when the ref called for a penalty shot against the Petes, Neilson pulled his goalie and put Stackhouse between the pipes. Stack charged the player moving in and made the "save." He had size and a superb shot. He was the product of the Bobby Orr influences on defencemen, and after stutter starts with California and Detroit he settled in with Pittsburgh in 1974 to play eight and a half seasons of excellent hockey. In March 1975, he tied a record by earning four assists in a period and six in a game, and he was an offensive force from the blueline. It wasn't until March 1979 that he finally registered a hat trick in a game. He retired in 1982 after 889 NHL games, and returned to Haliburton where he ran an electronics store and later taught at a Haliburton high school, where he continues to this day.

STACKHOUSE, Theodore "Ted"
b. New Glasgow, Nova Scotia, November 2, 1894
d. Mount Holly, New Jersey, November 24, 1975
One of the more obscure players, Stackhouse joined the army for action in the First World War prior to his pro career. He later played just a few games with the Toronto St. Pats and raised his family in New Jersey.

STAHAN, Frank "Butch"
b. Minnedosa, Manitoba, October 29, 1918
d. Ottawa, Ontario, May 25, 1995
The self-proclaimed Satchel Paige of hockey, Stahan was *definitely* born in Minnedosa but he was by no means born in 1918. For years he fibbed about his age to extend his career, claiming to be a number of years younger so he might play well past his perceived prime. He played 3 times for the Montreal Canadiens in the 1945 semifinals against Toronto, but played all over for some 20 years. He played years of senior hockey for Quebec and Ottawa, and in 1955 began a two-year stint as playing coach of Toledo. In his youth, he had been the welterweight champion of Canada in boxing circles, and his pugnacious attributes helped carry him through his puck-chasing career.

STAIOS, Steve
b. Hamilton, Ontario, July 28, 1973
Since being drafted by St. Louis in 1991, Staios worked his way into the NHL and has managed to stay there since becoming a regular, with Boston, late in the '95-'96 season. He has not been a Bruins player happily ever after, though. In fact, the defenceman has become something of a journeyman, though perhaps the three-year contract he signed with Edmonton in 2001 will ensure some stability to his career. He also had stays in Vancouver and Atlanta, the latter shortened by a serious groin injury in 1999-2000 that required surgery. With the Thrashers, Staios played both defence and right wing.

STAJDUHAR, Nick
b. Kitchener, Ontario, December 6, 1974
In his early days, Stajduhar was on top of the world. He won a gold medal at the World Juniors with Canada in 1994 after being a first-round draft choice by Edmonton the previous season. He was a defence-man both big and offensively talented, but as soon as he hit the pros, he stalled. He ended up playing just two games with the Oilers, and since then has spent

nearly a decade in every corner of the minor leagues. In 1999-2000 he led Flint to the UHL championship.

STALEY, Al
b. Regina, Saskatchewan, September 21, 1928
He played most of his hockey in Canada's west, but for one season Staley moved east. In 1948-49, he played for the New York Rovers and was called up to the Rangers for a game. He made history by recording an assist in that contest, making him a rare member of the one-game, one-point wonder club.

STAMLER, Lorne ("Scooter")
b. Winnipeg, Manitoba, August 9, 1951
Stamler played junior for the Toronto Marlies for two years, but a rough start to his pro aspirations convinced

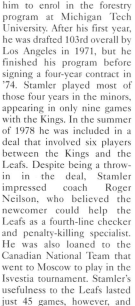

He played most of '79-'80 with the Jets, but again was on the move, signing as a free agent with the Islanders in 1980.
LORNE STAMLER

him to enrol in the forestry program at Michigan Tech University. After his first year, he was drafted 103rd overall by Los Angeles in 1971, but he finished his program before signing a four-year contract in '74. Stamler played most of those four years in the minors, appearing in only nine games with the Kings. In the summer of 1978 he was included in a deal that involved six players between the Kings and the Leafs. Despite being a throw-in in the deal, Stamler impressed coach Roger Neilson, who believed the newcomer could help the Leafs as a fourth-line checker and penalty-killing specialist. He was also loaned to the Canadian National Team that went to Moscow to play in the Isvestia tournament. Stamler's usefulness to the Leafs lasted just 45 games, however, and then he was claimed by the Winnipeg Jets in the Expansion Draft. He played most of '79-'80 with the Jets, but again was on the move, signing as a free agent with the Islanders in 1980. There he played four years with the farm team in Indianapolis, winning two Calder Cups and working the last two seasons as an assistant coach hoping to move up the Islanders' exec-utive ladder. Such was not the case, though, and Stamler wound up working for a cleaning business in Indy. Then, a Florida chemical company offered him a much better-paying job, and Stamler moved south, where he has been ever since. He opened his own business, has a staff of six, and plays as much golf as time permits, far from the hockey crowds of Long Island, Toronto, and Winnipeg.

Butch Stahan

ST. AMOUR, Martin
b. Montreal, Quebec, January 30, 1970
A game with the Oilers in 1992-93 assured St. Amour he'd get the alumni newsletter, but his greater contri-bution came with San Diego in the West Coast league. He joined the Gulls when the franchise began in 1995,

Jim Stanfield

and during his six years he won two scoring championships and led the team to three Taylor Cup championships. When he announced his retirement, the club honoured him with a Martin St. Amour Night and retired his number 18 to the rafters. He stayed on as an assistant coach, and also became head coach for the Gulls in roller hockey.

STANDING, George
b. Toronto, Ontario, August 3, 1941
A veteran of the Eastern league with Nashville, Standing played all of two games with the expansion North Stars in Minnesota after signing with them in 1967 during training camp. Outside of that small opportunity, he spent the majority of his time in the EHL until retiring in late 1971.

STANFIELD, Fred
b. Toronto, Ontario, May 4, 1944
The Sutters were almost eclipsed by the Stanfield Seven, for that is how many brothers played serious hockey in the 1960s. As things turned out, only Jack, Jim, and Fred made the NHL, allowing the six Sutters to set a miraculous family record. Fred had the finest career of his clan. He played junior for St. Catharines, which meant the Hawks had first dibs on his services, but they used him only sparingly and tossed him into the worst deal the club ever made. Chicago sent Stanfield, Phil Esposito, and Ken Hodge to Boston for Gilles Marotte, Pit Martin, and Jack Norris. Stanfield joined a great Boston team and played on a line with Johnny Bucyk and Johnny McKenzie, racking up 6 successive 20-goal seasons in as many years with the team. He also played the power-play point sometimes with Bobby Orr and was part of two Cup teams, in 1970 and '72. After he retired, he tried coaching junior, in Niagara Falls, but the rush he had as a player didn't translate to standing behind the bench and he moved on. He settled in Williamsville, New York, not far from Buffalo, where he played last in the NHL, and opened Stanfield's Office Furniture.

Ed Staniowski

Ed Stankiewicz

STANFIELD, Jack
b. Toronto, Ontario, May 30, 1942
In order, the complete Stanfield team: Jack was the oldest, a hustling left winger who specialized in killing penalties; Fred, of course, starred in the NHL; Jim made the NHL for a brief time; Joe played senior hockey in Toronto before becoming a fireman; Vic and Paul played junior B; and Gordie played junior B and later went to Germany to play with Vic. Gordie was a diabetic and was later killed in a car accident. Jack played his one NHL game with Chicago in the '66 playoffs. He was a minor-leaguer, but in 1972 he

The Sutters were almost eclipsed by the Stanfield Seven, for that is how many brothers played serious hockey in the 1960s.
FRED STANFIELD

joined Houston of the WHA and helped the Aeros win the Avco Cup. He made his home in Houston and stayed with the Apollos in the minor leagues, eventually becoming their assistant GM.

STANFIELD, Jim
b. Toronto, Ontario, January 1, 1947
One of the three Stanfield boys to make the NHL (seven played serious hockey), Jim is connected to the deal that saw brother Fred go from Chicago to Boston. Like Fred, Jim played junior in St. Catharines, meaning he was property of Chicago. After Fred got to the Bruins, Jim and Gilles Marotte (who went from Boston to Chicago in the previous deal) were traded with Dennis DeJordy to Los Angeles for Bill White, Gerry Desjardins, and Bryan Campbell. Jim played his only NHL games, seven in all, with the Kings but spent many years in the WHL. He ended his career in Spokane and stayed there, working for a brewery in the city.

STANIOWSKI, Ed
b. Moose Jaw, Saskatchewan, July 7, 1955
Rarely has a goalie had the kind of junior career Staniowski had, and certainly not with Regina. He began in 1971, and over the next three years he was his team's MVP each season. The Pats won the Memorial Cup in 1973-74 because of his goaltending and he was league MVP both that year and the next. He played for Canada at the unofficial World Juniors in 1975, the same year he was named the best junior in all of Canada. Over his 10-year NHL career, though, he enjoyed less success. He was primarily a backup in St. Louis, Winnipeg, and Hartford and many was the season he spent in the minors as well as the NHL. Staniowski represented Canada at the 1979 World Championships, the same year he won the Charlie Conacher Award for humanitarian efforts. After retiring, he settled in Regina and joined the Canadian Armed Forces. Today, he is a lieutenant-colonel with the Canadian Forces.

STANKIEWICZ, Ed ("Stanky")
b. Kitchener, Ontario, December 1, 1929
Being a boxer in the off-season had two advantages: one, it kept Stankiewicz in shape for the hockey season; two, it established long before he ever dropped the gloves his ability to take care of himself. He began his junior career in Oshawa, playing on a high-flyin' line with two other future NHLers, Glen Skov and Earl Reibel, in 1949-50. Stankiewicz saw his only NHL time with Detroit a few years later for 6 games in all, but he played in the minors for 13 seasons.

STANKIEWICZ, Myron ("Mike"/ "Stanky")
b. Kitchener, Ontario, December 4, 1935

Ed's younger brother, Mike was at the tail end of his career before he got a call to the NHL as a 33-year-old rookie with St. Louis. He had played much of his career in the AHL with Hershey where he had been a reliable 20-goal scorer for years. But in '68-'69 he played with both the Blues and the Flyers, and in 35 career games he scored nary a single goal and finished his career in the minors.

STANLEY, Allan ("Snowshoes"/ "Sam")
b. Timmins, Ontario, March 1, 1926

Surely one of the great unspectacular players in NHL history, Stanley was a superb defenceman who rarely looked superb but who almost never made a mistake and played his position perfectly. He was an awkward skater (ergo the nickname) and he was no whiz with the puck, but he was diligent as a checker and great in front of his own net. He was also a superb passer. All of these qualities were gleaned by Boston talent scouts who watched him play in Timmins. He didn't want to travel to Beantown for a tryout, but the team eventually convinced him to come, and then assigned him to the Olympics at age 17. From there he moved up to Providence and in 1948 he was with the Rangers after New York sacrificed a number of players to acquire him. Stanley got to Broadway amid great expectation from the fans. In his five seasons with the team he played true to character and eventually became team captain, but the fans wanted a heavy hitter. As a result, they booed him when he eased up on a hit and nicknamed him Sonja Henie, after the figure skater. The Rangers actually admitted the fans were why he was demoted to Vancouver of the WHL. It was the first time in league history that a captain had been sent to the minors. The next year, Stanley started with the Blueshirts but was quickly traded to Chicago. By this point, he was lucky just to be alive. In the summer of 1951, he had been slated to go on a fishing trip with another Timmins boy, Bill Barilko, but Stanley had to cancel at the last minute because of a dentist's appointment he couldn't change. Barilko was killed in a crash coming home from that trip. Stanley played two years with a Boston team that went to the finals both years, though he missed the big dance the first year because of an injured knee. By 1958, the Bruins thought the 32-year-old was finished, his knees too banged up and his skating never his strong suit to start with. Toronto took a chance on him, and he rewarded the Leafs with ten years of great defensive play, doing what he always did. He usually played on the blueline with Tim Horton, and the Leafs won four Cups

in the 1960s. He played 1 final year with Philadelphia, retiring in 1969 at the tender age of 43 after some 1,244 games. Stanley was one of the first players to operate his own hockey schools, and opened several in southern Ontario before starting a family resort. He was inducted into the Hockey Hall of Fame in 1981 in recognition of 21 outstanding seasons of NHL play.

STANLEY, Barney
b. Paisley, Ontario, June 1, 1893
d. Edmonton, Alberta, May 16, 1971

Stanley was best known out west, but it was in the heart of Ontario's dairy farmland that he first learned to skate. By the time he was 17, he had moved west to Medicine Hat to play hockey and from there had a successful career in Edmonton. Stanley played for the Vancouver Millionaires in 1915 when that team won its Stanley Cup, and spent most of his career in the west. Stanley's only NHL foray came in 1927-28 when he ws coaching the Black Hawks. He suited up for one game (getting his name in the NHL's record books), and at season's end was let go as coach. In 1929, Stanley returned to Edmonton to coach the Poolers. He worked for the Northern Alberta Dairy Pool, first as a sales manager and later as general manager, retiring in 1961. He was inducted into the Hockey Hall of Fame in 1962.

STANLEY, Daryl
b. Winnipeg, Manitoba, December 2, 1962

The litany of injuries and the accumulated ravages to his body are enough to make a strong man cringe. Stanley was never drafted but he wanted to play hockey, so he turned pro in the AHL with Maine after signing with Philadelphia and being assigned to the farm. He made his first appearance with the Flyers two years later, and in all he played three years in Philly and three more in Vancouver. He missed a large portion of the '85-'86 season after dislocating his neck and bruising his kidneys in a car accident. He later hurt and re-hurt his left ankle several times, dislocated his shoulder, hurt his back, twisted his knee, and tore tendons in a finger. By the time he retired in 1990, his body was plenty relieved. Stanley then went back to his land in Balmoral, Manitoba, and with his wife, C.C., started Stanley's Goose Camp. This was a large area where he outfitted waterfowl hunters and gave them plenty of acreage to explore and enjoy the outdoors.

STANOWSKI, Wally ("Wally the Hat"/ "The Whirling Dervish")
b. Winnipeg, Manitoba, April 28, 1919

When the St. Boniface Seals ventured east to Toronto to face Billy Taylor and Oshawa for the 1938 Memorial Cup, Stanowski seized the moment and outshone all

> **In the summer of 1951, he had been slated to go on a fishing trip with another Timmins boy, Bill Barilko, but Stanley had to cancel at the last minute.**
> **ALLAN STANLEY (LEFT)**

Myron Stankiewicz

Barney Stanley

Daryl Stanley

Mike Stapleton

Pat Stapleton

Sergei Starikov

Harold Starr

players. He had great speed for a defenceman, moved the puck well for a defenceman, and hit like you were meeting a brick wall. The Leafs moved him into their system almost immediately and for three years he was a mainstay with the team, winning the Cup in the spring of '42. He then joined the army and worked for two years as a physical training instructor out west, but upon discharge he returned to Maple Leaf Gardens where he picked up right where he had left off. In the next four years he won three more Cups, but when the Leafs gave him a chance to play in New York with old buddy Elwyn Morris he took the offer and finished his career with the Blueshirts of Broadway. He was sent down to Cincinnati in the IHL, but going back to get a puck he slipped and crashed into the end boards so hard that his leg went right through them. His leg was so badly broken he was forced to retire. He returned to Winnipeg, went into the meat packing business, and later worked as a sales rep for a heavy equipment operation, though he retired to Toronto later in life.

STANTON, Paul
b. Boston, Massachusetts, June 22, 1967
He couldn't have got much better of a start to a career than playing at the University of Wisconsin in the heyday of coach Bob Johnson. Stanton learned to play defence under Badger Bob and then after a year in the IHL (1989-90) he joined Pittsburgh in 1990 at the perfect time, for the Penguins won the Stanley Cup in the next two seasons. After one more season in the Igloo, though, he was on the move to Boston and Long Island, and at season's end he decided to head for Germany. Since 1995 he has played in the DEL and because of his skill, experience, and location he has also played at three World Championships for the U.S., a bronze in 1996 being his best result.

STAPLETON, Brian
b. Fort Erie, Ontario, December 25, 1951
Short but sweet. He came out of Brown University in the early 1970s, not the hotbed of college hockey, and he was never drafted. He signed with Washington, the worst pro team in the world, and he lasted just a single game. He played three years in the minors, in Dayton, and then retired.

STAPLETON, Mike
b. Sarnia, Ontario, May 5, 1966
By far the most successful son of a '72 Summit Series player, Mike has done dad, Pat, proud. He played for Canada at the 1986 WJC during his junior days in Cornwall, and turned pro with Chicago, the team that drafted him in 1984. Stapleton went on to play nearly 700 NHL games with 7 teams. A centre, he was by no means blessed with scoring ability but was a useful player nonetheless. In his 14 NHL seasons, though, he never made it past the first round of the playoffs, and by 2001 he had played himself into extinction. He signed with Espoo in the Finnish league, and a year later moved to Sweden to play with Leksand, and then back to Espoo.

STAPLETON, Pat ("Whitey")
b. Sarnia, Ontario, July 4, 1940
He was part of the greatest series in the history of hockey. Unfortunately, he has treated the most important artifact from that series with a mockery that defies understanding or sympathy. For years, Stapleton has claimed to have in his possession the puck from Paul Henderson's goal that won the 1972 Summit Series, yet he refuses to show it to anyone or take it to its rightful home at the Hockey Hall of Fame in Toronto. Instead, he has made a game of the souvenir to the point that, should he ever show a black disc to the world, the world would be wise to view the revelation with dubious regret. Stapleton began his career in the early 1960s with Boston, though he developed into a fine defenceman only a little later when he got to Chicago. Small and a good skater, he was paired on the blueline with Bill White, and they called themselves Mutt and Jeff. They were among the best pair of defencemen in the league, thus their invitation to Team Canada. He played in four All-Star Games and was named to the NHL's Second All-Star Team three times. Ironically, soon after the Summit Series, Hawks coach Billy Reay took Stapleton off the blueline and moved him to forward to take advantage of his offensive skills. At season's end, he moved to the WHA, signing with the Chicago Cougars as playing coach. He was named the league's best defenceman, and he and three teammates (Ralph Backstrom, Dave Dryden, and Rod Zaine) actually bought the team to keep it afloat. He retired from the WHA, and hockey, in 1978, and returned to his farm in Strathroy, Ontario, near Sarnia. He also formed Fundamentals in Action, a company intended to help both kids and adults apply hockey skills to life.

STARIKOV, Sergei
b. Chelyabinsk, Soviet Union (Russia), December 4, 1958
It was the best Soviet tandem on the blueline ever to wear the vaunted red sweater of CCCP. Starikov and Slava Fetisov formed a duo capable of inspiring offence, crushing defence, extreme resilience, and unparallelled endurance. For more than a decade, Starikov played virtually every international tournament with his partner, from the World Juniors in '77 and '78 to the Challenge Cup and Rendez-vous '87 and on through three Olympics, five World Championships, and a Canada Cup. In 1989, at age 31, his best years used by the Soviets, he was allowed to play for New Jersey with Fetisov, though their political differences couldn't be reconciled on the ice and Starikov lasted just 16 games. He played three and a half seasons in the minors, and has since stayed in the game coaching and running clinics.

STARR, Harold
b. Ottawa, Ontario, July 6, 1906
d. Ottawa, Ontario, September 25, 1981
A great athlete, Starr had a number of sports to choose from as far as a career was concerned. He was a professional wrestler for a time. He won championships with the Ottawa football club in the mid-1920s, and was a first-rate hockey player. He turned pro with the local Senators in 1929 and for the next six years played primarily in the NHL. After he retired, he went into the hotel business with partner Harry Viau, buying and running the Carleton Hotel in Ottawa for a number of decades. Quiet, he was legend in his city for his kindness as much as his athletic ability.

STARR, Wilf ("Twinkie")

b. St. Boniface, Manitoba, July 22, 1909

d. unknown

One of a small number of players to come out of the University of Manitoba, Starr played several years in the leagues that predated the AHL, the cream of the minor-league crop. He made it to the NHL with the Americans in 1932 and moved to the Red Wings a year later. He was in that system for three seasons, winning the IHL championship in '35-'36 with the Olympics. Starr finished his career in Providence.

STASIUK, Vic

b. Lethbridge, Alberta, May 23, 1929

The playing career can be neatly sectioned into two parts. The first, 1949-55, was full of team success but lacking in personal success. He started with Chicago and went to Detroit, and on paper he won three Cups with the Wings during their greatest years. He was shuffled in and out of the lineup, though, and was by no means one of the team's stars. When he was traded to Boston in the summer of '55, his playing took on greater meaning. He was put on a forward line with Bronco Horvath and Johnny Bucyk – all of Ukrainian heritage – and the Uke Line was born. This was no promotional stunt. The threesome developed into one of the league's top lines, and Stasiuk had 4 consecutive 20-goal seasons. He ended his NHL days in Boston and then was sent to the minors as a playing coach. During his prime, he also played semi-pro baseball in the summers back in Lethbridge and he owned a soft drink vending machine company.

There is no European player who has had a more profound impact on the NHL and international hockey.
PETER STASTNY

Coaching was dearer to him, though, and in 1969 he assumed duties as boss in Philadelphia, a tenure that ended after two stormy years. He had issued an edict against the five French-Canadian players on the team, forbidding them to speak anything but English any time, anywhere. The players simply ignored Stasiuk, who in turn lost respect and power as coach. He later coached in California and Vancouver, and after leaving hockey altogether he moved back to his 600-acre farm in Alberta to grow potatoes and corn. He later converted the farm into a golf course.

STASTNY, Anton

b. Bratislava, Czechoslovakia (Slovakia), August 5, 1959

Anton and brother Peter defected to Canada immediately after the 1980 Olympics in Lake Placid, joining the Quebec Nordiques. The next year, the third Stastny, Marian, also defected, and the NHL had the finest European line in league history. Anton, the left winger, played all of his 9 seasons with the Nordiques, averaging nearly 30 goals a season with the team. He played during the very peak of the Montreal-Quebec rivalry, though he was not a physical player. He returned to Europe in 1989 to finish his career, and after retiring he spent a good deal of time in Lausanne and other Swiss towns teaching hockey to kids at the house-league level.

STASTNY, Marian

b. Bratislava, Czechoslovakia (Slovakia), January 8, 1953

The oldest Stastny, Marian, had the shortest career in North America. He defected the year after his brothers, Anton and Peter, and the three formed a dynamic and high-scoring unit. He, too, played in the 1980 Olympics in Lake Placid, but previous to that he appeared in five World Championships and the inaugural Canada Cup in 1976. He won gold with the Czechs at the '76 and '77 WC, and silver the other three years. He finished his career in Toronto, but when he retired he returned to Quebec City, his adopted home. He opened Club de golf Marian Stastny and has been running it ever since.

STASTNY, Peter

b. Bratislava, Czechoslovakia (Slovakia), September 18, 1956

There is no European player who has had a more profound impact on the NHL and international hockey in the same lifetime, no player who has had as great an impact on his country's hockey program, and no player as giving of his time, experience, and knowledge. In the 1980s, the only player who recorded more points in the NHL was a guy named Gretzky. Stastny burst onto the hockey scene in 1976 when, at 19, he was a star on the Czech team in the World Championships. He helped the team to a stunning gold medal, made possible after Poland beat the Soviet Union 6-4 in the greatest international upset of all time. The next year, Stastny won another gold, and in the two subsequent WCs he won a pair of silver medals. The team had an awful performance in the 1980 Olympics in Lake Placid, but by age 24 Stastny was hands-down the best hockey player in Czechoslovakia. That summer, he took a trip to Austria with his brother, Anton, and they never went home. Instead, they flew to Quebec City where the Nordiques were awaiting their arrival. A year later, their brother Marian joined them, and for the first time three European brothers were playing on the same forward line in the NHL. Peter was the most skilled, and to watch him was to watch puck genius. He had all the skills one would expect from a star, and, like Gretzky, he had remarkable vision of the whole ice and wonderful anticipation. Like a grandmaster, he could see what was going to unfold three moves from the present. In his first NHL season, Stastny had 39 goals and 109 points and won the Calder Trophy, an honour that was a bit of a misnomer in that he had played pro in Europe for many years (the win inspired the league to change the rules for eligibility for the tro-

Vic Stasiuk

Anton Stastny

Marian Stastny

phy, but that should not denigrate his superb first season in North America). Incredibly, it was the first of six successive seasons he reached 100 points in a year. During this time, Stastny also created a stir when he took out Canadian citizenship and then played for Canada in the 1984 Canada Cup. It was a move that irked the Czechs, and it called into question national eligibility. However, there was no perestroika in sight in 1984, and for Stastny, he could not have believed he would ever set foot in Czechoslovakia again. He played nine and a half seasons with the Nordiques, establishing roots in Quebec City and learning English and French. He was traded to New Jersey and finished his career in St. Louis in 1995, but spent his later years more concerned with his homeland, which had, remarkably, become free and then split into Czech Republic and Slovakia.

A staunch nationalist, Stastny did whatever he could to help the Slovaks get on the hockey map. He represented his country at the 1994 Olympics in Lillehammer, and the next year he played for Slovakia in "B" pool of the world championships. They won the tournament, moving up to "A" pool the following year, after which the 39-year-old retired as a player. His work was not yet done, though. He worked with St. Louis as a scout, and became GM of the Slovak program, helping the team move up the ranks in "A" pool. He took the team to the Olympics in 1998 and 2002, and then at the 2002 World Championships became part of history when Slovakia won gold. The celebrations in Bratislava were extraordinary, and after years of work, the players, guided and inspired by their hero Stastny, had established Slovakia as a true hockey power, joining the big six as one of the top hockey nations on the planet. He was inducted into the Hockey Hall of Fame in 1998 and the IIHF Hall of Fame in 2000, a man whose accomplishments on ice are worthy of the epithet "great."

STASZAK, Ray
b. Philadelphia, Pennsylvania, December 1, 1962
The media dubbed him the Man of Steel. He didn't start skating until he was 13 and played junior B in Philadelphia with a team called the Bucks-Mont Glaciers. In the summers, he worked at a steel mill to save enough money to try out for the junior A Austin Mavericks in Minnesota, and from there he went to the University of Illinois-Chicago. That's when things started to get a little weird. No NHL team drafted him, yet he played well in college and had scouts drooling. They said he was big and strong, but his skating needed work. Teams started a bidding war, and he signed the richest rookie contract ever, a $1.3-million deal over five years arranged by his agent,

Rick St. Croix

Brian Burke. Only the Leafs showed no interest in acquiring the right winger. Staszak left college and joined the Red Wings, but the big league proved to be his kryptonite. In four games he registered a lone assist before being demoted. In the minors he suffered a serious groin injury that ended his season, and the year after he missed the entire season because of a torn rotator cuff. The Wings placed him on waivers, which he cleared, and then bought him out. Staszak retired a rich man, and likely the greatest rookie bust in the history of the NHL.

STAUBER, Robb
b. Duluth, Minnesota, November 25, 1967
The Hobey Baker Award is both a prize and a burden. Some players who win it go on to become stars in the NHL, but most do not. In 1988, Stauber was the first goalie to win the top honour in U.S. college playing for the University of Minnesota, but he went on to only a middling NHL career. He was, if nothing else, an innovator. In Los Angeles, he wore custom-designed pads and blocker that featured the king of clubs and spades, diamonds, and hearts on his pads and blocker. After retiring, he opened a goalie and golf school (figuring the two go hand in hand, so to speak) in Minnesota, and he invented something called the Staubar, an elastic device that is worn across a goalie's belly and attaches to the goalposts to develop positional play.

After retiring, he opened a goalie and golf school in Minnesota.
ROBB STAUBER

ST. CROIX, Rick
b. Kenora, Ontario, January 3, 1955
Every goalie aspires to be a starter, a number-one man, and to that end every goalie is prepared to start as number two, learn the ropes, and play himself into the top spot. St. Croix never really had the chance and from day one played himself into a reputation as a good backup. He joined Philadelphia in 1977 but for three years played the starter's role in the AHL, where he was a standout. When he got to the Flyers on a full-time basis, he was backup to Pete Peeters and then Pelle Lindbergh. He welcomed a trade to Toronto, but again he was backup to Mike Palmateer and then third behind the emerging duo of Allan Bester and Ken Wregget. After retiring in 1986, he started the Rick St. Croix School of Goaltending in Winnipeg and was later goalie coach for the Dallas Stars and Winnipeg Moose.

STEELE, Frank
b. Niagara Falls, Ontario, March 19, 1905
d. unknown
Christmas in 1930 was mighty fine for Steele, for that was the night he played his one and only NHL game. He had been playing in Detroit for the Olympics,

but he was called to the Wings for a game and returned to the IHL team right after. He played much of his career in the Motor City and across the river in Windsor.

STEEN, Anders
b. Nykoping, Sweden, April 28, 1955
After watching the success of Swede Anders Kallur with the Islanders, Winnipeg GM John Ferguson flew to the far reaches of Sweden to sign Steen, a big man with great hands and strong legs. Steen had been a star with Farjestads for years, and when he came to camp in 1980 with the Jets he looked impressive – until he strained knee ligaments and was out for a month. When he returned, he scored a goal in his first game and went on a mini-tear, but in half a season he wound up with just five goals and a ticket to the minors. After one season, Steen returned to Sweden to play, and later became a scout for St. Louis after hanging up the skates for good.

STEEN, Thomas
b. Grums, Sweden, June 8, 1960
The lines begin to blur with the Steen family. Thomas began playing in his native Sweden, becoming a star with Leksand and Farjestad with Hakan Loob. He won a silver medal at the 1981 World Championships, then played in that year's Canada Cup before joining the Winnipeg Jets right after. He played all 14 of his NHL years with the Jets, becoming the first Swedish captain of that team. Indeed, he was a leader. He was always among the team's top scorers, and his intelligent and responsible play was key to the team's success. He played in the 1984 Canada Cup on a line with Loob and Kent Nilsson, taking Tre Kronor on a surprise trip to the finals, where they lost to Canada. When he retired from the NHL in 1994, the Jets retired his number 25, an honour bestowed previously only on Bobby Hull. Steen played in Germany and later became an assistant coach with Vastra Frolunda. While he lived in Winnipeg, he had a son named Alexander who played much of his minor hockey in that city. The family returned to Sweden as Thomas retired and became an NHL scout, and young Alexander played for Frolunda. He was drafted by the Leafs in 2002, a Swede born in Canada playing in Sweden!

STEFAN, Greg
b. Brantford, Ontario, February 11, 1961
Gary Stefan was a goalie with Wayne Gretzky in house league in Brantford for a year, and when he left the team his brother, Greg, took over in net. By this time, Gretzky was a local phenom and would sometimes ask Stefan to wear his team jacket and sign autographs! Greg later played junior and then went on to the NHL, while Gary went to Britain and played for 20 years, earning induction into the British Ice Hockey Hall of Fame. Greg played his entire nine years in the NHL with Detroit throughout the 1980s, lean years by current Detroit standards. A product of Billy Smith's stick-swinging ways, Stefan was a hatchet man of note and players were punished if they encroached too closely on his crease. Stefan's career ended after he suffered another serious injury to his right knee. After retiring, he joined the Celebrity Players Tour as a golfer and he did work for the Wings as a TV analyst. He also worked as senior vice-president of Premier Sports Management. In 1992 he was inducted into the Brantford Hall of Fame.

STEFAN, Patrik
b. Pribram, Czechoslovakia (Czech Republic), September 16, 1980
There has been a long history of number-one draft choices becoming NHL busts, and so far Stefan fits into that category, though Atlanta is in some way to blame. The Thrashers made him the 1st-overall selection in 1999 despite his suffering two serious concussions in the IHL, where he opted to play instead of either home or Canadian junior. Since then, he has been slowed by a number of small injuries and has been outshone by Dany Heatley and Ilya Kovalchuk, two other high draft choices who have produced the goods early in their respective and collaborative careers.

STEFANIW, Morris
b. North Battleford, Saskatchewan, January 10, 1948
The staggering asterisk that was the '72-'73 season for Stefaniw might be easily explained or remain a hockey conundrum for all time. Yet here was a player in Nova Scotia, Montreal's farm team, who had never been drafted but was signed by Atlanta, sent to the Voyageurs on loan and tore the league apart. He became only the eighth AHLer to hit the 70-assist mark for the year, finishing with a league high of 71, playing on a line with two Habs prospects, Yvon Lambert and Tony Featherstone. Yet neither before nor after did Stefaniw come near the 30 goals he scored. He retired 3 years later, a minor leaguer who played just 13 games with the Flames.

STEFANSKI, Edward "Bud"
b. South Porcupine, Ontario, April 28, 1955
He played just two years with the Oshawa Generals (1973-75) but these left an indelible impression upon him. Stefanski turned pro in the IHL and these left a longtime player in the AHL, getting into a single game with the NHL Rangers along the way. After retiring, he started a career coaching in the OHL, a lengthy term of duty that continues to this day, most recently as head coach for the Barrie Colts.

STEIN, Phil
b. Toronto, Ontario, September 13, 1913
A minor leaguer who got and lost his break due to injury, Stein played all of one NHL game, for the Leafs. On January 18, 1940, he played in place of legendary Turk Broda, who was injured. Stein acquitted himself very well, playing to a 2-2 overtime tie with Detroit. He was slated to start a second game against the Americans two nights later, but in the warmup he was hit in the mouth by a shot, lost a number of teeth, and had to be replaced by Broda. He played all of the rest of his career in the minors, and when he retired he turned to his second love, baseball. Stein started the Leaside baseball league and helped develop Ron Taylor, future World Series winner. Stein was a sports director in Leaside for 12 years and manager of Leaside Memorial Gardens for 8, the arena where Frank Mahovlich's father was a famous and expert skate sharpener. Stein later worked as a sales rep for Hiram Walker distillery before retiring.

Anders Steen

Thomas Steen

Greg Stefan

Patrik Stefan

Phil Stein

Pete Stemkowski

Bob Stephenson

Ron Stern

STEMKOWSKI, Pete ("Stemmer"/ "The Magnetic Pole")
b. Winnipeg, Manitoba, August 25, 1943

Playing for the Leafs in the 1960s meant winning and winning some more. Stemkowski started by winning the Memorial Cup with the Marlies in 1964 and went on to play with Bob Pulford and Jim Pappin to help bring home the Cup in 1967. He was traded to Detroit with Frank Mahovlich in a multiplayer deal, but never got along with coach Ned Harkness and wound up going to the Rangers, though the Detroit view was that he wouldn't lose weight to get into playing shape. He had some of his finest years on Broadway, scoring a goal in triple overtime in the 1971 playoffs and recording three 20-goal seasons. He went to the Cup finals in '72 before losing to Boston. Everywhere he went he was known for his humour and relaxed attitude, attributes that were lacking one night in Long Island after he retired. He had made a bad business investment with bad people and offered an undercover officer $20,000 to break the wrists and ankles of the man whom Stemkowski thought owed him money. Stemkowski was charged with larceny and later sentenced to three years probation and ordered to undergo psychological therapy. Before and after, he was involved in Islanders telecasts and became sports director for a radio station that broadcast the team's games.

STENLUND, Vern
b. Thunder Bay, Ontario, April 11, 1956

It wasn't as a player that Stenlund has made his place in hockey. On that front, he played all of four games with Cleveland during the '76-'77 season coming out of London in the OHL. Rather, it was as a coach and writer. Stenlund crafted a number of books on developing hockey skills, and as a coach he has been active for almost 20 years. He was an assistant at the University of Windsor, and then moved to the OHL, principally with the Spits. He also coached junior B and later became an associate professor at U of W in the faculty of education, becoming the school's head coach of the hockey team in 2002. He also coached the Leamington Flyers

STEPHENSON, Bob
b. Saskatoon, Saskatchewan, February 1, 1954

He may have been born in nearby Saskatoon, but he lived in Outlook, a tiny spot on the map no bigger than a sesame seed. Stephenson attended St. F-X in Nova Scotia to get an education, but in 1977 he turned pro in the WHA. In all, he played just four years of hockey, including a few games with Hartford and the Leafs. After retiring, he went into politics in a big and small way. That is, he is the mayor of Outlook.

STEPHENSON, Wayne
b. Fort William, Ontario, January 29, 1945

For the first few years of his career, Stephenson played for Canada's National Team. He preferred to see the world than the NHL, and his time in Winnipeg, where the team was based, allowed him to study toward his degree in accounting. He played in goal for Canada at the 1968 Olympics in Grenoble and the next year at the World Championships, where he was given the nod in nets over Ken Dryden. He turned pro with St. Louis in 1972 and became a member of the Flyers in the fall of 1974. It was the best of times and the worst of times for him because he won the Cup in that first year with the team but he was forever the backup to Bernie Parent. When Parent missed '75-'76 with an injury, Stephenson played brilliantly on the year. He had a 40-10-13 record and played in the All-Star Game, but the year after he was a backup again. In 1977 he demanded a hefty pay raise to warm the bench, and when Philadelphia refused to acquiesce, he finished his accounting studies and had every intention of finding a job in that field. The Flyers gave in, but two years later he was traded to Washington where he got plenty of game time on an awful team. He again was miffed, though, when the Caps acquired Mike Palmateer, another man capable of being number one. Stephenson retired in 1981 because of a back injury that wouldn't go away. He settled in Milwaukee and worked as a commercial lender for Maine Bank and helped instruct kids in the finer arts and skills of the game.

Stephenson retired in 1981 because of a back injury that wouldn't go away.
WAYNE STEPHENSON

STERN, Ron
b. Ste. Agathe, Quebec, January 11, 1967

Like many a kid, Stern played his junior hockey in Quebec, with Longueuil. There was an awful difference, though. During his final season, while he was captain, his father, David, was killed by a car bombing. Stern struggled on and helped the Chevaliers win the 1987 Memorial Cup, and turned pro the next year. Stern had minimal hockey skills and maximal fighting skills. He made his way through the league as a tough guy, but unlike most, he persevered for 12 seasons. He played his best years with Calgary, where he was a fan favourite and the owner of two restaurants. But, after suffering serious knee injury, he missed all of '97-'98 and the Flames released him, figuring he was through. Not quite. He signed with San Jose and put his body through hell for two more seasons, retiring in 2000 only because of back and neck injuries that required surgery. He had survived 638 regular-season games.

STERNER, Ulf ("Uffe")
b. Deje, Sweden, February 11, 1941

Even before Salming and Hammarstrom in 1973, there was Sterner, the true pioneer, the first European-trained player to give the NHL a try. He had made his way into Tre Kronor history in 1962 when he scored two goals in a key 5-3 win over Canada at the World Championships, the first time his country had ever beaten the great power and only the third gold medal for the Swedes ever. He was a scorer and great passer who first played with the national team at age 17, the youngest ever to represent his country. In 1964, when he decided to try the NHL, he was a hero back home merely for making the effort. The Rangers signed him and sent him to St. Paul, where coach Fred Shero tried to get him used to physical, North American hockey, but Sterner played only four times for the Rangers.

He left after just one season, disliking the team and coaching. He returned to Sweden and continued his brilliant career, playing in five more World Championships and establishing his place as the best player ever developed in that country. He evidently learned something from North America, though, because in 1970 he was suspended for fighting in one international match and for punching a referee. He also played Team Canada in 1972 as it headed from Canada to Moscow during the Summit Series, and he was front and centre in a brawl-like atmosphere when he high-sticked Wayne Cashman, Sterner's stick going into Cashman's mouth and slicing his tongue for dozens of stitches. He later became a coach in Sweden and was inducted into the IIHF Hall of Fame in 2001.

STEVENS, John
b. Campbellton, New Brunswick, May 4, 1966

From down east, Stevens made his way to Oshawa to play junior, and from there he went on to Philadelphia, where he has been ever since. He played just a few games with the Flyers, spending most of his time in the minors, and after he signed with Hartford, it was déjà vu all over again, in the words of Yogi Berra. During his 13 years in the AHL, Stevens won 3 Calder Cups. He returned to the Flyers organization in 1996 and was named captain of the new Phantoms team, but his career was cut short by an eye injury suffered in December 1998. He was immediately named an assistant coach of the team, and the following summer he became the head man, a position he has held ever since.

STEVENS, Kevin
b. Brockton, Massachusetts, April 15, 1965

The common axiom in hockey is, never let the highs get too high or the lows get too low. Stevens managed both in one night. He was a Boston College graduate in 1987 and spent a year with the American National Team leading up to the 1988 Olympics in Calgary. He joined Pittsburgh after the Games and over the course of the next eight seasons developed into one of the finest power forwards in the league. He scored 40 goals or more in 4 successive years, including back-to-back 50-goal years when he had 123 and 111 points, respectively. He helped the team win two Stanley Cups, and with Ron Francis and Jaromir Jagr provided huge backup to the great Mario Lemieux. He missed much of the next year with a broken ankle, and then was traded to Boston in a payroll move. He quickly moved on to L.A. and the Rangers, and in New York his personal problems became public. On January 22, 2000, he was arrested after he picked up a prostitute, bought crack cocaine, and went back to his hotel, where he caused a ruckus and the police were called. At home, his pregnant wife was distraught by the news, and the story emerged that Stevens had had his share of similar troubles in Los Angeles. He checked into a clinic and enrolled in the NHLPA's assistance program, but the damage had been done despite his immense popularity throughout the league. He returned the following year but was a pale comparison to his former self, a self not many people, apparently, knew. In the fall of 2002, he retired and moved into the broadcast booth.

STEVENS, Mike
b. Kitchener, Ontario, December 30, 1965

It has been more than a decade since Stevens last played in the NHL, back in the 1980s when he spread his 23 games thin over 4 teams. The left winger scored only one goal, but he was signed and re-signed because of his physical play more than his prowess around the net. His last stop was a game with Toronto in 1990, after which he played in the AHL and IHL until 1997. At that point, he moved to Germany to play in the DEL, and has been there ever since.

STEVENS, Phil
b. St. Lambert, Ontario, February 15, 1893
d. Kelowna, British Columbia, April 8, 1968

A member of the Wanderers in the days of the NHA, Stevens stayed with the team when it joined the NHL, albeit briefly, and later played a few games for the Canadiens and Bruins. He passed the rest of his brief career in the minors, ending in California.

STEVENS, Scott
b. Kitchener, Ontario, April 1, 1964

It's this simple: Three years from the day he retires, Scott Stevens will be inducted into the Hockey Hall of Fame. While his brother, Mike, made but a small

Ulf Sterner

It's this simple: Three years from the day he retires, Scott Stevens will be inducted into the Hockey Hall of Fame.
SCOTT STEVENS

Kevin Stevens

Jeremy Stevenson

Shayne Stevenson

Turner Stevenson

Al Stewart

Bill Stewart

impression in the NHL, Scott has made a huge one. He started in 1982 as a rookie in Washington after the Caps selected him 5th overall, and ever since he has been a star defenceman in the league. First and foremost, he has earned a reputation as the hardest clean hitter in the game, most evident in his crushing shoulder to the head of Eric Lindros during the 2000 playoffs. In his early days, the Caps were hit-and-miss to make the playoffs, so Stevens augmented his season with four trips to the World Championships. His eight years in Washington came to an end in 1990 when he signed a $5.145-million deal over four years with St. Louis, a deal that changed hands only a year later. The Blues signed Brendan Shanahan the year after, but as compensation they lost Stevens to New Jersey. Since then, Stevens has captained one of the best teams of the last decade and led them to their first two Stanley Cups, in 1995 and again in 2000. In addition to his more than 1,400 NHL games, he has also played at the 1991 Canada Cup, 1996 World Cup, and 1998 Olympics for Team Canada, though he was left off the team that played at Salt Lake City in 2002. He has played in 13 All-Star Games, but amazingly his only individual award came from the most recent Cup win when he was named Conn Smythe Trophy winner. That year epitomized his brilliance. Stevens is a huge presence inside his own blueline. He has size and quickness and moves the puck well out of his own end, but his ability to hit with intimidating violence is what has always given him an edge. Players cutting over his blueline with their head down will be punished with clean open-ice checks and will, the next time, skate in a far more timorous soul. Truly, they don't make 'em like this any more.

STEVENSON, Doug
b. Regina, Saskatchewan, April 6, 1924
In 1944-45, Maurice Richard scored 50 goals in 50 games, many coming against subpar goalies while the NHL superstar puckstoppers were off at war. In game number 49, at home in Montreal, Richard had 49 goals and was facing a Chicago team that couldn't put Mike Karakas in net. He was injured, so the Hawks had to go with Stevenson. He lost the game 4-3, but Richard didn't score. Even more amazing, Stevenson stopped the Rocket on a penalty shot late in the game! In all, Stevenson played in only eight games during the war year, allowing nearly five goals each time out. He played out west for many years before retiring, but when he did he could always claim to have stopped the Rocket one-on-one at the Forum.

STEVENSON, Jeremy
b. San Bernardino, California, July 28, 1974
Refusing to sign with the team that drafts you is a crapshoot at best, as Stevenson found out. He was selected 60th overall by Winnipeg in 1992 but decided he could go higher, get a better deal, and improve over the 2 years he was playing while unsigned. He was dead wrong. In 1994, Anaheim drafted him a miserable 262nd overall, and his bargaining leverage was nil. Since then he's played tough guy for the Ducks and then Nashville, getting into a few games here and there but playing most of his time in the minors.

STEVENSON, Shayne
b. Newmarket, Ontario, October 26, 1970
When he retired in 2000, he had had enough. Not even 30, he had 5 concussions on his medical records, and the first-round draft choice in 1989 had done more than his share of being goaded into fighting and being taunted and putting up with intimidating hockey. Yet when he spoke out, the silence was deafening and the game continued apace. Just another concussion case. Just another guy who had played only a handful of NHL games and ended up in the Colonial league and Britain. Hardly counts as a voice at all.

STEVENSON, Turner ("T")
b. Prince George, British Columbia, May 18, 1972
After spending the first eight seasons of his career with Montreal, Stevenson wound up with a playoff team in New Jersey for the 2000-01 schedule. The rugged right winger had been a first-round draft choice by Montreal, but he quickly developed into a scrapper and fourth-liner who could contribute without being a detriment. As a junior, he won a gold with Canada at the 1992 WJC.

STEWART, Alan
b. Fort St. John, British Columbia, January 31, 1964
Plagued by serious injuries, Stewart got out of the game while he could still walk. He played most of his career in the New Jersey organization starting in 1983, but he was a minor leaguer who got only the occasional call to the Devils. He broke his leg in four places during training camp in 1989 and missed virtually the whole year, and two years later he suffered a knee injury that cost him another full year. He tried to make a brief comeback, but when he re-aggravated the knee, he retired.

STEWART, Bill
b. Toronto, Ontario, October 6, 1957
It's been an active and event-filled life, and Stewart isn't yet 50. He played junior in the OHL and joined Buffalo in 1977 as a rough-and-tumble defenceman. He moved on to St. Louis in the hopes of cracking the lineup, but in '81-'82 he took four severe blows to the head (two via pucks, two via sticks) which caused him headaches for a year and caused him to lose his place on the team. He got to the Leafs in the hopes of starting fresh, but he was demoted, threw a hissy fit, and that was the end of his time in Toronto. He started the '85-'86 season in the minors, but he was suspended for the foreseeable future when he fired a puck at a linesman. The North Stars immediately summoned him to the NHL – justice never transferred properly between the two leagues – and he played his final NHL games before going to Italy to start another career that lasted nine years. During that time he was allowed to play for the Azzurri internationally, and so Stewart appeared in two Olympics and two World Championships wearing the *tricolore*. When he returned to Canada, he began a coaching career that had as bizarre an ending as one could imagine. He started in the minors and came back to the OHL, eventually landing with the Islanders as an assistant and becoming head coach for part of the '98-'99 season. He ended up back in junior, coaching and managing Barrie, but he effectively lost his jobs when

he was discovered to be smuggling a Ukrainian-born player, Vladimir Chernenko, across the border in the luggage compartment of a bus. He resigned his position because U.S. Immigration would not permit him entry, making it difficult for him to carry out his duties. He still hopes to get back to the NHL as a coach.

STEWART, Blair
b. Winnipeg, Manitoba, March 15, 1953

These weren't the cuts and bruises that are the daily bread of pro hockey. No, siree. The injuries exacted on Stewart's body were devastating career-enders all, and in the end they won out. In the summer of 1974, he broke his leg in a car accident. Then he broke his foot after getting into a few games with Detroit and Washington. He broke his leg again two years later, and a year after that he suffered tears in both rotator cuffs. In 1981 he retired in one piece and became an entrepreneur. He started a telephone message service called Fan Phone Gift Package, in which a person's favourite star leaves a personalized wish on an answering machine (happy birthday, happy anniversary, etc.), and now in the age of the Internet, he has introduced ProWish, a service for the Web in which stars leave video-recorded messages for the same purposes.

Blair Stewart

STEWART, Bob ("Stewie")
b. Charlottetown, Prince Edward Island, November 10, 1950

He went from being a scoring defenceman in junior to a hard-hitting defender in the NHL, but unfortunately he played many years for bad teams and holds the NHL record for the worst career +/- statistic of all time, a -260. Stewart started his career in Boston, but after a few games he was traded to California. He became the Seals' best defenceman and team captain, but the Seals were an awful team that never made the playoffs during his five years with them. Stewart moved to Cleveland with the franchise and closed out his career in St. Louis and Pittsburgh, where he finally appeared in the playoffs before retiring.

STEWART, Cam ("Stew")
b. Kitchener, Ontario, September 18, 1971

Six concussions, game over. In the old days, loss of an eye was the horrible end to so many careers. Today, careers will end in greater and greater frequency because of post-concussion syndrome. Stewart started his NHL career with Boston in 1993 but played just 202 games in the big league, spending a good deal of time in the minors and an increasing amount of time on the injury list. On September 25, 2001, at training camp with Minnesota, he suffered his final head injury. Six months later, he still couldn't ride a stationary bike with-

He played on the Flying Forts line with Gus Bodnar and Bud Poile, all natives of Fort William.
GAYE STEWART

out severe headaches and nausea. He retired at 31, though not by choice.

STEWART, Charles
b. Carleton Place, Ontario, November 13, 1895
d. unknown

A tiny goalie who played most of his hockey in southern Ontario, Stewart was the main man between the pipes with Boston when the team joined the NHL in 1924. He remained with the Bruins for three increasingly more successful years, after which he retired.

STEWART, Gaye ("Punch"/ "Swish")
b. Fort William, Ontario, June 28, 1923

No player ever had the year Stewart did in 1941-42. He started the year as a junior, moved up to play senior hockey, then had a short stay in minor pro, and finally was called up to the Leafs and won the Stanley Cup. Then, he returned home to finish high school! The next year, Stewart scored 24 goals as a rookie and won the Calder Trophy. Not a bad start to his career, and never mind that he went off to join the army for two years. When he returned to the game, it was as though not a day had passed. His first year back he led the league in goals with 37 (to this day the last Leafs player to do so), and the next year he won another Cup. He played on the Flying Forts line with Gus Bodnar and Bud Poile, all natives of Fort William. He later did a tour of the Original Six, playing for every other team except Boston. After retiring, he coached Chicago's affiliate in Buffalo for a year and then became an NHL referee for two seasons. Stewart then joined the labour force, getting a job in sales and marketing with Molson Brewery, a job he held until 1988 when he retired. In his day, he was considered the fastest skater in the league, but he will go down in history for an act of violence caught in one of hockey's greatest photographs. In his rookie season, he and Jimmy Orlando clubbed each other about the head and face repeatedly until both were bloodied and semi-comatose. They were suspended and fined, and the image captured by Nat Turofsky is an unforgettable moment of an unconscionably violent act.

Bob Stewart

STEWART, Jack ("Black Jack")
b. Pilot Mound, Manitoba, May 6, 1917
d. Troy, Michigan, May 25, 1983

Stewart grew up on his family's wheat farm and learned to play hockey on outdoor rinks in the area. He was an outstanding player as a teen but didn't get a break until a Winnipeg businessman, Gene Houghton, recommended Stewart to a friend, James Norris, owner of the Wings. Stewart was assigned to Pittsburgh in 1937 and after just a year-and-a-half in the minors the Wings

Cam Stewart

Jack Stewart

called him up. He never went back. Right from the start he impressed coach and GM Jack Adams with a character that had "winner" written all over it. He was a deceptively fast skater, but there was nothing deceptive about his hitting, which was front and centre the most obviously impressive part of his game. He got his nickname when, apparently, a dazed opponent skated to the bench asking who hit him with a black jack. Before the war, Stewart was paired with the equally feared Jimmy Orlando on defence and, as Adams said, opponents seldom made it past those two. The Wings won the Cup in 1943, Stewart's fifth year in the league, and the first time he was named to the First All-Star Team. He then he left the game to join the war. He served as a Leading Aircraftman for the RCAF for two years, rejoining the Red Wings in 1945, teamed with Bill Quackenbush on the blue-line. After another five years, Stewart was part of the 1950 Cup-winning team and was then traded to Chicago. Rumour had it that Adams was aware of Stewart's deteriorating back, but regardless, his last two seasons were shortened – first by surgery and then by disability. On January 8, 1951, too pained by his back, Stewart retired. He then purchased the Chatham Maroons, a senior team, and decided to coach and play at that much lower level. He later coached in Kitchener and then with Pittsburgh in the AHL before serving as a judge at harness races at Wolverine Raceway outside Detroit. He retired to Florida but had to move back to Michigan to undergo treatment for cancer, the disease which finally took his life in 1983. He had been inducted into the Hockey Hall of Fame in 1964, and is still considered among the hardest-hitting defencemen the game has ever seen.

STEWART, Jim
b. Cambridge, Massachusetts, April 23, 1957
A great break turned into the worst night of his life. Goalie Stewart had a good training camp with Boston in 1979 as a walk-on, and the Bruins signed him to a contract. He started in the minors, but in January 1980 when Gerry Cheevers was injured and Gilles Gilbert had the flu, he was called up to start and another minor leaguer, Marco Baron, was called in as his backup. Well, Stewart allowed a goal on his first shot and five in the first period, and he was pulled. Baron went in and gave up two goals, and both were returned to the minors. Baron was later given another few chances over the years – Stewart was not.

STEWART, John
b. Eriksdale, Manitoba, May 16, 1950
After playing his junior hockey out west, Stewart made the Pittsburgh lineup in 1970 at his first camp, a prom-

John Stewart

ising 20-year-old on a young and not very good team. He played five years of NHL hockey, but not until year three did he play a full season. He had decent scoring ability but went to Atlanta and then California, not a good change. In 1975, Stewart left to play in the WHA for two years and ended his career in the minors.

STEWART, John ("J.C.")
b. Toronto, Ontario, January 2, 1954
Although Montreal drafted him in 1974, the Habs never really came close to using Stewart in a game. He signed with Cleveland of the WHA and spent five years in that league until it joined the NHL. At that time, he was claimed by Quebec in the Dispersal Draft of WHA players, and appeared in two NHL games with the Nordiques before ending his career back in the minors.

STEWART, Ken
b. Port Arthur, Ontario, March 29, 1913
d. unknown
Kenneth Laurence Stewart was no ordinary defenceman in the pre-war days. He was a leader, an explosive offensive player, and a gentleman. He played most of his hockey out west, reaching early prominence as a centre with Luscar in 1935-36. He switched to defence the year after and stayed there the rest of his career. He moved on to senior hockey in Lethbridge, where he played with future teammate Alex Kaleta, and in 1940-41 he not only was one of the league's top scorers but he became the team's playing coach in mid-season, taking the club to the Allan Cup semifinals. A year later, Chicago promoted him to the NHL for six games, and after

On January 3, 1931, Stewart set another record when he scored two goals in just four seconds.
NELS STEWART

that he entered the Royal Canadian Army Service Corps as a private. After the war, he played senior hockey again for a while before retiring.

STEWART, Nelson "Nels" ("Ol' Poison")
b. Montreal, Quebec, December 29, 1900
d. Wasaga Beach, Ontario, August 21, 1957
They just don't make nicknames like they used to. Ol' Poison earned his moniker because of his scoring ability and because, to a lesser degree, he had a mean streak. He grew up in the Beach area of Toronto with Hooley Smith, later to be a linemate, and was an outstanding all-round athlete. Stewart started his pro career at age 20 in Cleveland where he played for five years. When the USAHA ceased operations, he signed with the Montreal Maroons and there began a lengthy and successful career in the NHL; it started with a bang the likes of which has never been replicated. In his rookie season, he led the league with 34 goals, won the scoring title with 42 points, was named winner of the Hart Trophy, and helped the team to a Stanley Cup victory. He

played seven years with the Maroons, the last three rewarding because he played on the deadly S Line with Hooley Smith and Babe Siebert, the top-scoring line in the league. That first year as part of the threesome, 1929-30, Stewart won his second Hart Trophy. He later played with Boston and the New York Americans and reached the 20-goal mark nine times. He retired in 1940 having scored 324 career goals, tops in the league. It was a record that lasted until 1952 when Maurice Richard bettered it. On January 3, 1931, Stewart also set another record when he scored two goals in just four seconds. This lasted 64 years until Deron Quint of Winnipeg tied the mark in December 1995. Stewart returned to Toronto and worked as a sales rep for O'Keefe Breweries, eventually settling in Humberstone, Ontario. He was inducted into the Hockey Hall of Fame posthumously in 1962, having died of a heart attack in 1957 while vacationing on Georgian Bay.

STEWART, Paul ("Stewy")

b. Boston, Massachusetts, March 21, 1954

Believe it or not, Stewart began his hockey career on December 14, 1975, only after earning a degree from the University of Pennsylvania. In his first game with Binghamton he established his reputation as a fighter, and he never looked back. He was a goon of the first order, a player with very limited skills but a man who could throw punches on skates. He played a few games with the Nordiques in their first season in the NHL and retired soon after. He tried to find a job in the real world, but missed the game too much and decided to try his hand at refereeing. His grandfather, Bill,

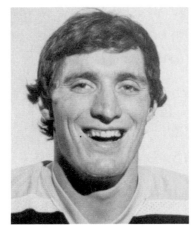

His grandfather, Bill, had coached the Black Hawks to the 1938 Stanley Cup.
PAUL STEWART

had coached the Black Hawks to the 1938 Stanley Cup and was later an umpire in baseball, so perhaps adjudication was in the genes. At any rate, Stewart worked his way up the ranks, eventually getting into the NHL in 1987. He developed a well-earned reputation as an official who called the game by "feel," one who let some infractions go in the name of flow and who let the fighters fight because he, and the fans, enjoyed a good and even one-on-one. Over the years, though, his ego got in the way and he refereed as if he were the star, not the players. He didn't judge by feel any more so much as he controlled the game, as was his wish. None of that mattered in February 1998, though, when doctors told him he had colon cancer. He likely wouldn't live to see the end of the year, they warned. Stewart was in top trim and underwent the chemotherapy with strength and resolve. He not only survived, he made his way back into the NHL and helped initiate a program called Hockey Fights Cancer. It was a truly remarkable recovery and comeback, a feel-good story of the ability of at least one man to meet the big C head on and come out a winner.

STEWART, Ralph ("Stewie")

b. Fort William, Ontario, December 2, 1948

At his best, he was the prototypical centre. He had a long reach and a long stride, was great on faceoffs, and was a superb penalty killer. In '73-'74, with the Islanders, he scored 23 goals, 5 of them short-handed. He started and ended his career with Vancouver, though he spent the bulk of his playing days in the Central league. Stewart was later inducted into the Northwestern Sports Hall of Fame.

Ralph Stewart

STEWART, Ron ("Stew")

b. Calgary, Alberta, July 11, 1932

If the Hockey Hall of Fame were to add a few players from the past to its roster of inductees, Stewart's name would be right there as a contender. He rose to prominence in '51-'52 during his final season of junior, a strange one to say the least. He started with the Marlies, went to Windsor for two games, and was traded to Barrie. He played for his fourth team of the season when Guelph acquired him, and with the Biltmores he won the Memorial Cup. That team included Andy Bathgate, Harry Howell, and Dean Prentice. Stewart played 21 years in the NHL, starting in 1952 with the Leafs, the team with which he spent his first 13 seasons. During that time, he was hailed as the finest all-round player in the league, a versatile man who could play defence one shift, left wing the next. He was a right winger by trade, and although he scored 20 goals only twice he was a role player extraordinaire. He was with the Toronto dynasty that won Cups in 1962, '63, and

Ron Stewart

'64, and he later played most of his days with the Rangers before finishing with the expansion Islanders. He went into coaching and led Springfield to the Calder Cup in '74-'75. He was named coach of the year and went on to coach the Rangers the year after. He later coached L.A. for a year before returning to Calgary to coach the Spurs in provincial junior play.

STEWART, Ryan

b. Houston, British Columbia, June 1, 1967

It looked for a while as though he was going to make the Jets, yet Stewart played just three games in '85-'86 with the team and spent the rest of his career in the minors and then Britain where he was a sensational scorer in a weak league.

STIENBURG, Trevor

b. Kingston, Ontario, May 13, 1966

A serious knee injury with Quebec in 1985 forced Stienburg to start his pro career slowly, and it wasn't until his fourth year that he played more than eight games with the team. He played the vast majority of

Trevor Stienburg

Cory Stillman

Andre St. Laurent

Dollard
St. Laurent

Martin St. Louis

Frank
St. Marseille

his career in the minors, and after retiring in 1994 he immediately began a coaching career down east, first with Dalhousie. He later led the East Hants Penguins in the Maritime provincial junior A league, and in 1997 Stienburg was named head coach of St. Mary's University hockey team.

STILES, Tony
b. Carstairs, Alberta, August 12, 1959
A graduate of Michigan Tech in 1982, Stiles played for Calgary soon after, but not for very long. He became a minor leaguer, but as the 1988 Olympics in Calgary approached he joined the National Team and played for Canada at the Games. He finished his career playing in Germany.

STILLMAN, Cory
b. Peterborough, Ontario, December 20, 1973
There was a great sense of expectation for Stillman in Calgary after the Flames drafted him 6th overall in 1992, and although he didn't develop into a true superstar he has made a name for himself as a solid centre in the NHL. He has had four 20-goal seasons in the league, though his first true playoffs came only after he was traded to St. Louis midway through the 2000-01 season. He took Peterborough to the Memorial Cup tournament in 1993 and lives there in the summer. He never played at the World Juniors but he did play for Canada at the 1999 World Championships, where he led the team in scoring.

ST. JACQUES, Bruno
b. Montreal, Quebec, August 22, 1980
Although he has become one of the more valuable and dependable players on the Philadelphia Phantoms, St. Jacques wants to take this AHL success to the NHL level. He has played only a few games with the Flyers, but the defenceman keeps working in the minors with the hope of being given another callup.

ST. LAURENT, Andre ("Ace")
b. Rouyn-Noranda, Quebec, February 16, 1953
His father, Frank, was the trainer for the Montreal Junior Canadiens, and his uncle, Dollard, was a longtime NHLer himself. It was under these circumstances that Andre made his way from those same Jr. Habs to the Islanders in 1973 to begin an 11-year NHL career. He scored 31 goals with Detroit 5 years later but was traded to Los Angeles to complete the fiasco of a deal that sent Dale McCourt to Detroit after he refused to go there in an earlier compensation ruling. St. Laurent ended his career in the minors and later played in Europe.

ST. LAURENT, Dollard ("Dolly")
b. Verdun, Quebec, May 12, 1929
For a long time St. Laurent was on top of the heap, playing for Montreal in the 1950s and winning Cups with regularity. He was the unspectacular defenceman, the unsung hero, the guy who did a flawless job in his own end but never played like a flashy star. He just won games, that's all. He joined the Habs for a few games in 1950-51 and made the team two years later, winning the Cup that first season and never looking back. He won three more championships before being traded to Chicago, and even there he brought a winning attitude

that helped the Hawks win the Cup in 1961. He frequently played with injury in the post-season, no more courageously than in 1955. He didn't miss a game of the playoffs, but between games he was in the hospital suffering from boils on his thighs that were so sore he could barely walk. He played a final season with Quebec in the AHL but wanted to make it back to the NHL until he suffered a broken leg and was forced to retire. He later coached the Verdun Pirates and played on a team from Montreal's Depression League organized by Maurice Richard that toured France. He settled in Montreal and ran his own insurance agency until retiring to LaSalle just outside the city.

ST. LAURENT, Sam
b. Arvida, Quebec, February 16, 1959
His pedigree was good, a goalie coming out of the Quebec league, but he was never drafted and played just 34 games in NHL nets over the years. St. Laurent signed first with Philadelphia in 1979, but it was more than six years before he saw his first NHL action, with New Jersey. He played four of his five years with Detroit after being traded by the Devils, but he appeared strictly on a callup basis and finished his career in the minors. He later became a goalie coach with the Rangers and Hartford Wolf Pack.

ST. LOUIS, Martin
b. Laval, Quebec, June 18, 1975
Although he never won the Hobey Baker Award, St. Louis was a three-time finalist in 1995, '96, and '97 with the University of Vermont. Still, he wasn't drafted and he signed with Calgary as a free agent in 1998, though the right winger played only a season and a half before being released. Tampa Bay signed him, and in 2001-02, his second with the Lightning, he was having a fine year when he broke his leg and missed a good part of the season. He rebounded in 2002-03, though, and proved that even at 5' 7" he still belongs in the NHL, not the minors.

ST. MARSEILLE, Frank
b. Levack, Ontario, December 14, 1939
The oldest of nine children born in a mining town, Frank made it out while others didn't. He had been a pipefitter and painter underground but saw in hockey a way of breathing the fresh air his father never did. Yet Frank came to every level of the game later than anyone else. At 23, he was still playing senior hockey, and he got his NHL chance with St. Louis only because his brother, Frederick, had written Scotty Bowman and told him to scout Frank in Port Huron of the IHL. Bowman not only liked what he saw, he called St. Marseille the Gordie Howe of the "I." In his almost six seasons in St. Louis starting in 1967, St. Marseille became the team's all-time leading scorer, and when he was traded to Los Angeles he was reunited with his brother, Frederick. He was a talented opera singer who had auditioned for the Met in New York, but to help pay the rent the powerful tenor sang the national anthem at Kings home games. St. Marseille scored at least 10 goals in every full season he played, but in the middle of '76-'77 he knew things were nearing an end so he accepted a demotion to the farm in Fort Worth, where he became a playing assistant coach. He later coached the Nova

Scotia Voyageurs for several years and returned to the Kings as an assistant. After returning to Canada he became a salesman for United Auto Parts.

STOCK, Philip Joseph "P.J."
b. Victoriaville, Quebec, May 26, 1975
Not even in junior was Stock much of a scorer, so his survival in the NHL has been for other reasons, namely fistic. Since starting with the Rangers in 1997, he has played for 4 teams and averaged a goal every 40 games or so. His penalty minutes are another matter. In that department, mostly in the minors, he has posted heavyweight numbers, and that is how he has endured.

STODDARD, John "Jack" ("Octopus"/ "Elbows")
b. Stoney Creek, Ontario, September 26, 1926
At 6'3" he was the tallest player in the NHL when he joined the Rangers in 1952, though he played just a season and a half with the Blueshirts, his only NHL team. He had a long reach and was a powerful man, the first regular to wear number 13 in league history. He didn't display his scoring prowess in the big league to quite the same degree he did in the AHL, where he was an annual 20-goal man. His pro career was delayed because of the war, and Stoddard played in Nova Scotia where he was a prison guard in the Canadian Navy stationed at Cornwallis. His teammates included Gaye Stewart, George Gee, and Joe Klukay, and after getting out Stoddard turned pro and began his road to the NHL. At the end of his career, he won an Allan Cup with Chatham in 1960. After retiring, he turned to coaching in Owen Sound, Elmira, and Woodstock. Stoddard worked for Schenley Distillers for 7 years and for Molson Brewery for 25 years before settling into a life of leisure.

STOJANOV, Alek
b. Windsor, Ontario, April 25, 1973
Ooh, this one hurts for Pittsburgh GM Craig Patrick, a wise and successful manager who didn't make too many bad trades – with this exception. Vancouver drafted Stojanov 7th overall in 1991 and in 62 games with the Canucks the right winger did not score a single goal. Nonetheless, Patrick acquired him on March 20, 1996 – for Markus Naslund, one of the best under-30 players in the NHL today. Stojanov? He scored twice with the Pens and most recently has been sighted playing with the New Mexico Scorpions. Ouch. It wasn't quite that simple, though. Along the way, he suffered a neck injury, three shoulder operations, and a painful injury to his public bone. He was given a tryout with the Ottawa Senators, and after being cut ended up in the minors en route to the Scorpions.

STOLTZ, Roland
b. Overkalix, Sweden, August 15, 1954
He never played a game in the minors, but that's because he came to the NHL from Swedish league play and returned there almost as quickly, some 14 games with Washington being his only North American foray. Stoltz played most of his career with Skelleftea in his 14 years, and his time with the Caps came right in the middle, during the '81-'82 season.

STONE, Steve
b. Toronto, Ontario, September 26, 1952
Two games with Vancouver was all Stone needed to become an NHL alumnus. He turned the trick on right wing for the Canucks in '73-'74 during his mostly (and brief) IHL career.

STORM, Jim
b. Milford, Michigan, February 5, 1971
Storm was a star with Michigan Tech in the early 1990s but that college success didn't carry over to the NHL. He played a full season with Hartford in '93-'94 and scored just six goals, and that led to part-time status before falling into the minors for good. Storm played his last hockey in 1997.

STORR, Jamie
b. Brampton, Ontario, December 28, 1975
One time early in his career with Los Angeles, Storr put an ad in a Japanese newspaper based in L.A. asking fans to identify the four NHLers who are of Japanese descent. The first 25 correct answers won tickets to a game. The answer? Paul and Steve Kariya, David Tanabe . . . and Storr. His full name gives it away: Jamie Ishio Storr. The Jamie comes from his father, the Ishio from his grandfather, an industrialist in Japan. Storr's father was a senior goalie who once had a tryout with the Leafs, but Jamie the son was the real deal. He had an outstanding junior career in Owen Sound and was named best goalie at the 1994 World Juniors before the Kings selected him 7th overall in 1994. Since then, he has played exclusively with the Kings, working his way into the lineup. He established himself as number one only fleetingly, though, before the team acquired Felix Potvin, relegating him to backup again.

STOTHERS, Mike
b. Toronto, Ontario, February 22, 1962
There was no way Stothers was ready to play in the NHL when the Flyers drafted him in 1980. Tall, he was just 18 and had yet to fill out, so he went back to junior and then played in the AHL for three years before he deemed himself ready. By that time, he had put on 33 pounds and was a strapping, mature young man. But in four seasons in Philly, he was either still in the minors

P.J. Stock

Jack Stoddard

Alek Stojanov

His full name gives it away: Jamie Ishio Storr. The Jamie comes from his father, the Ishio from his grandfather, an industrialist in Japan.
JAMIE STORR

or collecting dust in the press box for long stretches. He was a fighter by design, but the Flyers didn't want him for that and traded him to Toronto. Half a season later, he went back whence he came and played the rest of his career with the Philadelphia farm team in Hershey. Once he retired, he stayed with the Bears as an assistant coach, moving up to the Flyers in a similar role until he was hired as head coach of Owen Sound in the OHL.

STOUGHTON, Blaine ("Stash")
b. Gilbert Plains, Manitoba, March 13, 1953

Asked to name a 50-goal scorer in the NHL, most people would run out of names before they would think about including Stoughton's, though he completed the rare double of reaching the mark in both the NHL and WHA. In junior, he was a hellion with few equals. In Flin Flon, he was once suspended for 36 games for spearing an opponent in the head. Another time, he got five games for throwing his stick at a fan who dumped coffee on him. Worse yet, he was convicted of assault causing bodily harm after hitting a fan with his stick, for which he was convicted and given a three-month conditional discharge. But he could score. He was placid until provoked, ferocious when on the ice, and his shot was like a bolt of lightning. He began his career with Pittsburgh and Toronto, but in 1976 he moved to the WHA where he had a big season with Cincinnati. He was traded to New England and stayed with Hartford after the team joined the NHL, and in that first season he led the league with 56 goals. Two years later, he had 52, and he had two 40-goal seasons as well. His career petered out with the Rangers, after which he played in the South Florida Hockey League for fun. He became an executive in the WPHL and later returned to Manitoba where he owned and operated the Tween Lakes Motel in Dauphin.

Asked to name a 50-goal scorer in the NHL, most people would run out of names before they would think about including Stoughton's.
BLAINE STOUGHTON

STOYANOVICH, Steve
b. London, Ontario, May 2, 1957

After captaining the RPI college team, Stoyanovich went to the minors in the Islanders system but was traded to Hartford in 1983. He played just a few games with the Whalers and spent much of his career in Italy, never making it back to the NHL.

STRAIN, Neil
b. Kenora, Ontario, February 24, 1926
d. 1975

Of his 11 NHL goals, the first was most memorable. It came in his first game, playing for the Rangers and facing Detroit on November 19, 1952. He took a hard shot that hit Terry Sawchuk and went into the net – and forced Sawchuk out! Despite that grand entrance, Strain was neither a spectacular player nor robust. He could handle himself all right, but he stayed out of the penalty box and tried to play the game. This was his only NHL season, and he played most of his hockey out west, though he had played with Wally Hergesheimer in San Francisco previously. Strain delayed his pro career when he enlisted in the army at age 17 and for two and a half years served on corvettes and minesweepers.

STRAKA, Martin
b. Pizen, Czechoslovakia (Czech Republic), September 3, 1972

One of the most talented small men in the modern game, Straka had a year in 2001-02 that he would love to forget. Eleven games into the season, he broke his leg badly and needed a titanium rod inserted. Doctors told him he would miss a year, but four months later he was playing again. He shouldn't have bothered. A minute into his first game, he smashed his orbital bone (requiring insertion of a metal plate), eight days later he twisted his ankle, and finally his year was over. He needed two operations on the leg, and with time on his hands he worked with his company, which sold hockey sweaters throughout Europe. The previous year, he was one of the league's top scorers with Pittsburgh, recording 95 points. He had started with the Penguins in 1992, but after three seasons was on the move and played for three other teams before returning to the Igloo in 1998. In addition to his fine NHL career, he won Olympic gold with the Czechs at Nagano in 1998, played in the '96 World Cup, and also appeared in the WC and WJC, requisite tournaments for Europe's finest.

STRATE, Gord
b. Edmonton, Alberta, May 28, 1935

After the Detroit dynasty came to an end in the mid-1950s, the team went into a bit of a tailspin and fell on hard times. Strate was one of many defencemen the team tried, but he played just a few games over three years, though he played more than half of '57-'58. He ended in the minors.

STRATTON, Art
b. Winnipeg, Manitoba, October 8, 1935

On March 17, 1963, Stratton set an AHL record with Buffalo that may never be broken in any league, any time: He assisted on nine Bison goals. He went on to lead the league in assists that year, something he accomplished 5 times during his 21-year career that took him sporadically into the NHL. In the minors, he was a scoring champion, leader, all-star, MVP winner, and superstar with few rivals. In the NHL, he played a few

Gord Strate

Art Stratton

games with the Rangers here or Detroit there. With expansion, he played his only full season, split between Pittsburgh and Philadelphia. In 1974, he retired to coach at Syracuse, but when he was fired he started playing again, retiring only in 1976. He was later inducted into the Manitoba Sports Hall of Fame.

STROBEL, Art
b. Regina, Saskatchewan, November 28, 1922
He made it to the Rangers during the war because he played for the Rovers, but seven games in '43-'44 was the only NHL time this mighty mouse played. At 5'6" he was small even by contemporary standards, but no one pushed Strobel around without a bit of trouble. He played most of his hockey in Minneapolis.

STRONG, Ken
b. Toronto, Ontario, May 9, 1963
When the Leafs traded Darryl Sittler to Philadelphia on January 20, 1982, they received prospect Rich Costello, a draft choice, and future considerations. Those futures turned into a "player to be named later," and that turned out to be local boy Strong, who played his junior B in Streetsville. He made scant impression with the Leafs and spent the majority of his time in the minors until deciding that Europe was the route to go. Any player who plays three years in Italy qualifies to play for that country's national team, and under this odd loophole Strong appeared in three World Championships and the 1994 Olympics in Lillehammer for the Italians. Once retired, he returned to Toronto and coached the York Toros of the OHA. By day, he worked as a financial planner, and one son, Steve, named in honour of junior teammate Steve Yzerman, has turned into a fine young player.

In addition to his fine NHL career, he won Olympic gold with the Czechs at Nagano in 1998.
MARTIN STRAKA

STRUCH, David
b. Flin Flon, Manitoba, February 11, 1971
The NHL wouldn't have him and he wouldn't have the AHL, so Struch matched perfectly with Britain where there was a mutual regard. He played a few games with Calgary in the early 1990s and gave it a try in the minors, but in 1996 he accepted an offer to play in Austria and later transferred to Britain, where he continues to play.

STRUDWICK, Jason
b. Edmonton, Alberta, July 17, 1975
A defenceman with a difference, Strudwick was big and strong but he could also play inside his own blueline. He worked his way up from the minors to part-time work to full-time duty with Vancouver, and in the summer of 2002 he signed with Chicago, a team on the rise. He began his career with the Islanders until being traded to the Canucks for Gino Odjick.

STRUEBY, Todd
b. Lannigan, Saskatchewan, June 15, 1963
The five games he played with the Oilers in the glory days – when there was no chance of a merely good player making the team – pale in comparison to the 1982 World Juniors when Strueby and mates won a gold medal. He played extensively for the National Team, though to earn a living he also played in the minors and in Germany for years. After retiring, Strueby settled in Regina and became a police officer and years later came out of official retirement to play in the Allan Cup for the local Rangers, though they went winless in the four-team showdown captured by Powell River.

ST. SAUVEUR, Claude
b. Sherbrooke, Quebec, January 2, 1952
Years and years passed, but the fans didn't forget, and when the chance came to cast their vote, they made sure that St. Sauveur was inducted into the Roanoke Valley Hockey Hall of Fame. In 1972-73, in the Eastern league, he had scored 55 goals for the Rebels, and for that single season of great accomplishment he was immortalized in the minds and memories of the locals. He went on to play in the WHA where he made a name for himself because of his exceptional speed and quick shot, and he played just one full season in the NHL, 1975-76 with Atlanta, not enough to get him into the Hockey Hall of Fame. He scored 24 goals that year, spending half the time on the bench until he broke out in January with a 5-point night that convinced coach Fred Creighton to play him a regular shift. St. Sauveur, though, left for the WHA again and closed out his career outside the NHL.

STUART, Bill "Red" ("Ginger")
b. Sackville, New Brunswick, February 1, 1900
d. March 7, 1978
A defenceman in the early days of the NHL, Stuart played mostly with the Toronto St. Pats partnered with Harry Cameron. They helped bring the Cup home in 1921-22, and Stuart played five years with the team before being sold to Boston. He later played in Minneapolis in the American league.

STUART, Brad
b. Rocky Mountain House, Alberta, November 6, 1979
If the San Jose Sharks do anything of note in the coming few years with their terrific young roster, you can be sure Stuart will be in the thick of things. The team drafted him a lofty 3rd overall in 1998, and he went out and had a superb final season of junior. He won a silver medal with Canada at the WJC, he was named best defenceman in Canadian junior hockey, and he went to

Ken Strong

David Struch

Jason Strudwick

Todd Strueby

Bill Stuart

Herb Stuart

Jozef Stumpel

Bob Stumpf

Peter Sturgeon

Doug Sulliman

the Memorial Cup. That fall, he made the Sharks at age 19 and scored a goal in his first NHL game, against Calgary. He is blessed with size and speed, quickness and offensive ability. He has the potential – and, yes, potential is future hope more than present proof – to become one of the league's top defencemen.

STUART, Herb
b. Brantford, Ontario, March 30, 1899
d. unknown
In a long and successful career playing goal in senior hockey and then in the IHL, Stuart broke into the NHL ranks on three occasions with Detroit. On November 18, 1926, he played in a 2-0 loss to Boston, on February 16, 1927, he backstopped the Cougars to a 5-1 win over Toronto, and the next night he lost to Ottawa 2-1. Despite his fine play, though, he was not about to usurp Hap Holmes in the nets on a regular basis and he was back in the minors, with the Olympics, for the rest of his career.

STUMPEL, Jozef
b. Nitra, Czechoslovakia (Slovakia), July 20, 1972
One of the cream of the Slovakian crop, Stumpel has been an NHLer for a decade but has also contributed to the development of hockey in his homeland. He played the first six years of his career with Boston and ended up a Bruins player again during the 2001-02 season, and in between he played parts of five seasons with L.A. Not a superstar, he is nonetheless a hulking centre with good quickness who gives any team strength up the middle. He played for his country at the 2002 Olympics in Salt Lake City as well as at two World Championships and the '96 World Cup. He was also part of the history-making team that won gold at the 2002 Worlds in Sweden, the first time the country has risen to such prominence.

STUMPF, Bob
b. Milo, Alberta, April 25, 1953
Little came of Stumpf's foray into the world of pro hockey. He was drafted by the Flyers in 1973 but traded before he ever played a game on Broad Street, and he wound up appearing just a few times with St. Louis and Pittsburgh a year later.

STURGEON, Peter
b. Whitehorse, Yukon, February 12, 1954
When Don Cherry and the Mississauga Ice Dogs announced the appointment of Sturgeon as the team's first coach and GM in 1998, all was well. Not only did it not end well, though, it also ended quickly. The Cherry-Sturgeon tandem was not new. The two knew each other in the Boston system in the 1970s when Grapes was a high-flying head coach and Sturgeon had a bit part in the minors, trying to get a shot at the big time. When Cherry left for Colorado, he signed the left winger and put him in a few games, his only NHL appearances. Sturgeon retired in 1982 after a series of serious knee injuries left him unable to skate effectively. He spent his last season as a playing coach with Georgetown in senior hockey, helping the team to a Hardy Cup. His career as a coach was on. He later coached in Brampton and Milton and also started his own company, Pro-Bound Hockey Program, geared to

developing skills for players at all levels. The Ice Dogs had one of the worst seasons in the history of hockey in 1998-99, and Sturgeon was long gone by the time the season ended.

STURM, Marco
b. Dingolfing, West Germany, September 8, 1978
One of the few German-trained players to make it to the NHL, Sturm was a high draft choice by San Jose in 1996 based largely on his play in two World Junior performances. He joined the Sharks a year later and hasn't seen the minors yet, stepping into the centre ice role and adapting to the pace and speed of the big league. He scored a career-high 21 goals in 2001-02, a season capped by an appearance in the 2002 Olympics in Salt Lake City, his second Games (after 1998 in Nagano).

SUCHY, Radoslav ("Soosh")
b. Kezmarok, Slovakia, April 7, 1976
So far, Suchy is characterized as a tier-two Slovak, not quite up to Olympics snuff but still one of the country's elite players. He helped his country win a silver at the 2000 World Championships, and in NHL terms he signed with Phoenix in 1997 after never having been drafted. He went 2 full seasons and more than 130 games before scoring a goal in 2001-02 when the defenceman had four on the year.

SUIKKANEN, Kai
b. Parkano, Finland, June 29, 1959
Fresh on the heels of Jari Kurri's arrival in Edmonton in 1980, Suikkanen came to Buffalo a year later after being signed by the Sabres. Unfortunately for him, any and all parallels to Kurri's career end there. Suikkanen played a game in each of the next two years in Buffalo and midway through his third season in the AHL returned to Finland to continue his career, which didn't end until 1991. The only time he returned to North America was in 1988 for the Olympics in Calgary.

SULLIMAN, Doug
b. Glace Bay, Nova Scotia, August 29, 1959
Like many Canadian boys, Sulliman learned hockey on his backyard rink. He loved the game and played it well, and when he was recruited to play in the OHL he gladly accepted the opportunity. His play with Kitchener earned him a draft selection from the Rangers in 1979, and at his first camp he was put on a line with Ulf Nilsson and Anders Hedberg. After two seasons in which he split his time between the Blueshirts and the minors, Sulliman established himself as a creative and determined right winger. He was traded to Hartford and on to New Jersey, and in 4 of the next 5 seasons he scored at least 21 goals. He finished his career with the Flyers in 1990, by which time his knees had taken a beating. He had worn braces on both knees for years, and he knew when enough was enough. For many of his summers as a player, he worked on Wall Street. He eased into retirement by working as an assistant coach for the Devils for three years, but when he was offered the head coaching job of the Islanders farm team, he knew he had a decision to make. The desire to start all over again, to prove himself in the minors and work his way up as a coach, just wasn't

there. He left the game, settled in Rye Brook just outside Manhattan, and became a stockbroker on Wall Street, such a long way from a backyard rink in Nova Scotia.

SULLIVAN, Barry ("Big Ben")
b. Preston, Ontario, September 21, 1927

Even Sullivan wasn't sure when, how, or why he acquired the nickname Big Ben as a kid, but it grew to be appropriate later on. He was a goal scorer, so every time he got a goal, fans would shout and headlines would blare, "Big Ben strikes again!" He was tall and awkward and gangly, so he had deceptive speed. He had a tremendous shot, and in the post-war years he was a star in the AHL, notably with St. Louis. Sullivan played all of one NHL game, on February 3, 1948.

SULLIVAN, Bob
b. Noranda, Quebec, November 29, 1957

Through the quirks of minor pro hockey, Sullivan was an AHL rookie in 1981 at the age of 24 despite having played a number of seasons in the "I." In that "rookie" season, he set an AHL record when he recorded a point in his 25th consecutive game and went on to win rookie of the year honours. As a result, Hartford signed him in the summer, and for one glorious season Sullivan was a bona fide, full-time NHL left winger. He scored 18 goals, went back to the minors and then off to Europe, and never saw the big league again.

SULLIVAN, Brian
b. South Windsor, Connecticut, April 23, 1969

Electing to get an education before taking New Jersey up on their 1987 draft offer, Sullivan set off to Northeastern University to develop as a hockey player and earn a degree. He then entered the Devils system, playing in the minors before earning a two-game callup, his only NHL action. He spent the rest of his years in the minors, and when he retired in 1999 he became the director of community relations for the Cincinnati Cyclones in the IHL.

SULLIVAN, Frank ("Sully")
b. Toronto, Ontario, June 16, 1929

When you're named after a father who can talk about winning a gold medal at the 1928 Olympics, you're bound to prick up your ears in rapt attention and want to try to emulate dad. Frank Sr. played for the U of T Grads that won gold, and his son went on to a pro career that included NHL stops in Toronto and Chicago in the post-war years. But in what is without doubt the strangest and weirdest brother combination in NHL history, Frank Jr.'s brother, Peter, also played in the NHL. The strange and weird part is this: They were 2 of 9 children, and while Frank was born in 1929, Peter didn't see the light of day until 1951, and he didn't play in the NHL until 1979, *some 30 years* after his brother made his NHL debut! Frank played only eight NHL games but he was a star in the AHL. He retired from hockey in 1959… when Peter was only eight years old.

SULLIVAN, George "Red"
b. Peterborough, Ontario, December 24, 1929

Not many people were in the game as long as Sullivan. He began in 1949 with Boston playing centre, though he was considered meek and mild, a reputation he would later shed. Over the next five years, Sullivan played mostly in the minors, winning the scoring championship and setting an AHL record for assists (89) and points (119). The season previous, in a short stay with the Bruins, he established a team mark when he assisted on six Boston goals in a single game. At his best, he and Ed Kryzanowski were known as the team's top penalty killers. He was later sold to Chicago and traded to the Rangers, where he was only the fourth player to wear number 7 after Frank Boucher, Phil Watson, and Don Raleigh. He had his best years with the Rangers playing on a line with Andy Hebenton and Camille Henry, and Sullivan became adept at early "trash talk." His career more or less ended during a home-and-home series with Montreal. In the first game, he slew-footed Doug Harvey, and in the return game Harvey speared him viciously in the spleen. Sullivan played a short while later, but he never fully recovered from the injury and was forced to retire. The next phase of his career took him to coaching. He bossed the Rangers bench for four years in the 1960s and then turned to expansion teams in Pittsburgh and Washington. Sullivan then became a scout for a number of teams, including the NHL's Central Scouting Bureau, before retiring. He lived all his life in Peterborough and continues to do so today.

At his best, he and Ed Kryzanowski were known as the team's top penalty killers.
RED SULLIVAN

Bob Sullivan

Frank Sullivan

SULLIVAN, Mike
b. Marshfield, Massachusetts, February 27, 1968

During his career at Boston University, Sullivan had the chance to play with a number of distinguished mates, notably John Cullen, Tony Amonte, Scott Young, and Joe Sacco. He went on to make his NHL debut with the Sharks in 1991, and throughout an 11-year career he played for 4 teams. He never went deep into the playoffs, but he did play for the U.S. at the 1997 World Championships. The 2001-02 season was his last, and he became a rare example of a modern player who stepped right into a head coaching position when Providence hired him to lead the AHL Bruins for 2002-03.

Mike Sullivan

Peter Sullivan

SULLIVAN, Peter
b. Toronto, Ontario, July 25, 1951
This is, without a shadow of a doubt, the strangest and most difficult trivia question. There is a hockey player who won an Olympic gold medal. He had two sons who went on to play in the NHL, although he himself did not turn pro. One son made his NHL debut 21 years after the father won that gold. The other son made his NHL debut 51 years after his father won that gold. Name the three family members. It's no trick – it's only amazing. Frank Sullivan won gold in 1928 for Canada. His son Frank Jr. played for the Leafs in 1949, and another of his nine children, Peter, made his NHL debut in 1979 with the Winnipeg Jets. Peter had played in the AHL and WHA for years, helping the Jets to an Avco Cup in that league's final season. He played just a year and a half with the NHL Jets and then pursued a career in Switzerland where, after his first season, he was named the league's best import. He retired a few years later, but his trivia lineage will carry on forever.

Steve Sullivan

SULLIVAN, Steve ("Sully")
b. Timmins, Ontario, July 6, 1974
Not in any league at any level in any country during any era has there been such a hilarious coincidence as the one Sullivan was involved in during a game in Colorado the night of January 26, 2001. It was also one of his finest games, but that is almost a moot point in this play whose theme is comeuppance. Early in the game, Sullivan was hit in the face by a puck and cut. He was bleeding when the trainer came out to give him a towel, and as he skated to the bench a railside fan pointed to the cut and started laughing wildly, inappropriately, at the injury. Sullivan then scored 2 short-handed goals just 51 seconds apart to set a Chicago club record. Later in the game, Colorado goalie Patrick Roy cleared the puck around the glass, and the puck skittered into the crowd, hitting that same fan on the forehead and cutting him in virtually the exact way Sullivan had been earlier. As attendants came to the fan with a towel to soak up the blood, Sullivan skated by, pointed to his forehead, and laughed derisively. You can't write a fictional tale of coincidence and comeuppance better than that. Irrespective of that tale, the game defined the kind of player Sullivan is. Not big and strong, he is skilled, smart, and speedy. He has never failed to score at least 20 goals in any full season he played, and he leads by example. He has also played for Canada at the 2000 and 2001 World Championships.

SUMMANEN, Raimo
b. Jyvaskyla, Finland, March 2, 1962
Even though he was surrounded by greatness in the

Raimo Summanen

NHL, Summanen was never quite there. He played parts of four seasons with the Oilers in the 1980s but only rarely in the playoffs when all the fun was to be had. He played briefly with Vancouver as well, but Summanen left his most indelible mark playing internationally for his country. His finest accomplishment came in his final career, game when he helped Suomi win gold at the 1995 World Championships. He had also played in two Olympics, the 1987 and '91 Canada Cups, and three other WC. After retiring, he became a coach in the Finnish leagues.

SUMMERHILL, Bill "Pee Wee"
b. Toronto, Ontario, July 9, 1915
d. Toronto, Ontario, October 29, 1978
In the years leading up to the Second World War, Summerhill saw all of his NHL action, receiving a good long tryout with the Canadiens in 1938-39, his first full year. He spent increasing time in the minors, and his career changed course with the war when he joined the Canadian Dental Corps. In peacetime, he played several years in the AHL, but he never made it back to the big show.

SUNDBLAD, Niklas
b. Stockholm, Sweden, January 3, 1973
It's not a good sign when your first-round draft choice plays just two NHL games, but that was the fate assigned to Sundblad when he was selected by the Flames in 1991. He continued to play in Sweden for two years before venturing to Calgary's camp in 1993, but he spent three years in the minors with the exception of those two games. He then returned to Europe where he played in Sweden, Finland, and now Germany. He also played in the 1997 World Championships, winning a silver with a team that lost to Canada in the finals.

SUNDIN, Mats ("Weed"/"Sudden")
b. Bromma, Sweden, February 13, 1971
By turns enigmatic, brilliant, and frustrating, Sundin – on a given night – is one of the greatest players on the planet. On other nights, well . . . He was the most sensational junior player in Swedish hockey history when Quebec drafted him 1st overall in 1989, the first European to be chosen in that prestigious position. From that day to this, he has never scored fewer than 23 goals in a season, topping off with 47 goals and 114 points with the Nordiques in '92-'93. He played four full seasons with Quebec before being traded to Toronto in an enormous deal, the principal players being Sundin to the Leafs and captain and Leafs life force Wendel Clark to Quebec. It was a risky and sensational deal, trading the captain after his finest season

He is one of only three Swedes to win three World Championships gold medals.
MATS SUNDIN

in blue and white, but GM Cliff Fletcher felt he was getting one of the most skilled players in the game. The expectations for Sundin were heightened because of the godly status of Toronto's other principal Swede, Borje Salming, and Sundin was expected to fill that position as much as Clark's. He did, indeed, bring mesmerizing skill, but he also brought laconic play and a perplexing indifference to the rink. He is, perhaps, most favourably compared to Frank Mahovlich, whose easy-looking stride and skill belied the effort behind it. When Sundin was on his game, he brought fans from their seats, but too often he scored a goal, gave the big smile, and disappeared for the rest of the game. No killer instinct. What made matters more difficult for him was the emergence of Peter Forsberg in Colorado, who likely doesn't have the same puck skills but whose intensity has always seemed miles above Sundin's. Sundin slowly began to change in 1997 when he was named the first non-Canadian captain in Toronto's long NHL history. Over time, he developed a leadership quality over and above being the team's leading point getter, a style of play that culminated in the 2001 playoffs when he showed an ability and willingness to go the extra mile to win, to fight through checks and skate madly to the goal. In short, he finally was leading by example. Along the way, he has been an annual participant in the All-Star Game, but over and above his brilliant NHL career he has had an almost incomparable international career for Tre Kronor. He is one of only three Swedes (after Jonas Bergqvist and Sven Tumba) to win three World Championships gold medals (in 1991, '92, and '98) and he has never played better hockey than the early games of the 1996 World Cup. He played in both NHL Olympics (1998 and 2002), and he will go down in history as one of his country's greatest players.

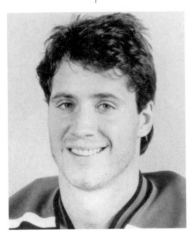

Sundstrom set a team record in February 1984 when he had a goal and six assists in a game.
PATRIK SUNDSTROM

SUNDIN, Ronnie
b. Ludvika, Sweden, October 3, 1970
Unrelated to Mats in both parents and skill, Ronnie is a modern one-game wonder who played for the Rangers a few years ago but is really a career member of Vastra Frolunda in Sweden, the team for which he continues to play and has been playing since 1992. He has also appeared in a number of World Championships for his country, though the defenceman is more steady than star, more reliable than hero. In 2003, though, he led Vastra Frolunda to the national championship and was named playoff MVP.

SUNDSTROM, Niklas ("Sunny")
b. Ornskoldsvik, Sweden, June 6, 1975
Unless something special happens during a player's NHL career, the allure and satisfaction of international play is so much greater at the end of the day. Sundstrom joined the Rangers in 1995 and has been a regular left winger in the NHL ever since, most recently with San Jose. He is a powerful left winger with scoring ability, but his achievements with Tre Kronor far outstrip his memories to date from the NHL. In 1993 he won a silver medal at the World Juniors, and the year after he won another silver, led the tournament in scoring, and was named the best forward. In 1996, he played in the World Cup. In 1998 and 2002, he played at the Olympics for Sweden, and he has also played in two World Championships.

SUNDSTROM, Patrik ("Sunny")
b. Skelleftea, Sweden, December 14, 1961
Who were the first set of Swedish twins to make it to the NHL? Patrik and Peter Sundstrom is the answer. Patrik is older, by about 20 minutes, and he made it to the NHL in 1982 with Vancouver. Almost instantly he became a star. He had plenty of international experience and exposure to the Canadian style of play, and he had just been named Swedish player of the year for '81-'82. He scored 23 goals as a rookie with the Canucks, and 38 the year after, and with Tony Tanti became half of one of the more dangerous pairs of forwards in the league. Their roles upended the stereotypes. Sundstrom was the biggest player on the team, and he was the net crasher while Tanti skated circles inside the blueline. Sundstrom set a team record in February 1984 when he had a goal and six assists in a game. After five years out west, he was traded to New Jersey, where he continued his dominating ways. On April 22, 1988, he set an NHL playoff record with eight points in a game (three goals, five assists), but his career was on a downswing soon after because of a chronic back injury (from all the aforementioned net crashing, among other things). He returned to Sweden for a final season of more relaxed play but was forced to retire at age 32 with plenty more hockey left in his legs and hands, but not his back.

SUNDSTROM, Peter
b. Skelleftea, Sweden, December 14, 1961
Two decades before the twin Sedins joined Vancouver, the Sundstroms were cavorting in the NHL. Peter started in New York with the Rangers, though in three years his reputation took a beating because his body didn't. He was labelled as skilled but soft, and by that third season he and coach Ted Sator were on the outs to the point that Sundstrom returned to Sweden to play. During his year and a half back home he helped the Swedes win gold at the 1987 World Championships, but his rights were traded

Peter Sundstrom

to Washington and he agreed to try North America one more time. Ironically, the Caps acquired him to replace Gaetan Duchesne on the checking line, playing with Bob Gould and Kelly Miller, and both Sundstrom's production and happiness dropped. In 1990, he returned home for good to resume his Swedish career, his success in the NHL tainted and muted by an adverse set of conditions.

SUOMI, Al
b. Eveleth, Minnesota, October 29, 1913

The only living member of the '36-'37 Chicago Black Hawks, Suomi started in pro hockey in a way every kid dreams of and almost no one realizes. He and two friends were playing shinny outdoors, and when they took a break a man walked up and asked them if they wanted a pro tryout in Chicago. Nothing to lose, they hopped on a bus an hour later, and sure enough Suomi was hired to play for a team called Chicago Baby-Ruth, a team that played before Hawks games and was formed merely to promote a candy bar of the same name. From there, Suomi was given a chance to play for Detroit in the old Michigan-Ontario Hockey League and he later got a tryout offer from the Hawks because of another promotion. Team owner Major Frederic McLaughlin was promising to field an all-American team, but the results toward the end of that '36-'37 season were only five games for Suomi, four of which were losses for the experiment gone bad. His NHL days done, he stayed in the city, played in a local league, and later became a referee for a short time. He spent most of his life as a welder, electrician, and handyman until retiring.

SUSHINSKY, Maxim
b. Leningrad, Soviet Union (Russia), July 1, 1974

The most recent trend in hockey has seen the elite Russian league try to reclaim some of its players from the NHL by offering semi-high contracts, in U.S. dollars, tax-free. It's working. Sushinsky played in Russia all his life until Minnesota drafted him in 2000. He came over to the Wild for the year, but after 30 games he returned to Russia instead of playing in the minors. Since then, he has accepted a generous offer from the team in Omsk, and has left Minnesota thinking it has wasted a draft pick who might choose never to play in North America again (should the Wild want him to return).

SUTER, Gary
b. Madison, Wisconsin, June 24, 1964

Who is the more famous Suter, Bob or his brother, Gary? Bob!? Yes, Bob, a little-known member of the 1980

Miracle on Ice team who never played in the NHL. Gary, of course, played 17 seasons in the league before retiring in 2002. He began with Calgary and stayed with that team for nine years, becoming one of the top offensive defencemen in the league. He won the Calder Trophy in '85-'86, and teamed with Al MacInnis on the power play point, the pair were a huge part of the Flames' run to the Cup finals in 1986 and Cup victory three years later. Suter scored 20 goals or more 3 times, peaking in '87-'88 when he had 91 points. He was a regular for Team USA in international competition, but was vilified for three egregious fouls during his career. In the 1987 Canada Cup, he slashed Andrei Lomakin of the Soviet Union so hard he broke his stick over his opponent's face, an infraction many said was the worst they had ever seen and would have earned a lengthy suspension had the incident taken place during an NHL game. In the 1991 Canada Cup, he cross-checked Wayne Gretzky from behind near the boards, and Gretzky was forced to miss the rest of the series. For that incident, though, Suter received due punishment because it was he who gave up the puck on a third-period power play in game two of the finals on which Steve Larmer scored the winning goal for Canada as Gretzky watched in a suit from the press box. And, in a January 1998 NHL game, he cross-checked Paul Kariya to the head after the Ducks star scored a goal, leading to a lengthy recovery from post-concussion syndrome that caused Kariya to miss the Olympics in Nagano a month later. Suter played in three All-Star Games and will, in due course, be inducted into the U.S. Hockey Hall of Fame for

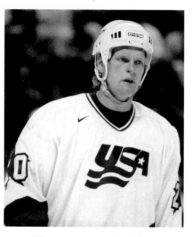

He was a regular for Team USA in international competition, but was vilified for three egregious fouls.
GARY SUTER

his long and successful career. For now, he has moved to Minaqua, Wisconsin, in the middle of nowhere, to settle into post-NHL life with his family.

SUTHERBY, Brian
b. Edmonton, Alberta, March 1, 1982

The path from junior to NHL is often fraught with contract problems. Washington drafted Sutherby in 2000, but that was only the first step in getting him on the team. It wasn't until October 1, 2001, that he signed a three-year contract with the Caps, and only then after having an excellent camp with the team. He played the first seven games with the Caps in the NHL and was then returned to junior in Moose Jaw to continue his progress.

SUTHERLAND, Bill
b. Regina, Saskatchewan, November 10, 1934

Before expansion, Sutherland played a grand total of two games in the NHL and more than a decade in the minors. After 1967, he was mostly an NHLer, starting with Philadelphia where he became part of team his-

Bill Sutherland

tory. Sutherland scored the first goal in Flyers history (on the road) and the first goal at the Spectrum en route to a 20-goal year as a 33-year-old rookie. He bounced around for four years before moving to the WHA to join the Jets, retiring in 1974. Sutherland did TV and radio work in hockey for five years and in 1979, when the team joined the NHL, he joined the team as an assistant coach. Late in the season he became head coach, and over the summer he was confirmed as the man behind the bench. This stint lasted just 29 games, though, as the Jets got off to a miserable 6-20-3 start and he was fired.

SUTHERLAND, Max
b. Grenfell, Saskatchewan, February 8, 1907
d. unknown

He played most of his hockey in the senior leagues and out west in the Pacific Coast league in the 1920s and 1930s, but Sutherland appeared twice for Boston in '31-'32 as a callup from the Boston Cubs.

SUTTER, Brent ("Pup")
b. Viking, Alberta, June 10, 1962

Sometimes they played on different teams. They had different levels and degrees of success. They came and went, one after the other. But the Sutters, the six men from a farm in Alberta, brothers all, who played in the NHL, came from the most remarkable family the world of sports has ever seen. Brent was no unique player within the family. What you say for him goes for all of them. He hated to lose. He worked hard for every shift and for every inch of ice. He was

He would play through pain that would hospitalize most men.
BRENT SUTTER

tough and skilled, and had his feet solidly on the ground. He would play through pain that would hospitalize most men. Brent was a first-round draft choice by the Islanders in 1980. He made his NHL entrance the next year playing with brother Duane, and the year after that they were part of a Cup team that repeated. He played more than 1,100 NHL games with just 2 teams, the Isles and Chicago, where he was coached by brother Darryl. Brent was one of the better scorers in the family. He had eleven 20-goal seasons, including 42 goals and 102 points in '84-'85, a year he started by helping Canada win the Canada Cup. He later played in the '87 and '91 Canada Cups as well. After retiring, he became coach, GM, and part owner of the Red Deer Rebels, leading the team to the Memorial Cup in 2001.

SUTTER, Brian
b. Viking, Alberta, October 7, 1956

He did everything he could for St. Louis except win the city its first Stanley Cup. When he joined the team in 1976, he was the first Sutter to play in the NHL and

he gave the league a taste of what was to come. Seven brothers lived in a two-bedroom house on a farm and Brian was the inspiration, the first out. He hated to lose a period let alone a game, exhibition or playoff. For 12 years he sacrificed his body to get the job done, and he scored his goals through determination and hard work, not because of a great shot or a quick release or a dipsy-doodle, one-on-one ability. He had two 40-goal seasons in his career. He led the team by example, by word, by glare and stare, when the need arose. He became the team captain, and when injuries slowed his battered body down, there was no rest: He became the team's coach, winning the Jack Adams Award in 1990-91. He later coached in Boston and after a brief retirement he returned to coach Calgary.

SUTTER, Darryl
b. Viking, Alberta, August 19, 1958

Another Sutter, another NHL career, another captain, another coach, another amazing story. Like Brian in St. Louis, Darryl played his whole career in Chicago but even more than any of his brothers, he suffered innumerable injuries that took a heavy toll. Surgery on a knee, a concussion, a cracked cheekbone, rib damage. After a while, he realized he couldn't captain a team from the trainer's table, and in 1987 he retired just eight seasons after entering the league. He stepped into a pair of coach's shoes and worked his way up, from assistant to coach on the farm to head coach of the Hawks in 1992. He stepped away from the game three years later to help raise his son who has Down's syndrome, but in 1997 he returned to coach in San Jose. In every year since he started in the NHL as a player in 1979, he has kept one incredible streak going: His team has never missed the playoffs, that is until he took over in Calgary during the 2002-03 season. Then, not even his career magic could carry the Flames into the post season.

SUTTER, Duane ("Dog")
b. Viking, Alberta, March 16, 1960

It's almost impossible to quantify tenacity within the context of the Sutter clan, but if one stands out for his ferocity and physical ability to play tough, it might just be Dog. He was fortunate enough to join the Islanders in 1979, and the Isles were fortunate enough to have him. In each of his first four years, the team won the Stanley Cup, in large measure due to his hard play and ability to mix it up, as they say. He played eight years in all with the team and three more with Chicago. When he retired in 1990, he kept the Sutter tradition going by staying in the game. First, he scouted for the Hawks, and then he became coach of the farm team in Indianapolis in 1992. He moved to the Panthers in 1995,

Brian Sutter

Darryl Sutter

Duane Sutter

Rich Sutter

Ron Sutter

Ken Sutton

Mark Suzor

Per Svartvadet

starting as a scout and becoming an assistant coach. Duane became a head coach – the fourth Sutter to do so – during the 2001-02 season, though he was later replaced by Mike Keenan. He became the team's director of player development. It seems only a matter of time, though, before all six brothers are head coaches.

SUTTER, Rich
b. Viking, Alberta, December 2, 1963
By the time Rich's draft year of 1982 rolled around, the league was knee-deep in Sutters and it was a *fait accompli* that any guy named Sutter born in Viking would be given a chance to prove he was not Sutter calibre. Nonetheless, Rich went 10th overall when Pittsburgh took him, perhaps a too-lofty selection and one based more on family reputation. He came out of Lethbridge, and being one of the youngest brothers he had had to do his share of self-defending in school and then in junior, where his family was already legend and Rich and his twin brother Ron had to prove themselves every night. Rich was a modest scorer but he could hit with the best of them, fight like a tornado, and bring to the dressing room the Sutter value of winning. Over his 13 years, though, he was traded 5 times, hardly typical NHL treatment for his family. He spent half his career in Philadelphia and the second half was a more nomadic existence. The closest he came to a Cup was with the Flyers in 1987 when they lost to Edmonton in the finals. He retired in 1995 and became a scout, most recently with the Minnesota Wild.

SUTTER, Ron
b. Viking, Alberta, December 2, 1963
His 1,093 NHL games represent the second-highest among the Sutters after Brent, though Ron was the least like his brothers in that he was cast almost from day one as a defensive specialist. Ron played half his career with the Flyers and with seven teams in all, and he has the distinction of being the last of the Sutters to retire, at the end of the 2001-02 season. This marked the end of 26 years with at least one Sutter in the league, and now it's a matter of time to see whether he joins the coaching ranks. Ron was captain in Philly, and only he and Brian never played for Chicago, a town that greatly admired the brothers' style of play.

SUTTON, Andy
b. Edmonton, Alberta, March 10, 1975
Undrafted, Sutton has played for the new teams since entering the league with San Jose as a free agent in 1998. He has gone on to skate with Minnesota and Atlanta, giving those teams important minutes as a

reliable and unspectacular defenceman. He graduated from Michigan Tech.

SUTTON, Ken
b. Edmonton, Alberta, November 5, 1969
There was a strange turn in Sutton's career path. He looked like he was going to become an NHL regular and since has proved not to be. He turned pro in 1989, and after a full year in the minors played a few games with Buffalo the next year. He played the better part of five full seasons in the NHL and then was relegated to the minors. Since 1997 he has been nothing more than a replacement and callup, though in 2000-01 he played the season with New Jersey, the team with which he has been affiliated most of the time since his career change. Along the way, he was named the best defenceman in the AHL for 1998-99. Perhaps his greatest claim to fame these days is that he is the first player the Devils have acquired on three separate occasions.

SUZOR, Mark
b. Windsor, Ontario, November 5, 1956
Fresh off back-to-back Stanley Cups, the brawling Flyers drafted Suzor in 1976, a defenceman out of Kingston who was – surprise, surprise – big and strong. Yet after just four games they traded him to Colorado for Barry Dean, who went on to play a year and a half with Philadelphia. Suzor played most of '77-'78 with the hapless Rockies and then went to Boston for Clayton Pachal. But Suzor never played with the Bruins, instead staying in the minors for the rest of his three years in pro hockey.

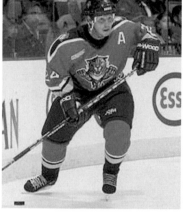

In 1992, he played at the Olympics in Albertville and the World Championships with Czechoslovakia.
ROBERT SVEHLA

SVARTVADET, Per
b. Solleftea, Sweden, May 17, 1975
The upshot of the deal to bring Svartvadet from Dallas to Atlanta won't be known for a while because he was acquired from the Stars for a draft choice in 1999 that Dallas used to select Justin Cox, a nascent talent still. Svartvadet has played well with the Thrashers since the trade, playing centre on a team desperate for quality players of every stripe. Although he was 18 when he was drafted, he continued to play in Sweden for another 6 years during which time he also won a silver at the '97 World Championships and bronze at the '95 WJC.

SVEHLA, Robert
b. Martin, Czechoslovakia (Slovakia), January 2, 1969
Florida caught a great break when Calgary drafted Svehla in 1992 and then refused to offer him a one-way contract. He stayed in Czechoslovakia, preferring league play to a possible career in the minors, and two years later the Flames gave up and traded him to the Panthers for a pair of draft choices. Oops. Svehla joined

Florida late in the '94-'95 season and almost immediately became the team's top defenceman. He could do everything. He hit hard and often; he blocked shots; he moved the puck speedily; he played with pain that sometimes made team doctors wince. For eight seasons, he was their leader, but when he threatened retirement in the summer of 2002 the Panthers gladly traded him to Toronto and got Dmitry Yushkevich in return. Outside the NHL, Svehla, like all other Slovaks, was fiercely proud of his young country. In fact, when he agreed to come to Toronto, he arranged to have the Leafs supply his home club of Trencin with much-needed money. In 1992, he played at the Olympics in Albertville and the World Championships with Czechoslovakia (where he was named best defenceman of the tournament), but since then Svehla has played for the Slovaks every chance he could get.

SVEJKOVSKY, Jaroslav

b. Plzen, Czechoslovakia (Czech Republic), October 1, 1976

A top prospect, Svejkovsky was named the AHL's rookie of the year in 1996-97, his first year of pro. Yet almost from the get-go he had injury problems, missing much of his first season with a serious ankle injury and year two with a concussion. The once-promising career ended in 2000 after just four seasons when Svejkovsky retired after another injury, this time serious damage to a knee.

SVENSSON, Leif

b. Harnosand, Sweden, July 8, 1951

Washington drooled when Svensson showed up to camp in 1978, a recent free agent signing. Paired with Rick Green on the blueline, he looked, management said, like a young and emerging Borje Salming. He had great skating ability and offensive creativity, and he was rock solid in his own end. Yet just a year and a half later, the pairing was finished. Svensson hurt his shoulder in January 1980, missed the rest of the year, and returned to Sweden in the summer, never to play in the NHL again.

SVENSSON, Magnus ("Sigge")

b. Tranas, Sweden, March 1, 1963

For those in Sweden, only 1994 matters when the name Svensson comes up. Late in the gold-medal game, Canada was beating the Swedes 2-1 with less than two minutes remaining when he tied the game with a slapshot from the blueline. Then, in the shootout, he contributed a goal to the gold-medal win. It was his finest hour. Svensson played almost all of his career in Leksand, but played parts of two years with Florida in the mid-1990s. He also played for Tre Kronor at the 1987 gold-medal win at the World

Championships, and at the '94 tournament he was named best defenceman. By the time he retired, he was a national hero in Sweden, his years with one club team and his international moments of brilliance his permanent points of reference in hockey hearts across the land.

SVOBODA, Jaroslav

b. Cervenka, Czechoslovakia (Czech Republic), June 1, 1980

Once Carolina drafted him in 1998, Svoboda came to Canada to play in the WHL. He played two seasons in Kootenay and then went to the minors, getting into his first game with the Hurricanes on March 11, 2002. He played 10 games down the stretch of the regular season and then became an ever more important part of the team as it went to the finals. Svoboda won a gold medal with the Czech Republic at the 2000 WJC.

SVOBODA, Petr

b. Most, Czechoslovakia (Czech Republic), February 14, 1966

Two conflicting facts about Svoboda's career stick out. The first is that he was the lone scorer in the gold-medal game at the 1998 Olympics in Nagano, his goal giving the Czechs their first championship in Olympic competition. The second is that Svoboda was 32 at the time of that win, and it was his first international competition. He had been playing a tournament with the Czechs in Germany in April 1984 when he defected, and upon arriving in Canada he lived with Montreal GM Serge Savard,

Svoboda lasted 17 years in the NHL and was the first Czech to play 1,000 NHL games.
PETR SVOBODA (b. 1966)

for it was the Habs that drafted him 5th overall. Another paradox: Svoboda lasted 17 years in the NHL and was the first Czech to play 1,000 NHL games. Yet, he was beset by injuries from the day he started in the league until the day he left. A series of injuries was forever taking him out of the lineup and convincing teams to trade him, but the mother of all hurts came on December 14, 2000, when he suffered a serious concussion. A year and a half later he was still feeling symptoms and he retired.

SVOBODA, Petr

b. Jihlava, Czechoslovakia (Czech Republic), June 20, 1980

Still very much a prospect with a few years left to show his stuff, Svoboda is in the Toronto system. He made his NHL debut on October 7, 2000, but was in St. John's most of the time, learning the North American game, until he finally played himself off the Leafs farm team. In November 2002, Svoboda went back to the Czech Republic to play for HC Trinec. He won a gold medal with the Czech juniors in 2000.

Jaroslav Svejkovsky

Leif Svensson

Garry Swain

George Swarbrick

Bill Sweeney

Bob Sweeney

Don Sweeney

SWAIN, Garry
b. Welland, Ontario, September 11, 1947
In Niagara Falls, Swain was a year-round success story. In 1967-68, he won the Memorial Cup with the Flyers, and in the summers he was a golf pro, winning the regional junior championship at one point. He turned pro with Pittsburgh the next fall but ended up stuck in the minors for a number of years until 1974, when he signed with New England of the WHA. Swain played three years in that league and then turned pro off the ice. He worked in both commercial and residential real estate and later worked in senior management with Heublein and Castle Construction Company. More recently, he has become a very successful management consultant.

SWANSON, Brian
b. Eagle River, Alaska, March 24, 1976
Coming out of Colorado College in 1999, Swanson had the goods. He was team MVP three times and an all-star every year, but no team drafted him and it wasn't until Edmonton signed him in the late fall that he had any NHL affiliation. Since then, Swanson has played mostly in the minors with only brief forays into the Oilers fold.

SWARBRICK, George
b. Moose Jaw, Saskatchewan, February 16, 1942
Expansion saved him from the anonymity of the minors, though during the Original Six days Swarbrick played for Canada at the 1964 Olympics in Innsbruck. When 1967 arrived, he was invited to California's camp and made the team as a right winger. He played for three teams over the next four years but ended his career in the lower leagues in 1977.

SWEENEY, Bill
b. Guelph, Ontario, January 30, 1937
d. 1991
Everyone said he was too slow, and perhaps he was for the NHL, where he played only four times. But in the AHL he was a scoring sensation. He was the first player in that league to win 3 successive scoring championships and first to have three successive 100-point seasons (1960-63). He won rookie of the year in '57-'58 and led the team to three consecutive Calder Cups (1959-62). Oddly enough, though, he was never voted the league's MVP before he retired, and only the Rangers ever gave him a shot in the NHL. A superb golfer, he was club pro at the Fairview Golf and Country Club in Guelph in the summers.

SWEENEY, Bob
b. Concord, Massachusetts, January 25, 1964
When Sweeney was at Boston College, his goalie was

He was one of the many pieces of the Dallas puzzle that fell into place in 1999 when the team won the Stanley Cup.
DARRYL SYDOR

Tom Barrasso. They both went on to the NHL, of course, and in Sweeney's second career game, in 1986, he scored his first goal for Boston – against Barrasso. Sweeney went on to play an even 10 years, twice going to the Cup finals (in 1988 and '90) and twice losing to Edmonton. He had a decent scoring touch over the years but in 1996 he found himself still craving to play, but no NHL team willing to take him on. He played in the minors for a year and then headed overseas, playing most of his career in the DEL before calling it quits in 2001.

SWEENEY, Don ("Sweens")
b. St. Stephen, New Brunswick, August 17, 1966
He may not have the name, skill, and ego of Ray Bourque, but Sweeney has been a devoted member of the Bruins for 14 Cup-less years on the blueline. He graduated from Harvard University in 1988 with a degree in economics and has been a Bruins player ever since. More defence than offence, Sweeney isn't big and isn't a power play quarterback, but he has been a dependable, top-six defenceman almost from day one. He's a rare example of having played more than 1,000 games with one team.

SWEENEY, Tim
b. Boston, Massachusetts, April 12, 1967
The surprise must have been great the first time Sweeney discovered his uncle's role in the Second World War. U.S. Army Air Corps General Charles Sweeney flew the B-29 plane that dropped the second atomic bomb on Japan. Kind of puts an NHL career into perspective pretty quickly. Tim was as much a minor leaguer as NHL regular, though he did play in the 1992 Olympics in Albertville for the U.S. He went on to become an amateur scout for the Minnesota Wild in 2001 after having retired from the game three years earlier.

SYDOR, Darryl
b. Edmonton, Alberta, May 13, 1972
Los Angeles made a huge mistake when it traded Sydor to Dallas midway through the '95-'96 season. He had been drafted in 1990 and the Kings expected him to be an offensive force from day one, but he wasn't. Instead, he learned to play defence in the NHL and developed his offensive skills more slowly. When he got to the Stars, he was mature and ready. Ever since, Sydor has been a pillar of strength on the team's blueline. He has combined great puck movement skills with power play efficiency and team leadership, and he was one of the many pieces of the Dallas puzzle that fell into place in 1999 when the team won the Stanley Cup and went to the finals

the year after. In junior, he won the Memorial Cup with Kamloops in 1992, the same year he won gold with Canada at the WJC. He has also played in two World Championships.

SYKES, Bob
b. Sudbury, Ontario, September 26, 1951
On February 12 and 15, 1975, Sykes played his only NHL games, with the Leafs, in a short pro career.

SYKES, Phil
b. Dawson Creek, British Columbia, March 18, 1959
Dawson Creek is nearer to heaven than a big city, and playing hockey there was an alternative to watching avalanches. In his teens, Sykes played in the Peace-Caribou Hockey League, not a major signpost on the way to the NHL. He went on to play at the University of North Dakota, but didn't go there on scholarship – he went there primarily for an education. In 1982, he signed with Los Angeles as a free agent, never really thinking about an extended pro career – but that's exactly what he got. He spent eight years in the Kings system and another three with Winnipeg. In '85-'86, he scored 20 goals, his best year, and when he retired in 1982 after 456 games, it was 456 more than he ever intended to play as a kid skating in God's country.

A centre, he went on to produce four 20-goal seasons on a club that preached defence.
PETR SYKORA (b. 1976)

SYKORA, Michal
b. Pardubice, Czechoslovakia (Czech Republic), July 5, 1973
A giant of a man even by today's standards (6'5" and 225 pounds), Sykora has gone from Czechoslovakia to North America and back in a decade. He played two years of junior in the WHL before joining San Jose in '93-'94, but after four mostly partial seasons he was on his way to Chicago and then Tampa Bay. He played his last NHL game in 1999 and has been back in the Czech Republic ever since. Sykora also won gold at the 2000 World Championships, and he played for the Czechs at both the World Cup in 1996 and the 2002 Olympics in Salt Lake City.

SYKORA, Petr ("Sykie")
b. Plzen, Czechoslovakia (Czech Republic), November 19, 1976
Following the lead of Radek Bonk, Sykora left the Czech Republic in early 1994 to play in the NHL and showcase his talents, even before he was drafted. New Jersey liked what he could do and selected him in '95, and Sykora has been with the team almost every day since. A centre, he went on to produce four 20-goal seasons on a club that preached defence, and he teamed with Patrik Elias and Jason Arnott to form the deadly A Line. He won a Cup with the Devils in 2000 and has played his entire career with the team. He

also has a wealth of international experience with the Czechs, winning gold at the 1999 World Championships and playing in the 2002 Olympics in Salt Lake City.

SYKORA, Petr
b. Pardubice, Czechoslovakia (Czech Republic), December 21, 1978
Unrelated to his countryman of the same name, this Sykora is younger and still a work in progress. He was a Detroit draft choice traded to Nashville, but apart from two games with the Predators he has played only in the minors and more recently at home with Pardubice. His chances of returning to the NHL are slim.

SYLVESTER, Dean
b. Hanson, Massachusetts, December 30, 1972
It took Sylvester a few years in the minors to convince the NHL to take him seriously, and although the ride didn't last long, it was a thrill all the same. In 1995 he signed with the Mysticks in Mobile in the East Coast league, and after three years he got into a single game with Buffalo. A trade to Atlanta gave him a longer stay in the league, but he hasn't been back since 2000.

SYLVESTRI, Don
b. Sudbury, Ontario, June 2, 1961
He played just one year of pro, unusual regardless of era or team or league. Sylvestri graduated from Clarkson College in 1984, and the year after played three games in goal for Boston and a few more down in the minors before retiring.

SZURA, Joe
b. Fort William, Ontario, December 18, 1938
What a way to start a pro career. In the same moment that Szura scored the first goal of his career, with the Montreal Royals in November 1959, he was cross-checked and broke his collarbone. Gone for six weeks. When he returned, Szura began a long and successful career in the minors that extended until 1974. Yet, unlike most stars in the minors, even in the AHL he was an unsung hero, a tall and skilled player who passed through the league year after year as a fine but unheralded centreman. He played most of his time with Cleveland, where he was usually among the top scorers, but he never won an individual trophy and only once did he make an All-Star Team (in '65-'66). He played two years in the WHA toward the end of his career, and his only NHL games came with Oakland in the team's first two seasons.

Bob Sykes

Phil Sykes

Michal Sykora

Dean Sylvester

Joe Szura

TABARACCI, Rick ("Tabby")

b. Toronto, Ontario, January 2, 1969

By the time he retired in 2001, not many goalies had been as well travelled as Tabby. He had played for seven NHL teams and even more teams in the minors, though rare was the season when he was the starting goalie. His best year in the NHL came in '96-'97 when he played in 50 games for Tampa Bay, and although he had a losing record on a lousy team, he had 4 shutouts and a GAA of just 2.75. For that, he was invited to play for Canada at the World Championships, his second of three appearances with the team (1992 and '99 were the others).

TAFT, John

b. Minneapolis, Minnesota, March 8, 1954

In the unenlightened days of pre-Miracle on Ice hockey in the U.S., international competition meant little to most Americans. So, it was of little historical consequence that the country finished fifth at the 1976 Olympics in Innsbruck, at which Taft played. Also not of note was the '75 World Championships, where Taft helped the team to a sixth-place finish. Taft came out of the University of Wisconsin and played just a few games with Detroit in '78-'79 before heading off to Salt Lake City to play in the Central League before retiring.

TAGLIANETTI, Peter ("Tags")

b. Framingham, Massachusetts, August 15, 1963

In the rafters of the Loring Arena in Framingham hangs Taglianetti's number 18 sweater, marking a sensational high school career that led to another fine career at Providence College (for which he was later inducted into that college's Athletic Hall of Fame). He played his first six NHL years with Winnipeg and made his way to Pittsburgh in time to win consecutive Cups in 1991 and '92. Taglianetti's style was marked by heavy, open-ice checks. He was a strong and mobile defenceman, and after his career was over he settled just outside Pittsburgh.

TAKKO, Kari

b. Uusikaupunki, Finland, June 23, 1962

Media fodder never came in more pre-packaged form than on November 22, 1990, when Takko was traded to Edmonton for Bruce Bell. The Takko-Bell trade made headlines that even disgusting orange cheese couldn't dissuade salivating editors everywhere from talking about. The Oilers acquired Takko to act as backup to Bill Ranford after Grant Fuhr was suspended, but when Fuhr returned, Ranford became backup, Takko became redundant and, instead of accepting a demotion, he retired and returned to play in Finland. He started his NHL career with Minnesota in 1985 but was never quite number-one material. He was a disciplined and positionally strong goalie, but his finest years were back in Europe, where the shots didn't come as fast and the traffic in front of the net wasn't quite so intense.

TALAFOUS, Dean

b. Duluth, Minnesota, August 25, 1953

After leading the University of Wisconsin to an NCAA championship in 1973, Talafous left the school a year later before completing his degree in physical education to turn pro with Atlanta. He later played with Minnesota where he had a number of fine seasons as an all-round, checking forward, and he ended in New York skating on a line with Phil Esposito and Don Maloney. He had played for the U.S. at the 1976 and '81 Canada Cups. On January 2, 1982, the Rangers traded him to Quebec with Jere Gillis for Robbie Ftorek. But, the team subsequently refused to offer him a long-term contract, and feeling his career was winding down anyway, he retired. The Nordiques were awarded Pat Hickey in the deal, and Talafous retreated to Apple Valley, Minnesota, where he ran a sporting goods store. He then took an active role as a coach, first as an assistant with U of Minnesota and later as head man in Alaska.

TALAKOSKI, Ron

b. Thunder Bay, Ontario, June 1, 1962

A two-sport athlete, Talakoski played football and hockey at the University of Manitoba in the mid-1980s, and the result was a player who turned pro in the Rangers organization. He played only a handful of games with the team, though, and after just two seasons in the minors returned to Thunder Bay to start a life in business.

TALBOT, Jean-Guy

b. Cap de la Madeleine, Quebec, July 11, 1932

Can a player be a part of one Cup team after another and still not be a Hall of Famer? Yes, and Talbot is exhibit A in the case. Over a career that lasted more than 1,000 games and 17 years, he won 7 Cups with Montreal as a steady and solid defenceman. Yet, he is not in the Hall of Fame. He played in seven All-Star Games (though mostly as a Cup champion) and was a First All-Star in '61-'62. After spending 13 seasons with Montreal, he finished his career by playing for Detroit, St. Louis, and Buffalo, and then became a coach for the Blues in 1972. He had played for Scotty Bowman in St. Louis, and, boy, there was some history there. In '51-'52, Talbot played for Trois-Rivières and Bowman for Montreal Jr. Canadiens. Talbot hit Bowman over the head with his stick, resulting in the end of Bowman's playing career and a one-year suspension. Talbot remained coach of the Blues for two years, and when he coached the Rangers in '77-'78 he made sartorial history by wearing a track suit behind the bench during games. After this one season, he retired to Trois-Rivières where he worked for Carling O'Keefe Breweries as a sales agent and promotions officer.

TALLAS, Robbie

b. Edmonton, Alberta, March 20, 1973

Given all the chance in the world to make it in goal for Boston, Tallas just didn't have it. The revolving door that has been the Bruins netminding situation could have been fixed by a series of strong outings at any point, but after five years Tallas was set free after compiling a 4-13-4 record in 1999-2000. He signed with Chicago, but again stuttered when he should have waxed poetic in the blue ice, and spent all of 2001-02 in the minors.

John Taft

Peter Taglianetti

Kari Takko

Jean-Guy Talbot

Rick Tabaracci
(opposite page)

Dale Tallon

Steve Tambellini

Chris Tamer

Alex Tanguay

TALLINDER, Henrik
b. Stockholm, Sweden, January 10, 1979
The reward for having such a good season on the blue-line with Rochester was to be called up for the last two games of Buffalo's regular season in 2001-02. Tallinder had been a quality defenceman for the Americans in his first year of pro in North America, and those two NHL games proved to be a nice launch to the start of the 2002-03 season when he made the Sabres at training camp. A good skater and clever puckhandler, his season was shortened by a shoulder injury.

TALLON, Dale
b. Noranda, Quebec, October 19, 1950
In 1970, a spin of the wheel gave Buffalo the 1st over-all choice in the draft and Vancouver, the other expansion team, the 2nd selection. Buffalo chose Gilbert Perreault; the Canucks took Tallon. He was supposed to be the next coming of Bobby Orr (any rushing defenceman was) and as such Tallon was a dis-appointment. Vancouver traded him to Chicago after his third season, and management there tried to get him to wear number 9, Bobby Hull's number after the Golden Jet had left for the WHA. Tallon, aghast, refused, of course, but in coming years he simply did-n't pan out as an offensive threat capable of controlling a game from the blueline. The one area he did com-pare to Orr was injuries, and Tallon incurred more than his fair share over the years. He retired in 1980 and turned to his second passion, golf. In 1969, he won the Canadian Junior Golf Championship, and he reacquired his amateur card after his NHL days. He later moved into the broadcast booth in Chicago and most recently has been the director of player person-nel for the Hawks.

TAMBELLINI, Steve
b. Trail, British Columbia, May 14, 1958
The town of Trail evokes hockey memories that are very specific and singular, and the Tambellini family is front and centre in that history. Steve's father, Addie, was a centre on the 1961 team that won gold at the World Championships, the last gold Canada would win until 1994. Steve, meanwhile, grew up to be a fine centre in his own right, having a fine NHL career but, in his father's footsteps, an even finer NHL career. An Islanders draft choice, he played for the team in 1979-80 when it won its first Stanley Cup. Over 10 years, he moved around, finished his career in Vancouver, and played for Canada in each of the big three interna-tional tournaments, culminating with the 1988 Olympics in Calgary. Tambellini settled into an administrative position with Vancouver after retiring. He worked his way up over a dozen years with the Canucks, from business operations to hockey opera-tions to, finally, vice-president of player personnel. He also acted as director of player personnel for Canada leading up to and including the 2002 Olympics in Salt Lake City, and in September 2002 he was named GM of Canada's national men's team for the coming sea-son, through to the 2003 World Championships.

TAMER, Chris
b. Dearborn, Michigan, November 17, 1970
An all-purpose defenceman, Tamer provides size and

ability on the blueline. He graduated from the University of Michigan in 1993, at which point he joined Pittsburgh. Since then, Tamer has established himself as a regular, first with the Penguins and later with the Rangers and Atlanta. He played for the U.S. at the 1999 World Championships.

TANABE, David
b. White Bear Lake, Minnesota, July 19, 1980
One of only a few NHL players of Japanese descent, Tanabe joined Carolina in 1999 after just one year of college hockey, making the leap from the University of Wisconsin to the NHL in one fell swoop. He scored a goal in his first game and after a rookie season split between the 'Canes and the minors, he's been an NHLer ever since. He played for the U.S. at the 2001 World Championships. The next year he played on the Young Guns game at the All-Star Game in Los Angeles.

TANCILL, Chris
b. Livonia, Michigan, February 7, 1968
Success came early and often for Tancill. He won an NCAA championship with the University of Wisconsin in 1990, where he was also named MVP of the final four. The next two years he won Calder Cup championships in the AHL while he was breaking in with Hartford and Detroit in the NHL. Tancill, though, was the proverbial small forward, and in his eight years in the league he was a part-timer who majored in the minors. His longest big-league stint was with San Jose in '95-'96, and after 1998 he decided to go to Europe to play. He has been there ever since, most recently with Zug, in Switzerland. As a result of his skill and Euro-play, he has also appeared in three World Championships for the U.S. along the way.

TANGUAY, Alex
b. Ste. Justine, Quebec, November 21, 1979
The game ain't what it used to be. Colorado drafted Tanguay in 1998 and invited him to camp that fall. He had but two years of junior under his belt, in Halifax, but he made the Avs based on his play with the pros. His agent and the team, though, could not agree on a contract, and instead of starting a highly promising career as an 18-year-old, he was back in junior. He fired that agent and got another, but just a few games later he suffered a severe concussion. From being an NHL-calibre player, Tanguay was now unable to walk around the block without pain. Over time, he recov-ered, and a year later he joined the Avs. He recorded points in each of his first five NHL games. Since then, he has developed into one of the best young players in the league, and in 2001 he was part of the Cup-winning team. Should the NHL be involved in the 2006 Olympics in Turino, Tanguay will be playing for Team Canada.

TANGUAY, Christian
b. Beauport, Quebec, August 4, 1962
There was such hope and promise when Tanguay was scoring in the Q league with Trois-Rivières, but the Nordiques called him up for just two games in 1981-82 and he never played himself into a position to

receive another invite. He played for another few years in the minors but no other team ever signed him or expressed interest in his services.

TANNAHILL, Don

b. Penetanguishene, Ontario, February 21, 1949
Everything came up roses for Tannahill in his first season with Vancouver, in 1972-73. He was the first Canucks rookie to score a hat trick, in December 1972, and he had 22 goals on the season. Midway through the next year, though, he hurt his back and required surgery. He had played his last NHL game. By the following training camp he had recovered enough to play in the WHA for three seasons, but that was the extent of his career. He retired and settled in California, where he became a real estate agent in Palm Springs.

TANNER, John

b. Cambridge, Ontario, March 17, 1971
A goalie can do or say whatever he wants. He can be a nut, unconventional, anti-social, spiteful, malicious, anything – as long as he stops the puck. If he doesn't do that, any and all negative attributes will bite him in the butt. Tanner came up through the OHL at a time when Ron Hextall was developing into a fine NHL goalie. Tanner was often compared to Hextall because of their mutual on-ice temper and temperament, their liking for wandering from the crease, using the stick as a sword as much as a puck catcher. But Hextall stopped the puck and Tanner didn't. Off the ice, he was either maligned or loathed, depending on whose version of the truth was more accurate. He earned a tie for Quebec in his first start but that was the only fine game he ever played. He made his way through the OHL and then the minor leagues, his final NHL record an unimpressive 2-11-5.

TANTI, Tony

b. Toronto, Ontario, September 7, 1963
Vancouver fans had to take the good with the bad. The good was having Tony Tanti in the lineup. The bad was having to watch him play in, without question, the ugliest sweaters in the history of the NHL, the old black with an orange "V" on the front. Tanti was drafted high by Chicago in 1981, but the Hawks gave up on the mammoth prospect after just three piddling games to acquire the more proven Curt Fraser. Tanti responded by scoring 45 goals in his first full season and averaged 40 in each of the next 4 years. He had played only one full season of junior, in Oshawa, but despite his great success with the Canucks the team struggled and rarely made the playoffs. As a result, Tanti played in four World Championships for Canada, and in 1992, once his NHL days were over,

he moved to Germany and played pro there for a few more years. Once retired, he settled in Vancouver and became a stock promoter.

TAPPER, Brad

b. Scarborough, Ontario, April 28, 1978
Undrafted through his years at RPI, Tapper signed as a free agent with Atlanta in the summer of 2000 and has struggled to make the team ever since. He's been called up for a few short stints, but the right winger has yet to stick with the expansion team.

TARDIF, Marc

b. Granby, Quebec, June 12, 1949
The physical strength of hockey players is matched only by their resolve to play the game, and this combination makes them athletes of incomparable determination. In the 1976 WHA playoffs, the Nordiques' great left winger Tardif was attacked by Rick Jodzio in one of the worst crimes ever committed on ice. Tardif was cross-checked unconscious by Jodzio, and as he lay on the ice the animal attacker continued to punch the prone player. Tardif did not instigate the attack, and he remained unconscious for half an hour, a dangerous length of time. For weeks afterward, he was still housebound as doctors feared for his ability to perform everyday tasks. Tardif had been a junior with the Canadiens and played his first four years of pro with the Habs, wining Cups in 1971 and '73 and establishing himself as one of the finest young stars in the league. But when he got an offer to triple his salary to play in the WHA, he packed his things and went to the L.A. Sharks and on to the Nordiques, where he became a local hero. In that '75-'76 regular season, he led the league in goals, assists, and points, and made a remarkable recovery not only to return to action later in the year but to continue to score. Nonetheless, he filed a lawsuit against Jodzio, though he himself came under scrutiny in 1979 over his contract with the Nordiques. He wanted his deal renegotiated, claiming that the $180,000 salary was predicated upon playing in the WHA. As the team was now entering the NHL, he wanted more money – and he got it. He had four more productive years with the team, and then his number 8 was retired to the rafters of Le Colisée. Tardif stayed in the city and worked his way up to vice-president of Laurier Pontiac Buick.

TARDIF, Patrice

b. Thetford Mines, Quebec, October 30, 1970
It was an expensive and short-lived deal for St. Louis when the Blues traded Tardif and two other players

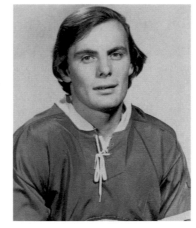

Tardif worked his way up to vice-president of Laurier Pontiac Buick.
MARC TARDIF

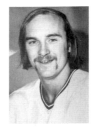

Don Tannahill

John Tanner

Tony Tanti

Mikhail Tatarinov

Dave Tataryn

Billy Taylor

Bob Taylor

and two draft choices to Los Angeles for Wayne Gretzky. Tardif had played just 50 games with the Blues, and he lasted only 15 more with the Kings before being relegated to the minors. He later went to Germany and then returned home to Thetford Mines to play senior hockey, but Tardif bailed on that team to return to Europe to play in Italy.

TARNSTROM, Dick
b. Sundbyberg, Sweden, January 20, 1975
The New York Islanders scraped the bottom of the barrel in 1994 when they drafted Tarnstrom 272nd overall, and the defenceman chose to stay with his club team, Solna, back home. Year after year passed, and Tarnstrom just stayed at home and carved out his proverbial career. Then, in 2001, he ventured to the Islanders. He played the full season, and played a regular shift, but in the summer the team put him on waivers and Pittsburgh claimed him.

TATARINOV, Mikhail
b. Angarsk, Soviet Union (Russia), July 16, 1966
When Washington acquired Tatarinov in 1990, the team felt comfortable that it had replaced a defenceman after the loss of Scott Stevens to free agency. Now, a dozen years and more later, Stevens has played about 1,000 more games than the Soviet, who retired in 1993. Tatarinov was allowed to leave the Soviet Union at age 24. That alone should have given the Caps a clue that he was not an elite player back home – but he wasn't incapable, either. He played a number of international tournaments with the CCCP and played for Dynamo in league play, during which time he accorded himself well. He played just two full seasons in the NHL, one with the Caps, a second with Quebec, before a back injury ended his '92-'93 season early. He reinjured the back early the year after and retired.

TATARYN, Dave
b. Sudbury, Ontario, July 17, 1950
In his heyday, he played all over the place, which was not a good thing. Tataryn backstopped Niagara Falls to the Memorial Cup in 1968, but instead of turning pro he went to university. He led U of T to a CIAU title in 1972 and late in his career won Allan Cups with both Petrolia (1981) and Cambridge (1983). In between, he played in all sorts of minor leagues, his only NHL games – two in all – coming with the Rangers. After retiring, he became a substitute teacher and worked on a farm, and then he opened his own goalie school, complete with residence, in Orton, Ontario. Taking on six students at a time, he worked on plastic ice and developed at least two NHLers, Robe Holland and Mike Moffat. He later became a goalie coach, most recently with the University of Waterloo.

TATCHELL, Spence
b. Lloydminster, Saskatchewan, July 16, 1924
Just a pup when he played his only game with the Rangers in '42-'43, Tatchell carried on to play many years in the Western league in British Columbia. He was later owned by the Canadiens but never made it back to the NHL.

TAYLOR, Billy ("Billy the Kid")
b. Winnipeg, Manitoba, May 3, 1919
d. Whitby, Ontario, June 12, 1990
The nickname was earned honestly. When Taylor was only 10, he was playing for Toronto St. James Church in minor bantam, where everyone else was 13. Over the years, his skills improved but he didn't grow that much, and by the time he was a pro he was downright small. Nonetheless, when he joined the Leafs in 1939 he was fresh off a Memorial Cup with Oshawa and one of the top Leafs prospects. Taylor made good on the talk. He developed into not only a good scorer but an excellent playmaker and during his five seasons with the Leafs he became an important centre on a team that won the Cup in 1942. Taylor's father had fought in the First World War and his health had been permanently damaged by poison gas. Not surprisingly, Billy joined the Canadian Infantry Corps and for two years was out of the NHL. Soon after, he was traded to Detroit and on to Boston, and that is when he was caught doing something no proud veteran could condone. In a series of tapped phone conversations, the FBI presented incontrovertible evidence that Taylor and Bruins teammate Don Gallinger had bet on hockey games, and not just as a third party but on games in which the Bruins were involved. NHL president Clarence Campbell acted swiftly and decisively, suspending both men for life, not only from the NHL but from involvement in the game anywhere, anyhow, forever. Taylor's life was completely ruined, but he had only himself to blame. He moved to Florida to escape the daily glare of the ban, but later returned to southern Ontario. Campbell lifted the ban in 1970, and Taylor coached in Owen Sound and later worked as a scout for Philadelphia and Washington. He received much sympathy for the extended punishment, but Campbell never had to worry about gambling again, and no one ever had to call into question the integrity of a game or wonder whether outcomes were fixed. Taylor died suddenly in 1990, his past disgrace long forgotten or unknown to the contemporary fan, his embarrassing legacy an indelible part of the NHL's history.

TAYLOR, Billy, Jr.
b. Winnipeg, Manitoba, October 14, 1942
Just a few months after winning the Stanley Cup in 1942, Billy Taylor and his wife had a bouncing boy they named Billy Jr. Just 18 years later, the kid would be in the NHL, though 18 years and two games later he would be out of it. Taylor had just a brief tryout with the Rangers, the team for whom his father played before being expelled for life from the game. The rest of his career passed in the minors, and even tough Minnesota claimed him in 1967, he never played for the North Stars or anyone else.

TAYLOR, Bob
b. Newton, Massachusetts, August 12, 1904
d. December 12, 1993
Taylor spent virtually his entire career in the minors in the northeastern United States, appearing in eight games with the Bruins in '29-'30. The tall winger failed to register a point, though, and was returned to the Can-Am league where he closed out his playing days.

TAYLOR, Bobby
b. Calgary, Alberta, January 24, 1945

At one time, Taylor was the highest-ranked goalie prospect in the Philadelphia system, but in 1972, the night he was going to make his debut, he pulled a hamstring muscle and ended up as Doug Favell's backup. Later in the year things took a turn for the worse when the team was involved in a disgusting brawl in Vancouver that moved into the stands. Taylor, goalie equipment and all, took part, at one point knocking down a police officer. He was charged with assault, and after being convicted in the summer was sentenced to 30 days in jail and fined $500. He stayed in the Flyers system for five years and ended his paying days with Pittsburgh. After retiring in 1976, he returned to Philly and worked as a colour analyst for the team's radio and television broadcasts.

TAYLOR, Chris
b. Stratford, Ontario, March 6, 1972

Turner Cup championships are great, but they are emblematic of IHL supremacy and represent a great distance from the NHL. Taylor's older brother, Tim, won the big silver with Detroit, but so far Chris has had to content himself with the IHL title. Since being drafted in 1990, he has gone from minors to NHL as often as any player, but as sure as he arrives, he knows there's a demotion waiting a few games later.

TAYLOR, Dave
b. Levack, Ontario, December 4, 1955

It's debatable as to which is more agonizing, being drafted hideously late in the proceedings or not being drafted at all. Regardless, Taylor is the reason players who fit into either category should ignore scouts and rely on their own confidence. Taylor went 210th overall in 1975 to Los Angeles after a very strong career with Clarkson College, and he went on to be one of the great success stories of all time based on this selection. He made the Kings in 1977 and scored 22 goals as a rookie, a figure he nearly doubled in year two playing on the Triple Crown line with Marcel Dionne and Charlie Simmer. In all, Taylor had six 30-goal seasons, and he was also considered the best defensively of that threesome. He later became the team captain, but resigned that position when Wayne Gretzky arrived in 1988. Taylor went to his only Cup finals in 1993, his second-last year in the league. He won both the Masterton and the King Clancy trophies in 1991 and played in four All-Star Games. Because the Kings were frequently spectators at playoff time, Taylor also played in three World Championships for Canada. In all, he played 1,111 games in the NHL, all with Los Angeles. He scored more than 1,000 points and was one of the most popular athletes in the city.

Taylor went to his only Cup finals in 1993, his second-last year in the league.
DAVE TAYLOR

He was the third player after Marcel Dionne and Rogie Vachon to have his number retired (18), and on April 22, 1997, he was named the team's vice-president and GM, positions he still holds.

TAYLOR, Harry
b. St. James, Manitoba, March 28, 1926

When he was eight years old, Taylor lost two teeth playing road hockey, which soured him on the game for five years. When he got back at it, he was as good as if he had been playing every day in the interim, and he worked his way up through leagues in Manitoba. He helped the Winnipeg team defeat the Marlies for the Memorial Cup in 1946 and joined the Leafs for a few games the year after. His only full season was '48-'49 when he helped the Leafs win the Cup, though he appeared only once in the playoffs. He also worked for the CPR in Winnipeg, a job he wanted to make full-time after his playing days. Taylor played a few games with Chicago but spent the rest of his career in the minors.

TAYLOR, Mark
b. Vancouver, British Columbia, January 26, 1958

The Mark in his name wasn't as important as the Taylor, for the surname linked back to a skater named Fred. Fred was better known as Cyclone, and Cyclone was one of the best skaters in the early years of the game. Mark was Cyclone's grandson, and although he was no Cyclone, he could play well enough to make the NHL for five years. Mark won an NCAA championship in 1980 with the University of North Dakota, and his years in the NHL were highlighted by a 24-goal season in '83-'84 with Pittsburgh. He went on to play in Europe for a number of years, and after retiring he returned to Vancouver. His father, Fred Jr., had long ago opened Cyclone Taylor Sports, an equipment store, and later Mark and his brother Rick took over the day-to-day operations of this Vancouver landmark that is now almost 50 years old.

TAYLOR, Ralph
b. Toronto, Ontario, October 2, 1905
d. July 3, 1976

He was an early member of Chicago, playing with the Hawks in 1927 until being traded to the Rangers early in 1930. Taylor, a defenceman, went on to play several more years in the American league after half a season with the Blueshirts, though he never made it back to the NHL. He played his final seasons in St. Louis and settled in that city, opening a sporting goods store.

TAYLOR, Ted
b. Oak Lake, Manitoba, February 25, 1942

Good things came in twos for Taylor, who won two AHL

Chris Taylor

Harry Taylor

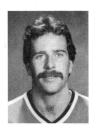
Mark Taylor

Ted Taylor

championships, two in the WHL, and two in the WHA. He was the textbook case of a player who appeared briefly in the Original Six days, and with expansion found a full-time job in the NHL. That, though, lasted just two years, in Vancouver, and in 1972 he moved to Houston to play with the Aeros and the Howe family. After retiring in 1978, Taylor returned to Oak Lake where he helped build and manage a local arena.

TAYLOR, Tim
b. Stratford, Ontario, February 6, 1969
Tim is the older brother of Chris, and Tim's wife is the sister of Chris's as well. Whereas Chris has had a fine minor-league career, Tim has legitimately sipped from the Cup as part of Detroit's '96-'97 team. Since then, though, he's moved on to Boston, New York, and Tampa Bay and has missed much of the last couple of years with injuries. His was no direct route to the NHL, either. He was drafted by Washington in 1988, traded to Vancouver, and signed by Detroit. He didn't play in his first NHL game until December 18, 1993, and his second game came nearly a year later. Since then, though, he's been a regular when healthy.

Tim Taylor

TEAL, Allan "Skip"
b. Ridgeway, Ontario, July 17, 1933
Separated by 16 years, Skip and Vic are a pair of brothers who made it to the NHL, Skip in 1954, Vic in 1973. Skip played a single game with the Bruins despite being a scoring sensation in the minors.

Vic Teal

TEAL, Jeff
b. Edina, Minnesota, May 30, 1960
His was a short career, culminating with a six-game stint with the Canadiens in '84-'85. Teal left the University of Minnesota in 1982 to play for Nova Scotia, the Montreal farm team, but his play never impressed more than that one tryout and he retired in 1985 after a little more than three years of pro.

TEAL, Vic ("Skeeter")
b. St. Catharines, Ontario, August 10, 1949
In 1938, Vic Teal Sr. moved from Fort Erie to St. Catharines to take a job as the engineer of the new Garden City Arena. He also coached minor hockey in the city, and over the years led the city to some 23 championships in age groups ranging from bantam to juvenile (14-18). As a result, the Vic Teal Memorial Tournament was started after his death, and his son, Vic Jr., also developed into a fine player. His much older brother had played during the Original Six, and Vic, like Skip, played just a single NHL game. He played for the Islanders in '73-'74 and played pro only until 1976.

Greg Tebbutt

TEBBUTT, Greg
b. North Vancouver, British Columbia, May 11, 1957
Discipline woes seemed to plague the talented defenceman and impeded his progress through the ranks. Tebbutt played in the last year of the WHA, but after just a couple of NHL games with Quebec the following year he was buried in the minors. By 1982 he worked his way back to the AHL, and set records for goals (28) and points (84) by a defenceman in that league, earning a contract with Pittsburgh. But in '83-'84, he fell out of favour with Baltimore coach Gene Ubriaco and was suspended, though he did play 24 games with the Pens that year. He was held without a single point and never made it back to the NHL, spending his final four years in the minors.

TENKRAT, Petr
b. Kladno, Czechoslovakia (Czech Republic), May 31, 1977
This low draft choice by Anaheim took an odd route to the NHL. Tenkrat was playing in his native Czech Republic, but after the Ducks called his name he played a year of pro in Finland before coming to North America. He never got much of a chance with Anaheim, but early in 2001-02 he was traded to Nashville where he recorded 24 points and stayed with the team most of the year.

TENO, Harvey
b. Windsor, Ontario, February 14, 1915
d. Windsor, Ontario, September 9, 1990
Harvey was one of two goaltending Teno brothers, but only he made it to the NHL. In the summer of 1936, the manager of the Atlantic City Seagulls called the Teno residence in Windsor and asked for the Teno goalie who had won a championship. It turned out that he wanted Charlie, but Harvey took the call and accepted the invite to try out for the team! Charlie had won the Allan Cup in 1937 with the Sudbury Frood-Tigers, but Harvey had won a Memorial Cup in 1934 with St. Mike's. Although Atlantic City got the wrong Teno, it got a great goalie who led the team to consecutive championships in his only two years there. During the '38-'39 season, Detroit goalie Normie Smith was suspended for refusing to play following a 2-0 loss to the Rangers. Teno got the call for 5 games in November 1938, winning twice and allowing 15 goals. Smith was then traded to Boston (and refused to report) for Tiny Thompson and Teno was sent back down to Pittsburgh of the AHL, where he played nine more years without another call to the NHL. While he played in Cleveland, he tutored a young goalie named John Kiszkan, who changed his name to Bower the next year. After retiring in 1948, Teno coached minor and junior hockey in Windsor

The center image caption

Skip played a single game with the Bruins.
SKIP TEAL

and established the Windsor Minor Hockey Association, which later developed players such as Ed Jovanovski. Teno also refereed in the OHA and IHL and founded the Windsor and District Hockey Referees' Association. He was inducted posthumously into the Windsor/Essex County Sports Hall of Fame.

TEPPER, Stephen
b. Santa Ana, California, March 10, 1969
Tepper graduated from the University of Maine in 1992, played a single game with Chicago the next year, and then played four years in the minors. He retired in 1996 to become the ticket manager for the Worcester Ice Cats, and he's been there ever since.

TERBENCHE, Paul
b. Port Hope, Ontario, September 16, 1945
It's difficult enough for a rookie to make the NHL, but when your coach tells you you're no longer a defenceman, but a forward, it makes the task all the tougher. That's what Terbenche faced when he made Chicago in 1967 and coach Billy Reay took him out of position. Terbenche stayed the year, but he had only three goals. He ended up in the minors until 1970, when Punch Imlach drafted him for the new team in Buffalo, but it was only in the last of four seasons with the Sabres that Terbenche stayed the season in the NHL. He later played in the WHA until it joined the NHL, and then he returned to Birmingham to play in the Central league with the Bulls.

Terreri won 2 Cups with the Devils and won 20 games on 3 occasions.
CHRIS TERRERI

TERRERI, Chris
b. Providence, Rhode Island, November 15, 1964
Not too many players can claim to have gone to Pilgrim High School. Terreri went on to have an outstanding college career at Providence, studying business management and taking the Friars to the NCAA final four in 1985. He was named MVP of that tournament and soon after made his debut with New Jersey. He spent most of the next two years working with the National Team toward a spot on the Olympic team for 1988, after which he joined the Devils full-time (he also played in four World Championships over the years). Terreri spent most of his career in New Jersey, playing as the number-one goalie for a few years while young Martin Brodeur developed, and then, toward the end of his career, as Brodeur's reliable and content backup. Along the way, Terreri won 2 Cups with the Devils and won 20 games on 3 occasions. He also spent two years each with San Jose and Chicago. After retiring, in 2001, he stayed with the Devils organization, becoming an assistant coach in Albany.

TERRION, Greg ("Tubby")
b. Marmora, Ontario, May 2, 1960
Los Angeles drafted him, and it with the Kings that he began his career in 1980, but Terrion will always be remembered as a Leafs forward. He was neither big nor talented, but he was determined and versatile and could fill one of a number of alternating roles. Terrion played six seasons for Toronto, checked and killed penalties, did anything to stay in the NHL. By 1988 his time had run out, and after a year in the minors he returned home. He went into partnership with his uncle on an Esso station on Highway 7 in Marmora, equidistant between Ottawa and Toronto.

TERRY, Bill
b. Toronto, Ontario, July 13, 1961
Four years at Michigan Tech didn't get Terry a sniff at the draft, and when he signed with Detroit as a free agent in 1986, the only perk was assignment to the minors. Minnesota later gave him five NHL games, but he soon went to Europe to play briefly before retiring.

TERTYSHNY, Dimitri
b. Chelyabinsk, Soviet Union (Russia), December 26, 1976
d. Okanagan Lake, British Columbia, July 23, 1999
Dying young is tragic enough, but dying as Tertyshny did is unjustly horrific. He and two AHL Russians were in Kelowna in the summer to run a hockey clinic, and were out on a boat relaxing. Tertyshny was at one end of the boat when a wave rocked it, sending him into the water. The boat ran over him, and the propeller sliced his throat. It was a gruesome way to die. His wife, back in Russia, was pregnant with their son but had not had time to tell him of the impending addition to their family. He died never knowing. Tertyshny had been a strong prospect with the Flyers, having just completed an impressive rookie season, his first pro year in North America. He may have become a star or a minor leaguer, but unjustly he was never given the chance to see which.

TESSIER, Orval
b. Cornwall, Ontario, June 30, 1933
Believe it or not, there was a bit of Wayne Gretzky in Tessier, even though the older of the two played but 59 NHL games away back when. He won the Memorial Cup in 1953 with Barrie and over the next eight years had but three quick callups with Montreal and Boston. He was a fine offensive centre, but accounted for just five goals in his career at the top level. But in 1959-60, with Kingston in the EPHL, he set a record for points when he collected 126, the most a player had ever registered in any pro league, any era. He kept plugging away in the minors until 1965 when

Paul Terbenche

Greg Terrion

Dimitri Tertyshny

Orval Tessier

he turned to coaching, where he had enormous success. Tessier won the Memorial Cup with Cornwall and later Kitchener, and in 1982 he was hired as new coach of Chicago. The Hawks earned 106 points on the year and he won the Jack Adams Award, but after the semifinals, in which the team lost to Edmonton, he made one of the most damaging comments an NHL coach has ever made. He said the players needed heart transplants, for their lack of effort, and although he later tried to backtrack from the comment, the damage had been done. He later returned to junior to coach before being hired by Colorado as a scout with the Avs.

Greg Theberge

TETARENKO, Joey
b. Prince Albert, Saskatchewan, March 3, 1978
Still working to establish himself at the NHL level, Tetarenko has split his time between Florida and the minors, though he missed much of 2001-02 with a serious jaw injury. He graduated from Portland of the WHL in 1998 and played for two years in the minors before getting a chance with the Panthers in 2000.

TEZIKOV, Alexei
b. Togliatti, Soviet Union (Russia), June 22, 1978
He did everything right to get to the NHL, but it hasn't worked out as he hoped it would. Tezikov, once drafted, played junior in Quebec and then went to the minors to work his way into the NHL. He's had a few chances, with Washington and Vancouver, but he has been a minor leaguer to date.

Mats Thelin

THEBERGE, Greg
b. Peterborough, Ontario, September 3, 1959
Lineage is a great place to start, but it alone cannot pass on the skill needed to be an NHLer. Not only was Theberge's grandfather Dit Clapper, one of the greatest Boston Bruins of all time, but the two lived together for 13 years, Dit encouraging the youngster when they went out to the frozen lakes around Peterborough to play whenever possible. Theberge, though, was considered too small when his draft year came along in 1979, and the Capitals, not the Bruins, selected him. He had won a Memorial Cup with his hometown Petes, and that stood him in good stead because the incoming Washington coach was Gary Green, the boss at Peterborough. He called up Theberge whenever occasion presented itself, but Theberge played just two full seasons with the team and a number more in the minors.

Jose Theodore

THELIN, Mats
b. Stockholm, Sweden, March 30, 1961
Boston drafted Thelin in 1981, but it was three years before he moved to North America to try the NHL. By that time, he had played at the 1984 Olympics in Sarajevo and later that year the Canada Cup, but Thelin was a smallish defenceman who had a tough time with the physical play of the league. After a healthy and solid rookie year, he suffered knee and foot injuries in successive seasons that kept him out of action for long periods, and in 1987 he returned home to continue his career with Stockholm in the Swedish league.

THELVEN, Michael
b. Stockholm, Sweden, January 7, 1961
At 24 and in the prime of life, Thelven left Sweden

Gaston Therrien

to play with Boston in the NHL. A mere five years later, he returned home hobbling, a shadow of his former, physically sound self. By 24, Thelven had been a veteran defenceman with Djurgarden, a member of the 1984 Olympic and Canada Cup teams for Tre Kronor, and one of the nation's best players. But in five years with the Bruins, he damaged his right knee so often there was little that hadn't been scraped, rearranged, removed, or diminished by the time he retired. There were other injuries, too, to his groin and a shoulder, but the knee did him in in the end.

THEODORE, Jose
b. Laval, Quebec, September 13, 1976
Only time will tell where that 2001-02 season fits in the history of the game, but for now it ranks as something special. Theodore had been with the Canadiens since being drafted in 1994, and made his NHL debut on February 21, 1996. Slowly but surely he developed as a backup, but in 2001-02 he had a superb year. He rose to be the team's starting goalie, had a record of 30-24-10 on a mediocre team, recorded seven shutouts, and had a 2.11 GAA. He almost single-handedly got the Canadiens into the playoffs for the first time in four years, and as a result was awarded the Hart and Vezina trophies, a remarkable double achievement that was the buzz of the 2002 NHL Awards night in Toronto. In the summer, the requisite contract demands upped Theodore's salary substantially, but whether that season was the start of a Hall of Fame career or an extraordinary blip on the Theodore landscape is yet to be determined. If 2002-03 is any indication, it's the latter.

THERIEN, Chris
b. Ottawa, Ontario, December 14, 1971
A large rock on the Philadelphia blueline, Therien joined the Flyers in 1994 after an active career as an amateur. He played on scholarship at Providence College and then for a year and a half stayed with Canada's National Team leading up to and including the 1994 Olympics in Lillehammer, winning a silver medal. Therien has played his entire career with the Flyers and is the prototypical player for the team – big, strong, immovable on the defence.

THERRIEN, Gaston
b. Montreal, Quebec, May 27, 1960
When the expansion Montreal Rocket hired Therrien as its coach for the Quebec league team in 1999, it also hired Danielle Sauvageau as his assistant, the first time a woman had held such a high-level position in men's hockey. Therrien has been a well-established coach in the Q since retiring as a player. He appeared with the Nordiques for three years in the early 1980s, but for the most part he was a minor leaguer who later played in Europe. Sauvageau later guided the women's national team to a gold medal at the 2002 Olympics in Salt Lake City, and Therrien has remained in the Q as a coach.

THIBAUDEAU, Gilles ("T-Bone"/ "Bud")
b. Montreal, Quebec, March 4, 1963
Thibaudeau didn't play traditional junior in his home

province, opting for minor pro instead. It worked in the short term insofar as he was named rookie of the year in the IHL for 1984-85 and the Canadiens signed him to a contract. But over the next five years he was a part-timer in the NHL, and by 1991 he decided to play in Europe. It wasn't until a decade later that he came home, to play senior hockey in Quebec.

THIBAULT, Jocelyn
b. Montreal, Quebec, January 12, 1975

It's pressure enough to play goal in Montreal, but imagine coming into the Canadiens fold in a trade that saw Patrick Roy go to the other team, in this case Colorado. After Roy threw his hissy fit in November 1995 and refused to play for the Habs again, the team traded him to the Avs and got Thibault in the deal. He went from backup on one team to expectant Cup winner on another. Montreal gave him plenty of opportunity to become a star, but after about three years of mediocrity he was traded to Chicago. Playing in a more relaxed atmosphere, Thibault shone. He played with a Hawks team much like the Habs, where goaltending was the difference between making the playoffs or not, but he quickly gave the team a chance to win every night with his play. As Chicago improves, Thibault now looks to be the difference between a long and short playoff year. He also has the distinction of winning the final game at both the Montreal Forum and Maple Leaf Gardens.

THIBEAULT, Lorrain
b. Charletone, Ontario,
October 2, 1918

A wartime player, Thibeault appeared briefly with Detroit and Montreal during a long career in minor pro and amateur hockey. He won the Calder Cup with the Buffalo Bisons in '43-'44 and finished his days in the Quebec league.

THIFFAULT, Leo
b. Drummondville, Quebec, December 16, 1944

The story sounds familiar, though the ending wasn't quite so perfect. Thiffault played for the Jr. Canadiens in the 1960s, and during the summer of expansion his rights were traded to Minnesota. But he didn't make the team and play years for them and become a star. Instead, he appeared in the 1968 playoffs for the team – five games in all – and never made it back. He retired soon after, having played in the minors for the majority of his career.

THOMAS, Cyril "Cy"
b. Dowlais, Wales, August 5, 1926

His was not a long career but Thomas was a throw-in in what was, to that date, the biggest deal in NHL history. The Leafs acquired Max Bentley and Thomas

from Chicago for five players – Gaye Stewart, Gus Bodnar, Bob Goldham, Bud Poile, and Ernie Dickens. The trade made the Leafs a Cup dynasty, though Thomas played but a few games with Toronto before being sent to the minors. He played most of the rest of his career out west.

THOMAS, Reg
b. Lambeth, Ontario, April 21, 1953

The WHA was like the bonds market. If things worked out well, they worked out very well. But, there was no guarantee. The NHL provided smaller contracts, but it was money in the bank. In 1972, Thomas could have signed with Chicago and played in the minors in the hopes of working his way into the NHL. Or, he could sign with the Los Angeles Sharks and be guaranteed a spot on the roster. He chose the Sharks, but the team soon moved to Detroit, then to Baltimore, and then to nowhere. Indianapolis claimed Thomas, and when that team folded he joined Cincinnati. In 1979, his WHA travels came to an end when the league joined the NHL and Thomas went to Quebec. Soon he was playing on a line with Robbie Ftorek and Jamie Hislop, but the high-scoring threesome didn't last too long because – according to inside word – management didn't want an all-English line to do so well. Thomas was soon in the minors. He bounced around, signed with other NHL teams, but never made it out of the minors. He returned to Lambeth, near Highway 4, where he and his wife ran a fruit and vegetable farm and raised four children, all of whom played hockey.

Thomas ran a fruit and vegetable farm and raised four children, all of whom played hockey.
REG THOMAS

it to Sarnia in the OHL, and a daughter also plays seriously, as do two smaller children. Behind the family house lies a full-sized rink that is the toast of the area in the winter.

THOMAS, Scott
b. Buffalo, New York, January 18, 1970

It's not so amazing that a 1989 draft choice is still playing hockey – there are plenty of longer-serving players – but what is interesting is that after a few games with Buffalo early in his career, Thomas seemed all but down and out when he got another chance. After leaving Clarkson University, he was given a couple of callups by the Sabres and then was buried in the minors, going quickly from the AHL to the "I" whence few return to tell tales of the game. Yet in the 2000-01 season he was recalled by Los Angeles and played 24 games for the Kings and another dozen in the playoffs, a nice bonus for a supposed minor leaguer. At season's end he played in Manchester, more or less signalling the end of his NHL days, but he had his moment on the ice and for that he must be pleased.

Gilles Thibaudeau

Jocelyn Thibault

Leo Thiffault

Cy Thomas

Scott Thomas

Wayne Thomas

Dave Thomlinson

Brent Thompson

Tiny Thompson

THOMAS, Steve ("Stumpy")

b. Stockport, England, July 15, 1963

No, the Hockey Hall of Fame won't be inducting him any time soon, but there aren't too many people in the world who can say they've scored 400 goals in the NHL. As Thomas carries on, he remains the last player from the Marlies to skate in the NHL, graduating from Toronto junior in 1984 to join his hometown Leafs. In his third season he scored 35 goals with a great and quick shot that was his trademark, but the Leafs sent him to Chicago with Rick Vaive for Ed Olczyk and Al Secord, a poor deal for the blue and white. With the Hawks, Thomas had a 40-goal season. He continued to score when he was healthy, but a serious abdominal and shoulder injury caused him to miss much of two seasons and he was traded to the Islanders. He recovered to play well and score often, but when he got to New Jersey defence was stressed above eating and breathing and his production tailed off badly. When he signed with the Leafs as a free agent in 1998, he was able to get back on track under Pat Quinn's scoring-minded style of play, but after a weak 2000-01 season, the Leafs let him walk away and sign with Chicago. Again, he missed much of the next year with injury, but soldiered on, and was later traded to Anaheim. In the 1990s, when his teams often missed the playoffs, Thomas had the chance to play in four World Championships, most notably in 1994 when he won a gold medal and two years later when he captained that team. He also won silver in 1991 and played in '92.

In his third season he scored 35 goals with a great and quick shot that was his trademark.
STEVE THOMAS

THOMAS, Wayne

b. Ottawa, Ontario, October 9, 1947

It always seemed that Thomas was a better goalie in reputation than he was ever given a chance to prove. He came out of the University of Wisconsin and turned pro with Montreal in 1970, and when he made his NHL debut on January 14, 1973, he earned a shutout. Yet that was enough to get him into just 10 games. The next year was his big chance. Ken Dryden sat out the season in a contract dispute, and Thomas played 42 games. His 23-12-5 record wasn't good enough to earn a single playoff assignment and the year after not only was Dryden back but Thomas was relegated to being the third goalie. That meant practising all the time and sitting in the press box for the entire year! He didn't play once. Montreal then traded him to Toronto for a first-round draft choice (they selected Peter Lee) and in Toronto he had a fine year. But again he was usurped by a star, Mike Palmateer, and Thomas was on the move again, to Broadway. He played the last four years of his career with the Rangers, and then turned to the management side of the game, starting as an assistant coach with that very team. He worked up to head coach of the farm team in Salt Lake City, and eventually became the vice-president and assistant GM in San Jose.

THOMLINSON, Dave

b. Edmonton, Alberta, October 22, 1966

It's every player's dream to be a free agent, provided there is interest around the league. Although Thomlinson was drafted by Toronto in 1985, the Leafs decided they couldn't use him and let him go. This started a trend whereby he signed as a free agent with four clubs in a span of six years, not so much because he was a star as because his contract expired and the team decided not to make him a new offer. Nonetheless, the offers were there but Thomlinson played a scant 42 games in 5 NHL seasons. He wound up in the "I" and after retiring returned to school at the University of Alberta.

THOMPSON, Brent

b. Calgary, Alberta, January 9, 1971

Since last playing in the NHL in 1996-97, Thompson has been the property of the Rangers, Florida, and Colorado without playing for any of those teams. Exclusively a minor leaguer now, he made his way to the NHL because of his penalty minutes, and he has kept a spot in the AHL for those same fistic reasons.

THOMPSON, Cecil "Tiny"

b. Sandon, British Columbia, May 31, 1903

d. Calgary, Alberta, February 9, 1981

An incredibly durable goalie and the brother of Paul Thompson, Tiny got his nickname more because of his minuscule goals-against average than his size. At 5'10" he was by no means the smallest tender in the league. He grew up in Calgary from the age of two, and it was in that city that he started to play organized hockey. He eventually moved to Duluth of the USAHA, but when the league folded in '24-'25, he joined Minneapolis and continued to play like a superstar. In 1928, he and Millers teammate Cooney Weiland went to Boston, and Thompson played so well in the Bruins' first game of the season that he unseated Hal Winkler as the starting goalie. And start he did. In his first ten seasons, he missed exactly one game. In the other nine seasons, he was the only goalie to play every game, and he led the league in wins five times, including his rookie season when he had 12 shutouts and a GAA of 1.15. On April 3, 1933, Thompson was in goal for the Bruins against Toronto in a playoff game that went into six overtimes. He allowed a goal to Ken Doraty in what was to date the longest NHL game ever played. Two years later, he made the record books again. He passed the puck to defenceman Babe Siebert who went the length of the ice to score, thus becoming the first goalie to be credited with an assist. In '37-'38, he and brother, Paul, were named to the First All-Star Team, the only brothers after Lionel and Charlie to achieve this distinction. His career with the Bruins ended similarly to how it began. He sat out two games because his eyes were bothering him, and a young goalie named Frank Brimsek replaced him. Brimsek played so well that Thompson was traded to Detroit, and it was there he played his last two NHL seasons. By the time he retired in 1940, Thompson had won four Vezina Trophies, more than any other goalie, and his 553 games played was far and away an NHL record. During the war he was a flight lieutenant in the RCAF, and after returning home he went back to Calgary where he worked as a western scout for Chicago. It was thanks to him that Cliff Korroll and Keith Magnuson, for instance, made it to the Hawks. Thompson was inducted into the Hockey Hall of Fame in 1959.

THOMPSON, Clifford
b. Winchester, Massachusetts, December 9, 1918
d. Boston, Massachusetts, February 6, 1997
After playing just three games for the Bruins in '41-'42, Thompson joined the U.S. Army. He served as a lieutenant with a tank destroyer unit, seeing action in France, Austria, and Germany. He was awarded two Bronze Stars, a Silver Star, and a Croix de Guerre. When he returned, he played for the Boston Olympics, but when Ed Kryzanowski was hurt, Thompson played ten games with the Bruins. He retired in 1950 and worked for the NHL as an official. During his playing days, Thompson was a mortician in the off season, but after his NHL association ended he settled in Reading, Massachusetts, where he became owner and president of New England Electrical Sales in nearby Charlestown.

THOMPSON, Errol ("Spud")
b. Summerside, Prince Edward Island, May 28, 1950
The near-glory days of the Leafs in the 1970s were at the heart of Thompson's career and popularity. He was drafted by Toronto in 1970 and over the next few years joined a young and talented nucleus of players that featured Darryl Sittler, Lanny McDonald, Borje Salming, Ian Turnbull, and Mike Palmateer. The Thompson-Sittler-McDonald line was one of the top-scoring threesomes in the league, and in '75-'76 Thompson had 43 goals. He was traded a short time later to Detroit when the Leafs became obsessed with acquiring Dan Maloney, a glorified goon whose contri-

bution to the team, in the context of the trade, was minimal. Thompson was known for his great backhand, but he retired in 1981 never having made it close to the Stanley Cup. After retiring, he returned down east and worked for Coca-Cola. For the last 17 years he has worked for Labatt as a sales rep.

THOMPSON, Ken
b. Oakengates, England, May 29, 1881
d. unknown
He played one and only one game, with the Montreal Wanderers before their arena burned down, during the NHL's first season. Little else is known about Thompson, although it appears that this was his last game of pro hockey.

Thompson made his fortune as majority owner of the Westgate Hotel.
PAUL THOMPSON

THOMPSON, Paul
b. Langdon, Alberta, November 2, 1906
d. Calgary, Alberta, September 13, 1991
The Thompson family moved to Calgary when Paul was five, and it was there that he and his brother, future Hall of Famer Tiny, learned to play the game with local teams. Paul turned pro with the Rangers for their first year, in 1926, signing for $3,500 a year. On the side, he appeared in ads for Cameo cigarettes, which paid $50 a week plus all he could smoke. Over the next 14 years Thompson played for only the Blueshirts and Chicago. He won three Stanley Cups during his career, one with the Rangers in 1928 and two with Chicago, in 1934 and '38. He was a skater and a scorer, starting in New York on the second line with Butch Keeling and Murray Murdoch. In Chicago, he led the Hawks in points for six straight seasons playing on a line usually with Doc Romnes and Mush March. He retired at 32 to coach the team and for six years, and one game in the seventh, he led the Hawks to good, but not great, records. He then moved to Kamloops. Thompson made his fortune as majority owner of the Westgate Hotel, though he also coached in town and managed the local arena. He returned to Calgary after selling his interest in the hotel, and watched his final years of games as the NHL expanded and changed forever. He died in hospital after a short illness.

THOMPSON, Rocky
b. Calgary, Alberta, August 8, 1977
A hard-nosed, tough-luck right winger, Thompson missed most of '98-'99 after suffering a serious concussion and taking months to recover. He started his second season with Calgary as a fan favourite who played much bigger than his skill might have allowed him, but the Flames traded him to Florida in 2000 and he has struggled to find a place in the Panthers lineup.

Errol Thompson

Bill Thoms

Floyd Thomson

THOMS, Bill
b. Newmarket, Ontario, March 5, 1910
d. Toronto, Ontario, December 26, 1964
After developing as a kid at home in Newmarket, Thoms ventured to the big city to play junior with the Marlies before making his NHL entrance with the local Leafs in '32-'33. As a centre, he was a terrific passer, though he was equally known for his accurate shot. In '35-'36 he led the NHL with 23 goals, but three years later he was traded to Chicago midway through the season. The Leafs may have thought Thoms was finished, but the Hawks got more life out of him by making the left-handed shot a right winger. The strategy worked, and Thoms was always among the team's top scorers. He retired after a few games with Boston in '44-'45 because of ill health and returned to Toronto. Thoms worked for the *Toronto Telegram* newspaper, but in September 1957 he suffered a heart attack. He recovered, but seven years later suffered a second, fatal attack at the age of 54.

THOMSON, Bill
b. Troon, Scotland, March 23, 1911
d. August 6, 1993
Not many early Olympians went on to play in the NHL, but Thoms did, for a short time. More important, he decided after the 1936 Olympics in Garmisch to turn pro, giving up his precious amateur status to seek a paying career as a puck carrier. He played only briefly with Detroit but spent more than a decade in the minors, mostly in the American league.

Thomson finished his career in Chicago in '57-'58 after being sold to the Hawks because of his involvement in the attempted formation of a players' association.
JIM THOMSON

and in his 12 seasons with the Leafs he played in 7 All-Star Games. A defenceman, he was paired for many years with Gus Mortson and the duo came to be called the Coal Dust Twins because in the summers Thomson ran a coal business and Mortson was his chief salesman. Thomson was superb in his own end and adept at moving the puck up to his forwards, but he was the bane of scorers. He once went 202 games without getting a goal, and in 787 career games he scored just 19 times. Even on the power play, his only job was to get the puck to the fella on the left point, Max Bentley, so he could do his thing. Thomson finished his career in Chicago in '57-'58 after being sold to the Hawks because of his involvement in the attempted formation of a players' association. It was a harsh fall given that at the start of the season he was appointed captain. Thomson returned to Toronto, established McKinnon Fuels (named using his wife's family's name), and worked the stock market with the best of them. In no short time he was likely the wealthiest ex-player in hockey.

THOMSON, Jim
b. Edmonton, Alberta, December 30, 1965
He played for 6 teams in 7 years, spread his 115 NHL games thin over the continent, and scored only 4 times, but Thomson was there. He started with Washington in 1986, then bounced from team to team with regularity and rapidity until the day he called it quite eight years later.

THOMSON, Floyd
b. Sudbury, Ontario, June 14, 1949
In 12 years of pro hockey, Thomson played exclusively in the St. Louis Blues system, an odd devotion given that he was by no means a regular from start to finish. In fact, Thomson was a full-time member of the NHL team for only five years, but when he wasn't with the big team he was in the minors – Kansas City or Salt Lake City – helping the farm team prosper. In '80-'81, he led the Golden Eagles to a CHL title, and a year later he retired.

THOMSON, Jim ("Jeems")
b. Winnipeg, Manitoba, February 23, 1927
d. Toronto, Ontario, May 18, 1991
He used to work as a busboy in the dining car of CPR trains, but when he developed his hockey skills, he became a passenger, not a servant. Thomson was a boy from out west who was recruited by the Leafs and sent to St. Mike's to play junior hockey. He played his first game for the Leafs in '45-'46, and the following season he made the team and never looked back. In 4 of his first 5 years the team won the Cup,

THOMSON, Rhys
b. Toronto, Ontario, August 9, 1918
d. Toronto, Ontario, October 12, 1993
Rhys Greenaway Thomson played a few games with Montreal and Toronto before joining the army as a Canadian Military Staff Clerk. He rose to the rank of sergeant during his two years in service, but when he was discharged his hockey days were more or less over. He lived the rest of his life in Toronto, eventually becoming president of Sheridan Equipment.

THORNBURY, Tom
b. Lindsay, Ontario, March 17, 1963
A Pittsburgh draft choice, Thornbury played his only 14 games in the NHL with the Penguins in '83-'84. He was later the property of Quebec and Calgary but played for neither team. Instead, he hung around the minors for a few years and then moved to Germany, where he played for many years as a scoring defenceman, something he had not been able to do much of in North America outside a fine year with Baltimore during the season he played with Pittsburgh.

Tom Thornbury

THORNTON, Joe
b. London, Ontario, July 2, 1979

In a stretch of a year and a half, Thornton won gold medals at the under-17, under-18, and World Junior tournaments, testament to his rising reputation as a teenager with a limitless future. Boston drafted him first overall in 1997, and the modern teen sensation with the spiffy watch called his friends right away to say hello. He then entered a heated contract battle with GM Harry Sinden before ever playing a game, and although his progress has been slow, his rise has been steady and his future greatness is almost assured. As a rookie, Thornton scored an embarrassing three goals and was far outperformed by fellow Bruins rookie Sergei Samsonov. In the off-season, he trained and gained needed strength to ready himself for year two, and he has become a prototypical power forward, capable of fighting off two or three men to make a pass or get to the net. He scored 16 goals the next year, 23 the year after, 37 the year after that. He learned to dominate, to play with a psychological strength and confidence that contributed to his physical attributes and blessed skill. Thornton has now outstripped Samsonov, and is the cornerstone of the next generation of Boston stars. He was a close miss for Canada's 2002 Olympics team, but he is a sure thing for 2006 if the NHL participates. His cousin, Scott, also plays in the NHL.

THORNTON, Scott ("Thorty")
b. London, Ontario, January 9, 1971

It has been a long trip from 1989, when his dream-team Leafs drafted him, to the present, when he started playing with San Jose and having the best years of his career. In a nutshell, Thornton has gotten better and better, pushing his prime back and developing later than most. He played his first few years with Toronto and the Oilers, seasons of frustration spent more in the minors. In 1993, the Oilers gave him a chance and he became an NHLer, a tough centre with two-way ability. He moved on to Montreal and Dallas, but when San Jose signed him in 2000 he joined one of the more talented young teams in the league. Now, it is a team ready to make a name for itself in the playoffs, and if that happens, it will be in part due to the play of Thornton, who scored a career-high 26 goals in 2001-02.

THORSTEINSON, Johann "Joe"
b. Winnipeg, Manitoba, March 19, 1905
d. Selkirk, Manitoba, August 24, 1948

The Thorsteinson clan moved to Selkirk when Joe was two, and that is where he learned how to play hockey. He played with a number of professional teams, mostly in the west, but he played four games with the New York Americans in '32-'33. After retiring, he became a coach, first for Fort Frances and then for Minnedosa. His father owned a photo business in Selkirk, and when he retired Joe took over the daily operations, though he also coached the Selkirk Junior B team.

THURIER, Fred
b. Granby, Quebec, January 11, 1916
d. Vero Beach, Florida, November 20, 1999

It wasn't a spectacular career, but Thurier did leave to go off to war and he did come back to play again. In his first go-round he played for the Americans and then joined the army with the Canadian Military Staff Clerks before playing for the Rangers in '44-'45, his one and only full season in the NHL. He then extended his career by playing for years in the American league with Cleveland, and by the time he retired he was the all-time points getter with 744. He was later inducted into both the Springfield Hockey Hall of Fame and the Cleveland Hockey Hall of Fame for his outstanding AHL career.

THURLBY, Tom
b. Kingston, Ontario, November 9, 1938

The bottom line was that he played for Oakland during the team's inaugural season after playing for the Seals in the WHL for many years leading up to expansion. He was 30 by the time he made his debut and didn't play pro hockey much longer after he was demoted.

THYER, Mario
b. Montreal, Quebec, September 29, 1966

Thyer left the University of Maine in 1989 to turn pro in the Minnesota organization, but the decision backfired inasmuch as he played only five games with the North Stars and only four seasons of pro. In Maine he proved to be heroic when he shattered his leg in three places early in the year and returned to the lineup during the playoffs. His career was shortened by injury, and he took the Stars to court seeking disability income, but he lost his case.

TIBBETTS, Billy
b. Boston, Massachusetts, October 14, 1974

The moral and ethical boundaries were stretched, perhaps beyond their limit, when Pittsburgh signed Tibbetts in April 2000. There have been players who get arrested and still have a career in the NHL, their crimes being drinking and driving, disorderly conduct, sometimes drug possession. Craig MacTavish spent a year in jail after killing a person while driving drunk, perhaps the worst crime ever committed by an active player. But in March 1994, Tibbetts pleaded guilty to raping a 15-year-old girl. A month later, he was convicted of assault and battery on a police officer,

He was 30 by the time he made his debut.
TOM THURLBY

Joe Thornton

Scott Thornton

Fred Thurier

Milan Tichy

Alex Tidey

Brad Tiley

Tom Tilley

disorderly conduct, and intimidating a witness. In July 1995 he was arrested and charged with assault and battery with a dangerous weapon and sentenced to two and a half years in prison. Previously, players committed a single offence, usually in a spontaneous moment. Tibbetts was a hard and tried criminal. He had a lengthy record, according to reports. Did he belong in the NHL? It certainly didn't do the Penguins or league any good to have him there, and he has been no star player besides. Prior to his convictions, he played no higher than East Coast league hockey, and in 71 NHL games through 2002 he scored 2 goals and accrued 257 penalty minutes.

TICHY, Milan
b. Plzen, Czechoslovakia (Czech Republic), September 22, 1969
By the time Tichy decided to come to North America in 1991, he was two years past his draft day with Chicago and at 22 believed he could play pro at the highest level. The Hawks thought differently and put him in the IHL for a year, then let him go in the Expansion Draft after only a few games with the parent club. He later played briefly for the Islanders but retired in 1996. Tichy became a regional scout for the Columbus Blue Jackets.

TIDEY, Alex
b. Vancouver, British Columbia, January 5, 1955
The lure of the WHA was too great for Tidey, who turned pro with San Diego in 1975. He went on to play just five more years of pro, though, and his NHL time was limited to a few games with Buffalo and Edmonton. The one Oilers perk was that those games came in 1979-80, the team's first year in the NHL and an early incarnation of one of the great offensive teams of all time. Lucky Tidey.

TIKKANEN, Esa ("Mr. T")
b. Helsinki, Finland, January 25, 1965
There was only one Tikkanen, a good and bad thing, his teammates might joke. When he was 16, he wanted to play in the NHL so badly that he moved to Regina to play junior hockey and learn the Canadian game. Edmonton drafted him in 1983 after he had returned home to play in his home league as well as international tournaments, and he joined the Oilers for the 1985 playoffs, when the team won the Stanley Cup. He played nine years with the Oilers and became a unique player. He was as determined a checker as there was in the game, but he also had plenty of scoring ability in him à la Derek Sanderson. He was a "trash talker" on ice, but his accent rendered much of what he said unintelligible and his patois came to be called Tiki-talki. He won four Cups with

the Oilers, none more special than 1990, which was accomplished without Wayne Gretzky. Like many players from those teams, Tikkanen joined the Rangers for '93-'94, the Cup won with many ex-Oilers in the lineup. It was his first of three stints with New York, and for the next six years the consistency of his first years was gone. He bounced from team to team, selling himself as a winner, a leader, and a pre-eminent checker, but his glory days were over. Despite his many accomplishments, he never won the Frank Selke Trophy and never played in an All-Star Game. He played in almost every international series he was eligible for, notably the 1998 Olympics in Nagano and five World Championships. He retired to Finland in 2000 to enjoy the good life of a hockey superstar, his dreams long since realized.

When he was 16, he wanted to play in the NHL so badly that he moved to Regina.
ESA TIKKANEN

TILEY, Brad
b. Markdale, Ontario, July 5, 1971
A star in the minors, Tiley has been classified more as a roster filler for the farm team than a prospective NHL defenceman. He turned pro in 1991 but had to wait six years to get into his first NHL game, with Phoenix, and after a few more games the pattern has repeated itself in Philadelphia. In 1999-2000, Tiley was named the AHL's best defenceman, but his offensive talents, so evident in the minors, have not given rise to a permanent spot with the Flyers.

TILLEY, Tom
b. Trenton, Ontario, March 28, 1965
It's a fact that he played his whole NHL career with St. Louis, but those 174 games represented but a small chunk of his total pro games and only once, in '88-'89, did he play a full season with the Blues. Tilley was a staple in the IHL for most of his career, playing nine years in all with, principally, the Chicago Wolves, his last team before retiring in 2001. He played for Canada at the 1995 World Championships, and his last NHL appearance was in '93-'94.

TIMANDER, Mattias
b. Solleftea, Sweden, April 16, 1974
It took Timander four years to go from the podium on draft day to his first game with the Bruins, and another four years and a trade to Columbus before he became an NHL regular. That's where he is today, a reliable defenceman for the expansion Blue Jackets, but he's getting plenty of ice time and learning the tricks of the trade. His rise to even marginal prominence in the NHL is admirable because he was selected 208th overall and the only international experience he had was with the junior team in 1994.

TIMGREN, Ray ("Golden Boy")
b. Windsor, Ontario, September 29, 1928
d. Lindsay, Ontario, November 25, 1999
Windsor is a tricky city. Fans can be devoted to their Leafs because Toronto is the great hockey capital and nearest Ontario team, but they can also swing to Detroit, their American neighbour just on the other side of the St. Clair River. Timgren leaned toward Leafland. He began his career with the Marlies after the war and made the NHL team in 1948. The team promptly won two Cups in his first three years, and he played four and a half seasons before being sent to Chicago. He finished his career in Toronto, and settled in the city where he went into teaching. When he retired from working life, he was a principal with the North York Board of Education. He moved to the quiet of Lindsay, Ontario, in 1996, where he passed away in hospital three years later.

Ray Timgren

TIMONEN, Kimmo
b. Kuopio, Finland, March 18, 1975
Being drafted 250th overall is not an encouraging sign for a player, but with time Timonen has become an NHLer over and above his fine international career. Los Angeles selected him in 1993, but it was with Nashville five years later that he made his debut. Not only has he survived with the team, he has become a fine offensive presence on their blueline, logging more than average minutes and anchoring the power play. He has also played in the two NHL Olympics (1998 and 2002) as well as four World Championships. His brother, Jussi, was drafted by Philadelphia in 2001.

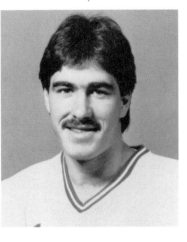

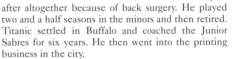

Tippett made his name in the NHL as a supreme checker.
DAVE TIPPETT

TINORDI, Mark
b. Red Deer, Alberta, May 9, 1966
While playing junior with Red Deer, Tinordi played like a bull. Big and tough, he had few offensive abilities, but he was a fine defenceman and could take care of himself. He was never drafted, and only Rangers scout Jack Fereira wanted anything to do with him. That's how Tinordi signed with New York in 1987, but when he got there he found out that the team wanted him to be an enforcer only. That's not what Fereira had envisioned, and not what Tinordi wanted. He was traded to Minnesota and later to Washington, where he played as he had in junior. He was a tough and solid defenceman, poised in his own end and nothing more, nothing fancy. He played in the 1992 All-Star Game and went to the Cup finals twice, once with the North Stars in 1991 and again with the Capitals in 1998. By the time he retired in 1999, he had earned league-wide respect for his play.

TIPPETT, Dave
b. Moosomin, Saskatchewan, August 25, 1961
Tippett's long and successful career will take an interesting turn now that he is head coach of Dallas. Named the new leader in 2002, the appointment marked a 20-year career in the game for Tippett, who started as a player at the University of North Dakota. He captained Canada's entry at the 1984 Olympics in Sarajevo and then signed with Hartford, the only team interested in the undrafted winger. The Whalers had watched him check Pat LaFontaine into the ice at Sarajevo and felt he was just the kind of player they needed. Tippett made his name in the NHL as a supreme checker and it was in that role that he was cast from start to finish of his playing days. He finished his career in the IHL in '94-'95, playing and coaching for Houston. The next year, he remained as assistant coach and a year later assumed head duties. His term with the Aeros climaxed in '98-'99 when the team won the Turner Cup, and on this strength he was made an assistant with Los Angeles. Ironically, the great checking player coached the Kings to the best power play in 2001-02, and in that summer the Stars offered him the top post.

Mark Tinordi

TITANIC, Morris
b. Toronto, Ontario, January 7, 1953
Titanic could not deliver on the promise of a 12th- overall draft choice, in large measure because of two serious injuries. In his rookie year, 1974-75, he suffered a bad knee injury and played just 17 games with the Sabres. The next year, he hurt his back, and missed the year after altogether because of back surgery. He played two and a half seasons in the minors and then retired. Titanic settled in Buffalo and coached the Junior Sabres for six years. He then went into the printing business in the city.

Morris Titanic

TITOV, German
b. Moscow, Soviet Union (Russia), October 16, 1965
His brother fell to his death off a balcony in Moscow. His father fell to his death off a balcony in Moscow. Welcome to the new Russia. Titov might be an exceptional hockey player, but he is part of a complex and sometimes frightening political landscape in the post-perestroika world of his homeland. He was drafted by Calgary when he was 27 and in his prime, having played for years in Khimik. Calgary selected him in 1993, just weeks after he helped his team win gold at the World Championships. He joined the Flames that fall and has been in the NHL ever since. He had 3 seasons of 22 goals or more in Calgary but has since gone on to play for 3 other teams, most recently Anaheim where he has tried to get his life back in order. He also

German Titov

Daniel Tkaczuk

Walt Tkaczuk

Mike Toal

helped Russia win a silver medal at the 1998 Olympics in Nagano.

TJARNQVIST, Daniel
b. Umea, Sweden, October 14, 1976
He made an immediate impact with Atlanta when he joined the team in 2001, but this was no rookie coming to camp. Tjarnqvist had been playing pro in Sweden since 1996, so here was an experienced defenceman who could help the expansion team quickly. He logged more than his fair share of ice time for the Thrashers and gave hope to the team for the future. Tjarnqvist finished that 2001-02 season by winning a bronze medal with Sweden at the World Championships. He had also played at the 2000 and 2001 WC and earlier at the 1995 and '96 World Juniors.

TKACHUK, Keith ("Walt")
b. Melrose, Massachusetts, March 28, 1972
He's brash and arrogant, strong, dominating, sometimes dirty. He's a superstar power forward, and you can take him or leave him. Regardless, he's likely to lead his team in goals and penalty minutes, though winning has been an elusive part of his game. He played for the U.S. at the 1998 Olympics in Nagano, a Games that was marred by the trashing by unidentified players of their rooms. He came home and called the experience a "waste of time," which is tough to argue given Team USA's fifth-place finish and horrendous behaviour. He also played in the 2002 Olympics in Salt Lake City, winning a silver, and the 1992 Olympics in Albertville.

He played on the successful World Cup team, but, of course, Tkachuk is, first and foremost, an NHLer. He has been in the league since 1992 and played most of his career with Winnipeg and Phoenix before being traded to St. Louis. He had two 50-goal seasons with the Jets, but he was stripped of his captaincy soon after being signed to a long-term contract. Although Tkachuk has never won an individual trophy, he has played in three All-Star Games. His brand of hockey is based on scoring and hitting, and he has established himself with a number of dirty hits and tough plays meant to intimidate the opposition. He might well reach the 500-goal mark and the 1,000-point plateau, though to date his teams have never advanced past the second round of the playoffs.

TKACZUK, Daniel
b. Toronto, Ontario, June 10, 1979
Unrelated to Walt, Daniel realized a dream when he scored his first NHL goal, with Calgary, on home ice in Toronto. He graduated from Barrie of the OHL but has spent most of his time developing in the minors.

**Although Tkachuk
has never won an individual
trophy, he has played
in three All-Star Games.**
KEITH TKACHUK

The best, or majority, of his career is still in the future.

TKACZUK, Walt
b. Emstedetten, Germany, September 29, 1947
The war affected everyone in one way or another. For the Tkaczuk family, the fighting changed everything. Father, Mike, was a miner in the Ukraine, but when the Germans took over the area, he and his wife were taken to a forced-labour camp in Emstedetten. They survived, and once peace was established started a family. Mike was given a chance to move halfway across the world, to South Porcupine, Ontario, to work in the mines, a chance he took in a heartbeat. His son, Walt, took an immediate liking to hockey, though he was by no means a superstar from day one. He was gangly and awkward, no ballerina on skates, but he was determined and focused. He made his way to junior with Kitchener and was called up to New York late in the '67-'68 season for a taste of the NHL. That was the start of 14 seasons and more than 1,000 NHL games, all with the Rangers. He grew and developed as a man, becoming one of the strongest players in the league. Playing on a line with Dave Balon and Bill Fairbairn, the threesome was dubbed the Bulldogs because of their physical strength and tenacious play. Tkaczuk had 5 successive 20-goal seasons at one point, but his career was cut short by a serious eye injury midway through the '80-'81 season. He remained with the team as an assistant coach for two years and later settled in Kitchener where he managed two stores that sold video games and computers. From there, he worked as a plastics salesman before developing a golf course in St. Mary's, Ontario, where he currently lives.

TOAL, Mike
b. Red Deer, Alberta, March 23, 1959
Edmonton used a number of players when it first joined the NHL in 1979, and Toal is among that group. He played three games for the team during his short career but three years later retired without getting another chance.

TOBLER, Ryan
b. Calgary, Alberta, May 13, 1976
Tobler's debut in the NHL had been in the works for a long time. He played for four WHL teams during his junior career, then started the lonely trek to the big time by turning pro in the minors without having been drafted. For more than four years he played in the IHL and AHL, eliciting interest along the way from Nashville and the Rangers. It wasn't until he signed with Tampa Bay in 2001, though, that he finally appeared in four games for the Lightning.

TOCCHET, Rick
b. Scarborough, Ontario, April 9, 1964

Game by game, goal by goal, Tocchet has moved through the years with the consistency of a certain battery that supposedly never stops. As a kid, all he ever wanted was to play in one game in the NHL, to prove that he could. Well, he's proved that, literally, more than a thousand times. He began his career in 1984 with Philadelphia and quickly became a tough and resilient power forward. He took the straight line to the net and hit whatever got in his way and pretty soon he was scoring 30, sometimes 40, goals a year. He played for Canada at the 1987 and '91 Canada Cups, but the Flyers traded him to Pittsburgh in February 1992, a great deal for him as the Pens went on to win the Cup. After that trade to the Igloo, Tocchet was on the move regularly. Injuries have slowed him down to the point that 2001-02 was a virtual write-off because of a serious knee injury, and his status as power forward slowly changed to be replaced by words such as gritty, grinder, and experienced winger. He retired in November 2002 because of his left knee, and joined Colorado as an assistant coach. Although he won't become a member of the Hockey Hall of Fame he certainly has left his mark on the NHL.

As a kid, all he ever wanted was to play in one game in the NHL, to prove that he could.
RICK TOCCHET

TODD, Kevin
b. Winnipeg, Manitoba, May 4, 1968

As a pro starting out in the New Jersey system, Todd played most of his first three years in the minors. He led the AHL in scoring in 1990-91 and was named league MVP that year, and in the fall he made the Devils as a bona fide NHLer. Over the course of the next seven seasons he moved around quite a bit and almost never appeared in the playoffs. Small, he was used as a checker, but his best year was his first, when he had 63 points with New Jersey. Todd finished his career in Europe before retiring.

TOMALTY, Glenn
b. Lachute, Quebec, July 23, 1954

A single game with the Jets soon after they joined the NHL in 1979 was the lone NHL story Tomalty will be able to tell the grandkids. He had a short pro career besides, never staying long enough anywhere to make a significant impact.

TOMLAK, Mike
b. Thunder Bay, Ontario, October 17, 1964

During his junior career in Cornwall, Tomlak was drafted by the Leafs in 1983. But rather than turn pro after junior, he enrolled at the University of Western Ontario and played four years in the CIAU. He was a dominant player with the Mustangs, setting all kinds of scoring records for the team and eventually being inducted into the school's hall of fame. Hartford signed him, and when he graduated Tomlak headed for Connecticut. Over the next four years he played 141 games with the Whalers, but didn't dominate. Big in CIAU terms is average in the NHL. Quick becomes slow and dominant becomes hopeful. Tomlak ended up in the minors where he fared better, though after 1994 he never made it back to the show.

TOMLINSON, Dave
b. North Vancouver, British Columbia, May 8, 1969

What's good for Mannheim is not necessarily what's good for Toronto. Tomlinson graduated from Boston University hoping to make the Leafs in 1991, but they played him only six times over two years before trading him. He played only a few more NHL games and spent most of his time in the minors until he accepted an offer to play for the Mannheim Eagles in 1996. He's been there ever since.

TOMLINSON, Kirk
b. Toronto, Ontario, May 2, 1968

He was one of the smallest goons the modern game has ever seen, but Tomlinson managed to take what little he had and turn it into a lifetime in the game that continues to this day. He played a single game with the North Stars in the 1980s during a minor-league career that took him all over the continent. No matter where he played, though, he found the penalty box quickly. After retiring in 1996, he turned to coaching, first as an assistant in the United league and then as a head coach, most recently with the Flint Generals.

TOMS, Jeff
b. Swift Current, Saskatchewan, June 4, 1974

It was third try lucky for Toms in junior. After losing in the Memorial Cup tournament with the Soo in 1991 and '92, the Greyhounds finally won it all in '93, springboarding Toms into the NHL. He started with Tampa on February 13, 1996, but has been a part-timer only ever since. In Florida for 2002-03, he is now on his sixth team, but the large left winger (6'5" and 210 pounds) has yet to make enough of an impact to become a regular.

TOMSON, John "Jack"
b. Uxbridge, England, January 31, 1918
d. Cloverdale, British Columbia, December 14, 2001

In the few years leading up to the Second World War, Tomson played a handful of games with the Americans, but once he joined the army his NHL days were over. He played in the Pacific Coast league out west and settled in B.C. after retiring, spending the rest of his life in that province.

Kevin Todd

Glenn Tomalty

Mike Tomlak

Kirk Tomlinson

Jeff Toms

John Tonelli

TONELLI, John

b. Milton, Ontario, March 23, 1957

There is pressure enough for a teenager who aspires to play in the NHL, but Tonelli compounded his efforts by going head-to-head with a decades-old contract he had signed with the OHL when he started to play junior with the Marlies in 1973. As his 18th birthday approached, he was being wooed by the WHA, knowing that the NHL didn't draft players until age 20. Tonelli left the Marlies on his birthday, but the Marlies took him to court, citing breach of contract which stipulated he was their property until age 20, when he would go on to the NHL. The WHA contended that at 18 he was an adult and free to do as he chose, and the courts sided with the upstart league, saying the contract was not negotiated in a fair manner. So there he was at 18 playing pro hockey in Houston on a line with Gordie and Marty Howe. Three years later, he moved to the NHL with the Islanders, the team that had drafted him, at age 20, in 1977. He played the first eight years of his career on Long Island, becoming part of the great nucleus of players that won four consecutive Stanley Cups. He was terrific in the corners, but also a bull in open ice, and as he gained confidence he developed into a dominating left winger. When he was invited to Team Canada's camp for the 1984 Canada Cup, he turned down the offer at first because he felt he wasn't good enough. After being convinced he was, he went on to collect nine points and was named tournament MVP. He then joined the Isles and had a career year, scoring 42 goals and recording 100 points. Tonelli was shocked when he was traded to Calgary on March 11, 1986, and over the last six years of his career he played for four teams. Although the Isles retired six numbers from that dynasty, Tonelli's isn't one of them. Yet, he remains one of the most important players from those years.

TOOKEY, Tim

b. Edmonton, Alberta, August 29, 1960

In his early teens, Tookey was the next big thing, but as he got older, enthusiasm for his talents dimmed. He started in the NHL with Washington in 1980 to begin a 15-year odyssey in pro hockey that was mostly AHL in nature. He played only a few games every now and then in the big time, but he became something of a legend in Hershey, where he spent much of his career. After retiring, he and Arnie Kullman were honoured by the Bears with a double retiring of their number 9 sweater. Tookey went on to coach junior B hockey in Indiana with the Central Penn Panthers.

Tim Tookey

Shane Toporowski

Zellio Toppazzini

He played the majority of his career in Boston, mostly during the dry years when the playoffs were only a dream.
JERRY TOPPAZZINI

TOOMEY, Sean

b. St. Paul, Minnesota, June 27, 1965

Being drafted out of high school in the U.S. is so misleading to a kid. He hasn't had the experience of junior hockey in Canada, and he hasn't played college hockey at the elite level in the U.S. Toomey went to the North Stars in 1983 but spent the next four years at the University of Minnesota-Duluth. At the end of his senior year, the Stars called him up for a game – and it turned out to be the only NHL game he ever played. After two years of pro, he retired.

TOPOROWSKI, Shayne ("Topper")

b. Paddockwood, Saskatchewan, August 6, 1975

Sometimes a goon isn't always a goon, or at least he has other, non-goon qualities that go unnoticed in the NHL. Toporowski came out of Prince Albert and played a few games with the Leafs in '96-'97, but for the most part he was cast as an enforcer. After about five years of fighting in the minors, he decided to go to Europe, signing with Espoo in 2000 and moving on to Britain. In 2001, he was signed by Lulea in Sweden, ironically to replace Mikael Renberg who had signed with the Leafs. He finished that season in Russia and continues his tour of the Continent far away from the fighting crowds in North America.

TOPPAZZINI, Jerry ("Topper")

b. Copper Cliff, Ontario, July 29, 1931

They're called battle scars for a reason, and if you played in the NHL for a dozen years during the Original Six, you had your share. Once, he was cross-checked in the face so hard by former teammate Ted Lindsay that doctors had to use photographs of him to reconstruct his face. In another year, he almost lost his right eye when he was poked with a stick. Through it all he kept coming back. He played the majority of his career in Boston, mostly during the dry years when the playoffs were only a dream. He was not as gifted a skater as his older brother, Zellio, but he was more determined. He finished his career in the minors with Port Huron of the IHL where he was a playing coach, and this led to work as a head coach in Springfield. He settled in Sudbury, where he coached the junior Wolves and ran a clothing store (à la Joe Ironstone). Topper later bought the Belvedere Hotel in town and worked part-time on Leafs radio broadcasts.

TOPPAZZINI, Zellio

b. Copper Cliff, Ontario, January 5, 1930

d. Providence, Rhode Island, April 1, 2001

In the summer of 2000, Toppazzini was named Rhode

Island Reds player of the century for his many years of service to hockey in Providence. Although he played a number of games in the NHL in the late 1940s and early 1950s, he was best remembered for his career in the AHL with the Reds. He played 12 years for the team and was an all-star right winger, and after retiring as a player he coached at Providence College. He led the AHL in scoring in 1955-56, the same year he led the team to the Calder Cup.

TORCHIA, Mike
b. Toronto, Ontario, February 23, 1972
They may have played on the same backyard rink together as kids in Toronto, but their careers have gone down different tines in that all important fork in the road. Eric Lindros was drafted 1st overall in 1991 and hasn't looked back; Torchia went 74th overall but played only 6 NHL games. The goalie played in the minors for years, and although he has been NHL property much of his career, he ended up going to Europe to play, most recently in Britain.

Mike Torchia

TORGAEV, Pavel
b. Gorky, Soviet Union (Russia), January 25, 1966
Torgaev wasn't drafted into the NHL until he was 28. He had spent the majority of his career playing in the Russian league in his hometown, but in 1995 he decided to try Calgary and see what all the NHL fuss was about. He played just half a season with the Flames before being sent to the minors, and Torgaev responded by trekking off to Switzerland to play. He returned briefly in 1999-2000, but when he was demoted again, this time by Tampa Bay, he was suspended. That was the last the NHL saw of the left winger who had played in the 1994 Olympics in Lillehammer.

TORKKI, Jari
b. Rauma, Finland, August 11, 1965
Like many a European player, the lure of North American hockey and the associated dollars went only as deep as the NHL. Without that cachet, there was little point in staying around. Torkki played 4 games with Chicago in 1988-89 but spent more than 15 years in the game, usually with his hometown club in Rauma. He later played in Germany and Italy, and after being out of the game for two years played briefly with Bracknell in 2001-02. Torkki also played at the 1988 Olympics in Calgary, a year after a strong showing in the World Championships. In all, he played two seasons in the IHL, and despite having some success he was neither intent to return to the NHL nor content riding buses to and from small-town America.

TORMANEN, Antti
b. Espoo, Finland, September 19, 1970
Another late draftee, Tormanen wasn't selected by Ottawa until he was 23, and he played less than one full season with the Senators. Before and after he played in the Finnish league, usually with Jokerit, but his greatest claim to fame is being part of Finland's 1995 World Championship team that won gold for the first time. He later played on three other WC teams as well as the bronze medal-winning 1998 Olympics team in Nagano.

TORRES, Raffi
b. Toronto, Ontario, October 8, 1981
The Islanders don't want to make a mistake with this young man's career. They drafted him 5th overall in 2000 with the expectations that he would one day be a superstar with the team. He played junior with Brampton and helped Canada win a bronze medal at the 2001 WJC, and the year after he got his feet wet in the NHL. Torres made the Islanders for the 2002-03 season, though he is still a long way from reaching his potential. A firecracker on ice, he still must prove he can contribute to the team offensively.

TOSKALA, Vesa
b. Tampere, Finland, May 20, 1977
Long after Toskala was drafted in 1995, he continued to play goal in Finland rather than come to the NHL. In 2000, he finally decided to give the big time a try, but has been in the minors with the exception of a 10-minute appearance for the Sharks.

Pavel Torgaev

Jari Torkki

TOUHEY, Bill
b. Ottawa, Ontario, March 23, 1906
d. Ottawa, Ontario, March 27, 1999
At the time of his death, Touhey was the last surviving original Senator. He had played five of his seven NHL seasons with the old Ottawa team, for which he was a decent scorer as a slight left winger. He played in the minors during his career, and retired to Ottawa where he played senior hockey until the war. Touhey coached the Ottawa RCAF Flyers to an Allan Cup in '41-'42 and then became successful in business. He owned and managed the Albion Hotel until selling it in the 1960s, and he was instrumental as an investor in the city getting the 67's as a franchise in the OHL. Golf was his other passion, and he played until his late eighties. He was inducted into the Ottawa Sports Hall of Fame in 1998.

TOUPIN, Jacques "Jack"
b. Trois-Rivières, Quebec, November 10, 1910
d. February 17, 1987
Toupin was a staple in the American league for years

Touhey coached the Ottawa RCAF Flyers to an Allan Cup in '41-'42.
BILL TOUHEY

Graeme Townshend

Larry Trader

Bob Trapp

Percy Traub

but got a wartime callup in '43-44 with Chicago. He scored a goal during his eight games, but went right back to the minors to finish out a long career there. He then returned to his hometown and opened a tavern, but in 1955 he became coach of the Lions, the new team in the Quebec Hockey League. Under his guidance, the team did surprisingly well, though Toupin did not remain in charge for long.

TOWNSEND, Art
b. Souris, Manitoba, October 9, 1905
d. Vancouver, British Columbia, August 5, 1971
The kid got a chance with Chicago during the team's first year in the NHL (1926-27) and then played in the minors for years, most frequently in western Canada. He went without a point in five games with the Hawks.

TOWNSHEND, Graeme
b. Kingston, Jamaica, October 2, 1965
He grew up in the Toronto area, but Townshend went on to play college hockey at RPI before signing with Boston in 1989. He had never been drafted, but after just a few games the Bruins let him go. From there he went on to the Islanders and the Senators with the same results, but he eventually found his niche in the IHL. After retiring, Townshend became coach in Macon and then with the Greensboro Generals of the ECHL.

TRADER, Larry
b. Barry's Bay, Ontario, July 7, 1963
There was plenty of potential in Trader when Detroit claimed him in 1981 while he was playing in London of the OHL. He was a defenceman with skill and quickness, and in four years in the minors he showed flashes of brilliance. Exhibit A in this regard was the 1986 AHL playoffs when he led the league in points and helped Adirondack capture the Calder Cup. That summer he was traded to St. Louis for Lee Norwood and soon enough the Blues passed him on to Montreal for Gaston Gingras. Trader never brought his great AHL game up to the NHL, though, and soon he was off to Italy to continue his career, which ended in 1993.

TRAINOR, Wes ("Bucko")
b. Charlottetown, Prince Edward Island, September 11, 1922
d. Charlottetown, Prince Edward Island, November 21, 1991
When he was still a teen, Trainor stopped playing hockey so he could fight in the war. He was a sergeant in the Royal Canadian Artillery, and only when he got out in one piece did he return to chasing the black disc around frozen waters. Soon after, he was given a decent chance by the Rangers, but after 17 games he

was returned to the minors. The Rangers sold him to Charlottetown of the Maritime Big Four league, and in his first season he was named the league's best player. He later played in Grand Falls, Newfoundland where he was called the godfather of hockey. Trainor coached numerous junior teams in that city, returning to Charlottetown in the early 1960s where he ran the local Forum for some 20 years.

TRAPP, Bob
b. Pembroke, Ontario, December 19, 1898
d. November 20, 1979
Back in 1926, the Hawks had to start somewhere, and Trapp was part of that beginning. He played defence for the Hawks for two seasons, though the team had limited success and he soon passed to the minors. Outside the NHL, Trapp played most of his time in Tulsa and Providence. Prior to his Chicago tenure he had played in Edmonton, going to the Stanley Cup finals against Ottawa in 1923.

TRAPP, Doug
b. Balcarres, Saskatchewan, November 28, 1965
A westerner through and through, Trapp played a few games with Buffalo during his three years in Rochester. He helped the Americans win the '87 Calder Cup but continued to play senior hockey out west while pursuing a coaching career. He led the Fort Knox Jr. B team at Fort Qu'Appelle for a number of years and more recently was an assistant with the Estevan Bruins. His father, Barry, has been a long-serving and successful scout with Canadian Hockey.

> **He played in Grand Falls, Newfoundland where he was called the godfather of hockey.**
> **WES TRAINOR**

TRAUB, Percy ("Puss")
b. Chesley, Ontario, August 23, 1896
d. May 1948
Percy Luthure Traub entered Canada's war efforts with the Artillery Depot in May 1918 but was discharged that December. He played hockey for years in Regina before joining Chicago for the first NHL season in 1926-27. He later played two seasons with Detroit during his brief career and then settled in Regina.

TRAVERSE, Patrick ("Travy")
b. Montreal, Quebec, March 14, 1974
One of Ottawa's original draft choices from that inaugural selection in 1992, Traverse attended five training camps with the team and every time was sent to the minors. He got one callup for a few games, but, disillusioned, went to Hershey as a free agent where his career got going again under coach Bob Hartley. Hartley moved on to Colorado and won a Cup, and Traverse was re-signed by Ottawa, where he played two years. After playing at the 2000 World

Championships for Canada, he had a busy 2000-01 season, playing for Anaheim, Boston, and Montreal. Like any modern Habs player, he suffered serious injuries. In his case, a knee and head injury caused him to miss most of 2001-02, though the big defenceman seems to have found a home, for a while, anyway.

TREBIL, Dan
b. Bloomington, Minnesota, April 10, 1974
A U of Minnesota grad in 1996, defenceman Trebil started his NHL days with Anaheim that fall. But over three seasons, his AHL time increased and NHL time decreased, which is not how things should work. He was traded to Pittsburgh, and there, too, has been used more as filler for the farm team than as a true NHL prospect. In 2001, he decided to try Europe, and spent the season in Sweden.

TREDWAY, Brock
b. Highland Creek, Ontario, June 23, 1959
Cornell University was where it was at for Tredway. From 1977 to '81 he was the star scorer, team captain, all-star, and MVP. In the NHL, that and a quarter got him a cup of coffee. Signed by L.A. after going undrafted, Tredway is the rarest of one-game wonders in that his lone appearance came in the play-offs in 1982. He played only briefly in the minors and later was inducted into Cornell's Sports Hall of Fame.

TREFILOV, Andrei
b. Kirovo-Chepetsk, Soviet Union (Russia), August 31, 1969
A goalie just doesn't get the same number of chances to make a team as a skater. As a result, he has to make the most of his chances, and he has to have excellent luck along the way. Trefilov was fortunate on neither count. In his NHL debut, with Calgary in 1992, he allowed five goals. The next year, he played better in a few more games, but the team didn't. When he signed as a free agent in Buffalo in 1995, he was consigned to the bench to admire Dominik Hasek. No matter how well he played for the Sabres – and he didn't play that well – he was never going to take the starter's role from the Dominator. In his last 14 starts, spread over 4 years, he won just once and allowed too many goals. Yet, his reputation was solid. He played in four World Championships for Russia and was backup at two Olympics (1992 and '98). He was even the main goalie for Russia at the '96 World Cup. Although he still plays in Germany, Trefilov saw the NHL last in 1999 and is almost certainly never going back as a goalie.

TREMBLAY, Brent
b. North Bay, Ontario, November 1, 1957
He wasn't NHL calibre, and he knew it, but in December 1979 Tremblay scored a goal in the league,

Tremblay rose to prominence in the 1965 playoffs when Jacques Laperriere was lost to injury.
J.C. TREMBLAY

and he beat Gordie Howe on the play to do it! That alone made his 10 games with Washington worth it.

TREMBLAY, Gilles
b. Montmorency, Quebec, December 17, 1938
There was a sense of incompleteness to Tremblay's career, cut short because of illness in his prime. He won the Memorial Cup with Hull-Ottawa in 1958-59 and joined the Canadiens in 1960. For most of his career on left wing Jean Béliveau was his centre and Bernie Geoffrion and then Yvan Cournoyer played the right side. He scored 32 goals in his first full season and had 5 years with 20 goals or more. Tremblay won three Cups with Montreal in the 1960s, but in 1969 he confirmed every suspicious person's worst fears. After getting a flu shot, not only did he contract flu but he also developed asthma he never got rid of. He moved into the broadcast booth for French-language television and also worked for Molson Brewery.

TREMBLAY, Jean-Claude "J.C."
b. Bagotville, Quebec, January 22, 1939
d. Montreal, Quebec, December 7, 1994
During his early days of junior in Hull-Ottawa, left winger J.C. Tremblay looked to the Canadiens and saw the depth of talent at his position. He immediately moved back to play defence and developed into one of the finest rushing defencemen of his day. From 1959 to '61 he received two lengthy callups to the Habs and so impressed management that by age 21 he was a star on a blueline deep in talent. He never scored that many goals, but his terrific stickhandling and superior ability to move the puck served the old adage that the best defence is a good offence – if the puck was not in the Montreal end, the team could not be scored upon. Tremblay rose to prominence in the 1965 playoffs when Jacques Laperriere was lost to injury. He picked up for his mate and dominated the semifinals against Chicago and the finals against the Red Wings, and he was runner-up in voting for the Conn Smythe Trophy. Three years later, he was runner-up to Bobby Orr for the Norris Trophy and in '70-'71 he broke Doug Harvey's team record for points by a defenceman when he registered 63 on the season. By 1972, Tremblay had done all he could do, so when the chance to play for Quebec in the WHA arose – sweetened by a lucrative contract, of course – he took it. He played all seven WHA seasons and retired just as the Nordiques joined the NHL in 1979. His number 3 was retired by the team. Tremblay then moved to Geneva, Switzerland, where he worked as a European scout for the Canadiens. When he became ill in late 1994 he returned to Montreal, passing away as a result of cancer of the kidney.

Brent Tremblay

Gilles Tremblay

TREMBLAY, Marcel
b. St. Boniface, Manitoba, July 4, 1914
d. unknown

He grew up in Manitoba and played his only games with the Canadiens before the Second World War, but the minor leaguer entered the army and never played after his discharge. In 10 games with Montreal, he recorded 2 assists.

TREMBLAY, Mario
b. Montreal, Quebec, February 9, 1956

There weren't too many third-line players in the NHL who were better at their job than Tremblay was at his, and the resultant five Stanley Cups were earned on merit and team play. Tremblay was a gritty menace. Playing on a line with Yvon Lambert and Doug Risebrough, the threesome had the ability to check the other team's top line into the ice, and at the same time outscore it. Tremblay averaged better than 20 goals a season for his dozen years in the league, all with Montreal, and he worked effectively killing penalties and on the power play. He was part of the late-1970s dynasty and won a final Cup in '85-'86, after which his battered body told him to stop. He later worked in Montreal for TV and radio, becoming a popular and controversial commentator. Five games into the '95-'96 season he replaced Jacques Demers as coach, but after two middling seasons he was replaced after being crushed by New Jersey in the opening round of the 1997 playoffs. Of course, his hiring was based largely on his being French-Canadian and his affiliation with the city, and he didn't find work in hockey again until former teammate Jacques Lemaire hired him as an assistant in Minnesota, a position he currently maintains.

Mario Tremblay

TREMBLAY, Nil
b. Matane, Quebec, July 26, 1923
d. unknown

A centre, Tremblay was a sensational scorer outside the NHL in senior leagues, but he was called up as an emergency replacement for only three games by Montreal, once in '44-'45 and twice the following season. He recorded an assist in his first game, and in '48-'49 won the Allan Cup with the Ottawa Senators.

TREMBLAY, Vince
b. Quebec City, Quebec, October 21, 1959

It was a deadly combination: playing for a bad team and not being able to stop the puck. Tremblay was supposed to be an up-and-comer when Toronto drafted him in 1979, someone to work with Mike Palmateer and develop into a number one on his own merit. Yet over the course of his five years in the NHL, Tremblay

Pascal Trepanier

allowed almost five goals a game, and that won't cut it in the Q let alone in the NHL. He played half a season in '81-'82, his only full year with any team, but soon was traded to Pittsburgh, where he didn't win a game and allowed 24 goals in 4 outings. He retired soon after.

TREMBLAY, Yannick
b. Pointe-aux-Trembles, Quebec, November 15, 1975

"Plans" are an important part of any team, and it's a simple, yet euphemistic word that carries the weight of many a career on its back. Tremblay has always been a very talented defenceman. He has all the proverbials in his favour – size, speed, mobility, puckhandling – but he never fit into Toronto's "plans" and was considered a minor leaguer who could come up to the Leafs when injury demanded a replacement. He always played well, never griped, but clearly grew frustrated. When Atlanta claimed him in 1999, he was set free, and with the Thrashers immediately established himself not just as one of the top players on the rock-bottom team but as a genuine NHL player who could make almost any team.

TREPANIER, Pascal
b. Gaspé, Quebec, September 4, 1973

The kind of defenceman every team needs but no team keeps, Trepanier will never be long out of work but he'll never command the big-ticket contract of his more high-profile brethren. He's twice been part of the Avalanche, no slouch of an organization there, and also played for Anaheim and now Nashville, at the other end of the skill scale.

Tremblay was supposed to be an up-and-comer when Toronto drafted him in 1979.
VINCE TREMBLAY

TRIMPER, Tim
b. Windsor, Ontario, September 28, 1959

It was a fortuitous and fruitful connection that helped Trimper get to the NHL. In '78-'79, he captained the Peterborough Petes to the Memorial Cup, a team guided by 24-year-old head coach Gary Green. The next year, Green became the youngest head coach in NHL history, with Chicago, and Green called on Trimper based on knowledge and experience from the Petes. Trimper was good in the corners, but playing on a line with Tom Lysiak and Rich Preston he didn't create the offence he had in junior when he set many Petes records. Trimper was traded to Winnipeg, but after two years he became a minor leaguer. He finished his career with Minnesota in 1985.

TRNKA, Pavel
b. Plzen, Czechoslovakia (Czech Republic), July 27, 1976

It's going to be decision day soon in Anaheim for Trnka, one of a number of still-young players who has yet to take the team into the playoffs (save a four-game sweep in 1999). He joined the Ducks in 1997 and has been on their blueline ever since, but a lack of results could mean a change of venue for Trnka. His only international experience was at the 1995 World Juniors for the Czechs, the year after he was drafted.

TROTTIER, Bryan ("Trotts")

b. Val Marie, Saskatchewan, July 17, 1956

When the WHA started operations in 1972, it sought to draft 18-year-olds, players two years younger than the NHL-imposed limit. The effect was going to be devastating to the NHL in that it might lose many young stars to a league that promised two years of pro pay before the NHL could, and although it wasn't until 1980 that all 18-year-olds were eligible to be drafted into the NHL, there were clandestine exceptions earlier on. Trottier, drafted in 1974 at 18 by the Islanders, was one such beast. But no sooner had the team selected him than it convinced him to stay in junior with Lethbridge another year to develop. The Isles even paid him a year's salary to do so, and the move was mutually beneficial. When Trottier hit the Islanders' training camp in the fall of 1975, he was a year older, bigger, and wiser. He was also clearly a superstar in the making. As a rookie, he set league records for assists (63) and points (95) while playing on a line with Clark Gillies and Billy Harris. He also won the Calder Trophy. The whole team had a mediocre '76-'77, but after that it was up, up, and away. Trottier had his first of five successive 100-point seasons on a new line with Gillies and scorer Mike Bossy, and not surprisingly he led the league in assists with 77.

He was a tenacious centre who worked well with the other two. Gillies was strictly a corner man who dug the puck out for the others; Bossy was the pure scorer with the quick release; and, Trottier was the beautiful passer and playmaker who had a great shot of his own to provide relief for Bossy. Trottier won his only Art Ross Trophy in '78-'79 just before Gretzky and Lemieux were to dominate the scoring for the next 15 years (he won the Hart Trophy that year as well). He led the team to the 1980 Stanley Cup, winning Conn Smythe Trophy honours as well, and the year after played for Team Canada at the 1981 Canada Cup. The Islanders went on to win four Cups in a row, but for the 1984 Canada Cup, Trottier stunned a country by declaring he would play for the U.S. His wife and children were American, and he had lived on Long Island for a number of years. There was more to it than that, though. Trottier was a mix of French, Irish, Cree, and Chippewa, and during his years in the WHL he felt the wrath of racism. His Indian identity card gave him full right to obtain U.S. citizenship, but during games in Montreal he was booed mercilessly by the crowd for

He was a slow skater but a brilliant stickhandler and passer.
DAVE TROTTIER

his perceived traitorous actions. After the Islanders dynasty, the team slowly waned and Trottier, who had grown with the team, also dimmed with it. He ended up signing with Pittsburgh in 1990, but as a defensive specialist who brought oodles of character and experience to a team near a Cup with its own group of stars including Lemieux and Jaromir Jagr. Trottier fit in perfectly and helped the team to two Cups in 1991 and '92. He then retired and returned to the Islanders as executive assistant to the president, but the desk job lacked appeal and challenge. He came back to play with the Penguins for half of '93-'94 and then stayed on with the team as an assistant coach. It was then he knew he had a new job: To do as coach what he had done as a player. In 1997, he assumed the head coaching job with Portland in the AHL, and a year after he went up to Colorado as an assistant. He was part of the Cup-winning team in 2000-01, and in the summer of 2002 finally got what he had been working for eight year for – an NHL head coaching job. The struggling, fumbling Rangers gave him his chance, but whether he can take a team of talented individuals and turn them into one cohesive unit is something only time will tell. Trottier was inducted into the Hockey Hall of Fame in 1997 in honour of his NHL seasons. He won six Stanley Cups, and his 1,425 career points puts him among the highest scorers in league history.

Bryan Trottier

TROTTIER, Dave

b. Pembroke, Ontario, June 25, 1906
d. Halifax, Nova Scotia, November 13, 1956

Few men have lived as rich and varied and successful a life as Trottier, who started out on ice and ended up in oil. Growing up in Toronto, he eventually played for the U of T Grads, coached by Conn Smythe and was chosen by the CAHA to represent Canada at the 1928 Olympics after having won the Allan Cup the previous year. Trottier et al. travelled to St. Moritz and destroyed the opposition, and the Grads returned as heroes. Some chose to turn professional; others did not. Trottier signed with Montreal Maroons for an astronomical price of $16,000 and went on to spend 10 of his 11 years with the team. He was a slow skater but a brilliant stickhandler and passer, and his NHL career culminated in 1935 when the Maroons went through the playoffs without a loss (five wins and two ties) en route to the Stanley Cup. Trottier played on the Blue Line with Russ Blinco and Earl Robinson and once scored 26 goals in a year, a fantastic number for that era. He was later traded to Detroit but by that time was working for an oil firm called McColl-Frontenac and retired from hockey after just a few games with the Wings. A short time later he accepted a transfer to Halifax, where he spent

Guy Trottier

the rest of his life. He played the occasional hockey game but became ever more interested in football, even serving a term as president of the Nova Scotia Football League. In fact, he passed away while watching a football game, his NHL legacy long since established, but his even greater accomplishment as a gold medallist in Olympic hockey the truest measure of his success.

TROTTIER, Guy ("The Mouse")
b. Hull, Quebec, April 1, 1941

As Isolde is to Tristan and Beatrice is to Dante, so is Trottier to Dayton, the team for which he starred and currently coaches. He joined the Gems in 1964 just days before the expansion team played its first game, but in 3 years he recorded record-setting numbers, culminating with a 71-goal and 135-point season. This prompted the Rangers to give him a two-game tryout, nothing more, and after two more sensational seasons with Buffalo in the AHL he signed with the Leafs. In two seasons with Toronto, though, the goals came few and far between and he ended up in the WHA. He later returned to Dayton and then in '75-'76 played for and coached the Buffalo Norsemen, leading to a full-time career as a coach. Appropriately, he returned to Dayton as an assistant, and continues in that capacity.

TROTTIER, Rocky
b. Climax, Saskatchewan, April 11, 1964

Unfortunately, because of his name and his draft position, Trottier goes down as a major NHL bust, through no fault of his own. The younger brother of Bryan, New Jersey was banking on the Trottier gene pool to produce a second Hall of Famer and selected Rocky 8th overall in 1982, way above the potential he had shown as a junior way west. He went on to play just 38 games for the Devils and a few innocuous years in the minors, coming nowhere near Bryan's accomplishments. Rocky eventually made his way to Indiana where he operated the TNT Hockey Academy, a school that used plastic ice.

Rocky Trottier

TRUDEL, Jean-Guy
b. Sudbury, Ontario, October 10, 1975

He has all the makings of a career minor leaguer, though he's still in his prime and stranger things have happened than to see a late bloomer make the NHL. To now, though, the undrafted winger has played only a few games with Phoenix before signing with Minnesota in the summer of 2002.

TRUDEL, Louis "Lou"
b. Salem, Massachusetts, July 21, 1912
d. Grand Rapids, Michigan, March 19, 1972

To say he was the first Massachusetts-born player to

Rene Trudell

have his name on the Cup is technically accurate, but it does something of a disservice to Bobby Carpenter, who was a Native and a true blue American. Trudel's parents came from Montreal, moving to witch country when Trudel Sr. got a job there. But soon after Louis was born, the family moved to Edmonton, where the hockey player grew up. In his early days he played for an outfit called the Edmonton Poolers, and in 1933 he joined Chicago, a team that won the Cup at season's end. Trudel won a second Cup with the Hawks four years later and finished his NHL tenure with three years in Montreal. Not a powerful player, he was good defensively and never stirred up trouble on the ice. He had a long career in the American league after his NHL days were over, and he later turned to coaching, first in Grand Rapids for three years and later in Milwaukee. He settled in Springfield and became a goal judge at Indians home games. He died of cancer.

Not a powerful player, he was good defensively and never stirred up trouble on the ice.
LOU TRUDEL

TRUDELL, Rene ("Trudy")
b. Mariapolis, Manitoba, January 31, 1919
d. March 19, 1972

A fine skater and stickhandler, Trudell could not deke around the Second World War. He had played senior hockey and ventured to Harringay, England, for a season, but in 1942 he put down his stick and took up arms, enrolling with the Canadian Dental Corps for almost four years. When he returned, he joined the Rangers and played two and a half seasons with the Blueshirts. Later in life he moved to San Francisco and opened a restaurant.

TSELIOS, Nikos
b. Oak Park, Illinois, January 20, 1979

At 6'5" and 210 pounds, Tselios is a ton larger than his distant relative, Chris Chelios, though they share the common trait of playing defence. But while Chelios is at the end of a long NHL career, Tselios (who never Americanized his Greek surname) is trying to get his started. Drafted by Carolina in 1997, he has played only a few games so far with the 'Canes.

TSULYGIN, Nikolai
b. Ufa, Soviet Union (Russia), May 29, 1975

The allure of a Russian name does not guarantee success, and if he's considered one of the country's best kept secrets, perhaps there's a reason. In this day and age, talent will out regardless of where it lives, so perhaps Anaheim thought it had scooped the other teams when it took Tsulygin 30th overall in 1993 while he was playing in Ufa, a city situated hundreds of kilometres due east of Moscow. Tsulygin has been playing pro almost ever since, but only 22 games in that time came with the Ducks in the NHL. He currently is right back where he started, playing in the Russian league.

TSYGUROV, Denis
b. Chelyabinsk, Soviet Union (Russia), February 26, 1971
Sometimes, the little bits and pieces (futures, draft choices, prospects) in a trade with the big names turn into something special, but most of the time they don't. Tsygurov didn't. He was drafted by Buffalo and played a few games with the Sabres in the early 1990s, but on February 14, 1995, he was traded to Los Angeles with Grant Fuhr and Philippe Boucher for Charlie Huddy, Robb Stauber, and a draft choice. Again, Tsygurov got into a few games, with the Kings, and pretty soon he was back playing in Russia. He retired in 2001.

TSYPLAKOV, Vladimir
b. Inta, Soviet Union (Russia), April 18, 1969
There is achievement, and then there is history. The one is satisfying; the other is breathtaking. Tsyplakov's achievements include playing in the NHL for six years, taking his regular turn on the left wing in L.A. and Buffalo, scoring some goals, making some plays. He had played for tiny Belarus at the 1998 Olympics in Nagano and two subsequent World Championships, but on Wednesday, February 20, 2002, he was part of history. That day, in a quarter-finals matchup, his Belarussians defeated Tre Kronor 4-3 on a late, fluky goal, one of the greatest upsets in Olympic hockey history. Tsyplakov had played that season in Russia, where he continues his post-NHL incarnation. And although Belarus lost to Russia for the bronze medal, that was still the most important game in that young country's history.

He won three Memorial Cups – an almost unheard of feat – with Kamloops in 1992, '94, and '95.
DARCY TUCKER

TUCKER, Darcy
b. Castor, Alberta, March 15, 1975
The number of players who had a comparable junior career to Tucker can be counted on a couple of fingers. He won three Memorial Cups – an almost unheard of feat - with Kamloops in 1992, '94, and '95. He also won a gold medal with Canada at the 1995 World Juniors. He turned pro in 1995 and was named rookie of the year after his first season in the AHL. He started in Montreal, went to Tampa Bay, and has established himself in the Blue and White of Toronto. Gritty, tough, small, marginally dirty, he is a presence, sometimes too reckless, sometimes effective. He yaps to the referees, charges the goalie, hits and gets hit along the fence. Love him or hate him he cannot be ignored. In 2001-02, he also upped his reputation by scoring 24 goals and 59 points, second on the team only to Mats Sundin. With the Leafs, he's doubly blessed because he plays with his brother-in-law, Shayne Corson, Tucker being married to Shannon Corson, Shayne's sister. Tucker learned his hockey on the frozen waters near the family farm in tiny Endiang, Alberta, and from there his rise to the NHL was meteoric.

TUCKER, John
b. Windsor, Ontario, September 29, 1964
As a kid, he could do it all and then some. As a junior, he could do almost all. As an NHLer, he could do some of it. Tucker came out of junior to join the Sabres in 1984 and never played in the minors. In his third year, he scored 31 times and looked to be quickly developing into a great star, yet that turned out to be his peak season. He settled in to become a solid centre good for 17 goals, and after 7 seasons in Buffalo he started to move around the league a bit more. He ended up playing in Europe and more recently in Japan before retiring in 2000. His uncle was Whit Tucker, a wide receiver in the CFL. Since 1990, Tucker has been running an eponymous hockey school every summer in various parts of Canada and the U.S.

TUCKER, Ted
b. Fort William, Ontario, May 7, 1949
In the late 1960s, Tucker was playing for the Jr. Canadiens and moved on to a nothing career in the lower levels of the minors. He got into goal for California in '73-'74 for three games, and for all of that he was extremely grateful in 1975 when he almost died. He was property of Toledo by this point, guarding the goal in the IHL, when he fell asleep at the wheel one night. He flipped the car, crashed through some poles, and wound up on death's door for three days. From the impact, much of his inner workings were rearranged or mangled: his heart was pushed under his lung, his stomach was rammed into where his heart had been, his left lung was punctured, his spleen was ruptured, and his esophagus was torn. Oh, yeah, and he broke some ribs. Three months later, he was in goal again, a medical miracle who defied doctors' more pessimistic conclusions. Tucker never made it back to the NHL, but he played a good while longer in the minors, a survivor, a battler of great courage – and luck.

TUDIN, Cornell "Conny"
b. Ottawa, Ontario, September 21, 1917
d. Ottawa, Ontario, October 24, 1988
Born in Overbrook, a suburb of Ottawa, Tudin grew up playing many sports well, though it was with the Ottawa Boys Club, as a hockey player, that he excelled. He left home to play at Harringay in '38-'39 on a mostly Canadian team, but with the war he returned home. He played four games with the Canadiens and then left hockey to enlist. Tudin served as a sergeant with the RCAF and after coming home had a long and

Denis Tsygurov

Ted Tucker

Conny Tudin

Rob Tudor

distinguished career playing senior hockey in his hometown. He won the Allan Cup in 1949 and was capable of playing both forward and defence. He had a reputation for being a first-rate penalty killer. After retiring, he continued to have an impact on the city's sporting scene. He played old-timers hockey and was a voracious golfer. Tudin was co-owner and president of the Rideau Glen Golf Club for 22 years (1955-77), and was also active in curling. The Ridgemont High School football team named its MVP award after Tudin, and he died tragically in a car accident while still a vibrant and healthy man of 71.

TUDOR, Rob
b. Cupar, Saskatchewan, June 30, 1956
By the time he retired, Tudor had only four NHL goals to his credit, but he was the all-time leader in goals in the CHL. Vancouver drafted him in 1976, but he played just a few games with the Canucks and later the Blues. However, with a number of teams in the Central league he was a prolific scorer. Early in the '83-'84 season, he scored his 192nd goal in that league and became the top career scorer, not enough of an achievement to get into the Hockey Hall of Fame, but enough to be proud of for a career well done.

TUER, Allan
b. North Battleford, Saskatchewan, July 19, 1963
Most players felt as if they would kill to get to the NHL, and Tuer certainly lived up to the French meaning of his name many nights as a goon with huge penalty minutes to his record. In Regina in the

Ron Tugnutt

WHL he spent more time in the box than most players on the ice, and when L.A. drafted him in 1981 it more or less reaffirmed the method to his madness. He played just a few games over the term of his NHL career, averaging four penalty minutes a game. In the minors, there was more fighting and mayhem, but by 1993 he had had enough.

TUGNUTT, Ron ("Tugger")
b. Scarborough, Ontario, October 22, 1967
Seven teams and counting, Tugnutt is one of the most well-travelled goalies in NHL history. He started with Quebec in 1987 and in each of his first four seasons worked more games until he was the number-one man in net for the Nordiques. Unfortunately, he had a dismal 12-29-10 record that year, and it wasn't until he joined Ottawa a number of years later that he was the starter again. In the interim, he played backup, and in '96-'97 he had his first season with a record above .500, his first of three in a row with the Senators that culminated with a selection to the 1999 All-Star Game. He ended that '98-'99 season with an incredible GAA of

Marko Tuomainen

1.79 to lead the league, the lowest average since Al Rollins' 1.77 in '50-'51. In the summer of 2000, he signed with Columbus, a veteran on a weak team, knowing he would be the team's main man.

TUOMAINEN, Marko
b. Kuopio, Finland, April 25, 1972
It's been a peripatetic career to date for Tuomainen, a Finn who took an unusual route to the NHL for a European by going to a U.S. college, Clarkson in his case. He was a prolific scorer there and played for Edmonton quickly in 1995, but after those four games he disappeared from the NHL atlas. He played in the minors, then went home, but, alas, that was not the last of him. Los Angeles dug out a contract for him in 1999, and he played all of the next season with the Kings. Since then, he's been downgraded to part-time duty there, and then with the Islanders, but he is a big right winger who just won't go away, and that means he just might be back for a while at some point.

TURCO, Marty
b. Sault Ste, Marie, Ontario, August 13, 1975
The main reason Dallas had no problem with star goalie Eddie Belfour signing with Toronto in the summer of 2002 was that his backup, Turco, had quietly proved to be as good a goalie and far more … emotionally reliable. He graduated from the University of Michigan and played for Michigan in the IHL before joining the Stars in 2000, and over his first two seasons had a superb aggregate record of 28-12-3. Whenever Belfour floundered, threw a fit, got arrested, or fought with the coach, Turco came in and played brilliantly steady and steadily brilliant. The starter's job is his to lose, but to date he has shown an ability to play well at the NHL level.

TURCOTTE, Alfie
b. Gary, Indiana, June 5, 1965
At the 1983 draft, Montreal GM Serge Savard commented on Turcotte's bravura performance at the previous Memorial Cup tournament and hailed the teenager as a superstar with as much talent and skill as Turcotte's good friend Pat LaFontaine. It didn't take long for the kid to prove the Senator wrong, for he showed up to his first training camp 20 pounds overweight. That meant a nice stay in the minors, but even worse, it meant a promotion to the Canadiens later in the year. That's when Turcotte showed all his many non-LaFontaine qualities. He later played with Winnipeg and Washington, but in 8 pro seasons in North America he played in just 112 games, scoring a grand total of 17 goals. In 1991, Turcotte moved to Europe to play and for seven years enjoyed new life in

For the last 20 years he has run the Turcotte Hockey School in the summers.
ALFIE TURCOTTE

a lesser-skilled environment. For the last 20 years he has run the Turcotte Hockey School in the summers, and since retiring he has worked as a skills coach for a number of NHL teams.

TURCOTTE, Darren
b. Boston, Massachusetts, May 2, 1968
In today's NHL, there is every chance in the world that Turcotte would have won the Calder Trophy for the rookie season he had with the Rangers. The trouble is – was – that when he started his first full season in '89-'90, he was up against Sergei Makarov and Igor Larionov, two senior members of the Soviet Union national teams but, technically, first-year NHLers. In his first four seasons, Turcotte developed into a great player with the Rangers, but his career changed completely in December 1993 when he blew out his knee and missed most of the year. He never scored more than 17 goals a year after that, his strength and speed were diminished, and his role changed. He also moved around the league, playing for six teams in his last seven seasons. When he destroyed his knee in November 1999, that more or less spelled the end of the line for him.

TUREK, Roman
b. Strakonice, Czechoslovakia (Czech Republic), May 21, 1970
It's a paradox, to say the least, but with one exception Turek has proved that he is both a great goalie and also one not yet capable of winning big. That exception came at the 1996 World Championships when he backstopped the Czechs to a gold medal. In fact, for a three-year period (1993-96), he was the country's top goalie at home, but when he joined Dallas in the NHL in 1996 as a 26-year-old pro, his career took on a different tone. He played so well behind Ed Belfour it was clear Dallas had two number-one goalies. The Stars opted to go with Belfour and traded Turek to St. Louis, but two excellent regular seasons also led to two early playoff exits for a team that was supposed to be fighting for a Cup. Turek had won the Cup with Dallas in 1999, but his contribution was more a technicality, for he was backup during the regular season and in the playoffs did not appear for even a minute of play. Frustrated, St. Louis traded him to Calgary during the 2001-02 season, and he played incredibly well. Does this mean he's a star when there is little at stake, but a sub-par performer at the ultimate level? Time will tell, but he can't answer much to the great what-have-you-done-for-me-lately question.

TURGEON, Pierre
b. Rouyn, Quebec, August 28, 1969
The modern NHL is full of illusions and magic tricks,

and things aren't all that they seem to be. It will be up to the Hockey Hall of Fame to separate the men from the boys and use criteria other than numbers for induction credentials, or else there might be too many Turgeons flooding the shrine. Turgeon was drafted first overall by Buffalo in 1987 and has recorded Hall of Fame numbers. He's played more than 1,000 games and recorded more than 1,000 points. He once scored 58 goals in a season, twice surpassed 100 points, and will likely hit the 500-goal mark before he retires. Yet for all those numbers he's done surprisingly little. He has had very little playoff success and has represented Canada not at all since the 1987 WJC (although he pitched for Canada at the 1982 Little League World Series). He's played in four All-Star Games and won one individual trophy, the Lady Byng in 1993, but the saying with him is that when the going gets tough, Turgeon gets going – right off the ice. In one sense, he's had a fantastic career; in another, he's come and almost gone without having made a Hall of Fame contribution. His brother, Sylvain, also played in the NHL.

TURGEON, Sylvain
b. Noranda, Quebec, January 17, 1965
Early in his career Turgeon suffered through an abdominal injury that eventually required surgery after years of pain and distraction, but even then he was scoring goals. His younger brother was drafted 1st overall in 1987, and Sylvain had gone 2nd overall four years earlier, to Hartford. He had his best years early, scoring 40, 31, and 45 goals his first 3 seasons, and then after serious surgery in '90-'91 to repair his hernia he was never the same player. He ended up playing in Europe, finishing his career in 2001 in Germany. Like his brother, playoff success all but passed him by and in 12 NHL seasons he appeared in only 36 playoff games.

TURLICK, Gord
b. Miskel, British Columbia, September 17, 1939
He made his career in Spokane through the 1960s, but Turlick made it to the NHL with Boston in '59-'60, playing two games right out of provincial junior hockey. He won the 1970 Allan Cup with the Jets toward the end of his career, the highlight of a long time playing the game.

TURNBULL, Ian ("Bull"/ "Hawk")
b. Montreal, Quebec, December 22, 1953
There was another Grapes in Toronto, in the 1970s, perhaps even as famous as Don Cherry himself. The other Grapes was a restaurant owned by Turnbull, and it said a good deal about the personality of its owner, someone laid back, casual, relaxed, someone who

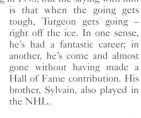

He made the history books in February 1977 when he scored five goals in a game, an NHL record for defencemen.
IAN TURNBULL

Darren Turcotte

Roman Turek

Pierre Turgeon

Sylvain Turgeon

Perry Turnbull

Bob Turner

loves good food, good drink, a late night. Turnbull was a tremendous talent gone to waste from lack of push, which in the end means, of course, that he wasn't such a great talent. He made the history books in February 1977 when he scored five goals in a game, an NHL record for defencemen. Yet over and above that, he could have been so much better than he was, and he gave evidence of that in the 1978 playoffs when his mate, Borje Salming, was lost with a serious eye injury. Turnbull stepped up and played as well as any defenceman in the league, but a career cannot be measured by a handful of games. Along with Salming, he was one of the top goal-scoring defencemen the Leafs ever had, and he was part of that talented nucleus in the late 1970s that could have gone farther but for the horrific duo of Harold Ballard and the second coming of Punch Imlach.

Turnbull was traded to L.A. in 1981 but was demoted before the end of the year and bought out at season's end. The Kings claimed he was overweight and didn't care; he countered by suing the team, looking for a two-thirds buyout to the one-third the team provided. He came back briefly in Pittsburgh, retired, and settled in sunny California, a state suited to his lifestyle. He has since worked as a real estate financier, his glory days all used up in one magical night when they could have, might have, gone on much longer.

TURNBULL, Perry
b. Bentley, Alberta, March 9, 1959

The shelf life of a power forward is often shorter than most players because of the extreme physical nature of their game and their need to score to augment their other abilities. Turnbull is one such beast, a tough forward who had 3 seasons of 32 goals or more but who eventually was worn down by the nature of his style of play. St. Louis drafted him 2nd overall in 1979, and for a while he did not disappoint. His teams never missed the playoffs in his nine-year career, nor did they advance far in the chase for the Cup. He finished his career in Europe, and then returned to the city of his greatest success, St. Louis, where he started a travel agency he runs to this day. He also became involved in the building of roller-hockey rinks and organizing in-line leagues in that city.

TURNBULL, Randy
b. Bentley, Alberta, February 7, 1962

This cousin of Perry had the same manual pedigree but not the same skill genes, for although he could fight with the best of them, he played only one game, with Calgary, during his final season of junior. The Flames never used him again after he graduated from Portland, and he played the rest of his short career in the minors.

TURNER, Bob
b. Regina, Saskatchewan, January 31, 1934

Turner is the only player in NHL history to win Stanley Cups in each of his first five years in the league. That, of course, was accomplished with Montreal during the great run between 1955 and '60. His blueline partner all those years was Hall of Famer Doug Harvey, but the Habs traded Turner to Chicago for a player named Fred Hilts who never played a single NHL game. After retiring, Turner returned to Regina and coached the junior Pats for 10 years, a tenure that culminated with a Memorial Cup victory in 1974. He later settled down to a life in business, opening his own insurance agency. His brother-in-law was Dunc Fisher, another NHLer.

TURNER, Brad
b. Winnipeg, Manitoba, May 25, 1968

Hockey can lead to many post-career opportunities, and Turner has been privvy to one in Hockeywood. He graduated from the University of Michigan in 1990 and played just three games with the Islanders. After a spell in the minors he went to Europe to continue his career, and one summer he returned home to Calgary when a phone call came from his brother-in-law who was working on a movie called *Mystery, Alaska*. Just like that, Turner became the hockey-scene coordinator and got a small part in the movie. When he retired, he moved to Vancouver, took some acting lessons, and has been involved in making movies with hockey themes ever since.

In January 2000 he was sentenced to 18 months in a federal prison for his role in a fraud scheme involving his mother.
DEAN TURNER

TURNER, Dean
b. Dearborn, Michigan, June 22, 1958

Dean Turner was much, much more than a hockey player, but that's not a good thing because in January 2000 he was sentenced to 18 months in a federal prison for his role in a fraud scheme involving his mother, the actress Marilyn Turner, and millions of dollars. The hockey part of his life was quick and simple. He played a game for the Rangers and was then traded to Don Cherry's Colorado team in 1979. The majority of his five years in pro was spent in the minors. After retiring, Turner's life became much more nefarious. He worked as a stockbroker for Dean Witter and by the late 1980s he and a partner, William Malek, convinced investors to support a company they owned, Lease Equities Inc. Millions of dollars were poured into the company, and Turner and Malek paid investors on a monthly basis, using new money to pay off old. All was fine until a bank called in a $4-million loan and their scam was revealed. Turner owed his mother more than $945,000 and she began legal action to wrest the funds from her son. Turner was eventually convicted of 3 counts of fraud while 16 others were dismissed and plunked in prison for his bilking practices.

TURNER, Joe
b. Windsor, Ontario, March 28, 1919
d. Holland, January 12, 1945

Prior to the war, Turner was a minor-league goalie who was not going to earn a regular spot in the NHL. But on February 12, 1942, Detroit's starter, Johnny Mowers, was injured, and Turner was called in from Indianapolis to replace him. He played the Leafs to a 3-3 tie, then joined the war effort. He wanted to go overseas, so instead of enlisting in his native Canada he joined the U.S. Marine Corps and was sent to Holland. He was killed in action in early 1945. In his honour, the new IHL named its championship trophy after him, and until the league's demise in 2001, the Turner Cup was presented annually to the league's playoff victors.

TUSTIN, Norm
b. Regina, Saskatchewan, January 3, 1919
d. August 16, 1998

Here was a case of the war ending a playing career. Tustin quickly worked his way up through the minors to make the Rangers in '41-'42, but he played half the season in New Haven and never got back to the NHL. At year's end, he enlisted with the RCAF, and upon discharge could reach no higher than the AHL.

TUTEN, Audley "Aut"
b. Enterprise, Alabama, January 14, 1914
d. Long Beach, California, May 7, 1994

'Bama has produced many fine athletes, but Tuten was the first hockeyist to hail from that state. "Hail," though, is a misnomer, because he was raised in Melville, Saskatchewan, hockey country. He turned pro with Hershey in the old Eastern league in 1934 and played parts of two seasons with Chicago during the war. He later joined the fighting himself and played only briefly thereafter.

TUTT, Brian
b. Swalwell, Alberta, June 9, 1962

Nineteen years in pro hockey is a long time, though Tutt managed to play just a few games in the NHL along the way. He was drafted by Philadelphia in 1980, but apart from that quick chance by the Caps he was never pursued by other teams. Tutt played in the minors for years and also in Europe, but his most memorable games came with Team Canada. He played at the 1992 Olympics in Albertville, winning a silver medal, and also at the 1992 and '95 World Championships. He retired in 2001 after a final season in North America.

TUTTLE, Steve
b. Vancouver, British Columbia, January 5, 1966

Coming out of the University of Wisconsin, Tuttle joined St. Louis at training camp in 1988 and made the team based on his scoring and skating. Unfortunately, his first year was tainted by one of the worst on-ice accidents in NHL history. On March 22, 1989, he and Buffalo defenceman Uwe Krupp were fighting for position in front of the Sabres goal when

Tuttle lost his balance and stepped on the throat of goalie Clint Malarchuk, severing his jugular vein. Only quick work by the training and medical staff saved Malarchuk's life, and Tuttle was plenty dazed by the incident. He played another year and a half with the Blues before ending up in the minors, and though he was later traded to Tampa Bay and Quebec, he never made it back to the NHL. He moved to Washington state and started his own computer business.

TUZZOLINO, Tony
b. Buffalo, New York, October 9, 1975

Since turning pro in 1997, Tuzzolino's NHL numbers are simple: one game with Anaheim, six with the Rangers, two with Boston. All the rest were of the minor-league variety, and the right winger doesn't seem to be in anybody's NHL plans so far.

TVERDOVSKY, Oleg
b. Donetsk, Soviet Union (Ukraine), May 18, 1976

Today, most people would likely take Ed Jovanovski over Tverdovsky on defence any day of the week, but leading up to the 1994 Draft, loyalties were split 50-50 across the NHL. As it turned out, Jovo went 1st and Oleg 2nd, but he was still a major prospect and Anaheim was happy to have landed him. Two years later, the Ducks were equally happy to package him off to Winnipeg to acquire Teemu Selanne, but interestingly enough the Ducks reacquired him in 1999 for Travis Green and a first-round draft choice. Tverdovsky represented Russia at the 1996 World Cup, the 2002 Olympics, and two World Championships, in 1996 and 2001.

TWIST, Tony
b. Sherwood Park, Alberta, May 9, 1968

Off the ice, things were more interesting than on it, and that's saying something. Twist spent the majority of his career in St. Louis, where he was the team's enforcer for 6 of his 10 years in the league. He also played for Quebec, but with the Blues he was not just a fighter but a devoted citizen who spent much of his free time helping children's charities. His career ended in July 1999 when he was hurt in a motorcycle accident. Soon he became embroiled in a fight with Todd McFarlane, creator of the comic book *Spawn*. In it, McFarlane introduced two characters, one named Joe Sakic, a bookkeeper to a mobster named Antonio Twistelli, a.k.a. Tony Twist. Twistelli was a violent Mafioso, and Twist the player took exception to the portrayal. He sued McFarlane and at one point was awarded $24.5-million, though the case was later thrown out of court in a Missouri appeals hearing.

Joe Turner

Norm Tustin

Aut Tuten

Steve Tuttle

Tony Twist

UBRIACO, Gene

b. Sault Ste. Marie, Ontario, December 26, 1937

Even though expansion gave Ubriaco a chance to play in the NHL, he knew pretty quickly he was a hanger-on more than an unidentified superstar. He played for St. Mike's in the 1950s, and for close to a decade played in the minors before Pittsburgh signed him in 1967. In all, he played less than three years in the NHL, retiring after the '69-'70 season to become a coach at Lake Superior State University. That, as it turned out, was his calling. He coached in the minors for years, winning honours every step of the way. In 1988, he took the NHL plunge, signing on as head man for Pittsburgh, but a year and a half later he was out the door after the team got off to a poor start. He went on to coach Italy at the 1992 Olympics in Albertville and soon after became director of hockey operations and assistant GM for the IHL's Chicago Wolves.

ULANOV, Igor

b. Krasnokamensk, Soviet Union (Russia), October 1, 1969

A defensive disturber along the lines of, say, Bryan Marchment or Darius Kasparaitis, Ulanov has been a solid NHLer since 1991, the year he was drafted by Winnipeg, the year he made the team at his first camp. What has been missing in his career is playoff activity, for wherever the well-travelled player has gone, the post-season has not necessarily followed. When he went to Florida in 2002, he joined his eighth team, yet he has appeared in only 39 playoff games over his 11-year career. He won't score many goals for his team, but he hits and blocks shots, does the dirty work that other players sometimes shy away from. And, playing on weak teams for the most part, Ulanov logs more than his share of ice time, proof positive that he can play at the elite level consistently.

ULLMAN, Norm

b. Provost, Alberta, December 26, 1935

He was one of the quietest men in the game and certainly the quietest 490-goal scorer the NHL has ever seen. Ullman was first scouted out west by Detroit bird-dog Clarence Mohr who signed him to a C-form and sent him to the Edmonton Flyers. Ullman was only 19 when he made the Wings in 1955, and over the years he became one of the most consistent and reliable men on the team. He scored 20 goals in a season 16 times, including 12 in a row from 1957 to 1969. Ullman had the pleasure and honour to play at various times on a line with Ted Lindsay and Gordie Howe, Howe and Alex Delvecchio, and Paul Henderson and Bruce MacGregor. The only blemish on his 1,410-game career was that he never won the Stanley Cup. He joined the Wings right after they had won four Cups in six years, but the team was on the downswing thereafter. Ullman developed into a great two-way player. On offence, he was master of the give-and-go, giving the puck to a winger after crossing the blueline, and then heading for the net to get the return pass. In his game, timing and positioning were everything. He wasn't flashy or fast, but he and the puck always arrived at the same place at the same time, and that often created a scoring chance. The media nicknamed him the Quiet Man because he shunned the spotlight and never said much, and GM Jack Adams comically called him Noisy for the same reasons. Although Ullman never won an individual award, he did lead the league in goals in '64-'65 with 42, the only time he reached 40 in his career. His career took a dramatic change in March 1968. He had become the NHLPA's president just a few weeks earlier, but as the team continued to play poorly, the Wings traded him with Paul Henderson, Floyd Smith, and Doug Barrie to Toronto for Frank Mahovlich, Carl Brewer, Garry Unger, and Pete Stemkowski. Ullman played the final seven-and-a-half years of his career with the Leafs, but it was a personally rewarding time on a tumultuous team. In '70-'71, he had a career-best 85 points, but in his years in Toronto the team never made it far in the playoffs. The Leafs gave up on him in 1975, but rather than retire at age 39 he accepted a chance to finish his career back home in Edmonton, in the WHA. He played with the Oilers for two years and then retired with 1,229 NHL points to his credit. Perhaps the finest compliment he had was that although he never won a Cup, he still played in 11 All-Star Games, a phenomenal achievement. Ullman was inducted into the Hockey Hall of Fame in 1982 and has continued to play in alumni and oldtimers' games. He settled in Toronto and became a sales rep for the Inter-Business Ribbon Company in Markham, Ontario.

ULMER, Jeff

b. Wilcox, Saskatchewan, April 27, 1977

An undrafted graduate of North Dakota in 1999, Ulmer played with the Canadian National Team to drum up some interest in his services. It worked only to the point that Houston in the "I" signed him, but that led to another signing in the summer of 2000 by the Rangers. He played 21 games on Broadway in 2000-01 but was traded to Ottawa a year later and has yet to see action with the Sens.

UNGER, Garry ("Iron Man")

b. Calgary, Alberta, December 7, 1947

Records are made to be broken, but lives are meant to be lived, so although Unger was a record-setter, he was happier late in his career when he found greater meaning to his existence. On February 24, 1968, he was in the Leafs system, called up to the parent club for a game to replace the injured Dave Keon. Unger played on a line with George Armstrong and Mike Walton, and didn't miss an NHL game until 11 years and 914 games later. He was traded to Detroit and then St. Louis, with whom he played the greatest number of games in the NHL's longest Iron Man streak. In fact, in '70-'71, when he went from the Wings to the Blues, he went one better, playing 79 games in the 78-game schedule. His streak ended as a member of Atlanta when, on December 22, 1979, coach Al MacNeil scratched him from the lineup. Unger was also a tremendous centre – he wasn't in the lineup for no reason. He had 8 consecutive 30-goal seasons, and at the end of his career he played in Britain, where he posted unbelievable numbers in what was comparatively a shinny league. In '86-'87, he played for the Peterborough Pirates, a second-tier

Gene Ubriaco

Igor Ulanov

Jeff Ulmer

Garry Unger

Norm Ullman
(opposite page)

Stefan Ustorf

team in the British league. In 30 games he scored 95 goals and had 238 points, an average of nearly 8 points a game! During his time with the Flames, though, he talked to Paul Henderson, a teammate, and discovered a devout belief in Christianity, one that helped him come to terms with his great skills vis-à-vis his sister, who was wheelchair bound. After retiring, Unger coached in Tulsa for years and later moved up to director of hockey operations with the team. His Iron Man streak, meanwhile, was broken by Doug Jarvis.

USTORF, Stefan

b. Kaufbeuren, Germany, January 3, 1974

Washington drafted him, later signed him as a free agent, and gave him his only NHL games in the mid-1990s. Beyond that, Ustorf was one of the most skilled players to come out of Germany and his contributions to the national team have been long and devoted. Ustorf has played in three Olympics (1994, 1998, and 2002), the 1996 World Cup, two World Championships, and three World Juniors. Although he has never won a medal with the lesser nation, he has kept the team in the elite division, an accomplishment in itself in a country where football dominates the sporting sensitivity.

VAANANEN, Ossi ("Oz")

b. Vantaa, Finland, August 18, 1980

Young yet experienced, Vaananen will be counted on by Phoenix to improve and grow into a top-flight defenceman. He has been a regular with the Coyotes since 2000 and has augmented his NHL time with appearances at all major international tournaments. He won a silver medal at the 2001 World Championships and played for Finland at the 2002 Olympics in Salt Lake City. Vaananen played at the 2003 All-Star Game in the Young Stars contest, but later that night he was struck by a car, injuring his knee and forcing him out of the lineup for the rest of the year.

VACHON, Nick

b. Montreal, Quebec, July 20, 1972

Son of Rogie, Nick was drafted by Toronto in 1990, but unlike his supremely talented dad, he played just one game six years later with the Islanders. He was a small centre, not a small goalie, retiring in 1998.

VACHON, Rogatien "Rogie"

b. Palmarolle, Quebec, September 8, 1945

The simple truth of the matter is that Vachon is likely the finest goalie (certainly of the modern era) not in the Hockey Hall of Fame. He began his stellar career with Montreal in '66-'67 as Gump Worsley's backup, but played so well that he took over in the playoffs. His lack of experience, though, led Toronto coach Punch Imlach to say in the finals that the team wasn't going to lose to a junior B goalie. Indeed, the Leafs did win the Cup, but Vachon proved his worth. He helped the Habs win three of the next four Cups, but his presence became redundant with the emergence of Ken Dryden, and the Habs sent Vachon to Los Angeles. For more than six years he was the undisputed starting goalie on the team, playing the lion's share of the games, taking the team to the playoffs, and giving the Kings a chance to win every night. His finest hour came at the 1976 Canada Cup when Vachon played every minute for his country en route to the championship and was named the team's MVP (though both he and Denis Potvin felt they should have been named tournament MVP, not Bobby Orr). Vachon stunned the Kings in the summer of 1978 when he signed as a free agent with Detroit. It was a move that also triggered lengthy legal action as L.A. was awarded Dale McCourt as compensation, and McCourt took the league to court to ensure he stayed with the Wings. Vachon closed out his career with Boston, and over his career he appeared in 795 games. He won 355 games, recorded 51 shutouts, and played in 3 All-Star Games. Although he never led the league in any statistical category, he won 20 games in a season 12 times and defied the experts who thought a goalie his size (5'7" and 170 pounds) could ever star in the NHL. After retiring in 1982, he stayed with the team and rose to become GM and chief operating officer. He retired as GM in 1991 but was appointed assistant to the president a short time later. His number 30 was retired by the team, and he remains one of the most popular hockey players to forge a career on the west coast.

VADNAIS, Carol

b. Montreal, Quebec, September 25, 1945

There are a number of important parts to Vadnais's career, but he is part of a great trivia question. When New Jersey released him at the end of the '82-'83 season, only he, Wayne Cashman, and Serge Savard had survived that long from their beginnings during the Original Six. Cashman and Savard outlasted Vadnais only on the technicality that their teams made the playoffs and the Devils didn't. He began in Montreal, playing a few games in '66-'67, his style of play greatly influenced by Bobby Orr. Vadnais liked to rush the puck, and he had the skating ability to do as much, though not to the extent Orr could, of course. He later played with Oakland, but his best years came with Boston and then the Rangers. He won the Cup in 1972 with Orr and the Bruins, and was involved in the biggest trade of the 1970s. On November 7, 1975, he and Phil Esposito were traded to the Rangers for Brad Park, Jean Ratelle, and Joe Zanussi. Vadnais played seven years with the Blueshirts, going to the finals in 1979. In all, he played more than 1,000 games, averaged a point every 2 games, and played in 6 All-Star Games. After retiring, he became an assistant coach with the Rangers and later head coach of Verdun in the Montreal system.

Carol Vadnais

VAIC, Lubomir

b. Spisska Nova Ves, Czechoslovakia (Slovakia), March 6, 1977

An important member of the Slovakian national team for years, Vaic appeared in the 2000 World Championships for his country after three appearances at the WJC. His only NHL time came with the Canucks, most recently in 1999-2000, and Vaic is now back in Europe playing in his homeland.

Lubomir Vaic

VAIL, Eric ("The Big Train")

b. Timmins, Ontario, September 16, 1953

Ability times ambition equals the true value of a player, and sadly a large number that might be ascribed to the first part of that equation is often offset by a decimal for the second part. Vail was a tremendous talent, a powerful forward with a quick and accurate shot. He had the skill to be a superstar – everyone associated with him felt that way – but he didn't take the pro game seriously. He floated rather than skated with purpose, coasted rather than pushed. He liked living large and being funny, and as soon as that reputation got the better of him, no number of goals could console GMs and scouts. He started with Atlanta in 1973, and in 7 seasons with that organization he averaged nearly 30 goals a year. The Flames finally had enough of his off-ice persona and traded him to Detroit, and the Wings buried him in the minors after trying to help him turn things around. At the 1977 World Championships, a violent, controversial tournament, Vail high-sticked Sergei Bobinov in a 1-1 game against the Soviet Union and Canada played a man short for 10 minutes. The team allowed two goals and went on to lose the game 8-1. Vail never made it past the first round of the playoffs, and by the time he retired in 1983, players talked about how sad his career was, not how much he had accomplished. He settled in Atlanta where he managed a nightclub, Timothy John's, and later

Eric Vail

Rogie Vachon
(opposite page)

Chris Valentine

Robert Valicevic

Jack Valiquette

Garry Valk

moved outside the city to Lawrenceville. In 2000, he was hired by the new Thrashers to work with the team in community relations and in-house game analysis, the older, mellower Vail being given a second chance.

VAIL, Melville ("Sparky")
b. Meaford, Ontario, July 5, 1906
d. unknown
Vail developed in Springfield under the aegis of the Rangers organization, playing his only NHL games with that team in '28-'29 and again the year after, perfectly ill-timed between Cup wins in 1928 and '33. He spent most of his career in the minors.

VAIVE, Rick ("Squid")
b. Ottawa, Ontario, May 14, 1959
Defence was never his main priority, but Vaive could score with the best of them. He made headlines at age 19 when he signed with Birmingham and played a year in the WHA, in '78-'79, joining Vancouver the following year when the league merged with the NHL. Vaive lasted only half a season with the Canucks when he was traded to Toronto, where he went on to have his best years. In '81-'82 he became the first player in team history to score 50 goals in a season (he finished with 54), and he replicated the feat in both of the next 2 years. His great, driving slapshot while racing down the right wing was his trademark as was his jostling for position in front of the enemy net on the power play. He led by example, and his determined play was often the only thing to cheer for at Maple Leaf Gardens toward the end of owner Harold Ballard's dismal tenure. Vaive was named team captain in 1981 but was stripped of the honour five years later when he slept in and missed a practice. While he was setting records as a player, the team was experiencing its worst years in club history, and Vaive was traded to Chicago in 1987 in a shakeup that had little positive effect. He finished his career in Buffalo, and by the time he was out of the NHL in 1992 he had accounted for 441 goals. He turned to coaching and ended in a number of leagues, most recently with the Mississauga Ice Dogs. In 2001-02, he returned to game action to join the Dundas Real McCoys as a ringer in the hopes of winning the prestigious Allan Cup, though his bid for a championship fell short. He went on to work for The Score and Leafs-TV, two digital channels.

VALENTINE, Chris
b. Belleville, Ontario, December 6, 1961
Unknown back home, Valentine is a legend in Dusseldorf, where he played most of his career. He began in the Q playing junior with Sorel, and his rookie season was a spectacular one. In '81-'82 with Washington he scored 30 goals and had 67 points, but in each of the next 2 years he dropped off dramatically to the point that the minors outstripped his NHL games played. In 1984, he signed with the German team and for the next dozen years led the league in scoring with Gretzky-like dominance. After he retired, the team hung his number 10 in the rafters of the Dusseldorf arena to acknowledge his great contribution to the team's four championships in the early 1990s.

VALICEVIC, Robert
b. Detroit, Michigan, January 6, 1971
He knew as a teen he was no superstar, so Valicevic went to Lake Superior State and got an education as well as hockey experience. He then played in the minors, while his drafting team, the Islanders, showed no interest in bringing him up. It wasn't until Nashville signed him that he debuted in the big tent, but after a season and a half he has since moved on to L.A. and Anaheim, his NHL career tenuous at best.

His determined play was often the only thing to cheer for at Maple Leaf Gardens.
RICK VAIVE

VALIQUETTE, Jack
b. St. Thomas, Ontario, March 18, 1954
It was a happy day for Valiquette when Toronto drafted him 13th overall in 1974, but it certainly stirred a great debate. He can't skate, said his detractors. Neither could Phil Esposito or Jean Béliveau at his age, his supporters shot back. Well, a quarter of a century later, the verdict is in, and Valiquette definitely still can't skate. He didn't do very much in his 4 years with the Leafs, and when he was traded to Colorado he did well enough to score 23 and 25 goals in consecutive seasons. When the Rockies sent him to the minors, he retired. He settled in Orillia, Ontario, and went into real estate, though he later operated his own sporting goods store. Most recently, Valiquette has worked for a produce company north of Toronto and is a frequent alumnus at Leafs games at the ACC.

VALIQUETTE, Stephen
b. Etobicoke, Ontario, August 20, 1977
With a 2-0-0 record in six career NHL games, Valiquette might go down as one of the few undefeated career goalies (or, at least, undefeated with the most appearances). His games came with the Islanders in 1999-2000 and he hasn't had a sniff of the NHL since. He's still in his prime, and at 6'5" is one of the tallest goalies ever to make it to the big time.

VALK, Garry
b. Edmonton, Alberta, November 27, 1967
Few players have earned their ice time the way Valk has, shift by shift, hit by hit, play by play. Not blessed

with talent, he has endured by sheer will of force and ambition, first with Vancouver and most recently with Toronto. He fills the role perfectly as a third-line checker, a penalty killer, a player who can adapt to a system and play within his means. He will score occasionally, avoid mistakes, and make big hits to get his team going. His biggest goal was an overtime score on May 17, 1999, for Toronto to eliminate Pittsburgh in game six of their conference semifinals. Each year, it becomes a bit harder for Valk to stay in the NHL, and though his career might end at any time, he's earned a pat on the back for a job well done.

VALLIS, Lindsay
b. Winnipeg, Manitoba, January 12, 1971

A modern Montreal bust, Vallis was drafted by the Habs 13th overall in 1989. That's star territory on draft day, but after four years in the minors the rewards at the NHL level translated to exactly one game. Montreal released him, and he made his way into the minors until he ended up with Asheville, the Siberia of hockey towns.

VAN ALLEN, Shaun ("Vanner")
b. Calgary, Alberta, August 29, 1967

If ever there were a utility forward, Van Allen is it. He's not a tough guy and not a scorer, but he won't hurt his team defensively and he can give the coach some minutes on the ice without costing his team the game. He started with Edmonton on February 18, 1991, and the next year in the minors Van Allen led the AHL in scoring. In the NHL, though, he has hit double digits for goals only once.

Beezer led the team to an improbable place in the 1996 Cup finals.
JOHN VANBIESBROUCK

VANBIESBROUCK, John ("Beezer")
b. Detroit, Michigan, September 4, 1963

Few American-born goalies have had the impact, longevity, and success of the man everyone called Beezer. He made his NHL debut with the Rangers in '81-'82 and within three seasons he was the team's starter, its promise in goal, its future. In '85-'86, he started 61 games and led the league with 31 wins, and over the years he won 20 games some 10 times. He eventually lost his starter's job to Mike Richter, and at that point was claimed by Florida in the Expansion Draft. The Panthers could not have made a wiser move. Beezer became a fan favourite and led the team to an improbable place in the 1996 Cup finals before losing to Colorado. He later signed a rich deal in Philadelphia, one that ultimately saw him deliver a disappointing performance. He retired, only to return briefly with New Jersey for a few games at the end of the 2001-02 season. Along the way, Vanbiesbrouck won the Vezina Trophy in

'83-'84 and played in three All-Star Games. He played in two Canada Cups and four World Championships, and made one appearance for the U.S. at the 1998 Olympics at Nagano. His 374 career wins ranks in the top 10 of all time, and he is a good bet to get into the Hockey Hall of Fame. Vanbiesbrouck returned to the Soo in 2002 to become coach and GM of the Greyhounds, his former junior team, although his tenure there ended controversially in March 2003 when he used a racial slur repeatedly to describe a black player on the team. Vanbiesbrouck resigned in disgrace and sold his ownership stake in the team.

VAN BOXMEER, John
b. Petrolia, Ontario, November 20, 1952

John Van Boxmeer

A life in hockey couldn't have got off to a better start than the one Van Boxmeer experienced. In 1972, he was drafted by the Canadiens, and then when Jacques Laperriere withdrew from Team Canada '72, Van Boxmeer was invited to practise with the team, though playing in games was an outside chance at best. He went on to play five seasons in the Canadiens organization but played only infrequently with the Habs, spending most of his time in the minors. He was up long enough in '75-'76 to get his name on that year's Cup, but he was later traded to Colorado and on to Buffalo. After retiring in 1984, Van Boxmeer started a coaching career that continues to this day. He started in the AHL with Rochester, staying almost a decade and winning the Calder Cup in '86-'87. He later joined Long Beach in the "I," and in the summer of 2002 the L.A. Kings hired him as an assistant, his first NHL stint in a suit.

VANDENBUSSCHE, Ryan
b. Simcoe, Ontario, February 28, 1973

Vandenbussche has one of the longest last names in NHL history, but during games he often plays the shortest of all his teammates. That's because he's primarily a fighter, so his coach in Chicago throws him over the boards for rough play, not goals and power plays, but that's how he's made his place on the team. He started out in the Toronto system in the early 1990s but was soon released and signed by the Rangers. Since 1999, Vandenbussche has been a regular with the Hawks.

Ryan Vandenbussche

VAN DORP, Wayne
b. Vancouver, British Columbia, May 19, 1961

Even before he hit the NHL, Van Dorp made history as the first pro to play for the Dutch national team. He played in "B" pool for the Dutchies at the 1986

Wayne Van Dorp

David Van Drunen

World Championships, automatically disqualifying him from ever playing for Team Canada. This was a concern for nether Van Dorp nor the aforementioned national program because the player was, for the most part, a goon. The chances of ever being asked to play for Canada were nil. Nonetheless, he made it to the NHL the following year and played a few games for the Cup-winning Oilers in '86-'87. He played only parts of four more years, his career more or less ended by two serious shoulder injuries, thus limiting his ability to fight. He ended in the minors and Europe, where the going wasn't as tough.

VAN DRUNEN, David
b. Sherwood Park, Alberta, January 31, 1976
Some players hope for the moon and are disappointed if they don't get there. Others hope only for a moment of glory and revel in it it moon-like satisfaction. Van Drunen knew he wasn't an NHL superstar. He attended Ottawa's camp in 1999 hoping to make the team, anyway, but on day one he ran into a wall called Andre Roy and spent the rest of camp on the trainer's table. Since then, he has been in the minors with a one-game exception, when he was called up to the Sens as an injury replacement. Ecstatic with his moment, he has played most of his time in Grand Rapids and Mobile.

VAN IMPE, Darren
b. Saskatoon, Saskatchewan, May 18, 1973

Ed Van Impe

Midway through the 2000-01 season, Van Impe underwent surgery on his right shoulder and missed the rest of the year. The Bruins gave up on him and put him on waivers with the intention of burying him in the minors, but the Rangers claimed him. Then Florida claimed him. Then the Panthers traded him to the Islanders, all in one season. He had spent three years with Anaheim and four with the Bruins, but the shoulder scared teams and he has been on the move ever since. His father's cousin, Ed Van Impe, also played in the NHL for a number of years.

VAN IMPE, Ed
b. Saskatoon, Saskatchewan, May 27, 1940
Hockey players are tough hombres, but even by those standards Van Impe raised a few eyebrows of admiration for his play. One night, he took a Wayne Muloin slapshot in the mouth, shattering a number of teeth and embedding shards of ivory in his gums. He needed stitches to close those cuts, and more to sew his tongue up, but, of course, he came back a few minutes later and finished the game. He played the final year of Original Six hockey with Chicago but the Flyers claimed him in the Expansion Draft. In his nine years with the Flyers he was a rock on defence, a great shotblocker and fine hitter. He couldn't skate well and his own shot couldn't shatter a mouthful of teeth, but no matter; he was effective and that was all that counted. He won two Cups with the Broad Street Bullies, in 1974 and '75, and finished his career discontentedly with Pittsburgh. Van Impe returned to Philadelphia, where he worked in the insurance brokerage business and as a TV colour commentator for Flyers home games.

Petri Varis

VAN RYN, Mike
b. London, Ontario, May 14, 1979
It's not a simple story, not as simple as New Jersey thought when they selected the University of Michigan player in the 1998 draft. Van Ryn circumvented the draft process for college students by leaving U of M and playing junior in Sarnia. The loophole was this: If a Canadian junior player is unsigned two years after being drafted, he becomes a free agent. But, if a U.S. collegian graduates from his program, he is still bound to the team that drafted him four years previous. Van Ryn left college to go to the OHL for the express purpose of becoming a free agent, but the Devils took him to court to try to retain his rights. The team failed, the player became a free agent, and St. Louis signed him in 2000. In his first game with the team, he hurt his shoulder and missed most of the year, though in 2001-02 he worked himself into the lineup quite nicely. Van Ryn also played two years with Canada's World Juniors in 1998 and '99.

VARADA, Vaclav
b. Vsetin, Czechoslovakia (Czech Republic),
April 26, 1976
He was traded to Buffalo by San Jose before ever having played a game with the Sharks, but since his NHL entrance in 1996 he has been a Sabres right winger. More versatile and reliable than budding star, Varada has some offensive ability but more than anything has been able to play within the team system that emphasizes defence and stopping the opponent before going on the attack. He represented the Czechs at the 2000 World Championships, his first international participation since the WJC in 1996.

VARIS, Petri
b. Varkaus, Finland, May 13, 1969
He was 28 years old by the time he played his lone NHL game, with Chicago, but by then Varis had had a long career in the Finnish league and had played for his country at the 1994 Olympics in Lillehammer. He went on to play in other European cities, most recently Switzerland, though his finest seasons came with Jokerit when he was the league's top scorer.

VARLAMOV, Sergei
b. Kiev, Soviet Union (Ukraine), July 21, 1978
Not only did Varlamov elect to play his junior hockey in Canada, he led the WHL in scoring for '97-'98 and was named player of the year in junior hockey in Canada. He signed with Calgary, but after four years of not doing very much in the system he was sent to St. Louis in a deal that brought Roman Turek to the Flames. Since then, it's been tabula rasa with the Blues, though he did play for the Ukraine at the 2002 Olympics in Salt Lake City.

VARVIO, Jarkko
b. Tampere, Finland, April 28, 1972
A staple in European hockey, Varvio played just a few games with Dallas soon after the team moved from Minnesota. He played two years in North America but has played mostly in Finland, though recently he has been relegated to lesser leagues in Germany. He has also played in two World Championships and two WJCs.

Jarkko Varvio

VASICEK, Josef
b. Havlickuv Brod, Czechoslovakia (Czech Republic), September 12, 1980

So far, so good for the youngster who came from the Czech Republic to play junior in the Soo. He was drafted by Carolina in 1998 at a propitious time, for he stepped into the lineup and became a regular in 2000. Vasicek was part of the 'Canes as the team went to the Cup finals in 2002, and the big centre is part of the young team that now must prove it can compete annually with the best.

VASILEVSKI, Alexander
b. Kiev, Soviet Union (Ukraine), January 8, 1975

At the 1993 Entry Draft, some 286 players were selected. Vasilevski was 15 from the end, so by the time his name was called there was no trip to the podium, no massaging of the baseball cap and donning of the sweater. St. Louis made the call, but the right winger played just four games with the Blues in a minor-league career. Unlike most, he played in North America's lesser leagues rather than return home as soon as it was evident he wasn't going to make the NHL as a regular.

VASILIEV, Alexei
b. Yaroslavl, Soviet Union (Russia), September 1, 1977

It's tough to know how much long-term damage was done, but when Vasiliev blew his knee out at his first training camp, with the Rangers, in 1997 he spent a year recovering and then became a minor leaguer. He played one game for the Blueshirts, but besides that he has been in the AHL, IHL, and, most recently, playing back home in Russia.

VASILJEVS, Herbert
b. Riga, Soviet Union (Latvia), May 27, 1976

Even though he came to the OHL as a teen to attract scouts' attention, Vasiljevs was not drafted and had to sign with Florida in 1996 for the purposes of filling the farm team roster. He has been called up for a few games by the Panthers, but they traded him to Atlanta where he has had longer NHL stays but only as a callup. The centre played for Latvia at the 2000 World Championships, helping the small nation to a respectable fifth-place finish. He was supposed to play for his country at the 2002 Olympics in Salt Lake City until a serious knee injury scuppered those plans.

VASILYEV, Andrei
b. Voskresensk, Soviet Union (Russia), March 30, 1972

To Germany go all good players when they are on their last legs or have something left to give to the game. That is where Vasilyev took his skills in 1999 after 5 years of North American pro yielded a scant 16 games with the Islanders and Coyotes. He had been an Isles draft choice, but even in the minors he showed only flashes of NHL potential. He won the Turner Cup in Utah in '95-'96.

VASKE, Dennis ("Bubba")
b. Rockford, Illinois, October 11, 1967

A concussion, by definition, is not a career-threatening injury. It is post-concussion syndrome – in other words, the inability to recover from a concussion – that will do you in. And it did in a stubborn and determined Vaske. He played all but 3 of his 235 NHL games with the Islanders, and at his best he played solid defence and did not worry about the offensive end of the ice. He missed a good part of '94-'95 with an ankle injury, and after signing a three-year deal with the team after a short holdout, he was hit from behind by Eric Lacroix of L.A. and suffered a concussion. That cost him the rest of the year. The next season, he injured his shoulder and missed the first part of the year. When he returned, he suffered concussion number two, and his year was done. The next year, a third head injury after just 19 games forced the Isles to tell him to retire. They let him go, but he was determined to play. He signed with Boston, despite warnings from doctors, but after three games had enough common sense to call it quits while his brain was still functioning.

Josef Vasicek

VASKO, Elmer "Moose"
b. Duparquet, Quebec, December 11, 1935
d. Chicago, Illinois, October 30, 1998

At 6'3" and 214 pounds, he stood tall and large in the six-team NHL. Fans around the league, especially at home in Chicago, chanted "Moose!" whenever he charged up the ice with the puck. Partnered with Pierre Pilote on the blueline, Vasko was one of the better rushing defencemen in the league and one of the most popular players in the game. When he built up a head of steam, stopping him was like hitting, well, a moose on the highway. He was instrumental in the revival of the Hawks, starting with the team in 1956 and playing 10 years, notably with the 1961 Cup team. He retired in 1966, but a year later was coerced out of retirement by Minnesota, where he played three final seasons. After retiring, he became director of player personnel for the Chicago Warriors of the USHL and later bought a liquor store in Chicago that he ran for years.

Alexei Vasiliev

VASKO, Rick
b. St. Catharines, Ontario, January 12, 1957

The nephew of the Moose made it to the NHL not long after uncle Elmer retired, Rick starting with Detroit in 1977. That's where parallels and similarities end, though, for the nephew played just a smattering of games for the Wings over three years. In 1979-80, he was named best defenceman in the AHL, with Adirondack, but that earned him not many more games in the NHL.

Dennis Vaske

VAUTOUR, Yvon
b. Saint John, New Brunswick, September 10, 1956

After having a decent first full year with Colorado in '80-'81, Vautour was wrecked by injuries the next season and never came close to that 15-goal year. In all, he played six partial years in the NHL before retiring in 1985. He returned home to Saint John and worked for Irving Oil Limited, though he started to coach more and more seriously, moving up to senior AAA. He went on to lead the Saint John midget AAA Flames at the national Air Canada Cup in 1998, and in 2000 he was hired by the NHL's Flames to act as an assistant with the AHL farm team in his city.

Moose Vasko

Rick Vasko

VAYDIK, Greg
b. Yellowknife, Northwest Territories, October 9, 1955

From Canada's Far North came a young man determined to play in the NHL. He travelled to Medicine Hat to play junior, and from there was drafted an improbable 7th overall by Chicago in 1975. For Vaydik, making the NHL was quite an accomplishment, but for the Hawks the use of a first-round draft choice for Vaydik was a real blunder. He played just five games with the Hawks and seven years in the minors.

VEISOR, Mike ("The Worm")
b. Toronto, Ontario, August 25, 1952

Throughout the 1970s there were two goalies who watched more games from the bench than any other in the history of the NHL – Michel Larocque in Montreal and Veisor in Chicago. In 12 seasons of pro, the goalie appeared in only 139 games, but in Chicago he was lucky to play 10 times a year behind durable starter Tony Esposito. During long stretches in the minors, Veisor impressed enough to be named CHL rookie of the year for '72-'73 and lead the league in wins three years later. His most active year was '80-'81 with Hartford when he got into 29 games, but his 6-13-6 record left something to be desired. After retiring in 1984, he settled in Hartford where he became a customer relations manager for Hoffman Toyota and played frequently in old-timers games.

Darren Veitch

Randy Velischek

Vic Venasky

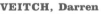

In 12 seasons of pro, the goalie appeared in only 139 games.
MIKE VEISOR

VEITCH, Darren
b. Saskatoon, Saskatchewan, April 24, 1960

What exactly qualifies a player as a celebrity? Perhaps it's a question famous and retired players ask when they see Veitch tee it up on the Celebrity Players Golf Tour, for he was no household name in the NHL but he's won more than his fair share of dough as a golfer in his second incarnation. In 511 games, Veitch played for 3 teams, starting in 1980 with Washington. He was a defensive defenceman who had a bit of offence in his stick, but by 1989 he was more or less out of the NHL loop. Nonetheless, he carried on in the minors for many years, retiring in 1999 only because he had a chance to get into broadcasting in Phoenix, the last stop on his NHL tour. From there he combined work in the booth and summers of golfing on the Celebrity Players Tour, when he can more than hold his own against players he couldn't touch, skill-wise, on the ice.

VELISCHEK, Randy
b. Montreal, Quebec, February 10, 1962

He rejected all offers from Verdun to play junior in the Q, instead opting to attend Providence College on scholarship. The plan was simple in that, after graduating, he wanted to play for Canada at the 1984 Olympics. He left Providence magna sum laude, but instead of doing the amateur ideal he turned quisling and signed a pro contract with Minnesota after GM Lou Nanne offered him a whole lotta money. But in 10 NHL years, Velischek did not develop into that first rank of defencemen the North Stars had hoped he would. In fact, within three years the team left him exposed in the Waiver Draft, and the Devils claimed him. He had five productive years in New Jersey, and later played for Quebec and then in the minors. He retired from hockey to take a job with the Devils as their radio commentator and has continued to work in the community outside the arena. He does charity work, runs clinics, and remains a visible and vibrant part of the organization.

VELLUCCI, Mike
b. Farmington, Michigan, August 11, 1966

A taste of the NHL gave way to a more realistic and longer-living dream of coaching. Two games with Hartford in '87-'88 got Vellucci into the record books as an alumnus, but after a number of years in the minors he decided to pursue the game using a chalkboard. He became coach of the Junior A Compuware Ambassadors in 1993, and over the next six years led the team to four league titles and two national championships. This led to a job with the Plymouth Whalers of the OHL, first as president and then as coach and GM as well. Not many men in the OHL have held all three jobs at once, but it is a tribute to Vellucci's reputation that he managed it at all.

VENASKY, Vic
b. Thunder Bay, Ontario, June 3, 1951

He led the NCAA in scoring his first year at the University of Denver, and would have repeated the effort in year two but for a knee injury. When he joined L.A. in 1972, he developed a serious and painful groin injury that plagued him for three years. He couldn't skate properly, spent much of the time in the minors, and didn't get better until he took karate classes one summer. Even then, though, his success was moderate. After seven seasons, the Kings bought out his contract, and Venasky retired soon after. He remained in southern California where he ran clinics for kids of all ages. The Vic Venasky Hockey School became hugely popular in that state, and he also did some scouting for junior and minor pro teams. He later became head coach for the UCLA team. He is the brother-in-law of Mike Murphy because his wife and Murphy's wife are sisters.

VENERUZZO, Gary
b. Fort William, Ontario, June 28, 1943

After playing junior with some fine Fort William teams in the early 1960s, Veneruzzo turned pro with Tulsa until 1967, when St. Louis claimed him. He played just 16 games with the Blues but made a name for himself in '71-'72 when he led the WHL in scoring with 41 goals. Included in that number was a league-record stretch of goals in 10 consecutive games. The next year he began a career in the WHA that included five teams in as many years.

VERBEEK, Pat
b. Sarnia, Ontario, May 24, 1964

The summer of 1985 was a time of mishaps and miracles. While on his farm in Forest, Ontario, Verbeek had the thumb on his left hand severed by an auger. His brother got him into a car to drive him to the hospital, but it ran out of gas. When they got there, they didn't have the thumb and had to phone their father, who was in Wyoming, Ontario, at the time, to go to Forest and look for the thumb in a bin of fertilizer. A six-hour operation promised no guarantees, yet three months later Verbeek was back with New Jersey as feisty as ever, ready to continue what has now been one of the longest careers in league history. Often referred to as the little ball of hate, Verbeek was an antagonistic forward, not small but pitbull ferocious. He fought and battled and pushed and shoved his way onto the Devils in 1983, and in his 20 years in the league he has scored more than 520 goals with the quietest fanfare of any player in that exclusive 500-goal club (or 1,000-point club, for that matter, of which he is also a member). In fact, Verbeek might one day find that he's the only player from that group not in the Hockey Hall of Fame after retiring. He never had a 100-point season, but he had four 40-goal years and another four 30-goal seasons. Yet it wasn't until 1999, after 17 NHL seasons, that he won his first Stanley Cup. It came with Dallas and added an exclamation point to a remarkable career. He has never won any personal honours in the NHL, though he did play in the All-Star Games of 1991 and '96.

Verbeek was an antagonistic forward, not small but pitbull ferocious.
PAT VERBEEK

VERMETTE, Mark
b. Cochenour, Ontario, October 3, 1967

In 3 years at Lake Superior State, Vermette increased his goal production from 1 to 19 to an NCAA-leading 45. In his first three NHL seasons, he increased production from none to one to three. In his four years with Quebec (1988-92), he didn't take advantage of the slim opportunities afforded him, and the result was a career in the minors. Once retired, though, he became GM of the Soo Indians of the NAJHL.

VERNON, Mike
b. Calgary, Alberta, February 24, 1963

Think of the name Vernon and one image darts into the mind's eye long before a second. It's the 1989 playoffs, and in the first round Vancouver is giving Calgary all it can handle. Game seven of the series goes into overtime, and there is Stan Smyl on a breakaway. He makes a fine wrist shot, and Vernon flicks out his glove like a snake does its tongue. The Flames go on to win the game, series, and Stanley Cup, and although Al MacInnis is named Conn Smythe Trophy winner, Vernon is a close second. That '88-'89 season was his seventh in the league, all with his hometown Flames. He started as a part-timer and worked his way into the starter's role, and in that Cup year won a league-best 37 games. He stayed in Calgary for 11 years, but when Detroit went looking for a goalie and offered Steve Chiasson in 1994, the Flames accepted and Vernon was on his way to another Cup-bound team. He had an odd experience with the Wings because he wasn't the number-one goalie in the regular season – that honour went to Chris Osgood – but in the playoffs coach Scotty Bowman went with the experienced netminder and sat Osgood. And so, in 1997, the Wings won the Cup for the first time since 1955, and Vernon won the Conn Smythe Trophy. He later bounced around before returning to Calgary, but it was not the fairy-tale reunion and happy ending either side had hoped for. Vernon retired in 2002 after a year in which he had a 2-9-1 record in just 18 games. Nevertheless, he won 385 games over his career and played in 6 All-Star Games. In 1983, he won a gold medal with Canada's juniors at the WJC.

VERRET, Claude
b. Lachine, Quebec, April 20, 1963

The '83-'84 season was Verret's first as a pro, and he won AHL rookie of the year honours as well as played in his first few NHL games. During one stretch he set an AHL record by getting points in 20 consecutive games, but although he improved the year after in the minors, his NHL time decreased and soon he was out of the loop for good. The balance of Verret's career passed in Europe. He was a longtime player in France and then Switzerland, and after retiring he coached at Thetford Mines.

VERSTRAETE, Leigh
b. Pincher Creek, Alberta, January 6, 1962

Here was a tough guy who put up monster penalty minutes in junior with Calgary. Toronto drafted him in 1982, and in six years he played only eight games with the Leafs. Most of his time came in St. Catharines and

Gary Veneruzzo

Mark Vermette

Mike Vernon

Claude Verret

Leigh Verstraete

**Dennis
Ververgaert**

Jim Vesey

Sid Veysey

Dennis Vial

Newmarket, where the Leafs had their farm teams, and on January 9, 1988, Verstraete broke his leg badly in a game with the Saints and never played again.

VERVERGAERT, Dennis
b. Hamilton, Ontario, March 30, 1953

You can do a lot worse as a teen player than be tutored by Bep Guidolin, as Ververgaert was in London. Yet because he was drafted 3rd overall in 1973 by Vancouver, the weight of great expectations was upon Ververgaert's shoulders when he joined the Canucks. Even though he averaged 26 goals in his first 5 seasons with the team, there was still a sense that he was a disappointment. Midway through the '78-'79 season, he was traded to Philadelphia after a series of run-ins with new coach Harry Neale, who wanted the scorer to assume some defensive responsibility. For all his personal success, his teams performed poorly in the playoffs or he wasn't part of the success. He played eight successful NHL regular seasons but played a grand total of only eight playoff games. After retiring, he settled outside Vancouver and worked in insurance, also remaining active in Canucks alumni.

VESEY, Jim
b. Columbus, Massachusetts, October 29, 1965

The all-time leading scorer out of Merrimack College, Vesey graduated in 1988 but couldn't make his way into an NHL career for very long. He had a brief tryout with St. Louis, but the Blues sent him to Boston and after just four games in '91-'92 he suffered a serious shoulder injury. He never made it back. Vesey spent the next three years in the minors and then retired, his Merrimack days the apogee of his playing career.

VEYSEY, Sid
b. Woodstock, New Brunswick, July 30, 1955

Any time a New Brunswicker makes it to the NHL, it's special, even if, as in Veysey's case, it's for only one game. His star turn in the NHL at centre came with Vancouver in '77-'78 two years after he was named rookie of the year in the "I." He returned to university in New Brunswick soon after and later played senior hockey in Saint John. He later moved to Nova Scotia, where he coached minor hockey in Bedford.

VÉZINA, Georges
("The Chicoutimi Cucumber")
b. Chicoutimi, Quebec, January 21, 1887
d. Chicoutimi, Quebec, March 27, 1926

When Joe Cattarinich watched the teenage Vézina play in an exhibition game in Chicoutimi, he knew he was seeing a goaltender of immense capability. Vézina had

played goal for years in his boots only, not learning how to skate until he was 18. In 1910, he was signed to the Montreal Canadiens at a salary of $800 for the year, and so began one of the greatest careers and streaks in all of hockey. From his first game with the Habs until his last some 16 seasons later, Vézina never missed a single game. He won the Cup with the Habs in 1916 after a five-game finals against the Portland Rosebuds, though the year after the team lost to Seattle in its quest to retain the sacred trophy. When the NHL was formed in 1917 to replace the NHA, Vézina remained in the Montreal nets. He led the NHL in wins and GAA that year, and recorded the first-ever shutout in the NHL. The next year, he played in the tragic finals against Seattle in which the series was cancelled because of the flu epidemic and the death of Joe Hall. He won one more Cup with Montreal in 1923-24, a year in which he led the league in GAA again with a 1.97 average. In all, Vézina played 367 consecutive regular season and playoff games for Montreal, earning the nickname Cucumber because of his cool demeanour under pressure. In the opening game of the '25-'26 season, though, his life took a dramatic turn for the worse. He came to training camp looking wan, and in the home opener he collapsed after playing just one period. Doctors diagnosed him with advanced tuberculosis and told him to get to the mountainous regions of his home in Chicoutimi right away. He had to leave without saying goodbye to his teammates, and passed away a few months later, his once-strong body wasted away by the ravages of the disease. In life, Vézina was unlucky. He had 22

In all, Vézina played 367 consecutive regular season and playoff games for Montreal.
GEORGES VÉZINA

children during his marriage to Marie Morin, but by the time he passed away only two had survived. The NHL honoured the great goalie by introducing a trophy named after him that would go to the best goalie in the league. George Hainsworth, the man who replaced Vézina in the Montreal net, was the first winner. Vézina was one of the inaugural 12 members inducted into the International (later Hockey) Hall of Fame when it was founded in 1945. Later, a private collector cut Vézina's pads up into tiny pieces to include in sets of hockey cards, one of the great travesties of the game – the polar opposite to the magnificent contribution Vézina made to the game.

VIAL, Dennis
b. Sault Ste. Marie, Ontario, April 10, 1969

Well after his NHL days were over, Vial signed in 1999 to play for Sheffield in the British league. In the NHL he was a goon, and in Britain he was part of the worst brawl in that country's history. It all began when Vial cross-checked Greg Hadden of Nottingham, and Vial in turn was nailed by Barry Nieckar. The benches emptied, 8 players were ejected, and a total of 404 penalty minutes were handed out in one period. In 242 career NHL games, Vial scored exactly 4 times. He did not appear in a single playoff game. After his season of infamy in Britain, he signed with a squad called the Columbia Inferno of the East Coast league.

VICKERS, Steve ("Sarge")
b. Toronto, Ontario, April 21, 1951
As a rookie, Vickers frequently wore a jacket with stripes on it. Ever-quick teammate Pete Stemkowski called him Sarge, and the name stuck for the rest of his career. The nickname was also a good luck charm, for Vickers counted 30 goals as a rookie and won Calder Trophy honours. He played every one of his 10 NHL years with the Rangers, coming closest to the Cup in 1979 when the Blueshirts lost to Montreal in the finals. He began his career as a left winger but soon switched to the right side, in part to take advantage of the angle afforded the left shooter, in part because he had an excellent backhand. Vickers set a club record when he had 3 goals and 7 points one night in an 11-4 victory over Washington. He peaked in his third season when he scored 41 times, but his career ended quietly when he was sent down to the AHL after 698 NHL games. He retired at the end of the '81-'82 season and has worked as a sales rep for the Yellow Pages since.

VIGIER, Jean-Pierre "J.P."
b. Notre Dame de Lourdes, Manitoba, September 11, 1976
Since making his NHL debut with Atlanta on February 7, 2001, at Toronto, Vigier has slowly made inroads into the NHL while proving to be a scorer in the minors. The Northern Michigan University graduate plays right wing, and although he's not likely to develop into a star at this late date, he might yet prove to be an NHL regular.

VIGNEAULT, Alain
b. Quebec City, Quebec, May 14, 1961
In the appalling circus of ignorance that is the Montreal hockey media, Vigneault didn't stand a chance, yet he was in many ways the finest coach the Habs have had since Scotty Bowman led the team to four Cups in the late 1970s. Like many a fine coach, his NHL playing days were nothing to brag about, a bunch of games with St. Louis in the early 1980s his only claim to fame in a short career. He started coaching junior in 1986 and for a decade was successful in the Quebec league, mostly with Hull, the team that hired him after Pat Burns left to become head coach of the Canadiens. Vigneault became Habs coach in 1997 and for more than three seasons kept an awful and injury-plagued team near

the .500 mark. Despite media pressure to fire him and fan impatience, he did a fine job with a minimum of working parts. In his first playoffs, the team upset Pittsburgh in the opening round, but in his second and third years the team failed to qualify. He was fired early in the 2000-01 season and started scouting for St. Louis, and he left with a class and dignity that belied the quality of the people reporting on the Habs. Vigneault returned to Montreal a year later to coach the Montreal Rocket of the QMJHL, playing its home games out of the Bell Centre before an average of 500 fans or so.

VIITAKOSKI, Vesa
b. Lappeenranta, Finland, February 13, 1971
Three years of minor pro was enough of a chance for Viitakoski. He played a few games with Calgary in that time (1993-96), but the rest of his career from start (1990) to today has passed almost exclusively in Finland. The big left winger showed some promise in the AHL but failed to impress Calgary coaches when he was called up to the NHL. Viitakoski played at the 2002 World Championships after a nine-year absence from that tournament, and early in his career he also played at two World Junior tournaments.

VILGRAIN, Claude
b. Port-au-Prince, Haiti, March 1, 1963
Because his father was working in Haiti at the time, Vilgrain goes down as the one and only NHLer born in that truly non-hockey land. He moved to Quebec City at age one, and by seven things were on track and his skates were on him in the winter like any other local boy. Vilgrain attended the University of Moncton and in 1986 joined the Canadian National Team for the purposes of playing at the 1988 Olympics in Calgary. After the Games, he joined Vancouver, but in all his years of pro his only full NHL season came in '91-'92 with New Jersey, when he had 19 goals. He also played for Philadelphia, but went to Europe and had a long second career in Swiss hockey.

VILLEMURE, Gilles
b. Trois-Rivières, Quebec, May 30, 1940
Summertime employment is a thing of the past, from the era when players earned thousands, not millions, per year. In those days, players generally sold cars, worked on golf courses, sold ads, or worked for breweries. But Villemure was likely the only harness racer in the off-hours of the summer, riding the trots at his home track in Trois-Rivières. He also trained horses, but once September rolled around he got out his goalie equipment and headed for the bright lights of New

Villemure was likely the only harness racer in the off-hours of the summer.
GILLES VILLEMURE

Steve Vickers

Alain Vigneault

Vesa Viitakoski

Claude Vilgrain

Daniel Vincelette

York. For years in the Original Six days he was a minor leaguer, a star in the WHL and AHL. He worked his way up to be Ed Giacomin's backup with the Rangers, and when Giacomin was claimed on waivers by Detroit Villemure became the starter. From 1970 to '73 he had an excellent record of 66-27-10 and led the team to the '72 Cup finals against Boston. He played in the All-Star Game each of those years and won the Vézina Trophy with Giacomin in '70-'71. Villemure retired in 1976 and pursued harness racing full-time, though in later years he worked as an electrician as well.

VINCELETTE, Daniel
b. Verdun, Quebec, August 1, 1967

In six years of pro, Vincelette, a left winger, played only his first two seasons full-time in the NHL, with Chicago. The Hawks drafted him out of Drummondville, where he established himself as a tough guy with some offensive skills, but with the Hawks he came in tough without the offence and it wasn't enough to stick around for too long. He played in the minors for a number of years and then went into coaching in Quebec, though his reputation took a beating during a game in the 2000-01 season. While working as an assistant under Joe Canale in Sherbrooke, the team was pelted by fans and the two coaches went into the crowd swinging sticks. They were both charged, and Vincelette pleaded guilty. He was given an unconditional discharge but fined $500. The next year, he was coach for the Granby Blitz, a semi-pro team.

Visheau played in a single game with Winnipeg shortly after being drafted by the team in 1992.
MARK VISHEAU

VIPOND, Pete
b. Oshawa, Ontario, December 8, 1949

Oakland drafted him in 1969, but the Seals barely got their money's worth. Vipond played just three games a few years later before retiring from the pro ranks and moving into the senior leagues for a short time.

VIRTA, Hannu
b. Turku, Finland, March 22, 1963

Imagine if your blessing and curse are one and the same – what a conundrum. Virta was scouted in Finland by Scotty Bowman, who saw the defenceman play in an exhibition game for which he had been given special exemption, Virta having been suspended for the year for violent play. Bowman drafted him for Buffalo in 1981, but in four seasons with the Sabres Virta's performance diminished rather than improved. Virta came to detest Bowman, and when he was called home to perform mandatory military duty, he left the team vowing never to return as long as Bowman was the coach. True to his word, Virta never played in the NHL again, but he spent

more than a decade playing back home. He appeared in seven World Championships, notably the historic gold-medal year of 1995, as well as the 1994 Olympics in Lillehammer, the 1996 World Cup, and the 1987 Canada Cup. By the time he retired in 1998, he was one of the most respected players in his country. He became an assistant coach with Turku, the Finnish club team for whom he had played so many years.

VIRTA, Tony ("Toka")
b. Hameenlinna, Finland, June 28, 1972

A longtime Finnish-league player, Virta was drafted in 2001 by Minnesota just days before his 29th birthday. He went on to play most of the 2001-02 season in the minors, though he did make eight appearances for the Wild. He won a silver with Suomi at the 2001 World Championships.

VIRTUE, Terry
b. Scarborough, Ontario, August 12, 1970

It wasn't until the late 1990s that Virtue played in the NHL, just reward for a career in the minors that doesn't promise a return to the NHL any time soon. He played four games for the Bruins and one more for the Rangers, but the tough defenceman has made a life of small-town USA, skating in places such as Wheeling, Roanoke, and Louisville. In 1994, he even played a summer season of roller hockey with the Atlanta Fire Ants.

VISHEAU, Mark
b. Burlington, Ontario, June 27, 1973

At 6'6" and 222 pounds, Visheau was not an easy defenceman to beat, but Mother Nature did what not many players could do. Visheau played in a single game with Winnipeg shortly after being drafted by the team in 1992 and then spent the next five years in the minors. He made a late impression with Los Angeles in 1998 and seemed to make the team full-time, but then he was felled by a congenital urinary tract obstruction. He required surgery, and never played again.

VISHNEVSKI, Vitaly ("Vish")
b. Kharkov, Soviet Union (Ukraine), March 18, 1980

The Mighty Ducks can't feel that they have got fair value to date for a 5th-overall draft choice in 1998 in the form of Vishnevski. He was named best defenceman at the 1999 WJC in Winnipeg and joined Anaheim the next season, but although he has proved to be a solid defenceman, he has yet to develop into a superstar. The best news, though, is that by the time he was 22 he had three years of NHL experience under his belt and two World Championships as well (1999 and 2001). His best days are still ahead, or so hope the Ducks.

Pete Vipond

Hannu Virta

Terry Virtue

Vitaly Vishnevski

VISNOVSKY, Lubomir

b. Topolcany, Czechoslovakia (Slovakia), August 11, 1976

Years of playing in his native Slovakia have prepared Visnovsky for the NHL, and since joining L.A. in 2000 he has been a solid member of the team's defence. More important, he also played for Slovakia at the 2002 Olympics in Salt Lake City, but true to the strength of the team, his services weren't needed for the World Championships later in the year when the country won a gold medal.

VITOLINSH, Harijs

b. Riga, Soviet Union (Latvia), April 30, 1968

When Latvia was under Soviet control, Vitolinsh was not among the CCCP's best players, but when the tiny amber-soaked nation became independent, Vitolinsh became a critical component to an emerging hockey power. He played at the 1993 World Championships when Latvia was in "C" pool, played two years later when they had climbed into "B" pool, and since 1997 has been a regular on the WC team since it emerged in "A" pool among the elite. He also played at the 2002 Olympics in Salt Lake City, but his eight WC appearances rank him among young Latvia's finest international players. His only NHL time came with Winnipeg in '93-'94.

VIVEIROS, Emanuel

b. St. Albert, Alberta, January 8, 1966

Time alters perspective and reinvents history. It makes the present look different in the past, and makes good seem not so good sometimes. When Viveiros played for Canada at the WJC in 1986, he was an Edmonton draft choice who had been traded to Minnesota and seemed to be moving up the ranks. Yet he played only a few games with the North Stars and in 1989 moved to Europe, settling in Austria where he became a star defenceman. However, under no circumstances could he play for Austria internationally, regardless of his heritage, regardless of how many years he had played and lived in Austria. Those games that he had played for Canada at the WJC ruled him ineligible to play at an IIHF-sanctioned event for another country, a rule that will soon change.

VLASAK, Tomas

b. Prague, Czechoslovakia (Czech Republic), February 1, 1975

He was in no hurry to rush to the NHL after Los Angeles drafted him in 1993, but until he came to North America he wasn't going to play for anyone else in the NHL. So, seven years later, when he decided to try the pro game, he played a few games for the Kings and a few more in the minors before L.A. released him. Vlasak retreated to Europe and has continued to play in more familiar climes, though most recently with Avangard Omsk in Russia.

VOKES, Ed

b. Quill Lake, Saskatchewan, 1904
d. unknown

In a short pro career in which Vokes played mainly in the hinterlands of California, the left winger also played a few games with Chicago in '30-'31 without registering a point.

VOKOUN, Tomas

b. Karlovy, Vary, Czechoslovakia (Czech Republic), July 2, 1976

Even though Vokoun is still in his prime, there are not many fans of the game who would remember that he made his NHL debut with Montreal. That inauspicious beginning occurred on February 6, 1997, at Philadelphia, but in the first period he was shelled for four goals and removed. It was a year and a half and another team removed before he made it back to the NHL, and he didn't make the same mistake he had in game one. Nashville claimed him in the 1998 Expansion Draft and he became the number-one goalie, sort of, with Mike Dunham, the pair forming a solid partnership in a situation that guaranteed them both plenty of action.

VOLCAN, Mickey

b. Edmonton, Alberta, March 3, 1962

One of the wonderful aspects of hockey is the unpredictable, the things that happen at a game that shouldn't, that come from nowhere and then disappear. Oddball situations, crazy moments, the bizarre, all are etched in memory and history. On January 15, 1983, Volcan was part of this history. He was playing for Hartford, and the Whalers were hosting New Jersey. A terrible storm delayed referee Ron Fournier and linesman Dan Marouelli (yes, he worked the lines a long time ago!) from arriving at the rink on time. The other linesman, Ron Foyt, took the orange band and acted as referee and the two linesmen positions were filled by injured players from the two teams! Volcan, out with a broken wrist, was the Whalers representative, and Garry Howatt, down with a bad knee, manned the lines on behalf of the Devils. Both handled themselves with tentative efficiency until the start of the second period when the NHL officials finally arrived. Volcan played just four part-time years in the NHL but played primarily in the minors. He later was a playing coach in Germany, and after some time away from the game resurfaced in the south. He was head coach of Arizona State University and an instructor for USA Hockey, and more recently has acted as a scout for the University of North Dakota.

VOLCHKOV, Alexandre

b. Moscow, Soviet Union (Russia), September 25, 1977

In the mid-1970s, Washington made some terrific draft blunders, but few compare to the one made in 1996 by the modern, quality Capitals. They chose Volchkov 4th overall, perhaps because the Russian name just sounded skilled and fast, but he went on to play a scant three games with the team. He was a centre with decent size, but the Caps badly misjudged his potential and after three poor seasons of pro he returned to his native Russia to play, not likely to return to the NHL.

VOLEK, David

b. Prague, Czechoslovakia (Czech Republic), June 18, 1966

The temptation began in 1984 when the Islanders drafted him. Then, there were performances at the 1987 Canada Cup and the Olympics in Calgary the year after, signs that Volek could play with the best. In the summer of 1988, he and his fiancée were permitted to leave Czechoslovakia to visit his parents in West Germany. He never returned. He joined the

Ed Vokes

Tomas Vokoun

Mickey Volcan

Alexandre Volchkov

David Volek

Doug Volmar

Phil Von Stefenelli

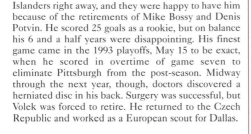

Jan Vopat

**Voss made history as
the one and only Calder Trophy
winner to be traded during
his first year of play.**
CARL VOSS

Islanders right away, and they were happy to have him because of the retirements of Mike Bossy and Denis Potvin. He scored 25 goals as a rookie, but on balance his 6 and a half years were disappointing. His finest game came in the 1993 playoffs, May 15 to be exact, when he scored in overtime of game seven to eliminate Pittsburgh from the post-season. Midway through the next year, though, doctors discovered a herniated disc in his back. Surgery was successful, but Volek was forced to retire. He returned to the Czech Republic and worked as a European scout for Dallas.

VOLMAR, Doug
b. Cleveland, Ohio, January 9, 1945
At the start, he was one of the best scorers the U.S. had ever produced. He spent '67-'68 with the National Team, playing in the 1968 Olympics in Grenoble, a sixth-place finish. The next year, he won IHL rookie of the year honours after scoring a league-record 63 goals. But in his four years in the NHL, he just couldn't score and his career trickled to an end.

VON ARX, Reto
b. Egerkingen, Switzerland, September 13, 1976
By the time the name Von Arx was uttered at the 2000 Entry Draft, cleaners had all but taken over the building and only the GMs were left to pack their belongings and head home. But for a Swiss player to be selected at all was huge news back home, and when Von Arx played 19 games with Chicago later that year, he made a name for himself as a rare Swiss entry into the NHL register and remains the only Swiss-born player to score a goal in the NHL. He has made a bigger name for himself off the ice, though. At the 1996 World Championships "B" pool, he was fined 5,000 francs for staying out long past his bedtime and having too good a time in too inappropriate a manner. In 2002, he was named to the Olympic team for La Suisse, but he and teammate Marcel Jenni, another star, stayed out until 7 a.m. one morning and were sent home by coach Ralph Kruger. Even worse, when a car came to their rooms to drive them to the airport, they had disappeared – gone to have more fun! The scandal in Switzerland was something to behold, but it didn't help Von Arx's chances of ever getting back to the NHL and a solid career.

VON STEFENELLI, Phil
b. Vancouver, British Columbia, April 10, 1969
A top student at Boston University, Von Stefenelli went on to play for the Bruins and Ottawa before establishing himself in Europe, principally Germany. He graduated from BU in 1991 and played in the minors, getting only scarce opportunity with Boston four years later.

VOPAT, Jan
b. Most, Czechoslovakia (Czech Republic), March 22, 1973
The last game of hockey Vopat ever played was on December 10, 1999. He wasn't old. He wasn't losing his skills or cut by a team. He wasn't injured, per se, and he hadn't lost his desire. He was, simply, a victim of "gunk," the term the hockey world has given to a horrible, debilitating skin disease caused by hockey equipment in combination with sweat. Tom Reid and Paul Gardner had to retire because of it. Rick Vaive and Grant Fuhr were able to recover from it and play. Like an allergy, it got worse and worse each time Vopat suffered from it. The gunk began as a rash, but it soon spread over his entire body except for his face. When he didn't play, there was no rash. When he did, it came back more and more quickly and got itchier and itchier to the point of insanity. He tried to combat it with creams and lotions, new soaps and different detergents, other clothes, and anything he could think of. He retired, was fine, tried a comeback with a team in Finland, and got the gunk again. His brother, Roman, also an NHLer, never has had the problem, but it ended Jan's career.

VOPAT, Roman
b. Litvinov, Czechoslovakia (Czech Republic), April 21, 1976
By the time he was 22 years old, Vopat had been owned by five NHL teams and played for four of them. Only a sub-NHL level of talent prevented him from continuing to move around the league to challenge Michel Petit's record of 10 career NHL teams. Indeed, Vopat's four-team travels came in just four years (1995-99), after which he returned to Europe when the Flyers released him.

VOROBIEV, Vladimir
b. Cherepovets, Soviet Union (Russia), October 2, 1972
Like many a Rangers or Oilers player in the 1990s, Vorobiev played for both those teams, though in his case the stay was short. He left Moscow to play near the Hudson, but after four years of mostly minors he retired and returned home.

VOSS, Carl
b. Chelsea, Massachusetts, January 6, 1907
d. Lake Park, Florida, September 13, 1994
It took a while for him to get to be a full-fledged rookie in the NHL, but once he did Voss made history as the one and only Calder Trophy winner to be traded during his first year of play. He was raised in southern Ontario and was a fine hockey and football player. He took the Kingston Frontenacs to the Memorial Cup in 1926, and the same year was also a halfback for Queen's University. He played for the Marlies the

Roman Vopat

next year and when Conn Smythe bought the Toronto St. Pats and renamed the team the Maple Leafs, Voss was the first man Smythe signed for his newly-named team. Over the next six seasons though, Voss was strictly a minor leaguer, with the exception of 14 games with the Leafs. He made the Rangers full-time in 1932, but after just a few games New York traded him to Detroit where he had an excellent year and won the Calder Trophy. Over the next six years, he was as well travelled as any, playing for six teams in a short period. In '37-'38, he started with the Maroons but ended with the Cup-winning Hawks, his last season in the league before a knee injury ended his career. Voss, though, was only just beginning his life in hockey. He joined CCM as its U.S. agent and sold hockey products throughout the country for a decade. He also refereed at many levels – the AHL, college, and in the California Hockey League. Voss replaced Jim Hendy as president of the USHL, a job which included the supervising of officials. When that league folded, Voss became manager and coach of the St. Louis Flyers in the AHL and continued to work with officials as a consultant. Finally, in 1950, he was offered his dream job, to work as referee-in-chief of NHL officials. He stayed in the position for 15 years during which time he improved the quality of officiating many times over. He ensured superior training for the zebras and scoured the minors for qualified referees and linesmen. He also streamlined their jobs so that teams could expect greater consistency from game to game, and he ran clinics at the junior level all across Canada to ensure the next generation of officials were being properly developed and encouraged. As a player, Voss was an early journeyman and third-line centre, but his work with officials was so outstanding that he was inducted into the Hockey Hall of Fame in 1974 as a Builder.

VRBATA, Radim ("Verb")
b. Boleslav, Czechoslovakia (Czech Republic), June 13, 1981

Few rookies had the impact Vrbata did with his team, Colorado, in 2001-02, and what a pleasant surprise he was to the Avs. He had been drafted a lowly 212th in 1999 during his junior career in the Q that saw him make a giant improvement in his final season. He played only a single game with Hershey in the 2001 playoffs before making Colorado in 2001, and the rookie scored 18 goals and finished seventh in rookie scoring for the year. Coach Bob Hartley used him more sparingly in the 2002 playoffs, a run that saw the Avs go to the Conference finals, but Vrbata might well become a surprise star in the league. He had an assist in his first career game, and a goal in his second.

VUJTEK, Vladimir
b. Ostrava, Czechoslovakia (Czech Republic), February 17, 1972

In a career that was all over the map, Vujtek took his hockey life in stride and with a dose of gratitude, for within one year he suffered two life-threatening injuries during play. One, at home, occurred in 1999 when he was elbowed in the head and knocked unconscious. Teammate Milos Holan had to put his stick in Vujtek's mouth and pull out his tongue as he suffered a seizure.

In '97-'98, he missed half a season with Epstein-Barr virus and returned home to recover. The year after his seizure, he joined Atlanta, but during an exhibition game he suffered a serious facial cut that required more than 200 stitches to close. He then affixed a visor to his helmet, but just a few games into the season the Thrashers released him and Vujtek returned to the Czech Republic to continue playing, happy just to be alive. He had played earlier in his career in Montreal and Edmonton, but again had returned home to play after unsuccessful forays with both teams.

VUKOTA, Mick
b. Saskatoon, Saskatchewan, September 14, 1966

After piling up 337 penalty minutes for Spokane in the WHL in '86-'87, Vukota was offered a contract by the Islanders, a team looking for a fourth-line goon. They got what they paid for, and Vukota spent the next several years beating opponents up – keeping them honest, in the parlance of the game – and taking his lumps. He was suspended twice for 10 games each, once for a last-second fight in a playoff game, another for coming off the bench to join in a melee. By the time he joined Tampa in 1997, he had fought his way to number one on the Islanders penalty list, and he kept on fighting with the Lightning and Canadiens until being sent to the minors. He retired in 2000 after two seasons in the "I" and no signs of NHL life.

VYAZMIKIN, Igor
b. Moscow, Soviet Union (Russia), January 8, 1966

In a long European career centred in his native Russia, Vyazmikin played four games with the Oilers in '90-'91. His only international experience came in 1986 with the Soviet juniors at the WJC, but he nonetheless played pro at one level or another for some 13 seasons.

VYBORNY, David
b. Jihlava, Czechoslovakia (Czech Republic), June 2, 1975

There was a slightly false start to Vyborny's NHL career, though in the meantime he established himself as one of the most successful modern players in the international game. Drafted by Edmonton in 1993, he came to the AHL a year later to play in the Oilers system, hoping to work his way into the lineup. Instead, he retreated, returning to the Czech Republic after a year in Cape Breton and spending five years far away from the NHL. Then, Columbus signed him in 2000 and he's been in the big league ever since. In the interim, though, he played in five consecutive World Championships, winning medals in each one: gold in 1996, bronze in 1997 and '98, and gold again in 1999 and 2000. He played again in 2002.

VYSHEDKEVICH, Sergei
b. Dedovsk, Soviet Union (Russia), January 3, 1975

The glorious and mellifluous Foster Hewitt was known to have problems pronouncing the names Enio Sclisizzi and Steve Wojciechowski (not to mention Cournoyer and Kharlamov), so Lord only knows what he would have done to Vyshedkevich. No worries, though, because the Russian defenceman played just a few games with Atlanta before returning to his homeland in 2001 after 5 years in the Devils and Thrashers systems that resulted in 30 NHL games.

Mick Vukota

Vladimir Vujtek

Sergei Vyshedkevich

WADDELL, Don
b. Detroit, Michigan, August 19, 1958

It's perfectly common for an NHL coach or GM to have had nothing more than a pedestrian playing career, but Waddell is the only one-game wonder to go on to better things in a suit. His lone game came with L.A. in 1980, soon after he had graduated from Northern Michigan University with a degree in business management. He played in the minors for eight years, having perhaps his best year in '81-'82 when he was named the IHL's best defenceman while skating for Saginaw. After retiring, he entered the fray again as coach almost immediately, starting with Flint in 1988. He built the expansion San Diego team in 1990, and five years later assumed a similar challenge with Orlando. In 1997, Waddell was assistant GM for Detroit, which won the Cup in his only season, and then he accepted the tough job of building the Atlanta Thrashers from scratch, a process that is years away from being completed.

WAITE, Frank
b. Fort Qu'Appelle, Saskatchewan, April 9, 1905
d. July 18, 1989

Waite played out west for a number of years before entering the minor pros of the east in 1926 when he joined Springfield. He played a few games with the Rangers a short time later, but moved around through the Can-Am and International leagues before retiring.

WAITE, Jimmy
b. Sherbrooke, Quebec, April 15, 1969

In retrospect, Chicago was crazy to draft Waite 8th overall in 1987. For starters, it was one of the highest choices ever used to select a goalie, but more to the point, the Hawks soon had Ed Belfour and Dominik Hasek in the fold. There was no room – none – for Waite. Yet he played 8 of his first 9 years with the Hawks, and later for Phoenix, but never appeared in more than 20 games in any season. The brightest moment of his career came near the start when he played for Canada at the 1988 World Juniors, leading the team to a gold medal and being named the tournament's best goalie. He has gone on to a continued career in the minors, first in the AHL and most recently in Germany.

WAKALUK, Darcy ("Lotsa Luck")
b. Pincher Creek, Alberta, March 14, 1966

On December 5, 1987, Wakaluk became the first AHL goalie to score a goal, an empty-net shot while playing for Rochester. The moment came near the start of his career, and over the course of the next few years he played his way into the NHL with Buffalo and then the Stars. His best year was '93-'94, when he had a record of 18-9-6 and also appeared in the playoffs, but that was the closest he came to being a bona fide starter. After retiring, he became a goalie consultant with Kamloops in the WHL, a position that turned into full-time assistant coach duties.

WAKELY, Ernie
b. Flin Flon, Manitoba, November 27, 1940

When Ernie Wakely made his pro debut with Winnipeg in 1960 he could not have envisioned that in 1979 he would still be blocking shots. Thankfully, by that time he was wearing a mask. He made his NHL debut in '62-63 with Montreal, and played his second NHL game more than six years later. Wakely made a name for himself starting in 1969 when he was traded to St. Louis and played as backup to Jacques Plante for a year, a year that saw him go to the All-Star Game and lead the league with a GAA of 2.11 over 30 appearances. The following season, Wakely inherited the great man's throne for a year and a half. Just as he was getting going, though, the Winnipeg Jets came a-calling, and the WHA dollars lured Wakely away from the NHL. He spent the rest of his days in the pirate league, making more money that he ever could have envisioned in the Original Six days.

WALKER, Gord
b. Castlegar, British Columbia, August 12, 1965

Walker began his career with a bang, scoring a goal in his first game, with the Rangers, in '86-'87. He played only a few games over two seasons, then repeated the pattern in Los Angeles, spending much of his time in the minors.

WALKER, Howard
b. Grande Prairie, Alberta, August 5, 1958

Like many a teen, Walker played provincial junior hockey (derogatorily referred to as Tier II hockey) in B.C. and then went to a U.S. college (University of North Dakota). He left after two years when Washington signed him to an NHL contract, but he played only one full season before finding his way to the minors. He retired in 1983.

WALKER, John "Jack"
b. Silver Mountain, Ontario, November 28, 1888
d. Seattle, Washington, February 16, 1950

The modest total of 80 games played in the NHL belies the quarter of a century Walker played hockey, winning Stanley Cups at numerous stops along the way. He played his early years in Port Arthur, winning city and intermediate championships before moving to the NHA in 1912. In his second season, he helped the Toronto Blueshirts win a Cup and he introduced the new league to his masterful hook check, a brilliant method of backchecking that made him the best defensive forward in the game, with the possible exception of Frank Nighbor. In 1915, Walker moved out west to play in the PCHA, starting what would become a lifelong affiliation with that part of the country. He helped the Seattle Metropolitans win the Cup in '16-'17 and stayed with the team until 1924. He transferred to Victoria, and lo and behold, the Cougars won a Cup. This marked the third Cup with the third team in the third league for Walker, a unique distinction, indeed. In 1926, when the WHL folded, he headed east to Detroit where he played two years with the Cougars. These were his only NHL games, for in 1928 he moved back west to play in Seattle again. At the close of his career, Walker moved down to California where he was a playing coach in Hollywood and Oakland. He retired in 1932 and moved back to Seattle where he taught the game to kids. Walker died in 1950 and was inducted into the Hockey Hall of Fame in 1960 for his contributions to the game for so long during hockey's formative years.

Jimmy Waite

Darcy Wakaluk

Gord Walker

Howard Walker

Jack Walker

Ernie Wakely
(opposite page)

Kurt Walker

Russ Walker

Scott Walker

Bob Wall

Peter Wallin

WALKER, Kurt
b. Weymouth, Massachusetts, June 10, 1954
The Leafs brought Walker up for the end of the '75-'76 season, a fighter who was there to go toe-to-toe with the Philadelphia goons in the playoffs. The year after, he made the team briefly but hurt his knee, missed much of the year, and had a tough time getting his job back as fighter. He played half a year in '77-'78, but his career was pretty much done by then.

WALKER, Russ
b. Red Deer, Alberta, May 24, 1953
In 1973, Walker had a simple choice: play in the WHA or in the NHL. He chose the more lucrative former option and signed with Cleveland, but after three years he moved to L.A. and the prestige of the NHL. He played only 17 games over 2 years, and when he retired in 1979 he settled in Saskatoon. Soon after, he started a real estate business that has proved successful for him.

WALKER, Scott
b. Cambridge, Ontario, July 19, 1973
As a junior, Walker made his mark as a fighter deluxe, a goon who looked for trouble, found it, and rolled around in it. This, in turn, got him into the NHL with Vancouver in 1994, but it wasn't until four years later when he went to Nashville that he blossomed as a player. He scored 15 goals that year and was asked to play at the World Championships for Canada. Two years later, he scored 25 times and was again in a red and white sweater at year's end at the WC. His world came crashing down in 2001-02, though, when he suffered a serious head injury and missed most of the year, his progress stopped in full flight.

WALL, Bob
b. Richmond Hill, Ontario, December 1, 1942
À la Red Kelly, Wall moved from defence to forward during the thick of his career, and he later switched back when he got to the NHL. Like many players of his vintage, he was a part-timer in the 1960s until expansion, after which his career took off. His early and few games came with Detroit, and L.A. gave him more meaningful work starting in 1967. He left the NHL in 1972 to join the WHA and retired four years later. He was later inducted into the Richmond Hill Sports Hall of Fame.

WALLIN, Jesse
b. Saskatoon, Saskatchewan, March 10, 1978
Two appearances for Canada's juniors in the late 1990s and Detroit choosing him could not have boded better for Wallin, yet he hasn't been able to do much with the chance yet. Just as he was working his way into the system, he suffered a serious groin injury that caused him to miss much of 2001-02. The first-round draft choice has plenty of work to do before he can crack the Red Wings blueline as a regular.

WALLIN, Niclas
b. Boden, Sweden, February 20, 1975
That first year was a real doozie. In his first game with Carolina, on October 7, 2000, he broke his wrist, and later in the year he hurt his shoulder and missed a few more games. In all, he was a healthy scratch (ironic, given his season) for 25 games, but in his sophomore year the defenceman took charge. He played most of the year and contributed to the team's phenomenal playoff run to the finals, his years of pro in Sweden helping him to play in the NHL on a nightly basis.

WALLIN, Peter
b. Stockholm, Sweden, April 30, 1957
After a Swedish-league game in Umea in the '80-'81 season, Wallin was charged and convicted of assault after knocking down an opponent. It was an unusual ruling in court but it didn't trigger a rash of similar charges (and convictions). Near the end of that season, he moved to New York to play for the Rangers, where tough play was more the norm, but he didn't show quite as violent a tenacity. He played a few games for the Blueshirts and all of the playoffs, and stayed half of the following year as well. He played most of his games in Sweden, though, and when he retired he went into coaching and later worked as a general manager, most significantly for Sweden at the 1999 and 2000 World Championships.

WALSER, Derrick
b. New Glasgow, Nova Scotia, May 12, 1978
Despite an excellent junior career, Walser couldn't attract flies after leaving the Quebec league in 1998. He had just been named not only best defenceman in the league but also best in all of Canadian junior hockey. Yet no team drafted him, and no team signed him. The reason was simple: 5'10" and 190 pounds. Too small, everyone reasoned. It wasn't until he went to Calgary's training camp in September that he was given even a slim hope of latching on to an NHL team. He played well and the Flames signed him to a contract. He has been in the minors ever since, but not with Calgary. Walser signed with Columbus in 2001 after realizing the Flames weren't going to call him up, and the Blue Jackets have given him two games in 2001-02, his only NHL time so far.

WALSH, James "Flat"
b. Kingston, Ontario, March 23, 1897
d. Kingston, Ontario, December 2, 1959
It was really only at the end of his long career that goalie Flat Walsh became a full-time cage guardian in the NHL. He spent most of his years in the Soo, a seven-year stint that culminated in a 1924 trip to the Allan Cup finals. Soon after he joined the Montreal Maroons, but it wasn't until 1929 that he assumed the role of starter. After retiring in 1933, he became manager of the Quebec City minor league team, and later returned to his native Kingston, where he went into private business and became famous for his second love, curling. He died after a two-week illness.

WALSH, Jim
b. Norfolk, Virginia, October 26, 1956
When you think hockey, the state of Virginia does not streak wildly through your head, but that was, in fact, Walsh's birthplace. He went on to attend Northeastern University where he played baseball, football, and hockey, though the last is what he pursued the most. He turned pro in 1979 in Rochester, but made only a slight impression when Buffalo called him up. Four years later,

he was out of the game and settled in Boston, running his own engineering and contracting firm. In 1991, he was inducted into Northeastern's Hall of Fame.

WALSH, Mike
b. New York, New York, April 3, 1962
Undaunted by not having been drafted in 1984 when he graduated from Colgate University, Walsh played in Sweden and worked his way into North American pro from the other side of the Atlantic. He came home after two years to sign with the Islanders and was assigned to Springfield in the AHL, but went on to play only a few games with the NHL team before being relegated to the AHL full-time. After retiring, he accepted a position as coach of the Tilton Rams, a New England prep school team.

WALTER, Ryan
b. New Westminster, British Columbia, April 23, 1958
Gritty and skilled, a leader and skater and winner before all, Walter played 1,000 games in the toughest league and then went on the air to tell all about it. His career can be neatly divided into three parts. His early years passed in the NHL with Washington, an awful team on which Walter quickly became a top player, from his rookie year in '78-'79 through his final year five seasons later. The Caps never made the playoffs, but as a result Walter played in three World Championships. When he was traded to Montreal, he made the playoffs every year and never again had occasion to go to the Worlds. He won a Cup in '85-'86, and then stage three of his career took him home to Vancouver. He played two seasons with the Canucks, used now mostly as a defensive player, then retired in 1993. He has since worked extensively as a TV broadcaster and analyst, and is also the director of National Training Rinks, a business that operates numerous arenas across Canada. In 2002, he was inducted into the B.C. Hockey Hall of Fame.

Walton married Candy Hoult, daughter of Jack, who was the ticket manager at Maple Leaf Gardens.
MIKE WALTON

WALTON, Bobby
b. Ottawa, Ontario, August 5, 1912
d. September 3, 1992
One of the lesser-known father-son combinations, Bobby preceded his son Mike into the NHL by playing four games for the Canadiens during the war. He had played in Kirkland Lake (where Mike was born) and later played in the NHL, but his minor accomplishments were long forgotten by most once Mike made a bigger splash in the NHL.

WALTON, Mike ("Shakey")
b. Kirkland Lake, Ontario, January 3, 1945
It's easy to look back now and laugh about a nickname rooted in psychological distress, but the truth was more serious at the time. Walton was part of the Maple Leafs family, both on and off the ice. He married Candy Hoult, daughter of Jack, who was the ticket manager at Maple Leaf Gardens and also the granddaughter of Conn Smythe. There were no favours for Walton as a result of this union, though, and his six-year tenure with the team was fraught with tension, anxiety, and depression. Despite being an excellent scorer and good team player, he had run-ins with coach Punch Imlach that were not unlike those between the coach and Frank Mahovlich. Walton was on the 1967 Cup team as a part-time player, but he was only too happy to be traded to Boston during the '70-'71 season. A year later, he won a second Cup with the Bruins and was finally able to enjoy the game in a more relaxed atmosphere. He later played in the WHA for three years, leading the league in scoring in his first year with the Minnesota Fighting Saints, '73-'74. After retiring from the game in 1980, Walton returned to Toronto and opened Shakey's, a west-end bar, and established himself in the real estate business. Ironically, even though he had six 20-goal seasons as a player, his 30 goals as a rookie in '67-'68 remained his finest year.

Ryan Walter

WALZ, Wes ("Walzy")
b. Calgary, Alberta, May 15, 1970
The great expansion of 1967 created a number of superb NHL careers, allowing many players buried in the minors to show their skills in the big tent. The various expansions in the 1990s that saw the league explode to 30 teams have done much the same thing. Case in point, Walz. Between 1989 and '96 he played in just 169 NHL games in a minor-league career, after which he went to Europe to play out what he assumed were his final years. But Minnesota signed him in 2000 and he has been a mainstay with the team ever since, becoming one of the best checkers and defensive forwards in the game. In 2000-01, he scored seven short-handed goals, second-best in the league, and at season's end he played for Canada at the World Championships. His other international tournament came in 1990 when he won gold at the WJC.

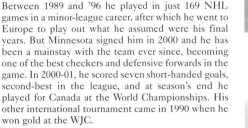

Bobby Walton

WAMSLEY, Rick ("Gump")
b. Simcoe, Ontario, May 25, 1959
In his early NHL years, Wamsley was tutored by the great Jacques Plante and for a short time could count himself among the better goalies in the game. He started with Montreal in 1980, not a good place to start because the team was just coming off four straight Stanley Cups and were expecting whoever played in goal to replace Ken Dryden save for save and win for

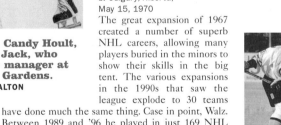

Wes Walz

Rick Wamsley

Gord Wappel

Aaron Ward

Dixon Ward

Jason Ward

Ron Ward

win. In four years, Wamsley had a great record of 72-36-16 but he was traded to St. Louis in 1984 and that was that. He had some good years with the Blues, but the team wasn't as strong and he was sent to Calgary with Rob Ramage in the deal that saw the Blues get Brett Hull and Steve Bozek. A short time later, he was involved in an even bigger deal, 10 players switching teams between the Flames and Leafs, and he ended his career in Toronto. He stayed on with the team as a goalie coach, and later went to Columbus as a consultant as well as coach. Wamsley also worked with a Toronto company that made goalie masks.

WAPPEL, Gord
b. Regina, Saskatchewan, July 26, 1958
Despite a fine, four-year career with Regina in the 1970s, Wappel could not translate his defence to the NHL when he had the chance. He played only fleetingly with the Atlanta/Calgary Flames during his five years of pro.

WARD, Aaron
b. Windsor, Ontario, January 17, 1973
Few players have worn the number of numbers Ward has worn. During his years with Detroit, he wore 61, 29, 8, 14, 38, 39, and 27. When he got to Carolina, he changed again – to number 4. He won the Cup with the Red Wings in 1997 and '98, and with the 'Canes came close to a third championship before losing to those Wings in the 2002 finals.

WARD, Dixon
b. Leduc, Alberta, September 23, 1968
After graduating from the University of North Dakota in 1992 with a degree in journalism that he vowed never to put to good use, Ward turned pro with Vancouver. He had been a high scorer at UND, and as a rookie with the Canucks he scored 22 goals. When he was traded to Toronto and on to Buffalo, though, he knew the way to a longer career was to become a defensive specialist, and to that end he gave up on scoring in favour of preventing goals. Along the way, he won the Calder Cup with Rochester in '95-'96 and was named playoff MVP. In the succeeding five years he played for the Sabres, but in 2001 Ward went to play in Switzerland.

WARD, Don
b. Sarnia, Ontario, October 19, 1935
Even though he played just a handful of games in the NHL, Ward was a legend with the Seattle Totems in the WHL, where he played some 11 seasons. He was always one of the largest players on the ice, and used that size to his advantage as a defenceman, and Chicago and Boston gave him some time in the late 1950s at the start of his career. After retiring in 1972, Ward went into coaching for a short time.

WARD, Ed
b. Edmonton, Alberta, November 10, 1969
Like a piece of music, Ward's career began slowly, reached its monumental peak, then trailed off quietly. Before the pro music began, though, he won an NCAA championship with Northern Michigan University in '90-'91 and then started with Quebec. It took him five

years and a trade, but in 1997 he was bona fide right winger with Calgary for two years before two future team changes left him dangling much of the time. He ended up in the minors and then in 2001 went to Sweden to play.

WARD, Jason
b. Chapleau, Ontario, January 16, 1979
Montreal hopes to see valuable return for their first-round draft choice of 1997, but those chances were hurt when Ward was injured in 2001, damaging his knee and forcing him to the press box for the rest of the season. He had won a silver medal with Canada's juniors in 1999 and had made some inroads with the Habs the following year, but after the knee injury Ward played all of 2001-02 in the minors.

WARD, Jimmy
b. Fort William, Ontario, September 1, 1906
d. Portland, Oregon, November 15, 1990
Some say he was the Bob Gainey of his day; others say he was so much better. Ward was a two-way player, someone who could create chances at one end and prevent them at the other, who could skate as fast as the best of them and hit hard as well. His 11 years with the Montreal Maroons was the longest tenure with the team, and he finished his career with the Habs in '38-'39 when the Maroons folded. Despite suffering a serious concussion in the '34-'35 season, Ward missed only a few games and led the team to the Stanley Cup. He settled in Portland and coached the Eagles in the PCHL for five years, after which he became a longtime salesman for a car dealership. In his later years he played golf almost every day.

WARD, Joe
b. Sarnia, Ontario, February 11, 1961
His father Don had been a star with Seattle in the WHL and made a small mark on the NHL, and Joe squeaked into the NHL during a very short pro career. He played four times for the old and not very good Colorado Rockies and retired from hockey altogether in 1983.

WARD, Lance
b. Lloydminster, Alberta, June 2, 1978
He gambled and lost at the draft, like almost every other kid in his position. New Jersey drafted him 10th overall in 1996 based on his career in Red Deer, where he was a tough defenceman. Ward decided not to sign with the Devils and re-entered the draft two years later. In 1998, Florida drafted him 63rd overall, and just like that his big fat contract hopes had been dashed. He has gone on to play a side role to Peter Worrell's leading-man marquee goon part. His brother, Blake, has been drafted by Colorado.

WARD, Ron
b. Cornwall, Ontario, September 12, 1944
Bad turned to good for Ward in the fall of 1967. He was dropped by Phoenix of the WHL and landed back with Tulsa, the team for which he had played the two previous seasons at the start of his career. He had an immediate impact with the Oilers during his second go-round, winning the scoring championship and scoring the winning goal in the playoffs for the Adams Cup. The

next year, he made it up to the AHL and was named rookie of the year, and from there he joined the Maple Leafs. He didn't last long, but he did play a full season for Vancouver two years later, after which time he played the rest of his career in the WHA. In the league's first year, Ward played for the New York Raiders and on the final day of the season led the scoring race by four points. He had scored 51 goals (and was the first to have a 5-goal game in that league) and finished with 118 points, but Philadelphia's Andre Lacroix had 6 points in his last game and bettered that total by 2 to take the scoring title. Ward went on to have some fine seasons in the league, but none as fine as that. He was also an exceptional lacrosse player. For two years he played in an all-Indian league outside Rochester, and he played with the Drummondville Athletics for seven seasons, winning the league championship six times. Ward later coached hockey at Brockville (provincial junior) and coached major junior in Drummondville for two years before moving to Florida to go into business. In 1988 he was inducted into the Cornwall Sports Hall of Fame.

WARE, Jeff
b. Toronto, Ontario, May 19, 1977
"Local boy makes good" would have made for lovely headlines in the Ware household, but Jeff made it with neither the Leafs nor any other NHL team. He was a high Toronto draft choice in 1995, and when he won a gold medal with Canada at the 1997 WJC, he looked to the future with a smile. But with the Leafs, Ware had trouble adjusting to the speed of the game and he tried to adapt in the minors. After three years, they sent him to Florida, but he played only six more games with the Panthers and has since become a regular in the AHL, most recently with Syracuse.

WARE, Mike
b. York, Ontario, March 22, 1967
Fighting was how he got to the NHL, but it didn't keep him on top for long. Ware played just a few games for the Oilers in '88-'89 and '89-'90, but they had a great team without him and kept him in the minors. He has played for many years in Britain, where he has become renowned as a tough captain, leader, and, of course, fighter.

WARES, Eddie
b. Calgary, Alberta, March 19, 1915
d. Calgary, Alberta, February 29, 1992
His best years came with Detroit, but no matter how much he talked about it later in life, no one remembered the Stanley Cup he won with the team as much as the one he had lost. He broke into the NHL with the Rangers in '36-'37, scoring two goals in his

only two games that year. After being traded to Detroit, though, his career took off. Wares played on a line with Don Grosso and Sid Abel and for a number of years the troika was the team's best. The Red Wings won the Cup in the spring of 1943, but the previous year it made the worst sort of history by winning the first three games of the finals against Toronto and losing the next four, an act of infamy still not replicated in the annals of the NHL. Wares went off to war for two years, and when he returned he played two seasons with Chicago. He ended his career in the minors, as a playing coach in Victoria and then in a senior league with Nelson. He refereed in the minors for three years and then returned to Calgary, where he ran a pool hall, sold insurance, and worked for Melcher's Distillery. In 1962, he was involved in a serious car accident near Lethbridge, his right leg broken in 10 places below the knee. He recovered, and in his later years sold tickets at Stampede Park. He represented Canada at the 1934 British Empire Games in track and field, and was inducted into the Alberta Sports Hall of Fame in 1980.

WARNER, Bob
b. Grimsby, Ontario, December 13, 1950
Yes, he made it to the NHL, with the Leafs in the mid-1970s, but the best years of his life were at St. Mary's University down east. He led the Huskies to three national championships, captaining the team his last two years. In 1999, he was inducted into the St. Mary's Sports Hall of Fame for his contributions to the school's athletics, regardless of his few games of pro in the minors beyond his Leafs days.

WARNER, Jim
b. Minneapolis, Minnesota, March 26, 1954
In 1974, the Amateur Draft saw 247 players added to NHL lists. Warner was the 245th player chosen, by the Rangers, before he had done anything to warrant being drafted at all. He had played in the World Junior tournament for the U.S. when it was an invitational affair, but his four years at Colorado College did not encourage the New Yorkers to push him onto the team. Warner played in three World Championships during his college days, and then signed with New England in the WHA in 1978. When that team became the Hartford Whalers and entered the NHL the following season, Warner followed, though he was soon in the minors. At season's end, he retired.

WARRENER, Rhett
b. Shaunavon, Saskatchewan, January 27, 1976
He was 19 when he turned pro with Florida in 1995, but the best thing the Panthers did that year was give him some time in the minors and lend him to Canada

Jeff Ware

Bob Warner

Jim Warner

Rhett Warrener

He broke into the NHL with the Rangers in '36-'37, scoring two goals in his only two games that year.
EDDIE WARES

Todd Warriner

Grant Warwick

Steve Washburn

Nick Wasnie

for the World Juniors. He won a gold with that team and acquired some confidence in his game from his rookie season, and since then he has been a front-line NHLer. Since March 1999 Warrener has been with Buffalo, and he helped the team advance to the Cup finals soon after arriving in town. He's not offensively gifted or quick with the puck, but he is solid in his own end and that has been his trademark.

WARRINER, Todd
b. Blenheim, Ontario, January 3, 1974
The accolades never stopped when Warriner was a junior, and the Nordiques responded by drafting him 4th overall in 1992. He took the '93-'94 season to play for the National Team and at the Olympics in Lillehammer, where he won a silver medal, and he was part of the big trade that saw Mats Sundin come to Toronto and Wendel Clark go to the Nordiques. With the Leafs, though, he just never developed. He never had that breakout game or time of maturity, never learned what kind of an NHL player he was. After playing parts of six years with Toronto, he was finally traded to Tampa Bay and he's been on the move steadily since. Nonetheless, he has one great claim to fame: He scored the first goal in the history of the Air Canada Centre, against Montreal on February 20, 1999.

WARWICK, Bill
b. Regina, Saskatchewan, November 17, 1924
The few games he played in the NHL, with the Rangers during the war, happened at the start of an incredible life and hockey journey. Bill, Grant, and Dickie were three hockey-playing brothers whose careers weaved in and out of each other's. In New York, Bill played with Grant (Dickie never made it to the NHL), though Grant went on to have a superior pro career while Bill played some 16 years in the minors. Bill played all over the U.S. for various teams in the AHL and USHL, but it was in Penticton in 1952 that things got most interesting. The Vees were a superb team, winning the Allan Cup in 1954 and featuring the three brothers. The team was selected by the CAHA to represent Canada at the 1955 World Championships, not just an honour but a heavy responsibility. Canada had lost in '54 to the Soviets, and the '55 team was expected to bring back gold to its rightful home. Thanks to the Warwick three, Canada did just that, hammering the Soviets 5-0 in the gold-medal game. The Vees came home with the tournament trophy held high, and then the Warwicks added their name to history by playing the most famous international prank. They had a cheap replica of the trophy made, and when the IIHF phoned the Vees to return the trophy for the '56 championships, the brothers sent the replica and

Bill played all over the U.S. for various teams in the AHL and USHL.
BILL WARWICK

kept the original in their Edmonton restaurant, which Bill has operated since retiring from puck chasing.

WARWICK, Grant ("Nobby")
b. Regina, Saskatchewan, October 11, 1921
d. Edmonton, Alberta, September 27, 1999
It was in large measure due to his great play for the Regina Rangers in '40-'41 en route to the Allan Cup that the Rangers wanted Warwick for their team the following year. Although he stood just 5'6" from the ground, he was a chunky 172 pounds, and with a low centre of gravity he was tough as nails to knock around. Warwick scored 16 goals as a rookie and proved right away he was an NHLer. He won the Calder Trophy, but at season's end was determined to join his father overseas. There was just one problem – he failed the medical. Doctors discovered he was half-deaf in one ear and that the eardrum of the other was punctured, so it was back to the NHL for him. He played another 8 years in the top loop, twice scoring 20 goals but never coming close to winning the Stanley Cup. He moved to Penticton, where he became a playing coach, setting all kinds of scoring records in the senior league. It was there he hooked up with his brothers, Bill and Dickie, and guided the Vees to an Allan Cup and then a gold medal at the 1955 World Championships, defeating the Soviets 5-0 in the final game. The three Warwicks settled in Edmonton, where they ran a popular and successful restaurant for many years.

WASHBURN, Steve
b. Ottawa, Ontario, April 10, 1975
It's not possible to get better coaching in junior than under the direction of Brian Kilrea of the Ottawa 67's, and Washburn was a fortunate pupil of the great coach. But when he turned pro, Washburn became a callup rather than a regular, with one exception in '97-'98 when he played most of the year with Florida. Before and after, with three other teams, he was a minor leaguer, and as a result he drifted overseas to continue playing in the DEL.

WASNIE, Nick
b. Selkirk, Manitoba, January 28, 1905
d. Winnipeg, Manitoba, May 26, 1991
After getting a taste of the NHL in '27-'28 with Chicago, Wasnie made a terrific impact with the Canadiens two years later. He was signed to replace Art Gagne on the top line with Howie Morenz and Aurel Joliat, and if you can't play with those two, well, you just can't play. The threesome did well together, leading the Habs to consecutive Stanley Cup victories. Wasnie played one more less successful with the team and ended his NHL days with three lesser teams – the Americans, Senators, and Eagles –

before finishing his skating in the minors. He returned to Manitoba and raised a family in Southeast Brainerd while operating a local grocery store. Wasnie was later inducted into the Manitoba Hockey Hall of Fame.

WATSON, Bill
b. Pine Falls, Manitoba, March 30, 1964

The Hobey Baker Award is such a prestigious personal honour for anyone attending U.S. college, but it comes in a currency by no means transferable to the NHL. Watson won the prize in 1985 after his third year with the University of Minnesota-Duluth, and he immediately left the school to sign with Chicago. He arrived with laurels and garlands, but after two full seasons it was clear his magic scoring stick was not working in the big tent. He retired soon after and became head coach at Saint Scholastica. In 1995 he was named an assistant coach at Western Michigan University, but three years later left to pursue other business interests.

WATSON, Bryan ("Bugsy")
b. Bancroft, Ontario, November 14, 1942

By the time he laid his stick and skates to rest in 1979, Watson was the most penalized player in the history of the NHL. He led the league in penalty box time only once ('71-'72), but he was near the top in many other of his 16 years in the league. He was a bit player in the Original Six era, but when the league opened to 12 teams in 1967, he found more employers willing to take him on. He was a small, tiger of a defenceman whose face looked like Gerry Cheevers' mask. Watson came close to the Cup only once, in his first full season, when Detroit went to the finals in 1966 against Montreal. He was one of five kids raised in Bancroft, but his father sent him to live with his grandparents in Peterborough so he could play serious junior hockey and have a chance at the big time. After retiring, he joined Edmonton as an assistant coach, and for 18 games in '80-'81 he was the head man. However, when one of the most potent lineups in the history of the game has a record of 4-9-5, the coach isn't likely to last long. Watson moved to Alexandria, Virginia, and opened Armand's, a successful sports bar.

WATSON, Dave
b. Kirkland Lake, Ontario, May 19, 1958

The excitement of leaving junior and attending his first NHL training camp was significantly dampened for Watson when he did some serious damage to his knee early on and missed the entire '78-'79 season recovering. Over the next two years, he never got on track and played just a few games with Colorado during a minor-league career.

WATSON, Harry ("Whipper")
b. Saskatoon, Saskatchewan, May 6, 1923

In the six-team NHL, rivalries dominated the game and hatred between players was common. The non-fraternization rule demanded that players on different teams not socialize, yet it was in this milieu that the large, harmless Watson lived as perhaps the nicest player in the game. He played all his minor and junior hockey in his hometown and developed into a hulking left winger who was as big a player there was, but who never used size to intimidate opponents. He turned pro with the Brooklyn Americans in 1941 at the ripe old age of 18, never having played a game in the minors. The Amerks lasted only one season and his rights were acquired by Detroit, and in his first year with the Wings he scored 13 goals and helped the team to a Cup. Watson then left the game to enlist in the army, and for two years he moved around the country performing a number of jobs while playing only a little hockey. In 1945, he returned to the Wings, but a year later he was traded to Toronto for Billy Taylor, a deal that changed his life and career. He played eight-and-a-half years with the Leafs, at first on a line with Syl Apps and Bill Ezinicki, scoring 20 goals four times. He rarely incurred a penalty, and his contributions to Toronto's four Cup efforts (between 1947 and '51) were significant. In 1948, he scored what turned out to be the Cup-winning goal, and in 1951 he assisted on Bill Barilko's historic overtime score. In fact, the huge number four is front and centre in the famous picture that captured the diving Barilko. The Leafs had wanted to convert Watson to defence when they acquired him, but his rather awkward performance in training camp convinced coach Hap Day against it. It was off ice that Watson distinguished himself. He frequently took players from other teams into his home after games so that they could spend the night and keep the hotel money for their own use, and he made friendships with opponents in a way that would have made NHL president Clarence Campbell cringe had he ever found out. He finished his career in Chicago and then went into coaching for a number of years. Watson started as playing coach with Buffalo in the AHL and later with St. Catharines in junior. In '62-'63, he guided the Windsor Bulldogs of senior glory to the Allan Cup, but his life in hockey didn't end there. He played oldtimer hockey for years and worked at hockey schools throughout the country. He was also treasurer of the Professional Hockey Players Golf Tournament, a charitable organization, and was the linchpin in alumni gatherings in Toronto for years. Watson ran his own bowling alley in Markham, Ontario, and owned his own sales agency there as well. He was inducted into the Hockey Hall of Fame as a Veteran Player in 1994, a

In 1948, he scored what turned out to be the Cup-winning goal.
HARRY WATSON

Bill Watson

Bryan Watson

Dave Watson

Jim Watson

fitting tribute to a man who enjoyed the game and shared his love for it with anyone around him.

WATSON, Jim ("Watty")
b. Malartic, Quebec, June 28, 1943
Watson made his first NHL appearance on January 29, 1964, with Detroit, and six and a half years later he scored his first goal. That was in part because he was a defenceman, and in part because he spent many of the intervening games and years outside the NHL. He played two full seasons with the Sabres their first two years in the league and then finished his career in the WHA.

WATSON, Jimmy
b. Smithers, British Columbia, August 19, 1952
It's amazing how resilient Watson was, right up until the end when his back simply couldn't give him any more. Watson joined his older brother, Joe, on the Philadelphia blue line in 1973 and for 10 years was part of the most violent team the game has ever known. He won two Cups with the Broad Street Bullies in 1974 and '75, and Watson thought he was being awarded an honour when he was named to play for Team Canada at the 1976 Canada Cup. Instead, he took a Gary Sargent slapshot in the face, breaking his cheekbone and jaw. He wasn't quite the same after that. Another combative chunk was taken from him three months later when the stick of St. Louis's Jerry Butler pecked him in the right eye. That retina never quite healed. And then came the backbreaker, literally. In January 1981 he required fusion in his back, and although the surgery was absolutely perfect the result was a back that could give him a healthy life but couldn't endure the rigours of the NHL. He retired and scouted for the team for a while, though he later became part of a homebuilding business in Philadelphia, his adopted home.

Jimmy Watson

WATSON, Joe
b. Smithers, British Columbia, July 6, 1943
Does it mean something or is it just awful coincidence that so many players from the brawling Philadelphia Flyers had their careers cut short because of injury? Bernie Parent, Barry Ashbee, Orest Kindrachuk, Jimmy Watson, and brother Joe all retired for reasons other than old age. In Joe's case, the injury occurred the year after the Flyers sold him to Colorado. Just 16 games into the '78-'79 season, Watson was hustling back into his own end to chase down an icing call. He was checked into the end boards by Wayne Babych and broke his leg in 13 places. His kneecap split in two. He was lucky to walk away months later with merely a limp. Watson had started with Boston but the

Watson was checked into the end boards by Wayne Babych and broke his leg in 13 places.
JOE WATSON

Bruins left him exposed in the Expansion Draft of 1967 and he spent the next 11 years with the Flyers. He won two Cups with the team, in 1974 and '75, but along the way fought anything and everything. He was one of several Flyers charged with varying degrees of assault for his actions off the ice during a playoff game in Toronto, though he also played in two All-Star Games (1974 and '77). After his injury, the Flyers hired him as an advance scout, though since then he has also worked in advertising for the Spectrum and First Union Center, the team's home building. He is currently senior account executive with the team.

WATSON, Phillipe "Phil"
b. Montreal, Quebec, April 24, 1914
d. Vancouver, British Columbia, February 1, 1991
The name Watson is testament to his Scottish father, but his given names, Phillipe Henri, are testament to his upbringing, which was entirely French. When he joined the Rangers in 1935, he didn't speak a word of English, and by the time he retired, he didn't speak much more. He was known for his language-oriented malapropisms, such as "lousy been-has" when referring to an older, detested opponent, but on skates he was sheer and smooth. In his prime, Watson played on a line with Lynn Patrick and Bryan Hextall, and the three led the Rangers to the Cup in 1940, its last for 54 years. He played his entire 13-year career with the Blueshirts with the exception of '43-'44 when he was loaned to Montreal so he could play and work around the wartime restrictions of the time. The Habs won the Cup that year. After retiring, he coached the Rangers through four mediocre seasons, but was known more for his temper than anything else. Frequently he would become so upset after a home loss that he would send the team out right after the game to go through a rigorous practice, much to the delight and befuddlement of fans exiting the building. He coached Boston for a year and a half and later worked as GM for Philadelphia and Vancouver in the WHA. He had a daughter, Jane, who was runner-up in a Miss California pageant and who stayed in Los Angeles to pursue acting. Watson devoted his later years primarily to fishing, and died of a heart attack while asleep at home.

WATT, Jim
b. Duluth, Minnesota, May 11, 1950
A goalie out of Michigan State, Watt played but a single period in an NHL net, with St. Louis in '73-'74. He surrendered two goals, returned to the minors, and retired a short time later.

Phil Watson

WATT, Mike
b. Seaforth, Ontario, March 31, 1976

It's not often a skater is traded straight up for a goalie, but in Watt's world anything is possible. Since playing in his first NHL game in 1997 with Edmonton, he has been the property of no fewer than five teams. He started with the Oilers but was traded to the Islanders for once-promising goalie Eric Fichaud, and from there Watt just kept changing teams.

WATTERS, Tim ("Muddy")
b. Kamloops, British Columbia, July 25, 1959

Underrated from the moment he started serious hockey until the day he retired, Watters nonetheless played 14 years in the NHL. The defenceman wasn't a slick puckhandler and didn't get many game-winning goals or first-star selections, but he was thoroughly dependable. He played all of his years with first Winnipeg and then Los Angeles, and when he finished playing in 1995 he went into coaching. Watters started as an assistant in Phoenix, where he had ended his pro days with the Roadrunners of the IHL. He then became the head coach for the Michigan Tech Huskies, a position he resigned from in the fall of 2000.

WATTS, Brian
b. Hagersville, Ontario, September 10, 1947

He was captain of Michigan Tech for '69-'70, his senior year, but it was five and a half years in the minors before Watt made it to the NHL. He played for Detroit four times – on March 21, 24, 30, and 31, 1976 – and soon was back in the minors to close out his career.

WEAVER, Mike
b. Bramalea, Ontario, May 2, 1978

Being a two-time champion of the Turner Cup with two different teams in consecutive years is something to be proud of, even if it isn't much beside Lord Stanley's bowl. Weaver played four years of college at Michigan State but wasn't drafted and signed with Atlanta. The Thrashers put him in the "I" with Orlando, and Weaver played an important role in the Solar Bears winning the league championship. In 2000-01, he had a short stay with the NHL team, but was sent to Chicago, again helping the team to a Turner Cup. He remains in the minors, a fringe NHL prospect hopeful of receiving that magical phone call from the parent team. But the question remains: can a 5'9" defenceman make it in the NHL?

WEBB, Steve
b. Peterborough, Ontario, April 20, 1975

Buffalo drafted him, but the Islanders signed him and played him, and Webb has been with the team since his first game on January 7, 1997. Webb is known more for his toughness than his offence, though he missed large parts of two seasons with a broken leg one year and a knee injury another.

WEBSTER, Aubrey
b. Kenora, Ontario, September 25, 1912
d. unknown

After a single game with the Philadelphia Quakers in '30-'31, Webster moved to Moncton and played for the Hawks when they won consecutive Allan Cups in 1933 and '34. This earned him another pro callup to Windsor, and from there he made a brief appearance with the Montreal Maroons. He played out west for a while but gave up playing to join the army. Webster served with the 1st Battalion of the Kenora Light Infantry, after which his hockey days were almost completely finished.

WEBSTER, Don
b. Toronto, Ontario, July 3, 1924
d. Fresno, California, April 12, 1978

Growing up in Toronto, Webster developed into a fine young player with the Toronto Marlies and played half a season with the Leafs during the war. The next year, he was assigned to Buffalo in the AHL, and while there he suffered a near-fatal and hideous injury. The boards used to be just that, slats of wood glued together. As such, there were bumps and gaps between each piece of wood. In one game, Roger Leger's stick got caught in the boards and broke, and that broken stick, acting like a spear, went through Webster's leg and up through his abdominal cavity. It was a gruesome sight, and doctors feared Webster might die as they worked frantically to remove the impaled shaft of wood. Amazingly, he recovered and returned to the game within a year, eventually settling in California. In 1953, he accepted a job with the new television station KJEO and for the next decade worked as operations manager of instructional TV for Fresno County Schools. He developed a great interest in youth sports and was president of Fresno High Spartan Football League. He also coached extensively in hockey, baseball, and soccer. Webster spent the last 14 months of his life fighting a brain tumour, to which he eventually succumbed, at home, at age 53.

WEBSTER, John
b. Toronto, Ontario, November 3, 1920

Older brother of Don, the centre from Toronto played 14 games with the Rangers in '49-'50 during his minor-league career. He spent most of his career in the American league.

WEBSTER, Tom ("Hawkeye")
b. Kirkland Lake, Ontario, October 4, 1948

Health issues were always front and centre in the life of Tom Webster, as a player and later as a coach. It all started in 1971. He had played a few games with Boston to get his feet wet, and then in '70-'71 he exploded for 30 goals with Detroit and looked to be developing into an NHL star. Then, in November, he hurt his back after 12 games and missed the rest of the season. He made a reasonably full recovery and played five and a half more years in the WHA, but the back pain returned and he required spinal fusion. He made a brief comeback a year and a half later before realizing life was more important than hockey, and then retired. Webster then began a long career as a coach. He coached in Windsor and then in Tulsa, where the team won the CHL championship despite playing the final half of the year and all of the playoffs on the road because the team had lost its home rink (for financial reasons). He was hired to coach the Rangers early in '86-'87, but had to quit after a short

Mike Watt

Tim Watters

Brian Watts

Don Webster

Tom Webster

time when an inner ear problem prevented him from flying. He later led L.A. for three years but was fired because of a poor playoff performance in 1992. Webster was head coach for Canada at the 1989 WJC and an assistant at the 1991 Canada Cup. He was later an assistant in Florida and Philadelphia.

WEEKES, Kevin

b. Toronto, Ontario, April 4, 1975

Kevin Weekes

Carl Weekes had been a member of the national cricket team of Barbados, but in 1974 he decided to move to Toronto and start a new, more promising life. The year after, his wife had a baby boy, and little Kevin quickly became fascinated with a goalie's hockey equipment. He went to school at St. Mike's before playing junior in Owen Sound, and when Florida drafted him in 1993 he was another step closer to realizing his NHL dream. In his first year with the Panthers, though, he had an awful 0-5-1 record in 11 appearances, and after a trade to Vancouver – horror of horrors – he again went winless in his first year, posting an 0-8-1 record in another 11 appearances. In fact, it was almost two years to the day from his first NHL game to his first NHL win, but since then he has steadied himself. He later played for the Islanders, Tampa Bay, and now Carolina, and Weekes might well become the most travelled goalie in NHL history by the time he retires.

WEEKS, Steve

b. Scarborough, Ontario, June 30, 1958

Steve Weeks

Along with (Hap) Day, (Mush) March, (Alan) May, (Bill) Friday, and (Don) Spring, Weeks is the starting goalie on the playful Temporal Team. In real life, he was a graduate of Northern Michigan University who played a dozen years in the NHL. His best season was his first full one, '81-'82, when he won 23 games in 49 appearances for the Rangers. In the summer of 1984 he was traded to Hartford in a move that guaranteed the Rangers a third-round draft choice in 1986, but a second-rounder if Weeks won 25 games over the next 2 seasons. He won 23. He later played for Vancouver and then three other teams in quick succession before retiring in 1993. Weeks became a goalie coach with Carolina and more recently has worked in the same capacity under Curt Fraser in Atlanta.

WEIGHT, Doug

b. Warren, Michigan, January 21, 1971

One of America's finest active players, Weight is both a solid scorer and one of the best playmakers the team has in international competition. In the NHL, he matured, developed, and rose to stardom in Edmonton, and once he was at his peak he bolted – or landed in a contractual situation that forced the Oilers to trade him – to

St. Louis. Weight started in 1991 with the Rangers, but the Blueshirts sacrificed their prized prospect two years later to acquire veteran Esa Tikkanen. Weight joined a young, fresh, rebuilding team that had superb skaters and loads of financial woes. In just his third full season with the team he recorded 104 points, a breakout year and one, in this day and age, he will not likely replicate. He helped the Oilers pull off a stunning upset of Dallas, their perennial playoff opponents, in 1997, and two years later was named team captain. By that time, though, he was considered a top player in the game, and the small-market Oilers could not afford to offer him a big-city contract. Instead, they traded him to the Blues in a multiplayer deal involving mostly prospects. Throughout his career, Weight has played for his country whenever he was available. He played in the 1991 WJC, and in two World Championships, as well as the championship World Cup team in 1996. He also appeared for the U.S. at the two NHL Olympics (1998 and 2002).

He helped the Oilers pull off a stunning upset of Dallas in 1997, and two years later was named team captain.
DOUG WEIGHT

WEILAND, Ralph "Cooney"

b. Egmondville, Ontario, November 5, 1904
d. New England, July 3, 1985

He was one of eight boys and a girl born to a father who worked as a cooper, making and repairing barrel staves at a sawmill in Egmondville, on the outskirts of Seaforth. Cooney played hockey on the Bayfield River, sometimes with his friends and family, sometimes by himself. He was called a River Rat, and those close to him always called him this in place of Cooney, another childhood nickname that replaced Ralph. Weiland sometimes worked at the sawmill to earn cash, but his greater preoccupation was to skate and stickhandle with a puck, dancing on frozen water with the disc stuck to his stick so that no one could take it from him. Cooney became so good that he went to Owen Sound to play junior, and in 1924 the Greys won the Memorial Cup. He turned pro with Minneapolis and three years later, in 1928, he joined the Boston Bruins. The small Weiland was put on a line with Dit Clapper and Dutch Gainor, two six-footers who formed the Dynamite Line, the top-scoring line in the league for three seasons. In '29-'30, Weiland set a modern-day record by scoring 43 goals in 44 games, the best average in the NHL. He also led the league in points with 73. Although he never quite had another season in which he averaged close to two points a game, he maintained a scoring pace that was the envy of most teams. He had won the Cup with the Bruins as a rookie in the spring of 1929, and after brief stints in Ottawa and Detroit he was back with the Bruins 1936 where he played the last four years of his career, winning a second Cup in his final season of '38-'39. Weiland then coached the team for two years, winning his third Cup in 1941, becoming the fastest to win a Cup first as a player ('39) and then coach (just two years later). His relations with GM Art Ross were never good, and a final falling out led him to leave the team in 1941. He immediately became coach of Hershey and then New Haven in the AHL, and in 1950 assumed coaching duties at Harvard University. It was an odd appointment for Weiland, who considered himself nothing more than a small-town Ontario boy far removed from the prestige of Ivy League society, but when the subject was hockey, he had few peers. He became famous for his fair and equal treatment of players, and over the course of an extraordinary 21 years won two ECAC championships and six Ivy league titles. He retired in 1971 with more than 300 wins to his credit, the same year he was inducted into the Hockey Hall of Fame. The next year he was given the Lester Patrick Award for his long and distinguished service to hockey in the United States. Weiland then moved to Florida where he spent the remaining years of his life.

WEINRICH, Eric
b. Roanoke, Virginia, December 19, 1966

By accident more than design, Weinrich has become something of a journeyman defenceman in the NHL. He ranks among that second tier of U.S.-born players who are highly skilled but not top 20. Before turning pro he played for his country at the 1988 Olympics in Calgary, and over the next three years developed into a fine young player with New Jersey, going from the minors to a full-time position on the Devils blueline. He played for the U.S. at the 1991 Canada Cup and emerged a true NHLer, but trades took him to Hartford and then Chicago in quick succession. Weinrich stayed with the Hawks for six seasons, though the team had troubles in the playoffs and he was traded again, to Montreal. In 2000, he was named team captain for part of the year after Saku Koivu was injured, but since then Weinrich has played for three more teams. He has also played in the 1996 World Cup and in five World Championships for the U.S.

WEIR, Stan ("Stash")
b. Ponoka, Alberta, March 17, 1952

Those who saw Stan Weir play junior in Medicine Hat in '70-'72 swore he was the best teenage player in the country. California certainly hoped so after they drafted him, but it was years before he achieved his apogee. He was a solid centre with the Seals and then Toronto, but he shone when he got to Edmonton in the WHA in 1978. In an exhibition game that first season, he had part of a finger cut off when he was slashed hard by an opponent, the offending stick slicing the finger and

Eric Weinrich

Weir's stick acting as the cutting board. Doctors had to stitch the severed part on after the game, but he made a full recovery. In that first year with the Oilers, Weir was the team's number-one centre, and the next year, the Oilers now in the NHL, he scored 33 goals while playing on the third line behind Wayne Gretzky and Ron Chipperfield. He retired in 1983 but later returned to play senior hockey in Ontario.

WEIR, Wally
b. Verdun, Quebec, June 3, 1954

That Weir once held the AHL record for most penalty minutes in a game with 54 spoke to his style of play. He played with the Nordiques in the WHA and in their first few years in the NHL when they had tremendous games against Montreal, and his toughness came in handy during those games, notably in 1982 during the team's march to the semifinals. He later played briefly in Hartford and Pittsburgh, and after retiring became a coach in Quebec minor hockey.

Stan Weir

WEISS, Stephen
b. Toronto, Ontario, April 3, 1983

The topsy-turvy 2001-02 season ended buoyantly for Weiss even though it had started sinkingly. He was at Florida's camp hoping to make the team when he suffered a groin injury and was sent back to his junior team in Plymouth. The Whalers were a top team, and Weiss was considered the best two-way player in junior hockey, but they were upset in the first round of the OHL playoffs. Ring, ring. The Panthers called him up to the NHL, and in his first game, on his 19th birthday, he scored a goal. That got his confidence up and his feet wet, but now he must develop and prove himself a regular, a tougher task for the 4th-overall selection at the 2001 Entry Draft.

WELLINGTON, Alex
b. Port Arthur, Ontario, August 4, 1893
d. unknown

Precious little information exists on the details of Wellington's life and career. He is credited with having played a single game with the Quebec Bulldogs in '19-'20 and that's about the extent of it.

WELLS, Chris
b. Calgary, Alberta, November 12, 1975

Contrary to scouts and coaches, size isn't everything. Wells stands 6'6" in his stocking feet, but he didn't have longevity in a career that started off in the NHL and has continued in the minors. He played most of his NHL time with Florida, but the Panthers eventually sent him down to the AHL and he has been lumbering around in other minor-pro leagues ever since.

Wally Weir

Chris Wells

In '29-'30, Weiland set a modern-day record by scoring 43 goals in 44 games.
COONEY WEILAND

Jay Wells

Cy Wentworth

Brad Werenka

Blake Wesley

WELLS, Jay
b. Paris, Ontario, May 18, 1959

The journey was a long one for Wells, but after 18 years he was ready to retire. This moment of realization came during the '96-'97 season with Tampa. He had played nearly 1,100 games and fought everyone there was to fight. He had won a Cup with the Rangers in 1994 and survived as a tough guy much longer than anyone might have imagined. He had suffered plenty of injuries along the way, but he left the game in good health. He never played in an All-Star Game or won any individual trophies. He just got the job done and moved on. Wells became an assistant coach in the AHL, first with Portland and then under Mike Foligno in Hershey.

WENSINK, John
b. Pincher Creek, Alberta, April 1, 1953

Even though he hardly established roots in St. Louis, he did plant them more firmly in the ground after his playing days. Wensink played a few games with the Blues in '73-'74, but just a short time later a serious spinal fusion operation put his career in jeopardy. Boston coach Don Cherry gave him a chance after the left winger had been out of the game for more than a year, putting him on a line with Peter McNab and Terry O'Reilly. Wensink was supposed to be a fighter, but he got pretty good at scoring, too, and during the '78-'79 season Wensink had 23 goals before the coach had a talk with him. Cherry apparently told Wensink to stop scoring and get back to fighting, a dictum that demoralized the player and eventually led to Wensink leaving the Bruins. He finished with New Jersey and retired in 1983, moving to St. Louis and establishing Wensink Construction. A year and a half later, though, he got a call from the Dutch team Nijmegen to play, and he jumped at the chance. He was of Dutch ancestry, had relatives in Holland, and his nephew, Bill Wensink, had played on that team for years. He was also brought in to combat Wayne Van Dorp, a goon who played for Groningen, but not much ever came of this duel. Wensink played hard but clean, and he became part of legend in that country when he apparently checked Theo van Gerwen of Eindhoven so hard that van Gerwen actually lost a skate! Wensink played for the rest of the season, two months, and then returned to St. Louis to run his business.

WENTWORTH, Marvin "Cy"
b. Grimsby, Ontario, January 24, 1905
d. Toronto, Ontario, October 10, 1982

In his 13 years of NHL hockey between the wars, Wentworth did everything but get into the Hockey Hall of Fame for his play. He was long regarded as the best defensive defenceman in the game. Not big, he used timing and the pokecheck to break up attacks, while his huge partner on the blueline, Taffy Abel, had no problem using his whole, and generous, body to prevent goals. Wentworth entered the league with Chicago in 1927, becoming captain in 1931. He later played for the two Montreal teams, winning his only Stanley Cup with the Maroons in 1935. He played in the two benefit games that pre-dated the All-Star Game, the Babe Seibert and Howie Morenz Games in 1937 and '39, respectively. After retiring, Wentworth settled in Toronto where he became a longtime worker for Labatt Breweries.

WERENKA, Brad
b. Two Hills, Alberta, February 12, 1969

He was by no means a star. Sometimes he was in the game, sometimes he was a healthy scratch, sometimes he was in the minors. But on December 29, 2000, he came off the ice not knowing where he was, another concussion victim, another player who, months later, still wasn't right. He retired at age 32 after less than eight years in the league. Werenka graduated from Northeastern Michigan University in 1991 with an NCAA championship and a degree in political science, a pre-law program he hoped to pick up later in his life. In his first five years of pro, he was a part-time player, but he realized another dream when he won a silver medal with Canada at the 1994 Olympics in Lillehammer. He had his longest stretch of regular ice time with Pittsburgh, though he was later dealt to Calgary where he suffered his career-ending injury. His cousin was Gary Bromley, and Werenka had learned to play on an outdoor rink his mother made every winter in Two Hills.

Wensink got a call from the Dutch team Nijmegen to play, and he jumped at the chance.
JOHN WENSINK

WESENBERG, Brian
b. Peterborough, Ontario, May 9, 1977

December 19, 1997, was a great night for Wesenberg. In his first full year of pro with Philadelphia's AHL affiliate, he had a goal and four assists to set a team record. That night and a fine season got him into just one game the next year with the Flyers, and he's been a minor leaguer ever since.

WESLEY, Blake
b. Red Deer, Alberta, July 10, 1959

Blake is one half of the Wesley brother combination that made the NHL, the other half being Glen. Their careers avoided each other perfectly, as Blake's last NHL season was '85-'86 and Glen's first was '87-'88. Both were big, physical defencemen, though Blake was the lesser of the two offensively. He graduated from junior in Portland to join Philadelphia in 1979 and for the better part of seven years was an NHL regular. He finished his career in the minors and then went into coaching, most recently with Tri-City and then back at his alma mater in Portland in 2001.

WESLEY, Glen
b. Red Deer, Alberta, October 2, 1968
Like his brother, Blake, Glen came out of the Portland junior system, but unlike Blake there was pressure on Glen to perform. He had been drafted a lofty 3rd overall by Boston in 1987, and not only was the 20-year-old expected to make the team at his first camp, he was expected to have an impact. Wesley was offensively gifted, and in his second year he scored 19 goals. In 1993, he scored a hat trick in a game, only the third Bruins defenceman to do so after Bobby Orr and Ray Bourque. In 1994, the Bruins traded him to Hartford for three first-round draft choices, a deal that turned out well for Boston, who selected Kyle McLaren (in 1995), Jonathan Aitken (in 1996), and Sergei Samsonov (in 1997). Hartford, though, got what it was looking for, and Wesley has been with the team ever since. He helped it develop from a club that missed the playoffs four years in a row to a team that went to the Cup finals in 2002. Wesley has quietly played more than 1,100 games and still has a number of years left in his legs, if his heart desires.

Glen Wesley

WESTCOTT, Duvie
b. Winnipeg, Manitoba, October 30, 1977
Coming out of St. Cloud State University in 2001, Westcott was undrafted, 23 years old, and unsure of his prospects for a career in hockey. Columbus took a chance on him, though, and he spent most of his first year as a pro in Syracuse. He made his NHL debut on March 16, 2002, but after four games he was back in the minors. That is where he began his second year of pro as well.

WESTFALL, Ed ("The Shadow"/ "18")
b. Belleville, Ontario, September 19, 1940
Quick! Name the only NHLer to win an Emmy Award. Answer: Ed Westfall. Explanation later. It isn't very often that a player will have two significant careers in the NHL, two distinct and successful periods in the league. Westfall joined the Bruins in 1961 and for the next 11 years became a crucial element in the team's Cup successes in 1970 and '72. He was a scorer, but coach Harry Sinden liked to use him as a checker, a shadow, and a penalty killer. He and Derek Sanderson were the best players short-handed in the league, and he scored more goals killing penalties than on the power play over the course of his

He was a scorer, but coach Harry Sinden liked to use him as a checker, a shadow, and a penalty killer.
ED WESTFALL

career with the Bruins. Then came 1972, and the Expansion Draft. The Islanders claimed him, and at 32 Westfall was transformed into another kind of a player based on another kind of situation. He was named the Isles' first team captain and scored the team's first-ever goal. He was relied on more for goals, worked the power play regularly, and helped establish the team as an up-and-comer before ultimate victory in 1980, by which time he had retired. Westfall played in four All-Star Games and won the Bill Masterton Trophy in 1977. He was also a licensed pilot, and during his years in New York he would fly to games from his home in Pelham, New Jersey, to a tiny airport near Nassau Coliseum. After hanging up the skates, he became a sportscaster and colour commentator, a job he has had now for more than 20 years and for which he won an Emmy.

WESTLUND, Tommy
b. Fors, Sweden, December 29, 1974
It wasn't until he was 24 that Westlund was drafted by Carolina while playing for Brynas, his Swedish club team, and another year still before he came to North America to play. He has since established himself in the Hurricanes lineup, though he missed half of 2001-02 with a bad back.

Tommy Westlund

WETZEL, Carl
b. Detroit, Michigan, December 12, 1938
Here, there, and everywhere was home for Wetzel. His NHL experience was limited to seven games in goal for Detroit and Minnesota, but that was just the top layer of a thick dossier of teams and leagues that encountered him at one time or another. He had a number of stints with the U.S. National Team in the late 1960s and early 1970s, playing in the 1967 and '71 World Championships. He played in the WHA and in Austria for a year and throughout the minors, never spending even 2 years in the same place during his 13 years of active duty. He later turned up as Washington's goalie coach in 1987.

Carl Wetzel

WHARRAM, Ken ("Whip")
b. North Bay, Ontario, July 2, 1933
Almost from the get-go, Wharram and Stan Mikita played together as if they were two halves of the same body. They played with Ted Lindsay and then Ab McDonald on the wing, and the Scooter Line was born. It was a speedy and skilled threesome that helped bring the Cup to Chicago in 1961, using Wharram's great stickhandling and passing abilities. He wasn't big, but he was a master evader of defencemen's checks, and he and Mikita communicated so well in the other team's end they had a language all their own. He recorded 7 straight 20-goal seasons, and had a career-high 39 in '63-'64, the year he was named a First Team

Ken Wharram

All-Star and won the Lady Byng Trophy. Wharram had such skinny ankles he had to have his skates specially made so he could skate properly. His career came to a sudden end at training camp in 1969 when he felt severe chest pains while taking off his skates after practice. Doctors called his condition myocarditis, and the heart attack-like symptoms forced Wharram to retire. He led a healthy life thereafter, returning to North Bay to work as a cabinetmaker and carpenter. In 1973, he moved to Chicago for a short time where he coached the Chicago Nordics of the Midwest Junior Hockey League, though he soon returned to North Bay to resume carpentry.

WHARTON, Len
b. Winnipeg, Manitoba,
December 13, 1927
One of the youngest Rangers ever to make an NHL appearance, Wharton played a single game for the Blueshirts during the '44-'45 season. He never made it back, spending the rest of his career in the minors. He later settled in Michigan.

WHEELDON, Simon
b. Vancouver, British Columbia,
August 30, 1966
From outcast to star, from NHLer to European, from Vancouver to Austria, Wheeldon has done a good deal of travelling in his day, which is by no means done. He hoped to make the NHL, but the truth was that after a few games with the Rangers and Jets between 1987 and '91, his chances were slim to none of ever getting back. In 1992, he moved to Austria, and has been there ever since, a star in league play and a national in world play. He represented Austria at the 1997 World Championships and since then has been a regular at IIHF events, including the 1998 Olympics in Nagano and the 2002 tournament in Salt Lake City. Most recently, he has taken his league play to the DEL.

WHELDON, Don
b. Falmouth, Massachusetts, December 28, 1954
d. Falmouth, Massachusetts, June 3, 1985
Dead at 30 under the most bizarre of circumstances. He and his wife were sleeping at home when a bolt of lightning hit the metal frame of their bed, killing Wheldon. He had been out of hockey since 1977 and had played two games with the Blues three years earlier.

WHELTON, Bill
b. Everett, Massachusetts, August 28, 1959
He left Boston University a year early to play in the Winnipeg system, but the Jets played him only twice

Don Wheldon

Bill Whelton

He later became a sales manager for a plumbing supply company in the city.
BILL WHITE

and Whelton spent the rest of his short career in the minors.

WHISTLE, Rob
b. Thunder Bay, Ontario, April 4, 1961
He had a pretty good idea he was never going to win the Stanley Cup solely on his own play, so Whistle left junior and went to Sir Wilfrid Laurier University. Ironically, during his years there he attracted NHL attention he hadn't while playing in Kitchener. He signed with the Rangers, played half the '85-'86 season, and two years later played briefly with St. Louis. Oddly, his statistics are unique for a defenceman in that he has more goals (seven) than assists (five) to show for his short career.

WHITE, Bill
b. Toronto, Ontario,
August 26, 1939
In the mid-1950s, White had no idea what hockey would have in store for him when he decided to try to become a professional. He played with the Marlies and turned pro in 1960, but spent most of the six-team NHL years in the hell that was Eddie Shore's Springfield. White and all his teammates went on strike to protest Shore's treatment of them, and he agreed to sell the club to Los Angeles, which was a double blessing for White: He was rid of Shore, and he found his route to the NHL. So there he was in 1967, a rookie at age 28, finally in the big league. He was traded to Chicago after two and a half excellent seasons, and formed a defensive partnership with Pat Stapleton, one of the finest around for years. Tall, slender, and bald, White looked the opposite of Stapleton, who was short, chunky, and possessed a full head of shockingly white hair. The two played most of the 1972 Summit Series together, and White's only goal of that series was huge, tying game eight 3-3 in the second period. His career came to an end in the 1976 playoffs, during the quarter-finals versus the Canadiens. White chased a puck into the corner followed closely by Doug Jarvis and Bob Gainey, and when the three collided White fell awkwardly into the boards and damaged his cervical nerves. It was months before he could use his right arm properly again. Midway through the next year, his playing days over, he became the Hawks' head coach, replacing the fired Billy Reay. He then coached the Marlies for a year but was loathed by his players because of his tough approach to the game. After one road loss, for instance, he scheduled a 3 a.m. practice. He was fired after a year and taught graphic arts at Danforth Technical School in Toronto. He later became a sales manager for a plumbing supply company in the city.

Rob Whistle

WHITE, Brian
b. Winchester, Massachusetts, February 7, 1976

Those two games he played with the Avalanche in '98-'99 look more special all the time, for the defenceman has seen nothing but the minors ever since. He signed with Anaheim in 2001, but the Ducks have yet to recall him.

WHITE, Colin
b. New Glasgow, Nova Scotia, December 12, 1977

The joke, of course, is that everyone down east is related, but in the context of White's hockey career, that's not far off the mark. When he was growing up, he was coached by Jon Sim's father. Sim won the Cup with Dallas in 1999 and took it home in the summer. He stopped by the White residence to show it off, White not having made the NHL by this time. The next year, though, White was called up by New Jersey late in the year and stuck around for the playoffs. He scored a game-winner in the Devils' series against Toronto, and the team went on to win the Cup. This time, it was White who got to bring the Cup home to show to Sim!

WHITE, Maurice "Moe"
b. Verdun, Quebec, July 28, 1919

Out of good comes reward – sometimes. White was having a harmless semi-pro career when he decided to join the army. He was assigned to Montreal, but soon after world peace had been restored the Canadiens called him up for four games. He went back to senior hockey with the Royals and played the rest of his days in Quebec and points east.

White was having a harmless semi-pro career when he decided to join the army.
MOE WHITE

WHITE, Peter
b. Montreal, Quebec, March 15, 1969

There is often a discrepancy between performance in the AHL and NHL, but rarely is it as profound and marked as in White's case. He played a handful of games with the Oilers, a single game with the Leafs, and a few more with the Flyers, but scattered in between were three scoring championships in the minors, amazingly each time with the exact same number of points. With Cape Breton, he had 105 points in '94-'95, and two years later with the Philadelphia Phantoms he again won the scoring title with 105. Just a year later, he won a third title – with 105 points. In the AHL, he has averaged well over a point a game; in the NHL, it's about one point every four games. His time in Philly was not all minor, though. White married the daughter of GM Bobby Clarke, and soon after Clarke let him go to Chicago as a free agent. No nepotism in the Clarke camp, that's for sure.

WHITE, Sherman ("Shermie")
b. Cape Tormentine, New Brunswick, May 12, 1923
d. unknown

White played his early hockey in the Amherst area before joining the RCAF. Once Corporal White returned to civilian life, he put down his gun, picked up his stick, and got back at the puck game. He played a few games with the Rangers during an AHL career centred in New Haven, and in 1951 he returned to Canada to play in a variety of senior leagues. He set numerous scoring records for his exploits, and his career carried him through 1964, by which time the 41-year-old had had enough. He was one of the all-time great New Brunswickers, even if his success in the NHL was minimal.

WHITE, Todd
b. Kanata, Ontario, May 21, 1975

"Local boy makes good" are the headlines to the Todd White story to date. Despite having an outstanding career at Clarkson University, he was never drafted. Chicago signed him, put him in the minors, and watched him win rookie of the year honours, but over the next four years White developed outside the NHL. He moved on to Philadelphia and Ottawa, never playing much in the NHL and looking like a minor-league lifer than a prospect. Then – and it's a big then – he made the Senators in 2001, and over the course of his first full season he scored 20 goals and had 50 points. Where did that come from? Ottawa hopes he can keep on doing it. If so, that's one smart free-agent signing by the Senators.

Colin White

WHITE, Tony
b. Grand Falls, Newfoundland, June 16, 1954

In Grand Falls, there were three options: work in the mines, work in the paper mill, or get the hell out. Fortunately, White could play hockey, and that meant happily saying sayonara to the mine and mill options. He turned pro in 1974 and had the misfortune to be drafted by the expansion Washington Capitals. In his first full year White scored a very respectable 25 goals from the port side. His production halved the year after, and from there he ended up in the minors.

WHITE, Wilfred "Tex"
b. Hillbrough, Ontario, June 26, 1900
d. December 2, 1949

White played for the Pittsburgh Yellowjackets in 1923, and two years later when the team entered the NHL as the Pirates, he was right there. He played in all five seasons the team was in existence, though the fourth was clipped by a few games near the end of the year when he was loaned to the New York Americans. He

Tony White

Bob Whitlock

later played a few games for another defunct team, in Philadelphia, after which he returned to the Yellowjackets which had, in the interval, left the NHL and joined the new IHL.

WHITELAW, Bob
b. Motherwell, Scotland, October 5, 1916

The one and only Scotsman ever scouted on his home turf, Whitelaw got to the NHL by the strangest means. His family emigrated to Winnipeg when he was seven, and he played hockey as a boy, like any other. But then he went to work in the mail-order department store in the city, and it was there he was offered a chance to return to the island and play hockey at Harringay, outside London. He accepted. Cut to Detroit. The Wings and Canadiens went to England to play a series of exhibition games in 1936, and once overseas Detroit GM Jack Adams was advised to watch the big Scot (who was really a Canadian now!). Adams liked what he saw and eventually put Motherwell in the Detroit system with Indianapolis, calling him up in 1940 for a few games. He played in the 1941 playoffs and a few games the year after, but that was the end of his NHL days.

WHITFIELD, Trent
b. Estevan, Saskatchewan, June 17, 1977

During his junior career in Spokane, Whitfield played for Canada at the 1997 World Junior Championships, winning a gold medal. Drafted by Boston the previous year, he didn't play in the NHL until Washington signed him and brought him up for the 2000 playoffs. Since then, the utility centre has had trouble staying in the league, spending most of his time in the minors.

WHITLOCK, Bob
b. Charlottetown, Prince Edward Island, July 16, 1949

Known to have one of the hardest shots around, that reputation didn't get Whitlock much ice time at the NHL level. One game, in fact. He played with Minnesota in '69-'70, and when the chance came in 1972 to step into the WHA, Whitlock happily took it. He later finished in the minors.

WHITMORE, Kay
b. Sudbury, Ontario, April 10, 1967

In '90-'91, Whitmore led the Springfield Indians to the Calder Cup, and for his bravura playoff performance was named MVP. It was the highlight of a career that has seen him become the property of eight NHL teams, though his career in the big league is more or less over. Like a big kid, Whitmore just plays and plays and plays. He turned pro in 1987 and played a few games for Hartford the following year,

Kay Whitmore

working his way up such that four years later he was their starting goalie. He was out of the NHL by 1995, but made a career in the minors and lo and behold Boston used him five times in the 2000-01 season when the Bruins were trying to find a goalie of some NHL stripe. Whitmore played a game with Calgary the following year, and as long as he keeps battling in the minors, he might get yet another NHL shot.

WHITNEY, Ray
b. Fort Saskatchewan, Alberta, May 8, 1972

Imagine the incredible story that could have unfolded in the 1999-2000 season that would have seen Ray Whitney score an NHL goal against his father, Floyd! It was never close to happening, yet it wasn't that improbable, either, given the circumstances. As a

As a kid, Ray was a stick boy for the Oilers.
RAY WHITNEY

kid, Ray was a stick boy for the Oilers, mostly because his dad was the team's practice goalie for more than 17 years. Ray's brother, Dean, went on to play pro as a goalie, though he never made the NHL, but Ray did make it, as a left winger. He played parts of six seasons with San Jose, starting in 1991, and later moved on to Edmonton and then Florida. Whitney had 3 outstanding seasons with the Panthers, scoring 32, 26, and 29 goals. During this time, his dad continued to work Oilers practices, though by day he was head of the canine unit of the Edmonton Police Department. During an Oilers home game, against Washington, not Florida, goalie Bill Ranford was hurt. Backup Tommy Salo came in, and then the Oilers activated Floyd Whitney. They signed him to a contract and had him dress in case he was needed! Ray later played for Columbus when the Panthers unwisely traded one of their top scorers.

WHYTE, Sean
b. Sudbury, Ontario, May 4, 1970

Whyte played his only games with Los Angeles in the early 1990s and was a minor leaguer besides. He was also an avid roller hockey player in the summers, and after he retired in 2001 he started his own business called Northern Edge Hockey School. He had been a regular on the skating school circuit through his career, both roller and ice hockey. Whyte also won a gold medal in roller hockey with Team Canada.

WICKENHEISER, Doug ("Wick")
b. Regina, Saskatchewan, March 30, 1961
d. St. Louis, Missouri, January 12, 1999

In July 1994, Wickenheiser discovered a cyst on his wrist. It was removed, and for three and a half years he remained healthy until he developed a tumour on his lung. Seven agonizing bouts of chemotherapy at Columbia Presbyterian Hospital in New York reduced it, and then cancers were found on his brain. In early 1999, Wickenheiser finally succumbed, his once-perfect hockey body ravaged by disease. He was a prairie boy who was drafted 1st overall by Montreal in 1980, a move for which the Habs were excoriated for years because they passed up on local boy Denis Savard, who went on to have a Hall of Fame career. Wick did not. He was a disappointment in Montreal and later St. Louis and everywhere else he played, but he was fine player regardless, just not the superstar the 1st-overall selection should suggest. The high point of his career came in St. Louis when he finished a great comeback on May 12, 1986. Down 5-2 in the third, the Blues stormed back to tie the game, and Wickenheiser scored the winner in overtime against Calgary. He played in the minors and overseas until that cyst was discovered in 1994, but his sister, Hayley, went on to become arguably the greatest woman hockey player on the planet. A devout Catholic and respected player and person, Doug's loss was felt profoundly throughout the hockey world.

WIDING, Juha ("Whitey")
b. Uleaborg, Finland, July 4, 1947
d. Kelowna, British Columbia, December 30, 1984
Technically, Widing was the first Finnish-born player to make the NHL, but his parents were Swedish and Juha was raised in Sweden. He and three Swedes were invited by Brandon's GM Jake Milford to attend the team's junior training camp in 1964, and Widing was impressive enough that he stayed. Like any other player, he worked his way up through the system and joined the New York Rangers in 1969. He was traded to L.A. after half a season and spent parts of eight years with the Kings. In the 1976 Canada Cup, he played for Team Sweden. After retiring, he settled on his farm in the Okanagan Valley, but was of ill health and after a lengthy battle died in a Kelowna hospital at age 37.

WIDMER, Jason
b. Calgary, Alberta, August 1, 1973
A western boy who came through Lethbridge to get to the NHL, Widmer played just seven NHL games in the mid-1990s. During his time in the minors, he was a solid defenceman, but early in 1999 he suffered an awful knee injury that eventually ended his career.

WIEBE, Art
b. Rosthern, Saskatchewan, September 28, 1911
d. Edmonton, Alberta, June 6, 1971
When Art Wiebe retired in 1942, he was done with hockey. He retreated to Vermilion, Alberta, to run his bakery, but by training camp he was getting calls from the Hawks. He finally agreed to rejoin the team, but he couldn't find a soul in town to take over the store. Finally, just before Christmas, his father agreed to run the business, and Art returned to the Windy City for a 10th season with the Hawks. The next year, the same thing happened! Wiebe joined Chicago during the '32-'33 season, and by the start of the following year was teamed on the blueline with Earl Seibert. They played together for seven years, helping the team win the Cup in '37-'38, and developing into one of the top partnerships in Black Hawks history. Wiebe settled in Edmonton in 1948 and began a career in oil that saw him become president of Regent Drilling Limited. He also coached hockey at the University of Alberta from 1951 to '53. Wiebe died in 1971 of cancer, but not before leaving his mark on the NHL.

WIEMER, Jason
b. Kimberley, British Columbia, April 14, 1976
The expectations of being drafted 8th overall were greater than what Wiemer was capable of delivering at the NHL level, though he has developed into a bona fide player. Tampa Bay selected him in 1994, and the 18-year-old jumped directly into the NHL without a single game of minor pro under his belt. He has now played for four teams as an all-purpose centre, though he's not the man to score 20 goals or quarterback the power play.

WIEMER, Jim
b. Sudbury, Ontario, January 9, 1961
Few part-time careers lasted as long as Wiemer's. He turned pro with Rochester in 1981 as a Buffalo draft choice, but over the next 14 seasons played only 325 NHL games. He had a full season with the Sabres, for instance, but it was years before he had another, with Boston. He won a Cup with Edmonton in 1988, though, really, he wasn't a member of the team that won, playing only 12 regular-season games and two more in the playoffs. Ironically, he ended his career back in Rochester, coming full circle as it were, a big and reliable defenceman who actually started his career as a forward. That makes his AHL defenceman of the year honours for '85-'86 all the more impressive.

WILCOX, Archie
b. Montreal, Quebec, May 9, 1900
d. Brockville, Ontario, August 27, 1993
During his defence days with the Montreal Maroons, Wilcox was most memorably paired with Lionel Conacher on the blueline, Wilcox's defensive abilities perfectly balanced with the Big Train's love of rushing the puck. Wilcox was a big man and a hard hitter, and he played six seasons during the 1930s. He later settled in Verdun, where he ran a successful business and became the town's alderman and councillor.

His sister, Hayley, went on to become arguably the greatest woman hockey player on the planet.
DOUG WICKENHEISER

Juha Widing

Art Wiebe

Jason Wiemer

Jim Wiemer

Archie Wilcox

Arch Wilder

Jim Wiley

Barry Wilkins

John Wilkinson

Brian Wilks

WILCOX, Barry
b. New Westminster, British Columbia, April 23, 1948
His was a short pro career that began in the Vancouver system in 1971. Wilcox was called up twice, most importantly during the '72-'73 season when he played 31 games. But twice Wilcox suffered bad breaks of his right arm, limiting his development, and he was out of hockey by 1976.

WILDER, Arch
b. Melville, Saskatchewan, April 30, 1917
d. Calgary, Alberta, December 24, 2002
Most of Wilder's playing career occurred before and after the war out west, but in 1937 he played in Detroit and attracted the attention of Red Wings master GM Jack Adams. Jolly Jack put Wilder in Indianapolis, and from there the left winger was called up to play a few games with the NHL team. He returned west before the war, and joined the RCAF as a flying instructor stationed in Saskatoon. He then played senior hockey for six years in Calgary, scoring the lone goal in a 1-0 game to give the local Stampeders the Allan Cup title in 1946. Wilder worked briefly for Lonestar Drilling as a commercial pilot, and in 1953 he joined Canadian Gulf Oil in Calgary, working for that company until his retirement in 1980.

WILEY, Jim
b. Sault Ste. Marie, Ontario, April 28, 1950
In the 1970s, Wiley thought he deserved more of an NHL shot than he ever got. In five years with Pittsburgh and Vancouver he was a minor leaguer most of the time, and by the time he retired in 1980 it was in Tulsa and not Vancouver that he said his goodbyes. Wiley has had a long and successful career as a coach since then. He has been in the San Jose system for a dozen years, a time that peaked in '95-'96 when he was an assistant with the NHL team and took over as head coach when Kevin Constantine was fired. After a 17-37-3 record, though, he went back to Lexington to coach the Men O' War team, returning to that city again in 2002 when the ECHL granted it an expansion team (the Men O' War having since left).

WILKIE, Bob
b. Calgary, Alberta, February 11, 1969
After achieving any player's two dreams – playing in the NHL and scoring a goal – the few games Wilkie had were all gravy. He won the Memorial Cup with Swift Current in 1989 and went into the Detroit system that fall, but most of the next decade passed in the minors. Wilkie knew where his career was, and a bad back made him think more carefully about the future. In his later years he became a playing coach, and when his back finally gave out he became a head coach in Anchorage. He also opened a small coffee house in Palmyra, Pennsylvania, called Java the Hut.

WILKIE, David
b. Ellensburgh, Washington, May 30, 1974
The Canadiens goofed when they drafted Wilkie in the first round in 1992. He had played junior in Kamloops and represented the U.S. at two World Juniors, but the defenceman never met his expectations. He was an offensive defenceman pre-NHL, but speed of the opposition and lack of confidence forced him to back off that part of his game and focus on defence first. He played one full season with the Habs, '96-'97, and by 1999 he was in the minors. In 2001 he signed with the Augusta Lynx of the ECHL as a playing assistant coach, and after a year he retired to become the director of player development and assistant coach for the team.

WILKINS, Barry
b. Toronto, Ontario, February 28, 1947
One injury after another felled Wilkins, but he kept scooping himself off the trainer's table and going out for more. Year after year his body seemed to find stray pucks and wayward sticks and corners of the boards to take him out. He started in Boston, but made history in Vancouver after the Canucks selected him in the Expansion Draft in 1970. Wilkins scored the first goal in team history, one of just five he counted all season. He later played for Pittsburgh, and in 1976 left the NHL to play in the WHA for two years.

WILKINSON, Derek
b. Lasalle, Ontario, July 29, 1974
Goalie Derek Wilkinson was fed to the wolves during his limited NHL days, the wolves being Tampa Bay, with whom he played a smattering of games in the 1990s. The Lightning were an awful team, and Wilkinson had a record of 3-12-3 during his years there. He played mostly in the minors and in 2000-01 finished his career in Britain. In the summer of 2002 he was hired as an assistant coach with the Charlotte Checkers.

WILKINSON, John
b. Ottawa, Ontario, July 9, 1911
d. Ottawa, Ontario, January 19, 1970
A wartime player and participant both, Wilkinson had a lengthy career in Ottawa punctuated by a nine-game stint with Boston in '43-'44. He also served with the Essex Scottish Regiment during the war, after which he retired and settled in Ottawa.

WILKINSON, Neil
b. Selkirk, Manitoba, August 15, 1967
A litany of injuries plagued Wilkinson throughout his playing days, and in the end serious problems with his abdomen and groin forced him to retire in 1999. He had played an even 10 years in the NHL by that time, and although he never won a Stanley Cup he did go to the finals with Minnesota in 1991. He later played four seasons with Pittsburgh, the team that beat the North Stars in those finals, though he never got that close to the Cup again.

WILKS, Brian
b. Toronto, Ontario, February 27, 1966
In December 1980, injuries to the Toronto Marlies forced the team to call up 14-year-old Wilks from grade 9 to play a game. He scored a goal against Windsor, and became the youngest player in the OHL since Bobby Orr was 14. Unfortunately, comparisons to number 4 end there. Wilks played most of his junior in Kitchener and then played parts

of four seasons with the L.A. Kings. He spent some time in the minors and then moved to Israel, where he continued to play. He represented Canada in hockey at the 1997 Maccabiah Games and other international tournaments.

WILLARD, Rod
b. New Liskeard, Ontario, May 1, 1960
November 17, 1982, will remain fixed in the Willard family history as the night Rod played for the Maple Leafs, his one and only foray into the NHL. Soon after he was sent to Chicago for Dave Snopek, but Willard never played for the Hawks and Snopek never hit the ice with Toronto. Willard retired after a short time in the minors.

WILLIAMS, Burton "Burr"
b. Okemah, Oklahoma,
August 30, 1909
d. February 12, 1981
Given the fact that he made his first NHL appearance with Detroit in '33-'34, it goes without saying that Williams was the first Oklahoman to make it to the NHL for quite some time. He recorded an assist in that first game and the year after played for St. Louis and Boston. He played in the American league for a few seasons after that, and in 26 total NHL games he had that lone assist to show for his time.

WILLIAMS, Darryl
b. Mt. Pearl, Newfoundland,
February 9, 1968
There aren't too many points on a map of North America that are farther from each other than Newfoundland and Los Angeles, but Williams made the trip thanks to hockey. He was a career fighter in the IHL, but played two games with the Kings in '92-'93. He retired in 1999 to become assistant coach of Long Beach, the team for which he had played the previous three seasons, and after one year he became head coach. In 2002, he moved to Cincinnati of the AHL as an assistant.

WILLIAMS, Dave "Tiger"
b. Weyburn, Saskatchewan, February 3, 1954
You know those mittens kids sometimes wear, the ones attached by a string to prevent them from getting lost all the time? Even those Williams probably managed to drop to the ground to start or finish a fight. By the time he got to Swift Current, he was the stuff of legend. By the time he was through with the NHL, he had kicked the stuffing out of that legend. Tiger was the most penalized player in NHL history, and since hanging up the gloves in 1988 no one has come along to take away his record. Amazingly, though, Williams could also play the game. He scored 20 goals in a season for 3 different teams, and had a personal-

best 35 goals with Vancouver in '80-'81, a season in which he also played in the All-Star Game. Today's goons are lucky to get five goals; the best get, maybe, a dozen. Nowhere was Tiger more popular than in Toronto, where his career began in 1974. He joined a team that was building toward a Stanley Cup, but he was one of many victims when Punch Imlach arrived on the scene in 1979. Williams and Jerry Butler were traded to Vancouver for Rick Vaive and Bill Derlago, a lopsided deal for the Leafs because of how well Vaive performed in Toronto. Tiger later played for Detroit, Los Angeles, and Hartford, and in all he had 241 goals (by comparison, Dave Schultz had 79). He led the league in penalty minutes 3 times and finished with 3,966 minutes, which doesn't include another 455 in the playoffs. He was loved for his fighting, but also for his tenacity and goal celebrations, which featured riding his stick a distance on the ice while waving his free arm. Despite his penalty minutes, he was rarely a dirty player, although he was once charged with assault for an incident in Toronto in which he broke his stick over Dennis Owchar's head (he was acquitted). He was also known for his quick tongue and acerbic wit, most famously during a playoff series against Pittsburgh in which he said the Penguins were "done like dinner." After retiring, Williams settled in Vancouver but didn't settle down. He ran a dry cleaners and later did well in real estate, but admitted the adjustment to post-NHL life was horribly difficult. He later played roller hockey for years, and despite being in his forties his

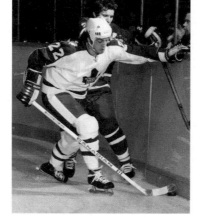

After retiring, Williams settled in Vancouver but didn't settle down.
TIGER WILLIAMS

feistiness didn't abate a jot. The Hanson brothers, of *Slap Shot* fame, campaigned to have Williams inducted into the Hockey Hall of Fame, though to date those efforts have not succeeded. Williams plays alumni events whenever possible, and he is to the next generation what Eddie Shack was before him – a much loved, somewhat skilled, brawling hockey nut.

WILLIAMS, David
b. Plainfield, New Jersey, August 25, 1967
Related by neither blood nor temperament to Tiger Williams, this David Williams was a Dartmouth College graduate in 1990. He played parts of four seasons with two expansion teams, San Jose and Anaheim, but was mostly a minor-league defenceman.

WILLIAMS, Fred ("Fats")
b. Saskatoon, Saskatchewan, July 1, 1956
In retrospect, it was a wasted pick, though at the time it made sense to Detroit when it selected him 4th overall in 1976. The Wings needed an all-purpose centre, and they were aware of Williams' abilities to

David Williams

Fred Williams

Justin Williams

Sean Williams

Tommy Williams

Shane Willis

skate on the power play, kill penalties, handle the puck, make plays, and score. They passed on Bernie Federko, Brian Sutter, Randy Carlyle, and a host of other future stars, and in Williams they got a player who appeared in only 44 games for the team. He was a minor leaguer the rest of the way, and in '80-'81 helped Maine win the Calder Cup.

WILLIAMS, Gord
b. Saskatoon, Saskatchewan, April 10, 1960
The younger brother of Fred, Gord had two one-game stints with Philadelphia in the early 1980s. He played his junior in Lethbridge before being drafted by the Flyers in 1979 and turning pro the following season.

WILLIAMS, Jason
b. London, Ontario, August 11, 1980
Undrafted, Williams has been slowly working his way into a Detroit lineup that is Stanley Cup successful and Hall of Fame intimidating. The youngster played junior in Peterborough, and time is still on his side as to whether he makes it or not.

WILLIAMS, Justin
b. Cobourg, Ontario, October 4, 1981
One of Philadelphia's bright young prospects, Williams has quickly worked his way into the Flyers lineup thanks to his hustle and tenacity. He debuted in 2000-01 and scored 12 goals, but the year after his confidence grew and as the season progressed he got more and more ice time. After the team was embarrassed in the first round of the playoffs against Ottawa, Williams flew to Sweden and joined Team Canada for the World Championships. He missed much of 2002-03, however, with a serious knee injury.

WILLIAMS, Sean
b. Oshawa, Ontario, January 28, 1968
In '87-'88, his final year of junior, Williams led the OHL in goals by scoring 58 times for Oshawa. This was sweet news for Chicago, which owned his NHL rights, but it was four years before he ever got a chance to play for the team and four years plus two games till his NHL career ended. He played the rest of his years in the minors.

WILLIAMS, Tommy
b. Duluth, Minnesota, April 17, 1940
d. Hudson, Massachusetts, February 8, 1992
A member of the U.S. Hockey Hall of Fame, Williams was inducted for good reason. He began his career as an amateur, helping the U.S. win a stunning gold at the 1960 Olympics in Squaw Valley. He turned pro later that year and joined Boston a season later. Amazingly, he was the only member of that 1960 team to play in the NHL. He played with the Bruins for eight years, during which time he was the only American-born player in the league. A right winger, he once scored 23 goals in a season, but was traded to Minnesota the season before the Bruins won the Cup. He started off well with the North Stars, but the '70-'71 season was created in hell and shipped to Williams' front porch. In November, he found his wife dead in their car, and was never able to determine if her death was a suicide or an accident. He started to fight with coach Jack Gordon and was suspended, and a trade to California didn't help him. Williams moved on to the WHA in 1972 to make a better paycheque and finished his career with the hopeless Washington Capitals their first two years in the league. His life turned around when he started to work for a large pipe manufacturing company and remarried, but in 1987 he was devastated again by the death of his 23-year-old son, Robert, who had been playing in the Bruins system. Tommy himself died early, the result of a heart attack suffered at home.

WILLIAMS, Tommy
b. Windsor, Ontario, February 7, 1951
The other Tommy, the east-coast Tommy, is better remembered and gets lots of ink, but this west-coast Tommy had his day in the sun as well. He played parts of three seasons with the Rangers, but it was clear he wasn't in their plans and it was in his best interest when the team sent him to Los Angeles. In the obscurity of California, Williams scored 114 goals in less than 6 seasons, topping off with 35 in '76-'77 during the heyday of the franchise. The Kings were never a playoff team, though, and Williams ended up in the minors, but he was no mean player at his peak.

WILLIAMS, Warren "Butch"
b. Duluth, Minnesota, September 11, 1952
Warren didn't have the personal problems that his brother Tommy had, nor did he have as long a hockey career. Butch played parts of three years in the mid-1970s, a time that culminated in his making Team USA for the 1976 Canada Cup. He also played in the 1977 World Championships before retiring. Williams returned home to Duluth, became manager of Fryberger Arena, and became active in coaching minor hockey.

WILLIS, Jordan
b. Kincardine, Ontario, February 28, 1975
In all likelihood, January 17, 1996, will go down as the one chance Willis had to play in the NHL. The goalie played a period of hockey (less a minute) and allowed a goal, but the 20-year-old went back to the minors and has been there ever since.

WILLIS, Shane
b. Edmonton, Alberta, June 13, 1977
Those who choose not to sign with the team that drafted them and opt to re-enter the draft do so at their own peril. Willis is another who was selected in a lower position his second time around, even though when Carolina took him in 1997 he had recently won a gold medal with Canada at the WJC. He was named the AHL's top rookie for '98-'99, and after another good year in the minors had a 20-goal season for the Hurricanes. After a poor start to the following year, though, he was traded to Tampa Bay.

WILLSIE, Brian
b. London, Ontario, March 16, 1978
After playing a single game with Colorado on January 9, 2000, Willsie felt ready to make the team

the following year. However, he hurt his back during training camp and missed almost half a season, and when he returned it was in Hershey where he led the team to the Calder Cup (while the Avs were winning the Stanley Cup). The year after, he was with the Avs, trying to establish himself as one of the bright young stars on a veteran team.

WILLSON, Don

b. Chatham, Ontario, January 1, 1914

In the years leading up to the war, Willson got into a few games with the Canadiens after returning from England, where he had been playing. He later played in the AHL and then in senior hockey, retiring soon after the war ended.

WILM, Clarke

b. Central Butte, Saskatchewan, October 24, 1976

Wilm has made the NHL strictly by the book. He went from junior in Saskatoon to the AHL in Saint John and made the Flames out of training camp in 1998. He has been a reliable third- or fourth-line player ever since, helping the team inch ever nearer the playoffs.

WILSON, Behn

b. Toronto, Ontario, December 19, 1958

In the off-hours, Wilson was a man who knew his Shakespeare and could recite – or intone – his Mikado. On the ice, he was a violent, unpredictable defenceman with the Flyers as the team was on the wane. The team had acquired a high draft choice from Pittsburgh in the hopes of getting Wilson in 1978, and he made the team that fall. In his five years with the Broad Street Bullies, Wilson had more than his share of fights and suspensions, but he was traded to Chicago and his hard hitting started to take its toll on his body. He suffered a back injury that forced him out of the game for a year in 1986, and less than a year later he aggravated the injury and was forced to retire. At his best, he was a tougher-than-tough defenceman; at his worst, he epitomized a second generation of Philadelphia goons in the shadow of the Cup wins in 1974 and '75.

WILSON, Bertwin "Bert" ("Beltin' Bert")

b. Orangeville, Ontario, October 17, 1949
d. Toronto, Ontario, February 28, 1992

Less than two years after Bill Masterton died after falling to the ice and hitting his head, Wilson almost replicated the fatal accident in a CHL game with Omaha in December 1969. He was skating hard to the net, was checked legally, and hit his head hard on the ice. He was taken off the ice unconscious and spent four days in hospital. The official diagnosis was a

severe concussion and scalp laceration; the layman's terminology was more direct – he was lucky to be alive. He recovered after a number of months and resumed his career, finally seeing the NHL in '73-'74 with the Rangers. The winger moved back to defence to get the most out of his career, which lasted eight years in the NHL and two final seasons in the minors. He died of stomach cancer at age 42.

WILSON, Bob

b. Sudbury, Ontario, February 18, 1934

Not to be confused with Chicago scout Bob Wilson, who worked at the same time this Bob Wilson played, he appeared in a single game with the Hawks in '53-'54. He then went on to a long and healthy career in the minors, primarily in the AHL.

Clarke Wilm

WILSON, Carey

b. Winnipeg, Manitoba, May 19, 1962

This is a story of the Wilson family, and it begins with Carey's father, Gerry. He was a fine teenaged player, but by the time he was 19 he had already had operations on both shoulders and his knees weren't much to kick over. He played three games with the Habs in the NHL, but his career was pretty much over because of his knees. So, he turned to sports medicine. He became a doctor and later took his family, Carey included, to Sweden where he, Gerry, learned all he could about the emerging field. In Sweden, the Wilsons met two fellows named Ulf Nilsson and Anders Hedberg, and when the family returned to Winnipeg, Gerry got a job as the Jets team

Bert Wilson

> **His right knee finally did him in, and he retired early in the '92-'93 season.**
> **CAREY WILSON**

Bob Wilson

doctor. He was important in bringing those two great Swedes to Canada to play in the WHA, and soon after Carey, hoping to follow in his father's footsteps, went to Dartmouth College to study pre-med. After two years, Carey decided to focus on hockey for the moment, so he moved to Finland in 1981 and played for Helsinki. Like a native, he also had a nine-to-five job, working in a shipping and receiving department. He did that for two years, developed as a player and got to know the language, then returned home to pursue the Olympic dream. That dream became reality when the average-scoring centre scored three goals in the first game of the 1984 Olympics in Sarajevo. After the tournament, he joined the Calgary Flames and for 5 years had at least 20 goals a season. Then the injuries came, and the good Lord rained down one after another on Carey's ever more battered body. His right knee finally did him in, and he retired early in the '92-'93 season. He never did emulate the Oilers' Randy Gregg and go into medicine, though. Instead, he started his own kids' hockey program year-round.

Cully Wilson

WILSON, Carol "Cully"

b. Winnipeg, Manitoba
d. Seattle, Washington, September 1962

It's difficult today to fully understand the abilities of tough guys, like Cully Wilson, from hockey's early days. Wilson would happily swing his stick mightily at an opponent's head, and upon getting out of the penalty box he was equally capable of making a tremendous play to score a goal. He played in an era long before terms such as *goon* or *enforcer* defined a player, but he was much more than that even though that's what got him notoriety. His real fame came as a fearless right winger. He starred with the Toronto Blueshirts in the NHA and with Seattle out west, winning a Cup with each team prior to the formation of the NHL. He joined the St. Pats in Toronto in 1919 and scored 20 goals in just 23 games. In all, he played 20 years of pro at a time when the NHL was not the only league around, and after retiring he settled in Seattle.

WILSON, Doug

b. Ottawa, Ontario, July 5, 1957

On paper, it looks simple. Born in Ottawa, he played junior in Ottawa. The reality, though, was that from ages three to six he lived in England, and later in Winnipeg, before returning to Ottawa. When Wilson did settle into the 67's lineup, he became one of the best defencemen that great franchise had ever seen. Chicago drafted him a lofty 6th overall in 1977, and this was one draft choice who did not disappoint. He apprenticed with Bobby Orr during Orr's short stay with the Hawks at the end of his career, and in no time at all Wilson was playing in Orr-like manner. In '81-'82, he scored 39 goals, the only defenceman other than Orr ever to score as many to that date. It was a season in which he was named to the First All-Star Team, won the Norris Trophy, and confirmed his status as one of the league's best. Wilson missed much of '87-'88 with a serious shoulder injury that doctors feared might end his career, but after successful surgery and rehab, he was back at it, scoring 23 goals 2 seasons later. He went to the Cup finals four times with the Hawks, though he never won, and played in seven All-Star Games. The last, in 1992, came as a member of San Jose, the team he chose to end his career with because of its youthful defence corps that he could work with almost like a playing assistant coach. San Jose was a good long-term fit for him, and he later returned to the organization. He was president of the NHLPA during his playing days, and during the lockout of '94-'95 he acted as honorary coach for the 99 All-Stars, the Wayne Gretzky team that played in Europe during this inactive NHL time. His first job after retiring was with the PA

In '81-'82, he scored 39 goals, the only defenceman other than Orr ever to score as many to that date.
DOUG WILSON

as coordinator of player relations and business development, and after four years he returned to the Sharks and became director of pro development for the team, a position he continues to hold. His number 7 was later retired by the 67's.

WILSON, Dune

b. Toronto, Ontario, March 22, 1948

Much as he loved the game, Wilson couldn't devote every waking minute to the game, and as a goalie he also absorbed losses better than most GMs would have liked. His character and personality earned him a reputation as a flake, though he was a perfectly competent stopper who had the misfortune to play goal on some very bad teams. Case in point, his first full year with the expansion Vancouver entry in '70-'71. Wilson had a GAA of 4.29, and his record was an embarrassing 3-25-2. In stops in Toronto and New York, he suffered a similar fate, being thrown to the wolves and then traded or released. His best year came with Pittsburgh in '76-'77 when he was a respectable 18-19-8, five of those wins coming with a shutout. Wilson was also a superb lacrosse player and golfer. He finished his playing days in Vancouver and then settled there to work as a longshoreman. He later relocated to Rossland, B.C., where he is a heavy equipment operator and consummate golfer. He also tends bar at the Rex Hotel in nearby Trail.

WILSON, Gerry (sometimes Jerry)

b. Edmonton, Alberta, April 10, 1937

Bobby Orr has nothing on this guy. He first had knee troubles at age seven. At 11, he had cartilage removed. By 18, he had had eight knee operations and cartilage removed four times. But he wanted to play hockey, and at 6'2" and 210 pounds, size was on his side. The Habs called him up for eight games and played him in three, but his knees simply gave out. Wilson returned to his home in Winnipeg and enrolled at U of Manitoba, where he became an orthopaedic doctor, learning all about his knees from the viewer's, not participant's, perspective. During his studies, he got a call from Punch Imlach in Toronto, offering him a contract and a chance to return. Wilson jumped at the opportunity, but when he could barely walk after only one practice, he knew his life did not have another day on ice in it. He studied science for four years, medicine another four, and orthopaedics for five before heading to Sweden for a year to study sports medicine. He later became team doctor for the Jets and helped the team acquire two great Swedes – Anders Hedberg and Ulf Nilsson – and his son, Carey, later had a fine hockey career of his own.

Dune Wilson

WILSON, Gord

b. Port Arthur, Ontario, August 13, 1932

Gordon "Phat" Wilson turned down an offer to play for the Bruins when he was in his prime, preferring to work in Port Arthur and play amateur hockey. He did, however, promise to send the Bruins any player he thought would make a great NHLer, and fulfilled that promise when he sent his son, Gord, to the B's in 1952. The young Wilson missed almost all of '53-'54 with a serious knee injury, but he was called up for the playoffs with Boston in 1955. He played in two games as centre to Ed Sandford and Fleming Mackell, and there was talk he was the big, lanky centre to replace Hall of Famer Milt Schmidt. He had a great shot, was a terrific stickhandler, could score like blazes, and came of good stock. Two years later, though, Wilson suffered another knee injury and never made it back to the NHL, his great hope and promise never realized.

WILSON, James "Hub"

b. Ottawa, Ontario, May 13, 1909
d. unknown

Wilson appeared in two regular-season games with the New York Americans in '31-'32 at the start of his career but played another decade in the American league without getting another shot at the NHL.

WILSON, Johnny ("Iron Man")

b. Kincardine, Ontario, June 14, 1929

The Wilson family migrated to Rouyn-Noranda when Johnny was quite small so his father could work in the mines. Johnny and brother, Larry, grew up with a shared love of hockey, and both had fine NHL careers. Johnny went from junior in Windsor to the Detroit system and started his career at the end of the '49-'50 season. His timing was impeccable, for the Wings went on to win the Cup that year, winning two best-of-seven series in the process. For Wilson, this marked not only the start of his career but also of a record 580 straight games, shattering Murray Murdoch's previous Iron Man record of 508. Wilson was a goal scorer in his Detroit years and won three more Cups (in 1952, '54, and '55) before moving on. He played for four of the six teams in the NHL, and at training camp in New York in 1961 he broke his collarbone and his games streak stopped. During the summers, Wilson worked for an Ontario brewery in sales, and when he retired in 1962 he moved to Owen Sound to work full-time for that company. He grew restless, though, and soon returned to the game as a coach, moving around North America with ease and frequency. Wilson coached at Princeton and in Cleveland as well as for numerous other minor-league teams. Through the 1970s he coached five NHL teams, including three years in Pittsburgh, his most successful stay. After leaving hockey, Wilson worked as a sales executive in manufacturing.

WILSON, Landon

b. St. Louis, Missouri, March 13, 1975

The comparisons to Cam Neely began early and continued often, but Wilson has not shown the heart and dedication needed to be another Neely, at least not yet. The son of former NHLer Rick, Landon grew up here, there, and everywhere, becoming an excellent football quarterback in his high school days. While at the University of North Dakota, he was drafted by the Leafs and then traded to Quebec in the big deal that sent Mats Sundin to Toronto in 1994. The Nordiques expected Wilson to make the team, but at his first training camp he broke a leg and couldn't skate until Christmas. He stayed with the team as it moved to Colorado, but the coaching staff was forever frustrated by his inconsistency and inability to raise his game to the next level. Since then, he has drifted to Boston and Phoenix, and it might just be that he has already reached his potential – it was just less than what admirers had anticipated.

Landon Wilson

He was all set to coach Adirondack for '79-'80 when he went jogging one day and collapsed, dying on the road of a heart attack.
LARRY WILSON

WILSON, Larry

b. Kincardine, Ontario, October 23, 1930
d. Queensbury, New York, August 16, 1979

An important part of the great Wilson hockey family, Larry made his own contributions in three ways. As an NHLer, he played for Detroit in the successful run to the 1950 Stanley Cup, his first of six seasons in the league. He spent most of his time in Chicago, but early in the '55-'56 season he was farmed to the minors, where stage two of his career took place. In all, Wilson played 19 years in the minors, mostly with Buffalo where the centreman was a regular 20-goal scorer. He finished his career in Dayton in 1970 and promptly took over as team coach, leading the Gems to Turner Cup championships in each of his first two seasons. Thus began phase three, as a coach, which took him to Providence, Richmond, and Baltimore until he landed with Detroit on an interim basis in '76-'77. He then returned to the minors, but tragedy struck in the summer of 1979. He was all set to coach Adirondack for '79-'80 when he went jogging one day and collapsed, dying on the road of a heart attack. He was 48. His brother, Johnny, also played and coached in the NHL, and Larry's four sons all played college hockey at Providence. One, Ron, went on to play in the NHL, and another, Randy, was a Detroit draft choice.

WILSON, Mike

b. Brampton, Ontario, February 26, 1975

Life got interesting for Wilson soon after being

Mike Wilson

Mitch Wilson

Murray Wilson

Rick Wilson

Roger Wilson

drafted by Vancouver in 1993. He, Michael Peca, and a first-round draft choice were traded to Buffalo for Alexander Mogilny and a fifth-round draft choice, and since then he's pushed on to Florida and Pittsburgh. Wilson is an intimidating presence, but the adage "the bigger they are, the harder they fall" holds true with him. At 6'6" he has done his fair share of pushing around, but has missed much of two recent seasons with serious shoulder troubles. His career hangs in the balance, awaiting his full recovery.

WILSON, Mitch
b. Kelowna, British Columbia, February 15, 1962
Some say that Wilson was, pound for pound, the toughest man in hockey. He played junior in Seattle, where he pounded the daylights out of any and all opponents, and New Jersey signed him as a free agent. He played just a few NHL games but made his living in the "I," mostly with Muskegon, and finished his career with the Louisville IceHawks of the ECHL. He stayed on with that team as an assistant coach for a short time, but eventually gravitated back to Seattle, where he became a tugboat operator.

WILSON, Murray
b. Toronto, Ontario, November 7, 1951
Born in Toronto and raised in Ottawa, when the family was in Canada, Murray and brother Doug were raised in a hockey environment by their Canadian Air Force dad, who moved the family to England for three years. Murray was a high Montreal draft pick, and made his debut in '72-'73, a Cup-winning season for the team. He played six seasons with the Habs, though he was plagued by serious injuries to a shoulder and knee (he had surgery on both knees at age 13 because of a football injury). He was traded to Los Angeles in 1978, a deal that was contingent upon him passing the team medical. He did, but a bad back limited his effectiveness. He cut his season short, but when doctors found out the extent of the damage, Wilson was forced to retire. He had to take the Kings to court to receive a disability payment of $230,000 because L.A. felt that Montreal should be on the hook for the payment since the injury began during Wilson's time with the Habs. An arbitrator begged to differ. Wilson returned to Ottawa where he worked as a leasing consultant with Turpin Pontiac-Buick and with agent Larry Kelly as a sports consultant.

WILSON, Rick
b. Prince Albert, Saskatchewan, August 10, 1950
As a defenceman, Wilson didn't have nearly the staying power and longevity he has had as a coach. He started with Montreal in the 1970s, but it was impossible at best to crack a Cup-winning lineup and the Habs traded him to St. Louis. He played three more seasons in the NHL and finished with a year in the minors before deciding on his future. When the chance came up in 1978 to be an assistant at his alma mater, University of North Dakota, he took it, and has been coaching ever since. He moved to junior as a head coach for eight years, and then to the NHL as an assistant. Since 1992 he has been with the Stars, first in Minnesota and then in Dallas, winning a Cup with the team in 1999.

WILSON, Rik
b. Long Beach, California, June 17, 1962
Of course, everyone in California has to be different, so Rick becomes Rik and instead of surfing decides to go to Kingston, Ontario, to play hockey. He played so well as an offensive defenceman that St. Louis drafted him 12th overall in 1980, but it took him a while to earn a spot in the lineup. For the better part of five years he was given a chance, then sent to the minors, until finally he was traded to Calgary, his point production and defensive play not what the Blues had been hoping for. Nothing different there. He played two games with the Flames and a few more with Chicago later, but Wilson's career turned minor pro in a hurry. He later played a bit in Europe before retiring, though he is co-owner (with numerous players) of the record for most assists in a period, with four.

WILSON, Roger
b. Sudbury, Ontario, September 18, 1946
After seven years in the minors, Wilson's NHL dream came true during the '74-'75 season when Chicago called him up for seven games. He was a tough guy in the Central and Eastern leagues, but never got into too much trouble with the Hawks. Wilson retired at the end of that season.

WILSON, Ron
b. Windsor, Ontario, May 28, 1955
Imagine the confusion in Toronto when the Leafs drafted Ron Wilson in 1975 and a year later another Ron Wilson (born in Toronto) was drafted by Montreal. The former actually played for the Leafs, but this Providence College graduate turned quisling on his country by becoming a successful head coach with various U.S. national teams. After spending most of his Leafs years in the minors, he played in Switzerland for a number of seasons and then found a nice loophole in NHL rules. For three years he played overseas and then joined Minnesota for the playoffs, a dual role that cannot be performed these days because the NHL stipulates that as soon as a player appears in a European league game he is no longer eligible for the NHL that season. Wilson retired in 1988 and has had three terms of coaching in the NHL, with Vancouver, Anaheim, and Washington. He took the Caps to the finals in 1998 but was fired in 2002, and along the way he led the U.S. to a World Cup victory over Canada in 1996. He also coached that team at the 1998 Olympics in Nagano. Most recently, he has worked at TSN, awaiting another head coaching position.

WILSON, Ron
b. Toronto, Ontario, May 13, 1956
Even while his NHL career was an ongoing concern, Wilson was an assistant coach in the minors, and when he retired, he got into the job full-time. He played junior with the Marlies in his native Toronto and joined Winnipeg in 1979, the Jets' first year in the NHL. Oddly, his best year was his rookie season, when he had 21 goals and 57 points, and over the course of his 14 years in the big league he saw periodic duty in the minors. Wilson played nine years in Winnipeg and four more in St. Louis, but for most of '88-'90 he was in the AHL, playing and working as an

assistant with Moncton. He ended his career in that capacity with Wheeling, and in 1996 became solely an assistant in Springfield. After four years he joined the Saint John Flames, helping the team to a 2000-01 Calder Cup championship.

WILSON, Ross "Lefty"

b. Toronto, Ontario, October 15, 1919
d. Marco Island, Florida, November 5, 2002

Never before and never again will a character like Wilson grace the NHL, a league that would have been the lesser without him. He was a rink rat, really, a trainer and practice goalie, nothing more, yet he played in three NHL games with three different teams as an emergency replacement. He played in the Detroit system until after the war when he joined the Red Wings. On the night of October 10, 1953, he replaced the injured Terry Sawchuk in the third period of a Detroit-Montreal game, and for the final 16 minutes he shut out the Habs. Stranger, though, were his next two appearances. On January 22, 1956, Toronto's Harry Lumley was injured and the Detroit employee had to play for his enemies, the Leafs! Detroit players were none too pleased by his shutout work for 13 minutes, though the Wings held on to their lead and won 4-1 anyway. On December 29, 1957, Boston's Don Simmons was injured early in the game, no laughing matter for the Wings. Wilson played brilliantly in a 2-2 tie (he allowed only 1 goal in 52 minutes) and, of course, no more bizarre a sight was there in the NHL than seeing Wilson head off the ice in a Boston sweater and go to the Detroit dressing room to clean up after the men he had just stoned all night! In 1958, he retired as Detroit's practice and replacement goalie to become the team's full-time trainer, inheriting the throne from the retiring Carl Mattson. Wilson stayed with the team for another quarter-century until being unceremoniously dumped by Mike Ilitch shortly after the pizza baron took control of the team.

WILSON, Wally

b. Berwick, Nova Scotia, May 25, 1921

After playing junior in Oshawa, Wilson didn't get very far before the war caught his patriotic attention. He played a year in the minors and then became a flight instructor for the RCAF. After discharge, Toronto put him into its system, but the Leafs sold the centre to Boston, where he played the '47-'48 season, his last in pro hockey.

WING, Murray

b. Thunder Bay, Ontario, October 14, 1950

On April 7, 1974, Wing got into his first and only NHL game, with Detroit, and recorded an assist. It came at the end of a season he had spent playing for the London Lions, Detroit's European experiment of a farm team. It was his last year of serious pro hockey, as Wing returned to Thunder Bay.

WINKLER, Harold "Hal"

b. Gretna, Manitoba, March 20, 1892
d. Winnipeg, Manitoba, May 30, 1956

One of the greatest goalies in the years immediately after the First World War, Winkler went on to make a dramatic entrance in the NHL in 1926 with the New York Rangers during their inaugural season. Previously, Winkler had played out west, and although he played just two NHL seasons, they were two for the record books. He recorded a shutout in his first game and had two in just eight games with the Blueshirts. Winkler was sold to Boston midway through the year, and it was with the B's he became a legend. In just 67 games over 2 years he had 19 shutouts. In his only full season, he played all 44 games and led the league with 15 blank sheets, still a single-season record for the Bruins. After retiring, Winkler returned to Winnipeg where he owned a mink farm and sold life insurance.

WINNES, Chris

b. Ridgefield, Connecticut, February 12, 1968

If there is a minor pro team for which Winnes hasn't played, it must be in a pretty small town or league because he has been everywhere and knows how far it is. Like many an American, Winnes chose college over Canadian junior (in his case, the University of New Hampshire) and turned pro with Boston. It became quickly apparent that he was bound for the minors, but as fate would have it he was traded and released, signed and moved on, more times than most circus acts. Nonetheless, the name of the game is to play, and that he has done for more than a decade now, regardless of where he calls home.

WISEMAN, Brian

b. Chatham, Ontario, July 13, 1971

His best year came when he was 10 years old. Wiseman scored 413 goals in 80 games at the atom level, and everyone was calling him the next Gretzky. But as the years went on, he didn't develop at that superstar pace, and the expectations were tremendous on a kid not yet a teenager. He wound up in junior B but his size became an ever more dispiriting factor as he remained 5'7" or 5'8". Nonetheless, Red Berenson had scouted Wiseman and offered him a full scholarship in 1990. After four years and a brief foray into the pro ranks, he returned the favour by rejoining the Wolverines after he retired. Along the way he

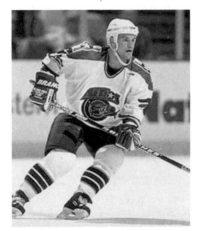

He played three games for the Leafs in '96-'97, but had his best years in the "I" with Houston.
BRIAN WISEMAN

Wally Wilson

Murray Wing

Chris Winnes

Eddie Wiseman

Jim Wiste

Jim Witherspoon

Brendan Witt

played three games for the Leafs in '96-'97, but had his best years in the "I" with Houston. In '98-'99, he led the league in scoring and was named MVP. He retired a year later, still in his prime, to take a job with U of M and later moved on to coach with the Houston Aeros.

WISEMAN, Eddie
b. Newcastle, New Brunswick, December 28, 1912
d. Red Deer, Alberta, May 4, 1977
Consistent and dependable were terms that needed to apply to any player in the six-team NHL, and Wiseman lived up to them. He started his career with Detroit in 1932 and for four years played regularly on the right wing. Although he played as long with the Americans, it was in Boston that he had his finest flourish. Playing on a line with Roy Conacher and Art Jackson, he led the league in playoff scoring in 1941 with six goals as the Bruins won the Cup. His career ended when he enlisted in the RCAF. He spent more than two years as a flying officer, and when he came out there were no NHL vacancies. Wiseman settled in Red Deer, Alberta, where he ran two very successful businesses in real estate and insurance, Robert-Wiseman Realty and Wiseman-Coupland Insurance Ltd.

WISTE, Jim
b. Moose Jaw, Saskatchewan, February 18, 1946
The University of Denver was as wonderful a place to play hockey as the old Colorado Rockies were nightmarish. Wiste falls into the former category as a result of the scholarship he was given in 1964 to play the game and get an education. How could he know then that the school would play such a prominent role in his life? He captained the '67-'68 team to a national championship in his senior year and then turned pro with Chicago. He got into only a few games and ended up in the minors and later the WHA, retiring in 1975. Wiste returned to Denver and bought the Campus Lounge, a bar/restaurant that is key to student life at U of D. In 2000, he was inducted into the university's athletic hall of fame for his four-year career in the 1960s, and the boy from Moose Jaw became as Denver as the snow in the mile-high mountains.

WITEHALL, Johan
b. Goteborg, Sweden, January 7, 1972
He came, he tried, he went home. He came from Swedish league hockey; he tried to make the Rangers in 1998 and the next three years; he returned to resume his European career when he made it with neither the New Yorkers nor the Canadiens, to whom he was sent during the 2000-01 season. He split 2002-03 between the Hamburg Freezers in Germany and Leksand back home in Sweden.

After leaving hockey, Woit worked as a grain trimmer, loading boats in Lake Superior harbour until retiring in the early 1980s.
BENNY WOIT

WITHERSPOON, Jim
b. Toronto, Ontario, October 3, 1951
Ohio State University has a renowned football program, but Witherspoon went there for hockey in 1970. Four years later, he was still undrafted, but later that summer Los Angeles signed him and put him in its system. A year and a half later he played his only two NHL games and was out of hockey just a short time later.

WITIUK, Steve
b. Winnipeg, Manitoba, January 8, 1929
In a 20-year pro career that ended in Spokane in 1969, Witiuk played half a season with Chicago in the early 1950s. He was a prolific scorer in the WHL, but in the NHL managed just three goals. Although he was later Leafs property, he never played for the Blue and White. He did, though, win a WHL championship with Calgary in '53-'54, and in 1997 he was inducted into the Manitoba Sports Hall of Fame.

WITT, Brendan
b. Humboldt, Saskatchewan, February 20, 1975
The advice given by agents is sometimes frightening for its lack of logic. Washington drafted Witt 11th overall in 1993, meaning the Caps considered him a top-flight prospect. The next year, he helped Canada win gold at the WJC, but after that final season of junior he sat out a full season in a contract dispute. Had he settled for less money and played, he might have developed into a superstar defenceman who could command a very high salary in his prime years. Instead, his growth and development were stunted for a year, and although he has been with the Caps ever since, he is by no means a top 10 defenceman in the league and he will never be considered a prime candidate for Team Canada. Solid, yes. Spectacular, no.

WOCHY, Steve
see **WOJCIECHOWSKI, Steve**

WOIT, Benedict "Benny"
b. Fort William, Ontario, January 7, 1928
Even in the six-team days when defencemen weren't supposed to score goals, Woit was famous for not scoring at all. In five full seasons plus bits of two others, he tallied a grand total of seven, often going dozens of games between scores. Nonetheless, he was the proverbial hard rock on the Detroit blueline during their greatest years. Woit developed on the farm in Indianapolis, and in 1951 made the Wings as a regular. He won three Cups in the next four years, and after being demoted to the minors became a playing coach. In '57-'58, he was a defensive coach for Rochester while

still playing for the team, and he later captained and coached in Providence and Clinton. After leaving hockey, Woit worked as a grain trimmer, loading boats in Lake Superior harbour until retiring in the early 1980s.

WOJCIECHOWSKI, Steve
(sometimes Steve Wochy)
b. Fort William, Ontario, December 25, 1922

In many ways, Foster Hewitt was the most powerful man in hockey during his time. He brought the game to the people, to Canadians from coast to coast who had no other means of connecting to hockey. So, when he decreed that the name Wojciechowski was unpronounceable, something had to be done. In the clearing of a throat, the name was shortened to Wochy. Wochy tried out for the New York Americans in 1939, but he was not yet ready for the pro grade. He played in Port Arthur and then enlisted in the army, a stint that lasted only a year because he was discharged with a stomach problem. Once he recovered, Wochy earned a tryout with Detroit, and in '44-'45 he made his NHL debut with the Wings. The right winger and sometime centreman set a team record for points by a rookie with 39, but it was to be his only full season in the league. He was sent to Indianapolis the next year, and the year after that he played his final five NHL games before becoming a star in the minors. He spent the next nine years in the AHL, mostly with Cleveland, and became known as one of the league's top goal getters. He never made it back to the NHL, though.

WOLANIN, Craig
("Wooly")
b. Grosse Pointe, Michigan, July 27, 1967

"Team" is a concept lived day by day. No finer example of this can be seen than in Edmonton. When Steve Smith scored an own goal that eliminated the Oilers from the 1986 Cup chase, he was supported by his teammates, and when they won the next year Wayne Gretzky handed the Cup to him before all other players to say all is forgiven. When Wolanin made a critical blunder with Colorado in the 1996 playoffs that led to a lost game against Chicago, goalie Patrick Roy told coach Marc Crawford not to play Wolanin for the rest of the playoffs. Crawford didn't, and for the next 13 games the 11-year veteran watched from the press box as the Avs went on to win the Cup. He was traded to lowly Tampa Bay in the summer. That '95-'96 season had been a painful one for Wolanin, who had serious shoulder surgery in the summer before joining the Lightning. He had been a 3rd-overall draft choice in 1985 by New Jersey, but his effectiveness was always represented by good team defence rather than great personal stats in goals and

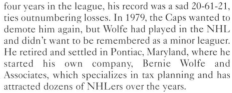

He was later named to the board of directors of the Catholic Social Services of Wayne County in his home state.
CRAIG WOLANIN

assists. He played for the U.S. at the 1991 Canada Cup and in two World Championships, but his last years were marred by injury. After the shoulder came lost years because of a knee injury, and he retired with a whimper rather than a bang. He was later named to the board of directors of the Catholic Social Services of Wayne County in his home state.

WOLF, Bennett
b. Kitchener, Ontario, October 23, 1959

He averaged more than four penalty minutes a game in his meagre NHL career, but that merely crystallized his role wherever he went. Wolf turned pro in 1979 and played only for the Penguins in the NHL, but in the AHL he was a ferocious and intimidating presence during his short career. Who's afraid of the big bad Wolf? Everyone. As he said, if the crowd isn't booing him (on the road), he's not doing his job.

WOLFE, Bernie
b. Montreal, Quebec, December 18, 1951

It was both a dream and a nightmare, playing in the NHL on the one hand, playing for Washington in the 1970s on the other. The Montreal-born goalie would never have had a chance to play for the Canadiens, so when the expansion Capitals wanted to sign him in 1974, he accepted. Wolfe started in the minors with Richmond, but such was the state of the team that in no time he was called up to face NHL rubber for 60, non-stop minutes. In his first season, Wolfe had a record of 5-23-7 and was hailed as the team's saviour. Over the course of his four years in the league, his record was a sad 20-61-21, ties outnumbering losses. In 1979, the Caps wanted to demote him again, but Wolfe had played in the NHL and didn't want to be remembered as a minor leaguer. He retired and settled in Pontiac, Maryland, where he started his own company, Bernie Wolfe and Associates, which specializes in tax planning and has attracted dozens of NHLers over the years.

WONG, Mike
b. Minneapolis, Minnesota, January 14, 1955

Centre Mike Wong played 22 games for Detroit in '75-'76 as a 20-year-old and only 3 and a half more years in the minors. He had played a year of junior in Montreal, after which the Wings drafted him, but it was clear he was not in the team's long-term plans when he was demoted.

WOOD, Alex
b. Falkirk, Scotland, January 15, 1911
d. Fort Wayne, Indiana, April 1979

The record books will show that Wood played a single

Bennett Wolf

Bernie Wolfe

Mike Wong

Alex Wood

Dody Wood

Randy Wood

Paul Woods

Jason Woolley

game in goal in the NHL, on January 31, 1937. He replaced Alfie Moore in the cage for the New York Americans in a 3-3 tie with the Maroons during his lengthy minor-league career, but had his greatest impact after he retired. Wood was raised in Ottawa. He was the first-ever coach of the Fort Wayne Komets in the new IHL, helping to establish the game and league in that city. He later coached Toledo, Louisville, and other teams, but made Fort Wayne his home for the rest of his days.

WOOD, Dody
b. Chetwynd, British Columbia, March 18, 1972
In 2001, after nine years in pro hockey, Wood decided to leave North America and play in Britain. He was a fighter who played all his NHL games with San Jose, though that comprised a mere 106 games over those years. He played mostly for the farm team in Kansas City, and when he was traded to New Jersey in 1997, a competitive team with no job openings for a goon, he knew his chances of returning to the NHL were slim. He averaged nearly five penalty minutes a game with the Sharks.

WOOD, Randy
b. Princeton, New Jersey, October 12, 1963
For many hockey players, the sport is the very fibre of life, the thing that gives meaning to waking up and staying sharp and earning a living. For Wood, it was ancillary. He was born in one great Ivy league town and went to school in another, New Haven (Yale University). He graduated in 1986 with a degree in economics and political science, but was also a pretty fair hockey player and decided to give that a try first. Over the course of 11 years, he was an altogether reliable and unspectacular forward, a utility man who could score and kill penalties and play a system and give 20 goals to the team per annum. He began and ended with the Islanders and in between appeared for Buffalo, Toronto, and Dallas. After retiring in 1997, he pursued education-oriented interests and became a successful investment banker in Manhattan.

WOOD, Robert
b. Lethbridge, Alberta, July 9, 1930
In a short career, Wood played one game with the Rangers in '50-'51 during the regular season and was never heard of again. He had been recruited by the Blueshirts in Alberta and played the rest of that season for the minor-league affiliate, the Rovers.

WOODLEY, Dan
b. Oklahoma City, Oklahoma, December 29, 1967
Drafting Woodley 7th overall in 1986 was not Vancouver's finest hour. Although Woodley had had a

good career in junior with Portland, he scored just two goals in five games for Vancouver and was soon traded to Montreal. The Habs never played him in the NHL, and for years Woodley roamed around the minors. He played roller hockey for the Vancouver Voodoo and re-signed with the Canucks in 1994, but never made it back with the team before retiring at season's end.

WOODS, Paul ("Woodsy")
b. Hespeler, Ontario, April 12, 1955
At first, it really was too good to be true. Woods was drafted by Montreal in 1975, and a year later attended his first training camp with the team after spending a year in the minors. Just a few minutes after stepping on the ice for the first time that season, Jim Roberts fell awkwardly on him and broke Woods' ankle. Montreal let him go after that season, Detroit claimed him, and it was with the Wings that he played all of his seven NHL seasons. Over the years, a bone spur in his hip and other injuries took away his best asset, his speed, and he retired midway through the '84-'85 season, which he spent in the minors. Woods was a great checker and penalty killer, but he played for the Wings at a low point in their history and never went far in the playoffs. He did play for Canada at the 1979 World Championships, though, one of his finer career moments. He later remained in Detroit where he worked in sales for Kord Industries in the car business. He also helped his family run a retirement home in Windsor.

> **In the summer of 1963, his life changed when he was traded to Montreal, a city that expected to win.**
> GUMP WORSLEY

WOOLLEY, Jason
b. Toronto, Ontario, July 27, 1969
A two-sport athlete in his teen years, Woolley played baseball and hockey at Michigan State University. In the summer of 1990, he won a bronze medal with Canada at the World Championships of baseball, just weeks after winning an NCAA championship with the hockey team at MSU. He spent all of '91-'92 with the Canadian National Team, winning a silver at the 1992 Olympics in Albertville, and then turned pro with Washington. A solid defenceman, Woolley also has offensive ability. He moved on to Florida and Pittsburgh before landing with Buffalo, his team of choice since 1997. He was part of the Sabres who went to the Cup finals in 1999 and has been one of their more reliable and consistent blueliners. In 1999, he was named one of the team's alternate captains.

WORRELL, Peter
b. Pierrefonds, Quebec, August 18, 1977
There are so many talented players in the international NHL these days that a great argument for fewer teams suggests there would be no room for detritus like Worrell to remain in the league. A goon

and disturber, his puck skills are minimal. In fact, his very efforts to try to score or create scoring chances are so close to zero it's amazing Florida has managed to keep him on its roster since 1997. In his final two seasons of junior, he accrued an odious 901 penalty minutes, and with the Panthers he has continued his brawling, mauling ways. He averages about four goals a year and more than four penalty minutes a game, and off the ice he is no angel, either. In the summer of 2001, he was charged with seven criminal violations having to do with driving, notably driving under the influence, leaving the scene of an accident, and kicking a police cruiser's window after arrest.

WORSLEY, Lorne "Gump"

b. Montreal, Quebec, May 14, 1929

The long and award-laden career of the Gumper might never have occurred had he played in the modern era, for his first coach likely would have sent him home and told him not to come back until he was in shape. Worsley was many things great in a goalie, but he was chunky even on a good day. He earned his nickname when Rangers teammate Phil Watson likened him to a comic-strip character of the same name, but it wasn't until he was 23 that the Gumper played in the NHL at all. From 1948 to 1952 he played with a series of minor-league teams, winning best goalie and rookie of the year honours with St. Paul of the USHL in '50-'51. He played the following year in the Pacific Coast league, and in '52-'53 the Rangers called him up. Worsley had an outstanding rookie season playing on a weak Rangers team. Despite his record of 13-29-8 he won the Calder Trophy, but the year after he was back in the minors, spending the entire season with Vancouver of the WHL. As a result, he holds the ignominious distinction of being the only Calder winner not to play a single NHL game in the year after winning. He was the best goalie in the WHL that year and the Rangers brought him up again the year after. He played three-and-a-half seasons before landing in the minors again, and he was up and down twice more during his 11 years in the New York system. He was above .500 only twice, but the team rarely made the playoffs and never made it to the finals during these years. In the summer of 1963, his life changed when he was traded to Montreal, a city that expected to win. But again, for his first two years he was mostly in the minors, though he was called up to the team toward the end of the '64-'65 season, a Cup-winning year for the Habs. Worsley had his best year in '65-'66 when he played 51 games and had a record of 29-14-6 and a GAA of 2.36. He shared the Vezina Trophy with Charlie Hodge that

year and won the Cup, and he split the duties in net for the next three-and-a-half seasons. He shared another Vezina in 1967-68 (with Rogie Vachon), but retired early in the '69-'70 season while sitting at O'Hare airport in Chicago. Back in 1949, he had been on a plane where one of the wings caught fire. The pilot had to perform an emergency landing, and since that time Worsley had had a terrible fear of flying. That day early in the '69-'70 season was harrowing for him because in the modern NHL of 12 teams air travel was a necessity and a constant. (Irony of ironies, one of his sons became a pilot in the Canadian Air Force!) The Gumper took the train home and vowed never to get on a plane again, but late in the season Minnesota GM Lou Nanne coaxed him out of retirement with a few incentives (such as $500 per win and $100 per shutout). Worsley stuck around another four years, but it was only in that last six games of his career that he wore a facemask. At 44, he finally hung up the pads and retired to the safety of Montreal, though he became a scout for the North Stars. He was inducted into the Hockey Hall of Fame in 1980.

Worters won the Hart Trophy in '28-'29, the first goalie so honoured.
ROY WORTERS

WORTERS, Roy ("Shrimp")

b. Toronto, Ontario, October 19, 1900
d. Toronto, Ontario, November 7, 1957

Blood, Worters used to say, was no reason to leave the nets. The only time a goalie had a right to complain was if he were hit in the eye such that his vision was blurred and he couldn't see the puck properly. At 5'3" and 125 pounds he was the lightest goalie ever to play the game – but he had the attitude of a giant. Worters grew up in Toronto with Lionel Conacher, and the two helped Parkdale win the Memorial Cup in 1920. The pair went down to Pittsburgh in 1923 to play for the Yellowjackets, and they stayed with the team, renamed the Pirates, when it joined the NHL in 1925. Despite playing on a poor team, Worters was astounding in goal. He was fearless and quick, and defied opponents to beat him with their hardest shots. He had 22 shutouts with Pittsburgh on a team that played all of two playoff games in that span, and in 1928 he was traded to the New York Americans, the team with which he spent the rest of his career. Worters won the Hart Trophy in '28-'29, the first goalie so honoured, after a year in which he had a record of 16-12-10 and a remarkable 1.15 GAA. Of those 16 wins, 13 came by shutout, an unheard of ratio. Two years later, he won the Vezina Trophy with a GAA of just 1.61, becoming the first goalie to win both the Hart and Vezina during his career. In his 12 years in the NHL, Worters played 484 regular season games and was as good a goalie as there ever was. But

Peter Worrell

the teams he represented were weak in the extreme, and he never won a Cup and made just 11 playoff appearances. After retiring, he returned to Toronto where he opened his own hotel just outside city limits. It was there many players past and present visited for a chat and a quiet, private drink or look at the day's racing form. He sold the hotel in the early 1950s and spent his final years battling throat cancer, eventually succumbing to the disease in 1957. Worters was inducted into the Hockey Hall of Fame in 1969.

WORTHY, Chris
b. Bristol, England, October 23, 1947

Chris Worthy

Rare is the goalie who can claim to have finished his junior career with quite the same flourish of the stick as Worthy. In '67-'68 in Flin Flon, he had a record of 47-8-5 and recorded 10 shutouts. From there he was traded by Detroit to Oakland with Howie Young, Doug Roberts, and Gary Jarrett for Bobby Baun and Ron Harris. Needless to say, that sparkling junior record could not be replicated with the hapless Seals. In 26 career games over 3 seasons, Worthy allowed 4.5 goals a game and sported a record of 5-10-4. He spent some time in the minors and then fled to the WHA, where he had better luck with the Oilers as a backup at the end of his career.

WORTMAN, Kevin
b. Saugus, Massachusetts, February 22, 1969

In the summer of 2002, Wortman suddenly retired from pro hockey because of unspecified family problems. He had been playing in Austria after two years in Germany and three in Finland, where he had established himself as a popular and skilled player. Wortman started his career in the Calgary system, but after only five games with the Flames and five years in the minors, he headed to Europe.

WOTTON, Mark
b. Foxwarren, Manitoba, November 16, 1973

A "sports hernia" is becoming an increasingly problematic injury for hockey players. Often misdiagnosed, it is painful and takes a long time to recover from, time most fringe players don't have. Wotton came out of Saskatoon in 1994 and played in the Vancouver system for five years. An offensive defenceman, he had no problem playing effectively in the minors, but could not make the Canucks on a full-time basis. In 1999, he signed with Dallas and was assigned to Kalamazoo, and that's when the real trouble began. A stomach pain was called a groin pull by the trainers, and Wotton struggled to finish the season. Doctors finally saw the hernia for what is was

and performed surgery, but Wotton didn't abide by the four-month recovery time and attended Stars training camp instead. This, of course, exacerbated his troubles, and a double hernia was discovered, requiring more surgery and a longer layoff. Finally, midway through 2001-02, he was back on the ice and pain-free, his recovery complete (and his fingers crossed), but he was still a ways away from a regular spot with Dallas.

WOYTOWICH, Bob ("Augie")
b. Winnipeg, Manitoba, August 8, 1941
d. Winnipeg, Manitoba, July 30, 1988

During his years in Pittsburgh, Woytowich was the most popular player on the team. He even had his own cheering section, called the Polish Army, which he laughed about because it was actually of Ukrainian descent. He began his career in Boston in 1964 and by a circuitous route in the summer of expansion he ended up with Minnesota and later the Penguins. Woytowich was an offensive defenceman who liked to go with the puck and get involved in scoring, but in his own end he was known for his long stick and pokechecking abilities. In 1972, he jumped at the chance to play for his native Jets when the WHA formed. After retiring, he settled into a job in the lumber business but was killed in a single-car accident in which his vehicle struck a light standard. Police fear he may have suffered a heart attack before the crash. He was just 46 years old.

In the lockout-shortened year of '94-'95, Wregget had a record of 25-9-2.
KEN WREGGET

Bob Woytowich

WREGGET, Ken
b. Brandon, Manitoba, March 25, 1964

The brave new beginning that was supposed to be Toronto in the early 1980s never came to be. Wregget, big and disciplined, and Alan Bester, small and quick, were supposed to be the goaltenders who would take the Leafs to the playoffs with a rebuilt team. Over six years, though, they proved unequal to the task, and the players in front of them didn't help matters any. Yet, it was 18 years later that Wregget played his final pro game. He was traded from the Leafs to Philadelphia and then on to Pittsburgh, and in his seven seasons with the Pens he won a Stanley Cup and had his finest years, now the mature goalie the Leafs had been hoping for. In the lockout-shortened year of '94-'95, Wregget had a record of 25-9-2, but he became more of a backup to Tom Barrasso, a backup who could take over at any time if the number-one man wasn't consistent. Wregget ended his career in Calgary and Detroit and finished with 225 total wins. He never played in an All-Star Game or won personal honours, but he was a goalie who survived much, much longer than most.

WREN, Bob

b. Preston, Ontario, September 16, 1974

In one generation there was Bruce Boudreau, in another there is now Bob Wren, a small player with terrific skills who has "minors" tattooed on his forehead. He has played a few games with Anaheim and Toronto, but in the AHL he has been a prolific scorer and occasional star. In '97-'98, he led the AHL with 42 goals and had 100 points, and although other years haven't been quite as sensational, Wren will have employment down below for as long as he wants.

WRIGHT, Jamie

b. Kitchener, Ontario, May 13, 1976

After winning a gold medal with Canada at the 1996 World Juniors, Wright turned pro in the Dallas system, though he could never make the team as anything more than a callup. He was traded to Calgary, a weaker team, which gave him a chance to play every night. It also gave him a chance to represent his country at the World Championships, which he did with pride in 2002. He scored the game-winning goal against the U.S. in a 2-1 preliminary-round win, one of the most important goals of his career so far.

WRIGHT, John

b. Toronto, Ontario, November 9, 1948

Success followed Wright everywhere, but the versatile athlete was not limited to hockey. He attended UCC in Toronto where he played football, and then played for the Marlies with whom he won the Memorial Cup in 1967. Although the Leafs had drafted him, he enrolled at U of T instead, taking a four-year program in phys ed. Under coach Tom Watt, Wright and the U of T Blues won the CIAU championship all four years, after which Wright's stock was at its peak. He signed a lucrative contract with the Canucks, but after a decent rookie season was on his way to St. Louis and then Kansas City. Wright was an accomplished golfer and sailor as well, and also worked at the Lakeshore Hockey School as an instructor.

WRIGHT, Keith

b. Aurora, Ontario, April 13, 1944

Montreal, the Rangers, Boston, and Philadelphia all owned his rights at some point, but only the Flyers, in their first season, gave Wright an NHL chance. He spent just a few seasons in the minors before retiring.

WRIGHT, Larry

b. Regina, Saskatchewan, October 8, 1951

Although he was a high draft choice by Philadelphia in 1971, Wright could muster only 4 goals in 104 NHL games. He played eight years of pro, five in the NHL, but only the '77-'78 season with Detroit was a full year without a long stay in the minors. He retired a year later.

WRIGHT, Tyler ("Ty")

b. Kamsack, Saskatchewan, April 6, 1973

A two-time member of the Canadian junior team at the WJC, Wright won gold in 1993 and saw his first NHL action with Edmonton. He was never able to work himself into the Oilers lineup, but when he was traded to Pittsburgh his career came to life a bit. He

has had his best years with Columbus, the team that claimed him in 2000. Wright scored 16 goals in 2000-01 and became an alternate captain, by now an experienced pro on a new team playing under difficult circumstances.

WYCHERLEY, Ralph ("Bus")

b. Saskatoon, Saskatchewan, February 26, 1920

Coming straight out of Brandon onto the New York Americans in 1940, Wycherley was counted on to score goals and fill in whenever he was needed. He was a bit of a disappointment in these regards, and after spending some time in the Canadian army he played in the minors where he fit the bill perfectly, scoring goals and becoming a star.

WYLIE, Bill ("Wiggie")

b. Galt, Ontario, July 15, 1928
d. November 24, 1983

If he ever weighed the 145 pounds he was supposed to have, it was because he stepped on a scale soaking wet and in his equipment. Yet Wylie wanted no admiration or any "pound-for-pound" praise of his talents. As he always said, in hockey, everyone is the same size. That was his attitude, and that was how he played – much bigger than he was. He played only a single game for the Rangers in '50-'51, but that was due reward for a forward who cut circles in the minors for years and years without complaint. He was most popular in Vancouver of the WHL and in Kitchener and Galt, where he finished his career. Wylie went into coaching almost immediately, in Galt and Preston. He led the Terriers to an Allan Cup in '70-'71 and had his best years as a coach with his hometown team.

WYLIE, Duane

b. Spokane, Washington, November 10, 1950

The Rangers drafted him in 1970 and then thought better of it and let him go. Chicago signed him two years later, and Wylie played all of his six years of pro in the Hawks system. During those years he played 14 games in the NHL, but he retired in 1978 without having made much of a mark with the team.

WYROZUB, Randy

b. Lacombe, Alberta, April 8, 1950

The wind was taken out of Wyrozub's sails in his rookie year with the expansion Buffalo Sabres thanks to two serious injuries. Early in '70-'71 he broke his collarbone and was out for a few weeks. Then, during practice near his return date, he was hit just above the eye by a puck and was gone another few weeks. He ended up in the minors, and over the next three years played only a few games with the Sabres. He later went to the WHA, but even there he was demoted and finished his career in the minors. He attended the University of Alberta, where he got a degree in education.

Bob Wren

John Wright

Keith Wright

Tyler Wright

Randy Wyrozub

YACHMENEV, Vitali
b. Chelyabinsk, Soviet Union (Russia), January 8, 1975
During his junior career in North Bay, Yachmenev became a local hero when he ran almost a mile to apprehend a burglar who had tried to rob his billet's home. He became an even greater hero for his scoring, his weak skating offset by his superb shot and toughness on the puck. He joined the L.A. Kings in 1995 and played on the right side to Wayne Gretzky's centre, and guess what? He became an NHL scorer. He had two goals in his first career game, in fact. The Kings were delighted, of course, but when Gretzky left the fold, guess what? Yachmenev could no longer score. In 1998, he was traded to Nashville for nothing more than future considerations. He has since tried to resurrect his career with the expansion team, far removed from the L.A. glitz of number 99.

YACKEL, Ken
b. St. Paul, Minnesota, March 5, 1932
d. July 12, 1991
Word has it that the University of Minnesota has never turned out a better athlete than Ken Yackel. Consider this: When he graduated, he had three offers. He could play pro football with the San Francisco 49ers; he could play baseball with the New York Yankees; or he could play pro hockey. He chose the third of these, of course, although he ended up playing just six games with the Bruins in '58-'59. He played in the AHL for two seasons, but reached his greatest heights with the Minneapolis Millers of the IHL. He was both playing coach and league-leading scorer with the team, and after retiring he became a coach and instructor full-time. He had won a silver medal with the U.S. at the 1952 Olympics in Oslo, and in 1965 he coached the National Team at the World Championships. He later coached briefly at U of M and then worked at a hockey school in the summer. In the winter, he worked for the John Mariucci Inner City Hockey Starter Association, a program that promoted the sport in St. Paul.

YAKE, Terry ("Yaker")
b. New Westminster, British Columbia, October 22, 1968
At the height of his powers, Yake was a checker who could score, a centre with good speed in place of size. He came out of Brandon in 1988, and over his first 5 years with Hartford played mostly in the minors until that last season, when he stayed the year and scored 22 goals. Anaheim claimed him that summer of 1993, and he followed up with a 21-goal season, though he never came close to that total again. He went to the minors, bounced around in the NHL, and finally ended up in Europe, playing in the DEL.

YAKUSHIN, Dmitri
b. Kharkov, Soviet Union (Ukraine), January 21, 1978
Excited by being drafted by the Leafs in 1996, Yakushin packed his bags and headed to Edmonton to play in the WHL that very fall. But after moving up to the AHL and getting into two games with the Leafs, he discovered the minors were his home and the NHL his visiting place. On that note, he returned to the Ukraine and played in a league there, his NHL days virtually over.

YAREMCHUK, Gary ("Weasel")
b. Edmonton, Alberta, August 15, 1961
Players who never make it with a team always ask only for a chance. Yaremchuk had four short chances with the Leafs in the early 1980s, but in 1985 he signed with Detroit hoping to get a longer shot than the dozen or so games the Leafs had given him. No such luck. The Wings kept him in the minors, and then Yaremchuk got on with things by going to Europe to play regularly. His brother, Ken, had much the same career.

YAREMCHUK, Ken ("Yammer")
b. Edmonton, Alberta, January 1, 1964
It's one thing to be told by a Cup-contending team that you don't fit into the long-term plans of the organization; it's quite another to be told the same thing by a marginally proficient team. Yaremchuk was drafted a lofty 7th overall by Chicago in 1982, a rank usually reserved for potential superstars. He had earned the selection based on two excellent seasons in Portland to close out his junior career, but his three years with Chicago were disappointing. He was sent to Toronto in 1986, but over the next three years couldn't earn a spot on the team come hell or high water. Yaremchuk, in fact, spent most of '87-'88 with Dave King and the National Team. At first, he didn't want to, but when the Leafs encouraged him to do so (read: we don't want you) he gave in and ended up having the experience of a lifetime at the 1988 Olympics in Calgary. He returned to the Leafs, but again was given the minor-league treatment. He then went to Europe and had a long and successful career with club teams there, notably in Switzerland where he spent most of his time scoring goals and enjoying playing every night.

YASHIN, Alexei
b. Sverdlovsk, Soviet Union (Russia), November 5, 1973
Perhaps never in the history of the NHL has a player alienated himself not only from fans but from teammates, GMs, and opponents alike. A magnificent player with a gargantuan ego and an agent to play his part perfectly, Yashin went from hero to hated in Ottawa with great rapidity. He joined the Senators in 1993 and proved to be a dynamic player who could score and pass with the best in the league. But as his reputation grew, so too did his self-importance, and in the summer of 1999 he and the team had a historic battle. Yashin's agent, Mark Gandler, demanded that his client's contract be renegotiated. The Senators, a team without deep pockets, refused, saying correctly that the player was under contract and there was no need or obligation to renegotiate. Gandler advised Yashin to sit out the year, but the Sens beat the money-grubbing duo to the punch by suspending him without pay. The year passed, and then Yashin sought to declare himself a free agent. The Senators countered by saying he still had a year left on his contract. He could sit out five years and still would have to play one final year, as per the contract, with the Sens before he was free. The case went to court, and the good guys won. Yashin was forced to play another season with the Sens, so he lost a full season of hockey and a full year's salary for absolutely nothing. He came back in excellent form and scored 40 goals, but in the playoffs got up to his usual, David Copperfield tricks

Vitali Yachmenev

Terry Yake

Dmitri Yakushin

Ken Yaremchuk

Gary Yaremchuk
(opposite page)

Trent Yawney

Alexei Yegorov

Stephane Yelle

– he disappeared. No goals in four games, and the Sens were out of the playoffs thanks, in large part, to Yashin's non-performance. In the summer, the inevitable happened. The Sens couldn't afford to sign the player and traded him to the Islanders, who quickly signed him to a mammoth 10-year contract worth $88-million. In the 2001-02 season, Yashin scored just 32 times, and then in the playoffs, voila! The team was eliminated, again by the Leafs. Yashin had failed yet again to take his team to the second round of the playoffs. He had been the first Russian captain of an NHL team in 1998, but after leaving the team he was replaced by Daniel Alfredsson. He has appeared at numerous international tournaments for Russia, but the man in the black turtleneck will go down in history for his grotesque attempts to break his contract in Ottawa. Ironically, it was not the first time he had tried to back out of a deal. He had "donated" $1-million to the National Arts Centre (NAC) in Ottawa, but then reneged on the agreement. He had wanted the NAC to promote more Russian music, but it was discovered only later that he wanted this done through his mother's business, Tatiana Entertainment. When the NAC refused, Yashin withdrew his putative donation.

YATES, Ross
b. Montreal, Quebec, June 18, 1959
Small, skilled players are often described in euphemism as a polite way of saying they are not NHL standard. Yates became known as a clever, playmaking centre, meaning small and quick and can't handle the rough going. Be that as it may, he had an outstanding career away from the NHL surrounding his seven games with Hartford in '83-'84. The previous year he led the AHL in assists and points and was named league MVP. He had graduated from Mount Allison University, but after four years in the Whalers system he decided to pursue a career in Europe. For 15 years Yates was first a star player and then a successful coach, mostly in Germany and Switzerland. He decided to return to North America in 2000 when the Syracuse Crunch offered him a job as assistant coach to the AHL affiliate of Columbus, and has been there ever since.

YAWNEY, Trent
b. Hudson Bay, Saskatchewan, September 29, 1965
Over a 12-year career, Yawney proved to be a strong skater on defence and a solid positional player, not spectacular but the kind of steadying force any team needs. He joined Chicago in 1987 and finished his career with the Hawks years later, playing with Calgary and St. Louis in between. The closest he came to the Cup was 1990 when the Hawks lost to Edmonton in

The man in the black turtleneck will go down in history for his grotesque attempts to break his contract in Ottawa.
ALEXEI YASHIN

the semifinals. After graduating from Saskatoon in 1985, Yawney spent most of the next three years with the Canadian National Team, which is how he learned his position so well. He played for Canada at the 1988 Olympics in Calgary before joining the Hawks. After suffering an arm injury midway through the '98-'99 season, Yawney decided he had had enough and retired, becoming an assistant coach with the team until season's end. He then assumed head coaching duties with the expansion Norfolk Admirals of the AHL and has been there ever since.

YEGOROV, Alexei
b. St. Petersburg, Soviet Union (Russia), May 21, 1975
d. unknown
As soon as it became clear that he might be drafted, Yegorov came to North America to play. In 1994, San Jose drafted him, but over the next 3 seasons he played only 11 games with the Sharks. He went home for a year, but then Atlanta claimed him in the 1999 Expansion Draft and returned. He didn't play a single game for the Thrashers, so he went home and later committed suicide under unknown circumstances.

YELLE, Stephane
b. Ottawa, Ontario, May 9, 1974
Before he made it to the NHL, Yelle could not have gotten any lower on the league's depth charts. Drafted way down the list by New Jersey in 1992, he was traded to Quebec two years later along with an 11th-round draft choice for an 11th-round draft choice. In other words, his street value as deemed by both teams equalled the difference between those club's selections in the *11th round!* In other words, as close to nil as possible. Yelle made the Avalanche (né Nordiques) in 1995 and has been with the team ever since. He helped the team win Cups in 1996 and 2001, and although he could never usurp Joe Sakic as the top centre, he was an important part of the team's success before being traded to Calgary at the start of the 2002-03 season. He is excellent on faceoffs, can check and kill penalties, and is sound defensively. Now, more than 500 NHL games later, his value is considerably more than the difference in position between two teams in the 11th round of the draft.

YEREMEYEV, Vitali
b. Ust-Kamenogorsk, Soviet Union (Kazakhstan), September 23, 1975
The highlight of Yeremeyev's career came at the 1998 Olympics in Nagano when he played goal for Kazakhstan, one of the new countries on the international hockey map. The team finished a surprisingly strong fifth, but Yeremeyev has not

followed that up with as much success in North America. He played four games for the Rangers in 2000-01 but allowed some four and a half goals a game and posted a 0-4-0 record. He started his career playing in Russian leagues, and after some time in the AHL that is where he gravitated in 2001-02. His return to North America is by no means guaranteed.

YLONEN, Juha
b. Helsinki, Finland, February 13, 1972
Although he was drafted by Winnipeg in 1991, Ylonen was in no great hurry to get to the NHL. In fact, it was five years before he joined the team, now in Phoenix and called the Coyotes. He had just played for Finland at the 1996 World Cup, the most recent in a string of international appearances. Most important, he won gold in 1995 at the World Championships, the first time ever his country had won the top spot. He played five years for Phoenix as a third-line centre, and also played at the two NHL Olympics, 1998 in Nagano and 2002 in Salt Lake City. Soon after returning from Salt Lake City, Ylonen was traded to Ottawa.

YONKMAN, Nolan
b. Punnicht, Saskatchewan, April 1, 1981
Still very much a work in progress, Yonkman is a young defenceman trying to develop in the Washington system and work himself into the Capitals lineup. He graduated from the WHL and has spent most of his time in the AHL with Portland. He played 11 games for the Caps in 2001-02 but started the next season back with the Pirates.

YORK, Harry
b. Ponoka, Alberta, April 16, 1974
In only four NHL seasons, York played for as many teams prior to retiring in 2000. He was never drafted, but St. Louis signed him in 1996, and in his rookie season he scored 14 goals. It was his best year.

YORK, Jason
b. Nepean, Ontario, May 20, 1970
There is something original or unique about every player, and in York's case it is that on January 30, 1999, the defenceman had 12 shots on goal. He was playing for Ottawa at the time, his team for five years where he established himself as one of its key players. He began his career with Detroit, developed with Anaheim, and matured with the Sens. The team made the playoffs every year he was with it before he re-signed with the Ducks as a free agent in 2001, and he is both a talented offensive player and a very solid workhorse in his own end of the ice.

In 2001-02 he started off strongly by playing on a line with Eric Lindros and Theo Fleury.
MIKE YORK

YORK, Mike ("Yorkie")
b. Pontiac, Michigan, January 3, 1978
During his four years at Michigan State, there wasn't much York didn't do. He was team captain, a two-time Hobey Baker Award finalist, the leading scorer, and CCHA player of the year. He also played for the U.S. in three World Junior Championships, and when he joined the Rangers in 1999 he had an immediate impact, scoring 26 goals. He faltered in his sophomore season with the Blueshirts, but in 2001-02 he started off strongly by playing on a line with Eric Lindros and Theo Fleury. For half a season, this was the league's dominant line, but it fell apart when Fleury could not control his own emotional and family problems and had to leave the team. The pair soldiered on, and York finished with a career-high 57 points, but there was so much more to be had from that season. Near the end of it, he was traded to Edmonton, a good fit for him because of his speed and offensive power. He went to a team with greater playoff promise, more youth, and better chemistry, but it will take more time to tell if he is going to develop into a top player.

YOUNG, B.J.
b. Anchorage, Alaska, July 23, 1977
Scott Gomez is not the only active player to come from Alaska, but Young has since returned whence he came whereas Gomez is now a bit of a star in the NHL. Young played junior in the WHL and was drafted by Detroit in 1997, but he played only a single game with the Wings in 1999-2000. He has played all his other games in the minors, and in 2001-02 he signed with Anchorage in the WCHL, returning home a pro with a sliver of hope of returning to the NHL.

YOUNG, Brian
b. Jasper, Alberta, October 2, 1958
In the 1970s, no hockey team had more success than the New Westminster Bruins, and Young was part of that success. He went to three straight Memorial Cup finals, winning in 1977 and '78. He also played for Team Canada at the 1978 WJC, a team that featured Wayne Gretzky, Mike Gartner, and many other future stars of the NHL. Young was not among that number. A Chicago draft choice, he played a few games with the Hawks during his three years in the minors, and then early in the '81-'82 season he went to Germany to play. He stayed overseas for nine years before retiring.

YOUNG, Carl Joshua "C.J."
b. Waban, Massachusetts, January 1, 1968
No, it didn't occur in the NHL, but it was a truly remarkable record all the same. On December 12, 1988, while playing for Harvard, Young scored 3

Juha Ylonen

Harry York

Jason York

B.J. Young

C.J. Young

Doug Young

Scott Young

short-handed goals in 49 seconds. This didn't translate to anything more than a fleetingly good reputation in the big league after he graduated in 1990, but still, it is a record worth bragging about. Young played half of the '92-'93 season split between Calgary and Boston and retired at the end of that year.

YOUNG, Doug
b. Medicine Hat, Alberta, October 1, 1908
d. May 15, 1990

A rock on Detroit's defence, Young played an even 10 seasons in the NHL starting in 1931. He was part of a nucleus of players who won the Cup with the Red Wings in 1936, and he should have won again a year later with the rest of the team. However, early in the '36-'37 season he crashed into the boards, broke his leg, and missed the year, including the playoffs. It was an atypical accident in that over his first five years Young missed only three games. He returned to the fold and closed out his career with two seasons in Montreal, but remained in the game for many years after. Young worked as an official, spending 17 years as a linesman in the NHL. He also acted as the referee-in-chief of the IHL, was active with the Detroit alumni, and ran clinics in Detroit. In 1971, he retired altogether and moved to Florida to enjoy a non-ice life for a change.

YOUNG, Howie ("Cowboy")
b. Toronto, Ontario, August 2, 1937
d. Thoreau, New Mexico, November 24, 1999

His parents were alcoholics, so he lived with his grandmother. She died before he turned 16, leaving him on his own. He turned to the bottle, and every day for the next 12 years he drank. He drank while he played junior and developed into a decent player and a ferocious fighter. He drank while he played for Detroit and Chicago in the early 1960s, a feat most sober people would have a tough time accomplishing. He drank every night, but when he was on the ice he was as bad a man as there was. He fought everyone and anyone. He fought because he was unhappy, because he wanted to make an impression, because that's how he could survive in the NHL. By 1964, though, no NHL team wanted an alcoholic. At 28, he was arrested for trying to break into his own apartment, and as he lay in his cell he vowed never to drink again. He went to an AA meeting, and kept his promise until the day he died. He continued to play hockey, but he fought less. He was in the minors now, most of the time, but made it back with, ironically, Detroit and Chicago, and Vancouver. He retired and came back, and didn't stop playing in the end until 1985, when he was 48 years old. Frank Sinatra liked

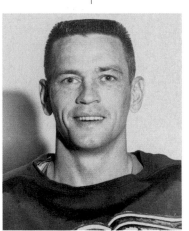

He fought because he was unhappy, because he wanted to make an impression, because that's how he could survive in the NHL.
HOWIE YOUNG

him and used him in a movie called *None But the Brave*. Young had one line – "Damn mosquitoes" – as he swatted an insect. He worked as a Brinks guard in Las Vegas and washed dishes, dug ditches, and drove buses and trucks. Finally, he and his third wife found peace in New Mexico. He drove kids to school for McKinley County and raised money to build a rink for the Navajo community, hoping, knowing, that one day a native kid from the area would go on to play in the NHL – and that kid would have Young to thank for it. He died of pancreatic cancer, having lived life, his interpretation of life, to the fullest.

YOUNG, Scott ("Fletch")
b. Clinton, Massachusetts, October 1, 1967

A model of terrific inconsistency, Young has had a long and industrious hockey career both in and out of the NHL. He went to Boston University in 1985 but left after two years when it became clear to him he could play the game at the highest level. He played at three WJCs for the U.S. and then spent most of '87-'88 with the National Team, including the 1988 Olympics in Calgary, his first of three Olympics. Young played his first four seasons of pro with Hartford and then was fortunate enough to be traded to Pittsburgh just weeks before the Pens won the Cup in 1991. He then rejoined the National Team, again with the intention of playing in the Olympics, after which he returned to the NHL with Quebec. He had two fine seasons of 30 and 26 goals, and when the club moved to Colorado he followed, winning another Cup in the spring of 1996. That fall, he won the World Cup with the U.S.. He had a bad season in Anaheim in '97-'98 when he scored just 13 times, but then he had 40 goals with St. Louis 3 years later, only to follow up with a disappointing year of 19 the next. During that season, he played again for the U.S., at the 2002 Olympics in Salt Lake City, where he won a silver medal. In the summer of 2002, Young signed with Dallas, where he played his 1,000th career game and scored his 300th career goal.

YOUNG, Tim
b. Scarborough, Ontario, February 22, 1955

Minnesota made a terrific deal in 1975 when it traded a second-round draft choice to Los Angeles for Young, who had yet to play in the NHL. In '75-'76, his rookie season, he had 51 points, and the year after he exploded for 95 points and played in the All-Star Game. Unfortunately, the achievements of that great year went to his head and he assumed everything would continue to go as easily for him in succeeding years. He was wrong. He continued to score 20 goals,

Tim Young

but struggled to come even moderately close to that second-year total, settling into a second-tier career rather than continuing to climb to the level of superstar. In January 1979, he scored five goals in a game, but soon was producing at half the pace he had expected. He ended his career in Winnipeg and Philadelphia.

YOUNG, Warren ("Warren Old")
b. Toronto, Ontario, January 11, 1956
Where did he come from? everyone asked when Young burst into the NHL in 1984. Where did he go to? everyone asks all these years later. Young is perhaps the most astounding 40-goal scorer story in the game. He came out of the mist and disappeared into the fog, but while he was visible he made a huge impression. In 1975, he accepted a scholarship offer from Michigan Tech, and four years later emerged with a business degree and a desire to play pro hockey. California drafted him in 1976, but he began his career in the minors. Over the next six years, he played just a few games with Minnesota and Pittsburgh, and had "minor leaguer" tattooed on his forehead. But at camp with the Penguins in 1984, he impressed the coaching staff, which felt he could contribute as a two-way player. He made the team. Young got the surprise of his life when he started to play alongside 18-year-old Mario Lemieux, and was even more surprised to see how immaculate were the hands and passes of the future Hall of Famer. Young scored 40 goals, a staggering, improbable number, except that anyone who played with Mario was going to score more than he ever dreamed possible. Young's descent, though, was swift. He signed a huge contract with Detroit in the summer, everyone figuring the 29-year-old was a late bloomer, but the Wings had no Mario and Young ended with 22 goals. A year later he had eight, and the year after that, in seven games, he had none. The decline was as swift as the ascent, but for one golden season Young was truly magnificent. He later coached the Louisville RiverFrogs of the ECHL.

YOUNG, Wendell
b. Halifax, Nova Scotia, August 1, 1963
By the time he retired in the summer of 2001, Young had accomplished what no other player ever had. He won a Memorial Cup (in 1981 with Kitchener), a Calder Cup (in 1988 with Hershey), a Turner Cup (in 1998 and 2000 with Chicago), and a Stanley Cup (in 1991 and '92 with Pittsburgh). Not a bad career for a marginal goalie who played more in the minors than in the NHL. Young's best years were his last, with the Wolves in the IHL. The team retired the goalie's number 1 and he assumed a job in the organization.

He was slated to play for his country at the 2002 Olympics in Salt Lake City, but in January, he was diagnosed with a blood clot in his leg.
DMITRY YUSHKEVICH

Additionally, he became a goalie coach with Calgary in the NHL.

YOUNGHANS, Tom
b. St. Paul, Minnesota, January 22, 1953
American players realize how precious is their knowledge and experience in the growth of the sport in their home state. They almost always return home after playing and try to help hockey develop, and in this regard Younghans is no different. He played in the NHL from 1976 to '82, mostly with Minnesota as a checker and penalty killer. He helped the Stars go to the semifinals in 1980, and also played in three World Championships and the 1981 Canada Cup for the U.S. When he retired, he returned to Minnesota and coached extensively in high schools.

YSEBAERT, Paul
b. Sarnia, Ontario, May 15, 1966
While attending Bowling Green University on scholarship, Ysebaert came to realize he could play pro hockey. When the chance to turn pro in 1987 came up, he didn't hesitate to leave his program and enter the Devils system, even though it was three years before he had a regular spot with the team. Just as quickly as he made it, he was traded to Detroit and developed into an excellent player, scoring 35 and 34 goals in consecutive seasons. He later moved on to Winnipeg and Chicago before settling into the final four years of his career with Tampa Bay in 1995. By the time he retired in 2000, after a final season in Switzerland, he was tired of the game and ready to move on. Unlike many players, he had something to go to right away – harness racing. During his days in Detroit he had become interested in McIntosh Stables, buying a few horses and following the circuit in southern Ontario with Bob Probert, with whom he invested in a few nags. The track has been his all-consuming interest since leaving hockey. He lives in Mooretown, Ontario, and goes to the stables in Windsor with enthusiasm and renewed energy.

YUSHKEVICH, Dmitry ("Tree") (formerly Dmitri)
b. Yaroslavl, Soviet Union (Russia), November 19, 1971
One of the elite defencemen in the game today, Yushkevich has been a devastating hitter and experienced presence on the blueline since 1992 when he joined Philadelphia. By that time he was already a successful player, having played at two WJC tournaments and won a gold medal with Russia at the 1992 Olympics in Albertville. He established himself with the Flyers immediately, but his best years were to come with Toronto after a trade to the Leafs in

Warren Young

Wendell Young

Tom Younghans

Paul Ysebaert

1995. For seven seasons he was the team's top defenceman, the player who logged most of the minutes, the man who became an assistant captain because of his play, demeanour, and leadership qualities. Yushkevich became a fan favourite for all of these reasons, and his international success continued as he played in both the 1996 World Cup and the 1998 Olympics in Nagano. But Yushkevich fell out of favour with management during the 2001-02 season. He was slated to play for his country at the 2002 Olympics in Salt Lake City, but in January, just days before the Games, he was diagnosed with a blood clot in his leg that kept him out the rest of the year. He took medication to thin his blood, and doctors cleared him to play. Yet the Leafs, fearful something awful might befall him during a game, refused to play him. In the summer, they traded him to Florida for Robert Svehla, citing not only the blood clot but also a bad knee as reasons to suspect his long-term health. Matters were made worse by the fact that his agent, the nefarious Mark Gandler, had a history of bad relations with the Leafs.

YZERMAN, Steve ("Stevie Y"/ "Stevie Wonderful")
b. Cranbrook, British Columbia, May 9, 1965

Regardless of league or era or teammates or any tangential considerations, Steve Yzerman will go down in history as one of the greatest players of all time. This is an unassailable fact, based on his character, play, and contributions to the game, that will ensure his induction into the Hockey Hall of Fame three years after he finally retires. At the age of 10, he moved to Nepean, Ontario, where he developed with a neighbour, Darren Pang, into a superstar from his earliest years. By the time he got to Peterborough in the OHL, he was a sensation, and two years later he was an 18-year-old NHLer. He had 39 goals and 87 points as a rookie, but lost the Calder Trophy to Tom Barrasso. By 1986, in his fourth season at 22, he became the youngest captain in league history, and now all these years later he is the longest-serving captain the NHL has even known. In '87-'88 he had a breakout season, scoring 50 goals and 102 points, his first of 6 successive seasons with more than 100 points. He peaked the next year with 155, but in the era of Gretzky and Lemieux, Yzerman never made the All-Star Team until 1999-2000. He also never won an individual trophy until that season, with two exceptions. In '88-'89, he was named winner of the Lester B. Pearson Award, the NHL's MVP as voted on by the players. Yzerman was devastated in 1987 and again in 1991 when coach Mike Keenan did not name him to the Canada Cup team for Canada, and although he continued to be the

third-best centre in the league and the best player to wear the Winged Wheel since Gordie Howe, Detroit never made deep forays into the playoffs. By the mid-1990s, it seemed Yzerman's career was going to take a turn. Trade talk and rumours heated up to the point that a deal was imminent, but the Wings balked at the last minute. If sometimes the best trade is the one you never make, then the non-deal to trade Yzerman was one of the best in team history. Detroit had excellent runs to the Cup in 1995 and '96, and then in '97 the miracle occurred and the Wings won the glorious trophy for the first time since 1955. When Yzerman held the Cup high above his shoulders, it was both team and personal triumph, a weight off the shoulders of the city and a deserving moment for one of the game's great players. As he had slowed down a bit, he had developed another part to his game as a two-way player, a great backchecker and face-off man, a team leader rather than just team-leading scorer. The Wings won the Cup again a year later, and Yzerman was named winner of the Conn Smythe Trophy. The team won again in 2002, and in many ways this was Yzerman's finest hour. He had played for Canada at the Olympics in February on a bad knee that got worse, and as the season came to an end he was almost without use of it. By the playoffs, he was hobbling off the ice after every shift, doubled over in pain and wracked by limited mobility. But he didn't miss a shift, and his teammates could play no less than their best when they saw how much the games meant to their fearless captain. Shortly after the celebrations and parade, he had that knee surgically reconstructed and missed many months before coming back to play late in the 2002-03 season. Yzerman won Olympic gold with Canada in 2002 to close out an international career that started late in some respects. He had played in three World Championships in his early NHL years when the Wings were bounced from the playoffs early, but his first big tournament was the 1996 World Cup and then the 1998 Olympics in Nagano. He is closing in on Gordie Howe as Detroit's all-time scorer and will leave the game as a captain, a champion, and a man devoted to the Wings, the team for whom he has played all of his more than 1,400 games. A gentleman and competitor, a man with great vision of the ice and a powerful shot, he is a perfect passer and as smart a player with the puck as has ever played.

> **He is a perfect passer and as smart a player with the puck as has ever played.**
> **STEVE YZERMAN**

ZABRANSKY, Libor
b. Brno, Czechoslovakia (Czech Republic), November 25, 1973

At one time, St. Louis considered him a prospect, but after half a season in '96-'97 the team changed its mind. Zabransky played two seasons and a bit in the minors, and then returned to Prague to play.

ZAHARKO, Miles
b. Mannville, Alberta, April 30, 1957

It was a big deal for Atlanta, but Zaharko found himself on the losing end. He had played all of '77-'78 with the Flames, but on June 13, 1979, GM Cliff Fletcher made a big trade that sent Zaharko, Tom Lysiak, Pat Ribble, Greg Fox, and Harold Phillipoff to Chicago for Ivan Boldirev, Phil Russell, and Darcy Rota. Zaharko played just one game with the Hawks that year and spent most of the next four years in the minors.

ZAINE, Rod
b. Ottawa, Ontario, May 18, 1946

While working on his degree in business communication at U of Ottawa, Zaine played hockey with Clinton of the EHL. He later played a number of games with Pittsburgh (in '70-'71) and Buffalo (the next year) and in 1972 he left the NHL to play for Chicago in the WHA.

ZALAPSKI, Zarley ("ZZ")
b. Edmonton, Alberta, April 22, 1968

If Bobby Orr had a dollar for every defenceman who was supposed to be the next incarnation of number 4, he'd be a rich man. The new star was called ZZ by teammates and ZZ Top by fans in Pittsburgh, but his dad called him Zarley after golfer Kermit Zarley. Zalapski brought all kinds of skill to the table as a teenager. He was fast and strong, smart with the puck, and a good stickhandler. The world was his oyster and the Penguins the first beneficiaries. But Zalapski delayed his NHL debut to play for Canada at the 1988 Olympics in Calgary. In fact, he spent most of 1985-88 with the National Team for just this reason. In December 1986, he was named best defenceman at the Izvestia tournament, and after Calgary he joined the Penguins. Unfortunately, there was quick disappointment. Turns out he wasn't the next Bobby Orr after all. He moved on to play for other teams, reaching a personal peak with Hartford when he scored 20 goals, but he simply wasn't a dominating player. His teams never went far in the playoffs, and although he was good on the power play he was not strong defensively. He ended up in the minors and finally in Europe, where he plays today.

ZAMUNER, Rob
b. Oakville, Ontario, September 17, 1969

Truly, men who think too much do more harm than good. Moving away from the Bard and toward the puck, no finer example can be cited than Canada's 1998 Olympic team. Sure, Wayne Gretzky might not have been strong on breakaways, but under no circumstances do you not select the most prolific scorer in the history of the game to participate in the shootout. Similarly, if you decide the team needs a checking forward (as GM Bobby Clarke did), you don't pick a Zamuner when you can pick a great player and ask him to be a checker for a few games. But what was Zamuner supposed to do when he was named to the Olympic team? Say no? Of course not. It was the absolute peak of his career, the reason one plays the game. He scored only one goal in that tournament, redirecting a brilliant pass from Gretzky off a faked slapshot on U.S. goalie Mike Richter. Zamuner isn't the reason Canada failed to win gold, but had his spot been taken by one of many stars in the league whose name was not on the roster... who knows? Zamuner was, in truth, one of the best checkers in the league. That was his specialty, and he had the size and tenacity to do his duty game in, game out. He had also won gold with Canada at the 1997 World Championships, so he knew the international game and the big ice surface. He had spent almost all of his career with Tampa Bay before Nagano, but since then has played for three teams.

ZANIER, Mike
b. Trail, British Columbia, August 22, 1962

In 1983, Zanier was living in Trail and receiving unemployment insurance. He wrote a letter to the 21 NHL teams asking for a tryout, and the only one that said yes was Edmonton. Zanier made his appearance at camp and was put into the Oilers system, and in the 1984 playoffs he was called up for two games as a backup goalie. He didn't play and didn't get his name on the Cup, but the Oilers did win and he did get a chance the next year. Zanier, first cousin of Steve Tambellini, appeared in three games and had a 1-1-1 record, and after two more years in the minors he went overseas to begin a long and successful career. Most of his time came with Italian teams and because he played there for so long he became eligible to play for the National Team. Zanier played goal at two World Championships for Italy as well as at the 1992 Olympics in Albertville, realizing a dream he never thought possible when he started out.

ZANUSSI, Joe
b. Rossland, British Columbia, September 25, 1947

Zanussi has a claim to fame, but he would rather not, thank you. On November 7, 1975, Brad Park, Jean Ratelle, and Zanussi were traded by the Rangers to Boston for Phil Esposito and Carol Vadnais. Four tremendous players (three future Hall of Famers, in fact) – and Zanussi. What was he doing there? How did he get there? He was a throw-in, an extra, a minor player added to a great trade. The result is that his name is known or forgotten daily in trivia contests and bars across the country, the other man involved in one of the great trades of the 1970s.

ZANUSSI, Ron ("Zoo")
b. Toronto, Ontario, August 31, 1956

Known as an aggressive player capable of hitting and banging along his right wing, Zanussi played with Minnesota and Toronto in his NHL years. He was drafted by the North Stars, who turned him into a banging checker, but late in the '80-'81 season he was traded to Toronto. As was the case with the North Stars, he spent more time in the minors than the NHL.

Libor Zabransky

Miles Zaharko

Zarley Zalapski

Rob Zamuner

Joe Zanussi

Rod Zaine
(opposite page)

Brad Zavisha

Richard Zednik

Jeff Zehr

Richard Zemlak

Jason Zent

ZAVISHA, Brad
b. Hines Creek, Alberta, January 4, 1972
After graduating from the WHL in 1992, Zavisha went to training camp in Edmonton only to suffer a season-ending knee injury. He played two games the next year for the team, and played in the minors the rest of his career before retiring in 1999.

ZEDNIK, Richard
b. Bystrica, Czechoslovakia (Slovakia), January 6, 1976
Drafted a lowly 249th overall in 1994, Zednik has proved far more skilled than that selection might suggest. He has been a fine skater in the NHL since 1995 when he joined the Capitals, though his offensive skills have been offset by injury problems. Zednik was traded to Montreal on March 13, 2001, to a team starved for goals. Internationally, he played for Slovakia at the 1996 WJC and later in the year at the World Cup. Most recently, he played at the 2001 World Championships.

ZEHR, Jeff
b. Woodstock, Ontario, December 10, 1978
Toward the end of his final season of junior, in Sarnia in 1999, Zehr dislocated his right kneecap. He required all summer to recover, but attended Boston's training camp with excitement, only to reinjure the area. Zehr missed most of that season, though he eventually did play four games for the Bruins. Those might prove to be his only NHL games. He has been in the ECHL ever since, and that same kneecap has caused him to miss large parts of subsequent seasons as well.

ZEIDEL, Larry ("The Rock")
b. Montreal, Quebec, June 1, 1928
In the old days, there was always a big fuss whenever a Jewish hockey player made it to the NHL, and Zeidel's case was no exception. One of the baddest men in the game, he came up to Detroit in '51-'52 and helped the Wings win the Cup. He played a few games the next year and most of the year after with Chicago, and then went to the minors where he was buried for the next 13 years. Zeidel spent most of his time in Hershey, but never gave up on a return to the NHL. To that end, he did a unique thing when expansion occurred in the summer of 1967. He put together a brochure on his career, complete with photos and information, and sent them to the 12 teams. Philadelphia responded positively and the 39-year-old was back in the top league. Late in that '67-'68 season he became involved in one of the ugliest incidents in league history. The Flyers were playing Boston in Toronto because the Spectrum roof had caved in. During the game, Zeidel high-sticked Eddie Shack and a stick-swinging duel occurred. Both players were badly hurt, and NHL president Clarence Campbell suspended them, Zeidel for four games (as the aggressor) and Shack for three (for retaliating). Early the next year, the Flyers demoted him, but Zeidel refused to go and decided to retire instead to become a stockbroker.

ZELEPUKIN, Valeri
b. Voskresensk, Soviet Union (Russia), September 17, 1968
Zelepukin was a low draft choice because at the time (1990) New Jersey had no idea if he would ever be able to travel to North America to play. A year later, though, he made the trip, and for six and a half seasons roamed the left wing for the Devils. He had three fine years and helped build the team into something close to a winner, but missed most of the lockout-shortened '94-'95 season because of a serious eye injury. He was able to return for the playoffs, which is what mattered most because the team won the Cup that spring. When New Jersey traded him to Edmonton, though, it began the end of his career as he passed through three teams on his way to the minors. He played for Russia at the 1996 World Cup and the 1998 Olympics in Nagano, his most recent international tournament.

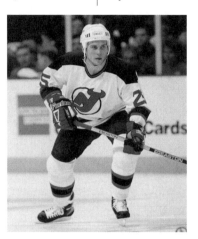

He played for Russia at the 1996 World Cup and the 1998 Olympics in Nagano.
VALERI ZELEPUKIN

ZEMLAK, Richard
b. Wynard, Saskatchewan, March 3, 1963
Few players travelled as much as Zemlak, an enforcer who fought in just about every league imaginable. In the WHL, he played for four teams as a junior. When he turned pro in 1981, he started with Salt Lake City and quickly moved on to Montana, Toledo, Muskegon, and on and on and on. He got his NHL start with Quebec in '86-'87 because the Nordiques had to match fist for fist and dropped glove for dropped glove with their arch-rivals, the Canadiens. From there, Zemlak kept moving to three other teams, all the while sprinkling his fighting throughout the minors. By the time he retired, he averaged four penalty minutes per game in the NHL, an average he maintained in the lesser leagues as well.

ZENIUK, Ed
b. Landis, Saskatchewan, March 8, 1933
The only NHL games Zeniuk played were on December 30, 1954, and January 9, 1955. He played junior hockey in Edmonton and only three seasons of pro, mostly out west.

ZENT, Jason
b. Buffalo, New York, April 15, 1971
Zent played for the U.S. at the 1989 WJC at the tender age of 17 and went on to play four years at the

University of Wisconsin. He graduated in 1994 and turned pro with Ottawa, but spent most of his six seasons in the minors. He did play 25 games with the Senators and another 2 with the Flyers, and after retiring returned to Massachusetts and became an assistant coach at Worcester Academy.

ZETTERSTROM, Lars
b. Stockholm, Sweden, November 6, 1953
Vancouver signed him as a free agent in 1978 after arranging (i.e., paying for) his release from his club team, Farjestads. It was an expensive deal, though, because Zetterstrom played only 14 games for the Canucks and a season in the minors before returning home. He won a silver medal with Tre Kronor at the 1977 World Championships, and also played at the WC in '78.

ZETTLER, Rob ("Zetts")
b. Sept Îles, Quebec, March 8, 1968
NHL trades and trips to the minors have been the two constants in Zettler's life, yet since turning pro in 1988 he was an active member of the hockey world until retiring in August 2002. The Soo Greyhound graduate started with Minnesota, his first of six teams, and he had to fight for every shift as he would every game and every year. Perhaps even Brad Marsh was a swifter, more graceful skater, but what Zettler lacked in speed he made up for in tenacity (and the occasional hook, clutch, grab, and block). In his 569 total games, he scored a total of 5 goals, once going 5 years and more than 200 games between markers! Yet he battled opponents in front of his net, went into the corners to tie up his man, and did all that coaches asked of him. He had to; that was how he survived. He put away his equipment and joined the broadcasting team for San Jose.

ZEZEL, Peter
b. Toronto, Ontario, April 22, 1965
A superb soccer player who gave up a chance to turn pro at the summer game, Zezel opted to play for the Toronto Marlies and look to the NHL. When he turned pro with Philadelphia in 1984, he began a 15-year career in the league. The sturdy centre had his best year in '86-'87, a year not coincidentally when the Flyers went to the finals. Zezel had 33 goals and 72 points in the regular season, his third year and the only time he went to the finals. He played for five other teams along the way, including three and a half seasons with his hometown Leafs. He was a terrific second- or third-line centre, good at both ends of the ice, and tenacious on the puck and away from the play. He was considered a character player, but his career came to an end somewhat controversially in Vancouver.

The Canucks traded him to Anaheim in March 1999 but Zezel refused to go. He had a niece in Toronto, Lilliann, who was dying from a rare form of cancer, and he wanted to be a short plane ride from her side. Anaheim would not be conducive to such a fast trip, so he retired. In October 2001, he himself became acutely ill. Feeling extremely weak, he called an ambulance and doctors later found he suffered from hemolytic anemia. It took him months to recover, but when he did he worked more heavily on his soccer and hockey camps and coached kids in the Toronto area.

ZHAMNOV, Alexei
b. Moscow, Soviet Union (Russia), October 1, 1970
What a perfect way to kill two birds with one stone. As a junior in Moscow, Zhamnov was coached by the great former player Valeri Vasiliev. Zhamnov also happened to fall in love with Vasiliev's daughter, Yelena, and so he got a great hockey education and a wife out of the same experience. He went on to play in the 1991 Canada Cup for CCCP and then at the 1992 Olympics in Albertville for Russia, winning a gold medal. He joined Winnipeg that fall and began an NHL career that has seen him produce 20 goals with uncanny consistency. He was traded to Chicago in 1996, the summer in which the Jets moved to Phoenix, and the Coyotes received Jeremy Roenick in the deal. Zhamnov promptly refused to report to camp without a new contract and eventually signed a five-year deal worth $15-million. He then went out and scored exactly 20 goals, as he has in 9 of his first 10 NHL seasons. He also played for Russia at both of the NHL Olympics, winning silver in 1998 and bronze in 2002.

ZHITNIK, Alexei
b. Kiev, Soviet Union (Russia), October 10, 1972
Like Alexei Zhamnov, Zhitnik won a gold medal at the 1992 Olympics in Albertville and then played in the NHL later that year. In Zhitnik's case, he joined Los Angeles where he had an immediate impact as a rushing, offensive-minded defenceman. He played just a little more than two years with the team before being traded in a multiplayer deal that saw Grant Fuhr go to the Kings. Zhitnik has been a Sabre ever since, though his point production has trailed off recently. He helped the team go to the 1999 Cup finals, though he has missed training camp twice because of contract disputes. Internationally, Zhitnik has played for Russia in four World Championships, the 1996 World Cup, the 1998 Olympics in Nagano, and two WJCs at the start of his successful career.

Lars Zetterstrom

Rob Zettler

Alexei Zhamnov

Alexei Zhitnik

He was a terrific second- or third-line centre, good at both ends of the ice.
PETER ZEZEL

Sergei Zholtok

Doug Zmolek

Rick Zombo

Dainius Zubrus

ZHOLTOK, Sergei ("Zholi")
b. Riga, Soviet Union (Latvia), February 12, 1972

For Zholtok, Sandis Ozolinsh, and other talented Latvian players, the National Team is the beef and the NHL merely the gravy. Zholtok started his career by playing for the Soviet Union, then for CIS (Commonwealth of Independent States) during the transition years, and finally for Latvia, an independent nation once again. He helped the team go from "B" pool to "A" pool in the World Championships and has played for his country every chance he has had. Like so many others, he joined the NHL in 1992, with Boston, but it wasn't until four years later with Ottawa that he played a full season and established himself as a quality player. The Sens let him go after two years, and he signed with the Canadiens with whom he scored a career-best 26 goals in 1999-2000. He started off poorly the year after, though, and the Habs sent him on to Edmonton and from there to Minnesota. He also played for Latvia at the 2002 World Championships with a nation now firmly ensconced in the top echelon of the international game.

ZIEGLER, Thomas
b. Zurich, Switzerland, June 9, 1978

Swiss-born players don't make the NHL by and large, and when Ziegler stepped on the ice on February 5, 2001, wearing a Tampa Bay sweater, he became just the sixth player from that tiny country to make it. He played only five games for the Lightning, though, and while the team liked his skills, he was told to build his slight 5'10", 174-pound body. Most of his finest games have come internationally, of course. He has played for La Suisse at the 1998 WJC and the 2000, 2001, and 2002 World Championships. Most of his league time has been spent at home in Switzerland, though he has also played a few AHL games in North America.

ZMOLEK, Doug
b. Rochester, Minnesota, November 3, 1970

Tough as nails without any scoring ability whatsoever, Zmolek made his living on the blueline and in front of his own goal. He played for four teams during his eight years in the league, but by the time he retired in 2000 he hadn't quite lived up to his 7th-overall selection in the 1989 draft. In fact, Minnesota let him go to San Jose without a fight even before he had played a game with the team, and over the years Zmolek endured his share of injuries to his increasingly banged-up body.

ZOBROSKY, Marty
b. Unknown

Little is known about Zobrosky, including the correct spelling of his name. It appears variously as Zobroski and Zoborosky, but one thing is certain: His lone NHL appearance came on December 31, 1944 when he wore number 7 for Chicago in a 6-2 loss to Detroit.

ZOMBO, Rick
b. Des Plaines, Illinois, May 8, 1963

It's tough to make a team when the coaches tell you beforehand that you're not in their plans, but in Zombo's case, he tried and tried and eventually succeeded. He had been through worse. Most of his three years at University of North Dakota (1981-84) were compromised by a bad knee, yet he impressed Detroit anyway come draft day. It took him three years in the minors, but Zombo finally made the Wings as a regular in 1987, and he played the next nine years in the NHL without a single trip to the AHL or the "I." He played many of those years with the Wings but later skated on the blueline for St. Louis and Boston, and when he retired in 1997 he returned to St. Louis where he coached the St. Louis Sting, a junior A team.

He won a Cup with the team in the spring of 1999, and played in three successive All-Star Games.
SERGEI ZUBOV

ZUBOV, Sergei ("Zubie")
b. Moscow, Soviet Union (Russia), July 22, 1970

By the time Zubov entered the NHL in 1992, he was 22 years old and in full stride. He had won Olympic gold near the start of the year and as soon as he joined the Rangers he had an impact as a terrific rushing defenceman. He skated fluidly. He made bullet, accurate passes. He made the transition from defence to offence lightning fast. He was key to the Rangers winning the Cup in '93-'94, but the Rangers were determined to trade him for offensive forwards. They failed to acquire Teemu Selanne, but they did get Luc Robitaille from Pittsburgh. Dallas made the smart trade, giving up Kevin Hatcher to get Zubov from the Penguins a year later, and since 1996 he has controlled the Stars blueline. He won a Cup with the team in the spring of 1999, signed a contract extension to run through 2005, and played in three successive All-Star Games in 1998, 1999, and 2000. He anchors the team's power play, plays almost half a game on average, and is key to the Dallas style of play at both ends of the ice.

ZUBRUS, Dainius
b. Elektrenai, Soviet Union (Lithuania), June 16, 1978

He was originally drafted by Philadelphia in 1996 using a draft choice the Flyers had acquired from Toronto in the deal that sent Dmitry Yushkevich to the Leafs, and when he joined the Flyers in 1996 Zubrus showed plenty of potential. The Flyers and later the Canadiens both gave up on him quickly, though, and it is Washington that has benefited from the mature play of the experienced winger. He had his best year in 2001-02 when he accumulated 43 points, and could well turn into a solid second-line player for the Caps. He played junior hockey in Ontario, but with NHL salaries as they are he has also been able to help the small hockey program in Lithuania as a sponsor of a club team, Druzhba 78.

ZUKE, Mike
b. Sault Ste. Marie, Ontario, April 16, 1954
Nobody ever had the college career that Zuke had at Michigan Tech. When he graduated in 1976, he led the school in every offensive category and ranked third all-time in the NCAA in points. He went on to play eight years in the NHL, the first five with St. Louis where he was an unspectacular yet efficient centre. He twice scored more than 22 goals in a season and was key to the team's power play, though he was never considered a star. Hartford claimed him in 1983, and he spent his last three years with the Whalers. Zuke was diminished over the years by a knee injury in his final season and three serious shoulder surgeries, which eventually convinced him to retire. In 1988 he was inducted into the Michigan Tech Sports Hall of Fame, and later worked with the Blues at the grassroots level.

ZUNICH, Rudy
b. Calumet, Michigan, November 24, 1910
d. Detroit, Michigan, March 13, 1974
Zunich played all of his hockey in Detroit, and as a result he was found by GM Jack Adams of the Red Wings. The defenceman was called up for two games during the war at the end of his career, and spent the rest of his life in the city.

ZYUZIN, Andrei
b. Ufa, Soviet Union (Russia), January 21, 1978
Although Zyuzin has become a solid NHLer, San Jose badly misjudged his worth when it selected him 2nd overall in the 1996 Draft. He joined the Sharks a year later and has since played for two other teams, but his has been a short and much-interrupted career. He left the team late in '98-'99 in a contract dispute, missed much of 1999-2000 with a shoulder injury, and in 2001-02 suffered a concussion and missed part of the year recovering from the head injury.

Mike Zuke

**PLAYERS INDUCTED INTO
THE HOCKEY HALL OF FAME
WHO NEVER PLAYED
IN THE NHL**

B

BAIN, Donald "Dan"

b. Belleville, Ontario, February 14, 1874
d. Winnipeg, Manitoba, August 15, 1962

Not only is Bain an inaugural member of the Hockey Hall of Fame (1945), he was a renowned athlete who was the best in every endeavour he chose to undertake. In 1887, at age 13, he was the three-mile rollerskating champion of Manitoba. A few years later, he was a gymnastics champion. Starting in 1894, he won three successive one-mile cycling titles. He was also a superb lacrosse player and a figure skating champion. But hockey was what ran in his veins and gave him his greatest thrills and successes. He first rose to prominence in 1895 playing with the Victorias in Winnipeg, and in February 1896 scored the winning goal in a 2-0 Victorias victory over the Montreal Vics to give his team the Stanley Cup. The Montreal team challenged their western counterparts a few months later, and despite Bain's two goals the east reclaimed the hallowed silverware. In 1899, Bain again led his team to a challenge of the Cup, albeit unsuccessful, but in 1900 he was the hero even though the Vics lost to the Montreal Shamrocks 11-10 in a total-goals series to win a second Cup. Bain counted four of his team's ten markers. In 1901, he led the team to its second Cup win and scored the winning goal in overtime, the first time the Cup had been won in such dramatic fashion. Bain also caused a stir when he played with a badly broken nose. He wore a special wooden facemask to protect his beak, and for years after he was called the "Masked Man." In 1902, the Vics defended their title but lost to the Montreal AAA just two months later. Bain retired from hockey in 1903 and devoted himself to trapshooting. Again he was without compare, winning first the Manitoba championship and then the title for all of Canada. He was named the country's best athlete of the last half of the 19th century and was also inducted into the Canadian and Manitoba Sports Halls of Fame.

BAKER, Hobart "Hobey"

b. Wissahickon, Pennsylvania, January 15, 1892
d. Toul, France, December 21, 1918

His full name was Hobart Amory Hare Baker, but everyone called him Hobey. He was the first great American hockey player, the stuff of legend – and his legend lives on. The Hobey Award is now given to the year's top player in U.S. college hockey. But as a youth, there were few options for an American to play the game. Baker learned quickly, and played at Princeton and later Yale. He was renowned for his stamina and great rushes to the point that the team became known as "Hobey Baker and six others." He was the best player in college hockey, a gentleman, and a highly successful student. But with no formal league in which to ply his skills he moved to New York and worked for the Morgan Bank on Wall Street. He joined the Saint Nicholas Skating Club and became its greatest star. When war broke out, Baker enlisted and was stationed at Mineola where he became an expert flyer. He went overseas in August 1917 and for several months did office work behind the lines, much to his frustration. At one point, he was sent into France to retrieve supplies, and showed such skill and daring that he was made captain and given a squadron of 20 lieutenants. Ironically, his life ended after he was called to come home. On one last routine flight he crashed and was killed. He was 26 years old. Baker was later inducted into the Hockey Hall of Fame, the U.S. Hockey Hall, and the Pro Football Hall of Fame. On his headstone reads appropriate testimony to his life: "You who seemed winged, even as a lad,/With that swift look of those who know the sky,/It was no blundering fate that stooped and bade/You break your wings, and fall to earth and die./I think some day you may have flown too high,/So that immortals saw you and were glad,/Watching the beauty of your spirits flame,/Until they loved and called you, and you came."

BOON, Richard "Dickie"

b. Montreal, Quebec, January 10, 1878
d. Montreal, Quebec, May 3, 1961

One of the first players to rise in hockey through a junior system, Boon went on to become one of hockey's legendary pioneers. He played for the Young Crystals in Montreal before moving up to the Monarchs and then the Montreal AAA juniors in 1900. The next year he joined the senior team and was part of the great Stanley Cup victory in 1902. Boon was a cover point and was likely the first to use the poke check as a method of checking a man and taking the puck. He never weighed more than 120 pounds, but like the rest of his team was tenacious and without fear. As a result of that '02 Cup win, the team was nicknamed the "Little Men of Iron," but the amateur team was soon on the outside looking in as the professionals began to buy and build superior squads. Boon retired as a player in 1905. He had become the manager of the Montreal Wanderers two years earlier and retained that post until January 1918 when the team's arena in Westmount burned down and the Wanderers ceased operations. He was the man who signed both Lester Patrick and Art Ross to their first contracts and guided the Redbands, as they were affectionately known, to three Cups – 1907, 1908, and 1910. After his hockey career ended, Boon focused his interests on the Boon-Strachan coal business and became one of Montreal's finest curlers. To this day, the Boon Trophy is one of the major bonspiel prizes at the Outremont Curling Club. Boon was inducted into the Hockey Hall of Fame in 1952, one of hockey's early great players and builders.

BOWIE, Russell ("Dubbie")

b. Montreal, Quebec, August 24, 1880
d. Montreal, Quebec, April 8, 1959

In the days when being an amateur made one proud, Bowie rejected the lure of money and professional hockey and remained true to the game his whole life. He played his entire career with the Montreal Victorias, winning a Cup with the team in 1898 while only 18 years old. A rover, he once scored 10 goals in a game, and in just 80 career games scored 234 times, an average of more than 3 a game! The Montreal Wanderers tried to induce him to turn pro with their team, going so far as to send a grand piano to his home as a signing bonus (Bowie was a fine pianist). He immediately ordered the piano removed and in 1909, when the fully pro National Hockey Association was formed, he retired. He continued to be active in the game for many years as a referee, and in 1945 Bowie was among the first men to be inducted into the Hockey Hall of Fame.

D

DAVIDSON, Allan "Scotty"

b. Kingston, Ontario, March 6, 1891
d. France, June 6, 1915

His coach and mentor was Captain James T. Sutherland, and it was because of him that Davidson developed into the best amateur player in Kingston. Davidson played with the Frontenacs starting in 1909, and led the team to two successive Ontario titles. He turned pro in Toronto in 1912 with the Blueshirts, and two years later was part of Jack Marshall's Cup-winning team. Davidson played the right wing with tenacity. He had a great shot and was a superb back checker, an attribute that served him well overseas during the war. With the 2nd Battalion in France, Davidson rescued an officer during a raid, but while carrying a wounded colleague to safety was shot in the back and killed. His name is commemorated on the Vimy Memorial. In 1950, Davidson took his place in the Hockey Hall of Fame.

DRINKWATER, Graham

b. Montreal, Quebec, February 22, 1875
d. Montreal, Quebec, September 25, 1946
Although he was not inducted into the Hockey Hall of Fame until four years after his death, Drinkwater was one of the finest players of the early days of hockey and also a successful businessman in Montreal after his skating days ended. He attended McGill University where he earned a science degree, but he was also a superb football and hockey player. He joined the Montreal AAA junior team and in 1895 signed with the Vics of Montreal where he won four Stanley Cups during his brief career. Drinkwater was team captain, and equally adept as a forward or defence player, thanks in large part to his superior skating abilities. He was a machinist in his youth, but in 1906 he joined the Fairbanks Morse Company, eventually becoming general manager and vice-president. He later became a director at Aldred and Co. and a member of the Montreal Stock Exchange, but he is best known in business circles as senior partner in the brokerage firm of Oswald and Drinkwater which he helped establish in 1921 and which occupied him until his death.

DUNDERDALE, Tommy

b. Benella, Australia, May 6, 1887
d. Winnipeg, Manitoba, December 15, 1960
It will likely be many a decade before another Australian-born man is inducted into the Hockey Hall of Fame. Dunderdale moved with his family to Ottawa when he was six, and soon after moved farther west to Winnipeg. It was, of course, in these cities that he first encountered skates and a hockey stick. He played in the fledgling NHA for two years, but when the Pacific Coast league began Dunderdale was lured to British Columbia by the Patrick brothers. He stayed there for 12 years, becoming the

league's all-time goal-scoring leader. He was an outstanding skater who played both rover and centre, but it was his stickhandling skills that separated him from the pack. Although he had fine league success, Dunderdale never won a Stanley Cup. He later coached and managed teams throughout North America, though he eventually settled in Winnipeg where he worked in private business until his death.

FARRELL, Art

b. Montreal, Quebec, February 8, 1877
d. Ste-Agathe-des-Monts, Quebec, February 7, 1909
His father was an alderman in Montreal, so Farrell grew up under favourable social circumstances. He was well educated and a fine athlete in his youth. He played hockey in high school and in 1897 he and some of his classmates joined the Montreal Shamrocks. The team introduced passing as a strategy of attack as opposed to the rugby style of advancing the puck that had long been in vogue. Farrell won two Cups with the Shamrocks but was equally famous in an historical context for having written the first books on hockey ever published. In 1899, he wrote *How to Play Ice Hockey*, and in succeeding years had two other volumes published. Once out of the game he went into the family's retail business, but in 1906 was confined to a sanitarium in Ste. Agathe to combat tuberculosis. He succumbed to the disease two and a half years later. Farrell was inducted into the Hockey Hall of Fame in 1965.

GARDNER, Jimmy

b. Montreal, Quebec, May 21, 1881
d. Montreal, Quebec, November 6, 1940
Four times did Gardner win the Stanley Cup in the early days of the trophy, twice with the Montreal AAA and another two with the Wanderers. Those first two came with the "Little

Men of Iron," the amateur team that won in 1902 and the next year. From there, the great left winger launched a peripatetic career that took him to Calumet, Michigan and out west to the PCHL in British Columbia before heading back to Montreal where he turned to the pro ranks of the east with the Wanderers. Gardner won Cups in 1909 and 1910 with the Redbands and after retiring remained very much in the game in a managerial capacity. He coached the Canadiens in 1915 for two seasons and then refereed in those parts of the world in which he had previously played. In 1924, he was named head coach of the Hamilton Tigers of the NHL and took the team to first place. But before the playoffs started, the players went on strike for more money, and the league disqualified the team. The Tigers withdrew from the league and Gardner continued to coach in the minors for several seasons. It wasn't until 1962 that he was inducted into the Hockey Hall of Fame, long after his death.

GILMOUR, Hamilton Livingstone "Billy"

b. Ottawa, Ontario, March 21, 1885
d. Montreal, Quebec, March 13, 1959
There were seven Gilmour brothers in all, and with their number came as much sadness and misfortune as glory. Allan was killed in World War I. Stuart drowned while still a boy. Suddie and Dave also died long before old age could catch up to them, though not before they had a chance to play with Billy for the Ottawa Silver Seven. Billy joined the team after graduating from McGill University and helped the vaunted Ottawas win three Stanley Cups. He retired in 1906 but returned a year later to Montreal, with the Victorias. However, he soon returned to his birthplace and helped the newly-named Senators win the Cup in 1909. He fought in the Great War and spent many years in Paris, barely making it out of the country with his daughter before the Germans invaded during the next war (his wife died young, in 1925). Gilmour ultimately settled in Montreal and was inducted into the Hockey Hall of Fame three years after his death.

GOHEEN, Francis Xavier "Moose"

b. White Bear Lake, Minnesota, February 9, 1894
d. White Bear Lake, Minnesota, November 13, 1979
A typical Canadian, Goheen learned to

play hockey outdoors near his home. He was an especially talented football, baseball, and hockey player, but it was with the puck that he became famous. He joined the St. Paul Athletic Club in 1915 and a year later helped the team win the McNaughton Trophy, emblematic of amateur supremacy in the U.S. After a second victory Goheen entered the war, but returned to the U.S. in 1920 and played at the Olympics. His country placed second behind Canada. By 1924, Goheen had a busy job in Minnesota working for the Northern States Power Co. As a result, he could not get away to play in the Olympics, though he continued to play for St. Paul until 1926 as an amateur and until 1932 as a professional. Goheen was offered NHL contracts by Toronto and Boston but preferred life in his home state to a hockey career. He was a rushing defenceman and likely the first to advocate full-time wearing of helmets as a safety measure. After his playing days, Goheen received three historic honours. In 1952, he was inducted into the Hockey Hall of Fame. Six years later he was named the finest hockey player ever to come out of Minnesota, and in 1973 was enshrined in the U.S. Hockey Hall of Fame.

GRANT, Mike

b. Montreal, Quebec, January 1874
d. Montreal, Quebec, August 20, 1955
A hockey man in all ways and at all levels, Grant was as comfortable on skates as most people are in slippers. At age 11, he won championships in three age groups of speed skating and soon took his skills with stick and puck to a commensurate level of success. He started out with the Crystals juniors in Montreal and progressively moved up to the Victorias where he captained the team to the Stanley Cup in 1895. Before the end of the century, the team had won the trophy five times in the challenge format. Because of his skating he played defence, and because of that, was hockey's first rusher of the puck from the back end. Grant retired in 1902 but returned to the game as a referee. He caused a sensation when he officiated one Cup game while wearing a derby hat, and later held many clinics and exhibitions in the U.S. to promote the game and its skills. Grant's father had been a blacksmith, and as a result Mike was a common figure at the racetrack. In retirement, Grant himself was a paddock judge for more than 40 years and was associated with numerous tracks in Ottawa and Montreal. He was

inducted into the Hockey Hall of Fame in 1950, and his son, Donald, later became the first president of the New York Mets, in 1962.

GRIFFIS, Silas "Si"

b. Onaga, Kansas, September 22, 1883
d. Vancouver, British Columbia, July 9, 1950
Kansas, if it knew what it had, could claim Griffis as a native son, but he grew up in Rat Portage (later Kenora) where he moved at age 18 months with his family. In his teens he was a terrific hockey player in the winter and oarsman in the summer, but hockey got the better of his attention and ambitions. Griffis was a large man but speedy and agile nonetheless. In an age of often ferocious play though, he was a gentlemanly giant. He started his career in 1900 and six years later was part of the Kenora Thistles – the smallest city ever to win the Stanley Cup. It was also the shortest Cup reign ever, Kenora holding the trophy for just 61 days before losing to the Montreal Wanderers. Griffis got married in 1906 and moved to Vancouver, though not before the good citizens of Kenora gave him a purse of gold in thanks, and tried to induce him to stay by offering him a big house. After four and a half years in Vancouver he came out of retirement to play for the Patricks in the PCHL. He played another seven years, until 1919, winning a second Cup, that one with the Vancouver Millionaires in 1915. After hanging up his blades for good, Griffis worked as the advertising manager for the *Vancouver News Herald*. He went on to become a senior executive for the *Vancouver Sun* and at the time of his death was with a business called McConnell, Eastman and Co. Ltd. He was inducted into the Hockey Hall of Fame in the summer of 1950, and just a week later passed away.

HERN, William Milton "Riley"

b. St. Mary's, Ontario, December 5, 1880
d. Montreal, Quebec, June 24, 1929
He was one of the earliest superstar goalies, a player who won seven championships in his first nine seasons of hockey, and a man respected throughout the business world in the years after he stopped stopping pucks for enjoyment. Hern played in Pittsburgh and Portage and a few

smaller places in between in his youth, but it was in 1906 when he joined the Montreal Wanderers that he earned a place in the game's history. Hern backstopped the Redbands to five Stanley Cups in the ensuing year before retiring in 1911 because of increased business successes. He had opened his own retail store on Peel Street in Montreal in 1908 and expanded to Toronto as well. He focused on Montreal by 1919 when he became closely associated with Spalding Athletic Goods, and also had business connections in boating and motoring. He was for many years president of the Ste. Rose Boating Club and every Christmas was responsible for organizing charity parties on behalf of the Children's Memorial Hospital. He died of what doctors called an "athlete's heart" – worn before its time – and left behind a wife and six children. Hern was inducted into the Hockey Hall of Fame in 1962.

HOOPER, Tom

b. Rat Portage (Kenora), Ontario, November 24, 1883
d. Vancouver, British Columbia, March 23, 1960
Hooper and boyhood friend Tommy Phillips were an unlikely pair to make Stanley Cup history. They were raised in a town of about 4,000 souls, but the two were so good that their high school hockey team defeated the senior team one year. They advanced to play locally and then in Manitoba, and for four years sought their dream of winning a Cup. But each year that they challenged, they lost. In 1903 it was to Ottawa; in 1905, Ottawa again; and finally, in January 1907, they beat the Montreal Wanderers 12-8 in a two-game, total-goals series. Hooper, a rover, scored three of the dozen goals in that series, but at year's end the team folded. He headed to Montreal where he played first for the AAA and then the Wanderers, winning his second Cup with that team three times in 1908 on various challenges. Hooper retired and settled out west. He was inducted into the Hockey Hall of Fame in 1962.

HUTTON, John Bower "Bouse"

b. Ottawa, Ontario, October 24, 1877
d. Ottawa, Ontario, October 27, 1962
Few athletes can boast the level of success in as many sports as Hutton. In one year alone he won three championships, starting with the Stanley Cup with the Silver Seven, continuing

with the lacrosse title with the Ottawa Nationals, and ending with the Dominion Rugby title with the Ottawa Rough Riders, precursors to the CFL team. Hutton was a first-rate baseball player in his youth and a champion lawn bowler in his post-hockey days, but it was as a goalie on ice that he achieved his greatest fame and glory. Four times he led the Canadian amateur ranks in goals-against average. He won the Cup in 1903 and '04 with the Ottawa team at which point he left hockey to play lacrosse full time. He played for Brantford, winning a Minto Cup and touring Britain with the team before heading back to Ottawa to coach hockey. After, he worked in the nation's capital with the post office and was a huge hockey fan until the day he died. In 1962, he was named to the Hockey Hall of Fame.

JOHNSON, Ernie "Moose"

b. Montreal, Quebec, February 26, 1886
d. White Rock, British Columbia, March 24, 1963

When he stretched his stick out in front, the distance was 99 inches from glove to tip of stick. Moose was famous for that long piece of timber in the days before length restrictions, but as a defenceman his poke check made it virtually impossible for forwards to get around him with any success. He was a big man, of course (the nickname), and he played much longer than the average star player of his day. He began in his hometown, winning four Stanley Cups with the Wanderers between 1905 and 1910. He moved out west to the PCHA in 1912 and continued to play in various leagues until 1931 when he was 45 years old. He had spent fine years in Portland and it was there he retired after his playing days. He served with the Union Pacific Railway in Oregon as a brakeman for 45 years, from his summer days as a player to full-time work after retiring. He finished with the railway in 1954 and resettled in White Rock, B.C. where he died two years after suffering a debilitating stroke. Perhaps most amazing of all in his lengthy career was that in 1900 he absorbed a 2,300-volt shock of electricity in an accident and lost two fingers on his right hand. He was likely the only great player to have such a career without the aid of two digits. Johnson was elected into the Hockey Hall of Fame in 1952.

L

LeSUEUR, Percy ("Perce"/ "Peerless Percy")

b. Quebec City, Quebec, November 21, 1881
d. Hamilton, Ontario, January 27, 1962

Fate strikes without warning or explanation, and no finer case for serendipity in the hockey world can be made than by LeSueur, who started as a right winger in Quebec. He worked as a bank clerk in the west and then took a similar post in Smiths Falls where he also played the wing for a local team. One day, the goaler became ill, and LeSueur volunteered to guard the cage. He never left. His team lost a Cup challenge to Ottawa in 1906, but he was so spectacular in defeat that the Senators asked him to play goal when they were, in turn, challenged by the Wanderers. He won two Cups with Ottawa and later played for Toronto before going off to war in 1916. He was discharged as a sergeant-major and turned to coaching. LeSueur was briefly with the Hamilton Tigers in the NHL, and was later the first manager of the Windsor Arena and Olympia in Detroit. He went on to manage the Peace Bridge Arena in Fort Erie and then returned to hockey with Buffalo in the IHL. He introduced the gauntlet glove to goalkeeping and designed a new net that was used in the NHA and NHL from 1912 to 1925. LeSueur was an original member of the famed Hot Stove League, and it was there his career in broadcasting evolved. He settled in Hamilton and worked in radio for some 20 years until retiring. Considered the finest goalie of his era, his finest honour might have come when he was named the starting goalie in the Hod Stuart Memorial Game in 1908, the first All-Star Game in hockey history. LeSueur was inducted into the Hockey Hall of Fame in 1961.

M

MARSHALL, Jack

b. St. Valier, Quebec, March 14, 1876
d. Montreal, Quebec, August 7, 1965

For most of his life Marshall held hockey's most prestigious record – having played on more Stanley Cup teams than any other man. He first won with the Winnipeg Victorias in 1901 and the following year with the Montreal AAA. In 1907 and 1910 he starred with the Montreal Wanderers' championship teams, and he closed out his miraculous record winning with the Toronto Blueshirts in 1914. To this day, he is the only man to have won the Cup with four different teams. His move from Winnipeg to Montreal sparked greater than passing interest because he also brought tube skates with him, the first time the east had seen such blades. Montreal was his home for life. He worked for the Macdonald Tobacco Company for half a century, and for many years was the only surviving member of the "Little Men of Iron" team of 1902. He was named to the Hockey Hall of Fame's honour roll in 1965.

MAXWELL, Fred "Steamer"

b. Winnipeg, Manitoba, May 19, 1890
d. Winnipeg, Manitoba, September 10, 1975

Maxwell's induction into the Hockey Hall of Fame as a player in 1962 was based on a short but successful burst on the hockey scene. He was given his nickname for his great speed as a skater, playing the rover position in the days of seven-man hockey. He developed with the Monarchs in his native Winnipeg in 1910 and played for only a few years, spurning any and all offers to turn professional. Teams in the NHA and PCHA tried to lure him with great cash contracts, but Maxwell preferred the Allan Cup to the Stanley Cup. He won the former with Winnipeg in 1915 and then retired as a player. After the war he turned to coaching, starting with the Winnipeg Falcons who won gold for Canada at the 1920 Olympics. He coached his former Monarchs and was then offered the best job in the game – bossing the bench of the Toronto Maple Leafs. But Maxwell demanded a three-year contract and Con Smythe wouldn't give it, so the Leafs took Dick Irvin and Maxwell stayed put in Manitoba. He later coached Canada to gold at the 1935 World Championships in Davos, Switzerland and throughout his life was an official in the yearly Memorial Cup and Allan Cup series of playoffs. In later years, he was also head of F.G. Maxwell Co. Ltd. in the lumber industry before retiring in 1967.

McGEE, Frank ("One-eyed Frank")

b. Ottawa, Ontario, 1881
d. Courcelette, France,
September 16, 1916

In the land where myth and legend meet reality, no one holds a more prominent place in the hockey department than Frank McGee. He came from a well-known family in Ottawa and developed into one of the city's finest hockey and football players, making his puck debut in 1903 by scoring two goals against the vaunted Montreal AAA team. He did this despite having the use of only one eye, the other having been damaged by a puck while he was playing with the Aberdeens a short time earlier. He played with Ottawa when the Silver Seven was at the height of its powers, becoming one of the league's best and most consistent scorers. A three-goal game was common for McGee. Four goals was not remarkable, and seven times did he score five goals in a game! He won Cups with the team in 1903, 1904, and 1905, the last of those providing the anecdote of mythological proportions that accompanies his name and Stanley Cup history. When a team from Dawson City travelled 3,000 miles to challenge Ottawa for the Cup, it marked the most lopsided series in Cup play. Ottawa won the first game 9-2, but after the Yukoners had a day's rest they became over-confident. In the next contest, McGee scored 14 goals, eight of them consecutively, and the Dawson City challenge was brutally crushed. He retired from hockey in 1907 but continued to play football until the start of the war when he enlisted. He told family that when it came time to take the eye exam, he put one hand over his bad eye and then changed hands, not eyes, in order to pass the test. He was wounded in action in December 1915, but once recovered insisted on returning to the front where he was killed in action. He was among the first men inducted into the Hockey Hall of Fame, in 1945, a man of courage, skill, and accomplishment.

McGIMSIE, Billy

b. Woodsville, Ontario, June 7, 1880
d. Calgary, Alberta, October 28, 1968

When McGimsie was a boy he was enamoured with a new trophy called the Stanley Cup. He vowed one day to win it, and to that end played hockey every spare moment. He moved to Rat Portage when he was just a year old, and wound up playing all his serious hockey at home. He played for the Thistles in the early 1900s when the team challenged for, and lost, the Cup to the mighty Silver Seven of Ottawa. But in 1907, playing for the team and city now known as Kenora, he centred his squad and upset the Montreal Wanderers for the trophy. Kenora was, and likely will forever be, the smallest city to win the Cup, and his dream realized, McGimsie was a happy man. On his way home from that Montreal series, the team played an exhibition game in Ottawa during which he dislocated his shoulder. He retired from hockey, moved to Calgary, and went into private business. His short but remarkable career was merit enough to place him in the Hockey Hall of Fame in 1962.

McNAMARA, George

b. Penetanguishene, Ontario,
August 26, 1886
d. Miami, Florida, March 10, 1952

George was the better player, but he and his brother, Howard, were more famous as a pair, called the "Dynamite Twins" because of their imposing size and physical presence on defence. They grew up in Sault Ste. Marie and began to play together in Halifax with the Crescents, where they were given their nickname. In 1914, the boys split when George played for the Toronto Blueshirts and Howard for the Montreal Canadiens in the NHA. George won his only Stanley Cup that season at Mutual Street Arena in Toronto. Two years later, Howard won with the Habs. George became a major in the 6th Railway Troops during the war. After retiring, he coached the Soo Greyhounds to an Allan Cup in 1924 and then he and Howard started McNamara Construction Co. Ltd. which became one of the largest and most successful firms in the country. George suffered a fatal heart attack while vacationing in Florida, and six years later he was inducted into the Hockey Hall of Fame.

MORAN, Patrick "Paddy"

b. Quebec City, Quebec, March 11, 1877
d. Quebec City, Quebec, January 14, 1966

He may have been a goalie in the old days when hockey was still developing, but much about his personality and style of play were modern. Moran was a standup goalie during an era when goalies weren't allowed to drop to their knees. He was known to wear a large sweater that he would unbutton just enough to cover a bit more net – the first exponent, as it were, of oversized equipment. Although there was no goal crease, he was also not averse to using his stick to hack and claim territory in front of his goal. He started out playing for the Sarsfield team in Quebec City and rose up through the ranks to play with the Bulldogs in 1905. He stayed with the team his entire career, winning consecutive Stanley Cups in 1912 and 1913. His goals-against average was never sparkling, but he was famous for playing his best in important games. When he retired in 1917, Moran stayed in his home town and worked for Canada Customs for the next 32 years. He was particularly proud of having built his own house with his hockey earnings, and remained a fan of the game his full and long life. He was inducted into the Hockey Hall of Fame in 1958.

P

PHILLIPS, Tommy ("Nibs")

b. Rat Portage (Kenora), Ontario,
May 22, 1883
d. Toronto, Ontario, November 30, 1923

In many ways Phillips was, in the modern vernacular, a complete player. He had great speed and a terrific shot, and he was also a backchecker without compare. He didn't play organized hockey until moving to Montreal in 1901 but soon earned a spot on the AAA team that went on to win the Stanley Cup in 1903. He was still just 19. Phillips moved back home to Rat Portage and played for the local team, losing the Cup challenge in 1905, but winning two years later. Ottawa recruited him and Phillips returned east, but the left winger at the time for the Senators was Alf Smith, no slouch himself. Phillips, a left shot, happily moved to the right side, thus becoming the first great forward to play his off-wing. Completing his Canadian tour of duty, he moved to British Columbia to play in the PCHA while also working in the lumber business. He passed away at age 40 in Toronto from an infection after the removal of a tooth.

PULFORD, Harvey

b. Toronto, Ontario, 1875
d. Ottawa, Ontario, October 31, 1940

Perhaps only Lionel Conacher was as fine an all-round athlete as Pulford, a man who played many sports for many years, a champion in everything he tried. In football, he played 16 years for the Rough Riders, winning four Dominion championships at the turn of the 20th century. In eight years of lacrosse, he was champion four times. From 1896 to 1898 he was the lightweight and then heavyweight boxing champ for eastern Canada, and in paddling and rowing he won almost too many titles to name. It was as a hockey player though, that he earned his greatest fame and glory, playing the game for some 17 years with Ottawa, his adopted home. Most significantly, Pulford anchored the Silver Seven defence when the team won three Stanley Cups, in 1902, 1904, and 1905, withstanding several challenges along the way. He was a leader and tremendous bodychecker, tough as nails but sporting and gentlemanly to boot. He retired from hockey in 1909 and worked in importing and insurance in Ottawa, but remained in sporting circles. In 1924, at age 49, he won a city squash championship. In later years, Pulford suffered from heart troubles and it was a heart attack that took his life in 1940. Five years later, one of Canada's greatest athletes was inducted into the Hockey Hall of Fame.

R

RANKIN, Frank
b. Stratford, Ontario, April 1, 1889
d. unknown

In later years, Frank Rankin was famous as the man who coached the Toronto Granites to Olympic gold in 1924. As a player though, he was a rover in the seven-man game who came up short at virtually every turn. He was part of three OHA champion teams with the Stratford juniors from 1906 to 1909, and he later captained an Eaton's team to two Allan Cup finals where the team lost to the powerful Winnipeg Victorias. Rankin then played for St. Mike's in Toronto, and again lost three consecutive provincial finals series. Nonetheless, Rankin was considered one of the finest rovers of his era and was inducted into the Hockey Hall of Fame in 1961.

RICHARDSON, George
b. Kingston, Ontario, September 14, 1886
d. Wulverghem, Belgium, February 9, 1916

On ice and in battle, no man accorded

himself with greater pride and dignity of purpose than George Taylor Richardson. A Hall of Famer in 1950, he won an Allan Cup with Queen's University in 1909, though he played the balance of his career with the 14th Regiment team in Kingston. His career was curtailed by a call-to-arms, and in enlisting he also sacrificed his position with his family's prosperous grain operations, James Richardson & Sons. He went overseas with the 2nd Canadian Infantry Battalion and was wounded at Langemarck. As soon as he was better he returned to the front where he fought for 10 months straight. He was shot in the hip during a night operation, was dragged back to his side, but died a short time later. On his deathbed he recited a passage from Kipling: "There is one task for all/One life for each to give/Who stand if freedom fall? Who die if England live."

ROBERTS, Gordon ("Doc")
b. Ottawa, Ontario, September 5, 1891
d. Oakland, California, September 2, 1966

A rare combination of academic intelligence and hockey acumen, Roberts was a skater and a doctor. He played with Ottawa in the NHA in 1910 but moved to Montreal to play for the Wanderers in order to study medicine at McGill University. He had terrific stamina on ice and was renowned for a shot that curved en route to the net. For six seasons he was one of the top scorers in the league. In 1916, he practised medicine in Vancouver and played in the PCHA for the local Millionaires, leading the league in scoring with 43 goals in just 23 games. The next year, his hospital work took him to Seattle, so he suited up with the Metropolitans. In 1925, Roberts had removed himself from hockey and the hockey world. He moved to Oakland and was a respected obstetrician for more than 40 years until his death. Five years later, he was inducted into the Hockey Hall of Fame for his skating exploits of a half a century earlier.

RUSSEL, Blair
b. Montreal, Quebec, September 17, 1880
d. Montreal, Quebec, December 7, 1961

Odd as it may seem in the 21st century, Russel preferred retirement to a career as a professional hockey player, a decision he was forced to make in 1909 when the dominant league of the day, the Eastern Canada Amateur Hockey Association, went pro. Russel played mostly with the Montreal Victorias

where his abilities were often overlooked because of teammate Russell Bowie. Together though, Russel and Russell were the best tandem in the ECAHA. Blair once scored seven goals in a game, and he was both a clean and a skillful player. In 1909, he had a choice to stay in the league as a pro or retire; he chose to remain a "pure" athlete and moved into business. Russel worked in investments in Montreal and passed away four years before being inducted into the Hockey Hall of Fame.

RUSSELL, Ernie
b. Montreal, Quebec, October 21, 1883
d. Montreal, Quebec, February 23, 1963

Playing centre or rover, Russell was a premier scorer in the early years of the 20th century in Montreal. He was a speedy and shifty offensive star who played on three Cup teams with the Wanderers, in 1907, 1908, and 1910. In that first season, Russell scored 42 goals in nine league games and recorded hat tricks in five successive games, an unheard of feat even in those days. Not surprisingly, the one year the Wanderers did not win the Cup in that stretch was the one year Russell did not play with the team. He was also a member of the Montreal AAA sports club, that too placed a team in the ECAHA, and because he refused to give up that membership he was expelled by the Redbands for a year. Upon his return, the team won the Cup again. He was made a member of the Hockey Hall of Fame in 1965.

RUTTAN, John Douglas "Jack"
b. Winnipeg, Manitoba, April 5, 1889
d. Winnipeg, Manitoba, January 7, 1973

Ruttan combined a lifetime playing hockey with a successful career, residing in Winnipeg his entire life. As a boy, he played for a series of local teams, from Armstrong's Point to St. John's College, and moved up to senior hockey in 1909. He helped the team win the title the next fall and by 1912-13 he was with the best team around, the Winnipeg Hockey Club. The team won the Allan Cup that season, and Ruttan played the rest of his career there. After retiring he coached the team. In 1926, he established Chipman Chemicals Limited, noted at first for weed control for the railway. He remained its president until 1955 and after retiring stayed on as a director. He was named to the Hockey Hall of Fame in 1962.

SCANLAN, Fred

b. unknown
d. unknown

The line of Harry Trihey, Art Farrell, and Fred Scanlan played for the Montreal Shamrocks and was the best forward combination of its day. Scanlan came to the team in 1987 and helped win Stanley Cups in 1899 and 1900. He moved out to Winnipeg to close out his career, retiring in 1903. Little is known of his life, but as a player he was considered the worker on that famous line. He had a good shot, but generally enabled Trihey and Farrell to work their magic around the net. He and Farrell were inducted into the Hockey Hall of Fame together in 1965 (Trihey had been so honoured in 1950).

SEIBERT, Oliver

b. Berlin (Kitchener), Ontario, March 18, 1881
d. Kitchener, Ontario, May 15, 1944

At one time, Oliver organized a team comprised only of family members. He and brothers Edward, Clarence, Nelson, Shannon, and Albert joined father, Frank, much to the delight of fans. Oliver was one of the finest pre-NHL skaters. He could move backwards faster than most players could forward, and was the first native of Berlin to become a professional hockey player when he joined a team in Sault Ste. Marie in 1904. Previously, he had played in the Western Ontario league where he developed a new shot, the wrist shot, that changed the way players moved in on goal and challenged the goalie. Seibert played pro for a number of years, and then returned to his home town to work as a locksmith for the rest of his days. His son, Earl, went on to a great career in the NHL, and together they became the first father-son combination to be inducted into the Hockey Hall of Fame, Oliver in 1961 and Earl two years later.

SMITH, Alf

b. Ottawa, Ontario, June 3, 1873
d. Ottawa, Ontario, August 21, 1953

He was the oldest of 11 hockey-playing brothers, and though Tommy was the better scorer and played longer it was Alf who likely had the greater glory. He moved his way up in Ottawa where he quickly earned a reputation as one of the toughest and meanest players

around. Smith played a year of pro in Pittsburgh and then retired for three years. He returned at age 30 to the local Silver Seven in 1902 and played right wing to Frank McGee on a team that won the Cup from 1903 through to 1906, four in all with hockey's first dynasty. The team later featured another brother, Harry. Alf played one final year in Pittsburgh and then began a lengthy career as a coach, a passion he developed while still playing. In 1909, he was behind the bench when the Ottawa Cliffsides captured the Allan Cup. Later, Smith coached all around, notably with the Senators and New York Americans in the NHL. He and Tommy were both inducted into the Hockey Hall of Fame, Alf in 1962 and Tommy 11 years later.

STUART, Bruce

b. Ottawa, Ontario, 1882
d. Ottawa, Ontario, October 28, 1961

A strong and dominating presence on ice was Stuart during the days of powerful teams in Ottawa and Montreal at the turn of the 20th century. He was a large man who could fight and score goals in equal measure. Bruce and brother, Hod, joined the Ottawa Senators in 1899 and played there for two seasons before joining the Bulldogs in Quebec. In 1902, Bruce left to play professionally in Pittsburgh and Houghton before joining the Wanderers in 1907. The team won the Stanley Cup in his first year, and the next year he captained the Senators to a second championship, in 1909. The Sens repeated their victory two years later, Stuart's last victory. He retired at season's end and coached in Ottawa while running a shoe store he had opened toward the end of his playing days. He remained its manager until 1952 when failing health confined him mostly to his bed. In 1961, Stuart used all his strength to attend his induction into the Hockey Hall of Fame, and just a few weeks later he passed away.

STUART, Hodgson "Hod"

b. Ottawa, Ontario, 1879
d. Belleville, Ontario, June 23, 1907

He was a sturdy man, a rock of a defenceman and a skilled skater to match, yet his life was cut short by a tragic accident. Like his brother Bruce, Hod played in the east and also ventured to the United States to play pro for a good contract. He was a tough but fair player, and after one particularly bloody game in Pittsburgh in 1906, he

immediately left and finished the season with the Montreal Wanderers, the team that had tried to recruit him at the start of the season. Stuart had played with his brother in Quebec, but it was in the late winter of 1907 that he won his only Stanley Cup when the Wanderers reclaimed the Cup from Kenora. Just a few months later, Stuart travelled to Belleville to oversee the construction of the Belleville Drill Shed, a contract his father had negotiated. Stuart went swimming one afternoon and dove off a dock into shallow water. His head struck a rock and he broke his neck. He was found a short while later floating in three feet of water. Stuart's death stunned the hockey world of eastern Canada and once the new season started plans were made to play a game for the benefit of Stuart's family. On January 2, 1908, the Hod Stuart Memorial Game was played, featuring the Wanderers against a league all-star team. The game raised $2,000 for his widow, and it was the first all-star contest in hockey history. Stuart was among the inaugural inductees into the Hockey Hall of Fame when that institution was started in 1945.

T

TAYLOR, Fred "Cyclone"

b. Tara, Ontario, June 23, 1883
d. Vancouver, British Columbia, June 10, 1979

Few players in the long history of hockey can claim the title of "best player never to play in the NHL" with more validity than Taylor. He was the best player of his era, the most exciting and most popular, but he had such a tremendous career out west in the Pacific Coast league that he had no reason to move east to the NHL after it formed in 1917. As a teen, he played for Listowel and Portage before turning pro with Houghton, Michigan in 1905. Two years later, he joined the Ottawa Senators, and in his first game scored five goals and demonstrated a skating ability that had no compare. He was, in short, a cyclone, and the nickname replaced his given name for the rest of his days. In 1910 he played for Renfrew and it was there that he scored a goal of mythical greatness as he apparently skated the length of the ice backwards to put the puck in the net! He was the highest paid player in the game and in his early career was a rushing defenceman, unparalleled in his use of strategy. He won two Stanley Cups, his first with Ottawa in 1909. When he reached a contractual impasse with the NHA he moved out west and played in Vancouver for the rest of his career. It was then that he was converted to forward, and even though he was 35 years old, won two successive scoring championships in the PCHA. After retiring, he stayed in Vancouver the rest of his life, working as the immigration commissioner for the federal government until retiring in 1959. He was named president of the PCHL in 1937 and served as a director for the British Columbia Hockey Benevolent Society from 1954 until his death. On July 1, 1946, King George VI conferred upon him the Order of the British Empire for his service in World War II. He was a charter member of the Hockey Hall of Fame in 1945 and was later inducted into the Canadian Sports Hall of Fame. He turned the sod to start construction of the new HHOF building in 1961, and dropped the puck at the Pacific Coliseum to begin play for Vancouver's NHL entry in 1970. Although he never played a minute in the NHL, Cyclone Taylor was one of the greatest players ever to master the sport of hockey.

TRETIAK, Vladislav

b. Dimitrovo, Soviet Union (Russia), April 25, 1952

No hockey player in the modern era has captivated the Canadian fan more than Tretiak, a goalie who never made it to the NHL because of politics, not ability. The Soviets may have been successful at keeping him away from the dollars and nets of NHL arenas, but they couldn't resist showing what they had. In 1963, the 11-year-old Tretiak played at the Children's Sports School, the early developmental level for top players. At age 17, he was on the top team in the country, the Central Red Army. And in 1972, at age 20, he proved to be as good as Ken Dryden and Tony Esposito at the Summit Series. Tretiak had been scouted before the tournament, and the verdict was that he was sloppy and had a weak glove hand. No one knew at the time that the night before the game he had been at a wedding and was playing badly hungover. Sure enough, over the course of the eight-game series, Tretiak established himself as a remarkable goalie with lightning reflexes, legs as quick as fingers and a glove hand that didn't permit a puck past. In ensuing years, he proved time and again to be

arguably the best goalie on the planet. In the famous New Year's Eve game at the Forum, December 31, 1975, the 3-3 tie between the Soviets and Canadiens was due to the efforts of Tretiak, whose team was outshot 38-13. In the 1981 Canada Cup finals, the only one Canada didn't win, Tretiak was astounding again. Internationally, his career is without compare. He won three Olympic gold medals, in 1972, 1976, and 1984. He won gold ten times at the World Championships, the Stanley Cup of tournaments for European nations, during which time the team was virtually unbeaten. He won 13 league titles with the Red Army and was named a First Team All-Star in 14 consecutive years. In 1978, he was given the Order of Lenin for his lifetime of service to Soviet hockey. His only blemish came at the 1980 Olympics when he was pulled in the game against the USA, the so-called "Miracle on Ice," which led to American gold. In 1983, the Canadiens drafted Tretiak in the hopes he might yet be released to the NHL in his declining years. The Soviets never acquiesced, and he retired after the Izvestia tournament in January 1985, tired of stopping pucks, but disappointed at never having had the chance to do so in North America. In 1989, he made history when the Hockey Hall of Fame inducted him, the first non-NHLer so chosen in the modern era. A year later, Chicago coach Mike Keenan hired him as a goalie coach, and it was in that capacity that Tretiak made it to the NHL. He tutored Ed Belfour who, in tribute, wore number 20. Like Jacques Plante, Tretiak was also a student of the game, and his book, *The Hockey I Love*, displays an understanding of the game that is far more sophisticated than the art of stopping pucks might at first blush suggest. He never played in the NHL but Tretiak's influence on the game has been undeniable, and some of the stops he made during his heyday were, well, unbelievable.

TRIHEY, Henry Judah "Harry"

b. Montreal, Quebec, December 25, 1877
d. Montreal, Quebec, December 9, 1942

Being a hockey player of the first order pales in comparison to the contributions Harry Trihey made to the city of Montreal during his full and successful life. A student at St. Mary's College, he subsequently entered McGill's law program. He led the school team to the

national rugby championship, and after graduating, played hockey for the Shamrocks. Trihey wasn't the fastest skater around but he did have a tremendous shot. He led the team to Stanley Cup victories in 1899 and 1900. On February 4, 1899, he scored ten goals in a single game, an all-time record bested only by Frank McGee. The Shamrocks lost the Cup in 1901 to Winnipeg and Trihey retired, but by then he had left his mark. He was credited with promoting team passing among the forwards rather than simply "lifting" the puck into the other end, as was common practice. In retirement, Trihey was active, generous, and successful. He practised law the rest of his life, and along the way distinguished himself in a variety of ways. In 1914, when war erupted, Colonel Trihey organized a military unit called the 55th Regiment Irish Canadian Rangers. He then took a full expeditionary force overseas, the 199th Battalion, Duchess of Connaught's Own Irish Canadian Rangers. He returned to the firm of Trihey and McManamy. From 1930 to 1935 he was a member of the Montreal Harbour Commission. He sat on numerous boards, wielded power in the business community, and was a life member of St. Mary's Hospital. In 1950, he was inducted into the Hockey Hall of Fame, a great hockey player, an even greater man.

WALSH, Marty

b. Kingston, Ontario, October 16, 1883
d. Gravenhurst, Ontario, March 27, 1915

It was rare for a member of Ottawa's early Cup teams to be born and raised outside the city, but Walsh was one such exception. He grew up in Kingston and as a teen attended Queen's University. He played hockey for the Queen's team and led it to challenge Ottawa for the Cup in 1906. The attempt failed, but Walsh distinguished himself even in defeat, and the next year became a professional with the Canadian Soo in the IHL. He broke his leg early in the season though, and the year after was lured to Ottawa by the Senators. In 1907-08, his first year, he scored seven goals in one game and led the league with 27 in just nine. He helped the team win the Cup in 1909, 1910, and 1911 during a period when his scoring exploits were the stuff of legend. In one challenge game against Port Arthur, on March 16, 1911, he scored 10 goals in an 11-4 victory. He retired in 1912 and moved out west to work as a paymaster in railway construction. He returned east but became very ill, spending his last days at the Gravenhurst Sanitarium before succumbing to either consumption or tuberculosis. He entered the Hockey Hall of Fame in 1962.

WATSON, Harry ("Moose")
b. St. John's, Newfoundland, July 14, 1898
d. London, Ontario, September 11, 1957
Of all the promising amateur hockey players in the early years of the NHL's existence, none was greater than Watson, yet he before all others shunned professionalism and never played for money. He spent the first few years of his life in England, but when his family settled finally in Toronto, he took to hockey with natural grace and ability. He played junior with St. Andrew's College and senior with Aura Lee in 1916-17, but stopped playing to join Canada's war efforts. Watson served with the Flying Corps, and upon his return played hockey again, with the Toronto Granites. They were the finest team in the land, a team that won the Allan Cup in 1922 and 1923, and was selected to represent Canada at the 1924 Olympic Winter Games in Chamonix, France. Watson set records at that tournament that will never be broken. In Canada's first game, against Czechoslovakia, he scored 11 goals. He had 6 against Sweden and then set the all-time scoring mark by registering 13 goals against Switzerland. In all, he had 36 goals in 5 games, including 3 in the 6-1 victory over the USA to give Canada the gold medal. The Granites returned to Toronto heroes. After the celebratory parade, linemates Dunc Munro and Hooley Smith turned pro. But no matter how much he was offered – including $30,000 a season by the Montreal Maroons – Watson steadfastly refused the greedy lure of money to play the sport he loved. Instead, he settled into a job with the Watson and McVittie Insurance Agency, a partnership he had established in 1921 and maintained until his death. He was inducted into the Hockey Hall of Fame as an amateur.

WESTWICK, Harry ("Rat")
b. Ottawa, Ontario, April 23, 1876
d. Ottawa, Ontario, April 3, 1957
Some described him as a player who could skate between two opponents standing side by side. Others said he was slippery and impossible to catch. Others, more plainly, said he looked like a rat on the ice. However he was pictured, the 130-pound goalie-turned-rover was a star in Ottawa both as a hockey player and a lacrosse star. On ice, he played for his hometown almost without cessation from 1895 to 1909. During these years he played on three Stanley Cup teams and scored more goals than any other on the team with the exception of the great Frank McGee. Westwick also played lacrosse from 1896 to 1904, winning three world championships. He also played football briefly with the Ottawa Rough Riders. After his playing days, Westwick stayed in the city and worked at the Federal Government Printing Bureau. He was inducted into the Hockey Hall of Fame in 1962.

WHITCROFT, Fred
b. Port Perry, Ontario, 1883
d. Vancouver, British Columbia, 1931
It wasn't until his family moved to Peterborough nine years after his birth that young Fred got his first taste of hockey, on the outdoor rink on Charlotte Street. His father was a foreman and as a teen Fred played junior for the local Colts, winning the championship in 1901. He stayed with the team for a number of years in the senior ranks, and impressed Tom Hooper of Kenora enough that when the Thistles were defending the Cup against a challenge from the Wanderers, Hooper enlisted the services of Whitcroft, a rover. The team lost and Whitcroft moved further west to Edmonton where he was part of two further unsuccessful challenges, in 1908 and 1910. He finished his career in the NHA playing for the Renfrew Creamery Kings and then returned to Edmonton to manage the team he had once played for. After a tenure of two seasons, he settled permanently in Vancouver, working in real estate and at the racetrack. He was inducted into the Hockey Hall of Fame in 1962.

WILSON, Gordon "Phat"
b. Port Arthur (Thunder Bay), Ontario, December 29, 1895
d. Port Arthur (Thunder Bay), Ontario, July 26, 1970
A lifelong resident of Port Arthur, Wilson spurned all offers to turn pro, though the name Gord Wilson does grace the annals of NHL history. Phat played kid hockey for the local church league and in 1918 joined the War Veterans Senior Hockey Club. In 1921-22, he ventured to Iroquois Falls where the team made it to the Allan Cup playoffs before losing to the eventual winners, Toronto Granites. Wilson returned home, and with the Port Arthur Seniors (erroneously called the Bearcats at that point in their history) won three Allan Cups, in 1925, 1926, and 1929. While the team's goalie, Lorne Chabot, and Wilson's defence partner, Bill Brydge, went on to sign NHL contracts, Wilson rejected the chance. He was working for the Port Arthur Utilities Commission, playing senior hockey, and was content. But he did tell Boston GM Art Ross that if he ever had a son who turned into a good player, Phat would send the boy to Boston. Years later, that's exactly what happened, and Gord Wilson Jr. played two games with the Bruins in '54-'55! Phat did, indeed, spend the rest of his life in Port Arthur. He retired from play in 1933 and was the co-founder of a girls hockey league. He was also president of the Port Arthur National Baseball League and coached senior hockey teams for a few years. He remained with the Utilities Commission for 35 years and was inducted into the Hockey Hall of Fame in 1962.

APPENDIX

NHL ROOKIES 2002-2003

#

ABID, Ramzi
b. Montreal, Quebec, March 24, 1980
A mid-round Phoenix draft choice in 2000, Abid made his NHL debut on November 12, 2002 to replace the injured Ladislav Nagy. He played just three minutes and was sent down the minors the next day. Like many a player who opted not to sign with the team that originally drafted him (Colorado, 28th overall in 1998), his second draft placement was considerably lower (85th). He missed most of his first season of pro, 2000-01, with a serious wrist injury.

ALLEN, Bobby
b. Braintree, Massachusetts, November 14, 1978
Drafted by Boston in 1998 but later traded to Edmonton, Allen entered the NHL with the Oilers on New Year's Eve 2002 and played just a few shifts. He graduated from Boston College in 2001 after four years, but the defenceman has yet to make an impact in the big tent.

ANDERSON, Craig
b. Park Ridge, Illinois, May 21, 1981
The sneaky little devil has made a mockery of the NHL, though all in the right spirit. When Anderson was 10, he took a trip to Sweden that left an indelible mark on him. As he grew up, he developed into an excellent goalie and was drafted by Calgary. The modern negotiating ploy of not signing and re-entering the draft appealed to him, and Chicago drafted him two years later. He had a fine junior career with Guelph in the OHL, and when he made his debut with the Hawks on November 30, 2002, his name on his sweater was spelled Andersson, in tribute to his fond memories as a boy. Will the league tell him to revert to the true spelling of his name? Stay tuned.

AULIN, Jared
b. Calgary, Alberta, March 15, 1982
Despite being called up for just one game by Los Angeles, on December 17, 2002, Aulin is a certain part of the Kings' future. He is a tough centre not afraid to go into the corners and play along the boards and has been willing to show his worth in the AHL without complaining.

#

BACKMAN, Christian
b. Alingsas, Sweden, April 28, 1980
It was four years from draft day in 1998 to the day Backman moved to North America after a successful career in the Swedish pro leagues, and St. Louis expects him to be one of their finer defencemen of the future. He made his NHL debut on February 11, 2003 and played just four games for the team during the regular season, but his ability to move the puck is what the Blues hope he will bring to the team in future years.

BARNEY, Scott
b. Oshawa, Ontario, March 27, 1979
January 25, 2003 was the successful culmination of overcoming years of pain, frustration, and devastation. Barney was drafted by Los Angeles in 1997, but one day in '99 he woke up in excruciating back pain. For the next three years, he couldn't walk for a quarter of an hour without agony and he couldn't even ride a stationary bike. Two operations, many doctors, and thousands of hours of determination later, he felt ready to try hockey again. He called the Kings and asked for a tryout, and he impressed the staff so much they signed him to a contract and assigned him to the minors. He made it to the NHL that January night, and with any luck he can keep it going in the years to come.

BARTOVIC, Milan
b. Trencin, Czechoslovakia (Slovakia), April 9, 1981
As soon as he was drafted by Buffalo in 1999, Bartovic moved to the Canadian west to play in the WHL. Two years later he was in the AHL, and on April 2, 2003 he made his NHL entry, a right winger with good speed and offensive ability.

BAYDA, Ryan
b. Saskatoon, Saskatchewan, December 9, 1980
Drafted by Carolina in 2000, Bayda couldn't have been happier to see the 'Canes go to the Cup finals in the spring of '02, but he couldn't have welcomed the chance to play during a tailspin that saw the team go from the finals to last place. Bayda left the University of North Dakota to turn pro after just three years of college, and on February 14, 2003 he played his first NHL game

on left wing with Ron Francis and Jeff O'Neill. He stayed the rest of the year and recorded 14 points. The team can only go up from 30th place next year.

BEAUCHEMIN, Francois
b. Sorel, Quebec, June 4, 1980
The road to the NHL was a twisty one for Beauchemin, who went from wearing a Montreal cap on draft day to finishing his junior career in the Q, going to the AHL, and sinking to the ECHL before getting his chance. On February 27, 2003, the Habs recalled him for a single game.

BERGERON, Marc-Andre
b. St. Louis de France, Quebec, October 13, 1980
Go figure. The player chosen as the best defenceman in Canadian junior for the 2000-01 season was never drafted, and it was only that summer that Edmonton signed Bergeron as a free agent. Only 5'9" he played considerably tougher than his height, making his debut with the Oil on March 11, 2003 and staying for a total of five games.

BLATNY, Zdenek
b. Brno, Czechoslovakia (Czech Republic), January 14, 1981
He was a decent scorer back in the Czech Republic, and an excellent scorer in the WHL, but since turning pro, Blatny has struggled, like many a teen phenom before him, to continue putting the puck in the net at the higher level. He made his debut with Atlanta on March 19, 2003 and played only four games, scoring nary a single point.

BOUCHARD, Pierre-Marc
b. Sherbrooke, Quebec, April 27, 1984
The sky is the limit for Bouchard, who made the NHL as an 18-year-old. He might be small, but his skill level is high and his intelligence on ice more than compensates for a lack of physical presence. He was player of the year in Canadian junior hockey for 2001-02, and the next fall he made Minnesota, the team that took him 8th overall at that summer's draft. Wisely, the Wild loaned him to the Canadian National Team for the World Junior Championships in Halifax, and he was one of the best players on ice, helping Canada win a silver medal. He returned to the Wild with greater confidence and can only become better and better.

BOUWMEESTER, Jay
b. Edmonton, Alberta,
September 27, 1983
Big, fast, mobile, smart, the kind of player to build a team around, Bouwmeester will certainly play in the NHL for a long time. Florida drafted him 3rd overall in 2002 and he made the team at training camp in the fall. He hasn't looked out of place yet. Bouwmeester was one of the youngest players ever to represent Canada at the WJC and is mature beyond his years. He developed with Medicine Hat in the WHL and coach Mike Keenan has worked him into the Panthers blueline corps with uncommon confidence. Bouwmeester is surely the kind of player who will one day win awards and Stanley Cups.

BYKOV, Dmitri
b. Izhevsk, Soviet Union (Russia),
May 5, 1977
Detroit drafted Bykov a lowly 258th overall in 2001 when he was already 24, and although he played briefly with the Wings in '02-'03, the defenceman will have a tough time cracking the Detroit lineup on a nightly basis.

C

CAJANEK, Peter
b. Gottwaldov, Czechoslovakia
(Czech Republic), August 18, 1975
As a 27-year-old rookie in 2002-03, Cajanek scored 9 goals in 51 games for St. Louis, though goals are not the only thing the centre brings to the table. He is also a solid defensive player with a bit of jam to his game, and at the 2002 Olympics in Salt Lake City he was the only non-NHLer on the Czech roster. Cajanek had played his whole career in the Czech Republic before being drafted by the Blues a lowly 253rd overall in 2001.

CAMMALLERI, Mike
b. Richmond Hill, Ontario, June 8, 1982
Despite taking the college route to the NHL, Cammalleri will have a hard time asserting himself in the NHL. He played for Canada at the World Juniors and was drafted by Los Angeles in 2001. He left the University of Michigan to turn pro but ended up in the minors to start the 2002-03 season. Cammalleri was recalled for a game on November 8,

2002 and recorded an assist but he is by no means a regular yet in the Kings lineup.

CARON, Sebastien
b. Amqui, Quebec, June 25, 1980
His timing couldn't be better. Caron, a goalie, was drafted by Pittsburgh in 1999, a team desperate for a solid netminder. Caron had a superb junior career in the Quebec league but struggled in two years in the AHL. He made his Penguins debut on January 11, 2003, stopping all 18 shots he faced over two periods, and in his few appearances made a strong impression.

CHEECHOO, Jonathan
b. Moose Factory, Ontario, July 15, 1980
Without doubt, one of the all-time great names in hockey! Cheechoo was a forceful presence in junior with Belleville but had a rough time when he got to San Jose for the 2002-03 season. He started slowly, wound up a fourth liner and then a healthy scratch, but worked his way back into the lineup and proved to be a legitimate right winger. He'll probably never score 50 goals or win the Selke Trophy, either, but he is a player of NHL calibre.

CHISTOV, Stanislav
b. Chelyabinsk, Soviet Union (Russia),
April 17, 1983
In his first NHL game, with Anaheim on October 10, 2002, Chistov became the youngest player in the league's history to register four points in his first game (a goal and three assists). Two games later, he was a healthy scratch because of poor play. Obviously, his talents lie somewhere in between those performances. Small and talented, like teammate Paul Kariya, he has to learn to play with intensity every shift. If he does, he will be an NHLer; if he doesn't, he'll become familiar with the press box and the minors.

COLAIACOVO, Carlo
b. Toronto, Ontario, January 27, 1983
The Leafs drafted him in 2001 and invited him to their training camp the next year to show him the ropes. Lo and behold, the teenager had such an outstanding camp he made the team, signed a multi-million-dollar contract and looked set for an NHL career. Whoa, Carlo! The Leafs got off to a slow start and didn't pay him for close to a month, and the team's awful showing put his place on the team in jeopardy. Coach and GM Pat Quinn sent him back to junior, and Colaiacovo wound up going to the

World Juniors and being one of the best players in the tournament. He narrowly missed becoming the first defenceman to lead the WJC in scoring, and returned to junior a better player. He'll be a regular with the Leafs one day – no doubt.

CORVO, Joe
b. Oak Park, Illinois, June 20, 1977
Gretzky, Orr, Lemieux, Howe – those are the guys who could afford to be cocky as teenagers and pre-NHLers because they could talk the talk and walk the walk. But when a mid-level draft choice out of college hockey can't come to terms with an NHL team and sits out a year to make a "statement," something is more wrong than right. When he did sign with Los Angeles, Corvo went down to the minors and was quickly arrested by police, further damaging his reputation. He made his NHL debut on December 15, 2002.

D

DAVISON, Rob
b. St. Catharines, Ontario, May 1, 1980
Big and tough, Davison is a defenceman who has been brought along slowly by San Jose since being drafted in 1998. He played with North Bay in the OHL for three years and in 2000 joined Kentucky of the AHL, coming to San Jose on March 9, 2003 and remaining the rest of the season.

DeFAUW, Brad
b. Edina, Minnesota, November 10, 1977
The group of players to score a goal in their NHL debut is a small one, but the number who scored *two* in their debut is even smaller. Add the name DeFauw to that list after he entered the league on March 10, 2003 and scored twice for Carolina in the first and third periods of a 6-5 win over Columbus.

DIMITRAKOS, Niko
b. Boston, Massachusetts, May 21, 1979
San Jose drafted Dimitrakos out of the University of Maine, and it was during his first year as pro that he got his first taste of the NHL, on February 12, 2003. He remained with the team the rest of the year, playing right wing and scoring an impressive 6 goals in 21 games.

DiPENTA, Joe
b. Barrie, Ontario, February 25, 1979
A large defenceman, DiPenta was here

and there before coming to the NHL. Florida drafted him, Philadelphia signed him as a free agent and then traded him to Atlanta, and the Thrashers finally gave him a chance on April 2, 2003. Three nights later, in his second game, he had a goal and an assist as the Thrashers' season drew to a close.

EMERY, Ray
b. Cayuga, Ontario, September 28, 1982
The Senators hope that they have a goalie of the future in Emery, a tall netminder drafted out of the OHL. He played a few minutes of relief on January 8, 2003, but his best years are still very much in the future.

EMINGER, Steve
b. Woodbridge, Ontario, October 31, 1983
Washington drafted Eminger 12th overall in 2002 and he made the team in the fall. A defenceman, he has immense potential. He can skate, shoot, pass, hit, but whether he can do all that on a regular basis in the NHL will be determined over the next few years. His partner on the Capitals blueline has been Calle Johansson, a 15-year NHLer and the perfect mentor for the teenager.

EXELBY, Garnet
b. Craik, Saskatchewan, August 16, 1981
Atlanta figured they had a surprise hit in Exelby when the team selected him a lowly 217th overall in 1999, and in the ensuing years he played better than that number might indicate. Solid positionally, he joined the Thrashers on March 11, 2003 and over the course of the rest of the season struggled with the speed of the game but eventually adjusted with more minutes.

FAHEY, Jim
b. Boston, Massachusetts, May 11, 1979
After graduating from Northeastern University in 2002, Fahey joined the San Jose organization and made his debut on December 12, 2002. If he has an impact, it will be a terrific success story in that he was drafted a distant 212th by the Sharks back in in 1998.

FEDOROV, Fedor
b. Moscow, Soviet Union (Russia), June 11, 1981
The younger brother of a great sibling always has a tough act to follow, especially when scouts say the younger is going to be better. In Fedor's case, that's unfair pressure because Sergei has been a superstar in the NHL since defecting to North America in 1990. Fedor has lived in Detroit since he was 13. He had his early hockey training in the Soviet Union and his more formative years under an NHL influence. Tampa Bay drafted him in 1999 and he declined to sign; two years later the Canucks selected him some 116 places closer to first overall (66th). He is considerably bigger than Sergei (6'3" and 220 pounds) and has the skill, but his career almost ended in 2001 when he was hit in the eye, suffered a detached retina, and almost lost sight in that organ. Fedorov made his debut with the Canucks early in the '02-'03 season, but he was sent to the minors and will need to impress management before earning regular ice time in the NHL.

FIBIGER, Jesse
b. Victoria, British Columbia, April 4, 1978
The Ducks drafted Fibiger after he had played just one year with the University of Minnesota-Duluth, but three years, unimpressed by his development, let him go. San Jose signed him, and on March 6, 2003 he made his NHL entrance to good effect, staying the year and establishing himself as a possible regular.

FIDDLER, Vernon
b. Edmonton, Alberta, May 9, 1980
Undrafted, Fiddler got to the NHL by dint of hard work and luck. After leaving the WHL, he went to the minors as a free agent, but when an ECHL team lets you go, there doesn't seem much reason for hope. Nonetheless, he signed with Nashville in the summer of 2002, was assigned to the AHL, and thanks to a string of injuries the Predators recalled him to the NHL.

FINLEY, Brian
b. Sault Ste. Marie, Ontario, July 13, 1981
The southpaw goalie played at the World Juniors for Canada and had a fine career in the OHL with Barrie. He was drafted a very lofty 6th overall by Nashville in 1999, but, as with so many modern goalies, suffered a serious groin injury that caused a major setback to his career and development. Finley didn't play a game in 2001-02, and in his NHL

entry, on New Year's Day 2003, he was anything but impressive. Nonetheless, he is young and still a first-rate prospect in the Predators' system.

FOSTER, Kurtis
b. Carp, Ontario, November 24, 1981
Another behemoth defenceman invading the NHL, Foster was one of many young Atlanta players to see some time once the playoffs were clearly out of reach in 2002-03. In his case, he started on March 31, 2003, getting in two games and whetting his appetite to ready himself for the next year.

FROLOV, Alexander
b. Moscow, Soviet Union (Russia), June 19, 1982
At 6'4" and just 191 pounds, he has some filling out to do, but Frolov is considered a skilled player by his bosses at the Los Angeles Kings. He played all his junior hockey back home and made the Kings out of training camp in September 2002. Frolov was part of the gold medal junior team for Russia in 2002.

GAMACHE, Simon
b. Montreal, Quebec, January 3, 1981
Size means so much to NHL scouts, and with a lack of it goes a commensurate lack of respect. In 2000, he was selected 290th overall by Atlanta in a draft in which 294 players were chosen. Yet Gamache went on to lead the Q in goals, assists, and points in both the regular season and Memorial Cup playdowns. He was the Canadian junior player of the year, and after a year and a half in the minors the Thrashers called him up for a game on March 7, 2003. He was held pointless in two games.

GAUSTAD, Paul
b. Fargo, North Dakota, February 3, 1982
Gaustad played a single game with Buffalo, on March 24, 2003. He is a large and imposing forward who played for Portland in the WHL before turning pro with the Sabres.

GERBER, Martin
b. Burgdorf, Switzerland, September 3, 1974
When Colorado's backup goalie David Aebischer had a rough go of it at the 2002 Olympics in Salt Lake City, it was Gerber who came in and did

an admirable job as replacement. Anaheim had drafted him in 2001 when he was already 27 and an established goalie in Sweden, and he played much of 2001-02 there. Gerber was made backup to J-S Giguere in Anaheim for 2002-03, an improbable rise if ever there was one.

GODARD, Eric
b. Vernon, British Columbia, March 7, 1980
Godard never made enough of an impression during his junior career in Lethbridge, but Florida signed him as a free agent at camp in 1999. He was sent to the minors and later traded to the Islanders before making his NHL debut, and it is his physical play more than soft hands that will earn him a place in any lineup in any league.

HAAKANA, Kari
b. Outokumpu, Finland, November 8, 1973
It wasn't until he was 30 years old that Haakana made his NHL debut, with Edmonton, after a lengthy career in Europe, mostly at home in Finland. A big defenceman, he went largely unnoticed by NHL scouts until the Oilers drafted him 248th overall in 2001, though since coming to North America that fall he has played primarily in the AHL with only a brief callup to Edmonton that lasted 13 games in '02-'03.

HAINSEY, Ron
b. Bolton, Connecticut, March 24, 1981
Montreal drafted him in the first round in 2000 and remains confident he will become a defenceman of the future for a team starved for reliable play in its own end. He's big and strong, but young, and still yet to develop to the point that he'll play every night at the Centre Bell. Hainsey was called up a couple of times in 2002-03 and accorded himself well, though the minors is still his place of perfect certainty for the time being.

HAYDAR, Darren
b. Toronto, Ontario, October 22, 1979
Not big but possessing plenty of speed and skill, Haydar had an outstanding college career at the University of New Hampshire (1998-2002) culminating in his senior year when he led the league

in assists and points. In his first NHL game, with Nashville, he learned an important NHL lesson – keep your head up. He suffered a concussion after a hit by Steve Poapst of Chicago, though he rallied to play some good hockey later in the year for the Hawks.

HECL, Radoslav
b. Partizanske, Czechoslovakia (Slovakia), October 11, 1974
Hecl was a veteran of the Slovak league when Buffalo decided to draft him in 2002 at age 27. He played much of the 2002-03 season in the minors for the Sabres, though he made his NHL entrance on November 30, 2002 against Toronto.

HEDSTROM, Jonathan
b. Skelleftea, Sweden, December 27, 1977
Toronto drafted him in 1997 but later traded him to Anaheim for two low draft choices in 2000. Up to 2002, Hedstrom played all of his hockey in Sweden, and his first year of pro in North America started off horribly when he suffered an eye injury in an AHL game. He regained his vision and played his first NHL game with the Ducks on December 3, 2002. A right winger, he is strong and determined and can score goals when the chances arise.

HEEREMA, Jeff
b. Thunder Bay, Ontario, January 17, 1980
A first-round draft choice by Carolina, Heerema will always remember his first NHL game. On January 17, 2003, he scored his team's only goal against New Jersey, and watched Joe Nieuwendyk score his 500th career goal for the Devils.

HEMSKY, Ales
b. Pardubice, Czechoslovakia (Czech Republic), August 13, 1983
At 17, Hemsky made the move from his homeland to the QMJHL to learn the Canadian game and to be a more visible player for scouts. He had a fine season and was selected by Edmonton in the first round of the 2001 draft; after one more season of junior he made the Oilers. Playing one season in a line with Marty Reasoner and Ethan Moreau, he improved with almost every game and impressed the coaching staff with his exceptional skills – raw but emerging talent.

HENRY, Alex
b. Elliot Lake, Ontario, October 18, 1979
What to make of Henry? At 6'6" and 225 pounds, he has the size to be an

intimidating defenceman. But after drafting him in 1998 and watching him in the AHL for three years, the Oilers cut him loose. Washington signed him in the hopes of getting something for nothing, but Henry has a ways to go before he can call himself an NHLer.

HENRY, Burke
b. Ste. Rose, Manitoba, January 21, 1979
The Rangers drafted him and the Flames acquired him and let him go, so it was left to Chicago to take a chance on the defenceman. He came out of the WHL known for his toughness more than his puck movement, making his first start with the Hawks on February 20, 2003.

HUET, Cristobal
b. St. Martin d'Heres, France, September 3, 1975
Few in Canada can understand how big a hero Huet is back in France, and all for the seemingly slightest of accomplishments. But Huet is the first native of France to play goal in the NHL, and after Philippe Bozon only the second France-born player to make the league. He played five years with Grenoble and four more in Lugano in the Swiss league, but Los Angeles drafted him on the recommendation of Jim Koleff, a friend of coach Andy Murray and a former coach at Lugano. Huet spent most of 2002-03 in the minors, but on February 20, 2003 he made his NHL debut. Five nights later he won his first game, and in the next he recorded a shutout. In 12 games on the season, Huet had a 4-4-1 record and an impressive GAA of 2.33. What he does from here is anybody's guess, but back in France it's all wonderful.

JANIK, Doug
b. Agawam, Massachusetts, March 26, 1980
A Buffalo draft choice from 1999, Janik is a solid, hard-hitting defenceman. He played six games for the missed-the-playoffs Sabres down the stretch of the 2002-03 season, starting with a game against Tampa Bay on March 14, 2003.

JOHANSSON, Mattias
b. Oskarshamn, Sweden, February 22, 1974
Johansson sports Elvis-style sideburns more 1970s than 21st century, but the

old rookie had a long career in Sweden before playing in the NHL. He was also part of Tre Kronor's team at the 2002 Olympics in Salt Lake City. He was drafted by Calgary, and it was with the Flames that he played most of the season before being traded to the Penguins near the deadline.

JOKELA, Mikko
b. Lappeenranta, Finland, March 4, 1980
Just as he was a late arrival to the NHL, he was also a late arrival to his first NHL game. Jokela was drafted in 1998 but stayed and played in Finland until 2001 when he moved to North America and played for Albany, New Jersey's farm team. He later signed with Vancouver and was recalled on February 18, 2003 for a game in Detroit. He arrive while the anthems were being sung, played five minutes, and had three shots on goal. He went back to the minors and, for now, calls Albany home.

KING, Jason
b. Corner Brook, Newfoundland, September 14, 1981
It wasn't for lack of scoring that King has yet to be given a long look in the NHL. In junior, with Halifax in the Q, he had seasons of 48 and 63 goals, the latter leading the league in 2001-02, but it was his lack of strength and physical ability that has hampered, or stalled, his progress. Nonetheless, Vancouver made the low draft choice a starter on March 17, 2003, playing on a line with Daniel and Henrik Sedin, and in eight games King had two assists.

KOBASEW, Chuck
b. Osoyoos, British Columbia, April 17, 1982
Everything players and scouts say about Kobasew points to one thing -- putting the puck in the net. He has a great shot and is effective in front of the goal. After his first score with the Flames in the 2002-03 season, he sent the puck to his best friend back in Osoyoos who was terminally ill with brain cancer. Kobasew played right wing on a line with Jarome Iginla in Calgary, and it seems only a matter of time before he scores in the NHL with the same frequency and consistency that he did in junior and college.

KOIVISTO, Tom
b. Turku, Finland, June 4, 1974
Koivisto was another older player to make his debut in 2002-03, in his case with St. Louis, the team that made him a late draft choice in 2002. He had played pro in Finland for a decade, but the small defenceman has by no means become a mainstay on the Blues' blueline just yet.

KOLTSOV, Konstantin
b. Minsk, Soviet Union (Belarus), April 17, 1981
Pittsburgh drafted him 18th overall in 1999, and he made his debut on January 28, 2003, an appropriate start considering the Penguins were pretty much an AHL team by that time of the year. Owner, captain, and Hall of Famer Mario Lemieux called Koltsov the fastest player in the game, and the youngster impressed with his speed during his two-game trial.

KOMISAREK, Mike
b. Islip Terrace, New York, January 19, 1982
Montreal has high hopes for Komisarek, a hulking defenceman out of the University of Michigan. He has size but can also move the puck quickly and effectively, and the Habs took him a lofty 7th overall in 2001. He played 21 games for the team in 2002-03 and did not look out of place on a team that often did during the year.

KRAFT, Ryan
b. Bottineau, North Dakota, November 7, 1975
Not a big man, Kraft doesn't have much time left as a prospect before he gets branded a minor leaguer. He was drafted by the Sharks way back in 1995, but after four years at the University of Minnesota and four more in the minors, he still hadn't seen the NHL. It wasn't until November 23, 2002 that San Jose gave him a chance – but that lasted all of seven games.

KRISTEK, Jaroslav
b. Zlin, Czechoslovakia (Czech Republic), March 16, 1980
It wasn't until he was drafted by Buffalo that Kristek came to North America to play. In 1998, the 18-year-old went to the WHL to finish his junior career and then played two years in the minors with Rochester of the American league. He was finally recalled by the Sabres for a game the night of January 10, 2003.

KURKA, Tomas
b. Most, Czechoslovakia (Czech Republic), December 14, 1981
Another young and small forward who can only benefit from any NHL attempt to cut down on obstruction, Kurka scored a goal in his first NHL game, February 26, 2003 for Carolina. He played junior back home with Litvinov before moving to North America to play pro in the AHL.

LEIGHTON, Mike
b. Petrolia, Ontario, May 19, 1981
Fewer than 20 goalies have recorded a shutout in their first NHL game, but only one has been involved in a 0-0 overtime tie to start his career. That historic night came on January 8, 2003 when Leighton and his Chicago mates skated to a scoreless tie against Phoenix.

LEOPOLD, Jordan
b. Golden Valley, Minnesota, August 3, 1980
Calgary had so much faith in the talents and abilities of this teenage defenceman that it traded star Derek Morris to Colorado to try to strengthen the team elsewhere. Leopold won the Hobey Baker Award in 2001-02 with the University of Minnesota and made the Flames at camp in the fall of 2002. However, he suffered a concussion toward the end of the exhibition season and missed the first month of the NHL year. When he returned, he quarterbacked the power-play point and was given every chance to use his offensive talents from the blueline. He wears number 4.

LOYNS, Lynn
b. Naicam, Saskatchewan, February 21, 1981
No one drafted him after a career with Spokane in the WHL, but San Jose signed Loyns as a free agent in 2001. He played a year in the AHL and then made the Sharks in 2002, impressing coach Darryl Sutter more than any other player at training camp. He was a healthy scratch for the first few weeks of the year, but when given a chance he proved his worth and has played semi-regularly ever since.

LUNDMARK, Jamie
b. Edmonton, Alberta, January 16, 1981
Being a rookie in the Rangers organization is not usually a good thing because the Blueshirts don't have a reputation for developing players; they like buying them already developed. Lundmark is a top-notch prospect, a centre who has NHL skills but who, in his early twenties, needs to play regularly and not have his mistakes booed by 18,200 louts at Madison Square Garden. Whether he can mature in that climate remains to be seen, but he could be a superstar in the league one day.

LUPASCHUK, Ross
b. Edmonton, Alberta, January 19, 1981
It was a deal made because of money, and it might turn into one of the most lopsided trades of the modern era. Pittsburgh sent Jaromir Jagr to Washington for Kris Beech, Michal Sivek, Lupaschuk, and future considerations. While Jagr continues to flourish as one of the game's dominant players, cumulatively, the young players acquired by Pittsburgh have not been playing to equal success. Lupaschuk first played on December 10, 2002 on defence but is still very much more a prospect than a player.

MacNEIL, Ian
b. Halifax, Nova Scotia, April 27, 1977
He was drafted at 18, like most Canadian hopefuls, but that was in 1995. The forward has been in the minors ever since, and his forays into the NHL came on December 18, 2002 and the following game when Philadelphia called him up to replace Jeremy Roenick who was serving a two-game suspension. After that, it was back to the minors for MacNeil.

MAJESKY, Ivan
b. Banska Bystrica, Czechoslovakia (Slovakia), September 2, 1976
Majesky was a key defenceman with the undermanned Slovak team in Salt Lake City in 2002, and the next fall he jumped into the NHL and played the full year for Florida. He had played pro in Europe for a number of years, but he still displayed skill and poise that even the Panthers had not expected; he played that way for the full 82 games of the season. His strength is his hitting

and positional play rather than offensive ability. He finished the season by helping his country win a bronze medal at the World Championships in Finland.

MALEC, Tomas
b. Skalica, Czechoslovakia (Slovakia), May 13, 1982
Florida drafted Malec and then traded him to Carolina as part of a package to acquire Sandis Ozolinsh. The 'Canes have been pleased ever since. Malec is a puck-handling defenceman who has size and a dirty mean streak going for him. He played his way up to the NHL from the minors, and in his first game with Carolina, on December 15, 2002, he recorded an assist. Since then, his stock has continued to rise within the organization.

MANNING, Paul
b. Red Deer, Alberta, April 15, 1979
Calgary drafted Manning in 1998 and then traded him to Columbus where he played in the minors after graduating from Colorado College. He made his debut with the Blue Jackets on January 4, 2003 and played well, suggesting the defenceman might well make the team sooner rather than later.

MAPLETOFT, Justin
b. Lloydminster, Saskatchewan, January 11, 1981
There is plenty of upside, as the expression has it, to Mapletoft. Drafted by the Islanders out of Red Deer, he helped the Rebels win the Memorial Cup in 2000-01, the same year he led the WHL in assists and points. What New York likes about him, aside from the points, though, is that he plays defence as well. After a year in the minors, Mapletoft played his first NHL games in '02-'03, including two in the playoffs, which ended early for the Isles. He is among the team's top prospects and will be given every chance to make the NHL at training camp in September 2003.

McDONNELL, Kent
b. Williamstown, Ontario, March 1, 1979
The gamble paid off to a slight degree. He was drafted by Carolina in 1997, 225th overall, but decided not to sign with the Hurricanes and re-entered the draft. Second time 'round McDonnell went marginally higher, 181st overall, to a better team, Detroit. But the Cup contenders traded him to one of the worst teams in the league, Columbus, for nothing more than future considerations, and it was under this

inauspicious cloud that he entered the NHL on April 2, 2003 as the '02-'03 season was drawing to a close. He was held off the scoresheet in three games.

McLEAN, Brett
b. Comox, British Columbia, August 14, 1978
Four teams owned McLean's rights before he made it to the NHL. Dallas drafted him in 1997, and over the next six years he played mostly in the minors under contract to Calgary, Minnesota, and Chicago. Perseverance pays though, and on December 10, 2002, the Hawks recalled the centreman to replace the injured Andrei Nikolishin.

McMORROW, Sean
b. Vancouver, British Columbia, January 19, 1982
In three years of junior, from 1999 to 2002, McMorrow played for six OHL teams. That has to be a record of some sort! The fighter was recalled for a March 22, 2003 dance with the Leafs at ACC, but he sat on the bench most of the night save for two innocuous shifts.

MILLER, Ryan
b. East Lansing, Michigan, July 17, 1980
Miller and East Lansing are synonymous, producing three fine players before Ryan: Kelly, Kevin, and Kip. Ryan is a cousin of that lot, and, to be different, a goalie. In his three years at Michigan State, he led the CCHA in shutouts and average each season, establishing a career record of 26 shutouts in total. He won the Hobey Baker Award in 2000-01, and in 2002 played for the U.S. at the World Championships in Sweden. Buffalo drafted him, and in his first NHL game he was stung for three goals in just one period. No matter. The Sabres feel he will be a superstar goalie, so they have him developing in Rochester. One day, they figure, he'll be as good as Dominik Hasek. That would be something, indeed.

MORRISONN, Shaone
b. Vancouver, British Columbia, December 23, 1982
He was drafted in the first round by Boston in 2001, and so far Morrisonn is on track to be at least a solid NHLer. He played his junior hockey with Kamloops and turned pro with the Bruins in 2002, starting in the AHL. Morrisonn played two NHL games, the first in Toronto on November 19, 2002, and did not look out of place with the team. A defenceman, he is a good skater who moves the puck well.

MROZIK, Rick

b. Duluth, Minnesota, January 2, 1975

A graduate of the University of Minnesota-Duluth, Mrozik has worked his way into the NHL slowly but surely. Drafted by Dallas in 1993, he languished in the minors before being traded to Washington after which he languished some more. In the summer of 2001, he signed with Calgary as a free agent, and in '02-'03 he got into two games for the Flames, his first NHL action.

MURPHY, Curtis

b. Kerrobert, Saskatchewan, December 3, 1975

The game's the thing, not the money and stardom. Murphy, never a great prospect, played hockey and pursued his education at the University of North Dakota. He was never drafted into the NHL but decided to play with Orlando in the IHL starting in 1998. Finally, in 2001, Minnesota signed him, and after yet another year in the minors played for the Wild on December 15, 2002. He's a small defenceman, but his precious NHL time to date is something that can never be taken from him.

N

NASH, Rick

b. Brampton, Ontario, June 16, 1984

There really isn't anything Nash can't do, at least not at any level he played in before the NHL. That's why Columbus made him the 1st overall selection at the 2002 Entry Draft and why he made the team at 18. He is an outstanding skater and superb stickhandler, the kind of winger who can beat a man one-on-one as opposed to outfighting a platoon in the corner to dig the puck free. In his rookie season, he proved an ability to score and play well in the NHL and it's only a matter of time before he develops into a star. Whether he can reach his peak in Predatorland is another story.

O

ORPIK, Brooks

b. San Francisco, California, September 26, 1980

The Bay City has the great bridge, fantastic seafood restaurants, rolling streets, and scenic streetcar routes. It can now claim a hockey player as well, though Orpik did well to leave and learn the game in more wintry climes such as Thayer Academy and Boston College. A defenceman, he was drafted by Pittsburgh and played his first game on December 10, 2002, in Toronto, his callup from the minors the result of numerous injuries to Penguins blueliners. He's a hitter, not a scorer, and he's in the right place at the right time.

OTT, Steve

b. Summerside, Prince Edward Island, August 19, 1982

He was drafted by Dallas in the first round in 2000 out of Windsor of the OHL, and turned pro in 2002. He spent most of that rookie season in the minors, though he did play a few games with the Stars, notably December 13, 2002, his first appearance in the big tent.

P

PAUL, Jeff

b. London, Ontario, March 1, 1978

A rough-and-tough defenceman, Paul was drafted by Chicago in 1996 but never got into a game with the Hawks. Instead, he was relegated to the minors where he spent the rest of his days playing in his physical style until Colorado signed him five years later. He got into a few games with the Avs in 2002-03.

PETTINEN, Tomi

b. Ylojarvi, Finland, June 17, 1977

Pettinen was minding his own business playing pro in Finland when the Islanders drafted him in 2000. He didn't move a muscle, but after his '01-'02 season, the Isles phoned and asked him to play a few games with Bridgeport in the AHL playoffs. Pettinen accepted, and decided to give the NHL a try. He spent all of the next year in the minors as well, but he did get the call for a game with the big club in 2002-03.

PIRJETA, Lasse

b. Oulu, Finland, April 4, 1974

Pirjeta's late entry into the NHL was enhanced by his being drafted by Columbus in 2002, a team desperate for skill and talent at every position. As a large and offensively-capable right winger, Pirjeta fit the bill to a T, but three games into the 2002-03 season he suffered a separated shoulder and missed a month. When he returned, he had some impact, scoring 11 goals and 21 points the rest of the way for the Blue Jackets.

PISANI, Fernando

b. Edmonton, Alberta, December 27, 1976

Pisani pursued his dreams of puck-chasing in his home province until going off to Providence College. He was drafted by his hometown in 1996 prior to starting at PC but it wasn't until 2002-03 that he finally made it to the NHL. He scored his first goal on February 5, 2003 in a 2-1 win over Anaheim.

R

RADULOV, Igor

b. Nizhny Tagil, Soviet Union (Russia), August 23, 1982

He had the speed and the skills, but even Chicago must have been surprised when Radulov scored five goals in his first seven NHL games. He started on March 23, 2003 and in his second game he scored twice and didn't let up for the rest of the short season. Radulov had played in Russia until 2001 when he joined the Mississauga Ice Dogs of the OHL.

REID, Brandon

b. Kirkland, Quebec, March 9, 1981

Reid helped Val d'Or to the Memorial Cup finals in 2001, a small, fleet scoring centreman drafted way down by Vancouver. He got an assist in his first game with the Canucks, on March 1, 2003, and in seven games had five points on one of the league's top offensive teams.

RUDKOWSKY, Cody

b. Willingdon, Alberta, July 21, 1978

He has worked all his life to make it to the NHL, and to date that has meant exactly a half-hour of stopping pucks in the world's best league. Rudkowsky came out of the WHL undrafted, but managed to sign with St. Louis in 1999 as a free agent. Since then, he has been recalled once in 2002-03 for that brief appearance, spending the rest of his time in the Blues' system.

RUPP, Mike

b. Cleveland, Ohio, January 13, 1980

Son of Duane, Mike is a whole lot bigger than Dad ever was. Junior stands in at 6'5" and 230 pounds, but he may have been given bad advice before getting to the NHL. The Islanders thought highly of him during his junior career with Erie and drafted him 9th overall in 1998, but Rupp never signed. Sure enough, two years later he was selected 76th overall by New Jersey, costing Rupp possible millions in contract revenue. Rupp has had little chance of cracking a Devils lineup replete with veterans who win most nights, and it wasn't until January 13, 2003 that he finally got into a game.

SAMUELSSON, Martin
b. Upplands, Vasby, Sweden,
January 25, 1982
Drafted by Boston, Samuelsson stayed in Sweden to play until the 2002-03 season when he finally decided it was time to try pro in North America. He spent most of that first season in the minors, and when he was called up on January 15, 2003 the right winger was put on a line with Brian Rolston and P-J Axelsson.

SANFORD, Curtis
b. Owen Sound, Ontario, October 5, 1979
His chance for NHL glory may have come and gone already. Sanford played junior in his hometown and was never drafted by the time he left the OHL. He hung around in the minors year after year, and when the St. Louis goalie situation was dire near the start of the '02-'03 season, he was put in net three times. He was then demoted to the minors, where he continues to stop pucks.

SAUER, Kurt
b. St. Cloud, Minnesota, January 16, 1981
Born in the heart of Hockey Country, USA, Sauer played junior in the WHL during which time he was signed by Colorado. Two years later, though, he was unsigned, and Anaheim swooped in to give him a contract. Sauer found a home with the Ducks and has been a regular player, sharing the dressing room with the likes of Kariya and Oates.

SCHMIDT, Chris
b. Beaverlodge, Alberta, March 1, 1976
An experienced centre in the Los Angeles system, Schmidt was drafted by the Kings in 1994 and has remained faithful to the team ever since. He finally got his just reward on February

11, 2003 when he was called up for ten games, having paid his dues in the form of seven years in the minors. He didn't manage to fish that important first-goal puck out of the net, so perhaps that will be a souvenir he collects before the CBA expires September 15, 2004.

SEIDENBERG, Denis
b. Schwenningen, West Germany,
July 18, 1981
Well, la-dee-da. Seidenberg came from Germany to take part in the Flyers' training camp to start the 2002-03 season, and he played so well he was in the lineup on opening night. The defenceman impressed coach Ken Hitchcock with his tremendous shot and ability to move the puck quickly and intelligently. Everything he does from here on in is gravy.

SEJNA, Peter
b. Liptovski Mikulas, Czechoslovakia (Slovakia), October 5, 1979
Sejna left his native Slovakia to play in North America and chase a dream, one he caught on the final day of the 2002-03 season. He played two years for Des Moines in the USHL and then attended Colorado College in 2001. He was a high-scoring left winger who led the WCHA in points the year after and was named player of the year. Sejna was also named a Hobey Baker Award finalist and then signed as a free agent with St. Louis. He made his debut on April 6, 2003, the Blues final game of the regular season, and in a 5-2 loss to the Avalanche Sejna scored a goal.

SEMENOV, Alexei
b. Murmansk, Soviet Union (Russia),
April 10, 1981
Game action is the only thing standing between Semenov and a spot with the Edmonton Oilers. He had an impressive training camp in the fall of 2002, and when he made his first appearance with the team on December 30, 2002, he did nothing wrong and many things right. For now, he's cutting his teeth (and losing them, too, no doubt) with Hamilton in the AHL.

SEVERSON, Cam
b. Canora, Saskatchewan,
January 15, 1978
Name a league and he's been there. Name a team and odds are he's played for or against it. Severson was drafted in 1997 by San Jose, but by the time he played his first NHL game, on March 30, 2003, he had skated just about everywhere. The Ducks signed him as a free agent in

the summer of 2002, and after playing in cities like Louisiana, Peoria, and Quad City, Severson was delighted to be a Mighty Duck for two games.

SHARP, Patrick
b. Thunder Bay, Ontario,
December 27, 1981
After two years at the University of Vermont Sharp decided to turn pro with the Flyers who had drafted him in 2001. He spent most of 2002-03 in the minors, but did make two appearances with the parent club during the season.

SIKLENKA, Mike
b. Meadow Lake, Saskatchewan,
December 18, 1979
On January 28, 2003, Siklenka signed a contract with the Flyers and played for the team that night, to date his only NHL contest. Injuries prompted the callup, surprising given that he was by no means the best player on the Phantoms, Philadelphia's AHL team. Not a goon but physical, he is strong on the puck but hardly a bundle of skill like Jaromir Jagr. Siklenka had done his time in the minors, but is likely to do more before he gets another dance in the big show.

SIVEK, Michal
b. Nachod, Czechoslovakia
(Czech Republic), January 21, 1981
Along with two other rookies – Kris Beech and Ross Lupaschuk – Sivek was a highly-touted prospect acquired by the Penguins when they traded Jaromir Jagr to Washington. And like the others, he has yet to prove he is even a third of a Jagr-like player. He played his first game on November 29, 2002 but has spent more time in the minors than the NHL.

SMIRNOV, Alexei
b. Tver, Soviet Union (Russia),
January 28, 1982
Anaheim sees nothing but good things from their 2000 first-round draft choice, but in 2002-03, his rookie season, Smirnov didn't see much playing time. A big left winger, he has shown signs of promise, though, and the Ducks are prepared to be very patient with their hopeful future star.

SMITHSON, Jerred
b. Vernon, British Columbia,
February 4, 1979
He played five years in the WHL, a rare feat, but partly his lengthy stay in the WHL was the result of never being drafted into the NHL. L.A. signed him in 2000, and on December 29, 2002, the

right winger made his first NHL appearance.

SOMIK, Radovan
b. Martin, Czechoslovakia (Slovakia), May 5, 1977
His skills were what drew Philadelphia to Somik in 1995 when the team first drafted the right winger; his experience was what drew the Flyers to finally play him some seven years later. In the interim, he played in Slovakia and represented his country at the 2002 Olympics in Salt Lake City. Unfortunately, his rookie season, 2002-03, passed haltingly because of a nagging and painful groin injury which kept forcing Somik out of the lineup.

SPEZZA, Jason
b. Mississauga, Ontario, June 13, 1983
Since he was 14 years old, Spezza was considered the next Gretzky, but as he got older he found it more and more difficult to live up to such untenable hype. He had a really good – but not staggeringly incredible – junior career, first with Don Cherry's Ice Dogs and then Windsor and Belleville, but when he went to Ottawa's camp in the fall of 2001 after being chosen 2nd overall in the summer draft, Spezza figured he'd never play anywhere else again other than the NHL. How wrong, how wrong was he. The Sens kept him late into that camp, giving him the impression he had made the team, but at the very end he was sent back to junior. Disappointed and upset, he threw a hissy fit before leaving. Nonetheless, he had a good year, and over the summer trained hard to ensure he'd make the team at his second camp as a 19-year-old. Nope. This time he was sent to the AHL. Early on, though, he was called up to Ottawa, and in his first game he had an assist. He stayed in the lineup for a short while as the big team went through a series of injuries, and although he proved to be a fine offensive talent, great passer, and effective skater on the power play, he was so weak defensively that coach Jacques Martin had no hesitation in sending him to the minors when he had a healthy lineup. Spezza played three times for Canada at the World Juniors, but it will take another year at least before he can prove he belongs with the world's best men.

STAJAN, Matt
b. Mississauga, Ontario, December 19, 1983
Wearing a reverse Dave Keon (i.e., number 41), Stajan closed his 2002-03

season in a most improbable manner. On Wednesday, April 2, 2003, his Belleville Bulls were eliminated from the OHL playoffs by St. Mike's. On Thursday, he signed a contract with the Leafs, the team that had drafted him the previous summer. On Friday, he was sent to St. John's to play his first pro game with the farm team Maple Leafs. On Saturday, he was told he'd be in the lineup that night at Air Canada Centre against Ottawa. And Saturday evening, on Hockey Night in Canada, he scored his first NHL goal, the Leafs' only goal in a 3-1 loss. It doesn't get any better than that.

STEPHENS, Charlie
b. London, Ontario, April 5, 1981
Few reputations have plummeted faster than Stephens's. In 1999, Washington selected him 31st overall in the draft. He never signed, and two years later Colorado took him as the 196th choice. He had been the top selection in the OHL draft in 1997, but that was then and now is a much less kind place for him. The Avs called him up for a few games, and although he didn't play poorly he didn't quite prove that he belonged in the company of Sakic, Forsberg, and Blake on a nightly basis.

STOLL, Jarret
b. Melville, Saskatchewan, June 25, 1982
The stats line for 2002-03 reads a simple four games played and one assist recorded, but that single digit was quite a piece of work. Stoll was drafted by Calgary in 2000 but didn't sign, re-entering in 2002 and being selected by provincial rivals, Edmonton. He won the Memorial Cup with Kootenay in 2001-02 and was called up by the Oilers for a look-see on January 29, 2003. On his first shift, his first touch of the puck, in fact, he sent linemate Jason Chimera in alone on goal with a perfect pass. Chimera scored, and Stoll had his first NHL point just seconds after joining the league. He has the size, the speed, the skill, the toughness to succeed. If he can work on the skating a bit, he could be with the Oil for more than a look-see next time up.

SURMA, Damian
b. Lincoln Park, Michigan, June 22, 1981
Carolina must have set some sort of record in 2002-03. During that nightmare-lousy season, the 'Canes gave a number of their youngsters and farmhands a taste of the NHL, and no fewer than five of those scored a goal in their first game! Surma was one of that

number. On March 18, 2003 against Ottawa, he scored in his lone NHL game to date.

SUROVY, Tomas
b. Banska Bystrica, Czechoslovakia (Slovakia), September 24, 1981
Another talented, young and untried European on the Pittsburgh roster, Surovy scored twice in his first 3 games and 4 times in 26 games in 2002-03 for Mario Lemieux. The skilled centre is sure to get plenty of opportunity to play on a team laden with less-than-NHL-calibre players, so he will have a real chance to prove himself.

SVITOV, Alexander
b. Omsk, Soviet Union (Russia), November 3, 1982
Svitov carved himself a reputation at the 2001 World Junior Championships as a dirty player who would be marked for life by his play. So far, his adversaries from Team Canada (who nicknamed him Spitov, for obvious reasons) who have gone on to the NHL have had little chance to enact payback because Svitov, a once surefire prospect, has hardly taken the pro ranks by storm. Tampa Bay chose him 3rd overall in '01, giving his future superstar status, but he struggled when he got to the Lightning and played himself into the minors.

T

TAFFE, Jeff
b. Hastings, Minnesota, February 19, 1981
St. Louis drafted him but traded him to Phoenix, and the Coyotes thought enough of Taffe to give him three games early in the 2002-03 season to show him what the NHL was like. The motivation has worked insofar as he has worked hard to take his scoring game to the next level, but he's back in the minors to learn defence and adjust to the size, strength, and speed of the pro game.

TELLQVIST, Mikael
b. Sundbyberg, Sweden, September 19, 1979
Training camp 2001 was supposed to be Tellqvist's moment. He was the top-rated minor-league goalie in the Leafs' system, and Glenn Healy, backup to Curtis Joseph at Air Canada Centre, had just retired. The spot was

Tellqvist's to lose – and he lost it. He had a lousy training camp and walk-on Corey Schwab was excellent, so Schwab got the job and Tellqvist was demoted. He was so upset he almost returned to Sweden, but he hung in there and had a decent year with the Baby Leafs. In 2002, he had a better training camp, but the Leafs by then had the excellent tandem of Eddie Belfour and Trevor Kidd. At one point, though, both were injured and Tellqvist had to replace Kidd in the third period of a game against Montreal on January 18, 2003. He allowed one goal and made several excellent saves, and the Leafs won the game in overtime, bringing a happy end to Tellqvist's first NHL game. He reasserted himself as a legitimate future NHLer, and went back to the AHL a better goalie.

THOMAS, Tim
b. Flint, Michigan, April 15, 1974
A bear hunter when he's not tending goal, Thomas is one of the best rookie stories for the 2002-03 season. He made his debut with Boston in October 2002 just a few months after finishing the previous year with Karpat Oulu, a Finnish team about an hour south of the Arctic Circle. He's played here, there, and everywhere, but the Bruins needed help and turned to Thomas; he stepped into the crease and helped the B's defeat Edmonton 4-3. He was a 28-year-old rookie, and for him to finally get to the NHL was a dream come true. How many games he'll play is another matter.

THORNTON, Shawn
b. Oshawa, Ontario, July 23, 1977
When the Leafs traded Thornton to Chicago for Marty Wilford on September 30, 2001, not too many radio talk shows were fielding calls to discuss the deal. It was minor league the whole way, except that when Thornton got to the Hawks he managed to fight well enough that the team let go veteran pugilist Bob Probert. Thornton's job is as simple as it is undesirable for most, but punching opponents up is what he does, and in the Hawks' estimation he does that very well.

TRIPP, John
b. Kingston, Ontario, May 4, 1977
It's tough for a kid to break into the Rangers at the best of times, but when the team is going poorly, better not to be there at all. Nonetheless, the minor leaguer played his first NHL game for the Blueshirts on January 8, 2003, and

collected two assists playing on a line with Mark Messier. He played a few more games, though, as the Rangers stumbled through another bad year.

U

UPSHALL, Scottie
b. Fort McMurray, Alberta, October 7, 1983
Aggressive, a pest, a skilled competitor, Upshall believes he'll be a star in the NHL some day soon. So do the Predators, the team that drafted him 6th overall in 2002 after his second strong season with Kamloops in the WHL. But Nashville returned him to junior at training camp, and Upshall ended up being captain for Canada's World Junior team in Halifax, winning a silver medal. He isn't big, but his chippiness and skills have led to comparisons to Darcy Tucker. Upshall played a few games with the Predators in '02-'03 to get his feet wet, but his career still has many games left in the NHL.

V

VANDERMEER, Jim
b. Caroline, Alberta, February 21, 1980
During a fine career with Red Deer in he WHL, Vandermeer found himself on the outside looking in until Philadelphia signed him as a free agent. The Flyers loved his in-your-face play, and as a defenceman he knows how to hit hard and clean. Vandermeer made his NHL debut on January 3, 2003, though he spent most of the season in the minors.

VEILLEUX, Stephane
b. Beaureville, Quebec, November 16, 1981
A solid, all-round player, Veilleux isn't blessed with gobs of talent but he is determined beyond his skills to make it. He was drafted by Minnesota and made a good fit during the 2002-03 season when Bill Muckalt was injured and he was called to replace him. He played in eleven consecutive games as a checker, doing his job on a Jacques Lemaire-coached team that specializes in players doing exactly what they're assigned.

VERNARSKY, Kris
b. Detroit, Michigan, April 5, 1982
Drafted by Toronto, Vernarsky was traded to Boston for Richard Jackman and made his debut with the Bruins on January 20, 2003. It was the best of nights and the worst of nights: he scored the tying goal in the third period for his team, but suffered an eye injury later in the game.

VOLCHENKOV, Anton
b. Moscow, Soviet Union (Russia), February 25, 1982
The Senators believe that the upside of Volchenkov is so positive that they kept him up for virtually all of 2002-03. A defenceman, he has ability to join the rush and get back into his own end in time, and has a physical side that the team very much needs. Young and still developing, the Sens expect him to be around many a year.

W

WALKER, Matt
b. Beaverlodge, Alberta, April 7, 1980
He seems to get bigger and stronger every day. Walker is now 6'3" and 236 pounds of strength on the St. Louis blueline, and although not a regular with the Blues he is being touted as such in the near future. He played his junior in Portland and was drafted in 1998.

WALLIN, Rickard
b. Stockholm, Sweden, April 19, 1980
He was drafted by Phoenix at age 18 in 1998, but Wallin continued to play in Sweden for another four years. By the time he came to North America, his rights had been traded to Minnesota, and he had an excellent camp with the Wild. Nonetheless, Wallin started in the minors and didn't make his NHL debut until December 2002, when the centre acquitted himself well.

WANVIG, Kyle
b. Calgary, Alberta, January 29, 1981
It has been an odd and event-filled ride for the young Wanvig so far. He has been drafted twice, once by Boston and then Minnesota. In between, he was traded to Boston for Jonas Hoglund, but the deal was nullified because of a faulty fax machine. So, still with Boston, he played in the WHL until the Wild acquired his

rights in the 2001 draft. The team sent him to Houston to develop, but he broke his ankle and missed half the season after playing the first half not knowing it was broken! Then, at training camp in 2002 he did nothing to impress coach Jacques Lemaire. Wanvig played a single game, on November 25, 2002, but has been in the minors ever since. The team wants him to play more physically, with more intensity and greater consistency. The rest is up to him.

WEINHANDL, Mattias
b. Ljungby, Sweden, June 1, 1980
Of German heritage, Weinhandl is, nonetheless, fully Swedish. Thus, he grew up in a hockey country and was drafted by the Islanders in 1999. Just a few months later, he was speared in the eye by Michal Travnicek in the Four Nations tournament and lost 90 percent of his vision on that side. Travnicek was suspended one year for the horrific spear, and Weinhandl set to making an extraordinary adjustment. On November 19, 2002, after three more years in the Swedish league, he was called up by the Islanders and played on a line with Brad Isbister and Alexei Yashin. He's been more or less a regular ever since, his recovery an amazing story of courage, his play a great story of skill.

WISEMAN, Chad
b. Burlington, Ontario, March 25, 1981
A low draft choice by San Jose in 2000, Wiseman went from the OHL to the AHL to the NHL in a year, though by no means is he in the big show to stay. The left winger didn't register a point in four games with the Sharks and didn't see much ice time, though he did get a chance to see what the NHL looks like up close.

Z

ZALESAK, Miroslav
b. Skalica, Czechoslovakia (Czech Republic), January 2, 1980
Fleet of foot, right winger Zalesak scored a goal in his first NHL game, with San Jose on March 11, 2003. He had played in Slovakia before heading to the Q in 1998, and from there he went to the AHL to develop in the Sharks' system.

ZETTERBERG, Henrik
b. Njurunda, Sweden, October 9, 1980
Despite his being drafted just 210th overall in 1999, Detroit believes it has in Zetterberg one of the best young players in the game. He played all his career in Sweden, including representing Tre Kronor at the 2002 Olympics in Salt Lake City, and the left winger has been compared to a young Peter Forsberg, someone who can work with the puck even in close quarters. Zetterberg made the Wings at camp in 2002 and for now the team doesn't consider the minors a league worthy of his skills.

ZIGOMANIS, Mike
b. North York, Ontario, January 17, 1981
Buffalo drafted him in 1999 but Zigomanis didn't sign until two years later when Carolina selected him. He played all his junior days in Kingston and developed into a skilled centreman with good offensive ability and a defensive sense of commitment. Zigomanis was called up by the 'Canes on February 26, 2003, and after another first gamer, Tomas Kurka, scored, Zigomanis did the same in his first NHL appearance. He stuck around for 19 games with the team which augurs well for '03-'04.

ZIZKA, Tomas
b. Sternberk, Czechoslovakia (Czech Republic), October 10, 1979
It wasn't until 2001, when he was 22, that Zizka left the familiar confines of Zlin to venture to the NHL side of hockey. He was drafted by Los Angeles and played for Manchester, the farm team, for most of 2001-03. But he was one of the top-scoring defencemen in the AHL and the Kings called him up on January 22, 2003. He had three assists in his ten-game tryout.

PHOTO CREDITS

All images in this book are courtesy of the
Hockey Hall of Fame and are taken from
the following collections:

Imperial Oil/Turovsky
Graphic Artists
Dave Sandford
Doug MacLellan
Lew Portnoy
DiMaggio Collection
O-Pee-Chee
HHOF Archives

ACKNOWLEDGEMENTS

Just listing the names of the many players and relatives who contributed their time and stories to these biographies would occupy many pages, so to all, a collective thanks.

Daily support came from a number of other sources, notably the Hockey Hall of Fame's Phil Pritchard, Craig Campbell, Tyler Wolosewich, Darren Boyko, Peter Jagla, Anthony Fusco, Geoff Fletcher, Izak Westgate, Marilyn Robbins, Margaret Lockhart, and Steve Poirier. Also Len Kotylo, Paul Patskou, Heather MacLean, Dennis Gibbons, Ray Mulley, Peter Borkowski, Michelle Putzel, Kelly McKay, Joseph Nieforth, Don Andrews, Ed Sweeney, Frank Selke, Carl Lavigne, and Jeff Davis.

A very special thanks goes to the phenomenal assistance of Szymon Szemberg and Kimmo Leinonen at the IIHF in Zurich.

Where would I be without the terrific efforts of everyone at Doubleday Canada, notably my editor, Christine Innes, publisher Maya Mavjee, and Suzanne Brandreth, as well as Susan Broadhurst and Valerie Applebee.

Special thanks to my agent, Dean Cooke, for his work in starting the project, and to his assistant, Samantha North. Collectively, without everyone's help, this mammoth undertaking could not have been so well managed or so carefully put together.

The author has made every effort to be as accurate and thorough as possible. Anyone with additional information is welcome to e-mail him at moydartpress@idirect.com with verifiable support to any additional information about a player's life in and/or out of hockey.